Presented to

By

....

Date

....

Occasion

....

....

*Your word is a lamp to guide my feet
and a light for my path.*

PSALM 119:105

everyday matters

BIBLE

for women

everyday matters

BIBLE

for women

*practical encouragement
to make every day matter*

{ NEW LIVING TRANSLATION }

Everyday Matters Bible for Women
© 2012 by Hendrickson Publishers Marketing, LLC
P. O. Box 3473
Peabody, Massachusetts 01961-3473

978-1-59856-705-2   Hardcover
978-1-61970-012-3   Rose Floral with Khaki Flexisoft

Interior design and typesetting by The Livingstone Corporation, Carol Stream, Illinois.

Cover design and interior art direction by Rusty Kinnunen.

Extra-biblical material supplied by Christianity Today and developed by Ginger Kolbaba and Kelli Trujillo in collaboration with CT contributors.

CHRISTIANITY ● **TODAY**

Produced with the assistance of The Livingstone Corporation and Christianity Today.
Project direction and research provided by Evelyn Bence, Jim Bolton, Ginger Kolbaba, JoHannah Reardon, Rusty Kinnunen, Mary McNeil, Rob Stone, Linda Taylor, and Ashley Taylor.

Printed in China

First Printing—September 2012

Contents

The Old Testament

The New Testament

contents

Books of the Bible in Alphabetical Order

Books of the New Testament are in *italics*.

A Note to Readers

The *Holy Bible,* New Living Translation, was first published in 1996. It quickly became one of the most popular Bible translations in the English-speaking world. While the NLT's influence was rapidly growing, the Bible Translation Committee determined that an additional investment in scholarly review and text refinement could make it even better. So shortly after its initial publication, the committee began an eight-year process with the purpose of increasing the level of the NLT's precision without sacrificing its easy-to-understand quality. This second-generation text was completed in 2004 and is reflected in this edition of the New Living Translation. An additional update with minor changes was subsequently introduced in 2007.

The goal of any Bible translation is to convey the meaning and content of the ancient Hebrew, Aramaic, and Greek texts as accurately as possible to contemporary readers. The challenge for our translators was to create a text that would communicate as clearly and powerfully to today's readers as the original texts did to readers and listeners in the ancient biblical world. The resulting translation is easy to read and understand, while also accurately communicating the meaning and content of the original biblical texts. The NLT is a general-purpose text especially good for study, devotional reading, and reading aloud in worship services.

We believe that the New Living Translation—which combines the latest biblical scholarship with a clear, dynamic writing style—will communicate God's word powerfully to all who read it. We publish it with the prayer that God will use it to speak his timeless truth to the church and the world in a fresh, new way.

The Publishers

October 2007

Introduction to the
New Living Translation

Translation Philosophy and Methodology

English Bible translations tend to be governed by one of two general translation theories. The first theory has been called "formal-equivalence," "literal," or "word-for-word" translation. According to this theory, the translator attempts to render each word of the original language into English and seeks to preserve the original syntax and sentence structure as much as possible in translation. The second theory has been called "dynamic-equivalence," "functional-equivalence," or "thought-for-thought" translation. The goal of this translation theory is to produce in English the closest natural equivalent of the message expressed by the original-language text, both in meaning and in style.

Both of these translation theories have their strengths. A formal-equivalence translation preserves aspects of the original text—including ancient idioms, term consistency, and original-language syntax—that are valuable for scholars and professional study. It allows a reader to trace formal elements of the original-language text through the English translation. A dynamic-equivalence translation, on the other hand, focuses on translating the message of the original-language text. It ensures that the meaning of the text is readily apparent to the contemporary reader. This allows the message to come through with immediacy, without requiring the reader to struggle with foreign idioms and awkward syntax. It also facilitates serious study of the text's message and clarity in both devotional and public reading.

The pure application of either of these translation philosophies would create translations at opposite ends of the translation spectrum. But in reality, all translations contain a mixture of these two philosophies. A purely formal-equivalence translation would be unintelligible in English, and a purely dynamic-equivalence translation would risk being unfaithful to the original. That is why translations shaped by dynamic-equivalence theory are usually quite literal when the original text is relatively clear, and the translations shaped by formal-equivalence theory are sometimes quite dynamic when the original text is obscure.

The translators of the New Living Translation set out to render the message of the original texts of Scripture into clear, contemporary English. As they did so, they kept the concerns of both formal-equivalence and dynamic-equivalence in mind. On the one hand, they translated as simply and literally as possible when that approach yielded an accurate, clear, and natural English text. Many words and phrases were rendered literally and consistently into English, preserving essential literary and rhetorical devices, ancient metaphors, and word choices that give structure to the text and provide echoes of meaning from one passage to the next.

On the other hand, the translators rendered the message more dynamically when the literal rendering was hard to understand, was misleading, or yielded archaic or foreign wording. They clarified difficult metaphors and terms to aid in the reader's understanding. The translators first struggled with the meaning of the words and phrases in the ancient context; then they rendered the message into clear, natural English. Their goal was to be both faithful to the ancient texts and eminently readable. The result is a translation that is both exegetically accurate and idiomatically powerful.

Translation Process and Team

To produce an accurate translation of the Bible into contemporary English, the translation team needed the skills necessary to enter into the thought patterns of the ancient authors and then to render their ideas, connotations, and effects into clear, contemporary English. To begin this process, qualified biblical scholars were needed to interpret the meaning of the original text and to check it against our base English translation. In order to guard against personal and theological biases, the scholars needed to represent a diverse group of evangelicals who would employ the best exegetical tools. Then to work alongside the scholars, skilled English stylists were needed to shape the text into clear, contemporary English.

With these concerns in mind, the Bible Translation Committee recruited teams of scholars that represented a broad spectrum of denominations, theological perspectives, and backgrounds within the worldwide evangelical community. (These scholars are listed at the end of this introduction.) Each book of the Bible was assigned to three different scholars with proven expertise in the book or group of books to be reviewed. Each of these scholars made a thorough review of a base translation and submitted suggested revisions to the appropriate Senior Translator. The Senior Translator then reviewed and summarized these suggestions and proposed a first-draft revision of the base text. This draft served as the basis for several additional phases of exegetical and stylistic committee review. Then the Bible Translation Committee jointly reviewed and approved every verse of the final translation.

Throughout the translation and editing process, the Senior Translators and their scholar teams were given a chance to review the editing done by the team of stylists. This ensured that exegetical errors would not be introduced late in the process and that the entire Bible Translation Committee was happy with the final result. By choosing a team of qualified scholars and skilled stylists and by setting up a process that allowed their interaction throughout the process, the New Living Translation has been refined to preserve the essential formal elements of the original biblical texts, while also creating a clear, understandable English text.

The New Living Translation was first published in 1996. Shortly after its initial publication, the Bible Translation Committee began a process of further committee review and translation refinement. The purpose of this continued revision was to increase the level of precision without sacrificing the text's easy-to-understand quality. This second-edition text was completed in 2004, and an additional update with minor changes was subsequently introduced in 2007. This printing of the New Living Translation reflects the updated 2007 text.

Written to Be Read Aloud

It is evident in Scripture that the biblical documents were written to be read aloud, often in public worship (see Nehemiah 8; Luke 4:16-20; 1 Timothy 4:13; Revelation 1:3). It is still the case today that more people will hear the Bible read aloud in church than are likely to read it for themselves. Therefore, a new translation must communicate with clarity and power when it is read publicly. Clarity was a primary goal for the NLT translators, not only to facilitate private reading and understanding, but also to ensure that it would be excellent for public reading and make an immediate and powerful impact on any listener.

The Texts behind the New Living Translation

The Old Testament translators used the Masoretic Text of the Hebrew Bible as represented in *Biblia Hebraica Stuttgartensia* (1977), with its extensive system of textual notes; this is an update of Rudolf Kittel's *Biblia Hebraica* (Stuttgart, 1937). The translators also further compared the Dead Sea Scrolls, the Septuagint and other Greek manuscripts, the Samaritan Pentateuch, the Syriac Peshitta, the Latin Vulgate, and any other versions or manuscripts that shed light on the meaning of difficult passages.

The New Testament translators used the two standard editions of the Greek New Testament: the *Greek New Testament,* published by the United Bible Societies (UBS, fourth revised edition,

1993), and *Novum Testamentum Graece,* edited by Nestle and Aland (NA, twenty-seventh edition, 1993). These two editions, which have the same text but differ in punctuation and textual notes, represent, for the most part, the best in modern textual scholarship. However, in cases where strong textual or other scholarly evidence supported the decision, the translators sometimes chose to differ from the UBS and NA Greek texts and followed variant readings found in other ancient witnesses. Significant textual variants of this sort are always noted in the textual notes of the New Living Translation.

Translation Issues

The translators have made a conscious effort to provide a text that can be easily understood by the typical reader of modern English. To this end, we sought to use only vocabulary and language structures in common use today. We avoided using language likely to become quickly dated or that reflects only a narrow subdialect of English, with the goal of making the New Living Translation as broadly useful and timeless as possible.

But our concern for readability goes beyond the concerns of vocabulary and sentence structure. We are also concerned about historical and cultural barriers to understanding the Bible, and we have sought to translate terms shrouded in history and culture in ways that can be immediately understood. To this end:

- We have converted ancient weights and measures (for example, "ephah" [a unit of dry volume] or "cubit" [a unit of length]) to modern English (American) equivalents, since the ancient measures are not generally meaningful to today's readers. Then in the textual footnotes we offer the literal Hebrew, Aramaic, or Greek measures, along with modern metric equivalents.

- Instead of translating ancient currency values literally, we have expressed them in common terms that communicate the message. For example, in the Old Testament, "ten shekels of silver" becomes "ten pieces of silver" to convey the intended message. In the New Testament, we have often translated the "denarius" as "the normal daily wage" to facilitate understanding. Then a footnote offers: "Greek *a denarius,* the payment for a full day's wage." In general, we give a clear English rendering and then state the literal Hebrew, Aramaic, or Greek in a textual footnote.

- Since the names of Hebrew months are unknown to most contemporary readers, and since the Hebrew lunar calendar fluctuates from year to year in relation to the solar calendar used today, we have looked for clear ways to communicate the time of year the Hebrew months (such as Abib) refer to. When an expanded or interpretive rendering is given in the text, a textual note gives the literal rendering. Where it is possible to define a specific ancient date in terms of our modern calendar, we use modern dates in the text. A textual footnote then gives the literal Hebrew date and states the rationale for our rendering. For example, Ezra 6:15 pinpoints the date when the postexilic Temple was completed in Jerusalem: "the third day of the month Adar." This was during the sixth year of King Darius's reign (that is, 515 B.C.). We have translated that date as March 12, with a footnote giving the Hebrew and identifying the year as 515 B.C.

- Since ancient references to the time of day differ from our modern methods of denoting time, we have used renderings that are instantly understandable to the modern reader. Accordingly, we have rendered specific times of day by using approximate equivalents in terms of our common "o'clock" system. On occasion, translations such as "at dawn the next morning" or "as the sun was setting" have been used when the biblical reference is more general.

- When the meaning of a proper name (or a wordplay inherent in a proper name) is relevant to the message of the text, its meaning is often illuminated with a textual footnote. For example, in Exodus 2:10 the text reads: "The princess named him Moses, for she explained, 'I lifted him out of the water.'" The accompanying footnote reads: "*Moses* sounds like a Hebrew term that means 'to lift out.'"

Sometimes, when the actual meaning of a name is clear, that meaning is included in parentheses within the text itself. For example, the text at Genesis 16:11 reads: "You are to name him Ishmael (*which means 'God hears'*), for the LORD has heard your cry of distress." Since the original hearers and readers would have instantly understood the meaning of the name "Ishmael," we have provided modern readers with the same information so they can experience the text in a similar way.

- Many words and phrases carry a great deal of cultural meaning that was obvious to the original readers but needs explanation in our own culture. For example, the phrase "they beat their breasts" (Luke 23:48) in ancient times meant that people were very upset, often in mourning. In our translation we chose to translate this phrase dynamically for clarity: "They went home *in deep sorrow*." Then we included a footnote with the literal Greek, which reads: "Greek *went home beating their breasts*." In other similar cases, however, we have sometimes chosen to illuminate the existing literal expression to make it immediately understandable. For example, here we might have expanded the literal Greek phrase to read: "They went home beating their breasts *in sorrow*." If we had done this, we would not have included a textual footnote, since the literal Greek clearly appears in translation.

- Metaphorical language is sometimes difficult for contemporary readers to understand, so at times we have chosen to translate or illuminate the meaning of a metaphor. For example, the ancient poet writes, "Your neck is *like* the tower of David" (Song of Songs 4:4). We have rendered it "Your neck is *as beautiful as* the tower of David" to clarify the intended positive meaning of the simile. Another example comes in Ecclesiastes 12:3, which can be literally rendered: "Remember him . . . when the grinding women cease because they are few, and the women who look through the windows see dimly." We have rendered it: "Remember him before your teeth—your few remaining servants—stop grinding; and before your eyes—the women looking through the windows—see dimly." We clarified such metaphors only when we believed a typical reader might be confused by the literal text.

- When the content of the original language text is poetic in character, we have rendered it in English poetic form. We sought to break lines in ways that clarify and highlight the relationships between phrases of the text. Hebrew poetry often uses parallelism, a literary form where a second phrase (or in some instances a third or fourth) echoes the initial phrase in some way. In Hebrew parallelism, the subsequent parallel phrases continue, while also furthering and sharpening, the thought expressed in the initial line or phrase. Whenever possible, we sought to represent these parallel phrases in natural poetic English.

- The Greek term *hoi Ioudaioi* is literally translated "the Jews" in many English translations. In the Gospel of John, however, this term doesn't always refer to the Jewish people generally. In some contexts, it refers more particularly to the Jewish religious leaders. We have attempted to capture the meaning in these different contexts by using terms such as "the people" (with a footnote: Greek *the Jewish people*) or "the religious leaders," where appropriate.

- One challenge we faced was how to translate accurately the ancient biblical text that was originally written in a context where male-oriented terms were used to refer to humanity generally. We needed to respect the nature of the ancient context while also trying to make the translation clear to a modern audience that tends to read male-oriented language as applying only to males. Often the original text, though using masculine nouns and pronouns, clearly intends that the message be applied to both men and women. A typical example is found in the New Testament letters, where the believers are called "brothers" (*adelphoi*). Yet it is clear from the content of these letters that they were addressed to all the believers—

male and female. Thus, we have usually translated this Greek word as "brothers and sisters" in order to represent the historical situation more accurately.

We have also been sensitive to passages where the text applies generally to human beings or to the human condition. In some instances we have used plural pronouns (they, them) in place of the masculine singular (he, him). For example, a traditional rendering of Proverbs 22:6 is: "Train up a child in the way he should go, and when he is old he will not turn from it." We have rendered it: "Direct your children onto the right path, and when they are older, they will not leave it." At times, we have also replaced third person pronouns with the second person to ensure clarity. A traditional rendering of Proverbs 26:27 is: "He who digs a pit will fall into it, and he who rolls a stone, it will come back on him." We have rendered it: "If you set a trap for others, you will get caught in it yourself. If you roll a boulder down on others, it will crush you instead."

We should emphasize, however, that all masculine nouns and pronouns used to represent God (for example, "Father") have been maintained without exception. All decisions of this kind have been driven by the concern to reflect accurately the intended meaning of the original texts of Scripture.

Lexical Consistency in Terminology

For the sake of clarity, we have translated certain original-language terms consistently, especially within synoptic passages and for commonly repeated rhetorical phrases, and within certain word categories such as divine names and non-theological technical terminology (e.g., liturgical, legal, cultural, zoological, and botanical terms). For theological terms, we have allowed a greater semantic range of acceptable English words or phrases for a single Hebrew or Greek word. We have avoided some theological terms that are not readily understood by many modern readers. For example, we avoided using words such as "justification" and "sanctification," which are carryovers from Latin translations. In place of these words, we have provided renderings such as "made right with God" and "made holy."

The Spelling of Proper Names

Many individuals in the Bible, especially the Old Testament, are known by more than one name (e.g., Uzziah/Azariah). For the sake of clarity, we have tried to use a single spelling for any one individual, footnoting the literal spelling whenever we differ from it. This is especially helpful in delineating the kings of Israel and Judah. King Joash/Jehoash of Israel has been consistently called Jehoash, while King Joash/Jehoash of Judah is called Joash. A similar distinction has been used to distinguish between Joram/Jehoram of Israel and Joram/Jehoram of Judah. All such decisions were made with the goal of clarifying the text for the reader. When the ancient biblical writers clearly had a theological purpose in their choice of a variant name (e.g., Esh-baal/Ishbosheth), the different names have been maintained with an explanatory footnote.

For the names Jacob and Israel, which are used interchangeably for both the individual patriarch and the nation, we generally render it "Israel" when it refers to the nation and "Jacob" when it refers to the individual. When our rendering of the name differs from the underlying Hebrew text, we provide a textual footnote, which includes this explanation: "The names 'Jacob' and 'Israel' are often interchanged throughout the Old Testament, referring sometimes to the individual patriarch and sometimes to the nation."

The Rendering of Divine Names

In the Old Testament, all appearances of 'el, 'elohim, or 'eloah have been translated "God," except where the context demands the translation "god(s)." We have generally rendered the tetragrammaton (YHWH) consistently as "the Lord," utilizing a form with small capitals that is common among English translations. This will distinguish it from the name *'adonai,* which we render "Lord." When *'adonai* and *YHWH* appear together, we have rendered it "Sovereign LORD." When *'elohim* and *YHWH* appear together, we have rendered it "LORD God." When *YH* (the short form of *YHWH*) and *YHWH* appear together, we have rendered it "LORD GOD." When *YHWH* appears with the term *tseba'oth,* we have rendered it "LORD of Heaven's Armies" to translate the meaning of the name. In a few cases, we have utilized the transliteration, *Yahweh,* when the personal character of the name is being invoked in contrast to another divine name or the name of some other god (for example, see Exodus 3:15; 6:2-3).

In the Gospels and Acts, the Greek word *christos* has been translated as "Messiah" when the context assumes a Jewish audience. When a Gentile audience can be assumed (which is consistently the case for the Epistles and Revelation), *christos* has been translated as "Christ." The Greek word *kurios* is consistently translated "Lord," except that it is translated "LORD" wherever the New Testament text explicitly quotes from the Old Testament, and the text there has it in small capitals.

Textual Footnotes

The New Living Translation provides several kinds of textual footnotes, all designated in the text with an asterisk:

- When for the sake of clarity the NLT renders a difficult or potentially confusing phrase dynamically, we generally give the literal rendering in a textual footnote. This allows the reader to see the literal source of our dynamic rendering and how our translation relates to other more literal translations. These notes are prefaced with "Hebrew," "Aramaic," or "Greek," identifying the language of the underlying source text. For example, in Acts 2:42 we translated the literal "breaking of bread" (from the Greek) as "the Lord's Supper" to clarify that this verse refers to the ceremonial practice of the church rather than just an ordinary meal. Then we attached a footnote to "the Lord's Supper," which reads: "Greek *the breaking of bread.*"

- Textual footnotes are also used to show alternative renderings, prefaced with the word "Or." These normally occur for passages where an aspect of the meaning is debated. On occasion, we also provide notes on words or phrases that represent a departure from long-standing tradition. These notes are prefaced with "Traditionally rendered." For example, the footnote to the translation "serious skin disease" at Leviticus 13:2 says: "Traditionally rendered *leprosy.* The Hebrew word used throughout this passage is used to describe various skin diseases."

- When our translators follow a textual variant that differs significantly from our standard Hebrew or Greek texts (listed earlier), we document that difference with a footnote. We also footnote cases when the NLT excludes a passage that is included in the Greek text known as the *Textus Receptus* (and familiar to readers through its translation in the King James Version). In such cases, we offer a translation of the excluded text in a footnote, even though it is generally recognized as a later addition to the Greek text and not part of the original Greek New Testament.

- All Old Testament passages that are quoted in the New Testament are identified by a textual footnote at the New Testament location. When the New Testament clearly quotes from the Greek translation of the Old Testament, and when it differs significantly in wording from the Hebrew text, we also place a textual footnote at the Old Testament location. This note includes a rendering of the Greek version, along with a cross-reference to the New Testament passage(s) where it is cited (for example, see notes on Psalms 8:2; 53:3; Proverbs 3:12).

- Some textual footnotes provide cultural and historical information on places, things, and people in the Bible that are probably obscure to modern readers. Such notes should aid the introduction to the New Living Translation

reader in understanding the message of the text. For example, in Acts 12:1, "King Herod" is named in this translation as "King Herod Agrippa" and is identified in a footnote as being "the nephew of Herod Antipas and a grandson of Herod the Great."

- When the meaning of a proper name (or a wordplay inherent in a proper name) is relevant to the meaning of the text, it is either illuminated with a textual footnote or included within parentheses in the text itself. For example, the footnote concerning the name "Eve" at Genesis 3:20 reads: "*Eve* sounds like a Hebrew term that means 'to give life.'" This wordplay in the Hebrew illuminates the meaning of the text, which goes on to say that Eve "would be the mother of all who live."

Cross-References

There are a number of different cross-referencing tools that appear in New Living Translation Bibles, and each offers a different level of help. All straight-text Bibles have the standard set of textual footnotes that include cross-references connecting New Testament texts to their related Old Testament sources. (See more on this above.)

Many NLT Bibles include an additional concise cross-reference system that places key cross-references at the ends of paragraphs, linking them to the associated verse or verses with a cross symbol within each paragraph. This space-efficient system, while not being obtrusive, offers many important key connections.

Larger study editions include a full-column cross-reference system, which allows space for a more comprehensive listing of cross-references. In this larger system, symbols differentiate between various kinds of cross-references. The parallel marker (///) designates a cross-referenced passage that is parallel in nature to the passage at hand. The asterisk (*) designates a cross-reference whose connection involves a direct quote from the other testament. Standard cross-references in this system appear unmarked.

In some study editions, we utilize an expanded full-column cross-reference system that has been enhanced by adding a system of Hebrew and Greek word studies. This tool, which takes 100 of the most significant Hebrew words in the Old Testament and 100 Greek words from the New Testament, creates a chain reference which points to key instances of these words so they can be studied in context. In the cross-reference system, each word is attached to a modified *Strong's* number, which points to a helpful key-word glossary at the back of the Bible.

As we submit this translation for publication, we recognize that any translation of the Scriptures is subject to limitations and imperfections. Anyone who has attempted to communicate the richness of God's Word into another language will realize it is impossible to make a perfect translation. Recognizing these limitations, we sought God's guidance and wisdom throughout this project. Now we pray that he will accept our efforts and use this translation for the benefit of the church and of all people.

We pray that the New Living Translation will overcome some of the barriers of history, culture, and language that have kept people from reading and understanding God's Word. We hope that readers unfamiliar with the Bible will find the words clear and easy to understand and that readers well versed in the Scriptures will gain a fresh perspective. We pray that readers will gain insight and wisdom for living, but most of all that they will meet the God of the Bible and be forever changed by knowing him.

The Bible Translation Committee

October 2007

BIBLE TRANSLATION TEAM
HOLY BIBLE,
NEW LIVING TRANSLATION

PENTATEUCH
Daniel I. Block, Senior Translator
Wheaton College

GENESIS
Allen Ross, *Beeson Divinity School, Samford University*
Gordon Wenham, *Trinity Theological College, Bristol*

EXODUS
Robert Bergen, *Hannibal-LaGrange College*
Daniel I. Block, *Wheaton College*
Eugene Carpenter, *Bethel College, Mishawaka, Indiana*

LEVITICUS
David Baker, *Ashland Theological Seminary*
Victor Hamilton, *Asbury College*
Kenneth Mathews, *Beeson Divinity School, Samford University*

NUMBERS
Dale A. Brueggemann, *Assemblies of God Division of Foreign Missions*
R. K. Harrison (deceased), *Wycliffe College*
Paul R. House, *Beeson Divinity School, Samford University*
Gerald L. Mattingly, *Johnson Bible College*

DEUTERONOMY
J. Gordon McConville, *University of Gloucester*
Eugene H. Merrill, *Dallas Theological Seminary*
John A. Thompson (deceased), *University of Melbourne*

HISTORICAL BOOKS
Barry J. Beitzel, Senior Translator
Trinity Evangelical Divinity School

JOSHUA, JUDGES
Carl E. Armerding, *Schloss Mittersill Study Centre*
Barry J. Beitzel, *Trinity Evangelical Divinity School*
Lawson Stone, *Asbury Theological Seminary*

1 & 2 SAMUEL
Robert Gordon, *Cambridge University*
V. Philips Long, *Regent College*
J. Robert Vannoy, *Biblical Theological Seminary*

1 & 2 KINGS
Bill T. Arnold, *Asbury Theological Seminary*
William H. Barnes, *North Central University*
Frederic W. Bush, *Fuller Theological Seminary*

1 & 2 CHRONICLES
Raymond B. Dillard (deceased), *Westminster Theological Seminary*
David A. Dorsey, *Evangelical School of Theology*
Terry Eves, *Erskine College*

RUTH, EZRA—ESTHER
William C. Williams, *Vanguard University*
H. G. M. Williamson, *Oxford University*

WISDOM BOOKS
Tremper Longman III, Senior Translator
Westmont College

JOB
August Konkel, *Providence Theological Seminary*
Tremper Longman III, *Westmont College*
Al Wolters, *Redeemer College*

PSALMS 1–75
Mark D. Futato, *Reformed Theological Seminary*
Douglas Green, *Westminster Theological Seminary*
Richard Pratt, *Reformed Theological Seminary*

PSALMS 76–150
David M. Howard Jr., *Bethel Theological Seminary*
Raymond C. Ortlund Jr., *Immanuel Church, Nashville, Tennessee*
Willem VanGemeren, *Trinity Evangelical Divinity School*

PROVERBS
Ted Hildebrandt, *Gordon College*
Richard Schultz, *Wheaton College*
Raymond C. Van Leeuwen, *Eastern College*

ECCLESIASTES, SONG OF SONGS
Daniel C. Fredericks, *Belhaven College*
David Hubbard (deceased), *Fuller Theological Seminary*
Tremper Longman III, *Westmont College*

PROPHETS
John N. Oswalt, Senior Translator
Wesley Biblical Seminary

ISAIAH
John N. Oswalt, *Wesley Biblical Seminary*
Gary Smith, *Union University*
John Walton, *Wheaton College*

JEREMIAH, LAMENTATIONS
G. Herbert Livingston, *Asbury Theological Seminary*
Elmer A. Martens, *Mennonite Brethren Biblical Seminary*

EZEKIEL
Daniel I. Block, *Wheaton College*
David H. Engelhard, *Calvin Theological Seminary*
David Thompson, *Asbury Theological Seminary*

DANIEL, HAGGAI—MALACHI
Joyce Baldwin Caine (deceased), *Trinity Theological College, Bristol*

Douglas Gropp, *Catholic University of America*
Roy Hayden, *Oral Roberts School of Theology*
Andrew Hill, *Wheaton College*
Tremper Longman III, *Westmont College*

HOSEA—ZEPHANIAH

Joseph Coleson, *Nazarene Theological Seminary*
Roy Hayden, *Oral Roberts School of Theology*
Andrew Hill, *Wheaton College*
Richard Patterson, *Liberty University*

GOSPELS AND ACTS

Grant R. Osborne, Senior Translator
Trinity Evangelical Divinity School

MATTHEW

Craig Blomberg, *Denver Seminary*
Donald A. Hagner, *Fuller Theological Seminary*
David Turner, *Grand Rapids Baptist Seminary*

MARK

Robert Guelich (deceased), *Fuller Theological Seminary*
George Guthrie, *Union University*
Grant R. Osborne, *Trinity Evangelical Divinity School*

LUKE

Darrell Bock, *Dallas Theological Seminary*
Scot McKnight, *North Park University*
Robert Stein, *The Southern Baptist Theological Seminary*

JOHN

Gary M. Burge, *Wheaton College*
Philip W. Comfort, *Coastal Carolina University*
Marianne Meye Thompson, *Fuller Theological Seminary*

ACTS

D. A. Carson, *Trinity Evangelical Divinity School*
William J. Larkin, *Columbia International University*
Roger Mohrlang, *Whitworth University*

LETTERS AND REVELATION

Norman R. Ericson, Senior Translator
Wheaton College

ROMANS, GALATIANS

Gerald Borchert, *Northern Baptist Theological Seminary*
Douglas J. Moo, *Wheaton College*
Thomas R. Schreiner, *The Southern Baptist Theological Seminary*

1 & 2 CORINTHIANS

Joseph Alexanian, *Trinity International University*
Linda Belleville, *Bethel College, Mishawaka, Indiana*
Douglas A. Oss, *Central Bible College*
Robert Sloan, *Houston Baptist University*

EPHESIANS—PHILEMON

Harold W. Hoehner (deceased), *Dallas Theological Seminary*
Moises Silva, *Gordon-Conwell Theological Seminary*
Klyne Snodgrass, *North Park Theological Seminary*

HEBREWS, JAMES, 1 & 2 PETER, JUDE

Peter Davids, *St. Stephen's University*
Norman R. Ericson, *Wheaton College*
William Lane (deceased), *Seattle Pacific University*
J. Ramsey Michaels, *S. W. Missouri State University*

1-3 JOHN, REVELATION

Greg Beale, *Westminster Theological Seminary*
Robert Mounce, *Whitworth University*
M. Robert Mulholland Jr., *Asbury Theological Seminary*

SPECIAL REVIEWERS

F. F. Bruce (deceased), *University of Manchester*
Kenneth N. Taylor (deceased), *Translator,* The Living Bible

COORDINATING TEAM

Mark D. Taylor, *Director and Chief Stylist*
Ronald A. Beers, *Executive Director and Stylist*
Mark R. Norton, *Managing Editor and O.T. Coordinating Editor*
Philip W. Comfort, *N.T. Coordinating Editor*
Daniel W. Taylor, *Bethel University, Senior Stylist*

Transforming Everyday Matters

into a
Life That Matters Every Day

Today's Christian woman is so busy handling the challenges of day-to-day life that it's easy to think of spending time with the Bible as yet another "should." Just the thought of it can be exhausting. But we know you want to spend time in the Word. We have good news for you: God gave us his Word to help make our lives *fuller*—not harder! He gives meaning to our lives, purpose to everything we do, and energy to thrive. He gives rest and reinvigoration, satisfaction, joy, and enjoyment. He wants our relationships to feed us, not drain us.

So we were excited when Christianity Today launched Kyria.com as a ministry to help women go deeper in their faith, making a difference in their own lives and the lives of others. And the best help we could offer was to focus on an aspect of the Christian walk that we had discovered many years before: spiritual disciplines that have been part of the Christian experience for centuries.

Spiritual disciplines may sound daunting. But in fact they are practices that allow us to focus and refocus our thoughts and priorities on discovering the heart of God, pursuing his heart with energy and excitement. We practice these disciplines in order for the Holy Spirit to work through us, granting us power and strength to do those things we cannot possibly do on our own.

Through the disciplines we also discover that God longs for us to be in intimate relationship with him, to "hang out" and revel in his love for us.

Spiritual practices help us shut out distractions (and still get everything done) and help us to dwell in God's presence and be aware of him in and with us every moment. In his book *Muscular Faith*, Ben Patterson likens the disciplines to spreading a sail. "They position you to receive what God is only too ready to give: himself and all that he is."

We heard of a woman who hated ironing in the days when that chore took up hours of every day. After years of feeling like her time was being eaten up by "shoulds" and depriving her of meaningful activities, she had a simple realization that changed her life. That day she began to use her "ironing time" as a time of prayer and fellowship with God. As she ironed her husband's shirts, she prayed for him. Ironing her daughter's dresses became a time to bathe her child in prayer. Every item on the ironing board became an opportunity for fellowship with God. The chore that had been so tedious became a precious part of her routine that nourished her.

The purpose of *Everyday Matters Bible for Women* is to help you use spiritual disciplines to make your everyday life fuller, richer and deeper. We have chosen to focus on twenty-four disciplines that are especially pertinent to this theme.

The Spiritual Disciplines

We've chosen practices that introduce the essentials of Christian spiritual formation. To help you navigate through the text, each of the twenty-four spiritual disciplines or practices is tagged with its own distinctive icon, shown here in this alphabetical summary.

Acceptance. We may be wives, mothers, friends, physicians, or teachers. Those are all roles we play. But they are not who we are at our core. At our core, we are children of God, created in his image, called and designed with special gifts, loved intensely and unconditionally "just because." God isn't as concerned with what we do as much as with who we are. Accepting that understanding is the first step to the freedom of living out God's call on our lives.

Bible Study and Meditation. We have amazing power and strength at our fingertips through understanding and applying God's Word to our lives. This discipline looks at the prayerful deliberation of and digging in to the Scriptures in more than just a cursory read.

Celebration. The writer of Hebrews tells us that Christ was anointed with the oil of joy. One of the ways Jesus drew others to him was his unreserved ability to celebrate, play, and rejoice in all things—including finding deep abiding joy in the moments of sorrow. Through this discipline, we too learn to live with unreserved delight and joy, to play, and to have a childlike exuberance and enjoyment of life, our world, and God's goodness.

Community. God created us to live out our faith within the context of the body of Christ. The Christian life is not meant to be journeyed alone. So through this discipline we learn to engage other believers through the common practices of worship, service, prayer, celebration, confession, and other activities with the shared goal of knowing and experiencing the triune God in a fuller, more complete way.

Confession. Repentance does not stop at the prayer of salvation; it is a continual honing and shaping of our character. Confession is bringing to light those things that keep us from experiencing the fullness of our relationship with God. We also practice repentence toward God and others by confessing our weaknesses and failures in order to receive forgiveness, mercy, restoration, and healing.

Contemplation. In a rush, rush world, our minds can become so filled with clutter that we lose the ability to focus on the eternal. The practice of contemplation allows us to have deliberate, prayerful reflection on God, his will, his world, and his works.

Faith. While God blesses us with a measure of faith, we must stretch and use it. The spiritual practice of growing our faith includes moving beyond and nurturing the expectations that God plants within us; it is about actively pursuing hope and a willingness to believe.

Fasting. Many of us think about fasting in terms of giving up food every once in a while when we're in a crisis. Yet biblical characters and our church mothers and fathers discovered a great power by fasting regularly. Here we look at fasting in terms of voluntarily denying or abstaining from a need, want, or desire (food, television, the Internet, etc.) to focus more clearly and intensely on connecting with God in a deeper, more profound way.

Forgiveness. Jesus was clear with his followers when he said if we want to be forgiven, we must forgive. Too often we focus on the pain of forgiving those who have hurt us. Yet that is only part of this practice. In this discipline we look at voluntarily receiving absolution from God, others, and ourselves, and releasing the same to others *and* ourselves.

Gratitude. How great is God's love and goodness toward us! As we realize more and more just who God is and what he thinks of us, his children, our hearts overflow with gratitude. This spiritual practice is about being more intentional in our thanksgiving than just a simple, "Thanks, God." It is about reflecting and offering a *deep* thankfulness for God's goodness and workings in our lives. Gratitude often reaps celebration.

Hospitality. Throughout the Bible, God commands us over and over to take notice of and care for those around us. More than just opening our homes to our friends or Bible study group for coffee, hospitality is a conscientious pursuit to welcome strangers and friends into our homes *and lives* and to make them feel loved and accepted.

Justice. God's heart is about seeking justice for those who have been wronged. As followers, then, our hearts also break, prompting us to become intentional about seeking and pursuing advocacy on behalf of those who have been mistreated.

Mentoring. We all have experiences that have helped us grow and given us wisdom. But their benefits are diminished if we do not share what we have learned. And how much insight we can gain as we seek wisdom from others who have traveled the road before us. From Naomi and Ruth to Mary and Elizabeth, we see models of mentoring throughout the Bible. In this practice we discover the importance of receiving and giving biblical, godly wisdom and insight in order to strengthen the body of Christ.

Outreach. Jesus told us to go into the world and share the gospel. So through this spiritual practice we model and testify to those outside the Christian faith, to introduce them to Jesus and the kingdom of God.

Prayer. It's easy to think that prayer is a mode of communication in which we talk, God listens, and then does what we desire! Prayer is much deeper and complex than that. It is a two-way connection and interaction between God and us. Prayer's multifaceted forms range from simple dialogue to deep intercession on behalf of others. It pursues the understanding of where God is working and how we can come alongside him in his work.

Reconciliation. Beyond confession and forgiveness, reconciliation is about pursuing peace on behalf of God's kingdom. It includes reconciling ourselves, others within the body of Christ, and those outside the body—in particular racial, ethnic, gender, and cultural reconnection. Reconciliation allows us to experience the unity that Jesus prayed about when he asked the Father to make his disciples one; it also refers to the reconciliation we have with God.

Sabbath and Rest. Even Jesus knew the importance of resting from activity and service. Some downtime can refresh us daily, allowing time for spiritual rejuvenation. Here we also practice the freedom of the fourth commandment, in which we observe a day that includes no work, a focus on God, and enjoying the want-tos.

Service. We honor God and others by making a difference in someone's life through thoughtful and loving help, advocacy, and compassion. Service is going beyond oneself to act for the good of others and to promote the work and heart of God in our communities and around the world.

Silence. Our world and lives are so noisy! In fact the noisier they are, the more difficult it is to hear the soft whisper of the Holy Spirit speaking into our lives. So we practice periods of quiet, in which we open ourselves to hearing what God is saying to us. When we close our minds to the distractions and sounds of life we can better hear God.

Simplicity. A traditional Shaker hymn says, "'Tis a gift to be simple, 'tis a gift to be free." Living out the spiritual practice of simplicity allows us to let go of anything that clutters our lives, minds, and souls, to pursue a single-minded focus on God. It includes pursuing modesty, humility, and unpretentiousness, and releasing our desire for status, comfort, and pride.

Solitude. While community is important and has a place, we also need to have solitary time with the Creator and Lover of our souls. Solitude is also closely connected to silence. It is removing oneself from all distractions or interactions with other people, to focus solely on God.

Stewardship. Proper management is one of the first responsibilities God called us to. In the Garden of Eden, God gave Adam and Eve control of the earth and everything in it, to be good stewards. Through this practice we take care of the things God has given us to manage—including time, money, creation, and relationships—in a way that honors him and his creation.

Submission. In our me-first culture it is difficult to move against that system and put others' needs before our own wants. Yet we follow a Savior who said, "Not my will, but yours, God." The daily act of submission means we continually refine an attitude of "yes, Lord," in our relationship with him and with others. We sacrifice our need to be in control and allow ourselves to be placed under the wisdom of those who will mentor and challenge us and nurture our growth.

Worship. One of the highest offerings we can give is pure worship. Through this practice we give ourselves fully over to the adoration of the greatness and glory of almighty God.

Each spiritual discipline is not mutually exclusive to the others, and they often overlap. For instance, stewardship and simplicity go hand in hand; celebration and gratitude have similarities; as do contemplation and prayer, silence and solitude. We've taken that into account and have cross-referenced them in the index. You'll quickly see how connected the disciplines are!

So Why Do We Practice the Spiritual Disciplines?

Because they help take us to a level of spiritual maturity that we can get to no other way. Pursuing these practices makes us more acutely aware of God's hand working behind the scenes in every aspect of our lives and in the world. These practices build our faith, make us stronger citizens of earth and heaven, and give us spiritual depth and wisdom.

We're so excited for you and the things you are going to learn and experience through these disciplines. They're truly life changing! From experience we can say that the initial conscious effort of practicing the spiritual disciplines can soon become habitual—an everyday matter, a lifelong experience.

As you put these disciplines into practice, may you be filled with the intense knowledge of God's presence. May you be overwhelmed by how much God has to say to you. May you never desire to live again without that knowledge. May you join all the saints and all creation as they proclaim, "Holy, holy, holy is the Lord God, the Almighty—the one who always was, who is, and who is still to come" (Revelation 4:8).

The editors,
Everyday Matters Bible for Women

How to Use This Bible

This Bible is specially designed for Christian women who sense that every day matters—not solely in terms of eternity, but also in terms of the here and now. They want to have a rich and deep relationship with Christ. They want to help expand the influence of his kingdom—not in their own strength but in strength that comes in and through the joy of the Lord. They want to serve him, but only by means that glorify him and along paths where he leads them personally. They know that they matter to God and that every day matters to them.

With these women in mind, our editorial team has carefully selected more than three hundred instructional and inspirational pieces to complement the biblical text of the New Living Translation. The supplementary articles, written by thoughtful contemporary authors, can help you apply the Word of God to your Christian walk. By sharing their insights—related to twenty-four spiritual disciplines or practices—these writers and the saints they cite become like companions, showing you that you are not alone on your journey.

To help you navigate through the text, each of the twenty-four spiritual disciplines or practices is tagged with its own distinctive icon. Each piece is placed immediately after a targeted Bible passage.

Four types of features appear throughout the biblical text, each providing insights and reflections regarding a particular spiritual discipline:

Everyday Matters. These two-page articles introduce major themes relevant to each spiritual discipline or focus on an essential part of understanding and practicing the discipline. Each spiritual discipline showcases two of these feature-length articles.

Everyday Profiles. We have included profiles of twenty-five women or groups of women who practiced or highlighted a particular discipline. It is easy to forget that the women in the Bible are not just story characters, but wives, mothers, warriors, and businesswomen who lived and experienced many of the same feelings, decisions, and challenges that we do today.

Everyday Q&A's. Each question-and-answer feature (two per discipline) delves into a puzzling aspect of the spiritual practice or offers some practical help in how to incorporate the discipline into your daily life.

Everyday Reflections. These "shorts," five to ten per discipline, touch on varied aspects of the practices. This feature highlights one of our intents: to showcase many writers and allow their voices to illustrate the possibilities for personalizing and applying God's Word to your own situation.

Practice by Practice

For readers interested in an in-depth look at the spiritual disciplines, we commend the comprehensive index that starts on page 1571.

The index list of twenty-four disciplines is organized alphabetically. This makes selections easy to find, but it does not suggest the order in which disciplines should be studied. Having said that, we see value in starting with the first alphabetical entry (Acceptance—of ourselves and our calling) and ending with the last (Worship—of our Lord). But that's as far as we take the alphabetical recommendation. You might want to intermingle the quiet and prayerful disciplines with those that are more active.

Discipline by discipline, or practice by practice, the four types of features are listed in our recommended order of reading: first the major articles (Everyday Matters), then the Everyday

Profiles of biblical women, followed by the Everyday Q&A's. The short Everyday Reflections could be read toward the end of your study of the discipline, or they could be interspersed among the previously mentioned features. Within each of the four feature categories, the individual articles are presented in biblical order, Genesis to Revelation. This schema is used for ease of reference, not necessarily as a recommended order or line-up for your reading or study.

Any articles listed in italics in the index are cross-referenced from other disciplines, because they are relevant to two practices.

On page 1587, you can find a list of all the contributors and brief biographies, cross-referenced to their articles.

You can study the disciplines at any pace, from one reading selection per day or session (again, we've selected more than three hundred!) to a more quickly paced discipline per day. This is your Bible; use it as you see fit.

Bible Study Basics

Whether you start in Genesis and read to Revelation or turn to the index and work through one discipline at a time, the best way to approach any Bible reading or topical study is first to pray. Ask God to give you clarity and discernment to hear only his message to you; ask God to clear your mind from distractions and to work in and through you as he chooses.

Then read the supplementary pieces as well as the biblical text cited in their headings and silently wait for God to speak through the writing. After you read a piece, ask God, What do you want to say to me through what I've read? What do you want me to learn? What do you want me to dwell on or do?

Sometimes you may feel that he's being silent. That's okay. Maybe he wants you to read and simply take it in; maybe he wants you to read and chew on it a few more times; maybe he wants you to soak it up, because he will bring it to mind later with a clear message for you.

Also try to discuss your reading and discoveries with other people—spiritual friends who can help you uncover or delight in God's Word and appreciate the value of practicing the spiritual disciplines. Sharing with others is a great way to encourage and build one another up. As Proverbs 27:17 notes, "As iron sharpens iron, so a friend sharpens a friend."

Other Options

Here are some suggestions for other ways to use this Bible:

- Read one of the pieces within a particular spiritual practice that you want to explore. Read the cited scriptural passage. In a quiet moment at day's end, consider how that passage affected you and your day's activities and priorities. Repeat this pattern daily, reading through the supplementary pieces of one spiritual practice, such as prayer, fasting, or justice, and then another.

- Choose one book (or more, if very short) of the Bible to read through in a week. Start with the introductory page, including the book's outline, to understand the overall themes and cultural context. Then divide the chapters to cover the entire week. How many, and which, spiritual practices are interwoven in the passages? Highlight the passages, biblical or supplementary, that speak to you. At the end of the week, go back through the book and read only the highlighted verses and paragraphs. Make those your prayer that God will use them to grow you spiritually.

- Choose a book of the Bible and do not read any of the supplementary material. As you read that book, note any evident spiritual practices (review the list of twenty-four). Consider their reasons and roles: For what reasons were they practiced by the biblical characters? And what purpose did they effect? What did the characters discover about themselves and God? Next go back and read the supplementary pieces placed alongside the biblical text. Which highlighted disciplines did you identify the first time through the book? Reflect on how you can practice those disciplines more fervently.

- For specific disciplines of interest, read through the Additional Scriptures of Note in the index that begins on page 1571. Note what the men and women of the Bible learned, or what they teach you, about spiritual growth. Journal any insights so you can refer back to them later. Note also the For Further Reading list on page 1600 for additional resources, many, not all, by the authors featured in these pages.

- Spend a longer amount of time (a month or a year) and work through the Bible or a particular spiritual practice with another person or a small group. For more ideas on studying together as a group, see "How to Use This Bible in a Small Group Study," on page 1569.

Living out the disciplines can be difficult (thus the name!), but don't grow discouraged. Keep focused and coming back to the Bible and its message, and God will bless, stretch, and grow you as he desires.

The
Old
Testament

Introduction to
Genesis

Background

Genesis is a Greek word that means "source," "origin," or "beginning." It comes from the first phrase of 1:1: "In the beginning" (*Bereshith* in Hebrew). Genesis is the book of beginnings, from the creation of the universe through the patriarchal era of Abraham, Isaac, and Jacob and his sons, the founding fathers of the people of Israel.

Genesis also is the first book of the Pentateuch (the Law), the five books of Moses. Genesis, Exodus, Leviticus, and Numbers are a continuous narrative, reviewed by the Book of Deuteronomy. Moses' authorship is supported by the Talmud and New Testament Scriptures (see Matthew 19:8; Mark 12:26; Luke 16:31; John 5:46–47).

Message

The Book of Genesis provides a reason for the rest of the Bible: God's plan to rescue the people he created after the fall of Adam and Eve (3:1–24). Because sin could not remain in the presence of a holy God, Adam and Eve and their descendants faced eternal separation from their Creator.

The first hint of God's plan to save people from sin by sending a Savior comes in 3:15, where God speaks to the Serpent: "And I will cause hostility between you and the woman, and between your offspring and her offspring. He will strike your head, and you will strike his heel." Out of the nations of people who scatter after the Tower of Babel (11:1–9), God chooses one family—that of Abraham, Isaac, and Jacob, whose name becomes Israel—through which his plan of salvation would come to fruition.

Time

While the narrative of Genesis extends from the beginning of the world to the death of Joseph (circa 1805 B.C.), the Book of Genesis was probably written between 1445 and 1406 B.C., while the people of Israel were camped in the wilderness.

Outline

Genesis

1 The Account of Creation

In the beginning God created the heavens and the earth.* ²The earth was formless and empty, and darkness covered the deep waters. And the Spirit of God was hovering over the surface of the waters.

³Then God said, "Let there be light," and there was light. ⁴And God saw that the light was good. Then he separated the light from the darkness. ⁵God called the light "day" and the darkness "night."

And evening passed and morning came, marking the first day.

⁶Then God said, "Let there be a space between the waters, to separate the waters of the heavens from the waters of the earth." ⁷And that is what happened. God made this space to separate the waters of the earth from the waters of the heavens. ⁸God called the space "sky."

And evening passed and morning came, marking the second day.

⁹Then God said, "Let the waters beneath the sky flow together into one place, so dry ground may appear." And that is what happened. ¹⁰God called the dry ground "land" and the waters "seas." And God saw that it was good. ¹¹Then God said, "Let the land sprout with vegetation—every sort of seed-bearing plant, and trees that grow seed-bearing fruit. These seeds will then produce the kinds of plants and trees from which they came." And that is what happened. ¹²The land produced vegetation—all sorts of seed-bearing plants, and trees with seed-bearing fruit. Their seeds produced plants and trees of the same kind. And God saw that it was good.

¹³And evening passed and morning came, marking the third day.

¹⁴Then God said, "Let lights appear in the sky to separate the day from the night. Let them be signs to mark the seasons, days, and years. ¹⁵Let these lights in the sky shine down on the earth." And that is what happened. ¹⁶God made two great lights—the larger one to govern the day, and the smaller one to govern the night. He also made the stars. ¹⁷God set these lights in the sky to light the earth, ¹⁸to govern the day and night, and to separate the light from the darkness. And God saw that it was good.

¹⁹And evening passed and morning came, marking the fourth day.

²⁰Then God said, "Let the waters swarm with fish and other life. Let the skies be filled with birds of every kind." ²¹So God created great sea creatures and every living thing that scurries and swarms in the water, and every sort of bird—each producing offspring of the same kind. And God saw that it was good. ²²Then God blessed them, saying, "Be fruitful and multiply. Let the fish fill the seas, and let the birds multiply on the earth."

²³And evening passed and morning came, marking the fifth day.

²⁴Then God said, "Let the earth produce every sort of animal, each produc-

---

1:1 Or *In the beginning when God created the heavens and the earth, . . .* Or *When God began to create the heavens and the earth, . . .*

ing offspring of the same kind—live-stock, small animals that scurry along the ground, and wild animals." And that is what happened. ²⁵God made all sorts of wild animals, livestock, and small animals, each able to produce offspring of the same kind. And God saw that it was good.

²⁶Then God said, "Let us make human beings* in our image, to be like us. They will reign over the fish in the sea, the birds in the sky, the livestock, all the wild animals on the earth, and the small animals that scurry along the ground."

²⁷ So God created human beings* in his own image.
In the image of God he created them;
male and female he created them.

²⁸Then God blessed them and said, "Be fruitful and multiply. Fill the earth and govern it. Reign over the fish in the sea, the birds in the sky, and all the animals that scurry along the ground."

²⁹Then God said, "Look! I have given you every seed-bearing plant throughout the earth and all the fruit trees for your food. ³⁰And I have given every green plant as food for all the wild animals, the birds in the sky, and the small animals that scurry along the ground—everything that has life." And that is what happened.

³¹Then God looked over all he had made, and he saw that it was very good!
And evening passed and morning came, marking the sixth day.

2 So the creation of the heavens and the earth and everything in them was completed. ²On the seventh day God had finished his work of creation, so he rested* from all his work. ³And God blessed the seventh day and declared it holy, because it was the day when he rested from all his work of creation.

⁴This is the account of the creation of the heavens and the earth.

The Man and Woman in Eden

When the LORD God made the earth and the heavens, ⁵neither wild plants nor grains were growing on the earth. For the LORD God had not yet sent rain to water the earth, and there were no people to cultivate the soil. ⁶Instead, springs* came up from the ground and watered all the land. ⁷Then the LORD God formed the man from the dust of the ground. He breathed the breath of life into the man's nostrils, and the man became a living person.

⁸Then the LORD God planted a garden in Eden in the east, and there he placed the man he had made. ⁹The LORD God made all sorts of trees grow up from the ground—trees that were beautiful and that produced delicious fruit. In the middle of the garden he placed the tree of life and the tree of the knowledge of good and evil.

¹⁰A river flowed from the land of Eden, watering the garden and then dividing into four branches. ¹¹The first branch, called the Pishon, flowed around the entire land of Havilah, where gold is found. ¹²The gold of that land is exceptionally pure; aromatic resin and onyx stone are also found there. ¹³The second branch, called the Gihon, flowed around the entire land of Cush. ¹⁴The third branch, called the Tigris, flowed east of the land of Asshur. The fourth branch is called the Euphrates.

¹⁵The LORD God placed the man in the Garden of Eden to tend and watch over it. ¹⁶But the LORD God warned him, "You may freely eat the fruit of every tree in the garden—¹⁷except the tree of the knowledge of good and evil. If you eat its fruit, you are sure to die."

¹⁸Then the LORD God said, "It is not good for the man to be alone. I will make a helper who is just right for him." ¹⁹So the LORD God formed from the ground all the wild animals and all the birds of the sky. He brought them to the man* to see what he would call them, and the man chose a name for each one. ²⁰He gave names to all the livestock, all the birds of the sky, and all the wild animals. But still there was no helper just right for him.

1:26 Or man; Hebrew reads adam.   1:27 Or the man; Hebrew reads ha-adam.   2:2 Or ceased; also in 2:3.   2:6 Or mist.   2:19 Or Adam, and so throughout the chapter.

²¹So the LORD God caused the man to fall into a deep sleep. While the man slept, the LORD God took out one of the man's ribs* and closed up the opening. ²²Then the LORD God made a woman from the rib, and he brought her to the man.

²³"At last!" the man exclaimed.

"This one is bone from my bone,
 and flesh from my flesh!
She will be called 'woman,'
 because she was taken from 'man.'"

²⁴This explains why a man leaves his father and mother and is joined to his wife, and the two are united into one.

The True Meaning of "Helper"

Acceptance

GENESIS 2:18–22

Genesis describes God creating Eve to be a "helper" for Adam. What does that really mean?

"Helper" in Genesis 2:20 is the Hebrew word *ezer*. Historically we've narrowed the word *ezer* to mean wife and mother, to indicate that a woman's role is to take on supportive duties for her husband. But is that actually what the word means? After all, when God used that word, Adam was in Eden. He didn't have a house, laundry, or meals that needed to be prepared. So what was she helping him with?

To put this idea into biblical context, we must realize that the word *ezer* occurs twenty-one times in the Old Testament. It's used just twice for the woman. But it's used three times for nations Israel turned to for military assistance, and sixteen times to describe God as Israel's helper. In these cases, the word has a strong military connotation: as Israel looked for "help" in battle; God as *ezer* is a shield and defense, standing sentry watch over his people.

So what insight can this give us about God's purpose when he created women?

When God said it wasn't good for the man to be alone, he wasn't speaking just about marriage. Genesis 1 and 2 are passages about God's vision for humanity. God created woman to come alongside the man in this battle of life. She watches his back; he watches hers. They're in this battle together.

The calling to be an *ezer* can excite and inspire us! We're called to be warriors for God's kingdom. We're called to be representatives of God, to speak and act for him. And God's calling for us starts when we're born. It's not something you can lose, and you don't have to wait for it to begin. You are God's image-bearer! It is not possible for you to live an insignificant life.

—*Carolyn Custis James*

For more on acceptance, see reading at Genesis 2:18–3:20.

2:21 Or *took a part of the man's side.*

²⁵Now the man and his wife were both naked, but they felt no shame.

3 The Man and Woman Sin

The serpent was the shrewdest of all the wild animals the LORD God had made. One day he asked the woman, "Did God really say you must not eat the fruit from any of the trees in the garden?"

²"Of course we may eat fruit from the trees in the garden," the woman replied. ³"It's only the fruit from the tree in the middle of the garden that we are not allowed to eat. God said, 'You must not eat it or even touch it; if you do, you will die.'"

⁴"You won't die!" the serpent replied to the woman. ⁵"God knows that your eyes will be opened as soon as you eat it, and you will be like God, knowing both good and evil."

⁶The woman was convinced. She saw that the tree was beautiful and its fruit looked delicious, and she wanted the wisdom it would give her. So she took some of the fruit and ate it. Then she gave some to her husband, who was with her, and he ate it, too. ⁷At that moment their eyes were opened, and they suddenly felt shame at their nakedness. So they sewed fig leaves together to cover themselves.

⁸When the cool evening breezes were blowing, the man* and his wife heard the LORD God walking about in the garden. So they hid from the LORD God among the

Eve: The Self before Sin

Acceptance

GENESIS 2:18-3:20

For a period of time, Eve experienced something that every other woman in human history longs for: a completely whole, healthy, and thriving sense of self. The world was without sin—without the distortions of low self-esteem and broken relationships. Eve lived in a world of beauty and truth, in intimate fellowship with God.

Picture Eve walking with her head held high, in confidence and security. Not racked by doubts, not scheming for attention, not constantly cataloging her faults and failings. She was a woman created by God and in his image, and she knew that it was a "very good" thing to be just who God made her to be (Genesis 1:31). She was free, confident, and at peace. Scripture tells us that she "felt no shame" (2:25).

What would it be like to truly feel *no shame* about who we are? We can only imagine it, because from that moment when Eve first sinned, the human "self" was broken. Now we each live with the damage sin has done, daily battling feelings of low self-worth, lack of confidence, hidden shame, painful body-image issues, and so much more.

Eve's life in Eden is a compelling model for us, giving us a picture of how God *intended* for us to live. To feel free, at peace, and happy as the women God uniquely made us to be. To have confidence, delight, and joy in the bodies and minds God has given to us. To walk in constant awareness of God's faithful, loving presence. To hold our heads high. To *feel no shame*. This is the self before sin. This is the self we will one day be again when we live with God in eternity. And this is the self God desires us to strive to be during this lifetime, as we choose to reject shame, comparison-itis, and the destructive lies of low self-esteem.

—*Kelli B. Trujillo*

For more on acceptance, see reading at Genesis 39:19-23.

3:8 Or *Adam,* and so throughout the chapter.

trees. ⁹Then the LORD God called to the man, "Where are you?"

¹⁰He replied, "I heard you walking in the garden, so I hid. I was afraid because I was naked."

¹¹"Who told you that you were naked?" the LORD God asked. "Have you eaten from the tree whose fruit I commanded you not to eat?"

¹²The man replied, "It was the woman you gave me who gave me the fruit, and I ate it."

¹³Then the LORD God asked the woman, "What have you done?"

"The serpent deceived me," she replied. "That's why I ate it."

¹⁴Then the LORD God said to the serpent,

"Because you have done this, you are
   cursed
more than all animals, domestic and
   wild.
You will crawl on your belly,
   groveling in the dust as long as you
   live.
¹⁵ And I will cause hostility between you
   and the woman,
and between your offspring and her
   offspring.
He will strike* your head,
   and you will strike his heel."

¹⁶Then he said to the woman,

"I will sharpen the pain of your
   pregnancy,
and in pain you will give birth.
And you will desire to control your
   husband,
   but he will rule over you.*"

¹⁷And to the man he said,

"Since you listened to your wife and ate
   from the tree
whose fruit I commanded you not to
   eat,
the ground is cursed because of you.
All your life you will struggle to
   scratch a living from it.
¹⁸ It will grow thorns and thistles for you,
   though you will eat of its grains.

¹⁹ By the sweat of your brow
   will you have food to eat
until you return to the ground
   from which you were made.
For you were made from dust,
   and to dust you will return."

Paradise Lost: God's Judgment

²⁰Then the man—Adam—named his wife Eve, because she would be the mother of all who live.* ²¹And the LORD God made clothing from animal skins for Adam and his wife.

²²Then the LORD God said, "Look, the human beings* have become like us, knowing both good and evil. What if they reach out, take fruit from the tree of life, and eat it? Then they will live forever!" ²³So the LORD God banished them from the Garden of Eden, and he sent Adam out to cultivate the ground from which he had been made. ²⁴After sending them out, the LORD God stationed mighty cherubim to the east of the Garden of Eden. And he placed a flaming sword that flashed back and forth to guard the way to the tree of life.

4 Cain and Abel

Now Adam* had sexual relations with his wife, Eve, and she became pregnant. When she gave birth to Cain, she said, "With the LORD's help, I have produced* a man!" ²Later she gave birth to his brother and named him Abel.

When they grew up, Abel became a shepherd, while Cain cultivated the ground. ³When it was time for the harvest, Cain presented some of his crops as a gift to the LORD. ⁴Abel also brought a gift—the best of the firstborn lambs from his flock. The LORD accepted Abel and his gift, ⁵but he did not accept Cain and his gift. This made Cain very angry, and he looked dejected.

⁶"Why are you so angry?" the LORD asked Cain. "Why do you look so dejected? ⁷You will be accepted if you do what is right. But if you refuse to do what is right, then watch out! Sin is crouching at the door, eager to control you. But you must subdue it and be its master."

3:15 Or *bruise;* also in 3:15b.   **3:16** Or *And though you will have desire for your husband, / he will rule over you.*   **3:20** *Eve* sounds like a Hebrew term that means "to give life."   **3:22** Or *the man;* Hebrew reads *ha-adam.*   **4:1a** Or *the man;* also in 4:25.   **4:1b** Or *I have acquired. Cain* sounds like a Hebrew term that can mean "produce" or "acquire."

Inner Conversation
GENESIS 4:1–7

R eflection is an inner conversation—a discourse we generate with ourselves and with God. During inner conversation, our engagement with other people is suspended. Yes, there's a time to love, serve, and care for other people. But a time of inner conversation is personal and private.

We get a sense of inner conversation when, in Psalms, the writer quizzes his deeper self: "Why am I discouraged? Why is my heart so sad?" (Psalm 42:5). Or when the writer invites God's attention: "Search me, O God, and know my heart" (Psalm 139:23).

Sometimes inner conversation originates with God. We see it in the words God uses to caution Cain: "Why are you so angry? . . . Why do you look so dejected?" (Genesis 4:6). We see it in the question God asks when Elijah flees to the wilderness in fear of Jezebel: "What are you doing here, Elijah?" (1 Kings 19:9). Then he tells him to slow down, sleep, eat, drink. What follows is a fascinating inner conversation in which Elijah's inaccurate perspective on things is repaired.

Paul is probably referring to inner conversation when he speaks of his "thorn in my flesh" and his frustration with it. "Three different times I begged the Lord to take it away" (2 Corinthians 12:7–8). But God didn't.

Sometimes I've imagined Moses' conversations with God. When Moses went to the Tent of Meeting, we are told that "the LORD would speak to Moses face to face, as one speaks to a friend" (Exodus 33:11). That sounds like inner conversation to me. Although God is great and mysterious and cannot be described in human terms, here is an exceptional description of conversation between Moses and God. It dares to describe God in intimate human language. But the purpose of the writer is not to make God seem like one of us but to express the way of inner conversation in which Moses is able to recalibrate his life and focus.

—Gordon MacDonald

For more on prayer, see reading at Judges 20:26–27.

---

⁸One day Cain suggested to his brother, "Let's go out into the fields."* And while they were in the field, Cain attacked his brother, Abel, and killed him.

⁹Afterward the LORD asked Cain, "Where is your brother? Where is Abel?"

"I don't know," Cain responded. "Am I my brother's guardian?"

¹⁰But the LORD said, "What have you done? Listen! Your brother's blood cries out to me from the ground! ¹¹Now you are cursed and banished from the ground, which has swallowed your brother's blood.

¹²No longer will the ground yield good crops for you, no matter how hard you work! From now on you will be a homeless wanderer on the earth."

¹³Cain replied to the LORD, "My punishment* is too great for me to bear! ¹⁴You have banished me from the land and from your presence; you have made me a homeless wanderer. Anyone who finds me will kill me!"

¹⁵The LORD replied, "No, for I will give a sevenfold punishment to anyone who kills you." Then the LORD put a mark on Cain to

4:8 As in Samaritan Pentateuch, Greek and Syriac versions, and Latin Vulgate; Masoretic Text lacks *"Let's go out into the fields."* **4:13** Or *My sin.*

warn anyone who might try to kill him. ¹⁶So Cain left the Lord's presence and settled in the land of Nod,* east of Eden.

The Descendants of Cain

¹⁷Cain had sexual relations with his wife, and she became pregnant and gave birth to Enoch. Then Cain founded a city, which he named Enoch, after his son. ¹⁸Enoch had a son named Irad. Irad became the father of* Mehujael. Mehujael became the father of Methushael. Methushael became the father of Lamech.

¹⁹Lamech married two women. The first was named Adah, and the second was Zillah. ²⁰Adah gave birth to Jabal, who was the first of those who raise livestock and live in tents. ²¹His brother's name was Jubal, the first of all who play the harp and flute. ²²Lamech's other wife, Zillah, gave birth to a son named Tubal-cain. He became an expert in forging tools of bronze and iron. Tubal-cain had a sister named Naamah. ²³One day Lamech said to his wives,

"Adah and Zillah, hear my voice;
    listen to me, you wives of Lamech.
I have killed a man who attacked me,
    a young man who wounded me.
²⁴ If someone who kills Cain is punished
        seven times,
    then the one who kills me will be
        punished seventy-seven times!"

The Birth of Seth

²⁵Adam had sexual relations with his wife again, and she gave birth to another son. She named him Seth,* for she said, "God has granted me another son in place of Abel, whom Cain killed." ²⁶When Seth grew up, he had a son and named him Enosh. At that time people first began to worship the Lord by name.

5 The Descendants of Adam

This is the written account of the descendants of Adam. When God created human beings,* he made them to be like himself. ²He created them male and female, and he blessed them and called them "human."

³When Adam was 130 years old, he became the father of a son who was just like him—in his very image. He named his son Seth. ⁴After the birth of Seth, Adam lived another 800 years, and he had other sons and daughters. ⁵Adam lived 930 years, and then he died.

⁶When Seth was 105 years old, he became the father of* Enosh. ⁷After the birth of* Enosh, Seth lived another 807 years, and he had other sons and daughters. ⁸Seth lived 912 years, and then he died.

⁹When Enosh was 90 years old, he became the father of Kenan. ¹⁰After the birth of Kenan, Enosh lived another 815 years, and he had other sons and daughters. ¹¹Enosh lived 905 years, and then he died.

¹²When Kenan was 70 years old, he became the father of Mahalalel. ¹³After the birth of Mahalalel, Kenan lived another 840 years, and he had other sons and daughters. ¹⁴Kenan lived 910 years, and then he died.

¹⁵When Mahalalel was 65 years old, he became the father of Jared. ¹⁶After the birth of Jared, Mahalalel lived another 830 years, and he had other sons and daughters. ¹⁷Mahalalel lived 895 years, and then he died.

¹⁸When Jared was 162 years old, he became the father of Enoch. ¹⁹After the birth of Enoch, Jared lived another 800 years, and he had other sons and daughters. ²⁰Jared lived 962 years, and then he died.

²¹When Enoch was 65 years old, he became the father of Methuselah. ²²After the birth of Methuselah, Enoch lived in close fellowship with God for another 300 years, and he had other sons and daughters. ²³Enoch lived 365 years, ²⁴walking in close fellowship with God. Then one day he disappeared, because God took him.

²⁵When Methuselah was 187 years old, he became the father of Lamech. ²⁶After the birth of Lamech, Methuselah lived another 782 years, and he had other sons and daughters. ²⁷Methuselah lived 969 years, and then he died.

4:16 Nod means "wandering." 4:18 Or the ancestor of, and so throughout the verse. 4:25 Seth probably means "granted"; the name may also mean "appointed." 5:1 Or man; Hebrew reads adam; similarly in 5:2. 5:6 Or the ancestor of; also in 5:9, 12, 15, 18, 21, 25. 5:7 Or the birth of this ancestor of; also in 5:10, 13, 16, 19, 22, 26.

²⁸When Lamech was 182 years old, he became the father of a son. ²⁹Lamech named his son Noah, for he said, "May he bring us relief* from our work and the painful labor of farming this ground that the LORD has cursed." ³⁰After the birth of Noah, Lamech lived another 595 years, and he had other sons and daughters. ³¹Lamech lived 777 years, and then he died.

³²By the time Noah was 500 years old, he was the father of Shem, Ham, and Japheth.

6 A World Gone Wrong

Then the people began to multiply on the earth, and daughters were born to them. ²The sons of God saw the beautiful women* and took any they wanted as their wives. ³Then the LORD said, "My Spirit will not put up with* humans for such a long time, for they are only mortal flesh. In the future, their normal lifespan will be no more than 120 years."

⁴In those days, and for some time after, giant Nephilites lived on the earth, for whenever the sons of God had intercourse with women, they gave birth to children who became the heroes and famous warriors of ancient times.

⁵The LORD observed the extent of human wickedness on the earth, and he saw that everything they thought or imagined was consistently and totally evil. ⁶So the LORD was sorry he had ever made them and put them on the earth. It broke his heart. ⁷And the LORD said, "I will wipe this human race I have created from the face of the earth. Yes, and I will destroy every living thing— all the people, the large animals, the small animals that scurry along the ground, and even the birds of the sky. I am sorry I ever made them." ⁸But Noah found favor with the LORD.

The Story of Noah

⁹This is the account of Noah and his family. Noah was a righteous man, the only blameless person living on earth at the time, and he walked in close fellowship with God. ¹⁰Noah was the father of three sons: Shem, Ham, and Japheth.

¹¹Now God saw that the earth had become corrupt and was filled with violence. ¹²God observed all this corruption in the world, for everyone on earth was corrupt. ¹³So God said to Noah, "I have decided to destroy all living creatures, for they have filled the earth with violence. Yes, I will wipe them all out along with the earth!

¹⁴"Build a large boat* from cypress wood* and waterproof it with tar, inside and out. Then construct decks and stalls throughout its interior. ¹⁵Make the boat 450 feet long, 75 feet wide, and 45 feet high.* ¹⁶Leave an 18-inch opening* below the roof all the way around the boat. Put the door on the side, and build three decks inside the boat— lower, middle, and upper.

¹⁷"Look! I am about to cover the earth with a flood that will destroy every living thing that breathes. Everything on earth will die. ¹⁸But I will confirm my covenant with you. So enter the boat—you and your wife and your sons and their wives. ¹⁹Bring a pair of every kind of animal—a male and a female—into the boat with you to keep them alive during the flood. ²⁰Pairs of every kind of bird, and every kind of animal, and every kind of small animal that scurries along the ground, will come to you to be kept alive. ²¹And be sure to take on board enough food for your family and for all the animals."

²²So Noah did everything exactly as God had commanded him.

7 The Flood Covers the Earth

When everything was ready, the LORD said to Noah, "Go into the boat with all your family, for among all the people of the earth, I can see that you alone are righteous. ²Take with you seven pairs—male and female—of each animal I have approved for eating and for sacrifice,* and take one pair of each of the others. ³Also take seven pairs of every kind of bird. There must be a male

---

5:29 *Noah* sounds like a Hebrew term that can mean "relief" or "comfort."   **6:2** Hebrew *daughters of men;* also in 6:4.   **6:3** Greek version reads *will not remain in.*   **6:14a** Traditionally rendered *an ark.*   **6:14b** Or *gopher wood.*   **6:15** Hebrew *300 cubits* [138 meters] *long, 50 cubits* [23 meters] *wide, and 30 cubits* [13.8 meters] *high.*   **6:16** Hebrew *an opening of 1 cubit* [46 centimeters].   **7:2** Hebrew *of each clean animal;* similarly in 7:8.

and a female in each pair to ensure that all life will survive on the earth after the flood. ⁴Seven days from now I will make the rains pour down on the earth. And it will rain for forty days and forty nights, until I have wiped from the earth all the living things I have created."

⁵So Noah did everything as the LORD commanded him.

⁶Noah was 600 years old when the flood covered the earth. ⁷He went on board the boat to escape the flood—he and his wife and his sons and their wives. ⁸With them were all the various kinds of animals—those approved for eating and for sacrifice and those that were not—along with all the birds and the small animals that scurry along the ground. ⁹They entered the boat in pairs, male and female, just as God had commanded Noah. ¹⁰After seven days, the waters of the flood came and covered the earth.

¹¹When Noah was 600 years old, on the seventeenth day of the second month, all the underground waters erupted from the earth, and the rain fell in mighty torrents from the sky. ¹²The rain continued to fall for forty days and forty nights.

¹³That very day Noah had gone into the boat with his wife and his sons—Shem, Ham, and Japheth—and their wives. ¹⁴With them in the boat were pairs of every kind of animal—domestic and wild, large and small—along with birds of every kind. ¹⁵Two by two they came into the boat, representing every living thing that breathes. ¹⁶A male and female of each kind entered, just as God had commanded Noah. Then the LORD closed the door behind them.

¹⁷For forty days the floodwaters grew deeper, covering the ground and lifting the boat high above the earth. ¹⁸As the waters rose higher and higher above the ground, the boat floated safely on the surface. ¹⁹Finally, the water covered even the highest mountains on the earth, ²⁰rising more than twenty-two feet* above the highest peaks. ²¹All the living things on earth died—birds, domestic animals, wild animals, small animals that scurry along the

ground, and all the people. ²²Everything that breathed and lived on dry land died. ²³God wiped out every living thing on the earth—people, livestock, small animals that scurry along the ground, and the birds of the sky. All were destroyed. The only people who survived were Noah and those with him in the boat. ²⁴And the floodwaters covered the earth for 150 days.

8 The Flood Recedes

But God remembered Noah and all the wild animals and livestock with him in the boat. He sent a wind to blow across the earth, and the floodwaters began to recede. ²The underground waters stopped flowing, and the torrential rains from the sky were stopped. ³So the floodwaters gradually receded from the earth. After 150 days, ⁴exactly five months from the time the flood began,* the boat came to rest on the mountains of Ararat. ⁵Two and a half months later,* as the waters continued to go down, other mountain peaks became visible.

⁶After another forty days, Noah opened the window he had made in the boat ⁷and released a raven. The bird flew back and forth until the floodwaters on the earth had dried up. ⁸He also released a dove to see if the water had receded and it could find dry ground. ⁹But the dove could find no place to land because the water still covered the ground. So it returned to the boat, and Noah held out his hand and drew the dove back inside. ¹⁰After waiting another seven days, Noah released the dove again. ¹¹This time the dove returned to him in the evening with a fresh olive leaf in its beak. Then Noah knew that the floodwaters were almost gone. ¹²He waited another seven days and then released the dove again. This time it did not come back.

¹³Noah was now 601 years old. On the first day of the new year, ten and a half months after the flood began,* the floodwaters had almost dried up from the earth. Noah lifted back the covering of the boat and saw that the surface of the ground was drying. ¹⁴Two more months went by,* and at last the earth was dry!

7:20 Hebrew *15 cubits* [6.9 meters]. **8:4** Hebrew *on the seventeenth day of the seventh month;* see 7:11. **8:5** Hebrew *On the first day of the tenth month;* see 7:11 and note on 8:4. **8:13** Hebrew *On the first day of the first month;* see 7:11. **8:14** Hebrew *The twenty-seventh day of the second month arrived;* see note on 8:13.

¹⁵ Then God said to Noah, ¹⁶ "Leave the boat, all of you—you and your wife, and your sons and their wives. ¹⁷ Release all the animals—the birds, the livestock, and the small animals that scurry along the ground—so they can be fruitful and multiply throughout the earth."

¹⁸ So Noah, his wife, and his sons and their wives left the boat. ¹⁹ And all of the large and small animals and birds came out of the boat, pair by pair.

²⁰ Then Noah built an altar to the LORD, and there he sacrificed as burnt offerings the animals and birds that had been approved for that purpose.* ²¹ And the LORD was pleased with the aroma of the sacrifice and said to himself, "I will never again curse the ground because of the human race, even though everything they think or imagine is bent toward evil from childhood. I will never again destroy all living things. ²² As long as the earth remains, there will be planting and harvest, cold and heat, summer and winter, day and night."

God Confirms His Covenant

9 Then God blessed Noah and his sons and told them, "Be fruitful and multiply. Fill the earth. ² All the animals of the earth, all the birds of the sky, all the small animals that scurry along the ground, and all the fish in the sea will look on you with fear and terror. I have placed them in your power. ³ I have given them to you for food, just as I have given you grain and vegetables. ⁴ But you must never eat any meat that still has the lifeblood in it.

⁵ "And I will require the blood of anyone who takes another person's life. If a wild animal kills a person, it must die. And anyone who murders a fellow human must die. ⁶ If anyone takes a human life, that person's life will also be taken by human hands. For God made human beings* in his own image. ⁷ Now be fruitful and multiply, and repopulate the earth."

⁸ Then God told Noah and his sons, ⁹ "I hereby confirm my covenant with you and your descendants, ¹⁰ and with all the animals that were on the boat with you—the birds, the livestock, and all the wild animals—every living creature on earth.

¹¹ Yes, I am confirming my covenant with you. Never again will floodwaters kill all living creatures; never again will a flood destroy the earth."

¹² Then God said, "I am giving you a sign of my covenant with you and with all living creatures, for all generations to come. ¹³ I have placed my rainbow in the clouds. It is the sign of my covenant with you and with all the earth. ¹⁴ When I send clouds over the earth, the rainbow will appear in the clouds, ¹⁵ and I will remember my covenant with you and with all living creatures. Never again will the floodwaters destroy all life. ¹⁶ When I see the rainbow in the clouds, I will remember the eternal covenant between God and every living creature on earth." ¹⁷ Then God said to Noah, "Yes, this rainbow is the sign of the covenant I am confirming with all the creatures on earth."

Noah's Sons

¹⁸ The sons of Noah who came out of the boat with their father were Shem, Ham, and Japheth. (Ham is the father of Canaan.) ¹⁹ From these three sons of Noah came all the people who now populate the earth.

²⁰ After the flood, Noah began to cultivate the ground, and he planted a vineyard. ²¹ One day he drank some wine he had made, and he became drunk and lay naked inside his tent. ²² Ham, the father of Canaan, saw that his father was naked and went outside and told his brothers. ²³ Then Shem and Japheth took a robe, held it over their shoulders, and backed into the tent to cover their father. As they did this, they looked the other way so they would not see him naked.

²⁴ When Noah woke up from his stupor, he learned what Ham, his youngest son, had done. ²⁵ Then he cursed Canaan, the son of Ham:

"May Canaan be cursed!
May he be the lowest of servants to his relatives."

²⁶ Then Noah said,

"May the LORD, the God of Shem, be blessed,
and may Canaan be his servant!

8:20 Hebrew *every clean animal and every clean bird.*   **9:6** Or *man;* Hebrew reads *ha-adam.*

27 May God expand the territory of
   Japheth!
   May Japheth share the prosperity of
   Shem,*
   and may Canaan be his servant."

28 Noah lived another 350 years after the great flood. 29 He lived 950 years, and then he died.

10 This is the account of the families of Shem, Ham, and Japheth, the three sons of Noah. Many children were born to them after the great flood.

Descendants of Japheth

2 The descendants of Japheth were Gomer, Magog, Madai, Javan, Tubal, Meshech, and Tiras.
3 The descendants of Gomer were Ashkenaz, Riphath, and Togarmah.
4 The descendants of Javan were Elishah, Tarshish, Kittim, and Rodanim.* 5 Their descendants became the seafaring peoples that spread out to various lands, each identified by its own language, clan, and national identity.

Descendants of Ham

6 The descendants of Ham were Cush, Mizraim, Put, and Canaan.
7 The descendants of Cush were Seba, Havilah, Sabtah, Raamah, and Sabteca. The descendants of Raamah were Sheba and Dedan.
   8 Cush was also the ancestor of Nimrod, who was the first heroic warrior on earth. 9 Since he was the greatest hunter in the world,* his name became proverbial. People would say, "This man is like Nimrod, the greatest hunter in the world." 10 He built his kingdom in the land of Babylonia,* with the cities of Babylon, Erech, Akkad, and Calneh. 11 From there he expanded his territory to Assyria,* building the cities of Nineveh, Rehoboth-ir, Calah, 12 and Resen (the great city located between Nineveh and Calah).

13 Mizraim was the ancestor of the Ludites, Anamites, Lehabites, Naphtuhites, 14 Pathrusites, Casluhites, and the Caphtorites, from whom the Philistines came.* 15 Canaan's oldest son was Sidon, the ancestor of the Sidonians. Canaan was also the ancestor of the Hittites,* 16 Jebusites, Amorites, Girgashites, 17 Hivites, Arkites, Sinites, 18 Arvadites, Zemarites, and Hamathites. The Canaanite clans eventually spread out, 19 and the territory of Canaan extended from Sidon in the north to Gerar and Gaza in the south, and east as far as Sodom, Gomorrah, Admah, and Zeboiim, near Lasha. 20 These were the descendants of Ham, identified by clan, language, territory, and national identity.

Descendants of Shem

21 Sons were also born to Shem, the older brother of Japheth.* Shem was the ancestor of all the descendants of Eber.
22 The descendants of Shem were Elam, Asshur, Arphaxad, Lud, and Aram.
23 The descendants of Aram were Uz, Hul, Gether, and Mash.
24 Arphaxad was the father of Shelah,* and Shelah was the father of Eber.
25 Eber had two sons. The first was named Peleg (which means "division"), for during his lifetime the people of the world were divided into different language groups. His brother's name was Joktan.
26 Joktan was the ancestor of Almodad, Sheleph, Hazarmaveth, Jerah, 27 Hadoram, Uzal, Diklah, 28 Obal, Abimael, Sheba, 29 Ophir, Havilah, and Jobab. All these were descendants of Joktan. 30 The territory they occupied extended from Mesha all the way to Sephar in the eastern mountains.
31 These were the descendants of Shem, identified by clan, language, territory, and national identity.

Conclusion

32 These are the clans that descended from Noah's sons, arranged by nation according

---

9:27 Hebrew *May he live in the tents of Shem.*   10:4 As in some Hebrew manuscripts and Greek version (see also 1 Chr 1:7); most Hebrew manuscripts read *Dodanim.*   10:9 Hebrew *a great hunter before the LORD;* also in 10:9b.   10:10 Hebrew *Shinar.*   10:11 Or *From that land Assyria went out.*   10:14 Hebrew *Casluhites, from whom the Philistines came, and Caphtorites.* Compare Jer 47:4; Amos 9:7.   10:15 Hebrew *ancestor of Heth.*   10:21 Or *Shem, whose older brother was Japheth.*   10:24 Greek version reads *Arphaxad was the father of Cainan, Cainan was the father of Shelah.* Compare Luke 3:36.

Restless Lives
GENESIS 11:1–9

Sabbath & Rest

Work hard, play hard. It's a mantra in corporate boardrooms, a slogan emblazoned on T-shirts. Forget long walks on the beach: *activity* is what's selling in our world today. Even in everyday conversation, it matters: we're expected to complain about being too busy. Imagine if you admitted to lounging all day; people would be shocked . . . and you'd probably feel embarrassed, maybe even ashamed.

Not having time to rest is today's forgivable sin—perhaps even an admired achievement. It reminds me of what Paul wrote when a man was grossly sinning, and the people were proud: "You are so proud of yourselves, but you should be mourning in sorrow and shame" (1 Corinthians 5:2).

I'm not so old school that I think we can revert back to the days when no one played baseball on Sunday. But making time to be still is essential to a healthy spiritual life.

Rest is more than having down time, and it's more than obeying the fourth commandment. God doesn't want us to toe the line; he wants our full heart—which means he calls us to rest in him *continually*, not just on Sunday afternoons. Remember, Christ came to fulfill the Law, not abolish it (Matthew 5:17).

Consider what rest really is. Isn't it being still before God, trusting him to provide and replenish? If we trusted him to provide and replenish every day of the week, in every detail of our lives, we would be more productive, more at peace, more rested than we can even imagine. In his book *Schedule Interrupted*, Mark Buchanan writes, "Pay attention to how God is afoot in the mystery of each moment, in its mad rush or maddening plod. He is present in both." What a wonderful God we have! It's a wonder rest isn't the easiest command to obey.

—*Heather Gemmen Wilson*

For more on Sabbath and rest, see reading at Exodus 33:12–14.

to their lines of descent. All the nations of the earth descended from these clans after the great flood.

11 The Tower of Babel

At one time all the people of the world spoke the same language and used the same words. [2]As the people migrated to the east, they found a plain in the land of Babylonia* and settled there.

[3]They began saying to each other, "Let's make bricks and harden them with fire." (In this region bricks were used instead of stone, and tar was used for mortar.) [4]Then they said, "Come, let's build a great city for ourselves with a tower that reaches into the sky. This will make us famous and keep us from being scattered all over the world."

[5]But the LORD came down to look at the city and the tower the people were building. [6]"Look!" he said. "The people are united, and they all speak the same language. After this, nothing they set out to do will be impossible for them! [7]Come, let's go down and confuse the people with different languages. Then they won't be able to understand each other."

[8]In that way, the LORD scattered them all over the world, and they stopped building the city. [9]That is why the city was called

11:2 Hebrew *Shinar.*

Babel,* because that is where the LORD confused the people with different languages. In this way he scattered them all over the world.

The Line of Descent from Shem to Abram

¹⁰This is the account of Shem's family.

Two years after the great flood, when Shem was 100 years old, he became the father of* Arphaxad. ¹¹After the birth of* Arphaxad, Shem lived another 500 years and had other sons and daughters. ¹²When Arphaxad was 35 years old, he became the father of Shelah. ¹³After the birth of Shelah, Arphaxad lived another 403 years and had other sons and daughters.* ¹⁴When Shelah was 30 years old, he became the father of Eber. ¹⁵After the birth of Eber, Shelah lived another 403 years and had other sons and daughters. ¹⁶When Eber was 34 years old, he became the father of Peleg. ¹⁷After the birth of Peleg, Eber lived another 430 years and had other sons and daughters. ¹⁸When Peleg was 30 years old, he became the father of Reu. ¹⁹After the birth of Reu, Peleg lived another 209 years and had other sons and daughters. ²⁰When Reu was 32 years old, he became the father of Serug. ²¹After the birth of Serug, Reu lived another 207 years and had other sons and daughters. ²²When Serug was 30 years old, he became the father of Nahor. ²³After the birth of Nahor, Serug lived another 200 years and had other sons and daughters. ²⁴When Nahor was 29 years old, he became the father of Terah. ²⁵After the birth of Terah, Nahor lived another 119 years and had other sons and daughters. ²⁶After Terah was 70 years old, he became the father of Abram, Nahor, and Haran.

The Family of Terah

²⁷This is the account of Terah's family. Terah was the father of Abram, Nahor, and Haran; and Haran was the father of Lot. ²⁸But Haran died in Ur of the Chaldeans, the land of his birth, while his father, Terah, was still living. ²⁹Meanwhile, Abram and Nahor both married. The name of Abram's wife was Sarai, and the name of Nahor's wife was Milcah. (Milcah and her sister Iscah were daughters of Nahor's brother Haran.) ³⁰But Sarai was unable to become pregnant and had no children.

³¹One day Terah took his son Abram, his daughter-in-law Sarai (his son Abram's wife), and his grandson Lot (his son Haran's child) and moved away from Ur of the Chaldeans. He was headed for the land of Canaan, but they stopped at Haran and settled there. ³²Terah lived for 205 years* and died while still in Haran.

12 The Call of Abram

The LORD had said to Abram, "Leave your native country, your relatives, and your father's family, and go to the land that I will show you. ²I will make you into a great nation. I will bless you and make you famous, and you will be a blessing to others. ³I will bless those who bless you and curse those who treat you with contempt. All the families on earth will be blessed through you."

⁴So Abram departed as the LORD had instructed, and Lot went with him. Abram was seventy-five years old when he left Haran. ⁵He took his wife, Sarai, his nephew Lot, and all his wealth—his livestock and all the people he had taken into his household at Haran—and headed for the land of Canaan. When they arrived in Canaan, ⁶Abram traveled through the land as far as Shechem. There he set up camp beside the oak of Moreh. At that time, the area was inhabited by Canaanites.

⁷Then the LORD appeared to Abram and said, "I will give this land to your descendants.*" And Abram built an altar there and dedicated it to the LORD, who had appeared to him. ⁸After that, Abram traveled south and set up camp in the hill country, with Bethel to the west and Ai to the

---

11:9 Or *Babylon. Babel* sounds like a Hebrew term that means "confusion."   **11:10** Or *the ancestor of;* also in 11:12, 14, 16, 18, 20, 22, 24.   **11:11** Or *the birth of this ancestor of;* also in 11:13, 15, 17, 19, 21, 23, 25.   **11:12-13** Greek version reads ¹²*When Arphaxad was 135 years old, he became the father of Cainan.* ¹³*After the birth of Cainan, Arphaxad lived another 430 years and had other sons and daughters, and then he died. When Cainan was 130 years old, he became the father of Shelah. After the birth of Shelah, Cainan lived another 330 years and had other sons and daughters, and then he died.* Compare Luke 3:35-36.   **11:32** Some ancient versions read *145 years;* compare 11:26 and 12:4.   **12:7** Hebrew *seed.*

east. There he built another altar and dedicated it to the LORD, and he worshiped the LORD. ⁹Then Abram continued traveling south by stages toward the Negev.

Abram and Sarai in Egypt

¹⁰At that time a severe famine struck the land of Canaan, forcing Abram to go down to Egypt, where he lived as a foreigner. ¹¹As he was approaching the border of Egypt, Abram said to his wife, Sarai, "Look, you are a very beautiful woman. ¹²When the Egyptians see you, they will say, 'This is his wife. Let's kill him; then we can have her!' ¹³So please tell them you are my sister. Then they will spare my life and treat me well because of their interest in you."

¹⁴And sure enough, when Abram arrived in Egypt, everyone noticed Sarai's beauty. ¹⁵When the palace officials saw her, they sang her praises to Pharaoh, their king, and Sarai was taken into his palace. ¹⁶Then Pharaoh gave Abram many gifts because of her—sheep, goats, cattle, male and female donkeys, male and female servants, and camels.

¹⁷But the LORD sent terrible plagues upon Pharaoh and his household because of Sarai, Abram's wife. ¹⁸So Pharaoh summoned Abram and accused him sharply. "What have you done to me?" he demanded. "Why didn't you tell me she was your wife? ¹⁹Why did you say, 'She is my sister,' and allow me to take her as my wife? Now then, here is your wife. Take her and get out of here!" ²⁰Pharaoh ordered some of his men to escort them, and he sent Abram out of the country, along with his wife and all his possessions.

13 Abram and Lot Separate

So Abram left Egypt and traveled north into the Negev, along with his wife and Lot and all that they owned. ²(Abram was very rich in livestock, silver, and gold.) ³From the Negev, they continued traveling by stages toward Bethel, and they pitched their tents between Bethel and Ai, where they had camped before. ⁴This was the same place where Abram had built the altar, and there he worshiped the LORD again.

⁵Lot, who was traveling with Abram, had also become very wealthy with flocks of sheep and goats, herds of cattle, and many tents. ⁶But the land could not support both Abram and Lot with all their flocks and herds living so close together. ⁷So disputes broke out between the herdsmen of Abram and Lot. (At that time Canaanites and Perizzites were also living in the land.)

⁸Finally Abram said to Lot, "Let's not allow this conflict to come between us or our herdsmen. After all, we are close relatives! ⁹The whole countryside is open to you. Take your choice of any section of the land you want, and we will separate. If you want the land to the left, then I'll take the land on the right. If you prefer the land on the right, then I'll go to the left."

¹⁰Lot took a long look at the fertile plains of the Jordan Valley in the direction of Zoar. The whole area was well watered everywhere, like the garden of the LORD or the beautiful land of Egypt. (This was before the LORD destroyed Sodom and Gomorrah.) ¹¹Lot chose for himself the whole Jordan Valley to the east of them. He went there with his flocks and servants and parted company with his uncle Abram. ¹²So Abram settled in the land of Canaan, and Lot moved his tents to a place near Sodom and settled among the cities of the plain. ¹³But the people of this area were extremely wicked and constantly sinned against the LORD.

¹⁴After Lot had gone, the LORD said to Abram, "Look as far as you can see in every direction—north and south, east and west. ¹⁵I am giving all this land, as far as you can see, to you and your descendants* as a permanent possession. ¹⁶And I will give you so many descendants that, like the dust of the earth, they cannot be counted! ¹⁷Go and walk through the land in every direction, for I am giving it to you."

¹⁸So Abram moved his camp to Hebron and settled near the oak grove belonging to Mamre. There he built another altar to the LORD.

14 Abram Rescues Lot

About this time war broke out in the region. King Amraphel of Babylonia,* King Arioch of Ellasar, King Kedorlaomer

---

13:15 Hebrew *seed;* also in 13:16.   **14:1** Hebrew *Shinar;* also in 14:9.

of Elam, and King Tidal of Goiim ²fought against King Bera of Sodom, King Birsha of Gomorrah, King Shinab of Admah, King Shemeber of Zeboiim, and the king of Bela (also called Zoar).

³This second group of kings joined forces in Siddim Valley (that is, the valley of the Dead Sea*). ⁴For twelve years they had been subject to King Kedorlaomer, but in the thirteenth year they rebelled against him.

⁵One year later Kedorlaomer and his allies arrived and defeated the Rephaites at Ashteroth-karnaim, the Zuzites at Ham, the Emites at Shaveh-kiriathaim, ⁶and the Horites at Mount Seir, as far as El-paran at the edge of the wilderness. ⁷Then they turned back and came to En-mishpat (now called Kadesh) and conquered all the territory of the Amalekites, and also the Amorites living in Hazazon-tamar.

⁸Then the rebel kings of Sodom, Gomorrah, Admah, Zeboiim, and Bela (also called Zoar) prepared for battle in the valley of the Dead Sea.* ⁹They fought against King Kedorlaomer of Elam, King Tidal of Goiim, King Amraphel of Babylonia, and King Arioch of Ellasar—four kings against five. ¹⁰As it happened, the valley of the Dead Sea was filled with tar pits. And as the army of the kings of Sodom and Gomorrah fled, some fell into the tar pits, while the rest escaped into the mountains. ¹¹The victorious invaders then plundered Sodom and Gomorrah and headed for home, taking with them all the spoils of war and the food supplies. ¹²They also captured Lot—Abram's nephew who lived in Sodom—and carried off everything he owned.

¹³But one of Lot's men escaped and reported everything to Abram the Hebrew, who was living near the oak grove belonging to Mamre the Amorite. Mamre and his relatives, Eshcol and Aner, were Abram's allies.

¹⁴When Abram heard that his nephew Lot had been captured, he mobilized the 318 trained men who had been born into his household. Then he pursued Kedorlaomer's army until he caught up with them

at Dan. ¹⁵There he divided his men and attacked during the night. Kedorlaomer's army fled, but Abram chased them as far as Hobah, north of Damascus. ¹⁶Abram recovered all the goods that had been taken, and he brought back his nephew Lot with his possessions and all the women and other captives.

Melchizedek Blesses Abram

¹⁷After Abram returned from his victory over Kedorlaomer and all his allies, the king of Sodom went out to meet him in the valley of Shaveh (that is, the King's Valley).

¹⁸And Melchizedek, the king of Salem and a priest of God Most High,* brought Abram some bread and wine. ¹⁹Melchizedek blessed Abram with this blessing:

"Blessed be Abram by God Most High,
    Creator of heaven and earth.
²⁰ And blessed be God Most High,
    who has defeated your enemies for
        you."

Then Abram gave Melchizedek a tenth of all the goods he had recovered.

²¹The king of Sodom said to Abram, "Give back my people who were captured. But you may keep for yourself all the goods you have recovered."

²²Abram replied to the king of Sodom, "I solemnly swear to the LORD, God Most High, Creator of heaven and earth, ²³that I will not take so much as a single thread or sandal thong from what belongs to you. Otherwise you might say, 'I am the one who made Abram rich.' ²⁴I will accept only what my young warriors have already eaten, and I request that you give a fair share of the goods to my allies—Aner, Eshcol, and Mamre."

15 The LORD's Covenant Promise to Abram

Some time later, the LORD spoke to Abram in a vision and said to him, "Do not be afraid, Abram, for I will protect you, and your reward will be great."

²But Abram replied, "O Sovereign LORD, what good are all your blessings when I

14:3 Hebrew *Salt Sea.*   **14:8** Hebrew *Siddim Valley* (see 14:3); also in 14:10.   **14:18** Hebrew *El-Elyon;* also in 14:19, 20, 22.

don't even have a son? Since you've given me no children, Eliezer of Damascus, a servant in my household, will inherit all my wealth. ³You have given me no descendants of my own, so one of my servants will be my heir."

⁴Then the LORD said to him, "No, your servant will not be your heir, for you will have a son of your own who will be your heir." ⁵Then the LORD took Abram outside and said to him, "Look up into the sky and count the stars if you can. That's how many descendants you will have!"

⁶And Abram believed the LORD, and the LORD counted him as righteous because of his faith.

⁷Then the LORD told him, "I am the LORD who brought you out of Ur of the Chaldeans to give you this land as your possession."

⁸But Abram replied, "O Sovereign LORD, how can I be sure that I will actually possess it?"

⁹The LORD told him, "Bring me a three-year-old heifer, a three-year-old female goat, a three-year-old ram, a turtledove, and a young pigeon." ¹⁰So Abram presented all these to him and killed them. Then he cut each animal down the middle and laid the halves side by side; he did not, however, cut the birds in half. ¹¹Some vultures swooped down to eat the carcasses, but Abram chased them away.

¹²As the sun was going down, Abram fell into a deep sleep, and a terrifying darkness came down over him. ¹³Then the LORD said to Abram, "You can be sure that your descendants will be strangers in a foreign land, where they will be oppressed as slaves for 400 years. ¹⁴But I will punish the nation that enslaves them, and in the end they will come away with great wealth. ¹⁵(As for you, you will die in peace and be buried at a ripe old age.) ¹⁶After four generations your descendants will return here to this land, for the sins of the Amorites do not yet warrant their destruction."

¹⁷After the sun went down and darkness fell, Abram saw a smoking firepot and a flaming torch pass between the halves of the carcasses. ¹⁸So the LORD made a covenant with Abram that day and said, "I have given this land to your descendants, all the way from the border of Egypt* to the great Euphrates River—¹⁹the land now occupied by the Kenites, Kenizzites, Kadmonites, ²⁰Hittites, Perizzites, Rephaites, ²¹Amorites, Canaanites, Girgashites, and Jebusites."

16 The Birth of Ishmael

Now Sarai, Abram's wife, had not been able to bear children for him. But she had an Egyptian servant named Hagar. ²So Sarai said to Abram, "The LORD has prevented me from having children. Go and sleep with my servant. Perhaps I can have children through her." And Abram agreed with Sarai's proposal. ³So Sarai, Abram's wife, took Hagar the Egyptian servant and gave her to Abram as a wife. (This happened ten years after Abram had settled in the land of Canaan.)

⁴So Abram had sexual relations with Hagar, and she became pregnant. But when Hagar knew she was pregnant, she began to treat her mistress, Sarai, with contempt. ⁵Then Sarai said to Abram, "This is all your fault! I put my servant into your arms, but now that she's pregnant she treats me with contempt. The LORD will show who's wrong—you or me!"

⁶Abram replied, "Look, she is your servant, so deal with her as you see fit." Then Sarai treated Hagar so harshly that she finally ran away.

⁷The angel of the LORD found Hagar beside a spring of water in the wilderness, along the road to Shur. ⁸The angel said to her, "Hagar, Sarai's servant, where have you come from, and where are you going?"

"I'm running away from my mistress, Sarai," she replied.

⁹The angel of the LORD said to her, "Return to your mistress, and submit to her authority." ¹⁰Then he added, "I will give you more descendants than you can count."

¹¹And the angel also said, "You are now pregnant and will give birth to a son. You are to name him Ishmael (which means 'God hears'), for the LORD has heard your cry of distress. ¹²This son of yours will be a wild man, as untamed as a wild donkey! He will

---

15:18 Hebrew *the river of Egypt,* referring either to an eastern branch of the Nile River or to the Brook of Egypt in the Sinai (see Num 34:5).

raise his fist against everyone, and everyone will be against him. Yes, he will live in open hostility against all his relatives."

¹³Thereafter, Hagar used another name to refer to the LORD, who had spoken to her. She said, "You are the God who sees me."* She also said, "Have I truly seen the One who sees me?" ¹⁴So that well was named Beer-lahai-roi (which means "well of the Living One who sees me"). It can still be found between Kadesh and Bered.

¹⁵So Hagar gave Abram a son, and Abram named him Ishmael. ¹⁶Abram was eighty-six years old when Ishmael was born.

Solitude

Hagar: Encountering the God Who Sees Us

GENESIS 16

Hagar was an Egyptian slave who served Abram's wife, Sarai. As a slave Hagar was like a piece of property; she didn't have "rights" or a say-so in her destiny.

When Sarai was unable to become pregnant, she forced Hagar to have sexual relations with Abram. Then when Hagar became pregnant, she responded by treating Sarai with contempt (Genesis 16:4). Sarai reacted so harshly that Hagar ran away.

How frightened Hagar must have felt. Pregnant, homeless, alone in the wilderness. Yet the angel of the Lord found Hagar there. He commanded her to return and submit to Sarai (16:7–9). Then he comforted her with the news that her son would have many descendants and that she was to name him Ishmael, which means "God hears."

After that Hagar addressed God differently. She called God "El-roi," which means "You are the God who sees me." She obeyed the angel's commands and returned to Sarai and Abram.

There are times of solitude that we choose—perhaps time alone during a weekend retreat or an early morning prayer time. But there are also experiences of solitude that we do not choose, when our aloneness is thrust upon us. Perhaps we're in a hospital bed or a lonely and empty house or a broken-down car in the middle of nowhere. During these times we can feel ignored, isolated, abandoned.

When we're surrounded by people, faith can sometimes seem easier; we see and experience God working through the words, actions, and comfort that others may provide. But being alone can be a test of faith: it's just you and God . . . and perhaps you wonder if he is even really there at all.

In a painful and lonely moment, Hagar experienced God's presence in a profound way. She came to know God as the One who hears and sees us, even when no one else is around.

Being alone, whether by choice or by force, can provide a unique opportunity to experience God's presence. An angel may not speak to us directly, but we can listen, watch, and remember the profound truth: God hears us. God sees us. God is present with us.

—Joy-Elizabeth Lawrence

For more on solitude, see reading at 1 Chronicles 17.

17 Abram Is Named Abraham

When Abram was ninety-nine years old, the LORD appeared to him and said, "I am El-Shaddai—'God Almighty.' Serve me faithfully and live a blameless life. ²I will make a covenant with you, by which I will guarantee to give you countless descendants."

³At this, Abram fell face down on the ground. Then God said to him, ⁴"This is my covenant with you: I will make you the father of a multitude of nations! ⁵What's more, I am changing your name. It will no longer be Abram. Instead, you will be called Abraham,* for you will be the father of many nations. ⁶I will make you extremely fruitful. Your descendants will become many nations, and kings will be among them!

⁷"I will confirm my covenant with you and your descendants* after you, from generation to generation. This is the everlasting covenant: I will always be your God and the God of your descendants after you. ⁸And I will give the entire land of Canaan, where you now live as a foreigner, to you and your descendants. It will be their possession forever, and I will be their God."

The Mark of the Covenant

⁹Then God said to Abraham, "Your responsibility is to obey the terms of the covenant. You and all your descendants have this continual responsibility. ¹⁰This is the covenant that you and your descendants must keep: Each male among you must be circumcised. ¹¹You must cut off the flesh of your foreskin as a sign of the covenant between me and you. ¹²From generation to generation, every male child must be circumcised on the eighth day after his birth. This applies not only to members of your family but also to the servants born in your household and the foreign-born servants whom you have purchased. ¹³All must be circumcised. Your bodies will bear the mark of my everlasting covenant. ¹⁴Any male who fails to be circumcised will be cut off from the covenant family for breaking the covenant."

Sarai Is Named Sarah

¹⁵Then God said to Abraham, "Regarding Sarai, your wife—her name will no longer be Sarai. From now on her name will be Sarah.* ¹⁶And I will bless her and give you a son from her! Yes, I will bless her richly, and she will become the mother of many nations. Kings of nations will be among her descendants."

¹⁷Then Abraham bowed down to the ground, but he laughed to himself in disbelief. "How could I become a father at the age of 100?" he thought. "And how can Sarah have a baby when she is ninety years old?" ¹⁸So Abraham said to God, "May Ishmael live under your special blessing!"

¹⁹But God replied, "No—Sarah, your wife, will give birth to a son for you. You will name him Isaac,* and I will confirm my covenant with him and his descendants as an everlasting covenant. ²⁰As for Ishmael, I will bless him also, just as you have asked. I will make him extremely fruitful and multiply his descendants. He will become the father of twelve princes, and I will make him a great nation. ²¹But my covenant will be confirmed with Isaac, who will be born to you and Sarah about this time next year." ²²When God had finished speaking, he left Abraham.

²³On that very day Abraham took his son, Ishmael, and every male in his household, including those born there and those he had bought. Then he circumcised them, cutting off their foreskins, just as God had told him. ²⁴Abraham was ninety-nine years old when he was circumcised, ²⁵and Ishmael, his son, was thirteen. ²⁶Both Abraham and his son, Ishmael, were circumcised on that same day, ²⁷along with all the other men and boys of the household, whether they were born there or bought as servants. All were circumcised with him.

18 A Son Is Promised to Sarah

The LORD appeared again to Abraham near the oak grove belonging to Mamre. One day Abraham was sitting at the entrance to his tent during the hottest part of the day. ²He looked up and noticed

---

17:5 *Abram* means "exalted father"; *Abraham* sounds like a Hebrew term that means "father of many." **17:7** Hebrew *seed;* also in 17:7b, 8, 9, 10, 19. **17:15** *Sarai* and *Sarah* both mean "princess"; the change in spelling may reflect the difference in dialect between Ur and Canaan. **17:19** *Isaac* means "he laughs."

Hospitality versus Entertaining

GENESIS 18:1–8

S everal years ago my wife and I read a book that helped us put hospitality in its proper perspective. In *Open Heart, Open Home* by Karen Burton Mains, we learned that hospitality is not the same as "entertaining." Entertainment is what we do to call attention to ourselves. It is a performance that expects applause. When we entertain, we hope people will say, "Wow!"

Hospitality, on the other hand, is helping people feel welcome in our home even though the house is not camera ready. When we express hospitality, we hope people will say, "It sure is comfortable being here."

So we swallowed hard and invited people into our humble abode with its hand-me-down furnishings, determined that what we didn't have in decor would be compensated for with what we could offer: sincere interest in people who longed for friendship and acceptance. We've learned the joy of welcoming folks for a simple supper of soup and bread or take-out pizza. We use paper plates and concentrate on conversation rather than fine china. Laughter and good company can be much more nourishing than a fancy meal!

Since we focus more on people than on our modest possessions, hospitality has become more rewarding. As we've opened our home to others, we've been strengthened by sharing what we have.

—Greg Asimakoupoulos

For more on hospitality, see reading at 2 Kings 4:8–37.

three men standing nearby. When he saw them, he ran to meet them and welcomed them, bowing low to the ground.

³"My lord," he said, "if it pleases you, stop here for a while. ⁴Rest in the shade of this tree while water is brought to wash your feet. ⁵And since you've honored your servant with this visit, let me prepare some food to refresh you before you continue on your journey."

"All right," they said. "Do as you have said."

⁶So Abraham ran back to the tent and said to Sarah, "Hurry! Get three large measures* of your best flour, knead it into dough, and bake some bread." ⁷Then Abraham ran out to the herd and chose a tender calf and gave it to his servant, who quickly prepared it. ⁸When the food was ready, Abraham took some yogurt and milk and

the roasted meat, and he served it to the men. As they ate, Abraham waited on them in the shade of the trees.

⁹"Where is Sarah, your wife?" the visitors asked.

"She's inside the tent," Abraham replied.

¹⁰Then one of them said, "I will return to you about this time next year, and your wife, Sarah, will have a son!"

Sarah was listening to this conversation from the tent. ¹¹Abraham and Sarah were both very old by this time, and Sarah was long past the age of having children. ¹²So she laughed silently to herself and said, "How could a worn-out woman like me enjoy such pleasure, especially when my master—my husband—is also so old?"

¹³Then the LORD said to Abraham, "Why did Sarah laugh? Why did she say, 'Can an old

---

18:6 Hebrew *3 seahs*, about half a bushel or 18 liters.

woman like me have a baby?' ¹⁴Is anything too hard for the LORD? I will return about this time next year, and Sarah will have a son."

¹⁵Sarah was afraid, so she denied it, saying, "I didn't laugh."

But the LORD said, "No, you did laugh."

Abraham Intercedes for Sodom

¹⁶Then the men got up from their meal and looked out toward Sodom. As they left, Abraham went with them to send them on their way.

¹⁷"Should I hide my plan from Abra-ham?" the LORD asked. ¹⁸"For Abraham will certainly become a great and mighty nation, and all the nations of the earth will be blessed through him. ¹⁹I have singled him out so that he will direct his sons and their families to keep the way of the LORD by doing what is right and just. Then I will do for Abraham all that I have promised."

²⁰So the LORD told Abraham, "I have heard a great outcry from Sodom and Gomorrah, because their sin is so flagrant. ²¹I am going down to see if their actions are as wicked as I have heard. If not, I want to know."

Sarah: Laughing Her Way to Hope

GENESIS 18:9-15

We've all done it. We, like Sarah, have laughed at God. Maybe you haven't exactly laughed. Maybe your doubt has come out in tears, depression, or a fading sense of hope. Maybe you've just stopped letting yourself believe that the good promises of God will play out in your life.

As Sarah stood in her tent, cleaning up after dinner, she overheard one of her guests telling her husband that she, an old, barren woman, would have a child within the year. Her response was to laugh—not a joyful giggle of delight, but a cold, pained laugh of disbelief, an expression of her long years of disappointment (Genesis 18:12).

We know that laugh, don't we? We know that bitterness, that sorrow, that absent hope. We wait for love, children, peace, fulfillment, joy, and yet they so often seem to elude us.

Sarah longed for a child, and there was likely a time when she believed God would honor that longing. But that didn't happen . . . and Sarah's heart shut down a little. She had thought God was good and giving, but maybe she'd been wrong. So she adjusted her hope and expectations and toned down her belief in a gracious God.

Like so many of us when we're worn down by pain, Sarah found herself disappointed in God.

But then, long after she had settled for a lesser version of God, someone came along to tell her she'd been right to hope, that she'd been right to expect God's care and kindness. Even then she didn't dare hope. Instead, she scoffed and hid her small vision of God.

We know how this story ends—with a baby named Isaac who was the start of a trajectory that led to the birth of Jesus. Neither Isaac nor Jesus meant the end of pain, sorrow, or bitterness, but they are reminders that we are right to believe in a good and loving God. Isaac was a sign that God was bigger than Sarah's disappointment and sorrow. Jesus, the ultimate display of God's love for the world, is ours.

—Carla Barnhill

For more on faith, see reading at Exodus 2:1-10.

²² The other men turned and headed toward Sodom, but the LORD remained with Abraham. ²³ Abraham approached him and said, "Will you sweep away both the righteous and the wicked? ²⁴ Suppose you find fifty righteous people living there in the city—will you still sweep it away and not spare it for their sakes? ²⁵ Surely you wouldn't do such a thing, destroying the righteous along with the wicked. Why, you would be treating the righteous and the wicked exactly the same! Surely you wouldn't do that! Should not the Judge of all the earth do what is right?"

²⁶ And the LORD replied, "If I find fifty righteous people in Sodom, I will spare the entire city for their sake."

²⁷ Then Abraham spoke again. "Since I have begun, let me speak further to my Lord, even though I am but dust and ashes. ²⁸ Suppose there are only forty-five righteous people rather than fifty? Will you destroy the whole city for lack of five?"

And the LORD said, "I will not destroy it if I find forty-five righteous people there."

²⁹ Then Abraham pressed his request further. "Suppose there are only forty?"

And the LORD replied, "I will not destroy it for the sake of the forty."

³⁰ "Please don't be angry, my Lord," Abraham pleaded. "Let me speak—suppose only thirty righteous people are found?"

And the LORD replied, "I will not destroy it if I find thirty."

³¹ Then Abraham said, "Since I have dared to speak to the Lord, let me continue—suppose there are only twenty?"

And the LORD replied, "Then I will not destroy it for the sake of the twenty."

³² Finally, Abraham said, "Lord, please don't be angry with me if I speak one more time. Suppose only ten are found there?"

And the LORD replied, "Then I will not destroy it for the sake of the ten."

³³ When the LORD had finished his conversation with Abraham, he went on his way, and Abraham returned to his tent.

19 Sodom and Gomorrah Destroyed

That evening the two angels came to the entrance of the city of Sodom. Lot was sitting there, and when he saw them, he stood up to meet them. Then he welcomed them and bowed with his face to the ground. ² "My lords," he said, "come to my home to wash your feet, and be my guests for the night. You may then get up early in the morning and be on your way again."

"Oh no," they replied. "We'll just spend the night out here in the city square."

³ But Lot insisted, so at last they went home with him. Lot prepared a feast for them, complete with fresh bread made without yeast, and they ate. ⁴ But before they retired for the night, all the men of Sodom, young and old, came from all over the city and surrounded the house. ⁵ They shouted to Lot, "Where are the men who came to spend the night with you? Bring them out to us so we can have sex with them!"

⁶ So Lot stepped outside to talk to them, shutting the door behind him. ⁷ "Please, my brothers," he begged, "don't do such a wicked thing. ⁸ Look, I have two virgin daughters. Let me bring them out to you, and you can do with them as you wish. But please, leave these men alone, for they are my guests and are under my protection."

⁹ "Stand back!" they shouted. "This fellow came to town as an outsider, and now he's acting like our judge! We'll treat you far worse than those other men!" And they lunged toward Lot to break down the door.

¹⁰ But the two angels* reached out, pulled Lot into the house, and bolted the door. ¹¹ Then they blinded all the men, young and old, who were at the door of the house, so they gave up trying to get inside.

¹² Meanwhile, the angels questioned Lot. "Do you have any other relatives here in the city?" they asked. "Get them out of this place—your sons-in-law, sons, daughters, or anyone else. ¹³ For we are about to destroy this city completely. The outcry against this place is so great it has reached the LORD, and he has sent us to destroy it."

¹⁴ So Lot rushed out to tell his daughters' fiancés, "Quick, get out of the city! The LORD is about to destroy it." But the young men thought he was only joking.

¹⁵ At dawn the next morning the angels became insistent. "Hurry," they said to Lot.

19:10 Hebrew *men;* also in 19:12, 16.

"Take your wife and your two daughters who are here. Get out right now, or you will be swept away in the destruction of the city!"

¹⁶When Lot still hesitated, the angels seized his hand and the hands of his wife and two daughters and rushed them to safety outside the city, for the LORD was merciful. ¹⁷When they were safely out of the city, one of the angels ordered, "Run for your lives! And don't look back or stop anywhere in the valley! Escape to the mountains, or you will be swept away!"

¹⁸"Oh no, my lord!" Lot begged. ¹⁹"You have been so gracious to me and saved my life, and you have shown such great kindness. But I cannot go to the mountains. Disaster would catch up to me there, and I would soon die. ²⁰See, there is a small village nearby. Please let me go there instead; don't you see how small it is? Then my life will be saved."

²¹"All right," the angel said, "I will grant your request. I will not destroy the little village. ²²But hurry! Escape to it, for I can do nothing until you arrive there." (This explains why that village was known as Zoar, which means "little place.")

²³Lot reached the village just as the sun was rising over the horizon. ²⁴Then the LORD rained down fire and burning sulfur from the sky on Sodom and Gomorrah. ²⁵He utterly destroyed them, along with the other cities and villages of the plain, wiping out all the people and every bit of vegetation. ²⁶But Lot's wife looked back as she was following behind him, and she turned into a pillar of salt.

²⁷Abraham got up early that morning and hurried out to the place where he had stood in the LORD's presence. ²⁸He looked out across the plain toward Sodom and Gomorrah and watched as columns of smoke rose from the cities like smoke from a furnace.

²⁹But God had listened to Abraham's request and kept Lot safe, removing him from the disaster that engulfed the cities on the plain.

Lot and His Daughters

³⁰Afterward Lot left Zoar because he was afraid of the people there, and he went to live in a cave in the mountains with his two daughters. ³¹One day the older daughter said to her sister, "There are no men left anywhere in this entire area, so we can't get married like everyone else. And our father will soon be too old to have children. ³²Come, let's get him drunk with wine, and then we will have sex with him. That way we will preserve our family line through our father."

³³So that night they got him drunk with wine, and the older daughter went in and had intercourse with her father. He was unaware of her lying down or getting up again.

³⁴The next morning the older daughter said to her younger sister, "I had sex with our father last night. Let's get him drunk with wine again tonight, and you go in and have sex with him. That way we will preserve our family line through our father." ³⁵So that night they got him drunk with wine again, and the younger daughter went in and had intercourse with him. As before, he was unaware of her lying down or getting up again.

³⁶As a result, both of Lot's daughters became pregnant by their own father. ³⁷When the older daughter gave birth to a son, she named him Moab.* He became the ancestor of the nation now known as the Moabites. ³⁸When the younger daughter gave birth to a son, she named him Ben-ammi.* He became the ancestor of the nation now known as the Ammonites.

20 Abraham Deceives Abimelech

Abraham moved south to the Negev and lived for a while between Kadesh and Shur, and then he moved on to Gerar. While living there as a foreigner, ²Abraham introduced his wife, Sarah, by saying, "She is my sister." So King Abimelech of Gerar sent for Sarah and had her brought to him at his palace.

³But that night God came to Abimelech in a dream and told him, "You are a dead man, for that woman you have taken is already married!"

⁴But Abimelech had not slept with her yet, so he said, "Lord, will you destroy an

19:37 *Moab* sounds like a Hebrew term that means "from father."   19:38 *Ben-ammi* means "son of my kinsman."

innocent nation? ⁵Didn't Abraham tell me, 'She is my sister'? And she herself said, 'Yes, he is my brother.' I acted in complete innocence! My hands are clean."

⁶In the dream God responded, "Yes, I know you are innocent. That's why I kept you from sinning against me, and why I did not let you touch her. ⁷Now return the woman to her husband, and he will pray for you, for he is a prophet. Then you will live. But if you don't return her to him, you can be sure that you and all your people will die."

⁸Abimelech got up early the next morning and quickly called all his servants together. When he told them what had happened, his men were terrified. ⁹Then Abimelech called for Abraham. "What have you done to us?" he demanded. "What crime have I committed that deserves treatment like this, making me and my kingdom guilty of this great sin? No one should ever do what you have done! ¹⁰Whatever possessed you to do such a thing?"

¹¹Abraham replied, "I thought, 'This is a godless place. They will want my wife and will kill me to get her.' ¹²And she really is my sister, for we both have the same father, but different mothers. And I married her. ¹³When God called me to leave my father's home and to travel from place to place, I told her, 'Do me a favor. Wherever we go, tell the people that I am your brother.' "

¹⁴Then Abimelech took some of his sheep and goats, cattle, and male and female servants, and he presented them to Abraham. He also returned his wife, Sarah, to him. ¹⁵Then Abimelech said, "Look over my land and choose any place where you would like to live." ¹⁶And he said to Sarah, "Look, I am giving your 'brother' 1,000 pieces of silver* in the presence of all these witnesses. This is to compensate you for any wrong I may have done to you. This will settle any claim against me, and your reputation is cleared."

¹⁷Then Abraham prayed to God, and God healed Abimelech, his wife, and his female servants, so they could have children. ¹⁸For the LORD had caused all the women to be infertile because of what happened with Abraham's wife, Sarah.

21 The Birth of Isaac

The LORD kept his word and did for Sarah exactly what he had promised. ²She became pregnant, and she gave birth to a son for Abraham in his old age. This happened at just the time God had said it would. ³And Abraham named their son Isaac. ⁴Eight days after Isaac was born, Abraham circumcised him as God had commanded. ⁵Abraham was 100 years old when Isaac was born.

⁶And Sarah declared, "God has brought me laughter.* All who hear about this will laugh with me. ⁷Who would have said to Abraham that Sarah would nurse a baby? Yet I have given Abraham a son in his old age!"

Hagar and Ishmael Are Sent Away

⁸When Isaac grew up and was about to be weaned, Abraham prepared a huge feast to celebrate the occasion. ⁹But Sarah saw Ishmael—the son of Abraham and her Egyptian servant Hagar—making fun of her son, Isaac.* ¹⁰So she turned to Abraham and demanded, "Get rid of that slave woman and her son. He is not going to share the inheritance with my son, Isaac. I won't have it!"

¹¹This upset Abraham very much because Ishmael was his son. ¹²But God told Abraham, "Do not be upset over the boy and your servant. Do whatever Sarah tells you, for Isaac is the son through whom your descendants will be counted. ¹³But I will also make a nation of the descendants of Hagar's son because he is your son, too."

¹⁴So Abraham got up early the next morning, prepared food and a container of water, and strapped them on Hagar's shoulders. Then he sent her away with their son, and she wandered aimlessly in the wilderness of Beersheba.

¹⁵When the water was gone, she put the boy in the shade of a bush. ¹⁶Then she went and sat down by herself about a hundred yards* away. "I don't want to watch the boy die," she said, as she burst into tears.

¹⁷But God heard the boy crying, and the angel of God called to Hagar from heaven,

20:16 Hebrew *1,000 [shekels] of silver,* about 25 pounds or 11.4 kilograms in weight. 21:6 The name *Isaac* means "he laughs." 21:9 As in Greek version and Latin Vulgate; Hebrew lacks *of her son, Isaac.* 21:16 Hebrew *a bowshot.*

"Hagar, what's wrong? Do not be afraid! God has heard the boy crying as he lies there. ¹⁸ Go to him and comfort him, for I will make a great nation from his descendants."

¹⁹ Then God opened Hagar's eyes, and she saw a well full of water. She quickly filled her water container and gave the boy a drink.

²⁰ And God was with the boy as he grew up in the wilderness. He became a skillful archer, ²¹ and he settled in the wilderness of Paran. His mother arranged for him to marry a woman from the land of Egypt.

Abraham's Covenant with Abimelech

²² About this time, Abimelech came with Phicol, his army commander, to visit Abraham. "God is obviously with you, helping you in everything you do," Abimelech said. ²³ "Swear to me in God's name that you will never deceive me, my children, or any of my descendants. I have been loyal to you, so now swear that you will be loyal to me and to this country where you are living as a foreigner."

²⁴ Abraham replied, "Yes, I swear to it!" ²⁵ Then Abraham complained to Abimelech about a well that Abimelech's servants had taken by force from Abraham's servants.

²⁶ "This is the first I've heard of it," Abimelech answered. "I have no idea who is responsible. You have never complained about this before."

²⁷ Abraham then gave some of his sheep, goats, and cattle to Abimelech, and they made a treaty. ²⁸ But Abraham also took seven additional female lambs and set them off by themselves. ²⁹ Abimelech asked, "Why have you set these seven apart from the others?"

³⁰ Abraham replied, "Please accept these seven lambs to show your agreement that I dug this well." ³¹ Then he named the place Beersheba (which means "well of the oath"), because that was where they had sworn the oath.

³² After making their covenant at Beersheba, Abimelech left with Phicol, the commander of his army, and they returned home to the land of the Philistines. ³³ Then Abraham planted a tamarisk tree at Beersheba,

and there he worshiped the LORD, the Eternal God.* ³⁴ And Abraham lived as a foreigner in Philistine country for a long time.

22 Abraham's Faith Tested

Some time later, God tested Abraham's faith. "Abraham!" God called.

"Yes," he replied. "Here I am."

² "Take your son, your only son—yes, Isaac, whom you love so much—and go to the land of Moriah. Go and sacrifice him as a burnt offering on one of the mountains, which I will show you."

³ The next morning Abraham got up early. He saddled his donkey and took two of his servants with him, along with his son, Isaac. Then he chopped wood for a fire for a burnt offering and set out for the place God had told him about. ⁴ On the third day of their journey, Abraham looked up and saw the place in the distance. ⁵ "Stay here with the donkey," Abraham told the servants. "The boy and I will travel a little farther. We will worship there, and then we will come right back."

⁶ So Abraham placed the wood for the burnt offering on Isaac's shoulders, while he himself carried the fire and the knife. As the two of them walked on together, ⁷ Isaac turned to Abraham and said, "Father?"

"Yes, my son?" Abraham replied.

"We have the fire and the wood," the boy said, "but where is the sheep for the burnt offering?"

⁸ "God will provide a sheep for the burnt offering, my son," Abraham answered. And they both walked on together.

⁹ When they arrived at the place where God had told him to go, Abraham built an altar and arranged the wood on it. Then he tied his son, Isaac, and laid him on the altar on top of the wood. ¹⁰ And Abraham picked up the knife to kill his son as a sacrifice. ¹¹ At that moment the angel of the LORD called to him from heaven, "Abraham! Abraham!"

"Yes," Abraham replied. "Here I am!"

¹² "Don't lay a hand on the boy!" the angel said. "Do not hurt him in any way, for now I know that you truly fear God. You have not withheld from me even your son, your only son."

21:33 Hebrew *El-Olam.*

Submission for the Strong Willed

GENESIS 22:1-18

Submission can be difficult for all of us, but perhaps it is especially difficult for natural leaders—for those God has called and gifted as visionaries, course charters, and influencers of others. Good leaders often have a strong will.

There is a fundamental difference between a surrendered will and a weak will. Jesus taught us to pray, "Your will be done" (Matthew 6:10), and Jesus himself surrendered his will as he determined to go to the Cross (Matthew 26:39). That meant he placed it in submission to his Father, to the mission his Father gave him, and to the service of sacrificial love. But that did *not* mean he was weak willed. To the contrary, it required a tremendous exertion of moral courage to defy power, authorities, and influences that tugged on him from all sides trying to divert him from his calling.

Having a determined, indomitable, and strong sense of will is not the same as sheer stubbornness. Stubbornness lacks precisely the humility that makes learning possible and it gives conviction the flexibility needed to achieve ultimate goals. And it is not egotism, which seeks to gain control for the gratification of the self.

At its heart, a good leader's indomitable will involves a sense of commitment; a binding of oneself to a task, cause, or value so intensely that mere external forces are not allowed to sway or deter. At its best, in the words of Gerald May, it involves not willfulness but willingness—a giving of my will in the service of a greater mission.

Our sense of will can be dangerous when it veers toward stubbornness or egotism—or it can be buoyed by divine strength when our will is submitted fully to God's leading. I've found that, amazingly, the One who demands the most surrender of my will is the One who wants and makes my will to be its strongest and best.

—*John Ortberg*

For more on submission, see reading at Genesis 50:14-21.

[13] Then Abraham looked up and saw a ram caught by its horns in a thicket. So he took the ram and sacrificed it as a burnt offering in place of his son. [14] Abraham named the place Yahweh-Yireh (which means "the LORD will provide"). To this day, people still use that name as a proverb: "On the mountain of the LORD it will be provided."

[15] Then the angel of the LORD called again to Abraham from heaven. [16] "This is what the LORD says: Because you have obeyed me and have not withheld even your son, your only son, I swear by my own name that [17] I will certainly bless you. I will multiply your descendants* beyond number, like the stars in the sky and the sand on the seashore. Your descendants will conquer the cities of their enemies. [18] And through your descendants all the nations of the earth will be blessed—all because you have obeyed me."

[19] Then they returned to the servants and traveled back to Beersheba, where Abraham continued to live.

22:17 Hebrew seed; also in 22:17b, 18.

²⁰Soon after this, Abraham heard that Milcah, his brother Nahor's wife, had borne Nahor eight sons. ²¹The oldest was named Uz, the next oldest was Buz, followed by Kemuel (the ancestor of the Arameans), ²²Kesed, Hazo, Pildash, Jidlaph, and Bethuel. ²³(Bethuel became the father of Rebekah.) In addition to these eight sons from Milcah, ²⁴Nahor had four other children from his concubine Reumah. Their names were Tebah, Gaham, Tahash, and Maacah.

23 The Burial of Sarah

When Sarah was 127 years old, ²she died at Kiriath-arba (now called Hebron) in the land of Canaan. There Abraham mourned and wept for her.

³Then, leaving her body, he said to the Hittite elders, ⁴"Here I am, a stranger and a foreigner among you. Please sell me a piece of land so I can give my wife a proper burial."

⁵The Hittites replied to Abraham, ⁶"Listen, my lord, you are an honored prince among us. Choose the finest of our tombs and bury her there. No one here will refuse to help you in this way."

⁷Then Abraham bowed low before the Hittites ⁸and said, "Since you are willing to help me in this way, be so kind as to ask Ephron son of Zohar ⁹to let me buy his cave at Machpelah, down at the end of his field. I will pay the full price in the presence of witnesses, so I will have a permanent burial place for my family."

¹⁰Ephron was sitting there among the others, and he answered Abraham as the others listened, speaking publicly before all the Hittite elders of the town. ¹¹"No, my lord," he said to Abraham, "please listen to me. I will give you the field and the cave. Here in the presence of my people, I give it to you. Go and bury your dead."

¹²Abraham again bowed low before the citizens of the land, ¹³and he replied to Ephron as everyone listened. "No, listen to me. I will buy it from you. Let me pay the full price for the field so I can bury my dead there."

¹⁴Ephron answered Abraham, ¹⁵"My lord, please listen to me. The land is worth 400 pieces* of silver, but what is that between friends? Go ahead and bury your dead."

¹⁶So Abraham agreed to Ephron's price and paid the amount he had suggested—400 pieces of silver, weighed according to the market standard. The Hittite elders witnessed the transaction.

¹⁷So Abraham bought the plot of land belonging to Ephron at Machpelah, near Mamre. This included the field itself, the cave that was in it, and all the surrounding trees. ¹⁸It was transferred to Abraham as his permanent possession in the presence of the Hittite elders at the city gate. ¹⁹Then Abraham buried his wife, Sarah, there in Canaan, in the cave of Machpelah, near Mamre (also called Hebron). ²⁰So the field and the cave were transferred from the Hittites to Abraham for use as a permanent burial place.

24 A Wife for Isaac

Abraham was now a very old man, and the LORD had blessed him in every way. ²One day Abraham said to his oldest servant, the man in charge of his household, "Take an oath by putting your hand under my thigh. ³Swear by the LORD, the God of heaven and earth, that you will not allow my son to marry one of these local Canaanite women. ⁴Go instead to my homeland, to my relatives, and find a wife there for my son Isaac."

⁵The servant asked, "But what if I can't find a young woman who is willing to travel so far from home? Should I then take Isaac there to live among your relatives in the land you came from?"

⁶"No!" Abraham responded. "Be careful never to take my son there. ⁷For the LORD, the God of heaven, who took me from my father's house and my native land, solemnly promised to give this land to my descendants.* He will send his angel ahead of you, and he will see to it that you find a wife there for my son. ⁸If she is unwilling to come back with you, then you are free from this oath of mine. But under no circumstances are you to take my son there."

⁹So the servant took an oath by putting

23:15 Hebrew *400 shekels*, about 10 pounds or 4.6 kilograms in weight; also in 23:16.   **24:7** Hebrew *seed*; also in 24:60.

his hand under the thigh of his master, Abraham. He swore to follow Abraham's instructions. ¹⁰Then he loaded ten of Abraham's camels with all kinds of expensive gifts from his master, and he traveled to distant Aram-naharaim. There he went to the town where Abraham's brother Nahor had settled. ¹¹He made the camels kneel beside a well just outside the town. It was evening, and the women were coming out to draw water.

¹²"O LORD, God of my master, Abraham," he prayed. "Please give me success today, and show unfailing love to my master, Abraham. ¹³See, I am standing here beside this spring, and the young women of the town are coming out to draw water. ¹⁴This is my request. I will ask one of them, 'Please give me a drink from your jug.' If she says, 'Yes, have a drink, and I will water your camels, too!'—let her be the one you have selected as Isaac's wife. This is how I will know that you have shown unfailing love to my master."

¹⁵Before he had finished praying, he saw a young woman named Rebekah coming out with her water jug on her shoulder. She was the daughter of Bethuel, who was the son of Abraham's brother Nahor and his wife, Milcah. ¹⁶Rebekah was very beautiful and old enough to be married, but she was still a virgin. She went down to the spring, filled her jug, and came up again. ¹⁷Running over to her, the servant said, "Please give me a little drink of water from your jug."

¹⁸"Yes, my lord," she answered, "have a drink." And she quickly lowered her jug from her shoulder and gave him a drink. ¹⁹When she had given him a drink, she said, "I'll draw water for your camels, too, until they have had enough to drink." ²⁰So she quickly emptied her jug into the watering trough and ran back to the well to draw water for all his camels.

²¹The servant watched her in silence, wondering whether or not the LORD had given him success in his mission. ²²Then at last, when the camels had finished drinking, he took out a gold ring for her nose and two large gold bracelets* for her wrists.

²³"Whose daughter are you?" he asked. "And please tell me, would your father have any room to put us up for the night?"

²⁴"I am the daughter of Bethuel," she replied. "My grandparents are Nahor and Milcah. ²⁵Yes, we have plenty of straw and feed for the camels, and we have room for guests."

²⁶The man bowed low and worshiped the LORD. ²⁷"Praise the LORD, the God of my master, Abraham," he said. "The LORD has shown unfailing love and faithfulness to my master, for he has led me straight to my master's relatives."

²⁸The young woman ran home to tell her family everything that had happened. ²⁹Now Rebekah had a brother named Laban, who ran out to meet the man at the spring. ³⁰He had seen the nose-ring and the bracelets on his sister's wrists, and had heard Rebekah tell what the man had said. So he rushed out to the spring, where the man was still standing beside his camels. ³¹Laban said to him, "Come and stay with us, you who are blessed by the LORD! Why are you standing here outside the town when I have a room all ready for you and a place prepared for the camels?"

³²So the man went home with Laban, and Laban unloaded the camels, gave him straw for their bedding, fed them, and provided water for the man and the camel drivers to wash their feet. ³³Then food was served. But Abraham's servant said, "I don't want to eat until I have told you why I have come."

"All right," Laban said, "tell us."

³⁴"I am Abraham's servant," he explained. ³⁵"And the LORD has greatly blessed my master; he has become a wealthy man. The LORD has given him flocks of sheep and goats, herds of cattle, a fortune in silver and gold, and many male and female servants and camels and donkeys.

³⁶"When Sarah, my master's wife, was very old, she gave birth to my master's son, and my master has given him everything he owns. ³⁷And my master made me take an oath. He said, 'Do not allow my son to marry one of these local Canaanite women. ³⁸Go instead to my father's house, to my relatives, and find a wife there for my son.'

24:22 Hebrew *a gold nose-ring weighing a half shekel* [0.2 ounces or 6 grams] *and two gold bracelets weighing 10 shekels* [4 ounces or 114 grams].

[39]"But I said to my master, 'What if I can't find a young woman who is willing to go back with me?' [40]He responded, 'The LORD, in whose presence I have lived, will send his angel with you and will make your mission successful. Yes, you must find a wife for my son from among my relatives, from my father's family. [41]Then you will have fulfilled your obligation. But if you go to my relatives and they refuse to let her go with you, you will be free from my oath.'

[42]"So today when I came to the spring, I prayed this prayer: 'O LORD, God of my master, Abraham, please give me success on this mission. [43]See, I am standing here beside this spring. This is my request. When a young woman comes to draw water, I will say to her, "Please give me a little drink of water from your jug." [44]If she says, "Yes, have a drink, and I will draw water for your camels, too," let her be the one you have selected to be the wife of my master's son.'

[45]"Before I had finished praying in my heart, I saw Rebekah coming out with her water jug on her shoulder. She went down to the spring and drew water. So I said to her, 'Please give me a drink.' [46]She quickly lowered her jug from her shoulder and said, 'Yes, have a drink, and I will water your camels, too!' So I drank, and then she watered the camels.

[47]"Then I asked, 'Whose daughter are you?' She replied, 'I am the daughter of Bethuel, and my grandparents are Nahor and Milcah.' So I put the ring on her nose, and the bracelets on her wrists.

[48]"Then I bowed low and worshiped the LORD. I praised the LORD, the God of my master, Abraham, because he had led me straight to my master's niece to be his son's wife. [49]So tell me—will you or won't you show unfailing love and faithfulness to my master? Please tell me yes or no, and then I'll know what to do next."

[50]Then Laban and Bethuel replied, "The LORD has obviously brought you here, so there is nothing we can say. [51]Here is Rebekah; take her and go. Yes, let her be the wife of your master's son, as the LORD has directed."

[52]When Abraham's servant heard their answer, he bowed down to the ground and worshiped the LORD. [53]Then he brought out silver and gold jewelry and clothing and presented them to Rebekah. He also gave expensive presents to her brother and mother. [54]Then they ate their meal, and the servant and the men with him stayed there overnight.

But early the next morning, Abraham's servant said, "Send me back to my master."

[55]"But we want Rebekah to stay with us at least ten days," her brother and mother said. "Then she can go."

[56]But he said, "Don't delay me. The LORD has made my mission successful; now send me back so I can return to my master."

[57]"Well," they said, "we'll call Rebekah and ask her what she thinks." [58]So they called Rebekah. "Are you willing to go with this man?" they asked her.

And she replied, "Yes, I will go."

[59]So they said good-bye to Rebekah and sent her away with Abraham's servant and his men. The woman who had been Rebekah's childhood nurse went along with her. [60]They gave her this blessing as she parted:

"Our sister, may you become
    the mother of many millions!
May your descendants be strong
    and conquer the cities of their
        enemies."

[61]Then Rebekah and her servant girls mounted the camels and followed the man. So Abraham's servant took Rebekah and went on his way.

[62]Meanwhile, Isaac, whose home was in the Negev, had returned from Beer-lahai-roi. [63]One evening as he was walking and meditating in the fields, he looked up and saw the camels coming. [64]When Rebekah looked up and saw Isaac, she quickly dismounted from her camel. [65]"Who is that man walking through the fields to meet us?" she asked the servant.

And he replied, "It is my master." So Rebekah covered her face with her veil. [66]Then the servant told Isaac everything he had done.

[67]And Isaac brought Rebekah into his mother Sarah's tent, and she became his wife. He loved her deeply, and she was a special comfort to him after the death of his mother.

25 The Death of Abraham

Abraham married another wife, whose name was Keturah. ²She gave birth to Zimran, Jokshan, Medan, Midian, Ishbak, and Shuah. ³Jokshan was the father of Sheba and Dedan. Dedan's descendants were the Asshurites, Letushites, and Leummites. ⁴Midian's sons were Ephah, Epher, Hanoch, Abida, and Eldaah. These were all descendants of Abraham through Keturah.

⁵Abraham gave everything he owned to his son Isaac. ⁶But before he died, he gave gifts to the sons of his concubines and sent them off to a land in the east, away from Isaac.

⁷Abraham lived for 175 years, ⁸and he died at a ripe old age, having lived a long and satisfying life. He breathed his last and joined his ancestors in death. ⁹His sons Isaac and Ishmael buried him in the cave of Machpelah, near Mamre, in the field of Ephron son of Zohar the Hittite. ¹⁰This was the field Abraham had purchased from the Hittites and where he had buried his wife Sarah. ¹¹After Abraham's death, God blessed his son Isaac, who settled near Beer-lahai-roi in the Negev.

Ishmael's Descendants

¹²This is the account of the family of Ishmael, the son of Abraham through Hagar, Sarah's Egyptian servant. ¹³Here is a list, by their names and clans, of Ishmael's descendants: The oldest was Nebaioth, followed by Kedar, Adbeel, Mibsam, ¹⁴Mishma, Dumah, Massa, ¹⁵Hadad, Tema, Jetur, Naphish, and Kedemah. ¹⁶These twelve sons of Ishmael became the founders of twelve tribes named after them, listed according to the places they settled and camped. ¹⁷Ishmael lived for 137 years. Then he breathed his last and joined his ancestors in death. ¹⁸Ishmael's descendants occupied the region from Havilah to Shur, which is east of Egypt in the direction of Asshur. There they lived in open hostility toward all their relatives.*

The Births of Esau and Jacob

¹⁹This is the account of the family of Isaac, the son of Abraham. ²⁰When Isaac was forty years old, he married Rebekah, the daughter of Bethuel the Aramean from Paddanaram and the sister of Laban the Aramean.

²¹Isaac pleaded with the LORD on behalf of his wife, because she was unable to have children. The LORD answered Isaac's prayer, and Rebekah became pregnant with twins. ²²But the two children struggled with each other in her womb. So she went to ask the LORD about it. "Why is this happening to me?" she asked.

²³And the LORD told her, "The sons in your womb will become two nations. From the very beginning, the two nations will be rivals. One nation will be stronger than the other; and your older son will serve your younger son."

²⁴And when the time came to give birth, Rebekah discovered that she did indeed have twins! ²⁵The first one was very red at birth and covered with thick hair like a fur coat. So they named him Esau.* ²⁶Then the other twin was born with his hand grasping Esau's heel. So they named him Jacob.* Isaac was sixty years old when the twins were born.

Esau Sells His Birthright

²⁷As the boys grew up, Esau became a skillful hunter. He was an outdoorsman, but Jacob had a quiet temperament, preferring to stay at home. ²⁸Isaac loved Esau because he enjoyed eating the wild game Esau brought home, but Rebekah loved Jacob.

²⁹One day when Jacob was cooking some stew, Esau arrived home from the wilderness exhausted and hungry. ³⁰Esau said to Jacob, "I'm starved! Give me some of that red stew!" (This is how Esau got his other name, Edom, which means "red.")

³¹"All right," Jacob replied, "but trade me your rights as the firstborn son."

³²"Look, I'm dying of starvation!" said Esau. "What good is my birthright to me now?"

³³But Jacob said, "First you must swear that your birthright is mine." So Esau swore an oath, thereby selling all his rights as the firstborn to his brother, Jacob.

³⁴Then Jacob gave Esau some bread and

25:18 The meaning of the Hebrew is uncertain. **25:25** *Esau* sounds like a Hebrew term that means "hair." **25:26** *Jacob* sounds like the Hebrew words for "heel" and "deceiver."

lentil stew. Esau ate the meal, then got up and left. He showed contempt for his rights as the firstborn.

26 Isaac Deceives Abimelech

A severe famine now struck the land, as had happened before in Abraham's time. So Isaac moved to Gerar, where Abimelech, king of the Philistines, lived.

²The LORD appeared to Isaac and said, "Do not go down to Egypt, but do as I tell you. ³Live here as a foreigner in this land, and I will be with you and bless you. I hereby confirm that I will give all these lands to you and your descendants,* just as I solemnly promised Abraham, your father. ⁴I will cause your descendants to become as numerous as the stars of the sky, and I will give them all these lands. And through your descendants all the nations of the earth will be blessed. ⁵I will do this because Abraham listened to me and obeyed all my requirements, commands, decrees, and instructions." ⁶So Isaac stayed in Gerar.

⁷When the men who lived there asked Isaac about his wife, Rebekah, he said, "She is my sister." He was afraid to say, "She is my wife." He thought, "They will kill me to get her, because she is so beautiful." ⁸But some time later, Abimelech, king of the Philistines, looked out his window and saw Isaac caressing Rebekah.

⁹Immediately, Abimelech called for Isaac and exclaimed, "She is obviously your wife! Why did you say, 'She is my sister'?"

"Because I was afraid someone would kill me to get her from me," Isaac replied.

¹⁰"How could you do this to us?" Abimelech exclaimed. "One of my people might easily have taken your wife and slept with her, and you would have made us guilty of great sin."

¹¹Then Abimelech issued a public proclamation: "Anyone who touches this man or his wife will be put to death!"

Conflict over Water Rights

¹²When Isaac planted his crops that year, he harvested a hundred times more grain than he planted, for the LORD blessed him. ¹³He became a very rich man, and his wealth continued to grow. ¹⁴He acquired so many flocks of sheep and goats, herds of cattle, and servants that the Philistines became jealous of him. ¹⁵So the Philistines filled up all of Isaac's wells with dirt. These were the wells that had been dug by the servants of his father, Abraham.

¹⁶Finally, Abimelech ordered Isaac to leave the country. "Go somewhere else," he said, "for you have become too powerful for us."

¹⁷So Isaac moved away to the Gerar Valley, where he set up their tents and settled down. ¹⁸He reopened the wells his father had dug, which the Philistines had filled in after Abraham's death. Isaac also restored the names Abraham had given them.

¹⁹Isaac's servants also dug in the Gerar Valley and discovered a well of fresh water. ²⁰But then the shepherds from Gerar came and claimed the spring. "This is our water," they said, and they argued over it with Isaac's herdsmen. So Isaac named the well Esek (which means "argument"). ²¹Isaac's men then dug another well, but again there was a dispute over it. So Isaac named it Sitnah (which means "hostility"). ²²Abandoning that one, Isaac moved on and dug another well. This time there was no dispute over it, so Isaac named the place Rehoboth (which means "open space"), for he said, "At last the LORD has created enough space for us to prosper in this land."

²³From there Isaac moved to Beersheba, ²⁴where the LORD appeared to him on the night of his arrival. "I am the God of your father, Abraham," he said. "Do not be afraid, for I am with you and will bless you. I will multiply your descendants, and they will become a great nation. I will do this because of my promise to Abraham, my servant." ²⁵Then Isaac built an altar there and worshiped the LORD. He set up his camp at that place, and his servants dug another well.

Isaac's Covenant with Abimelech

²⁶One day King Abimelech came from Gerar with his adviser, Ahuzzath, and also Phicol, his army commander. ²⁷"Why have you come here?" Isaac asked. "You obviously hate me, since you kicked me off your land."

26:3 Hebrew *seed*; also in 26:4, 24.

They replied, "We can plainly see that the Lord is with you. So we want to enter into a sworn treaty with you. Let's make a covenant. ²⁹Swear that you will not harm us, just as we have never troubled you. We have always treated you well, and we sent you away from us in peace. And now look how the Lord has blessed you!"

³⁰So Isaac prepared a covenant feast to celebrate the treaty, and they ate and drank together. ³¹Early the next morning, they each took a solemn oath not to interfere with each other. Then Isaac sent them home again, and they left him in peace.

³²That very day Isaac's servants came and told him about a new well they had dug. "We've found water!" they exclaimed. ³³So Isaac named the well Shibah (which means "oath"). And to this day the town that grew up there is called Beersheba (which means "well of the oath").

³⁴At the age of forty, Esau married two Hittite wives: Judith, the daughter of Beeri, and Basemath, the daughter of Elon. ³⁵But Esau's wives made life miserable for Isaac and Rebekah.

27 Jacob Steals Esau's Blessing

One day when Isaac was old and turning blind, he called for Esau, his older son, and said, "My son."

"Yes, Father?" Esau replied.

²"I am an old man now," Isaac said, "and I don't know when I may die. ³Take your bow and a quiver full of arrows, and go out into the open country to hunt some wild game for me. ⁴Prepare my favorite dish, and bring it here for me to eat. Then I will pronounce the blessing that belongs to you, my first-born son, before I die."

⁵But Rebekah overheard what Isaac had said to his son Esau. So when Esau left to hunt for the wild game, ⁶she said to her son Jacob, "Listen. I overheard your father say to Esau, ⁷'Bring me some wild game and prepare me a delicious meal. Then I will bless you in the Lord's presence before I die.' ⁸Now, my son, listen to me. Do exactly as I tell you. ⁹Go out to the flocks, and bring me two fine young goats. I'll use them to prepare your father's favorite dish. ¹⁰Then take the food to your father so he can eat it and bless you before he dies."

¹¹"But look," Jacob replied to Rebekah, "my brother, Esau, is a hairy man, and my skin is smooth. ¹²What if my father touches me? He'll see that I'm trying to trick him, and then he'll curse me instead of blessing me."

¹³But his mother replied, "Then let the curse fall on me, my son! Just do what I tell you. Go out and get the goats for me!"

¹⁴So Jacob went out and got the young goats for his mother. Rebekah took them and prepared a delicious meal, just the way Isaac liked it. ¹⁵Then she took Esau's favorite clothes, which were there in the house, and gave them to her younger son, Jacob. ¹⁶She covered his arms and the smooth part of his neck with the skin of the young goats. ¹⁷Then she gave Jacob the delicious meal, including freshly baked bread.

¹⁸So Jacob took the food to his father. "My father?" he said.

"Yes, my son," Isaac answered. "Who are you—Esau or Jacob?"

¹⁹Jacob replied, "It's Esau, your firstborn son. I've done as you told me. Here is the wild game. Now sit up and eat it so you can give me your blessing."

²⁰Isaac asked, "How did you find it so quickly, my son?"

"The Lord your God put it in my path!" Jacob replied.

²¹Then Isaac said to Jacob, "Come closer so I can touch you and make sure that you really are Esau." ²²So Jacob went closer to his father, and Isaac touched him. "The voice is Jacob's, but the hands are Esau's," Isaac said. ²³But he did not recognize Jacob, because Jacob's hands felt hairy just like Esau's. So Isaac prepared to bless Jacob. ²⁴"But are you really my son Esau?" he asked.

"Yes, I am," Jacob replied.

²⁵Then Isaac said, "Now, my son, bring me the wild game. Let me eat it, and then I will give you my blessing." So Jacob took the food to his father, and Isaac ate it. He also drank the wine that Jacob served him. ²⁶Then Isaac said to Jacob, "Please come a little closer and kiss me, my son."

²⁷So Jacob went over and kissed him. And when Isaac caught the smell of his clothes, he was finally convinced, and he blessed his son. He said, "Ah! The smell of my son is

like the smell of the outdoors, which the
LORD has blessed!

²⁸ "From the dew of heaven
and the richness of the earth,
may God always give you abundant
harvests of grain
and bountiful new wine.
²⁹ May many nations become your
servants,
and may they bow down to you.
May you be the master over your
brothers,
and may your mother's sons bow
down to you.
All who curse you will be cursed,
and all who bless you will be blessed."

³⁰ As soon as Isaac had finished blessing Jacob, and almost before Jacob had left his father, Esau returned from his hunt. ³¹ Esau prepared a delicious meal and brought it to his father. Then he said, "Sit up, my father, and eat my wild game so you can give me your blessing."

³² But Isaac asked him, "Who are you?"

Esau replied, "It's your son, your firstborn son, Esau."

³³ Isaac began to tremble uncontrollably and said, "Then who just served me wild game? I have already eaten it, and I blessed him just before you came. And yes, that blessing must stand!"

³⁴ When Esau heard his father's words, he let out a loud and bitter cry. "Oh my father, what about me? Bless me, too!" he begged.

³⁵ But Isaac said, "Your brother was here, and he tricked me. He has taken away your blessing."

³⁶ Esau exclaimed, "No wonder his name is Jacob, for now he has cheated me twice.* First he took my rights as the firstborn, and now he has stolen my blessing. Oh, haven't you saved even one blessing for me?"

³⁷ Isaac said to Esau, "I have made Jacob your master and have declared that all his brothers will be his servants. I have guaranteed him an abundance of grain and wine— what is left for me to give you, my son?"

³⁸ Esau pleaded, "But do you have only one blessing? Oh my father, bless me, too!" Then Esau broke down and wept.

³⁹ Finally, his father, Isaac, said to him,

"You will live away from the richness of
the earth,
and away from the dew of the heaven
above.
⁴⁰ You will live by your sword,
and you will serve your brother.
But when you decide to break free,
you will shake his yoke from your
neck."

Jacob Flees to Paddan-Aram

⁴¹ From that time on, Esau hated Jacob because their father had given Jacob the blessing. And Esau began to scheme: "I will soon be mourning my father's death. Then I will kill my brother, Jacob."

⁴² But Rebekah heard about Esau's plans. So she sent for Jacob and told him, "Listen, Esau is consoling himself by plotting to kill you. ⁴³ So listen carefully, my son. Get ready and flee to my brother, Laban, in Haran. ⁴⁴ Stay there with him until your brother cools off. ⁴⁵ When he calms down and forgets what you have done to him, I will send for you to come back. Why should I lose both of you in one day?"

⁴⁶ Then Rebekah said to Isaac, "I'm sick and tired of these local Hittite women! I would rather die than see Jacob marry one of them."

28 So Isaac called for Jacob, blessed him, and said, "You must not marry any of these Canaanite women. ² Instead, go at once to Paddan-aram, to the house of your grandfather Bethuel, and marry one of your uncle Laban's daughters. ³ May God Almighty* bless you and give you many children. And may your descendants multiply and become many nations! ⁴ May God pass on to you and your descendants* the blessings he promised to Abraham. May you own this land where you are now living as a foreigner, for God gave this land to Abraham."

⁵ So Isaac sent Jacob away, and he went to Paddan-aram to stay with his uncle Laban, his mother's brother, the son of Bethuel the Aramean.

⁶ Esau knew that his father, Isaac, had

blessed Jacob and sent him to Paddan-aram to find a wife, and that he had warned Jacob, "You must not marry a Canaanite woman." ⁷He also knew that Jacob had obeyed his parents and gone to Paddan-aram. ⁸It was now very clear to Esau that his father did not like the local Canaanite women. ⁹So Esau visited his uncle Ishmael's family and married one of Ishmael's daughters, in addition to the wives he already had. His new wife's name was Mahalath. She was the sister of Nebaioth and the daughter of Ishmael, Abraham's son.

Jacob's Dream at Bethel

¹⁰Meanwhile, Jacob left Beersheba and traveled toward Haran. ¹¹At sundown he arrived at a good place to set up camp and stopped there for the night. Jacob found a stone to rest his head against and lay down to sleep. ¹²As he slept, he dreamed of a stairway that reached from the earth up to heaven. And he saw the angels of God going up and down the stairway.

¹³At the top of the stairway stood the Lord, and he said, "I am the Lord, the God of your grandfather Abraham, and the God of your father, Isaac. The ground you are lying on belongs to you. I am giving it to you and your descendants. ¹⁴Your descendants will be as numerous as the dust of the earth! They will spread out in all directions—to the west and the east, to the north and the south. And all the families of the earth will be blessed through you and your descendants. ¹⁵What's more, I am with you, and I will protect you wherever you go. One day I will bring you back to this land. I will not leave you until I have finished giving you everything I have promised you."

¹⁶Then Jacob awoke from his sleep and said, "Surely the Lord is in this place, and I wasn't even aware of it!" ¹⁷But he was also afraid and said, "What an awesome place this is! It is none other than the house of God, the very gateway to heaven!"

¹⁸The next morning Jacob got up very early. He took the stone he had rested his head against, and he set it upright as a memorial pillar. Then he poured olive oil over it. ¹⁹He named that place Bethel (which means "house of God"), although it was previously called Luz.

²⁰Then Jacob made this vow: "If God will indeed be with me and protect me on this journey, and if he will provide me with food and clothing, ²¹and if I return safely to my father's home, then the Lord will certainly be my God. ²²And this memorial pillar I have set up will become a place for worshiping God, and I will present to God a tenth of everything he gives me."

29 Jacob Arrives at Paddan-Aram

Then Jacob hurried on, finally arriving in the land of the east. ²He saw a well in the distance. Three flocks of sheep and goats lay in an open field beside it, waiting to be watered. But a heavy stone covered the mouth of the well.

³It was the custom there to wait for all the flocks to arrive before removing the stone and watering the animals. Afterward the stone would be placed back over the mouth of the well. ⁴Jacob went over to the shepherds and asked, "Where are you from, my friends?"

"We are from Haran," they answered.

⁵"Do you know a man there named Laban, the grandson of Nahor?" he asked.

"Yes, we do," they replied.

⁶"Is he doing well?" Jacob asked.

"Yes, he's well," they answered. "Look, here comes his daughter Rachel with the flock now."

⁷Jacob said, "Look, it's still broad daylight—too early to round up the animals. Why don't you water the sheep and goats so they can get back out to pasture?"

⁸"We can't water the animals until all the flocks have arrived," they replied. "Then the shepherds move the stone from the mouth of the well, and we water all the sheep and goats."

⁹Jacob was still talking with them when Rachel arrived with her father's flock, for she was a shepherd. ¹⁰And because Rachel was his cousin—the daughter of Laban, his mother's brother—and because the sheep and goats belonged to his uncle Laban, Jacob went over to the well and moved the stone from its mouth and watered his uncle's flock. ¹¹Then Jacob kissed Rachel, and he

wept aloud. ¹²He explained to Rachel that he was her cousin on her father's side—the son of her aunt Rebekah. So Rachel quickly ran and told her father, Laban.

¹³As soon as Laban heard that his nephew Jacob had arrived, he ran out to meet him. He embraced and kissed him and brought him home. When Jacob had told him his story, ¹⁴Laban exclaimed, "You really are my own flesh and blood!"

Jacob Marries Leah and Rachel

After Jacob had stayed with Laban for about a month, ¹⁵Laban said to him, "You shouldn't work for me without pay just because we are relatives. Tell me how much your wages should be."

¹⁶Now Laban had two daughters. The older daughter was named Leah, and the younger one was Rachel. ¹⁷There was no sparkle in Leah's eyes,* but Rachel had a beautiful figure and a lovely face. ¹⁸Since Jacob was in love with Rachel, he told her father, "I'll work for you for seven years if you'll give me Rachel, your younger daughter, as my wife."

¹⁹"Agreed!" Laban replied. "I'd rather give her to you than to anyone else. Stay and work with me." ²⁰So Jacob worked seven

Leah: Grateful for What She Had

GENESIS 29:16–35

From the moment she appears in Scripture, Leah is compared to, and eclipsed by, her younger sister, Rachel. Genesis 29:17 says, "There was no sparkle in Leah's eyes, but Rachel had a beautiful figure and a lovely face." So she must have experienced the heartache of feeling unloved and unattractive.

Even Leah's future husband, Jacob, had eyes only for Rachel. He worked for his uncle seven years in return for Rachel's hand in marriage, yet when the wedding night came, Jacob was so blinded by love he didn't notice the bride sharing his bed wasn't Rachel. This cruel deception was Leah's father's idea, and her new husband, Jacob, clearly "loved [Rachel] much more than Leah" (29:30). Meanwhile Leah was yoked to a man who didn't choose her, love her, or want her.

Yet God noticed Leah. He cared for Leah. And he took away her pain as only he could: "He enabled her to have children" (29:31). The Lord showed Leah she had value in her society and was indeed loved—if not by her father or Jacob, then surely by her heavenly Father. Leah gave birth to three sons in a row; her hopes pinned on winning Jacob's love: "Surely this time my husband will feel affection for me" (29:34). But after the birth of each son, not a word was heard from Jacob. When God blessed her womb a fourth time, something happened inside Leah's heart. Three times she'd turned to a weak man for love. This time she turned to a strong God. "Once again Leah became pregnant and gave birth to another son. . . . [And] she said, 'Now I will praise the LORD!'" (29:35).

What a woman! Instead of blaming God for what she didn't have, Leah thanked God for what she *did* have: four healthy children and the Lord's unfailing favor. Leah had many reasons to become bitter and angry. Instead she chose to see God's goodness and faithfulness in her life and to praise him for them.

—Liz Curtis Higgs

For more on gratitude, see reading at Exodus 16:1–18.

29:17 Or *Leah had dull eyes*, or *Leah had soft eyes*. The meaning of the Hebrew is uncertain.

years to pay for Rachel. But his love for her was so strong that it seemed to him but a few days.

²¹ Finally, the time came for him to marry her. "I have fulfilled my agreement," Jacob said to Laban. "Now give me my wife so I can sleep with her."

²² So Laban invited everyone in the neighborhood and prepared a wedding feast. ²³ But that night, when it was dark, Laban took Leah to Jacob, and he slept with her. ²⁴ (Laban had given Leah a servant, Zilpah, to be her maid.)

²⁵ But when Jacob woke up in the morning—it was Leah! "What have you done to me?" Jacob raged at Laban. "I worked seven years for Rachel! Why have you tricked me?"

²⁶ "It's not our custom here to marry off a younger daughter ahead of the firstborn," Laban replied. ²⁷ "But wait until the bridal week is over, then we'll give you Rachel, too—provided you promise to work another seven years for me."

²⁸ So Jacob agreed to work seven more years. A week after Jacob had married Leah, Laban gave him Rachel, too. ²⁹ (Laban gave Rachel a servant, Bilhah, to be her maid.) ³⁰ So Jacob slept with Rachel, too, and he loved her much more than Leah. He then stayed and worked for Laban the additional seven years.

Jacob's Many Children

³¹ When the LORD saw that Leah was unloved, he enabled her to have children, but Rachel could not conceive. ³² So Leah became pregnant and gave birth to a son. She named him Reuben,* for she said, "The LORD has noticed my misery, and now my husband will love me."

³³ She soon became pregnant again and gave birth to another son. She named him Simeon,* for she said, "The LORD heard that I was unloved and has given me another son."

³⁴ Then she became pregnant a third time and gave birth to another son. She named him Levi,* for she said, "Surely this time my husband will feel affection for me, since I have given him three sons!"

³⁵ Once again Leah became pregnant and gave birth to another son. She named him Judah,* for she said, "Now I will praise the LORD!" And then she stopped having children.

30 When Rachel saw that she wasn't having any children for Jacob, she became jealous of her sister. She pleaded with Jacob, "Give me children, or I'll die!"

² Then Jacob became furious with Rachel. "Am I God?" he asked. "He's the one who has kept you from having children!"

³ Then Rachel told him, "Take my maid, Bilhah, and sleep with her. She will bear children for me,* and through her I can have a family, too." ⁴ So Rachel gave her servant, Bilhah, to Jacob as a wife, and he slept with her. ⁵ Bilhah became pregnant and presented him with a son. ⁶ Rachel named him Dan,* for she said, "God has vindicated me! He has heard my request and given me a son." ⁷ Then Bilhah became pregnant again and gave Jacob a second son. ⁸ Rachel named him Naphtali,* for she said, "I have struggled hard with my sister, and I'm winning!"

⁹ Meanwhile, Leah realized that she wasn't getting pregnant anymore, so she took her servant, Zilpah, and gave her to Jacob as a wife. ¹⁰ Soon Zilpah presented him with a son. ¹¹ Leah named him Gad,* for she said, "How fortunate I am!" ¹² Then Zilpah gave Jacob a second son. ¹³ And Leah named him Asher,* for she said, "What joy is mine! Now the other women will celebrate with me."

¹⁴ One day during the wheat harvest, Reuben found some mandrakes growing in a field and brought them to his mother, Leah. Rachel begged Leah, "Please give me some of your son's mandrakes."

¹⁵ But Leah angrily replied, "Wasn't it enough that you stole my husband? Now will you steal my son's mandrakes, too?"

Rachel answered, "I will let Jacob sleep with you tonight if you give me some of the mandrakes."

¹⁶ So that evening, as Jacob was coming home from the fields, Leah went out to

---

29:32 Reuben means "Look, a son!" It also sounds like the Hebrew for "He has seen my misery."   **29:33** Simeon probably means "one who hears."   **29:34** Levi sounds like a Hebrew term that means "being attached" or "feeling affection for."   **29:35** Judah is related to the Hebrew term for "praise."   **30:3** Hebrew bear children on my knees.   **30:6** Dan means "he judged" or "he vindicated."   **30:8** Naphtali means "my struggle."   **30:11** Gad means "good fortune."   **30:13** Asher means "happy."

meet him. "You must come and sleep with me tonight!" she said. "I have paid for you with some mandrakes that my son found." So that night he slept with Leah. ¹⁷ And God answered Leah's prayers. She became pregnant again and gave birth to a fifth son for Jacob. ¹⁸ She named him Issachar,* for she said, "God has rewarded me for giving my servant to my husband as a wife." ¹⁹ Then Leah became pregnant again and gave birth to a sixth son for Jacob. ²⁰ She named him Zebulun,* for she said, "God has given me a good reward. Now my husband will treat me with respect, for I have given him six sons." ²¹ Later she gave birth to a daughter and named her Dinah.

²² Then God remembered Rachel's plight and answered her prayers by enabling her to have children. ²³ She became pregnant and gave birth to a son. "God has removed my disgrace," she said. ²⁴ And she named him Joseph,* for she said, "May the LORD add yet another son to my family."

Jacob's Wealth Increases

²⁵ Soon after Rachel had given birth to Joseph, Jacob said to Laban, "Please release me so I can go home to my own country. ²⁶ Let me take my wives and children, for I have earned them by serving you, and let me be on my way. You certainly know how hard I have worked for you."

²⁷ "Please listen to me," Laban replied. "I have become wealthy, for* the LORD has blessed me because of you. ²⁸ Tell me how much I owe you. Whatever it is, I'll pay it."

²⁹ Jacob replied, "You know how hard I've worked for you, and how your flocks and herds have grown under my care. ³⁰ You had little indeed before I came, but your wealth has increased enormously. The LORD has blessed you through everything I've done. But now, what about me? When can I start providing for my own family?"

³¹ "What wages do you want?" Laban asked again.

Jacob replied, "Don't give me anything. Just do this one thing, and I'll continue to tend and watch over your flocks. ³² Let me inspect your flocks today and remove all the sheep and goats that are speckled or spotted, along with all the black sheep. Give these to me as my wages. ³³ In the future, when you check on the animals you have given me as my wages, you'll see that I have been honest. If you find in my flock any goats without speckles or spots, or any sheep that are not black, you will know that I have stolen them from you."

³⁴ "All right," Laban replied. "It will be as you say." ³⁵ But that very day Laban went out and removed the male goats that were streaked and spotted, all the female goats that were speckled and spotted or had white patches, and all the black sheep. He placed them in the care of his own sons, ³⁶ who took them a three-days' journey from where Jacob was. Meanwhile, Jacob stayed and cared for the rest of Laban's flock.

³⁷ Then Jacob took some fresh branches from poplar, almond, and plane trees and peeled off strips of bark, making white streaks on them. ³⁸ Then he placed these peeled branches in the watering troughs where the flocks came to drink, for that was where they mated. ³⁹ And when they mated in front of the white-streaked branches, they gave birth to young that were streaked, speckled, and spotted. ⁴⁰ Jacob separated those lambs from Laban's flock. And at mating time he turned the flock to face Laban's animals that were streaked or black. This is how he built his own flock instead of increasing Laban's.

⁴¹ Whenever the stronger females were ready to mate, Jacob would place the peeled branches in the watering troughs in front of them. Then they would mate in front of the branches. ⁴² But he didn't do this with the weaker ones, so the weaker lambs belonged to Laban, and the stronger ones were Jacob's. ⁴³ As a result, Jacob became very wealthy, with large flocks of sheep and goats, female and male servants, and many camels and donkeys.

31 Jacob Flees from Laban

But Jacob soon learned that Laban's sons were grumbling about him. "Jacob has robbed our father of everything!" they said.

30:18 *Issachar* sounds like a Hebrew term that means "reward." **30:20** *Zebulun* probably means "honor." **30:24** *Joseph* means "may he add." **30:27** Or *I have learned by divination that.*

"He has gained all his wealth at our father's expense." ²And Jacob began to notice a change in Laban's attitude toward him.

³Then the LORD said to Jacob, "Return to the land of your father and grandfather and to your relatives there, and I will be with you."

⁴So Jacob called Rachel and Leah out to the field where he was watching his flock. ⁵He said to them, "I have noticed that your father's attitude toward me has changed. But the God of my father has been with me. ⁶You know how hard I have worked for your father, ⁷but he has cheated me, changing my wages ten times. But God has not allowed him to do me any harm. ⁸For if he said, 'The speckled animals will be your wages,' the whole flock began to produce speckled young. And when he changed his mind and said, 'The striped animals will be your wages,' then the whole flock produced striped young. ⁹In this way, God has taken your father's animals and given them to me.

¹⁰"One time during the mating season, I had a dream and saw that the male goats mating with the females were streaked, speckled, and spotted. ¹¹Then in my dream, the angel of God said to me, 'Jacob!' And I replied, 'Yes, here I am.'

¹²"The angel said, 'Look up, and you will see that only the streaked, speckled, and spotted males are mating with the females of your flock. For I have seen how Laban has treated you. ¹³I am the God who appeared to you at Bethel,* the place where you anointed the pillar of stone and made your vow to me. Now get ready and leave this country and return to the land of your birth.'"

¹⁴Rachel and Leah responded, "That's fine with us! We won't inherit any of our father's wealth anyway. ¹⁵He has reduced our rights to those of foreign women. And after he sold us, he wasted the money you paid him for us. ¹⁶All the wealth God has given you from our father legally belongs to us and our children. So go ahead and do whatever God has told you."

¹⁷So Jacob put his wives and children on camels, ¹⁸and he drove all his livestock in front of him. He packed all the belongings he had acquired in Paddan-aram and set out for the land of Canaan, where his father, Isaac, lived. ¹⁹At the time they left, Laban was some distance away, shearing his sheep. Rachel stole her father's household idols and took them with her. ²⁰Jacob outwitted Laban the Aramean, for they set out secretly and never told Laban they were leaving. ²¹So Jacob took all his possessions with him and crossed the Euphrates River,* heading for the hill country of Gilead.

Laban Pursues Jacob

²²Three days later, Laban was told that Jacob had fled. ²³So he gathered a group of his relatives and set out in hot pursuit. He caught up with Jacob seven days later in the hill country of Gilead. ²⁴But the previous night God had appeared to Laban the Aramean in a dream and told him, "I'm warning you—leave Jacob alone!"

²⁵Laban caught up with Jacob as he was camped in the hill country of Gilead, and he set up his camp not far from Jacob's. ²⁶"What do you mean by deceiving me like this?" Laban demanded. "How dare you drag my daughters away like prisoners of war? ²⁷Why did you slip away secretly? Why did you deceive me? And why didn't you say you wanted to leave? I would have given you a farewell feast, with singing and music, accompanied by tambourines and harps. ²⁸Why didn't you let me kiss my daughters and grandchildren and tell them good-bye? You have acted very foolishly! ²⁹I could destroy you, but the God of your father appeared to me last night and warned me, 'Leave Jacob alone!' ³⁰I can understand your feeling that you must go, and your intense longing for your father's home. But why have you stolen my gods?"

³¹"I rushed away because I was afraid," Jacob answered. "I thought you would take your daughters from me by force. ³²But as for your gods, see if you can find them, and let the person who has taken them die! And if you find anything else that belongs to you, identify it before all these relatives of ours, and I will give it back!" But Jacob did

---

31:13 As in Greek version and an Aramaic Targum; Hebrew reads *the God of Bethel*. **31:21** Hebrew *the river*.

not know that Rachel had stolen the household idols.

[33] Laban went first into Jacob's tent to search there, then into Leah's, and then the tents of the two servant wives—but he found nothing. Finally, he went into Rachel's tent. [34] But Rachel had taken the household idols and hidden them in her camel saddle, and now she was sitting on them. When Laban had thoroughly searched her tent without finding them, [35] she said to her father, "Please, sir, forgive me if I don't get up for you. I'm having my monthly period." So Laban continued his search, but he could not find the household idols.

[36] Then Jacob became very angry, and he challenged Laban. "What's my crime?" he demanded. "What have I done wrong to make you chase after me as though I were a criminal? [37] You have rummaged through everything I own. Now show me what you found that belongs to you! Set it out here in front of us, before our relatives, for all to see. Let them judge between us!

[38] "For twenty years I have been with you, caring for your flocks. In all that time your sheep and goats never miscarried. In all those years I never used a single ram of yours for food. [39] If any were attacked and killed by wild animals, I never showed you the carcass and asked you to reduce the count of your flock. No, I took the loss myself! You made me pay for every stolen animal, whether it was taken in broad daylight or in the dark of night.

[40] "I worked for you through the scorching heat of the day and through cold and sleepless nights. [41] Yes, for twenty years I slaved in your house! I worked for fourteen years earning your two daughters, and then six more years for your flock. And you changed my wages ten times! [42] In fact, if the God of my father had not been on my side—the God of Abraham and the fearsome God of Isaac*—you would have sent me away empty-handed. But God has seen your abuse and my hard work. That is why he appeared to you last night and rebuked you!"

Jacob's Treaty with Laban

[43] Then Laban replied to Jacob, "These women are my daughters, these children are my grandchildren, and these flocks are my flocks—in fact, everything you see is mine. But what can I do now about my daughters and their children? [44] So come, let's make a covenant, you and I, and it will be a witness to our commitment."

[45] So Jacob took a stone and set it up as a monument. [46] Then he told his family members, "Gather some stones." So they gathered stones and piled them in a heap. Then Jacob and Laban sat down beside the pile of stones to eat a covenant meal. [47] To commemorate the event, Laban called the place Jegar-sahadutha (which means "witness pile" in Aramaic), and Jacob called it Galeed (which means "witness pile" in Hebrew).

[48] Then Laban declared, "This pile of stones will stand as a witness to remind us of the covenant we have made today." This explains why it was called Galeed— "Witness Pile." [49] But it was also called Mizpah (which means "watchtower"), for Laban said, "May the LORD keep watch between us to make sure that we keep this covenant when we are out of each other's sight. [50] If you mistreat my daughters or if you marry other wives, God will see it even if no one else does. He is a witness to this covenant between us.

[51] "See this pile of stones," Laban continued, "and see this monument I have set between us. [52] They stand between us as witnesses of our vows. I will never pass this pile of stones to harm you, and you must never pass these stones or this monument to harm me. [53] I call on the God of our ancestors—the God of your grandfather Abraham and the God of my grandfather Nahor—to serve as a judge between us."

So Jacob took an oath before the fearsome God of his father, Isaac,* to respect the boundary line. [54] Then Jacob offered a sacrifice to God there on the mountain and invited everyone to a covenant feast. After they had eaten, they spent the night on the mountain.

[55] *Laban got up early the next morning, and he kissed his grandchildren and his daughters and blessed them. Then he left and returned home.

31:42 Or and the Fear of Isaac.   **31:53** Or the Fear of his father, Isaac.   **31:55** Verse 31:55 is numbered 32:1 in Hebrew text.

32

¹*As Jacob started on his way again, angels of God came to meet him. ²When Jacob saw them, he exclaimed, "This is God's camp!" So he named the place Mahanaim.*

Jacob Sends Gifts to Esau

³Then Jacob sent messengers ahead to his brother, Esau, who was living in the region of Seir in the land of Edom. ⁴He told them, "Give this message to my master Esau: 'Humble greetings from your servant Jacob. Until now I have been living with Uncle Laban, ⁵and now I own cattle, donkeys, flocks of sheep and goats, and many servants, both men and women. I have sent these messengers to inform my lord of my coming, hoping that you will be friendly to me.'"

⁶After delivering the message, the messengers returned to Jacob and reported, "We met your brother, Esau, and he is already on his way to meet you—with an army of 400 men!" ⁷Jacob was terrified at the news. He divided his household, along with the flocks and herds and camels, into two groups. ⁸He thought, "If Esau meets one group and attacks it, perhaps the other group can escape."

⁹Then Jacob prayed, "O God of my grandfather Abraham, and God of my father, Isaac—O LORD, you told me, 'Return to your own land and to your relatives.' And you promised me, 'I will treat you kindly.' ¹⁰I am not worthy of all the unfailing love and faithfulness you have shown to me, your servant. When I left home and crossed the Jordan River, I owned nothing except a walking stick. Now my household fills two large camps! ¹¹O LORD, please rescue me from the hand of my brother, Esau. I am afraid that he is coming to attack me, along with my wives and children. ¹²But you promised me, 'I will surely treat you kindly, and I will multiply your descendants until they become as numerous as the sands along the seashore—too many to count.'"

¹³Jacob stayed where he was for the night. Then he selected these gifts from his possessions to present to his brother, Esau: ¹⁴200 female goats, 20 male goats, 200 ewes, 20 rams, ¹⁵30 female camels with their young, 40 cows, 10 bulls, 20 female donkeys, and 10 male donkeys. ¹⁶He divided these animals into herds and assigned each to different servants. Then he told his servants, "Go ahead of me with the animals, but keep some distance between the herds."

¹⁷He gave these instructions to the men leading the first group: "When my brother, Esau, meets you, he will ask, 'Whose servants are you? Where are you going? Who owns these animals?' ¹⁸You must reply, 'They belong to your servant Jacob, but they are a gift for his master Esau. Look, he is coming right behind us.'"

¹⁹Jacob gave the same instructions to the second and third herdsmen and to all who followed behind the herds: "You must say the same thing to Esau when you meet him. ²⁰And be sure to say, 'Look, your servant Jacob is right behind us.'"

Jacob thought, "I will try to appease him by sending gifts ahead of me. When I see him in person, perhaps he will be friendly to me." ²¹So the gifts were sent on ahead, while Jacob himself spent that night in the camp.

Jacob Wrestles with God

²²During the night Jacob got up and took his two wives, his two servant wives, and his eleven sons and crossed the Jabbok River with them. ²³After taking them to the other side, he sent over all his possessions.

²⁴This left Jacob all alone in the camp, and a man came and wrestled with him until the dawn began to break. ²⁵When the man saw that he would not win the match, he touched Jacob's hip and wrenched it out of its socket. ²⁶Then the man said, "Let me go, for the dawn is breaking!"

But Jacob said, "I will not let you go unless you bless me."

²⁷"What is your name?" the man asked.

He replied, "Jacob."

²⁸"Your name will no longer be Jacob," the man told him. "From now on you will be called Israel,* because you have fought with God and with men and have won."

²⁹"Please tell me your name," Jacob said.

"Why do you want to know my name?" the man replied. Then he blessed Jacob there.

32:1 Verses 32:1-32 are numbered 32:2-33 in Hebrew text.　**32:2** *Mahanaim* means "two camps."　**32:28** *Jacob* sounds like the Hebrew words for "heel" and "deceiver." *Israel* means "God fights."

³⁰Jacob named the place Peniel (which means "face of God"), for he said, "I have seen God face to face, yet my life has been spared." ³¹The sun was rising as Jacob left Peniel,* and he was limping because of the injury to his hip. ³²(Even today the people of Israel don't eat the tendon near the hip socket because of what happened that night when the man strained the tendon of Jacob's hip.)

33 Jacob and Esau Make Peace

Then Jacob looked up and saw Esau coming with his 400 men. So he divided the children among Leah, Rachel, and his two servant wives. ²He put the servant wives and their children at the front, Leah and her children next, and Rachel and Joseph last. ³Then Jacob went on ahead. As he approached his brother, he bowed to the ground seven times before him. ⁴Then Esau ran to meet him and embraced him, threw his arms around his neck, and kissed him. And they both wept.

⁵Then Esau looked at the women and children and asked, "Who are these people with you?"

"These are the children God has graciously given to me, your servant," Jacob replied. ⁶Then the servant wives came forward with their children and bowed before him. ⁷Next came Leah with her children, and they bowed before him. Finally, Joseph and Rachel came forward and bowed before him.

⁸"And what were all the flocks and herds I met as I came?" Esau asked.

Jacob replied, "They are a gift, my lord, to ensure your friendship."

⁹"My brother, I have plenty," Esau answered. "Keep what you have for yourself."

¹⁰But Jacob insisted, "No, if I have found favor with you, please accept this gift from me. And what a relief to see your friendly smile. It is like seeing the face of God! ¹¹Please take this gift I have brought you, for God has been very gracious to me. I have more than enough." And because Jacob insisted, Esau finally accepted the gift.

¹²"Well," Esau said, "let's be going. I will lead the way."

¹³But Jacob replied, "You can see, my lord, that some of the children are very young, and the flocks and herds have their young, too. If they are driven too hard, even for one day, all the animals could die. ¹⁴Please, my lord, go ahead of your servant. We will follow slowly, at a pace that is comfortable for the livestock and the children. I will meet you at Seir."

¹⁵"All right," Esau said, "but at least let me assign some of my men to guide and protect you."

Jacob responded, "That's not necessary. It's enough that you've received me warmly, my lord!"

¹⁶So Esau turned around and started back to Seir that same day. ¹⁷Jacob, on the other hand, traveled on to Succoth. There he built himself a house and made shelters for his livestock. That is why the place was named Succoth (which means "shelters").

¹⁸Later, having traveled all the way from Paddan-aram, Jacob arrived safely at the town of Shechem, in the land of Canaan. There he set up camp outside the town. ¹⁹Jacob bought the plot of land where he camped from the family of Hamor, the father of Shechem, for 100 pieces of silver.* ²⁰And there he built an altar and named it El-Elohe-Israel.*

34 Revenge against Shechem

One day Dinah, the daughter of Jacob and Leah, went to visit some of the young women who lived in the area. ²But when the local prince, Shechem son of Hamor the Hivite, saw Dinah, he seized her and raped her. ³But then he fell in love with her, and he tried to win her affection with tender words. ⁴He said to his father, Hamor, "Get me this young girl. I want to marry her."

⁵Soon Jacob heard that Shechem had defiled his daughter, Dinah. But since his sons were out in the fields herding his livestock, he said nothing until they returned. ⁶Hamor, Shechem's father, came to discuss the matter with Jacob. ⁷Meanwhile, Jacob's sons had come in from the field as soon as they heard what had happened. They were

32:31 Hebrew *Penuel*, a variant spelling of Peniel. 33:19 Hebrew *100 kesitahs*; the value or weight of the kesitah is no longer known. 33:20 *El-Elohe-Israel* means "God, the God of Israel."

shocked and furious that their sister had been raped. Shechem had done a disgraceful thing against Jacob's family,* something that should never be done.

⁸Hamor tried to speak with Jacob and his sons. "My son Shechem is truly in love with your daughter," he said. "Please let him marry her. ⁹In fact, let's arrange other marriages, too. You give us your daughters for our sons, and we will give you our daughters for your sons. ¹⁰And you may live among us; the land is open to you! Settle here and trade with us. And feel free to buy property in the area."

¹¹Then Shechem himself spoke to Dinah's father and brothers. "Please be kind to me, and let me marry her," he begged. "I will give you whatever you ask. ¹²No matter what dowry or gift you demand, I will gladly pay it—just give me the girl as my wife."

¹³But since Shechem had defiled their sister, Dinah, Jacob's sons responded deceitfully to Shechem and his father, Hamor. ¹⁴They said to them, "We couldn't possibly allow this, because you're not circumcised. It would be a disgrace for our sister to marry a man like you! ¹⁵But here is a solution. If every man among you will be circumcised like we are, ¹⁶then we will give you our daughters, and we'll take your daughters for ourselves. We will live among you and become one people. ¹⁷But if you don't agree to be circumcised, we will take her and be on our way."

¹⁸Hamor and his son Shechem agreed to their proposal. ¹⁹Shechem wasted no time in acting on this request, for he wanted Jacob's daughter desperately. Shechem was a highly respected member of his family, ²⁰and he went with his father, Hamor, to present this proposal to the leaders at the town gate.

²¹"These men are our friends," they said. "Let's invite them to live here among us and trade freely. Look, the land is large enough to hold them. We can take their daughters as wives and let them marry ours. ²²But they will consider staying here and becoming one people with us only if all of our men are circumcised, just as they are. ²³But if we do this, all their livestock and possessions will eventually be ours. Come, let's agree to their terms and let them settle here among us."

²⁴So all the men in the town council agreed with Hamor and Shechem, and every male in the town was circumcised. ²⁵But three days later, when their wounds were still sore, two of Jacob's sons, Simeon and Levi, who were Dinah's full brothers, took their swords and entered the town without opposition. Then they slaughtered every male there, ²⁶including Hamor and his son Shechem. They killed them with their swords, then took Dinah from Shechem's house and returned to their camp.

²⁷Meanwhile, the rest of Jacob's sons arrived. Finding the men slaughtered, they plundered the town because their sister had been defiled there. ²⁸They seized all the flocks and herds and donkeys—everything they could lay their hands on, both inside the town and outside in the fields. ²⁹They looted all their wealth and plundered their houses. They also took all their little children and wives and led them away as captives.

³⁰Afterward Jacob said to Simeon and Levi, "You have ruined me! You've made me stink among all the people of this land—among all the Canaanites and Perizzites. We are so few that they will join forces and crush us. I will be ruined, and my entire household will be wiped out!"

³¹"But why should we let him treat our sister like a prostitute?" they retorted angrily.

35 Jacob's Return to Bethel

Then God said to Jacob, "Get ready and move to Bethel and settle there. Build an altar there to the God who appeared to you when you fled from your brother, Esau."

²So Jacob told everyone in his household, "Get rid of all your pagan idols, purify yourselves, and put on clean clothing. ³We are now going to Bethel, where I will build an altar to the God who answered my prayers when I was in distress. He has been with me wherever I have gone."

⁴So they gave Jacob all their pagan idols and earrings, and he buried them under

---

34:7 Hebrew *a disgraceful thing in Israel.*

the great tree near Shechem. ⁵As they set out, a terror from God spread over the people in all the towns of that area, so no one attacked Jacob's family.

⁶Eventually, Jacob and his household arrived at Luz (also called Bethel) in Canaan. ⁷Jacob built an altar there and named the place El-bethel (which means "God of Bethel"), because God had appeared to him there when he was fleeing from his brother, Esau.

⁸Soon after this, Rebekah's old nurse, Deborah, died. She was buried beneath the oak tree in the valley below Bethel. Ever since, the tree has been called Allon-bacuth (which means "oak of weeping").

⁹Now that Jacob had returned from Paddan-aram, God appeared to him again at Bethel. God blessed him, ¹⁰saying, "Your name is Jacob, but you will not be called Jacob any longer. From now on your name will be Israel."* So God renamed him Israel.

¹¹Then God said, "I am El-Shaddai—'God Almighty.' Be fruitful and multiply. You will become a great nation, even many nations. Kings will be among your descendants! ¹²And I will give you the land I once gave to Abraham and Isaac. Yes, I will give it to you and your descendants after you." ¹³Then God went up from the place where he had spoken to Jacob.

¹⁴Jacob set up a stone pillar to mark the place where God had spoken to him. Then he poured wine over it as an offering to God and anointed the pillar with olive oil. ¹⁵And Jacob named the place Bethel (which means "house of God"), because God had spoken to him there.

The Deaths of Rachel and Isaac

¹⁶Leaving Bethel, Jacob and his clan moved on toward Ephrath. But Rachel went into labor while they were still some distance away. Her labor pains were intense. ¹⁷After a very hard delivery, the midwife finally exclaimed, "Don't be afraid—you have another son!" ¹⁸Rachel was about to die, but with her last breath she named the baby Ben-oni (which means "son of my sorrow"). The baby's father, however, called

him Benjamin (which means "son of my right hand"). ¹⁹So Rachel died and was buried on the way to Ephrath (that is, Bethlehem). ²⁰Jacob set up a stone monument over Rachel's grave, and it can be seen there to this day.

²¹Then Jacob* traveled on and camped beyond Migdal-eder. ²²While he was living there, Reuben had intercourse with Bilhah, his father's concubine, and Jacob soon heard about it.

These are the names of the twelve sons of Jacob:

²³The sons of Leah were Reuben (Jacob's oldest son), Simeon, Levi, Judah, Issachar, and Zebulun.

²⁴The sons of Rachel were Joseph and Benjamin.

²⁵The sons of Bilhah, Rachel's servant, were Dan and Naphtali.

²⁶The sons of Zilpah, Leah's servant, were Gad and Asher.

These are the names of the sons who were born to Jacob at Paddan-aram.

²⁷So Jacob returned to his father, Isaac, in Mamre, which is near Kiriath-arba (now called Hebron), where Abraham and Isaac had both lived as foreigners. ²⁸Isaac lived for 180 years. ²⁹Then he breathed his last and died at a ripe old age, joining his ancestors in death. And his sons, Esau and Jacob, buried him.

36 Descendants of Esau

This is the account of the descendants of Esau (also known as Edom). ²Esau married two young women from Canaan: Adah, the daughter of Elon the Hittite; and Oholibamah, the daughter of Anah and granddaughter of Zibeon the Hivite. ³He also married his cousin Basemath, who was the daughter of Ishmael and the sister of Nebaioth. ⁴Adah gave birth to a son named Eliphaz for Esau. Basemath gave birth to a son named Reuel. ⁵Oholibamah gave birth to sons named Jeush, Jalam, and Korah. All these sons were born to Esau in the land of Canaan.

⁶Esau took his wives, his children, and his

35:10 *Jacob* sounds like the Hebrew words for "heel" and "deceiver." *Israel* means "God fights." **35:21** Hebrew *Israel;* also in 35:22a. The names "Jacob" and "Israel" are often interchanged throughout the Old Testament, referring sometimes to the individual patriarch and sometimes to the nation.

entire household, along with his livestock and cattle—all the wealth he had acquired in the land of Canaan—and moved away from his brother, Jacob. ⁷There was not enough land to support them both because of all the livestock and possessions they had acquired. ⁸So Esau (also known as Edom) settled in the hill country of Seir.

⁹This is the account of Esau's descendants, the Edomites, who lived in the hill country of Seir.

¹⁰These are the names of Esau's sons: Eliphaz, the son of Esau's wife Adah; and Reuel, the son of Esau's wife Basemath.
¹¹The descendants of Eliphaz were Teman, Omar, Zepho, Gatam, and Kenaz. ¹²Timna, the concubine of Esau's son Eliphaz, gave birth to a son named Amalek. These are the descendants of Esau's wife Adah.
¹³The descendants of Reuel were Nahath, Zerah, Shammah, and Mizzah. These are the descendants of Esau's wife Basemath.
¹⁴Esau also had sons through Oholibamah, the daughter of Anah and granddaughter of Zibeon. Their names were Jeush, Jalam, and Korah.

¹⁵These are the descendants of Esau who became the leaders of various clans:

The descendants of Esau's oldest son, Eliphaz, became the leaders of the clans of Teman, Omar, Zepho, Kenaz, ¹⁶Korah, Gatam, and Amalek. These are the clan leaders in the land of Edom who descended from Eliphaz. All these were descendants of Esau's wife Adah.
¹⁷The descendants of Esau's son Reuel became the leaders of the clans of Nahath, Zerah, Shammah, and Mizzah. These are the clan leaders in the land of Edom who descended from Reuel. All these were descendants of Esau's wife Basemath.
¹⁸The descendants of Esau and his wife Oholibamah became the leaders of the clans of Jeush, Jalam, and Korah. These are the clan leaders who descended from Esau's wife Oholibamah, the daughter of Anah.
¹⁹These are the clans descended from Esau (also known as Edom), identified by their clan leaders.

Original Peoples of Edom

²⁰These are the names of the tribes that descended from Seir the Horite. They lived in the land of Edom: Lotan, Shobal, Zibeon, Anah, ²¹Dishon, Ezer, and Dishan. These were the Horite clan leaders, the descendants of Seir, who lived in the land of Edom.

²²The descendants of Lotan were Hori and Hemam. Lotan's sister was named Timna.
²³The descendants of Shobal were Alvan, Manahath, Ebal, Shepho, and Onam.
²⁴The descendants of Zibeon were Aiah and Anah. (This is the Anah who discovered the hot springs in the wilderness while he was grazing his father's donkeys.)
²⁵The descendants of Anah were his son, Dishon, and his daughter, Oholibamah.
²⁶The descendants of Dishon* were Hemdan, Eshban, Ithran, and Keran.
²⁷The descendants of Ezer were Bilhan, Zaavan, and Akan.
²⁸The descendants of Dishan were Uz and Aran.
²⁹So these were the leaders of the Horite clans: Lotan, Shobal, Zibeon, Anah, ³⁰Dishon, Ezer, and Dishan. The Horite clans are named after their clan leaders, who lived in the land of Seir.

Rulers of Edom

³¹These are the kings who ruled in the land of Edom before any king ruled over the Israelites*:

³²Bela son of Beor, who ruled in Edom from his city of Dinhabah.
³³When Bela died, Jobab son of Zerah from Bozrah became king in his place.
³⁴When Jobab died, Husham from the land of the Temanites became king in his place.
³⁵When Husham died, Hadad son of Bedad became king in his place and ruled from the city of Avith. He was the one who defeated the Midianites in the land of Moab.

36:26 Hebrew *Dishan,* a variant spelling of Dishon; compare 36:21, 28.   **36:31** Or *before an Israelite king ruled over them.*

³⁶When Hadad died, Samlah from the city of Masrekah became king in his place. ³⁷When Samlah died, Shaul from the city of Rehoboth-on-the-River became king in his place. ³⁸When Shaul died, Baal-hanan son of Acbor became king in his place. ³⁹When Baal-hanan son of Acbor died, Hadad* became king in his place and ruled from the city of Pau. His wife was Mehetabel, the daughter of Matred and granddaughter of Me-zahab.

⁴⁰These are the names of the leaders of the clans descended from Esau, who lived in the places named for them: Timna, Alvah, Jetheth, ⁴¹Oholibamah, Elah, Pinon, ⁴²Kenaz, Teman, Mibzar, ⁴³Magdiel, and Iram. These are the leaders of the clans of Edom, listed according to their settlements in the land they occupied. They all descended from Esau, the ancestor of the Edomites.

37 Joseph's Dreams

So Jacob settled again in the land of Canaan, where his father had lived as a foreigner.

²This is the account of Jacob and his family. When Joseph was seventeen years old, he often tended his father's flocks. He worked for his half brothers, the sons of his father's wives Bilhah and Zilpah. But Joseph reported to his father some of the bad things his brothers were doing.

³Jacob* loved Joseph more than any of his other children because Joseph had been born to him in his old age. So one day Jacob had a special gift made for Joseph—a beautiful robe.* ⁴But his brothers hated Joseph because their father loved him more than the rest of them. They couldn't say a kind word to him.

⁵One night Joseph had a dream, and when he told his brothers about it, they hated him more than ever. ⁶"Listen to this dream," he said. ⁷"We were out in the field, tying up bundles of grain. Suddenly my bundle stood up, and your bundles all gathered around and bowed low before mine!"

⁸His brothers responded, "So you think you will be our king, do you? Do you actually think you will reign over us?" And they hated him all the more because of his dreams and the way he talked about them.

⁹Soon Joseph had another dream, and again he told his brothers about it. "Listen, I have had another dream," he said. "The sun, moon, and eleven stars bowed low before me!"

¹⁰This time he told the dream to his father as well as to his brothers, but his father scolded him. "What kind of dream is that?" he asked. "Will your mother and I and your brothers actually come and bow to the ground before you?" ¹¹But while his brothers were jealous of Joseph, his father wondered what the dreams meant.

¹²Soon after this, Joseph's brothers went to pasture their father's flocks at Shechem. ¹³When they had been gone for some time, Jacob said to Joseph, "Your brothers are pasturing the sheep at Shechem. Get ready, and I will send you to them."

"I'm ready to go," Joseph replied.

¹⁴"Go and see how your brothers and the flocks are getting along," Jacob said. "Then come back and bring me a report." So Jacob sent him on his way, and Joseph traveled to Shechem from their home in the valley of Hebron.

¹⁵When he arrived there, a man from the area noticed him wandering around the countryside. "What are you looking for?" he asked.

¹⁶"I'm looking for my brothers," Joseph replied. "Do you know where they are pasturing their sheep?"

¹⁷"Yes," the man told him. "They have moved on from here, but I heard them say, 'Let's go on to Dothan.'" So Joseph followed his brothers to Dothan and found them there.

Joseph Sold into Slavery

¹⁸When Joseph's brothers saw him coming, they recognized him in the distance. As he approached, they made plans to kill him. ¹⁹"Here comes the dreamer!" they said. ²⁰"Come on, let's kill him and throw him

---

36:39 As in some Hebrew manuscripts, Samaritan Pentateuch, and Syriac version (see also 1 Chr 1:50); most Hebrew manuscripts read *Hadar.* **37:3a** Hebrew *Israel;* also in 37:13. See note on 35:21. **37:3b** Traditionally rendered *a coat of many colors.* The exact meaning of the Hebrew is uncertain.

into one of these cisterns. We can tell our father, 'A wild animal has eaten him.' Then we'll see what becomes of his dreams!"

²¹ But when Reuben heard of their scheme, he came to Joseph's rescue. "Let's not kill him," he said. ²² "Why should we shed any blood? Let's just throw him into this empty cistern here in the wilderness. Then he'll die without our laying a hand on him." Reuben was secretly planning to rescue Joseph and return him to his father.

²³ So when Joseph arrived, his brothers ripped off the beautiful robe he was wearing. ²⁴ Then they grabbed him and threw him into the cistern. Now the cistern was empty; there was no water in it. ²⁵ Then, just as they were sitting down to eat, they looked up and saw a caravan of camels in the distance coming toward them. It was a group of Ishmaelite traders taking a load of gum, balm, and aromatic resin from Gilead down to Egypt.

²⁶ Judah said to his brothers, "What will we gain by killing our brother? We'd have to cover up the crime.* ²⁷ Instead of hurting him, let's sell him to those Ishmaelite traders. After all, he is our brother—our own flesh and blood!" And his brothers agreed. ²⁸ So when the Ishmaelites, who were Midianite traders, came by, Joseph's brothers pulled him out of the cistern and sold him to them for twenty pieces* of silver. And the traders took him to Egypt.

²⁹ Some time later, Reuben returned to get Joseph out of the cistern. When he discovered that Joseph was missing, he tore his clothes in grief. ³⁰ Then he went back to his brothers and lamented, "The boy is gone! What will I do now?"

³¹ Then the brothers killed a young goat and dipped Joseph's robe in its blood. ³² They sent the beautiful robe to their father with this message: "Look at what we found. Doesn't this robe belong to your son?"

³³ Their father recognized it immediately. "Yes," he said, "it is my son's robe. A wild animal must have eaten him. Joseph has clearly been torn to pieces!" ³⁴ Then Jacob tore his clothes and dressed himself in burlap. He mourned deeply for his son for a long time. ³⁵ His family all tried to comfort him, but he refused to be comforted. "I will go to my grave* mourning for my son," he would say, and then he would weep.

³⁶ Meanwhile, the Midianite traders* arrived in Egypt, where they sold Joseph to Potiphar, an officer of Pharaoh, the king of Egypt. Potiphar was captain of the palace guard.

38 Judah and Tamar

About this time, Judah left home and moved to Adullam, where he stayed with a man named Hirah. ² There he saw a Canaanite woman, the daughter of Shua, and he married her. When he slept with her, ³ she became pregnant and gave birth to a son, and he named the boy Er. ⁴ Then she became pregnant again and gave birth to another son, and she named him Onan. ⁵ And when she gave birth to a third son, she named him Shelah. At the time of Shelah's birth, they were living at Kezib.

⁶ In the course of time, Judah arranged for his firstborn son, Er, to marry a young woman named Tamar. ⁷ But Er was a wicked man in the LORD's sight, so the LORD took his life. ⁸ Then Judah said to Er's brother Onan, "Go and marry Tamar, as our law requires of the brother of a man who has died. You must produce an heir for your brother."

⁹ But Onan was not willing to have a child who would not be his own heir. So whenever he had intercourse with his brother's wife, he spilled the semen on the ground. This prevented her from having a child who would belong to his brother. ¹⁰ But the LORD considered it evil for Onan to deny a child to his dead brother. So the LORD took Onan's life, too.

¹¹ Then Judah said to Tamar, his daughter-in-law, "Go back to your parents' home and remain a widow until my son Shelah is old enough to marry you." (But Judah didn't really intend to do this because he was afraid Shelah would also die, like his two brothers.) So Tamar went back to live in her father's home.

¹² Some years later Judah's wife died.

37:26 Hebrew *cover his blood.* **37:28** Hebrew *20 shekels,* about 8 ounces or 228 grams in weight. **37:35** Hebrew *go down to Sheol.* **37:36** Hebrew *the Medanites.* The relationship between the Midianites and Medanites is unclear; compare 37:28. See also 25:2.

After the time of mourning was over, Judah and his friend Hirah the Adullamite went up to Timnah to supervise the shearing of his sheep. [13] Someone told Tamar, "Look, your father-in-law is going up to Timnah to shear his sheep."

[14] Tamar was aware that Shelah had grown up, but no arrangements had been made for her to come and marry him. So she changed out of her widow's clothing and covered herself with a veil to disguise herself. Then she sat beside the road at the entrance to the village of Enaim, which is on the road to Timnah. [15] Judah noticed her and thought she was a prostitute, since she had covered her face. [16] So he stopped and propositioned her. "Let me have sex with you," he said, not realizing that she was his own daughter-in-law.

"How much will you pay to have sex with me?" Tamar asked.

[17] "I'll send you a young goat from my flock," Judah promised.

"But what will you give me to guarantee that you will send the goat?" she asked.

[18] "What kind of guarantee do you want?" he replied.

She answered, "Leave me your identification seal and its cord and the walking stick you are carrying." So Judah gave them to her. Then he had intercourse with her, and she became pregnant. [19] Afterward she went back home, took off her veil, and put on her widow's clothing as usual.

[20] Later Judah asked his friend Hirah the Adullamite to take the young goat to the woman and to pick up the things he had given her as his guarantee. But Hirah couldn't find her. [21] So he asked the men who lived there, "Where can I find the shrine prostitute who was sitting beside the road at the entrance to Enaim?"

"We've never had a shrine prostitute here," they replied.

[22] So Hirah returned to Judah and told him, "I couldn't find her anywhere, and the men of the village claim they've never had a shrine prostitute there."

[23] "Then let her keep the things I gave her," Judah said. "I sent the young goat as we agreed, but you couldn't find her. We'd be the laughingstock of the village if we went back again to look for her."

[24] About three months later, Judah was told, "Tamar, your daughter-in-law, has acted like a prostitute. And now, because of this, she's pregnant."

"Bring her out, and let her be burned!" Judah demanded.

[25] But as they were taking her out to kill her, she sent this message to her father-in-law: "The man who owns these things made me pregnant. Look closely. Whose seal and cord and walking stick are these?"

[26] Judah recognized them immediately and said, "She is more righteous than I am, because I didn't arrange for her to marry my son Shelah." And Judah never slept with Tamar again.

[27] When the time came for Tamar to give birth, it was discovered that she was carrying twins. [28] While she was in labor, one of the babies reached out his hand. The midwife grabbed it and tied a scarlet string around the child's wrist, announcing, "This one came out first." [29] But then he pulled back his hand, and out came his brother! "What!" the midwife exclaimed. "How did you break out first?" So he was named Perez.* [30] Then the baby with the scarlet string on his wrist was born, and he was named Zerah.*

39 Joseph in Potiphar's House

When Joseph was taken to Egypt by the Ishmaelite traders, he was purchased by Potiphar, an Egyptian officer. Potiphar was captain of the guard for Pharaoh, the king of Egypt.

[2] The LORD was with Joseph, so he succeeded in everything he did as he served in the home of his Egyptian master. [3] Potiphar noticed this and realized that the LORD was with Joseph, giving him success in everything he did. [4] This pleased Potiphar, so he soon made Joseph his personal attendant. He put him in charge of his entire household and everything he owned. [5] From the day Joseph was put in charge of his master's household and property, the LORD began to bless Potiphar's household for Joseph's sake.

38:29 Perez means "breaking out." **38:30** Zerah means "scarlet" or "brightness."

All his household affairs ran smoothly, and his crops and livestock flourished. ⁶So Potiphar gave Joseph complete administrative responsibility over everything he owned. With Joseph there, he didn't worry about a thing—except what kind of food to eat!

Joseph was a very handsome and well-built young man, ⁷and Potiphar's wife soon began to look at him lustfully. "Come and sleep with me," she demanded.

⁸But Joseph refused. "Look," he told her, "my master trusts me with everything in his entire household. ⁹No one here has more authority than I do. He has held back nothing from me except you, because you are his wife. How could I do such a wicked thing? It would be a great sin against God."

¹⁰She kept putting pressure on Joseph day after day, but he refused to sleep with her, and he kept out of her way as much as possible. ¹¹One day, however, no one else was around when he went in to do his work. ¹²She came and grabbed him by his cloak, demanding, "Come on, sleep with me!" Joseph tore himself away, but he left his cloak in her hand as he ran from the house.

¹³When she saw that she was holding his cloak and he had fled, ¹⁴she called out to her servants. Soon all the men came running. "Look!" she said. "My husband has brought this Hebrew slave here to make fools of us! He came into my room to rape me, but I screamed. ¹⁵When he heard me scream, he ran outside and got away, but he left his cloak behind with me."

¹⁶She kept the cloak with her until her husband came home. ¹⁷Then she told him her story. "That Hebrew slave you've brought into our house tried to come in and fool around with me," she said. ¹⁸"But when I screamed, he ran outside, leaving his cloak with me!"

Joseph Put in Prison

¹⁹Potiphar was furious when he heard his wife's story about how Joseph had treated her. ²⁰So he took Joseph and threw him into the prison where the king's prisoners were held, and there he remained. ²¹But the LORD was with Joseph in the prison and showed him his faithful love. And the LORD made Joseph a favorite with the prison warden. ²²Before long, the warden put Joseph in charge of all the other prisoners and over everything that happened in the prison. ²³The warden had no more worries, because Joseph took care of everything. The LORD was with him and caused everything he did to succeed.

40 Joseph Interprets Two Dreams

Some time later, Pharaoh's chief cup-bearer and chief baker offended their royal master. ²Pharaoh became angry with these two officials, ³and he put them in the prison where Joseph was, in the palace of the captain of the guard. ⁴They remained in prison for quite some time, and the captain of the guard assigned them to Joseph, who looked after them.

⁵While they were in prison, Pharaoh's cup-bearer and baker each had a dream one night, and each dream had its own meaning. ⁶When Joseph saw them the next morning, he noticed that they both looked upset. ⁷"Why do you look so worried today?" he asked them.

⁸And they replied, "We both had dreams last night, but no one can tell us what they mean."

"Interpreting dreams is God's business," Joseph replied. "Go ahead and tell me your dreams."

⁹So the chief cup-bearer told Joseph his dream first. "In my dream," he said, "I saw a grapevine in front of me. ¹⁰The vine had three branches that began to bud and blossom, and soon it produced clusters of ripe grapes. ¹¹I was holding Pharaoh's wine cup in my hand, so I took a cluster of grapes and squeezed the juice into the cup. Then I placed the cup in Pharaoh's hand."

¹²"This is what the dream means," Joseph said. "The three branches represent three days. ¹³Within three days Pharaoh will lift you up and restore you to your position as his chief cup-bearer. ¹⁴And please remember me and do me a favor when things go well for you. Mention me to Pharaoh, so he might let me out of this place. ¹⁵For I was kidnapped from my homeland, the land of the Hebrews, and now I'm here in prison, but I did nothing to deserve it."

¹⁶When the chief baker saw that Joseph had given the first dream such a positive interpretation, he said to Joseph, "I had a

Your Calling May Change

GENESIS 39:19-23

Acceptance

It's important to figure out what God is calling us to do in each phase of life—because that calling can change. For example, I wasn't supposed to be doing what I'm doing *now* when I was in my twenties. What God called me to do in my twenties was different even from what he had for me to do in my thirties.

Yet sometimes we can get locked in to a sense of calling and think, *This is what I'm supposed to do with the rest of my life.* But we need to hold that sense of direction loosely in our hands because it's really up to God; he could change the direction he's leading us at any moment.

God has a call for you in *this* particular season—and he may call you to something different in the next season. But what remains constant is our yes to God; through all the stages of our lives, we can say to God, *I will do whatever you ask, whenever you ask, however you ask, in whatever manner you ask.* Our surrender to him is constant—and *he* fills in the details of what we're supposed to be doing during each stage.

Every season has both limitations and joys that are present only in that season; we're wise to recognize our current limitations and also to find and celebrate the joys. For example, mothers of young kids can feel limited. They may desire to use their gifts in a ministry or leadership opportunity, but instead much of their time and energy is spent parenting. If you're a young mom who's struggling with this stage of life, I know you're itching to get out there and save the world or to use your gift to the best of your ability. You're *dying* to do that. But be careful, because those moments with your children are fleeting, and they will never come again.

Whatever stage you're in, trust God with this season of your life; accept its limits, but also relish its joys.

—*Kay Warren*

For more on acceptance, see reading at Genesis 41:1–46.

---

dream, too. In my dream there were three baskets of white pastries stacked on my head. [17]The top basket contained all kinds of pastries for Pharaoh, but the birds came and ate them from the basket on my head."

[18]"This is what the dream means," Joseph told him. "The three baskets also represent three days. [19]Three days from now Pharaoh will lift you up and impale your body on a pole. Then birds will come and peck away at your flesh."

[20]Pharaoh's birthday came three days later, and he prepared a banquet for all his officials and staff. He summoned* his chief cup-bearer and chief baker to join the other officials. [21]He then restored the chief cup-bearer to his former position, so he could again hand Pharaoh his cup. [22]But Pharaoh impaled the chief baker, just as Joseph had predicted when he interpreted his dream. [23]Pharaoh's chief cup-bearer, however, forgot all about Joseph, never giving him another thought.

41 Pharaoh's Dreams

Two full years later, Pharaoh dreamed that he was standing on the bank of the Nile River. [2]In his dream he saw

---

40:20 Hebrew *He lifted up the head of.*

More Influence than You Realize

GENESIS 41:1-46

Acceptance

All women are kingdom participants. We're eternal beings whom Jesus wants to mold into his image. We need to step up to that without apology, without fear, without compromise, and with great obedience to Christ. It starts with reframing how we see ourselves. You may be in a carpool; you're influencing the children in your car. You may be in a grocery store; you're influencing the checkout person. You may be in corporate America; you're influencing those around you. You don't need to wait to become a woman of influence; you already *are* one.

Too often *leadership* can be a loaded word. Many women are uncomfortable being leaders. There are so many preconceived notions about what leadership means in our world or in the Bible. But it's really about making a difference, influencing, imparting, contributing, guiding, and shining (Philippians 2:15).

What's freeing is that it's not our light we're shining. When we come into relationship with Jesus, his light comes into us. And God's light will shine out of us—even through the cracks in our humanity—to provide a source of hope and light for those around us.

—*Elisa Morgan*

For more on acceptance, see reading at Exodus 4:1-17.

seven fat, healthy cows come up out of the river and begin grazing in the marsh grass. ³Then he saw seven more cows come up behind them from the Nile, but these were scrawny and thin. These cows stood beside the fat cows on the riverbank. ⁴Then the scrawny, thin cows ate the seven healthy, fat cows! At this point in the dream, Pharaoh woke up.

⁵But he fell asleep again and had a second dream. This time he saw seven heads of grain, plump and beautiful, growing on a single stalk. ⁶Then seven more heads of grain appeared, but these were shriveled and withered by the east wind. ⁷And these thin heads swallowed up the seven plump, well-formed heads! Then Pharaoh woke up again and realized it was a dream.

⁸The next morning Pharaoh was very disturbed by the dreams. So he called for all the magicians and wise men of Egypt. When Pharaoh told them his dreams, not one of them could tell him what they meant.

⁹Finally, the king's chief cup-bearer spoke up. "Today I have been reminded of my failure," he told Pharaoh. ¹⁰"Some time ago, you were angry with the chief baker and me, and you imprisoned us in the palace of the captain of the guard. ¹¹One night the chief baker and I each had a dream, and each dream had its own meaning. ¹²There was a young Hebrew man with us in the prison who was a slave of the captain of the guard. We told him our dreams, and he told us what each of our dreams meant. ¹³And everything happened just as he had predicted. I was restored to my position as cup-bearer, and the chief baker was executed and impaled on a pole."

¹⁴Pharaoh sent for Joseph at once, and he was quickly brought from the prison. After he shaved and changed his clothes, he went in and stood before Pharaoh. ¹⁵Then Pharaoh said to Joseph, "I had a dream last night, and no one here can tell me what it means. But I have heard that when you hear about a dream you can interpret it."

¹⁶"It is beyond my power to do this," Joseph

replied. "But God can tell you what it means and set you at ease."

[17] So Pharaoh told Joseph his dream. "In my dream," he said, "I was standing on the bank of the Nile River, [18] and I saw seven fat, healthy cows come up out of the river and begin grazing in the marsh grass. [19] But then I saw seven sick-looking cows, scrawny and thin, come up after them. I've never seen such sorry-looking animals in all the land of Egypt. [20] These thin, scrawny cows ate the seven fat cows. [21] But afterward you wouldn't have known it, for they were still as thin and scrawny as before! Then I woke up.

[22] "Then I fell asleep again, and I had another dream. This time I saw seven heads of grain, full and beautiful, growing on a single stalk. [23] Then seven more heads of grain appeared, but these were blighted, shriveled, and withered by the east wind. [24] And the shriveled heads swallowed the seven healthy heads. I told these dreams to the magicians, but no one could tell me what they mean."

[25] Joseph responded, "Both of Pharaoh's dreams mean the same thing. God is telling Pharaoh in advance what he is about to do. [26] The seven healthy cows and the seven healthy heads of grain both represent seven years of prosperity. [27] The seven thin, scrawny cows that came up later and the seven thin heads of grain, withered by the east wind, represent seven years of famine.

[28] "This will happen just as I have described it, for God has revealed to Pharaoh in advance what he is about to do. [29] The next seven years will be a period of great prosperity throughout the land of Egypt. [30] But afterward there will be seven years of famine so great that all the prosperity will be forgotten in Egypt. Famine will destroy the land. [31] This famine will be so severe that even the memory of the good years will be erased. [32] As for having two similar dreams, it means that these events have been decreed by God, and he will soon make them happen.

[33] "Therefore, Pharaoh should find an intelligent and wise man and put him in charge of the entire land of Egypt. [34] Then Pharaoh should appoint supervisors over the land and let them collect one-fifth of all the crops during the seven good years. [35] Have them gather all the food produced in the good years that are just ahead and bring it to Pharaoh's storehouses. Store it away, and guard it so there will be food in the cities. [36] That way there will be enough to eat when the seven years of famine come to the land of Egypt. Otherwise this famine will destroy the land."

Joseph Made Ruler of Egypt

[37] Joseph's suggestions were well received by Pharaoh and his officials. [38] So Pharaoh asked his officials, "Can we find anyone else like this man so obviously filled with the spirit of God?" [39] Then Pharaoh said to Joseph, "Since God has revealed the meaning of the dreams to you, clearly no one else is as intelligent or wise as you are. [40] You will be in charge of my court, and all my people will take orders from you. Only I, sitting on my throne, will have a rank higher than yours."

[41] Pharaoh said to Joseph, "I hereby put you in charge of the entire land of Egypt." [42] Then Pharaoh removed his signet ring from his hand and placed it on Joseph's finger. He dressed him in fine linen clothing and hung a gold chain around his neck. [43] Then he had Joseph ride in the chariot reserved for his second-in-command. And wherever Joseph went, the command was shouted, "Kneel down!" So Pharaoh put Joseph in charge of all Egypt. [44] And Pharaoh said to him, "I am Pharaoh, but no one will lift a hand or foot in the entire land of Egypt without your approval."

[45] Then Pharaoh gave Joseph a new Egyptian name, Zaphenath-paneah.* He also gave him a wife, whose name was Asenath. She was the daughter of Potiphera, the priest of On.* So Joseph took charge of the entire land of Egypt. [46] He was thirty years old when he began serving in the court of Pharaoh, the king of Egypt. And when Joseph left Pharaoh's presence, he inspected the entire land of Egypt.

[47] As predicted, for seven years the land produced bumper crops. [48] During those

---

41:45a *Zaphenath-paneah* probably means "God speaks and lives."   **41:45b** Greek version reads *of Heliopolis*; also in 41:50.

years, Joseph gathered all the crops grown in Egypt and stored the grain from the surrounding fields in the cities. [49]He piled up huge amounts of grain like sand on the seashore. Finally, he stopped keeping records because there was too much to measure.

[50]During this time, before the first of the famine years, two sons were born to Joseph and his wife, Asenath, the daughter of Potiphera, the priest of On. [51]Joseph named his older son Manasseh,* for he said, "God has made me forget all my troubles and everyone in my father's family." [52]Joseph named his second son Ephraim,* for he said, "God has made me fruitful in this land of my grief."

[53]At last the seven years of bumper crops throughout the land of Egypt came to an end. [54]Then the seven years of famine began, just as Joseph had predicted. The famine also struck all the surrounding countries, but throughout Egypt there was plenty of food. [55]Eventually, however, the famine spread throughout the land of Egypt as well. And when the people cried out to Pharaoh for food, he told them, "Go to Joseph, and do whatever he tells you." [56]So with severe famine everywhere, Joseph opened up the storehouses and distributed grain to the Egyptians, for the famine was severe throughout the land of Egypt. [57]And people from all around came to Egypt to buy grain from Joseph because the famine was severe throughout the world.

42 Joseph's Brothers Go to Egypt

When Jacob heard that grain was available in Egypt, he said to his sons, "Why are you standing around looking at one another? [2]I have heard there is grain in Egypt. Go down there, and buy enough grain to keep us alive. Otherwise we'll die."

[3]So Joseph's ten older brothers went down to Egypt to buy grain. [4]But Jacob wouldn't let Joseph's younger brother, Benjamin, go with them, for fear some harm might come to him. [5]So Jacob's* sons arrived in Egypt along with others to buy food, for the famine was in Canaan as well.

[6]Since Joseph was governor of all Egypt and in charge of selling grain to all the people, it was to him that his brothers came. When they arrived, they bowed before him with their faces to the ground. [7]Joseph recognized his brothers instantly, but he pretended to be a stranger and spoke harshly to them. "Where are you from?" he demanded.

"From the land of Canaan," they replied. "We have come to buy food."

[8]Although Joseph recognized his brothers, they didn't recognize him. [9]And he remembered the dreams he'd had about them many years before. He said to them, "You are spies! You have come to see how vulnerable our land has become."

[10]"No, my lord!" they exclaimed. "Your servants have simply come to buy food. [11]We are all brothers—members of the same family. We are honest men, sir! We are not spies!"

[12]"Yes, you are!" Joseph insisted. "You have come to see how vulnerable our land has become."

[13]"Sir," they said, "there are actually twelve of us. We, your servants, are all brothers, sons of a man living in the land of Canaan. Our youngest brother is back there with our father right now, and one of our brothers is no longer with us."

[14]But Joseph insisted, "As I said, you are spies! [15]This is how I will test your story. I swear by the life of Pharaoh that you will never leave Egypt unless your youngest brother comes here! [16]One of you must go and get your brother. I'll keep the rest of you here in prison. Then we'll find out whether or not your story is true. By the life of Pharaoh, if it turns out that you don't have a younger brother, then I'll know you are spies."

[17]So Joseph put them all in prison for three days. [18]On the third day Joseph said to them, "I am a God-fearing man. If you do as I say, you will live. [19]If you really are honest men, choose one of your brothers to remain in prison. The rest of you may go home with grain for your starving families. [20]But you must bring your youngest brother back to me. This will prove that you are telling the truth, and you will not die." To this they agreed.

41:51 Manasseh sounds like a Hebrew term that means "causing to forget."   **41:52** Ephraim sounds like a Hebrew term that means "fruitful."   **42:5** Hebrew Israel's. See note on 35:21.

²¹Speaking among themselves, they said, "Clearly we are being punished because of what we did to Joseph long ago. We saw his anguish when he pleaded for his life, but we wouldn't listen. That's why we're in this trouble."

²²"Didn't I tell you not to sin against the boy?" Reuben asked. "But you wouldn't listen. And now we have to answer for his blood!"

²³Of course, they didn't know that Joseph understood them, for he had been speaking to them through an interpreter. ²⁴Now he turned away from them and began to weep. When he regained his composure, he spoke to them again. Then he chose Simeon from among them and had him tied up right before their eyes.

²⁵Joseph then ordered his servants to fill the men's sacks with grain, but he also gave secret instructions to return each brother's payment at the top of his sack. He also gave them supplies for their journey home. ²⁶So the brothers loaded their donkeys with the grain and headed for home.

²⁷But when they stopped for the night and one of them opened his sack to get grain for his donkey, he found his money in the top of his sack. ²⁸"Look!" he exclaimed to his brothers. "My money has been returned; it's here in my sack!" Then their hearts sank. Trembling, they said to each other, "What has God done to us?"

²⁹When the brothers came to their father, Jacob, in the land of Canaan, they told him everything that had happened to them. ³⁰"The man who is governor of the land spoke very harshly to us," they told him. "He accused us of being spies scouting the land. ³¹But we said, 'We are honest men, not spies. ³²We are twelve brothers, sons of one father. One brother is no longer with us, and the youngest is at home with our father in the land of Canaan.'

³³"Then the man who is governor of the land told us, 'This is how I will find out if you are honest men. Leave one of your brothers here with me, and take grain for your starving families and go on home. ³⁴But you must bring your youngest brother back to me. Then I will know you are honest men and not spies. Then I will give you

back your brother, and you may trade freely in the land.'"

³⁵As they emptied out their sacks, there in each man's sack was the bag of money he had paid for the grain! The brothers and their father were terrified when they saw the bags of money. ³⁶Jacob exclaimed, "You are robbing me of my children! Joseph is gone! Simeon is gone! And now you want to take Benjamin, too. Everything is going against me!"

³⁷Then Reuben said to his father, "You may kill my two sons if I don't bring Benjamin back to you. I'll be responsible for him, and I promise to bring him back."

³⁸But Jacob replied, "My son will not go down with you. His brother Joseph is dead, and he is all I have left. If anything should happen to him on your journey, you would send this grieving, white-haired man to his grave.*"

43 The Brothers Return to Egypt

But the famine continued to ravage the land of Canaan. ²When the grain they had brought from Egypt was almost gone, Jacob said to his sons, "Go back and buy us a little more food."

³But Judah said, "The man was serious when he warned us, 'You won't see my face again unless your brother is with you.' ⁴If you send Benjamin with us, we will go down and buy more food. ⁵But if you don't let Benjamin go, we won't go either. Remember, the man said, 'You won't see my face again unless your brother is with you.'"

⁶"Why were you so cruel to me?" Jacob* moaned. "Why did you tell him you had another brother?"

⁷"The man kept asking us questions about our family," they replied. "He asked, 'Is your father still alive? Do you have another brother?' So we answered his questions. How could we know he would say, 'Bring your brother down here'?"

⁸Judah said to his father, "Send the boy with me, and we will be on our way. Otherwise we will all die of starvation—and not only we, but you and our little ones. ⁹I personally guarantee his safety. You may hold me responsible if I don't bring him back to

you. Then let me bear the blame forever. [10]If we hadn't wasted all this time, we could have gone and returned twice by now."

[11]So their father, Jacob, finally said to them, "If it can't be avoided, then at least do this. Pack your bags with the best products of this land. Take them down to the man as gifts—balm, honey, gum, aromatic resin, pistachio nuts, and almonds. [12]Also take double the money that was put back in your sacks, as it was probably someone's mistake. [13]Then take your brother, and go back to the man. [14]May God Almighty* give you mercy as you go before the man, so that he will release Simeon and let Benjamin return. But if I must lose my children, so be it."

[15]So the men packed Jacob's gifts and double the money and headed off with Benjamin. They finally arrived in Egypt and presented themselves to Joseph. [16]When Joseph saw Benjamin with them, he said to the manager of his household, "These men will eat with me this noon. Take them inside the palace. Then go slaughter an animal, and prepare a big feast." [17]So the man did as Joseph told him and took them into Joseph's palace.

[18]The brothers were terrified when they saw that they were being taken into Joseph's house. "It's because of the money someone put in our sacks last time we were here," they said. "He plans to pretend that we stole it. Then he will seize us, make us slaves, and take our donkeys."

A Feast at Joseph's Palace

[19]The brothers approached the manager of Joseph's household and spoke to him at the entrance to the palace. [20]"Sir," they said, "we came to Egypt once before to buy food. [21]But as we were returning home, we stopped for the night and opened our sacks. Then we discovered that each man's money—the exact amount paid—was in the top of his sack! Here it is; we have brought it back with us. [22]We also have additional money to buy more food. We have no idea who put our money in our sacks."

[23]"Relax. Don't be afraid," the household manager told them. "Your God, the God of your father, must have put this treasure into your sacks. I know I received your payment." Then he released Simeon and brought him out to them.

[24]The manager then led the men into Joseph's palace. He gave them water to wash their feet and provided food for their donkeys. [25]They were told they would be eating there, so they prepared their gifts for Joseph's arrival at noon.

[26]When Joseph came home, they gave him the gifts they had brought him, then bowed low to the ground before him. [27]After greeting them, he asked, "How is your father, the old man you spoke about? Is he still alive?"

[28]"Yes," they replied. "Our father, your servant, is alive and well." And they bowed low again.

[29]Then Joseph looked at his brother Benjamin, the son of his own mother. "Is this your youngest brother, the one you told me about?" Joseph asked. "May God be gracious to you, my son." [30]Then Joseph hurried from the room because he was overcome with emotion for his brother. He went into his private room, where he broke down and wept. [31]After washing his face, he came back out, keeping himself under control. Then he ordered, "Bring out the food!"

[32]The waiters served Joseph at his own table, and his brothers were served at a separate table. The Egyptians who ate with Joseph sat at their own table, because Egyptians despise Hebrews and refuse to eat with them. [33]Joseph told each of his brothers where to sit, and to their amazement, he seated them according to age, from oldest to youngest. [34]And Joseph filled their plates with food from his own table, giving Benjamin five times as much as he gave the others. So they feasted and drank freely with him.

44 Joseph's Silver Cup

When his brothers were ready to leave, Joseph gave these instructions to his palace manager: "Fill each of their sacks with as much grain as they can carry, and put each man's money back into his sack. [2]Then put my personal silver cup at the top

---

43:14 Hebrew *El-Shaddai.*

of the youngest brother's sack, along with the money for his grain." So the manager did as Joseph instructed him.

³ The brothers were up at dawn and were sent on their journey with their loaded donkeys. ⁴ But when they had gone only a short distance and were barely out of the city, Joseph said to his palace manager, "Chase after them and stop them. When you catch up with them, ask them, 'Why have you repaid my kindness with such evil? ⁵ Why have you stolen my master's silver cup,* which he uses to predict the future? What a wicked thing you have done!'"

⁶ When the palace manager caught up with the men, he spoke to them as he had been instructed.

⁷ "What are you talking about?" the brothers responded. "We are your servants and would never do such a thing! ⁸ Didn't we return the money we found in our sacks? We brought it back all the way from the land of Canaan. Why would we steal silver or gold from your master's house? ⁹ If you find his cup with any one of us, let that man die. And all the rest of us, my lord, will be your slaves."

¹⁰ "That's fair," the man replied. "But only the one who stole the cup will be my slave. The rest of you may go free."

¹¹ They all quickly took their sacks from the backs of their donkeys and opened them. ¹² The palace manager searched the brothers' sacks, from the oldest to the youngest. And the cup was found in Benjamin's sack! ¹³ When the brothers saw this, they tore their clothing in despair. Then they loaded their donkeys again and returned to the city.

¹⁴ Joseph was still in his palace when Judah and his brothers arrived, and they fell to the ground before him. ¹⁵ "What have you done?" Joseph demanded. "Don't you know that a man like me can predict the future?"

¹⁶ Judah answered, "Oh, my lord, what can we say to you? How can we explain this? How can we prove our innocence? God is punishing us for our sins. My lord, we have all returned to be your slaves—all of us, not just our brother who had your cup in his sack."

¹⁷ "No," Joseph said. "I would never do such a thing! Only the man who stole the cup will be my slave. The rest of you may go back to your father in peace."

Judah Speaks for His Brothers

¹⁸ Then Judah stepped forward and said, "Please, my lord, let your servant say just one word to you. Please, do not be angry with me, even though you are as powerful as Pharaoh himself.

¹⁹ "My lord, previously you asked us, your servants, 'Do you have a father or a brother?' ²⁰ And we responded, 'Yes, my lord, we have a father who is an old man, and his youngest son is a child of his old age. His full brother is dead, and he alone is left of his mother's children, and his father loves him very much.'

²¹ "And you said to us, 'Bring him here so I can see him with my own eyes.' ²² But we said to you, 'My lord, the boy cannot leave his father, for his father would die.' ²³ But you told us, 'Unless your youngest brother comes with you, you will never see my face again.'

²⁴ "So we returned to your servant, our father, and told him what you had said. ²⁵ Later, when he said, 'Go back again and buy us more food,' ²⁶ we replied, 'We can't go unless you let our youngest brother go with us. We'll never get to see the man's face unless our youngest brother is with us.'

²⁷ "Then my father said to us, 'As you know, my wife had two sons, ²⁸ and one of them went away and never returned. Doubtless he was torn to pieces by some wild animal. I have never seen him since. ²⁹ Now if you take his brother away from me, and any harm comes to him, you will send this grieving, white-haired man to his grave.*'

³⁰ "And now, my lord, I cannot go back to my father without the boy. Our father's life is bound up in the boy's life. ³¹ If he sees that the boy is not with us, our father will die. We, your servants, will indeed be responsible for sending that grieving, white-haired man to his grave. ³² My lord, I guaranteed to my father that I would take care of the boy. I told him, 'If I don't bring him back to you, I will bear the blame forever.'

44:5 As in Greek version; Hebrew lacks this phrase.   **44:29** Hebrew *to Sheol*; also in 44:31.

Service

Seeing Faces behind the Needs

GENESIS 45:1-15

When I began volunteering at a food pantry, I had a vague sort of guilt about world hunger, brought on by newspaper headlines about children dying from malnutrition. Volunteering at the food pantry seemed like a salve for my conscience.

Yet I've learned that if you volunteer to feel good, you'll work a few shifts, then give it up. The work isn't easy; not everyone we serve is grateful. There are hard days that shatter our lofty ideals about fighting hunger.

Despite the challenges, there are clients whose stories stick in my mind. The suburban mom who thanked me and "God blessed" me more times in fifteen minutes than I could count. The kind, elderly man from Florence who cracked jokes and laughed at my attempts to speak a few words of Italian as we selected pasta and cannellini beans. The mother of the refugee family of six who showed palpable relief as she loaded her basket with rice, beans, and vegetables. That month, she could feed her family. Her smile said "thank you" in every language.

Serving the hungry is changing me. Now when I donate food, I instinctively put healthy, quality items in my bag, rather than unwanted leftovers. I think about Jesus' words in Matthew 25:35: "For I was hungry, and you fed me. I was thirsty, and you gave me a drink. I was a stranger, and you invited me into your home." Instead of a vague notion of "the hungry," I see the Muslim woman with the shy, dark-haired four-year-old boy who has the most luminous eyes I've ever seen. The badly injured Asian woman unable to work but cheerful and smiling nonetheless. The neatly dressed professional man who was laid off but has kept his dignity.

Now when I think of the hungry, I no longer see headlines, but faces. And that has made all the difference.

—Cindy Crosby

For more on service, see reading at Deuteronomy 17:1-13.

³³"So please, my lord, let me stay here as a slave instead of the boy, and let the boy return with his brothers. ³⁴For how can I return to my father if the boy is not with me? I couldn't bear to see the anguish this would cause my father!"

45 Joseph Reveals His Identity

Joseph could stand it no longer. There were many people in the room, and he said to his attendants, "Out, all of you!" So he was alone with his brothers when he told them who he was. ²Then he broke down and wept. He wept so loudly the Egyptians could hear him, and word of it quickly carried to Pharaoh's palace.

³"I am Joseph!" he said to his brothers. "Is my father still alive?" But his brothers were speechless! They were stunned to realize that Joseph was standing there in front of them. ⁴"Please, come closer," he said to them. So they came closer. And he said again, "I am Joseph, your brother, whom you sold into slavery in Egypt. ⁵But don't be upset, and don't be angry with yourselves for selling me to this place. It was God who sent me here ahead of you to preserve your lives. ⁶This famine that has ravaged the

land for two years will last five more years, and there will be neither plowing nor harvesting. [7]God has sent me ahead of you to keep you and your families alive and to preserve many survivors.* [8]So it was God who sent me here, not you! And he is the one who made me an adviser* to Pharaoh—the manager of his entire palace and the governor of all Egypt.

[9]"Now hurry back to my father and tell him, 'This is what your son Joseph says: God has made me master over all the land of Egypt. So come down to me immediately! [10]You can live in the region of Goshen, where you can be near me with all your children and grandchildren, your flocks and herds, and everything you own. [11]I will take care of you there, for there are still five years of famine ahead of us. Otherwise you, your household, and all your animals will starve.'"

[12]Then Joseph added, "Look! You can see for yourselves, and so can my brother Benjamin, that I really am Joseph! [13]Go tell my father of my honored position here in Egypt. Describe for him everything you have seen, and then bring my father here quickly." [14]Weeping with joy, he embraced Benjamin, and Benjamin did the same. [15]Then Joseph kissed each of his brothers and wept over them, and after that they began talking freely with him.

Pharaoh Invites Jacob to Egypt

[16]The news soon reached Pharaoh's palace: "Joseph's brothers have arrived!" Pharaoh and his officials were all delighted to hear this.

[17]Pharaoh said to Joseph, "Tell your brothers, 'This is what you must do: Load your pack animals, and hurry back to the land of Canaan. [18]Then get your father and all of your families, and return here to me. I will give you the very best land in Egypt, and you will eat from the best that the land produces.'"

[19]Then Pharaoh said to Joseph, "Tell your brothers, 'Take wagons from the land of Egypt to carry your little children and your wives, and bring your father here. [20]Don't worry about your personal belongings, for the best of all the land of Egypt is yours.'"

[21]So the sons of Jacob* did as they were told. Joseph provided them with wagons, as Pharaoh had commanded, and he gave them supplies for the journey. [22]And he gave each of them new clothes—but to Benjamin he gave five changes of clothes and 300 pieces* of silver. [23]He also sent his father ten male donkeys loaded with the finest products of Egypt, and ten female donkeys loaded with grain and bread and other supplies he would need on his journey.

[24]So Joseph sent his brothers off, and as they left, he called after them, "Don't quarrel about all this along the way!" [25]And they left Egypt and returned to their father, Jacob, in the land of Canaan.

[26]"Joseph is still alive!" they told him. "And he is governor of all the land of Egypt!" Jacob was stunned at the news—he couldn't believe it. [27]But when they repeated to Jacob everything Joseph had told them, and when he saw the wagons Joseph had sent to carry him, their father's spirits revived.

[28]Then Jacob exclaimed, "It must be true! My son Joseph is alive! I must go and see him before I die."

46 Jacob's Journey to Egypt

So Jacob* set out for Egypt with all his possessions. And when he came to Beersheba, he offered sacrifices to the God of his father, Isaac. [2]During the night God spoke to him in a vision. "Jacob! Jacob!" he called.

"Here I am," Jacob replied.

[3]"I am God,* the God of your father," the voice said. "Do not be afraid to go down to Egypt, for there I will make your family into a great nation. [4]I will go with you down to Egypt, and I will bring you back again. You will die in Egypt, but Joseph will be with you to close your eyes."

[5]So Jacob left Beersheba, and his sons took him to Egypt. They carried him and their little ones and their wives in the wagons Pharaoh had provided for them. [6]They also took all their livestock and all the personal belongings they had acquired in the

45:7 Or and to save you with an extraordinary rescue. The meaning of the Hebrew is uncertain.   45:8 Hebrew a father.   45:21 Hebrew Israel; also in 45:28. See note on 35:21.   45:22 Hebrew 300 shekels, about 7.5 pounds or 3.4 kilograms in weight.   46:1 Hebrew Israel; also in 46:29, 30. See note on 35:21.   46:3 Hebrew I am El.

land of Canaan. So Jacob and his entire family went to Egypt—[7]sons and grandsons, daughters and granddaughters—all his descendants.

[8]These are the names of the descendants of Israel—the sons of Jacob—who went to Egypt:

Reuben was Jacob's oldest son. [9]The sons of Reuben were Hanoch, Pallu, Hezron, and Carmi.

[10]The sons of Simeon were Jemuel, Jamin, Ohad, Jakin, Zohar, and Shaul. (Shaul's mother was a Canaanite woman.)

[11]The sons of Levi were Gershon, Kohath, and Merari.

[12]The sons of Judah were Er, Onan, Shelah, Perez, and Zerah (though Er and Onan had died in the land of Canaan). The sons of Perez were Hezron and Hamul.

[13]The sons of Issachar were Tola, Puah,* Jashub,* and Shimron.

[14]The sons of Zebulun were Sered, Elon, and Jahleel.

[15]These were the sons of Leah and Jacob who were born in Paddan-aram, in addition to their daughter, Dinah. The number of Jacob's descendants (male and female) through Leah was thirty-three.

[16]The sons of Gad were Zephon,* Haggi, Shuni, Ezbon, Eri, Arodi, and Areli.

[17]The sons of Asher were Imnah, Ishvah, Ishvi, and Beriah. Their sister was Serah. Beriah's sons were Heber and Malkiel.

[18]These were the sons of Zilpah, the servant given to Leah by her father, Laban. The number of Jacob's descendants through Zilpah was sixteen.

[19]The sons of Jacob's wife Rachel were Joseph and Benjamin.

[20]Joseph's sons, born in the land of Egypt, were Manasseh and Ephraim. Their mother was Asenath, daughter of Potiphera, the priest of On.*

[21]Benjamin's sons were Bela, Beker, Ashbel, Gera, Naaman, Ehi, Rosh, Muppim, Huppim, and Ard.

[22]These were the sons of Rachel and Jacob. The number of Jacob's descendants through Rachel was fourteen.

[23]The son of Dan was Hushim.

[24]The sons of Naphtali were Jahzeel, Guni, Jezer, and Shillem.

[25]These were the sons of Bilhah, the servant given to Rachel by her father, Laban. The number of Jacob's descendants through Bilhah was seven.

[26]The total number of Jacob's direct descendants who went with him to Egypt, not counting his sons' wives, was sixty-six. [27]In addition, Joseph had two sons* who were born in Egypt. So altogether, there were seventy* members of Jacob's family in the land of Egypt.

Jacob's Family Arrives in Goshen

[28]As they neared their destination, Jacob sent Judah ahead to meet Joseph and get directions to the region of Goshen. And when they finally arrived there, [29]Joseph prepared his chariot and traveled to Goshen to meet his father, Jacob. When Joseph arrived, he embraced his father and wept, holding him for a long time. [30]Finally, Jacob said to Joseph, "Now I am ready to die, since I have seen your face again and know you are still alive."

[31]And Joseph said to his brothers and to his father's entire family, "I will go to Pharaoh and tell him, 'My brothers and my father's entire family have come to me from the land of Canaan. [32]These men are shepherds, and they raise livestock. They have brought with them their flocks and herds and everything they own.'"

[33]Then he said, "When Pharaoh calls for you and asks you about your occupation, [34]you must tell him, 'We, your servants, have raised livestock all our lives, as our ancestors have always done.' When you tell him this, he will let you live here in the region of Goshen, for the Egyptians despise shepherds."

47 Jacob Blesses Pharaoh

Then Joseph went to see Pharaoh and told him, "My father and my brothers have arrived from the land of Canaan. They have come with all their flocks and herds

---

46:13a As in Syriac version and Samaritan Pentateuch (see also 1 Chr 7:1); Hebrew reads *Puvah*. **46:13b** As in some Greek manuscripts and Samaritan Pentateuch (see also Num 26:24; 1 Chr 7:1); Hebrew reads *Iob*. **46:16** As in Greek version and Samaritan Pentateuch (see also Num 26:15); Hebrew reads *Ziphion*. **46:20** Greek version reads *of Heliopolis*. **46:27a** Greek version reads *nine sons*, probably including Joseph's grandsons through Ephraim and Manasseh (see 1 Chr 7:14-20). **46:27b** Greek version reads *seventy-five*; see note on Exod 1:5.

and possessions, and they are now in the region of Goshen."

²Joseph took five of his brothers with him and presented them to Pharaoh. ³And Pharaoh asked the brothers, "What is your occupation?"

They replied, "We, your servants, are shepherds, just like our ancestors. ⁴We have come to live here in Egypt for a while, for there is no pasture for our flocks in Canaan. The famine is very severe there. So please, we request permission to live in the region of Goshen."

⁵Then Pharaoh said to Joseph, "Now that your father and brothers have joined you here, ⁶choose any place in the entire land of Egypt for them to live. Give them the best land of Egypt. Let them live in the region of Goshen. And if any of them have special skills, put them in charge of my livestock, too."

⁷Then Joseph brought in his father, Jacob, and presented him to Pharaoh. And Jacob blessed Pharaoh.

⁸"How old are you?" Pharaoh asked him.

⁹Jacob replied, "I have traveled this earth for 130 hard years. But my life has been short compared to the lives of my ancestors." ¹⁰Then Jacob blessed Pharaoh again before leaving his court.

¹¹So Joseph assigned the best land of Egypt—the region of Rameses—to his father and his brothers, and he settled them there, just as Pharaoh had commanded. ¹²And Joseph provided food for his father and his brothers in amounts appropriate to the number of their dependents, including the smallest children.

Joseph's Leadership in the Famine

¹³Meanwhile, the famine became so severe that all the food was used up, and people were starving throughout the lands of Egypt and Canaan. ¹⁴By selling grain to the people, Joseph eventually collected all the money in Egypt and Canaan, and he put the money in Pharaoh's treasury. ¹⁵When the people of Egypt and Canaan ran out of money, all the Egyptians came to Joseph. "Our money is gone!" they cried. "But please give us food, or we will die before your very eyes!"

¹⁶Joseph replied, "Since your money is gone, bring me your livestock. I will give you food in exchange for your livestock." ¹⁷So they brought their livestock to Joseph in exchange for food. In exchange for their horses, flocks of sheep and goats, herds of cattle, and donkeys, Joseph provided them with food for another year.

¹⁸But that year ended, and the next year they came again and said, "We cannot hide the truth from you, my lord. Our money is gone, and all our livestock and cattle are yours. We have nothing left to give but our bodies and our land. ¹⁹Why should we die before your very eyes? Buy us and our land in exchange for food; we offer our land and ourselves as slaves for Pharaoh. Just give us grain so we may live and not die, and so the land does not become empty and desolate."

²⁰So Joseph bought all the land of Egypt for Pharaoh. All the Egyptians sold him their fields because the famine was so severe, and soon all the land belonged to Pharaoh. ²¹As for the people, he made them all slaves,* from one end of Egypt to the other. ²²The only land he did not buy was the land belonging to the priests. They received an allotment of food directly from Pharaoh, so they didn't need to sell their land.

²³Then Joseph said to the people, "Look, today I have bought you and your land for Pharaoh. I will provide you with seed so you can plant the fields. ²⁴Then when you harvest it, one-fifth of your crop will belong to Pharaoh. You may keep the remaining four-fifths as seed for your fields and as food for you, your households, and your little ones."

²⁵"You have saved our lives!" they exclaimed. "May it please you, my lord, to let us be Pharaoh's servants." ²⁶Joseph then issued a decree still in effect in the land of Egypt, that Pharaoh should receive one-fifth of all the crops grown on his land. Only the land belonging to the priests was not given to Pharaoh.

²⁷Meanwhile, the people of Israel settled in the region of Goshen in Egypt. There they acquired property, and they were fruitful, and their population grew rapidly. ²⁸Jacob lived for seventeen years after his arrival in Egypt, so he lived 147 years in all.

47:21 As in Greek version and Samaritan Pentateuch; Hebrew reads *he moved them all into the towns.*

[29] As the time of his death drew near, Jacob* called for his son Joseph and said to him, "Please do me this favor. Put your hand under my thigh and swear that you will treat me with unfailing love by honoring this last request: Do not bury me in Egypt. [30] When I die, please take my body out of Egypt and bury me with my ancestors."

So Joseph promised, "I will do as you ask."

[31] "Swear that you will do it," Jacob insisted. So Joseph gave his oath, and Jacob bowed humbly at the head of his bed.*

48 Jacob Blesses Manasseh and Ephraim

One day not long after this, word came to Joseph, "Your father is failing rapidly." So Joseph went to visit his father, and he took with him his two sons, Manasseh and Ephraim.

[2] When Joseph arrived, Jacob was told, "Your son Joseph has come to see you." So Jacob* gathered his strength and sat up in his bed.

[3] Jacob said to Joseph, "God Almighty* appeared to me at Luz in the land of Canaan and blessed me. [4] He said to me, 'I will make you fruitful, and I will multiply your descendants. I will make you a multitude of nations. And I will give this land of Canaan to your descendants* after you as an everlasting possession.'

[5] "Now I am claiming as my own sons these two boys of yours, Ephraim and Manasseh, who were born here in the land of Egypt before I arrived. They will be my sons, just as Reuben and Simeon are. [6] But any children born to you in the future will be your own, and they will inherit land within the territories of their brothers Ephraim and Manasseh.

[7] "Long ago, as I was returning from Paddan-aram, Rachel died in the land of Canaan. We were still on the way, some distance from Ephrath (that is, Bethlehem). So with great sorrow I buried her there beside the road to Ephrath."

[8] Then Jacob looked over at the two boys. "Are these your sons?" he asked.

[9] "Yes," Joseph told him, "these are the sons God has given me here in Egypt."

And Jacob said, "Bring them closer to me, so I can bless them."

[10] Jacob was half blind because of his age and could hardly see. So Joseph brought the boys close to him, and Jacob kissed and embraced them. [11] Then Jacob said to Joseph, "I never thought I would see your face again, but now God has let me see your children, too!"

[12] Joseph moved the boys, who were at their grandfather's knees, and he bowed with his face to the ground. [13] Then he positioned the boys in front of Jacob. With his right hand he directed Ephraim toward Jacob's left hand, and with his left hand he put Manasseh at Jacob's right hand. [14] But Jacob crossed his arms as he reached out to lay his hands on the boys' heads. He put his right hand on the head of Ephraim, though he was the younger boy, and his left hand on the head of Manasseh, though he was the firstborn. [15] Then he blessed Joseph and said,

"May the God before whom my
grandfather Abraham
and my father, Isaac, walked—
the God who has been my shepherd
all my life, to this very day,
[16] the Angel who has redeemed me from
all harm—
may he bless these boys.
May they preserve my name
and the names of Abraham and Isaac.
And may their descendants multiply
greatly
throughout the earth."

[17] But Joseph was upset when he saw that his father placed his right hand on Ephraim's head. So Joseph lifted it to move it from Ephraim's head to Manasseh's head. [18] "No, my father," he said. "This one is the firstborn. Put your right hand on his head."

[19] But his father refused. "I know, my son; I know," he replied. "Manasseh will also become a great people, but his younger brother will become even greater. And his descendants will become a multitude of nations."

²⁰So Jacob blessed the boys that day with this blessing: "The people of Israel will use your names when they give a blessing. They will say, 'May God make you as prosperous as Ephraim and Manasseh.'" In this way, Jacob put Ephraim ahead of Manasseh.

²¹Then Jacob said to Joseph, "Look, I am about to die, but God will be with you and will take you back to Canaan, the land of your ancestors. ²²And beyond what I have given your brothers, I am giving you an extra portion of the land* that I took from the Amorites with my sword and bow."

49 Jacob's Last Words to His Sons

Then Jacob called together all his sons and said, "Gather around me, and I will tell you what will happen to each of you in the days to come.

² "Come and listen, you sons of Jacob;
 listen to Israel, your father.

³ "Reuben, you are my firstborn, my
  strength,
 the child of my vigorous youth.
 You are first in rank and first in
  power.
⁴ But you are as unruly as a flood,
 and you will be first no longer.
For you went to bed with my wife;
 you defiled my marriage couch.

⁵ "Simeon and Levi are two of a kind;
 their weapons are instruments of
  violence.
⁶ May I never join in their meetings;
 may I never be a party to their
  plans.
For in their anger they murdered men,
 and they crippled oxen just for sport.
⁷ A curse on their anger, for it is fierce;
 a curse on their wrath, for it is cruel.
I will scatter them among the
  descendants of Jacob;
 I will disperse them throughout
  Israel.

⁸ "Judah, your brothers will praise you.
 You will grasp your enemies by the
  neck.
 All your relatives will bow before you.

⁹ Judah, my son, is a young lion
 that has finished eating its prey.
Like a lion he crouches and lies down;
 like a lioness—who dares to rouse
  him?
¹⁰ The scepter will not depart from Judah,
 nor the ruler's staff from his
  descendants,*
until the coming of the one to whom it
  belongs,*
 the one whom all nations will honor.
¹¹ He ties his foal to a grapevine,
 the colt of his donkey to a choice vine.
He washes his clothes in wine,
 his robes in the blood of grapes.
¹² His eyes are darker than wine,
 and his teeth are whiter than milk.

¹³ "Zebulun will settle by the seashore
 and will be a harbor for ships;
 his borders will extend to Sidon.

¹⁴ "Issachar is a sturdy donkey,
 resting between two saddlepacks.*
¹⁵ When he sees how good the
  countryside is
 and how pleasant the land,
he will bend his shoulder to the load
 and submit himself to hard labor.

¹⁶ "Dan will govern his people,
 like any other tribe in Israel.
¹⁷ Dan will be a snake beside the road,
 a poisonous viper along the path
that bites the horse's hooves
 so its rider is thrown off.

¹⁸ I trust in you for salvation, O LORD!

¹⁹ "Gad will be attacked by marauding
  bands,
 but he will attack them when they
  retreat.

²⁰ "Asher will dine on rich foods
 and produce food fit for kings.

²¹ "Naphtali is a doe set free
 that bears beautiful fawns.

²² "Joseph is the foal of a wild donkey,
 the foal of a wild donkey at a spring—
 one of the wild donkeys on the ridge.*
²³ Archers attacked him savagely;
 they shot at him and harassed him.

48:22 Or *an extra ridge of land.* The meaning of the Hebrew is uncertain. **49:10a** Hebrew *from between his feet.* **49:10b** Or *until tribute is brought to him and the peoples obey;* traditionally rendered *until Shiloh comes.* **49:14** Or *sheepfolds,* or *hearths.* **49:22** Or *Joseph is a fruitful tree, / a fruitful tree beside a spring. / His branches reach over the wall.* The meaning of the Hebrew is uncertain.

24 But his bow remained taut,
  and his arms were strengthened
  by the hands of the Mighty One of Jacob,
  by the Shepherd, the Rock of Israel.
25 May the God of your father help you;
  may the Almighty bless you
  with the blessings of the heavens above,
  and blessings of the watery depths
    below,
  and blessings of the breasts and
    womb.
26 May the blessings of your father
  surpass the blessings of the ancient
    mountains,*
  reaching to the heights of the eternal
    hills.
  May these blessings rest on the head of
    Joseph,
  who is a prince among his brothers.

27 "Benjamin is a ravenous wolf,
  devouring his enemies in the morning
  and dividing his plunder in the
    evening."

28 These are the twelve tribes of Israel, and this is what their father said as he told his sons good-bye. He blessed each one with an appropriate message.

Jacob's Death and Burial

29 Then Jacob instructed them, "Soon I will die and join my ancestors. Bury me with my father and grandfather in the cave in the field of Ephron the Hittite. 30 This is the cave in the field of Machpelah, near Mamre in Canaan, that Abraham bought from Ephron the Hittite as a permanent burial site. 31 There Abraham and his wife Sarah are buried. There Isaac and his wife, Rebekah, are buried. And there I buried Leah. 32 It is the plot of land and the cave that my grandfather Abraham bought from the Hittites."

33 When Jacob had finished this charge to his sons, he drew his feet into the bed, breathed his last, and joined his ancestors in death.

50 Joseph threw himself on his father and wept over him and kissed him. 2 Then Joseph told the physicians who served him to embalm his father's body; so Jacob*

was embalmed. 3 The embalming process took the usual forty days. And the Egyptians mourned his death for seventy days.

4 When the period of mourning was over, Joseph approached Pharaoh's advisers and said, "Please do me this favor and speak to Pharaoh on my behalf. 5 Tell him that my father made me swear an oath. He said to me, 'Listen, I am about to die. Take my body back to the land of Canaan, and bury me in the tomb I prepared for myself.' So please allow me to go and bury my father. After his burial, I will return without delay."

6 Pharaoh agreed to Joseph's request. "Go and bury your father, as he made you promise," he said. 7 So Joseph went up to bury his father. He was accompanied by all of Pharaoh's officials, all the senior members of Pharaoh's household, and all the senior officers of Egypt. 8 Joseph also took his entire household and his brothers and their households. But they left their little children and flocks and herds in the land of Goshen. 9 A great number of chariots and charioteers accompanied Joseph.

10 When they arrived at the threshing floor of Atad, near the Jordan River, they held a very great and solemn memorial service, with a seven-day period of mourning for Joseph's father. 11 The local residents, the Canaanites, watched them mourning at the threshing floor of Atad. Then they renamed that place (which is near the Jordan) Abel-mizraim,* for they said, "This is a place of deep mourning for these Egyptians."

12 So Jacob's sons did as he had commanded them. 13 They carried his body to the land of Canaan and buried him in the cave in the field of Machpelah, near Mamre. This is the cave that Abraham had bought as a permanent burial site from Ephron the Hittite.

Joseph Reassures His Brothers

14 After burying Jacob, Joseph returned to Egypt with his brothers and all who had accompanied him to his father's burial. 15 But now that their father was dead, Joseph's brothers became fearful. "Now Joseph will show his anger and pay us back for all the wrong we did to him," they said.

49:26 Or of my ancestors.   50:2 Hebrew Israel. See note on 35:21.   50:11 Abel-mizraim means "mourning of the Egyptians."

In the Midst of Difficulties

GENESIS 50:14-21

Joseph is a great example of submission. In the midst of his difficulties in Egypt (Genesis 39-50), he trusted God with his suffering, betrayal, and injustice. We see this in the names he chose for his children. Manasseh means "God has made me forget all my troubles," and Ephraim means "God has made me fruitful in this land of my grief" (Genesis 41:51-52).

Joseph believed in God's goodness, which is what we all must do. And we must realize that God's goodness might include some things that we may not necessarily label as good. Yet God's nature is the essence of goodness. And when we belong to him, we can trust that whatever he allows he will use for good. Joseph exemplified this wise perspective when he said to his brothers, "You intended to harm me, but God intended it all for good" (Genesis 50:20). That trust in God's goodness is what makes it possible for us to submit to the hard, dark things he sometimes allows us to experience. Whatever God allows to happen, we can give ourselves over to his goodness, gladly knowing that he can and will use it for good.

—Nancy Guthrie

[16] So they sent this message to Joseph: "Before your father died, he instructed us [17] to say to you: 'Please forgive your brothers for the great wrong they did to you—for their sin in treating you so cruelly.' So we, the servants of the God of your father, beg you to forgive our sin." When Joseph received the message, he broke down and wept. [18] Then his brothers came and threw themselves down before Joseph. "Look, we are your slaves!" they said.

[19] But Joseph replied, "Don't be afraid of me. Am I God, that I can punish you? [20] You intended to harm me, but God intended it all for good. He brought me to this position so I could save the lives of many people. [21] No, don't be afraid. I will continue to take care of you and your children." So he reassured them by speaking kindly to them.

The Death of Joseph

[22] So Joseph and his brothers and their families continued to live in Egypt. Joseph lived to the age of 110. [23] He lived to see three generations of descendants of his son Ephraim, and he lived to see the birth of the children of Manasseh's son Makir, whom he claimed as his own.*

[24] "Soon I will die," Joseph told his brothers, "but God will surely come to help you and lead you out of this land of Egypt. He will bring you back to the land he solemnly promised to give to Abraham, to Isaac, and to Jacob."

[25] Then Joseph made the sons of Israel swear an oath, and he said, "When God comes to help you and lead you back, you must take my bones with you." [26] So Joseph died at the age of 110. The Egyptians embalmed him, and his body was placed in a coffin in Egypt.

50:23 Hebrew *who were born on Joseph's knees.*

Introduction to
Exodus

Background

The word *exodus*, the Latin form of the Greek word *exodos,* means "exit" and is the major event of the Book of Exodus. The story begins centuries after the close of Genesis. The Hebrew people are in Egypt, where a new pharaoh arises who does not remember all that Joseph did for the nation. Instead, he sees foreign people growing in numbers within his borders. Fearing an uprising, Pharaoh enslaves the people and even goes so far as to kill the male newborns. After four hundred years of slavery, God responds to the cries of his people. He sends them Moses, his chosen leader, and proceeds miraculously to bring his people out of Egypt.

Testimony to Moses' authorship of the Book of Exodus comes from Joshua 8:31, Malachi 4:4, Jesus' disciples (John 1:45), the apostle Paul (Romans 10:5), and Jesus himself (Mark 7:10; 12:26; Luke 2:22; John 5:46–47; 7:19–23).

Message

Seen throughout Genesis as the Creator and Provider, God now reveals to Moses that he is to be called I Am Who I Am (3:14; 34:6–7—expressed as Lord) and that he wants to make a covenant with the people he rescued from bondage. In the story of the Passover—a substitutionary lamb being killed—the stage is set for the Exodus. Millennia later the apostle Paul refers to Jesus as "our Passover Lamb" who "has been sacrificed for us" (1 Corinthians 5:7).

God proves that he is merciful and willing to forgive when the people grumble about the hardships of the wilderness; he provides water and daily sustenance of manna and quail. On Mount Sinai, God establishes a code of living. He gives the law and provides the design for the tabernacle where he will dwell and be worshiped.

Time

First Kings 6:1 hooks the date of Solomon's construction of the Jerusalem temple to that of the Exodus from Egypt; calculating backward one can date the Exodus to circa 1445 B.C. As is true of Genesis and the other books of the Pentateuch, the Book of Exodus was probably written between 1445 and 1406 B.C.

Outline

Exodus

1 The Israelites in Egypt

These are the names of the sons of Israel (that is, Jacob) who moved to Egypt with their father, each with his family: ²Reuben, Simeon, Levi, Judah, ³Issachar, Zebulun, Benjamin, ⁴Dan, Naphtali, Gad, and Asher. ⁵In all, Jacob had seventy* descendants in Egypt, including Joseph, who was already there.

⁶In time, Joseph and all of his brothers died, ending that entire generation. ⁷But their descendants, the Israelites, had many children and grandchildren. In fact, they multiplied so greatly that they became extremely powerful and filled the land.

⁸Eventually, a new king came to power in Egypt who knew nothing about Joseph or what he had done. ⁹He said to his people, "Look, the people of Israel now outnumber us and are stronger than we are. ¹⁰We must make a plan to keep them from growing even more. If we don't, and if war breaks out, they will join our enemies and fight against us. Then they will escape from the country.*"

¹¹So the Egyptians made the Israelites their slaves. They appointed brutal slave drivers over them, hoping to wear them down with crushing labor. They forced them to build the cities of Pithom and Rameses as supply centers for the king. ¹²But the more the Egyptians oppressed them, the more the Israelites multiplied and spread, and the more alarmed the Egyptians became. ¹³So the Egyptians worked the people of Israel without mercy. ¹⁴They made their lives bitter, forcing them to mix mortar and make bricks and do all the work in the fields. They were ruthless in all their demands.

¹⁵Then Pharaoh, the king of Egypt, gave this order to the Hebrew midwives, Shiphrah and Puah: ¹⁶"When you help the Hebrew women as they give birth, watch as they deliver.* If the baby is a boy, kill him; if it is a girl, let her live." ¹⁷But because the midwives feared God, they refused to obey the king's orders. They allowed the boys to live, too.

¹⁸So the king of Egypt called for the midwives. "Why have you done this?" he demanded. "Why have you allowed the boys to live?"

¹⁹"The Hebrew women are not like the Egyptian women," the midwives replied. "They are more vigorous and have their babies so quickly that we cannot get there in time."

²⁰So God was good to the midwives, and the Israelites continued to multiply, growing more and more powerful. ²¹And because the midwives feared God, he gave them families of their own.

²²Then Pharaoh gave this order to all his people: "Throw every newborn Hebrew boy into the Nile River. But you may let the girls live."

2 The Birth of Moses

About this time, a man and woman from the tribe of Levi got married. ²The woman became pregnant and gave birth to a son. She saw that he was a special baby and kept him hidden for three months. ³But when she could no longer

---

1:5 Dead Sea Scrolls and Greek version read *seventy-five*; see notes on Gen 46:27.　**1:10** Or *will take the country.*
1:16 Hebrew *look upon the two stones*; perhaps the reference is to a birthstool.

hide him, she got a basket made of papyrus reeds and waterproofed it with tar and pitch. She put the baby in the basket and laid it among the reeds along the bank of the Nile River. ⁴The baby's sister then stood at a distance, watching to see what would happen to him.

⁵Soon Pharaoh's daughter came down to bathe in the river, and her attendants walked along the riverbank. When the princess saw the basket among the reeds, she sent her maid to get it for her. ⁶When the princess opened it, she saw the baby. The little boy was crying, and she felt sorry for him. "This must be one of the Hebrew children," she said.

⁷Then the baby's sister approached the princess. "Should I go and find one of the Hebrew women to nurse the baby for you?" she asked.

⁸"Yes, do!" the princess replied. So the girl went and called the baby's mother.

⁹"Take this baby and nurse him for me," the princess told the baby's mother. "I will

Shiphrah and Puah:
Defying Pharaoh, Doing What's Right
EXODUS 1:15-22

Shiphrah and Puah were Hebrew midwives who lived under oppressive slavery in Egypt. They were accustomed to suffering. But when Pharaoh gave Shiphrah and Puah his ultimatum to kill all the Hebrew boys (Exodus 1:16), they faced a choice. They knew the consequences of disobeying a powerfully ruthless ruler. Their livelihoods and lives were on the line. They could save others or save themselves. "But because the midwives feared God, they refused to obey the king's orders" (1:17).

The fear of God gave the midwives a greater strength to see beyond their interests and act wisely; they embodied the words the psalmist would one day write: "Fear of the LORD is the foundation of true wisdom" (Psalm 111:10). Their godly fear translated into love. The choice was not easy, but they fearlessly followed the truth and selflessly chose the path of service, no matter the consequences. They let the boys live.

Other brutal realities may have confronted them. If they didn't kill the boys, would someone else be forced to do it? What would happen to the living babies? Were they destined to be hunted down and murdered by Pharaoh's soldiers? In the face of complex circumstances, the midwives' experience reminds us that we can control only our own actions; we are responsible for our own choices.

They were undaunted however indignant the king might be. They deceived Pharaoh with a savvy response to his questioning (1:18-19). Was it wrong for them to lie? This issue too is complex, but we can see that they saved countless lives; they honored a greater Truth in their choice to disobey Pharaoh. God blessed their faithful obedience to him by giving them families of their own (1:21).

Shiphrah and Puah's decision to work against injustice inspires us to take a stand. In the wake of their civil disobedience an unlikely leader would rise and deliver the people out of slavery. And an unlikely Savior would eventually come and deliver the world from sin. One whose first cries from a manger and final cries from the cross still echo with justice and truth.

—Amie Hollmann

For more on justice, see reading at Deuteronomy 24:17-21.

Letting Go
EXODUS 2:1–10

Her back was against a wall. When she realized her three-month-old son, Moses, was now too large (and probably too loud) to continue to hide him from the soldiers ordered to kill all the Hebrew infant boys, Jochebed did the unthinkable: she placed him in a basket and set him among the reeds of the powerful Nile. As a mother I cannot imagine what it was like for Jochebed in that moment of painful desperation. Yet somehow she willed herself to choose to place her child in God's hands.

Jochebed's painful, faith-filled decision provides us with a powerful image of surrender. Sometimes trusting God means we must utterly let go. Sometimes faith requires us to do the unthinkable, to risk it all, to step into a situation in which we are completely powerless with the hope that God will bear us up in it. Faith, as musician Charles Hayes reminds us, asks us to put all our "burdens, problems," and unanswered questions "*all* in his hands!" When we face a crisis, faith invites us to let go of our illusions of power and affirm that God is in control and we are not. Faith asks us to trust and rely entirely on God to work *his* will in the situation.

Wholehearted surrender is the hard, but necessary, part of trust. As we rely on God's power more than our own, we're able with freedom to say, "Your will be done."

—*Kelli B. Trujillo*

For more on faith, see reading at 2 Kings 6:8–23.

pay you for your help." So the woman took her baby home and nursed him.

¹⁰ Later, when the boy was older, his mother brought him back to Pharaoh's daughter, who adopted him as her own son. The princess named him Moses,* for she explained, "I lifted him out of the water."

Moses Escapes to Midian
¹¹ Many years later, when Moses had grown up, he went out to visit his own people, the Hebrews, and he saw how hard they were forced to work. During his visit, he saw an Egyptian beating one of his fellow Hebrews. ¹² After looking in all directions to make sure no one was watching, Moses killed the Egyptian and hid the body in the sand.

¹³ The next day, when Moses went out to visit his people again, he saw two Hebrew men fighting. "Why are you beating up your friend?" Moses said to the one who had started the fight.

¹⁴ The man replied, "Who appointed you to be our prince and judge? Are you going to kill me as you killed that Egyptian yesterday?"

Then Moses was afraid, thinking, "Everyone knows what I did." ¹⁵ And sure enough, Pharaoh heard what had happened, and he tried to kill Moses. But Moses fled from Pharaoh and went to live in the land of Midian.

When Moses arrived in Midian, he sat down beside a well. ¹⁶ Now the priest of Midian had seven daughters who came as usual to draw water and fill the water troughs for their father's flocks. ¹⁷ But some other shepherds came and chased them away. So Moses jumped up and rescued the girls from the shepherds. Then he drew water for their flocks.

2:10 *Moses* sounds like a Hebrew term that means "to lift out."

Look Again

EXODUS 3:1-6

Do you ever wonder why some things are invisible to us? I can walk down a street and look right through people. Not until they say my name do I actually see them.

Or a child can stand in front of the refrigerator and ask, "Where's the salsa?" And we have to hand it to him—when it was right in front of his nose the whole time.

I also miss hearing things. I tell my husband, "You didn't tell me!"

He replies, "Oh, but I did."

It's an irony, I suppose, but even the sighted and hearing can be blind and deaf.

This irony runs deeply through the pages of Scripture. I recently stumbled on a passage that framed this all too well: "Listen, you who are deaf! Look and see, you blind! . . . You hear with your ears, but *don't really listen*" (Isaiah 42:18, 20, italics added). Other translations say, "You pay no attention." God puts a premium on the simple disciplines of seeing and hearing. These two qualities—a seeing eye, a hearing ear—represent a heart awake to God.

Moses learned to pay attention and so heard from God. One day while herding sheep in the wilderness of Midian, he noticed a bush. It seemed to be on fire, but it wasn't burning up. The desert is a strange place—the shimmering heat, light, solitude—it can all play tricks on you. Mirages happen. Moses could have thought, *Why bother? It's just a trick of the eye.* But Moses turned his mind from the sheep. "'This is amazing,' Moses said to himself. 'Why isn't that bush burning up? I must go see it'" (Exodus 3:3).

This single act of paying attention to something in nature—a burning bush—changed his life. "When the LORD saw Moses coming to *take a closer look*, God called to him from the middle of bush" (Exodus 3:4, italics added). When God called, "Moses! Moses!" Moses paid attention and said, "Here I am!"

This discipline of seeing and hearing is available to all Christians as we seek to be present and attentive to our lives. "Come to me with your ears wide open. Listen, and you will find life" (Isaiah 55:3). Jesus echoed this same idea when he said, "Anyone with ears to hear should listen and understand" (Mark 4:9).

It's not enough just to have eyes and ears. We need to *learn* how to hear and see God's presence and his guidance for us. The world isn't short of revelation or even myriads of transcendences. But we have habits that sabotage these two basic senses.

We don't expect to hear or see anything. We've been there; done that. We're just having coffee with a friend. We're going to church again. We aren't expecting divine messages. We aren't expecting to see into anyone's soul. Yet C. S. Lewis reminds us, God is walking this world incognito. The question is whether or not we are awake and expecting God to show up.

We multitask. People who multitask aren't really present to others. I became aware of this one day as I was talking on the phone and typing on my laptop at the same time. The caller started to cry, and I couldn't figure out what I'd missed. Pulled up short, I knew I had to change. Now when the phone rings, I put my hand on the receiver and pray, "Lord, help me be present."

We hurry into our future so fast we fail to live in the present. In fact, the present is just a crack between the past and the future. No one can meet God or a friend in the future. The only time you have for relationship is the present moment. Slow down. Say no. Live the life you've been given.

God calls you by name, just as he called Moses or Samuel or Martha. Are you present? Do you think that kind of calling doesn't happen these days? Are you tuned in or out? Can you imagine the God who dreamed you up before the morning stars sang together still has things to reveal to you?

Paul writes in Ephesians 1:17-19: "[I pray] asking God . . . to give you spiritual wisdom and insight so that you might grow in your knowledge of God. I pray that your hearts will be flooded with light. . . . I also pray that you will understand the incredible greatness of God's power for us who believe him."

God's presence is all around you—his guidance, his truth, his leading in your life are available to you. Are you looking? Are you listening?

—*Adele Ahlberg Calhoun*

For more on contemplation, see reading at Job 42:1-5.

¹⁸When the girls returned to Reuel, their father, he asked, "Why are you back so soon today?"

¹⁹"An Egyptian rescued us from the shepherds," they answered. "And then he drew water for us and watered our flocks."

²⁰"Then where is he?" their father asked. "Why did you leave him there? Invite him to come and eat with us."

²¹Moses accepted the invitation, and he settled there with him. In time, Reuel gave Moses his daughter Zipporah to be his wife. ²²Later she gave birth to a son, and Moses named him Gershom,* for he explained, "I have been a foreigner in a foreign land."

²³Years passed, and the king of Egypt died. But the Israelites continued to groan under their burden of slavery. They cried out for help, and their cry rose up to God. ²⁴God heard their groaning, and he remembered his covenant promise to Abraham, Isaac, and Jacob. ²⁵He looked down on the people of Israel and knew it was time to act.*

3 Moses and the Burning Bush

One day Moses was tending the flock of his father-in-law, Jethro,* the priest of Midian. He led the flock far into the wilderness and came to Sinai,* the mountain of God. ²There the angel of the LORD appeared to him in a blazing fire from the middle of a bush. Moses stared in amazement. Though the bush was engulfed in flames, it didn't burn up. ³"This is amazing," Moses said to himself. "Why isn't that bush burning up? I must go see it."

⁴When the LORD saw Moses coming to take a closer look, God called to him from the middle of the bush, "Moses! Moses!"

"Here I am!" Moses replied.

⁵"Do not come any closer," the LORD warned. "Take off your sandals, for you are standing on holy ground. ⁶I am the God of your father*—the God of Abraham, the God of Isaac, and the God of Jacob." When Moses heard this, he covered his face because he was afraid to look at God.

⁷Then the LORD told him, "I have certainly seen the oppression of my people in Egypt. I have heard their cries of distress because of their harsh slave drivers. Yes, I am aware of their suffering. ⁸So I have come down to rescue them from the power of the Egyptians and lead them out of Egypt into their own fertile and spacious land. It is a land flowing with milk and honey—the land where the Canaanites, Hittites, Amorites, Perizzites, Hivites, and Jebusites now live. ⁹Look! The cry of the people of Israel has reached me, and I have seen how harshly the Egyptians abuse them. ¹⁰Now go, for I am sending you to Pharaoh. You must lead my people Israel out of Egypt."

¹¹But Moses protested to God, "Who am I to appear before Pharaoh? Who am I to lead the people of Israel out of Egypt?"

¹²God answered, "I will be with you. And this is your sign that I am the one who has sent you: When you have brought the people out of Egypt, you will worship God at this very mountain."

¹³But Moses protested, "If I go to the people of Israel and tell them, 'The God of your ancestors has sent me to you,' they will ask me, 'What is his name?' Then what should I tell them?"

¹⁴God replied to Moses, "I AM WHO I AM.* Say this to the people of Israel: I AM has sent me to you." ¹⁵God also said to Moses, "Say this to the people of Israel: Yahweh,* the God of your ancestors—the God of Abraham, the God of Isaac, and the God of Jacob—has sent me to you.

This is my eternal name,
my name to remember for all generations.

¹⁶"Now go and call together all the elders of Israel. Tell them, 'The LORD, the God of your ancestors—the God of Abraham, Isaac, and Jacob—has appeared to me. He told me, "I have been watching closely, and I see how the Egyptians are treating you. ¹⁷I have promised to rescue you from your oppression in Egypt. I will lead you to a land flowing with milk and honey—the land where the Canaanites, Hittites, Amorites, Perizzites, Hivites, and Jebusites now live."'

2:22 Gershom sounds like a Hebrew term that means "a foreigner there."   2:25 Or and acknowledged his obligation to help them.
3:1a Moses' father-in-law went by two names, Jethro and Reuel.   3:1b Hebrew Horeb, another name for Sinai.   3:6 Greek version reads your fathers.   3:14 Or I WILL BE WHAT I WILL BE.   3:15 Yahweh is a transliteration of the proper name YHWH that is sometimes rendered "Jehovah"; in this translation it is usually rendered "the LORD" (note the use of small capitals).

¹⁸ "The elders of Israel will accept your message. Then you and the elders must go to the king of Egypt and tell him, 'The LORD, the God of the Hebrews, has met with us. So please let us take a three-day journey into the wilderness to offer sacrifices to the LORD, our God.'

¹⁹ "But I know that the king of Egypt will not let you go unless a mighty hand forces him.* ²⁰ So I will raise my hand and strike the Egyptians, performing all kinds of miracles among them. Then at last he will let you go. ²¹ And I will cause the Egyptians to look favorably on you. They will give you gifts when you go so you will not leave empty-handed. ²² Every Israelite woman will ask for articles of silver and gold and fine clothing from her Egyptian neighbors and from the foreign women in their houses. You will dress your sons and daughters with these, stripping the Egyptians of their wealth."

Signs of the LORD's Power

4 But Moses protested again, "What if they won't believe me or listen to me? What if they say, 'The LORD never appeared to you'?"

² Then the LORD asked him, "What is that in your hand?"

"A shepherd's staff," Moses replied.

³ "Throw it down on the ground," the LORD told him. So Moses threw down the staff, and it turned into a snake! Moses jumped back.

⁴ Then the LORD told him, "Reach out and grab its tail." So Moses reached out and grabbed it, and it turned back into a shepherd's staff in his hand.

⁵ "Perform this sign," the LORD told him. "Then they will believe that the LORD, the God of their ancestors—the God of Abraham, the God of Isaac, and the God of Jacob—really has appeared to you."

⁶ Then the LORD said to Moses, "Now put your hand inside your cloak." So Moses put his hand inside his cloak, and when he took it out again, his hand was white as snow with a severe skin disease.* ⁷ "Now put your hand back into your cloak," the LORD said. So Moses put his hand back in, and when he took it out again, it was as healthy as the rest of his body.

⁸ The LORD said to Moses, "If they do not believe you and are not convinced by the first miraculous sign, they will be convinced by the second sign. ⁹ And if they don't believe you or listen to you even after these two signs, then take some water from the Nile River and pour it out on the dry ground. When you do, the water from the Nile will turn to blood on the ground."

¹⁰ But Moses pleaded with the LORD, "O Lord, I'm not very good with words. I never have been, and I'm not now, even though you have spoken to me. I get tongue-tied, and my words get tangled."

¹¹ Then the LORD asked Moses, "Who makes a person's mouth? Who decides whether people speak or do not speak, hear or do not hear, see or do not see? Is it not I, the LORD? ¹² Now go! I will be with you as you speak, and I will instruct you in what to say."

¹³ But Moses again pleaded, "Lord, please! Send anyone else."

¹⁴ Then the LORD became angry with Moses. "All right," he said. "What about your brother, Aaron the Levite? I know he speaks well. And look! He is on his way to meet you now. He will be delighted to see you. ¹⁵ Talk to him, and put the words in his mouth. I will be with both of you as you speak, and I will instruct you both in what to do. ¹⁶ Aaron will be your spokesman to the people. He will be your mouthpiece, and you will stand in the place of God for him, telling him what to say. ¹⁷ And take your shepherd's staff with you, and use it to perform the miraculous signs I have shown you."

Moses Returns to Egypt

¹⁸ So Moses went back home to Jethro, his father-in-law. "Please let me return to my relatives in Egypt," Moses said. "I don't even know if they are still alive."

"Go in peace," Jethro replied.

¹⁹ Before Moses left Midian, the LORD said to him, "Return to Egypt, for all those who wanted to kill you have died."

²⁰ So Moses took his wife and sons, put

3:19 As in Greek and Latin versions; Hebrew reads *will not let you go, not by a mighty hand.* **4:6** Or *with leprosy.* The Hebrew word used here can describe various skin diseases.

When Fears Hold You Back

EXODUS 4:1-17

Acceptance

Have you ever heard God's call to serve and responded, "Is there *anyone else* who can do it?"

I relate to the fear and inadequacy Moses expressed when God called him to lead the Hebrew slaves out of Egypt (Exodus 3–4). Like Moses, I sometimes focus on the task God would have me accept. This causes me to interpret the question, "Will you serve?" as meaning, "Do you possess the qualifications and ability to best perform this job?"

Terrified, I try to bow out, using Moses' excuses: I'm a nobody; my authority will be questioned (3:11, 13). "What if they won't believe me or listen to me?" (4:1).

God responded to Moses' self-doubt with abundant provision. First, God served as Moses' speechwriter, assuring him Israel's leaders would take heed of God's own words. God further equipped Moses with physical evidence—not just one but *three* signs. While Moses acknowledged this provision, he still believed his inadequacy (he'd never been a good public speaker) inevitably would cause him to fail.

Fear can cause us to minimize God's provision and even doubt God's ability. When we fixate on our lack, we essentially tell God, *You aren't enough. My weakness trumps your strength.*

This wrongheaded focus is due to misunderstanding the purpose of God's call: it's never about accomplishing a task for God's benefit. God has the means to work without human involvement. As Moses would discover, God can single-handedly drown an army in the sea and feed a nation by dropping food from the sky. Further, human resistance to God's will is irrelevant. "Who makes a person's mouth? Who decides whether people speak or do not speak, hear or do not hear, see or do not see? Is it not I, the LORD?" (4:11). Whatever God desires, it will be accomplished.

Hearing God's call gauges our understanding of *his* strength rather than our assessment of our own. Do we believe God is strong enough to compensate for our lack—of faith, ability, training, resources? Our bad habits, our lack of emotional stability, a clean history, or a picture-perfect life? To accept God's call is to proclaim that God conquers all (Philippians 4:13).

—*Holly Vicente Robaina*

For more on acceptance, see reading at Judges 6:11-16.

them on a donkey, and headed back to the land of Egypt. In his hand he carried the staff of God.

²¹ And the LORD told Moses, "When you arrive back in Egypt, go to Pharaoh and perform all the miracles I have empowered you to do. But I will harden his heart so he will refuse to let the people go. ²² Then you will tell him, 'This is what the LORD says: Israel is my firstborn son. ²³ I commanded you, "Let my son go, so he can worship me." But since you have refused, I will now kill your firstborn son!'"

²⁴ On the way to Egypt, at a place where Moses and his family had stopped for the night, the LORD confronted him and was about to kill him. ²⁵ But Moses' wife, Zipporah, took a flint knife and circumcised her son. She touched his feet* with the foreskin and said, "Now you are a bride-

---

4:25 The Hebrew word for "feet" may refer here to the male sex organ.

groom of blood to me." ²⁶(When she said "a bridegroom of blood," she was referring to the circumcision.) After that, the LORD left him alone.

²⁷Now the LORD had said to Aaron, "Go out into the wilderness to meet Moses." So Aaron went and met Moses at the mountain of God, and he embraced him. ²⁸Moses then told Aaron everything the LORD had commanded him to say. And he told him about the miraculous signs the LORD had commanded him to perform.

²⁹Then Moses and Aaron returned to Egypt and called all the elders of Israel together. ³⁰Aaron told them everything the LORD had told Moses, and Moses performed the miraculous signs as they watched. ³¹Then the people of Israel were convinced that the LORD had sent Moses and Aaron. When they heard that the LORD was concerned about them and had seen their misery, they bowed down and worshiped.

5 Moses and Aaron Speak to Pharaoh

After this presentation to Israel's leaders, Moses and Aaron went and spoke to Pharaoh. They told him, "This is what the LORD, the God of Israel, says: Let my people go so they may hold a festival in my honor in the wilderness."

²"Is that so?" retorted Pharaoh. "And who is the LORD? Why should I listen to him and let Israel go? I don't know the LORD, and I will not let Israel go."

³But Aaron and Moses persisted. "The God of the Hebrews has met with us," they declared. "So let us take a three-day journey into the wilderness so we can offer sacrifices to the LORD our God. If we don't, he will kill us with a plague or with the sword."

⁴Pharaoh replied, "Moses and Aaron, why are you distracting the people from their tasks? Get back to work! ⁵Look, there are many of your people in the land, and you are stopping them from their work."

Making Bricks without Straw

⁶That same day Pharaoh sent this order to the Egyptian slave drivers and the Israelite foremen: ⁷"Do not supply any more straw for making bricks. Make the people get it

themselves! ⁸But still require them to make the same number of bricks as before. Don't reduce the quota. They are lazy. That's why they are crying out, 'Let us go and offer sacrifices to our God.' ⁹Load them down with more work. Make them sweat! That will teach them to listen to lies!"

¹⁰So the slave drivers and foremen went out and told the people: "This is what Pharaoh says: I will not provide any more straw for you. ¹¹Go and get it yourselves. Find it wherever you can. But you must produce just as many bricks as before!" ¹²So the people scattered throughout the land of Egypt in search of stubble to use as straw.

¹³Meanwhile, the Egyptian slave drivers continued to push hard. "Meet your daily quota of bricks, just as you did when we provided you with straw!" they demanded. ¹⁴Then they whipped the Israelite foremen they had put in charge of the work crews. "Why haven't you met your quotas either yesterday or today?" they demanded.

¹⁵So the Israelite foremen went to Pharaoh and pleaded with him. "Please don't treat your servants like this," they begged. ¹⁶"We are given no straw, but the slave drivers still demand, 'Make bricks!' We are being beaten, but it isn't our fault! Your own people are to blame!"

¹⁷But Pharaoh shouted, "You're just lazy! Lazy! That's why you're saying, 'Let us go and offer sacrifices to the LORD.' ¹⁸Now get back to work! No straw will be given to you, but you must still produce the full quota of bricks."

¹⁹The Israelite foremen could see that they were in serious trouble when they were told, "You must not reduce the number of bricks you make each day." ²⁰As they left Pharaoh's court, they confronted Moses and Aaron, who were waiting outside for them. ²¹The foremen said to them, "May the LORD judge and punish you for making us stink before Pharaoh and his officials. You have put a sword into their hands, an excuse to kill us!"

²²Then Moses went back to the LORD and protested, "Why have you brought all this trouble on your own people, Lord? Why did you send me? ²³Ever since I came to

Pharaoh as your spokesman, he has been even more brutal to your people. And you have done nothing to rescue them!"

6 Promises of Deliverance

Then the LORD told Moses, "Now you will see what I will do to Pharaoh. When he feels the force of my strong hand, he will let the people go. In fact, he will force them to leave his land!"

²And God said to Moses, "I am Yahweh—'the LORD.'* ³I appeared to Abraham, to Isaac, and to Jacob as El-Shaddai—'God Almighty'*—but I did not reveal my name, Yahweh, to them. ⁴And I reaffirmed my covenant with them. Under its terms, I promised to give them the land of Canaan, where they were living as foreigners. ⁵You can be sure that I have heard the groans of the people of Israel, who are now slaves to the Egyptians. And I am well aware of my covenant with them.

⁶"Therefore, say to the people of Israel: 'I am the LORD. I will free you from your oppression and will rescue you from your slavery in Egypt. I will redeem you with a powerful arm and great acts of judgment. ⁷I will claim you as my own people, and I will be your God. Then you will know that I am the LORD your God who has freed you from your oppression in Egypt. ⁸I will bring you into the land I swore to give to Abraham, Isaac, and Jacob. I will give it to you as your very own possession. I am the LORD!'"

⁹So Moses told the people of Israel what the LORD had said, but they refused to listen anymore. They had become too discouraged by the brutality of their slavery.

¹⁰Then the LORD said to Moses, ¹¹"Go back to Pharaoh, the king of Egypt, and tell him to let the people of Israel leave his country."

¹²"But LORD!" Moses objected. "My own people won't listen to me anymore. How can I expect Pharaoh to listen? I'm such a clumsy speaker!*"

¹³But the LORD spoke to Moses and Aaron and gave them orders for the Israelites and for Pharaoh, the king of Egypt. The LORD commanded Moses and Aaron to lead the people of Israel out of Egypt.

The Ancestors of Moses and Aaron

¹⁴These are the ancestors of some of the clans of Israel:

The sons of Reuben, Israel's oldest son, were Hanoch, Pallu, Hezron, and Carmi. Their descendants became the clans of Reuben.

¹⁵The sons of Simeon were Jemuel, Jamin, Ohad, Jakin, Zohar, and Shaul. (Shaul's mother was a Canaanite woman.) Their descendants became the clans of Simeon.

¹⁶These are the descendants of Levi, as listed in their family records: The sons of Levi were Gershon, Kohath, and Merari. (Levi lived to be 137 years old.)

¹⁷The descendants of Gershon included Libni and Shimei, each of whom became the ancestor of a clan.

¹⁸The descendants of Kohath included Amram, Izhar, Hebron, and Uzziel. (Kohath lived to be 133 years old.)

¹⁹The descendants of Merari included Mahli and Mushi.

These are the clans of the Levites, as listed in their family records.

²⁰Amram married his father's sister Jochebed, and she gave birth to his sons, Aaron and Moses. (Amram lived to be 137 years old.)

²¹The sons of Izhar were Korah, Nepheg, and Zicri.

²²The sons of Uzziel were Mishael, Elzaphan, and Sithri.

²³Aaron married Elisheba, the daughter of Amminadab and sister of Nahshon, and she gave birth to his sons, Nadab, Abihu, Eleazar, and Ithamar.

²⁴The sons of Korah were Assir, Elkanah, and Abiasaph. Their descendants became the clans of Korah.

²⁵Eleazar son of Aaron married one of the daughters of Putiel, and she gave birth to his son, Phinehas.

These are the ancestors of the Levite families, listed according to their clans.

6:2 *Yahweh* is a transliteration of the proper name *YHWH* that is sometimes rendered "Jehovah"; in this translation it is usually rendered "the LORD" (note the use of small capitals). **6:3** *El-Shaddai*, which means "God Almighty," is the name for God used in Gen 17:1; 28:3; 35:11; 43:14; 48:3. **6:12** Hebrew *I have uncircumcised lips*; also in 6:30.

26 The Aaron and Moses named in this list are the same ones to whom the LORD said, "Lead the people of Israel out of the land of Egypt like an army." 27 It was Moses and Aaron who spoke to Pharaoh, the king of Egypt, about leading the people of Israel out of Egypt.

28 When the LORD spoke to Moses in the land of Egypt, 29 he said to him, "I am the LORD! Tell Pharaoh, the king of Egypt, everything I am telling you." 30 But Moses argued with the LORD, saying, "I can't do it! I'm such a clumsy speaker! Why should Pharaoh listen to me?"

7 Aaron's Staff Becomes a Serpent

Then the LORD said to Moses, "Pay close attention to this. I will make you seem like God to Pharaoh, and your brother, Aaron, will be your prophet. 2 Tell Aaron everything I command you, and Aaron must command Pharaoh to let the people of Israel leave his country. 3 But I will make Pharaoh's heart stubborn so I can multiply my miraculous signs and wonders in the land of Egypt. 4 Even then Pharaoh will refuse to listen to you. So I will bring down my fist on Egypt. Then I will rescue my forces—my people, the Israelites—from the land of Egypt with great acts of judgment. 5 When I raise my powerful hand and bring out the Israelites, the Egyptians will know that I am the LORD."

6 So Moses and Aaron did just as the LORD had commanded them. 7 Moses was eighty years old, and Aaron was eighty-three when they made their demands to Pharaoh.

8 Then the LORD said to Moses and Aaron, 9 "Pharaoh will demand, 'Show me a miracle.' When he does this, say to Aaron, 'Take your staff and throw it down in front of Pharaoh, and it will become a serpent.*'"

10 So Moses and Aaron went to Pharaoh and did what the LORD had commanded them. Aaron threw down his staff before Pharaoh and his officials, and it became a serpent! 11 Then Pharaoh called in his own wise men and sorcerers, and these Egyptian magicians did the same thing with their magic. 12 They threw down their staffs, which also became serpents! But then Aaron's staff swallowed up their staffs. 13 Pharaoh's heart, however, remained hard. He still refused to listen, just as the LORD had predicted.

A Plague of Blood

14 Then the LORD said to Moses, "Pharaoh's heart is stubborn,* and he still refuses to let the people go. 15 So go to Pharaoh in the morning as he goes down to the river. Stand on the bank of the Nile and meet him there. Be sure to take along the staff that turned into a snake. 16 Then announce to him, 'The LORD, the God of the Hebrews, has sent me to tell you, "Let my people go, so they can worship me in the wilderness." Until now, you have refused to listen to him. 17 So this is what the LORD says: "I will show you that I am the LORD." Look! I will strike the water of the Nile with this staff in my hand, and the river will turn to blood. 18 The fish in it will die, and the river will stink. The Egyptians will not be able to drink any water from the Nile.'"

19 Then the LORD said to Moses: "Tell Aaron, 'Take your staff and raise your hand over the waters of Egypt—all its rivers, canals, ponds, and all the reservoirs. Turn all the water to blood. Everywhere in Egypt the water will turn to blood, even the water stored in wooden bowls and stone pots.'"

20 So Moses and Aaron did just as the LORD commanded them. As Pharaoh and all of his officials watched, Aaron raised his staff and struck the water of the Nile. Suddenly, the whole river turned to blood! 21 The fish in the river died, and the water became so foul that the Egyptians couldn't drink it. There was blood everywhere throughout the land of Egypt. 22 But again the magicians of Egypt used their magic, and they, too, turned water into blood. So Pharaoh's heart remained hard. He refused to listen to Moses and Aaron, just as the LORD had predicted. 23 Pharaoh returned to his palace and put the whole thing out of his mind. 24 Then all the Egyptians dug along the riverbank to find drinking water, for they couldn't drink the water from the Nile.

25 Seven days passed from the time the LORD struck the Nile.

7:9 Hebrew *tannin*, which elsewhere refers to a sea monster. Greek version translates it "dragon."   7:14 Hebrew *heavy*.

8 A Plague of Frogs

¹*Then the LORD said to Moses, "Go back to Pharaoh and announce to him, 'This is what the LORD says: Let my people go, so they can worship me. ²If you refuse to let them go, I will send a plague of frogs across your entire land. ³The Nile River will swarm with frogs. They will come up out of the river and into your palace, even into your bedroom and onto your bed! They will enter the houses of your officials and your people. They will even jump into your ovens and your kneading bowls. ⁴Frogs will jump on you, your people, and all your officials.'"

⁵*Then the LORD said to Moses, "Tell Aaron, 'Raise the staff in your hand over all the rivers, canals, and ponds of Egypt, and bring up frogs over all the land.'" ⁶So Aaron raised his hand over the waters of Egypt, and frogs came up and covered the whole land! ⁷But the magicians were able to do the same thing with their magic. They, too, caused frogs to come up on the land of Egypt.

⁸Then Pharaoh summoned Moses and Aaron and begged, "Plead with the LORD to take the frogs away from me and my people. I will let your people go, so they can offer sacrifices to the LORD."

⁹"You set the time!" Moses replied. "Tell me when you want me to pray for you, your officials, and your people. Then you and your houses will be rid of the frogs. They will remain only in the Nile River."

¹⁰"Do it tomorrow," Pharaoh said.

"All right," Moses replied, "it will be as you have said. Then you will know that there is no one like the LORD our God. ¹¹The frogs will leave you and your houses, your officials, and your people. They will remain only in the Nile River."

¹²So Moses and Aaron left Pharaoh's palace, and Moses cried out to the LORD about the frogs he had inflicted on Pharaoh. ¹³And the LORD did just what Moses had predicted. The frogs in the houses, the courtyards, and the fields all died. ¹⁴The Egyptians piled them into great heaps, and a terrible stench filled the land. ¹⁵But when Pharaoh saw that relief had come, he became stubborn.* He refused to listen to Moses and Aaron, just as the LORD had predicted.

A Plague of Gnats

¹⁶So the LORD said to Moses, "Tell Aaron, 'Raise your staff and strike the ground. The dust will turn into swarms of gnats throughout the land of Egypt.'" ¹⁷So Moses and Aaron did just as the LORD had commanded them. When Aaron raised his hand and struck the ground with his staff, gnats infested the entire land, covering the Egyptians and their animals. All the dust in the land of Egypt turned into gnats. ¹⁸Pharaoh's magicians tried to do the same thing with their secret arts, but this time they failed. And the gnats covered everyone, people and animals alike.

¹⁹"This is the finger of God!" the magicians exclaimed to Pharaoh. But Pharaoh's heart remained hard. He wouldn't listen to them, just as the LORD had predicted.

A Plague of Flies

²⁰Then the LORD told Moses, "Get up early in the morning and stand in Pharaoh's way as he goes down to the river. Say to him, 'This is what the LORD says: Let my people go, so they can worship me. ²¹If you refuse, then I will send swarms of flies on you, your officials, your people, and all the houses. The Egyptian homes will be filled with flies, and the ground will be covered with them. ²²But this time I will spare the region of Goshen, where my people live. No flies will be found there. Then you will know that I am the LORD and that I am present even in the heart of your land. ²³I will make a clear distinction between* my people and your people. This miraculous sign will happen tomorrow.'"

²⁴And the LORD did just as he had said. A thick swarm of flies filled Pharaoh's palace and the houses of his officials. The whole land of Egypt was thrown into chaos by the flies.

²⁵Pharaoh called for Moses and Aaron. "All right! Go ahead and offer sacrifices to your God," he said. "But do it here in this land."

8:1 Verses 8:1-4 are numbered 7:26-29 in Hebrew text.   8:5 Verses 8:5-32 are numbered 8:1-28 in Hebrew text.   8:15 Hebrew *made his heart heavy;* also in 8:32.   8:23 As in Greek and Latin versions; Hebrew reads *I will set redemption between.*

²⁶But Moses replied, "That wouldn't be right. The Egyptians detest the sacrifices that we offer to the LORD our God. Look, if we offer our sacrifices here where the Egyptians can see us, they will stone us. ²⁷We must take a three-day trip into the wilderness to offer sacrifices to the LORD our God, just as he has commanded us."

²⁸"All right, go ahead," Pharaoh replied. "I will let you go into the wilderness to offer sacrifices to the LORD your God. But don't go too far away. Now hurry and pray for me."

²⁹Moses answered, "As soon as I leave you, I will pray to the LORD, and tomorrow the swarms of flies will disappear from you and your officials and all your people. But I am warning you, Pharaoh, don't lie to us again and refuse to let the people go to sacrifice to the LORD."

³⁰So Moses left Pharaoh's palace and pleaded with the LORD to remove all the flies. ³¹And the LORD did as Moses asked and caused the swarms of flies to disappear from Pharaoh, his officials, and his people. Not a single fly remained. ³²But Pharaoh again became stubborn and refused to let the people go.

9 A Plague against Livestock

"Go back to Pharaoh," the LORD commanded Moses. "Tell him, 'This is what the LORD, the God of the Hebrews, says: Let my people go, so they can worship me. ²If you continue to hold them and refuse to let them go, ³the hand of the LORD will strike all your livestock—your horses, donkeys, camels, cattle, sheep, and goats—with a deadly plague. ⁴But the LORD will again make a distinction between the livestock of the Israelites and that of the Egyptians. Not a single one of Israel's animals will die! ⁵The LORD has already set the time for the plague to begin. He has declared that he will strike the land tomorrow.'"

⁶And the LORD did just as he had said. The next morning all the livestock of the Egyptians died, but the Israelites didn't lose a single animal. ⁷Pharaoh sent his officials to investigate, and they discovered that the Israelites had not lost a single animal! But even so, Pharaoh's heart remained stubborn,* and he still refused to let the people go.

A Plague of Festering Boils

⁸Then the LORD said to Moses and Aaron, "Take handfuls of soot from a brick kiln, and have Moses toss it into the air while Pharaoh watches. ⁹The ashes will spread like fine dust over the whole land of Egypt, causing festering boils to break out on people and animals throughout the land."

¹⁰So they took soot from a brick kiln and went and stood before Pharaoh. As Pharaoh watched, Moses threw the soot into the air, and boils broke out on people and animals alike. ¹¹Even the magicians were unable to stand before Moses, because the boils had broken out on them and all the Egyptians. ¹²But the LORD hardened Pharaoh's heart, and just as the LORD had predicted to Moses, Pharaoh refused to listen.

A Plague of Hail

¹³Then the LORD said to Moses, "Get up early in the morning and stand before Pharaoh. Tell him, 'This is what the LORD, the God of the Hebrews, says: Let my people go, so they can worship me. ¹⁴If you don't, I will send more plagues on you* and your officials and your people. Then you will know that there is no one like me in all the earth. ¹⁵By now I could have lifted my hand and struck you and your people with a plague to wipe you off the face of the earth. ¹⁶But I have spared you for a purpose—to show you my power* and to spread my fame throughout the earth. ¹⁷But you still lord it over my people and refuse to let them go. ¹⁸So tomorrow at this time I will send a hailstorm more devastating than any in all the history of Egypt. ¹⁹Quick! Order your livestock and servants to come in from the fields to find shelter. Any person or animal left outside will die when the hail falls.'"

²⁰Some of Pharaoh's officials were afraid because of what the LORD had said. They quickly brought their servants and livestock in from the fields. ²¹But those who paid no attention to the word of the LORD left theirs out in the open.

9:7 Hebrew *heavy.*   **9:14** Hebrew *on your heart.*   **9:16** Greek version reads *to display my power in you;* compare Rom 9:17.

²²Then the LORD said to Moses, "Lift your hand toward the sky so hail may fall on the people, the livestock, and all the plants throughout the land of Egypt."

²³So Moses lifted his staff toward the sky, and the LORD sent thunder and hail, and lightning flashed toward the earth. The LORD sent a tremendous hailstorm against all the land of Egypt. ²⁴Never in all the history of Egypt had there been a storm like that, with such devastating hail and continuous lightning. ²⁵It left all of Egypt in ruins. The hail struck down everything in the open field—people, animals, and plants alike. Even the trees were destroyed. ²⁶The only place without hail was the region of Goshen, where the people of Israel lived.

²⁷Then Pharaoh quickly summoned Moses and Aaron. "This time I have sinned," he confessed. "The LORD is the righteous one, and my people and I are wrong. ²⁸Please beg the LORD to end this terrifying thunder and hail. We've had enough. I will let you go; you don't need to stay any longer."

²⁹"All right," Moses replied. "As soon as I leave the city, I will lift my hands and pray to the LORD. Then the thunder and hail will stop, and you will know that the earth belongs to the LORD. ³⁰But I know that you and your officials still do not fear the LORD God."

³¹(All the flax and barley were ruined by the hail, because the barley had formed heads and the flax was budding. ³²But the wheat and the emmer wheat were spared, because they had not yet sprouted from the ground.)

³³So Moses left Pharaoh's court and went out of the city. When he lifted his hands to the LORD, the thunder and hail stopped, and the downpour ceased. ³⁴But when Pharaoh saw that the rain, hail, and thunder had stopped, he and his officials sinned again, and Pharaoh again became stubborn.* ³⁵Because his heart was hard, Pharaoh refused to let the people leave, just as the LORD had predicted through Moses.

10 A Plague of Locusts

Then the LORD said to Moses, "Return to Pharaoh and make your demands again. I have made him and his officials stubborn* so I can display my miraculous signs among them. ²I've also done it so you can tell your children and grandchildren about how I made a mockery of the Egyptians and about the signs I displayed among them—and so you will know that I am the LORD."

³So Moses and Aaron went to Pharaoh and said, "This is what the LORD, the God of the Hebrews, says: How long will you refuse to submit to me? Let my people go, so they can worship me. ⁴If you refuse, watch out! For tomorrow I will bring a swarm of locusts on your country. ⁵They will cover the land so that you won't be able to see the ground. They will devour what little is left of your crops after the hailstorm, including all the trees growing in the fields. ⁶They will overrun your palaces and the homes of your officials and all the houses in Egypt. Never in the history of Egypt have your ancestors seen a plague like this one!" And with that, Moses turned and left Pharaoh.

⁷Pharaoh's officials now came to Pharaoh and appealed to him. "How long will you let this man hold us hostage? Let the men go to worship the LORD their God! Don't you realize that Egypt lies in ruins?"

⁸So Moses and Aaron were brought back to Pharaoh. "All right," he told them, "go and worship the LORD your God. But who exactly will be going with you?"

⁹Moses replied, "We will all go—young and old, our sons and daughters, and our flocks and herds. We must all join together in celebrating a festival to the LORD."

¹⁰Pharaoh retorted, "The LORD will certainly need to be with you if I let you take your little ones! I can see through your evil plan. ¹¹Never! Only the men may go and worship the LORD, since that is what you requested." And Pharaoh threw them out of the palace.

¹²Then the LORD said to Moses, "Raise your hand over the land of Egypt to bring on the locusts. Let them cover the land and devour every plant that survived the hailstorm."

¹³So Moses raised his staff over Egypt, and the LORD caused an east wind to blow over the land all that day and through the night. When morning arrived, the east

---

9:34 Hebrew *made his heart heavy.*   10:1 Hebrew *have made his heart and his officials' hearts heavy.*

wind had brought the locusts. [14]And the locusts swarmed over the whole land of Egypt, settling in dense swarms from one end of the country to the other. It was the worst locust plague in Egyptian history, and there has never been another one like it. [15]For the locusts covered the whole country and darkened the land. They devoured every plant in the fields and all the fruit on the trees that had survived the hailstorm. Not a single leaf was left on the trees and plants throughout the land of Egypt.

[16]Pharaoh quickly summoned Moses and Aaron. "I have sinned against the LORD your God and against you," he confessed. [17]"Forgive my sin, just this once, and plead with the LORD your God to take away this death from me."

[18]So Moses left Pharaoh's court and pleaded with the LORD. [19]The LORD responded by shifting the wind, and the strong west wind blew the locusts into the Red Sea.* Not a single locust remained in all the land of Egypt. [20]But the LORD hardened Pharaoh's heart again, so he refused to let the people go.

A Plague of Darkness

[21]Then the LORD said to Moses, "Lift your hand toward heaven, and the land of Egypt will be covered with a darkness so thick you can feel it." [22]So Moses lifted his hand to the sky, and a deep darkness covered the entire land of Egypt for three days. [23]During all that time the people could not see each other, and no one moved. But there was light as usual where the people of Israel lived.

[24]Finally, Pharaoh called for Moses. "Go and worship the LORD," he said. "But leave your flocks and herds here. You may even take your little ones with you."

[25]"No," Moses said, "you must provide us with animals for sacrifices and burnt offerings to the LORD our God. [26]All our livestock must go with us, too; not a hoof can be left behind. We must choose our sacrifices for the LORD our God from among these animals. And we won't know how we are to worship the LORD until we get there."

[27]But the LORD hardened Pharaoh's heart once more, and he would not let them go. [28]"Get out of here!" Pharaoh shouted at Moses. "I'm warning you. Never come back to see me again! The day you see my face, you will die!"

[29]"Very well," Moses replied. "I will never see your face again."

11 Death for Egypt's Firstborn

Then the LORD said to Moses, "I will strike Pharaoh and the land of Egypt with one more blow. After that, Pharaoh will let you leave this country. In fact, he will be so eager to get rid of you that he will force you all to leave. [2]Tell all the Israelite men and women to ask their Egyptian neighbors for articles of silver and gold." [3](Now the LORD had caused the Egyptians to look favorably on the people of Israel. And Moses was considered a very great man in the land of Egypt, respected by Pharaoh's officials and the Egyptian people alike.)

[4]Moses had announced to Pharaoh, "This is what the LORD says: At midnight tonight I will pass through the heart of Egypt. [5]All the firstborn sons will die in every family in Egypt, from the oldest son of Pharaoh, who sits on his throne, to the oldest son of his lowliest servant girl who grinds the flour. Even the firstborn of all the livestock will die. [6]Then a loud wail will rise throughout the land of Egypt, a wail like no one has heard before or will ever hear again. [7]But among the Israelites it will be so peaceful that not even a dog will bark. Then you will know that the LORD makes a distinction between the Egyptians and the Israelites. [8]All the officials of Egypt will run to me and fall to the ground before me. 'Please leave!' they will beg. 'Hurry! And take all your followers with you.' Only then will I go!" Then, burning with anger, Moses left Pharaoh.

[9]Now the LORD had told Moses earlier, "Pharaoh will not listen to you, but then I will do even more mighty miracles in the land of Egypt." [10]Moses and Aaron performed these miracles in Pharaoh's presence, but the LORD hardened Pharaoh's heart, and he wouldn't let the Israelites leave the country.

10:19 Hebrew *sea of reeds*.

12 The First Passover

While the Israelites were still in the land of Egypt, the LORD gave the following instructions to Moses and Aaron: 2 "From now on, this month will be the first month of the year for you. 3 Announce to the whole community of Israel that on the tenth day of this month each family must choose a lamb or a young goat for a sacrifice, one animal for each household. 4 If a family is too small to eat a whole animal, let them share with another family in the neighborhood. Divide the animal according to the size of each family and how much they can eat. 5 The animal you select must be a one-year-old male, either a sheep or a goat, with no defects.

6 "Take special care of this chosen animal until the evening of the fourteenth day of this first month. Then the whole assembly of the community of Israel must slaughter their lamb or young goat at twilight. 7 They are to take some of the blood and smear it on the sides and top of the doorframes of the houses where they eat the animal. 8 That same night they must roast the meat over a fire and eat it along with bitter salad greens and bread made without yeast. 9 Do not eat any of the meat raw or boiled in water. The whole animal—including the head, legs, and internal organs—must be roasted over a fire. 10 Do not leave any of it until the next morning. Burn whatever is not eaten before morning.

11 "These are your instructions for eating this meal: Be fully dressed,* wear your sandals, and carry your walking stick in your hand. Eat the meal with urgency, for this is the LORD's Passover. 12 On that night I will pass through the land of Egypt and strike down every firstborn son and firstborn male animal in the land of Egypt. I will execute judgment against all the gods of Egypt, for I am the LORD! 13 But the blood on your doorposts will serve as a sign, marking the houses where you are staying. When I see the blood, I will pass over you. This plague of death will not touch you when I strike the land of Egypt.

14 "This is a day to remember. Each year, from generation to generation, you must celebrate it as a special festival to the LORD. This is a law for all time. 15 For seven days the bread you eat must be made without yeast. On the first day of the festival, remove every trace of yeast from your homes. Anyone who eats bread made with yeast during the seven days of the festival will be cut off from the community of Israel. 16 On the first day of the festival and again on the seventh day, all the people must observe an official day for holy assembly. No work of any kind may be done on these days except in the preparation of food.

17 "Celebrate this Festival of Unleavened Bread, for it will remind you that I brought your forces out of the land of Egypt on this very day. This festival will be a permanent law for you; celebrate this day from generation to generation. 18 The bread you eat must be made without yeast from the evening of the fourteenth day of the first month until the evening of the twenty-first day of that month. 19 During those seven days, there must be no trace of yeast in your homes. Anyone who eats anything made with yeast during this week will be cut off from the community of Israel. These regulations apply both to the foreigners living among you and to the native-born Israelites. 20 During those days you must not eat anything made with yeast. Wherever you live, eat only bread made without yeast."

21 Then Moses called all the elders of Israel together and said to them, "Go, pick out a lamb or young goat for each of your families, and slaughter the Passover animal. 22 Drain the blood into a basin. Then take a bundle of hyssop branches and dip it into the blood. Brush the hyssop across the top and sides of the doorframes of your houses. And no one may go out through the door until morning. 23 For the LORD will pass through the land to strike down the Egyptians. But when he sees the blood on the top and sides of the doorframe, the LORD will pass over your home. He will not permit his death angel to enter your house and strike you down.

24 "Remember, these instructions are a permanent law that you and your descendants must observe forever. 25 When you

---

12:11 Hebrew *Bind up your loins.*

enter the land the LORD has promised to give you, you will continue to observe this ceremony. ²⁶Then your children will ask, 'What does this ceremony mean?' ²⁷And you will reply, 'It is the Passover sacrifice to the LORD, for he passed over the houses of the Israelites in Egypt. And though he struck the Egyptians, he spared our families.'" When Moses had finished speaking, all the people bowed down to the ground and worshiped.

²⁸So the people of Israel did just as the LORD had commanded through Moses and Aaron. ²⁹And that night at midnight, the LORD struck down all the firstborn sons in the land of Egypt, from the firstborn son of Pharaoh, who sat on his throne, to the firstborn son of the prisoner in the dungeon. Even the firstborn of their livestock were killed. ³⁰Pharaoh and all his officials and all the people of Egypt woke up during the night, and loud wailing was heard throughout the land of Egypt. There was not a single house where someone had not died.

Israel's Exodus from Egypt

³¹Pharaoh sent for Moses and Aaron during the night. "Get out!" he ordered. "Leave my people—and take the rest of the Israelites with you! Go and worship the LORD as you have requested. ³²Take your flocks and herds, as you said, and be gone. Go, but bless me as you leave." ³³All the Egyptians urged the people of Israel to get out of the land as quickly as possible, for they thought, "We will all die!"

³⁴The Israelites took their bread dough before yeast was added. They wrapped their kneading boards in their cloaks and carried them on their shoulders. ³⁵And the people of Israel did as Moses had instructed; they asked the Egyptians for clothing and articles of silver and gold. ³⁶The LORD caused the Egyptians to look favorably on the Israelites, and they gave the Israelites whatever they asked for. So they stripped the Egyptians of their wealth!

³⁷That night the people of Israel left Rameses and started for Succoth. There were about 600,000 men,* plus all the women and children. ³⁸A rabble of non-Israelites went with them, along with great flocks and herds of livestock. ³⁹For bread they baked flat cakes from the dough without yeast they had brought from Egypt. It was made without yeast because the people were driven out of Egypt in such a hurry that they had no time to prepare the bread or other food.

⁴⁰The people of Israel had lived in Egypt* for 430 years. ⁴¹In fact, it was on the last day of the 430th year that all the LORD's forces left the land. ⁴²On this night the LORD kept his promise to bring his people out of the land of Egypt. So this night belongs to him, and it must be commemorated every year by all the Israelites, from generation to generation.

Instructions for the Passover

⁴³Then the LORD said to Moses and Aaron, "These are the instructions for the festival of Passover. No outsiders are allowed to eat the Passover meal. ⁴⁴But any slave who has been purchased may eat it if he has been circumcised. ⁴⁵Temporary residents and hired servants may not eat it. ⁴⁶Each Passover lamb must be eaten in one house. Do not carry any of its meat outside, and do not break any of its bones. ⁴⁷The whole community of Israel must celebrate this Passover festival.

⁴⁸"If there are foreigners living among you who want to celebrate the LORD's Passover, let all their males be circumcised. Only then may they celebrate the Passover with you like any native-born Israelite. But no uncircumcised male may ever eat the Passover meal. ⁴⁹This instruction applies to everyone, whether a native-born Israelite or a foreigner living among you."

⁵⁰So all the people of Israel followed all the LORD's commands to Moses and Aaron. ⁵¹On that very day the LORD brought the people of Israel out of the land of Egypt like an army.

13 Dedication of the Firstborn

Then the LORD said to Moses, ²"Dedicate to me every firstborn among the Israelites. The first offspring to be born, of both humans and animals, belongs to me."

12:37 Or *fighting men;* Hebrew reads *men on foot.* **12:40** Samaritan Pentateuch reads *in Canaan and Egypt;* Greek version reads *in Egypt and Canaan.*

³So Moses said to the people, "This is a day to remember forever—the day you left Egypt, the place of your slavery. Today the LORD has brought you out by the power of his mighty hand. (Remember, eat no food containing yeast.) ⁴On this day in early spring, in the month of Abib,* you have been set free. ⁵You must celebrate this event in this month each year after the LORD brings you into the land of the Canaanites, Hittites, Amorites, Hivites, and Jebusites. (He swore to your ancestors that he would give you this land—a land flowing with milk and honey.) ⁶For seven days the bread you eat must be made without yeast. Then on the seventh day, celebrate a feast to the LORD. ⁷Eat bread without yeast during those seven days. In fact, there must be no yeast bread or any yeast at all found within the borders of your land during this time.

⁸"On the seventh day you must explain to your children, 'I am celebrating what the LORD did for me when I left Egypt.' ⁹This annual festival will be a visible sign to you, like a mark branded on your hand or your forehead. Let it remind you always to recite this teaching of the LORD: 'With a strong hand, the LORD rescued you from Egypt.'* ¹⁰So observe the decree of this festival at the appointed time each year.

¹¹"This is what you must do when the LORD fulfills the promise he swore to you and to your ancestors. When he gives you the land where the Canaanites now live, ¹²you must present all firstborn sons and firstborn male animals to the LORD, for they belong to him. ¹³A firstborn donkey may be bought back from the LORD by presenting a lamb or young goat in its place. But if you do not buy it back, you must break its neck. However, you must buy back every firstborn son.

¹⁴"And in the future, your children will ask you, 'What does all this mean?' Then you will tell them, 'With the power of his mighty hand, the LORD brought us out of Egypt, the place of our slavery. ¹⁵Pharaoh stubbornly refused to let us go, so the LORD killed all the firstborn males throughout the land of Egypt, both people and animals.

That is why I now sacrifice all the firstborn males to the LORD—except that the firstborn sons are always bought back.' ¹⁶This ceremony will be like a mark branded on your hand or your forehead. It is a reminder that the power of the LORD's mighty hand brought us out of Egypt."

Israel's Wilderness Detour

¹⁷When Pharaoh finally let the people go, God did not lead them along the main road that runs through Philistine territory, even though that was the shortest route to the Promised Land. God said, "If the people are faced with a battle, they might change their minds and return to Egypt." ¹⁸So God led them in a roundabout way through the wilderness toward the Red Sea.* Thus the Israelites left Egypt like an army ready for battle.*

¹⁹Moses took the bones of Joseph with him, for Joseph had made the sons of Israel swear to do this. He said, "God will certainly come to help you. When he does, you must take my bones with you from this place."

²⁰The Israelites left Succoth and camped at Etham on the edge of the wilderness. ²¹The LORD went ahead of them. He guided them during the day with a pillar of cloud, and he provided light at night with a pillar of fire. This allowed them to travel by day or by night. ²²And the LORD did not remove the pillar of cloud or pillar of fire from its place in front of the people.

14 Then the LORD gave these instructions to Moses: ²"Order the Israelites to turn back and camp by Pi-hahiroth between Migdol and the sea. Camp there along the shore, across from Baal-zephon. ³Then Pharaoh will think, 'The Israelites are confused. They are trapped in the wilderness!' ⁴And once again I will harden Pharaoh's heart, and he will chase after you.* I have planned this in order to display my glory through Pharaoh and his whole army. After this the Egyptians will know that I am the LORD!" So the Israelites camped there as they were told.

13:4 Hebrew *On this day in the month of Abib.* This first month of the ancient Hebrew lunar calendar usually occurs within the months of March and April.   13:9 Or *Let it remind you always to keep the instructions of the LORD on the tip of your tongue, because with a strong hand, the LORD rescued you from Egypt.*   13:18a Hebrew *sea of reeds.*   13:18b Greek version reads *left Egypt in the fifth generation.*   14:4 Hebrew *after them.*

The Egyptians Pursue Israel

⁵When word reached the king of Egypt that the Israelites had fled, Pharaoh and his officials changed their minds. "What have we done, letting all those Israelite slaves get away?" they asked. ⁶So Pharaoh harnessed his chariot and called up his troops. ⁷He took with him 600 of Egypt's best chariots, along with the rest of the chariots of Egypt, each with its commander. ⁸The LORD hardened the heart of Pharaoh, the king of Egypt, so he chased after the people of Israel, who had left with fists raised in defiance. ⁹The Egyptians chased after them with all the forces in Pharaoh's army—all his horses and chariots, his charioteers, and his troops. The Egyptians caught up with the people of Israel as they were camped beside the shore near Pi-hahiroth, across from Baal-zephon.

¹⁰As Pharaoh approached, the people of Israel looked up and panicked when they saw the Egyptians overtaking them. They cried out to the LORD, ¹¹and they said to Moses, "Why did you bring us out here to die in the wilderness? Weren't there enough graves for us in Egypt? What have you done to us? Why did you make us leave Egypt? ¹²Didn't we tell you this would happen while we were still in Egypt? We said, 'Leave us alone! Let us be slaves to the Egyptians. It's better to be a slave in Egypt than a corpse in the wilderness!'"

¹³But Moses told the people, "Don't be afraid. Just stand still and watch the LORD rescue you today. The Egyptians you see today will never be seen again. ¹⁴The LORD himself will fight for you. Just stay calm."

Escape through the Red Sea

¹⁵Then the LORD said to Moses, "Why are you crying out to me? Tell the people to get moving! ¹⁶Pick up your staff and raise your hand over the sea. Divide the water so the Israelites can walk through the middle of the sea on dry ground. ¹⁷And I will harden the hearts of the Egyptians, and they will charge in after the Israelites. My great glory will be displayed through Pharaoh and his troops, his chariots, and his charioteers. ¹⁸When my glory is displayed through them, all Egypt will see my glory and know that I am the LORD!"

¹⁹Then the angel of God, who had been leading the people of Israel, moved to the rear of the camp. The pillar of cloud also moved from the front and stood behind them. ²⁰The cloud settled between the Egyptian and Israelite camps. As darkness fell, the cloud turned to fire, lighting up the night. But the Egyptians and Israelites did not approach each other all night.

²¹Then Moses raised his hand over the sea, and the LORD opened up a path through the water with a strong east wind. The wind blew all that night, turning the seabed into dry land. ²²So the people of Israel walked through the middle of the sea on dry ground, with walls of water on each side!

²³Then the Egyptians—all of Pharaoh's horses, chariots, and charioteers—chased them into the middle of the sea. ²⁴But just before dawn the LORD looked down on the Egyptian army from the pillar of fire and cloud, and he threw their forces into total confusion. ²⁵He twisted* their chariot wheels, making their chariots difficult to drive. "Let's get out of here—away from these Israelites!" the Egyptians shouted. "The LORD is fighting for them against Egypt!"

²⁶When all the Israelites had reached the other side, the LORD said to Moses, "Raise your hand over the sea again. Then the waters will rush back and cover the Egyptians and their chariots and charioteers." ²⁷So as the sun began to rise, Moses raised his hand over the sea, and the water rushed back into its usual place. The Egyptians tried to escape, but the LORD swept them into the sea. ²⁸Then the waters returned and covered all the chariots and charioteers—the entire army of Pharaoh. Of all the Egyptians who had chased the Israelites into the sea, not a single one survived.

²⁹But the people of Israel had walked through the middle of the sea on dry ground, as the water stood up like a wall on both sides. ³⁰That is how the LORD rescued Israel from the hand of the Egyptians that day. And the Israelites saw the bodies of the Egyptians washed up on the seashore. ³¹When the people of Israel saw the mighty

---

14:25 As in Greek version, Samaritan Pentateuch, and Syriac version; Hebrew reads *He removed.*

power that the Lord had unleashed against the Egyptians, they were filled with awe before him. They put their faith in the Lord and in his servant Moses.

15 A Song of Deliverance

Then Moses and the people of Israel sang this song to the Lord:

"I will sing to the Lord,
    for he has triumphed gloriously;
he has hurled both horse and rider
    into the sea.
2 The Lord is my strength and my song;
    he has given me victory.
This is my God, and I will praise him—
    my father's God, and I will exalt him!
3 The Lord is a warrior;
    Yahweh* is his name!
4 Pharaoh's chariots and army
    he has hurled into the sea.
The finest of Pharaoh's officers
    are drowned in the Red Sea.*
5 The deep waters gushed over them;
    they sank to the bottom like a stone.

6 "Your right hand, O Lord,
    is glorious in power.
Your right hand, O Lord,
    smashes the enemy.
7 In the greatness of your majesty,
    you overthrow those who rise against
        you.
You unleash your blazing fury;
    it consumes them like straw.
8 At the blast of your breath,
    the waters piled up!
The surging waters stood straight like a
    wall;
    in the heart of the sea the deep waters
        became hard.

9 "The enemy boasted, 'I will chase them
    and catch up with them.
I will plunder them
    and consume them.
I will flash my sword;
    my powerful hand will destroy them.'
10 But you blew with your breath,
    and the sea covered them.
They sank like lead
    in the mighty waters.

11 "Who is like you among the gods,
    O Lord—
glorious in holiness,
awesome in splendor,
    performing great wonders?
12 You raised your right hand,
    and the earth swallowed our enemies.

13 "With your unfailing love you lead
    the people you have redeemed.
In your might, you guide them
    to your sacred home.
14 The peoples hear and tremble;
    anguish grips those who live in
        Philistia.
15 The leaders of Edom are terrified;
    the nobles of Moab tremble.
All who live in Canaan melt away;
16   terror and dread fall upon them.
The power of your arm
    makes them lifeless as stone
until your people pass by, O Lord,
    until the people you purchased
        pass by.
17 You will bring them in and plant them
    on your own mountain—
    the place, O Lord, reserved for your
        own dwelling,
    the sanctuary, O Lord, that your hands
        have established.
18 The Lord will reign forever and ever!"

19 When Pharaoh's horses, chariots, and charioteers rushed into the sea, the Lord brought the water crashing down on them. But the people of Israel had walked through the middle of the sea on dry ground! 20 Then Miriam the prophet, Aaron's sister, took a tambourine and led all the women as they played their tambourines and danced. 21 And Miriam sang this song:

"Sing to the Lord,
    for he has triumphed gloriously;
he has hurled both horse and rider
    into the sea."

Bitter Water at Marah

22 Then Moses led the people of Israel away from the Red Sea, and they moved out into the desert of Shur. They traveled in this desert for three days without finding any

---

15:3 Yahweh is a transliteration of the proper name YHWH that is sometimes rendered "Jehovah"; in this translation it is usually rendered "the Lord" (note the use of small capitals).   15:4 Hebrew sea of reeds; also in 15:22.

Complain, Complain

EXODUS 16:1-18

Gratitude

I blamed God for all my problems, from not having enough time to the cost of gas. Criticism became part of my everyday language.

Then as I was studying the Israelites' journey through the desert, it hit me: they complained for forty years and never saw the Promised Land. Although God had performed many miracles in the wilderness, they refused to trust him.

I realized my own complaints weren't only negative words, they were grumblings against God. He's much bigger than any problem I face, and in his strength I can overcome anything. When I complain, it lets God know I don't trust him. As with the manna and quail, I was graciously given the necessities in life. I had a job, food, and clothing, but I was too busy looking at the bigger problems.

So I decided to give up complaining. I renew my mind daily by giving thanks, such as my house may need repair, but I have a house. The more confidence I have in God, the less dissatisfied I feel. First Timothy 6:6 says, "True godliness with contentment is itself great wealth." God's promises can be mine. I just need the right attitude.

—*Linda Manes*

For more on gratitude, see reading at 2 Samuel 22:47-51.

water. ²³When they came to the oasis of Marah, the water was too bitter to drink. So they called the place Marah (which means "bitter").

²⁴ Then the people complained and turned against Moses. "What are we going to drink?" they demanded. ²⁵ So Moses cried out to the LORD for help, and the LORD showed him a piece of wood. Moses threw it into the water, and this made the water good to drink.

It was there at Marah that the LORD set before them the following decree as a standard to test their faithfulness to him. ²⁶ He said, "If you will listen carefully to the voice of the LORD your God and do what is right in his sight, obeying his commands and keeping all his decrees, then I will not make you suffer any of the diseases I sent on the Egyptians; for I am the LORD who heals you."

²⁷ After leaving Marah, the Israelites trav- eled on to the oasis of Elim, where they found twelve springs and seventy palm trees. They camped there beside the water.

16 Manna and Quail from Heaven

Then the whole community of Israel set out from Elim and journeyed into the wilderness of Sin,* between Elim and Mount Sinai. They arrived there on the fif- teenth day of the second month, one month after leaving the land of Egypt.* ²There, too, the whole community of Israel complained about Moses and Aaron.

³ "If only the LORD had killed us back in Egypt," they moaned. "There we sat around pots filled with meat and ate all the bread we wanted. But now you have brought us into this wilderness to starve us all to death."

⁴ Then the LORD said to Moses, "Look, I'm going to rain down food from heaven for you. Each day the people can go out and

---

16:1a The geographical name *Sin* is related to *Sinai* and should not be confused with the English word *sin*.   **16:1b** The Exodus had occurred on the fifteenth day of the first month (see Num 33:3).

pick up as much food as they need for that day. I will test them in this to see whether or not they will follow my instructions. ⁵On the sixth day they will gather food, and when they prepare it, there will be twice as much as usual."

⁶So Moses and Aaron said to all the people of Israel, "By evening you will realize it was the LORD who brought you out of the land of Egypt. ⁷In the morning you will see the glory of the LORD, because he has heard your complaints, which are against him, not against us. What have we done that you should complain about us?" ⁸Then Moses added, "The LORD will give you meat to eat in the evening and bread to satisfy you in the morning, for he has heard all your complaints against him. What have we done? Yes, your complaints are against the LORD, not against us."

⁹Then Moses said to Aaron, "Announce this to the entire community of Israel: 'Present yourselves before the LORD, for he has heard your complaining.'" ¹⁰And as Aaron spoke to the whole community of Israel, they looked out toward the wilderness. There they could see the awesome glory of the LORD in the cloud.

¹¹Then the LORD said to Moses, ¹²"I have heard the Israelites' complaints. Now tell them, 'In the evening you will have meat to eat, and in the morning you will have all the bread you want. Then you will know that I am the LORD your God.'"

¹³That evening vast numbers of quail flew in and covered the camp. And the next morning the area around the camp was wet with dew. ¹⁴When the dew evaporated, a flaky substance as fine as frost blanketed the ground. ¹⁵The Israelites were puzzled when they saw it. "What is it?" they asked each other. They had no idea what it was.

And Moses told them, "It is the food the LORD has given you to eat. ¹⁶These are the LORD's instructions: Each household should gather as much as it needs. Pick up two quarts* for each person in your tent."

¹⁷So the people of Israel did as they were told. Some gathered a lot, some only a little. ¹⁸But when they measured it out,* everyone had just enough. Those who gathered a lot

had nothing left over, and those who gathered only a little had enough. Each family had just what it needed.

¹⁹Then Moses told them, "Do not keep any of it until morning." ²⁰But some of them didn't listen and kept some of it until morning. But by then it was full of maggots and had a terrible smell. Moses was very angry with them.

²¹After this the people gathered the food morning by morning, each family according to its need. And as the sun became hot, the flakes they had not picked up melted and disappeared. ²²On the sixth day, they gathered twice as much as usual—four quarts* for each person instead of two. Then all the leaders of the community came and asked Moses for an explanation. ²³He told them, "This is what the LORD commanded: Tomorrow will be a day of complete rest, a holy Sabbath day set apart for the LORD. So bake or boil as much as you want today, and set aside what is left for tomorrow."

²⁴So they put some aside until morning, just as Moses had commanded. And in the morning the leftover food was wholesome and good, without maggots or odor. ²⁵Moses said, "Eat this food today, for today is a Sabbath day dedicated to the LORD. There will be no food on the ground today. ²⁶You may gather the food for six days, but the seventh day is the Sabbath. There will be no food on the ground that day."

²⁷Some of the people went out anyway on the seventh day, but they found no food. ²⁸The LORD asked Moses, "How long will these people refuse to obey my commands and instructions? ²⁹They must realize that the Sabbath is the LORD's gift to you. That is why he gives you a two-day supply on the sixth day, so there will be enough for two days. On the Sabbath day you must each stay in your place. Do not go out to pick up food on the seventh day." ³⁰So the people did not gather any food on the seventh day.

³¹The Israelites called the food manna.* It was white like coriander seed, and it tasted like honey wafers.

³²Then Moses said, "This is what the LORD has commanded: Fill a two-quart container with manna to preserve it for

---

16:16 Hebrew 1 omer [2 liters]; also in 16:32, 33.   **16:18** Hebrew measured it with an omer.   **16:22** Hebrew 2 omers [4 liters].   **16:31** Manna means "What is it?" See 16:15.

your descendants. Then later generations will be able to see the food I gave you in the wilderness when I set you free from Egypt."

33 Moses said to Aaron, "Get a jar and fill it with two quarts of manna. Then put it in a sacred place before the LORD to preserve it for all future generations." 34 Aaron did just as the LORD had commanded Moses. He eventually placed it in the Ark of the Covenant—in front of the stone tablets inscribed with the terms of the covenant.* 35 So the people of Israel ate manna for forty years until they arrived at the land where they would settle. They ate manna until they came to the border of the land of Canaan.

36 The container used to measure the manna was an omer, which was one-tenth of an ephah; it held about two quarts.*

17 Water from the Rock

At the LORD's command, the whole community of Israel left the wilderness of Sin* and moved from place to place. Eventually they camped at Rephidim, but there was no water there for the people to drink. 2 So once more the people complained against Moses. "Give us water to drink!" they demanded.

"Quiet!" Moses replied. "Why are you complaining against me? And why are you testing the LORD?"

3 But tormented by thirst, they continued to argue with Moses. "Why did you bring us out of Egypt? Are you trying to kill us, our children, and our livestock with thirst?"

4 Then Moses cried out to the LORD, "What should I do with these people? They are ready to stone me!"

5 The LORD said to Moses, "Walk out in front of the people. Take your staff, the one you used when you struck the water of the Nile, and call some of the elders of Israel to join you. 6 I will stand before you on the rock at Mount Sinai.* Strike the rock, and water will come gushing out. Then the people will be able to drink." So Moses struck the rock as he was told, and water gushed out as the elders looked on.

7 Moses named the place Massah (which means "test") and Meribah (which means "arguing") because the people of Israel argued with Moses and tested the LORD by saying, "Is the LORD here with us or not?"

Israel Defeats the Amalekites

8 While the people of Israel were still at Rephidim, the warriors of Amalek attacked them. 9 Moses commanded Joshua, "Choose some men to go out and fight the army of Amalek for us. Tomorrow, I will stand at the top of the hill, holding the staff of God in my hand."

10 So Joshua did what Moses had commanded and fought the army of Amalek. Meanwhile, Moses, Aaron, and Hur climbed to the top of a nearby hill. 11 As long as Moses held up the staff in his hand, the Israelites had the advantage. But whenever he dropped his hand, the Amalekites gained the advantage. 12 Moses' arms soon became so tired he could no longer hold them up. So Aaron and Hur found a stone for him to sit on. Then they stood on each side of Moses, holding up his hands. So his hands held steady until sunset. 13 As a result, Joshua overwhelmed the army of Amalek in battle.

14 After the victory, the LORD instructed Moses, "Write this down on a scroll as a permanent reminder, and read it aloud to Joshua: I will erase the memory of Amalek from under heaven." 15 Moses built an altar there and named it Yahweh-Nissi (which means "the LORD is my banner"). 16 He said, "They have raised their fist against the LORD's throne, so now* the LORD will be at war with Amalek generation after generation."

18 Jethro's Visit to Moses

Moses' father-in-law, Jethro, the priest of Midian, heard about everything God had done for Moses and his people, the Israelites. He heard especially about how the LORD had rescued them from Egypt.

2 Earlier, Moses had sent his wife, Zipporah, and his two sons back to Jethro, who had taken them in. 3 (Moses' first son

---

16:34 Hebrew *He placed it in front of the Testimony;* see note on 25:16.   **16:36** Hebrew *An omer is one-tenth of an ephah.*   **17:1** The geographical name *Sin* is related to *Sinai* and should not be confused with the English word *sin.*   **17:6** Hebrew *Horeb,* another name for Sinai.   **17:16** Or *Hands have been lifted up to the LORD's throne, and now.*

was named Gershom,* for Moses had said when the boy was born, "I have been a foreigner in a foreign land." ⁴His second son was named Eliezer,* for Moses had said, "The God of my ancestors was my helper; he rescued me from the sword of Pharaoh.") ⁵Jethro, Moses' father-in-law, now came to visit Moses in the wilderness. He brought Moses' wife and two sons with him, and they arrived while Moses and the people were camped near the mountain of God. ⁶Jethro had sent a message to Moses, saying, "I, Jethro, your father-in-law, am coming to see you with your wife and your two sons."

⁷ So Moses went out to meet his father-in-law. He bowed low and kissed him. They asked about each other's welfare and then went into Moses' tent. ⁸Moses told his father-in-law everything the LORD had done to Pharaoh and Egypt on behalf of Israel. He also told about all the hardships they had experienced along the way and how the LORD had rescued his people from all their troubles. ⁹Jethro was delighted when he heard about all the good things the LORD had done for Israel as he rescued them from the hand of the Egyptians.

¹⁰"Praise the LORD," Jethro said, "for he has rescued you from the Egyptians and from Pharaoh. Yes, he has rescued Israel from the powerful hand of Egypt! ¹¹I know now that the LORD is greater than all other gods, because he rescued his people from the oppression of the proud Egyptians." ¹² Then Jethro, Moses' father-in-law, brought a burnt offering and sacrifices to God. Aaron and all the elders of Israel came out and joined him in a sacrificial meal in God's presence.

Jethro's Wise Advice

¹³The next day, Moses took his seat to hear the people's disputes against each other. They waited before him from morning till evening. ¹⁴When Moses' father-in-law saw all that Moses was doing for the people, he asked, "What are you really accomplishing here? Why are you trying to do all this alone while everyone stands around you from morning till evening?"

¹⁵ Moses replied, "Because the people come to me to get a ruling from God. ¹⁶When a dispute arises, they come to me, and I am the one who settles the case between the quarreling parties. I inform the people of God's decrees and give them his instructions."

¹⁷"This is not good!" Moses' father-in-law exclaimed. ¹⁸"You're going to wear yourself out—and the people, too. This job is too heavy a burden for you to handle all by yourself. ¹⁹Now listen to me, and let me give you a word of advice, and may God be with you. You should continue to be the people's representative before God, bringing their disputes to him. ²⁰Teach them God's decrees, and give them his instructions. Show them how to conduct their lives. ²¹But select from all the people some capable, honest men who fear God and hate bribes. Appoint them as leaders over groups of one thousand, one hundred, fifty, and ten. ²²They should always be available to solve the people's common disputes, but have them bring the major cases to you. Let the leaders decide the smaller matters themselves. They will help you carry the load, making the task easier for you. ²³If you follow this advice, and if God commands you to do so, then you will be able to endure the pressures, and all these people will go home in peace."

²⁴Moses listened to his father-in-law's advice and followed his suggestions. ²⁵He chose capable men from all over Israel and appointed them as leaders over the people. He put them in charge of groups of one thousand, one hundred, fifty, and ten. ²⁶These men were always available to solve the people's common disputes. They brought the major cases to Moses, but they took care of the smaller matters themselves.

²⁷Soon after this, Moses said good-bye to his father-in-law, who returned to his own land.

19 The LORD Reveals Himself at Sinai

Exactly two months after the Israelites left Egypt,* they arrived in the wilderness of Sinai. ²After breaking camp

---

18:3 Gershom sounds like a Hebrew term that means "a foreigner there."   **18:4** Eliezer means "God is my helper."   **19:1** Hebrew In the third month after the Israelites left Egypt, on the very day, i.e., two lunar months to the day after leaving Egypt. Compare Num 33:3.

at Rephidim, they came to the wilderness of Sinai and set up camp there at the base of Mount Sinai.

³Then Moses climbed the mountain to appear before God. The LORD called to him from the mountain and said, "Give these instructions to the family of Jacob; announce it to the descendants of Israel: ⁴'You have seen what I did to the Egyptians. You know how I carried you on eagles' wings and brought you to myself. ⁵Now if you will obey me and keep my covenant, you will be my own special treasure from among all the peoples on earth; for all the earth belongs to me. ⁶And you will be my kingdom of priests, my holy nation.' This is the message you must give to the people of Israel."

⁷So Moses returned from the mountain and called together the elders of the people and told them everything the LORD had commanded him. ⁸And all the people responded together, "We will do everything the LORD has commanded." So Moses brought the people's answer back to the LORD.

⁹Then the LORD said to Moses, "I will come to you in a thick cloud, Moses, so the people themselves can hear me when I speak with you. Then they will always trust you."

Moses told the LORD what the people had said. ¹⁰Then the LORD told Moses, "Go down and prepare the people for my arrival. Consecrate them today and tomorrow, and have them wash their clothing. ¹¹Be sure they are ready on the third day, for on that day the LORD will come down on Mount Sinai as all the people watch. ¹²Mark off a boundary all around the mountain. Warn the people, 'Be careful! Do not go up on the mountain or even touch its boundaries. Anyone who touches the mountain will certainly be put to death. ¹³No hand may touch the person or animal that crosses the boundary; instead, stone them or shoot them with arrows. They must be put to death.' However, when the ram's horn sounds a long blast, then the people may go up on the mountain.*"

¹⁴So Moses went down to the people. He consecrated them for worship, and they washed their clothes. ¹⁵He told them, "Get ready for the third day, and until then abstain from having sexual intercourse."

¹⁶On the morning of the third day, thunder roared and lightning flashed, and a dense cloud came down on the mountain. There was a long, loud blast from a ram's horn, and all the people trembled. ¹⁷Moses led them out from the camp to meet with God, and they stood at the foot of the mountain. ¹⁸All of Mount Sinai was covered with smoke because the LORD had descended on it in the form of fire. The smoke billowed into the sky like smoke from a brick kiln, and the whole mountain shook violently. ¹⁹As the blast of the ram's horn grew louder and louder, Moses spoke, and God thundered his reply. ²⁰The LORD came down on the top of Mount Sinai and called Moses to the top of the mountain. So Moses climbed the mountain.

²¹Then the LORD told Moses, "Go back down and warn the people not to break through the boundaries to see the LORD, or they will die. ²²Even the priests who regularly come near to the LORD must purify themselves so that the LORD does not break out and destroy them."

²³"But LORD," Moses protested, "the people cannot come up to Mount Sinai. You already warned us. You told me, 'Mark off a boundary all around the mountain to set it apart as holy.'"

²⁴But the LORD said, "Go down and bring Aaron back up with you. In the meantime, do not let the priests or the people break through to approach the LORD, or he will break out and destroy them."

²⁵So Moses went down to the people and told them what the LORD had said.

20 Ten Commandments for the Covenant Community

Then God gave the people all these instructions*:

²"I am the LORD your God, who rescued you from the land of Egypt, the place of your slavery.

³"You must not have any other god but me.

⁴"You must not make for yourself an idol

19:13 Or *up to the mountain.*   **20:1** Hebrew *all these words.*

Worship

Worshiping with Your Heart and Mind

EXODUS 19:10–20

There's an old joke among Myers-Briggs users. Question: what happens when a passionate, hyperexpressive, exquisitely emotional feeler meets a logical, hyperrational, Mr. Spock-type thinker?

Answer: they get married.

Too often deep thinking and profound feeling never meet in the one place they're most needed: in worship. How can we worship in ways that both engage the mind and touch the heart?

Some churches specialize in generating emotion. The platform people are experts at moving worshipers to laughter or tears. Attendees gradually learn to evaluate the service in terms of the emotion they feel.

In time, however, the law of diminishing returns sets in. Prayers are offered in highly emotive style and bathed in background music. Stories have to get more dramatic, songs more sentimental, preaching more histrionic, to keep people having intense emotional experiences.

Such worship is often shallow, sometimes artificial, and rarely reflective. Little attention is given to worshiping with the mind. It produces people who have little depth or rootedness. They may develop a "misdirected zeal" for God that isn't backed up by knowledge (Romans 10:2). They become worship junkies, searching for whichever church can supply the best rush.

Like the beloved character in *The Wizard of Oz*, this is Scarecrow worship: it would be better if it only had a brain.

On the other hand, some churches focus keenly on cognitive correctness. They recite great creeds, distribute reams of exegetical information, craft careful prayers ahead of time. And yet the heart and spirit are not seized with the wonder and passion that characterize those in Scripture who must fall on their faces when they encounter the living God. No one is ever so moved that she actually moves.

This is tragic because, as Dallas Willard writes, "To handle the things of God without worship is always to falsify them."

Those who attend such services may be competent to spot theological error, but the unspoken truth is they're also a little bored. Their worship is dry—it doesn't connect with their deepest hurts and desires. Rarely does it generate awe or healing and never raucous joy.

This is *Oz*-like Tin Man worship: if it only had a heart.

Unfortunately many of us have the tendency to approach worship as consumers. The focus is on my experience, sitting back with arms folded and saying to those leading worship, "Wow me." Do something to grab my attention, catch my interest. We assume worship is like watching a movie; it's something I critique afterward.

But can you imagine the Israelites, freshly delivered from slavery, before a mountain that trembles violently with the presence of God (Exodus 19), muttering, "We're leaving because we're not singing the songs we like. Like that tambourine song, how come they don't do that tambourine song anymore?"

"I don't like it when Moses leads worship; Aaron's better."

"This is too formal—all that smoke and mystery. I like casual worship."

"It was okay, except for Miriam's dance—too wild, not enough reverence. And I don't like the tambourine."

No, Scripture doesn't read like that. The people were filled with awe, wonder, trembling, hope, and fear, because there in the middle of nowhere, before this bunch of ex-slaves, was God.

In our day—when the beauty of liturgical traditions, the freedom of charismatic expression, and the intellectual rigor of the Reformation are being cross-fertilized—we have a wonderful opportunity to pursue worship that balances intellect and passion. We can move beyond a consumer mentality and step into worship fully engaged, using both our hearts and our minds.

How can you seize the opportunity to truly worship when you gather with your church family?

First, prepare yourself to worship. Football players prepare for the big game. Salespeople prepare for a big pitch. And worshipers should prepare to worship, both mind and heart. Prepare at home and even in the car en route to the service.

Then when you're at church, commit to invest yourself fully, regardless of how you feel. Too often in corporate worship people experience what psychologists speak of as mindlessness. They go on autopilot. They wait for something to grab their attention. Instead, we need to say to God, "I'm fully present—listening, praising, confessing, responding—every moment of worship. I offer myself fully to you."

The single most important aspect of balanced worship is to fully devote both your intellect and your emotions in your focus on God. When this happens, moments will come when you feel and understand God in ways no one could have planned.

—Pam Howell and John Ortberg

For more on worship, see reading at Exodus 32:1–8.

of any kind or an image of anything in the heavens or on the earth or in the sea. ⁵You must not bow down to them or worship them, for I, the LORD your God, am a jealous God who will not tolerate your affection for any other gods. I lay the sins of the parents upon their children; the entire family is affected— even children in the third and fourth generations of those who reject me. ⁶But I lavish unfailing love for a thousand generations on those* who love me and obey my commands.

⁷"You must not misuse the name of the LORD your God. The LORD will not let you go unpunished if you misuse his name.

⁸"Remember to observe the Sabbath day by keeping it holy. ⁹You have six days each week for your ordinary work, ¹⁰but the seventh day is a Sabbath day of rest dedicated to the LORD your God. On that day no one in your household may do any work. This includes you, your sons and daughters, your male and female servants, your livestock, and any foreigners living among you. ¹¹For in six days the LORD made the heavens, the earth, the sea, and everything in them; but on the seventh day he rested. That is why the LORD blessed the Sabbath day and set it apart as holy.

¹²"Honor your father and mother. Then you will live a long, full life in the land the LORD your God is giving you.

¹³"You must not murder.

¹⁴"You must not commit adultery.

¹⁵"You must not steal.

¹⁶"You must not testify falsely against your neighbor.

¹⁷"You must not covet your neighbor's house. You must not covet your neighbor's wife, male or female servant, ox or donkey, or anything else that belongs to your neighbor."

¹⁸When the people heard the thunder and the loud blast of the ram's horn, and when they saw the flashes of lightning and the smoke billowing from the mountain, they stood at a distance, trembling with fear.

¹⁹And they said to Moses, "You speak to us, and we will listen. But don't let God speak directly to us, or we will die!"

²⁰"Don't be afraid," Moses answered them, "for God has come in this way to test you, and so that your fear of him will keep you from sinning!"

²¹As the people stood in the distance, Moses approached the dark cloud where God was.

Proper Use of Altars

²²And the LORD said to Moses, "Say this to the people of Israel: You saw for yourselves that I spoke to you from heaven. ²³Remember, you must not make any idols of silver or gold to rival me.

²⁴"Build for me an altar made of earth, and offer your sacrifices to me—your burnt offerings and peace offerings, your sheep and goats, and your cattle. Build my altar wherever I cause my name to be remembered, and I will come to you and bless you. ²⁵If you use stones to build my altar, use only natural, uncut stones. Do not shape the stones with a tool, for that would make the altar unfit for holy use. ²⁶And do not approach my altar by going up steps. If you do, someone might look up under your clothing and see your nakedness.

21 Fair Treatment of Slaves

"These are the regulations you must present to Israel.

²"If you buy a Hebrew slave, he may serve for no more than six years. Set him free in the seventh year, and he will owe you nothing for his freedom. ³If he was single when he became your slave, he shall leave single. But if he was married before he became a slave, then his wife must be freed with him.

⁴"If his master gave him a wife while he was a slave and they had sons or daughters, then only the man will be free in the seventh year, but his wife and children will still belong to his master. ⁵But the slave may declare, 'I love my master, my wife, and my children. I don't want to go free.' ⁶If he does this, his master must present him before God.* Then his master must take him to the door or doorpost and publicly pierce

his ear with an awl. After that, the slave will serve his master for life.

7 "When a man sells his daughter as a slave, she will not be freed at the end of six years as the men are. 8 If she does not satisfy her owner, he must allow her to be bought back again. But he is not allowed to sell her to foreigners, since he is the one who broke the contract with her. 9 But if the slave's owner arranges for her to marry his son, he may no longer treat her as a slave but as a daughter.

10 "If a man who has married a slave wife takes another wife for himself, he must not neglect the rights of the first wife to food, clothing, and sexual intimacy. 11 If he fails in any of these three obligations, she may leave as a free woman without making any payment.

Cases of Personal Injury

12 "Anyone who assaults and kills another person must be put to death. 13 But if it was simply an accident permitted by God, I will appoint a place of refuge where the slayer can run for safety. 14 However, if someone deliberately kills another person, then the slayer must be dragged even from my altar and be put to death.

15 "Anyone who strikes father or mother must be put to death.

16 "Kidnappers must be put to death, whether they are caught in possession of their victims or have already sold them as slaves.

17 "Anyone who dishonors* father or mother must be put to death.

18 "Now suppose two men quarrel, and one hits the other with a stone or fist, and the injured person does not die but is confined to bed. 19 If he is later able to walk outside again, even with a crutch, the assailant will not be punished but must compensate his victim for lost wages and provide for his full recovery.

20 "If a man beats his male or female slave with a club and the slave dies as a result, the owner must be punished. 21 But if the slave recovers within a day or two, then the owner shall not be punished, since the slave is his property.

22 "Now suppose two men are fighting, and in the process they accidentally strike a pregnant woman so she gives birth prematurely.* If no further injury results, the man who struck the woman must pay the amount of compensation the woman's husband demands and the judges approve. 23 But if there is further injury, the punishment must match the injury: a life for a life, 24 an eye for an eye, a tooth for a tooth, a hand for a hand, a foot for a foot, 25 a burn for a burn, a wound for a wound, a bruise for a bruise.

26 "If a man hits his male or female slave in the eye and the eye is blinded, he must let the slave go free to compensate for the eye. 27 And if a man knocks out the tooth of his male or female slave, he must let the slave go free to compensate for the tooth.

28 "If an ox* gores a man or woman to death, the ox must be stoned, and its flesh may not be eaten. In such a case, however, the owner will not be held liable. 29 But suppose the ox had a reputation for goring, and the owner had been informed but failed to keep it under control. If the ox then kills someone, it must be stoned, and the owner must also be put to death. 30 However, the dead person's relatives may accept payment to compensate for the loss of life. The owner of the ox may redeem his life by paying whatever is demanded.

31 "The same regulation applies if the ox gores a boy or a girl. 32 But if the ox gores a slave, either male or female, the animal's owner must pay the slave's owner thirty silver coins,* and the ox must be stoned.

33 "Suppose someone digs or uncovers a pit and fails to cover it, and then an ox or a donkey falls into it. 34 The owner of the pit must pay full compensation to the owner of the animal, but then he gets to keep the dead animal.

35 "If someone's ox injures a neighbor's ox and the injured ox dies, then the two owners must sell the live ox and divide the price equally between them. They must also divide the dead animal. 36 But if the ox had a reputation for goring, yet its owner failed to keep it under control, he must pay full compensation—a live ox for the dead one—but he may keep the dead ox.

21:17 Greek version reads *Anyone who speaks disrespectfully of*. Compare Matt 15:4; Mark 7:10. **21:22** Or *so she has a miscarriage;* Hebrew reads *so her children come out*. **21:28** Or *bull, or cow;* also in 21:29-36. **21:32** Hebrew *30 shekels of silver,* about 12 ounces or 342 grams in weight.

22 Protection of Property

¹*"If someone steals an ox* or sheep and then kills or sells it, the thief must pay back five oxen for each ox stolen, and four sheep for each sheep stolen.

²*"If a thief is caught in the act of breaking into a house and is struck and killed in the process, the person who killed the thief is not guilty of murder. ³But if it happens in daylight, the one who killed the thief is guilty of murder.

"A thief who is caught must pay in full for everything he stole. If he cannot pay, he must be sold as a slave to pay for his theft. ⁴If someone steals an ox or a donkey or a sheep and it is found in the thief's possession, then the thief must pay double the value of the stolen animal.

⁵"If an animal is grazing in a field or vineyard and the owner lets it stray into someone else's field to graze, then the animal's owner must pay compensation from the best of his own grain or grapes.

⁶"If you are burning thornbushes and the fire gets out of control and spreads into another person's field, destroying the sheaves or the uncut grain or the whole crop, the one who started the fire must pay for the lost crop.

⁷"Suppose someone leaves money or goods with a neighbor for safekeeping, and they are stolen from the neighbor's house. If the thief is caught, the compensation is double the value of what was stolen. ⁸But if the thief is not caught, the neighbor must appear before God,* who will determine if he stole the property.

⁹"Suppose there is a dispute between two people who both claim to own a particular ox, donkey, sheep, article of clothing, or any lost property. Both parties must come before God, and the person whom God declares* guilty must pay double compensation to the other.

¹⁰"Now suppose someone leaves a donkey, ox, sheep, or any other animal with a neighbor for safekeeping, but it dies or is injured or gets away, and no one sees what happened. ¹¹The neighbor must then take an oath in the presence of the LORD. If the LORD confirms that the neighbor did not steal the property, the owner must accept the verdict, and no payment will be required. ¹²But if the animal was indeed stolen, the guilty person must pay compensation to the owner. ¹³If it was torn to pieces by a wild animal, the remains of the carcass must be shown as evidence, and no compensation will be required.

¹⁴"If someone borrows an animal from a neighbor and it is injured or dies when the owner is absent, the person who borrowed it must pay full compensation. ¹⁵But if the owner was present, no compensation is required. And no compensation is required if the animal was rented, for this loss is covered by the rental fee.

Social Responsibility

¹⁶"If a man seduces a virgin who is not engaged to anyone and has sex with her, he must pay the customary bride price and marry her. ¹⁷But if her father refuses to let him marry her, the man must still pay him an amount equal to the bride price of a virgin.

¹⁸"You must not allow a sorceress to live.

¹⁹"Anyone who has sexual relations with an animal must certainly be put to death.

²⁰"Anyone who sacrifices to any god other than the LORD must be destroyed.*

²¹"You must not mistreat or oppress foreigners in any way. Remember, you yourselves were once foreigners in the land of Egypt.

²²"You must not exploit a widow or an orphan. ²³If you exploit them in any way and they cry out to me, then I will certainly hear their cry. ²⁴My anger will blaze against you, and I will kill you with the sword. Then your wives will be widows and your children fatherless.

²⁵"If you lend money to any of my people who are in need, do not charge interest as a money lender would. ²⁶If you take your neighbor's cloak as security for a loan, you must return it before sunset. ²⁷This coat may be the only blanket your neighbor has. How can a person sleep without it? If you do not return it and your neighbor cries out to me for help, then I will hear, for I am merciful.

22:1a Verse 22:1 is numbered 21:37 in Hebrew text. 22:1b Or *bull, or cow;* also in 22:4, 9, 10. 22:2 Verses 22:2-31 are numbered 22:1-30 in Hebrew text. 22:8 Or *before the judges.* 22:9 Or *before the judges, and the person whom the judges declare.* 22:20 The Hebrew term used here refers to the complete consecration of things or people to the LORD, either by destroying them or by giving them as an offering.

28"You must not dishonor God or curse any of your rulers.

29"You must not hold anything back when you give me offerings from your crops and your wine.

"You must give me your firstborn sons.

30"You must also give me the firstborn of your cattle, sheep, and goats. But leave the newborn animal with its mother for seven days; then give it to me on the eighth day.

31"You must be my holy people. Therefore, do not eat any animal that has been torn up and killed by wild animals. Throw it to the dogs.

23 A Call for Justice

"You must not pass along false rumors. You must not cooperate with evil people by lying on the witness stand.

2"You must not follow the crowd in doing wrong. When you are called to testify in a dispute, do not be swayed by the crowd to twist justice. 3And do not slant your testimony in favor of a person just because that person is poor.

4"If you come upon your enemy's ox or donkey that has strayed away, take it back to its owner. 5If you see that the donkey of someone who hates you has collapsed under its load, do not walk by. Instead, stop and help.

6"In a lawsuit, you must not deny justice to the poor.

7"Be sure never to charge anyone falsely with evil. Never sentence an innocent or blameless person to death, for I never declare a guilty person to be innocent.

8"Take no bribes, for a bribe makes you ignore something that you clearly see. A bribe makes even a righteous person twist the truth.

9"You must not oppress foreigners. You know what it's like to be a foreigner, for you yourselves were once foreigners in the land of Egypt.

10"Plant and harvest your crops for six years, 11but let the land be renewed and lie uncultivated during the seventh year. Then let the poor among you harvest whatever grows on its own. Leave the rest for wild animals to eat. The same applies to your vineyards and olive groves.

12"You have six days each week for your ordinary work, but on the seventh day you must stop working. This gives your ox and your donkey a chance to rest. It also allows your slaves and the foreigners living among you to be refreshed.

13"Pay close attention to all my instructions. You must not call on the name of any other gods. Do not even speak their names.

Three Annual Festivals

14"Each year you must celebrate three festivals in my honor. 15First, celebrate the Festival of Unleavened Bread. For seven days the bread you eat must be made without yeast, just as I commanded you. Celebrate this festival annually at the appointed time in early spring, in the month of Abib,* for that is the anniversary of your departure from Egypt. No one may appear before me without an offering.

16"Second, celebrate the Festival of Harvest,* when you bring me the first crops of your harvest.

"Finally, celebrate the Festival of the Final Harvest* at the end of the harvest season, when you have harvested all the crops from your fields. 17At these three times each year, every man in Israel must appear before the Sovereign, the LORD.

18"You must not offer the blood of my sacrificial offerings together with any baked goods containing yeast. And do not leave the fat from the festival offerings until the next morning.

19"As you harvest your crops, bring the very best of the first harvest to the house of the LORD your God.

"You must not cook a young goat in its mother's milk.

A Promise of the LORD's Presence

20"See, I am sending an angel before you to protect you on your journey and lead you safely to the place I have prepared for you. 21Pay close attention to him, and obey his

---

23:15 Hebrew *appointed time in the month of Abib.* This first month of the ancient Hebrew lunar calendar usually occurs within the months of March and April. **23:16a** Or *Festival of Weeks.* This was later called the Festival of Pentecost (see Acts 2:1). It is celebrated today as Shavuot (or Shabuoth). **23:16b** Or *Festival of Ingathering.* This was later called the Festival of Shelters or Festival of Tabernacles (see Lev 23:33-36). It is celebrated today as Sukkot (or Succoth).

The Faith-Shaping Power of Festivals and Feasts

EXODUS 23:14–19

A steady, ongoing, and life-transforming rhythm: season by season, year by year, God's people honored him through traditional celebrations. Marching farmers, homeless slaves, flatbread eaten in haste, beautiful fruits in baskets: these are just a few elements in a trilogy of biblical harvest festivals described in Scripture. In these celebrations everything is brought to the table through these festivals: suffering, triumph, sorrow, joy, struggle, comfort, ugliness, beauty, emptiness, plenty, separation, community, death, and life.

This trilogy of Old Testament festivals begins with Passover, which coincides with the barley harvest (Leviticus 23:5–8; Deuteronomy 16:1–8). If you remember the story in Exodus 12, Passover commemorates the night God struck down all the firstborn in Egypt, except in the households that had painted blood on the doorposts as a sign that they should be "passed over." The end of the story is life for those who listened, but overall this festival is fairly dark in its celebratory elements: flatbread, a slaughtered lamb, and additional items like bitter herbs and parsley dipped in salt water.

Seven weeks later in the Jewish calendar, the tone changes considerably, with the coming of the Feast of Weeks, or *Shavuot*, which Christians will recognize as coinciding with Pentecost (Leviticus 23:15–22; Deuteronomy 16:9–12). The wheat harvest had begun. Flatbread gave over to fat loaves, waved before the Lord. Farmers who had tied ribbons on branches budding with first fruits now harvested these fruits and began a march toward Jerusalem. They sang, danced, trailed behind flute players, and carried their baskets of beautiful fruits toward the temple.

Upon arrival at the temple, this rowdy crowd was greeted with priestly song—the Levites welcoming pilgrims and accepting the sacrifice of first fruits. With joy the farmers presented their gifts, reciting these lines: "So the LORD brought us out of Egypt with a strong hand and powerful arm, with overwhelming terror, and with miraculous signs and wonders. He brought us to this place and gave us this land flowing with milk and honey! And now, O LORD, I have brought you the first portion of the harvest you have given me from the ground" (Deuteronomy 26:8–10).

The deliverance that began with Passover was more fully experienced in Shavuot, as the fruits of freedom were recognized and shared. God's people celebrated the Source of their gifts, received in one hand while releasing with the other—a full-circle picture of gratitude and thanks.

Finally, this trilogy of harvest celebrations ended each year with *Sukkot*, the Festival of Booths, which coincided with the fruit harvest (Leviticus 23:33-43; Deuteronomy 16:13-17). People built booths or *sukkot*, which means "coverings, shelters," and they slept and ate in them. These temporary structures called to mind the wandering of homeless, escaped Israelite slaves in the desert, where they depended fully on God for their sustenance in an unstable life of struggle and impermanence. Although Sukkot commemorated a fragile time, its emphasis was on rejoicing.

Imagine for a moment the effect it would have on a person growing up and living within the annual rhythm of these biblical festivals. Year after year, to recall the stories of God's blessings and deliverance, and at the same time to feel a part of God's ongoing story. To affirm, over and over with one's community, that *this is who we are* and *this is what we believe.* To shape one's very sense of time around remembering, and remembering again, all that God in his goodness has provided.

What can we learn from these joyful marching farmers, homeless slaves, and people spared in the passing-over? To begin, we might remember that all aspects of life—suffering and joy, struggle and comfort, ugliness and beauty, and so on— are welcome and dealt with at the table of celebration.

We might also remember that God is generous and good; he delights in our own experiences of joy as we acknowledge his goodness to us. We, like the farmers and the booth dwellers, can freely receive beauty and abundance in one hand while we sacrificially release gifts with the other; we can daily choose ways to concretely manifest such acceptance and generosity.

And we can also allow ourselves to consider how our own patterns and rituals of celebration form and shape our sense of who we are. Through our celebration of holidays and everyday blessings, we can solidify our sense of identity within the people of God. We can consciously choose to recall, over and over, who God is and all he's done for us. We can affirm, *Yes, this is who I am,* and, *yes, this is what I believe.*

—L. L. Barkat

For more on celebration, see reading at Ruth 4:13-18.

instructions. Do not rebel against him, for he is my representative, and he will not forgive your rebellion. ²²But if you are careful to obey him, following all my instructions, then I will be an enemy to your enemies, and I will oppose those who oppose you. ²³For my angel will go before you and bring you into the land of the Amorites, Hittites, Perizzites, Canaanites, Hivites, and Jebusites, so you may live there. And I will destroy them completely. ²⁴You must not worship the gods of these nations or serve them in any way or imitate their evil practices. Instead, you must utterly destroy them and smash their sacred pillars.

²⁵"You must serve only the LORD your God. If you do, I* will bless you with food and water, and I will protect you from illness. ²⁶There will be no miscarriages or infertility in your land, and I will give you long, full lives.

²⁷"I will send my terror ahead of you and create panic among all the people whose lands you invade. I will make all your enemies turn and run. ²⁸I will send terror* ahead of you to drive out the Hivites, Canaanites, and Hittites. ²⁹But I will not drive them out in a single year, because the land would become desolate and the wild animals would multiply and threaten you. ³⁰I will drive them out a little at a time until your population has increased enough to take possession of the land. ³¹And I will fix your boundaries from the Red Sea to the Mediterranean Sea,* and from the eastern wilderness to the Euphrates River.* I will hand over to you the people now living in the land, and you will drive them out ahead of you.

³²"Make no treaties with them or their gods. ³³They must not live in your land, or they will cause you to sin against me. If you serve their gods, you will be caught in the trap of idolatry."

24

Israel Accepts the LORD's Covenant
Then the LORD instructed Moses: "Come up here to me, and bring along Aaron, Nadab, Abihu, and seventy of Israel's elders. All of you must worship from a distance. ²Only Moses is allowed to come near to the LORD. The others must not come near, and none of the other people are allowed to climb up the mountain with him."

³Then Moses went down to the people and repeated all the instructions and regulations the LORD had given him. All the people answered with one voice, "We will do everything the LORD has commanded."

⁴Then Moses carefully wrote down all the LORD's instructions. Early the next morning Moses got up and built an altar at the foot of the mountain. He also set up twelve pillars, one for each of the twelve tribes of Israel. ⁵Then he sent some of the young Israelite men to present burnt offerings and to sacrifice bulls as peace offerings to the LORD. ⁶Moses drained half the blood from these animals into basins. The other half he splattered against the altar.

⁷Then he took the Book of the Covenant and read it aloud to the people. Again they all responded, "We will do everything the LORD has commanded. We will obey."

⁸Then Moses took the blood from the basins and splattered it over the people, declaring, "Look, this blood confirms the covenant the LORD has made with you in giving you these instructions."

⁹Then Moses, Aaron, Nadab, Abihu, and the seventy elders of Israel climbed up the mountain. ¹⁰There they saw the God of Israel. Under his feet there seemed to be a surface of brilliant blue lapis lazuli, as clear as the sky itself. ¹¹And though these nobles of Israel gazed upon God, he did not destroy them. In fact, they ate a covenant meal, eating and drinking in his presence!

¹²Then the LORD said to Moses, "Come up to me on the mountain. Stay there, and I will give you the tablets of stone on which I have inscribed the instructions and commands so you can teach the people." ¹³So Moses and his assistant Joshua set out, and Moses climbed up the mountain of God. ¹⁴Moses told the elders, "Stay here and wait for us until we come back. Aaron and Hur are here with you. If anyone has a dispute while I am gone, consult with them."

¹⁵Then Moses climbed up the mountain, and the cloud covered it. ¹⁶And the glory

---

23:25 As in Greek and Latin versions; Hebrew reads *he.*   **23:28** Often rendered *the hornet.* The meaning of the Hebrew is uncertain.   **23:31a** Hebrew *from the sea of reeds to the sea of the Philistines.*   **23:31b** Hebrew *from the wilderness to the river.*

of the LORD settled down on Mount Sinai, and the cloud covered it for six days. On the seventh day the LORD called to Moses from inside the cloud. [17]To the Israelites at the foot of the mountain, the glory of the LORD appeared at the summit like a consuming fire. [18]Then Moses disappeared into the cloud as he climbed higher up the mountain. He remained on the mountain forty days and forty nights.

25 Offerings for the Tabernacle

The LORD said to Moses, [2]"Tell the people of Israel to bring me their sacred offerings. Accept the contributions from all whose hearts are moved to offer them. [3]Here is a list of sacred offerings you may accept from them:

gold, silver, and bronze;
[4] blue, purple, and scarlet thread;
fine linen and goat hair for cloth;
[5] tanned ram skins and fine goatskin leather;
acacia wood;
[6] olive oil for the lamps;
spices for the anointing oil and the fragrant incense;
[7] onyx stones, and other gemstones to be set in the ephod and the priest's chestpiece.

[8]"Have the people of Israel build me a holy sanctuary so I can live among them. [9]You must build this Tabernacle and its furnishings exactly according to the pattern I will show you.

Plans for the Ark of the Covenant

[10]"Have the people make an Ark of acacia wood—a sacred chest 45 inches long, 27 inches wide, and 27 inches high.* [11]Overlay it inside and outside with pure gold, and run a molding of gold all around it. [12]Cast four gold rings and attach them to its four feet, two rings on each side. [13]Make poles from acacia wood, and overlay them with gold. [14]Insert the poles into the rings at the sides of the Ark to carry it. [15]These carrying poles must stay inside the rings; never

remove them. [16]When the Ark is finished, place inside it the stone tablets inscribed with the terms of the covenant,* which I will give to you.

[17]"Then make the Ark's cover—the place of atonement—from pure gold. It must be 45 inches long and 27 inches wide.* [18]Then make two cherubim from hammered gold, and place them on the two ends of the atonement cover. [19]Mold the cherubim on each end of the atonement cover, making it all of one piece of gold. [20]The cherubim will face each other and look down on the atonement cover. With their wings spread above it, they will protect it. [21]Place inside the Ark the stone tablets inscribed with the terms of the covenant, which I will give to you. Then put the atonement cover on top of the Ark. [22]I will meet with you there and talk to you from above the atonement cover between the gold cherubim that hover over the Ark of the Covenant.* From there I will give you my commands for the people of Israel.

Plans for the Table

[23]"Then make a table of acacia wood, 36 inches long, 18 inches wide, and 27 inches high.* [24]Overlay it with pure gold and run a gold molding around the edge. [25]Decorate it with a 3-inch border* all around, and run a gold molding along the border. [26]Make four gold rings for the table and attach them at the four corners next to the four legs. [27]Attach the rings near the border to hold the poles that are used to carry the table. [28]Make these poles from acacia wood, and overlay them with gold. [29]Make special containers of pure gold for the table—bowls, pans, pitchers, and jars—to be used in pouring out liquid offerings. [30]Place the Bread of the Presence on the table to remain before me at all times.

Plans for the Lampstand

[31]"Make a lampstand of pure, hammered gold. Make the entire lampstand and its decorations of one piece—the base, center stem, lamp cups, buds, and petals. [32]Make it

---

25:10 Hebrew 2.5 cubits [115 centimeters] long, 1.5 cubits [69 centimeters] wide, and 1.5 cubits high.   25:16 Hebrew Place inside the Ark the Testimony; similarly in 25:21. The Hebrew word for "testimony" refers to the terms of the LORD's covenant with Israel as written on stone tablets, and also to the covenant itself.   25:17 Hebrew 2.5 cubits [115 centimeters] long and 1.5 cubits [69 centimeters] wide.   25:22 Or Ark of the Testimony.   25:23 Hebrew 2 cubits [92 centimeters] long, 1 cubit [46 centimeters] wide, and 1.5 cubits [69 centimeters] high.   25:25 Hebrew a border of a handbreadth [8 centimeters].

with six branches going out from the center stem, three on each side. ³³Each of the six branches will have three lamp cups shaped like almond blossoms, complete with buds and petals. ³⁴Craft the center stem of the lampstand with four lamp cups shaped like almond blossoms, complete with buds and petals. ³⁵There will also be an almond bud beneath each pair of branches where the six branches extend from the center stem. ³⁶The almond buds and branches must all be of one piece with the center stem, and they must be hammered from pure gold. ³⁷Then make the seven lamps for the lampstand, and set them so they reflect their light forward. ³⁸The lamp snuffers and trays must also be made of pure gold. ³⁹You will need seventy-five pounds* of pure gold for the lampstand and its accessories.

⁴⁰"Be sure that you make everything according to the pattern I have shown you here on the mountain.

26 Plans for the Tabernacle

"Make the Tabernacle from ten curtains of finely woven linen. Decorate the curtains with blue, purple, and scarlet thread and with skillfully embroidered cherubim. ²These ten curtains must all be exactly the same size—42 feet long and 6 feet wide.* ³Join five of these curtains together to make one long curtain, then join the other five into a second long curtain. ⁴Put loops of blue yarn along the edge of the last curtain in each set. ⁵The fifty loops along the edge of one curtain are to match the fifty loops along the edge of the other curtain. ⁶Then make fifty gold clasps and fasten the long curtains together with the clasps. In this way, the Tabernacle will be made of one continuous piece.

⁷"Make eleven curtains of goat-hair cloth to serve as a tent covering for the Tabernacle. ⁸These eleven curtains must all be exactly the same size—45 feet long and 6 feet wide.* ⁹Join five of these curtains together to make one long curtain, and join the other six into a second long curtain. Allow 3 feet of material from the second set of curtains to hang over the front*

of the sacred tent. ¹⁰Make fifty loops for one edge of each large curtain. ¹¹Then make fifty bronze clasps, and fasten the loops of the long curtains with the clasps. In this way, the tent covering will be made of one continuous piece. ¹²The remaining 3 feet* of this tent covering will be left to hang over the back of the Tabernacle. ¹³Allow 18 inches* of remaining material to hang down over each side, so the Tabernacle is completely covered. ¹⁴Complete the tent covering with a protective layer of tanned ram skins and a layer of fine goatskin leather.

¹⁵"For the framework of the Tabernacle, construct frames of acacia wood. ¹⁶Each frame must be 15 feet high and 27 inches wide,* ¹⁷with two pegs under each frame. Make all the frames identical. ¹⁸Make twenty of these frames to support the curtains on the south side of the Tabernacle. ¹⁹Also make forty silver bases—two bases under each frame, with the pegs fitting securely into the bases. ²⁰For the north side of the Tabernacle, make another twenty frames, ²¹with their forty silver bases, two bases under each frame. ²²Make six frames for the rear—the west side of the Tabernacle—²³along with two additional frames to reinforce the rear corners of the Tabernacle. ²⁴These corner frames will be matched at the bottom and firmly attached at the top with a single ring, forming a single corner unit. Make both of these corner units the same way. ²⁵So there will be eight frames at the rear of the Tabernacle, set in sixteen silver bases—two bases under each frame.

²⁶"Make crossbars of acacia wood to link the frames, five crossbars for the north side of the Tabernacle ²⁷and five for the south side. Also make five crossbars for the rear of the Tabernacle, which will face west. ²⁸The middle crossbar, attached halfway up the frames, will run all the way from one end of the Tabernacle to the other. ²⁹Overlay the frames with gold, and make gold rings to hold the crossbars. Overlay the crossbars with gold as well.

³⁰"Set up this Tabernacle according to the pattern you were shown on the mountain.

³¹"For the inside of the Tabernacle, make a special curtain of finely woven linen. Decorate it with blue, purple, and scarlet thread and with skillfully embroidered cherubim. ³²Hang this curtain on gold hooks attached to four posts of acacia wood. Overlay the posts with gold, and set them in four silver bases. ³³Hang the inner curtain from clasps, and put the Ark of the Covenant* in the room behind it. This curtain will separate the Holy Place from the Most Holy Place.

³⁴"Then put the Ark's cover—the place of atonement—on top of the Ark of the Covenant inside the Most Holy Place. ³⁵Place the table outside the inner curtain on the north side of the Tabernacle, and place the lampstand across the room on the south side.

³⁶"Make another curtain for the entrance to the sacred tent. Make it of finely woven linen and embroider it with exquisite designs, using blue, purple, and scarlet thread. ³⁷Craft five posts from acacia wood. Overlay them with gold, and hang the curtain from them with gold hooks. Cast five bronze bases for the posts.

27 Plans for the Altar of Burnt Offering

"Using acacia wood, construct a square altar 7½ feet wide, 7½ feet long, and 4½ feet high.* ²Make horns for each of its four corners so that the horns and altar are all one piece. Overlay the altar with bronze. ³Make ash buckets, shovels, basins, meat forks, and firepans, all of bronze. ⁴Make a bronze grating for it, and attach four bronze rings at its four corners. ⁵Install the grating halfway down the side of the altar, under the ledge. ⁶For carrying the altar, make poles from acacia wood, and overlay them with bronze. ⁷Insert the poles through the rings on the two sides of the altar. ⁸The altar must be hollow, made from planks. Build it just as you were shown on the mountain.

Plans for the Courtyard

⁹"Then make the courtyard for the Tabernacle, enclosed with curtains made of finely woven linen. On the south side, make the curtains 150 feet long.* ¹⁰They will be held up by twenty posts set securely in twenty bronze bases. Hang the curtains with silver hooks and rings. ¹¹Make the curtains the same on the north side—150 feet of curtains held up by twenty posts set securely in bronze bases. Hang the curtains with silver hooks and rings. ¹²The curtains on the west end of the courtyard will be 75 feet long,* supported by ten posts set into ten bases. ¹³The east end of the courtyard, the front, will also be 75 feet long. ¹⁴The courtyard entrance will be on the east end, flanked by two curtains. The curtain on the right side will be 22½ feet long,* supported by three posts set into three bases. ¹⁵The curtain on the left side will also be 22½ feet long, supported by three posts set into three bases.

¹⁶"For the entrance to the courtyard, make a curtain that is 30 feet long.* Make it from finely woven linen, and decorate it with beautiful embroidery in blue, purple, and scarlet thread. Support it with four posts, each securely set in its own base. ¹⁷All the posts around the courtyard must have silver rings and hooks and bronze bases. ¹⁸So the entire courtyard will be 150 feet long and 75 feet wide, with curtain walls 7½ feet high,* made from finely woven linen. The bases for the posts will be made of bronze.

¹⁹"All the articles used in the rituals of the Tabernacle, including all the tent pegs used to support the Tabernacle and the courtyard curtains, must be made of bronze.

Light for the Tabernacle

²⁰"Command the people of Israel to bring you pure oil of pressed olives for the light, to keep the lamps burning continually. ²¹The lampstand will stand in the Tabernacle, in front of the inner curtain that shields the Ark of the Covenant.* Aaron and his sons must keep the lamps burning in the LORD's presence all night. This is a permanent law for the people of Israel, and it must be observed from generation to generation.

26:33 Or *Ark of the Testimony*; also in 26:34.   **27:1** Hebrew *5 cubits* [2.3 meters] *wide, 5 cubits long, a square, and 3 cubits* [1.4 meters] *high.* **27:9** Hebrew *100 cubits* [46 meters]; also in 27:11.   **27:12** Hebrew *50 cubits* [23 meters]; also in 27:13.   **27:14** Hebrew *15 cubits* [6.9 meters]; also in 27:15.   **27:16** Hebrew *20 cubits* [9.2 meters].   **27:18** Hebrew *100 cubits* [46 meters] *long and 50 by 50* [23 meters] *wide and 5 cubits* [2.3 meters] *high.*   **27:21** Hebrew *in the Tent of Meeting, outside the inner curtain that is in front of the Testimony.* See note on 25:16.

28 Clothing for the Priests

"Call for your brother, Aaron, and his sons, Nadab, Abihu, Eleazar, and Ithamar. Set them apart from the rest of the people of Israel so they may minister to me and be my priests. ²Make sacred garments for Aaron that are glorious and beautiful. ³Instruct all the skilled craftsmen whom I have filled with the spirit of wisdom. Have them make garments for Aaron that will distinguish him as a priest set apart for my service. ⁴These are the garments they are to make: a chestpiece, an ephod, a robe, a patterned tunic, a turban, and a sash. They are to make these sacred garments for your brother, Aaron, and his sons to wear when they serve me as priests. ⁵So give them fine linen cloth, gold thread, and blue, purple, and scarlet thread.

Design of the Ephod

⁶"The craftsmen must make the ephod of finely woven linen and skillfully embroider it with gold and with blue, purple, and scarlet thread. ⁷It will consist of two pieces, front and back, joined at the shoulders with two shoulder-pieces. ⁸The decorative sash will be made of the same materials: finely woven linen embroidered with gold and with blue, purple, and scarlet thread.

⁹"Take two onyx stones, and engrave on them the names of the tribes of Israel. ¹⁰Six names will be on each stone, arranged in the order of the births of the original sons of Israel. ¹¹Engrave these names on the two stones in the same way a jeweler engraves a seal. Then mount the stones in settings of gold filigree. ¹²Fasten the two stones on the shoulder-pieces of the ephod as a reminder that Aaron represents the people of Israel. Aaron will carry these names on his shoulders as a constant reminder whenever he goes before the LORD. ¹³Make the settings of gold filigree, ¹⁴then braid two cords of pure gold and attach them to the filigree settings on the shoulders of the ephod.

Design of the Chestpiece

¹⁵"Then, with great skill and care, make a chestpiece to be worn for seeking a decision from God.* Make it to match the ephod, using finely woven linen embroidered with gold and with blue, purple, and scarlet thread. ¹⁶Make the chestpiece of a single piece of cloth folded to form a pouch nine inches* square. ¹⁷Mount four rows of gemstones* on it. The first row will contain a red carnelian, a pale-green peridot, and an emerald. ¹⁸The second row will contain a turquoise, a blue lapis lazuli, and a white moonstone. ¹⁹The third row will contain an orange jacinth, an agate, and a purple amethyst. ²⁰The fourth row will contain a blue-green beryl, an onyx, and a green jasper. All these stones will be set in gold filigree. ²¹Each stone will represent one of the twelve sons of Israel, and the name of that tribe will be engraved on it like a seal.

²²"To attach the chestpiece to the ephod, make braided cords of pure gold thread. ²³Then make two gold rings and attach them to the top corners of the chestpiece. ²⁴Tie the two gold cords to the two rings on the chestpiece. ²⁵Tie the other ends of the cords to the gold settings on the shoulder-pieces of the ephod. ²⁶Then make two more gold rings and attach them to the inside edges of the chestpiece next to the ephod. ²⁷And make two more gold rings and attach them to the front of the ephod, below the shoulder-pieces, just above the knot where the decorative sash is fastened to the ephod. ²⁸Then attach the bottom rings of the chestpiece to the rings on the ephod with blue cords. This will hold the chestpiece securely to the ephod above the decorative sash.

²⁹"In this way, Aaron will carry the names of the tribes of Israel on the sacred chestpiece* over his heart when he goes into the Holy Place. This will be a continual reminder that he represents the people when he comes before the LORD. ³⁰Insert the Urim and Thummim into the sacred chestpiece so they will be carried over Aaron's heart when he goes into the LORD's presence. In this way, Aaron will always carry over his heart the objects used to determine the LORD's will for his people whenever he goes in before the LORD.

28:15 Hebrew *a chestpiece for decision.* 28:16 Hebrew *1 span* [23 centimeters]. 28:17 The identification of some of these gemstones is uncertain. 28:29 Hebrew *the chestpiece for decision;* also in 28:30. See 28:15.

Additional Clothing for the Priests

[31] "Make the robe that is worn with the ephod from a single piece of blue cloth, [32] with an opening for Aaron's head in the middle of it. Reinforce the opening with a woven collar* so it will not tear. [33] Make pomegranates out of blue, purple, and scarlet yarn, and attach them to the hem of the robe, with gold bells between them. [34] The gold bells and pomegranates are to alternate all around the hem. [35] Aaron will wear this robe whenever he ministers before the LORD, and the bells will tinkle as he goes in and out of the LORD's presence in the Holy Place. If he wears it, he will not die.

[36] "Next make a medallion of pure gold, and engrave it like a seal with these words: HOLY TO THE LORD. [37] Attach the medallion with a blue cord to the front of Aaron's turban, where it must remain. [38] Aaron must wear it on his forehead so he may take on himself any guilt of the people of Israel when they consecrate their sacred offerings. He must always wear it on his forehead so the LORD will accept the people.

[39] "Weave Aaron's patterned tunic from fine linen cloth. Fashion the turban from this linen as well. Also make a sash, and decorate it with colorful embroidery.

[40] "For Aaron's sons, make tunics, sashes, and special head coverings that are glorious and beautiful. [41] Clothe your brother, Aaron, and his sons with these garments, and then anoint and ordain them. Consecrate them so they can serve as my priests. [42] Also make linen undergarments for them, to be worn next to their bodies, reaching from their hips to their thighs. [43] These must be worn whenever Aaron and his sons enter the Tabernacle* or approach the altar in the Holy Place to perform their priestly duties. Then they will not incur guilt and die. This is a permanent law for Aaron and all his descendants after him.

29 Dedication of the Priests

"This is the ceremony you must follow when you consecrate Aaron and his sons to serve me as priests: Take a young bull and two rams with no defects. [2] Then, using choice wheat flour and no yeast, make loaves of bread, thin cakes mixed with olive oil, and wafers spread with oil. [3] Place them all in a single basket, and present them at the entrance of the Tabernacle, along with the young bull and the two rams.

[4] "Present Aaron and his sons at the entrance of the Tabernacle,* and wash them with water. [5] Dress Aaron in his priestly garments—the tunic, the robe worn with the ephod, the ephod itself, and the chestpiece. Then wrap the decorative sash of the ephod around him. [6] Place the turban on his head, and fasten the sacred medallion to the turban. [7] Then anoint him by pouring the anointing oil over his head. [8] Next present his sons, and dress them in their tunics. [9] Wrap the sashes around the waists of Aaron and his sons, and put their special head coverings on them. Then the right to the priesthood will be theirs by law forever. In this way, you will ordain Aaron and his sons.

[10] "Bring the young bull to the entrance of the Tabernacle, where Aaron and his sons will lay their hands on its head. [11] Then slaughter the bull in the LORD's presence at the entrance of the Tabernacle. [12] Put some of its blood on the horns of the altar with your finger, and pour out the rest at the base of the altar. [13] Take all the fat around the internal organs, the long lobe of the liver, and the two kidneys and the fat around them, and burn it all on the altar. [14] Then take the rest of the bull, including its hide, meat, and dung, and burn it outside the camp as a sin offering.

[15] "Next Aaron and his sons must lay their hands on the head of one of the rams. [16] Then slaughter the ram, and splatter its blood against all sides of the altar. [17] Cut the ram into pieces, and wash off the internal organs and the legs. Set them alongside the head and the other pieces of the body, [18] then burn the entire animal on the altar. This is a burnt offering to the LORD; it is a pleasing aroma, a special gift presented to the LORD.

[19] "Now take the other ram, and have Aaron and his sons lay their hands on its

---

28:32 The meaning of the Hebrew is uncertain. **28:43** Hebrew *Tent of Meeting.* **29:4** Hebrew *Tent of Meeting;* also in 29:10, 11, 30, 32, 42, 44.

head. ²⁰Then slaughter it, and apply some of its blood to the right earlobes of Aaron and his sons. Also put it on the thumbs of their right hands and the big toes of their right feet. Splatter the rest of the blood against all sides of the altar. ²¹Then take some of the blood from the altar and some of the anointing oil, and sprinkle it on Aaron and his sons and on their garments. In this way, they and their garments will be set apart as holy.

²²"Since this is the ram for the ordination of Aaron and his sons, take the fat of the ram, including the fat of the broad tail, the fat around the internal organs, the long lobe of the liver, and the two kidneys and the fat around them, along with the right thigh. ²³Then take one round loaf of bread, one thin cake mixed with olive oil, and one wafer from the basket of bread without yeast that was placed in the LORD's presence. ²⁴Put all these in the hands of Aaron and his sons to be lifted up as a special offering to the LORD. ²⁵Afterward take the various breads from their hands, and burn them on the altar along with the burnt offering. It is a pleasing aroma to the LORD, a special gift for him. ²⁶Then take the breast of Aaron's ordination ram, and lift it up in the LORD's presence as a special offering to him. Then keep it as your own portion.

²⁷"Set aside the portions of the ordination ram that belong to Aaron and his sons. This includes the breast and the thigh that were lifted up before the LORD as a special offering. ²⁸In the future, whenever the people of Israel lift up a peace offering, a portion of it must be set aside for Aaron and his descendants. This is their permanent right, and it is a sacred offering from the Israelites to the LORD.

²⁹"Aaron's sacred garments must be preserved for his descendants who succeed him, and they will wear them when they are anointed and ordained. ³⁰The descendant who succeeds him as high priest will wear these clothes for seven days as he ministers in the Tabernacle and the Holy Place.

³¹"Take the ram used in the ordination ceremony, and boil its meat in a sacred place. ³²Then Aaron and his sons will eat this meat, along with the bread in the basket, at the Tabernacle entrance. ³³They alone may eat the meat and bread used for their purification* in the ordination ceremony. No one else may eat them, for these things are set apart and holy. ³⁴If any of the ordination meat or bread remains until the morning, it must be burned. It may not be eaten, for it is holy.

³⁵"This is how you will ordain Aaron and his sons to their offices, just as I have commanded you. The ordination ceremony will go on for seven days. ³⁶Each day you must sacrifice a young bull as a sin offering to purify them, making them right with the LORD.* Afterward, cleanse the altar by purifying it*; make it holy by anointing it with oil. ³⁷Purify the altar, and consecrate it every day for seven days. After that, the altar will be absolutely holy, and whatever touches it will become holy.

³⁸"These are the sacrifices you are to offer regularly on the altar. Each day, offer two lambs that are a year old, ³⁹one in the morning and the other in the evening. ⁴⁰With one of them, offer two quarts of choice flour mixed with one quart of pure oil of pressed olives; also, offer one quart of wine* as a liquid offering. ⁴¹Offer the other lamb in the evening, along with the same offerings of flour and wine as in the morning. It will be a pleasing aroma, a special gift presented to the LORD.

⁴²"These burnt offerings are to be made each day from generation to generation. Offer them in the LORD's presence at the Tabernacle entrance; there I will meet with you and speak with you. ⁴³I will meet the people of Israel there, in the place made holy by my glorious presence. ⁴⁴Yes, I will consecrate the Tabernacle and the altar, and I will consecrate Aaron and his sons to serve me as priests. ⁴⁵Then I will live among the people of Israel and be their God, ⁴⁶and they will know that I am the LORD their God. I am the one who brought them out of the land of Egypt so that I could live among them. I am the LORD their God.

29:33 Or *their atonement.* **29:36a** Or *to make atonement.* **29:36b** Or *by making atonement for it;* similarly in 29:37. **29:40** Hebrew *¹⁄₁₀ of an ephah* [2.2 liters] *of choice flour . . . ¼ of a hin* [1 liter] *of pure oil . . . ¼ of a hin of wine.*

30 Plans for the Incense Altar

"Then make another altar of acacia wood for burning incense. ²Make it 18 inches square and 36 inches high,* with horns at the corners carved from the same piece of wood as the altar itself. ³Overlay the top, sides, and horns of the altar with pure gold, and run a gold molding around the entire altar. ⁴Make two gold rings, and attach them on opposite sides of the altar below the gold molding to hold the carrying poles. ⁵Make the poles of acacia wood and overlay them with gold. ⁶Place the incense altar just outside the inner curtain that shields the Ark of the Covenant,* in front of the Ark's cover—the place of atonement—that covers the tablets inscribed with the terms of the covenant.* I will meet with you there.

⁷"Every morning when Aaron maintains the lamps, he must burn fragrant incense on the altar. ⁸And each evening when he lights the lamps, he must again burn incense in the LORD's presence. This must be done from generation to generation. ⁹Do not offer any unholy incense on this altar, or any burnt offerings, grain offerings, or liquid offerings.

¹⁰"Once a year Aaron must purify* the altar by smearing its horns with blood from the offering made to purify the people from their sin. This will be a regular, annual event from generation to generation, for this is the LORD's most holy altar."

Money for the Tabernacle

¹¹Then the LORD said to Moses, ¹²"Whenever you take a census of the people of Israel, each man who is counted must pay a ransom for himself to the LORD. Then no plague will strike the people as you count them. ¹³Each person who is counted must give a small piece of silver as a sacred offering to the LORD. (This payment is half a shekel,* based on the sanctuary shekel, which equals twenty gerahs.) ¹⁴All who have reached their twentieth birthday must give this sacred offering to the LORD. ¹⁵When this offering is given to the LORD to purify your lives, making you right with him,* the rich must not give more than the specified amount, and the poor must not give less. ¹⁶Receive this ransom money from the Israelites, and use it for the care of the Tabernacle.* It will bring the Israelites to the LORD's attention, and it will purify your lives."

Plans for the Washbasin

¹⁷Then the LORD said to Moses, ¹⁸"Make a bronze washbasin with a bronze stand. Place it between the Tabernacle and the altar, and fill it with water. ¹⁹Aaron and his sons will wash their hands and feet there. ²⁰They must wash with water whenever they go into the Tabernacle to appear before the LORD and when they approach the altar to burn up their special gifts to the LORD—or they will die! ²¹They must always wash their hands and feet, or they will die. This is a permanent law for Aaron and his descendants, to be observed from generation to generation."

The Anointing Oil

²²Then the LORD said to Moses, ²³"Collect choice spices—12½ pounds of pure myrrh, 6¼ pounds of fragrant cinnamon, 6¼ pounds of fragrant calamus,* ²⁴and 12½ pounds of cassia*—as measured by the weight of the sanctuary shekel. Also get one gallon of olive oil.* ²⁵Like a skilled incense maker, blend these ingredients to make a holy anointing oil. ²⁶Use this sacred oil to anoint the Tabernacle, the Ark of the Covenant, ²⁷the table and all its utensils, the lampstand and all its accessories, the incense altar, ²⁸the altar of burnt offering and all its utensils, and the washbasin with its stand. ²⁹Consecrate them to make them absolutely holy. After this, whatever touches them will also become holy.

³⁰"Anoint Aaron and his sons also, consecrating them to serve me as priests. ³¹And say to the people of Israel, 'This holy anointing oil is reserved for me from generation to generation. ³²It must never be used to anoint anyone else, and you must never

---

30:2 Hebrew *1 cubit* [46 centimeters] *long and 1 cubit wide, a square, and 2 cubits* [92 centimeters] *high.* 30:6a Or *Ark of the Testimony;* also in 30:26. 30:6b Hebrew *that covers the Testimony;* see note on 25:16. 30:10 Or *make atonement for;* also in 30:10b. 30:13 Or *0.2 ounces, or 6 grams.* 30:15 Or *to make atonement for your lives;* similarly in 30:16. 30:16 Hebrew *Tent of Meeting;* also in 30:18, 20, 26, 36. 30:23 Hebrew *500 shekels* [5.7 kilograms] *of pure myrrh, 250 shekels* [2.9 kilograms] *of fragrant cinnamon, 250 shekels of fragrant calamus.* 30:24a Hebrew *500 shekels* [5.7 kilograms] *of cassia.* 30:24b Hebrew *1 hin* [3.8 liters] *of olive oil.*

make any blend like it for yourselves. It is holy, and you must treat it as holy. ³³Anyone who makes a blend like it or anoints someone other than a priest will be cut off from the community.'"

The Incense

³⁴Then the LORD said to Moses, "Gather fragrant spices—resin droplets, mollusk shell, and galbanum—and mix these fragrant spices with pure frankincense, weighed out in equal amounts. ³⁵Using the usual techniques of the incense maker, blend the spices together and sprinkle them with salt to produce a pure and holy incense. ³⁶Grind some of the mixture into a very fine powder and put it in front of the Ark of the Covenant,* where I will meet with you in the Tabernacle. You must treat this incense as most holy. ³⁷Never use this formula to make this incense for yourselves. It is reserved for the LORD, and you must treat it as holy. ³⁸Anyone who makes incense like this for personal use will be cut off from the community."

31 Craftsmen: Bezalel and Oholiab

Then the LORD said to Moses, ²"Look, I have specifically chosen Bezalel son of Uri, grandson of Hur, of the tribe of Judah. ³I have filled him with the Spirit of God, giving him great wisdom, ability, and expertise in all kinds of crafts. ⁴He is a master craftsman, expert in working with gold, silver, and bronze. ⁵He is skilled in engraving and mounting gemstones and in carving wood. He is a master at every craft!

⁶"And I have personally appointed Oholiab son of Ahisamach, of the tribe of Dan, to be his assistant. Moreover, I have given special skill to all the gifted craftsmen so they can make all the things I have commanded you to make:

⁷ the Tabernacle;*
   the Ark of the Covenant;*
   the Ark's cover—the place of atonement;
   all the furnishings of the Tabernacle;
⁸ the table and its utensils;
   the pure gold lampstand with all its
      accessories;
   the incense altar;

⁹ the altar of burnt offering with all its
   utensils;
   the washbasin with its stand;
¹⁰ the beautifully stitched garments—the
      sacred garments for Aaron the priest,
      and the garments for his sons to wear
      as they minister as priests;
¹¹ the anointing oil;
   the fragrant incense for the Holy Place.

The craftsmen must make everything as I have commanded you."

Instructions for the Sabbath

¹²The LORD then gave these instructions to Moses: ¹³"Tell the people of Israel: 'Be careful to keep my Sabbath day, for the Sabbath is a sign of the covenant between me and you from generation to generation. It is given so you may know that I am the LORD, who makes you holy. ¹⁴You must keep the Sabbath day, for it is a holy day for you. Anyone who desecrates it must be put to death; anyone who works on that day will be cut off from the community. ¹⁵You have six days each week for your ordinary work, but the seventh day must be a Sabbath day of complete rest, a holy day dedicated to the LORD. Anyone who works on the Sabbath must be put to death. ¹⁶The people of Israel must keep the Sabbath day by observing it from generation to generation. This is a covenant obligation for all time. ¹⁷It is a permanent sign of my covenant with the people of Israel. For in six days the LORD made heaven and earth, but on the seventh day he stopped working and was refreshed.'"

¹⁸When the LORD finished speaking with Moses on Mount Sinai, he gave him the two stone tablets inscribed with the terms of the covenant,* written by the finger of God.

32 The Gold Calf

When the people saw how long it was taking Moses to come back down the mountain, they gathered around Aaron. "Come on," they said, "make us some gods who can lead us. We don't know what happened to this fellow Moses, who brought us here from the land of Egypt."

30:36 Hebrew *in front of the Testimony*; see note on 25:16.   31:7a Hebrew *the Tent of Meeting*.   31:7b Hebrew *the Ark of the Testimony*.
31:18 Hebrew *the two tablets of the Testimony*; see note on 25:16.

Rooting Out Idol Worship

EXODUS 32:1-8

It's easy for us to look at the Israelites and their fall into idol worship with a mixture of disdain and incredulity. How could they bow before a golden calf when God had pushed walls of water aside for them, showered them with daily food, led them with a cloud by day and a fire by night?

Idolatry is one of the most frequently discussed problems in the Bible. God clearly forbade idolatry in the Ten Commandments (Exodus 20:3-5). Jesus also indirectly addressed this issue when he taught, "You must love the LORD your God with all your heart, all your soul, and all your mind" (Matthew 22:37). In other words, don't love anything or anyone else best of all.

Though we may shrink in horror from the notion of literal idols of wood or stone, or cluck our tongues disapprovingly over obvious modern-day idolatries, we too fall into idol worship when something—*anything*—other than God becomes the focus of our hearts. Paul calls this covetousness or greed, and he warned, "You can be sure that no . . . greedy person will inherit the Kingdom of Christ and of God. For a greedy person is an idolater, worshiping the things of this world" (Ephesians 5:5).

This type of idolatry begins when the seed of dissatisfaction plants itself within our hearts. We feel unhappy about something in our lives, we covet something "better," and our hearts become divided as our internal focus shifts from God to something else. Recognizing our own inner drives and longings that lead us into idolatry can help immeasurably as we seek to root out idol worship from our lives. As we face these inner desires in honesty before God, we can pray like David, "Grant me purity of heart, so that I may honor you" (Psalm 86:11) and ask God to help us live in wholehearted devotion to him alone.

—*Lauretta Patterson*

For more on worship, see reading at Judges 5.

²So Aaron said, "Take the gold rings from the ears of your wives and sons and daughters, and bring them to me."
³All the people took the gold rings from their ears and brought them to Aaron. ⁴Then Aaron took the gold, melted it down, and molded it into the shape of a calf. When the people saw it, they exclaimed, "O Israel, these are the gods who brought you out of the land of Egypt!"
⁵Aaron saw how excited the people were, so he built an altar in front of the calf. Then he announced, "Tomorrow will be a festival to the LORD!"
⁶The people got up early the next morning to sacrifice burnt offerings and peace offerings. After this, they celebrated with feasting and drinking, and they indulged in pagan revelry.

⁷The LORD told Moses, "Quick! Go down the mountain! Your people whom you brought from the land of Egypt have corrupted themselves. ⁸How quickly they have turned away from the way I commanded them to live! They have melted down gold and made a calf, and they have bowed down and sacrificed to it. They are saying, 'These are your gods, O Israel, who brought you out of the land of Egypt.'"

⁹Then the LORD said, "I have seen how stubborn and rebellious these people are. ¹⁰Now leave me alone so my fierce anger

can blaze against them, and I will destroy them. Then I will make you, Moses, into a great nation."

[11] But Moses tried to pacify the LORD his God. "O LORD!" he said. "Why are you so angry with your own people whom you brought from the land of Egypt with such great power and such a strong hand? [12] Why let the Egyptians say, 'Their God rescued them with the evil intention of slaughtering them in the mountains and wiping them from the face of the earth'? Turn away from your fierce anger. Change your mind about this terrible disaster you have threatened against your people! [13] Remember your servants Abraham, Isaac, and Jacob.* You bound yourself with an oath to them, saying, 'I will make your descendants as numerous as the stars of heaven. And I will give them all of this land that I have promised to your descendants, and they will possess it forever.'"

[14] So the LORD changed his mind about the terrible disaster he had threatened to bring on his people.

[15] Then Moses turned and went down the mountain. He held in his hands the two stone tablets inscribed with the terms of the covenant.* They were inscribed on both sides, front and back. [16] These tablets were God's work; the words on them were written by God himself.

[17] When Joshua heard the boisterous noise of the people shouting below them, he exclaimed to Moses, "It sounds like war in the camp!"

[18] But Moses replied, "No, it's not a shout of victory nor the wailing of defeat. I hear the sound of a celebration."

[19] When they came near the camp, Moses saw the calf and the dancing, and he burned with anger. He threw the stone tablets to the ground, smashing them at the foot of the mountain. [20] He took the calf they had made and burned it. Then he ground it into powder, threw it into the water, and forced the people to drink it.

[21] Finally, he turned to Aaron and demanded, "What did these people do to you to make you bring such terrible sin upon them?"

[22] "Don't get so upset, my lord," Aaron replied. "You yourself know how evil these people are. [23] They said to me, 'Make us gods who will lead us. We don't know what happened to this fellow Moses, who brought us here from the land of Egypt.' [24] So I told them, 'Whoever has gold jewelry, take it off.' When they brought it to me, I simply threw it into the fire—and out came this calf!"

[25] Moses saw that Aaron had let the people get completely out of control, much to the amusement of their enemies.* [26] So he stood at the entrance to the camp and shouted, "All of you who are on the LORD's side, come here and join me." And all the Levites gathered around him.

[27] Moses told them, "This is what the LORD, the God of Israel, says: Each of you, take your swords and go back and forth from one end of the camp to the other. Kill everyone—even your brothers, friends, and neighbors." [28] The Levites obeyed Moses' command, and about 3,000 people died that day.

[29] Then Moses told the Levites, "Today you have ordained yourselves* for the service of the LORD, for you obeyed him even though it meant killing your own sons and brothers. Today you have earned a blessing."

Moses Intercedes for Israel

[30] The next day Moses said to the people, "You have committed a terrible sin, but I will go back up to the LORD on the mountain. Perhaps I will be able to obtain forgiveness* for your sin."

[31] So Moses returned to the LORD and said, "Oh, what a terrible sin these people have committed. They have made gods of gold for themselves. [32] But now, if you will only forgive their sin—but if not, erase my name from the record you have written!"

[33] But the LORD replied to Moses, "No, I will erase the name of everyone who has sinned against me. [34] Now go, lead the people to the place I told you about. Look! My

---

32:13 Hebrew *Israel*. The names "Jacob" and "Israel" are often interchanged throughout the Old Testament, referring sometimes to the individual patriarch and sometimes to the nation. 32:15 Hebrew *the two tablets of the Testimony*; see note on 25:16. 32:25 Or *out of control, and they mocked anyone who opposed them*. The meaning of the Hebrew is unclear. 32:29 As in Greek and Latin versions; Hebrew reads *Today ordain yourselves*. 32:30 Or *to make atonement*.

angel will lead the way before you. And when I come to call the people to account, I will certainly hold them responsible for their sins."

³⁵Then the LORD sent a great plague upon the people because they had worshiped the calf Aaron had made.

33

The LORD said to Moses, "Get going, you and the people you brought up from the land of Egypt. Go up to the land I swore to give to Abraham, Isaac, and Jacob. I told them, 'I will give this land to your descendants.' ²And I will send an angel before you to drive out the Canaanites, Amorites, Hittites, Perizzites, Hivites, and Jebusites. ³Go up to this land that flows with milk and honey. But I will not travel among you, for you are a stubborn and rebellious people. If I did, I would surely destroy you along the way."

⁴When the people heard these stern words, they went into mourning and stopped wearing their jewelry and fine clothes. ⁵For the LORD had told Moses to tell them, "You are a stubborn and rebellious people. If I were to travel with you for even a moment, I would destroy you. Remove your jewelry and fine clothes while I decide what to do with you." ⁶So from the time they left Mount Sinai,* the Israelites wore no more jewelry or fine clothes.

⁷It was Moses' practice to take the Tent of Meeting* and set it up some distance from the camp. Everyone who wanted to make a request of the LORD would go to the Tent of Meeting outside the camp.

⁸Whenever Moses went out to the Tent of Meeting, all the people would get up and stand in the entrances of their own tents. They would all watch Moses until he disappeared inside. ⁹As he went into the tent, the pillar of cloud would come down and hover at its entrance while the LORD spoke with Moses. ¹⁰When the people saw the cloud standing at the entrance of the tent, they would stand and bow down in front of their own tents. ¹¹Inside the Tent of Meeting, the LORD would speak to Moses face to face, as one speaks to a friend. Afterward Moses would return to the camp, but the young man who assisted him, Joshua son of Nun, would remain behind in the Tent of Meeting.

Moses Sees the LORD's Glory

¹²One day Moses said to the LORD, "You have been telling me, 'Take these people up to the Promised Land.' But you haven't told me whom you will send with me. You have told me, 'I know you by name, and I look favorably on you.' ¹³If it is true that you look favorably on me, let me know your ways so I may understand you more fully and continue to enjoy your favor. And remember that this nation is your very own people."

¹⁴The LORD replied, "I will personally go with you, Moses, and I will give you rest—everything will be fine for you."

¹⁵Then Moses said, "If you don't personally go with us, don't make us leave this place. ¹⁶How will anyone know that you look favorably on me—on me and on your people—if you don't go with us? For your presence among us sets your people and me apart from all other people on the earth."

¹⁷The LORD replied to Moses, "I will indeed do what you have asked, for I look favorably on you, and I know you by name."

¹⁸Moses responded, "Then show me your glorious presence."

¹⁹The LORD replied, "I will make all my goodness pass before you, and I will call out my name, Yahweh,* before you. For I will show mercy to anyone I choose, and I will show compassion to anyone I choose. ²⁰But you may not look directly at my face, for no one may see me and live." ²¹The LORD continued, "Look, stand near me on this rock. ²²As my glorious presence passes by, I will hide you in the crevice of the rock and cover you with my hand until I have passed by. ²³Then I will remove my hand and let you see me from behind. But my face will not be seen."

34

A New Copy of the Covenant

Then the LORD told Moses, "Chisel out two stone tablets like the first ones. I will write on them the same words that

---

33:6 Hebrew *Horeb,* another name for Sinai.   **33:7** This "Tent of Meeting" is different from the Tabernacle described in chapters 26 and 36.   **33:19** *Yahweh* is a transliteration of the proper name *YHWH* that is sometimes rendered "Jehovah"; in this translation it is usually rendered "the LORD" (note the use of small capitals).

Sabbath & Rest

God Knows What We Need

EXODUS 33:12-14

Moses came to God with a problem. He'd led God's people out of Egypt; he'd received the Ten Commandments; he'd found God's people worshiping a golden calf and had sought God's forgiveness for their sins. And now another task lay before him: he was to lead God's people on the trek to the Promised Land.

He asked God for help. How would he do it? Who would help him?

God responded to Moses by answering a question Moses didn't even ask, by identifying a need Moses didn't voice. "I will personally go with you, Moses, and *I will give you rest*" (Exodus 33:14, italics added).

God's presence, God's rest—ultimately we all, like Moses, desperately need them.

God created us with a need for rest. God called rest *holy* (Genesis 2:3), and he crafted daily (sundown) and weekly (Sabbath) rhythms for his people that involved rest.

I don't know much about you, but I can guess that you—like Moses—need rest.

Yet in our busy world, we regard taking it easy as something only for the wealthy and the lazy. The rest of us have work, families, young children, sick relatives, churches, hobbies, and vacation time we're storing up. We do not have time to rest.

Most of us believe rest is for the weary and faint, the overwhelmed, the sick or depressed. We rest because we're forced into it, not because we're invited.

Or perhaps we turn down God's invitation to rest because we're not sure what true rest would look like. How do you rest in the clutter of home? Isn't true rest like good sex, something you have to go on vacation to find?

No.

The reason most of us don't rest is because we're not convinced rest is as spiritual as God made it out to be.

It's easier to pray, fast, or give to the poor than to rest. I can point to that time as productive, focused, self-disciplined. It's easier to attend church, take a missionary trip, even to love my enemy than it is to rest.

Like Moses, we may not realize how deeply we *need* rest. We may not recognize that rest—pure, physical rest and emotional refreshment—is connected to the health of our souls.

So what might true rest look like for you? Ask yourself, "What feels like work to me?"

Then make a list. Here's what mine includes:

- writing
- responding to e-mails
- designing a PowerPoint presentation
- laundry
- dusting
- cleaning toilets
- washing dishes
- *any* cleaning
- going online
- shopping

Then comes the fun question: what would I do if all my work was done? Of course this requires a stretch of the imagination, but visualize that all the items on the first list were completed. An empty inbox, a paper turned in, a sparkling toilet, a clear counter, stocked shelves.

Now what?

A nap!

Okay, take it.

When you wake up, fight the urge to feel guilty, and ask yourself *again*, "What would I do if all my work was done?"

My answers:

- take a walk
- spontaneously play with my son, even if it means crawling around the house and getting dog hair all over my knees
- take a long, hot bath
- sit on the porch in the rocking chair
- read poetry over lunch
- slowly, carefully make macaroni and cheese
- sketch
- pray
- read Scripture slowly, maybe just two verses

Most of the time, rest doesn't come handed to us on a platter. We have to choose it. And choosing rest means consciously overlooking the things that working women everywhere feel obliged to fix or guilty about not fixing: crumb-covered floors, piles of snow, foody dishes, overflowing inboxes, ringing phones.

Rest means listening to God's promise to Moses and letting it speak to our souls: *I will be with you. I will give you rest.*

Will we live a life that chooses to receive and enjoy this gift from God?

Take a nap. Be refreshed. Enjoy God's presence with you as you rest.

—*Jonalyn Fincher*

For more on Sabbath and rest, see reading at Deuteronomy 5:12–15.

were on the tablets you smashed. ²Be ready in the morning to climb up Mount Sinai and present yourself to me on the top of the mountain. ³No one else may come with you. In fact, no one is to appear anywhere on the mountain. Do not even let the flocks or herds graze near the mountain."

⁴So Moses chiseled out two tablets of stone like the first ones. Early in the morning he climbed Mount Sinai as the LORD had commanded him, and he carried the two stone tablets in his hands.

⁵Then the LORD came down in a cloud and stood there with him; and he called out his own name, Yahweh.* ⁶The LORD passed in front of Moses, calling out,

"Yahweh!* The LORD!
The God of compassion and mercy!
I am slow to anger
and filled with unfailing love and
faithfulness.
⁷ I lavish unfailing love to a thousand
generations.*
I forgive iniquity, rebellion, and sin.
But I do not excuse the guilty.
I lay the sins of the parents upon their
children and grandchildren;
the entire family is affected—
even children in the third and fourth
generations."

⁸Moses immediately threw himself to the ground and worshiped. ⁹And he said, "O Lord, if it is true that I have found favor with you, then please travel with us. Yes, this is a stubborn and rebellious people, but please forgive our iniquity and our sins. Claim us as your own special possession."

¹⁰The LORD replied, "Listen, I am making a covenant with you in the presence of all your people. I will perform miracles that have never been performed anywhere in all the earth or in any nation. And all the people around you will see the power of the LORD—the awesome power I will display for you. ¹¹But listen carefully to everything I command you today. Then I will go ahead of you and drive out the Amorites, Canaanites, Hittites, Perizzites, Hivites, and Jebusites.

¹²"Be very careful never to make a treaty with the people who live in the land where you are going. If you do, you will follow their evil ways and be trapped. ¹³Instead, you must break down their pagan altars, smash their sacred pillars, and cut down their Asherah poles. ¹⁴You must worship no other gods, for the LORD, whose very name is Jealous, is a God who is jealous about his relationship with you.

¹⁵"You must not make a treaty of any kind with the people living in the land. They lust after their gods, offering sacrifices to them. They will invite you to join them in their sacrificial meals, and you will go with them. ¹⁶Then you will accept their daughters, who sacrifice to other gods, as wives for your sons. And they will seduce your sons to commit adultery against me by worshiping other gods. ¹⁷You must not make any gods of molten metal for yourselves.

¹⁸"You must celebrate the Festival of Unleavened Bread. For seven days the bread you eat must be made without yeast, just as I commanded you. Celebrate this festival annually at the appointed time in early spring, in the month of Abib,* for that is the anniversary of your departure from Egypt.

¹⁹"The firstborn of every animal belongs to me, including the firstborn males from your herds of cattle and your flocks of sheep and goats. ²⁰A firstborn donkey may be bought back from the LORD by presenting a lamb or young goat in its place. But if you do not buy it back, you must break its neck. However, you must buy back every firstborn son.

"No one may appear before me without an offering.

²¹"You have six days each week for your ordinary work, but on the seventh day you must stop working, even during the seasons of plowing and harvest.

²²"You must celebrate the Festival of Harvest* with the first crop of the wheat harvest, and celebrate the Festival of the Final Harvest* at the end of the harvest season.

34:5 Yahweh is a transliteration of the proper name YHWH that is sometimes rendered "Jehovah"; in this translation it is usually rendered "the LORD" (note the use of small capitals). **34:6** See note on 34:5. **34:7** Hebrew for thousands. **34:18** Hebrew appointed time in the month of Abib. This first month of the ancient Hebrew lunar calendar usually occurs within the months of March and April. **34:22a** Hebrew Festival of Weeks; compare 23:16. This was later called the Festival of Pentecost. It is celebrated today as Shavuot (or Shabuoth). **34:22b** Or Festival of Ingathering. This was later called the Festival of Shelters or Festival of Tabernacles (see Lev 23:33-36). It is celebrated today as Sukkot (or Succoth).

23 Three times each year every man in Israel must appear before the Sovereign, the LORD, the God of Israel. 24 I will drive out the other nations ahead of you and expand your territory, so no one will covet and conquer your land while you appear before the LORD your God three times each year.

25 "You must not offer the blood of my sacrificial offerings together with any baked goods containing yeast. And none of the meat of the Passover sacrifice may be kept over until the next morning.

26 "As you harvest your crops, bring the very best of the first harvest to the house of the LORD your God.

"You must not cook a young goat in its mother's milk."

27 Then the LORD said to Moses, "Write down all these instructions, for they represent the terms of the covenant I am making with you and with Israel."

28 Moses remained there on the mountain with the LORD forty days and forty nights. In all that time he ate no bread and drank no water. And the LORD* wrote the terms of the covenant—the Ten Commandments*—on the stone tablets.

29 When Moses came down Mount Sinai carrying the two stone tablets inscribed with the terms of the covenant,* he wasn't aware that his face had become radiant because he had spoken to the LORD. 30 So when Aaron and the people of Israel saw the radiance of Moses' face, they were afraid to come near him.

31 But Moses called out to them and asked Aaron and all the leaders of the community to come over, and he talked with them. 32 Then all the people of Israel approached him, and Moses gave them all the instructions the LORD had given him on Mount Sinai. 33 When Moses finished speaking with them, he covered his face with a veil. 34 But whenever he went into the Tent of Meeting to speak with the LORD, he would remove the veil until he came out again. Then he would give the people whatever instructions the LORD had given him, 35 and the people of Israel would see the radiant glow of his face. So he would put the veil over his face until he returned to speak with the LORD.

35 Instructions for the Sabbath

Then Moses called together the whole community of Israel and told them, "These are the instructions the LORD has commanded you to follow. 2 You have six days each week for your ordinary work, but the seventh day must be a Sabbath day of complete rest, a holy day dedicated to the LORD. Anyone who works on that day must be put to death. 3 You must not even light a fire in any of your homes on the Sabbath."

Offerings for the Tabernacle

4 Then Moses said to the whole community of Israel, "This is what the LORD has commanded: 5 Take a sacred offering for the LORD. Let those with generous hearts present the following gifts to the LORD:

gold, silver, and bronze;
6 blue, purple, and scarlet thread;
fine linen and goat hair for cloth;
7 tanned ram skins and fine goatskin leather;
acacia wood;
8 olive oil for the lamps;
spices for the anointing oil and the fragrant incense;
9 onyx stones, and other gemstones to be set in the ephod and the priest's chestpiece.

10 "Come, all of you who are gifted craftsmen. Construct everything that the LORD has commanded:

11 the Tabernacle and its sacred tent, its covering, clasps, frames, crossbars, posts, and bases;
12 the Ark and its carrying poles;
the Ark's cover—the place of atonement;
the inner curtain to shield the Ark;
13 the table, its carrying poles, and all its utensils;
the Bread of the Presence;
14 for light, the lampstand, its accessories, the lamp cups, and the olive oil for lighting;
15 the incense altar and its carrying poles;
the anointing oil and fragrant incense;
the curtain for the entrance of the Tabernacle;

34:28a Hebrew he.　34:28b Hebrew the ten words.　34:29 Hebrew the two tablets of the Testimony; see note on 25:16.

16 the altar of burnt offering;
the bronze grating of the altar and its
carrying poles and utensils;
the washbasin with its stand;
17 the curtains for the walls of the
courtyard;
the posts and their bases;
the curtain for the entrance to the
courtyard;
18 the tent pegs of the Tabernacle and
courtyard and their ropes;
19 the beautifully stitched garments for the
priests to wear while ministering in
the Holy Place—the sacred garments
for Aaron the priest, and the garments
for his sons to wear as they minister as
priests."

20 So the whole community of Israel left Moses and returned to their tents. 21 All whose hearts were stirred and whose spirits were moved came and brought their sacred offerings to the LORD. They brought all the materials needed for the Tabernacle,* for the performance of its rituals, and for the sacred garments. 22 Both men and women came, all whose hearts were willing. They brought to the LORD their offerings of gold—brooches, earrings, rings from their fingers, and necklaces. They presented gold objects of every kind as a special offering to the LORD. 23 All those who owned the following items willingly brought them: blue, purple, and scarlet thread; fine linen and goat hair for cloth; and tanned ram skins and fine goatskin leather. 24 And all who had silver and bronze objects gave them as a sacred offering to the LORD. And those who had acacia wood brought it for use in the project.

25 All the women who were skilled in sewing and spinning prepared blue, purple, and scarlet thread, and fine linen cloth. 26 All the women who were willing used their skills to spin the goat hair into yarn. 27 The leaders brought onyx stones and the special gemstones to be set in the ephod and the priest's chestpiece. 28 They also brought spices and olive oil for the light, the anointing oil, and the fragrant incense. 29 So the people of Israel—every man and woman who was eager to help in the work the LORD had given them through Moses—

brought their gifts and gave them freely to the LORD.

30 Then Moses told the people of Israel, "The LORD has specifically chosen Bezalel son of Uri, grandson of Hur, of the tribe of Judah. 31 The LORD has filled Bezalel with the Spirit of God, giving him great wisdom, ability, and expertise in all kinds of crafts. 32 He is a master craftsman, expert in working with gold, silver, and bronze. 33 He is skilled in engraving and mounting gemstones and in carving wood. He is a master at every craft. 34 And the LORD has given both him and Oholiab son of Ahisamach, of the tribe of Dan, the ability to teach their skills to others. 35 The LORD has given them special skills as engravers, designers, embroiderers in blue, purple, and scarlet thread on fine linen cloth, and weavers. They excel as craftsmen and as designers.

36 "The LORD has gifted Bezalel, Oholiab, and the other skilled craftsmen with wisdom and ability to perform any task involved in building the sanctuary. Let them construct and furnish the Tabernacle, just as the LORD has commanded."

2 So Moses summoned Bezalel and Oholiab and all the others who were specially gifted by the LORD and were eager to get to work. 3 Moses gave them the materials donated by the people of Israel as sacred offerings for the completion of the sanctuary. But the people continued to bring additional gifts each morning. 4 Finally the craftsmen who were working on the sanctuary left their work. 5 They went to Moses and reported, "The people have given more than enough materials to complete the job the LORD has commanded us to do!"

6 So Moses gave the command, and this message was sent throughout the camp: "Men and women, don't prepare any more gifts for the sanctuary. We have enough!" So the people stopped bringing their sacred offerings. 7 Their contributions were more than enough to complete the whole project.

Building the Tabernacle

8 The skilled craftsmen made ten curtains of finely woven linen for the Tabernacle. Then Bezalel* decorated the curtains with blue,

purple, and scarlet thread and with skillfully embroidered cherubim. ⁹All ten curtains were exactly the same size—42 feet long and 6 feet wide.* ¹⁰Five of these curtains were joined together to make one long curtain, and the other five were joined to make a second long curtain. ¹¹He made fifty loops of blue yarn and put them along the edge of the last curtain in each set. ¹²The fifty loops along the edge of one curtain matched the fifty loops along the edge of the other curtain. ¹³Then he made fifty gold clasps and fastened the long curtains together with the clasps. In this way, the Tabernacle was made of one continuous piece.

¹⁴He made eleven curtains of goat-hair cloth to serve as a tent covering for the Tabernacle. ¹⁵These eleven curtains were all exactly the same size—45 feet long and 6 feet wide.* ¹⁶Bezalel joined five of these curtains together to make one long curtain, and the other six were joined to make a second long curtain. ¹⁷He made fifty loops for the edge of each large curtain. ¹⁸He also made fifty bronze clasps to fasten the long curtains together. In this way, the tent covering was made of one continuous piece. ¹⁹He completed the tent covering with a layer of tanned ram skins and a layer of fine goatskin leather.

²⁰For the framework of the Tabernacle, Bezalel constructed frames of acacia wood. ²¹Each frame was 15 feet high and 27 inches wide,* ²²with two pegs under each frame. All the frames were identical. ²³He made twenty of these frames to support the curtains on the south side of the Tabernacle. ²⁴He also made forty silver bases—two bases under each frame, with the pegs fitting securely into the bases. ²⁵For the north side of the Tabernacle, he made another twenty frames, ²⁶with their forty silver bases, two bases under each frame. ²⁷He made six frames for the rear—the west side of the Tabernacle—²⁸along with two additional frames to reinforce the rear corners of the Tabernacle. ²⁹These corner frames were matched at the bottom and firmly attached at the top with a single ring, forming a single corner unit. Both of these cor-

ner units were made the same way. ³⁰So there were eight frames at the rear of the Tabernacle, set in sixteen silver bases—two bases under each frame.

³¹Then he made crossbars of acacia wood to link the frames, five crossbars for the north side of the Tabernacle ³²and five for the south side. He also made five crossbars for the rear of the Tabernacle, which faced west. ³³He made the middle crossbar to attach halfway up the frames; it ran all the way from one end of the Tabernacle to the other. ³⁴He overlaid the frames with gold and made gold rings to hold the crossbars. Then he overlaid the crossbars with gold as well.

³⁵For the inside of the Tabernacle, Bezalel made a special curtain of finely woven linen. He decorated it with blue, purple, and scarlet thread and with skillfully embroidered cherubim. ³⁶For the curtain, he made four posts of acacia wood and four gold hooks. He overlaid the posts with gold and set them in four silver bases.

³⁷Then he made another curtain for the entrance to the sacred tent. He made it of finely woven linen and embroidered it with exquisite designs using blue, purple, and scarlet thread. ³⁸This curtain was hung on gold hooks attached to five posts. The posts with their decorated tops and hooks were overlaid with gold, and the five bases were cast from bronze.

37 Building the Ark of the Covenant

Next Bezalel made the Ark of acacia wood—a sacred chest 45 inches long, 27 inches wide, and 27 inches high.* ²He overlaid it inside and outside with pure gold, and he ran a molding of gold all around it. ³He cast four gold rings and attached them to its four feet, two rings on each side. ⁴Then he made poles from acacia wood and overlaid them with gold. ⁵He inserted the poles into the rings at the sides of the Ark to carry it.

⁶Then he made the Ark's cover—the place of atonement—from pure gold. It was 45 inches long and 27 inches wide.* ⁷He made two cherubim from hammered gold and placed them on the two ends of

---

36:9 Hebrew 28 cubits [12.9 meters] long and 4 cubits [1.8 meters] wide.   36:15 Hebrew 30 cubits [13.8 meters] long and 4 cubits [1.8 meters] wide.   36:21 Hebrew 10 cubits [4.6 meters] high and 1.5 cubits [69 centimeters] wide.   37:1 Hebrew 2.5 cubits [115 centimeters] long, 1.5 cubits [69 centimeters] wide, and 1.5 cubits high.   37:6 Hebrew 2.5 cubits [115 centimeters] long and 1.5 cubits [69 centimeters] wide.

the atonement cover. ⁸He molded the cherubim on each end of the atonement cover, making it all of one piece of gold. ⁹The cherubim faced each other and looked down on the atonement cover. With their wings spread above it, they protected it.

Building the Table

¹⁰Then Bezalel* made the table of acacia wood, 36 inches long, 18 inches wide, and 27 inches high.* ¹¹He overlaid it with pure gold and ran a gold molding around the edge. ¹²He decorated it with a 3-inch border* all around, and he ran a gold molding along the border. ¹³Then he cast four gold rings for the table and attached them at the four corners next to the four legs. ¹⁴The rings were attached near the border to hold the poles that were used to carry the table. ¹⁵He made these poles from acacia wood and overlaid them with gold. ¹⁶Then he made special containers of pure gold for the table—bowls, pans, jars, and pitchers—to be used in pouring out liquid offerings.

Building the Lampstand

¹⁷Then Bezalel made the lampstand of pure, hammered gold. He made the entire lampstand and its decorations of one piece—the base, center stem, lamp cups, buds, and petals. ¹⁸The lampstand had six branches going out from the center stem, three on each side. ¹⁹Each of the six branches had three lamp cups shaped like almond blossoms, complete with buds and petals. ²⁰The center stem of the lampstand was crafted with four lamp cups shaped like almond blossoms, complete with buds and petals. ²¹There was an almond bud beneath each pair of branches where the six branches extended from the center stem, all made of one piece. ²²The almond buds and branches were all of one piece with the center stem, and they were hammered from pure gold.

²³He also made seven lamps for the lampstand, lamp snuffers, and trays, all of pure gold. ²⁴The entire lampstand, along with its accessories, was made from seventy-five pounds* of pure gold.

Building the Incense Altar

²⁵Then Bezalel made the incense altar of acacia wood. It was 18 inches square and 36 inches high,* with horns at the corners carved from the same piece of wood as the altar itself. ²⁶He overlaid the top, sides, and horns of the altar with pure gold, and he ran a gold molding around the entire altar. ²⁷He made two gold rings and attached them on opposite sides of the altar below the gold molding to hold the carrying poles. ²⁸He made the poles of acacia wood and overlaid them with gold.

²⁹Then he made the sacred anointing oil and the fragrant incense, using the techniques of a skilled incense maker.

38 Building the Altar of Burnt Offering

Next Bezalel* used acacia wood to construct the square altar of burnt offering. It was 7½ feet wide, 7½ feet long, and 4½ feet high.* ²He made horns for each of its four corners so that the horns and altar were all one piece. He overlaid the altar with bronze. ³Then he made all the altar utensils of bronze—the ash buckets, shovels, basins, meat forks, and firepans. ⁴Next he made a bronze grating and installed it halfway down the side of the altar, under the ledge. ⁵He cast four rings and attached them to the corners of the bronze grating to hold the carrying poles. ⁶He made the poles from acacia wood and overlaid them with bronze. ⁷He inserted the poles through the rings on the sides of the altar. The altar was hollow and was made from planks.

Building the Washbasin

⁸Bezalel made the bronze washbasin and its bronze stand from bronze mirrors donated by the women who served at the entrance of the Tabernacle.*

Building the Courtyard

⁹Then Bezalel made the courtyard, which was enclosed with curtains made of finely woven linen. On the south side the curtains were 150 feet long.* ¹⁰They were held up by twenty posts set securely in twenty bronze

---

37:10a Hebrew *he;* also in 37:17, 25.   **37:10b** Hebrew *2 cubits* [92 centimeters] *long, 1 cubit* [46 centimeters] *wide, and 1.5 cubits* [69 centimeters] *high.*   **37:12** Hebrew *a border of a handbreadth* [8 centimeters].   **37:24** Hebrew *1 talent* [34 kilograms].
37:25 Hebrew *1 cubit* [46 centimeters] *long and 1 cubit wide, a square, and 2 cubits* [92 centimeters] *high.*   **38:1a** Hebrew *he;* also in 38:8, 9.
38:1b Hebrew *5 cubits* [2.3 meters] *wide, 5 cubits long, a square, and 3 cubits* [1.4 meters] *high.*   **38:8** Hebrew *Tent of Meeting;* also in 38:30.
38:9 Hebrew *100 cubits* [46 meters]; also in 38:11.

bases. He hung the curtains with silver hooks and rings. ¹¹He made a similar set of curtains for the north side—150 feet of curtains held up by twenty posts set securely in bronze bases. He hung the curtains with silver hooks and rings. ¹²The curtains on the west end of the courtyard were 75 feet long,* hung with silver hooks and rings and supported by ten posts set into ten bases. ¹³The east end, the front, was also 75 feet long.

¹⁴The courtyard entrance was on the east end, flanked by two curtains. The curtain on the right side was 22½ feet long* and was supported by three posts set into three bases. ¹⁵The curtain on the left side was also 22½ feet long and was supported by three posts set into three bases. ¹⁶All the curtains used in the courtyard were made of finely woven linen. ¹⁷Each post had a bronze base, and all the hooks and rings were silver. The tops of the posts of the courtyard were overlaid with silver, and the rings to hold up the curtains were made of silver.

¹⁸He made the curtain for the entrance to the courtyard of finely woven linen, and he decorated it with beautiful embroidery in blue, purple, and scarlet thread. It was 30 feet long, and its height was 7½ feet,* just like the curtains of the courtyard walls. ¹⁹It was supported by four posts, each set securely in its own bronze base. The tops of the posts were overlaid with silver, and the hooks and rings were also made of silver. ²⁰All the tent pegs used in the Tabernacle and courtyard were made of bronze.

Inventory of Materials

²¹This is an inventory of the materials used in building the Tabernacle of the Covenant.* The Levites compiled the figures, as Moses directed, and Ithamar son of Aaron the priest served as recorder. ²²Bezalel son of Uri, grandson of Hur, of the tribe of Judah, made everything just as the LORD had commanded Moses. ²³He was assisted by Oholiab son of Ahisamach, of the tribe of Dan, a craftsman expert at engraving, designing, and embroidering with blue, purple, and scarlet thread on fine linen cloth.

²⁴The people brought special offerings of gold totaling 2,193 pounds,* as measured by the weight of the sanctuary shekel. This gold was used throughout the Tabernacle.

²⁵The whole community of Israel gave 7,545 pounds* of silver, as measured by the weight of the sanctuary shekel. ²⁶This silver came from the tax collected from each man registered in the census. (The tax is one beka, which is half a shekel,* based on the sanctuary shekel.) The tax was collected from 603,550 men who had reached their twentieth birthday. ²⁷The hundred bases for the frames of the sanctuary walls and for the posts supporting the inner curtain required 7,500 pounds of silver, about 75 pounds for each base.* ²⁸The remaining 45 pounds* of silver was used to make the hooks and rings and to overlay the tops of the posts.

²⁹The people also brought as special offerings 5,310 pounds* of bronze, ³⁰which was used for casting the bases for the posts at the entrance to the Tabernacle, and for the bronze altar with its bronze grating and all the altar utensils. ³¹Bronze was also used to make the bases for the posts that supported the curtains around the courtyard, the bases for the curtain at the entrance of the courtyard, and all the tent pegs for the Tabernacle and the courtyard.

39 Clothing for the Priests

The craftsmen made beautiful sacred garments of blue, purple, and scarlet cloth—clothing for Aaron to wear while ministering in the Holy Place, just as the LORD had commanded Moses.

Making the Ephod

²Bezalel* made the ephod of finely woven linen and embroidered it with gold and with blue, purple, and scarlet thread. ³He made gold thread by hammering out thin sheets of gold and cutting it into fine strands. With great skill and care, he worked it into the

---

38:12 Hebrew 50 cubits [23 meters]; also in 38:13.   38:14 Hebrew 15 cubits [6.9 meters]; also in 38:15.   38:18 Hebrew 20 cubits [9.2 meters] long and 5 cubits [2.3 meters] high.   38:21 Hebrew the Tabernacle, the Tabernacle of the Testimony.   38:24 Hebrew 29 talents and 730 shekels [994 kilograms]. Each shekel weighed about 0.4 ounces.   38:25 Hebrew 100 talents and 1,775 shekels [3,420 kilograms].   38:26 Or 0.2 ounces, or 6 grams.   38:27 Hebrew 100 talents [3,400 kilograms] of silver, 1 talent [34 kilograms] for each base.   38:28 Hebrew 1,775 shekels [20.2 kilograms].   38:29 Hebrew 70 talents and 2,400 shekels [2,407 kilograms].   39:2 Hebrew He; also in 39:8, 22.

fine linen with the blue, purple, and scarlet thread.

[4] The ephod consisted of two pieces, front and back, joined at the shoulders with two shoulder-pieces. [5] The decorative sash was made of the same materials: finely woven linen embroidered with gold and with blue, purple, and scarlet thread, just as the LORD had commanded Moses. [6] They mounted the two onyx stones in settings of gold filigree. The stones were engraved with the names of the tribes of Israel, just as a seal is engraved. [7] He fastened these stones on the shoulder-pieces of the ephod as a reminder that the priest represents the people of Israel. All this was done just as the LORD had commanded Moses.

Making the Chestpiece

[8] Bezalel made the chestpiece with great skill and care. He made it to match the ephod, using finely woven linen embroidered with gold and with blue, purple, and scarlet thread. [9] He made the chestpiece of a single piece of cloth folded to form a pouch nine inches* square. [10] They mounted four rows of gemstones* on it. The first row contained a red carnelian, a pale-green peridot, and an emerald. [11] The second row contained a turquoise, a blue lapis lazuli, and a white moonstone. [12] The third row contained an orange jacinth, an agate, and a purple amethyst. [13] The fourth row contained a blue-green beryl, an onyx, and a green jasper. All these stones were set in gold filigree. [14] Each stone represented one of the twelve sons of Israel, and the name of that tribe was engraved on it like a seal.

[15] To attach the chestpiece to the ephod, they made braided cords of pure gold thread. [16] They also made two settings of gold filigree and two gold rings and attached them to the top corners of the chestpiece. [17] They tied the two gold cords to the rings on the chestpiece. [18] They tied the other ends of the cords to the gold settings on the shoulder-pieces of the ephod. [19] Then they made two more gold rings and attached them to the inside edges of the chestpiece next to the ephod. [20] Then they made two more gold rings and attached them to the front of the ephod, below the shoulder-pieces, just above the knot where the decorative sash was fastened to the ephod. [21] They attached the bottom rings of the chestpiece to the rings on the ephod with blue cords. In this way, the chestpiece was held securely to the ephod above the decorative sash. All this was done just as the LORD had commanded Moses.

Additional Clothing for the Priests

[22] Bezalel made the robe that is worn with the ephod from a single piece of blue woven cloth, [23] with an opening for Aaron's head in the middle of it. The opening was reinforced with a woven collar* so it would not tear. [24] They made pomegranates of blue, purple, and scarlet yarn, and attached them to the hem of the robe. [25] They also made bells of pure gold and placed them between the pomegranates along the hem of the robe, [26] with bells and pomegranates alternating all around the hem. This robe was to be worn whenever the priest ministered before the LORD, just as the LORD had commanded Moses.

[27] They made tunics for Aaron and his sons from fine linen cloth. [28] The turban and the special head coverings were made of fine linen, and the undergarments were also made of finely woven linen. [29] The sashes were made of finely woven linen and embroidered with blue, purple, and scarlet thread, just as the LORD had commanded Moses.

[30] Finally, they made the sacred medallion—the badge of holiness—of pure gold. They engraved it like a seal with these words: HOLY TO THE LORD. [31] They attached the medallion with a blue cord to Aaron's turban, just as the LORD had commanded Moses.

Moses Inspects the Work

[32] And so at last the Tabernacle* was finished. The Israelites had done everything just as the LORD had commanded Moses. [33] And they brought the entire Tabernacle to Moses:

39:9 Hebrew *1 span* [23 centimeters].   **39:10** The identification of some of these gemstones is uncertain.   **39:23** The meaning of the Hebrew is uncertain.   **39:32** Hebrew *the Tabernacle, the Tent of Meeting;* also in 39:40.

the sacred tent with all its furnishings, clasps, frames, crossbars, posts, and bases;

[34] the tent coverings of tanned ram skins and fine goatskin leather; the inner curtain to shield the Ark;

[35] the Ark of the Covenant* and its carrying poles; the Ark's cover—the place of atonement;

[36] the table and all its utensils; the Bread of the Presence;

[37] the pure gold lampstand with its symmetrical lamp cups, all its accessories, and the olive oil for lighting;

[38] the gold altar; the anointing oil and fragrant incense; the curtain for the entrance of the sacred tent;

[39] the bronze altar; the bronze grating and its carrying poles and utensils; the washbasin with its stand;

[40] the curtains for the walls of the courtyard; the posts and their bases; the curtain for the entrance to the courtyard; the ropes and tent pegs; all the furnishings to be used in worship at the Tabernacle;

[41] the beautifully stitched garments for the priests to wear while ministering in the Holy Place—the sacred garments for Aaron the priest, and the garments for his sons to wear as they minister as priests.

[42] So the people of Israel followed all of the LORD's instructions to Moses. [43] Then Moses inspected all their work. When he found it had been done just as the LORD had commanded him, he blessed them.

40 The Tabernacle Completed

Then the LORD said to Moses, [2] "Set up the Tabernacle* on the first day of the new year.* [3] Place the Ark of the Covenant* inside, and install the inner curtain to enclose the Ark within the Most Holy Place. [4] Then bring in the table, and arrange the utensils on it. And bring in the lampstand, and set up the lamps.

[5] "Place the gold incense altar in front of the Ark of the Covenant. Then hang the curtain at the entrance of the Tabernacle. [6] Place the altar of burnt offering in front of the Tabernacle entrance. [7] Set the washbasin between the Tabernacle* and the altar, and fill it with water. [8] Then set up the courtyard around the outside of the tent, and hang the curtain for the courtyard entrance.

[9] "Take the anointing oil and anoint the Tabernacle and all its furnishings to consecrate them and make them holy. [10] Anoint the altar of burnt offering and its utensils to consecrate them. Then the altar will become absolutely holy. [11] Next anoint the washbasin and its stand to consecrate them.

[12] "Present Aaron and his sons at the entrance of the Tabernacle, and wash them with water. [13] Dress Aaron with the sacred garments and anoint him, consecrating him to serve me as a priest. [14] Then present his sons and dress them in their tunics. [15] Anoint them as you did their father, so they may also serve me as priests. With their anointing, Aaron's descendants are set apart for the priesthood forever, from generation to generation."

[16] Moses proceeded to do everything just as the LORD had commanded him. [17] So the Tabernacle was set up on the first day of the first month of the second year. [18] Moses erected the Tabernacle by setting down its bases, inserting the frames, attaching the crossbars, and setting up the posts. [19] Then he spread the coverings over the Tabernacle framework and put on the protective layers, just as the LORD had commanded him.

[20] He took the stone tablets inscribed with the terms of the covenant and placed them* inside the Ark. Then he attached the carrying poles to the Ark, and he set the Ark's cover—the place of atonement—on top of it. [21] Then he brought the Ark of the Covenant into the Tabernacle and hung the inner curtain to shield it from view, just as the LORD had commanded him.

39:35 Or *Ark of the Testimony.*   **40:2a** Hebrew *the Tabernacle, the Tent of Meeting;* also in 40:6, 29.   **40:2b** Hebrew *the first day of the first month.* This day of the ancient Hebrew lunar calendar occurred in March or April.   **40:3** Or *Ark of the Testimony;* also in 40:5, 21.
40:7 Hebrew *Tent of Meeting;* also in 40:12, 22, 24, 26, 30, 32, 34, 35.   **40:20** Hebrew *He placed the Testimony;* see note on 25:16.

²²Next Moses placed the table in the Tabernacle, along the north side of the Holy Place, just outside the inner curtain. ²³And he arranged the Bread of the Presence on the table before the LORD, just as the LORD had commanded him.

²⁴He set the lampstand in the Tabernacle across from the table on the south side of the Holy Place. ²⁵Then he lit the lamps in the LORD's presence, just as the LORD had commanded him. ²⁶He also placed the gold incense altar in the Tabernacle, in the Holy Place in front of the inner curtain. ²⁷On it he burned the fragrant incense, just as the LORD had commanded him.

²⁸He hung the curtain at the entrance of the Tabernacle, ²⁹and he placed the altar of burnt offering near the Tabernacle entrance. On it he offered a burnt offering and a grain offering, just as the LORD had commanded him.

³⁰Next Moses placed the washbasin between the Tabernacle and the altar. He filled it with water so the priests could wash themselves. ³¹Moses and Aaron and Aaron's sons used water from it to wash their hands and feet. ³²Whenever they approached the altar and entered the Tabernacle, they washed themselves, just as the LORD had commanded Moses.

³³Then he hung the curtains forming the courtyard around the Tabernacle and the altar. And he set up the curtain at the entrance of the courtyard. So at last Moses finished the work.

The LORD's Glory Fills the Tabernacle

³⁴Then the cloud covered the Tabernacle, and the glory of the LORD filled the Tabernacle. ³⁵Moses could no longer enter the Tabernacle because the cloud had settled down over it, and the glory of the LORD filled the Tabernacle.

³⁶Now whenever the cloud lifted from the Tabernacle, the people of Israel would set out on their journey, following it. ³⁷But if the cloud did not rise, they remained where they were until it lifted. ³⁸The cloud of the LORD hovered over the Tabernacle during the day, and at night fire glowed inside the cloud so the whole family of Israel could see it. This continued throughout all their journeys.

Leviticus

Background

Leviticus is a book of laws that show God's people how to live. With the tabernacle as their focal point, these laws emphasize perfection. They stipulate perfect animals for sacrifices, the exclusion of those with skin ailments from worship, priests without physical challenges chosen to serve, and so forth. These laws reflect the perfection of God himself: "You must be holy because I, the LORD your God, am holy" (19:2).

From the Greek, the title *Leviticus* means "of or relating to the Levites"—the tribe from which priests came—and the book centers on tabernacle worship. The title in Hebrew, *Wayyiqra,* refers to the first word in 1:1: "The LORD called."

About fifty-five times in Leviticus, God is described as giving the law to Moses (e.g., 1:1; 4:1; 6:1; 8:1; 11:1; 12:1; 13:1), who is credited as being the author of the book.

Message

For the tribes of Israel, God creates a system of worship that reflects his holiness and reminds the people of their sinfulness. God requires various kinds of sacrificial offerings to atone for sins. These offerings—usually an unblemished animal that is killed—constantly remind the givers of the ultimate consequence of sin (death) and their dependence upon God for forgiveness and life itself.

The Old Testament sacrificial system foreshadows the sacrifice to come—that of the Savior, Jesus. His perfect sacrifice as "the Lamb of God who takes away the sin of the world" (John 1:29) fulfilled all sacrifices.

Time

The events of Leviticus take place over the course of about a month. Like the other books of the Pentateuch, the Book of Leviticus was probably written between 1445 and 1406 B.C., while the people of Israel were camped in the wilderness.

Outline

Leviticus

1 Procedures for the Burnt Offering

The LORD called to Moses from the Tabernacle* and said to him, [2]"Give the following instructions to the people of Israel. When you present an animal as an offering to the LORD, you may take it from your herd of cattle or your flock of sheep and goats.

[3]"If the animal you present as a burnt offering is from the herd, it must be a male with no defects. Bring it to the entrance of the Tabernacle so you* may be accepted by the LORD. [4]Lay your hand on the animal's head, and the LORD will accept its death in your place to purify you, making you right with him.* [5]Then slaughter the young bull in the LORD's presence, and Aaron's sons, the priests, will present the animal's blood by splattering it against all sides of the altar that stands at the entrance to the Tabernacle. [6]Then skin the animal and cut it into pieces. [7]The sons of Aaron the priest will build a wood fire on the altar. [8]They will arrange the pieces of the offering, including the head and fat, on the wood burning on the altar. [9]But the internal organs and the legs must first be washed with water. Then the priest will burn the entire sacrifice on the altar as a burnt offering. It is a special gift, a pleasing aroma to the LORD.

[10]"If the animal you present as a burnt offering is from the flock, it may be either a sheep or a goat, but it must be a male with no defects. [11]Slaughter the animal on the north side of the altar in the LORD's presence, and Aaron's sons, the priests, will splatter its blood against all sides of the altar. [12]Then cut the animal in pieces, and the priests will arrange the pieces of the offering, including the head and fat, on the wood burning on the altar. [13]But the internal organs and the legs must first be washed with water. Then the priest will burn the entire sacrifice on the altar as a burnt offering. It is a special gift, a pleasing aroma to the LORD.

[14]"If you present a bird as a burnt offering to the LORD, choose either a turtle-dove or a young pigeon. [15]The priest will take the bird to the altar, wring off its head, and burn it on the altar. But first he must drain its blood against the side of the altar. [16]The priest must also remove the crop and the feathers* and throw them in the ashes on the east side of the altar. [17]Then, grasping the bird by its wings, the priest will tear the bird open, but without tearing it apart. Then he will burn it as a burnt offering on the wood burning on the altar. It is a special gift, a pleasing aroma to the LORD.

2 Procedures for the Grain Offering

"When you present grain as an offering to the LORD, the offering must consist of choice flour. You are to pour olive oil on it, sprinkle it with frankincense, [2]and bring it to Aaron's sons, the priests. The priest will scoop out a handful of the flour moistened with oil, together with all the frankincense, and burn this representative portion on the altar. It is a special gift, a pleasing aroma to the LORD. [3]The rest of the grain offering will then be given to Aaron and

---

1:1 Hebrew *Tent of Meeting;* also in 1:3, 5.   1:3 Or *it.*   1:4 Or *to make atonement for you.*   1:16 Or *the crop and its contents.* The meaning of the Hebrew is uncertain.

his sons. This offering will be considered a most holy part of the special gifts presented to the LORD.

[4] "If your offering is a grain offering baked in an oven, it must be made of choice flour, but without any yeast. It may be presented in the form of thin cakes mixed with olive oil or wafers spread with olive oil. [5] If your grain offering is cooked on a griddle, it must be made of choice flour mixed with olive oil but without any yeast. [6] Break it in pieces and pour olive oil on it; it is a grain offering. [7] If your grain offering is prepared in a pan, it must be made of choice flour and olive oil.

[8] "No matter how a grain offering for the LORD has been prepared, bring it to the priest, who will present it at the altar. [9] The priest will take a representative portion of the grain offering and burn it on the altar. It is a special gift, a pleasing aroma to the LORD. [10] The rest of the grain offering will then be given to Aaron and his sons as their food. This offering will be considered a most holy part of the special gifts presented to the LORD.

[11] "Do not use yeast in preparing any of the grain offerings you present to the LORD, because no yeast or honey may be burned as a special gift presented to the LORD. [12] You may add yeast and honey to an offering of the first crops of your harvest, but these must never be offered on the altar as a pleasing aroma to the LORD. [13] Season all your grain offerings with salt to remind you of God's eternal covenant. Never forget to add salt to your grain offerings.

[14] "If you present a grain offering to the LORD from the first portion of your harvest, bring fresh grain that is coarsely ground and roasted on a fire. [15] Put olive oil on this grain offering, and sprinkle it with frankincense. [16] The priest will take a representative portion of the grain moistened with oil, together with all the frankincense, and burn it as a special gift presented to the LORD.

3 Procedures for the Peace Offering

"If you present an animal from the herd as a peace offering to the LORD, it may be a male or a female, but it must have no defects. [2] Lay your hand on the animal's head, and slaughter it at the entrance of the Tabernacle.* Then Aaron's sons, the priests, will splatter its blood against all sides of the altar. [3] The priest must present part of this peace offering as a special gift to the LORD. This includes all the fat around the internal organs, [4] the two kidneys and the fat around them near the loins, and the long lobe of the liver. These must be removed with the kidneys, [5] and Aaron's sons will burn them on top of the burnt offering on the wood burning on the altar. It is a special gift, a pleasing aroma to the LORD.

[6] "If you present an animal from the flock as a peace offering to the LORD, it may be a male or a female, but it must have no defects. [7] If you present a sheep as your offering, bring it to the LORD, [8] lay your hand on its head, and slaughter it in front of the Tabernacle. Aaron's sons will then splatter the sheep's blood against all sides of the altar. [9] The priest must present the fat of this peace offering as a special gift to the LORD. This includes the fat of the broad tail cut off near the backbone, all the fat around the internal organs, [10] the two kidneys and the fat around them near the loins, and the long lobe of the liver. These must be removed with the kidneys, [11] and the priest will burn them on the altar. It is a special gift of food presented to the LORD.

[12] "If you present a goat as your offering, bring it to the LORD, [13] lay your hand on its head, and slaughter it in front of the Tabernacle. Aaron's sons will then splatter the goat's blood against all sides of the altar. [14] The priest must present part of this offering as a special gift to the LORD. This includes all the fat around the internal organs, [15] the two kidneys and the fat around them near the loins, and the long lobe of the liver. These must be removed with the kidneys, [16] and the priest will burn them on the altar. It is a special gift of food, a pleasing aroma to the LORD. All the fat belongs to the LORD.

[17] "You must never eat any fat or blood. This is a permanent law for you, and it must be observed from generation to generation, wherever you live."

3:2 Hebrew *Tent of Meeting;* also in 3:8, 13.

4 Procedures for the Sin Offering

Then the LORD said to Moses, [2]"Give the following instructions to the people of Israel. This is how you are to deal with those who sin unintentionally by doing anything that violates one of the LORD's commands.

[3]"If the high priest* sins, bringing guilt upon the entire community, he must give a sin offering for the sin he has committed. He must present to the LORD a young bull with no defects. [4]He must bring the bull to the LORD at the entrance of the Tabernacle,* lay his hand on the bull's head, and slaughter it before the LORD. [5]The high priest will then take some of the bull's blood into the Tabernacle, [6]dip his finger in the blood, and sprinkle it seven times before the LORD in front of the inner curtain of the sanctuary. [7]The priest will then put some of the blood on the horns of the altar for fragrant incense that stands in the LORD's presence inside the Tabernacle. He will pour out the rest of the bull's blood at the base of the altar for burnt offerings at the entrance of the Tabernacle. [8]Then the priest must remove all the fat of the bull to be offered as a sin offering. This includes all the fat around the internal organs, [9]the two kidneys and the fat around them near the loins, and the long lobe of the liver. He must remove these along with the kidneys, [10]just as he does with cattle offered as a peace offering, and burn them on the altar of burnt offerings. [11]But he must take whatever is left of the bull—its hide, meat, head, legs, internal organs, and dung—[12]and carry it away to a place outside the camp that is ceremonially clean, the place where the ashes are dumped. There, on the ash heap, he will burn it on a wood fire.

[13]"If the entire Israelite community sins by violating one of the LORD's commands, but the people don't realize it, they are still guilty. [14]When they become aware of their sin, the people must bring a young bull as an offering for their sin and present it before the Tabernacle. [15]The elders of the community must then lay their hands on the bull's head and slaughter it before the LORD. [16]The high priest will then take some of the bull's blood into the Tabernacle, [17]dip his finger in the blood, and sprinkle it seven times before the LORD in front of the inner curtain. [18]He will then put some of the blood on the horns of the altar for fragrant incense that stands in the LORD's presence inside the Tabernacle. He will pour out the rest of the blood at the base of the altar for burnt offerings at the entrance of the Tabernacle. [19]Then the priest must remove all the animal's fat and burn it on the altar, [20]just as he does with the bull offered as a sin offering for the high priest. Through this process, the priest will purify the people, making them right with the LORD,* and they will be forgiven. [21]Then the priest must take what is left of the bull and carry it outside the camp and burn it there, just as is done with the sin offering for the high priest. This offering is for the sin of the entire congregation of Israel.

[22]"If one of Israel's leaders sins by violating one of the commands of the LORD his God but doesn't realize it, he is still guilty. [23]When he becomes aware of his sin, he must bring as his offering a male goat with no defects. [24]He must lay his hand on the goat's head and slaughter it at the place where burnt offerings are slaughtered before the LORD. This is an offering for his sin. [25]Then the priest will dip his finger in the blood of the sin offering and put it on the horns of the altar for burnt offerings. He will pour out the rest of the blood at the base of the altar. [26]Then he must burn all the goat's fat on the altar, just as he does with the peace offering. Through this process, the priest will purify the leader from his sin, making him right with the LORD, and he will be forgiven.

[27]"If any of the common people sin by violating one of the LORD's commands, but they don't realize it, they are still guilty. [28]When they become aware of their sin, they must bring as an offering for their sin a female goat with no defects. [29]They must lay a hand on the head of the sin offering and slaughter it at the place where burnt offerings are slaughtered. [30]Then the priest will dip his finger in the blood and put it on the horns of the altar for burnt offerings. He will pour out the rest of the blood at the

---

4:3 Hebrew *the anointed priest;* also in 4:5, 16.   **4:4** Hebrew *Tent of Meeting;* also in 4:5, 7, 14, 16, 18.   **4:20** Or *will make atonement for the people;* similarly in 4:26, 31, 35.

base of the altar. ³¹Then he must remove all the goat's fat, just as he does with the fat of the peace offering. He will burn the fat on the altar, and it will be a pleasing aroma to the Lord. Through this process, the priest will purify the people, making them right with the Lord, and they will be forgiven.

³²"If the people bring a sheep as their sin offering, it must be a female with no defects. ³³They must lay a hand on the head of the sin offering and slaughter it at the place where burnt offerings are slaughtered. ³⁴Then the priest will dip his finger in the blood of the sin offering and put it on the horns of the altar for burnt offerings. He will pour out the rest of the blood at the base of the altar. ³⁵Then he must remove all the sheep's fat, just as he does with the fat of a sheep presented as a peace offering. He will burn the fat on the altar on top of the special gifts presented to the Lord. Through this process, the priest will purify the people from their sin, making them right with the Lord, and they will be forgiven.

Sins Requiring a Sin Offering

5 "If you are called to testify about something you have seen or that you know about, it is sinful to refuse to testify, and you will be punished for your sin.

²"Or suppose you unknowingly touch something that is ceremonially unclean, such as the carcass of an unclean animal. When you realize what you have done, you must admit your defilement and your guilt. This is true whether it is a wild animal, a domestic animal, or an animal that scurries along the ground.

³"Or suppose you unknowingly touch something that makes a person unclean. When you realize what you have done, you must admit your guilt.

⁴"Or suppose you make a foolish vow of any kind, whether its purpose is for good or for bad. When you realize its foolishness, you must admit your guilt.

⁵"When you become aware of your guilt in any of these ways, you must confess your sin. ⁶Then you must bring to the Lord as the penalty for your sin a female from the flock, either a sheep or a goat. This is a sin offering with which the priest will purify you from your sin, making you right with the Lord.*

⁷"But if you cannot afford to bring a sheep, you may bring to the Lord two turtledoves or two young pigeons as the penalty for your sin. One of the birds will be for a sin offering, and the other for a burnt offering. ⁸You must bring them to the priest, who will present the first bird as the sin offering. He will wring its neck but without severing its head from the body. ⁹Then he will sprinkle some of the blood of the sin offering against the sides of the altar, and the rest of the blood will be drained out at the base of the altar. This is an offering for sin. ¹⁰The priest will then prepare the second bird as a burnt offering, following all the procedures that have been prescribed. Through this process the priest will purify you from your sin, making you right with the Lord, and you will be forgiven.

¹¹"If you cannot afford to bring two turtledoves or two young pigeons, you may bring two quarts* of choice flour for your sin offering. Since it is an offering for sin, you must not moisten it with olive oil or put any frankincense on it. ¹²Take the flour to the priest, who will scoop out a handful as a representative portion. He will burn it on the altar on top of the special gifts presented to the Lord. It is an offering for sin. ¹³Through this process, the priest will purify those who are guilty of any of these sins, making them right with the Lord, and they will be forgiven. The rest of the flour will belong to the priest, just as with the grain offering."

Procedures for the Guilt Offering

¹⁴Then the Lord said to Moses, ¹⁵"If one of you commits a sin by unintentionally defiling the Lord's sacred property, you must bring a guilt offering to the Lord. The offering must be your own ram with no defects, or you may buy one of equal value with silver, as measured by the weight of the sanctuary shekel.* ¹⁶You must make

---

5:6 Or *will make atonement for you for your sin;* similarly in 5:10, 13, 16, 18.   **5:11** Hebrew *¹⁄₁₀ of an ephah* [2.2 liters].   **5:15** Each shekel was about 0.4 ounces or 11 grams in weight.

restitution for the sacred property you have harmed by paying for the loss, plus an additional 20 percent. When you give the payment to the priest, he will purify you with the ram sacrificed as a guilt offering, making you right with the LORD, and you will be forgiven.

¹⁷"Suppose you sin by violating one of the LORD's commands. Even if you are unaware of what you have done, you are guilty and will be punished for your sin. ¹⁸For a guilt offering, you must bring to the priest your own ram with no defects, or you may buy one of equal value. Through this process the priest will purify you from your unintentional sin, making you right with the LORD, and you will be forgiven. ¹⁹This is a guilt offering, for you have been guilty of an offense against the LORD."

6 Sins Requiring a Guilt Offering

¹*Then the LORD said to Moses, ²"Suppose one of you sins against your associate and is unfaithful to the LORD. Suppose you cheat in a deal involving a security deposit, or you steal or commit fraud, ³or you find lost property and lie about it, or you lie while swearing to tell the truth, or you commit any other such sin. ⁴If you have sinned in any of these ways, you are guilty. You must give back whatever you stole, or the money you took by extortion, or the security deposit, or the lost property you found, ⁵or anything obtained by swearing falsely. You must make restitution by paying the full price plus an additional 20 percent to the person you have harmed. On the same day you must present a guilt offering. ⁶As a guilt offering to the LORD, you must bring to the priest your own ram with no defects, or you may buy one of equal value. ⁷Through this process, the priest will purify you before the LORD, making you right with him,* and you will be forgiven for any of these sins you have committed."

Further Instructions for the Burnt Offering

⁸*Then the LORD said to Moses, ⁹"Give Aaron and his sons the following instructions regarding the burnt offering. The burnt offering must be left on top of the altar until the next morning, and the fire on the altar must be kept burning all night. ¹⁰In the morning, after the priest on duty has put on his official linen clothing and linen undergarments, he must clean out the ashes of the burnt offering and put them beside the altar. ¹¹Then he must take off these garments, change back into his regular clothes, and carry the ashes outside the camp to a place that is ceremonially clean. ¹²Meanwhile, the fire on the altar must be kept burning; it must never go out. Each morning the priest will add fresh wood to the fire and arrange the burnt offering on it. He will then burn the fat of the peace offerings on it. ¹³Remember, the fire must be kept burning on the altar at all times. It must never go out.

Further Instructions for the Grain Offering

¹⁴"These are the instructions regarding the grain offering. Aaron's sons must present this offering to the LORD in front of the altar. ¹⁵The priest on duty will take from the grain offering a handful of the choice flour moistened with olive oil, together with all the frankincense. He will burn this representative portion on the altar as a pleasing aroma to the LORD. ¹⁶Aaron and his sons may eat the rest of the flour, but it must be baked without yeast and eaten in a sacred place within the courtyard of the Tabernacle.* ¹⁷Remember, it must never be prepared with yeast. I have given it to the priests as their share of the special gifts presented to me. Like the sin offering and the guilt offering, it is most holy. ¹⁸Any of Aaron's male descendants may eat from the special gifts presented to the LORD. This is their permanent right from generation to generation. Anyone or anything that touches these offerings will become holy."

Procedures for the Ordination Offering

¹⁹Then the LORD said to Moses, ²⁰"On the day Aaron and his sons are anointed, they must present to the LORD a grain offering of two quarts* of choice flour, half to be offered in the morning and half to be

---

6:1 Verses 6:1-7 are numbered 5:20-26 in Hebrew text. **6:7** Or *will make atonement for you before the LORD.* **6:8** Verses 6:8-30 are numbered 6:1-23 in Hebrew text. **6:16** Hebrew *Tent of Meeting;* also in 6:26, 30. **6:20** Hebrew ¹⁄₁₀ *of an ephah* [2.2 liters].

offered in the evening. ²¹It must be carefully mixed with olive oil and cooked on a griddle. Then slice* this grain offering and present it as a pleasing aroma to the LORD. ²²In each generation, the high priest* who succeeds Aaron must prepare this same offering. It belongs to the LORD and must be burned up completely. This is a permanent law. ²³All such grain offerings of a priest must be burned up entirely. None of it may be eaten."

Further Instructions for the Sin Offering

²⁴Then the LORD said to Moses, ²⁵"Give Aaron and his sons the following instructions regarding the sin offering. The animal given as an offering for sin is a most holy offering, and it must be slaughtered in the LORD's presence at the place where the burnt offerings are slaughtered. ²⁶The priest who offers the sacrifice as a sin offering must eat his portion in a sacred place within the courtyard of the Tabernacle. ²⁷Anyone or anything that touches the sacrificial meat will become holy. If any of the sacrificial blood spatters on a person's clothing, the soiled garment must be washed in a sacred place. ²⁸If a clay pot is used to boil the sacrificial meat, it must then be broken. If a bronze pot is used, it must be scoured and thoroughly rinsed with water. ²⁹Any male from a priest's family may eat from this offering; it is most holy. ³⁰But the offering for sin may not be eaten if its blood was brought into the Tabernacle as an offering for purification* in the Holy Place. It must be completely burned with fire.

7 Further Instructions for the Guilt Offering

"These are the instructions for the guilt offering. It is most holy. ²The animal sacrificed as a guilt offering must be slaughtered at the place where the burnt offerings are slaughtered, and its blood must be splattered against all sides of the altar. ³The priest will then offer all its fat on the altar, including the fat of the broad tail, the fat around the internal organs, ⁴the two kidneys and the fat around them near the

loins, and the long lobe of the liver. These are to be removed with the kidneys, ⁵and the priests will burn them on the altar as a special gift presented to the LORD. This is the guilt offering. ⁶Any male from a priest's family may eat the meat. It must be eaten in a sacred place, for it is most holy.

⁷"The same instructions apply to both the guilt offering and the sin offering. Both belong to the priest who uses them to purify someone, making that person right with the LORD.* ⁸In the case of the burnt offering, the priest may keep the hide of the sacrificed animal. ⁹Any grain offering that has been baked in an oven, prepared in a pan, or cooked on a griddle belongs to the priest who presents it. ¹⁰All other grain offerings, whether made of dry flour or flour moistened with olive oil, are to be shared equally among all the priests, the descendants of Aaron.

Further Instructions for the Peace Offering

¹¹"These are the instructions regarding the different kinds of peace offerings that may be presented to the LORD. ¹²If you present your peace offering as an expression of thanksgiving, the usual animal sacrifice must be accompanied by various kinds of bread made without yeast—thin cakes mixed with olive oil, wafers spread with oil, and cakes made of choice flour mixed with olive oil. ¹³This peace offering of thanksgiving must also be accompanied by loaves of bread made with yeast. ¹⁴One of each kind of bread must be presented as a gift to the LORD. It will then belong to the priest who splatters the blood of the peace offering against the altar. ¹⁵The meat of the peace offering of thanksgiving must be eaten on the same day it is offered. None of it may be saved for the next morning.

¹⁶"If you bring an offering to fulfill a vow or as a voluntary offering, the meat must be eaten on the same day the sacrifice is offered, but whatever is left over may be eaten on the second day. ¹⁷Any meat left over until the third day must be completely burned up. ¹⁸If any of the meat from the peace offering is eaten on the third day,

---

6:21 The meaning of this Hebrew term is uncertain.   **6:22** Hebrew *the anointed priest.*   **6:30** Or *an offering to make atonement.*   **7:7** Or *to make atonement.*

the person who presented it will not be accepted by the LORD. You will receive no credit for offering it. By then the meat will be contaminated; if you eat it, you will be punished for your sin.

[19] "Meat that touches anything ceremonially unclean may not be eaten; it must be completely burned up. The rest of the meat may be eaten, but only by people who are ceremonially clean. [20] If you are ceremonially unclean and you eat meat from a peace offering that was presented to the LORD, you will be cut off from the community. [21] If you touch anything that is unclean (whether it is human defilement or an unclean animal or any other unclean, detestable thing) and then eat meat from a peace offering presented to the LORD, you will be cut off from the community."

The Forbidden Blood and Fat

[22] Then the LORD said to Moses, [23] "Give the following instructions to the people of Israel. You must never eat fat, whether from cattle, sheep, or goats. [24] The fat of an animal found dead or torn to pieces by wild animals must never be eaten, though it may be used for any other purpose. [25] Anyone who eats fat from an animal presented as a special gift to the LORD will be cut off from the community. [26] No matter where you live, you must never consume the blood of any bird or animal. [27] Anyone who consumes blood will be cut off from the community."

A Portion for the Priests

[28] Then the LORD said to Moses, [29] "Give the following instructions to the people of Israel. When you present a peace offering to the LORD, bring part of it as a gift to the LORD. [30] Present it to the LORD with your own hands as a special gift to the LORD. Bring the fat of the animal, together with the breast, and lift up the breast as a special offering to the LORD. [31] Then the priest will burn the fat on the altar, but the breast will belong to Aaron and his descendants. [32] Give the right thigh of your peace offering to the priest as a gift. [33] The right thigh must always be given to the priest who offers the blood and the fat of the peace offering. [34] For I have reserved the breast of the

special offering and the right thigh of the sacred offering for the priests. It is the permanent right of Aaron and his descendants to share in the peace offerings brought by the people of Israel. [35] This is their rightful share. The special gifts presented to the LORD have been reserved for Aaron and his descendants from the time they were set apart to serve the LORD as priests. [36] On the day they were anointed, the LORD commanded the Israelites to give these portions to the priests as their permanent share from generation to generation."

[37] These are the instructions for the burnt offering, the grain offering, the sin offering, and the guilt offering, as well as the ordination offering and the peace offering. [38] The LORD gave these instructions to Moses on Mount Sinai when he commanded the Israelites to present their offerings to the LORD in the wilderness of Sinai.

8 Ordination of the Priests

Then the LORD said to Moses, [2] "Bring Aaron and his sons, along with their sacred garments, the anointing oil, the bull for the sin offering, the two rams, and the basket of bread made without yeast, [3] and call the entire community of Israel together at the entrance of the Tabernacle.*"

[4] So Moses followed the LORD's instructions, and the whole community assembled at the Tabernacle entrance. [5] Moses announced to them, "This is what the LORD has commanded us to do!" [6] Then he presented Aaron and his sons and washed them with water. [7] He put the official tunic on Aaron and tied the sash around his waist. He dressed him in the robe, placed the ephod on him, and attached the ephod securely with its decorative sash. [8] Then Moses placed the chestpiece on Aaron and put the Urim and the Thummim inside it. [9] He placed the turban on Aaron's head and attached the gold medallion—the badge of holiness—to the front of the turban, just as the LORD had commanded him.

[10] Then Moses took the anointing oil and anointed the Tabernacle and everything in it, making them holy. [11] He sprinkled the oil on the altar seven times, anointing it and all its utensils, as well as the washbasin and its

---

8:3 Hebrew *Tent of Meeting;* also in 8:4, 31, 33, 35.

stand, making them holy. ¹²Then he poured some of the anointing oil on Aaron's head, anointing him and making him holy for his work. ¹³Next Moses presented Aaron's sons. He clothed them in their tunics, tied their sashes around them, and put their special head coverings on them, just as the LORD had commanded him.

¹⁴Then Moses presented the bull for the sin offering. Aaron and his sons laid their hands on the bull's head, ¹⁵and Moses slaughtered it. Moses took some of the blood, and with his finger he put it on the four horns of the altar to purify it. He poured out the rest of the blood at the base of the altar. Through this process, he made the altar holy by purifying it.* ¹⁶Then Moses took all the fat around the internal organs, the long lobe of the liver, and the two kidneys and the fat around them, and he burned it all on the altar. ¹⁷He took the rest of the bull, including its hide, meat, and dung, and burned it on a fire outside the camp, just as the LORD had commanded him.

¹⁸Then Moses presented the ram for the burnt offering. Aaron and his sons laid their hands on the ram's head, ¹⁹and Moses slaughtered it. Then Moses took the ram's blood and splattered it against all sides of the altar. ²⁰Then he cut the ram into pieces, and he burned the head, some of its pieces, and the fat on the altar. ²¹After washing the internal organs and the legs with water, Moses burned the entire ram on the altar as a burnt offering. It was a pleasing aroma, a special gift presented to the LORD, just as the LORD had commanded him.

²²Then Moses presented the other ram, which was the ram of ordination. Aaron and his sons laid their hands on the ram's head, ²³and Moses slaughtered it. Then Moses took some of its blood and applied it to the lobe of Aaron's right ear, the thumb of his right hand, and the big toe of his right foot. ²⁴Next Moses presented Aaron's sons and applied some of the blood to the lobes of their right ears, the thumbs of their right hands, and the big toes of their right feet. He then splattered the rest of the blood against all sides of the altar.

²⁵Next Moses took the fat, including the fat of the broad tail, the fat around the internal organs, the long lobe of the liver, and the two kidneys and the fat around them, along with the right thigh. ²⁶On top of these he placed a thin cake of bread made without yeast, a cake of bread mixed with olive oil, and a wafer spread with olive oil. All these were taken from the basket of bread made without yeast that was placed in the LORD's presence. ²⁷He put all these in the hands of Aaron and his sons, and he lifted them up as a special offering to the LORD. ²⁸Moses then took all the offerings back from them and burned them on the altar on top of the burnt offering. This was the ordination offering. It was a pleasing aroma, a special gift presented to the LORD. ²⁹Then Moses took the breast and lifted it up as a special offering to the LORD. This was Moses' portion of the ram of ordination, just as the LORD had commanded him.

³⁰Next Moses took some of the anointing oil and some of the blood that was on the altar, and he sprinkled them on Aaron and his garments and on his sons and their garments. In this way, he made Aaron and his sons and their garments holy.

³¹Then Moses said to Aaron and his sons, "Boil the remaining meat of the offerings at the Tabernacle entrance, and eat it there, along with the bread that is in the basket of offerings for the ordination, just as I commanded when I said, 'Aaron and his sons will eat it.' ³²Any meat or bread that is left over must then be burned up. ³³You must not leave the Tabernacle entrance for seven days, for that is when the ordination ceremony will be completed. ³⁴Everything we have done today was commanded by the LORD in order to purify you, making you right with him.* ³⁵Now stay at the entrance of the Tabernacle day and night for seven days, and do everything the LORD requires. If you fail to do this, you will die, for this is what the LORD has commanded." ³⁶So Aaron and his sons did everything the LORD had commanded through Moses.

9 The Priests Begin Their Work

After the ordination ceremony, on the eighth day, Moses called together Aaron and his sons and the elders of Israel. ²He said to Aaron, "Take a young bull for a sin

---

8:15 Or by making atonement for it; or that offerings for purification might be made on it.   **8:34** Or to make atonement for you.

offering and a ram for a burnt offering, both without defects, and present them to the Lord. ³Then tell the Israelites, 'Take a male goat for a sin offering, and take a calf and a lamb, both a year old and without defects, for a burnt offering. ⁴Also take a bull* and a ram for a peace offering and flour moistened with olive oil for a grain offering. Present all these offerings to the Lord because the Lord will appear to you today.'"

⁵So the people presented all these things at the entrance of the Tabernacle,* just as Moses had commanded. Then the whole community came forward and stood before the Lord. ⁶And Moses said, "This is what the Lord has commanded you to do so that the glory of the Lord may appear to you."

⁷Then Moses said to Aaron, "Come to the altar and sacrifice your sin offering and your burnt offering to purify yourself and the people. Then present the offerings of the people to purify them, making them right with the Lord,* just as he has commanded."

⁸So Aaron went to the altar and slaughtered the calf as a sin offering for himself. ⁹His sons brought him the blood, and he dipped his finger in it and put it on the horns of the altar. He poured out the rest of the blood at the base of the altar. ¹⁰Then he burned on the altar the fat, the kidneys, and the long lobe of the liver from the sin offering, just as the Lord had commanded Moses. ¹¹The meat and the hide, however, he burned outside the camp.

¹²Next Aaron slaughtered the animal for the burnt offering. His sons brought him the blood, and he splattered it against all sides of the altar. ¹³Then they handed him each piece of the burnt offering, including the head, and he burned them on the altar. ¹⁴Then he washed the internal organs and the legs and burned them on the altar along with the rest of the burnt offering.

¹⁵Next Aaron presented the offerings of the people. He slaughtered the people's goat and presented it as an offering for their sin, just as he had first done with the offering for his own sin. ¹⁶Then he presented the burnt offering and sacrificed it in the prescribed way. ¹⁷He also presented the grain offering, burning a handful of the flour mixture on the altar, in addition to the regular burnt offering for the morning.

¹⁸Then Aaron slaughtered the bull and the ram for the people's peace offering. His sons brought him the blood, and he splattered it against all sides of the altar. ¹⁹Then he took the fat of the bull and the ram—the fat of the broad tail and from around the internal organs—along with the kidneys and the long lobes of the livers. ²⁰He placed these fat portions on top of the breasts of these animals and burned them on the altar. ²¹Aaron then lifted up the breasts and right thighs as a special offering to the Lord, just as Moses had commanded.

²²After that, Aaron raised his hands toward the people and blessed them. Then, after presenting the sin offering, the burnt offering, and the peace offering, he stepped down from the altar. ²³Then Moses and Aaron went into the Tabernacle, and when they came back out, they blessed the people again, and the glory of the Lord appeared to the whole community. ²⁴Fire blazed forth from the Lord's presence and consumed the burnt offering and the fat on the altar. When the people saw this, they shouted with joy and fell face down on the ground.

10 The Sin of Nadab and Abihu

Aaron's sons Nadab and Abihu put coals of fire in their incense burners and sprinkled incense over them. In this way, they disobeyed the Lord by burning before him the wrong kind of fire, different than he had commanded. ²So fire blazed forth from the Lord's presence and burned them up, and they died there before the Lord.

³Then Moses said to Aaron, "This is what the Lord meant when he said,

'I will display my holiness
    through those who come near me.
I will display my glory
    before all the people.'"

And Aaron was silent.

⁴Then Moses called for Mishael and Elzaphan, Aaron's cousins, the sons of Aaron's uncle Uzziel. He said to them, "Come forward and carry away the bodies of your

---

9:4 Or *cow*; also in 9:18, 19.   **9:5** Hebrew *Tent of Meeting*; also in 9:23.   **9:7** Or *to make atonement for them.*

relatives from in front of the sanctuary to a place outside the camp." [5] So they came forward and picked them up by their garments and carried them out of the camp, just as Moses had commanded.

[6] Then Moses said to Aaron and his sons Eleazar and Ithamar, "Do not show grief by leaving your hair uncombed* or by tearing your clothes. If you do, you will die, and the LORD's anger will strike the whole community of Israel. However, the rest of the Israelites, your relatives, may mourn because of the LORD's fiery destruction of Nadab and Abihu. [7] But you must not leave the entrance of the Tabernacle* or you will die, for you have been anointed with the LORD's anointing oil." So they did as Moses commanded.

Instructions for Priestly Conduct
[8] Then the LORD said to Aaron, [9] "You and your descendants must never drink wine or any other alcoholic drink before going into the Tabernacle. If you do, you will die. This is a permanent law for you, and it must be observed from generation to generation. [10] You must distinguish between what is sacred and what is common, between what is ceremonially unclean and what is clean. [11] And you must teach the Israelites all the decrees that the LORD has given them through Moses."

[12] Then Moses said to Aaron and his remaining sons, Eleazar and Ithamar, "Take what is left of the grain offering after a portion has been presented as a special gift to the LORD, and eat it beside the altar. Make sure it contains no yeast, for it is most holy. [13] You must eat it in a sacred place, for it has been given to you and your descendants as your portion of the special gifts presented to the LORD. These are the commands I have been given. [14] But the breast and thigh that were lifted up as a special offering may be eaten in any place that is ceremonially clean. These parts have been given to you and your descendants as your portion of the peace offerings presented by the people of Israel. [15] You must lift up the thigh and breast as a special offering to the LORD, along with the fat of the special gifts. These

parts will belong to you and your descendants as your permanent right, just as the LORD has commanded."

[16] Moses then asked them what had happened to the goat of the sin offering. When he discovered it had been burned up, he became very angry with Eleazar and Ithamar, Aaron's remaining sons. [17] "Why didn't you eat the sin offering in the sacred area?" he demanded. "It is a holy offering! The LORD has given it to you to remove the guilt of the community and to purify the people, making them right with the LORD.* [18] Since the animal's blood was not brought into the Holy Place, you should have eaten the meat in the sacred area as I ordered you."

[19] Then Aaron answered Moses, "Today my sons presented both their sin offering and their burnt offering to the LORD. And yet this tragedy has happened to me. If I had eaten the people's sin offering on such a tragic day as this, would the LORD have been pleased?" [20] And when Moses heard this, he was satisfied.

11 Ceremonially Clean and Unclean Animals

Then the LORD said to Moses and Aaron, [2] "Give the following instructions to the people of Israel.

"Of all the land animals, these are the ones you may use for food. [3] You may eat any animal that has completely split hooves and chews the cud. [4] You may not, however, eat the following animals* that have split hooves or that chew the cud, but not both. The camel chews the cud but does not have split hooves, so it is ceremonially unclean for you. [5] The hyrax* chews the cud but does not have split hooves, so it is unclean. [6] The hare chews the cud but does not have split hooves, so it is unclean. [7] The pig has evenly split hooves but does not chew the cud, so it is unclean. [8] You may not eat the meat of these animals or even touch their carcasses. They are ceremonially unclean for you.

[9] "Of all the marine animals, these are ones you may use for food. You may eat anything from the water if it has both fins and scales, whether taken from salt water

or from streams. ¹⁰But you must never eat animals from the sea or from rivers that do not have both fins and scales. They are detestable to you. This applies both to little creatures that live in shallow water and to all creatures that live in deep water. ¹¹They will always be detestable to you. You must never eat their meat or even touch their dead bodies. ¹²Any marine animal that does not have both fins and scales is detestable to you.

¹³"These are the birds that are detestable to you. You must never eat them: the griffon vulture, the bearded vulture, the black vulture, ¹⁴the kite, falcons of all kinds, ¹⁵ravens of all kinds, ¹⁶the eagle owl, the short-eared owl, the seagull, hawks of all kinds, ¹⁷the little owl, the cormorant, the great owl, ¹⁸the barn owl, the desert owl, the Egyptian vulture, ¹⁹the stork, herons of all kinds, the hoopoe, and the bat.

²⁰"You must not eat winged insects that walk along the ground; they are detestable to you. ²¹You may, however, eat winged insects that walk along the ground and have jointed legs so they can jump. ²²The insects you are permitted to eat include all kinds of locusts, bald locusts, crickets, and grasshoppers. ²³All other winged insects that walk along the ground are detestable to you.

²⁴"The following creatures will make you ceremonially unclean. If any of you touch their carcasses, you will be defiled until evening. ²⁵If you pick up their carcasses, you must wash your clothes, and you will remain defiled until evening.

²⁶"Any animal that has split hooves that are not evenly divided or that does not chew the cud is unclean for you. If you touch the carcass of such an animal, you will be defiled. ²⁷Of the animals that walk on all fours, those that have paws are unclean. If you touch the carcass of such an animal, you will be defiled until evening. ²⁸If you pick up its carcass, you must wash your clothes, and you will remain defiled until evening. These animals are unclean for you.

²⁹"Of the small animals that scurry along the ground, these are unclean for you: the mole rat, the rat, large lizards of all kinds, ³⁰the gecko, the monitor lizard, the common lizard, the sand lizard, and the chameleon. ³¹All these small animals are unclean for you. If any of you touch the dead body of such an animal, you will be defiled until evening. ³²If such an animal dies and falls on something, that object will be unclean. This is true whether the object is made of wood, cloth, leather, or burlap. Whatever its use, you must dip it in water, and it will remain defiled until evening. After that, it will be ceremonially clean and may be used again.

³³"If such an animal falls into a clay pot, everything in the pot will be defiled, and the pot must be smashed. ³⁴If the water from such a container spills on any food, the food will be defiled. And any beverage in such a container will be defiled. ³⁵Any object on which the carcass of such an animal falls will be defiled. If it is an oven or hearth, it must be destroyed, for it is defiled, and you must treat it accordingly.

³⁶"However, if the carcass of such an animal falls into a spring or a cistern, the water will still be clean. But anyone who touches the carcass will be defiled. ³⁷If the carcass falls on seed grain to be planted in the field, the seed will still be considered clean. ³⁸But if the seed is wet when the carcass falls on it, the seed will be defiled.

³⁹"If an animal you are permitted to eat dies and you touch its carcass, you will be defiled until evening. ⁴⁰If you eat any of its meat or carry away its carcass, you must wash your clothes, and you will remain defiled until evening.

⁴¹"All small animals that scurry along the ground are detestable, and you must never eat them. ⁴²This includes all animals that slither along on their bellies, as well as those with four legs and those with many feet. All such animals that scurry along the ground are detestable, and you must never eat them. ⁴³Do not defile yourselves by touching them. You must not make yourselves ceremonially unclean because of them. ⁴⁴For I am the LORD your God. You must consecrate yourselves and be holy, because I am holy. So do not defile yourselves with any of these small animals that scurry along the ground. ⁴⁵For I, the LORD, am the one who brought you up from the land of Egypt, that I might be your God. Therefore, you must be holy because I am holy.

⁴⁶"These are the instructions regarding land animals, birds, marine creatures, and animals that scurry along the ground. ⁴⁷By these instructions you will know what is unclean and clean, and which animals may be eaten and which may not be eaten."

12 Purification after Childbirth

The LORD said to Moses, ²"Give the following instructions to the people of Israel. If a woman becomes pregnant and gives birth to a son, she will be ceremonially unclean for seven days, just as she is unclean during her menstrual period. ³On the eighth day the boy's foreskin must be circumcised. ⁴After waiting thirty-three days, she will be purified from the bleeding of childbirth. During this time of purification, she must not touch anything that is set apart as holy. And she must not enter the sanctuary until her time of purification is over. ⁵If a woman gives birth to a daughter, she will be ceremonially unclean for two weeks, just as she is unclean during her menstrual period. After waiting sixty-six days, she will be purified from the bleeding of childbirth.

⁶"When the time of purification is completed for either a son or a daughter, the woman must bring a one-year-old lamb for a burnt offering and a young pigeon or turtledove for a purification offering. She must bring her offerings to the priest at the entrance of the Tabernacle.* ⁷The priest will then present them to the LORD to purify her.* Then she will be ceremonially clean again after her bleeding at childbirth. These are the instructions for a woman after the birth of a son or a daughter.

⁸"If a woman cannot afford to bring a lamb, she must bring two turtledoves or two young pigeons. One will be for the burnt offering and the other for the purification offering. The priest will sacrifice them to purify her, and she will be ceremonially clean."

13 Serious Skin Diseases

The LORD said to Moses and Aaron, ²"If anyone has a swelling or a rash or discolored skin that might develop into a serious skin disease,* that person must be brought to Aaron the priest or to one of his sons.* ³The priest will examine the affected area of the skin. If the hair in the affected area has turned white and the problem appears to be more than skin-deep, it is a serious skin disease, and the priest who examines it must pronounce the person ceremonially unclean.

⁴"But if the affected area of the skin is only a white discoloration and does not appear to be more than skin-deep, and if the hair on the spot has not turned white, the priest will quarantine the person for seven days. ⁵On the seventh day the priest will make another examination. If he finds the affected area has not changed and the problem has not spread on the skin, the priest will quarantine the person for seven more days. ⁶On the seventh day the priest will make another examination. If he finds the affected area has faded and has not spread, the priest will pronounce the person ceremonially clean. It was only a rash. The person's clothing must be washed, and the person will be ceremonially clean. ⁷But if the rash continues to spread after the person has been examined by the priest and has been pronounced clean, the infected person must return to be examined again. ⁸If the priest finds that the rash has spread, he must pronounce the person ceremonially unclean, for it is indeed a skin disease.

⁹"Anyone who develops a serious skin disease must go to the priest for an examination. ¹⁰If the priest finds a white swelling on the skin, and some hair on the spot has turned white, and there is an open sore in the affected area, ¹¹it is a chronic skin disease, and the priest must pronounce the person ceremonially unclean. In such cases the person need not be quarantined, for it is obvious that the skin is defiled by the disease.

¹²"Now suppose the disease has spread all over the person's skin, covering the body from head to foot. ¹³When the priest examines the infected person and finds that the disease covers the entire body, he will pronounce the person ceremonially clean. Since the skin has turned completely white, the person is clean. ¹⁴But if any open sores

---

12:6 Hebrew *Tent of Meeting.*   **12:7** Or *to make atonement for her;* also in 12:8.   **13:2a** Traditionally rendered *leprosy.* The Hebrew word used throughout this passage is used to describe various skin diseases.   **13:2b** Or *one of his descendants.*

appear, the infected person will be pronounced ceremonially unclean. ¹⁵The priest must make this pronouncement as soon as he sees an open sore, since open sores indicate the presence of a skin disease. ¹⁶However, if the open sores heal and turn white like the rest of the skin, the person must return to the priest ¹⁷for another examination. If the affected areas have indeed turned white, the priest will then pronounce the person ceremonially clean by declaring, 'You are clean!'

¹⁸"If anyone has a boil on the skin that has started to heal, ¹⁹but a white swelling or a reddish white spot develops in its place, that person must go to the priest to be examined. ²⁰If the priest examines it and finds it to be more than skin-deep, and if the hair in the affected area has turned white, the priest must pronounce the person ceremonially unclean. The boil has become a serious skin disease. ²¹But if the priest finds no white hair on the affected area and the problem appears to be no more than skin-deep and has faded, the priest must quarantine the person for seven days. ²²If during that time the affected area spreads on the skin, the priest must pronounce the person ceremonially unclean, because it is a serious disease. ²³But if the area grows no larger and does not spread, it is merely the scar from the boil, and the priest will pronounce the person ceremonially clean.

²⁴"If anyone has suffered a burn on the skin and the burned area changes color, becoming either reddish white or shiny white, ²⁵the priest must examine it. If he finds that the hair in the affected area has turned white and the problem appears to be more than skin-deep, a skin disease has broken out in the burn. The priest must then pronounce the person ceremonially unclean, for it is clearly a serious skin disease. ²⁶But if the priest finds no white hair on the affected area and the problem appears to be no more than skin-deep and has faded, the priest must quarantine the infected person for seven days. ²⁷On the seventh day the priest must examine the person again. If the affected area has spread on the skin, the priest must pronounce that person ceremonially unclean, for it is

clearly a serious skin disease. ²⁸But if the affected area has not changed or spread on the skin and has faded, it is simply a swelling from the burn. The priest will then pronounce the person ceremonially clean, for it is only the scar from the burn.

²⁹"If anyone, either a man or woman, has a sore on the head or chin, ³⁰the priest must examine it. If he finds it is more than skin-deep and has fine yellow hair on it, the priest must pronounce the person ceremonially unclean. It is a scabby sore of the head or chin. ³¹If the priest examines the scabby sore and finds that it is only skin-deep but there is no black hair on it, he must quarantine the person for seven days. ³²On the seventh day the priest must examine the sore again. If he finds that the scabby sore has not spread, and there is no yellow hair on it, and it appears to be only skin-deep, ³³the person must shave off all hair except the hair on the affected area. Then the priest must quarantine the person for another seven days. ³⁴On the seventh day he will examine the sore again. If it has not spread and appears to be no more than skin-deep, the priest will pronounce the person ceremonially clean. The person's clothing must be washed, and the person will be ceremonially clean. ³⁵But if the scabby sore begins to spread after the person is pronounced clean, ³⁶the priest must do another examination. If he finds that the sore has spread, the priest does not need to look for yellow hair. The infected person is ceremonially unclean. ³⁷But if the color of the scabby sore does not change and black hair has grown on it, it has healed. The priest will then pronounce the person ceremonially clean.

³⁸"If anyone, either a man or woman, has shiny white patches on the skin, ³⁹the priest must examine the affected area. If he finds that the shiny patches are only pale white, this is a harmless skin rash, and the person is ceremonially clean.

⁴⁰"If a man loses his hair and his head becomes bald, he is still ceremonially clean. ⁴¹And if he loses hair on his forehead, he simply has a bald forehead; he is still clean. ⁴²However, if a reddish white sore appears on the bald area at the top or back of his

head, this is a skin disease. ⁴³The priest must examine him, and if he finds swelling around the reddish white sore anywhere on the man's head and it looks like a skin disease, ⁴⁴the man is indeed infected with a skin disease and is unclean. The priest must pronounce him ceremonially unclean because of the sore on his head.

⁴⁵"Those who suffer from a serious skin disease must tear their clothing and leave their hair uncombed.* They must cover their mouth and call out, 'Unclean! Unclean!' ⁴⁶As long as the serious disease lasts, they will be ceremonially unclean. They must live in isolation in their place outside the camp.

Treatment of Contaminated Clothing

⁴⁷"Now suppose mildew* contaminates some woolen or linen clothing, ⁴⁸woolen or linen fabric, the hide of an animal, or anything made of leather. ⁴⁹If the contaminated area in the clothing, the animal hide, the fabric, or the leather article has turned greenish or reddish, it is contaminated with mildew and must be shown to the priest. ⁵⁰After examining the affected spot, the priest will put the article in quarantine for seven days. ⁵¹On the seventh day the priest must inspect it again. If the contaminated area has spread, the clothing or fabric or leather is clearly contaminated by a serious mildew and is ceremonially unclean. ⁵²The priest must burn the item—the clothing, the woolen or linen fabric, or piece of leather—for it has been contaminated by a serious mildew. It must be completely destroyed by fire.

⁵³"But if the priest examines it and finds that the contaminated area has not spread in the clothing, the fabric, or the leather, ⁵⁴the priest will order the object to be washed and then quarantined for seven more days. ⁵⁵Then the priest must examine the object again. If he finds that the contaminated area has not changed color after being washed, even if it did not spread, the object is defiled. It must be completely burned up, whether the contaminated spot* is on the inside or outside. ⁵⁶But if the priest examines it and finds that the contaminated area has faded after being washed, he must cut the spot from the clothing, the fabric, or the leather. ⁵⁷If the spot later reappears on the clothing, the fabric, or the leather article, the mildew is clearly spreading, and the contaminated object must be burned up. ⁵⁸But if the spot disappears from the clothing, the fabric, or the leather article after it has been washed, it must be washed again; then it will be ceremonially clean.

⁵⁹"These are the instructions for dealing with mildew that contaminates woolen or linen clothing or fabric or anything made of leather. This is how the priest will determine whether these items are ceremonially clean or unclean."

14 Cleansing from Skin Diseases

And the LORD said to Moses, ²"The following instructions are for those seeking ceremonial purification from a skin disease.* Those who have been healed must be brought to the priest, ³who will examine them at a place outside the camp. If the priest finds that someone has been healed of a serious skin disease, ⁴he will perform a purification ceremony, using two live birds that are ceremonially clean, a stick of cedar,* some scarlet yarn, and a hyssop branch. ⁵The priest will order that one bird be slaughtered over a clay pot filled with fresh water. ⁶He will take the live bird, the cedar stick, the scarlet yarn, and the hyssop branch, and dip them into the blood of the bird that was slaughtered over the fresh water. ⁷The priest will then sprinkle the blood of the dead bird seven times on the person being purified of the skin disease. When the priest has purified the person, he will release the live bird in the open field to fly away.

⁸"The persons being purified must then wash their clothes, shave off all their hair, and bathe themselves in water. Then they will be ceremonially clean and may return to the camp. However, they must remain outside their tents for seven days. ⁹On the seventh day they must again shave all the hair from their heads, including the hair

13:45 Or and uncover their heads.   13:47 Traditionally rendered leprosy. The Hebrew term used throughout this passage is the same term used for the various skin diseases described in 13:1-46.   13:55 The meaning of the Hebrew is uncertain.   14:2 Traditionally rendered leprosy; see note on 13:2a.   14:4 Or juniper; also in 14:6, 49, 51.

of the beard and eyebrows. They must also wash their clothes and bathe themselves in water. Then they will be ceremonially clean.

¹⁰"On the eighth day each person being purified must bring two male lambs and a one-year-old female lamb, all with no defects, along with a grain offering of six quarts* of choice flour moistened with olive oil, and a cup* of olive oil. ¹¹Then the officiating priest will present that person for purification, along with the offerings, before the LORD at the entrance of the Tabernacle.* ¹²The priest will take one of the male lambs and the olive oil and present them as a guilt offering, lifting them up as a special offering before the LORD. ¹³He will then slaughter the male lamb in the sacred area where sin offerings and burnt offerings are slaughtered. As with the sin offering, the guilt offering belongs to the priest. It is a most holy offering. ¹⁴The priest will then take some of the blood of the guilt offering and apply it to the lobe of the right ear, the thumb of the right hand, and the big toe of the right foot of the person being purified.

¹⁵"Then the priest will pour some of the olive oil into the palm of his own left hand. ¹⁶He will dip his right finger into the oil in his palm and sprinkle some of it with his finger seven times before the LORD. ¹⁷The priest will then apply some of the oil in his palm over the blood from the guilt offering that is on the lobe of the right ear, the thumb of the right hand, and the big toe of the right foot of the person being purified. ¹⁸The priest will apply the oil remaining in his hand to the head of the person being purified. Through this process, the priest will purify* the person before the LORD.

¹⁹"Then the priest must present the sin offering to purify the person who was cured of the skin disease. After that, the priest will slaughter the burnt offering ²⁰and offer it on the altar along with the grain offering. Through this process, the priest will purify the person who was healed, and the person will be ceremonially clean.

²¹"But anyone who is too poor and cannot afford these offerings may bring one male lamb for a guilt offering, to be lifted up as a special offering for purification. The person must also bring two quarts* of choice flour moistened with olive oil for the grain offering and a cup of olive oil. ²²The offering must also include two turtledoves or two young pigeons, whichever the person can afford. One of the pair must be used for the sin offering and the other for a burnt offering. ²³On the eighth day of the purification ceremony, the person being purified must bring the offerings to the priest in the LORD's presence at the entrance of the Tabernacle. ²⁴The priest will take the lamb for the guilt offering, along with the olive oil, and lift them up as a special offering to the LORD. ²⁵Then the priest will slaughter the lamb for the guilt offering. He will take some of its blood and apply it to the lobe of the right ear, the thumb of the right hand, and the big toe of the right foot of the person being purified.

²⁶"The priest will also pour some of the olive oil into the palm of his own left hand. ²⁷He will dip his right finger into the oil in his palm and sprinkle some of it seven times before the LORD. ²⁸The priest will then apply some of the oil in his palm over the blood from the guilt offering that is on the lobe of the right ear, the thumb of the right hand, and the big toe of the right foot of the person being purified. ²⁹The priest will apply the oil remaining in his hand to the head of the person being purified. Through this process, the priest will purify the person before the LORD.

³⁰"Then the priest will offer the two turtledoves or the two young pigeons, whichever the person can afford. ³¹One of them is for a sin offering and the other for a burnt offering, to be presented along with the grain offering. Through this process, the priest will purify the person before the LORD. ³²These are the instructions for purification for those who have recovered from a serious skin disease but who cannot afford to bring the offerings normally required for the ceremony of purification."

Treatment of Contaminated Houses

³³Then the LORD said to Moses and Aaron, ³⁴"When you arrive in Canaan, the land I am giving you as your own possession, I

14:10a Hebrew ³⁄₁₀ of an ephah [6.6 liters].   14:10b Hebrew 1 log [0.3 liters]; also in 14:21.   14:11 Hebrew Tent of Meeting; also in 14:23.
14:18 Or will make atonement for; similarly in 14:19, 20, 21, 29, 31, 53.   14:21 Hebrew ¹⁄₁₀ of an ephah [2.2 liters].

may contaminate some of the houses in your land with mildew.* ³⁵The owner of such a house must then go to the priest and say, 'It appears that my house has some kind of mildew.' ³⁶Before the priest goes in to inspect the house, he must have the house emptied so nothing inside will be pronounced ceremonially unclean. ³⁷Then the priest will go in and examine the mildew on the walls. If he finds greenish or reddish streaks and the contamination appears to go deeper than the wall's surface, ³⁸the priest will step outside the door and put the house in quarantine for seven days. ³⁹On the seventh day the priest must return for another inspection. If he finds that the mildew on the walls of the house has spread, ⁴⁰the priest must order that the stones from those areas be removed. The contaminated material will then be taken outside the town to an area designated as ceremonially unclean. ⁴¹Next the inside walls of the entire house must be scraped thoroughly and the scrapings dumped in the unclean place outside the town. ⁴²Other stones will be brought in to replace the ones that were removed, and the walls will be replastered.

⁴³"But if the mildew reappears after all the stones have been replaced and the house has been scraped and replastered, ⁴⁴the priest must return and inspect the house again. If he finds that the mildew has spread, the walls are clearly contaminated with a serious mildew, and the house is defiled. ⁴⁵It must be torn down, and all its stones, timbers, and plaster must be carried out of town to the place designated as ceremonially unclean. ⁴⁶Those who enter the house during the period of quarantine will be ceremonially unclean until evening, ⁴⁷and all who sleep or eat in the house must wash their clothing.

⁴⁸"But if the priest returns for his inspection and finds that the mildew has not reappeared in the house after the fresh plastering, he will pronounce it clean because the mildew is clearly gone. ⁴⁹To purify the house the priest must take two birds, a stick of cedar, some scarlet yarn, and a hyssop branch. ⁵⁰He will slaughter one of the birds over a clay pot filled with fresh water. ⁵¹He will take the cedar stick, the hyssop branch, the scarlet yarn, and the live bird, and dip them into the blood of the slaughtered bird and into the fresh water. Then he will sprinkle the house seven times. ⁵²When the priest has purified the house in exactly this way, ⁵³he will release the live bird in the open fields outside the town. Through this process, the priest will purify the house, and it will be ceremonially clean.

⁵⁴"These are the instructions for dealing with serious skin diseases,* including scabby sores; ⁵⁵and mildew,* whether on clothing or in a house; ⁵⁶and a swelling on the skin, a rash, or discolored skin. ⁵⁷This procedure will determine whether a person or object is ceremonially clean or unclean.

"These are the instructions regarding skin diseases and mildew."

15 Bodily Discharges

The Lord said to Moses and Aaron, ²"Give the following instructions to the people of Israel.

"Any man who has a bodily discharge is ceremonially unclean. ³This defilement is caused by his discharge, whether the discharge continues or stops. In either case the man is unclean. ⁴Any bed on which the man with the discharge lies and anything on which he sits will be ceremonially unclean. ⁵So if you touch the man's bed, you must wash your clothes and bathe yourself in water, and you will remain unclean until evening. ⁶If you sit where the man with the discharge has sat, you must wash your clothes and bathe yourself in water, and you will remain unclean until evening. ⁷If you touch the man with the discharge, you must wash your clothes and bathe yourself in water, and you will remain unclean until evening. ⁸If the man spits on you, you must wash your clothes and bathe yourself in water, and you will remain unclean until evening. ⁹Any saddle blanket on which the man rides will be ceremonially unclean. ¹⁰If you touch anything that was under the man, you will be unclean until evening. You must wash your clothes and bathe yourself in water, and you will remain unclean until evening. ¹¹If the man touches you without first rinsing his hands, you must wash your clothes and bathe yourself in water, and you will remain unclean until evening. ¹²Any clay pot the man touches must be broken, and any wooden utensil he touches must be rinsed with water.

¹³"When the man with the discharge is healed, he must count off seven days for the period of purification. Then he must wash his clothes and bathe himself in fresh water, and he will be ceremonially clean. ¹⁴On the eighth day he must get two turtledoves or two young pigeons and come before the LORD at the entrance of the Tabernacle* and give his offerings to the priest. ¹⁵The priest will offer one bird for a sin offering and the other for a burnt offering. Through this process, the priest will purify* the man before the LORD for his discharge.

¹⁶"Whenever a man has an emission of semen, he must bathe his entire body in water, and he will remain ceremonially unclean until the next evening.* ¹⁷Any clothing or leather with semen on it must be washed in water, and it will remain unclean until evening. ¹⁸After a man and a woman have sexual intercourse, they must each bathe in water, and they will remain unclean until the next evening.

¹⁹"Whenever a woman has her menstrual period, she will be ceremonially unclean for seven days. Anyone who touches her during that time will be unclean until evening. ²⁰Anything on which the woman lies or sits during the time of her period will be unclean. ²¹If any of you touch her bed, you must wash your clothes and bathe yourself in water, and you will remain unclean until evening. ²²If you touch any object she has sat on, you must wash your clothes and bathe yourself in water, and you will remain unclean until evening. ²³This includes her bed or any other object she has sat on; you will be unclean until evening if you touch it. ²⁴If a man has sexual intercourse with her and her blood touches him, her menstrual impurity will be transmitted to him. He will remain unclean for seven days, and any bed on which he lies will be unclean.

²⁵"If a woman has a flow of blood for many days that is unrelated to her men-

strual period, or if the blood continues beyond the normal period, she is ceremonially unclean. As during her menstrual period, the woman will be unclean as long as the discharge continues. ²⁶Any bed she lies on and any object she sits on during that time will be unclean, just as during her normal menstrual period. ²⁷If any of you touch these things, you will be ceremonially unclean. You must wash your clothes and bathe yourself in water, and you will remain unclean until evening.

²⁸"When the woman's bleeding stops, she must count off seven days. Then she will be ceremonially clean. ²⁹On the eighth day she must bring two turtledoves or two young pigeons and present them to the priest at the entrance of the Tabernacle. ³⁰The priest will offer one for a sin offering and the other for a burnt offering. Through this process, the priest will purify her before the LORD for the ceremonial impurity caused by her bleeding.

³¹"This is how you will guard the people of Israel from ceremonial uncleanness. Otherwise they would die, for their impurity would defile my Tabernacle that stands among them. ³²These are the instructions for dealing with anyone who has a bodily discharge—a man who is unclean because of an emission of semen ³³or a woman during her menstrual period. It applies to any man or woman who has a bodily discharge, and to a man who has sexual intercourse with a woman who is ceremonially unclean."

16 The Day of Atonement

The LORD spoke to Moses after the death of Aaron's two sons, who died after they entered the LORD's presence and burned the wrong kind of fire before him. ²The LORD said to Moses, "Warn your brother, Aaron, not to enter the Most Holy Place behind the inner curtain whenever he chooses; if he does, he will die. For the Ark's cover—the place of atonement—is there, and I myself am present in the cloud above the atonement cover.

³"When Aaron enters the sanctuary area, he must follow these instructions fully. He

---

15:14 Hebrew *Tent of Meeting;* also in 15:29.   **15:15** Or *will make atonement for;* also in 15:30.   **15:16** Hebrew *until evening;* also in 15:18.

must bring a young bull for a sin offering and a ram for a burnt offering. [4] He must put on his linen tunic and the linen undergarments worn next to his body. He must tie the linen sash around his waist and put the linen turban on his head. These are sacred garments, so he must bathe himself in water before he puts them on. [5] Aaron must take from the community of Israel two male goats for a sin offering and a ram for a burnt offering.

[6] "Aaron will present his own bull as a sin offering to purify himself and his family, making them right with the LORD.* [7] Then he must take the two male goats and present them to the LORD at the entrance of the Tabernacle.* [8] He is to cast sacred lots to determine which goat will be reserved as an offering to the LORD and which will carry the sins of the people to the wilderness of Azazel. [9] Aaron will then present as a sin offering the goat chosen by lot for the LORD. [10] The other goat, the scapegoat chosen by lot to be sent away, will be kept alive, standing before the LORD. When it is sent away to Azazel in the wilderness, the people will be purified and made right with the LORD.*

[11] "Aaron will present his own bull as a sin offering to purify himself and his family, making them right with the LORD. After he has slaughtered the bull as a sin offering, [12] he will fill an incense burner with burning coals from the altar that stands before the LORD. Then he will take two handfuls of fragrant powdered incense and will carry the burner and the incense behind the inner curtain. [13] There in the LORD's presence he will put the incense on the burning coals so that a cloud of incense will rise over the Ark's cover—the place of atonement—that rests on the Ark of the Covenant.* If he follows these instructions, he will not die. [14] Then he must take some of the blood of the bull, dip his finger in it, and sprinkle it on the east side of the atonement cover. He must sprinkle blood seven times with his finger in front of the atonement cover.

[15] "Then Aaron must slaughter the first goat as a sin offering for the people and carry its blood behind the inner curtain. There he will sprinkle the goat's blood over the atonement cover and in front of it, just as he did with the bull's blood. [16] Through this process, he will purify* the Most Holy Place, and he will do the same for the entire Tabernacle, because of the defiling sin and rebellion of the Israelites. [17] No one else is allowed inside the Tabernacle when Aaron enters it for the purification ceremony in the Most Holy Place. No one may enter until he comes out again after purifying himself, his family, and all the congregation of Israel, making them right with the LORD.

[18] "Then Aaron will come out to purify the altar that stands before the LORD. He will do this by taking some of the blood from the bull and the goat and putting it on each of the horns of the altar. [19] Then he must sprinkle the blood with his finger seven times over the altar. In this way, he will cleanse it from Israel's defilement and make it holy.

[20] "When Aaron has finished purifying the Most Holy Place and the Tabernacle and the altar, he must present the live goat. [21] He will lay both of his hands on the goat's head and confess over it all the wickedness, rebellion, and sins of the people of Israel. In this way, he will transfer the people's sins to the head of the goat. Then a man specially chosen for the task will drive the goat into the wilderness. [22] As the goat goes into the wilderness, it will carry all the people's sins upon itself into a desolate land.

[23] "When Aaron goes back into the Tabernacle, he must take off the linen garments he was wearing when he entered the Most Holy Place, and he must leave the garments there. [24] Then he must bathe himself with water in a sacred place, put on his regular garments, and go out to sacrifice a burnt offering for himself and a burnt offering for the people. Through this process, he will purify himself and the people, making them right with the LORD. [25] He must then burn all the fat of the sin offering on the altar.

16:6 Or *to make atonement for himself and his family;* similarly in 16:11, 17b, 24, 34.   **16:7** Hebrew *Tent of Meeting;* also in 16:16, 17, 20, 23, 33.   **16:10** Or *wilderness, it will make atonement for the people.*   **16:13** Hebrew *that is above the Testimony.* The Hebrew word for "testimony" refers to the terms of the LORD's covenant with Israel as written on stone tablets, which were kept in the Ark, and also to the covenant itself.   **16:16** Or *make atonement for;* similarly in 16:17a, 18, 20, 27, 33.

Atonement and Reconciliation
LEVITICUS 16:20–25

On November 3, 1979, five protest marchers in Greensboro, North Carolina, were killed by the Ku Klux Klan and the American Nazi Party in an event known as the Greensboro Massacre. Despite two criminal trials, no one was ever convicted of the murders.

More than twenty years later, in 2005, a group called the Greensboro Truth and Reconciliation Commission sought to bring healing to this still-open wound in their community. Through the testimony of eyewitnesses and the careful assessment of evidence, the commission found that the burden of blame for this tragedy lay not only on the shoulders of the shooters but also on the greater community that had allowed violent rhetoric and blind-eyed ignorance to rule the day.

What the work of this commission—and the Truth and Reconciliation Commissions in places like South Africa and Liberia that inspired it—shows us is that reconciliation is not only about finding the "bad guys." It's about speaking the truth, no matter how ugly it is. It's about digging for the roots of evil and bringing them into the light so they can be named and destroyed. It's about recognizing what went wrong and agreeing to try again.

That's the kind of reconciliation to which God called the nation of Israel, to which God continues to call us. As God gave detailed instructions for the Day of Atonement (Leviticus 16), the idea was not just to make Aaron, the chosen representative of the people, jump through a bunch of bizarre, random hoops. God asked for a long process that would give the people time to recall their sin, to dig deep, to reflect. Instead of rushing in to the temple to get a quick dose of forgiveness, Aaron had to put time, effort, and thought into this act of communal repentance.

Justice and reconciliation—for churches, nations, individuals—are never quick. They demand far more than apologies. True atonement requires us to take our time and figure out what went wrong. It asks us to pace ourselves and look beyond the surface of our sin to figure out how to create real change. And it demands we lay all of our failings at the feet of our gracious, compassionate God.

—Carla Barnhill

For more on reconciliation, see reading at Leviticus 19:18.

26"The man chosen to drive the scapegoat into the wilderness of Azazel must wash his clothes and bathe himself in water. Then he may return to the camp.

27"The bull and the goat presented as sin offerings, whose blood Aaron takes into the Most Holy Place for the purification ceremony, will be carried outside the camp. The animals' hides, internal organs, and dung are all to be burned. 28The man who burns them must wash his clothes and bathe himself in water before returning to the camp.

29"On the tenth day of the appointed month in early autumn,* you must deny yourselves.* Neither native-born Israelites nor foreigners living among you may do any kind of work. This is a permanent law for you. 30On that day offerings of purifi-

16:29a Hebrew On the tenth day of the seventh month. This day in the ancient Hebrew lunar calendar occurred in September or October.
16:29b Or must fast; also in 16:31.

cation will be made for you,* and you will be purified in the LORD's presence from all your sins. ³¹It will be a Sabbath day of complete rest for you, and you must deny yourselves. This is a permanent law for you. ³²In future generations, the purification* ceremony will be performed by the priest who has been anointed and ordained to serve as high priest in place of his ancestor Aaron. He will put on the holy linen garments ³³and purify the Most Holy Place, the Tabernacle, the altar, the priests, and the entire congregation. ³⁴This is a permanent law for you, to purify the people of Israel from their sins, making them right with the LORD once each year."

Moses followed all these instructions exactly as the LORD had commanded him.

17 Prohibitions against Eating Blood

Then the LORD said to Moses, ²"Give the following instructions to Aaron and his sons and all the people of Israel. This is what the LORD has commanded.

³"If any native Israelite sacrifices a bull* or a lamb or a goat anywhere inside or outside the camp ⁴instead of bringing it to the entrance of the Tabernacle* to present it as an offering to the LORD, that person will be as guilty as a murderer.* Such a person has shed blood and will be cut off from the community. ⁵The purpose of this rule is to stop the Israelites from sacrificing animals in the open fields. It will ensure that they bring their sacrifices to the priest at the entrance of the Tabernacle, so he can present them to the LORD as peace offerings. ⁶Then the priest will be able to splatter the blood against the LORD's altar at the entrance of the Tabernacle, and he will burn the fat as a pleasing aroma to the LORD. ⁷The people must no longer be unfaithful to the LORD by offering sacrifices to the goat idols.* This is a permanent law for them, to be observed from generation to generation.

⁸"Give them this command as well. If any native Israelite or foreigner living among you offers a burnt offering or a sacrifice ⁹but does not bring it to the entrance of the Tabernacle to offer it to the LORD, that person will be cut off from the community.

¹⁰"And if any native Israelite or foreigner living among you eats or drinks blood in any form, I will turn against that person and cut him off from the community of your people, ¹¹for the life of the body is in its blood. I have given you the blood on the altar to purify you, making you right with the LORD.* It is the blood, given in exchange for a life, that makes purification possible. ¹²That is why I have said to the people of Israel, 'You must never eat or drink blood—neither you nor the foreigners living among you.'

¹³"And if any native Israelite or foreigner living among you goes hunting and kills an animal or bird that is approved for eating, he must drain its blood and cover it with earth. ¹⁴The life of every creature is in its blood. That is why I have said to the people of Israel, 'You must never eat or drink blood, for the life of any creature is in its blood.' So whoever consumes blood will be cut off from the community.

¹⁵"And if any native-born Israelites or foreigners eat the meat of an animal that died naturally or was torn up by wild animals, they must wash their clothes and bathe themselves in water. They will remain ceremonially unclean until evening, but then they will be clean. ¹⁶But if they do not wash their clothes and bathe themselves, they will be punished for their sin."

18 Forbidden Sexual Practices

Then the LORD said to Moses, ²"Give the following instructions to the people of Israel. I am the LORD your God. ³So do not act like the people in Egypt, where you used to live, or like the people of Canaan, where I am taking you. You must not imitate their way of life. ⁴You must obey all my regulations and be careful to obey my decrees, for I am the LORD your God. ⁵If you obey my decrees and my regulations, you will find life through them. I am the LORD.

⁶"You must never have sexual relations with a close relative, for I am the LORD.

⁷"Do not violate your father by having sexual relations with your mother. She is your mother; you must not have sexual relations with her.

⁸"Do not have sexual relations with any of your father's wives, for this would violate your father.

⁹"Do not have sexual relations with your sister or half sister, whether she is your father's daughter or your mother's daughter, whether she was born into your household or someone else's.

¹⁰"Do not have sexual relations with your granddaughter, whether she is your son's daughter or your daughter's daughter, for this would violate yourself.

¹¹"Do not have sexual relations with your stepsister, the daughter of any of your father's wives, for she is your sister.

¹²"Do not have sexual relations with your father's sister, for she is your father's close relative.

¹³"Do not have sexual relations with your mother's sister, for she is your mother's close relative.

¹⁴"Do not violate your uncle, your father's brother, by having sexual relations with his wife, for she is your aunt.

¹⁵"Do not have sexual relations with your daughter-in-law; she is your son's wife, so you must not have sexual relations with her.

¹⁶"Do not have sexual relations with your brother's wife, for this would violate your brother.

¹⁷"Do not have sexual relations with both a woman and her daughter. And do not take* her granddaughter, whether her son's daughter or her daughter's daughter, and have sexual relations with her. They are close relatives, and this would be a wicked act.

¹⁸"While your wife is living, do not marry her sister and have sexual relations with her, for they would be rivals.

¹⁹"Do not have sexual relations with a woman during her period of menstrual impurity.

²⁰"Do not defile yourself by having sexual intercourse with your neighbor's wife.

²¹"Do not permit any of your children to be offered as a sacrifice to Molech, for you must not bring shame on the name of your God. I am the LORD.

²²"Do not practice homosexuality, having sex with another man as with a woman. It is a detestable sin.

²³"A man must not defile himself by having sex with an animal. And a woman must not offer herself to a male animal to have intercourse with it. This is a perverse act.

²⁴"Do not defile yourselves in any of these ways, for the people I am driving out before you have defiled themselves in all these ways. ²⁵Because the entire land has become defiled, I am punishing the people who live there. I will cause the land to vomit them out. ²⁶You must obey all my decrees and regulations. You must not commit any of these detestable sins. This applies both to native-born Israelites and to the foreigners living among you.

²⁷"All these detestable activities are practiced by the people of the land where I am taking you, and this is how the land has become defiled. ²⁸So do not defile the land and give it a reason to vomit you out, as it will vomit out the people who live there now. ²⁹Whoever commits any of these detestable sins will be cut off from the community of Israel. ³⁰So obey my instructions, and do not defile yourselves by committing any of these detestable practices that were committed by the people who lived in the land before you. I am the LORD your God."

19 Holiness in Personal Conduct

The LORD also said to Moses, ²"Give the following instructions to the entire community of Israel. You must be holy because I, the LORD your God, am holy.

³"Each of you must show great respect for your mother and father, and you must always observe my Sabbath days of rest. I am the LORD your God.

⁴"Do not put your trust in idols or make metal images of gods for yourselves. I am the LORD your God.

⁵"When you sacrifice a peace offering to the LORD, offer it properly so you* will be accepted by God. ⁶The sacrifice must be eaten on the same day you offer it or on the next day. Whatever is left over until the third day must be completely burned up. ⁷If any of the sacrifice is eaten on the third day, it will be contaminated, and I will not accept it. ⁸Anyone who eats it on the third day will be punished for defiling what is holy to the LORD and will be cut off from the community.

18:17 Or do not marry. 19:5 Or it.

Loving the "Other"

LEVITICUS 19:18

Reconciliation

I'm usually "the Every"; I'm used to fitting in just about everywhere. I have a mix of Caucasian, Filipino, Mexican, and Native American ancestry. I generally feel comfortable around people of every ethnicity.

That is, until someone makes me feel I'm "the Other."

I've been told, "You're not really Asian." I've been called a Spanish slur reserved for Latina women who've betrayed their culture. When I was in third grade, a skinhead shouted at me, "Don't you wish you were white?" Recently a complete stranger in a store snarled, "Why don't you go back where you came from?" The hurtful message sent to the Other is: *you're not like us; you don't belong.*

You'd hope folks wouldn't be made to feel like the Other within the Christian community. Unfortunately hurts happen here too. Too often the plight of the Other is ignored. Slights, insensitivities, jokes, or just plain insults against the Other are minimized, treated as "no big deal." But we err when we trust our own assessment of whether something is hurtful—when we think, *They shouldn't be hurt. I wouldn't be.* That's like telling the Other, "It's your fault for not being like me."

Jesus embraced the Other in his society: women, children, lepers, the poor, prostitutes, Samaritans, and tax collectors. The early church leaders struggled to bridge the differences between Jews and Gentiles. As a church today, we too need to recognize the wounds of the Other and not dismiss their pain. To love our neighbor as ourselves is a profound undertaking because it requires a respect and consideration that doesn't come naturally (Leviticus 19:18; Mark 12:28-31). It begins with submission: giving up my rights to meet another's needs.

—Holly Vicente Robaina

For more on reconciliation, see reading at Isaiah 9:1-7.

⁹"When you harvest the crops of your land, do not harvest the grain along the edges of your fields, and do not pick up what the harvesters drop. ¹⁰It is the same with your grape crop—do not strip every last bunch of grapes from the vines, and do not pick up the grapes that fall to the ground. Leave them for the poor and the foreigners living among you. I am the LORD your God.

¹¹"Do not steal.

"Do not deceive or cheat one another.

¹²"Do not bring shame on the name of your God by using it to swear falsely. I am the LORD.

¹³"Do not defraud or rob your neighbor.

"Do not make your hired workers wait until the next day to receive their pay.

¹⁴"Do not insult the deaf or cause the blind to stumble. You must fear your God; I am the LORD.

¹⁵"Do not twist justice in legal matters by favoring the poor or being partial to the rich and powerful. Always judge people fairly.

¹⁶"Do not spread slanderous gossip among your people.*

"Do not stand idly by when your neighbor's life is threatened. I am the LORD.

¹⁷"Do not nurse hatred in your heart for any of your relatives.* Confront people

---

19:16 Hebrew *Do not act as a merchant toward your own people.*   **19:17** Hebrew *for your brother.*

directly so you will not be held guilty for their sin.

¹⁸"Do not seek revenge or bear a grudge against a fellow Israelite, but love your neighbor as yourself. I am the LORD.

¹⁹"You must obey all my decrees.

"Do not mate two different kinds of animals. Do not plant your field with two different kinds of seed. Do not wear clothing woven from two different kinds of thread.

²⁰"If a man has sex with a slave girl whose freedom has never been purchased but who is committed to become another man's wife, he must pay full compensation to her master. But since she is not a free woman, neither the man nor the woman will be put to death. ²¹The man, however, must bring a ram as a guilt offering and present it to the LORD at the entrance of the Tabernacle.* ²²The priest will then purify him* before the LORD with the ram of the guilt offering, and the man's sin will be forgiven.

²³"When you enter the land and plant fruit trees, leave the fruit unharvested for the first three years and consider it forbidden.* Do not eat it. ²⁴In the fourth year the entire crop must be consecrated to the LORD as a celebration of praise. ²⁵Finally, in the fifth year you may eat the fruit. If you follow this pattern, your harvest will increase. I am the LORD your God.

²⁶"Do not eat meat that has not been drained of its blood.

"Do not practice fortune-telling or witchcraft.

²⁷"Do not trim off the hair on your temples or trim your beards.

²⁸"Do not cut your bodies for the dead, and do not mark your skin with tattoos. I am the LORD.

²⁹"Do not defile your daughter by making her a prostitute, or the land will be filled with prostitution and wickedness.

³⁰"Keep my Sabbath days of rest, and show reverence toward my sanctuary. I am the LORD.

³¹"Do not defile yourselves by turning to mediums or to those who consult the spirits of the dead. I am the LORD your God.

³²"Stand up in the presence of the elderly, and show respect for the aged. Fear your God. I am the LORD.

³³"Do not take advantage of foreigners who live among you in your land. ³⁴Treat them like native-born Israelites, and love them as you love yourself. Remember that you were once foreigners living in the land of Egypt. I am the LORD your God.

³⁵"Do not use dishonest standards when measuring length, weight, or volume. ³⁶Your scales and weights must be accurate. Your containers for measuring dry materials or liquids must be accurate.* I am the LORD your God who brought you out of the land of Egypt.

³⁷"You must be careful to keep all of my decrees and regulations by putting them into practice. I am the LORD."

20 Punishments for Disobedience

The LORD said to Moses, ²"Give the people of Israel these instructions, which apply both to native Israelites and to the foreigners living in Israel.

"If any of them offer their children as a sacrifice to Molech, they must be put to death. The people of the community must stone them to death. ³I myself will turn against them and cut them off from the community, because they have defiled my sanctuary and brought shame on my holy name by offering their children to Molech. ⁴And if the people of the community ignore those who offer their children to Molech and refuse to execute them, ⁵I myself will turn against them and their families and will cut them off from the community. This will happen to all who commit spiritual prostitution by worshiping Molech.

⁶"I will also turn against those who commit spiritual prostitution by putting their trust in mediums or in those who consult the spirits of the dead. I will cut them off from the community. ⁷So set yourselves apart to be holy, for I am the LORD your God. ⁸Keep all my decrees by putting them into practice, for I am the LORD who makes you holy.

⁹"Anyone who dishonors* father or mother must be put to death. Such a person is guilty of a capital offense.

19:21 Hebrew Tent of Meeting.   **19:22** Or make atonement for him.   **19:23** Hebrew consider it uncircumcised.   **19:36** Hebrew Use an honest ephah [a dry measure] and an honest hin [a liquid measure].   **20:9** Greek version reads Anyone who speaks disrespectfully of. Compare Matt 15:4; Mark 7:10.

¹⁰"If a man commits adultery with his neighbor's wife, both the man and the woman who have committed adultery must be put to death.

¹¹"If a man violates his father by having sex with one of his father's wives, both the man and the woman must be put to death, for they are guilty of a capital offense.

¹²"If a man has sex with his daughter-in-law, both must be put to death. They have committed a perverse act and are guilty of a capital offense.

¹³"If a man practices homosexuality, having sex with another man as with a woman, both men have committed a detestable act. They must both be put to death, for they are guilty of a capital offense.

¹⁴"If a man marries both a woman and her mother, he has committed a wicked act. The man and both women must be burned to death to wipe out such wickedness from among you.

¹⁵"If a man has sex with an animal, he must be put to death, and the animal must be killed.

¹⁶"If a woman presents herself to a male animal to have intercourse with it, she and the animal must both be put to death. You must kill both, for they are guilty of a capital offense.

¹⁷"If a man marries his sister, the daughter of either his father or his mother, and they have sexual relations, it is a shameful disgrace. They must be publicly cut off from the community. Since the man has violated his sister, he will be punished for his sin.

¹⁸"If a man has sexual relations with a woman during her menstrual period, both of them must be cut off from the community, for together they have exposed the source of her blood flow.

¹⁹"Do not have sexual relations with your aunt, whether your mother's sister or your father's sister. This would dishonor a close relative. Both parties are guilty and will be punished for their sin.

²⁰"If a man has sex with his uncle's wife, he has violated his uncle. Both the man and woman will be punished for their sin, and they will die childless.

²¹"If a man marries his brother's wife, it is an act of impurity. He has violated his brother, and the guilty couple will remain childless.

²²"You must keep all my decrees and regulations by putting them into practice; otherwise the land to which I am bringing you as your new home will vomit you out. ²³Do not live according to the customs of the people I am driving out before you. It is because they do these shameful things that I detest them. ²⁴But I have promised you, 'You will possess their land because I will give it to you as your possession— a land flowing with milk and honey.' I am the LORD your God, who has set you apart from all other people.

²⁵"You must therefore make a distinction between ceremonially clean and unclean animals, and between clean and unclean birds. You must not defile yourselves by eating any unclean animal or bird or creature that scurries along the ground. I have identified them as being unclean for you. ²⁶You must be holy because I, the LORD, am holy. I have set you apart from all other people to be my very own.

²⁷"Men and women among you who act as mediums or who consult the spirits of the dead must be put to death by stoning. They are guilty of a capital offense."

21 Instructions for the Priests

The LORD said to Moses, "Give the following instructions to the priests, the descendants of Aaron.

"A priest must not make himself ceremonially unclean by touching the dead body of a relative. ²The only exceptions are his closest relatives—his mother or father, son or daughter, brother, ³or his virgin sister who depends on him because she has no husband. ⁴But a priest must not defile himself and make himself unclean for someone who is related to him only by marriage.

⁵"The priests must not shave their heads or trim their beards or cut their bodies. ⁶They must be set apart as holy to their God and must never bring shame on the name of God. They must be holy, for they are the ones who present the special gifts to the LORD, gifts of food for their God.

⁷"Priests may not marry a woman defiled

by prostitution, and they may not marry a woman who is divorced from her husband, for the priests are set apart as holy to their God. [8] You must treat them as holy because they offer up food to your God. You must consider them holy because I, the LORD, am holy, and I make you holy.

[9] "If a priest's daughter defiles herself by becoming a prostitute, she also defiles her father's holiness, and she must be burned to death.

[10] "The high priest has the highest rank of all the priests. The anointing oil has been poured on his head, and he has been ordained to wear the priestly garments. He must never leave his hair uncombed* or tear his clothing. [11] He must not defile himself by going near a dead body. He may not make himself ceremonially unclean even for his father or mother. [12] He must not defile the sanctuary of his God by leaving it to attend to a dead person, for he has been made holy by the anointing oil of his God. I am the LORD.

[13] "The high priest may marry only a virgin. [14] He may not marry a widow, a woman who is divorced, or a woman who has defiled herself by prostitution. She must be a virgin from his own clan, [15] so that he will not dishonor his descendants among his clan, for I am the LORD who makes him holy."

[16] Then the LORD said to Moses, [17] "Give the following instructions to Aaron: In all future generations, none of your descendants who has any defect will qualify to offer food to his God. [18] No one who has a defect qualifies, whether he is blind, lame, disfigured, deformed, [19] or has a broken foot or arm, [20] or is hunchbacked or dwarfed, or has a defective eye, or skin sores or scabs, or damaged testicles. [21] No descendant of Aaron who has a defect may approach the altar to present special gifts to the LORD. Since he has a defect, he may not approach the altar to offer food to his God. [22] However, he may eat from the food offered to God, including the holy offerings and the most holy offerings. [23] Yet because of his physical defect, he may not enter the room behind the inner curtain or approach the altar, for this would defile my holy places. I am the LORD who makes them holy."

[24] So Moses gave these instructions to Aaron and his sons and to all the Israelites.

22 The LORD said to Moses, [2] "Tell Aaron and his sons to be very careful with the sacred gifts that the Israelites set apart for me, so they do not bring shame on my holy name. I am the LORD. [3] Give them the following instructions.

"In all future generations, if any of your descendants is ceremonially unclean when he approaches the sacred offerings that the people of Israel consecrate to the LORD, he must be cut off from my presence. I am the LORD.

[4] "If any of Aaron's descendants has a skin disease* or any kind of discharge that makes him ceremonially unclean, he may not eat from the sacred offerings until he has been pronounced clean. He also becomes unclean by touching a corpse, or by having an emission of semen, [5] or by touching a small animal that is unclean, or by touching someone who is ceremonially unclean for any reason. [6] The man who is defiled in any of these ways will remain unclean until evening. He may not eat from the sacred offerings until he has bathed himself in water. [7] When the sun goes down, he will be ceremonially clean again and may eat from the sacred offerings, for this is his food. [8] He may not eat an animal that has died a natural death or has been torn apart by wild animals, for this would defile him. I am the LORD.

[9] "The priests must follow my instructions carefully. Otherwise they will be punished for their sin and will die for violating my instructions. I am the LORD who makes them holy.

[10] "No one outside a priest's family may eat the sacred offerings. Even guests and hired workers in a priest's home are not allowed to eat them. [11] However, if the priest buys a slave for himself, the slave may eat from the sacred offerings. And if his slaves have children, they also may share his food. [12] If a priest's daughter marries someone outside the priestly family, she may no longer eat the sacred offerings. [13] But if she becomes

---

21:10 Or *never uncover his head.*   **22:4** Traditionally rendered *leprosy;* see note on 13:2a.

a widow or is divorced and has no children to support her, and she returns to live in her father's home as in her youth, she may eat her father's food again. Otherwise, no one outside a priest's family may eat the sacred offerings.

[14]"Any such person who eats the sacred offerings without realizing it must pay the priest for the amount eaten, plus an additional 20 percent. [15]The priests must not let the Israelites defile the sacred offerings brought to the LORD [16]by allowing unauthorized people to eat them. This would bring guilt upon them and require them to pay compensation. I am the LORD who makes them holy."

Worthy and Unworthy Offerings

[17]And the LORD said to Moses, [18]"Give Aaron and his sons and all the Israelites these instructions, which apply both to native Israelites and to the foreigners living among you.

"If you present a gift as a burnt offering to the LORD, whether it is to fulfill a vow or is a voluntary offering, [19]you* will be accepted only if your offering is a male animal with no defects. It may be a bull, a ram, or a male goat. [20]Do not present an animal with defects, because the LORD will not accept it on your behalf.

[21]"If you present a peace offering to the LORD from the herd or the flock, whether it is to fulfill a vow or is a voluntary offering, you must offer a perfect animal. It may have no defect of any kind. [22]You must not offer an animal that is blind, crippled, or injured, or that has a wart, a skin sore, or scabs. Such animals must never be offered on the altar as special gifts to the LORD. [23]If a bull* or lamb has a leg that is too long or too short, it may be offered as a voluntary offering, but it may not be offered to fulfill a vow. [24]If an animal has damaged testicles or is castrated, you may not offer it to the LORD. You must never do this in your own land, [25]and you must not accept such an animal from foreigners and then offer it as a sacrifice to your God. Such animals will not be accepted on your behalf, for they are mutilated or defective."

[26]And the LORD said to Moses, [27]"When a calf or lamb or goat is born, it must be left with its mother for seven days. From the eighth day on, it will be acceptable as a special gift to the LORD. [28]But you must not slaughter a mother animal and her offspring on the same day, whether from the herd or the flock. [29]When you bring a thanksgiving offering to the LORD, sacrifice it properly so you will be accepted. [30]Eat the entire sacrificial animal on the day it is presented. Do not leave any of it until the next morning. I am the LORD.

[31]"You must faithfully keep all my commands by putting them into practice, for I am the LORD. [32]Do not bring shame on my holy name, for I will display my holiness among the people of Israel. I am the LORD who makes you holy. [33]It was I who rescued you from the land of Egypt, that I might be your God. I am the LORD."

23 The Appointed Festivals

The LORD said to Moses, [2]"Give the following instructions to the people of Israel. These are the LORD's appointed festivals, which you are to proclaim as official days for holy assembly.

[3]"You have six days each week for your ordinary work, but the seventh day is a Sabbath day of complete rest, an official day for holy assembly. It is the LORD's Sabbath day, and it must be observed wherever you live.

[4]"In addition to the Sabbath, these are the LORD's appointed festivals, the official days for holy assembly that are to be celebrated at their proper times each year.

Passover and the Festival of Unleavened Bread

[5]"The LORD's Passover begins at sundown on the fourteenth day of the first month.* [6]On the next day, the fifteenth day of the month, you must begin celebrating the Festival of Unleavened Bread. This festival to the LORD continues for seven days, and during that time the bread you eat must be made without yeast. [7]On the first day of the festival, all the people must stop their ordinary work and observe an official day for holy assembly. [8]For seven days you must

---

22:19 Or it.   **22:23** Or cow.   **23:5** This day in the ancient Hebrew lunar calendar occurred in late March, April, or early May.

present special gifts to the LORD. On the seventh day the people must again stop all their ordinary work to observe an official day for holy assembly."

Celebration of First Harvest

⁹Then the LORD said to Moses, ¹⁰"Give the following instructions to the people of Israel. When you enter the land I am giving you and you harvest its first crops, bring the priest a bundle of grain from the first cutting of your grain harvest. ¹¹On the day after the Sabbath, the priest will lift it up before the LORD so it may be accepted on your behalf. ¹²On that same day you must sacrifice a one-year-old male lamb with no defects as a burnt offering to the LORD. ¹³With it you must present a grain offering consisting of four quarts* of choice flour moistened with olive oil. It will be a special gift, a pleasing aroma to the LORD. You must also offer one quart* of wine as a liquid offering. ¹⁴Do not eat any bread or roasted grain or fresh kernels on that day until you bring this offering to your God. This is a permanent law for you, and it must be observed from generation to generation wherever you live.

The Festival of Harvest

¹⁵"From the day after the Sabbath—the day you bring the bundle of grain to be lifted up as a special offering—count off seven full weeks. ¹⁶Keep counting until the day after the seventh Sabbath, fifty days later. Then present an offering of new grain to the LORD. ¹⁷From wherever you live, bring two loaves of bread to be lifted up before the LORD as a special offering. Make these loaves from four quarts of choice flour, and bake them with yeast. They will be an offering to the LORD from the first of your crops. ¹⁸Along with the bread, present seven one-year-old male lambs with no defects, one young bull, and two rams as burnt offerings to the LORD. These burnt offerings, together with the grain offerings and liquid offerings, will be a special gift, a pleasing aroma to the LORD. ¹⁹Then you must offer one male goat as a sin offering and two one-year-old male lambs as a peace offering.

²⁰"The priest will lift up the two lambs as a special offering to the LORD, together with the loaves representing the first of your crops. These offerings, which are holy to the LORD, belong to the priests. ²¹That same day will be proclaimed an official day for holy assembly, a day on which you do no ordinary work. This is a permanent law for you, and it must be observed from generation to generation wherever you live.*

²²"When you harvest the crops of your land, do not harvest the grain along the edges of your fields, and do not pick up what the harvesters drop. Leave it for the poor and the foreigners living among you. I am the LORD your God."

The Festival of Trumpets

²³The LORD said to Moses, ²⁴"Give the following instructions to the people of Israel. On the first day of the appointed month in early autumn,* you are to observe a day of complete rest. It will be an official day for holy assembly, a day commemorated with loud blasts of a trumpet. ²⁵You must do no ordinary work on that day. Instead, you are to present special gifts to the LORD."

The Day of Atonement

²⁶Then the LORD said to Moses, ²⁷"Be careful to celebrate the Day of Atonement on the tenth day of that same month—nine days after the Festival of Trumpets.* You must observe it as an official day for holy assembly, a day to deny yourselves* and present special gifts to the LORD. ²⁸Do no work during that entire day because it is the Day of Atonement, when offerings of purification are made for you, making you right with* the LORD your God. ²⁹All who do not deny themselves that day will be cut off from God's people. ³⁰And I will destroy anyone among you who does any work on that day. ³¹You must not do any work at all! This is a permanent law for you, and it must

---

23:13a Hebrew ²⁄₁₀ of an ephah [4.4 liters]; also in 23:17.   23:13b Hebrew ¼ of a hin [1 liter].   23:21 This celebration, called the Festival of Harvest or the Festival of Weeks, was later called the Festival of Pentecost (see Acts 2:1). It is celebrated today as Shavuot (or Shabuoth).   23:24 Hebrew On the first day of the seventh month. This day in the ancient Hebrew lunar calendar occurred in September or October. This festival is celebrated today as Rosh Hashanah, the Jewish new year.   23:27a Hebrew on the tenth day of the seventh month; see 23:24 and the note there. This day in the ancient Hebrew lunar calendar occurred in September or October. It is celebrated today as Yom Kippur.   23:27b Or to fast; similarly in 23:29, 32.   23:28 Or when atonement is made for you before.

Rest and Self-Denial?

LEVITICUS 23:32

When I dream about rest, I picture some pampered, paradisial setting. Perhaps it's a breezy moment on a peaceful, sunny beach. Maybe it's sleeping in on a fluffy, feather bed in a quiet room (with no children coming in to wake me). *Rest* brings to mind feeling comfortable and at ease.

Yet in Leviticus we find what may strike us as a strange pairing: rest and self-denial. In descriptions of how God's people were to observe the Day of Atonement, we find this instruction: "It will be a Sabbath day of complete rest for you, and you must deny yourselves" (Leviticus 16:31; see also 23:32). *The Jewish Publication Society Torah Commentary* on Leviticus explains that "the idiom *'innah nefesh* ["deny yourself"] always connotes fasting." It's the same idea used to describe fasting in Isaiah 58:3 and Psalm 35:13. Ancient rabbinical teachings interpret this self-denial to involve five forms of fasting or abstention: "from food and drink, bathing, use of oil or unguent on the body, wearing leather shoes, and sexual intercourse." This fasting led to a day of "complete rest"—literally *shabbat shabbaton,* a repetition of the word for *Sabbath,* making this a doubly emphasized superlative. Somehow the self-denial of fasting is linked with true rest of the soul.

This counterintuitive rest that fasting brings—whether it be fasting from food, sexual expression, or other modern-day appetites like television watching, Internet surfing, or make-up—is nearly the opposite of the comfortable, pampered rest I daydream about. God offers us a completely different rest: a rest that comes, paradoxically, when our appetites and comforts are not satisfied but are stripped away; when we are left raw and real, vulnerable and maybe even weak—but when what's left is just us and God, nothing else in the way. It's a rest that may not "feel" good—but that *is* good.

—*Kelli B. Trujillo*

For more on fasting, see reading at Deuteronomy 8:1–5.

be observed from generation to generation wherever you live. ³²This will be a Sabbath day of complete rest for you, and on that day you must deny yourselves. This day of rest will begin at sundown on the ninth day of the month and extend until sundown on the tenth day."

The Festival of Shelters

³³And the LORD said to Moses, ³⁴"Give the following instructions to the people of Israel. Begin celebrating the Festival of Shelters* on the fifteenth day of the appointed month—five days after the Day of Atonement.* This festival to the LORD will last for seven days. ³⁵On the first day of the festival you must proclaim an official day for holy assembly, when you do no ordinary work. ³⁶For seven days you must present special gifts to the LORD. The eighth day is another holy day on which you present your special gifts to the LORD. This will be a solemn occasion, and no ordinary work may be done that day.

³⁷("These are the LORD's appointed festivals. Celebrate them each year as official days for holy assembly by presenting special gifts to the LORD—burnt offerings,

---

23:34a Or *Festival of Booths,* or *Festival of Tabernacles.* This was earlier called the Festival of the Final Harvest or Festival of Ingathering (see Exod 23:16b). It is celebrated today as Sukkot (or Succoth). **23:34b** Hebrew *on the fifteenth day of the seventh month;* see 23:27a and the note there.

grain offerings, sacrifices, and liquid offerings—each on its proper day. [38] These festivals must be observed in addition to the LORD's regular Sabbath days, and the offerings are in addition to your personal gifts, the offerings you give to fulfill your vows, and the voluntary offerings you present to the LORD.)

[39] "Remember that this seven-day festival to the LORD—the Festival of Shelters—begins on the fifteenth day of the appointed month,* after you have harvested all the produce of the land. The first day and the eighth day of the festival will be days of complete rest. [40] On the first day gather branches from magnificent trees*—palm fronds, boughs from leafy trees, and willows that grow by the streams. Then celebrate with joy before the LORD your God for seven days. [41] You must observe this festival to the LORD for seven days every year. This is a permanent law for you, and it must be observed in the appointed month* from generation to generation. [42] For seven days you must live outside in little shelters. All native-born Israelites must live in shelters. [43] This will remind each new generation of Israelites that I made their ancestors live in shelters when I rescued them from the land of Egypt. I am the LORD your God."

[44] So Moses gave the Israelites these instructions regarding the annual festivals of the LORD.

24 Pure Oil and Holy Bread

The LORD said to Moses, [2] "Command the people of Israel to bring you pure oil of pressed olives for the light, to keep the lamps burning continually. [3] This is the lampstand that stands in the Tabernacle, in front of the inner curtain that shields the Ark of the Covenant.* Aaron must keep the lamps burning in the LORD's presence all night. This is a permanent law for you, and it must be observed from generation to generation. [4] Aaron and the priests must tend the lamps on the pure gold lampstand continually in the LORD's presence.

[5] "You must bake twelve loaves of bread from choice flour, using four quarts* of flour for each loaf. [6] Place the bread before the LORD on the pure gold table, and arrange the loaves in two rows, with six loaves in each row. [7] Put some pure frankincense near each row to serve as a representative offering, a special gift presented to the LORD. [8] Every Sabbath day this bread must be laid out before the LORD. The bread is to be received from the people of Israel as a requirement of the eternal covenant. [9] The loaves of bread will belong to Aaron and his descendants, who must eat them in a sacred place, for they are most holy. It is the permanent right of the priests to claim this portion of the special gifts presented to the LORD."

An Example of Just Punishment

[10] One day a man who had an Israelite mother and an Egyptian father came out of his tent and got into a fight with one of the Israelite men. [11] During the fight, this son of an Israelite woman blasphemed the Name of the LORD* with a curse. So the man was brought to Moses for judgment. His mother was Shelomith, the daughter of Dibri of the tribe of Dan. [12] They kept the man in custody until the LORD's will in the matter should become clear to them.

[13] Then the LORD said to Moses, [14] "Take the blasphemer outside the camp, and tell all those who heard the curse to lay their hands on his head. Then let the entire community stone him to death. [15] Say to the people of Israel: Those who curse their God will be punished for their sin. [16] Anyone who blasphemes the Name of the LORD must be stoned to death by the whole community of Israel. Any native-born Israelite or foreigner among you who blasphemes the Name of the LORD must be put to death.

[17] "Anyone who takes another person's life must be put to death.

[18] "Anyone who kills another person's animal must pay for it in full—a live animal for the animal that was killed.

[19] "Anyone who injures another person must be dealt with according to the injury inflicted—[20] a fracture for a fracture, an eye for an eye, a tooth for a tooth. Whatever

---

23:39 Hebrew on the fifteenth day of the seventh month.   23:40 Or gather fruit from majestic trees.   23:41 Hebrew the seventh month.
24:3 Hebrew in the Tent of Meeting, outside the inner curtain of the Testimony; see note on 16:13.   24:5 Hebrew ⅖ of an ephah
[4.4 liters].   24:11 Hebrew the Name; also in 24:16b.

anyone does to injure another person must be paid back in kind.

²¹"Whoever kills an animal must pay for it in full, but whoever kills another person must be put to death.

²²"This same standard applies both to native-born Israelites and to the foreigners living among them. I am the LORD your God."

²³After Moses gave all these instructions to the Israelites, they took the blasphemer outside the camp and stoned him to death. The Israelites did just as the LORD had commanded Moses.

25 The Sabbath Year

While Moses was on Mount Sinai, the LORD said to him, ²"Give the following instructions to the people of Israel. When you have entered the land I am giving you, the land itself must observe a Sabbath rest before the LORD every seventh year. ³For six years you may plant your fields and prune your vineyards and harvest your crops, ⁴but during the seventh year the land must have a Sabbath year of complete rest. It is the LORD's Sabbath. Do not plant your fields or prune your vineyards during that year. ⁵And don't store away the crops that grow on their own or gather the grapes from your unpruned vines. The land must have a year of complete rest. ⁶But you may eat whatever the land produces on its own during its Sabbath. This applies to you, your male and female servants, your hired workers, and the temporary residents who live with you. ⁷Your livestock and the wild animals in your land will also be allowed to eat what the land produces.

The Year of Jubilee

⁸"In addition, you must count off seven Sabbath years, seven sets of seven years, adding up to forty-nine years in all. ⁹Then on the Day of Atonement in the fiftieth year,* blow the ram's horn loud and long throughout the land. ¹⁰Set this year apart as holy, a time to proclaim freedom throughout the land for all who live there. It will be a jubilee year for you, when each of you may return to the land that belonged

to your ancestors and return to your own clan. ¹¹This fiftieth year will be a jubilee for you. During that year you must not plant your fields or store away any of the crops that grow on their own, and don't gather the grapes from your unpruned vines. ¹²It will be a jubilee year for you, and you must keep it holy. But you may eat whatever the land produces on its own. ¹³In the Year of Jubilee each of you may return to the land that belonged to your ancestors.

¹⁴"When you make an agreement with your neighbor to buy or sell property, you must not take advantage of each other. ¹⁵When you buy land from your neighbor, the price you pay must be based on the number of years since the last jubilee. The seller must set the price by taking into account the number of years remaining until the next Year of Jubilee. ¹⁶The more years until the next jubilee, the higher the price; the fewer years, the lower the price. After all, the person selling the land is actually selling you a certain number of harvests. ¹⁷Show your fear of God by not taking advantage of each other. I am the LORD your God.

¹⁸"If you want to live securely in the land, follow my decrees and obey my regulations. ¹⁹Then the land will yield large crops, and you will eat your fill and live securely in it. ²⁰But you might ask, 'What will we eat during the seventh year, since we are not allowed to plant or harvest crops that year?' ²¹Be assured that I will send my blessing for you in the sixth year, so the land will produce a crop large enough for three years. ²²When you plant your fields in the eighth year, you will still be eating from the large crop of the sixth year. In fact, you will still be eating from that large crop when the new crop is harvested in the ninth year.

Redemption of Property

²³"The land must never be sold on a permanent basis, for the land belongs to me. You are only foreigners and tenant farmers working for me.

²⁴"With every purchase of land you must grant the seller the right to buy it back. ²⁵If one of your fellow Israelites falls into

poverty and is forced to sell some family land, then a close relative should buy it back for him. ²⁶If there is no close relative to buy the land, but the person who sold it gets enough money to buy it back, ²⁷he then has the right to redeem it from the one who bought it. The price of the land will be discounted according to the number of years until the next Year of Jubilee. In this way the original owner can then return to the land. ²⁸But if the original owner cannot afford to buy back the land, it will remain with the new owner until the next Year of Jubilee. In the jubilee year, the land must be returned to the original owners so they can return to their family land.

²⁹"Anyone who sells a house inside a walled town has the right to buy it back for a full year after its sale. During that year, the seller retains the right to buy it back. ³⁰But if it is not bought back within a year, the sale of the house within the walled town cannot be reversed. It will become the permanent property of the buyer. It will not be returned to the original owner in the Year of Jubilee. ³¹But a house in a village—a settlement without fortified walls—will be treated like property in the countryside. Such a house may be bought back at any time, and it must be returned to the original owner in the Year of Jubilee.

³²"The Levites always have the right to buy back a house they have sold within the towns allotted to them. ³³And any property that is sold by the Levites—all houses within the Levitical towns—must be returned in the Year of Jubilee. After all, the houses in the towns reserved for the Levites are the only property they own in all Israel. ³⁴The open pastureland around the Levitical towns may never be sold. It is their permanent possession.

Redemption of the Poor and Enslaved

³⁵"If one of your fellow Israelites falls into poverty and cannot support himself, support him as you would a foreigner or a temporary resident and allow him to live with you. ³⁶Do not charge interest or make a profit at his expense. Instead, show your fear of God by letting him live with you as your relative. ³⁷Remember, do not charge interest on money you lend him or make a profit on food you sell him. ³⁸I am the LORD your God, who brought you out of the land of Egypt to give you the land of Canaan and to be your God.

³⁹"If one of your fellow Israelites falls into poverty and is forced to sell himself to you, do not treat him as a slave. ⁴⁰Treat him instead as a hired worker or as a temporary resident who lives with you, and he will serve you only until the Year of Jubilee. ⁴¹At that time he and his children will no longer be obligated to you, and they will return to their clans and go back to the land originally allotted to their ancestors. ⁴²The people of Israel are my servants, whom I brought out of the land of Egypt, so they must never be sold as slaves. ⁴³Show your fear of God by not treating them harshly.

⁴⁴"However, you may purchase male and female slaves from among the nations around you. ⁴⁵You may also purchase the children of temporary residents who live among you, including those who have been born in your land. You may treat them as your property, ⁴⁶passing them on to your children as a permanent inheritance. You may treat them as slaves, but you must never treat your fellow Israelites this way.

⁴⁷"Suppose a foreigner or temporary resident becomes rich while living among you. If any of your fellow Israelites fall into poverty and are forced to sell themselves to such a foreigner or to a member of his family, ⁴⁸they still retain the right to be bought back, even after they have been purchased. They may be bought back by a brother, ⁴⁹an uncle, or a cousin. In fact, anyone from the extended family may buy them back. They may also redeem themselves if they have prospered. ⁵⁰They will negotiate the price of their freedom with the person who bought them. The price will be based on the number of years from the time they were sold until the next Year of Jubilee—whatever it would cost to hire a worker for that period of time. ⁵¹If many years still remain until the jubilee, they will repay the proper proportion of what they received when they sold themselves. ⁵²If only a few years remain until the Year of Jubilee, they will repay a small amount for their redemption. ⁵³The foreigner must treat them as workers hired on a yearly basis. You must

not allow a foreigner to treat any of your fellow Israelites harshly. ⁵⁴If any Israelites have not been bought back by the time the Year of Jubilee arrives, they and their children must be set free at that time. ⁵⁵For the people of Israel belong to me. They are my servants, whom I brought out of the land of Egypt. I am the LORD your God.

26

Blessings for Obedience

"Do not make idols or set up carved images, or sacred pillars, or sculptured stones in your land so you may worship them. I am the LORD your God. ²You must keep my Sabbath days of rest and show reverence for my sanctuary. I am the LORD.

³"If you follow my decrees and are careful to obey my commands, ⁴I will send you the seasonal rains. The land will then yield its crops, and the trees of the field will produce their fruit. ⁵Your threshing season will overlap with the grape harvest, and your grape harvest will overlap with the season of planting grain. You will eat your fill and live securely in your own land.

⁶"I will give you peace in the land, and you will be able to sleep with no cause for fear. I will rid the land of wild animals and keep your enemies out of your land. ⁷In fact, you will chase down your enemies and slaughter them with your swords. ⁸Five of you will chase a hundred, and a hundred of you will chase ten thousand! All your enemies will fall beneath your sword.

⁹"I will look favorably upon you, making you fertile and multiplying your people. And I will fulfill my covenant with you. ¹⁰You will have such a surplus of crops that you will need to clear out the old grain to make room for the new harvest! ¹¹I will live among you, and I will not despise you. ¹²I will walk among you; I will be your God, and you will be my people. ¹³I am the LORD your God, who brought you out of the land of Egypt so you would no longer be their slaves. I broke the yoke of slavery from your neck so you can walk with your heads held high.

Punishments for Disobedience

¹⁴"However, if you do not listen to me or obey all these commands, ¹⁵and if you break my covenant by rejecting my decrees, treating my regulations with contempt, and refusing to obey my commands, ¹⁶I will punish you. I will bring sudden terrors upon you—wasting diseases and burning fevers that will cause your eyes to fail and your life to ebb away. You will plant your crops in vain because your enemies will eat them. ¹⁷I will turn against you, and you will be defeated by your enemies. Those who hate you will rule over you, and you will run even when no one is chasing you!

¹⁸"And if, in spite of all this, you still disobey me, I will punish you seven times over for your sins. ¹⁹I will break your proud spirit by making the skies as unyielding as iron and the earth as hard as bronze. ²⁰All your work will be for nothing, for your land will yield no crops, and your trees will bear no fruit.

²¹"If even then you remain hostile toward me and refuse to obey me, I will inflict disaster on you seven times over for your sins. ²²I will send wild animals that will rob you of your children and destroy your livestock. Your numbers will dwindle, and your roads will be deserted.

²³"And if you fail to learn the lesson and continue your hostility toward me, ²⁴then I myself will be hostile toward you. I will personally strike you with calamity seven times over for your sins. ²⁵I will send armies against you to carry out the curse of the covenant you have broken. When you run to your towns for safety, I will send a plague to destroy you there, and you will be handed over to your enemies. ²⁶I will destroy your food supply, so that ten women will need only one oven to bake bread for their families. They will ration your food by weight, and though you have food to eat, you will not be satisfied.

²⁷"If in spite of all this you still refuse to listen and still remain hostile toward me, ²⁸then I will give full vent to my hostility. I myself will punish you seven times over for your sins. ²⁹Then you will eat the flesh of your own sons and daughters. ³⁰I will destroy your pagan shrines and knock down your places of worship. I will leave your lifeless corpses piled on top of your lifeless idols,* and I will despise you. ³¹I will make

---

26:30 The Hebrew term (literally *round things*) probably alludes to dung.

your cities desolate and destroy your places of pagan worship. I will take no pleasure in your offerings that should be a pleasing aroma to me. ³²Yes, I myself will devastate your land, and your enemies who come to occupy it will be appalled at what they see. ³³I will scatter you among the nations and bring out my sword against you. Your land will become desolate, and your cities will lie in ruins. ³⁴Then at last the land will enjoy its neglected Sabbath years as it lies desolate while you are in exile in the land of your enemies. Then the land will finally rest and enjoy the Sabbaths it missed. ³⁵As long as the land lies in ruins, it will enjoy the rest you never allowed it to take every seventh year while you lived in it.

³⁶"And for those of you who survive, I will demoralize you in the land of your enemies. You will live in such fear that the sound of a leaf driven by the wind will send you fleeing. You will run as though fleeing from a sword, and you will fall even when no one pursues you. ³⁷Though no one is chasing you, you will stumble over each other as though fleeing from a sword. You will have no power to stand up against your enemies. ³⁸You will die among the foreign nations and be devoured in the land of your enemies. ³⁹Those of you who survive will waste away in your enemies' lands because of their sins and the sins of their ancestors.

⁴⁰"But at last my people will confess their sins and the sins of their ancestors for betraying me and being hostile toward me. ⁴¹When I have turned their hostility back on them and brought them to the land of their enemies, then at last their stubborn hearts will be humbled, and they will pay for their sins. ⁴²Then I will remember my covenant with Jacob and my covenant with Isaac and my covenant with Abraham, and I will remember the land. ⁴³For the land must be abandoned to enjoy its years of Sabbath rest as it lies deserted. At last the people will pay for their sins, for they have continually rejected my regulations and despised my decrees.

⁴⁴"But despite all this, I will not utterly reject or despise them while they are in exile in the land of their enemies. I will not cancel my covenant with them by wiping them out, for I am the LORD their God. ⁴⁵For their sakes I will remember my ancient covenant with their ancestors, whom I brought out of the land of Egypt in the sight of all the nations, that I might be their God. I am the LORD."

⁴⁶These are the decrees, regulations, and instructions that the LORD gave through Moses on Mount Sinai as evidence of the relationship between himself and the Israelites.

27 Redemption of Gifts Offered to the LORD

The LORD said to Moses, ²"Give the following instructions to the people of Israel. If anyone makes a special vow to dedicate someone to the LORD by paying the value of that person, ³here is the scale of values to be used. A man between the ages of twenty and sixty is valued at fifty shekels* of silver, as measured by the sanctuary shekel. ⁴A woman of that age is valued at thirty shekels* of silver. ⁵A boy between the ages of five and twenty is valued at twenty shekels of silver; a girl of that age is valued at ten shekels* of silver. ⁶A boy between the ages of one month and five years is valued at five shekels of silver; a girl of that age is valued at three shekels* of silver. ⁷A man older than sixty is valued at fifteen shekels of silver; a woman of that age is valued at ten shekels* of silver. ⁸If you desire to make such a vow but cannot afford to pay the required amount, take the person to the priest. He will determine the amount for you to pay based on what you can afford.

⁹"If your vow involves giving an animal that is acceptable as an offering to the LORD, any gift to the LORD will be considered holy. ¹⁰You may not exchange or substitute it for another animal—neither a good animal for a bad one nor a bad animal for a good one. But if you do exchange one animal for another, then both the original animal and its substitute will be considered holy. ¹¹If your vow involves an unclean animal—one that is not acceptable as an

---

27:3 Or 20 ounces [570 grams]. 27:4 Or 12 ounces [342 grams]. 27:5 Or A boy . . . 8 ounces [228 grams] of silver; a girl . . . 4 ounces [114 grams]. 27:6 Or A boy . . . 2 ounces [57 grams] of silver; a girl . . . 1.2 ounces [34 grams]. 27:7 Or A man . . . 6 ounces [171 grams] of silver; a woman . . . 4 ounces [114 grams].

offering to the LORD—then you must bring the animal to the priest. ¹²He will assess its value, and his assessment will be final, whether high or low. ¹³If you want to buy back the animal, you must pay the value set by the priest, plus 20 percent.

¹⁴"If someone dedicates a house to the LORD, the priest will come to assess its value. The priest's assessment will be final, whether high or low. ¹⁵If the person who dedicated the house wants to buy it back, he must pay the value set by the priest, plus 20 percent. Then the house will again be his.

¹⁶"If someone dedicates to the LORD a piece of his family property, its value will be assessed according to the amount of seed required to plant it—fifty shekels of silver for a field planted with five bushels of barley seed.* ¹⁷If the field is dedicated to the LORD in the Year of Jubilee, then the entire assessment will apply. ¹⁸But if the field is dedicated after the Year of Jubilee, the priest will assess the land's value in proportion to the number of years left until the next Year of Jubilee. Its assessed value is reduced each year. ¹⁹If the person who dedicated the field wants to buy it back, he must pay the value set by the priest, plus 20 percent. Then the field will again be legally his. ²⁰But if he does not want to buy it back, and it is sold to someone else, the field can no longer be bought back. ²¹When the field is released in the Year of Jubilee, it will be holy, a field specially set apart* for the LORD. It will become the property of the priests.

²²"If someone dedicates to the LORD a field he has purchased but which is not part of his family property, ²³the priest will assess its value based on the number of years left until the next Year of Jubilee. On that day he must give the assessed value of the land as a sacred donation to the LORD. ²⁴In the Year of Jubilee the field must be returned to the person from whom he purchased it, the one who inherited it as family property. ²⁵(All the payments must be measured by the weight of the sanctuary shekel,* which equals twenty gerahs.)

²⁶"You may not dedicate a firstborn animal to the LORD, for the firstborn of your cattle, sheep, and goats already belong to him. ²⁷However, you may buy back the firstborn of a ceremonially unclean animal by paying the priest's assessment of its worth, plus 20 percent. If you do not buy it back, the priest will sell it at its assessed value.

²⁸"However, anything specially set apart for the LORD—whether a person, an animal, or family property—must never be sold or bought back. Anything devoted in this way has been set apart as holy, and it belongs to the LORD. ²⁹No person specially set apart for destruction may be bought back. Such a person must be put to death.

³⁰"One-tenth of the produce of the land, whether grain from the fields or fruit from the trees, belongs to the LORD and must be set apart to him as holy. ³¹If you want to buy back the LORD's tenth of the grain or fruit, you must pay its value, plus 20 percent. ³²Count off every tenth animal from your herds and flocks and set them apart for the LORD as holy. ³³You may not pick and choose between good and bad animals, and you may not substitute one for another. But if you do exchange one animal for another, then both the original animal and its substitute will be considered holy and cannot be bought back."

³⁴These are the commands that the LORD gave through Moses on Mount Sinai for the Israelites.

Introduction to

Numbers

Background

In Hebrew, the title for the Book of Numbers comes from the fifth word in the first verse: *bemidbar*, meaning "desert"—a fitting title for Israel's wilderness wanderings. The book's English title comes from the Greek Septuagint translation, where the title refers to the census in chapters 1 and 26.

Several New Testament passages attest to Moses' authorship of the Book of Numbers, including Acts 7, 1 Corinthians 10, and Hebrews 3–4. Within the book itself, God speaks directly to Moses more than eighty times. For example, "At the LORD's direction, Moses kept a written record of their progress" (33:2). Though Numbers allocates lands of Canaan to various tribes, the text does not show the people of Israel leaving Moab and crossing the Jordan.

Message

Chapters 13–14 serve as a literal turning point in Israel's trek from Egypt to the Promised Land. After the spies return from the land and bring their report, the people's complaints, fear, and refusal to trust God for the conquest provoke his anger and discipline.

God takes faith seriously. The people who have seen his great miracles, from the plagues on Egypt to the parting of the Red Sea, are the same ones who now rebel in fear of the fortified cities and giant people. They do not trust that God will do for them what he has done before. What are the consequences of their sin? An about-face back into the wilderness to wander for forty years until the entire adult generation that left Egypt dies. Only their children and two faithful spies—Joshua and Caleb—are allowed to enter the Promised Land.

Time

The events of Numbers unfold over thirty-nine years of Israel's wilderness wanderings. As is true of Genesis and the other books of the Pentateuch, the Book of Numbers was probably written by Moses between 1445 and 1406 B.C.

Outline

Numbers

1 Registration of Israel's Troops

A year after Israel's departure from Egypt, the LORD spoke to Moses in the Tabernacle* in the wilderness of Sinai. On the first day of the second month* of that year he said, ²"From the whole community of Israel, record the names of all the warriors by their clans and families. List all the men ³twenty years old or older who are able to go to war. You and Aaron must register the troops, ⁴and you will be assisted by one family leader from each tribe.

⁵"These are the tribes and the names of the leaders who will assist you:

Tribe	Leader
Reuben	Elizur son of Shedeur
⁶ Simeon	Shelumiel son of Zurishaddai
⁷ Judah	Nahshon son of Amminadab
⁸ Issachar	Nethanel son of Zuar
⁹ Zebulun	Eliab son of Helon
¹⁰ Ephraim son of Joseph	Elishama son of Ammihud
Manasseh son of Joseph	Gamaliel son of Pedahzur
¹¹ Benjamin	Abidan son of Gideoni
¹² Dan	Ahiezer son of Ammishaddai
¹³ Asher	Pagiel son of Ocran
¹⁴ Gad	Eliasaph son of Deuel
¹⁵ Naphtali	Ahira son of Enan

¹⁶These are the chosen leaders of the community, the leaders of their ancestral tribes, the heads of the clans of Israel."

¹⁷So Moses and Aaron called together these chosen leaders, ¹⁸and they assembled the whole community of Israel on that very day.* All the people were registered according to their ancestry by their clans and families. The men of Israel who were twenty years old or older were listed one by one, ¹⁹just as the LORD had commanded Moses. So Moses recorded their names in the wilderness of Sinai.

²⁰⁻²¹This is the number of men twenty years old or older who were able to go to war, as their names were listed in the records of their clans and families*:

Tribe	Number
Reuben (Jacob's* oldest son)	46,500
²²⁻²³ Simeon	59,300
²⁴⁻²⁵ Gad	45,650
²⁶⁻²⁷ Judah	74,600
²⁸⁻²⁹ Issachar	54,400
³⁰⁻³¹ Zebulun	57,400

1:1a Hebrew *the Tent of Meeting.*   **1:1b** This day in the ancient Hebrew lunar calendar occurred in April or May.
1:18 Hebrew *on the first day of the second month;* see 1:1.   **1:20-21a** In the Hebrew text, this sentence (*This is the number of men twenty years old or older who were able to go to war, as their names were listed in the records of their clans and families*) is repeated in 1:22, 24, 26, 28, 30, 32, 34, 36, 38, 40, 42.   **1:20-21b** Hebrew *Israel's.* The names "Jacob" and "Israel" are often interchanged throughout the Old Testament, referring sometimes to the individual patriarch and sometimes to the nation.

32-33	Ephraim son of Joseph	40,500
34-35	Manasseh son of Joseph	32,200
36-37	Benjamin.	35,400
38-39	Dan	62,700
40-41	Asher.	41,500
42-43	Naphtali	53,400

⁴⁴These were the men registered by Moses and Aaron and the twelve leaders of Israel, all listed according to their ancestral descent. ⁴⁵They were registered by families—all the men of Israel who were twenty years old or older and able to go to war. ⁴⁶The total number was 603,550.

⁴⁷But this total did not include the Levites. ⁴⁸For the LORD had said to Moses, ⁴⁹"Do not include the tribe of Levi in the registration; do not count them with the rest of the Israelites. ⁵⁰Put the Levites in charge of the Tabernacle of the Covenant,* along with all its furnishings and equipment. They must carry the Tabernacle and all its furnishings as you travel, and they must take care of it and camp around it. ⁵¹Whenever it is time for the Tabernacle to move, the Levites will take it down. And when it is time to stop, they will set it up again. But any unauthorized person who goes too near the Tabernacle must be put to death. ⁵²Each tribe of Israel will camp in a designated area with its own family banner. ⁵³But the Levites will camp around the Tabernacle of the Covenant to protect the community of Israel from the LORD's anger. The Levites are responsible to stand guard around the Tabernacle."

⁵⁴So the Israelites did everything just as the LORD had commanded Moses.

2 Organization for Israel's Camp

Then the LORD gave these instructions to Moses and Aaron: ²"When the Israelites set up camp, each tribe will be assigned its own area. The tribal divisions will camp beneath their family banners on all four sides of the Tabernacle,* but at some distance from it.

³-⁴"The divisions of Judah, Issachar, and Zebulun are to camp toward the sunrise on the east side of the Tabernacle, beneath their family banners. These are the names

of the tribes, their leaders, and the numbers of their registered troops:

Tribe	Leader	Number
Judah	Nahshon son of Amminadab	74,600
5-6 Issachar	Nethanel son of Zuar	54,400
7-8 Zebulun	Eliab son of Helon	57,400

⁹So the total of all the troops on Judah's side of the camp is 186,400. These three tribes are to lead the way whenever the Israelites travel to a new campsite.

¹⁰-¹¹"The divisions of Reuben, Simeon, and Gad are to camp on the south side of the Tabernacle, beneath their family banners. These are the names of the tribes, their leaders, and the numbers of their registered troops:

Tribe	Leader	Number
Reuben	Elizur son of Shedeur	46,500
12-13 Simeon	Shelumiel son of Zurishaddai	59,300
14-15 Gad	Eliasaph son of Deuel*	45,650

¹⁶So the total of all the troops on Reuben's side of the camp is 151,450. These three tribes will be second in line whenever the Israelites travel.

¹⁷"Then the Tabernacle, carried by the Levites, will set out from the middle of the camp. All the tribes are to travel in the same order that they camp, each in position under the appropriate family banner.

¹⁸-¹⁹"The divisions of Ephraim, Manasseh, and Benjamin are to camp on the west side of the Tabernacle, beneath their family banners. These are the names of the tribes, their leaders, and the numbers of their registered troops:

Tribe	Leader	Number
Ephraim	Elishama son of Ammihud	40,500
20-21 Manasseh	Gamaliel son of Pedahzur	32,200
22-23 Benjamin	Abidan son of Gideoni	35,400

1:50 Or *Tabernacle of the Testimony;* also in 1:53.   **2:2** Hebrew *the Tent of Meeting;* also in 2:17.   **2:14-15** As in many Hebrew manuscripts, Samaritan Pentateuch, and Latin Vulgate (see also 1:14); most Hebrew manuscripts read *son of Reuel.*

[24] So the total of all the troops on Ephraim's side of the camp is 108,100. These three tribes will be third in line whenever the Israelites travel.

[25-26] "The divisions of Dan, Asher, and Naphtali are to camp on the north side of the Tabernacle, beneath their family banners. These are the names of the tribes, their leaders, and the numbers of their registered troops:

Tribe	Leader	Number
Dan	Ahiezer son of Ammishaddai	62,700
[27-28] Asher	Pagiel son of Ocran	41,500
[29-30] Naphtali	Ahira son of Enan	53,400

[31] So the total of all the troops on Dan's side of the camp is 157,600. These three tribes will be last, marching under their banners whenever the Israelites travel."

[32] In summary, the troops of Israel listed by their families totaled 603,550. [33] But as the LORD had commanded, the Levites were not included in this registration. [34] So the people of Israel did everything as the LORD had commanded Moses. Each clan and family set up camp and marched under their banners exactly as the LORD had instructed them.

3 Levites Appointed for Service

This is the family line of Aaron and Moses as it was recorded when the LORD spoke to Moses on Mount Sinai: [2] The names of Aaron's sons were Nadab (the oldest), Abihu, Eleazar, and Ithamar. [3] These sons of Aaron were anointed and ordained to minister as priests. [4] But Nadab and Abihu died in the LORD's presence in the wilderness of Sinai when they burned before the LORD the wrong kind of fire, different than he had commanded. Since they had no sons, this left only Eleazar and Ithamar to serve as priests with their father, Aaron.

[5] Then the LORD said to Moses, [6] "Call forward the tribe of Levi, and present them to Aaron the priest to serve as his assistants. [7] They will serve Aaron and the whole community, performing their sacred duties in and around the Tabernacle.* [8] They will also maintain all the furnishings of the sacred tent,* serving in the Tabernacle on behalf of all the Israelites. [9] Assign the Levites to Aaron and his sons. They have been given from among all the people of Israel to serve as their assistants. [10] Appoint Aaron and his sons to carry out the duties of the priesthood. But any unauthorized person who goes too near the sanctuary must be put to death."

[11] And the LORD said to Moses, [12] "Look, I have chosen the Levites from among the Israelites to serve as substitutes for all the firstborn sons of the people of Israel. The Levites belong to me, [13] for all the firstborn males are mine. On the day I struck down all the firstborn sons of the Egyptians, I set apart for myself all the firstborn in Israel, both of people and of animals. They are mine; I am the LORD."

Registration of the Levites

[14] The LORD spoke again to Moses in the wilderness of Sinai. He said, [15] "Record the names of the members of the tribe of Levi by their families and clans. List every male who is one month old or older." [16] So Moses listed them, just as the LORD had commanded.

[17] Levi had three sons, whose names were Gershon, Kohath, and Merari.
[18] The clans descended from Gershon were named after two of his descendants, Libni and Shimei.
[19] The clans descended from Kohath were named after four of his descendants, Amram, Izhar, Hebron, and Uzziel.
[20] The clans descended from Merari were named after two of his descendants, Mahli and Mushi.
These were the Levite clans, listed according to their family groups.

[21] The descendants of Gershon were composed of the clans descended from Libni and Shimei. [22] There were 7,500 males one month old or older among these Gershonite clans. [23] They were assigned the area to the west of the Tabernacle for their camp. [24] The leader of the Gershonite clans was Eliasaph son of Lael. [25] These two clans were responsible to care for the Tabernacle,

---

3:7 Hebrew *around the Tent of Meeting, doing service at the Tabernacle.*   **3:8** Hebrew *the Tent of Meeting;* also in 3:25.

including the sacred tent with its layers of coverings, the curtain at its entrance, ²⁶the curtains of the courtyard that surrounded the Tabernacle and altar, the curtain at the courtyard entrance, the ropes, and all the equipment related to their use.

²⁷The descendants of Kohath were composed of the clans descended from Amram, Izhar, Hebron, and Uzziel. ²⁸There were 8,600* males one month old or older among these Kohathite clans. They were responsible for the care of the sanctuary, ²⁹and they were assigned the area south of the Tabernacle for their camp. ³⁰The leader of the Kohathite clans was Elizaphan son of Uzziel. ³¹These four clans were responsible for the care of the Ark, the table, the lampstand, the altars, the various articles used in the sanctuary, the inner curtain, and all the equipment related to their use. ³²Eleazar, son of Aaron the priest, was the chief administrator over all the Levites, with special responsibility for the oversight of the sanctuary.

³³The descendants of Merari were composed of the clans descended from Mahli and Mushi. ³⁴There were 6,200 males one month old or older among these Merarite clans. ³⁵They were assigned the area north of the Tabernacle for their camp. The leader of the Merarite clans was Zuriel son of Abihail. ³⁶These two clans were responsible for the care of the frames supporting the Tabernacle, the crossbars, the pillars, the bases, and all the equipment related to their use. ³⁷They were also responsible for the posts of the courtyard and all their bases, pegs, and ropes.

³⁸The area in front of the Tabernacle, in the east toward the sunrise,* was reserved for the tents of Moses and of Aaron and his sons, who had the final responsibility for the sanctuary on behalf of the people of Israel. Anyone other than a priest or Levite who went too near the sanctuary was to be put to death.

³⁹When Moses and Aaron counted the Levite clans at the LORD's command, the total number was 22,000 males one month old or older.

Redeeming the Firstborn Sons

⁴⁰Then the LORD said to Moses, "Now count all the firstborn sons in Israel who are one month old or older, and make a list of their names. ⁴¹The Levites must be reserved for me as substitutes for the firstborn sons of Israel; I am the LORD. And the Levites' livestock must be reserved for me as substitutes for the firstborn livestock of the whole nation of Israel."

⁴²So Moses counted the firstborn sons of the people of Israel, just as the LORD had commanded. ⁴³The number of firstborn sons who were one month old or older was 22,273.

⁴⁴Then the LORD said to Moses, ⁴⁵"Take the Levites as substitutes for the firstborn sons of the people of Israel. And take the livestock of the Levites as substitutes for the firstborn livestock of the people of Israel. The Levites belong to me; I am the LORD. ⁴⁶There are 273 more firstborn sons of Israel than there are Levites. To redeem these extra firstborn sons, ⁴⁷collect five pieces of silver* for each of them (each piece weighing the same as the sanctuary shekel, which equals twenty gerahs). ⁴⁸Give the silver to Aaron and his sons as the redemption price for the extra firstborn sons."

⁴⁹So Moses collected the silver for redeeming the firstborn sons of Israel who exceeded the number of Levites. ⁵⁰He collected 1,365 pieces of silver* on behalf of these firstborn sons of Israel (each piece weighing the same as the sanctuary shekel). ⁵¹And Moses gave the silver for the redemption to Aaron and his sons, just as the LORD had commanded.

4 Duties of the Kohathite Clan

Then the LORD said to Moses and Aaron, ²"Record the names of the members of the clans and families of the Kohathite division of the tribe of Levi. ³List all the men between the ages of thirty and fifty who are eligible to serve in the Tabernacle.* ⁴"The duties of the Kohathites at the Tabernacle will relate to the most sacred objects. ⁵When the camp moves, Aaron and his sons must enter the Tabernacle first

---

3:28 Some Greek manuscripts read *8,300;* see total in 3:39. **3:38** Hebrew *toward the sunrise, in front of the Tent of Meeting.* **3:47** Hebrew *5 shekels* [2 ounces or 57 grams]. **3:50** Hebrew *1,365 shekels* [34 pounds or 15.5 kilograms]. **4:3** Hebrew *the Tent of Meeting;* also in 4:4, 15, 23, 25, 28, 30, 31, 33, 35, 37, 39, 41, 43, 47.

to take down the inner curtain and cover the Ark of the Covenant* with it. 6 Then they must cover the inner curtain with fine goatskin leather and spread over that a single piece of blue cloth. Finally, they must put the carrying poles of the Ark in place.

7 "Next they must spread a blue cloth over the table where the Bread of the Presence is displayed, and on the cloth they will place the bowls, pans, jars, pitchers, and the special bread. 8 They must spread a scarlet cloth over all of this, and finally a covering of fine goatskin leather on top of the scarlet cloth. Then they must insert the carrying poles into the table.

9 "Next they must cover the lampstand with a blue cloth, along with its lamps, lamp snuffers, trays, and special jars of olive oil. 10 Then they must cover the lampstand and its accessories with fine goatskin leather and place the bundle on a carrying frame.

11 "Next they must spread a blue cloth over the gold incense altar and cover this cloth with fine goatskin leather. Then they must attach the carrying poles to the altar. 12 They must take all the remaining furnishings of the sanctuary and wrap them in a blue cloth, cover them with fine goatskin leather, and place them on the carrying frame.

13 "They must remove the ashes from the altar for sacrifices and cover the altar with a purple cloth. 14 All the altar utensils— the firepans, meat forks, shovels, basins, and all the containers—must be placed on the cloth, and a covering of fine goatskin leather must be spread over them. Finally, they must put the carrying poles in place. 15 The camp will be ready to move when Aaron and his sons have finished covering the sanctuary and all the sacred articles. The Kohathites will come and carry these things to the next destination. But they must not touch the sacred objects, or they will die. So these are the things from the Tabernacle that the Kohathites must carry.

16 "Eleazar son of Aaron the priest will be responsible for the oil of the lampstand, the fragrant incense, the daily grain offering, and the anointing oil. In fact, Eleazar will be responsible for the entire Tabernacle and everything in it, including the sanctuary and its furnishings."

17 Then the LORD said to Moses and Aaron, 18 "Do not let the Kohathite clans be destroyed from among the Levites! 19 This is what you must do so they will live and not die when they approach the most sacred objects. Aaron and his sons must always go in with them and assign a specific duty or load to each person. 20 The Kohathites must never enter the sanctuary to look at the sacred objects for even a moment, or they will die."

Duties of the Gershonite Clan

21 And the LORD said to Moses, 22 "Record the names of the members of the clans and families of the Gershonite division of the tribe of Levi. 23 List all the men between the ages of thirty and fifty who are eligible to serve in the Tabernacle.

24 "These Gershonite clans will be responsible for general service and carrying loads. 25 They must carry the curtains of the Tabernacle, the Tabernacle itself with its coverings, the outer covering of fine goatskin leather, and the curtain for the Tabernacle entrance. 26 They are also to carry the curtains for the courtyard walls that surround the Tabernacle and altar, the curtain across the courtyard entrance, the ropes, and all the equipment related to their use. The Gershonites are responsible for all these items. 27 Aaron and his sons will direct the Gershonites regarding all their duties, whether it involves moving the equipment or doing other work. They must assign the Gershonites responsibility for the loads they are to carry. 28 So these are the duties assigned to the Gershonite clans at the Tabernacle. They will be directly responsible to Ithamar son of Aaron the priest.

Duties of the Merarite Clan

29 "Now record the names of the members of the clans and families of the Merarite division of the tribe of Levi. 30 List all the men between the ages of thirty and fifty who are eligible to serve in the Tabernacle.

31 "Their only duty at the Tabernacle will be to carry loads. They will carry the frames

---

4:5 Or Ark of the Testimony.

of the Tabernacle, the crossbars, the posts, and the bases; ³²also the posts for the courtyard walls with their bases, pegs, and ropes; and all the accessories and everything else related to their use. Assign the various loads to each man by name. ³³So these are the duties of the Merarite clans at the Tabernacle. They are directly responsible to Ithamar son of Aaron the priest."

Summary of the Registration

³⁴So Moses, Aaron, and the other leaders of the community listed the members of the Kohathite division by their clans and families. ³⁵The list included all the men between thirty and fifty years of age who were eligible for service in the Tabernacle, ³⁶and the total number came to 2,750. ³⁷So this was the total of all those from the Kohathite clans who were eligible to serve at the Tabernacle. Moses and Aaron listed them, just as the Lord had commanded through Moses.

³⁸The Gershonite division was also listed by its clans and families. ³⁹The list included all the men between thirty and fifty years of age who were eligible for service in the Tabernacle, ⁴⁰and the total number came to 2,630. ⁴¹So this was the total of all those from the Gershonite clans who were eligible to serve at the Tabernacle. Moses and Aaron listed them, just as the Lord had commanded.

⁴²The Merarite division was also listed by its clans and families. ⁴³The list included all the men between thirty and fifty years of age who were eligible for service in the Tabernacle, ⁴⁴and the total number came to 3,200. ⁴⁵So this was the total of all those from the Merarite clans who were eligible for service. Moses and Aaron listed them, just as the Lord had commanded through Moses.

⁴⁶So Moses, Aaron, and the leaders of Israel listed all the Levites by their clans and families. ⁴⁷All the men between thirty and fifty years of age who were eligible for service in the Tabernacle and for its transportation ⁴⁸numbered 8,580. ⁴⁹When their names were recorded, as the Lord had commanded through Moses, each man was assigned his task and told what to carry.

And so the registration was completed, just as the Lord had commanded Moses.

5 Purity in Israel's Camp

The Lord gave these instructions to Moses: ²"Command the people of Israel to remove from the camp anyone who has a skin disease* or a discharge, or who has become ceremonially unclean by touching a dead person. ³This command applies to men and women alike. Remove them so they will not defile the camp in which I live among them." ⁴So the Israelites did as the Lord had commanded Moses and removed such people from the camp.

⁵Then the Lord said to Moses, ⁶"Give the following instructions to the people of Israel: If any of the people—men or women—betray the Lord by doing wrong to another person, they are guilty. ⁷They must confess their sin and make full restitution for what they have done, adding an additional 20 percent and returning it to the person who was wronged. ⁸But if the person who was wronged is dead, and there are no near relatives to whom restitution can be made, the payment belongs to the Lord and must be given to the priest. Those who are guilty must also bring a ram as a sacrifice, and they will be purified and made right with the Lord.* ⁹All the sacred offerings that the Israelites bring to a priest will belong to him. ¹⁰Each priest may keep all the sacred donations that he receives."

Protecting Marital Faithfulness

¹¹And the Lord said to Moses, ¹²"Give the following instructions to the people of Israel.

"Suppose a man's wife goes astray, and she is unfaithful to her husband ¹³and has sex with another man, but neither her husband nor anyone else knows about it. She has defiled herself, even though there was no witness and she was not caught in the act. ¹⁴If her husband becomes jealous and is suspicious of his wife and needs to know whether or not she has defiled herself, ¹⁵the husband must bring his wife to the priest. He must also bring an offering of two quarts* of barley flour to be presented

---

5:2 Traditionally rendered leprosy. The Hebrew word used here describes various skin diseases. **5:8** Or bring a ram for atonement, which will make atonement for them. **5:15** Hebrew ¹⁄₁₀ of an ephah [2.2 liters].

on her behalf. Do not mix it with olive oil or frankincense, for it is a jealousy offering—an offering to prove whether or not she is guilty.

16 "The priest will then present her to stand trial before the LORD. 17 He must take some holy water in a clay jar and pour into it dust he has taken from the Tabernacle floor. 18 When the priest has presented the woman before the LORD, he must unbind her hair and place in her hands the offering of proof—the jealousy offering to determine whether her husband's suspicions are justified. The priest will stand before her, holding the jar of bitter water that brings a curse to those who are guilty. 19 The priest will then put the woman under oath and say to her, 'If no other man has had sex with you, and you have not gone astray and defiled yourself while under your husband's authority, may you be immune from the effects of this bitter water that brings on the curse. 20 But if you have gone astray by being unfaithful to your husband, and have defiled yourself by having sex with another man—'

21 "At this point the priest must put the woman under oath by saying, 'May the people know that the LORD's curse is upon you when he makes you infertile, causing your womb to shrivel* and your abdomen to swell. 22 Now may this water that brings the curse enter your body and cause your abdomen to swell and your womb to shrivel.*' And the woman will be required to say, 'Yes, let it be so.' 23 And the priest will write these curses on a piece of leather and wash them off into the bitter water. 24 He will make the woman drink the bitter water that brings on the curse. When the water enters her body, it will cause bitter suffering if she is guilty.

25 "The priest will take the jealousy offering from the woman's hand, lift it up before the LORD, and carry it to the altar. 26 He will take a handful of the flour as a token portion and burn it on the altar, and he will require the woman to drink the water. 27 If she has defiled herself by being unfaithful to her husband, the water that brings on the curse will cause bitter suffering. Her abdo-

men will swell and her womb will shrink,* and her name will become a curse among her people. 28 But if she has not defiled herself and is pure, then she will be unharmed and will still be able to have children.

29 "This is the ritual law for dealing with suspicion. If a woman goes astray and defiles herself while under her husband's authority, 30 or if a man becomes jealous and is suspicious that his wife has been unfaithful, the husband must present his wife before the LORD, and the priest will apply this entire ritual law to her. 31 The husband will be innocent of any guilt in this matter, but his wife will be held accountable for her sin."

6 Nazirite Laws

Then the LORD said to Moses, 2 "Give the following instructions to the people of Israel.

"If any of the people, either men or women, take the special vow of a Nazirite, setting themselves apart to the LORD in a special way, 3 they must give up wine and other alcoholic drinks. They must not use vinegar made from wine or from other alcoholic drinks, they must not drink fresh grape juice, and they must not eat grapes or raisins. 4 As long as they are bound by their Nazirite vow, they are not allowed to eat or drink anything that comes from a grapevine—not even the grape seeds or skins.

5 "They must never cut their hair throughout the time of their vow, for they are holy and set apart to the LORD. Until the time of their vow has been fulfilled, they must let their hair grow long. 6 And they must not go near a dead body during the entire period of their vow to the LORD. 7 Even if the dead person is their own father, mother, brother, or sister, they must not defile themselves, for the hair on their head is the symbol of their separation to God. 8 This requirement applies as long as they are set apart to the LORD.

9 "If someone falls dead beside them, the hair they have dedicated will be defiled. They must wait for seven days and then shave their heads. Then they will be cleansed from their defilement. 10 On the

---

5:21 Hebrew *when he causes your thigh to waste away.*   **5:22** Hebrew *and your thigh to waste away.*   **5:27** Hebrew *and her thigh will waste away.*

Community

Community, Solitude, and the Presence of God

Living in community—whether it's a church family, an immediate or extended family, or a group of friends or co-workers—requires that we constantly see the face of God in others. The blessing in Numbers 6:22-26 reminds us to see God's blessing on the blessed, to see the face and peace of God reflected on the other person. In times of disagreement—real or imagined, minuscule or gigantic—we need to see God's face to remind us of the greater calling God has for us. Then we're invited to turn this prayer around: "May God help me bless you; may God help me to be gracious to you; may God help me to turn my face toward you and give you peace."

Of course our blessing is nothing compared to God's! But by praying this prayer and seeking to live this blessing we invite God's Spirit to generate the graciousness and peace that we're unable to muster up ourselves. Living out this blessing in community requires that we intentionally take time *away* from that community; in solitude, we may pray this blessing upon our own lives and seek God's peace in the quietness. These times away from others remind us that true community isn't just ourselves and others. True community includes God, who turns us toward one another and, in the process, to himself.

—Joy-Elizabeth Lawrence

For more on Community, see reading at Numbers 12.

eighth day they must bring two turtle-doves or two young pigeons to the priest at the entrance of the Tabernacle.* ¹¹The priest will offer one of the birds for a sin offering and the other for a burnt offering. In this way, he will purify them* from the guilt they incurred through contact with the dead body. Then they must reaffirm their commitment and let their hair begin to grow again. ¹²The days of their vow that were completed before their defilement no longer count. They must rededicate themselves to the LORD as a Nazirite for the full term of their vow, and each must bring a one-year-old male lamb for a guilt offering.

¹³"This is the ritual law for Nazirites. At the conclusion of their time of separation as Nazirites, they must each go to the entrance of the Tabernacle ¹⁴and offer their sacrifices to the LORD: a one-year-old male lamb without defect for a burnt offering, a one-year-old female lamb without defect for a sin offering, a ram without defect for a peace offering, ¹⁵a basket of bread made without yeast—cakes of choice flour mixed with olive oil and wafers spread with olive oil—along with their prescribed grain offerings and liquid offerings. ¹⁶The priest will present these offerings before the LORD: first the sin offering and the burnt offering; ¹⁷then the ram for a peace offering, along with the basket of bread made without yeast. The priest must also present the prescribed grain offering and liquid offering to the LORD.

¹⁸"Then the Nazirites will shave their heads at the entrance of the Tabernacle. They will take the hair that had been dedicated and place it on the fire beneath the peace-offering sacrifice. ¹⁹After the Nazirite's head has been shaved, the priest will take for each of them the boiled shoulder

---

6:10 Hebrew *the Tent of Meeting*; also in 6:13, 18. **6:11** Or *make atonement for them.*

of the ram, and he will take from the basket a cake and a wafer made without yeast. He will put them all into the Nazirite's hands. ²⁰Then the priest will lift them up as a special offering before the Lord. These are holy portions for the priest, along with the breast of the special offering and the thigh of the sacred offering that are lifted up before the Lord. After this ceremony the Nazirites may again drink wine.

²¹"This is the ritual law of the Nazirites, who vow to bring these offerings to the Lord. They may also bring additional offerings if they can afford it. And they must be careful to do whatever they vowed when they set themselves apart as Nazirites."

The Priestly Blessing

²²Then the Lord said to Moses, ²³"Tell Aaron and his sons to bless the people of Israel with this special blessing:

²⁴ 'May the Lord bless you
and protect you.
²⁵ May the Lord smile on you
and be gracious to you.
²⁶ May the Lord show you his favor
and give you his peace.'

²⁷Whenever Aaron and his sons bless the people of Israel in my name, I myself will bless them."

7 Offerings of Dedication

On the day Moses set up the Tabernacle, he anointed it and set it apart as holy. He also anointed and set apart all its furnishings and the altar with its utensils. ²Then the leaders of Israel—the tribal leaders who had registered the troops—came and brought their offerings. ³Together they brought six large wagons and twelve oxen. There was a wagon for every two leaders and an ox for each leader. They presented these to the Lord in front of the Tabernacle. ⁴Then the Lord said to Moses, ⁵"Receive their gifts, and use these oxen and wagons for transporting the Tabernacle.* Distribute them among the Levites according to the work they have to do." ⁶So Moses

took the wagons and oxen and presented them to the Levites. ⁷He gave two wagons and four oxen to the Gershonite division for their work, ⁸and he gave four wagons and eight oxen to the Merarite division for their work. All their work was done under the leadership of Ithamar son of Aaron the priest. ⁹But he gave none of the wagons or oxen to the Kohathite division, since they were required to carry the sacred objects of the Tabernacle on their shoulders.

¹⁰The leaders also presented dedication gifts for the altar at the time it was anointed. They each placed their gifts before the altar. ¹¹The Lord said to Moses, "Let one leader bring his gift each day for the dedication of the altar."

¹²On the first day Nahshon son of Amminadab, leader of the tribe of Judah, presented his offering.

¹³His offering consisted of a silver platter weighing 3¼ pounds and a silver basin weighing 1¾ pounds* (as measured by the weight of the sanctuary shekel). These were both filled with grain offerings of choice flour moistened with olive oil. ¹⁴He also brought a gold container weighing four ounces,* which was filled with incense. ¹⁵He brought a young bull, a ram, and a one-year-old male lamb for a burnt offering, ¹⁶and a male goat for a sin offering. ¹⁷For a peace offering he brought two bulls, five rams, five male goats, and five one-year-old male lambs. This was the offering brought by Nahshon son of Amminadab.

¹⁸On the second day Nethanel son of Zuar, leader of the tribe of Issachar, presented his offering.

¹⁹His offering consisted of a silver platter weighing 3¼ pounds and a silver basin weighing 1¾ pounds (as measured by the weight of the sanctuary shekel). These were both filled with grain offerings of choice flour moistened with olive oil. ²⁰He also brought a gold container weighing four ounces, which was filled with incense. ²¹He brought a young bull, a ram, and a one-year-old

---

7:5 Hebrew *the Tent of Meeting;* also in 7:89. **7:13** Hebrew *silver platter weighing 130 shekels* [1.5 kilograms] *and a silver basin weighing 70 shekels* [800 grams]; also in 7:19, 25, 31, 37, 43, 49, 55, 61, 67, 73, 79, 85. **7:14** Hebrew *10 shekels* [114 grams]; also in 7:20, 26, 32, 38, 44, 50, 56, 62, 68, 74, 80, 86.

male lamb for a burnt offering, ²²and a male goat for a sin offering. ²³For a peace offering he brought two bulls, five rams, five male goats, and five one-year-old male lambs. This was the offering brought by Nethanel son of Zuar.

²⁴On the third day Eliab son of Helon, leader of the tribe of Zebulun, presented his offering.

²⁵His offering consisted of a silver platter weighing 3¼ pounds and a silver basin weighing 1¾ pounds (as measured by the weight of the sanctuary shekel). These were both filled with grain offerings of choice flour moistened with olive oil. ²⁶He also brought a gold container weighing four ounces, which was filled with incense. ²⁷He brought a young bull, a ram, and a one-year-old male lamb for a burnt offering, ²⁸and a male goat for a sin offering. ²⁹For a peace offering he brought two bulls, five rams, five male goats, and five one-year-old male lambs. This was the offering brought by Eliab son of Helon.

³⁰On the fourth day Elizur son of Shedeur, leader of the tribe of Reuben, presented his offering.

³¹His offering consisted of a silver platter weighing 3¼ pounds and a silver basin weighing 1¾ pounds (as measured by the weight of the sanctuary shekel). These were both filled with grain offerings of choice flour moistened with olive oil. ³²He also brought a gold container weighing four ounces, which was filled with incense. ³³He brought a young bull, a ram, and a one-year-old male lamb for a burnt offering, ³⁴and a male goat for a sin offering. ³⁵For a peace offering he brought two bulls, five rams, five male goats, and five one-year-old male lambs. This was the offering brought by Elizur son of Shedeur.

³⁶On the fifth day Shelumiel son of Zuri-shaddai, leader of the tribe of Simeon, presented his offering.

³⁷His offering consisted of a silver platter weighing 3¼ pounds and a silver basin weighing 1¾ pounds (as measured by the weight of the sanctuary shekel). These were both filled with grain offerings of choice flour moistened with olive oil. ³⁸He also brought a gold container weighing four ounces, which was filled with incense. ³⁹He brought a young bull, a ram, and a one-year-old male lamb for a burnt offering, ⁴⁰and a male goat for a sin offering. ⁴¹For a peace offering he brought two bulls, five rams, five male goats, and five one-year-old male lambs. This was the offering brought by Shelumiel son of Zurishaddai.

⁴²On the sixth day Eliasaph son of Deuel, leader of the tribe of Gad, presented his offering.

⁴³His offering consisted of a silver platter weighing 3¼ pounds and a silver basin weighing 1¾ pounds (as measured by the weight of the sanctuary shekel). These were both filled with grain offerings of choice flour moistened with olive oil. ⁴⁴He also brought a gold container weighing four ounces, which was filled with incense. ⁴⁵He brought a young bull, a ram, and a one-year-old male lamb for a burnt offering, ⁴⁶and a male goat for a sin offering. ⁴⁷For a peace offering he brought two bulls, five rams, five male goats, and five one-year-old male lambs. This was the offering brought by Eliasaph son of Deuel.

⁴⁸On the seventh day Elishama son of Ammihud, leader of the tribe of Ephraim, presented his offering.

⁴⁹His offering consisted of a silver platter weighing 3¼ pounds and a silver basin weighing 1¾ pounds (as measured by the weight of the sanctuary shekel). These were both filled with grain offerings of choice flour moistened with olive oil. ⁵⁰He also brought a gold container weighing four ounces, which was filled with incense. ⁵¹He brought a young bull, a ram, and a one-year-old male lamb for a burnt offering, ⁵²and a male goat for a sin offering. ⁵³For a peace offering he brought two bulls, five rams, five male goats, and five one-year-old male lambs. This was the offering brought by Elishama son of Ammihud.

⁵⁴On the eighth day Gamaliel son of Pedahzur, leader of the tribe of Manasseh, presented his offering.

⁵⁵His offering consisted of a silver platter weighing 3¼ pounds and a silver basin weighing 1¾ pounds (as measured by the weight of the sanctuary shekel). These were both filled with grain offerings of choice flour moistened with olive oil. ⁵⁶He also brought a gold container weighing four ounces, which was filled with incense. ⁵⁷He brought a young bull, a ram, and a one-year-old male lamb for a burnt offering, ⁵⁸and a male goat for a sin offering. ⁵⁹For a peace offering he brought two bulls, five rams, five male goats, and five one-year-old male lambs. This was the offering brought by Gamaliel son of Pedahzur.

⁶⁰On the ninth day Abidan son of Gideoni, leader of the tribe of Benjamin, presented his offering.

⁶¹His offering consisted of a silver platter weighing 3¼ pounds and a silver basin weighing 1¾ pounds (as measured by the weight of the sanctuary shekel). These were both filled with grain offerings of choice flour moistened with olive oil. ⁶²He also brought a gold container weighing four ounces, which was filled with incense. ⁶³He brought a young bull, a ram, and a one-year-old male lamb for a burnt offering, ⁶⁴and a male goat for a sin offering. ⁶⁵For a peace offering he brought two bulls, five rams, five male goats, and five one-year-old male lambs. This was the offering brought by Abidan son of Gideoni.

⁶⁶On the tenth day Ahiezer son of Ammishaddai, leader of the tribe of Dan, presented his offering.

⁶⁷His offering consisted of a silver platter weighing 3¼ pounds and a silver basin weighing 1¾ pounds (as measured by the weight of the sanctuary shekel). These were both filled with grain offerings of choice flour moistened with olive oil. ⁶⁸He also brought a gold container weighing four ounces, which was filled with incense. ⁶⁹He brought a young bull, a ram, and a one-year-old male lamb for a burnt offering, ⁷⁰and a male goat for a sin offering. ⁷¹For a peace offering he brought two bulls, five rams, five male goats, and five one-year-old male lambs. This was the offering brought by Ahiezer son of Ammishaddai.

⁷²On the eleventh day Pagiel son of Ocran, leader of the tribe of Asher, presented his offering.

⁷³His offering consisted of a silver platter weighing 3¼ pounds and a silver basin weighing 1¾ pounds (as measured by the weight of the sanctuary shekel). These were both filled with grain offerings of choice flour moistened with olive oil. ⁷⁴He also brought a gold container weighing four ounces, which was filled with incense. ⁷⁵He brought a young bull, a ram, and a one-year-old male lamb for a burnt offering, ⁷⁶and a male goat for a sin offering. ⁷⁷For a peace offering he brought two bulls, five rams, five male goats, and five one-year-old male lambs. This was the offering brought by Pagiel son of Ocran.

⁷⁸On the twelfth day Ahira son of Enan, leader of the tribe of Naphtali, presented his offering.

⁷⁹His offering consisted of a silver platter weighing 3¼ pounds and a silver basin weighing 1¾ pounds (as measured by the weight of the sanctuary shekel). These were both filled with grain offerings of choice flour moistened with olive oil. ⁸⁰He also brought a gold container weighing four ounces, which was filled with incense. ⁸¹He brought a young bull, a ram, and a one-year-old male lamb for a burnt offering, ⁸²and a male goat for a sin offering. ⁸³For a peace offering he brought two bulls, five rams, five male goats, and five one-year-old male lambs. This was the offering brought by Ahira son of Enan.

⁸⁴So this was the dedication offering brought by the leaders of Israel at the time the altar was anointed: twelve silver platters, twelve silver basins, and twelve gold incense containers. ⁸⁵Each silver platter weighed 3¼ pounds, and each silver basin weighed 1¾ pounds. The total weight of the silver was 60 pounds* (as measured by

7:85 Hebrew *2,400 shekels* [27.6 kilograms].

the weight of the sanctuary shekel). [86] Each of the twelve gold containers that was filled with incense weighed four ounces (as measured by the weight of the sanctuary shekel). The total weight of the gold was three pounds.* [87] Twelve young bulls, twelve rams, and twelve one-year-old male lambs were donated for the burnt offerings, along with their prescribed grain offerings. Twelve male goats were brought for the sin offerings. [88] Twenty-four bulls, sixty rams, sixty male goats, and sixty one-year-old male lambs were donated for the peace offerings. This was the dedication offering for the altar after it was anointed.

[89] Whenever Moses went into the Tabernacle to speak with the LORD, he heard the voice speaking to him from between the two cherubim above the Ark's cover—the place of atonement—that rests on the Ark of the Covenant.* The LORD spoke to him from there.

8 Preparing the Lamps

The LORD said to Moses, [2] "Give Aaron the following instructions: When you set up the seven lamps in the lampstand, place them so their light shines forward in front of the lampstand." [3] So Aaron did this. He set up the seven lamps so they reflected their light forward, just as the LORD had commanded Moses. [4] The entire lampstand, from its base to its decorative blossoms, was made of beaten gold. It was built according to the exact design the LORD had shown Moses.

The Levites Dedicated

[5] Then the LORD said to Moses, [6] "Now set the Levites apart from the rest of the people of Israel and make them ceremonially clean. [7] Do this by sprinkling them with the water of purification, and have them shave their entire body and wash their clothing. Then they will be ceremonially clean. [8] Have them bring a young bull and a grain offering of choice flour moistened with olive oil, along with a second young bull for a sin offering. [9] Then assemble the whole community of Israel, and present the Levites at the entrance of the Tabernacle.* [10] When

you present the Levites before the LORD, the people of Israel must lay their hands on them. [11] Raising his hands, Aaron must then present the Levites to the LORD as a special offering from the people of Israel, thus dedicating them to the LORD's service.

[12] "Next the Levites will lay their hands on the heads of the young bulls. Present one as a sin offering and the other as a burnt offering to the LORD, to purify the Levites and make them right with the LORD.* [13] Then have the Levites stand in front of Aaron and his sons, and raise your hands and present them as a special offering to the LORD. [14] In this way, you will set the Levites apart from the rest of the people of Israel, and the Levites will belong to me. [15] After this, they may go into the Tabernacle to do their work, because you have purified them and presented them as a special offering.

[16] "Of all the people of Israel, the Levites are reserved for me. I have claimed them for myself in place of all the firstborn sons of the Israelites; I have taken the Levites as their substitutes. [17] For all the firstborn males among the people of Israel are mine, both of people and of animals. I set them apart for myself on the day I struck down all the firstborn sons of the Egyptians. [18] Yes, I have claimed the Levites in place of all the firstborn sons of Israel. [19] And of all the Israelites, I have assigned the Levites to Aaron and his sons. They will serve in the Tabernacle on behalf of the Israelites and make sacrifices to purify* the people so no plague will strike them when they approach the sanctuary."

[20] So Moses, Aaron, and the whole community of Israel dedicated the Levites, carefully following all the LORD's instructions to Moses. [21] The Levites purified themselves from sin and washed their clothes, and Aaron lifted them up and presented them to the LORD as a special offering. He then offered a sacrifice to purify them and make them right with the LORD.* [22] After that the Levites went into the Tabernacle to perform their duties, assisting Aaron and his sons. So they carried out all the commands that the LORD gave Moses concerning the Levites.

7:86 Hebrew *120 shekels* [1.4 kilograms].   7:89 Or *Ark of the Testimony.*   8:9 Hebrew *the Tent of Meeting;* also in 8:15, 19, 22, 24, 26.
8:12 Or *to make atonement for the Levites.*   8:19 Or *make atonement for.*   8:21 Or *then made atonement for them to purify them.*

²³ The LORD also instructed Moses, ²⁴"This is the rule the Levites must follow: They must begin serving in the Tabernacle at the age of twenty-five, ²⁵and they must retire at the age of fifty. ²⁶After retirement they may assist their fellow Levites by serving as guards at the Tabernacle, but they may not officiate in the service. This is how you must assign duties to the Levites."

9 The Second Passover

A year after Israel's departure from Egypt, the LORD spoke to Moses in the wilderness of Sinai. In the first month* of that year he said, ²"Tell the Israelites to celebrate the Passover at the prescribed time, ³at twilight on the fourteenth day of the first month.* Be sure to follow all my decrees and regulations concerning this celebration."

⁴So Moses told the people to celebrate the Passover ⁵in the wilderness of Sinai as twilight fell on the fourteenth day of the month. And they celebrated the festival there, just as the LORD had commanded Moses. ⁶But some of the men had been ceremonially defiled by touching a dead body, so they could not celebrate the Passover that day. They came to Moses and Aaron that day ⁷and said, "We have become ceremonially unclean by touching a dead body. But why should we be prevented from presenting the LORD's offering at the proper time with the rest of the Israelites?"

⁸Moses answered, "Wait here until I have received instructions for you from the LORD."

⁹This was the LORD's reply to Moses. ¹⁰"Give the following instructions to the people of Israel: If any of the people now or in future generations are ceremonially unclean at Passover time because of touching a dead body, or if they are on a journey and cannot be present at the ceremony, they may still celebrate the LORD's Passover. ¹¹They must offer the Passover sacrifice one month later, at twilight on the fourteenth day of the second month.* They must eat the Passover lamb at that time with bitter salad greens and bread made without yeast. ¹²They must not leave any of the lamb until the next morning, and they must not break any of its bones. They must follow all the normal regulations concerning the Passover.

¹³"But those who neglect to celebrate the Passover at the regular time, even though they are ceremonially clean and not away on a trip, will be cut off from the community of Israel. If they fail to present the LORD's offering at the proper time, they will suffer the consequences of their guilt. ¹⁴And if foreigners living among you want to celebrate the Passover to the LORD, they must follow these same decrees and regulations. The same laws apply both to native-born Israelites and to the foreigners living among you."

The Fiery Cloud

¹⁵On the day the Tabernacle was set up, the cloud covered it.* But from evening until morning the cloud over the Tabernacle looked like a pillar of fire. ¹⁶This was the regular pattern—at night the cloud that covered the Tabernacle had the appearance of fire. ¹⁷Whenever the cloud lifted from over the sacred tent, the people of Israel would break camp and follow it. And wherever the cloud settled, the people of Israel would set up camp. ¹⁸In this way, they traveled and camped at the LORD's command wherever he told them to go. Then they remained in their camp as long as the cloud stayed over the Tabernacle. ¹⁹If the cloud remained over the Tabernacle for a long time, the Israelites stayed and performed their duty to the LORD. ²⁰Sometimes the cloud would stay over the Tabernacle for only a few days, so the people would stay for only a few days, as the LORD commanded. Then at the LORD's command they would break camp and move on. ²¹Sometimes the cloud stayed only overnight and lifted the next morning. But day or night, when the cloud lifted, the people broke camp and moved on. ²²Whether the cloud stayed above the Tabernacle for two days, a month, or a year, the people of Israel stayed in camp and did not move on. But as soon as it lifted, they broke camp and moved on.

9:1 The first month of the ancient Hebrew lunar calendar usually occurs within the months of March and April.   **9:3** This day in the ancient Hebrew lunar calendar occurred in late March, April, or early May.   **9:11** This day in the ancient Hebrew lunar calendar occurred in late April, May, or early June.   **9:15** Hebrew *covered the Tabernacle, the Tent of the Testimony.*

²³So they camped or traveled at the LORD's command, and they did whatever the LORD told them through Moses.

10 The Silver Trumpets

Now the LORD said to Moses, ²"Make two trumpets of hammered silver for calling the community to assemble and for signaling the breaking of camp. ³When both trumpets are blown, everyone must gather before you at the entrance of the Tabernacle.* ⁴But if only one trumpet is blown, then only the leaders—the heads of the clans of Israel—must present themselves to you.

⁵"When you sound the signal to move on, the tribes camped on the east side of the Tabernacle must break camp and move forward. ⁶When you sound the signal a second time, the tribes camped on the south will follow. You must sound short blasts as the signal for moving on. ⁷But when you call the people to an assembly, blow the trumpets with a different signal. ⁸Only the priests, Aaron's descendants, are allowed to blow the trumpets. This is a permanent law for you, to be observed from generation to generation.

⁹"When you arrive in your own land and go to war against your enemies who attack you, sound the alarm with the trumpets. Then the LORD your God will remember you and rescue you from your enemies. ¹⁰Blow the trumpets in times of gladness, too, sounding them at your annual festivals and at the beginning of each month. And blow the trumpets over your burnt offerings and peace offerings. The trumpets will remind the LORD your God of his covenant with you. I am the LORD your God."

The Israelites Leave Sinai

¹¹In the second year after Israel's departure from Egypt—on the twentieth day of the second month*—the cloud lifted from the Tabernacle of the Covenant.* ¹²So the Israelites set out from the wilderness of Sinai and traveled on from place to place until the cloud stopped in the wilderness of Paran.

¹³When the people set out for the first time, following the instructions the LORD had given through Moses, ¹⁴Judah's troops led the way. They marched behind their banner, and their leader was Nahshon son of Amminadab. ¹⁵They were joined by the troops of the tribe of Issachar, led by Nethanel son of Zuar, ¹⁶and the troops of the tribe of Zebulun, led by Eliab son of Helon.

¹⁷Then the Tabernacle was taken down, and the Gershonite and Merarite divisions of the Levites were next in the line of march, carrying the Tabernacle with them. ¹⁸Reuben's troops went next, marching behind their banner. Their leader was Elizur son of Shedeur. ¹⁹They were joined by the troops of the tribe of Simeon, led by Shelumiel son of Zurishaddai, ²⁰and the troops of the tribe of Gad, led by Eliasaph son of Deuel.

²¹Next came the Kohathite division of the Levites, carrying the sacred objects from the Tabernacle. Before they arrived at the next camp, the Tabernacle would already be set up at its new location. ²²Ephraim's troops went next, marching behind their banner. Their leader was Elishama son of Ammihud. ²³They were joined by the troops of the tribe of Manasseh, led by Gamaliel son of Pedahzur, ²⁴and the troops of the tribe of Benjamin, led by Abidan son of Gideoni.

²⁵Dan's troops went last, marching behind their banner and serving as the rear guard for all the tribal camps. Their leader was Ahiezer son of Ammishaddai. ²⁶They were joined by the troops of the tribe of Asher, led by Pagiel son of Ocran, ²⁷and the troops of the tribe of Naphtali, led by Ahira son of Enan.

²⁸This was the order in which the Israelites marched, division by division.

²⁹One day Moses said to his brother-in-law, Hobab son of Reuel the Midianite, "We are on our way to the place the LORD promised us, for he said, 'I will give it to you.' Come with us and we will treat you well, for the LORD has promised wonderful blessings for Israel!"

³⁰But Hobab replied, "No, I will not go. I must return to my own land and family."

³¹"Please don't leave us," Moses pleaded.

10:3 Hebrew *Tent of Meeting.* **10:11a** This day in the ancient Hebrew lunar calendar occurred in late April, May, or early June. **10:11b** Or *Tabernacle of the Testimony.*

"You know the places in the wilderness where we should camp. Come, be our guide. ³²If you do, we'll share with you all the blessings the LORD gives us."

³³They marched for three days after leaving the mountain of the LORD, with the Ark of the LORD's Covenant moving ahead of them to show them where to stop and rest. ³⁴As they moved on each day, the cloud of the LORD hovered over them. ³⁵And whenever the Ark set out, Moses would shout, "Arise, O LORD, and let your enemies be scattered! Let them flee before you!" ³⁶And when the Ark was set down, he would say, "Return, O LORD, to the countless thousands of Israel!"

11 The People Complain to Moses

Soon the people began to complain about their hardship, and the LORD heard everything they said. Then the LORD's anger blazed against them, and he sent a fire to rage among them, and he destroyed some of the people in the outskirts of the camp. ²Then the people screamed to Moses for help, and when he prayed to the LORD, the fire stopped. ³After that, the area was known as Taberah (which means "the place of burning"), because fire from the LORD had burned among them there.

⁴Then the foreign rabble who were traveling with the Israelites began to crave the good things of Egypt. And the people of Israel also began to complain. "Oh, for some meat!" they exclaimed. ⁵"We remember the fish we used to eat for free in Egypt. And we had all the cucumbers, melons, leeks, onions, and garlic we wanted. ⁶But now our appetites are gone. All we ever see is this manna!"

⁷The manna looked like small coriander seeds, and it was pale yellow like gum resin. ⁸The people would go out and gather it from the ground. They made flour by grinding it with hand mills or pounding it in mortars. Then they boiled it in a pot and made it into flat cakes. These cakes tasted like pastries baked with olive oil. ⁹The manna came down on the camp with the dew during the night.

¹⁰Moses heard all the families standing in the doorways of their tents whining, and the LORD became extremely angry. Moses was also very aggravated. ¹¹And Moses said to the LORD, "Why are you treating me, your servant, so harshly? Have mercy on me! What did I do to deserve the burden of all these people? ¹²Did I give birth to them? Did I bring them into the world? Why did you tell me to carry them in my arms like a mother carries a nursing baby? How can I carry them to the land you swore to give their ancestors? ¹³Where am I supposed to get meat for all these people? They keep whining to me, saying, 'Give us meat to eat!' ¹⁴I can't carry all these people by myself! The load is far too heavy! ¹⁵If this is how you intend to treat me, just go ahead and kill me. Do me a favor and spare me this misery!"

Moses Chooses Seventy Leaders

¹⁶Then the LORD said to Moses, "Gather before me seventy men who are recognized as elders and leaders of Israel. Bring them to the Tabernacle* to stand there with you. ¹⁷I will come down and talk to you there. I will take some of the Spirit that is upon you, and I will put the Spirit upon them also. They will bear the burden of the people along with you, so you will not have to carry it alone.

¹⁸"And say to the people, 'Purify yourselves, for tomorrow you will have meat to eat. You were whining, and the LORD heard you when you cried, "Oh, for some meat! We were better off in Egypt!" Now the LORD will give you meat, and you will have to eat it. ¹⁹And it won't be for just a day or two, or for five or ten or even twenty. ²⁰You will eat it for a whole month until you gag and are sick of it. For you have rejected the LORD, who is here among you, and you have whined to him, saying, "Why did we ever leave Egypt?"'"

²¹But Moses responded to the LORD, "There are 600,000 foot soldiers here with me, and yet you say, 'I will give them meat for a whole month!' ²²Even if we butchered all our flocks and herds, would that satisfy them? Even if we caught all the fish in the sea, would that be enough?"

²³Then the LORD said to Moses, "Has my arm lost its power? Now you will see whether or not my word comes true!"

²⁴So Moses went out and reported the LORD's words to the people. He gathered the seventy elders and stationed them around the Tabernacle.* ²⁵And the LORD came down in the cloud and spoke to Moses. Then he gave the seventy elders the same Spirit that was upon Moses. And when the Spirit rested upon them, they prophesied. But this never happened again. ²⁶Two men, Eldad and Medad, had stayed behind in the camp. They were listed among the elders, but they had not gone out to the Tabernacle. Yet the Spirit rested upon them as well, so they prophesied there in the camp. ²⁷A young man ran and reported to Moses, "Eldad and Medad are prophesying in the camp!"

²⁸Joshua son of Nun, who had been Moses' assistant since his youth, protested, "Moses, my master, make them stop!"

²⁹But Moses replied, "Are you jealous for my sake? I wish that all the LORD's people were prophets and that the LORD would put his Spirit upon them all!" ³⁰Then Moses returned to the camp with the elders of Israel.

The LORD Sends Quail

³¹Now the LORD sent a wind that brought quail from the sea and let them fall all around the camp. For miles in every direction there were quail flying about three feet above the ground.* ³²So the people went out and caught quail all that day and throughout the night and all the next day, too. No one gathered less than fifty bushels*! They spread the quail all around the camp to dry. ³³But while they were gorging themselves on the meat—while it was still in their mouths—the anger of the LORD blazed against the people, and he struck them with a severe plague. ³⁴So that place was called Kibroth-hattaavah (which means "graves of gluttony") because there they buried the people who had craved meat from Egypt. ³⁵From Kibroth-hattaavah the Israelites traveled to Hazeroth, where they stayed for some time.

12 The Complaints of Miriam and Aaron

While they were at Hazeroth, Miriam and Aaron criticized Moses because he had married a Cushite woman. ²They said, "Has the LORD spoken only through Moses? Hasn't he spoken through us, too?" But the LORD heard them. ³(Now Moses was very humble—more humble than any other person on earth.)

⁴So immediately the LORD called to Moses, Aaron, and Miriam and said, "Go out to the Tabernacle,* all three of you!" So the three of them went to the Tabernacle. ⁵Then the LORD descended in the pillar of cloud and stood at the entrance of the Tabernacle.* "Aaron and Miriam!" he called, and they stepped forward. ⁶And the LORD said to them, "Now listen to what I say:

"If there were prophets among you,
  I, the LORD, would reveal myself in
    visions.
  I would speak to them in dreams.
⁷ But not with my servant Moses.
  Of all my house, he is the one I trust.
⁸ I speak to him face to face,
  clearly, and not in riddles!
  He sees the LORD as he is.
So why were you not afraid
  to criticize my servant Moses?"

⁹The LORD was very angry with them, and he departed. ¹⁰As the cloud moved from above the Tabernacle, there stood Miriam, her skin as white as snow from leprosy.* When Aaron saw what had happened to her, ¹¹he cried out to Moses, "Oh, my master! Please don't punish us for this sin we have so foolishly committed. ¹²Don't let her be like a stillborn baby, already decayed at birth."

¹³So Moses cried out to the LORD, "O God, I beg you, please heal her!"

¹⁴But the LORD said to Moses, "If her father had done nothing more than spit in her face, wouldn't she be defiled for seven days? So keep her outside the camp for seven days, and after that she may be accepted back." ¹⁵So Miriam was kept outside the camp

---

11:24 Hebrew *the tent;* also in 11:26.   **11:31** Or *there were quail 3 feet* [2 cubits or 92 centimeters] *deep on the ground.*   **11:32** Hebrew *10 homers* [1.8 kiloliters].   **12:4** Hebrew *the Tent of Meeting.*   **12:5** Hebrew *the tent;* also in 12:10.   **12:10** Or *with a skin disease.* The Hebrew word used here can describe various skin diseases.

for seven days, and the people waited until she was brought back before they traveled again. ¹⁶Then they left Hazeroth and camped in the wilderness of Paran.

13 Twelve Scouts Explore Canaan

The LORD now said to Moses, ²"Send out men to explore the land of Canaan, the land I am giving to the Israelites. Send one leader from each of the twelve ancestral

tribes." ³So Moses did as the LORD commanded him. He sent out twelve men, all tribal leaders of Israel, from their camp in the wilderness of Paran. ⁴These were the tribes and the names of their leaders:

Tribe	Leader
Reuben	Shammua son of Zaccur
⁵ Simeon	Shaphat son of Hori
⁶ Judah	Caleb son of Jephunneh
⁷ Issachar	Igal son of Joseph

Miriam: The Destructive Power of Complaining
NUMBERS 12

Every time we meet Miriam in Scripture, it's in the context of family. In Exodus 2 she is the sister who anxiously watches her baby brother, Moses, float down the river in a basket. And in Exodus 15 as she and Moses together sing praise to God for the astounding victory he gave Israel by parting the Red Sea, we get a sense they are in complete accord with each other.

However, the next time we meet Miriam, she has switched her allegiance to her older brother, Aaron, and they have ganged up against Moses, complaining and criticizing him because he married a woman who was not a Hebrew (Numbers 12).

Why was this family squabble included in Scripture? Because Moses was the respected leader of the group and his siblings' rebellion against him could potentially ripple through the entire community of God's people.

So God, the best of fathers, settled this score by declaring Moses in the right. Not only that, but he gave Miriam the severe punishment of leprosy. When Moses pled her case, the Lord insisted it was a fair punishment, and banished her from the community for the seven days that she had the skin disease.

God's harsh treatment of Miriam's rebellion and complaining reveals how highly God values unity among his people. Miriam's punishment was severe because the *danger* was severe: the cohesion of the group was at stake. This painful experience undoubtedly taught Miriam a life-changing lesson.

Like Miriam we can often be tempted to focus on the things we don't like and let our tongues turn to criticism. Will we give voice to critiques or complaints, even if our words threaten the unity of God's people?

We don't have to stay mired in the struggle against complaining; if we seek his help, God can change both our tongues and our spirits. Though Miriam struggled with the temptation to judge, critique, and complain, we can also see that God worked in her spirit and used her in powerful ways. In Micah 6:4 the Lord says, "For I brought you out of Egypt and redeemed you from slavery. I sent Moses, Aaron, and Miriam to help you." In the end she gets as much credit as Moses for her part in God's redemption of his people.

—JoHannah Reardon

For more on community, see reading at Job 20.

⁸ Ephraim . . . . Hoshea son of Nun
⁹ Benjamin . . . . Palti son of Raphu
¹⁰ Zebulun . . . . Gaddiel son of Sodi
¹¹ Manasseh son of
      Joseph . . . . Gaddi son of Susi
¹² Dan . . . . Ammiel son of Gemalli
¹³ Asher . . . . . . Sethur son of Michael
¹⁴ Naphtali . . . . . . Nahbi son of Vophsi
¹⁵ Gad . . . . Geuel son of Maki

¹⁶ These are the names of the men Moses sent out to explore the land. (Moses called Hoshea son of Nun by the name Joshua.)

¹⁷ Moses gave the men these instructions as he sent them out to explore the land: "Go north through the Negev into the hill country. ¹⁸ See what the land is like, and find out whether the people living there are strong or weak, few or many. ¹⁹ See what kind of land they live in. Is it good or bad? Do their towns have walls, or are they unprotected like open camps? ²⁰ Is the soil fertile or poor? Are there many trees? Do your best to bring back samples of the crops you see." (It happened to be the season for harvesting the first ripe grapes.)

²¹ So they went up and explored the land from the wilderness of Zin as far as Rehob, near Lebo-hamath. ²² Going north, they passed through the Negev and arrived at Hebron, where Ahiman, Sheshai, and Talmai—all descendants of Anak—lived. (The ancient town of Hebron was founded seven years before the Egyptian city of Zoan.) ²³ When they came to the valley of Eshcol, they cut down a branch with a single cluster of grapes so large that it took two of them to carry it on a pole between them! They also brought back samples of the pomegranates and figs. ²⁴ That place was called the valley of Eshcol (which means "cluster"), because of the cluster of grapes the Israelite men cut there.

The Scouting Report

²⁵ After exploring the land for forty days, the men returned ²⁶ to Moses, Aaron, and the whole community of Israel at Kadesh in the wilderness of Paran. They reported to the whole community what they had seen and showed them the fruit they had taken from the land. ²⁷ This was their report

to Moses: "We entered the land you sent us to explore, and it is indeed a bountiful country—a land flowing with milk and honey. Here is the kind of fruit it produces. ²⁸ But the people living there are powerful, and their towns are large and fortified. We even saw giants there, the descendants of Anak! ²⁹ The Amalekites live in the Negev, and the Hittites, Jebusites, and Amorites live in the hill country. The Canaanites live along the coast of the Mediterranean Sea* and along the Jordan Valley."

³⁰ But Caleb tried to quiet the people as they stood before Moses. "Let's go at once to take the land," he said. "We can certainly conquer it!"

³¹ But the other men who had explored the land with him disagreed. "We can't go up against them! They are stronger than we are!" ³² So they spread this bad report about the land among the Israelites: "The land we traveled through and explored will devour anyone who goes to live there. All the people we saw were huge. ³³ We even saw giants* there, the descendants of Anak. Next to them we felt like grasshoppers, and that's what they thought, too!"

14

The People Rebel

Then the whole community began weeping aloud, and they cried all night. ² Their voices rose in a great chorus of protest against Moses and Aaron. "If only we had died in Egypt, or even here in the wilderness!" they complained. ³ "Why is the LORD taking us to this country only to have us die in battle? Our wives and our little ones will be carried off as plunder! Wouldn't it be better for us to return to Egypt?" ⁴ Then they plotted among themselves, "Let's choose a new leader and go back to Egypt!"

⁵ Then Moses and Aaron fell face down on the ground before the whole community of Israel. ⁶ Two of the men who had explored the land, Joshua son of Nun and Caleb son of Jephunneh, tore their clothing. ⁷ They said to all the people of Israel, "The land we traveled through and explored is a wonderful land! ⁸ And if the LORD is pleased with us, he will bring us safely into that land and

---

13:29 Hebrew *the sea.*   **13:33** Hebrew *nephilim.*

give it to us. It is a rich land flowing with milk and honey. [9] Do not rebel against the LORD, and don't be afraid of the people of the land. They are only helpless prey to us! They have no protection, but the LORD is with us! Don't be afraid of them!"

[10] But the whole community began to talk about stoning Joshua and Caleb. Then the glorious presence of the LORD appeared to all the Israelites at the Tabernacle.* [11] And the LORD said to Moses, "How long will these people treat me with contempt? Will they never believe me, even after all the miraculous signs I have done among them? [12] I will disown them and destroy them with a plague. Then I will make you into a nation greater and mightier than they are!"

Moses Intercedes for the People

[13] But Moses objected. "What will the Egyptians think when they hear about it?" he asked the LORD. "They know full well the power you displayed in rescuing your people from Egypt. [14] Now if you destroy them, the Egyptians will send a report to the inhabitants of this land, who have already heard that you live among your people. They know, LORD, that you have appeared to your people face to face and that your pillar of cloud hovers over them. They know that you go before them in the pillar of cloud by day and the pillar of fire by night. [15] Now if you slaughter all these people with a single blow, the nations that have heard of your fame will say, [16] 'The LORD was not able to bring them into the land he swore to give them, so he killed them in the wilderness.'

[17] "Please, Lord, prove that your power is as great as you have claimed. For you said, [18] 'The LORD is slow to anger and filled with unfailing love, forgiving every kind of sin and rebellion. But he does not excuse the guilty. He lays the sins of the parents upon their children; the entire family is affected— even children in the third and fourth generations.' [19] In keeping with your magnificent, unfailing love, please pardon the sins of this people, just as you have forgiven them ever since they left Egypt."

[20] Then the LORD said, "I will pardon them as you have requested. [21] But as surely as I live, and as surely as the earth is filled with the LORD's glory, [22] not one of these people will ever enter that land. They have all seen my glorious presence and the miraculous signs I performed both in Egypt and in the wilderness, but again and again they have tested me by refusing to listen to my voice. [23] They will never even see the land I swore to give their ancestors. None of those who have treated me with contempt will ever see it. [24] But my servant Caleb has a different attitude than the others have. He has remained loyal to me, so I will bring him into the land he explored. His descendants will possess their full share of that land. [25] Now turn around, and don't go on toward the land where the Amalekites and Canaanites live. Tomorrow you must set out for the wilderness in the direction of the Red Sea.*"

The LORD Punishes the Israelites

[26] Then the LORD said to Moses and Aaron, [27] "How long must I put up with this wicked community and its complaints about me? Yes, I have heard the complaints the Israelites are making against me. [28] Now tell them this: 'As surely as I live, declares the LORD, I will do to you the very things I heard you say. [29] You will all drop dead in this wilderness! Because you complained against me, every one of you who is twenty years old or older and was included in the registration will die. [30] You will not enter and occupy the land I swore to give you. The only exceptions will be Caleb son of Jephunneh and Joshua son of Nun.

[31] "'You said your children would be carried off as plunder. Well, I will bring them safely into the land, and they will enjoy what you have despised. [32] But as for you, you will drop dead in this wilderness. [33] And your children will be like shepherds, wandering in the wilderness for forty years. In this way, they will pay for your faithlessness, until the last of you lies dead in the wilderness.

[34] "'Because your men explored the land for forty days, you must wander in the wilderness for forty years—a year for each day,

14:10 Hebrew *the Tent of Meeting.*   **14:25** Hebrew *sea of reeds.*

suffering the consequences of your sins. Then you will discover what it is like to have me for an enemy.' ³⁵I, the LORD, have spoken! I will certainly do these things to every member of the community who has conspired against me. They will be destroyed here in this wilderness, and here they will die!"

³⁶The ten men Moses had sent to explore the land—the ones who incited rebellion against the LORD with their bad report—³⁷were struck dead with a plague before the LORD. ³⁸Of the twelve who had explored the land, only Joshua and Caleb remained alive.

³⁹When Moses reported the LORD's words to all the Israelites, the people were filled with grief. ⁴⁰Then they got up early the next morning and went to the top of the range of hills. "Let's go," they said. "We realize that we have sinned, but now we are ready to enter the land the LORD has promised us."

⁴¹But Moses said, "Why are you now disobeying the LORD's orders to return to the wilderness? It won't work. ⁴²Do not go up into the land now. You will only be crushed by your enemies because the LORD is not with you. ⁴³When you face the Amalekites and Canaanites in battle, you will be slaughtered. The LORD will abandon you because you have abandoned the LORD."

⁴⁴But the people defiantly pushed ahead toward the hill country, even though neither Moses nor the Ark of the LORD's Covenant left the camp. ⁴⁵Then the Amalekites and the Canaanites who lived in those hills came down and attacked them and chased them back as far as Hormah.

15 Laws concerning Offerings

Then the LORD told Moses, ²"Give the following instructions to the people of Israel.

"When you finally settle in the land I am giving you, ³you will offer special gifts as a pleasing aroma to the LORD. These gifts may take the form of a burnt offering, a sacrifice to fulfill a vow, a voluntary offering, or an offering at any of your annual festivals, and they may be taken from your herds of cattle or your flocks of sheep and goats.

⁴When you present these offerings, you must also give the LORD a grain offering of two quarts* of choice flour mixed with one quart* of olive oil. ⁵For each lamb offered as a burnt offering or a special sacrifice, you must also present one quart of wine as a liquid offering.

⁶"If the sacrifice is a ram, give a grain offering of four quarts* of choice flour mixed with a third of a gallon* of olive oil, ⁷and give a third of a gallon of wine as a liquid offering. This will be a pleasing aroma to the LORD.

⁸"When you present a young bull as a burnt offering or as a sacrifice to fulfill a vow or as a peace offering to the LORD, ⁹you must also give a grain offering of six quarts* of choice flour mixed with two quarts* of olive oil, ¹⁰and give two quarts of wine as a liquid offering. This will be a special gift, a pleasing aroma to the LORD.

¹¹"Each sacrifice of a bull, ram, lamb, or young goat should be prepared in this way. ¹²Follow these instructions with each offering you present. ¹³All of you native-born Israelites must follow these instructions when you offer a special gift as a pleasing aroma to the LORD. ¹⁴And if any foreigners visit you or live among you and want to present a special gift as a pleasing aroma to the LORD, they must follow these same procedures. ¹⁵Native-born Israelites and foreigners are equal before the LORD and are subject to the same decrees. This is a permanent law for you, to be observed from generation to generation. ¹⁶The same instructions and regulations will apply both to you and to the foreigners living among you."

¹⁷Then the LORD said to Moses, ¹⁸"Give the following instructions to the people of Israel.

"When you arrive in the land where I am taking you, ¹⁹and you eat the crops that grow there, you must set some aside as a sacred offering to the LORD. ²⁰Present a cake from the first of the flour you grind, and set it aside as a sacred offering, as you do with the first grain from the threshing floor. ²¹Throughout the generations to come, you are to present a sacred offering

---

15:4a Hebrew ¹⁄₁₀ of an ephah [2.2 liters].   **15:4b** Hebrew ¼ of a hin [1 liter]; also in 15:5.   **15:6a** Hebrew ²⁄₁₀ of an ephah [4.4 liters].
15:6b Hebrew ⅓ of a hin [1.3 liters]; also in 15:7.   **15:9a** Hebrew ³⁄₁₀ of an ephah [6.6 liters].   **15:9b** Hebrew ½ of a hin [2 liters]; also in 15:10.

to the LORD each year from the first of your ground flour.

²²"But suppose you unintentionally fail to carry out all these commands that the LORD has given you through Moses. ²³And suppose your descendants in the future fail to do everything the LORD has commanded through Moses. ²⁴If the mistake was made unintentionally, and the community was unaware of it, the whole community must present a young bull for a burnt offering as a pleasing aroma to the LORD. It must be offered along with its prescribed grain offering and liquid offering and with one male goat for a sin offering. ²⁵With it the priest will purify the whole community of Israel, making them right with the LORD,* and they will be forgiven. For it was an unintentional sin, and they have corrected it with their offerings to the LORD— the special gift and the sin offering. ²⁶The whole community of Israel will be forgiven, including the foreigners living among you, for all the people were involved in the sin.

²⁷"If one individual commits an unintentional sin, the guilty person must bring a one-year-old female goat for a sin offering. ²⁸The priest will sacrifice it to purify* the guilty person before the LORD, and that person will be forgiven. ²⁹These same instructions apply both to native-born Israelites and to the foreigners living among you.

³⁰"But those who brazenly violate the LORD's will, whether native-born Israelites or foreigners, have blasphemed the LORD, and they must be cut off from the community. ³¹Since they have treated the LORD's word with contempt and deliberately disobeyed his command, they must be completely cut off and suffer the punishment for their guilt."

Penalty for Breaking the Sabbath

³²One day while the people of Israel were in the wilderness, they discovered a man gathering wood on the Sabbath day. ³³The people who found him doing this took him before Moses, Aaron, and the rest of the community. ³⁴They held him in custody because they did not know what to do with him. ³⁵Then the LORD said to Moses, "The man must be put to death! The whole community must stone him outside the camp." ³⁶So the whole community took the man outside the camp and stoned him to death, just as the LORD had commanded Moses.

Tassels on Clothing

³⁷Then the LORD said to Moses, ³⁸"Give the following instructions to the people of Israel: Throughout the generations to come you must make tassels for the hems of your clothing and attach them with a blue cord. ³⁹When you see the tassels, you will remember and obey all the commands of the LORD instead of following your own desires and defiling yourselves, as you are prone to do. ⁴⁰The tassels will help you remember that you must obey all my commands and be holy to your God. ⁴¹I am the LORD your God who brought you out of the land of Egypt that I might be your God. I am the LORD your God!"

16 Korah's Rebellion

One day Korah son of Izhar, a descendant of Kohath son of Levi, conspired with Dathan and Abiram, the sons of Eliab, and On son of Peleth, from the tribe of Reuben. ²They incited a rebellion against Moses, along with 250 other leaders of the community, all prominent members of the assembly. ³They united against Moses and Aaron and said, "You have gone too far! The whole community of Israel has been set apart by the LORD, and he is with all of us. What right do you have to act as though you are greater than the rest of the LORD's people?"

⁴When Moses heard what they were saying, he fell face down on the ground. ⁵Then he said to Korah and his followers, "Tomorrow morning the LORD will show us who belongs to him* and who is holy. The LORD will allow only those whom he selects to enter his own presence. ⁶Korah, you and all your followers must prepare your incense burners. ⁷Light fires in them tomorrow, and burn incense before the LORD. Then we will see whom the LORD chooses as his holy one. You Levites are the ones who have gone too far!"

⁸Then Moses spoke again to Korah: "Now

15:25 Or *will make atonement for the whole community of Israel.*   **15:28** Or *to make atonement for.*   **16:5** Greek version reads *God has visited and knows those who are his.* Compare 2 Tim 2:19.

listen, you Levites! ⁹Does it seem insignificant to you that the God of Israel has chosen you from among all the community of Israel to be near him so you can serve in the LORD's Tabernacle and stand before the people to minister to them? ¹⁰Korah, he has already given this special ministry to you and your fellow Levites. Are you now demanding the priesthood as well? ¹¹The LORD is the one you and your followers are really revolting against! For who is Aaron that you are complaining about him?"

¹²Then Moses summoned Dathan and Abiram, the sons of Eliab, but they replied, "We refuse to come before you! ¹³Isn't it enough that you brought us out of Egypt, a land flowing with milk and honey, to kill us here in this wilderness, and that you now treat us like your subjects? ¹⁴What's more, you haven't brought us into another land flowing with milk and honey. You haven't given us a new homeland with fields and vineyards. Are you trying to fool these men?* We will not come."

¹⁵Then Moses became very angry and said to the LORD, "Do not accept their grain offerings! I have not taken so much as a donkey from them, and I have never hurt a single one of them." ¹⁶And Moses said to Korah, "You and all your followers must come here tomorrow and present yourselves before the LORD. Aaron will also be here. ¹⁷You and each of your 250 followers must prepare an incense burner and put incense on it, so you can all present them before the LORD. Aaron will also bring his incense burner." ¹⁸So each of these men prepared an incense burner, lit the fire, and placed incense on it. Then they all stood at the entrance of the Tabernacle* with Moses and Aaron. ¹⁹Meanwhile, Korah had stirred up the entire community against Moses and Aaron, and they all gathered at the Tabernacle entrance. Then the glorious presence of the LORD appeared to the whole community, ²⁰and the LORD said to Moses and Aaron, ²¹"Get away from all these people so that I may instantly destroy them!"

²²But Moses and Aaron fell face down on the ground. "O God," they pleaded, "you are the God who gives breath to all creatures. Must you be angry with all the people when only one man sins?"

²³And the LORD said to Moses, ²⁴"Then tell all the people to get away from the tents of Korah, Dathan, and Abiram."

²⁵So Moses got up and rushed over to the tents of Dathan and Abiram, followed by the elders of Israel. ²⁶"Quick!" he told the people. "Get away from the tents of these wicked men, and don't touch anything that belongs to them. If you do, you will be destroyed for their sins." ²⁷So all the people stood back from the tents of Korah, Dathan, and Abiram. Then Dathan and Abiram came out and stood at the entrances of their tents, together with their wives and children and little ones.

²⁸And Moses said, "This is how you will know that the LORD has sent me to do all these things that I have done—for I have not done them on my own. ²⁹If these men die a natural death, or if nothing unusual happens, then the LORD has not sent me. ³⁰But if the LORD does something entirely new and the ground opens its mouth and swallows them and all their belongings, and they go down alive into the grave,* then you will know that these men have shown contempt for the LORD."

³¹He had hardly finished speaking the words when the ground suddenly split open beneath them. ³²The earth opened its mouth and swallowed the men, along with their households and all their followers who were standing with them, and everything they owned. ³³So they went down alive into the grave, along with all their belongings. The earth closed over them, and they all vanished from among the people of Israel. ³⁴All the people around them fled when they heard their screams. "The earth will swallow us, too!" they cried. ³⁵Then fire blazed forth from the LORD and burned up the 250 men who were offering incense.

³⁶*And the LORD said to Moses, ³⁷"Tell Eleazar son of Aaron the priest to pull all the incense burners from the fire, for they are holy. Also tell him to scatter the burning coals. ³⁸Take the incense burners of these men who have sinned at the cost of

---

16:14 Hebrew *Are you trying to put out the eyes of these men?* 16:18 Hebrew *the Tent of Meeting;* also in 16:19, 42, 43, 50. 16:30 Hebrew *into Sheol;* also in 16:33. 16:36 Verses 16:36-50 are numbered 17:1-15 in Hebrew text.

their lives, and hammer the metal into a thin sheet to overlay the altar. Since these burners were used in the Lord's presence, they have become holy. Let them serve as a warning to the people of Israel."

³⁹ So Eleazar the priest collected the 250 bronze incense burners that had been used by the men who died in the fire, and he hammered them into a thin sheet to overlay the altar. ⁴⁰ This would warn the Israelites that no unauthorized person—no one who was not a descendant of Aaron—should ever enter the Lord's presence to burn incense. If anyone did, the same thing would happen to him as happened to Korah and his followers. So the Lord's instructions to Moses were carried out.

⁴¹ But the very next morning the whole community of Israel began muttering again against Moses and Aaron, saying, "You have killed the Lord's people!" ⁴² As the community gathered to protest against Moses and Aaron, they turned toward the Tabernacle and saw that the cloud had covered it, and the glorious presence of the Lord appeared.

⁴³ Moses and Aaron came and stood in front of the Tabernacle, ⁴⁴ and the Lord said to Moses, ⁴⁵ "Get away from all these people so that I can instantly destroy them!" But Moses and Aaron fell face down on the ground.

⁴⁶ And Moses said to Aaron, "Quick, take an incense burner and place burning coals on it from the altar. Lay incense on it, and carry it out among the people to purify them and make them right with the Lord.* The Lord's anger is blazing against them— the plague has already begun."

⁴⁷ Aaron did as Moses told him and ran out among the people. The plague had already begun to strike down the people, but Aaron burned the incense and purified* the people. ⁴⁸ He stood between the dead and the living, and the plague stopped. ⁴⁹ But 14,700 people died in that plague, in addition to those who had died in the affair involving Korah. ⁵⁰ Then because the plague had stopped, Aaron returned to Moses at the entrance of the Tabernacle.

17 The Budding of Aaron's Staff

¹*Then the Lord said to Moses, ²"Tell the people of Israel to bring you twelve wooden staffs, one from each leader of Israel's ancestral tribes, and inscribe each leader's name on his staff. ³ Inscribe Aaron's name on the staff of the tribe of Levi, for there must be one staff for the leader of each ancestral tribe. ⁴ Place these staffs in the Tabernacle in front of the Ark containing the tablets of the Covenant,* where I meet with you. ⁵ Buds will sprout on the staff belonging to the man I choose. Then I will finally put an end to the people's murmuring and complaining against you."

⁶ So Moses gave the instructions to the people of Israel, and each of the twelve tribal leaders, including Aaron, brought Moses a staff. ⁷ Moses placed the staffs in the Lord's presence in the Tabernacle of the Covenant.* ⁸ When he went into the Tabernacle of the Covenant the next day, he found that Aaron's staff, representing the tribe of Levi, had sprouted, budded, blossomed, and produced ripe almonds!

⁹ When Moses brought all the staffs out from the Lord's presence, he showed them to the people. Each man claimed his own staff. ¹⁰ And the Lord said to Moses: "Place Aaron's staff permanently before the Ark of the Covenant* to serve as a warning to rebels. This should put an end to their complaints against me and prevent any further deaths." ¹¹ So Moses did as the Lord commanded him.

¹² Then the people of Israel said to Moses, "Look, we are doomed! We are dead! We are ruined! ¹³ Everyone who even comes close to the Tabernacle of the Lord dies. Are we all doomed to die?"

18 Duties of Priests and Levites

Then the Lord said to Aaron: "You, your sons, and your relatives from the tribe of Levi will be held responsible for any offenses related to the sanctuary. But you and your sons alone will be held responsible for violations connected with the priesthood.

16:46 Or to make atonement for them.   **16:47** Or and made atonement for.   **17:1** Verses 17:1-13 are numbered 17:16-28 in Hebrew text.
17:4 Hebrew in the Tent of Meeting before the Testimony. The Hebrew word for "testimony" refers to the terms of the Lord's covenant with Israel as written on stone tablets, which were kept in the Ark, and also to the covenant itself.   **17:7** Or Tabernacle of the Testimony; also in 17:8.
17:10 Hebrew before the Testimony; see note on 17:4.

2 "Bring your relatives of the tribe of Levi—your ancestral tribe—to assist you and your sons as you perform the sacred duties in front of the Tabernacle of the Covenant.* 3 But as the Levites go about all their assigned duties at the Tabernacle, they must be careful not to go near any of the sacred objects or the altar. If they do, both you and they will die. 4 The Levites must join you in fulfilling their responsibilities for the care and maintenance of the Tabernacle,* but no unauthorized person may assist you.

5 "You yourselves must perform the sacred duties inside the sanctuary and at the altar. If you follow these instructions, the LORD's anger will never again blaze against the people of Israel. 6 I myself have chosen your fellow Levites from among the Israelites to be your special assistants. They are a gift to you, dedicated to the LORD for service in the Tabernacle. 7 But you and your sons, the priests, must personally handle all the priestly rituals associated with the altar and with everything behind the inner curtain. I am giving you the priesthood as your special privilege of service. Any unauthorized person who comes too near the sanctuary will be put to death."

Support for the Priests and Levites

8 The LORD gave these further instructions to Aaron: "I myself have put you in charge of all the holy offerings that are brought to me by the people of Israel. I have given all these consecrated offerings to you and your sons as your permanent share. 9 You are allotted the portion of the most holy offerings that is not burned on the fire. This portion of all the most holy offerings—including the grain offerings, sin offerings, and guilt offerings—will be most holy, and it belongs to you and your sons. 10 You must eat it as a most holy offering. All the males may eat of it, and you must treat it as most holy.

11 "All the sacred offerings and special offerings presented to me when the Israelites lift them up before the altar also belong to you. I have given them to you and to your sons and daughters as your permanent share. Any member of your family who is ceremonially clean may eat of these offerings.

12 "I also give you the harvest gifts brought by the people as offerings to the LORD—the best of the olive oil, new wine, and grain. 13 All the first crops of their land that the people present to the LORD belong to you. Any member of your family who is ceremonially clean may eat this food.

14 "Everything in Israel that is specially set apart for the LORD* also belongs to you.

15 "The firstborn of every mother, whether human or animal, that is offered to the LORD will be yours. But you must always redeem your firstborn sons and the firstborn of ceremonially unclean animals. 16 Redeem them when they are one month old. The redemption price is five pieces of silver* (as measured by the weight of the sanctuary shekel, which equals twenty gerahs).

17 "However, you may not redeem the firstborn of cattle, sheep, or goats. They are holy and have been set apart for the LORD. Sprinkle their blood on the altar, and burn their fat as a special gift, a pleasing aroma to the LORD. 18 The meat of these animals will be yours, just like the breast and right thigh that are presented by lifting them up as a special offering before the altar. 19 Yes, I am giving you all these holy offerings that the people of Israel bring to the LORD. They are for you and your sons and daughters, to be eaten as your permanent share. This is an eternal and unbreakable covenant* between the LORD and you, and it also applies to your descendants."

20 And the LORD said to Aaron, "You priests will receive no allotment of land or share of property among the people of Israel. I am your share and your allotment. 21 As for the tribe of Levi, your relatives, I will compensate them for their service in the Tabernacle. Instead of an allotment of land, I will give them the tithes from the entire land of Israel.

22 "From now on, no Israelites except priests or Levites may approach the Tabernacle. If they come too near, they will be

---

18:2 Or Tabernacle of the Testimony.   18:4 Hebrew the Tent of Meeting; also in 18:6, 21, 22, 23, 31.   18:14 The Hebrew term used here refers to the complete consecration of things or people to the LORD, either by destroying them or by giving them as an offering.   18:16 Hebrew 5 shekels [2 ounces or 57 grams] of silver.   18:19 Hebrew a covenant of salt.

Stewardship

Why 10 Percent?

NUMBERS 18:20-21

Some Christians are rigid in their view of tithing, with a hard and fast commitment to giving an exact 10 percent. Others view the percentage as a guideline, while still others consider us to be free from the laws of the Old Testament, including tithing. So who came up with the 10 percent amount? Why should we take this figure as authoritative? *Is* tithing just another form of legalism?

Here, as in most churchly matters, a bit of history can go a long way in helping us understand the the tithe.

Most tithing discussions begin with the Old Testament precedent, first recorded in Genesis 14:20. After winning an astounding victory in battle and retrieving his nephew Lot along with all his lost possessions, Abram thanked God by giving Melchizedek one-tenth of all he had.

Then in Numbers 18:21, we find tithing included in the Mosaic Law. Its purpose was to provide for the Levites, whom God wanted to concentrate on priestly duties.

While the New Testament contains no explicit command to tithe, many have argued that this relationship between the Levites and the other tribes of Israel prefigures how Christians should provide for their ministers. This view of tithing, known as parallelism, gained prominence in the church around the sixth century.

The early church's views on tithing foreshadowed many of today's financial stewardship debates. The Eastern Church began tithing out of obligation, because they believed Jesus' conversation with the rich young man demanded sacrificial generosity (Mark 10:17-25). Clement of Alexandria and Irenaeus pleaded with the church to surpass even the Old Testament tithe since Christ had freed them from the law.

Later church leaders—John Chrysostom, Cyprian, Origen, and Augustine among them—complained from time to time that their followers lacked Christian charity. Chrysostom even shamed his stingy church for marveling at those who tithed. He contrasted their amazement with the dutiful giving of Old Testament Jews.

Research of modern-day Christians, sadly, reveals a similar stinginess; many of us don't give generously to the church. Perhaps we ought to try to emulate the words of seventeenth-century John Bunyan, "There was a man, some called him mad; The more he gave, the more he had."

—Collin Hansen

For more on stewardship, see reading at 1 Chronicles 29:1-20.

judged guilty and will die. ²³Only the Levites may serve at the Tabernacle, and they will be held responsible for any offenses against it. This is a permanent law for you, to be observed from generation to generation. The Levites will receive no allotment of land among the Israelites, ²⁴because I have given them the Israelites' tithes, which have been presented as sacred offerings to the LORD. This will be the Levites' share. That is why I said they would receive no allotment of land among the Israelites."

25 The Lord also told Moses, 26 "Give these instructions to the Levites: When you receive from the people of Israel the tithes I have assigned as your allotment, give a tenth of the tithes you receive—a tithe of the tithe—to the Lord as a sacred offering. 27 The Lord will consider this offering to be your harvest offering, as though it were the first grain from your own threshing floor or wine from your own winepress. 28 You must present one-tenth of the tithe received from the Israelites as a sacred offering to the Lord. This is the Lord's sacred portion, and you must present it to Aaron the priest. 29 Be sure to give to the Lord the best portions of the gifts given to you.

30 "Also, give these instructions to the Levites: When you present the best part as your offering, it will be considered as though it came from your own threshing floor or winepress. 31 You Levites and your families may eat this food anywhere you wish, for it is your compensation for serving in the Tabernacle. 32 You will not be considered guilty for accepting the Lord's tithes if you give the best portion to the priests. But be careful not to treat the holy gifts of the people of Israel as though they were common. If you do, you will die."

19 The Water of Purification

The Lord said to Moses and Aaron, 2 "Here is another legal requirement commanded by the Lord: Tell the people of Israel to bring you a red heifer, a perfect animal that has no defects and has never been yoked to a plow. 3 Give it to Eleazar the priest, and it will be taken outside the camp and slaughtered in his presence. 4 Eleazar will take some of its blood on his finger and sprinkle it seven times toward the front of the Tabernacle.* 5 As Eleazar watches, the heifer must be burned—its hide, meat, blood, and dung. 6 Eleazar the priest must then take a stick of cedar,* a hyssop branch, and some scarlet yarn and throw them into the fire where the heifer is burning.

7 "Then the priest must wash his clothes and bathe himself in water. Afterward he may return to the camp, though he will remain ceremonially unclean until evening.

8 The man who burns the animal must also wash his clothes and bathe himself in water, and he, too, will remain unclean until evening. 9 Then someone who is ceremonially clean will gather up the ashes of the heifer and deposit them in a purified place outside the camp. They will be kept there for the community of Israel to use in the water for the purification ceremony. This ceremony is performed for the removal of sin. 10 The man who gathers up the ashes of the heifer must also wash his clothes, and he will remain ceremonially unclean until evening. This is a permanent law for the people of Israel and any foreigners who live among them.

11 "All those who touch a dead human body will be ceremonially unclean for seven days. 12 They must purify themselves on the third and seventh days with the water of purification; then they will be purified. But if they do not do this on the third and seventh days, they will continue to be unclean even after the seventh day. 13 All those who touch a dead body and do not purify themselves in the proper way defile the Lord's Tabernacle, and they will be cut off from the community of Israel. Since the water of purification was not sprinkled on them, their defilement continues.

14 "This is the ritual law that applies when someone dies inside a tent: All those who enter that tent and those who were inside when the death occurred will be ceremonially unclean for seven days. 15 Any open container in the tent that was not covered with a lid is also defiled. 16 And if someone in an open field touches the corpse of someone who was killed with a sword or who died a natural death, or if someone touches a human bone or a grave, that person will be defiled for seven days.

17 "To remove the defilement, put some of the ashes from the burnt purification offering in a jar, and pour fresh water over them. 18 Then someone who is ceremonially clean must take a hyssop branch and dip it into the water. That person must sprinkle the water on the tent, on all the furnishings in the tent, and on the people who were in the tent; also on the person who touched a

human bone, or touched someone who was killed or who died naturally, or touched a grave. ¹⁹On the third and seventh days the person who is ceremonially clean must sprinkle the water on those who are defiled. Then on the seventh day the people being cleansed must wash their clothes and bathe themselves, and that evening they will be cleansed of their defilement.

²⁰"But those who become defiled and do not purify themselves will be cut off from the community, for they have defiled the sanctuary of the LORD. Since the water of purification has not been sprinkled on them, they remain defiled. ²¹This is a permanent law for the people. Those who sprinkle the water of purification must afterward wash their clothes, and anyone who then touches the water used for purification will remain defiled until evening. ²²Anything and anyone that a defiled person touches will be ceremonially unclean until evening."

20 Moses Strikes the Rock

In the first month of the year,* the whole community of Israel arrived in the wilderness of Zin and camped at Kadesh. While they were there, Miriam died and was buried.

²There was no water for the people to drink at that place, so they rebelled against Moses and Aaron. ³The people blamed Moses and said, "If only we had died in the LORD's presence with our brothers! ⁴Why have you brought the congregation of the LORD's people into this wilderness to die, along with all our livestock? ⁵Why did you make us leave Egypt and bring us here to this terrible place? This land has no grain, no figs, no grapes, no pomegranates, and no water to drink!"

⁶Moses and Aaron turned away from the people and went to the entrance of the Tabernacle,* where they fell face down on the ground. Then the glorious presence of the LORD appeared to them, ⁷and the LORD said to Moses, ⁸"You and Aaron must take the staff and assemble the entire community. As the people watch, speak to the rock over there, and it will pour out its water.

You will provide enough water from the rock to satisfy the whole community and their livestock."

⁹So Moses did as he was told. He took the staff from the place where it was kept before the LORD. ¹⁰Then he and Aaron summoned the people to come and gather at the rock. "Listen, you rebels!" he shouted. "Must we bring you water from this rock?" ¹¹Then Moses raised his hand and struck the rock twice with the staff, and water gushed out. So the entire community and their livestock drank their fill.

¹²But the LORD said to Moses and Aaron, "Because you did not trust me enough to demonstrate my holiness to the people of Israel, you will not lead them into the land I am giving them!" ¹³This place was known as the waters of Meribah (which means "arguing") because there the people of Israel argued with the LORD, and there he demonstrated his holiness among them.

Edom Refuses Israel Passage

¹⁴While Moses was at Kadesh, he sent ambassadors to the king of Edom with this message:

"This is what your relatives, the people of Israel, say: You know all the hardships we have been through. ¹⁵Our ancestors went down to Egypt, and we lived there a long time, and we and our ancestors were brutally mistreated by the Egyptians. ¹⁶But when we cried out to the LORD, he heard us and sent an angel who brought us out of Egypt. Now we are camped at Kadesh, a town on the border of your land. ¹⁷Please let us travel through your land. We will be careful not to go through your fields and vineyards. We won't even drink water from your wells. We will stay on the king's road and never leave it until we have passed through your territory."

¹⁸But the king of Edom said, "Stay out of my land, or I will meet you with an army!"

¹⁹The Israelites answered, "We will stay on the main road. If our livestock drink your water, we will pay for it. Just let us pass through your country. That's all we ask."

20:1 The first month of the ancient Hebrew lunar calendar usually occurs within the months of March and April. The number of years since leaving Egypt is not specified. **20:6** Hebrew *the Tent of Meeting.*

²⁰ But the king of Edom replied, "Stay out! You may not pass through our land." With that he mobilized his army and marched out against them with an imposing force. ²¹ Because Edom refused to allow Israel to pass through their country, Israel was forced to turn around.

The Death of Aaron

²² The whole community of Israel left Kadesh and arrived at Mount Hor. ²³ There, on the border of the land of Edom, the LORD said to Moses and Aaron, ²⁴ "The time has come for Aaron to join his ancestors in death. He will not enter the land I am giving the people of Israel, because the two of you rebelled against my instructions concerning the water at Meribah. ²⁵ Now take Aaron and his son Eleazar up Mount Hor. ²⁶ There you will remove Aaron's priestly garments and put them on Eleazar, his son. Aaron will die there and join his ancestors."

²⁷ So Moses did as the LORD commanded. The three of them went up Mount Hor together as the whole community watched. ²⁸ At the summit, Moses removed the priestly garments from Aaron and put them on Eleazar, Aaron's son. Then Aaron died there on top of the mountain, and Moses and Eleazar went back down. ²⁹ When the people realized that Aaron had died, all Israel mourned for him thirty days.

21 Victory over the Canaanites

The Canaanite king of Arad, who lived in the Negev, heard that the Israelites were approaching on the road through Atharim. So he attacked the Israelites and took some of them as prisoners. ² Then the people of Israel made this vow to the LORD: "If you will hand these people over to us, we will completely destroy* all their towns." ³ The LORD heard the Israelites' request and gave them victory over the Canaanites. The Israelites completely destroyed them and their towns, and the place has been called Hormah* ever since.

The Bronze Snake

⁴ Then the people of Israel set out from Mount Hor, taking the road to the Red Sea* to go around the land of Edom. But the people grew impatient with the long journey, ⁵ and they began to speak against God and Moses. "Why have you brought us out of Egypt to die here in the wilderness?" they complained. "There is nothing to eat here and nothing to drink. And we hate this horrible manna!"

⁶ So the LORD sent poisonous snakes among the people, and many were bitten and died. ⁷ Then the people came to Moses and cried out, "We have sinned by speaking against the LORD and against you. Pray that the LORD will take away the snakes." So Moses prayed for the people.

⁸ Then the LORD told him, "Make a replica of a poisonous snake and attach it to a pole. All who are bitten will live if they simply look at it!" ⁹ So Moses made a snake out of bronze and attached it to a pole. Then anyone who was bitten by a snake could look at the bronze snake and be healed!

Israel's Journey to Moab

¹⁰ The Israelites traveled next to Oboth and camped there. ¹¹ Then they went on to Iye-abarim, in the wilderness on the eastern border of Moab. ¹² From there they traveled to the valley of Zered Brook and set up camp. ¹³ Then they moved out and camped on the far side of the Arnon River, in the wilderness adjacent to the territory of the Amorites. The Arnon is the boundary line between the Moabites and the Amorites. ¹⁴ For this reason *The Book of the Wars of the LORD* speaks of "the town of Waheb in the area of Suphah, and the ravines of the Arnon River, ¹⁵ and the ravines that extend as far as the settlement of Ar on the border of Moab."

¹⁶ From there the Israelites traveled to Beer,* which is the well where the LORD said to Moses, "Assemble the people, and I will give them water." ¹⁷ There the Israelites sang this song:

"Spring up, O well!
 Yes, sing its praises!
¹⁸ Sing of this well,
  which princes dug,
 which great leaders hollowed out
  with their scepters and staffs."

21:2 The Hebrew term used here refers to the complete consecration of things or people to the LORD, either by destroying them or by giving them as an offering; also in 21:3. **21:3** *Hormah* means "destruction." **21:4** Hebrew *sea of reeds.* **21:16** *Beer* means "well."

Then the Israelites left the wilderness and proceeded on through Mattanah, [19]Nahaliel, and Bamoth. [20]After that they went to the valley in Moab where Pisgah Peak overlooks the wasteland.*

Victory over Sihon and Og

[21]The Israelites sent ambassadors to King Sihon of the Amorites with this message:

[22]"Let us travel through your land. We will be careful not to go through your fields and vineyards. We won't even drink water from your wells. We will stay on the king's road until we have passed through your territory."

[23]But King Sihon refused to let them cross his territory. Instead, he mobilized his entire army and attacked Israel in the wilderness, engaging them in battle at Jahaz. [24]But the Israelites slaughtered them with their swords and occupied their land from the Arnon River to the Jabbok River. They went only as far as the Ammonite border because the boundary of the Ammonites was fortified.* [25]So Israel captured all the towns of the Amorites and settled in them, including the city of Heshbon and its surrounding villages. [26]Heshbon had been the capital of King Sihon of the Amorites. He had defeated a former Moabite king and seized all his land as far as the Arnon River. [27]Therefore, the ancient poets wrote this about him:

"Come to Heshbon and let it be rebuilt!
  Let the city of Sihon be restored.
[28] A fire flamed forth from Heshbon,
  a blaze from the city of Sihon.
It burned the city of Ar in Moab;
  it destroyed the rulers of the Arnon
    heights.
[29] What sorrow awaits you, O people of
    Moab!
  You are finished, O worshipers of
    Chemosh!
Chemosh has left his sons as refugees,
  his daughters as captives of Sihon, the
    Amorite king.
[30] We have utterly destroyed them,
  from Heshbon to Dibon.

We have completely wiped them out
  as far away as Nophah and Medeba.*"

[31]So the people of Israel occupied the territory of the Amorites. [32]After Moses sent men to explore the Jazer area, they captured all the towns in the region and drove out the Amorites who lived there. [33]Then they turned and marched up the road to Bashan, but King Og of Bashan and all his people attacked them at Edrei. [34]The LORD said to Moses, "Do not be afraid of him, for I have handed him over to you, along with all his people and his land. Do the same to him as you did to King Sihon of the Amorites, who ruled in Heshbon." [35]And Israel killed King Og, his sons, and all his subjects; not a single survivor remained. Then Israel occupied their land.

22 Balak Sends for Balaam

Then the people of Israel traveled to the plains of Moab and camped east of the Jordan River, across from Jericho. [2]Balak son of Zippor, the Moabite king, had seen everything the Israelites did to the Amorites. [3]And when the people of Moab saw how many Israelites there were, they were terrified. [4]The king of Moab said to the elders of Midian, "This mob will devour everything in sight, like an ox devours grass in the field!"

So Balak, king of Moab, [5]sent messengers to call Balaam son of Beor, who was living in his native land of Pethor* near the Euphrates River.* His message said:

"Look, a vast horde of people has arrived from Egypt. They cover the face of the earth and are threatening me. [6]Please come and curse these people for me because they are too powerful for me. Then perhaps I will be able to conquer them and drive them from the land. I know that blessings fall on any people you bless, and curses fall on people you curse."

[7]Balak's messengers, who were elders of Moab and Midian, set out with money to pay Balaam to place a curse upon Israel.* They went to Balaam and delivered Balak's

21:20 Or overlooks Jeshimon.   21:24 Or because the terrain of the Ammonite frontier was rugged; Hebrew reads because the boundary of the Ammonites was strong.   21:30 Or until fire spread to Medeba. The meaning of the Hebrew is uncertain.   22:5a Or who was at Pethor in the land of the Amavites.   22:5b Hebrew the river.   22:7 Hebrew set out with the money of divination in their hand.

message to him. ⁸"Stay here overnight," Balaam said. "In the morning I will tell you whatever the LORD directs me to say." So the officials from Moab stayed there with Balaam.

⁹That night God came to Balaam and asked him, "Who are these men visiting you?"

¹⁰Balaam said to God, "Balak son of Zippor, king of Moab, has sent me this message: ¹¹'Look, a vast horde of people has arrived from Egypt, and they cover the face of the earth. Come and curse these people for me. Then perhaps I will be able to stand up to them and drive them from the land.'"

¹²But God told Balaam, "Do not go with them. You are not to curse these people, for they have been blessed!"

¹³The next morning Balaam got up and told Balak's officials, "Go on home! The LORD will not let me go with you."

¹⁴So the Moabite officials returned to King Balak and reported, "Balaam refused to come with us." ¹⁵Then Balak tried again. This time he sent a larger number of even more distinguished officials than those he had sent the first time. ¹⁶They went to Balaam and delivered this message to him:

"This is what Balak son of Zippor says: Please don't let anything stop you from coming to help me. ¹⁷I will pay you very well and do whatever you tell me. Just come and curse these people for me!"

¹⁸But Balaam responded to Balak's messengers, "Even if Balak were to give me his palace filled with silver and gold, I would be powerless to do anything against the will of the LORD my God. ¹⁹But stay here one more night, and I will see if the LORD has anything else to say to me."

²⁰That night God came to Balaam and told him, "Since these men have come for you, get up and go with them. But do only what I tell you to do."

Balaam and His Donkey

²¹So the next morning Balaam got up, saddled his donkey, and started off with the Moabite officials. ²²But God was angry that Balaam was going, so he sent the angel of the LORD to stand in the road to block his way. As Balaam and two servants were riding along, ²³Balaam's donkey saw the angel of the LORD standing in the road with a drawn sword in his hand. The donkey bolted off the road into a field, but Balaam beat it and turned it back onto the road. ²⁴Then the angel of the LORD stood at a place where the road narrowed between two vineyard walls. ²⁵When the donkey saw the angel of the LORD, it tried to squeeze by and crushed Balaam's foot against the wall. So Balaam beat the donkey again. ²⁶Then the angel of the LORD moved farther down the road and stood in a place too narrow for the donkey to get by at all. ²⁷This time when the donkey saw the angel, it lay down under Balaam. In a fit of rage Balaam beat the animal again with his staff.

²⁸Then the LORD gave the donkey the ability to speak. "What have I done to you that deserves your beating me three times?" it asked Balaam.

²⁹"You have made me look like a fool!" Balaam shouted. "If I had a sword with me, I would kill you!"

³⁰"But I am the same donkey you have ridden all your life," the donkey answered. "Have I ever done anything like this before?"

"No," Balaam admitted.

³¹Then the LORD opened Balaam's eyes, and he saw the angel of the LORD standing in the roadway with a drawn sword in his hand. Balaam bowed his head and fell face down on the ground before him.

³²"Why did you beat your donkey those three times?" the angel of the LORD demanded. "Look, I have come to block your way because you are stubbornly resisting me. ³³Three times the donkey saw me and shied away; otherwise, I would certainly have killed you by now and spared the donkey."

³⁴Then Balaam confessed to the angel of the LORD, "I have sinned. I didn't realize you were standing in the road to block my way. I will return home if you are against my going."

³⁵But the angel of the LORD told Balaam, "Go with these men, but say only what I tell you to say." So Balaam went on with Balak's officials. ³⁶When King Balak heard that Balaam was on the way, he went out to meet him at a Moabite town on the Arnon River at the farthest border of his land.

³⁷"Didn't I send you an urgent invitation? Why didn't you come right away?" Balak asked Balaam. "Didn't you believe me when I said I would reward you richly?"

³⁸Balaam replied, "Look, now I have come, but I have no power to say whatever I want. I will speak only the message that God puts in my mouth." ³⁹Then Balaam accompanied Balak to Kiriath-huzoth, ⁴⁰where the king sacrificed cattle and sheep. He sent portions of the meat to Balaam and the officials who were with him. ⁴¹The next morning Balak took Balaam up to Bamoth-baal. From there he could see some of the people of Israel spread out below him.

23 Balaam Blesses Israel

Then Balaam said to King Balak, "Build me seven altars here, and prepare seven young bulls and seven rams for me to sacrifice." ²Balak followed his instructions, and the two of them sacrificed a young bull and a ram on each altar.

³Then Balaam said to Balak, "Stand here by your burnt offerings, and I will go to see if the LORD will respond to me. Then I will tell you whatever he reveals to me." So Balaam went alone to the top of a bare hill, ⁴and God met him there. Balaam said to him, "I have prepared seven altars and have sacrificed a young bull and a ram on each altar."

⁵The LORD gave Balaam a message for King Balak. Then he said, "Go back to Balak and give him my message."

⁶So Balaam returned and found the king standing beside his burnt offerings with all the officials of Moab. ⁷This was the message Balaam delivered:

"Balak summoned me to come from Aram;
    the king of Moab brought me from the eastern hills.
'Come,' he said, 'curse Jacob for me!
    Come and announce Israel's doom.'
⁸ But how can I curse those
    whom God has not cursed?
How can I condemn those
    whom the LORD has not condemned?
⁹ I see them from the cliff tops;
    I watch them from the hills.

I see a people who live by themselves,
    set apart from other nations.
¹⁰ Who can count Jacob's descendants, as numerous as dust?
    Who can count even a fourth of Israel's people?
Let me die like the righteous;
    let my life end like theirs."

¹¹Then King Balak demanded of Balaam, "What have you done to me? I brought you to curse my enemies. Instead, you have blessed them!"

¹²But Balaam replied, "I will speak only the message that the LORD puts in my mouth."

Balaam's Second Message

¹³Then King Balak told him, "Come with me to another place. There you will see another part of the nation of Israel, but not all of them. Curse at least that many!" ¹⁴So Balak took Balaam to the plateau of Zophim on Pisgah Peak. He built seven altars there and offered a young bull and a ram on each altar.

¹⁵Then Balaam said to the king, "Stand here by your burnt offerings while I go over there to meet the LORD."

¹⁶And the LORD met Balaam and gave him a message. Then he said, "Go back to Balak and give him my message."

¹⁷So Balaam returned and found the king standing beside his burnt offerings with all the officials of Moab. "What did the LORD say?" Balak asked eagerly.

¹⁸This was the message Balaam delivered:

"Rise up, Balak, and listen!
    Hear me, son of Zippor.
¹⁹ God is not a man, so he does not lie.
    He is not human, so he does not change his mind.
Has he ever spoken and failed to act?
    Has he ever promised and not carried it through?
²⁰ Listen, I received a command to bless;
    God has blessed, and I cannot reverse it!
²¹ No misfortune is in his plan for Jacob;
    no trouble is in store for Israel.
For the LORD their God is with them;
    he has been proclaimed their king.

²² God brought them out of Egypt;
   for them he is as strong as a wild ox.
²³ No curse can touch Jacob;
   no magic has any power against Israel.
For now it will be said of Jacob,
   'What wonders God has done for
    Israel!'
²⁴ These people rise up like a lioness,
   like a majestic lion rousing itself.
They refuse to rest
   until they have feasted on prey,
   drinking the blood of the
    slaughtered!"

²⁵ Then Balak said to Balaam, "Fine, but if you won't curse them, at least don't bless them!"

²⁶ But Balaam replied to Balak, "Didn't I tell you that I can do only what the LORD tells me?"

Balaam's Third Message

²⁷ Then King Balak said to Balaam, "Come, I will take you to one more place. Perhaps it will please God to let you curse them from there."

²⁸ So Balak took Balaam to the top of Mount Peor, overlooking the wasteland.* ²⁹ Balaam again told Balak, "Build me seven altars, and prepare seven young bulls and seven rams for me to sacrifice." ³⁰ So Balak did as Balaam ordered and offered a young bull and a ram on each altar.

24 By now Balaam realized that the LORD was determined to bless Israel, so he did not resort to divination as before. Instead, he turned and looked out toward the wilderness, ² where he saw the people of Israel camped, tribe by tribe. Then the Spirit of God came upon him, ³ and this is the message he delivered:

"This is the message of Balaam son of
   Beor,
   the message of the man whose eyes
    see clearly,
⁴ the message of one who hears the words
   of God,
   who sees a vision from the Almighty,
   who bows down with eyes wide open:
⁵ How beautiful are your tents, O Jacob;
   how lovely are your homes, O Israel!

⁶ They spread before me like palm groves,*
   like gardens by the riverside.
They are like tall trees planted by the
   LORD,
   like cedars beside the waters.
⁷ Water will flow from their buckets;
   their offspring have all they need.
Their king will be greater than Agag;
   their kingdom will be exalted.
⁸ God brought them out of Egypt;
   for them he is as strong as a wild ox.
He devours all the nations that oppose
   him,
   breaking their bones in pieces,
   shooting them with arrows.
⁹ Like a lion, Israel crouches and lies down;
   like a lioness, who dares to arouse her?
Blessed is everyone who blesses you,
   O Israel,
   and cursed is everyone who curses you."

¹⁰ King Balak flew into a rage against Balaam. He angrily clapped his hands and shouted, "I called you to curse my enemies! Instead, you have blessed them three times. ¹¹ Now get out of here! Go back home! I promised to reward you richly, but the LORD has kept you from your reward."

¹² Balaam told Balak, "Don't you remember what I told your messengers? I said, ¹³ 'Even if Balak were to give me his palace filled with silver and gold, I would be powerless to do anything against the will of the LORD.' I told you that I could say only what the LORD says! ¹⁴ Now I am returning to my own people. But first let me tell you what the Israelites will do to your people in the future."

Balaam's Final Messages

¹⁵ This is the message Balaam delivered:

"This is the message of Balaam son of
   Beor,
   the message of the man whose eyes
    see clearly,
¹⁶ the message of one who hears the words
   of God,
   who has knowledge from the Most High,
who sees a vision from the Almighty,
   who bows down with eyes wide open:
¹⁷ I see him, but not here and now.
   I perceive him, but far in the distant
    future.

23:28 Or overlooking Jeshimon.   **24:6** Or like a majestic valley.

A star will rise from Jacob;
  a scepter will emerge from Israel.
It will crush the foreheads of Moab's
    people,
  cracking the skulls of the people of
    Sheth.
[18] Edom will be taken over,
  and Seir, its enemy, will be conquered,
    while Israel marches on in triumph.
[19] A ruler will rise in Jacob
  who will destroy the survivors of Ir."

[20] Then Balaam looked over toward the people of Amalek and delivered this message:

"Amalek was the greatest of nations,
  but its destiny is destruction!"

[21] Then he looked over toward the Kenites and delivered this message:

"Your home is secure;
  your nest is set in the rocks.
[22] But the Kenites will be destroyed
  when Assyria* takes you captive."

[23] Balaam concluded his messages by saying:

"Alas, who can survive
  unless God has willed it?
[24] Ships will come from the coasts of
    Cyprus*;
  they will oppress Assyria and afflict
    Eber,
  but they, too, will be utterly destroyed."

[25] Then Balaam and Balak returned to their homes.

25 Moab Seduces Israel

While the Israelites were camped at Acacia Grove,* some of the men defiled themselves by having* sexual relations with local Moabite women. [2] These women invited them to attend sacrifices to their gods, so the Israelites feasted with them and worshiped the gods of Moab. [3] In this way, Israel joined in the worship of Baal of Peor, causing the LORD's anger to blaze against his people.

[4] The LORD issued the following command to Moses: "Seize all the ringleaders and execute them before the LORD in broad daylight, so his fierce anger will turn away from the people of Israel."

[5] So Moses ordered Israel's judges, "Each of you must put to death the men under your authority who have joined in worshiping Baal of Peor."

[6] Just then one of the Israelite men brought a Midianite woman into his tent, right before the eyes of Moses and all the people, as everyone was weeping at the entrance of the Tabernacle.* [7] When Phinehas son of Eleazar and grandson of Aaron the priest saw this, he jumped up and left the assembly. He took a spear [8] and rushed after the man into his tent. Phinehas thrust the spear all the way through the man's body and into the woman's stomach. So the plague against the Israelites was stopped, [9] but not before 24,000 people had died.

[10] Then the LORD said to Moses, [11] "Phinehas son of Eleazar and grandson of Aaron the priest has turned my anger away from the Israelites by being as zealous among them as I was. So I stopped destroying all Israel as I had intended to do in my zealous anger. [12] Now tell him that I am making my special covenant of peace with him. [13] In this covenant, I give him and his descendants a permanent right to the priesthood, for in his zeal for me, his God, he purified the people of Israel, making them right with me.*"

[14] The Israelite man killed with the Midianite woman was named Zimri son of Salu, the leader of a family from the tribe of Simeon. [15] The woman's name was Cozbi; she was the daughter of Zur, the leader of a Midianite clan.

[16] Then the LORD said to Moses, [17] "Attack the Midianites and destroy them, [18] because they assaulted you with deceit and tricked you into worshiping Baal of Peor, and because of Cozbi, the daughter of a Midianite leader, who was killed at the time of the plague because of what happened at Peor."

26 The Second Registration of Israel's Troops

After the plague had ended, the LORD said to Moses and to Eleazar son of Aaron the priest, [2] "From the whole community of

24:22 Hebrew Asshur; also in 24:24. 24:24 Hebrew Kittim. 25:1a Hebrew Shittim. 25:1b As in Greek version; Hebrew reads some of the men began having. 25:6 Hebrew the Tent of Meeting. 25:13 Or he made atonement for the people of Israel.

Israel, record the names of all the warriors by their families. List all the men twenty years old or older who are able to go to war."

³So there on the plains of Moab beside the Jordan River, across from Jericho, Moses and Eleazar the priest issued these instructions to the leaders of Israel: ⁴"List all the men of Israel twenty years old and older, just as the LORD commanded Moses."

This is the record of all the descendants of Israel who came out of Egypt.

The Tribe of Reuben

⁵These were the clans descended from the sons of Reuben, Jacob's* oldest son:

The Hanochite clan, named after their ancestor Hanoch.

The Palluite clan, named after their ancestor Pallu.

⁶ The Hezronite clan, named after their ancestor Hezron.

The Carmite clan, named after their ancestor Carmi.

⁷These were the clans of Reuben. Their registered troops numbered 43,730.

⁸Pallu was the ancestor of Eliab, ⁹and Eliab was the father of Nemuel, Dathan, and Abiram. This Dathan and Abiram are the same community leaders who conspired with Korah against Moses and Aaron, rebelling against the LORD. ¹⁰But the earth opened up its mouth and swallowed them with Korah, and fire devoured 250 of their followers. This served as a warning to the entire nation of Israel. ¹¹However, the sons of Korah did not die that day.

The Tribe of Simeon

¹²These were the clans descended from the sons of Simeon:

The Jemuelite clan, named after their ancestor Jemuel.*

The Jaminite clan, named after their ancestor Jamin.

The Jakinite clan, named after their ancestor Jakin.

¹³ The Zoharite clan, named after their ancestor Zohar.*

The Shaulite clan, named after their ancestor Shaul.

¹⁴These were the clans of Simeon. Their registered troops numbered 22,200.

The Tribe of Gad

¹⁵These were the clans descended from the sons of Gad:

The Zephonite clan, named after their ancestor Zephon.

The Haggite clan, named after their ancestor Haggi.

The Shunite clan, named after their ancestor Shuni.

¹⁶ The Oznite clan, named after their ancestor Ozni.

The Erite clan, named after their ancestor Eri.

¹⁷ The Arodite clan, named after their ancestor Arodi.*

The Arelite clan, named after their ancestor Areli.

¹⁸These were the clans of Gad. Their registered troops numbered 40,500.

The Tribe of Judah

¹⁹Judah had two sons, Er and Onan, who had died in the land of Canaan. ²⁰These were the clans descended from Judah's surviving sons:

The Shelanite clan, named after their ancestor Shelah.

The Perezite clan, named after their ancestor Perez.

The Zerahite clan, named after their ancestor Zerah.

²¹These were the subclans descended from the Perezites:

The Hezronites, named after their ancestor Hezron.

The Hamulites, named after their ancestor Hamul.

²²These were the clans of Judah. Their registered troops numbered 76,500.

The Tribe of Issachar

²³These were the clans descended from the sons of Issachar:

The Tolaite clan, named after their ancestor Tola.

The Puite clan, named after their ancestor Puah.*

26:5 Hebrew *Israel's;* see note on 1:20-21b.   26:12 As in Syriac version (see also Gen 46:10; Exod 6:15); Hebrew reads *Nemuelite . . . Nemuel.*   26:13 As in parallel texts at Gen 46:10 and Exod 6:15; Hebrew reads *Zerahite . . . Zerah.*   26:17 As in Samaritan Pentateuch and Greek and Syriac versions (see also Gen 46:16); Hebrew reads *Arod.*   26:23 As in Samaritan Pentateuch, Greek and Syriac versions, and Latin Vulgate (see also 1 Chr 7:1); Hebrew reads *The Punite clan, named after its ancestor Puvah.*

²⁴ The Jashubite clan, named after their ancestor Jashub.

The Shimronite clan, named after their ancestor Shimron.

²⁵ These were the clans of Issachar. Their registered troops numbered 64,300.

The Tribe of Zebulun

²⁶ These were the clans descended from the sons of Zebulun:

The Seredite clan, named after their ancestor Sered.

The Elonite clan, named after their ancestor Elon.

The Jahleelite clan, named after their ancestor Jahleel.

²⁷ These were the clans of Zebulun. Their registered troops numbered 60,500.

The Tribe of Manasseh

²⁸ Two clans were descended from Joseph through Manasseh and Ephraim.

²⁹ These were the clans descended from Manasseh:

The Makirite clan, named after their ancestor Makir.

The Gileadite clan, named after their ancestor Gilead, Makir's son.

³⁰ These were the subclans descended from the Gileadites:

The Iezerites, named after their ancestor Iezer.

The Helekites, named after their ancestor Helek.

³¹ The Asrielites, named after their ancestor Asriel.

The Shechemites, named after their ancestor Shechem.

³² The Shemidaites, named after their ancestor Shemida.

The Hepherites, named after their ancestor Hepher.

³³ (One of Hepher's descendants, Zelophehad, had no sons, but his daughters' names were Mahlah, Noah, Hoglah, Milcah, and Tirzah.)

³⁴ These were the clans of Manasseh. Their registered troops numbered 52,700.

The Tribe of Ephraim

³⁵ These were the clans descended from the sons of Ephraim:

The Shuthelahite clan, named after their ancestor Shuthelah.

The Bekerite clan, named after their ancestor Beker.

The Tahanite clan, named after their ancestor Tahan.

³⁶ This was the subclan descended from the Shuthelahites:

The Eranites, named after their ancestor Eran.

³⁷ These were the clans of Ephraim. Their registered troops numbered 32,500.

These clans of Manasseh and Ephraim were all descendants of Joseph.

The Tribe of Benjamin

³⁸ These were the clans descended from the sons of Benjamin:

The Belaite clan, named after their ancestor Bela.

The Ashbelite clan, named after their ancestor Ashbel.

The Ahiramite clan, named after their ancestor Ahiram.

³⁹ The Shuphamite clan, named after their ancestor Shupham.*

The Huphamite clan, named after their ancestor Hupham.

⁴⁰ These were the subclans descended from the Belaites:

The Ardites, named after their ancestor Ard.*

The Naamites, named after their ancestor Naaman.

⁴¹ These were the clans of Benjamin. Their registered troops numbered 45,600.

The Tribe of Dan

⁴² These were the clans descended from the sons of Dan:

The Shuhamite clan, named after their ancestor Shuham.

⁴³ These were the Shuhamite clans of Dan. Their registered troops numbered 64,400.

26:39 As in some Hebrew manuscripts, Samaritan Pentateuch, Greek and Syriac versions, and Latin Vulgate; most Hebrew manuscripts read *Shephupham.* **26:40** As in Samaritan Pentateuch, some Greek manuscripts, and Latin Vulgate; Hebrew lacks *named after their ancestor Ard.*

The Tribe of Asher

⁴⁴These were the clans descended from the sons of Asher:

The Imnite clan, named after their ancestor Imnah.

The Ishvite clan, named after their ancestor Ishvi.

The Beriite clan, named after their ancestor Beriah.

⁴⁵These were the subclans descended from the Beriites:

The Heberites, named after their ancestor Heber.

The Malkielites, named after their ancestor Malkiel.

⁴⁶Asher also had a daughter named Serah.

⁴⁷These were the clans of Asher. Their registered troops numbered 53,400.

The Tribe of Naphtali

⁴⁸These were the clans descended from the sons of Naphtali:

The Jahzeelite clan, named after their ancestor Jahzeel.

The Gunite clan, named after their ancestor Guni.

⁴⁹ The Jezerite clan, named after their ancestor Jezer.

The Shillemite clan, named after their ancestor Shillem.

⁵⁰These were the clans of Naphtali. Their registered troops numbered 45,400.

Results of the Registration

⁵¹In summary, the registered troops of all Israel numbered 601,730.

⁵²Then the Lord said to Moses, ⁵³"Divide the land among the tribes, and distribute the grants of land in proportion to the tribes' populations, as indicated by the number of names on the list. ⁵⁴Give the larger tribes more land and the smaller tribes less land, each group receiving a grant in proportion to the size of its population. ⁵⁵But you must assign the land by lot, and give land to each ancestral tribe according to the number of names on the list. ⁵⁶Each grant of land must be assigned by lot among the larger and smaller tribal groups."

The Tribe of Levi

⁵⁷This is the record of the Levites who were counted according to their clans:

The Gershonite clan, named after their ancestor Gershon.

The Kohathite clan, named after their ancestor Kohath.

The Merarite clan, named after their ancestor Merari.

⁵⁸The Libnites, the Hebronites, the Mahlites, the Mushites, and the Korahites were all subclans of the Levites.

Now Kohath was the ancestor of Amram, ⁵⁹and Amram's wife was named Jochebed. She also was a descendant of Levi, born among the Levites in the land of Egypt. Amram and Jochebed became the parents of Aaron, Moses, and their sister, Miriam. ⁶⁰To Aaron were born Nadab, Abihu, Eleazar, and Ithamar. ⁶¹But Nadab and Abihu died when they burned before the Lord the wrong kind of fire, different than he had commanded.

⁶²The men from the Levite clans who were one month old or older numbered 23,000. But the Levites were not included in the registration of the rest of the people of Israel because they were not given an allotment of land when it was divided among the Israelites.

⁶³So these are the results of the registration of the people of Israel as conducted by Moses and Eleazar the priest on the plains of Moab beside the Jordan River, across from Jericho. ⁶⁴Not one person on this list had been among those listed in the previous registration taken by Moses and Aaron in the wilderness of Sinai. ⁶⁵For the Lord had said of them, "They will all die in the wilderness." Not one of them survived except Caleb son of Jephunneh and Joshua son of Nun.

27 The Daughters of Zelophehad

One day a petition was presented by the daughters of Zelophehad—Mahlah, Noah, Hoglah, Milcah, and Tirzah. Their father, Zelophehad, was a descendant of Hepher son of Gilead, son of Makir, son of Manasseh, son of Joseph. ²These women stood before Moses, Eleazar the priest, the tribal leaders, and the entire community at the entrance of the Tabernacle.* ³"Our

27:2 Hebrew *the Tent of Meeting.*

father died in the wilderness," they said. "He was not among Korah's followers, who rebelled against the LORD; he died because of his own sin. But he had no sons. ⁴Why should the name of our father disappear from his clan just because he had no sons? Give us property along with the rest of our relatives."

⁵So Moses brought their case before the LORD. ⁶And the LORD replied to Moses, ⁷"The claim of the daughters of Zelophehad is legitimate. You must give them a grant of land along with their father's relatives. Assign them the property that would have been given to their father.

⁸"And give the following instructions to the people of Israel: If a man dies and has no son, then give his inheritance to his daughters. ⁹And if he has no daughter either, transfer his inheritance to his brothers. ¹⁰If he has no brothers, give his inheritance to his father's brothers. ¹¹But if his father has no brothers, give his inheritance to the nearest relative in his clan. This is a legal requirement for the people of Israel, just as the LORD commanded Moses."

Joshua Chosen to Lead Israel

¹²One day the LORD said to Moses, "Climb one of the mountains east of the river,* and look out over the land I have given the people of Israel. ¹³After you have seen it, you will die like your brother, Aaron, ¹⁴for you both rebelled against my instructions in the wilderness of Zin. When the people of Israel rebelled, you failed to demonstrate my holiness to them at the waters." (These are the waters of Meribah at Kadesh* in the wilderness of Zin.)

¹⁵Then Moses said to the LORD, ¹⁶"O LORD, you are the God who gives breath to all creatures. Please appoint a new man as leader for the community. ¹⁷Give them someone who will guide them wherever they go and will lead them into battle, so the community of the LORD will not be like sheep without a shepherd."

¹⁸The LORD replied, "Take Joshua son of Nun, who has the Spirit in him, and lay your hands on him. ¹⁹Present him to Eleazar the priest before the whole community, and

publicly commission him to lead the people. ²⁰Transfer some of your authority to him so the whole community of Israel will obey him. ²¹When direction from the LORD is needed, Joshua will stand before Eleazar the priest, who will use the Urim—one of the sacred lots cast before the LORD—to determine his will. This is how Joshua and the rest of the community of Israel will determine everything they should do."

²²So Moses did as the LORD commanded. He presented Joshua to Eleazar the priest and the whole community. ²³Moses laid his hands on him and commissioned him to lead the people, just as the LORD had commanded through Moses.

28 The Daily Offerings

The LORD said to Moses, ²"Give these instructions to the people of Israel: The offerings you present as special gifts are a pleasing aroma to me; they are my food. See to it that they are brought at the appointed times and offered according to my instructions.

³"Say to the people: This is the special gift you must present to the LORD as your daily burnt offering. You must offer two one-year-old male lambs with no defects. ⁴Sacrifice one lamb in the morning and the other in the evening. ⁵With each lamb you must offer a grain offering of two quarts* of choice flour mixed with one quart* of pure oil of pressed olives. ⁶This is the regular burnt offering instituted at Mount Sinai as a special gift, a pleasing aroma to the LORD. ⁷Along with it you must present the proper liquid offering of one quart of alcoholic drink with each lamb, poured out in the Holy Place as an offering to the LORD. ⁸Offer the second lamb in the evening with the same grain offering and liquid offering. It, too, is a special gift, a pleasing aroma to the LORD.

The Sabbath Offerings

⁹"On the Sabbath day, sacrifice two one-year-old male lambs with no defects. They must be accompanied by a grain offering of four quarts* of choice flour moistened with olive oil, and a liquid offering. ¹⁰This is the

---

27:12 Or *the mountains of Abarim.*　**27:14** Hebrew *waters of Meribath-kadesh.*　**28:5a** Hebrew ⅒ *of an ephah* [2.2 liters]; also in 28:13, 21, 29.　**28:5b** Hebrew ¼ *of a hin* [1 liter]; also in 28:7.　**28:9** Hebrew ²⁄₁₀ *of an ephah* [4.4 liters]; also in 28:12, 20, 28.

burnt offering to be presented each Sabbath day, in addition to the regular burnt offering and its accompanying liquid offering.

The Monthly Offerings

[11] "On the first day of each month, present an extra burnt offering to the LORD of two young bulls, one ram, and seven one-year-old male lambs, all with no defects. [12] These must be accompanied by grain offerings of choice flour moistened with olive oil—six quarts* with each bull, four quarts with the ram, [13] and two quarts with each lamb. This burnt offering will be a special gift, a pleasing aroma to the LORD. [14] You must also present a liquid offering with each sacrifice: two quarts* of wine for each bull, a third of a gallon* for the ram, and one quart* for each lamb. Present this monthly burnt offering on the first day of each month throughout the year.

[15] "On the first day of each month, you must also offer one male goat for a sin offering to the LORD. This is in addition to the regular burnt offering and its accompanying liquid offering.

Offerings for the Passover

[16] "On the fourteenth day of the first month,* you must celebrate the LORD's Passover. [17] On the following day—the fifteenth day of the month—a joyous, seven-day festival will begin, but no bread made with yeast may be eaten. [18] The first day of the festival will be an official day for holy assembly, and no ordinary work may be done on that day. [19] As a special gift you must present a burnt offering to the LORD—two young bulls, one ram, and seven one-year-old male lambs, all with no defects. [20] These will be accompanied by grain offerings of choice flour moistened with olive oil—six quarts with each bull, four quarts with the ram, [21] and two quarts with each of the seven lambs. [22] You must also offer a male goat as a sin offering to purify yourselves and make yourselves right with the LORD.*

[23] Present these offerings in addition to your regular morning burnt offering. [24] On each of the seven days of the festival, this is how you must prepare the food offering that is presented as a special gift, a pleasing aroma to the LORD. These will be offered in addition to the regular burnt offerings and liquid offerings. [25] The seventh day of the festival will be another official day for holy assembly, and no ordinary work may be done on that day.

Offerings for the Festival of Harvest

[26] "At the Festival of Harvest,* when you present the first of your new grain to the LORD, you must call an official day for holy assembly, and you may do no ordinary work on that day. [27] Present a special burnt offering on that day as a pleasing aroma to the LORD. It will consist of two young bulls, one ram, and seven one-year-old male lambs. [28] These will be accompanied by grain offerings of choice flour moistened with olive oil—six quarts with each bull, four quarts with the ram, [29] and two quarts with each of the seven lambs. [30] Also, offer one male goat to purify yourselves and make yourselves right with the LORD. [31] Prepare these special burnt offerings, along with their liquid offerings, in addition to the regular burnt offering and its accompanying grain offering. Be sure that all the animals you sacrifice have no defects.

29 Offerings for the Festival of Trumpets

"Celebrate the Festival of Trumpets each year on the first day of the appointed month in early autumn.* You must call an official day for holy assembly, and you may do no ordinary work. [2] On that day you must present a burnt offering as a pleasing aroma to the LORD. It will consist of one young bull, one ram, and seven one-year-old male lambs, all with no defects. [3] These must be accompanied by grain offerings of choice flour moistened with olive oil—six quarts* with the bull, four quarts* with

28:12 Hebrew ³⁄₁₀ of an ephah [6.6 liters]; also in 28:20, 28. 28:14a Hebrew ½ of a hin [2 liters]. 28:14b Hebrew ⅓ of a hin [1.3 liters]. 28:14c Hebrew ¼ of a hin [1 liter]. 28:16 This day in the ancient Hebrew lunar calendar occurred in late March, April, or early May. 28:22 Or to make atonement for yourselves; also in 28:30. 28:26 Hebrew Festival of Weeks. This was later called the Festival of Pentecost (see Acts 2:1). It is celebrated today as Shavuot (or Shabuoth). 29:1 Hebrew the first day of the seventh month. This day in the ancient Hebrew lunar calendar occurred in September or October. This festival is celebrated today as Rosh Hashanah, the Jewish new year. 29:3a Hebrew ³⁄₁₀ of an ephah [6.6 liters]; also in 29:9, 14. 29:3b Hebrew ²⁄₁₀ of an ephah [4.4 liters]; also in 29:9, 14.

the ram, [4]and two quarts* with each of the seven lambs. [5]In addition, you must sacrifice a male goat as a sin offering to purify yourselves and make yourselves right with the LORD.* [6]These special sacrifices are in addition to your regular monthly and daily burnt offerings, and they must be given with their prescribed grain offerings and liquid offerings. These offerings are given as a special gift to the LORD, a pleasing aroma to him.

Offerings for the Day of Atonement

[7]"Ten days later, on the tenth day of the same month,* you must call another holy assembly. On that day, the Day of Atonement, the people must go without food and must do no ordinary work. [8]You must present a burnt offering as a pleasing aroma to the LORD. It will consist of one young bull, one ram, and seven one-year-old male lambs, all with no defects. [9]These offerings must be accompanied by the prescribed grain offerings of choice flour moistened with olive oil—six quarts of choice flour with the bull, four quarts of choice flour with the ram, [10]and two quarts of choice flour with each of the seven lambs. [11]You must also sacrifice one male goat for a sin offering. This is in addition to the sin offering of atonement and the regular daily burnt offering with its grain offering, and their accompanying liquid offerings.

Offerings for the Festival of Shelters

[12]"Five days later, on the fifteenth day of the same month,* you must call another holy assembly of all the people, and you may do no ordinary work on that day. It is the beginning of the Festival of Shelters,* a seven-day festival to the LORD. [13]On the first day of the festival, you must present a burnt offering as a special gift, a pleasing aroma to the LORD. It will consist of thirteen young bulls, two rams, and fourteen one-year-old male lambs, all with no defects. [14]Each of these offerings must be accompanied by a grain offering of choice flour moistened with olive oil—six quarts for each of the thirteen

bulls, four quarts for each of the two rams, [15]and two quarts for each of the fourteen lambs. [16]You must also sacrifice a male goat as a sin offering, in addition to the regular burnt offering with its accompanying grain offering and liquid offering.

[17]"On the second day of this seven-day festival, sacrifice twelve young bulls, two rams, and fourteen one-year-old male lambs, all with no defects. [18]Each of these offerings of bulls, rams, and lambs must be accompanied by its prescribed grain offering and liquid offering. [19]You must also sacrifice a male goat as a sin offering, in addition to the regular burnt offering with its accompanying grain offering and liquid offering.

[20]"On the third day of the festival, sacrifice eleven young bulls, two rams, and fourteen one-year-old male lambs, all with no defects. [21]Each of these offerings of bulls, rams, and lambs must be accompanied by its prescribed grain offering and liquid offering. [22]You must also sacrifice a male goat as a sin offering, in addition to the regular burnt offering with its accompanying grain offering and liquid offering.

[23]"On the fourth day of the festival, sacrifice ten young bulls, two rams, and fourteen one-year-old male lambs, all with no defects. [24]Each of these offerings of bulls, rams, and lambs must be accompanied by its prescribed grain offering and liquid offering. [25]You must also sacrifice a male goat as a sin offering, in addition to the regular burnt offering with its accompanying grain offering and liquid offering.

[26]"On the fifth day of the festival, sacrifice nine young bulls, two rams, and fourteen one-year-old male lambs, all with no defects. [27]Each of these offerings of bulls, rams, and lambs must be accompanied by its prescribed grain offering and liquid offering. [28]You must also sacrifice a male goat as a sin offering, in addition to the regular burnt offering with its accompanying grain offering and liquid offering.

[29]"On the sixth day of the festival, sacrifice eight young bulls, two rams, and fourteen one-year-old male lambs, all with no

---

29:4 Hebrew ⅒ of an ephah [2.2 liters]; also in 29:10, 15.　**29:5** Or to make atonement for yourselves.　**29:7** Hebrew On the tenth day of the seventh month; see 29:1 and the note there. This day in the ancient Hebrew lunar calendar occurred in September or October. It is celebrated today as Yom Kippur.　**29:12a** Hebrew On the fifteenth day of the seventh month; see 29:1, 7 and the notes there. This day in the ancient Hebrew lunar calendar occurred in late September, October, or early November.　**29:12b** Or Festival of Booths, or Festival of Tabernacles. This was earlier called the Festival of the Final Harvest or Festival of Ingathering (see Exod 23:16b). It is celebrated today as Sukkot (or Succoth).

defects. [30]Each of these offerings of bulls, rams, and lambs must be accompanied by its prescribed grain offering and liquid offering. [31]You must also sacrifice a male goat as a sin offering, in addition to the regular burnt offering with its accompanying grain offering and liquid offering.

[32]"On the seventh day of the festival, sacrifice seven young bulls, two rams, and fourteen one-year-old male lambs, all with no defects. [33]Each of these offerings of bulls, rams, and lambs must be accompanied by its prescribed grain offering and liquid offering. [34]You must also sacrifice one male goat as a sin offering, in addition to the regular burnt offering with its accompanying grain offering and liquid offering.

[35]"On the eighth day of the festival, proclaim another holy day. You must do no ordinary work on that day. [36]You must present a burnt offering as a special gift, a pleasing aroma to the LORD. It will consist of one young bull, one ram, and seven one-year-old male lambs, all with no defects. [37]Each of these offerings must be accompanied by its prescribed grain offering and liquid offering. [38]You must also sacrifice one male goat as a sin offering, in addition to the regular burnt offering with its accompanying grain offering and liquid offering.

[39]"You must present these offerings to the LORD at your annual festivals. These are in addition to the sacrifices and offerings you present in connection with vows, or as voluntary offerings, burnt offerings, grain offerings, liquid offerings, or peace offerings."

[40]*So Moses gave all of these instructions to the people of Israel as the LORD had commanded him.

30 Laws concerning Vows

[1]*Then Moses summoned the leaders of the tribes of Israel and told them, "This is what the LORD has commanded: [2]A man who makes a vow to the LORD or makes a pledge under oath must never break it. He must do exactly what he said he would do.

[3]"If a young woman makes a vow to the LORD or a pledge under oath while she is still living at her father's home, [4]and her father hears of the vow or pledge and does not object to it, then all her vows and pledges will stand. [5]But if her father refuses to let her fulfill the vow or pledge on the day he hears of it, then all her vows and pledges will become invalid. The LORD will forgive her because her father would not let her fulfill them.

[6]"Now suppose a young woman makes a vow or binds herself with an impulsive pledge and later marries. [7]If her husband learns of her vow or pledge and does not object on the day he hears of it, her vows and pledges will stand. [8]But if her husband refuses to accept her vow or impulsive pledge on the day he hears of it, he nullifies her commitments, and the LORD will forgive her. [9]If, however, a woman is a widow or is divorced, she must fulfill all her vows and pledges.

[10]"But suppose a woman is married and living in her husband's home when she makes a vow or binds herself with a pledge. [11]If her husband hears of it and does not object to it, her vow or pledge will stand. [12]But if her husband refuses to accept it on the day he hears of it, her vow or pledge will be nullified, and the LORD will forgive her. [13]So her husband may either confirm or nullify any vows or pledges she makes to deny herself. [14]But if he does not object on the day he hears of it, then he is agreeing to all her vows and pledges. [15]If he waits more than a day and then tries to nullify a vow or pledge, he will be punished for her guilt."

[16]These are the regulations the LORD gave Moses concerning relationships between a man and his wife, and between a father and a young daughter who still lives at home.

31 Conquest of the Midianites

Then the LORD said to Moses, [2]"On behalf of the people of Israel, take revenge on the Midianites for leading them into idolatry. After that, you will die and join your ancestors."

[3]So Moses said to the people, "Choose some men, and arm them to fight the LORD's war of revenge against Midian. [4]From each tribe of Israel, send 1,000 men into battle."

29:40 Verse 29:40 is numbered 30:1 in Hebrew text.   **30:1** Verses 30:1-16 are numbered 30:2-17 in Hebrew text.

[5] So they chose 1,000 men from each tribe of Israel, a total of 12,000 men armed for battle. [6] Then Moses sent them out, 1,000 men from each tribe, and Phinehas son of Eleazar the priest led them into battle. They carried along the holy objects of the sanctuary and the trumpets for sounding the charge. [7] They attacked Midian as the LORD had commanded Moses, and they killed all the men. [8] All five of the Midianite kings—Evi, Rekem, Zur, Hur, and Reba—died in the battle. They also killed Balaam son of Beor with the sword.

[9] Then the Israelite army captured the Midianite women and children and seized their cattle and flocks and all their wealth as plunder. [10] They burned all the towns and villages where the Midianites had lived. [11] After they had gathered the plunder and captives, both people and animals, [12] they brought them all to Moses and Eleazar the priest, and to the whole community of Israel, which was camped on the plains of Moab beside the Jordan River, across from Jericho. [13] Moses, Eleazar the priest, and all the leaders of the community went to meet them outside the camp. [14] But Moses was furious with all the generals and captains* who had returned from the battle.

[15] "Why have you let all the women live?" he demanded. [16] "These are the very ones who followed Balaam's advice and caused the people of Israel to rebel against the LORD at Mount Peor. They are the ones who caused the plague to strike the LORD's people. [17] So kill all the boys and all the women who have had intercourse with a man. [18] Only the young girls who are virgins may live; you may keep them for yourselves. [19] And all of you who have killed anyone or touched a dead body must stay outside the camp for seven days. You must purify yourselves and your captives on the third and seventh days. [20] Purify all your clothing, too, and everything made of leather, goat hair, or wood."

[21] Then Eleazar the priest said to the men who were in the battle, "The LORD has given Moses this legal requirement: [22] Anything made of gold, silver, bronze, iron, tin, or lead—[23] that is, all metals that do not burn—must be passed through fire in order to be made ceremonially pure. These metal objects must then be further purified with the water of purification. But everything that burns must be purified by the water alone. [24] On the seventh day you must wash your clothes and be purified. Then you may return to the camp."

Division of the Plunder

[25] And the LORD said to Moses, [26] "You and Eleazar the priest and the family leaders of each tribe are to make a list of all the plunder taken in the battle, including the people and animals. [27] Then divide the plunder into two parts, and give half to the men who fought the battle and half to the rest of the people. [28] From the army's portion, first give the LORD his share of the plunder—one of every 500 of the prisoners and of the cattle, donkeys, sheep, and goats. [29] Give this share of the army's half to Eleazar the priest as an offering to the LORD. [30] From the half that belongs to the people of Israel, take one of every fifty of the prisoners and of the cattle, donkeys, sheep, goats, and other animals. Give this share to the Levites, who are in charge of maintaining the LORD's Tabernacle." [31] So Moses and Eleazar the priest did as the LORD commanded Moses.

[32] The plunder remaining from everything the fighting men had taken totaled 675,000 sheep and goats, [33] 72,000 cattle, [34] 61,000 donkeys, [35] and 32,000 virgin girls. [36] Half of the plunder was given to the fighting men. It totaled 337,500 sheep and goats, [37] of which 675 were the LORD's share; [38] 36,000 cattle, of which 72 were the LORD's share; [39] 30,500 donkeys, of which 61 were the LORD's share; [40] and 16,000 virgin girls, of whom 32 were the LORD's share. [41] Moses gave all the LORD's share to Eleazar the priest, just as the LORD had directed him.

[42] Half of the plunder belonged to the people of Israel, and Moses separated it from the half belonging to the fighting men. [43] It totaled 337,500 sheep and goats, [44] 36,000 cattle, [45] 30,500 donkeys, [46] and 16,000 virgin girls. [47] From the half-share given to the people, Moses took one of every fifty prisoners and animals and gave them to the

---

31:14 Hebrew *the commanders of thousands, and the commanders of hundreds;* also in 31:48, 52, 54.

Levites, who maintained the LORD's Tabernacle. All this was done as the LORD had commanded Moses.

⁴⁸Then all the generals and captains came to Moses ⁴⁹and said, "We, your servants, have accounted for all the men who went out to battle under our command; not one of us is missing! ⁵⁰So we are presenting the items of gold we captured as an offering to the LORD from our share of the plunder—armbands, bracelets, rings, earrings, and necklaces. This will purify our lives before the LORD and make us right with him.*"

⁵¹So Moses and Eleazar the priest received the gold from all the military commanders—all kinds of jewelry and crafted objects. ⁵²In all, the gold that the generals and captains presented as a gift to the LORD weighed about 420 pounds.* ⁵³All the fighting men had taken some of the plunder for themselves. ⁵⁴So Moses and Eleazar the priest accepted the gifts from the generals and captains and brought the gold to the Tabernacle* as a reminder to the LORD that the people of Israel belong to him.

32 The Tribes East of the Jordan

The tribes of Reuben and Gad owned vast numbers of livestock. So when they saw that the lands of Jazer and Gilead were ideally suited for their flocks and herds, ²they came to Moses, Eleazar the priest, and the other leaders of the community. They said, ³"Notice the towns of Ataroth, Dibon, Jazer, Nimrah, Heshbon, Elealeh, Sibmah,* Nebo, and Beon. ⁴The LORD has conquered this whole area for the community of Israel, and it is ideally suited for all our livestock. ⁵If we have found favor with you, please let us have this land as our property instead of giving us land across the Jordan River."

⁶"Do you intend to stay here while your brothers go across and do all the fighting?" Moses asked the men of Gad and Reuben. ⁷"Why do you want to discourage the rest of the people of Israel from going across to the land the LORD has given them? ⁸Your ancestors did the same thing when I sent them from Kadesh-barnea to explore the land. ⁹After they went up to the valley of Eshcol and explored the land, they discouraged the people of Israel from entering the land the LORD was giving them. ¹⁰Then the LORD was very angry with them, and he vowed, ¹¹'Of all those I rescued from Egypt, no one who is twenty years old or older will ever see the land I swore to give to Abraham, Isaac, and Jacob, for they have not obeyed me wholeheartedly. ¹²The only exceptions are Caleb son of Jephunneh the Kenizzite and Joshua son of Nun, for they have wholeheartedly followed the LORD.'

¹³"The LORD was angry with Israel and made them wander in the wilderness for forty years until the entire generation that sinned in the LORD's sight had died. ¹⁴But here you are, a brood of sinners, doing exactly the same thing! You are making the LORD even angrier with Israel. ¹⁵If you turn away from him like this and he abandons them again in the wilderness, you will be responsible for destroying this entire nation!"

¹⁶But they approached Moses and said, "We simply want to build pens for our livestock and fortified towns for our wives and children. ¹⁷Then we will arm ourselves and lead our fellow Israelites into battle until we have brought them safely to their land. Meanwhile, our families will stay in the fortified towns we build here, so they will be safe from any attacks by the local people. ¹⁸We will not return to our homes until all the people of Israel have received their portions of land. ¹⁹But we do not claim any of the land on the other side of the Jordan. We would rather live here on the east side and accept this as our grant of land."

²⁰Then Moses said, "If you keep your word and arm yourselves for the LORD's battles, ²¹and if your troops cross the Jordan and keep fighting until the LORD has driven out his enemies, ²²then you may return when the LORD has conquered the land. You will have fulfilled your duty to the LORD and to the rest of the people of Israel. And the land on the east side of the Jordan will be your property from the LORD. ²³But if you fail to keep your word, then you will have sinned against the LORD, and you may be sure that your sin will find you out. ²⁴Go ahead and build towns for your families

---

31:50 Or will make atonement for our lives before the LORD.   31:52 Hebrew 16,750 shekels [191 kilograms].   31:54 Hebrew the Tent of Meeting.   32:3 As in Samaritan Pentateuch and Greek version (see also 32:38); Hebrew reads Sebam.

and pens for your flocks, but do everything you have promised."

25 Then the men of Gad and Reuben replied, "We, your servants, will follow your instructions exactly. 26 Our children, wives, flocks, and cattle will stay here in the towns of Gilead. 27 But all who are able to bear arms will cross over to fight for the LORD, just as you have said."

28 So Moses gave orders to Eleazar the priest, Joshua son of Nun, and the leaders of the clans of Israel. 29 He said, "The men of Gad and Reuben who are armed for battle must cross the Jordan with you to fight for the LORD. If they do, give them the land of Gilead as their property when the land is conquered. 30 But if they refuse to arm themselves and cross over with you, then they must accept land with the rest of you in the land of Canaan."

31 The tribes of Gad and Reuben said again, "We are your servants, and we will do as the LORD has commanded! 32 We will cross the Jordan into Canaan fully armed to fight for the LORD, but our property will be here on this side of the Jordan."

33 So Moses assigned land to the tribes of Gad, Reuben, and half the tribe of Manasseh son of Joseph. He gave them the territory of King Sihon of the Amorites and the land of King Og of Bashan—the whole land with its cities and surrounding lands.

34 The descendants of Gad built the towns of Dibon, Ataroth, Aroer, 35 Atroth-shophan, Jazer, Jogbehah, 36 Beth-nimrah, and Beth-haran. These were all fortified towns with pens for their flocks.

37 The descendants of Reuben built the towns of Heshbon, Elealeh, Kiriathaim, 38 Nebo, Baal-meon, and Sibmah. They changed the names of some of the towns they conquered and rebuilt.

39 Then the descendants of Makir of the tribe of Manasseh went to Gilead and conquered it, and they drove out the Amorites living there. 40 So Moses gave Gilead to the Makirites, descendants of Manasseh, and they settled there. 41 The people of Jair, another clan of the tribe of Manasseh, captured many of the towns in Gilead and changed the name of that region to the Towns of Jair.* 42 Meanwhile, a man named Nobah captured the town of Kenath and its surrounding villages, and he renamed that area Nobah after himself.

33 Remembering Israel's Journey

This is the route the Israelites followed as they marched out of Egypt under the leadership of Moses and Aaron. 2 At the LORD's direction, Moses kept a written record of their progress. These are the stages of their march, identified by the different places where they stopped along the way.

3 They set out from the city of Rameses in early spring—on the fifteenth day of the first month*—on the morning after the first Passover celebration. The people of Israel left defiantly, in full view of all the Egyptians. 4 Meanwhile, the Egyptians were burying all their firstborn sons, whom the LORD had killed the night before. The LORD had defeated the gods of Egypt that night with great acts of judgment!

5 After leaving Rameses, the Israelites set up camp at Succoth.

6 Then they left Succoth and camped at Etham on the edge of the wilderness.

7 They left Etham and turned back toward Pi-hahiroth, opposite Baal-zephon, and camped near Migdol.

8 They left Pi-hahiroth and crossed the Red Sea* into the wilderness beyond. Then they traveled for three days into the Etham wilderness and camped at Marah.

9 They left Marah and camped at Elim, where there were twelve springs of water and seventy palm trees.

10 They left Elim and camped beside the Red Sea.*

11 They left the Red Sea and camped in the wilderness of Sin.*

12 They left the wilderness of Sin and camped at Dophkah.

13 They left Dophkah and camped at Alush.

14 They left Alush and camped at Rephidim, where there was no water for the people to drink.

15 They left Rephidim and camped in the wilderness of Sinai.

32:41 Hebrew *Havvoth-jair.* 33:3 This day in the ancient Hebrew lunar calendar occurred in late March, April, or early May. 33:8 Hebrew *the sea.* 33:10 Hebrew *sea of reeds;* also in 33:11. 33:11 The geographical name *Sin* is related to *Sinai* and should not be confused with the English word *sin.*

16 They left the wilderness of Sinai and camped at Kibroth-hattaavah.

17 They left Kibroth-hattaavah and camped at Hazeroth.

18 They left Hazeroth and camped at Rithmah.

19 They left Rithmah and camped at Rimmon-perez.

20 They left Rimmon-perez and camped at Libnah.

21 They left Libnah and camped at Rissah.

22 They left Rissah and camped at Kehelathah.

23 They left Kehelathah and camped at Mount Shepher.

24 They left Mount Shepher and camped at Haradah.

25 They left Haradah and camped at Makheloth.

26 They left Makheloth and camped at Tahath.

27 They left Tahath and camped at Terah.

28 They left Terah and camped at Mithcah.

29 They left Mithcah and camped at Hashmonah.

30 They left Hashmonah and camped at Moseroth.

31 They left Moseroth and camped at Bene-jaakan.

32 They left Bene-jaakan and camped at Hor-haggidgad.

33 They left Hor-haggidgad and camped at Jotbathah.

34 They left Jotbathah and camped at Abronah.

35 They left Abronah and camped at Ezion-geber.

36 They left Ezion-geber and camped at Kadesh in the wilderness of Zin.

37 They left Kadesh and camped at Mount Hor, at the border of Edom. 38 While they were at the foot of Mount Hor, Aaron the priest was directed by the LORD to go up the mountain, and there he died. This happened in midsummer, on the first day of the fifth month* of the fortieth year after Israel's departure from Egypt. 39 Aaron was 123 years old when he died there on Mount Hor.

40 At that time the Canaanite king of Arad, who lived in the Negev in the land of Canaan, heard that the people of Israel were approaching his land.

41 Meanwhile, the Israelites left Mount Hor and camped at Zalmonah.

42 Then they left Zalmonah and camped at Punon.

43 They left Punon and camped at Oboth.

44 They left Oboth and camped at Iye-abarim on the border of Moab.

45 They left Iye-abarim* and camped at Dibon-gad.

46 They left Dibon-gad and camped at Almon-diblathaim.

47 They left Almon-diblathaim and camped in the mountains east of the river,* near Mount Nebo.

48 They left the mountains east of the river and camped on the plains of Moab beside the Jordan River, across from Jericho. 49 Along the Jordan River they camped from Beth-jeshimoth as far as the meadows of Acacia* on the plains of Moab.

50 While they were camped near the Jordan River on the plains of Moab opposite Jericho, the LORD said to Moses, 51 "Give the following instructions to the people of Israel: When you cross the Jordan River into the land of Canaan, 52 you must drive out all the people living there. You must destroy all their carved and molten images and demolish all their pagan shrines. 53 Take possession of the land and settle in it, because I have given it to you to occupy. 54 You must distribute the land among the clans by sacred lot and in proportion to their size. A larger portion of land will be allotted to each of the larger clans, and a smaller portion will be allotted to each of the smaller clans. The decision of the sacred lot is final. In this way, the portions of land will be divided among your ancestral tribes. 55 But if you fail to drive out the people who live in the land, those who remain will be like splinters in your eyes and thorns in your sides. They will harass you in the land where you live. 56 And I will do to you what I had planned to do to them."

34 Boundaries of the Land

Then the LORD said to Moses, 2 "Give these instructions to the Israelites: When you come into the land of Canaan, which

---

33:38 This day in the ancient Hebrew lunar calendar occurred in July or August.   33:45 As in 33:44; Hebrew reads Iyim, another name for Iye-abarim.   33:47 Or the mountains of Abarim; also in 33:48.   33:49 Hebrew as far as Abel-shittim.

I am giving you as your special possession, these will be the boundaries. ³The southern portion of your country will extend from the wilderness of Zin, along the edge of Edom. The southern boundary will begin on the east at the Dead Sea.* ⁴It will then run south past Scorpion Pass* in the direction of Zin. Its southernmost point will be Kadesh-barnea, from which it will go to Hazar-addar, and on to Azmon. ⁵From Azmon the boundary will turn toward the Brook of Egypt and end at the Mediterranean Sea.*

⁶"Your western boundary will be the coastline of the Mediterranean Sea.

⁷"Your northern boundary will begin at the Mediterranean Sea and run east to Mount Hor, ⁸then to Lebo-hamath, and on through Zedad ⁹and Ziphron to Hazarenan. This will be your northern boundary.

¹⁰"The eastern boundary will start at Hazar-enan and run south to Shepham, ¹¹then down to Riblah on the east side of Ain. From there the boundary will run down along the eastern edge of the Sea of Galilee,* ¹²and then along the Jordan River to the Dead Sea. These are the boundaries of your land."

¹³Then Moses told the Israelites, "This territory is the homeland you are to divide among yourselves by sacred lot. The LORD has commanded that the land be divided among the nine and a half remaining tribes. ¹⁴The families of the tribes of Reuben, Gad, and half the tribe of Manasseh have already received their grants of land ¹⁵on the east side of the Jordan River, across from Jericho toward the sunrise."

Leaders to Divide the Land

¹⁶And the LORD said to Moses, ¹⁷"Eleazar the priest and Joshua son of Nun are the men designated to divide the grants of land among the people. ¹⁸Enlist one leader from each tribe to help them with the task. ¹⁹These are the tribes and the names of the leaders:

Tribe	Leader
Judah	Caleb son of Jephunneh
²⁰ Simeon	Shemuel son of Ammihud
²¹ Benjamin	Elidad son of Kislon
²² Dan	Bukki son of Jogli
²³ Manasseh son of Joseph	Hanniel son of Ephod
²⁴ Ephraim son of Joseph	Kemuel son of Shiphtan
²⁵ Zebulun	Elizaphan son of Parnach
²⁶ Issachar	Paltiel son of Azzan
²⁷ Asher	Ahihud son of Shelomi
²⁸ Naphtali	Pedahel son of Ammihud

²⁹These are the men the LORD has appointed to divide the grants of land in Canaan among the Israelites."

35 Towns for the Levites

While Israel was camped beside the Jordan on the plains of Moab across from Jericho, the LORD said to Moses, ²"Command the people of Israel to give to the Levites from their property certain towns to live in, along with the surrounding pasturelands. ³These towns will be for the Levites to live in, and the surrounding lands will provide pasture for their cattle, flocks, and other livestock. ⁴The pastureland assigned to the Levites around these towns will extend 1,500 feet* from the town walls in every direction. ⁵Measure off 3,000 feet* outside the town walls in every direction—east, south, west, north—with the town at the center. This area will serve as the larger pastureland for the towns.

⁶"Six of the towns you give the Levites will be cities of refuge, where a person who has accidentally killed someone can flee for safety. In addition, give them forty-two other towns. ⁷In all, forty-eight towns with the surrounding pastureland will be given to the Levites. ⁸These towns will come from the property of the people of Israel. The larger tribes will give more towns to the Levites, while the smaller tribes will give fewer. Each tribe will give property in proportion to the size of its land."

Cities of Refuge

⁹The LORD said to Moses, ¹⁰"Give the following instructions to the people of Israel.

"When you cross the Jordan into the land of Canaan, ¹¹designate cities of refuge to

---

34:3 Hebrew *Salt Sea;* also in 34:12. **34:4** Or *the ascent of Akrabbim.* **34:5** Hebrew *the sea;* also in 34:6, 7. **34:11** Hebrew *Sea of Kinnereth.* **35:4** Hebrew *1,000 cubits* [460 meters]. **35:5** Hebrew *2,000 cubits* [920 meters].

which people can flee if they have killed someone accidentally. ¹²These cities will be places of protection from a dead person's relatives who want to avenge the death. The slayer must not be put to death before being tried by the community. ¹³Designate six cities of refuge for yourselves, ¹⁴three on the east side of the Jordan River and three on the west in the land of Canaan. ¹⁵These cities are for the protection of Israelites, foreigners living among you, and traveling merchants. Anyone who accidentally kills someone may flee there for safety.

¹⁶"But if someone strikes and kills another person with a piece of iron, it is murder, and the murderer must be executed. ¹⁷Or if someone with a stone in his hand strikes and kills another person, it is murder, and the murderer must be put to death. ¹⁸Or if someone strikes and kills another person with a wooden object, it is murder, and the murderer must be put to death. ¹⁹The victim's nearest relative is responsible for putting the murderer to death. When they meet, the avenger must put the murderer to death. ²⁰So if someone hates another person and pushes him or throws a dangerous object at him and he dies, it is murder. ²¹Or if someone hates another person and hits him with a fist and he dies, it is murder. In such cases, the avenger must put the murderer to death when they meet.

²²"But suppose someone pushes another person without having shown previous hostility, or throws something that unintentionally hits another person, ²³or accidentally drops a huge stone on someone, though they were not enemies, and the person dies. ²⁴If this should happen, the community must follow these regulations in making a judgment between the slayer and the avenger, the victim's nearest relative: ²⁵The community must protect the slayer from the avenger and must escort the slayer back to live in the city of refuge to which he fled. There he must remain until the death of the high priest, who was anointed with the sacred oil.

²⁶"But if the slayer ever leaves the limits of the city of refuge, ²⁷and the avenger finds him outside the city and kills him, it will not be considered murder. ²⁸The slayer should have stayed inside the city of refuge until the death of the high priest. But after the death of the high priest, the slayer may return to his own property. ²⁹These are legal requirements for you to observe from generation to generation, wherever you may live.

³⁰"All murderers must be put to death, but only if evidence is presented by more than one witness. No one may be put to death on the testimony of only one witness. ³¹Also, you must never accept a ransom payment for the life of someone judged guilty of murder and subject to execution; murderers must always be put to death. ³²And never accept a ransom payment from someone who has fled to a city of refuge, allowing a slayer to return to his property before the death of the high priest. ³³This will ensure that the land where you live will not be polluted, for murder pollutes the land. And no sacrifice except the execution of the murderer can purify the land from murder.* ³⁴You must not defile the land where you live, for I live there myself. I am the LORD, who lives among the people of Israel."

36 Women Who Inherit Property

Then the heads of the clans of Gilead—descendants of Makir, son of Manasseh, son of Joseph—came to Moses and the family leaders of Israel with a petition. ²They said, "Sir, the LORD instructed you to divide the land by sacred lot among the people of Israel. You were told by the LORD to give the grant of land owned by our brother Zelophehad to his daughters. ³But if they marry men from another tribe, their grants of land will go with them to the tribe into which they marry. In this way, the total area of our tribal land will be reduced. ⁴Then when the Year of Jubilee comes, their portion of land will be added to that of the new tribe, causing it to be lost forever to our ancestral tribe."

⁵So Moses gave the Israelites this command from the LORD: "The claim of the men of the tribe of Joseph is legitimate. ⁶This is what the LORD commands concerning the daughters of Zelophehad: Let them marry

---

35:33 Or *can make atonement for murder.*

anyone they like, as long as it is within their own ancestral tribe. [7]None of the territorial land may pass from tribe to tribe, for all the land given to each tribe must remain within the tribe to which it was first allotted. [8]The daughters throughout the tribes of Israel who are in line to inherit property must marry within their tribe, so that all the Israelites will keep their ancestral property. [9]No grant of land may pass from one tribe to another; each tribe of Israel must keep its allotted portion of land."

[10]The daughters of Zelophehad did as the LORD commanded Moses. [11]Mahlah, Tirzah, Hoglah, Milcah, and Noah all married cousins on their father's side. [12]They married into the clans of Manasseh son of Joseph. Thus, their inheritance of land remained within their ancestral tribe.

[13]These are the commands and regulations that the LORD gave to the people of Israel through Moses while they were camped on the plains of Moab beside the Jordan River across from Jericho.

Introduction to
Deuteronomy

Background

The Israelites have wandered in the desert for forty years. A previous approach to their Promised Land four decades earlier led to rebellion and fear. God punished his people by refusing to give them the land. Instead, they wander until the generation that left Egypt has died. God will fulfill his promise to their children and grandchildren. Now those children have grown to adulthood themselves and once again stand poised to enter the land. Moses gathers them for a final speech, a reminder of where they have come from and what God has planned for their futures.

Moses is the presumed author of all but the last chapter of Deuteronomy—his obituary—which was probably written by his successor, Joshua.

Deuteronomy is the last book of the Pentateuch. Its title comes from the Greek word *deuteronomion,* which means a "repetition of the law" and refers to a phrase in 17:18. The Hebrew title repeated the text's first phrase: "This book records the words." The New Testament quotes from Deuteronomy some eighty times, including three of Jesus' scriptural rebuttals during his desert temptation (see Matthew 4 and Luke 4).

Message

Although Moses is still blessed with health, God reveals that his death is imminent (32:48–52). Due to his sin (Numbers 20:1–13), Moses is not able to enter the Promised Land; he will see it from the mountain and then die. His final task is to remind the people of the covenant they made with God.

This book contains three discourses of Moses, including his final words to the people he has led for forty years. Moses reminds his people of their history and their heritage. This new generation, Moses warns, would do well to learn from the mistakes of their parents. The beloved leader of the children of Israel lays out clearly what God expects. The series of blessings for obedience and curses for disobedience (28:1–68) will be lived out vividly in the coming historical books that recount the reigns of various kings of Israel and Judah.

Time

Deuteronomy was probably written in 1406 B.C.

Outline

Deuteronomy

1 Introduction to Moses' First Address

These are the words that Moses spoke to all the people of Israel while they were in the wilderness east of the Jordan River. They were camped in the Jordan Valley* near Suph, between Paran on one side and Tophel, Laban, Hazeroth, and Di-zahab on the other.

²Normally it takes only eleven days to travel from Mount Sinai* to Kadesh-barnea, going by way of Mount Seir. ³But forty years after the Israelites left Egypt, on the first day of the eleventh month,* Moses addressed the people of Israel, telling them everything the LORD had commanded him to say. ⁴This took place after he had defeated King Sihon of the Amorites, who had ruled in Heshbon, and King Og of Bashan, who had ruled in Ashtaroth and Edrei.

⁵While the Israelites were in the land of Moab east of the Jordan River, Moses carefully explained the LORD's instructions as follows.

The Command to Leave Sinai

⁶"When we were at Mount Sinai, the LORD our God said to us, 'You have stayed at this mountain long enough. ⁷It is time to break camp and move on. Go to the hill country of the Amorites and to all the neighboring regions—the Jordan Valley, the hill country, the western foothills,* the Negev, and the coastal plain. Go to the land of the Canaanites and to Lebanon, and all the way to the great Euphrates River. ⁸Look, I am giving all this land to you! Go in and occupy it, for it is the land the LORD swore to give to your ancestors Abraham, Isaac, and Jacob, and to all their descendants.'"

Moses Appoints Leaders from Each Tribe

⁹Moses continued, "At that time I told you, 'You are too great a burden for me to carry all by myself. ¹⁰The LORD your God has increased your population, making you as numerous as the stars! ¹¹And may the LORD, the God of your ancestors, multiply you a thousand times more and bless you as he promised! ¹²But you are such a heavy load to carry! How can I deal with all your problems and bickering? ¹³Choose some well-respected men from each tribe who are known for their wisdom and understanding, and I will appoint them as your leaders.'

¹⁴"Then you responded, 'Your plan is a good one.' ¹⁵So I took the wise and respected men you had selected from your tribes and appointed them to serve as judges and officials over you. Some were responsible for a thousand people, some for a hundred, some for fifty, and some for ten.

¹⁶"At that time I instructed the judges, 'You must hear the cases of your fellow Israelites and the foreigners living among you. Be perfectly fair in your decisions ¹⁷and impartial in your judgments. Hear the cases of those who are poor as well as those who are rich. Don't be afraid of anyone's anger, for the decision

---

1:1 Hebrew *the Arabah;* also in 1:7. **1:2** Hebrew *Horeb,* another name for Sinai; also in 1:6, 19. **1:3** Hebrew *In the fortieth year, on the first day of the eleventh month.* This day in the ancient Hebrew lunar calendar occurred in January or February. **1:7** Hebrew *the Shephelah.*

you make is God's decision. Bring me any cases that are too difficult for you, and I will handle them.'

¹⁸"At that time I gave you instructions about everything you were to do.

Scouts Explore the Land

¹⁹"Then, just as the LORD our God commanded us, we left Mount Sinai and traveled through the great and terrifying wilderness, as you yourselves remember, and headed toward the hill country of the Amorites. When we arrived at Kadesh-barnea, ²⁰I said to you, 'You have now reached the hill country of the Amorites that the LORD our God is giving us. ²¹Look! He has placed the land in front of you. Go and occupy it as the LORD, the God of your ancestors, has promised you. Don't be afraid! Don't be discouraged!'

²²"But you all came to me and said, 'First, let's send out scouts to explore the land for us. They will advise us on the best route to take and which towns we should enter.'

²³"This seemed like a good idea to me, so I chose twelve scouts, one from each of your tribes. ²⁴They headed for the hill country and came to the valley of Eshcol and explored it. ²⁵They picked some of its fruit and brought it back to us. And they reported, 'The land the LORD our God has given us is indeed a good land.'

Israel's Rebellion against the LORD

²⁶"But you rebelled against the command of the LORD your God and refused to go in. ²⁷You complained in your tents and said, 'The LORD must hate us. That's why he has brought us here from Egypt—to hand us over to the Amorites to be slaughtered. ²⁸Where can we go? Our brothers have demoralized us with their report. They tell us, "The people of the land are taller and more powerful than we are, and their towns are large, with walls rising high into the sky! We even saw giants there—the descendants of Anak!"'

²⁹"But I said to you, 'Don't be shocked or afraid of them! ³⁰The LORD your God is going ahead of you. He will fight for you, just as you saw him do in Egypt. ³¹And you saw how the LORD your God cared for you

all along the way as you traveled through the wilderness, just as a father cares for his child. Now he has brought you to this place.'

³²"But even after all he did, you refused to trust the LORD your God, ³³who goes before you looking for the best places to camp, guiding you with a pillar of fire by night and a pillar of cloud by day.

³⁴"When the LORD heard your complaining, he became very angry. So he solemnly swore, ³⁵'Not one of you from this wicked generation will live to see the good land I swore to give your ancestors, ³⁶except Caleb son of Jephunneh. He will see this land because he has followed the LORD completely. I will give to him and his descendants some of the very land he explored during his scouting mission.'

³⁷"And the LORD was also angry with me because of you. He said to me, 'Moses, not even you will enter the Promised Land! ³⁸Instead, your assistant, Joshua son of Nun, will lead the people into the land. Encourage him, for he will lead Israel as they take possession of it. ³⁹I will give the land to your little ones—your innocent children. You were afraid they would be captured, but they will be the ones who occupy it. ⁴⁰As for you, turn around now and go on back through the wilderness toward the Red Sea.*'

⁴¹"Then you confessed, 'We have sinned against the LORD! We will go into the land and fight for it, as the LORD our God has commanded us.' So your men strapped on their weapons, thinking it would be easy to attack the hill country.

⁴²"But the LORD told me to tell you, 'Do not attack, for I am not with you. If you go ahead on your own, you will be crushed by your enemies.'

⁴³"This is what I told you, but you would not listen. Instead, you again rebelled against the LORD's command and arrogantly went into the hill country to fight. ⁴⁴But the Amorites who lived there came out against you like a swarm of bees. They chased and battered you all the way from Seir to Hormah. ⁴⁵Then you returned and wept before the LORD, but he refused to listen. ⁴⁶So you stayed there at Kadesh for a long time.

1:40 Hebrew *sea of reeds.*

2 Remembering Israel's Wanderings

"Then we turned around and headed back across the wilderness toward the Red Sea,* just as the LORD had instructed me, and we wandered around in the region of Mount Seir for a long time.

2"Then at last the LORD said to me, 3'You have been wandering around in this hill country long enough; turn to the north. 4Give these orders to the people: "You will pass through the country belonging to your relatives the Edomites, the descendants of Esau, who live in Seir. The Edomites will feel threatened, so be careful. 5Do not bother them, for I have given them all the hill country around Mount Seir as their property, and I will not give you even one square foot of their land. 6If you need food to eat or water to drink, pay them for it. 7For the LORD your God has blessed you in everything you have done. He has watched your every step through this great wilderness. During these forty years, the LORD your God has been with you, and you have lacked nothing."'

8"So we bypassed the territory of our relatives, the descendants of Esau, who live in Seir. We avoided the road through the Arabah Valley that comes up from Elath and Ezion-geber.

"Then as we turned north along the desert route through Moab, 9the LORD warned us, 'Do not bother the Moabites, the descendants of Lot, or start a war with them. I have given them Ar as their property, and I will not give you any of their land.'"

10(A race of giants called the Emites had once lived in the area of Ar. They were as strong and numerous and tall as the Anakites, another race of giants. 11Both the Emites and the Anakites are also known as the Rephaites, though the Moabites call them Emites. 12In earlier times the Horites had lived in Seir, but they were driven out and displaced by the descendants of Esau, just as Israel drove out the people of Canaan when the LORD gave Israel their land.)

13Moses continued, "Then the LORD said to us, 'Get moving. Cross the Zered Brook.' So we crossed the brook.

14"Thirty-eight years passed from the time we first left Kadesh-barnea until we finally crossed the Zered Brook! By then, all the men old enough to fight in battle had died in the wilderness, as the LORD had vowed would happen. 15The LORD struck them down until they had all been eliminated from the community.

16"When all the men of fighting age had died, 17the LORD said to me, 18'Today you will cross the border of Moab at Ar 19and enter the land of the Ammonites, the descendants of Lot. But do not bother them or start a war with them. I have given the land of Ammon to them as their property, and I will not give you any of their land.'"

20(That area was once considered the land of the Rephaites, who had lived there, though the Ammonites call them Zamzummites. 21They were also as strong and numerous and tall as the Anakites. But the LORD destroyed them so the Ammonites could occupy their land. 22He had done the same for the descendants of Esau who lived in Seir, for he destroyed the Horites so they could settle there in their place. The descendants of Esau live there to this day. 23A similar thing happened when the Caphtorites from Crete* invaded and destroyed the Avvites, who had lived in villages in the area of Gaza.)

24Moses continued, "Then the LORD said, 'Now get moving! Cross the Arnon Gorge. Look, I will hand over to you Sihon the Amorite, king of Heshbon, and I will give you his land. Attack him and begin to occupy the land. 25Beginning today I will make people throughout the earth terrified because of you. When they hear reports about you, they will tremble with dread and fear.'"

Victory over Sihon of Heshbon

26Moses continued, "From the wilderness of Kedemoth I sent ambassadors to King Sihon of Heshbon with this proposal of peace:

27'Let us travel through your land. We will stay on the main road and won't turn off into the fields on either side. 28Sell us food to eat and water to drink, and we will pay for it. All we want is permission to pass through your land.

²⁹The descendants of Esau who live in Seir allowed us to go through their country, and so did the Moabites, who live in Ar. Let us pass through until we cross the Jordan into the land the LORD our God is giving us.'

³⁰"But King Sihon of Heshbon refused to allow us to pass through, because the LORD your God made Sihon stubborn and defiant so he could help you defeat him, as he has now done.

³¹"Then the LORD said to me, 'Look, I have begun to hand King Sihon and his land over to you. Begin now to conquer and occupy his land.'

³²"Then King Sihon declared war on us and mobilized his forces at Jahaz. ³³But the LORD our God handed him over to us, and we crushed him, his sons, and all his people. ³⁴We conquered all his towns and completely destroyed* everyone—men, women, and children. Not a single person was spared. ³⁵We took all the livestock as plunder for ourselves, along with anything of value from the towns we ransacked.

³⁶"The LORD our God also helped us conquer Aroer on the edge of the Arnon Gorge, and the town in the gorge, and the whole area as far as Gilead. No town had walls too strong for us. ³⁷However, we avoided the land of the Ammonites all along the Jabbok River and the towns in the hill country—all the places the LORD our God had commanded us to leave alone.

3 Victory over Og of Bashan

"Next we turned and headed for the land of Bashan, where King Og and his entire army attacked us at Edrei. ²But the LORD told me, 'Do not be afraid of him, for I have given you victory over Og and his entire army, and I will give you all his land. Treat him just as you treated King Sihon of the Amorites, who ruled in Heshbon.'

³"So the LORD our God handed King Og and all his people over to us, and we killed them all. Not a single person survived. ⁴We conquered all sixty of his towns—the entire Argob region in his kingdom of Bashan. Not a single town escaped our conquest. ⁵These towns were all fortified with high walls and barred gates. We also took many unwalled villages at the same time. ⁶We completely destroyed* the kingdom of Bashan, just as we had destroyed King Sihon of Heshbon. We destroyed all the people in every town we conquered—men, women, and children alike. ⁷But we kept all the livestock for ourselves and took plunder from all the towns.

⁸"So we took the land of the two Amorite kings east of the Jordan River—all the way from the Arnon Gorge to Mount Hermon. ⁹(Mount Hermon is called Sirion by the Sidonians, and the Amorites call it Senir.) ¹⁰We had now conquered all the cities on the plateau and all Gilead and Bashan, as far as the towns of Salecah and Edrei, which were part of Og's kingdom in Bashan. ¹¹(King Og of Bashan was the last survivor of the giant Rephaites. His bed was made of iron and was more than thirteen feet long and six feet wide.* It can still be seen in the Ammonite city of Rabbah.)

Land Division East of the Jordan

¹²"When we took possession of this land, I gave to the tribes of Reuben and Gad the territory beyond Aroer along the Arnon Gorge, plus half of the hill country of Gilead with its towns. ¹³Then I gave the rest of Gilead and all of Bashan—Og's former kingdom—to the half-tribe of Manasseh. (This entire Argob region of Bashan used to be known as the land of the Rephaites. ¹⁴Jair, a leader from the tribe of Manasseh, conquered the whole Argob region in Bashan, all the way to the border of the Geshurites and Maacathites. Jair renamed this region after himself, calling it the Towns of Jair,* as it is still known today.) ¹⁵I gave Gilead to the clan of Makir. ¹⁶But I also gave part of Gilead to the tribes of Reuben and Gad. The area I gave them extended from the middle of the Arnon Gorge in the south to the Jabbok River on the Ammonite frontier. ¹⁷They also received the Jordan Valley, all the way from the Sea of Galilee down to the Dead Sea,* with the Jordan River serving as

---

2:34 The Hebrew term used here refers to the complete consecration of things or people to the LORD, either by destroying them or by giving them as an offering. 3:6 The Hebrew term used here refers to the complete consecration of things or people to the LORD, either by destroying them or by giving them as an offering; also in 3:6b. 3:11 Hebrew 9 cubits [4.1 meters] long and 4 cubits [1.8 meters] wide. 3:14 Hebrew Havvoth-jair. 3:17 Hebrew from Kinnereth to the Sea of the Arabah, the Salt Sea.

the western boundary. To the east were the slopes of Pisgah.

¹⁸"At that time I gave this command to the tribes that would live east of the Jordan: 'Although the LORD your God has given you this land as your property, all your fighting men must cross the Jordan ahead of your Israelite relatives, armed and ready to assist them. ¹⁹Your wives, children, and numerous livestock, however, may stay behind in the towns I have given you. ²⁰When the LORD has given security to the rest of the Israelites, as he has to you, and when they occupy the land the LORD your God is giving them across the Jordan River, then you may all return here to the land I have given you.'

Moses Forbidden to Enter the Land

²¹"At that time I gave Joshua this charge: 'You have seen for yourself everything the LORD your God has done to these two kings. He will do the same to all the kingdoms on the west side of the Jordan. ²²Do not be afraid of the nations there, for the LORD your God will fight for you.'

²³"At that time I pleaded with the LORD and said, ²⁴'O Sovereign LORD, you have only begun to show your greatness and the strength of your hand to me, your servant. Is there any god in heaven or on earth who can perform such great and mighty deeds as you do? ²⁵Please let me cross the Jordan to see the wonderful land on the other side, the beautiful hill country and the Lebanon mountains.'

²⁶"But the LORD was angry with me because of you, and he would not listen to me. 'That's enough!' he declared. 'Speak of it no more. ²⁷But go up to Pisgah Peak, and look over the land in every direction. Take a good look, but you may not cross the Jordan River. ²⁸Instead, commission Joshua and encourage and strengthen him, for he will lead the people across the Jordan. He will give them all the land you now see before you as their possession.' ²⁹So we stayed in the valley near Beth-peor.

4 Moses Urges Israel to Obey

"And now, Israel, listen carefully to these decrees and regulations that I am about to teach you. Obey them so that you

may live, so you may enter and occupy the land that the LORD, the God of your ancestors, is giving you. ²Do not add to or subtract from these commands I am giving you. Just obey the commands of the LORD your God that I am giving you.

³"You saw for yourself what the LORD did to you at Baal-peor. There the LORD your God destroyed everyone who had worshiped Baal, the god of Peor. ⁴But all of you who were faithful to the LORD your God are still alive today—every one of you.

⁵"Look, I now teach you these decrees and regulations just as the LORD my God commanded me, so that you may obey them in the land you are about to enter and occupy. ⁶Obey them completely, and you will display your wisdom and intelligence among the surrounding nations. When they hear all these decrees, they will exclaim, 'How wise and prudent are the people of this great nation!' ⁷For what great nation has a god as near to them as the LORD our God is near to us whenever we call on him? ⁸And what great nation has decrees and regulations as righteous and fair as this body of instructions that I am giving you today?

⁹"But watch out! Be careful never to forget what you yourself have seen. Do not let these memories escape from your mind as long as you live! And be sure to pass them on to your children and grandchildren. ¹⁰Never forget the day when you stood before the LORD your God at Mount Sinai,* where he told me, 'Summon the people before me, and I will personally instruct them. Then they will learn to fear me as long as they live, and they will teach their children to fear me also.'

¹¹"You came near and stood at the foot of the mountain, while flames from the mountain shot into the sky. The mountain was shrouded in black clouds and deep darkness. ¹²And the LORD spoke to you from the heart of the fire. You heard the sound of his words but didn't see his form; there was only a voice. ¹³He proclaimed his covenant—the Ten Commandments*—which he commanded you to keep, and which he wrote on two stone tablets. ¹⁴It was at that time that the LORD commanded me to teach you his decrees and regulations so

4:10 Hebrew *Horeb*, another name for Sinai; also in 4:15.   **4:13** Hebrew *the ten words*.

you would obey them in the land you are about to enter and occupy.

A Warning against Idolatry

¹⁵"But be very careful! You did not see the LORD's form on the day he spoke to you from the heart of the fire at Mount Sinai. ¹⁶So do not corrupt yourselves by making an idol in any form—whether of a man or a woman, ¹⁷an animal on the ground, a bird in the sky, ¹⁸a small animal that scurries along the ground, or a fish in the deepest sea. ¹⁹And when you look up into the sky and see the sun, moon, and stars—all the forces of heaven—don't be seduced into worshiping them. The LORD your God gave them to all the peoples of the earth. ²⁰Remember that the LORD rescued you from the iron-smelting furnace of Egypt in order to make you his very own people and his special possession, which is what you are today.

²¹"But the LORD was angry with me because of you. He vowed that I would not cross the Jordan River into the good land the LORD your God is giving you as your special possession. ²²You will cross the Jordan to occupy the land, but I will not. Instead, I will die here on the east side of the river. ²³So be careful not to break the covenant the LORD your God has made with you. Do not make idols of any shape or form, for the LORD your God has forbidden this. ²⁴The LORD your God is a devouring fire; he is a jealous God.

²⁵"In the future, when you have children and grandchildren and have lived in the land a long time, do not corrupt yourselves by making idols of any kind. This is evil in the sight of the LORD your God and will arouse his anger. ²⁶Today I call on heaven and earth as witnesses against you. If you break my covenant, you will quickly disappear from the land you are crossing the Jordan to occupy. You will live there only a short time; then you will be utterly destroyed. ²⁷For the LORD will scatter you among the nations, where only a few of you will survive. ²⁸There, in a foreign land, you will worship idols made from wood and stone—gods that neither see nor hear nor eat nor smell. ²⁹But from there you will search again for the LORD your God. And if you search for him with all your heart and soul, you will find him.

³⁰"In the distant future, when you are suffering all these things, you will finally return to the LORD your God and listen to what he tells you. ³¹For the LORD your God is a merciful God; he will not abandon you or destroy you or forget the solemn covenant he made with your ancestors.

There Is Only One God

³²"Now search all of history, from the time God created people on the earth until now, and search from one end of the heavens to the other. Has anything as great as this ever been seen or heard before? ³³Has any nation ever heard the voice of God* speaking from fire—as you did—and survived? ³⁴Has any other god dared to take a nation for himself out of another nation by means of trials, miraculous signs, wonders, war, a strong hand, a powerful arm, and terrifying acts? Yet that is what the LORD your God did for you in Egypt, right before your eyes.

³⁵"He showed you these things so you would know that the LORD is God and there is no other. ³⁶He let you hear his voice from heaven so he could instruct you. He let you see his great fire here on earth so he could speak to you from it. ³⁷Because he loved your ancestors, he chose to bless their descendants, and he personally brought you out of Egypt with a great display of power. ³⁸He drove out nations far greater than you, so he could bring you in and give you their land as your special possession, as it is today.

³⁹"So remember this and keep it firmly in mind: The LORD is God both in heaven and on earth, and there is no other. ⁴⁰If you obey all the decrees and commands I am giving you today, all will be well with you and your children. I am giving you these instructions so you will enjoy a long life in the land the LORD your God is giving you for all time."

Eastern Cities of Refuge

⁴¹Then Moses set apart three cities of refuge east of the Jordan River. ⁴²Anyone who

---

4:33 Or voice of a god.

killed another person unintentionally, without previous hostility, could flee there to live in safety. ⁴³ These were the cities: Bezer on the wilderness plateau for the tribe of Reuben; Ramoth in Gilead for the tribe of Gad; Golan in Bashan for the tribe of Manasseh.

Introduction to Moses' Second Address

⁴⁴ This is the body of instruction that Moses presented to the Israelites. ⁴⁵ These are the laws, decrees, and regulations that Moses gave to the people of Israel when they left Egypt, ⁴⁶ and as they camped in the valley near Beth-peor east of the Jordan River. (This land was formerly occupied by the Amorites under King Sihon, who ruled from Heshbon. But Moses and the Israelites destroyed him and his people when they came up from Egypt. ⁴⁷ Israel took possession of his land and that of King Og of Bashan—the two Amorite kings east of the Jordan. ⁴⁸ So Israel conquered the entire area from Aroer at the edge of the Arnon Gorge all the way to Mount Sirion,* also called Mount Hermon. ⁴⁹ And they conquered the eastern bank of the Jordan River as far south as the Dead Sea,* below the slopes of Pisgah.)

5 Ten Commandments for the Covenant Community

Moses called all the people of Israel together and said, "Listen carefully, Israel. Hear the decrees and regulations I am giving you today, so you may learn them and obey them!

² "The LORD our God made a covenant with us at Mount Sinai.* ³ The LORD did not make this covenant with our ancestors, but with all of us who are alive today. ⁴ At the mountain the LORD spoke to you face to face from the heart of the fire. ⁵ I stood as an intermediary between you and the LORD, for you were afraid of the fire and did not want to approach the mountain. He spoke to me, and I passed his words on to you. This is what he said:

⁶ "I am the LORD your God, who rescued you from the land of Egypt, the place of your slavery.

⁷ "You must not have any other god but me.

⁸ "You must not make for yourself an idol of any kind, or an image of anything in the heavens or on the earth or in the sea. ⁹ You must not bow down to them or worship them, for I, the LORD your God, am a jealous God who will not tolerate your affection for any other gods. I lay the sins of the parents upon their children; the entire family is affected—even children in the third and fourth generations of those who reject me. ¹⁰ But I lavish unfailing love for a thousand generations on those* who love me and obey my commands.

¹¹ "You must not misuse the name of the LORD your God. The LORD will not let you go unpunished if you misuse his name.

¹² "Observe the Sabbath day by keeping it holy, as the LORD your God has commanded you. ¹³ You have six days each week for your ordinary work, ¹⁴ but the seventh day is a Sabbath day of rest dedicated to the LORD your God. On that day no one in your household may do any work. This includes you, your sons and daughters, your male and female servants, your oxen and donkeys and other livestock, and any foreigners living among you. All your male and female servants must rest as you do. ¹⁵ Remember that you were once slaves in Egypt, but the LORD your God brought you out with his strong hand and powerful arm. That is why the LORD your God has commanded you to rest on the Sabbath day.

¹⁶ "Honor your father and mother, as the LORD your God commanded you. Then you will live a long, full life in the land the LORD your God is giving you.

¹⁷ "You must not murder.

¹⁸ "You must not commit adultery.

¹⁹ "You must not steal.

²⁰ "You must not testify falsely against your neighbor.

²¹ "You must not covet your neighbor's wife. You must not covet your neighbor's house or land, male or female servant, ox or donkey, or anything else that belongs to your neighbor.

4:48 As in Syriac version (see also 3:9); Hebrew reads *Mount Sion*. 4:49 Hebrew *took the Arabah on the east side of the Jordan as far as the sea of the Arabah*. 5:2 Hebrew *Horeb*, another name for Sinai. 5:10 Hebrew *for thousands of those*.

Sabbath & Rest

What Does It Mean to Keep the Sabbath Holy?

DEUTERONOMY 5:12-15

Shabbat candles, braided challah bread, prayer, family time. In Jewish communities, Sabbaths are truly set apart from the rest of the week. (Indeed, the Hebrew word for *holy*—as in, "Remember to observe the Sabbath day by keeping it holy" [Exodus 20:8]—means, literally, "set apart.") When I practiced Judaism, I would begin my Sabbath with a relaxed Friday night dinner, followed by a day of worship, rest, and celebration. During the Sabbath day, I didn't think about my schoolwork, spend any money, ride in a car, or watch television.

Then I became a Christian. Although I went to church on Sunday mornings, the day never seemed quite as holy. As often as not, I wound up at the shopping mall on Sunday afternoon.

Of course, Christians aren't bound by Old Testament Sabbath directives. Twice in his epistles, the apostle Paul made it clear that Sabbath observance, like other external signs of piety, is insufficient for salvation. As he wrote to the Colossians, "So don't let anyone condemn you . . . for not celebrating certain holy days or new moon ceremonies or Sabbaths. For these rules are only shadows of the reality yet to come. And Christ himself is that reality" (Colossians 2:16-17). And Jesus, when rebuked by the Pharisees for plucking grain from a field on the Sabbath, criticized those who made a fetish of Sabbath observance, insisting, "The Sabbath was made to meet the needs of people, and not people to meet the requirements of the Sabbath" (Mark 2:27).

But Jesus never said to forget the Sabbath completely. Keeping the Sabbath is one of the Ten Commandments after all! And through the ages Christians have seen the wisdom of devoting one full day to rest and praise. There's an old Puritan saying, "Good Sabbaths make good Christians."

But honoring the Sabbath was perhaps easier in Puritan New England, where almost everyone took the Sabbath seriously. Shops weren't open on Sundays, businesses closed their doors, and everyone headed to church. Sabbaths are much more difficult in contemporary America. In fact, in a society that values busyness and productivity, observing the Sabbath is downright countercultural.

That's not to say contemporary society doesn't encourage us to relax. To the contrary, most secular women's magazines, television talk shows, and advertisements aimed at women instruct us to indulge ourselves. While there's nothing wrong with the occasional bubble bath, "me-days" aren't quite the same thing as Sabbaths. The key to the Sabbath isn't merely rest. Rather, it's that in our rest we turn our attention to God, whose rest our Sabbath mirrors.

So how, in our hectic world, can we set apart a day truly given over to rest and reverence?

I've found it helpful to mark the beginning of the Sabbath. On Saturday evenings I gather with friends for an unhurried time of food, fellowship, and prayer.

I also have taken inspiration from the two commandments that govern Jewish Sabbath observance: to not work on the Sabbath and to be joyful. On Sundays I don't shop; I don't grade papers; I try not to make any plans for the week ahead. I also try not to check e-mail or my cell phone on the Sabbath, which may sound like a small thing. But those are implements that connect us to our work, and they put me in this state of very low-grade, constant tension that someone is trying to get a hold of me. Instead, I try to do things that will give me and God joy. I take long walks with friends. I take extra time for Bible study.

The way into Christian Sabbath observance isn't so much about rules as orientation: away from the busyness of the week and toward the Creator who rested. In this we may find a true sense of *Shabbat shalom*, Sabbath peace.

—*Lauren F. Winner*

For more on Sabbath and rest, see reading at Psalm 23.

²²"The LORD spoke these words to all of you assembled there at the foot of the mountain. He spoke with a loud voice from the heart of the fire, surrounded by clouds and deep darkness. This was all he said at that time, and he wrote his words on two stone tablets and gave them to me.

²³"But when you heard the voice from the heart of the darkness, while the mountain was blazing with fire, all your tribal leaders and elders came to me. ²⁴They said, 'Look, the LORD our God has shown us his glory and greatness, and we have heard his voice from the heart of the fire. Today we have seen that God can speak to us humans, and yet we live! ²⁵But now, why should we risk death again? If the LORD our God speaks to us again, we will certainly die and be consumed by this awesome fire. ²⁶Can any living thing hear the voice of the living God from the heart of the fire as we did and yet survive? ²⁷Go yourself and listen to what the LORD our God says. Then come and tell us everything he tells you, and we will listen and obey.'

²⁸"The LORD heard the request you made to me. And he said, 'I have heard what the people said to you, and they are right. ²⁹Oh, that they would always have hearts like this, that they might fear me and obey all my commands! If they did, they and their descendants would prosper forever. ³⁰Go and tell them, "Return to your tents." ³¹But you stand here with me so I can give you all my commands, decrees, and regulations. You must teach them to the people so they can obey them in the land I am giving them as their possession.'"

³²So Moses told the people, "You must be careful to obey all the commands of the LORD your God, following his instructions in every detail. ³³Stay on the path that the LORD your God has commanded you to follow. Then you will live long and prosperous lives in the land you are about to enter and occupy.

6 A Call for Wholehearted Commitment

"These are the commands, decrees, and regulations that the LORD your God commanded me to teach you. You must obey them in the land you are about to enter and occupy, ²and you and your children and grandchildren must fear the LORD your God as long as you live. If you obey all his decrees and commands, you will enjoy a long life. ³Listen closely, Israel, and be careful to obey. Then all will go well with you, and you will have many children in the land flowing with milk and honey, just as the LORD, the God of your ancestors, promised you.

⁴"Listen, O Israel! The LORD is our God, the LORD alone.* ⁵And you must love the LORD your God with all your heart, all your soul, and all your strength. ⁶And you must commit yourselves wholeheartedly to these commands that I am giving you today. ⁷Repeat them again and again to your children. Talk about them when you are at home and when you are on the road, when you are going to bed and when you are getting up. ⁸Tie them to your hands and wear them on your forehead as reminders. ⁹Write them on the doorposts of your house and on your gates.

¹⁰"The LORD your God will soon bring you into the land he swore to give you when he made a vow to your ancestors Abraham, Isaac, and Jacob. It is a land with large, prosperous cities that you did not build. ¹¹The houses will be richly stocked with goods you did not produce. You will draw water from cisterns you did not dig, and you will eat from vineyards and olive trees you did not plant. When you have eaten your fill in this land, ¹²be careful not to forget the LORD, who rescued you from slavery in the land of Egypt. ¹³You must fear the LORD your God and serve him. When you take an oath, you must use only his name.

¹⁴"You must not worship any of the gods of neighboring nations, ¹⁵for the LORD your God, who lives among you, is a jealous God. His anger will flare up against you, and he will wipe you from the face of the earth. ¹⁶You must not test the LORD your God as you did when you complained at Massah. ¹⁷You must diligently obey the commands of the LORD your God—all the laws and decrees he has given you. ¹⁸Do what is right and good in the LORD's sight, so all will

---

6:4 Or The LORD our God is one LORD; or The LORD our God, the LORD is one; or The LORD is our God, the LORD is one.

go well with you. Then you will enter and occupy the good land that the LORD swore to give your ancestors. ¹⁹You will drive out all the enemies living in the land, just as the LORD said you would.

²⁰"In the future your children will ask you, 'What is the meaning of these laws, decrees, and regulations that the LORD our God has commanded us to obey?'

²¹"Then you must tell them, 'We were Pharaoh's slaves in Egypt, but the LORD brought us out of Egypt with his strong hand. ²²The LORD did miraculous signs and wonders before our eyes, dealing terrifying blows against Egypt and Pharaoh and all his people. ²³He brought us out of Egypt so he could give us this land he had sworn to give our ancestors. ²⁴And the LORD our God commanded us to obey all these decrees and to fear him so he can continue to bless us and preserve our lives, as he has done to this day. ²⁵For we will be counted as righteous when we obey all the commands the LORD our God has given us.'

7 The Privilege of Holiness

"When the LORD your God brings you into the land you are about to enter and occupy, he will clear away many nations ahead of you: the Hittites, Girgashites, Amorites, Canaanites, Perizzites, Hivites, and Jebusites. These seven nations are greater and more numerous than you. ²When the LORD your God hands these nations over to you and you conquer them, you must completely destroy* them. Make no treaties with them and show them no mercy. ³You must not intermarry with them. Do not let your daughters and sons marry their sons and daughters, ⁴for they will lead your children away from me to worship other gods. Then the anger of the LORD will burn against you, and he will quickly destroy you. ⁵This is what you must do. You must break down their pagan altars and shatter their sacred pillars. Cut down their Asherah poles and burn their idols. ⁶For you are a holy people, who belong to the LORD your God. Of all the people on earth, the LORD your God has chosen you to be his own special treasure.

⁷"The LORD did not set his heart on you and choose you because you were more numerous than other nations, for you were the smallest of all nations! ⁸Rather, it was simply that the LORD loves you, and he was keeping the oath he had sworn to your ancestors. That is why the LORD rescued you with such a strong hand from your slavery and from the oppressive hand of Pharaoh, king of Egypt. ⁹Understand, therefore, that the LORD your God is indeed God. He is the faithful God who keeps his covenant for a thousand generations and lavishes his unfailing love on those who love him and obey his commands. ¹⁰But he does not hesitate to punish and destroy those who reject him. ¹¹Therefore, you must obey all these commands, decrees, and regulations I am giving you today.

¹²"If you listen to these regulations and faithfully obey them, the LORD your God will keep his covenant of unfailing love with you, as he promised with an oath to your ancestors. ¹³He will love you and bless you, and he will give you many children. He will give fertility to your land and your animals. When you arrive in the land he swore to give your ancestors, you will have large harvests of grain, new wine, and olive oil, and great herds of cattle, sheep, and goats. ¹⁴You will be blessed above all the nations of the earth. None of your men or women will be childless, and all your livestock will bear young. ¹⁵And the LORD will protect you from all sickness. He will not let you suffer from the terrible diseases you knew in Egypt, but he will inflict them on all your enemies!

¹⁶"You must destroy all the nations the LORD your God hands over to you. Show them no mercy, and do not worship their gods, or they will trap you. ¹⁷Perhaps you will think to yourselves, 'How can we ever conquer these nations that are so much more powerful than we are?' ¹⁸But don't be afraid of them! Just remember what the LORD your God did to Pharaoh and to all the land of Egypt. ¹⁹Remember the great terrors the LORD your God sent against them. You saw it all with your own eyes! And remember the miraculous signs and

---

7:2 The Hebrew term used here refers to the complete consecration of things or people to the LORD, either by destroying them or by giving them as an offering; also in 7:26.

A Clearer Focus

DEUTERONOMY 8:1-5

After recently completing a forty-day fast involving a restricted diet, I've found that my mind has been marvelously focused. The first focus is on what a slave I can be to food. Am I sad? I eat. Am I happy? Eat. Tired? Eat. Angry, depressed, bored? Eat, eat, eat. Do we have a social occasion? We must eat.

I was surprised, then exhilarated at how free I was during the fast. What began as a command quickly became a permission. The permission? To not have to live on the level of my appetites. As the fast came to an end, I actually became afraid to go back to eating normally, fearful I might lose the freedom I'd gained. (So far, so good.)

Second, my mind was marvelously focused on the fact that gluttony is about more than mere volume of food. It can express itself also as an inordinate interest in the *experience* of food, making taste buds promiscuous and stomachs ravenous for novelty and variety. At first the foods I restricted myself to made the prospect of a meal boring. Beans again? Another salad? But the fast focused my mind on the simple goodness of God's creation. I rediscovered how good a mere carrot can be. Or a bare slice of bread or a crisp apple. With simplicity comes gratitude and joy.

Which leads to the third and most marvelous focus the fast brought to my mind: food is ultimately not about food, but about God. The meaning of hunger—indeed, of all desire—is to point us to God. Scripture records how God intentionally allowed his people to feel hunger so that they'd learn to seek him for their true sustenance (Deuteronomy 8:3). We shouldn't be too quick to make hunger go away, for it can teach us much about our frailty, need, and emptiness apart from God. A little hunger never hurt anyone, but its absence will.

—*Ben Patterson*

For more on fasting, see reading at 2 Chronicles 20:1-9.

wonders, and the strong hand and powerful arm with which he brought you out of Egypt. The LORD your God will use this same power against all the people you fear. [20] And then the LORD your God will send terror* to drive out the few survivors still hiding from you!

[21] "No, do not be afraid of those nations, for the LORD your God is among you, and he is a great and awesome God. [22] The LORD your God will drive those nations out ahead of you little by little. You will not clear them away all at once, otherwise the wild animals would multiply too quickly for you. [23] But the LORD your God will hand them over to you. He will throw them into complete confusion until they are destroyed. [24] He will put their kings in your power, and you will erase their names from the face of the earth. No one will be able to stand against you, and you will destroy them all.

[25] "You must burn their idols in fire, and you must not covet the silver or gold that covers them. You must not take it or it will become a trap to you, for it is detestable to the LORD your God. [26] Do not bring any detestable objects into your home, for then you will be destroyed, just like them. You must utterly detest such things, for they are set apart for destruction.

7:20 Often rendered *the hornet*. The meaning of the Hebrew is uncertain.

8 A Call to Remember and Obey

"Be careful to obey all the commands I am giving you today. Then you will live and multiply, and you will enter and occupy the land the LORD swore to give your ancestors. 2Remember how the LORD your God led you through the wilderness for these forty years, humbling you and testing you to prove your character, and to find out whether or not you would obey his commands. 3Yes, he humbled you by letting you go hungry and then feeding you with manna, a food previously unknown to you and your ancestors. He did it to teach you that people do not live by bread alone; rather, we live by every word that comes from the mouth of the LORD. 4For all these forty years your clothes didn't wear out, and your feet didn't blister or swell. 5Think about it: Just as a parent disciplines a child, the LORD your God disciplines you for your own good.

6"So obey the commands of the LORD your God by walking in his ways and fearing him. 7For the LORD your God is bringing you into a good land of flowing streams and pools of water, with fountains and springs that gush out in the valleys and hills. 8It is a land of wheat and barley; of grapevines, fig trees, and pomegranates; of olive oil and honey. 9It is a land where food is plentiful and nothing is lacking. It is a land where iron is as common as stone, and copper is abundant in the hills. 10When you have eaten your fill, be sure to praise the LORD your God for the good land he has given you.

11"But that is the time to be careful! Beware that in your plenty you do not forget the LORD your God and disobey his commands, regulations, and decrees that I am giving you today. 12For when you have become full and prosperous and have built fine homes to live in, 13and when your flocks and herds have become very large and your silver and gold have multiplied along with everything else, be careful! 14Do not become proud at that time and forget the LORD your God, who rescued you from slavery in the land of Egypt. 15Do not forget that he led you through the great and terrifying wilderness with its poison-

ous snakes and scorpions, where it was so hot and dry. He gave you water from the rock! 16He fed you with manna in the wilderness, a food unknown to your ancestors. He did this to humble you and test you for your own good. 17He did all this so you would never say to yourself, 'I have achieved this wealth with my own strength and energy.' 18Remember the LORD your God. He is the one who gives you power to be successful, in order to fulfill the covenant he confirmed to your ancestors with an oath.

19"But I assure you of this: If you ever forget the LORD your God and follow other gods, worshiping and bowing down to them, you will certainly be destroyed. 20Just as the LORD has destroyed other nations in your path, you also will be destroyed if you refuse to obey the LORD your God.

9 Victory by God's Grace

"Listen, O Israel! Today you are about to cross the Jordan River to take over the land belonging to nations much greater and more powerful than you. They live in cities with walls that reach to the sky! 2The people are strong and tall—descendants of the famous Anakite giants. You've heard the saying, 'Who can stand up to the Anakites?' 3But recognize today that the LORD your God is the one who will cross over ahead of you like a devouring fire to destroy them. He will subdue them so that you will quickly conquer them and drive them out, just as the LORD has promised.

4"After the LORD your God has done this for you, don't say in your hearts, 'The LORD has given us this land because we are such good people!' No, it is because of the wickedness of the other nations that he is pushing them out of your way. 5It is not because you are so good or have such integrity that you are about to occupy their land. The LORD your God will drive these nations out ahead of you only because of their wickedness, and to fulfill the oath he swore to your ancestors Abraham, Isaac, and Jacob. 6You must recognize that the LORD your God is not giving you this good land because you are good, for you are not—you are a stubborn people.

Remembering the Gold Calf

7"Remember and never forget how angry you made the LORD your God out in the wilderness. From the day you left Egypt until now, you have been constantly rebelling against him. 8Even at Mount Sinai* you made the LORD so angry he was ready to destroy you. 9This happened when I was on the mountain receiving the tablets of stone inscribed with the words of the covenant that the LORD had made with you. I was there for forty days and forty nights, and all that time I ate no food and drank no water. 10The LORD gave me the two tablets on which God had written with his own finger all the words he had spoken to you from the heart of the fire when you were assembled at the mountain.

11"At the end of the forty days and nights, the LORD handed me the two stone tablets inscribed with the words of the covenant. 12Then the LORD said to me, 'Get up! Go down immediately, for the people you brought out of Egypt have corrupted themselves. How quickly they have turned away from the way I commanded them to live! They have melted gold and made an idol for themselves!'

13"The LORD also said to me, 'I have seen how stubborn and rebellious these people are. 14Leave me alone so I may destroy them and erase their name from under heaven. Then I will make a mighty nation of your descendants, a nation larger and more powerful than they are.'

15"So while the mountain was blazing with fire I turned and came down, holding in my hands the two stone tablets inscribed with the terms of the covenant. 16There below me I could see that you had sinned against the LORD your God. You had melted gold and made a calf idol for yourselves. How quickly you had turned away from the path the LORD had commanded you to follow! 17So I took the stone tablets and threw them to the ground, smashing them before your eyes.

18"Then, as before, I threw myself down before the LORD for forty days and nights. I ate no bread and drank no water because of the great sin you had committed by doing what the LORD hated, provoking him to anger. 19I feared that the furious anger of the LORD, which turned him against you, would drive him to destroy you. But again he listened to me. 20The LORD was so angry with Aaron that he wanted to destroy him, too. But I prayed for Aaron, and the LORD spared him. 21I took your sin—the calf you had made—and I melted it down in the fire and ground it into fine dust. Then I threw the dust into the stream that flows down the mountain.

22"You also made the LORD angry at Taberah,* Massah,* and Kibroth-hattaavah.* 23And at Kadesh-barnea the LORD sent you out with this command: 'Go up and take over the land I have given you.' But you rebelled against the command of the LORD your God and refused to put your trust in him or obey him. 24Yes, you have been rebelling against the LORD as long as I have known you.

25"That is why I threw myself down before the LORD for forty days and nights—for the LORD said he would destroy you. 26I prayed to the LORD and said, 'O Sovereign LORD, do not destroy them. They are your own people. They are your special possession, whom you redeemed from Egypt by your mighty power and your strong hand. 27Please overlook the stubbornness and the awful sin of these people, and remember instead your servants Abraham, Isaac, and Jacob. 28If you destroy these people, the Egyptians will say, "The Israelites died because the LORD wasn't able to bring them to the land he had promised to give them." Or they might say, "He destroyed them because he hated them; he deliberately took them into the wilderness to slaughter them." 29But they are your people and your special possession, whom you brought out of Egypt by your great strength and powerful arm.'

10 A New Copy of the Covenant

"At that time the LORD said to me, 'Chisel out two stone tablets like the first ones. Also make a wooden Ark—a sacred chest to store them in. Come up to me on the mountain, 2and I will write on the tablets the same words that were on the ones you smashed. Then place the tablets in the Ark.'

9:8 Hebrew *Horeb,* another name for Sinai.   9:22a *Taberah* means "place of burning." See Num 11:1-3.   9:22b *Massah* means "place of testing." See Exod 17:1-7.   9:22c *Kibroth-hattaavah* means "graves of gluttony." See Num 11:31-34.

3"So I made an Ark of acacia wood and cut two stone tablets like the first two. Then I went up the mountain with the tablets in my hand. 4Once again the LORD wrote the Ten Commandments* on the tablets and gave them to me. They were the same words the LORD had spoken to you from the heart of the fire on the day you were assembled at the foot of the mountain. 5Then I turned and came down the mountain and placed the tablets in the Ark of the Covenant, which I had made, just as the LORD commanded me. And the tablets are still there in the Ark."

6(The people of Israel set out from the wells of the people of Jaakan* and traveled to Moserah, where Aaron died and was buried. His son Eleazar ministered as high priest in his place. 7Then they journeyed to Gudgodah, and from there to Jotbathah, a land with many brooks and streams. 8At that time the LORD set apart the tribe of Levi to carry the Ark of the LORD's Covenant, and to stand before the LORD as his ministers, and to pronounce blessings in his name. These are their duties to this day. 9That is why the Levites have no share of property or possession of land among the other Israelite tribes. The LORD himself is their special possession, as the LORD your God told them.)

10"As for me, I stayed on the mountain in the LORD's presence for forty days and nights, as I had done the first time. And once again the LORD listened to my pleas and agreed not to destroy you. 11Then the LORD said to me, 'Get up and resume the journey, and lead the people to the land I swore to give to their ancestors, so they may take possession of it.'

A Call to Love and Obedience

12"And now, Israel, what does the LORD your God require of you? He requires only that you fear the LORD your God, and live in a way that pleases him, and love him and serve him with all your heart and soul. 13And you must always obey the LORD's commands and decrees that I am giving you today for your own good.

14"Look, the highest heavens and the earth and everything in it all belong to the LORD your God. 15Yet the LORD chose your ancestors as the objects of his love. And he chose you, their descendants, above all other nations, as is evident today. 16Therefore, change your hearts* and stop being stubborn.

17"For the LORD your God is the God of gods and Lord of lords. He is the great God, the mighty and awesome God, who shows no partiality and cannot be bribed. 18He ensures that orphans and widows receive justice. He shows love to the foreigners living among you and gives them food and clothing. 19So you, too, must show love to foreigners, for you yourselves were once foreigners in the land of Egypt. 20You must fear the LORD your God and worship him and cling to him. Your oaths must be in his name alone. 21He alone is your God, the only one who is worthy of your praise, the one who has done these mighty miracles that you have seen with your own eyes. 22When your ancestors went down into Egypt, there were only seventy of them. But now the LORD your God has made you as numerous as the stars in the sky!

11 "You must love the LORD your God and obey all his requirements, decrees, regulations, and commands. 2Keep in mind that I am not talking now to your children, who have never experienced the discipline of the LORD your God or seen his greatness and his strong hand and powerful arm. 3They didn't see the miraculous signs and wonders he performed in Egypt against Pharaoh and all his land. 4They didn't see what the LORD did to the armies of Egypt and to their horses and chariots—how he drowned them in the Red Sea* as they were chasing you. He destroyed them, and they have not recovered to this very day!

5"Your children didn't see how the LORD cared for you in the wilderness until you arrived here. 6They didn't see what he did to Dathan and Abiram (the sons of Eliab, a descendant of Reuben) when the earth opened its mouth in the Israelite camp and swallowed them, along with their households and tents and every living thing that belonged to them. 7But you have seen the

---

10:4 Hebrew *the ten words.* **10:6** Or *set out from Beeroth of Bene-jaakan.* **10:16** Hebrew *circumcise the foreskin of your hearts.* **11:4** Hebrew *sea of reeds.*

LORD perform all these mighty deeds with your own eyes!

The Blessings of Obedience

8 "Therefore, be careful to obey every command I am giving you today, so you may have strength to go in and take over the land you are about to enter. 9 If you obey, you will enjoy a long life in the land the LORD swore to give to your ancestors and to you, their descendants—a land flowing with milk and honey! 10 For the land you are about to enter and take over is not like the land of Egypt from which you came, where you planted your seed and made irrigation ditches with your foot as in a vegetable garden. 11 Rather, the land you will soon take over is a land of hills and valleys with plenty of rain—12 a land that the LORD your God cares for. He watches over it through each season of the year!

13 "If you carefully obey all the commands I am giving you today, and if you love the LORD your God and serve him with all your heart and soul, 14 then he will send the rains in their proper seasons—the early and late rains—so you can bring in your harvests of grain, new wine, and olive oil. 15 He will give you lush pastureland for your livestock, and you yourselves will have all you want to eat.

16 "But be careful. Don't let your heart be deceived so that you turn away from the LORD and serve and worship other gods. 17 If you do, the LORD's anger will burn against you. He will shut up the sky and hold back the rain, and the ground will fail to produce its harvests. Then you will quickly die in that good land the LORD is giving you.

18 "So commit yourselves wholeheartedly to these words of mine. Tie them to your hands and wear them on your forehead as reminders. 19 Teach them to your children. Talk about them when you are at home and when you are on the road, when you are going to bed and when you are getting up. 20 Write them on the doorposts of your house and on your gates, 21 so that as long as the sky remains above the earth, you and your children may flourish in the land the LORD swore to give your ancestors.

22 "Be careful to obey all these commands I am giving you. Show love to the LORD your God by walking in his ways and holding tightly to him. 23 Then the LORD will drive out all the nations ahead of you, though they are much greater and stronger than you, and you will take over their land. 24 Wherever you set foot, that land will be yours. Your frontiers will stretch from the wilderness in the south to Lebanon in the north, and from the Euphrates River in the east to the Mediterranean Sea in the west.* 25 No one will be able to stand against you, for the LORD your God will cause the people to fear and dread you, as he promised, wherever you go in the whole land.

26 "Look, today I am giving you the choice between a blessing and a curse! 27 You will be blessed if you obey the commands of the LORD your God that I am giving you today. 28 But you will be cursed if you reject the commands of the LORD your God and turn away from him and worship gods you have not known before.

29 "When the LORD your God brings you into the land and helps you take possession of it, you must pronounce the blessing at Mount Gerizim and the curse at Mount Ebal. 30 (These two mountains are west of the Jordan River in the land of the Canaanites who live in the Jordan Valley,* near the town of Gilgal, not far from the oaks of Moreh.) 31 For you are about to cross the Jordan River to take over the land the LORD your God is giving you. When you take that land and are living in it, 32 you must be careful to obey all the decrees and regulations I am giving you today.

12 The LORD's Chosen Place for Worship

"These are the decrees and regulations you must be careful to obey when you live in the land that the LORD, the God of your ancestors, is giving you. You must obey them as long as you live.

2 "When you drive out the nations that live there, you must destroy all the places where they worship their gods—high on the mountains, up on the hills, and under every green tree. 3 Break down their altars

---

11:24 Hebrew to the western sea.   11:30 Hebrew the Arabah.

and smash their sacred pillars. Burn their Asherah poles and cut down their carved idols. Completely erase the names of their gods!

⁴"Do not worship the LORD your God in the way these pagan peoples worship their gods. ⁵Rather, you must seek the LORD your God at the place of worship he himself will choose from among all the tribes— the place where his name will be honored. ⁶There you will bring your burnt offerings, your sacrifices, your tithes, your sacred offerings, your offerings to fulfill a vow, your voluntary offerings, and your offerings of the firstborn animals of your herds and flocks. ⁷There you and your families will feast in the presence of the LORD your God, and you will rejoice in all you have accomplished because the LORD your God has blessed you.

⁸"Your pattern of worship will change. Today all of you are doing as you please, ⁹because you have not yet arrived at the place of rest, the land the LORD your God is giving you as your special possession. ¹⁰But you will soon cross the Jordan River and live in the land the LORD your God is giving you. When he gives you rest from all your enemies and you're living safely in the land, ¹¹you must bring everything I command you—your burnt offerings, your sacrifices, your tithes, your sacred offerings, and your offerings to fulfill a vow—to the designated place of worship, the place the LORD your God chooses for his name to be honored.

¹²"You must celebrate there in the presence of the LORD your God with your sons and daughters and all your servants. And remember to include the Levites who live in your towns, for they will receive no allotment of land among you. ¹³Be careful not to sacrifice your burnt offerings just anywhere you like. ¹⁴You may do so only at the place the LORD will choose within one of your tribal territories. There you must offer your burnt offerings and do everything I command you.

¹⁵"But you may butcher your animals and eat their meat in any town whenever you want. You may freely eat the animals with which the LORD your God blesses you. All of you, whether ceremonially clean or unclean, may eat that meat, just as you now eat gazelle and deer. ¹⁶But you must not consume the blood. You must pour it out on the ground like water.

¹⁷"But you may not eat your offerings in your hometown—neither the tithe of your grain and new wine and olive oil, nor the firstborn of your flocks and herds, nor any offering to fulfill a vow, nor your voluntary offerings, nor your sacred offerings. ¹⁸You must eat these in the presence of the LORD your God at the place he will choose. Eat them there with your children, your servants, and the Levites who live in your towns, celebrating in the presence of the LORD your God in all you do. ¹⁹And be very careful never to neglect the Levites as long as you live in your land.

²⁰"When the LORD your God expands your territory as he has promised, and you have the urge to eat meat, you may freely eat meat whenever you want. ²¹It might happen that the designated place of worship— the place the LORD your God chooses for his name to be honored—is a long way from your home. If so, you may butcher any of the cattle, sheep, or goats the LORD has given you, and you may freely eat the meat in your hometown, as I have commanded you. ²²Anyone, whether ceremonially clean or unclean, may eat that meat, just as you do now with gazelle and deer. ²³But never consume the blood, for the blood is the life, and you must not consume the lifeblood with the meat. ²⁴Instead, pour out the blood on the ground like water. ²⁵Do not consume the blood, so that all may go well with you and your children after you, because you will be doing what pleases the LORD.

²⁶"Take your sacred gifts and your offerings given to fulfill a vow to the place the LORD chooses. ²⁷You must offer the meat and blood of your burnt offerings on the altar of the LORD your God. The blood of your other sacrifices must be poured out on the altar of the LORD your God, but you may eat the meat. ²⁸Be careful to obey all my commands, so that all will go well with you and your children after you, because you will be doing what is good and pleasing to the LORD your God.

²⁹"When the LORD your God goes ahead

of you and destroys the nations and you drive them out and live in their land, ³⁰do not fall into the trap of following their customs and worshiping their gods. Do not inquire about their gods, saying, 'How do these nations worship their gods? I want to follow their example.' ³¹You must not worship the LORD your God the way the other nations worship their gods, for they perform for their gods every detestable act that the LORD hates. They even burn their sons and daughters as sacrifices to their gods.

³²*"So be careful to obey all the commands I give you. You must not add anything to them or subtract anything from them.

13 A Warning against Idolatry

¹*"Suppose there are prophets among you or those who dream dreams about the future, and they promise you signs or miracles, ²and the predicted signs or miracles occur. If they then say, 'Come, let us worship other gods'—gods you have not known before—³do not listen to them. The LORD your God is testing you to see if you truly love him with all your heart and soul. ⁴Serve only the LORD your God and fear him alone. Obey his commands, listen to his voice, and cling to him. ⁵The false prophets or visionaries who try to lead you astray must be put to death, for they encourage rebellion against the LORD your God, who redeemed you from slavery and brought you out of the land of Egypt. Since they try to lead you astray from the way the LORD your God commanded you to live, you must put them to death. In this way you will purge the evil from among you.

⁶"Suppose someone secretly entices you—even your brother, your son or daughter, your beloved wife, or your closest friend—and says, 'Let us go worship other gods'—gods that neither you nor your ancestors have known. ⁷They might suggest that you worship the gods of peoples who live nearby or who come from the ends of the earth. ⁸But do not give in or listen. Have no pity, and do not spare or protect them. ⁹You must put them to death! Strike

the first blow yourself, and then all the people must join in. ¹⁰Stone the guilty ones to death because they have tried to draw you away from the LORD your God, who rescued you from the land of Egypt, the place of slavery. ¹¹Then all Israel will hear about it and be afraid, and no one will act so wickedly again.

¹²"When you begin living in the towns the LORD your God is giving you, you may hear ¹³that scoundrels among you are leading their fellow citizens astray by saying, 'Let us go worship other gods'—gods you have not known before. ¹⁴In such cases, you must examine the facts carefully. If you find that the report is true and such a detestable act has been committed among you, ¹⁵you must attack that town and completely destroy* all its inhabitants, as well as all the livestock. ¹⁶Then you must pile all the plunder in the middle of the open square and burn it. Burn the entire town as a burnt offering to the LORD your God. That town must remain a ruin forever; it may never be rebuilt. ¹⁷Keep none of the plunder that has been set apart for destruction. Then the LORD will turn from his fierce anger and be merciful to you. He will have compassion on you and make you a large nation, just as he swore to your ancestors.

¹⁸"The LORD your God will be merciful only if you listen to his voice and keep all his commands that I am giving you today, doing what pleases him.

14 Ceremonially Clean and Unclean Animals

"Since you are the people of the LORD your God, never cut yourselves or shave the hair above your foreheads in mourning for the dead. ²You have been set apart as holy to the LORD your God, and he has chosen you from all the nations of the earth to be his own special treasure.

³"You must not eat any detestable animals that are ceremonially unclean. ⁴These are the animals* you may eat: the ox, the sheep, the goat, ⁵the deer, the gazelle, the roe deer, the wild goat, the addax, the antelope, and the mountain sheep.

12:32 Verse 12:32 is numbered 13:1 in Hebrew text. **13:1** Verses 13:1-18 are numbered 13:2-19 in Hebrew text. **13:15** The Hebrew term used here refers to the complete consecration of things or people to the LORD, either by destroying them or by giving them as an offering; similarly in 13:17. **14:4** The identification of some of the animals and birds listed in this chapter is uncertain.

6 "You may eat any animal that has completely split hooves and chews the cud, 7 but if the animal doesn't have both, it may not be eaten. So you may not eat the camel, the hare, or the hyrax.* They chew the cud but do not have split hooves, so they are ceremonially unclean for you. 8 And you may not eat the pig. It has split hooves but does not chew the cud, so it is ceremonially unclean for you. You may not eat the meat of these animals or even touch their carcasses.

9 "Of all the marine animals, you may eat whatever has both fins and scales. 10 You may not, however, eat marine animals that do not have both fins and scales. They are ceremonially unclean for you.

11 "You may eat any bird that is ceremonially clean. 12 These are the birds you may not eat: the griffon vulture, the bearded vulture, the black vulture, 13 the kite, the falcon, buzzards of all kinds, 14 ravens of all kinds, 15 the eagle owl, the short-eared owl, the seagull, hawks of all kinds, 16 the little owl, the great owl, the barn owl, 17 the desert owl, the Egyptian vulture, the cormorant, 18 the stork, herons of all kinds, the hoopoe, and the bat.

19 "All winged insects that walk along the ground are ceremonially unclean for you and may not be eaten. 20 But you may eat any winged bird or insect that is ceremonially clean.

21 "You must not eat anything that has died a natural death. You may give it to a foreigner living in your town, or you may sell it to a stranger. But do not eat it yourselves, for you are set apart as holy to the LORD your God.

"You must not cook a young goat in its mother's milk.

The Giving of Tithes

22 "You must set aside a tithe of your crops— one-tenth of all the crops you harvest each year. 23 Bring this tithe to the designated place of worship—the place the LORD your God chooses for his name to be honored— and eat it there in his presence. This applies to your tithes of grain, new wine, olive oil, and the firstborn males of your flocks and herds. Doing this will teach you always to fear the LORD your God.

24 "Now when the LORD your God blesses you with a good harvest, the place of worship he chooses for his name to be honored might be too far for you to bring the tithe. 25 If so, you may sell the tithe portion of your crops and herds, put the money in a pouch, and go to the place the LORD your God has chosen. 26 When you arrive, you may use the money to buy any kind of food you want— cattle, sheep, goats, wine, or other alcoholic drink. Then feast there in the presence of the LORD your God and celebrate with your household. 27 And do not neglect the Levites in your town, for they will receive no allotment of land among you.

28 "At the end of every third year, bring the entire tithe of that year's harvest and store it in the nearest town. 29 Give it to the Levites, who will receive no allotment of land among you, as well as to the foreigners living among you, the orphans, and the widows in your towns, so they can eat and be satisfied. Then the LORD your God will bless you in all your work.

15 Release for Debtors

"At the end of every seventh year you must cancel the debts of everyone who owes you money. 2 This is how it must be done. Everyone must cancel the loans they have made to their fellow Israelites. They must not demand payment from their neighbors or relatives, for the LORD's time of release has arrived. 3 This release from debt, however, applies only to your fellow Israelites— not to the foreigners living among you.

4 "There should be no poor among you, for the LORD your God will greatly bless you in the land he is giving you as a special possession. 5 You will receive this blessing if you are careful to obey all the commands of the LORD your God that I am giving you today. 6 The LORD your God will bless you as he has promised. You will lend money to many nations but will never need to borrow. You will rule many nations, but they will not rule over you.

7 "But if there are any poor Israelites in your towns when you arrive in the land the LORD your God is giving you, do not be hard-hearted or tightfisted toward them. 8 Instead, be generous and lend them

14:7 Or coney, or rock badger.

whatever they need. ⁹Do not be mean-spirited and refuse someone a loan because the year for canceling debts is close at hand. If you refuse to make the loan and the needy person cries out to the LORD, you will be considered guilty of sin. ¹⁰Give generously to the poor, not grudgingly, for the LORD your God will bless you in everything you do. ¹¹There will always be some in the land who are poor. That is why I am commanding you to share freely with the poor and with other Israelites in need.

Release for Hebrew Slaves

¹²"If a fellow Hebrew sells himself or herself to be your servant* and serves you for six years, in the seventh year you must set that servant free.

¹³"When you release a male servant, do not send him away empty-handed. ¹⁴Give him a generous farewell gift from your flock, your threshing floor, and your winepress. Share with him some of the bounty with which the LORD your God has blessed you. ¹⁵Remember that you were once slaves in the land of Egypt and the LORD your God redeemed you! That is why I am giving you this command.

¹⁶"But suppose your servant says, 'I will not leave you,' because he loves you and your family, and he has done well with you. ¹⁷In that case, take an awl and push it through his earlobe into the door. After that, he will be your servant for life. And do the same for your female servants.

¹⁸"You must not consider it a hardship when you release your servants. Remember that for six years they have given you services worth double the wages of hired workers, and the LORD your God will bless you in all you do.

Sacrificing Firstborn Male Animals

¹⁹"You must set aside for the LORD your God all the firstborn males from your flocks and herds. Do not use the firstborn of your herds to work your fields, and do not shear the firstborn of your flocks. ²⁰Instead, you and your family must eat these animals in the presence of the LORD your God each year at the place he chooses. ²¹But if this firstborn animal has any defect, such as lameness or blindness, or if anything else is wrong with it, you must not sacrifice it to the LORD your God. ²²Instead, use it for food for your family in your hometown. Anyone, whether ceremonially clean or unclean, may eat it, just as anyone may eat a gazelle or deer. ²³But you must not consume the blood. You must pour it out on the ground like water.

16 Passover and the Festival of Unleavened Bread

"In honor of the LORD your God, celebrate the Passover each year in the early spring, in the month of Abib,* for that was the month in which the LORD your God brought you out of Egypt by night. ²Your Passover sacrifice may be from either the flock or the herd, and it must be sacrificed to the LORD your God at the designated place of worship—the place he chooses for his name to be honored. ³Eat it with bread made without yeast. For seven days the bread you eat must be made without yeast, as when you escaped from Egypt in such a hurry. Eat this bread—the bread of suffering—so that as long as you live you will remember the day you departed from Egypt. ⁴Let no yeast be found in any house throughout your land for those seven days. And when you sacrifice the Passover lamb on the evening of the first day, do not let any of the meat remain until the next morning.

⁵"You may not sacrifice the Passover in just any of the towns that the LORD your God is giving you. ⁶You must offer it only at the designated place of worship—the place the LORD your God chooses for his name to be honored. Sacrifice it there in the evening as the sun goes down on the anniversary of your exodus from Egypt. ⁷Roast the lamb and eat it in the place the LORD your God chooses. Then you may go back to your tents the next morning. ⁸For the next six days you may not eat any bread made with yeast. On the seventh day proclaim another holy day in honor of the LORD your God, and no work may be done on that day.

15:12 Or *If a Hebrew man or woman is sold to you.* **16:1** Hebrew *Observe the month of Abib, and keep the Passover unto the LORD your God.* Abib, the first month of the ancient Hebrew lunar calendar, usually occurs within the months of March and April.

The Festival of Harvest

[9] "Count off seven weeks from when you first begin to cut the grain at the time of harvest. [10] Then celebrate the Festival of Harvest* to honor the LORD your God. Bring him a voluntary offering in proportion to the blessings you have received from him. [11] This is a time to celebrate before the LORD your God at the designated place of worship he will choose for his name to be honored. Celebrate with your sons and daughters, your male and female servants, the Levites from your towns, and the foreigners, orphans, and widows who live among you. [12] Remember that you were once slaves in Egypt, so be careful to obey all these decrees.

The Festival of Shelters

[13] "You must observe the Festival of Shelters* for seven days at the end of the harvest season, after the grain has been threshed and the grapes have been pressed. [14] This festival will be a happy time of celebrating with your sons and daughters, your male and female servants, and the Levites, foreigners, orphans, and widows from your towns. [15] For seven days you must celebrate this festival to honor the LORD your God at the place he chooses, for it is he who blesses you with bountiful harvests and gives you success in all your work. This festival will be a time of great joy for all.

[16] "Each year every man in Israel must celebrate these three festivals: the Festival of Unleavened Bread, the Festival of Harvest, and the Festival of Shelters. On each of these occasions, all men must appear before the LORD your God at the place he chooses, but they must not appear before the LORD without a gift for him. [17] All must give as they are able, according to the blessings given to them by the LORD your God.

Justice for the People

[18] "Appoint judges and officials for yourselves from each of your tribes in all the towns the LORD your God is giving you. They must judge the people fairly. [19] You must never twist justice or show partiality. Never accept a bribe, for bribes blind the eyes of the wise and corrupt the decisions of the godly. [20] Let true justice prevail, so you may live and occupy the land that the LORD your God is giving you.

[21] "You must never set up a wooden Asherah pole beside the altar you build for the LORD your God. [22] And never set up sacred pillars for worship, for the LORD your God hates them.

17 "Never sacrifice sick or defective cattle, sheep, or goats to the LORD your God, for he detests such gifts.

[2] "When you begin living in the towns the LORD your God is giving you, a man or woman among you might do evil in the sight of the LORD your God and violate the covenant. [3] For instance, they might serve other gods or worship the sun, the moon, or any of the stars—the forces of heaven—which I have strictly forbidden. [4] When you hear about it, investigate the matter thoroughly. If it is true that this detestable thing has been done in Israel, [5] then the man or woman who has committed such an evil act must be taken to the gates of the town and stoned to death. [6] But never put a person to death on the testimony of only one witness. There must always be two or three witnesses. [7] The witnesses must throw the first stones, and then all the people may join in. In this way, you will purge the evil from among you.

[8] "Suppose a case arises in a local court that is too hard for you to decide—for instance, whether someone is guilty of murder or only of manslaughter, or a difficult lawsuit, or a case involving different kinds of assault. Take such legal cases to the place the LORD your God will choose, [9] and present them to the Levitical priests or the judge on duty at that time. They will hear the case and declare the verdict. [10] You must carry out the verdict they announce and the sentence they prescribe at the place the LORD chooses. You must do exactly what they say. [11] After they have interpreted the law and declared their verdict, the sentence they impose must be fully executed; do not

---

16:10 Hebrew *Festival of Weeks;* also in 16:16. This was later called the Festival of Pentecost (see Acts 2:1). It is celebrated today as Shavuot (or Shabuoth). **16:13** Or *Festival of Booths,* or *Festival of Tabernacles;* also in 16:16. This was earlier called the Festival of the Final Harvest or Festival of Ingathering (see Exod 23:16b). It is celebrated today as Sukkot (or Succoth).

Service

The Significance of All We Do

DEUTERONOMY 17:1-13

Throughout my life I've come to realize that serving the Lord is often full of twists and turns and sometimes even turbulence—and that how we serve him is multidimensional.

After seminary I served on the staff of a church in Texas in a variety of ministries I loved. I worked with teenage girls, led a weekly Bible study, was involved with the music, and spent a lot of time in one-on-one ministry with young singles. Then my marriage transplanted me to Pennsylvania where, to support my husband's academic studies, I switched from ministry to hospital administration and eventually worked my way into management, computers, and software development. Ministry opportunities were scarce. Much as I enjoyed what I was doing, it felt like a detour—as though I'd stepped away from my service to God.

When our daughter was three, we uprooted again and moved to Oxford, England, for a four-year stint while my husband pursued doctoral studies and I supported our family with my software development business. I was in the middle of what turned out to be a thirteen-year hiatus from official ministry. My energies centered on family concerns and working with my clients. I didn't have much time or energy left for anything else, and I still remember a sense of guilt that I wasn't *really* serving the Lord.

But during those years, the words of a friend freed me to think differently about what constitutes service to God. "Sometimes your family is your ministry." Her words validated the significance of everything I was doing at that time. Even though I wasn't leading a Bible study or volunteering at our church, what I was doing was indeed serving God. It was a significant segue for me between official, recognized ways of service and a much larger vision of what serving God entails. In fact, her comment wasn't nearly expansive enough to encompass the *vast possibilities* God has in mind when he entrusts us with gifts and opportunities and calls us to serve him.

The call to serve God doesn't begin with Jesus issuing the Great Commission (Matthew 28:18-20). It begins at the beginning, when God creates his image-bearers—male and female (Genesis 1-2). That single act elevates *everything we do* to the lofty level of service for God. As I wrote in my book *Half the Church,* creating us as his image-bearers "places us at the center of what God is doing in the world—not as spectators, but as kingdom agents and as leaders with responsibility for what is happening around us."

Implicit in our identity as image-bearers is the call to represent him—to be his eyes, ears, hands, voice. God is counting on us to pay attention, to hear the cries of the hurting and the oppressed, to notice when things aren't the way he wants them to be, and to act on his behalf in putting things right.

Bottom line, it means anywhere we go, anything we do holds the possibility of service to God—from creating culture and stewarding the earth's resources to freeing the captives, feeding the hungry, relieving the oppressed, going to work, or rocking your baby to sleep at night. According to Jesus, the slightest, most mundane, behind-the-scenes act of kindness doesn't go unnoticed, even though the world may not detect anything significant going on. He said, "If anyone gives you even a cup of water because you belong to the Messiah, I tell you the truth, that person will surely be rewarded" (Mark 9:41). The potential for ministry is limitless.

That notion proved true for an elderly friend when she was admitted to an extended-care facility. After a life of active ministry and service in foreign missions, she lamented to me, "I thought my life was over when I came here." She felt she had been put on the shelf and was waiting to die. But then it dawned on her that, although she was no longer in a foreign land, God still had kingdom work for her to do. "I looked around and realized there is a mission field here no one is doing anything about." My dear friend lived and died *serving the Lord.*

—*Carolyn Custis James*

For more on service, see reading at Joshua 2.

modify it in any way. [12] Anyone arrogant enough to reject the verdict of the judge or of the priest who represents the LORD your God must die. In this way you will purge the evil from Israel. [13] Then everyone else will hear about it and be afraid to act so arrogantly.

Guidelines for a King

[14] "You are about to enter the land the LORD your God is giving you. When you take it over and settle there, you may think, 'We should select a king to rule over us like the other nations around us.' [15] If this happens, be sure to select as king the man the LORD your God chooses. You must appoint a fellow Israelite; he may not be a foreigner.

[16] "The king must not build up a large stable of horses for himself or send his people to Egypt to buy horses, for the LORD has told you, 'You must never return to Egypt.' [17] The king must not take many wives for himself, because they will turn his heart away from the LORD. And he must not accumulate large amounts of wealth in silver and gold for himself.

[18] "When he sits on the throne as king, he must copy for himself this body of instruction on a scroll in the presence of the Levitical priests. [19] He must always keep that copy with him and read it daily as long as he lives. That way he will learn to fear the LORD his God by obeying all the terms of these instructions and decrees. [20] This regular reading will prevent him from becoming proud and acting as if he is above his fellow citizens. It will also prevent him from turning away from these commands in the smallest way. And it will ensure that he and his descendants will reign for many generations in Israel.

18 Gifts for the Priests and Levites

"Remember that the Levitical priests—that is, the whole of the tribe of Levi—will receive no allotment of land among the other tribes in Israel. Instead, the priests and Levites will eat from the special gifts given to the LORD, for that is their share. [2] They will have no land of their own among the Israelites. The LORD himself is their special possession, just as he promised them.

[3] "These are the parts the priests may claim as their share from the cattle, sheep, and goats that the people bring as offerings: the shoulder, the cheeks, and the stomach. [4] You must also give to the priests the first share of the grain, the new wine, the olive oil, and the wool at shearing time. [5] For the LORD your God chose the tribe of Levi out of all your tribes to minister in the LORD's name forever.

[6] "Suppose a Levite chooses to move from his town in Israel, wherever he is living, to the place the LORD chooses for worship. [7] He may minister there in the name of the LORD his God, just like all his fellow Levites who are serving the LORD there. [8] He may eat his share of the sacrifices and offerings, even if he also receives support from his family.

A Call to Holy Living

[9] "When you enter the land the LORD your God is giving you, be very careful not to imitate the detestable customs of the nations living there. [10] For example, never sacrifice your son or daughter as a burnt offering.* And do not let your people practice fortune-telling, or use sorcery, or interpret omens, or engage in witchcraft, [11] or cast spells, or function as mediums or psychics, or call forth the spirits of the dead. [12] Anyone who does these things is detestable to the LORD. It is because the other nations have done these detestable things that the LORD your God will drive them out ahead of you. [13] But you must be blameless before the LORD your God. [14] The nations you are about to displace consult sorcerers and fortune-tellers, but the LORD your God forbids you to do such things."

True and False Prophets

[15] Moses continued, "The LORD your God will raise up for you a prophet like me from among your fellow Israelites. You must listen to him. [16] For this is what you yourselves requested of the LORD your God when you were assembled at Mount Sinai.* You said, 'Don't let us hear the voice of the LORD our

---

18:10 Or *never make your son or daughter pass through the fire.*   18:16 Hebrew *Horeb,* another name for Sinai.

God anymore or see this blazing fire, for we will die.'

¹⁷"Then the LORD said to me, 'What they have said is right. ¹⁸I will raise up a prophet like you from among their fellow Israelites. I will put my words in his mouth, and he will tell the people everything I command him. ¹⁹I will personally deal with anyone who will not listen to the messages the prophet proclaims on my behalf. ²⁰But any prophet who falsely claims to speak in my name or who speaks in the name of another god must die.'

²¹"But you may wonder, 'How will we know whether or not a prophecy is from the LORD?' ²²If the prophet speaks in the LORD's name but his prediction does not happen or come true, you will know that the LORD did not give that message. That prophet has spoken without my authority and need not be feared.

19 Cities of Refuge

"When the LORD your God destroys the nations whose land he is giving you, you will take over their land and settle in their towns and homes. ²Then you must set apart three cities of refuge in the land the LORD your God is giving you. ³Survey the territory,* and divide the land the LORD your God is giving you into three districts, with one of these cities in each district. Then anyone who has killed someone can flee to one of the cities of refuge for safety.

⁴"If someone kills another person unintentionally, without previous hostility, the slayer may flee to any of these cities to live in safety. ⁵For example, suppose someone goes into the forest with a neighbor to cut wood. And suppose one of them swings an ax to chop down a tree, and the ax head flies off the handle, killing the other person. In such cases, the slayer may flee to one of the cities of refuge to live in safety.

⁶"If the distance to the nearest city of refuge is too far, an enraged avenger might be able to chase down and kill the person who caused the death. Then the slayer would die unfairly, since he had never shown hostility toward the person who died. ⁷That is why I am commanding you to set aside three cities of refuge.

⁸"And if the LORD your God enlarges your territory, as he swore to your ancestors, and gives you all the land he promised them, ⁹you must designate three additional cities of refuge. (He will give you this land if you are careful to obey all the commands I have given you—if you always love the LORD your God and walk in his ways.) ¹⁰That way you will prevent the death of innocent people in the land the LORD your God is giving you as your special possession. You will not be held responsible for the death of innocent people.

¹¹"But suppose someone is hostile toward a neighbor and deliberately ambushes and murders him and then flees to one of the cities of refuge. ¹²In that case, the elders of the murderer's hometown must send agents to the city of refuge to bring him back and hand him over to the dead person's avenger to be put to death. ¹³Do not feel sorry for that murderer! Purge from Israel the guilt of murdering innocent people; then all will go well with you.

Concern for Justice

¹⁴"When you arrive in the land the LORD your God is giving you as your special possession, you must never steal anyone's land by moving the boundary markers your ancestors set up to mark their property.

¹⁵"You must not convict anyone of a crime on the testimony of only one witness. The facts of the case must be established by the testimony of two or three witnesses.

¹⁶"If a malicious witness comes forward and accuses someone of a crime, ¹⁷then both the accuser and accused must appear before the LORD by coming to the priests and judges in office at that time. ¹⁸The judges must investigate the case thoroughly. If the accuser has brought false charges against his fellow Israelite, ¹⁹you must impose on the accuser the sentence he intended for the other person. In this way, you will purge such evil from among you. ²⁰Then the rest of the people will hear about it and be afraid to do such an evil thing. ²¹You must show no pity for the guilty! Your rule should be life for life, eye for eye, tooth for tooth, hand for hand, foot for foot.

19:3 Or *Keep the roads in good repair.*

20 Regulations concerning War

"When you go out to fight your enemies and you face horses and chariots and an army greater than your own, do not be afraid. The LORD your God, who brought you out of the land of Egypt, is with you! ²When you prepare for battle, the priest must come forward to speak to the troops. ³He will say to them, 'Listen to me, all you men of Israel! Do not be afraid as you go out to fight your enemies today! Do not lose heart or panic or tremble before them. ⁴For the LORD your God is going with you! He will fight for you against your enemies, and he will give you victory!'

⁵"Then the officers of the army must address the troops and say, 'Has anyone here just built a new house but not yet dedicated it? If so, you may go home! You might be killed in the battle, and someone else would dedicate your house. ⁶Has anyone here just planted a vineyard but not yet eaten any of its fruit? If so, you may go home! You might die in battle, and someone else would eat the first fruit. ⁷Has anyone here just become engaged to a woman but not yet married her? Well, you may go home and get married! You might die in the battle, and someone else would marry her.'

⁸"Then the officers will also say, 'Is anyone here afraid or worried? If you are, you may go home before you frighten anyone else.' ⁹When the officers have finished speaking to their troops, they will appoint the unit commanders.

¹⁰"As you approach a town to attack it, you must first offer its people terms for peace. ¹¹If they accept your terms and open the gates to you, then all the people inside will serve you in forced labor. ¹²But if they refuse to make peace and prepare to fight, you must attack the town. ¹³When the LORD your God hands the town over to you, use your swords to kill every man in the town. ¹⁴But you may keep for yourselves all the women, children, livestock, and other plunder. You may enjoy the plunder from your enemies that the LORD your God has given you.

¹⁵"But these instructions apply only to distant towns, not to the towns of the nations in the land you will enter. ¹⁶In those towns that the LORD your God is giving you as a special possession, destroy every living thing. ¹⁷You must completely destroy* the Hittites, Amorites, Canaanites, Perizzites, Hivites, and Jebusites, just as the LORD your God has commanded you. ¹⁸This will prevent the people of the land from teaching you to imitate their detestable customs in the worship of their gods, which would cause you to sin deeply against the LORD your God.

¹⁹"When you are attacking a town and the war drags on, you must not cut down the trees with your axes. You may eat the fruit, but do not cut down the trees. Are the trees your enemies, that you should attack them? ²⁰You may only cut down trees that you know are not valuable for food. Use them to make the equipment you need to attack the enemy town until it falls.

21 Cleansing for Unsolved Murder

"When you are in the land the LORD your God is giving you, someone may be found murdered in a field, and you don't know who committed the murder. ²In such a case, your elders and judges must measure the distance from the site of the crime to the nearby towns. ³When the nearest town has been determined, that town's elders must select from the herd a young cow that has never been trained or yoked to a plow. ⁴They must lead it down to a valley that has not been plowed or planted and that has a stream running through it. There in the valley they must break the young cow's neck. ⁵Then the Levitical priests must step forward, for the LORD your God has chosen them to minister before him and to pronounce blessings in the LORD's name. They are to decide all legal and criminal cases.

⁶"The elders of the town must wash their hands over the young cow whose neck was broken. ⁷Then they must say, 'Our hands did not shed this person's blood, nor did we see it happen. ⁸O LORD, forgive your people Israel whom you have redeemed. Do not charge your people with the guilt of murdering an innocent person.' Then they will be absolved of the guilt of this person's

---

20:17 The Hebrew term used here refers to the complete consecration of things or people to the LORD, either by destroying them or by giving them as an offering.

blood. ⁹By following these instructions, you will do what is right in the LORD's sight and will cleanse the guilt of murder from your community.

Marriage to a Captive Woman

¹⁰"Suppose you go out to war against your enemies and the LORD your God hands them over to you, and you take some of them as captives. ¹¹And suppose you see among the captives a beautiful woman, and you are attracted to her and want to marry her. ¹²If this happens, you may take her to your home, where she must shave her head, cut her nails, ¹³and change the clothes she was wearing when she was captured. She will stay in your home, but let her mourn for her father and mother for a full month. Then you may marry her, and you will be her husband and she will be your wife. ¹⁴But if you marry her and she does not please you, you must let her go free. You may not sell her or treat her as a slave, for you have humiliated her.

Rights of the Firstborn

¹⁵"Suppose a man has two wives, but he loves one and not the other, and both have given him sons. And suppose the firstborn son is the son of the wife he does not love. ¹⁶When the man divides his inheritance, he may not give the larger inheritance to his younger son, the son of the wife he loves, as if he were the firstborn son. ¹⁷He must recognize the rights of his oldest son, the son of the wife he does not love, by giving him a double portion. He is the first son of his father's virility, and the rights of the first-born belong to him.

Dealing with a Rebellious Son

¹⁸"Suppose a man has a stubborn and rebellious son who will not obey his father or mother, even though they discipline him. ¹⁹In such a case, the father and mother must take the son to the elders as they hold court at the town gate. ²⁰The parents must say to the elders, 'This son of ours is stubborn and rebellious and refuses to obey. He is a glutton and a drunkard.' ²¹Then all the men of his town must stone him to death.

In this way, you will purge this evil from among you, and all Israel will hear about it and be afraid.

Various Regulations

²²"If someone has committed a crime worthy of death and is executed and hung on a tree,* ²³the body must not remain hanging from the tree overnight. You must bury the body that same day, for anyone who is hung* is cursed in the sight of God. In this way, you will prevent the defilement of the land the LORD your God is giving you as your special possession.

22 ¹"If you see your neighbor's ox or sheep or goat wandering away, don't ignore your responsibility.* Take it back to its owner. ²If its owner does not live nearby or you don't know who the owner is, take it to your place and keep it until the owner comes looking for it. Then you must return it. ³Do the same if you find your neighbor's donkey, clothing, or anything else your neighbor loses. Don't ignore your responsibility.

⁴"If you see that your neighbor's donkey or ox has collapsed on the road, do not look the other way. Go and help your neighbor get it back on its feet!

⁵"A woman must not put on men's clothing, and a man must not wear women's clothing. Anyone who does this is detestable in the sight of the LORD your God.

⁶"If you happen to find a bird's nest in a tree or on the ground, and there are young ones or eggs in it with the mother sitting in the nest, do not take the mother with the young. ⁷You may take the young, but let the mother go, so that you may prosper and enjoy a long life.

⁸"When you build a new house, you must build a railing around the edge of its flat roof. That way you will not be considered guilty of murder if someone falls from the roof.

⁹"You must not plant any other crop between the rows of your vineyard. If you do, you are forbidden to use either the grapes from the vineyard or the other crop.

¹⁰"You must not plow with an ox and a donkey harnessed together.

¹¹ "You must not wear clothing made of wool and linen woven together.

¹² "You must put four tassels on the hem of the cloak with which you cover yourself—on the front, back, and sides.

Regulations for Sexual Purity

¹³ "Suppose a man marries a woman, but after sleeping with her, he turns against her ¹⁴ and publicly accuses her of shameful conduct, saying, 'When I married this woman, I discovered she was not a virgin.' ¹⁵ Then the woman's father and mother must bring the proof of her virginity to the elders as they hold court at the town gate. ¹⁶ Her father must say to them, 'I gave my daughter to this man to be his wife, and now he has turned against her. ¹⁷ He has accused her of shameful conduct, saying, "I discovered that your daughter was not a virgin." But here is the proof of my daughter's virginity.' Then they must spread her bed sheet before the elders. ¹⁸ The elders must then take the man and punish him. ¹⁹ They must also fine him 100 pieces of silver,* which he must pay to the woman's father because he publicly accused a virgin of Israel of shameful conduct. The woman will then remain the man's wife, and he may never divorce her.

²⁰ "But suppose the man's accusations are true, and he can show that she was not a virgin. ²¹ The woman must be taken to the door of her father's home, and there the men of the town must stone her to death, for she has committed a disgraceful crime in Israel by being promiscuous while living in her parents' home. In this way, you will purge this evil from among you.

²² "If a man is discovered committing adultery, both he and the woman must die. In this way, you will purge Israel of such evil.

²³ "Suppose a man meets a young woman, a virgin who is engaged to be married, and he has sexual intercourse with her. If this happens within a town, ²⁴ you must take both of them to the gates of that town and stone them to death. The woman is guilty because she did not scream for help. The man must die because he violated another man's wife. In this way, you will purge this evil from among you.

²⁵ "But if the man meets the engaged woman out in the country, and he rapes her, then only the man must die. ²⁶ Do nothing to the young woman; she has committed no crime worthy of death. She is as innocent as a murder victim. ²⁷ Since the man raped her out in the country, it must be assumed that she screamed, but there was no one to rescue her.

²⁸ "Suppose a man has intercourse with a young woman who is a virgin but is not engaged to be married. If they are discovered, ²⁹ he must pay her father fifty pieces of silver.* Then he must marry the young woman because he violated her, and he may never divorce her as long as he lives.

³⁰* "A man must not marry his father's former wife, for this would violate his father.

23 Regulations concerning Worship

¹* "If a man's testicles are crushed or his penis is cut off, he may not be admitted to the assembly of the LORD.

² "If a person is illegitimate by birth, neither he nor his descendants for ten generations may be admitted to the assembly of the LORD.

³ "No Ammonite or Moabite or any of their descendants for ten generations may be admitted to the assembly of the LORD. ⁴ These nations did not welcome you with food and water when you came out of Egypt. Instead, they hired Balaam son of Beor from Pethor in distant Aram-naharaim to curse you. ⁵ But the LORD your God refused to listen to Balaam. He turned the intended curse into a blessing because the LORD your God loves you. ⁶ As long as you live, you must never promote the welfare and prosperity of the Ammonites or Moabites.

⁷ "Do not detest the Edomites or the Egyptians, because the Edomites are your relatives and you lived as foreigners among the Egyptians. ⁸ The third generation of Edomites and Egyptians may enter the assembly of the LORD.

Miscellaneous Regulations

⁹ "When you go to war against your enemies, be sure to stay away from anything that is impure.

¹⁰ "Any man who becomes ceremonially

22:19 Hebrew *100 shekels of silver*, about 2.5 pounds or 1.1 kilograms in weight.   **22:29** Hebrew *50 shekels of silver*, about 1.25 pounds or 570 grams in weight.   **22:30** Verse 22:30 is numbered 23:1 in Hebrew text.   **23:1** Verses 23:1-25 are numbered 23:2-26 in Hebrew text.

defiled because of a nocturnal emission must leave the camp and stay away all day. ¹¹Toward evening he must bathe himself, and at sunset he may return to the camp.

¹²"You must have a designated area outside the camp where you can go to relieve yourself. ¹³Each of you must have a spade as part of your equipment. Whenever you relieve yourself, dig a hole with the spade and cover the excrement. ¹⁴The camp must be holy, for the LORD your God moves around in your camp to protect you and to defeat your enemies. He must not see any shameful thing among you, or he will turn away from you.

¹⁵"If slaves should escape from their masters and take refuge with you, you must not hand them over to their masters. ¹⁶Let them live among you in any town they choose, and do not oppress them.

¹⁷"No Israelite, whether man or woman, may become a temple prostitute. ¹⁸When you are bringing an offering to fulfill a vow, you must not bring to the house of the LORD your God any offering from the earnings of a prostitute, whether a man* or a woman, for both are detestable to the LORD your God.

¹⁹"Do not charge interest on the loans you make to a fellow Israelite, whether you loan money, or food, or anything else. ²⁰You may charge interest to foreigners, but you may not charge interest to Israelites, so that the LORD your God may bless you in everything you do in the land you are about to enter and occupy.

²¹"When you make a vow to the LORD your God, be prompt in fulfilling whatever you promised him. For the LORD your God demands that you promptly fulfill all your vows, or you will be guilty of sin. ²²However, it is not a sin to refrain from making a vow. ²³But once you have voluntarily made a vow, be careful to fulfill your promise to the LORD your God.

²⁴"When you enter your neighbor's vineyard, you may eat your fill of grapes, but you must not carry any away in a basket. ²⁵And when you enter your neighbor's field of grain, you may pluck the heads of grain with your hand, but you must not harvest it with a sickle.

24 "Suppose a man marries a woman but she does not please him. Having discovered something wrong with her, he writes her a letter of divorce, hands it to her, and sends her away from his house. ²When she leaves his house, she is free to marry another man. ³But if the second husband also turns against her and divorces her, or if he dies, ⁴the first husband may not marry her again, for she has been defiled. That would be detestable to the LORD. You must not bring guilt upon the land the LORD your God is giving you as a special possession.

⁵"A newly married man must not be drafted into the army or be given any other official responsibilities. He must be free to spend one year at home, bringing happiness to the wife he has married.

⁶"It is wrong to take a set of millstones, or even just the upper millstone, as security for a loan, for the owner uses it to make a living.

⁷"If anyone kidnaps a fellow Israelite and treats him as a slave or sells him, the kidnapper must die. In this way, you will purge the evil from among you.

⁸"In all cases involving serious skin diseases,* be careful to follow the instructions of the Levitical priests; obey all the commands I have given them. ⁹Remember what the LORD your God did to Miriam as you were coming from Egypt.

¹⁰"If you lend anything to your neighbor, do not enter his house to pick up the item he is giving as security. ¹¹You must wait outside while he goes in and brings it out to you. ¹²If your neighbor is poor and gives you his cloak as security for a loan, do not keep the cloak overnight. ¹³Return the cloak to its owner by sunset so he can stay warm through the night and bless you, and the LORD your God will count you as righteous.

¹⁴"Never take advantage of poor and destitute laborers, whether they are fellow Israelites or foreigners living in your towns. ¹⁵You must pay them their wages each day before sunset because they are poor and are counting on it. If you don't, they might cry out to the LORD against you, and it would be counted against you as sin.

23:18 Hebrew *a dog.* **24:8** Traditionally rendered *leprosy.* The Hebrew word used here can describe various skin diseases.

Reflecting God's Love of Justice

DEUTERONOMY 24:17-21

God is the essence of justice: "He is the great God, the mighty and awesome God, who shows no partiality and cannot be bribed. He ensures that orphans and widows receive justice. He shows love to the foreigners living among you and gives them food and clothing" (Deuteronomy 10:17-18). God's sense of justice involves making sure that even the most typically overlooked members of society have everything they need and are being treated with love and dignity.

And God, from the beginning, has called his people to live justly. "You, too, must show love to foreigners," he commands (10:19). He created laws that would make his people distinct from the other nations: his people were to reflect his love of justice. From mandating a day of Sabbath so that laborers and servants won't be overworked (Deuteronomy 5:14), to instructing farmers not to glean the edges of their fields so that immigrants and the poor can have a source of food (Deuteronomy 24:19), God's desire is that his people join in on caring for the struggling in this world.

His desire is the same for us. God has shown us that our task is to act justly, love mercy, and to walk humbly in all God's ways (Micah 6:8). Orienting our lives to serve sacrificially the needs of others is to love justice as God does. From caring about the treatment of the workers who pick our produce or sew our clothing, to working to end the trafficking of women into sex-slavery, to fighting for struggling single mothers in our community, God invites us to help make things right in the world. God invites us to act justly.

—*Julie Clawson*

For more on justice, see reading at Nehemiah 5.

---

¹⁶"Parents must not be put to death for the sins of their children, nor children for the sins of their parents. Those deserving to die must be put to death for their own crimes.

¹⁷"True justice must be given to foreigners living among you and to orphans, and you must never accept a widow's garment as security for her debt. ¹⁸Always remember that you were slaves in Egypt and that the LORD your God redeemed you from your slavery. That is why I have given you this command.

¹⁹"When you are harvesting your crops and forget to bring in a bundle of grain from your field, don't go back to get it. Leave it for the foreigners, orphans, and widows. Then the LORD your God will bless you in all you do. ²⁰When you beat the olives from your olive trees, don't go over the boughs twice. Leave the remaining olives for the foreigners, orphans, and widows. ²¹When you gather the grapes in your vineyard, don't glean the vines after they are picked. Leave the remaining grapes for the foreigners, orphans, and widows. ²²Remember that you were slaves in the land of Egypt. That is why I am giving you this command.

25 "Suppose two people take a dispute to court, and the judges declare that one is right and the other is wrong. ²If the person in the wrong is sentenced to be flogged, the judge must command him to lie down and be beaten in his presence with the number of lashes appropriate to the crime. ³But never give more than forty lashes; more than forty lashes would publicly humiliate your neighbor.

⁴"You must not muzzle an ox to keep it from eating as it treads out the grain.

⁵"If two brothers are living together on the same property and one of them dies without a son, his widow may not be married to anyone from outside the family. Instead, her husband's brother should marry her and have intercourse with her to fulfill the duties of a brother-in-law. ⁶The first son she bears to him will be considered the son of the dead brother, so that his name will not be forgotten in Israel.

⁷"But if the man refuses to marry his brother's widow, she must go to the town gate and say to the elders assembled there, 'My husband's brother refuses to preserve his brother's name in Israel—he refuses to fulfill the duties of a brother-in-law by marrying me.' ⁸The elders of the town will then summon him and talk with him. If he still refuses and says, 'I don't want to marry her,' ⁹the widow must walk over to him in the presence of the elders, pull his sandal from his foot, and spit in his face. Then she must declare, 'This is what happens to a man who refuses to provide his brother with children.' ¹⁰Ever afterward in Israel his family will be referred to as 'the family of the man whose sandal was pulled off'!

¹¹"If two Israelite men get into a fight and the wife of one tries to rescue her husband by grabbing the testicles of the other man, ¹²you must cut off her hand. Show her no pity.

¹³"You must use accurate scales when you weigh out merchandise, ¹⁴and you must use full and honest measures. ¹⁵Yes, always use honest weights and measures, so that you may enjoy a long life in the land the LORD your God is giving you. ¹⁶All who cheat with dishonest weights and measures are detestable to the LORD your God.

¹⁷"Never forget what the Amalekites did to you as you came from Egypt. ¹⁸They attacked you when you were exhausted and weary, and they struck down those who were straggling behind. They had no fear of God. ¹⁹Therefore, when the LORD your God has given you rest from all your enemies in the land he is giving you as a special possession, you must destroy the Amalekites and erase their memory from under heaven. Never forget this!

26 Harvest Offerings and Tithes

"When you enter the land the LORD your God is giving you as a special possession and you have conquered it and settled there, ²put some of the first produce from each crop you harvest into a basket and bring it to the designated place of worship—the place the LORD your God chooses for his name to be honored. ³Go to the priest in charge at that time and say to him, 'With this gift I acknowledge to the LORD your God that I have entered the land he swore to our ancestors he would give us.' ⁴The priest will then take the basket from your hand and set it before the altar of the LORD your God.

⁵"You must then say in the presence of the LORD your God, 'My ancestor Jacob was a wandering Aramean who went to live as a foreigner in Egypt. His family arrived few in number, but in Egypt they became a large and mighty nation. ⁶When the Egyptians oppressed and humiliated us by making us their slaves, ⁷we cried out to the LORD, the God of our ancestors. He heard our cries and saw our hardship, toil, and oppression. ⁸So the LORD brought us out of Egypt with a strong hand and powerful arm, with overwhelming terror, and with miraculous signs and wonders. ⁹He brought us to this place and gave us this land flowing with milk and honey! ¹⁰And now, O LORD, I have brought you the first portion of the harvest you have given me from the ground.' Then place the produce before the LORD your God, and bow to the ground in worship before him. ¹¹Afterward you may go and celebrate because of all the good things the LORD your God has given to you and your household. Remember to include the Levites and the foreigners living among you in the celebration.

¹²"Every third year you must offer a special tithe of your crops. In this year of the special tithe you must give your tithes to the Levites, foreigners, orphans, and widows, so that they will have enough to eat in your towns. ¹³Then you must declare in the presence of the LORD your God, 'I have taken the sacred gift from my house and have given it to the Levites, foreigners, orphans, and widows, just as you commanded me. I

have not violated or forgotten any of your commands. ¹⁴I have not eaten any of it while in mourning; I have not handled it while I was ceremonially unclean; and I have not offered any of it to the dead. I have obeyed the LORD my God and have done everything you commanded me. ¹⁵Now look down from your holy dwelling place in heaven and bless your people Israel and the land you swore to our ancestors to give us—a land flowing with milk and honey.'

A Call to Obey the LORD's Commands

¹⁶"Today the LORD your God has commanded you to obey all these decrees and regulations. So be careful to obey them wholeheartedly. ¹⁷You have declared today that the LORD is your God. And you have promised to walk in his ways, and to obey his decrees, commands, and regulations, and to do everything he tells you. ¹⁸The LORD has declared today that you are his people, his own special treasure, just as he promised, and that you must obey all his commands. ¹⁹And if you do, he will set you high above all the other nations he has made. Then you will receive praise, honor, and renown. You will be a nation that is holy to the LORD your God, just as he promised."

27 The Altar on Mount Ebal

Then Moses and the leaders of Israel gave this charge to the people: "Obey all these commands that I am giving you today. ²When you cross the Jordan River and enter the land the LORD your God is giving you, set up some large stones and coat them with plaster. ³Write this whole body of instruction on them when you cross the river to enter the land the LORD your God is giving you—a land flowing with milk and honey, just as the LORD, the God of your ancestors, promised you. ⁴When you cross the Jordan, set up these stones at Mount Ebal and coat them with plaster, as I am commanding you today. ⁵"Then build an altar there to the LORD your God, using natural, uncut stones. You must not shape the stones with an iron tool. ⁶Build the altar of uncut stones, and use it to offer burnt offerings to the LORD your God. ⁷Also sacrifice peace offerings on it,

and celebrate by feasting there before the LORD your God. ⁸You must clearly write all these instructions on the stones coated with plaster."

⁹Then Moses and the Levitical priests addressed all Israel as follows: "O Israel, be quiet and listen! Today you have become the people of the LORD your God. ¹⁰So you must obey the LORD your God by keeping all these commands and decrees that I am giving you today."

Curses from Mount Ebal

¹¹That same day Moses also gave this charge to the people: ¹²"When you cross the Jordan River, the tribes of Simeon, Levi, Judah, Issachar, Joseph, and Benjamin must stand on Mount Gerizim to proclaim a blessing over the people. ¹³And the tribes of Reuben, Gad, Asher, Zebulun, Dan, and Naphtali must stand on Mount Ebal to proclaim a curse.

¹⁴"Then the Levites will shout to all the people of Israel:

¹⁵'Cursed is anyone who carves or casts an idol and secretly sets it up. These idols, the work of craftsmen, are detestable to the LORD.'

And all the people will reply, 'Amen.'

¹⁶'Cursed is anyone who dishonors father or mother.'

And all the people will reply, 'Amen.'

¹⁷'Cursed is anyone who steals property from a neighbor by moving a boundary marker.'

And all the people will reply, 'Amen.'

¹⁸'Cursed is anyone who leads a blind person astray on the road.'

And all the people will reply, 'Amen.'

¹⁹'Cursed is anyone who denies justice to foreigners, orphans, or widows.'

And all the people will reply, 'Amen.'

²⁰'Cursed is anyone who has sexual intercourse with one of his father's wives, for he has violated his father.'

And all the people will reply, 'Amen.'

²¹'Cursed is anyone who has sexual intercourse with an animal.'

And all the people will reply, 'Amen.'

When Scripture Doesn't Transform

DEUTERONOMY 28:1-14

Cindy participated in the Bible study I led for three years. She accumulated a lot of knowledge. But her life never changed. I've puzzled a lot over people like Cindy who interact with Scripture, but never seem to be transformed by it. Why does this happen?

Sometimes it's because the person is focused purely on *accumulating knowledge*. This kind of person comes to the Scriptures with an analytical eye rather than by humbly asking God to transform her life. While she may take pride in mastering the text, she doesn't know how to let the text master her.

Others come to Scripture with *arrogance*, expecting the Word of God to prove their point. This kind of person may have already decided what she wants the Bible to teach. She may have been taught such ideas as a child, been drawn to the Bible because it preserves the lifestyle she wants, or because it gives her power in certain choices. This person seeks to use the Bible as a proof text and to gain ammunition for the battles of life.

And some read the Bible *through the lens of their own personal baggage*. My friend Cindy's biggest problem was that she'd already decided God was a killjoy; she didn't trust him with her life. Therefore she came to Bible study because she wanted friendship, not because she wanted to be transformed by God. Until she truly believed that God was her only hope for joy and fulfillment, she would never be able to believe a word he said.

As we come to Scripture, we'd do well to ask ourselves: *do I come to Scripture with these preconceived ideas or off-base expectations?* It can be easy to fall unknowingly into one of these patterns; as we seek to be transformed by God's Word, we can begin by inviting him to help us check our motives.

—JoHannah Reardon

For more on Bible study and meditation, see reading at Joshua 1:7-9.

22'Cursed is anyone who has sexual intercourse with his sister, whether she is the daughter of his father or his mother.'

And all the people will reply, 'Amen.'

23'Cursed is anyone who has sexual intercourse with his mother-in-law.'

And all the people will reply, 'Amen.'

24'Cursed is anyone who attacks a neighbor in secret.'

And all the people will reply, 'Amen.'

25'Cursed is anyone who accepts payment to kill an innocent person.'

And all the people will reply, 'Amen.'

26'Cursed is anyone who does not affirm and obey the terms of these instructions.'

And all the people will reply, 'Amen.'

28 Blessings for Obedience

"If you fully obey the LORD your God and carefully keep all his commands that I am giving you today, the LORD your God will set you high above all the nations of the world. 2You will experience all these blessings if you obey the LORD your God:

3 Your towns and your fields
will be blessed.

⁴ Your children and your crops
　　will be blessed.
The offspring of your herds and flocks
　　will be blessed.
⁵ Your fruit baskets and breadboards
　　will be blessed.
⁶ Wherever you go and whatever you do,
　　you will be blessed.

⁷ "The LORD will conquer your enemies when they attack you. They will attack you from one direction, but they will scatter from you in seven!

⁸ "The LORD will guarantee a blessing on everything you do and will fill your storehouses with grain. The LORD your God will bless you in the land he is giving you.

⁹ "If you obey the commands of the LORD your God and walk in his ways, the LORD will establish you as his holy people as he swore he would do. ¹⁰ Then all the nations of the world will see that you are a people claimed by the LORD, and they will stand in awe of you.

¹¹ "The LORD will give you prosperity in the land he swore to your ancestors to give you, blessing you with many children, numerous livestock, and abundant crops. ¹² The LORD will send rain at the proper time from his rich treasury in the heavens and will bless all the work you do. You will lend to many nations, but you will never need to borrow from them. ¹³ If you listen to these commands of the LORD your God that I am giving you today, and if you carefully obey them, the LORD will make you the head and not the tail, and you will always be on top and never at the bottom. ¹⁴ You must not turn away from any of the commands I am giving you today, nor follow after other gods and worship them.

Curses for Disobedience

¹⁵ "But if you refuse to listen to the LORD your God and do not obey all the commands and decrees I am giving you today, all these curses will come and overwhelm you:

¹⁶ Your towns and your fields
　　will be cursed.
¹⁷ Your fruit baskets and breadboards
　　will be cursed.

¹⁸ Your children and your crops
　　will be cursed.
The offspring of your herds and flocks
　　will be cursed.
¹⁹ Wherever you go and whatever you do,
　　you will be cursed.

²⁰ "The LORD himself will send on you curses, confusion, and frustration in everything you do, until at last you are completely destroyed for doing evil and abandoning me. ²¹ The LORD will afflict you with diseases until none of you are left in the land you are about to enter and occupy. ²² The LORD will strike you with wasting diseases, fever, and inflammation, with scorching heat and drought, and with blight and mildew. These disasters will pursue you until you die. ²³ The skies above will be as unyielding as bronze, and the earth beneath will be as hard as iron. ²⁴ The LORD will change the rain that falls on your land into powder, and dust will pour down from the sky until you are destroyed.

²⁵ "The LORD will cause you to be defeated by your enemies. You will attack your enemies from one direction, but you will scatter from them in seven! You will be an object of horror to all the kingdoms of the earth. ²⁶ Your corpses will be food for all the scavenging birds and wild animals, and no one will be there to chase them away.

²⁷ "The LORD will afflict you with the boils of Egypt and with tumors, scurvy, and the itch, from which you cannot be cured. ²⁸ The LORD will strike you with madness, blindness, and panic. ²⁹ You will grope around in broad daylight like a blind person groping in the darkness, but you will not find your way. You will be oppressed and robbed continually, and no one will come to save you.

³⁰ "You will be engaged to a woman, but another man will sleep with her. You will build a house, but someone else will live in it. You will plant a vineyard, but you will never enjoy its fruit. ³¹ Your ox will be butchered before your eyes, but you will not eat a single bite of the meat. Your donkey will be taken from you, never to be returned. Your sheep and goats will be given to your enemies, and no one will be there to help you. ³² You will watch as your sons and daughters are taken away as

slaves. Your heart will break for them, but you won't be able to help them. ³³A foreign nation you have never heard about will eat the crops you worked so hard to grow. You will suffer under constant oppression and harsh treatment. ³⁴You will go mad because of all the tragedy you see around you. ³⁵The LORD will cover your knees and legs with incurable boils. In fact, you will be covered from head to foot.

³⁶"The LORD will exile you and your king to a nation unknown to you and your ancestors. There in exile you will worship gods of wood and stone! ³⁷You will become an object of horror, ridicule, and mockery among all the nations to which the LORD sends you.

³⁸"You will plant much but harvest little, for locusts will eat your crops. ³⁹You will plant vineyards and care for them, but you will not drink the wine or eat the grapes, for worms will destroy the vines. ⁴⁰You will grow olive trees throughout your land, but you will never use the olive oil, for the fruit will drop before it ripens. ⁴¹You will have sons and daughters, but you will lose them, for they will be led away into captivity. ⁴²Swarms of insects will destroy your trees and crops.

⁴³"The foreigners living among you will become stronger and stronger, while you become weaker and weaker. ⁴⁴They will lend money to you, but you will not lend to them. They will be the head, and you will be the tail!

⁴⁵"If you refuse to listen to the LORD your God and to obey the commands and decrees he has given you, all these curses will pursue and overtake you until you are destroyed. ⁴⁶These horrors will serve as a sign and warning among you and your descendants forever. ⁴⁷If you do not serve the LORD your God with joy and enthusiasm for the abundant benefits you have received, ⁴⁸you will serve your enemies whom the LORD will send against you. You will be left hungry, thirsty, naked, and lacking in everything. The LORD will put an iron yoke on your neck, oppressing you harshly until he has destroyed you.

⁴⁹"The LORD will bring a distant nation against you from the end of the earth, and it will swoop down on you like a vulture. It is a nation whose language you do not understand, ⁵⁰a fierce and heartless nation that shows no respect for the old and no pity for the young. ⁵¹Its armies will devour your livestock and crops, and you will be destroyed. They will leave you no grain, new wine, olive oil, calves, or lambs, and you will starve to death. ⁵²They will attack your cities until all the fortified walls in your land—the walls you trusted to protect you—are knocked down. They will attack all the towns in the land the LORD your God has given you.

⁵³"The siege and terrible distress of the enemy's attack will be so severe that you will eat the flesh of your own sons and daughters, whom the LORD your God has given you. ⁵⁴The most tenderhearted man among you will have no compassion for his own brother, his beloved wife, and his surviving children. ⁵⁵He will refuse to share with them the flesh he is devouring—the flesh of one of his own children—because he has nothing else to eat during the siege and terrible distress that your enemy will inflict on all your towns. ⁵⁶The most tender and delicate woman among you—so delicate she would not so much as touch the ground with her foot—will be selfish toward the husband she loves and toward her own son or daughter. ⁵⁷She will hide from them the afterbirth and the new baby she has borne, so that she herself can secretly eat them. She will have nothing else to eat during the siege and terrible distress that your enemy will inflict on all your towns.

⁵⁸"If you refuse to obey all the words of instruction that are written in this book, and if you do not fear the glorious and awesome name of the LORD your God, ⁵⁹then the LORD will overwhelm you and your children with indescribable plagues. These plagues will be intense and without relief, making you miserable and unbearably sick. ⁶⁰He will afflict you with all the diseases of Egypt that you feared so much, and you will have no relief. ⁶¹The LORD will afflict you with every sickness and plague there is, even those not mentioned in this Book of Instruction, until you are destroyed. ⁶²Though you become as numerous as the stars in the sky, few of you will be left

because you would not listen to the LORD your God.

63 "Just as the LORD has found great pleasure in causing you to prosper and multiply, the LORD will find pleasure in destroying you. You will be torn from the land you are about to enter and occupy. 64 For the LORD will scatter you among all the nations from one end of the earth to the other. There you will worship foreign gods that neither you nor your ancestors have known, gods made of wood and stone! 65 There among those nations you will find no peace or place to rest. And the LORD will cause your heart to tremble, your eyesight to fail, and your soul to despair. 66 Your life will constantly hang in the balance. You will live night and day in fear, unsure if you will survive. 67 In the morning you will say, 'If only it were night!' And in the evening you will say, 'If only it were morning!' For you will be terrified by the awful horrors you see around you. 68 Then the LORD will send you back to Egypt in ships, to a destination I promised you would never see again. There you will offer to sell yourselves to your enemies as slaves, but no one will buy you."

29

1 *These are the terms of the covenant the LORD commanded Moses to make with the Israelites while they were in the land of Moab, in addition to the covenant he had made with them at Mount Sinai.*

Moses Reviews the Covenant

2 *Moses summoned all the Israelites and said to them, "You have seen with your own eyes everything the LORD did in the land of Egypt to Pharaoh and to all his servants and to his whole country—3 all the great tests of strength, the miraculous signs, and the amazing wonders. 4 But to this day the LORD has not given you minds that understand, nor eyes that see, nor ears that hear! 5 For forty years I led you through the wilderness, yet your clothes and sandals did not wear out. 6 You ate no bread and drank no wine or other alcoholic drink, but he gave you food so you would know that he is the LORD your God.

7 "When we came here, King Sihon of Heshbon and King Og of Bashan came out to fight against us, but we defeated them. 8 We took their land and gave it to the tribes of Reuben and Gad and to the half-tribe of Manasseh as their grant of land.

9 "Therefore, obey the terms of this covenant so that you will prosper in everything you do. 10 All of you—tribal leaders, elders, officers, all the men of Israel—are standing today in the presence of the LORD your God. 11 Your little ones and your wives are with you, as well as the foreigners living among you who chop your wood and carry your water. 12 You are standing here today to enter into the covenant of the LORD your God. The LORD is making this covenant, including the curses. 13 By entering into the covenant today, he will establish you as his people and confirm that he is your God, just as he promised you and as he swore to your ancestors Abraham, Isaac, and Jacob.

14 "But you are not the only ones with whom I am making this covenant with its curses. 15 I am making this covenant both with you who stand here today in the presence of the LORD our God, and also with the future generations who are not standing here today.

16 "You remember how we lived in the land of Egypt and how we traveled through the lands of enemy nations as we left. 17 You have seen their detestable practices and their idols* made of wood, stone, silver, and gold. 18 I am making this covenant with you so that no one among you—no man, woman, clan, or tribe—will turn away from the LORD our God to worship these gods of other nations, and so that no root among you bears bitter and poisonous fruit.

19 "Those who hear the warnings of this curse should not congratulate themselves, thinking, 'I am safe, even though I am following the desires of my own stubborn heart.' This would lead to utter ruin. 20 The LORD will never pardon such people. Instead his anger and jealousy will burn against them. All the curses written in this book will come down on them, and the LORD will erase their names from under heaven. 21 The LORD will separate

---

29:1a Verse 29:1 is numbered 28:69 in Hebrew text. **29:1b** Hebrew *Horeb*, another name for Sinai. **29:2** Verses 29:2-29 are numbered 29:1-28 in Hebrew text. **29:17** The Hebrew term (literally *round things*) probably alludes to dung.

them from all the tribes of Israel, to pour out on them all the curses of the covenant recorded in this Book of Instruction.

22 "Then the generations to come, both your own descendants and the foreigners who come from distant lands, will see the devastation of the land and the diseases the Lord inflicts on it. 23 They will exclaim, 'The whole land is devastated by sulfur and salt. It is a wasteland with nothing planted and nothing growing, not even a blade of grass. It is like the cities of Sodom and Gomorrah, Admah and Zeboiim, which the Lord destroyed in his intense anger.'

24 "And all the surrounding nations will ask, 'Why has the Lord done this to this land? Why was he so angry?'

25 "And the answer will be, 'This happened because the people of the land abandoned the covenant that the Lord, the God of their ancestors, made with them when he brought them out of the land of Egypt. 26 Instead, they turned away to serve and worship gods they had not known before, gods that were not from the Lord. 27 That is why the Lord's anger has burned against this land, bringing down on it every curse recorded in this book. 28 In great anger and fury the Lord uprooted his people from their land and banished them to another land, where they still live today!'

29 "The Lord our God has secrets known to no one. We are not accountable for them, but we and our children are accountable forever for all that he has revealed to us, so that we may obey all the terms of these instructions.

30 A Call to Return to the Lord

"In the future, when you experience all these blessings and curses I have listed for you, and when you are living among the nations to which the Lord your God has exiled you, take to heart all these instructions. 2 If at that time you and your children return to the Lord your God, and if you obey with all your heart and all your soul all the commands I have given you today, 3 then the Lord your God will restore your fortunes. He will have mercy on you and gather you back from all the nations where

he has scattered you. 4 Even though you are banished to the ends of the earth, the Lord your God will gather you from there and bring you back again. 5 The Lord your God will return you to the land that belonged to your ancestors, and you will possess that land again. Then he will make you even more prosperous and numerous than your ancestors!

6 "The Lord your God will change your heart* and the hearts of all your descendants, so that you will love him with all your heart and soul and so you may live! 7 The Lord your God will inflict all these curses on your enemies and on those who hate and persecute you. 8 Then you will again obey the Lord and keep all his commands that I am giving you today.

9 "The Lord your God will then make you successful in everything you do. He will give you many children and numerous livestock, and he will cause your fields to produce abundant harvests, for the Lord will again delight in being good to you as he was to your ancestors. 10 The Lord your God will delight in you if you obey his voice and keep the commands and decrees written in this Book of Instruction, and if you turn to the Lord your God with all your heart and soul.

The Choice of Life or Death

11 "This command I am giving you today is not too difficult for you to understand, and it is not beyond your reach. 12 It is not kept in heaven, so distant that you must ask, 'Who will go up to heaven and bring it down so we can hear it and obey?' 13 It is not kept beyond the sea, so far away that you must ask, 'Who will cross the sea to bring it to us so we can hear it and obey?' 14 No, the message is very close at hand; it is on your lips and in your heart so that you can obey it.

15 "Now listen! Today I am giving you a choice between life and death, between prosperity and disaster. 16 For I command you this day to love the Lord your God and to keep his commands, decrees, and regulations by walking in his ways. If you do this, you will live and multiply, and the

---

30:6 Hebrew *circumcise your heart.*

When God Says No

DEUTERONOMY 31:1–3

I was recently presented with an amazing opportunity that would be great for my career. It felt like a dream come true!

But after I prayed about it, it just didn't feel right. I didn't feel at peace about it; I became sure God was not leading me in that direction.

Though everything in me wanted to say yes, eventually I said no.

Some friends questioned my decision. Couldn't this opportunity be an answer to prayer? Did I *really* hear from God, or was it just my own feelings?

God often speaks to us through other Christians, and so I felt tempted to take their counsel. Yet deep down I had a clear sense of conviction that, in this case, my well-meaning friends were mistaken: I knew I'd heard from God and I needed to obey him. God was asking me to surrender my (and my friends') desires for my life and submit myself to his plan, even if it didn't seem logical.

As Christians we know obeying God is essential, and we desire to follow God's lead rather than our own ambitions. But what about when God says no to a dream? When it's really tough—when these truths move from the realm of theology and into our real lives—we're tempted to look for loopholes. Did God *really* say no?

Yet many times in Scripture we clearly see God answering no: when God didn't allow Moses to enter the Promised Land (Numbers 20:12; Deuteronomy 31:3); when David pleaded with God for his son's life (2 Samuel 12:14–23); when Jesus asked to be spared the suffering of the Cross (Matthew 26:39); when Paul sought for his "thorn in the flesh" to be taken away (2 Corinthians 12:7–10).

When we're in a healthy relationship with God, we *know* God's character. We recognize his voice. We may not understand why God calls us to do or not do certain things, but we choose to listen to him above our own desires. We choose to trust him—and to obey.

—*Heather Gemmen Wilson*

For more on submission, see reading at Judges 13:1–13.

LORD your God will bless you and the land you are about to enter and occupy.

17 "But if your heart turns away and you refuse to listen, and if you are drawn away to serve and worship other gods, 18 then I warn you now that you will certainly be destroyed. You will not live a long, good life in the land you are crossing the Jordan to occupy.

19 "Today I have given you the choice between life and death, between blessings and curses. Now I call on heaven and earth to witness the choice you make. Oh, that you would choose life, so that you and your descendants might live! 20 You can make this choice by loving the LORD your God, obeying him, and committing yourself firmly to him. This* is the key to your life. And if you love and obey the LORD, you will live long in the land the LORD swore to give your ancestors Abraham, Isaac, and Jacob."

31 Joshua Becomes Israel's Leader

When Moses had finished giving these instructions* to all the people of Israel, 2 he said, "I am now 120 years old, and I am no longer able to lead you. The LORD

30:20 Or *He.*   **31:1** As in Dead Sea Scrolls and Greek version; Masoretic Text reads *Moses went and spoke.*

has told me, 'You will not cross the Jordan River.' ³But the Lord your God himself will cross over ahead of you. He will destroy the nations living there, and you will take possession of their land. Joshua will lead you across the river, just as the Lord promised.

⁴"The Lord will destroy the nations living in the land, just as he destroyed Sihon and Og, the kings of the Amorites. ⁵The Lord will hand over to you the people who live there, and you must deal with them as I have commanded you. ⁶So be strong and courageous! Do not be afraid and do not panic before them. For the Lord your God will personally go ahead of you. He will neither fail you nor abandon you."

⁷Then Moses called for Joshua, and as all Israel watched, he said to him, "Be strong and courageous! For you will lead these people into the land that the Lord swore to their ancestors he would give them. You are the one who will divide it among them as their grants of land. ⁸Do not be afraid or discouraged, for the Lord will personally go ahead of you. He will be with you; he will neither fail you nor abandon you."

Public Reading of the Book of Instruction

⁹So Moses wrote this entire body of instruction in a book and gave it to the priests, who carried the Ark of the Lord's Covenant, and to the elders of Israel. ¹⁰Then Moses gave them this command: "At the end of every seventh year, the Year of Release, during the Festival of Shelters, ¹¹you must read this Book of Instruction to all the people of Israel when they assemble before the Lord your God at the place he chooses. ¹²Call them all together—men, women, children, and the foreigners living in your towns—so they may hear this Book of Instruction and learn to fear the Lord your God and carefully obey all the terms of these instructions. ¹³Do this so that your children who have not known these instructions will hear them and will learn to fear the Lord your God. Do this as long as you live in the land you are crossing the Jordan to occupy."

Israel's Disobedience Predicted

¹⁴Then the Lord said to Moses, "The time has come for you to die. Call Joshua and present yourselves at the Tabernacle,* so that I may commission him there." So Moses and Joshua went and presented themselves at the Tabernacle. ¹⁵And the Lord appeared to them in a pillar of cloud that stood at the entrance to the sacred tent.

¹⁶The Lord said to Moses, "You are about to die and join your ancestors. After you are gone, these people will begin to worship foreign gods, the gods of the land where they are going. They will abandon me and break my covenant that I have made with them. ¹⁷Then my anger will blaze forth against them. I will abandon them, hiding my face from them, and they will be devoured. Terrible trouble will come down on them, and on that day they will say, 'These disasters have come down on us because God is no longer among us!' ¹⁸At that time I will hide my face from them on account of all the evil they commit by worshiping other gods.

¹⁹"So write down the words of this song, and teach it to the people of Israel. Help them learn it, so it may serve as a witness for me against them. ²⁰For I will bring them into the land I swore to give their ancestors—a land flowing with milk and honey. There they will become prosperous, eat all the food they want, and become fat. But they will begin to worship other gods; they will despise me and break my covenant. ²¹And when great disasters come down on them, this song will stand as evidence against them, for it will never be forgotten by their descendants. I know the intentions of these people, even now before they have entered the land I swore to give them."

²²So that very day Moses wrote down the words of the song and taught it to the Israelites.

²³Then the Lord commissioned Joshua son of Nun with these words: "Be strong and courageous, for you must bring the people of Israel into the land I swore to give them. I will be with you."

²⁴When Moses had finished writing this entire body of instruction in a book, ²⁵he gave this command to the Levites who carried the Ark of the Lord's Covenant: ²⁶"Take this Book of Instruction and place it beside the Ark of the Covenant of the

---

31:14 Hebrew *Tent of Meeting;* also in 31:14b.

LORD your God, so it may remain there as a witness against the people of Israel. ²⁷For I know how rebellious and stubborn you are. Even now, while I am still alive and am here with you, you have rebelled against the LORD. How much more rebellious will you be after my death!

²⁸"Now summon all the elders and officials of your tribes, so that I can speak to them directly and call heaven and earth to witness against them. ²⁹I know that after my death you will become utterly corrupt and will turn from the way I have commanded you to follow. In the days to come, disaster will come down on you, for you will do what is evil in the LORD's sight, making him very angry with your actions."

The Song of Moses

³⁰So Moses recited this entire song publicly to the assembly of Israel:

32

¹ "Listen, O heavens, and I will speak!
   Hear, O earth, the words that I say!
² Let my teaching fall on you like rain;
   let my speech settle like dew.
Let my words fall like rain on tender grass,
   like gentle showers on young plants.
³ I will proclaim the name of the LORD;
   how glorious is our God!
⁴ He is the Rock; his deeds are perfect.
   Everything he does is just and fair.
He is a faithful God who does no wrong;
   how just and upright he is!

⁵ "But they have acted corruptly toward him;
   when they act so perversely,
are they really his children?*
They are a deceitful and twisted generation.
⁶ Is this the way you repay the LORD,
   you foolish and senseless people?
Isn't he your Father who created you?
   Has he not made you and established you?
⁷ Remember the days of long ago;
   think about the generations past.

Ask your father, and he will inform you.
   Inquire of your elders, and they will tell you.
⁸ When the Most High assigned lands to the nations,
   when he divided up the human race,
he established the boundaries of the peoples
   according to the number in his heavenly court.*

⁹ "For the people of Israel belong to the LORD;
   Jacob is his special possession.
¹⁰ He found them in a desert land,
   in an empty, howling wasteland.
He surrounded them and watched over them;
   he guarded them as he would guard his own eyes.*
¹¹ Like an eagle that rouses her chicks
   and hovers over her young,
so he spread his wings to take them up
   and carried them safely on his pinions.
¹² The LORD alone guided them;
   they followed no foreign gods.
¹³ He let them ride over the highlands
   and feast on the crops of the fields.
He nourished them with honey from the rock
   and olive oil from the stony ground.
¹⁴ He fed them yogurt from the herd
   and milk from the flock,
   together with the fat of lambs.
He gave them choice rams from Bashan, and goats,
   together with the choicest wheat.
You drank the finest wine,
   made from the juice of grapes.

¹⁵ "But Israel* soon became fat and unruly;
   the people grew heavy, plump, and stuffed!
Then they abandoned the God who had made them;
   they made light of the Rock of their salvation.
¹⁶ They stirred up his jealousy by worshiping foreign gods;
   they provoked his fury with detestable deeds.

¹⁷ They offered sacrifices to demons, which
are not God,
to gods they had not known before,
to new gods only recently arrived,
to gods their ancestors had never
feared.
¹⁸ You neglected the Rock who had
fathered you;
you forgot the God who had given you
birth.

¹⁹ "The LORD saw this and drew back,
provoked to anger by his own sons
and daughters.
²⁰ He said, 'I will abandon them;
then see what becomes of them.
For they are a twisted generation,
children without integrity.
²¹ They have roused my jealousy by
worshiping things that are not God;
they have provoked my anger with
their useless idols.
Now I will rouse their jealousy through
people who are not even a people;
I will provoke their anger through the
foolish Gentiles.
²² For my anger blazes forth like fire
and burns to the depths of the grave.*
It devours the earth and all its crops
and ignites the foundations of the
mountains.
²³ I will heap disasters upon them
and shoot them down with my arrows.
²⁴ I will weaken them with famine,
burning fever, and deadly disease.
I will send the fangs of wild beasts
and poisonous snakes that glide in the
dust.
²⁵ Outside, the sword will bring death,
and inside, terror will strike
both young men and young women,
both infants and the aged.
²⁶ I would have annihilated them,
wiping out even the memory of them.
²⁷ But I feared the taunt of Israel's enemy,
who might misunderstand and say,
"Our own power has triumphed!
The LORD had nothing to do with this!"'

²⁸ "But Israel is a senseless nation;
the people are foolish, without
understanding.

²⁹ Oh, that they were wise and could
understand this!
Oh, that they might know their fate!
³⁰ How could one person chase a thousand
of them,
and two people put ten thousand to
flight,
unless their Rock had sold them,
unless the LORD had given them up?
³¹ But the rock of our enemies is not like
our Rock,
as even they recognize.*
³² Their vine grows from the vine of Sodom,
from the vineyards of Gomorrah.
Their grapes are poison,
and their clusters are bitter.
³³ Their wine is the venom of serpents,
the deadly poison of cobras.

³⁴ "The LORD says, 'Am I not storing up
these things,
sealing them away in my treasury?
³⁵ I will take revenge; I will pay them back.
In due time their feet will slip.
Their day of disaster will arrive,
and their destiny will overtake them.'

³⁶ "Indeed, the LORD will give justice to his
people,
and he will change his mind about* his
servants,
when he sees their strength is gone
and no one is left, slave or free.
³⁷ Then he will ask, 'Where are their gods,
the rocks they fled to for refuge?
³⁸ Where now are those gods,
who ate the fat of their sacrifices
and drank the wine of their offerings?
Let those gods arise and help you!
Let them provide you with shelter!
³⁹ Look now; I myself am he!
There is no other god but me!
I am the one who kills and gives life;
I am the one who wounds and heals;
no one can be rescued from my
powerful hand!
⁴⁰ Now I raise my hand to heaven
and declare, "As surely as I live,
⁴¹ when I sharpen my flashing sword
and begin to carry out justice,
I will take revenge on my enemies
and repay those who reject me.

32:22 Hebrew of *Sheol.*   **32:31** The meaning of the Hebrew is uncertain. Greek version reads *our enemies are fools.*   **32:36** Or *will take revenge for.*

42 I will make my arrows drunk with blood,
　　and my sword will devour flesh—
　　　the blood of the slaughtered and the
　　　　captives,
　　　and the heads of the enemy leaders." '

43 "Rejoice with him, you heavens,
　　and let all of God's angels worship
　　　him.*
　Rejoice with his people, you nations,
　　and let all the angels be strengthened
　　　in him.*
　For he will avenge the blood of his
　　servants;
　　he will take revenge against his
　　　enemies.
　He will repay those who hate him*
　　and cleanse the land for his people."

44 So Moses came with Joshua* son of
Nun and recited all the words of this song
to the people.

45 When Moses had finished reciting all
these words to the people of Israel, 46 he
added: "Take to heart all the words of
warning I have given you today. Pass them
on as a command to your children so they
will obey every word of these instructions.
47 These instructions are not empty words—
they are your life! By obeying them you will
enjoy a long life in the land you will occupy
when you cross the Jordan River."

Moses' Death Foretold

48 That same day the LORD said to Moses,
49 "Go to Moab, to the mountains east of
the river,* and climb Mount Nebo, which
is across from Jericho. Look out across the
land of Canaan, the land I am giving to the
people of Israel as their own special possession. 50 Then you will die there on the
mountain. You will join your ancestors,
just as Aaron, your brother, died on Mount
Hor and joined his ancestors. 51 For both of
you betrayed me with the Israelites at the
waters of Meribah at Kadesh* in the wilderness of Zin. You failed to demonstrate my
holiness to the people of Israel there. 52 So
you will see the land from a distance, but
you may not enter the land I am giving to
the people of Israel."

33 Moses Blesses the People

This is the blessing that Moses, the
man of God, gave to the people of Israel
before his death:

2 "The LORD came from Mount Sinai
　　and dawned upon us* from Mount
　　　Seir;
　he shone forth from Mount Paran
　　and came from Meribah-kadesh
　　with flaming fire at his right hand.*
3 Indeed, he loves his people;*
　　all his holy ones are in his hands.
　They follow in his steps
　　and accept his teaching.
4 Moses gave us the LORD's instruction,
　　the special possession of the people of
　　　Israel.*
5 The LORD became king in Israel*—
　　when the leaders of the people
　　　assembled,
　　when the tribes of Israel gathered as
　　　one."

6 Moses said this about the tribe of Reuben:*

"Let the tribe of Reuben live and not die
　out,
　　though they are few in number."

7 Moses said this about the tribe of Judah:

"O LORD, hear the cry of Judah
　　and bring them together as a people.
　Give them strength to defend their
　　cause;
　help them against their enemies!"

8 Moses said this about the tribe of Levi:

"O LORD, you have given your Thummim
　and Urim—the sacred lots—
　　to your faithful servants the Levites.*
You put them to the test at Massah
　and struggled with them at the waters
　　of Meribah.

32:43a As in Dead Sea Scrolls and Greek version; Masoretic Text lacks the first two lines. Compare Heb 1:6.   32:43b As in Greek version;
Hebrew text lacks this line.   32:43c As in Dead Sea Scrolls and Greek version; Masoretic Text lacks this line.   32:44 Hebrew *Hoshea*,
a variant name for Joshua.   32:49 Hebrew *the mountains of Abarim*.   32:51 Hebrew *waters of Meribath-kadesh*.   33:2a As in Greek and
Syriac versions; Hebrew reads *upon them*.   33:2b Or *came from myriads of holy ones, from the south, from his mountain slopes*. The meaning of
the Hebrew is uncertain.   33:3 As in Greek version; Hebrew reads *Indeed, lover of the peoples*.   33:4 Hebrew *of Jacob*. The names "Jacob"
and "Israel" are often interchanged throughout the Old Testament, referring sometimes to the individual patriarch and sometimes to the
nation.   33:5 Hebrew *in Jeshurun*, a term of endearment for Israel.   33:6 Hebrew lacks *Moses said this about the tribe of Reuben*.   33:8 As in
Greek version; Hebrew lacks *the Levites*.

⁹ The Levites obeyed your word
   and guarded your covenant.
They were more loyal to you
   than to their own parents.
They ignored their relatives
   and did not acknowledge their own
      children.
¹⁰ They teach your regulations to Jacob;
   they give your instructions to Israel.
They present incense before you
   and offer whole burnt offerings on the
      altar.
¹¹ Bless the ministry of the Levites,
      O Lord,
   and accept all the work of their hands.
Hit their enemies where it hurts the most;
   strike down their foes so they never
      rise again."

¹² Moses said this about the tribe of Benjamin:

"The people of Benjamin are loved by
      the Lord
   and live in safety beside him.
He surrounds them continuously
   and preserves them from every harm."

¹³ Moses said this about the tribes of Joseph:

"May their land be blessed by the Lord
   with the precious gift of dew from the
      heavens
   and water from beneath the earth;
¹⁴ with the rich fruit that grows in the sun,
   and the rich harvest produced each
      month;
¹⁵ with the finest crops of the ancient
      mountains,
   and the abundance from the
      everlasting hills;
¹⁶ with the best gifts of the earth and its
      bounty,
   and the favor of the one who appeared
      in the burning bush.
May these blessings rest on Joseph's
      head,
   crowning the brow of the prince
      among his brothers.
¹⁷ Joseph has the majesty of a young bull;
   he has the horns of a wild ox.
He will gore distant nations,
   driving them to the ends of the earth.

This is my blessing for the multitudes of
      Ephraim
   and the thousands of Manasseh."

¹⁸ Moses said this about the tribes of
Zebulun and Issachar*:

"May the people of Zebulun prosper in
      their travels.
   May the people of Issachar prosper at
      home in their tents.
¹⁹ They summon the people to the
      mountain
   to offer proper sacrifices there.
They benefit from the riches of the sea
   and the hidden treasures in the sand."

²⁰ Moses said this about the tribe of Gad:

"Blessed is the one who enlarges Gad's
      territory!
   Gad is poised there like a lion
   to tear off an arm or a head.
²¹ The people of Gad took the best land for
      themselves;
   a leader's share was assigned to them.
When the leaders of the people were
      assembled,
   they carried out the Lord's justice
   and obeyed his regulations for Israel."

²² Moses said this about the tribe of Dan:

"Dan is a lion's cub,
   leaping out from Bashan."

²³ Moses said this about the tribe of Naphtali:

"O Naphtali, you are rich in favor
   and full of the Lord's blessings;
   may you possess the west and the
      south."

²⁴ Moses said this about the tribe of Asher:

"May Asher be blessed above other sons;
   may he be esteemed by his brothers;
   may he bathe his feet in olive oil.
²⁵ May the bolts of your gates be of iron
      and bronze;
   may you be secure all your days."

²⁶ "There is no one like the God of Israel.*
   He rides across the heavens to help
      you,
   across the skies in majestic splendor.

33:18 Hebrew lacks and Issachar.   33:26 Hebrew of Jeshurun, a term of endearment for Israel.

²⁷ The eternal God is your refuge,
   and his everlasting arms are under
      you.
He drives out the enemy before you;
   he cries out, 'Destroy them!'
²⁸ So Israel will live in safety,
   prosperous Jacob in security,
in a land of grain and new wine,
   while the heavens drop down dew.
²⁹ How blessed you are, O Israel!
   Who else is like you, a people saved by
      the LORD?
He is your protecting shield
   and your triumphant sword!
Your enemies will cringe before you,
   and you will stomp on their backs!"

34 The Death of Moses

Then Moses went up to Mount Nebo from the plains of Moab and climbed Pisgah Peak, which is across from Jericho. And the LORD showed him the whole land, from Gilead as far as Dan; ²all the land of Naphtali; the land of Ephraim and Manasseh; all the land of Judah, extending to the Mediterranean Sea*; ³the Negev; the Jordan Valley with Jericho—the city of palms—as far as Zoar. ⁴Then the LORD said to Moses, "This is the land I promised on oath to Abraham, Isaac, and Jacob when I said, 'I will give it to your descendants.' I have now allowed you to see it with your own eyes, but you will not enter the land."

⁵So Moses, the servant of the LORD, died there in the land of Moab, just as the LORD had said. ⁶The LORD buried him* in a valley near Beth-peor in Moab, but to this day no one knows the exact place. ⁷Moses was 120 years old when he died, yet his eyesight was clear, and he was as strong as ever. ⁸The people of Israel mourned for Moses on the plains of Moab for thirty days, until the customary period of mourning was over.

⁹Now Joshua son of Nun was full of the spirit of wisdom, for Moses had laid his hands on him. So the people of Israel obeyed him, doing just as the LORD had commanded Moses.

¹⁰There has never been another prophet in Israel like Moses, whom the LORD knew face to face. ¹¹The LORD sent him to perform all the miraculous signs and wonders in the land of Egypt against Pharaoh, and all his servants, and his entire land. ¹²With mighty power, Moses performed terrifying acts in the sight of all Israel.

34:2 Hebrew *the western sea.*   **34:6** Hebrew *He buried him;* Samaritan Pentateuch and some Greek manuscripts read *They buried him.*

Introduction to

Joshua

Background

Moses has given his final speech (the Book of Deuteronomy) and now he, too, is
dead. His chosen successor, Joshua, has taken the mantle of leadership. He was
one of the twelve spies who scouted the land forty years earlier (Numbers 14:26–
30). Although he and Caleb trusted God, the rest of the people did not. So Joshua
has been trudging through the wilderness these many decades along with the
disobedient people, trusting that God would remember his promise to keep him
alive to take the land (Numbers 14:30). The time has finally come.

Although the book is named after its chief character, the name Joshua (*Yeshua*)
is also another name for Jesus. Joshua the son of Nun was originally called Hoshea,
which means "salvation." Moses gives him the name Joshua (see Numbers 13:16;
Deuteronomy 32:44), meaning "the LORD saves."

Historically, the book has been attributed to Joshua. The book itself testifies to
this fact: "Joshua recorded these things in the Book of God's Instructions" (24:26).
The last section, Joshua's obituary (24:29–33), may have been written by the priest
Eleazar or his son Phinehas.

Message

God's promise to Abraham to provide a land for his people (Genesis 15:12–21)
comes to fulfillment as the people of Israel begin the long process of conquering
the land of Canaan. A series of battles and victories commence, culminating in
a division of the land east and west of the Jordan River. God always keeps his
promises. Despite the people's sins and setbacks, God works to accomplish his
plans. The long-range plans are not forgotten either, for the faithful woman from
Jericho—Rahab—becomes an ancestor of Jesus Christ (Matthew 1:5).

The Book of Joshua is about courage, faith, and God's faithfulness in keeping his
promises.

Time

Much of the book seems to have been written during the time of Israel's conquest
of Canaan (1406–1380 B.C.). Joshua died in 1380 B.C.

Outline

Joshua

1 The LORD's Charge to Joshua

After the death of Moses the LORD's servant, the LORD spoke to Joshua son of Nun, Moses' assistant. He said, [2]"Moses my servant is dead. Therefore, the time has come for you to lead these people, the Israelites, across the Jordan River into the land I am giving them. [3]I promise you what I promised Moses: 'Wherever you set foot, you will be on land I have given you—[4]from the Negev wilderness in the south to the Lebanon mountains in the north, from the Euphrates River in the east to the Mediterranean Sea* in the west, including all the land of the Hittites.' [5]No one will be able to stand against you as long as you live. For I will be with you as I was with Moses. I will not fail you or abandon you.

[6]"Be strong and courageous, for you are the one who will lead these people to possess all the land I swore to their ancestors I would give them. [7]Be strong and very courageous. Be careful to obey all the instructions Moses gave you. Do not deviate from them, turning either to the right or to the left. Then you will be successful in everything you do. [8]Study this Book of Instruction continually. Meditate on it day and night so you will be sure to obey everything written in it. Only then will you prosper and succeed in all you do. [9]This is my command— be strong and courageous! Do not be afraid or discouraged. For the LORD your God is with you wherever you go."

Joshua's Charge to the Israelites

[10]Joshua then commanded the officers of Israel, [11]"Go through the camp and tell the people to get their provisions ready. In three days you will cross the Jordan River and take possession of the land the LORD your God is giving you."

[12]Then Joshua called together the tribes of Reuben, Gad, and the half-tribe of Manasseh. He told them, [13]"Remember what Moses, the servant of the LORD, commanded you: 'The LORD your God is giving you a place of rest. He has given you this land.' [14]Your wives, children, and livestock may remain here in the land Moses assigned to you on the east side of the Jordan River. But your strong warriors, fully armed, must lead the other tribes across the Jordan to help them conquer their territory. Stay with them [15]until the LORD gives them rest, as he has given you rest, and until they, too, possess the land the LORD your God is giving them. Only then may you return and settle here on the east side of the Jordan River in the land that Moses, the servant of the LORD, assigned to you."

[16]They answered Joshua, "We will do whatever you command us, and we will go wherever you send us. [17]We will obey you just as we obeyed Moses. And may the LORD your God be with you as he was with Moses. [18]Anyone who rebels against your orders and does not obey your words and everything you command will be put to death. So be strong and courageous!"

1:4 Hebrew *the Great Sea.*

2 Rahab Protects the Spies

Then Joshua secretly sent out two spies from the Israelite camp at Acacia Grove.* He instructed them, "Scout out the land on the other side of the Jordan River, especially around Jericho." So the two men set out and came to the house of a prostitute named Rahab and stayed there that night.

²But someone told the king of Jericho, "Some Israelites have come here tonight to spy out the land." ³So the king of Jericho sent orders to Rahab: "Bring out the men who have come into your house, for they have come here to spy out the whole land."

⁴Rahab had hidden the two men, but she replied, "Yes, the men were here earlier, but I didn't know where they were from. ⁵They left the town at dusk, as the gates were about to close. I don't know where they went. If you hurry, you can probably catch up with them." ⁶(Actually, she had taken them up to the roof and hidden them beneath bundles

Rahab: An Unlikely Servant
JOSHUA 2

Word had spread in Jericho about God's miraculous work in freeing the Hebrews from Egypt decades earlier. The city knew Joshua and his forces were approaching—and they were overcome with fear by what they'd heard about the Hebrew God.

When the two Hebrew spies came to Rahab's door, we can only imagine what went through her mind. As a prostitute, she was used to receiving male visitors into her home. But these men were enemies, threatening her people.

Yet she chose to hide them—and when the king sought them out, she lied in order to keep them safe.

Rahab could have captured those men in her house; she could have betrayed them to the king and gained his favor. But instead, she arranged the spies' hiding place; organized a doomed pursuit for her kinsmen timed to lock them out (Joshua 2:7); instructed the Israelites when, where, and how long to flee (2:16); and negotiated her and her family's safety (2:12-13).

And God honored her by keeping her and her entire family safe (Joshua 6:22-25). Rahab backed these spies because of a basic faith that "the LORD your God is the supreme God of the heavens above and the earth below" (2:11). Because of her actions, Rahab is named alongside heroes of faith like Noah, Abraham, Joseph, and Moses in Hebrews 11:31. And James 2:25 cites her faith-driven choice as an example of righteousness. But in that initial moment when we see her standing on her roof, looking down at the spies hiding under her bundles of flax, she doesn't look like a typical servant, does she? Courageous, yes—but a servant?

Yet Rahab shows us that servanthood involves courage and faith. It asks us to risk, to give, to sacrifice to a point beyond what is comfortable. Rahab chose the spies' safety and well-being over her own; she picked their needs over her own allegiances. She chose their God over her king, even though it could have cost her everything. Rahab served and saved—and in the end found the people of Israel serving and saving her.

—Jonalyn Fincher

For more on service, see reading at 2 Samuel 9.

2:1 Hebrew *Shittim*.

Meeting God in Scripture

JOSHUA 1:7-9

When I became a Christian, I knew absolutely nothing about the Bible. The person who led me to Christ told me I should read my Bible every day, so I began at the beginning the way I'd read every other book. Halfway through Genesis I wondered when it was going to start talking about Jesus. Someone kindly explained the difference between the Old and New Testaments, gave me a ton of Bible studies, and I was off and running.

Because I came from such a clueless background, I devoured the Bible. My heart overflowed with the truth I found in Deuteronomy 32:1-3: "Listen, O heavens, and I will speak! Hear, O earth, the words that I say! Let my teaching fall on you like rain; let my speech settle like dew. Let my words fall like rain on tender grass, like gentle showers on young plants. I will proclaim the name of the LORD; how glorious is our God!"

The reason these verses spoke (and still speak) so powerfully to me was because this book I was reading for the first time was painting a picture of God. Before this all I knew of God were popular societal platitudes that were long on political correctness but short on details; God was a fuzzy, benevolent being that didn't bother much with humans.

But the Bible revealed a specific and extremely involved God. As I read, it was truly like discovering the pearl Jesus talked about in Matthew 13:46—so valuable that it was worth selling everything to have it. I marveled over and over as I read. This book was telling me who God was! No wonder I couldn't tear myself away.

The more I studied God's Word, the more I grew to love him. And the more I grew to love him, the more I was drawn to immerse myself in Scripture. It was a wonderful cycle that Deuteronomy 6:1-9 alludes to: wholehearted love for God means that I want to know him, which in turn gives me a hunger for his Word and a desire to immerse every part of my life in that cycle. I began to live life through the filter of Scripture, which helped me live it through the filter of God's point of view and be intimately in touch with him.

Scripture, rather than the ideas of culture or even our own opinions and feelings, is the essential starting point and authoritative foundation for our understanding of who God is and what God is like. God's Word ought to be, writes Eugene Peterson in *Eat This Book*, "at the center [of our minds] as the text for living the Christian life deeply and well." First Corinthians 15:27–28 emphasizes this preeminent place God's Word is to have in our hearts and lives: "For the Scriptures say, 'God has put all things under his authority.' . . . so that God, who gave his Son authority over all things, will be utterly supreme over everything everywhere." After a lifetime of reading the Scriptures, this is still what I long for: to make the Scriptures, and thus God, my authority for living so that I can live the Christian life deeply and well.

Not only is this necessary, it's delightful! Nothing is better than being able to walk in the light rather than groping in the dark. I read a passage like 2 Peter 1:18–19, and my heart soars. "We ourselves heard that voice from heaven when we were with him on the holy mountain. Because of that experience, we have even greater confidence in the message proclaimed by the prophets. You must pay close attention to what they wrote, for their words are like a lamp shining in a dark place—until the Day dawns, and Christ the Morning Star shines in your hearts."

As a young woman, Scripture gave me the foundation to build my entire life upon—a mission that extended even to my grandchildren, a then-distant thought that is now upon me. Joshua 1:8 says, "Study this Book of Instruction continually. Meditate on it day and night so you will be sure to obey everything written in it. Only then will you prosper and succeed in all you do." Meditating on God's Word day and night has helped me make my way in the minefields of life. But most of all it has been the means to know a great and awesome God.

—JoHannah Reardon

For more on Bible study and meditation, see reading at 2 Chronicles 34:22–29.

of flax she had laid out.) ⁷So the king's men went looking for the spies along the road leading to the shallow crossings of the Jordan River. And as soon as the king's men had left, the gate of Jericho was shut.

⁸Before the spies went to sleep that night, Rahab went up on the roof to talk with them. ⁹"I know the LORD has given you this land," she told them. "We are all afraid of you. Everyone in the land is living in terror. ¹⁰For we have heard how the LORD made a dry path for you through the Red Sea* when you left Egypt. And we know what you did to Sihon and Og, the two Amorite kings east of the Jordan River, whose people you completely destroyed.* ¹¹No wonder our hearts have melted in fear! No one has the courage to fight after hearing such things. For the LORD your God is the supreme God of the heavens above and the earth below.

¹²"Now swear to me by the LORD that you will be kind to me and my family since I have helped you. Give me some guarantee that ¹³when Jericho is conquered, you will let me live, along with my father and mother, my brothers and sisters, and all their families."

¹⁴"We offer our own lives as a guarantee for your safety," the men agreed. "If you don't betray us, we will keep our promise and be kind to you when the LORD gives us the land."

¹⁵Then, since Rahab's house was built into the town wall, she let them down by a rope through the window. ¹⁶"Escape to the hill country," she told them. "Hide there for three days from the men searching for you. Then, when they have returned, you can go on your way."

¹⁷Before they left, the men told her, "We will be bound by the oath we have taken only if you follow these instructions. ¹⁸When we come into the land, you must leave this scarlet rope hanging from the window through which you let us down. And all your family members—your father, mother, brothers, and all your relatives—must be here inside the house. ¹⁹If they go out into the street and are killed, it will not be our fault. But if anyone lays a hand on people inside this house, we will accept

the responsibility for their death. ²⁰If you betray us, however, we are not bound by this oath in any way."

²¹"I accept your terms," she replied. And she sent them on their way, leaving the scarlet rope hanging from the window.

²²The spies went up into the hill country and stayed there three days. The men who were chasing them searched everywhere along the road, but they finally returned without success.

²³Then the two spies came down from the hill country, crossed the Jordan River, and reported to Joshua all that had happened to them. ²⁴"The LORD has given us the whole land," they said, "for all the people in the land are terrified of us."

3 The Israelites Cross the Jordan

Early the next morning Joshua and all the Israelites left Acacia Grove* and arrived at the banks of the Jordan River, where they camped before crossing. ²Three days later the Israelite officers went through the camp, ³giving these instructions to the people: "When you see the Levitical priests carrying the Ark of the Covenant of the LORD your God, move out from your positions and follow them. ⁴Since you have never traveled this way before, they will guide you. Stay about a half mile* behind them, keeping a clear distance between you and the Ark. Make sure you don't come any closer."

⁵Then Joshua told the people, "Purify yourselves, for tomorrow the LORD will do great wonders among you."

⁶In the morning Joshua said to the priests, "Lift up the Ark of the Covenant and lead the people across the river." And so they started out and went ahead of the people.

⁷The LORD told Joshua, "Today I will begin to make you a great leader in the eyes of all the Israelites. They will know that I am with you, just as I was with Moses. ⁸Give this command to the priests who carry the Ark of the Covenant: 'When you reach the banks of the Jordan River, take a few steps into the river and stop there.'"

⁹So Joshua told the Israelites, "Come and listen to what the LORD your God says. ¹⁰Today you will know that the living God

---

2:10a Hebrew *sea of reeds.*   2:10b The Hebrew term used here refers to the complete consecration of things or people to the LORD, either by destroying them or by giving them as an offering.   3:1 Hebrew *Shittim.*   3:4 Hebrew *about 2,000 cubits* [920 meters].

is among you. He will surely drive out the Canaanites, Hittites, Hivites, Perizzites, Girgashites, Amorites, and Jebusites ahead of you. ¹¹Look, the Ark of the Covenant, which belongs to the Lord of the whole earth, will lead you across the Jordan River! ¹²Now choose twelve men from the tribes of Israel, one from each tribe. ¹³The priests will carry the Ark of the LORD, the Lord of all the earth. As soon as their feet touch the water, the flow of water will be cut off upstream, and the river will stand up like a wall."

¹⁴So the people left their camp to cross the Jordan, and the priests who were carrying the Ark of the Covenant went ahead of them. ¹⁵It was the harvest season, and the Jordan was overflowing its banks. But as soon as the feet of the priests who were carrying the Ark touched the water at the river's edge, ¹⁶the water above that point began backing up a great distance away at a town called Adam, which is near Zarethan. And the water below that point flowed on to the Dead Sea* until the riverbed was dry. Then all the people crossed over near the town of Jericho.

¹⁷Meanwhile, the priests who were carrying the Ark of the LORD's Covenant stood on dry ground in the middle of the riverbed as the people passed by. They waited there until the whole nation of Israel had crossed the Jordan on dry ground.

4 Memorials to the Jordan Crossing

When all the people had crossed the Jordan, the LORD said to Joshua, ²"Now choose twelve men, one from each tribe. ³Tell them, 'Take twelve stones from the very place where the priests are standing in the middle of the Jordan. Carry them out and pile them up at the place where you will camp tonight.'"

⁴So Joshua called together the twelve men he had chosen—one from each of the tribes of Israel. ⁵He told them, "Go into the middle of the Jordan, in front of the Ark of the LORD your God. Each of you must pick up one stone and carry it out on your shoulder—twelve stones in all, one for each of the twelve tribes of Israel. ⁶We will use these stones to build a memorial. In the future your children will

ask you, 'What do these stones mean?' ⁷Then you can tell them, 'They remind us that the Jordan River stopped flowing when the Ark of the LORD's Covenant went across.' These stones will stand as a memorial among the people of Israel forever."

⁸So the men did as Joshua had commanded them. They took twelve stones from the middle of the Jordan River, one for each tribe, just as the LORD had told Joshua. They carried them to the place where they camped for the night and constructed the memorial there.

⁹Joshua also set up another pile of twelve stones in the middle of the Jordan, at the place where the priests who carried the Ark of the Covenant were standing. And they are there to this day.

¹⁰The priests who were carrying the Ark stood in the middle of the river until all of the LORD's commands that Moses had given to Joshua were carried out. Meanwhile, the people hurried across the riverbed. ¹¹And when everyone was safely on the other side, the priests crossed over with the Ark of the LORD as the people watched.

¹²The armed warriors from the tribes of Reuben, Gad, and the half-tribe of Manasseh led the Israelites across the Jordan, just as Moses had directed. ¹³These armed men—about 40,000 strong—were ready for battle, and the LORD was with them as they crossed over to the plains of Jericho.

¹⁴That day the LORD made Joshua a great leader in the eyes of all the Israelites, and for the rest of his life they revered him as much as they had revered Moses.

¹⁵The LORD had said to Joshua, ¹⁶"Command the priests carrying the Ark of the Covenant* to come up out of the riverbed." ¹⁷So Joshua gave the command. ¹⁸As soon as the priests carrying the Ark of the LORD's Covenant came up out of the riverbed and their feet were on high ground, the water of the Jordan returned and overflowed its banks as before.

¹⁹The people crossed the Jordan on the tenth day of the first month.* Then they camped at Gilgal, just east of Jericho. ²⁰It was there at Gilgal that Joshua piled up the twelve stones taken from the Jordan River.

3:16 Hebrew *the sea of the Arabah, the Salt Sea.* **4:16** Hebrew *Ark of the Testimony.* **4:19** This day in the ancient Hebrew lunar calendar occurred in late March, April, or early May.

[21] Then Joshua said to the Israelites, "In the future your children will ask, 'What do these stones mean?' [22] Then you can tell them, 'This is where the Israelites crossed the Jordan on dry ground.' [23] For the LORD your God dried up the river right before your eyes, and he kept it dry until you were all across, just as he did at the Red Sea* when he dried it up until we had all crossed over. [24] He did this so all the nations of the earth might know that the LORD's hand is powerful, and so you might fear the LORD your God forever."

5 When all the Amorite kings west of the Jordan and all the Canaanite kings who lived along the Mediterranean coast* heard how the LORD had dried up the Jordan River so the people of Israel could cross, they lost heart and were paralyzed with fear because of them.

Israel Reestablishes Covenant Ceremonies

[2] At that time the LORD told Joshua, "Make flint knives and circumcise this second generation of Israelites.*" [3] So Joshua made flint knives and circumcised the entire male population of Israel at Gibeath-haaraloth.*

[4] Joshua had to circumcise them because all the men who were old enough to fight in battle when they left Egypt had died in the wilderness. [5] Those who left Egypt had all been circumcised, but none of those born after the Exodus, during the years in the wilderness, had been circumcised. [6] The Israelites had traveled in the wilderness for forty years until all the men who were old enough to fight in battle when they left Egypt had died. For they had disobeyed the LORD, and the LORD vowed he would not let them enter the land he had sworn to give us—a land flowing with milk and honey. [7] So Joshua circumcised their sons—those who had grown up to take their fathers' places—for they had not been circumcised on the way to the Promised Land. [8] After all the males had been circumcised, they rested in the camp until they were healed.

[9] Then the LORD said to Joshua, "Today I have rolled away the shame of your slavery in Egypt." So that place has been called Gilgal* to this day.

[10] While the Israelites were camped at Gilgal on the plains of Jericho, they celebrated Passover on the evening of the fourteenth day of the first month.* [11] The very next day they began to eat unleavened bread and roasted grain harvested from the land. [12] No manna appeared on the day they first ate from the crops of the land, and it was never seen again. So from that time on the Israelites ate from the crops of Canaan.

The LORD's Commander Confronts Joshua

[13] When Joshua was near the town of Jericho, he looked up and saw a man standing in front of him with sword in hand. Joshua went up to him and demanded, "Are you friend or foe?"

[14] "Neither one," he replied. "I am the commander of the LORD's army."

At this, Joshua fell with his face to the ground in reverence. "I am at your command," Joshua said. "What do you want your servant to do?"

[15] The commander of the LORD's army replied, "Take off your sandals, for the place where you are standing is holy." And Joshua did as he was told.

6 The Fall of Jericho

Now the gates of Jericho were tightly shut because the people were afraid of the Israelites. No one was allowed to go out or in. [2] But the LORD said to Joshua, "I have given you Jericho, its king, and all its strong warriors. [3] You and your fighting men should march around the town once a day for six days. [4] Seven priests will walk ahead of the Ark, each carrying a ram's horn. On the seventh day you are to march around the town seven times, with the priests blowing the horns. [5] When you hear the priests give one long blast on the rams' horns, have all the people shout as loud as they can. Then the walls of the town will collapse, and the people can charge straight into the town."

[6] So Joshua called together the priests and said, "Take up the Ark of the LORD's

4:23 Hebrew *sea of reeds.* **5:1** Hebrew *along the sea.* **5:2** Or *circumcise the Israelites a second time.* **5:3** *Gibeath-haaraloth* means "hill of foreskins." **5:9** *Gilgal* sounds like the Hebrew word *galal,* meaning "to roll." **5:10** This day in the ancient Hebrew lunar calendar occurred in late March, April, or early May.

Covenant, and assign seven priests to walk in front of it, each carrying a ram's horn." ⁷Then he gave orders to the people: "March around the town, and the armed men will lead the way in front of the Ark of the LORD."

⁸After Joshua spoke to the people, the seven priests with the rams' horns started marching in the presence of the LORD, blowing the horns as they marched. And the Ark of the LORD's Covenant followed behind them. ⁹Some of the armed men marched in front of the priests with the horns and some behind the Ark, with the priests continually blowing the horns. ¹⁰"Do not shout; do not even talk," Joshua commanded. "Not a single word from any of you until I tell you to shout. Then shout!" ¹¹So the Ark of the LORD was carried around the town once that day, and then everyone returned to spend the night in the camp.

¹²Joshua got up early the next morning, and the priests again carried the Ark of the LORD. ¹³The seven priests with the rams' horns marched in front of the Ark of the LORD, blowing their horns. Again the armed men marched both in front of the priests with the horns and behind the Ark of the LORD. All this time the priests were blowing their horns. ¹⁴On the second day they again marched around the town once and returned to the camp. They followed this pattern for six days.

¹⁵On the seventh day the Israelites got up at dawn and marched around the town as they had done before. But this time they went around the town seven times. ¹⁶The seventh time around, as the priests sounded the long blast on their horns, Joshua commanded the people, "Shout! For the LORD has given you the town! ¹⁷Jericho and everything in it must be completely destroyed* as an offering to the LORD. Only Rahab the prostitute and the others in her house will be spared, for she protected our spies.

¹⁸"Do not take any of the things set apart for destruction, or you yourselves will be completely destroyed, and you will bring trouble on the camp of Israel. ¹⁹Everything made from silver, gold, bronze, or iron is sacred to the LORD and must be brought into his treasury."

²⁰When the people heard the sound of the rams' horns, they shouted as loud as they could. Suddenly, the walls of Jericho collapsed, and the Israelites charged straight into the town and captured it. ²¹They completely destroyed everything in it with their swords—men and women, young and old, cattle, sheep, goats, and donkeys.

²²Meanwhile, Joshua said to the two spies, "Keep your promise. Go to the prostitute's house and bring her out, along with all her family."

²³The men who had been spies went in and brought out Rahab, her father, mother, brothers, and all the other relatives who were with her. They moved her whole family to a safe place near the camp of Israel.

²⁴Then the Israelites burned the town and everything in it. Only the things made from silver, gold, bronze, or iron were kept for the treasury of the LORD's house. ²⁵So Joshua spared Rahab the prostitute and her relatives who were with her in the house, because she had hidden the spies Joshua sent to Jericho. And she lives among the Israelites to this day.

²⁶At that time Joshua invoked this curse:

"May the curse of the LORD fall on
     anyone
   who tries to rebuild the town of
     Jericho.
At the cost of his firstborn son,
   he will lay its foundation.
At the cost of his youngest son,
   he will set up its gates."

²⁷So the LORD was with Joshua, and his reputation spread throughout the land.

7 Ai Defeats the Israelites

But Israel violated the instructions about the things set apart for the LORD.* A man named Achan had stolen some of these dedicated things, so the LORD was very angry with the Israelites. Achan was the son of Carmi, a descendant of Zimri* son of Zerah, of the tribe of Judah.

6:17 The Hebrew term used here refers to the complete consecration of things or people to the LORD, either by destroying them or by giving them as an offering; similarly in 6:18, 21. 7:1a The Hebrew term used here refers to the complete consecration of things or people to the LORD, either by destroying them or by giving them as an offering; similarly in 7:11, 12, 13, 15. 7:1b As in parallel text at 1 Chr 2:6; Hebrew reads Zabdi. Also in 7:17, 18.

Overcoming Confession's Obstacles

JOSHUA 7:1–22

Shame and fear are two of the biggest obstacles to confessing our sins to other Christians. We're all broken people, but to admit that reveals our weakness and imperfection. In addition, we fear being judged. The church should be the safest place for people to confess, but too often we don't feel safe confessing there because we're afraid we'll be rejected.

As we choose to practice the discipline of confession, we must remember that the shame and fear we experience simply are not the truth. Both are diametrically opposed to what the gospel is. The *Scripture* is truth. *Grace* is truth. So as difficult as it may seem, we have to do the opposite of what our fear tells us. Fear wants to keep the bad things hidden and encourages us to live with shame, lacking purpose, holiness, and purity. But that's not what God intended for us.

Although the fear that holds us back from confession isn't going to go away, we can still act courageously. Confession doesn't ever get *easier*, but it does become more natural as we begin to experience the fullness of God's forgiveness and grace.

—Anne Jackson

For more on confession, see reading at 2 Samuel 24.

²Joshua sent some of his men from Jericho to spy out the town of Ai, east of Bethel, near Beth-aven. ³When they returned, they told Joshua, "There's no need for all of us to go up there; it won't take more than two or three thousand men to attack Ai. Since there are so few of them, don't make all our people struggle to go up there."

⁴So approximately 3,000 warriors were sent, but they were soundly defeated. The men of Ai ⁵chased the Israelites from the town gate as far as the quarries,* and they killed about thirty-six who were retreating down the slope. The Israelites were paralyzed with fear at this turn of events, and their courage melted away.

⁶Joshua and the elders of Israel tore their clothing in dismay, threw dust on their heads, and bowed face down to the ground before the Ark of the LORD until evening. ⁷Then Joshua cried out, "Oh, Sovereign LORD, why did you bring us across the Jordan River if you are going to let the Amo-

rites kill us? If only we had been content to stay on the other side! ⁸Lord, what can I say now that Israel has fled from its enemies? ⁹For when the Canaanites and all the other people living in the land hear about it, they will surround us and wipe our name off the face of the earth. And then what will happen to the honor of your great name?"

¹⁰But the LORD said to Joshua, "Get up! Why are you lying on your face like this? ¹¹Israel has sinned and broken my covenant! They have stolen some of the things that I commanded must be set apart for me. And they have not only stolen them but have lied about it and hidden the things among their own belongings. ¹²That is why the Israelites are running from their enemies in defeat. For now Israel itself has been set apart for destruction. I will not remain with you any longer unless you destroy the things among you that were set apart for destruction.

¹³"Get up! Command the people to purify themselves in preparation for tomorrow.

7:5 Or *as far as Shebarim.*

For this is what the LORD, the God of Israel, says: Hidden among you, O Israel, are things set apart for the LORD. You will never defeat your enemies until you remove these things from among you.

14 "In the morning you must present yourselves by tribes, and the LORD will point out the tribe to which the guilty man belongs. That tribe must come forward with its clans, and the LORD will point out the guilty clan. That clan will then come forward, and the LORD will point out the guilty family. Finally, each member of the guilty family must come forward one by one. 15 The one who has stolen what was set apart for destruction will himself be burned with fire, along with everything he has, for he has broken the covenant of the LORD and has done a horrible thing in Israel."

Achan's Sin

16 Early the next morning Joshua brought the tribes of Israel before the LORD, and the tribe of Judah was singled out. 17 Then the clans of Judah came forward, and the clan of Zerah was singled out. Then the families of Zerah came forward, and the family of Zimri was singled out. 18 Every member of Zimri's family was brought forward person by person, and Achan was singled out.

19 Then Joshua said to Achan, "My son, give glory to the LORD, the God of Israel, by telling the truth. Make your confession and tell me what you have done. Don't hide it from me."

20 Achan replied, "It is true! I have sinned against the LORD, the God of Israel. 21 Among the plunder I saw a beautiful robe from Babylon,* 200 silver coins,* and a bar of gold weighing more than a pound.* I wanted them so much that I took them. They are hidden in the ground beneath my tent, with the silver buried deeper than the rest."

22 So Joshua sent some men to make a search. They ran to the tent and found the stolen goods hidden there, just as Achan had said, with the silver buried beneath the rest. 23 They took the things from the tent and brought them to Joshua and all the Israelites. Then they laid them on the ground in the presence of the LORD.

24 Then Joshua and all the Israelites took Achan, the silver, the robe, the bar of gold, his sons, daughters, cattle, donkeys, sheep, goats, tent, and everything he had, and they brought them to the valley of Achor. 25 Then Joshua said to Achan, "Why have you brought trouble on us? The LORD will now bring trouble on you." And all the Israelites stoned Achan and his family and burned their bodies. 26 They piled a great heap of stones over Achan, which remains to this day. That is why the place has been called the Valley of Trouble* ever since. So the LORD was no longer angry.

8 The Israelites Defeat Ai

Then the LORD said to Joshua, "Do not be afraid or discouraged. Take all your fighting men and attack Ai, for I have given you the king of Ai, his people, his town, and his land. 2 You will destroy them as you destroyed Jericho and its king. But this time you may keep the plunder and the livestock for yourselves. Set an ambush behind the town."

3 So Joshua and all the fighting men set out to attack Ai. Joshua chose 30,000 of his best warriors and sent them out at night 4 with these orders: "Hide in ambush close behind the town and be ready for action. 5 When our main army attacks, the men of Ai will come out to fight as they did before, and we will run away from them. 6 We will let them chase us until we have drawn them away from the town. For they will say, 'The Israelites are running away from us as they did before.' Then, while we are running from them, 7 you will jump up from your ambush and take possession of the town, for the LORD your God will give it to you. 8 Set the town on fire, as the LORD has commanded. You have your orders."

9 So they left and went to the place of ambush between Bethel and the west side of Ai. But Joshua remained among the people in the camp that night. 10 Early the next morning Joshua roused his men and started toward Ai, accompanied by the elders of Israel. 11 All the fighting men who were with Joshua marched in front of the town and camped on the north side of Ai, with a valley between them and the town.

¹²That night Joshua sent 5,000 men to lie in ambush between Bethel and Ai, on the west side of the town. ¹³So they stationed the main army north of the town and the ambush west of the town. Joshua himself spent that night in the valley.

¹⁴When the king of Ai saw the Israelites across the valley, he and all his army hurried out early in the morning and attacked the Israelites at a place overlooking the Jordan Valley.* But he didn't realize there was an ambush behind the town. ¹⁵Joshua and the Israelite army fled toward the wilderness as though they were badly beaten. ¹⁶Then all the men in the town were called out to chase after them. In this way, they were lured away from the town. ¹⁷There was not a man left in Ai or Bethel* who did not chase after the Israelites, and the town was left wide open.

¹⁸Then the LORD said to Joshua, "Point the spear in your hand toward Ai, for I will hand the town over to you." Joshua did as he was commanded. ¹⁹As soon as Joshua gave this signal, all the men in ambush jumped up from their position and poured into the town. They quickly captured it and set it on fire.

²⁰When the men of Ai looked behind them, smoke from the town was filling the sky, and they had nowhere to go. For the Israelites who had fled in the direction of the wilderness now turned on their pursuers. ²¹When Joshua and all the other Israelites saw that the ambush had succeeded and that smoke was rising from the town, they turned and attacked the men of Ai. ²²Meanwhile, the Israelites who were inside the town came out and attacked the enemy from the rear. So the men of Ai were caught in the middle, with Israelite fighters on both sides. Israel attacked them, and not a single person survived or escaped. ²³Only the king of Ai was taken alive and brought to Joshua.

²⁴When the Israelite army finished chasing and killing all the men of Ai in the open fields, they went back and finished off everyone inside. ²⁵So the entire population of Ai, including men and women, was wiped out that day—12,000 in all. ²⁶For Joshua kept holding out his spear until everyone who

had lived in Ai was completely destroyed.* ²⁷Only the livestock and the treasures of the town were not destroyed, for the Israelites kept these as plunder for themselves, as the LORD had commanded Joshua. ²⁸So Joshua burned the town of Ai,* and it became a permanent mound of ruins, desolate to this very day.

²⁹Joshua impaled the king of Ai on a sharpened pole and left him there until evening. At sunset the Israelites took down the body, as Joshua commanded, and threw it in front of the town gate. They piled a great heap of stones over him that can still be seen today.

The LORD's Covenant Renewed

³⁰Then Joshua built an altar to the LORD, the God of Israel, on Mount Ebal. ³¹He followed the commands that Moses the LORD's servant had written in the Book of Instruction: "Make me an altar from stones that are uncut and have not been shaped with iron tools."* Then on the altar they presented burnt offerings and peace offerings to the LORD. ³²And as the Israelites watched, Joshua copied onto the stones of the altar* the instructions Moses had given them.

³³Then all the Israelites—foreigners and native-born alike—along with the elders, officers, and judges, were divided into two groups. One group stood in front of Mount Gerizim, the other in front of Mount Ebal. Each group faced the other, and between them stood the Levitical priests carrying the Ark of the LORD's Covenant. This was all done according to the commands that Moses, the servant of the LORD, had previously given for blessing the people of Israel.

³⁴Joshua then read to them all the blessings and curses Moses had written in the Book of Instruction. ³⁵Every word of every command that Moses had ever given was read to the entire assembly of Israel, including the women and children and the foreigners who lived among them.

9 The Gibeonites Deceive Israel

Now all the kings west of the Jordan River heard about what had happened. These were the kings of the Hittites, Amo-

---

8:14 Hebrew *the Arabah.*   8:17 Some manuscripts lack *or Bethel.*   8:26 The Hebrew term used here refers to the complete consecration of things or people to the LORD, either by destroying them or by giving them as an offering.   8:28 *Ai* means "ruin."   8:31 Exod 20:25; Deut 27:5-6.   8:32 Hebrew *onto the stones.*

rites, Canaanites, Perizzites, Hivites, and Jebusites, who lived in the hill country, in the western foothills,* and along the coast of the Mediterranean Sea* as far north as the Lebanon mountains. ²These kings combined their armies to fight as one against Joshua and the Israelites.

³But when the people of Gibeon heard what Joshua had done to Jericho and Ai, ⁴they resorted to deception to save themselves. They sent ambassadors to Joshua, loading their donkeys with weathered saddlebags and old, patched wineskins. ⁵They put on worn-out, patched sandals and ragged clothes. And the bread they took with them was dry and moldy. ⁶When they arrived at the camp of Israel at Gilgal, they told Joshua and the men of Israel, "We have come from a distant land to ask you to make a peace treaty with us."

⁷The Israelites replied to these Hivites, "How do we know you don't live nearby? For if you do, we cannot make a treaty with you."

⁸They replied, "We are your servants."

"But who are you?" Joshua demanded. "Where do you come from?"

⁹They answered, "Your servants have come from a very distant country. We have heard of the might of the LORD your God and of all he did in Egypt. ¹⁰We have also heard what he did to the two Amorite kings east of the Jordan River—King Sihon of Heshbon and King Og of Bashan (who lived in Ashtaroth). ¹¹So our elders and all our people instructed us, 'Take supplies for a long journey. Go meet with the people of Israel and tell them, "We are your servants; please make a treaty with us."'

¹²"This bread was hot from the ovens when we left our homes. But now, as you can see, it is dry and moldy. ¹³These wineskins were new when we filled them, but now they are old and split open. And our clothing and sandals are worn out from our very long journey."

¹⁴So the Israelites examined their food, but they did not consult the LORD. ¹⁵Then Joshua made a peace treaty with them and guaranteed their safety, and the leaders of the community ratified their agreement with a binding oath.

¹⁶Three days after making the treaty, they learned that these people actually lived nearby! ¹⁷The Israelites set out at once to investigate and reached their towns in three days. The names of these towns were Gibeon, Kephirah, Beeroth, and Kiriath-jearim. ¹⁸But the Israelites did not attack the towns, for the Israelite leaders had made a vow to them in the name of the LORD, the God of Israel.

The people of Israel grumbled against their leaders because of the treaty. ¹⁹But the leaders replied, "Since we have sworn an oath in the presence of the LORD, the God of Israel, we cannot touch them. ²⁰This is what we must do. We must let them live, for divine anger would come upon us if we broke our oath. ²¹Let them live." So they made them woodcutters and water carriers for the entire community, as the Israelite leaders directed.

²²Joshua called together the Gibeonites and said, "Why did you lie to us? Why did you say that you live in a distant land when you live right here among us? ²³May you be cursed! From now on you will always be servants who cut wood and carry water for the house of my God."

²⁴They replied, "We did it because we—your servants—were clearly told that the LORD your God commanded his servant Moses to give you this entire land and to destroy all the people living in it. So we feared greatly for our lives because of you. That is why we have done this. ²⁵Now we are at your mercy—do to us whatever you think is right."

²⁶So Joshua did not allow the people of Israel to kill them. ²⁷But that day he made the Gibeonites the woodcutters and water carriers for the community of Israel and for the altar of the LORD—wherever the LORD would choose to build it. And that is what they do to this day.

10 Israel Defeats the Southern Armies

Adoni-zedek, king of Jerusalem, heard that Joshua had captured and completely destroyed* Ai and killed its king, just as he had destroyed the town of Jericho and killed its king. He also learned that the

9:1a Hebrew the Shephelah. 9:1b Hebrew the Great Sea. 10:1 The Hebrew term used here refers to the complete consecration of things or people to the LORD, either by destroying them or by giving them as an offering; also in 10:28, 35, 37, 39, 40.

Gibeonites had made peace with Israel and were now their allies. ²He and his people became very afraid when they heard all this because Gibeon was a large town—as large as the royal cities and larger than Ai. And the Gibeonite men were strong warriors.

³So King Adoni-zedek of Jerusalem sent messengers to several other kings: Hoham of Hebron, Piram of Jarmuth, Japhia of Lachish, and Debir of Eglon. ⁴"Come and help me destroy Gibeon," he urged them, "for they have made peace with Joshua and the people of Israel." ⁵So these five Amorite kings combined their armies for a united attack. They moved all their troops into place and attacked Gibeon.

⁶The men of Gibeon quickly sent messengers to Joshua at his camp in Gilgal. "Don't abandon your servants now!" they pleaded. "Come at once! Save us! Help us! For all the Amorite kings who live in the hill country have joined forces to attack us."

⁷So Joshua and his entire army, including his best warriors, left Gilgal and set out for Gibeon. ⁸"Do not be afraid of them," the LORD said to Joshua, "for I have given you victory over them. Not a single one of them will be able to stand up to you."

⁹Joshua traveled all night from Gilgal and took the Amorite armies by surprise. ¹⁰The LORD threw them into a panic, and the Israelites slaughtered great numbers of them at Gibeon. Then the Israelites chased the enemy along the road to Beth-horon, killing them all along the way to Azekah and Makkedah. ¹¹As the Amorites retreated down the road from Beth-horon, the LORD destroyed them with a terrible hailstorm from heaven that continued until they reached Azekah. The hail killed more of the enemy than the Israelites killed with the sword.

¹²On the day the LORD gave the Israelites victory over the Amorites, Joshua prayed to the LORD in front of all the people of Israel. He said,

"Let the sun stand still over Gibeon,
   and the moon over the valley of
      Aijalon."

¹³So the sun stood still and the moon stayed in place until the nation of Israel had defeated its enemies.

Is this event not recorded in *The Book of Jashar**? The sun stayed in the middle of the sky, and it did not set as on a normal day.* ¹⁴There has never been a day like this one before or since, when the LORD answered such a prayer. Surely the LORD fought for Israel that day!

¹⁵Then Joshua and the Israelite army returned to their camp at Gilgal.

Joshua Kills the Five Southern Kings

¹⁶During the battle the five kings escaped and hid in a cave at Makkedah. ¹⁷When Joshua heard that they had been found, ¹⁸he issued this command: "Cover the opening of the cave with large rocks, and place guards at the entrance to keep the kings inside. ¹⁹The rest of you continue chasing the enemy and cut them down from the rear. Don't give them a chance to get back to their towns, for the LORD your God has given you victory over them."

²⁰So Joshua and the Israelite army continued the slaughter and completely crushed the enemy. They totally wiped out the five armies except for a tiny remnant that managed to reach their fortified towns. ²¹Then the Israelites returned safely to Joshua in the camp at Makkedah. After that, no one dared to speak even a word against Israel.

²²Then Joshua said, "Remove the rocks covering the opening of the cave, and bring the five kings to me." ²³So they brought the five kings out of the cave—the kings of Jerusalem, Hebron, Jarmuth, Lachish, and Eglon. ²⁴When they brought them out, Joshua told the commanders of his army, "Come and put your feet on the kings' necks." And they did as they were told.

²⁵"Don't ever be afraid or discouraged," Joshua told his men. "Be strong and courageous, for the LORD is going to do this to all of your enemies." ²⁶Then Joshua killed each of the five kings and impaled them on five sharpened poles, where they hung until evening.

²⁷As the sun was going down, Joshua gave instructions for the bodies of the kings to be taken down from the poles and thrown into the cave where they had been hiding. Then they covered the opening of the cave

---

10:13a Or *The Book of the Upright.*   **10:13b** Or *did not set for about a whole day.*

with a pile of large rocks, which remains to this very day.

Israel Destroys the Southern Towns

²⁸ That same day Joshua captured and destroyed the town of Makkedah. He killed everyone in it, including the king, leaving no survivors. He destroyed them all, and he killed the king of Makkedah as he had killed the king of Jericho. ²⁹ Then Joshua and the Israelites went to Libnah and attacked it. ³⁰ There, too, the LORD gave them the town and its king. He killed everyone in it, leaving no survivors. Then Joshua killed the king of Libnah as he had killed the king of Jericho.

³¹ From Libnah, Joshua and the Israelites went to Lachish and attacked it. ³² Here again, the LORD gave them Lachish. Joshua took it on the second day and killed everyone in it, just as he had done at Libnah. ³³ During the attack on Lachish, King Horam of Gezer arrived with his army to help defend the town. But Joshua's men killed him and his army, leaving no survivors.

³⁴ Then Joshua and the Israelite army went on to Eglon and attacked it. ³⁵ They captured it that day and killed everyone in it. He completely destroyed everyone, just as he had done at Lachish. ³⁶ From Eglon, Joshua and the Israelite army went up to Hebron and attacked it. ³⁷ They captured the town and killed everyone in it, including its king, leaving no survivors. They did the same thing to all of its surrounding villages. And just as he had done at Eglon, he completely destroyed the entire population.

³⁸ Then Joshua and the Israelites turned back and attacked Debir. ³⁹ He captured the town, its king, and all of its surrounding villages. He completely destroyed everyone in it, leaving no survivors. He did to Debir and its king just what he had done to Hebron and to Libnah and its king.

⁴⁰ So Joshua conquered the whole region—the kings and people of the hill country, the Negev, the western foothills,* and the mountain slopes. He completely destroyed everyone in the land, leaving no survivors, just as the LORD, the God of

Israel, had commanded. ⁴¹ Joshua slaughtered them from Kadesh-barnea to Gaza and from the region around the town of Goshen up to Gibeon. ⁴² Joshua conquered all these kings and their land in a single campaign, for the LORD, the God of Israel, was fighting for his people.

⁴³ Then Joshua and the Israelite army returned to their camp at Gilgal.

11 Israel Defeats the Northern Armies

When King Jabin of Hazor heard what had happened, he sent messages to the following kings: King Jobab of Madon; the king of Shimron; the king of Acshaph; ² all the kings of the northern hill country; the kings in the Jordan Valley south of Galilee*; the kings in the Galilean foothills*; the kings of Naphoth-dor on the west; ³ the kings of Canaan, both east and west; the kings of the Amorites, the Hittites, the Perizzites, the Jebusites in the hill country, and the Hivites in the towns on the slopes of Mount Hermon in the land of Mizpah.

⁴ All these kings came out to fight. Their combined armies formed a vast horde. And with all their horses and chariots, they covered the landscape like the sand on the seashore. ⁵ The kings joined forces and established their camp around the water near Merom to fight against Israel.

⁶ Then the LORD said to Joshua, "Do not be afraid of them. By this time tomorrow I will hand all of them over to Israel as dead men. Then you must cripple their horses and burn their chariots."

⁷ So Joshua and all his fighting men traveled to the water near Merom and attacked suddenly. ⁸ And the LORD gave them victory over their enemies. The Israelites chased them as far as Greater Sidon and Misrephoth-maim, and eastward into the valley of Mizpah, until not one enemy warrior was left alive. ⁹ Then Joshua crippled the horses and burned all the chariots, as the LORD had instructed.

¹⁰ Joshua then turned back and captured Hazor and killed its king. (Hazor had at one time been the capital of all these kingdoms.) ¹¹ The Israelites completely destroyed* every

---

10:40 Hebrew *the Shephelah*.   **11:2a** Hebrew *in the Arabah south of Kinnereth*.   **11:2b** Hebrew *the Shephelah;* also in 11:16.   **11:11** The Hebrew term used here refers to the complete consecration of things or people to the LORD, either by destroying them or by giving them as an offering; also in 11:12, 20, 21.

living thing in the city, leaving no survivors. Not a single person was spared. And then Joshua burned the city.

¹²Joshua slaughtered all the other kings and their people, completely destroying them, just as Moses, the servant of the LORD, had commanded. ¹³But the Israelites did not burn any of the towns built on mounds except Hazor, which Joshua burned. ¹⁴And the Israelites took all the plunder and live-stock of the ravaged towns for themselves. But they killed all the people, leaving no survivors. ¹⁵As the LORD had commanded his servant Moses, so Moses commanded Joshua. And Joshua did as he was told, care-fully obeying all the commands that the LORD had given to Moses.

¹⁶So Joshua conquered the entire region— the hill country, the entire Negev, the whole area around the town of Goshen, the west-ern foothills, the Jordan Valley,* the moun-tains of Israel, and the Galilean foothills. ¹⁷The Israelite territory now extended all the way from Mount Halak, which leads up to Seir in the south, as far north as Baal-gad at the foot of Mount Hermon in the valley of Lebanon. Joshua killed all the kings of those territories, ¹⁸waging war for a long time to accomplish this. ¹⁹No one in this region made peace with the Israelites except the Hivites of Gibeon. All the oth-ers were defeated. ²⁰For the LORD hard-ened their hearts and caused them to fight the Israelites. So they were completely destroyed without mercy, as the LORD had commanded Moses.

²¹During this period Joshua destroyed all the descendants of Anak, who lived in the hill country of Hebron, Debir, Anab, and the entire hill country of Judah and Israel. He killed them all and completely destroyed their towns. ²²None of the descendants of Anak were left in all the land of Israel, though some still remained in Gaza, Gath, and Ashdod.

²³So Joshua took control of the entire land, just as the LORD had instructed Moses. He gave it to the people of Israel as their special possession, dividing the land among the tribes. So the land finally had rest from war.

Kings Defeated East of the Jordan

12 These are the kings east of the Jordan River who had been killed by the Israelites and whose land was taken. Their territory extended from the Arnon Gorge to Mount Hermon and included all the land east of the Jordan Valley.*

²King Sihon of the Amorites, who lived in Heshbon, was defeated. His kingdom included Aroer, on the edge of the Arnon Gorge, and extended from the middle of the Arnon Gorge to the Jabbok River, which serves as a border for the Ammonites. This territory included the southern half of the territory of Gilead. ³Sihon also controlled the Jordan Valley and regions to the east— from as far north as the Sea of Galilee to as far south as the Dead Sea,* including the road to Beth-jeshimoth and southward to the slopes of Pisgah.

⁴King Og of Bashan, the last of the Repha-ites, lived at Ashtaroth and Edrei. ⁵He ruled a territory stretching from Mount Hermon to Salecah in the north and to all of Bashan in the east, and westward to the borders of the kingdoms of Geshur and Maacah. This territory included the northern half of Gil-ead, as far as the boundary of King Sihon of Heshbon.

⁶Moses, the servant of the LORD, and the Israelites had destroyed the people of King Sihon and King Og. And Moses gave their land as a possession to the tribes of Reuben, Gad, and the half-tribe of Manasseh.

Kings Defeated West of the Jordan

⁷The following is a list of the kings that Joshua and the Israelite armies defeated on the west side of the Jordan, from Baal-gad in the valley of Lebanon to Mount Halak, which leads up to Seir. (Joshua gave this land to the tribes of Israel as their pos-session, ⁸including the hill country, the western foothills,* the Jordan Valley, the mountain slopes, the Judean wilderness, and the Negev. The people who lived in this region were the Hittites, the Amorites, the Canaanites, the Perizzites, the Hivites, and the Jebusites.) These are the kings Israel defeated:

11:16 Hebrew *the Shephelah, the Arabah.* **12:1** Hebrew *the Arabah;* also in 12:3, 8. **12:3** Hebrew *from the Sea of Kinnereth to the Sea of the Arabah, which is the Salt Sea.* **12:8** Hebrew *the Shephelah.*

⁹ The king of Jericho
   The king of Ai, near Bethel
¹⁰ The king of Jerusalem
   The king of Hebron
¹¹ The king of Jarmuth
   The king of Lachish
¹² The king of Eglon
   The king of Gezer
¹³ The king of Debir
   The king of Geder
¹⁴ The king of Hormah
   The king of Arad
¹⁵ The king of Libnah
   The king of Adullam
¹⁶ The king of Makkedah
   The king of Bethel
¹⁷ The king of Tappuah
   The king of Hepher
¹⁸ The king of Aphek
   The king of Lasharon
¹⁹ The king of Madon
   The king of Hazor
²⁰ The king of Shimron-meron
   The king of Acshaph
²¹ The king of Taanach
   The king of Megiddo
²² The king of Kedesh
   The king of Jokneam in Carmel
²³ The king of Dor in the town of Naphoth-
   dor*
   The king of Goyim in Gilgal*
²⁴ The king of Tirzah.

In all, thirty-one kings were defeated.

13 The Land Yet to Be Conquered

When Joshua was an old man, the LORD said to him, "You are growing old, and much land remains to be conquered. ²This is the territory that remains: all the regions of the Philistines and the Geshurites, ³and the larger territory of the Canaanites, extending from the stream of Shihor on the border of Egypt, northward to the boundary of Ekron. It includes the territory of the five Philistine rulers of Gaza, Ashdod, Ashkelon, Gath, and Ekron. The land of the Avvites ⁴in the south also remains to be conquered. In the north, the following area has not yet been conquered: all the land of the Canaanites, including Mearah (which belongs to the Sidonians), stretching north-ward to Aphek on the border of the Amorites; ⁵the land of the Gebalites and all of the Lebanon mountain area to the east, from Baal-gad below Mount Hermon to Lebo-hamath; ⁶and all the hill country from Lebanon to Misrephoth-maim, including all the land of the Sidonians.

"I myself will drive these people out of the land ahead of the Israelites. So be sure to give this land to Israel as a special possession, just as I have commanded you. ⁷Include all this territory as Israel's possession when you divide this land among the nine tribes and the half-tribe of Manasseh."

The Land Divided East of the Jordan

⁸Half the tribe of Manasseh and the tribes of Reuben and Gad had already received their grants of land on the east side of the Jordan, for Moses, the servant of the LORD, had previously assigned this land to them.

⁹Their territory extended from Aroer on the edge of the Arnon Gorge (including the town in the middle of the gorge) to the plain beyond Medeba, as far as Dibon. ¹⁰It also included all the towns of King Sihon of the Amorites, who had reigned in Heshbon, and extended as far as the borders of Ammon. ¹¹It included Gilead, the territory of the kingdoms of Geshur and Maacah, all of Mount Hermon, all of Bashan as far as Salecah, ¹²and all the territory of King Og of Bashan, who had reigned in Ashtaroth and Edrei. King Og was the last of the Rephaites, for Moses had attacked them and driven them out. ¹³But the Israelites failed to drive out the people of Geshur and Maacah, so they continue to live among the Israelites to this day.

An Allotment for the Tribe of Levi

¹⁴Moses did not assign any allotment of land to the tribe of Levi. Instead, as the LORD had promised them, their allotment came from the offerings burned on the altar to the LORD, the God of Israel.

The Land Given to the Tribe of Reuben

¹⁵Moses had assigned the following area to the clans of the tribe of Reuben.

12:23a Hebrew *Naphath-dor,* a variant spelling of Naphoth-dor. **12:23b** Greek version reads *Goyim in Galilee.*

16Their territory extended from Aroer on the edge of the Arnon Gorge (including the town in the middle of the gorge) to the plain beyond Medeba. 17It included Heshbon and the other towns on the plain—Dibon, Bamoth-baal, Beth-baal-meon, 18Jahaz, Kedemoth, Mephaath, 19Kiriathaim, Sibmah, Zereth-shahar on the hill above the valley, 20Beth-peor, the slopes of Pisgah, and Beth-jeshimoth.

21The land of Reuben also included all the towns of the plain and the entire kingdom of Sihon. Sihon was the Amorite king who had reigned in Heshbon and was killed by Moses along with the leaders of Midian—Evi, Rekem, Zur, Hur, and Reba—princes living in the region who were allied with Sihon. 22The Israelites had also killed Balaam son of Beor, who used magic to tell the future. 23The Jordan River marked the western boundary for the tribe of Reuben. The towns and their surrounding villages in this area were given as a homeland to the clans of the tribe of Reuben.

The Land Given to the Tribe of Gad

24Moses had assigned the following area to the clans of the tribe of Gad.

25Their territory included Jazer, all the towns of Gilead, and half of the land of Ammon, as far as the town of Aroer just west of* Rabbah. 26It extended from Heshbon to Ramath-mizpeh and Betonim, and from Mahanaim to the territory of Lo-debar.* 27In the valley were Beth-haram, Beth-nimrah, Succoth, Zaphon, and the rest of the kingdom of King Sihon of Heshbon. The western boundary ran along the Jordan River, extended as far north as the tip of the Sea of Galilee,* and then turned eastward. 28The towns and their surrounding villages in this area were given as a homeland to the clans of the tribe of Gad.

The Land Given to the Half-Tribe of Manasseh

29Moses had assigned the following area to the clans of the half-tribe of Manasseh.

30Their territory extended from Mahanaim, including all of Bashan, all the former kingdom of King Og, and the sixty towns of Jair in Bashan. 31It also included half of Gilead and King Og's royal cities of Ashtaroth and Edrei. All this was given to the clans of the descendants of Makir, who was Manasseh's son.

32These are the allotments Moses had made while he was on the plains of Moab, across the Jordan River, east of Jericho. 33But Moses gave no allotment of land to the tribe of Levi, for the LORD, the God of Israel, had promised that he himself would be their allotment.

14 The Land Divided West of the Jordan

The remaining tribes of Israel received land in Canaan as allotted by Eleazar the priest, Joshua son of Nun, and the tribal leaders. 2These nine and a half tribes received their grants of land by means of sacred lots, in accordance with the LORD's command through Moses. 3Moses had already given a grant of land to the two and a half tribes on the east side of the Jordan River, but he had given the Levites no such allotment. 4The descendants of Joseph had become two separate tribes—Manasseh and Ephraim. And the Levites were given no land at all, only towns to live in with surrounding pasturelands for their livestock and all their possessions. 5So the land was distributed in strict accordance with the LORD's commands to Moses.

Caleb Requests His Land

6A delegation from the tribe of Judah, led by Caleb son of Jephunneh the Kenizzite, came to Joshua at Gilgal. Caleb said to Joshua, "Remember what the LORD said to Moses, the man of God, about you and me when we were at Kadesh-barnea. 7I was forty years old when Moses, the servant of the LORD, sent me from Kadesh-barnea to explore the land of Canaan. I returned and gave an honest report, 8but my brothers who went with me frightened the people from entering the Promised Land. For

---

13:25 Hebrew *in front of.* **13:26** Hebrew *Li-debir,* apparently a variant spelling of Lo-debar (compare 2 Sam 9:4; 17:27; Amos 6:13).
13:27 Hebrew *Sea of Kinnereth.*

my part, I wholeheartedly followed the LORD my God. ⁹So that day Moses solemnly promised me, 'The land of Canaan on which you were just walking will be your grant of land and that of your descendants forever, because you wholeheartedly followed the LORD my God.'

¹⁰"Now, as you can see, the LORD has kept me alive and well as he promised for all these forty-five years since Moses made this promise—even while Israel wandered in the wilderness. Today I am eighty-five years old. ¹¹I am as strong now as I was when Moses sent me on that journey, and I can still travel and fight as well as I could then. ¹²So give me the hill country that the LORD promised me. You will remember that as scouts we found the descendants of Anak living there in great, walled towns. But if the LORD is with me, I will drive them out of the land, just as the LORD said."

¹³So Joshua blessed Caleb son of Jephunneh and gave Hebron to him as his portion of land. ¹⁴Hebron still belongs to the descendants of Caleb son of Jephunneh the Kenizzite because he wholeheartedly followed the LORD, the God of Israel. ¹⁵(Previously Hebron had been called Kiriath-arba. It had been named after Arba, a great hero of the descendants of Anak.)

And the land had rest from war.

15 The Land Given to the Tribe of Judah

The allotment for the clans of the tribe of Judah reached southward to the border of Edom, as far south as the wilderness of Zin.

²The southern boundary began at the south bay of the Dead Sea,* ³ran south of Scorpion Pass* into the wilderness of Zin, and then went south of Kadesh-barnea to Hezron. Then it went up to Addar, where it turned toward Karka. ⁴From there it passed to Azmon until it finally reached the Brook of Egypt, which it followed to the Mediterranean Sea.* This was their* southern boundary.

⁵The eastern boundary extended along the Dead Sea to the mouth of the Jordan River.

The northern boundary began at the bay where the Jordan River empties into the Dead Sea, ⁶went up from there to Beth-hoglah, then proceeded north of Beth-arabah to the Stone of Bohan. (Bohan was Reuben's son.) ⁷From that point it went through the valley of Achor to Debir, turning north toward Gilgal, which is across from the slopes of Adummim on the south side of the valley. From there the boundary extended to the springs at En-shemesh and on to En-rogel. ⁸The boundary then passed through the valley of Ben-Hinnom, along the southern slopes of the Jebusites, where the city of Jerusalem is located. Then it went west to the top of the mountain above the valley of Hinnom, and on up to the northern end of the valley of Rephaim. ⁹From there the boundary extended from the top of the mountain to the spring at the waters of Nephtoah,* and from there to the towns on Mount Ephron. Then it turned toward Baalah (that is, Kiriath-jearim). ¹⁰The boundary circled west of Baalah to Mount Seir, passed along to the town of Kesalon on the northern slope of Mount Jearim, and went down to Beth-shemesh and on to Timnah. ¹¹The boundary then proceeded to the slope of the hill north of Ekron, where it turned toward Shikkeron and Mount Baalah. It passed Jabneel and ended at the Mediterranean Sea.

¹²The western boundary was the shoreline of the Mediterranean Sea.*

These are the boundaries for the clans of the tribe of Judah.

The Land Given to Caleb

¹³The LORD commanded Joshua to assign some of Judah's territory to Caleb son of Jephunneh. So Caleb was given the town of Kiriath-arba (that is, Hebron), which had been named after Anak's ancestor. ¹⁴Caleb drove out the three groups of Anakites—the descendants of Sheshai, Ahiman, and Talmai, the sons of Anak.

¹⁵From there he went to fight against the people living in the town of Debir (formerly

15:2 Hebrew *the Salt Sea;* also in 15:5.   **15:3** Hebrew *Akrabbim.*   **15:4a** Hebrew *the sea;* also in 15:11.   **15:4b** Hebrew *your.*   **15:9** Or *the spring at Me-nephtoah.*   **15:12** Hebrew *the Great Sea;* also in 15:47.

called Kiriath-sepher). [16]Caleb said, "I will give my daughter Acsah in marriage to the one who attacks and captures Kiriath-sepher." [17]Othniel, the son of Caleb's brother Kenaz, was the one who conquered it, so Acsah became Othniel's wife.

[18]When Acsah married Othniel, she urged him* to ask her father for a field. As she got down off her donkey, Caleb asked her, "What's the matter?"

[19]She said, "Give me another gift. You have already given me land in the Negev; now please give me springs of water, too." So Caleb gave her the upper and lower springs.

The Towns Allotted to Judah

[20]This was the homeland allocated to the clans of the tribe of Judah.

[21]The towns of Judah situated along the borders of Edom in the extreme south were Kabzeel, Eder, Jagur, [22]Kinah, Dimonah, Adadah, [23]Kedesh, Hazor, Ithnan, [24]Ziph, Telem, Bealoth, [25]Hazor-hadattah, Kerioth-hezron (that is, Hazor), [26]Amam, Shema, Moladah, [27]Hazar-gaddah, Heshmon, Beth-pelet, [28]Hazar-shual, Beersheba, Biziothiah, [29]Baalah, Iim, Ezem, [30]Eltolad, Kesil, Hormah, [31]Ziklag, Madmannah, Sansannah, [32]Lebaoth, Shilhim, Ain, and Rimmon—twenty-nine towns with their surrounding villages.

[33]The following towns situated in the western foothills* were also given to Judah: Eshtaol, Zorah, Ashnah, [34]Zanoah, En-gannim, Tappuah, Enam, [35]Jarmuth, Adullam, Socoh, Azekah, [36]Shaaraim, Adithaim, Gederah, and Gederothaim—fourteen towns with their surrounding villages.

[37]Also included were Zenan, Hadashah, Migdal-gad, [38]Dilean, Mizpeh, Joktheel, [39]Lachish, Bozkath, Eglon, [40]Cabbon, Lahmam, Kitlish, [41]Gederoth, Beth-dagon, Naamah, and Makkedah—sixteen towns with their surrounding villages.

[42]Besides these, there were Libnah, Ether, Ashan, [43]Iphtah, Ashnah, Nezib, [44]Keilah, Aczib, and Mareshah—nine towns with their surrounding villages.

[45]The territory of the tribe of Judah also included Ekron and its surrounding settlements and villages. [46]From Ekron the boundary extended west and included the towns near Ashdod with their surrounding villages. [47]It also included Ashdod with its surrounding settlements and villages and Gaza with its settlements and villages, as far as the Brook of Egypt and along the coast of the Mediterranean Sea.

[48]Judah also received the following towns in the hill country: Shamir, Jattir, Socoh, [49]Dannah, Kiriath-sannah (that is, Debir), [50]Anab, Eshtemoh, Anim, [51]Goshen, Holon, and Giloh—eleven towns with their surrounding villages.

[52]Also included were the towns of Arab, Dumah, Eshan, [53]Janim, Beth-tappuah, Aphekah, [54]Humtah, Kiriath-arba (that is, Hebron), and Zior—nine towns with their surrounding villages.

[55]Besides these, there were Maon, Carmel, Ziph, Juttah, [56]Jezreel, Jokdeam, Zanoah, [57]Kain, Gibeah, and Timnah—ten towns with their surrounding villages.

[58]In addition, there were Halhul, Beth-zur, Gedor, [59]Maarath, Beth-anoth, and Eltekon—six towns with their surrounding villages.

[60]There were also Kiriath-baal (that is, Kiriath-jearim) and Rabbah—two towns with their surrounding villages.

[61]In the wilderness there were the towns of Beth-arabah, Middin, Secacah, [62]Nibshan, the City of Salt, and En-gedi—six towns with their surrounding villages.

[63]But the tribe of Judah could not drive out the Jebusites, who lived in the city of Jerusalem, so the Jebusites live there among the people of Judah to this day.

16 The Land Given to Ephraim and West Manasseh

The allotment for the descendants of Joseph extended from the Jordan River near Jericho, east of the springs of Jericho, through the wilderness and into the hill country of Bethel. [2]From Bethel (that is, Luz)* it ran over to Ataroth in the ter-

---

15:18 Some Greek manuscripts read *he urged her.* **15:33** Hebrew *the Shephelah.* **16:2** As in Greek version (also see 18:13); Hebrew reads *From Bethel to Luz.*

ritory of the Arkites. ³Then it descended westward to the territory of the Japhletites as far as Lower Beth-horon, then to Gezer and over to the Mediterranean Sea.*

⁴This was the homeland allocated to the families of Joseph's sons, Manasseh and Ephraim.

The Land Given to Ephraim

⁵The following territory was given to the clans of the tribe of Ephraim.

The boundary of their homeland began at Ataroth-addar in the east. From there it ran to Upper Beth-horon, ⁶then on to the Mediterranean Sea. From Micmethath on the north, the boundary curved eastward past Taanath-shiloh to the east of Janoah. ⁷From Janoah it turned southward to Ataroth and Naarah, touched Jericho, and ended at the Jordan River. ⁸From Tappuah the boundary extended westward, following the Kanah Ravine to the Mediterranean Sea. This is the homeland allocated to the clans of the tribe of Ephraim.

⁹In addition, some towns with their surrounding villages in the territory allocated to the half-tribe of Manasseh were set aside for the tribe of Ephraim. ¹⁰They did not drive the Canaanites out of Gezer, however, so the people of Gezer live as slaves among the people of Ephraim to this day.

17 The Land Given to West Manasseh

The next allotment of land was given to the half-tribe of Manasseh, the descendants of Joseph's older son. Makir, the firstborn son of Manasseh, was the father of Gilead. Because his descendants were experienced soldiers, the regions of Gilead and Bashan on the east side of the Jordan had already been given to them. ²So the allotment on the west side of the Jordan was for the remaining families within the clans of the tribe of Manasseh: Abiezer, Helek, Asriel, Shechem, Hepher, and Shemida. These clans represent the male descendants of Manasseh son of Joseph.

³However, Zelophehad, a descendant of Hepher son of Gilead, son of Makir, son of Manasseh, had no sons. He had only daughters, whose names were Mahlah, Noah, Hoglah, Milcah, and Tirzah. ⁴These women came to Eleazar the priest, Joshua son of Nun, and the Israelite leaders and said, "The LORD commanded Moses to give us a grant of land along with the men of our tribe."

So Joshua gave them a grant of land along with their uncles, as the LORD had commanded. ⁵As a result, Manasseh's total allocation came to ten parcels of land, in addition to the land of Gilead and Bashan across the Jordan River, ⁶because the female descendants of Manasseh received a grant of land along with the male descendants. (The land of Gilead was given to the rest of the male descendants of Manasseh.)

⁷The boundary of the tribe of Manasseh extended from the border of Asher to Micmethath, near Shechem. Then the boundary went south from Micmethath to the settlement near the spring of Tappuah. ⁸The land surrounding Tappuah belonged to Manasseh, but the town of Tappuah itself, on the border of Manasseh's territory, belonged to the tribe of Ephraim. ⁹From the spring of Tappuah, the boundary of Manasseh followed the Kanah Ravine to the Mediterranean Sea.* Several towns south of the ravine were inside Manasseh's territory, but they actually belonged to the tribe of Ephraim. ¹⁰In general, however, the land south of the ravine belonged to Ephraim, and the land north of the ravine belonged to Manasseh. Manasseh's boundary ran along the northern side of the ravine and ended at the Mediterranean Sea. North of Manasseh was the territory of Asher, and to the east was the territory of Issachar.

¹¹The following towns within the territory of Issachar and Asher, however, were given to Manasseh: Beth-shan,* Ibleam, Dor (that is, Naphoth-dor),* Endor, Taanach, and Megiddo, each with their surrounding settlements.

16:3 Hebrew *the sea;* also in 16:6, 8. **17:9** Hebrew *the sea;* also in 17:10. **17:11a** Hebrew *Beth-shean,* a variant spelling of Beth-shan; also in 17:16. **17:11b** The meaning of the Hebrew here is uncertain.

¹²But the descendants of Manasseh were unable to occupy these towns. They could not drive out the Canaanites who continued to live there. ¹³Later, however, when the Israelites became strong enough, they forced the Canaanites to work as slaves. But they did not drive them out of the land.

¹⁴The descendants of Joseph came to Joshua and asked, "Why have you given us only one portion of land as our homeland when the LORD has blessed us with so many people?"

¹⁵Joshua replied, "If there are so many of you, and if the hill country of Ephraim is not large enough for you, clear out land for yourselves in the forest where the Perizzites and Rephaites live."

¹⁶The descendants of Joseph responded, "It's true that the hill country is not large enough for us. But all the Canaanites in the lowlands have iron chariots, both those in Beth-shan and its surrounding settlements and those in the valley of Jezreel. They are too strong for us."

¹⁷Then Joshua said to the tribes of Ephraim and Manasseh, the descendants of Joseph, "Since you are so large and strong, you will be given more than one portion. ¹⁸The forests of the hill country will be yours as well. Clear as much of the land as you wish, and take possession of its farthest corners. And you will drive out the Canaanites from the valleys, too, even though they are strong and have iron chariots."

18 The Allotments of the Remaining Land

Now that the land was under Israelite control, the entire community of Israel gathered at Shiloh and set up the Tabernacle.* ²But there remained seven tribes who had not yet been allotted their grants of land.

³Then Joshua asked them, "How long are you going to wait before taking possession of the remaining land the LORD, the God of your ancestors, has given to you? ⁴Select three men from each tribe, and I will send them out to explore the land and map it out. They will then return to me with a written report of their proposed divisions of their new homeland. ⁵Let them divide the land into seven sections, excluding Judah's territory in the south and Joseph's territory in the north. ⁶And when you record the seven divisions of the land and bring them to me, I will cast sacred lots in the presence of the LORD our God to assign land to each tribe.

⁷"The Levites, however, will not receive any allotment of land. Their role as priests of the LORD is their allotment. And the tribes of Gad, Reuben, and the half-tribe of Manasseh won't receive any more land, for they have already received their grant of land, which Moses, the servant of the LORD, gave them on the east side of the Jordan River."

⁸As the men started on their way to map out the land, Joshua commanded them, "Go and explore the land and write a description of it. Then return to me, and I will assign the land to the tribes by casting sacred lots here in the presence of the LORD at Shiloh." ⁹The men did as they were told and mapped the entire territory into seven sections, listing the towns in each section. They made a written record and then returned to Joshua in the camp at Shiloh. ¹⁰And there at Shiloh, Joshua cast sacred lots in the presence of the LORD to determine which tribe should have each section.

The Land Given to Benjamin

¹¹The first allotment of land went to the clans of the tribe of Benjamin. It lay between the territory assigned to the tribes of Judah and Joseph.

¹²The northern boundary of Benjamin's land began at the Jordan River, went north of the slope of Jericho, then west through the hill country and the wilderness of Beth-aven. ¹³From there the boundary went south to Luz (that is, Bethel) and proceeded down to Atarothaddar on the hill that lies south of Lower Beth-horon.

¹⁴The boundary then made a turn and swung south along the western edge of the hill facing Beth-horon, ending at the village of Kiriath-baal (that is, Kiriathjearim), a town belonging to the tribe of Judah. This was the western boundary.

¹⁵The southern boundary began at

18:1 Hebrew Tent of Meeting.

the outskirts of Kiriath-jearim. From that western point it ran* to the spring at the waters of Nephtoah,* [16]and down to the base of the mountain beside the valley of Ben-Hinnom, at the northern end of the valley of Rephaim. From there it went down the valley of Hinnom, crossing south of the slope where the Jebusites lived, and continued down to En-rogel. [17]From En-rogel the boundary proceeded in a northerly direction and came to En-shemesh and on to Geliloth (which is across from the slopes of Adummim). Then it went down to the Stone of Bohan. (Bohan was Reuben's son.) [18]From there it passed along the north side of the slope overlooking the Jordan Valley.* The border then went down into the valley, [19]ran past the north slope of Beth-hoglah, and ended at the north bay of the Dead Sea,* which is the southern end of the Jordan River. This was the southern boundary.

[20]The eastern boundary was the Jordan River.

These were the boundaries of the homeland allocated to the clans of the tribe of Benjamin.

The Towns Given to Benjamin

[21]These were the towns given to the clans of the tribe of Benjamin.

Jericho, Beth-hoglah, Emek-keziz, [22]Betharabah, Zemaraim, Bethel, [23]Avvim, Parah, Ophrah, [24]Kephar-ammoni, Ophni, and Geba—twelve towns with their surrounding villages. [25]Also Gibeon, Ramah, Beeroth, [26]Mizpah, Kephirah, Mozah, [27]Rekem, Irpeel, Taralah, [28]Zela, Haeleph, Jebus (that is, Jerusalem), Gibeah, and Kiriath*—fourteen towns with their surrounding villages.

This was the homeland allocated to the clans of the tribe of Benjamin.

19 The Land Given to Simeon

The second allotment of land went to the clans of the tribe of Simeon. Their homeland was surrounded by Judah's territory.

[2]Simeon's homeland included Beersheba, Sheba, Moladah, [3]Hazar-shual, Balah, Ezem, [4]Eltolad, Bethul, Hormah, [5]Ziklag, Beth-marcaboth, Hazar-susah, [6]Beth-lebaoth, and Sharuhen—thirteen towns with their surrounding villages. [7]It also included Ain, Rimmon, Ether, and Ashan—four towns with their villages, [8]including all the surrounding villages as far south as Baalath-beer (also known as Ramah of the Negev).

This was the homeland allocated to the clans of the tribe of Simeon. [9]Their allocation of land came from part of what had been given to Judah because Judah's territory was too large for them. So the tribe of Simeon received an allocation within the territory of Judah.

The Land Given to Zebulun

[10]The third allotment of land went to the clans of the tribe of Zebulun.

The boundary of Zebulun's homeland started at Sarid. [11]From there it went west, going past Maralah, touching Dabbesheth, and proceeding to the brook east of Jokneam. [12]In the other direction, the boundary went east from Sarid to the border of Kisloth-tabor, and from there to Daberath and up to Japhia. [13]Then it continued east to Gath-hepher, Eth-kazin, and Rimmon and turned toward Neah. [14]The northern boundary of Zebulun passed Hannathon and ended at the valley of Iphtah-el. [15]The towns in these areas included Kattath, Nahalal, Shimron, Idalah, and Bethlehem—twelve towns with their surrounding villages.

[16]The homeland allocated to the clans of the tribe of Zebulun included these towns and their surrounding villages.

The Land Given to Issachar

[17]The fourth allotment of land went to the clans of the tribe of Issachar.

[18]Its boundaries included the following towns: Jezreel, Kesulloth, Shunem, [19]Hapharaim, Shion, Anaharath,

---

18:15a Or *From there it went to Mozah.* The meaning of the Hebrew is uncertain.   **18:15b** Or *the spring at Me-nephtoah.*   **18:18** Hebrew *overlooking the Arabah,* or *overlooking Beth-arabah.*   **18:19** Hebrew *Salt Sea.*   **18:28** Some Greek manuscripts read *Kiriath-jearim.*

Rabbith, Kishion, Ebez, ²¹Remeth, En-gannim, En-haddah, and Beth-pazzez. ²²The boundary also touched Tabor, Shahazumah, and Beth-shemesh, ending at the Jordan River—sixteen towns with their surrounding villages.

²³The homeland allocated to the clans of the tribe of Issachar included these towns and their surrounding villages.

The Land Given to Asher

²⁴The fifth allotment of land went to the clans of the tribe of Asher.

²⁵Its boundaries included these towns: Helkath, Hali, Beten, Acshaph, ²⁶Allam-melech, Amad, and Mishal. The boundary on the west touched Carmel and Shihor-libnath, ²⁷then it turned east toward Beth-dagon, and ran as far as Zebulun in the valley of Iphtah-el, going north to Beth-emek and Neiel. It then continued north to Cabul, ²⁸Abdon,* Rehob, Ham-mon, Kanah, and as far as Greater Sidon. ²⁹Then the boundary turned toward Ramah and the fortress of Tyre, where it turned toward Hosah and came to the Mediterranean Sea.* The territory also included Mehebel, Aczib, ³⁰Ummah, Aphek, and Rehob—twenty-two towns with their surrounding villages.

³¹The homeland allocated to the clans of the tribe of Asher included these towns and their surrounding villages.

The Land Given to Naphtali

³²The sixth allotment of land went to the clans of the tribe of Naphtali.

³³Its boundary ran from Heleph, from the oak at Zaanannim, and extended across to Adami-nekeb, Jabneel, and as far as Lakkum, ending at the Jordan River. ³⁴The western boundary ran past Aznoth-tabor, then to Hukkok, and touched the border of Zebulun in the south, the border of Asher on the west, and the Jordan River* on the east. ³⁵The fortified towns included in this territory were Ziddim, Zer, Hammath, Rakkath,

Kinnereth, ³⁶Adamah, Ramah, Hazor, ³⁷Kedesh, Edrei, En-hazor, ³⁸Yiron, Migdal-el, Horem, Beth-anath, and Beth-shemesh—nineteen towns with their surrounding villages.

³⁹The homeland allocated to the clans of the tribe of Naphtali included these towns and their surrounding villages.

The Land Given to Dan

⁴⁰The seventh allotment of land went to the clans of the tribe of Dan.

⁴¹The land allocated as their homeland included the following towns: Zorah, Eshtaol, Ir-shemesh, ⁴²Shaalabbin, Aija-lon, Ithlah, ⁴³Elon, Timnah, Ekron, ⁴⁴Eltekeh, Gibbethon, Baalath, ⁴⁵Jehud, Bene-berak, Gath-rimmon, ⁴⁶Me-jarkon, Rakkon, and the territory across from Joppa.

⁴⁷But the tribe of Dan had trouble taking possession of their land,* so they attacked the town of Laish.* They captured it, slaughtered its people, and settled there. They renamed the town Dan after their ancestor.

⁴⁸The homeland allocated to the clans of the tribe of Dan included these towns and their surrounding villages.

The Land Given to Joshua

⁴⁹After all the land was divided among the tribes, the Israelites gave a piece of land to Joshua as his allocation. ⁵⁰For the LORD had said he could have any town he wanted. He chose Timnath-serah in the hill country of Ephraim. He rebuilt the town and lived there.

⁵¹These are the territories that Eleazar the priest, Joshua son of Nun, and the tribal leaders allocated as grants of land to the tribes of Israel by casting sacred lots in the presence of the LORD at the entrance of the Tabernacle* at Shiloh. So the division of the land was completed.

20 The Cities of Refuge

The LORD said to Joshua, ²"Now tell the Israelites to designate the cities of ref-uge, as I instructed Moses. ³Anyone who

---

19:28 As in some Hebrew manuscripts (see also 21:30); most Hebrew manuscripts read *Ebron.*   19:29 Hebrew *the sea.*   19:34 Hebrew *and Judah at the Jordan River.*   19:47a Or *had trouble holding on to their land.*   19:47b Hebrew *Leshem,* a variant spelling of Laish.   19:51 Hebrew *Tent of Meeting.*

kills another person accidentally and unintentionally can run to one of these cities; they will be places of refuge from relatives seeking revenge for the person who was killed.

⁴"Upon reaching one of these cities, the one who caused the death will appear before the elders at the city gate and present his case. They must allow him to enter the city and give him a place to live among them. ⁵If the relatives of the victim come to avenge the killing, the leaders must not release the slayer to them, for he killed the other person unintentionally and without previous hostility. ⁶But the slayer must stay in that city and be tried by the local assembly, which will render a judgment. And he must continue to live in that city until the death of the high priest who was in office at the time of the accident. After that, he is free to return to his own home in the town from which he fled."

⁷The following cities were designated as cities of refuge: Kedesh of Galilee, in the hill country of Naphtali; Shechem, in the hill country of Ephraim; and Kiriath-arba (that is, Hebron), in the hill country of Judah. ⁸On the east side of the Jordan River, across from Jericho, the following cities were designated: Bezer, in the wilderness plain of the tribe of Reuben; Ramoth in Gilead, in the territory of the tribe of Gad; and Golan in Bashan, in the land of the tribe of Manasseh. ⁹These cities were set apart for all the Israelites as well as the foreigners living among them. Anyone who accidentally killed another person could take refuge in one of these cities. In this way, they could escape being killed in revenge prior to standing trial before the local assembly.

21 The Towns Given to the Levites

Then the leaders of the tribe of Levi came to consult with Eleazar the priest, Joshua son of Nun, and the leaders of the other tribes of Israel. ²They came to them at Shiloh in the land of Canaan and said, "The LORD commanded Moses to give us towns to live in and pasturelands for our livestock." ³So by the command of the LORD the people of Israel gave the Levites the following towns and pasturelands out of their own grants of land.

⁴The descendants of Aaron, who were members of the Kohathite clan within the tribe of Levi, were allotted thirteen towns that were originally assigned to the tribes of Judah, Simeon, and Benjamin. ⁵The other families of the Kohathite clan were allotted ten towns from the tribes of Ephraim, Dan, and the half-tribe of Manasseh.

⁶The clan of Gershon was allotted thirteen towns from the tribes of Issachar, Asher, Naphtali, and the half-tribe of Manasseh in Bashan.

⁷The clan of Merari was allotted twelve towns from the tribes of Reuben, Gad, and Zebulun.

⁸So the Israelites obeyed the LORD's command to Moses and assigned these towns and pasturelands to the Levites by casting sacred lots.

⁹The Israelites gave the following towns from the tribes of Judah and Simeon ¹⁰to the descendants of Aaron, who were members of the Kohathite clan within the tribe of Levi, since the sacred lot fell to them first: ¹¹Kiriath-arba (that is, Hebron), in the hill country of Judah, along with its surrounding pasturelands. (Arba was an ancestor of Anak.) ¹²But the open fields beyond the town and the surrounding villages were given to Caleb son of Jephunneh as his possession.

¹³The following towns with their pasturelands were given to the descendants of Aaron the priest: Hebron (a city of refuge for those who accidentally killed someone), Libnah, ¹⁴Jattir, Eshtemoa, ¹⁵Holon, Debir, ¹⁶Ain, Juttah, and Beth-shemesh—nine towns from these two tribes.

¹⁷From the tribe of Benjamin the priests were given the following towns with their pasturelands: Gibeon, Geba, ¹⁸Anathoth, and Almon—four towns. ¹⁹So in all, thirteen towns with their pasturelands were given to the priests, the descendants of Aaron.

²⁰The rest of the Kohathite clan from the tribe of Levi was allotted the following towns and pasturelands from the tribe of Ephraim: ²¹Shechem in the hill country of Ephraim (a city of refuge for those who accidentally killed someone), Gezer, ²²Kibzaim, and Beth-horon—four towns.

²³The following towns and pasturelands were allotted to the priests from the tribe of Dan: Eltekeh, Gibbethon, ²⁴Aijalon, and Gath-rimmon—four towns.

²⁵The half-tribe of Manasseh allotted the following towns with their pasturelands to the priests: Taanach and Gath-rimmon—two towns. ²⁶So in all, ten towns with their pasturelands were given to the rest of the Kohathite clan.

²⁷The descendants of Gershon, another clan within the tribe of Levi, received the following towns with their pasturelands from the half-tribe of Manasseh: Golan in Bashan (a city of refuge for those who accidentally killed someone) and Be-eshterah—two towns.

²⁸From the tribe of Issachar they received the following towns with their pasturelands: Kishion, Daberath, ²⁹Jarmuth, and En-gannim—four towns.

³⁰From the tribe of Asher they received the following towns with their pasturelands: Mishal, Abdon, ³¹Helkath, and Rehob—four towns.

³²From the tribe of Naphtali they received the following towns with their pasturelands: Kedesh in Galilee (a city of refuge for those who accidentally killed someone), Hammoth-dor, and Kartan—three towns. ³³So in all, thirteen towns with their pasturelands were allotted to the clan of Gershon.

³⁴The rest of the Levites—the Merari clan—were given the following towns with their pasturelands from the tribe of Zebulun: Jokneam, Kartah, ³⁵Dimnah, and Nahalal—four towns.

³⁶From the tribe of Reuben they received the following towns with their pasturelands: Bezer, Jahaz,* ³⁷Kedemoth, and Mephaath—four towns.

³⁸From the tribe of Gad they received the following towns with their pasturelands: Ramoth in Gilead (a city of refuge for those who accidentally killed someone), Mahanaim, ³⁹Heshbon, and Jazer—four towns. ⁴⁰So in all, twelve towns were allotted to the clan of Merari.

⁴¹The total number of towns and pasturelands within Israelite territory given to the Levites came to forty-eight. ⁴²Every one of these towns had pasturelands surrounding it.

⁴³So the LORD gave to Israel all the land he had sworn to give their ancestors, and they took possession of it and settled there. ⁴⁴And the LORD gave them rest on every side, just as he had solemnly promised their ancestors. None of their enemies could stand against them, for the LORD helped them conquer all their enemies. ⁴⁵Not a single one of all the good promises the LORD had given to the family of Israel was left unfulfilled; everything he had spoken came true.

22 The Eastern Tribes Return Home

Then Joshua called together the tribes of Reuben, Gad, and the half-tribe of Manasseh. ²He told them, "You have done as Moses, the servant of the LORD, commanded you, and you have obeyed every order I have given you. ³During all this time you have not deserted the other tribes. You have been careful to obey the commands of the LORD your God right up to the present day. ⁴And now the LORD your God has given the other tribes rest, as he promised them. So go back home to the land that Moses, the servant of the LORD, gave you as your possession on the east side of the Jordan River. ⁵But be very careful to obey all the commands and the instructions that Moses gave to you. Love the LORD your God, walk in all his ways, obey his commands, hold firmly to him, and serve him with all your heart and all your soul." ⁶So Joshua blessed them and sent them away, and they went home.

⁷Moses had given the land of Bashan, east of the Jordan River, to the half-tribe of Manasseh. (The other half of the tribe was given land west of the Jordan.) As Joshua sent them away and blessed them, ⁸he said to them, "Go back to your homes with the great wealth you have taken from your enemies—the vast herds of livestock, the silver, gold, bronze, and iron, and the large supply of clothing. Share the plunder with your relatives."

⁹So the men of Reuben, Gad, and the half-tribe of Manasseh left the rest of Israel at

---

21:36 Hebrew *Jahzah*, a variant spelling of Jahaz.

Shiloh in the land of Canaan. They started the journey back to their own land of Gilead, the territory that belonged to them according to the LORD's command through Moses.

The Eastern Tribes Build an Altar

¹⁰But while they were still in Canaan, and when they came to a place called Geliloth* near the Jordan River, the men of Reuben, Gad, and the half-tribe of Manasseh stopped to build a large and imposing altar.

¹¹The rest of Israel heard that the people of Reuben, Gad, and the half-tribe of Manasseh had built an altar at Geliloth at the edge of the land of Canaan, on the west side of the Jordan River. ¹²So the whole community of Israel gathered at Shiloh and prepared to go to war against them. ¹³First, however, they sent a delegation led by Phinehas son of Eleazar, the priest, to talk with the tribes of Reuben, Gad, and the half-tribe of Manasseh. ¹⁴In this delegation were ten leaders of Israel, one from each of the ten tribes, and each the head of his family within the clans of Israel.

¹⁵When they arrived in the land of Gilead, they said to the tribes of Reuben, Gad, and the half-tribe of Manasseh, ¹⁶"The whole community of the LORD demands to know why you are betraying the God of Israel. How could you turn away from the LORD and build an altar for yourselves in rebellion against him? ¹⁷Was our sin at Peor not enough? To this day we are not fully cleansed of it, even after the plague that struck the entire community of the LORD. ¹⁸And yet today you are turning away from following the LORD. If you rebel against the LORD today, he will be angry with all of us tomorrow.

¹⁹"If you need the altar because the land you possess is defiled, then join us in the LORD's land, where the Tabernacle of the LORD is situated, and share our land with us. But do not rebel against the LORD or against us by building an altar other than the one true altar of the LORD our God. ²⁰Didn't divine anger fall on the entire community of Israel when Achan, a member of the clan of Zerah, sinned by stealing the things set apart for the LORD*? He was not the only one who died because of his sin."

²¹Then the people of Reuben, Gad, and the half-tribe of Manasseh answered the heads of the clans of Israel: ²²"The LORD, the Mighty One, is God! The LORD, the Mighty One, is God! He knows the truth, and may Israel know it, too! We have not built the altar in treacherous rebellion against the LORD. If we have done so, do not spare our lives this day. ²³If we have built an altar for ourselves to turn away from the LORD or to offer burnt offerings or grain offerings or peace offerings, may the LORD himself punish us.

²⁴"The truth is, we have built this altar because we fear that in the future your descendants will say to ours, 'What right do you have to worship the LORD, the God of Israel? ²⁵The LORD has placed the Jordan River as a barrier between our people and you people of Reuben and Gad. You have no claim to the LORD.' So your descendants may prevent our descendants from worshiping the LORD.

²⁶"So we decided to build the altar, not for burnt offerings or sacrifices, ²⁷but as a memorial. It will remind our descendants and your descendants that we, too, have the right to worship the LORD at his sanctuary with our burnt offerings, sacrifices, and peace offerings. Then your descendants will not be able to say to ours, 'You have no claim to the LORD.'

²⁸"If they say this, our descendants can reply, 'Look at this copy of the LORD's altar that our ancestors made. It is not for burnt offerings or sacrifices; it is a reminder of the relationship both of us have with the LORD.' ²⁹Far be it from us to rebel against the LORD or turn away from him by building our own altar for burnt offerings, grain offerings, or sacrifices. Only the altar of the LORD our God that stands in front of the Tabernacle may be used for that purpose."

³⁰When Phinehas the priest and the leaders of the community—the heads of the clans of Israel—heard this from the tribes of Reuben, Gad, and the half-tribe of Manasseh, they were satisfied. ³¹Phinehas son of Eleazar, the priest, replied to them, "Today we know the LORD is among us because you have not committed this treachery against the LORD as we thought. Instead, you have

Signs of Fruitful Mentoring
JOSHUA 23

How do we know if our efforts to mentor another person are effective? To evaluate the fruitfulness of a mentoring relationship, we can look for these characteristics:

- Trust and confidence. All the cards are on the table. Anything given in confidence should be held in confidence.
- Unvarnished truth. We should come to the place in the relationship where we can be direct. My two great mentors never had to preface the truth or hedge their statements with me.
- Climbs and plateaus. We progress by climbing, then plateauing for assimilation, then climbing again, plateauing again—repeating the process as long as we live. Don't stop when you reach a comfortable plateau.
- Character development. The mentor teaches, but the Spirit changes character. Although I've mentored actively for more than forty years, I cannot claim any success in improving character in adults. Character improves only through spiritual experience.
- Mentoree initiation. The mentoree is responsible for all contact. The mentoree controls the continuation of the relationship. Sometimes a mentoring relationship becomes nonproductive and should end. I accept this as normal.
- Joy in the doing. A mentor has accomplished great good when she has taught the individual the joy of accomplishment. That has become so much a part of my life that when I get low, I immediately start to do something that I feel will be worthwhile. And the joy of living returns.

—Fred Smith

For more on mentoring, see reading at 1 Samuel 3:1-14.

rescued Israel from being destroyed by the hand of the Lord."

³² Then Phinehas son of Eleazar, the priest, and the other leaders left the tribes of Reuben and Gad in Gilead and returned to the land of Canaan to tell the Israelites what had happened. ³³ And all the Israelites were satisfied and praised God and spoke no more of war against Reuben and Gad.

³⁴ The people of Reuben and Gad named the altar "Witness,"* for they said, "It is a witness between us and them that the Lord is our God, too."

23 Joshua's Final Words to Israel
The years passed, and the Lord had given the people of Israel rest from all their enemies. Joshua, who was now very old, ² called together all the elders, lead-ers, judges, and officers of Israel. He said to them, "I am now a very old man. ³ You have seen everything the Lord your God has done for you during my lifetime. The Lord your God has fought for you against your enemies. ⁴ I have allotted to you as your homeland all the land of the nations yet unconquered, as well as the land of those we have already conquered—from the Jordan River to the Mediterranean Sea* in the west. ⁵ This land will be yours, for the Lord your God will himself drive out all the people living there now. You will take possession of their land, just as the Lord your God promised you.

⁶ "So be very careful to follow everything Moses wrote in the Book of Instruction. Do not deviate from it, turning either to the right or to the left. ⁷ Make sure you

22:34 Some manuscripts lack this word.   23:4 Hebrew *the Great Sea.*

do not associate with the other people still remaining in the land. Do not even mention the names of their gods, much less swear by them or serve them or worship them. ⁸Rather, cling tightly to the Lord your God as you have done until now.

⁹"For the Lord has driven out great and powerful nations for you, and no one has yet been able to defeat you. ¹⁰Each one of you will put to flight a thousand of the enemy, for the Lord your God fights for you, just as he has promised. ¹¹So be very careful to love the Lord your God.

¹²"But if you turn away from him and cling to the customs of the survivors of these nations remaining among you, and if you intermarry with them, ¹³then know for certain that the Lord your God will no longer drive them out of your land. Instead, they will be a snare and a trap to you, a whip for your backs and thorny brambles in your eyes, and you will vanish from this good land the Lord your God has given you.

¹⁴"Soon I will die, going the way of everything on earth. Deep in your hearts you know that every promise of the Lord your God has come true. Not a single one has failed! ¹⁵But as surely as the Lord your God has given you the good things he promised, he will also bring disaster on you if you disobey him. He will completely destroy you from this good land he has given you. ¹⁶If you break the covenant of the Lord your God by worshiping and serving other gods, his anger will burn against you, and you will quickly vanish from the good land he has given you."

24 The Lord's Covenant Renewed

Then Joshua summoned all the tribes of Israel to Shechem, including their elders, leaders, judges, and officers. So they came and presented themselves to God.

²Joshua said to the people, "This is what the Lord, the God of Israel, says: Long ago your ancestors, including Terah, the father of Abraham and Nahor, lived beyond the Euphrates River,* and they worshiped other gods. ³But I took your ancestor Abraham from the land beyond the Euphrates and led him into the land of Canaan. I gave him

many descendants through his son Isaac. ⁴To Isaac I gave Jacob and Esau. To Esau I gave the mountains of Seir, while Jacob and his children went down into Egypt.

⁵"Then I sent Moses and Aaron, and I brought terrible plagues on Egypt; and afterward I brought you out as a free people. ⁶But when your ancestors arrived at the Red Sea,* the Egyptians chased after you with chariots and charioteers. ⁷When your ancestors cried out to the Lord, I put darkness between you and the Egyptians. I brought the sea crashing down on the Egyptians, drowning them. With your very own eyes you saw what I did. Then you lived in the wilderness for many years.

⁸"Finally, I brought you into the land of the Amorites on the east side of the Jordan. They fought against you, but I destroyed them before you. I gave you victory over them, and you took possession of their land. ⁹Then Balak son of Zippor, king of Moab, started a war against Israel. He summoned Balaam son of Beor to curse you, ¹⁰but I would not listen to him. Instead, I made Balaam bless you, and so I rescued you from Balak.

¹¹"When you crossed the Jordan River and came to Jericho, the men of Jericho fought against you, as did the Amorites, the Perizzites, the Canaanites, the Hittites, the Girgashites, the Hivites, and the Jebusites. But I gave you victory over them. ¹²And I sent terror* ahead of you to drive out the two kings of the Amorites. It was not your swords or bows that brought you victory. ¹³I gave you land you had not worked on, and I gave you towns you did not build—the towns where you are now living. I gave you vineyards and olive groves for food, though you did not plant them.

¹⁴"So fear the Lord and serve him wholeheartedly. Put away forever the idols your ancestors worshiped when they lived beyond the Euphrates River and in Egypt. Serve the Lord alone. ¹⁵But if you refuse to serve the Lord, then choose today whom you will serve. Would you prefer the gods your ancestors served beyond the Euphrates? Or will it be the gods of the Amorites

---

24:2 Hebrew *the river*; also in 24:3, 14, 15.   24:6 Hebrew *sea of reeds*.   24:12 Often rendered *the hornet*. The meaning of the Hebrew is uncertain.

in whose land you now live? But as for me and my family, we will serve the LORD."

¹⁶ The people replied, "We would never abandon the LORD and serve other gods. ¹⁷ For the LORD our God is the one who rescued us and our ancestors from slavery in the land of Egypt. He performed mighty miracles before our very eyes. As we traveled through the wilderness among our enemies, he preserved us. ¹⁸ It was the LORD who drove out the Amorites and the other nations living here in the land. So we, too, will serve the LORD, for he alone is our God."

¹⁹ Then Joshua warned the people, "You are not able to serve the LORD, for he is a holy and jealous God. He will not forgive your rebellion and your sins. ²⁰ If you abandon the LORD and serve other gods, he will turn against you and destroy you, even though he has been so good to you."

²¹ But the people answered Joshua, "No, we will serve the LORD!"

²² "You are a witness to your own decision," Joshua said. "You have chosen to serve the LORD."

"Yes," they replied, "we are witnesses to what we have said."

²³ "All right then," Joshua said, "destroy the idols among you, and turn your hearts to the LORD, the God of Israel."

²⁴ The people said to Joshua, "We will serve the LORD our God. We will obey him alone."

²⁵ So Joshua made a covenant with the people that day at Shechem, committing them to follow the decrees and regulations of the LORD. ²⁶ Joshua recorded these things in the Book of God's Instructions. As a reminder of their agreement, he took a huge stone and rolled it beneath the terebinth tree beside the Tabernacle of the LORD.

²⁷ Joshua said to all the people, "This stone has heard everything the LORD said to us. It will be a witness to testify against you if you go back on your word to God."

²⁸ Then Joshua sent all the people away to their own homelands.

Leaders Buried in the Promised Land

²⁹ After this, Joshua son of Nun, the servant of the LORD, died at the age of 110. ³⁰ They buried him in the land he had been allocated, at Timnath-serah in the hill country of Ephraim, north of Mount Gaash.

³¹ The people of Israel served the LORD throughout the lifetime of Joshua and of the elders who outlived him—those who had personally experienced all that the LORD had done for Israel.

³² The bones of Joseph, which the Israelites had brought along with them when they left Egypt, were buried at Shechem, in the parcel of ground Jacob had bought from the sons of Hamor for 100 pieces of silver.* This land was located in the territory allotted to the descendants of Joseph.

³³ Eleazar son of Aaron also died. He was buried in the hill country of Ephraim, in the town of Gibeah, which had been given to his son Phinehas.

24:32 Hebrew *100 kesitahs;* the value or weight of the kesitah is no longer known.

Introduction to

Judges

Background

The conquest of the land that began so promisingly with Joshua is never really completed. After the initial conquest of key cities, such as Jericho, the land was divided among Israel's tribes, and it was up to each tribe to conquer its own area. The first chapter of the Book of Judges describes how each tribe "failed to drive out" (1:21) the inhabitants of the land as God commanded. In time these idol-worshiping nations became the downfall of God's people.

The period of the judges lasted more than four hundred years, from the death of Joshua to the time of Samuel (see Acts 13:20).

Historically the prophet Samuel was believed to have written the Book of Judges. However, his authorship is uncertain.

Message

After the death of Joshua, the constant refrain "the Israelites did evil in the LORD's sight" (2:11; 3:7, 12; 4:1; 6:1; 10:6; 13:1) shows Israel's departure from its former holiness. A vicious cycle carries throughout the book: first, the people sin, provoking God's wrath. As a result God allows their enemies to attack. The people cry out to God. God raises up a faithful and courageous judge—a military leader and counselor—to lead the people against their enemies. After victory is secured, the people sin, and the cycle begins again. God remains faithful, but sin always has consequences.

Time

The Book of Judges was probably written between 1043 and 1004 B.C. The phrase "in those days Israel had no king" (17:6; 18:1; 19:1; 21:25) implies that the book was written after the monarchy was established.

Outline

Judges

1 Judah and Simeon Conquer the Land

After the death of Joshua, the Israelites asked the LORD, "Which tribe should go first to attack the Canaanites?"

² The LORD answered, "Judah, for I have given them victory over the land."

³ The men of Judah said to their relatives from the tribe of Simeon, "Join with us to fight against the Canaanites living in the territory allotted to us. Then we will help you conquer your territory." So the men of Simeon went with Judah.

⁴ When the men of Judah attacked, the LORD gave them victory over the Canaanites and Perizzites, and they killed 10,000 enemy warriors at the town of Bezek. ⁵ While at Bezek they encountered King Adoni-bezek and fought against him, and the Canaanites and Perizzites were defeated. ⁶ Adoni-bezek escaped, but the Israelites soon captured him and cut off his thumbs and big toes.

⁷ Adoni-bezek said, "I once had seventy kings with their thumbs and big toes cut off, eating scraps from under my table. Now God has paid me back for what I did to them." They took him to Jerusalem, and he died there.

⁸ The men of Judah attacked Jerusalem and captured it, killing all its people and setting the city on fire. ⁹ Then they went down to fight the Canaanites living in the hill country, the Negev, and the western foothills.* ¹⁰ Judah marched against the Canaanites in Hebron (formerly called Kiriath-arba), defeating the forces of Sheshai, Ahiman, and Talmai.

¹¹ From there they went to fight against the people living in the town of Debir (formerly called Kiriath-sepher). ¹² Caleb said, "I will give my daughter Acsah in marriage to the one who attacks and captures Kiriath-sepher." ¹³ Othniel, the son of Caleb's younger brother, Kenaz, was the one who conquered it, so Acsah became Othniel's wife.

¹⁴ When Acsah married Othniel, she urged him* to ask her father for a field. As she got down off her donkey, Caleb asked her, "What's the matter?"

¹⁵ She said, "Let me have another gift. You have already given me land in the Negev; now please give me springs of water, too." So Caleb gave her the upper and lower springs.

¹⁶ When the tribe of Judah left Jericho—the city of palms—the Kenites, who were descendants of Moses' father-in-law, traveled with them into the wilderness of Judah. They settled among the people there, near the town of Arad in the Negev.

¹⁷ Then Judah joined with Simeon to fight against the Canaanites living in Zephath, and they completely destroyed* the town. So the town was named Hormah.* ¹⁸ In addition, Judah captured the towns of Gaza, Ashkelon, and Ekron, along with their surrounding territories.

Israel Fails to Conquer the Land

¹⁹ The LORD was with the people of Judah, and they took possession of the hill country. But they failed to drive out the people living in the plains, who had iron

---

1:9 Hebrew *the Shephelah.*   **1:14** Greek version and Latin Vulgate read *he urged her.*   **1:17a** The Hebrew term used here refers to the complete consecration of things or people to the LORD, either by destroying them or by giving them as an offering.   **1:17b** *Hormah* means "destruction."

chariots. ²⁰The town of Hebron was given to Caleb as Moses had promised. And Caleb drove out the people living there, who were descendants of the three sons of Anak.

²¹The tribe of Benjamin, however, failed to drive out the Jebusites, who were living in Jerusalem. So to this day the Jebusites live in Jerusalem among the people of Benjamin.

²²The descendants of Joseph attacked the town of Bethel, and the LORD was with them. ²³They sent men to scout out Bethel (formerly known as Luz). ²⁴They confronted a man coming out of the town and said to him, "Show us a way into the town, and we will have mercy on you." ²⁵So he showed them a way in, and they killed everyone in the town except that man and his family. ²⁶Later the man moved to the land of the Hittites, where he built a town. He named it Luz, which is its name to this day.

²⁷The tribe of Manasseh failed to drive out the people living in Beth-shan,* Taanach, Dor, Ibleam, Megiddo, and all their surrounding settlements, because the Canaanites were determined to stay in that region. ²⁸When the Israelites grew stronger, they forced the Canaanites to work as slaves, but they never did drive them completely out of the land.

²⁹The tribe of Ephraim failed to drive out the Canaanites living in Gezer, so the Canaanites continued to live there among them.

³⁰The tribe of Zebulun failed to drive out the residents of Kitron and Nahalol, so the Canaanites continued to live among them. But the Canaanites were forced to work as slaves for the people of Zebulun.

³¹The tribe of Asher failed to drive out the residents of Acco, Sidon, Ahlab, Aczib, Helbah, Aphik, and Rehob. ³²Instead, the people of Asher moved in among the Canaanites, who controlled the land, for they failed to drive them out.

³³Likewise, the tribe of Naphtali failed to drive out the residents of Beth-shemesh and Beth-anath. Instead, they moved in among the Canaanites, who controlled the land. Nevertheless, the people of Beth-shemesh and Beth-anath were forced to work as slaves for the people of Naphtali.

³⁴As for the tribe of Dan, the Amorites forced them back into the hill country and would not let them come down into the plains. ³⁵The Amorites were determined to stay in Mount Heres, Aijalon, and Shaalbim, but when the descendants of Joseph became stronger, they forced the Amorites to work as slaves. ³⁶The boundary of the Amorites ran from Scorpion Pass* to Sela and continued upward from there.

2 The LORD's Messenger Comes to Bokim

The angel of the LORD went up from Gilgal to Bokim and said to the Israelites, "I brought you out of Egypt into this land that I swore to give your ancestors, and I said I would never break my covenant with you. ²For your part, you were not to make any covenants with the people living in this land; instead, you were to destroy their altars. But you disobeyed my command. Why did you do this? ³So now I declare that I will no longer drive out the people living in your land. They will be thorns in your sides,* and their gods will be a constant temptation to you."

⁴When the angel of the LORD finished speaking to all the Israelites, the people wept loudly. ⁵So they called the place Bokim (which means "weeping"), and they offered sacrifices there to the LORD.

The Death of Joshua

⁶After Joshua sent the people away, each of the tribes left to take possession of the land allotted to them. ⁷And the Israelites served the LORD throughout the lifetime of Joshua and the leaders who outlived him—those who had seen all the great things the LORD had done for Israel.

⁸Joshua son of Nun, the servant of the LORD, died at the age of 110. ⁹They buried him in the land he had been allocated, at Timnath-serah* in the hill country of Ephraim, north of Mount Gaash.

Israel Disobeys the LORD

¹⁰After that generation died, another generation grew up who did not acknowledge the LORD or remember the mighty things he had done for Israel.

1:27 Hebrew *Beth-shean,* a variant spelling of Beth-shan.   **1:36** Hebrew *Akrabbim.*   **2:3** Hebrew *They will be in your sides;* compare Num 33:55.
2:9 As in parallel text at Josh 24:30; Hebrew reads *Timnath-heres,* a variant spelling of Timnath-serah.

¹¹The Israelites did evil in the LORD's sight and served the images of Baal. ¹²They abandoned the LORD, the God of their ancestors, who had brought them out of Egypt. They went after other gods, worshiping the gods of the people around them. And they angered the LORD. ¹³They abandoned the LORD to serve Baal and the images of Ashtoreth. ¹⁴This made the LORD burn with anger against Israel, so he handed them over to raiders who stole their possessions. He turned them over to their enemies all around, and they were no longer able to resist them. ¹⁵Every time Israel went out to battle, the LORD fought against them, causing them to be defeated, just as he had warned. And the people were in great distress.

The LORD Rescues His People

¹⁶Then the LORD raised up judges to rescue the Israelites from their attackers. ¹⁷Yet Israel did not listen to the judges but prostituted themselves by worshiping other gods. How quickly they turned away from the path of their ancestors, who had walked in obedience to the LORD's commands.

¹⁸Whenever the LORD raised up a judge over Israel, he was with that judge and rescued the people from their enemies throughout the judge's lifetime. For the LORD took pity on his people, who were burdened by oppression and suffering. ¹⁹But when the judge died, the people returned to their corrupt ways, behaving worse than those who had lived before them. They went after other gods, serving and worshiping them. And they refused to give up their evil practices and stubborn ways.

²⁰So the LORD burned with anger against Israel. He said, "Because these people have violated my covenant, which I made with their ancestors, and have ignored my commands, ²¹I will no longer drive out the nations that Joshua left unconquered when he died. ²²I did this to test Israel—to see whether or not they would follow the ways of the LORD as their ancestors did." ²³That is why the LORD left those nations in place. He did not quickly drive them out or allow Joshua to conquer them all.

3 The Nations Left in Canaan

These are the nations that the LORD left in the land to test those Israelites who had not experienced the wars of Canaan. ²He did this to teach warfare to generations of Israelites who had no experience in battle. ³These are the nations: the Philistines (those living under the five Philistine rulers), all the Canaanites, the Sidonians, and the Hivites living in the mountains of Lebanon from Mount Baal-hermon to Lebo-hamath. ⁴These people were left to test the Israelites—to see whether they would obey the commands the LORD had given to their ancestors through Moses.

⁵So the people of Israel lived among the Canaanites, Hittites, Amorites, Perizzites, Hivites, and Jebusites, ⁶and they intermarried with them. Israelite sons married their daughters, and Israelite daughters were given in marriage to their sons. And the Israelites served their gods.

Othniel Becomes Israel's Judge

⁷The Israelites did evil in the LORD's sight. They forgot about the LORD their God, and they served the images of Baal and the Asherah poles. ⁸Then the LORD burned with anger against Israel, and he turned them over to King Cushan-rishathaim of Aram-naharaim.* And the Israelites served Cushan-rishathaim for eight years.

⁹But when the people of Israel cried out to the LORD for help, the LORD raised up a rescuer to save them. His name was Othniel, the son of Caleb's younger brother, Kenaz. ¹⁰The Spirit of the LORD came upon him, and he became Israel's judge. He went to war against King Cushan-rishathaim of Aram, and the LORD gave Othniel victory over him. ¹¹So there was peace in the land for forty years. Then Othniel son of Kenaz died.

Ehud Becomes Israel's Judge

¹²Once again the Israelites did evil in the LORD's sight, and the LORD gave King Eglon of Moab control over Israel because of their evil. ¹³Eglon enlisted the Ammonites and Amalekites as allies, and then he went out and defeated Israel, taking possession

---

3:8 *Aram-naharaim* means "Aram of the two rivers," thought to have been located between the Euphrates and Balih Rivers in northwestern Mesopotamia.

of Jericho, the city of palms. ¹⁴And the Israelites served Eglon of Moab for eighteen years.

¹⁵But when the people of Israel cried out to the LORD for help, the LORD again raised up a rescuer to save them. His name was Ehud son of Gera, a left-handed man of the tribe of Benjamin. The Israelites sent Ehud to deliver their tribute money to King Eglon of Moab. ¹⁶So Ehud made a double-edged dagger that was about a foot* long, and he strapped it to his right thigh, keeping it hidden under his clothing. ¹⁷He brought the tribute money to Eglon, who was very fat.

¹⁸After delivering the payment, Ehud started home with those who had helped carry the tribute. ¹⁹But when Ehud reached the stone idols near Gilgal, he turned back. He came to Eglon and said, "I have a secret message for you."

So the king commanded his servants, "Be quiet!" and he sent them all out of the room.

²⁰Ehud walked over to Eglon, who was sitting alone in a cool upstairs room. And Ehud said, "I have a message from God for you!" As King Eglon rose from his seat, ²¹Ehud reached with his left hand, pulled out the dagger strapped to his right thigh, and plunged it into the king's belly. ²²The dagger went so deep that the handle disappeared beneath the king's fat. So Ehud did not pull out the dagger, and the king's bowels emptied.* ²³Then Ehud closed and locked the doors of the room and escaped down the latrine.*

²⁴After Ehud was gone, the king's servants returned and found the doors to the upstairs room locked. They thought he might be using the latrine in the room, ²⁵so they waited. But when the king didn't come out after a long delay, they became concerned and got a key. And when they opened the doors, they found their master dead on the floor.

²⁶While the servants were waiting, Ehud escaped, passing the stone idols on his way to Seirah. ²⁷When he arrived in the hill country of Ephraim, Ehud sounded a call to arms. Then he led a band of Israelites down from the hills.

²⁸"Follow me," he said, "for the LORD has given you victory over Moab your enemy." So they followed him. And the Israelites took control of the shallow crossings of the Jordan River across from Moab, preventing anyone from crossing.

²⁹They attacked the Moabites and killed about 10,000 of their strongest and most able-bodied warriors. Not one of them escaped. ³⁰So Moab was conquered by Israel that day, and there was peace in the land for eighty years.

Shamgar Becomes Israel's Judge

³¹After Ehud, Shamgar son of Anath rescued Israel. He once killed 600 Philistines with an ox goad.

4 Deborah Becomes Israel's Judge

After Ehud's death, the Israelites again did evil in the LORD's sight. ²So the LORD turned them over to King Jabin of Hazor, a Canaanite king. The commander of his army was Sisera, who lived in Harosheth-haggoyim. ³Sisera, who had 900 iron chariots, ruthlessly oppressed the Israelites for twenty years. Then the people of Israel cried out to the LORD for help.

⁴Deborah, the wife of Lappidoth, was a prophet who was judging Israel at that time. ⁵She would sit under the Palm of Deborah, between Ramah and Bethel in the hill country of Ephraim, and the Israelites would go to her for judgment. ⁶One day she sent for Barak son of Abinoam, who lived in Kedesh in the land of Naphtali. She said to him, "This is what the LORD, the God of Israel, commands you: Call out 10,000 warriors from the tribes of Naphtali and Zebulun at Mount Tabor. ⁷And I will call out Sisera, commander of Jabin's army, along with his chariots and warriors, to the Kishon River. There I will give you victory over him."

⁸Barak told her, "I will go, but only if you go with me."

⁹"Very well," she replied, "I will go with you. But you will receive no honor in this venture, for the LORD's victory over Sisera will be at the hands of a woman." So Deborah went with Barak to Kedesh. ¹⁰At Kedesh, Barak called together the tribes of Zebulun and Naphtali, and 10,000 warriors went up with him. Deborah also went with him.

3:16 Hebrew *gomed*, the length of which is uncertain.   **3:22** Or *and it came out behind.*   **3:23** Or *and went out through the porch;* the meaning of the Hebrew is uncertain.

¹¹Now Heber the Kenite, a descendant of Moses' brother-in-law* Hobab, had moved away from the other members of his tribe and pitched his tent by the oak of Zaanannim near Kedesh.

¹²When Sisera was told that Barak son of Abinoam had gone up to Mount Tabor, ¹³he called for all 900 of his iron chariots and all of his warriors, and they marched from Harosheth-haggoyim to the Kishon River.

¹⁴Then Deborah said to Barak, "Get ready! This is the day the LORD will give you victory over Sisera, for the LORD is marching ahead of you." So Barak led his 10,000 warriors down the slopes of Mount Tabor into battle. ¹⁵When Barak attacked, the LORD threw Sisera and all his chariots and warriors into a panic. Sisera leaped down from his chariot and escaped on foot. ¹⁶Then Barak chased the chariots and the enemy army all the way to Harosheth-haggoyim,

Deborah: Recognizing the True Object of Worship

JUDGES 5

Scripture's account of Deborah doesn't explain how a woman living within a patriarchal society was chosen to be a judge—a very significant cultural, religious, and political figure. We don't know much about her leadership style or the types of responses she received from others. Though we know she was a prophetess, only one of her prophecies is recorded. We don't know any details about her family life except for the name of her husband.

But this is what we do know: the Israelites had been under the thumb of the Canaanites for more than twenty years. The Canaanites had a significant advantage, including more than nine hundred iron chariots (Judges 4:2-3). Yet God, through Deborah, promised to give his people victory (4:6-7). Despite this assurance Barak, the commander of the Israelite army, refused to fight unless Deborah went with him into battle—so she did (4:8-9). And despite all rational expectations, the Canaanites were *defeated* by the Israelite army. God empowered the Israelites, and he used a woman name Jael to assassinate the Canaanite commander, Sisera.

After the battle Deborah sang a victory song (Judges 5). She could have sung about the strengths of women or about her own valor and leadership skills, but she doesn't. Instead, her song tells the story of what happened, mentioning specific names and places, but it ultimately gives God credit for fighting the battle. "LORD, when you set out from Seir and marched across the fields of Edom, the earth trembled, and the cloudy skies poured down rain. The mountains quaked in the presence of the LORD, the God of Mount Sinai—in the presence of the LORD, the God of Israel" (5:4-5).

Worship is about God, not us. In her book *Reaching Out without Dumbing Down*, theologian Marva Dawn writes about the importance of God being both the *subject* and *object* in our worship: "The gifts of worship flow from God the subject and return to God as the object of our reverence." Deborah's song makes a perfect example of how this is done. *God has done this great act*, her song proclaims. *Praise him!*

—Joy-Elizabeth Lawrence

For more on worship, see reading at 2 Samuel 6:16-22.

4:11 Or *father-in-law.*

killing all of Sisera's warriors. Not a single one was left alive.

¹⁷ Meanwhile, Sisera ran to the tent of Jael, the wife of Heber the Kenite, because Heber's family was on friendly terms with King Jabin of Hazor. ¹⁸ Jael went out to meet Sisera and said to him, "Come into my tent, sir. Come in. Don't be afraid." So he went into her tent, and she covered him with a blanket.

¹⁹ "Please give me some water," he said. "I'm thirsty." So she gave him some milk from a leather bag and covered him again.

²⁰ "Stand at the door of the tent," he told her. "If anybody comes and asks you if there is anyone here, say no."

²¹ But when Sisera fell asleep from exhaustion, Jael quietly crept up to him with a hammer and tent peg in her hand. Then she drove the tent peg through his temple and into the ground, and so he died.

²² When Barak came looking for Sisera, Jael went out to meet him. She said, "Come, and I will show you the man you are looking for." So he followed her into the tent and found Sisera lying there dead, with the tent peg through his temple.

²³ So on that day Israel saw God defeat Jabin, the Canaanite king. ²⁴ And from that time on Israel became stronger and stronger against King Jabin until they finally destroyed him.

5 The Song of Deborah

On that day Deborah and Barak son of Abinoam sang this song:

² "Israel's leaders took charge,
  and the people gladly followed.
Praise the LORD!

³ "Listen, you kings!
  Pay attention, you mighty rulers!
For I will sing to the LORD.
  I will make music to the LORD, the
    God of Israel.

⁴ "LORD, when you set out from Seir
  and marched across the fields of
    Edom,
the earth trembled,
  and the cloudy skies poured down
    rain.

⁵ The mountains quaked in the presence
    of the LORD,
  the God of Mount Sinai—
in the presence of the LORD,
  the God of Israel.

⁶ "In the days of Shamgar son of Anath,
  and in the days of Jael,
people avoided the main roads,
  and travelers stayed on winding
    pathways.

⁷ There were few people left in the villages
    of Israel*—
  until Deborah arose as a mother for
    Israel.

⁸ When Israel chose new gods,
  war erupted at the city gates.
Yet not a shield or spear could be seen
  among forty thousand warriors in
    Israel!

⁹ My heart is with the commanders of
    Israel,
  with those who volunteered for war.
Praise the LORD!

¹⁰ "Consider this, you who ride on fine
    donkeys,
  you who sit on fancy saddle blankets,
  and you who walk along the road.

¹¹ Listen to the village musicians*
  gathered at the watering holes.
They recount the righteous victories of
    the LORD
  and the victories of his villagers in
    Israel.
Then the people of the LORD
  marched down to the city gates.

¹² "Wake up, Deborah, wake up!
  Wake up, wake up, and sing a song!
Arise, Barak!
  Lead your captives away, son of
    Abinoam!

¹³ "Down from Tabor marched the few
    against the nobles.
The people of the LORD marched
  down against mighty warriors.

¹⁴ They came down from Ephraim—
  a land that once belonged to the
    Amalekites;
they followed you, Benjamin, with
  your troops.

5:7 The meaning of the Hebrew is uncertain.   **5:11** The meaning of the Hebrew is uncertain.

From Makir the commanders marched
down;
from Zebulun came those who carry a
commander's staff.
¹⁵ The princes of Issachar were with
Deborah and Barak.
They followed Barak, rushing into the
valley.
But in the tribe of Reuben
there was great indecision.
¹⁶ Why did you sit at home among the
sheepfolds—
to hear the shepherds whistle for their
flocks?
Yes, in the tribe of Reuben
there was great indecision.
¹⁷ Gilead remained east of the Jordan.
And why did Dan stay home?
Asher sat unmoved at the seashore,
remaining in his harbors.
¹⁸ But Zebulun risked his life,
as did Naphtali, on the heights of the
battlefield.

¹⁹ "The kings of Canaan came and fought,
at Taanach near Megiddo's springs,
but they carried off no silver treasures.
²⁰ The stars fought from heaven.
The stars in their orbits fought against
Sisera.
²¹ The Kishon River swept them away—
that ancient torrent, the Kishon.
March on with courage, my soul!
²² Then the horses' hooves hammered the
ground,
the galloping, galloping of Sisera's
mighty steeds.
²³ 'Let the people of Meroz be cursed,' said
the angel of the LORD.
'Let them be utterly cursed,
because they did not come to help the
LORD—
to help the LORD against the mighty
warriors.'

²⁴ "Most blessed among women is Jael,
the wife of Heber the Kenite.
May she be blessed above all women
who live in tents.
²⁵ Sisera asked for water,
and she gave him milk.
In a bowl fit for nobles,
she brought him yogurt.

²⁶ Then with her left hand she reached for
a tent peg,
and with her right hand for the
workman's hammer.
She struck Sisera with the hammer,
crushing his head.
With a shattering blow, she pierced his
temples.
²⁷ He sank, he fell,
he lay still at her feet.
And where he sank,
there he died.

²⁸ "From the window Sisera's mother
looked out.
Through the window she watched for
his return, saying,
'Why is his chariot so long in coming?
Why don't we hear the sound of
chariot wheels?'
²⁹ "Her wise women answer,
and she repeats these words to herself:
³⁰ 'They must be dividing the captured
plunder—
with a woman or two for every man.
There will be colorful robes for Sisera,
and colorful, embroidered robes
for me.
Yes, the plunder will include
colorful robes embroidered on both
sides.'

³¹ "LORD, may all your enemies die like
Sisera!
But may those who love you rise like
the sun in all its power!"

Then there was peace in the land for forty
years.

6 Gideon Becomes Israel's Judge

The Israelites did evil in the LORD's
sight. So the LORD handed them over to the
Midianites for seven years. ² The Midianites
were so cruel that the Israelites made hiding places for themselves in the mountains, caves, and strongholds. ³ Whenever
the Israelites planted their crops, maraud-
ers from Midian, Amalek, and the people
of the east would attack Israel, ⁴ camping in
the land and destroying crops as far away
as Gaza. They left the Israelites with nothing to eat, taking all the sheep, goats, cattle,

Discover Your Calling

JUDGES 6:11-16

Acceptance

What would you say if someone asked you to state in a few sentences who you are?

The reality is that a person's calling is tied inextricably to his or her identity and isn't always easily stated. Like a diamond, one's character and personality have many different facets. Discerning, accepting, and pursuing one's calling is an ongoing process of discovery. For me, as I learn more about myself and become more of a whole person, the vision of my life's purpose becomes clearer. I believe that as we intentionally seek God and his will, he stirs up a sense of calling within us.

Make a six-month commitment to think and pray specifically about your life purpose. Each day ask the Lord to give you discernment and direction about his plans for you. Ponder your heart's desires. What motivates you? Fascinates you? Moves you? Look at your life and think of things—activities, awards, projects, and so on—of which you are proud. Is there a connecting factor, motivation, or theme?

After praying, waiting on the Lord, keeping a journal, and exploring activities and areas of interest, talk to a trusted two or three others about what you have learned. Tell them the direction in which you would like to head. Ask them if your vision squares with what they know of you. Then listen to their responses, asking God to highlight the truth and discard the rest.

As God's beloved children we are called and chosen to love and glorify him always. This is our highest purpose; this is our most glorious command. And we follow a Father who loves to lead us down the path to life—the road that will bring him the most glory and us the most fruitfulness, joy, and peace.

—*Amy Boucher Pye*

For more on acceptance, see reading at Nehemiah 1.

and donkeys. ⁵These enemy hordes, coming with their livestock and tents, were as thick as locusts; they arrived on droves of camels too numerous to count. And they stayed until the land was stripped bare. ⁶So Israel was reduced to starvation by the Midianites. Then the Israelites cried out to the LORD for help.

⁷When they cried out to the LORD because of Midian, ⁸the LORD sent a prophet to the Israelites. He said, "This is what the LORD, the God of Israel, says: I brought you up out of slavery in Egypt. ⁹I rescued you from the Egyptians and from all who oppressed you. I drove out your enemies and gave you their land. ¹⁰I told you, 'I am the LORD your God.

You must not worship the gods of the Amorites, in whose land you now live.' But you have not listened to me."

¹¹Then the angel of the LORD came and sat beneath the great tree at Ophrah, which belonged to Joash of the clan of Abiezer. Gideon son of Joash was threshing wheat at the bottom of a winepress to hide the grain from the Midianites. ¹²The angel of the LORD appeared to him and said, "Mighty hero, the LORD is with you!"

¹³"Sir," Gideon replied, "if the LORD is with us, why has all this happened to us? And where are all the miracles our ancestors told us about? Didn't they say, 'The LORD brought us up out of Egypt'? But now

the LORD has abandoned us and handed us over to the Midianites."

¹⁴Then the LORD turned to him and said, "Go with the strength you have, and rescue Israel from the Midianites. I am sending you!"

¹⁵"But Lord," Gideon replied, "how can I rescue Israel? My clan is the weakest in the whole tribe of Manasseh, and I am the least in my entire family!"

¹⁶The LORD said to him, "I will be with you. And you will destroy the Midianites as if you were fighting against one man."

¹⁷Gideon replied, "If you are truly going to help me, show me a sign to prove that it is really the LORD speaking to me. ¹⁸Don't go away until I come back and bring my offering to you."

He answered, "I will stay here until you return."

¹⁹Gideon hurried home. He cooked a young goat, and with a basket* of flour he baked some bread without yeast. Then, carrying the meat in a basket and the broth in a pot, he brought them out and presented them to the angel, who was under the great tree.

²⁰The angel of God said to him, "Place the meat and the unleavened bread on this rock, and pour the broth over it." And Gideon did as he was told. ²¹Then the angel of the LORD touched the meat and bread with the tip of the staff in his hand, and fire flamed up from the rock and consumed all he had brought. And the angel of the LORD disappeared.

²²When Gideon realized that it was the angel of the LORD, he cried out, "Oh, Sovereign LORD, I'm doomed! I have seen the angel of the LORD face to face!"

²³"It is all right," the LORD replied. "Do not be afraid. You will not die." ²⁴And Gideon built an altar to the LORD there and named it Yahweh-Shalom (which means "the LORD is peace"). The altar remains in Ophrah in the land of the clan of Abiezer to this day.

²⁵That night the LORD said to Gideon, "Take the second bull from your father's herd, the one that is seven years old. Pull down your father's altar to Baal, and cut down the Asherah pole standing beside

it. ²⁶Then build an altar to the LORD your God here on this hilltop sanctuary, laying the stones carefully. Sacrifice the bull as a burnt offering on the altar, using as fuel the wood of the Asherah pole you cut down."

²⁷So Gideon took ten of his servants and did as the LORD had commanded. But he did it at night because he was afraid of the other members of his father's household and the people of the town.

²⁸Early the next morning, as the people of the town began to stir, someone discovered that the altar of Baal had been broken down and that the Asherah pole beside it had been cut down. In their place a new altar had been built, and on it were the remains of the bull that had been sacrificed. ²⁹The people said to each other, "Who did this?" And after asking around and making a careful search, they learned that it was Gideon, the son of Joash.

³⁰"Bring out your son," the men of the town demanded of Joash. "He must die for destroying the altar of Baal and for cutting down the Asherah pole."

³¹But Joash shouted to the mob that confronted him, "Why are you defending Baal? Will you argue his case? Whoever pleads his case will be put to death by morning! If Baal truly is a god, let him defend himself and destroy the one who broke down his altar!" ³²From then on Gideon was called Jerub-baal, which means "Let Baal defend himself," because he broke down Baal's altar.

Gideon Asks for a Sign

³³Soon afterward the armies of Midian, Amalek, and the people of the east formed an alliance against Israel and crossed the Jordan, camping in the valley of Jezreel. ³⁴Then the Spirit of the LORD took possession of Gideon. He blew a ram's horn as a call to arms, and the men of the clan of Abiezer came to him. ³⁵He also sent messengers throughout Manasseh, Asher, Zebulun, and Naphtali, summoning their warriors, and all of them responded.

³⁶Then Gideon said to God, "If you are truly going to use me to rescue Israel as you promised, ³⁷prove it to me in this way. I will put a wool fleece on the threshing floor

6:19 Hebrew an ephah [20 quarts or 22 liters].

tonight. If the fleece is wet with dew in the morning but the ground is dry, then I will know that you are going to help me rescue Israel as you promised." ³⁸ And that is just what happened. When Gideon got up early the next morning, he squeezed the fleece and wrung out a whole bowlful of water.

³⁹ Then Gideon said to God, "Please don't be angry with me, but let me make one more request. Let me use the fleece for one more test. This time let the fleece remain dry while the ground around it is wet with dew." ⁴⁰ So that night God did as Gideon asked. The fleece was dry in the morning, but the ground was covered with dew.

7 Gideon Defeats the Midianites

So Jerub-baal (that is, Gideon) and his army got up early and went as far as the spring of Harod. The armies of Midian were camped north of them in the valley near the hill of Moreh. ²The LORD said to Gideon, "You have too many warriors with you. If I let all of you fight the Midianites, the Israelites will boast to me that they saved themselves by their own strength. ³Therefore, tell the people, 'Whoever is timid or afraid may leave this mountain* and go home.'" So 22,000 of them went home, leaving only 10,000 who were willing to fight.

⁴But the LORD told Gideon, "There are still too many! Bring them down to the spring, and I will test them to determine who will go with you and who will not." ⁵When Gideon took his warriors down to the water, the LORD told him, "Divide the men into two groups. In one group put all those who cup water in their hands and lap it up with their tongues like dogs. In the other group put all those who kneel down and drink with their mouths in the stream." ⁶Only 300 of the men drank from their hands. All the others got down on their knees and drank with their mouths in the stream.

⁷The LORD told Gideon, "With these 300 men I will rescue you and give you victory over the Midianites. Send all the others home." ⁸So Gideon collected the provisions and rams' horns of the other warriors and sent them home. But he kept the 300 men with him.

The Midianite camp was in the valley just below Gideon. ⁹That night the LORD said, "Get up! Go down into the Midianite camp, for I have given you victory over them! ¹⁰But if you are afraid to attack, go down to the camp with your servant Purah. ¹¹Listen to what the Midianites are saying, and you will be greatly encouraged. Then you will be eager to attack."

So Gideon took Purah and went down to the edge of the enemy camp. ¹²The armies of Midian, Amalek, and the people of the east had settled in the valley like a swarm of locusts. Their camels were like grains of sand on the seashore—too many to count! ¹³Gideon crept up just as a man was telling his companion about a dream. The man said, "I had this dream, and in my dream a loaf of barley bread came tumbling down into the Midianite camp. It hit a tent, turned it over, and knocked it flat!"

¹⁴His companion answered, "Your dream can mean only one thing—God has given Gideon son of Joash, the Israelite, victory over Midian and all its allies!"

¹⁵When Gideon heard the dream and its interpretation, he bowed in worship before the LORD.* Then he returned to the Israelite camp and shouted, "Get up! For the LORD has given you victory over the Midianite hordes!" ¹⁶He divided the 300 men into three groups and gave each man a ram's horn and a clay jar with a torch in it.

¹⁷Then he said to them, "Keep your eyes on me. When I come to the edge of the camp, do just as I do. ¹⁸As soon as I and those with me blow the rams' horns, blow your horns, too, all around the entire camp, and shout, 'For the LORD and for Gideon!'"

¹⁹It was just after midnight,* after the changing of the guard, when Gideon and the 100 men with him reached the edge of the Midianite camp. Suddenly, they blew the rams' horns and broke their clay jars. ²⁰Then all three groups blew their horns and broke their jars. They held the blazing torches in their left hands and the horns in their right hands, and they all shouted, "A sword for the LORD and for Gideon!"

²¹Each man stood at his position around the camp and watched as all the Midianites

---

7:3 Hebrew *may leave Mount Gilead.* The identity of Mount Gilead is uncertain in this context. It is perhaps used here as another name for Mount Gilboa. **7:15** As in Greek version; Hebrew reads *he bowed.* **7:19** Hebrew *at the beginning of the second watch.*

rushed around in a panic, shouting as they ran to escape. ²²When the 300 Israelites blew their rams' horns, the LORD caused the warriors in the camp to fight against each other with their swords. Those who were not killed fled to places as far away as Beth-shittah near Zererah and to the border of Abel-meholah near Tabbath.

²³Then Gideon sent for the warriors of Naphtali, Asher, and Manasseh, who joined in chasing the army of Midian. ²⁴Gideon also sent messengers throughout the hill country of Ephraim, saying, "Come down to attack the Midianites. Cut them off at the shallow crossings of the Jordan River at Beth-barah."

So all the men of Ephraim did as they were told. ²⁵They captured Oreb and Zeeb, the two Midianite commanders, killing Oreb at the rock of Oreb, and Zeeb at the winepress of Zeeb. And they continued to chase the Midianites. Afterward the Israelites brought the heads of Oreb and Zeeb to Gideon, who was by the Jordan River.

8 Gideon Kills Zebah and Zalmunna

Then the people of Ephraim asked Gideon, "Why have you treated us this way? Why didn't you send for us when you first went out to fight the Midianites?" And they argued heatedly with Gideon.

²But Gideon replied, "What have I accomplished compared to you? Aren't even the leftover grapes of Ephraim's harvest better than the entire crop of my little clan of Abiezer? ³God gave you victory over Oreb and Zeeb, the commanders of the Midianite army. What have I accomplished compared to that?" When the men of Ephraim heard Gideon's answer, their anger subsided.

⁴Gideon then crossed the Jordan River with his 300 men, and though exhausted, they continued to chase the enemy. ⁵When they reached Succoth, Gideon asked the leaders of the town, "Please give my warriors some food. They are very tired. I am chasing Zebah and Zalmunna, the kings of Midian."

⁶But the officials of Succoth replied, "Catch Zebah and Zalmunna first, and then we will feed your army."

⁷So Gideon said, "After the LORD gives me victory over Zebah and Zalmunna, I will return and tear your flesh with the thorns and briers from the wilderness."

⁸From there Gideon went up to Peniel* and again asked for food, but he got the same answer. ⁹So he said to the people of Peniel, "After I return in victory, I will tear down this tower."

¹⁰By this time Zebah and Zalmunna were in Karkor with 15,000 warriors—all that remained of the allied armies of the east, for 120,000 had already been killed. ¹¹Gideon circled around by the caravan route east of Nobah and Jogbehah, taking the Midianite army by surprise. ¹²Zebah and Zalmunna, the two Midianite kings, fled, but Gideon chased them down and captured all their warriors.

¹³After this, Gideon returned from the battle by way of Heres Pass. ¹⁴There he captured a young man from Succoth and demanded that he write down the names of all the seventy-seven officials and elders in the town. ¹⁵Gideon then returned to Succoth and said to the leaders, "Here are Zebah and Zalmunna. When we were here before, you taunted me, saying, 'Catch Zebah and Zalmunna first, and then we will feed your exhausted army.'" ¹⁶Then Gideon took the elders of the town and taught them a lesson, punishing them with thorns and briers from the wilderness. ¹⁷He also tore down the tower of Peniel and killed all the men in the town.

¹⁸Then Gideon asked Zebah and Zalmunna, "The men you killed at Tabor—what were they like?"

"Like you," they replied. "They all had the look of a king's son."

¹⁹"They were my brothers, the sons of my own mother!" Gideon exclaimed. "As surely as the LORD lives, I wouldn't kill you if you hadn't killed them."

²⁰Turning to Jether, his oldest son, he said, "Kill them!" But Jether did not draw his sword, for he was only a boy and was afraid.

²¹Then Zebah and Zalmunna said to Gideon, "Be a man! Kill us yourself!" So Gideon killed them both and took the royal ornaments from the necks of their camels.

8:8 Hebrew *Penuel*, a variant spelling of Peniel; also in 8:9, 17.

Gideon's Sacred Ephod

22 Then the Israelites said to Gideon, "Be our ruler! You and your son and your grandson will be our rulers, for you have rescued us from Midian."

23 But Gideon replied, "I will not rule over you, nor will my son. The LORD will rule over you! 24 However, I do have one request—that each of you give me an earring from the plunder you collected from your fallen enemies." (The enemies, being Ishmaelites, all wore gold earrings.)

25 "Gladly!" they replied. They spread out a cloak, and each one threw in a gold earring he had gathered from the plunder. 26 The weight of the gold earrings was forty-three pounds,* not including the royal ornaments and pendants, the purple clothing worn by the kings of Midian, or the chains around the necks of their camels.

27 Gideon made a sacred ephod from the gold and put it in Ophrah, his hometown. But soon all the Israelites prostituted themselves by worshiping it, and it became a trap for Gideon and his family.

28 That is the story of how the people of Israel defeated Midian, which never recovered. Throughout the rest of Gideon's lifetime—about forty years—there was peace in the land.

29 Then Gideon* son of Joash returned home. 30 He had seventy sons born to him, for he had many wives. 31 He also had a concubine in Shechem, who gave birth to a son, whom he named Abimelech. 32 Gideon died when he was very old, and he was buried in the grave of his father, Joash, at Ophrah in the land of the clan of Abiezer.

33 As soon as Gideon died, the Israelites prostituted themselves by worshiping the images of Baal, making Baal-berith their god. 34 They forgot the LORD their God, who had rescued them from all their enemies surrounding them. 35 Nor did they show any loyalty to the family of Jerub-baal (that is, Gideon), despite all the good he had done for Israel.

9 Abimelech Rules over Shechem

One day Gideon's* son Abimelech went to Shechem to visit his uncles—his mother's brothers. He said to them and to the rest of his mother's family, 2 "Ask the leading citizens of Shechem whether they want to be ruled by all seventy of Gideon's sons or by one man. And remember that I am your own flesh and blood!"

3 So Abimelech's uncles gave his message to all the citizens of Shechem on his behalf. And after listening to this proposal, the people of Shechem decided in favor of Abimelech because he was their relative. 4 They gave him seventy silver coins from the temple of Baal-berith, which he used to hire some reckless troublemakers who agreed to follow him. 5 He went to his father's home at Ophrah, and there, on one stone, they killed all seventy of his half brothers, the sons of Gideon.* But the youngest brother, Jotham, escaped and hid.

6 Then all the leading citizens of Shechem and Beth-millo called a meeting under the oak beside the pillar* at Shechem and made Abimelech their king.

Jotham's Parable

7 When Jotham heard about this, he climbed to the top of Mount Gerizim and shouted,

"Listen to me, citizens of Shechem!
    Listen to me if you want God to listen
        to you!
8 Once upon a time the trees decided to
        choose a king.
    First they said to the olive tree,
        'Be our king!'
9 But the olive tree refused, saying,
    'Should I quit producing the olive oil
        that blesses both God and people,
    just to wave back and forth over the
        trees?'

10 "Then they said to the fig tree,
    'You be our king!'
11 But the fig tree also refused, saying,
    'Should I quit producing my sweet fruit
    just to wave back and forth over the
        trees?'

12 "Then they said to the grapevine,
    'You be our king!'
13 But the grapevine also refused, saying,
    'Should I quit producing the wine
        that cheers both God and people,

8:26 Hebrew 1,700 shekels [19.4 kilograms].   8:29 Hebrew Jerub-baal; see 6:32.   9:1 Hebrew Jerub-baal's (see 6:32); also in 9:2, 24.
9:5 Hebrew Jerub-baal (see 6:32); also in 9:16, 19, 28, 57.   9:6 The meaning of the Hebrew is uncertain.

just to wave back and forth over the trees?'

¹⁴ "Then all the trees finally turned to the thornbush and said,
'Come, you be our king!'
¹⁵ And the thornbush replied to the trees,
'If you truly want to make me your king,
come and take shelter in my shade.
If not, let fire come out from me
and devour the cedars of Lebanon.'"

¹⁶Jotham continued, "Now make sure you have acted honorably and in good faith by making Abimelech your king, and that you have done right by Gideon and all of his descendants. Have you treated him with the honor he deserves for all he accomplished? ¹⁷For he fought for you and risked his life when he rescued you from the Midianites. ¹⁸But today you have revolted against my father and his descendants, killing his seventy sons on one stone. And you have chosen his slave woman's son, Abimelech, to be your king just because he is your relative.

¹⁹"If you have acted honorably and in good faith toward Gideon and his descendants today, then may you find joy in Abimelech, and may he find joy in you. ²⁰But if you have not acted in good faith, then may fire come out from Abimelech and devour the leading citizens of Shechem and Beth-millo; and may fire come out from the citizens of Shechem and Beth-millo and devour Abimelech!"

²¹Then Jotham escaped and lived in Beer because he was afraid of his brother Abimelech.

Shechem Rebels against Abimelech

²²After Abimelech had ruled over Israel for three years, ²³God sent a spirit that stirred up trouble between Abimelech and the leading citizens of Shechem, and they revolted. ²⁴God was punishing Abimelech for murdering Gideon's seventy sons, and the citizens of Shechem for supporting him in this treachery of murdering his brothers. ²⁵The citizens of Shechem set an ambush for Abimelech on the hilltops and robbed everyone who passed that way. But someone warned Abimelech about their plot.

²⁶One day Gaal son of Ebed moved to Shechem with his brothers and gained the confidence of the leading citizens of Shechem. ²⁷During the annual harvest festival at Shechem, held in the temple of the local god, the wine flowed freely, and everyone began cursing Abimelech. ²⁸"Who is Abimelech?" Gaal shouted. "He's not a true son of Shechem,* so why should we be his servants? He's merely the son of Gideon, and this Zebul is merely his deputy. Serve the true sons of Hamor, the founder of Shechem. Why should we serve Abimelech? ²⁹If I were in charge here, I would get rid of Abimelech. I would say* to him, 'Get some soldiers, and come out and fight!'"

³⁰But when Zebul, the leader of the city, heard what Gaal was saying, he was furious. ³¹He sent messengers to Abimelech in Arumah,* telling him, "Gaal son of Ebed and his brothers have come to live in Shechem, and now they are inciting the city to rebel against you. ³²Come by night with an army and hide out in the fields. ³³In the morning, as soon as it is daylight, attack the city. When Gaal and those who are with him come out against you, you can do with them as you wish."

³⁴So Abimelech and all his men went by night and split into four groups, stationing themselves around Shechem. ³⁵Gaal was standing at the city gates when Abimelech and his army came out of hiding. ³⁶When Gaal saw them, he said to Zebul, "Look, there are people coming down from the hilltops!"

Zebul replied, "It's just the shadows on the hills that look like men."

³⁷But again Gaal said, "No, people are coming down from the hills.* And another group is coming down the road past the Diviners' Oak.*"

³⁸Then Zebul turned on him and asked, "Now where is that big mouth of yours? Wasn't it you that said, 'Who is Abimelech, and why should we be his servants?' The men you mocked are right outside the city! Go out and fight them!"

³⁹So Gaal led the leading citizens of Shechem into battle against Abimelech. ⁴⁰But Abimelech chased him, and many of She-

9:28 Hebrew *Who is Shechem?* 9:29 As in Greek version; Hebrew reads *And he said.* 9:31 Or *in secret*; Hebrew reads *in Tormah*; compare 9:41. 9:37a Or *the center of the land.* 9:37b Hebrew *Elon-meonenim.*

chem's men were wounded and fell along the road as they retreated to the city gate. ⁴¹Abimelech returned to Arumah, and Zebul drove Gaal and his brothers out of Shechem.

⁴²The next day the people of Shechem went out into the fields to battle. When Abimelech heard about it, ⁴³he divided his men into three groups and set an ambush in the fields. When Abimelech saw the people coming out of the city, he and his men jumped up from their hiding places and attacked them. ⁴⁴Abimelech and his group stormed the city gate to keep the men of Shechem from getting back in, while Abimelech's other two groups cut them down in the fields. ⁴⁵The battle went on all day before Abimelech finally captured the city. He killed the people, leveled the city, and scattered salt all over the ground.

⁴⁶When the leading citizens who lived in the tower of Shechem heard what had happened, they ran and hid in the temple of Baal-berith.* ⁴⁷Someone reported to Abimelech that the citizens had gathered in the temple, ⁴⁸so he led his forces to Mount Zalmon. He took an ax and chopped some branches from a tree, then put them on his shoulder. "Quick, do as I have done!" he told his men. ⁴⁹So each of them cut down some branches, following Abimelech's example. They piled the branches against the walls of the temple and set them on fire. So all the people who had lived in the tower of Shechem died—about 1,000 men and women.

⁵⁰Then Abimelech attacked the town of Thebez and captured it. ⁵¹But there was a strong tower inside the town, and all the men and women—the entire population— fled to it. They barricaded themselves in and climbed up to the roof of the tower. ⁵²Abimelech followed them to attack the tower. But as he prepared to set fire to the entrance, ⁵³a woman on the roof dropped a millstone that landed on Abimelech's head and crushed his skull.

⁵⁴He quickly said to his young armor bearer, "Draw your sword and kill me! Don't let it be said that a woman killed Abimelech!" So the young man ran him through with his sword, and he died. ⁵⁵When Abimelech's men saw that he was dead, they disbanded and returned to their homes.

⁵⁶In this way, God punished Abimelech for the evil he had done against his father by murdering his seventy brothers. ⁵⁷God also punished the men of Shechem for all their evil. So the curse of Jotham son of Gideon was fulfilled.

10 Tola Becomes Israel's Judge

After Abimelech died, Tola son of Puah, son of Dodo, was the next person to rescue Israel. He was from the tribe of Issachar but lived in the town of Shamir in the hill country of Ephraim. ²He judged Israel for twenty-three years. When he died, he was buried in Shamir.

Jair Becomes Israel's Judge

³After Tola died, Jair from Gilead judged Israel for twenty-two years. ⁴His thirty sons rode around on thirty donkeys, and they owned thirty towns in the land of Gilead, which are still called the Towns of Jair.* ⁵When Jair died, he was buried in Kamon.

The Ammonites Oppress Israel

⁶Again the Israelites did evil in the LORD's sight. They served the images of Baal and Ashtoreth, and the gods of Aram, Sidon, Moab, Ammon, and Philistia. They abandoned the LORD and no longer served him at all. ⁷So the LORD burned with anger against Israel, and he turned them over to the Philistines and the Ammonites, ⁸who began to oppress them that year. For eighteen years they oppressed all the Israelites east of the Jordan River in the land of the Amorites (that is, in Gilead). ⁹The Ammonites also crossed to the west side of the Jordan and attacked Judah, Benjamin, and Ephraim.

The Israelites were in great distress. ¹⁰Finally, they cried out to the LORD for help, saying, "We have sinned against you because we have abandoned you as our God and have served the images of Baal."

¹¹The LORD replied, "Did I not rescue you from the Egyptians, the Amorites, the Ammonites, the Philistines, ¹²the Sidonians, the Amalekites, and the Maonites? When

---

9:46 Hebrew *El-berith*, another name for Baal-berith; compare 9:4. 10:4 Hebrew *Havvoth-jair*.

they oppressed you, you cried out to me for help, and I rescued you. ¹³Yet you have abandoned me and served other gods. So I will not rescue you anymore. ¹⁴Go and cry out to the gods you have chosen! Let them rescue you in your hour of distress!"

¹⁵But the Israelites pleaded with the LORD and said, "We have sinned. Punish us as you see fit, only rescue us today from our enemies." ¹⁶Then the Israelites put aside their foreign gods and served the LORD. And he was grieved by their misery.

¹⁷At that time the armies of Ammon had gathered for war and were camped in Gilead, and the people of Israel assembled and camped at Mizpah. ¹⁸The leaders of Gilead said to each other, "Whoever attacks the Ammonites first will become ruler over all the people of Gilead."

11 Jephthah Becomes Israel's Judge

Now Jephthah of Gilead was a great warrior. He was the son of Gilead, but his mother was a prostitute. ²Gilead's wife also had several sons, and when these half brothers grew up, they chased Jephthah off the land. "You will not get any of our father's inheritance," they said, "for you are the son of a prostitute." ³So Jephthah fled from his brothers and lived in the land of Tob. Soon he had a band of worthless rebels following him.

⁴At about this time, the Ammonites began their war against Israel. ⁵When the Ammonites attacked, the elders of Gilead sent for Jephthah in the land of Tob. The elders said, ⁶"Come and be our commander! Help us fight the Ammonites!"

⁷But Jephthah said to them, "Aren't you the ones who hated me and drove me from my father's house? Why do you come to me now when you're in trouble?"

⁸"Because we need you," the elders replied. "If you lead us in battle against the Ammonites, we will make you ruler over all the people of Gilead."

⁹Jephthah said to the elders, "Let me get this straight. If I come with you and if the LORD gives me victory over the Ammonites, will you really make me ruler over all the people?"

¹⁰"The LORD is our witness," the elders replied. "We promise to do whatever you say."

¹¹So Jephthah went with the elders of Gilead, and the people made him their ruler and commander of the army. At Mizpah, in the presence of the LORD, Jephthah repeated what he had said to the elders.

¹²Then Jephthah sent messengers to the king of Ammon, asking, "Why have you come out to fight against my land?"

¹³The king of Ammon answered Jephthah's messengers, "When the Israelites came out of Egypt, they stole my land from the Arnon River to the Jabbok River and all the way to the Jordan. Now then, give back the land peaceably."

¹⁴Jephthah sent this message back to the Ammonite king:

¹⁵"This is what Jephthah says: Israel did not steal any land from Moab or Ammon. ¹⁶When the people of Israel arrived at Kadesh on their journey from Egypt after crossing the Red Sea,* ¹⁷they sent messengers to the king of Edom asking for permission to pass through his land. But their request was denied. Then they asked the king of Moab for similar permission, but he wouldn't let them pass through either. So the people of Israel stayed in Kadesh.

¹⁸"Finally, they went around Edom and Moab through the wilderness. They traveled along Moab's eastern border and camped on the other side of the Arnon River. But they never once crossed the Arnon River into Moab, for the Arnon was the border of Moab.

¹⁹"Then Israel sent messengers to King Sihon of the Amorites, who ruled from Heshbon, asking for permission to cross through his land to get to their destination. ²⁰But King Sihon didn't trust Israel to pass through his land. Instead, he mobilized his army at Jahaz and attacked them. ²¹But the LORD, the God of Israel, gave his people victory over King Sihon. So Israel took control of all the land of the Amorites, who lived in that region, ²²from the Arnon River to the Jabbok

11:16 Hebrew *sea of reeds.*

River, and from the eastern wilderness to the Jordan.

²³"So you see, it was the LORD, the God of Israel, who took away the land from the Amorites and gave it to Israel. Why, then, should we give it back to you? ²⁴You keep whatever your god Chemosh gives you, and we will keep whatever the LORD our God gives us. ²⁵Are you any better than Balak son of Zippor, king of Moab? Did he try to make a case against Israel for disputed land? Did he go to war against them?

²⁶"Israel has been living here for 300 years, inhabiting Heshbon and its surrounding settlements, all the way to Aroer and its settlements, and in all the towns along the Arnon River. Why have you made no effort to recover it before now? ²⁷Therefore, I have not sinned against you. Rather, you have wronged me by attacking me. Let the LORD, who is judge, decide today which of us is right—Israel or Ammon."

²⁸But the king of Ammon paid no attention to Jephthah's message.

Jephthah's Vow

²⁹At that time the Spirit of the LORD came upon Jephthah, and he went throughout the land of Gilead and Manasseh, including Mizpah in Gilead, and from there he led an army against the Ammonites. ³⁰And Jephthah made a vow to the LORD. He said, "If you give me victory over the Ammonites, ³¹I will give to the LORD whatever comes out of my house to meet me when I return in triumph. I will sacrifice it as a burnt offering."

³²So Jephthah led his army against the Ammonites, and the LORD gave him victory. ³³He crushed the Ammonites, devastating about twenty towns from Aroer to an area near Minnith and as far away as Abel-keramim. In this way Israel defeated the Ammonites.

³⁴When Jephthah returned home to Mizpah, his daughter came out to meet him, playing on a tambourine and dancing for joy. She was his one and only child; he had no other sons or daughters. ³⁵When he saw her, he tore his clothes in anguish. "Oh, my daughter!" he cried out. "You have completely destroyed me! You've brought disaster on me! For I have made a vow to the LORD, and I cannot take it back."

³⁶And she said, "Father, if you have made a vow to the LORD, you must do to me what you have vowed, for the LORD has given you a great victory over your enemies, the Ammonites. ³⁷But first let me do this one thing: Let me go up and roam in the hills and weep with my friends for two months, because I will die a virgin."

³⁸"You may go," Jephthah said. And he sent her away for two months. She and her friends went into the hills and wept because she would never have children. ³⁹When she returned home, her father kept the vow he had made, and she died a virgin.

So it has become a custom in Israel ⁴⁰for young Israelite women to go away for four days each year to lament the fate of Jephthah's daughter.

12 Ephraim Fights with Jephthah

Then the people of Ephraim mobilized an army and crossed over the Jordan River to Zaphon. They sent this message to Jephthah: "Why didn't you call for us to help you fight against the Ammonites? We are going to burn down your house with you in it!"

²Jephthah replied, "I summoned you at the beginning of the dispute, but you refused to come! You failed to help us in our struggle against Ammon. ³So when I realized you weren't coming, I risked my life and went to battle without you, and the LORD gave me victory over the Ammonites. So why have you now come to fight me?"

⁴The people of Ephraim responded, "You men of Gilead are nothing more than fugitives from Ephraim and Manasseh." So Jephthah gathered all the men of Gilead and attacked the men of Ephraim and defeated them.

⁵Jephthah captured the shallow crossings of the Jordan River, and whenever a fugitive from Ephraim tried to go back across, the men of Gilead would challenge him. "Are you a member of the tribe of Ephraim?" they would ask. If the man said, "No, I'm not," ⁶they would tell him to say "Shibboleth." If he was from Ephraim, he would say

"Sibboleth," because people from Ephraim cannot pronounce the word correctly. Then they would take him and kill him at the shallow crossings of the Jordan. In all, 42,000 Ephraimites were killed at that time.

⁷Jephthah judged Israel for six years. When he died, he was buried in one of the towns of Gilead.

Ibzan Becomes Israel's Judge

⁸After Jephthah died, Ibzan from Bethlehem judged Israel. ⁹He had thirty sons and thirty daughters. He sent his daughters to marry men outside his clan, and he brought in thirty young women from outside his clan to marry his sons. Ibzan judged Israel for seven years. ¹⁰When he died, he was buried at Bethlehem.

Elon Becomes Israel's Judge

¹¹After Ibzan died, Elon from the tribe of Zebulun judged Israel for ten years. ¹²When he died, he was buried at Aijalon in Zebulun.

Abdon Becomes Israel's Judge

¹³After Elon died, Abdon son of Hillel, from Pirathon, judged Israel. ¹⁴He had forty sons and thirty grandsons, who rode on seventy donkeys. He judged Israel for eight years. ¹⁵When he died, he was buried at Pirathon in Ephraim, in the hill country of the Amalekites.

13 The Birth of Samson

Again the Israelites did evil in the LORD's sight, so the LORD handed them over to the Philistines, who oppressed them for forty years.

²In those days a man named Manoah from the tribe of Dan lived in the town of Zorah. His wife was unable to become pregnant, and they had no children. ³The angel of the LORD appeared to Manoah's wife and said, "Even though you have been unable to have children, you will soon become pregnant and give birth to a son. ⁴So be careful; you must not drink wine or any other alcoholic drink nor eat any forbidden food.* ⁵You will become pregnant and give birth to a son, and his hair must never be cut. For he will be dedicated to God as a Nazirite

from birth. He will begin to rescue Israel from the Philistines."

⁶The woman ran and told her husband, "A man of God appeared to me! He looked like one of God's angels, terrifying to see. I didn't ask where he was from, and he didn't tell me his name. ⁷But he told me, 'You will become pregnant and give birth to a son. You must not drink wine or any other alcoholic drink nor eat any forbidden food. For your son will be dedicated to God as a Nazirite from the moment of his birth until the day of his death.'"

⁸Then Manoah prayed to the LORD, saying, "Lord, please let the man of God come back to us again and give us more instructions about this son who is to be born."

⁹God answered Manoah's prayer, and the angel of God appeared once again to his wife as she was sitting in the field. But her husband, Manoah, was not with her. ¹⁰So she quickly ran and told her husband, "The man who appeared to me the other day is here again!"

¹¹Manoah ran back with his wife and asked, "Are you the man who spoke to my wife the other day?"

"Yes," he replied, "I am."

¹²So Manoah asked him, "When your words come true, what kind of rules should govern the boy's life and work?"

¹³The angel of the LORD replied, "Be sure your wife follows the instructions I gave her. ¹⁴She must not eat grapes or raisins, drink wine or any other alcoholic drink, or eat any forbidden food."

¹⁵Then Manoah said to the angel of the LORD, "Please stay here until we can prepare a young goat for you to eat."

¹⁶"I will stay," the angel of the LORD replied, "but I will not eat anything. However, you may prepare a burnt offering as a sacrifice to the LORD." (Manoah didn't realize it was the angel of the LORD.)

¹⁷Then Manoah asked the angel of the LORD, "What is your name? For when all this comes true, we want to honor you."

¹⁸"Why do you ask my name?" the angel of the LORD replied. "It is too wonderful for you to understand."

¹⁹Then Manoah took a young goat and a grain offering and offered it on a rock as a

---

13:4 Hebrew *any unclean thing;* also in 13:7, 14.

Submission

Obeying in the "Little Things"

JUDGES 13:1–13

Manoah's wife had an amazing encounter with an angel and received astonishing news: though she was barren, she would miraculously become pregnant! God granted her deep desire to become a mother . . . and he had amazing plans for her son.

But the angel also enumerated specific instructions she was to follow concerning her prenatal diet and her son's diet and personal grooming. He also commanded that her son be dedicated to the Lord as a Nazirite. (Nazirites were people who observed certain fasts and outward signs representing a special dedication to God; see Numbers 6 for more details.)

God both *blessed* Manoah's wife and also *required* something from her: obedience. She had an important part to play in God's plan for her son, Samson, and the angel wanted her to make sure she understood how important her obedience was, reiterating to Manoah, "Be sure your wife follows the instructions I gave her" (Judges 13:13).

God's call to Samson's mother wasn't a vague and general call to try to do her best; he asked specific things of her and desired her to obey him even in the littlest detail. Like her, we too can cultivate an attitude that says, *God, I'll obey your rules and submit to your leading, even in small matters.*

These "small matters" tend to fill our daily lives—and they may, in fact, be harder to obey than the "big" issues. For example, will we speak kindly when we're irritated or avoid white lies? Will we keep ourselves from gossiping or turn away from lustful thoughts? Will we follow the Spirit's nudging that we apologize about something "minor" we said or did?

Submission, often misunderstood as weakness, actually requires a strength and determination. We live with a sense that God requires something of us—and we live determined to follow the instructions God gives us.

—*Kelli B. Trujillo*

For more on submission, see reading at 1 Samuel 20.

sacrifice to the Lord. And as Manoah and his wife watched, the Lord did an amazing thing. [20] As the flames from the altar shot up toward the sky, the angel of the Lord ascended in the fire. When Manoah and his wife saw this, they fell with their faces to the ground.

[21] The angel did not appear again to Manoah and his wife. Manoah finally realized it was the angel of the Lord, [22] and he said to his wife, "We will certainly die, for we have seen God!"

[23] But his wife said, "If the Lord were going to kill us, he wouldn't have accepted our burnt offering and grain offering. He wouldn't have appeared to us and told us this wonderful thing and done these miracles."

[24] When her son was born, she named him Samson. And the Lord blessed him as he grew up. [25] And the Spirit of the Lord began to stir him while he lived in Mahaneh-dan, which is located between the towns of Zorah and Eshtaol.

14 Samson's Riddle

One day when Samson was in Timnah, one of the Philistine women caught his eye. [2] When he returned home, he told his father and mother, "A young Philistine woman in Timnah caught my eye. I want to marry her. Get her for me."

³His father and mother objected. "Isn't there even one woman in our tribe or among all the Israelites you could marry?" they asked. "Why must you go to the pagan Philistines to find a wife?"

But Samson told his father, "Get her for me! She looks good to me." ⁴His father and mother didn't realize the LORD was at work in this, creating an opportunity to work against the Philistines, who ruled over Israel at that time.

⁵As Samson and his parents were going down to Timnah, a young lion suddenly attacked Samson near the vineyards of Timnah. ⁶At that moment the Spirit of the LORD came powerfully upon him, and he ripped the lion's jaws apart with his bare hands. He did it as easily as if it were a young goat. But he didn't tell his father or mother about it. ⁷When Samson arrived in Timnah, he talked with the woman and was very pleased with her.

⁸Later, when he returned to Timnah for the wedding, he turned off the path to look at the carcass of the lion. And he found that a swarm of bees had made some honey in the carcass. ⁹He scooped some of the honey into his hands and ate it along the way. He also gave some to his father and mother, and they ate it. But he didn't tell them he had taken the honey from the carcass of the lion.

¹⁰As his father was making final arrangements for the marriage, Samson threw a party at Timnah, as was the custom for elite young men. ¹¹When the bride's parents* saw him, they selected thirty young men from the town to be his companions.

¹²Samson said to them, "Let me tell you a riddle. If you solve my riddle during these seven days of the celebration, I will give you thirty fine linen robes and thirty sets of festive clothing. ¹³But if you can't solve it, then you must give me thirty fine linen robes and thirty sets of festive clothing."

"All right," they agreed, "let's hear your riddle."

¹⁴So he said:

"Out of the one who eats came something to eat;
out of the strong came something sweet."

Three days later they were still trying to figure it out. ¹⁵On the fourth* day they said to Samson's wife, "Entice your husband to explain the riddle for us, or we will burn down your father's house with you in it. Did you invite us to this party just to make us poor?"

¹⁶So Samson's wife came to him in tears and said, "You don't love me; you hate me! You have given my people a riddle, but you haven't told me the answer."

"I haven't even given the answer to my father or mother," he replied. "Why should I tell you?" ¹⁷So she cried whenever she was with him and kept it up for the rest of the celebration. At last, on the seventh day he told her the answer because she was tormenting him with her nagging. Then she explained the riddle to the young men.

¹⁸So before sunset of the seventh day, the men of the town came to Samson with their answer:

"What is sweeter than honey?
What is stronger than a lion?"

Samson replied, "If you hadn't plowed with my heifer, you wouldn't have solved my riddle!"

¹⁹Then the Spirit of the LORD came powerfully upon him. He went down to the town of Ashkelon, killed thirty men, took their belongings, and gave their clothing to the men who had solved his riddle. But Samson was furious about what had happened, and he went back home to live with his father and mother. ²⁰So his wife was given in marriage to the man who had been Samson's best man at the wedding.

15 Samson's Vengeance on the Philistines

Later on, during the wheat harvest, Samson took a young goat as a present to his wife. He said, "I'm going into my wife's room to sleep with her," but her father wouldn't let him in.

²"I truly thought you must hate her," her father explained, "so I gave her in marriage to your best man. But look, her younger

14:11 Hebrew they. 14:15 As in Greek version; Hebrew reads seventh.

sister is even more beautiful than she is. Marry her instead."

³Samson said, "This time I cannot be blamed for everything I am going to do to you Philistines." ⁴Then he went out and caught 300 foxes. He tied their tails together in pairs, and he fastened a torch to each pair of tails. ⁵Then he lit the torches and let the foxes run through the grain fields of the Philistines. He burned all their grain to the ground, including the sheaves and the uncut grain. He also destroyed their vineyards and olive groves.

⁶"Who did this?" the Philistines demanded.

"Samson," was the reply, "because his father-in-law from Timnah gave Samson's wife to be married to his best man." So the Philistines went and got the woman and her father and burned them to death.

⁷"Because you did this," Samson vowed, "I won't rest until I take my revenge on you!" ⁸So he attacked the Philistines with great fury and killed many of them. Then he went to live in a cave in the rock of Etam.

⁹The Philistines retaliated by setting up camp in Judah and spreading out near the town of Lehi. ¹⁰The men of Judah asked the Philistines, "Why are you attacking us?"

The Philistines replied, "We've come to capture Samson. We've come to pay him back for what he did to us."

¹¹So 3,000 men of Judah went down to get Samson at the cave in the rock of Etam. They said to Samson, "Don't you realize the Philistines rule over us? What are you doing to us?"

But Samson replied, "I only did to them what they did to me."

¹²But the men of Judah told him, "We have come to tie you up and hand you over to the Philistines."

"All right," Samson said. "But promise that you won't kill me yourselves."

¹³"We will only tie you up and hand you over to the Philistines," they replied. "We won't kill you." So they tied him up with two new ropes and brought him up from the rock.

¹⁴As Samson arrived at Lehi, the Philistines came shouting in triumph. But the Spirit of the LORD came powerfully upon Samson, and he snapped the ropes on his arms as if they were burnt strands of flax, and they fell from his wrists. ¹⁵Then he found the jawbone of a recently killed donkey. He picked it up and killed 1,000 Philistines with it. ¹⁶Then Samson said,

"With the jawbone of a donkey,
    I've piled them in heaps!
With the jawbone of a donkey,
    I've killed a thousand men!"

¹⁷When he finished his boasting, he threw away the jawbone; and the place was named Jawbone Hill.*

¹⁸Samson was now very thirsty, and he cried out to the LORD, "You have accomplished this great victory by the strength of your servant. Must I now die of thirst and fall into the hands of these pagans?" ¹⁹So God caused water to gush out of a hollow in the ground at Lehi, and Samson was revived as he drank. Then he named that place "The Spring of the One Who Cried Out,"* and it is still in Lehi to this day.

²⁰Samson judged Israel for twenty years during the period when the Philistines dominated the land.

16 Samson Carries Away Gaza's Gates

One day Samson went to the Philistine town of Gaza and spent the night with a prostitute. ²Word soon spread* that Samson was there, so the men of Gaza gathered together and waited all night at the town gates. They kept quiet during the night, saying to themselves, "When the light of morning comes, we will kill him."

³But Samson stayed in bed only until midnight. Then he got up, took hold of the doors of the town gate, including the two posts, and lifted them up, bar and all. He put them on his shoulders and carried them all the way to the top of the hill across from Hebron.

Samson and Delilah

⁴Some time later Samson fell in love with a woman named Delilah, who lived in the valley of Sorek. ⁵The rulers of the Philistines went to her and said, "Entice Samson

---

15:17 Hebrew *Ramath-lehi*.   15:19 Hebrew *En-hakkore*.   16:2 As in Greek and Syriac versions and Latin Vulgate; Hebrew lacks *Word soon spread*.

to tell you what makes him so strong and how he can be overpowered and tied up securely. Then each of us will give you 1,100 pieces* of silver."

⁶So Delilah said to Samson, "Please tell me what makes you so strong and what it would take to tie you up securely."

⁷Samson replied, "If I were tied up with seven new bowstrings that have not yet been dried, I would become as weak as anyone else."

⁸So the Philistine rulers brought Delilah seven new bowstrings, and she tied Samson up with them. ⁹She had hidden some men in one of the inner rooms of her house, and she cried out, "Samson! The Philistines have come to capture you!" But Samson snapped the bowstrings as a piece of string snaps when it is burned by a fire. So the secret of his strength was not discovered.

¹⁰Afterward Delilah said to him, "You've been making fun of me and telling me lies! Now please tell me how you can be tied up securely."

¹¹Samson replied, "If I were tied up with brand-new ropes that had never been used, I would become as weak as anyone else."

¹²So Delilah took new ropes and tied him up with them. The men were hiding in the inner room as before, and again Delilah cried out, "Samson! The Philistines have come to capture you!" But again Samson snapped the ropes from his arms as if they were thread.

¹³Then Delilah said, "You've been making fun of me and telling me lies! Now tell me how you can be tied up securely."

Samson replied, "If you were to weave the seven braids of my hair into the fabric on your loom and tighten it with the loom shuttle, I would become as weak as anyone else."

So while he slept, Delilah wove the seven braids of his hair into the fabric. ¹⁴Then she tightened it with the loom shuttle.* Again she cried out, "Samson! The Philistines have come to capture you!" But Samson woke up, pulled back the loom shuttle, and yanked his hair away from the loom and the fabric.

¹⁵Then Delilah pouted, "How can you tell me, 'I love you,' when you don't share your secrets with me? You've made fun of me three times now, and you still haven't told me what makes you so strong!" ¹⁶She tormented him with her nagging day after day until he was sick to death of it.

¹⁷Finally, Samson shared his secret with her. "My hair has never been cut," he confessed, "for I was dedicated to God as a Nazirite from birth. If my head were shaved, my strength would leave me, and I would become as weak as anyone else."

¹⁸Delilah realized he had finally told her the truth, so she sent for the Philistine rulers. "Come back one more time," she said, "for he has finally told me his secret." So the Philistine rulers returned with the money in their hands. ¹⁹Delilah lulled Samson to sleep with his head in her lap, and then she called in a man to shave off the seven locks of his hair. In this way she began to bring him down,* and his strength left him.

²⁰Then she cried out, "Samson! The Philistines have come to capture you!"

When he woke up, he thought, "I will do as before and shake myself free." But he didn't realize the LORD had left him.

²¹So the Philistines captured him and gouged out his eyes. They took him to Gaza, where he was bound with bronze chains and forced to grind grain in the prison.

²²But before long, his hair began to grow back.

Samson's Final Victory

²³The Philistine rulers held a great festival, offering sacrifices and praising their god, Dagon. They said, "Our god has given us victory over our enemy Samson!"

²⁴When the people saw him, they praised their god, saying, "Our god has delivered our enemy to us! The one who killed so many of us is now in our power!"

²⁵Half drunk by now, the people demanded, "Bring out Samson so he can amuse us!" So he was brought from the prison to amuse them, and they had him stand between the pillars supporting the roof.

²⁶Samson said to the young servant who

16:5 Hebrew *1,100 shekels*, about 28 pounds or 12.5 kilograms in weight.   **16:13-14** As in Greek version and Latin Vulgate; Hebrew lacks *I would become as weak as anyone else. / So while he slept, Delilah wove the seven braids of his hair into the fabric.* ¹⁴*Then she tightened it with the loom shuttle.*   **16:19** Or *she began to torment him.* Greek version reads *He began to grow weak.*

was leading him by the hand, "Place my hands against the pillars that hold up the temple. I want to rest against them." ²⁷Now the temple was completely filled with people. All the Philistine rulers were there, and there were about 3,000 men and women on the roof who were watching as Samson amused them.

²⁸Then Samson prayed to the LORD, "Sovereign LORD, remember me again. O God, please strengthen me just one more time. With one blow let me pay back the Philistines for the loss of my two eyes." ²⁹Then Samson put his hands on the two center pillars that held up the temple. Pushing against them with both hands, ³⁰he prayed, "Let me die with the Philistines." And the temple crashed down on the Philistine rulers and all the people. So he killed more people when he died than he had during his entire lifetime.

³¹Later his brothers and other relatives went down to get his body. They took him back home and buried him between Zorah and Eshtaol, where his father, Manoah, was buried. Samson had judged Israel for twenty years.

17 Micah's Idols

There was a man named Micah, who lived in the hill country of Ephraim. ²One day he said to his mother, "I heard you place a curse on the person who stole 1,100 pieces* of silver from you. Well, I have the money. I was the one who took it."

"The LORD bless you for admitting it," his mother replied. ³He returned the money to her, and she said, "I now dedicate these silver coins to the LORD. In honor of my son, I will have an image carved and an idol cast."

⁴So when he returned the money to his mother, she took 200 silver coins and gave them to a silversmith, who made them into an image and an idol. And these were placed in Micah's house. ⁵Micah set up a shrine for the idol, and he made a sacred ephod and some household idols. Then he installed one of his sons as his personal priest.

⁶In those days Israel had no king; all the people did whatever seemed right in their own eyes.

⁷One day a young Levite, who had been living in Bethlehem in Judah, arrived in that area. ⁸He had left Bethlehem in search of another place to live, and as he traveled, he came to the hill country of Ephraim. He happened to stop at Micah's house as he was traveling through. ⁹"Where are you from?" Micah asked him.

He replied, "I am a Levite from Bethlehem in Judah, and I am looking for a place to live."

¹⁰"Stay here with me," Micah said, "and you can be a father and priest to me. I will give you ten pieces* of silver a year, plus a change of clothes and your food." ¹¹The Levite agreed to this, and the young man became like one of Micah's sons.

¹²So Micah installed the Levite as his personal priest, and he lived in Micah's house. ¹³"I know the LORD will bless me now," Micah said, "because I have a Levite serving as my priest."

18 Idolatry in the Tribe of Dan

Now in those days Israel had no king. And the tribe of Dan was trying to find a place where they could settle, for they had not yet moved into the land assigned to them when the land was divided among the tribes of Israel. ²So the men of Dan chose from their clans five capable warriors from the towns of Zorah and Eshtaol to scout out a land for them to settle in.

When these warriors arrived in the hill country of Ephraim, they came to Micah's house and spent the night there. ³While at Micah's house, they recognized the young Levite's accent, so they went over and asked him, "Who brought you here, and what are you doing in this place? Why are you here?" ⁴He told them about his agreement with Micah and that he had been hired as Micah's personal priest.

⁵Then they said, "Ask God whether or not our journey will be successful."

⁶"Go in peace," the priest replied. "For the LORD is watching over your journey."

⁷So the five men went on to the town of Laish, where they noticed the people living carefree lives, like the Sidonians; they were peaceful and secure.* The people were also

17:2 Hebrew 1,100 shekels, about 28 pounds or 12.5 kilograms in weight. 17:10 Hebrew 10 shekels, about 4 ounces or 114 grams in weight. 18:7 The meaning of the Hebrew is uncertain.

wealthy because their land was very fertile. And they lived a great distance from Sidon and had no allies nearby.

[8] When the men returned to Zorah and Eshtaol, their relatives asked them, "What did you find?"

[9] The men replied, "Come on, let's attack them! We have seen the land, and it is very good. What are you waiting for? Don't hesitate to go and take possession of it. [10] When you get there, you will find the people living carefree lives. God has given us a spacious and fertile land, lacking in nothing!"

[11] So 600 men from the tribe of Dan, armed with weapons of war, set out from Zorah and Eshtaol. [12] They camped at a place west of Kiriath-jearim in Judah, which is called Mahaneh-dan* to this day. [13] Then they went on from there into the hill country of Ephraim and came to the house of Micah.

[14] The five men who had scouted out the land around Laish explained to the others, "These buildings contain a sacred ephod, as well as some household idols, a carved image, and a cast idol. What do you think you should do?" [15] Then the five men turned off the road and went over to Micah's house, where the young Levite lived, and greeted him kindly. [16] As the 600 armed warriors from the tribe of Dan stood at the entrance of the gate, [17] the five scouts entered the shrine and removed the carved image, the sacred ephod, the household idols, and the cast idol. Meanwhile, the priest was standing at the gate with the 600 armed warriors.

[18] When the priest saw the men carrying all the sacred objects out of Micah's shrine, he said, "What are you doing?"

[19] "Be quiet and come with us," they said. "Be a father and priest to all of us. Isn't it better to be a priest for an entire tribe and clan of Israel than for the household of just one man?"

[20] The young priest was quite happy to go with them, so he took along the sacred ephod, the household idols, and the carved image. [21] They turned and started on their way again, placing their children, livestock, and possessions in front of them.

[22] When the people from the tribe of Dan were quite a distance from Micah's house, the people who lived near Micah came chasing after them. [23] They were shouting as they caught up with them. The men of Dan turned around and said to Micah, "What's the matter? Why have you called these men together and chased after us like this?"

[24] "What do you mean, 'What's the matter?'" Micah replied. "You've taken away all the gods I have made, and my priest, and I have nothing left!"

[25] The men of Dan said, "Watch what you say! There are some short-tempered men around here who might get angry and kill you and your family." [26] So the men of Dan continued on their way. When Micah saw that there were too many of them for him to attack, he turned around and went home.

[27] Then, with Micah's idols and his priest, the men of Dan came to the town of Laish, whose people were peaceful and secure. They attacked with swords and burned the town to the ground. [28] There was no one to rescue the people, for they lived a great distance from Sidon and had no allies nearby. This happened in the valley near Beth-rehob.

Then the people of the tribe of Dan rebuilt the town and lived there. [29] They renamed the town Dan after their ancestor, Israel's son, but it had originally been called Laish.

[30] Then they set up the carved image, and they appointed Jonathan son of Gershom, son of Moses,* as their priest. This family continued as priests for the tribe of Dan until the Exile. [31] So Micah's carved image was worshiped by the tribe of Dan as long as the Tabernacle of God remained at Shiloh.

19 The Levite and His Concubine

Now in those days Israel had no king. There was a man from the tribe of Levi living in a remote area of the hill country of Ephraim. One day he brought home a woman from Bethlehem in Judah to be his concubine. [2] But she became angry with him* and returned to her father's home in Bethlehem.

After about four months, [3] her husband

18:12 Mahaneh-dan means "the camp of Dan." **18:30** As in an ancient Hebrew tradition, some Greek manuscripts, and Latin Vulgate; Masoretic Text reads son of Manasseh. **19:2** Or she was unfaithful to him.

set out for Bethlehem to speak personally to her and persuade her to come back. He took with him a servant and a pair of donkeys. When he arrived at* her father's house, her father saw him and welcomed him. ⁴Her father urged him to stay awhile, so he stayed three days, eating, drinking, and sleeping there.

⁵On the fourth day the man was up early, ready to leave, but the woman's father said to his son-in-law, "Have something to eat before you go." ⁶So the two men sat down together and had something to eat and drink. Then the woman's father said, "Please stay another night and enjoy yourself." ⁷The man got up to leave, but his father-in-law kept urging him to stay, so he finally gave in and stayed the night.

⁸On the morning of the fifth day he was up early again, ready to leave, and again the woman's father said, "Have something to eat; then you can leave later this afternoon." So they had another day of feasting. ⁹Later, as the man and his concubine and servant were preparing to leave, his father-in-law said, "Look, it's almost evening. Stay the night and enjoy yourself. Tomorrow you can get up early and be on your way."

¹⁰But this time the man was determined to leave. So he took his two saddled donkeys and his concubine and headed in the direction of Jebus (that is, Jerusalem). ¹¹It was late in the day when they neared Jebus, and the man's servant said to him, "Let's stop at this Jebusite town and spend the night there."

¹²"No," his master said, "we can't stay in this foreign town where there are no Israelites. Instead, we will go on to Gibeah. ¹³Come on, let's try to get as far as Gibeah or Ramah, and we'll spend the night in one of those towns." ¹⁴So they went on. The sun was setting as they came to Gibeah, a town in the land of Benjamin, ¹⁵so they stopped there to spend the night. They rested in the town square, but no one took them in for the night.

¹⁶That evening an old man came home from his work in the fields. He was from the hill country of Ephraim, but he was living in Gibeah, where the people were from the tribe of Benjamin. ¹⁷When he saw the travelers sitting in the town square, he asked them where they were from and where they were going.

¹⁸"We have been in Bethlehem in Judah," the man replied. "We are on our way to a remote area in the hill country of Ephraim, which is my home. I traveled to Bethlehem, and now I'm returning home.* But no one has taken us in for the night, ¹⁹even though we have everything we need. We have straw and feed for our donkeys and plenty of bread and wine for ourselves."

²⁰"You are welcome to stay with me," the old man said. "I will give you anything you might need. But whatever you do, don't spend the night in the square." ²¹So he took them home with him and fed the donkeys. After they washed their feet, they ate and drank together.

²²While they were enjoying themselves, a crowd of troublemakers from the town surrounded the house. They began beating at the door and shouting to the old man, "Bring out the man who is staying with you so we can have sex with him."

²³The old man stepped outside to talk to them. "No, my brothers, don't do such an evil thing. For this man is a guest in my house, and such a thing would be shameful. ²⁴Here, take my virgin daughter and this man's concubine. I will bring them out to you, and you can abuse them and do whatever you like. But don't do such a shameful thing to this man."

²⁵But they wouldn't listen to him. So the Levite took hold of his concubine and pushed her out the door. The men of the town abused her all night, taking turns raping her until morning. Finally, at dawn they let her go. ²⁶At daybreak the woman returned to the house where her husband was staying. She collapsed at the door of the house and lay there until it was light.

²⁷When her husband opened the door to leave, there lay his concubine with her hands on the threshold. ²⁸He said, "Get up! Let's go!" But there was no answer.* So he put her body on his donkey and took her home.

²⁹When he got home, he took a knife and cut his concubine's body into twelve

19:3 As in Greek version; Hebrew reads When she brought him to.   19:18 As in Greek version (see also 19:29); Hebrew reads now I'm going to the Tabernacle of the Lord.   19:28 Greek version adds for she was dead.

pieces. Then he sent one piece to each tribe throughout all the territory of Israel.

³⁰Everyone who saw it said, "Such a horrible crime has not been committed in all the time since Israel left Egypt. Think about it! What are we going to do? Who's going to speak up?"

20 Israel's War with Benjamin

Then all the Israelites were united as one man, from Dan in the north to Beersheba in the south, including those from across the Jordan in the land of Gilead. The entire community assembled in the presence of the LORD at Mizpah. ²The leaders of all the people and all the tribes of Israel—400,000 warriors armed with swords—took their positions in the assembly of the people of God. ³(Word soon reached the land of Benjamin that the other tribes had gone up to Mizpah.) The Israelites then asked how this terrible crime had happened.

⁴The Levite, the husband of the woman who had been murdered, said, "My concubine and I came to spend the night in Gibeah, a town that belongs to the people of Benjamin. ⁵That night some of the leading citizens of Gibeah surrounded the house, planning to kill me, and they raped my concubine until she was dead. ⁶So I cut her body into twelve pieces and sent the pieces throughout the territory assigned to Israel, for these men have committed a terrible and shameful crime. ⁷Now then, all of you—the entire community of Israel— must decide here and now what should be done about this!"

⁸And all the people rose to their feet in unison and declared, "None of us will return home! No, not even one of us! ⁹Instead, this is what we will do to Gibeah; we will draw lots to decide who will attack it. ¹⁰One-tenth of the men* from each tribe will be chosen to supply the warriors with food, and the rest of us will take revenge on Gibeah* of Benjamin for this shameful thing they have done in Israel." ¹¹So all the Israelites were completely united, and they gathered together to attack the town.

¹²The Israelites sent messengers to the tribe of Benjamin, saying, "What a terrible thing has been done among you! ¹³Give up those evil men, those troublemakers from Gibeah, so we can execute them and purge Israel of this evil."

But the people of Benjamin would not listen. ¹⁴Instead, they came from their towns and gathered at Gibeah to fight the Israelites. ¹⁵In all, 26,000 of their warriors armed with swords arrived in Gibeah to join the 700 elite troops who lived there. ¹⁶Among Benjamin's elite troops, 700 were left-handed, and each of them could sling a rock and hit a target within a hairsbreadth without missing. ¹⁷Israel had 400,000 experienced soldiers armed with swords, not counting Benjamin's warriors.

¹⁸Before the battle the Israelites went to Bethel and asked God, "Which tribe should go first to attack the people of Benjamin?"

The LORD answered, "Judah is to go first."

¹⁹So the Israelites left early the next morning and camped near Gibeah. ²⁰Then they advanced toward Gibeah to attack the men of Benjamin. ²¹But Benjamin's warriors, who were defending the town, came out and killed 22,000 Israelites on the battlefield that day.

²²But the Israelites encouraged each other and took their positions again at the same place they had fought the previous day. ²³For they had gone up to Bethel and wept in the presence of the LORD until evening. They had asked the LORD, "Should we fight against our relatives from Benjamin again?"

And the LORD had said, "Go out and fight against them."

²⁴So the next day they went out again to fight against the men of Benjamin, ²⁵but the men of Benjamin killed another 18,000 Israelites, all of whom were experienced with the sword.

²⁶Then all the Israelites went up to Bethel and wept in the presence of the LORD and fasted until evening. They also brought burnt offerings and peace offerings to the LORD. ²⁷The Israelites went up seeking direction from the LORD. (In those days the Ark of the Covenant of God was in Bethel, ²⁸and Phinehas son of Eleazar and grandson of Aaron

---

20:10a Hebrew *10 men from every hundred, 100 men from every thousand, and 1,000 men from every 10,000.*   20:10b Hebrew *Geba*, in this case a variant spelling of *Gibeah*; also in 20:33.

Praying Together

JUDGES 20:26-27

Many of us think of prayer as an individual discipline—something best done between us and God, all alone. Sure, we pray together at church or perhaps at Bible studies, but when a need for prayer arises, we tend to think about *solitude* rather than *community*.

And yet corporate prayer—praying together—has a long, important history in our faith tradition. People in the Old Testament prayed together: "Then all the Israelites went up to Bethel and wept in the presence of the LORD and fasted until evening. . . . The Israelites went up seeking direction from the LORD" (Judges 20:26-27). Time and again in Scripture we see examples like this. And the plural pronouns in the Lord's Prayer seem to indicate Jesus had corporate prayer in mind when he taught us how to pray (Matthew 6:9-13). We see this promise that in Christian community we can experience Jesus' presence in a unique way: "For where two or three gather together as my followers, I am there among them" (Matthew 18:20).

So why do we not consider prayer together more often? For one, we may fear becoming like the Pharisees who Jesus warns will be "severely punished" for hypocritically "making long prayers in public" (Mark 12:38-40). Another reason might be a rightful fear that prayer groups are thinly veiled gossip sessions or, conversely, bragging sessions.

While these are concerns to guard against, praying together offers too much to be pushed aside. When we pray together—with humble, open, vulnerable hearts—we gain intimacy with one another as we go before God.

But corporate prayer does something else: when words escape us or we don't even know how to pray, others can pray *for* us. We powerfully experience the grace of God through our Christian community as we allow others to carry our prayer burdens.

In fact, almost nothing else can duplicate the bonds of a trusted community of believers who together lift their worries and brokenness to our merciful, redeeming God.

—*Caryn Rivadeneira*

For more on prayer, see reading at 1 Samuel 1.

was the priest.) The Israelites asked the LORD, "Should we fight against our relatives from Benjamin again, or should we stop?"

The LORD said, "Go! Tomorrow I will hand them over to you."

29 So the Israelites set an ambush all around Gibeah. 30 They went out on the third day and took their positions at the same place as before. 31 When the men of Benjamin came out to attack, they were drawn away from the town. And as they had done before, they began to kill the Israelites. About thirty Israelites died in the open fields and along the roads, one leading to Bethel and the other leading back to Gibeah.

32 Then the warriors of Benjamin shouted, "We're defeating them as we did before!" But the Israelites had planned in advance to run away so that the men of Benjamin would chase them along the roads and be drawn away from the town.

33 When the main group of Israelite warriors reached Baal-tamar, they turned and took up their positions. Meanwhile, the

Israelites hiding in ambush to the west* of Gibeah jumped up to fight. ³⁴There were 10,000 elite Israelite troops who advanced against Gibeah. The fighting was so heavy that Benjamin didn't realize the impending disaster. ³⁵So the LORD helped Israel defeat Benjamin, and that day the Israelites killed 25,100 of Benjamin's warriors, all of whom were experienced swordsmen. ³⁶Then the men of Benjamin saw that they were beaten.

The Israelites had retreated from Benjamin's warriors in order to give those hiding in ambush more room to maneuver against Gibeah. ³⁷Then those who were hiding rushed in from all sides and killed everyone in the town. ³⁸They had arranged to send up a large cloud of smoke from the town as a signal. ³⁹When the Israelites saw the smoke, they turned and attacked Benjamin's warriors.

By that time Benjamin's warriors had killed about thirty Israelites, and they shouted, "We're defeating them as we did in the first battle!" ⁴⁰But when the warriors of Benjamin looked behind them and saw the smoke rising into the sky from every part of the town, ⁴¹the men of Israel turned and attacked. At this point the men of Benjamin became terrified, because they realized disaster was close at hand. ⁴²So they turned around and fled before the Israelites toward the wilderness. But they couldn't escape the battle, and the people who came out of the nearby towns were also killed.* ⁴³The Israelites surrounded the men of Benjamin and chased them relentlessly, finally overtaking them east of Gibeah.* ⁴⁴That day 18,000 of Benjamin's strongest warriors died in battle. ⁴⁵The survivors fled into the wilderness toward the rock of Rimmon, but Israel killed 5,000 of them along the road. They continued the chase until they had killed another 2,000 near Gidom.

⁴⁶So that day the tribe of Benjamin lost 25,000 strong warriors armed with swords, ⁴⁷leaving only 600 men who escaped to the rock of Rimmon, where they lived for four months. ⁴⁸And the Israelites returned and slaughtered every living thing in all the towns—the people, the livestock, and everything they found. They also burned down all the towns they came to.

21 Israel Provides Wives for Benjamin

The Israelites had vowed at Mizpah, "We will never give our daughters in marriage to a man from the tribe of Benjamin." ²Now the people went to Bethel and sat in the presence of God until evening, weeping loudly and bitterly. ³"O LORD, God of Israel," they cried out, "why has this happened in Israel? Now one of our tribes is missing from Israel!"

⁴Early the next morning the people built an altar and presented their burnt offerings and peace offerings on it. ⁵Then they said, "Who among the tribes of Israel did not join us at Mizpah when we held our assembly in the presence of the LORD?" At that time they had taken a solemn oath in the LORD's presence, vowing that anyone who refused to come would be put to death.

⁶The Israelites felt sorry for their brother Benjamin and said, "Today one of the tribes of Israel has been cut off. ⁷How can we find wives for the few who remain, since we have sworn by the LORD not to give them our daughters in marriage?"

⁸So they asked, "Who among the tribes of Israel did not join us at Mizpah when we assembled in the presence of the LORD?" And they discovered that no one from Jabesh-gilead had attended the assembly. ⁹For after they counted all the people, no one from Jabesh-gilead was present.

¹⁰So the assembly sent 12,000 of their best warriors to Jabesh-gilead with orders to kill everyone there, including women and children. ¹¹"This is what you are to do," they said. "Completely destroy* all the males and every woman who is not a virgin." ¹²Among the residents of Jabesh-gilead they found 400 young virgins who had never slept with a man, and they brought them to the camp at Shiloh in the land of Canaan.

¹³The Israelite assembly sent a peace delegation to the remaining people of Benjamin who were living at the rock of Rimmon. ¹⁴Then the men of Benjamin returned to

---

20:33 As in Greek and Syriac versions and Latin Vulgate; Hebrew reads *hiding in the open space*. **20:42** Or *battle, for the people from the nearby towns also came out and killed them.* **20:43** The meaning of the Hebrew is uncertain. **21:11** The Hebrew term used here refers to the complete consecration of things or people to the LORD, either by destroying them or by giving them as an offering.

their homes, and the 400 women of Jabesh-gilead who had been spared were given to them as wives. But there were not enough women for all of them.

¹⁵ The people felt sorry for Benjamin because the LORD had made this gap among the tribes of Israel. ¹⁶ So the elders of the assembly asked, "How can we find wives for the few who remain, since the women of the tribe of Benjamin are dead? ¹⁷ There must be heirs for the survivors so that an entire tribe of Israel is not wiped out. ¹⁸ But we cannot give them our own daughters in marriage because we have sworn with a solemn oath that anyone who does this will fall under God's curse."

¹⁹ Then they thought of the annual festival of the LORD held in Shiloh, south of Lebonah and north of Bethel, along the east side of the road that goes from Bethel to Shechem. ²⁰ They told the men of Benjamin who still needed wives, "Go and hide in the vineyards. ²¹ When you see the young women of Shiloh come out for their dances, rush out from the vineyards, and each of you can take one of them home to the land of Benjamin to be your wife! ²² And when their fathers and brothers come to us in protest, we will tell them, 'Please be sympathetic. Let them have your daughters, for we didn't find wives for all of them when we destroyed Jabesh-gilead. And you are not guilty of breaking the vow since you did not actually give your daughters to them in marriage.'"

²³ So the men of Benjamin did as they were told. Each man caught one of the women as she danced in the celebration and carried her off to be his wife. They returned to their own land, and they rebuilt their towns and lived in them.

²⁴ Then the people of Israel departed by tribes and families, and they returned to their own homes.

²⁵ In those days Israel had no king; all the people did whatever seemed right in their own eyes.

Introduction to

Ruth

Background

This beautiful story of loyalty and redemption is a quiet interlude during the turbulent time of the judges. The book's title is taken from the name of the main character, Ruth, a young widow of Moab. Her name means "friendship," a quality shown in her loyalty to her mother-in-law, Naomi.

The author of Ruth is unknown. While some scholars name Samuel as a probable author, it is unlikely that he wrote the book, since David's partial genealogy is given in the last chapter of Ruth. The inclusion of the genealogy points to the book's having been written during David's reign.

Message

Love, loyalty, faithfulness, and redemption are themes in this short book. Boaz's act as a kinsman-redeemer prefigures the redemption that Christ will bring to all people. Boaz redeems land owned by Naomi, marries Ruth, and has a child to keep the family name alive. When all seems hopeless for the widows who returned empty-handed from a foreign land, God breaks through with his mercy and protection.

Ruth herself is an example of Christlike faithfulness. Although she is not an Israelite, but a foreigner from Moab, her fidelity earns her a place in the family line of David and Jesus (Matthew 1:5).

Time

Ruth died around 1125 B.C. The Book of Ruth was likely written between 980 and 960 B.C.

Outline

Ruth

1 Elimelech Moves His Family to Moab

In the days when the judges ruled in Israel, a severe famine came upon the land. So a man from Bethlehem in Judah left his home and went to live in the country of Moab, taking his wife and two sons with him. ²The man's name was Elimelech, and his wife was Naomi. Their two sons were Mahlon and Kilion. They were Ephrathites from Bethlehem in the land of Judah. And when they reached Moab, they settled there.

³Then Elimelech died, and Naomi was left with her two sons. ⁴The two sons married Moabite women. One married a woman named Orpah, and the other a woman named Ruth. But about ten years later, ⁵both Mahlon and Kilion died. This left Naomi alone, without her two sons or her husband.

Naomi and Ruth Return

⁶Then Naomi heard in Moab that the LORD had blessed his people in Judah by giving them good crops again. So Naomi and her daughters-in-law got ready to leave Moab to return to her homeland. ⁷With her two daughters-in-law she set out from the place where she had been living, and they took the road that would lead them back to Judah.

⁸But on the way, Naomi said to her two daughters-in-law, "Go back to your mothers' homes. And may the LORD reward you for your kindness to your husbands and to me. ⁹May the LORD bless you with the security of another marriage." Then she kissed them good-bye, and they all broke down and wept.

¹⁰"No," they said. "We want to go with you to your people."

¹¹But Naomi replied, "Why should you go on with me? Can I still give birth to other sons who could grow up to be your husbands? ¹²No, my daughters, return to your parents' homes, for I am too old to marry again. And even if it were possible, and I were to get married tonight and bear sons, then what? ¹³Would you wait for them to grow up and refuse to marry someone else? No, of course not, my daughters! Things are far more bitter for me than for you, because the LORD himself has raised his fist against me."

¹⁴And again they wept together, and Orpah kissed her mother-in-law good-bye. But Ruth clung tightly to Naomi. ¹⁵"Look," Naomi said to her, "your sister-in-law has gone back to her people and to her gods. You should do the same."

¹⁶But Ruth replied, "Don't ask me to leave you and turn back. Wherever you go, I will go; wherever you live, I will live. Your people will be my people, and your God will be my God. ¹⁷Wherever you die, I will die, and there I will be buried. May the LORD punish me severely if I allow anything but death to separate us!" ¹⁸When Naomi saw that Ruth was determined to go with her, she said nothing more.

¹⁹So the two of them continued on their journey. When they came to Bethlehem, the entire town was excited by their arrival. "Is it really Naomi?" the women asked.

²⁰"Don't call me Naomi," she responded. "Instead, call me Mara,* for the

---

1:20 *Naomi* means "pleasant"; *Mara* means "bitter."

Almighty has made life very bitter for me. [21]I went away full, but the LORD has brought me home empty. Why call me Naomi when the LORD has caused me to suffer* and the Almighty has sent such tragedy upon me?"

[22]So Naomi returned from Moab, accompanied by her daughter-in-law Ruth, the young Moabite woman. They arrived in Bethlehem in late spring, at the beginning of the barley harvest.

2 Ruth Works in Boaz's Field

Now there was a wealthy and influential man in Bethlehem named Boaz, who was a relative of Naomi's husband, Elimelech.

[2]One day Ruth the Moabite said to Naomi, "Let me go out into the harvest fields to pick up the stalks of grain left behind by anyone who is kind enough to let me do it."

Naomi replied, "All right, my daughter, go ahead." [3]So Ruth went out to gather grain behind the harvesters. And as it happened, she found herself working in a field that belonged to Boaz, the relative of her father-in-law, Elimelech.

[4]While she was there, Boaz arrived from Bethlehem and greeted the harvesters. "The LORD be with you!" he said.

"The LORD bless you!" the harvesters replied.

[5]Then Boaz asked his foreman, "Who is that young woman over there? Who does she belong to?"

[6]And the foreman replied, "She is the young woman from Moab who came back with Naomi. [7]She asked me this morning if she could gather grain behind the harvesters. She has been hard at work ever since, except for a few minutes' rest in the shelter."

[8]Boaz went over and said to Ruth, "Listen, my daughter. Stay right here with us when you gather grain; don't go to any other fields. Stay right behind the young women working in my field. [9]See which part of the field they are harvesting, and then follow them. I have warned the young men not to treat you roughly. And when you are thirsty, help yourself to the water they have drawn from the well."

[10]Ruth fell at his feet and thanked him warmly. "What have I done to deserve such kindness?" she asked. "I am only a foreigner."

[11]"Yes, I know," Boaz replied. "But I also know about everything you have done for your mother-in-law since the death of your husband. I have heard how you left your father and mother and your own land to live here among complete strangers. [12]May the LORD, the God of Israel, under whose wings you have come to take refuge, reward you fully for what you have done."

[13]"I hope I continue to please you, sir," she replied. "You have comforted me by speaking so kindly to me, even though I am not one of your workers."

[14]At mealtime Boaz called to her, "Come over here, and help yourself to some food. You can dip your bread in the sour wine." So she sat with his harvesters, and Boaz gave her some roasted grain to eat. She ate all she wanted and still had some left over.

[15]When Ruth went back to work again, Boaz ordered his young men, "Let her gather grain right among the sheaves without stopping her. [16]And pull out some heads of barley from the bundles and drop them on purpose for her. Let her pick them up, and don't give her a hard time!"

[17]So Ruth gathered barley there all day, and when she beat out the grain that evening, it filled an entire basket.* [18]She carried it back into town and showed it to her mother-in-law. Ruth also gave her the roasted grain that was left over from her meal.

[19]"Where did you gather all this grain today?" Naomi asked. "Where did you work? May the LORD bless the one who helped you!"

So Ruth told her mother-in-law about the man in whose field she had worked. She said, "The man I worked with today is named Boaz."

[20]"May the LORD bless him!" Naomi told her daughter-in-law. "He is showing his kindness to us as well as to your dead husband.* That man is one of our closest relatives, one of our family redeemers."

[21]Then Ruth* said, "What's more, Boaz even told me to come back and stay with his harvesters until the entire harvest is completed."

1:21 Or has testified against me. **2:17** Hebrew it was about an ephah [20 quarts or 22 liters]. **2:20** Hebrew to the living and to the dead. **2:21** Hebrew Ruth the Moabite.

²²"Good!" Naomi exclaimed. "Do as he said, my daughter. Stay with his young women right through the whole harvest. You might be harassed in other fields, but you'll be safe with him."

²³So Ruth worked alongside the women in Boaz's fields and gathered grain with them until the end of the barley harvest. Then she continued working with them through the wheat harvest in early summer. And all the while she lived with her mother-in-law.

3 Ruth at the Threshing Floor

One day Naomi said to Ruth, "My daughter, it's time that I found a permanent home for you, so that you will be provided for. ²Boaz is a close relative of ours, and he's been very kind by letting you gather grain with his young women. Tonight he will be winnowing barley at the threshing floor. ³Now do as I tell you—take a bath and put on perfume and dress in your nicest clothes. Then go to the threshing floor, but don't let Boaz see you until he has finished eating and drinking. ⁴Be sure to notice where he lies down; then go and uncover his feet and lie down there. He will tell you what to do."

⁵"I will do everything you say," Ruth replied. ⁶So she went down to the threshing floor that night and followed the instructions of her mother-in-law.

⁷After Boaz had finished eating and drinking and was in good spirits, he lay down at the far end of the pile of grain and went to sleep. Then Ruth came quietly, uncovered his feet, and lay down. ⁸Around midnight Boaz suddenly woke up and turned over. He was surprised to find a woman lying at his feet! ⁹"Who are you?" he asked.

"I am your servant Ruth," she replied. "Spread the corner of your covering over me, for you are my family redeemer."

¹⁰"The LORD bless you, my daughter!" Boaz exclaimed. "You are showing even more family loyalty now than you did before, for you have not gone after a younger man, whether rich or poor. ¹¹Now don't worry about a thing, my daughter. I will do what is necessary, for everyone in town knows you are a virtuous woman. ¹²But

while it's true that I am one of your family redeemers, there is another man who is more closely related to you than I am. ¹³Stay here tonight, and in the morning I will talk to him. If he is willing to redeem you, very well. Let him marry you. But if he is not willing, then as surely as the LORD lives, I will redeem you myself! Now lie down here until morning."

¹⁴So Ruth lay at Boaz's feet until the morning, but she got up before it was light enough for people to recognize each other. For Boaz had said, "No one must know that a woman was here at the threshing floor." ¹⁵Then Boaz said to her, "Bring your cloak and spread it out." He measured six scoops* of barley into the cloak and placed it on her back. Then he* returned to the town.

¹⁶When Ruth went back to her mother-in-law, Naomi asked, "What happened, my daughter?"

Ruth told Naomi everything Boaz had done for her, ¹⁷and she added, "He gave me these six scoops of barley and said, 'Don't go back to your mother-in-law empty-handed.'"

¹⁸Then Naomi said to her, "Just be patient, my daughter, until we hear what happens. The man won't rest until he has settled things today."

4 Boaz Marries Ruth

Boaz went to the town gate and took a seat there. Just then the family redeemer he had mentioned came by, so Boaz called out to him, "Come over here and sit down, friend. I want to talk to you." So they sat down together. ²Then Boaz called ten leaders from the town and asked them to sit as witnesses. ³And Boaz said to the family redeemer, "You know Naomi, who came back from Moab. She is selling the land that belonged to our relative Elimelech. ⁴I thought I should speak to you about it so that you can redeem it if you wish. If you want the land, then buy it here in the presence of these witnesses. But if you don't want it, let me know right away, because I am next in line to redeem it after you."

The man replied, "All right, I'll redeem it."

⁵Then Boaz told him, "Of course, your

3:15a Hebrew *six measures,* an unknown quantity. **3:15b** Most Hebrew manuscripts read *he;* many Hebrew manuscripts, Syriac version, and Latin Vulgate read *she.*

purchase of the land from Naomi also requires that you marry Ruth, the Moabite widow. That way she can have children who will carry on her husband's name and keep the land in the family."

⁶"Then I can't redeem it," the family redeemer replied, "because this might endanger my own estate. You redeem the land; I cannot do it."

⁷Now in those days it was the custom in Israel for anyone transferring a right of purchase to remove his sandal and hand it to the other party. This publicly validated the transaction. ⁸So the other family redeemer drew off his sandal as he said to Boaz, "You buy the land."

⁹Then Boaz said to the elders and to the crowd standing around, "You are witnesses that today I have bought from Naomi all the property of Elimelech, Kilion, and Mahlon. ¹⁰And with the land I have acquired Ruth, the Moabite widow of Mahlon, to be my

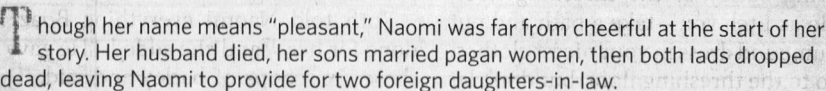

Naomi: Celebration . . . Eventually

RUTH 4:13-18

Though her name means "pleasant," Naomi was far from cheerful at the start of her story. Her husband died, her sons married pagan women, then both lads dropped dead, leaving Naomi to provide for two foreign daughters-in-law.

Naomi offered a bitter explanation for her plight: "The LORD himself has raised his fist against me" (Ruth 1:13). Negativity rolled off the woman in waves.

Yet it's clear something good happened. Naomi began to praise God, rather than blame him. When she heard of Boaz's kindness to her daughter-in-law, Naomi responded, "May the LORD bless him!" (2:20). Sounds like celebration to me.

Naomi was practicing what the New Testament calls "a continual sacrifice of praise" (Hebrews 13:15). Praising God when it costs you something, when it isn't easy but it's right. That's where the discipline comes in. The psalmist of the Old Testament well knew the challenge of celebrating when it hurts: "Why am I discouraged? Why is my heart so sad? I will put my hope in God! I will praise him again—my Savior and my God!" (Psalm 43:5).

I will praise him again. A decision, a discipline. When we lift our eyes from the pain of the moment to the promise of the future, our hearts and minds lift as well, giving us the strength to go on.

In Naomi's case, she began to put Ruth's happiness above her own: "My daughter, it's time that I found a permanent home for you, so that you will be provided for" (Ruth 3:1). And when Ruth found that home and bore a son, the women of Bethlehem said to Naomi, "Praise the LORD, who has now provided a redeemer for your family!" (4:14). Naomi's joy was obvious as she "took the baby and cuddled him to her breast" (4:16).

Happy endings seldom come easily. They are hard won through daily commitment to finding joy in the midst of junk and celebrating, delighting in, the good rather than whining about the bad. Embrace them both, and you'll discover the delicious fruit of this divine discipline: peace.

—Liz Curtis Higgs

For more on celebration, see reading at Esther 9:20-32.

wife. This way she can have a son to carry on the family name of her dead husband and to inherit the family property here in his hometown. You are all witnesses today."

¹¹ Then the elders and all the people standing in the gate replied, "We are witnesses! May the LORD make this woman who is coming into your home like Rachel and Leah, from whom all the nation of Israel descended! May you prosper in Ephrathah and be famous in Bethlehem. ¹² And may the LORD give you descendants by this young woman who will be like those of our ancestor Perez, the son of Tamar and Judah."

The Descendants of Boaz

¹³ So Boaz took Ruth into his home, and she became his wife. When he slept with her, the LORD enabled her to become pregnant, and she gave birth to a son. ¹⁴ Then the women of the town said to Naomi, "Praise the LORD, who has now provided a redeemer for your family! May this child be famous in Israel. ¹⁵ May he restore your youth and care for you in your old age. For he is the son of your daughter-in-law who loves you and has been better to you than seven sons!"

¹⁶ Naomi took the baby and cuddled him to her breast. And she cared for him as if he were her own. ¹⁷ The neighbor women said, "Now at last Naomi has a son again!" And they named him Obed. He became the father of Jesse and the grandfather of David.

¹⁸ This is the genealogical record of their ancestor Perez:

Perez was the father of Hezron.
¹⁹ Hezron was the father of Ram.
Ram was the father of Amminadab.
²⁰ Amminadab was the father of Nahshon.
Nahshon was the father of Salmon.*
²¹ Salmon was the father of Boaz.
Boaz was the father of Obed.
²² Obed was the father of Jesse.
Jesse was the father of David.

4:20 As in some Greek manuscripts (see also 4:21); Hebrew reads *Salma*.

Introduction to

1 Samuel

Background

First Samuel describes a turning point for the tribes of Israel: the theocracy—a nation ruled by God under his appointed judges—becomes a monarchy. The prophet Samuel is the last judge. He is chosen by God to anoint the first king, Saul.

The books of 1 and 2 Samuel were originally one narrative in the Hebrew Scriptures but are divided in the Greek Septuagint version. Although both books bear the name of the prophet Samuel, he may have written only part of 1 Samuel. Because 1 Chronicles 29:29 mentions "*The Record of Nathan the Prophet*, and . . . *The Record of Gad the Seer*," Nathan and Gad have also been proposed as contributors to 1 Samuel.

Message

The old saying "be careful what you wish for" speaks to this period in Israel's history. Other nations have kings. When the people of Israel demand a king, God gives them one but warns them of the cost (8:10–18). This demand for a king is not merely a rejection of Samuel's leadership; the people are rejecting God himself (8:7). They do not want an unseen God as their leader; they want a king so they can "be like the nations around us. Our king will judge us and lead us into battle" (8:20).

While Saul has a kingly bearing, his flagrant disobedience eventually leads God to anoint "a man after his own heart" (13:14)—David. This young shepherd boy kills a giant, succeeds in battle, and eludes Saul for many years before the king's death allows him to ascend the throne.

Time

The narrative of 1 Samuel covers the period from before Samuel's birth until the death of Saul (1105–1011 B.C.). First and 2 Samuel, however, were compiled between 931 and 722 B.C.

Outline

1 Samuel

1 Elkanah and His Family

There was a man named Elkanah who lived in Ramah in the region of Zuph* in the hill country of Ephraim. He was the son of Jeroham, son of Elihu, son of Tohu, son of Zuph, of Ephraim. ²Elkanah had two wives, Hannah and Peninnah. Peninnah had children, but Hannah did not.

³Each year Elkanah would travel to Shiloh to worship and sacrifice to the LORD of Heaven's Armies at the Tabernacle. The priests of the LORD at that time were the two sons of Eli—Hophni and Phinehas. ⁴On the days Elkanah presented his sacrifice, he would give portions of the meat to Peninnah and each of her children. ⁵And though he loved Hannah, he would give her only one choice portion* because the LORD had given her no children. ⁶So Peninnah would taunt Hannah and make fun of her because the LORD had kept her from having children. ⁷Year after year it was the same—Peninnah would taunt Hannah as they went to the Tabernacle.* Each time, Hannah would be reduced to tears and would not even eat.

⁸"Why are you crying, Hannah?" Elkanah would ask. "Why aren't you eating? Why be downhearted just because you have no children? You have me—isn't that better than having ten sons?"

Hannah's Prayer for a Son

⁹Once after a sacrificial meal at Shiloh, Hannah got up and went to pray. Eli the priest was sitting at his customary place beside the entrance of the Tabernacle.* ¹⁰Hannah was in deep anguish, crying bitterly as she prayed to the LORD. ¹¹And she made this vow: "O LORD of Heaven's Armies, if you will look upon my sorrow and answer my prayer and give me a son, then I will give him back to you. He will be yours for his entire lifetime, and as a sign that he has been dedicated to the LORD, his hair will never be cut.*"

¹²As she was praying to the LORD, Eli watched her. ¹³Seeing her lips moving but hearing no sound, he thought she had been drinking. ¹⁴"Must you come here drunk?" he demanded. "Throw away your wine!"

¹⁵"Oh no, sir!" she replied. "I haven't been drinking wine or anything stronger. But I am very discouraged, and I was pouring out my heart to the LORD. ¹⁶Don't think I am a wicked woman! For I have been praying out of great anguish and sorrow."

¹⁷"In that case," Eli said, "go in peace! May the God of Israel grant the request you have asked of him."

¹⁸"Oh, thank you, sir!" she exclaimed. Then she went back and began to eat again, and she was no longer sad.

Samuel's Birth and Dedication

¹⁹The entire family got up early the next morning and went to worship the LORD once more. Then they returned home to Ramah. When Elkanah slept

---

1:1 As in Greek version; Hebrew reads in Ramathaim-zophim; compare 1:19.   1:5 Or And because he loved Hannah, he would give her a choice portion. The meaning of the Hebrew is uncertain.   1:7 Hebrew the house of the LORD; also in 1:24.   1:9 Hebrew the Temple of the LORD.   1:11 Some manuscripts add He will drink neither wine nor intoxicants.

with Hannah, the LORD remembered her plea, ²⁰and in due time she gave birth to a son. She named him Samuel,* for she said, "I asked the LORD for him."

²¹ The next year Elkanah and his family went on their annual trip to offer a sacrifice to the LORD. ²²But Hannah did not go. She told her husband, "Wait until the boy is weaned. Then I will take him to the Tabernacle and leave him there with the LORD permanently.*"

²³ "Whatever you think is best," Elkanah agreed. "Stay here for now, and may the LORD help you keep your promise." So she stayed home and nursed the boy until he was weaned.

²⁴ When the child was weaned, Hannah took him to the Tabernacle in Shiloh. They brought along a three-year-old bull* for the sacrifice and a basket* of flour and some wine. ²⁵ After sacrificing the bull, they brought the boy to Eli. ²⁶ "Sir, do you

Hannah: Bargaining with God

1 SAMUEL 1

Poor Hannah. She was married to a man who had another wife besides her. And this other wife, Peninnah, had children, while Hannah had none. To make matters worse, Peninnah liked to remind Hannah of her barren state. The Bible says she "would taunt Hannah and make fun of her" (1 Samuel 1:6). This went on for years. Finally she could stand it no more, and while visiting the tabernacle, she poured out her heart to God. In her pleading she bargained with God in a radical deal: if God would give her a child, she would give the child back to him for his service. She would raise him until he was weaned then give him to the priest to raise. Not exactly a healthy, balanced, and pure perspective.

But God answered her envious, competitive, bargaining prayer. It goes against everything we've considered about the "right" way to pray. Yet Hannah shows us that God does answer requests based on mixed motives and bargained vows.

The Bible is clear that wrong motives can hinder our prayers (James 4:3) and that God's favor can't be bought (Deuteronomy 10:17). So why did God answer Hannah's prayer? In his book *Fixing Abraham*, Chris Tiegreen suggests it's because God is "much more responsive to honest dysfunction than to beautiful but dishonest masks. . . . And God is always looking for real. . . . [Hannah] was real with her need and never attempted to base her appeal on her innocence or worthiness to get her desire met."

When God granted her desired request, Hannah responded with a song of gratitude (1 Samuel 2) that is comparable to Mary's Magnificat in Luke 1:46-55.

Of course God doesn't answer every prayer that's prayed selfishly. But through Hannah we learn that God is interested in communicating with us at a real, gut-honest level. And sometimes he even uses our desperation to set up his own plans—in Hannah's case, to accomplish a larger purpose for an entire nation to follow him.

—*Ginger Kolbaba*

For more on prayer, see reading at 2 Samuel 12:13-25.

1:20 *Samuel* sounds like the Hebrew term for "asked of God" or "heard by God."   **1:22** Some manuscripts add *I will offer him as a Nazirite for all time.*   **1:24a** As in Dead Sea Scrolls, Greek and Syriac versions; Masoretic Text reads *three bulls.*   **1:24b** Hebrew *and an ephah* [20 quarts or 22 liters].

remember me?" Hannah asked. "I am the woman who stood here several years ago praying to the LORD. [27] I asked the LORD to give me this boy, and he has granted my request. [28] Now I am giving him to the LORD, and he will belong to the LORD his whole life." And they* worshiped the LORD there.

2 Hannah's Prayer of Praise

Then Hannah prayed:

"My heart rejoices in the LORD!
  The LORD has made me strong.*
Now I have an answer for my enemies;
  I rejoice because you rescued me.
[2] No one is holy like the LORD!
  There is no one besides you;
  there is no Rock like our God.

[3] "Stop acting so proud and haughty!
  Don't speak with such arrogance!
For the LORD is a God who knows what
    you have done;
  he will judge your actions.
[4] The bow of the mighty is now broken,
  and those who stumbled are now strong.
[5] Those who were well fed are now
    starving,
  and those who were starving are now
    full.
The childless woman now has seven
    children,
  and the woman with many children
    wastes away.
[6] The LORD gives both death and life;
  he brings some down to the grave* but
    raises others up.
[7] The LORD makes some poor and others
    rich;
  he brings some down and lifts
    others up.
[8] He lifts the poor from the dust
  and the needy from the garbage dump.
He sets them among princes,
  placing them in seats of honor.
For all the earth is the LORD's,
  and he has set the world in order.
[9] "He will protect his faithful ones,
  but the wicked will disappear in
    darkness.

No one will succeed by strength alone.
[10] Those who fight against the LORD will
    be shattered.
He thunders against them from heaven;
  the LORD judges throughout the earth.
He gives power to his king;
  he increases the strength* of his
    anointed one."

[11] Then Elkanah returned home to Ramah without Samuel. And the boy served the LORD by assisting Eli the priest.

Eli's Wicked Sons

[12] Now the sons of Eli were scoundrels who had no respect for the LORD [13] or for their duties as priests. Whenever anyone offered a sacrifice, Eli's sons would send over a servant with a three-pronged fork. While the meat of the sacrificed animal was still boiling, [14] the servant would stick the fork into the pot and demand that whatever it brought up be given to Eli's sons. All the Israelites who came to worship at Shiloh were treated this way. [15] Sometimes the servant would come even before the animal's fat had been burned on the altar. He would demand raw meat before it had been boiled so that it could be used for roasting.

[16] The man offering the sacrifice might reply, "Take as much as you want, but the fat must be burned first." Then the servant would demand, "No, give it to me now, or I'll take it by force." [17] So the sin of these young men was very serious in the LORD's sight, for they treated the LORD's offerings with contempt.

[18] But Samuel, though he was only a boy, served the LORD. He wore a linen garment like that of a priest.* [19] Each year his mother made a small coat for him and brought it to him when she came with her husband for the sacrifice. [20] Before they returned home, Eli would bless Elkanah and his wife and say, "May the LORD give you other children to take the place of this one she gave to the LORD.*" [21] And the LORD gave Hannah three sons and two daughters. Meanwhile, Samuel grew up in the presence of the LORD.

[22] Now Eli was very old, but he was aware

1:28 Hebrew *he.*   **2:1** Hebrew *has exalted my horn.*   **2:6** Hebrew *to Sheol.*   **2:10** Hebrew *he exalts the horn.*   **2:18** Hebrew *He wore a linen ephod.*   **2:20** As in Dead Sea Scrolls and Greek version; Masoretic Text reads *this one he requested of the LORD.*

of what his sons were doing to the people of Israel. He knew, for instance, that his sons were seducing the young women who assisted at the entrance of the Tabernacle.* ²³Eli said to them, "I have been hearing reports from all the people about the wicked things you are doing. Why do you keep sinning? ²⁴You must stop, my sons! The reports I hear among the Lord's people are not good. ²⁵If someone sins against another person, God* can mediate for the guilty party. But if someone sins against the Lord, who can intercede?" But Eli's sons wouldn't listen to their father, for the Lord was already planning to put them to death.

²⁶Meanwhile, the boy Samuel grew taller and grew in favor with the Lord and with the people.

A Warning for Eli's Family

²⁷One day a man of God came to Eli and gave him this message from the Lord: "I revealed myself* to your ancestors when the people of Israel were slaves in Egypt. ²⁸I chose your ancestor Aaron* from among all the tribes of Israel to be my priest, to offer sacrifices on my altar, to burn incense, and to wear the priestly vest* as he served me. And I assigned the sacrificial offerings to you priests. ²⁹So why do you scorn my sacrifices and offerings? Why do you give your sons more honor than you give me—for you and they have become fat from the best offerings of my people Israel!

³⁰"Therefore, the Lord, the God of Israel, says: I promised that your branch of the tribe of Levi* would always be my priests. But I will honor those who honor me, and I will despise those who think lightly of me. ³¹The time is coming when I will put an end to your family, so it will no longer serve as my priests. All the members of your family will die before their time. None will reach old age. ³²You will watch with envy as I pour out prosperity on the people of Israel. But no members of your family will ever live out their days. ³³Those who survive will live in sadness and grief, and their children will die a violent death.* ³⁴And to prove that what I have said will come true, I will cause

your two sons, Hophni and Phinehas, to die on the same day!

³⁵"Then I will raise up a faithful priest who will serve me and do what I desire. I will establish his family, and they will be priests to my anointed kings forever. ³⁶Then all of your surviving family will bow before him, begging for money and food. 'Please,' they will say, 'give us jobs among the priests so we will have enough to eat.'"

3 The Lord Speaks to Samuel

Meanwhile, the boy Samuel served the Lord by assisting Eli. Now in those days messages from the Lord were very rare, and visions were quite uncommon.

²One night Eli, who was almost blind by now, had gone to bed. ³The lamp of God had not yet gone out, and Samuel was sleeping in the Tabernacle* near the Ark of God. ⁴Suddenly the Lord called out, "Samuel!"

"Yes?" Samuel replied. "What is it?" ⁵He got up and ran to Eli. "Here I am. Did you call me?"

"I didn't call you," Eli replied. "Go back to bed." So he did.

⁶Then the Lord called out again, "Samuel!"

Again Samuel got up and went to Eli. "Here I am. Did you call me?"

"I didn't call you, my son," Eli said. "Go back to bed."

⁷Samuel did not yet know the Lord because he had never had a message from the Lord before. ⁸So the Lord called a third time, and once more Samuel got up and went to Eli. "Here I am. Did you call me?"

Then Eli realized it was the Lord who was calling the boy. ⁹So he said to Samuel, "Go and lie down again, and if someone calls again, say, 'Speak, Lord, your servant is listening.'" So Samuel went back to bed.

¹⁰And the Lord came and called as before, "Samuel! Samuel!"

And Samuel replied, "Speak, your servant is listening."

¹¹Then the Lord said to Samuel, "I am about to do a shocking thing in Israel. ¹²I am going to carry out all my threats against

---

2:22 Hebrew *Tent of Meeting*. Some manuscripts lack this entire sentence. **2:25** Or *the judges*. **2:27** As in Greek and Syriac versions; Hebrew reads *Did I reveal myself?* **2:28a** Hebrew *your father*. **2:28b** Hebrew *an ephod*. **2:30** Hebrew *that your house and your father's house*. **2:33** As in Dead Sea Scrolls, which read *die by the sword*; Masoretic Text reads *die like mortals*. **3:3** Hebrew *the Temple of the Lord*.

Mentors Help Us Hear God's Voice
1 SAMUEL 3:1-14

In 1 Samuel 3 young Samuel hears from God—but it takes Eli, who's older, wiser, and more mature, to help him discern that he's truly hearing God's voice. All of us need an Eli in our lives—a spiritual mentor who has been walking in faith longer than we have. Someone who can help us hear and respond rightly to God.

A good mentor should be someone who's able to discern God's voice and understand God's Word—someone who has a fervent prayer life, who studies and is clearly obedient to God's Word. As you study Scripture and seek to hear God's voice, you can go to this person and say, "Here's what I sense God saying to me. What do you think?"

Without mentors, Christians can easily take a verse of Scripture out of context and go off in the wrong direction like a misguided arrow. When we face big decisions and are trying to follow God's leading, we go to our mentors and ask them to pray with us and help us discern God's will. God often uses them to give us a sense of confirmation that yes, indeed, God is speaking to us.

—Priscilla Shirer

For more on mentoring, see reading at 1 Samuel 23:15-29.

Eli and his family, from beginning to end. [13] I have warned him that judgment is coming upon his family forever, because his sons are blaspheming God* and he hasn't disciplined them. [14] So I have vowed that the sins of Eli and his sons will never be forgiven by sacrifices or offerings."

Samuel Speaks for the LORD

[15] Samuel stayed in bed until morning, then got up and opened the doors of the Tabernacle* as usual. He was afraid to tell Eli what the LORD had said to him. [16] But Eli called out to him, "Samuel, my son."

"Here I am," Samuel replied.

[17] "What did the LORD say to you? Tell me everything. And may God strike you and even kill you if you hide anything from me!" [18] So Samuel told Eli everything; he didn't hold anything back. "It is the LORD's will," Eli replied. "Let him do what he thinks best."

[19] As Samuel grew up, the LORD was with him, and everything Samuel said proved to be reliable. [20] And all Israel, from Dan in the north to Beersheba in the south, knew that Samuel was confirmed as a prophet of the LORD. [21] The LORD continued to appear at Shiloh and gave messages to Samuel there at the Tabernacle. [4:1] And Samuel's words went out to all the people of Israel.

4 The Philistines Capture the Ark

At that time Israel was at war with the Philistines. The Israelite army was camped near Ebenezer, and the Philistines were at Aphek. [2] The Philistines attacked and defeated the army of Israel, killing 4,000 men. [3] After the battle was over, the troops retreated to their camp, and the elders of Israel asked, "Why did the LORD allow us to be defeated by the Philistines?" Then they said, "Let's bring the Ark of the Covenant of the LORD from Shiloh. If we carry it into battle with us, it* will save us from our enemies."

3:13 As in Greek version; Hebrew reads *his sons have made themselves contemptible.*   **3:15** Hebrew *the house of the LORD.*   **4:3** Or *he.*

⁴So they sent men to Shiloh to bring the Ark of the Covenant of the LORD of Heaven's Armies, who is enthroned between the cherubim. Hophni and Phinehas, the sons of Eli, were also there with the Ark of the Covenant of God. ⁵When all the Israelites saw the Ark of the Covenant of the LORD coming into the camp, their shout of joy was so loud it made the ground shake!

⁶"What's going on?" the Philistines asked. "What's all the shouting about in the Hebrew camp?" When they were told it was because the Ark of the LORD had arrived, ⁷they panicked. "The gods have* come into their camp!" they cried. "This is a disaster! We have never had to face anything like this before! ⁸Help! Who can save us from these mighty gods of Israel? They are the same gods who destroyed the Egyptians with plagues when Israel was in the wilderness. ⁹Fight as never before, Philistines! If you don't, we will become the Hebrews' slaves just as they have been ours! Stand up like men and fight!"

¹⁰So the Philistines fought desperately, and Israel was defeated again. The slaughter was great; 30,000 Israelite soldiers died that day. The survivors turned and fled to their tents. ¹¹The Ark of God was captured, and Hophni and Phinehas, the two sons of Eli, were killed.

The Death of Eli

¹²A man from the tribe of Benjamin ran from the battlefield and arrived at Shiloh later that same day. He had torn his clothes and put dust on his head to show his grief. ¹³Eli was waiting beside the road to hear the news of the battle, for his heart trembled for the safety of the Ark of God. When the messenger arrived and told what had happened, an outcry resounded throughout the town.

¹⁴"What is all the noise about?" Eli asked.

The messenger rushed over to Eli, ¹⁵who was ninety-eight years old and blind. ¹⁶He said to Eli, "I have just come from the battlefield—I was there this very day."

"What happened, my son?" Eli demanded.

¹⁷"Israel has been defeated by the Philis-

tines," the messenger replied. "The people have been slaughtered, and your two sons, Hophni and Phinehas, were also killed. And the Ark of God has been captured."

¹⁸When the messenger mentioned what had happened to the Ark of God, Eli fell backward from his seat beside the gate. He broke his neck and died, for he was old and overweight. He had been Israel's judge for forty years.

¹⁹Eli's daughter-in-law, the wife of Phinehas, was pregnant and near her time of delivery. When she heard that the Ark of God had been captured and that her father-in-law and husband were dead, she went into labor and gave birth. ²⁰She died in childbirth, but before she passed away the midwives tried to encourage her. "Don't be afraid," they said. "You have a baby boy!" But she did not answer or pay attention to them.

²¹She named the child Ichabod (which means "Where is the glory?"), for she said, "Israel's glory is gone." She named him this because the Ark of God had been captured and because her father-in-law and husband were dead. ²²Then she said, "The glory has departed from Israel, for the Ark of God has been captured."

5 The Ark in Philistia

After the Philistines captured the Ark of God, they took it from the battleground at Ebenezer to the town of Ashdod. ²They carried the Ark of God into the temple of Dagon and placed it beside an idol of Dagon. ³But when the citizens of Ashdod went to see it the next morning, Dagon had fallen with his face to the ground in front of the Ark of the LORD! So they took Dagon and put him in his place again. ⁴But the next morning the same thing happened— Dagon had fallen face down before the Ark of the LORD again. This time his head and hands had broken off and were lying in the doorway. Only the trunk of his body was left intact. ⁵That is why to this day neither the priests of Dagon nor anyone who enters the temple of Dagon in Ashdod will step on its threshold.

4:7 Or A god has.

⁶Then the LORD's heavy hand struck the people of Ashdod and the nearby villages with a plague of tumors.* ⁷When the people realized what was happening, they cried out, "We can't keep the Ark of the God of Israel here any longer! He is against us! We will all be destroyed along with Dagon, our god." ⁸So they called together the rulers of the Philistine towns and asked, "What should we do with the Ark of the God of Israel?"

The rulers discussed it and replied, "Move it to the town of Gath." So they moved the Ark of the God of Israel to Gath. ⁹But when the Ark arrived at Gath, the LORD's heavy hand fell on its men, young and old; he struck them with a plague of tumors, and there was a great panic.

¹⁰So they sent the Ark of God to the town of Ekron, but when the people of Ekron saw it coming they cried out, "They are bringing the Ark of the God of Israel here to kill us, too!" ¹¹The people summoned the Philistine rulers again and begged them, "Please send the Ark of the God of Israel back to its own country, or it* will kill us all." For the deadly plague from God had already begun, and great fear was sweeping across the town. ¹²Those who didn't die were afflicted with tumors; and the cry from the town rose to heaven.

6 The Philistines Return the Ark

The Ark of the LORD remained in Philistine territory seven months in all. ²Then the Philistines called in their priests and diviners and asked them, "What should we do about the Ark of the LORD? Tell us how to return it to its own country."

³"Send the Ark of the God of Israel back with a gift," they were told. "Send a guilt offering so the plague will stop. Then, if you are healed, you will know it was his hand that caused the plague."

⁴"What sort of guilt offering should we send?" they asked.

And they were told, "Since the plague has struck both you and your five rulers, make five gold tumors and five gold rats, just like those that have ravaged your land. ⁵Make these things to show honor to the God of Israel. Perhaps then he will stop afflicting you, your gods, and your land. ⁶Don't be stubborn and rebellious as Pharaoh and the Egyptians were. By the time God was finished with them, they were eager to let Israel go.

⁷"Now build a new cart, and find two cows that have just given birth to calves. Make sure the cows have never been yoked to a cart. Hitch the cows to the cart, but shut their calves away from them in a pen. ⁸Put the Ark of the LORD on the cart, and beside it place a chest containing the gold rats and gold tumors you are sending as a guilt offering. Then let the cows go wherever they want. ⁹If they cross the border of our land and go to Beth-shemesh, we will know it was the LORD who brought this great disaster upon us. If they don't, we will know it was not his hand that caused the plague. It came simply by chance."

¹⁰So these instructions were carried out. Two cows were hitched to the cart, and their newborn calves were shut up in a pen. ¹¹Then the Ark of the LORD and the chest containing the gold rats and gold tumors were placed on the cart. ¹²And sure enough, without veering off in other directions, the cows went straight along the road toward Beth-shemesh, lowing as they went. The Philistine rulers followed them as far as the border of Beth-shemesh.

¹³The people of Beth-shemesh were harvesting wheat in the valley, and when they saw the Ark, they were overjoyed! ¹⁴The cart came into the field of a man named Joshua and stopped beside a large rock. So the people broke up the wood of the cart for a fire and killed the cows and sacrificed them to the LORD as a burnt offering. ¹⁵Several men of the tribe of Levi lifted the Ark of the LORD and the chest containing the gold rats and gold tumors from the cart and placed them on the large rock. Many sacrifices and burnt offerings were offered to the LORD that day by the people of Beth-shemesh. ¹⁶The five Philistine rulers watched all this and then returned to Ekron that same day.

¹⁷The five gold tumors sent by the Philistines as a guilt offering to the LORD were

---

5:6 Greek version and Latin Vulgate read *tumors; and rats appeared in their land, and death and destruction were throughout the city.*   **5:11** Or *he.*

gifts from the rulers of Ashdod, Gaza, Ashkelon, Gath, and Ekron. ¹⁸The five gold rats represented the five Philistine towns and their surrounding villages, which were controlled by the five rulers. The large rock at Beth-shemesh, where they set the Ark of the LORD, still stands in the field of Joshua as a witness to what happened there.

The Ark Moved to Kiriath-Jearim

¹⁹But the LORD killed seventy men* from Beth-shemesh because they looked into the Ark of the LORD. And the people mourned greatly because of what the LORD had done. ²⁰"Who is able to stand in the presence of the LORD, this holy God?" they cried out. "Where can we send the Ark from here?"

²¹So they sent messengers to the people at Kiriath-jearim and told them, "The Philistines have returned the Ark of the LORD. Come here and get it!"

7 So the men of Kiriath-jearim came to get the Ark of the LORD. They took it to the hillside home of Abinadab and ordained Eleazar, his son, to be in charge of it. ²The Ark remained in Kiriath-jearim for a long time—twenty years in all. During that time all Israel mourned because it seemed the LORD had abandoned them.

Samuel Leads Israel to Victory

³Then Samuel said to all the people of Israel, "If you are really serious about wanting to return to the LORD, get rid of your foreign gods and your images of Ashtoreth. Determine to obey only the LORD; then he will rescue you from the Philistines." ⁴So the Israelites got rid of their images of Baal and Ashtoreth and worshiped only the LORD.

⁵Then Samuel told them, "Gather all of Israel to Mizpah, and I will pray to the LORD for you." ⁶So they gathered at Mizpah and, in a great ceremony, drew water from a well and poured it out before the LORD. They also went without food all day and confessed that they had sinned against the LORD. (It was at Mizpah that Samuel became Israel's judge.)

⁷When the Philistine rulers heard that Israel had gathered at Mizpah, they mobilized their army and advanced. The Israelites were badly frightened when they learned that the Philistines were approaching. ⁸"Don't stop pleading with the LORD our God to save us from the Philistines!" they begged Samuel. ⁹So Samuel took a young lamb and offered it to the LORD as a whole burnt offering. He pleaded with the LORD to help Israel, and the LORD answered him.

¹⁰Just as Samuel was sacrificing the burnt offering, the Philistines arrived to attack Israel. But the LORD spoke with a mighty voice of thunder from heaven that day, and the Philistines were thrown into such confusion that the Israelites defeated them. ¹¹The men of Israel chased them from Mizpah to a place below Beth-car, slaughtering them all along the way.

¹²Samuel then took a large stone and placed it between the towns of Mizpah and Jeshanah.* He named it Ebenezer (which means "the stone of help"), for he said, "Up to this point the LORD has helped us!"

¹³So the Philistines were subdued and didn't invade Israel again for some time. And throughout Samuel's lifetime, the LORD's powerful hand was raised against the Philistines. ¹⁴The Israelite villages near Ekron and Gath that the Philistines had captured were restored to Israel, along with the rest of the territory that the Philistines had taken. And there was peace between Israel and the Amorites in those days.

¹⁵Samuel continued as Israel's judge for the rest of his life. ¹⁶Each year he traveled around, setting up his court first at Bethel, then at Gilgal, and then at Mizpah. He judged the people of Israel at each of these places. ¹⁷Then he would return to his home at Ramah, and he would hear cases there, too. And Samuel built an altar to the LORD at Ramah.

8 Israel Requests a King

As Samuel grew old, he appointed his sons to be judges over Israel. ²Joel and Abijah, his oldest sons, held court in Beersheba. ³But they were not like their father, for they were greedy for money. They accepted bribes and perverted justice.

6:19 As in a few Hebrew manuscripts; most Hebrew manuscripts read *70 men, 50,000 men.* Perhaps the text should be understood to read *the LORD killed 70 men and 50 oxen.* **7:12** As in Greek and Syriac versions; Hebrew reads *Shen.*

⁴Finally, all the elders of Israel met at Ramah to discuss the matter with Samuel. ⁵"Look," they told him, "you are now old, and your sons are not like you. Give us a king to judge us like all the other nations have."

⁶Samuel was displeased with their request and went to the LORD for guidance. ⁷"Do everything they say to you," the LORD replied, "for it is me they are rejecting, not you. They don't want me to be their king any longer. ⁸Ever since I brought them from Egypt they have continually abandoned me and followed other gods. And now they are giving you the same treatment. ⁹Do as they ask, but solemnly warn them about the way a king will reign over them."

Samuel Warns against a Kingdom

¹⁰So Samuel passed on the LORD's warning to the people who were asking him for a king. ¹¹"This is how a king will reign over you," Samuel said. "The king will draft your sons and assign them to his chariots and his charioteers, making them run before his chariots. ¹²Some will be generals and captains in his army,* some will be forced to plow in his fields and harvest his crops, and some will make his weapons and chariot equipment. ¹³The king will take your daughters from you and force them to cook and bake and make perfumes for him. ¹⁴He will take away the best of your fields and vineyards and olive groves and give them to his own officials. ¹⁵He will take a tenth of your grain and your grape harvest and distribute it among his officers and attendants. ¹⁶He will take your male and female slaves and demand the finest of your cattle* and donkeys for his own use. ¹⁷He will demand a tenth of your flocks, and you will be his slaves. ¹⁸When that day comes, you will beg for relief from this king you are demanding, but then the LORD will not help you."

¹⁹But the people refused to listen to Samuel's warning. "Even so, we still want a king," they said. ²⁰"We want to be like the nations around us. Our king will judge us and lead us into battle."

²¹So Samuel repeated to the LORD what the people had said, ²²and the LORD replied, "Do as they say, and give them a king." Then Samuel agreed and sent the people home.

9 Saul Meets Samuel

There was a wealthy, influential man named Kish from the tribe of Benjamin. He was the son of Abiel, son of Zeror, son of Becorath, son of Aphiah, of the tribe of Benjamin. ²His son Saul was the most handsome man in Israel—head and shoulders taller than anyone else in the land.

³One day Kish's donkeys strayed away, and he told Saul, "Take a servant with you, and go look for the donkeys." ⁴So Saul took one of the servants and traveled through the hill country of Ephraim, the land of Shalishah, the Shaalim area, and the entire land of Benjamin, but they couldn't find the donkeys anywhere.

⁵Finally, they entered the region of Zuph, and Saul said to his servant, "Let's go home. By now my father will be more worried about us than about the donkeys!"

⁶But the servant said, "I've just thought of something! There is a man of God who lives here in this town. He is held in high honor by all the people because everything he says comes true. Let's go find him. Perhaps he can tell us which way to go."

⁷"But we don't have anything to offer him," Saul replied. "Even our food is gone, and we don't have a thing to give him."

⁸"Well," the servant said, "I have one small silver piece.* We can at least offer it to the man of God and see what happens!" ⁹(In those days if people wanted a message from God, they would say, "Let's go and ask the seer," for prophets used to be called seers.)

¹⁰"All right," Saul agreed, "let's try it!" So they started into the town where the man of God lived.

¹¹As they were climbing the hill to the town, they met some young women coming out to draw water. So Saul and his servant asked, "Is the seer here today?"

¹²"Yes," they replied. "Stay right on this road. He is at the town gates. He has just arrived to take part in a public sacrifice up at the place of worship. ¹³Hurry and catch him before he goes up there to eat. The guests

---

8:12 Hebrew *commanders of thousands and commanders of fifties.* **8:16** As in Greek version; Hebrew reads *young men.* **9:8** Hebrew *¼ shekel of silver,* about 0.1 ounces or 3 grams in weight.

won't begin eating until he arrives to bless the food."

¹⁴So they entered the town, and as they passed through the gates, Samuel was coming out toward them to go up to the place of worship.

¹⁵Now the Lord had told Samuel the previous day, ¹⁶"About this time tomorrow I will send you a man from the land of Benjamin. Anoint him to be the leader of my people, Israel. He will rescue them from the Philistines, for I have looked down on my people in mercy and have heard their cry."

¹⁷When Samuel saw Saul, the Lord said, "That's the man I told you about! He will rule my people."

¹⁸Just then Saul approached Samuel at the gateway and asked, "Can you please tell me where the seer's house is?"

¹⁹"I am the seer!" Samuel replied. "Go up to the place of worship ahead of me. We will eat there together, and in the morning I'll tell you what you want to know and send you on your way. ²⁰And don't worry about those donkeys that were lost three days ago, for they have been found. And I am here to tell you that you and your family are the focus of all Israel's hopes."

²¹Saul replied, "But I'm only from the tribe of Benjamin, the smallest tribe in Israel, and my family is the least important of all the families of that tribe! Why are you talking like this to me?"

²²Then Samuel brought Saul and his servant into the hall and placed them at the head of the table, honoring them above the thirty special guests. ²³Samuel then instructed the cook to bring Saul the finest cut of meat, the piece that had been set aside for the guest of honor. ²⁴So the cook brought in the meat and placed it before Saul. "Go ahead and eat it," Samuel said. "I was saving it for you even before I invited these others!" So Saul ate with Samuel that day.

²⁵When they came down from the place of worship and returned to town, Samuel took Saul up to the roof of the house and prepared a bed for him there.* ²⁶At daybreak the next morning, Samuel called to Saul, "Get up! It's time you were on your way." So Saul

got ready, and he and Samuel left the house together. ²⁷When they reached the edge of town, Samuel told Saul to send his servant on ahead. After the servant was gone, Samuel said, "Stay here, for I have received a special message for you from God."

10 Samuel Anoints Saul as King

Then Samuel took a flask of olive oil and poured it over Saul's head. He kissed Saul and said, "I am doing this because the Lord has appointed you to be the ruler over Israel, his special possession.* ²When you leave me today, you will see two men beside Rachel's tomb at Zelzah, on the border of Benjamin. They will tell you that the donkeys have been found and that your father has stopped worrying about them and is now worried about you. He is asking, 'Have you seen my son?'

³"When you get to the oak of Tabor, you will see three men coming toward you who are on their way to worship God at Bethel. One will be bringing three young goats, another will have three loaves of bread, and the third will be carrying a wineskin full of wine. ⁴They will greet you and offer you two of the loaves, which you are to accept.

⁵"When you arrive at Gibeah of God,* where the garrison of the Philistines is located, you will meet a band of prophets coming down from the place of worship. They will be playing a harp, a tambourine, a flute, and a lyre, and they will be prophesying. ⁶At that time the Spirit of the Lord will come powerfully upon you, and you will prophesy with them. You will be changed into a different person. ⁷After these signs take place, do what must be done, for God is with you. ⁸Then go down to Gilgal ahead of me. I will join you there to sacrifice burnt offerings and peace offerings. You must wait for seven days until I arrive and give you further instructions."

Samuel's Signs Are Fulfilled

⁹As Saul turned and started to leave, God gave him a new heart, and all Samuel's signs were fulfilled that day. ¹⁰When Saul and his servant arrived at Gibeah, they saw

---

9:25 As in Greek version; Hebrew reads and talked with him there. **10:1** Greek version reads over Israel. And you will rule over the Lord's people and save them from their enemies around them. This will be the sign to you that the Lord has appointed you to be leader over his special possession. **10:5** Hebrew Gibeath-elohim.

a group of prophets coming toward them. Then the Spirit of God came powerfully upon Saul, and he, too, began to prophesy. [11] When those who knew Saul heard about it, they exclaimed, "What? Is even Saul a prophet? How did the son of Kish become a prophet?"

[12] And one of those standing there said, "Can anyone become a prophet, no matter who his father is?"* So that is the origin of the saying "Is even Saul a prophet?"

[13] When Saul had finished prophesying, he went up to the place of worship. [14] "Where have you been?" Saul's uncle asked him and his servant.

"We were looking for the donkeys," Saul replied, "but we couldn't find them. So we went to Samuel to ask him where they were."

[15] "Oh? And what did he say?" his uncle asked.

[16] "He told us that the donkeys had already been found," Saul replied. But Saul didn't tell his uncle what Samuel said about the kingdom.

Saul Is Acclaimed King

[17] Later Samuel called all the people of Israel to meet before the LORD at Mizpah. [18] And he said, "This is what the LORD, the God of Israel, has declared: I brought you from Egypt and rescued you from the Egyptians and from all of the nations that were oppressing you. [19] But though I have rescued you from your misery and distress, you have rejected your God today and have said, 'No, we want a king instead!' Now, therefore, present yourselves before the LORD by tribes and clans."

[20] So Samuel brought all the tribes of Israel before the LORD, and the tribe of Benjamin was chosen by lot. [21] Then he brought each family of the tribe of Benjamin before the LORD, and the family of the Matrites was chosen. And finally Saul son of Kish was chosen from among them. But when they looked for him, he had disappeared! [22] So they asked the LORD, "Where is he?"

And the LORD replied, "He is hiding among the baggage." [23] So they found him and brought him out, and he stood head and shoulders above anyone else.

[24] Then Samuel said to all the people, "This is the man the LORD has chosen as your king. No one in all Israel is like him!"

And all the people shouted, "Long live the king!"

[25] Then Samuel told the people what the rights and duties of a king were. He wrote them down on a scroll and placed it before the LORD. Then Samuel sent the people home again.

[26] When Saul returned to his home at Gibeah, a group of men whose hearts God had touched went with him. [27] But there were some scoundrels who complained, "How can this man save us?" And they scorned him and refused to bring him gifts. But Saul ignored them.

[Nahash, king of the Ammonites, had been grievously oppressing the people of Gad and Reuben who lived east of the Jordan River. He gouged out the right eye of each of the Israelites living there, and he didn't allow anyone to come and rescue them. In fact, of all the Israelites east of the Jordan, there wasn't a single one whose right eye Nahash had not gouged out. But there were 7,000 men who had escaped from the Ammonites, and they had settled in Jabesh-gilead.]*

11 Saul Defeats the Ammonites

About a month later,* King Nahash of Ammon led his army against the Israelite town of Jabesh-gilead. But all the citizens of Jabesh asked for peace. "Make a treaty with us, and we will be your servants," they pleaded.

[2] "All right," Nahash said, "but only on one condition. I will gouge out the right eye of every one of you as a disgrace to all Israel!"

[3] "Give us seven days to send messengers throughout Israel!" replied the elders of Jabesh. "If no one comes to save us, we will agree to your terms."

[4] When the messengers came to Gibeah of Saul and told the people about their plight, everyone broke into tears. [5] Saul had been plowing a field with his oxen, and when he returned to town, he asked, "What's the matter? Why is everyone crying?" So they told him about the message from Jabesh.

10:12 Hebrew said, "Who is their father?" **10:27** This paragraph, which is not included in the Masoretic Text, is found in Dead Sea Scroll 4QSamᵃ. **11:1** As in Greek version; Hebrew lacks About a month later.

⁶Then the Spirit of God came powerfully upon Saul, and he became very angry. ⁷He took two oxen and cut them into pieces and sent the messengers to carry them throughout Israel with this message: "This is what will happen to the oxen of anyone who refuses to follow Saul and Samuel into battle!" And the LORD made the people afraid of Saul's anger, and all of them came out together as one. ⁸When Saul mobilized them at Bezek, he found that there were 300,000 men from Israel and 30,000* men from Judah.

⁹So Saul sent the messengers back to Jabesh-gilead to say, "We will rescue you by noontime tomorrow!" There was great joy throughout the town when that message arrived!

¹⁰The men of Jabesh then told their enemies, "Tomorrow we will come out to you, and you can do to us whatever you wish." ¹¹But before dawn the next morning, Saul arrived, having divided his army into three detachments. He launched a surprise attack against the Ammonites and slaughtered them the whole morning. The remnant of their army was so badly scattered that no two of them were left together.

¹²Then the people exclaimed to Samuel, "Now where are those men who said, 'Why should Saul rule over us?' Bring them here, and we will kill them!"

¹³But Saul replied, "No one will be executed today, for today the LORD has rescued Israel!"

¹⁴Then Samuel said to the people, "Come, let us all go to Gilgal to renew the kingdom." ¹⁵So they all went to Gilgal, and in a solemn ceremony before the LORD they made Saul king. Then they offered peace offerings to the LORD, and Saul and all the Israelites were filled with joy.

12 Samuel's Farewell Address

Then Samuel addressed all Israel: "I have done as you asked and given you a king. ²Your king is now your leader. I stand here before you—an old, gray-haired man—and my sons serve you. I have served as your leader from the time I was a boy to this very day. ³Now testify against me in the presence of the LORD and before his anointed one. Whose ox or donkey have I stolen? Have I ever cheated any of you? Have I ever oppressed you? Have I ever taken a bribe and perverted justice? Tell me and I will make right whatever I have done wrong."

⁴"No," they replied, "you have never cheated or oppressed us, and you have never taken even a single bribe."

⁵"The LORD and his anointed one are my witnesses today," Samuel declared, "that my hands are clean."

"Yes, he is a witness," they replied.

⁶"It was the LORD who appointed Moses and Aaron," Samuel continued. "He brought your ancestors out of the land of Egypt. ⁷Now stand here quietly before the LORD as I remind you of all the great things the LORD has done for you and your ancestors.

⁸"When the Israelites were* in Egypt and cried out to the LORD, he sent Moses and Aaron to rescue them from Egypt and to bring them into this land. ⁹But the people soon forgot about the LORD their God, so he handed them over to Sisera, the commander of Hazor's army, and also to the Philistines and to the king of Moab, who fought against them.

¹⁰"Then they cried to the LORD again and confessed, 'We have sinned by turning away from the LORD and worshiping the images of Baal and Ashtoreth. But we will worship you and you alone if you will rescue us from our enemies.' ¹¹Then the LORD sent Gideon,* Bedan,* Jephthah, and Samuel* to save you, and you lived in safety.

¹²"But when you were afraid of Nahash, the king of Ammon, you came to me and said that you wanted a king to reign over you, even though the LORD your God was already your king. ¹³All right, here is the king you have chosen. You asked for him, and the LORD has granted your request.

¹⁴"Now if you fear and worship the LORD and listen to his voice, and if you do not rebel against the LORD's commands, then both you and your king will show that you recognize the LORD as your God. ¹⁵But if you rebel against the LORD's commands

---

11:8 Dead Sea Scrolls and Greek version read *70,000*. **12:8** Hebrew *When Jacob was*. The names "Jacob" and "Israel" are often interchanged throughout the Old Testament, referring sometimes to the individual patriarch and sometimes to the nation. **12:11a** Hebrew *Jerub-baal*, another name for Gideon; see Judg 6:32. **12:11b** Greek and Syriac versions read *Barak*. **12:11c** Greek and Syriac versions read *Samson*.

and refuse to listen to him, then his hand will be as heavy upon you as it was upon your ancestors.

[16]"Now stand here and see the great thing the LORD is about to do. [17]You know that it does not rain at this time of the year during the wheat harvest. I will ask the LORD to send thunder and rain today. Then you will realize how wicked you have been in asking the LORD for a king!"

[18]So Samuel called to the LORD, and the LORD sent thunder and rain that day. And all the people were terrified of the LORD and of Samuel. [19]"Pray to the LORD your God for us, or we will die!" they all said to Samuel. "For now we have added to our sins by asking for a king."

[20]"Don't be afraid," Samuel reassured them. "You have certainly done wrong, but make sure now that you worship the LORD with all your heart, and don't turn your back on him. [21]Don't go back to worshiping worthless idols that cannot help or rescue you—they are totally useless! [22]The LORD will not abandon his people, because that would dishonor his great name. For it has pleased the LORD to make you his very own people.

[23]"As for me, I will certainly not sin against the LORD by ending my prayers for you. And I will continue to teach you what is good and right. [24]But be sure to fear the LORD and faithfully serve him. Think of all the wonderful things he has done for you. [25]But if you continue to sin, you and your king will be swept away."

13 Continued War with Philistia

Saul was thirty* years old when he became king, and he reigned for forty-two years.*

[2]Saul selected 3,000 special troops from the army of Israel and sent the rest of the men home. He took 2,000 of the chosen men with him to Micmash and the hill country of Bethel. The other 1,000 went with Saul's son Jonathan to Gibeah in the land of Benjamin.

[3]Soon after this, Jonathan attacked and defeated the garrison of Philistines at Geba. The news spread quickly among the Philistines. So Saul blew the ram's horn through-out the land, saying, "Hebrews, hear this! Rise up in revolt!" [4]All Israel heard the news that Saul had destroyed the Philistine garrison at Geba and that the Philistines now hated the Israelites more than ever. So the entire Israelite army was summoned to join Saul at Gilgal.

[5]The Philistines mustered a mighty army of 3,000* chariots, 6,000 charioteers, and as many warriors as the grains of sand on the seashore! They camped at Micmash east of Beth-aven. [6]The men of Israel saw what a tight spot they were in; and because they were hard pressed by the enemy, they tried to hide in caves, thickets, rocks, holes, and cisterns. [7]Some of them crossed the Jordan River and escaped into the land of Gad and Gilead.

Saul's Disobedience and Samuel's Rebuke

Meanwhile, Saul stayed at Gilgal, and his men were trembling with fear. [8]Saul waited there seven days for Samuel, as Samuel had instructed him earlier, but Samuel still didn't come. Saul realized that his troops were rapidly slipping away. [9]So he demanded, "Bring me the burnt offering and the peace offerings!" And Saul sacrificed the burnt offering himself.

[10]Just as Saul was finishing with the burnt offering, Samuel arrived. Saul went out to meet and welcome him, [11]but Samuel said, "What is this you have done?"

Saul replied, "I saw my men scattering from me, and you didn't arrive when you said you would, and the Philistines are at Micmash ready for battle. [12]So I said, 'The Philistines are ready to march against us at Gilgal, and I haven't even asked for the LORD's help!' So I felt compelled to offer the burnt offering myself before you came."

[13]"How foolish!" Samuel exclaimed. "You have not kept the command the LORD your God gave you. Had you kept it, the LORD would have established your kingdom over Israel forever. [14]But now your kingdom must end, for the LORD has sought out a man after his own heart. The LORD has already appointed him to be the leader of his people, because you have not kept the LORD's command."

13:1a As in a few Greek manuscripts; the number is missing in the Hebrew. **13:1b** Hebrew *reigned . . . and two*; the number is incomplete in the Hebrew. Compare Acts 13:21. **13:5** As in Greek and Syriac versions; Hebrew reads *30,000*.

Israel's Military Disadvantage

¹⁵Samuel then left Gilgal and went on his way, but the rest of the troops went with Saul to meet the army. They went up from Gilgal to Gibeah in the land of Benjamin.* When Saul counted the men who were still with him, he found only 600 were left! ¹⁶Saul and Jonathan and the troops with them were staying at Geba in the land of Benjamin. The Philistines set up their camp at Micmash. ¹⁷Three raiding parties soon left the camp of the Philistines. One went north toward Ophrah in the land of Shual, ¹⁸another went west to Beth-horon, and the third moved toward the border above the valley of Zeboim near the wilderness.

¹⁹There were no blacksmiths in the land of Israel in those days. The Philistines wouldn't allow them for fear they would make swords and spears for the Hebrews. ²⁰So whenever the Israelites needed to sharpen their plowshares, picks, axes, or sickles,* they had to take them to a Philistine blacksmith. ²¹(The charges were as follows: a quarter of an ounce of silver* for sharpening a plowshare or a pick, and an eighth of an ounce* for sharpening an ax, a sickle, or an ox goad.) ²²So on the day of the battle none of the people of Israel had a sword or spear, except for Saul and Jonathan.

²³The pass at Micmash had meanwhile been secured by a contingent of the Philistine army.

14 Jonathan's Daring Plan

One day Jonathan said to his armor bearer, "Come on, let's go over to where the Philistines have their outpost." But Jonathan did not tell his father what he was doing.

²Meanwhile, Saul and his 600 men were camped on the outskirts of Gibeah, around the pomegranate tree* at Migron. ³Among Saul's men was Ahijah the priest, who was wearing the ephod, the priestly vest. Ahijah was the son of Ichabod's brother Ahitub, son of Phinehas, son of Eli, the priest of the LORD who had served at Shiloh.

No one realized that Jonathan had left the Israelite camp. ⁴To reach the Philistine outpost, Jonathan had to go down between two rocky cliffs that were called Bozez and Seneh. ⁵The cliff on the north was in front of Micmash, and the one on the south was in front of Geba. ⁶"Let's go across to the outpost of those pagans," Jonathan said to his armor bearer. "Perhaps the LORD will help us, for nothing can hinder the LORD. He can win a battle whether he has many warriors or only a few!"

⁷"Do what you think is best," the armor bearer replied. "I'm with you completely, whatever you decide."

⁸"All right then," Jonathan told him. "We will cross over and let them see us. ⁹If they say to us, 'Stay where you are or we'll kill you,' then we will stop and not go up to them. ¹⁰But if they say, 'Come on up and fight,' then we will go up. That will be the LORD's sign that he will help us defeat them."

¹¹When the Philistines saw them coming, they shouted, "Look! The Hebrews are crawling out of their holes!" ¹²Then the men from the outpost shouted to Jonathan, "Come on up here, and we'll teach you a lesson!"

"Come on, climb right behind me," Jonathan said to his armor bearer, "for the LORD will help us defeat them!"

¹³So they climbed up using both hands and feet, and the Philistines fell before Jonathan, and his armor bearer killed those who came behind them. ¹⁴They killed some twenty men in all, and their bodies were scattered over about half an acre.* ¹⁵Suddenly, panic broke out in the Philistine army, both in the camp and in the field, including even the outposts and raiding parties. And just then an earthquake struck, and everyone was terrified.

Israel Defeats the Philistines

¹⁶Saul's lookouts in Gibeah of Benjamin saw a strange sight—the vast army of Philistines began to melt away in every direction. ¹⁷"Call the roll and find out who's missing," Saul ordered. And when they checked, they found that Jonathan and his armor bearer were gone.

¹⁸Then Saul shouted to Ahijah, "Bring the ephod here!" For at that time Ahijah was wearing the ephod in front of the Israelites.*

13:15 As in Greek version; Hebrew reads *Samuel then left Gilgal and went to Gibeah in the land of Benjamin.* 13:20 As in Greek version; Hebrew reads *or plowshares.* 13:21a Hebrew *1 pim* [8 grams]. 13:21b Hebrew *⅓ of a shekel* [4 grams]. 14:2 Or *around the rock of Rimmon;* compare Judg 20:45, 47; 21:13. 14:14 Hebrew *half a yoke;* a "yoke" was the amount of land plowed by a pair of yoked oxen in one day. 14:18 As in some Greek manuscripts; Hebrew reads *"Bring the Ark of God."* For at that time the Ark of God was with the Israelites.

[19] But while Saul was talking to the priest, the confusion in the Philistine camp grew louder and louder. So Saul said to the priest, "Never mind; let's get going!"*

[20] Then Saul and all his men rushed out to the battle and found the Philistines killing each other. There was terrible confusion everywhere. [21] Even the Hebrews who had previously gone over to the Philistine army revolted and joined in with Saul, Jonathan, and the rest of the Israelites. [22] Likewise, the men of Israel who were hiding in the hill country of Ephraim joined the chase when they saw the Philistines running away. [23] So the LORD saved Israel that day, and the battle continued to rage even beyond Beth-aven.

Saul's Foolish Oath

[24] Now the men of Israel were pressed to exhaustion that day, because Saul had placed them under an oath, saying, "Let a curse fall on anyone who eats before evening—before I have full revenge on my enemies." So no one ate anything all day, [25] even though they had all found honeycomb on the ground in the forest. [26] They didn't dare touch the honey because they all feared the oath they had taken.

[27] But Jonathan had not heard his father's command, and he dipped the end of his stick into a piece of honeycomb and ate the honey. After he had eaten it, he felt refreshed.* [28] But one of the men saw him and said, "Your father made the army take a strict oath that anyone who eats food today will be cursed. That is why everyone is weary and faint."

[29] "My father has made trouble for us all!" Jonathan exclaimed. "A command like that only hurts us. See how refreshed I am now that I have eaten this little bit of honey. [30] If the men had been allowed to eat freely from the food they found among our enemies, think how many more Philistines we could have killed!"

[31] They chased and killed the Philistines all day from Micmash to Aijalon, growing more and more faint. [32] That evening they rushed for the battle plunder and butchered the sheep, goats, cattle, and calves, but they ate them without draining the blood. [33] Someone reported to Saul, "Look, the men are sinning against the LORD by eating meat that still has blood in it."

"That is very wrong," Saul said. "Find a large stone and roll it over here. [34] Then go out among the troops and tell them, 'Bring the cattle, sheep, and goats here to me. Kill them here, and drain the blood before you eat them. Do not sin against the LORD by eating meat with the blood still in it.'"

So that night all the troops brought their animals and slaughtered them there. [35] Then Saul built an altar to the LORD; it was the first of the altars he built to the LORD.

[36] Then Saul said, "Let's chase the Philistines all night and plunder them until sunrise. Let's destroy every last one of them."

His men replied, "We'll do whatever you think is best."

But the priest said, "Let's ask God first."

[37] So Saul asked God, "Should we go after the Philistines? Will you help us defeat them?" But God made no reply that day.

[38] Then Saul said to the leaders, "Something's wrong! I want all my army commanders to come here. We must find out what sin was committed today. [39] I vow by the name of the LORD who rescued Israel that the sinner will surely die, even if it is my own son Jonathan!" But no one would tell him what the trouble was.

[40] Then Saul said, "Jonathan and I will stand over here, and all of you stand over there."

And the people responded to Saul, "Whatever you think is best."

[41] Then Saul prayed, "O LORD, God of Israel, please show us who is guilty and who is innocent.*" Then they cast sacred lots, and Jonathan and Saul were chosen as the guilty ones, and the people were declared innocent.

[42] Then Saul said, "Now cast lots again and choose between me and Jonathan." And Jonathan was shown to be the guilty one.

[43] "Tell me what you have done," Saul demanded of Jonathan.

"I tasted a little honey," Jonathan admitted. "It was only a little bit on the end of my stick. Does that deserve death?"

14:19 Hebrew *Withdraw your hand.*   **14:27** Or *his eyes brightened;* similarly in 14:29.   **14:41** Greek version adds *If the fault is with me or my son Jonathan, respond with Urim; but if the men of Israel are at fault, respond with Thummim.*

44 "Yes, Jonathan," Saul said, "you must die! May God strike me and even kill me if you do not die for this."

45 But the people broke in and said to Saul, "Jonathan has won this great victory for Israel. Should he die? Far from it! As surely as the LORD lives, not one hair on his head will be touched, for God helped him do a great deed today." So the people rescued Jonathan, and he was not put to death.

46 Then Saul called back the army from chasing the Philistines, and the Philistines returned home.

Saul's Military Successes

47 Now when Saul had secured his grasp on Israel's throne, he fought against his enemies in every direction—against Moab, Ammon, Edom, the kings of Zobah, and the Philistines. And wherever he turned, he was victorious.* 48 He performed great deeds and conquered the Amalekites, saving Israel from all those who had plundered them.

49 Saul's sons included Jonathan, Ishbosheth,* and Malkishua. He also had two daughters: Merab, who was older, and Michal. 50 Saul's wife was Ahinoam, the daughter of Ahimaaz. The commander of Saul's army was Abner, the son of Saul's uncle Ner. 51 Saul's father, Kish, and Abner's father, Ner, were both sons of Abiel.

52 The Israelites fought constantly with the Philistines throughout Saul's lifetime. So whenever Saul observed a young man who was brave and strong, he drafted him into his army.

15 Saul Destroys the Amalekites

One day Samuel said to Saul, "It was the LORD who told me to anoint you as king of his people, Israel. Now listen to this message from the LORD! 2 This is what the LORD of Heaven's Armies has declared: I have decided to settle accounts with the nation of Amalek for opposing Israel when they came from Egypt. 3 Now go and completely destroy* the entire Amalekite nation—men, women, children, babies, cattle, sheep, goats, camels, and donkeys."

4 So Saul mobilized his army at Telaim.

There were 200,000 soldiers from Israel and 10,000 men from Judah. 5 Then Saul and his army went to a town of the Amalekites and lay in wait in the valley. 6 Saul sent this warning to the Kenites: "Move away from where the Amalekites live, or you will die with them. For you showed kindness to all the people of Israel when they came up from Egypt." So the Kenites packed up and left.

7 Then Saul slaughtered the Amalekites from Havilah all the way to Shur, east of Egypt. 8 He captured Agag, the Amalekite king, but completely destroyed everyone else. 9 Saul and his men spared Agag's life and kept the best of the sheep and goats, the cattle, the fat calves, and the lambs—everything, in fact, that appealed to them. They destroyed only what was worthless or of poor quality.

The LORD Rejects Saul

10 Then the LORD said to Samuel, 11 "I am sorry that I ever made Saul king, for he has not been loyal to me and has refused to obey my command." Samuel was so deeply moved when he heard this that he cried out to the LORD all night.

12 Early the next morning Samuel went to find Saul. Someone told him, "Saul went to the town of Carmel to set up a monument to himself; then he went on to Gilgal."

13 When Samuel finally found him, Saul greeted him cheerfully. "May the LORD bless you," he said. "I have carried out the LORD's command!"

14 "Then what is all the bleating of sheep and goats and the lowing of cattle I hear?" Samuel demanded.

15 "It's true that the army spared the best of the sheep, goats, and cattle," Saul admitted. "But they are going to sacrifice them to the LORD your God. We have destroyed everything else."

16 Then Samuel said to Saul, "Stop! Listen to what the LORD told me last night!"

"What did he tell you?" Saul asked.

17 And Samuel told him, "Although you may think little of yourself, are you not the leader of the tribes of Israel? The LORD has anointed you king of Israel. 18 And the LORD sent you on a mission and told you,

---

14:47 As in Greek version; Hebrew reads *he acted wickedly.*   14:49 Hebrew *Ishvi,* a variant name for Ishbosheth; also known as Esh-baal.
15:3 The Hebrew term used here refers to the complete consecration of things or people to the LORD, either by destroying them or by giving them as an offering; also in 15:8, 9, 15, 18, 20, 21.

To Obey Is to Listen
1 SAMUEL 15:22

As a mother of four who was juggling part-time work, family responsibilities, ministry opportunities, other relationships, and multiple varied commitments, I had become something of a multitasking expert. But my perspective on multitasking radically changed when I called an Episcopal monk to get a quote for a story I was writing.

He told me that his work, as a monk, was simply to listen to God. He'd taken a vow, he said.

"A vow to listen?"

"A vow of obedience. To obey is to listen," he said. He told me that the word's etymology reveals that *obedience* is less about complying with rules and more about listening. Deep listening.

The Hebrew word is *shama*: "to hear, to listen." Samuel uses the word, declaring that "Obedience is better than sacrifice, and submission is better than offering the fat of rams" (1 Samuel 15:22).

In Greek the word is *hupakouo* or "to listen under."

The Latin for obedience is *oboedire*: "to hear or listen toward."

In Old English it's *herknen*. So the monk said, to obey God is to listen deeply to him—or hearken to his voice.

He explained why monks so often practice silence: "It's not that there's nothing to be said; it's that there is so much to be heard." This silence stands in strong opposition to a culture that is "obsessed with multitasking."

"Multitasking has been normalized. It is costly to the soul," he said.

Ouch.

His closing advice spoke directly to me: "Do one thing at a time."

Since talking to him, I've been weaning myself from my multitasking habit. The more I practice the lost art of doing one thing at a time, the more I hear the voice of God. Offering peace and clarity. Nudging me to interact with a person. Infusing me with an idea. Reminding me of his presence.

—Jennifer Grant

For more on silence, see reading at 1 Kings 19:9–13.

'Go and completely destroy the sinners, the Amalekites, until they are all dead.' ¹⁹Why haven't you obeyed the LORD? Why did you rush for the plunder and do what was evil in the LORD's sight?"

²⁰"But I did obey the LORD," Saul insisted. "I carried out the mission he gave me. I brought back King Agag, but I destroyed everyone else. ²¹Then my troops brought in the best of the sheep, goats, cattle, and plunder to sacrifice to the LORD your God in Gilgal."

²²But Samuel replied,

"What is more pleasing to the LORD:
your burnt offerings and sacrifices
or your obedience to his voice?

Listen! Obedience is better than
 sacrifice,
 and submission is better than offering
 the fat of rams.
23 Rebellion is as sinful as witchcraft,
 and stubbornness as bad as
 worshiping idols.
So because you have rejected the
 command of the LORD,
 he has rejected you as king."

Saul Pleads for Forgiveness

24 Then Saul admitted to Samuel, "Yes, I
have sinned. I have disobeyed your instructions and the LORD's command, for I was
afraid of the people and did what they
demanded. 25 But now, please forgive my sin
and come back with me so that I may worship the LORD."

26 But Samuel replied, "I will not go back
with you! Since you have rejected the
LORD's command, he has rejected you as
king of Israel."

27 As Samuel turned to go, Saul tried to
hold him back and tore the hem of his robe.
28 And Samuel said to him, "The LORD has
torn the kingdom of Israel from you today
and has given it to someone else—one
who is better than you. 29 And he who is
the Glory of Israel will not lie, nor will he
change his mind, for he is not human that
he should change his mind!"

30 Then Saul pleaded again, "I know I have
sinned. But please, at least honor me before
the elders of my people and before Israel by
coming back with me so that I may worship
the LORD your God." 31 So Samuel finally
agreed and went back with him, and Saul
worshiped the LORD.

Samuel Executes King Agag

32 Then Samuel said, "Bring King Agag
to me." Agag arrived full of hope, for he
thought, "Surely the worst is over, and I
have been spared!"* 33 But Samuel said, "As
your sword has killed the sons of many
mothers, now your mother will be childless." And Samuel cut Agag to pieces before
the LORD at Gilgal.

34 Then Samuel went home to Ramah,
and Saul returned to his house at Gibeah

of Saul. 35 Samuel never went to meet with
Saul again, but he mourned constantly for
him. And the LORD was sorry he had ever
made Saul king of Israel.

16 Samuel Anoints David as King

Now the LORD said to Samuel, "You
have mourned long enough for Saul. I have
rejected him as king of Israel, so fill your
flask with olive oil and go to Bethlehem.
Find a man named Jesse who lives there,
for I have selected one of his sons to be my
king."

2 But Samuel asked, "How can I do that? If
Saul hears about it, he will kill me."

"Take a heifer with you," the LORD replied,
"and say that you have come to make a sacrifice to the LORD. 3 Invite Jesse to the sacrifice, and I will show you which of his sons
to anoint for me."

4 So Samuel did as the LORD instructed.
When he arrived at Bethlehem, the elders
of the town came trembling to meet him.
"What's wrong?" they asked. "Do you come
in peace?"

5 "Yes," Samuel replied. "I have come to
sacrifice to the LORD. Purify yourselves and
come with me to the sacrifice." Then Samuel performed the purification rite for Jesse
and his sons and invited them to the sacrifice, too.

6 When they arrived, Samuel took one
look at Eliab and thought, "Surely this is the
LORD's anointed!"

7 But the LORD said to Samuel, "Don't
judge by his appearance or height, for I have
rejected him. The LORD doesn't see things
the way you see them. People judge by outward appearance, but the LORD looks at the
heart."

8 Then Jesse told his son Abinadab to
step forward and walk in front of Samuel.
But Samuel said, "This is not the one the
LORD has chosen." 9 Next Jesse summoned
Shimea,* but Samuel said, "Neither is this
the one the LORD has chosen." 10 In the same
way all seven of Jesse's sons were presented
to Samuel. But Samuel said to Jesse, "The
LORD has not chosen any of these." 11 Then
Samuel asked, "Are these all the sons you
have?"

15:32 Dead Sea Scrolls and Greek version read *Agag arrived hesitantly, for he thought, "Surely this is the bitterness of death."* **16:9** Hebrew
Shammah, a variant spelling of Shimea; compare 1 Chr 2:13; 20:7.

"There is still the youngest," Jesse replied. "But he's out in the fields watching the sheep and goats."

"Send for him at once," Samuel said. "We will not sit down to eat until he arrives."

12 So Jesse sent for him. He was dark and handsome, with beautiful eyes.

And the LORD said, "This is the one; anoint him."

13 So as David stood there among his brothers, Samuel took the flask of olive oil he had brought and anointed David with the oil. And the Spirit of the LORD came powerfully upon David from that day on. Then Samuel returned to Ramah.

David Serves in Saul's Court

14 Now the Spirit of the LORD had left Saul, and the LORD sent a tormenting spirit* that filled him with depression and fear.

15 Some of Saul's servants said to him, "A tormenting spirit from God is troubling you. 16 Let us find a good musician to play the harp whenever the tormenting spirit troubles you. He will play soothing music, and you will soon be well again."

17 "All right," Saul said. "Find me someone who plays well, and bring him here."

18 One of the servants said to Saul, "One of Jesse's sons from Bethlehem is a talented harp player. Not only that—he is a brave warrior, a man of war, and has good judgment. He is also a fine-looking young man, and the LORD is with him."

19 So Saul sent messengers to Jesse to say, "Send me your son David, the shepherd."

20 Jesse responded by sending David to Saul, along with a young goat, a donkey loaded with bread, and a wineskin full of wine.

21 So David went to Saul and began serving him. Saul loved David very much, and David became his armor bearer.

22 Then Saul sent word to Jesse asking, "Please let David remain in my service, for I am very pleased with him."

23 And whenever the tormenting spirit from God troubled Saul, David would play the harp. Then Saul would feel better, and the tormenting spirit would go away.

17 Goliath Challenges the Israelites

The Philistines now mustered their army for battle and camped between Socoh in Judah and Azekah at Ephes-dammim. 2 Saul countered by gathering his Israelite troops near the valley of Elah. 3 So the Philistines and Israelites faced each other on opposite hills, with the valley between them.

4 Then Goliath, a Philistine champion from Gath, came out of the Philistine ranks to face the forces of Israel. He was over nine feet* tall! 5 He wore a bronze helmet, and his bronze coat of mail weighed 125 pounds.* 6 He also wore bronze leg armor, and he carried a bronze javelin on his shoulder. 7 The shaft of his spear was as heavy and thick as a weaver's beam, tipped with an iron spearhead that weighed 15 pounds.* His armor bearer walked ahead of him carrying a shield.

8 Goliath stood and shouted a taunt across to the Israelites. "Why are you all coming out to fight?" he called. "I am the Philistine champion, but you are only the servants of Saul. Choose one man to come down here and fight me! 9 If he kills me, then we will be your slaves. But if I kill him, you will be our slaves! 10 I defy the armies of Israel today! Send me a man who will fight me!" 11 When Saul and the Israelites heard this, they were terrified and deeply shaken.

Jesse Sends David to Saul's Camp

12 Now David was the son of a man named Jesse, an Ephrathite from Bethlehem in the land of Judah. Jesse was an old man at that time, and he had eight sons. 13 Jesse's three oldest sons—Eliab, Abinadab, and Shimea*—had already joined Saul's army to fight the Philistines. 14 David was the youngest son. David's three oldest brothers stayed with Saul's army, 15 but David went back and forth so he could help his father with the sheep in Bethlehem.

16 For forty days, every morning and evening, the Philistine champion strutted in front of the Israelite army.

17 One day Jesse said to David, "Take this basket* of roasted grain and these ten loaves of bread, and carry them quickly to

your brothers. ¹⁸And give these ten cuts of cheese to their captain. See how your brothers are getting along, and bring back a report on how they are doing.*" ¹⁹David's brothers were with Saul and the Israelite army at the valley of Elah, fighting against the Philistines.

²⁰So David left the sheep with another shepherd and set out early the next morning with the gifts, as Jesse had directed him. He arrived at the camp just as the Israelite army was leaving for the battlefield with shouts and battle cries. ²¹Soon the Israelite and Philistine forces stood facing each other, army against army. ²²David left his things with the keeper of supplies and hurried out to the ranks to greet his brothers. ²³As he was talking with them, Goliath, the Philistine champion from Gath, came out from the Philistine ranks. Then David heard him shout his usual taunt to the army of Israel.

²⁴As soon as the Israelite army saw him, they began to run away in fright. ²⁵"Have you seen the giant?" the men asked. "He comes out each day to defy Israel. The king has offered a huge reward to anyone who kills him. He will give that man one of his daughters for a wife, and the man's entire family will be exempted from paying taxes!"

²⁶David asked the soldiers standing nearby, "What will a man get for killing this Philistine and ending his defiance of Israel? Who is this pagan Philistine anyway, that he is allowed to defy the armies of the living God?"

²⁷And these men gave David the same reply. They said, "Yes, that is the reward for killing him."

²⁸But when David's oldest brother, Eliab, heard David talking to the men, he was angry. "What are you doing around here anyway?" he demanded. "What about those few sheep you're supposed to be taking care of? I know about your pride and deceit. You just want to see the battle!"

²⁹"What have I done now?" David replied. "I was only asking a question!" ³⁰He walked over to some others and asked them the same thing and received the same answer. ³¹Then David's question was reported to King Saul, and the king sent for him.

David Kills Goliath

³²"Don't worry about this Philistine," David told Saul. "I'll go fight him!"

³³"Don't be ridiculous!" Saul replied. "There's no way you can fight this Philistine and possibly win! You're only a boy, and he's been a man of war since his youth."

³⁴But David persisted. "I have been taking care of my father's sheep and goats," he said. "When a lion or a bear comes to steal a lamb from the flock, ³⁵I go after it with a club and rescue the lamb from its mouth. If the animal turns on me, I catch it by the jaw and club it to death. ³⁶I have done this to both lions and bears, and I'll do it to this pagan Philistine, too, for he has defied the armies of the living God! ³⁷The LORD who rescued me from the claws of the lion and the bear will rescue me from this Philistine!"

Saul finally consented. "All right, go ahead," he said. "And may the LORD be with you!"

³⁸Then Saul gave David his own armor—a bronze helmet and a coat of mail. ³⁹David put it on, strapped the sword over it, and took a step or two to see what it was like, for he had never worn such things before.

"I can't go in these," he protested to Saul. "I'm not used to them." So David took them off again. ⁴⁰He picked up five smooth stones from a stream and put them into his shepherd's bag. Then, armed only with his shepherd's staff and sling, he started across the valley to fight the Philistine.

⁴¹Goliath walked out toward David with his shield bearer ahead of him, ⁴²sneering in contempt at this ruddy-faced boy. ⁴³"Am I a dog," he roared at David, "that you come at me with a stick?" And he cursed David by the names of his gods. ⁴⁴"Come over here, and I'll give your flesh to the birds and wild animals!" Goliath yelled.

⁴⁵David replied to the Philistine, "You come to me with sword, spear, and javelin, but I come to you in the name of the LORD of Heaven's Armies—the God of the armies of Israel, whom you have defied. ⁴⁶Today the LORD will conquer you, and I will kill you and cut off your head. And then I will give the dead bodies of your men to the birds

---

17:18 Hebrew *and take their pledge.*

and wild animals, and the whole world will know that there is a God in Israel! ⁴⁷And everyone assembled here will know that the LORD rescues his people, but not with sword and spear. This is the LORD's battle, and he will give you to us!"

⁴⁸As Goliath moved closer to attack, David quickly ran out to meet him. ⁴⁹Reaching into his shepherd's bag and taking out a stone, he hurled it with his sling and hit the Philistine in the forehead. The stone sank in, and Goliath stumbled and fell face down on the ground.

⁵⁰So David triumphed over the Philistine with only a sling and a stone, for he had no sword. ⁵¹Then David ran over and pulled Goliath's sword from its sheath. David used it to kill him and cut off his head.

Israel Routs the Philistines

When the Philistines saw that their champion was dead, they turned and ran. ⁵²Then the men of Israel and Judah gave a great shout of triumph and rushed after the Philistines, chasing them as far as Gath* and the gates of Ekron. The bodies of the dead and wounded Philistines were strewn all along the road from Shaaraim, as far as Gath and Ekron. ⁵³Then the Israelite army returned and plundered the deserted Philistine camp. ⁵⁴(David took the Philistine's head to Jerusalem, but he stored the man's armor in his own tent.)

⁵⁵As Saul watched David go out to fight the Philistine, he asked Abner, the commander of his army, "Abner, whose son is this young man?"

"I really don't know," Abner declared.

⁵⁶"Well, find out who he is!" the king told him.

⁵⁷As soon as David returned from killing Goliath, Abner brought him to Saul with the Philistine's head still in his hand. ⁵⁸"Tell me about your father, young man," Saul said.

And David replied, "His name is Jesse, and we live in Bethlehem."

18 Saul Becomes Jealous of David

After David had finished talking with Saul, he met Jonathan, the king's son. There was an immediate bond between them, for Jonathan loved David. ²From that day on Saul kept David with him and wouldn't let him return home. ³And Jonathan made a solemn pact with David, because he loved him as he loved himself. ⁴Jonathan sealed the pact by taking off his robe and giving it to David, together with his tunic, sword, bow, and belt.

⁵Whatever Saul asked David to do, David did it successfully. So Saul made him a commander over the men of war, an appointment that was welcomed by the people and Saul's officers alike.

⁶When the victorious Israelite army was returning home after David had killed the Philistine, women from all the towns of Israel came out to meet King Saul. They sang and danced for joy with tambourines and cymbals.* ⁷This was their song:

"Saul has killed his thousands,
and David his ten thousands!"

⁸This made Saul very angry. "What's this?" he said. "They credit David with ten thousands and me with only thousands. Next they'll be making him their king!" ⁹So from that time on Saul kept a jealous eye on David.

¹⁰The very next day a tormenting spirit* from God overwhelmed Saul, and he began to rave in his house like a madman. David was playing the harp, as he did each day. But Saul had a spear in his hand, ¹¹and he suddenly hurled it at David, intending to pin him to the wall. But David escaped him twice.

¹²Saul was then afraid of David, for the LORD was with David and had turned away from Saul. ¹³Finally, Saul sent him away and appointed him commander over 1,000 men, and David faithfully led his troops into battle.

¹⁴David continued to succeed in everything he did, for the LORD was with him. ¹⁵When Saul recognized this, he became even more afraid of him. ¹⁶But all Israel and Judah loved David because he was so successful at leading his troops into battle.

17:52 As in some Greek manuscripts; Hebrew reads *a valley.*   **18:6** The type of instrument represented by the word *cymbals* is uncertain.   **18:10** Or *an evil spirit.*

David Marries Saul's Daughter

¹⁷ One day Saul said to David, "I am ready to give you my older daughter, Merab, as your wife. But first you must prove yourself to be a real warrior by fighting the LORD's battles." For Saul thought, "I'll send him out against the Philistines and let them kill him rather than doing it myself."

¹⁸ "Who am I, and what is my family in Israel that I should be the king's son-in-law?" David exclaimed. "My father's family is nothing!" ¹⁹ So* when the time came for Saul to give his daughter Merab in marriage to David, he gave her instead to Adriel, a man from Meholah.

²⁰ In the meantime, Saul's daughter Michal had fallen in love with David, and Saul was delighted when he heard about it. ²¹ "Here's another chance to see him killed by the Philistines!" Saul said to himself. But to David he said, "Today you have a second chance to become my son-in-law!"

²² Then Saul told his men to say to David, "The king really likes you, and so do we. Why don't you accept the king's offer and become his son-in-law?"

²³ When Saul's men said these things to David, he replied, "How can a poor man from a humble family afford the bride price for the daughter of a king?"

²⁴ When Saul's men reported this back to the king, ²⁵ he told them, "Tell David that all I want for the bride price is 100 Philistine foreskins! Vengeance on my enemies is all I really want." But what Saul had in mind was that David would be killed in the fight.

²⁶ David was delighted to accept the offer. Before the time limit expired, ²⁷ he and his men went out and killed 200 Philistines. Then David fulfilled the king's requirement by presenting all their foreskins to him. So Saul gave his daughter Michal to David to be his wife.

²⁸ When Saul realized that the LORD was with David and how much his daughter Michal loved him, ²⁹ Saul became even more afraid of him, and he remained David's enemy for the rest of his life.

³⁰ Every time the commanders of the Philistines attacked, David was more successful against them than all the rest of Saul's officers. So David's name became very famous.

19 Saul Tries to Kill David

Saul now urged his servants and his son Jonathan to assassinate David. But Jonathan, because of his strong affection for David, ²told him what his father was planning. "Tomorrow morning," he warned him, "you must find a hiding place out in the fields. ³ I'll ask my father to go out there with me, and I'll talk to him about you. Then I'll tell you everything I can find out."

⁴ The next morning Jonathan spoke with his father about David, saying many good things about him. "The king must not sin against his servant David," Jonathan said. "He's never done anything to harm you. He has always helped you in any way he could. ⁵ Have you forgotten about the time he risked his life to kill the Philistine giant and how the LORD brought a great victory to all Israel as a result? You were certainly happy about it then. Why should you murder an innocent man like David? There is no reason for it at all!"

⁶ So Saul listened to Jonathan and vowed, "As surely as the LORD lives, David will not be killed."

⁷ Afterward Jonathan called David and told him what had happened. Then he brought David to Saul, and David served in the court as before.

⁸ War broke out again after that, and David led his troops against the Philistines. He attacked them with such fury that they all ran away.

⁹ But one day when Saul was sitting at home, with spear in hand, the tormenting spirit* from the LORD suddenly came upon him again. As David played his harp, ¹⁰ Saul hurled his spear at David. But David dodged out of the way, and leaving the spear stuck in the wall, he fled and escaped into the night.

Michal Saves David's Life

¹¹ Then Saul sent troops to watch David's house. They were told to kill David when he came out the next morning. But Michal, David's wife, warned him, "If you don't

---

18:19 Or But.　**19:9** Or evil spirit.

escape tonight, you will be dead by morning." ¹²So she helped him climb out through a window, and he fled and escaped. ¹³Then she took an idol* and put it in his bed, covered it with blankets, and put a cushion of goat's hair at its head.

¹⁴When the troops came to arrest David, she told them he was sick and couldn't get out of bed.

¹⁵But Saul sent the troops back to get David. He ordered, "Bring him to me in his bed so I can kill him!" ¹⁶But when they came to carry David out, they discovered that it was only an idol in the bed with a cushion of goat's hair at its head.

¹⁷"Why have you betrayed me like this and let my enemy escape?" Saul demanded of Michal.

"I had to," Michal replied. "He threatened to kill me if I didn't help him."

¹⁸So David escaped and went to Ramah to see Samuel, and he told him all that Saul had done to him. Then Samuel took David with him to live at Naioth. ¹⁹When the report reached Saul that David was at Naioth in Ramah, ²⁰he sent troops to capture him. But when they arrived and saw Samuel leading a group of prophets who were prophesying, the Spirit of God came upon Saul's men, and they also began to prophesy. ²¹When Saul heard what had happened, he sent other troops, but they, too, prophesied! The same thing happened a third time. ²²Finally, Saul himself went to Ramah and arrived at the great well in Secu. "Where are Samuel and David?" he demanded.

"They are at Naioth in Ramah," someone told him.

²³But on the way to Naioth in Ramah the Spirit of God came even upon Saul, and he, too, began to prophesy all the way to Naioth! ²⁴He tore off his clothes and lay naked on the ground all day and all night, prophesying in the presence of Samuel. The people who were watching exclaimed, "What? Is even Saul a prophet?"

20 Jonathan Helps David

David now fled from Naioth in Ramah and found Jonathan. "What have I done?" he exclaimed. "What is my crime? How have I offended your father that he is so determined to kill me?"

²"That's not true!" Jonathan protested. "You're not going to die. He always tells me everything he's going to do, even the little things. I know my father wouldn't hide something like this from me. It just isn't so!"

³Then David took an oath before Jonathan and said, "Your father knows perfectly well about our friendship, so he has said to himself, 'I won't tell Jonathan—why should I hurt him?' But I swear to you that I am only a step away from death! I swear it by the LORD and by your own soul!"

⁴"Tell me what I can do to help you," Jonathan exclaimed.

⁵David replied, "Tomorrow we celebrate the new moon festival. I've always eaten with the king on this occasion, but tomorrow I'll hide in the field and stay there until the evening of the third day. ⁶If your father asks where I am, tell him I asked permission to go home to Bethlehem for an annual family sacrifice. ⁷If he says, 'Fine!' you will know all is well. But if he is angry and loses his temper, you will know he is determined to kill me. ⁸Show me this loyalty as my sworn friend—for we made a solemn pact before the LORD—or kill me yourself if I have sinned against your father. But please don't betray me to him!"

⁹"Never!" Jonathan exclaimed. "You know that if I had the slightest notion my father was planning to kill you, I would tell you at once."

¹⁰Then David asked, "How will I know whether or not your father is angry?"

¹¹"Come out to the field with me," Jonathan replied. And they went out there together. ¹²Then Jonathan told David, "I promise by the LORD, the God of Israel, that by this time tomorrow, or the next day at the latest, I will talk to my father and let you know at once how he feels about you. If he speaks favorably about you, I will let you know. ¹³But if he is angry and wants you killed, may the LORD strike me and even kill me if I don't warn you so you can escape and live. May the LORD be with you as he used to be with my father. ¹⁴And may you treat me with the faithful love of the LORD as long as I live. But if I die, ¹⁵treat my family with this faithful love, even when the LORD destroys all your enemies from the face of the earth."

19:13 Hebrew teraphim; also in 19:16.

Submitting to a Friend's Wisdom

1 Samuel 20

Had I been pursuing a lifestyle of submission some years ago, I could have saved myself the heartache of dating a man I knew wasn't right for me. Although a friend and a family member both gently yet firmly told me their concerns, I chose stubbornly to ignore them. I wanted to make my own decisions. In retrospect I see that my hardheaded refusal to submit to loved ones' wisdom led to several months of pain.

Learning to depend on others leads to seeking out honest input from them. Recently I sensed God nudging me to seek accountability in a specific difficult situation, so I talked it over with a wise friend. She loves God and loves me. She gently guided me to respond to the tough situation differently from how I'd planned. Allowing her to glimpse raw places in my soul and asking her to speak truth into those areas made me feel uncomfortable and exposed. But after that evening's stretching conversation, we both sensed we'd entered a deeper level of trust in our friendship. By submitting to her, I bestowed on my friend the authority to bring light into my decisions and relationships. And I grew wiser and stronger as I allowed myself to submit to her godly advice.

—Stephanie Voiland

For more on submission, see reading at 1 Kings 17.

¹⁶ So Jonathan made a solemn pact with David,* saying, "May the LORD destroy all your enemies!" ¹⁷ And Jonathan made David reaffirm his vow of friendship again, for Jonathan loved David as he loved himself.

¹⁸ Then Jonathan said, "Tomorrow we celebrate the new moon festival. You will be missed when your place at the table is empty. ¹⁹ The day after tomorrow, toward evening, go to the place where you hid before, and wait there by the stone pile.* ²⁰ I will come out and shoot three arrows to the side of the stone pile as though I were shooting at a target. ²¹ Then I will send a boy to bring the arrows back. If you hear me tell him, 'They're on this side,' then you will know, as surely as the LORD lives, that all is well, and there is no trouble. ²² But if I tell him, 'Go farther—the arrows are still ahead of you,' then it will mean that you must leave immediately, for the LORD is sending you away. ²³ And may the LORD make us

keep our promises to each other, for he has witnessed them."

²⁴ So David hid himself in the field, and when the new moon festival began, the king sat down to eat. ²⁵ He sat at his usual place against the wall, with Jonathan sitting opposite him* and Abner beside him. But David's place was empty. ²⁶ Saul didn't say anything about it that day, for he said to himself, "Something must have made David ceremonially unclean." ²⁷ But when David's place was empty again the next day, Saul asked Jonathan, "Why hasn't the son of Jesse been here for the meal either yesterday or today?"

²⁸ Jonathan replied, "David earnestly asked me if he could go to Bethlehem. ²⁹ He said, 'Please let me go, for we are having a family sacrifice. My brother demanded that I be there. So please let me get away to see my brothers.' That's why he isn't here at the king's table."

20:16 Hebrew with the house of David.   **20:19** Hebrew the stone Ezel. The meaning of the Hebrew is uncertain.   **20:25** As in Greek version; Hebrew reads with Jonathan standing.

³⁰Saul boiled with rage at Jonathan. "You stupid son of a whore!"* he swore at him. "Do you think I don't know that you want him to be king in your place, shaming yourself and your mother? ³¹As long as that son of Jesse is alive, you'll never be king. Now go and get him so I can kill him!"

³²"But why should he be put to death?" Jonathan asked his father. "What has he done?" ³³Then Saul hurled his spear at Jonathan, intending to kill him. So at last Jonathan realized that his father was really determined to kill David.

³⁴Jonathan left the table in fierce anger and refused to eat on that second day of the festival, for he was crushed by his father's shameful behavior toward David.

³⁵The next morning, as agreed, Jonathan went out into the field and took a young boy with him to gather his arrows. ³⁶"Start running," he told the boy, "so you can find the arrows as I shoot them." So the boy ran, and Jonathan shot an arrow beyond him. ³⁷When the boy had almost reached the arrow, Jonathan shouted, "The arrow is still ahead of you. ³⁸Hurry, hurry, don't wait." So the boy quickly gathered up the arrows and ran back to his master. ³⁹He, of course, suspected nothing; only Jonathan and David understood the signal. ⁴⁰Then Jonathan gave his bow and arrows to the boy and told him to take them back to town.

⁴¹As soon as the boy was gone, David came out from where he had been hiding near the stone pile.* Then David bowed three times to Jonathan with his face to the ground. Both of them were in tears as they embraced each other and said good-bye, especially David.

⁴²At last Jonathan said to David, "Go in peace, for we have sworn loyalty to each other in the LORD's name. The LORD is the witness of a bond between us and our children forever." Then David left, and Jonathan returned to the town.*

21 David Runs from Saul

¹*David went to the town of Nob to see Ahimelech the priest. Ahimelech trembled when he saw him. "Why are you alone?" he asked. "Why is no one with you?"

²"The king has sent me on a private matter," David said. "He told me not to tell anyone why I am here. I have told my men where to meet me later. ³Now, what is there to eat? Give me five loaves of bread or anything else you have."

⁴"We don't have any regular bread," the priest replied. "But there is the holy bread, which you can have if your young men have not slept with any women recently."

⁵"Don't worry," David replied. "I never allow my men to be with women when they are on a campaign. And since they stay clean even on ordinary trips, how much more on this one!"

⁶Since there was no other food available, the priest gave him the holy bread—the Bread of the Presence that was placed before the LORD in the Tabernacle. It had just been replaced that day with fresh bread.

⁷Now Doeg the Edomite, Saul's chief herdsman, was there that day, having been detained before the LORD.*

⁸David asked Ahimelech, "Do you have a spear or sword? The king's business was so urgent that I didn't even have time to grab a weapon!"

⁹"I only have the sword of Goliath the Philistine, whom you killed in the valley of Elah," the priest replied. "It is wrapped in a cloth behind the ephod. Take that if you want it, for there is nothing else here."

"There is nothing like it!" David replied. "Give it to me!"

¹⁰So David escaped from Saul and went to King Achish of Gath. ¹¹But the officers of Achish were unhappy about his being there. "Isn't this David, the king of the land?" they asked. "Isn't he the one the people honor with dances, singing,

'Saul has killed his thousands,
 and David his ten thousands'?"

¹²David heard these comments and was very afraid of what King Achish of Gath might do to him. ¹³So he pretended to be insane, scratching on doors and drooling down his beard.

¹⁴Finally, King Achish said to his men, "Must you bring me a madman? ¹⁵We already have enough of them around here! Why should I let someone like this be my guest?"

20:30 Hebrew *You son of a perverse and rebellious woman.* **20:41** As in Greek version; Hebrew reads *near the south edge.* **20:42** This sentence is numbered 21:1 in Hebrew text. **21:1** Verses 21:1-15 are numbered 21:2-16 in Hebrew text. **21:7** The meaning of the Hebrew is uncertain.

22 David at the Cave of Adullam

So David left Gath and escaped to the cave of Adullam. Soon his brothers and all his other relatives joined him there. ²Then others began coming—men who were in trouble or in debt or who were just discontented—until David was the captain of about 400 men.

³Later David went to Mizpeh in Moab, where he asked the king, "Please allow my father and mother to live here with you until I know what God is going to do for me." ⁴So David's parents stayed in Moab with the king during the entire time David was living in his stronghold.

⁵One day the prophet Gad told David, "Leave the stronghold and return to the land of Judah." So David went to the forest of Hereth.

⁶The news of his arrival in Judah soon reached Saul. At the time, the king was sitting beneath the tamarisk tree on the hill at Gibeah, holding his spear and surrounded by his officers.

⁷"Listen here, you men of Benjamin!" Saul shouted to his officers when he heard the news. "Has that son of Jesse promised every one of you fields and vineyards? Has he promised to make you all generals and captains in his army?* ⁸Is that why you have conspired against me? For not one of you told me when my own son made a solemn pact with the son of Jesse. You're not even sorry for me. Think of it! My own son—encouraging him to kill me, as he is trying to do this very day!"

⁹Then Doeg the Edomite, who was standing there with Saul's men, spoke up. "When I was at Nob," he said, "I saw the son of Jesse talking to the priest, Ahimelech son of Ahitub. ¹⁰Ahimelech consulted the LORD for him. Then he gave him food and the sword of Goliath the Philistine."

The Slaughter of the Priests

¹¹King Saul immediately sent for Ahimelech and all his family, who served as priests at Nob. ¹²When they arrived, Saul shouted at him, "Listen to me, you son of Ahitub!"

"What is it, my king?" Ahimelech asked.

¹³"Why have you and the son of Jesse conspired against me?" Saul demanded. "Why did you give him food and a sword? Why have you consulted God for him? Why have you encouraged him to kill me, as he is trying to do this very day?"

¹⁴"But sir," Ahimelech replied, "is anyone among all your servants as faithful as David, your son-in-law? Why, he is the captain of your bodyguard and a highly honored member of your household! ¹⁵This was certainly not the first time I had consulted God for him! May the king not accuse me and my family in this matter, for I knew nothing at all of any plot against you."

¹⁶"You will surely die, Ahimelech, along with your entire family!" the king shouted. ¹⁷And he ordered his bodyguards, "Kill these priests of the LORD, for they are allies and conspirators with David! They knew he was running away from me, but they didn't tell me!" But Saul's men refused to kill the LORD's priests.

¹⁸Then the king said to Doeg, "You do it." So Doeg the Edomite turned on them and killed them that day, eighty-five priests in all, still wearing their priestly garments. ¹⁹Then he went to Nob, the town of the priests, and killed the priests' families—men and women, children and babies—and all the cattle, donkeys, sheep, and goats.

²⁰Only Abiathar, one of the sons of Ahimelech, escaped and fled to David. ²¹When he told David that Saul had killed the priests of the LORD, ²²David exclaimed, "I knew it! When I saw Doeg the Edomite there that day, I knew he was sure to tell Saul. Now I have caused the death of all your father's family. ²³Stay here with me, and don't be afraid. I will protect you with my own life, for the same person wants to kill us both."

23 David Protects the Town of Keilah

One day news came to David that the Philistines were at Keilah stealing grain from the threshing floors. ²David asked the LORD, "Should I go and attack them?"

"Yes, go and save Keilah," the LORD told him.

³But David's men said, "We're afraid even here in Judah. We certainly don't want to go to Keilah to fight the whole Philistine army!"

22:7 Hebrew commanders of thousands and commanders of hundreds?

Spiritual Direction
1 SAMUEL 23:15-29

Mentoring

Spiritual direction is a practice in which, with the help of another, you try to listen to your own heart and to God's. It's about intention and attention: I desire to hear God, so with another believer, I'm going to make space to give him my attention. Together we ask ourselves, *How is God with me right now? What is God saying to me? Is God pleased with me?* Spiritual direction gives us a place to talk out loud and confidentially ask these questions of discernment.

In talking about spiritual direction, Eugene Peterson says, "The Christian community has acquired wisdom through the centuries that provides guidance." Spiritual direction is grounded within the Christian community and the wisdom that God gives. It is rooted firmly in Christian theology, prayer, spirituality, and Scripture.

Practicing spiritual direction in the context of Christian community is one way to heighten our awareness of our journeys, to ask for grace to make gentle adjustments. Through spiritual direction, whether formal or informal, we can together invite the Holy Spirit to guide our prayer, reflections, and lives.

—*Jeannette Bakke*

For more on mentoring, see reading at Proverbs 1.

⁴So David asked the LORD again, and again the LORD replied, "Go down to Keilah, for I will help you conquer the Philistines."

⁵So David and his men went to Keilah. They slaughtered the Philistines and took all their livestock and rescued the people of Keilah. ⁶Now when Abiathar son of Ahimelech fled to David at Keilah, he brought the ephod with him.

⁷Saul soon learned that David was at Keilah. "Good!" he exclaimed. "We've got him now! God has handed him over to me, for he has trapped himself in a walled town!" ⁸So Saul mobilized his entire army to march to Keilah and besiege David and his men.

⁹But David learned of Saul's plan and told Abiathar the priest to bring the ephod and ask the LORD what he should do. ¹⁰Then David prayed, "O LORD, God of Israel, I have heard that Saul is planning to come and destroy Keilah because I am here. ¹¹Will the leaders of Keilah betray me to him?*

And will Saul actually come as I have heard? O LORD, God of Israel, please tell me."

And the LORD said, "He will come."

¹²Again David asked, "Will the leaders of Keilah betray me and my men to Saul?"

And the LORD replied, "Yes, they will betray you."

David Hides in the Wilderness

¹³So David and his men—about 600 of them now—left Keilah and began roaming the countryside. Word soon reached Saul that David had escaped, so he didn't go to Keilah after all. ¹⁴David now stayed in the strongholds of the wilderness and in the hill country of Ziph. Saul hunted him day after day, but God didn't let Saul find him.

¹⁵One day near Horesh, David received the news that Saul was on the way to Ziph to search for him and kill him. ¹⁶Jonathan went to find David and encouraged him to stay strong in his faith in God. ¹⁷"Don't be afraid," Jonathan reassured him. "My father

23:11 Some manuscripts lack the first sentence of 23:11.

will never find you! You are going to be the king of Israel, and I will be next to you, as my father, Saul, is well aware." [18] So the two of them renewed their solemn pact before the LORD. Then Jonathan returned home, while David stayed at Horesh.

[19] But now the men of Ziph went to Saul in Gibeah and betrayed David to him. "We know where David is hiding," they said. "He is in the strongholds of Horesh on the hill of Hakilah, which is in the southern part of Jeshimon. [20] Come down whenever you're ready, O king, and we will catch him and hand him over to you!"

[21] "The LORD bless you," Saul said. "At last someone is concerned about me! [22] Go and check again to be sure of where he is staying and who has seen him there, for I know that he is very crafty. [23] Discover his hiding places, and come back when you are sure. Then I'll go with you. And if he is in the area at all, I'll track him down, even if I have to search every hiding place in Judah!" [24] So the men of Ziph returned home ahead of Saul.

Meanwhile, David and his men had moved into the wilderness of Maon in the Arabah Valley south of Jeshimon. [25] When David heard that Saul and his men were searching for him, he went even farther into the wilderness to the great rock, and he remained there in the wilderness of Maon. But Saul kept after him in the wilderness.

[26] Saul and David were now on opposite sides of a mountain. Just as Saul and his men began to close in on David and his men, [27] an urgent message reached Saul that the Philistines were raiding Israel again. [28] So Saul quit chasing David and returned to fight the Philistines. Ever since that time, the place where David was camped has been called the Rock of Escape.* [29]*David then went to live in the strongholds of En-gedi.

24 David Spares Saul's Life

[1]*After Saul returned from fighting the Philistines, he was told that David had gone into the wilderness of En-gedi. [2] So Saul chose 3,000 elite troops from all Israel and went to search for David and his men near the rocks of the wild goats.

[3] At the place where the road passes some sheepfolds, Saul went into a cave to relieve himself. But as it happened, David and his men were hiding farther back in that very cave!

[4] "Now's your opportunity!" David's men whispered to him. "Today the LORD is telling you, 'I will certainly put your enemy into your power, to do with as you wish.'" So David crept forward and cut off a piece of the hem of Saul's robe.

[5] But then David's conscience began bothering him because he had cut Saul's robe. [6] "The LORD knows I shouldn't have done that to my lord the king," he said to his men. "The LORD forbid that I should do this to my lord the king and attack the LORD's anointed one, for the LORD himself has chosen him." [7] So David restrained his men and did not let them kill Saul.

After Saul had left the cave and gone on his way, [8] David came out and shouted after him, "My lord the king!" And when Saul looked around, David bowed low before him.

[9] Then he shouted to Saul, "Why do you listen to the people who say I am trying to harm you? [10] This very day you can see with your own eyes it isn't true. For the LORD placed you at my mercy back there in the cave. Some of my men told me to kill you, but I spared you. For I said, 'I will never harm the king—he is the LORD's anointed one.' [11] Look, my father, at what I have in my hand. It is a piece of the hem of your robe! I cut it off, but I didn't kill you. This proves that I am not trying to harm you and that I have not sinned against you, even though you have been hunting for me to kill me.

[12] "May the LORD judge between us. Perhaps the LORD will punish you for what you are trying to do to me, but I will never harm you. [13] As that old proverb says, 'From evil people come evil deeds.' So you can be sure I will never harm you. [14] Who is the king of Israel trying to catch anyway? Should he spend his time chasing one who is as worthless as a dead dog or a single flea? [15] May the LORD therefore judge which of us is right and punish the guilty one. He is my advocate, and he will rescue me from your power!"

23:28 Hebrew *Sela-hammahlekoth*.   23:29 Verse 23:29 is numbered 24:1 in Hebrew text.   24:1 Verses 24:1-22 are numbered 24:2-23 in Hebrew text.

[16] When David had finished speaking, Saul called back, "Is that really you, my son David?" Then he began to cry. [17] And he said to David, "You are a better man than I am, for you have repaid me good for evil. [18] Yes, you have been amazingly kind to me today, for when the LORD put me in a place where you could have killed me, you didn't do it. [19] Who else would let his enemy get away when he had him in his power? May the LORD reward you well for the kindness you have shown me today. [20] And now I realize that you are surely going to be king, and that the kingdom of Israel will flourish under your rule. [21] Now swear to me by the LORD that when that happens you will not kill my family and destroy my line of descendants!"

[22] So David promised this to Saul with an oath. Then Saul went home, but David and his men went back to their stronghold.

25 The Death of Samuel

Now Samuel died, and all Israel gathered for his funeral. They buried him at his house in Ramah.

Nabal Angers David

Then David moved down to the wilderness of Maon.* [2] There was a wealthy man from Maon who owned property near the town of Carmel. He had 3,000 sheep and 1,000 goats, and it was sheep-shearing time. [3] This man's name was Nabal, and his wife, Abigail, was a sensible and beautiful woman. But Nabal, a descendant of Caleb, was crude and mean in all his dealings.

[4] When David heard that Nabal was shearing his sheep, [5] he sent ten of his young men to Carmel with this message for Nabal: [6] "Peace and prosperity to you, your family, and everything you own! [7] I am told that it is sheep-shearing time. While your shepherds stayed among us near Carmel, we never harmed them, and nothing was ever stolen from them. [8] Ask your own men, and they will tell you this is true. So would you be kind to us, since we have come at a time of celebration? Please share any provisions you might have on hand with us

and with your friend David." [9] David's young men gave this message to Nabal in David's name, and they waited for a reply.

[10] "Who is this fellow David?" Nabal sneered to the young men. "Who does this son of Jesse think he is? There are lots of servants these days who run away from their masters. [11] Should I take my bread and my water and my meat that I've slaughtered for my shearers and give it to a band of outlaws who come from who knows where?"

[12] So David's young men returned and told him what Nabal had said. [13] "Get your swords!" was David's reply as he strapped on his own. Then 400 men started off with David, and 200 remained behind to guard their equipment.

[14] Meanwhile, one of Nabal's servants went to Abigail and told her, "David sent messengers from the wilderness to greet our master, but he screamed insults at them. [15] These men have been very good to us, and we never suffered any harm from them. Nothing was stolen from us the whole time they were with us. [16] In fact, day and night they were like a wall of protection to us and the sheep. [17] You need to know this and figure out what to do, for there is going to be trouble for our master and his whole family. He's so ill-tempered that no one can even talk to him!"

[18] Abigail wasted no time. She quickly gathered 200 loaves of bread, two wineskins full of wine, five sheep that had been slaughtered, nearly a bushel* of roasted grain, 100 clusters of raisins, and 200 fig cakes. She packed them on donkeys [19] and said to her servants, "Go on ahead. I will follow you shortly." But she didn't tell her husband Nabal what she was doing.

[20] As she was riding her donkey into a mountain ravine, she saw David and his men coming toward her. [21] David had just been saying, "A lot of good it did to help this fellow. We protected his flocks in the wilderness, and nothing he owned was lost or stolen. But he has repaid me evil for good. [22] May God strike me and kill me* if even one man of his household is still alive tomorrow morning!"

25:1 As in Greek version (see also 25:2); Hebrew reads *Paran*.   **25:18** Hebrew *5 seahs* [30 liters].   **25:22** As in Greek version; Hebrew reads *May God strike and kill the enemies of David*.

Forgiveness

Choosing Forgiveness over Bitterness

1 SAMUEL 25:23-38

It's a dramatic scene: an angry David tells his men to grab their swords as he straps on his own. They rush off, stomping and ranting, to kill Nabal—the man who snubbed their kindness. But then they see her: Abigail, Nabal's "sensible and beautiful" wife (1 Samuel 25:3). At first she's on a donkey, approaching them in the ravine. Next, she's on the ground, bowing at David's feet.

"I accept all blame in this matter, my lord," she says. "Please listen to what I have to say. I know Nabal is a wicked and ill-tempered man; please don't pay any attention to him. He is a fool, just as his name suggests" (25:23-25). She then asks David for forgiveness, on behalf of her wicked husband.

At that moment David faces a choice: to forgive or stay bitter. To accept the gifts of grace Abigail has brought or to carry on and kill everyone in Nabal's household.

While perhaps not this extreme, we all face this same decision every day. Every time someone hurts, offends, or wrongs us in big ways or small, we face a choice: forgive and accept the fruits of grace or carry on with the destruction that our bitterness brings.

David chose forgiveness, but it couldn't have been easy. It never is. Harnessing our bitterness feels like power, like we're in control. And yet the truth is that bitterness controls *us*. Under its influence, we make foolish, even dangerous, choices.

Perhaps this is why David thanked God for Abigail's own "good sense." Perhaps he realized that Nabal's wife must have waged her own personal war against bitterness—after all, she'd spent years *married* to this foolish man. Yet she chose to risk her own neck to protect her wicked husband against an army of men. David saw the wisdom and the healing power of her gracious spirit—and responded in kind.

—*Caryn Rivadeneira*

For more on forgiveness, see reading at 2 Samuel 18.

Abigail Intercedes for Nabal

23 When Abigail saw David, she quickly got off her donkey and bowed low before him. 24 She fell at his feet and said, "I accept all blame in this matter, my lord. Please listen to what I have to say. 25 I know Nabal is a wicked and ill-tempered man; please don't pay any attention to him. He is a fool, just as his name suggests.* But I never even saw the young men you sent.

26 "Now, my lord, as surely as the LORD lives and you yourself live, since the LORD has kept you from murdering and taking vengeance into your own hands, let all your enemies and those who try to harm you be as cursed as Nabal is. 27 And here is a present that I, your servant, have brought to you and your young men. 28 Please forgive me if I have offended you in any way. The LORD will surely reward you with a lasting dynasty, for you are fighting the LORD's battles. And you have not done wrong throughout your entire life.

25:25 The name *Nabal* means "fool."

29 "Even when you are chased by those who seek to kill you, your life is safe in the care of the LORD your God, secure in his treasure pouch! But the lives of your enemies will disappear like stones shot from a sling! 30 When the LORD has done all he promised and has made you leader of Israel, 31 don't let this be a blemish on your record. Then your conscience won't have to bear the staggering burden of needless bloodshed and vengeance. And when the LORD has done these great things for you, please remember me, your servant!"

32 David replied to Abigail, "Praise the LORD, the God of Israel, who has sent you to meet me today! 33 Thank God for your good sense! Bless you for keeping me from murder and from carrying out vengeance with my own hands. 34 For I swear by the LORD, the God of Israel, who has kept me from hurting you, that if you had not hurried out to meet me, not one of Nabal's men would still be alive tomorrow morning." 35 Then David accepted her present and told her, "Return home in peace. I have heard what you said. We will not kill your husband."

36 When Abigail arrived home, she found that Nabal was throwing a big party and was celebrating like a king. He was very drunk, so she didn't tell him anything about her meeting with David until dawn the next day. 37 In the morning when Nabal was sober, his wife told him what had happened. As a result he had a stroke,* and he lay paralyzed on his bed like a stone. 38 About ten days later, the LORD struck him, and he died.

David Marries Abigail

39 When David heard that Nabal was dead, he said, "Praise the LORD, who has avenged the insult I received from Nabal and has kept me from doing it myself. Nabal has received the punishment for his sin." Then David sent messengers to Abigail to ask her to become his wife.

40 When the messengers arrived at Carmel, they told Abigail, "David has sent us to take you back to marry him."

41 She bowed low to the ground and responded, "I, your servant, would be happy to marry David. I would even be willing to become a slave, washing the feet of his servants!" 42 Quickly getting ready, she took along five of her servant girls as attendants, mounted her donkey, and went with David's messengers. And so she became his wife. 43 David also married Ahinoam from Jezreel, making both of them his wives. 44 Saul, meanwhile, had given his daughter Michal, David's wife, to a man from Gallim named Palti son of Laish.

26 David Spares Saul Again

Now some men from Ziph came to Saul at Gibeah to tell him, "David is hiding on the hill of Hakilah, which overlooks Jeshimon."

2 So Saul took 3,000 of Israel's elite troops and went to hunt him down in the wilderness of Ziph. 3 Saul camped along the road beside the hill of Hakilah, near Jeshimon, where David was hiding. When David learned that Saul had come after him into the wilderness, 4 he sent out spies to verify the report of Saul's arrival.

5 David slipped over to Saul's camp one night to look around. Saul and Abner son of Ner, the commander of his army, were sleeping inside a ring formed by the slumbering warriors. 6 "Who will volunteer to go in there with me?" David asked Ahimelech the Hittite and Abishai son of Zeruiah, Joab's brother.

"I'll go with you," Abishai replied. 7 So David and Abishai went right into Saul's camp and found him asleep, with his spear stuck in the ground beside his head. Abner and the soldiers were lying asleep around him.

8 "God has surely handed your enemy over to you this time!" Abishai whispered to David. "Let me pin him to the ground with one thrust of the spear; I won't need to strike twice!"

9 "No!" David said. "Don't kill him. For who can remain innocent after attacking the LORD's anointed one? 10 Surely the LORD will strike Saul down someday, or he will die of old age or in battle. 11 The LORD forbid that I should kill the one he has

---

25:37 Hebrew *his heart failed him.*

anointed! But take his spear and that jug of water beside his head, and then let's get out of here!"

¹²So David took the spear and jug of water that were near Saul's head. Then he and Abishai got away without anyone seeing them or even waking up, because the LORD had put Saul's men into a deep sleep. ¹³David climbed the hill opposite the camp until he was at a safe distance. ¹⁴Then he shouted down to the soldiers and to Abner son of Ner, "Wake up, Abner!"

"Who is it?" Abner demanded.

¹⁵"Well, Abner, you're a great man, aren't you?" David taunted. "Where in all Israel is there anyone as mighty? So why haven't you guarded your master the king when someone came to kill him? ¹⁶This isn't good at all! I swear by the LORD that you and your men deserve to die, because you failed to protect your master, the LORD's anointed! Look around! Where are the king's spear and the jug of water that were beside his head?"

¹⁷Saul recognized David's voice and called out, "Is that you, my son David?"

And David replied, "Yes, my lord the king. ¹⁸Why are you chasing me? What have I done? What is my crime? ¹⁹But now let my lord the king listen to his servant. If the LORD has stirred you up against me, then let him accept my offering. But if this is simply a human scheme, then may those involved be cursed by the LORD. For they have driven me from my home, so I can no longer live among the LORD's people, and they have said, 'Go, worship pagan gods.' ²⁰Must I die on foreign soil, far from the presence of the LORD? Why has the king of Israel come out to search for a single flea? Why does he hunt me down like a partridge on the mountains?"

²¹Then Saul confessed, "I have sinned. Come back home, my son, and I will no longer try to harm you, for you valued my life today. I have been a fool and very, very wrong."

²²"Here is your spear, O king," David replied. "Let one of your young men come over and get it. ²³The LORD gives his own reward for doing good and for being loyal, and I refused to kill you even when the LORD placed you in my power, for you are the LORD's anointed one. ²⁴Now may the

LORD value my life, even as I have valued yours today. May he rescue me from all my troubles."

²⁵And Saul said to David, "Blessings on you, my son David. You will do many heroic deeds, and you will surely succeed." Then David went away, and Saul returned home.

27 David among the Philistines

But David kept thinking to himself, "Someday Saul is going to get me. The best thing I can do is escape to the Philistines. Then Saul will stop hunting for me in Israelite territory, and I will finally be safe."

²So David took his 600 men and went over and joined Achish son of Maoch, the king of Gath. ³David and his men and their families settled there with Achish at Gath. David brought his two wives along with him—Ahinoam from Jezreel and Abigail, Nabal's widow from Carmel. ⁴Word soon reached Saul that David had fled to Gath, so he stopped hunting for him.

⁵One day David said to Achish, "If it is all right with you, we would rather live in one of the country towns instead of here in the royal city."

⁶So Achish gave him the town of Ziklag (which still belongs to the kings of Judah to this day), ⁷and they lived there among the Philistines for a year and four months.

⁸David and his men spent their time raiding the Geshurites, the Girzites, and the Amalekites—people who had lived near Shur, toward the land of Egypt, since ancient times. ⁹David did not leave one person alive in the villages he attacked. He took the sheep, goats, cattle, donkeys, camels, and clothing before returning home to see King Achish.

¹⁰"Where did you make your raid today?" Achish would ask.

And David would reply, "Against the south of Judah, the Jerahmeelites, and the Kenites."

¹¹No one was left alive to come to Gath and tell where he had really been. This happened again and again while he was living among the Philistines. ¹²Achish believed David and thought to himself, "By now the people of Israel must hate him bitterly. Now he will have to stay here and serve me forever!"

28 Saul Consults a Medium

About that time the Philistines mustered their armies for another war with Israel. King Achish told David, "You and your men will be expected to join me in battle."

²"Very well!" David agreed. "Now you will see for yourself what we can do."

Then Achish told David, "I will make you my personal bodyguard for life."

³Meanwhile, Samuel had died, and all Israel had mourned for him. He was buried in Ramah, his hometown. And Saul had banned from the land of Israel all mediums and those who consult the spirits of the dead.

⁴The Philistines set up their camp at Shunem, and Saul gathered all the army of Israel and camped at Gilboa. ⁵When Saul saw the vast Philistine army, he became frantic with fear. ⁶He asked the LORD what he should do, but the LORD refused to answer him, either by dreams or by sacred lots* or by the prophets. ⁷Saul then said to his advisers, "Find a woman who is a medium, so I can go and ask her what to do."

His advisers replied, "There is a medium at Endor."

⁸So Saul disguised himself by wearing ordinary clothing instead of his royal robes. Then he went to the woman's home at night, accompanied by two of his men. "I have to talk to a man who has died," he said. "Will you call up his spirit for me?"

⁹"Are you trying to get me killed?" the woman demanded. "You know that Saul has outlawed all the mediums and all who consult the spirits of the dead. Why are you setting a trap for me?"

¹⁰But Saul took an oath in the name of the LORD and promised, "As surely as the LORD lives, nothing bad will happen to you for doing this."

¹¹Finally, the woman said, "Well, whose spirit do you want me to call up?"

"Call up Samuel," Saul replied.

¹²When the woman saw Samuel, she screamed, "You've deceived me! You are Saul!"

¹³"Don't be afraid!" the king told her. "What do you see?"

"I see a god* coming up out of the earth," she said.

¹⁴"What does he look like?" Saul asked.

"He is an old man wrapped in a robe," she replied. Saul realized it was Samuel, and he fell to the ground before him.

¹⁵"Why have you disturbed me by calling me back?" Samuel asked Saul.

"Because I am in deep trouble," Saul replied. "The Philistines are at war with me, and God has left me and won't reply by prophets or dreams. So I have called for you to tell me what to do."

¹⁶But Samuel replied, "Why ask me, since the LORD has left you and has become your enemy? ¹⁷The LORD has done just as he said he would. He has torn the kingdom from you and given it to your rival, David. ¹⁸The LORD has done this to you today because you refused to carry out his fierce anger against the Amalekites. ¹⁹What's more, the LORD will hand you and the army of Israel over to the Philistines tomorrow, and you and your sons will be here with me. The LORD will bring down the entire army of Israel in defeat."

²⁰Saul fell full length on the ground, paralyzed with fright because of Samuel's words. He was also faint with hunger, for he had eaten nothing all day and all night.

²¹When the woman saw how distraught he was, she said, "Sir, I obeyed your command at the risk of my life. ²²Now do what I say, and let me give you a little something to eat so you can regain your strength for the trip back."

²³But Saul refused to eat anything. Then his advisers joined the woman in urging him to eat, so he finally yielded and got up from the ground and sat on the couch.

²⁴The woman had been fattening a calf, so she hurried out and killed it. She took some flour, kneaded it into dough and baked unleavened bread. ²⁵She brought the meal to Saul and his advisers, and they ate it. Then they went out into the night.

29 The Philistines Reject David

The entire Philistine army now mobilized at Aphek, and the Israelites camped at the spring in Jezreel. ²As the Philistine rulers

---

28:6 Hebrew by *Urim.*   **28:13** Or *gods.*

were leading out their troops in groups of hundreds and thousands, David and his men marched at the rear with King Achish. ³But the Philistine commanders demanded, "What are these Hebrews doing here?"

And Achish told them, "This is David, the servant of King Saul of Israel. He's been with me for years, and I've never found a single fault in him from the day he arrived until today."

⁴But the Philistine commanders were angry. "Send him back to the town you've given him!" they demanded. "He can't go into the battle with us. What if he turns against us in battle and becomes our adversary? Is there any better way for him to reconcile himself with his master than by handing our heads over to him? ⁵Isn't this the same David about whom the women of Israel sing in their dances,

'Saul has killed his thousands,
    and David his ten thousands'?"

⁶So Achish finally summoned David and said to him, "I swear by the LORD that you have been a trustworthy ally. I think you should go with me into battle, for I've never found a single flaw in you from the day you arrived until today. But the other Philistine rulers won't hear of it. ⁷Please don't upset them, but go back quietly."

⁸"What have I done to deserve this treatment?" David demanded. "What have you ever found in your servant, that I can't go and fight the enemies of my lord the king?"

⁹But Achish insisted, "As far as I'm concerned, you're as perfect as an angel of God. But the Philistine commanders are afraid to have you with them in the battle. ¹⁰Now get up early in the morning, and leave with your men as soon as it gets light."

¹¹So David and his men headed back into the land of the Philistines, while the Philistine army went on to Jezreel.

30 David Destroys the Amalekites

Three days later, when David and his men arrived home at their town of Ziklag, they found that the Amalekites had made a raid into the Negev and Ziklag; they had crushed Ziklag and burned it to the ground. ²They had carried off the women and children and everyone else but without killing anyone.

³When David and his men saw the ruins and realized what had happened to their families, ⁴they wept until they could weep no more. ⁵David's two wives, Ahinoam from Jezreel and Abigail, the widow of Nabal from Carmel, were among those captured. ⁶David was now in great danger because all his men were very bitter about losing their sons and daughters, and they began to talk of stoning him. But David found strength in the LORD his God.

⁷Then he said to Abiathar the priest, "Bring me the ephod!" So Abiathar brought it. ⁸Then David asked the LORD, "Should I chase after this band of raiders? Will I catch them?"

And the LORD told him, "Yes, go after them. You will surely recover everything that was taken from you!"

⁹So David and his 600 men set out, and they came to the brook Besor. ¹⁰But 200 of the men were too exhausted to cross the brook, so David continued the pursuit with 400 men.

¹¹Along the way they found an Egyptian man in a field and brought him to David. They gave him some bread to eat and water to drink. ¹²They also gave him part of a fig cake and two clusters of raisins, for he hadn't had anything to eat or drink for three days and nights. Before long his strength returned.

¹³"To whom do you belong, and where do you come from?" David asked him.

"I am an Egyptian—the slave of an Amalekite," he replied. "My master abandoned me three days ago because I was sick. ¹⁴We were on our way back from raiding the Kerethites in the Negev, the territory of Judah, and the land of Caleb, and we had just burned Ziklag."

¹⁵"Will you lead me to this band of raiders?" David asked.

The young man replied, "If you take an oath in God's name that you will not kill me or give me back to my master, then I will guide you to them."

¹⁶So he led David to them, and they found the Amalekites spread out across the fields, eating and drinking and danc-

ing with joy because of the vast amount of plunder they had taken from the Philistines and the land of Judah. ¹⁷David and his men rushed in among them and slaughtered them throughout that night and the entire next day until evening. None of the Amalekites escaped except 400 young men who fled on camels. ¹⁸David got back everything the Amalekites had taken, and he rescued his two wives. ¹⁹Nothing was missing: small or great, son or daughter, nor anything else that had been taken. David brought everything back. ²⁰He also recovered all the flocks and herds, and his men drove them ahead of the other livestock. "This plunder belongs to David!" they said.

²¹Then David returned to the brook Besor and met up with the 200 men who had been left behind because they were too exhausted to go with him. They went out to meet David and his men, and David greeted them joyfully. ²²But some evil troublemakers among David's men said, "They didn't go with us, so they can't have any of the plunder we recovered. Give them their wives and children, and tell them to be gone."

²³But David said, "No, my brothers! Don't be selfish with what the LORD has given us. He has kept us safe and helped us defeat the band of raiders that attacked us. ²⁴Who will listen when you talk like this? We share and share alike—those who go to battle and those who guard the equipment." ²⁵From then on David made this a decree and regulation for Israel, and it is still followed today.

²⁶When he arrived at Ziklag, David sent part of the plunder to the elders of Judah, who were his friends. "Here is a present for you, taken from the LORD's enemies," he said. ²⁷The gifts were sent to the people of the following towns David had visited: Bethel, Ramoth-negev, Jattir, ²⁸Aroer, Siphmoth, Eshtemoa, ²⁹Racal,* the towns of the Jerahmeelites, the towns of the Kenites, ³⁰Hormah, Bor-ashan, Athach, ³¹Hebron, and all the other places David and his men had visited.

31 The Death of Saul

Now the Philistines attacked Israel, and the men of Israel fled before them. Many were slaughtered on the slopes of Mount Gilboa. ²The Philistines closed in on Saul and his sons, and they killed three of his sons—Jonathan, Abinadab, and Malkishua. ³The fighting grew very fierce around Saul, and the Philistine archers caught up with him and wounded him severely.

⁴Saul groaned to his armor bearer, "Take your sword and kill me before these pagan Philistines come to run me through and taunt and torture me."

But his armor bearer was afraid and would not do it. So Saul took his own sword and fell on it. ⁵When his armor bearer realized that Saul was dead, he fell on his own sword and died beside the king. ⁶So Saul, his three sons, his armor bearer, and his troops all died together that same day.

⁷When the Israelites on the other side of the Jezreel Valley and beyond the Jordan saw that the Israelite army had fled and that Saul and his sons were dead, they abandoned their towns and fled. So the Philistines moved in and occupied their towns.

⁸The next day, when the Philistines went out to strip the dead, they found the bodies of Saul and his three sons on Mount Gilboa. ⁹So they cut off Saul's head and stripped off his armor. Then they proclaimed the good news of Saul's death in their pagan temple and to the people throughout the land of Philistia. ¹⁰They placed his armor in the temple of the Ashtoreths, and they fastened his body to the wall of the city of Beth-shan.

¹¹But when the people of Jabesh-gilead heard what the Philistines had done to Saul, ¹²all their mighty warriors traveled through the night to Beth-shan and took the bodies of Saul and his sons down from the wall. They brought them to Jabesh, where they burned the bodies. ¹³Then they took their bones and buried them beneath the tamarisk tree at Jabesh, and they fasted for seven days.

30:29 Greek version reads Carmel.

Introduction to

2 Samuel

Background

King Saul and his son Jonathan are dead. At the beginning of 2 Samuel, David hears the news, mourns their passing, and is anointed king over Judah and then over all of Israel. The rest of the book recounts the reign of David.

First and 2 Samuel were originally one narrative in the Hebrew Scriptures but divided in the Septuagint. The compiler of 2 Samuel was probably a member of a school of prophets.

Message

The first half of 2 Samuel details King David's amassing power; the second half shows his sad decline. The turning point is David's illicit relationship with Bathsheba and its subsequent cover-up. God sends the prophet Nathan to confront David. Although David acknowledges and repents of his sin, consequences remain. As Nathan prophesies, "From this time on, your family will live by the sword" (12:10). David's family endures endless turmoil: his son Amnon's rape of Tamar, his half-sister; Absalom's conspiracy to murder Amnon; and Absalom's rebellion. Despite David's shortcomings, the heart of the book testifies to God's faithfulness to the Davidic covenant (7:4–17). Here God promises that David's dynasty will last forever: "Your house and your kingdom will continue before me for all time, and your throne will be secure forever" (7:16). This promise is fulfilled in a descendant of David—Jesus Christ, who will reign forever.

Time

David's reign in Hebron began in 1011 B.C. He ruled all of Israel from 1004 until 971 B.C.

Outline

2 Samuel

1 David Learns of Saul's Death

After the death of Saul, David returned from his victory over the Amalekites and spent two days in Ziklag. ²On the third day a man arrived from Saul's army camp. He had torn his clothes and put dirt on his head to show that he was in mourning. He fell to the ground before David in deep respect.

³"Where have you come from?" David asked.

"I escaped from the Israelite camp," the man replied.

⁴"What happened?" David demanded. "Tell me how the battle went."

The man replied, "Our entire army fled from the battle. Many of the men are dead, and Saul and his son Jonathan are also dead."

⁵"How do you know Saul and Jonathan are dead?" David demanded of the young man.

⁶The man answered, "I happened to be on Mount Gilboa, and there was Saul leaning on his spear with the enemy chariots and charioteers closing in on him. ⁷When he turned and saw me, he cried out for me to come to him. 'How can I help?' I asked him.

⁸"He responded, 'Who are you?'

"'I am an Amalekite,' I told him.

⁹"Then he begged me, 'Come over here and put me out of my misery, for I am in terrible pain and want to die.'

¹⁰"So I killed him," the Amalekite told David, "for I knew he couldn't live. Then I took his crown and his armband, and I have brought them here to you, my lord."

¹¹David and his men tore their clothes in sorrow when they heard the news. ¹²They mourned and wept and fasted all day for Saul and his son Jonathan, and for the LORD's army and the nation of Israel, because they had died by the sword that day.

¹³Then David said to the young man who had brought the news, "Where are you from?"

And he replied, "I am a foreigner, an Amalekite, who lives in your land."

¹⁴"Why were you not afraid to kill the LORD's anointed one?" David asked.

¹⁵Then David said to one of his men, "Kill him!" So the man thrust his sword into the Amalekite and killed him. ¹⁶"You have condemned yourself," David said, "for you yourself confessed that you killed the LORD's anointed one."

David's Song for Saul and Jonathan

¹⁷Then David composed a funeral song for Saul and Jonathan, ¹⁸and he commanded that it be taught to the people of Judah. It is known as the Song of the Bow, and it is recorded in *The Book of Jashar.**

¹⁹ Your pride and joy, O Israel, lies dead on the hills!
   Oh, how the mighty heroes have fallen!
²⁰ Don't announce the news in Gath,
      don't proclaim it in the streets of Ashkelon,

1:18 Or *The Book of the Upright.*

or the daughters of the Philistines will
rejoice
and the pagans will laugh in triumph.

²¹ O mountains of Gilboa,
let there be no dew or rain upon you,
nor fruitful fields producing offerings
of grain.*
For there the shield of the mighty heroes
was defiled;
the shield of Saul will no longer be
anointed with oil.

²² The bow of Jonathan was powerful,
and the sword of Saul did its mighty
work.
They shed the blood of their enemies
and pierced the bodies of mighty
heroes.

²³ How beloved and gracious were Saul
and Jonathan!
They were together in life and in
death.
They were swifter than eagles,
stronger than lions.

²⁴ O women of Israel, weep for Saul,
for he dressed you in luxurious scarlet
clothing,
in garments decorated with gold.

²⁵ Oh, how the mighty heroes have fallen
in battle!
Jonathan lies dead on the hills.

²⁶ How I weep for you, my brother
Jonathan!
Oh, how much I loved you!
And your love for me was deep,
deeper than the love of women!

²⁷ Oh, how the mighty heroes have fallen!
Stripped of their weapons, they lie dead.

2 David Anointed King of Judah

After this, David asked the LORD,
"Should I move back to one of the towns
of Judah?"

"Yes," the LORD replied.

Then David asked, "Which town should
I go to?"

"To Hebron," the LORD answered.

²David's two wives were Ahinoam from
Jezreel and Abigail, the widow of Nabal
from Carmel. So David and his wives ³and
his men and their families all moved to
Judah, and they settled in the villages near
Hebron. ⁴Then the men of Judah came to
David and anointed him king over the peo-
ple of Judah.

When David heard that the men of
Jabesh-gilead had buried Saul, ⁵he sent
them this message: "May the LORD bless
you for being so loyal to your master Saul
and giving him a decent burial. ⁶May the
LORD be loyal to you in return and reward
you with his unfailing love! And I, too, will
reward you for what you have done. ⁷Now
that Saul is dead, I ask you to be my strong
and loyal subjects like the people of Judah,
who have anointed me as their new king."

Ishbosheth Proclaimed King of Israel

⁸But Abner son of Ner, the commander of
Saul's army, had already gone to Mahanaim
with Saul's son Ishbosheth.* ⁹There he proclaimed Ishbosheth king over Gilead, Jezreel, Ephraim, Benjamin, the land of the
Ashurites, and all the rest of Israel.

¹⁰Ishbosheth, Saul's son, was forty years
old when he became king, and he ruled
from Mahanaim for two years. Meanwhile, the people of Judah remained loyal
to David. ¹¹David made Hebron his capital,
and he ruled as king of Judah for seven and
a half years.

War between Israel and Judah

¹²One day Abner led Ishbosheth's troops
from Mahanaim to Gibeon. ¹³About the
same time, Joab son of Zeruiah led David's
troops out and met them at the pool of Gibeon. The two groups sat down there, facing
each other from opposite sides of the pool.

¹⁴Then Abner suggested to Joab, "Let's
have a few of our warriors fight hand to
hand here in front of us."

"All right," Joab agreed. ¹⁵So twelve men
were chosen to fight from each side—twelve
men of Benjamin representing Ishbosheth
son of Saul, and twelve representing David.
¹⁶Each one grabbed his opponent by the
hair and thrust his sword into the other's
side so that all of them died. So this place
at Gibeon has been known ever since as the
Field of Swords.*

1:21 The meaning of the Hebrew is uncertain.   **2:8** *Ishbosheth* is another name for Esh-baal.   **2:16** Hebrew *Helkath-hazzurim*.

[17] A fierce battle followed that day, and Abner and the men of Israel were defeated by the forces of David.

The Death of Asahel

[18] Joab, Abishai, and Asahel—the three sons of Zeruiah—were among David's forces that day. Asahel could run like a gazelle, [19] and he began chasing Abner. He pursued him relentlessly, not stopping for anything. [20] When Abner looked back and saw him coming, he called out, "Is that you, Asahel?"

"Yes, it is," he replied.

[21] "Go fight someone else!" Abner warned. "Take on one of the younger men, and strip him of his weapons." But Asahel kept right on chasing Abner.

[22] Again Abner shouted to him, "Get away from here! I don't want to kill you. How could I ever face your brother Joab again?"

[23] But Asahel refused to turn back, so Abner thrust the butt end of his spear through Asahel's stomach, and the spear came out through his back. He stumbled to the ground and died there. And everyone who came by that spot stopped and stood still when they saw Asahel lying there.

[24] When Joab and Abishai found out what had happened, they set out after Abner. The sun was just going down as they arrived at the hill of Ammah near Giah, along the road to the wilderness of Gibeon. [25] Abner's troops from the tribe of Benjamin regrouped there at the top of the hill to take a stand.

[26] Abner shouted down to Joab, "Must we always be killing each other? Don't you realize that bitterness is the only result? When will you call off your men from chasing their Israelite brothers?"

[27] Then Joab said, "God only knows what would have happened if you hadn't spoken, for we would have chased you all night if necessary." [28] So Joab blew the ram's horn, and his men stopped chasing the troops of Israel.

[29] All that night Abner and his men retreated through the Jordan Valley.* They crossed the Jordan River, traveling all through the morning,* and didn't stop until they arrived at Mahanaim.

[30] Meanwhile, Joab and his men also returned home. When Joab counted his casualties, he discovered that only 19 men were missing in addition to Asahel. [31] But 360 of Abner's men had been killed, all from the tribe of Benjamin. [32] Joab and his men took Asahel's body to Bethlehem and buried him there in his father's tomb. Then they traveled all night and reached Hebron at daybreak.

3 That was the beginning of a long war between those who were loyal to Saul and those loyal to David. As time passed David became stronger and stronger, while Saul's dynasty became weaker and weaker.

David's Sons Born in Hebron

[2] These are the sons who were born to David in Hebron:

The oldest was Amnon, whose mother was Ahinoam from Jezreel.
[3] The second was Daniel,* whose mother was Abigail, the widow of Nabal from Carmel.
The third was Absalom, whose mother was Maacah, the daughter of Talmai, king of Geshur.
[4] The fourth was Adonijah, whose mother was Haggith.
The fifth was Shephatiah, whose mother was Abital.
[5] The sixth was Ithream, whose mother was Eglah, David's wife.

These sons were all born to David in Hebron.

Abner Joins Forces with David

[6] As the war between the house of Saul and the house of David went on, Abner became a powerful leader among those loyal to Saul. [7] One day Ishbosheth,* Saul's son, accused Abner of sleeping with one of his father's concubines, a woman named Rizpah, daughter of Aiah.

[8] Abner was furious. "Am I some Judean dog to be kicked around like this?" he shouted. "After all I have done for your father, Saul, and his family and friends by not handing you over to David, is this my reward—that you find fault with me about this woman?

2:29a Hebrew *the Arabah.*   **2:29b** Or *continued on through the Bithron.* The meaning of the Hebrew is uncertain.   **3:3** As in parallel text at 1 Chr 3:1 (see also Greek version, which reads *Daluia,* and Dead Sea Scrolls, which read *Dan[iel]*); Hebrew reads *Kileab.*   **3:7** *Ishbosheth* is another name for Esh-baal.

⁹May God strike me and even kill me if I don't do everything I can to help David get what the LORD has promised him! ¹⁰I'm going to take Saul's kingdom and give it to David. I will establish the throne of David over Israel as well as Judah, all the way from Dan in the north to Beersheba in the south." ¹¹Ishbosheth didn't dare say another word because he was afraid of what Abner might do.

¹²Then Abner sent messengers to David, saying, "Doesn't the entire land belong to you? Make a solemn pact with me, and I will help turn over all of Israel to you."

¹³"All right," David replied, "but I will not negotiate with you unless you bring back my wife Michal, Saul's daughter, when you come."

¹⁴David then sent this message to Ishbosheth, Saul's son: "Give me back my wife Michal, for I bought her with the lives* of 100 Philistines."

¹⁵So Ishbosheth took Michal away from her husband, Palti* son of Laish. ¹⁶Palti followed along behind her as far as Bahurim, weeping as he went. Then Abner told him, "Go back home!" So Palti returned.

¹⁷Meanwhile, Abner had consulted with the elders of Israel. "For some time now," he told them, "you have wanted to make David your king. ¹⁸Now is the time! For the LORD has said, 'I have chosen David to save my people Israel from the hands of the Philistines and from all their other enemies.'" ¹⁹Abner also spoke with the men of Benjamin. Then he went to Hebron to tell David that all the people of Israel and Benjamin had agreed to support him.

²⁰When Abner and twenty of his men came to Hebron, David entertained them with a great feast. ²¹Then Abner said to David, "Let me go and call an assembly of all Israel to support my lord the king. They will make a covenant with you to make you their king, and you will rule over everything your heart desires." So David sent Abner safely on his way.

Joab Murders Abner

²²But just after David had sent Abner away in safety, Joab and some of David's troops returned from a raid, bringing much plunder with them. ²³When Joab arrived, he was told that Abner had just been there visiting the king and had been sent away in safety.

²⁴Joab rushed to the king and demanded, "What have you done? What do you mean by letting Abner get away? ²⁵You know perfectly well that he came to spy on you and find out everything you're doing!"

²⁶Joab then left David and sent messengers to catch up with Abner, asking him to return. They found him at the well of Sirah and brought him back, though David knew nothing about it. ²⁷When Abner arrived back at Hebron, Joab took him aside at the gateway as if to speak with him privately. But then he stabbed Abner in the stomach and killed him in revenge for killing his brother Asahel.

²⁸When David heard about it, he declared, "I vow by the LORD that I and my kingdom are forever innocent of this crime against Abner son of Ner. ²⁹Joab and his family are the guilty ones. May the family of Joab be cursed in every generation with a man who has open sores or leprosy* or who walks on crutches* or dies by the sword or begs for food!"

³⁰So Joab and his brother Abishai killed Abner because Abner had killed their brother Asahel at the battle of Gibeon.

David Mourns Abner's Death

³¹Then David said to Joab and all those who were with him, "Tear your clothes and put on burlap. Mourn for Abner." And King David himself walked behind the procession to the grave. ³²They buried Abner in Hebron, and the king and all the people wept at his graveside. ³³Then the king sang this funeral song for Abner:

"Should Abner have died as fools die?
³⁴ Your hands were not bound;
   your feet were not chained.
 No, you were murdered—
   the victim of a wicked plot."

All the people wept again for Abner. ³⁵David had refused to eat anything on the day of the funeral, and now everyone

---

3:14 Hebrew *the foreskins.*   **3:15** As in 1 Sam 25:44; Hebrew reads *Paltiel,* a variant spelling of Palti.   **3:29a** Or *or a contagious skin disease.* The Hebrew word used here can describe various skin diseases.   **3:29b** Or *who is effeminate;* Hebrew reads *who handles a spindle.*

begged him to eat. But David had made a vow, saying, "May God strike me and even kill me if I eat anything before sundown."

³⁶ This pleased the people very much. In fact, everything the king did pleased them! ³⁷ So everyone in Judah and all Israel understood that David was not responsible for Abner's murder.

³⁸ Then King David said to his officials, "Don't you realize that a great commander has fallen today in Israel? ³⁹ And even though I am the anointed king, these two sons of Zeruiah—Joab and Abishai—are too strong for me to control. So may the LORD repay these evil men for their evil deeds."

4 The Murder of Ishbosheth

When Ishbosheth,* Saul's son, heard about Abner's death at Hebron, he lost all courage, and all Israel became paralyzed with fear. ²Now there were two brothers, Baanah and Recab, who were captains of Ishbosheth's raiding parties. They were sons of Rimmon, a member of the tribe of Benjamin who lived in Beeroth. The town of Beeroth is now part of Benjamin's territory ³because the original people of Beeroth fled to Gittaim, where they still live as foreigners.

⁴(Saul's son Jonathan had a son named Mephibosheth,* who was crippled as a child. He was five years old when the report came from Jezreel that Saul and Jonathan had been killed in battle. When the child's nurse heard the news, she picked him up and fled. But as she hurried away, she dropped him, and he became crippled.)

⁵One day Recab and Baanah, the sons of Rimmon from Beeroth, went to Ishbosheth's house around noon as he was taking his midday rest. ⁶The doorkeeper, who had been sifting wheat, became drowsy and fell asleep. So Recab and Baanah slipped past her.* ⁷They went into the house and found Ishbosheth sleeping on his bed. They struck and killed him and cut off his head. Then, taking his head with them, they fled across the Jordan Valley* through the night. ⁸When they arrived at Hebron, they presented Ishbosheth's head to David. "Look!" they exclaimed to the king. "Here is the head of Ishbosheth, the son of your enemy Saul who tried to kill you. Today the LORD has given my lord the king revenge on Saul and his entire family!"

⁹But David said to Recab and Baanah, "The LORD, who saves me from all my enemies, is my witness. ¹⁰Someone once told me, 'Saul is dead,' thinking he was bringing me good news. But I seized him and killed him at Ziklag. That's the reward I gave him for his news! ¹¹How much more should I reward evil men who have killed an innocent man in his own house and on his own bed? Shouldn't I hold you responsible for his blood and rid the earth of you?"

¹²So David ordered his young men to kill them, and they did. They cut off their hands and feet and hung their bodies beside the pool in Hebron. Then they took Ishbosheth's head and buried it in Abner's tomb in Hebron.

5 David Becomes King of All Israel

Then all the tribes of Israel went to David at Hebron and told him, "We are your own flesh and blood. ²In the past,* when Saul was our king, you were the one who really led the forces of Israel. And the LORD told you, 'You will be the shepherd of my people Israel. You will be Israel's leader.'"

³So there at Hebron, King David made a covenant before the LORD with all the elders of Israel. And they anointed him king of Israel.

⁴David was thirty years old when he began to reign, and he reigned forty years in all. ⁵He had reigned over Judah from Hebron for seven years and six months, and from Jerusalem he reigned over all Israel and Judah for thirty-three years.

David Captures Jerusalem

⁶David then led his men to Jerusalem to fight against the Jebusites, the original inhabitants of the land who were living there. The Jebusites taunted David, saying, "You'll never get in here! Even the blind and lame could keep you out!" For the Jebusites

---

4:1 Ishbosheth is another name for Esh-baal.   **4:4** Mephibosheth is another name for Merib-baal.   **4:6** As in Greek version; Hebrew reads So they went into the house pretending to fetch wheat, but they stabbed him in the stomach. Then Recab and Baanah escaped.   **4:7** Hebrew the Arabah.   **5:2** Or For some time.

thought they were safe. [7] But David captured the fortress of Zion, which is now called the City of David.

[8] On the day of the attack, David said to his troops, "I hate those 'lame' and 'blind' Jebusites.* Whoever attacks them should strike by going into the city through the water tunnel.*" That is the origin of the saying, "The blind and the lame may not enter the house."*

[9] So David made the fortress his home, and he called it the City of David. He extended the city, starting at the supporting terraces* and working inward. [10] And David became more and more powerful, because the LORD God of Heaven's Armies was with him.

[11] Then King Hiram of Tyre sent messengers to David, along with cedar timber and carpenters and stonemasons, and they built David a palace. [12] And David realized that the LORD had confirmed him as king over Israel and had blessed his kingdom for the sake of his people Israel.

[13] After moving from Hebron to Jerusalem, David married more concubines and wives, and they had more sons and daughters. [14] These are the names of David's sons who were born in Jerusalem: Shammua, Shobab, Nathan, Solomon, [15] Ibhar, Elishua, Nepheg, Japhia, [16] Elishama, Eliada, and Eliphelet.

David Conquers the Philistines

[17] When the Philistines heard that David had been anointed king of Israel, they mobilized all their forces to capture him. But David was told they were coming, so he went into the stronghold. [18] The Philistines arrived and spread out across the valley of Rephaim. [19] So David asked the LORD, "Should I go out to fight the Philistines? Will you hand them over to me?"

The LORD replied to David, "Yes, go ahead. I will certainly hand them over to you."

[20] So David went to Baal-perazim and defeated the Philistines there. "The LORD did it!" David exclaimed. "He burst through my enemies like a raging flood!" So he named

that place Baal-perazim (which means "the Lord who bursts through"). [21] The Philistines had abandoned their idols there, so David and his men confiscated them.

[22] But after a while the Philistines returned and again spread out across the valley of Rephaim. [23] And again David asked the LORD what to do. "Do not attack them straight on," the LORD replied. "Instead, circle around behind and attack them near the poplar* trees. [24] When you hear a sound like marching feet in the tops of the poplar trees, be on the alert! That will be the signal that the LORD is moving ahead of you to strike down the Philistine army." [25] So David did what the LORD commanded, and he struck down the Philistines all the way from Gibeon* to Gezer.

6 Moving the Ark to Jerusalem

Then David again gathered all the elite troops in Israel, 30,000 in all. [2] He led them to Baalah of Judah* to bring back the Ark of God, which bears the name of the LORD of Heaven's Armies,* who is enthroned between the cherubim. [3] They placed the Ark of God on a new cart and brought it from Abinadab's house, which was on a hill. Uzzah and Ahio, Abinadab's sons, were guiding the cart as it left the house, [4] carrying the Ark of God. Ahio walked in front of the Ark. [5] David and all the people of Israel were celebrating before the LORD, singing songs* and playing all kinds of musical instruments—lyres, harps, tambourines, castanets, and cymbals.

[6] But when they arrived at the threshing floor of Nacon, the oxen stumbled, and Uzzah reached out his hand and steadied the Ark of God. [7] Then the LORD's anger was aroused against Uzzah, and God struck him dead because of this.* So Uzzah died right there beside the Ark of God.

[8] David was angry because the LORD's anger had burst out against Uzzah. He named that place Perez-uzzah (which means "to burst out against Uzzah"), as it is still called today.

5:8a Or Those 'lame' and 'blind' Jebusites hate me. 5:8b Or with scaling hooks. The meaning of the Hebrew is uncertain. 5:8c The meaning of this saying is uncertain. 5:9 Hebrew the millo. The meaning of the Hebrew is uncertain. 5:23 Or aspen, or balsam; also in 5:24. The exact identification of this tree is uncertain. 5:25 As in Greek version (see also 1 Chr 14:16); Hebrew reads Geba. 6:2a Baalah of Judah is another name for Kiriath-jearim; compare 1 Chr 13:6. 6:2b Or the Ark of God where the Name is proclaimed—the name of the LORD of Heaven's Armies. 6:5 As in Dead Sea Scrolls and Greek version (see also 1 Chr 13:8); Masoretic Text reads before the LORD with all manner of cypress wood. 6:7 As in Dead Sea Scrolls; Masoretic Text reads because of his irreverence.

Dance of the God-Struck

2 SAMUEL 6:16–22

Second Samuel 6 presents us with an odd and startling story. It begins when David wants to make the ark of the covenant a symbol of his royal authority. Bringing the ark "home" to Jerusalem is not primarily a political gesture. It is primarily worship. By this, David makes a powerful statement: God is king in this kingdom, lord of this land. The king acknowledges the King beyond him, above him, to whom he owes all fealty. So David brings the ark to Jerusalem—and he dances in worship. Choreographed by yearning and wonder, this is the dance of the God-struck, the God-smitten.

A messy argument erupts in David's household afterward. His wife Michal has decided to stay home. Maybe—and the text hints at this—she is making a statement. For Michal commits the principal act of those who disapprove: she merely watches, distant, judging. "When she saw King David leaping and dancing before the LORD, she was filled with contempt for him" (6:16).

David barely gets in the door before Michal, cold with contempt and hot with scorn, sarcastically declares, "How distinguished the king of Israel looked today" (6:20). Michal seems to believe that the chief end of humanity is to uphold its own reputation. Religion is fine, in its place. But worship? Worship is a dicey thing, because modesty and moderation are Michal's watchwords, and worship always threatens them, always wants to push beyond them.

So God struck Michal barren—and her example teaches us a valuable lesson about God. God is not the safe-keeper of our reputations; and our main job on this earth is not to keep ourselves from embarrassment. We must come before the King, dignified or undignified, robed or disrobed, and worship with all our might.

Occasionally we get glimpses of Deepest Reality—of God. Glimpsing it can make you do funny things. You can become stony still. Or giddily happy. Or chokingly afraid. It can calm you with uncanny peace or disrupt you with implacable dread. It can make you, simultaneously, not yourself and fully yourself. It can make kings dance.

—Mark Buchanan

For more on worship, see reading at 2 Chronicles 29:25–36.

⁹David was now afraid of the LORD, and he asked, "How can I ever bring the Ark of the LORD back into my care?" ¹⁰So David decided not to move the Ark of the LORD into the City of David. Instead, he took it to the house of Obed-edom of Gath. ¹¹The Ark of the LORD remained there in Obed-edom's house for three months, and the LORD blessed Obed-edom and his entire household.

¹²Then King David was told, "The LORD has blessed Obed-edom's household and everything he has because of the Ark of God." So David went there and brought the Ark of God from the house of Obed-edom to the City of David with a great celebration. ¹³After the men who were carrying the Ark of the LORD had gone six steps, David sacrificed a bull and a fattened calf. ¹⁴And David danced before the LORD with all his might, wearing a priestly garment.* ¹⁵So

6:14 Hebrew *a linen ephod.*

David and all the people of Israel brought up the Ark of the LORD with shouts of joy and the blowing of rams' horns.

Michal's Contempt for David

[16] But as the Ark of the LORD entered the City of David, Michal, the daughter of Saul, looked down from her window. When she saw King David leaping and dancing before the LORD, she was filled with contempt for him.

[17] They brought the Ark of the LORD and set it in its place inside the special tent David had prepared for it. And David sacrificed burnt offerings and peace offerings to the LORD. [18] When he had finished his sacrifices, David blessed the people in the name of the LORD of Heaven's Armies. [19] Then he gave to every Israelite man and woman in the crowd a loaf of bread, a cake of dates,* and a cake of raisins. Then all the people returned to their homes.

[20] When David returned home to bless his own family, Michal, the daughter of Saul, came out to meet him. She said in disgust, "How distinguished the king of Israel looked today, shamelessly exposing himself to the servant girls like any vulgar person might do!"

[21] David retorted to Michal, "I was dancing before the LORD, who chose me above your father and all his family! He appointed me as the leader of Israel, the people of the LORD, so I celebrate before the LORD. [22] Yes, and I am willing to look even more foolish than this, even to be humiliated in my own eyes! But those servant girls you mentioned will indeed think I am distinguished!" [23] So Michal, the daughter of Saul, remained childless throughout her entire life.

7 The LORD's Covenant Promise to David

When King David was settled in his palace and the LORD had given him rest from all the surrounding enemies, [2] the king summoned Nathan the prophet. "Look," David said, "I am living in a beautiful cedar palace,* but the Ark of God is out there in a tent!"

[3] Nathan replied to the king, "Go ahead and do whatever you have in mind, for the LORD is with you."

[4] But that same night the LORD said to Nathan,

[5] "Go and tell my servant David, 'This is what the LORD has declared: Are you the one to build a house for me to live in? [6] I have never lived in a house, from the day I brought the Israelites out of Egypt until this very day. I have always moved from one place to another with a tent and a Tabernacle as my dwelling. [7] Yet no matter where I have gone with the Israelites, I have never once complained to Israel's tribal leaders, the shepherds of my people Israel. I have never asked them, "Why haven't you built me a beautiful cedar house?"'

[8] "Now go and say to my servant David, 'This is what the LORD of Heaven's Armies has declared: I took you from tending sheep in the pasture and selected you to be the leader of my people Israel. [9] I have been with you wherever you have gone, and I have destroyed all your enemies before your eyes. Now I will make your name as famous as anyone who has ever lived on the earth! [10] And I will provide a homeland for my people Israel, planting them in a secure place where they will never be disturbed. Evil nations won't oppress them as they've done in the past, [11] starting from the time I appointed judges to rule my people Israel. And I will give you rest from all your enemies.

"'Furthermore, the LORD declares that he will make a house for you—a dynasty of kings! [12] For when you die and are buried with your ancestors, I will raise up one of your descendants, your own offspring, and I will make his kingdom strong. [13] He is the one who will build a house—a temple—for my name. And I will secure his royal throne forever. [14] I will be his father, and he will be my son. If he sins, I will correct and discipline him with the rod, like any father would do. [15] But my favor will not be taken from him as I took it from Saul, whom I removed from your sight. [16] Your house and your kingdom will continue before me* for all time, and your throne will be secure forever.'"

6:19 Or *a portion of meat.* The meaning of the Hebrew is uncertain. 7:2 Hebrew *a house of cedar.* 7:16 As in Greek version and some Hebrew manuscripts; Masoretic Text reads *before you.*

[17] So Nathan went back to David and told him everything the LORD had said in this vision.

David's Prayer of Thanks

[18] Then King David went in and sat before the LORD and prayed,

"Who am I, O Sovereign LORD, and what is my family, that you have brought me this far? [19] And now, Sovereign LORD, in addition to everything else, you speak of giving your servant a lasting dynasty! Do you deal with everyone this way, O Sovereign LORD?*

[20] "What more can I say to you? You know what your servant is really like, Sovereign LORD. [21] Because of your promise and according to your will, you have done all these great things and have made them known to your servant.

[22] "How great you are, O Sovereign LORD! There is no one like you. We have never even heard of another God like you! [23] What other nation on earth is like your people Israel? What other nation, O God, have you redeemed from slavery to be your own people? You made a great name for yourself when you redeemed your people from Egypt. You performed awesome miracles and drove out the nations and gods that stood in their way.* [24] You made Israel your very own people forever, and you, O LORD, became their God.

[25] "And now, O LORD God, I am your servant; do as you have promised concerning me and my family. Confirm it as a promise that will last forever. [26] And may your name be honored forever so that everyone will say, 'The LORD of Heaven's Armies is God over Israel!' And may the house of your servant David continue before you forever.

[27] "O LORD of Heaven's Armies, God of Israel, I have been bold enough to pray this prayer to you because you have revealed all this to your servant, saying, 'I will build a house for you—a dynasty of kings!' [28] For you are God, O Sovereign LORD. Your words are truth, and you have promised these good things to your servant. [29] And now, may it please you to bless the house of your servant, so that it may continue forever before you. For you have spoken, and when you grant a blessing to your servant, O Sovereign LORD, it is an eternal blessing!"

8 David's Military Victories

After this, David defeated and subdued the Philistines by conquering Gath, their largest town.* [2] David also conquered the land of Moab. He made the people lie down on the ground in a row, and he measured them off in groups with a length of rope. He measured off two groups to be executed for every one group to be spared. The Moabites who were spared became David's subjects and paid him tribute money.

[3] David also destroyed the forces of Hadadezer son of Rehob, king of Zobah, when Hadadezer marched out to strengthen his control along the Euphrates River. [4] David captured 1,000 chariots, 7,000 charioteers,* and 20,000 foot soldiers. He crippled all the chariot horses except enough for 100 chariots.

[5] When Arameans from Damascus arrived to help King Hadadezer, David killed 22,000 of them. [6] Then he placed several army garrisons in Damascus, the Aramean capital, and the Arameans became David's subjects and paid him tribute money. So the LORD made David victorious wherever he went.

[7] David brought the gold shields of Hadadezer's officers to Jerusalem, [8] along with a large amount of bronze from Hadadezer's towns of Tebah* and Berothai.

[9] When King Toi of Hamath heard that David had destroyed the entire army of Hadadezer, [10] he sent his son Joram to congratulate King David for his successful campaign. Hadadezer and Toi had been enemies and were often at war. Joram presented David with many gifts of silver, gold, and bronze.

[11] King David dedicated all these gifts

7:19 Or *This is your instruction for all humanity, O Sovereign LORD.* **7:23** As in Greek version (see also 1 Chr 17:21); Hebrew reads *You made a great name for yourself and performed awesome miracles for your land. You did this in the sight of your people, whom you redeemed from Egypt, from nations and their gods.* **8:1** Hebrew *by conquering Metheg-ammah,* a name that means "the bridle," possibly referring to the size of the town or the tribute money taken from it. Compare 1 Chr 18:1. **8:4** As in Dead Sea Scrolls and Greek version (see also 1 Chr 18:4); Masoretic Text reads *captured 1,700 charioteers.* **8:8** As in some Greek manuscripts (see also 1 Chr 18:8); Hebrew reads *Betah.*

Jump in with Your Heart

2 SAMUEL 9

One day about a decade ago, I picked up a news magazine, and it was a moment that changed my life forever. I read an article about AIDS in Africa. At that time I didn't care at all about the issue of AIDS. I really had a hard heart.

When I began to read that article and saw the awful photos of people suffering terribly, I tried to cover the pictures so I could just read the text. But right in the middle of the article were words that jumped to my attention: *twelve million children orphaned in Africa due to AIDS.* The words rocked me—and I threw the magazine down, hardly believing it was true.

For days all I could see in my mind were those pictures. It was as if I could hear the cries of those children and the parents who were dying and leaving them behind. No matter how I tried, I couldn't get away from it. Over the next month God kept bringing it to my mind; he was convicting me and calling me to serve.

After about a month of being haunted by the terrible reality of the AIDS crisis, I realized I'd come to a fork in the road: I could either ignore this sense of conviction and go on leading a comfortable life, or I could jump off the precipice and into an unknown future by saying, *Yes, God, I will do something about that.*

When you find yourself touched on an emotional level—when you sense God is tugging on your heart or convicting you, I encourage you to say *yes* to God. Don't hold back. Don't overthink it or analyze all the what-ifs—just jump in with your heart. From there, take time to get educated: listen to what others have to say, glean wisdom from others, and get training. Be the best servant you can be!

—*Kay Warren*

For more on service, see reading at Psalm 139:13–16.

to the LORD, as he did with the silver and gold from the other nations he had defeated—[12] from Edom,* Moab, Ammon, Philistia, and Amalek—and from Hadadezer son of Rehob, king of Zobah.

[13] So David became even more famous when he returned from destroying 18,000 Edomites* in the Valley of Salt. [14] He placed army garrisons throughout Edom, and all the Edomites became David's subjects. In fact, the LORD made David victorious wherever he went.

[15] So David reigned over all Israel and did what was just and right for all his people. [16] Joab son of Zeruiah was commander of the army. Jehoshaphat son of Ahilud was the royal historian. [17] Zadok son of Ahitub and Ahimelech son of Abiathar were the priests. Seraiah was the court secretary. [18] Benaiah son of Jehoiada was captain of the king's bodyguard.* And David's sons served as priestly leaders.*

9 David's Kindness to Mephibosheth

One day David asked, "Is anyone in Saul's family still alive—anyone to whom I can show kindness for Jonathan's sake?" [2] He summoned a man named Ziba, who had been one of Saul's servants. "Are you Ziba?" the king asked.

"Yes sir, I am," Ziba replied.

[3] The king then asked him, "Is anyone still alive from Saul's family? If so, I want to show God's kindness to them."

8:12 As in a few Hebrew manuscripts and Greek and Syriac versions (see also 8:14; 1 Chr 18:11); most Hebrew manuscripts read *Aram*.
8:13 As in a few Hebrew manuscripts and Greek and Syriac versions (see also 8:14; 1 Chr 18:12); most Hebrew manuscripts read *Arameans*.
8:18a Hebrew *of the Kerethites and Pelethites*.   **8:18b** Hebrew *David's sons were priests;* compare parallel text at 1 Chr 18:17.

Ziba replied, "Yes, one of Jonathan's sons is still alive. He is crippled in both feet."

⁴"Where is he?" the king asked.

"In Lo-debar," Ziba told him, "at the home of Makir son of Ammiel."

⁵So David sent for him and brought him from Makir's home. ⁶His name was Mephibosheth*; he was Jonathan's son and Saul's grandson. When he came to David, he bowed low to the ground in deep respect. David said, "Greetings, Mephibosheth."

Mephibosheth replied, "I am your servant."

⁷"Don't be afraid!" David said. "I intend to show kindness to you because of my promise to your father, Jonathan. I will give you all the property that once belonged to your grandfather Saul, and you will eat here with me at the king's table!"

⁸Mephibosheth bowed respectfully and exclaimed, "Who is your servant, that you should show such kindness to a dead dog like me?"

⁹Then the king summoned Saul's servant Ziba and said, "I have given your master's grandson everything that belonged to Saul and his family. ¹⁰You and your sons and servants are to farm the land for him to produce food for your master's household.* But Mephibosheth, your master's grandson, will eat here at my table." (Ziba had fifteen sons and twenty servants.)

¹¹Ziba replied, "Yes, my lord the king; I am your servant, and I will do all that you have commanded." And from that time on, Mephibosheth ate regularly at David's table,* like one of the king's own sons.

¹²Mephibosheth had a young son named Mica. From then on, all the members of Ziba's household were Mephibosheth's servants. ¹³And Mephibosheth, who was crippled in both feet, lived in Jerusalem and ate regularly at the king's table.

10 David Defeats the Ammonites

Some time after this, King Nahash* of the Ammonites died, and his son Hanun became king. ²David said, "I am going to show loyalty to Hanun just as his father, Nahash, was always loyal to me." So David sent ambassadors to express sympathy to Hanun about his father's death.

But when David's ambassadors arrived in the land of Ammon, ³the Ammonite commanders said to Hanun, their master, "Do you really think these men are coming here to honor your father? No! David has sent them to spy out the city so they can come in and conquer it!" ⁴So Hanun seized David's ambassadors and shaved off half of each man's beard, cut off their robes at the buttocks, and sent them back to David in shame.

⁵When David heard what had happened, he sent messengers to tell the men, "Stay at Jericho until your beards grow out, and then come back." For they felt deep shame because of their appearance.

⁶When the people of Ammon realized how seriously they had angered David, they sent and hired 20,000 Aramean foot soldiers from the lands of Beth-rehob and Zobah, 1,000 from the king of Maacah, and 12,000 from the land of Tob. ⁷When David heard about this, he sent Joab and all his warriors to fight them. ⁸The Ammonite troops came out and drew up their battle lines at the entrance of the city gate, while the Arameans from Zobah and Rehob and the men from Tob and Maacah positioned themselves to fight in the open fields.

⁹When Joab saw that he would have to fight on both the front and the rear, he chose some of Israel's elite troops and placed them under his personal command to fight the Arameans in the fields. ¹⁰He left the rest of the army under the command of his brother Abishai, who was to attack the Ammonites. ¹¹"If the Arameans are too strong for me, then come over and help me," Joab told his brother. "And if the Ammonites are too strong for you, I will come and help you. ¹²Be courageous! Let us fight bravely for our people and the cities of our God. May the LORD's will be done."

¹³When Joab and his troops attacked, the Arameans began to run away. ¹⁴And when the Ammonites saw the Arameans running, they ran from Abishai and retreated into the city. After the battle was over, Joab returned to Jerusalem.

¹⁵The Arameans now realized that they were no match for Israel. So when they regrouped, ¹⁶they were joined by additional Aramean troops summoned by Hadadezer from the other side of the Euphrates River.* These troops arrived at Helam under the command of Shobach, the commander of Hadadezer's forces.

¹⁷When David heard what was happening, he mobilized all Israel, crossed the Jordan River, and led the army to Helam. The Arameans positioned themselves in battle formation and fought against David. ¹⁸But again the Arameans fled from the Israelites. This time David's forces killed 700 charioteers and 40,000 foot soldiers,* including Shobach, the commander of their army. ¹⁹When all the kings allied with Hadadezer saw that they had been defeated by Israel, they surrendered to Israel and became their subjects. After that, the Arameans were afraid to help the Ammonites.

11 David and Bathsheba

In the spring of the year,* when kings normally go out to war, David sent Joab and the Israelite army to fight the Ammonites. They destroyed the Ammonite army and laid siege to the city of Rabbah. However, David stayed behind in Jerusalem.

²Late one afternoon, after his midday rest, David got out of bed and was walking on the roof of the palace. As he looked out over the city, he noticed a woman of unusual beauty taking a bath. ³He sent someone to find out who she was, and he was told, "She is Bathsheba, the daughter of Eliam and the wife of Uriah the Hittite." ⁴Then David sent messengers to get her; and when she came to the palace, he slept with her. She had just completed the purification rites after having her menstrual period. Then she returned home. ⁵Later, when Bathsheba discovered that she was pregnant, she sent David a message, saying, "I'm pregnant."

⁶Then David sent word to Joab: "Send me Uriah the Hittite." So Joab sent him to David. ⁷When Uriah arrived, David asked him how Joab and the army were getting along and how the war was progressing. ⁸Then he told Uriah, "Go on home and relax.*" David even sent a gift to Uriah after he had left the palace. ⁹But Uriah didn't go home. He slept that night at the palace entrance with the king's palace guard.

¹⁰When David heard that Uriah had not gone home, he summoned him and asked, "What's the matter? Why didn't you go home last night after being away for so long?"

¹¹Uriah replied, "The Ark and the armies of Israel and Judah are living in tents,* and Joab and my master's men are camping in the open fields. How could I go home to wine and dine and sleep with my wife? I swear that I would never do such a thing."

¹²"Well, stay here today," David told him, "and tomorrow you may return to the army." So Uriah stayed in Jerusalem that day and the next. ¹³Then David invited him to dinner and got him drunk. But even then he couldn't get Uriah to go home to his wife. Again he slept at the palace entrance with the king's palace guard.

David Arranges for Uriah's Death

¹⁴So the next morning David wrote a letter to Joab and gave it to Uriah to deliver. ¹⁵The letter instructed Joab, "Station Uriah on the front lines where the battle is fiercest. Then pull back so that he will be killed." ¹⁶So Joab assigned Uriah to a spot close to the city wall where he knew the enemy's strongest men were fighting. ¹⁷And when the enemy soldiers came out of the city to fight, Uriah the Hittite was killed along with several other Israelite soldiers.

¹⁸Then Joab sent a battle report to David. ¹⁹He told his messenger, "Report all the news of the battle to the king. ²⁰But he might get angry and ask, 'Why did the troops go so close to the city? Didn't they know there would be shooting from the walls? ²¹Wasn't Abimelech son of Gideon* killed at Thebez by a woman who threw a millstone down on him from the wall? Why would you get so close to the wall?' Then tell him, 'Uriah the Hittite was killed, too.'"

10:16 Hebrew *the river.* **10:18** As in some Greek manuscripts (see also 1 Chr 19:18); Hebrew reads *charioteers.* **11:1** Hebrew *At the turn of the year.* The first day of the year in the ancient Hebrew lunar calendar occurred in March or April. **11:8** Hebrew *and wash your feet,* an expression that may also have a connotation of ritualistic washing. **11:11** Or *at Succoth.* **11:21** Hebrew *son of Jerub-besheth.* Jerub-besheth is a variation on the name Jerub-baal, which is another name for Gideon; see Judg 6:32.

²²So the messenger went to Jerusalem and gave a complete report to David. ²³"The enemy came out against us in the open fields," he said. "And as we chased them back to the city gate, ²⁴the archers on the wall shot arrows at us. Some of the king's men were killed, including Uriah the Hittite."

²⁵"Well, tell Joab not to be discouraged," David said. "The sword devours this one today and that one tomorrow! Fight harder next time, and conquer the city!"

²⁶When Uriah's wife heard that her husband was dead, she mourned for him. ²⁷When the period of mourning was over, David sent for her and brought her to the palace, and she became one of his wives. Then she gave birth to a son. But the LORD was displeased with what David had done.

12 Nathan Rebukes David

So the LORD sent Nathan the prophet to tell David this story: "There were two men in a certain town. One was rich, and one was poor. ²The rich man owned a great many sheep and cattle. ³The poor man owned nothing but one little lamb he had bought. He raised that little lamb, and it grew up with his children. It ate from the man's own plate and drank from his cup. He cuddled it in his arms like a baby daughter. ⁴One day a guest arrived at the home of the rich man. But instead of killing an animal from his own flock or herd, he took the poor man's lamb and killed it and prepared it for his guest."

⁵David was furious. "As surely as the LORD lives," he vowed, "any man who would do such a thing deserves to die! ⁶He must repay four lambs to the poor man for the one he stole and for having no pity."

⁷Then Nathan said to David, "You are that man! The LORD, the God of Israel, says: I anointed you king of Israel and saved you from the power of Saul. ⁸I gave you your master's house and his wives and the kingdoms of Israel and Judah. And if that had not been enough, I would have given you much, much more. ⁹Why, then, have you despised the word of the LORD and done this horrible deed? For you have murdered Uriah the Hittite with the sword of the Ammonites and stolen his wife. ¹⁰From this time on, your family will live by the sword because you have despised me by taking Uriah's wife to be your own.

¹¹"This is what the LORD says: Because of what you have done, I will cause your own household to rebel against you. I will give your wives to another man before your very eyes, and he will go to bed with them in public view. ¹²You did it secretly, but I will make this happen to you openly in the sight of all Israel."

David Confesses His Guilt

¹³Then David confessed to Nathan, "I have sinned against the LORD."

Nathan replied, "Yes, but the LORD has forgiven you, and you won't die for this sin. ¹⁴Nevertheless, because you have shown utter contempt for the LORD* by doing this, your child will die."

¹⁵After Nathan returned to his home, the LORD sent a deadly illness to the child of David and Uriah's wife. ¹⁶David begged God to spare the child. He went without food and lay all night on the bare ground. ¹⁷The elders of his household pleaded with him to get up and eat with them, but he refused.

¹⁸Then on the seventh day the child died. David's advisers were afraid to tell him. "He wouldn't listen to reason while the child was ill," they said. "What drastic thing will he do when we tell him the child is dead?"

¹⁹When David saw them whispering, he realized what had happened. "Is the child dead?" he asked.

"Yes," they replied, "he is dead."

²⁰Then David got up from the ground, washed himself, put on lotions,* and changed his clothes. He went to the Tabernacle and worshiped the LORD. After that, he returned to the palace and was served food and ate.

²¹His advisers were amazed. "We don't understand you," they told him. "While the child was still living, you wept and refused to eat. But now that the child is dead, you have stopped your mourning and are eating again."

²²David replied, "I fasted and wept while the child was alive, for I said, 'Perhaps the

12:14 As in Dead Sea Scrolls; Masoretic Text reads *the LORD's enemies.* **12:20** Hebrew *anointed himself.*

Prayer for Healing
2 SAMUEL 12:13–25

James 5:14–15 urges us to respond to illness with prayer, assuring us that "a prayer offered in faith will heal the sick." But we also know from Scripture this isn't a guarantee. Consider the prayers of King David in 2 Samuel 12. He fasted and prayed seven days, begging God to spare his dying child. In verse 22, David said, "Perhaps the LORD will be gracious to me and let the child live." *Perhaps.* Or as the New International Version translates it, "Who knows?" When his child died, though, David got up and worshiped God anyway.

We each know the pain and disappointment of unanswered prayers for healing. It's difficult to understand why one person is healed or spared suffering and another isn't—yet perhaps this simply isn't ours to know.

Many amazing healings are recorded in Scripture. We even see that Lazarus was raised from the dead! But some ten or twenty years later, Lazarus died again. In this broken world, suffering and death are inevitable. In the meantime we pray. Even in the face of doubt, we can boldly ask God for a miracle. We pray and plead, and with open and upturned hands we join with David in saying, "Who knows?"

—Nancy Ortberg

For more on prayer, see reading at 1 Kings 8:22–53.

LORD will be gracious to me and let the child live.' ²³ But why should I fast when he is dead? Can I bring him back again? I will go to him one day, but he cannot return to me."

²⁴ Then David comforted Bathsheba, his wife, and slept with her. She became pregnant and gave birth to a son, and David* named him Solomon. The LORD loved the child ²⁵ and sent word through Nathan the prophet that they should name him Jedidiah (which means "beloved of the LORD"), as the LORD had commanded.*

David Captures Rabbah

²⁶ Meanwhile, Joab was fighting against Rabbah, the capital of Ammon, and he captured the royal fortifications.* ²⁷ Joab sent messengers to tell David, "I have fought against Rabbah and captured its water supply.* ²⁸ Now bring the rest of the army and capture the city. Otherwise, I will capture it and get credit for the victory."

²⁹ So David gathered the rest of the army and went to Rabbah, and he fought against it and captured it. ³⁰ David removed the crown from the king's head,* and it was placed on his own head. The crown was made of gold and set with gems, and it weighed seventy-five pounds.* David took a vast amount of plunder from the city. ³¹ He also made slaves of the people of Rabbah and forced them to labor with* saws, iron picks, and iron axes, and to work in the brick kilns.* That is how he dealt with the people of all the Ammonite towns. Then David and all the army returned to Jerusalem.

13 The Rape of Tamar

Now David's son Absalom had a beautiful sister named Tamar. And Amnon, her

---

12:24 Hebrew *he*; an alternate Hebrew reading and some Hebrew manuscripts read *she*.   **12:25** As in Greek version; Hebrew reads *because of the LORD*.   **12:26** Or *the royal city*.   **12:27** Or *captured the city of water*.   **12:30a** Or *from the head of Milcom* (as in Greek version). Milcom, also called Molech, was the god of the Ammonites.   **12:30b** Hebrew *1 talent* [34 kilograms].   **12:31a** Or *He also brought out the people of Rabbah and put them under*.   **12:31b** Or *and he made them pass through the brick kilns*.

half brother, fell desperately in love with her. [2] Amnon became so obsessed with Tamar that he became ill. She was a virgin, and Amnon thought he could never have her.

[3] But Amnon had a very crafty friend—his cousin Jonadab. He was the son of David's brother Shimea.* [4] One day Jonadab said to Amnon, "What's the trouble? Why should the son of a king look so dejected morning after morning?"

So Amnon told him, "I am in love with Tamar, my brother Absalom's sister."

[5] "Well," Jonadab said, "I'll tell you what to do. Go back to bed and pretend you are ill. When your father comes to see you, ask him to let Tamar come and prepare some food for you. Tell him you'll feel better if she prepares it as you watch and feeds you with her own hands."

[6] So Amnon lay down and pretended to be sick. And when the king came to see him, Amnon asked him, "Please let my sister Tamar come and cook my favorite dish* as I watch. Then I can eat it from her own hands." [7] So David agreed and sent Tamar to Amnon's house to prepare some food for him.

[8] When Tamar arrived at Amnon's house, she went to the place where he was lying down so he could watch her mix some dough. Then she baked his favorite dish for him. [9] But when she set the serving tray before him, he refused to eat. "Everyone get out of here," Amnon told his servants. So they all left.

[10] Then he said to Tamar, "Now bring the food into my bedroom and feed it to me here." So Tamar took his favorite dish to him. [11] But as she was feeding him, he grabbed her and demanded, "Come to bed with me, my darling sister."

[12] "No, my brother!" she cried. "Don't be foolish! Don't do this to me! Such wicked things aren't done in Israel. [13] Where could I go in my shame? And you would be called one of the greatest fools in Israel. Please, just speak to the king about it, and he will let you marry me."

[14] But Amnon wouldn't listen to her, and since he was stronger than she was, he raped her. [15] Then suddenly Amnon's love turned to hate, and he hated her even more than he had loved her. "Get out of here!" he snarled at her.

[16] "No, no!" Tamar cried. "Sending me away now is worse than what you've already done to me."

But Amnon wouldn't listen to her. [17] He shouted for his servant and demanded, "Throw this woman out, and lock the door behind her!"

[18] So the servant put her out and locked the door behind her. She was wearing a long, beautiful robe,* as was the custom in those days for the king's virgin daughters. [19] But now Tamar tore her robe and put ashes on her head. And then, with her face in her hands, she went away crying.

[20] Her brother Absalom saw her and asked, "Is it true that Amnon has been with you? Well, my sister, keep quiet for now, since he's your brother. Don't you worry about it." So Tamar lived as a desolate woman in her brother Absalom's house.

[21] When King David heard what had happened, he was very angry.* [22] And though Absalom never spoke to Amnon about this, he hated Amnon deeply because of what he had done to his sister.

Absalom's Revenge on Amnon

[23] Two years later, when Absalom's sheep were being sheared at Baal-hazor near Ephraim, Absalom invited all the king's sons to come to a feast. [24] He went to the king and said, "My sheep-shearers are now at work. Would the king and his servants please come to celebrate the occasion with me?"

[25] The king replied, "No, my son. If we all came, we would be too much of a burden on you." Absalom pressed him, but the king would not come, though he gave Absalom his blessing.

[26] "Well, then," Absalom said, "if you can't come, how about sending my brother Amnon with us?"

"Why Amnon?" the king asked. [27] But Absalom kept on pressing the king until he finally agreed to let all his sons attend, including Amnon. So Absalom prepared a feast fit for a king.*

13:3 Hebrew *Shimeah* (also in 13:32), a variant spelling of Shimea; compare 1 Chr 2:13. **13:6** Or *a couple of cakes;* also in 13:8, 10. **13:18** Or *a robe with sleeves,* or *an ornamented robe.* The meaning of the Hebrew is uncertain. **13:21** Dead Sea Scrolls and Greek version add *But he did not punish his son Amnon, because he loved him, for he was his firstborn.* **13:27** As in Greek and Latin versions (compare also Dead Sea Scrolls); the Hebrew text lacks this sentence.

²⁸Absalom told his men, "Wait until Amnon gets drunk; then at my signal, kill him! Don't be afraid. I'm the one who has given the command. Take courage and do it!" ²⁹So at Absalom's signal they murdered Amnon. Then the other sons of the king jumped on their mules and fled.

³⁰As they were on the way back to Jerusalem, this report reached David: "Absalom has killed all the king's sons; not one is left alive!" ³¹The king got up, tore his robe, and threw himself on the ground. His advisers also tore their clothes in horror and sorrow.

³²But just then Jonadab, the son of David's brother Shimea, arrived and said, "No, don't believe that all the king's sons have been killed! It was only Amnon! Absalom has been plotting this ever since Amnon raped his sister Tamar. ³³No, my lord the king, your sons aren't all dead! It was only Amnon." ³⁴Meanwhile Absalom escaped.

Then the watchman on the Jerusalem wall saw a great crowd coming down the hill on the road from the west. He ran to tell the king, "I see a crowd of people coming from the Horonaim road along the side of the hill."*

³⁵"Look!" Jonadab told the king. "There they are now! The king's sons are coming, just as I said."

³⁶They soon arrived, weeping and sobbing, and the king and all his servants wept bitterly with them. ³⁷And David mourned many days for his son Amnon.

Absalom fled to his grandfather, Talmai son of Ammihud, the king of Geshur. ³⁸He stayed there in Geshur for three years. ³⁹And King David,* now reconciled to Amnon's death, longed to be reunited with his son Absalom.*

14 Joab Arranges for Absalom's Return

Joab realized how much the king longed to see Absalom. ²So he sent for a woman from Tekoa who had a reputation for great wisdom. He said to her, "Pretend you are in mourning; wear mourning clothes and don't put on lotions.* Act like a woman who has been mourning for the dead for a long time. ³Then go to the king and tell him the story I am about to tell you." Then Joab told her what to say.

⁴When the woman from Tekoa approached the king, she bowed with her face to the ground in deep respect and cried out, "O king! Help me!"

⁵"What's the trouble?" the king asked.

"Alas, I am a widow!" she replied. "My husband is dead. ⁶My two sons had a fight out in the field. And since no one was there to stop it, one of them was killed. ⁷Now the rest of the family is demanding, 'Let us have your son. We will execute him for murdering his brother. He doesn't deserve to inherit his family's property.' They want to extinguish the only coal I have left, and my husband's name and family will disappear from the face of the earth."

⁸"Leave it to me," the king told her. "Go home, and I'll see to it that no one touches him."

⁹"Oh, thank you, my lord the king," the woman from Tekoa replied. "If you are criticized for helping me, let the blame fall on me and on my father's house, and let the king and his throne be innocent."

¹⁰"If anyone objects," the king said, "bring him to me. I can assure you he will never complain again!"

¹¹Then she said, "Please swear to me by the LORD your God that you won't let anyone take vengeance against my son. I want no more bloodshed."

"As surely as the LORD lives," he replied, "not a hair on your son's head will be disturbed!"

¹²"Please allow me to ask one more thing of my lord the king," she said.

"Go ahead and speak," he responded.

¹³She replied, "Why don't you do as much for the people of God as you have promised to do for me? You have convicted yourself in making this decision, because you have refused to bring home your own banished son. ¹⁴All of us must die eventually. Our lives are like water spilled out on the ground, which cannot be gathered up again. But God does not just sweep life away; instead, he devises ways to bring us back when we have been separated from him.

¹⁵"I have come to plead with my lord the

13:34 As in Greek version; Hebrew lacks this sentence.   **13:39a** Dead Sea Scrolls and Greek version read *And the spirit of the king.*
13:39b Or *no longer felt a need to go out after Absalom.*   **14:2** Hebrew *don't anoint yourself with oil.*

king because people have threatened me. I said to myself, 'Perhaps the king will listen to me [16]and rescue us from those who would cut us off from the inheritance* God has given us. [17]Yes, my lord the king will give us peace of mind again.' I know that you are like an angel of God in discerning good from evil. May the LORD your God be with you."

[18]"I must know one thing," the king replied, "and tell me the truth."

"Yes, my lord the king," she responded.

[19]"Did Joab put you up to this?"

And the woman replied, "My lord the king, how can I deny it? Nobody can hide anything from you. Yes, Joab sent me and told me what to say. [20]He did it to place the matter before you in a different light. But you are as wise as an angel of God, and you understand everything that happens among us!"

[21]So the king sent for Joab and told him, "All right, go and bring back the young man Absalom."

[22]Joab bowed with his face to the ground in deep respect and said, "At last I know that I have gained your approval, my lord the king, for you have granted me this request!"

[23]Then Joab went to Geshur and brought Absalom back to Jerusalem. [24]But the king gave this order: "Absalom may go to his own house, but he must never come into my presence." So Absalom did not see the king.

Absalom Reconciled to David

[25]Now Absalom was praised as the most handsome man in all Israel. He was flawless from head to foot. [26]He cut his hair only once a year, and then only because it was so heavy. When he weighed it out, it came to five pounds!* [27]He had three sons and one daughter. His daughter's name was Tamar, and she was very beautiful.

[28]Absalom lived in Jerusalem for two years, but he never got to see the king. [29]Then Absalom sent for Joab to ask him to intercede for him, but Joab refused to come. Absalom sent for him a second time, but again Joab refused to come. [30]So Absa-

lom said to his servants, "Go and set fire to Joab's barley field, the field next to mine." So they set his field on fire, as Absalom had commanded.

[31]Then Joab came to Absalom at his house and demanded, "Why did your servants set my field on fire?"

[32]And Absalom replied, "Because I wanted you to ask the king why he brought me back from Geshur if he didn't intend to see me. I might as well have stayed there. Let me see the king; if he finds me guilty of anything, then let him kill me."

[33]So Joab told the king what Absalom had said. Then at last David summoned Absalom, who came and bowed low before the king, and the king kissed him.

15 Absalom's Rebellion

After this, Absalom bought a chariot and horses, and he hired fifty bodyguards to run ahead of him. [2]He got up early every morning and went out to the gate of the city. When people brought a case to the king for judgment, Absalom would ask where in Israel they were from, and they would tell him their tribe. [3]Then Absalom would say, "You've really got a strong case here! It's too bad the king doesn't have anyone to hear it. [4]I wish I were the judge. Then everyone could bring their cases to me for judgment, and I would give them justice!"

[5]When people tried to bow before him, Absalom wouldn't let them. Instead, he took them by the hand and kissed them. [6]Absalom did this with everyone who came to the king for judgment, and so he stole the hearts of all the people of Israel.

[7]After four years,* Absalom said to the king, "Let me go to Hebron to offer a sacrifice to the LORD and fulfill a vow I made to him. [8]For while your servant was at Geshur in Aram, I promised to sacrifice to the LORD in Hebron* if he would bring me back to Jerusalem."

[9]"All right," the king told him. "Go and fulfill your vow."

So Absalom went to Hebron. [10]But while he was there, he sent secret messengers to all the tribes of Israel to stir up a rebellion against the king. "As soon as you hear the

---

14:16 Or the property; or the people.   **14:26** Hebrew 200 shekels [2.3 kilograms] by the royal standard.   **15:7** As in Greek and Syriac versions; Hebrew reads forty years.   **15:8** As in some Greek manuscripts; Hebrew lacks in Hebron.

ram's horn," his message read, "you are to say, 'Absalom has been crowned king in Hebron.'" [11] He took 200 men from Jerusalem with him as guests, but they knew nothing of his intentions. [12] While Absalom was offering the sacrifices, he sent for Ahithophel, one of David's counselors who lived in Giloh. Soon many others also joined Absalom, and the conspiracy gained momentum.

David Escapes from Jerusalem

[13] A messenger soon arrived in Jerusalem to tell David, "All Israel has joined Absalom in a conspiracy against you!"

[14] "Then we must flee at once, or it will be too late!" David urged his men. "Hurry! If we get out of the city before Absalom arrives, both we and the city of Jerusalem will be spared from disaster."

[15] "We are with you," his advisers replied. "Do what you think is best."

[16] So the king and all his household set out at once. He left no one behind except ten of his concubines to look after the palace. [17] The king and all his people set out on foot, pausing at the last house [18] to let all the king's men move past to lead the way. There were 600 men from Gath who had come with David, along with the king's bodyguard.*

[19] Then the king turned and said to Ittai, a leader of the men from Gath, "Why are you coming with us? Go on back to King Absalom, for you are a guest in Israel, a foreigner in exile. [20] You arrived only recently, and should I force you today to wander with us? I don't even know where we will go. Go on back and take your kinsmen with you, and may the LORD show you his unfailing love and faithfulness.*"

[21] But Ittai said to the king, "I vow by the LORD and by your own life that I will go wherever my lord the king goes, no matter what happens—whether it means life or death."

[22] David replied, "All right, come with us." So Ittai and all his men and their families went along.

[23] Everyone cried loudly as the king and his followers passed by. They crossed the Kidron Valley and then went out toward the wilderness.

[24] Zadok and all the Levites also came along, carrying the Ark of the Covenant of God. They set down the Ark of God, and Abiathar offered sacrifices* until everyone had passed out of the city.

[25] Then the king instructed Zadok to take the Ark of God back into the city. "If the LORD sees fit," David said, "he will bring me back to see the Ark and the Tabernacle* again. [26] But if he is through with me, then let him do what seems best to him."

[27] The king also told Zadok the priest, "Look,* here is my plan. You and Abiathar* should return quietly to the city with your son Ahimaaz and Abiathar's son Jonathan. [28] I will stop at the shallows of the Jordan River* and wait there for a report from you." [29] So Zadok and Abiathar took the Ark of God back to the city and stayed there.

[30] David walked up the road to the Mount of Olives, weeping as he went. His head was covered and his feet were bare as a sign of mourning. And the people who were with him covered their heads and wept as they climbed the hill. [31] When someone told David that his adviser Ahithophel was now backing Absalom, David prayed, "O LORD, let Ahithophel give Absalom foolish advice!"

[32] When David reached the summit of the Mount of Olives where people worshiped God, Hushai the Arkite was waiting there for him. Hushai had torn his clothing and put dirt on his head as a sign of mourning. [33] But David told him, "If you go with me, you will only be a burden. [34] Return to Jerusalem and tell Absalom, 'I will now be your adviser, O king, just as I was your father's adviser in the past.' Then you can frustrate and counter Ahithophel's advice. [35] Zadok and Abiathar, the priests, will be there. Tell them about the plans being made in the king's palace, [36] and they will send their sons Ahimaaz and Jonathan to tell me what is going on."

[37] So David's friend Hushai returned to Jerusalem, getting there just as Absalom arrived.

15:18 Hebrew *the Kerethites and Pelethites.* **15:20** As in Greek version; Hebrew reads *and may unfailing love and faithfulness go with you.* **15:24** Or *Abiathar went up.* **15:25** Hebrew *and his dwelling place.* **15:27a** As in Greek version; Hebrew reads *Are you a seer?* or *Do you see?* **15:27b** Hebrew lacks *and Abiathar;* compare 15:29. **15:28** Hebrew *at the crossing points of the wilderness.*

16 David and Ziba

When David had gone a little beyond the summit of the Mount of Olives, Ziba, the servant of Mephibosheth,* was waiting there for him. He had two donkeys loaded with 200 loaves of bread, 100 clusters of raisins, 100 bunches of summer fruit, and a wineskin full of wine.

²"What are these for?" the king asked Ziba.

Ziba replied, "The donkeys are for the king's people to ride on, and the bread and summer fruit are for the young men to eat. The wine is for those who become exhausted in the wilderness."

³"And where is Mephibosheth, Saul's grandson?" the king asked him.

"He stayed in Jerusalem," Ziba replied. "He said, 'Today I will get back the kingdom of my grandfather Saul.'"

⁴"In that case," the king told Ziba, "I give you everything Mephibosheth owns."

"I bow before you," Ziba replied. "May I always be pleasing to you, my lord the king."

Shimei Curses David

⁵As King David came to Bahurim, a man came out of the village cursing them. It was Shimei son of Gera, from the same clan as Saul's family. ⁶He threw stones at the king and the king's officers and all the mighty warriors who surrounded him. ⁷"Get out of here, you murderer, you scoundrel!" he shouted at David. ⁸"The LORD is paying you back for all the bloodshed in Saul's clan. You stole his throne, and now the LORD has given it to your son Absalom. At last you will taste some of your own medicine, for you are a murderer!"

⁹"Why should this dead dog curse my lord the king?" Abishai son of Zeruiah demanded. "Let me go over and cut off his head!"

¹⁰"No!" the king said. "Who asked your opinion, you sons of Zeruiah! If the LORD has told him to curse me, who are you to stop him?"

¹¹Then David said to Abishai and to all his servants, "My own son is trying to kill me. Doesn't this relative of Saul* have even more reason to do so? Leave him alone and

let him curse, for the LORD has told him to do it. ¹²And perhaps the LORD will see that I am being wronged and will bless me because of these curses today." ¹³So David and his men continued down the road, and Shimei kept pace with them on a nearby hillside, cursing as he went and throwing stones at David and tossing dust into the air.

¹⁴The king and all who were with him grew weary along the way, so they rested when they reached the Jordan River.*

Ahithophel Advises Absalom

¹⁵Meanwhile, Absalom and all the army of Israel arrived at Jerusalem, accompanied by Ahithophel. ¹⁶When David's friend Hushai the Arkite arrived, he went immediately to see Absalom. "Long live the king!" he exclaimed. "Long live the king!"

¹⁷"Is this the way you treat your friend David?" Absalom asked him. "Why aren't you with him?"

¹⁸"I'm here because I belong to the man who is chosen by the LORD and by all the men of Israel," Hushai replied. ¹⁹"And anyway, why shouldn't I serve you? Just as I was your father's adviser, now I will be your adviser!"

²⁰Then Absalom turned to Ahithophel and asked him, "What should I do next?"

²¹Ahithophel told him, "Go and sleep with your father's concubines, for he has left them here to look after the palace. Then all Israel will know that you have insulted your father beyond hope of reconciliation, and they will throw their support to you." ²²So they set up a tent on the palace roof where everyone could see it, and Absalom went in and had sex with his father's concubines.

²³Absalom followed Ahithophel's advice, just as David had done. For every word Ahithophel spoke seemed as wise as though it had come directly from the mouth of God.

17 Now Ahithophel urged Absalom, "Let me choose 12,000 men to start out after David tonight. ²I will catch up with him while he is weary and discouraged. He

---

16:1 Mephibosheth is another name for Merib-baal.   16:11 Hebrew this Benjaminite.   16:14 As in Greek version (see also 17:16); Hebrew reads when they reached their destination.

and his troops will panic, and everyone will run away. Then I will kill only the king, ³and I will bring all the people back to you as a bride returns to her husband. After all, it is only one man's life that you seek.* Then you will be at peace with all the people." ⁴This plan seemed good to Absalom and to all the elders of Israel.

Hushai Counters Ahithophel's Advice

⁵But then Absalom said, "Bring in Hushai the Arkite. Let's see what he thinks about this." ⁶When Hushai arrived, Absalom told him what Ahithophel had said. Then he asked, "What is your opinion? Should we follow Ahithophel's advice? If not, what do you suggest?"

⁷"Well," Hushai replied to Absalom, "this time Ahithophel has made a mistake. ⁸You know your father and his men; they are mighty warriors. Right now they are as enraged as a mother bear who has been robbed of her cubs. And remember that your father is an experienced man of war. He won't be spending the night among the troops. ⁹He has probably already hidden in some pit or cave. And when he comes out and attacks and a few of your men fall, there will be panic among your troops, and the word will spread that Absalom's men are being slaughtered. ¹⁰Then even the bravest soldiers, though they have the heart of a lion, will be paralyzed with fear. For all Israel knows what a mighty warrior your father is and how courageous his men are.

¹¹"I recommend that you mobilize the entire army of Israel, bringing them from as far away as Dan in the north and Beersheba in the south. That way you will have an army as numerous as the sand on the seashore. And I advise that you personally lead the troops. ¹²When we find David, we'll fall on him like dew that falls on the ground. Then neither he nor any of his men will be left alive. ¹³And if David were to escape into some town, you will have all Israel there at your command. Then we can take ropes and drag the walls of the town into the nearest valley until every stone is torn down."

¹⁴Then Absalom and all the men of Israel said, "Hushai's advice is better than Ahithophel's." For the LORD had determined to defeat the counsel of Ahithophel, which really was the better plan, so that he could bring disaster on Absalom!

Hushai Warns David to Escape

¹⁵Hushai told Zadok and Abiathar, the priests, what Ahithophel had said to Absalom and the elders of Israel and what he himself had advised instead. ¹⁶"Quick!" he told them. "Find David and urge him not to stay at the shallows of the Jordan River* tonight. He must go across at once into the wilderness beyond. Otherwise he will die and his entire army with him."

¹⁷Jonathan and Ahimaaz had been staying at En-rogel so as not to be seen entering and leaving the city. Arrangements had been made for a servant girl to bring them the message they were to take to King David. ¹⁸But a boy spotted them at En-rogel, and he told Absalom about it. So they quickly escaped to Bahurim, where a man hid them down inside a well in his courtyard. ¹⁹The man's wife put a cloth over the top of the well and scattered grain on it to dry in the sun; so no one suspected they were there.

²⁰When Absalom's men arrived, they asked her, "Have you seen Ahimaaz and Jonathan?"

The woman replied, "They were here, but they crossed over the brook." Absalom's men looked for them without success and returned to Jerusalem.

²¹Then the two men crawled out of the well and hurried on to King David. "Quick!" they told him, "cross the Jordan tonight!" And they told him how Ahithophel had advised that he be captured and killed. ²²So David and all the people with him went across the Jordan River during the night, and they were all on the other bank before dawn.

²³When Ahithophel realized that his advice had not been followed, he saddled his donkey, went to his hometown, set his affairs in order, and hanged himself. He died there and was buried in the family tomb.

17:3 As in Greek version; Hebrew reads *like the return of all is the man whom you seek.*   **17:16** Hebrew *at the crossing points of the wilderness.*

²⁴David soon arrived at Mahanaim. By now, Absalom had mobilized the entire army of Israel and was leading his troops across the Jordan River. ²⁵Absalom had appointed Amasa as commander of his army, replacing Joab, who had been commander under David. (Amasa was Joab's cousin. His father was Jether,* an Ishmaelite.* His mother, Abigail daughter of Nahash, was the sister of Joab's mother, Zeruiah.) ²⁶Absalom and the Israelite army set up camp in the land of Gilead.

²⁷When David arrived at Mahanaim, he was warmly greeted by Shobi son of Nahash, who came from Rabbah of the Ammonites, and by Makir son of Ammiel from Lo-debar, and by Barzillai of Gilead from Rogelim. ²⁸They brought sleeping mats, cooking pots, serving bowls, wheat and barley, flour and roasted grain, beans, lentils, ²⁹honey, butter, sheep, goats, and cheese for David and those who were with him. For they said, "You must all be very hungry and tired and thirsty after your long march through the wilderness."

18 Absalom's Defeat and Death

David now mustered the men who were with him and appointed generals and captains* to lead them. ²He sent the troops out in three groups, placing one group under Joab, one under Joab's brother Abishai son of Zeruiah, and one under Ittai, the man from Gath. The king told his troops, "I am going out with you."

³But his men objected strongly. "You must not go," they urged. "If we have to turn and run—and even if half of us die—it will make no difference to Absalom's troops; they will be looking only for you. You are worth 10,000 of us,* and it is better that you stay here in the town and send help if we need it."

⁴"If you think that's the best plan, I'll do it," the king answered. So he stood alongside the gate of the town as all the troops marched out in groups of hundreds and of thousands.

⁵And the king gave this command to Joab, Abishai, and Ittai: "For my sake, deal gently with young Absalom." And all the troops heard the king give this order to his commanders.

⁶So the battle began in the forest of Ephraim, ⁷and the Israelite troops were beaten back by David's men. There was a great slaughter that day, and 20,000 men laid down their lives. ⁸The battle raged all across the countryside, and more men died because of the forest than were killed by the sword.

⁹During the battle, Absalom happened to come upon some of David's men. He tried to escape on his mule, but as he rode beneath the thick branches of a great tree, his hair* got caught in the tree. His mule kept going and left him dangling in the air. ¹⁰One of David's men saw what had happened and told Joab, "I saw Absalom dangling from a great tree."

¹¹"What?" Joab demanded. "You saw him there and didn't kill him? I would have rewarded you with ten pieces of silver* and a hero's belt!"

¹²"I would not kill the king's son for even a thousand pieces of silver,*" the man replied to Joab. "We all heard the king say to you and Abishai and Ittai, 'For my sake, please spare young Absalom.' ¹³And if I had betrayed the king by killing his son—and the king would certainly find out who did it—you yourself would be the first to abandon me."

¹⁴"Enough of this nonsense," Joab said. Then he took three daggers and plunged them into Absalom's heart as he dangled, still alive, in the great tree. ¹⁵Ten of Joab's young armor bearers then surrounded Absalom and killed him.

¹⁶Then Joab blew the ram's horn, and his men returned from chasing the army of Israel. ¹⁷They threw Absalom's body into a deep pit in the forest and piled a great heap of stones over it. And all Israel fled to their homes.

¹⁸During his lifetime, Absalom had built a monument to himself in the King's Valley, for he said, "I have no son to carry on

---

17:25a Hebrew *Ithra*, a variant spelling of Jether.   **17:25b** As in some Greek manuscripts (see also 1 Chr 2:17); Hebrew reads *an Israelite*. **18:1** Hebrew *appointed commanders of thousands and commanders of hundreds*.   **18:3** As in two Hebrew manuscripts and some Greek and Latin manuscripts; most Hebrew manuscripts read *Now there are 10,000 like us.*   **18:9** Hebrew *his head*.   **18:11** Hebrew *10 shekels of silver*, about 4 ounces or 114 grams in weight.   **18:12** Hebrew *1,000 shekels*, about 25 pounds or 11.4 kilograms in weight.

Forgiveness

Forgiving
When It Seems
Impossible

2 Samuel 18

We were living as missionaries in Europe when we received a life-shattering telephone call. Our twenty-three-year-old son, Tim, had been murdered. He'd suffered at least three close-range bullet wounds in the back of his head, shot by a man named Mike.

As we left to return to the States, a close friend said to me, "Remember, Dianne, God is good. Hold on to this."

Instinctively I responded, "No! I will *never* say, 'My son's been murdered,' and, 'God is good,' in the same sentence!"

My life felt destroyed. My firstborn son had been brutally murdered. *Why* would a good God allow this to happen?

Slowly the facts about what happened that night emerged. Tim's co-worker Donna had an abusive husband. One night Tim offered to give her a ride home. When her enraged husband, Mike, saw them together, he shot Donna five times, then shot Tim. Donna lived—with disabilities. Our son was dead.

Mike pled guilty to first-degree murder; he was sentenced to life in prison.

Since Tim's murder, I've been on a long and difficult road of forgiveness and growth in my faith. Forgiveness, at first, seemed impossible, and even repugnant, to me. Affirming God's goodness felt beyond my abilities.

But a point came at which I realized I had a decision to make: would I trust God or reject him? Even though I had no feelings of forgiveness, God brought me to the point where I could pray, "God, in your strength, I choose to forgive this man." I've had to repeat that prayer over and over, especially as I've experienced the pain of seeing my husband and children go through terrible times of grief. When my family suffered, or we'd learn something new about the murder, I'd have to choose to forgive again.

That first year I felt I'd done all God expected of me. My husband and children were on their own journey toward forgiveness, and I couldn't push them. But as the anniversary of Tim's murder approached, I felt convinced God wanted me to do more. I asked my brother Bill to find out where Mike was so I could contact him. Bill had to go to great lengths to get Mike's address; the prison system doesn't trust the victim's family members with that information.

{ ❖ }

My brother initiated contact with Mike. Eventually I prayerfully and tearfully sent a letter to him through Bill. Mike responded, expressing sorrow for what he'd done. Mike was repentant but didn't feel he deserved God's forgiveness.

I don't know what God will lead me to do in the future. I've done all he's asked, and I'm committed to obey whatever else he wants. If my husband seeks to visit Mike, I'm willing to go along and face him, but I don't believe I could do it on my own.

I know, both from the Bible and from personal experience, that God's command to forgive as he forgives us is for *my* good—it brings release from the destructive forces of bitterness and anger.

Obviously forgiveness doesn't excuse the terrible crime of murder, nor does it mean that Mike doesn't deserve his punishment. It in no way diminishes the horror that this one man's choice wreaked in my life and the lives of my loved ones. For me forgiveness means that I choose to release my "right" for revenge or judgment. Scripture calls us to leave the issue of revenge in God's hands and assures us of his justice (Romans 12:19). Repeatedly I reaffirm that Mike is in God's hands—and I pray he'll experience not just God's justice, but also God's love and forgiveness.

Has my pain gone away? No. I don't expect ever to be free from the pain of losing my son. As another grieving parent expressed, "It never becomes easy, but it does become more bearable." But I don't grieve as someone without hope (1 Thessalonians 4:13). I know that Tim, who asked Jesus to be his Savior when he was four years old, is in heaven and that someday I'll see him again.

Ultimately I'm able to have this hope because Jesus rose from the dead. Though I will not see my son again in this world, and though that reality is still painful, Christ's resurrection gives me a hope that's beyond this earthly life. The same power that raised Jesus from the grave that early Sunday morning is the very power that saved me from my sin and changed my (and my son's) destination from hell to heaven. It's that power that enables me to have hope in the midst of despair and this world's evil.

We've permanently engraved Tim's tombstone, "Life is not fair, but God is good." My cry of "why?" is engulfed in the goodness of God—my reason for life and hope.

—*Dianne Collard*

For more on forgiveness, see reading at 2 Kings 5:1–19.

my name." He named the monument after himself, and it is known as Absalom's Monument to this day.

David Mourns Absalom's Death

¹⁹Then Zadok's son Ahimaaz said, "Let me run to the king with the good news that the LORD has rescued him from his enemies."

²⁰"No," Joab told him, "it wouldn't be good news to the king that his son is dead. You can be my messenger another time, but not today."

²¹Then Joab said to a man from Ethiopia,* "Go tell the king what you have seen." The man bowed and ran off.

²²But Ahimaaz continued to plead with Joab, "Whatever happens, please let me go, too."

"Why should you go, my son?" Joab replied. "There will be no reward for your news."

²³"Yes, but let me go anyway," he begged.

Joab finally said, "All right, go ahead." So Ahimaaz took the less demanding route by way of the plain and ran to Mahanaim ahead of the Ethiopian.

²⁴While David was sitting between the inner and outer gates of the town, the watchman climbed to the roof of the gateway by the wall. As he looked, he saw a lone man running toward them. ²⁵He shouted the news down to David, and the king replied, "If he is alone, he has news."

As the messenger came closer, ²⁶the watchman saw another man running toward them. He shouted down, "Here comes another one!"

The king replied, "He also will have news."

²⁷"The first man runs like Ahimaaz son of Zadok," the watchman said.

"He is a good man and comes with good news," the king replied.

²⁸Then Ahimaaz cried out to the king, "Everything is all right!" He bowed before the king with his face to the ground and said, "Praise to the LORD your God, who has handed over the rebels who dared to stand against my lord the king."

²⁹"What about young Absalom?" the king demanded. "Is he all right?"

Ahimaaz replied, "When Joab told me to come, there was a lot of commotion. But I didn't know what was happening."

³⁰"Wait here," the king told him. So Ahimaaz stepped aside.

³¹Then the man from Ethiopia arrived and said, "I have good news for my lord the king. Today the LORD has rescued you from all those who rebelled against you."

³²"What about young Absalom?" the king demanded. "Is he all right?"

And the Ethiopian replied, "May all of your enemies, my lord the king, both now and in the future, share the fate of that young man!"

³³*The king was overcome with emotion. He went up to the room over the gateway and burst into tears. And as he went, he cried, "O my son Absalom! My son, my son Absalom! If only I had died instead of you! O Absalom, my son, my son."

19 Joab Rebukes the King

¹*Word soon reached Joab that the king was weeping and mourning for Absalom. ²As all the people heard of the king's deep grief for his son, the joy of that day's victory was turned into deep sadness. ³They crept back into the town that day as though they were ashamed and had deserted in battle. ⁴The king covered his face with his hands and kept on crying, "O my son Absalom! O Absalom, my son, my son!"

⁵Then Joab went to the king's room and said to him, "We saved your life today and the lives of your sons, your daughters, and your wives and concubines. Yet you act like this, making us feel ashamed of ourselves. ⁶You seem to love those who hate you and hate those who love you. You have made it clear today that your commanders and troops mean nothing to you. It seems that if Absalom had lived and all of us had died, you would be pleased. ⁷Now go out there and congratulate your troops, for I swear by the LORD that if you don't go out, not a single one of them will remain here tonight. Then you will be worse off than ever before."

⁸So the king went out and took his seat at the town gate, and as the news spread throughout the town that he was there, everyone went to him.

18:21 Hebrew from Cush; similarly in 18:23, 31, 32.   18:33 Verse 18:33 is numbered 19:1 in Hebrew text.   19:1 Verses 19:1-43 are numbered 19:2-44 in Hebrew text.

Meanwhile, the Israelites who had supported Absalom fled to their homes. 9And throughout all the tribes of Israel there was much discussion and argument going on. The people were saying, "The king rescued us from our enemies and saved us from the Philistines, but Absalom chased him out of the country. 10Now Absalom, whom we anointed to rule over us, is dead. Why not ask David to come back and be our king again?"

11Then King David sent Zadok and Abiathar, the priests, to say to the elders of Judah, "Why are you the last ones to welcome back the king into his palace? For I have heard that all Israel is ready. 12You are my relatives, my own tribe, my own flesh and blood! So why are you the last ones to welcome back the king?" 13And David told them to tell Amasa, "Since you are my own flesh and blood, like Joab, may God strike me and even kill me if I do not appoint you as commander of my army in his place."

14Then Amasa* convinced all the men of Judah, and they responded unanimously. They sent word to the king, "Return to us, and bring back all who are with you."

David's Return to Jerusalem

15So the king started back to Jerusalem. And when he arrived at the Jordan River, the people of Judah came to Gilgal to meet him and escort him across the river. 16Shimei son of Gera, the man from Bahurim in Benjamin, hurried across with the men of Judah to welcome King David. 17A thousand other men from the tribe of Benjamin were with him, including Ziba, the chief servant of the house of Saul, and Ziba's fifteen sons and twenty servants. They rushed down to the Jordan to meet the king. 18They crossed the shallows of the Jordan to bring the king's household across the river, helping him in every way they could.

David's Mercy to Shimei

As the king was about to cross the river, Shimei fell down before him. 19"My lord the king, please forgive me," he pleaded. "Forget the terrible thing your servant did when you left Jerusalem. May the king put it out

of his mind. 20I know how much I sinned. That is why I have come here today, the very first person in all Israel* to greet my lord the king."

21Then Abishai son of Zeruiah said, "Shimei should die, for he cursed the LORD's anointed king!"

22"Who asked your opinion, you sons of Zeruiah!" David exclaimed. "Why have you become my adversary* today? This is not a day for execution but for celebration! Today I am once again the king of Israel!" 23Then, turning to Shimei, David vowed, "Your life will be spared."

David's Kindness to Mephibosheth

24Now Mephibosheth,* Saul's grandson, came down from Jerusalem to meet the king. He had not cared for his feet, trimmed his beard, or washed his clothes since the day the king left Jerusalem. 25"Why didn't you come with me, Mephibosheth?" the king asked him.

26Mephibosheth replied, "My lord the king, my servant Ziba deceived me. I told him, 'Saddle my donkey* so I can go with the king.' For as you know I am crippled. 27Ziba has slandered me by saying that I refused to come. But I know that my lord the king is like an angel of God, so do what you think is best. 28All my relatives and I could expect only death from you, my lord, but instead you have honored me by allowing me to eat at your own table! What more can I ask?"

29"You've said enough," David replied. "I've decided that you and Ziba will divide your land equally between you."

30"Give him all of it," Mephibosheth said. "I am content just to have you safely back again, my lord the king!"

David's Kindness to Barzillai

31Barzillai of Gilead had come down from Rogelim to escort the king across the Jordan. 32He was very old, about eighty, and very wealthy. He was the one who had provided food for the king during his stay in Mahanaim. 33"Come across with me and live in Jerusalem," the king said to Barzillai. "I will take care of you there."

19:14 Or David; Hebrew reads he.   19:20 Hebrew in the house of Joseph.   19:22 Or my prosecutor.   19:24 Mephibosheth is another name for Merib-baal.   19:26 As in Greek, Syriac, and Latin versions; Hebrew reads I will saddle a donkey for myself.

[34]"No," he replied, "I am far too old to go with the king to Jerusalem. [35]I am eighty years old today, and I can no longer enjoy anything. Food and wine are no longer tasty, and I cannot hear the singers as they sing. I would only be a burden to my lord the king. [36]Just to go across the Jordan River with the king is all the honor I need! [37]Then let me return again to die in my own town, where my father and mother are buried. But here is your servant, my son Kimham. Let him go with my lord the king and receive whatever you want to give him."

[38]"Good," the king agreed. "Kimham will go with me, and I will help him in any way you would like. And I will do for you anything you want." [39]So all the people crossed the Jordan with the king. After David had blessed Barzillai and kissed him, Barzillai returned to his own home.

[40]The king then crossed over to Gilgal, taking Kimham with him. All the troops of Judah and half the troops of Israel escorted the king on his way.

An Argument over the King

[41]But all the men of Israel complained to the king, "The men of Judah stole the king and didn't give us the honor of helping take you, your household, and all your men across the Jordan."

[42]The men of Judah replied, "The king is one of our own kinsmen. Why should this make you angry? We haven't eaten any of the king's food or received any special favors!"

[43]"But there are ten tribes in Israel," the others replied. "So we have ten times as much right to the king as you do. What right do you have to treat us with such contempt? Weren't we the first to speak of bringing him back to be our king again?" The argument continued back and forth, and the men of Judah spoke even more harshly than the men of Israel.

20 The Revolt of Sheba

There happened to be a troublemaker there named Sheba son of Bicri, a man from the tribe of Benjamin. Sheba blew a ram's horn and began to chant:

"Down with the dynasty of David!
    We have no interest in the son of Jesse.
Come on, you men of Israel,
    back to your homes!"

[2]So all the men of Israel deserted David and followed Sheba son of Bicri. But the men of Judah stayed with their king and escorted him from the Jordan River to Jerusalem.

[3]When David came to his palace in Jerusalem, he took the ten concubines he had left to look after the palace and placed them in seclusion. Their needs were provided for, but he no longer slept with them. So each of them lived like a widow until she died.

[4]Then the king told Amasa, "Mobilize the army of Judah within three days, and report back at that time." [5]So Amasa went out to notify Judah, but it took him longer than the time he had been given.

[6]Then David said to Abishai, "Sheba son of Bicri is going to hurt us more than Absalom did. Quick, take my troops and chase after him before he gets into a fortified town where we can't reach him."

[7]So Abishai and Joab,* together with the king's bodyguard* and all the mighty warriors, set out from Jerusalem to go after Sheba. [8]As they arrived at the great stone in Gibeon, Amasa met them. Joab was wearing his military tunic with a dagger strapped to his belt. As he stepped forward to greet Amasa, he slipped the dagger from its sheath.*

[9]"How are you, my cousin?" Joab said and took him by the beard with his right hand as though to kiss him. [10]Amasa didn't notice the dagger in his left hand, and Joab stabbed him in the stomach with it so that his insides gushed out onto the ground. Joab did not need to strike again, and Amasa soon died. Joab and his brother Abishai left him lying there and continued after Sheba.

[11]One of Joab's young men shouted to Amasa's troops, "If you are for Joab and David, come and follow Joab." [12]But Amasa lay in his blood in the middle of the road, and Joab's man saw that everyone was stopping to stare at him. So he pulled him off the road into a field and threw a cloak over

---

20:7a Hebrew *So Joab's men.*   **20:7b** Hebrew *the Kerethites and Pelethites;* also in 20:23.   **20:8** Hebrew *As he stepped forward, it fell out.*

him. ¹³With Amasa's body out of the way, everyone went on with Joab to capture Sheba son of Bicri.

¹⁴Meanwhile, Sheba traveled through all the tribes of Israel and eventually came to the town of Abel-beth-maacah. All the members of his own clan, the Bicrites,* assembled for battle and followed him into the town. ¹⁵When Joab's forces arrived, they attacked Abel-beth-maacah. They built a siege ramp against the town's fortifications and began battering down the wall. ¹⁶But a wise woman in the town called out to Joab, "Listen to me, Joab. Come over here so I can talk to you." ¹⁷As he approached, the woman asked, "Are you Joab?"

"I am," he replied.

So she said, "Listen carefully to your servant."

"I'm listening," he said.

¹⁸Then she continued, "There used to be a saying, 'If you want to settle an argument, ask advice at the town of Abel.' ¹⁹I am one who is peace loving and faithful in Israel. But you are destroying an important town in Israel.* Why do you want to devour what belongs to the LORD?"

²⁰And Joab replied, "Believe me, I don't want to devour or destroy your town! ²¹That's not my purpose. All I want is a man named Sheba son of Bicri from the hill country of Ephraim, who has revolted against King David. If you hand over this one man to me, I will leave the town in peace."

"All right," the woman replied, "we will throw his head over the wall to you." ²²Then the woman went to all the people with her wise advice, and they cut off Sheba's head and threw it out to Joab. So he blew the ram's horn and called his troops back from the attack. They all returned to their homes, and Joab returned to the king at Jerusalem.

²³Now Joab was the commander of the army of Israel. Benaiah son of Jehoiada was captain of the king's bodyguard. ²⁴Adoniram* was in charge of the labor force. Jehoshaphat son of Ahilud was the royal historian. ²⁵Sheva was the court secretary. Zadok and Abiathar were the priests. ²⁶And Ira, a descendant of Jair, was David's personal priest.

21 David Avenges the Gibeonites

There was a famine during David's reign that lasted for three years, so David asked the LORD about it. And the LORD said, "The famine has come because Saul and his family are guilty of murdering the Gibeonites."

²So the king summoned the Gibeonites. They were not part of Israel but were all that was left of the nation of the Amorites. The people of Israel had sworn not to kill them, but Saul, in his zeal for Israel and Judah, had tried to wipe them out. ³David asked them, "What can I do for you? How can I make amends so that you will bless the LORD's people again?"

⁴"Well, money can't settle this matter between us and the family of Saul," the Gibeonites replied. "Neither can we demand the life of anyone in Israel."

"What can I do then?" David asked. "Just tell me and I will do it for you."

⁵Then they replied, "It was Saul who planned to destroy us, to keep us from having any place at all in the territory of Israel. ⁶So let seven of Saul's sons be handed over to us, and we will execute them before the LORD at Gibeon, on the mountain of the LORD.*"

"All right," the king said, "I will do it." ⁷The king spared Jonathan's son Mephibosheth,* who was Saul's grandson, because of the oath David and Jonathan had sworn before the LORD. ⁸But he gave them Saul's two sons Armoni and Mephibosheth, whose mother was Rizpah daughter of Aiah. He also gave them the five sons of Saul's daughter Merab,* the wife of Adriel son of Barzillai from Meholah. ⁹The men of Gibeon executed them on the mountain before the LORD. So all seven of them died together at the beginning of the barley harvest.

¹⁰Then Rizpah daughter of Aiah, the mother of two of the men, spread burlap on a rock and stayed there the entire harvest

---

20:14 As in Greek and Latin versions; Hebrew reads *All the Berites.*   20:19 Hebrew *a town that is a mother in Israel.*   20:24 As in Greek version (see also 1 Kgs 4:6; 5:14); Hebrew reads *Adoram.*   21:6 As in Greek version (see also 21:9); Hebrew reads *at Gibeah of Saul, the chosen of the LORD.*   21:7 *Mephibosheth* is another name for Merib-baal.   21:8 As in a few Hebrew and Greek manuscripts and Syriac version (see also 1 Sam 18:19); most Hebrew manuscripts read *Michal.*

season. She prevented the scavenger birds from tearing at their bodies during the day and stopped wild animals from eating them at night. [11] When David learned what Rizpah, Saul's concubine, had done, [12] he went to the people of Jabesh-gilead and retrieved the bones of Saul and his son Jonathan. (When the Philistines had killed Saul and Jonathan on Mount Gilboa, the people of Jabesh-gilead stole their bodies from the public square of Beth-shan, where the Philistines had hung them.) [13] So David obtained the bones of Saul and Jonathan, as well as the bones of the men the Gibeonites had executed.

[14] Then the king ordered that they bury the bones in the tomb of Kish, Saul's father, at the town of Zela in the land of Benjamin. After that, God ended the famine in the land.

Battles against Philistine Giants

[15] Once again the Philistines were at war with Israel. And when David and his men were in the thick of battle, David became weak and exhausted. [16] Ishbi-benob was a descendant of the giants*; his bronze spearhead weighed more than seven pounds,* and he was armed with a new sword. He had cornered David and was about to kill him. [17] But Abishai son of Zeruiah came to David's rescue and killed the Philistine. Then David's men declared, "You are not going out to battle with us again! Why risk snuffing out the light of Israel?"

[18] After this, there was another battle against the Philistines at Gob. As they fought, Sibbecai from Hushah killed Saph, another descendant of the giants.

[19] During another battle at Gob, Elhanan son of Jair* from Bethlehem killed the brother of Goliath of Gath.* The handle of his spear was as thick as a weaver's beam!

[20] In another battle with the Philistines at Gath, they encountered a huge man with six fingers on each hand and six toes on each foot, twenty-four in all, who was also a descendant of the giants. [21] But when he defied and taunted Israel, he was killed

by Jonathan, the son of David's brother Shimea.*

[22] These four Philistines were descendants of the giants of Gath, but David and his warriors killed them.

22 David's Song of Praise

David sang this song to the LORD on the day the LORD rescued him from all his enemies and from Saul. [2] He sang:

"The LORD is my rock, my fortress, and my savior;
[3]   my God is my rock, in whom I find protection.
He is my shield, the power that saves me, and my place of safety.
He is my refuge, my savior, the one who saves me from violence.
[4] I called on the LORD, who is worthy of praise,
    and he saved me from my enemies.

[5] "The waves of death overwhelmed me; floods of destruction swept over me.
[6] The grave* wrapped its ropes around me; death laid a trap in my path.
[7] But in my distress I cried out to the LORD;
    yes, I cried to my God for help.
He heard me from his sanctuary; my cry reached his ears.

[8] "Then the earth quaked and trembled. The foundations of the heavens shook;
    they quaked because of his anger.
[9] Smoke poured from his nostrils; fierce flames leaped from his mouth. Glowing coals blazed forth from him.
[10] He opened the heavens and came down; dark storm clouds were beneath his feet.
[11] Mounted on a mighty angelic being,* he flew,
    soaring* on the wings of the wind.
[12] He shrouded himself in darkness, veiling his approach with dense rain clouds.
[13] A great brightness shone around him, and burning coals* blazed forth.

21:16a Or *a descendant of the Rapha;* also in 21:18, 20, 22.   **21:16b** Hebrew *300 shekels* [3.4 kilograms].   **21:19a** As in parallel text at 1 Chr 20:5; Hebrew reads *son of Jaare-oregim.*   **21:19b** As in parallel text at 1 Chr 20:5; Hebrew reads *killed Goliath of Gath.*   **21:21** As in parallel text at 1 Chr 20:7; Hebrew reads *Shimei,* a variant spelling of Shimea.   **22:6** Hebrew *Sheol.*   **22:11a** Hebrew *a cherub.*   **22:11b** As in some Hebrew manuscripts (see also Ps 18:10); other Hebrew manuscripts read *appearing.*   **22:13** Or *and lightning bolts.*

¹⁴ The LORD thundered from heaven;
　　the voice of the Most High resounded.
¹⁵ He shot arrows and scattered his
　　　enemies;
　　his lightning flashed, and they were
　　　confused.
¹⁶ Then at the command of the LORD,
　　at the blast of his breath,
　　the bottom of the sea could be seen,
　　and the foundations of the earth were
　　　laid bare.
¹⁷ "He reached down from heaven and
　　　rescued me;
　　he drew me out of deep waters.
¹⁸ He rescued me from my powerful enemies,
　　from those who hated me and were too
　　　strong for me.
¹⁹ They attacked me at a moment when I
　　　was in distress,
　　but the LORD supported me.
²⁰ He led me to a place of safety;
　　he rescued me because he delights
　　　in me.
²¹ The LORD rewarded me for doing right;
　　he restored me because of my
　　　innocence.
²² For I have kept the ways of the LORD;
　　I have not turned from my God to
　　　follow evil.
²³ I have followed all his regulations;
　　I have never abandoned his decrees.
²⁴ I am blameless before God;
　　I have kept myself from sin.
²⁵ The LORD rewarded me for doing right.
　　He has seen my innocence.

²⁶ "To the faithful you show yourself
　　　faithful;
　　to those with integrity you show
　　　integrity.
²⁷ To the pure you show yourself pure,
　　but to the wicked you show yourself
　　　hostile.
²⁸ You rescue the humble,
　　but your eyes watch the proud and
　　　humiliate them.
²⁹ O LORD, you are my lamp.
　　The LORD lights up my darkness.
³⁰ In your strength I can crush an army;
　　with my God I can scale any wall.

³¹ "God's way is perfect.
　　All the LORD's promises prove true.
　　He is a shield for all who look to him
　　　for protection.
³² For who is God except the LORD?
　　Who but our God is a solid rock?
³³ God is my strong fortress,
　　and he makes my way perfect.
³⁴ He makes me as surefooted as a deer,
　　enabling me to stand on mountain
　　　heights.
³⁵ He trains my hands for battle;
　　he strengthens my arm to draw a
　　　bronze bow.
³⁶ You have given me your shield of victory;
　　your help* has made me great.
³⁷ You have made a wide path for my feet
　　to keep them from slipping.

³⁸ "I chased my enemies and destroyed
　　　them;
　　I did not stop until they were
　　　conquered.
³⁹ I consumed them;
　　I struck them down so they did not
　　　get up;
　　they fell beneath my feet.
⁴⁰ You have armed me with strength for
　　　the battle;
　　you have subdued my enemies under
　　　my feet.
⁴¹ You placed my foot on their necks.
　　I have destroyed all who hated me.
⁴² They looked for help, but no one came
　　to their rescue.
　　They even cried to the LORD, but he
　　　refused to answer.
⁴³ I ground them as fine as the dust of the
　　　earth;
　　I trampled them* in the gutter like dirt.

⁴⁴ "You gave me victory over my accusers.
　　You preserved me as the ruler over
　　　nations;
　　people I don't even know now
　　　serve me.
⁴⁵ Foreign nations cringe before me;
　　as soon as they hear of me, they submit.
⁴⁶ They all lose their courage
　　and come trembling* from their
　　　strongholds.

22:36 As in Dead Sea Scrolls (see also Ps 18:35); Masoretic Text reads *your answering.* 　22:43 As in Dead Sea Scrolls (see also Ps 18:42); Masoretic Text reads *I crushed and trampled them.* 　22:46 As in parallel text at Ps 18:45; Hebrew reads *come girding themselves.*

47 "The LORD lives! Praise to my Rock!
   May God, the Rock of my salvation, be
   exalted!
48 He is the God who pays back those who
   harm me;
   he brings down the nations under me
49 and delivers me from my enemies.
   You hold me safe beyond the reach of
   my enemies;
   you save me from violent opponents.
50 For this, O LORD, I will praise you
   among the nations;
   I will sing praises to your name.
51 You give great victories to your king;

you show unfailing love to your
   anointed,
to David and all his descendants
   forever."

23 David's Last Words

These are the last words of David:

"David, the son of Jesse, speaks—
   David, the man who was raised up so
   high,
David, the man anointed by the God of
   Jacob,
   David, the sweet psalmist of Israel.*

Q&A { A Lifestyle of Gratitude } Gratitude

2 SAMUEL 22:47–51

How can I make practicing gratitude a lifestyle?

The spiritual discipline of gratitude is really about a change of heart. For me it began as I asked myself what I really wanted to become in life. Who did I want to be? I realized I didn't want to be a whiner—instead, I wanted to be a contented, life-giving person. So I began to take bad attitudes captive (2 Corinthians 10:5) and say, "Thank you, God." I made the decision to acknowledge God's presence and worship him.

Picture your heart and soul like a garden. Whatever you sow, water, fertilize, and care for, *that's* what will grow. Gratitude and joy are what I want to grow, so those are the things I intentionally care for and cultivate. I'm clear about planting the seeds, plucking the weeds, and intentionally guarding my heart against those things that kill my joy and gratefulness. It's hard work, but it bears the fruit of joy.

I have two daily habits that plant the seeds of gratitude in my life. I don't get out of bed until I've told God what I'm grateful for, and every night I don't close my eyes until I thank God for what he's done that day.

Gratitude doesn't just "happen." We need a plan; we need to form purposeful habits. It takes constant vigilance—and that's why it's called the *discipline* of gratitude.

—Sally Clarkson

For more on gratitude, see reading at Job 12.

23:1 Or *the favorite subject of the songs of Israel; or the favorite of the Strong One of Israel.*

2 "The Spirit of the LORD speaks
through me;
his words are upon my tongue.
3 The God of Israel spoke.
The Rock of Israel said to me:
'The one who rules righteously,
who rules in the fear of God,
4 is like the light of morning at sunrise,
like a morning without clouds,
like the gleaming of the sun
on new grass after rain.'

5 "Is it not my family God has chosen?
Yes, he has made an everlasting
covenant with me.
His agreement is arranged and
guaranteed in every detail.
He will ensure my safety and success.
6 But the godless are like thorns to be
thrown away,
for they tear the hand that touches
them.
7 One must use iron tools to chop them
down;
they will be totally consumed by fire."

David's Mightiest Warriors

8 These are the names of David's mightiest warriors. The first was Jashobeam the Hacmonite,* who was leader of the Three*— the three mightiest warriors among David's men. He once used his spear to kill 800 enemy warriors in a single battle.*

9 Next in rank among the Three was Eleazar son of Dodai, a descendant of Ahoah. Once Eleazar and David stood together against the Philistines when the entire Israelite army had fled. 10 He killed Philistines until his hand was too tired to lift his sword, and the LORD gave him a great victory that day. The rest of the army did not return until it was time to collect the plunder!

11 Next in rank was Shammah son of Agee from Harar. One time the Philistines gathered at Lehi and attacked the Israelites in a field full of lentils. The Israelite army fled, 12 but Shammah* held his ground in the middle of the field and beat back the Philistines. So the LORD brought about a great victory.

13 Once during the harvest, when David was at the cave of Adullam, the Philistine army was camped in the valley of Rephaim. The Three (who were among the Thirty— an elite group among David's fighting men) went down to meet him there. 14 David was staying in the stronghold at the time, and a Philistine detachment had occupied the town of Bethlehem.

15 David remarked longingly to his men, "Oh, how I would love some of that good water from the well by the gate in Bethlehem." 16 So the Three broke through the Philistine lines, drew some water from the well by the gate in Bethlehem, and brought it back to David. But he refused to drink it. Instead, he poured it out as an offering to the LORD. 17 "The LORD forbid that I should drink this!" he exclaimed. "This water is as precious as the blood of these men* who risked their lives to bring it to me." So David did not drink it. These are examples of the exploits of the Three.

David's Thirty Mighty Men

18 Abishai son of Zeruiah, the brother of Joab, was the leader of the Thirty.* He once used his spear to kill 300 enemy warriors in a single battle. It was by such feats that he became as famous as the Three. 19 Abishai was the most famous of the Thirty* and was their commander, though he was not one of the Three.

20 There was also Benaiah son of Jehoiada, a valiant warrior* from Kabzeel. He did many heroic deeds, which included killing two champions* of Moab. Another time, on a snowy day, he chased a lion down into a pit and killed it. 21 Once, armed only with a club, he killed a great Egyptian warrior who was armed with a spear. Benaiah wrenched the spear from the Egyptian's hand and killed him with it. 22 Deeds like these made Benaiah as famous as the Three mightiest warriors. 23 He was more honored than the other members of the Thirty, though he was not one of the Three. And David made him captain of his bodyguard.

24 Other members of the Thirty included:

23:8a As in parallel text at 1 Chr 11:11; Hebrew reads *Josheb-basshebeth the Tahkemonite.* 23:8b As in Greek and Latin versions (see also 1 Chr 11:11); the meaning of the Hebrew is uncertain. 23:8c As in some Greek manuscripts (see also 1 Chr 11:11); the meaning of the Hebrew is uncertain, though it might be rendered *the Three. It was Adino the Eznite who killed 800 men at one time.* 23:12 Hebrew *he.* 23:17 Hebrew *Shall I drink the blood of these men?* 23:18 As in a few Hebrew manuscripts and Syriac version; most Hebrew manuscripts read *the Three.* 23:19 As in Syriac version; Hebrew reads *the Three.* 23:20a Or *son of Jehoiada, son of Ish-hai.* 23:20b Hebrew *two of Ariel.*

Asahel, Joab's brother;
Elhanan son of Dodo from Bethlehem;
25 Shammah from Harod;
Elika from Harod;
26 Helez from Pelon*;
Ira son of Ikkesh from Tekoa;
27 Abiezer from Anathoth;
Sibbecai* from Hushah;
28 Zalmon from Ahoah;
Maharai from Netophah;
29 Heled* son of Baanah from Netophah;
Ithai* son of Ribai from Gibeah (in the
land of Benjamin);
30 Benaiah from Pirathon;
Hurai* from Nahale-gaash*;
31 Abi-albon from Arabah;
Azmaveth from Bahurim;
32 Eliahba from Shaalbon;
the sons of Jashen;
Jonathan 33son of Shagee* from Harar;
Ahiam son of Sharar from Harar;
34 Eliphelet son of Ahasbai from Maacah;
Eliam son of Ahithophel from Giloh;
35 Hezro from Carmel;
Paarai from Arba;
36 Igal son of Nathan from Zobah;
Bani from Gad;
37 Zelek from Ammon;
Naharai from Beeroth, Joab's armor
bearer;
38 Ira from Jattir;
Gareb from Jattir;
39 Uriah the Hittite.

There were thirty-seven in all.

24 David Takes a Census

Once again the anger of the LORD
burned against Israel, and he caused David
to harm them by taking a census. "Go and
count the people of Israel and Judah," the
LORD told him.

2 So the king said to Joab and the commanders* of the army, "Take a census of all
the tribes of Israel—from Dan in the north
to Beersheba in the south—so I may know
how many people there are."

3 But Joab replied to the king, "May the
LORD your God let you live to see a hundred times as many people as there are
now! But why, my lord the king, do you
want to do this?"

4 But the king insisted that they take the
census, so Joab and the commanders of
the army went out to count the people of
Israel. 5 First they crossed the Jordan and
camped at Aroer, south of the town in the
valley, in the direction of Gad. Then they
went on to Jazer, 6 then to Gilead in the
land of Tahtim-hodshi* and to Dan-jaan
and around to Sidon. 7 Then they came to
the fortress of Tyre, and all the towns of the
Hivites and Canaanites. Finally, they went
south to Judah* as far as Beersheba.

8 Having gone through the entire land for
nine months and twenty days, they returned
to Jerusalem. 9 Joab reported the number
of people to the king. There were 800,000
capable warriors in Israel who could handle
a sword, and 500,000 in Judah.

Judgment for David's Sin

10 But after he had taken the census, David's
conscience began to bother him. And he
said to the LORD, "I have sinned greatly by
taking this census. Please forgive my guilt,
LORD, for doing this foolish thing."

11 The next morning the word of the LORD
came to the prophet Gad, who was David's
seer. This was the message: 12 "Go and say
to David, 'This is what the LORD says: I will
give you three choices. Choose one of these
punishments, and I will inflict it on you.'"

13 So Gad came to David and asked him,
"Will you choose three* years of famine
throughout your land, three months of
fleeing from your enemies, or three days of
severe plague throughout your land? Think
this over and decide what answer I should
give the LORD who sent me."

14 "I'm in a desperate situation!" David
replied to Gad. "But let us fall into the
hands of the LORD, for his mercy is great.
Do not let me fall into human hands."

15 So the LORD sent a plague upon Israel
that morning, and it lasted for three days.*

23:26 As in parallel text at 1 Chr 11:27 (see also 1 Chr 27:10); Hebrew reads from Palti. 23:27 As in some Greek manuscripts (see also
1 Chr 11:29); Hebrew reads Mebunnai. 23:29a As in some Hebrew manuscripts (see also 1 Chr 11:30); most Hebrew manuscripts read
Heleb. 23:29b As in parallel text at 1 Chr 11:31; Hebrew reads Ittai. 23:30a As in some Greek manuscripts (see also 1 Chr 11:32);
Hebrew reads Hiddai. 23:30b Or from the ravines of Gaash. 23:33 As in parallel text at 1 Chr 11:34; Hebrew reads Jonathan, Shammah;
some Greek manuscripts read Jonathan son of Shammah. 24:2 As in Greek version (see also 24:4 and 1 Chr 21:2); Hebrew reads Joab the
commander. 24:6 Greek version reads to Gilead and to Kadesh in the land of the Hittites. 24:7 Or they went to the Negev of Judah. 24:13 As
in Greek version (see also 1 Chr 21:12); Hebrew reads seven. 24:15 Hebrew for the designated time.

The Gift of Guilt

2 SAMUEL 24

Love means never having to say you're sorry," proclaimed a sappy romance novel from the 1970s. I've come to believe the opposite, that love means precisely having to say you're sorry. A sense of guilt, vastly underappreciated, deserves our gratitude, for only such a powerful force can nudge us toward repentance and reconciliation with those we've harmed.

Yet guilt represents danger as well. I've known Christians who go through life with hyperattention to defects. Some raised in oppressive environments go through life afraid, heads down, fleeing anything that might be perceived as pleasure, and terrified that they're somehow offending one of God's laws.

Martin Luther, in his early days as a monk, would daily wear out his confessors with as many as six straight hours of introspection about minuscule sins and unhealthy thoughts. "My son, God is not angry with you: it is you who are angry with God," said one of his exasperated advisers. Luther eventually came to agree that his fear of sinning actually showed a lack of faith, both in his ability to live purely in an impure world and in Christ's provision for his sin. "To diagnose smallpox you do not have to probe each pustule, nor do you heal each separately," he concluded.

We must learn to discriminate between false guilt inherited from parents, church, or society and true guilt as a response to breaking God's laws clearly revealed in the Bible. True guilt has a directional movement, first pointing backward to the sin and then pointing forward to repentance. Guilt serves its designed purpose only if it presses us toward the God who promises forgiveness and restoration. Guilt is only a symptom; we listen to it because it drives us toward the cure.

—*Philip Yancey*

For more on confession, see reading at Psalm 51.

A total of 70,000 people died throughout the nation, from Dan in the north to Beersheba in the south. [16] But as the angel was preparing to destroy Jerusalem, the LORD relented and said to the death angel, "Stop! That is enough!" At that moment the angel of the LORD was by the threshing floor of Araunah the Jebusite.

[17] When David saw the angel, he said to the LORD, "I am the one who has sinned and done wrong! But these people are as innocent as sheep—what have they done? Let your anger fall against me and my family."

David Builds an Altar

[18] That day Gad came to David and said to him, "Go up and build an altar to the LORD on the threshing floor of Araunah the Jebusite."

[19] So David went up to do what the LORD had commanded him. [20] When Araunah saw the king and his men coming toward him, he came and bowed before the king with his face to the ground. [21] "Why have you come, my lord the king?" Araunah asked.

David replied, "I have come to buy your threshing floor and to build an altar to the LORD there, so that he will stop the plague."

[22] "Take it, my lord the king, and use it as you wish," Araunah said to David. "Here are oxen for the burnt offering, and you can use the threshing boards and ox yokes for wood to build a fire on the altar. [23] I will give it

all to you, Your Majesty, and may the LORD your God accept your sacrifice."

²⁴But the king replied to Araunah, "No, I insist on buying it, for I will not present burnt offerings to the LORD my God that have cost me nothing." So David paid him fifty pieces of silver* for the threshing floor and the oxen.

²⁵David built an altar there to the LORD and sacrificed burnt offerings and peace offerings. And the LORD answered his prayer for the land, and the plague on Israel was stopped.

24:24 Hebrew *50 shekels of silver*, about 20 ounces or 570 grams in weight.

Introduction to
1 Kings

Background

The Book of 1 Kings starts with the death of David, followed by Solomon ruling over a united Israel; it ends with the nation as divided as his heart. Through the building of the temple, along with unsurpassed wealth and wisdom from God, Solomon leads Israel to a true golden age. Yet this wisest of kings allows his foreign wives to sway him toward idolatry. At Solomon's death, the united kingdom of Israel divides into two nations—Israel, in the north, and Judah, in the south. The northern kingdom is home to ten of the twelve tribes, and a capital is set up in Samaria. The southern kingdom has two tribes—Judah and Benjamin—and maintains the former capital at Jerusalem.

First and 2 Kings were originally one book but were divided in the Greek Septuagint version. While the author of 1 and 2 Kings is unknown, the prophet Jeremiah is on the list of possible candidates.

Message

The themes of kingship and covenants are prominent throughout 1 and 2 Kings. The rulers who follow God are clearly delineated from those who don't by the phrase "he did what was evil in the LORD's sight" (15:34). In other words, such kings do not honor the covenants the people of Israel had historically made with God. The writer of 1 Kings shows the gradual moral decline from the reigns of Rehoboam to Jehoshaphat (in Judah) and from Jeroboam to Ahaziah (in Israel). God is not silent, however. He speaks through the prophets, particularly Elijah, constantly calling his people back to himself and caring for those who remain faithful in times of great turmoil and ungodly leadership. The contest on Mount Carmel in which Elijah challenges the prophets of Baal provides the people an unmistakable display of God's great power.

Time

First Kings covers events from 970 B.C. to circa 850 B.C.

Outline

1 Kings

1 David in His Old Age

King David was now very old, and no matter how many blankets covered him, he could not keep warm. ²So his advisers told him, "Let us find a young virgin to wait on you and look after you, my lord. She will lie in your arms and keep you warm."

³So they searched throughout the land of Israel for a beautiful girl, and they found Abishag from Shunem and brought her to the king. ⁴The girl was very beautiful, and she looked after the king and took care of him. But the king had no sexual relations with her.

Adonijah Claims the Throne

⁵About that time David's son Adonijah, whose mother was Haggith, began boasting, "I will make myself king." So he provided himself with chariots and charioteers and recruited fifty men to run in front of him. ⁶Now his father, King David, had never disciplined him at any time, even by asking, "Why are you doing that?" Adonijah had been born next after Absalom, and he was very handsome.

⁷Adonijah took Joab son of Zeruiah and Abiathar the priest into his confidence, and they agreed to help him become king. ⁸But Zadok the priest, Benaiah son of Jehoiada, Nathan the prophet, Shimei, Rei, and David's personal bodyguard refused to support Adonijah.

⁹Adonijah went to the Stone of Zoheleth* near the spring of En-rogel, where he sacrificed sheep, cattle, and fattened calves. He invited all his brothers—the other sons of King David—and all the royal officials of Judah. ¹⁰But he did not invite Nathan the prophet or Benaiah or the king's bodyguard or his brother Solomon.

¹¹Then Nathan went to Bathsheba, Solomon's mother, and asked her, "Haven't you heard that Haggith's son, Adonijah, has made himself king, and our lord David doesn't even know about it? ¹²If you want to save your own life and the life of your son Solomon, follow my advice. ¹³Go at once to King David and say to him, 'My lord the king, didn't you make a vow and say to me, "Your son Solomon will surely be the next king and will sit on my throne"? Why then has Adonijah become king?' ¹⁴And while you are still talking with him, I will come and confirm everything you have said."

¹⁵So Bathsheba went into the king's bedroom. (He was very old now, and Abishag was taking care of him.) ¹⁶Bathsheba bowed down before the king.

"What can I do for you?" he asked her.

¹⁷She replied, "My lord, you made a vow before the LORD your God when you said to me, 'Your son Solomon will surely be the next king and will sit on my throne.' ¹⁸But instead, Adonijah has made himself king, and my lord the king does not even know about it. ¹⁹He has sacrificed many cattle, fattened calves, and sheep, and he has invited all the king's sons to attend the celebration. He also invited Abiathar the priest and Joab, the commander of the army. But he

---

1:9 Or *to the Serpent's Stone;* Greek version supports reading *Zoheleth* as a proper name.

did not invite your servant Solomon. ²⁰And now, my lord the king, all Israel is waiting for you to announce who will become king after you. ²¹If you do not act, my son Solomon and I will be treated as criminals as soon as my lord the king has died."

²²While she was still speaking with the king, Nathan the prophet arrived. ²³The king's officials told him, "Nathan the prophet is here to see you."

Nathan went in and bowed before the king with his face to the ground. ²⁴Nathan asked, "My lord the king, have you decided that Adonijah will be the next king and that he will sit on your throne? ²⁵Today he has sacrificed many cattle, fattened calves, and sheep, and he has invited all the king's sons to attend the celebration. He also invited the commanders of the army and Abiathar the priest. They are feasting and drinking with him and shouting, 'Long live King Adonijah!' ²⁶But he did not invite me or Zadok the priest or Benaiah or your servant Solomon. ²⁷Has my lord the king really done this without letting any of his officials know who should be the next king?"

David Makes Solomon King

²⁸King David responded, "Call Bathsheba!" So she came back in and stood before the king. ²⁹And the king repeated his vow: "As surely as the LORD lives, who has rescued me from every danger, ³⁰your son Solomon will be the next king and will sit on my throne this very day, just as I vowed to you before the LORD, the God of Israel."

³¹Then Bathsheba bowed down with her face to the ground before the king and exclaimed, "May my lord King David live forever!"

³²Then King David ordered, "Call Zadok the priest, Nathan the prophet, and Benaiah son of Jehoiada." When they came into the king's presence, ³³the king said to them, "Take Solomon and my officials down to Gihon Spring. Solomon is to ride on my own mule. ³⁴There Zadok the priest and Nathan the prophet are to anoint him king over Israel. Blow the ram's horn and shout, 'Long live King Solomon!' ³⁵Then escort him back here, and he will sit on my throne. He will succeed me as king, for I have appointed him to be ruler over Israel and Judah."

³⁶"Amen!" Benaiah son of Jehoiada replied. "May the LORD, the God of my lord the king, decree that it happen. ³⁷And may the LORD be with Solomon as he has been with you, my lord the king, and may he make Solomon's reign even greater than yours!"

³⁸So Zadok the priest, Nathan the prophet, Benaiah son of Jehoiada, and the king's bodyguard* took Solomon down to Gihon Spring, with Solomon riding on King David's own mule. ³⁹There Zadok the priest took the flask of olive oil from the sacred tent and anointed Solomon with the oil. Then they sounded the ram's horn and all the people shouted, "Long live King Solomon!" ⁴⁰And all the people followed Solomon into Jerusalem, playing flutes and shouting for joy. The celebration was so joyous and noisy that the earth shook with the sound.

⁴¹Adonijah and his guests heard the celebrating and shouting just as they were finishing their banquet. When Joab heard the sound of the ram's horn, he asked, "What's going on? Why is the city in such an uproar?"

⁴²And while he was still speaking, Jonathan son of Abiathar the priest arrived. "Come in," Adonijah said to him, "for you are a good man. You must have good news."

⁴³"Not at all!" Jonathan replied. "Our lord King David has just declared Solomon king! ⁴⁴The king sent him down to Gihon Spring with Zadok the priest, Nathan the prophet, and Benaiah son of Jehoiada, protected by the king's bodyguard. They had him ride on the king's own mule, ⁴⁵and Zadok and Nathan have anointed him at Gihon Spring as the new king. They have just returned, and the whole city is celebrating and rejoicing. That's what all the noise is about. ⁴⁶What's more, Solomon is now sitting on the royal throne as king. ⁴⁷And all the royal officials have gone to King David and congratulated him, saying, 'May your God make Solomon's fame even greater than your own, and may Solomon's reign be even greater than yours!' Then the

---

1:38 Hebrew *the Kerethites and Pelethites;* also in 1:44.

king bowed his head in worship as he lay in his bed, ⁴⁸and he said, 'Praise the LORD, the God of Israel, who today has chosen a successor to sit on my throne while I am still alive to see it.'"

⁴⁹Then all of Adonijah's guests jumped up in panic from the banquet table and quickly scattered. ⁵⁰Adonijah was afraid of Solomon, so he rushed to the sacred tent and grabbed on to the horns of the altar. ⁵¹Word soon reached Solomon that Adonijah had seized the horns of the altar in fear, and that he was pleading, "Let King Solomon swear today that he will not kill me!"

⁵²Solomon replied, "If he proves himself to be loyal, not a hair on his head will be touched. But if he makes trouble, he will die." ⁵³So King Solomon summoned Adonijah, and they brought him down from the altar. He came and bowed respectfully before King Solomon, who dismissed him, saying, "Go on home."

2 David's Final Instructions to Solomon

As the time of King David's death approached, he gave this charge to his son Solomon:

²"I am going where everyone on earth must someday go. Take courage and be a man. ³Observe the requirements of the LORD your God, and follow all his ways. Keep the decrees, commands, regulations, and laws written in the Law of Moses so that you will be successful in all you do and wherever you go. ⁴If you do this, then the LORD will keep the promise he made to me. He told me, 'If your descendants live as they should and follow me faithfully with all their heart and soul, one of them will always sit on the throne of Israel.'

⁵"And there is something else. You know what Joab son of Zeruiah did to me when he murdered my two army commanders, Abner son of Ner and Amasa son of Jether. He pretended that it was an act of war, but it was done in a time of peace,* staining his belt and sandals with innocent blood.* ⁶Do with him what you think best, but don't let him grow old and go to his grave in peace.*

⁷"Be kind to the sons of Barzillai of Gil-

ead. Make them permanent guests at your table, for they took care of me when I fled from your brother Absalom.

⁸"And remember Shimei son of Gera, the man from Bahurim in Benjamin. He cursed me with a terrible curse as I was fleeing to Mahanaim. When he came down to meet me at the Jordan River, I swore by the LORD that I would not kill him. ⁹But that oath does not make him innocent. You are a wise man, and you will know how to arrange a bloody death for him.*"

¹⁰Then David died and was buried with his ancestors in the City of David. ¹¹David had reigned over Israel for forty years, seven of them in Hebron and thirty-three in Jerusalem. ¹²Solomon became king and sat on the throne of David his father, and his kingdom was firmly established.

Solomon Establishes His Rule

¹³One day Adonijah, whose mother was Haggith, came to see Bathsheba, Solomon's mother. "Have you come with peaceful intentions?" she asked him.

"Yes," he said, "I come in peace. ¹⁴In fact, I have a favor to ask of you."

"What is it?" she asked.

¹⁵He replied, "As you know, the kingdom was rightfully mine; all Israel wanted me to be the next king. But the tables were turned, and the kingdom went to my brother instead; for that is the way the LORD wanted it. ¹⁶So now I have just one favor to ask of you. Please don't turn me down."

"What is it?" she asked.

¹⁷He replied, "Speak to King Solomon on my behalf, for I know he will do anything you request. Ask him to let me marry Abishag, the girl from Shunem."

¹⁸"All right," Bathsheba replied. "I will speak to the king for you."

¹⁹So Bathsheba went to King Solomon to speak on Adonijah's behalf. The king rose from his throne to meet her, and he bowed down before her. When he sat down on his throne again, the king ordered that a throne be brought for his mother, and she sat at his right hand.

²⁰"I have one small request to make of

2:5a Or *He murdered them during a time of peace as revenge for deaths they had caused in time of war.*   **2:5b** As in some Greek and Old Latin manuscripts; Hebrew reads *with the blood of war.*   **2:6** Hebrew *don't let his white head go down to Sheol in peace.*   **2:9** Hebrew *how to bring his white head down to Sheol in blood.*

you," she said. "I hope you won't turn me down."

"What is it, my mother?" he asked. "You know I won't refuse you."

²¹"Then let your brother Adonijah marry Abishag, the girl from Shunem," she replied.

²²"How can you possibly ask me to give Abishag to Adonijah?" King Solomon demanded. "You might as well ask me to give him the kingdom! You know that he is my older brother, and that he has Abiathar the priest and Joab son of Zeruiah on his side."

²³Then King Solomon made a vow before the LORD: "May God strike me and even kill me if Adonijah has not sealed his fate with this request. ²⁴The LORD has confirmed me and placed me on the throne of my father, David; he has established my dynasty as he promised. So as surely as the LORD lives, Adonijah will die this very day!" ²⁵So King Solomon ordered Benaiah son of Jehoiada to execute him, and Adonijah was put to death.

²⁶Then the king said to Abiathar the priest, "Go back to your home in Anathoth. You deserve to die, but I will not kill you now, because you carried the Ark of the Sovereign LORD for David my father and you shared all his hardships." ²⁷So Solomon deposed Abiathar from his position as priest of the LORD, thereby fulfilling the prophecy the LORD had given at Shiloh concerning the descendants of Eli.

²⁸Joab had not joined Absalom's earlier rebellion, but he had joined Adonijah's rebellion. So when Joab heard about Adonijah's death, he ran to the sacred tent of the LORD and grabbed on to the horns of the altar. ²⁹When this was reported to King Solomon, he sent Benaiah son of Jehoiada to execute him.

³⁰Benaiah went to the sacred tent of the LORD and said to Joab, "The king orders you to come out!"

But Joab answered, "No, I will die here."

So Benaiah returned to the king and told him what Joab had said.

³¹"Do as he said," the king replied. "Kill him there beside the altar and bury him. This will remove the guilt of Joab's senseless murders from me and from my father's family. ³²The LORD will repay him* for the murders of two men who were more righteous and better than he. For my father knew nothing about the deaths of Abner son of Ner, commander of the army of Israel, and of Amasa son of Jether, commander of the army of Judah. ³³May their blood be on Joab and his descendants forever, and may the LORD grant peace forever to David, his descendants, his dynasty, and his throne."

³⁴So Benaiah son of Jehoiada returned to the sacred tent and killed Joab, and he was buried at his home in the wilderness. ³⁵Then the king appointed Benaiah to command the army in place of Joab, and he installed Zadok the priest to take the place of Abiathar.

³⁶The king then sent for Shimei and told him, "Build a house here in Jerusalem and live there. But don't step outside the city to go anywhere else. ³⁷On the day you so much as cross the Kidron Valley, you will surely die; and your blood will be on your own head."

³⁸Shimei replied, "Your sentence is fair; I will do whatever my lord the king commands." So Shimei lived in Jerusalem for a long time.

³⁹But three years later two of Shimei's slaves ran away to King Achish son of Maacah of Gath. When Shimei learned where they were, ⁴⁰he saddled his donkey and went to Gath to search for them. When he found them, he brought them back to Jerusalem.

⁴¹Solomon heard that Shimei had left Jerusalem and had gone to Gath and returned. ⁴²So the king sent for Shimei and demanded, "Didn't I make you swear by the LORD and warn you not to go anywhere else or you would surely die? And you replied, 'The sentence is fair; I will do as you say.' ⁴³Then why haven't you kept your oath to the LORD and obeyed my command?"

⁴⁴The king also said to Shimei, "You certainly remember all the wicked things you did to my father, David. May the LORD now bring that evil on your own head. ⁴⁵But may I, King Solomon, receive the LORD's blessings, and may one of David's descendants always sit on this throne in the presence of

the LORD." ⁴⁶Then, at the king's command, Benaiah son of Jehoiada took Shimei outside and killed him.

So the kingdom was now firmly in Solomon's grip.

3 Solomon Asks for Wisdom

Solomon made an alliance with Pharaoh, the king of Egypt, and married one of his daughters. He brought her to live in the City of David until he could finish building his palace and the Temple of the LORD and the wall around the city. ²At that time the people of Israel sacrificed their offerings at local places of worship, for a temple honoring the name of the LORD had not yet been built.

³Solomon loved the LORD and followed all the decrees of his father, David, except that Solomon, too, offered sacrifices and burned incense at the local places of worship. ⁴The most important of these places of worship was at Gibeon, so the king went there and sacrificed 1,000 burnt offerings. ⁵That night the LORD appeared to Solomon in a dream, and God said, "What do you want? Ask, and I will give it to you!"

⁶Solomon replied, "You showed faithful love to your servant my father, David, because he was honest and true and faithful to you. And you have continued your faithful love to him today by giving him a son to sit on his throne.

⁷"Now, O LORD my God, you have made me king instead of my father, David, but I am like a little child who doesn't know his way around. ⁸And here I am in the midst of your own chosen people, a nation so great and numerous they cannot be counted! ⁹Give me an understanding heart so that I can govern your people well and know the difference between right and wrong. For who by himself is able to govern this great people of yours?"

¹⁰The Lord was pleased that Solomon had asked for wisdom. ¹¹So God replied, "Because you have asked for wisdom in governing my people with justice and have not asked for a long life or wealth or the death of your enemies—¹²I will give you what you asked for! I will give you a wise and understanding heart such as no one else has had or ever will have! ¹³And I will also give you

what you did not ask for—riches and fame! No other king in all the world will be compared to you for the rest of your life! ¹⁴And if you follow me and obey my decrees and my commands as your father, David, did, I will give you a long life."

¹⁵Then Solomon woke up and realized it had been a dream. He returned to Jerusalem and stood before the Ark of the Lord's Covenant, where he sacrificed burnt offerings and peace offerings. Then he invited all his officials to a great banquet.

Solomon Judges Wisely

¹⁶Some time later two prostitutes came to the king to have an argument settled. ¹⁷"Please, my lord," one of them began, "this woman and I live in the same house. I gave birth to a baby while she was with me in the house. ¹⁸Three days later this woman also had a baby. We were alone; there were only two of us in the house.

¹⁹"But her baby died during the night when she rolled over on it. ²⁰Then she got up in the night and took my son from beside me while I was asleep. She laid her dead child in my arms and took mine to sleep beside her. ²¹And in the morning when I tried to nurse my son, he was dead! But when I looked more closely in the morning light, I saw that it wasn't my son at all."

²²Then the other woman interrupted, "It certainly was your son, and the living child is mine."

"No," the first woman said, "the living child is mine, and the dead one is yours." And so they argued back and forth before the king.

²³Then the king said, "Let's get the facts straight. Both of you claim the living child is yours, and each says that the dead one belongs to the other. ²⁴All right, bring me a sword." So a sword was brought to the king.

²⁵Then he said, "Cut the living child in two, and give half to one woman and half to the other!"

²⁶Then the woman who was the real mother of the living child, and who loved him very much, cried out, "Oh no, my lord! Give her the child—please do not kill him!"

But the other woman said, "All right, he will be neither yours nor mine; divide him between us!"

27 Then the king said, "Do not kill the child, but give him to the woman who wants him to live, for she is his mother!"

28 When all Israel heard the king's decision, the people were in awe of the king, for they saw the wisdom God had given him for rendering justice.

4 Solomon's Officials and Governors

King Solomon now ruled over all Israel, 2 and these were his high officials:

Azariah son of Zadok was the priest.
3 Elihoreph and Ahijah, the sons of Shisha, were court secretaries.
Jehoshaphat son of Ahilud was the royal historian.
4 Benaiah son of Jehoiada was commander of the army.
Zadok and Abiathar were priests.
5 Azariah son of Nathan was in charge of the district governors.
Zabud son of Nathan, a priest, was a trusted adviser to the king.
6 Ahishar was manager of the palace property.
Adoniram son of Abda was in charge of the labor force.

7 Solomon also had twelve district governors who were over all Israel. They were responsible for providing food for the king's household. Each of them arranged provisions for one month of the year. 8 These are the names of the twelve governors:

Ben-hur, in the hill country of Ephraim.
9 Ben-deker, in Makaz, Shaalbim, Beth-shemesh, and Elon-bethhanan.
10 Ben-hesed, in Arubboth, including Socoh and all the land of Hepher.
11 Ben-abinadab, in all of Naphoth-dor.* (He was married to Taphath, one of Solomon's daughters.)
12 Baana son of Ahilud, in Taanach and Megiddo, all of Beth-shan* near Zarethan below Jezreel, and all the territory from Beth-shan to Abel-meholah and over to Jokmeam.
13 Ben-geber, in Ramoth-gilead, including the Towns of Jair (named for Jair of the tribe of Manasseh*) in Gilead, and in the Argob region of Bashan, including sixty large fortified towns with bronze bars on their gates.
14 Ahinadab son of Iddo, in Mahanaim.
15 Ahimaaz, in Naphtali. (He was married to Basemath, another of Solomon's daughters.)
16 Baana son of Hushai, in Asher and in Aloth.
17 Jehoshaphat son of Paruah, in Issachar.
18 Shimei son of Ela, in Benjamin.
19 Geber son of Uri, in the land of Gilead,* including the territories of King Sihon of the Amorites and King Og of Bashan.
There was also one governor over the land of Judah.*

Solomon's Prosperity and Wisdom

20 The people of Judah and Israel were as numerous as the sand on the seashore. They were very contented, with plenty to eat and drink. 21*Solomon ruled over all the kingdoms from the Euphrates River* in the north to the land of the Philistines and the border of Egypt in the south. The conquered peoples of those lands sent tribute money to Solomon and continued to serve him throughout his lifetime.

22 The daily food requirements for Solomon's palace were 150 bushels of choice flour and 300 bushels of meal*; 23 also 10 oxen from the fattening pens, 20 pasture-fed cattle, 100 sheep or goats, as well as deer, gazelles, roe deer, and choice poultry.*

24 Solomon's dominion extended over all the kingdoms west of the Euphrates River, from Tiphsah to Gaza. And there was peace on all his borders. 25 During the lifetime of Solomon, all of Judah and Israel lived in peace and safety. And from Dan in the north to Beersheba in the south, each family had its own home and garden.*

26 Solomon had 4,000* stalls for his chariot horses, and he had 12,000 horses.*

27 The district governors faithfully provided food for King Solomon and his court;

4:11 Hebrew *Naphath-dor*, a variant spelling of Naphoth-dor. **4:12** Hebrew *Beth-shean*, a variant spelling of Beth-shan; also in 4:12b. **4:13** Hebrew *Jair son of Manasseh*; compare 1 Chr 2:22. **4:19a** Greek version reads *of Gad*; compare 4:13. **4:19b** As in some Greek manuscripts; Hebrew lacks *of Judah*. The meaning of the Hebrew is uncertain. **4:21a** Verses 4:21-34 are numbered 5:1-14 in Hebrew text. **4:21b** Hebrew *the river*; also in 4:24. **4:22** Hebrew *30 cors* [5.5 kiloliters] *of choice flour and 60 cors* [11 kiloliters] *of meal.* **4:23** Or *and fattened geese.* **4:25** Hebrew *each family lived under its own grapevine and under its own fig tree.* **4:26a** As in some Greek manuscripts (see also 2 Chr 9:25); Hebrew reads *40,000.* **4:26b** Or *12,000 charioteers.*

each made sure nothing was lacking during the month assigned to him. [28] They also brought the necessary barley and straw for the royal horses in the stables.

[29] God gave Solomon very great wisdom and understanding, and knowledge as vast as the sands of the seashore. [30] In fact, his wisdom exceeded that of all the wise men of the East and the wise men of Egypt. [31] He was wiser than anyone else, including Ethan the Ezrahite and the sons of Mahol—Heman, Calcol, and Darda. His fame spread throughout all the surrounding nations. [32] He composed some 3,000 proverbs and wrote 1,005 songs. [33] He could speak with authority about all kinds of plants, from the great cedar of Lebanon to the tiny hyssop that grows from cracks in a wall. He could also speak about animals, birds, small creatures, and fish. [34] And kings from every nation sent their ambassadors to listen to the wisdom of Solomon.

5 Preparations for Building the Temple

[1]*King Hiram of Tyre had always been a loyal friend of David. When Hiram learned that David's son Solomon was the new king of Israel, he sent ambassadors to congratulate him.

[2] Then Solomon sent this message back to Hiram:

[3] "You know that my father, David, was not able to build a Temple to honor the name of the LORD his God because of the many wars waged against him by surrounding nations. He could not build until the LORD gave him victory over all his enemies. [4] But now the LORD my God has given me peace on every side; I have no enemies, and all is well. [5] So I am planning to build a Temple to honor the name of the LORD my God, just as he had instructed my father, David. For the LORD told him, 'Your son, whom I will place on your throne, will build the Temple to honor my name.'

[6] "Therefore, please command that cedars from Lebanon be cut for me. Let my men work alongside yours, and I will pay your men whatever wages you ask. As you know, there is no one among us who can cut timber like you Sidonians!"

[7] When Hiram received Solomon's message, he was very pleased and said, "Praise the LORD today for giving David a wise son to be king of the great nation of Israel." [8] Then he sent this reply to Solomon:

"I have received your message, and I will supply all the cedar and cypress timber you need. [9] My servants will bring the logs from the Lebanon mountains to the Mediterranean Sea* and make them into rafts and float them along the coast to whatever place you choose. Then we will break the rafts apart so you can carry the logs away. You can pay me by supplying me with food for my household."

[10] So Hiram supplied as much cedar and cypress timber as Solomon desired. [11] In return, Solomon sent him an annual payment of 100,000 bushels* of wheat for his household and 110,000 gallons* of pure olive oil. [12] So the LORD gave wisdom to Solomon, just as he had promised. And Hiram and Solomon made a formal alliance of peace.

[13] Then King Solomon conscripted a labor force of 30,000 men from all Israel. [14] He sent them to Lebanon in shifts, 10,000 every month, so that each man would be one month in Lebanon and two months at home. Adoniram was in charge of this labor force. [15] Solomon also had 70,000 common laborers, 80,000 quarry workers in the hill country, [16] and 3,600* foremen to supervise the work. [17] At the king's command, they quarried large blocks of high-quality stone and shaped them to make the foundation of the Temple. [18] Men from the city of Gebal helped Solomon's and Hiram's builders prepare the timber and stone for the Temple.

6 Solomon Builds the Temple

It was in midspring, in the month of Ziv,* during the fourth year of Solomon's reign, that he began to construct the Temple of the LORD. This was 480 years after

---

5:1 Verses 5:1-18 are numbered 5:15-32 in Hebrew text. **5:9** Hebrew *the sea.* **5:11a** Hebrew *20,000 cors* [3,640 kiloliters]. **5:11b** As in Greek version, which reads *20,000 baths* [420 kiloliters] (see also 2 Chr 2:10); Hebrew reads *20 cors,* about 800 gallons or 3.6 kiloliters in volume. **5:16** As in some Greek manuscripts (see also 2 Chr 2:2, 18); Hebrew reads *3,300.* **6:1** Hebrew *It was in the month of Ziv, which is the second month.* This month of the ancient Hebrew lunar calendar usually occurs within the months of April and May.

the people of Israel were rescued from their slavery in the land of Egypt.

²The Temple that King Solomon built for the LORD was 90 feet long, 30 feet wide, and 45 feet high.* ³The entry room at the front of the Temple was 30 feet* wide, running across the entire width of the Temple. It projected outward 15 feet* from the front of the Temple. ⁴Solomon also made narrow recessed windows throughout the Temple.

⁵He built a complex of rooms against the outer walls of the Temple, all the way around the sides and rear of the building. ⁶The complex was three stories high, the bottom floor being 7½ feet wide, the second floor 9 feet wide, and the top floor 10½ feet wide.* The rooms were connected to the walls of the Temple by beams resting on ledges built out from the wall. So the beams were not inserted into the walls themselves.

⁷The stones used in the construction of the Temple were finished at the quarry, so there was no sound of hammer, ax, or any other iron tool at the building site.

⁸The entrance to the bottom floor* was on the south side of the Temple. There were winding stairs going up to the second floor, and another flight of stairs between the second and third floors. ⁹After completing the Temple structure, Solomon put in a ceiling made of cedar beams and planks. ¹⁰As already stated, he built a complex of rooms on three sides of the building, attached to the Temple walls by cedar timbers. Each story of the complex was 7½ feet* high.

¹¹Then the LORD gave this message to Solomon: ¹²"Concerning this Temple you are building, if you keep all my decrees and regulations and obey all my commands, I will fulfill through you the promise I made to your father, David. ¹³I will live among the Israelites and will never abandon my people Israel."

The Temple's Interior

¹⁴So Solomon finished building the Temple. ¹⁵The entire inside, from floor to ceiling, was paneled with wood. He paneled the walls and ceilings with cedar, and he used planks of cypress for the floors. ¹⁶He partitioned off an inner sanctuary—the Most Holy Place—at the far end of the Temple. It was 30 feet deep and was paneled with cedar from floor to ceiling. ¹⁷The main room of the Temple, outside the Most Holy Place, was 60 feet* long. ¹⁸Cedar paneling completely covered the stone walls throughout the Temple, and the paneling was decorated with carvings of gourds and open flowers.

¹⁹He prepared the inner sanctuary at the far end of the Temple, where the Ark of the LORD's Covenant would be placed. ²⁰This inner sanctuary was 30 feet long, 30 feet wide, and 30 feet high. He overlaid the inside with solid gold. He also overlaid the altar made of cedar.* ²¹Then Solomon overlaid the rest of the Temple's interior with solid gold, and he made gold chains to protect the entrance* to the Most Holy Place. ²²So he finished overlaying the entire Temple with gold, including the altar that belonged to the Most Holy Place.

²³He made two cherubim of wild olive* wood, each 15 feet* tall, and placed them in the inner sanctuary. ²⁴The wingspan of each of the cherubim was 15 feet, each wing being 7½ feet* long. ²⁵The two cherubim were identical in shape and size; ²⁶each was 15 feet tall. ²⁷He placed them side by side in the inner sanctuary of the Temple. Their outspread wings reached from wall to wall, while their inner wings touched at the center of the room. ²⁸He overlaid the two cherubim with gold.

²⁹He decorated all the walls of the inner sanctuary and the main room with carvings of cherubim, palm trees, and open flowers. ³⁰He overlaid the floor in both rooms with gold.

³¹For the entrance to the inner sanctuary, he made double doors of wild olive wood with five-sided doorposts.* ³²These double doors were decorated with carvings of cherubim, palm trees, and open flowers. The

---

6:2 Hebrew 60 cubits [27.6 meters] long, 20 cubits [9.2 meters] wide, and 30 cubits [13.8 meters] high.   **6:3a** Hebrew 20 cubits [9.2 meters]; also in 6:16, 20.   **6:3b** Hebrew 10 cubits [4.6 meters].   **6:6** Hebrew the bottom floor being 5 cubits [2.3 meters] wide, the second floor 6 cubits [2.8 meters] wide, and the top floor 7 cubits [3.2 meters] wide.   **6:8** As in Greek version; Hebrew reads middle floor.   **6:10** Hebrew 5 cubits [2.3 meters].   **6:17** Hebrew 40 cubits [18.4 meters].   **6:20** Or overlaid the altar with cedar. The meaning of the Hebrew is uncertain.   **6:21** Or to draw curtains across. The meaning of the Hebrew is uncertain.   **6:23a** Or pine; Hebrew reads oil tree; also in 6:31, 33.   **6:23b** Hebrew 10 cubits [4.6 meters]; also in 6:24, 25.   **6:24** Hebrew 5 cubits [2.3 meters].   **6:31** The meaning of the Hebrew is uncertain.

doors, including the decorations of cherubim and palm trees, were overlaid with gold. ³³Then he made four-sided doorposts of wild olive wood for the entrance to the Temple. ³⁴There were two folding doors of cypress wood, and each door was hinged to fold back upon itself. ³⁵These doors were decorated with carvings of cherubim, palm trees, and open flowers—all overlaid evenly with gold.

³⁶The walls of the inner courtyard were built so that there was one layer of cedar beams between every three layers of finished stone.

³⁷The foundation of the LORD's Temple was laid in midspring, in the month of Ziv,* during the fourth year of Solomon's reign. ³⁸The entire building was completed in every detail by midautumn, in the month of Bul,* during the eleventh year of his reign. So it took seven years to build the Temple.

7 Solomon Builds His Palace

Solomon also built a palace for himself, and it took him thirteen years to complete the construction.

²One of Solomon's buildings was called the Palace of the Forest of Lebanon. It was 150 feet long, 75 feet wide, and 45 feet high.* There were four rows of cedar pillars, and great cedar beams rested on the pillars. ³The hall had a cedar roof. Above the beams on the pillars were forty-five side rooms,* arranged in three tiers of fifteen each. ⁴On each end of the long hall were three rows of windows facing each other. ⁵All the doorways and doorposts* had rectangular frames and were arranged in sets of three, facing each other.

⁶Solomon also built the Hall of Pillars, which was 75 feet long and 45 feet wide.* There was a porch in front, along with a canopy supported by pillars.

⁷Solomon also built the throne room, known as the Hall of Justice, where he sat to hear legal matters. It was paneled with cedar from floor to ceiling.* ⁸Solomon's living quarters surrounded a courtyard behind this hall, and they were constructed the same way. He also built similar living quarters for Pharaoh's daughter, whom he had married.

⁹From foundation to eaves, all these buildings were built from huge blocks of high-quality stone, cut with saws and trimmed to exact measure on all sides. ¹⁰Some of the huge foundation stones were 15 feet long, and some were 12 feet* long. ¹¹The blocks of high-quality stone used in the walls were also cut to measure, and cedar beams were also used. ¹²The walls of the great courtyard were built so that there was one layer of cedar beams between every three layers of finished stone, just like the walls of the inner courtyard of the LORD's Temple with its entry room.

Furnishings for the Temple

¹³King Solomon then asked for a man named Huram* to come from Tyre. ¹⁴He was half Israelite, since his mother was a widow from the tribe of Naphtali, and his father had been a craftsman in bronze from Tyre. Huram was extremely skillful and talented in any work in bronze, and he came to do all the metal work for King Solomon.

¹⁵Huram cast two bronze pillars, each 27 feet tall and 18 feet in circumference.* ¹⁶For the tops of the pillars he cast bronze capitals, each 7½ feet* tall. ¹⁷Each capital was decorated with seven sets of latticework and interwoven chains. ¹⁸He also encircled the latticework with two rows of pomegranates to decorate the capitals over the pillars. ¹⁹The capitals on the columns inside the entry room were shaped like water lilies, and they were six feet* tall. ²⁰The capitals on the two pillars had 200 pomegranates in two rows around them, beside the rounded surface next to the latticework. ²¹Huram set the pillars at the entrance of the Temple, one toward the south and one toward the north. He named the one on the south Jakin, and

6:37 Hebrew *was laid in the month of Ziv.* This month of the ancient Hebrew lunar calendar usually occurs within the months of April and May. 6:38 Hebrew *by the month of Bul, which is the eighth month.* This month of the ancient Hebrew lunar calendar usually occurs within the months of October and November. 7:2 Hebrew *100 cubits* [46 meters], *50 cubits* [23 meters] *wide, and 50 cubits* [13.5 meters] *high.* 7:3 Or *45 rafters,* or *45 beams,* or *45 pillars.* The architectural details in 7:2-6 can be interpreted in many different ways. 7:5 Greek version reads *windows.* 7:6 Hebrew *50 cubits* [23 meters] *long and 30 cubits* [13.8 meters] *wide.* 7:7 As in Syriac version and Latin Vulgate; Hebrew reads *from floor to floor.* 7:10 Hebrew *10 cubits* [4.6 meters] . . . *8 cubits* [3.7 meters]. 7:13 Hebrew *Hiram* (also in 7:40, 45); compare 2 Chr 2:13. This is not the same person mentioned in 5:1. 7:15 Hebrew *18 cubits* [8.3 meters] *tall and 12 cubits* [5.5 meters] *in circumference.* 7:16 Hebrew *5 cubits* [2.3 meters]. 7:19 Hebrew *4 cubits* [1.8 meters]; also in 7:38.

the one on the north Boaz.* ²²The capitals on the pillars were shaped like water lilies. And so the work on the pillars was finished.

²³Then Huram cast a great round basin, 15 feet across from rim to rim, called the Sea. It was 7½ feet deep and about 45 feet in circumference.* ²⁴It was encircled just below its rim by two rows of decorative gourds. There were about six gourds per foot* all the way around, and they were cast as part of the basin.

²⁵The Sea was placed on a base of twelve bronze oxen,* all facing outward. Three faced north, three faced west, three faced south, and three faced east, and the Sea rested on them. ²⁶The walls of the Sea were about three inches* thick, and its rim flared out like a cup and resembled a water lily blossom. It could hold about 11,000 gallons* of water.

²⁷Huram also made ten bronze water carts, each 6 feet long, 6 feet wide, and 4½ feet tall.* ²⁸They were constructed with side panels braced with crossbars. ²⁹Both the panels and the crossbars were decorated with carved lions, oxen, and cherubim. Above and below the lions and oxen were wreath decorations. ³⁰Each of these carts had four bronze wheels and bronze axles. There were supporting posts for the bronze basins at the corners of the carts; these supports were decorated on each side with carvings of wreaths. ³¹The top of each cart had a rounded frame for the basin. It projected 1½ feet* above the cart's top like a round pedestal, and its opening was 2¼ feet* across; it was decorated on the outside with carvings of wreaths. The panels of the carts were square, not round. ³²Under the panels were four wheels that were connected to axles that had been cast as one unit with the cart. The wheels were 2¼ feet in diameter ³³and were similar to chariot wheels. The axles, spokes, rims, and hubs were all cast from molten bronze.

³⁴There were handles at each of the four corners of the carts, and these, too, were cast as one unit with the cart. ³⁵Around the top of each cart was a rim nine inches wide.* The corner supports and side panels were cast as one unit with the cart. ³⁶Carvings of cherubim, lions, and palm trees decorated the panels and corner supports wherever there was room, and there were wreaths all around. ³⁷All ten water carts were the same size and were made alike, for each was cast from the same mold.

³⁸Huram also made ten smaller bronze basins, one for each cart. Each basin was six feet across and could hold 220 gallons* of water. ³⁹He set five water carts on the south side of the Temple and five on the north side. The great bronze basin called the Sea was placed near the southeast corner of the Temple. ⁴⁰He also made the necessary washbasins, shovels, and bowls.

So at last Huram completed everything King Solomon had assigned him to make for the Temple of the LORD:

⁴¹ the two pillars;
the two bowl-shaped capitals on top of the pillars;
the two networks of interwoven chains that decorated the capitals;
⁴² the 400 pomegranates that hung from the chains on the capitals (two rows of pomegranates for each of the chain networks that decorated the capitals on top of the pillars);
⁴³ the ten water carts holding the ten basins;
⁴⁴ the Sea and the twelve oxen under it;
⁴⁵ the ash buckets, the shovels, and the bowls.

Huram made all these things of burnished bronze for the Temple of the LORD, just as King Solomon had directed. ⁴⁶The king had them cast in clay molds in the Jordan Valley between Succoth and Zarethan. ⁴⁷Solomon did not weigh all these things because there were so many; the weight of the bronze could not be measured.

⁴⁸Solomon also made all the furnishings of the Temple of the LORD:

the gold altar;
the gold table for the Bread of the Presence;

7:21 Jakin probably means "he establishes"; Boaz probably means "in him is strength." **7:23** Hebrew 10 cubits [4.6 meters] across.... 5 cubits [2.3 meters] deep and 30 cubits [13.8 meters] in circumference. **7:24** Or 20 gourds per meter; Hebrew reads 10 per cubit. **7:25** Hebrew 12 oxen; compare 2 Kgs 16:17, which specifies bronze oxen. **7:26a** Hebrew a handbreadth [8 centimeters]. **7:26b** Hebrew 2,000 baths [42 kiloliters]. **7:27** Hebrew 4 cubits [1.8 meters] long, 4 cubits wide, and 3 cubits [1.4 meters] high. **7:31a** Hebrew a cubit [46 centimeters]. **7:31b** Hebrew 1½ cubits [69 centimeters]; also in 7:32. **7:35** Hebrew half a cubit wide [23 centimeters]. **7:38** Hebrew 40 baths [840 liters].

[49] the lampstands of solid gold, five on the south and five on the north, in front of the Most Holy Place;

the flower decorations, lamps, and tongs—all of gold;

[50] the small bowls, lamp snuffers, bowls, dishes, and incense burners—all of solid gold;

the doors for the entrances to the Most Holy Place and the main room of the Temple, with their fronts overlaid with gold.

[51] So King Solomon finished all his work on the Temple of the LORD. Then he brought all the gifts his father, David, had dedicated—the silver, the gold, and the various articles—and he stored them in the treasuries of the LORD's Temple.

8 The Ark Brought to the Temple

Solomon then summoned to Jerusalem the elders of Israel and all the heads of the tribes—the leaders of the ancestral families of the Israelites. They were to bring the Ark of the LORD's Covenant to the Temple from its location in the City of David, also known as Zion. [2] So all the men of Israel assembled before King Solomon at the annual Festival of Shelters, which is held in early autumn in the month of Ethanim.*

[3] When all the elders of Israel arrived, the priests picked up the Ark. [4] The priests and Levites brought up the Ark of the LORD along with the special tent* and all the sacred items that had been in it. [5] There, before the Ark, King Solomon and the entire community of Israel sacrificed so many sheep, goats, and cattle that no one could keep count!

[6] Then the priests carried the Ark of the LORD's Covenant into the inner sanctuary of the Temple—the Most Holy Place—and placed it beneath the wings of the cherubim. [7] The cherubim spread their wings over the Ark, forming a canopy over the Ark and its carrying poles. [8] These poles were so long that their ends could be seen from the Temple's main room—the Holy Place—but not from the outside. They are still there to this day. [9] Nothing was in the Ark except the two stone tablets that Moses had placed in it at Mount Sinai,* where the LORD made a covenant with the people of Israel when they left the land of Egypt.

[10] When the priests came out of the Holy Place, a thick cloud filled the Temple of the LORD. [11] The priests could not continue their service because of the cloud, for the glorious presence of the LORD filled the Temple.

Solomon Praises the LORD

[12] Then Solomon prayed, "O LORD, you have said that you would live in a thick cloud of darkness. [13] Now I have built a glorious Temple for you, a place where you can live forever!*"

[14] Then the king turned around to the entire community of Israel standing before him and gave this blessing: [15] "Praise the LORD, the God of Israel, who has kept the promise he made to my father, David. For he told my father, [16] 'From the day I brought my people Israel out of Egypt, I have never chosen a city among any of the tribes of Israel as the place where a Temple should be built to honor my name. But I have chosen David to be king over my people Israel.'"

[17] Then Solomon said, "My father, David, wanted to build this Temple to honor the name of the LORD, the God of Israel. [18] But the LORD told him, 'You wanted to build the Temple to honor my name. Your intention is good, [19] but you are not the one to do it. One of your own sons will build the Temple to honor me.'

[20] "And now the LORD has fulfilled the promise he made, for I have become king in my father's place, and I now sit on the throne of Israel, just as the LORD promised. I have built this Temple to honor the name of the LORD, the God of Israel. [21] And I have prepared a place there for the Ark, which contains the covenant that the LORD made with our ancestors when he brought them out of Egypt."

8:2 Hebrew *at the festival in the month Ethanim, which is the seventh month.* The Festival of Shelters began on the fifteenth day of the seventh month of the ancient Hebrew lunar calendar. This day occurred in late September, October, or early November.   **8:4** Hebrew *the Tent of Meeting;* i.e., the tent mentioned in 2 Sam 6:17 and 1 Chr 16:1.   **8:9** Hebrew *at Horeb,* another name for Sinai.   **8:13** Some Greek texts add the line *Is this not written in the Book of Jashar?*

Solomon's Prayer of Dedication

22 Then Solomon stood before the altar of the LORD in front of the entire community of Israel. He lifted his hands toward heaven, 23 and he prayed,

"O LORD, God of Israel, there is no God like you in all of heaven above or on the earth below. You keep your covenant and show unfailing love to all who walk before you in wholehearted devotion. 24 You have kept your promise to your servant David, my father. You made that promise with your own mouth, and with your own hands you have fulfilled it today.

25 "And now, O LORD, God of Israel, carry out the additional promise you made to your servant David, my father. For you said to him, 'If your descendants guard their behavior and faithfully follow me as you have done, one of them will always sit on the throne of Israel.' 26 Now, O God of Israel, fulfill this promise to your servant David, my father.

27 "But will God really live on earth? Why, even the highest heavens cannot contain you. How much less this Temple I have built! 28 Nevertheless, listen to my prayer and my plea, O LORD my God. Hear the cry and the prayer that your servant is making to you today. 29 May you watch over this Temple night and day, this place where you have said, 'My name will be there.' May you always hear the prayers I make toward this place. 30 May you hear the humble and earnest requests from me and your people Israel when we pray toward this place. Yes, hear us from heaven where you live, and when you hear, forgive.

31 "If someone wrongs another person and is required to take an oath of innocence in front of your altar in this Temple, 32 then hear from heaven and judge between your servants—the accuser and the accused. Punish the guilty as they deserve. Acquit the innocent because of their innocence.

33 "If your people Israel are defeated by their enemies because they have sinned against you, and if they turn to you and acknowledge your name and pray to you here in this Temple, 34 then hear from heaven and forgive the sin of your people Israel and return them to this land you gave their ancestors.

35 "If the skies are shut up and there is no rain because your people have sinned against you, and if they pray toward this Temple and acknowledge your name and turn from their sins because you have punished them, 36 then hear from heaven and forgive the sins of your servants, your people Israel. Teach them to follow the right path, and send rain on your land that you have given to your people as their special possession.

37 "If there is a famine in the land or a plague or crop disease or attacks of locusts or caterpillars, or if your people's enemies are in the land besieging their towns—whatever disaster or disease there is—38 and if your people Israel pray about their troubles, raising their hands toward this Temple, 39 then hear from heaven where you live, and forgive. Give your people what their actions deserve, for you alone know each human heart. 40 Then they will fear you as long as they live in the land you gave to our ancestors.

41 "In the future, foreigners who do not belong to your people Israel will hear of you. They will come from distant lands because of your name, 42 for they will hear of your great name and your strong hand and your powerful arm. And when they pray toward this Temple, 43 then hear from heaven where you live, and grant what they ask of you. In this way, all the people of the earth will come to know and fear you, just as your own people Israel do. They, too, will know that this Temple I have built honors your name.

44 "If your people go out where you send them to fight their enemies, and if they pray to the LORD by turning toward this city you have chosen and toward this Temple I have built to honor your name, 45 then hear their prayers from heaven and uphold their cause.

46 "If they sin against you—and who has never sinned?—you might become angry with them and let their enemies conquer them and take them captive to their

When I Have No Words

1 KINGS 8:22-53

I was raised on prayer. Some of my earliest memories involve praying at bedtime with my mother at my side: "God bless my sister, my brother, my dad . . ." right down to the names of the gerbils in their cage. In church and at mealtimes, I was taught to pray spontaneously—to "talk" to God from the heart and tell him what's on my mind. And I had plenty to say . . . until my late thirties when the words evaporated.

When I tried to pray, I found I had nothing to say. With this new state of affairs came doubt. *Did my prayers really do anything? Was anyone listening?*

So I stopped praying.

The weeks stretched into months. I felt a darkness, a void, in my life without prayer. Eventually, help came from an unexpected quarter: ancient Christians and their written prayers.

It started simply. About the same time I found myself unable to pray, we joined a church that regularly said the Lord's Prayer together. Every week I prayed it aloud with my faith community—people I loved, those I disliked, men and women who were strangers to me. An odd thing happened: I began to feel a link to the roots of my faith, stretching back to those early disciples and Christians who prayed the same prayer centuries ago.

This connection with the Lord's Prayer opened more possibilities. I looked up other ancient prayers, mostly from the early church. All I had to do was speak them to God; they gave me words when I had no words of my own.

My days began with Scripture and this ancient prayer for the morning: "Lord God, almighty and everlasting Father, you have brought me in safety to this new day: preserve me with your mighty power, that I may not fall into sin, nor be overcome by adversity; and in all I do direct me to the fulfilling of your purpose; through Jesus Christ my Lord. Amen."

I found reassurance in this daily plea for help—especially inviting God to give me direction. Before bed, I read from *The Book of Common Prayer*: "Keep watch, dear Lord, with those who work, or watch, or weep this night, and give your angels charge over those who sleep. Tend the sick, Lord Christ; give rest to the weary, bless the dying, soothe the suffering, pity the afflicted, shield the joyous; and all for your love's sake. Amen."

The rote prayers that I had formerly put aside as "meaningless repetition" surprisingly became a lifeline for me, drawing me closer to God and helping me relax in the knowledge of his care.

As I rested in this framework of prayer, I discovered that great men and women of the Christian faith often wrestled with the same doubts, frustrations, and "dark nights of the soul" that I was struggling with. They had questions; they were unsure, and this was reflected in their prayers. Augustine of Hippo prayed: "Father, I am seeking: I am hesitant and uncertain, but will you, O God, watch over each step of mine, and guide me?"

I discovered Gregory of Nazianzus's fourth-century prayer of personal repentance, which concludes with this request: "Kindle for me your light, O Christ, restore me by your presence." These prayers served as a starting place for me to find my own words of repentance and confession again—stumbling, halting, imperfect words—because I longed for the light to return.

At first I read and spoke these ancient prayers only at rising and at bedtime. But I found other prayers that were helpful at specific moments; especially at times of anxiety and fear. For example, Columba, a sixth-century Irish missionary, gave me this easily memorized prayer: "Alone with none but thee, my God, I journey on my way. What need I fear, when thou art near, O King of night and day? More safe am I within thy hand than if a host did round me stand."

As I prayed Columba's words, I found myself calmer, less afraid, more assured through these pleas for God's presence from Christians who also knew fear and worry.

Recently I've found words of my own to pray again. I've learned to pray in ways without voicing words as well: journaling, walking, drawing. But I rest assured, knowing that if I ever find myself unable to pray, I am surrounded by a mighty band of ancient Christians. These ancients are ready to prop me up, to let their words stand in for mine, and help bring light into any darkness that might come my way.

—*Cindy Crosby*

For more on prayer, see reading at 2 Kings 20:1-10.

land far away or near. ⁴⁷But in that land of exile, they might turn to you in repentance and pray, 'We have sinned, done evil, and acted wickedly.' ⁴⁸If they turn to you with their whole heart and soul in the land of their enemies and pray toward the land you gave to their ancestors—toward this city you have chosen, and toward this Temple I have built to honor your name—⁴⁹then hear their prayers and their petition from heaven where you live, and uphold their cause. ⁵⁰Forgive your people who have sinned against you. Forgive all the offenses they have committed against you. Make their captors merciful to them, ⁵¹for they are your people—your special possession—whom you brought out of the iron-smelting furnace of Egypt.

⁵²"May your eyes be open to my requests and to the requests of your people Israel. May you hear and answer them whenever they cry out to you. ⁵³For when you brought our ancestors out of Egypt, O Sovereign LORD, you told your servant Moses that you had set Israel apart from all the nations of the earth to be your own special possession."

The Dedication of the Temple

⁵⁴When Solomon finished making these prayers and petitions to the LORD, he stood up in front of the altar of the LORD, where he had been kneeling with his hands raised toward heaven. ⁵⁵He stood and in a loud voice blessed the entire congregation of Israel:

⁵⁶"Praise the LORD who has given rest to his people Israel, just as he promised. Not one word has failed of all the wonderful promises he gave through his servant Moses. ⁵⁷May the LORD our God be with us as he was with our ancestors; may he never leave us or abandon us. ⁵⁸May he give us the desire to do his will in everything and to obey all the commands, decrees, and regulations that he gave our ancestors. ⁵⁹And may these words that I have prayed in the presence of the LORD be before him constantly, day and night, so that the LORD our God may give

justice to me and to his people Israel, according to each day's needs. ⁶⁰Then people all over the earth will know that the LORD alone is God and there is no other. ⁶¹And may you be completely faithful to the LORD our God. May you always obey his decrees and commands, just as you are doing today."

⁶²Then the king and all Israel with him offered sacrifices to the LORD. ⁶³Solomon offered to the LORD a peace offering of 22,000 cattle and 120,000 sheep and goats. And so the king and all the people of Israel dedicated the Temple of the LORD.

⁶⁴That same day the king consecrated the central area of the courtyard in front of the LORD's Temple. He offered burnt offerings, grain offerings, and the fat of peace offerings there, because the bronze altar in the LORD's presence was too small to hold all the burnt offerings, grain offerings, and the fat of the peace offerings.

⁶⁵Then Solomon and all Israel celebrated the Festival of Shelters* in the presence of the LORD our God. A large congregation had gathered from as far away as Lebo-hamath in the north and the Brook of Egypt in the south. The celebration went on for fourteen days in all—seven days for the dedication of the altar and seven days for the Festival of Shelters.* ⁶⁶After the festival was over,* Solomon sent the people home. They blessed the king and went to their homes joyful and glad because the LORD had been good to his servant David and to his people Israel.

9 The LORD's Response to Solomon

So Solomon finished building the Temple of the LORD, as well as the royal palace. He completed everything he had planned to do. ²Then the LORD appeared to Solomon a second time, as he had done before at Gibeon. ³The LORD said to him,

"I have heard your prayer and your petition. I have set this Temple apart to be holy—this place you have built where my name will be honored forever. I will always watch over it, for it is dear to my heart. ⁴"As for you, if you will follow me with integrity and godliness, as David your

---

8:65a Hebrew *the festival;* see note on 8:2.   8:65b Hebrew *seven days and seven days, fourteen days;* compare parallel text at 2 Chr 7:8-10.
8:66 Hebrew *On the eighth day,* probably referring to the day following the seven-day Festival of Shelters; compare parallel text at 2 Chr 7:9-10.

father did, obeying all my commands, decrees, and regulations, ⁵then I will establish the throne of your dynasty over Israel forever. For I made this promise to your father, David: 'One of your descendants will always sit on the throne of Israel.'

⁶"But if you or your descendants abandon me and disobey the commands and decrees I have given you, and if you serve and worship other gods, ⁷then I will uproot Israel from this land that I have given them. I will reject this Temple that I have made holy to honor my name. I will make Israel an object of mockery and ridicule among the nations. ⁸And though this Temple is impressive now, all who pass by will be appalled and will shake their heads in amazement. They will ask, 'Why did the LORD do such terrible things to this land and to this Temple?'

⁹"And the answer will be, 'Because his people abandoned the LORD their God, who brought their ancestors out of Egypt, and they worshiped other gods instead and bowed down to them. That is why the LORD has brought all these disasters on them.'"

Solomon's Agreement with Hiram

¹⁰It took Solomon twenty years to build the LORD's Temple and his own royal palace. At the end of that time, ¹¹he gave twenty towns in the land of Galilee to King Hiram of Tyre. (Hiram had previously provided all the cedar and cypress timber and gold that Solomon had requested.) ¹²But when Hiram came from Tyre to see the towns Solomon had given him, he was not at all pleased with them. ¹³"What kind of towns are these, my brother?" he asked. So Hiram called that area Cabul (which means "worthless"), as it is still known today. ¹⁴Nevertheless, Hiram paid* Solomon 9,000 pounds* of gold.

Solomon's Many Achievements

¹⁵This is the account of the forced labor that King Solomon conscripted to build the LORD's Temple, the royal palace, the supporting terraces,* the wall of Jerusalem, and the cities of Hazor, Megiddo, and Gezer. ¹⁶(Pharaoh, the king of Egypt, had attacked and captured Gezer, killing the Canaanite population and burning it down. He gave the city to his daughter as a wedding gift when she married Solomon. ¹⁷So Solomon rebuilt the city of Gezer.) He also built up the towns of Lower Beth-horon, ¹⁸Baalath, and Tamar* in the wilderness within his land. ¹⁹He built towns as supply centers and constructed towns where his chariots and horses* could be stationed. He built everything he desired in Jerusalem and Lebanon and throughout his entire realm.

²⁰There were still some people living in the land who were not Israelites, including Amorites, Hittites, Perizzites, Hivites, and Jebusites. ²¹These were descendants of the nations whom the people of Israel had not completely destroyed.* So Solomon conscripted them for his labor force, and they serve in the labor force to this day. ²²But Solomon did not conscript any of the Israelites for forced labor. Instead, he assigned them to serve as fighting men, government officials, officers and captains in his army, commanders of his chariots, and charioteers. ²³Solomon appointed 550 of them to supervise the people working on his various projects.

²⁴Solomon moved his wife, Pharaoh's daughter, from the City of David to the new palace he had built for her. Then he constructed the supporting terraces.

²⁵Three times each year Solomon presented burnt offerings and peace offerings on the altar he had built for the LORD. He also burned incense to the LORD. And so he finished the work of building the Temple.

²⁶King Solomon also built a fleet of ships at Ezion-geber, a port near Elath* in the land of Edom, along the shore of the Red Sea.* ²⁷Hiram sent experienced crews of sailors to sail the ships with Solomon's men. ²⁸They sailed to Ophir and brought back to Solomon some sixteen tons* of gold.

9:14a Or For Hiram had paid.   9:14b Hebrew 120 talents [4,000 kilograms].   9:15 Hebrew the millo; also in 9:24. The meaning of the Hebrew is uncertain.   9:18 An alternate reading in the Masoretic Text reads Tadmor.   9:19 Or and charioteers.   9:21 The Hebrew term used here refers to the complete consecration of things or people to the LORD, either by destroying them or by giving them as an offering.   9:26a As in Greek version (see also 2 Kgs 14:22; 16:6); Hebrew reads Eloth, a variant spelling of Elath.   9:26b Hebrew sea of reeds.   9:28 Hebrew 420 talents [14 metric tons].

10 Visit of the Queen of Sheba

When the queen of Sheba heard of Solomon's fame, which brought honor to the name of the LORD,* she came to test him with hard questions. ²She arrived in Jerusalem with a large group of attendants and a great caravan of camels loaded with spices, large quantities of gold, and precious jewels. When she met with Solomon, she talked with him about everything she had on her mind. ³Solomon had answers for all her questions; nothing was too hard for the king to explain to her. ⁴When the queen of Sheba realized how very wise Solomon was, and when she saw the palace he had built, ⁵she was overwhelmed. She was also amazed at the food on his tables, the organization of his officials and their splendid clothing, the cup-bearers, and the burnt offerings Solomon made at the Temple of the LORD.

⁶She exclaimed to the king, "Everything I heard in my country about your achievements* and wisdom is true! ⁷I didn't believe what was said until I arrived here and saw it with my own eyes. In fact, I had not heard the half of it! Your wisdom and prosperity are far beyond what I was told. ⁸How happy your people* must be! What a privilege for your officials to stand here day after day, listening to your wisdom! ⁹Praise the LORD your God, who delights in you and has placed you on the throne of Israel. Because of the LORD's eternal love for Israel, he has made you king so you can rule with justice and righteousness."

¹⁰Then she gave the king a gift of 9,000 pounds* of gold, great quantities of spices, and precious jewels. Never again were so many spices brought in as those the queen of Sheba gave to King Solomon.

¹¹(In addition, Hiram's ships brought gold from Ophir, and they also brought rich cargoes of red sandalwood* and precious jewels. ¹²The king used the sandalwood to make railings for the Temple of the LORD and the royal palace, and to construct lyres and harps for the musicians. Never before or since has there been such a supply of sandalwood.)

¹³King Solomon gave the queen of Sheba whatever she asked for, besides all the customary gifts he had so generously given. Then she and all her attendants returned to their own land.

Solomon's Wealth and Splendor

¹⁴Each year Solomon received about 25 tons* of gold. ¹⁵This did not include the additional revenue he received from merchants and traders, all the kings of Arabia, and the governors of the land.

¹⁶King Solomon made 200 large shields of hammered gold, each weighing more than fifteen pounds.* ¹⁷He also made 300 smaller shields of hammered gold, each weighing nearly four pounds.* The king placed these shields in the Palace of the Forest of Lebanon.

¹⁸Then the king made a huge throne, decorated with ivory and overlaid with fine gold. ¹⁹The throne had six steps and a rounded back. There were armrests on both sides of the seat, and the figure of a lion stood on each side of the throne. ²⁰There were also twelve other lions, one standing on each end of the six steps. No other throne in all the world could be compared with it!

²¹All of King Solomon's drinking cups were solid gold, as were all the utensils in the Palace of the Forest of Lebanon. They were not made of silver, for silver was considered worthless in Solomon's day!

²²The king had a fleet of trading ships* that sailed with Hiram's fleet. Once every three years the ships returned, loaded with gold, silver, ivory, apes, and peacocks.*

²³So King Solomon became richer and wiser than any other king on earth. ²⁴People from every nation came to consult him and to hear the wisdom God had given him. ²⁵Year after year everyone who visited brought him gifts of silver and gold, clothing, weapons, spices, horses, and mules.

²⁶Solomon built up a huge force of chariots and horses.* He had 1,400 chariots and 12,000 horses. He stationed some of them in the chariot cities and some near him in Jerusalem. ²⁷The king made silver as plentiful in Jerusalem as stone. And valu-

---

10:1 Or which was due to the name of the LORD. The meaning of the Hebrew is uncertain.   10:6 Hebrew your words.   10:8 Greek and Syriac versions and Latin Vulgate read your wives.   10:10 Hebrew 120 talents [4,000 kilograms].   10:11 Hebrew almug wood; also in 10:12.   10:14 Hebrew 666 talents [23 metric tons].   10:16 Hebrew 600 [shekels] of gold [6.8 kilograms].   10:17 Hebrew 3 minas [1.8 kilograms].   10:22a Hebrew fleet of ships of Tarshish.   10:22b Or and baboons.   10:26 Or charioteers; also in 10:26b.

able cedar timber was as common as the sycamore-fig trees that grow in the foothills of Judah.* [28] Solomon's horses were imported from Egypt* and from Cilicia*; the king's traders acquired them from Cilicia at the standard price. [29] At that time chariots from Egypt could be purchased for 600 pieces of silver,* and horses for 150 pieces of silver.* They were then exported to the kings of the Hittites and the kings of Aram.

11 Solomon's Many Wives

Now King Solomon loved many foreign women. Besides Pharaoh's daughter, he married women from Moab, Ammon, Edom, Sidon, and from among the Hittites. [2] The LORD had clearly instructed the people of Israel, "You must not marry them, because they will turn your hearts to their gods." Yet Solomon insisted on loving them anyway. [3] He had 700 wives of royal birth and 300 concubines. And in fact, they did turn his heart away from the LORD.

[4] In Solomon's old age, they turned his heart to worship other gods instead of being completely faithful to the LORD his God, as his father, David, had been. [5] Solomon worshiped Ashtoreth, the goddess of the Sidonians, and Molech,* the detestable god of the Ammonites. [6] In this way, Solomon did what was evil in the LORD's sight; he refused to follow the LORD completely, as his father, David, had done.

[7] On the Mount of Olives, east of Jerusalem,* he even built a pagan shrine for Chemosh, the detestable god of Moab, and another for Molech, the detestable god of the Ammonites. [8] Solomon built such shrines for all his foreign wives to use for burning incense and sacrificing to their gods.

[9] The LORD was very angry with Solomon, for his heart had turned away from the LORD, the God of Israel, who had appeared to him twice. [10] He had warned Solomon specifically about worshiping other gods, but Solomon did not listen to the LORD's command. [11] So now the LORD said to him, "Since you have not kept my covenant and have disobeyed my decrees, I will surely tear the kingdom away from you and give it to one of your servants. [12] But for the sake of your father, David, I will not do this while you are still alive. I will take the kingdom away from your son. [13] And even so, I will not take away the entire kingdom; I will let him be king of one tribe, for the sake of my servant David and for the sake of Jerusalem, my chosen city."

Solomon's Adversaries

[14] Then the LORD raised up Hadad the Edomite, a member of Edom's royal family, to be Solomon's adversary. [15] Years before, David had defeated Edom. Joab, his army commander, had stayed to bury some of the Israelite soldiers who had died in battle. While there, they killed every male in Edom. [16] Joab and the army of Israel had stayed there for six months, killing them.

[17] But Hadad and a few of his father's royal officials escaped and headed for Egypt. (Hadad was just a boy at the time.) [18] They set out from Midian and went to Paran, where others joined them. Then they traveled to Egypt and went to Pharaoh, who gave them a home, food, and some land. [19] Pharaoh grew very fond of Hadad, and he gave him his wife's sister in marriage—the sister of Queen Tahpenes. [20] She bore him a son named Genubath. Tahpenes raised him* in Pharaoh's palace among Pharaoh's own sons.

[21] When the news reached Hadad in Egypt that David and his commander Joab were both dead, he said to Pharaoh, "Let me return to my own country."

[22] "Why?" Pharaoh asked him. "What do you lack here that makes you want to go home?"

"Nothing," he replied. "But even so, please let me return home."

[23] God also raised up Rezon son of Eliada as Solomon's adversary. Rezon had fled from his master, King Hadadezer of Zobah, [24] and had become the leader of a gang of rebels. After David conquered Hadadezer, Rezon and his men fled to Damascus, where he became king. [25] Rezon was Israel's

---

10:27 Hebrew *the Shephelah.* **10:28a** Possibly *Muzur,* a district near Cilicia; also in 10:29. **10:28b** Hebrew *Kue,* probably another name for Cilicia. **10:29a** Hebrew *600 [shekels] of silver,* about 15 pounds or 6.8 kilograms in weight. **10:29b** Hebrew *150 [shekels],* about 3.8 pounds or 1.7 kilograms in weight. **11:5** Hebrew *Milcom,* a variant spelling of Molech; also in 11:33. **11:7** Hebrew *On the mountain east of Jerusalem.* **11:20** As in Greek version; Hebrew reads *weaned him.*

Simplicity

Two of Me
1 KINGS 11:1–13

Simplicity has become a cool, trendy topic. *Real Simple* magazine, for example, will tell you how to organize your closets, unclutter your garage, and even how to leave your high-pressure job in the city and move to Montana to start a lavender farm, which then finds amazing success and eventually goes public, requiring another downsizing. The popular message is this: embracing simplicity will make your life more manageable and more enjoyable.

But simplicity, from a biblical perspective, is not about making our lives more manageable. Did Moses' life become less complex after the burning bush? Did Esther's decision to follow God make her life easier? Consider Joseph and Mary. Did submitting to God make their young lives more manageable? Hardly. And we shouldn't forget the apostle Paul. Few would argue that the persecution he endured was a manageable lifestyle. These examples, and many others, reveal that for God's people the opposite of simplicity is not complexity. It's duplicity.

What does it mean to be duplicitous? The root word gives us a clue. A *duplicate* is a representation or copy of an original. When the word is attributed to human behavior, it means the persona we present to others is a double, a fake. The "real" us exists somewhere, but we are presenting a duplicate in our stead. While we recoil at the thought of deliberate duplicity (the hypocrisy of the Pharisees comes to mind), we have to face the subtle and destructive force of culturally acceptable duplicity every day. This temptation usually revolves around the need for more—more time, more energy, more money, more accomplishments, even more of us.

How many of us, in our stressed-out moments, have uttered, "If only there were more of me to go around . . ." or, "I just need a few more hours in the day!"? In those moments we are tempted to live duplicitously.

As difficult as it has been for me to admit, this kind of duplicity is the root of many evils in my life. I have often operated from a false self; when I feel the pull to be more confident, put together, successful, spiritual, hard working, or organized than I really am, I am tempted by duplicity. And when I succumb to that temptation, everyone around me suffers. Moving away from duplicity means practicing a new spiritual discipline—the discipline of simplicity.

I have found that practicing simplicity means determining who I really am, identifying the boundaries of my true self, and then making decisions and presenting myself to others grounded in that truth. Romans 12:3 challenges us to be sober minded in our assessment of ourselves. When we wrongly pursue opportunities, commitments, or avenues of ministry God never had in mind when he designed us, or when we refuse to use the gifts we have been given, we're not being honest about ourselves.

In an important sense, simplicity is not only about what we have and possess but also about how we determine what we will give. In 2 Corinthians 9:7 Paul says we should give what we decide in our hearts to give, not reluctantly or under compulsion, because God loves a cheerful giver. This verse is often applied to financial giving, but I believe it applies to any resource we give away, including our time, energy, or skills. During one particularly overextended time, most of my "gives" were reluctant or under compulsion. I felt I *had* to help, *had* to serve, or *had* to solve the problem. But when we attempt to give what we do not have, we cross a boundary and trespass into joylessness.

When an opportunity to give (time, money, service, etc.) arises, practicing simplicity means starting with self-examination. "Do I have it in my heart to give?" If that answer is no, then something else, something duplicitous, is behind the motivation to say yes. A critical step toward simplicity involves defining and respecting the boundary lines that shape our lives; I've learned I honor God when I recognize the outer limits of my time, energy, relational capacity, and gifting—and when I choose to live healthily within those limits.

Moving from duplicity to simplicity requires a new way of life—one marked by defining boundaries, being honest about how God has gifted and formed us, and keeping accounts of what we are truly capable of giving. As we travel down this path, we might discover life's complexity actually increasing as we step out in obedience. But we can learn to rest even amid the complexity if our interior life is one of quietness, trust, and rest with God.

—*Mindy Caliguire*

For more on simplicity, see reading at 2 Kings 4:1–7.

bitter adversary for the rest of Solomon's reign, and he made trouble, just as Hadad did. Rezon hated Israel intensely and continued to reign in Aram.

Jeroboam Rebels against Solomon

26 Another rebel leader was Jeroboam son of Nebat, one of Solomon's own officials. He came from the town of Zeredah in Ephraim, and his mother was Zeruah, a widow.

27 This is the story behind his rebellion. Solomon was rebuilding the supporting terraces* and repairing the walls of the city of his father, David. 28 Jeroboam was a very capable young man, and when Solomon saw how industrious he was, he put him in charge of the labor force from the tribes of Ephraim and Manasseh, the descendants of Joseph.

29 One day as Jeroboam was leaving Jerusalem, the prophet Ahijah from Shiloh met him along the way. Ahijah was wearing a new cloak. The two of them were alone in a field, 30 and Ahijah took hold of the new cloak he was wearing and tore it into twelve pieces. 31 Then he said to Jeroboam, "Take ten of these pieces, for this is what the LORD, the God of Israel, says: 'I am about to tear the kingdom from the hand of Solomon, and I will give ten of the tribes to you! 32 But I will leave him one tribe for the sake of my servant David and for the sake of Jerusalem, which I have chosen out of all the tribes of Israel. 33 For Solomon has* abandoned me and worshiped Ashtoreth, the goddess of the Sidonians; Chemosh, the god of Moab; and Molech, the god of the Ammonites. He has not followed my ways and done what is pleasing in my sight. He has not obeyed my decrees and regulations as David his father did.

34 "'But I will not take the entire kingdom from Solomon at this time. For the sake of my servant David, the one whom I chose and who obeyed my commands and decrees, I will keep Solomon as leader for the rest of his life. 35 But I will take the kingdom away from his son and give ten of the tribes to you. 36 His son will have one tribe so that the descendants of David my servant will continue to reign, shining like a lamp in Jerusalem, the city I have chosen

to be the place for my name. 37 And I will place you on the throne of Israel, and you will rule over all that your heart desires. 38 If you listen to what I tell you and follow my ways and do whatever I consider to be right, and if you obey my decrees and commands, as my servant David did, then I will always be with you. I will establish an enduring dynasty for you as I did for David, and I will give Israel to you. 39 Because of Solomon's sin I will punish the descendants of David—though not forever.'"

40 Solomon tried to kill Jeroboam, but he fled to King Shishak of Egypt and stayed there until Solomon died.

Summary of Solomon's Reign

41 The rest of the events in Solomon's reign, including all his deeds and his wisdom, are recorded in *The Book of the Acts of Solomon*. 42 Solomon ruled in Jerusalem over all Israel for forty years. 43 When he died, he was buried in the City of David, named for his father. Then his son Rehoboam became the next king.

12 The Northern Tribes Revolt

Rehoboam went to Shechem, where all Israel had gathered to make him king. 2 When Jeroboam son of Nebat heard of this, he returned from Egypt,* for he had fled to Egypt to escape from King Solomon. 3 The leaders of Israel summoned him, and Jeroboam and the whole assembly of Israel went to speak with Rehoboam. 4 "Your father was a hard master," they said. "Lighten the harsh labor demands and heavy taxes that your father imposed on us. Then we will be your loyal subjects."

5 Rehoboam replied, "Give me three days to think this over. Then come back for my answer." So the people went away.

6 Then King Rehoboam discussed the matter with the older men who had counseled his father, Solomon. "What is your advice?" he asked. "How should I answer these people?"

7 The older counselors replied, "If you are willing to be a servant to these people today and give them a favorable answer, they will always be your loyal subjects."

11:27 Hebrew *the millo.* The meaning of the Hebrew is uncertain. 11:33 As in Greek, Syriac, and Latin Vulgate; Hebrew reads *For they have.* 12:2 As in Greek version and Latin Vulgate (see also 2 Chr 10:2); Hebrew reads *he lived in Egypt.*

⁸But Rehoboam rejected the advice of the older men and instead asked the opinion of the young men who had grown up with him and were now his advisers. ⁹"What is your advice?" he asked them. "How should I answer these people who want me to lighten the burdens imposed by my father?"

¹⁰The young men replied, "This is what you should tell those complainers who want a lighter burden: 'My little finger is thicker than my father's waist! ¹¹Yes, my father laid heavy burdens on you, but I'm going to make them even heavier! My father beat you with whips, but I will beat you with scorpions!'"

¹²Three days later Jeroboam and all the people returned to hear Rehoboam's decision, just as the king had ordered. ¹³But Rehoboam spoke harshly to the people, for he rejected the advice of the older counselors ¹⁴and followed the counsel of his younger advisers. He told the people, "My father laid heavy burdens on you, but I'm going to make them even heavier! My father beat you with whips, but I will beat you with scorpions!"

¹⁵So the king paid no attention to the people. This turn of events was the will of the LORD, for it fulfilled the LORD's message to Jeroboam son of Nebat through the prophet Ahijah from Shiloh.

¹⁶When all Israel realized that the king had refused to listen to them, they responded,

"Down with the dynasty of David!
    We have no interest in the son of Jesse.
Back to your homes, O Israel!
    Look out for your own house,
        O David!"

So the people of Israel returned home. ¹⁷But Rehoboam continued to rule over the Israelites who lived in the towns of Judah.

¹⁸King Rehoboam sent Adoniram,* who was in charge of the labor force, to restore order, but the people of Israel stoned him to death. When this news reached King Rehoboam, he quickly jumped into his chariot and fled to Jerusalem. ¹⁹And to this day the northern tribes of Israel have refused to be ruled by a descendant of David.

²⁰When the people of Israel learned of Jeroboam's return from Egypt, they called an assembly and made him king over all Israel. So only the tribe of Judah remained loyal to the family of David.

Shemaiah's Prophecy

²¹When Rehoboam arrived at Jerusalem, he mobilized the men of Judah and the tribe of Benjamin—180,000 select troops—to fight against the men of Israel and to restore the kingdom to himself.

²²But God said to Shemaiah, the man of God, ²³"Say to Rehoboam son of Solomon, king of Judah, and to all the people of Judah and Benjamin, and to the rest of the people, ²⁴'This is what the LORD says: Do not fight against your relatives, the Israelites. Go back home, for what has happened is my doing!'" So they obeyed the message of the LORD and went home, as the LORD had commanded.

Jeroboam Makes Gold Calves

²⁵Jeroboam then built up the city of Shechem in the hill country of Ephraim, and it became his capital. Later he went and built up the town of Peniel.*

²⁶Jeroboam thought to himself, "Unless I am careful, the kingdom will return to the dynasty of David. ²⁷When these people go to Jerusalem to offer sacrifices at the Temple of the LORD, they will again give their allegiance to King Rehoboam of Judah. They will kill me and make him their king instead."

²⁸So on the advice of his counselors, the king made two gold calves. He said to the people,* "It is too much trouble for you to worship in Jerusalem. Look, Israel, these are the gods who brought you out of Egypt!"

²⁹He placed these calf idols in Bethel and in Dan—at either end of his kingdom. ³⁰But this became a great sin, for the people worshiped the idols, traveling as far north as Dan to worship the one there.

³¹Jeroboam also erected buildings at the pagan shrines and ordained priests from the common people—those who were not from the priestly tribe of Levi. ³²And Jeroboam instituted a religious festival in

---

12:18 As in some Greek manuscripts and Syriac version (see also 4:6; 5:14); Hebrew reads *Adoram.* **12:25** Hebrew *Penuel,* a variant spelling of Peniel. **12:28** Hebrew *to them.*

Bethel, held on the fifteenth day of the eighth month,* in imitation of the annual Festival of Shelters in Judah. There at Bethel he himself offered sacrifices to the calves he had made, and he appointed priests for the pagan shrines he had made. ³³So on the fifteenth day of the eighth month, a day that he himself had designated, Jeroboam offered sacrifices on the altar at Bethel. He instituted a religious festival for Israel, and he went up to the altar to burn incense.

13 A Prophet Denounces Jeroboam

At the LORD's command, a man of God from Judah went to Bethel, arriving there just as Jeroboam was approaching the altar to burn incense. ²Then at the LORD's command, he shouted, "O altar, altar! This is what the LORD says: A child named Josiah will be born into the dynasty of David. On you he will sacrifice the priests from the pagan shrines who come here to burn incense, and human bones will be burned on you." ³That same day the man of God gave a sign to prove his message. He said, "The LORD has promised to give this sign: This altar will split apart, and its ashes will be poured out on the ground."

⁴When King Jeroboam heard the man of God speaking against the altar at Bethel, he pointed at him and shouted, "Seize that man!" But instantly the king's hand became paralyzed in that position, and he couldn't pull it back. ⁵At the same time a wide crack appeared in the altar, and the ashes poured out, just as the man of God had predicted in his message from the LORD.

⁶The king cried out to the man of God, "Please ask the LORD your God to restore my hand again!" So the man of God prayed to the LORD, and the king's hand was restored and he could move it again.

⁷Then the king said to the man of God, "Come to the palace with me and have something to eat, and I will give you a gift."

⁸But the man of God said to the king, "Even if you gave me half of everything you own, I would not go with you. I would not eat or drink anything in this place. ⁹For the LORD gave me this command: 'You must

not eat or drink anything while you are there, and do not return to Judah by the same way you came.'" ¹⁰So he left Bethel and went home another way.

¹¹As it happened, there was an old prophet living in Bethel, and his sons* came home and told him what the man of God had done in Bethel that day. They also told their father what the man had said to the king. ¹²The old prophet asked them, "Which way did he go?" So they showed their father* which road the man of God had taken. ¹³"Quick, saddle the donkey," the old man said. So they saddled the donkey for him, and he mounted it.

¹⁴Then he rode after the man of God and found him sitting under a great tree. The old prophet asked him, "Are you the man of God who came from Judah?"

"Yes, I am," he replied.

¹⁵Then he said to the man of God, "Come home with me and eat some food."

¹⁶"No, I cannot," he replied. "I am not allowed to eat or drink anything here in this place. ¹⁷For the LORD gave me this command: 'You must not eat or drink anything while you are there, and do not return to Judah by the same way you came.'"

¹⁸But the old prophet answered, "I am a prophet, too, just as you are. And an angel gave me this command from the LORD: 'Bring him home with you so he can have something to eat and drink.'" But the old man was lying to him. ¹⁹So they went back together, and the man of God ate and drank at the prophet's home.

²⁰Then while they were sitting at the table, a command from the LORD came to the old prophet. ²¹He cried out to the man of God from Judah, "This is what the LORD says: You have defied the word of the LORD and have disobeyed the command the LORD your God gave you. ²²You came back to this place and ate and drank where he told you not to eat or drink. Because of this, your body will not be buried in the grave of your ancestors."

²³After the man of God had finished eating and drinking, the old prophet saddled his own donkey for him, ²⁴and the man of

---

12:32 This day of the ancient Hebrew lunar calendar occurred in late October or early November, exactly one month after the annual Festival of Shelters in Judah (see Lev 23:34). **13:11** As in Greek version; Hebrew reads *son*. **13:12** As in Greek version; Hebrew reads *They had seen*.

God started off again. But as he was traveling along, a lion came out and killed him. His body lay there on the road, with the donkey and the lion standing beside it. ²⁵People who passed by saw the body lying in the road and the lion standing beside it, and they went and reported it in Bethel, where the old prophet lived.

²⁶When the prophet heard the report, he said, "It is the man of God who disobeyed the LORD's command. The LORD has fulfilled his word by causing the lion to attack and kill him."

²⁷Then the prophet said to his sons, "Saddle a donkey for me." So they saddled a donkey, ²⁸and he went out and found the body lying in the road. The donkey and lion were still standing there beside it, for the lion had not eaten the body nor attacked the donkey. ²⁹So the prophet laid the body of the man of God on the donkey and took it back to the town to mourn over him and bury him. ³⁰He laid the body in his own grave, crying out in grief, "Oh, my brother!"

³¹Afterward the prophet said to his sons, "When I die, bury me in the grave where the man of God is buried. Lay my bones beside his bones. ³²For the message the LORD told him to proclaim against the altar in Bethel and against the pagan shrines in the towns of Samaria will certainly come true."

³³But even after this, Jeroboam did not turn from his evil ways. He continued to choose priests from the common people. He appointed anyone who wanted to become a priest for the pagan shrines. ³⁴This became a great sin and resulted in the utter destruction of Jeroboam's dynasty from the face of the earth.

14 Ahijah's Prophecy against Jeroboam

At that time Jeroboam's son Abijah became very sick. ²So Jeroboam told his wife, "Disguise yourself so that no one will recognize you as my wife. Then go to the prophet Ahijah at Shiloh—the man who told me I would become king. ³Take him a gift of ten loaves of bread, some cakes, and a jar of honey, and ask him what will happen to the boy."

⁴So Jeroboam's wife went to Ahijah's home at Shiloh. He was an old man now and could no longer see. ⁵But the LORD had told Ahijah, "Jeroboam's wife will come here, pretending to be someone else. She will ask you about her son, for he is very sick. Give her the answer I give you."

⁶So when Ahijah heard her footsteps at the door, he called out, "Come in, wife of Jeroboam! Why are you pretending to be someone else?" Then he told her, "I have bad news for you. ⁷Give your husband, Jeroboam, this message from the LORD, the God of Israel: 'I promoted you from the ranks of the common people and made you ruler over my people Israel. ⁸I ripped the kingdom away from the family of David and gave it to you. But you have not been like my servant David, who obeyed my commands and followed me with all his heart and always did whatever I wanted. ⁹You have done more evil than all who lived before you. You have made other gods for yourself and have made me furious with your gold calves. And since you have turned your back on me, ¹⁰I will bring disaster on your dynasty and will destroy every one of your male descendants, slave and free alike, anywhere in Israel. I will burn up your royal dynasty as one burns up trash until it is all gone. ¹¹The members of Jeroboam's family who die in the city will be eaten by dogs, and those who die in the field will be eaten by vultures. I, the LORD, have spoken.'"

¹²Then Ahijah said to Jeroboam's wife, "Go on home, and when you enter the city, the child will die. ¹³All Israel will mourn for him and bury him. He is the only member of your family who will have a proper burial, for this child is the only good thing that the LORD, the God of Israel, sees in the entire family of Jeroboam.

¹⁴"In addition, the LORD will raise up a king over Israel who will destroy the family of Jeroboam. This will happen today, even now! ¹⁵Then the LORD will shake Israel like a reed whipped about in a stream. He will uproot the people of Israel from this good land that he gave their ancestors and will scatter them beyond the Euphrates River,* for they have angered the LORD with the

---

14:15 Hebrew *the river.*

Asherah poles they have set up for worship. [16]He will abandon Israel because Jeroboam sinned and made Israel sin along with him."

[17]So Jeroboam's wife returned to Tirzah, and the child died just as she walked through the door of her home. [18]And all Israel buried him and mourned for him, as the LORD had promised through the prophet Ahijah.

[19]The rest of the events in Jeroboam's reign, including all his wars and how he ruled, are recorded in *The Book of the History of the Kings of Israel.* [20]Jeroboam reigned in Israel twenty-two years. When Jeroboam died, his son Nadab became the next king.

Rehoboam Rules in Judah

[21]Meanwhile, Rehoboam son of Solomon was king in Judah. He was forty-one years old when he became king, and he reigned seventeen years in Jerusalem, the city the LORD had chosen from among all the tribes of Israel as the place to honor his name. Rehoboam's mother was Naamah, an Ammonite woman.

[22]During Rehoboam's reign, the people of Judah did what was evil in the LORD's sight, provoking his anger with their sin, for it was even worse than that of their ancestors. [23]For they also built for themselves pagan shrines and set up sacred pillars and Asherah poles on every high hill and under every green tree. [24]There were even male and female shrine prostitutes throughout the land. The people imitated the detestable practices of the pagan nations the LORD had driven from the land ahead of the Israelites.

[25]In the fifth year of King Rehoboam's reign, King Shishak of Egypt came up and attacked Jerusalem. [26]He ransacked the treasuries of the LORD's Temple and the royal palace; he stole everything, including all the gold shields Solomon had made. [27]King Rehoboam later replaced them with bronze shields as substitutes, and he entrusted them to the care of the commanders of the guard who protected the entrance to the royal palace. [28]Whenever the king went to the Temple of the LORD, the guards would also take the shields and then return them to the guardroom.

[29]The rest of the events in Rehoboam's reign and everything he did are recorded in *The Book of the History of the Kings of Judah.* [30]There was constant war between Rehoboam and Jeroboam. [31]When Rehoboam died, he was buried among his ancestors in the City of David. His mother was Naamah, an Ammonite woman. Then his son Abijam* became the next king.

15 Abijam Rules in Judah

Abijam* began to rule over Judah in the eighteenth year of Jeroboam's reign in Israel. [2]He reigned in Jerusalem three years. His mother was Maacah, the daughter of Absalom.*

[3]He committed the same sins as his father before him, and he was not faithful to the LORD his God, as his ancestor David had been. [4]But for David's sake, the LORD his God allowed his descendants to continue ruling, shining like a lamp, and he gave Abijam a son to rule after him in Jerusalem. [5]For David had done what was pleasing in the LORD's sight and had obeyed the LORD's commands throughout his life, except in the affair concerning Uriah the Hittite.

[6]There was war between Abijam and Jeroboam* throughout Abijam's reign. [7]The rest of the events in Abijam's reign and everything he did are recorded in *The Book of the History of the Kings of Judah.* There was constant war between Abijam and Jeroboam. [8]When Abijam died, he was buried in the City of David. Then his son Asa became the next king.

Asa Rules in Judah

[9]Asa began to rule over Judah in the twentieth year of Jeroboam's reign in Israel. [10]He reigned in Jerusalem forty-one years. His grandmother* was Maacah, the daughter of Absalom.

[11]Asa did what was pleasing in the LORD's sight, as his ancestor David had done. [12]He banished the male and female shrine prostitutes from the land and got rid of all the idols* his ancestors had made. [13]He even deposed his grandmother Maacah from her position as queen mother because she

14:31 Also known as *Abijah.*   **15:1** Also known as *Abijah.*   **15:2** Hebrew *Abishalom* (also in 15:10), a variant spelling of Absalom; compare 2 Chr 11:20.   **15:6** As in a few Hebrew and Greek manuscripts; most Hebrew manuscripts read *between Rehoboam and Jeroboam.*   **15:10** Or *The queen mother;* Hebrew reads *His mother* (also in 15:13); compare 15:2.   **15:12** The Hebrew term (literally *round things*) probably alludes to dung.

had made an obscene Asherah pole. He cut down her obscene pole and burned it in the Kidron Valley. ¹⁴Although the pagan shrines were not removed, Asa's heart remained completely faithful to the LORD throughout his life. ¹⁵He brought into the Temple of the LORD the silver and gold and the various items that he and his father had dedicated.

¹⁶There was constant war between King Asa of Judah and King Baasha of Israel. ¹⁷King Baasha of Israel invaded Judah and fortified Ramah in order to prevent anyone from entering or leaving King Asa's territory in Judah.

¹⁸Asa responded by removing all the silver and gold that was left in the treasuries of the Temple of the LORD and the royal palace. He sent it with some of his officials to Ben-hadad son of Tabrimmon, son of Hezion, the king of Aram, who was ruling in Damascus, along with this message:

¹⁹"Let there be a treaty* between you and me like the one between your father and my father. See, I am sending you a gift of silver and gold. Break your treaty with King Baasha of Israel so that he will leave me alone."

²⁰Ben-hadad agreed to King Asa's request and sent the commanders of his army to attack the towns of Israel. They conquered the towns of Ijon, Dan, Abel-beth-maacah, and all Kinnereth, and all the land of Naphtali. ²¹As soon as Baasha of Israel heard what was happening, he abandoned his project of fortifying Ramah and withdrew to Tirzah. ²²Then King Asa sent an order throughout Judah, requiring that everyone, without exception, help to carry away the building stones and timbers that Baasha had been using to fortify Ramah. Asa used these materials to fortify the town of Geba in Benjamin and the town of Mizpah.

²³The rest of the events in Asa's reign—the extent of his power, everything he did, and the names of the cities he built—are recorded in *The Book of the History of the Kings of Judah.* In his old age his feet became diseased. ²⁴When Asa died, he was buried with his ancestors in the City of David.

Then Jehoshaphat, Asa's son, became the next king.

Nadab Rules in Israel

²⁵Nadab son of Jeroboam began to rule over Israel in the second year of King Asa's reign in Judah. He reigned in Israel two years. ²⁶But he did what was evil in the LORD's sight and followed the example of his father, continuing the sins that Jeroboam had led Israel to commit.

²⁷Then Baasha son of Ahijah, from the tribe of Issachar, plotted against Nadab and assassinated him while he and the Israelite army were laying siege to the Philistine town of Gibbethon. ²⁸Baasha killed Nadab in the third year of King Asa's reign in Judah, and he became the next king of Israel.

²⁹He immediately slaughtered all the descendants of King Jeroboam, so that not one of the royal family was left, just as the LORD had promised concerning Jeroboam by the prophet Ahijah from Shiloh. ³⁰This was done because Jeroboam had provoked the anger of the LORD, the God of Israel, by the sins he had committed and the sins he had led Israel to commit.

³¹The rest of the events in Nadab's reign and everything he did are recorded in *The Book of the History of the Kings of Israel.*

Baasha Rules in Israel

³²There was constant war between King Asa of Judah and King Baasha of Israel. ³³Baasha son of Ahijah began to rule over all Israel in the third year of King Asa's reign in Judah. Baasha reigned in Tirzah twenty-four years. ³⁴But he did what was evil in the LORD's sight and followed the example of Jeroboam, continuing the sins that Jeroboam had led Israel to commit.

16 This message from the LORD was delivered to King Baasha by the prophet Jehu son of Hanani: ²"I lifted you out of the dust to make you ruler of my people Israel, but you have followed the evil example of Jeroboam. You have provoked my anger by causing my people Israel to sin. ³So now I will destroy you and your

---

15:19 As in Greek version; Hebrew reads *There is a treaty.*

family, just as I destroyed the descendants of Jeroboam son of Nebat. ⁴The members of Baasha's family who die in the city will be eaten by dogs, and those who die in the field will be eaten by vultures."

⁵The rest of the events in Baasha's reign and the extent of his power are recorded in *The Book of the History of the Kings of Israel.* ⁶When Baasha died, he was buried in Tirzah. Then his son Elah became the next king.

⁷The message from the LORD against Baasha and his family came through the prophet Jehu son of Hanani. It was delivered because Baasha had done what was evil in the LORD's sight (just as the family of Jeroboam had done), and also because Baasha had destroyed the family of Jeroboam. The LORD's anger was provoked by Baasha's sins.

Elah Rules in Israel

⁸Elah son of Baasha began to rule over Israel in the twenty-sixth year of King Asa's reign in Judah. He reigned in the city of Tirzah for two years.

⁹Then Zimri, who commanded half of the royal chariots, made plans to kill him. One day in Tirzah, Elah was getting drunk at the home of Arza, the supervisor of the palace. ¹⁰Zimri walked in and struck him down and killed him. This happened in the twenty-seventh year of King Asa's reign in Judah. Then Zimri became the next king.

¹¹Zimri immediately killed the entire royal family of Baasha, leaving him not even a single male child. He even destroyed distant relatives and friends. ¹²So Zimri destroyed the dynasty of Baasha as the LORD had promised through the prophet Jehu. ¹³This happened because of all the sins Baasha and his son Elah had committed, and because of the sins they led Israel to commit. They provoked the anger of the LORD, the God of Israel, with their worthless idols.

¹⁴The rest of the events in Elah's reign and everything he did are recorded in *The Book of the History of the Kings of Israel.*

Zimri Rules in Israel

¹⁵Zimri began to rule over Israel in the twenty-seventh year of King Asa's reign in Judah, but his reign in Tirzah lasted only seven days. The army of Israel was then attacking the Philistine town of Gibbethon. ¹⁶When they heard that Zimri had committed treason and had assassinated the king, that very day they chose Omri, commander of the army, as the new king of Israel. ¹⁷So Omri led the entire army of Israel up from Gibbethon to attack Tirzah, Israel's capital. ¹⁸When Zimri saw that the city had been taken, he went into the citadel of the palace and burned it down over himself and died in the flames. ¹⁹For he, too, had done what was evil in the LORD's sight. He followed the example of Jeroboam in all the sins he had committed and led Israel to commit.

²⁰The rest of the events in Zimri's reign and his conspiracy are recorded in *The Book of the History of the Kings of Israel.*

Omri Rules in Israel

²¹But now the people of Israel were split into two factions. Half the people tried to make Tibni son of Ginath their king, while the other half supported Omri. ²²But Omri's supporters defeated the supporters of Tibni. So Tibni was killed, and Omri became the next king.

²³Omri began to rule over Israel in the thirty-first year of King Asa's reign in Judah. He reigned twelve years in all, six of them in Tirzah. ²⁴Then Omri bought the hill now known as Samaria from its owner, Shemer, for 150 pounds of silver.* He built a city on it and called the city Samaria in honor of Shemer.

²⁵But Omri did what was evil in the LORD's sight, even more than any of the kings before him. ²⁶He followed the example of Jeroboam son of Nebat in all the sins he had committed and led Israel to commit. The people provoked the anger of the LORD, the God of Israel, with their worthless idols.

²⁷The rest of the events in Omri's reign, the extent of his power, and everything he did are recorded in *The Book of the History of the Kings of Israel.* ²⁸When Omri died, he was buried in Samaria. Then his son Ahab became the next king.

16:24 Hebrew *for 2 talents* [68 kilograms] *of silver.*

Ahab Rules in Israel

²⁹Ahab son of Omri began to rule over Israel in the thirty-eighth year of King Asa's reign in Judah. He reigned in Samaria twenty-two years. ³⁰But Ahab son of Omri did what was evil in the LORD's sight, even more than any of the kings before him. ³¹And as though it were not enough to follow the example of Jeroboam, he married Jezebel, the daughter of King Ethbaal of the Sidonians, and he began to bow down in worship of Baal. ³²First Ahab built a temple and an altar for Baal in Samaria. ³³Then he set up an Asherah pole. He did more to provoke the anger of the LORD, the God of Israel, than any of the other kings of Israel before him.

³⁴It was during his reign that Hiel, a man from Bethel, rebuilt Jericho. When he laid its foundations, it cost him the life of his oldest son, Abiram. And when he completed it and set up its gates, it cost him the life of his youngest son, Segub.* This all happened according to the message from the LORD concerning Jericho spoken by Joshua son of Nun.

17 Elijah Fed by Ravens

Now Elijah, who was from Tishbe in Gilead, told King Ahab, "As surely as the LORD, the God of Israel, lives—the God I serve—there will be no dew or rain during the next few years until I give the word!"

²Then the LORD said to Elijah, ³"Go to the east and hide by Kerith Brook, near where it enters the Jordan River. ⁴Drink from the brook and eat what the ravens bring you, for I have commanded them to bring you food."

⁵So Elijah did as the LORD told him and camped beside Kerith Brook, east of the Jordan. ⁶The ravens brought him bread and meat each morning and evening, and he drank from the brook. ⁷But after a while the brook dried up, for there was no rainfall anywhere in the land.

The Widow at Zarephath

⁸Then the LORD said to Elijah, ⁹"Go and live in the village of Zarephath, near the city of Sidon. I have instructed a widow there to feed you."

¹⁰So he went to Zarephath. As he arrived at the gates of the village, he saw a widow gathering sticks, and he asked her, "Would you please bring me a little water in a cup?" ¹¹As she was going to get it, he called to her, "Bring me a bite of bread, too."

¹²But she said, "I swear by the LORD your God that I don't have a single piece of bread in the house. And I have only a handful of flour left in the jar and a little cooking oil in the bottom of the jug. I was just gathering a few sticks to cook this last meal, and then my son and I will die."

¹³But Elijah said to her, "Don't be afraid! Go ahead and do just what you've said, but make a little bread for me first. Then use what's left to prepare a meal for yourself and your son. ¹⁴For this is what the LORD, the God of Israel, says: There will always be flour and olive oil left in your containers until the time when the LORD sends rain and the crops grow again!"

¹⁵So she did as Elijah said, and she and Elijah and her family continued to eat for many days. ¹⁶There was always enough flour and olive oil left in the containers, just as the LORD had promised through Elijah.

¹⁷Some time later the woman's son became sick. He grew worse and worse, and finally he died. ¹⁸Then she said to Elijah, "O man of God, what have you done to me? Have you come here to point out my sins and kill my son?"

¹⁹But Elijah replied, "Give me your son." And he took the child's body from her arms, carried him up the stairs to the room where he was staying, and laid the body on his bed. ²⁰Then Elijah cried out to the LORD, "O LORD my God, why have you brought tragedy to this widow who has opened her home to me, causing her son to die?"

²¹And he stretched himself out over the child three times and cried out to the LORD, "O LORD my God, please let this child's life return to him." ²²The LORD heard Elijah's prayer, and the life of the child returned, and he revived! ²³Then Elijah brought him down from the upper room and gave him to his mother. "Look!" he said. "Your son is alive!"

²⁴Then the woman told Elijah, "Now I

16:34 An ancient Hebrew scribal tradition reads *He killed his oldest son when he laid its foundations, and he killed his youngest son when he set up its gates.*

know for sure that you are a man of God, and that the LORD truly speaks through you."

18 The Contest on Mount Carmel

Later on, in the third year of the drought, the LORD said to Elijah, "Go and present yourself to King Ahab. Tell him that I will soon send rain!" ²So Elijah went to appear before Ahab.

Meanwhile, the famine had become very severe in Samaria. ³So Ahab summoned Obadiah, who was in charge of the palace.

(Obadiah was a devoted follower of the LORD. ⁴Once when Jezebel had tried to kill all the LORD's prophets, Obadiah had hidden 100 of them in two caves. He put fifty prophets in each cave and supplied them with food and water.) ⁵Ahab said to Obadiah, "We must check every spring and valley in the land to see if we can find enough grass to save at least some of my horses and mules." ⁶So they divided the land between them. Ahab went one way by himself, and Obadiah went another way by himself.

Submission

The Widow of Zarephath:
Ridiculous Obedience

1 KINGS 17

The story of Elijah and the widow of Zarephath is told from one perspective only: Elijah's. The first thing we learn about her is what the Lord tells Elijah: "I have instructed a widow [in Zarephath] to feed you" (1 Kings 17:9).

But consider things from the widow's perspective: Elijah arrives and, before she's even finished with her chore of picking up sticks, he's asked her to get him a drink of water. Then, before she's even had an opportunity to go get the water, he's asked her to also bring him some bread.

To complicate matters, there's a famine, and she doesn't have enough food for herself and her son to live on, much less an additional guest. Though hospitality was a strong cultural norm of the day, this woman didn't have anything to be hospitable with. "I swear by the LORD your God that I don't have a single piece of bread in the house," she tells him. "I was just gathering a few sticks to cook this last meal, and then my son and I will die" (17:12).

Imagine if you had only enough food for one final meal with a beloved family member. What would you do? Would you obey God? Would you give it to a stranger?

Sometimes submitting to God is like following a recipe that looks like it won't work. Anyone who cooks knows what it's like to look in the flour bin and see just a quarter cup left (which is certainly not enough to make much of anything!). But despite the seemingly untrustworthy recipe—even though all her rational thought and motherly instincts tell her it cannot possibly serve three people for many days—the widow obeys God's instructions.

Obedience to God isn't easy. Sometimes it requires sacrifice—even when it may mean death.

But in this case, it didn't. In a miraculous way, God came through for this widow, her son, and Elijah. Her difficult choice to obey, even when all seemed lost, opened an opportunity for God to show her how faithful and trustworthy he is.

—Joy-Elizabeth Lawrence

For more on submission, see reading at Psalm 119:129-144.

⁷As Obadiah was walking along, he suddenly saw Elijah coming toward him. Obadiah recognized him at once and bowed low to the ground before him. "Is it really you, my lord Elijah?" he asked.

⁸"Yes, it is," Elijah replied. "Now go and tell your master, 'Elijah is here.'"

⁹"Oh, sir," Obadiah protested, "what harm have I done to you that you are sending me to my death at the hands of Ahab? ¹⁰For I swear by the LORD your God that the king has searched every nation and kingdom on earth from end to end to find you. And each time he was told, 'Elijah isn't here,' King Ahab forced the king of that nation to swear to the truth of his claim. ¹¹And now you say, 'Go and tell your master, "Elijah is here."' ¹²But as soon as I leave you, the Spirit of the LORD will carry you away to who knows where. When Ahab comes and cannot find you, he will kill me. Yet I have been a true servant of the LORD all my life. ¹³Has no one told you, my lord, about the time when Jezebel was trying to kill the LORD's prophets? I hid 100 of them in two caves and supplied them with food and water. ¹⁴And now you say, 'Go and tell your master, "Elijah is here."' Sir, if I do that, Ahab will certainly kill me."

¹⁵But Elijah said, "I swear by the LORD Almighty, in whose presence I stand, that I will present myself to Ahab this very day."

¹⁶So Obadiah went to tell Ahab that Elijah had come, and Ahab went out to meet Elijah. ¹⁷When Ahab saw him, he exclaimed, "So, is it really you, you troublemaker of Israel?"

¹⁸"I have made no trouble for Israel," Elijah replied. "You and your family are the troublemakers, for you have refused to obey the commands of the LORD and have worshiped the images of Baal instead. ¹⁹Now summon all Israel to join me at Mount Carmel, along with the 450 prophets of Baal and the 400 prophets of Asherah who are supported by Jezebel.*"

²⁰So Ahab summoned all the people of Israel and the prophets to Mount Carmel. ²¹Then Elijah stood in front of them and said, "How much longer will you waver, hobbling between two opinions? If the LORD is God, follow him! But if Baal is God, then follow him!" But the people were completely silent.

²²Then Elijah said to them, "I am the only prophet of the LORD who is left, but Baal has 450 prophets. ²³Now bring two bulls. The prophets of Baal may choose whichever one they wish and cut it into pieces and lay it on the wood of their altar, but without setting fire to it. I will prepare the other bull and lay it on the wood on the altar, but not set fire to it. ²⁴Then call on the name of your god, and I will call on the name of the LORD. The god who answers by setting fire to the wood is the true God!" And all the people agreed.

²⁵Then Elijah said to the prophets of Baal, "You go first, for there are many of you. Choose one of the bulls, and prepare it and call on the name of your god. But do not set fire to the wood."

²⁶So they prepared one of the bulls and placed it on the altar. Then they called on the name of Baal from morning until noontime, shouting, "O Baal, answer us!" But there was no reply of any kind. Then they danced, hobbling around the altar they had made.

²⁷About noontime Elijah began mocking them. "You'll have to shout louder," he scoffed, "for surely he is a god! Perhaps he is daydreaming, or is relieving himself.* Or maybe he is away on a trip, or is asleep and needs to be wakened!"

²⁸So they shouted louder, and following their normal custom, they cut themselves with knives and swords until the blood gushed out. ²⁹They raved all afternoon until the time of the evening sacrifice, but still there was no sound, no reply, no response.

³⁰Then Elijah called to the people, "Come over here!" They all crowded around him as he repaired the altar of the LORD that had been torn down. ³¹He took twelve stones, one to represent each of the tribes of Israel,* ³²and he used the stones to rebuild the altar in the name of the LORD. Then he dug a trench around the altar large enough to hold about three gallons.* ³³He piled wood on the altar, cut the bull into pieces, and laid the pieces on the wood.

18:19 Hebrew *who eat at Jezebel's table.*   **18:27** Or *is busy somewhere else, or is engaged in business.*   **18:31** Hebrew *each of the tribes of the sons of Jacob to whom the LORD had said, "Your name will be Israel."*   **18:32** Hebrew *2 seahs [12 liters] of seed.*

Then he said, "Fill four large jars with water, and pour the water over the offering and the wood."

34 After they had done this, he said, "Do the same thing again!" And when they were finished, he said, "Now do it a third time!" So they did as he said, 35 and the water ran around the altar and even filled the trench.

36 At the usual time for offering the evening sacrifice, Elijah the prophet walked up to the altar and prayed, "O LORD, God of Abraham, Isaac, and Jacob,* prove today that you are God in Israel and that I am your servant. Prove that I have done all this at your command. 37 O LORD, answer me! Answer me so these people will know that you, O LORD, are God and that you have brought them back to yourself."

38 Immediately the fire of the LORD flashed down from heaven and burned up the young bull, the wood, the stones, and the dust. It even licked up all the water in the trench! 39 And when all the people saw it, they fell face down on the ground and cried out, "The LORD—he is God! Yes, the LORD is God!"

40 Then Elijah commanded, "Seize all the prophets of Baal. Don't let a single one escape!" So the people seized them all, and Elijah took them down to the Kishon Valley and killed them there.

Elijah Prays for Rain

41 Then Elijah said to Ahab, "Go get something to eat and drink, for I hear a mighty rainstorm coming!"

42 So Ahab went to eat and drink. But Elijah climbed to the top of Mount Carmel and bowed low to the ground and prayed with his face between his knees.

43 Then he said to his servant, "Go and look out toward the sea."

The servant went and looked, then returned to Elijah and said, "I didn't see anything."

Seven times Elijah told him to go and look. 44 Finally the seventh time, his servant told him, "I saw a little cloud about the size of a man's hand rising from the sea."

Then Elijah shouted, "Hurry to Ahab and tell him, 'Climb into your chariot and go back home. If you don't hurry, the rain will stop you!'"

45 And soon the sky was black with clouds. A heavy wind brought a terrific rainstorm, and Ahab left quickly for Jezreel. 46 Then the LORD gave special strength to Elijah. He tucked his cloak into his belt* and ran ahead of Ahab's chariot all the way to the entrance of Jezreel.

19 Elijah Flees to Sinai

When Ahab got home, he told Jezebel everything Elijah had done, including the way he had killed all the prophets of Baal. 2 So Jezebel sent this message to Elijah: "May the gods strike me and even kill me if by this time tomorrow I have not killed you just as you killed them."

3 Elijah was afraid and fled for his life. He went to Beersheba, a town in Judah, and he left his servant there. 4 Then he went on alone into the wilderness, traveling all day. He sat down under a solitary broom tree and prayed that he might die. "I have had enough, LORD," he said. "Take my life, for I am no better than my ancestors who have already died."

5 Then he lay down and slept under the broom tree. But as he was sleeping, an angel touched him and told him, "Get up and eat!" 6 He looked around and there beside his head was some bread baked on hot stones and a jar of water! So he ate and drank and lay down again.

7 Then the angel of the LORD came again and touched him and said, "Get up and eat some more, or the journey ahead will be too much for you."

8 So he got up and ate and drank, and the food gave him enough strength to travel forty days and forty nights to Mount Sinai,* the mountain of God. 9 There he came to a cave, where he spent the night.

The LORD Speaks to Elijah

But the LORD said to him, "What are you doing here, Elijah?"

10 Elijah replied, "I have zealously served the LORD God Almighty. But the people of Israel have broken their covenant with you,

---

18:36 Hebrew and Israel. The names "Jacob" and "Israel" are often interchanged throughout the Old Testament, referring sometimes to the individual patriarch and sometimes to the nation. 18:46 Hebrew He bound up his loins. 19:8 Hebrew to Horeb, another name for Sinai.

Listening for the Whisper

1 KINGS 19:9-13

I'm a sucker for spectacle. I've gone to my share of religious extravaganzas—from Christmas programs to evangelistic crusades. There is something wonderful about sitting with a large crowd of believers praising God. It harkens to the kingdom of heaven, the vision of the 144,000 worshiping the Lamb (Revelation 14:1–3).

But the problem with religious spectacle is that the steady, repeated, raucous noise will eventually make us hard of hearing. And that will make it impossible to hear God's normal tone of voice. He is not usually found in earthquake, wind, and fire, but in the small whisper, heard only by those who enter with Elijah into the dark cave.

This whisper is difficult to hear in the din of our culture and religious life. It is also frightening even to try to listen for it, because to do so we must, like Elijah, enter the dark cave from whence the whisper emerges. That means stepping into mystery.

When you try to practice Elijah-like spirituality, says the author of *The Cloud of Unknowing*, you will at first feel a "darkness about your mind, or as it were *a cloud of unknowing.* You will seem to know nothing and feel nothing except a naked intent toward God in the depths of your being. Try as you might, this darkness and this cloud will remain between you and your God. You will feel frustrated, for your mind will be unable to grasp him, and your heart will not relish the delight of his love."

Withdrawal from the noise and glitter of religious spectacle sounds like a formula for spiritual suicide; how am I even going to experience God without the pounding of the music and electricity of the crowd and inspirational message of the dynamic preacher? But eventually, says this author, if "you hope to feel and see God as he is in himself, it must be within this darkness and this cloud."

Regularly retiring to the dark cave, to the fearful quiet of silent prayer and meditation, to listen to the whisper is the first step in breaking free from addiction to religious spectacle. The darkness of mystery and silence opens up whole new vistas for us and gives us the ears to hear the whisper.

—Mark Galli

For more on silence, see reading at Psalm 46:10.

torn down your altars, and killed every one of your prophets. I am the only one left, and now they are trying to kill me, too."

[11] "Go out and stand before me on the mountain," the LORD told him. And as Elijah stood there, the LORD passed by, and a mighty windstorm hit the mountain. It was such a terrible blast that the rocks were torn loose, but the LORD was not in the wind. After the wind there was an earthquake, but the LORD was not in the earthquake. [12] And after the earthquake there was a fire, but the LORD was not in the fire. And after the fire there was the sound of a gentle whisper. [13] When Elijah heard it, he wrapped his face in his cloak and went out and stood at the entrance of the cave.

And a voice said, "What are you doing here, Elijah?"

[14] He replied again, "I have zealously served the LORD God Almighty. But the people of Israel have broken their covenant

with you, torn down your altars, and killed every one of your prophets. I am the only one left, and now they are trying to kill me, too."

15 Then the LORD told him, "Go back the same way you came, and travel to the wilderness of Damascus. When you arrive there, anoint Hazael to be king of Aram. 16 Then anoint Jehu grandson of Nimshi* to be king of Israel, and anoint Elisha son of Shaphat from the town of Abel-meholah to replace you as my prophet. 17 Anyone who escapes from Hazael will be killed by Jehu, and those who escape Jehu will be killed by Elisha! 18 Yet I will preserve 7,000 others in Israel who have never bowed down to Baal or kissed him!"

The Call of Elisha

19 So Elijah went and found Elisha son of Shaphat plowing a field. There were twelve teams of oxen in the field, and Elisha was plowing with the twelfth team. Elijah went over to him and threw his cloak across his shoulders and then walked away. 20 Elisha left the oxen standing there, ran after Elijah, and said to him, "First let me go and kiss my father and mother good-bye, and then I will go with you!"

Elijah replied, "Go on back, but think about what I have done to you."

21 So Elisha returned to his oxen and slaughtered them. He used the wood from the plow to build a fire to roast their flesh. He passed around the meat to the townspeople, and they all ate. Then he went with Elijah as his assistant.

20 Ben-Hadad Attacks Samaria

About that time King Ben-hadad of Aram mobilized his army, supported by the chariots and horses of thirty-two allied kings. They went to besiege Samaria, the capital of Israel, and launched attacks against it. 2 Ben-hadad sent messengers into the city to relay this message to King Ahab of Israel: "This is what Ben-hadad says: 3 'Your silver and gold are mine, and so are your wives and the best of your children!'"

4 "All right, my lord the king," Israel's king replied. "All that I have is yours!"

5 Soon Ben-hadad's messengers returned again and said, "This is what Ben-hadad says: 'I have already demanded that you give me your silver, gold, wives, and children. 6 But about this time tomorrow I will send my officials to search your palace and the homes of your people. They will take away everything you consider valuable!'"

7 Then Ahab summoned all the elders of the land and said to them, "Look how this man is stirring up trouble! I already agreed with his demand that I give him my wives and children and silver and gold."

8 "Don't give in to any more demands," all the elders and the people advised.

9 So Ahab told the messengers from Ben-hadad, "Say this to my lord the king: 'I will give you everything you asked for the first time, but I cannot accept this last demand of yours.'" So the messengers returned to Ben-hadad with that response.

10 Then Ben-hadad sent this message to Ahab: "May the gods strike me and even kill me if there remains enough dust from Samaria to provide even a handful for each of my soldiers."

11 The king of Israel sent back this answer: "A warrior putting on his sword for battle should not boast like a warrior who has already won."

12 Ahab's reply reached Ben-hadad and the other kings as they were drinking in their tents.* "Prepare to attack!" Ben-hadad commanded his officers. So they prepared to attack the city.

Ahab's Victory over Ben-Hadad

13 Then a certain prophet came to see King Ahab of Israel and told him, "This is what the LORD says: Do you see all these enemy forces? Today I will hand them all over to you. Then you will know that I am the LORD."

14 Ahab asked, "How will he do it?"

And the prophet replied, "This is what the LORD says: The troops of the provincial commanders will do it."

"Should we attack first?" Ahab asked.

"Yes," the prophet answered.

15 So Ahab mustered the troops of the 232 provincial commanders. Then he

called out the rest of the army of Israel, some 7,000 men. [16] About noontime, as Ben-hadad and the thirty-two allied kings were still in their tents drinking themselves into a stupor, [17] the troops of the provincial commanders marched out of the city as the first contingent.

As they approached, Ben-hadad's scouts reported to him, "Some troops are coming from Samaria."

[18] "Take them alive," Ben-hadad commanded, "whether they have come for peace or for war."

[19] But Ahab's provincial commanders and the entire army had now come out to fight. [20] Each Israelite soldier killed his Aramean opponent, and suddenly the entire Aramean army panicked and fled. The Israelites chased them, but King Ben-hadad and a few of his charioteers escaped on horses. [21] However, the king of Israel destroyed the other horses and chariots and slaughtered the Arameans.

[22] Afterward the prophet said to King Ahab, "Get ready for another attack. Begin making plans now, for the king of Aram will come back next spring.*"

Ben-Hadad's Second Attack

[23] After their defeat, Ben-hadad's officers said to him, "The Israelite gods are gods of the hills; that is why they won. But we can beat them easily on the plains. [24] Only this time replace the kings with field commanders! [25] Recruit another army like the one you lost. Give us the same number of horses, chariots, and men, and we will fight against them on the plains. There's no doubt that we will beat them." So King Ben-hadad did as they suggested.

[26] The following spring he called up the Aramean army and marched out against Israel, this time at Aphek. [27] Israel then mustered its army, set up supply lines, and marched out for battle. But the Israelite army looked like two little flocks of goats in comparison to the vast Aramean forces that filled the countryside!

[28] Then the man of God went to the king of Israel and said, "This is what the LORD says: The Arameans have said, 'The LORD is a god of the hills and not of the plains.' So I will defeat this vast army for you. Then you will know that I am the LORD."

[29] The two armies camped opposite each other for seven days, and on the seventh day the battle began. The Israelites killed 100,000 Aramean foot soldiers in one day. [30] The rest fled into the town of Aphek, but the wall fell on them and killed another 27,000. Ben-hadad fled into the town and hid in a secret room.

[31] Ben-hadad's officers said to him, "Sir, we have heard that the kings of Israel are merciful. So let's humble ourselves by wearing burlap around our waists and putting ropes on our heads, and surrender to the king of Israel. Then perhaps he will let you live."

[32] So they put on burlap and ropes, and they went to the king of Israel and begged, "Your servant Ben-hadad says, 'Please let me live!'"

The king of Israel responded, "Is he still alive? He is my brother!"

[33] The men took this as a good sign and quickly picked up on his words. "Yes," they said, "your brother Ben-hadad!"

"Go and get him," the king of Israel told them. And when Ben-hadad arrived, Ahab invited him up into his chariot.

[34] Ben-hadad told him, "I will give back the towns my father took from your father, and you may establish places of trade in Damascus, as my father did in Samaria."

Then Ahab said, "I will release you under these conditions." So they made a new treaty, and Ben-hadad was set free.

A Prophet Condemns Ahab

[35] Meanwhile, the LORD instructed one of the group of prophets to say to another man, "Hit me!" But the man refused to hit the prophet. [36] Then the prophet told him, "Because you have not obeyed the voice of the LORD, a lion will kill you as soon as you leave me." And when he had gone, a lion did attack and kill him.

[37] Then the prophet turned to another man and said, "Hit me!" So he struck the prophet and wounded him.

20:22 Hebrew at the turn of the year; similarly in 20:26. The first day of the year in the ancient Hebrew lunar calendar occurred in March or April.

[38] The prophet placed a bandage over his eyes to disguise himself and then waited beside the road for the king. [39] As the king passed by, the prophet called out to him, "Sir, I was in the thick of battle, and suddenly a man brought me a prisoner. He said, 'Guard this man; if for any reason he gets away, you will either die or pay a fine of seventy-five pounds* of silver!' [40] But while I was busy doing something else, the prisoner disappeared!"

"Well, it's your own fault," the king replied. "You have brought the judgment on yourself."

[41] Then the prophet quickly pulled the bandage from his eyes, and the king of Israel recognized him as one of the prophets. [42] The prophet said to him, "This is what the LORD says: Because you have spared the man I said must be destroyed,* now you must die in his place, and your people will die instead of his people." [43] So the king of Israel went home to Samaria angry and sullen.

21 Naboth's Vineyard

Now there was a man named Naboth, from Jezreel, who owned a vineyard in Jezreel beside the palace of King Ahab of Samaria. [2] One day Ahab said to Naboth, "Since your vineyard is so convenient to my palace, I would like to buy it to use as a vegetable garden. I will give you a better vineyard in exchange, or if you prefer, I will pay you for it."

[3] But Naboth replied, "The LORD forbid that I should give you the inheritance that was passed down by my ancestors."

[4] So Ahab went home angry and sullen because of Naboth's answer. The king went to bed with his face to the wall and refused to eat!

[5] "What's the matter?" his wife Jezebel asked him. "What's made you so upset that you're not eating?"

[6] "I asked Naboth to sell me his vineyard or trade it, but he refused!" Ahab told her.

[7] "Are you the king of Israel or not?" Jezebel demanded. "Get up and eat something, and don't worry about it. I'll get you Naboth's vineyard!"

[8] So she wrote letters in Ahab's name, sealed them with his seal, and sent them to the elders and other leaders of the town where Naboth lived. [9] In her letters she commanded: "Call the citizens together for fasting and prayer, and give Naboth a place of honor. [10] And then seat two scoundrels across from him who will accuse him of cursing God and the king. Then take him out and stone him to death."

[11] So the elders and other town leaders followed the instructions Jezebel had written in the letters. [12] They called for a fast and put Naboth at a prominent place before the people. [13] Then the two scoundrels came and sat down across from him. And they accused Naboth before all the people, saying, "He cursed God and the king." So he was dragged outside the town and stoned to death. [14] The town leaders then sent word to Jezebel, "Naboth has been stoned to death."

[15] When Jezebel heard the news, she said to Ahab, "You know the vineyard Naboth wouldn't sell you? Well, you can have it now! He's dead!" [16] So Ahab immediately went down to the vineyard of Naboth to claim it.

[17] But the LORD said to Elijah,* [18] "Go down to meet King Ahab of Israel, who rules in Samaria. He will be at Naboth's vineyard in Jezreel, claiming it for himself. [19] Give him this message: 'This is what the LORD says: Wasn't it enough that you killed Naboth? Must you rob him, too? Because you have done this, dogs will lick your blood at the very place where they licked the blood of Naboth!'"

[20] "So, my enemy, you have found me!" Ahab exclaimed to Elijah.

"Yes," Elijah answered, "I have come because you have sold yourself to what is evil in the LORD's sight. [21] So now the LORD says, 'I will bring disaster on you and consume you. I will destroy every one of your male descendants, slave and free alike, anywhere in Israel! [22] I am going to destroy your family as I did the family of Jeroboam son of Nebat and the family of Baasha son of Ahijah, for you have made me very angry and have led Israel into sin.'

20:39 Hebrew *1 talent* [34 kilograms].   20:42 The Hebrew term used here refers to the complete consecration of things or people to the LORD, either by destroying them or by giving them as an offering.   21:17 Hebrew *Elijah the Tishbite;* also in 21:28.

²³"And regarding Jezebel, the LORD says, 'Dogs will eat Jezebel's body at the plot of land in Jezreel.*'

²⁴"The members of Ahab's family who die in the city will be eaten by dogs, and those who die in the field will be eaten by vultures."

²⁵(No one else so completely sold himself to what was evil in the LORD's sight as Ahab did under the influence of his wife Jezebel. ²⁶His worst outrage was worshiping idols* just as the Amorites had done—the people whom the LORD had driven out from the land ahead of the Israelites.)

²⁷But when Ahab heard this message, he tore his clothing, dressed in burlap, and fasted. He even slept in burlap and went about in deep mourning.

²⁸Then another message from the LORD came to Elijah: ²⁹"Do you see how Ahab has humbled himself before me? Because he has done this, I will not do what I promised during his lifetime. It will happen to his sons; I will destroy his dynasty."

22 Jehoshaphat and Ahab

For three years there was no war between Aram and Israel. ²Then during the third year, King Jehoshaphat of Judah went to visit King Ahab of Israel. ³During the visit, the king of Israel said to his officials, "Do you realize that the town of Ramoth-gilead belongs to us? And yet we've done nothing to recapture it from the king of Aram!"

⁴Then he turned to Jehoshaphat and asked, "Will you join me in battle to recover Ramoth-gilead?"

Jehoshaphat replied to the king of Israel, "Why, of course! You and I are as one. My troops are your troops, and my horses are your horses." ⁵Then Jehoshaphat added, "But first let's find out what the LORD says."

⁶So the king of Israel summoned the prophets, about 400 of them, and asked them, "Should I go to war against Ramoth-gilead, or should I hold back?"

They all replied, "Yes, go right ahead! The Lord will give the king victory."

⁷But Jehoshaphat asked, "Is there not also a prophet of the LORD here? We should ask him the same question."

⁸The king of Israel replied to Jehoshaphat, "There is one more man who could consult the LORD for us, but I hate him. He never prophesies anything but trouble for me! His name is Micaiah son of Imlah."

Jehoshaphat replied, "That's not the way a king should talk! Let's hear what he has to say."

⁹So the king of Israel called one of his officials and said, "Quick! Bring Micaiah son of Imlah."

Micaiah Prophesies against Ahab

¹⁰King Ahab of Israel and King Jehoshaphat of Judah, dressed in their royal robes, were sitting on thrones at the threshing floor near the gate of Samaria. All of Ahab's prophets were prophesying there in front of them. ¹¹One of them, Zedekiah son of Kenaanah, made some iron horns and proclaimed, "This is what the LORD says: With these horns you will gore the Arameans to death!"

¹²All the other prophets agreed. "Yes," they said, "go up to Ramoth-gilead and be victorious, for the LORD will give the king victory!"

¹³Meanwhile, the messenger who went to get Micaiah said to him, "Look, all the prophets are promising victory for the king. Be sure that you agree with them and promise success."

¹⁴But Micaiah replied, "As surely as the LORD lives, I will say only what the LORD tells me to say."

¹⁵When Micaiah arrived before the king, Ahab asked him, "Micaiah, should we go to war against Ramoth-gilead, or should we hold back?"

Micaiah replied sarcastically, "Yes, go up and be victorious, for the LORD will give the king victory!"

¹⁶But the king replied sharply, "How many times must I demand that you speak only the truth to me when you speak for the LORD?"

¹⁷Then Micaiah told him, "In a vision I saw all Israel scattered on the mountains, like sheep without a shepherd. And the LORD said, 'Their master has been killed.* Send them home in peace.'"

21:23 As in several Hebrew manuscripts, Syriac, and Latin Vulgate (see also 2 Kgs 9:26, 36); most Hebrew manuscripts read *at the city wall.* **21:26** The Hebrew term (literally *round things*) probably alludes to dung. **22:17** Hebrew *These people have no master.*

¹⁸"Didn't I tell you?" the king of Israel exclaimed to Jehoshaphat. "He never prophesies anything but trouble for me."

¹⁹Then Micaiah continued, "Listen to what the LORD says! I saw the LORD sitting on his throne with all the armies of heaven around him, on his right and on his left. ²⁰And the LORD said, 'Who can entice Ahab to go into battle against Ramoth-gilead so he can be killed?'

"There were many suggestions, ²¹and finally a spirit approached the LORD and said, 'I can do it!'

²²"'How will you do this?' the LORD asked.

"And the spirit replied, 'I will go out and inspire all of Ahab's prophets to speak lies.'

"'You will succeed,' said the LORD. 'Go ahead and do it.'

²³"So you see, the LORD has put a lying spirit in the mouths of all your prophets. For the LORD has pronounced your doom."

²⁴Then Zedekiah son of Kenaanah walked up to Micaiah and slapped him across the face. "Since when did the Spirit of the LORD leave me to speak to you?" he demanded.

²⁵And Micaiah replied, "You will find out soon enough when you are trying to hide in some secret room!"

²⁶"Arrest him!" the king of Israel ordered. "Take him back to Amon, the governor of the city, and to my son Joash. ²⁷Give them this order from the king: 'Put this man in prison, and feed him nothing but bread and water until I return safely from the battle!'"

²⁸But Micaiah replied, "If you return safely, it will mean that the LORD has not spoken through me!" Then he added to those standing around, "Everyone mark my words!"

The Death of Ahab

²⁹So King Ahab of Israel and King Jehoshaphat of Judah led their armies against Ramoth-gilead. ³⁰The king of Israel said to Jehoshaphat, "As we go into battle, I will disguise myself so no one will recognize me, but you wear your royal robes." So the king of Israel disguised himself, and they went into battle.

³¹Meanwhile, the king of Aram had is-sued these orders to his thirty-two chariot commanders: "Attack only the king of Israel. Don't bother with anyone else!" ³²So when the Aramean chariot commanders saw Jehoshaphat in his royal robes, they went after him. "There is the king of Israel!" they shouted. But when Jehoshaphat called out, ³³the chariot commanders realized he was not the king of Israel, and they stopped chasing him.

³⁴An Aramean soldier, however, randomly shot an arrow at the Israelite troops and hit the king of Israel between the joints of his armor. "Turn the horses* and get me out of here!" Ahab groaned to the driver of his chariot. "I'm badly wounded!"

³⁵The battle raged all that day, and the king remained propped up in his chariot facing the Arameans. The blood from his wound ran down to the floor of his chariot, and as evening arrived he died. ³⁶Just as the sun was setting, the cry ran through his troops: "We're done for! Run for your lives!"

³⁷So the king died, and his body was taken to Samaria and buried there. ³⁸Then his chariot was washed beside the pool of Samaria, and dogs came and licked his blood at the place where the prostitutes bathed,* just as the LORD had promised.

³⁹The rest of the events in Ahab's reign and everything he did, including the story of the ivory palace and the towns he built, are recorded in *The Book of the History of the Kings of Israel.* ⁴⁰So Ahab died, and his son Ahaziah became the next king.

Jehoshaphat Rules in Judah

⁴¹Jehoshaphat son of Asa began to rule over Judah in the fourth year of King Ahab's reign in Israel. ⁴²Jehoshaphat was thirty-five years old when he became king, and he reigned in Jerusalem twenty-five years. His mother was Azubah, the daughter of Shilhi.

⁴³Jehoshaphat was a good king, following the example of his father, Asa. He did what was pleasing in the LORD's sight. *During his reign, however, he failed to remove all the pagan shrines, and the people still offered sacrifices and burned incense there. ⁴⁴Jehoshaphat also made peace with the king of Israel.

22:34 Hebrew *Turn your hand.*   22:38 Or *his blood, and the prostitutes bathed* [in it]; or *his blood, and they washed his armor.*   22:43 Verses 22:43b-53 are numbered 22:44-54 in Hebrew text.

⁴⁵ The rest of the events in Jehoshaphat's reign, the extent of his power, and the wars he waged are recorded in *The Book of the History of the Kings of Judah.* ⁴⁶ He banished from the land the rest of the male and female shrine prostitutes, who still continued their practices from the days of his father, Asa.

⁴⁷ (There was no king in Edom at that time, only a deputy.)

⁴⁸ Jehoshaphat also built a fleet of trading ships* to sail to Ophir for gold. But the ships never set sail, for they met with disaster in their home port of Ezion-geber. ⁴⁹ At one time Ahaziah son of Ahab had proposed to Jehoshaphat, "Let my men sail with your men in the ships." But Jehoshaphat refused the request.

⁵⁰ When Jehoshaphat died, he was buried with his ancestors in the City of David. Then his son Jehoram became the next king.

Ahaziah Rules in Israel

⁵¹ Ahaziah son of Ahab began to rule over Israel in the seventeenth year of King Jehoshaphat's reign in Judah. He reigned in Samaria two years. ⁵² But he did what was evil in the LORD's sight, following the example of his father and mother and the example of Jeroboam son of Nebat, who had led Israel to sin. ⁵³ He served Baal and worshiped him, provoking the anger of the LORD, the God of Israel, just as his father had done.

22:48 Hebrew *fleet of ships of Tarshish.*

2 Kings

Background

Second Kings picks up where 1 Kings leaves off. It covers the reigns of twelve kings of Israel (the northern kingdom), from Ahaziah through Hoshea, and fifteen kings and one queen of Judah (the southern kingdom), from Jehoram through Zedekiah. While the northern kingdom has no godly kings, Judah experiences ups and downs as good rulers follow evil ones. Eventually the northern kingdom falls to the Assyrians and its people are taken into exile. Judah's few good rulers temporarily give the nation stability, but eventually that nation too succumbs—to the Babylonians.

While the author of 1 and 2 Kings is unknown, the prophet Jeremiah is on the list of possible candidates.

Message

Many parents have stated, "This will hurt me more than it hurts you" when disciplining a wayward child. God grieves as he judges his sinful people for their idolatry. As good kings follow bad ones, God consistently calls the people to himself, sending prophets to show them their rampant evil and sinfulness. Elisha, Hosea, and Amos speak for God to the northern kingdom; Isaiah, Jeremiah, Joel, Micah, Habakkuk, and Zephaniah speak to the southern kingdom. God never leaves his people without hope, without strength, or without his presence. But make no mistake—sin will be judged. These nations learn that lesson the hard way.

Time

The events of 2 Kings take place between circa 850 and 586 B.C.

Outline

2 Kings

1 Elijah Confronts King Ahaziah

After King Ahab's death, the land of Moab rebelled against Israel.
²One day Israel's new king, Ahaziah, fell through the latticework of an upper room at his palace in Samaria and was seriously injured. So he sent messengers to the temple of Baal-zebub, the god of Ekron, to ask whether he would recover.

³But the angel of the LORD told Elijah, who was from Tishbe, "Go and confront the messengers of the king of Samaria and ask them, 'Is there no God in Israel? Why are you going to Baal-zebub, the god of Ekron, to ask whether the king will recover? ⁴Now, therefore, this is what the LORD says: You will never leave the bed you are lying on; you will surely die.'" So Elijah went to deliver the message.

⁵When the messengers returned to the king, he asked them, "Why have you returned so soon?"

⁶They replied, "A man came up to us and told us to go back to the king and give him this message. 'This is what the LORD says: Is there no God in Israel? Why are you sending men to Baal-zebub, the god of Ekron, to ask whether you will recover? Therefore, because you have done this, you will never leave the bed you are lying on; you will surely die.'"

⁷"What sort of man was he?" the king demanded. "What did he look like?"

⁸They replied, "He was a hairy man,* and he wore a leather belt around his waist."

"Elijah from Tishbe!" the king exclaimed.

⁹Then he sent an army captain with fifty soldiers to arrest him. They found him sitting on top of a hill. The captain said to him, "Man of God, the king has commanded you to come down with us."

¹⁰But Elijah replied to the captain, "If I am a man of God, let fire come down from heaven and destroy you and your fifty men!" Then fire fell from heaven and killed them all.

¹¹So the king sent another captain with fifty men. The captain said to him, "Man of God, the king demands that you come down at once."

¹²Elijah replied, "If I am a man of God, let fire come down from heaven and destroy you and your fifty men!" And again the fire of God fell from heaven and killed them all.

¹³Once more the king sent a third captain with fifty men. But this time the captain went up the hill and fell to his knees before Elijah. He pleaded with him, "O man of God, please spare my life and the lives of these, your fifty servants. ¹⁴See how the fire from heaven came down and destroyed the first two groups. But now please spare my life!"

¹⁵Then the angel of the LORD said to Elijah, "Go down with him, and don't be afraid of him." So Elijah got up and went with him to the king.

¹⁶And Elijah said to the king, "This is what the LORD says: Why did you send messengers to Baal-zebub, the god of Ekron, to ask whether you will recover? Is there no God in Israel to answer your question? Therefore, because you have

---

1:8 Or *He was wearing clothing made of hair.*

done this, you will never leave the bed you are lying on; you will surely die."

[17] So Ahaziah died, just as the LORD had promised through Elijah. Since Ahaziah did not have a son to succeed him, his brother Joram* became the next king. This took place in the second year of the reign of Jehoram son of Jehoshaphat, king of Judah.

[18] The rest of the events in Ahaziah's reign are recorded in *The Book of the History of the Kings of Israel*.

2 Elijah Taken into Heaven

When the LORD was about to take Elijah up to heaven in a whirlwind, Elijah and Elisha were traveling from Gilgal. [2] And Elijah said to Elisha, "Stay here, for the LORD has told me to go to Bethel."

But Elisha replied, "As surely as the LORD lives and you yourself live, I will never leave you!" So they went down together to Bethel.

[3] The group of prophets from Bethel came to Elisha and asked him, "Did you know that the LORD is going to take your master away from you today?"

"Of course I know," Elisha answered. "But be quiet about it."

[4] Then Elijah said to Elisha, "Stay here, for the LORD has told me to go to Jericho."

But Elisha replied again, "As surely as the LORD lives and you yourself live, I will never leave you." So they went on together to Jericho.

[5] Then the group of prophets from Jericho came to Elisha and asked him, "Did you know that the LORD is going to take your master away from you today?"

"Of course I know," Elisha answered. "But be quiet about it."

[6] Then Elijah said to Elisha, "Stay here, for the LORD has told me to go to the Jordan River."

But again Elisha replied, "As surely as the LORD lives and you yourself live, I will never leave you." So they went on together.

[7] Fifty men from the group of prophets also went and watched from a distance as Elijah and Elisha stopped beside the Jordan River. [8] Then Elijah folded his cloak together and struck the water with it. The river divided, and the two of them went across on dry ground!

[9] When they came to the other side, Elijah said to Elisha, "Tell me what I can do for you before I am taken away."

And Elisha replied, "Please let me inherit a double share of your spirit and become your successor."

[10] "You have asked a difficult thing," Elijah replied. "If you see me when I am taken from you, then you will get your request. But if not, then you won't."

[11] As they were walking along and talking, suddenly a chariot of fire appeared, drawn by horses of fire. It drove between the two men, separating them, and Elijah was carried by a whirlwind into heaven. [12] Elisha saw it and cried out, "My father! My father! I see the chariots and charioteers of Israel!" And as they disappeared from sight, Elisha tore his clothes in distress.

[13] Elisha picked up Elijah's cloak, which had fallen when he was taken up. Then Elisha returned to the bank of the Jordan River. [14] He struck the water with Elijah's cloak and cried out, "Where is the LORD, the God of Elijah?" Then the river divided, and Elisha went across.

[15] When the group of prophets from Jericho saw from a distance what happened, they exclaimed, "Elijah's spirit rests upon Elisha!" And they went to meet him and bowed to the ground before him. [16] "Sir," they said, "just say the word and fifty of our strongest men will search the wilderness for your master. Perhaps the Spirit of the LORD has left him on some mountain or in some valley."

"No," Elisha said, "don't send them." [17] But they kept urging him until they shamed him into agreeing, and he finally said, "All right, send them." So fifty men searched for three days but did not find Elijah. [18] Elisha was still at Jericho when they returned. "Didn't I tell you not to go?" he asked.

Elisha's First Miracles

[19] One day the leaders of the town of Jericho visited Elisha. "We have a problem, my lord," they told him. "This town is located in pleasant surroundings, as you can see. But the water is bad, and the land is unproductive."

[20] Elisha said, "Bring me a new bowl with

1:17 Hebrew *Jehoram*, a variant spelling of Joram.

salt in it." So they brought it to him. ²¹Then he went out to the spring that supplied the town with water and threw the salt into it. And he said, "This is what the LORD says: I have purified this water. It will no longer cause death or infertility.*" ²²And the water has remained pure ever since, just as Elisha said.

²³Elisha left Jericho and went up to Bethel. As he was walking along the road, a group of boys from the town began mocking and making fun of him. "Go away, baldy!" they chanted. "Go away, baldy!" ²⁴Elisha turned around and looked at them, and he cursed them in the name of the LORD. Then two bears came out of the woods and mauled forty-two of them. ²⁵From there Elisha went to Mount Carmel and finally returned to Samaria.

3 War between Israel and Moab

Ahab's son Joram* began to rule over Israel in the eighteenth year of King Jehoshaphat's reign in Judah. He reigned in Samaria twelve years. ²He did what was evil in the LORD's sight, but not to the same extent as his father and mother. He at least tore down the sacred pillar of Baal that his father had set up. ³Nevertheless, he continued in the sins that Jeroboam son of Nebat had committed and led the people of Israel to commit.

⁴King Mesha of Moab was a sheep breeder. He used to pay the king of Israel an annual tribute of 100,000 lambs and the wool of 100,000 rams. ⁵But after Ahab's death, the king of Moab rebelled against the king of Israel. ⁶So King Joram promptly mustered the army of Israel and marched from Samaria. ⁷On the way, he sent this message to King Jehoshaphat of Judah: "The king of Moab has rebelled against me. Will you join me in battle against him?"

And Jehoshaphat replied, "Why, of course! You and I are as one. My troops are your troops, and my horses are your horses." ⁸Then Jehoshaphat asked, "What route will we take?"

"We will attack from the wilderness of Edom," Joram replied.

⁹The king of Edom and his troops joined them, and all three armies traveled along a roundabout route through the wilderness for seven days. But there was no water for the men or their animals.

¹⁰"What should we do?" the king of Israel cried out. "The LORD has brought the three of us here to let the king of Moab defeat us."

¹¹But King Jehoshaphat of Judah asked, "Is there no prophet of the LORD with us? If there is, we can ask the LORD what to do through him."

One of King Joram's officers replied, "Elisha son of Shaphat is here. He used to be Elijah's personal assistant.*"

¹²Jehoshaphat said, "Yes, the LORD speaks through him." So the kings of Israel, Judah, and Edom went to consult with Elisha.

¹³"Why are you coming to me?"* Elisha asked the king of Israel. "Go to the pagan prophets of your father and mother!"

But King Joram of Israel said, "No! For it was the LORD who called us three kings here—only to be defeated by the king of Moab!"

¹⁴Elisha replied, "As surely as the LORD Almighty lives, whom I serve, I wouldn't even bother with you except for my respect for King Jehoshaphat of Judah. ¹⁵Now bring me someone who can play the harp."

While the harp was being played, the power* of the LORD came upon Elisha, ¹⁶and he said, "This is what the LORD says: This dry valley will be filled with pools of water! ¹⁷You will see neither wind nor rain, says the LORD, but this valley will be filled with water. You will have plenty for yourselves and your cattle and other animals. ¹⁸But this is only a simple thing for the LORD, for he will make you victorious over the army of Moab! ¹⁹You will conquer the best of their towns, even the fortified ones. You will cut down all their good trees, stop up all their springs, and ruin all their good land with stones."

²⁰The next day at about the time when the morning sacrifice was offered, water suddenly appeared! It was flowing from the direction of Edom, and soon there was water everywhere.

2:21 Or or make the land unproductive; Hebrew reads or barrenness.   3:1 Hebrew Jehoram, a variant spelling of Joram; also in 3:6.
3:11 Hebrew He used to pour water on the hands of Elijah.   3:13 Hebrew What is there in common between you and me?   3:15 Hebrew the hand.

²¹Meanwhile, when the people of Moab heard about the three armies marching against them, they mobilized every man who was old enough to strap on a sword, and they stationed themselves along their border. ²²But when they got up the next morning, the sun was shining across the water, making it appear red to the Moabites—like blood. ²³"It's blood!" the Moabites exclaimed. "The three armies must have attacked and killed each other! Let's go, men of Moab, and collect the plunder!"

²⁴But when the Moabites arrived at the Israelite camp, the army of Israel rushed out and attacked them until they turned and ran. The army of Israel chased them into the land of Moab, destroying everything as they went.* ²⁵They destroyed the towns, covered their good land with stones, stopped up all the springs, and cut down all the good trees. Finally, only Kir-hareseth and its stone walls were left, but men with slings surrounded and attacked it.

²⁶When the king of Moab saw that he was losing the battle, he led 700 of his swordsmen in a desperate attempt to break through the enemy lines near the king of Edom, but they failed. ²⁷Then the king of Moab took his oldest son, who would have been the next king, and sacrificed him as a burnt offering on the wall. So there was great anger against Israel,* and the Israelites withdrew and returned to their own land.

Elisha Helps a Poor Widow

4 One day the widow of a member of the group of prophets came to Elisha and cried out, "My husband who served you is dead, and you know how he feared the LORD. But now a creditor has come, threatening to take my two sons as slaves."

²"What can I do to help you?" Elisha asked. "Tell me, what do you have in the house?"

"Nothing at all, except a flask of olive oil," she replied.

³And Elisha said, "Borrow as many empty jars as you can from your friends and neighbors. ⁴Then go into your house with your sons and shut the door behind you. Pour olive oil from your flask into the jars, setting each one aside when it is filled."

⁵So she did as she was told. Her sons kept bringing jars to her, and she filled one after another. ⁶Soon every container was full to the brim!

"Bring me another jar," she said to one of her sons.

"There aren't any more!" he told her. And then the olive oil stopped flowing.

⁷When she told the man of God what had happened, he said to her, "Now sell the olive oil and pay your debts, and you and your sons can live on what is left over."

Elisha and the Woman from Shunem

⁸One day Elisha went to the town of Shunem. A wealthy woman lived there, and she urged him to come to her home for a meal. After that, whenever he passed that way, he would stop there for something to eat.

⁹She said to her husband, "I am sure this man who stops in from time to time is a holy man of God. ¹⁰Let's build a small room for him on the roof and furnish it with a bed, a table, a chair, and a lamp. Then he will have a place to stay whenever he comes by."

¹¹One day Elisha returned to Shunem, and he went up to this upper room to rest. ¹²He said to his servant Gehazi, "Tell the woman from Shunem I want to speak to her." When she appeared, ¹³Elisha said to Gehazi, "Tell her, 'We appreciate the kind concern you have shown us. What can we do for you? Can we put in a good word for you to the king or to the commander of the army?'"

"No," she replied, "my family takes good care of me."

¹⁴Later Elisha asked Gehazi, "What can we do for her?"

Gehazi replied, "She doesn't have a son, and her husband is an old man."

¹⁵"Call her back again," Elisha told him. When the woman returned, Elisha said to her as she stood in the doorway, ¹⁶"Next year at this time you will be holding a son in your arms!"

"No, my lord!" she cried. "O man of God, don't deceive me and get my hopes up like that."

¹⁷But sure enough, the woman soon became pregnant. And at that time the fol-

---

3:24 The meaning of the Hebrew is uncertain.   3:27 Or *So Israel's anger was great.* The meaning of the Hebrew is uncertain.

Simplicity

Simple Trust

2 KINGS 4:1–7

H er cry was one of desperation: widowed and in debt, her two sons about to be taken as slaves to repay what was owed, she was at the end of her rope. She cried out to Elisha for help. She had only one possession of any value left: a flask of olive oil.

And God stepped in, working powerfully to rescue her sons from indentured servitude. The oil was multiplied. She was provided for. She learned a lesson in trust that she undoubtedly carried with her for the rest of her life.

For me too it was during times when I was poorest in physical possessions that I was richest in faith—and I saw God do remarkable things. While my husband traveled for his nonprofit job, I was stuck at home, carless, with preschoolers. One day we both felt led to pray for another car that we couldn't afford. That night a friend said, "An associate wants to give her car away. Do you know anyone who needs it?" That car got us through the next three years of seminary. When our family ran out of funds during seminary and didn't even have grocery money, we again trusted God. A check came in the mail from a woman I'd met only once.

Sometimes when we live in financial comfort, we miss seeing God provide in amazing ways. His provision becomes more matter-of-fact to us than miraculous. Jesus challenged his followers, "I tell you not to worry about everyday life—whether you have enough food and drink, or enough clothes to wear" (Matthew 6:25). When we embrace this teaching, we can experience freedom from the attachment and addiction to material things, and we can learn how to trust God in a profound way. And this practice of trusting God is of infinitely more value than being comfortable.

—JoHannah Reardon

For more on simplicity, see reading at Psalm 34.

lowing year she had a son, just as Elisha had said.

¹⁸ One day when her child was older, he went out to help his father, who was working with the harvesters. ¹⁹ Suddenly he cried out, "My head hurts! My head hurts!"

His father said to one of the servants, "Carry him home to his mother."

²⁰ So the servant took him home, and his mother held him on her lap. But around noontime he died. ²¹ She carried him up and laid him on the bed of the man of God, then shut the door and left him there. ²² She sent a message to her husband: "Send one of the servants and a donkey so that I can hurry to the man of God and come right back."

²³ "Why go today?" he asked. "It is neither a new moon festival nor a Sabbath."

But she said, "It will be all right."

²⁴ So she saddled the donkey and said to the servant, "Hurry! Don't slow down unless I tell you to."

²⁵ As she approached the man of God at Mount Carmel, Elisha saw her in the distance. He said to Gehazi, "Look, the woman from Shunem is coming. ²⁶ Run out to meet her and ask her, 'Is everything all right with you, your husband, and your child?'"

"Yes," the woman told Gehazi, "everything is fine."

²⁷ But when she came to the man of God at the mountain, she fell to the ground before him and caught hold of his feet. Gehazi

Hospitality

God's Radical Hospitality
2 KINGS 4:8–37

It was with great pride that I learned my niece Isabel was selected to play the part of Mary in her preschool's *Las Posadas* celebration. With her long black hair, bright brown eyes, and olive skin, Isabel was the picture-perfect Mary. She and "Joseph" led the other children in a miniature version of the Mexican holiday that is now celebrated in both Protestant and Catholic Latino communities across the Americas. Las Posadas is a remembrance of Mary and Joseph's sojourn to crowded Bethlehem in which there was no place for them to stay (Luke 2:7). A traditional Las Posadas procession imagines and magnifies what their experience may have been like, as people playing the roles of Mary and Joseph go door to door throughout a neighborhood acting out their search for a place to stay. In song they request, "In the name of God, we ask those who dwell here, to give some travelers lodging this evening." But over and over, as the ritual goes, they are told there is no room. They are turned away. They are left on the outside, as doors close in their faces.

In Scripture we find a counterbalance to this story of doors closing to Mary and Joseph. Second Kings 4 describes an opposite picture of exuberant, generous, and intentional hospitality in which a woman from Shunem went out of her way to extend hospitality to the prophet Elisha. First, "she urged [Elisha] to come to her home for a meal" (4:8)—a dinner he repeated many times, as he returned again and again for sustenance and company. Then she took the initiative to go even further, explaining her idea to her husband: "Let's build a small room for him on the roof and furnish it with a bed, a table, a chair, and a lamp. Then he will have a place to stay whenever he comes by" (4:10).

Elisha was so appreciative of her hospitality that he, through the power of God, promised her the miracle of a son. She did give birth to a son, and Scripture indicates that she and her family had an ongoing, close relationship with their regular houseguest Elisha. In the rest of the story, through both tragedy and another miracle, we observe the deepening, honest friendship between Elisha and this woman who opened her home and her life to him, offering him a place of safety and refreshment during his exhausting and important prophetic ministry.

In one story, doors are closed. In the other, the door is flung wide open. The meal is repeatedly served. The guest room is constructed. The invitation stands open.

These stories ask me some pointed questions that I'd prefer to ignore: *Which story do I most often live out? Do I live with an open door, an open hand, and an open heart, ready to welcome and minister to others? Or do I live as one without room in my life or heart to minister to those in need? Do I live in a way that invites or rejects?*

"The need for shelter, for *posada*, is a fundamental human need," writes Ana María Pineda in *Practicing Our Faith*. "None of us ever knows for sure when we might be uprooted and cast upon the mercy of others." A key to living in God-honoring hospitality is the realization that the wanderer at the door could be *me*.

God used this idea to guide his people toward a culture of hospitality. They had been enslaved by the Egyptians; they poignantly knew what it was to need care and kindness and be treated harshly instead. God reminded them of this fact when he instructed them, "Do not take advantage of foreigners who live among you in your land. Treat them like native-born Israelites, and *love them as you love yourself. Remember that you were once foreigners living in the land of Egypt.* I am the LORD your God" (Leviticus 19:33–34, italics added). This is the very passage that Jesus quoted from when he spoke what has become known as the Golden Rule (Matthew 7:12; Luke 6:31).

In God's radical hospitality, we don't see an outsider or stranger at our door; we see ourselves. We consciously choose to love and care for them as we'd desire to be cared for. A hot meal. A kind word. A hug. A listening ear. Space and time just to be.

"Offering hospitality is a moral imperative," writes Pineda. "It emerges from knowing the hospitality God has shown us." God has welcomed us sinners in, with open arms, tremendous blessings, generous grace. He shelters us under his wings (Psalm 91:4). Like the woman from Shunem, may we respond as people who go above and beyond in our willingness and effort to minister to those journeying among us.

—*Kelli B. Trujillo*

For more on hospitality, see reading at Psalm 36:5–9.

began to push her away, but the man of God said, "Leave her alone. She is deeply troubled, but the LORD has not told me what it is."

²⁸ Then she said, "Did I ask you for a son, my lord? And didn't I say, 'Don't deceive me and get my hopes up'?"

²⁹ Then Elisha said to Gehazi, "Get ready to travel*; take my staff and go! Don't talk to anyone along the way. Go quickly and lay the staff on the child's face."

³⁰ But the boy's mother said, "As surely as the LORD lives and you yourself live, I won't go home unless you go with me." So Elisha returned with her.

³¹ Gehazi hurried on ahead and laid the staff on the child's face, but nothing happened. There was no sign of life. He returned to meet Elisha and told him, "The child is still dead."

³² When Elisha arrived, the child was indeed dead, lying there on the prophet's bed. ³³ He went in alone and shut the door behind him and prayed to the LORD. ³⁴ Then he lay down on the child's body, placing his mouth on the child's mouth, his eyes on the child's eyes, and his hands on the child's hands. And as he stretched out on him, the child's body began to grow warm again! ³⁵ Elisha got up, walked back and forth across the room once, and then stretched himself out again on the child. This time the boy sneezed seven times and opened his eyes!

³⁶ Then Elisha summoned Gehazi. "Call the child's mother!" he said. And when she came in, Elisha said, "Here, take your son!" ³⁷ She fell at his feet and bowed before him, overwhelmed with gratitude. Then she took her son in her arms and carried him downstairs.

Miracles during a Famine

³⁸ Elisha now returned to Gilgal, and there was a famine in the land. One day as the group of prophets was seated before him, he said to his servant, "Put a large pot on the fire, and make some stew for the rest of the group."

³⁹ One of the young men went out into the field to gather herbs and came back with a pocketful of wild gourds. He shred-ded them and put them into the pot without realizing they were poisonous. ⁴⁰ Some of the stew was served to the men. But after they had eaten a bite or two they cried out, "Man of God, there's poison in this stew!" So they would not eat it.

⁴¹ Elisha said, "Bring me some flour." Then he threw it into the pot and said, "Now it's all right; go ahead and eat." And then it did not harm them.

⁴² One day a man from Baal-shalishah brought the man of God a sack of fresh grain and twenty loaves of barley bread made from the first grain of his harvest. Elisha said, "Give it to the people so they can eat."

⁴³ "What?" his servant exclaimed. "Feed a hundred people with only this?"

But Elisha repeated, "Give it to the people so they can eat, for this is what the LORD says: Everyone will eat, and there will even be some left over!" ⁴⁴ And when they gave it to the people, there was plenty for all and some left over, just as the LORD had promised.

5 The Healing of Naaman

The king of Aram had great admiration for Naaman, the commander of his army, because through him the LORD had given Aram great victories. But though Naaman was a mighty warrior, he suffered from leprosy.*

² At this time Aramean raiders had invaded the land of Israel, and among their captives was a young girl who had been given to Naaman's wife as a maid. ³ One day the girl said to her mistress, "I wish my master would go to see the prophet in Samaria. He would heal him of his leprosy."

⁴ So Naaman told the king what the young girl from Israel had said. ⁵ "Go and visit the prophet," the king of Aram told him. "I will send a letter of introduction for you to take to the king of Israel." So Naaman started out, carrying as gifts 750 pounds of silver, 150 pounds of gold,* and ten sets of clothing. ⁶ The letter to the king of Israel said: "With this letter I present my servant Naaman. I want you to heal him of his leprosy."

⁷ When the king of Israel read the letter, he tore his clothes in dismay and said, "This

---

4:29 Hebrew *Bind up your loins.* 5:1 Or *from a contagious skin disease.* The Hebrew word used here and throughout this passage can describe various skin diseases. 5:5 Hebrew *10 talents* [340 kilograms] *of silver, 6,000 shekels* [68 kilograms] *of gold.*

man sends me a leper to heal! Am I God, that I can give life and take it away? I can see that he's just trying to pick a fight with me."

⁸But when Elisha, the man of God, heard that the king of Israel had torn his clothes in dismay, he sent this message to him: "Why are you so upset? Send Naaman to me, and he will learn that there is a true prophet here in Israel."

⁹So Naaman went with his horses and chariots and waited at the door of Elisha's house. ¹⁰But Elisha sent a messenger out to him with this message: "Go and wash yourself seven times in the Jordan River. Then your skin will be restored, and you will be healed of your leprosy."

¹¹But Naaman became angry and stalked away. "I thought he would certainly come out to meet me!" he said. "I expected him to wave his hand over the leprosy and call on the name of the LORD his God and heal me! ¹²Aren't the rivers of Damascus, the Abana

Naaman's Servant: Showing Kindness to Her Captor

2 KINGS 5:1-19

Forgiveness

In our day we find slavery detestable. But in the ancient world, people were often treated as property and plunder. Families were ripped apart. Children taken. Parents killed. Lives destroyed. Can you imagine what this kind of violence would do to your body, to your spirit, to your faith in a God who promises he holds all things in his hands?

We know little about the "young girl" of 2 Kings 5. We know she worked as a maid for the wife of Naaman, the commander of an army that opposed the Israelites. We know Naaman "owned" this young girl because she'd been taken captive during the violence of war, ripped from her family and everything else she knew. It's possible that her family was killed in the raid. She would have every reason to be embittered, angry, and hateful toward her new master—and even toward God.

But what we see in Scripture is a young girl who expressed profound compassion and simple faith. When she learned of Naaman's skin disease, she told his wife about a healer and prophet who could cure him.

What transpired in her mind when she chose mercy and kindness over revenge? What motivated her to seek *good* for this man, her master and captor? Though Scripture doesn't describe her internal struggle, her actions show us a great deal about her heart: she had chosen forgiveness.

The painful process of forgiveness involves letting God strip away our desires for vengeance in surrender to God's justice. But that process always leads to great fruit. For this young girl, her simple suggestion led to Naaman's healing and created an opportunity for the entire household to encounter the truth about the one true God.

In her simple faith and compassionate spirit, Naaman's servant girl exemplified a heart surrendered to God. Her example shows us that God seeks our obedience in matters of the heart and in simple acts of service. And beyond just thoughts of forgiveness, she embodies for us a choice to actively do good to those who have harmed us.

—Nicole Unice

For more on forgiveness, see reading at Isaiah 43:14-25.

and the Pharpar, better than any of the rivers of Israel? Why shouldn't I wash in them and be healed?" So Naaman turned and went away in a rage.

¹³But his officers tried to reason with him and said, "Sir,* if the prophet had told you to do something very difficult, wouldn't you have done it? So you should certainly obey him when he says simply, 'Go and wash and be cured!'" ¹⁴So Naaman went down to the Jordan River and dipped himself seven times, as the man of God had instructed him. And his skin became as healthy as the skin of a young child's, and he was healed!

¹⁵Then Naaman and his entire party went back to find the man of God. They stood before him, and Naaman said, "Now I know that there is no God in all the world except in Israel. So please accept a gift from your servant."

¹⁶But Elisha replied, "As surely as the LORD lives, whom I serve, I will not accept any gifts." And though Naaman urged him to take the gift, Elisha refused.

¹⁷Then Naaman said, "All right, but please allow me to load two of my mules with earth from this place, and I will take it back home with me. From now on I will never again offer burnt offerings or sacrifices to any other god except the LORD. ¹⁸However, may the LORD pardon me in this one thing: When my master the king goes into the temple of the god Rimmon to worship there and leans on my arm, may the LORD pardon me when I bow, too."

¹⁹"Go in peace," Elisha said. So Naaman started home again.

The Greed of Gehazi

²⁰But Gehazi, the servant of Elisha, the man of God, said to himself, "My master should not have let this Aramean get away without accepting any of his gifts. As surely as the LORD lives, I will chase after him and get something from him." ²¹So Gehazi set off after Naaman.

When Naaman saw Gehazi running after him, he climbed down from his chariot and went to meet him. "Is everything all right?" Naaman asked.

²²"Yes," Gehazi said, "but my master has sent me to tell you that two young prophets from the hill country of Ephraim have just arrived. He would like 75 pounds* of silver and two sets of clothing to give to them."

²³"By all means, take twice as much* silver," Naaman insisted. He gave him two sets of clothing, tied up the money in two bags, and sent two of his servants to carry the gifts for Gehazi. ²⁴But when they arrived at the citadel,* Gehazi took the gifts from the servants and sent the men back. Then he went and hid the gifts inside the house.

²⁵When he went in to his master, Elisha asked him, "Where have you been, Gehazi?"

"I haven't been anywhere," he replied.

²⁶But Elisha asked him, "Don't you realize that I was there in spirit when Naaman stepped down from his chariot to meet you? Is this the time to receive money and clothing, olive groves and vineyards, sheep and cattle, and male and female servants? ²⁷Because you have done this, you and your descendants will suffer from Naaman's leprosy forever." When Gehazi left the room, he was covered with leprosy; his skin was white as snow.

6 The Floating Ax Head

One day the group of prophets came to Elisha and told him, "As you can see, this place where we meet with you is too small. ²Let's go down to the Jordan River, where there are plenty of logs. There we can build a new place for us to meet."

"All right," he told them, "go ahead."

³"Please come with us," someone suggested.

"I will," he said. ⁴So he went with them.

When they arrived at the Jordan, they began cutting down trees. ⁵But as one of them was cutting a tree, his ax head fell into the river. "Oh, sir!" he cried. "It was a borrowed ax!"

⁶"Where did it fall?" the man of God asked. When he showed him the place, Elisha cut a stick and threw it into the water at that spot. Then the ax head floated to the surface. ⁷"Grab it," Elisha said. And the man reached out and grabbed it.

5:13 Hebrew *My father.* **5:22** Hebrew *1 talent* [34 kilograms]. **5:23** Hebrew *take 2 talents* [68 kilograms]. **5:24** Hebrew *the Ophel.*

Expecting God to Act

2 KINGS 6:8-23

Throughout the Bible we see that the people were going about their daily lives while God was busily, quietly working in the background.

One of my favorite examples is a story of Elisha's faith in action. In 2 Kings 6 the Arameans are at war with Israel, and they surround and outnumber Elisha's camp. One of Elisha's servants discovers it and desperately cries, "What will we do now?" (6:15).

And Elisha responds, "Don't be afraid!" (6:16). In other words, have faith that our God is going to take care of us; it will work out.

But the servant still anguishes over the circumstances. He focuses only on what he can actually see. (How often do we do this in our circumstances?) But Elisha's faith proves strong, as he prays for God to open the servant's eyes. And the servant receives a glimpse of the spiritual world: there, spread out across the hillside, is a great angelic army ready to fight for them!

Sometimes we can focus our "faith" on the immediate circumstances we can see. Worry, fear, anxiety, complaints, and everything else blind us to God's ever-vigilant hand at work on our behalf. But God calls us to live *as though* we see him working, *as though* we see that army of angels ready to fight for us.

That's the power of faith: that we live as more than overcomers because we know God is working on our behalf always.

—*Ginger Kolbaba*

For more on faith, see reading at 1 Chronicles 16:34.

Elisha Traps the Arameans

⁸When the king of Aram was at war with Israel, he would confer with his officers and say, "We will mobilize our forces at such and such a place."

⁹But immediately Elisha, the man of God, would warn the king of Israel, "Do not go near that place, for the Arameans are planning to mobilize their troops there." ¹⁰So the king of Israel would send word to the place indicated by the man of God. Time and again Elisha warned the king, so that he would be on the alert there.

¹¹The king of Aram became very upset over this. He called his officers together and demanded, "Which of you is the traitor? Who has been informing the king of Israel of my plans?"

¹²"It's not us, my lord the king," one of the officers replied. "Elisha, the prophet in Israel, tells the king of Israel even the words you speak in the privacy of your bedroom!"

¹³"Go and find out where he is," the king commanded, "so I can send troops to seize him."

And the report came back: "Elisha is at Dothan." ¹⁴So one night the king of Aram sent a great army with many chariots and horses to surround the city.

¹⁵When the servant of the man of God got up early the next morning and went outside, there were troops, horses, and chariots everywhere. "Oh, sir, what will we do now?" the young man cried to Elisha.

¹⁶"Don't be afraid!" Elisha told him. "For there are more on our side than on theirs!" ¹⁷Then Elisha prayed, "O LORD, open his eyes and let him see!" The LORD opened the

young man's eyes, and when he looked up, he saw that the hillside around Elisha was filled with horses and chariots of fire.

18 As the Aramean army advanced toward him, Elisha prayed, "O LORD, please make them blind." So the LORD struck them with blindness as Elisha had asked.

19 Then Elisha went out and told them, "You have come the wrong way! This isn't the right city! Follow me, and I will take you to the man you are looking for." And he led them to the city of Samaria.

20 As soon as they had entered Samaria, Elisha prayed, "O LORD, now open their eyes and let them see." So the LORD opened their eyes, and they discovered that they were in the middle of Samaria.

21 When the king of Israel saw them, he shouted to Elisha, "My father, should I kill them? Should I kill them?"

22 "Of course not!" Elisha replied. "Do we kill prisoners of war? Give them food and drink and send them home again to their master."

23 So the king made a great feast for them and then sent them home to their master. After that, the Aramean raiders stayed away from the land of Israel.

Ben-Hadad Besieges Samaria

24 Some time later, however, King Ben-hadad of Aram mustered his entire army and besieged Samaria. 25 As a result, there was a great famine in the city. The siege lasted so long that a donkey's head sold for eighty pieces of silver, and a cup of dove's dung sold for five pieces* of silver.

26 One day as the king of Israel was walking along the wall of the city, a woman called to him, "Please help me, my lord the king!"

27 He answered, "If the LORD doesn't help you, what can I do? I have neither food from the threshing floor nor wine from the press to give you." 28 But then the king asked, "What is the matter?"

She replied, "This woman said to me: 'Come on, let's eat your son today, then we will eat my son tomorrow.' 29 So we cooked my son and ate him. Then the next day I

said to her, 'Kill your son so we can eat him,' but she has hidden her son."

30 When the king heard this, he tore his clothes in despair. And as the king walked along the wall, the people could see that he was wearing burlap under his robe next to his skin. 31 "May God strike me and even kill me if I don't separate Elisha's head from his shoulders this very day," the king vowed.

32 Elisha was sitting in his house with the elders of Israel when the king sent a messenger to summon him. But before the messenger arrived, Elisha said to the elders, "A murderer has sent a man to cut off my head. When he arrives, shut the door and keep him out. We will soon hear his master's steps following him."

33 While Elisha was still saying this, the messenger arrived. And the king* said, "All this misery is from the LORD! Why should I wait for the LORD any longer?"

7 Elisha replied, "Listen to this message from the LORD! This is what the LORD says: By this time tomorrow in the markets of Samaria, five quarts of choice flour will cost only one piece of silver,* and ten quarts of barley grain will cost only one piece of silver.*"

2 The officer assisting the king said to the man of God, "That couldn't happen even if the LORD opened the windows of heaven!"

But Elisha replied, "You will see it happen with your own eyes, but you won't be able to eat any of it!"

Lepers Visit the Enemy Camp

3 Now there were four men with leprosy* sitting at the entrance of the city gates. "Why should we sit here waiting to die?" they asked each other. 4 "We will starve if we stay here, but with the famine in the city, we will starve if we go back there. So we might as well go out and surrender to the Aramean army. If they let us live, so much the better. But if they kill us, we would have died anyway."

5 So at twilight they set out for the camp of the Arameans. But when they came to the edge of the camp, no one was there! 6 For

---

6:25 Hebrew *sold for 80 shekels* [2 pounds, or 0.9 kilograms] *of silver, and ¼ of a cab* [0.3 liters] *of dove's dung sold for 5 shekels* [2 ounces, or 57 grams]. *Dove's dung* may be a variety of wild vegetable.   **6:33** Hebrew *he.*   **7:1a** Hebrew *1 seah* [6 liters] *of choice flour will cost 1 shekel* [0.4 ounces, or 11 grams]; also in 7:16, 18.   **7:1b** Hebrew *2 seahs* [12 liters] *of barley grain will cost 1 shekel* [0.4 ounces, or 11 grams]; also in 7:16, 18.   **7:3** Or *with a contagious skin disease.* The Hebrew word used here and throughout this passage can describe various skin diseases.

the Lord had caused the Aramean army to hear the clatter of speeding chariots and the galloping of horses and the sounds of a great army approaching. "The king of Israel has hired the Hittites and Egyptians* to attack us!" they cried to one another. [7] So they panicked and ran into the night, abandoning their tents, horses, donkeys, and everything else, as they fled for their lives.

[8] When the lepers arrived at the edge of the camp, they went into one tent after another, eating and drinking wine; and they carried off silver and gold and clothing and hid it. [9] Finally, they said to each other, "This is not right. This is a day of good news, and we aren't sharing it with anyone! If we wait until morning, some calamity will certainly fall upon us. Come on, let's go back and tell the people at the palace."

[10] So they went back to the city and told the gatekeepers what had happened. "We went out to the Aramean camp," they said, "and no one was there! The horses and donkeys were tethered and the tents were all in order, but there wasn't a single person around!" [11] Then the gatekeepers shouted the news to the people in the palace.

Israel Plunders the Camp

[12] The king got out of bed in the middle of the night and told his officers, "I know what has happened. The Arameans know we are starving, so they have left their camp and have hidden in the fields. They are expecting us to leave the city, and then they will take us alive and capture the city."

[13] One of his officers replied, "We had better send out scouts to check into this. Let them take five of the remaining horses. If something happens to them, it will be no worse than if they stay here and die with the rest of us."

[14] So two chariots with horses were prepared, and the king sent scouts to see what had happened to the Aramean army. [15] They went all the way to the Jordan River, following a trail of clothing and equipment that the Arameans had thrown away in their mad rush to escape. The scouts returned and told the king about it. [16] Then the people of Samaria rushed out and plundered the Aramean camp. So it was true that five quarts of choice flour were sold that day for one piece of silver, and ten quarts of barley grain were sold for one piece of silver, just as the Lord had promised. [17] The king appointed his officer to control the traffic at the gate, but he was knocked down and trampled to death as the people rushed out.

So everything happened exactly as the man of God had predicted when the king came to his house. [18] The man of God had said to the king, "By this time tomorrow in the markets of Samaria, five quarts of choice flour will cost one piece of silver, and ten quarts of barley grain will cost one piece of silver." [19] The king's officer had replied, "That couldn't happen even if the Lord opened the windows of heaven!" And the man of God had said, "You will see it happen with your own eyes, but you won't be able to eat any of it!" [20] And so it was, for the people trampled him to death at the gate!

8 The Woman from Shunem Returns Home

Elisha had told the woman whose son he had brought back to life, "Take your family and move to some other place, for the Lord has called for a famine on Israel that will last for seven years." [2] So the woman did as the man of God instructed. She took her family and settled in the land of the Philistines for seven years.

[3] After the famine ended she returned from the land of the Philistines, and she went to see the king about getting back her house and land. [4] As she came in, the king was talking with Gehazi, the servant of the man of God. The king had just said, "Tell me some stories about the great things Elisha has done." [5] And Gehazi was telling the king about the time Elisha had brought a boy back to life. At that very moment, the mother of the boy walked in to make her appeal to the king about her house and land.

"Look, my lord the king!" Gehazi exclaimed. "Here is the woman now, and this is her son— the very one Elisha brought back to life!"

[6] "Is this true?" the king asked her. And she told him the story. So he directed one of his officials to see that everything she had

---

7:6 Possibly *and the people of Muzur*, a district near Cilicia.

lost was restored to her, including the value of any crops that had been harvested during her absence.

Hazael Murders Ben-Hadad

[7] Elisha went to Damascus, the capital of Aram, where King Ben-hadad lay sick. When someone told the king that the man of God had come, [8] the king said to Hazael, "Take a gift to the man of God. Then tell him to ask the LORD, 'Will I recover from this illness?'"

[9] So Hazael loaded down forty camels with the finest products of Damascus as a gift for Elisha. He went to him and said, "Your servant Ben-hadad, the king of Aram, has sent me to ask, 'Will I recover from this illness?'"

[10] And Elisha replied, "Go and tell him, 'You will surely recover.' But actually the LORD has shown me that he will surely die!" [11] Elisha stared at Hazael* with a fixed gaze until Hazael became uneasy.* Then the man of God started weeping.

[12] "What's the matter, my lord?" Hazael asked him.

Elisha replied, "I know the terrible things you will do to the people of Israel. You will burn their fortified cities, kill their young men with the sword, dash their little children to the ground, and rip open their pregnant women!"

[13] Hazael responded, "How could a nobody like me* ever accomplish such great things?"

Elisha answered, "The LORD has shown me that you are going to be the king of Aram."

[14] When Hazael left Elisha and went back, the king asked him, "What did Elisha tell you?"

And Hazael replied, "He told me that you will surely recover."

[15] But the next day Hazael took a blanket, soaked it in water, and held it over the king's face until he died. Then Hazael became the next king of Aram.

Jehoram Rules in Judah

[16] Jehoram son of King Jehoshaphat of Judah began to rule over Judah in the fifth year of the reign of Joram son of Ahab, king of Israel. [17] Jehoram was thirty-two years old when he became king, and he reigned in Jerusalem eight years. [18] But Jehoram followed the example of the kings of Israel and was as wicked as King Ahab, for he had married one of Ahab's daughters. So Jehoram did what was evil in the LORD's sight. [19] But the LORD did not want to destroy Judah, for he had made a covenant with David and promised that his descendants would continue to rule, shining like a lamp forever.

[20] During Jehoram's reign, the Edomites revolted against Judah and crowned their own king. [21] So Jehoram* went with all his chariots to attack the town of Zair.* The Edomites surrounded him and his chariot commanders, but he went out at night and attacked them* under cover of darkness. But Jehoram's army deserted him and fled to their homes. [22] So Edom has been independent from Judah to this day. The town of Libnah also revolted about that same time.

[23] The rest of the events in Jehoram's reign and everything he did are recorded in *The Book of the History of the Kings of Judah.* [24] When Jehoram died, he was buried with his ancestors in the City of David. Then his son Ahaziah became the next king.

Ahaziah Rules in Judah

[25] Ahaziah son of Jehoram began to rule over Judah in the twelfth year of the reign of Joram son of Ahab, king of Israel.

[26] Ahaziah was twenty-two years old when he became king, and he reigned in Jerusalem one year. His mother was Athaliah, a granddaughter of King Omri of Israel. [27] Ahaziah followed the evil example of King Ahab's family. He did what was evil in the LORD's sight, just as Ahab's family had done, for he was related by marriage to the family of Ahab.

[28] Ahaziah joined Joram son of Ahab, the king of Israel, in his war against King Hazael of Aram at Ramoth-gilead. When the Arameans wounded King Joram in the battle, [29] he returned to Jezreel to recover from the wounds he had received at Ramoth.* Because Joram was wounded, King Ahaziah of Judah went to Jezreel to visit him.

8:11a Hebrew *He stared at him.* 8:11b The meaning of the Hebrew is uncertain. 8:13 Hebrew *a dog.* 8:21a Hebrew *Joram,* a variant spelling of Jehoram; also in 8:23, 24. 8:21b Greek version reads *Seir.* 8:21c Or *he went out and escaped.* The meaning of the Hebrew is uncertain. 8:29 Hebrew *Ramah,* a variant spelling of Ramoth.

9 Jehu Anointed King of Israel

Meanwhile, Elisha the prophet had summoned a member of the group of prophets. "Get ready to travel,"* he told him, "and take this flask of olive oil with you. Go to Ramoth-gilead, ²and find Jehu son of Jehoshaphat, son of Nimshi. Call him into a private room away from his friends, ³and pour the oil over his head. Say to him, 'This is what the LORD says: I anoint you to be the king over Israel.' Then open the door and run for your life!"

⁴So the young prophet did as he was told and went to Ramoth-gilead. ⁵When he arrived there, he found Jehu sitting around with the other army officers. "I have a message for you, Commander," he said.

"For which one of us?" Jehu asked.

"For you, Commander," he replied.

⁶So Jehu left the others and went into the house. Then the young prophet poured the oil over Jehu's head and said, "This is what the LORD, the God of Israel, says: I anoint you king over the LORD's people, Israel. ⁷You are to destroy the family of Ahab, your master. In this way, I will avenge the murder of my prophets and all the LORD's servants who were killed by Jezebel. ⁸The entire family of Ahab must be wiped out. I will destroy every one of his male descendants, slave and free alike, anywhere in Israel. ⁹I will destroy the family of Ahab as I destroyed the families of Jeroboam son of Nebat and of Baasha son of Ahijah. ¹⁰Dogs will eat Ahab's wife Jezebel at the plot of land in Jezreel, and no one will bury her." Then the young prophet opened the door and ran.

¹¹Jehu went back to his fellow officers, and one of them asked him, "What did that madman want? Is everything all right?"

"You know how a man like that babbles on," Jehu replied.

¹²"You're hiding something," they said. "Tell us."

So Jehu told them, "He said to me, 'This is what the LORD says: I have anointed you to be king over Israel.'"

¹³Then they quickly spread out their cloaks on the bare steps and blew the ram's horn, shouting, "Jehu is king!"

Jehu Kills Joram and Ahaziah

¹⁴So Jehu son of Jehoshaphat, son of Nimshi, led a conspiracy against King Joram. (Now Joram had been with the army at Ramoth-gilead, defending Israel against the forces of King Hazael of Aram. ¹⁵But King Joram* was wounded in the fighting and returned to Jezreel to recover from his wounds.) So Jehu told the men with him, "If you want me to be king, don't let anyone leave town and go to Jezreel to report what we have done."

¹⁶Then Jehu got into a chariot and rode to Jezreel to find King Joram, who was lying there wounded. King Ahaziah of Judah was there, too, for he had gone to visit him. ¹⁷The watchman on the tower of Jezreel saw Jehu and his company approaching, so he shouted to Joram, "I see a company of troops coming!"

"Send out a rider to ask if they are coming in peace," King Joram ordered.

¹⁸So a horseman went out to meet Jehu and said, "The king wants to know if you are coming in peace."

Jehu replied, "What do you know about peace? Fall in behind me!"

The watchman called out to the king, "The messenger has met them, but he's not returning."

¹⁹So the king sent out a second horseman. He rode up to them and said, "The king wants to know if you come in peace."

Again Jehu answered, "What do you know about peace? Fall in behind me!"

²⁰The watchman exclaimed, "The messenger has met them, but he isn't returning either! It must be Jehu son of Nimshi, for he's driving like a madman."

²¹"Quick! Get my chariot ready!" King Joram commanded.

Then King Joram of Israel and King Ahaziah of Judah rode out in their chariots to meet Jehu. They met him at the plot of land that had belonged to Naboth of Jezreel. ²²King Joram demanded, "Do you come in peace, Jehu?"

Jehu replied, "How can there be peace as long as the idolatry and witchcraft of your mother, Jezebel, are all around us?"

²³Then King Joram turned the horses

9:1 Hebrew *Bind up your loins.*   **9:15** Hebrew *Jehoram,* a variant spelling of Joram; also in 9:17, 21, 22, 23, 24.

around* and fled, shouting to King Ahaziah, "Treason, Ahaziah!" ²⁴But Jehu drew his bow and shot Joram between the shoulders. The arrow pierced his heart, and he sank down dead in his chariot.

²⁵Jehu said to Bidkar, his officer, "Throw him into the plot of land that belonged to Naboth of Jezreel. Do you remember when you and I were riding along behind his father, Ahab? The LORD pronounced this message against him: ²⁶'I solemnly swear that I will repay him here on this plot of land, says the LORD, for the murder of Naboth and his sons that I saw yesterday.' So throw him out on Naboth's property, just as the LORD said."

²⁷When King Ahaziah of Judah saw what was happening, he fled along the road to Beth-haggan. Jehu rode after him, shouting, "Shoot him, too!" So they shot Ahaziah in his chariot at the Ascent of Gur, near Ibleam. He was able to go on as far as Megiddo, but he died there. ²⁸His servants took him by chariot to Jerusalem, where they buried him with his ancestors in the City of David. ²⁹Ahaziah had become king over Judah in the eleventh year of the reign of Joram son of Ahab.

The Death of Jezebel

³⁰When Jezebel, the queen mother, heard that Jehu had come to Jezreel, she painted her eyelids and fixed her hair and sat at a window. ³¹When Jehu entered the gate of the palace, she shouted at him, "Have you come in peace, you murderer? You're just like Zimri, who murdered his master!"*

³²Jehu looked up and saw her at the window and shouted, "Who is on my side?" And two or three eunuchs looked out at him. ³³"Throw her down!" Jehu yelled. So they threw her out the window, and her blood spattered against the wall and on the horses. And Jehu trampled her body under his horses' hooves.

³⁴Then Jehu went into the palace and ate and drank. Afterward he said, "Someone go and bury this cursed woman, for she is the daughter of a king." ³⁵But when they went out to bury her, they found only her skull, her feet, and her hands.

³⁶When they returned and told Jehu, he stated, "This fulfills the message from the LORD, which he spoke through his servant Elijah from Tishbe: 'At the plot of land in Jezreel, dogs will eat Jezebel's body. ³⁷Her remains will be scattered like dung on the plot of land in Jezreel, so that no one will be able to recognize her.'"

10 Jehu Kills Ahab's Family

Ahab had seventy sons living in the city of Samaria. So Jehu wrote letters and sent them to Samaria, to the elders and officials of the city,* and to the guardians of King Ahab's sons. He said, ²"The king's sons are with you, and you have at your disposal chariots, horses, a fortified city, and weapons. As soon as you receive this letter, ³select the best qualified of your master's sons to be your king, and prepare to fight for Ahab's dynasty."

⁴But they were paralyzed with fear and said, "We've seen that two kings couldn't stand against this man! What can we do?"

⁵So the palace and city administrators, together with the elders and the guardians of the king's sons, sent this message to Jehu: "We are your servants and will do anything you tell us. We will not make anyone king; do whatever you think is best."

⁶Jehu responded with a second letter: "If you are on my side and are going to obey me, bring the heads of your master's sons to me at Jezreel by this time tomorrow." Now the seventy sons of the king were being cared for by the leaders of Samaria, where they had been raised since childhood. ⁷When the letter arrived, the leaders killed all seventy of the king's sons. They placed their heads in baskets and presented them to Jehu at Jezreel.

⁸A messenger went to Jehu and said, "They have brought the heads of the king's sons."

So Jehu ordered, "Pile them in two heaps at the entrance of the city gate, and leave them there until morning."

⁹In the morning he went out and spoke to the crowd that had gathered around them. "You are not to blame," he told them. "I am the one who conspired against my master

---

9:23 Hebrew *turned his hands.* **9:31** See 1 Kgs 16:9-10, where Zimri killed his master, King Elah. **10:1** As in some Greek manuscripts and Latin Vulgate (see also 10:6); Hebrew reads *of Jezreel.*

and killed him. But who killed all these? ¹⁰You can be sure that the message of the LORD that was spoken concerning Ahab's family will not fail. The LORD declared through his servant Elijah that this would happen." ¹¹Then Jehu killed all who were left of Ahab's relatives living in Jezreel and all his important officials, his personal friends, and his priests. So Ahab was left without a single survivor.

¹²Then Jehu set out for Samaria. Along the way, while he was at Beth-eked of the Shepherds, ¹³he met some relatives of King Ahaziah of Judah. "Who are you?" he asked them.

And they replied, "We are relatives of King Ahaziah. We are going to visit the sons of King Ahab and the sons of the queen mother."

¹⁴"Take them alive!" Jehu shouted to his men. And they captured all forty-two of them and killed them at the well of Beth-eked. None of them escaped.

¹⁵When Jehu left there, he met Jehonadab son of Recab, who was coming to meet him. After they had greeted each other, Jehu said to him, "Are you as loyal to me as I am to you?"

"Yes, I am," Jehonadab replied.

"If you are," Jehu said, "then give me your hand." So Jehonadab put out his hand, and Jehu helped him into the chariot. ¹⁶Then Jehu said, "Now come with me, and see how devoted I am to the LORD." So Jehonadab rode along with him.

¹⁷When Jehu arrived in Samaria, he killed everyone who was left there from Ahab's family, just as the LORD had promised through Elijah.

Jehu Kills the Priests of Baal

¹⁸Then Jehu called a meeting of all the people of the city and said to them, "Ahab's worship of Baal was nothing compared to the way I will worship him! ¹⁹Therefore, summon all the prophets and worshipers of Baal, and call together all his priests. See to it that every one of them comes, for I am going to offer a great sacrifice to Baal. Anyone who fails to come will be put to death." But Jehu's cunning plan was to destroy all the worshipers of Baal.

²⁰Then Jehu ordered, "Prepare a solemn assembly to worship Baal!" So they did. ²¹He sent messengers throughout all Israel summoning those who worshiped Baal. They all came—not a single one remained behind—and they filled the temple of Baal from one end to the other. ²²And Jehu instructed the keeper of the wardrobe, "Be sure that every worshiper of Baal wears one of these robes." So robes were given to them.

²³Then Jehu went into the temple of Baal with Jehonadab son of Recab. Jehu said to the worshipers of Baal, "Make sure no one who worships the LORD is here—only those who worship Baal." ²⁴So they were all inside the temple to offer sacrifices and burnt offerings. Now Jehu had stationed eighty of his men outside the building and had warned them, "If you let anyone escape, you will pay for it with your own life."

²⁵As soon as Jehu had finished sacrificing the burnt offering, he commanded his guards and officers, "Go in and kill all of them. Don't let a single one escape!" So they killed them all with their swords, and the guards and officers dragged their bodies outside.* Then Jehu's men went into the innermost fortress* of the temple of Baal. ²⁶They dragged out the sacred pillar* used in the worship of Baal and burned it. ²⁷They smashed the sacred pillar and wrecked the temple of Baal, converting it into a public toilet, as it remains to this day.

²⁸In this way, Jehu destroyed every trace of Baal worship from Israel. ²⁹He did not, however, destroy the gold calves at Bethel and Dan, with which Jeroboam son of Nebat had caused Israel to sin.

³⁰Nonetheless the LORD said to Jehu, "You have done well in following my instructions to destroy the family of Ahab. Therefore, your descendants will be kings of Israel down to the fourth generation." ³¹But Jehu did not obey the Law of the LORD, the God of Israel, with all his heart. He refused to turn from the sins that Jeroboam had led Israel to commit.

The Death of Jehu

³²At about that time the LORD began to cut down the size of Israel's territory. King

---

10:25a Or they left their bodies lying there; or they threw them out into the outermost court.   **10:25b** Hebrew city.   **10:26** As in Greek and Syriac versions and Latin Vulgate; Hebrew reads sacred pillars.

Hazael conquered several sections of the country ³³east of the Jordan River, including all of Gilead, Gad, Reuben, and Manasseh. He conquered the area from the town of Aroer by the Arnon Gorge to as far north as Gilead and Bashan.

³⁴The rest of the events in Jehu's reign—everything he did and all his achievements—are recorded in *The Book of the History of the Kings of Israel.*

³⁵When Jehu died, he was buried in Samaria. Then his son Jehoahaz became the next king. ³⁶In all, Jehu reigned over Israel from Samaria for twenty-eight years.

11 Queen Athaliah Rules in Judah

When Athaliah, the mother of King Ahaziah of Judah, learned that her son was dead, she began to destroy the rest of the royal family. ²But Ahaziah's sister Jehosheba, the daughter of King Jehoram,* took Ahaziah's infant son, Joash, and stole him away from among the rest of the king's children, who were about to be killed. She put Joash and his nurse in a bedroom to hide him from Athaliah, so the child was not murdered. ³Joash remained hidden in the Temple of the LORD for six years while Athaliah ruled over the land.

Revolt against Athaliah

⁴In the seventh year of Athaliah's reign, Jehoiada the priest summoned the commanders, the Carite mercenaries, and the palace guards to come to the Temple of the LORD. He made a solemn pact with them and made them swear an oath of loyalty there in the LORD's Temple; then he showed them the king's son.

⁵Jehoiada told them, "This is what you must do. A third of you who are on duty on the Sabbath are to guard the royal palace itself. ⁶Another third of you are to stand guard at the Sur Gate. And the final third must stand guard behind the palace guard. These three groups will all guard the palace. ⁷The other two units who are off duty on the Sabbath must stand guard for the king at the LORD's Temple. ⁸Form a bodyguard around the king and keep your weapons in hand.

Kill anyone who tries to break through. Stay with the king wherever he goes."

⁹So the commanders did everything as Jehoiada the priest ordered. The commanders took charge of the men reporting for duty that Sabbath, as well as those who were going off duty. They brought them all to Jehoiada the priest, ¹⁰and he supplied them with the spears and small shields that had once belonged to King David and were stored in the Temple of the LORD. ¹¹The palace guards stationed themselves around the king, with their weapons ready. They formed a line from the south side of the Temple around to the north side and all around the altar.

¹²Then Jehoiada brought out Joash, the king's son, placed the crown on his head, and presented him with a copy of God's laws.* They anointed him and proclaimed him king, and everyone clapped their hands and shouted, "Long live the king!"

The Death of Athaliah

¹³When Athaliah heard all the noise made by the palace guards and the people, she hurried to the LORD's Temple to see what was happening. ¹⁴When she arrived, she saw the newly crowned king standing in his place of authority by the pillar, as was the custom at times of coronation. The commanders and trumpeters were surrounding him, and people from all over the land were rejoicing and blowing trumpets. When Athaliah saw all this, she tore her clothes in despair and shouted, "Treason! Treason!"

¹⁵Then Jehoiada the priest ordered the commanders who were in charge of the troops, "Take her to the soldiers in front of the Temple,* and kill anyone who tries to rescue her." For the priest had said, "She must not be killed in the Temple of the LORD." ¹⁶So they seized her and led her out to the gate where horses enter the palace grounds, and she was killed there.

Jehoiada's Religious Reforms

¹⁷Then Jehoiada made a covenant between the LORD and the king and the people that they would be the LORD's people. He also

---

11:2 Hebrew *Joram,* a variant spelling of Jehoram. **11:12** Or *a copy of the covenant.* **11:15** Or *Bring her out from between the ranks;* or *Take her out of the Temple precincts.* The meaning of the Hebrew is uncertain.

made a covenant between the king and the people. ¹⁸And all the people of the land went over to the temple of Baal and tore it down. They demolished the altars and smashed the idols to pieces, and they killed Mattan the priest of Baal in front of the altars.

Jehoiada the priest stationed guards at the Temple of the LORD. ¹⁹Then the commanders, the Carite mercenaries, the palace guards, and all the people of the land escorted the king from the Temple of the LORD. They went through the gate of the guards and into the palace, and the king took his seat on the royal throne. ²⁰So all the people of the land rejoiced, and the city was peaceful because Athaliah had been killed at the king's palace.

²¹*Joash* was seven years old when he became king.

12 Joash Repairs the Temple

¹*Joash* began to rule over Judah in the seventh year of King Jehu's reign in Israel. He reigned in Jerusalem forty years. His mother was Zibiah from Beersheba. ²All his life Joash did what was pleasing in the LORD's sight because Jehoiada the priest instructed him. ³Yet even so, he did not destroy the pagan shrines, and the people still offered sacrifices and burned incense there.

⁴One day King Joash said to the priests, "Collect all the money brought as a sacred offering to the LORD's Temple, whether it is a regular assessment, a payment of vows, or a voluntary gift. ⁵Let the priests take some of that money to pay for whatever repairs are needed at the Temple."

⁶But by the twenty-third year of Joash's reign, the priests still had not repaired Temple. ⁷So King Joash called for Jehoiada and the other priests and asked them, "Why haven't you repaired the Temple? Don't use any more money for your own needs. From now on, it must all be spent on Temple repairs." ⁸So the priests agreed not to accept any more money from the people, and they also agreed to let others take responsibility for repairing the Temple.

⁹Then Jehoiada the priest bored a hole in the lid of a large chest and set it on the right-hand side of the altar at the entrance of the Temple of the LORD. The priests guarding the entrance put all of the people's contributions into the chest. ¹⁰Whenever the chest became full, the court secretary and the high priest counted the money that had been brought to the LORD's Temple and put it into bags. ¹¹Then they gave the money to the construction supervisors, who used it to pay the people working on the LORD's Temple—the carpenters, the builders, ¹²the masons, and the stonecutters. They also used the money to buy the timber and the finished stone needed for repairing the LORD's Temple, and they paid any other expenses related to the Temple's restoration.

¹³The money brought to the Temple was not used for making silver bowls, lamp snuffers, basins, trumpets, or other articles of gold or silver for the Temple of the LORD. ¹⁴It was paid to the workmen, who used it for the Temple repairs. ¹⁵No accounting of this money was required from the construction supervisors, because they were honest and trustworthy men. ¹⁶However, the money that was contributed for guilt offerings and sin offerings was not brought into the LORD's Temple. It was given to the priests for their own use.

The End of Joash's Reign

¹⁷About this time King Hazael of Aram went to war against Gath and captured it. Then he turned to attack Jerusalem. ¹⁸King Joash collected all the sacred objects that Jehoshaphat, Jehoram, and Ahaziah, the previous kings of Judah, had dedicated, along with what he himself had dedicated. He sent them all to Hazael, along with all the gold in the treasuries of the LORD's Temple and the royal palace. So Hazael called off his attack on Jerusalem.

¹⁹The rest of the events in Joash's reign and everything he did are recorded in *The Book of the History of the Kings of Judah.*

²⁰Joash's officers plotted against him and assassinated him at Beth-millo on the road to Silla. ²¹The assassins were Jozacar* son

---

11:21a Verse 11:21 is numbered 12:1 in Hebrew text. **11:21b** Hebrew *Jehoash,* a variant spelling of Joash. **12:1a** Verses 12:1-21 are numbered 12:2-22 in Hebrew text. **12:1b** Hebrew *Jehoash,* a variant spelling of Joash; also in 12:2, 4, 6, 7, 18. **12:21** As in Greek and Syriac versions; Hebrew reads *Jozabad.*

of Shimeath and Jehozabad son of Shomer—both trusted advisers. Joash was buried with his ancestors in the City of David. Then his son Amaziah became the next king.

13 Jehoahaz Rules in Israel

Jehoahaz son of Jehu began to rule over Israel in the twenty-third year of King Joash's reign in Judah. He reigned in Samaria seventeen years. ²But he did what was evil in the LORD's sight. He followed the example of Jeroboam son of Nebat, continuing the sins that Jeroboam had led Israel to commit. ³So the LORD was very angry with Israel, and he allowed King Hazael of Aram and his son Ben-hadad to defeat them repeatedly.

⁴Then Jehoahaz prayed for the LORD's help, and the LORD heard his prayer, for he could see how severely the king of Aram was oppressing Israel. ⁵So the LORD provided someone to rescue the Israelites from the tyranny of the Arameans. Then Israel lived in safety again as they had in former days. ⁶But they continued to sin, following the evil example of Jeroboam. They also allowed the Asherah pole in Samaria to remain standing. ⁷Finally, Jehoahaz's army was reduced to 50 charioteers, 10 chariots, and 10,000 foot soldiers. The king of Aram had killed the others, trampling them like dust under his feet.

⁸The rest of the events in Jehoahaz's reign—everything he did and the extent of his power—are recorded in *The Book of the History of the Kings of Israel.* ⁹When Jehoahaz died, he was buried in Samaria. Then his son Jehoash* became the next king.

Jehoash Rules in Israel

¹⁰Jehoash son of Jehoahaz began to rule over Israel in the thirty-seventh year of King Joash's reign in Judah. He reigned in Samaria sixteen years. ¹¹But he did what was evil in the LORD's sight. He refused to turn from the sins that Jeroboam son of Nebat had led Israel to commit.

¹²The rest of the events in Jehoash's reign and everything he did, including the extent of his power and his war with King Amaziah of Judah, are recorded in *The Book of the History of the Kings of Israel.* ¹³When Jehoash died, he was buried in Samaria with the kings of Israel. Then his son Jeroboam II became the next king.

Elisha's Final Prophecy

¹⁴When Elisha was in his last illness, King Jehoash of Israel visited him and wept over him. "My father! My father! I see the chariots and charioteers of Israel!" he cried.

¹⁵Elisha told him, "Get a bow and some arrows." And the king did as he was told. ¹⁶Elisha told him, "Put your hand on the bow," and Elisha laid his own hands on the king's hands.

¹⁷Then he commanded, "Open that eastern window," and he opened it. Then he said, "Shoot!" So he shot an arrow. Elisha proclaimed, "This is the LORD's arrow, an arrow of victory over Aram, for you will completely conquer the Arameans at Aphek."

¹⁸Then he said, "Now pick up the other arrows and strike them against the ground." So the king picked them up and struck the ground three times. ¹⁹But the man of God was angry with him. "You should have struck the ground five or six times!" he exclaimed. "Then you would have beaten Aram until it was entirely destroyed. Now you will be victorious only three times."

²⁰Then Elisha died and was buried.

Groups of Moabite raiders used to invade the land each spring. ²¹Once when some Israelites were burying a man, they spied a band of these raiders. So they hastily threw the corpse into the tomb of Elisha and fled. But as soon as the body touched Elisha's bones, the dead man revived and jumped to his feet!

²²King Hazael of Aram had oppressed Israel during the entire reign of King Jehoahaz. ²³But the LORD was gracious and merciful to the people of Israel, and they were not totally destroyed. He pitied them because of his covenant with Abraham, Isaac, and Jacob. And to this day he still has not completely destroyed them or banished them from his presence.

²⁴King Hazael of Aram died, and his son

13:9 Hebrew *Joash,* a variant spelling of Jehoash; also in 13:10, 12, 13, 14, 25.

Ben-hadad became the next king. ²⁵Then Jehoash son of Jehoahaz recaptured from Ben-hadad son of Hazael the towns that had been taken from Jehoash's father, Jehoahaz. Jehoash defeated Ben-hadad on three occasions, and he recovered the Israelite towns.

14 Amaziah Rules in Judah

Amaziah son of Joash began to rule over Judah in the second year of the reign of King Jehoash* of Israel. ²Amaziah was twenty-five years old when he became king, and he reigned in Jerusalem twenty-nine years. His mother was Jehoaddin from Jerusalem. ³Amaziah did what was pleasing in the LORD's sight, but not like his ancestor David. Instead, he followed the example of his father, Joash. ⁴Amaziah did not destroy the pagan shrines, and the people still offered sacrifices and burned incense there.

⁵When Amaziah was well established as king, he executed the officials who had assassinated his father. ⁶However, he did not kill the children of the assassins, for he obeyed the command of the LORD as written by Moses in the Book of the Law: "Parents must not be put to death for the sins of their children, nor children for the sins of their parents. Those deserving to die must be put to death for their own crimes."*

⁷Amaziah also killed 10,000 Edomites in the Valley of Salt. He also conquered Sela and changed its name to Joktheel, as it is called to this day.

⁸One day Amaziah sent messengers with this challenge to Israel's king Jehoash, the son of Jehoahaz and grandson of Jehu: "Come and meet me in battle!"*

⁹But King Jehoash of Israel replied to King Amaziah of Judah with this story: "Out in the Lebanon mountains, a thistle sent a message to a mighty cedar tree: 'Give your daughter in marriage to my son.' But just then a wild animal of Lebanon came by and stepped on the thistle, crushing it!

¹⁰"You have indeed defeated Edom, and you are very proud of it. But be content with your victory and stay at home! Why stir up trouble that will only bring disaster on you and the people of Judah?"

¹¹But Amaziah refused to listen, so King Jehoash of Israel mobilized his army against King Amaziah of Judah. The two armies drew up their battle lines at Beth-shemesh in Judah. ¹²Judah was routed by the army of Israel, and its army scattered and fled for home. ¹³King Jehoash of Israel captured Judah's king, Amaziah son of Joash and grandson of Ahaziah, at Beth-shemesh. Then he marched to Jerusalem, where he demolished 600 feet* of Jerusalem's wall, from the Ephraim Gate to the Corner Gate. ¹⁴He carried off all the gold and silver and all the articles from the Temple of the LORD. He also seized the treasures from the royal palace, along with hostages, and then returned to Samaria.

¹⁵The rest of the events in Jehoash's reign and everything he did, including the extent of his power and his war with King Amaziah of Judah, are recorded in *The Book of the History of the Kings of Israel*. ¹⁶When Jehoash died, he was buried in Samaria with the kings of Israel. And his son Jeroboam II became the next king.

¹⁷King Amaziah of Judah lived for fifteen years after the death of King Jehoash of Israel. ¹⁸The rest of the events in Amaziah's reign are recorded in *The Book of the History of the Kings of Judah*.

¹⁹There was a conspiracy against Amaziah's life in Jerusalem, and he fled to Lachish. But his enemies sent assassins after him, and they killed him there. ²⁰They brought his body back to Jerusalem on a horse, and he was buried with his ancestors in the City of David.

²¹All the people of Judah had crowned Amaziah's sixteen-year-old son, Uzziah,* as king in place of his father, Amaziah. ²²After his father's death, Uzziah rebuilt the town of Elath and restored it to Judah.

Jeroboam II Rules in Israel

²³Jeroboam II, the son of Jehoash, began to rule over Israel in the fifteenth year of King Amaziah's reign in Judah. Jeroboam reigned in Samaria forty-one years. ²⁴He did what was evil in the LORD's sight. He refused to turn from the sins that Jeroboam son of Nebat had led Israel to commit. ²⁵Jeroboam II recovered the territories of

---

14:1 Hebrew *Joash,* a variant spelling of Jehoash; also in 14:13, 23, 27.   **14:6** Deut 24:16.   **14:8** Hebrew *Come, let us look one another in the face.*   **14:13** Hebrew *400 cubits* [180 meters].   **14:21** Hebrew *Azariah,* a variant spelling of Uzziah.

Israel between Lebo-hamath and the Dead Sea,* just as the LORD, the God of Israel, had promised through Jonah son of Amittai, the prophet from Gath-hepher.

²⁶For the LORD saw the bitter suffering of everyone in Israel, and that there was no one in Israel, slave or free, to help them. ²⁷And because the LORD had not said he would blot out the name of Israel completely, he used Jeroboam II, the son of Jehoash, to save them.

²⁸The rest of the events in the reign of Jeroboam II and everything he did—including the extent of his power, his wars, and how he recovered for Israel both Damascus and Hamath, which had belonged to Judah*—are recorded in *The Book of the History of the Kings of Israel.* ²⁹When Jeroboam II died, he was buried in Samaria* with the kings of Israel. Then his son Zechariah became the next king.

15 Uzziah Rules in Judah

Uzziah* son of Amaziah began to rule over Judah in the twenty-seventh year of the reign of King Jeroboam II of Israel. ²He was sixteen years old when he became king, and he reigned in Jerusalem fifty-two years. His mother was Jecoliah from Jerusalem.

³He did what was pleasing in the LORD's sight, just as his father, Amaziah, had done. ⁴But he did not destroy the pagan shrines, and the people still offered sacrifices and burned incense there. ⁵The LORD struck the king with leprosy,* which lasted until the day he died. He lived in isolation in a separate house. The king's son Jotham was put in charge of the royal palace, and he governed the people of the land.

⁶The rest of the events in Uzziah's reign and everything he did are recorded in *The Book of the History of the Kings of Judah.* ⁷When Uzziah died, he was buried with his ancestors in the City of David. And his son Jotham became the next king.

Zechariah Rules in Israel

⁸Zechariah son of Jeroboam II began to rule over Israel in the thirty-eighth year of King Uzziah's reign in Judah. He reigned in Samaria six months. ⁹Zechariah did what was evil in the LORD's sight, as his ancestors had done. He refused to turn from the sins that Jeroboam son of Nebat had led Israel to commit. ¹⁰Then Shallum son of Jabesh conspired against Zechariah, assassinated him in public,* and became the next king.

¹¹The rest of the events in Zechariah's reign are recorded in *The Book of the History of the Kings of Israel.* ¹²So the LORD's message to Jehu came true: "Your descendants will be kings of Israel down to the fourth generation."

Shallum Rules in Israel

¹³Shallum son of Jabesh began to rule over Israel in the thirty-ninth year of King Uzziah's reign in Judah. Shallum reigned in Samaria only one month. ¹⁴Then Menahem son of Gadi went to Samaria from Tirzah and assassinated him, and he became the next king.

¹⁵The rest of the events in Shallum's reign, including his conspiracy, are recorded in *The Book of the History of the Kings of Israel.*

Menahem Rules in Israel

¹⁶At that time Menahem destroyed the town of Tappuah* and all the surrounding countryside as far as Tirzah, because its citizens refused to surrender the town. He killed the entire population and ripped open the pregnant women.

¹⁷Menahem son of Gadi began to rule over Israel in the thirty-ninth year of King Uzziah's reign in Judah. He reigned in Samaria ten years. ¹⁸But Menahem did what was evil in the LORD's sight. During his entire reign, he refused to turn from the sins that Jeroboam son of Nebat had led Israel to commit.

¹⁹Then King Tiglath-pileser* of Assyria invaded the land. But Menahem paid him thirty-seven tons* of silver to gain his support in tightening his grip on royal power. ²⁰Menahem extorted the money from the rich of Israel, demanding that each of

14:25 Hebrew *the sea of the Arabah.* **14:28** Or *to Yaudi.* The meaning of the Hebrew is uncertain. **14:29** As in some Greek manuscripts; Hebrew lacks *he was buried in Samaria.* **15:1** Hebrew *Azariah,* a variant spelling of Uzziah; also in 15:6, 7, 8, 17, 23, 27. **15:5** Or *with a contagious skin disease.* The Hebrew word used here and throughout this passage can describe various skin diseases. **15:10** Or *at Ibleam.* **15:16** As in some Greek manuscripts; other Greek manuscripts read *at Ibleam.* Hebrew reads *Tiphsah.* **15:19a** Hebrew *Pul,* another name for Tiglath-pileser. **15:19b** Hebrew *1,000 talents* [34 metric tons].

them pay fifty pieces* of silver to the king of Assyria. So the king of Assyria turned from attacking Israel and did not stay in the land.

²¹ The rest of the events in Menahem's reign and everything he did are recorded in *The Book of the History of the Kings of Israel.* ²² When Menahem died, his son Pekahiah became the next king.

Pekahiah Rules in Israel

²³ Pekahiah son of Menahem began to rule over Israel in the fiftieth year of King Uzziah's reign in Judah. He reigned in Samaria two years. ²⁴ But Pekahiah did what was evil in the LORD's sight. He refused to turn from the sins that Jeroboam son of Nebat had led Israel to commit.

²⁵ Then Pekah son of Remaliah, the commander of Pekahiah's army, conspired against him. With fifty men from Gilead, Pekah assassinated the king, along with Argob and Arieh, in the citadel of the palace at Samaria. And Pekah reigned in his place.

²⁶ The rest of the events in Pekahiah's reign and everything he did are recorded in *The Book of the History of the Kings of Israel.*

Pekah Rules in Israel

²⁷ Pekah son of Remaliah began to rule over Israel in the fifty-second year of King Uzziah's reign in Judah. He reigned in Samaria twenty years. ²⁸ But Pekah did what was evil in the LORD's sight. He refused to turn from the sins that Jeroboam son of Nebat had led Israel to commit.

²⁹ During Pekah's reign, King Tiglath-pileser of Assyria attacked Israel again, and he captured the towns of Ijon, Abel-beth-maacah, Janoah, Kedesh, and Hazor. He also conquered the regions of Gilead, Galilee, and all of Naphtali, and he took the people to Assyria as captives. ³⁰ Then Hoshea son of Elah conspired against Pekah and assassinated him. He began to rule over Israel in the twentieth year of Jotham son of Uzziah.

³¹ The rest of the events in Pekah's reign and everything he did are recorded in *The Book of the History of the Kings of Israel.*

Jotham Rules in Judah

³² Jotham son of Uzziah began to rule over Judah in the second year of King Pekah's reign in Israel. ³³ He was twenty-five years old when he became king, and he reigned in Jerusalem sixteen years. His mother was Jerusha, the daughter of Zadok.

³⁴ Jotham did what was pleasing in the LORD's sight. He did everything his father, Uzziah, had done. ³⁵ But he did not destroy the pagan shrines, and the people still offered sacrifices and burned incense there. He rebuilt the upper gate of the Temple of the LORD.

³⁶ The rest of the events in Jotham's reign and everything he did are recorded in *The Book of the History of the Kings of Judah.* ³⁷ In those days the LORD began to send King Rezin of Aram and King Pekah of Israel to attack Judah. ³⁸ When Jotham died, he was buried with his ancestors in the City of David. And his son Ahaz became the next king.

16 Ahaz Rules in Judah

Ahaz son of Jotham began to rule over Judah in the seventeenth year of King Pekah's reign in Israel. ² Ahaz was twenty years old when he became king, and he reigned in Jerusalem sixteen years. He did not do what was pleasing in the sight of the LORD his God, as his ancestor David had done. ³ Instead, he followed the example of the kings of Israel, even sacrificing his own son in the fire.* In this way, he followed the detestable practices of the pagan nations the LORD had driven from the land ahead of the Israelites. ⁴ He offered sacrifices and burned incense at the pagan shrines and on the hills and under every green tree.

⁵ Then King Rezin of Aram and King Pekah of Israel came up to attack Jerusalem. They besieged Ahaz but could not conquer him. ⁶ At that time the king of Edom* recovered the town of Elath for Edom.* He drove out the people of Judah and sent Edomites* to live there, as they do to this day.

⁷ King Ahaz sent messengers to King Tiglath-pileser of Assyria with this message: "I am your servant and your vassal.*

15:20 Hebrew *50 shekels* [20 ounces, or 570 grams].   **16:3** Or *even making his son pass through the fire.*   **16:6a** As in Latin Vulgate; Hebrew reads *Rezin king of Aram.*   **16:6b** As in Latin Vulgate; Hebrew reads *Aram.*   **16:6c** As in Greek version, Latin Vulgate, and an alternate reading of the Masoretic Text; the other alternate reads *Arameans.*   **16:7** Hebrew *your son.*

Come up and rescue me from the attacking armies of Aram and Israel." [8] Then Ahaz took the silver and gold from the Temple of the LORD and the palace treasury and sent it as a payment to the Assyrian king. [9] So the king of Assyria attacked the Aramean capital of Damascus and led its population away as captives, resettling them in Kir. He also killed King Rezin.

[10] King Ahaz then went to Damascus to meet with King Tiglath-pileser of Assyria. While he was there, he took special note of the altar. Then he sent a model of the altar to Uriah the priest, along with its design in full detail. [11] Uriah followed the king's instructions and built an altar just like it, and it was ready before the king returned from Damascus. [12] When the king returned, he inspected the altar and made offerings on it. [13] He presented a burnt offering and a grain offering, he poured out a liquid offering, and he sprinkled the blood of peace offerings on the altar.

[14] Then King Ahaz removed the old bronze altar from its place in front of the LORD's Temple, between the entrance and the new altar, and placed it on the north side of the new altar. [15] He told Uriah the priest, "Use the new altar* for the morning sacrifices of burnt offering, the evening grain offering, the king's burnt offering and grain offering, and the burnt offerings of all the people, as well as their grain offerings and liquid offerings. Sprinkle the blood from all the burnt offerings and sacrifices on the new altar. The bronze altar will be for my personal use only." [16] Uriah the priest did just as King Ahaz commanded him.

[17] Then the king removed the side panels and basins from the portable water carts. He also removed the great bronze basin called the Sea from the backs of the bronze oxen and placed it on the stone pavement. [18] In deference to the king of Assyria, he also removed the canopy that had been constructed inside the palace for use on the Sabbath day,* as well as the king's outer entrance to the Temple of the LORD.

[19] The rest of the events in Ahaz's reign and everything he did are recorded in *The Book of the History of the Kings of Judah.*

[20] When Ahaz died, he was buried with his ancestors in the City of David. Then his son Hezekiah became the next king.

17 Hoshea Rules in Israel

Hoshea son of Elah began to rule over Israel in the twelfth year of King Ahaz's reign in Judah. He reigned in Samaria nine years. [2] He did what was evil in the LORD's sight, but not to the same extent as the kings of Israel who ruled before him.

[3] King Shalmaneser of Assyria attacked King Hoshea, so Hoshea was forced to pay heavy tribute to Assyria. [4] But Hoshea stopped paying the annual tribute and conspired against the king of Assyria by asking King So of Egypt* to help him shake free of Assyria's power. When the king of Assyria discovered this treachery, he seized Hoshea and put him in prison.

Samaria Falls to Assyria

[5] Then the king of Assyria invaded the entire land, and for three years he besieged the city of Samaria. [6] Finally, in the ninth year of King Hoshea's reign, Samaria fell, and the people of Israel were exiled to Assyria. They were settled in colonies in Halah, along the banks of the Habor River in Gozan, and in the cities of the Medes.

[7] This disaster came upon the people of Israel because they worshiped other gods. They sinned against the LORD their God, who had brought them safely out of Egypt and had rescued them from the power of Pharaoh, the king of Egypt. [8] They had followed the practices of the pagan nations the LORD had driven from the land ahead of them, as well as the practices the kings of Israel had introduced. [9] The people of Israel had also secretly done many things that were not pleasing to the LORD their God. They built pagan shrines for themselves in all their towns, from the smallest outpost to the largest walled city. [10] They set up sacred pillars and Asherah poles at the top of every hill and under every green tree. [11] They offered sacrifices on all the hilltops, just like the nations the LORD had driven from the land ahead of them. So the people of Israel had done many evil things,

---

16:15 Hebrew *the great altar.*   16:18 The meaning of the Hebrew is uncertain.   17:4 Or *by asking the king of Egypt at Sais.*

arousing the LORD's anger. ¹²Yes, they worshiped idols,* despite the LORD's specific and repeated warnings.

¹³Again and again the LORD had sent his prophets and seers to warn both Israel and Judah: "Turn from all your evil ways. Obey my commands and decrees—the entire law that I commanded your ancestors to obey, and that I gave you through my servants the prophets."

¹⁴But the Israelites would not listen. They were as stubborn as their ancestors who had refused to believe in the LORD their God. ¹⁵They rejected his decrees and the covenant he had made with their ancestors, and they despised all his warnings. They worshiped worthless idols, so they became worthless themselves. They followed the example of the nations around them, disobeying the LORD's command not to imitate them.

¹⁶They rejected all the commands of the LORD their God and made two calves from metal. They set up an Asherah pole and worshiped Baal and all the forces of heaven. ¹⁷They even sacrificed their own sons and daughters in the fire.* They consulted fortune-tellers and practiced sorcery and sold themselves to evil, arousing the LORD's anger.

¹⁸Because the LORD was very angry with Israel, he swept them away from his presence. Only the tribe of Judah remained in the land. ¹⁹But even the people of Judah refused to obey the commands of the LORD their God, for they followed the evil practices that Israel had introduced. ²⁰The LORD rejected all the descendants of Israel. He punished them by handing them over to their attackers until he had banished Israel from his presence.

²¹For when the LORD* tore Israel away from the kingdom of David, they chose Jeroboam son of Nebat as their king. But Jeroboam drew Israel away from following the LORD and made them commit a great sin. ²²And the people of Israel persisted in all the evil ways of Jeroboam. They did not turn from these sins ²³until the LORD finally swept them away from his presence, just as all his prophets had warned. So Israel was exiled from their land to Assyria, where they remain to this day.

Foreigners Settle in Israel

²⁴The king of Assyria transported groups of people from Babylon, Cuthah, Avva, Hamath, and Sepharvaim and resettled them in the towns of Samaria, replacing the people of Israel. They took possession of Samaria and lived in its towns. ²⁵But since these foreign settlers did not worship the LORD when they first arrived, the LORD sent lions among them, which killed some of them.

²⁶So a message was sent to the king of Assyria: "The people you have sent to live in the towns of Samaria do not know the religious customs of the God of the land. He has sent lions among them to destroy them because they have not worshiped him correctly."

²⁷The king of Assyria then commanded, "Send one of the exiled priests back to Samaria. Let him live there and teach the new residents the religious customs of the God of the land." ²⁸So one of the priests who had been exiled from Samaria returned to Bethel and taught the new residents how to worship the LORD.

²⁹But these various groups of foreigners also continued to worship their own gods. In town after town where they lived, they placed their idols at the pagan shrines that the people of Samaria had built. ³⁰Those from Babylon worshiped idols of their god Succoth-benoth. Those from Cuthah worshiped their god Nergal. And those from Hamath worshiped Ashima. ³¹The Avvites worshiped their gods Nibhaz and Tartak. And the people from Sepharvaim even burned their own children as sacrifices to their gods Adrammelech and Anammelech.

³²These new residents worshiped the LORD, but they also appointed from among themselves all sorts of people as priests to offer sacrifices at their places of worship. ³³And though they worshiped the LORD, they continued to follow their own gods according to the religious customs of the nations from which they came. ³⁴And this is still going on today. They continue to follow their former practices instead

---

17:12 The Hebrew term (literally *round things*) probably alludes to dung. **17:17** Or *They even made their sons and daughters pass through the fire.* **17:21** Hebrew *he;* compare 1 Kgs 11:31-32.

of truly worshiping the Lord and obeying the decrees, regulations, instructions, and commands he gave the descendants of Jacob, whose name he changed to Israel. ³⁵For the Lord had made a covenant with the descendants of Jacob and commanded them: "Do not worship any other gods or bow before them or serve them or offer sacrifices to them. ³⁶But worship only the Lord, who brought you out of Egypt with great strength and a powerful arm. Bow down to him alone, and offer sacrifices only to him. ³⁷Be careful at all times to obey the decrees, regulations, instructions, and commands that he wrote for you. You must not worship other gods. ³⁸Do not forget the covenant I made with you, and do not worship other gods. ³⁹You must worship only the Lord your God. He is the one who will rescue you from all your enemies."

⁴⁰But the people would not listen and continued to follow their former practices. ⁴¹So while these new residents worshiped the Lord, they also worshiped their idols. And to this day their descendants do the same.

18 Hezekiah Rules in Judah

Hezekiah son of Ahaz began to rule over Judah in the third year of King Hoshea's reign in Israel. ²He was twenty-five years old when he became king, and he reigned in Jerusalem twenty-nine years. His mother was Abijah,* the daughter of Zechariah. ³He did what was pleasing in the Lord's sight, just as his ancestor David had done. ⁴He removed the pagan shrines, smashed the sacred pillars, and cut down the Asherah poles. He broke up the bronze serpent that Moses had made, because the people of Israel had been offering sacrifices to it. The bronze serpent was called Nehushtan.*

⁵Hezekiah trusted in the Lord, the God of Israel. There was no one like him among all the kings of Judah, either before or after his time. ⁶He remained faithful to the Lord in everything, and he carefully obeyed all the commands the Lord had given Moses. ⁷So the Lord was with him, and Heze-

kiah was successful in everything he did. He revolted against the king of Assyria and refused to pay him tribute. ⁸He also conquered the Philistines as far distant as Gaza and its territory, from their smallest outpost to their largest walled city.

⁹During the fourth year of Hezekiah's reign, which was the seventh year of King Hoshea's reign in Israel, King Shalmaneser of Assyria attacked the city of Samaria and began a siege against it. ¹⁰Three years later, during the sixth year of King Hezekiah's reign and the ninth year of King Hoshea's reign in Israel, Samaria fell. ¹¹At that time the king of Assyria exiled the Israelites to Assyria and placed them in colonies in Halah, along the banks of the Habor River in Gozan, and in the cities of the Medes. ¹²For they refused to listen to the Lord their God and obey him. Instead, they violated his covenant—all the laws that Moses the Lord's servant had commanded them to obey.

Assyria Invades Judah

¹³In the fourteenth year of King Hezekiah's reign,* King Sennacherib of Assyria came to attack the fortified towns of Judah and conquered them. ¹⁴King Hezekiah sent this message to the king of Assyria at Lachish: "I have done wrong. I will pay whatever tribute money you demand if you will only withdraw." The king of Assyria then demanded a settlement of more than eleven tons of silver and one ton of gold.* ¹⁵To gather this amount, King Hezekiah used all the silver stored in the Temple of the Lord and in the palace treasury. ¹⁶Hezekiah even stripped the gold from the doors of the Lord's Temple and from the doorposts he had overlaid with gold, and he gave it all to the Assyrian king.

¹⁷Nevertheless, the king of Assyria sent his commander in chief, his field commander, and his chief of staff* from Lachish with a huge army to confront King Hezekiah in Jerusalem. The Assyrians took up a position beside the aqueduct that feeds water into the upper pool, near the road leading to the field where cloth is washed.*

18:2 As in parallel text at 2 Chr 29:1; Hebrew reads *Abi,* a variant spelling of Abijah. **18:4** *Nehushtan* sounds like the Hebrew terms that mean "snake," "bronze," and "unclean thing." **18:13** The fourteenth year of Hezekiah's reign was 701 B.C. **18:14** Hebrew *300 talents* [10 metric tons] *of silver and 30 talents* [1 metric ton] *of gold.* **18:17a** Or *the rabshakeh;* also in 18:19, 26, 27, 28, 37. **18:17b** Or *bleached.*

18 They summoned King Hezekiah, but the king sent these officials to meet with them: Eliakim son of Hilkiah, the palace administrator; Shebna the court secretary; and Joah son of Asaph, the royal historian.

Sennacherib Threatens Jerusalem

19 Then the Assyrian king's chief of staff told them to give this message to Hezekiah:

"This is what the great king of Assyria says: What are you trusting in that makes you so confident? 20 Do you think that mere words can substitute for military skill and strength? Who are you counting on, that you have rebelled against me? 21 On Egypt? If you lean on Egypt, it will be like a reed that splinters beneath your weight and pierces your hand. Pharaoh, the king of Egypt, is completely unreliable!

22 "But perhaps you will say to me, 'We are trusting in the LORD our God!' But isn't he the one who was insulted by Hezekiah? Didn't Hezekiah tear down his shrines and altars and make everyone in Judah and Jerusalem worship only at the altar here in Jerusalem?

23 "I'll tell you what! Strike a bargain with my master, the king of Assyria. I will give you 2,000 horses if you can find that many men to ride on them! 24 With your tiny army, how can you think of challenging even the weakest contingent of my master's troops, even with the help of Egypt's chariots and charioteers? 25 What's more, do you think we have invaded your land without the LORD's direction? The LORD himself told us, 'Attack this land and destroy it!' "

26 Then Eliakim son of Hilkiah, Shebna, and Joah said to the Assyrian chief of staff, "Please speak to us in Aramaic, for we understand it well. Don't speak in Hebrew,* for the people on the wall will hear."

27 But Sennacherib's chief of staff replied, "Do you think my master sent this message only to you and your master? He wants all the people to hear it, for when we put this city under siege, they will suffer along with you. They will be so hungry and thirsty that they will eat their own dung and drink their own urine."

28 Then the chief of staff stood and shouted in Hebrew to the people on the wall, "Listen to this message from the great king of Assyria! 29 This is what the king says: Don't let Hezekiah deceive you. He will never be able to rescue you from my power. 30 Don't let him fool you into trusting in the LORD by saying, 'The LORD will surely rescue us. This city will never fall into the hands of the Assyrian king!'

31 "Don't listen to Hezekiah! These are the terms the king of Assyria is offering: Make peace with me—open the gates and come out. Then each of you can continue eating from your own grapevine and fig tree and drinking from your own well. 32 Then I will arrange to take you to another land like this one—a land of grain and new wine, bread and vineyards, olive groves and honey. Choose life instead of death!

"Don't listen to Hezekiah when he tries to mislead you by saying, 'The LORD will rescue us!' 33 Have the gods of any other nations ever saved their people from the king of Assyria? 34 What happened to the gods of Hamath and Arpad? And what about the gods of Sepharvaim, Hena, and Ivvah? Did any god rescue Samaria from my power? 35 What god of any nation has ever been able to save its people from my power? So what makes you think that the LORD can rescue Jerusalem from me?"

36 But the people were silent and did not utter a word because Hezekiah had commanded them, "Do not answer him."

37 Then Eliakim son of Hilkiah, the palace administrator; Shebna the court secretary; and Joah son of Asaph, the royal historian, went back to Hezekiah. They tore their clothes in despair, and they went in to see the king and told him what the Assyrian chief of staff had said.

19 Hezekiah Seeks the LORD's Help

When King Hezekiah heard their report, he tore his clothes and put on burlap and went into the Temple of the LORD. 2 And he sent Eliakim the palace administrator, Shebna the court secretary, and

---

18:26 Hebrew *in the dialect of Judah;* also in 18:28.

the leading priests, all dressed in burlap, to the prophet Isaiah son of Amoz. ³They told him, "This is what King Hezekiah says: Today is a day of trouble, insults, and disgrace. It is like when a child is ready to be born, but the mother has no strength to deliver the baby. ⁴But perhaps the LORD your God has heard the Assyrian chief of staff,* sent by the king to defy the living God, and will punish him for his words. Oh, pray for those of us who are left!"

⁵After King Hezekiah's officials delivered the king's message to Isaiah, ⁶the prophet replied, "Say to your master, 'This is what the LORD says: Do not be disturbed by this blasphemous speech against me from the Assyrian king's messengers. ⁷Listen! I myself will move against him,* and the king will receive a message that he is needed at home. So he will return to his land, where I will have him killed with a sword.'"

⁸Meanwhile, the Assyrian chief of staff left Jerusalem and went to consult the king of Assyria, who had left Lachish and was attacking Libnah.

⁹Soon afterward King Sennacherib received word that King Tirhakah of Ethiopia* was leading an army to fight against him. Before leaving to meet the attack, he sent messengers back to Hezekiah in Jerusalem with this message:

¹⁰"This message is for King Hezekiah of Judah. Don't let your God, in whom you trust, deceive you with promises that Jerusalem will not be captured by the king of Assyria. ¹¹You know perfectly well what the kings of Assyria have done wherever they have gone. They have completely destroyed everyone who stood in their way! Why should you be any different? ¹²Have the gods of other nations rescued them—such nations as Gozan, Haran, Rezeph, and the people of Eden who were in Tel-assar? My predecessors destroyed them all! ¹³What happened to the king of Hamath and the king of Arpad? What happened to the kings of Sepharvaim, Hena, and Ivvah?"

¹⁴After Hezekiah received the letter from the messengers and read it, he went up to the LORD's Temple and spread it out before the LORD. ¹⁵And Hezekiah prayed this prayer before the LORD: "O LORD, God of Israel, you are enthroned between the mighty cherubim! You alone are God of all the kingdoms of the earth. You alone created the heavens and the earth. ¹⁶Bend down, O LORD, and listen! Open your eyes, O LORD, and see! Listen to Sennacherib's words of defiance against the living God.

¹⁷"It is true, LORD, that the kings of Assyria have destroyed all these nations. ¹⁸And they have thrown the gods of these nations into the fire and burned them. But of course the Assyrians could destroy them! They were not gods at all—only idols of wood and stone shaped by human hands. ¹⁹Now, O LORD our God, rescue us from his power; then all the kingdoms of the earth will know that you alone, O LORD, are God."

Isaiah Predicts Judah's Deliverance

²⁰Then Isaiah son of Amoz sent this message to Hezekiah: "This is what the LORD, the God of Israel, says: I have heard your prayer about King Sennacherib of Assyria. ²¹And the LORD has spoken this word against him:

"The virgin daughter of Zion
   despises you and laughs at you.
The daughter of Jerusalem
   shakes her head in derision as you flee.

²² "Whom have you been defying and
      ridiculing?
   Against whom did you raise your
      voice?
At whom did you look with such
      haughty eyes?
   It was the Holy One of Israel!
²³ By your messengers you have defied the
      Lord.
   You have said, 'With my many chariots
I have conquered the highest
      mountains—
   yes, the remotest peaks of Lebanon.
I have cut down its tallest cedars
   and its finest cypress trees.
I have reached its farthest corners
   and explored its deepest forests.

19:4 Or the rabshakeh; also in 19:8.   19:7 Hebrew I will put a spirit in him.   19:9 Hebrew of Cush.

24 I have dug wells in many foreign lands
and refreshed myself with their water.
With the sole of my foot
I stopped up all the rivers of Egypt!'

25 "But have you not heard?
I decided this long ago.
Long ago I planned it,
and now I am making it happen.
I planned for you to crush fortified cities
into heaps of rubble.
26 That is why their people have so little
power
and are so frightened and confused.
They are as weak as grass,
as easily trampled as tender green
shoots.
They are like grass sprouting on a
housetop,
scorched before it can grow lush and
tall.

27 "But I know you well—
where you stay
and when you come and go.
I know the way you have raged
against me.
28 And because of your raging against me
and your arrogance, which I have
heard for myself,
I will put my hook in your nose
and my bit in your mouth.
I will make you return
by the same road on which you
came."

29 Then Isaiah said to Hezekiah, "Here is the proof that what I say is true:

"This year you will eat only what grows
up by itself,
and next year you will eat what springs
up from that.
But in the third year you will plant crops
and harvest them;
you will tend vineyards and eat their
fruit.
30 And you who are left in Judah,
who have escaped the ravages of the
siege,
will put roots down in your own soil
and will grow up and flourish.

31 For a remnant of my people will spread
out from Jerusalem,
a group of survivors from Mount
Zion.
The passionate commitment of the
LORD of Heaven's Armies*
will make this happen!

32 "And this is what the LORD says about the king of Assyria:

"His armies will not enter Jerusalem.
They will not even shoot an arrow at it.
They will not march outside its gates
with their shields
nor build banks of earth against its
walls.
33 The king will return to his own country
by the same road on which he came.
He will not enter this city,
says the LORD.
34 For my own honor and for the sake of
my servant David,
I will defend this city and protect it."

35 That night the angel of the LORD went out to the Assyrian camp and killed 185,000 Assyrian soldiers. When the surviving Assyrians* woke up the next morning, they found corpses everywhere. 36 Then King Sennacherib of Assyria broke camp and returned to his own land. He went home to his capital of Nineveh and stayed there.

37 One day while he was worshiping in the temple of his god Nisroch, his sons* Adrammelech and Sharezer killed him with their swords. They then escaped to the land of Ararat, and another son, Esarhaddon, became the next king of Assyria.

20 Hezekiah's Sickness and Recovery

About that time Hezekiah became deathly ill, and the prophet Isaiah son of Amoz went to visit him. He gave the king this message: "This is what the LORD says: Set your affairs in order, for you are going to die. You will not recover from this illness."

2 When Hezekiah heard this, he turned his face to the wall and prayed to the LORD, 3 "Remember, O LORD, how I have always been faithful to you and have served you

---

19:31 As in Greek and Syriac versions, Latin Vulgate, and an alternate reading of the Masoretic Text (see also Isa 37:32); the other alternate reads *the LORD*. 19:35 Hebrew *When they*. 19:37 As in Greek version and an alternate reading of the Masoretic Text (see also Isa 37:38); the other alternate reading lacks *his sons*.

single-mindedly, always doing what pleases you." Then he broke down and wept bitterly.

⁴But before Isaiah had left the middle courtyard,* this message came to him from the LORD: ⁵"Go back to Hezekiah, the leader of my people. Tell him, 'This is what the LORD, the God of your ancestor David, says: I have heard your prayer and seen your tears. I will heal you, and three days from now you will get out of bed and go to the Temple of the LORD. ⁶I will add fifteen years to your life, and I will rescue you and this city from the king of Assyria. I

Praying for the Impossible

2 KINGS 20:1–10

How can I pray in the face of tragedy?

When I heard that my friend Lynn had been diagnosed with a quick-spreading cancer, it took a week to set in. At times I couldn't even think about her grim prognosis. But I knew I should pray.

We've all experienced times when tragedy strikes us dumb—a devastating illness, a marriage falling apart, a child born with a disability, miscarriage or infertility, chronic unemployment. Although we care deeply, it's hard to know just *how* to pray. We may even wonder if it's worth asking for a miracle that seems unlikely.

At those times we must remember that God *invites* us to bring him our requests (Hebrews 4:16; Ephesians 3:12), even those about seemingly impossible situations. Scripture assures us that "with God everything is possible" (Matthew 19:26). Yet as we pray, we must always keep in mind that, as Ole Hallesby says, "When God says yes, it is because he loves us, and when God says no, it is because he loves us."

In my prayers for Lynn, I asked God to heal her. Yet neither fervent prayer nor doctors' care reversed her cancer. My prayers for Lynn began to change. I asked that God would ease her pain. Eventually I prayed that God would take her home, which he did.

Should I feel cheated? In some ways, that is a natural reaction. But I also believe that God wants us to ask (Matthew 7:7), to persevere in prayer (Luke 18:1–8), and to believe (Matthew 21:22). I cannot say I fully *understand* how prayers are answered. Ultimately, though, I believe our prayers must be colored by our view of God: he is sovereign. Each time we pray, we trust him as the One who holds the answers—whatever they might be—to our prayers.

—Becky Tirabassi

For more on prayer, see reading at Psalm 55.

20:4 As in Greek version and an alternate reading in the Masoretic Text; the other alternate reads *the middle of the city.*

will defend this city for my own honor and for the sake of my servant David.'"

⁷Then Isaiah said, "Make an ointment from figs." So Hezekiah's servants spread the ointment over the boil, and Hezekiah recovered!

⁸Meanwhile, Hezekiah had said to Isaiah, "What sign will the LORD give to prove that he will heal me and that I will go to the Temple of the LORD three days from now?"

⁹Isaiah replied, "This is the sign from the LORD to prove that he will do as he promised. Would you like the shadow on the sundial to go forward ten steps or backward ten steps?*"

¹⁰"The shadow always moves forward," Hezekiah replied, "so that would be easy. Make it go ten steps backward instead." ¹¹So Isaiah the prophet asked the LORD to do this, and he caused the shadow to move ten steps backward on the sundial* of Ahaz!

Envoys from Babylon

¹²Soon after this, Merodach-baladan son of Baladan, king of Babylon, sent Hezekiah his best wishes and a gift, for he had heard that Hezekiah had been very sick. ¹³Hezekiah received the Babylonian envoys and showed them everything in his treasure-houses—the silver, the gold, the spices, and the aromatic oils. He also took them to see his armory and showed them everything in his royal treasuries! There was nothing in his palace or kingdom that Hezekiah did not show them.

¹⁴Then Isaiah the prophet went to King Hezekiah and asked him, "What did those men want? Where were they from?"

Hezekiah replied, "They came from the distant land of Babylon."

¹⁵"What did they see in your palace?" Isaiah asked.

"They saw everything," Hezekiah replied. "I showed them everything I own—all my royal treasuries."

¹⁶Then Isaiah said to Hezekiah, "Listen to this message from the LORD: ¹⁷The time is coming when everything in your palace—all the treasures stored up by your ancestors until now—will be carried off to Babylon. Nothing will be left, says the LORD. ¹⁸Some

of your very own sons will be taken away into exile. They will become eunuchs who will serve in the palace of Babylon's king."

¹⁹Then Hezekiah said to Isaiah, "This message you have given me from the LORD is good." For the king was thinking, "At least there will be peace and security during my lifetime."

²⁰The rest of the events in Hezekiah's reign, including the extent of his power and how he built a pool and dug a tunnel* to bring water into the city, are recorded in *The Book of the History of the Kings of Judah.* ²¹Hezekiah died, and his son Manasseh became the next king.

21 Manasseh Rules in Judah

Manasseh was twelve years old when he became king, and he reigned in Jerusalem fifty-five years. His mother was Hephzibah. ²He did what was evil in the LORD's sight, following the detestable practices of the pagan nations that the LORD had driven from the land ahead of the Israelites. ³He rebuilt the pagan shrines his father, Hezekiah, had destroyed. He constructed altars for Baal and set up an Asherah pole, just as King Ahab of Israel had done. He also bowed before all the powers of the heavens and worshiped them.

⁴He built pagan altars in the Temple of the LORD, the place where the LORD had said, "My name will remain in Jerusalem forever." ⁵He built these altars for all the powers of the heavens in both courtyards of the LORD's Temple. ⁶Manasseh also sacrificed his own son in the fire.* He practiced sorcery and divination, and he consulted with mediums and psychics. He did much that was evil in the LORD's sight, arousing his anger.

⁷Manasseh even made a carved image of Asherah and set it up in the Temple, the very place where the LORD had told David and his son Solomon: "My name will be honored forever in this Temple and in Jerusalem—the city I have chosen from among all the tribes of Israel. ⁸If the Israelites will be careful to obey my commands—all the laws my servant Moses gave them—I will not send them into exile from this land

---

20:9 Or *The shadow on the sundial has gone forward ten steps; do you want it to go backward ten steps?*   **20:11** Hebrew *the steps.*
20:20 Hebrew *watercourse.*   **21:6** Or *also made his son pass through the fire.*

that I gave their ancestors." [9]But the people refused to listen, and Manasseh led them to do even more evil than the pagan nations that the LORD had destroyed when the people of Israel entered the land.

[10]Then the LORD said through his servants the prophets: [11]"King Manasseh of Judah has done many detestable things. He is even more wicked than the Amorites, who lived in this land before Israel. He has caused the people of Judah to sin with his idols.* [12]So this is what the LORD, the God of Israel, says: I will bring such disaster on Jerusalem and Judah that the ears of those who hear about it will tingle with horror. [13]I will judge Jerusalem by the same standard I used for Samaria and the same measure* I used for the family of Ahab. I will wipe away the people of Jerusalem as one wipes a dish and turns it upside down. [14]Then I will reject even the remnant of my own people who are left, and I will hand them over as plunder for their enemies. [15]For they have done great evil in my sight and have angered me ever since their ancestors came out of Egypt."

[16]Manasseh also murdered many innocent people until Jerusalem was filled from one end to the other with innocent blood. This was in addition to the sin that he caused the people of Judah to commit, leading them to do evil in the LORD's sight.

[17]The rest of the events in Manasseh's reign and everything he did, including the sins he committed, are recorded in *The Book of the History of the Kings of Judah.* [18]When Manasseh died, he was buried in the palace garden, the garden of Uzza. Then his son Amon became the next king.

Amon Rules in Judah

[19]Amon was twenty-two years old when he became king, and he reigned in Jerusalem two years. His mother was Meshullemeth, the daughter of Haruz from Jotbah. [20]He did what was evil in the LORD's sight, just as his father, Manasseh, had done. [21]He followed the example of his father, worshiping the same idols his father had worshiped. [22]He abandoned the LORD, the God

of his ancestors, and he refused to follow the LORD's ways.

[23]Then Amon's own officials conspired against him and assassinated him in his palace. [24]But the people of the land killed all those who had conspired against King Amon, and they made his son Josiah the next king.

[25]The rest of the events in Amon's reign and what he did are recorded in *The Book of the History of the Kings of Judah.* [26]He was buried in his tomb in the garden of Uzza. Then his son Josiah became the next king.

22 Josiah Rules in Judah

Josiah was eight years old when he became king, and he reigned in Jerusalem thirty-one years. His mother was Jedidah, the daughter of Adaiah from Bozkath. [2]He did what was pleasing in the LORD's sight and followed the example of his ancestor David. He did not turn away from doing what was right.

[3]In the eighteenth year of his reign, King Josiah sent Shaphan son of Azaliah and grandson of Meshullam, the court secretary, to the Temple of the LORD. He told him, [4]"Go to Hilkiah the high priest and have him count the money the gatekeepers have collected from the people at the LORD's Temple. [5]Entrust this money to the men assigned to supervise the Temple's restoration. Then they can use it to pay workers to repair the Temple of the LORD. [6]They will need to hire carpenters, builders, and masons. Also have them buy the timber and the finished stone needed to repair the Temple. [7]But don't require the construction supervisors to keep account of the money they receive, for they are honest and trustworthy men."

Hilkiah Discovers God's Law

[8]Hilkiah the high priest said to Shaphan the court secretary, "I have found the Book of the Law in the LORD's Temple!" Then Hilkiah gave the scroll to Shaphan, and he read it.

[9]Shaphan went to the king and reported, "Your officials have turned over the money collected at the Temple of the LORD to the workers and supervisors at the Temple."

¹⁰Shaphan also told the king, "Hilkiah the priest has given me a scroll." So Shaphan read it to the king.

¹¹When the king heard what was written in the Book of the Law, he tore his clothes in despair. ¹²Then he gave these orders to Hilkiah the priest, Ahikam son of Shaphan, Acbor son of Micaiah, Shaphan the court secretary, and Asaiah the king's personal adviser: ¹³"Go to the Temple and speak to the LORD for me and for the people and for all Judah. Inquire about the words written in this scroll that has been found. For the LORD's great anger is burning against us because our ancestors have not obeyed the words in this scroll. We have not been doing everything it says we must do."

¹⁴So Hilkiah the priest, Ahikam, Acbor, Shaphan, and Asaiah went to the New Quarter* of Jerusalem to consult with the prophet Huldah. She was the wife of Shallum son of Tikvah, son of Harhas, the keeper of the Temple wardrobe.

¹⁵She said to them, "The LORD, the God of Israel, has spoken! Go back and tell the man who sent you, ¹⁶'This is what the LORD says: I am going to bring disaster on this city* and its people. All the words written in the scroll that the king of Judah has read will come true. ¹⁷For my people have abandoned me and offered sacrifices to pagan gods, and I am very angry with them for everything they have done. My anger will burn against this place, and it will not be quenched.'

¹⁸"But go to the king of Judah who sent you to seek the LORD and tell him: 'This is what the LORD, the God of Israel, says concerning the message you have just heard: ¹⁹You were sorry and humbled yourself before the LORD when you heard what I said against this city and its people—that this land would be cursed and become desolate. You tore your clothing in despair and wept before me in repentance. And I have indeed heard you, says the LORD. ²⁰So I will not send the promised disaster until after you have died and been buried in peace. You will not see the disaster I am going to bring on this city.'"

So they took her message back to the king.

23 Josiah's Religious Reforms

Then the king summoned all the elders of Judah and Jerusalem. ²And the king went up to the Temple of the LORD with all the people of Judah and Jerusalem, along with the priests and the prophets— all the people from the least to the greatest. There the king read to them the entire Book of the Covenant that had been found in the LORD's Temple. ³The king took his place of authority beside the pillar and renewed the covenant in the LORD's presence. He pledged to obey the LORD by keeping all his commands, laws, and decrees with all his heart and soul. In this way, he confirmed all the terms of the covenant that were written in the scroll, and all the people pledged themselves to the covenant.

⁴Then the king instructed Hilkiah the high priest and the priests of the second rank and the Temple gatekeepers to remove from the LORD's Temple all the articles that were used to worship Baal, Asherah, and all the powers of the heavens. The king had all these things burned outside Jerusalem on the terraces of the Kidron Valley, and he carried the ashes away to Bethel. ⁵He did away with the idolatrous priests, who had been appointed by the previous kings of Judah, for they had offered sacrifices at the pagan shrines throughout Judah and even in the vicinity of Jerusalem. They had also offered sacrifices to Baal, and to the sun, the moon, the constellations, and to all the powers of the heavens. ⁶The king removed the Asherah pole from the LORD's Temple and took it outside Jerusalem to the Kidron Valley, where he burned it. Then he ground the ashes of the pole to dust and threw the dust over the graves of the people. ⁷He also tore down the living quarters of the male and female shrine prostitutes that were inside the Temple of the LORD, where the women wove coverings for the Asherah pole.

⁸Josiah brought to Jerusalem all the priests who were living in other towns of Judah. He also defiled the pagan shrines, where they had offered sacrifices—all the way from Geba to Beersheba. He destroyed the shrines at the entrance to the gate of Joshua, the governor of Jerusalem. This gate

---

22:14 Or *the Second Quarter,* a newer section of Jerusalem. Hebrew reads *the Mishneh.*   **22:16** Hebrew *this place;* also in 22:19, 20.

was located to the left of the city gate as one enters the city. ⁹The priests who had served at the pagan shrines were not allowed* to serve at the LORD's altar in Jerusalem, but they were allowed to eat unleavened bread with the other priests.

¹⁰Then the king defiled the altar of Topheth in the valley of Ben-Hinnom, so no one could ever again use it to sacrifice a son or daughter in the fire* as an offering to Molech. ¹¹He removed from the entrance of the LORD's Temple the horse statues that the former kings of Judah had dedicated to the sun. They were near the quarters of Nathan-melech the eunuch, an officer of the court.* The king also burned the chariots dedicated to the sun.

¹²Josiah tore down the altars that the kings of Judah had built on the palace roof above the upper room of Ahaz. The king destroyed the altars that Manasseh had built in the two courtyards of the LORD's Temple. He smashed them to bits* and scattered the pieces in the Kidron Valley. ¹³The king also desecrated the pagan shrines east of Jerusalem, to the south of the Mount of Corruption, where King Solomon of Israel had built shrines for Ashtoreth, the detestable goddess of the Sidonians; and for Chemosh, the detestable god of the Moabites; and for Molech,* the vile god of the Ammonites. ¹⁴He smashed the sacred pillars and cut down the Asherah poles. Then he desecrated these places by scattering human bones over them.

¹⁵The king also tore down the altar at Bethel—the pagan shrine that Jeroboam son of Nebat had made when he caused Israel to sin. He burned down the shrine and ground it to dust, and he burned the Asherah pole. ¹⁶Then Josiah turned around and noticed several tombs in the side of the hill. He ordered that the bones be brought out, and he burned them on the altar at Bethel to desecrate it. (This happened just as the LORD had promised through the man of God when Jeroboam stood beside the altar at the festival.)

Then Josiah turned and looked up at the tomb of the man of God* who had predicted these things. ¹⁷"What is that monument over there?" Josiah asked.

And the people of the town told him, "It is the tomb of the man of God who came from Judah and predicted the very things that you have just done to the altar at Bethel!"

¹⁸Josiah replied, "Leave it alone. Don't disturb his bones." So they did not burn his bones or those of the old prophet from Samaria.

¹⁹Then Josiah demolished all the buildings at the pagan shrines in the towns of Samaria, just as he had done at Bethel. They had been built by the various kings of Israel and had made the LORD* very angry. ²⁰He executed the priests of the pagan shrines on their own altars, and he burned human bones on the altars to desecrate them. Finally, he returned to Jerusalem.

Josiah Celebrates Passover

²¹King Josiah then issued this order to all the people: "You must celebrate the Passover to the LORD your God, as required in this Book of the Covenant." ²²There had not been a Passover celebration like that since the time when the judges ruled in Israel, nor throughout all the years of the kings of Israel and Judah. ²³This Passover was celebrated to the LORD in Jerusalem in the eighteenth year of King Josiah's reign.

²⁴Josiah also got rid of the mediums and psychics, the household gods, the idols,* and every other kind of detestable practice, both in Jerusalem and throughout the land of Judah. He did this in obedience to the laws written in the scroll that Hilkiah the priest had found in the LORD's Temple. ²⁵Never before had there been a king like Josiah, who turned to the LORD with all his heart and soul and strength, obeying all the laws of Moses. And there has never been a king like him since.

²⁶Even so, the LORD was very angry with Judah because of all the wicked things Manasseh had done to provoke him. ²⁷For the LORD said, "I will also banish Judah from my presence just as I have banished

---

23:9 Hebrew *did not come up.* 23:10 Or *to make a son or daughter pass through the fire.* 23:11 The meaning of the Hebrew is uncertain. 23:12 Or *He quickly removed them.* 23:13 Hebrew *Milcom,* a variant spelling of Molech. 23:16 As in Greek version; Hebrew lacks *when Jeroboam stood beside the altar at the festival. Then Josiah turned and looked up at the tomb of the man of God.* 23:19 As in Greek and Syriac versions and Latin Vulgate; Hebrew lacks *the LORD.* 23:24 The Hebrew term (literally *round things*) probably alludes to dung.

Israel. And I will reject my chosen city of Jerusalem and the Temple where my name was to be honored."

²⁸The rest of the events in Josiah's reign and all his deeds are recorded in *The Book of the History of the Kings of Judah.*

²⁹While Josiah was king, Pharaoh Neco, king of Egypt, went to the Euphrates River to help the king of Assyria. King Josiah and his army marched out to fight him,* but King Neco* killed him when they met at Megiddo. ³⁰Josiah's officers took his body back in a chariot from Megiddo to Jerusalem and buried him in his own tomb. Then the people of the land anointed Josiah's son Jehoahaz and made him the next king.

Jehoahaz Rules in Judah

³¹Jehoahaz was twenty-three years old when he became king, and he reigned in Jerusalem three months. His mother was Hamutal, the daughter of Jeremiah from Libnah. ³²He did what was evil in the LORD's sight, just as his ancestors had done.

³³Pharaoh Neco put Jehoahaz in prison at Riblah in the land of Hamath to prevent him from ruling* in Jerusalem. He also demanded that Judah pay 7,500 pounds of silver and 75 pounds of gold* as tribute.

Jehoiakim Rules in Judah

³⁴Pharaoh Neco then installed Eliakim, another of Josiah's sons, to reign in place of his father, and he changed Eliakim's name to Jehoiakim. Jehoahaz was taken to Egypt as a prisoner, where he died.

³⁵In order to get the silver and gold demanded as tribute by Pharaoh Neco, Jehoiakim collected a tax from the people of Judah, requiring them to pay in proportion to their wealth.

³⁶Jehoiakim was twenty-five years old when he became king, and he reigned in Jerusalem eleven years. His mother was Zebidah, the daughter of Pedaiah from Rumah. ³⁷He did what was evil in the LORD's sight, just as his ancestors had done.

24 During Jehoiakim's reign, King Nebuchadnezzar of Babylon invaded the land of Judah. Jehoiakim surrendered

and paid him tribute for three years but then rebelled. ²Then the LORD sent bands of Babylonian,* Aramean, Moabite, and Ammonite raiders against Judah to destroy it, just as the LORD had promised through his prophets. ³These disasters happened to Judah because of the LORD's command. He had decided to banish Judah from his presence because of the many sins of Manasseh, ⁴who had filled Jerusalem with innocent blood. The LORD would not forgive this.

⁵The rest of the events in Jehoiakim's reign and all his deeds are recorded in *The Book of the History of the Kings of Judah.* ⁶When Jehoiakim died, his son Jehoiachin became the next king.

⁷The king of Egypt did not venture out of his country after that, for the king of Babylon captured the entire area formerly claimed by Egypt—from the Brook of Egypt to the Euphrates River.

Jehoiachin Rules in Judah

⁸Jehoiachin was eighteen years old when he became king, and he reigned in Jerusalem three months. His mother was Nehushta, the daughter of Elnathan from Jerusalem. ⁹Jehoiachin did what was evil in the LORD's sight, just as his father had done.

¹⁰During Jehoiachin's reign, the officers of King Nebuchadnezzar of Babylon came up against Jerusalem and besieged it. ¹¹Nebuchadnezzar himself arrived at the city during the siege. ¹²Then King Jehoiachin, along with the queen mother, his advisers, his commanders, and his officials, surrendered to the Babylonians.

In the eighth year of Nebuchadnezzar's reign, he took Jehoiachin prisoner. ¹³As the LORD had said beforehand, Nebuchadnezzar carried away all the treasures from the LORD's Temple and the royal palace. He stripped away* all the gold objects that King Solomon of Israel had placed in the Temple. ¹⁴King Nebuchadnezzar took all of Jerusalem captive, including all the commanders and the best of the soldiers, craftsmen, and artisans—10,000 in all. Only the poorest people were left in the land.

¹⁵Nebuchadnezzar led King Jehoiachin away as a captive to Babylon, along with the

---

23:29a Or *Josiah went out to meet him.*   **23:29b** Hebrew *he.*   **23:33a** The meaning of the Hebrew is uncertain.   **23:33b** Hebrew *100 talents* [3,400 kilograms] *of silver and 1 talent* [34 kilograms] *of gold.*   **24:2** Or *Chaldean.*   **24:13** Or *He cut apart.*

queen mother, his wives and officials, and all Jerusalem's elite. ¹⁶He also exiled 7,000 of the best troops and 1,000 craftsmen and artisans, all of whom were strong and fit for war. ¹⁷Then the king of Babylon installed Mattaniah, Jehoiachin's* uncle, as the next king, and he changed Mattaniah's name to Zedekiah.

Zedekiah Rules in Judah

¹⁸Zedekiah was twenty-one years old when he became king, and he reigned in Jerusalem eleven years. His mother was Hamutal, the daughter of Jeremiah from Libnah. ¹⁹But Zedekiah did what was evil in the LORD's sight, just as Jehoiakim had done. ²⁰These things happened because of the LORD's anger against the people of Jerusalem and Judah, until he finally banished them from his presence and sent them into exile.

The Fall of Jerusalem

Zedekiah rebelled against the king of Babylon.

25 So on January 15,* during the ninth year of Zedekiah's reign, King Nebuchadnezzar of Babylon led his entire army against Jerusalem. They surrounded the city and built siege ramps against its walls. ²Jerusalem was kept under siege until the eleventh year of King Zedekiah's reign.

³By July 18 in the eleventh year of Zedekiah's reign,* the famine in the city had become very severe, and the last of the food was entirely gone. ⁴Then a section of the city wall was broken down, and all the soldiers fled. Since the city was surrounded by the Babylonians,* they waited for nightfall. Then they slipped through the gate between the two walls behind the king's garden and headed toward the Jordan Valley.*

⁵But the Babylonian* troops chased the king and caught him on the plains of Jericho, for his men had all deserted him

and scattered. ⁶They took him to the king of Babylon at Riblah, where they pronounced judgment upon Zedekiah. ⁷They made Zedekiah watch as they slaughtered his sons. Then they gouged out Zedekiah's eyes, bound him in bronze chains, and led him away to Babylon.

The Temple Destroyed

⁸On August 14 of that year,* which was the nineteenth year of King Nebuchadnezzar's reign, Nebuzaradan, the captain of the guard and an official of the Babylonian king, arrived in Jerusalem. ⁹He burned down the Temple of the LORD, the royal palace, and all the houses of Jerusalem. He destroyed all the important buildings* in the city. ¹⁰Then he supervised the entire Babylonian army as they tore down the walls of Jerusalem on every side. ¹¹Nebuzaradan, the captain of the guard, then took as exiles the rest of the people who remained in the city, the defectors who had declared their allegiance to the king of Babylon, and the rest of the population. ¹²But the captain of the guard allowed some of the poorest people to stay behind in Judah to care for the vineyards and fields.

¹³The Babylonians broke up the bronze pillars in front of the LORD's Temple, the bronze water carts, and the great bronze basin called the Sea, and they carried all the bronze away to Babylon. ¹⁴They also took all the ash buckets, shovels, lamp snuffers, dishes, and all the other bronze articles used for making sacrifices at the Temple. ¹⁵Nebuzaradan, the captain of the guard, also took the incense burners and basins, and all the other articles made of pure gold or silver.

¹⁶The weight of the bronze from the two pillars, the Sea, and the water carts was too great to be measured. These things had been made for the LORD's Temple in the days of King Solomon. ¹⁷Each of the pillars was 27 feet* tall. The bronze capital on top of each pillar was 7½ feet* high and was

---

24:17 Hebrew *his*. **25:1** Hebrew *on the tenth day of the tenth month*, of the ancient Hebrew lunar calendar. A number of events in 2 Kings can be cross-checked with dates in surviving Babylonian records and related accurately to our modern calendar. This day was January 15, 588 B.C. **25:3** Hebrew *By the ninth day of the [fourth] month* [in the eleventh year of Zedekiah's reign] (compare Jer 52:6 and the note there). This day was July 18, 586 B.C.; also see note on 25:1. **25:4a** Or *the Chaldeans*; also in 25:13, 25, 26. **25:4b** Hebrew the *Arabah*. **25:5** Or *Chaldean*; also in 25:10, 24. **25:8** Hebrew *On the seventh day of the fifth month*, of the ancient Hebrew lunar calendar. This day was August 14, 586 B.C.; also see note on 25:1. **25:9** Or *destroyed the houses of all the important people*. **25:17a** Hebrew *18 cubits* [8.1 meters]. **25:17b** As in parallel texts at 1 Kgs 7:16, 2 Chr 3:15, and Jer 52:22, all of which read *5 cubits* [2.3 meters]; Hebrew reads *3 cubits*, which is 4.5 feet or 1.4 meters.

decorated with a network of bronze pomegranates all the way around. ¹⁸Nebuzaradan, the captain of the guard, took with him as prisoners Seraiah the high priest, Zephaniah the priest of the second rank, and the three chief gatekeepers. ¹⁹And from among the people still hiding in the city, he took an officer who had been in charge of the Judean army; five of the king's personal advisers; the army commander's chief secretary, who was in charge of recruitment; and sixty other citizens. ²⁰Nebuzaradan, the captain of the guard, took them all to the king of Babylon at Riblah. ²¹And there at Riblah, in the land of Hamath, the king of Babylon had them all put to death. So the people of Judah were sent into exile from their land.

Gedaliah Governs in Judah

²²Then King Nebuchadnezzar appointed Gedaliah son of Ahikam and grandson of Shaphan as governor over the people he had left in Judah. ²³When all the army commanders and their men learned that the king of Babylon had appointed Gedaliah as governor, they went to see him at Mizpah. These included Ishmael son of Nethaniah, Johanan son of Kareah, Seraiah son of Tanhumeth the Netophathite, and Jezaniah* son of the Maacathite, and all their men.

²⁴Gedaliah vowed to them that the Babylonian officials meant them no harm. "Don't be afraid of them. Live in the land and serve the king of Babylon, and all will go well for you," he promised.

²⁵But in midautumn of that year,* Ishmael son of Nethaniah and grandson of Elishama, who was of the royal family, went to Mizpah with ten men and killed Gedaliah. He also killed all the Judeans and Babylonians who were with Gedaliah at Mizpah.

²⁶Then all the people of Judah, from the least to the greatest, as well as the army commanders, fled in panic to Egypt, for they were afraid of what the Babylonians would do to them.

Hope for Israel's Royal Line

²⁷In the thirty-seventh year of the exile of King Jehoiachin of Judah, Evil-merodach ascended to the Babylonian throne. He was kind to* Jehoiachin and released him from prison on April 2 of that year.* ²⁸He spoke kindly to Jehoiachin and gave him a higher place than all the other exiled kings in Babylon. ²⁹He supplied Jehoiachin with new clothes to replace his prison garb and allowed him to dine in the king's presence for the rest of his life. ³⁰So the Babylonian king gave him a regular food allowance as long as he lived.

25:23 As in parallel text at Jer 40:8; Hebrew reads *Jaazaniah*, a variant spelling of Jezaniah.   25:25 Hebrew *in the seventh month*, of the ancient Hebrew lunar calendar. This month occurred within the months of October and November 586 B.C.; also see note on 25:1. 25:27a Hebrew *He raised the head of.*   25:27b Hebrew *on the twenty-seventh day of the twelfth month*, of the ancient Hebrew lunar calendar. This day was April 2, 561 B.C.; also see note on 25:1.

Introduction to

1 Chronicles

Background

While the Chronicles cover many of the same events as the books of the Kings, the two accounts aren't mirror images. First Chronicles follows the family line of David starting with Adam. It provides God's perspective on the events occurring in Israel during the reign of King David, including details of David's preparations for the building of the temple. The prophet Nathan tells him not to construct the temple, but that does not stop him from putting plans, alliances, and supplies in place for the one who would.

The priest-scribe Ezra is believed to be the author of 1 and 2 Chronicles. The books originally were one book, called *Dibre Hayyamim* or "The Words of the Days," but were divided in the Greek Septuagint translation, where they were titled "Of Things Omitted." The "things omitted" are events not included in 1 and 2 Samuel and 1 and 2 Kings. The name Chronicles comes from the Latin Vulgate, which called the book "The Chronicles of the Whole of Sacred History."

Message

The Babylonian captivity is virtually over and the Medo-Persian emperor Cyrus allows exiles to return home. Ezra leads a group of exiles back to Jerusalem around 457 B.C. He serves as a spiritual leader for the discouraged people who return to a destroyed city, dismantled wall, and ravaged temple. After years of exile, the remnant back in Jerusalem needs hope and a sense of national identity. Ezra writes to give the people hope: God will continue to be faithful to his promises to them. First and 2 Chronicles demonstrate God's loving involvement in the lives of his people.

Time

The genealogies of 1 Chronicles extend from Adam to 538 B.C., when the first group of exiles was allowed to return to Jerusalem. The Book of 1 Chronicles covers events to the end of the reign of David in 971 B.C. Ezra probably completed the books of 1 and 2 Chronicles between 450 and 430 B.C.

Outline

1 Chronicles

1 From Adam to Noah's Sons

The descendants of Adam were Seth, Enosh, [2]Kenan, Mahalalel, Jared, [3]Enoch, Methuselah, Lamech, [4]and Noah.

The sons of Noah were* Shem, Ham, and Japheth.

Descendants of Japheth

[5]The descendants of Japheth were Gomer, Magog, Madai, Javan, Tubal, Meshech, and Tiras.

[6]The descendants of Gomer were Ashkenaz, Riphath,* and Togarmah.

[7]The descendants of Javan were Elishah, Tarshish, Kittim, and Rodanim.

Descendants of Ham

[8]The descendants of Ham were Cush, Mizraim,* Put, and Canaan.

[9]The descendants of Cush were Seba, Havilah, Sabtah, Raamah, and Sabteca. The descendants of Raamah were Sheba and Dedan. [10]Cush was also the ancestor of Nimrod, who was the first heroic warrior on earth.

[11]Mizraim was the ancestor of the Ludites, Anamites, Lehabites, Naphtuhites, [12]Pathrusites, Casluhites, and the Caphtorites, from whom the Philistines came.*

[13]Canaan's oldest son was Sidon, the ancestor of the Sidonians. Canaan was also the ancestor of the Hittites,* [14]Jebusites, Amorites, Girgashites, [15]Hivites, Arkites, Sinites, [16]Arvadites, Zemarites, and Hamathites.

Descendants of Shem

[17]The descendants of Shem were Elam, Asshur, Arphaxad, Lud, and Aram. The descendants of Aram were* Uz, Hul, Gether, and Mash.*

[18]Arphaxad was the father of Shelah.

Shelah was the father of Eber.

[19]Eber had two sons. The first was named Peleg (which means "division"), for during his lifetime the people of the world were divided into different language groups. His brother's name was Joktan.

[20]Joktan was the ancestor of Almodad, Sheleph, Hazarmaveth, Jerah, [21]Hadoram, Uzal, Diklah, [22]Obal,* Abimael, Sheba, [23]Ophir, Havilah, and Jobab. All these were descendants of Joktan.

[24]So this is the family line descended from Shem: Arphaxad, Shelah,* [25]Eber, Peleg, Reu, [26]Serug, Nahor, Terah, [27]and Abram, later known as Abraham.

Descendants of Abraham

[28]The sons of Abraham were Isaac and Ishmael. [29]These are their genealogical records:

1:4 As in Greek version (see also Gen 5:3-32); Hebrew lacks *The sons of Noah were*. **1:6** As in some Hebrew manuscripts and Greek version (see also Gen 10:3); most Hebrew manuscripts read *Diphath*. **1:8** Or *Egypt;* also in 1:11. **1:12** Hebrew *Casluhites, from whom the Philistines came, Caphtorites*. See Jer 47:4; Amos 9:7. **1:13** Hebrew *ancestor of Heth*. **1:17a** As in one Hebrew manuscript and some Greek manuscripts (see also Gen 10:23); most Hebrew manuscripts lack *The descendants of Aram were*. **1:17b** As in parallel text at Gen 10:23; Hebrew reads *and Meshech*. **1:22** As in some Hebrew manuscripts and Syriac version (see also Gen 10:28); most Hebrew manuscripts read *Ebal*. **1:24** Some Greek manuscripts read *Arphaxad, Cainan, Shelah*. See notes on Gen 10:24; 11:12-13.

The sons of Ishmael were Nebaioth (the oldest), Kedar, Adbeel, Mibsam, ³⁰Mishma, Dumah, Massa, Hadad, Tema, ³¹Jetur, Naphish, and Kedemah. These were the sons of Ishmael.

³²The sons of Keturah, Abraham's concubine, were Zimran, Jokshan, Medan, Midian, Ishbak, and Shuah. The sons of Jokshan were Sheba and Dedan. ³³The sons of Midian were Ephah, Epher, Hanoch, Abida, and Eldaah.

All these were descendants of Abraham through his concubine Keturah.

Descendants of Isaac

³⁴Abraham was the father of Isaac. The sons of Isaac were Esau and Israel.*

Descendants of Esau

³⁵The sons of Esau were Eliphaz, Reuel, Jeush, Jalam, and Korah. ³⁶The descendants of Eliphaz were Teman, Omar, Zepho,* Gatam, Kenaz, and Amalek, who was born to Timna.* ³⁷The descendants of Reuel were Nahath, Zerah, Shammah, and Mizzah.

Original Peoples of Edom

³⁸The descendants of Seir were Lotan, Shobal, Zibeon, Anah, Dishon, Ezer, and Dishan. ³⁹The descendants of Lotan were Hori and Hemam.* Lotan's sister was named Timna. ⁴⁰The descendants of Shobal were Alvan,* Manahath, Ebal, Shepho,* and Onam. The descendants of Zibeon were Aiah and Anah. ⁴¹The son of Anah was Dishon. The descendants of Dishon were Hemdan,* Eshban, Ithran, and Keran. ⁴²The descendants of Ezer were Bilhan, Zaavan, and Akan.* The descendants of Dishan* were Uz and Aran.

Rulers of Edom

⁴³These are the kings who ruled in the land of Edom before any king ruled over the Israelites*:

Bela son of Beor, who ruled from his city of Dinhabah. ⁴⁴When Bela died, Jobab son of Zerah from Bozrah became king in his place. ⁴⁵When Jobab died, Husham from the land of the Temanites became king in his place. ⁴⁶When Husham died, Hadad son of Bedad became king in his place and ruled from the city of Avith. He was the one who destroyed the Midianite army in the land of Moab. ⁴⁷When Hadad died, Samlah from the city of Masrekah became king in his place. ⁴⁸When Samlah died, Shaul from the city of Rehoboth-on-the-River became king in his place. ⁴⁹When Shaul died, Baal-hanan son of Acbor became king in his place. ⁵⁰When Baal-hanan died, Hadad became king in his place and ruled from the city of Pau.* His wife was Mehetabel, the daughter of Matred and granddaughter of Me-zahab. ⁵¹Then Hadad died.

The clan leaders of Edom were Timna, Alvah,* Jetheth, ⁵²Oholibamah, Elah, Pinon, ⁵³Kenaz, Teman, Mibzar, ⁵⁴Magdiel, and Iram. These are the clan leaders of Edom.

2 Descendants of Israel

The sons of Israel* were Reuben, Simeon, Levi, Judah, Issachar, Zebulun, ²Dan, Joseph, Benjamin, Naphtali, Gad, and Asher.

Descendants of Judah

³Judah had three sons from Bathshua, a Canaanite woman. Their names were Er, Onan, and Shelah. But the LORD saw that the oldest son, Er, was a wicked

---

1:34 *Israel* is the name that God gave to Jacob.   **1:36a** As in many Hebrew manuscripts and a few Greek manuscripts (see also Gen 36:11); most Hebrew manuscripts read *Zephi*.   **1:36b** As in some Greek manuscripts (see also Gen 36:12); Hebrew reads *Kenaz, Timna, and Amalek*.   **1:39** As in parallel text at Gen 36:22; Hebrew reads *and Homam*.   **1:40a** As in many Hebrew manuscripts and a few Greek manuscripts (see also Gen 36:23); most Hebrew manuscripts read *Alian*.   **1:40b** As in some Hebrew manuscripts (see also Gen 36:23); most Hebrew manuscripts read *Shephi*.   **1:41** As in many Hebrew manuscripts and some Greek manuscripts (see also Gen 36:26); most Hebrew manuscripts read *Hamran*.   **1:42a** As in many Hebrew and Greek manuscripts (see also Gen 36:27); most Hebrew manuscripts read *Jaakan*.   **1:42b** Hebrew *Dishon;* compare 1:38 and parallel text at Gen 36:28.   **1:43** Or *before an Israelite king ruled over them*.   **1:50** As in many Hebrew manuscripts, some Greek manuscripts, Syriac version, and Latin Vulgate (see also Gen 36:39); most Hebrew manuscripts read *Pai*.   **1:51** As in parallel text at Gen 36:40; Hebrew reads *Aliah*.   **2:1** *Israel* is the name that God gave to Jacob.

man, so he killed him. ⁴Later Judah had twin sons from Tamar, his widowed daughter-in-law. Their names were Perez and Zerah. So Judah had five sons in all.

⁵The sons of Perez were Hezron and Hamul.

⁶The sons of Zerah were Zimri, Ethan, Heman, Calcol, and Darda*—five in all.

⁷The son of Carmi (a descendant of Zimri) was Achan,* who brought disaster on Israel by taking plunder that had been set apart for the LORD.*

⁸The son of Ethan was Azariah.

From Judah's Grandson Hezron to David

⁹The sons of Hezron were Jerahmeel, Ram, and Caleb.*

¹⁰ Ram was the father of Amminadab. Amminadab was the father of Nahshon, a leader of Judah.

¹¹ Nahshon was the father of Salmon.* Salmon was the father of Boaz.

¹² Boaz was the father of Obed. Obed was the father of Jesse.

¹³Jesse's first son was Eliab, his second was Abinadab, his third was Shimea, ¹⁴his fourth was Nethanel, his fifth was Raddai, ¹⁵his sixth was Ozem, and his seventh was David.

¹⁶Their sisters were named Zeruiah and Abigail. Zeruiah had three sons named Abishai, Joab, and Asahel. ¹⁷Abigail married a man named Jether, an Ishmaelite, and they had a son named Amasa.

Other Descendants of Hezron

¹⁸Hezron's son Caleb had sons from his wife Azubah and from Jerioth.* Her sons were named Jesher, Shobab, and Ardon. ¹⁹After Azubah died, Caleb married Ephrathah,* and they had a son named Hur. ²⁰Hur was the father of Uri. Uri was the father of Bezalel.

²¹When Hezron was sixty years old, he married Gilead's sister, the daughter of Makir. They had a son named Segub. ²²Segub was the father of Jair, who ruled twenty-three towns in the land of Gilead. ²³(But Geshur and Aram captured the Towns of Jair* and also took Kenath and its sixty surrounding villages.) All these were descendants of Makir, the father of Gilead.

²⁴Soon after Hezron died in the town of Caleb-ephrathah, his wife Abijah gave birth to a son named Ashhur (the father of* Tekoa).

Descendants of Hezron's Son Jerahmeel

²⁵The sons of Jerahmeel, the oldest son of Hezron, were Ram (the firstborn), Bunah, Oren, Ozem, and Ahijah. ²⁶Jerahmeel had a second wife named Atarah. She was the mother of Onam.

²⁷The sons of Ram, the oldest son of Jerahmeel, were Maaz, Jamin, and Eker.

²⁸The sons of Onam were Shammai and Jada.

The sons of Shammai were Nadab and Abishur.

²⁹The sons of Abishur and his wife Abihail were Ahban and Molid.

³⁰The sons of Nadab were Seled and Appaim. Seled died without children, ³¹but Appaim had a son named Ishi. The son of Ishi was Sheshan. Sheshan had a descendant named Ahlai.

³²The sons of Jada, Shammai's brother, were Jether and Jonathan. Jether died without children, ³³but Jonathan had two sons named Peleth and Zaza.

These were all descendants of Jerahmeel.

³⁴Sheshan had no sons, though he did have daughters. He also had an Egyptian servant named Jarha. ³⁵Sheshan gave one of his daughters to be the wife of Jarha, and they had a son named Attai.

³⁶ Attai was the father of Nathan. Nathan was the father of Zabad.

³⁷ Zabad was the father of Ephlal. Ephlal was the father of Obed.

³⁸ Obed was the father of Jehu. Jehu was the father of Azariah.

³⁹ Azariah was the father of Helez. Helez was the father of Eleasah.

2:6 As in many Hebrew manuscripts, some Greek manuscripts, and Syriac version (see also 1 Kgs 4:31); Hebrew reads Dara.   2:7a Hebrew Achar; compare Josh 7:1. Achar means "disaster."   2:7b The Hebrew term used here refers to the complete consecration of things or people to the LORD, either by destroying them or by giving them as an offering.   2:9 Hebrew Kelubai, a variant spelling of Caleb; compare 2:18.   2:11 As in Greek version (see also Ruth 4:20); Hebrew reads Salma.   2:18 Or Caleb had a daughter named Jerioth from his wife, Azubah. The meaning of the Hebrew is uncertain.   2:19 Hebrew Ephrath, a variant spelling of Ephrathah; compare 2:50 and 4:4.   2:23 Or captured Havvoth-jair.   2:24 Or the founder of; also in 2:42, 45, 49.

40 Eleasah was the father of Sismai. Sismai was the father of Shallum. 41 Shallum was the father of Jekamiah. Jekamiah was the father of Elishama.

Descendants of Hezron's Son Caleb

42 The descendants of Caleb, the brother of Jerahmeel, included Mesha (the first-born), who became the father of Ziph. Caleb's descendants also included the sons of Mareshah, the father of Hebron.* 43 The sons of Hebron were Korah, Tappuah, Rekem, and Shema. 44 Shema was the father of Raham. Raham was the father of Jorkeam. Rekem was the father of Shammai. 45 The son of Shammai was Maon. Maon was the father of Beth-zur. 46 Caleb's concubine Ephah gave birth to Haran, Moza, and Gazez. Haran was the father of Gazez.

47 The sons of Jahdai were Regem, Jotham, Geshan, Pelet, Ephah, and Shaaph. 48 Another of Caleb's concubines, Maacah, gave birth to Sheber and Tirhanah. 49 She also gave birth to Shaaph (the father of Madmannah) and Sheva (the father of Macbenah and Gibea). Caleb also had a daughter named Acsah. 50 These were all descendants of Caleb.

Descendants of Caleb's Son Hur

The sons of Hur, the oldest son of Caleb's wife Ephrathah, were Shobal (the founder of Kiriath-jearim), 51 Salma (the founder of Bethlehem), and Hareph (the founder of Beth-gader). 52 The descendants of Shobal (the founder of Kiriath-jearim) were Haroeh, half the Manahathites, 53 and the families of Kiriath-jearim—the Ithrites, Puthites, Shumathites, and Mishraites, from whom came the people of Zorah and Eshtaol. 54 The descendants of Salma were the people of Bethlehem, the Netophathites, Atroth-beth-joab, the other half of the Manahathites, the Zorites, 55 and the families of scribes living at Jabez— the Tirathites, Shimeathites, and Sucathites. All these were Kenites who descended from Hammath, the father of the family of Recab.*

3 Descendants of David

These are the sons of David who were born in Hebron:

The oldest was Amnon, whose mother was Ahinoam from Jezreel.
The second was Daniel, whose mother was Abigail from Carmel.
2 The third was Absalom, whose mother was Maacah, the daughter of Talmai, king of Geshur.
The fourth was Adonijah, whose mother was Haggith.
3 The fifth was Shephatiah, whose mother was Abital.
The sixth was Ithream, whose mother was Eglah, David's wife.

4 These six sons were born to David in Hebron, where he reigned seven and a half years.

Then David reigned another thirty-three years in Jerusalem. 5 The sons born to David in Jerusalem included Shammua,* Shobab, Nathan, and Solomon. Their mother was Bathsheba,* the daughter of Ammiel. 6 David also had nine other sons: Ibhar, Elishua,* Elpelet,* 7 Nogah, Nepheg, Japhia, 8 Elishama, Eliada, and Eliphelet.

9 These were the sons of David, not including his sons born to his concubines. Their sister was named Tamar.

Descendants of Solomon

10 The descendants of Solomon were Rehoboam, Abijah, Asa, Jehoshaphat, 11 Jehoram,* Ahaziah, Joash, 12 Amaziah, Uzziah,* Jotham, 13 Ahaz, Hezekiah, Manasseh, 14 Amon, and Josiah. 15 The sons of Josiah were Johanan (the oldest), Jehoiakim (the second), Zedekiah (the third), and Jehoahaz* (the fourth). 16 The successors of Jehoiakim were his son Jehoiachin and his brother Zedekiah.*

Descendants of Jehoiachin

17 The sons of Jehoiachin,* who was taken prisoner by the Babylonians, were

---

2:42 Or who founded Hebron. The meaning of the Hebrew is uncertain. 2:55 Or the founder of Beth-recab. 3:5a As in Syriac version (see also 14:4; 2 Sam 5:14); Hebrew reads Shimea. 3:5b Hebrew Bathshua, a variant spelling of Bathsheba. 3:6a As in some Hebrew and Greek manuscripts (see also 14:5-7 and 2 Sam 5:15); most Hebrew manuscripts read Elishama. 3:6b Hebrew Eliphelet; compare parallel text at 14:5-7. 3:11 Hebrew Joram, a variant spelling of Jehoram. 3:12 Hebrew Azariah, a variant spelling of Uzziah. 3:15 Hebrew Shallum, another name for Jehoahaz. 3:16 Hebrew The sons of Jehoiakim were his son Jeconiah [a variant spelling of Jehoiachin] and his son Zedekiah. 3:17 Hebrew Jeconiah, a variant spelling of Jehoiachin.

Shealtiel, ¹⁸Malkiram, Pedaiah, Shenazzar, Jekamiah, Hoshama, and Nedabiah.
¹⁹The sons of Pedaiah were Zerubbabel and Shimei.

The sons of Zerubbabel were Meshullam and Hananiah. (Their sister was Shelomith.) ²⁰His five other sons were Hashubah, Ohel, Berekiah, Hasadiah, and Jushab-hesed.

²¹The sons of Hananiah were Pelatiah and Jeshaiah. Jeshaiah's son was Rephaiah. Rephaiah's son was Arnan. Arnan's son was Obadiah. Obadiah's son was Shecaniah.

²²The descendants of Shecaniah were Shemaiah and his sons, Hattush, Igal, Bariah, Neariah, and Shaphat—six in all.

²³The sons of Neariah were Elioenai, Hizkiah, and Azrikam—three in all.

²⁴The sons of Elioenai were Hodaviah, Eliashib, Pelaiah, Akkub, Johanan, Delaiah, and Anani—seven in all.

4 Other Descendants of Judah

The descendants of Judah were Perez, Hezron, Carmi, Hur, and Shobal.

²Shobal's son Reaiah was the father of Jahath. Jahath was the father of Ahumai and Lahad. These were the families of the Zorathites.

³The descendants of* Etam were Jezreel, Ishma, Idbash, their sister Hazzelelponi, ⁴Penuel (the father of* Gedor), and Ezer (the father of Hushah). These were the descendants of Hur (the firstborn of Ephrathah), the ancestor of Bethlehem.

⁵Ashhur (the father of Tekoa) had two wives, named Helah and Naarah. ⁶Naarah gave birth to Ahuzzam, Hepher, Temeni, and Haahashtari. ⁷Helah gave birth to Zereth, Izhar,* Ethnan, ⁸and Koz, who became the ancestor of Anub, Zobebah, and all the families of Aharhel son of Harum.

⁹There was a man named Jabez who was more honorable than any of his brothers. His mother named him Jabez* because his birth had been so painful. ¹⁰He was the one who prayed to the God

of Israel, "Oh, that you would bless me and expand my territory! Please be with me in all that I do, and keep me from all trouble and pain!" And God granted him his request.

¹¹Kelub (the brother of Shuhah) was the father of Mehir. Mehir was the father of Eshton. ¹²Eshton was the father of Beth-rapha, Paseah, and Tehinnah. Tehinnah was the father of Ir-nahash. These were the descendants of Recah.

¹³The sons of Kenaz were Othniel and Seraiah. Othniel's sons were Hathath and Meonothai.* ¹⁴Meonothai was the father of Ophrah. Seraiah was the father of Joab, the founder of the Valley of Craftsmen,* so called because they were craftsmen.

¹⁵The sons of Caleb son of Jephunneh were Iru, Elah, and Naam. The son of Elah was Kenaz.

¹⁶The sons of Jehallelel were Ziph, Ziphah, Tiria, and Asarel.

¹⁷The sons of Ezrah were Jether, Mered, Epher, and Jalon. One of Mered's wives became* the mother of Miriam, Shammai, and Ishbah (the father of Eshtemoa). ¹⁸He married a woman from Judah, who became the mother of Jered (the father of Gedor), Heber (the father of Soco), and Jekuthiel (the father of Zanoah). Mered also married Bithia, a daughter of Pharaoh, and she bore him children.

¹⁹Hodiah's wife was the sister of Naham. One of her sons was the father of Keilah the Garmite, and another was the father of Eshtemoa the Maacathite.

²⁰The sons of Shimon were Amnon, Rinnah, Ben-hanan, and Tilon.

The descendants of Ishi were Zoheth and Ben-zoheth.

Descendants of Judah's Son Shelah

²¹Shelah was one of Judah's sons. The descendants of Shelah were Er (the father of Lecah); Laadah (the father of Mareshah); the families of linen workers at Beth-ashbea; ²²Jokim; the men of

---

4:3 As in Greek version; Hebrew reads *father of.* The meaning of the Hebrew is uncertain. **4:4** Or *the founder of;* also in 4:5, 12, 14, 17, 18, and perhaps other instances where the text reads *the father of.* **4:7** As in an alternate reading in the Masoretic Text (see also Latin Vulgate); the other alternate and the Greek version read *Zohar.* **4:9** *Jabez* sounds like a Hebrew word meaning "distress" or "pain." **4:13** As in some Greek manuscripts and Latin Vulgate; Hebrew lacks *and Meonothai.* **4:14** Or *Joab, the father of Ge-harashim.* **4:17** Or *Jether's wife became;* Hebrew reads *She became.*

Cozeba; and Joash and Saraph, who ruled over Moab and Jashubi-lehem. These names all come from ancient records. ²³They were the pottery makers who lived in Netaim and Gederah. They lived there and worked for the king.

Descendants of Simeon

²⁴The sons of Simeon were Jemuel,* Jamin, Jarib, Zohar,* and Shaul. ²⁵The descendants of Shaul were Shallum, Mibsam, and Mishma. ²⁶The descendants of Mishma were Hammuel, Zaccur, and Shimei. ²⁷Shimei had sixteen sons and six daughters, but none of his brothers had large families. So Simeon's tribe never grew as large as the tribe of Judah. ²⁸They lived in Beersheba, Moladah, Hazar-shual, ²⁹Bilhah, Ezem, Tolad, ³⁰Bethuel, Hormah, Ziklag, ³¹Beth-marcaboth, Hazar-susim, Beth-biri, and Shaaraim. These towns were under their control until the time of King David. ³²Their descendants also lived in Etam, Ain, Rimmon, Token, and Ashan—five towns ³³and their surrounding villages as far away as Baalath.* This was their territory, and these names are listed in their genealogical records. ³⁴Other descendants of Simeon included Meshobab, Jamlech, Joshah son of Amaziah, ³⁵Joel, Jehu son of Joshibiah, son of Seraiah, son of Asiel, ³⁶Elioenai, Jaakobah, Jeshohaiah, Asaiah, Adiel, Jesimiel, Benaiah, ³⁷and Ziza son of Shiphi, son of Allon, son of Jedaiah, son of Shimri, son of Shemaiah.

³⁸These were the names of some of the leaders of Simeon's wealthy clans. Their families grew, ³⁹and they traveled to the region of Gerar,* in the east part of the valley, seeking pastureland for their flocks. ⁴⁰They found lush pastures there, and the land was quiet and peaceful. Some of Ham's descendants had been living in that region. ⁴¹But during the reign of King Hezekiah of Judah, these leaders of Simeon invaded the region and completely destroyed* the homes of the descendants of Ham and of the Meunites. No trace of them remains today. They killed everyone who lived there and took the land for themselves, because they wanted its good pastureland for their flocks. ⁴²Five hundred of these invaders from the tribe of Simeon went to Mount Seir, led by Pelatiah, Neariah, Rephaiah, and Uzziel—all sons of Ishi. ⁴³They destroyed the few Amalekites who had survived, and they have lived there ever since.

5 Descendants of Reuben

The oldest son of Israel* was Reuben. But since he dishonored his father by sleeping with one of his father's concubines, his birthright was given to the sons of his brother Joseph. For this reason, Reuben is not listed in the genealogical records as the firstborn son. ²The descendants of Judah became the most powerful tribe and provided a ruler for the nation,* but the birthright belonged to Joseph.

³The sons of Reuben, the oldest son of Israel, were Hanoch, Pallu, Hezron, and Carmi.

⁴The descendants of Joel were Shemaiah, Gog, Shimei, ⁵Micah, Reaiah, Baal, ⁶and Beerah. Beerah was the leader of the Reubenites when they were taken into captivity by King Tiglath-pileser* of Assyria. ⁷Beerah's* relatives are listed in their genealogical records by their clans: Jeiel (the leader), Zechariah, ⁸and Bela son of Azaz, son of Shema, son of Joel.

The Reubenites lived in the area that stretches from Aroer to Nebo and Baal-meon. ⁹And since they had so many livestock in the land of Gilead, they spread east toward the edge of the desert that stretches to the Euphrates River. ¹⁰During the reign of Saul, the Reubenites defeated the Hagrites in battle. Then they moved into the Hagrite settlements all along the eastern edge of Gilead.

4:24a As in Syriac version (see also Gen 46:10; Exod 6:15); Hebrew reads *Nemuel*.   4:24b As in parallel texts at Gen 46:10 and Exod 6:15; Hebrew reads *Zerah*.   4:33 As in some Greek manuscripts (see also Josh 19:8); Hebrew reads *Baal*.   4:39 As in Greek version; Hebrew reads *Gedor*.   4:41 The Hebrew term used here refers to the complete consecration of things or people to the LORD, either by destroying them or by giving them as an offering.   5:1 *Israel* is the name that God gave to Jacob.   5:2 Or *and from Judah came a prince*.   5:6 Hebrew *Tilgath-pilneser*, a variant spelling of Tiglath-pileser; also in 5:26.   5:7 Hebrew *His*.

Descendants of Gad

¹¹ Next to the Reubenites, the descendants of Gad lived in the land of Bashan as far east as Salecah. ¹² Joel was the leader in the land of Bashan, and Shapham was second-in-command, followed by Janai and Shaphat.

¹³ Their relatives, the leaders of seven other clans, were Michael, Meshullam, Sheba, Jorai, Jacan, Zia, and Eber. ¹⁴ These were all descendants of Abihail son of Huri, son of Jaroah, son of Gilead, son of Michael, son of Jeshishai, son of Jahdo, son of Buz. ¹⁵ Ahi son of Abdiel, son of Guni, was the leader of their clans.

¹⁶ The Gadites lived in the land of Gilead, in Bashan and its villages, and throughout all the pasturelands of Sharon. ¹⁷ All of these were listed in the genealogical records during the days of King Jotham of Judah and King Jeroboam of Israel.

The Tribes East of the Jordan

¹⁸ There were 44,760 capable warriors in the armies of Reuben, Gad, and the half-tribe of Manasseh. They were all skilled in combat and armed with shields, swords, and bows. ¹⁹ They waged war against the Hagrites, the Jeturites, the Naphishites, and the Nodabites. ²⁰ They cried out to God during the battle, and he answered their prayer because they trusted in him. So the Hagrites and all their allies were defeated. ²¹ The plunder taken from the Hagrites included 50,000 camels, 250,000 sheep and goats, 2,000 donkeys, and 100,000 captives. ²² Many of the Hagrites were killed in the battle because God was fighting against them. The people of Reuben, Gad, and Manasseh lived in their land until they were taken into exile.

²³ The half-tribe of Manasseh was very large and spread through the land from Bashan to Baal-hermon, Senir, and Mount Hermon. ²⁴ These were the leaders of their clans: Epher,* Ishi, Eliel, Azriel, Jeremiah, Hodaviah, and Jahdiel. These men had a great reputation as mighty warriors and leaders of their clans.

²⁵ But these tribes were unfaithful to the God of their ancestors. They worshiped the gods of the nations that God had destroyed. ²⁶ So the God of Israel caused King Pul of Assyria (also known as Tiglath-pileser) to invade the land and take away the people of Reuben, Gad, and the half-tribe of Manasseh as captives. The Assyrians exiled them to Halah, Habor, Hara, and the Gozan River, where they remain to this day.

6 The Priestly Line

¹* The sons of Levi were Gershon, Kohath, and Merari.
² The descendants of Kohath included Amram, Izhar, Hebron, and Uzziel.
³ The children of Amram were Aaron, Moses, and Miriam.
The sons of Aaron were Nadab, Abihu, Eleazar, and Ithamar.
⁴ Eleazar was the father of Phinehas. Phinehas was the father of Abishua.
⁵ Abishua was the father of Bukki. Bukki was the father of Uzzi.
⁶ Uzzi was the father of Zerahiah. Zerahiah was the father of Meraioth.
⁷ Meraioth was the father of Amariah. Amariah was the father of Ahitub.
⁸ Ahitub was the father of Zadok. Zadok was the father of Ahimaaz.
⁹ Ahimaaz was the father of Azariah. Azariah was the father of Johanan.
¹⁰ Johanan was the father of Azariah, the high priest at the Temple* built by Solomon in Jerusalem.
¹¹ Azariah was the father of Amariah. Amariah was the father of Ahitub.
¹² Ahitub was the father of Zadok. Zadok was the father of Shallum.
¹³ Shallum was the father of Hilkiah. Hilkiah was the father of Azariah.
¹⁴ Azariah was the father of Seraiah. Seraiah was the father of Jehozadak,
¹⁵ who went into exile when the LORD sent the people of Judah and Jerusalem into captivity under Nebuchadnezzar.

The Levite Clans

¹⁶* The sons of Levi were Gershon,* Kohath, and Merari.
¹⁷ The descendants of Gershon included Libni and Shimei.

5:24 As in Greek version and Latin Vulgate; Hebrew reads and Epher.   6:1 Verses 6:1-15 are numbered 5:27-41 in Hebrew text.   6:10 Hebrew the house.   6:16a Verses 6:16-81 are numbered 6:1-66 in Hebrew text.   6:16b Hebrew Gershom, a variant spelling of Gershon (see 6:1); also in 6:17, 20, 43, 62, 71.

18 The descendants of Kohath included Amram, Izhar, Hebron, and Uzziel. 19 The descendants of Merari included Mahli and Mushi.

The following were the Levite clans, listed according to their ancestral descent:

20 The descendants of Gershon included Libni, Jahath, Zimmah, 21 Joah, Iddo, Zerah, and Jeatherai.

22 The descendants of Kohath included Amminadab, Korah, Assir, 23 Elkanah, Abiasaph,* Assir, 24 Tahath, Uriel, Uzziah, and Shaul. 25 The descendants of Elkanah included Amasai, Ahimoth, 26 Elkanah, Zophai, Nahath, 27 Eliab, Jeroham, Elkanah, and Samuel.* 28 The sons of Samuel were Joel* (the older) and Abijah (the second). 29 The descendants of Merari included Mahli, Libni, Shimei, Uzzah, 30 Shimea, Haggiah, and Asaiah.

The Temple Musicians

31 David assigned the following men to lead the music at the house of the LORD after the Ark was placed there. 32 They ministered with music at the Tabernacle* until Solomon built the Temple of the LORD in Jerusalem. They carried out their work, following all the regulations handed down to them. 33 These are the men who served, along with their sons:

Heman the musician was from the clan of Kohath. His genealogy was traced back through Joel, Samuel, 34 Elkanah, Jeroham, Eliel, Toah, 35 Zuph, Elkanah, Mahath, Amasai, 36 Elkanah, Joel, Azariah, Zephaniah, 37 Tahath, Assir, Abiasaph, Korah, 38 Izhar, Kohath, Levi, and Israel.* 39 Heman's first assistant was Asaph from the clan of Gershon.* Asaph's genealogy was traced back through Berekiah, Shimea, 40 Michael, Baaseiah, Malkijah, 41 Ethni, Zerah, Adaiah, 42 Ethan, Zimmah, Shimei, 43 Jahath, Gershon, and Levi.

44 Heman's second assistant was Ethan from the clan of Merari. Ethan's genealogy was traced back through Kishi, Abdi, Malluch, 45 Hashabiah, Amaziah, Hilkiah, 46 Amzi, Bani, Shemer, 47 Mahli, Mushi, Merari, and Levi.

48 Their fellow Levites were appointed to various other tasks in the Tabernacle, the house of God.

Aaron's Descendants

49 Only Aaron and his descendants served as priests. They presented the offerings on the altar of burnt offering and the altar of incense, and they performed all the other duties related to the Most Holy Place. They made atonement for Israel by doing everything that Moses, the servant of God, had commanded them.

50 The descendants of Aaron were Eleazar, Phinehas, Abishua, 51 Bukki, Uzzi, Zerahiah, 52 Meraioth, Amariah, Ahitub, 53 Zadok, and Ahimaaz.

Territory for the Levites

54 This is a record of the towns and territory assigned by means of sacred lots to the descendants of Aaron, who were from the clan of Kohath. 55 This territory included Hebron and its surrounding pasturelands in Judah, 56 but the fields and outlying areas belonging to the city were given to Caleb son of Jephunneh. 57 So the descendants of Aaron were given the following towns, each with its pasturelands: Hebron (a city of refuge),* Libnah, Jattir, Eshtemoa, 58 Holon,* Debir, 59 Ain,* Juttah,* and Beth-shemesh. 60 And from the territory of Benjamin they were given Gibeon,* Geba, Alemeth, and Anathoth, each with its pasturelands. So thirteen towns were given to the descendants of Aaron. 61 The remaining descendants of Kohath received ten towns from the territory of the half-tribe of Manasseh by means of sacred lots.

62 The descendants of Gershon received by sacred lots thirteen towns from the ter-

ritories of Issachar, Asher, Naphtali, and from the Bashan area of Manasseh, east of the Jordan.

⁶³The descendants of Merari received by sacred lots twelve towns from the territories of Reuben, Gad, and Zebulun.

⁶⁴So the people of Israel assigned all these towns and pasturelands to the Levites. ⁶⁵The towns in the territories of Judah, Simeon, and Benjamin, mentioned above, were assigned to them by means of sacred lots.

⁶⁶The descendants of Kohath were given the following towns from the territory of Ephraim, each with its pasturelands: ⁶⁷Shechem (a city of refuge in the hill country of Ephraim),* Gezer, ⁶⁸Jokmeam, Bethhoron, ⁶⁹Aijalon, and Gath-rimmon. ⁷⁰The remaining descendants of Kohath were assigned the towns of Aner and Bileam from the territory of the half-tribe of Manasseh, each with its pasturelands.

⁷¹The descendants of Gershon received the towns of Golan (in Bashan) and Ashtaroth from the territory of the half-tribe of Manasseh, each with its pasturelands. ⁷²From the territory of Issachar, they were given Kedesh, Daberath, ⁷³Ramoth, and Anem, each with its pasturelands. ⁷⁴From the territory of Asher, they received Mashal, Abdon, ⁷⁵Hukok, and Rehob, each with its pasturelands. ⁷⁶From the territory of Naphtali, they were given Kedesh in Galilee, Hammon, and Kiriathaim, each with its pasturelands.

⁷⁷The remaining descendants of Merari received the towns of Jokneam, Kartah,* Rimmon,* and Tabor from the territory of Zebulun, each with its pasturelands. ⁷⁸From the territory of Reuben, east of the Jordan River opposite Jericho, they received Bezer (a desert town), Jahaz,* ⁷⁹Kedemoth, and Mephaath, each with its pasturelands. ⁸⁰And from the territory of Gad, they received Ramoth in Gilead, Mahanaim, ⁸¹Heshbon, and Jazer, each with its pasturelands.

7 Descendants of Issachar

The four sons of Issachar were Tola, Puah, Jashub, and Shimron.

²The sons of Tola were Uzzi, Rephaiah, Jeriel, Jahmai, Ibsam, and Shemuel. Each of them was the leader of an ancestral clan. At the time of King David, the total number of mighty warriors listed in the records of these clans was 22,600.

³The son of Uzzi was Izrahiah. The sons of Izrahiah were Michael, Obadiah, Joel, and Isshiah. These five became the leaders of clans. ⁴All of them had many wives and many sons, so the total number of men available for military service among their descendants was 36,000.

⁵The total number of mighty warriors from all the clans of the tribe of Issachar was 87,000. All of them were listed in their genealogical records.

Descendants of Benjamin

⁶Three of Benjamin's sons were Bela, Beker, and Jediael.

⁷The five sons of Bela were Ezbon, Uzzi, Uzziel, Jerimoth, and Iri. Each of them was the leader of an ancestral clan. The total number of mighty warriors from these clans was 22,034, as listed in their genealogical records.

⁸The sons of Beker were Zemirah, Joash, Eliezer, Elioenai, Omri, Jeremoth, Abijah, Anathoth, and Alemeth. ⁹Each of them was the leader of an ancestral clan. The total number of mighty warriors and leaders from these clans was 20,200, as listed in their genealogical records.

¹⁰The son of Jediael was Bilhan. The sons of Bilhan were Jeush, Benjamin, Ehud, Kenaanah, Zethan, Tarshish, and Ahishahar. ¹¹Each of them was the leader of an ancestral clan. From these clans the total number of mighty warriors ready for war was 17,200.

¹²The sons of Ir were Shuppim and Huppim. Hushim was the son of Aher.

Descendants of Naphtali

¹³The sons of Naphtali were Jahzeel,* Guni, Jezer, and Shillem.* They were all descendants of Jacob's concubine Bilhah.

6:66-67 As in parallel text at Josh 21:21. Hebrew text reads *were given the cities of refuge: Shechem in the hill country of Ephraim, and the following towns, each with its pasturelands.* **6:77a** As in Greek version (see also Josh 21:34); Hebrew lacks *Jokneam, Kartah.* **6:77b** As in Greek version (see also Josh 19:13); Hebrew reads *Rimmono.* **6:78** Hebrew *Jahzah,* a variant spelling of Jahaz. **7:13a** As in parallel text at Gen 46:24; Hebrew reads *Jahziel,* a variant spelling of Jahzeel. **7:13b** As in some Hebrew and Greek manuscripts (see also Gen 46:24; Num 26:49); most Hebrew manuscripts read *Shallum.*

Descendants of Manasseh

¹⁴The descendants of Manasseh through his Aramean concubine included Asriel. She also bore Makir, the father of Gilead. ¹⁵Makir found wives for* Huppim and Shuppim. Makir had a sister named Maacah. One of his descendants was Zelophehad, who had only daughters. ¹⁶Makir's wife, Maacah, gave birth to a son whom she named Peresh. His brother's name was Sheresh. The sons of Peresh were Ulam and Rakem. ¹⁷The son of Ulam was Bedan. All these were considered Gileadites, descendants of Makir son of Manasseh.

¹⁸Makir's sister Hammoleketh gave birth to Ishhod, Abiezer, and Mahlah. ¹⁹The sons of Shemida were Ahian, Shechem, Likhi, and Aniam.

Descendants of Ephraim

²⁰The descendants of Ephraim were Shuthelah, Bered, Tahath, Eleadah, Tahath, ²¹Zabad, Shuthelah, Ezer, and Elead. These two were killed trying to steal livestock from the local farmers near Gath. ²²Their father, Ephraim, mourned for them a long time, and his relatives came to comfort him. ²³Afterward Ephraim slept with his wife, and she became pregnant and gave birth to a son. Ephraim named him Beriah* because of the tragedy his family had suffered. ²⁴He had a daughter named Sheerah. She built the towns of Lower and Upper Beth-horon and Uzzen-sheerah.

²⁵The descendants of Ephraim included Rephah, Resheph, Telah, Tahan, ²⁶Ladan, Ammihud, Elishama, ²⁷Nun, and Joshua.

²⁸The descendants of Ephraim lived in the territory that included Bethel and its surrounding towns to the south, Naaran to the east, Gezer and its villages to the west, and Shechem and its surrounding villages to the north as far as Ayyah and its towns. ²⁹Along the border of Manasseh were the towns of Beth-shan,* Taanach, Megiddo, Dor, and their surrounding villages. The descendants of Joseph son of Israel* lived in these towns.

Descendants of Asher

³⁰The sons of Asher were Imnah, Ishvah, Ishvi, and Beriah. They had a sister named Serah. ³¹The sons of Beriah were Heber and Malkiel (the father of Birzaith). ³²The sons of Heber were Japhlet, Shomer, and Hotham. They had a sister named Shua. ³³The sons of Japhlet were Pasach, Bimhal, and Ashvath. ³⁴The sons of Shomer were Ahi,* Rohgah, Hubbah, and Aram. ³⁵The sons of his brother Helem* were Zophah, Imna, Shelesh, and Amal. ³⁶The sons of Zophah were Suah, Harnepher, Shual, Beri, Imrah, ³⁷Bezer, Hod, Shamma, Shilshah, Ithran,* and Beera. ³⁸The sons of Jether were Jephunneh, Pispah, and Ara. ³⁹The sons of Ulla were Arah, Hanniel, and Rizia.

⁴⁰Each of these descendants of Asher was the head of an ancestral clan. They were all select men—mighty warriors and outstanding leaders. The total number of men available for military service was 26,000, as listed in their genealogical records.

8 Descendants of Benjamin

Benjamin's first son was Bela, the second was Ashbel, the third was Aharah, ²the fourth was Nohah, and the fifth was Rapha. ³The sons of Bela were Addar, Gera, Abihud,* ⁴Abishua, Naaman, Ahoah, ⁵Gera, Shephuphan, and Huram. ⁶The sons of Ehud, leaders of the clans living at Geba, were exiled to Manahath. ⁷Ehud's sons were Naaman, Ahijah, and Gera. Gera, who led them into exile, was the father of Uzza and Ahihud.* ⁸After Shaharaim divorced his wives Hushim and Baara, he had children in the land of Moab. ⁹His wife Hodesh gave birth to Jobab, Zibia, Mesha, Malcam, ¹⁰Jeuz, Sakia, and Mirmah. These sons all became the leaders of clans. ¹¹Shaharaim's wife Hushim had already

---

7:15 Or *Makir took a wife from.* The meaning of the Hebrew is uncertain.   7:23 *Beriah* sounds like a Hebrew term meaning "tragedy" or "misfortune."   7:29a Hebrew *Beth-shean,* a variant spelling of Beth-shan.   7:29b *Israel* is the name that God gave to Jacob.   7:34 Or *The sons of Shomer, his brother, were.*   7:35 Possibly another name for *Hotham;* compare 7:32.   7:37 Possibly another name for *Jether;* compare 7:38.   8:3 Possibly *Gera the father of Ehud;* compare 8:6.   8:7 Or *Gera, that is Heglam, was the father of Uzza and Ahihud.*

given birth to Abitub and Elpaal. 12 The sons of Elpaal were Eber, Misham, Shemed (who built the towns of Ono and Lod and their nearby villages), 13 Beriah, and Shema. They were the leaders of the clans living in Aijalon, and they drove out the inhabitants of Gath.

14 Ahio, Shashak, Jeremoth, 15 Zebadiah, Arad, Eder, 16 Michael, Ishpah, and Joha were the sons of Beriah.

17 Zebadiah, Meshullam, Hizki, Heber, 18 Ishmerai, Izliah, and Jobab were the sons of Elpaal.

19 Jakim, Zicri, Zabdi, 20 Elienai, Zillethai, Eliel, 21 Adaiah, Beraiah, and Shimrath were the sons of Shimei.

22 Ishpan, Eber, Eliel, 23 Abdon, Zicri, Hanan, 24 Hananiah, Elam, Anthothijah, 25 Iphdeiah, and Penuel were the sons of Shashak.

26 Shamsherai, Shehariah, Athaliah, 27 Jaareshiah, Elijah, and Zicri were the sons of Jeroham.

28 These were the leaders of the ancestral clans; they were listed in their genealogical records, and they all lived in Jerusalem.

The Family of Saul

29 Jeiel* (the father of* Gibeon) lived in the town of Gibeon. His wife's name was Maacah, 30 and his oldest son was named Abdon. Jeiel's other sons were Zur, Kish, Baal, Ner,* Nadab, 31 Gedor, Ahio, Zechariah,* 32 and Mikloth, who was the father of Shimeam.* All these families lived near each other in Jerusalem.

33 Ner was the father of Kish.
Kish was the father of Saul.
Saul was the father of Jonathan, Malkishua, Abinadab, and Esh-baal.

34 Jonathan was the father of Merib-baal.
Merib-baal was the father of Micah.

35 Micah was the father of Pithon, Melech, Tahrea,* and Ahaz.

36 Ahaz was the father of Jadah.*
Jadah was the father of Alemeth, Azmaveth, and Zimri.
Zimri was the father of Moza.

37 Moza was the father of Binea.

Binea was the father of Rephaiah.*
Rephaiah was the father of Eleasah.
Eleasah was the father of Azel.

38 Azel had six sons: Azrikam, Bokeru, Ishmael, Sheariah, Obadiah, and Hanan. These were the sons of Azel.

39 Azel's brother Eshek had three sons: the first was Ulam, the second was Jeush, and the third was Eliphelet. 40 Ulam's sons were all mighty warriors and expert archers. They had many sons and grandsons—150 in all.

All these were descendants of Benjamin.

9 So all Israel was listed in the genealogical records in *The Book of the Kings of Israel.*

The Returning Exiles

The people of Judah were exiled to Babylon because they were unfaithful to the LORD. 2 The first of the exiles to return to their property in their former towns were priests, Levites, Temple servants, and other Israelites. 3 Some of the people from the tribes of Judah, Benjamin, Ephraim, and Manasseh came and settled in Jerusalem.

4 One family that returned was that of Uthai son of Ammihud, son of Omri, son of Imri, son of Bani, a descendant of Perez son of Judah.

5 Others returned from the Shilonite clan, including Asaiah (the oldest) and his sons.

6 From the Zerahite clan, Jeuel returned with his relatives.
In all, 690 families from the tribe of Judah returned.

7 From the tribe of Benjamin came Sallu son of Meshullam, son of Hodaviah, son of Hassenuah; 8 Ibneiah son of Jeroham; Elah son of Uzzi, son of Micri; and Meshullam son of Shephatiah, son of Reuel, son of Ibnijah.

9 These men were all leaders of clans, and they were listed in their genealogical records. In all, 956 families from the tribe of Benjamin returned.

8:29a As in some Greek manuscripts (see also 9:35); Hebrew lacks *Jeiel.* 8:29b Or *the founder of.* 8:30 As in some Greek manuscripts (see also 9:36); Hebrew lacks *Ner.* 8:31 As in parallel text at 9:37; Hebrew reads *Zeker,* a variant spelling of Zechariah. 8:32 As in parallel text at 9:38; Hebrew reads *Shimeah,* a variant spelling of Shimeam. 8:35 As in parallel text at 9:41; Hebrew reads *Tarea,* a variant spelling of Tahrea. 8:36 As in parallel text at 9:42; Hebrew reads *Jehoaddah,* a variant spelling of Jadah. 8:37 As in parallel text at 9:43; Hebrew reads *Raphah,* a variant spelling of Rephaiah.

The Returning Priests

[10] Among the priests who returned were Jedaiah, Jehoiarib, Jakin, [11] Azariah son of Hilkiah, son of Meshullam, son of Zadok, son of Meraioth, son of Ahitub. Azariah was the chief officer of the house of God.

[12] Other returning priests were Adaiah son of Jeroham, son of Pashhur, son of Malkijah, and Maasai son of Adiel, son of Jahzerah, son of Meshullam, son of Meshillemith, son of Immer.

[13] In all, 1,760 priests returned. They were heads of clans and very able men. They were responsible for ministering at the house of God.

The Returning Levites

[14] The Levites who returned were Shemaiah son of Hasshub, son of Azrikam, son of Hashabiah, a descendant of Merari; [15] Bakbakkar; Heresh; Galal; Mattaniah son of Mica, son of Zicri, son of Asaph; [16] Obadiah son of Shemaiah, son of Galal, son of Jeduthun; and Berekiah son of Asa, son of Elkanah, who lived in the area of Netophah.

[17] The gatekeepers who returned were Shallum, Akkub, Talmon, Ahiman, and their relatives. Shallum was the chief gatekeeper. [18] Prior to this time, they were responsible for the King's Gate on the east side. These men served as gatekeepers for the camps of the Levites. [19] Shallum was the son of Kore, a descendant of Abiasaph,* from the clan of Korah. He and his relatives, the Korahites, were responsible for guarding the entrance to the sanctuary, just as their ancestors had guarded the Tabernacle in the camp of the LORD.

[20] Phinehas son of Eleazar had been in charge of the gatekeepers in earlier times, and the LORD had been with him. [21] And later Zechariah son of Meshelemiah was responsible for guarding the entrance to the Tabernacle.*

[22] In all, there were 212 gatekeepers in those days, and they were listed according to the genealogies in their villages. David and Samuel the seer had appointed their ancestors because they were reliable men. [23] These gatekeepers and their descendants, by their divisions, were responsible for guarding the entrance to the house of the LORD when that house was a tent. [24] The gatekeepers were stationed on all four sides—east, west, north, and south. [25] Their relatives in the villages came regularly to share their duties for seven-day periods.

[26] The four chief gatekeepers, all Levites, were trusted officials, for they were responsible for the rooms and treasuries at the house of God. [27] They would spend the night around the house of God, since it was their duty to guard it and to open the gates every morning.

[28] Some of the gatekeepers were assigned to care for the various articles used in worship. They checked them in and out to avoid any loss. [29] Others were responsible for the furnishings, the items in the sanctuary, and the supplies, such as choice flour, wine, olive oil, frankincense, and spices. [30] But it was the priests who blended the spices. [31] Mattithiah, a Levite and the oldest son of Shallum the Korahite, was entrusted with baking the bread used in the offerings. [32] And some members of the clan of Kohath were in charge of preparing the bread to be set on the table each Sabbath day.

[33] The musicians, all prominent Levites, lived at the Temple. They were exempt from other responsibilities since they were on duty at all hours. [34] All these men lived in Jerusalem. They were the heads of Levite families and were listed as prominent leaders in their genealogical records.

King Saul's Family Tree

[35] Jeiel (the father of* Gibeon) lived in the town of Gibeon. His wife's name was Maacah, [36] and his oldest son was named Abdon. Jeiel's other sons were Zur, Kish, Baal, Ner, Nadab, [37] Gedor, Ahio, Zechariah, and Mikloth. [38] Mikloth was the father of Shimeam. All these families lived near each other in Jerusalem.

[39] Ner was the father of Kish.
Kish was the father of Saul.
Saul was the father of Jonathan, Malkishua, Abinadab, and Esh-baal.

9:19 Hebrew *Ebiasaph,* a variant spelling of Abiasaph; compare Exod 6:24.   **9:21** Hebrew *Tent of Meeting.*   **9:35** Or *the founder of.*

⁴⁰ Jonathan was the father of Merib-baal.
Merib-baal was the father of Micah.

⁴¹ The sons of Micah were Pithon, Melech, Tahrea, and Ahaz.*

⁴² Ahaz was the father of Jadah.*
Jadah was the father of Alemeth, Azmaveth, and Zimri.
Zimri was the father of Moza.

⁴³ Moza was the father of Binea.
Binea's son was Rephaiah.
Rephaiah's son was Eleasah.
Eleasah's son was Azel.

⁴⁴ Azel had six sons, whose names were Azrikam, Bokeru, Ishmael, Sheariah, Obadiah, and Hanan. These were the sons of Azel.

10 The Death of King Saul

Now the Philistines attacked Israel, and the men of Israel fled before them. Many were slaughtered on the slopes of Mount Gilboa. ²The Philistines closed in on Saul and his sons, and they killed three of his sons—Jonathan, Abinadab, and Malkishua. ³The fighting grew very fierce around Saul, and the Philistine archers caught up with him and wounded him.

⁴Saul groaned to his armor bearer, "Take your sword and kill me before these pagan Philistines come to taunt and torture me."

But his armor bearer was afraid and would not do it. So Saul took his own sword and fell on it. ⁵When his armor bearer realized that Saul was dead, he fell on his own sword and died. ⁶So Saul and his three sons died there together, bringing his dynasty to an end.

⁷When all the Israelites in the Jezreel Valley saw that their army had fled and that Saul and his sons were dead, they abandoned their towns and fled. So the Philistines moved in and occupied their towns.

⁸The next day, when the Philistines went out to strip the dead, they found the bodies of Saul and his sons on Mount Gilboa. ⁹So they stripped off Saul's armor and cut off his head. Then they proclaimed the good news of Saul's death before their idols and to the people throughout the land of Philistia. ¹⁰They placed his armor in the temple of their gods, and they fastened his head to the temple of Dagon.

¹¹But when everyone in Jabesh-gilead heard about everything the Philistines had done to Saul, ¹²all their mighty warriors brought the bodies of Saul and his sons back to Jabesh. Then they buried their bones beneath the great tree at Jabesh, and they fasted for seven days.

¹³So Saul died because he was unfaithful to the LORD. He failed to obey the LORD's command, and he even consulted a medium ¹⁴instead of asking the LORD for guidance. So the LORD killed him and turned the kingdom over to David son of Jesse.

11 David Becomes King of All Israel

Then all Israel gathered before David at Hebron and told him, "We are your own flesh and blood. ²In the past,* even when Saul was king, you were the one who really led the forces of Israel. And the LORD your God told you, 'You will be the shepherd of my people Israel. You will be the leader of my people Israel.'"

³So there at Hebron, David made a covenant before the LORD with all the elders of Israel. And they anointed him king of Israel, just as the LORD had promised through Samuel.

David Captures Jerusalem

⁴Then David and all Israel went to Jerusalem (or Jebus, as it used to be called), where the Jebusites, the original inhabitants of the land, were living. ⁵The people of Jebus taunted David, saying, "You'll never get in here!" But David captured the fortress of Zion, which is now called the City of David.

⁶David had said to his troops, "Whoever is first to attack the Jebusites will become the commander of my armies!" And Joab, the son of David's sister Zeruiah, was first to attack, so he became the commander of David's armies.

⁷David made the fortress his home, and that is why it is called the City of David. ⁸He extended the city from the supporting terraces* to the surrounding area, while Joab

---

9:41 As in Syriac version and Latin Vulgate (see also 8:35); Hebrew lacks *and Ahaz*. **9:42** As in some Hebrew manuscripts and Greek version (see also 8:36); Hebrew reads *Jarah*. **11:2** Or *For some time*. **11:8** Hebrew *the millo*. The meaning of the Hebrew is uncertain.

rebuilt the rest of Jerusalem. ⁹And David became more and more powerful, because the LORD of Heaven's Armies was with him.

David's Mightiest Warriors

¹⁰These are the leaders of David's mighty warriors. Together with all Israel, they decided to make David their king, just as the LORD had promised concerning Israel.

¹¹Here is the record of David's mightiest warriors: The first was Jashobeam the Hacmonite, who was leader of the Three—the mightiest warriors among David's men.* He once used his spear to kill 300 enemy warriors in a single battle.

¹²Next in rank among the Three was Eleazar son of Dodai,* a descendant of Ahoah. ¹³He was with David in the battle against the Philistines at Pas-dammim. The battle took place in a field full of barley, and the Israelite army fled. ¹⁴But Eleazar and David* held their ground in the middle of the field and beat back the Philistines. So the LORD saved them by giving them a great victory.

¹⁵Once when David was at the rock near the cave of Adullam, the Philistine army was camped in the valley of Rephaim. The Three (who were among the Thirty—an elite group among David's fighting men) went down to meet him there. ¹⁶David was staying in the stronghold at the time, and a Philistine detachment had occupied the town of Bethlehem.

¹⁷David remarked longingly to his men, "Oh, how I would love some of that good water from the well by the gate in Bethlehem." ¹⁸So the Three broke through the Philistine lines, drew some water from the well by the gate in Bethlehem, and brought it back to David. But David refused to drink it. Instead, he poured it out as an offering to the LORD. ¹⁹"God forbid that I should drink this!" he exclaimed. "This water is as precious as the blood of these men* who risked their lives to bring it to me." So David did not drink it. These are examples of the exploits of the Three.

David's Thirty Mighty Men

²⁰Abishai, the brother of Joab, was the leader of the Thirty.* He once used his spear to kill 300 enemy warriors in a single battle. It was by such feats that he became as famous as the Three. ²¹Abishai was the most famous of the Thirty and was their commander, though he was not one of the Three.

²²There was also Benaiah son of Jehoiada, a valiant warrior from Kabzeel. He did many heroic deeds, which included killing two champions* of Moab. Another time, on a snowy day, he chased a lion down into a pit and killed it. ²³Once, armed only with a club, he killed an Egyptian warrior who was 7½ feet* tall and whose spear was as thick as a weaver's beam. Benaiah wrenched the spear from the Egyptian's hand and killed him with it. ²⁴Deeds like these made Benaiah as famous as the three mightiest warriors. ²⁵He was more honored than the other members of the Thirty, though he was not one of the Three. And David made him captain of his bodyguard.

²⁶David's mighty warriors also included:

Asahel, Joab's brother;
Elhanan son of Dodo from Bethlehem;
²⁷ Shammah from Harod;*
Helez from Pelon;
²⁸ Ira son of Ikkesh from Tekoa;
Abiezer from Anathoth;
²⁹ Sibbecai from Hushah;
Zalmon* from Ahoah;
³⁰ Maharai from Netophah;
Heled son of Baanah from Netophah;
³¹ Ithai son of Ribai from Gibeah (in the land of Benjamin);
Benaiah from Pirathon;
³² Hurai from near Nahale-gaash*;
Abi-albon* from Arabah;
³³ Azmaveth from Bahurim*;
Eliahba from Shaalbon;
³⁴ the sons of Jashen* from Gizon;
Jonathan son of Shagee from Harar;
³⁵ Ahiam son of Sharar* from Harar;
Eliphal son of Ur;

11:11 As in some Greek manuscripts (see also 2 Sam 23:8); Hebrew reads *leader of the Thirty*, or *leader of the captains*. 11:12 As in parallel text at 2 Sam 23:9 (see also 1 Chr 27:4); Hebrew reads *Dodo*, a variant spelling of Dodai. 11:14 Hebrew *they*. 11:19 Hebrew *Shall I drink the lifeblood of these men?* 11:20 As in Syriac version; Hebrew reads *the Three*; also in 11:21. 11:22 Or *two sons of Ariel*. 11:23 Hebrew *5 cubits* [2.3 meters]. 11:27 As in parallel text at 2 Sam 23:25; Hebrew reads *Shammoth from Haror*. 11:29 As in parallel text at 2 Sam 23:28; Hebrew reads *Ilai*. 11:32a Or *from the ravines of Gaash*. 11:32b As in parallel text at 2 Sam 23:31; Hebrew reads *Abiel*. 11:33 As in parallel text at 2 Sam 23:31; Hebrew reads *Baharum*. 11:34 As in parallel text at 2 Sam 23:32; Hebrew reads *sons of Hashem*. 11:35 As in parallel text at 2 Sam 23:33; Hebrew reads *son of Sacar*.

³⁶ Hepher from Mekerah;
Ahijah from Pelon;
³⁷ Hezro from Carmel;
Paarai* son of Ezbai;
³⁸ Joel, the brother of Nathan;
Mibhar son of Hagri;
³⁹ Zelek from Ammon;
Naharai from Beeroth, Joab's armor
bearer;
⁴⁰ Ira from Jattir;
Gareb from Jattir;
⁴¹ Uriah the Hittite;
Zabad son of Ahlai;
⁴² Adina son of Shiza, the Reubenite leader
who had thirty men with him;
⁴³ Hanan son of Maacah;
Joshaphat from Mithna;
⁴⁴ Uzzia from Ashtaroth;
Shama and Jeiel, the sons of Hotham,
from Aroer;
⁴⁵ Jediael son of Shimri;
Joha, his brother, from Tiz;
⁴⁶ Eliel from Mahavah;
Jeribai and Joshaviah, the sons of
Elnaam;
Ithmah from Moab;
⁴⁷ Eliel and Obed;
Jaasiel from Zobah.*

12 Warriors Join David's Army

The following men joined David at Ziklag while he was hiding from Saul son of Kish. They were among the warriors who fought beside David in battle. ² All of them were expert archers, and they could shoot arrows or sling stones with their left hand as well as their right. They were all relatives of Saul from the tribe of Benjamin. ³ Their leader was Ahiezer son of Shemaah from Gibeah; his brother Joash was second-in-command. These were the other warriors:

Jeziel and Pelet, sons of Azmaveth;
Beracah;
Jehu from Anathoth;
⁴ Ishmaiah from Gibeon, a famous
warrior and leader among the Thirty;
*Jeremiah, Jahaziel, Johanan, and
Jozabad from Gederah;
⁵ Eluzai, Jerimoth, Bealiah, Shemariah,
and Shephatiah from Haruph;

⁶ Elkanah, Isshiah, Azarel, Joezer, and
Jashobeam, who were Korahites;
⁷ Joelah and Zebadiah, sons of Jeroham
from Gedor.

⁸ Some brave and experienced warriors from the tribe of Gad also defected to David while he was at the stronghold in the wilderness. They were expert with both shield and spear, as fierce as lions and as swift as deer on the mountains.

⁹ Ezer was their leader.
Obadiah was second.
Eliab was third.
¹⁰ Mishmannah was fourth.
Jeremiah was fifth.
¹¹ Attai was sixth.
Eliel was seventh.
¹² Johanan was eighth.
Elzabad was ninth.
¹³ Jeremiah was tenth.
Macbannai was eleventh.

¹⁴ These warriors from Gad were army commanders. The weakest among them could take on a hundred regular troops, and the strongest could take on a thousand! ¹⁵ These were the men who crossed the Jordan River during its seasonal flooding at the beginning of the year and drove out all the people living in the lowlands on both the east and west banks.

¹⁶ Others from Benjamin and Judah came to David at the stronghold. ¹⁷ David went out to meet them and said, "If you have come in peace to help me, we are friends. But if you have come to betray me to my enemies when I am innocent, then may the God of our ancestors see it and punish you."

¹⁸ Then the Spirit came upon Amasai, the leader of the Thirty, and he said,

"We are yours, David!
We are on your side, son of Jesse.
Peace and prosperity be with you,
and success to all who help you,
for your God is the one who helps
you."

So David let them join him, and he made them officers over his troops.

¹⁹ Some men from Manasseh defected

11:37 As in parallel text at 2 Sam 23:35; Hebrew reads *Naarai*.   **11:47** Or *the Mezobaite*.   **12:4** Verses 12:4b-40 are numbered 12:5-41 in Hebrew text.

from the Israelite army and joined David when he set out with the Philistines to fight against Saul. But as it turned out, the Philistine rulers refused to let David and his men go with them. After much discussion, they sent them back, for they said, "It will cost us our heads if David switches loyalties to Saul and turns against us."

20 Here is a list of the men from Manasseh who defected to David as he was returning to Ziklag: Adnah, Jozabad, Jediael, Michael, Jozabad, Elihu, and Zillethai. Each commanded 1,000 troops from the tribe of Manasseh. 21 They helped David chase down bands of raiders, for they were all brave and able warriors who became commanders in his army. 22 Day after day more men joined David until he had a great army, like the army of God.

23 These are the numbers of armed warriors who joined David at Hebron. They were all eager to see David become king instead of Saul, just as the LORD had promised.

24 From the tribe of Judah, there were 6,800 warriors armed with shields and spears.

25 From the tribe of Simeon, there were 7,100 brave warriors.

26 From the tribe of Levi, there were 4,600 warriors. 27 This included Jehoiada, leader of the family of Aaron, who had 3,700 under his command. 28 This also included Zadok, a brave young warrior, with 22 members of his family who were all officers.

29 From the tribe of Benjamin, Saul's relatives, there were 3,000 warriors. Most of the men from Benjamin had remained loyal to Saul until this time.

30 From the tribe of Ephraim, there were 20,800 brave warriors, each highly respected in his own clan.

31 From the half-tribe of Manasseh west of the Jordan, 18,000 men were designated by name to help David become king.

32 From the tribe of Issachar, there were 200 leaders of the tribe with their relatives. All these men understood the signs of the times and knew the best course for Israel to take.

33 From the tribe of Zebulun, there were 50,000 skilled warriors. They were fully armed and prepared for battle and completely loyal to David.

34 From the tribe of Naphtali, there were 1,000 officers and 37,000 warriors armed with shields and spears.

35 From the tribe of Dan, there were 28,600 warriors, all prepared for battle.

36 From the tribe of Asher, there were 40,000 trained warriors, all prepared for battle.

37 From the east side of the Jordan River— where the tribes of Reuben and Gad and the half-tribe of Manasseh lived—there were 120,000 troops armed with every kind of weapon.

38 All these men came in battle array to Hebron with the single purpose of making David the king over all Israel. In fact, everyone in Israel agreed that David should be their king. 39 They feasted and drank with David for three days, for preparations had been made by their relatives for their arrival. 40 And people from as far away as Issachar, Zebulun, and Naphtali brought food on donkeys, camels, mules, and oxen. Vast supplies of flour, fig cakes, clusters of raisins, wine, olive oil, cattle, sheep, and goats were brought to the celebration. There was great joy throughout the land of Israel.

13 David Attempts to Move the Ark

David consulted with all his officials, including the generals and captains of his army.* 2 Then he addressed the entire assembly of Israel as follows: "If you approve and if it is the will of the LORD our God, let us send messages to all the Israelites throughout the land, including the priests and Levites in their towns and pasturelands. Let us invite them to come and join us. 3 It is time to bring back the Ark of our God, for we neglected it during the reign of Saul."

4 The whole assembly agreed to this, for the people could see it was the right thing to do. 5 So David summoned all Israel, from the Shihor Brook of Egypt in the south all the way to the town of Lebo-hamath in the north, to join in bringing the Ark of God

13:1 Hebrew the commanders of thousands and of hundreds.

from Kiriath-jearim. ⁶Then David and all Israel went to Baalah of Judah (also called Kiriath-jearim) to bring back the Ark of God, which bears the name* of the LORD who is enthroned between the cherubim. ⁷They placed the Ark of God on a new cart and brought it from Abinadab's house. Uzzah and Ahio were guiding the cart. ⁸David and all Israel were celebrating before God with all their might, singing songs and playing all kinds of musical instruments—lyres, harps, tambourines, cymbals, and trumpets.

⁹But when they arrived at the threshing floor of Nacon,* the oxen stumbled, and Uzzah reached out his hand to steady the Ark. ¹⁰Then the LORD's anger was aroused against Uzzah, and he struck him dead because he had laid his hand on the Ark. So Uzzah died there in the presence of God.

¹¹David was angry because the LORD's anger had burst out against Uzzah. He named that place Perez-uzzah (which means "to burst out against Uzzah"), as it is still called today.

¹²David was now afraid of God, and he asked, "How can I ever bring the Ark of God back into my care?" ¹³So David did not move the Ark into the City of David. Instead, he took it to the house of Obed-edom of Gath. ¹⁴The Ark of God remained there in Obed-edom's house for three months, and the LORD blessed the household of Obed-edom and everything he owned.

14 David's Palace and Family

Then King Hiram of Tyre sent messengers to David, along with cedar timber, and stonemasons and carpenters to build him a palace. ²And David realized that the LORD had confirmed him as king over Israel and had greatly blessed his kingdom for the sake of his people Israel.

³Then David married more wives in Jerusalem, and they had more sons and daughters. ⁴These are the names of David's sons who were born in Jerusalem: Shammua, Shobab, Nathan, Solomon, ⁵Ibhar, Elishua, Elpelet, ⁶Nogah, Nepheg, Japhia, ⁷Elishama, Eliada,* and Eliphelet.

David Conquers the Philistines

⁸When the Philistines heard that David had been anointed king over all Israel, they mobilized all their forces to capture him. But David was told they were coming, so he marched out to meet them. ⁹The Philistines arrived and made a raid in the valley of Rephaim. ¹⁰So David asked God, "Should I go out to fight the Philistines? Will you hand them over to me?"

The LORD replied, "Yes, go ahead. I will hand them over to you."

¹¹So David and his troops went up to Baal-perazim and defeated the Philistines there. "God did it!" David exclaimed. "He used me to burst through my enemies like a raging flood!" So they named that place Baal-perazim (which means "the Lord who bursts through"). ¹²The Philistines had abandoned their gods there, so David gave orders to burn them.

¹³But after a while the Philistines returned and raided the valley again. ¹⁴And once again David asked God what to do. "Do not attack them straight on," God replied. "Instead, circle around behind and attack them near the poplar* trees. ¹⁵When you hear a sound like marching feet in the tops of the poplar trees, go out and attack! That will be the signal that God is moving ahead of you to strike down the Philistine army." ¹⁶So David did what God commanded, and they struck down the Philistine army all the way from Gibeon to Gezer.

¹⁷So David's fame spread everywhere, and the LORD caused all the nations to fear David.

15 Preparing to Move the Ark

David now built several buildings for himself in the City of David. He also prepared a place for the Ark of God and set up a special tent for it. ²Then he commanded, "No one except the Levites may carry the Ark of God. The LORD has chosen them to carry the Ark of the LORD and to serve him forever."

³Then David summoned all Israel to Jerusalem to bring the Ark of the LORD to the place he had prepared for it. ⁴This is the number of the descendants of Aaron (the

---

13:6 Or the Ark of God, where the Name is proclaimed—the name. **13:9** As in parallel text at 2 Sam 6:6; Hebrew reads Kidon. **14:7** Hebrew Beeliada, a variant spelling of Eliada; compare 3:8 and parallel text at 2 Sam 5:16. **14:14** Or aspen, or balsam; also in 14:15. The exact identification of this tree is uncertain.

priests) and the Levites who were called together:

⁵From the clan of Kohath, 120, with Uriel as their leader.

⁶From the clan of Merari, 220, with Asaiah as their leader.

⁷From the clan of Gershon,* 130, with Joel as their leader.

⁸From the descendants of Elizaphan, 200, with Shemaiah as their leader.

⁹From the descendants of Hebron, 80, with Eliel as their leader.

¹⁰From the descendants of Uzziel, 112, with Amminadab as their leader.

¹¹ Then David summoned the priests, Zadok and Abiathar, and these Levite leaders: Uriel, Asaiah, Joel, Shemaiah, Eliel, and Amminadab. ¹²He said to them, "You are the leaders of the Levite families. You must purify yourselves and all your fellow Levites, so you can bring the Ark of the LORD, the God of Israel, to the place I have prepared for it. ¹³Because you Levites did not carry the Ark the first time, the anger of the LORD our God burst out against us. We failed to ask God how to move it properly." ¹⁴So the priests and the Levites purified themselves in order to bring the Ark of the LORD, the God of Israel, to Jerusalem. ¹⁵Then the Levites carried the Ark of God on their shoulders with its carrying poles, just as the LORD had instructed Moses.

¹⁶David also ordered the Levite leaders to appoint a choir of Levites who were singers and musicians to sing joyful songs to the accompaniment of harps, lyres, and cymbals. ¹⁷So the Levites appointed Heman son of Joel along with his fellow Levites: Asaph son of Berekiah, and Ethan son of Kushaiah from the clan of Merari. ¹⁸The following men were chosen as their assistants: Zechariah, Jaaziel,* Shemiramoth, Jehiel, Unni, Eliab, Benaiah, Maaseiah, Mattithiah, Eliphelehu, Mikneiah, and the gatekeepers—Obed-edom and Jeiel. ¹⁹The musicians Heman, Asaph, and Ethan were chosen to sound the bronze cymbals. ²⁰Zechariah, Aziel, Shemiramoth, Jehiel, Unni, Eliab, Maaseiah, and Benaiah were chosen to play the harps.* ²¹Mattithiah, Eliphelehu, Mikneiah, Obed-edom, Jeiel, and Azaziah were chosen to play the lyres.* ²²Kenaniah, the head Levite, was chosen as the choir leader because of his skill.

²³Berekiah and Elkanah were chosen to guard* the Ark. ²⁴Shebaniah, Joshaphat, Nethanel, Amasai, Zechariah, Benaiah, and Eliezer—all of whom were priests—were chosen to blow the trumpets as they marched in front of the Ark of God. Obed-edom and Jehiah were chosen to guard the Ark.

Moving the Ark to Jerusalem

²⁵Then David and the elders of Israel and the generals of the army* went to the house of Obed-edom to bring the Ark of the LORD's Covenant up to Jerusalem with a great celebration. ²⁶And because God was clearly helping the Levites as they carried the Ark of the LORD's Covenant, they sacrificed seven bulls and seven rams.

²⁷David was dressed in a robe of fine linen, as were all the Levites who carried the Ark, and also the singers, and Kenaniah the choir leader. David was also wearing a priestly garment.* ²⁸So all Israel brought up the Ark of the LORD's Covenant with shouts of joy, the blowing of rams' horns and trumpets, the crashing of cymbals, and loud playing on harps and lyres.

²⁹But as the Ark of the LORD's Covenant entered the City of David, Michal, the daughter of Saul, looked down from her window. When she saw King David skipping about and laughing with joy, she was filled with contempt for him.

16 They brought the Ark of God and placed it inside the special tent David had prepared for it. And they presented burnt offerings and peace offerings to God. ²When he had finished his sacrifices, David blessed the people in the name of the LORD. ³Then he gave to every man and woman in all Israel a loaf of bread, a cake of dates,* and a cake of raisins.

15:7 Hebrew *Gershom*, a variant spelling of Gershon. 15:18 As in several Hebrew manuscripts and Greek version (see also parallel lists in 15:20; 16:5); Masoretic Text reads *Zechariah ben Jaaziel*. 15:20 Hebrew adds *according to Alamoth*, which is probably a musical term. The meaning of the Hebrew is uncertain. 15:21 Hebrew adds *according to the Sheminith*, which is probably a musical term. The meaning of the Hebrew is uncertain. 15:23 Hebrew *chosen as gatekeepers for;* also in 15:24. 15:25 Hebrew *the commanders of thousands*. 15:27 Hebrew *a linen ephod*. 16:3 Or *a portion of meat*. The meaning of the Hebrew is uncertain.

⁴David appointed the following Levites to lead the people in worship before the Ark of the LORD—to invoke his blessings, to give thanks, and to praise the LORD, the God of Israel. ⁵Asaph, the leader of this group, sounded the cymbals. Second to him was Zechariah, followed by Jeiel, Shemiramoth, Jehiel, Mattithiah, Eliab, Benaiah, Obed-edom, and Jeiel. They played the harps and lyres. ⁶The priests, Benaiah and Jahaziel, played the trumpets regularly before the Ark of God's Covenant.

David's Song of Praise

⁷On that day David gave to Asaph and his fellow Levites this song of thanksgiving to the LORD:

⁸ Give thanks to the LORD and proclaim
     his greatness.
   Let the whole world know what he has
     done.
⁹ Sing to him; yes, sing his praises.
   Tell everyone about his wonderful
     deeds.
¹⁰ Exult in his holy name;
    rejoice, you who worship the LORD.
¹¹ Search for the LORD and for his strength;
    continually seek him.
¹² Remember the wonders he has
     performed,
    his miracles, and the rulings he has
     given,
¹³ you children of his servant Israel,
    you descendants of Jacob, his chosen
     ones.

¹⁴ He is the LORD our God.
    His justice is seen throughout the land.
¹⁵ Remember his covenant forever—
    the commitment he made to a
     thousand generations.
¹⁶ This is the covenant he made with
     Abraham
    and the oath he swore to Isaac.
¹⁷ He confirmed it to Jacob as a decree,
    and to the people of Israel as a
     never-ending covenant:
¹⁸ "I will give you the land of Canaan
    as your special possession."

¹⁹ He said this when you were few in
     number,
    a tiny group of strangers in Canaan.

²⁰ They wandered from nation to nation,
    from one kingdom to another.
²¹ Yet he did not let anyone oppress them.
    He warned kings on their behalf:
²² "Do not touch my chosen people,
    and do not hurt my prophets."

²³ Let the whole earth sing to the LORD!
    Each day proclaim the good news that
     he saves.
²⁴ Publish his glorious deeds among the
     nations.
    Tell everyone about the amazing
     things he does.
²⁵ Great is the LORD! He is most worthy of
     praise!
    He is to be feared above all gods.
²⁶ The gods of other nations are mere idols,
    but the LORD made the heavens!
²⁷ Honor and majesty surround him;
    strength and joy fill his dwelling.

²⁸ O nations of the world, recognize the
     LORD,
    recognize that the LORD is glorious
     and strong.
²⁹ Give to the LORD the glory he deserves!
    Bring your offering and come into his
     presence.
   Worship the LORD in all his holy
     splendor.
³⁰   Let all the earth tremble before him.
    The world stands firm and cannot be
     shaken.

³¹ Let the heavens be glad, and the earth
     rejoice!
    Tell all the nations, "The LORD reigns!"
³² Let the sea and everything in it shout his
     praise!
    Let the fields and their crops burst out
     with joy!
³³ Let the trees of the forest rustle with
     praise,
    for the LORD is coming to judge the
     earth.

³⁴ Give thanks to the LORD, for he is good!
    His faithful love endures forever.
³⁵ Cry out, "Save us, O God of our
     salvation!
    Gather and rescue us from among the
     nations,
   so we can thank your holy name
    and rejoice and praise you."

Believing God Is Good

1 CHRONICLES 16:34

When my oldest son, Kirby, was born, my list of regular worries expanded to include abductions, food allergies, and the pond in our backyard. I feared something would happen to him. I'd always told the Lord, "Your will, not mine. Take me, make me, break me." But when Kirby was born, it seemed impossible to say, "Take *him*, make *him*, break *him*." I didn't trust God at that level.

I began to wade into a period of doubt. I just had so many big questions: If God were sovereign, why *did* so many bad things happen? How much does prayer impact these situations? I was frustrated and afraid. I didn't even pick up my Bible for about a year.

It wasn't that I doubted God's existence; I just wasn't sure about his character. It was difficult to understand his sovereignty in the face of awful things that happen in our world.

But after a year, I got sick of myself. I realized the fruit of my anger, bitterness, cynicism, and fear is anger, bitterness, cynicism, fear, and *death*.

I finally picked up my Bible again. I started reading in Job and flipped over to Psalms. I couldn't get enough. And I haven't stopped since. Something broke open inside me.

The Lord helped me gain a greater understanding of his nature. Psalm 34:8 invites us to "taste and see that the LORD is good." I know I'll have questions and struggles in the future. Although I don't have all the answers, I feel better equipped to handle the questions as I cling to this essential goodness of God.

Michael Card, in his wonderful book *A Sacred Sorrow*, says doubts can actually be a profound statement of faith because they represent a person saying she won't let go of a good God in the face of the profound evil she's seeing. In fact, despite our depravity and selfishness, God uses us to heal this broken world. That's pretty amazing.

—*Sara Groves*

For more on faith, see reading at Job 38:25-33.

³⁶ Praise the LORD, the God of Israel, who lives from everlasting to everlasting!

And all the people shouted "Amen!" and praised the LORD.

Worship at Jerusalem and Gibeon

³⁷ David arranged for Asaph and his fellow Levites to serve regularly before the Ark of the LORD's Covenant, doing whatever needed to be done each day. ³⁸ This group included Obed-edom (son of Jeduthun), Hosah, and sixty-eight other Levites as gatekeepers.

³⁹ Meanwhile, David stationed Zadok the priest and his fellow priests at the Tabernacle of the LORD at the place of worship in Gibeon, where they continued to minister before the LORD. ⁴⁰ They sacrificed the regular burnt offerings to the LORD each morning and evening on the altar set aside for that purpose, obeying everything written in the Law of the LORD, as he had commanded Israel. ⁴¹ David also appointed Heman, Jeduthun, and the others chosen by name to give thanks to the LORD, for "his faithful love endures forever." ⁴² They used their trumpets, cymbals, and other

instruments to accompany their songs of praise to God.* And the sons of Jeduthun were appointed as gatekeepers.

⁴³Then all the people returned to their homes, and David turned and went home to bless his own family.

17 The Lord's Covenant Promise to David

When David was settled in his palace, he summoned Nathan the prophet. "Look," David said, "I am living in a beautiful cedar palace,* but the Ark of the Lord's Covenant is out there under a tent!"

²Nathan replied to David, "Do whatever you have in mind, for God is with you."

³But that same night God said to Nathan,

⁴"Go and tell my servant David, 'This is what the Lord has declared: You are not the one to build a house for me to live in. ⁵I have never lived in a house, from the day I brought the Israelites out of Egypt until this very day. My home has always been a tent, moving from one place to another in a Tabernacle. ⁶Yet no matter where I have gone with the Israelites, I have never once complained to Israel's leaders,* the shepherds of my people. I have never asked them, "Why haven't you built me a beautiful cedar house?"'

⁷"Now go and say to my servant David, 'This is what the Lord of Heaven's Armies has declared: I took you from tending sheep in the pasture and selected you to be the leader of my people Israel. ⁸I have been with you wherever you have gone, and I have destroyed all your enemies before your eyes. Now I will make your name as famous as anyone who has ever lived on the earth! ⁹And I will provide a homeland for my people Israel, planting them in a secure place where they will never be disturbed. Evil nations won't oppress them as they've done in the past, ¹⁰starting from the time I appointed judges to rule my people Israel. And I will defeat all your enemies.

"'Furthermore, I declare that the Lord will build a house for you—a dynasty of kings! ¹¹For when you die and join your ancestors, I will raise up one of your descendants, one of your sons, and I will make his kingdom strong. ¹²He is the one who will build a house—a temple—for me. And I will secure his throne forever. ¹³I will be his father, and he will be my son. I will never take my favor from him as I took it from the one who ruled before you. ¹⁴I will confirm him as king over my house and my kingdom for all time, and his throne will be secure forever.'"

¹⁵So Nathan went back to David and told him everything the Lord had said in this vision.

David's Prayer of Thanks

¹⁶Then King David went in and sat before the Lord and prayed,

"Who am I, O Lord God, and what is my family, that you have brought me this far? ¹⁷And now, O God, in addition to everything else, you speak of giving your servant a lasting dynasty! You speak as though I were someone very great,* O Lord God!

¹⁸"What more can I say to you about the way you have honored me? You know what your servant is really like. ¹⁹For the sake of your servant, O Lord, and according to your will, you have done all these great things and have made them known.

²⁰O Lord, there is no one like you. We have never even heard of another God like you! ²¹What other nation on earth is like your people Israel? What other nation, O God, have you redeemed from slavery to be your own people? You made a great name for yourself when you redeemed your people from Egypt. You performed awesome miracles and drove out the nations that stood in their way. ²²You chose Israel to be your very own people forever, and you, O Lord, became their God.

²³"And now, O Lord, I am your servant; do as you have promised concerning me and my family. May it be a

---

16:42 Or to accompany the sacred music; or to accompany singing to God.   **17:1** Hebrew a house of cedar.   **17:6** As in Greek version (see also 2 Sam 7:7); Hebrew reads judges.   **17:17** The meaning of the Hebrew is uncertain.

Solitude

Leading through Solitude

1 CHRONICLES 17

Recently as I prepared to leave for a retreat I was leading for a group of pastors and hospital chaplains, I realized how tired I was, how desperate I was for intimacy with God, and how much I needed the very things into which I would be guiding others that day.

After twenty-five years in ministry, I had learned to pay attention to such inner dynamics and knew not to wait for a "better" time. When the retreat was over, I left immediately for my own retreat destination to enter into twenty-four hours of solitude and silence.

That choice alone changed the tenor of the week and the whole month that followed. In solitude I was able to be with God and with what was true about me in utter privacy. There was time and space to attend to what was real in my own life—to celebrate the joys, grieve the losses, sit with my questions, attend to my loneliness, shed my tears—and allow God to be with me in those places.

This was not primarily a time for problem solving or fixing—because not everything can be fixed or solved. It was a time just to "keep still" and wait for God to accomplish what was most needed in my life. It was a deep kind of rest.

One of my most important disciplines as a person in ministry is a constant rhythm of solitude and community, stillness and action, engagement and retreat. I need times when I am not "on" and do not have to be any particular way for anyone, times when I can be alone in God's presence for my own soul's sake.

One of the most sobering truths about life in leadership is that I can be busy and look important, yet be out of touch with that place in the center of my being where I know who I am in God and what he has called me to do—that place where I am responsive to the voice of God above all others'. When this happens, I am at the mercy of all manner of external and internal forces, tossed and turned by others' expectations and my inner compulsions. This inner emptiness then becomes the source of frenetic activity that is untethered from any kind of grounding in God. This is not a good situation for a leader to be in.

Over the years I have learned that my greatest need as a human being and as a spiritual leader is to experience God's unconditional love and presence beyond all that I do for him. I need to hear a voice that is not my own speaking those things that I most need to hear. In the regular practice of solitude, God's unconditional love and presence become the bedrock of my being, the unshakable foundation of my true identity and calling. God's transforming presence experienced in solitude is deeply restorative, enlivening my leadership and enabling me to bring fresh energy and deeper wisdom to the responsibilities before me.

There is rarely a good time for extended solitude in the life of a leader; there is only the right time. On many occasions, when my spirit has been willing but my schedule has been weak, Emilie Griffin's words, from her book *Wilderness Time*, have provided a kick in the you-know-what:

> When there is no time to do it, that's when you most need to unclutter the calendar and go apart to pray. When the gridlock in your schedule relentlessly forbids it is the time you most need retreat. That is when your heart beats against the prison walls of your enslavement and says, "Yes, Lord, I want to spend time with you."

—*Ruth Haley Barton*

For more on solitude, see reading at Psalm 16.

promise that will last forever. ²⁴And may your name be established and honored forever so that everyone will say, 'The LORD of Heaven's Armies, the God of Israel, is Israel's God!' And may the house of your servant David continue before you forever.

²⁵"O my God, I have been bold enough to pray to you because you have revealed to your servant that you will build a house for him—a dynasty of kings! ²⁶For you are God, O LORD. And you have promised these good things to your servant. ²⁷And now, it has pleased you to bless the house of your servant, so that it will continue forever before you. For when you grant a blessing, O LORD, it is an eternal blessing!"

18 David's Military Victories

After this, David defeated and subdued the Philistines by conquering Gath and its surrounding towns. ²David also conquered the land of Moab, and the Moabites who were spared became David's subjects and paid him tribute money.

³David also destroyed the forces of Hadadezer, king of Zobah, as far as Hamath,* when Hadadezer marched out to strengthen his control along the Euphrates River. ⁴David captured 1,000 chariots, 7,000 charioteers, and 20,000 foot soldiers. He crippled all the chariot horses except enough for 100 chariots.

⁵When Arameans from Damascus arrived to help King Hadadezer, David killed 22,000 of them. ⁶Then he placed several army garrisons* in Damascus, the Aramean capital, and the Arameans became David's subjects and paid him tribute money. So the LORD made David victorious wherever he went.

⁷David brought the gold shields of Hadadezer's officers to Jerusalem, ⁸along with a large amount of bronze from Hadadezer's towns of Tebah* and Cun. Later Solomon melted the bronze and molded it into the great bronze basin called the Sea, the pillars, and the various bronze articles used at the Temple.

⁹When King Toi* of Hamath heard that David had destroyed the entire army of King Hadadezer of Zobah, ¹⁰he sent his son Joram* to congratulate King David for his successful campaign. Hadadezer and Toi had been enemies and were often at war. Joram presented David with many gifts of gold, silver, and bronze.

¹¹King David dedicated all these gifts to the LORD, along with the silver and gold he had taken from the other nations—from Edom, Moab, Ammon, Philistia, and Amalek.

¹²Abishai son of Zeruiah destroyed 18,000 Edomites in the Valley of Salt. ¹³He placed army garrisons in Edom, and all the Edomites became David's subjects. In fact, the LORD made David victorious wherever he went.

¹⁴So David reigned over all Israel and did what was just and right for all his people. ¹⁵Joab son of Zeruiah was commander of the army. Jehoshaphat son of Ahilud was the royal historian. ¹⁶Zadok son of Ahitub and Ahimelech* son of Abiathar were the priests. Seraiah* was the court secretary. ¹⁷Benaiah son of Jehoiada was captain of the king's bodyguard.* And David's sons served as the king's chief assistants.

19 David Defeats the Ammonites

Some time after this, King Nahash of the Ammonites died, and his son Hanun* became king. ²David said, "I am going to show loyalty to Hanun because his father, Nahash, was always loyal to me." So David sent messengers to express sympathy to Hanun about his father's death.

But when David's ambassadors arrived in the land of Ammon, ³the Ammonite commanders said to Hanun, "Do you really think these men are coming here to honor your father? No! David has sent them to spy out the land so they can come in and conquer it!" ⁴So Hanun seized David's ambassadors and shaved them, cut off their robes

---

18:3 The meaning of the Hebrew is uncertain. 18:6 As in Greek version and Latin Vulgate (see also 2 Sam 8:6); Hebrew lacks several army garrisons. 18:8 Hebrew reads Tibhath, a variant spelling of Tebah; compare parallel text at 2 Sam 8:8. 18:9 As in parallel text at 2 Sam 8:9; Hebrew reads Tou; also in 18:10. 18:10 As in parallel text at 2 Sam 8:10; Hebrew reads Hadoram, a variant spelling of Joram. 18:16a As in some Hebrew manuscripts, Syriac version, and Latin Vulgate (see also 2 Sam 8:17); most Hebrew manuscripts read Abimelech. 18:16b As in parallel text at 2 Sam 8:17; Hebrew reads Shavsha. 18:17 Hebrew of the Kerethites and Pelethites. 19:1 As in parallel text at 2 Sam 10:1; Hebrew lacks Hanun.

at the buttocks, and sent them back to David in shame.

⁵When David heard what had happened to the men, he sent messengers to tell them, "Stay at Jericho until your beards grow out, and then come back." For they felt deep shame because of their appearance.

⁶When the people of Ammon realized how seriously they had angered David, Hanun and the Ammonites sent 75,000 pounds* of silver to hire chariots and charioteers from Aram-naharaim, Aram-maacah, and Zobah. ⁷They also hired 32,000 chariots and secured the support of the king of Maacah and his army. These forces camped at Medeba, where they were joined by the Ammonite troops that Hanun had recruited from his own towns. ⁸When David heard about this, he sent Joab and all his warriors to fight them. ⁹The Ammonite troops came out and drew up their battle lines at the entrance of the city, while the other kings positioned themselves to fight in the open fields.

¹⁰When Joab saw that he would have to fight on both the front and the rear, he chose some of Israel's elite troops and placed them under his personal command to fight the Arameans in the fields. ¹¹He left the rest of the army under the command of his brother Abishai, who was to attack the Ammonites. ¹²"If the Arameans are too strong for me, then come over and help me," Joab told his brother. "And if the Ammonites are too strong for you, I will help you. ¹³Be courageous! Let us fight bravely for our people and the cities of our God. May the LORD's will be done."

¹⁴When Joab and his troops attacked, the Arameans began to run away. ¹⁵And when the Ammonites saw the Arameans running, they also ran from Abishai and retreated into the city. Then Joab returned to Jerusalem.

¹⁶The Arameans now realized that they were no match for Israel, so they sent messengers and summoned additional Aramean troops from the other side of the Euphrates River.* These troops were under

the command of Shobach,* the commander of Hadadezer's forces.

¹⁷When David heard what was happening, he mobilized all Israel, crossed the Jordan River, and positioned his troops in battle formation. Then David engaged the Arameans in battle, and they fought against him. ¹⁸But again the Arameans fled from the Israelites. This time David's forces killed 7,000 charioteers and 40,000 foot soldiers, including Shobach, the commander of their army. ¹⁹When Hadadezer's allies saw that they had been defeated by Israel, they surrendered to David and became his subjects. After that, the Arameans were no longer willing to help the Ammonites.

20 David Captures Rabbah

In the spring of the year,* when kings normally go out to war, Joab led the Israelite army in successful attacks against the land of the Ammonites. In the process he laid siege to the city of Rabbah. However, David stayed behind in Jerusalem.

²When David arrived at Rabbah, he removed the crown from the king's head,* and it was placed on his own head. The crown was made of gold and set with gems, and he found that it weighed seventy-five pounds.* David took a vast amount of plunder from the city. ³He also made slaves of the people of Rabbah and forced them to labor with saws, iron picks, and iron axes.* That is how David dealt with the people of all the Ammonite towns. Then David and all the army returned to Jerusalem.

Battles against Philistine Giants

⁴After this, war broke out with the Philistines at Gezer. As they fought, Sibbecai from Hushah killed Saph,* a descendant of the giants,* and so the Philistines were subdued.

⁵During another battle with the Philistines, Elhanan son of Jair killed Lahmi, the brother of Goliath of Gath. The handle of Lahmi's spear was as thick as a weaver's beam!

⁶In another battle with the Philistines

19:6 Hebrew 1,000 talents [34,000 kilograms].   **19:16a** Hebrew the river.   **19:16b** As in parallel text at 2 Sam 10:16; Hebrew reads Shophach; also in 19:18.   **20:1** Hebrew At the turn of the year. The first day of the year in the ancient Hebrew lunar calendar occurred in March or April.   **20:2a** Or from the head of Milcom (as in Greek version and Latin Vulgate). Milcom, also called Molech, was the god of the Ammonites.   **20:2b** Hebrew 1 talent [34 kilograms].   **20:3** As in parallel text at 2 Sam 12:31; Hebrew reads and cut them with saws, iron picks, and saws.   **20:4a** As in parallel text at 2 Sam 21:18; Hebrew reads Sippai.   **20:4b** Hebrew descendant of the Rephaites; also in 20:6, 8.

at Gath, they encountered a huge man with six fingers on each hand and six toes on each foot, twenty-four in all, who was also a descendant of the giants. [7] But when he defied and taunted Israel, he was killed by Jonathan, the son of David's brother Shimea.

[8] These Philistines were descendants of the giants of Gath, but David and his warriors killed them.

21 David Takes a Census

Satan rose up against Israel and caused David to take a census of the people of Israel. [2] So David said to Joab and the commanders of the army, "Take a census of all the people of Israel—from Beersheba in the south to Dan in the north—and bring me a report so I may know how many there are."

[3] But Joab replied, "May the LORD increase the number of his people a hundred times over! But why, my lord the king, do you want to do this? Are they not all your servants? Why must you cause Israel to sin?"

[4] But the king insisted that they take the census, so Joab traveled throughout all Israel to count the people. Then he returned to Jerusalem [5] and reported the number of people to David. There were 1,100,000 warriors in all Israel who could handle a sword, and 470,000 in Judah. [6] But Joab did not include the tribes of Levi and Benjamin in the census because he was so distressed at what the king had made him do.

Judgment for David's Sin

[7] God was very displeased with the census, and he punished Israel for it. [8] Then David said to God, "I have sinned greatly by taking this census. Please forgive my guilt for doing this foolish thing."

[9] Then the LORD spoke to Gad, David's seer. This was the message: [10] "Go and say to David, 'This is what the LORD says: I will give you three choices. Choose one of these punishments, and I will inflict it on you.'"

[11] So Gad came to David and said, "These are the choices the LORD has given you. [12] You may choose three years of famine, three months of destruction by the sword of your enemies, or three days of severe plague as the angel of the LORD brings devastation throughout the land of Israel. Decide what answer I should give the LORD who sent me."

[13] "I'm in a desperate situation!" David replied to Gad. "But let me fall into the hands of the LORD, for his mercy is very great. Do not let me fall into human hands."

[14] So the LORD sent a plague upon Israel, and 70,000 people died as a result. [15] And God sent an angel to destroy Jerusalem. But just as the angel was preparing to destroy it, the LORD relented and said to the death angel, "Stop! That is enough!" At that moment the angel of the LORD was standing by the threshing floor of Araunah* the Jebusite.

[16] David looked up and saw the angel of the LORD standing between heaven and earth with his sword drawn, reaching out over Jerusalem. So David and the leaders of Israel put on burlap to show their deep distress and fell face down on the ground. [17] And David said to God, "I am the one who called for the census! I am the one who has sinned and done wrong! But these people are as innocent as sheep—what have they done? O LORD my God, let your anger fall against me and my family, but do not destroy your people."

David Builds an Altar

[18] Then the angel of the LORD told Gad to instruct David to go up and build an altar to the LORD on the threshing floor of Araunah the Jebusite. [19] So David went up to do what the LORD had commanded him through Gad. [20] Araunah, who was busy threshing wheat at the time, turned and saw the angel there. His four sons, who were with him, ran away and hid. [21] When Araunah saw David approaching, he left his threshing floor and bowed before David with his face to the ground.

[22] David said to Araunah, "Let me buy this threshing floor from you at its full price. Then I will build an altar to the LORD there, so that he will stop the plague."

[23] "Take it, my lord the king, and use it as

21:15 As in parallel text at 2 Sam 24:16; Hebrew reads *Ornan*, another name for Araunah; also in 21:18-28.

you wish," Araunah said to David. "I will give the oxen for the burnt offerings, and the threshing boards for wood to build a fire on the altar, and the wheat for the grain offering. I will give it all to you."

²⁴But King David replied to Araunah, "No, I insist on buying it for the full price. I will not take what is yours and give it to the LORD. I will not present burnt offerings that have cost me nothing!" ²⁵So David gave Araunah 600 pieces of gold* in payment for the threshing floor.

²⁶David built an altar there to the LORD and sacrificed burnt offerings and peace offerings. And when David prayed, the LORD answered him by sending fire from heaven to burn up the offering on the altar. ²⁷Then the LORD spoke to the angel, who put the sword back into its sheath.

²⁸When David saw that the LORD had answered his prayer, he offered sacrifices there at Araunah's threshing floor. ²⁹At that time the Tabernacle of the LORD and the altar of burnt offering that Moses had made in the wilderness were located at the place of worship in Gibeon. ³⁰But David was not able to go there to inquire of God, because he was terrified by the drawn sword of the angel of the LORD.

22 Then David said, "This will be the location for the Temple of the LORD God and the place of the altar for Israel's burnt offerings!"

Preparations for the Temple

²So David gave orders to call together the foreigners living in Israel, and he assigned them the task of preparing finished stone for building the Temple of God. ³David provided large amounts of iron for the nails that would be needed for the doors in the gates and for the clamps, and he gave more bronze than could be weighed. ⁴He also provided innumerable cedar logs, for the men of Tyre and Sidon had brought vast amounts of cedar to David.

⁵David said, "My son Solomon is still young and inexperienced. And since the Temple to be built for the LORD must be a magnificent structure, famous and glorious throughout the world, I will begin making preparations for it now." So David collected vast amounts of building materials before his death.

⁶Then David sent for his son Solomon and instructed him to build a Temple for the LORD, the God of Israel. ⁷"My son, I wanted to build a Temple to honor the name of the LORD my God," David told him. ⁸"But the LORD said to me, 'You have killed many men in the battles you have fought. And since you have shed so much blood in my sight, you will not be the one to build a Temple to honor my name. ⁹But you will have a son who will be a man of peace. I will give him peace with his enemies in all the surrounding lands. His name will be Solomon,* and I will give peace and quiet to Israel during his reign. ¹⁰He is the one who will build a Temple to honor my name. He will be my son, and I will be his father. And I will secure the throne of his kingdom over Israel forever.'

¹¹"Now, my son, may the LORD be with you and give you success as you follow his directions in building the Temple of the LORD your God. ¹²And may the LORD give you wisdom and understanding, that you may obey the Law of the LORD your God as you rule over Israel. ¹³For you will be successful if you carefully obey the decrees and regulations that the LORD gave to Israel through Moses. Be strong and courageous; do not be afraid or lose heart!

¹⁴"I have worked hard to provide materials for building the Temple of the LORD— nearly 4,000 tons of gold, 40,000 tons of silver,* and so much iron and bronze that it cannot be weighed. I have also gathered timber and stone for the walls, though you may need to add more. ¹⁵You have a large number of skilled stonemasons and carpenters and craftsmen of every kind. ¹⁶You have expert goldsmiths and silversmiths and workers of bronze and iron. Now begin the work, and may the LORD be with you!"

¹⁷Then David ordered all the leaders of Israel to assist Solomon in this project. ¹⁸"The LORD your God is with you," he

---

21:25 Hebrew *600 shekels of gold*, about 15 pounds or 6.8 kilograms in weight. **22:9** *Solomon* sounds like and is probably derived from the Hebrew word for "peace." **22:14** Hebrew *100,000 talents* [3,400 metric tons] *of gold, 1,000,000 talents* [34,000 metric tons] *of silver*.

declared. "He has given you peace with the surrounding nations. He has handed them over to me, and they are now subject to the LORD and his people. [19]Now seek the LORD your God with all your heart and soul. Build the sanctuary of the LORD God so that you can bring the Ark of the LORD's Covenant and the holy vessels of God into the Temple built to honor the LORD's name."

23 Duties of the Levites

When David was an old man, he appointed his son Solomon to be king over Israel. [2]David summoned all the leaders of Israel, together with the priests and Levites. [3]All the Levites who were thirty years old or older were counted, and the total came to 38,000. [4]Then David said, "From all the Levites, 24,000 will supervise the work at the Temple of the LORD. Another 6,000 will serve as officials and judges. [5]Another 4,000 will work as gatekeepers, and 4,000 will praise the LORD with the musical instruments I have made." [6]Then David divided the Levites into divisions named after the clans descended from the three sons of Levi—Gershon, Kohath, and Merari.

The Gershonites

[7]The Gershonite family units were defined by their lines of descent from Libni* and Shimei, the sons of Gershon. [8]Three of the descendants of Libni were Jehiel (the family leader), Zetham, and Joel. [9]These were the leaders of the family of Libni.

Three of the descendants of Shimei were Shelomoth, Haziel, and Haran. [10]Four other descendants of Shimei were Jahath, Ziza,* Jeush, and Beriah. [11]Jahath was the family leader, and Ziza was next. Jeush and Beriah were counted as a single family because neither had many sons.

The Kohathites

[12]Four of the descendants of Kohath were Amram, Izhar, Hebron, and Uzziel. [13]The sons of Amram were Aaron and Moses. Aaron and his descendants were set apart to dedicate the most holy things, to offer sacrifices in the LORD's presence, to serve the LORD, and to pronounce blessings in his name forever.

[14]As for Moses, the man of God, his sons were included with the tribe of Levi. [15]The sons of Moses were Gershom and Eliezer. [16]The descendants of Gershom included Shebuel, the family leader. [17]Eliezer had only one son, Rehabiah, the family leader. Rehabiah had numerous descendants.

[18]The descendants of Izhar included Shelomith, the family leader.

[19]The descendants of Hebron included Jeriah (the family leader), Amariah (the second), Jahaziel (the third), and Jekameam (the fourth).

[20]The descendants of Uzziel included Micah (the family leader) and Isshiah (the second).

The Merarites

[21]The descendants of Merari included Mahli and Mushi.

The sons of Mahli were Eleazar and Kish. [22]Eleazar died with no sons, only daughters. His daughters married their cousins, the sons of Kish.

[23]Three of the descendants of Mushi were Mahli, Eder, and Jerimoth.

[24]These were the descendants of Levi by clans, the leaders of their family groups, registered carefully by name. Each had to be twenty years old or older to qualify for service in the house of the LORD. [25]For David said, "The LORD, the God of Israel, has given us peace, and he will always live in Jerusalem. [26]Now the Levites will no longer need to carry the Tabernacle and its furnishings from place to place." [27]In accordance with David's final instructions, all the Levites twenty years old or older were registered for service.

[28]The work of the Levites was to assist the priests, the descendants of Aaron, as they served at the house of the LORD. They also took care of the courtyards and side rooms, helped perform the ceremonies of purification, and served in many other ways in the house of God. [29]They were in charge of the sacred bread that was set out on the table,

---

23:7 Hebrew *Ladan* (also in 23:8, 9), a variant spelling of Libni; compare 6:17. **23:10** As in Greek version and Latin Vulgate (see also 23:11); Hebrew reads *Zina*.

the choice flour for the grain offerings, the wafers made without yeast, the cakes cooked in olive oil, and the other mixed breads. They were also responsible to check all the weights and measures. ³⁰ And each morning and evening they stood before the LORD to sing songs of thanks and praise to him. ³¹ They assisted with the burnt offerings that were presented to the LORD on Sabbath days, at new moon celebrations, and at all the appointed festivals. The required number of Levites served in the LORD's presence at all times, following all the procedures they had been given.

³² And so, under the supervision of the priests, the Levites watched over the Tabernacle and the Temple* and faithfully carried out their duties of service at the house of the LORD.

24 Duties of the Priests

This is how Aaron's descendants, the priests, were divided into groups for service. The sons of Aaron were Nadab, Abihu, Eleazar, and Ithamar. ²But Nadab and Abihu died before their father, and they had no sons. So only Eleazar and Ithamar were left to carry on as priests.

³With the help of Zadok, who was a descendant of Eleazar, and of Ahimelech, who was a descendant of Ithamar, David divided Aaron's descendants into groups according to their various duties. ⁴Eleazar's descendants were divided into sixteen groups and Ithamar's into eight, for there were more family leaders among the descendants of Eleazar.

⁵All tasks were assigned to the various groups by means of sacred lots so that no preference would be shown, for there were many qualified officials serving God in the sanctuary from among the descendants of both Eleazar and Ithamar. ⁶Shemaiah son of Nethanel, a Levite, acted as secretary and wrote down the names and assignments in the presence of the king, the officials, Zadok the priest, Ahimelech son of Abiathar, and the family leaders of the priests and Levites. The descendants of Eleazar and Ithamar took turns casting lots.

⁷ The first lot fell to Jehoiarib.
The second lot fell to Jedaiah.
⁸ The third lot fell to Harim.
The fourth lot fell to Seorim.
⁹ The fifth lot fell to Malkijah.
The sixth lot fell to Mijamin.
¹⁰ The seventh lot fell to Hakkoz.
The eighth lot fell to Abijah.
¹¹ The ninth lot fell to Jeshua.
The tenth lot fell to Shecaniah.
¹² The eleventh lot fell to Eliashib.
The twelfth lot fell to Jakim.
¹³ The thirteenth lot fell to Huppah.
The fourteenth lot fell to Jeshebeab.
¹⁴ The fifteenth lot fell to Bilgah.
The sixteenth lot fell to Immer.
¹⁵ The seventeenth lot fell to Hezir.
The eighteenth lot fell to Happizzez.
¹⁶ The nineteenth lot fell to Pethahiah.
The twentieth lot fell to Jehezkel.
¹⁷ The twenty-first lot fell to Jakin.
The twenty-second lot fell to Gamul.
¹⁸ The twenty-third lot fell to Delaiah.
The twenty-fourth lot fell to Maaziah.

¹⁹ Each group carried out its appointed duties in the house of the LORD according to the procedures established by their ancestor Aaron in obedience to the commands of the LORD, the God of Israel.

Family Leaders among the Levites

²⁰ These were the other family leaders descended from Levi:

From the descendants of Amram, the leader was Shebuel.*
From the descendants of Shebuel, the leader was Jehdeiah.
²¹ From the descendants of Rehabiah, the leader was Isshiah.
²² From the descendants of Izhar, the leader was Shelomith.*
From the descendants of Shelomith, the leader was Jahath.
²³ From the descendants of Hebron, Jeriah was the leader,* Amariah was second, Jahaziel was third, and Jekameam was fourth.
²⁴ From the descendants of Uzziel, the leader was Micah.

23:32 Hebrew *the Tent of Meeting and the sanctuary.* **24:20** Hebrew *Shubael* (also in 24:20b), a variant spelling of Shebuel; compare 23:16 and 26:24. **24:22** Hebrew *Shelomoth* (also in 24:22b), a variant spelling of Shelomith; compare 23:18. **24:23** Hebrew *From the descendants of Jeriah;* compare 23:19.

From the descendants of Micah, the leader was Shamir, ²⁵along with Isshiah, the brother of Micah.

From the descendants of Isshiah, the leader was Zechariah.

²⁶ From the descendants of Merari, the leaders were Mahli and Mushi.

From the descendants of Jaaziah, the leader was Beno.

²⁷ From the descendants of Merari through Jaaziah, the leaders were Beno, Shoham, Zaccur, and Ibri.

²⁸ From the descendants of Mahli, the leader was Eleazar, though he had no sons.

²⁹ From the descendants of Kish, the leader was Jerahmeel.

³⁰ From the descendants of Mushi, the leaders were Mahli, Eder, and Jerimoth.

These were the descendants of Levi in their various families. ³¹ Like the descendants of Aaron, they were assigned to their duties by means of sacred lots, without regard to age or rank. Lots were drawn in the presence of King David, Zadok, Ahimelech, and the family leaders of the priests and the Levites.

25 Duties of the Musicians

David and the army commanders then appointed men from the families of Asaph, Heman, and Jeduthun to proclaim God's messages to the accompaniment of lyres, harps, and cymbals. Here is a list of their names and their work:

²From the sons of Asaph, there were Zaccur, Joseph, Nethaniah, and Asarelah. They worked under the direction of their father, Asaph, who proclaimed God's messages by the king's orders.

³From the sons of Jeduthun, there were Gedaliah, Zeri, Jeshaiah, Shimei,* Hashabiah, and Mattithiah, six in all. They worked under the direction of their father, Jeduthun, who proclaimed God's messages to the accompaniment of the lyre, offering thanks and praise to the LORD.

⁴From the sons of Heman, there were Bukkiah, Mattaniah, Uzziel, Shubael,* Jerimoth, Hananiah, Hanani, Eliathah, Giddalti, Romamti-ezer, Joshbekashah, Mallothi, Hothir, and Mahazioth. ⁵All these were the sons of Heman, the king's seer, for God had honored him with fourteen sons and three daughters.

⁶All these men were under the direction of their fathers as they made music at the house of the LORD. Their responsibilities included the playing of cymbals, harps, and lyres at the house of God. Asaph, Jeduthun, and Heman reported directly to the king. ⁷They and their families were all trained in making music before the LORD, and each of them—288 in all—was an accomplished musician. ⁸The musicians were appointed to their term of service by means of sacred lots, without regard to whether they were young or old, teacher or student.

⁹ The first lot fell to Joseph of the Asaph clan and twelve of his sons and relatives.*

The second lot fell to Gedaliah and twelve of his sons and relatives.

¹⁰ The third lot fell to Zaccur and twelve of his sons and relatives.

¹¹ The fourth lot fell to Zeri* and twelve of his sons and relatives.

¹² The fifth lot fell to Nethaniah and twelve of his sons and relatives.

¹³ The sixth lot fell to Bukkiah and twelve of his sons and relatives.

¹⁴ The seventh lot fell to Asarelah* and twelve of his sons and relatives.

¹⁵ The eighth lot fell to Jeshaiah and twelve of his sons and relatives.

¹⁶ The ninth lot fell to Mattaniah and twelve of his sons and relatives.

¹⁷ The tenth lot fell to Shimei and twelve of his sons and relatives.

¹⁸ The eleventh lot fell to Uzziel* and twelve of his sons and relatives.

¹⁹ The twelfth lot fell to Hashabiah and twelve of his sons and relatives.

²⁰ The thirteenth lot fell to Shubael and twelve of his sons and relatives.

²¹ The fourteenth lot fell to Mattithiah and

25:3 As in one Hebrew manuscript and some Greek manuscripts (see also 25:17); most Hebrew manuscripts lack *Shimei*. **25:4** Hebrew *Shebuel*, a variant spelling of Shubael; compare 25:20. **25:9** As in Greek version; Hebrew lacks *and twelve of his sons and relatives*. **25:11** Hebrew *Izri*, a variant spelling of Zeri; compare 25:3. **25:14** Hebrew *Jesarelah*, a variant spelling of Asarelah; compare 25:2. **25:18** Hebrew *Azarel*, a variant spelling of Uzziel; compare 25:4.

twelve of his sons and relatives. ²²The fifteenth lot fell to Jerimoth* and twelve of his sons and relatives. ²³The sixteenth lot fell to Hananiah and twelve of his sons and relatives. ²⁴The seventeenth lot fell to Joshbekashah* and twelve of his sons and relatives. ²⁵The eighteenth lot fell to Hanani and twelve of his sons and relatives. ²⁶The nineteenth lot fell to Mallothi and twelve of his sons and relatives. ²⁷The twentieth lot fell to Eliathah and twelve of his sons and relatives. ²⁸The twenty-first lot fell to Hothir and twelve of his sons and relatives. ²⁹The twenty-second lot fell to Giddalti and twelve of his sons and relatives. ³⁰The twenty-third lot fell to Mahazioth and twelve of his sons and relatives. ³¹The twenty-fourth lot fell to Romamti-ezer and twelve of his sons and relatives.

26 Duties of the Gatekeepers
These are the divisions of the gatekeepers:

From the Korahites, there was Meshelemiah son of Kore, of the family of Abiasaph.* ²The sons of Meshelemiah were Zechariah (the oldest), Jediael (the second), Zebadiah (the third), Jathniel (the fourth), ³Elam (the fifth), Jehohanan (the sixth), and Eliehoenai (the seventh). ⁴The sons of Obed-edom, also gatekeepers, were Shemaiah (the oldest), Jehozabad (the second), Joah (the third), Sacar (the fourth), Nethanel (the fifth), ⁵Ammiel (the sixth), Issachar (the seventh), and Peullethai (the eighth). God had richly blessed Obed-edom.

⁶Obed-edom's son Shemaiah had sons with great ability who earned positions of great authority in the clan. ⁷Their names were Othni, Rephael, Obed, and Elzabad. Their relatives, Elihu and Semakiah, were also very capable men. ⁸All of these descendants of Obed-edom, including their sons and grandsons—sixty-two of them in all—were very capable men, well qualified for their work. ⁹Meshelemiah's eighteen sons and relatives were also very capable men.

¹⁰Hosah, of the Merari clan, appointed Shimri as the leader among his sons, though he was not the oldest. ¹¹His other sons included Hilkiah (the second), Tebaliah (the third), and Zechariah (the fourth). Hosah's sons and relatives, who served as gatekeepers, numbered thirteen in all.

¹²These divisions of the gatekeepers were named for their family leaders, and like the other Levites, they served at the house of the LORD. ¹³They were assigned by families for guard duty at the various gates, without regard to age or training, for it was all decided by means of sacred lots.

¹⁴The responsibility for the east gate went to Meshelemiah* and his group. The north gate was assigned to his son Zechariah, a man of unusual wisdom. ¹⁵The south gate went to Obed-edom, and his sons were put in charge of the storehouse. ¹⁶Shuppim and Hosah were assigned the west gate and the gateway leading up to the Temple.* Guard duties were divided evenly. ¹⁷Six Levites were assigned each day to the east gate, four to the north gate, four to the south gate, and two pairs at the storehouse. ¹⁸Six were assigned each day to the west gate, four to the gateway leading up to the Temple, and two to the courtyard.*

¹⁹These were the divisions of the gatekeepers from the clans of Korah and Merari.

Treasurers and Other Officials
²⁰Other Levites, led by Ahijah, were in charge of the treasuries of the house of God and the treasuries of the gifts dedicated to the LORD. ²¹From the family of Libni* in the clan of Gershon, Jehiel* was the leader. ²²The sons of Jehiel, Zetham and his brother Joel, were in charge of the treasuries of the house of the LORD.

25:22 Hebrew *Jeremoth*, a variant spelling of Jerimoth; compare 25:4. **25:24** Hebrew *Joshbekasha*, a variant spelling of Joshbekashah; compare 25:4. **26:1** As in Greek version (see also Exod 6:24); Hebrew reads *Asaph*. **26:14** Hebrew *Shelemiah*, a variant spelling of Meshelemiah; compare 26:2. **26:16** Or *the gate of Shalleketh on the upper road* (also in 26:18). The meaning of the Hebrew is uncertain. **26:18** Or *the colonnade*. The meaning of the Hebrew is uncertain. **26:21a** Hebrew *Ladan*, a variant spelling of Libni; compare 6:17. **26:21b** Hebrew *Jehieli* (also in 26:22), a variant spelling of Jehiel; compare 23:8.

²³These are the leaders that descended from Amram, Izhar, Hebron, and Uzziel:

²⁴From the clan of Amram, Shebuel was a descendant of Gershom son of Moses. He was the chief officer of the treasuries. ²⁵His relatives through Eliezer were Rehabiah, Jeshaiah, Joram, Zicri, and Shelomoth. ²⁶Shelomoth and his relatives were in charge of the treasuries containing the gifts that King David, the family leaders, and the generals and captains* and other officers of the army had dedicated to the LORD. ²⁷These men dedicated some of the plunder they had gained in battle to maintain the house of the LORD. ²⁸Shelomoth* and his relatives also cared for the gifts dedicated to the LORD by Samuel the seer, Saul son of Kish, Abner son of Ner, and Joab son of Zeruiah. All the other dedicated gifts were in their care, too.

²⁹From the clan of Izhar came Kenaniah. He and his sons were given administrative responsibilities* over Israel as officials and judges.

³⁰From the clan of Hebron came Hashabiah. He and his relatives—1,700 capable men—were put in charge of the Israelite lands west of the Jordan River. They were responsible for all matters related to the things of the LORD and the service of the king in that area.

³¹Also from the clan of Hebron came Jeriah,* who was the leader of the Hebronites according to the genealogical records. (In the fortieth year of David's reign, a search was made in the records, and capable men from the clan of Hebron were found at Jazer in the land of Gilead.) ³²There were 2,700 capable men among the relatives of Jeriah. King David sent them to the east side of the Jordan River and put them in charge of the tribes of Reuben and Gad and the half-tribe of Manasseh. They were responsible for all matters related to God and to the king.

27 Military Commanders and Divisions

This is the list of Israelite generals and captains,* and their officers, who served the king by supervising the army divisions that were on duty each month of the year. Each division served for one month and had 24,000 troops.

²Jashobeam son of Zabdiel was commander of the first division of 24,000 troops, which was on duty during the first month. ³He was a descendant of Perez and was in charge of all the army officers for the first month.

⁴Dodai, a descendant of Ahoah, was commander of the second division of 24,000 troops, which was on duty during the second month. Mikloth was his chief officer.

⁵Benaiah son of Jehoiada the priest was commander of the third division of 24,000 troops, which was on duty during the third month. ⁶This was the Benaiah who commanded David's elite military group known as the Thirty. His son Ammizabad was his chief officer.

⁷Asahel, the brother of Joab, was commander of the fourth division of 24,000 troops, which was on duty during the fourth month. Asahel was succeeded by his son Zebadiah.

⁸Shammah* the Izrahite was commander of the fifth division of 24,000 troops, which was on duty during the fifth month.

⁹Ira son of Ikkesh from Tekoa was commander of the sixth division of 24,000 troops, which was on duty during the sixth month.

¹⁰Helez, a descendant of Ephraim from Pelon, was commander of the seventh division of 24,000 troops, which was on duty during the seventh month.

¹¹Sibbecai, a descendant of Zerah from Hushah, was commander of the eighth division of 24,000 troops, which was on duty during the eighth month.

¹²Abiezer from Anathoth in the territory of Benjamin was commander of the ninth division of 24,000 troops, which was on duty during the ninth month.

¹³Maharai, a descendant of Zerah from Netophah, was commander of the tenth division of 24,000 troops, which was on duty during the tenth month.

26:26 Hebrew *the commanders of thousands and of hundreds.* 26:28 Hebrew *Shelomith,* a variant spelling of Shelomoth. 26:29 Or *were given outside work;* or *were given work away from the Temple area.* 26:31 Hebrew *Jerijah,* a variant spelling of Jeriah; compare 23:19. 27:1 Hebrew *commanders of thousands and of hundreds.* 27:8 Hebrew *Shamhuth,* a variant spelling of Shammah; compare 11:27 and 2 Sam 23:25.

[14]Benaiah from Pirathon in Ephraim was commander of the eleventh division of 24,000 troops, which was on duty during the eleventh month.

[15]Heled,* a descendant of Othniel from Netophah, was commander of the twelfth division of 24,000 troops, which was on duty during the twelfth month.

Leaders of the Tribes

[16]The following were the tribes of Israel and their leaders:

Tribe	Leader
Reuben	Eliezer son of Zicri
Simeon	Shephatiah son of Maacah
[17] Levi	Hashabiah son of Kemuel
Aaron (the priests)	Zadok
[18] Judah	Elihu (a brother of David)
Issachar	Omri son of Michael
[19] Zebulun	Ishmaiah son of Obadiah
Naphtali	Jeremoth son of Azriel
[20] Ephraim	Hoshea son of Azaziah
Manasseh (west)	Joel son of Pedaiah
[21] Manasseh in Gilead (east)	Iddo son of Zechariah
Benjamin	Jaasiel son of Abner
[22] Dan	Azarel son of Jeroham

These were the leaders of the tribes of Israel.

[23]When David took his census, he did not count those who were younger than twenty years of age, because the Lord had promised to make the Israelites as numerous as the stars in heaven. [24]Joab son of Zeruiah began the census but never finished it because* the anger of God fell on Israel. The total number was never recorded in King David's official records.

Officials of David's Kingdom

[25]Azmaveth son of Adiel was in charge of the palace treasuries.

Jonathan son of Uzziah was in charge of the regional treasuries throughout the towns, villages, and fortresses of Israel.

[26]Ezri son of Kelub was in charge of the field workers who farmed the king's lands.

[27]Shimei from Ramah was in charge of the king's vineyards.

Zabdi from Shepham was responsible for the grapes and the supplies of wine.

[28]Baal-hanan from Geder was in charge of the king's olive groves and sycamore-fig trees in the foothills of Judah.*

Joash was responsible for the supplies of olive oil.

[29]Shitrai from Sharon was in charge of the cattle on the Sharon Plain.

Shaphat son of Adlai was responsible for the cattle in the valleys.

[30]Obil the Ishmaelite was in charge of the camels.

Jehdeiah from Meronoth was in charge of the donkeys.

[31]Jaziz the Hagrite was in charge of the king's flocks of sheep and goats.

All these officials were overseers of King David's property.

[32]Jonathan, David's uncle, was a wise counselor to the king, a man of great insight, and a scribe. Jehiel the Hacmonite was responsible for teaching the king's sons. [33]Ahithophel was the royal adviser. Hushai the Arkite was the king's friend. [34]Ahithophel was succeeded by Jehoiada son of Benaiah and by Abiathar. Joab was commander of the king's army.

28 David's Instructions to Solomon

David summoned all the officials of Israel to Jerusalem—the leaders of the tribes, the commanders of the army divisions, the other generals and captains,* the overseers of the royal property and livestock, the palace officials, the mighty men, and all the other brave warriors in the kingdom. [2]David rose to his feet and said: "My brothers and my people! It was my desire to build a temple where the Ark of the Lord's Covenant, God's footstool, could rest permanently. I made the necessary preparations for building it, [3]but God said to me, 'You must not build a temple to honor my name, for you are a warrior and have shed much blood.'

[4]"Yet the Lord, the God of Israel, has chosen me from among all my father's family to be king over Israel forever. For he has chosen the tribe of Judah to rule, and from

among the families of Judah he chose my father's family. And from among my father's sons the LORD was pleased to make me king over all Israel. ⁵And from among my sons—for the LORD has given me many—he chose Solomon to succeed me on the throne of Israel and to rule over the LORD's kingdom. ⁶He said to me, 'Your son Solomon will build my Temple and its courtyards, for I have chosen him as my son, and I will be his father. ⁷And if he continues to obey my commands and regulations as he does now, I will make his kingdom last forever.'

⁸"So now, with God as our witness, and in the sight of all Israel—the LORD's assembly—I give you this charge. Be careful to obey all the commands of the LORD your God, so that you may continue to possess this good land and leave it to your children as a permanent inheritance.

⁹"And Solomon, my son, learn to know the God of your ancestors intimately. Worship and serve him with your whole heart and a willing mind. For the LORD sees every heart and knows every plan and thought. If you seek him, you will find him. But if you forsake him, he will reject you forever. ¹⁰So take this seriously. The LORD has chosen you to build a Temple as his sanctuary. Be strong, and do the work."

¹¹Then David gave Solomon the plans for the Temple and its surroundings, including the entry room, the storerooms, the upstairs rooms, the inner rooms, and the inner sanctuary—which was the place of atonement. ¹²David also gave Solomon all the plans he had in mind* for the courtyards of the LORD's Temple, the outside rooms, the treasuries, and the rooms for the gifts dedicated to the LORD. ¹³The king also gave Solomon the instructions concerning the work of the various divisions of priests and Levites in the Temple of the LORD. And he gave specifications for the items in the Temple that were to be used for worship.

¹⁴David gave instructions regarding how much gold and silver should be used to make the items needed for service. ¹⁵He told Solomon the amount of gold needed for the gold lampstands and lamps, and the amount of silver for the silver lampstands and lamps, depending on how each would be used. ¹⁶He designated the amount of gold for the table on which the Bread of the Presence would be placed and the amount of silver for other tables.

¹⁷David also designated the amount of gold for the solid gold meat hooks used to handle the sacrificial meat and for the basins, pitchers, and dishes, as well as the amount of silver for every dish. ¹⁸He designated the amount of refined gold for the altar of incense. Finally, he gave him a plan for the LORD's "chariot"—the gold cherubim* whose wings were stretched out over the Ark of the LORD's Covenant. ¹⁹"Every part of this plan," David told Solomon, "was given to me in writing from the hand of the LORD.*"

²⁰Then David continued, "Be strong and courageous, and do the work. Don't be afraid or discouraged, for the LORD God, my God, is with you. He will not fail you or forsake you. He will see to it that all the work related to the Temple of the LORD is finished correctly. ²¹The various divisions of priests and Levites will serve in the Temple of God. Others with skills of every kind will volunteer, and the officials and the entire nation are at your command."

29 Gifts for Building the Temple

Then King David turned to the entire assembly and said, "My son Solomon, whom God has clearly chosen as the next king of Israel, is still young and inexperienced. The work ahead of him is enormous, for the Temple he will build is not for mere mortals—it is for the LORD God himself! ²Using every resource at my command, I have gathered as much as I could for building the Temple of my God. Now there is enough gold, silver, bronze, iron, and wood, as well as great quantities of onyx, other precious stones, costly jewels, and all kinds of fine stone and marble.

³"And now, because of my devotion to the Temple of my God, I am giving all of my own private treasures of gold and silver to help in the construction. This is in addition to the building materials I have already

---

28:12 Or the plans of the spirit that was with him. 28:18 Hebrew for the gold cherub chariot. 28:19 Or was written under the direction of the LORD.

"Little" Money Decisions

1 CHRONICLES 29:1-20

I often wonder about stewardship in my daily decisions. For example, my husband and I are in the middle of remodeling our kitchen, which brings up stewardship questions. How big of an oven do we really need? Should we spend the extra 20 percent to get the backsplash tile I *really* want? And when do we say, "The cheaper version is good enough, and we'd rather do other things with our money"?

I'm not sure we've made all the right decisions, but at least my husband and I are having that conversation. We were debating whether or not to move an exterior wall, which added 25 percent to the overall cost of the remodel. We prayed about it and weren't sure what to do. We talked to three families we really respect, and they gave us good input. So stewardship decisions aren't something we do solely on our own. We need to ask others to give input about how we're stewarding our time and money, because we can't always see the materialism that is blinding us.

Every dollar we spend is a stewardship decision. I used to think only big purchases mattered. Now I think that whether or not I go out to lunch is, in some ways, a kingdom decision. We should be mindful of others and try to fund and create systems that offer hope, freedom, and the gospel to people. They're all wrapped together.

—*Kara Powell*

For more on stewardship, see reading at Psalm 24.

collected for his holy Temple. ⁴I am donating more than 112 tons of gold* from Ophir and 262 tons of refined silver* to be used for overlaying the walls of the buildings ⁵and for the other gold and silver work to be done by the craftsmen. Now then, who will follow my example and give offerings to the LORD today?"

⁶Then the family leaders, the leaders of the tribes of Israel, the generals and captains of the army,* and the king's administrative officers all gave willingly. ⁷For the construction of the Temple of God, they gave about 188 tons of gold,* 10,000 gold coins,* 375 tons of silver,* 675 tons of bronze,* and 3,750 tons of iron.* ⁸They also contributed numerous precious stones, which were deposited in the treasury of the house of the LORD under the care of Jehiel, a descendant of Gershon. ⁹The people rejoiced over the offerings, for they had given freely and wholeheartedly to the LORD, and King David was filled with joy.

David's Prayer of Praise

¹⁰Then David praised the LORD in the presence of the whole assembly:

"O LORD, the God of our ancestor Israel,* may you be praised forever and ever! ¹¹Yours, O LORD, is the greatness, the power, the glory, the victory, and the majesty. Everything in the heavens and on earth is yours, O LORD, and this is your kingdom. We adore you as the one who is over all things. ¹²Wealth and honor come from you alone, for you rule over everything. Power and might are in

29:4a Hebrew *3,000 talents* [102 metric tons] *of gold.*   29:4b Hebrew *7,000 talents* [238 metric tons] *of silver.*   29:6 Hebrew *the commanders of thousands and commanders of hundreds.*   29:7a Hebrew *5,000 talents* [170 metric tons] *of gold.*   29:7b Hebrew *10,000 darics* [a Persian coin] *of gold,* about 185 pounds or 84 kilograms in weight.   29:7c Hebrew *10,000 talents* [340 metric tons] *of silver.*   29:7d Hebrew *18,000 talents* [612 metric tons] *of bronze.*   29:7e Hebrew *100,000 talents* [3,400 metric tons] *of iron.*   29:10 *Israel* is the name that God gave to Jacob.

your hand, and at your discretion people are made great and given strength.

¹³"O our God, we thank you and praise your glorious name! ¹⁴But who am I, and who are my people, that we could give anything to you? Everything we have has come from you, and we give you only what you first gave us! ¹⁵We are here for only a moment, visitors and strangers in the land as our ancestors were before us. Our days on earth are like a passing shadow, gone so soon without a trace.

¹⁶"O LORD our God, even this material we have gathered to build a Temple to honor your holy name comes from you! It all belongs to you! ¹⁷I know, my God, that you examine our hearts and rejoice when you find integrity there. You know I have done all this with good motives, and I have watched your people offer their gifts willingly and joyously.

¹⁸"O LORD, the God of our ancestors Abraham, Isaac, and Israel, make your people always want to obey you. See to it that their love for you never changes. ¹⁹Give my son Solomon the wholehearted desire to obey all your commands, laws, and decrees, and to do everything necessary to build this Temple, for which I have made these preparations."

²⁰Then David said to the whole assembly, "Give praise to the LORD your God!" And the entire assembly praised the LORD, the God of their ancestors, and they bowed low and knelt before the LORD and the king.

Solomon Named as King

²¹The next day they brought 1,000 bulls, 1,000 rams, and 1,000 male lambs as burnt offerings to the LORD. They also brought liquid offerings and many other sacrifices on behalf of all Israel. ²²They feasted and drank in the LORD's presence with great joy that day.

And again they crowned David's son Solomon as their new king. They anointed him before the LORD as their leader, and they anointed Zadok as priest. ²³So Solomon took the throne of the LORD in place of his father, David, and he succeeded in everything, and all Israel obeyed him. ²⁴All the officials, the warriors, and the sons of King David pledged their loyalty to King Solomon. ²⁵And the LORD exalted Solomon in the sight of all Israel, and he gave Solomon greater royal splendor than any king in Israel before him.

Summary of David's Reign

²⁶So David son of Jesse reigned over all Israel. ²⁷He reigned over Israel for forty years, seven of them in Hebron and thirty-three in Jerusalem. ²⁸He died at a ripe old age, having enjoyed long life, wealth, and honor. Then his son Solomon ruled in his place.

²⁹All the events of King David's reign, from beginning to end, are written in *The Record of Samuel the Seer, The Record of Nathan the Prophet,* and *The Record of Gad the Seer.* ³⁰These accounts include the mighty deeds of his reign and everything that happened to him and to Israel and to all the surrounding kingdoms.

Introduction to
2 Chronicles

Background

The events described in 2 Chronicles follow in the footsteps of those recounted in 1 Chronicles. While much of the material in 2 Chronicles seems to repeat 2 Kings, 2 Chronicles covers only the history of the southern kingdom of Judah. The importance of worship is the focus of 2 Chronicles, and the author reminds his readers of the special place of the temple in their spiritual lives.

The priest-scribe Ezra is believed to be the author of this book. (See the introduction to 1 Chronicles for more information.) Second Chronicles was compiled from a number of sources that are noted throughout the book.

Message

Second Chronicles emphasizes the centrality of temple worship. The temple symbolizes God's presence. This book begins and ends with the temple: from its construction to the edict by Cyrus of Persia for its rebuilding.

The newly returned exiles from Babylon are struggling to rebuild their temple, their city, and their lives. God's covenant with the family line of David (2 Samuel 7:1–29) remains sure, even though the people have failed and been severely punished. Second Chronicles repeatedly teaches that whenever God's people forsake him, he withdraws his blessings. But he is always ready and willing to forgive and restore.

Time

The Book of 2 Chronicles covers events from 971 to 515 B.C.

Outline

2 Chronicles

1 Solomon Asks for Wisdom

Solomon son of David took firm control of his kingdom, for the LORD his God was with him and made him very powerful.

²Solomon called together all the leaders of Israel—the generals and captains of the army,* the judges, and all the political and clan leaders. ³Then he led the entire assembly to the place of worship in Gibeon, for God's Tabernacle* was located there. (This was the Tabernacle that Moses, the LORD's servant, had made in the wilderness.)

⁴David had already moved the Ark of God from Kiriath-jearim to the tent he had prepared for it in Jerusalem. ⁵But the bronze altar made by Bezalel son of Uri and grandson of Hur was there* at Gibeon in front of the Tabernacle of the LORD. So Solomon and the people gathered in front of it to consult the LORD.* ⁶There in front of the Tabernacle, Solomon went up to the bronze altar in the LORD's presence and sacrificed 1,000 burnt offerings on it.

⁷That night God appeared to Solomon and said, "What do you want? Ask, and I will give it to you!"

⁸Solomon replied to God, "You showed faithful love to David, my father, and now you have made me king in his place. ⁹O LORD God, please continue to keep your promise to David my father, for you have made me king over a people as numerous as the dust of the earth! ¹⁰Give me the wisdom and knowledge to lead them properly,* for who could possibly govern this great people of yours?"

¹¹God said to Solomon, "Because your greatest desire is to help your people, and you did not ask for wealth, riches, fame, or even the death of your enemies or a long life, but rather you asked for wisdom and knowledge to properly govern my people—¹²I will certainly give you the wisdom and knowledge you requested. But I will also give you wealth, riches, and fame such as no other king has had before you or will ever have in the future!"

¹³Then Solomon returned to Jerusalem from the Tabernacle at the place of worship in Gibeon, and he reigned over Israel.

¹⁴Solomon built up a huge force of chariots and horses.* He had 1,400 chariots and 12,000 horses. He stationed some of them in the chariot cities and some near him in Jerusalem. ¹⁵The king made silver and gold as plentiful in Jerusalem as stone. And valuable cedar timber was as common as the sycamore-fig trees that grow in the foothills of Judah.* ¹⁶Solomon's horses were imported from Egypt* and from Cilicia*; the king's traders acquired them from Cilicia at the standard price. ¹⁷At that time chariots from Egypt could be purchased for 600 pieces of silver,* and horses for 150 pieces of silver.* They were then exported to the kings of the Hittites and the kings of Aram.

1:2 Hebrew *the commanders of thousands and of hundreds.* **1:3** Hebrew *Tent of Meeting;* also in 1:6, 13. **1:5a** As in Greek version and Latin Vulgate, and some Hebrew manuscripts. Masoretic Text reads *he placed.* **1:5b** Hebrew *to consult him.* **1:10** Hebrew *to go out and come in before this people.* **1:14** Or *charioteers;* also in 1:14b. **1:15** Hebrew *the Shephelah.* **1:16a** Possibly *Muzur,* a district near Cilicia; also in 1:17. **1:16b** Hebrew *Kue,* probably another name for Cilicia. **1:17a** Hebrew *600 [shekels] of silver,* about 15 pounds or 6.8 kilograms in weight. **1:17b** Hebrew *150 [shekels],* about 3.8 pounds or 1.7 kilograms in weight.

2 Preparations for Building the Temple

1 *Solomon decided to build a Temple to honor the name of the LORD, and also a royal palace for himself. 2 *He enlisted a force of 70,000 laborers, 80,000 men to quarry stone in the hill country, and 3,600 foremen.

3 Solomon also sent this message to King Hiram* at Tyre:

"Send me cedar logs as you did for my father, David, when he was building his palace. 4 I am about to build a Temple to honor the name of the LORD my God. It will be a place set apart to burn fragrant incense before him, to display the special sacrificial bread, and to sacrifice burnt offerings each morning and evening, on the Sabbaths, at new moon celebrations, and at the other appointed festivals of the LORD our God. He has commanded Israel to do these things forever.

5 "This must be a magnificent Temple because our God is greater than all other gods. 6 But who can really build him a worthy home? Not even the highest heavens can contain him! So who am I to consider building a Temple for him, except as a place to burn sacrifices to him?

7 "So send me a master craftsman who can work with gold, silver, bronze, and iron, as well as with purple, scarlet, and blue cloth. He must be a skilled engraver who can work with the craftsmen of Judah and Jerusalem who were selected by my father, David.

8 "Also send me cedar, cypress, and red sandalwood* logs from Lebanon, for I know that your men are without equal at cutting timber in Lebanon. I will send my men to help them. 9 An immense amount of timber will be needed, for the Temple I am going to build will be very large and magnificent. 10 In payment for your woodcutters, I will send 100,000 bushels of crushed wheat, 100,000 bushels of barley,* 110,000 gallons of wine, and 110,000 gallons of olive oil.*"

11 King Hiram sent this letter of reply to Solomon:

"It is because the LORD loves his people that he has made you their king! 12 Praise the LORD, the God of Israel, who made the heavens and the earth! He has given King David a wise son, gifted with skill and understanding, who will build a Temple for the LORD and a royal palace for himself.

13 "I am sending you a master craftsman named Huram-abi, who is extremely talented. 14 His mother is from the tribe of Dan in Israel, and his father is from Tyre. He is skillful at making things from gold, silver, bronze, and iron, and he also works with stone and wood. He can work with purple, blue, and scarlet cloth and fine linen. He is also an engraver and can follow any design given to him. He will work with your craftsmen and those appointed by my lord David, your father.

15 "Send along the wheat, barley, olive oil, and wine that my lord has mentioned. 16 We will cut whatever timber you need from the Lebanon mountains and will float the logs in rafts down the coast of the Mediterranean Sea* to Joppa. From there you can transport the logs up to Jerusalem."

17 Solomon took a census of all foreigners in the land of Israel, like the census his father had taken, and he counted 153,600. 18 He assigned 70,000 of them as common laborers, 80,000 as quarry workers in the hill country, and 3,600 as foremen.

3 Solomon Builds the Temple

So Solomon began to build the Temple of the LORD in Jerusalem on Mount Moriah, where the LORD had appeared to David, his father. The Temple was built on the threshing floor of Araunah* the Jebusite, the site that David had selected. 2 The construction began in midspring,* during the fourth year of Solomon's reign.

2:1 Verse 2:1 is numbered 1:18 in Hebrew text. 2:2 Verses 2:2-18 are numbered 2:1-17 in Hebrew text. 2:3 Hebrew *Huram,* a variant spelling of Hiram; also in 2:11. 2:8 Or *juniper;* Hebrew reads *algum,* perhaps a variant spelling of *almug;* compare 9:10-11 and parallel text at 1 Kgs 10:11-12. 2:10a Hebrew *20,000 cors* [3,640 kiloliters] *of crushed wheat, 20,000 cors of barley.* 2:10b Hebrew *20,000 baths* [420 kiloliters] *of wine, and 20,000 baths of olive oil.* 2:16 Hebrew *the sea.* 3:1 Hebrew reads *Ornan,* a variant spelling of Araunah; compare 2 Sam 24:16. 3:2 Hebrew *on the second day of the second month.* This day of the ancient Hebrew lunar calendar occurred in April or May.

³These are the dimensions Solomon used for the foundation of the Temple of God (using the old standard of measurement).* It was 90 feet long and 30 feet wide.* ⁴The entry room at the front of the Temple was 30 feet* wide, running across the entire width of the Temple, and 30 feet* high. He overlaid the inside with pure gold.

⁵He paneled the main room of the Temple with cypress wood, overlaid it with fine gold, and decorated it with carvings of palm trees and chains. ⁶He decorated the walls of the Temple with beautiful jewels and with gold from the land of Parvaim. ⁷He overlaid the beams, thresholds, walls, and doors throughout the Temple with gold, and he carved figures of cherubim on the walls.

⁸He made the Most Holy Place 30 feet wide, corresponding to the width of the Temple, and 30 feet deep. He overlaid its interior with 23 tons* of fine gold. ⁹The gold nails that were used weighed 20 ounces* each. He also overlaid the walls of the upper rooms with gold.

¹⁰He made two figures shaped like cherubim, overlaid them with gold, and placed them in the Most Holy Place. ¹¹The total wingspan of the two cherubim standing side by side was 30 feet. One wing of the first figure was 7½ feet* long, and it touched the Temple wall. The other wing, also 7½ feet long, touched one of the wings of the second figure. ¹²In the same way, the second figure had one wing 7½ feet long that touched the opposite wall. The other wing, also 7½ feet long, touched the wing of the first figure. ¹³So the wingspan of the two cherubim side by side was 30 feet. They stood on their feet and faced out toward the main room of the Temple.

¹⁴Across the entrance of the Most Holy Place he hung a curtain made of fine linen, decorated with blue, purple, and scarlet thread and embroidered with figures of cherubim.

¹⁵For the front of the Temple, he made two pillars that were 27 feet* tall, each topped by a capital extending upward another 7½ feet. ¹⁶He made a network of interwoven chains and used them to decorate the tops of the pillars. He also made 100 decorative pomegranates and attached them to the chains. ¹⁷Then he set up the two pillars at the entrance of the Temple, one to the south of the entrance and the other to the north. He named the one on the south Jakin, and the one on the north Boaz.*

4 Furnishings for the Temple

Solomon* also made a bronze altar 30 feet long, 30 feet wide, and 15 feet high.* ²Then he cast a great round basin, 15 feet across from rim to rim, called the Sea. It was 7½ feet deep and about 45 feet in circumference.* ³It was encircled just below its rim by two rows of figures that resembled oxen. There were about six oxen per foot* all the way around, and they were cast as part of the basin.

⁴The Sea was placed on a base of twelve bronze oxen, all facing outward. Three faced north, three faced west, three faced south, and three faced east, and the Sea rested on them. ⁵The walls of the Sea were about three inches* thick, and its rim flared out like a cup and resembled a water lily blossom. It could hold about 16,500 gallons* of water.

⁶He also made ten smaller basins for washing the utensils for the burnt offerings. He set five on the south side and five on the north. But the priests washed themselves in the Sea.

⁷He then cast ten gold lampstands according to the specifications that had been given, and he put them in the Temple. Five were placed against the south wall, and five were placed against the north wall.

⁸He also built ten tables and placed them in the Temple, five along the south wall and five along the north wall. Then he molded 100 gold basins.

3:3a The "old standard of measurement" was a cubit equal to 18 inches [46 centimeters]. The new standard was a cubit of approximately 21 inches [53 centimeters]. **3:3b** Hebrew *60 cubits* [27.6 meters] *long and 20 cubits* [9.2 meters] *wide.* **3:4a** Hebrew *20 cubits* [9.2 meters]; also in 3:8, 11, 13. **3:4b** As in some Greek and Syriac manuscripts, which read *20 cubits* [9.2 meters]; Hebrew reads *120 [cubits],* which is 180 feet or 55 meters. **3:8** Hebrew *600 talents* [20.4 metric tons]. **3:9** Hebrew *50 shekels* [570 grams]. **3:11** Hebrew *5 cubits* [2.3 meters]; also in 3:11b, 12, 15. **3:15** As in Syriac version (see also 1 Kgs 7:15; 2 Kgs 25:17; Jer 52:21), which reads *18 cubits* [8.3 meters]; Hebrew reads *35 cubits,* which is 52.5 feet or 16.5 meters. **3:17** *Jakin* probably means "he establishes"; *Boaz* probably means "in him is strength." **4:1a** Or *Huram-abi;* Hebrew reads *He.* **4:1b** Hebrew *20 cubits* [9.2 meters] *long, 20 cubits wide, and 10 cubits* [4.6 meters] *high.* **4:2** Hebrew *10 cubits* [4.6 meters] *across . . . 5 cubits* [2.3 meters] *deep and 30 cubits* [13.8 meters] *in circumference.* **4:3** Or *20 oxen per meter;* Hebrew reads *10 per cubit.* **4:5a** Hebrew *a handbreadth* [8 centimeters]. **4:5b** Hebrew *3,000 baths* [63 kiloliters].

⁹He then built a courtyard for the priests, and also the large outer courtyard. He made doors for the courtyard entrances and overlaid them with bronze. ¹⁰The great bronze basin called the Sea was placed near the southeast corner of the Temple.

¹¹Huram-abi also made the necessary washbasins, shovels, and bowls.

So at last Huram-abi completed everything King Solomon had assigned him to make for the Temple of God:

¹² the two pillars;

the two bowl-shaped capitals on top of the pillars;

the two networks of interwoven chains that decorated the capitals;

¹³ the 400 pomegranates that hung from the chains on the capitals (two rows of pomegranates for each of the chain networks that decorated the capitals on top of the pillars);

¹⁴ the water carts holding the basins;

¹⁵ the Sea and the twelve oxen under it;

¹⁶ the ash buckets, the shovels, the meat hooks, and all the related articles.

Huram-abi made all these things of burnished bronze for the Temple of the LORD, just as King Solomon had directed. ¹⁷The king had them cast in clay molds in the Jordan Valley between Succoth and Zarethan.* ¹⁸Solomon used such great quantities of bronze that its weight could not be determined.

¹⁹Solomon also made all the furnishings for the Temple of God:

the gold altar;

the tables for the Bread of the Presence;

²⁰ the lampstands and their lamps of solid gold, to burn in front of the Most Holy Place as prescribed;

²¹ the flower decorations, lamps, and tongs—all of the purest gold;

²² the lamp snuffers, bowls, dishes, and incense burners—all of solid gold;

the doors for the entrances to the Most Holy Place and the main room of the Temple, overlaid with gold.

5 So Solomon finished all his work on the Temple of the LORD. Then he brought all the gifts his father, David, had dedicated—the silver, the gold, and the various articles—and he stored them in the treasuries of the Temple of God.

The Ark Brought to the Temple

²Solomon then summoned to Jerusalem the elders of Israel and all the heads of tribes—the leaders of the ancestral families of Israel. They were to bring the Ark of the LORD's Covenant to the Temple from its location in the City of David, also known as Zion. ³So all the men of Israel assembled before the king at the annual Festival of Shelters, which is held in early autumn.*

⁴When all the elders of Israel arrived, the Levites picked up the Ark. ⁵The priests and Levites brought up the Ark along with the special tent* and all the sacred items that had been in it. ⁶There, before the Ark, King Solomon and the entire community of Israel sacrificed so many sheep, goats, and cattle that no one could keep count!

⁷Then the priests carried the Ark of the LORD's Covenant into the inner sanctuary of the Temple—the Most Holy Place—and placed it beneath the wings of the cherubim. ⁸The cherubim spread their wings over the Ark, forming a canopy over the Ark and its carrying poles. ⁹These poles were so long that their ends could be seen from the Temple's main room—the Holy Place*—but not from the outside. They are still there to this day. ¹⁰Nothing was in the Ark except the two stone tablets that Moses had placed in it at Mount Sinai,* where the LORD made a covenant with the people of Israel when they left Egypt.

¹¹Then the priests left the Holy Place. All the priests who were present had purified themselves, whether or not they were on duty that day. ¹²And the Levites who were musicians—Asaph, Heman, Jeduthun, and all their sons and brothers—were dressed in fine linen robes and stood at the east side of the altar playing cymbals, lyres, and harps. They were joined by 120 priests who

---

4:17 As in parallel text at 1 Kgs 7:46; Hebrew reads *Zeredah.* **5:3** Hebrew *at the festival that is in the seventh month.* The Festival of Shelters began on the fifteenth day of the seventh month of the ancient Hebrew lunar calendar. This day occurred in late September, October, or early November. **5:5** Hebrew *the Tent of Meeting;* i.e., the tent mentioned in 2 Sam 6:17 and 1 Chr 16:1. **5:9** As in some Hebrew manuscripts and Greek version (see also 1 Kgs 8:8); Masoretic Text reads *from the Ark in front of the Most Holy Place.* **5:10** Hebrew *Horeb,* another name for Sinai.

were playing trumpets. ¹³ The trumpeters and singers performed together in unison to praise and give thanks to the Lord. Accompanied by trumpets, cymbals, and other instruments, they raised their voices and praised the Lord with these words:

"He is good!
His faithful love endures forever!"

At that moment a thick cloud filled the Temple of the Lord. ¹⁴ The priests could not continue their service because of the cloud, for the glorious presence of the Lord filled the Temple of God.

6 Solomon Praises the Lord

Then Solomon prayed, "O Lord, you have said that you would live in a thick cloud of darkness. ²Now I have built a glorious Temple for you, a place where you can live forever!"

³Then the king turned around to the entire community of Israel standing before him and gave this blessing: ⁴"Praise the Lord, the God of Israel, who has kept the promise he made to my father, David. For he told my father, ⁵'From the day I brought my people out of the land of Egypt, I have never chosen a city among any of the tribes of Israel as the place where a Temple should be built to honor my name. Nor have I chosen a king to lead my people Israel. ⁶But now I have chosen Jerusalem as the place for my name to be honored, and I have chosen David to be king over my people Israel.'"

⁷Then Solomon said, "My father, David, wanted to build this Temple to honor the name of the Lord, the God of Israel. ⁸But the Lord told him, 'You wanted to build the Temple to honor my name. Your intention is good, ⁹but you are not the one to do it. One of your own sons will build the Temple to honor me.'

¹⁰"And now the Lord has fulfilled the promise he made, for I have become king in my father's place, and now I sit on the throne of Israel, just as the Lord promised. I have built this Temple to honor the name of the Lord, the God of Israel. ¹¹There I have placed the Ark, which contains the covenant that the Lord made with the people of Israel."

Solomon's Prayer of Dedication

¹²Then Solomon stood before the altar of the Lord in front of the entire community of Israel, and he lifted his hands in prayer. ¹³Now Solomon had made a bronze platform 7½ feet long, 7½ feet wide, and 4½ feet high* and had placed it at the center of the Temple's outer courtyard. He stood on the platform, and then he knelt in front of the entire community of Israel and lifted his hands toward heaven. ¹⁴He prayed,

"O Lord, God of Israel, there is no God like you in all of heaven and earth. You keep your covenant and show unfailing love to all who walk before you in wholehearted devotion. ¹⁵You have kept your promise to your servant David, my father. You made that promise with your own mouth, and with your own hands you have fulfilled it today.

¹⁶"And now, O Lord, God of Israel, carry out the additional promise you made to your servant David, my father. For you said to him, 'If your descendants guard their behavior and faithfully follow my Law as you have done, one of them will always sit on the throne of Israel.' ¹⁷Now, O Lord, God of Israel, fulfill this promise to your servant David.

¹⁸"But will God really live on earth among people? Why, even the highest heavens cannot contain you. How much less this Temple I have built! ¹⁹Nevertheless, listen to my prayer and my plea, O Lord my God. Hear the cry and the prayer that your servant is making to you. ²⁰May you watch over this Temple day and night, this place where you have said you would put your name. May you always hear the prayers I make toward this place. ²¹May you hear the humble and earnest requests from me and your people Israel when we pray toward this place. Yes, hear us from heaven where you live, and when you hear, forgive.

²²"If someone wrongs another person and is required to take an oath

---

of innocence in front of your altar at this Temple, ²³then hear from heaven and judge between your servants— the accuser and the accused. Pay back the guilty as they deserve. Acquit the innocent because of their innocence.

²⁴"If your people Israel are defeated by their enemies because they have sinned against you, and if they turn back and acknowledge your name and pray to you here in this Temple, ²⁵then hear from heaven and forgive the sin of your people Israel and return them to this land you gave to them and to their ancestors.

²⁶"If the skies are shut up and there is no rain because your people have sinned against you, and if they pray toward this Temple and acknowledge your name and turn from their sins because you have punished them, ²⁷then hear from heaven and forgive the sins of your servants, your people Israel. Teach them to follow the right path, and send rain on your land that you have given to your people as their special possession.

²⁸"If there is a famine in the land or a plague or crop disease or attacks of locusts or caterpillars, or if your people's enemies are in the land besieging their towns—whatever disaster or disease there is—²⁹and if your people Israel pray about their troubles or sorrow, raising their hands toward this Temple, ³⁰then hear from heaven where you live, and forgive. Give your people what their actions deserve, for you alone know each human heart. ³¹Then they will fear you and walk in your ways as long as they live in the land you gave to our ancestors.

³²"In the future, foreigners who do not belong to your people Israel will hear of you. They will come from distant lands when they hear of your great name and your strong hand and your powerful arm. And when they pray toward this Temple, ³³then hear from heaven where you live, and grant what they ask of you. In this way, all the people of the earth will come to know and fear you, just as your own people Israel do. They, too, will know that this Temple I have built honors your name.

³⁴"If your people go out where you send them to fight their enemies, and if they pray to you by turning toward this city you have chosen and toward this Temple I have built to honor your name, ³⁵then hear their prayers from heaven and uphold their cause.

³⁶"If they sin against you—and who has never sinned?—you might become angry with them and let their enemies conquer them and take them captive to a foreign land far away or near. ³⁷But in that land of exile, they might turn to you in repentance and pray, 'We have sinned, done evil, and acted wickedly.' ³⁸If they turn to you with their whole heart and soul in the land of their captivity and pray toward the land you gave to their ancestors—toward this city you have chosen, and toward this Temple I have built to honor your name—³⁹then hear their prayers and their petitions from heaven where you live, and uphold their cause. Forgive your people who have sinned against you.

⁴⁰"O my God, may your eyes be open and your ears attentive to all the prayers made to you in this place.

⁴¹ "And now arise, O Lord God, and
enter your resting place,
along with the Ark, the symbol of
your power.
May your priests, O Lord God, be
clothed with salvation;
may your loyal servants rejoice in
your goodness.
⁴² O Lord God, do not reject the king
you have anointed.
Remember your unfailing love for
your servant David."

7 The Dedication of the Temple

When Solomon finished praying, fire flashed down from heaven and burned up the burnt offerings and sacrifices, and the glorious presence of the Lord filled the Temple. ²The priests could not enter the Temple of the Lord because the glorious presence of the Lord filled it. ³When all the people of Israel saw the fire coming down and the glorious presence of the Lord filling the Temple, they fell face down on the ground and worshiped and praised the Lord, saying,

"He is good!
His faithful love endures forever!"

[4]Then the king and all the people offered sacrifices to the LORD. [5]King Solomon offered a sacrifice of 22,000 cattle and 120,000 sheep and goats. And so the king and all the people dedicated the Temple of God. [6]The priests took their assigned positions, and so did the Levites who were singing, "His faithful love endures forever!" They accompanied the singing with music from the instruments King David had made for praising the LORD. Across from the Levites, the priests blew the trumpets, while all Israel stood.

[7]Solomon then consecrated the central area of the courtyard in front of the LORD's Temple. He offered burnt offerings and the fat of peace offerings there, because the bronze altar he had built could not hold all the burnt offerings, grain offerings, and sacrificial fat.

[8]For the next seven days Solomon and all Israel celebrated the Festival of Shelters.* A large congregation had gathered from as far away as Lebo-hamath in the north and the Brook of Egypt in the south. [9]On the eighth day they had a closing ceremony, for they had celebrated the dedication of the altar for seven days and the Festival of Shelters for seven days. [10]Then at the end of the celebration,* Solomon sent the people home. They were all joyful and glad because the LORD had been so good to David and to Solomon and to his people Israel.

The LORD's Response to Solomon

[11]So Solomon finished the Temple of the LORD, as well as the royal palace. He completed everything he had planned to do in the construction of the Temple and the palace. [12]Then one night the LORD appeared to Solomon and said,

"I have heard your prayer and have chosen this Temple as the place for making sacrifices. [13]At times I might shut up the heavens so that no rain falls, or command grasshoppers to devour your crops, or send plagues among you. [14]Then if my people who are called by my name will humble themselves and pray and seek my face and turn from their wicked ways, I will hear from heaven and will forgive their sins and restore their land. [15]My eyes will be open and my ears attentive to every prayer made in this place. [16]For I have chosen this Temple and set it apart to be holy—a place where my name will be honored forever. I will always watch over it, for it is dear to my heart.

[17]"As for you, if you faithfully follow me as David your father did, obeying all my commands, decrees, and regulations, [18]then I will establish the throne of your dynasty. For I made this covenant with your father, David, when I said, 'One of your descendants will always rule over Israel.'

[19]"But if you or your descendants abandon me and disobey the decrees and commands I have given you, and if you serve and worship other gods, [20]then I will uproot the people from this land that I have given them. I will reject this Temple that I have made holy to honor my name. I will make it an object of mockery and ridicule among the nations. [21]And though this Temple is impressive now, all who pass by will be appalled. They will ask, 'Why did the LORD do such terrible things to this land and to this Temple?'

[22]"And the answer will be, 'Because his people abandoned the LORD, the God of their ancestors, who brought them out of Egypt, and they worshiped other gods instead and bowed down to them. That is why he has brought all these disasters on them.'"

8 Solomon's Many Achievements

It took Solomon twenty years to build the LORD's Temple and his own royal palace. At the end of that time, [2]Solomon turned his attention to rebuilding the towns that King Hiram* had given him, and he settled Israelites in them. [3]Solomon also fought against the town of Hamath-zobah and conquered it. [4]He rebuilt Tadmor in the wilderness and built

---

7:8 Hebrew the festival (also in 7:9); see note on 5:3.   7:10 Hebrew Then on the twenty-third day of the seventh month. This day of the ancient Hebrew lunar calendar occurred in October or early November.   8:2 Hebrew Huram, a variant spelling of Hiram; also in 8:18.

towns in the region of Hamath as supply centers. ⁵He fortified the towns of Upper Beth-horon and Lower Beth-horon, rebuilding their walls and installing barred gates. ⁶He also rebuilt Baalath and other supply centers and constructed towns where his chariots and horses* could be stationed. He built everything he desired in Jerusalem and Lebanon and throughout his entire realm.

⁷There were still some people living in the land who were not Israelites, including the Hittites, Amorites, Perizzites, Hivites, and Jebusites. ⁸These were descendants of the nations whom the people of Israel had not destroyed. So Solomon conscripted them for his labor force, and they serve in the labor force to this day. ⁹But Solomon did not conscript any of the Israelites for his labor force. Instead, he assigned them to serve as fighting men, officers in his army, commanders of his chariots, and charioteers. ¹⁰King Solomon appointed 250 of them to supervise the people.

¹¹Solomon moved his wife, Pharaoh's daughter, from the City of David to the new palace he had built for her. He said, "My wife must not live in King David's palace, for the Ark of the LORD has been there, and it is holy ground."

¹²Then Solomon presented burnt offerings to the LORD on the altar he had built for him in front of the entry room of the Temple. ¹³He offered the sacrifices for the Sabbaths, the new moon festivals, and the three annual festivals—the Passover celebration, the Festival of Harvest,* and the Festival of Shelters—as Moses had commanded.

¹⁴In assigning the priests to their duties, Solomon followed the regulations of his father, David. He also assigned the Levites to lead the people in praise and to assist the priests in their daily duties. And he assigned the gatekeepers to their gates by their divisions, following the commands of David, the man of God. ¹⁵Solomon did not deviate in any way from David's commands concerning the priests and Levites and the treasuries.

¹⁶So Solomon made sure that all the work related to building the Temple of the LORD was carried out, from the day its foundation was laid to the day of its completion.

¹⁷Later Solomon went to Ezion-geber and Elath,* ports along the shore of the Red Sea* in the land of Edom. ¹⁸Hiram sent him ships commanded by his own officers and manned by experienced crews of sailors. These ships sailed to Ophir with Solomon's men and brought back to Solomon almost seventeen tons* of gold.

9 Visit of the Queen of Sheba

When the queen of Sheba heard of Solomon's fame, she came to Jerusalem to test him with hard questions. She arrived with a large group of attendants and a great caravan of camels loaded with spices, large quantities of gold, and precious jewels. When she met with Solomon, she talked with him about everything she had on her mind. ²Solomon had answers for all her questions; nothing was too hard for him to explain to her. ³When the queen of Sheba realized how wise Solomon was, and when she saw the palace he had built, ⁴she was overwhelmed. She was also amazed at the food on his tables, the organization of his officials and their splendid clothing, the cup-bearers and their robes, and the burnt offerings Solomon made at the Temple of the LORD.

⁵She exclaimed to the king, "Everything I heard in my country about your achievements* and wisdom is true! ⁶I didn't believe what was said until I arrived here and saw it with my own eyes. In fact, I had not heard the half of your great wisdom! It is far beyond what I was told. ⁷How happy your people must be! What a privilege for your officials to stand here day after day, listening to your wisdom! ⁸Praise the LORD your God, who delights in you and has placed you on the throne as king to rule for him. Because God loves Israel and desires this kingdom to last forever, he has made you king over them so you can rule with justice and righteousness."

⁹Then she gave the king a gift of 9,000

---

pounds* of gold, great quantities of spices, and precious jewels. Never before had there been spices as fine as those the queen of Sheba gave to King Solomon.

¹⁰(In addition, the crews of Hiram and Solomon brought gold from Ophir, and they also brought red sandalwood* and precious jewels. ¹¹The king used the sandalwood to make steps* for the Temple of the LORD and the royal palace, and to construct lyres and harps for the musicians. Never before had such beautiful things been seen in Judah.)

¹²King Solomon gave the queen of Sheba whatever she asked for—gifts of greater value than the gifts she had given him. Then she and all her attendants returned to their own land.

Solomon's Wealth and Splendor

¹³Each year Solomon received about 25 tons* of gold. ¹⁴This did not include the additional revenue he received from merchants and traders. All the kings of Arabia and the governors of the provinces also brought gold and silver to Solomon.

¹⁵King Solomon made 200 large shields of hammered gold, each weighing more than 15 pounds.* ¹⁶He also made 300 smaller shields of hammered gold, each weighing more than 7½ pounds.* The king placed these shields in the Palace of the Forest of Lebanon.

¹⁷Then the king made a huge throne, decorated with ivory and overlaid with pure gold. ¹⁸The throne had six steps, with a footstool of gold. There were armrests on both sides of the seat, and the figure of a lion stood on each side of the throne. ¹⁹There were also twelve other lions, one standing on each end of the six steps. No other throne in all the world could be compared with it!

²⁰All of King Solomon's drinking cups were solid gold, as were all the utensils in the Palace of the Forest of Lebanon. They were not made of silver, for silver was considered worthless in Solomon's day!

²¹The king had a fleet of trading ships* manned by the sailors sent by Hiram.*

Once every three years the ships returned, loaded with gold, silver, ivory, apes, and peacocks.*

²²So King Solomon became richer and wiser than any other king on earth. ²³Kings from every nation came to consult him and to hear the wisdom God had given him. ²⁴Year after year everyone who visited brought him gifts of silver and gold, clothing, weapons, spices, horses, and mules.

²⁵Solomon had 4,000 stalls for his horses and chariots, and he had 12,000 horses.* He stationed some of them in the chariot cities, and some near him in Jerusalem. ²⁶He ruled over all the kings from the Euphrates River* in the north to the land of the Philistines and the border of Egypt in the south. ²⁷The king made silver as plentiful in Jerusalem as stone. And valuable cedar timber was as common as the sycamore-fig trees that grow in the foothills of Judah.* ²⁸Solomon's horses were imported from Egypt* and many other countries.

Summary of Solomon's Reign

²⁹The rest of the events of Solomon's reign, from beginning to end, are recorded in *The Record of Nathan the Prophet,* and *The Prophecy of Ahijah from Shiloh,* and also in *The Visions of Iddo the Seer,* concerning Jeroboam son of Nebat. ³⁰Solomon ruled in Jerusalem over all Israel for forty years. ³¹When he died, he was buried in the City of David, named for his father. Then his son Rehoboam became the next king.

10 The Northern Tribes Revolt

Rehoboam went to Shechem, where all Israel had gathered to make him king. ²When Jeroboam son of Nebat heard of this, he returned from Egypt, for he had fled to Egypt to escape from King Solomon. ³The leaders of Israel summoned him, and Jeroboam and all Israel went to speak with Rehoboam. ⁴"Your father was a hard master," they said. "Lighten the harsh labor demands and heavy taxes that your father imposed on us. Then we will be your loyal subjects."

9:9 Hebrew *120 talents* [4,000 kilograms].   **9:10** Hebrew *algum wood* (also in 9:11); perhaps a variant spelling of *almug.* Compare parallel text at 1 Kgs 10:11-12.   **9:11** Or *gateways.* The meaning of the Hebrew is uncertain.   **9:13** Hebrew *666 talents* [23 metric tons]. **9:15** Hebrew *600 [shekels] of hammered gold* [6.8 kilograms].   **9:16** Hebrew *300 [shekels] of gold* [3.4 kilograms].   **9:21a** Hebrew *fleet of ships that could sail to Tarshish.*   **9:21b** Hebrew *Huram,* a variant spelling of Hiram.   **9:21c** Or *and baboons.*   **9:25** Or *12,000 charioteers.*   **9:26** Hebrew *the river.*   **9:27** Hebrew *the Shephelah.*   **9:28** Possibly *Muzur,* a district near Cilicia.

⁵Rehoboam replied, "Come back in three days for my answer." So the people went away.

⁶Then King Rehoboam discussed the matter with the older men who had counseled his father, Solomon. "What is your advice?" he asked. "How should I answer these people?"

⁷The older counselors replied, "If you are good to these people and do your best to please them and give them a favorable answer, they will always be your loyal subjects."

⁸But Rehoboam rejected the advice of the older men and instead asked the opinion of the young men who had grown up with him and were now his advisers. ⁹"What is your advice?" he asked them. "How should I answer these people who want me to lighten the burdens imposed by my father?"

¹⁰The young men replied, "This is what you should tell those complainers who want a lighter burden: 'My little finger is thicker than my father's waist! ¹¹Yes, my father laid heavy burdens on you, but I'm going to make them even heavier! My father beat you with whips, but I will beat you with scorpions!'"

¹²Three days later Jeroboam and all the people returned to hear Rehoboam's decision, just as the king had ordered. ¹³But Rehoboam spoke harshly to them, for he rejected the advice of the older counselors ¹⁴and followed the counsel of his younger advisers. He told the people, "My father laid* heavy burdens on you, but I'm going to make them even heavier! My father beat you with whips, but I will beat you with scorpions!"

¹⁵So the king paid no attention to the people. This turn of events was the will of God, for it fulfilled the LORD's message to Jeroboam son of Nebat through the prophet Ahijah from Shiloh.

¹⁶When all Israel realized* that the king had refused to listen to them, they responded,

"Down with the dynasty of David!
We have no interest in the son of Jesse.

Back to your homes, O Israel!
Look out for your own house,
O David!"

So all the people of Israel returned home. ¹⁷But Rehoboam continued to rule over the Israelites who lived in the towns of Judah.

¹⁸King Rehoboam sent Adoniram,* who was in charge of the labor force, to restore order, but the people of Israel stoned him to death. When this news reached King Rehoboam, he quickly jumped into his chariot and fled to Jerusalem. ¹⁹And to this day the northern tribes of Israel have refused to be ruled by a descendant of David.

11 Shemaiah's Prophecy

When Rehoboam arrived at Jerusalem, he mobilized the men of Judah and Benjamin—180,000 select troops—to fight against Israel and to restore the kingdom to himself.

²But the LORD said to Shemaiah, the man of God, ³"Say to Rehoboam son of Solomon, king of Judah, and to all the Israelites in Judah and Benjamin: ⁴'This is what the LORD says: Do not fight against your relatives. Go back home, for what has happened is my doing!'" So they obeyed the message of the LORD and did not fight against Jeroboam.

Rehoboam Fortifies Judah

⁵Rehoboam remained in Jerusalem and fortified various towns for the defense of Judah. ⁶He built up Bethlehem, Etam, Tekoa, ⁷Beth-zur, Soco, Adullam, ⁸Gath, Mareshah, Ziph, ⁹Adoraim, Lachish, Azekah, ¹⁰Zorah, Aijalon, and Hebron. These became the fortified towns of Judah and Benjamin. ¹¹Rehoboam strengthened their defenses and stationed commanders in them, and he stored supplies of food, olive oil, and wine. ¹²He also put shields and spears in these towns as a further safety measure. So only Judah and Benjamin remained under his control.

¹³But all the priests and Levites living among the northern tribes of Israel

---

10:14 As in Greek version and many Hebrew manuscripts (see also 1 Kgs 12:14); Masoretic Text reads *I will lay.* **10:16** As in Syriac version, Latin Vulgate, and many Hebrew manuscripts (see also 1 Kgs 12:16); Masoretic Text lacks *realized.* **10:18** Hebrew *Hadoram,* a variant spelling of Adoniram; compare 1 Kgs 4:6; 5:14; 12:18.

sided with Rehoboam. [14] The Levites even abandoned their pasturelands and property and moved to Judah and Jerusalem, because Jeroboam and his sons would not allow them to serve the LORD as priests. [15] Jeroboam appointed his own priests to serve at the pagan shrines, where they worshiped the goat and calf idols he had made. [16] From all the tribes of Israel, those who sincerely wanted to worship the LORD, the God of Israel, followed the Levites to Jerusalem, where they could offer sacrifices to the LORD, the God of their ancestors. [17] This strengthened the kingdom of Judah, and for three years they supported Rehoboam son of Solomon, for during those years they faithfully followed in the footsteps of David and Solomon.

Rehoboam's Family

[18] Rehoboam married his cousin Mahalath, the daughter of David's son Jerimoth and of Abihail, the daughter of Eliab son of Jesse. [19] Mahalath had three sons—Jeush, Shemariah, and Zaham.

[20] Later Rehoboam married another cousin, Maacah, the daughter of Absalom. Maacah gave birth to Abijah, Attai, Ziza, and Shelomith. [21] Rehoboam loved Maacah more than any of his other wives and concubines. In all, he had eighteen wives and sixty concubines, and they gave birth to twenty-eight sons and sixty daughters.

[22] Rehoboam appointed Maacah's son Abijah as leader among the princes, making it clear that he would be the next king. [23] Rehoboam also wisely gave responsibilities to his other sons and stationed some of them in the fortified towns throughout the land of Judah and Benjamin. He provided them with generous provisions, and he found many wives for them.

12 Egypt Invades Judah

But when Rehoboam was firmly established and strong, he abandoned the Law of the LORD, and all Israel followed him in this sin. [2] Because they were unfaithful to the LORD, King Shishak of Egypt came up and attacked Jerusalem in the fifth year of King Rehoboam's reign. [3] He came with 1,200 chariots, 60,000 horses,* and a countless army of foot soldiers, including Libyans, Sukkites, and Ethiopians.* [4] Shishak conquered Judah's fortified towns and then advanced to attack Jerusalem.

[5] The prophet Shemaiah then met with Rehoboam and Judah's leaders, who had all fled to Jerusalem because of Shishak. Shemaiah told them, "This is what the LORD says: You have abandoned me, so I am abandoning you to Shishak."

[6] Then the leaders of Israel and the king humbled themselves and said, "The LORD is right in doing this to us!"

[7] When the LORD saw their change of heart, he gave this message to Shemaiah: "Since the people have humbled themselves, I will not completely destroy them and will soon give them some relief. I will not use Shishak to pour out my anger on Jerusalem. [8] But they will become his subjects, so they will know the difference between serving me and serving earthly rulers."

[9] So King Shishak of Egypt came up and attacked Jerusalem. He ransacked the treasuries of the LORD's Temple and the royal palace; he stole everything, including all the gold shields Solomon had made. [10] King Rehoboam later replaced them with bronze shields as substitutes, and he entrusted them to the care of the commanders of the guard who protected the entrance to the royal palace. [11] Whenever the king went to the Temple of the LORD, the guards would also take the shields and then return them to the guardroom. [12] Because Rehoboam humbled himself, the LORD's anger was turned away, and he did not destroy him completely. There were still some good things in the land of Judah.

Summary of Rehoboam's Reign

[13] King Rehoboam firmly established himself in Jerusalem and continued to rule. He was forty-one years old when he became king, and he reigned seventeen years in Jerusalem, the city the LORD had chosen from among all the tribes of Israel as the place to honor his name. Rehoboam's mother was Naamah, a woman from

12:3a Or *charioteers,* or *horsemen.* **12:3b** Hebrew *and Cushites.*

Ammon. ¹⁴But he was an evil king, for he did not seek the LORD with all his heart.

¹⁵The rest of the events of Rehoboam's reign, from beginning to end, are recorded in *The Record of Shemaiah the Prophet* and *The Record of Iddo the Seer*, which are part of the genealogical record. Rehoboam and Jeroboam were continually at war with each other. ¹⁶When Rehoboam died, he was buried in the City of David. Then his son Abijah became the next king.

13 Abijah's War with Jeroboam

Abijah began to rule over Judah in the eighteenth year of Jeroboam's reign in Israel. ²He reigned in Jerusalem three years. His mother was Maacah,* the daughter of Uriel from Gibeah.

Then war broke out between Abijah and Jeroboam. ³Judah, led by King Abijah, fielded 400,000 select warriors, while Jeroboam mustered 800,000 select troops from Israel.

⁴When the army of Judah arrived in the hill country of Ephraim, Abijah stood on Mount Zemaraim and shouted to Jeroboam and all Israel: "Listen to me! ⁵Don't you realize that the LORD, the God of Israel, made a lasting covenant* with David, giving him and his descendants the throne of Israel forever? ⁶Yet Jeroboam son of Nebat, a mere servant of David's son Solomon, rebelled against his master. ⁷Then a whole gang of scoundrels joined him, defying Solomon's son Rehoboam when he was young and inexperienced and could not stand up to them.

⁸"Do you really think you can stand against the kingdom of the LORD that is led by the descendants of David? You may have a vast army, and you have those gold calves that Jeroboam made as your gods. ⁹But you have chased away the priests of the LORD (the descendants of Aaron) and the Levites, and you have appointed your own priests, just like the pagan nations. You let anyone become a priest these days! Whoever comes to be dedicated with a young bull and seven rams can become a priest of these so-called gods of yours!

¹⁰"But as for us, the LORD is our God, and we have not abandoned him. Only the descendants of Aaron serve the LORD as priests, and the Levites alone may help them in their work. ¹¹They present burnt offerings and fragrant incense to the LORD every morning and evening. They place the Bread of the Presence on the holy table, and they light the gold lampstand every evening. We are following the instructions of the LORD our God, but you have abandoned him. ¹²So you see, God is with us. He is our leader. His priests blow their trumpets and lead us into battle against you. O people of Israel, do not fight against the LORD, the God of your ancestors, for you will not succeed!"

¹³Meanwhile, Jeroboam had secretly sent part of his army around behind the men of Judah to ambush them. ¹⁴When Judah realized that they were being attacked from the front and the rear, they cried out to the LORD for help. Then the priests blew the trumpets, ¹⁵and the men of Judah began to shout. At the sound of their battle cry, God defeated Jeroboam and all Israel and routed them before Abijah and the army of Judah.

¹⁶The Israelite army fled from Judah, and God handed them over to Judah in defeat. ¹⁷Abijah and his army inflicted heavy losses on them; 500,000 of Israel's select troops were killed that day. ¹⁸So Judah defeated Israel on that occasion because they trusted in the LORD, the God of their ancestors. ¹⁹Abijah and his army pursued Jeroboam's troops and captured some of his towns, including Bethel, Jeshanah, and Ephron, along with their surrounding villages.

²⁰So Jeroboam of Israel never regained his power during Abijah's lifetime, and finally the LORD struck him down and he died. ²¹Meanwhile, Abijah of Judah grew more and more powerful. He married fourteen wives and had twenty-two sons and sixteen daughters.

²²The rest of the events of Abijah's reign, including his words and deeds, are recorded in *The Commentary of Iddo the Prophet.*

13:2 As in most Greek manuscripts and Syriac version (see also 2 Chr 11:20-21; 1 Kgs 15:2); Hebrew reads *Micaiah,* a variant spelling of Maacah. **13:5** Hebrew *a covenant of salt.*

14 Early Years of Asa's Reign

¹*When Abijah died, he was buried in the City of David. Then his son Asa became the next king. There was peace in the land for ten years. ²*Asa did what was pleasing and good in the sight of the LORD his God. ³He removed the foreign altars and the pagan shrines. He smashed the sacred pillars and cut down the Asherah poles. ⁴He commanded the people of Judah to seek the LORD, the God of their ancestors, and to obey his law and his commands. ⁵Asa also removed the pagan shrines, as well as the incense altars from every one of Judah's towns. So Asa's kingdom enjoyed a period of peace. ⁶During those peaceful years, he was able to build up the fortified towns throughout Judah. No one tried to make war against him at this time, for the LORD was giving him rest from his enemies.

⁷Asa told the people of Judah, "Let us build towns and fortify them with walls, towers, gates, and bars. The land is still ours because we sought the LORD our God, and he has given us peace on every side." So they went ahead with these projects and brought them to completion.

⁸King Asa had an army of 300,000 warriors from the tribe of Judah, armed with large shields and spears. He also had an army of 280,000 warriors from the tribe of Benjamin, armed with small shields and bows. Both armies were composed of well-trained fighting men.

⁹Once an Ethiopian* named Zerah attacked Judah with an army of 1,000,000 men* and 300 chariots. They advanced to the town of Mareshah, ¹⁰so Asa deployed his armies for battle in the valley north of Mareshah.* ¹¹Then Asa cried out to the LORD his God, "O LORD, no one but you can help the powerless against the mighty! Help us, O LORD our God, for we trust in you alone. It is in your name that we have come against this vast horde. O LORD, you are our God; do not let mere men prevail against you!"

¹²So the LORD defeated the Ethiopians* in the presence of Asa and the army of Judah, and the enemy fled. ¹³Asa and his army pursued them as far as Gerar, and so many Ethiopians fell that they were unable to rally. They were destroyed by the LORD and his army, and the army of Judah carried off a vast amount of plunder.

¹⁴While they were at Gerar, they attacked all the towns in that area, and terror from the LORD came upon the people there. As a result, a vast amount of plunder was taken from these towns, too. ¹⁵They also attacked the camps of herdsmen and captured many sheep, goats, and camels before finally returning to Jerusalem.

15 Asa's Religious Reforms

Then the Spirit of God came upon Azariah son of Oded, ²and he went out to meet King Asa as he was returning from the battle. "Listen to me, Asa!" he shouted. "Listen, all you people of Judah and Benjamin! The LORD will stay with you as long as you stay with him! Whenever you seek him, you will find him. But if you abandon him, he will abandon you. ³For a long time Israel was without the true God, without a priest to teach them, and without the Law to instruct them. ⁴But whenever they were in trouble and turned to the LORD, the God of Israel, and sought him out, they found him.

⁵"During those dark times, it was not safe to travel. Problems troubled the people of every land. ⁶Nation fought against nation, and city against city, for God was troubling them with every kind of problem. ⁷But as for you, be strong and courageous, for your work will be rewarded."

⁸When Asa heard this message from Azariah the prophet,* he took courage and removed all the detestable idols from the land of Judah and Benjamin and in the towns he had captured in the hill country of Ephraim. And he repaired the altar of the LORD, which stood in front of the entry room of the LORD's Temple.

⁹Then Asa called together all the people of Judah and Benjamin, along with the people of Ephraim, Manasseh, and Simeon who had settled among them. For many from Israel had moved to Judah during

---

14:1 Verse 14:1 is numbered 13:23 in Hebrew text.   **14:2** Verses 14:2-15 are numbered 14:1-14 in Hebrew text.   **14:9a** Hebrew *a Cushite.*
14:9b Or *an army of thousands and thousands;* Hebrew reads *an army of a thousand thousands.*   **14:10** Or *in the Zephathah Valley near Mareshah.*
14:12 Hebrew *Cushites;* also in 14:13.   **15:8** As in Syriac version and Latin Vulgate (see also 15:1); Hebrew reads *from Oded the prophet.*

Asa's reign when they saw that the LORD his God was with him. ¹⁰The people gathered at Jerusalem in late spring,* during the fifteenth year of Asa's reign.

¹¹On that day they sacrificed to the LORD 700 cattle and 7,000 sheep and goats from the plunder they had taken in the battle. ¹²Then they entered into a covenant to seek the LORD, the God of their ancestors, with all their heart and soul. ¹³They agreed that anyone who refused to seek the LORD, the God of Israel, would be put to death—whether young or old, man or woman. ¹⁴They shouted out their oath of loyalty to the LORD with trumpets blaring and rams' horns sounding. ¹⁵All in Judah were happy about this covenant, for they had entered into it with all their heart. They earnestly sought after God, and they found him. And the LORD gave them rest from their enemies on every side.

¹⁶King Asa even deposed his grandmother* Maacah from her position as queen mother because she had made an obscene Asherah pole. He cut down her obscene pole, broke it up, and burned it in the Kidron Valley. ¹⁷Although the pagan shrines were not removed from Israel, Asa's heart remained completely faithful throughout his life. ¹⁸He brought into the Temple of God the silver and gold and the various items that he and his father had dedicated.

¹⁹So there was no more war until the thirty-fifth year of Asa's reign.

16 Final Years of Asa's Reign

In the thirty-sixth year of Asa's reign, King Baasha of Israel invaded Judah and fortified Ramah in order to prevent anyone from entering or leaving King Asa's territory in Judah.

²Asa responded by removing the silver and gold from the treasuries of the Temple of the LORD and the royal palace. He sent it to King Ben-hadad of Aram, who was ruling in Damascus, along with this message:

³"Let there be a treaty* between you and me like the one between your father and my father. See, I am sending you silver and gold. Break your treaty with King Baasha of Israel so that he will leave me alone."

⁴Ben-hadad agreed to King Asa's request and sent the commanders of his army to attack the towns of Israel. They conquered the towns of Ijon, Dan, Abel-beth-maacah,* and all the store cities in Naphtali. ⁵As soon as Baasha of Israel heard what was happening, he abandoned his project of fortifying Ramah and stopped all work on it. ⁶Then King Asa called out all the men of Judah to carry away the building stones and timbers that Baasha had been using to fortify Ramah. Asa used these materials to fortify the towns of Geba and Mizpah.

⁷At that time Hanani the seer came to King Asa and told him, "Because you have put your trust in the king of Aram instead of in the LORD your God, you missed your chance to destroy the army of the king of Aram. ⁸Don't you remember what happened to the Ethiopians* and Libyans and their vast army, with all of their chariots and charioteers?* At that time you relied on the LORD, and he handed them over to you. ⁹The eyes of the LORD search the whole earth in order to strengthen those whose hearts are fully committed to him. What a fool you have been! From now on you will be at war."

¹⁰Asa became so angry with Hanani for saying this that he threw him into prison and put him in stocks. At that time Asa also began to oppress some of his people.

Summary of Asa's Reign

¹¹The rest of the events of Asa's reign, from beginning to end, are recorded in *The Book of the Kings of Judah and Israel.* ¹²In the thirty-ninth year of his reign, Asa developed a serious foot disease. Yet even with the severity of his disease, he did not seek the LORD's help but turned only to his physicians. ¹³So he died in the forty-first year of his reign. ¹⁴He was buried in the tomb he had carved out for himself in the City of David. He was laid on a bed perfumed with sweet spices and fragrant ointments,

---

15:10 Hebrew *in the third month.* This month of the ancient Hebrew lunar calendar usually occurs within the months of May and June. **15:16** Hebrew *his mother.* **16:3** As in Greek version; Hebrew reads *There is a treaty.* **16:4** As in parallel text at 1 Kgs 15:20; Hebrew reads *Abel-maim,* another name for Abel-beth-maacah. **16:8a** Hebrew *Cushites.* **16:8b** Or *and horsemen?*

and the people built a huge funeral fire in his honor.

17 Jehoshaphat Rules in Judah

Then Jehoshaphat, Asa's son, became the next king. He strengthened Judah to stand against any attack from Israel. ²He stationed troops in all the fortified towns of Judah, and he assigned additional garrisons to the land of Judah and to the towns of Ephraim that his father, Asa, had captured.

³The LORD was with Jehoshaphat because he followed the example of his father's early years* and did not worship the images of Baal. ⁴He sought his father's God and obeyed his commands instead of following the evil practices of the kingdom of Israel. ⁵So the LORD established Jehoshaphat's control over the kingdom of Judah. All the people of Judah brought gifts to Jehoshaphat, so he became very wealthy and highly esteemed. ⁶He was deeply committed to* the ways of the LORD. He removed the pagan shrines and Asherah poles from Judah.

⁷In the third year of his reign Jehoshaphat sent his officials to teach in all the towns of Judah. These officials included Ben-hail, Obadiah, Zechariah, Nethanel, and Micaiah. ⁸He sent Levites along with them, including Shemaiah, Nethaniah, Zebadiah, Asahel, Shemiramoth, Jehonathan, Adonijah, Tobijah, and Tob-adonijah. He also sent out the priests Elishama and Jehoram. ⁹They took copies of the Book of the Law of the LORD and traveled around through all the towns of Judah, teaching the people.

¹⁰Then the fear of the LORD fell over all the surrounding kingdoms so that none of them wanted to declare war on Jehoshaphat. ¹¹Some of the Philistines brought him gifts and silver as tribute, and the Arabs brought 7,700 rams and 7,700 male goats.

¹²So Jehoshaphat became more and more powerful and built fortresses and storage cities throughout Judah. ¹³He stored numerous supplies in Judah's towns and stationed an army of seasoned troops at Jerusalem. ¹⁴His army was enrolled according to ancestral clans.

From Judah there were 300,000 troops organized in units of 1,000, under the command of Adnah. ¹⁵Next in command was Jehohanan, who commanded 280,000 troops. ¹⁶Next was Amasiah son of Zicri, who volunteered for the LORD's service, with 200,000 troops under his command.

¹⁷From Benjamin there were 200,000 troops equipped with bows and shields. They were under the command of Eliada, a veteran soldier. ¹⁸Next in command was Jehozabad, who commanded 180,000 armed men.

¹⁹These were the troops stationed in Jerusalem to serve the king, besides those Jehoshaphat stationed in the fortified towns throughout Judah.

18 Jehoshaphat and Ahab

Jehoshaphat enjoyed great riches and high esteem, and he made an alliance with Ahab of Israel by having his son marry Ahab's daughter. ²A few years later he went to Samaria to visit Ahab, who prepared a great banquet for him and his officials. They butchered great numbers of sheep, goats, and cattle for the feast. Then Ahab enticed Jehoshaphat to join forces with him to recover Ramoth-gilead.

³"Will you go with me to Ramoth-gilead?" King Ahab of Israel asked King Jehoshaphat of Judah.

Jehoshaphat replied, "Why, of course! You and I are as one, and my troops are your troops. We will certainly join you in battle." ⁴Then Jehoshaphat added, "But first let's find out what the LORD says."

⁵So the king of Israel summoned the prophets, 400 of them, and asked them, "Should we go to war against Ramoth-gilead, or should I hold back?"

They all replied, "Yes, go right ahead! God will give the king victory."

⁶But Jehoshaphat asked, "Is there not also a prophet of the LORD here? We should ask him the same question."

⁷The king of Israel replied to Jehoshaphat, "There is one more man who could consult the LORD for us, but I hate him. He never prophesies anything but trouble for me! His name is Micaiah son of Imlah."

Jehoshaphat replied, "That's not the way

17:3 Some Hebrew manuscripts read *the example of his father, David.*   17:6 Hebrew *His heart was courageous in.*

a king should talk! Let's hear what he has to say."

[8] So the king of Israel called one of his officials and said, "Quick! Bring Micaiah son of Imlah."

Micaiah Prophesies against Ahab

[9] King Ahab of Israel and King Jehoshaphat of Judah, dressed in their royal robes, were sitting on thrones at the threshing floor near the gate of Samaria. All of Ahab's prophets were prophesying there in front of them. [10] One of them, Zedekiah son of Kenaanah, made some iron horns and proclaimed, "This is what the LORD says: With these horns you will gore the Arameans to death!"

[11] All the other prophets agreed. "Yes," they said, "go up to Ramoth-gilead and be victorious, for the LORD will give the king victory!"

[12] Meanwhile, the messenger who went to get Micaiah said to him, "Look, all the prophets are promising victory for the king. Be sure that you agree with them and promise success."

[13] But Micaiah replied, "As surely as the LORD lives, I will say only what my God says."

[14] When Micaiah arrived before the king, Ahab asked him, "Micaiah, should we go to war against Ramoth-gilead, or should I hold back?"

Micaiah replied sarcastically, "Yes, go up and be victorious, for you will have victory over them!"

[15] But the king replied sharply, "How many times must I demand that you speak only the truth to me when you speak for the LORD?"

[16] Then Micaiah told him, "In a vision I saw all Israel scattered on the mountains, like sheep without a shepherd. And the LORD said, 'Their master has been killed.* Send them home in peace.'"

[17] "Didn't I tell you?" the king of Israel exclaimed to Jehoshaphat. "He never prophesies anything but trouble for me."

[18] Then Micaiah continued, "Listen to what the LORD says! I saw the LORD sitting on his throne with all the armies of heaven around him, on his right and on his left. [19] And the LORD said, 'Who can entice King Ahab of Israel to go into battle against Ramoth-gilead so he can be killed?'

"There were many suggestions, [20] and finally a spirit approached the LORD and said, 'I can do it!'

"'How will you do this?' the LORD asked.

[21] "And the spirit replied, 'I will go out and inspire all of Ahab's prophets to speak lies.'

"'You will succeed,' said the LORD. 'Go ahead and do it.'

[22] "So you see, the LORD has put a lying spirit in the mouths of your prophets. For the LORD has pronounced your doom."

[23] Then Zedekiah son of Kenaanah walked up to Micaiah and slapped him across the face. "Since when did the Spirit of the LORD leave me to speak to you?" he demanded.

[24] And Micaiah replied, "You will find out soon enough when you are trying to hide in some secret room!"

[25] "Arrest him!" the king of Israel ordered. "Take him back to Amon, the governor of the city, and to my son Joash. [26] Give them this order from the king: 'Put this man in prison, and feed him nothing but bread and water until I return safely from the battle!'"

[27] But Micaiah replied, "If you return safely, it will mean that the LORD has not spoken through me!" Then he added to those standing around, "Everyone mark my words!"

The Death of Ahab

[28] So King Ahab of Israel and King Jehoshaphat of Judah led their armies against Ramoth-gilead. [29] The king of Israel said to Jehoshaphat, "As we go into battle, I will disguise myself so no one will recognize me, but you wear your royal robes." So the king of Israel disguised himself, and they went into battle.

[30] Meanwhile, the king of Aram had issued these orders to his chariot commanders: "Attack only the king of Israel! Don't bother with anyone else." [31] So when the Aramean chariot commanders saw Jehoshaphat in his royal robes, they went after him. "There is the king of Israel!" they shouted. But Jehoshaphat called out, and the LORD saved

18:16 Hebrew *These people have no master.*

him. God helped him by turning the attackers away from him. ³²As soon as the chariot commanders realized he was not the king of Israel, they stopped chasing him.

³³An Aramean soldier, however, randomly shot an arrow at the Israelite troops and hit the king of Israel between the joints of his armor. "Turn the horses* and get me out of here!" Ahab groaned to the driver of the chariot. "I'm badly wounded!"

³⁴The battle raged all that day, and the king of Israel propped himself up in his chariot facing the Arameans. In the evening, just as the sun was setting, he died.

19 Jehoshaphat Appoints Judges

When King Jehoshaphat of Judah arrived safely home in Jerusalem, ²Jehu son of Hanani the seer went out to meet him. "Why should you help the wicked and love those who hate the LORD?" he asked the king. "Because of what you have done, the LORD is very angry with you. ³Even so, there is some good in you, for you have removed the Asherah poles throughout the land, and you have committed yourself to seeking God."

⁴Jehoshaphat lived in Jerusalem, but he went out among the people, traveling from Beersheba to the hill country of Ephraim, encouraging the people to return to the LORD, the God of their ancestors. ⁵He appointed judges throughout the nation in all the fortified towns, ⁶and he said to them, "Always think carefully before pronouncing judgment. Remember that you do not judge to please people but to please the LORD. He will be with you when you render the verdict in each case. ⁷Fear the LORD and judge with integrity, for the LORD our God does not tolerate perverted justice, partiality, or the taking of bribes."

⁸In Jerusalem, Jehoshaphat appointed some of the Levites and priests and clan leaders in Israel to serve as judges for cases involving the LORD's regulations and for civil disputes. ⁹These were his instructions to them: "You must always act in the fear of the LORD, with faithfulness and an undivided heart. ¹⁰Whenever a case comes

to you from fellow citizens in an outlying town, whether a murder case or some other violation of God's laws, commands, decrees, or regulations, you must warn them not to sin against the LORD, so that he will not be angry with you and them. Do this and you will not be guilty.

¹¹"Amariah the high priest will have final say in all cases involving the LORD. Zebadiah son of Ishmael, a leader from the tribe of Judah, will have final say in all civil cases. The Levites will assist you in making sure that justice is served. Take courage as you fulfill your duties, and may the LORD be with those who do what is right."

20 War with Surrounding Nations

After this, the armies of the Moabites, Ammonites, and some of the Meunites* declared war on Jehoshaphat. ²Messengers came and told Jehoshaphat, "A vast army from Edom* is marching against you from beyond the Dead Sea.* They are already at Hazazon-tamar." (This was another name for En-gedi.)

³Jehoshaphat was terrified by this news and begged the LORD for guidance. He also ordered everyone in Judah to begin fasting. ⁴So people from all the towns of Judah came to Jerusalem to seek the LORD's help.

⁵Jehoshaphat stood before the community of Judah and Jerusalem in front of the new courtyard at the Temple of the LORD. ⁶He prayed, "O LORD, God of our ancestors, you alone are the God who is in heaven. You are ruler of all the kingdoms of the earth. You are powerful and mighty; no one can stand against you! ⁷O our God, did you not drive out those who lived in this land when your people Israel arrived? And did you not give this land forever to the descendants of your friend Abraham? ⁸Your people settled here and built this Temple to honor your name. ⁹They said, 'Whenever we are faced with any calamity such as war,* plague, or famine, we can come to stand in your presence before this Temple where your name is honored. We can cry out to you to save us, and you will hear us and rescue us.'

¹⁰"And now see what the armies of Am-

18:33 Hebrew *Turn your hand.* **20:1** As in some Greek manuscripts (see also 26:7); Hebrew repeats *Ammonites.* **20:2a** As in one Hebrew manuscript; most Hebrew manuscripts and ancient versions read *Aram.* **20:2b** Hebrew *the sea.* **20:9** Or *sword of judgment;* or *sword, judgment.*

Turning Off the News

2 CHRONICLES 20:1–9

I'm a news junkie. I like knowing what's going on in the world.

But a drawback came several years ago when I found myself feeling more irritable, frustrated, and discouraged after I listened to the news. Slowly I realized that there was a correlation between my listening to the news and my emotional state.

As I thought and prayed about it, I felt God calling me to give up the news and devote that time to prayer.

It was tough to go cold turkey! But that fast allowed me to clear my mind and emotions, to focus on the hope of Christ rather than the hopelessness of the world.

Once the fast was over, I was eager to go back to the news but now was grateful it didn't hold quite the control over me any longer.

I've often fasted from food and other things during different seasons of my life and for numerous reasons. And I've been amazed each time by how much more clearly I hear God's voice and direction. For me, fasting feels like prayer on steroids. As we fast, we experience a wonderful delight as we taste and see the goodness of God (Psalm 34:8).

—*Ginger Kolbaba*

For more on fasting, see reading at Ezra 8:21–23.

mon, Moab, and Mount Seir are doing. You would not let our ancestors invade those nations when Israel left Egypt, so they went around them and did not destroy them. ¹¹Now see how they reward us! For they have come to throw us out of your land, which you gave us as an inheritance. ¹²O our God, won't you stop them? We are powerless against this mighty army that is about to attack us. We do not know what to do, but we are looking to you for help."

¹³As all the men of Judah stood before the LORD with their little ones, wives, and children, ¹⁴the Spirit of the LORD came upon one of the men standing there. His name was Jahaziel son of Zechariah, son of Benaiah, son of Jeiel, son of Mattaniah, a Levite who was a descendant of Asaph.

¹⁵He said, "Listen, all you people of Judah and Jerusalem! Listen, King Jehoshaphat! This is what the LORD says: Do not be afraid! Don't be discouraged by this mighty army, for the battle is not yours, but God's.

¹⁶Tomorrow, march out against them. You will find them coming up through the ascent of Ziz at the end of the valley that opens into the wilderness of Jeruel. ¹⁷But you will not even need to fight. Take your positions; then stand still and watch the LORD's victory. He is with you, O people of Judah and Jerusalem. Do not be afraid or discouraged. Go out against them tomorrow, for the LORD is with you!"

¹⁸Then King Jehoshaphat bowed low with his face to the ground. And all the people of Judah and Jerusalem did the same, worshiping the LORD. ¹⁹Then the Levites from the clans of Kohath and Korah stood to praise the LORD, the God of Israel, with a very loud shout.

²⁰Early the next morning the army of Judah went out into the wilderness of Tekoa. On the way Jehoshaphat stopped and said, "Listen to me, all you people of Judah and Jerusalem! Believe in the LORD your God, and you will be able to stand

firm. Believe in his prophets, and you will succeed."

²¹ After consulting the people, the king appointed singers to walk ahead of the army, singing to the LORD and praising him for his holy splendor. This is what they sang:

"Give thanks to the LORD;
    his faithful love endures forever!"

²² At the very moment they began to sing and give praise, the LORD caused the armies of Ammon, Moab, and Mount Seir to start fighting among themselves. ²³ The armies of Moab and Ammon turned against their allies from Mount Seir and killed every one of them. After they had destroyed the army of Seir, they began attacking each other. ²⁴ So when the army of Judah arrived at the lookout point in the wilderness, all they saw were dead bodies lying on the ground as far as they could see. Not a single one of the enemy had escaped.

²⁵ King Jehoshaphat and his men went out to gather the plunder. They found vast amounts of equipment, clothing,* and other valuables—more than they could carry. There was so much plunder that it took them three days just to collect it all! ²⁶ On the fourth day they gathered in the Valley of Blessing,* which got its name that day because the people praised and thanked the LORD there. It is still called the Valley of Blessing today.

²⁷ Then all the men returned to Jerusalem, with Jehoshaphat leading them, overjoyed that the LORD had given them victory over their enemies. ²⁸ They marched into Jerusalem to the music of harps, lyres, and trumpets, and they proceeded to the Temple of the LORD.

²⁹ When all the surrounding kingdoms heard that the LORD himself had fought against the enemies of Israel, the fear of God came over them. ³⁰ So Jehoshaphat's kingdom was at peace, for his God had given him rest on every side.

Summary of Jehoshaphat's Reign

³¹ So Jehoshaphat ruled over the land of Judah. He was thirty-five years old when he became king, and he reigned in Jerusalem twenty-five years. His mother was Azubah, the daughter of Shilhi.

³² Jehoshaphat was a good king, following the ways of his father, Asa. He did what was pleasing in the LORD's sight. ³³ During his reign, however, he failed to remove all the pagan shrines, and the people never fully committed themselves to follow the God of their ancestors.

³⁴ The rest of the events of Jehoshaphat's reign, from beginning to end, are recorded in *The Record of Jehu Son of Hanani*, which is included in *The Book of the Kings of Israel*.

³⁵ Some time later King Jehoshaphat of Judah made an alliance with King Ahaziah of Israel, who was very wicked.* ³⁶ Together they built a fleet of trading ships* at the port of Ezion-geber. ³⁷ Then Eliezer son of Dodavahu from Mareshah prophesied against Jehoshaphat. He said, "Because you have allied yourself with King Ahaziah, the LORD will destroy your work." So the ships met with disaster and never put out to sea.*

21 Jehoram Rules in Judah

When Jehoshaphat died, he was buried with his ancestors in the City of David. Then his son Jehoram became the next king.

² Jehoram's brothers—the other sons of Jehoshaphat—were Azariah, Jehiel, Zechariah, Azariahu, Michael, and Shephatiah; all these were the sons of Jehoshaphat king of Judah.* ³ Their father had given each of them valuable gifts of silver, gold, and costly items, and also some of Judah's fortified towns. However, he designated Jehoram as the next king because he was the oldest. ⁴ But when Jehoram had become solidly established as king, he killed all his brothers and some of the other leaders of Judah.

⁵ Jehoram was thirty-two years old when he became king, and he reigned in Jerusalem eight years. ⁶ But Jehoram followed the example of the kings of Israel and was as wicked as King Ahab, for he had married one of Ahab's daughters. So Jehoram did what was evil in the LORD's sight. ⁷ But

---

20:25 As in some Hebrew manuscripts and Latin Vulgate; most Hebrew manuscripts read *corpses*. **20:26** Hebrew *valley of Beracah*. **20:35** Or *who made him do what was wicked*. **20:36** Hebrew *fleet of ships that could go to Tarshish*. **20:37** Hebrew *never set sail for Tarshish*. **21:2** Masoretic Text reads *of Israel*; also in 21:4. The author of Chronicles sees Judah as representative of the true Israel. (Some Hebrew manuscripts, Greek and Syriac versions, and Latin Vulgate read of *Judah*.)

the LORD did not want to destroy David's dynasty, for he had made a covenant with David and promised that his descendants would continue to rule, shining like a lamp forever.

⁸During Jehoram's reign, the Edomites revolted against Judah and crowned their own king. ⁹So Jehoram went out with his full army and all his chariots. The Edomites surrounded him and his chariot commanders, but he went out at night and attacked them* under cover of darkness. ¹⁰Even so, Edom has been independent from Judah to this day. The town of Libnah also revolted about that same time. All this happened because Jehoram had abandoned the LORD, the God of his ancestors. ¹¹He had built pagan shrines in the hill country of Judah and had led the people of Jerusalem and Judah to give themselves to pagan gods and to go astray.

¹²Then Elijah the prophet wrote Jehoram this letter:

"This is what the LORD, the God of your ancestor David, says: You have not followed the good example of your father, Jehoshaphat, or your grandfather King Asa of Judah. ¹³Instead, you have been as evil as the kings of Israel. You have led the people of Jerusalem and Judah to worship idols, just as King Ahab did in Israel. And you have even killed your own brothers, men who were better than you. ¹⁴So now the LORD is about to strike you, your people, your children, your wives, and all that is yours with a heavy blow. ¹⁵You yourself will suffer with a severe intestinal disease that will get worse each day until your bowels come out."

¹⁶Then the LORD stirred up the Philistines and the Arabs, who lived near the Ethiopians,* to attack Jehoram. ¹⁷They marched against Judah, broke down its defenses, and carried away everything of value in the royal palace, including the king's sons and his wives. Only his youngest son, Ahaziah,* was spared.

¹⁸After all this, the LORD struck Jehoram with the severe intestinal disease. ¹⁹The disease grew worse and worse, and at the end of two years it caused his bowels to come out, and he died in agony. His people did not build a great funeral fire to honor him as they had done for his ancestors.

²⁰Jehoram was thirty-two years old when he became king, and he reigned in Jerusalem eight years. No one was sorry when he died. They buried him in the City of David, but not in the royal cemetery.

22 Ahaziah Rules in Judah

Then the people of Jerusalem made Ahaziah, Jehoram's youngest son, their next king, since the marauding bands who came with the Arabs* had killed all the older sons. So Ahaziah son of Jehoram reigned as king of Judah.

²Ahaziah was twenty-two* years old when he became king, and he reigned in Jerusalem one year. His mother was Athaliah, a granddaughter of King Omri. ³Ahaziah also followed the evil example of King Ahab's family, for his mother encouraged him in doing wrong. ⁴He did what was evil in the LORD's sight, just as Ahab's family had done. They even became his advisers after the death of his father, and they led him to ruin.

⁵Following their evil advice, Ahaziah joined King Joram,* the son of King Ahab of Israel, in his war against King Hazael of Aram at Ramoth-gilead. When the Arameans wounded Joram in the battle, ⁶he returned to Jezreel to recover from the wounds he had received at Ramoth.* Because Joram was wounded, King Ahaziah* of Judah went to Jezreel to visit him. ⁷But God had decided that this visit would be Ahaziah's downfall. While he was there, Ahaziah went out with Joram to meet Jehu grandson of Nimshi,* whom the LORD had appointed to destroy the dynasty of Ahab.

⁸While Jehu was executing judgment against the family of Ahab, he happened to

---

21:9 Or *he went out and escaped.* The meaning of the Hebrew is uncertain. **21:16** Hebrew *the Cushites.* **21:17** Hebrew *Jehoahaz,* a variant spelling of Ahaziah; compare 22:1. **22:1** Or *marauding bands of Arabs.* **22:2** As in some Greek manuscripts and Syriac version (see also 2 Kgs 8:26); Hebrew reads *forty-two.* **22:5** Hebrew *Jehoram,* a variant spelling of Joram; also in 22:6, 7. **22:6a** Hebrew *Ramah,* a variant spelling of Ramoth. **22:6b** As in some Hebrew manuscripts, Greek and Syriac versions, and Latin Vulgate (see also 2 Kgs 8:29); most Hebrew manuscripts read *Azariah.* **22:7** Hebrew *descendant of Nimshi;* compare 2 Kgs 9:2, 14.

meet some of Judah's officials and Ahaziah's relatives* who were traveling with Ahaziah. So Jehu killed them all. ⁹ Then Jehu's men searched for Ahaziah, and they found him hiding in the city of Samaria. They brought him to Jehu, who killed him. Ahaziah was given a decent burial because the people said, "He was the grandson of Jehoshaphat—a man who sought the LORD with all his heart." But none of the surviving members of Ahaziah's family was capable of ruling the kingdom.

Queen Athaliah Rules in Judah

¹⁰ When Athaliah, the mother of King Ahaziah of Judah, learned that her son was dead, she began to destroy the rest of Judah's royal family. ¹¹ But Ahaziah's sister Jehosheba,* the daughter of King Jehoram, took Ahaziah's infant son, Joash, and stole him away from among the rest of the king's children, who were about to be killed. She put Joash and his nurse in a bedroom. In this way, Jehosheba, wife of Jehoiada the priest and sister of Ahaziah, hid the child so that Athaliah could not murder him. ¹² Joash remained hidden in the Temple of God for six years while Athaliah ruled over the land.

23 Revolt against Athaliah

In the seventh year of Athaliah's reign, Jehoiada the priest decided to act. He summoned his courage and made a pact with five army commanders: Azariah son of Jeroham, Ishmael son of Jehohanan, Azariah son of Obed, Maaseiah son of Adaiah, and Elishaphat son of Zicri. ² These men traveled secretly throughout Judah and summoned the Levites and clan leaders in all the towns to come to Jerusalem. ³ They all gathered at the Temple of God, where they made a solemn pact with Joash, the young king.

Jehoiada said to them, "Here is the king's son! The time has come for him to reign! The LORD has promised that a descendant of David will be our king. ⁴ This is what you must do. When you priests and Levites come on duty on the Sabbath, a third of you will serve as gatekeepers. ⁵ Another third

will go over to the royal palace, and the final third will be at the Foundation Gate. Everyone else should stay in the courtyards of the LORD's Temple. ⁶ Remember, only the priests and Levites on duty may enter the Temple of the LORD, for they are set apart as holy. The rest of the people must obey the LORD's instructions and stay outside. ⁷ You Levites, form a bodyguard around the king and keep your weapons in hand. Kill anyone who tries to enter the Temple. Stay with the king wherever he goes."

⁸ So the Levites and all the people of Judah did everything as Jehoiada the priest ordered. The commanders took charge of the men reporting for duty that Sabbath, as well as those who were going off duty. Jehoiada the priest did not let anyone go home after their shift ended. ⁹ Then Jehoiada supplied the commanders with the spears and the large and small shields that had once belonged to King David and were stored in the Temple of God. ¹⁰ He stationed all the people around the king, with their weapons ready. They formed a line from the south side of the Temple around to the north side and all around the altar.

¹¹ Then Jehoiada and his sons brought out Joash, the king's son, placed the crown on his head, and presented him with a copy of God's laws.* They anointed him and proclaimed him king, and everyone shouted, "Long live the king!"

The Death of Athaliah

¹² When Athaliah heard the noise of the people running and the shouts of praise to the king, she hurried to the LORD's Temple to see what was happening. ¹³ When she arrived, she saw the newly crowned king standing in his place of authority by the pillar at the Temple entrance. The commanders and trumpeters were surrounding him, and people from all over the land were rejoicing and blowing trumpets. Singers with musical instruments were leading the people in a great celebration. When Athaliah saw all this, she tore her clothes in despair and shouted, "Treason! Treason!"

¹⁴ Then Jehoiada the priest ordered the commanders who were in charge of the

---

troops, "Take her to the soldiers in front of the Temple,* and kill anyone who tries to rescue her." For the priest had said, "She must not be killed in the Temple of the LORD." ¹⁵So they seized her and led her out to the entrance of the Horse Gate on the palace grounds, and they killed her there.

Jehoiada's Religious Reforms

¹⁶Then Jehoiada made a covenant between himself and the king and the people that they would be the LORD's people. ¹⁷And all the people went over to the temple of Baal and tore it down. They demolished the altars and smashed the idols, and they killed Mattan the priest of Baal in front of the altars.

¹⁸Jehoiada now put the priests and Levites in charge of the Temple of the LORD, following all the directions given by David. He also commanded them to present burnt offerings to the LORD, as prescribed by the Law of Moses, and to sing and rejoice as David had instructed. ¹⁹He also stationed gatekeepers at the gates of the LORD's Temple to keep out those who for any reason were ceremonially unclean.

²⁰Then the commanders, nobles, rulers, and all the people of the land escorted the king from the Temple of the LORD. They went through the upper gate and into the palace, and they seated the king on the royal throne. ²¹So all the people of the land rejoiced, and the city was peaceful because Athaliah had been killed.

24 Joash Repairs the Temple

Joash was seven years old when he became king, and he reigned in Jerusalem forty years. His mother was Zibiah from Beersheba. ²Joash did what was pleasing in the LORD's sight throughout the lifetime of Jehoiada the priest. ³Jehoiada chose two wives for Joash, and he had sons and daughters.

⁴At one point Joash decided to repair and restore the Temple of the LORD. ⁵He summoned the priests and Levites and gave them these instructions: "Go to all the towns of Judah and collect the required annual offerings, so that we can repair the Temple of your God. Do not delay!" But the Levites did not act immediately.

⁶So the king called for Jehoiada the high priest and asked him, "Why haven't you demanded that the Levites go out and collect the Temple taxes from the towns of Judah and from Jerusalem? Moses, the servant of the LORD, levied this tax on the community of Israel in order to maintain the Tabernacle of the Covenant.*"

⁷Over the years the followers of wicked Athaliah had broken into the Temple of God, and they had used all the dedicated things from the Temple of the LORD to worship the images of Baal.

⁸So now the king ordered a chest to be made and set outside the gate leading to the Temple of the LORD. ⁹Then a proclamation was sent throughout Judah and Jerusalem, telling the people to bring to the LORD the tax that Moses, the servant of God, had required of the Israelites in the wilderness. ¹⁰This pleased all the leaders and the people, and they gladly brought their money and filled the chest with it.

¹¹Whenever the chest became full, the Levites would carry it to the king's officials. Then the court secretary and an officer of the high priest would come and empty the chest and take it back to the Temple again. This went on day after day, and a large amount of money was collected. ¹²The king and Jehoiada gave the money to the construction supervisors, who hired masons and carpenters to restore the Temple of the LORD. They also hired metalworkers, who made articles of iron and bronze for the LORD's Temple.

¹³The men in charge of the renovation worked hard and made steady progress. They restored the Temple of God according to its original design and strengthened it. ¹⁴When all the repairs were finished, they brought the remaining money to the king and Jehoiada. It was used to make various articles for the Temple of the LORD—articles for worship services and for burnt offerings, including ladles and other articles made of gold and silver. And the burnt offerings were sacrificed continually in the Temple of the LORD during the lifetime of Jehoiada the priest.

23:14 Or *Bring her out from between the ranks;* or *Take her out of the Temple precincts.* The meaning of the Hebrew is uncertain. **24:6** Hebrew *Tent of the Testimony.*

[15] Jehoiada lived to a very old age, finally dying at 130. [16] He was buried among the kings in the City of David, because he had done so much good in Israel for God and his Temple.

Jehoiada's Reforms Reversed

[17] But after Jehoiada's death, the leaders of Judah came and bowed before King Joash and persuaded him to listen to their advice. [18] They decided to abandon the Temple of the LORD, the God of their ancestors, and they worshiped Asherah poles and idols instead! Because of this sin, divine anger fell on Judah and Jerusalem. [19] Yet the LORD sent prophets to bring them back to him. The prophets warned them, but still the people would not listen.

[20] Then the Spirit of God came upon Zechariah son of Jehoiada the priest. He stood before the people and said, "This is what God says: Why do you disobey the LORD's commands and keep yourselves from prospering? You have abandoned the LORD, and now he has abandoned you!" [21] Then the leaders plotted to kill Zechariah, and King Joash ordered that they stone him to death in the courtyard of the LORD's Temple. [22] That was how King Joash repaid Jehoiada for his loyalty—by killing his son. Zechariah's last words as he died were, "May the LORD see what they are doing and avenge my death!"

The End of Joash's Reign

[23] In the spring of the year* the Aramean army marched against Joash. They invaded Judah and Jerusalem and killed all the leaders of the nation. Then they sent all the plunder back to their king in Damascus. [24] Although the Arameans attacked with only a small army, the LORD helped them conquer the much larger army of Judah. The people of Judah had abandoned the LORD, the God of their ancestors, so judgment was carried out against Joash.

[25] The Arameans withdrew, leaving Joash severely wounded. But his own officials plotted to kill him for murdering the son* of Jehoiada the priest. They assassinated him as he lay in bed. Then he was buried in the City of David, but not in the royal cemetery. [26] The assassins were Jozacar,* the son of an Ammonite woman named Shimeath, and Jehozabad, the son of a Moabite woman named Shomer.*

[27] The account of the sons of Joash, the prophecies about him, and the record of his restoration of the Temple of God are written in *The Commentary on the Book of the Kings.* His son Amaziah became the next king.

25 Amaziah Rules in Judah

Amaziah was twenty-five years old when he became king, and he reigned in Jerusalem twenty-nine years. His mother was Jehoaddin* from Jerusalem. [2] Amaziah did what was pleasing in the LORD's sight, but not wholeheartedly.

[3] When Amaziah was well established as king, he executed the officials who had assassinated his father. [4] However, he did not kill the children of the assassins, for he obeyed the command of the LORD as written by Moses in the Book of the Law: "Parents must not be put to death for the sins of their children, nor children for the sins of their parents. Those deserving to die must be put to death for their own crimes."*

[5] Then Amaziah organized the army, assigning generals and captains* for all Judah and Benjamin. He took a census and found that he had an army of 300,000 select troops, twenty years old and older, all trained in the use of spear and shield. [6] He also paid about 7,500 pounds* of silver to hire 100,000 experienced fighting men from Israel.

[7] But a man of God came to him and said, "Your Majesty, do not hire troops from Israel, for the LORD is not with Israel. He will not help those people of Ephraim! [8] If you let them go with your troops into battle, you will be defeated by the enemy no matter how well you fight. God will overthrow you, for he has the power to help you or to trip you up."

[9] Amaziah asked the man of God, "But

24:23 Hebrew *At the turn of the year.* The first day of the year in the ancient Hebrew lunar calendar occurred in March or April. **24:25** As in Greek version and Latin Vulgate; Hebrew reads *sons.* **24:26a** As in parallel text at 2 Kgs 12:21; Hebrew reads *Zabad.* **24:26b** As in parallel text at 2 Kgs 12:21; Hebrew reads *Shimrith,* a variant spelling of *Shomer.* **25:1** As in parallel text at 2 Kgs 14:2; Hebrew reads *Jehoaddan,* a variant spelling of *Jehoaddin.* **25:4** Deut 24:16. **25:5** Hebrew *commanders of thousands and commanders of hundreds.* **25:6** Hebrew *100 talents* [3,400 kilograms].

what about all that silver I paid to hire the army of Israel?"

The man of God replied, "The LORD is able to give you much more than this!" [10] So Amaziah discharged the hired troops and sent them back to Ephraim. This made them very angry with Judah, and they returned home in a great rage.

[11] Then Amaziah summoned his courage and led his army to the Valley of Salt, where they killed 10,000 Edomite troops from Seir. [12] They captured another 10,000 and took them to the top of a cliff and threw them off, dashing them to pieces on the rocks below.

[13] Meanwhile, the hired troops that Amaziah had sent home raided several of the towns of Judah between Samaria and Beth-horon. They killed 3,000 people and carried off great quantities of plunder.

[14] When King Amaziah returned from slaughtering the Edomites, he brought with him idols taken from the people of Seir. He set them up as his own gods, bowed down in front of them, and offered sacrifices to them! [15] This made the LORD very angry, and he sent a prophet to ask, "Why do you turn to gods who could not even save their own people from you?"

[16] But the king interrupted him and said, "Since when have I made you the king's counselor? Be quiet now before I have you killed!"

So the prophet stopped with this warning: "I know that God has determined to destroy you because you have done this and have refused to accept my counsel."

[17] After consulting with his advisers, King Amaziah of Judah sent this challenge to Israel's king Jehoash,* the son of Jehoahaz and grandson of Jehu: "Come and meet me in battle!"*

[18] But King Jehoash of Israel replied to King Amaziah of Judah with this story: "Out in the Lebanon mountains, a thistle sent a message to a mighty cedar tree: 'Give your daughter in marriage to my son.' But just then a wild animal of Lebanon came by and stepped on the thistle, crushing it!

[19] "You are saying, 'I have defeated Edom,' and you are very proud of it. But my advice is to stay at home. Why stir up trouble that will only bring disaster on you and the people of Judah?"

[20] But Amaziah refused to listen, for God was determined to destroy him for turning to the gods of Edom. [21] So King Jehoash of Israel mobilized his army against King Amaziah of Judah. The two armies drew up their battle lines at Beth-shemesh in Judah. [22] Judah was routed by the army of Israel, and its army scattered and fled for home. [23] King Jehoash of Israel captured Judah's king, Amaziah son of Joash and grandson of Ahaziah, at Beth-shemesh. Then he brought him to Jerusalem, where he demolished 600 feet* of Jerusalem's wall, from the Ephraim Gate to the Corner Gate. [24] He carried off all the gold and silver and all the articles from the Temple of God that had been in the care of Obed-edom. He also seized the treasures of the royal palace, along with hostages, and then returned to Samaria.

[25] King Amaziah of Judah lived on for fifteen years after the death of King Jehoash of Israel. [26] The rest of the events in Amaziah's reign, from beginning to end, are recorded in *The Book of the Kings of Judah and Israel.* [27] After Amaziah turned away from the LORD, there was a conspiracy against his life in Jerusalem, and he fled to Lachish. But his enemies sent assassins after him, and they killed him there. [28] They brought his body back on a horse, and he was buried with his ancestors in the City of David.*

26 Uzziah Rules in Judah

All the people of Judah had crowned Amaziah's sixteen-year-old son, Uzziah, as king in place of his father. [2] After his father's death, Uzziah rebuilt the town of Elath* and restored it to Judah.

[3] Uzziah was sixteen years old when he became king, and he reigned in Jerusalem fifty-two years. His mother was Jecoliah from Jerusalem. [4] He did what was pleasing in the LORD's sight, just as his father, Amaziah,

---

25:17a Hebrew *Joash,* a variant spelling of Jehoash; also in 25:18, 21, 23, 25. **25:17b** Hebrew *Come, let us look one another in the face.* **25:23** Hebrew *400 cubits* [180 meters]. **25:28** As in some Hebrew manuscripts and other ancient versions (see also 2 Kgs 14:20); most Hebrew manuscripts read *the city of Judah.* **26:2** As in Greek version (see also 2 Kgs 14:22; 16:6); Hebrew reads *Eloth,* a variant spelling of Elath.

had done. [5]Uzziah sought God during the days of Zechariah, who taught him to fear God.* And as long as the king sought guidance from the LORD, God gave him success.

[6]Uzziah declared war on the Philistines and broke down the walls of Gath, Jabneh, and Ashdod. Then he built new towns in the Ashdod area and in other parts of Philistia. [7]God helped him in his wars against the Philistines, his battles with the Arabs of Gur,* and his wars with the Meunites. [8]The Meunites* paid annual tribute to him, and his fame spread even to Egypt, for he had become very powerful.

[9]Uzziah built fortified towers in Jerusalem at the Corner Gate, at the Valley Gate, and at the angle in the wall. [10]He also constructed forts in the wilderness and dug many water cisterns, because he kept great herds of livestock in the foothills of Judah* and on the plains. He was also a man who loved the soil. He had many workers who cared for his farms and vineyards, both on the hillsides and in the fertile valleys.

[11]Uzziah had an army of well-trained warriors, ready to march into battle, unit by unit. This army had been mustered and organized by Jeiel, the secretary of the army, and his assistant, Maaseiah. They were under the direction of Hananiah, one of the king's officials. [12]These regiments of mighty warriors were commanded by 2,600 clan leaders. [13]The army consisted of 307,500 men, all elite troops. They were prepared to assist the king against any enemy.

[14]Uzziah provided the entire army with shields, spears, helmets, coats of mail, bows, and sling stones. [15]And he built structures on the walls of Jerusalem, designed by experts to protect those who shot arrows and hurled large stones* from the towers and the corners of the wall. His fame spread far and wide, for the LORD gave him marvelous help, and he became very powerful.

Uzziah's Sin and Punishment

[16]But when he had become powerful, he also became proud, which led to his downfall. He sinned against the LORD his God by entering the sanctuary of the LORD's Temple and personally burning incense on the incense altar. [17]Azariah the high priest went in after him with eighty other priests of the LORD, all brave men. [18]They confronted King Uzziah and said, "It is not for you, Uzziah, to burn incense to the LORD. That is the work of the priests alone, the descendants of Aaron who are set apart for this work. Get out of the sanctuary, for you have sinned. The LORD God will not honor you for this!"

[19]Uzziah, who was holding an incense burner, became furious. But as he was standing there raging at the priests before the incense altar in the LORD's Temple, leprosy* suddenly broke out on his forehead. [20]When Azariah the high priest and all the other priests saw the leprosy, they rushed him out. And the king himself was eager to get out because the LORD had struck him. [21]So King Uzziah had leprosy until the day he died. He lived in isolation in a separate house, for he was excluded from the Temple of the LORD. His son Jotham was put in charge of the royal palace, and he governed the people of the land.

[22]The rest of the events of Uzziah's reign, from beginning to end, are recorded by the prophet Isaiah son of Amoz. [23]When Uzziah died, he was buried with his ancestors; his grave was in a nearby burial field belonging to the kings, for the people said, "He had leprosy." And his son Jotham became the next king.

27 Jotham Rules in Judah

Jotham was twenty-five years old when he became king, and he reigned in Jerusalem sixteen years. His mother was Jerusha, the daughter of Zadok.

[2]Jotham did what was pleasing in the LORD's sight. He did everything his father, Uzziah, had done, except that Jotham did not sin by entering the Temple of the LORD. But the people continued in their corrupt ways.

[3]Jotham rebuilt the upper gate of the Temple of the LORD. He also did extensive rebuilding on the wall at the hill of Ophel. [4]He built towns in the hill country

---

26:5 As in Syriac and Greek versions; Hebrew reads *who instructed him in divine visions*.   26:7 As in Greek version; Hebrew reads *Gur-baal*.   26:8 As in Greek version; Hebrew reads *Ammonites*. Compare 26:7.   26:10 Hebrew *the Shephelah*.   26:15 Or *to shoot arrows and hurl large stones*.   26:19 Or *a contagious skin disease*. The Hebrew word used here and throughout this passage can describe various skin diseases.

of Judah and constructed fortresses and towers in the wooded areas. [5]Jotham went to war against the Ammonites and conquered them. Over the next three years he received from them an annual tribute of 7,500 pounds* of silver, 50,000 bushels of wheat, and 50,000 bushels of barley.*

[6]King Jotham became powerful because he was careful to live in obedience to the LORD his God.

[7]The rest of the events of Jotham's reign, including all his wars and other activities, are recorded in *The Book of the Kings of Israel and Judah.* [8]He was twenty-five years old when he became king, and he reigned in Jerusalem sixteen years. [9]When Jotham died, he was buried in the City of David. And his son Ahaz became the next king.

28 Ahaz Rules in Judah

Ahaz was twenty years old when he became king, and he reigned in Jerusalem sixteen years. He did not do what was pleasing in the sight of the LORD, as his ancestor David had done. [2]Instead, he followed the example of the kings of Israel. He cast metal images for the worship of Baal. [3]He offered sacrifices in the valley of Ben-Hinnom, even sacrificing his own sons in the fire.* In this way, he followed the detestable practices of the pagan nations the LORD had driven from the land ahead of the Israelites. [4]He offered sacrifices and burned incense at the pagan shrines and on the hills and under every green tree.

[5]Because of all this, the LORD his God allowed the king of Aram to defeat Ahaz and to exile large numbers of his people to Damascus. The armies of the king of Israel also defeated Ahaz and inflicted many casualties on his army. [6]In a single day Pekah son of Remaliah, Israel's king, killed 120,000 of Judah's troops, all of them experienced warriors, because they had abandoned the LORD, the God of their ancestors. [7]Then Zicri, a warrior from Ephraim, killed Maaseiah, the king's son; Azrikam, the king's palace commander; and Elkanah, the king's second-in-command. [8]The armies of Israel captured 200,000 women and children from Judah and seized tremendous amounts of plunder, which they took back to Samaria.

[9]But a prophet of the LORD named Oded was there in Samaria when the army of Israel returned home. He went out to meet them and said, "The LORD, the God of your ancestors, was angry with Judah and let you defeat them. But you have gone too far, killing them without mercy, and all heaven is disturbed. [10]And now you are planning to make slaves of these people from Judah and Jerusalem. What about your own sins against the LORD your God? [11]Listen to me and return these prisoners you have taken, for they are your own relatives. Watch out, because now the LORD's fierce anger has been turned against you!"

[12]Then some of the leaders of Israel*— Azariah son of Jehohanan, Berekiah son of Meshillemoth, Jehizkiah son of Shallum, and Amasa son of Hadlai—agreed with this and confronted the men returning from battle. [13]"You must not bring the prisoners here!" they declared. "We cannot afford to add to our sins and guilt. Our guilt is already great, and the LORD's fierce anger is already turned against Israel."

[14]So the warriors released the prisoners and handed over the plunder in the sight of the leaders and all the people. [15]Then the four men just mentioned by name came forward and distributed clothes from the plunder to the prisoners who were naked. They provided clothing and sandals to wear, gave them enough food and drink, and dressed their wounds with olive oil. They put those who were weak on donkeys and took all the prisoners back to their own people in Jericho, the city of palms. Then they returned to Samaria.

Ahaz Closes the Temple

[16]At that time King Ahaz of Judah asked the king of Assyria for help. [17]The armies of Edom had again invaded Judah and taken captives. [18]And the Philistines had raided towns located in the foothills of Judah* and in the Negev of Judah. They had already captured and occupied Beth-shemesh, Aijalon, Gederoth, Soco with its villages, Timnah with its villages, and Gimzo with its villages.

27:5a Hebrew *100 talents* [3,400 kilograms]. **27:5b** Hebrew *10,000 cors* [1,820 kiloliters] *of wheat, and 10,000 cors of barley.* **28:3** Or even making his sons pass through the fire. **28:12** Hebrew *Ephraim,* referring to the northern kingdom of Israel. **28:18** Hebrew *the Shephelah.*

[19] The LORD was humbling Judah because of King Ahaz of Judah,* for he had encouraged his people to sin and had been utterly unfaithful to the LORD.

[20] So when King Tiglath-pileser* of Assyria arrived, he attacked Ahaz instead of helping him. [21] Ahaz took valuable items from the LORD's Temple, the royal palace, and from the homes of his officials and gave them to the king of Assyria as tribute. But this did not help him.

[22] Even during this time of trouble, King Ahaz continued to reject the LORD. [23] He offered sacrifices to the gods of Damascus who had defeated him, for he said, "Since these gods helped the kings of Aram, they will help me, too, if I sacrifice to them." But instead, they led to his ruin and the ruin of all Judah.

[24] The king took the various articles from the Temple of God and broke them into pieces. He shut the doors of the LORD's Temple so that no one could worship there, and he set up altars to pagan gods in every corner of Jerusalem. [25] He made pagan shrines in all the towns of Judah for offering sacrifices to other gods. In this way, he aroused the anger of the LORD, the God of his ancestors.

[26] The rest of the events of Ahaz's reign and everything he did, from beginning to end, are recorded in *The Book of the Kings of Judah and Israel.* [27] When Ahaz died, he was buried in Jerusalem but not in the royal cemetery of the kings of Judah. Then his son Hezekiah became the next king.

29 Hezekiah Rules in Judah

Hezekiah was twenty-five years old when he became the king of Judah, and he reigned in Jerusalem twenty-nine years. His mother was Abijah, the daughter of Zechariah. [2] He did what was pleasing in the LORD's sight, just as his ancestor David had done.

Hezekiah Reopens the Temple

[3] In the very first month of the first year of his reign, Hezekiah reopened the doors of the Temple of the LORD and repaired them. [4] He summoned the priests and Levites to meet him at the courtyard east of the Temple. [5] He said to them, "Listen to me, you Levites! Purify yourselves, and purify the Temple of the LORD, the God of your ancestors. Remove all the defiled things from the sanctuary. [6] Our ancestors were unfaithful and did what was evil in the sight of the LORD our God. They abandoned the LORD and his dwelling place; they turned their backs on him. [7] They also shut the doors to the Temple's entry room, and they snuffed out the lamps. They stopped burning incense and presenting burnt offerings at the sanctuary of the God of Israel.

[8] "That is why the LORD's anger has fallen upon Judah and Jerusalem. He has made them an object of dread, horror, and ridicule, as you can see with your own eyes. [9] Because of this, our fathers have been killed in battle, and our sons and daughters and wives have been captured. [10] But now I will make a covenant with the LORD, the God of Israel, so that his fierce anger will turn away from us. [11] My sons, do not neglect your duties any longer! The LORD has chosen you to stand in his presence, to minister to him, and to lead the people in worship and present offerings to him."

[12] Then these Levites got right to work:

From the clan of Kohath: Mahath son of Amasai and Joel son of Azariah.
From the clan of Merari: Kish son of Abdi and Azariah son of Jehallelel.
From the clan of Gershon: Joah son of Zimmah and Eden son of Joah.
[13] From the family of Elizaphan: Shimri and Jeiel.
From the family of Asaph: Zechariah and Mattaniah.
[14] From the family of Heman: Jehiel and Shimei.
From the family of Jeduthun: Shemaiah and Uzziel.

[15] These men called together their fellow Levites, and they all purified themselves. Then they began to cleanse the Temple of the LORD, just as the king had commanded. They were careful to follow all the LORD's instructions in their work. [16] The priests went into the sanctuary of the Temple of

---

28:19 Masoretic Text reads *of Israel;* also in 28:23, 27. The author of Chronicles sees Judah as representative of the true Israel. (Some Hebrew manuscripts and Greek version read *of Judah.*) **28:20** Hebrew *Tilgath-pileser,* a variant spelling of Tiglath-pileser.

Worship

Wasting Time in Worship
2 CHRONICLES 29:25-36

When people try to do something and it doesn't work, they say, "That was a royal waste of time." True worship *is* a waste of time because it's not utilitarian, even though churches try to make worship utilitarian. But whenever we expect worship to produce something on our terms, we've lost the freedom, the total abandonment in God's presence.

Worship isn't about getting some particular desired result in a congregation or in our individual lives. A utilitarian perspective will prevent us from entering into true worship. But if we give up our ulterior agendas, we can go in the presence of God ready to receive what God wants to happen. And then God surprises us. There is a splendor in worshiping God—in getting to know God in all his fullness.

Yet worship in its own way does yield results: as we live in worship, we're able to truly be the church for the world. Worship forms and shapes us so that, rather than trying to *do* church, we're able to actually *be* the church. For example, worship can form me into a more generous person, because in worship I constantly see the generosity of God. Or worship can nurture and grow patience and graciousness in me as I spend time focusing on and praising God for the grace and patience he shows to me and the rest of humankind. Worship changes my perspective; it changes who I am.

—*Marva Dawn*

For more on worship, see reading at Psalm 25.

the LORD to cleanse it, and they took out to the Temple courtyard all the defiled things they found. From there the Levites carted it all out to the Kidron Valley.

[17] They began the work in early spring, on the first day of the new year,* and in eight days they had reached the entry room of the LORD's Temple. Then they purified the Temple of the LORD itself, which took another eight days. So the entire task was completed in sixteen days.

The Temple Rededication

[18] Then the Levites went to King Hezekiah and gave him this report: "We have cleansed the entire Temple of the LORD, the altar of burnt offering with all its utensils, and the table of the Bread of the Presence with all its utensils. [19] We have also recovered all the items discarded by King Ahaz when he was unfaithful and closed the Temple. They are now in front of the altar of the LORD, purified and ready for use."

[20] Early the next morning King Hezekiah gathered the city officials and went to the Temple of the LORD. [21] They brought seven bulls, seven rams, and seven male lambs as a burnt offering, together with seven male goats as a sin offering for the kingdom, for the Temple, and for Judah. The king commanded the priests, who were descendants of Aaron, to sacrifice the animals on the altar of the LORD.

[22] So they killed the bulls, and the priests took the blood and sprinkled it on the altar. Next they killed the rams and sprinkled their blood on the altar. And finally, they did the same with the male lambs. [23] The male goats for the sin offering were then brought before the king and the assembly of

---

29:17 Hebrew *on the first day of the first month.* This day in the ancient Hebrew lunar calendar occurred in March or early April, 715 B.C.

people, who laid their hands on them. [24] The priests then killed the goats as a sin offering and sprinkled their blood on the altar to make atonement for the sins of all Israel. The king had specifically commanded that this burnt offering and sin offering should be made for all Israel.

[25] King Hezekiah then stationed the Levites at the Temple of the LORD with cymbals, lyres, and harps. He obeyed all the commands that the LORD had given to King David through Gad, the king's seer, and the prophet Nathan. [26] The Levites then took their positions around the Temple with the instruments of David, and the priests took their positions with the trumpets.

[27] Then Hezekiah ordered that the burnt offering be placed on the altar. As the burnt offering was presented, songs of praise to the LORD were begun, accompanied by the trumpets and other instruments of David, the former king of Israel. [28] The entire assembly worshiped the LORD as the singers sang and the trumpets blew, until all the burnt offerings were finished. [29] Then the king and everyone with him bowed down in worship. [30] King Hezekiah and the officials ordered the Levites to praise the LORD with the psalms written by David and by Asaph the seer. So they offered joyous praise and bowed down in worship.

[31] Then Hezekiah declared, "Now that you have consecrated yourselves to the LORD, bring your sacrifices and thanksgiving offerings to the Temple of the LORD." So the people brought their sacrifices and thanksgiving offerings, and all whose hearts were willing brought burnt offerings, too. [32] The people brought to the LORD 70 bulls, 100 rams, and 200 male lambs for burnt offerings. [33] They also brought 600 cattle and 3,000 sheep and goats as sacred offerings.

[34] But there were too few priests to prepare all the burnt offerings. So their relatives the Levites helped them until the work was finished and more priests had been purified, for the Levites had been more conscientious about purifying themselves than the priests had been. [35] There was an abundance of burnt offerings, along with the usual liquid offerings, and a great deal of fat from the many peace offerings.

So the Temple of the LORD was restored to service. [36] And Hezekiah and all the people rejoiced because of what God had done for the people, for everything had been accomplished so quickly.

30 Preparations for Passover

King Hezekiah now sent word to all Israel and Judah, and he wrote letters of invitation to the people of Ephraim and Manasseh. He asked everyone to come to the Temple of the LORD at Jerusalem to celebrate the Passover of the LORD, the God of Israel. [2] The king, his officials, and all the community of Jerusalem decided to celebrate Passover a month later than usual.* [3] They were unable to celebrate it at the prescribed time because not enough priests could be purified by then, and the people had not yet assembled at Jerusalem.

[4] This plan for keeping the Passover seemed right to the king and all the people. [5] So they sent a proclamation throughout all Israel, from Beersheba in the south to Dan in the north, inviting everyone to come to Jerusalem to celebrate the Passover of the LORD, the God of Israel. The people had not been celebrating it in great numbers as required in the Law.

[6] At the king's command, runners were sent throughout Israel and Judah. They carried letters that said:

"O people of Israel, return to the LORD, the God of Abraham, Isaac, and Israel,* so that he will return to the few of us who have survived the conquest of the Assyrian kings. [7] Do not be like your ancestors and relatives who abandoned the LORD, the God of their ancestors, and became an object of derision, as you yourselves can see. [8] Do not be stubborn, as they were, but submit yourselves to the LORD. Come to his Temple, which he has set apart as holy forever. Worship the LORD your God so that his fierce anger will turn away from you. [9] "For if you return to the LORD, your relatives and your children will be

---

30:2 Hebrew *in the second month.* Passover was normally observed in the first month (of the ancient Hebrew lunar calendar). **30:6** *Israel* is the name that God gave to Jacob.

treated mercifully by their captors, and they will be able to return to this land. For the LORD your God is gracious and merciful. If you return to him, he will not continue to turn his face from you."

Celebration of Passover

[10] The runners went from town to town throughout Ephraim and Manasseh and as far as the territory of Zebulun. But most of the people just laughed at the runners and made fun of them. [11] However, some people from Asher, Manasseh, and Zebulun humbled themselves and went to Jerusalem.

[12] At the same time, God's hand was on the people in the land of Judah, giving them all one heart to obey the orders of the king and his officials, who were following the word of the LORD. [13] So a huge crowd assembled at Jerusalem in midspring* to celebrate the Festival of Unleavened Bread. [14] They set to work and removed the pagan altars from Jerusalem. They took away all the incense altars and threw them into the Kidron Valley.

[15] On the fourteenth day of the second month, one month later than usual,* the people slaughtered the Passover lamb. This shamed the priests and Levites, so they purified themselves and brought burnt offerings to the Temple of the LORD. [16] Then they took their places at the Temple as prescribed in the Law of Moses, the man of God. The Levites brought the sacrificial blood to the priests, who then sprinkled it on the altar. [17] Since many of the people had not purified themselves, the Levites had to slaughter their Passover lamb for them, to set them apart for the LORD. [18] Most of those who came from Ephraim, Manasseh, Issachar, and Zebulun had not purified themselves. But King Hezekiah prayed for them, and they were allowed to eat the Passover meal anyway, even though this was contrary to the requirements of the Law. For Hezekiah said, "May the LORD, who is good, pardon those [19] who decide to follow the LORD, the God of their ancestors, even though they are not properly cleansed for the ceremony." [20] And the LORD listened to Hezekiah's prayer and healed the people.

[21] So the people of Israel who were present in Jerusalem joyously celebrated the Festival of Unleavened Bread for seven days. Each day the Levites and priests sang to the LORD, accompanied by loud instruments.* [22] Hezekiah encouraged all the Levites regarding the skill they displayed as they served the LORD. The celebration continued for seven days. Peace offerings were sacrificed, and the people gave thanks to the LORD, the God of their ancestors.

[23] The entire assembly then decided to continue the festival another seven days, so they celebrated joyfully for another week. [24] King Hezekiah gave the people 1,000 bulls and 7,000 sheep and goats for offerings, and the officials donated 1,000 bulls and 10,000 sheep and goats. Meanwhile, many more priests purified themselves.

[25] The entire assembly of Judah rejoiced, including the priests, the Levites, all who came from the land of Israel, the foreigners who came to the festival, and all those who lived in Judah. [26] There was great joy in the city, for Jerusalem had not seen a celebration like this one since the days of Solomon, King David's son. [27] Then the priests and Levites stood and blessed the people, and God heard their prayer from his holy dwelling in heaven.

31 Hezekiah's Religious Reforms

When the festival ended, the Israelites who attended went to all the towns of Judah, Benjamin, Ephraim, and Manasseh, and they smashed all the sacred pillars, cut down the Asherah poles, and removed the pagan shrines and altars. After this, the Israelites returned to their own towns and homes.

[2] Hezekiah then organized the priests and Levites into divisions to offer the burnt offerings and peace offerings, and to worship and give thanks and praise to the LORD at the gates of the Temple. [3] The king also made a personal contribution of animals for the daily morning and evening burnt offerings, the weekly Sabbath festivals, the monthly new moon festivals, and the annual festivals as prescribed in the Law

---

30:13 Hebrew *in the second month.* The second month of the ancient Hebrew lunar calendar usually occurs within the months of April and May.   **30:15** Hebrew *On the fourteenth day of the second month.* Passover normally began on the fourteenth day of the first month (see Lev 23:5).   **30:21** Or *sang to the LORD with all their strength.*

of the LORD. ⁴In addition, he required the people in Jerusalem to bring a portion of their goods to the priests and Levites, so they could devote themselves fully to the Law of the LORD.

⁵When the people of Israel heard these requirements, they responded generously by bringing the first share of their grain, new wine, olive oil, honey, and all the produce of their fields. They brought a large quantity—a tithe of all they produced. ⁶The people who had moved to Judah from Israel, and the people of Judah themselves, brought in the tithes of their cattle, sheep, and goats and a tithe of the things that had been dedicated to the LORD their God, and they piled them up in great heaps. ⁷They began piling them up in late spring, and the heaps continued to grow until early autumn.* ⁸When Hezekiah and his officials came and saw these huge piles, they thanked the LORD and his people Israel!

⁹"Where did all this come from?" Hezekiah asked the priests and Levites.

¹⁰And Azariah the high priest, from the family of Zadok, replied, "Since the people began bringing their gifts to the LORD's Temple, we have had enough to eat and plenty to spare. The LORD has blessed his people, and all this is left over."

¹¹Hezekiah ordered that storerooms be prepared in the Temple of the LORD. When this was done, ¹²the people faithfully brought all the tithes and gifts to the Temple. Conaniah the Levite was put in charge, assisted by his brother Shimei. ¹³The supervisors under them were Jehiel, Azaziah, Nahath, Asahel, Jerimoth, Jozabad, Eliel, Ismakiah, Mahath, and Benaiah. These appointments were made by King Hezekiah and Azariah, the chief official in the Temple of God.

¹⁴Kore son of Imnah the Levite, who was the gatekeeper at the East Gate, was put in charge of distributing the voluntary offerings given to God, the gifts, and the things that had been dedicated to the LORD. ¹⁵His faithful assistants were Eden, Miniamin, Jeshua, Shemaiah, Amariah, and Shecaniah. They distributed the gifts among the families of priests in their towns by their divisions, dividing the gifts fairly among old and young alike. ¹⁶They distributed the gifts to all males three years old or older, regardless of their place in the genealogical records. The distribution went to all who would come to the LORD's Temple to perform their daily duties according to their divisions. ¹⁷They distributed gifts to the priests who were listed by their families in the genealogical records, and to the Levites twenty years old or older who were listed according to their jobs and their divisions. ¹⁸Food allotments were also given to the families of all those listed in the genealogical records, including their little babies, wives, sons, and daughters. For they had all been faithful in purifying themselves.

¹⁹As for the priests, the descendants of Aaron, who were living in the open villages around the towns, men were appointed by name to distribute portions to every male among the priests and to all the Levites listed in the genealogical records.

²⁰In this way, King Hezekiah handled the distribution throughout all Judah, doing what was pleasing and good in the sight of the LORD his God. ²¹In all that he did in the service of the Temple of God and in his efforts to follow God's laws and commands, Hezekiah sought his God wholeheartedly. As a result, he was very successful.

32 Assyria Invades Judah

After Hezekiah had faithfully carried out this work, King Sennacherib of Assyria invaded Judah. He laid siege to the fortified towns, giving orders for his army to break through their walls. ²When Hezekiah realized that Sennacherib also intended to attack Jerusalem, ³he consulted with his officials and military advisers, and they decided to stop the flow of the springs outside the city. ⁴They organized a huge work crew to stop the flow of the springs, cutting off the brook that ran through the fields. For they said, "Why should the kings of Assyria come here and find plenty of water?"

⁵Then Hezekiah worked hard at repairing all the broken sections of the wall, erecting

---

31:7 Hebrew *in the third month . . . until the seventh month.* The third month of the ancient Hebrew lunar calendar usually occurs within the months of May and June; the seventh month usually occurs within September and October.

towers, and constructing a second wall outside the first. He also reinforced the supporting terraces* in the City of David and manufactured large numbers of weapons and shields. ⁶He appointed military officers over the people and assembled them before him in the square at the city gate. Then Hezekiah encouraged them by saying: ⁷"Be strong and courageous! Don't be afraid or discouraged because of the king of Assyria or his mighty army, for there is a power far greater on our side! ⁸He may have a great army, but they are merely men. We have the LORD our God to help us and to fight our battles for us!" Hezekiah's words greatly encouraged the people.

Sennacherib Threatens Jerusalem

⁹While King Sennacherib of Assyria was still besieging the town of Lachish, he sent his officers to Jerusalem with this message for Hezekiah and all the people in the city:

¹⁰"This is what King Sennacherib of Assyria says: What are you trusting in that makes you think you can survive my siege of Jerusalem? ¹¹Hezekiah has said, 'The LORD our God will rescue us from the king of Assyria.' Surely Hezekiah is misleading you, sentencing you to death by famine and thirst! ¹²Don't you realize that Hezekiah is the very person who destroyed all the LORD's shrines and altars? He commanded Judah and Jerusalem to worship only at the altar at the Temple and to offer sacrifices on it alone.

¹³"Surely you must realize what I and the other kings of Assyria before me have done to all the people of the earth! Were any of the gods of those nations able to rescue their people from my power? ¹⁴Which of their gods was able to rescue its people from the destructive power of my predecessors? What makes you think your God can rescue you from me? ¹⁵Don't let Hezekiah deceive you! Don't let him fool you like this! I say it again—no god of any nation or kingdom has ever yet been able to rescue his people from me or my ancestors. How much less will your God rescue you from my power!"

¹⁶And Sennacherib's officers further mocked the LORD God and his servant Hezekiah, heaping insult upon insult. ¹⁷The king also sent letters scorning the LORD, the God of Israel. He wrote, "Just as the gods of all the other nations failed to rescue their people from my power, so the God of Hezekiah will also fail." ¹⁸The Assyrian officials who brought the letters shouted this in Hebrew* to the people gathered on the walls of the city, trying to terrify them so it would be easier to capture the city. ¹⁹These officers talked about the God of Jerusalem as though he were one of the pagan gods, made by human hands.

²⁰Then King Hezekiah and the prophet Isaiah son of Amoz cried out in prayer to God in heaven. ²¹And the LORD sent an angel who destroyed the Assyrian army with all its commanders and officers. So Sennacherib was forced to return home in disgrace to his own land. And when he entered the temple of his god, some of his own sons killed him there with a sword.

²²That is how the LORD rescued Hezekiah and the people of Jerusalem from King Sennacherib of Assyria and from all the others who threatened them. So there was peace throughout the land. ²³From then on King Hezekiah became highly respected among all the surrounding nations, and many gifts for the LORD arrived at Jerusalem, with valuable presents for King Hezekiah, too.

Hezekiah's Sickness and Recovery

²⁴About that time Hezekiah became deathly ill. He prayed to the LORD, who healed him and gave him a miraculous sign. ²⁵But Hezekiah did not respond appropriately to the kindness shown him, and he became proud. So the LORD's anger came against him and against Judah and Jerusalem. ²⁶Then Hezekiah humbled himself and repented of his pride, as did the people of Jerusalem. So the LORD's anger did not fall on them during Hezekiah's lifetime.

²⁷Hezekiah was very wealthy and highly honored. He built special treasury buildings for his silver, gold, precious stones, and spices, and for his shields and other valuable items. ²⁸He also constructed many

---

32:5 Hebrew *the millo.* The meaning of the Hebrew is uncertain.　**32:18** Hebrew *in the dialect of Judah.*

storehouses for his grain, new wine, and olive oil; and he made many stalls for his cattle and pens for his flocks of sheep and goats. ²⁹He built many towns and acquired vast flocks and herds, for God had given him great wealth. ³⁰He blocked up the upper spring of Gihon and brought the water down through a tunnel to the west side of the City of David. And so he succeeded in everything he did.

³¹However, when ambassadors arrived from Babylon to ask about the remarkable events that had taken place in the land, God withdrew from Hezekiah in order to test him and to see what was really in his heart.

Summary of Hezekiah's Reign

³²The rest of the events in Hezekiah's reign and his acts of devotion are recorded in *The Vision of the Prophet Isaiah Son of Amoz,* which is included in *The Book of the Kings of Judah and Israel.* ³³When Hezekiah died, he was buried in the upper area of the royal cemetery, and all Judah and Jerusalem honored him at his death. And his son Manasseh became the next king.

33 Manasseh Rules in Judah

Manasseh was twelve years old when he became king, and he reigned in Jerusalem fifty-five years. ²He did what was evil in the LORD's sight, following the detestable practices of the pagan nations that the LORD had driven from the land ahead of the Israelites. ³He rebuilt the pagan shrines his father, Hezekiah, had broken down. He constructed altars for the images of Baal and set up Asherah poles. He also bowed before all the powers of the heavens and worshiped them.

⁴He built pagan altars in the Temple of the LORD, the place where the LORD had said, "My name will remain in Jerusalem forever." ⁵He built these altars for all the powers of the heavens in both courtyards of the LORD's Temple. ⁶Manasseh also sacrificed his own sons in the fire* in the valley of Ben-Hinnom. He practiced sorcery, divination, and witchcraft, and he consulted with mediums and psychics. He did much that was evil in the LORD's sight, arousing his anger.

⁷Manasseh even took a carved idol he had made and set it up in God's Temple, the very place where God had told David and his son Solomon: "My name will be honored forever in this Temple and in Jerusalem—the city I have chosen from among all the tribes of Israel. ⁸If the Israelites will be careful to obey my commands—all the laws, decrees, and regulations given through Moses—I will not send them into exile from this land that I set aside for your ancestors." ⁹But Manasseh led the people of Judah and Jerusalem to do even more evil than the pagan nations that the LORD had destroyed when the people of Israel entered the land.

¹⁰The LORD spoke to Manasseh and his people, but they ignored all his warnings. ¹¹So the LORD sent the commanders of the Assyrian armies, and they took Manasseh prisoner. They put a ring through his nose, bound him in bronze chains, and led him away to Babylon. ¹²But while in deep distress, Manasseh sought the LORD his God and sincerely humbled himself before the God of his ancestors. ¹³And when he prayed, the LORD listened to him and was moved by his request. So the LORD brought Manasseh back to Jerusalem and to his kingdom. Then Manasseh finally realized that the LORD alone is God!

¹⁴After this Manasseh rebuilt the outer wall of the City of David, from west of the Gihon Spring in the Kidron Valley to the Fish Gate, and continuing around the hill of Ophel. He built the wall very high. And he stationed his military officers in all of the fortified towns of Judah. ¹⁵Manasseh also removed the foreign gods and the idol from the LORD's Temple. He tore down all the altars he had built on the hill where the Temple stood and all the altars that were in Jerusalem, and he dumped them outside the city. ¹⁶Then he restored the altar of the LORD and sacrificed peace offerings and thanksgiving offerings on it. He also encouraged the people of Judah to worship the LORD, the God of Israel. ¹⁷However, the people still sacrificed at the pagan shrines, though only to the LORD their God.

¹⁸The rest of the events of Manasseh's reign, his prayer to God, and the words the

---

33:6 Or *also made his sons pass through the fire.*

seers spoke to him in the name of the LORD, the God of Israel, are recorded in *The Book of the Kings of Israel.* ¹⁹Manasseh's prayer, the account of the way God answered him, and an account of all his sins and unfaithfulness are recorded in *The Record of the Seers.** It includes a list of the locations where he built pagan shrines and set up Asherah poles and idols before he humbled himself and repented. ²⁰When Manasseh died, he was buried in his palace. Then his son Amon became the next king.

Amon Rules in Judah

²¹Amon was twenty-two years old when he became king, and he reigned in Jerusalem two years. ²²He did what was evil in the LORD's sight, just as his father, Manasseh, had done. He worshiped and sacrificed to all the idols his father had made. ²³But unlike his father, he did not humble himself before the LORD. Instead, Amon sinned even more.

²⁴Then Amon's own officials conspired against him and assassinated him in his palace. ²⁵But the people of the land killed all those who had conspired against King Amon, and they made his son Josiah the next king.

34 Josiah Rules in Judah

Josiah was eight years old when he became king, and he reigned in Jerusalem thirty-one years. ²He did what was pleasing in the LORD's sight and followed the example of his ancestor David. He did not turn away from doing what was right.

³During the eighth year of his reign, while he was still young, Josiah began to seek the God of his ancestor David. Then in the twelfth year he began to purify Judah and Jerusalem, destroying all the pagan shrines, the Asherah poles, and the carved idols and cast images. ⁴He ordered that the altars of Baal be demolished and that the incense altars which stood above them be broken down. He also made sure that the Asherah poles, the carved idols, and the cast images were smashed and scattered over the graves of those who had sacrificed to them. ⁵He burned the bones of the pagan

priests on their own altars, and so he purified Judah and Jerusalem.

⁶He did the same thing in the towns of Manasseh, Ephraim, and Simeon, even as far as Naphtali, and in the regions* all around them. ⁷He destroyed the pagan altars and the Asherah poles, and he crushed the idols into dust. He cut down all the incense altars throughout the land of Israel. Finally, he returned to Jerusalem.

⁸In the eighteenth year of his reign, after he had purified the land and the Temple, Josiah appointed Shaphan son of Azaliah, Maaseiah the governor of Jerusalem, and Joah son of Joahaz, the royal historian, to repair the Temple of the LORD his God. ⁹They gave Hilkiah the high priest the money that had been collected by the Levites who served as gatekeepers at the Temple of God. The gifts were brought by people from Manasseh, Ephraim, and from all the remnant of Israel, as well as from all Judah, Benjamin, and the people of Jerusalem.

¹⁰He entrusted the money to the men assigned to supervise the restoration of the LORD's Temple. Then they paid the workers who did the repairs and renovation of the Temple. ¹¹They hired carpenters and builders, who purchased finished stone for the walls and timber for the rafters and beams. They restored what earlier kings of Judah had allowed to fall into ruin.

¹²The workers served faithfully under the leadership of Jahath and Obadiah, Levites of the Merarite clan, and Zechariah and Meshullam, Levites of the Kohathite clan. Other Levites, all of whom were skilled musicians, ¹³were put in charge of the laborers of the various trades. Still others assisted as secretaries, officials, and gatekeepers.

Hilkiah Discovers God's Law

¹⁴While they were bringing out the money collected at the LORD's Temple, Hilkiah the priest found the Book of the Law of the LORD that was written by Moses. ¹⁵Hilkiah said to Shaphan the court secretary, "I have found the Book of the Law in the LORD's Temple!" Then Hilkiah gave the scroll to Shaphan.

¹⁶Shaphan took the scroll to the king

and reported, "Your officials are doing everything they were assigned to do. [17] The money that was collected at the Temple of the LORD has been turned over to the supervisors and workmen." [18] Shaphan also told the king, "Hilkiah the priest has given me a scroll." So Shaphan read it to the king.

[19] When the king heard what was written in the Law, he tore his clothes in despair. [20] Then he gave these orders to Hilkiah, Ahikam son of Shaphan, Acbor son of Micaiah,* Shaphan the court secretary, and Asaiah the king's personal adviser: [21] "Go to the Temple and speak to the LORD for me

Huldah: Leading Others to Obey God's Word

2 CHRONICLES 34:22-29

During the turbulent times of the kings, rulers ping-ponged from indulgence to repentance, often with each generation outdoing the R-rated romp of the past. But King Josiah was different; he "did what was pleasing in the LORD's sight" (2 Chronicles 34:2).

Josiah put teams to work, restoring God's temple. Amid the rubble, the Book of the Law was found (34:14) . . . and it didn't contain good news. The Scripture made it clear that the people's sin would not go unpunished.

Josiah humbly "tore his clothes in despair" (34:19). Then he sent Hilkiah the priest to "inquire about the words written in the scroll that has been found" (34:21). Hilkiah sought the counsel of a prophetess he knew and trusted: Huldah.

Unlike so many others, Huldah had not abandoned God. Instead, she had been called to serve—and amid uncertain times, Huldah spoke with authority on God's behalf, attentive to his voice.

Huldah's words to Hilkiah were direct and clear: "The LORD, the God of Israel, has spoken! Go back and tell the man who sent you, 'This is what the LORD says . . .'" (34:23-24). She didn't have good news either: God's declarations in the scroll would come true.

At a crucial time, Huldah spoke truth and helped the people face a situation that was only getting worse because of their disobedience. And directed by God, she leveled her harsh words with hope, delivering a difficult message with clarity and conviction while offering a small comfort: the faithful king, Josiah, would die before seeing the calamity that was to come.

God used Huldah to help his people find their way back to a path of obedience. Both Josiah's humility and Huldah's honesty gave God's people a place to start again. With Huldah's counsel, the people renewed their covenant with God (34:31).

God calls us, like Huldah, to be attentive to his Word and believe its truth. And as we read the Bible, we need to surround ourselves with others like Huldah who know God's Word, who can help us understand it, and who can keep us on the path of obedience. And we can embrace and respond to the truth of God's Word; we can seek to obey it as Josiah did, "with all his heart and soul" (34:31).

—Amie Hollmann

For more on Bible study and meditation, see reading at Nehemiah 8:1-8.

34:20 As in parallel text at 2 Kgs 22:12; Hebrew reads *Abdon son of Micah.*

and for all the remnant of Israel and Judah. Inquire about the words written in the scroll that has been found. For the Lord's great anger has been poured out on us because our ancestors have not obeyed the word of the Lord. We have not been doing everything this scroll says we must do."

²²So Hilkiah and the other men went to the New Quarter* of Jerusalem to consult with the prophet Huldah. She was the wife of Shallum son of Tikvah, son of Harhas,* the keeper of the Temple wardrobe.

²³She said to them, "The Lord, the God of Israel, has spoken! Go back and tell the man who sent you, ²⁴'This is what the Lord says: I am going to bring disaster on this city* and its people. All the curses written in the scroll that was read to the king of Judah will come true. ²⁵For my people have abandoned me and offered sacrifices to pagan gods, and I am very angry with them for everything they have done. My anger will be poured out on this place, and it will not be quenched.'

²⁶"But go to the king of Judah who sent you to seek the Lord and tell him: 'This is what the Lord, the God of Israel, says concerning the message you have just heard: ²⁷You were sorry and humbled yourself before God when you heard his words against this city and its people. You humbled yourself and tore your clothing in despair and wept before me in repentance. And I have indeed heard you, says the Lord. ²⁸So I will not send the promised disaster until after you have died and been buried in peace. You yourself will not see the disaster I am going to bring on this city and its people.'"

So they took her message back to the king.

Josiah's Religious Reforms

²⁹Then the king summoned all the elders of Judah and Jerusalem. ³⁰And the king went up to the Temple of the Lord with all the people of Judah and Jerusalem, along with the priests and the Levites—all the people from the greatest to the least. There the king read to them the entire Book of the Cov-

enant that had been found in the Lord's Temple. ³¹The king took his place of authority beside the pillar and renewed the covenant in the Lord's presence. He pledged to obey the Lord by keeping all his commands, laws, and decrees with all his heart and soul. He promised to obey all the terms of the covenant that were written in the scroll. ³²And he required everyone in Jerusalem and the people of Benjamin to make a similar pledge. The people of Jerusalem did so, renewing their covenant with God, the God of their ancestors.

³³So Josiah removed all detestable idols from the entire land of Israel and required everyone to worship the Lord their God. And throughout the rest of his lifetime, they did not turn away from the Lord, the God of their ancestors.

35 Josiah Celebrates Passover

Then Josiah announced that the Passover of the Lord would be celebrated in Jerusalem, and so the Passover lamb was slaughtered on the fourteenth day of the first month.* ²Josiah also assigned the priests to their duties and encouraged them in their work at the Temple of the Lord. ³He issued this order to the Levites, who were to teach all Israel and who had been set apart to serve the Lord: "Put the holy Ark in the Temple that was built by Solomon son of David, the king of Israel. You no longer need to carry it back and forth on your shoulders. Now spend your time serving the Lord your God and his people Israel. ⁴Report for duty according to the family divisions of your ancestors, following the directions of King David of Israel and the directions of his son Solomon.

⁵"Then stand in the sanctuary at the place appointed for your family division and help the families assigned to you as they bring their offerings to the Temple. ⁶Slaughter the Passover lambs, purify yourselves, and prepare to help those who come. Follow all the directions that the Lord gave through Moses."

⁷Then Josiah provided 30,000 lambs and young goats for the people's Passover

---

34:22a Or *the Second Quarter,* a newer section of Jerusalem. Hebrew reads *the Mishneh.* 34:22b As in parallel text at 2 Kgs 22:14; Hebrew reads *son of Tokhath, son of Hasrah.* 34:24 Hebrew *this place;* also in 34:27, 28. 35:1 This day in the ancient Hebrew lunar calendar was April 5, 622 b.c.

offerings, along with 3,000 cattle, all from the king's own flocks and herds. ⁸ The king's officials also made willing contributions to the people, priests, and Levites. Hilkiah, Zechariah, and Jehiel, the administrators of God's Temple, gave the priests 2,600 lambs and young goats and 300 cattle as Passover offerings. ⁹ The Levite leaders—Conaniah and his brothers Shemaiah and Nethanel, as well as Hashabiah, Jeiel, and Jozabad—gave 5,000 lambs and young goats and 500 cattle to the Levites for their Passover offerings.

¹⁰ When everything was ready for the Passover celebration, the priests and the Levites took their places, organized by their divisions, as the king had commanded. ¹¹ The Levites then slaughtered the Passover lambs and presented the blood to the priests, who sprinkled the blood on the altar while the Levites prepared the animals. ¹² They divided the burnt offerings among the people by their family groups, so they could offer them to the LORD as prescribed in the Book of Moses. They did the same with the cattle. ¹³ Then they roasted the Passover lambs as prescribed; and they boiled the holy offerings in pots, kettles, and pans, and brought them out quickly so the people could eat them.

¹⁴ Afterward the Levites prepared Passover offerings for themselves and for the priests—the descendants of Aaron—because the priests had been busy from morning till night offering the burnt offerings and the fat portions. The Levites took responsibility for all these preparations.

¹⁵ The musicians, descendants of Asaph, were in their assigned places, following the commands that had been given by David, Asaph, Heman, and Jeduthun, the king's seer. The gatekeepers guarded the gates and did not need to leave their posts of duty, for their Passover offerings were prepared for them by their fellow Levites.

¹⁶ The entire ceremony for the LORD's Passover was completed that day. All the burnt offerings were sacrificed on the altar of the LORD, as King Josiah had commanded. ¹⁷ All the Israelites present in Jerusalem celebrated Passover and the Festival of Unleavened Bread for seven days. ¹⁸ Never since the time of the prophet Samuel had there been such a Passover. None of the kings of Israel had ever kept a Passover as Josiah did, involving all the priests and Levites, all the people of Jerusalem, and people from all over Judah and Israel. ¹⁹ This Passover celebration took place in the eighteenth year of Josiah's reign.

Josiah Dies in Battle

²⁰ After Josiah had finished restoring the Temple, King Neco of Egypt led his army up from Egypt to do battle at Carchemish on the Euphrates River, and Josiah and his army marched out to fight him.* ²¹ But King Neco sent messengers to Josiah with this message:

"What do you want with me, king of Judah? I have no quarrel with you today! I am on my way to fight another nation, and God has told me to hurry! Do not interfere with God, who is with me, or he will destroy you."

²² But Josiah refused to listen to Neco, to whom God had indeed spoken, and he would not turn back. Instead, he disguised himself and led his army into battle on the plain of Megiddo. ²³ But the enemy archers hit King Josiah with their arrows and wounded him. He cried out to his men, "Take me from the battle, for I am badly wounded!"

²⁴ So they lifted Josiah out of his chariot and placed him in another chariot. Then they brought him back to Jerusalem, where he died. He was buried there in the royal cemetery. And all Judah and Jerusalem mourned for him. ²⁵ The prophet Jeremiah composed funeral songs for Josiah, and to this day choirs still sing these sad songs about his death. These songs of sorrow have become a tradition and are recorded in *The Book of Laments.*

²⁶ The rest of the events of Josiah's reign and his acts of devotion (carried out according to what was written in the Law of the LORD), ²⁷ from beginning to end—all are recorded in *The Book of the Kings of Israel and Judah.*

35:20 Or *Josiah went out to meet him.*

36 Jehoahaz Rules in Judah

Then the people of the land took Josiah's son Jehoahaz and made him the next king in Jerusalem.

²Jehoahaz* was twenty-three years old when he became king, and he reigned in Jerusalem three months.

³Then he was deposed by the king of Egypt, who demanded that Judah pay 7,500 pounds of silver and 75 pounds of gold* as tribute.

Jehoiakim Rules in Judah

⁴The king of Egypt then installed Eliakim, the brother of Jehoahaz, as the next king of Judah and Jerusalem, and he changed Eliakim's name to Jehoiakim. Then Neco took Jehoahaz to Egypt as a prisoner.

⁵Jehoiakim was twenty-five years old when he became king, and he reigned in Jerusalem eleven years. He did what was evil in the sight of the Lord his God.

⁶Then King Nebuchadnezzar of Babylon came to Jerusalem and captured it, and he bound Jehoiakim in bronze chains and led him away to Babylon. ⁷Nebuchadnezzar also took some of the treasures from the Temple of the Lord, and he placed them in his palace* in Babylon.

⁸The rest of the events in Jehoiakim's reign, including all the evil things he did and everything found against him, are recorded in *The Book of the Kings of Israel and Judah.* Then his son Jehoiachin became the next king.

Jehoiachin Rules in Judah

⁹Jehoiachin was eighteen* years old when he became king, and he reigned in Jerusalem three months and ten days. Jehoiachin did what was evil in the Lord's sight.

¹⁰In the spring of the year* King Nebuchadnezzar took Jehoiachin to Babylon. Many treasures from the Temple of the Lord were also taken to Babylon at that time. And Nebuchadnezzar installed Jehoiachin's uncle,* Zedekiah, as the next king in Judah and Jerusalem.

Zedekiah Rules in Judah

¹¹Zedekiah was twenty-one years old when he became king, and he reigned in Jerusalem eleven years. ¹²He did what was evil in the sight of the Lord his God, and he refused to humble himself when the prophet Jeremiah spoke to him directly from the Lord. ¹³He also rebelled against King Nebuchadnezzar, even though he had taken an oath of loyalty in God's name. Zedekiah was a hard and stubborn man, refusing to turn to the Lord, the God of Israel.

¹⁴Likewise, all the leaders of the priests and the people became more and more unfaithful. They followed all the pagan practices of the surrounding nations, desecrating the Temple of the Lord that had been consecrated in Jerusalem.

¹⁵The Lord, the God of their ancestors, repeatedly sent his prophets to warn them, for he had compassion on his people and his Temple. ¹⁶But the people mocked these messengers of God and despised their words. They scoffed at the prophets until the Lord's anger could no longer be restrained and nothing could be done.

The Fall of Jerusalem

¹⁷So the Lord brought the king of Babylon against them. The Babylonians* killed Judah's young men, even chasing after them into the Temple. They had no pity on the people, killing both young men and young women, the old and the infirm. God handed all of them over to Nebuchadnezzar. ¹⁸The king took home to Babylon all the articles, large and small, used in the Temple of God, and the treasures from both the Lord's Temple and from the palace of the king and his officials. ¹⁹Then his army burned the Temple of God, tore down the walls of Jerusalem, burned all the palaces, and completely destroyed everything of value.* ²⁰The few who survived were taken as exiles to Babylon, and they became servants to the king and his sons until the kingdom of Persia came to power.

²¹So the message of the Lord spoken

36:2 Hebrew *Joahaz*, a variant spelling of Jehoahaz; also in 36:4.   36:3 Hebrew *100 talents* [3,400 kilograms] *of silver and 1 talent* [34 kilograms] *of gold.*   36:7 Or *temple.*   36:9 As in one Hebrew manuscript, some Greek manuscripts, and Syriac version (see also 2 Kgs 24:8); most Hebrew manuscripts read *eight.*   36:10a Hebrew *At the turn of the year.* The first day of this year in the ancient Hebrew lunar calendar was April 13, 597 B.C.   36:10b As in parallel text at 2 Kgs 24:17; Hebrew reads *brother,* or *relative.*   36:17 Or *Chaldeans.*   36:19 Or *destroyed all the valuable articles from the Temple.*

through Jeremiah was fulfilled. The land finally enjoyed its Sabbath rest, lying desolate until the seventy years were fulfilled, just as the prophet had said.

Cyrus Allows the Exiles to Return

²²In the first year of King Cyrus of Persia,* the LORD fulfilled the prophecy he had given through Jeremiah.* He stirred the heart of Cyrus to put this proclamation in writing and to send it throughout his kingdom:

²³"This is what King Cyrus of Persia says:

"The LORD, the God of heaven, has given me all the kingdoms of the earth. He has appointed me to build him a Temple at Jerusalem, which is in Judah. Any of you who are the LORD's people may go there for this task. And may the LORD your God be with you!"

36:22a The first year of Cyrus's reign over Babylon was 538 B.C. 36:22b See Jer 25:11-12; 29:10.

Introduction to

Ezra

Background

The Book of Ezra is in step with the chronology of 2 Chronicles. The second exodus of God's people begins as God fulfills his promise to return his people to their land (Jeremiah 29:10) after their seventy-year exile. The first part of this exilic return addresses the leadership and work under Zerubbabel, the governor appointed to rebuild the temple. Halfway through the book, almost sixty years later, the priest-scribe Ezra returns with silver, gold, and other items for use in the temple, as well as priests to offer sacrifices.

Ezra, a priest and descendant of Aaron (7:1–5), is believed to be the author of this book. The sections of the book written in the first person (7:28–9:15) give credence to his authorship. Historically, the books of Ezra and Nehemiah were believed to be one document.

Message

The Book of Ezra is a testament to God's faithfulness. After the once-conquering Babylonians were conquered by the Medo-Persians (Daniel 5:30), the Persian king Cyrus issues a decree allowing the people of Israel to return home. This action had been prophesied by Isaiah (44:28)—down to the name of the king: "When I say of Cyrus, 'He is my shepherd,' he will certainly do as I say. He will command, 'Rebuild Jerusalem'; he will say, 'Restore the Temple.'" Nothing takes God by surprise: nothing is outside of his control.

Time

The Book of Ezra was probably written between 457 and 444 B.C. Its events dovetail with the books of Esther and Nehemiah: the events in Esther occur during the period covered in the first six chapters of Ezra; the events of Nehemiah take place during the period recounted in Ezra chapters 7–10.

Outline

Ezra

1 Cyrus Allows the Exiles to Return

In the first year of King Cyrus of Persia,* the LORD fulfilled the prophecy he had given through Jeremiah.* He stirred the heart of Cyrus to put this proclamation in writing and to send it throughout his kingdom:

²"This is what King Cyrus of Persia says:

"The LORD, the God of heaven, has given me all the kingdoms of the earth. He has appointed me to build him a Temple at Jerusalem, which is in Judah. ³Any of you who are his people may go to Jerusalem in Judah to rebuild this Temple of the LORD, the God of Israel, who lives in Jerusalem. And may your God be with you! ⁴Wherever this Jewish remnant is found, let their neighbors contribute toward their expenses by giving them silver and gold, supplies for the journey, and livestock, as well as a voluntary offering for the Temple of God in Jerusalem."

⁵Then God stirred the hearts of the priests and Levites and the leaders of the tribes of Judah and Benjamin to go to Jerusalem to rebuild the Temple of the LORD. ⁶And all their neighbors assisted by giving them articles of silver and gold, supplies for the journey, and livestock. They gave them many valuable gifts in addition to all the voluntary offerings.

⁷King Cyrus himself brought out the articles that King Nebuchadnezzar had taken from the LORD's Temple in Jerusalem and had placed in the temple of his own gods. ⁸Cyrus directed Mithredath, the treasurer of Persia, to count these items and present them to Sheshbazzar, the leader of the exiles returning to Judah.* ⁹This is a list of the items that were returned:

gold basins	30
silver basins	1,000
silver incense burners*	29
¹⁰ gold bowls	30
silver bowls	410
other items	1,000

¹¹In all, there were 5,400 articles of gold and silver. Sheshbazzar brought all of these along when the exiles went from Babylon to Jerusalem.

2 Exiles Who Returned with Zerubbabel

Here is the list of the Jewish exiles of the provinces who returned from their captivity. King Nebuchadnezzar had deported them to Babylon, but now they returned to Jerusalem and the other towns in Judah where they originally lived. ²Their leaders were Zerubbabel, Jeshua, Nehemiah, Seraiah, Reelaiah, Mordecai, Bilshan, Mispar, Bigvai, Rehum, and Baanah.

This is the number of the men of Israel who returned from exile:

³ The family of Parosh	2,172

1:1a The first year of Cyrus's reign over Babylon was 538 B.C. 1:1b See Jer 25:11-12; 29:10. 1:8 Hebrew Sheshbazzar, the prince of Judah. 1:9 The meaning of this Hebrew word is uncertain.

4 The family of Shephatiah 372
5 The family of Arah 775
6 The family of Pahath-moab
  (descendants of Jeshua and Joab) . 2,812
7 The family of Elam 1,254
8 The family of Zattu 945
9 The family of Zaccai 760
10 The family of Bani. 642
11 The family of Bebai 623
12 The family of Azgad. 1,222
13 The family of Adonikam 666
14 The family of Bigvai. 2,056
15 The family of Adin 454
16 The family of Ater
  (descendants of Hezekiah). 98
17 The family of Bezai 323
18 The family of Jorah 112
19 The family of Hashum 223
20 The family of Gibbar 95
21 The people of Bethlehem. 123
22 The people of Netophah 56
23 The people of Anathoth 128
24 The people of Beth-azmaveth*. 42
25 The people of Kiriath-jearim,*
  Kephirah, and Beeroth. 743
26 The people of Ramah and Geba . . . 621
27 The people of Micmash. 122
28 The people of Bethel and Ai 223
29 The citizens of Nebo 52
30 The citizens of Magbish 156
31 The citizens of West Elam*. 1,254
32 The citizens of Harim. 320
33 The citizens of Lod, Hadid,
  and Ono 725
34 The citizens of Jericho 345
35 The citizens of Senaah 3,630

36 These are the priests who returned from exile:
  The family of Jedaiah (through the
  line of Jeshua) 973
37 The family of Immer 1,052
38 The family of Pashhur. 1,247
39 The family of Harim. 1,017

40 These are the Levites who returned from exile:
  The families of Jeshua and Kadmiel
  (descendants of Hodaviah) 74
41 The singers of the family of Asaph . 128
42 The gatekeepers of the families of

Shallum, Ater, Talmon, Akkub,
Hatita, and Shobai 139

43 The descendants of the following Temple servants returned from exile:
  Ziha, Hasupha, Tabbaoth,
44 Keros, Siaha, Padon,
45 Lebanah, Hagabah, Akkub,
46 Hagab, Shalmai,* Hanan,
47 Giddel, Gahar, Reaiah,
48 Rezin, Nekoda, Gazzam,
49 Uzza, Paseah, Besai,
50 Asnah, Meunim, Nephusim,
51 Bakbuk, Hakupha, Harhur,
52 Bazluth, Mehida, Harsha,
53 Barkos, Sisera, Temah,
54 Neziah, and Hatipha.

55 The descendants of these servants of King Solomon returned from exile:
  Sotai, Hassophereth, Peruda,
56 Jaalah, Darkon, Giddel,
57 Shephatiah, Hattil, Pokereth-hazzebaim, and Ami.

58 In all, the Temple servants and the descendants of Solomon's servants numbered 392.

59 Another group returned at this time from the towns of Tel-melah, Tel-harsha, Kerub, Addan, and Immer. However, they could not prove that they or their families were descendants of Israel. 60 This group included the families of Delaiah, Tobiah, and Nekoda—a total of 652 people.

61 Three families of priests—Hobaiah, Hakkoz, and Barzillai—also returned. (This Barzillai had married a woman who was a descendant of Barzillai of Gilead, and he had taken her family name.) 62 They searched for their names in the genealogical records, but they were not found, so they were disqualified from serving as priests. 63 The governor told them not to eat the priests' share of food from the sacrifices until a priest could consult the LORD about the matter by using the Urim and Thummim—the sacred lots.

64 So a total of 42,360 people returned to Judah, 65 in addition to 7,337 servants and 200 singers, both men and women. 66 They took with them 736 horses, 245 mules, 67 435 camels, and 6,720 donkeys.

2:24 As in parallel text at Neh 7:28; Hebrew reads *Azmaveth*. **2:25** As in some Hebrew manuscripts and Greek version (see also Neh 7:29); Hebrew reads *Kiriath-arim*. **2:31** Or *of the other Elam*. **2:46** As in an alternate reading of the Masoretic Text (see also Neh 7:48); the other alternate reads *Shamlai*.

⁶⁸When they arrived at the Temple of the LORD in Jerusalem, some of the family leaders made voluntary offerings toward the rebuilding of God's Temple on its original site, ⁶⁹and each leader gave as much as he could. The total of their gifts came to 61,000 gold coins,* 6,250 pounds* of silver, and 100 robes for the priests.

⁷⁰So the priests, the Levites, the singers, the gatekeepers, the Temple servants, and some of the common people settled in villages near Jerusalem. The rest of the people returned to their own towns throughout Israel.

3 The Altar Is Rebuilt

In early autumn,* when the Israelites had settled in their towns, all the people assembled in Jerusalem with a unified purpose. ²Then Jeshua son of Jehozadak* joined his fellow priests and Zerubbabel son of Shealtiel with his family in rebuilding the altar of the God of Israel. They wanted to sacrifice burnt offerings on it, as instructed in the Law of Moses, the man of God. ³Even though the people were afraid of the local residents, they rebuilt the altar at its old site. Then they began to sacrifice burnt offerings on the altar to the LORD each morning and evening.

⁴They celebrated the Festival of Shelters as prescribed in the Law, sacrificing the number of burnt offerings specified for each day of the festival. ⁵They also offered the regular burnt offerings and the offerings required for the new moon celebrations and the annual festivals as prescribed by the LORD. The people also gave voluntary offerings to the LORD. ⁶Fifteen days before the Festival of Shelters began,* the priests had begun to sacrifice burnt offerings to the LORD. This was even before they had started to lay the foundation of the LORD's Temple.

The People Begin to Rebuild the Temple

⁷Then the people hired masons and carpenters and bought cedar logs from the people of Tyre and Sidon, paying them with food, wine, and olive oil. The logs were brought down from the Lebanon mountains and floated along the coast of the Mediterranean Sea* to Joppa, for King Cyrus had given permission for this.

⁸The construction of the Temple of God began in midspring,* during the second year after they arrived in Jerusalem. The work force was made up of everyone who had returned from exile, including Zerubbabel son of Shealtiel, Jeshua son of Jehozadak and his fellow priests, and all the Levites. The Levites who were twenty years old or older were put in charge of rebuilding the LORD's Temple. ⁹The workers at the Temple of God were supervised by Jeshua with his sons and relatives, and Kadmiel and his sons, all descendants of Hodaviah.* They were helped in this task by the Levites of the family of Henadad.

¹⁰When the builders completed the foundation of the LORD's Temple, the priests put on their robes and took their places to blow their trumpets. And the Levites, descendants of Asaph, clashed their cymbals to praise the LORD, just as King David had prescribed. ¹¹With praise and thanks, they sang this song to the LORD:

"He is so good!
His faithful love for Israel endures forever!"

Then all the people gave a great shout, praising the LORD because the foundation of the LORD's Temple had been laid. ¹²But many of the older priests, Levites, and other leaders who had seen the first Temple wept aloud when they saw the new Temple's foundation. The others, however, were shouting for joy. ¹³The joyful shouting and weeping mingled together in a loud noise that could be heard far in the distance.

4 Enemies Oppose the Rebuilding

The enemies of Judah and Benjamin heard that the exiles were rebuilding a

---

2:69a Hebrew *61,000 darics of gold*, about 1,100 pounds or 500 kilograms in weight. **2:69b** Hebrew *5,000 minas* [3,000 kilograms]. **3:1** Hebrew *In the seventh month*. The year is not specified, so it may have been during Cyrus's first year (538 B.C.) or second year (537 B.C.). The seventh month of the ancient Hebrew lunar calendar occurred within the months of September/October 538 B.C. and October/ November 537 B.C. **3:2** Hebrew *Jozadak*, a variant spelling of Jehozadak; also in 3:8. **3:6** Hebrew *On the first day of the seventh month*. This day in the ancient Hebrew lunar calendar occurred in September or October. The Festival of Shelters began on the fifteenth day of the seventh month. **3:7** Hebrew *the sea*. **3:8** Hebrew *in the second month*. This month in the ancient Hebrew lunar calendar occurred within the months of April and May 536 B.C. **3:9** Hebrew *sons of Judah* (i.e., *bene Yehudah*). *Bene* might also be read here as the proper name Binnui; *Yehudah* is probably another name for Hodaviah. Compare 2:40; Neh 7:43; 1 Esdras 5:58.

Temple to the LORD, the God of Israel. ²So they approached Zerubbabel and the other leaders and said, "Let us build with you, for we worship your God just as you do. We have sacrificed to him ever since King Esarhaddon of Assyria brought us here."

³But Zerubbabel, Jeshua, and the other leaders of Israel replied, "You may have no part in this work. We alone will build the Temple for the LORD, the God of Israel, just as King Cyrus of Persia commanded us."

⁴Then the local residents tried to discourage and frighten the people of Judah to keep them from their work. ⁵They bribed agents to work against them and to frustrate their plans. This went on during the entire reign of King Cyrus of Persia and lasted until King Darius of Persia took the throne.*

Later Opposition under Xerxes and Artaxerxes

⁶Years later when Xerxes* began his reign, the enemies of Judah wrote a letter of accusation against the people of Judah and Jerusalem.

⁷Even later, during the reign of King Artaxerxes of Persia,* the enemies of Judah, led by Bishlam, Mithredath, and Tabeel, sent a letter to Artaxerxes in the Aramaic language, and it was translated for the king.

⁸*Rehum the governor and Shimshai the court secretary wrote the letter, telling King Artaxerxes about the situation in Jerusalem. ⁹They greeted the king for all their colleagues—the judges and local leaders, the people of Tarpel, the Persians, the Babylonians, and the people of Erech and Susa (that is, Elam). ¹⁰They also sent greetings from the rest of the people whom the great and noble Ashurbanipal* had deported and relocated in Samaria and throughout the neighboring lands of the province west of the Euphrates River.*

¹¹This is a copy of their letter:

"To King Artaxerxes, from your loyal subjects in the province west of the Euphrates River.

¹²"The king should know that the Jews who came here to Jerusalem from Babylon are rebuilding this rebellious and evil city. They have already laid the foundation and will soon finish its walls. ¹³And the king should know that if this city is rebuilt and its walls are completed, it will be much to your disadvantage, for the Jews will then refuse to pay their tribute, customs, and tolls to you.

¹⁴"Since we are your loyal subjects* and do not want to see the king dishonored in this way, we have sent the king this information. ¹⁵We suggest that a search be made in your ancestors' records, where you will discover what a rebellious city this has been in the past. In fact, it was destroyed because of its long and troublesome history of revolt against the kings and countries who controlled it. ¹⁶We declare to the king that if this city is rebuilt and its walls are completed, the province west of the Euphrates River will be lost to you."

¹⁷Then King Artaxerxes sent this reply:

"To Rehum the governor, Shimshai the court secretary, and their colleagues living in Samaria and throughout the province west of the Euphrates River. Greetings.

¹⁸"The letter you sent has been translated and read to me. ¹⁹I ordered a search of the records and have found that Jerusalem has indeed been a hotbed of insurrection against many kings. In fact, rebellion and revolt are normal there! ²⁰Powerful kings have ruled over Jerusalem and the entire province west of the Euphrates River, receiving tribute, customs, and tolls. ²¹Therefore, issue orders to have these men stop their work. That city must not be rebuilt except at my express command. ²²Be diligent, and don't neglect this matter, for we must not permit the situation to harm the king's interests."

²³When this letter from King Artaxerxes was read to Rehum, Shimshai, and their colleagues, they hurried to Jerusalem. Then, with a show of strength, they forced the Jews to stop building.

4:5 Darius reigned 521–486 B.C.   **4:6** Hebrew *Ahasuerus*, another name for Xerxes. He reigned 486–465 B.C.   **4:7** Artaxerxes reigned 465–424 B.C.   **4:8** The original text of 4:8–6:18 is in Aramaic.   **4:10a** Aramaic *Osnappar*, another name for Ashurbanipal.   **4:10b** Aramaic *the province beyond the river*; also in 4:11, 16, 17, 20.   **4:14** Aramaic *Since we eat the salt of the palace.*

The Rebuilding Resumes

²⁴So the work on the Temple of God in Jerusalem had stopped, and it remained at a standstill until the second year of the reign of King Darius of Persia.*

5 At that time the prophets Haggai and Zechariah son of Iddo prophesied to the Jews in Judah and Jerusalem. They prophesied in the name of the God of Israel who was over them. ²Zerubbabel son of Shealtiel and Jeshua son of Jehozadak* responded by starting again to rebuild the Temple of God in Jerusalem. And the prophets of God were with them and helped them.

³But Tattenai, governor of the province west of the Euphrates River,* and Shethar-bozenai and their colleagues soon arrived in Jerusalem and asked, "Who gave you permission to rebuild this Temple and restore this structure?" ⁴They also asked for the names of all the men working on the Temple. ⁵But because their God was watching over them, the leaders of the Jews were not prevented from building until a report was sent to Darius and he returned his decision.

Tattenai's Letter to King Darius

⁶This is a copy of the letter that Tattenai the governor, Shethar-bozenai, and the other officials of the province west of the Euphrates River sent to King Darius:

⁷"To King Darius. Greetings.

⁸"The king should know that we went to the construction site of the Temple of the great God in the province of Judah. It is being rebuilt with specially prepared stones, and timber is being laid in its walls. The work is going forward with great energy and success.

⁹"We asked the leaders, 'Who gave you permission to rebuild this Temple and restore this structure?' ¹⁰And we demanded their names so that we could tell you who the leaders were.

¹¹"This was their answer: 'We are the servants of the God of heaven and earth, and we are rebuilding the Temple that was built here many years ago by a great king of Israel. ¹²But because our ancestors angered the God of heaven, he abandoned them to King Nebuchadnezzar of Babylon,* who destroyed this Temple and exiled the people to Babylonia. ¹³However, King Cyrus of Babylon,* during the first year of his reign, issued a decree that the Temple of God should be rebuilt. ¹⁴King Cyrus returned the gold and silver cups that Nebuchadnezzar had taken from the Temple of God in Jerusalem and had placed in the temple of Babylon. These cups were taken from that temple and presented to a man named Sheshbazzar, whom King Cyrus appointed as governor of Judah. ¹⁵The king instructed him to return the cups to their place in Jerusalem and to rebuild the Temple of God there on its original site. ¹⁶So this Sheshbazzar came and laid the foundations of the Temple of God in Jerusalem. The people have been working on it ever since, though it is not yet completed.'

¹⁷"Therefore, if it pleases the king, we request that a search be made in the royal archives of Babylon to discover whether King Cyrus ever issued a decree to rebuild God's Temple in Jerusalem. And then let the king send us his decision in this matter."

Darius Approves the Rebuilding

6 So King Darius issued orders that a search be made in the Babylonian archives, which were stored in the treasury. ²But it was at the fortress at Ecbatana in the province of Media that a scroll was found. This is what it said:

"Memorandum:

³"In the first year of King Cyrus's reign, a decree was sent out concerning the Temple of God at Jerusalem.

"Let the Temple be rebuilt on the site where Jews used to offer their sacrifices, using the original foundations. Its height will be ninety feet, and its width will be ninety feet.* ⁴Every three layers of

---

4:24 The second year of Darius's reign was 520 B.C. The narrative started in 4:1-5 is resumed at verse 24. **5:2** Aramaic *Jozadak*, a variant spelling of Jehozadak. **5:3** Aramaic *the province beyond the river;* also in 5:6. **5:12** Aramaic *Nebuchadnezzar the Chaldean.* **5:13** King Cyrus of Persia is here identified as the king of Babylon because Persia had conquered the Babylonian Empire. **6:3** Aramaic *Its height will be 60 cubits* [27.6 meters], *and its width will be 60 cubits.* It is commonly held that this verse should be emended to read: "Its height will be 30 cubits [45 feet, or 13.8 meters], its length will be 60 cubits [90 feet, or 27.6 meters], and its width will be 20 cubits [30 feet, or 9.2 meters]"; compare 1 Kgs 6:2. The emendation regarding the width is supported by the Syriac version.

specially prepared stones will be topped by a layer of timber. All expenses will be paid by the royal treasury. [5]Furthermore, the gold and silver cups, which were taken to Babylon by Nebuchadnezzar from the Temple of God in Jerusalem, must be returned to Jerusalem and put back where they belong. Let them be taken back to the Temple of God."

[6]So King Darius sent this message:

"Now therefore, Tattenai, governor of the province west of the Euphrates River,* and Shethar-bozenai, and your colleagues and other officials west of the Euphrates River—stay away from there! [7]Do not disturb the construction of the Temple of God. Let it be rebuilt on its original site, and do not hinder the governor of Judah and the elders of the Jews in their work.

[8]"Moreover, I hereby decree that you are to help these elders of the Jews as they rebuild this Temple of God. You must pay the full construction costs, without delay, from my taxes collected in the province west of the Euphrates River so that the work will not be interrupted.

[9]"Give the priests in Jerusalem whatever is needed in the way of young bulls, rams, and male lambs for the burnt offerings presented to the God of heaven. And without fail, provide them with as much wheat, salt, wine, and olive oil as they need each day. [10]Then they will be able to offer acceptable sacrifices to the God of heaven and pray for the welfare of the king and his sons.

[11]"Those who violate this decree in any way will have a beam pulled from their house. Then they will be tied to it and flogged, and their house will be reduced to a pile of rubble.* [12]May the God who has chosen the city of Jerusalem as the place to honor his name destroy any king or nation that violates this command and destroys this Temple.

"I, Darius, have issued this decree. Let it be obeyed with all diligence."

The Temple's Dedication

[13]Tattenai, governor of the province west of the Euphrates River, and Shethar-bozenai and their colleagues complied at once with the command of King Darius. [14]So the Jewish elders continued their work, and they were greatly encouraged by the preaching of the prophets Haggai and Zechariah son of Iddo. The Temple was finally finished, as had been commanded by the God of Israel and decreed by Cyrus, Darius, and Artaxerxes, the kings of Persia. [15]The Temple was completed on March 12,* during the sixth year of King Darius's reign.

[16]The Temple of God was then dedicated with great joy by the people of Israel, the priests, the Levites, and the rest of the people who had returned from exile. [17]During the dedication ceremony for the Temple of God, 100 young bulls, 200 rams, and 400 male lambs were sacrificed. And 12 male goats were presented as a sin offering for the twelve tribes of Israel. [18]Then the priests and Levites were divided into their various divisions to serve at the Temple of God in Jerusalem, as prescribed in the Book of Moses.

Celebration of Passover

[19]On April 21* the returned exiles celebrated Passover. [20]The priests and Levites had purified themselves and were ceremonially clean. So they slaughtered the Passover lamb for all the returned exiles, for their fellow priests, and for themselves. [21]The Passover meal was eaten by the people of Israel who had returned from exile and by the others in the land who had turned from their immoral customs to worship the LORD, the God of Israel. [22]Then they celebrated the Festival of Unleavened Bread for seven days. There was great joy throughout the land because the LORD had caused the king of Assyria* to be favorable to them, so that he helped them to rebuild the Temple of God, the God of Israel.

6:6 Aramaic *the province beyond the river;* also in 6:6b, 8, 13.   6:11 Aramaic *a dunghill.*   6:15 Aramaic *on the third day of the month Adar,* of the ancient Hebrew lunar calendar. A number of events in Ezra can be cross-checked with dates in surviving Persian records and related accurately to our modern calendar. This day was March 12, 515 B.C.   6:19 Hebrew *On the fourteenth day of the first month,* of the ancient Hebrew lunar calendar. This day was April 21, 515 B.C.; also see note on 6:15.   6:22 King Darius of Persia is here identified as the king of Assyria because Persia had conquered the Babylonian Empire, which included the earlier Assyrian Empire.

7 Ezra Arrives in Jerusalem

Many years later, during the reign of King Artaxerxes of Persia,* there was a man named Ezra. He was the son* of Seraiah, son of Azariah, son of Hilkiah, ²son of Shallum, son of Zadok, son of Ahitub, ³son of Amariah, son of Azariah, son* of Meraioth, ⁴son of Zerahiah, son of Uzzi, son of Bukki, ⁵son of Abishua, son of Phinehas, son of Eleazar, son of Aaron the high priest.* ⁶This Ezra was a scribe who was well versed in the Law of Moses, which the LORD, the God of Israel, had given to the people of Israel. He came up to Jerusalem from Babylon, and the king gave him everything he asked for, because the gracious hand of the LORD his God was on him. ⁷Some of the people of Israel, as well as some of the priests, Levites, singers, gatekeepers, and Temple servants, traveled up to Jerusalem with him in the seventh year of King Artaxerxes' reign.

⁸Ezra arrived in Jerusalem in August* of that year. ⁹He had arranged to leave Babylon on April 8, the first day of the new year,* and he arrived at Jerusalem on August 4,* for the gracious hand of his God was on him. ¹⁰This was because Ezra had determined to study and obey the Law of the LORD and to teach those decrees and regulations to the people of Israel.

Artaxerxes' Letter to Ezra

¹¹King Artaxerxes had given a copy of the following letter to Ezra, the priest and scribe who studied and taught the commands and decrees of the LORD to Israel:

¹²*"From Artaxerxes, the king of kings, to Ezra the priest, the teacher of the law of the God of heaven. Greetings.

¹³"I decree that any of the people of Israel in my kingdom, including the priests and Levites, may volunteer to return to Jerusalem with you. ¹⁴I and my council of seven hereby instruct you to conduct an inquiry into the situation in Judah and Jerusalem, based on your God's law, which is in your hand. ¹⁵We also commission you to take with you silver and gold, which we are freely presenting as an offering to the God of Israel who lives in Jerusalem.

¹⁶"Furthermore, you are to take any silver and gold that you may obtain from the province of Babylon, as well as the voluntary offerings of the people and the priests that are presented for the Temple of their God in Jerusalem. ¹⁷These donations are to be used specifically for the purchase of bulls, rams, male lambs, and the appropriate grain offerings and liquid offerings, all of which will be offered on the altar of the Temple of your God in Jerusalem. ¹⁸Any silver and gold that is left over may be used in whatever way you and your colleagues feel is the will of your God.

¹⁹"But as for the cups we are entrusting to you for the service of the Temple of your God, deliver them all to the God of Jerusalem. ²⁰If you need anything else for your God's Temple or for any similar needs, you may take it from the royal treasury.

²¹"I, Artaxerxes the king, hereby send this decree to all the treasurers in the province west of the Euphrates River*: 'You are to give Ezra, the priest and teacher of the law of the God of heaven, whatever he requests of you. ²²You are to give him up to 7,500 pounds* of silver, 500 bushels* of wheat, 550 gallons of wine, 550 gallons of olive oil,* and an unlimited supply of salt. ²³Be careful to provide whatever the God of heaven demands for his Temple, for why should we risk bringing God's anger against the realm of the king and his sons? ²⁴I also decree that no priest, Levite, singer, gatekeeper, Temple servant, or other worker in this Temple of God will be required to pay tribute, customs, or tolls of any kind.'

²⁵"And you, Ezra, are to use the wisdom your God has given you to appoint

---

7:1a Artaxerxes reigned 465–424 B.C.   7:1b Or *descendant*; see 1 Chr 6:14.   7:3 Or *descendant*; see 1 Chr 6:6-10.   7:5 Or *the first priest*.
7:8 Hebrew *in the fifth month*. This month in the ancient Hebrew lunar calendar occurred within the months of August and September 458 B.C.   7:9a Hebrew *on the first day of the first month*, of the ancient Hebrew lunar calendar. This day was April 8, 458 B.C.; also see note on 6:15.   7:9b Hebrew *on the first day of the fifth month*, of the ancient Hebrew lunar calendar. This day was August 4, 458 B.C.; also see note on 6:15.   7:12 The original text of 7:12-26 is in Aramaic.   7:21 Aramaic *the province beyond the river*; also in 7:25.   7:22a Aramaic *100 talents* [3,400 kilograms].   7:22b Aramaic *100 cors* [18.2 kiloliters].   7:22c Aramaic *100 baths* [2.1 kiloliters] *of wine, 100 baths of olive oil.*

magistrates and judges who know your God's laws to govern all the people in the province west of the Euphrates River. Teach the law to anyone who does not know it. ²⁶ Anyone who refuses to obey the law of your God and the law of the king will be punished immediately, either by death, banishment, confiscation of goods, or imprisonment."

Ezra Praises the LORD

²⁷ Praise the LORD, the God of our ancestors, who made the king want to beautify the Temple of the LORD in Jerusalem! ²⁸ And praise him for demonstrating such unfailing love to me by honoring me before the king, his council, and all his mighty nobles! I felt encouraged because the gracious hand of the LORD my God was on me. And I gathered some of the leaders of Israel to return with me to Jerusalem.

8 Exiles Who Returned with Ezra

Here is a list of the family leaders and the genealogies of those who came with me from Babylon during the reign of King Artaxerxes:

² From the family of Phinehas: Gershom.
From the family of Ithamar: Daniel.
From the family of David: Hattush, ³ a descendant of Shecaniah.
From the family of Parosh: Zechariah and 150 other men were registered.

⁴ From the family of Pahath-moab: Eliehoenai son of Zerahiah and 200 other men.

⁵ From the family of Zattu*: Shecaniah son of Jahaziel and 300 other men.

⁶ From the family of Adin: Ebed son of Jonathan and 50 other men.

⁷ From the family of Elam: Jeshaiah son of Athaliah and 70 other men.

⁸ From the family of Shephatiah: Zebadiah son of Michael and 80 other men.

⁹ From the family of Joab: Obadiah son of Jehiel and 218 other men.

¹⁰ From the family of Bani*: Shelomith son of Josiphiah and 160 other men.

¹¹ From the family of Bebai: Zechariah son of Bebai and 28 other men.

¹² From the family of Azgad: Johanan son of Hakkatan and 110 other men.

¹³ From the family of Adonikam, who came later*: Eliphelet, Jeuel, Shemaiah, and 60 other men.

¹⁴ From the family of Bigvai: Uthai, Zaccur,* and 70 other men.

Ezra's Journey to Jerusalem

¹⁵ I assembled the exiles at the Ahava Canal, and we camped there for three days while I went over the lists of the people and the priests who had arrived. I found that not one Levite had volunteered to come along. ¹⁶ So I sent for Eliezer, Ariel, Shemaiah, Elnathan, Jarib, Elnathan, Nathan, Zechariah, and Meshullam, who were leaders of the people. I also sent for Joiarib and Elnathan, who were men of discernment. ¹⁷ I sent them to Iddo, the leader of the Levites at Casiphia, to ask him and his relatives and the Temple servants to send us ministers for the Temple of God at Jerusalem.

¹⁸ Since the gracious hand of our God was on us, they sent us a man named Sherebiah, along with eighteen of his sons and brothers. He was a very astute man and a descendant of Mahli, who was a descendant of Levi son of Israel.* ¹⁹ They also sent Hashabiah, together with Jeshaiah from the descendants of Merari, and twenty of his sons and brothers, ²⁰ and 220 Temple servants. The Temple servants were assistants to the Levites—a group of Temple workers first instituted by King David and his officials. They were all listed by name.

²¹ And there by the Ahava Canal, I gave orders for all of us to fast and humble ourselves before our God. We prayed that he would give us a safe journey and protect us, our children, and our goods as we traveled. ²² For I was ashamed to ask the king for soldiers and horsemen* to accompany us and protect us from enemies along the way. After all, we had told the king, "Our God's hand of protection is on all who worship him, but his fierce anger rages against those who abandon him." ²³ So we fasted and earnestly prayed that our God would take care of us, and he heard our prayer.

8:5 As in some Greek manuscripts (see also 1 Esdras 8:32); Hebrew lacks *Zattu*. **8:10** As in some Greek manuscripts (see also 1 Esdras 8:36); Hebrew lacks *Bani*. **8:13** Or *who were the last of his family*. **8:14** As in Greek and Syriac versions and an alternate reading of the Masoretic Text; the other alternate reads *Zabbud*. **8:18** *Israel* is the name that God gave to Jacob. **8:22** Or *charioteers*.

²⁴ I appointed twelve leaders of the priests—Sherebiah, Hashabiah, and ten other priests—²⁵ to be in charge of transporting the silver, the gold, the gold bowls, and the other items that the king, his council, his officials, and all the people of Israel had presented for the Temple of God. ²⁶ I weighed the treasure as I gave it to them and found the totals to be as follows:

24 tons* of silver,
7,500 pounds* of silver articles,
7,500 pounds of gold,

²⁷ 20 gold bowls, equal in value to 1,000 gold coins,*
2 fine articles of polished bronze, as precious as gold.

²⁸ And I said to these priests, "You and these treasures have been set apart as holy to the LORD. This silver and gold is a voluntary offering to the LORD, the God of our ancestors. ²⁹ Guard these treasures well until you present them to the leading priests, the Levites, and the leaders of Israel, who will weigh them at the storerooms of the LORD's

Q&A — When Should We Fast?

EZRA 8:21–23

When should we fast?

Disciplining our bodies and stilling our minds through fasting cause something mysterious and beyond description to take place. It brings mental clarity and reminds us how vulnerable and dependent we are on God, as we listen closely to him. When we fast, we're reminded of Jesus' forty-day fast. It was then that Jesus said, "People do not live by bread alone, but by every word that comes from the mouth of God" (Matthew 4:4).

In the Scriptures people often fasted purposefully—with a specific reason in mind. For example, people would fast when someone was experiencing private affliction, such as David who fasted when his child was ill (2 Samuel 12:15-17), and when danger was approaching, such as when Esther fasted as she prepared for her dangerous meeting with King Xerxes (Esther 4:15-16). Other reasons people fasted were the ordination of ministers (Acts 13:2-3); confession of sin (1 Samuel 7:6; Nehemiah 9:1-2); seeking humility (Psalm 35:13); to discern God's will and direction (Ezra 8:21-23); to seek healing (Isaiah 58:6-8); to request God's intervention (2 Chronicles 20:3); in obedience to the direction of a leader (Jonah 3:6-10).

We can learn more and orient our thinking about it by seriously studying these and other biblical texts. But also, it's important to learn about fasting by *doing* it; I'm a big believer in the power of the experience. Fasting is an *essential* spiritual discipline that spurs us toward maturity in Christ.

—*Alise Barrymore*

For more on fasting, see reading at Esther 4:7–5:2.

8:26a Hebrew *650 talents* [22 metric tons]. **8:26b** Hebrew *100 talents* [3,400 kilograms]; also in 8:26c. **8:27** Hebrew *1,000 darics*, about 19 pounds or 8.6 kilograms in weight.

Temple in Jerusalem." ³⁰So the priests and the Levites accepted the task of transporting these treasures of silver and gold to the Temple of our God in Jerusalem.

³¹We broke camp at the Ahava Canal on April 19* and started off to Jerusalem. And the gracious hand of our God protected us and saved us from enemies and bandits along the way. ³²So we arrived safely in Jerusalem, where we rested for three days.

³³On the fourth day after our arrival, the silver, gold, and other valuables were weighed at the Temple of our God and entrusted to Meremoth son of Uriah the priest and to Eleazar son of Phinehas, along with Jozabad son of Jeshua and Noadiah son of Binnui—both of whom were Levites. ³⁴Everything was accounted for by number and weight, and the total weight was officially recorded.

³⁵Then the exiles who had come out of captivity sacrificed burnt offerings to the God of Israel. They presented twelve bulls for all the people of Israel, as well as ninety-six rams and seventy-seven male lambs. They also offered twelve male goats as a sin offering. All this was given as a burnt offering to the LORD. ³⁶The king's decrees were delivered to his highest officers and the governors of the province west of the Euphrates River,* who then cooperated by supporting the people and the Temple of God.

9 Ezra's Prayer concerning Intermarriage

When these things had been done, the Jewish leaders came to me and said, "Many of the people of Israel, and even some of the priests and Levites, have not kept themselves separate from the other peoples living in the land. They have taken up the detestable practices of the Canaanites, Hittites, Perizzites, Jebusites, Ammonites, Moabites, Egyptians, and Amorites. ²For the men of Israel have married women from these people and have taken them as wives for their sons. So the holy race has become polluted by these mixed marriages. Worse yet, the leaders and officials have led the way in this outrage."

³When I heard this, I tore my cloak and my shirt, pulled hair from my head and beard, and sat down utterly shocked. ⁴Then all who trembled at the words of the God of Israel came and sat with me because of this outrage committed by the returned exiles. And I sat there utterly appalled until the time of the evening sacrifice.

⁵At the time of the sacrifice, I stood up from where I had sat in mourning with my clothes torn. I fell to my knees and lifted my hands to the LORD my God. ⁶I prayed,

"O my God, I am utterly ashamed; I blush to lift up my face to you. For our sins are piled higher than our heads, and our guilt has reached to the heavens. ⁷From the days of our ancestors until now, we have been steeped in sin. That is why we and our kings and our priests have been at the mercy of the pagan kings of the land. We have been killed, captured, robbed, and disgraced, just as we are today.

⁸"But now we have been given a brief moment of grace, for the LORD our God has allowed a few of us to survive as a remnant. He has given us security in this holy place. Our God has brightened our eyes and granted us some relief from our slavery. ⁹For we were slaves, but in his unfailing love our God did not abandon us in our slavery. Instead, he caused the kings of Persia to treat us favorably. He revived us so we could rebuild the Temple of our God and repair its ruins. He has given us a protective wall in Judah and Jerusalem.

¹⁰"And now, O our God, what can we say after all of this? For once again we have abandoned your commands! ¹¹Your servants the prophets warned us when they said, 'The land you are entering to possess is totally defiled by the detestable practices of the people living there. From one end to the other, the land is filled with corruption. ¹²Don't let your daughters marry their sons! Don't take their daughters as wives for your sons. Don't ever promote the peace and prosperity of those nations.

8:31 Hebrew *on the twelfth day of the first month,* of the ancient Hebrew lunar calendar. This day was April 19, 458 B.C.; also see note on 6:15.
8:36 Hebrew *the province beyond the river.*

If you follow these instructions, you will be strong and will enjoy the good things the land produces, and you will leave this prosperity to your children forever.'

¹³"Now we are being punished because of our wickedness and our great guilt. But we have actually been punished far less than we deserve, for you, our God, have allowed some of us to survive as a remnant. ¹⁴But even so, we are again breaking your commands and intermarrying with people who do these detestable things. Won't your anger be enough to destroy us, so that even this little remnant no longer survives? ¹⁵O LORD, God of Israel, you are just. We come before you in our guilt as nothing but an escaped remnant, though in such a condition none of us can stand in your presence."

10 The People Confess Their Sin

While Ezra prayed and made this confession, weeping and lying face down on the ground in front of the Temple of God, a very large crowd of people from Israel—men, women, and children—gathered and wept bitterly with him. ²Then Shecaniah son of Jehiel, a descendant of Elam, said to Ezra, "We have been unfaithful to our God, for we have married these pagan women of the land. But in spite of this there is hope for Israel. ³Let us now make a covenant with our God to divorce our pagan wives and to send them away with their children. We will follow the advice given by you and by the others who respect the commands of our God. Let it be done according to the Law of God. ⁴Get up, for it is your duty to tell us how to proceed in setting things straight. We are behind you, so be strong and take action."

⁵So Ezra stood up and demanded that the leaders of the priests and the Levites and all the people of Israel swear that they would do as Shecaniah had said. And they all swore a solemn oath. ⁶Then Ezra left the front of the Temple of God and went to the room of Jehohanan son of Eliashib.

He spent the night* there without eating or drinking anything. He was still in mourning because of the unfaithfulness of the returned exiles.

⁷Then a proclamation was made throughout Judah and Jerusalem that all the exiles should come to Jerusalem. ⁸Those who failed to come within three days would, if the leaders and elders so decided, forfeit all their property and be expelled from the assembly of the exiles.

⁹Within three days, all the people of Judah and Benjamin had gathered in Jerusalem. This took place on December 19,* and all the people were sitting in the square before the Temple of God. They were trembling both because of the seriousness of the matter and because it was raining. ¹⁰Then Ezra the priest stood and said to them: "You have committed a terrible sin. By marrying pagan women, you have increased Israel's guilt. ¹¹So now confess your sin to the LORD, the God of your ancestors, and do what he demands. Separate yourselves from the people of the land and from these pagan women."

¹²Then the whole assembly raised their voices and answered, "Yes, you are right; we must do as you say!" ¹³Then they added, "This isn't something that can be done in a day or two, for many of us are involved in this extremely sinful affair. And this is the rainy season, so we cannot stay out here much longer. ¹⁴Let our leaders act on behalf of us all. Let everyone who has a pagan wife come at a scheduled time, accompanied by the leaders and judges of his city, so that the fierce anger of our God concerning this affair may be turned away from us."

¹⁵Only Jonathan son of Asahel and Jahzeiah son of Tikvah opposed this course of action, and they were supported by Meshullam and Shabbethai the Levite.

¹⁶So this was the plan they followed. Ezra selected leaders to represent their families, designating each of the representatives by name. On December 29,* the leaders sat down to investigate the matter. ¹⁷By March 27, the first day of the new year,*

10:6 As in parallel text at 1 Esdras 9:2; Hebrew reads *He went.*   10:9 Hebrew *on the twentieth day of the ninth month,* of the ancient Hebrew lunar calendar. This day was December 19, 458 B.C.; also see note on 6:15.   10:16 Hebrew *On the first day of the tenth month,* of the ancient Hebrew lunar calendar. This day was December 29, 458 B.C.; also see note on 6:15.   10:17 Hebrew *By the first day of the first month,* of the ancient Hebrew lunar calendar. This day was March 27, 457 B.C.; also see note on 6:15.

they had finished dealing with all the men who had married pagan wives.

Those Guilty of Intermarriage

[18] These are the priests who had married pagan wives:

From the family of Jeshua son of Jehozadak* and his brothers: Maaseiah, Eliezer, Jarib, and Gedaliah. [19] They vowed to divorce their wives, and they each acknowledged their guilt by offering a ram as a guilt offering.

[20] From the family of Immer: Hanani and Zebadiah.

[21] From the family of Harim: Maaseiah, Elijah, Shemaiah, Jehiel, and Uzziah.

[22] From the family of Pashhur: Elioenai, Maaseiah, Ishmael, Nethanel, Jozabad, and Elasah.

[23] These are the Levites who were guilty: Jozabad, Shimei, Kelaiah (also called Kelita), Pethahiah, Judah, and Eliezer.

[24] This is the singer who was guilty: Eliashib.

These are the gatekeepers who were guilty: Shallum, Telem, and Uri.

[25] These are the other people of Israel who were guilty:

From the family of Parosh: Ramiah, Izziah, Malkijah, Mijamin, Eleazar, Hashabiah,* and Benaiah.

[26] From the family of Elam: Mattaniah, Zechariah, Jehiel, Abdi, Jeremoth, and Elijah.

[27] From the family of Zattu: Elioenai, Eliashib, Mattaniah, Jeremoth, Zabad, and Aziza.

[28] From the family of Bebai: Jehohanan, Hananiah, Zabbai, and Athlai.

[29] From the family of Bani: Meshullam, Malluch, Adaiah, Jashub, Sheal, and Jeremoth.

[30] From the family of Pahath-moab: Adna, Kelal, Benaiah, Maaseiah, Mattaniah, Bezalel, Binnui, and Manasseh.

[31] From the family of Harim: Eliezer, Ishijah, Malkijah, Shemaiah, Shimeon, [32] Benjamin, Malluch, and Shemariah.

[33] From the family of Hashum: Mattenai, Mattattah, Zabad, Eliphelet, Jeremai, Manasseh, and Shimei.

[34] From the family of Bani: Maadai, Amram, Uel, [35] Benaiah, Bedeiah, Keluhi, [36] Vaniah, Meremoth, Eliashib, [37] Mattaniah, Mattenai, and Jaasu.

[38] From the family of Binnui*: Shimei, [39] Shelemiah, Nathan, Adaiah, [40] Macnadebai, Shashai, Sharai, [41] Azarel, Shelemiah, Shemariah, [42] Shallum, Amariah, and Joseph.

[43] From the family of Nebo: Jeiel, Mattithiah, Zabad, Zebina, Jaddai, Joel, and Benaiah.

[44] Each of these men had a pagan wife, and some even had children by these wives.*

10:18 Hebrew *Jozadak*, a variant spelling of Jehozadak.   **10:25** As in parallel text at 1 Esdras 9:26; Hebrew reads *Malkijah*.   **10:37-38** As in Greek version; Hebrew reads *Jaasu*, [38]*Bani, Binnui*.   **10:44** Or *and they sent them away with their children*. The meaning of the Hebrew is uncertain.

Introduction to
Nehemiah

Background

The story of Nehemiah and the rebuilding of the wall around the city of Jerusalem is a staple in Sunday-school classes. At the beginning of his text, Nehemiah lives in exile in the Persian Empire. His trustworthiness is evident through his profession as cupbearer to King Artaxerxes, the stepson of Queen Esther. At Nehemiah's request, in 445 B.C. Artaxerxes allows him to return to Jerusalem to oversee the rebuilding of its gates and walls.

At least part of this book was written by Nehemiah. For more information about the relationship between the books of Ezra and Nehemiah, see the introduction to the Book of Ezra.

Message

While Ezra addresses the spiritual restoration of God's people and the rebuilding of the temple, Nehemiah's task is to ensure the city's security by rebuilding its wall. In ancient times, a city without a wall had no defense. Nehemiah's courageous leadership and his faith in God, exemplified by his prayer life, allow the job to continue despite constant harassment from the locals. The people work together and the wall is completed in a mere fifty-two days—a feat by any standards. With God's guidance and good planning, nothing is impossible. Nehemiah serves as governor, raising awareness of the needs of the poor, the importance of keeping the Sabbath and of bringing tithes to the Lord. In 433 B.C. Nehemiah is recalled to Artaxerxes but again asks for and receives permission to return to Jerusalem (13:6), where he serves a second term as governor.

Time

See the introduction to the Book of Ezra. The events in Nehemiah start in 445 B.C. and continue for at least twelve years. Nehemiah arrives in Jerusalem in the twentieth year of the reign of Artaxerxes. The prophet Malachi was a contemporary of Nehemiah.

Outline

Nehemiah

1 These are the memoirs of Nehemiah son of Hacaliah.

Nehemiah's Concern for Jerusalem

In late autumn, in the month of Kislev, in the twentieth year of King Artaxerxes' reign,* I was at the fortress of Susa. ²Hanani, one of my brothers, came to visit me with some other men who had just arrived from Judah. I asked them about the Jews who had returned there from captivity and about how things were going in Jerusalem.

³They said to me, "Things are not going well for those who returned to the province of Judah. They are in great trouble and disgrace. The wall of Jerusalem has been torn down, and the gates have been destroyed by fire."

⁴When I heard this, I sat down and wept. In fact, for days I mourned, fasted, and prayed to the God of heaven. ⁵Then I said,

"O Lord, God of heaven, the great and awesome God who keeps his covenant of unfailing love with those who love him and obey his commands, ⁶listen to my prayer! Look down and see me praying night and day for your people Israel. I confess that we have sinned against you. Yes, even my own family and I have sinned! ⁷We have sinned terribly by not obeying the commands, decrees, and regulations that you gave us through your servant Moses.

⁸"Please remember what you told your servant Moses: 'If you are unfaithful to me, I will scatter you among the nations. ⁹But if you return to me and obey my commands and live by them, then even if you are exiled to the ends of the earth, I will bring you back to the place I have chosen for my name to be honored.'

¹⁰"The people you rescued by your great power and strong hand are your servants. ¹¹O Lord, please hear my prayer! Listen to the prayers of those of us who delight in honoring you. Please grant me success today by making the king favorable to me.* Put it into his heart to be kind to me."

In those days I was the king's cup-bearer.

2 Nehemiah Goes to Jerusalem

Early the following spring, in the month of Nisan,* during the twentieth year of King Artaxerxes' reign, I was serving the king his wine. I had never before appeared sad in his presence. ²So the king asked me, "Why are you looking so sad? You don't look sick to me. You must be deeply troubled."

Then I was terrified, ³but I replied, "Long live the king! How can I not be sad? For the city where my ancestors are buried is in ruins, and the gates have been destroyed by fire."

1:1 Hebrew *In the month of Kislev of the twentieth year.* A number of dates in the book of Nehemiah can be cross-checked with dates in surviving Persian records and related accurately to our modern calendar. This month of the ancient Hebrew lunar calendar occurred within the months of November and December 446 B.C. The *twentieth year* probably refers to the reign of King Artaxerxes I; compare 2:1; 5:14.   **1:11** Hebrew *today in the sight of this man.*   **2:1** Hebrew *In the month of Nisan.* This month of the ancient Hebrew lunar calendar occurred within the months of April and May 445 B.C.

Acceptance

The Dream Tucked Away in Your Heart
NEHEMIAH 1

Did you have a secret wish as a child, something you longed to do "someday" when you grew up? Me too. I wanted to write a novel.

When you make such a bold confession at age ten, people hide their smiles. "Is that so? Good luck, honey," they comment.

I bought a ruled notebook with a fake marble cover and began my first novel, *The Mountain Cabin Mystery*. Ten juvenile mysteries poured from my pencil before I "grew up" and went off to college, storing my fiction hopes in a cardboard box in my parents' attic. Those notebooks—and my dream—gathered dust while I went on with real life.

But God didn't forget, not for one patient minute.

He nudged me year after year—just as he may be tugging at your heart right now—whispering, *What are you waiting for? Open your gift.* Scripture tells us that every good gift is from our Father (James 1:17); you can be sure whatever gifts were tucked in your young heart came from the hand of God.

Often we display our gifts proudly as children, then we hide them in adulthood, hoping no one will ask us, "Do you draw? Can you play the piano? Do you know how to sew?"

"Not really," we murmur, fearing risk, dreading failure, convinced those things we loved to do as kids were nothing but child's play, when in truth they were a gift from God, placed in our small hands with big expectations.

The Lord knew, long before I knew him, that I would become a storyteller someday. It took thirty-five years from my first pretend novel to the release of my first published one. Just as I'd hidden that box in the attic for safekeeping, God had stored that dream deep inside a corner of my heart and waited for me to find it again.

What about you? Don't wait another minute. Open your gift; it's never too late for a child's dream to see the light of day.

—Liz Curtis Higgs

For more on acceptance, see reading at Job 2:1–10.

⁴The king asked, "Well, how can I help you?"

With a prayer to the God of heaven, ⁵I replied, "If it please the king, and if you are pleased with me, your servant, send me to Judah to rebuild the city where my ancestors are buried."

⁶The king, with the queen sitting beside him, asked, "How long will you be gone? When will you return?" After I told him how long I would be gone, the king agreed to my request.

⁷I also said to the king, "If it please the king, let me have letters addressed to the governors of the province west of the Euphrates River,* instructing them to let me travel safely through their territories on my way to Judah. ⁸And please give me a letter addressed to Asaph, the manager of the king's forest, instructing him to give me timber. I will

2:7 Hebrew *the province beyond the river;* also in 2:9.

need it to make beams for the gates of the Temple fortress, for the city walls, and for a house for myself." And the king granted these requests, because the gracious hand of God was on me.

⁹When I came to the governors of the province west of the Euphrates River, I delivered the king's letters to them. The king, I should add, had sent along army officers and horsemen* to protect me. ¹⁰But when Sanballat the Horonite and Tobiah the Ammonite official heard of my arrival, they were very displeased that someone had come to help the people of Israel.

Nehemiah Inspects Jerusalem's Wall

¹¹So I arrived in Jerusalem. Three days later, ¹²I slipped out during the night, taking only a few others with me. I had not told anyone about the plans God had put in my heart for Jerusalem. We took no pack animals with us except the donkey I was riding. ¹³After dark I went out through the Valley Gate, past the Jackal's Well,* and over to the Dung Gate to inspect the broken walls and burned gates. ¹⁴Then I went to the Fountain Gate and to the King's Pool, but my donkey couldn't get through the rubble. ¹⁵So, though it was still dark, I went up the Kidron Valley* instead, inspecting the wall before I turned back and entered again at the Valley Gate.

¹⁶The city officials did not know I had been out there or what I was doing, for I had not yet said anything to anyone about my plans. I had not yet spoken to the Jewish leaders—the priests, the nobles, the officials, or anyone else in the administration. ¹⁷But now I said to them, "You know very well what trouble we are in. Jerusalem lies in ruins, and its gates have been destroyed by fire. Let us rebuild the wall of Jerusalem and end this disgrace!" ¹⁸Then I told them about how the gracious hand of God had been on me, and about my conversation with the king.

They replied at once, "Yes, let's rebuild the wall!" So they began the good work.

¹⁹But when Sanballat, Tobiah, and Geshem the Arab heard of our plan, they scoffed contemptuously. "What are you doing? Are you rebelling against the king?" they asked.

²⁰I replied, "The God of heaven will help us succeed. We, his servants, will start rebuilding this wall. But you have no share, legal right, or historic claim in Jerusalem."

3 Rebuilding the Wall of Jerusalem

Then Eliashib the high priest and the other priests started to rebuild at the Sheep Gate. They dedicated it and set up its doors, building the wall as far as the Tower of the Hundred, which they dedicated, and the Tower of Hananel. ²People from the town of Jericho worked next to them, and beyond them was Zaccur son of Imri.

³The Fish Gate was built by the sons of Hassenaah. They laid the beams, set up its doors, and installed its bolts and bars. ⁴Meremoth son of Uriah and grandson of Hakkoz repaired the next section of wall. Beside him were Meshullam son of Berekiah and grandson of Meshezabel, and then Zadok son of Baana. ⁵Next were the people from Tekoa, though their leaders refused to work with the construction supervisors.

⁶The Old City Gate* was repaired by Joiada son of Paseah and Meshullam son of Besodeiah. They laid the beams, set up its doors, and installed its bolts and bars. ⁷Next to them were Melatiah from Gibeon, Jadon from Meronoth, people from Gibeon, and people from Mizpah, the headquarters of the governor of the province west of the Euphrates River.* ⁸Next was Uzziel son of Harhaiah, a goldsmith by trade, who also worked on the wall. Beyond him was Hananiah, a manufacturer of perfumes. They left out a section of Jerusalem as they built the Broad Wall.*

⁹Rephaiah son of Hur, the leader of half the district of Jerusalem, was next to them on the wall. ¹⁰Next Jedaiah son of Harumaph repaired the wall across from his own house, and next to him was Hattush son of Hashabneiah. ¹¹Then came Malkijah son of Harim and Hasshub son of Pahath-moab, who repaired another section of the wall and the Tower of the Ovens. ¹²Shallum son of Hallohesh and his daughters repaired the next section. He was the leader of the other half of the district of Jerusalem.

¹³The Valley Gate was repaired by the

people from Zanoah, led by Hanun. They set up its doors and installed its bolts and bars. They also repaired the 1,500 feet* of wall to the Dung Gate.

¹⁴ The Dung Gate was repaired by Malkijah son of Recab, the leader of the Beth-hakkerem district. He rebuilt it, set up its doors, and installed its bolts and bars.

¹⁵ The Fountain Gate was repaired by Shallum* son of Col-hozeh, the leader of the Mizpah district. He rebuilt it, roofed it, set up its doors, and installed its bolts and bars. Then he repaired the wall of the pool of Siloam* near the king's garden, and he rebuilt the wall as far as the stairs that descend from the City of David. ¹⁶ Next to him was Nehemiah son of Azbuk, the leader of half the district of Beth-zur. He rebuilt the wall from a place across from the tombs of David's family as far as the water reservoir and the House of the Warriors.

¹⁷ Next to him, repairs were made by a group of Levites working under the supervision of Rehum son of Bani. Then came Hashabiah, the leader of half the district of Keilah, who supervised the building of the wall on behalf of his own district. ¹⁸ Next down the line were his countrymen led by Binnui* son of Henadad, the leader of the other half of the district of Keilah.

¹⁹ Next to them, Ezer son of Jeshua, the leader of Mizpah, repaired another section of wall across from the ascent to the armory near the angle in the wall. ²⁰ Next to him was Baruch son of Zabbai, who zealously repaired an additional section from the angle to the door of the house of Eliashib the high priest. ²¹ Meremoth son of Uriah and grandson of Hakkoz rebuilt another section of the wall extending from the door of Eliashib's house to the end of the house.

²² The next repairs were made by the priests from the surrounding region. ²³ After them, Benjamin and Hasshub repaired the section across from their house, and Azariah son of Maaseiah and grandson of Ananiah repaired the section across from his house. ²⁴ Next was Binnui son of Henadad, who rebuilt another section of the wall

from Azariah's house to the angle and the corner. ²⁵ Palal son of Uzai carried on the work from a point opposite the angle and the tower that projects up from the king's upper house beside the court of the guard. Next to him were Pedaiah son of Parosh, ²⁶ with the Temple servants living on the hill of Ophel, who repaired the wall as far as a point across from the Water Gate to the east and the projecting tower. ²⁷ Then came the people of Tekoa, who repaired another section across from the great projecting tower and over to the wall of Ophel.

²⁸ Above the Horse Gate, the priests repaired the wall. Each one repaired the section immediately across from his own house. ²⁹ Next Zadok son of Immer also rebuilt the wall across from his own house, and beyond him was Shemaiah son of Shecaniah, the gatekeeper of the East Gate. ³⁰ Next Hananiah son of Shelemiah and Hanun, the sixth son of Zalaph, repaired another section, while Meshullam son of Berekiah rebuilt the wall across from where he lived. ³¹ Malkijah, one of the goldsmiths, repaired the wall as far as the housing for the Temple servants and merchants, across from the Inspection Gate. Then he continued as far as the upper room at the corner. ³² The other goldsmiths and merchants repaired the wall from that corner to the Sheep Gate.

4 Enemies Oppose the Rebuilding

¹ *Sanballat was very angry when he learned that we were rebuilding the wall. He flew into a rage and mocked the Jews, ²saying in front of his friends and the Samarian army officers, "What does this bunch of poor, feeble Jews think they're doing? Do they think they can build the wall in a single day by just offering a few sacrifices?* Do they actually think they can make something of stones from a rubbish heap—and charred ones at that?"

³ Tobiah the Ammonite, who was standing beside him, remarked, "That stone wall would collapse if even a fox walked along the top of it!"

⁴ Then I prayed, "Hear us, our God, for we are being mocked. May their scoffing

---

3:13 Hebrew *1,000 cubits* [450 meters].   **3:15a** As in Syriac version; Hebrew reads *Shallun.*   **3:15b** Hebrew *pool of Shelah,* another name for the pool of Siloam.   **3:18** As in a few Hebrew manuscripts, some Greek manuscripts, and Syriac version (see also 3:24; 10:9); most Hebrew manuscripts read *Bavvai.*   **4:1** Verses 4:1-6 are numbered 3:33-38 in Hebrew text.   **4:2** The meaning of the Hebrew is uncertain.

fall back on their own heads, and may they themselves become captives in a foreign land! ⁵Do not ignore their guilt. Do not blot out their sins, for they have provoked you to anger here in front of* the builders."

⁶At last the wall was completed to half its height around the entire city, for the people had worked with enthusiasm.

⁷*But when Sanballat and Tobiah and the Arabs, Ammonites, and Ashdodites heard that the work was going ahead and that the gaps in the wall of Jerusalem were being repaired, they were furious. ⁸They all made plans to come and fight against Jerusalem and throw us into confusion. ⁹But we prayed to our God and guarded the city day and night to protect ourselves.

¹⁰Then the people of Judah began to complain, "The workers are getting tired, and there is so much rubble to be moved. We will never be able to build the wall by ourselves."

¹¹Meanwhile, our enemies were saying, "Before they know what's happening, we will swoop down on them and kill them and end their work."

¹²The Jews who lived near the enemy came and told us again and again, "They will come from all directions and attack us!"* ¹³So I placed armed guards behind the lowest parts of the wall in the exposed areas. I stationed the people to stand guard by families, armed with swords, spears, and bows.

¹⁴Then as I looked over the situation, I called together the nobles and the rest of the people and said to them, "Don't be afraid of the enemy! Remember the Lord, who is great and glorious, and fight for your brothers, your sons, your daughters, your wives, and your homes!"

¹⁵When our enemies heard that we knew of their plans and that God had frustrated them, we all returned to our work on the wall. ¹⁶But from then on, only half my men worked while the other half stood guard with spears, shields, bows, and coats of mail. The leaders stationed themselves behind the people of Judah ¹⁷who were building the wall. The laborers carried on their work with one hand supporting their load and one hand holding a weapon. ¹⁸All the builders had a sword belted to their side. The trumpeter stayed with me to sound the alarm.

¹⁹Then I explained to the nobles and officials and all the people, "The work is very spread out, and we are widely separated from each other along the wall. ²⁰When you hear the blast of the trumpet, rush to wherever it is sounding. Then our God will fight for us!"

²¹We worked early and late, from sunrise to sunset. And half the men were always on guard. ²²I also told everyone living outside the walls to stay in Jerusalem. That way they and their servants could help with guard duty at night and work during the day. ²³During this time, none of us—not I, nor my relatives, nor my servants, nor the guards who were with me—ever took off our clothes. We carried our weapons with us at all times, even when we went for water.*

5 Nehemiah Defends the Oppressed

About this time some of the men and their wives raised a cry of protest against their fellow Jews. ²They were saying, "We have such large families. We need more food to survive."

³Others said, "We have mortgaged our fields, vineyards, and homes to get food during the famine."

⁴And others said, "We have had to borrow money on our fields and vineyards to pay our taxes. ⁵We belong to the same family as those who are wealthy, and our children are just like theirs. Yet we must sell our children into slavery just to get enough money to live. We have already sold some of our daughters, and we are helpless to do anything about it, for our fields and vineyards are already mortgaged to others."

⁶When I heard their complaints, I was very angry. ⁷After thinking it over, I spoke out against these nobles and officials. I told them, "You are hurting your own relatives by charging interest when they borrow money!" Then I called a public meeting to deal with the problem.

⁸At the meeting I said to them, "We are

4:5 Or *for they have thrown insults in the face of.* **4:7** Verses 4:7-23 are numbered 4:1-17 in Hebrew text. **4:12** The meaning of the Hebrew is uncertain. **4:23** Or *Each carried his weapon in his right hand.* Hebrew reads *Each his weapon the water.* The meaning of the Hebrew is uncertain.

doing all we can to redeem our Jewish relatives who have had to sell themselves to pagan foreigners, but you are selling them back into slavery again. How often must we redeem them?" And they had nothing to say in their defense.

⁹Then I pressed further, "What you are doing is not right! Should you not walk in the fear of our God in order to avoid being mocked by enemy nations? ¹⁰I myself, as well as my brothers and my workers, have been lending the people money and grain, but now let us stop this business of charging interest. ¹¹You must restore their fields, vineyards, olive groves, and homes to them

this very day. And repay the interest you charged when you lent them money, grain, new wine, and olive oil."

¹²They replied, "We will give back everything and demand nothing more from the people. We will do as you say." Then I called the priests and made the nobles and officials swear to do what they had promised.

¹³I shook out the folds of my robe and said, "If you fail to keep your promise, may God shake you like this from your homes and from your property!"

The whole assembly responded, "Amen," and they praised the LORD. And the people did as they had promised.

Just Purchases
NEHEMIAH 5

I know money "talks." How can I spend money justly?

My justice journey started with a deliberate choice to buy only fair trade coffee. I'd read reports that coffee farmers around the world were being cheated of their wages for the coffee they grew. They could no longer send their children to school and were struggling even to put food on the table. By purchasing fair trade coffee I knew that the farmers were paid a decent wage for their work, allowed to have a say in how the coffee was grown, and were not abused or threatened as they worked. Sure, it cost me a little more, but I realized that my morning cup of coffee was a justice issue.

From there I researched other purchasing options. I learned the clothes I wear often are made by children in abusive sweatshops, that the cell phone I use may have connections to guerrilla squads that terrorize and rape women, that the chocolate I eat may have been grown by children trafficked into slavery, and that the energy I use has helped to destroy communities in Appalachia and Nigeria.

Our lives are connected to people around the world; often our choices about what we consume or participate in inadvertently contribute to the harm of others. If we want to seek justice for others, we can start by (slowly) changing our spending habits. Even in the small things, we can pursue justice and compassion.

—Julie Clawson

For more on justice, see reading at Isaiah 1:17.

¹⁴For the entire twelve years that I was governor of Judah—from the twentieth year to the thirty-second year of the reign of King Artaxerxes*—neither I nor my officials drew on our official food allowance. ¹⁵The former governors, in contrast, had laid heavy burdens on the people, demanding a daily ration of food and wine, besides forty pieces* of silver. Even their assistants took advantage of the people. But because I feared God, I did not act that way.

¹⁶I also devoted myself to working on the wall and refused to acquire any land. And I required all my servants to spend time working on the wall. ¹⁷I asked for nothing, even though I regularly fed 150 Jewish officials at my table, besides all the visitors from other lands! ¹⁸The provisions I paid for each day included one ox, six choice sheep or goats, and a large number of poultry. And every ten days we needed a large supply of all kinds of wine. Yet I refused to claim the governor's food allowance because the people already carried a heavy burden.

¹⁹Remember, O my God, all that I have done for these people, and bless me for it.

6 Continued Opposition to Rebuilding

Sanballat, Tobiah, Geshem the Arab, and the rest of our enemies found out that I had finished rebuilding the wall and that no gaps remained—though we had not yet set up the doors in the gates. ²So Sanballat and Geshem sent a message asking me to meet them at one of the villages* in the plain of Ono.

But I realized they were plotting to harm me, ³so I replied by sending this message to them: "I am engaged in a great work, so I can't come. Why should I stop working to come and meet with you?"

⁴Four times they sent the same message, and each time I gave the same reply. ⁵The fifth time, Sanballat's servant came with an open letter in his hand, ⁶and this is what it said:

"There is a rumor among the surrounding nations, and Geshem* tells me it is true, that you and the Jews are planning to rebel and that is why you are building the wall. According to his reports, you plan to be their king. ⁷He also reports that you have appointed prophets in Jerusalem to proclaim about you, 'Look! There is a king in Judah!'

"You can be very sure that this report will get back to the king, so I suggest that you come and talk it over with me."

⁸I replied, "There is no truth in any part of your story. You are making up the whole thing."

⁹They were just trying to intimidate us, imagining that they could discourage us and stop the work. So I continued the work with even greater determination.*

¹⁰Later I went to visit Shemaiah son of Delaiah and grandson of Mehetabel, who was confined to his home. He said, "Let us meet together inside the Temple of God and bolt the doors shut. Your enemies are coming to kill you tonight."

¹¹But I replied, "Should someone in my position run from danger? Should someone in my position enter the Temple to save his life? No, I won't do it!" ¹²I realized that God had not spoken to him, but that he had uttered this prophecy against me because Tobiah and Sanballat had hired him. ¹³They were hoping to intimidate me and make me sin. Then they would be able to accuse and discredit me.

¹⁴Remember, O my God, all the evil things that Tobiah and Sanballat have done. And remember Noadiah the prophet and all the prophets like her who have tried to intimidate me.

The Builders Complete the Wall

¹⁵So on October 2* the wall was finished—just fifty-two days after we had begun. ¹⁶When our enemies and the surrounding nations heard about it, they were frightened and humiliated. They realized this work had been done with the help of our God.

¹⁷During those fifty-two days, many letters went back and forth between Tobiah and the nobles of Judah. ¹⁸For many in

---

5:14 That is, 445–433 b.c.   **5:15** Hebrew *40 shekels* [1 pound, or 456 grams].   **6:2** As in Greek version; Hebrew reads *at Kephirim.*
6:6 Hebrew *Gashmu,* a variant spelling of Geshem.   **6:9** As in Greek version; Hebrew reads *But now to strengthen my hands.*   **6:15** Hebrew *on the twenty-fifth day of the month Elul,* of the ancient Hebrew lunar calendar. This day was October 2, 445 b.c.; also see note on 1:1.

Judah had sworn allegiance to him because his father-in-law was Shecaniah son of Arah, and his son Jehohanan was married to the daughter of Meshullam son of Berekiah. ¹⁹They kept telling me about Tobiah's good deeds, and then they told him everything I said. And Tobiah kept sending threatening letters to intimidate me.

7 After the wall was finished and I had set up the doors in the gates, the gatekeepers, singers, and Levites were appointed. ²I gave the responsibility of governing Jerusalem to my brother Hanani, along with Hananiah, the commander of the fortress, for he was a faithful man who feared God more than most. ³I said to them, "Do not leave the gates open during the hottest part of the day.* And even while the gatekeepers are on duty, have them shut and bar the doors. Appoint the residents of Jerusalem to act as guards, everyone on a regular watch. Some will serve at sentry posts and some in front of their own homes."

Nehemiah Registers the People
⁴At that time the city was large and spacious, but the population was small, and none of the houses had been rebuilt. ⁵So my God gave me the idea to call together all the nobles and leaders of the city, along with the ordinary citizens, for registration. I had found the genealogical record of those who had first returned to Judah. This is what was written there:

⁶Here is the list of the Jewish exiles of the provinces who returned from their captivity. King Nebuchadnezzar had deported them to Babylon, but now they returned to Jerusalem and the other towns in Judah where they originally lived. ⁷Their leaders were Zerubbabel, Jeshua, Nehemiah, Seraiah,* Reelaiah,* Nahamani, Mordecai, Bilshan, Mispar,* Bigvai, Rehum,* and Baanah.

This is the number of the men of Israel who returned from exile:

⁸ The family of Parosh 2,172
⁹ The family of Shephatiah 372
¹⁰ The family of Arah 652
¹¹ The family of Pahath-moab
   (descendants of Jeshua
   and Joab) 2,818
¹² The family of Elam 1,254
¹³ The family of Zattu 845
¹⁴ The family of Zaccai 760
¹⁵ The family of Bani* 648
¹⁶ The family of Bebai 628
¹⁷ The family of Azgad 2,322
¹⁸ The family of Adonikam 667
¹⁹ The family of Bigvai 2,067
²⁰ The family of Adin 655
²¹ The family of Ater
   (descendants of Hezekiah) 98
²² The family of Hashum 328
²³ The family of Bezai 324
²⁴ The family of Jorah* 112
²⁵ The family of Gibbar* 95
²⁶ The people of Bethlehem
   and Netophah. 188
²⁷ The people of Anathoth 128
²⁸ The people of Beth-azmaveth 42
²⁹ The people of Kiriath-jearim,
   Kephirah, and Beeroth. 743
³⁰ The people of Ramah and Geba. . 621
³¹ The people of Micmash 122
³² The people of Bethel and Ai 123
³³ The people of West Nebo*. 52
³⁴ The citizens of West Elam* . . . 1,254
³⁵ The citizens of Harim 320
³⁶ The citizens of Jericho 345
³⁷ The citizens of Lod, Hadid,
   and Ono 721
³⁸ The citizens of Senaah 3,930

³⁹These are the priests who returned from exile:
   The family of Jedaiah
   (through the line of Jeshua) . . . 973
⁴⁰ The family of Immer 1,052
⁴¹ The family of Pashhur 1,247
⁴² The family of Harim 1,017

⁴³These are the Levites who returned from exile:
   The families of Jeshua and Kadmiel
   (descendants of Hodaviah*). . . . 74

7:3 Or *Keep the gates of Jerusalem closed until the sun is hot.* **7:7a** As in parallel text at Ezra 2:2; Hebrew reads *Azariah.* **7:7b** As in parallel text at Ezra 2:2; Hebrew reads *Raamiah.* **7:7c** As in parallel text at Ezra 2:2; Hebrew reads *Mispereth.* **7:7d** As in parallel text at Ezra 2:2; Hebrew reads *Nehum.* **7:15** As in parallel text at Ezra 2:10; Hebrew reads *Binnui.* **7:24** As in parallel text at Ezra 2:18; Hebrew reads *Hariph.* **7:25** As in parallel text at Ezra 2:20; Hebrew reads *Gibeon.* **7:33** Or *of the other Nebo.* **7:34** Or *of the other Elam.* **7:43** As in parallel text at Ezra 2:40; Hebrew reads *Hodevah.*

⁴⁴ The singers of the family
of Asaph. 148
⁴⁵ The gatekeepers of the families of
Shallum, Ater, Talmon, Akkub,
Hatita, and Shobai 138

⁴⁶ The descendants of the following Temple servants returned from exile:
Ziha, Hasupha, Tabbaoth,
⁴⁷ Keros, Siaha,* Padon,
⁴⁸ Lebanah, Hagabah, Shalmai,
⁴⁹ Hanan, Giddel, Gahar,
⁵⁰ Reaiah, Rezin, Nekoda,
⁵¹ Gazzam, Uzza, Paseah,
⁵² Besai, Meunim, Nephusim,*
⁵³ Bakbuk, Hakupha, Harhur,
⁵⁴ Bazluth,* Mehida, Harsha,
⁵⁵ Barkos, Sisera, Temah,
⁵⁶ Neziah, and Hatipha.

⁵⁷ The descendants of these servants of King Solomon returned from exile:
Sotai, Hassophereth, Peruda,*
⁵⁸ Jaalah,* Darkon, Giddel,
⁵⁹ Shephatiah, Hattil, Pokereth-hazzebaim, and Ami.*

⁶⁰ In all, the Temple servants and the descendants of Solomon's servants numbered 392.

⁶¹ Another group returned at this time from the towns of Tel-melah, Tel-harsha, Kerub, Addan,* and Immer. However, they could not prove that they or their families were descendants of Israel. ⁶² This group included the families of Delaiah, Tobiah, and Nekoda—a total of 642 people. ⁶³ Three families of priests—Hobaiah, Hakkoz, and Barzillai—also returned. (This Barzillai had married a woman who was a descendant of Barzillai of Gilead, and he had taken her family name.) ⁶⁴ They searched for their names in the genealogical records, but they were not found, so they were disqualified from serving as priests.

⁶⁵ The governor told them not to eat the priests' share of food from the sacrifices until a priest could consult the LORD about the matter by using the Urim and Thummim—the sacred lots.

⁶⁶ So a total of 42,360 people returned to Judah, ⁶⁷ in addition to 7,337 servants and 245 singers, both men and women. ⁶⁸ They took with them 736 horses, 245 mules,* ⁶⁹ 435 camels, and 6,720 donkeys.

⁷⁰ Some of the family leaders gave gifts for the work. The governor gave to the treasury 1,000 gold coins,* 50 gold basins, and 530 robes for the priests. ⁷¹ The other leaders gave to the treasury a total of 20,000 gold coins* and some 2,750 pounds* of silver for the work. ⁷² The rest of the people gave 20,000 gold coins, about 2,500 pounds* of silver, and 67 robes for the priests.

⁷³ So the priests, the Levites, the gatekeepers, the singers, the Temple servants, and some of the common people settled near Jerusalem. The rest of the people returned to their own towns throughout Israel.

8 Ezra Reads the Law

In October,* when the Israelites had settled in their towns, ^{8:1} all the people assembled with a unified purpose at the square just inside the Water Gate. They asked Ezra the scribe to bring out the Book of the Law of Moses, which the LORD had given for Israel to obey.

² So on October 8* Ezra the priest brought the Book of the Law before the assembly, which included the men and women and all the children old enough to understand. ³ He faced the square just inside the Water Gate from early morning until noon and read aloud to everyone who could understand. All the people listened closely to the Book of the Law.

⁴ Ezra the scribe stood on a high wooden

7:47 As in parallel text at Ezra 2:44; Hebrew reads *Sia*.   **7:52** As in parallel text at Ezra 2:50; Hebrew reads *Nephushesim*.   **7:54** As in parallel text at Ezra 2:52; Hebrew reads *Bazlith*.   **7:57** As in parallel text at Ezra 2:55; Hebrew reads *Sotai, Sophereth, Perida*.   **7:58** As in parallel text at Ezra 2:56; Hebrew reads *Jaala*.   **7:59** As in parallel text at Ezra 2:57; Hebrew reads *Amon*.   **7:61** As in parallel text at Ezra 2:59; Hebrew reads *Addon*.   **7:68** As in some Hebrew manuscripts (see also Ezra 2:66); most Hebrew manuscripts lack this verse. Verses 7:69-73 are numbered 7:68-72 in Hebrew text.   **7:70** Hebrew *1,000 darics of gold*, about 19 pounds or 8.6 kilograms in weight.   **7:71a** Hebrew *20,000 darics of gold*, about 375 pounds or 170 kilograms in weight; also in 7:72.   **7:71b** Hebrew *2,200 minas* [1,300 kilograms].   **7:72** Hebrew *2,000 minas* [1,200 kilograms].   **7:73** Hebrew *in the seventh month*. This month of the ancient Hebrew lunar calendar occurred within the months of October and November 445 B.C.   **8:2** Hebrew *on the first day of the seventh month*, of the ancient Hebrew lunar calendar. This day was October 8, 445 B.C.; also see note on 1:1.

Devoted Listening to Scripture

NEHEMIAH 8:1-8

A woman once told me that I should offer a fill-in-the-blank worksheet when I speak. "Busy women don't want to listen too hard," she said. "We just want to fill in the blanks."

Her comment bothers me. Not only because she underestimated the abilities of busy women, but also because this woman wanted to stifle an important spiritual and intellectual discipline: that of critical, Spirit-led *listening*. Especially when it's listening to teaching or preaching from the Word of God.

According to Acts 2:42, believers in the early church "devoted themselves to the apostles' teaching." This didn't mean they tuned in only long enough to figure out what words were missing from an apostle's key point number 1. They were devoted. *Devout listeners.* They believed Jesus when he said, "Anyone who accepts your message is also accepting me" (Luke 10:16).

Being a devoted listener to Bible teaching and preaching means more than passively absorbing what we hear. Devout listeners know that Christ is present and that what we hear could change our lives. That said, it also means that we listen with critical, curious ears, eager to learn and discover more. And it means that we also keep our eyes toward Christ and our ears tuned to what the Holy Spirit might want to convict us on or challenge us with.

To do this may mean we listen to preaching and teaching with our eyes closed, in contemplative meditation. Or it may mean we listen with a pen and paper in hand, scribbling down thoughts, questions, or promptings of the Spirit. Or it may mean that we go home and read, pray, or discuss what we've heard. It might mean all three. Or more.

Whatever it looks like for us—as unique individuals with different personalities and affinities—the discipline of devoted listening means we listen, understanding that Christ is present and that God is at work.

—*Caryn Rivadeneira*

For more on Bible study and meditation, see reading at Psalm 1.

platform that had been made for the occasion. To his right stood Mattithiah, Shema, Anaiah, Uriah, Hilkiah, and Maaseiah. To his left stood Pedaiah, Mishael, Malkijah, Hashum, Hashbaddanah, Zechariah, and Meshullam. ⁵Ezra stood on the platform in full view of all the people. When they saw him open the book, they all rose to their feet.

⁶Then Ezra praised the LORD, the great God, and all the people chanted, "Amen! Amen!" as they lifted their hands. Then they bowed down and worshiped the LORD with their faces to the ground.

⁷The Levites—Jeshua, Bani, Sherebiah, Jamin, Akkub, Shabbethai, Hodiah, Maaseiah, Kelita, Azariah, Jozabad, Hanan, and Pelaiah—then instructed the people in the Law while everyone remained in their places. ⁸They read from the Book of the Law of God and clearly explained the meaning of what was being read, helping the people understand each passage.

⁹Then Nehemiah the governor, Ezra the priest and scribe, and the Levites who were interpreting for the people said to them, "Don't mourn or weep on such a day as this! For today is a sacred day before the

LORD your God." For the people had all been weeping as they listened to the words of the Law.

¹⁰And Nehemiah* continued, "Go and celebrate with a feast of rich foods and sweet drinks, and share gifts of food with people who have nothing prepared. This is a sacred day before our Lord. Don't be dejected and sad, for the joy of the LORD is your strength!"

¹¹And the Levites, too, quieted the people, telling them, "Hush! Don't weep! For this is a sacred day." ¹²So the people went away to eat and drink at a festive meal, to share gifts of food, and to celebrate with great joy because they had heard God's words and understood them.

The Festival of Shelters

¹³On October 9* the family leaders of all the people, together with the priests and Levites, met with Ezra the scribe to go over the Law in greater detail. ¹⁴As they studied the Law, they discovered that the LORD had commanded through Moses that the Israelites should live in shelters during the festival to be held that month.* ¹⁵He had said that a proclamation should be made throughout their towns and in Jerusalem, telling the people to go to the hills to get branches from olive, wild olive,* myrtle, palm, and other leafy trees. They were to use these branches to make shelters in which they would live during the festival, as prescribed in the Law.

¹⁶So the people went out and cut branches and used them to build shelters on the roofs of their houses, in their courtyards, in the courtyards of God's Temple, or in the squares just inside the Water Gate and the Ephraim Gate. ¹⁷So everyone who had returned from captivity lived in these shelters during the festival, and they were all filled with great joy! The Israelites had not celebrated like this since the days of Joshua* son of Nun.

¹⁸Ezra read from the Book of the Law of God on each of the seven days of the festival. Then on the eighth day they held a solemn assembly, as was required by law.

9 The People Confess Their Sins

On October 31* the people assembled again, and this time they fasted and dressed in burlap and sprinkled dust on their heads. ²Those of Israelite descent separated themselves from all foreigners as they confessed their own sins and the sins of their ancestors. ³They remained standing in place for three hours* while the Book of the Law of the LORD their God was read aloud to them. Then for three more hours they confessed their sins and worshiped the LORD their God. ⁴The Levites—Jeshua, Bani, Kadmiel, Shebaniah, Bunni, Sherebiah, Bani, and Kenani—stood on the stairway of the Levites and cried out to the LORD their God with loud voices.

⁵Then the leaders of the Levites—Jeshua, Kadmiel, Bani, Hashabneiah, Sherebiah, Hodiah, Shebaniah, and Pethahiah—called out to the people: "Stand up and praise the LORD your God, for he lives from everlasting to everlasting!" Then they prayed:

"May your glorious name be praised! May it be exalted above all blessing and praise!

⁶"You alone are the LORD. You made the skies and the heavens and all the stars. You made the earth and the seas and everything in them. You preserve them all, and the angels of heaven worship you.

⁷"You are the LORD God, who chose Abram and brought him from Ur of the Chaldeans and renamed him Abraham. ⁸When he had proved himself faithful, you made a covenant with him to give him and his descendants the land of the Canaanites, Hittites, Amorites, Perizzites, Jebusites, and Girgashites. And you have done what you promised, for you are always true to your word.

⁹"You saw the misery of our ancestors in Egypt, and you heard their cries from beside the Red Sea.* ¹⁰You displayed miraculous signs and wonders against Pharaoh, his officials, and all his people, for you knew how arrogantly they were

8:10 Hebrew *he.* **8:13** Hebrew *On the second day,* of the seventh month of the ancient Hebrew lunar calendar. This day was October 9, 445 B.C.; also see notes on 1:1 and 8:2. **8:14** Hebrew *in the seventh month.* This month of the ancient Hebrew lunar calendar usually occurs within the months of September and October. See Lev 23:39-43. **8:15** Or *pine;* Hebrew reads *oil tree.* **8:17** Hebrew *Jeshua,* a variant spelling of Joshua. **9:1** Hebrew *On the twenty-fourth day of that same month,* the seventh month of the ancient Hebrew lunar calendar. This day was October 31, 445 B.C.; also see notes on 1:1 and 8:2. **9:3** Hebrew *for a quarter of a day.* **9:9** Hebrew *sea of reeds.*

treating our ancestors. You have a glorious reputation that has never been forgotten. [11] You divided the sea for your people so they could walk through on dry land! And then you hurled their enemies into the depths of the sea. They sank like stones beneath the mighty waters. [12] You led our ancestors by a pillar of cloud during the day and a pillar of fire at night so that they could find their way.

[13] "You came down at Mount Sinai and spoke to them from heaven. You gave them regulations and instructions that were just, and decrees and commands that were good. [14] You instructed them concerning your holy Sabbath. And you commanded them, through Moses your servant, to obey all your commands, decrees, and instructions.

[15] "You gave them bread from heaven when they were hungry and water from the rock when they were thirsty. You commanded them to go and take possession of the land you had sworn to give them.

[16] "But our ancestors were proud and stubborn, and they paid no attention to your commands. [17] They refused to obey and did not remember the miracles you had done for them. Instead, they became stubborn and appointed a leader to take them back to their slavery in Egypt! But you are a God of forgiveness, gracious and merciful, slow to become angry, and rich in unfailing love. You did not abandon them, [18] even when they made an idol shaped like a calf and said, 'This is your god who brought you out of Egypt!' They committed terrible blasphemies.

[19] "But in your great mercy you did not abandon them to die in the wilderness. The pillar of cloud still led them forward by day, and the pillar of fire showed them the way through the night. [20] You sent your good Spirit to instruct them, and you did not stop giving them manna from heaven or water for their thirst. [21] For forty years you sustained them in the wilderness, and they lacked nothing. Their clothes did not wear out, and their feet did not swell!

[22] "Then you helped our ancestors conquer kingdoms and nations, and you placed your people in every corner of the land.* They took over the land of King Sihon of Heshbon and the land of King Og of Bashan. [23] You made their descendants as numerous as the stars in the sky and brought them into the land you had promised to their ancestors.

[24] "They went in and took possession of the land. You subdued whole nations before them. Even the Canaanites, who inhabited the land, were powerless! Your people could deal with these nations and their kings as they pleased. [25] Our ancestors captured fortified cities and fertile land. They took over houses full of good things, with cisterns already dug and vineyards and olive groves and fruit trees in abundance. So they ate until they were full and grew fat and enjoyed themselves in all your blessings.

[26] "But despite all this, they were disobedient and rebelled against you. They turned their backs on your Law, they killed your prophets who warned them to return to you, and they committed terrible blasphemies. [27] So you handed them over to their enemies, who made them suffer. But in their time of trouble they cried to you, and you heard them from heaven. In your great mercy, you sent them liberators who rescued them from their enemies.

[28] "But as soon as they were at peace, your people again committed evil in your sight, and once more you let their enemies conquer them. Yet whenever your people turned and cried to you again for help, you listened once more from heaven. In your wonderful mercy, you rescued them many times!

[29] "You warned them to return to your Law, but they became proud and obstinate and disobeyed your commands. They did not follow your regulations, by which people will find life if only they obey. They stubbornly turned their backs on you and refused to listen. [30] In your love, you were patient with them for many years. You sent your Spirit, who warned them through the prophets. But

still they wouldn't listen! So once again you allowed the peoples of the land to conquer them. ³¹But in your great mercy, you did not destroy them completely or abandon them forever. What a gracious and merciful God you are!

³²"And now, our God, the great and mighty and awesome God, who keeps his covenant of unfailing love, do not let all the hardships we have suffered seem insignificant to you. Great trouble has come upon us and upon our kings and leaders and priests and prophets and ancestors—all of your people—from the days when the kings of Assyria first triumphed over us until now. ³³Every time you punished us you were being just. We have sinned greatly, and you gave us only what we deserved. ³⁴Our kings, leaders, priests, and ancestors did not obey your Law or listen to the warnings in your commands and laws. ³⁵Even while they had their own kingdom, they did not serve you, though you showered your goodness on them. You gave them a large, fertile land, but they refused to turn from their wickedness.

³⁶"So now today we are slaves in the land of plenty that you gave our ancestors for their enjoyment! We are slaves here in this good land. ³⁷The lush produce of this land piles up in the hands of the kings whom you have set over us because of our sins. They have power over us and our livestock. We serve them at their pleasure, and we are in great misery."

The People Agree to Obey

³⁸*The people responded, "In view of all this,* we are making a solemn promise and putting it in writing. On this sealed document are the names of our leaders and Levites and priests."

10

¹*The document was ratified and sealed with the following names:

The governor:
Nehemiah son of Hacaliah, and also Zedekiah.
²The following priests:

Seraiah, Azariah, Jeremiah, ³Pashhur, Amariah, Malkijah, ⁴Hattush, Shebaniah, Malluch, ⁵Harim, Meremoth, Obadiah, ⁶Daniel, Ginnethon, Baruch, ⁷Meshullam, Abijah, Mijamin, ⁸Maaziah, Bilgai, and Shemaiah. These were the priests.
⁹The following Levites:
Jeshua son of Azaniah, Binnui from the family of Henadad, Kadmiel, ¹⁰and their fellow Levites: Shebaniah, Hodiah, Kelita, Pelaiah, Hanan, ¹¹Mica, Rehob, Hashabiah, ¹²Zaccur, Sherebiah, Shebaniah, ¹³Hodiah, Bani, and Beninu.
¹⁴The following leaders:
Parosh, Pahath-moab, Elam, Zattu, Bani, ¹⁵Bunni, Azgad, Bebai, ¹⁶Adonijah, Bigvai, Adin, ¹⁷Ater, Hezekiah, Azzur, ¹⁸Hodiah, Hashum, Bezai, ¹⁹Hariph, Anathoth, Nebai, ²⁰Magpiash, Meshullam, Hezir, ²¹Meshezabel, Zadok, Jaddua, ²²Pelatiah, Hanan, Anaiah, ²³Hoshea, Hananiah, Hasshub, ²⁴Hallohesh, Pilha, Shobek, ²⁵Rehum, Hashabnah, Maaseiah, ²⁶Ahiah, Hanan, Anan, ²⁷Malluch, Harim, and Baanah.

The Vow of the People

²⁸Then the rest of the people—the priests, Levites, gatekeepers, singers, Temple servants, and all who had separated themselves from the pagan people of the land in order to obey the Law of God, together with their wives, sons, daughters, and all who were old enough to understand—²⁹joined their leaders and bound themselves with an oath. They swore a curse on themselves if they failed to obey the Law of God as issued by his servant Moses. They solemnly promised to carefully follow all the commands, regulations, and decrees of the Lord our Lord:

³⁰"We promise not to let our daughters marry the pagan people of the land, and not to let our sons marry their daughters.
³¹"We also promise that if the people of the land should bring any merchandise or grain to be sold on the Sabbath or on any other holy day, we will refuse to buy it. Every seventh year we will let our land rest, and we will cancel all debts owed to us.

9:38a Verse 9:38 is numbered 10:1 in Hebrew text.   9:38b Or *In spite of all this.*   10:1 Verses 10:1-39 are numbered 10:2-40 in Hebrew text.

³²"In addition, we promise to obey the command to pay the annual Temple tax of one-eighth of an ounce of silver* for the care of the Temple of our God. ³³This will provide for the Bread of the Presence; for the regular grain offerings and burnt offerings; for the offerings on the Sabbaths, the new moon celebrations, and the annual festivals; for the holy offerings; and for the sin offerings to make atonement for Israel. It will provide for everything necessary for the work of the Temple of our God.

³⁴"We have cast sacred lots to determine when—at regular times each year—the families of the priests, Levites, and the common people should bring wood to God's Temple to be burned on the altar of the LORD our God, as is written in the Law.

³⁵"We promise to bring the first part of every harvest to the LORD's Temple year after year—whether it be a crop from the soil or from our fruit trees. ³⁶We agree to give God our oldest sons and the firstborn of all our herds and flocks, as prescribed in the Law. We will present them to the priests who minister in the Temple of our God. ³⁷We will store the produce in the storerooms of the Temple of our God. We will bring the best of our flour and other grain offerings, the best of our fruit, and the best of our new wine and olive oil. And we promise to bring to the Levites a tenth of everything our land produces, for it is the Levites who collect the tithes in all our rural towns.

³⁸"A priest—a descendant of Aaron— will be with the Levites as they receive these tithes. And a tenth of all that is collected as tithes will be delivered by the Levites to the Temple of our God and placed in the storerooms. ³⁹The people and the Levites must bring these offerings of grain, new wine, and olive oil to the storerooms and place them in the sacred containers near the ministering priests, the gatekeepers, and the singers.

"We promise together not to neglect the Temple of our God."

11 The People Occupy Jerusalem

The leaders of the people were living in Jerusalem, the holy city. A tenth of the people from the other towns of Judah and Benjamin were chosen by sacred lots to live there, too, while the rest stayed where they were. ²And the people commended everyone who volunteered to resettle in Jerusalem.

³Here is a list of the names of the provincial officials who came to live in Jerusalem. (Most of the people, priests, Levites, Temple servants, and descendants of Solomon's servants continued to live in their own homes in the various towns of Judah, ⁴but some of the people from Judah and Benjamin resettled in Jerusalem.)

From the tribe of Judah:
Athaiah son of Uzziah, son of Zechariah, son of Amariah, son of Shephatiah, son of Mahalalel, of the family of Perez. ⁵Also Maaseiah son of Baruch, son of Col-hozeh, son of Hazaiah, son of Adaiah, son of Joiarib, son of Zechariah, of the family of Shelah.* ⁶There were 468 descendants of Perez who lived in Jerusalem—all outstanding men. ⁷From the tribe of Benjamin:
Sallu son of Meshullam, son of Joed, son of Pedaiah, son of Kolaiah, son of Maaseiah, son of Ithiel, son of Jeshaiah. ⁸After him were Gabbai and Sallai and a total of 928 relatives. ⁹Their chief officer was Joel son of Zicri, who was assisted by Judah son of Hassenuah, second-in-command over the city.

¹⁰From the priests:
Jedaiah son of Joiarib; Jakin; ¹¹and Seraiah son of Hilkiah, son of Meshullam, son of Zadok, son of Meraioth, son of Ahitub, the supervisor of the Temple of God. ¹²Also 822 of their associates, who worked at the Temple. Also Adaiah son of Jeroham, son of Pelaliah, son of Amzi, son of Zechariah, son of Pashhur, son of Malkijah, ¹³along with 242 of his associates, who were heads of their families. Also Amashsai son of Azarel, son of Ahzai, son of Meshillemoth, son of Immer, ¹⁴and 128 of his* outstanding associates. Their chief officer was Zabdiel son of Haggedolim.

10:32 Hebrew *tax of ⅓ of a shekel* [4 grams].   **11:5** Hebrew *son of the Shilonite.*   **11:14** As in Greek version; Hebrew reads *their.*

¹⁵From the Levites:

Shemaiah son of Hasshub, son of Azrikam, son of Hashabiah, son of Bunni. ¹⁶Also Shabbethai and Jozabad, who were in charge of the work outside the Temple of God. ¹⁷Also Mattaniah son of Mica, son of Zabdi, a descendant of Asaph, who led in thanksgiving and prayer. Also Bakbukiah, who was Mattaniah's assistant, and Abda son of Shammua, son of Galal, son of Jeduthun. ¹⁸In all, there were 284 Levites in the holy city.

¹⁹From the gatekeepers:

Akkub, Talmon, and 172 of their associates, who guarded the gates.

²⁰The other priests, Levites, and the rest of the Israelites lived wherever their family inheritance was located in any of the towns of Judah. ²¹The Temple servants, however, whose leaders were Ziha and Gishpa, all lived on the hill of Ophel.

²²The chief officer of the Levites in Jerusalem was Uzzi son of Bani, son of Hashabiah, son of Mattaniah, son of Mica, a descendant of Asaph, whose family served as singers at God's Temple. ²³Their daily responsibilities were carried out according to the terms of a royal command.

²⁴Pethahiah son of Meshezabel, a descendant of Zerah son of Judah, was the royal adviser in all matters of public administration.

²⁵As for the surrounding villages with their open fields, some of the people of Judah lived in Kiriath-arba with its settlements, Dibon with its settlements, and Jekabzeel with its villages. ²⁶They also lived in Jeshua, Moladah, Beth-pelet, ²⁷Hazar-shual, Beersheba with its settlements, ²⁸Ziklag, and Meconah with its settlements. ²⁹They also lived in En-rimmon, Zorah, Jarmuth, ³⁰Zanoah, and Adullam with their surrounding villages. They also lived in Lachish with its nearby fields and Azekah with its surrounding villages. So the people of Judah were living all the way from Beersheba in the south to the valley of Hinnom.

³¹Some of the people of Benjamin lived at Geba, Micmash, Aija, and Bethel with its settlements. ³²They also lived in Anathoth, Nob, Ananiah, ³³Hazor, Ramah, Gittaim, ³⁴Hadid, Zeboim, Neballat, ³⁵Lod, Ono, and the Valley of Craftsmen.* ³⁶Some of the Levites who lived in Judah were sent to live with the tribe of Benjamin.

12 A History of the Priests and Levites

Here is the list of the priests and Levites who returned with Zerubbabel son of Shealtiel and Jeshua the high priest:

Seraiah, Jeremiah, Ezra,
² Amariah, Malluch, Hattush,
³ Shecaniah, Harim,* Meremoth,
⁴ Iddo, Ginnethon,* Abijah,
⁵ Miniamin, Moadiah,* Bilgah,
⁶ Shemaiah, Joiarib, Jedaiah,
⁷ Sallu, Amok, Hilkiah, and Jedaiah.

These were the leaders of the priests and their associates in the days of Jeshua.

⁸The Levites who returned with them were Jeshua, Binnui, Kadmiel, Sherebiah, Judah, and Mattaniah, who with his associates was in charge of the songs of thanksgiving. ⁹Their associates, Bakbukiah and Unni, stood opposite them during the service.

¹⁰ Jeshua the high priest was the father of Joiakim.
Joiakim was the father of Eliashib.
Eliashib was the father of Joiada.
¹¹ Joiada was the father of Johanan.*
Johanan was the father of Jaddua.

¹²Now when Joiakim was high priest, the family leaders of the priests were as follows:

Meraiah was leader of the family of Seraiah.
Hananiah was leader of the family of Jeremiah.
¹³ Meshullam was leader of the family of Ezra.
Jehohanan was leader of the family of Amariah.
¹⁴ Jonathan was leader of the family of Malluch.*

11:35 Or *and Ge-harashim.* **12:3** Hebrew *Rehum;* compare 7:42; 12:15; Ezra 2:39. **12:4** As in some Hebrew manuscripts and Latin Vulgate (see also 12:16); most Hebrew manuscripts read *Ginnethoi.* **12:5** Hebrew *Mijamin, Maadiah;* compare 12:17. **12:11** Hebrew *Jonathan;* compare 12:22. **12:14a** As in Greek version (see also 10:4; 12:2); Hebrew reads *Malluchi.*

Joseph was leader of the family of
Shecaniah.*

¹⁵ Adna was leader of the family of Harim.
Helkai was leader of the family of
Meremoth.*

¹⁶ Zechariah was leader of the family of
Iddo.
Meshullam was leader of the family of
Ginnethon.

¹⁷ Zicri was leader of the family of Abijah.
There was also a* leader of the family of
Miniamin.
Piltai was leader of the family of
Moadiah.

¹⁸ Shammua was leader of the family of
Bilgah.
Jehonathan was leader of the family of
Shemaiah.

¹⁹ Mattenai was leader of the family of
Joiarib.
Uzzi was leader of the family of Jedaiah.

²⁰ Kallai was leader of the family of Sallu.*
Eber was leader of the family of Amok.

²¹ Hashabiah was leader of the family of
Hilkiah.
Nethanel was leader of the family of
Jedaiah.

²²A record of the Levite families was kept during the years when Eliashib, Joiada, Johanan, and Jaddua served as high priest. Another record of the priests was kept during the reign of Darius the Persian.* ²³A record of the heads of the Levite families was kept in *The Book of History* down to the days of Johanan, the grandson* of Eliashib.

²⁴These were the family leaders of the Levites: Hashabiah, Sherebiah, Jeshua, Binnui,* Kadmiel, and other associates, who stood opposite them during the ceremonies of praise and thanksgiving, one section responding to the other, as commanded by David, the man of God. ²⁵This included Mattaniah, Bakbukiah, and Obadiah.

Meshullam, Talmon, and Akkub were the gatekeepers in charge of the storerooms at the gates. ²⁶These all served in the days of Joiakim son of Jeshua, son of Jehozadak,*

and in the days of Nehemiah the governor and of Ezra the priest and scribe.

Dedication of Jerusalem's Wall

²⁷For the dedication of the new wall of Jerusalem, the Levites throughout the land were asked to come to Jerusalem to assist in the ceremonies. They were to take part in the joyous occasion with their songs of thanksgiving and with the music of cymbals, harps, and lyres. ²⁸The singers were brought together from the region around Jerusalem and from the villages of the Netophathites. ²⁹They also came from Beth-gilgal and the rural areas near Geba and Azmaveth, for the singers had built their own settlements around Jerusalem. ³⁰The priests and Levites first purified themselves; then they purified the people, the gates, and the wall.

³¹I led the leaders of Judah to the top of the wall and organized two large choirs to give thanks. One of the choirs proceeded southward* along the top of the wall to the Dung Gate. ³²Hoshaiah and half the leaders of Judah followed them, ³³along with Azariah, Ezra, Meshullam, ³⁴Judah, Benjamin, Shemaiah, and Jeremiah. ³⁵Then came some priests who played trumpets, including Zechariah son of Jonathan, son of Shemaiah, son of Mattaniah, son of Micaiah, son of Zaccur, a descendant of Asaph. ³⁶And Zechariah's colleagues were Shemaiah, Azarel, Milalai, Gilalai, Maai, Nethanel, Judah, and Hanani. They used the musical instruments prescribed by David, the man of God. Ezra the scribe led this procession. ³⁷At the Fountain Gate they went straight up the steps on the ascent of the city wall toward the City of David. They passed the house of David and then proceeded to the Water Gate on the east.

³⁸The second choir giving thanks went northward* around the other way to meet them. I followed them, together with the other half of the people, along the top of the wall past the Tower of the Ovens to the Broad Wall, ³⁹then past the Ephraim Gate to the Old City Gate,* past the Fish Gate

12:14b As in many Hebrew manuscripts, some Greek manuscripts, and Syriac version (see also 12:3); most Hebrew manuscripts read *Shebaniah.* 12:15 As in some Greek manuscripts (see also 12:3); Hebrew reads *Meraioth.* 12:17 Hebrew lacks the name of this family leader. 12:20 Hebrew *Sallai;* compare 12:7. 12:22 *Darius the Persian* is probably Darius II, who reigned 423–404 B.C., or possibly Darius III, who reigned 336–331 B.C. 12:23 Hebrew *descendant;* compare 12:10-11. 12:24 Hebrew *son of* (i.e., *ben*), which should probably be read here as the proper name Binnui; compare Ezra 3:9 and the note there. 12:26 Hebrew *Jozadak,* a variant spelling of Jehozadak. 12:31 Hebrew *to the right.* 12:38 Hebrew *to the left.* 12:39 Or *the Mishneh Gate,* or *the Jeshanah Gate.*

and the Tower of Hananel, and on to the Tower of the Hundred. Then we continued on to the Sheep Gate and stopped at the Guard Gate.

⁴⁰The two choirs that were giving thanks then proceeded to the Temple of God, where they took their places. So did I, together with the group of leaders who were with me. ⁴¹We went together with the trumpet-playing priests—Eliakim, Maaseiah, Miniamin, Micaiah, Elioenai, Zechariah, and Hananiah—⁴²and the singers—Maaseiah, Shemaiah, Eleazar, Uzzi, Jehohanan, Malkijah, Elam, and Ezer. They played and sang loudly under the direction of Jezrahiah the choir director.

⁴³Many sacrifices were offered on that joyous day, for God had given the people cause for great joy. The women and children also participated in the celebration, and the joy of the people of Jerusalem could be heard far away.

Provisions for Temple Worship

⁴⁴On that day men were appointed to be in charge of the storerooms for the offerings, the first part of the harvest, and the tithes. They were responsible to collect from the fields outside the towns the portions required by the Law for the priests and Levites. For all the people of Judah took joy in the priests and Levites and their work. ⁴⁵They performed the service of their God and the service of purification, as commanded by David and his son Solomon, and so did the singers and the gatekeepers. ⁴⁶The custom of having choir directors to lead the choirs in hymns of praise and thanksgiving to God began long ago in the days of David and Asaph. ⁴⁷So now, in the days of Zerubbabel and of Nehemiah, all Israel brought a daily supply of food for the singers, the gatekeepers, and the Levites. The Levites, in turn, gave a portion of what they received to the priests, the descendants of Aaron.

13 Nehemiah's Various Reforms

On that same day, as the Book of Moses was being read to the people, the passage was found that said no Ammonite or Moabite should ever be permitted to enter the assembly of God.* ²For they had not provided the Israelites with food and water in the wilderness. Instead, they hired Balaam to curse them, though our God turned the curse into a blessing. ³When this passage of the Law was read, all those of foreign descent were immediately excluded from the assembly.

⁴Before this had happened, Eliashib the priest, who had been appointed as supervisor of the storerooms of the Temple of our God and who was also a relative of Tobiah, ⁵had converted a large storage room and placed it at Tobiah's disposal. The room had previously been used for storing the grain offerings, the frankincense, various articles for the Temple, and the tithes of grain, new wine, and olive oil (which were prescribed for the Levites, the singers, and the gatekeepers), as well as the offerings for the priests.

⁶I was not in Jerusalem at that time, for I had returned to King Artaxerxes of Babylon in the thirty-second year of his reign,* though I later asked his permission to return. ⁷When I arrived back in Jerusalem, I learned about Eliashib's evil deed in providing Tobiah with a room in the courtyards of the Temple of God. ⁸I became very upset and threw all of Tobiah's belongings out of the room. ⁹Then I demanded that the rooms be purified, and I brought back the articles for God's Temple, the grain offerings, and the frankincense.

¹⁰I also discovered that the Levites had not been given their prescribed portions of food, so they and the singers who were to conduct the worship services had all returned to work their fields. ¹¹I immediately confronted the leaders and demanded, "Why has the Temple of God been neglected?" Then I called all the Levites back again and restored them to their proper duties. ¹²And once more all the people of Judah began bringing their tithes of grain, new wine, and olive oil to the Temple storerooms.

¹³I assigned supervisors for the storerooms: Shelemiah the priest, Zadok the scribe, and Pedaiah, one of the Levites. And

---

13:1 See Deut 23:3-6. **13:6** King Artaxerxes of Persia is here identified as the king of Babylon because Persia had conquered the Babylonian Empire. The thirty-second year of Artaxerxes was 433 B.C.

I appointed Hanan son of Zaccur and grandson of Mattaniah as their assistant. These men had an excellent reputation, and it was their job to make honest distributions to their fellow Levites.

[14]Remember this good deed, O my God, and do not forget all that I have faithfully done for the Temple of my God and its services.

[15]In those days I saw men of Judah treading out their winepresses on the Sabbath. They were also bringing in grain, loading it on donkeys, and bringing their wine, grapes, figs, and all sorts of produce to Jerusalem to sell on the Sabbath. So I rebuked them for selling their produce on that day. [16]Some men from Tyre, who lived in Jerusalem, were bringing in fish and all kinds of merchandise. They were selling it on the Sabbath to the people of Judah—and in Jerusalem at that!

[17]So I confronted the nobles of Judah. "Why are you profaning the Sabbath in this evil way?" I asked. [18]"Wasn't it just this sort of thing that your ancestors did that caused our God to bring all this trouble upon us and our city? Now you are bringing even more wrath upon Israel by permitting the Sabbath to be desecrated in this way!"

[19]Then I commanded that the gates of Jerusalem should be shut as darkness fell every Friday evening,* not to be opened until the Sabbath ended. I sent some of my own servants to guard the gates so that no merchandise could be brought in on the Sabbath day. [20]The merchants and tradesmen with a variety of wares camped outside Jerusalem once or twice. [21]But I spoke sharply to them and said, "What are you doing out here, camping around the wall? If you do this again, I will arrest you!" And that was the last time they came on the Sabbath. [22]Then I commanded the Levites to purify themselves and to guard the gates in order to preserve the holiness of the Sabbath.

Remember this good deed also, O my God! Have compassion on me according to your great and unfailing love.

[23]About the same time I realized that some of the men of Judah had married women from Ashdod, Ammon, and Moab. [24]Furthermore, half their children spoke the language of Ashdod or of some other people and could not speak the language of Judah at all. [25]So I confronted them and called down curses on them. I beat some of them and pulled out their hair. I made them swear in the name of God that they would not let their children intermarry with the pagan people of the land.

[26]"Wasn't this exactly what led King Solomon of Israel into sin?" I demanded. "There was no king from any nation who could compare to him, and God loved him and made him king over all Israel. But even he was led into sin by his foreign wives. [27]How could you even think of committing this sinful deed and acting unfaithfully toward God by marrying foreign women?"

[28]One of the sons of Joiada son of Eliashib the high priest had married a daughter of Sanballat the Horonite, so I banished him from my presence.

[29]Remember them, O my God, for they have defiled the priesthood and the solemn vows of the priests and Levites.

[30]So I purged out everything foreign and assigned tasks to the priests and Levites, making certain that each knew his work. [31]I also made sure that the supply of wood for the altar and the first portions of the harvest were brought at the proper times.

Remember this in my favor, O my God.

Introduction to

Esther

Background

The compelling and intriguing story of Esther has been the subject of movies and novels. Set aside the fairy-tale aspects and one sees a darker story: a genocide plot proposed by Haman, the king's appointed number-two man, but counteracted by someone not mentioned in the book—God. Esther is God's instrument in the salvation of his people.

The author of the Book of Esther is unknown. It is named after its main character, Esther, whose Hebrew name was *Hadassah* (2:7), which means "myrtle." The name Esther comes from the Persian word *ester*, which means "star." The Feast of Purim (9:26) is still celebrated in the Jewish community in the early spring.

Message

The theme of divine providence is evident throughout the book—from the deposing of Vashti to the ascension of Esther, through plots overheard and foiled, and even to the book the king reads because he can't sleep. The plot to destroy all Jews sounds eerily similar to events even in the past century. Esther, a young Jewish woman raised by her relative Mordecai, becomes a queen to the Persian king "for such a time as this" (4:14). God uses his beautiful servant to stop the plot of Haman and to save his people.

Time

The events of Esther take place in the period between Zerubbabel's journey to Jerusalem and Ezra's return. Ahasuerus (Xerxes) ruled Persia for twenty years, from circa 486 to 464 B.C. The feast in which Vashti was deposed took place about 480 B.C. (See also the introduction to the Book of Ezra.)

Outline

I. Birth of a Plot
   A. Esther becomes queen   1:1–2:23
   B. Haman's plot   3:1–15

II. Exposure of a Plot
   A. Appeal to Esther   4:1–17
   B. Esther goes before the king   5:1–14
   C. Mordecai honored   6:1–14
   D. Haman's execution   7:1–10

III. Defeat of a Plot
   A. The king's decree   8:1–17
   B. The Feast of Purim   9:1–32
   C. Promotion of Mordecai   10:1–3

Esther

1 The King's Banquet

These events happened in the days of King Xerxes,* who reigned over 127 provinces stretching from India to Ethiopia.* ²At that time Xerxes ruled his empire from his royal throne at the fortress of Susa. ³In the third year of his reign, he gave a banquet for all his nobles and officials. He invited all the military officers of Persia and Media as well as the princes and nobles of the provinces. ⁴The celebration lasted 180 days—a tremendous display of the opulent wealth of his empire and the pomp and splendor of his majesty.

⁵When it was all over, the king gave a banquet for all the people, from the greatest to the least, who were in the fortress of Susa. It lasted for seven days and was held in the courtyard of the palace garden. ⁶The courtyard was beautifully decorated with white cotton curtains and blue hangings, which were fastened with white linen cords and purple ribbons to silver rings embedded in marble pillars. Gold and silver couches stood on a mosaic pavement of porphyry, marble, mother-of-pearl, and other costly stones. ⁷Drinks were served in gold goblets of many designs, and there was an abundance of royal wine, reflecting the king's generosity. ⁸By edict of the king, no limits were placed on the drinking, for the king had instructed all his palace officials to serve each man as much as he wanted.

⁹At the same time, Queen Vashti gave a banquet for the women in the royal palace of King Xerxes.

Queen Vashti Deposed

¹⁰On the seventh day of the feast, when King Xerxes was in high spirits because of the wine, he told the seven eunuchs who attended him—Mehuman, Biztha, Harbona, Bigtha, Abagtha, Zethar, and Carcas—¹¹to bring Queen Vashti to him with the royal crown on her head. He wanted the nobles and all the other men to gaze on her beauty, for she was a very beautiful woman. ¹²But when they conveyed the king's order to Queen Vashti, she refused to come. This made the king furious, and he burned with anger.

¹³He immediately consulted with his wise advisers, who knew all the Persian laws and customs, for he always asked their advice. ¹⁴The names of these men were Carshena, Shethar, Admatha, Tarshish, Meres, Marsena, and Memucan—seven nobles of Persia and Media. They met with the king regularly and held the highest positions in the empire.

¹⁵"What must be done to Queen Vashti?" the king demanded. "What penalty does the law provide for a queen who refuses to obey the king's orders, properly sent through his eunuchs?"

¹⁶Memucan answered the king and his nobles, "Queen Vashti has wronged not only the king but also every noble and citizen throughout your empire. ¹⁷Women everywhere will begin to despise their husbands when they learn that Queen Vashti has refused to appear before the king. ¹⁸Before this day is out,

---

1:1a Hebrew *Ahasuerus*, another name for Xerxes; also throughout the book of Esther. Xerxes reigned 486–465 B.C.
1:1b Hebrew *to Cush*.

the wives of all the king's nobles throughout Persia and Media will hear what the queen did and will start treating their husbands the same way. There will be no end to their contempt and anger.

[19]"So if it please the king, we suggest that you issue a written decree, a law of the Persians and Medes that cannot be revoked. It should order that Queen Vashti be forever banished from the presence of King Xerxes, and that the king should choose another queen more worthy than she. [20]When this decree is published throughout the king's vast empire, husbands everywhere, whatever their rank, will receive proper respect from their wives!"

[21]The king and his nobles thought this made good sense, so he followed Memucan's counsel. [22]He sent letters to all parts of the empire, to each province in its own script and language, proclaiming that every man should be the ruler of his own home and should say whatever he pleases.*

2 Esther Becomes Queen

But after Xerxes' anger had subsided, he began thinking about Vashti and what she had done and the decree he had made. [2]So his personal attendants suggested, "Let us search the empire to find beautiful young virgins for the king. [3]Let the king appoint agents in each province to bring these beautiful young women into the royal harem at the fortress of Susa. Hegai, the king's eunuch in charge of the harem, will see that they are all given beauty treatments. [4]After that, the young woman who most pleases the king will be made queen instead of Vashti." This advice was very appealing to the king, so he put the plan into effect.

[5]At that time there was a Jewish man in the fortress of Susa whose name was Mordecai son of Jair. He was from the tribe of Benjamin and was a descendant of Kish and Shimei. [6]His family* had been among those who, with King Jehoiachin* of Judah, had been exiled from Jerusalem to Babylon by King Nebuchadnezzar. [7]This man had a very beautiful and lovely young cousin,

Hadassah, who was also called Esther. When her father and mother died, Mordecai adopted her into his family and raised her as his own daughter.

[8]As a result of the king's decree, Esther, along with many other young women, was brought to the king's harem at the fortress of Susa and placed in Hegai's care. [9]Hegai was very impressed with Esther and treated her kindly. He quickly ordered a special menu for her and provided her with beauty treatments. He also assigned her seven maids specially chosen from the king's palace, and he moved her and her maids into the best place in the harem.

[10]Esther had not told anyone of her nationality and family background, because Mordecai had directed her not to do so. [11]Every day Mordecai would take a walk near the courtyard of the harem to find out about Esther and what was happening to her.

[12]Before each young woman was taken to the king's bed, she was given the prescribed twelve months of beauty treatments—six months with oil of myrrh, followed by six months with special perfumes and ointments. [13]When it was time for her to go to the king's palace, she was given her choice of whatever clothing or jewelry she wanted to take from the harem. [14]That evening she was taken to the king's private rooms, and the next morning she was brought to the second harem,* where the king's wives lived. There she would be under the care of Shaashgaz, the king's eunuch in charge of the concubines. She would never go to the king again unless he had especially enjoyed her and requested her by name.

[15]Esther was the daughter of Abihail, who was Mordecai's uncle. (Mordecai had adopted his younger cousin Esther.) When it was Esther's turn to go to the king, she accepted the advice of Hegai, the eunuch in charge of the harem. She asked for nothing except what he suggested, and she was admired by everyone who saw her.

[16]Esther was taken to King Xerxes at the royal palace in early winter* of the seventh

---

1:22 Or *and should speak in the language of his own people.*   **2:6a** Hebrew *He.*   **2:6b** Hebrew *Jeconiah,* a variant spelling of Jehoiachin.   **2:14** Or *to another part of the harem.*   **2:16** Hebrew *in the tenth month, the month of Tebeth.* A number of dates in the book of Esther can be cross-checked with dates in surviving Persian records and related accurately to our modern calendar. This month of the ancient Hebrew lunar calendar occurred within the months of December 479 B.C. and January 478 B.C.

year of his reign. ¹⁷And the king loved Esther more than any of the other young women. He was so delighted with her that he set the royal crown on her head and declared her queen instead of Vashti. ¹⁸To celebrate the occasion, he gave a great banquet in Esther's honor for all his nobles and officials, declaring a public holiday for the provinces and giving generous gifts to everyone.

¹⁹Even after all the young women had been transferred to the second harem* and Mordecai had become a palace official,* ²⁰Esther continued to keep her family background and nationality a secret. She was still following Mordecai's directions, just as she did when she lived in his home.

Mordecai's Loyalty to the King

²¹One day as Mordecai was on duty at the king's gate, two of the king's eunuchs, Bigthana* and Teresh—who were guards at the door of the king's private quarters—became angry at King Xerxes and plotted to assassinate him. ²²But Mordecai heard about the plot and gave the information to Queen Esther. She then told the king about it and gave Mordecai credit for the report. ²³When an investigation was made and Mordecai's story was found to be true, the two men were impaled on a sharpened pole. This was all recorded in *The Book of the History of King Xerxes' Reign.*

3 Haman's Plot against the Jews

Some time later King Xerxes promoted Haman son of Hammedatha the Agagite over all the other nobles, making him the most powerful official in the empire. ²All the king's officials would bow down before Haman to show him respect whenever he passed by, for so the king had commanded. But Mordecai refused to bow down or show him respect.

³Then the palace officials at the king's gate asked Mordecai, "Why are you disobeying the king's command?" ⁴They spoke to him day after day, but still he refused to comply with the order. So they spoke to Haman about this to see if he would tolerate Mordecai's conduct, since Mordecai had told them he was a Jew.

⁵When Haman saw that Mordecai would not bow down or show him respect, he was filled with rage. ⁶He had learned of Mordecai's nationality, so he decided it was not enough to lay hands on Mordecai alone. Instead, he looked for a way to destroy all the Jews throughout the entire empire of Xerxes.

⁷So in the month of April,* during the twelfth year of King Xerxes' reign, lots were cast in Haman's presence (the lots were called *purim*) to determine the best day and month to take action. And the day selected was March 7, nearly a year later.*

⁸Then Haman approached King Xerxes and said, "There is a certain race of people scattered through all the provinces of your empire who keep themselves separate from everyone else. Their laws are different from those of any other people, and they refuse to obey the laws of the king. So it is not in the king's interest to let them live. ⁹If it please the king, issue a decree that they be destroyed, and I will give 10,000 large sacks* of silver to the government administrators to be deposited in the royal treasury."

¹⁰The king agreed, confirming his decision by removing his signet ring from his finger and giving it to Haman son of Hammedatha the Agagite, the enemy of the Jews. ¹¹The king said, "The money and the people are both yours to do with as you see fit."

¹²So on April 17* the king's secretaries were summoned, and a decree was written exactly as Haman dictated. It was sent to the king's highest officers, the governors of the respective provinces, and the nobles of each province in their own scripts and languages. The decree was written in the name of King Xerxes and sealed with the king's signet ring. ¹³Dispatches were sent by swift messengers into all the provinces of the empire, giving the order that all Jews—young and old, including women and children—must be killed, slaughtered, and annihilated on a single day. This was

---

2:19a The meaning of the Hebrew is uncertain. **2:19b** Hebrew *and Mordecai was sitting in the gate of the king.* **2:21** Hebrew *Bigthan;* compare 6:2. **3:7a** Hebrew *in the first month, the month of Nisan.* This month of the ancient Hebrew lunar calendar occurred within the months of April and May 474 B.C.; also see note on 2:16. **3:7b** As in 3:13, which reads *the thirteenth day of the twelfth month, the month of Adar;* Hebrew reads *in the twelfth month,* of the ancient Hebrew lunar calendar. The date selected was March 7, 473 B.C.; also see note on 2:16. **3:9** Hebrew *10,000 talents,* about 375 tons or 340 metric tons in weight. **3:12** Hebrew *On the thirteenth day of the first month,* of the ancient Hebrew lunar calendar. This day was April 17, 474 B.C.; also see note on 2:16.

scheduled to happen on March 7 of the next year.* The property of the Jews would be given to those who killed them.

¹⁴A copy of this decree was to be issued as law in every province and proclaimed to all peoples, so that they would be ready to do their duty on the appointed day. ¹⁵At the king's command, the decree went out by swift messengers, and it was also proclaimed in the fortress of Susa. Then the king and Haman sat down to drink, but the city of Susa fell into confusion.

4 Mordecai Requests Esther's Help

When Mordecai learned about all that had been done, he tore his clothes, put on burlap and ashes, and went out into the city, crying with a loud and bitter wail. ²He went as far as the gate of the palace, for no one was allowed to enter the palace gate while wearing clothes of mourning. ³And as news of the king's decree reached all the provinces, there was great mourning among the Jews. They fasted, wept, and wailed, and many people lay in burlap and ashes.

⁴When Queen Esther's maids and eunuchs came and told her about Mordecai, she was deeply distressed. She sent clothing to him to replace the burlap, but he refused it. ⁵Then Esther sent for Hathach, one of the king's eunuchs who had been appointed as her attendant. She ordered him to go to Mordecai and find out what was troubling him and why he was in mourning. ⁶So Hathach went out to Mordecai in the square in front of the palace gate.

⁷Mordecai told him the whole story, including the exact amount of money Haman had promised to pay into the royal treasury for the destruction of the Jews. ⁸Mordecai gave Hathach a copy of the decree issued in Susa that called for the death of all Jews. He asked Hathach to show it to Esther and explain the situation to her. He also asked Hathach to direct her to go to the king to beg for mercy and plead for her people. ⁹So Hathach returned to Esther with Mordecai's message.

¹⁰Then Esther told Hathach to go back and relay this message to Mordecai: ¹¹"All the king's officials and even the people in the provinces know that anyone who appears before the king in his inner court without being invited is doomed to die unless the king holds out his gold scepter. And the king has not called for me to come to him for thirty days." ¹²So Hathach* gave Esther's message to Mordecai.

¹³Mordecai sent this reply to Esther: "Don't think for a moment that because you're in the palace you will escape when all other Jews are killed. ¹⁴If you keep quiet at a time like this, deliverance and relief for the Jews will arise from some other place, but you and your relatives will die. Who knows if perhaps you were made queen for just such a time as this?"

¹⁵Then Esther sent this reply to Mordecai: ¹⁶"Go and gather together all the Jews of Susa and fast for me. Do not eat or drink for three days, night or day. My maids and I will do the same. And then, though it is against the law, I will go in to see the king. If I must die, I must die." ¹⁷So Mordecai went away and did everything as Esther had ordered him.

5 Esther's Request to the King

On the third day of the fast, Esther put on her royal robes and entered the inner court of the palace, just across from the king's hall. The king was sitting on his royal throne, facing the entrance. ²When he saw Queen Esther standing there in the inner court, he welcomed her and held out the gold scepter to her. So Esther approached and touched the end of the scepter.

³Then the king asked her, "What do you want, Queen Esther? What is your request? I will give it to you, even if it is half the kingdom!"

⁴And Esther replied, "If it please the king, let the king and Haman come today to a banquet I have prepared for the king."

⁵The king turned to his attendants and said, "Tell Haman to come quickly to a banquet, as Esther has requested." So the king and Haman went to Esther's banquet.

⁶And while they were drinking wine, the king said to Esther, "Now tell me what you

really want. What is your request? I will give it to you, even if it is half the kingdom!"

⁷Esther replied, "This is my request and deepest wish. ⁸If I have found favor with the king, and if it pleases the king to grant my request and do what I ask, please come with Haman tomorrow to the banquet I will prepare for you. Then I will explain what this is all about."

Haman's Plan to Kill Mordecai

⁹Haman was a happy man as he left the banquet! But when he saw Mordecai sitting at the palace gate, not standing up or trembling nervously before him, Haman became furious. ¹⁰However, he restrained himself and went on home.

Then Haman gathered together his friends and Zeresh, his wife, ¹¹and boasted to them about his great wealth and his many children. He bragged about the honors the king had given him and how he had been promoted over all the other nobles and officials. ¹²Then Haman added, "And that's not all! Queen Esther invited only me and the king himself to the banquet she prepared for us.

Esther: Weakness That Leads to Strength

ESTHER 4:7–5:2

Marked by humble beginnings as a Jewish orphan and exile, Esther rose to prominence when a series of unpredictable events elevated her to the status of queen. But when King Xerxes ordered a province-wide genocide of the Jewish people, Esther was confronted with a choice that would change the course of history. Would she use her influence to plead mercy for her people? To speak to the king without his consent could mean a death sentence—yet to remain quiet ensured death of her beloved cousin Mordecai and the ultimate betrayal of her heritage.

It was in this moment of need that Esther called for every Jew in the kingdom to fast for divine intervention.

For Esther fasting was a sign of humble contrition before God. It was an individual consecration for strength in the face of death and a community cry to God for his intercession. Because of her strength built through fasting, when Esther faced the king, she did so with determination, courage, and grace—and she changed the fate of an entire nation.

Both the Old and New Testaments highlight examples of people abstaining from food or drink in order to find strength to carry out God's will. Although we rarely face life-and-death decisions as Esther did, we do need courage in many situations. We discipline our outward behavior to sharpen an inward reality: nothing can nourish and sustain us like the love of Christ and the power of the Holy Spirit. As we experience physical weakness brought on by fasting, we are drawn closer to the Source of true power in every situation: Christ in us (Colossians 1:27).

When Esther fasted, she was strengthened. That same power is available to us. Although we may not have an entire nation under our charge, we all face life-changing decisions. When we fast, the pang of hunger compels us to pray without ceasing. When confronted with choices that exceed our capacity, through fasting, we draw near to a God who will sustain us with his strength.

—*Nicole Unice*

For more on fasting, see reading at Isaiah 26:8–9.

And she has invited me to dine with her and the king again tomorrow!" ¹³Then he added, "But this is all worth nothing as long as I see Mordecai the Jew just sitting there at the palace gate."

¹⁴So Haman's wife, Zeresh, and all his friends suggested, "Set up a sharpened pole that stands seventy-five feet* tall, and in the morning ask the king to impale Mordecai on it. When this is done, you can go on your merry way to the banquet with the king." This pleased Haman, and he ordered the pole set up.

6 The King Honors Mordecai

That night the king had trouble sleeping, so he ordered an attendant to bring the book of the history of his reign so it could be read to him. ²In those records he discovered an account of how Mordecai had exposed the plot of Bigthana and Teresh, two of the eunuchs who guarded the door to the king's private quarters. They had plotted to assassinate King Xerxes.

³"What reward or recognition did we ever give Mordecai for this?" the king asked.

His attendants replied, "Nothing has been done for him."

⁴"Who is that in the outer court?" the king inquired. As it happened, Haman had just arrived in the outer court of the palace to ask the king to impale Mordecai on the pole he had prepared.

⁵So the attendants replied to the king, "Haman is out in the court."

"Bring him in," the king ordered. ⁶So Haman came in, and the king said, "What should I do to honor a man who truly pleases me?"

Haman thought to himself, "Whom would the king wish to honor more than me?" ⁷So he replied, "If the king wishes to honor someone, ⁸he should bring out one of the king's own royal robes, as well as a horse that the king himself has ridden—one with a royal emblem on its head. ⁹Let the robes and the horse be handed over to one of the king's most noble officials. And let him see that the man whom the king wishes to honor is dressed in the king's robes and led through the city square on the king's horse. Have the

official shout as they go, 'This is what the king does for someone he wishes to honor!'"

¹⁰"Excellent!" the king said to Haman. "Quick! Take the robes and my horse, and do just as you have said for Mordecai the Jew, who sits at the gate of the palace. Leave out nothing you have suggested!"

¹¹So Haman took the robes and put them on Mordecai, placed him on the king's own horse, and led him through the city square, shouting, "This is what the king does for someone he wishes to honor!" ¹²Afterward Mordecai returned to the palace gate, but Haman hurried home dejected and completely humiliated.

¹³When Haman told his wife, Zeresh, and all his friends what had happened, his wise advisers and his wife said, "Since Mordecai—this man who has humiliated you—is of Jewish birth, you will never succeed in your plans against him. It will be fatal to continue opposing him."

¹⁴While they were still talking, the king's eunuchs arrived and quickly took Haman to the banquet Esther had prepared.

7 The King Executes Haman

So the king and Haman went to Queen Esther's banquet. ²On this second occasion, while they were drinking wine, the king again said to Esther, "Tell me what you want, Queen Esther. What is your request? I will give it to you, even if it is half the kingdom!"

³Queen Esther replied, "If I have found favor with the king, and if it pleases the king to grant my request, I ask that my life and the lives of my people will be spared. ⁴For my people and I have been sold to those who would kill, slaughter, and annihilate us. If we had merely been sold as slaves, I could remain quiet, for that would be too trivial a matter to warrant disturbing the king."

⁵"Who would do such a thing?" King Xerxes demanded. "Who would be so presumptuous as to touch you?"

⁶Esther replied, "This wicked Haman is our adversary and our enemy." Haman grew pale with fright before the king and queen. ⁷Then the king jumped to his feet in a rage and went out into the palace garden.

5:14 Hebrew *50 cubits* [22.5 meters].

Haman, however, stayed behind to plead for his life with Queen Esther, for he knew that the king intended to kill him. [8] In despair he fell on the couch where Queen Esther was reclining, just as the king was returning from the palace garden.

The king exclaimed, "Will he even assault the queen right here in the palace, before my very eyes?" And as soon as the king spoke, his attendants covered Haman's face, signaling his doom.

[9] Then Harbona, one of the king's eunuchs, said, "Haman has set up a sharpened pole that stands seventy-five feet* tall in his own courtyard. He intended to use it to impale Mordecai, the man who saved the king from assassination."

"Then impale Haman on it!" the king ordered. [10] So they impaled Haman on the pole he had set up for Mordecai, and the king's anger subsided.

8 A Decree to Help the Jews

On that same day King Xerxes gave the property of Haman, the enemy of the Jews, to Queen Esther. Then Mordecai was brought before the king, for Esther had told the king how they were related. [2] The king took off his signet ring—which he had taken back from Haman—and gave it to Mordecai. And Esther appointed Mordecai to be in charge of Haman's property.

[3] Then Esther went again before the king, falling down at his feet and begging him with tears to stop the evil plot devised by Haman the Agagite against the Jews. [4] Again the king held out the gold scepter to Esther. So she rose and stood before him.

[5] Esther said, "If it please the king, and if I have found favor with him, and if he thinks it is right, and if I am pleasing to him, let there be a decree that reverses the orders of Haman son of Hammedatha the Agagite, who ordered that Jews throughout all the king's provinces should be destroyed. [6] For how can I endure to see my people and my family slaughtered and destroyed?"

[7] Then King Xerxes said to Queen Esther and Mordecai the Jew, "I have given Esther the property of Haman, and he has been impaled on a pole because he tried to destroy the Jews. [8] Now go ahead and send a message to the Jews in the king's name, telling them whatever you want, and seal it with the king's signet ring. But remember that whatever has already been written in the king's name and sealed with his signet ring can never be revoked."

[9] So on June 25* the king's secretaries were summoned, and a decree was written exactly as Mordecai dictated. It was sent to the Jews and to the highest officers, the governors, and the nobles of all the 127 provinces stretching from India to Ethiopia.* The decree was written in the scripts and languages of all the peoples of the empire, including that of the Jews. [10] The decree was written in the name of King Xerxes and sealed with the king's signet ring. Mordecai sent the dispatches by swift messengers, who rode fast horses especially bred for the king's service.

[11] The king's decree gave the Jews in every city authority to unite to defend their lives. They were allowed to kill, slaughter, and annihilate anyone of any nationality or province who might attack them or their children and wives, and to take the property of their enemies. [12] The day chosen for this event throughout all the provinces of King Xerxes was March 7 of the next year.*

[13] A copy of this decree was to be issued as law in every province and proclaimed to all peoples, so that the Jews would be ready to take revenge on their enemies on the appointed day. [14] So urged on by the king's command, the messengers rode out swiftly on fast horses bred for the king's service. The same decree was also proclaimed in the fortress of Susa.

[15] Then Mordecai left the king's presence, wearing the royal robe of blue and white, the great crown of gold, and an outer cloak of fine linen and purple. And the people of Susa celebrated the new decree. [16] The Jews were filled with joy and gladness and were honored everywhere. [17] In every province and city, wherever the king's decree arrived, the Jews rejoiced and had a great celebration and declared a public festival and holiday. And many of the people of

---

7:9 Hebrew 50 cubits [22.5 meters]. **8:9a** Hebrew on the twenty-third day of the third month, the month of Sivan, of the ancient Hebrew lunar calendar. This day was June 25, 474 b.c.; also see note on 2:16. **8:9b** Hebrew to Cush. **8:12** Hebrew the thirteenth day of the twelfth month, the month of Adar, of the ancient Hebrew lunar calendar. The date selected was March 7, 473 b.c.; also see note on 2:16.

the land became Jews themselves, for they feared what the Jews might do to them.

9 The Victory of the Jews

So on March 7* the two decrees of the king were put into effect. On that day, the enemies of the Jews had hoped to overpower them, but quite the opposite happened. It was the Jews who overpowered their enemies. ²The Jews gathered in their cities throughout all the king's provinces to attack anyone who tried to harm them. But no one could make a stand against them, for everyone was afraid of them. ³And all the nobles of the provinces, the highest officers, the governors, and the royal officials helped the Jews for fear of Mordecai. ⁴For Mordecai had been promoted in the king's palace, and his fame spread throughout all the provinces as he became more and more powerful.

⁵So the Jews went ahead on the appointed day and struck down their enemies with the sword. They killed and annihilated their enemies and did as they pleased with those who hated them. ⁶In the fortress of Susa itself, the Jews killed 500 men. ⁷They also killed Parshandatha, Dalphon, Aspatha, ⁸Poratha, Adalia, Aridatha, ⁹Parmashta, Arisai, Aridai, and Vaizatha—¹⁰the ten sons of Haman son of Hammedatha, the enemy of the Jews. But they did not take any plunder.

¹¹That very day, when the king was informed of the number of people killed in the fortress of Susa, ¹²he called for Queen Esther. He said, "The Jews have killed 500 men in the fortress of Susa alone, as well as Haman's ten sons. If they have done that here, what has happened in the rest of the provinces? But now, what more do you want? It will be granted to you; tell me and I will do it."

¹³Esther responded, "If it please the king, give the Jews in Susa permission to do again tomorrow as they have done today, and let the bodies of Haman's ten sons be impaled on a pole."

¹⁴So the king agreed, and the decree was announced in Susa. And they impaled the bodies of Haman's ten sons. ¹⁵Then the Jews at Susa gathered together on March 8* and killed 300 more men, and again they took no plunder.

¹⁶Meanwhile, the other Jews throughout the king's provinces had gathered together to defend their lives. They gained relief from all their enemies, killing 75,000 of those who hated them. But they did not take any plunder. ¹⁷This was done throughout the provinces on March 7, and on March 8 they rested,* celebrating their victory with a day of feasting and gladness. ¹⁸(The Jews at Susa killed their enemies on March 7 and again on March 8, then rested on March 9,* making that their day of feasting and gladness.) ¹⁹So to this day, rural Jews living in remote villages celebrate an annual festival and holiday on the appointed day in late winter,* when they rejoice and send gifts of food to each other.

The Festival of Purim

²⁰Mordecai recorded these events and sent letters to the Jews near and far, throughout all the provinces of King Xerxes, ²¹calling on them to celebrate an annual festival on these two days.* ²²He told them to celebrate these days with feasting and gladness and by giving gifts of food to each other and presents to the poor. This would commemorate a time when the Jews gained relief from their enemies, when their sorrow was turned into gladness and their mourning into joy.

²³So the Jews accepted Mordecai's proposal and adopted this annual custom. ²⁴Haman son of Hammedatha the Agagite, the enemy of the Jews, had plotted to crush and destroy them on the date determined by casting lots (the lots were called *purim*). ²⁵But when Esther came before the king, he issued a decree causing Haman's evil plot to backfire, and Haman and his sons were impaled on a sharpened pole. ²⁶That is why this celebration is called Purim, because it is the ancient word for casting lots.

So because of Mordecai's letter and because of what they had experienced, ²⁷the Jews throughout the realm agreed to

9:1 Hebrew *on the thirteenth day of the twelfth month, the month of Adar,* of the ancient Hebrew lunar calendar. This day was March 7, 473 B.C.; also see note on 2:16.   **9:15** Hebrew *the fourteenth day of the month of Adar,* of the Hebrew lunar calendar. This day was March 8, 473 B.C.; also see note on 2:16.   **9:17** Hebrew *on the thirteenth day of the month of Adar, and on the fourteenth day they rested.* These days were March 7 and 8, 473 B.C.; also see note on 2:16.   **9:18** Hebrew *killed their enemies on the thirteenth day and the fourteenth day, and then rested on the fifteenth day,* of the Hebrew month of Adar.   **9:19** Hebrew *on the fourteenth day of the month of Adar.* This day of the Hebrew lunar calendar occurs in February or March.   **9:21** Hebrew *on the fourteenth and fifteenth days of Adar,* of the Hebrew lunar calendar.

Celebration

Celebration and Worship

ESTHER 9:20-32

Like many Christian practices and disciplines, celebration and worship naturally intertwine in our lives and in our expressions of praise and thanks. We worship God in a spirit of celebration; we celebrate from a heart of worship.

So what's the difference between worship and celebration? Dallas Willard, in *The Spirit of the Disciplines,* explains, "In worship we engage ourselves with, dwell upon, and express the greatness, beauty, and goodness of God." Whereas in celebration, as Willard describes it, "we enjoy ourselves, our life, our world, in conjunction with our faith and confidence in God's greatness, beauty, and goodness."

In a most basic sense, worship is when we acknowledge and express praise to God for who he *is*—for his character, for his power and grandeur, for his very God-ness. And in celebration, we enjoy and thank God for what he *does* in our lives. As we recall the works of God in Scripture, in history, and in our own faith journey, we celebrate. As we sing of Christ's redeeming work on the cross and as we tell our own stories of experiencing his grace, we celebrate. As we marvel at his divine fingerprints marking the beauty of the created world, we celebrate. As we laugh, smile, eat, and make merry with friends and family, we celebrate the goodness of God expressed through the gift of the people we love.

—*Kelli B. Trujillo*

For more on celebration, see reading at Psalm 27:1-6.

inaugurate this tradition and to pass it on to their descendants and to all who became Jews. They declared they would never fail to celebrate these two prescribed days at the appointed time each year. [28] These days would be remembered and kept from generation to generation and celebrated by every family throughout the provinces and cities of the empire. This Festival of Purim would never cease to be celebrated among the Jews, nor would the memory of what happened ever die out among their descendants.

[29] Then Queen Esther, the daughter of Abihail, along with Mordecai the Jew, wrote another letter putting the queen's full authority behind Mordecai's letter to establish the Festival of Purim. [30] Letters wishing peace and security were sent to the Jews throughout the 127 provinces of the empire of Xerxes. [31] These letters established the Festival of Purim—an annual celebration of these days at the appointed time, decreed by both Mordecai the Jew and Queen

Esther. (The people decided to observe this festival, just as they had decided for themselves and their descendants to establish the times of fasting and mourning.) [32] So the command of Esther confirmed the practices of Purim, and it was all written down in the records.

10 The Greatness of Xerxes and Mordecai

King Xerxes imposed a tribute throughout his empire, even to the distant coastlands. [2] His great achievements and the full account of the greatness of Mordecai, whom the king had promoted, are recorded in *The Book of the History of the Kings of Media and Persia.* [3] Mordecai the Jew became the prime minister, with authority next to that of King Xerxes himself. He was very great among the Jews, who held him in high esteem, because he continued to work for the good of his people and to speak up for the welfare of all their descendants.

Introduction to

Job

Background

Why does God allow suffering and evil in the world? This question is debated in the pages of the Book of Job—the story of a godly man who suffers greatly. By addressing these questions, the book is classified among the biblical Wisdom Books.

The Book of Job may be the oldest book of the Bible. While the author is unknown, several people have been considered as possibilities: Moses, Elihu, Solomon, Isaiah, Hezekiah, Jeremiah, Baruch, and even Ezra. The Hebrew word for Job might mean "persecuted one."

Message

God's sovereignty is the prominent theme of the Book of Job. God allows Satan to afflict Job, a righteous man, with everything short of death. Job's suffering becomes the subject of vigorous debate between Job and his friends, Eliphaz, Bildad, Zophar, and Elihu. Finally God offers a rebuttal by providing a stunning series of rhetorical questions showcasing his power and authority.

Time

While no one knows when the story of Job took place, the cultural setting suggests a possible date during the time of the patriarchs, between 2100 and 1900 B.C.

Outline

Job

1 Prologue

There once was a man named Job who lived in the land of Uz. He was blameless—a man of complete integrity. He feared God and stayed away from evil. ²He had seven sons and three daughters. ³He owned 7,000 sheep, 3,000 camels, 500 teams of oxen, and 500 female donkeys. He also had many servants. He was, in fact, the richest person in that entire area.

⁴Job's sons would take turns preparing feasts in their homes, and they would also invite their three sisters to celebrate with them. ⁵When these celebrations ended—sometimes after several days—Job would purify his children. He would get up early in the morning and offer a burnt offering for each of them. For Job said to himself, "Perhaps my children have sinned and have cursed God in their hearts." This was Job's regular practice.

Job's First Test

⁶One day the members of the heavenly court* came to present themselves before the LORD, and the Accuser, Satan,* came with them. ⁷"Where have you come from?" the LORD asked Satan.

Satan answered the LORD, "I have been patrolling the earth, watching everything that's going on."

⁸Then the LORD asked Satan, "Have you noticed my servant Job? He is the finest man in all the earth. He is blameless—a man of complete integrity. He fears God and stays away from evil."

⁹Satan replied to the LORD, "Yes, but Job has good reason to fear God. ¹⁰You have always put a wall of protection around him and his home and his property. You have made him prosper in everything he does. Look how rich he is! ¹¹But reach out and take away everything he has, and he will surely curse you to your face!"

¹²"All right, you may test him," the LORD said to Satan. "Do whatever you want with everything he possesses, but don't harm him physically." So Satan left the LORD's presence.

¹³One day when Job's sons and daughters were feasting at the oldest brother's house, ¹⁴a messenger arrived at Job's home with this news: "Your oxen were plowing, with the donkeys feeding beside them, ¹⁵when the Sabeans raided us. They stole all the animals and killed all the farmhands. I am the only one who escaped to tell you."

¹⁶While he was still speaking, another messenger arrived with this news: "The fire of God has fallen from heaven and burned up your sheep and all the shepherds. I am the only one who escaped to tell you."

¹⁷While he was still speaking, a third messenger arrived with this news: "Three bands of Chaldean raiders have stolen your camels and killed your servants. I am the only one who escaped to tell you."

¹⁸While he was still speaking, another messenger arrived with this news: "Your sons and daughters were feasting in their oldest brother's home. ¹⁹Sud-

---

1:6a Hebrew *the sons of God.*   **1:6b** Hebrew *and the satan;* similarly throughout this chapter.

Purposeful Living in the Midst of Pain
JOB 2:1-10

Acceptance

Years ago I went through a very difficult period: my family fell apart, my sense of identity was stripped away. I was left with no sense of purpose. The angst of that purposelessness almost tore me apart. I was yearning for a life that had significance.

During those painful years, I lived in manic mode; I numbed my pain with overspending, travel, and work. It didn't occur to me that numbing my pain had *become* my purpose. I had no idea how much my past influenced my everyday life. I needed to put my anger, regret, bitterness, and pain behind me before I could focus on the race God set before me. It took me years to hear God's voice over the noise and confusion in which I lived. Thankfully, God used other Christians to speak into my life and help me, eventually, to seek out and understand God's purpose and calling for me.

I love the way God takes any willing Christian—no matter how broken or scarred her past—and weaves every thread of her life into his kingdom-building plan! He doesn't shy away from our hurts and failures but specializes in hope, second chances, and resurrections. I never imagined that my tough experiences would give me the substance I now need to minister to others. Our ordinary routines and daily roles—no matter what they are—can provide incredible opportunities to help others become more like Christ.

Purposeful living is about hope. If you can hang onto the hope that God does have a plan for your life, as the Bible promises in Jeremiah 29:11, you'll make it through the tough days of the unknown, and later, the tough days of fulfilling the bold purposes God assigns you.

—Katie Brazelton

For more on acceptance, see reading at Matthew 15:21-28.

denly, a powerful wind swept in from the wilderness and hit the house on all sides. The house collapsed, and all your children are dead. I am the only one who escaped to tell you."

[20]Job stood up and tore his robe in grief. Then he shaved his head and fell to the ground to worship. [21]He said,

"I came naked from my mother's womb,
  and I will be naked when I leave.
The LORD gave me what I had,
  and the LORD has taken it away.
Praise the name of the LORD!"

[22]In all of this, Job did not sin by blaming God.

2 Job's Second Test
One day the members of the heavenly court* came again to present themselves before the LORD, and the Accuser, Satan,* came with them. [2]"Where have you come from?" the LORD asked Satan.

Satan answered the LORD, "I have been patrolling the earth, watching everything that's going on."

[3]Then the LORD asked Satan, "Have you noticed my servant Job? He is the finest man in all the earth. He is blameless—a man of complete integrity. He fears God and stays away from evil. And he has maintained his integrity, even though you urged me to harm him without cause."

2:1a Hebrew *the sons of God.*   **2:1b** Hebrew *and the satan;* similarly throughout this chapter.

⁴Satan replied to the Lord, "Skin for skin! A man will give up everything he has to save his life. ⁵But reach out and take away his health, and he will surely curse you to your face!"

⁶"All right, do with him as you please," the Lord said to Satan. "But spare his life." ⁷So Satan left the Lord's presence, and he struck Job with terrible boils from head to foot.

⁸Job scraped his skin with a piece of broken pottery as he sat among the ashes. ⁹His wife said to him, "Are you still trying to maintain your integrity? Curse God and die."

¹⁰But Job replied, "You talk like a foolish woman. Should we accept only good things from the hand of God and never anything bad?" So in all this, Job said nothing wrong.

Job's Three Friends Share His Anguish

¹¹When three of Job's friends heard of the tragedy he had suffered, they got together and traveled from their homes to comfort and console him. Their names were Eliphaz the Temanite, Bildad the Shuhite, and Zophar the Naamathite. ¹²When they saw Job from a distance, they scarcely recognized him. Wailing loudly, they tore their robes and threw dust into the air over their heads to show their grief. ¹³Then they sat on the ground with him for seven days and nights. No one said a word to Job, for they saw that his suffering was too great for words.

3 Job's First Speech

At last Job spoke, and he cursed the day of his birth. ²He said:

³ "Let the day of my birth be erased,
  and the night I was conceived.
⁴ Let that day be turned to darkness.
  Let it be lost even to God on high,
  and let no light shine on it.
⁵ Let the darkness and utter gloom claim
    that day for its own.
  Let a black cloud overshadow it,
  and let the darkness terrify it.
⁶ Let that night be blotted off the calendar,
  never again to be counted among the
    days of the year,
  never again to appear among the
    months.

⁷ Let that night be childless.
  Let it have no joy.
⁸ Let those who are experts at cursing—
  whose cursing could rouse
    Leviathan*—
  curse that day.
⁹ Let its morning stars remain dark.
  Let it hope for light, but in vain;
  may it never see the morning light.
¹⁰ Curse that day for failing to shut my
    mother's womb,
  for letting me be born to see all this
    trouble.

¹¹ "Why wasn't I born dead?
  Why didn't I die as I came from the
    womb?
¹² Why was I laid on my mother's lap?
  Why did she nurse me at her breasts?
¹³ Had I died at birth, I would now be at
    peace.
  I would be asleep and at rest.
¹⁴ I would rest with the world's kings and
    prime ministers,
  whose great buildings now lie in ruins.
¹⁵ I would rest with princes, rich in gold,
  whose palaces were filled with silver.
¹⁶ Why wasn't I buried like a stillborn child,
  like a baby who never lives to see the
    light?
¹⁷ For in death the wicked cause no trouble,
  and the weary are at rest.
¹⁸ Even captives are at ease in death,
  with no guards to curse them.
¹⁹ Rich and poor are both there,
  and the slave is free from his master.

²⁰ "Oh, why give light to those in misery,
  and life to those who are bitter?
²¹ They long for death, and it won't come.
  They search for death more eagerly
    than for hidden treasure.
²² They're filled with joy when they finally
    die,
  and rejoice when they find the grave.
²³ Why is life given to those with no future,
  those God has surrounded with
    difficulties?
²⁴ I cannot eat for sighing;
  my groans pour out like water.
²⁵ What I always feared has happened to me.
  What I dreaded has come true.

3:8 The identification of Leviathan is disputed, ranging from an earthly creature to a mythical sea monster in ancient literature.

²⁶ I have no peace, no quietness.
   I have no rest; only trouble comes."

4 Eliphaz's First Response to Job

Then Eliphaz the Temanite replied to Job:

² "Will you be patient and let me say a word?
   For who could keep from speaking out?

³ "In the past you have encouraged many people;
   you have strengthened those who were weak.

⁴ Your words have supported those who were falling;
   you encouraged those with shaky knees.

⁵ But now when trouble strikes, you lose heart.
   You are terrified when it touches you.

⁶ Doesn't your reverence for God give you confidence?
   Doesn't your life of integrity give you hope?

⁷ "Stop and think! Do the innocent die?
   When have the upright been destroyed?

⁸ My experience shows that those who plant trouble
   and cultivate evil will harvest the same.

⁹ A breath from God destroys them.
   They vanish in a blast of his anger.

¹⁰ The lion roars and the wildcat snarls,
   but the teeth of strong lions will be broken.

¹¹ The fierce lion will starve for lack of prey,
   and the cubs of the lioness will be scattered.

¹² "This truth was given to me in secret,
   as though whispered in my ear.

¹³ It came to me in a disturbing vision at night,
   when people are in a deep sleep.

¹⁴ Fear gripped me,
   and my bones trembled.

¹⁵ A spirit* swept past my face,
   and my hair stood on end.*

¹⁶ The spirit stopped, but I couldn't see its shape.
   There was a form before my eyes.

In the silence I heard a voice say,
¹⁷ 'Can a mortal be innocent before God?
   Can anyone be pure before the Creator?'

¹⁸ "If God does not trust his own angels
   and has charged his messengers with foolishness,

¹⁹ how much less will he trust people made of clay!
   They are made of dust, crushed as easily as a moth.

²⁰ They are alive in the morning but dead by evening,
   gone forever without a trace.

²¹ Their tent-cords are pulled and the tent collapses,
   and they die in ignorance.

5 Eliphaz's Response Continues

¹ "Cry for help, but will anyone answer you?
   Which of the angels* will help you?

² Surely resentment destroys the fool,
   and jealousy kills the simple.

³ I have seen that fools may be successful for the moment,
   but then comes sudden disaster.

⁴ Their children are abandoned far from help;
   they are crushed in court with no one to defend them.

⁵ The hungry devour their harvest,
   even when it is guarded by brambles.*
   The thirsty pant after their wealth.

⁶ But evil does not spring from the soil,
   and trouble does not sprout from the earth.

⁷ People are born for trouble
   as readily as sparks fly up from a fire.

⁸ "If I were you, I would go to God
   and present my case to him.

⁹ He does great things too marvelous to understand.
   He performs countless miracles.

¹⁰ He gives rain for the earth
   and water for the fields.

¹¹ He gives prosperity to the poor
   and protects those who suffer.

¹² He frustrates the plans of schemers
   so the work of their hands will not succeed.

4:15a Or *wind;* also in 4:16.   **4:15b** Or *its wind sent shivers up my spine.*   **5:1** Hebrew *the holy ones.*   **5:5** The meaning of the Hebrew for this phrase is uncertain.

¹³ He traps the wise in their own cleverness
  so their cunning schemes are
    thwarted.
¹⁴ They find it is dark in the daytime,
  and they grope at noon as if it were
    night.
¹⁵ He rescues the poor from the cutting
    words of the strong,
  and rescues them from the clutches of
    the powerful.
¹⁶ And so at last the poor have hope,
  and the snapping jaws of the wicked
    are shut.

¹⁷ "But consider the joy of those corrected
    by God!
  Do not despise the discipline of the
    Almighty when you sin.
¹⁸ For though he wounds, he also
    bandages.
  He strikes, but his hands also heal.
¹⁹ From six disasters he will rescue you;
  even in the seventh, he will keep you
    from evil.
²⁰ He will save you from death in time of
    famine,
  from the power of the sword in time
    of war.
²¹ You will be safe from slander
  and have no fear when destruction
    comes.
²² You will laugh at destruction and
    famine;
  wild animals will not terrify you.
²³ You will be at peace with the stones of
    the field,
  and its wild animals will be at peace
    with you.
²⁴ You will know that your home is safe.
  When you survey your possessions,
    nothing will be missing.
²⁵ You will have many children;
  your descendants will be as plentiful
    as grass!
²⁶ You will go to the grave at a ripe old age,
  like a sheaf of grain harvested at the
    proper time!

²⁷ "We have studied life and found all this
    to be true.
  Listen to my counsel, and apply it to
    yourself."

6 Job's Second Speech: A Response to Eliphaz

Then Job spoke again:

² "If my misery could be weighed
  and my troubles be put on the scales,
³ they would outweigh all the sands of the
    sea.
  That is why I spoke impulsively.
⁴ For the Almighty has struck me down
    with his arrows.
  Their poison infects my spirit.
  God's terrors are lined up against me.
⁵ Don't I have a right to complain?
  Don't wild donkeys bray when they
    find no grass,
  and oxen bellow when they have no
    food?
⁶ Don't people complain about unsalted
    food?
  Does anyone want the tasteless white
    of an egg?*
⁷ My appetite disappears when I look at it;
  I gag at the thought of eating it!

⁸ "Oh, that I might have my request,
  that God would grant my desire.
⁹ I wish he would crush me.
  I wish he would reach out his hand
    and kill me.
¹⁰ At least I can take comfort in this:
    Despite the pain,
  I have not denied the words of the
    Holy One.
¹¹ But I don't have the strength to endure.
  I have nothing to live for.
¹² Do I have the strength of a stone?
  Is my body made of bronze?
¹³ No, I am utterly helpless,
  without any chance of success.

¹⁴ "One should be kind to a fainting friend,
  but you accuse me without any fear of
    the Almighty.*
¹⁵ My brothers, you have proved as
    unreliable as a seasonal brook
  that overflows its banks in the spring
¹⁶   when it is swollen with ice and melting
    snow.
¹⁷ But when the hot weather arrives, the
    water disappears.
  The brook vanishes in the heat.

6:6 Or the tasteless juice of the mallow plant?   6:14 Or friend, / or he might lose his fear of the Almighty.

¹⁸ The caravans turn aside to be refreshed,
    but there is nothing to drink, so they
    die.
¹⁹ The caravans from Tema search for this
    water;
    the travelers from Sheba hope to find it.
²⁰ They count on it but are disappointed.
    When they arrive, their hopes are
    dashed.
²¹ You, too, have given no help.
    You have seen my calamity, and you
    are afraid.
²² But why? Have I ever asked you for a
    gift?
    Have I begged for anything of yours
    for myself?
²³ Have I asked you to rescue me from my
    enemies,
    or to save me from ruthless people?
²⁴ Teach me, and I will keep quiet.
    Show me what I have done wrong.
²⁵ Honest words can be painful,
    but what do your criticisms amount to?
²⁶ Do you think your words are convincing
    when you disregard my cry of
    desperation?
²⁷ You would even send an orphan into
    slavery*
    or sell a friend.
²⁸ Look at me!
    Would I lie to your face?
²⁹ Stop assuming my guilt,
    for I have done no wrong.
³⁰ Do you think I am lying?
    Don't I know the difference between
    right and wrong?

7 ¹ "Is not all human life a struggle?
    Our lives are like that of a hired hand,
² like a worker who longs for the shade,
    like a servant waiting to be paid.
³ I, too, have been assigned months of
    futility,
    long and weary nights of misery.
⁴ Lying in bed, I think, 'When will it be
    morning?'
    But the night drags on, and I toss till
    dawn.
⁵ My body is covered with maggots and
    scabs.
    My skin breaks open, oozing with pus.

Job Cries Out to God

⁶ "My days fly faster than a weaver's
    shuttle.
    They end without hope.
⁷ O God, remember that my life is but a
    breath,
    and I will never again feel happiness.
⁸ You see me now, but not for long.
    You will look for me, but I will be gone.
⁹ Just as a cloud dissipates and vanishes,
    those who die* will not come back.
¹⁰ They are gone forever from their home—
    never to be seen again.

¹¹ "I cannot keep from speaking.
    I must express my anguish.
    My bitter soul must complain.
¹² Am I a sea monster or a dragon
    that you must place me under guard?
¹³ I think, 'My bed will comfort me,
    and sleep will ease my misery,'
¹⁴ but then you shatter me with dreams
    and terrify me with visions.
¹⁵ I would rather be strangled—
    rather die than suffer like this.
¹⁶ I hate my life and don't want to go on
    living.
    Oh, leave me alone for my few
    remaining days.

¹⁷ "What are people, that you should make
    so much of us,
    that you should think of us so often?
¹⁸ For you examine us every morning
    and test us every moment.
¹⁹ Why won't you leave me alone,
    at least long enough for me to swallow!
²⁰ If I have sinned, what have I done to you,
    O watcher of all humanity?
    Why make me your target?
    Am I a burden to you?
²¹ Why not just forgive my sin
    and take away my guilt?
    For soon I will lie down in the dust and
    die.
    When you look for me, I will be gone."

Bildad's First Response to Job

8 Then Bildad the Shuhite replied to Job:

² "How long will you go on like this?
    You sound like a blustering wind.

6:27 Hebrew *even gamble over an orphan.*   **7:9** Hebrew *who go down to Sheol.*

³ Does God twist justice?
Does the Almighty twist what is
right?
⁴ Your children must have sinned against
him,
so their punishment was well
deserved.
⁵ But if you pray to God
and seek the favor of the Almighty,
⁶ and if you are pure and live with
integrity,
he will surely rise up and restore your
happy home.
⁷ And though you started with little,
you will end with much.

⁸ "Just ask the previous generation.
Pay attention to the experience of our
ancestors.
⁹ For we were born but yesterday and
know nothing.
Our days on earth are as fleeting as a
shadow.
¹⁰ But those who came before us will teach
you.
They will teach you the wisdom of old.

¹¹ "Can papyrus reeds grow tall without a
marsh?
Can marsh grass flourish without
water?
¹² While they are still flowering, not ready
to be cut,
they begin to wither more quickly
than grass.
¹³ The same happens to all who forget God.
The hopes of the godless evaporate.
¹⁴ Their confidence hangs by a thread.
They are leaning on a spider's web.
¹⁵ They cling to their home for security,
but it won't last.
They try to hold it tight, but it will not
endure.
¹⁶ The godless seem like a lush plant
growing in the sunshine,
its branches spreading across the
garden.
¹⁷ Its roots grow down through a pile of
stones;
it takes hold on a bed of rocks.
¹⁸ But when it is uprooted,
it's as though it never existed!

¹⁹ That's the end of its life,
and others spring up from the earth to
replace it.

²⁰ "But look, God will not reject a person
of integrity,
nor will he lend a hand to the wicked.
²¹ He will once again fill your mouth with
laughter
and your lips with shouts of joy.
²² Those who hate you will be clothed with
shame,
and the home of the wicked will be
destroyed."

9 Job's Third Speech: A Response to Bildad

Then Job spoke again:

² "Yes, I know all this is true in principle.
But how can a person be declared
innocent in God's sight?
³ If someone wanted to take God to court,*
would it be possible to answer him
even once in a thousand times?
⁴ For God is so wise and so mighty.
Who has ever challenged him
successfully?

⁵ "Without warning, he moves the
mountains,
overturning them in his anger.
⁶ He shakes the earth from its place,
and its foundations tremble.
⁷ If he commands it, the sun won't rise
and the stars won't shine.
⁸ He alone has spread out the heavens
and marches on the waves of the sea.
⁹ He made all the stars—the Bear and
Orion,
the Pleiades and the constellations of
the southern sky.
¹⁰ He does great things too marvelous to
understand.
He performs countless miracles.

¹¹ "Yet when he comes near, I cannot see
him.
When he moves by, I do not see him go.
¹² If he snatches someone in death, who
can stop him?
Who dares to ask, 'What are you
doing?'

9:3 Or *If God wanted to take someone to court.*

¹³ And God does not restrain his anger.
Even the monsters of the sea* are
crushed beneath his feet.

¹⁴ "So who am I, that I should try to answer
God
or even reason with him?

¹⁵ Even if I were right, I would have no
defense.
I could only plead for mercy.

¹⁶ And even if I summoned him and he
responded,
I'm not sure he would listen to me.

¹⁷ For he attacks me with a storm
and repeatedly wounds me without
cause.

¹⁸ He will not let me catch my breath,
but fills me instead with bitter
sorrows.

¹⁹ If it's a question of strength, he's the
strong one.
If it's a matter of justice, who dares to
summon him to court?

²⁰ Though I am innocent, my own mouth
would pronounce me guilty.
Though I am blameless, it* would
prove me wicked.

²¹ "I am innocent,
but it makes no difference to me—
I despise my life.

²² Innocent or wicked, it is all the same to
God.
That's why I say, 'He destroys both the
blameless and the wicked.'

²³ When a plague* sweeps through,
he laughs at the death of the innocent.

²⁴ The whole earth is in the hands of the
wicked,
and God blinds the eyes of the judges.
If he's not the one who does it, who is?

²⁵ "My life passes more swiftly than a
runner.
It flees away without a glimpse of
happiness.

²⁶ It disappears like a swift papyrus boat,
like an eagle swooping down on its
prey.

²⁷ If I decided to forget my complaints,
to put away my sad face and be
cheerful,

²⁸ I would still dread all the pain,
for I know you will not find me
innocent, O God.

²⁹ Whatever happens, I will be found guilty.
So what's the use of trying?

³⁰ Even if I were to wash myself with soap
and clean my hands with lye,

³¹ you would plunge me into a muddy
ditch,
and my own filthy clothing would
hate me.

³² "God is not a mortal like me,
so I cannot argue with him or take
him to trial.

³³ If only there were a mediator between us,
someone who could bring us together.

³⁴ The mediator could make God stop
beating me,
and I would no longer live in terror of
his punishment.

³⁵ Then I could speak to him without fear,
but I cannot do that in my own
strength.

10 Job Frames His Plea to God

¹ "I am disgusted with my life.
Let me complain freely.
My bitter soul must complain.

² I will say to God, 'Don't simply condemn
me—
tell me the charge you are bringing
against me.

³ What do you gain by oppressing me?
Why do you reject me, the work of
your own hands,
while smiling on the schemes of the
wicked?

⁴ Are your eyes like those of a human?
Do you see things only as people see
them?

⁵ Is your lifetime only as long as ours?
Is your life so short

⁶ that you must quickly probe for my guilt
and search for my sin?

⁷ Although you know I am not guilty,
no one can rescue me from your hands.

⁸ "'You formed me with your hands; you
made me,
yet now you completely destroy me.

9:13 Hebrew *the helpers of Rahab,* the name of a mythical sea monster that represents chaos in ancient literature.   **9:20** Or *he.*   **9:23** Or
disaster.

⁹ Remember that you made me from
dust—
will you turn me back to dust so soon?
¹⁰ You guided my conception
and formed me in the womb.*
¹¹ You clothed me with skin and flesh,
and you knit my bones and sinews
together.
¹² You gave me life and showed me your
unfailing love.
My life was preserved by your care.

¹³ "'Yet your real motive—
your true intent—
¹⁴ was to watch me, and if I sinned,
you would not forgive my guilt.
¹⁵ If I am guilty, too bad for me;
and even if I'm innocent, I can't hold
my head high,
because I am filled with shame and
misery.
¹⁶ And if I hold my head high, you hunt me
like a lion
and display your awesome power
against me.
¹⁷ Again and again you witness against me.
You pour out your growing anger on me
and bring fresh armies against me.

¹⁸ "'Why, then, did you deliver me from
my mother's womb?
Why didn't you let me die at birth?
¹⁹ It would be as though I had never existed,
going directly from the womb to the
grave.
²⁰ I have only a few days left, so leave me
alone,
that I may have a moment of comfort
²¹ before I leave—never to return—
for the land of darkness and utter
gloom.
²² It is a land as dark as midnight,
a land of gloom and confusion,
where even the light is dark as
midnight.'"

11 Zophar's First Response to Job

Then Zophar the Naamathite replied
to Job:

² "Shouldn't someone answer this torrent
of words?

Is a person proved innocent just by a
lot of talking?
³ Should I remain silent while you
babble on?
When you mock God, shouldn't
someone make you ashamed?
⁴ You claim, 'My beliefs are pure,'
and 'I am clean in the sight of God.'
⁵ If only God would speak;
if only he would tell you what he
thinks!
⁶ If only he would tell you the secrets of
wisdom,
for true wisdom is not a simple matter.
Listen! God is doubtless punishing you
far less than you deserve!

⁷ "Can you solve the mysteries of God?
Can you discover everything about the
Almighty?
⁸ Such knowledge is higher than the
heavens—
and who are you?
It is deeper than the underworld*—
what do you know?
⁹ It is broader than the earth
and wider than the sea.
¹⁰ If God comes and puts a person in
prison
or calls the court to order, who can
stop him?
¹¹ For he knows those who are false,
and he takes note of all their sins.
¹² An empty-headed person won't become
wise
any more than a wild donkey can bear
a human child.*

¹³ "If only you would prepare your heart
and lift up your hands to him in
prayer!
¹⁴ Get rid of your sins,
and leave all iniquity behind you.
¹⁵ Then your face will brighten with
innocence.
You will be strong and free of fear.
¹⁶ You will forget your misery;
it will be like water flowing away.
¹⁷ Your life will be brighter than the
noonday.
Even darkness will be as bright as
morning.

10:10 Hebrew *You poured me out like milk / and curdled me like cheese.*   11:8 Hebrew *than Sheol.*   11:12 Or *than a wild male donkey can bear a tame colt.*

Why Me?

JOB 12

J ust about every trouble possible happened to Job. And how did he respond? With authentic gratitude. He struggled, ached, grieved, and yet in the midst of it all, he praised God.

The American military has a motto: "Do the harder right." It's easy to be grateful when life is good and things are going along nicely. But the harder right means we practice thanking God when everything within us screams, "Why me?"

I've come to realize the question shouldn't be, "Why me?" but, "Why *not* me?"

The interesting thing about asking that question is that it changes my perspective. My eyes move from myself and my current circumstance to the bigger picture of eternity and how God wants to shape me into the image of Jesus.

When I embrace that question, not only do I mature, but I'm also able to empathize with, love, and care for those with similar troubles.

As I practice doing "the harder right" and being thankful for what God has blessed me with, when the troubles come, I hope my natural inclination will become, "Why *not* me? Thank you, God, for this circumstance too. In the midst of it, help me to honor you and bless others."

—*Ginger Kolbaba*

For more on gratitude, see reading at Psalm 95.

---

18 Having hope will give you courage.
    You will be protected and will rest in
      safety.
19 You will lie down unafraid,
    and many will look to you for help.
20 But the wicked will be blinded.
    They will have no escape.
    Their only hope is death."

12 Job's Fourth Speech: A Response to Zophar

Then Job spoke again:

2 "You people really know everything,
      don't you?
    And when you die, wisdom will die
      with you!
3 Well, I know a few things myself—
    and you're no better than I am.
    Who doesn't know these things you've
      been saying?
4 Yet my friends laugh at me,

for I call on God and expect an answer.
    I am a just and blameless man,
      yet they laugh at me.
5 People who are at ease mock those in
      trouble.
    They give a push to people who are
      stumbling.
6 But robbers are left in peace,
    and those who provoke God live in
      safety—
    though God keeps them in his power.

7 "Just ask the animals, and they will teach
      you.
    Ask the birds of the sky, and they will
      tell you.
8 Speak to the earth, and it will instruct
      you.
    Let the fish in the sea speak to you.
9 For they all know
    that my disaster* has come from the
      hand of the LORD.

12:9 Hebrew *that this*.

¹⁰ For the life of every living thing is in his
    hand,
    and the breath of every human being.
¹¹ The ear tests the words it hears
    just as the mouth distinguishes
    between foods.
¹² Wisdom belongs to the aged,
    and understanding to the old.

¹³ "But true wisdom and power are found
    in God;
    counsel and understanding are his.
¹⁴ What he destroys cannot be rebuilt.
    When he puts someone in prison,
    there is no escape.
¹⁵ If he holds back the rain, the earth
    becomes a desert.
    If he releases the waters, they flood
    the earth.
¹⁶ Yes, strength and wisdom are his;
    deceivers and deceived are both in his
    power.
¹⁷ He leads counselors away, stripped of
    good judgment;
    wise judges become fools.
¹⁸ He removes the royal robe of kings.
    They are led away with ropes around
    their waist.
¹⁹ He leads priests away, stripped of status;
    he overthrows those with long years
    in power.
²⁰ He silences the trusted adviser
    and removes the insight of the elders.
²¹ He pours disgrace upon princes
    and disarms the strong.

²² "He uncovers mysteries hidden in darkness;
    he brings light to the deepest gloom.
²³ He builds up nations, and he destroys
    them.
    He expands nations, and he abandons
    them.
²⁴ He strips kings of understanding
    and leaves them wandering in a
    pathless wasteland.
²⁵ They grope in the darkness without a
    light.
    He makes them stagger like drunkards.

13 Job Wants to Argue His Case with God

¹ "Look, I have seen all this with my own
    eyes

and heard it with my own ears, and
    now I understand.
² I know as much as you do.
    You are no better than I am.
³ As for me, I would speak directly to the
    Almighty.
    I want to argue my case with God
    himself.
⁴ As for you, you smear me with lies.
    As physicians, you are worthless quacks.
⁵ If only you could be silent!
    That's the wisest thing you could do.
⁶ Listen to my charge;
    pay attention to my arguments.

⁷ "Are you defending God with lies?
    Do you make your dishonest
    arguments for his sake?
⁸ Will you slant your testimony in his
    favor?
    Will you argue God's case for him?
⁹ What will happen when he finds out
    what you are doing?
    Can you fool him as easily as you fool
    people?
¹⁰ No, you will be in trouble with him
    if you secretly slant your testimony in
    his favor.
¹¹ Doesn't his majesty terrify you?
    Doesn't your fear of him overwhelm
    you?
¹² Your platitudes are as valuable as ashes.
    Your defense is as fragile as a clay pot.

¹³ "Be silent now and leave me alone.
    Let me speak, and I will face the
    consequences.
¹⁴ Yes, I will take my life in my hands
    and say what I really think.
¹⁵ God might kill me, but I have no other
    hope.*
    I am going to argue my case with him.
¹⁶ But this is what will save me—I am not
    godless.
    If I were, I could not stand before him.

¹⁷ "Listen closely to what I am about to say.
    Hear me out.
¹⁸ I have prepared my case;
    I will be proved innocent.
¹⁹ Who can argue with me over this?
    And if you prove me wrong, I will
    remain silent and die.

13:15 An alternate reading in the Masoretic Text reads *God might kill me, but I hope in him.*

Job Asks How He Has Sinned

20 "O God, grant me these two things,
and then I will be able to face you.
21 Remove your heavy hand from me,
and don't terrify me with your
awesome presence.
22 Now summon me, and I will answer!
Or let me speak to you, and you reply.
23 Tell me, what have I done wrong?
Show me my rebellion and my sin.
24 Why do you turn away from me?
Why do you treat me as your enemy?
25 Would you terrify a leaf blown by the
wind?
Would you chase dry straw?

26 "You write bitter accusations against me
and bring up all the sins of my youth.
27 You put my feet in stocks.
You examine all my paths.
You trace all my footprints.
28 I waste away like rotting wood,
like a moth-eaten coat.

14 1 "How frail is humanity!
How short is life, how full of
trouble!
2 We blossom like a flower and then wither.
Like a passing shadow, we quickly
disappear.
3 Must you keep an eye on such a frail
creature
and demand an accounting from me?
4 Who can bring purity out of an impure
person?
No one!
5 You have decided the length of our lives.
You know how many months we will
live,
and we are not given a minute longer.
6 So leave us alone and let us rest!
We are like hired hands, so let us
finish our work in peace.

7 "Even a tree has more hope!
If it is cut down, it will sprout again
and grow new branches.
8 Though its roots have grown old in the
earth
and its stump decays,
9 at the scent of water it will bud
and sprout again like a new seedling.

10 "But when people die, their strength is
gone.
They breathe their last, and then
where are they?
11 As water evaporates from a lake
and a river disappears in drought,
12 people are laid to rest and do not rise
again.
Until the heavens are no more, they
will not wake up
nor be roused from their sleep.

13 "I wish you would hide me in the
grave*
and forget me there until your anger
has passed.
But mark your calendar to think of me
again!
14 Can the dead live again?
If so, this would give me hope through
all my years of struggle,
and I would eagerly await the release
of death.
15 You would call and I would answer,
and you would yearn for me, your
handiwork.
16 For then you would guard my steps,
instead of watching for my sins.
17 My sins would be sealed in a pouch,
and you would cover my guilt.

18 "But instead, as mountains fall and
crumble
and as rocks fall from a cliff,
19 as water wears away the stones
and floods wash away the soil,
so you destroy people's hope.
20 You always overpower them, and they
pass from the scene.
You disfigure them in death and send
them away.
21 They never know if their children grow
up in honor
or sink to insignificance.
22 They suffer painfully;
their life is full of trouble."

15 Eliphaz's Second Response to Job

Then Eliphaz the Temanite replied:

2 "A wise man wouldn't answer with such
empty talk!
You are nothing but a windbag.

14:13 Hebrew *in Sheol.*

3 The wise don't engage in empty chatter.
 What good are such words?
4 Have you no fear of God,
 no reverence for him?
5 Your sins are telling your mouth what to
 say.
 Your words are based on clever
 deception.
6 Your own mouth condemns you, not I.
 Your own lips testify against you.

7 "Were you the first person ever born?
 Were you born before the hills were
 made?
8 Were you listening at God's secret
 council?
 Do you have a monopoly on wisdom?
9 What do you know that we don't?
 What do you understand that we do
 not?
10 On our side are aged, gray-haired men
 much older than your father!

11 "Is God's comfort too little for you?
 Is his gentle word not enough?
12 What has taken away your reason?
 What has weakened your vision,*
13 that you turn against God
 and say all these evil things?
14 Can any mortal be pure?
 Can anyone born of a woman be just?
15 Look, God does not even trust the
 angels.*
 Even the heavens are not absolutely
 pure in his sight.
16 How much less pure is a corrupt and
 sinful person
 with a thirst for wickedness!

17 "If you will listen, I will show you.
 I will answer you from my own
 experience.
18 And it is confirmed by the reports of
 wise men
 who have heard the same thing from
 their fathers—
19 from those to whom the land was given
 long before any foreigners arrived.
20 "The wicked writhe in pain throughout
 their lives.
 Years of trouble are stored up for the
 ruthless.

21 The sound of terror rings in their ears,
 and even on good days they fear the
 attack of the destroyer.
22 They dare not go out into the darkness
 for fear they will be murdered.
23 They wander around, saying, 'Where can
 I find bread?'*
 They know their day of destruction is
 near.
24 That dark day terrifies them.
 They live in distress and anguish,
 like a king preparing for battle.
25 For they shake their fists at God,
 defying the Almighty.
26 Holding their strong shields,
 they defiantly charge against him.

27 "These wicked people are heavy and
 prosperous;
 their waists bulge with fat.
28 But their cities will be ruined.
 They will live in abandoned houses
 that are ready to tumble down.
29 Their riches will not last,
 and their wealth will not endure.
 Their possessions will no longer
 spread across the horizon.
30 "They will not escape the darkness.
 The burning sun will wither their
 shoots,
 and the breath of God will destroy
 them.
31 Let them no longer fool themselves by
 trusting in empty riches,
 for emptiness will be their only
 reward.
32 Like trees, they will be cut down in the
 prime of life;
 their branches will never again be
 green.
33 They will be like a vine whose grapes are
 harvested too early,
 like an olive tree that loses its
 blossoms before the fruit can form.
34 For the godless are barren.
 Their homes, enriched through
 bribery, will burn.
35 They conceive trouble and give birth to
 evil.
 Their womb produces deceit."

15:12 Or *Why do your eyes flash with anger;* Hebrew reads *Why do your eyes blink.* **15:15** Hebrew *the holy ones.* **15:23** Greek version reads *He is appointed to be food for a vulture.*

16 Job's Fifth Speech: A Response to Eliphaz

Then Job spoke again:

2 "I have heard all this before.
   What miserable comforters you are!
3 Won't you ever stop blowing hot air?
   What makes you keep on talking?
4 I could say the same things if you were
      in my place.
   I could spout off criticism and shake
      my head at you.
5 But if it were me, I would encourage you.
   I would try to take away your grief.
6 Instead, I suffer if I defend myself,
   and I suffer no less if I refuse to speak.

7 "O God, you have ground me down
   and devastated my family.
8 As if to prove I have sinned, you've
      reduced me to skin and bones.
   My gaunt flesh testifies against me.
9 God hates me and angrily tears me
      apart.
   He snaps his teeth at me
   and pierces me with his eyes.
10 People jeer and laugh at me.
   They slap my cheek in contempt.
   A mob gathers against me.
11 God has handed me over to sinners.
   He has tossed me into the hands of the
      wicked.

12 "I was living quietly until he shattered me.
   He took me by the neck and broke me
      in pieces.
   Then he set me up as his target,
13   and now his archers surround me.
   His arrows pierce me without mercy.
   The ground is wet with my blood.*
14 Again and again he smashes against me,
   charging at me like a warrior.
15 I wear burlap to show my grief.
   My pride lies in the dust.
16 My eyes are red with weeping;
   dark shadows circle my eyes.
17 Yet I have done no wrong,
   and my prayer is pure.

18 "O earth, do not conceal my blood.
   Let it cry out on my behalf.
19 Even now my witness is in heaven.
   My advocate is there on high.

20 My friends scorn me,
   but I pour out my tears to God.
21 I need someone to mediate between
      God and me,
   as a person mediates between friends.
22 For soon I must go down that road
   from which I will never return.

17 Job Continues to Defend His Innocence

1 "My spirit is crushed,
   and my life is nearly snuffed out.
   The grave is ready to receive me.
2 I am surrounded by mockers.
   I watch how bitterly they taunt me.

3 "You must defend my innocence, O God,
   since no one else will stand up for me.
4 You have closed their minds to
      understanding,
   but do not let them triumph.
5 They betray their friends for their own
      advantage,
   so let their children faint with hunger.

6 "God has made a mockery of me among
      the people;
   they spit in my face.
7 My eyes are swollen with weeping,
   and I am but a shadow of my former
      self.
8 The virtuous are horrified when they
      see me.
   The innocent rise up against the
      ungodly.
9 The righteous keep moving forward,
   and those with clean hands become
      stronger and stronger.

10 "As for all of you, come back with a
      better argument,
   though I still won't find a wise man
      among you.
11 My days are over.
   My hopes have disappeared.
   My heart's desires are broken.
12 These men say that night is day;
   they claim that the darkness is light.
13 What if I go to the grave*
   and make my bed in darkness?
14 What if I call the grave my father,
   and the maggot my mother or my
      sister?

16:13 Hebrew *my gall.*   **17:13** Hebrew *to Sheol;* also in 17:16.

¹⁵ Where then is my hope?
Can anyone find it?
¹⁶ No, my hope will go down with me to
the grave.
We will rest together in the dust!"

18 Bildad's Second Response to Job

Then Bildad the Shuhite replied:

² "How long before you stop talking?
Speak sense if you want us to answer!
³ Do you think we are mere animals?
Do you think we are stupid?
⁴ You may tear out your hair in anger,
but will that destroy the earth?
Will it make the rocks tremble?

⁵ "Surely the light of the wicked will be
snuffed out.
The sparks of their fire will not glow.
⁶ The light in their tent will grow dark.
The lamp hanging above them will be
quenched.
⁷ The confident stride of the wicked will
be shortened.
Their own schemes will be their
downfall.
⁸ The wicked walk into a net.
They fall into a pit.
⁹ A trap grabs them by the heel.
A snare holds them tight.
¹⁰ A noose lies hidden on the ground.
A rope is stretched across their path.

¹¹ "Terrors surround the wicked
and trouble them at every step.
¹² Hunger depletes their strength,
and calamity waits for them to
stumble.
¹³ Disease eats their skin;
death devours their limbs.
¹⁴ They are torn from the security of their
homes
and are brought down to the king of
terrors.
¹⁵ The homes of the wicked will burn
down;
burning sulfur rains on their houses.
¹⁶ Their roots will dry up,
and their branches will wither.
¹⁷ All memory of their existence will fade
from the earth;
no one will remember their names.

¹⁸ They will be thrust from light into
darkness,
driven from the world.
¹⁹ They will have neither children nor
grandchildren,
nor any survivor in the place where
they lived.
²⁰ People in the west are appalled at their
fate;
people in the east are horrified.
²¹ They will say, 'This was the home of a
wicked person,
the place of one who rejected God.'"

19 Job's Sixth Speech: A Response to Bildad

Then Job spoke again:

² "How long will you torture me?
How long will you try to crush me
with your words?
³ You have already insulted me ten times.
You should be ashamed of treating me
so badly.
⁴ Even if I have sinned,
that is my concern, not yours.
⁵ You think you're better than I am,
using my humiliation as evidence of
my sin.
⁶ But it is God who has wronged me,
capturing me in his net.*

⁷ "I cry out, 'Help!' but no one answers me.
I protest, but there is no justice.
⁸ God has blocked my way so I cannot
move.
He has plunged my path into
darkness.
⁹ He has stripped me of my honor
and removed the crown from my
head.
¹⁰ He has demolished me on every side,
and I am finished.
He has uprooted my hope like a fallen
tree.
¹¹ His fury burns against me;
he counts me as an enemy.
¹² His troops advance.
They build up roads to attack me.
They camp all around my tent.

¹³ "My relatives stay far away,
and my friends have turned against me.

19:6 Or *for I am like a city under siege.*

¹⁴ My family is gone,
and my close friends have forgotten me.
¹⁵ My servants and maids consider me a
stranger.
I am like a foreigner to them.
¹⁶ When I call my servant, he doesn't
come;
I have to plead with him!
¹⁷ My breath is repulsive to my wife.
I am rejected by my own family.
¹⁸ Even young children despise me.
When I stand to speak, they turn their
backs on me.
¹⁹ My close friends detest me.
Those I loved have turned against me.
²⁰ I have been reduced to skin and bones
and have escaped death by the skin of
my teeth.

²¹ "Have mercy on me, my friends, have
mercy,
for the hand of God has struck me.
²² Must you also persecute me, like God
does?
Haven't you chewed me up enough?

²³ "Oh, that my words could be recorded.
Oh, that they could be inscribed on a
monument,
²⁴ carved with an iron chisel and filled with
lead,
engraved forever in the rock.

²⁵ "But as for me, I know that my
Redeemer lives,
and he will stand upon the earth at last.
²⁶ And after my body has decayed,
yet in my body I will see God!*
²⁷ I will see him for myself.
Yes, I will see him with my own eyes.
I am overwhelmed at the thought!

²⁸ "How dare you go on persecuting me,
saying, 'It's his own fault'?
²⁹ You should fear punishment yourselves,
for your attitude deserves punishment.
Then you will know that there is
indeed a judgment."

20 Zophar's Second Response to Job
Then Zophar the Naamathite replied:

² "I must reply
because I am greatly disturbed.

³ I've had to endure your insults,
but now my spirit prompts me to
reply.

⁴ "Don't you realize that from the
beginning of time,
ever since people were first placed on
the earth,
⁵ the triumph of the wicked has been
short lived
and the joy of the godless has been
only temporary?
⁶ Though the pride of the godless reaches
to the heavens
and their heads touch the clouds,
⁷ yet they will vanish forever,
thrown away like their own dung.
Those who knew them will ask,
'Where are they?'
⁸ They will fade like a dream and not be
found.
They will vanish like a vision in the
night.
⁹ Those who once saw them will see them
no more.
Their families will never see them
again.
¹⁰ Their children will beg from the poor,
for they must give back their stolen
riches.
¹¹ Though they are young,
their bones will lie in the dust.

¹² "They enjoyed the sweet taste of
wickedness,
letting it melt under their tongue.
¹³ They savored it,
holding it long in their mouths.
¹⁴ But suddenly the food in their bellies
turns sour,
a poisonous venom in their stomach.
¹⁵ They will vomit the wealth they
swallowed.
God won't let them keep it down.
¹⁶ They will suck the poison of cobras.
The viper will kill them.
¹⁷ They will never again enjoy streams of
olive oil
or rivers of milk and honey.
¹⁸ They will give back everything they
worked for.
Their wealth will bring them no joy.

19:26 Or *without my body I will see God.* The meaning of the Hebrew is uncertain.

Community

Comforting Those Who Mourn
JOB 20

I've watched my parents suffer through a cancer diagnosis and a rare neurological disease. I have tried to offer comfort, and I've watched others do the same. Sometimes our words have been balms. Sometimes they have been hand grenades, like the platitudes and wrong-headed theology Job's "friends" spoke to him in his pain and suffering.

Sometimes, though well-intentioned, we offer words that invalidate others' pain. With a bombastic mix of well-meaning fervor and unconscious impatience, we attempt to rush our wounded friend to closure. Classic well-meaning platitudes include "It will all work out in the end," "Time heals all wounds," and glib recitations of Romans 8:28: "God causes everything to work together. . . ."

Or we may offer some sort of formula—some rational, uniform explanation that we think can be applied to all suffering. This approach suggests that affliction is either discipline from God or an attack from Satan, and that the right degree of repentance—or faith—will turn things around.

And of course there are the common "forced meaning" reactions. "God has a reason for everything," we claim, and then we try to ram horrible tragedies into redemptive molds—suggesting that cancer, rape, and earthquakes are wake-up calls, strange expressions of grace in God's epic story. But are these platitudes actually comforting . . . or true?

So what *can* we do to build community among those who hurt? There's a piece of advice attributed to Miles Davis: "Think of a note and don't play it." As a musician, I understand: allow for space in the music, don't always rush in, and *listen*. Sometimes the most helpful thing we can do is *think* of a truth and embody it rather than say it. Only when we acknowledge the present pain—and the mysteries that likely shroud its cause—do we earn the right to affirm God's goodness in the midst of it. And only when we mourn—for ourselves, for one another, and for a world groaning for redemption—can we be comforted . . . and be a comfort.

—*Carolyn Arends*

For more on community, see reading at Psalm 133.

---

[19] For they oppressed the poor and left
  them destitute.
  They foreclosed on their homes.
[20] They were always greedy and never
  satisfied.
  Nothing remains of all the things they
  dreamed about.
[21] Nothing is left after they finish gorging
  themselves.
  Therefore, their prosperity will not
  endure.

[22] "In the midst of plenty, they will run into
  trouble
  and be overcome by misery.
[23] May God give them a bellyful of trouble.
  May God rain down his anger upon
  them.
[24] When they try to escape an iron
  weapon,
  a bronze-tipped arrow will pierce
  them.
[25] The arrow is pulled from their back,

and the arrowhead glistens with
    blood.*
The terrors of death are upon them.
26 Their treasures will be thrown into
    deepest darkness.
A wildfire will devour their goods,
    consuming all they have left.
27 The heavens will reveal their guilt,
    and the earth will testify against them.
28 A flood will sweep away their house.
    God's anger will descend on them in
    torrents.
29 This is the reward that God gives the
    wicked.
    It is the inheritance decreed by God."

21 Job's Seventh Speech: A Response to Zophar

Then Job spoke again:

2 "Listen closely to what I am saying.
    That's one consolation you can
    give me.
3 Bear with me, and let me speak.
    After I have spoken, you may resume
    mocking me.

4 "My complaint is with God, not with
    people.
    I have good reason to be so impatient.
5 Look at me and be stunned.
    Put your hand over your mouth in
    shock.
6 When I think about what I am saying, I
    shudder.
    My body trembles.

7 "Why do the wicked prosper,
    growing old and powerful?
8 They live to see their children grow up
    and settle down,
    and they enjoy their grandchildren.
9 Their homes are safe from every fear,
    and God does not punish them.
10 Their bulls never fail to breed.
    Their cows bear calves and never
    miscarry.
11 They let their children frisk about like
    lambs.
    Their little ones skip and dance.
12 They sing with tambourine and harp.
    They celebrate to the sound of the
    flute.

13 They spend their days in prosperity,
    then go down to the grave* in peace.
14 And yet they say to God, 'Go away.
    We want no part of you and your ways.
15 Who is the Almighty, and why should
    we obey him?
    What good will it do us to pray?'
16 (They think their prosperity is of their
    own doing,
    but I will have nothing to do with that
    kind of thinking.)

17 "Yet the light of the wicked never seems
    to be extinguished.
    Do they ever have trouble?
    Does God distribute sorrows to them
    in anger?
18 Are they driven before the wind like
    straw?
    Are they carried away by the storm
    like chaff?
    Not at all!

19 "'Well,' you say, 'at least God will punish
    their children!'
    But I say he should punish the ones
    who sin,
    so that they understand his judgment.
20 Let them see their destruction with their
    own eyes.
    Let them drink deeply of the anger of
    the Almighty.
21 For they will not care what happens to
    their family
    after they are dead.

22 "But who can teach a lesson to God,
    since he judges even the most
    powerful?
23 One person dies in prosperity,
    completely comfortable and secure,
24 the picture of good health,
    vigorous and fit.
25 Another person dies in bitter poverty,
    never having tasted the good life.
26 But both are buried in the same dust,
    both eaten by the same maggots.

27 "Look, I know what you're thinking.
    I know the schemes you plot
    against me.
28 You will tell me of rich and wicked
    people

20:25 Hebrew *with gall.*   **21:13** Hebrew *to Sheol.*

whose houses have vanished because of their sins.

²⁹ But ask those who have been around,
and they will tell you the truth.

³⁰ Evil people are spared in times of calamity
and are allowed to escape disaster.

³¹ No one criticizes them openly
or pays them back for what they have done.

³² When they are carried to the grave,
an honor guard keeps watch at their tomb.

³³ A great funeral procession goes to the cemetery.
Many pay their respects as the body is laid to rest,
and the earth gives sweet repose.

³⁴ "How can your empty clichés comfort me?
All your explanations are lies!"

22 Eliphaz's Third Response to Job

Then Eliphaz the Temanite replied:

² "Can a person do anything to help God?
Can even a wise person be helpful to him?

³ Is it any advantage to the Almighty if you are righteous?
Would it be any gain to him if you were perfect?

⁴ Is it because you're so pious that he accuses you
and brings judgment against you?

⁵ No, it's because of your wickedness!
There's no limit to your sins.

⁶ "For example, you must have lent money to your friend
and demanded clothing as security.
Yes, you stripped him to the bone.

⁷ You must have refused water for the thirsty
and food for the hungry.

⁸ You probably think the land belongs to the powerful
and only the privileged have a right to it!

⁹ You must have sent widows away empty-handed
and crushed the hopes of orphans.

¹⁰ That is why you are surrounded by traps
and tremble from sudden fears.

¹¹ That is why you cannot see in the darkness,
and waves of water cover you.

¹² "God is so great—higher than the heavens,
higher than the farthest stars.

¹³ But you reply, 'That's why God can't see what I am doing!
How can he judge through the thick darkness?

¹⁴ For thick clouds swirl about him, and he cannot see us.
He is way up there, walking on the vault of heaven.'

¹⁵ "Will you continue on the old paths where evil people have walked?

¹⁶ They were snatched away in the prime of life,
the foundations of their lives washed away.

¹⁷ For they said to God, 'Leave us alone!
What can the Almighty do to us?'

¹⁸ Yet he was the one who filled their homes with good things,
so I will have nothing to do with that kind of thinking.

¹⁹ "The righteous will be happy to see the wicked destroyed,
and the innocent will laugh in contempt.

²⁰ They will say, 'See how our enemies have been destroyed.
The last of them have been consumed in the fire.'

²¹ "Submit to God, and you will have peace;
then things will go well for you.

²² Listen to his instructions,
and store them in your heart.

²³ If you return to the Almighty, you will be restored—
so clean up your life.

²⁴ If you give up your lust for money
and throw your precious gold into the river,

²⁵ the Almighty himself will be your treasure.
He will be your precious silver!

26 "Then you will take delight in the Almighty
    and look up to God.
27 You will pray to him, and he will hear
    you,
        and you will fulfill your vows to him.
28 You will succeed in whatever you choose
    to do,
        and light will shine on the road ahead
        of you.
29 If people are in trouble and you say,
    'Help them,'
        God will save them.
30 Even sinners will be rescued;
    they will be rescued because your
    hands are pure."

23 Job's Eighth Speech: A Response to Eliphaz

Then Job spoke again:

2 "My complaint today is still a bitter one,
    and I try hard not to groan aloud.
3 If only I knew where to find God,
    I would go to his court.
4 I would lay out my case
    and present my arguments.
5 Then I would listen to his reply
    and understand what he says to me.
6 Would he use his great power to argue
    with me?
        No, he would give me a fair hearing.
7 Honest people can reason with him,
    so I would be forever acquitted by my
    judge.
8 I go east, but he is not there.
    I go west, but I cannot find him.
9 I do not see him in the north, for he is
    hidden.
        I look to the south, but he is concealed.

10 "But he knows where I am going.
    And when he tests me, I will come out
    as pure as gold.
11 For I have stayed on God's paths;
    I have followed his ways and not
    turned aside.
12 I have not departed from his commands,
    but have treasured his words more
    than daily food.
13 But once he has made his decision, who
    can change his mind?
        Whatever he wants to do, he does.
14 So he will do to me whatever he has
    planned.

He controls my destiny.
15 No wonder I am so terrified in his
    presence.
        When I think of it, terror grips me.
16 God has made me sick at heart;
    the Almighty has terrified me.
17 Darkness is all around me;
    thick, impenetrable darkness is
    everywhere.

24 Job Asks Why the Wicked Are Not Punished

1 "Why doesn't the Almighty bring the
    wicked to judgment?
        Why must the godly wait for him in
        vain?
2 Evil people steal land by moving the
    boundary markers.
        They steal livestock and put them in
        their own pastures.
3 They take the orphan's donkey
    and demand the widow's ox as
    security for a loan.
4 The poor are pushed off the path;
    the needy must hide together for safety.
5 Like wild donkeys in the wilderness,
    the poor must spend all their time
    looking for food,
        searching even in the desert for food
        for their children.
6 They harvest a field they do not own,
    and they glean in the vineyards of the
    wicked.
7 All night they lie naked in the cold,
    without clothing or covering.
8 They are soaked by mountain showers,
    and they huddle against the rocks for
    want of a home.

9 "The wicked snatch a widow's child from
    her breast,
        taking the baby as security for a loan.
10 The poor must go about naked, without
    any clothing.
        They harvest food for others while
        they themselves are starving.
11 They press out olive oil without being
    allowed to taste it,
        and they tread in the winepress as
        they suffer from thirst.
12 The groans of the dying rise from the city,
    and the wounded cry for help,
        yet God ignores their moaning.

13 "Wicked people rebel against the light.
    They refuse to acknowledge its ways
    or stay in its paths.
14 The murderer rises in the early dawn
    to kill the poor and needy;
    at night he is a thief.
15 The adulterer waits for the twilight,
    saying, 'No one will see me then.'
    He hides his face so no one will know
    him.
16 Thieves break into houses at night
    and sleep in the daytime.
    They are not acquainted with the light.
17 The black night is their morning.
    They ally themselves with the terrors
    of the darkness.

18 "But they disappear like foam down a
    river.
    Everything they own is cursed,
    and they are afraid to enter their own
    vineyards.
19 The grave* consumes sinners
    just as drought and heat consume snow.
20 Their own mothers will forget them.
    Maggots will find them sweet to eat.
    No one will remember them.
    Wicked people are broken like a tree
    in the storm.
21 They cheat the woman who has no son
    to help her.
    They refuse to help the needy widow.

22 "God, in his power, drags away the rich.
    They may rise high, but they have no
    assurance of life.
23 They may be allowed to live in security,
    but God is always watching them.
24 And though they are great now,
    in a moment they will be gone like all
    others,
    cut off like heads of grain.
25 Can anyone claim otherwise?
    Who can prove me wrong?"

25 Bildad's Third Response to Job
Then Bildad the Shuhite replied:

2 "God is powerful and dreadful.
    He enforces peace in the heavens.
3 Who is able to count his heavenly army?
    Doesn't his light shine on all the earth?

4 How can a mortal be innocent before
    God?
    Can anyone born of a woman be
    pure?
5 God is more glorious than the moon;
    he shines brighter than the stars.
6 In comparison, people are maggots;
    we mortals are mere worms."

26 Job's Ninth Speech: A Response to Bildad
Then Job spoke again:

2 "How you have helped the powerless!
    How you have saved the weak!
3 How you have enlightened my stupidity!
    What wise advice you have offered!
4 Where have you gotten all these wise
    sayings?
    Whose spirit speaks through you?

5 "The dead tremble—
    those who live beneath the waters.
6 The underworld* is naked in God's
    presence.
    The place of destruction* is
    uncovered.
7 God stretches the northern sky over
    empty space
    and hangs the earth on nothing.
8 He wraps the rain in his thick clouds,
    and the clouds don't burst with the
    weight.
9 He covers the face of the moon,*
    shrouding it with his clouds.
10 He created the horizon when he
    separated the waters;
    he set the boundary between day and
    night.
11 The foundations of heaven tremble;
    they shudder at his rebuke.
12 By his power the sea grew calm.
    By his skill he crushed the great sea
    monster.*
13 His Spirit made the heavens beautiful,
    and his power pierced the gliding
    serpent.
14 These are just the beginning of all that
    he does,
    merely a whisper of his power.
    Who, then, can comprehend the
    thunder of his power?"

24:19 Hebrew *Sheol.* 26:6a Hebrew *Sheol.* 26:6b Hebrew *Abaddon.* 26:9 Or *covers his throne.* 26:12 Hebrew *Rahab,* the name of a
mythical sea monster that represents chaos in ancient literature.

27 Job's Final Speech
Job continued speaking:

[2] "I vow by the living God, who has taken
away my rights,
by the Almighty who has embittered
my soul—
[3] As long as I live,
while I have breath from God,
[4] my lips will speak no evil,
and my tongue will speak no lies.
[5] I will never concede that you are right;
I will defend my integrity until I die.
[6] I will maintain my innocence without
wavering.
My conscience is clear for as long as
I live.

[7] "May my enemy be punished like the
wicked,
my adversary like those who do evil.
[8] For what hope do the godless have when
God cuts them off
and takes away their life?
[9] Will God listen to their cry
when trouble comes upon them?
[10] Can they take delight in the Almighty?
Can they call to God at any time?
[11] I will teach you about God's power.
I will not conceal anything concerning
the Almighty.
[12] But you have seen all this,
yet you say all these useless things
to me.

[13] "This is what the wicked will receive
from God;
this is their inheritance from the
Almighty.
[14] They may have many children,
but the children will die in war or
starve to death.
[15] Those who survive will die of a plague,
and not even their widows will mourn
them.

[16] "Evil people may have piles of money
and may store away mounds of
clothing.
[17] But the righteous will wear that clothing,
and the innocent will divide that
money.
[18] The wicked build houses as fragile as a
spider's web,*

as flimsy as a shelter made of
branches.
[19] The wicked go to bed rich
but wake to find that all their wealth
is gone.
[20] Terror overwhelms them like a flood,
and they are blown away in the storms
of the night.
[21] The east wind carries them away, and
they are gone.
It sweeps them away.
[22] It whirls down on them without mercy.
They struggle to flee from its power.
[23] But everyone jeers at them
and mocks them.

28 Job Speaks of Wisdom and Understanding

[1] "People know where to mine silver
and how to refine gold.
[2] They know where to dig iron from the
earth
and how to smelt copper from rock.
[3] They know how to shine light in the
darkness
and explore the farthest regions of the
earth
as they search in the dark for ore.
[4] They sink a mine shaft into the earth
far from where anyone lives.
They descend on ropes, swinging back
and forth.
[5] Food is grown on the earth above,
but down below, the earth is melted as
by fire.
[6] Here the rocks contain precious lapis
lazuli,
and the dust contains gold.
[7] These are treasures no bird of prey can
see,
no falcon's eye observe.
[8] No wild animal has walked upon these
treasures;
no lion has ever set his paw there.
[9] People know how to tear apart flinty
rocks
and overturn the roots of mountains.
[10] They cut tunnels in the rocks
and uncover precious stones.
[11] They dam up the trickling streams
and bring to light the hidden
treasures.

27:18 As in Greek and Syriac versions (see also 8:14); Hebrew reads *a moth.*

¹² "But do people know where to find
wisdom?
Where can they find understanding?
¹³ No one knows where to find it,
for it is not found among the living.
¹⁴ 'It is not here,' says the ocean.
'Nor is it here,' says the sea.
¹⁵ It cannot be bought with gold.
It cannot be purchased with silver.
¹⁶ It's worth more than all the gold of Ophir,
greater than precious onyx or lapis
lazuli.
¹⁷ Wisdom is more valuable than gold and
crystal.
It cannot be purchased with jewels
mounted in fine gold.
¹⁸ Coral and jasper are worthless in trying
to get it.
The price of wisdom is far above
rubies.
¹⁹ Precious peridot from Ethiopia* cannot
be exchanged for it.
It's worth more than the purest gold.

²⁰ "But do people know where to find
wisdom?
Where can they find understanding?
²¹ It is hidden from the eyes of all
humanity.
Even the sharp-eyed birds in the sky
cannot discover it.
²² Destruction* and Death say,
'We've heard only rumors of where
wisdom can be found.'

²³ "God alone understands the way to
wisdom;
he knows where it can be found,
²⁴ for he looks throughout the whole earth
and sees everything under the
heavens.
²⁵ He decided how hard the winds should
blow
and how much rain should fall.
²⁶ He made the laws for the rain
and laid out a path for the lightning.
²⁷ Then he saw wisdom and evaluated it.
He set it in place and examined it
thoroughly.
²⁸ And this is what he says to all humanity:
'The fear of the Lord is true wisdom;
to forsake evil is real understanding.'"

29 Job Speaks of His Former Blessings

Job continued speaking:

² "I long for the years gone by
when God took care of me,
³ when he lit up the way before me
and I walked safely through the
darkness.
⁴ When I was in my prime,
God's friendship was felt in my home.
⁵ The Almighty was still with me,
and my children were around me.
⁶ My cows produced milk in abundance,
and my groves poured out streams of
olive oil.

⁷ "Those were the days when I went to the
city gate
and took my place among the honored
leaders.
⁸ The young stepped aside when they
saw me,
and even the aged rose in respect at
my coming.
⁹ The princes stood in silence
and put their hands over their mouths.
¹⁰ The highest officials of the city stood
quietly,
holding their tongues in respect.

¹¹ "All who heard me praised me.
All who saw me spoke well of me.
¹² For I assisted the poor in their need
and the orphans who required help.
¹³ I helped those without hope, and they
blessed me.
And I caused the widows' hearts to
sing for joy.
¹⁴ Everything I did was honest.
Righteousness covered me like a robe,
and I wore justice like a turban.
¹⁵ I served as eyes for the blind
and feet for the lame.
¹⁶ I was a father to the poor
and assisted strangers who needed help.
¹⁷ I broke the jaws of godless oppressors
and plucked their victims from their
teeth.

¹⁸ "I thought, 'Surely I will die surrounded
by my family
after a long, good life.*

28:19 Hebrew *from Cush.*   28:22 Hebrew *Abaddon.*   29:18 Hebrew *after I have counted my days like sand.*

¹⁹ For I am like a tree whose roots reach
  the water,
  whose branches are refreshed with the
  dew.
²⁰ New honors are constantly bestowed
  on me,
  and my strength is continually
  renewed.'

²¹ "Everyone listened to my advice.
  They were silent as they waited for me
  to speak.
²² And after I spoke, they had nothing to
  add,
  for my counsel satisfied them.
²³ They longed for me to speak as people
  long for rain.
  They drank my words like a refreshing
  spring rain.
²⁴ When they were discouraged, I smiled at
  them.
  My look of approval was precious to
  them.
²⁵ Like a chief, I told them what to do.
  I lived like a king among his troops
  and comforted those who mourned.

30 Job Speaks of His Anguish

¹ "But now I am mocked by people
  younger than I,
  by young men whose fathers are not
  worthy to run with my sheepdogs.
² A lot of good they are to me—
  those worn-out wretches!
³ They are gaunt with hunger
  and flee to the deserts,
  to desolate and gloomy wastelands.
⁴ They pluck wild greens from among the
  bushes
  and eat from the roots of broom trees.
⁵ They are driven from human society,
  and people shout at them as if they
  were thieves.
⁶ So now they live in frightening ravines,
  in caves and among the rocks.
⁷ They sound like animals howling among
  the bushes,
  huddled together beneath the nettles.
⁸ They are nameless fools,
  outcasts from society.

⁹ "And now they mock me with vulgar
  songs!
  They taunt me!

¹⁰ They despise me and won't come near me,
  except to spit in my face.
¹¹ For God has cut my bowstring.
  He has humbled me,
  so they have thrown off all restraint.
¹² These outcasts oppose me to my face.
  They send me sprawling
  and lay traps in my path.
¹³ They block my road
  and do everything they can to
  destroy me.
  They know I have no one to help me.
¹⁴ They come at me from all directions.
  They jump on me when I am down.
¹⁵ I live in terror now.
  My honor has blown away in the wind,
  and my prosperity has vanished like a
  cloud.

¹⁶ "And now my life seeps away.
  Depression haunts my days.
¹⁷ At night my bones are filled with pain,
  which gnaws at me relentlessly.
¹⁸ With a strong hand, God grabs my shirt.
  He grips me by the collar of my coat.
¹⁹ He has thrown me into the mud.
  I'm nothing more than dust and ashes.

²⁰ "I cry to you, O God, but you don't
  answer.
  I stand before you, but you don't even
  look.
²¹ You have become cruel toward me.
  You use your power to persecute me.
²² You throw me into the whirlwind
  and destroy me in the storm.
²³ And I know you are sending me to my
  death—
  the destination of all who live.

²⁴ "Surely no one would turn against the
  needy
  when they cry for help in their trouble.
²⁵ Did I not weep for those in trouble?
  Was I not deeply grieved for the
  needy?
²⁶ So I looked for good, but evil came
  instead.
  I waited for the light, but darkness fell.
²⁷ My heart is troubled and restless.
  Days of suffering torment me.
²⁸ I walk in gloom, without sunlight.
  I stand in the public square and cry
  for help.

²⁹ Instead, I am considered a brother to jackals
  and a companion to owls.
³⁰ My skin has turned dark,
  and my bones burn with fever.
³¹ My harp plays sad music,
  and my flute accompanies those who weep.

31 Job's Final Protest of Innocence

¹ "I made a covenant with my eyes
  not to look with lust at a young woman.
² For what has God above chosen for us?
  What is our inheritance from the Almighty on high?
³ Isn't it calamity for the wicked
  and misfortune for those who do evil?
⁴ Doesn't he see everything I do
  and every step I take?

⁵ "Have I lied to anyone
  or deceived anyone?
⁶ Let God weigh me on the scales of justice,
  for he knows my integrity.
⁷ If I have strayed from his pathway,
  or if my heart has lusted for what my eyes have seen,
  or if I am guilty of any other sin,
⁸ then let someone else eat the crops I have planted.
  Let all that I have planted be uprooted.

⁹ "If my heart has been seduced by a woman,
  or if I have lusted for my neighbor's wife,
¹⁰ then let my wife belong to* another man;
  let other men sleep with her.
¹¹ For lust is a shameful sin,
  a crime that should be punished.
¹² It is a fire that burns all the way to hell.*
  It would wipe out everything I own.

¹³ "If I have been unfair to my male or female servants
  when they brought their complaints to me,
¹⁴ how could I face God?
  What could I say when he questioned me?

¹⁵ For God created both me and my servants.
  He created us both in the womb.

¹⁶ "Have I refused to help the poor,
  or crushed the hopes of widows?
¹⁷ Have I been stingy with my food
  and refused to share it with orphans?
¹⁸ No, from childhood I have cared for orphans like a father,
  and all my life I have cared for widows.
¹⁹ Whenever I saw the homeless without clothes
  and the needy with nothing to wear,
²⁰ did they not praise me
  for providing wool clothing to keep them warm?

²¹ "If I raised my hand against an orphan,
  knowing the judges would take my side,
²² then let my shoulder be wrenched out of place!
  Let my arm be torn from its socket!
²³ That would be better than facing God's judgment.
  For if the majesty of God opposes me, what hope is there?

²⁴ "Have I put my trust in money
  or felt secure because of my gold?
²⁵ Have I gloated about my wealth
  and all that I own?

²⁶ "Have I looked at the sun shining in the skies,
  or the moon walking down its silver pathway,
²⁷ and been secretly enticed in my heart
  to throw kisses at them in worship?
²⁸ If so, I should be punished by the judges,
  for it would mean I had denied the God of heaven.

²⁹ "Have I ever rejoiced when disaster struck my enemies,
  or become excited when harm came their way?
³⁰ No, I have never sinned by cursing anyone
  or by asking for revenge.

³¹ "My servants have never said,
  'He let others go hungry.'

31:10 Hebrew *grind for*. **31:12** Hebrew *to Abaddon*.

³² I have never turned away a stranger
   but have opened my doors to
      everyone.

³³ "Have I tried to hide my sins like other
      people do,
   concealing my guilt in my heart?

³⁴ Have I feared the crowd
   or the contempt of the masses,
   so that I kept quiet and stayed
      indoors?

³⁵ "If only someone would listen to me!
   Look, I will sign my name to my
      defense.
   Let the Almighty answer me.
   Let my accuser write out the charges
      against me.

³⁶ I would face the accusation proudly.
   I would wear it like a crown.

³⁷ For I would tell him exactly what I have
      done.
   I would come before him like a prince.

³⁸ "If my land accuses me
   and all its furrows cry out together,

³⁹ or if I have stolen its crops
   or murdered its owners,

⁴⁰ then let thistles grow on that land
      instead of wheat,
   and weeds instead of barley."

Job's words are ended.

32 Elihu Responds to Job's Friends

Job's three friends refused to reply further to him because he kept insisting on his innocence. ²Then Elihu son of Barakel the Buzite, of the clan of Ram, became angry. He was angry because Job refused to admit that he had sinned and that God was right in punishing him. ³He was also angry with Job's three friends, for they made God* appear to be wrong by their inability to answer Job's arguments. ⁴Elihu had waited for the others to speak to Job because they were older than he. ⁵But when he saw that they had no further reply, he spoke out angrily. ⁶Elihu son of Barakel the Buzite said,

"I am young and you are old,
   so I held back from telling you what I
      think.

⁷ I thought, 'Those who are older should
      speak,
   for wisdom comes with age.'

⁸ But there is a spirit* within people,
   the breath of the Almighty within them,
   that makes them intelligent.

⁹ Sometimes the elders are not wise.
   Sometimes the aged do not
      understand justice.

¹⁰ So listen to me,
   and let me tell you what I think.

¹¹ "I have waited all this time,
   listening very carefully to your
      arguments,
   listening to you grope for words.

¹² I have listened,
   but not one of you has refuted Job
   or answered his arguments.

¹³ And don't tell me, 'He is too wise for us.
   Only God can convince him.'

¹⁴ If Job had been arguing with me,
   I would not answer with your kind of
      logic!

¹⁵ You sit there baffled,
   with nothing more to say.

¹⁶ Should I continue to wait, now that you
      are silent?
   Must I also remain silent?

¹⁷ No, I will say my piece.
   I will speak my mind.

¹⁸ For I am full of pent-up words,
   and the spirit within me urges me on.

¹⁹ I am like a cask of wine without a vent,
   like a new wineskin ready to burst!

²⁰ I must speak to find relief,
   so let me give my answers.

²¹ I won't play favorites
   or try to flatter anyone.

²² For if I tried flattery,
   my Creator would soon destroy me.

33 Elihu Presents His Case against Job

¹ "Listen to my words, Job;
   pay attention to what I have to say.

² Now that I have begun to speak,
   let me continue.

³ I speak with all sincerity;
   I speak the truth.

⁴ For the Spirit of God has made me,
   and the breath of the Almighty gives
      me life.

32:3 As in ancient Hebrew scribal tradition; the Masoretic Text reads *Job*. **32:8** Or *Spirit*; also in 32:18.

5 Answer me, if you can;
    make your case and take your stand.
6 Look, you and I both belong to God.
    I, too, was formed from clay.
7 So you don't need to be afraid of me.
    I won't come down hard on you.

8 "You have spoken in my hearing,
    and I have heard your very words.
9 You said, 'I am pure; I am without sin;
    I am innocent; I have no guilt.
10 God is picking a quarrel with me,
    and he considers me his enemy.
11 He puts my feet in the stocks
    and watches my every move.'

12 "But you are wrong, and I will show you
        why.
    For God is greater than any human
        being.
13 So why are you bringing a charge against
        him?
    Why say he does not respond to
        people's complaints?
14 For God speaks again and again,
    though people do not recognize it.
15 He speaks in dreams, in visions of the
        night,
    when deep sleep falls on people
        as they lie in their beds.
16 He whispers in their ears
    and terrifies them with warnings.
17 He makes them turn from doing wrong;
    he keeps them from pride.
18 He protects them from the grave,
    from crossing over the river of death.

19 "Or God disciplines people with pain on
        their sickbeds,
    with ceaseless aching in their bones.
20 They lose their appetite
    for even the most delicious food.
21 Their flesh wastes away,
    and their bones stick out.
22 They are at death's door;
    the angels of death wait for them.

23 "But if an angel from heaven appears—
    a special messenger to intercede for a
        person
    and declare that he is upright—
24 he will be gracious and say,
    'Rescue him from the grave,
    for I have found a ransom for his life.'

25 Then his body will become as healthy as
        a child's,
    firm and youthful again.
26 When he prays to God,
    he will be accepted.
    And God will receive him with joy
        and restore him to good standing.
27 He will declare to his friends,
    'I sinned and twisted the truth,
        but it was not worth it.*
28 God rescued me from the grave,
    and now my life is filled with light.'

29 "Yes, God does these things
    again and again for people.
30 He rescues them from the grave
    so they may enjoy the light of life.
31 Mark this well, Job. Listen to me,
    for I have more to say.
32 But if you have anything to say, go
        ahead.
    Speak, for I am anxious to see you
        justified.
33 But if not, then listen to me.
    Keep silent and I will teach you
        wisdom!"

34 Elihu Accuses Job of Arrogance
Then Elihu said:

2 "Listen to me, you wise men.
    Pay attention, you who have
        knowledge.
3 Job said, 'The ear tests the words it hears
    just as the mouth distinguishes
        between foods.'
4 So let us discern for ourselves what is
        right;
    let us learn together what is good.
5 For Job also said, 'I am innocent,
    but God has taken away my rights.
6 I am innocent, but they call me a liar.
    My suffering is incurable, though I
        have not sinned.'

7 "Tell me, has there ever been a man like
        Job,
    with his thirst for irreverent talk?
8 He chooses evil people as companions.
    He spends his time with wicked men.
9 He has even said, 'Why waste time
    trying to please God?'

33:27 Greek version reads *but he [God] did not punish me as my sin deserved.*

10 "Listen to me, you who have
    understanding.
        Everyone knows that God doesn't sin!
        The Almighty can do no wrong.
11 He repays people according to their
    deeds.
        He treats people as they deserve.
12 Truly, God will not do wrong.
        The Almighty will not twist justice.
13 Did someone else put the world in his
    care?
        Who set the whole world in place?
14 If God were to take back his spirit
        and withdraw his breath,
15 all life would cease,
        and humanity would turn again to
        dust.

16 "Now listen to me if you are wise.
        Pay attention to what I say.
17 Could God govern if he hated justice?
        Are you going to condemn the
        almighty judge?
18 For he says to kings, 'You are wicked,'
        and to nobles, 'You are unjust.'
19 He doesn't care how great a person
        may be,
        and he pays no more attention to the
        rich than to the poor.
        He made them all.
20 In a moment they die.
        In the middle of the night they pass
        away;
        the mighty are removed without
        human hand.

21 "For God watches how people live;
        he sees everything they do.
22 No darkness is thick enough
        to hide the wicked from his eyes.
23 We don't set the time
        when we will come before God in
        judgment.
24 He brings the mighty to ruin without
        asking anyone,
        and he sets up others in their place.
25 He knows what they do,
        and in the night he overturns and
        destroys them.
26 He strikes them down because they are
        wicked,
        doing it openly for all to see.
27 For they turned away from following
        him.

They have no respect for any of his
        ways.
28 They cause the poor to cry out, catching
        God's attention.
        He hears the cries of the needy.
29 But if he chooses to remain quiet,
        who can criticize him?
        When he hides his face, no one can find
        him,
        whether an individual or a nation.
30 He prevents the godless from ruling
        so they cannot be a snare to the
        people.

31 "Why don't people say to God, 'I have
        sinned,
        but I will sin no more'?
32 Or 'I don't know what evil I have done—
        tell me.
        If I have done wrong, I will stop at
        once'?

33 "Must God tailor his justice to your
        demands?
        But you have rejected him!
        The choice is yours, not mine.
        Go ahead, share your wisdom with us.
34 After all, bright people will tell me,
        and wise people will hear me say,
35 'Job speaks out of ignorance;
        his words lack insight.'
36 Job, you deserve the maximum penalty
        for the wicked way you have talked.
37 For you have added rebellion to your sin;
        you show no respect,
        and you speak many angry words
        against God."

35 Elihu Reminds Job of God's Justice
Then Elihu said:

2 "Do you think it is right for you to claim,
        'I am righteous before God'?
3 For you also ask, 'What's in it for me?
        What's the use of living a righteous
        life?'

4 "I will answer you
        and all your friends, too.
5 Look up into the sky,
        and see the clouds high above you.
6 If you sin, how does that affect God?
        Even if you sin again and again,
        what effect will it have on him?

⁷ If you are good, is this some great gift to
  him?
    What could you possibly give him?
⁸ No, your sins affect only people like
  yourself,
    and your good deeds also affect only
    humans.

⁹ "People cry out when they are
  oppressed.
    They groan beneath the power of the
    mighty.
¹⁰ Yet they don't ask, 'Where is God my
  Creator,
    the one who gives songs in the night?
¹¹ Where is the one who makes us smarter
  than the animals
    and wiser than the birds of the sky?'
¹² And when they cry out, God does not
  answer
    because of their pride.
¹³ But it is wrong to say God doesn't listen,
    to say the Almighty isn't concerned.
¹⁴ You say you can't see him,
    but he will bring justice if you will only
    wait.*
¹⁵ You say he does not respond to sinners
  with anger
    and is not greatly concerned about
    wickedness.*
¹⁶ But you are talking nonsense, Job.
    You have spoken like a fool."

36 Elihu continued speaking:

² "Let me go on, and I will show you the
  truth.
    For I have not finished defending God!
³ I will present profound arguments
    for the righteousness of my Creator.
⁴ I am telling you nothing but the truth,
    for I am a man of great knowledge.

⁵ "God is mighty, but he does not despise
  anyone!
    He is mighty in both power and
    understanding.
⁶ He does not let the wicked live
    but gives justice to the afflicted.
⁷ He never takes his eyes off the innocent,

but he sets them on thrones with
  kings
    and exalts them forever.
⁸ If they are bound in chains
    and caught up in a web of trouble,
⁹ he shows them the reason.
    He shows them their sins of pride.
¹⁰ He gets their attention
    and commands that they turn from
    evil.
¹¹ "If they listen and obey God,
    they will be blessed with prosperity
    throughout their lives.
    All their years will be pleasant.
¹² But if they refuse to listen to him,
    they will be killed by the sword*
    and die from lack of understanding.
¹³ For the godless are full of resentment.
    Even when he punishes them,
    they refuse to cry out to him for help.
¹⁴ They die when they are young,
    after wasting their lives in immoral
    living.
¹⁵ But by means of their suffering, he
  rescues those who suffer.
    For he gets their attention through
    adversity.

¹⁶ "God is leading you away from danger,
  Job,
    to a place free from distress.
    He is setting your table with the best
    food.
¹⁷ But you are obsessed with whether the
  godless will be judged.
    Don't worry, judgment and justice will
    be upheld.
¹⁸ But watch out, or you may be seduced
  by wealth.*
    Don't let yourself be bribed into sin.
¹⁹ Could all your wealth*
    or all your mighty efforts
    keep you from distress?
²⁰ Do not long for the cover of night,
    for that is when people will be
    destroyed.*
²¹ Be on guard! Turn back from evil,
    for God sent this suffering
    to keep you from a life of evil.

35:13-14 These verses can also be translated as follows: ¹³*Indeed, God doesn't listen to their empty plea; / the Almighty is not concerned. /* ¹⁴*How
much less will he listen when you say you don't see him, / and that your case is before him and you're waiting for justice.* **35:15** As in Greek and
Latin versions; the meaning of this Hebrew word is uncertain. **36:12** Or *they will cross the river* [of death]. **36:18** Or *But don't let your anger
lead you to mockery.* **36:19** Or *Could all your cries for help.* **36:16-20** The meaning of the Hebrew in this passage is uncertain.

Elihu Reminds Job of God's Power

22 "Look, God is all-powerful.
  Who is a teacher like him?
23 No one can tell him what to do,
  or say to him, 'You have done wrong.'
24 Instead, glorify his mighty works,
  singing songs of praise.
25 Everyone has seen these things,
  though only from a distance.

26 "Look, God is greater than we can
    understand.
  His years cannot be counted.
27 He draws up the water vapor
  and then distills it into rain.
28 The rain pours down from the clouds,
  and everyone benefits.
29 Who can understand the spreading of
    the clouds
  and the thunder that rolls forth from
    heaven?
30 See how he spreads the lightning around
    him
  and how it lights up the depths of the
    sea.
31 By these mighty acts he nourishes* the
    people,
  giving them food in abundance.
32 He fills his hands with lightning bolts
  and hurls each at its target.
33 The thunder announces his presence;
  the storm announces his indignant
    anger.*

37 ¹ "My heart pounds as I think of
    this.
  It trembles within me.
2 Listen carefully to the thunder of God's
    voice
  as it rolls from his mouth.
3 It rolls across the heavens,
  and his lightning flashes in every
    direction.
4 Then comes the roaring of the thunder—
  the tremendous voice of his majesty.
  He does not restrain it when he speaks.
5 God's voice is glorious in the thunder.
  We can't even imagine the greatness of
    his power.

6 "He directs the snow to fall on the earth
  and tells the rain to pour down.

7 Then everyone stops working
  so they can watch his power.
8 The wild animals take cover
  and stay inside their dens.
9 The stormy wind comes from its chamber,
  and the driving winds bring the cold.
10 God's breath sends the ice,
  freezing wide expanses of water.
11 He loads the clouds with moisture,
  and they flash with his lightning.
12 The clouds churn about at his direction.
  They do whatever he commands
    throughout the earth.
13 He makes these things happen either to
    punish people
  or to show his unfailing love.

14 "Pay attention to this, Job.
  Stop and consider the wonderful
    miracles of God!
15 Do you know how God controls the
    storm
  and causes the lightning to flash from
    his clouds?
16 Do you understand how he moves the
    clouds
  with wonderful perfection and skill?
17 When you are sweltering in your clothes
  and the south wind dies down and
    everything is still,
18 he makes the skies reflect the heat like a
    bronze mirror.
  Can you do that?

19 "So teach the rest of us what to say to
    God.
  We are too ignorant to make our own
    arguments.
20 Should God be notified that I want to
    speak?
  Can people even speak when they are
    confused?*
21 We cannot look at the sun,
  for it shines brightly in the sky
  when the wind clears away the clouds.
22 So also, golden splendor comes from the
    mountain of God.*
  He is clothed in dazzling splendor.
23 We cannot imagine the power of the
    Almighty;
  but even though he is just and righteous,
  he does not destroy us.

36:31 Or he governs.   36:33 Or even the cattle know when a storm is coming. The meaning of the Hebrew is uncertain.   37:20 Or speak without being swallowed up?   37:22 Or from the north; or from the abode.

²⁴ No wonder people everywhere fear him.
    All who are wise show him
        reverence."

38 The Lord Challenges Job

Then the Lord answered Job from the whirlwind:

² "Who is this that questions my wisdom
    with such ignorant words?
³ Brace yourself like a man,
    because I have some questions for
        you,
    and you must answer them.

⁴ "Where were you when I laid the
    foundations of the earth?
    Tell me, if you know so much.
⁵ Who determined its dimensions
    and stretched out the surveying line?
⁶ What supports its foundations,
    and who laid its cornerstone
⁷ as the morning stars sang together
    and all the angels* shouted for joy?

⁸ "Who kept the sea inside its boundaries
    as it burst from the womb,
⁹ and as I clothed it with clouds
    and wrapped it in thick darkness?
¹⁰ For I locked it behind barred gates,
    limiting its shores.
¹¹ I said, 'This far and no farther will you
        come.
    Here your proud waves must stop!'

¹² "Have you ever commanded the
        morning to appear
    and caused the dawn to rise in the
        east?
¹³ Have you made daylight spread to the
        ends of the earth,
    to bring an end to the night's
        wickedness?
¹⁴ As the light approaches,
    the earth takes shape like clay pressed
        beneath a seal;
    it is robed in brilliant colors.*
¹⁵ The light disturbs the wicked
    and stops the arm that is raised in
        violence.

¹⁶ "Have you explored the springs from
        which the seas come?
    Have you explored their depths?

¹⁷ Do you know where the gates of death
        are located?
    Have you seen the gates of utter gloom?
¹⁸ Do you realize the extent of the earth?
    Tell me about it if you know!

¹⁹ "Where does light come from,
    and where does darkness go?
²⁰ Can you take each to its home?
    Do you know how to get there?
²¹ But of course you know all this!
    For you were born before it was all
        created,
    and you are so very experienced!

²² "Have you visited the storehouses of the
        snow
    or seen the storehouses of hail?
²³ (I have reserved them as weapons for the
        time of trouble,
    for the day of battle and war.)
²⁴ Where is the path to the source of light?
    Where is the home of the east wind?

²⁵ "Who created a channel for the torrents
        of rain?
    Who laid out the path for the
        lightning?
²⁶ Who makes the rain fall on barren land,
    in a desert where no one lives?
²⁷ Who sends rain to satisfy the parched
        ground
    and make the tender grass spring up?

²⁸ "Does the rain have a father?
    Who gives birth to the dew?
²⁹ Who is the mother of the ice?
    Who gives birth to the frost from the
        heavens?
³⁰ For the water turns to ice as hard as
        rock,
    and the surface of the water freezes.

³¹ "Can you direct the movement of the
        stars—
    binding the cluster of the Pleiades
    or loosening the cords of Orion?
³² Can you direct the sequence of the
        seasons
    or guide the Bear with her cubs across
        the heavens?
³³ Do you know the laws of the universe?
    Can you use them to regulate the
        earth?

38:7 Hebrew *the sons of God.*   **38:14** Or *its features stand out like folds in a robe.*

34 "Can you shout to the clouds
   and make it rain?
35 Can you make lightning appear
   and cause it to strike as you direct?
36 Who gives intuition to the heart
   and instinct to the mind?
37 Who is wise enough to count all the
   clouds?
   Who can tilt the water jars of heaven
38 when the parched ground is dry
   and the soil has hardened into clods?

39 "Can you stalk prey for a lioness
   and satisfy the young lions' appetites
40 as they lie in their dens
   or crouch in the thicket?
41 Who provides food for the ravens
   when their young cry out to God
   and wander about in hunger?

39 The Lord's Challenge Continues

1 "Do you know when the wild
   goats give birth?
   Have you watched as deer are born in
   the wild?
2 Do you know how many months they
   carry their young?
   Are you aware of the time of their
   delivery?
3 They crouch down to give birth to their
   young
   and deliver their offspring.
4 Their young grow up in the open fields,
   then leave home and never return.

5 "Who gives the wild donkey its
   freedom?
   Who untied its ropes?
6 I have placed it in the wilderness;
   its home is the wasteland.
7 It hates the noise of the city
   and has no driver to shout at it.
8 The mountains are its pastureland,
   where it searches for every blade of
   grass.

9 "Will the wild ox consent to being
   tamed?
   Will it spend the night in your stall?
10 Can you hitch a wild ox to a plow?
   Will it plow a field for you?
11 Given its strength, can you trust it?
   Can you leave and trust the ox to do
   your work?

12 Can you rely on it to bring home your
   grain
   and deliver it to your threshing floor?

13 "The ostrich flaps her wings grandly,
   but they are no match for the feathers
   of the stork.
14 She lays her eggs on top of the earth,
   letting them be warmed in the dust.
15 She doesn't worry that a foot might
   crush them
   or a wild animal might destroy them.
16 She is harsh toward her young,
   as if they were not her own.
   She doesn't care if they die.
17 For God has deprived her of wisdom.
   He has given her no understanding.
18 But whenever she jumps up to run,
   she passes the swiftest horse with its
   rider.

19 "Have you given the horse its strength
   or clothed its neck with a flowing
   mane?
20 Did you give it the ability to leap like a
   locust?
   Its majestic snorting is terrifying!
21 It paws the earth and rejoices in its
   strength
   when it charges out to battle.
22 It laughs at fear and is unafraid.
   It does not run from the sword.
23 The arrows rattle against it,
   and the spear and javelin flash.
24 It paws the ground fiercely
   and rushes forward into battle when
   the ram's horn blows.
25 It snorts at the sound of the horn.
   It senses the battle in the distance.
   It quivers at the captain's commands
   and the noise of battle.

26 "Is it your wisdom that makes the hawk
   soar
   and spread its wings toward the
   south?
27 Is it at your command that the eagle
   rises
   to the heights to make its nest?
28 It lives on the cliffs,
   making its home on a distant, rocky
   crag.
29 From there it hunts its prey,
   keeping watch with piercing eyes.

Choosing Hope

JOB 38:25-33

I t's 2 degrees outside, and my mailbox is overflowing with lilies and tomatoes. Pictures of them, that is. Seed catalogs.

I love how they arrive in the dead of winter—so much promise for just pennies a packet. In all the catalogs, warm colors proliferate: reds, oranges, yellows. A kaleidoscope of hot peppers on one page, zinnias like fireworks on the next. I soak up colors, the butter yellows of sweet corn, the bright pinks of impatiens, the deep greens of basil.

Outside, it's difficult to think about planting anything. Fourteen inches of snow have obliterated all signs of my backyard garden. My bird feeders are empty and silent. Steam curls up invitingly from the heated birdbath, but there are no takers.

Planting a garden and caring for it is a spiritual act of faith for me. These seed catalogs invite me to dream and hope, even in the dead of winter. I can dream of planting flowers to attract butterflies or hummingbirds. I can conjure up a garden of herbs specifically for tea. I might recreate the tallgrass prairie or a wildflower meadow on my little plot or grow paste tomatoes to make special Italian dishes. Each page is another possibility.

When you watch a seed crack the earth, put out leaves, then blossom and fruit into food for your family, it gives you hope. When you see a dry husk sprout and become a beautiful pinwheel of color, it prompts you to dream. A garden is an act of defiance; a determination to focus on new life and beauty in the midst of a world in crisis. It's a blow struck for believing things will change for the better.

When Job wondered why bad things happened, God answered his questions with a tour through the wonders of nature: "Who created a channel for the torrents of rain? Who laid out the path for the lightning? . . . Who sends rain to satisfy the parched ground and make the tender grass spring up? . . . Can you direct the movement of the stars? . . . Can you direct the sequence of the seasons? . . . Do you know the laws of the universe? Can you use them to regulate the earth?" (38:25-33). The God who created all these wonders is the God I can go to when I'm afraid.

I can't control a plummeting economy, unrest in the Middle East, or the injuries and illnesses of loved ones. I don't understand the injustices and calamities of the world, trumpeted in bold newspaper headlines each morning, but I know the God who loves me—and who made all the wonders of the outdoors—is holding me close to his heart. I can choose my response: "Where do I put my hope? My only hope is in you" (Psalm 39:7). I can confidently cry out, "When I am afraid, I will put my trust in you" (56:3).

I'm also reminded of Matthew 6:27: "Can all your worries add a single moment to your life?" I don't want my life to be defined by worry and fear; I don't want my garden to be choked with "weeds." I want to put down deep roots of faith, to grow and to bloom, and to reach toward sunlight and warmth. I want to plant a garden for the future, one that is seeded with contentment, joy, and hope for what might be.

I make out my seed list, adding some flowers and herbs here, crossing off a few vegetables there. Drawing the outline of where the new roses will go, mentally shifting the iris to another spot by the pond. I can't shift my worries so easily, but each time I choose to plan a garden, it brings me one step closer. I dream, and I choose to believe . . . and to hope.

—*Cindy Crosby*

For more on faith, see reading at Psalm 42.

³⁰ Its young gulp down blood.
 Where there's a carcass, there you'll
  find it."

40

Then the LORD said to Job,

² "Do you still want to argue with the
   Almighty?
 You are God's critic, but do you have
  the answers?"

Job Responds to the LORD

³ Then Job replied to the LORD,

⁴ "I am nothing—how could I ever find
   the answers?
 I will cover my mouth with my hand.
⁵ I have said too much already.
 I have nothing more to say."

The LORD Challenges Job Again

⁶ Then the LORD answered Job from the
whirlwind:

⁷ "Brace yourself like a man,
  because I have some questions for
   you,
  and you must answer them.

⁸ "Will you discredit my justice
  and condemn me just to prove you are
   right?
⁹ Are you as strong as God?
  Can you thunder with a voice like his?
¹⁰ All right, put on your glory and
   splendor,
  your honor and majesty.
¹¹ Give vent to your anger.
  Let it overflow against the proud.
¹² Humiliate the proud with a glance;
  walk on the wicked where they stand.
¹³ Bury them in the dust.
  Imprison them in the world of the dead.
¹⁴ Then even I would praise you,
  for your own strength would save you.

¹⁵ "Take a look at Behemoth,*
  which I made, just as I made you.
  It eats grass like an ox.
¹⁶ See its powerful loins
  and the muscles of its belly.

¹⁷ Its tail is as strong as a cedar.
  The sinews of its thighs are knit tightly
   together.
¹⁸ Its bones are tubes of bronze.
  Its limbs are bars of iron.
¹⁹ It is a prime example of God's
   handiwork,
  and only its Creator can threaten it.
²⁰ The mountains offer it their best food,
  where all the wild animals play.
²¹ It lies under the lotus plants,*
  hidden by the reeds in the marsh.
²² The lotus plants give it shade
  among the willows beside the stream.
²³ It is not disturbed by the raging river,
  not concerned when the swelling
   Jordan rushes around it.
²⁴ No one can catch it off guard
  or put a ring in its nose and lead it
   away.

41

The LORD's Challenge Continues

¹* "Can you catch Leviathan* with a
   hook
  or put a noose around its jaw?
² Can you tie it with a rope through the
   nose
  or pierce its jaw with a spike?
³ Will it beg you for mercy
  or implore you for pity?
⁴ Will it agree to work for you,
  to be your slave for life?
⁵ Can you make it a pet like a bird,
  or give it to your little girls to play with?
⁶ Will merchants try to buy it
  to sell it in their shops?
⁷ Will its hide be hurt by spears
  or its head by a harpoon?
⁸ If you lay a hand on it,
  you will certainly remember the battle
   that follows.
  You won't try that again!
⁹* No, it is useless to try to capture it.
  The hunter who attempts it will be
   knocked down.
¹⁰ And since no one dares to disturb it,
  who then can stand up to me?
¹¹ Who has given me anything that I need
   to pay back?
  Everything under heaven is mine.

40:15 The identification of Behemoth is disputed, ranging from an earthly creature to a mythical sea monster in ancient literature.
40:21 Or *bramble bushes;* also in 40:22.   **41:1a** Verses 41:1-8 are numbered 40:25-32 in Hebrew text.   **41:1b** The identification of Leviathan is disputed, ranging from an earthly creature to a mythical sea monster in ancient literature.   **41:9** Verses 41:9-34 are numbered 41:1-26 in Hebrew text.

¹² "I want to emphasize Leviathan's
  limbs
  and its enormous strength and
  graceful form.
¹³ Who can strip off its hide,
  and who can penetrate its double layer
  of armor?*
¹⁴ Who could pry open its jaws?
  For its teeth are terrible!
¹⁵ Its scales are like rows of shields
  tightly sealed together.
¹⁶ They are so close together
  that no air can get between them.
¹⁷ Each scale sticks tight to the next.
  They interlock and cannot be
  penetrated.

¹⁸ "When it sneezes, it flashes light!
  Its eyes are like the red of dawn.
¹⁹ Lightning leaps from its mouth;
  flames of fire flash out.
²⁰ Smoke streams from its nostrils
  like steam from a pot heated over
  burning rushes.
²¹ Its breath would kindle coals,
  for flames shoot from its mouth.

²² "The tremendous strength in Leviathan's
  neck
  strikes terror wherever it goes.
²³ Its flesh is hard and firm
  and cannot be penetrated.
²⁴ Its heart is hard as rock,
  hard as a millstone.
²⁵ When it rises, the mighty are afraid,
  gripped by terror.
²⁶ No sword can stop it,
  no spear, dart, or javelin.
²⁷ Iron is nothing but straw to that
  creature,
  and bronze is like rotten wood.
²⁸ Arrows cannot make it flee.
  Stones shot from a sling are like bits
  of grass.
²⁹ Clubs are like a blade of grass,
  and it laughs at the swish of javelins.
³⁰ Its belly is covered with scales as sharp
  as glass.
  It plows up the ground as it drags
  through the mud.

³¹ "Leviathan makes the water boil with its
  commotion.

It stirs the depths like a pot of
  ointment.
³² The water glistens in its wake,
  making the sea look white.
³³ Nothing on earth is its equal,
  no other creature so fearless.
³⁴ Of all the creatures, it is the proudest.
  It is the king of beasts."

42 Job Responds to the LORD
Then Job replied to the LORD:

² "I know that you can do anything,
  and no one can stop you.
³ You asked, 'Who is this that questions
  my wisdom with such ignorance?'
  It is I—and I was talking about things I
  knew nothing about,
  things far too wonderful for me.
⁴ You said, 'Listen and I will speak!
  I have some questions for you,
  and you must answer them.'
⁵ I had only heard about you before,
  but now I have seen you with my own
  eyes.
⁶ I take back everything I said,
  and I sit in dust and ashes to show my
  repentance."

Conclusion: The LORD Blesses Job
⁷ After the LORD had finished speaking to
Job, he said to Eliphaz the Temanite: "I am
angry with you and your two friends, for
you have not spoken accurately about me,
as my servant Job has. ⁸ So take seven bulls
and seven rams and go to my servant Job
and offer a burnt offering for yourselves.
My servant Job will pray for you, and I will
accept his prayer on your behalf. I will not
treat you as you deserve, for you have not
spoken accurately about me, as my servant
Job has." ⁹ So Eliphaz the Temanite, Bildad
the Shuhite, and Zophar the Naamathite
did as the LORD commanded them, and the
LORD accepted Job's prayer.

¹⁰ When Job prayed for his friends, the
LORD restored his fortunes. In fact, the
LORD gave him twice as much as before!
¹¹ Then all his brothers, sisters, and former friends came and feasted with him
in his home. And they consoled him and
comforted him because of all the trials the

41:13 As in Greek version; Hebrew reads *its bridle?*

The Prayer of Quiet

JOB 42:1-5

Contemplation

Sometimes we come to God with much to say. Sometimes we come to him without words, unable to speak because of pain or turmoil in our lives. And sometimes we *choose* wordlessness; we turn to God in a prayer of silent focus on his presence, his truth. This is the essence of contemplative prayer.

Teresa of Avila called this "the prayer of quiet," saying it revives a "desolate and very dry" heart, leading the "servants of love" to a union with God that is like "rain that comes down abundantly from heaven to soak and saturate the whole garden" of the soul.

Another medieval Christian, the anonymous author of a classic work on contemplative prayer titled *The Cloud of Unknowing*, describes this type of prayer this way: "You only need a naked intent for God. When you long for him, that's enough. . . . Through God's grace, our minds can explore, understand, and reflect on creation and even on God's own works, but we can't think our way to God. That's why I'm willing to abandon everything I know, to love the one thing I cannot think. He can be loved, but not thought. By love, God can be embraced."

This ancient Christian discipline of listening in prayer, of contemplation, rather than speaking helps us learn to rest in and experience God's presence, as we build his "temple" in our hearts. There, in this holy sanctuary, we move beyond simple conversation with Christ to have deep communion with him. We hear and are healed by the eloquence of divine stillness, as John of the Cross says, "Silence is God's *first* language."

Writing as a Christian steeped in contemplative prayer, the tenth-century English Benedictine abbot Ælfric of Eynsham reminds us that such prayer is transformative: "The love that loves God is not idle. Instead, it is strong and works great things always. And if love isn't willing to work, then it isn't love." In contemplation we come to know the God of love better, and then, as Christ's friends—empowered by his Spirit—we become more loving ourselves.

—*Carmen Acevedo Butcher*

For more on contemplation, see reading at Psalm 8.

LORD had brought against him. And each of them brought him a gift of money* and a gold ring.

¹²So the LORD blessed Job in the second half of his life even more than in the beginning. For now he had 14,000 sheep, 6,000 camels, 1,000 teams of oxen, and 1,000 female donkeys. ¹³He also gave Job seven more sons and three more daughters. ¹⁴He named his first daughter Jemimah, the second Keziah, and the third Keren-happuch. ¹⁵In all the land no women were as lovely as the daughters of Job. And their father put them into his will along with their brothers.

¹⁶Job lived 140 years after that, living to see four generations of his children and grandchildren. ¹⁷Then he died, an old man who had lived a long, full life.

42:11 Hebrew *a kesitah;* the value or weight of the kesitah is no longer known.

Introduction to
Psalms

Background

Psalms is the songbook, or psalter, of the Bible. Unlike other books of the Old Testament, Psalms does not follow one continuous narrative. Instead, its poems and prayers capture many different moments in a believer's relationship with God.

King David wrote many of the psalms in response to events in his life (see, e.g., 18:1–50; 51:1–19) or to be performed in the temple. Other psalmists are mentioned, including Asaph, a priest who led the temple music service (50:1–23; 73:1–83:18), the sons of Korah, a guild of singers and composers (42:1–11; 44:1–49:20; 84:1–85:13; 87:1–7), Solomon (72:1–20; 127:1–5), Moses (90:1–17), Heman, a wise man (88:1–18), and Ethan, a wise man (89:1–52). These psalmists employ different types of verse and various literary devices: there are psalms to be accompanied by musical instruments; contemplative poems; alphabetical acrostics (37:1–40; 119:1–176); creation psalms (8:1–9; 19:1–14); an exodus account (78:1–72); psalms of penitence (6:1–10; 25:1–22; 32:1–11; 38:1–22; 51:1–19); pilgrimage psalms (120:1–134:3); and messianic psalms.

Message

The Book of Psalms lifts the veil of Old Testament narrative to reveal how God works in the inner life of his chosen people. Its themes range from praise to lament, war to peace, and from jubilation to judgment. The psalmists' pleas for God's deliverance, their impassioned cries for his vengeance, and their delight in his salvation seen and promised all illustrate what it means to be "after [God's] own heart" (1 Samuel 13:14).

Time

The Book of Psalms was composed and compiled through generations of Israel's history, over a period extending from the days of Moses to the rebuilding of the nation under Ezra (1410–430 B.C.). The outline given here is from early Hebrew manuscripts, which present the collection in five sections or "books."

Outline

Psalms

Book One (Psalms 1–41)

1 ¹ Oh, the joys of those who do not
    follow the advice of the wicked,
or stand around with sinners,
    or join in with mockers.
² But they delight in the law of the LORD,
    meditating on it day and night.
³ They are like trees planted along the riverbank,
    bearing fruit each season.
Their leaves never wither,
    and they prosper in all they do.

⁴ But not the wicked!
    They are like worthless chaff, scattered by the wind.
⁵ They will be condemned at the time of judgment.
    Sinners will have no place among the godly.
⁶ For the LORD watches over the path of the godly,
    but the path of the wicked leads to destruction.

2 ¹ Why are the nations so angry?
    Why do they waste their time with futile plans?
² The kings of the earth prepare for battle;
    the rulers plot together
against the LORD
    and against his anointed one.
³ "Let us break their chains," they cry,
    "and free ourselves from slavery to God."

⁴ But the one who rules in heaven laughs.
    The Lord scoffs at them.
⁵ Then in anger he rebukes them,
    terrifying them with his fierce fury.
⁶ For the Lord declares, "I have placed my chosen king on the throne
    in Jerusalem,* on my holy mountain."

⁷ The king proclaims the LORD's decree:
    "The LORD said to me, 'You are my son.*
    Today I have become your Father.*
⁸ Only ask, and I will give you the nations as your inheritance,
    the whole earth as your possession.
⁹ You will break* them with an iron rod
    and smash them like clay pots.'"

2:6 Hebrew *on Zion.*   **2:7a** Or *Son;* also in 2:12.   **2:7b** Or *Today I reveal you as my son.*   **2:9** Greek version reads *rule.*
Compare Rev 2:27.

Lectio Divina

PSALM 1

Scripture meditation has historically been called *lectio divina* or "sacred reading." It's a way of reverentially listening to God's Word, of diving deep into Scripture rather than skimming. In lectio divina, we experience joy as we delight in God's Word, meditating on it and fully immersing ourselves in it (Psalm 1:1–2). Lectio divina is a way of allowing the mind to "descend" into the heart, so that both mind and heart might be drawn into the deep love and goodness of God. It's like enjoying a lovingly prepared holiday meal at Grandmother's house as opposed to zipping through a drive-through restaurant before charging to the next errand.

To practice lectio divina, pick a Bible verse or short passage. Take your time and read the verse unrushed, over and over. You might want to memorize it or take the words with you everywhere on a slip of paper. The point is to keep the words in front of you and let the Lord speak to you. When a word or phrase from Scripture stands out, stay with it awhile. Pay attention to how it makes you feel. Sit with it. Let it lead you into quietness or simple contemplative prayer.

Or if you'd prefer a more formal approach, you could follow the pattern outlined for us in church history. In its classic form, lectio comprises four elements, although there are many variations with different wording and emphasis:
- *lectio* (reading with a listening spirit)
- *meditatio* (reflecting on what we are "hearing")
- *oratio* (praying in response to this hearing)
- *contemplatio* (contemplating what we will carry forward into our lives)

We can also refer to these basic elements of lectio as *listening, reflecting, praying,* and *obeying.* When these elements are combined—regardless of sequence, for they overlap and intermingle in a circular rather than a linear way—they lead our human spirit into a dynamic interaction with the Holy Spirit.

—*Richard J. Foster and Carmen Acevedo Butcher*

For more on Bible study and meditation, see reading at Psalm 19:7–10.

---

10 Now then, you kings, act wisely!
 Be warned, you rulers of the
 earth!
11 Serve the LORD with reverent fear,
 and rejoice with trembling.
12 Submit to God's royal son,* or he will
 become angry,
 and you will be destroyed in the midst
 of all your activities—
 for his anger flares up in an instant.
 But what joy for all who take refuge in
 him!

3 *A psalm of David, regarding the time David fled from his son Absalom.*

1 O LORD, I have so many enemies;
 so many are against me.
2 So many are saying,
 "God will never rescue him!"

*Interlude**

3 But you, O LORD, are a shield
 around me;
 you are my glory, the one who holds
 my head high.

2:12 The meaning of the Hebrew is uncertain. **3:2** Hebrew *Selah.* The meaning of this word is uncertain, though it is probably a musical or literary term. It is rendered *Interlude* throughout the Psalms.

⁴ I cried out to the LORD,
 and he answered me from his holy
  mountain. *Interlude*

⁵ I lay down and slept,
 yet I woke up in safety,
 for the LORD was watching over me.
⁶ I am not afraid of ten thousand enemies
 who surround me on every side.

⁷ Arise, O LORD!
 Rescue me, my God!
 Slap all my enemies in the face!
 Shatter the teeth of the wicked!
⁸ Victory comes from you, O LORD.
 May you bless your people. *Interlude*

4 *For the choir director: A psalm of
 David, to be accompanied by stringed
instruments.*

¹ Answer me when I call to you,
 O God who declares me innocent.
 Free me from my troubles.
 Have mercy on me and hear my
  prayer.

² How long will you people ruin my
  reputation?
 How long will you make groundless
  accusations?
 How long will you continue your lies?
   Interlude
³ You can be sure of this:
 The LORD set apart the godly for
  himself.
 The LORD will answer when I call to
  him.

⁴ Don't sin by letting anger control you.
 Think about it overnight and remain
  silent. *Interlude*
⁵ Offer sacrifices in the right spirit,
 and trust the LORD.

⁶ Many people say, "Who will show us
  better times?"
 Let your face smile on us, LORD.
⁷ You have given me greater joy
 than those who have abundant
  harvests of grain and new wine.
⁸ In peace I will lie down and sleep,
 for you alone, O LORD, will keep me
  safe.

5 *For the choir director: A psalm of
 David, to be accompanied by the flute.*

¹ O LORD, hear me as I pray;
 pay attention to my groaning.
² Listen to my cry for help, my King and
  my God,
 for I pray to no one but you.
³ Listen to my voice in the morning, LORD.
 Each morning I bring my requests to
  you and wait expectantly.

⁴ O God, you take no pleasure in
  wickedness;
 you cannot tolerate the sins of the
  wicked.
⁵ Therefore, the proud may not stand in
  your presence,
 for you hate all who do evil.
⁶ You will destroy those who tell lies.
 The LORD detests murderers and
  deceivers.

⁷ Because of your unfailing love, I can
  enter your house;
 I will worship at your Temple with
  deepest awe.
⁸ Lead me in the right path, O LORD,
 or my enemies will conquer me.
 Make your way plain for me to follow.

⁹ My enemies cannot speak a truthful
  word.
 Their deepest desire is to destroy
  others.
 Their talk is foul, like the stench from an
  open grave.
 Their tongues are filled with flattery.*
¹⁰ O God, declare them guilty.
 Let them be caught in their own traps.
 Drive them away because of their many
  sins,
 for they have rebelled against you.

¹¹ But let all who take refuge in you
  rejoice;
 let them sing joyful praises forever.
 Spread your protection over them,
 that all who love your name may be
  filled with joy.
¹² For you bless the godly, O LORD;
 you surround them with your shield
  of love.

5:9 Greek version reads *with lies.* Compare Rom 3:13.

6 For the choir director: A psalm of David, to be accompanied by an eight-stringed instrument.*

¹ O LORD, don't rebuke me in your anger
    or discipline me in your rage.
² Have compassion on me, LORD, for I am weak.
    Heal me, LORD, for my bones are in agony.
³ I am sick at heart.
    How long, O LORD, until you restore me?

⁴ Return, O LORD, and rescue me.
    Save me because of your unfailing love.
⁵ For the dead do not remember you.
    Who can praise you from the grave?*

⁶ I am worn out from sobbing.
    All night I flood my bed with weeping,
    drenching it with my tears.
⁷ My vision is blurred by grief;
    my eyes are worn out because of all my enemies.

⁸ Go away, all you who do evil,
    for the LORD has heard my weeping.
⁹ The LORD has heard my plea;
    the LORD will answer my prayer.
¹⁰ May all my enemies be disgraced and terrified.
    May they suddenly turn back in shame.

7 A psalm of David, which he sang to the LORD concerning Cush of the tribe of Benjamin.

¹ I come to you for protection, O LORD my God.
    Save me from my persecutors—
    rescue me!
² If you don't, they will maul me like a lion,
    tearing me to pieces with no one to rescue me.
³ O LORD my God, if I have done wrong
    or am guilty of injustice,
⁴ if I have betrayed a friend
    or plundered my enemy without cause,

⁵ then let my enemies capture me.
    Let them trample me into the ground
    and drag my honor in the dust.

Interlude

⁶ Arise, O LORD, in anger!
    Stand up against the fury of my enemies!
    Wake up, my God, and bring justice!
⁷ Gather the nations before you.
    Rule over them from on high.
⁸   The LORD judges the nations.
Declare me righteous, O LORD,
    for I am innocent, O Most High!
⁹ End the evil of those who are wicked,
    and defend the righteous.
For you look deep within the mind and heart,
    O righteous God.

¹⁰ God is my shield,
    saving those whose hearts are true and right.
¹¹ God is an honest judge.
    He is angry with the wicked every day.
¹² If a person does not repent,
    God* will sharpen his sword;
    he will bend and string his bow.
¹³ He will prepare his deadly weapons
    and shoot his flaming arrows.
¹⁴ The wicked conceive evil;
    they are pregnant with trouble
    and give birth to lies.
¹⁵ They dig a deep pit to trap others,
    then fall into it themselves.
¹⁶ The trouble they make for others
    backfires on them.
    The violence they plan falls on their own heads.

¹⁷ I will thank the LORD because he is just;
    I will sing praise to the name of the LORD Most High.

8 For the choir director: A psalm of David, to be accompanied by a stringed instrument.*

¹ O LORD, our Lord, your majestic name fills the earth!
    Your glory is higher than the heavens.

6:TITLE Hebrew *with stringed instruments; according to the sheminith.* 6:5 Hebrew *from Sheol?* 7:12 Hebrew *he.* 8:TITLE Hebrew *according to the gittith.*

Back to the Garden?

PSALM 8

Contemplation

"When my soul is dry and thirsty and my body tense from too much desk work, airports, and boardrooms, an infallible solution is garden work," writes Luci Shaw in *Water My Soul*.

In this contemplative time of quiet labor in dirt and sun, Shaw experiences renewed spiritual sustenance. When she's done gardening, she finds that "God has rehydrated, *rejuiced* my spirit, and my heart sings the song of the Gardener."

For me too the yard and garden become a spiritual retreat of sorts. Time spent watching dragonflies light on the arrowhead leaves in my tiny pond is time set apart for solitude. Planting prairie plants is contemplation. Reading on the porch behind a screen of old roses is occasion for self-examination. And whacking my dandelion-riddled lawn with my push mower is sweaty meditation.

Orthodox theologian Vigen Guroian writes in *The Fragrance of God* that the act of gardening brings him closer to God. "I spend more time on my knees in the garden than in holy sanctuary." In the garden we encounter symbols that point us to God and that "testify not only to [God's] existence but also to the goodness of his Creation." The raw beauty we encounter can transform us. Gardening can be true soul work, Guroian writes; as we garden, in quietness with God and colaboring with him in his created world, we're practicing an act of spiritual formation.

Let's dig deep into the dirt. Nurture seedlings. Prune vines. Stop and smell the proverbial roses. Sit in the shade of a beech tree and admire the backlighting of the leaves. Let's learn the names of the birds that come to our feeders, the wildflowers that spring up by the woodpile. With dirt under our fingernails, with wind-whipped hair and sun-warmed back, let us join God in the garden. With sore muscles but focused hearts, we can contemplate his beauty, his truth, his created world in a profoundly real way as we dig into the soil that he's made, as we nurture stalks and vines and tendrils that he's sustaining and growing. The spiritual journey starts at no better place than in the garden.

—*Cindy Crosby*

For more on contemplation, see reading at Psalm 37:7.

---

[2] You have taught children and infants
to tell of your strength,*
silencing your enemies
and all who oppose you.

[3] When I look at the night sky and see the
work of your fingers—
the moon and the stars you set in
place—
[4] what are mere mortals that you should
think about them,
human beings that you should care for
them?*
[5] Yet you made them only a little lower
than God*
and crowned them* with glory and
honor.
[6] You gave them charge of everything you
made,
putting all things under their authority—
[7] the flocks and the herds
and all the wild animals,

8:2 Greek version reads *to give you praise.* Compare Matt 21:16.   **8:4** Hebrew *what is man that you should think of him, / the son of man that you should care for him?*   **8:5a** Or *Yet you made them only a little lower than the angels;* Hebrew reads *Yet you made him* [i.e., man] *a little lower than Elohim.*   **8:5b** Hebrew *him* [i.e., man]; similarly in 8:6.

⁸ the birds in the sky, the fish in the sea,
and everything that swims the ocean
currents.
⁹ O Lord, our Lord, your majestic name
fills the earth!

9 *For the choir director: A psalm of David,
to be sung to the tune "Death of the Son."*

¹ I will praise you, Lord, with all my heart;
I will tell of all the marvelous things
you have done.
² I will be filled with joy because of you.
I will sing praises to your name,
O Most High.

³ My enemies retreated;
they staggered and died when you
appeared.
⁴ For you have judged in my favor;
from your throne you have judged
with fairness.
⁵ You have rebuked the nations and
destroyed the wicked;
you have erased their names forever.
⁶ The enemy is finished, in endless ruins;
the cities you uprooted are now
forgotten.

⁷ But the Lord reigns forever,
executing judgment from his throne.
⁸ He will judge the world with justice
and rule the nations with fairness.
⁹ The Lord is a shelter for the oppressed,
a refuge in times of trouble.
¹⁰ Those who know your name trust in you,
for you, O Lord, do not abandon
those who search for you.

¹¹ Sing praises to the Lord who reigns in
Jerusalem.*
Tell the world about his unforgettable
deeds.
¹² For he who avenges murder cares for the
helpless.
He does not ignore the cries of those
who suffer.

¹³ Lord, have mercy on me.
See how my enemies torment me.
Snatch me back from the jaws of
death.

¹⁴ Save me so I can praise you publicly at
Jerusalem's gates,
so I can rejoice that you have
rescued me.
¹⁵ The nations have fallen into the pit they
dug for others.
Their own feet have been caught in
the trap they set.
¹⁶ The Lord is known for his justice.
The wicked are trapped by their own
deeds.   *Quiet Interlude**

¹⁷ The wicked will go down to the grave.*
This is the fate of all the nations who
ignore God.
¹⁸ But the needy will not be ignored
forever;
the hopes of the poor will not always
be crushed.

¹⁹ Arise, O Lord!
Do not let mere mortals defy you!
Judge the nations!
²⁰ Make them tremble in fear, O Lord.
Let the nations know they are merely
human.   *Interlude*

10 ¹ O Lord, why do you stand so far
away?
Why do you hide when I am in trouble?
² The wicked arrogantly hunt down the
poor.
Let them be caught in the evil they
plan for others.
³ For they brag about their evil desires;
they praise the greedy and curse the
Lord.

⁴ The wicked are too proud to seek God.
They seem to think that God is dead.
⁵ Yet they succeed in everything they do.
They do not see your punishment
awaiting them.
They sneer at all their enemies.
⁶ They think, "Nothing bad will ever
happen to us!
We will be free of trouble forever!"

⁷ Their mouths are full of cursing, lies,
and threats.*
Trouble and evil are on the tips of
their tongues.

9:11 Hebrew *Zion;* also in 9:14.   **9:16** Hebrew *Higgaion Selah.* The meaning of this phrase is uncertain.   **9:17** Hebrew *to Sheol.*   **10:7** Greek
version reads *cursing and bitterness.* Compare Rom 3:14.

8 They lurk in ambush in the villages,
    waiting to murder innocent people.
    They are always searching for helpless
        victims.
9 Like lions crouched in hiding,
    they wait to pounce on the helpless.
    Like hunters they capture the
        helpless
    and drag them away in nets.
10 Their helpless victims are crushed;
    they fall beneath the strength of the
        wicked.
11 The wicked think, "God isn't
        watching us!
    He has closed his eyes and won't even
        see what we do!"

12 Arise, O LORD!
    Punish the wicked, O God!
    Do not ignore the helpless!
13 Why do the wicked get away with
        despising God?
    They think, "God will never call us to
        account."
14 But you see the trouble and grief they
        cause.
    You take note of it and punish them.
    The helpless put their trust in you.
    You defend the orphans.

15 Break the arms of these wicked, evil
        people!
    Go after them until the last one is
        destroyed.
16 The LORD is king forever and ever!
    The godless nations will vanish from
        the land.
17 LORD, you know the hopes of the
        helpless.
    Surely you will hear their cries and
        comfort them.
18 You will bring justice to the orphans and
        the oppressed,
    so mere people can no longer terrify
        them.

11 For the choir director: A psalm of
    David.

1 I trust in the LORD for protection.
    So why do you say to me,
    "Fly like a bird to the mountains for
        safety!

2 The wicked are stringing their bows
    and fitting their arrows on the
        bowstrings.
    They shoot from the shadows
        at those whose hearts are right.
3 The foundations of law and order have
        collapsed.
    What can the righteous do?"

4 But the LORD is in his holy Temple;
    the LORD still rules from heaven.
    He watches everyone closely,
    examining every person on
        earth.
5 The LORD examines both the righteous
        and the wicked.
    He hates those who love violence.
6 He will rain down blazing coals and
        burning sulfur on the wicked,
    punishing them with scorching
        winds.
7 For the righteous LORD loves justice.
    The virtuous will see his face.

12 For the choir director: A psalm of
    David, to be accompanied by an
eight-stringed instrument.*

1 Help, O LORD, for the godly are fast
        disappearing!
    The faithful have vanished from the
        earth!
2 Neighbors lie to each other,
    speaking with flattering lips and
        deceitful hearts.
3 May the LORD cut off their flattering
        lips
    and silence their boastful
        tongues.
4 They say, "We will lie to our hearts'
        content.
    Our lips are our own—who can
        stop us?"

5 The LORD replies, "I have seen violence
        done to the helpless,
    and I have heard the groans of the
        poor.
    Now I will rise up to rescue them,
    as they have longed for me to do."
6 The LORD's promises are pure,
    like silver refined in a furnace,
    purified seven times over.

12:TITLE Hebrew according to the sheminith.

⁷ Therefore, Lᴏʀᴅ, we know you will
  protect the oppressed,
  preserving them forever from this
  lying generation,
⁸ even though the wicked strut about,
  and evil is praised throughout the land.

13 *For the choir director: A psalm of
David.*

¹ O Lᴏʀᴅ, how long will you forget me?
  Forever?
  How long will you look the other way?
² How long must I struggle with anguish
  in my soul,
  with sorrow in my heart every day?
  How long will my enemy have the
  upper hand?

³ Turn and answer me, O Lᴏʀᴅ my God!
  Restore the sparkle to my eyes, or I
  will die.
⁴ Don't let my enemies gloat, saying, "We
  have defeated him!"
  Don't let them rejoice at my downfall.

⁵ But I trust in your unfailing love.
  I will rejoice because you have
  rescued me.
⁶ I will sing to the Lᴏʀᴅ
  because he is good to me.

14 *For the choir director: A psalm of
David.*

¹ Only fools say in their hearts,
  "There is no God."
  They are corrupt, and their actions are
  evil;
  not one of them does good!

² The Lᴏʀᴅ looks down from heaven
  on the entire human race;
  he looks to see if anyone is truly wise,
  if anyone seeks God.
³ But no, all have turned away;
  all have become corrupt.*
  No one does good,
  not a single one!

⁴ Will those who do evil never learn?
  They eat up my people like bread
  and wouldn't think of praying to the
  Lᴏʀᴅ.

⁵ Terror will grip them,
  for God is with those who obey him.
⁶ The wicked frustrate the plans of the
  oppressed,
  but the Lᴏʀᴅ will protect his people.

⁷ Who will come from Mount Zion to
  rescue Israel?
  When the Lᴏʀᴅ restores his people,
  Jacob will shout with joy, and Israel
  will rejoice.

15 *A psalm of David.*

¹ Who may worship in your sanctuary,
  Lᴏʀᴅ?
  Who may enter your presence on your
  holy hill?
² Those who lead blameless lives and do
  what is right,
  speaking the truth from sincere hearts.
³ Those who refuse to gossip
  or harm their neighbors
  or speak evil of their friends.
⁴ Those who despise flagrant sinners,
  and honor the faithful followers of the
  Lᴏʀᴅ,
  and keep their promises even when it
  hurts.
⁵ Those who lend money without charging
  interest,
  and who cannot be bribed to lie about
  the innocent.
  Such people will stand firm forever.

16 *A psalm* of David.*

¹ Keep me safe, O God,
  for I have come to you for refuge.

² I said to the Lᴏʀᴅ, "You are my Master!
  Every good thing I have comes from
  you."
³ The godly people in the land
  are my true heroes!
  I take pleasure in them!
⁴ Troubles multiply for those who chase
  after other gods.
  I will not take part in their sacrifices
  of blood
  or even speak the names of their gods.

14:3 Greek version reads *have become useless.* Compare Rom 3:12.　**16:TITLE** Hebrew *miktam.* This may be a literary or musical term.

Solitude

Getting Away with God

PSALM 16

Years ago while I was working at a church, the senior pastor mandated monthly personal retreats for all staff members. My hungry heart eyed the potential of a few quiet hours—but at the same time, I felt strangely anxious, fearful that I'd be unable to attend to the quiet things of God for that length of time.

My pastor shared three phrases of encouragement as I set out for my first retreat. *Rest well. Listen closely. Produce nothing.*

I've taken personal retreats of solitude again and again throughout the years. They've nourished my faith and enabled me to weather the challenges of a growing ministry, the loss of two children, the birth of a child with spina bifida, and the long goodbye to my mom who died of Alzheimer's.

These retreats have helped me enjoy the gift of stillness. Stillness offers me the distinct beauty of hearing God whisper my name, as only he can. The words *quiet, alone,* and *undistracted* do not describe the vast majority of my waking hours. It is in this mixture, however, that God often makes himself known.

My retreats of solitude—often now just a few hours on a Saturday afternoon—are a time when I can just be. I listen. I follow no agenda, yet each time God tenderly renews my mind and refreshes my soul. Sometimes God offers an explosion of insight; other times his presence is like a gentle breeze.

—*Brenda Jank*

For more on solitude, see reading at Isaiah 55.

⁵ Lord, you alone are my inheritance, my
  cup of blessing.
    You guard all that is mine.
⁶ The land you have given me is a pleasant
  land.
    What a wonderful inheritance!

⁷ I will bless the Lord who guides me;
    even at night my heart instructs me.
⁸ I know the Lord is always with me.
    I will not be shaken, for he is right
    beside me.

⁹ No wonder my heart is glad, and I
  rejoice.*
    My body rests in safety.
¹⁰ For you will not leave my soul among
  the dead*
    or allow your holy one* to rot in the
    grave.

¹¹ You will show me the way of life,
    granting me the joy of your
    presence
    and the pleasures of living with you
    forever.*

17 *A prayer of David.*

¹ O Lord, hear my plea for justice.
    Listen to my cry for help.
  Pay attention to my prayer,
    for it comes from honest lips.
² Declare me innocent,
    for you see those who do right.

³ You have tested my thoughts and
    examined my heart in the night.
  You have scrutinized me and found
    nothing wrong.

16:9 Greek version reads *and my tongue shouts his praises.* Compare Acts 2:26.   **16:10a** Hebrew *in Sheol.*   **16:10b** Or *your Holy One.*
16:11 Greek version reads *You have shown me the way of life, / and you will fill me with the joy of your presence.* Compare Acts 2:28.

I am determined not to sin in what I
say.
⁴ I have followed your commands,
which keep me from following cruel
and evil people.
⁵ My steps have stayed on your path;
I have not wavered from following
you.

⁶ I am praying to you because I know you
will answer, O God.
Bend down and listen as I pray.
⁷ Show me your unfailing love in
wonderful ways.
By your mighty power you rescue
those who seek refuge from their
enemies.
⁸ Guard me as you would guard your own
eyes.*
Hide me in the shadow of your
wings.
⁹ Protect me from wicked people who
attack me,
from murderous enemies who
surround me.
¹⁰ They are without pity.
Listen to their boasting!
¹¹ They track me down and
surround me,
watching for the chance to throw me
to the ground.
¹² They are like hungry lions, eager to tear
me apart—
like young lions hiding in ambush.

¹³ Arise, O LORD!
Stand against them, and bring them to
their knees!
Rescue me from the wicked with your
sword!
¹⁴ By the power of your hand, O LORD,
destroy those who look to this world
for their reward.
But satisfy the hunger of your treasured
ones.
May their children have plenty,
leaving an inheritance for their
descendants.
¹⁵ Because I am righteous, I will see
you.
When I awake, I will see you face to
face and be satisfied.

18 *For the choir director: A psalm of
David, the servant of the LORD. He
sang this song to the LORD on the day the
LORD rescued him from all his enemies and
from Saul. He sang:*

¹ I love you, LORD;
you are my strength.
² The LORD is my rock, my fortress, and
my savior;
my God is my rock, in whom I find
protection.
He is my shield, the power that saves me,
and my place of safety.
³ I called on the LORD, who is worthy of
praise,
and he saved me from my enemies.

⁴ The ropes of death entangled me;
floods of destruction swept over me.
⁵ The grave* wrapped its ropes
around me;
death laid a trap in my path.
⁶ But in my distress I cried out to the LORD;
yes, I prayed to my God for help.
He heard me from his sanctuary;
my cry to him reached his ears.

⁷ Then the earth quaked and trembled.
The foundations of the mountains
shook;
they quaked because of his anger.
⁸ Smoke poured from his nostrils;
fierce flames leaped from his mouth.
Glowing coals blazed forth from him.
⁹ He opened the heavens and came down;
dark storm clouds were beneath his
feet.
¹⁰ Mounted on a mighty angelic being,* he
flew,
soaring on the wings of the wind.
¹¹ He shrouded himself in darkness,
veiling his approach with dark rain
clouds.
¹² Thick clouds shielded the brightness
around him
and rained down hail and burning
coals.*
¹³ The LORD thundered from heaven;
the voice of the Most High resounded
amid the hail and burning coals.
¹⁴ He shot his arrows and scattered his
enemies;

17:8 Hebrew *as the pupil of your eye.*   **18:5** Hebrew *Sheol.*   **18:10** Hebrew *a cherub.*   **18:12** Or *and lightning bolts;* also in 18:13.

his lightning flashed, and they were
greatly confused.
¹⁵ Then at your command, O LORD,
at the blast of your breath,
the bottom of the sea could be seen,
and the foundations of the earth were
laid bare.

¹⁶ He reached down from heaven and
rescued me;
he drew me out of deep waters.
¹⁷ He rescued me from my powerful
enemies,
from those who hated me and were
too strong for me.
¹⁸ They attacked me at a moment when I
was in distress,
but the LORD supported me.
¹⁹ He led me to a place of safety;
he rescued me because he delights
in me.
²⁰ The LORD rewarded me for doing right;
he restored me because of my
innocence.
²¹ For I have kept the ways of the LORD;
I have not turned from my God to
follow evil.
²² I have followed all his regulations;
I have never abandoned his decrees.
²³ I am blameless before God;
I have kept myself from sin.
²⁴ The LORD rewarded me for doing right.
He has seen my innocence.

²⁵ To the faithful you show yourself faithful;
to those with integrity you show
integrity.
²⁶ To the pure you show yourself pure,
but to the wicked you show yourself
hostile.
²⁷ You rescue the humble,
but you humiliate the proud.
²⁸ You light a lamp for me.
The LORD, my God, lights up my
darkness.
²⁹ In your strength I can crush an army;
with my God I can scale any wall.

³⁰ God's way is perfect.
All the LORD's promises prove true.
He is a shield for all who look to him
for protection.
³¹ For who is God except the LORD?
Who but our God is a solid rock?

³² God arms me with strength,
and he makes my way perfect.
³³ He makes me as surefooted as a deer,
enabling me to stand on mountain
heights.
³⁴ He trains my hands for battle;
he strengthens my arm to draw a
bronze bow.
³⁵ You have given me your shield of victory.
Your right hand supports me;
your help has made me great.
³⁶ You have made a wide path for my feet
to keep them from slipping.

³⁷ I chased my enemies and caught them;
I did not stop until they were
conquered.
³⁸ I struck them down so they could not
get up;
they fell beneath my feet.
³⁹ You have armed me with strength for
the battle;
you have subdued my enemies under
my feet.
⁴⁰ You placed my foot on their necks.
I have destroyed all who hated me.
⁴¹ They called for help, but no one came to
their rescue.
They even cried to the LORD, but he
refused to answer.
⁴² I ground them as fine as dust in the wind.
I swept them into the gutter like dirt.
⁴³ You gave me victory over my accusers.
You appointed me ruler over nations;
people I don't even know now
serve me.
⁴⁴ As soon as they hear of me, they submit;
foreign nations cringe before me.
⁴⁵ They all lose their courage
and come trembling from their
strongholds.

⁴⁶ The LORD lives! Praise to my Rock!
May the God of my salvation be exalted!
⁴⁷ He is the God who pays back those who
harm me;
he subdues the nations under me
⁴⁸ and rescues me from my enemies.
You hold me safe beyond the reach of
my enemies;
you save me from violent opponents.
⁴⁹ For this, O LORD, I will praise you
among the nations;
I will sing praises to your name.

Treating the Bible as Sacred

PSALM 19:7-10

We were running late for church one Sunday during a visit to Pakistan, so when our driver dropped us off in front of the church building, I hastily and absent-mindedly set my Bible on the van floor and stepped out. Inside the church we sang worship songs, then the minister asked us to open our Bibles. Mine, I remembered, was on the van floor, so I just listened.

Later that evening our Pakistani host took me aside and said, "You shouldn't have done that. They are watching to see how we act—how we treat our holy book. What you did . . . they see that as disrespectful. It is a reflection on us as Christians here."

That night I tearfully berated myself for being thoughtless. I knew it would be offensive to set a Qur'an on the floor, yet setting my Bible on the van floor seemed inconsequential.

Was he implying that I undervalued my Bible? I chilled. That couldn't be true. Of course I esteemed my Bible. However, I realized my carelessness that morning certainly wasn't oozing with reverence.

Had I become too casual and complacent in my treatment of the Word of God? I pictured my beloved books back home and winced. I knew I would never leave my treasured old hardback copy of *The Secret Garden* in a place where it could be kicked or maimed. Sadly I realized it was true. I had become lazy in my treatment of my Bible.

Psalm 19:7-10 links reverence for God with an attitude that honors and appreciates God's Word. John Stoughton said, "The Bible among [other] books is as a diamond among precious stones." That difficult conversation in Pakistan convicted me that I needed to show more respect for this precious diamond. Not out of a sense of duty—but out of love for the Author and his words.

—Janice Sheridan

For more on Bible study and meditation, see reading at Psalm 119:9-16.

---

50 You give great victories to your king;
   you show unfailing love to your
      anointed,
   to David and all his descendants forever.

19 For the choir director: A psalm of David.

1 The heavens proclaim the glory of God.
   The skies display his craftsmanship.
2 Day after day they continue to speak;
   night after night they make him known.
3 They speak without a sound or word;
   their voice is never heard.*

4 Yet their message has gone throughout
      the earth,
   and their words to all the world.

God has made a home in the heavens for
      the sun.
5 It bursts forth like a radiant bridegroom
      after his wedding.
   It rejoices like a great athlete eager to
      run the race.
6 The sun rises at one end of the heavens
   and follows its course to the other
      end.
   Nothing can hide from its heat.

19:3 Or *There is no speech or language where their voice is not heard.*

7 The instructions of the LORD are perfect,
      reviving the soul.
  The decrees of the LORD are
      trustworthy,
      making wise the simple.
8 The commandments of the LORD are
      right,
      bringing joy to the heart.
  The commands of the LORD are clear,
      giving insight for living.
9 Reverence for the LORD is pure,
      lasting forever.
  The laws of the LORD are true;
      each one is fair.
10 They are more desirable than gold,
      even the finest gold.
  They are sweeter than honey,
      even honey dripping from the comb.
11 They are a warning to your servant,
      a great reward for those who obey them.

12 How can I know all the sins lurking in
      my heart?
  Cleanse me from these hidden faults.
13 Keep your servant from deliberate sins!
      Don't let them control me.
  Then I will be free of guilt
      and innocent of great sin.

14 May the words of my mouth
      and the meditation of my heart
  be pleasing to you,
      O LORD, my rock and my redeemer.

20 *For the choir director: A psalm of David.*

1 In times of trouble, may the LORD
      answer your cry.
  May the name of the God of Jacob
      keep you safe from all harm.
2 May he send you help from his sanctuary
      and strengthen you from Jerusalem.*
3 May he remember all your gifts
      and look favorably on your burnt
      offerings.   *Interlude*

4 May he grant your heart's desires
      and make all your plans succeed.
5 May we shout for joy when we hear of
      your victory
      and raise a victory banner in the name
      of our God.
  May the LORD answer all your prayers.

6 Now I know that the LORD rescues his
      anointed king.
  He will answer him from his holy heaven
      and rescue him by his great power.
7 Some nations boast of their chariots and
      horses,
      but we boast in the name of the LORD
      our God.
8 Those nations will fall down and collapse,
      but we will rise up and stand firm.

9 Give victory to our king, O LORD!
      Answer our cry for help.

21 *For the choir director: A psalm of David.*

1 How the king rejoices in your strength,
      O LORD!
  He shouts with joy because you give
      him victory.
2 For you have given him his heart's desire;
      you have withheld nothing he
      requested.   *Interlude*

3 You welcomed him back with success
      and prosperity.
  You placed a crown of finest gold on
      his head.
4 He asked you to preserve his life,
      and you granted his request.
  The days of his life stretch on forever.
5 Your victory brings him great honor,
      and you have clothed him with
      splendor and majesty.
6 You have endowed him with eternal
      blessings
      and given him the joy of your presence.
7 For the king trusts in the LORD.
  The unfailing love of the Most High
      will keep him from stumbling.

8 You will capture all your enemies.
  Your strong right hand will seize all
      who hate you.
9 You will throw them in a flaming furnace
      when you appear.
  The LORD will consume them in his anger;
      fire will devour them.
10 You will wipe their children from the
      face of the earth;
      they will never have descendants.
11 Although they plot against you,
      their evil schemes will never succeed.

20:2 Hebrew *Zion.*

¹² For they will turn and run
    when they see your arrows aimed at
        them.
¹³ Rise up, O Lord, in all your power.
    With music and singing we celebrate
        your mighty acts.

22 *For the choir director: A psalm of David, to be sung to the tune "Doe of the Dawn."*

¹ My God, my God, why have you
    abandoned me?
    Why are you so far away when I groan
        for help?
² Every day I call to you, my God, but you
    do not answer.
    Every night you hear my voice, but I
        find no relief.

³ Yet you are holy,
    enthroned on the praises of Israel.
⁴ Our ancestors trusted in you,
    and you rescued them.
⁵ They cried out to you and were saved.
    They trusted in you and were never
        disgraced.

⁶ But I am a worm and not a man.
    I am scorned and despised by all!
⁷ Everyone who sees me mocks me.
    They sneer and shake their heads,
        saying,
⁸ "Is this the one who relies on the Lord?
    Then let the Lord save him!
    If the Lord loves him so much,
    let the Lord rescue him!"

⁹ Yet you brought me safely from my
    mother's womb
    and led me to trust you at my mother's
        breast.
¹⁰ I was thrust into your arms at my birth.
    You have been my God from the
        moment I was born.
¹¹ Do not stay so far from me,
    for trouble is near,
    and no one else can help me.
¹² My enemies surround me like a herd of
    bulls;
    fierce bulls of Bashan have hemmed
        me in!
¹³ Like lions they open their jaws against me,
    roaring and tearing into their prey.

¹⁴ My life is poured out like water,
    and all my bones are out of joint.
    My heart is like wax,
        melting within me.
¹⁵ My strength has dried up like sunbaked
    clay.
    My tongue sticks to the roof of my
        mouth.
    You have laid me in the dust and left
        me for dead.
¹⁶ My enemies surround me like a pack of
    dogs;
    an evil gang closes in on me.
    They have pierced my hands and feet.
¹⁷ I can count all my bones.
    My enemies stare at me and gloat.
¹⁸ They divide my garments among
    themselves
    and throw dice* for my clothing.

¹⁹ O Lord, do not stay far away!
    You are my strength; come quickly to
        my aid!
²⁰ Save me from the sword;
    spare my precious life from these dogs.
²¹ Snatch me from the lion's jaws
    and from the horns of these wild oxen.

²² I will proclaim your name to my
    brothers and sisters.*
    I will praise you among your
        assembled people.
²³ Praise the Lord, all you who fear him!
    Honor him, all you descendants of
        Jacob!
    Show him reverence, all you
        descendants of Israel!
²⁴ For he has not ignored or belittled the
    suffering of the needy.
    He has not turned his back on them,
    but has listened to their cries for help.

²⁵ I will praise you in the great assembly.
    I will fulfill my vows in the presence of
        those who worship you.
²⁶ The poor will eat and be satisfied.
    All who seek the Lord will praise him.
    Their hearts will rejoice with
        everlasting joy.
²⁷ The whole earth will acknowledge the
    Lord and return to him.
    All the families of the nations will bow
        down before him.

22:18 Hebrew *cast lots.*   **22:22** Hebrew *my brothers.*

Sabbath & Rest

A God-Paced Life

PSALM 23

Our lives are often jam packed with responsibilities, commitments, relationships, and ministries. Yet is a busy, hectic, overscheduled, and underrested life really what God has in mind for us?

Rather than living at the frenetic pace championed by our culture (and sometimes also by our churches), we are called to live a God-paced life. A life that models his priorities; that breathes his values; that allows space and time for spiritual refreshment, emotional enjoyment, and physical rest.

Psalm 23 paints a picture of what a God-paced life can be like. When the Lord is our Shepherd, we have everything we need, so we don't have to worry. In that psalm God tells me to "rest in green meadows" and that he "leads me beside peaceful streams" and "renews my strength." Leading a God-paced life means allowing the Lord to be our guide so that we can go on the right paths that honor his name.

We can take our schedules, commitments, and relational demands before God and sincerely ask, *Lord, what is it you want me to focus on? How best can I take time to rest?*

We can say to him (and this can be difficult), *Shepherd, give me the courage to give up those things that prevent me from living a God-paced life.*

Rather than always feeling compelled to do more—even doing more good things, such as ministry to others—we can seek to honor God by aiming to discover and focus on the specific things he's called us to, and letting go of all the rest. Ephesians 2:10 reminds us that God created us "in Christ Jesus, so we can do the good things he planned for us long ago." We seek to do what God has planned for us, to walk on the path he has for us, and to do it at the pace he has for us. As we abide in Christ and allow him to guide us in what we do, we're free to turn away from the "do-everything" pace of our culture and live a truly God-paced life.

—Cynthia Heald

For more on Sabbath and rest, see reading at Psalm 121.

28 For royal power belongs to the LORD.
  He rules all the nations.

29 Let the rich of the earth feast and worship.
  Bow before him, all who are mortal,
  all whose lives will end as dust.
30 Our children will also serve him.
  Future generations will hear about the
    wonders of the Lord.
31 His righteous acts will be told to those
    not yet born.
  They will hear about everything he has
    done.

23 *A psalm of David.*

1 The LORD is my shepherd;
  I have all that I need.
2 He lets me rest in green meadows;
  he leads me beside peaceful streams.
3 He renews my strength.
  He guides me along right paths,
    bringing honor to his name.
4 Even when I walk
    through the darkest valley,*
  I will not be afraid,

23:4 Or *the dark valley of death.*

for you are close beside me.
Your rod and your staff
  protect and comfort me.
⁵ You prepare a feast for me
  in the presence of my enemies.
You honor me by anointing my head
  with oil.
My cup overflows with blessings.
⁶ Surely your goodness and unfailing love
  will pursue me

all the days of my life,
  and I will live in the house of the LORD
  forever.

24 *A psalm of David.*

¹ The earth is the LORD's, and everything
  in it.
The world and all its people belong to
  him.

Stewardship and Entitlement
PSALM 24

I hear about recycling and other "green" issues, but they seem so guilt inducing and political. How can I respond in a God-honoring way?

When I hear news about global warming, oil spills, wastefulness, I wonder, *Should I be proactive or prudent—especially with global destruction on the line?*

Then I think about my grandmother. You could say she was eco-friendly. Decades before caring about the environment was in vogue, she set her thermostat low and pulled on a sweater. She reused glass jars and tin cans for canning, baking, and crafts. She patched old clothes. When those became threadbare, she recycled the material to make rugs and potholders.

But Grandma never faced the two great threats of today: excessiveness and entitlement. I can afford to buy disposable tableware, hand wipes, cameras, cell phones, and plenty of other one-use items. How does this abundance affect my attitude toward possessions—and life? Will I become ungrateful for what's used but still serviceable? Do I become more self-sufficient rather than God-dependent when I obtain whatever I want, whenever I want it?

Two spiritual disciplines can offer clarity as we face the convoluted issue of environmental degradation: simplicity and stewardship. Simplicity says, *I don't need to buy a new wardrobe every season to feel pretty. I don't need to leave every light on in my house to feel safe. I don't need to drive a gas-guzzling car to feel empowered.* If I realize I don't need those things to feel good about myself, maybe I'll look to God more often for my value. Stewardship similarly reminds us, "The earth is the LORD's and everything in it" (Psalm 24:1). It tells us, *Everything I have is on loan from God, so being careful with his stuff shows him respect.*

My grandmother's stewardship was an expression of gratitude to God. And from her, I've learned it's about common sense: when we reduce, reuse, recycle—we're being proactive, prudent, *and* grateful.

—Holly Vicente Robaina

For more on stewardship, see reading at Psalm 50:7-15.

2 For he laid the earth's foundation on the
seas
and built it on the ocean depths.

3 Who may climb the mountain of the
LORD?
Who may stand in his holy place?
4 Only those whose hands and hearts are
pure,
who do not worship idols
and never tell lies.
5 They will receive the LORD's blessing
and have a right relationship with God
their savior.
6 Such people may seek you
and worship in your presence, O God
of Jacob. *Interlude*

7 Open up, ancient gates!
Open up, ancient doors,
and let the King of glory enter.
8 Who is the King of glory?
The LORD, strong and mighty;
the LORD, invincible in battle.
9 Open up, ancient gates!
Open up, ancient doors,
and let the King of glory enter.
10 Who is the King of glory?
The LORD of Heaven's Armies—
he is the King of glory. *Interlude*

25 * *A psalm of David.*

1 O* LORD, I give my life to you.
2 I trust in you, my God!
Do not let me be disgraced,
or let my enemies rejoice in my defeat.
3 No one who trusts in you will ever be
disgraced,
but disgrace comes to those who try to
deceive others.

4 Show me the right path, O LORD;
point out the road for me to follow.
5 Lead me by your truth and teach me,
for you are the God who saves me.
All day long I put my hope in you.
6 Remember, O LORD, your compassion
and unfailing love,
which you have shown from long ages
past.
7 Do not remember the rebellious sins of
my youth.

Remember me in the light of your
unfailing love,
for you are merciful, O LORD.

8 The LORD is good and does what is right;
he shows the proper path to those
who go astray.
9 He leads the humble in doing right,
teaching them his way.
10 The LORD leads with unfailing love and
faithfulness
all who keep his covenant and obey
his demands.

11 For the honor of your name, O LORD,
forgive my many, many sins.
12 Who are those who fear the LORD?
He will show them the path they
should choose.
13 They will live in prosperity,
and their children will inherit the land.
14 The LORD is a friend to those who fear
him.
He teaches them his covenant.
15 My eyes are always on the LORD,
for he rescues me from the traps of my
enemies.

16 Turn to me and have mercy,
for I am alone and in deep distress.
17 My problems go from bad to worse.
Oh, save me from them all!
18 Feel my pain and see my trouble.
Forgive all my sins.
19 See how many enemies I have
and how viciously they hate me!
20 Protect me! Rescue my life from them!
Do not let me be disgraced, for in you
I take refuge.
21 May integrity and honesty protect me,
for I put my hope in you.

22 O God, ransom Israel
from all its troubles.

26 *A psalm of David.*

1 Declare me innocent, O LORD,
for I have acted with integrity;
I have trusted in the LORD without
wavering.
2 Put me on trial, LORD, and cross-
examine me.

---

25 This psalm is a Hebrew acrostic poem; each verse begins with a successive letter of the Hebrew alphabet.

Test my motives and my heart.

³ For I am always aware of your unfailing love,
and I have lived according to your truth.

⁴ I do not spend time with liars
or go along with hypocrites.

⁵ I hate the gatherings of those who do evil,

and I refuse to join in with the wicked.

⁶ I wash my hands to declare my innocence.
I come to your altar, O LORD,

⁷ singing a song of thanksgiving
and telling of all your wonders.

⁸ I love your sanctuary, LORD,
the place where your glorious presence dwells.

Q&A — Balancing Fear and Friendship in Worship

PSALM 25

We're told to fear God, and yet we're also told he's our friend. So how do we balance the two sides in our worship?

Christianity claims a unique place among the world's religions. Our faith tells of a God before whom the strongest saints took off their shoes, bowed down, fell on their faces, repented in dust and ashes. At the same time, it tells of a God who came to earth as a baby, who showed tender mercies to children and the weak, who taught us to call him "Abba," who loved and was loved. God inspires at once awe and love, fear and friendship.

I welcome the sense of celebration, joy, and intimacy in much of the popular worship music. Yet I wonder what we're missing when we seek to reduce the distance between creature and Creator, a distance expressed so eloquently by Job, Isaiah, and the psalmists. John, the disciple Jesus loved, who had lain against Jesus' breast, records in Revelation that he fell at his feet as though dead when Jesus appeared in full glory.

Jewish ethicist Abraham Heschel made the observation, "Awe, unlike fear, does not make us shrink from the awe-inspiring object, but, on the contrary, draws us near to it." And Martin Luther was said to pray with the reverence of addressing God and the boldness of addressing a friend.

Psalm 25:14 says, "The LORD is a friend to those who fear him." Authentic worship encompasses both friendship with God and fear of God. It is the proper response when a holy God extends to flawed human beings an invitation to intimacy. In the Old Testament, the primary Hebrew word for worship means "to bow down in reverence and submission." And in the New Testament, the most common Greek word for worship means "to come forward to kiss." Between those two—or combining both—lies our best approach to God.

—*Philip Yancey*

For more on worship, see reading at Psalm 29.

Celebration

Joy Brings Strength

PSALM 27:1-6

In Nehemiah 8 God's people were weighed down by a heavy sense of conviction. The priest Ezra had just read to them from God's Law; in earnest sorrow and repentance, the people began to weep in response (8:9). Nehemiah commanded them, "Go and celebrate with a feast of rich foods and sweet drinks. . . . Don't be dejected and sad, for *the joy of the LORD is your strength*!" (8:10, italics added).

But how can joy be strength? Whether we define it as something physical, emotional, or spiritual, how does joy fit into the definition?

The Hebrew word translated as *strength* (*ma'oz*) is often used in Scripture to describe a refuge or shelter. That same term describes a mountain stronghold in Judges 6:26. It's also used figuratively to describe God as a place of refuge or defense in Psalm 27:1: "The LORD is my fortress, protecting me from danger, so why should I tremble?"

But this is the point: joy and celebration, especially when done in the presence of God, give us a sense of comfort that leads to strength for our everyday tasks. Joy encourages us to face whatever is before us with a new sense of vigor. Nehemiah knew that finding joy in God—and choosing celebration over sorrow—was what would give God's people the courage and determination to live in obedience to God's law. The same is true for us. Living a life that honors God requires strength—the strength to obey, the determination to resist temptation, the courage to persevere in faith. It may seem counterintuitive, but we can build up that strength through times of pure joy and delight. As we celebrate God's goodness and enjoy his presence, we're empowered to hold tight to that goodness during dark times. When temptation, doubt, or loneliness assails us, our faith is strong enough to stand the test.

—George Rehberg

For more on celebration, see reading at Psalm 100.

9 Don't let me suffer the fate of sinners.
  Don't condemn me along with
    murderers.
10 Their hands are dirty with evil schemes,
  and they constantly take bribes.
11 But I am not like that; I live with integrity.
  So redeem me and show me mercy.
12 Now I stand on solid ground,
  and I will publicly praise the LORD.

27 *A psalm of David.*

1 The LORD is my light and my salvation—
  so why should I be afraid?
The LORD is my fortress, protecting me
    from danger,
  so why should I tremble?
2 When evil people come to devour me,
  when my enemies and foes attack me,
  they will stumble and fall.
3 Though a mighty army surrounds me,
  my heart will not be afraid.
Even if I am attacked,
  I will remain confident.

4 The one thing I ask of the LORD—
    the thing I seek most—
is to live in the house of the LORD all the
    days of my life,
  delighting in the LORD's perfections
  and meditating in his Temple.
5 For he will conceal me there when
    troubles come;

he will hide me in his sanctuary.
He will place me out of reach on a
high rock.
⁶ Then I will hold my head high
above my enemies who surround me.
At his sanctuary I will offer sacrifices
with shouts of joy,
singing and praising the LORD with
music.

⁷ Hear me as I pray, O LORD.
Be merciful and answer me!
⁸ My heart has heard you say, "Come and
talk with me."
And my heart responds, "LORD, I am
coming."
⁹ Do not turn your back on me.
Do not reject your servant in anger.
You have always been my helper.
Don't leave me now; don't abandon me,
O God of my salvation!
¹⁰ Even if my father and mother abandon me,
the LORD will hold me close.

¹¹ Teach me how to live, O LORD.
Lead me along the right path,
for my enemies are waiting for me.
¹² Do not let me fall into their hands.
For they accuse me of things I've never
done;
with every breath they threaten me
with violence.
¹³ Yet I am confident I will see the LORD's
goodness
while I am here in the land of the living.

¹⁴ Wait patiently for the LORD.
Be brave and courageous.
Yes, wait patiently for the LORD.

28 *A psalm of David.*

¹ I pray to you, O LORD, my rock.
Do not turn a deaf ear to me.
For if you are silent,
I might as well give up and die.
² Listen to my prayer for mercy
as I cry out to you for help,
as I lift my hands toward your holy
sanctuary.

³ Do not drag me away with the wicked—
with those who do evil—

those who speak friendly words to their
neighbors
while planning evil in their hearts.
⁴ Give them the punishment they so richly
deserve!
Measure it out in proportion to their
wickedness.
Pay them back for all their evil deeds!
Give them a taste of what they have
done to others.
⁵ They care nothing for what the LORD
has done
or for what his hands have made.
So he will tear them down,
and they will never be rebuilt!

⁶ Praise the LORD!
For he has heard my cry for mercy.
⁷ The LORD is my strength and shield.
I trust him with all my heart.
He helps me, and my heart is filled with
joy.
I burst out in songs of thanksgiving.

⁸ The LORD gives his people strength.
He is a safe fortress for his anointed
king.
⁹ Save your people!
Bless Israel, your special possession.*
Lead them like a shepherd,
and carry them in your arms forever.

29 *A psalm of David.*

¹ Honor the LORD, you heavenly beings*;
honor the LORD for his glory and
strength.
² Honor the LORD for the glory of his name.
Worship the LORD in the splendor of
his holiness.

³ The voice of the LORD echoes above the
sea.
The God of glory thunders.
The LORD thunders over the mighty
sea.
⁴ The voice of the LORD is powerful;
the voice of the LORD is majestic.
⁵ The voice of the LORD splits the mighty
cedars;
the LORD shatters the cedars of
Lebanon.

28:9 Hebrew *Bless your inheritance.*   29:1 Hebrew *you sons of God.*

What's Your Worship Language?

PSALM 29

Music speaks to me. I composed (quite cheesy) worship songs on my keyboard as a ten-year-old. As a young adult, some of my deepest expressions of faith were words I belted out loudly while clapping to the backbeat with my university gospel choir. Today I can hardly sing a full stanza of a hymn in church without tears welling up in my eyes. Music seems to be a language God made me to hear and speak.

For others, music is like a foreign tongue. Tone-deaf singers, the rhythmically challenged, and those who just aren't "into" music may often feel left out in our churches, which often narrowly use *worship* as a code word for singing.

Yet the Bible is peopled with a variety of types of worshipers: some used art, others ritual, still others offerings or acts of service or bold proclamation. As Gary Thomas points out in *Sacred Pathways*, "Our temperaments will cause us to be more comfortable in some of these expressions than others—and that's perfectly acceptable to God. . . . By worshiping God according to the way he made us, we are affirming his work as Creator."

Thomas identifies several biblical avenues of expressing worship, including interacting with nature, using your five senses, employing ritual and symbol, spending time in solitude and simplicity, activism and service, celebration, and employing one's mind.

So if music isn't your native worship-language, how about a walk outside? Or what about wrestling with a calculus equation and marveling over it with God? Or how about worshiping God by fighting injustice or volunteering?

God made you—and that includes forming your unique temperament and personality. He knows that some things just "fit" you better than others. God's desire is that you respond to him in worship that's natural, instinctive, and authentically who you are.

—*Kelli B. Trujillo*

For more on worship, see reading at Psalm 148.

---

⁶ He makes Lebanon's mountains skip like a calf;
   he makes Mount Hermon* leap like a young wild ox.
⁷ The voice of the LORD strikes with bolts of lightning.
⁸ The voice of the LORD makes the barren wilderness quake;
   the LORD shakes the wilderness of Kadesh.
⁹ The voice of the LORD twists mighty oaks*
   and strips the forests bare.

In his Temple everyone shouts, "Glory!"

¹⁰ The LORD rules over the floodwaters.
   The LORD reigns as king forever.
¹¹ The LORD gives his people strength.
   The LORD blesses them with peace.

30 *A psalm of David. A song for the dedication of the Temple.*

¹ I will exalt you, LORD, for you rescued me.
   You refused to let my enemies triumph over me.

29:6 Hebrew *Sirion*, another name for Mount Hermon.   **29:9** Or *causes the deer to writhe in labor.*

² O LORD my God, I cried to you for
     help,
  and you restored my health.
³ You brought me up from the grave,*
     O LORD.
  You kept me from falling into the pit
     of death.

⁴ Sing to the LORD, all you godly ones!
     Praise his holy name.
⁵ For his anger lasts only a moment,
     but his favor lasts a lifetime!
  Weeping may last through the night,
     but joy comes with the morning.

⁶ When I was prosperous, I said,
     "Nothing can stop me now!"
⁷ Your favor, O LORD, made me as secure
     as a mountain.
  Then you turned away from me, and I
     was shattered.

⁸ I cried out to you, O LORD.
     I begged the Lord for mercy, saying,
⁹ "What will you gain if I die,
     if I sink into the grave?
  Can my dust praise you?
     Can it tell of your faithfulness?
¹⁰ Hear me, LORD, and have mercy on me.
     Help me, O LORD."

¹¹ You have turned my mourning into
     joyful dancing.
  You have taken away my clothes of
     mourning and clothed me with joy,
¹² that I might sing praises to you and not
     be silent.
  O LORD my God, I will give you
     thanks forever!

31
*For the choir director: A psalm of
David.*

¹ O LORD, I have come to you for
     protection;
  don't let me be disgraced.
  Save me, for you do what is right.
² Turn your ear to listen to me;
     rescue me quickly.
  Be my rock of protection,
     a fortress where I will be safe.
³ You are my rock and my fortress.
  For the honor of your name, lead me
     out of this danger.

⁴ Pull me from the trap my enemies set
     for me,
  for I find protection in you alone.
⁵ I entrust my spirit into your hand.
  Rescue me, LORD, for you are a
     faithful God.

⁶ I hate those who worship worthless idols.
     I trust in the LORD.
⁷ I will be glad and rejoice in your
     unfailing love,
  for you have seen my troubles,
     and you care about the anguish of my
     soul.
⁸ You have not handed me over to my
     enemies
  but have set me in a safe place.

⁹ Have mercy on me, LORD, for I am in
     distress.
  Tears blur my eyes.
  My body and soul are withering away.
¹⁰ I am dying from grief;
     my years are shortened by sadness.
  Sin has drained my strength;
     I am wasting away from within.
¹¹ I am scorned by all my enemies
     and despised by my neighbors—
  even my friends are afraid to come
     near me.
  When they see me on the street,
     they run the other way.
¹² I am ignored as if I were dead,
     as if I were a broken pot.
¹³ I have heard the many rumors about me,
     and I am surrounded by terror.
  My enemies conspire against me,
     plotting to take my life.

¹⁴ But I am trusting you, O LORD,
     saying, "You are my God!"
¹⁵ My future is in your hands.
  Rescue me from those who hunt me
     down relentlessly.
¹⁶ Let your favor shine on your servant.
     In your unfailing love, rescue me.
¹⁷ Don't let me be disgraced, O LORD,
     for I call out to you for help.
  Let the wicked be disgraced;
     let them lie silent in the grave.*
¹⁸ Silence their lying lips—
     those proud and arrogant lips that
     accuse the godly.

30:3 Hebrew *from Sheol.*   **31:17** Hebrew *in Sheol.*

¹⁹ How great is the goodness
  you have stored up for those who fear
    you.
  You lavish it on those who come to you
    for protection,
  blessing them before the watching
    world.
²⁰ You hide them in the shelter of your
    presence,
  safe from those who conspire against
    them.
  You shelter them in your presence,
    far from accusing tongues.

²¹ Praise the LORD,
  for he has shown me the wonders of
    his unfailing love.
  He kept me safe when my city was
    under attack.
²² In panic I cried out,
  "I am cut off from the LORD!"
  But you heard my cry for mercy
    and answered my call for help.

²³ Love the LORD, all you godly ones!
  For the LORD protects those who are
    loyal to him,
  but he harshly punishes the arrogant.
²⁴ So be strong and courageous,
  all you who put your hope in the
    LORD!

32 A psalm* of David.

¹ Oh, what joy for those
  whose disobedience is forgiven,
  whose sin is put out of sight!
² Yes, what joy for those
  whose record the LORD has cleared of
    guilt,*
  whose lives are lived in complete
    honesty!
³ When I refused to confess my sin,
  my body wasted away,
  and I groaned all day long.
⁴ Day and night your hand of discipline
    was heavy on me.
  My strength evaporated like water in
    the summer heat.   *Interlude*

⁵ Finally, I confessed all my sins to you
  and stopped trying to hide my guilt.

I said to myself, "I will confess my
    rebellion to the LORD."
  And you forgave me! All my guilt is
    gone.   *Interlude*

⁶ Therefore, let all the godly pray to you
    while there is still time,
  that they may not drown in the
    floodwaters of judgment.
⁷ For you are my hiding place;
  you protect me from trouble.
  You surround me with songs of
    victory.   *Interlude*

⁸ The LORD says, "I will guide you along
    the best pathway for your life.
  I will advise you and watch over you.
⁹ Do not be like a senseless horse or
    mule
  that needs a bit and bridle to keep it
    under control."

¹⁰ Many sorrows come to the wicked,
  but unfailing love surrounds those
    who trust the LORD.
¹¹ So rejoice in the LORD and be glad, all
    you who obey him!
  Shout for joy, all you whose hearts are
    pure!

33 ¹ Let the godly sing for joy to the
    LORD;
  it is fitting for the pure to praise him.
² Praise the LORD with melodies on the
    lyre;
  make music for him on the ten-
    stringed harp.
³ Sing a new song of praise to him;
  play skillfully on the harp, and sing
    with joy.
⁴ For the word of the LORD holds true,
  and we can trust everything he does.
⁵ He loves whatever is just and good;
  the unfailing love of the LORD fills the
    earth.
⁶ The LORD merely spoke,
  and the heavens were created.
  He breathed the word,
  and all the stars were born.
⁷ He assigned the sea its boundaries
  and locked the oceans in vast
    reservoirs.

32:TITLE Hebrew *maskil*. This may be a literary or musical term.   **32:2** Greek version reads *of sin.* Compare Rom 4:7.

⁸ Let the whole world fear the LORD,
and let everyone stand in awe of him.
⁹ For when he spoke, the world began!
It appeared at his command.

¹⁰ The LORD frustrates the plans of the
nations
and thwarts all their schemes.
¹¹ But the LORD's plans stand firm
forever;
his intentions can never be shaken.

¹² What joy for the nation whose God is
the LORD,
whose people he has chosen as his
inheritance.

¹³ The LORD looks down from heaven
and sees the whole human race.
¹⁴ From his throne he observes
all who live on the earth.
¹⁵ He made their hearts,
so he understands everything they do.
¹⁶ The best-equipped army cannot save a
king,
nor is great strength enough to save a
warrior.
¹⁷ Don't count on your warhorse to give
you victory—
for all its strength, it cannot save you.

¹⁸ But the LORD watches over those who
fear him,
those who rely on his unfailing love.
¹⁹ He rescues them from death
and keeps them alive in times of
famine.

²⁰ We put our hope in the LORD.
He is our help and our shield.
²¹ In him our hearts rejoice,
for we trust in his holy name.
²² Let your unfailing love surround us,
LORD,
for our hope is in you alone.

34 *A psalm of David, regarding the
time he pretended to be insane in
front of Abimelech, who sent him away.*

¹ I will praise the LORD at all times.
I will constantly speak his praises.
² I will boast only in the LORD;
let all who are helpless take heart.

³ Come, let us tell of the LORD's greatness;
let us exalt his name together.
⁴ I prayed to the LORD, and he
answered me.
He freed me from all my fears.
⁵ Those who look to him for help will be
radiant with joy;
no shadow of shame will darken their
faces.
⁶ In my desperation I prayed, and the
LORD listened;
he saved me from all my troubles.
⁷ For the angel of the LORD is a guard;
he surrounds and defends all who fear
him.

⁸ Taste and see that the LORD is good.
Oh, the joys of those who take refuge
in him!
⁹ Fear the LORD, you his godly people,
for those who fear him will have all
they need.
¹⁰ Even strong young lions sometimes go
hungry,
but those who trust in the LORD will
lack no good thing.

¹¹ Come, my children, and listen to me,
and I will teach you to fear the LORD.
¹² Does anyone want to live a life
that is long and prosperous?
¹³ Then keep your tongue from speaking
evil
and your lips from telling lies!
¹⁴ Turn away from evil and do good.
Search for peace, and work to
maintain it.

¹⁵ The eyes of the LORD watch over those
who do right;
his ears are open to their cries for help.
¹⁶ But the LORD turns his face against
those who do evil;
he will erase their memory from the
earth.
¹⁷ The LORD hears his people when they
call to him for help.
He rescues them from all their
troubles.
¹⁸ The LORD is close to the brokenhearted;
he rescues those whose spirits are
crushed.

---

34 This psalm is a Hebrew acrostic poem; each verse begins with a successive letter of the Hebrew alphabet.

Simplicity

Lacking No Good Thing
PSALM 34

My kitchen drawer is filled with so many gadgets that I can't find the one I need when I'm searching through the tangle of sharp blades. I have too much . . . but I still want more.

"More" is the caustic mantra of our society that defines us by our possessions. In an article in *Sojourners*, William Cavanaugh defines our condition in the relentless search for "something else." Distinguishing shopping from buying, he notes, "It is this restlessness—the moving on to shopping for something else no matter what one has just purchased—that sets the spiritual tone for consumerism."

Must-haves become has-beens. Trends die and fads fade. The endless treadmill of greed keeps us chasing after the next thing instead of cultivating contentment as God intends.

The curious truth is that the discipline of simplicity opens us to possibility, not scarcity. Greed keeps us stuck and selfishly turned inward. Simplicity is a constant *yes* to the call of the larger life of generosity.

Simplicity quiets the voice of "if only." ("If only I had X-Y-Z, I would be happy!") Simplicity helps us define our world on God's terms and offers a proper perspective to the richness we have materially and spiritually. There is always enough. In God's economy of simplicity, the basket of fish multiplies. The jar of oil overflows. Water is turned into wine. The banquet feast is shared with a stranger.

Simplicity is not about going without but going with God through the beautiful journey of a life lived in the simple abundance of grace.

"More!" is replaced with "there is enough" as our mantra—one we can repeat with confidence even in difficult times. As the psalmist rejoices, "Those who fear him will have all they need. . . . Those who trust in the LORD will lack no good thing" (Psalm 34:9-10).

—*Amie Hollmann*

For more on simplicity, see reading at Psalm 116:7.

¹⁹ The righteous person faces many troubles,
  but the LORD comes to the rescue each time.
²⁰ For the LORD protects the bones of the righteous;
  not one of them is broken!
²¹ Calamity will surely overtake the wicked,
  and those who hate the righteous will be punished.
²² But the LORD will redeem those who serve him.

No one who takes refuge in him will be condemned.

35 *A psalm of David.*

¹ O LORD, oppose those who oppose me.
  Fight those who fight against me.
² Put on your armor, and take up your shield.
  Prepare for battle, and come to my aid.
³ Lift up your spear and javelin
  against those who pursue me.

Let me hear you say,
  "I will give you victory!"
⁴ Bring shame and disgrace on those
    trying to kill me;
  turn them back and humiliate those
    who want to harm me.
⁵ Blow them away like chaff in the wind—
  a wind sent by the angel of the LORD.
⁶ Make their path dark and slippery,
  with the angel of the LORD pursuing
    them.
⁷ I did them no wrong, but they laid a trap
    for me.
  I did them no wrong, but they dug a
    pit to catch me.
⁸ So let sudden ruin come upon them!
  Let them be caught in the trap they set
    for me!
  Let them be destroyed in the pit they
    dug for me.

⁹ Then I will rejoice in the LORD.
  I will be glad because he rescues me.
¹⁰ With every bone in my body I will praise
    him:
  "LORD, who can compare with you?
  Who else rescues the helpless from the
    strong?
  Who else protects the helpless and
    poor from those who rob them?"

¹¹ Malicious witnesses testify against me.
  They accuse me of crimes I know
    nothing about.
¹² They repay me evil for good.
  I am sick with despair.
¹³ Yet when they were ill, I grieved for them.
  I denied myself by fasting for them,
  but my prayers returned unanswered.
¹⁴ I was sad, as though they were my
    friends or family,
  as if I were grieving for my own
    mother.
¹⁵ But they are glad now that I am in
    trouble;
  they gleefully join together against me.
  I am attacked by people I don't even
    know;
  they slander me constantly.
¹⁶ They mock me and call me names;
  they snarl at me.

¹⁷ How long, O Lord, will you look on and
    do nothing?

Rescue me from their fierce attacks.
  Protect my life from these lions!
¹⁸ Then I will thank you in front of the
    great assembly.
  I will praise you before all the people.
¹⁹ Don't let my treacherous enemies rejoice
    over my defeat.
  Don't let those who hate me without
    cause gloat over my sorrow.
²⁰ They don't talk of peace;
  they plot against innocent people who
    mind their own business.
²¹ They shout, "Aha! Aha!
  With our own eyes we saw him do it!"

²² O LORD, you know all about this.
  Do not stay silent.
  Do not abandon me now, O Lord.
²³ Wake up! Rise to my defense!
  Take up my case, my God and my
    Lord.
²⁴ Declare me not guilty, O LORD my God,
  for you give justice.
  Don't let my enemies laugh about me
    in my troubles.
²⁵ Don't let them say, "Look, we got what
    we wanted!
  Now we will eat him alive!"

²⁶ May those who rejoice at my troubles
    be humiliated and disgraced.
  May those who triumph over me
    be covered with shame and dishonor.
²⁷ But give great joy to those who came to
    my defense.
  Let them continually say, "Great is the
    LORD,
  who delights in blessing his servant
    with peace!"
²⁸ Then I will proclaim your justice,
  and I will praise you all day long.

36

For the choir director: A psalm of
David, the servant of the LORD.

¹ Sin whispers to the wicked, deep within
    their hearts.
  They have no fear of God at all.
² In their blind conceit,
  they cannot see how wicked they
    really are.
³ Everything they say is crooked and
    deceitful.
  They refuse to act wisely or do good.

Accepting God's Hospitality
PSALM 36:5-9

As I've worked to practice the spiritual discipline of hospitality, I've discovered that it ultimately begins with opening myself to receive *God's* hospitality toward me (Psalm 36:5-9). I know a lot of Christians who know God loves them but don't realize that God likes them too. God invites us; he draws us in. He accepts us. He offers us freedom, grace, warmth. With God, we can be truly ourselves.

It's wonderful to have a specific time of prayer. It's also wonderful just to "waste time" with God, to come to him with no agenda, to spend time with him as one does with a friend. But when I find myself too drained to be hospitable, it's usually because I haven't wasted time with God, just soaking in the understanding that he loves *and* likes me. Unless I connect with God's love for me, and see myself being hosted by God, I have little to give others.

—*Michele Hershberger*

For more on hospitality, see reading at Proverbs 18:20-21.

---

⁴ They lie awake at night, hatching sinful
plots.
　Their actions are never good.
　They make no attempt to turn from
　　evil.

⁵ Your unfailing love, O LORD, is as vast as
　the heavens;
　your faithfulness reaches beyond the
　clouds.
⁶ Your righteousness is like the mighty
　mountains,
　your justice like the ocean depths.
　You care for people and animals alike,
　　O LORD.
⁷ 　How precious is your unfailing love,
　O God!
　All humanity finds shelter
　in the shadow of your wings.
⁸ You feed them from the abundance of
　your own house,
　letting them drink from your river of
　delights.
⁹ For you are the fountain of life,
　the light by which we see.

¹⁰ Pour out your unfailing love on those
　who love you;
　give justice to those with honest
　hearts.
¹¹ Don't let the proud trample me

or the wicked push me around.
¹² Look! Those who do evil have fallen!
　They are thrown down, never to rise
　again.

37* *A psalm of David.*

¹ Don't worry about the wicked
　or envy those who do wrong.
² For like grass, they soon fade away.
　Like spring flowers, they soon wither.

³ Trust in the LORD and do good.
　Then you will live safely in the land
　　and prosper.
⁴ Take delight in the LORD,
　and he will give you your heart's
　　desires.

⁵ Commit everything you do to the LORD.
　Trust him, and he will help you.
⁶ He will make your innocence radiate like
　the dawn,
　and the justice of your cause will shine
　like the noonday sun.

⁷ Be still in the presence of the LORD,
　and wait patiently for him to act.
　Don't worry about evil people who
　prosper
　or fret about their wicked schemes.

37 This psalm is a Hebrew acrostic poem; each stanza begins with a successive letter of the Hebrew alphabet.

Centering on God
PSALM 37:7

I spent a summer determined to strengthen my prayer life. My first attempts began the way many begin: I tried praying *more*.

Rising earlier and taking more time, however, only provided part of my answer. I still found myself distracted. A friend gave me a book on intimate prayer that instructed me to just stop thinking: if thoughts distracted me from listening to God, I should tell my brain to stop it. He made it sound simple, so I tried it. I told my mind to stop thinking.

I might as well have told my lungs to stop breathing.

While that technique may work for others, it didn't work for me. I needed to find another way to center my mind.

During a spiritual retreat in the quiet confines of a convent that same summer, I learned about contemplative prayer. I spent three days learning from a fourteenth-century volume, written by an anonymous monk, about "centering prayer." The goal of centering prayer is to enter totally into God's presence, discovering communion with him through focusing our attention on him alone. It is also called a "prayer of consent"—this kind of prayer is focused on stillness in God's presence and complete submission to him (Psalms 37:7; 46:10).

Centering prayer teaches that, instead of an irritated reaction to unwanted, distracting thoughts that interrupt our prayer focus, we can use a sacred word to gently brush the pesky thoughts away. Commonly used words include *God*, *Jesus*, *love*, *peace*, and *trust*. *Yes* became my sacred word. I chose it because it implies submission to whatever God has for me. When I was practicing centering prayer and distracting thoughts came along, I simply thought, *Yes*.

For years I bemoaned the fact that God didn't seem to talk to me much. I was so diverted by to-do lists that I couldn't hear the gentle whisperings of God. Centering prayer has helped me to quiet my spirit and has improved my spiritual hearing.

—*Kathy Callahan-Howell*

For more on contemplation, see reading at Proverbs 3:32.

8 Stop being angry!
    Turn from your rage!
Do not lose your temper—
    it only leads to harm.
9 For the wicked will be destroyed,
    but those who trust in the LORD will
        possess the land.

10 Soon the wicked will disappear.
    Though you look for them, they will
        be gone.
11 The lowly will possess the land
    and will live in peace and prosperity.

12 The wicked plot against the godly;
    they snarl at them in defiance.
13 But the Lord just laughs,
    for he sees their day of judgment
        coming.

14 The wicked draw their swords
    and string their bows
to kill the poor and the oppressed,
    to slaughter those who do right.
15 But their swords will stab their own
        hearts,
    and their bows will be broken.

16 It is better to be godly and have little
than to be evil and rich.
17 For the strength of the wicked will be
shattered,
but the LORD takes care of the godly.
18 Day by day the LORD takes care of the
innocent,
and they will receive an inheritance
that lasts forever.
19 They will not be disgraced in hard times;
even in famine they will have more
than enough.

20 But the wicked will die.
The LORD's enemies are like flowers in
a field—
they will disappear like smoke.

21 The wicked borrow and never repay,
but the godly are generous givers.
22 Those the LORD blesses will possess the
land,
but those he curses will die.

23 The LORD directs the steps of the godly.
He delights in every detail of their
lives.
24 Though they stumble, they will never fall,
for the LORD holds them by the hand.

25 Once I was young, and now I am old.
Yet I have never seen the godly
abandoned
or their children begging for bread.
26 The godly always give generous loans to
others,
and their children are a blessing.

27 Turn from evil and do good,
and you will live in the land forever.
28 For the LORD loves justice,
and he will never abandon the godly.

He will keep them safe forever,
but the children of the wicked will die.
29 The godly will possess the land
and will live there forever.

30 The godly offer good counsel;
they teach right from wrong.
31 They have made God's law their own,
so they will never slip from his path.

32 The wicked wait in ambush for the
godly,
looking for an excuse to kill them.

33 But the LORD will not let the wicked
succeed
or let the godly be condemned when
they are put on trial.

34 Put your hope in the LORD.
Travel steadily along his path.
He will honor you by giving you the land.
You will see the wicked destroyed.

35 I have seen wicked and ruthless people
flourishing like a tree in its native soil.
36 But when I looked again, they were gone!
Though I searched for them, I could
not find them!

37 Look at those who are honest and good,
for a wonderful future awaits those
who love peace.
38 But the rebellious will be destroyed;
they have no future.

39 The LORD rescues the godly;
he is their fortress in times of trouble.
40 The LORD helps them,
rescuing them from the wicked.
He saves them,
and they find shelter in him.

38 A psalm of David, asking God to remember him.

1 O LORD, don't rebuke me in your anger
or discipline me in your rage!
2 Your arrows have struck deep,
and your blows are crushing me.
3 Because of your anger, my whole body is
sick;
my health is broken because of my sins.
4 My guilt overwhelms me—
it is a burden too heavy to bear.
5 My wounds fester and stink
because of my foolish sins.
6 I am bent over and racked with pain.
All day long I walk around filled with
grief.
7 A raging fever burns within me,
and my health is broken.
8 I am exhausted and completely crushed.
My groans come from an anguished
heart.

9 You know what I long for, Lord;
you hear my every sigh.
10 My heart beats wildly, my strength fails,
and I am going blind.

¹¹ My loved ones and friends stay away,
    fearing my disease.
  Even my own family stands at a distance.
¹² Meanwhile, my enemies lay traps to
    kill me.
  Those who wish me harm make plans
    to ruin me.
  All day long they plan their treachery.
¹³ But I am deaf to all their threats.
  I am silent before them as one who
    cannot speak.
¹⁴ I choose to hear nothing,
  and I make no reply.
¹⁵ For I am waiting for you, O LORD.
  You must answer for me, O Lord my
    God.
¹⁶ I prayed, "Don't let my enemies gloat
    over me
  or rejoice at my downfall."

¹⁷ I am on the verge of collapse,
  facing constant pain.
¹⁸ But I confess my sins;
  I am deeply sorry for what I have done.
¹⁹ I have many aggressive enemies;
  they hate me without reason.
²⁰ They repay me evil for good
  and oppose me for pursuing good.
²¹ Do not abandon me, O LORD.
  Do not stand at a distance, my God.
²² Come quickly to help me,
  O Lord my savior.

39

For Jeduthun, the choir director: A psalm of David.

¹ I said to myself, "I will watch what I do
  and not sin in what I say.
I will hold my tongue
  when the ungodly are around me."
² But as I stood there in silence—
  not even speaking of good things—
  the turmoil within me grew worse.
³ The more I thought about it,
  the hotter I got,
  igniting a fire of words:
⁴ "LORD, remind me how brief my time on
    earth will be.
  Remind me that my days are
    numbered—
  how fleeting my life is.
⁵ You have made my life no longer than
  the width of my hand.

My entire lifetime is just a moment to
    you;
  at best, each of us is but a breath."
                    Interlude

⁶ We are merely moving shadows,
  and all our busy rushing ends in nothing.
We heap up wealth,
  not knowing who will spend it.
⁷ And so, Lord, where do I put my hope?
  My only hope is in you.
⁸ Rescue me from my rebellion.
  Do not let fools mock me.
⁹ I am silent before you; I won't say a word,
  for my punishment is from you.
¹⁰ But please stop striking me!
  I am exhausted by the blows from
    your hand.
¹¹ When you discipline us for our sins,
  you consume like a moth what is
    precious to us.
  Each of us is but a breath.   *Interlude*

¹² Hear my prayer, O LORD!
  Listen to my cries for help!
  Don't ignore my tears.
For I am your guest—
  a traveler passing through,
  as my ancestors were before me.
¹³ Leave me alone so I can smile again
  before I am gone and exist no more.

40

For the choir director: A psalm of David.

¹ I waited patiently for the LORD to help me,
  and he turned to me and heard my cry.
² He lifted me out of the pit of despair,
  out of the mud and the mire.
He set my feet on solid ground
  and steadied me as I walked along.
³ He has given me a new song to sing,
  a hymn of praise to our God.
Many will see what he has done and be
    amazed.
  They will put their trust in the LORD.

⁴ Oh, the joys of those who trust the LORD,
  who have no confidence in the proud
  or in those who worship idols.
⁵ O LORD my God, you have performed
    many wonders for us.
  Your plans for us are too numerous to
    list.
  You have no equal.

If I tried to recite all your wonderful
    deeds,
    I would never come to the end of them.
⁶ You take no delight in sacrifices or
    offerings.
    Now that you have made me listen, I
    finally understand*—
    you don't require burnt offerings or
    sin offerings.
⁷ Then I said, "Look, I have come.
    As is written about me in the Scriptures:
⁸ I take joy in doing your will, my God,
    for your instructions are written on
    my heart."

⁹ I have told all your people about your
    justice.
    I have not been afraid to speak out,
    as you, O LORD, well know.
¹⁰ I have not kept the good news of your
    justice hidden in my heart;
    I have talked about your faithfulness
    and saving power.
    I have told everyone in the great assembly
    of your unfailing love and faithfulness.

¹¹ LORD, don't hold back your tender
    mercies from me.
    Let your unfailing love and
    faithfulness always protect me.
¹² For troubles surround me—
    too many to count!
    My sins pile up so high
    I can't see my way out.
    They outnumber the hairs on my head.
    I have lost all courage.

¹³ Please, LORD, rescue me!
    Come quickly, LORD, and help me.
¹⁴ May those who try to destroy me
    be humiliated and put to shame.
    May those who take delight in my
    trouble
    be turned back in disgrace.
¹⁵ Let them be horrified by their shame,
    for they said, "Aha! We've got him now!"

¹⁶ But may all who search for you
    be filled with joy and gladness in you.
    May those who love your salvation
    repeatedly shout, "The LORD is great!"
¹⁷ As for me, since I am poor and needy,
    let the Lord keep me in his thoughts.

You are my helper and my savior.
    O my God, do not delay.

41 *For the choir director: A psalm of
David.*

¹ Oh, the joys of those who are kind to the
    poor!
    The LORD rescues them when they are
    in trouble.
² The LORD protects them
    and keeps them alive.
    He gives them prosperity in the land
    and rescues them from their enemies.
³ The LORD nurses them when they are
    sick
    and restores them to health.

⁴ "O LORD," I prayed, "have mercy on me.
    Heal me, for I have sinned against
    you."
⁵ But my enemies say nothing but evil
    about me.
    "How soon will he die and be
    forgotten?" they ask.
⁶ They visit me as if they were my friends,
    but all the while they gather gossip,
    and when they leave, they spread it
    everywhere.
⁷ All who hate me whisper about me,
    imagining the worst.
⁸ "He has some fatal disease," they say.
    "He will never get out of that bed!"
⁹ Even my best friend, the one I trusted
    completely,
    the one who shared my food, has
    turned against me.

¹⁰ LORD, have mercy on me.
    Make me well again, so I can pay them
    back!
¹¹ I know you are pleased with me,
    for you have not let my enemies
    triumph over me.
¹² You have preserved my life because I am
    innocent;
    you have brought me into your
    presence forever.

¹³ Praise the LORD, the God of Israel,
    who lives from everlasting to
    everlasting.
    Amen and amen!

40:6 Greek text reads *You have given me a body.* Compare Heb 10:5.

Dark Nights of the Soul
PSALM 42

John of the Cross, a sixteenth-century Spanish monk who deeply loved Christ, experienced a prolonged period of intense spiritual darkness, which he described in *Dark Night of the Soul.* Many mature, committed Christians have experienced similar "dark nights" in which prayers seem purposeless, worship seems empty, and God seems not to respond despite our longing for intimacy with him.

I don't know about you, but my usual response to the dark is to switch on the biggest spotlight I can find. But perhaps true transformation requires periods of darkness; perhaps it takes place even in dim and murky places.

Read only a few of the psalms, and you see this theme played out: disorientation and doubt are gestational to faith. Consider the trust displayed by the downcast and disturbed soul in Psalm 42:3–5. Enveloped in a seemingly infinite expanse of questions, the uncertain pilgrim stretches forward to know and see beyond himself. Beyond the tangible. Just as darkness is the womb of being, so it is the beginning of faith.

You may be in a period of deep questioning in which God may seem distant or unreachable. I encourage you to embrace your *now*: this obscure and murky place. Because in this now, you can live in unprecedented, unfettered honesty. Instead of reaching for the nearest spotlight, reach for your journal and begin saying those things you haven't even dared whisper. Or reach for a paintbrush, a sketch pad, the piano, or your camera. Paint, scribble, compose, or picture this strange, new world you inhabit, this landscape in which you feel an utter misfit. This is your gestation into new life. Just as the psalmist journeyed forward through his darkness, you can join him in saying, "Why am I discouraged? Why is my heart so sad? I will put my hope in God! I will praise him again—my Savior and my God!" (42:5–6).

—*Sally Morgenthaler*

For more on faith, see reading at Psalm 111.

Book Two (Psalms 42–72)

42 *For the choir director: A psalm* of the descendants of Korah.*

¹ As the deer longs for streams of water,
so I long for you, O God.
² I thirst for God, the living God.
When can I go and stand before him?
³ Day and night I have only tears for food,
while my enemies continually taunt me, saying,
"Where is this God of yours?"
⁴ My heart is breaking
as I remember how it used to be:

I walked among the crowds of worshipers,
leading a great procession to the house of God,
singing for joy and giving thanks amid the sound of a great celebration!

⁵ Why am I discouraged?
Why is my heart so sad?
I will put my hope in God!
I will praise him again—
my Savior and ⁶my God!

Now I am deeply discouraged,
but I will remember you—

42:TITLE Hebrew *maskil*. This may be a literary or musical term.

even from distant Mount Hermon, the
source of the Jordan,
from the land of Mount Mizar.
[7] I hear the tumult of the raging seas
as your waves and surging tides sweep
over me.
[8] But each day the LORD pours his
unfailing love upon me,
and through each night I sing his songs,
praying to God who gives me life.

[9] "O God my rock," I cry,
"Why have you forgotten me?
Why must I wander around in grief,
oppressed by my enemies?"
[10] Their taunts break my bones.
They scoff, "Where is this God of yours?"

[11] Why am I discouraged?
Why is my heart so sad?
I will put my hope in God!
I will praise him again—
my Savior and my God!

43 [1] Declare me innocent, O God!
Defend me against these
ungodly people.
Rescue me from these unjust liars.
[2] For you are God, my only safe haven.
Why have you tossed me aside?
Why must I wander around in grief,
oppressed by my enemies?
[3] Send out your light and your truth;
let them guide me.
Let them lead me to your holy mountain,
to the place where you live.
[4] There I will go to the altar of God,
to God—the source of all my joy.
I will praise you with my harp,
O God, my God!

[5] Why am I discouraged?
Why is my heart so sad?
I will put my hope in God!
I will praise him again—
my Savior and my God!

44 For the choir director: A psalm* of
the descendants of Korah.

[1] O God, we have heard it with our own
ears—
our ancestors have told us

of all you did in their day,
in days long ago:
[2] You drove out the pagan nations by your
power
and gave all the land to our ancestors.
You crushed their enemies
and set our ancestors free.
[3] They did not conquer the land with their
swords;
it was not their own strong arm that
gave them victory.
It was your right hand and strong arm
and the blinding light from your face
that helped them,
for you loved them.

[4] You are my King and my God.
You command victories for Israel.*
[5] Only by your power can we push back
our enemies;
only in your name can we trample our
foes.
[6] I do not trust in my bow;
I do not count on my sword to save me.
[7] You are the one who gives us victory
over our enemies;
you disgrace those who hate us.
[8] O God, we give glory to you all day long
and constantly praise your name.

Interlude

[9] But now you have tossed us aside in
dishonor.
You no longer lead our armies to battle.
[10] You make us retreat from our enemies
and allow those who hate us to
plunder our land.
[11] You have butchered us like sheep
and scattered us among the nations.
[12] You sold your precious people for a
pittance,
making nothing on the sale.
[13] You let our neighbors mock us.
We are an object of scorn and derision
to those around us.
[14] You have made us the butt of their jokes;
they shake their heads at us in scorn.
[15] We can't escape the constant
humiliation;
shame is written across our faces.
[16] All we hear are the taunts of our mockers.
All we see are our vengeful enemies.

44:TITLE Hebrew *maskil*. This may be a literary or musical term.　**44:4** Hebrew *for Jacob*. The names "Jacob" and "Israel" are often
interchanged throughout the Old Testament, referring sometimes to the individual patriarch and sometimes to the nation.

17 All this has happened though we have
      not forgotten you.
   We have not violated your covenant.
18 Our hearts have not deserted you.
   We have not strayed from your path.
19 Yet you have crushed us in the jackal's
      desert home.
   You have covered us with darkness
      and death.
20 If we had forgotten the name of our God
      or spread our hands in prayer to
      foreign gods,
21 God would surely have known it,
   for he knows the secrets of every heart.
22 But for your sake we are killed every day;
   we are being slaughtered like sheep.

23 Wake up, O Lord! Why do you sleep?
   Get up! Do not reject us forever.
24 Why do you look the other way?
   Why do you ignore our suffering and
      oppression?
25 We collapse in the dust,
   lying face down in the dirt.
26 Rise up! Help us!
   Ransom us because of your unfailing
      love.

45 *For the choir director: A love song to
      be sung to the tune "Lilies." A psalm**
of the descendants of Korah.

1 Beautiful words stir my heart.
   I will recite a lovely poem about the
      king,
   for my tongue is like the pen of a
      skillful poet.

2 You are the most handsome of all.
   Gracious words stream from your lips.
   God himself has blessed you forever.
3 Put on your sword, O mighty warrior!
   You are so glorious, so majestic!
4 In your majesty, ride out to victory,
   defending truth, humility, and justice.
   Go forth to perform awe-inspiring
      deeds!
5 Your arrows are sharp, piercing your
      enemies' hearts.
   The nations fall beneath your feet.

6 Your throne, O God,* endures forever
   and ever.

You rule with a scepter of justice.
7 You love justice and hate evil.
   Therefore God, your God, has
      anointed you,
   pouring out the oil of joy on you more
      than on anyone else.
8 Myrrh, aloes, and cassia perfume your
      robes.
   In ivory palaces the music of strings
      entertains you.
9 Kings' daughters are among your noble
      women.
   At your right side stands the queen,
      wearing jewelry of finest gold from
      Ophir!

10 Listen to me, O royal daughter; take to
      heart what I say.
   Forget your people and your family far
      away.
11 For your royal husband delights in your
      beauty;
   honor him, for he is your lord.
12 The princess of Tyre* will shower you
      with gifts.
   The wealthy will beg your favor.
13 The bride, a princess, looks glorious
   in her golden gown.
14 In her beautiful robes, she is led to the
      king,
   accompanied by her bridesmaids.
15 What a joyful and enthusiastic procession
   as they enter the king's palace!

16 Your sons will become kings like their
      father.
   You will make them rulers over many
      lands.
17 I will bring honor to your name in every
      generation.
   Therefore, the nations will praise you
      forever and ever.

46 *For the choir director: A song of the
      descendants of Korah, to be sung by
soprano voices.**

1 God is our refuge and strength,
   always ready to help in times of
      trouble.
2 So we will not fear when earthquakes
      come

45:TITLE Hebrew *maskil.* This may be a literary or musical term.   **45:6** Or *Your divine throne.*   **45:12** Hebrew *The daughter of Tyre.*
46:TITLE Hebrew *according to alamoth.*

Silence

Finding Friendship with God in Silence

PSALM 46:10

Who doesn't yearn to know in her very marrow that God is her friend? Who doesn't want more peace? And who wouldn't like to handle life's difficulties and pain with equanimity?

In Christ surely such impossible-sounding desires are possible. In one of the most beautiful Gospel chapters, John 15, Jesus opens his heart to his disciples. He tells them that he loves them, that they are his friends, and that he is always with them: "I have loved you even as the Father has loved me. Remain in my love. . . . I no longer call you slaves, because a master doesn't confide in his slaves. Now you are my *friends*" (15:9, 15, italics added).

Jesus says the same to us: "Now you are my friends." If we consider the awesome intimacy of Christ's friendship, we can discover the truth of Saint Augustine's words: "God is closer to your soul than you are yourself."

Silence is an ancient spiritual discipline that helps us nurture our friendship with God. Silence merely means shutting our mouths for a moment, which is always hard for this particular middle-aged Cuban woman, wife, mother, and professor to do.

Psalm 46:10 can frame our understanding of this discipline: "Be still, and know that I am God!" How would our world change if we practiced what silence teaches? When we look into church history, we discover that the ancient Christian mystics teach us our lives can be transformed when we are still and quiet regularly. In a sermon the thirteenth-century Benedictine nun Umiltà of Faenza says, "Those who want to be able to listen well to God's speaking must enclose themselves in great silence." As we spend time in quietness with God, we are able to listen to the rich, soul-making silence that is divine love.

In the fourteenth-century masterpiece on prayer *The Cloud of Unknowing*, an anonymous English monk tells us that communing with God is easy; we need only *a nakid entente* ("a naked intent"). If we desire with all our hearts to be close to God, that is enough, he says, and he encourages us simply to try sitting quietly before God: "Be bold."

The fourteenth-century Christian mystic Catherine of Siena also knew the sustaining joys that come from the profound place of silence within her soul. "Sweet eternal will of God, you've taught us how to find you. If we asked our kind, loving Savior and most merciful Father: 'How can we find you?' God would tell us: 'If you want to find and experience the fruit of my will, always live in the cell of your soul.'"

And Saint Augustine reminds us in his *Confessions* that we must get alone with God daily:

> If you could calm your body's loud demands—if you could blind your point of view; if you could silence noise and dreams and language and symbols and everything that does not last forever . . . if you could listen only to your Maker speak, not through anything but himself: then we would hear Being, the unmoving Wisdom. And if we could sustain this not-thinking for any length of time, it would swallow us up into unspeakable delights of the soul, and we would know what Jesus meant when he told the parable of the talents, giving this invitation: 'Enter into the joy of your master' (Matthew 25:23).

In *The Herald of Divine Love*, the thirteenth-century nun Gertrude the Great shows us how simple it is to be alone with God and what an antidote it is to the human reality of acute loneliness:

> One day not long after Easter I went to the garden before Prime and sat down beside the pond. I began thinking what a pleasant place it was. . . . I loved the quiet, hidden tranquility of this secluded place. I asked myself what else I needed to complete my joy there in such an excellent spot, and I realized I needed a friend. I needed someone intimate, sweet, wise, and fun to share my solitude. Then you, God, led me in meditation back to yourself, the source of unimaginable joy.

Though silence can be difficult at times, it leads us to experience God's divine love. In taking time to be alone and quiet with Christ, I can know in my inmost being that God is my friend.

—*Carmen Acevedo Butcher*

For more on silence, see reading at Psalm 62:1–2.

and the mountains crumble into the
sea.
³ Let the oceans roar and foam.
Let the mountains tremble as the
waters surge!   *Interlude*

⁴ A river brings joy to the city of our God,
the sacred home of the Most High.
⁵ God dwells in that city; it cannot be
destroyed.
From the very break of day, God will
protect it.
⁶ The nations are in chaos,
and their kingdoms crumble!
God's voice thunders,
and the earth melts!
⁷ The LORD of Heaven's Armies is here
among us;
the God of Israel* is our fortress.
Interlude

⁸ Come, see the glorious works of the
LORD:
See how he brings destruction upon
the world.
⁹ He causes wars to end throughout the
earth.
He breaks the bow and snaps the spear;
he burns the shields with fire.
¹⁰ "Be still, and know that I am God!
I will be honored by every nation.
I will be honored throughout the
world."
¹¹ The LORD of Heaven's Armies is here
among us;
the God of Israel is our fortress.
Interlude

47 *For the choir director: A psalm of
the descendants of Korah.*

¹ Come, everyone! Clap your hands!
Shout to God with joyful praise!
² For the LORD Most High is awesome.
He is the great King of all the earth.
³ He subdues the nations before us,
putting our enemies beneath our feet.
⁴ He chose the Promised Land as our
inheritance,
the proud possession of Jacob's
descendants, whom he loves.
Interlude

⁵ God has ascended with a mighty shout.
The LORD has ascended with trumpets
blaring.
⁶ Sing praises to God, sing praises;
sing praises to our King, sing praises!
⁷ For God is the King over all the earth.
Praise him with a psalm.*
⁸ God reigns above the nations,
sitting on his holy throne.
⁹ The rulers of the world have gathered
together
with the people of the God of
Abraham.
For all the kings of the earth belong to
God.
He is highly honored everywhere.

48 *A song. A psalm of the descendants
of Korah.*

¹ How great is the LORD,
how deserving of praise,
in the city of our God,
which sits on his holy mountain!
² It is high and magnificent;
the whole earth rejoices to see it!
Mount Zion, the holy mountain,*
is the city of the great King!
³ God himself is in Jerusalem's towers,
revealing himself as its defender.

⁴ The kings of the earth joined forces
and advanced against the city.
⁵ But when they saw it, they were stunned;
they were terrified and ran away.
⁶ They were gripped with terror
and writhed in pain like a woman in
labor.
⁷ You destroyed them like the mighty
ships of Tarshish
shattered by a powerful east wind.

⁸ We had heard of the city's glory,
but now we have seen it ourselves—
the city of the LORD of Heaven's
Armies.
It is the city of our God;
he will make it safe forever.   *Interlude*

⁹ O God, we meditate on your unfailing
love
as we worship in your Temple.

46:7 Hebrew *of Jacob;* also in 46:11. See note on 44:4.   47:7 Hebrew *maskil.* This may be a literary or musical term.   48:2 Or *Mount Zion, in
the far north;* Hebrew reads *Mount Zion, the heights of Zaphon.*

¹⁰ As your name deserves, O God,
  you will be praised to the ends of the
    earth.
  Your strong right hand is filled with
    victory.
¹¹ Let the people on Mount Zion rejoice.
  Let all the towns of Judah be glad
    because of your justice.
¹² Go, inspect the city of Jerusalem.*
  Walk around and count the many
    towers.
¹³ Take note of the fortified walls,
  and tour all the citadels,
that you may describe them
  to future generations.
¹⁴ For that is what God is like.
  He is our God forever and ever,
  and he will guide us until we die.

49

*For the choir director: A psalm of
the descendants of Korah.*

¹ Listen to this, all you people!
  Pay attention, everyone in the world!
² High and low,
  rich and poor—listen!
³ For my words are wise,
  and my thoughts are filled with
    insight.
⁴ I listen carefully to many proverbs
  and solve riddles with inspiration from
    a harp.

⁵ Why should I fear when trouble comes,
  when enemies surround me?
⁶ They trust in their wealth
  and boast of great riches.
⁷ Yet they cannot redeem themselves from
    death*
  by paying a ransom to God.
⁸ Redemption does not come so easily,
  for no one can ever pay enough
⁹ to live forever
  and never see the grave.

¹⁰ Those who are wise must finally die,
  just like the foolish and senseless,
  leaving all their wealth behind.
¹¹ The grave is their eternal home,
  where they will stay forever.
They may name their estates after
  themselves,

¹² but their fame will not last.
  They will die, just like animals.
¹³ This is the fate of fools,
  though they are remembered as being
    wise.*   *Interlude*

¹⁴ Like sheep, they are led to the grave,*
  where death will be their shepherd.
In the morning the godly will rule over
  them.
  Their bodies will rot in the grave,
  far from their grand estates.
¹⁵ But as for me, God will redeem my life.
  He will snatch me from the power of
    the grave.   *Interlude*

¹⁶ So don't be dismayed when the wicked
    grow rich
  and their homes become ever more
    splendid.
¹⁷ For when they die, they take nothing
    with them.
  Their wealth will not follow them into
    the grave.
¹⁸ In this life they consider themselves
    fortunate
  and are applauded for their success.
¹⁹ But they will die like all before them
  and never again see the light of day.
²⁰ People who boast of their wealth don't
    understand;
  they will die, just like animals.

50

A psalm of Asaph.

¹ The LORD, the Mighty One, is God,
    and he has spoken;
he has summoned all humanity
  from where the sun rises to where it
    sets.
² From Mount Zion, the perfection of
    beauty,
  God shines in glorious radiance.
³ Our God approaches,
    and he is not silent.
Fire devours everything in his way,
  and a great storm rages around him.
⁴ He calls on the heavens above and earth
    below
  to witness the judgment of his
    people.

48:12 Hebrew *Zion*.   **49:7** Or *no one can redeem the life of another.*   **49:13** The meaning of the Hebrew is uncertain.   **49:14** Hebrew *Sheol;*
also in 49:14b, 15.

Stewardship

More than Caretakers

PSALM 50:7-15

"All the world is mine and everything in it" (Psalm 50:12). Everything I have ultimately belongs to God. My money, house, yard, car, dog, children, and marriage belong to God. My job, hobbies, relationships, gifts, talents, mind, heart, soul, body, and time belong to God. And the breath he gives me in each moment belongs to him. *I* belong to him. I'm merely the manager of the resources he's placed under my stewardship.

So what does it mean to live as if we truly *believe* that everything belongs to God?

The answer varies based on our unique callings, but all of us are accountable to God for the way we employ what he gives us. And he wants us to be much more than just caretakers. In Matthew 25:14-30 Jesus told the story of three servants. When the master went away, he expected his servants to invest what he'd given them, to take some risks, and to return to the master more than he'd given. When he returned, the master praised the two servants who had invested and produced a return on the money he'd given them. He rebuked the third servant, but not for squandering his money. No, it was for choosing to keep it safe. The servant had protected it—and that wasn't good enough.

As stewards, we have no right to squander, hoard, treasure, ignore, abuse, or merely protect what God has entrusted to us. We're obligated to *use* these gifts as God would want. God gives us gifts not merely for our pleasure, but for his pleasure and glory—which may bring us pleasure as well. Or it may require us to painfully loosen our grasp on something or someone we'd like to protect and hold on to. Rather than possessiveness, stewardship requires gratitude. Rather than a sense of entitlement, God calls us to responsibility. How selfish we are to think God's gifts are ours to do with as we please—or to ignore.

—*Amy Simpson*

For more on stewardship, see reading at Hosea 4:3.

5 "Bring my faithful people to me—
  those who made a covenant with me
    by giving sacrifices."
6 Then let the heavens proclaim his justice,
  for God himself will be the judge.
                              Interlude
7 "O my people, listen as I speak.
  Here are my charges against you,
    O Israel:
  I am God, your God!
8 I have no complaint about your sacrifices
  or the burnt offerings you constantly
    offer.
9 But I do not need the bulls from your
    barns
  or the goats from your pens.

10 For all the animals of the forest are mine,
  and I own the cattle on a thousand
    hills.
11 I know every bird on the mountains,
  and all the animals of the field are mine.
12 If I were hungry, I would not tell you,
  for all the world is mine and
    everything in it.
13 Do I eat the meat of bulls?
  Do I drink the blood of goats?
14 Make thankfulness your sacrifice to God,
  and keep the vows you made to the
    Most High.
15 Then call on me when you are in trouble,
  and I will rescue you,
  and you will give me glory."

Grace amid the Vices

PSALM 51

The point of confession and spiritual self-examination isn't, thankfully, just to beat ourselves up and feel guilty. Confession is a way of naming the problem, admitting it, and saying, *Look, there's this mess, Lord, and I'm not going to clean it up on my own. I'm not able, nor am I entirely willing, to let go of these things without some serious divine assistance.* We confess our sins, receive absolution (forgiveness), and seek to make things right. The spiritual discipline of confession is a way of counterforming the self—of *rightly* forming the self.

That said, it can be dangerous to become scrupulous—obsessed with scrutinizing our sin. We should not fall into a works-righteousness approach to faith. But the opposite danger is to neglect sanctification, because we've overemphasized justification: "Oh, you're justified; oh good, you're done. Now you can sit on the couch and relax." No, justification is the *beginning* of the project, not the end.

As we make progress in our spiritual lives, we see how deeply the things we're struggling with are rooted. Sanctification implies that progress isn't only possible but also *expected*, and that becoming more and more like Christ is a journey and a destination.

—*Rebecca Konyndyk DeYoung*

For more on confession, see reading at Psalm 139.

16 But God says to the wicked:
"Why bother reciting my decrees
and pretending to obey my covenant?
17 For you refuse my discipline
and treat my words like trash.
18 When you see thieves, you approve of them,
and you spend your time with adulterers.
19 Your mouth is filled with wickedness,
and your tongue is full of lies.
20 You sit around and slander your brother—
your own mother's son.
21 While you did all this, I remained silent,
and you thought I didn't care.
But now I will rebuke you,
listing all my charges against you.
22 Repent, all of you who forget me,
or I will tear you apart,
and no one will help you.
23 But giving thanks is a sacrifice that truly honors me.

If you keep to my path,
I will reveal to you the salvation of God."

51 *For the choir director: A psalm of David, regarding the time Nathan the prophet came to him after David had committed adultery with Bathsheba.*

1 Have mercy on me, O God,
because of your unfailing love.
Because of your great compassion,
blot out the stain of my sins.
2 Wash me clean from my guilt.
Purify me from my sin.
3 For I recognize my rebellion;
it haunts me day and night.
4 Against you, and you alone, have I sinned;
I have done what is evil in your sight.
You will be proved right in what you say,
and your judgment against me is just.*
5 For I was born a sinner—

51:4 Greek version reads *and you will win your case in court.* Compare Rom 3:4.

yes, from the moment my mother
  conceived me.
⁶ But you desire honesty from the womb,*
  teaching me wisdom even there.

⁷ Purify me from my sins,* and I will be
  clean;
  wash me, and I will be whiter than snow.
⁸ Oh, give me back my joy again;
  you have broken me—
  now let me rejoice.
⁹ Don't keep looking at my sins.
  Remove the stain of my guilt.
¹⁰ Create in me a clean heart, O God.
  Renew a loyal spirit within me.
¹¹ Do not banish me from your presence,
  and don't take your Holy Spirit*
  from me.

¹² Restore to me the joy of your salvation,
  and make me willing to obey you.
¹³ Then I will teach your ways to rebels,
  and they will return to you.
¹⁴ Forgive me for shedding blood, O God
  who saves;
  then I will joyfully sing of your
  forgiveness.
¹⁵ Unseal my lips, O Lord,
  that my mouth may praise you.

¹⁶ You do not desire a sacrifice, or I would
  offer one.
  You do not want a burnt offering.
¹⁷ The sacrifice you desire is a broken spirit.
  You will not reject a broken and
  repentant heart, O God.
¹⁸ Look with favor on Zion and help her;
  rebuild the walls of Jerusalem.
¹⁹ Then you will be pleased with sacrifices
  offered in the right spirit—
  with burnt offerings and whole burnt
  offerings.
  Then bulls will again be sacrificed on
  your altar.

52 *For the choir director: A psalm* of
David, regarding the time Doeg the
Edomite said to Saul, "David has gone to
see Ahimelech."*

¹ Why do you boast about your crimes,
  great warrior?

Don't you realize God's justice
  continues forever?
² All day long you plot destruction.
  Your tongue cuts like a sharp razor;
  you're an expert at telling lies.
³ You love evil more than good
  and lies more than truth.   *Interlude*

⁴ You love to destroy others with your
  words,
  you liar!
⁵ But God will strike you down once and
  for all.
  He will pull you from your home
  and uproot you from the land of the
  living.   *Interlude*

⁶ The righteous will see it and be amazed.
  They will laugh and say,
⁷ "Look what happens to mighty warriors
  who do not trust in God.
  They trust their wealth instead
  and grow more and more bold in their
  wickedness."

⁸ But I am like an olive tree, thriving in
  the house of God.
  I will always trust in God's unfailing
  love.
⁹ I will praise you forever, O God,
  for what you have done.
  I will trust in your good name
  in the presence of your faithful people.

53 *For the choir director: A meditation;
a psalm* of David.*

¹ Only fools say in their hearts,
  "There is no God."
  They are corrupt, and their actions are
  evil;
  not one of them does good!

² God looks down from heaven
  on the entire human race;
  he looks to see if anyone is truly wise,
  if anyone seeks God.
³ But no, all have turned away;
  all have become corrupt.*
  No one does good,
  not a single one!

⁴ Will those who do evil never learn?

51:6 Or *from the heart;* Hebrew reads *in the inward parts.*   **51:7** Hebrew *Purify me with the hyssop branch.*   **51:11** Or *your spirit of holiness.*
52:TITLE Hebrew *maskil.* This may be a literary or musical term.   **53:TITLE** Hebrew *According to mahalath; a maskil.* These may be literary or
musical terms.   **53:3** Greek version reads *have become useless.* Compare Rom 3:12.

They eat up my people like bread
and wouldn't think of praying to God.
⁵ Terror will grip them,
terror like they have never known
before.
God will scatter the bones of your enemies.
You will put them to shame, for God
has rejected them.

⁶ Who will come from Mount Zion to
rescue Israel?
When God restores his people,
Jacob will shout with joy, and Israel
will rejoice.

54

For the choir director: A psalm*
of David, regarding the time the
Ziphites came and said to Saul, "We know
where David is hiding." To be accompanied
by stringed instruments.

¹ Come with great power, O God, and
rescue me!
Defend me with your might.
² Listen to my prayer, O God.
Pay attention to my plea.
³ For strangers are attacking me;
violent people are trying to kill me.
They care nothing for God.   *Interlude*

⁴ But God is my helper.
The Lord keeps me alive!
⁵ May the evil plans of my enemies be
turned against them.
Do as you promised and put an end to
them.

⁶ I will sacrifice a voluntary offering to you;
I will praise your name, O Lord,
for it is good.
⁷ For you have rescued me from my
troubles
and helped me to triumph over my
enemies.

55

For the choir director: A psalm*
of David, to be accompanied by
stringed instruments.

¹ Listen to my prayer, O God.
Do not ignore my cry for help!
² Please listen and answer me,
for I am overwhelmed by my troubles.

³ My enemies shout at me,
making loud and wicked threats.
They bring trouble on me
and angrily hunt me down.

⁴ My heart pounds in my chest.
The terror of death assaults me.
⁵ Fear and trembling overwhelm me,
and I can't stop shaking.
⁶ Oh, that I had wings like a dove;
then I would fly away and rest!
⁷ I would fly far away
to the quiet of the wilderness.
Interlude

⁸ How quickly I would escape—
far from this wild storm of hatred.

⁹ Confuse them, Lord, and frustrate their
plans,
for I see violence and conflict in the city.
¹⁰ Its walls are patrolled day and night
against invaders,
but the real danger is wickedness
within the city.
¹¹ Everything is falling apart;
threats and cheating are rampant in
the streets.

¹² It is not an enemy who taunts me—
I could bear that.
It is not my foes who so arrogantly
insult me—
I could have hidden from them.
¹³ Instead, it is you—my equal,
my companion and close friend.
¹⁴ What good fellowship we once enjoyed
as we walked together to the house of
God.

¹⁵ Let death stalk my enemies;
let the grave* swallow them alive,
for evil makes its home within them.

¹⁶ But I will call on God,
and the Lord will rescue me.
¹⁷ Morning, noon, and night
I cry out in my distress,
and the Lord hears my voice.
¹⁸ He ransoms me and keeps me safe
from the battle waged against me,
though many still oppose me.
¹⁹ God, who has ruled forever,
will hear me and humble them.
Interlude

54:title Hebrew *maskil.* This may be a literary or musical term.   55:title Hebrew *maskil.* This may be a literary or musical term.
55:15 Hebrew *let Sheol.*

Honest to God
PSALM 55

I was twelve when I realized I was truly a Christian. I was in catechism class, and I misunderstood my teacher, thinking she said, "You *can't* talk to God anywhere you want."

"What are you talking about?" I blurted. "I talk to God all the time—in bed, on the bus, outside, even in the bathtub!" I continued my impassioned theological tantrum until I noticed everyone was laughing.

Being able to talk to God—prayer—is what makes our religion a relationship. My faith as a twelve-year-old was rooted in this idea that we *can* connect intimately with our heavenly Father anytime and anywhere. Perhaps what is even more profound is that we can talk to him about *anything*.

Psalms, a collection of prayers, is filled with passionate cries to God. "Listen to my prayer, O God. Do not ignore my cry for help! Please listen and answer me, for I am overwhelmed by my troubles" (Psalm 55:1-2). Some psalms express torment of heart; others are jubilant words of praise or thanks; others reveal peace, fear, anger, or grief. Scripture invites us to draw upon the full range of human emotion in our prayers. We can be real, raw, and honest with God.

And it makes sense. God created us to be in an intimate relationship with him. If we were required to hold back certain emotions, the relationship would be rendered false and our prayers would become mere pretense. Consider what riled Jesus the most: the pretension of the Pharisees. "What sorrow awaits you teachers of religious law and you Pharisees. Hypocrites! For you are like whitewashed tombs—beautiful on the outside but filled on the inside with dead people's bones and all sorts of impurity" (Matthew 23:27). God wants us to come to him with integrity, not to present a nice front and keep the real stuff—pain, guilt, frustration, loneliness, confusion—hidden away. In prayer he invites us, like the psalmists, to come to him with our honest thoughts and feelings.

—*Heather Gemmen Wilson*

For more on prayer, see reading at Psalm 91.

For my enemies refuse to change their
  ways;
    they do not fear God.
²⁰ As for my companion, he betrayed his
    friends;
    he broke his promises.
²¹ His words are as smooth as butter,
    but in his heart is war.
  His words are as soothing as lotion,
    but underneath are
      daggers!

²² Give your burdens to the LORD,
    and he will take care of you.

He will not permit the godly to slip
    and fall.
²³ But you, O God, will send the wicked
    down to the pit of destruction.
  Murderers and liars will die young,
    but I am trusting you to save me.

56 *For the choir director: A psalm* of David, regarding the time the Philistines seized him in Gath. To be sung to the tune "Dove on Distant Oaks."*

¹ O God, have mercy on me,
    for people are hounding me.

56:TITLE Hebrew *miktam*. This may be a literary or musical term.

My foes attack me all day long.
² I am constantly hounded by those who
slander me,
and many are boldly attacking me.
³ But when I am afraid,
I will put my trust in you.
⁴ I praise God for what he has promised.
I trust in God, so why should I be
afraid?
What can mere mortals do to me?

⁵ They are always twisting what I say;
they spend their days plotting to
harm me.
⁶ They come together to spy on me—
watching my every step, eager to kill me.
⁷ Don't let them get away with their
wickedness;
in your anger, O God, bring them down.

⁸ You keep track of all my sorrows.*
You have collected all my tears in your
bottle.
You have recorded each one in your
book.

⁹ My enemies will retreat when I call to
you for help.
This I know: God is on my side!
¹⁰ I praise God for what he has promised;
yes, I praise the LORD for what he has
promised.
¹¹ I trust in God, so why should I be afraid?
What can mere mortals do to me?

¹² I will fulfill my vows to you, O God,
and will offer a sacrifice of thanks for
your help.
¹³ For you have rescued me from death;
you have kept my feet from slipping.
So now I can walk in your presence,
O God,
in your life-giving light.

57 *For the choir director: A psalm* of
David, regarding the time he fled
from Saul and went into the cave. To be
sung to the tune "Do Not Destroy!"*

¹ Have mercy on me, O God, have mercy!
I look to you for protection.
I will hide beneath the shadow of your
wings

until the danger passes by.
² I cry out to God Most High,*
to God who will fulfill his purpose
for me.
³ He will send help from heaven to
rescue me,
disgracing those who hound me.
Interlude
My God will send forth his unfailing
love and faithfulness.

⁴ I am surrounded by fierce lions
who greedily devour human prey—
whose teeth pierce like spears and
arrows,
and whose tongues cut like swords.

⁵ Be exalted, O God, above the highest
heavens!
May your glory shine over all the earth.

⁶ My enemies have set a trap for me.
I am weary from distress.
They have dug a deep pit in my path,
but they themselves have fallen into it.
Interlude

⁷ My heart is confident in you, O God;
my heart is confident.
No wonder I can sing your praises!
⁸ Wake up, my heart!
Wake up, O lyre and harp!
I will wake the dawn with my song.
⁹ I will thank you, Lord, among all the
people.
I will sing your praises among the
nations.
¹⁰ For your unfailing love is as high as the
heavens.
Your faithfulness reaches to the clouds.
¹¹ Be exalted, O God, above the highest
heavens.
May your glory shine over all the
earth.

58 *For the choir director: A psalm* of
David, to be sung to the tune "Do
Not Destroy!"*

¹ Justice—do you rulers* know the
meaning of the word?
Do you judge the people fairly?

2 No! You plot injustice in your hearts.
    You spread violence throughout the
        land.
3 These wicked people are born sinners;
    even from birth they have lied and
        gone their own way.
4 They spit venom like deadly snakes;
    they are like cobras that refuse to listen,
5 ignoring the tunes of the snake charmers,
    no matter how skillfully they play.

6 Break off their fangs, O God!
    Smash the jaws of these lions, O LORD!
7 May they disappear like water into
        thirsty ground.
    Make their weapons useless in their
        hands.*
8 May they be like snails that dissolve into
        slime,
    like a stillborn child who will never see
        the sun.
9 God will sweep them away, both young
        and old,
    faster than a pot heats over burning
        thorns.

10 The godly will rejoice when they see
        injustice avenged.
    They will wash their feet in the blood
        of the wicked.
11 Then at last everyone will say,
    "There truly is a reward for those who
        live for God;
    surely there is a God who judges justly
        here on earth."

59 For the choir director: A psalm* of
    David, regarding the time Saul sent
soldiers to watch David's house in order
to kill him. To be sung to the tune "Do Not
Destroy!"

1 Rescue me from my enemies, O God.
    Protect me from those who have come
        to destroy me.
2 Rescue me from these criminals;
    save me from these murderers.
3 They have set an ambush for me.
    Fierce enemies are out there waiting,
        LORD,
    though I have not sinned or offended
        them.

4 I have done nothing wrong,
    yet they prepare to attack me.
    Wake up! See what is happening and
        help me!
5 O LORD God of Heaven's Armies, the
        God of Israel,
    wake up and punish those hostile
        nations.
    Show no mercy to wicked traitors.
                                        Interlude

6 They come out at night,
    snarling like vicious dogs
    as they prowl the streets.
7 Listen to the filth that comes from their
        mouths;
    their words cut like swords.
    "After all, who can hear us?" they sneer.
8 But LORD, you laugh at them.
    You scoff at all the hostile nations.
9 You are my strength; I wait for you to
        rescue me,
    for you, O God, are my fortress.
10 In his unfailing love, my God will stand
        with me.
    He will let me look down in triumph
        on all my enemies.

11 Don't kill them, for my people soon
        forget such lessons;
    stagger them with your power, and
        bring them to their knees,
    O Lord our shield.
12 Because of the sinful things they say,
    because of the evil that is on their lips,
    let them be captured by their pride,
        their curses, and their lies.
13 Destroy them in your anger!
    Wipe them out completely!
    Then the whole world will know
        that God reigns in Israel.*   Interlude

14 My enemies come out at night,
    snarling like vicious dogs
    as they prowl the streets.
15 They scavenge for food
    but go to sleep unsatisfied.*

16 But as for me, I will sing about your power.
    Each morning I will sing with joy
        about your unfailing love.
    For you have been my refuge,
        a place of safety when I am in distress.

58:7 Or Let them be trodden down and wither like grass. The meaning of the Hebrew is uncertain.   59:TITLE Hebrew miktam. This may be a
literary or musical term.   59:13 Hebrew in Jacob. See note on 44:4.   59:15 Or and growl if they don't get enough.

¹⁷ O my Strength, to you I sing praises,
    for you, O God, are my refuge,
    the God who shows me unfailing love.

60 *For the choir director: A psalm* of David useful for teaching, regarding the time David fought Aram-naharaim and Aram-zobah, and Joab returned and killed 12,000 Edomites in the Valley of Salt. To be sung to the tune "Lily of the Testimony."*

¹ You have rejected us, O God, and
    broken our defenses.
  You have been angry with us; now
    restore us to your favor.
² You have shaken our land and split it
    open.
  Seal the cracks, for the land trembles.
³ You have been very hard on us,
    making us drink wine that sent us
    reeling.
⁴ But you have raised a banner for those
    who fear you—
  a rallying point in the face of attack.
               Interlude

⁵ Now rescue your beloved people.
  Answer and save us by your power.
⁶ God has promised this by his holiness*:
  "I will divide up Shechem with joy.
  I will measure out the valley of Succoth.
⁷ Gilead is mine,
    and Manasseh, too.
  Ephraim, my helmet, will produce my
    warriors,
  and Judah, my scepter, will produce
    my kings.
⁸ But Moab, my washbasin, will become
    my servant,
  and I will wipe my feet on Edom
  and shout in triumph over Philistia."

⁹ Who will bring me into the fortified
    city?
  Who will bring me victory over Edom?
¹⁰ Have you rejected us, O God?
  Will you no longer march with our
    armies?
¹¹ Oh, please help us against our enemies,
  for all human help is useless.
¹² With God's help we will do mighty
    things,
  for he will trample down our foes.

61 *For the choir director: A psalm of David, to be accompanied by stringed instruments.*

¹ O God, listen to my cry!
  Hear my prayer!
² From the ends of the earth,
  I cry to you for help
  when my heart is overwhelmed.
  Lead me to the towering rock of safety,
³ for you are my safe refuge,
  a fortress where my enemies cannot
    reach me.
⁴ Let me live forever in your sanctuary,
  safe beneath the shelter of your wings!
               Interlude

⁵ For you have heard my vows, O God.
  You have given me an inheritance
    reserved for those who fear your
    name.
⁶ Add many years to the life of the king!
  May his years span the generations!
⁷ May he reign under God's protection
    forever.
  May your unfailing love and
    faithfulness watch over him.
⁸ Then I will sing praises to your name
    forever
  as I fulfill my vows each day.

62 *For Jeduthun, the choir director: A psalm of David.*

¹ I wait quietly before God,
  for my victory comes from him.
² He alone is my rock and my salvation,
  my fortress where I will never be shaken.

³ So many enemies against one man—
  all of them trying to kill me.
  To them I'm just a broken-down wall
  or a tottering fence.
⁴ They plan to topple me from my high
    position.
  They delight in telling lies about me.
  They praise me to my face
  but curse me in their hearts. *Interlude*

⁵ Let all that I am wait quietly before God,
  for my hope is in him.
⁶ He alone is my rock and my salvation,
  my fortress where I will not be shaken.
⁷ My victory and honor come from God
  alone.

60:TITLE Hebrew *miktam*. This may be a literary or musical term.   **60:6** Or *in his sanctuary.*

He is my refuge, a rock where no
  enemy can reach me.
⁸ O my people, trust in him at all times.
  Pour out your heart to him,
  for God is our refuge.   *Interlude*

⁹ Common people are as worthless as a
    puff of wind,
  and the powerful are not what they
    appear to be.
  If you weigh them on the scales,
    together they are lighter than a breath
    of air.

¹⁰ Don't make your living by extortion
  or put your hope in stealing.

And if your wealth increases,
    don't make it the center of your life.

¹¹ God has spoken plainly,
    and I have heard it many times:
  Power, O God, belongs to you;
¹²   unfailing love, O Lord, is yours.
  Surely you repay all people
    according to what they have done.

63 *A psalm of David, regarding a time
when David was in the wilderness of
Judah.*

¹ O God, you are my God;
    I earnestly search for you.

  **Hearing
from God**
PSALM 62:1–2

What if I don't "hear" anything from God during silence?

Sometimes we can hear God's voice when we're with others. Perhaps
something hits us in a sermon, or a friend says just the right thing at the right
time. But beyond hearing God speak through others, ultimately we need to
seek to hear directly from him. We need time to be quiet and alone with God
in order to hear the unique message or leading that's meant just for us. So we
"wait quietly before God" (Psalm 62:1). We turn to him in silence and do our
best to be present as we listen for his voice.

But let me be honest: most often when I'm in times of silence, I don't "hear"
anything. If we expect great gems each time we meet with God, we'll be
terribly disappointed and lose interest. Instead, we can approach times
of silence with an attitude that says, *God, I just want to be in your presence
because I love you. Tell me anything you want me to know; I'm listening. But if
there isn't anything I need to know right now, just help me to enjoy being with you.*

At times when I don't seem to hear God leading me in my spirit, I turn
directly to his Word where I can *always* hear from him. I may read a passage
like Psalm 63, Matthew 5:1-16, or Colossians 3:1-17 and quietly, prayerfully
think about the passage as I sit with God.

During times when we cannot "hear" God, perhaps his message is simply:
just be.

—JoHannah Reardon

For more on silence, see reading at Psalm 73.

My soul thirsts for you;
my whole body longs for you
in this parched and weary land
where there is no water.
² I have seen you in your sanctuary
and gazed upon your power and glory.
³ Your unfailing love is better than life itself;
how I praise you!
⁴ I will praise you as long as I live,
lifting up my hands to you in prayer.
⁵ You satisfy me more than the richest
feast.
I will praise you with songs of joy.

⁶ I lie awake thinking of you,
meditating on you through the night.
⁷ Because you are my helper,
I sing for joy in the shadow of your
wings.
⁸ I cling to you;
your strong right hand holds me
securely.

⁹ But those plotting to destroy me will
come to ruin.
They will go down into the depths of
the earth.
¹⁰ They will die by the sword
and become the food of jackals.
¹¹ But the king will rejoice in God.
All who trust in him will praise him,
while liars will be silenced.

64 *For the choir director: A psalm of David.*

¹ O God, listen to my complaint.
Protect my life from my enemies'
threats.
² Hide me from the plots of this evil mob,
from this gang of wrongdoers.
³ They sharpen their tongues like swords
and aim their bitter words like arrows.
⁴ They shoot from ambush at the innocent,
attacking suddenly and fearlessly.
⁵ They encourage each other to do evil
and plan how to set their traps in secret.
"Who will ever notice?" they ask.
⁶ As they plot their crimes, they say,
"We have devised the perfect plan!"
Yes, the human heart and mind are
cunning.

⁷ But God himself will shoot them with
his arrows,

suddenly striking them down.
⁸ Their own tongues will ruin them,
and all who see them will shake their
heads in scorn.
⁹ Then everyone will be afraid;
they will proclaim the mighty acts of
God
and realize all the amazing things he
does.
¹⁰ The godly will rejoice in the LORD
and find shelter in him.
And those who do what is right
will praise him.

65 *For the choir director: A song. A psalm of David.*

¹ What mighty praise, O God,
belongs to you in Zion.
We will fulfill our vows to you,
²   for you answer our prayers.
All of us must come to you.
³ Though we are overwhelmed by our sins,
you forgive them all.
⁴ What joy for those you choose to bring
near,
those who live in your holy courts.
What festivities await us
inside your holy Temple.

⁵ You faithfully answer our prayers with
awesome deeds,
O God our savior.
You are the hope of everyone on earth,
even those who sail on distant seas.
⁶ You formed the mountains by your
power
and armed yourself with mighty
strength.
⁷ You quieted the raging oceans
with their pounding waves
and silenced the shouting of the nations.
⁸ Those who live at the ends of the earth
stand in awe of your wonders.
From where the sun rises to where it sets,
you inspire shouts of joy.

⁹ You take care of the earth and water it,
making it rich and fertile.
The river of God has plenty of water;
it provides a bountiful harvest of grain,
for you have ordered it so.
¹⁰ You drench the plowed ground with
rain,

melting the clods and leveling the
ridges.
You soften the earth with showers
and bless its abundant crops.
¹¹ You crown the year with a bountiful
harvest;
even the hard pathways overflow with
abundance.
¹² The grasslands of the wilderness become
a lush pasture,
and the hillsides blossom with joy.
¹³ The meadows are clothed with flocks of
sheep,
and the valleys are carpeted with grain.
They all shout and sing for joy!

66
For the choir director: A song. A psalm.

¹ Shout joyful praises to God, all the earth!
²   Sing about the glory of his name!
Tell the world how glorious he is.
³ Say to God, "How awesome are your
deeds!
Your enemies cringe before your
mighty power.
⁴ Everything on earth will worship you;
they will sing your praises,
shouting your name in glorious songs."
Interlude

⁵ Come and see what our God has done,
what awesome miracles he performs
for people!
⁶ He made a dry path through the Red Sea,*
and his people went across on foot.
There we rejoiced in him.
⁷ For by his great power he rules forever.
He watches every movement of the
nations;
let no rebel rise in defiance. *Interlude*

⁸ Let the whole world bless our God
and loudly sing his praises.
⁹ Our lives are in his hands,
and he keeps our feet from stumbling.
¹⁰ You have tested us, O God;
you have purified us like silver.
¹¹ You captured us in your net
and laid the burden of slavery on our
backs.
¹² Then you put a leader over us.*
We went through fire and flood,

but you brought us to a place of great
abundance.
¹³ Now I come to your Temple with burnt
offerings
to fulfill the vows I made to you—
¹⁴ yes, the sacred vows that I made
when I was in deep trouble.
¹⁵ That is why I am sacrificing burnt
offerings to you—
the best of my rams as a pleasing
aroma,
and a sacrifice of bulls and male goats.
Interlude

¹⁶ Come and listen, all you who fear God,
and I will tell you what he did for me.
¹⁷ For I cried out to him for help,
praising him as I spoke.
¹⁸ If I had not confessed the sin in my heart,
the Lord would not have listened.
¹⁹ But God did listen!
He paid attention to my prayer.
²⁰ Praise God, who did not ignore my
prayer
or withdraw his unfailing love from me.

67
For the choir director: A song. A psalm, to be accompanied by stringed instruments.

¹ May God be merciful and bless us.
May his face smile with favor on us.
Interlude

² May your ways be known throughout
the earth,
your saving power among people
everywhere.
³ May the nations praise you, O God.
Yes, may all the nations praise you.
⁴ Let the whole world sing for joy,
because you govern the nations with
justice
and guide the people of the whole
world. *Interlude*

⁵ May the nations praise you, O God.
Yes, may all the nations praise you.
⁶ Then the earth will yield its harvests,
and God, our God, will richly bless us.
⁷ Yes, God will bless us,
and people all over the world will fear
him.

66:6 Hebrew *the sea.* 66:12 Or *You made people ride over our heads.*

68

For the choir director: A song. A psalm of David.

¹ Rise up, O God, and scatter your
    enemies.
  Let those who hate God run for their
    lives.
² Blow them away like smoke.
  Melt them like wax in a fire.
  Let the wicked perish in the presence
    of God.
³ But let the godly rejoice.
  Let them be glad in God's presence.
  Let them be filled with joy.
⁴ Sing praises to God and to his name!
  Sing loud praises to him who rides the
    clouds.
  His name is the LORD—
  rejoice in his presence!

⁵ Father to the fatherless, defender of
    widows—
  this is God, whose dwelling is holy.
⁶ God places the lonely in families;
  he sets the prisoners free and gives
    them joy.
  But he makes the rebellious live in a sun-
    scorched land.

⁷ O God, when you led your people out
    from Egypt,
  when you marched through the dry
    wasteland,   *Interlude*
⁸ the earth trembled, and the heavens
    poured down rain
  before you, the God of Sinai,
  before God, the God of Israel.
⁹ You sent abundant rain, O God,
  to refresh the weary land.
¹⁰ There your people finally settled,
  and with a bountiful harvest, O God,
  you provided for your needy people.

¹¹ The Lord gives the word,
  and a great army* brings the good news.
¹² Enemy kings and their armies flee,
  while the women of Israel divide the
    plunder.
¹³ Even those who lived among the
    sheepfolds found treasures—
  doves with wings of silver
  and feathers of gold.
¹⁴ The Almighty scattered the enemy kings
like a blowing snowstorm on Mount
    Zalmon.

¹⁵ The mountains of Bashan are majestic,
  with many peaks stretching high into
    the sky.
¹⁶ Why do you look with envy, O rugged
    mountains,
  at Mount Zion, where God has chosen
    to live,
  where the LORD himself will live
    forever?

¹⁷ Surrounded by unnumbered thousands
    of chariots,
  the Lord came from Mount Sinai into
    his sanctuary.
¹⁸ When you ascended to the heights,
  you led a crowd of captives.
  You received gifts from the people,
  even from those who rebelled against
    you.
  Now the LORD God will live among us
    there.

¹⁹ Praise the Lord; praise God our savior!
  For each day he carries us in his arms.
                                Interlude
²⁰ Our God is a God who saves!
  The Sovereign LORD rescues us from
    death.

²¹ But God will smash the heads of his
    enemies,
  crushing the skulls of those who love
    their guilty ways.
²² The Lord says, "I will bring my enemies
    down from Bashan;
  I will bring them up from the depths
    of the sea.
²³ You, my people, will wash your feet in
    their blood,
  and even your dogs will get their share!"

²⁴ Your procession has come into view,
    O God—
  the procession of my God and King as
    he goes into the sanctuary.
²⁵ Singers are in front, musicians behind;
  between them are young women
    playing tambourines.
²⁶ Praise God, all you people of Israel;
  praise the LORD, the source of Israel's
    life.

68:11 Or *a host of women.*

²⁷ Look, the little tribe of Benjamin leads
the way.
Then comes a great throng of rulers
from Judah
and all the rulers of Zebulun and
Naphtali.
²⁸ Summon your might, O God.
Display your power, O God, as you
have in the past.
²⁹ The kings of the earth are bringing
tribute
to your Temple in Jerusalem.
³⁰ Rebuke these enemy nations—
these wild animals lurking in the
reeds,
this herd of bulls among the weaker
calves.
Make them bring bars of silver in
humble tribute.
Scatter the nations that delight in war.
³¹ Let Egypt come with gifts of precious
metals*;
let Ethiopia* bow in submission to
God.
³² Sing to God, you kingdoms of the earth.
Sing praises to the Lord.   *Interlude*
³³ Sing to the one who rides across the
ancient heavens,
his mighty voice thundering from the
sky.
³⁴ Tell everyone about God's power.
His majesty shines down on Israel;
his strength is mighty in the heavens.
³⁵ God is awesome in his sanctuary.
The God of Israel gives power and
strength to his people.

Praise be to God!

69 *For the choir director: A psalm of
David, to be sung to the tune "Lilies."*

¹ Save me, O God,
for the floodwaters are up to my neck.
² Deeper and deeper I sink into the mire;
I can't find a foothold.
I am in deep water,
and the floods overwhelm me.
³ I am exhausted from crying for help;
my throat is parched.
My eyes are swollen with weeping,
waiting for my God to help me.

⁴ Those who hate me without cause
outnumber the hairs on my head.
Many enemies try to destroy me with
lies,
demanding that I give back what I
didn't steal.
⁵ O God, you know how foolish I am;
my sins cannot be hidden from you.
⁶ Don't let those who trust in you be
ashamed because of me,
O Sovereign LORD of Heaven's
Armies.
Don't let me cause them to be
humiliated,
O God of Israel.
⁷ For I endure insults for your sake;
humiliation is written all over my face.
⁸ Even my own brothers pretend they
don't know me;
they treat me like a stranger.

⁹ Passion for your house has consumed me,
and the insults of those who insult you
have fallen on me.
¹⁰ When I weep and fast,
they scoff at me.
¹¹ When I dress in burlap to show sorrow,
they make fun of me.
¹² I am the favorite topic of town gossip,
and all the drunks sing about me.

¹³ But I keep praying to you, LORD,
hoping this time you will show me
favor.
In your unfailing love, O God,
answer my prayer with your sure
salvation.
¹⁴ Rescue me from the mud;
don't let me sink any deeper!
Save me from those who hate me,
and pull me from these deep waters.
¹⁵ Don't let the floods overwhelm me,
or the deep waters swallow me,
or the pit of death devour me.

¹⁶ Answer my prayers, O LORD,
for your unfailing love is wonderful.
Take care of me,
for your mercy is so plentiful.
¹⁷ Don't hide from your servant;
answer me quickly, for I am in deep
trouble!

68:31a Or *of rich cloth.*   **68:31b** Hebrew *Cush.*

¹⁸ Come and redeem me;
    free me from my enemies.
¹⁹ You know of my shame, scorn, and
    disgrace.
    You see all that my enemies are doing.
²⁰ Their insults have broken my heart,
    and I am in despair.
    If only one person would show some pity;
    if only one would turn and comfort me.
²¹ But instead, they give me poison* for
    food;
    they offer me sour wine for my thirst.

²² Let the bountiful table set before them
    become a snare
    and their prosperity become a trap.*
²³ Let their eyes go blind so they cannot see,
    and make their bodies shake
    continually.*
²⁴ Pour out your fury on them;
    consume them with your burning anger.
²⁵ Let their homes become desolate
    and their tents be deserted.
²⁶ To the one you have punished, they add
    insult to injury;
    they add to the pain of those you have
    hurt.
²⁷ Pile their sins up high,
    and don't let them go free.
²⁸ Erase their names from the Book of Life;
    don't let them be counted among the
    righteous.

²⁹ I am suffering and in pain.
    Rescue me, O God, by your saving
    power.
³⁰ Then I will praise God's name with
    singing,
    and I will honor him with thanksgiving.
³¹ For this will please the LORD more than
    sacrificing cattle,
    more than presenting a bull with its
    horns and hooves.
³² The humble will see their God at work
    and be glad.
    Let all who seek God's help be
    encouraged.
³³ For the LORD hears the cries of the needy;
    he does not despise his imprisoned
    people.

³⁴ Praise him, O heaven and earth,
    the seas and all that move in them.
³⁵ For God will save Jerusalem*
    and rebuild the towns of Judah.
    His people will live there
    and settle in their own land.
³⁶ The descendants of those who obey him
    will inherit the land,
    and those who love him will live there
    in safety.

70 *For the choir director: A psalm of David, asking God to remember him.*

¹ Please, God, rescue me!
    Come quickly, LORD, and help me.
² May those who try to kill me
    be humiliated and put to shame.
    May those who take delight in my
    trouble
    be turned back in disgrace.
³ Let them be horrified by their shame,
    for they said, "Aha! We've got him
    now!"
⁴ But may all who search for you
    be filled with joy and gladness in you.
    May those who love your salvation
    repeatedly shout, "God is great!"
⁵ But as for me, I am poor and needy;
    please hurry to my aid, O God.
    You are my helper and my savior;
    O LORD, do not delay.

71 ¹ O LORD, I have come to you for
    protection;
    don't let me be disgraced.
² Save me and rescue me,
    for you do what is right.
    Turn your ear to listen to me,
    and set me free.
³ Be my rock of safety
    where I can always hide.
    Give the order to save me,
    for you are my rock and my fortress.
⁴ My God, rescue me from the power of
    the wicked,
    from the clutches of cruel oppressors.
⁵ O Lord, you alone are my hope.
    I've trusted you, O LORD, from
    childhood.

69:21 Or *gall.* **69:22** Greek version reads *Let their bountiful table set before them become a snare, / a trap that makes them think all is well. / Let their blessings cause them to stumble, / and let them get what they deserve.* Compare Rom 11:9. **69:23** Greek version reads *and let their backs be bent forever.* Compare Rom 11:10. **69:35** Hebrew *Zion.*

⁶ Yes, you have been with me from birth;
    from my mother's womb you have
        cared for me.
    No wonder I am always praising you!
⁷ My life is an example to many,
    because you have been my strength
        and protection.
⁸ That is why I can never stop praising you;
    I declare your glory all day long.
⁹ And now, in my old age, don't set me aside.
    Don't abandon me when my strength
        is failing.
¹⁰ For my enemies are whispering
        against me.
    They are plotting together to kill me.
¹¹ They say, "God has abandoned him.
    Let's go and get him,
    for no one will help him now."

¹² O God, don't stay away.
    My God, please hurry to help me.
¹³ Bring disgrace and destruction on my
        accusers.
    Humiliate and shame those who want
        to harm me.
¹⁴ But I will keep on hoping for your help;
    I will praise you more and more.
¹⁵ I will tell everyone about your
        righteousness.
    All day long I will proclaim your
        saving power,
    though I am not skilled with words.*
¹⁶ I will praise your mighty deeds,
    O Sovereign LORD.
    I will tell everyone that you alone are
        just.

¹⁷ O God, you have taught me from my
        earliest childhood,
    and I constantly tell others about the
        wonderful things you do.
¹⁸ Now that I am old and gray,
    do not abandon me, O God.
    Let me proclaim your power to this new
        generation,
    your mighty miracles to all who come
        after me.
¹⁹ Your righteousness, O God, reaches to
        the highest heavens.
    You have done such wonderful things.
    Who can compare with you, O God?

²⁰ You have allowed me to suffer much
        hardship,
    but you will restore me to life again
    and lift me up from the depths of the
        earth.
²¹ You will restore me to even greater honor
    and comfort me once again.

²² Then I will praise you with music on the
        harp,
    because you are faithful to your
        promises, O my God.
    I will sing praises to you with a lyre,
    O Holy One of Israel.
²³ I will shout for joy and sing your praises,
    for you have ransomed me.
²⁴ I will tell about your righteous deeds
    all day long,
    for everyone who tried to hurt me
    has been shamed and humiliated.

72 *A psalm of Solomon.*

¹ Give your love of justice to the king,
    O God,
    and righteousness to the king's son.
² Help him judge your people in the right
        way;
    let the poor always be treated fairly.
³ May the mountains yield prosperity for
        all,
    and may the hills be fruitful.
⁴ Help him to defend the poor,
    to rescue the children of the needy,
    and to crush their oppressors.
⁵ May they fear you* as long as the sun
        shines,
    as long as the moon remains in the sky.
    Yes, forever!

⁶ May the king's rule be refreshing like
        spring rain on freshly cut grass,
    like the showers that water the earth.
⁷ May all the godly flourish during his reign.
    May there be abundant prosperity
    until the moon is no more.
⁸ May he reign from sea to sea,
    and from the Euphrates River* to the
        ends of the earth.
⁹ Desert nomads will bow before him;
    his enemies will fall before him in the
        dust.

71:15 Or *though I cannot count it.*   **72:5** Greek version reads *May they endure.*   **72:8** Hebrew *the river.*

¹⁰ The western kings of Tarshish and other
distant lands
will bring him tribute.
The eastern kings of Sheba and Seba
will bring him gifts.
¹¹ All kings will bow before him,
and all nations will serve him.

¹² He will rescue the poor when they cry to
him;
he will help the oppressed, who have
no one to defend them.
¹³ He feels pity for the weak and the needy,
and he will rescue them.
¹⁴ He will redeem them from oppression
and violence,
for their lives are precious to him.

¹⁵ Long live the king!
May the gold of Sheba be given to him.
May the people always pray for him
and bless him all day long.
¹⁶ May there be abundant grain throughout
the land,
flourishing even on the hilltops.
May the fruit trees flourish like the trees
of Lebanon,
and may the people thrive like grass in
a field.
¹⁷ May the king's name endure forever;
may it continue as long as the sun shines.
May all nations be blessed through him
and bring him praise.

¹⁸ Praise the LORD God, the God of Israel,
who alone does such wonderful
things.
¹⁹ Praise his glorious name forever!
Let the whole earth be filled with his
glory.
Amen and amen!

²⁰ (This ends the prayers of David son of
Jesse.)

BOOK THREE (Psalms 73–89)

73 *A psalm of Asaph.*

¹ Truly God is good to Israel,
to those whose hearts are pure.
² But as for me, I almost lost my footing.
My feet were slipping, and I was
almost gone.

³ For I envied the proud
when I saw them prosper despite their
wickedness.
⁴ They seem to live such painless lives;
their bodies are so healthy and strong.
⁵ They don't have troubles like other people;
they're not plagued with problems like
everyone else.
⁶ They wear pride like a jeweled necklace
and clothe themselves with cruelty.
⁷ These fat cats have everything
their hearts could ever wish for!
⁸ They scoff and speak only evil;
in their pride they seek to crush others.
⁹ They boast against the very heavens,
and their words strut throughout the
earth.
¹⁰ And so the people are dismayed and
confused,
drinking in all their words.
¹¹ "What does God know?" they ask.
"Does the Most High even know
what's happening?"
¹² Look at these wicked people—
enjoying a life of ease while their
riches multiply.

¹³ Did I keep my heart pure for nothing?
Did I keep myself innocent for no
reason?
¹⁴ I get nothing but trouble all day long;
every morning brings me pain.

¹⁵ If I had really spoken this way to others,
I would have been a traitor to your
people.
¹⁶ So I tried to understand why the wicked
prosper.
But what a difficult task it is!
¹⁷ Then I went into your sanctuary, O God,
and I finally understood the destiny of
the wicked.
¹⁸ Truly, you put them on a slippery path
and send them sliding over the cliff to
destruction.
¹⁹ In an instant they are destroyed,
completely swept away by terrors.
²⁰ When you arise, O Lord,
you will laugh at their silly ideas
as a person laughs at dreams in the
morning.

²¹ Then I realized that my heart was bitter,
and I was all torn up inside.

Silence and Self-Pity
PSALM 73

P salm 73 is a powerful illustration of what happens when we enter into silence before the Lord. The author, Asaph, recounts his internal consternation as he watches the wicked prosper. It doesn't seem fair to him that such a rebellious lot not only get away with their depravity but are seemingly rewarded for it. "They seem to live such painless lives; their bodies are so healthy and strong. They don't have troubles like other people; they're not plagued with problems like everyone else" (73:4–5).

Meanwhile Asaph tries his best to lead a righteous life, and what does he get for it? Nothing. "Did I keep my heart pure for nothing? Did I keep myself innocent for no reason?" (73:13).

I recognize this kind of self-pity. When I wallow in it, I ultimately find myself in freefall, like Asaph, spiraling downward toward the pit of despair.

But everything changes when we enter the sanctuary of God. It is there, Asaph continues in verse 17, that understanding comes. When we remove ourselves from the dwelling of self-absorbed humanity and enter purposefully into the presence of God, the "aha" moment happens. Proper perspective is restored. Clarity dawns. Our skewed perceptions are made right.

Most of us are exposed to a myriad of voices every day, and the great majority of them would try to convince us to think in ways that are contrary to the principles that reign in the kingdom of God. Removing ourselves and entering into "the sanctuary," through silence and solitude, help us sit attentively before the True Voice and be turned 'round right again. What once made us anxious is now released into loving hands. Our anger turns into repentance. Our agitation is replaced by peace—peace that the world cannot give.

—Tracy Balzer

For more on silence, see reading at Psalm 77:11-15.

---

22 I was so foolish and ignorant—
  I must have seemed like a senseless
    animal to you.
23 Yet I still belong to you;
  you hold my right hand.
24 You guide me with your counsel,
  leading me to a glorious destiny.
25 Whom have I in heaven but you?
  I desire you more than anything on
    earth.
26 My health may fail, and my spirit may
    grow weak,
  but God remains the strength of my
    heart;
  he is mine forever.

27 Those who desert him will perish,
  for you destroy those who abandon
    you.
28 But as for me, how good it is to be near
    God!
  I have made the Sovereign LORD my
    shelter,
  and I will tell everyone about the
    wonderful things you do.

74 A psalm* of Asaph.

1 O God, why have you rejected us so long?
  Why is your anger so intense against
    the sheep of your own pasture?

74:TITLE Hebrew *maskil*. This may be a literary or musical term.

² Remember that we are the people you
   chose long ago,
   the tribe you redeemed as your own
   special possession!
And remember Jerusalem,* your home
   here on earth.

³ Walk through the awful ruins of the city;
   see how the enemy has destroyed your
   sanctuary.

⁴ There your enemies shouted their
   victorious battle cries;
   there they set up their battle
   standards.

⁵ They swung their axes
   like woodcutters in a forest.

⁶ With axes and picks,
   they smashed the carved paneling.

⁷ They burned your sanctuary to the
   ground.
   They defiled the place that bears your
   name.

⁸ Then they thought, "Let's destroy
   everything!"
   So they burned down all the places
   where God was worshiped.

⁹ We no longer see your miraculous signs.
   All the prophets are gone,
   and no one can tell us when it will end.

¹⁰ How long, O God, will you allow our
    enemies to insult you?
    Will you let them dishonor your name
    forever?

¹¹ Why do you hold back your strong right
    hand?
    Unleash your powerful fist and
    destroy them.

¹² You, O God, are my king from ages past,
    bringing salvation to the earth.

¹³ You split the sea by your strength
    and smashed the heads of the sea
    monsters.

¹⁴ You crushed the heads of Leviathan*
    and let the desert animals eat him.

¹⁵ You caused the springs and streams to
    gush forth,
    and you dried up rivers that never run
    dry.

¹⁶ Both day and night belong to you;
    you made the starlight* and the sun.

¹⁷ You set the boundaries of the earth,
    and you made both summer and winter.

¹⁸ See how these enemies insult you, LORD.
    A foolish nation has dishonored your
    name.

¹⁹ Don't let these wild beasts destroy your
    turtledoves.
    Don't forget your suffering people
    forever.

²⁰ Remember your covenant promises,
    for the land is full of darkness and
    violence!

²¹ Don't let the downtrodden be humiliated
    again.
    Instead, let the poor and needy praise
    your name.

²² Arise, O God, and defend your cause.
    Remember how these fools insult you
    all day long.

²³ Don't overlook what your enemies have
    said
    or their growing uproar.

75

For the choir director: A psalm of
Asaph. A song to be sung to the tune
"Do Not Destroy!"

¹ We thank you, O God!
   We give thanks because you are near.
   People everywhere tell of your
   wonderful deeds.

² God says, "At the time I have planned,
   I will bring justice against the wicked.

³ When the earth quakes and its people
   live in turmoil,
   I am the one who keeps its
   foundations firm.   *Interlude*

⁴ "I warned the proud, 'Stop your
   boasting!'
   I told the wicked, 'Don't raise your fists!

⁵ Don't raise your fists in defiance at the
   heavens
   or speak with such arrogance.'"

⁶ For no one on earth—from east or west,
   or even from the wilderness—
   should raise a defiant fist.*

⁷ It is God alone who judges;
   he decides who will rise and who will
   fall.

74:2 Hebrew *Mount Zion.*   74:14 The identification of Leviathan is disputed, ranging from an earthly creature to a mythical sea monster in ancient literature.   74:16 Or *moon;* Hebrew reads *light.*   75:6 Hebrew *should lift.*

8 For the LORD holds a cup in his hand
   that is full of foaming wine mixed with
     spices.
 He pours out the wine in judgment,
   and all the wicked must drink it,
     draining it to the dregs.

9 But as for me, I will always proclaim
   what God has done;
 I will sing praises to the God of Jacob.
10 For God says, "I will break the strength
   of the wicked,
   but I will increase the power of the
     godly."

76 *For the choir director: A psalm of
Asaph. A song to be accompanied by
stringed instruments.*

1 God is honored in Judah;
   his name is great in Israel.
2 Jerusalem* is where he lives;
   Mount Zion is his home.
3 There he has broken the fiery arrows of
     the enemy,
   the shields and swords and weapons of
     war.   *Interlude*

4 You are glorious and more majestic
   than the everlasting mountains.*
5 Our boldest enemies have been
     plundered.
 They lie before us in the sleep of
     death.
 No warrior could lift a hand against us.
6 At the blast of your breath, O God of
     Jacob,
   their horses and chariots lay still.

7 No wonder you are greatly feared!
 Who can stand before you when your
     anger explodes?
8 From heaven you sentenced your
     enemies;
   the earth trembled and stood silent
     before you.
9 You stand up to judge those who do evil,
     O God,
   and to rescue the oppressed of the
     earth.   *Interlude*
10 Human defiance only enhances your
     glory,
   for you use it as a weapon.*

11 Make vows to the LORD your God, and
   keep them.
 Let everyone bring tribute to the
   Awesome One.
12 For he breaks the pride of princes,
   and the kings of the earth fear him.

77 *For Jeduthun, the choir director: A
psalm of Asaph.*

1 I cry out to God; yes, I shout.
 Oh, that God would listen to me!
2 When I was in deep trouble,
   I searched for the Lord.
 All night long I prayed, with hands lifted
     toward heaven,
   but my soul was not comforted.
3 I think of God, and I moan,
   overwhelmed with longing for his
     help.   *Interlude*

4 You don't let me sleep.
 I am too distressed even to pray!
5 I think of the good old days,
   long since ended,
6 when my nights were filled with joyful
     songs.
 I search my soul and ponder the
     difference now.
7 Has the Lord rejected me forever?
 Will he never again be kind to me?
8 Is his unfailing love gone forever?
 Have his promises permanently failed?
9 Has God forgotten to be gracious?
 Has he slammed the door on his
     compassion?   *Interlude*

10 And I said, "This is my fate;
   the Most High has turned his hand
     against me."
11 But then I recall all you have done,
     O LORD;
   I remember your wonderful deeds of
     long ago.
12 They are constantly in my thoughts.
   I cannot stop thinking about your
     mighty works.

13 O God, your ways are holy.
 Is there any god as mighty as you?
14 You are the God of great wonders!
 You demonstrate your awesome
   power among the nations.

76:2 Hebrew *Salem*, another name for Jerusalem.   76:4 As in Greek version; Hebrew reads *than mountains filled with beasts of prey.*
76:10 The meaning of the Hebrew is uncertain.

¹⁵ By your strong arm, you redeemed your
people,
the descendants of Jacob and Joseph.
Interlude

¹⁶ When the Red Sea* saw you, O God,
its waters looked and trembled!
The sea quaked to its very depths.
¹⁷ The clouds poured down rain;
the thunder rumbled in the sky.
Your arrows of lightning flashed.

¹⁸ Your thunder roared from the whirlwind;
the lightning lit up the world!
The earth trembled and shook.
¹⁹ Your road led through the sea,
your pathway through the mighty
waters—
a pathway no one knew was there!
²⁰ You led your people along that road like
a flock of sheep,
with Moses and Aaron as their
shepherds.

Q&A | Entering into Silence
PSALM 77:11–15

Practicing silence can be intimidating. How can I get started?

Ease into it. Intentionally set aside a few hours in nature or a peaceful indoor spot for a retreat of silence. Making the transition from a busy world to a quiet time will be a challenge. It can be like walking to our cars after attending a rock concert. Our ears are still buzzing from the intense amplification, and we can't hear so well. In the same way, when first entering into silence, we can't expect that our attention to God will immediately be acute. A few slow, deep breaths can help with that transition.

During your time of silence, you will be attacked by a barrage of thoughts and mental distractions that will threaten to throw you off. So have a pen and pad of paper nearby as you settle in your quiet spot, then simply write every distracting thought that comes into your head. By writing them down, you can be assured that all of those important items will not be forgotten; they can be accessed later when your silent time is over.

From this point on the only thing you need to "do" in your silent time is to remind yourself of the purpose of this time: to listen, pay attention, and rest in the love of God. If you'd like, use Scripture to guide silent prayers as you seek to listen to God's voice. Take a walk and observe the glories of creation and the delightful mosaic of humanity. Jot down a long chain of the blessings in your life. There are *many* ways to enjoy silence and to let God heal you through it.

Seeing the truth about ourselves and about God during periods of silence sets us free to be healthy, whole, and of better service to the world. Silence puts us in our place, reminding us that God is God and we are not.

—*Tracy Balzer*

For more on silence, see reading at Psalm 131.

77:16 Hebrew *the waters*.

78 A psalm* of Asaph.

1 O my people, listen to my instructions.
  Open your ears to what I am saying,
2 for I will speak to you in a parable.
  I will teach you hidden lessons from our
    past—
3   stories we have heard and known,
  stories our ancestors handed down
    to us.
4 We will not hide these truths from our
    children;
  we will tell the next generation
  about the glorious deeds of the LORD,
    about his power and his mighty
    wonders.
5 For he issued his laws to Jacob;
  he gave his instructions to Israel.
  He commanded our ancestors
    to teach them to their children,
6 so the next generation might know them—
    even the children not yet born—
  and they in turn will teach their own
    children.
7 So each generation should set its hope
    anew on God,
  not forgetting his glorious miracles
    and obeying his commands.
8 Then they will not be like their ancestors—
    stubborn, rebellious, and unfaithful,
  refusing to give their hearts to God.

9 The warriors of Ephraim, though armed
    with bows,
  turned their backs and fled on the day
    of battle.
10 They did not keep God's covenant
  and refused to live by his instructions.
11 They forgot what he had done—
  the great wonders he had shown them,
12 the miracles he did for their ancestors
  on the plain of Zoan in the land of
    Egypt.
13 For he divided the sea and led them
    through,
  making the water stand up like walls!
14 In the daytime he led them by a cloud,
  and all night by a pillar of fire.
15 He split open the rocks in the wilderness
  to give them water, as from a gushing
    spring.

16 He made streams pour from the rock,
  making the waters flow down like a
    river!
17 Yet they kept on sinning against him,
  rebelling against the Most High in the
    desert.
18 They stubbornly tested God in their
    hearts,
  demanding the foods they craved.
19 They even spoke against God himself,
    saying,
  "God can't give us food in the
    wilderness.
20 Yes, he can strike a rock so water gushes
    out,
  but he can't give his people bread and
    meat."
21 When the LORD heard them, he was
    furious.
  The fire of his wrath burned against
    Jacob.
  Yes, his anger rose against Israel,
22 for they did not believe God
  or trust him to care for them.
23 But he commanded the skies to open;
  he opened the doors of heaven.
24 He rained down manna for them to eat;
  he gave them bread from heaven.
25 They ate the food of angels!
  God gave them all they could hold.
26 He released the east wind in the heavens
  and guided the south wind by his
    mighty power.
27 He rained down meat as thick as dust—
  birds as plentiful as the sand on the
    seashore!
28 He caused the birds to fall within their
    camp
  and all around their tents.
29 The people ate their fill.
  He gave them what they craved.
30 But before they satisfied their craving,
  while the meat was yet in their mouths,
31 the anger of God rose against them,
  and he killed their strongest men.
  He struck down the finest of Israel's
    young men.

32 But in spite of this, the people kept
    sinning.
  Despite his wonders, they refused to
    trust him.

78:TITLE Hebrew *maskil*. This may be a literary or musical term.

³³ So he ended their lives in failure,
  their years in terror.
³⁴ When God began killing them,
  they finally sought him.
  They repented and took God seriously.
³⁵ Then they remembered that God was
    their rock,
  that God Most High* was their
    redeemer.
³⁶ But all they gave him was lip service;
  they lied to him with their tongues.
³⁷ Their hearts were not loyal to him.
  They did not keep his covenant.
³⁸ Yet he was merciful and forgave their sins
  and did not destroy them all.
  Many times he held back his anger
  and did not unleash his fury!
³⁹ For he remembered that they were
    merely mortal,
  gone like a breath of wind that never
    returns.

⁴⁰ Oh, how often they rebelled against him
    in the wilderness
  and grieved his heart in that dry
    wasteland.
⁴¹ Again and again they tested God's
    patience
  and provoked the Holy One of Israel.
⁴² They did not remember his power
  and how he rescued them from their
    enemies.
⁴³ They did not remember his miraculous
    signs in Egypt,
  his wonders on the plain of Zoan.
⁴⁴ For he turned their rivers into blood,
  so no one could drink from the streams.
⁴⁵ He sent vast swarms of flies to consume
    them
  and hordes of frogs to ruin them.
⁴⁶ He gave their crops to caterpillars;
  their harvest was consumed by
    locusts.
⁴⁷ He destroyed their grapevines with hail
  and shattered their sycamore-figs with
    sleet.
⁴⁸ He abandoned their cattle to the hail,
  their livestock to bolts of lightning.
⁴⁹ He loosed on them his fierce anger—
  all his fury, rage, and hostility.
  He dispatched against them
  a band of destroying angels.

⁵⁰ He turned his anger against them;
  he did not spare the Egyptians' lives
  but ravaged them with the plague.
⁵¹ He killed the oldest son in each Egyptian
    family,
  the flower of youth throughout the
    land of Egypt.*
⁵² But he led his own people like a flock of
    sheep,
  guiding them safely through the
    wilderness.
⁵³ He kept them safe so they were not afraid;
  but the sea covered their enemies.
⁵⁴ He brought them to the border of his
    holy land,
  to this land of hills he had won for
    them.
⁵⁵ He drove out the nations before them;
  he gave them their inheritance by lot.
  He settled the tribes of Israel into their
    homes.

⁵⁶ But they kept testing and rebelling
    against God Most High.
  They did not obey his laws.
⁵⁷ They turned back and were as faithless
    as their parents.
  They were as undependable as a
    crooked bow.
⁵⁸ They angered God by building shrines to
    other gods;
  they made him jealous with their idols.
⁵⁹ When God heard them, he was very
    angry,
  and he completely rejected Israel.
⁶⁰ Then he abandoned his dwelling at Shiloh,
  the Tabernacle where he had lived
    among the people.
⁶¹ He allowed the Ark of his might to be
    captured;
  he surrendered his glory into enemy
    hands.
⁶² He gave his people over to be butchered
    by the sword,
  because he was so angry with his own
    people—his special possession.
⁶³ Their young men were killed by fire;
  their young women died before
    singing their wedding songs.
⁶⁴ Their priests were slaughtered,
  and their widows could not mourn
    their deaths.

78:35 Hebrew *El-Elyon*. 78:51 Hebrew *in the tents of Ham*.

⁶⁵ Then the Lord rose up as though waking
from sleep,
like a warrior aroused from a drunken
stupor.
⁶⁶ He routed his enemies
and sent them to eternal shame.
⁶⁷ But he rejected Joseph's descendants;
he did not choose the tribe of
Ephraim.
⁶⁸ He chose instead the tribe of Judah,
and Mount Zion, which he loved.
⁶⁹ There he built his sanctuary as high as
the heavens,
as solid and enduring as the earth.
⁷⁰ He chose his servant David,
calling him from the sheep pens.
⁷¹ He took David from tending the ewes
and lambs
and made him the shepherd of Jacob's
descendants—
God's own people, Israel.
⁷² He cared for them with a true heart
and led them with skillful hands.

79 *A psalm of Asaph.*

¹ O God, pagan nations have conquered
your land,
your special possession.
They have defiled your holy Temple
and made Jerusalem a heap of ruins.
² They have left the bodies of your
servants
as food for the birds of heaven.
The flesh of your godly ones
has become food for the wild animals.
³ Blood has flowed like water all around
Jerusalem;
no one is left to bury the dead.
⁴ We are mocked by our neighbors,
an object of scorn and derision to
those around us.

⁵ O Lord, how long will you be angry
with us? Forever?
How long will your jealousy burn like
fire?
⁶ Pour out your wrath on the nations that
refuse to acknowledge you—
on kingdoms that do not call upon
your name.

⁷ For they have devoured your people
Israel,*
making the land a desolate
wilderness.
⁸ Do not hold us guilty for the sins of our
ancestors!
Let your compassion quickly meet our
needs,
for we are on the brink of despair.

⁹ Help us, O God of our salvation!
Help us for the glory of your name.
Save us and forgive our sins
for the honor of your name.
¹⁰ Why should pagan nations be allowed to
scoff,
asking, "Where is their God?"
Show us your vengeance against the
nations,
for they have spilled the blood of your
servants.
¹¹ Listen to the moaning of the prisoners.
Demonstrate your great power by
saving those condemned to die.

¹² O Lord, pay back our neighbors seven
times
for the scorn they have hurled at you.
¹³ Then we your people, the sheep of your
pasture,
will thank you forever and ever,
praising your greatness from
generation to generation.

80 *For the choir director: A psalm of Asaph, to be sung to the tune "Lilies of the Covenant."*

¹ Please listen, O Shepherd of Israel,
you who lead Joseph's descendants like
a flock.
O God, enthroned above the cherubim,
display your radiant glory
² to Ephraim, Benjamin, and Manasseh.
Show us your mighty power.
Come to rescue us!

³ Turn us again to yourself, O God.
Make your face shine down upon us.
Only then will we be saved.
⁴ O Lord God of Heaven's Armies,
how long will you be angry with our
prayers?

79:7 Hebrew *devoured Jacob.* See note on 44:4.

⁵ You have fed us with sorrow
  and made us drink tears by the
  bucketful.
⁶ You have made us the scorn* of
  neighboring nations.
  Our enemies treat us as a joke.

⁷ Turn us again to yourself, O God of
  Heaven's Armies.
  Make your face shine down upon us.
  Only then will we be saved.
⁸ You brought us from Egypt like a
  grapevine;
  you drove away the pagan nations and
  transplanted us into your land.
⁹ You cleared the ground for us,
  and we took root and filled the land.
¹⁰ Our shade covered the mountains;
  our branches covered the mighty
  cedars.
¹¹ We spread our branches west to the
  Mediterranean Sea;
  our shoots spread east to the
  Euphrates River.*
¹² But now, why have you broken down our
  walls
  so that all who pass by may steal our
  fruit?
¹³ The wild boar from the forest devours it,
  and the wild animals feed on it.

¹⁴ Come back, we beg you, O God of
  Heaven's Armies.
  Look down from heaven and see our
  plight.
  Take care of this grapevine
¹⁵ that you yourself have planted,
  this son you have raised for yourself.
¹⁶ For we are chopped up and burned by
  our enemies.
  May they perish at the sight of your
  frown.
¹⁷ Strengthen the man you love,
  the son of your choice.
¹⁸ Then we will never abandon you again.
  Revive us so we can call on your name
  once more.

¹⁹ Turn us again to yourself, O LORD God
  of Heaven's Armies.
  Make your face shine down upon us.
  Only then will we be saved.

81

*For the choir director: A psalm of
Asaph, to be accompanied by a
stringed instrument.*

¹ Sing praises to God, our strength.
  Sing to the God of Jacob.
² Sing! Beat the tambourine.
  Play the sweet lyre and the harp.
³ Blow the ram's horn at new moon,
  and again at full moon to call a festival!
⁴ For this is required by the decrees of
  Israel;
  it is a regulation of the God of Jacob.
⁵ He made it a law for Israel*
  when he attacked Egypt to set us free.

I heard an unknown voice say,
⁶ "Now I will take the load from your
  shoulders;
  I will free your hands from their heavy
  tasks.
⁷ You cried to me in trouble, and I saved
  you;
  I answered out of the thundercloud
  and tested your faith when there was
  no water at Meribah.   *Interlude*

⁸ "Listen to me, O my people, while I give
  you stern warnings.
  O Israel, if you would only listen to me!
⁹ You must never have a foreign god;
  you must not bow down before a false
  god.
¹⁰ For it was I, the LORD your God,
  who rescued you from the land of Egypt.
  Open your mouth wide, and I will fill
  it with good things.

¹¹ "But no, my people wouldn't listen.
  Israel did not want me around.
¹² So I let them follow their own stubborn
  desires,
  living according to their own ideas.
¹³ Oh, that my people would listen to me!
  Oh, that Israel would follow me,
  walking in my paths!
¹⁴ How quickly I would then subdue their
  enemies!
  How soon my hands would be upon
  their foes!
¹⁵ Those who hate the LORD would cringe
  before him;
  they would be doomed forever.

80:6 As in Syriac version; Hebrew reads *the strife.*   **80:11** Hebrew *west to the sea, . . . east to the river.*   **81:TITLE** Hebrew *according to the gittith.*   **81:5** Hebrew *for Joseph.*

16 But I would feed you with the finest
wheat.
I would satisfy you with wild honey
from the rock."

82 A psalm of Asaph.

1 God presides over heaven's court;
he pronounces judgment on the
heavenly beings:
2 "How long will you hand down unjust
decisions
by favoring the wicked?   *Interlude*

3 "Give justice to the poor and the orphan;
uphold the rights of the oppressed and
the destitute.
4 Rescue the poor and helpless;
deliver them from the grasp of evil
people.
5 But these oppressors know nothing;
they are so ignorant!
They wander about in darkness,
while the whole world is shaken to the
core.
6 I say, 'You are gods;
you are all children of the Most High.
7 But you will die like mere mortals
and fall like every other ruler.'"
8 Rise up, O God, and judge the earth,
for all the nations belong to you.

83 A song. A psalm of Asaph.

1 O God, do not be silent!
Do not be deaf.
Do not be quiet, O God.
2 Don't you hear the uproar of your
enemies?
Don't you see that your arrogant
enemies are rising up?
3 They devise crafty schemes against your
people;
they conspire against your precious
ones.
4 "Come," they say, "let us wipe out Israel
as a nation.
We will destroy the very memory of
its existence."
5 Yes, this was their unanimous decision.

They signed a treaty as allies against
you—
6 these Edomites and Ishmaelites;
Moabites and Hagrites;
7 Gebalites, Ammonites, and Amalekites;
and people from Philistia and Tyre.
8 Assyria has joined them, too,
and is allied with the descendants of
Lot.   *Interlude*

9 Do to them as you did to the Midianites
and as you did to Sisera and Jabin at
the Kishon River.
10 They were destroyed at Endor,
and their decaying corpses fertilized
the soil.
11 Let their mighty nobles die as Oreb and
Zeeb did.
Let all their princes die like Zebah and
Zalmunna,
12 for they said, "Let us seize for our
own use
these pasturelands of God!"
13 O my God, scatter them like
tumbleweed,
like chaff before the wind!
14 As a fire burns a forest
and as a flame sets mountains ablaze,
15 chase them with your fierce storm;
terrify them with your tempest.
16 Utterly disgrace them
until they submit to your name,
O Lord.
17 Let them be ashamed and terrified
forever.
Let them die in disgrace.
18 Then they will learn that you alone are
called the Lord,
that you alone are the Most High,
supreme over all the earth.

84 For the choir director: A psalm of the descendants of Korah, to be accompanied by a stringed instrument.*

1 How lovely is your dwelling place,
O Lord of Heaven's Armies.
2 I long, yes, I faint with longing
to enter the courts of the Lord.
With my whole being, body and soul,
I will shout joyfully to the living God.
3 Even the sparrow finds a home,

84:TITLE Hebrew *according to the gittith.*

and the swallow builds her nest and
    raises her young
at a place near your altar,
    O Lord of Heaven's Armies, my King
        and my God!
⁴ What joy for those who can live in your
        house,
    always singing your praises.   *Interlude*

⁵ What joy for those whose strength
        comes from the Lord,
    who have set their minds on a
        pilgrimage to Jerusalem.
⁶ When they walk through the Valley of
        Weeping,*
    it will become a place of refreshing
        springs.
    The autumn rains will clothe it with
        blessings.
⁷ They will continue to grow stronger,
    and each of them will appear before
        God in Jerusalem.*

⁸ O Lord God of Heaven's Armies, hear
        my prayer.
    Listen, O God of Jacob.   *Interlude*

⁹ O God, look with favor upon the king,
        our shield!
    Show favor to the one you have
        anointed.
¹⁰ A single day in your courts
    is better than a thousand anywhere
        else!
    I would rather be a gatekeeper in the
        house of my God
    than live the good life in the homes of
        the wicked.
¹¹ For the Lord God is our sun and our
        shield.
    He gives us grace and glory.
    The Lord will withhold no good
        thing
    from those who do what is right.
¹² O Lord of Heaven's Armies,
    what joy for those who trust in you.

85 *For the choir director: A psalm of the
descendants of Korah.*

¹ Lord, you poured out blessings on your
        land!
    You restored the fortunes of Israel.*

² You forgave the guilt of your people—
    yes, you covered all their sins.   *Interlude*
³ You held back your fury.
    You kept back your blazing anger.
⁴ Now restore us again, O God of our
        salvation.
    Put aside your anger against us once
        more.
⁵ Will you be angry with us always?
    Will you prolong your wrath to all
        generations?
⁶ Won't you revive us again,
    so your people can rejoice in you?
⁷ Show us your unfailing love, O Lord,
    and grant us your salvation.

⁸ I listen carefully to what God the Lord
        is saying,
    for he speaks peace to his faithful
        people.
    But let them not return to their foolish
        ways.
⁹ Surely his salvation is near to those who
        fear him,
    so our land will be filled with his glory.

¹⁰ Unfailing love and truth have met
        together.
    Righteousness and peace have kissed!
¹¹ Truth springs up from the earth,
    and righteousness smiles down from
        heaven.
¹² Yes, the Lord pours down his blessings.
    Our land will yield its bountiful
        harvest.
¹³ Righteousness goes as a herald before
        him,
    preparing the way for his steps.

86 *A prayer of David.*

¹ Bend down, O Lord, and hear my prayer;
    answer me, for I need your help.
² Protect me, for I am devoted to you.
    Save me, for I serve you and trust you.
    You are my God.
³ Be merciful to me, O Lord,
    for I am calling on you constantly.
⁴ Give me happiness, O Lord,
    for I give myself to you.

84:6 Or *Valley of Poplars;* Hebrew reads *valley of Baca.*   **84:7** Hebrew *Zion.*   **85:1** Hebrew *of Jacob.* See note on 44:4.

⁵ O Lord, you are so good, so ready to
    forgive,
  so full of unfailing love for all who ask
    for your help.
⁶ Listen closely to my prayer, O LORD;
  hear my urgent cry.
⁷ I will call to you whenever I'm in trouble,
  and you will answer me.

⁸ No pagan god is like you, O Lord.
  None can do what you do!
⁹ All the nations you made
  will come and bow before you, Lord;
  they will praise your holy name.
¹⁰ For you are great and perform wonderful
    deeds.
  You alone are God.

¹¹ Teach me your ways, O LORD,
  that I may live according to your truth!
  Grant me purity of heart,
  so that I may honor you.
¹² With all my heart I will praise you,
    O Lord my God.
  I will give glory to your name forever,
¹³ for your love for me is very great.
  You have rescued me from the depths
    of death.*

¹⁴ O God, insolent people rise up
    against me;
  a violent gang is trying to kill me.
  You mean nothing to them.
¹⁵ But you, O Lord,
  are a God of compassion and mercy,
  slow to get angry
  and filled with unfailing love and
    faithfulness.
¹⁶ Look down and have mercy on me.
  Give your strength to your servant;
  save me, the son of your servant.
¹⁷ Send me a sign of your favor.
  Then those who hate me will be put to
    shame,
  for you, O LORD, help and comfort me.

87 *A song. A psalm of the descendants
of Korah.*

¹ On the holy mountain
  stands the city founded by the LORD.

² He loves the city of Jerusalem
  more than any other city in Israel.*
³ O city of God,
  what glorious things are said of you!
                              Interlude

⁴ I will count Egypt* and Babylon among
    those who know me—
  also Philistia and Tyre, and even
    distant Ethiopia.*
  They have all become citizens of
    Jerusalem!
⁵ Regarding Jerusalem* it will be said,
  "Everyone enjoys the rights of
    citizenship there."
  And the Most High will personally
    bless this city.
⁶ When the LORD registers the nations, he
    will say,
  "They have all become citizens of
    Jerusalem."   *Interlude*

⁷ The people will play flutes* and sing,
  "The source of my life springs from
    Jerusalem!"

88 *For the choir director: A psalm of the
descendants of Korah. A song to be
sung to the tune "The Suffering of Affliction."
A psalm* of Heman the Ezrahite.*

¹ O LORD, God of my salvation,
  I cry out to you by day.
  I come to you at night.
² Now hear my prayer;
  listen to my cry.
³ For my life is full of troubles,
  and death* draws near.
⁴ I am as good as dead,
  like a strong man with no strength left.
⁵ They have left me among the dead,
  and I lie like a corpse in a grave.
  I am forgotten,
  cut off from your care.
⁶ You have thrown me into the lowest pit,
  into the darkest depths.
⁷ Your anger weighs me down;
  with wave after wave you have
    engulfed me.   *Interlude*

⁸ You have driven my friends away
  by making me repulsive to them.

86:13 Hebrew *of Sheol.* **87:2** Hebrew *He loves the gates of Zion more than all the dwellings of Jacob.* See note on 44:4. **87:4a** Hebrew *Rahab,*
the name of a mythical sea monster that represents chaos in ancient literature. The name is used here as a poetic name for Egypt.
87:4b Hebrew *Cush.* **87:5** Hebrew *Zion.* **87:7** Or *will dance.* **88:TITLE** Hebrew *maskil.* This may be a literary or musical term.
88:3 Hebrew *Sheol.*

I am in a trap with no way of escape.
9 My eyes are blinded by my tears.
Each day I beg for your help, O Lord;
I lift my hands to you for mercy.
10 Are your wonderful deeds of any use to
the dead?
Do the dead rise up and praise you?
Interlude

11 Can those in the grave declare your
unfailing love?
Can they proclaim your faithfulness in
the place of destruction?*
12 Can the darkness speak of your
wonderful deeds?
Can anyone in the land of
forgetfulness talk about your
righteousness?
13 O Lord, I cry out to you.
I will keep on pleading day by day.
14 O Lord, why do you reject me?
Why do you turn your face
from me?

15 I have been sick and close to death since
my youth.
I stand helpless and desperate before
your terrors.
16 Your fierce anger has overwhelmed me.
Your terrors have paralyzed me.
17 They swirl around me like floodwaters
all day long.
They have engulfed me completely.
18 You have taken away my companions
and loved ones.
Darkness is my closest friend.

89 *A psalm* of Ethan the Ezrahite.

1 I will sing of the Lord's unfailing love
forever!
Young and old will hear of your
faithfulness.
2 Your unfailing love will last forever.
Your faithfulness is as enduring as the
heavens.

3 The Lord said, "I have made a covenant
with David, my chosen servant.
I have sworn this oath to him:
4 'I will establish your descendants as
kings forever;

they will sit on your throne from now
until eternity.'" *Interlude*
5 All heaven will praise your great
wonders, Lord;
myriads of angels will praise you for
your faithfulness.
6 For who in all of heaven can compare
with the Lord?
What mightiest angel is anything like
the Lord?
7 The highest angelic powers stand in awe
of God.
He is far more awesome than all who
surround his throne.
8 O Lord God of Heaven's Armies!
Where is there anyone as mighty as
you, O Lord?
You are entirely faithful.

9 You rule the oceans.
You subdue their storm-tossed waves.
10 You crushed the great sea monster.*
You scattered your enemies with your
mighty arm.
11 The heavens are yours, and the earth is
yours;
everything in the world is yours—you
created it all.
12 You created north and south.
Mount Tabor and Mount Hermon
praise your name.
13 Powerful is your arm!
Strong is your hand!
Your right hand is lifted high in
glorious strength.
14 Righteousness and justice are the
foundation of your throne.
Unfailing love and truth walk before
you as attendants.
15 Happy are those who hear the joyful call
to worship,
for they will walk in the light of your
presence, Lord.
16 They rejoice all day long in your
wonderful reputation.
They exult in your righteousness.
17 You are their glorious strength.
It pleases you to make us strong.
18 Yes, our protection comes from the Lord,
and he, the Holy One of Israel, has
given us our king.

88:11 Hebrew *in Abaddon?* **89:TITLE** Hebrew *maskil.* This may be a literary or musical term. **89:10** Hebrew *Rahab,* the name of a mythical
sea monster that represents chaos in ancient literature.

¹⁹ Long ago you spoke in a vision to your
faithful people.
You said, "I have raised up a warrior.
I have selected him from the common
people to be king.
²⁰ I have found my servant David.
I have anointed him with my holy oil.
²¹ I will steady him with my hand;
with my powerful arm I will make him
strong.
²² His enemies will not defeat him,
nor will the wicked overpower him.
²³ I will beat down his adversaries before
him
and destroy those who hate him.
²⁴ My faithfulness and unfailing love will
be with him,
and by my authority he will grow in
power.
²⁵ I will extend his rule over the sea,
his dominion over the rivers.
²⁶ And he will call out to me, 'You are my
Father,
my God, and the Rock of my salvation.'
²⁷ I will make him my firstborn son,
the mightiest king on earth.
²⁸ I will love him and be kind to him forever;
my covenant with him will never end.
²⁹ I will preserve an heir for him;
his throne will be as endless as the
days of heaven.
³⁰ But if his descendants forsake my
instructions
and fail to obey my regulations,
³¹ if they do not obey my decrees
and fail to keep my commands,
³² then I will punish their sin with the rod,
and their disobedience with beating.
³³ But I will never stop loving him
nor fail to keep my promise to him.
³⁴ No, I will not break my covenant;
I will not take back a single word I said.
³⁵ I have sworn an oath to David,
and in my holiness I cannot lie:
³⁶ His dynasty will go on forever;
his kingdom will endure as the sun.
³⁷ It will be as eternal as the moon,
my faithful witness in the sky!"

Interlude

³⁸ But now you have rejected him and cast
him off.

You are angry with your anointed
king.
³⁹ You have renounced your covenant with
him;
you have thrown his crown in the dust.
⁴⁰ You have broken down the walls
protecting him
and ruined every fort defending him.
⁴¹ Everyone who comes along has robbed
him,
and he has become a joke to his
neighbors.
⁴² You have strengthened his enemies
and made them all rejoice.
⁴³ You have made his sword useless
and refused to help him in battle.
⁴⁴ You have ended his splendor
and overturned his throne.
⁴⁵ You have made him old before his time
and publicly disgraced him.   *Interlude*

⁴⁶ O LORD, how long will this go on?
Will you hide yourself forever?
How long will your anger burn like fire?
⁴⁷ Remember how short my life is,
how empty and futile this human
existence!
⁴⁸ No one can live forever; all will die.
No one can escape the power of the
grave.*   *Interlude*

⁴⁹ Lord, where is your unfailing love?
You promised it to David with a
faithful pledge.
⁵⁰ Consider, Lord, how your servants are
disgraced!
I carry in my heart the insults of so
many people.
⁵¹ Your enemies have mocked me, O LORD;
they mock your anointed king
wherever he goes.

⁵² Praise the LORD forever!
Amen and amen!

BOOK FOUR (Psalms 90–106)

90 *A prayer of Moses, the man of God.*

¹ Lord, through all the generations
you have been our home!
² Before the mountains were born,

89:48 Hebrew of *Sheol.*

before you gave birth to the earth and
the world,
from beginning to end, you are God.

³ You turn people back to dust, saying,
"Return to dust, you mortals!"
⁴ For you, a thousand years are as a
passing day,
as brief as a few night hours.
⁵ You sweep people away like dreams that
disappear.
They are like grass that springs up in
the morning.
⁶ In the morning it blooms and flourishes,
but by evening it is dry and withered.
⁷ We wither beneath your anger;
we are overwhelmed by your fury.
⁸ You spread out our sins before you—
our secret sins—and you see them all.
⁹ We live our lives beneath your wrath,
ending our years with a groan.

¹⁰ Seventy years are given to us!
Some even live to eighty.
But even the best years are filled with
pain and trouble;
soon they disappear, and we fly away.
¹¹ Who can comprehend the power of your
anger?
Your wrath is as awesome as the fear
you deserve.
¹² Teach us to realize the brevity of life,
so that we may grow in wisdom.

¹³ O LORD, come back to us!
How long will you delay?
Take pity on your servants!
¹⁴ Satisfy us each morning with your
unfailing love,
so we may sing for joy to the end of
our lives.
¹⁵ Give us gladness in proportion to our
former misery!
Replace the evil years with good.
¹⁶ Let us, your servants, see you work again;
let our children see your glory.
¹⁷ And may the Lord our God show us his
approval
and make our efforts successful.
Yes, make our efforts successful!

91 ¹ Those who live in the shelter of the
Most High
will find rest in the shadow of the
Almighty.

² This I declare about the LORD:
He alone is my refuge, my place of
safety;
he is my God, and I trust him.
³ For he will rescue you from every trap
and protect you from deadly disease.
⁴ He will cover you with his feathers.
He will shelter you with his wings.
His faithful promises are your armor
and protection.
⁵ Do not be afraid of the terrors of the
night,
nor the arrow that flies in the day.
⁶ Do not dread the disease that stalks in
darkness,
nor the disaster that strikes at midday.
⁷ Though a thousand fall at your side,
though ten thousand are dying around
you,
these evils will not touch you.
⁸ Just open your eyes,
and see how the wicked are punished.

⁹ If you make the LORD your refuge,
if you make the Most High your shelter,
¹⁰ no evil will conquer you;
no plague will come near your home.
¹¹ For he will order his angels
to protect you wherever you go.
¹² They will hold you up with their hands
so you won't even hurt your foot on a
stone.
¹³ You will trample upon lions and cobras;
you will crush fierce lions and
serpents under your feet!

¹⁴ The LORD says, "I will rescue those who
love me.
I will protect those who trust in my
name.
¹⁵ When they call on me, I will answer;
I will be with them in trouble.
I will rescue and honor them.
¹⁶ I will reward them with a long life
and give them my salvation."

92 *A psalm. A song to be sung on the
Sabbath Day.*

¹ It is good to give thanks to the LORD,
to sing praises to the Most High.
² It is good to proclaim your unfailing love
in the morning,
your faithfulness in the evening,

³ accompanied by the ten-stringed harp
and the melody of the lyre.

⁴ You thrill me, LORD, with all you have
done for me!
I sing for joy because of what you have
done.

⁵ O LORD, what great works you do!
And how deep are your thoughts.

⁶ Only a simpleton would not know,
and only a fool would not understand
this:

⁷ Though the wicked sprout like weeds
and evildoers flourish,
they will be destroyed forever.

⁸ But you, O LORD, will be exalted forever.

⁹ Your enemies, LORD, will surely perish;
all evildoers will be scattered.

¹⁰ But you have made me as strong as a
wild ox.
You have anointed me with the finest
oil.

¹¹ My eyes have seen the downfall of my
enemies;
my ears have heard the defeat of my
wicked opponents.

¹² But the godly will flourish like palm
trees
and grow strong like the cedars of
Lebanon.

¹³ For they are transplanted to the LORD's
own house.

Persistence in Prayer
PSALM 91

How do I know if I should keep praying about a specific request or if I should stop and simply trust the situation to God?

Scripture certainly exhorts us to be persistent in prayer. In Luke 11, for example, Jesus tells a parable about a man who comes to his friend's house at midnight and asks for bread. Jesus explains, "I tell you this—though he won't do it for friendship's sake, if you keep knocking long enough, he will get up and give you whatever you need" (11:8). Jesus calls us to be bold and persistent in our prayers. He also goes on in Luke 11 to urge us to keep on asking, seeking, and knocking in prayer.

But persistence isn't simply about repeating the same request over and over until we get the answer we desire. The blessing of persistence in prayer is that it brings us, over and over, into the presence of God. We form a pattern of coming to him. We can say to him, *Here I am, Lord, again. You know my prayer, and because you do, I'm not going to ask it again, but I am going to enjoy your rest. I'm going to enjoy your peace.*

Psalm 91:1 says, "Those who live in the shelter of the Most High will find rest in the shadow of the Almighty." That's what we need—resting in God's presence—more than anything else. We pray fervently; we labor so hard in our spiritual lives and in our prayer requests, but perhaps what we ultimately need at times is simply to be quiet and rest in God's presence. These times of rest, quietness, and trust should play a key part in our persistent prayers.

—Patricia Raybon

For more on prayer, see reading at Ezekiel 22:30.

They flourish in the courts of our God.
14 Even in old age they will still produce
fruit;
they will remain vital and green.
15 They will declare, "The LORD is just!
He is my rock!
There is no evil in him!"

93
1 The LORD is king! He is robed in
majesty.
Indeed, the LORD is robed in majesty
and armed with strength.
The world stands firm
and cannot be shaken.
2 Your throne, O LORD, has stood from
time immemorial.
You yourself are from the everlasting
past.
3 The floods have risen up, O LORD.
The floods have roared like thunder;
the floods have lifted their pounding
waves.
4 But mightier than the violent raging of
the seas,
mightier than the breakers on the
shore—
the LORD above is mightier than these!
5 Your royal laws cannot be changed.
Your reign, O LORD, is holy forever
and ever.

94
1 O LORD, the God of vengeance,
O God of vengeance, let your
glorious justice shine forth!
2 Arise, O judge of the earth.
Give the proud what they deserve.
3 How long, O LORD?
How long will the wicked be allowed
to gloat?
4 How long will they speak with
arrogance?
How long will these evil people boast?
5 They crush your people, LORD,
hurting those you claim as your own.
6 They kill widows and foreigners
and murder orphans.
7 "The LORD isn't looking," they say,
"and besides, the God of Israel*
doesn't care."
8 Think again, you fools!

When will you finally catch on?
9 Is he deaf—the one who made your
ears?
Is he blind—the one who formed your
eyes?
10 He punishes the nations—won't he also
punish you?
He knows everything—doesn't he also
know what you are doing?
11 The LORD knows people's thoughts;
he knows they are worthless!
12 Joyful are those you discipline, LORD,
those you teach with your
instructions.
13 You give them relief from troubled times
until a pit is dug to capture the
wicked.
14 The LORD will not reject his people;
he will not abandon his special
possession.
15 Judgment will again be founded on
justice,
and those with virtuous hearts will
pursue it.
16 Who will protect me from the wicked?
Who will stand up for me against
evildoers?
17 Unless the LORD had helped me,
I would soon have settled in the
silence of the grave.
18 I cried out, "I am slipping!"
but your unfailing love, O LORD,
supported me.
19 When doubts filled my mind,
your comfort gave me renewed hope
and cheer.
20 Can unjust leaders claim that God is on
their side—
leaders whose decrees permit
injustice?
21 They gang up against the righteous
and condemn the innocent to death.
22 But the LORD is my fortress;
my God is the mighty rock where I
hide.
23 God will turn the sins of evil people
back on them.
He will destroy them for their sins.
The LORD our God will destroy
them.

94:7 Hebrew of *Jacob*. See note on 44:4.

Leading Others in Thanksgiving
PSALM 95

The Roman philosopher Cicero was on to something when he said, "Gratitude is not only the greatest of virtues but the parent of all the others." It's also the basic Christian attitude. Paul says: "Be thankful in all circumstances, for this is God's will for you who belong to Christ Jesus" (1 Thessalonians 5:18).

That might seem a challenge during a season of economic trouble and political unrest. But consider the example of German pastor Martin Rinckart, who served a town that became a refuge for political and military fugitives during the Thirty Years' War. The situation in Eilenburg was bad even before the Black Plague arrived in 1637. One pastor fled. Rinckart buried another two on the same day. The only pastor remaining, he conducted funeral services for as many as 50 people a day and 4,480 within one year.

Yet Rinckart is best known for writing, in the midst of the war, the great hymn that triumphantly proclaims this:

> Now thank we all our God,
> With heart and hands and voices
> Who wondrous things has done,
> In whom this world rejoices;
> Who from our mothers' arms
> Has blessed us on our way
> With countless gifts of love,
> And still is ours today.

Rinckart maintained a faith characterized by trust and gratitude in the face of great hardships. But he also moved beyond his own private gratitude to lead others in expressing thanksgiving. Through his hymn lyrics, he reminded those he pastored that though they were enduring unbearable suffering, God's rich love for them was still abundant. Rinckart ministered to hurting people not only by sharing their sorrows but also by giving them words to sing their own thanks. Like Rinckart, through our example and our words, we can lead others in giving thanks. We can draw others into gratitude, inviting, "Come, let us sing to the Lord! . . . Let us come to him with thanksgiving" (Psalm 95:1-2).

—Mollie Ziegler Hemingway

For more on gratitude, see reading at Psalm 106:1-12.

95 ¹ Come, let us sing to the Lord!
Let us shout joyfully to the Rock of our salvation.
² Let us come to him with thanksgiving.
Let us sing psalms of praise to him.
³ For the Lord is a great God,
a great King above all gods.
⁴ He holds in his hands the depths of the earth
and the mightiest mountains.
⁵ The sea belongs to him, for he made it.
His hands formed the dry land, too.

⁶ Come, let us worship and bow down.
Let us kneel before the Lord our maker,
⁷ for he is our God.
We are the people he watches over,
the flock under his care.

If only you would listen to his voice today!
8 The Lord says, "Don't harden your
hearts as Israel did at Meribah,
as they did at Massah in the
wilderness.
9 For there your ancestors tested and tried
my patience,
even though they saw everything I did.
10 For forty years I was angry with them,
and I said,
'They are a people whose hearts turn
away from me.
They refuse to do what I tell them.'
11 So in my anger I took an oath:
'They will never enter my place of rest.'"

96 1 Sing a new song to the Lord!
Let the whole earth sing to the
Lord!
2 Sing to the Lord; praise his name.
Each day proclaim the good news that
he saves.
3 Publish his glorious deeds among the
nations.
Tell everyone about the amazing
things he does.
4 Great is the Lord! He is most worthy of
praise!
He is to be feared above all gods.
5 The gods of other nations are mere idols,
but the Lord made the heavens!
6 Honor and majesty surround him;
strength and beauty fill his sanctuary.

7 O nations of the world, recognize the
Lord;
recognize that the Lord is glorious
and strong.
8 Give to the Lord the glory he deserves!
Bring your offering and come into his
courts.
9 Worship the Lord in all his holy splendor.
Let all the earth tremble before him.
10 Tell all the nations, "The Lord reigns!"
The world stands firm and cannot be
shaken.
He will judge all peoples fairly.

11 Let the heavens be glad, and the earth
rejoice!
Let the sea and everything in it shout
his praise!
12 Let the fields and their crops burst out
with joy!

Let the trees of the forest rustle with
praise
13 before the Lord, for he is coming!
He is coming to judge the earth.
He will judge the world with justice,
and the nations with his truth.

97 1 The Lord is king!
Let the earth rejoice!
Let the farthest coastlands be glad.
2 Dark clouds surround him.
Righteousness and justice are the
foundation of his throne.
3 Fire spreads ahead of him
and burns up all his foes.
4 His lightning flashes out across the world.
The earth sees and trembles.
5 The mountains melt like wax before the
Lord,
before the Lord of all the earth.
6 The heavens proclaim his righteousness;
every nation sees his glory.
7 Those who worship idols are disgraced—
all who brag about their worthless
gods—
for every god must bow to him.
8 Jerusalem* has heard and rejoiced,
and all the towns of Judah are glad
because of your justice, O Lord!
9 For you, O Lord, are supreme over all
the earth;
you are exalted far above all gods.

10 You who love the Lord, hate evil!
He protects the lives of his godly
people
and rescues them from the power of
the wicked.
11 Light shines on the godly,
and joy on those whose hearts are
right.
12 May all who are godly rejoice in the Lord
and praise his holy name!

98 *A psalm.*

1 Sing a new song to the Lord,
for he has done wonderful deeds.
His right hand has won a mighty victory;
his holy arm has shown his saving
power!

97:8 Hebrew *Zion.*

2 The LORD has announced his victory
and has revealed his righteousness to
every nation!
3 He has remembered his promise to love
and be faithful to Israel.
The ends of the earth have seen the
victory of our God.

4 Shout to the LORD, all the earth;
break out in praise and sing for joy!
5 Sing your praise to the LORD with the
harp,
with the harp and melodious song,
6 with trumpets and the sound of the
ram's horn.
Make a joyful symphony before the
LORD, the King!

7 Let the sea and everything in it shout his
praise!
Let the earth and all living things
join in.
8 Let the rivers clap their hands in glee!
Let the hills sing out their songs of joy
9 before the LORD.
For the LORD is coming to judge the
earth.
He will judge the world with justice,
and the nations with fairness.

99

1 The LORD is king!
Let the nations tremble!
He sits on his throne between the
cherubim.
Let the whole earth quake!
2 The LORD sits in majesty in Jerusalem,*
exalted above all the nations.
3 Let them praise your great and awesome
name.
Your name is holy!
4 Mighty King, lover of justice,
you have established fairness.
You have acted with justice
and righteousness throughout Israel.*
5 Exalt the LORD our God!
Bow low before his feet, for he is holy!

6 Moses and Aaron were among his
priests;
Samuel also called on his name.
They cried to the LORD for help,
and he answered them.

7 He spoke to Israel from the pillar of
cloud,
and they followed the laws and
decrees he gave them.
8 O LORD our God, you answered them.
You were a forgiving God to them,
but you punished them when they
went wrong.

9 Exalt the LORD our God,
and worship at his holy mountain in
Jerusalem,
for the LORD our God is holy!

100 *A psalm of thanksgiving.*

1 Shout with joy to the LORD, all the earth!
2 Worship the LORD with gladness.
Come before him, singing with joy.
3 Acknowledge that the LORD is God!
He made us, and we are his.*
We are his people, the sheep of his
pasture.
4 Enter his gates with thanksgiving;
go into his courts with praise.
Give thanks to him and praise his name.
5 For the LORD is good.
His unfailing love continues forever,
and his faithfulness continues to each
generation.

101 *A psalm of David.*

1 I will sing of your love and justice, LORD.
I will praise you with songs.
2 I will be careful to live a blameless life—
when will you come to help me?
I will lead a life of integrity
in my own home.
3 I will refuse to look at
anything vile and vulgar.
I hate all who deal crookedly;
I will have nothing to do with them.
4 I will reject perverse ideas
and stay away from every evil.
5 I will not tolerate people who slander
their neighbors.
I will not endure conceit and pride.

6 I will search for faithful people
to be my companions.

99:2 Hebrew *Zion.* 99:4 Hebrew *Jacob.* See note on 44:4. 100:3 As in an alternate reading in the Masoretic Text; the other alternate and some ancient versions read *and not we ourselves.*

Only those who are above reproach
　　will be allowed to serve me.
7 I will not allow deceivers to serve in my
　　house,
　　and liars will not stay in my presence.
8 My daily task will be to ferret out the
　　wicked
　　and free the city of the LORD from
　　their grip.

102 *A prayer of one overwhelmed with
trouble, pouring out problems
before the LORD.*

1 LORD, hear my prayer!
　　Listen to my plea!
2 Don't turn away from me
　　in my time of distress.
　　Bend down to listen,

Q&A · Joyful Living in a Dark World

Celebration

PSALM 100

How can we be joyful when it seems as though the world is falling apart?

World hunger is only worsening. Nuclear threats grow daily. Human trafficking is expanding. Billions are mired not just in poverty of material needs but also poverty of spirit. Who in their right mind can talk about joy? Empathy, yes. But to put on joy when so many are dressed in the rags of anxiety, grief, and despair? It would be scandalous.

Yet the gospel itself *is* a scandal because it announces joy right when everything is falling apart. "Don't be afraid!" the angel tells the quaking shepherds. "I bring you good news that will bring great joy to all people" (Luke 2:10). The church's God-given mission to the world is no different. "Do not be afraid!" we're to announce to a world shivering in the dark. "We bring good news of a great joy—for everyone!"

"It is astonishing," wrote Karl Barth, "how many references there are in the Old and New Testaments to delight, joy, bliss, exultation, merry-making, and rejoicing, and how emphatically these are demanded" of us. Indeed, from "Shout with joy to the LORD, all the earth!" (Psalm 100:1) to "Always be full of joy in the Lord. I say it again—rejoice!" (Philippians 4:4)—and dozens of places before and after and in between—Scripture urges us to lead joy-filled lives.

There is certainly a time to ponder the sobering reality of evil in our world. But G. K. Chesterton knew well the greater truth—which is why the Bible harped on it so. A person is only fully human, he says, "when joy is the fundamental thing in him, and grief the superficial. Melancholy should be an innocent interlude, a tender and fugitive frame of mind; praise should be the permanent pulsation of the soul. Pessimism is at best an emotional half holiday; joy is the uproarious labor by which all things live."

—Mark Galli

For more on celebration, see reading at Psalm 113.

and answer me quickly when I call to
you.
³ For my days disappear like smoke,
and my bones burn like red-hot coals.
⁴ My heart is sick, withered like grass,
and I have lost my appetite.
⁵ Because of my groaning,
I am reduced to skin and bones.
⁶ I am like an owl in the desert,
like a little owl in a far-off wilderness.
⁷ I lie awake,
lonely as a solitary bird on the roof.
⁸ My enemies taunt me day after day.
They mock and curse me.
⁹ I eat ashes for food.
My tears run down into my drink
¹⁰ because of your anger and wrath.
For you have picked me up and
thrown me out.
¹¹ My life passes as swiftly as the evening
shadows.
I am withering away like grass.

¹² But you, O LORD, will sit on your throne
forever.
Your fame will endure to every
generation.
¹³ You will arise and have mercy on
Jerusalem*—
and now is the time to pity her,
now is the time you promised to help.
¹⁴ For your people love every stone in her
walls
and cherish even the dust in her
streets.
¹⁵ Then the nations will tremble before the
LORD.
The kings of the earth will tremble
before his glory.
¹⁶ For the LORD will rebuild Jerusalem.
He will appear in his glory.
¹⁷ He will listen to the prayers of the
destitute.
He will not reject their pleas.

¹⁸ Let this be recorded for future
generations,
so that a people not yet born will
praise the LORD.
¹⁹ Tell them the LORD looked down
from his heavenly sanctuary.
He looked down to earth from heaven

²⁰ to hear the groans of the prisoners,
to release those condemned to die.
²¹ And so the LORD's fame will be
celebrated in Zion,
his praises in Jerusalem,
²² when multitudes gather together
and kingdoms come to worship the
LORD.

²³ He broke my strength in midlife,
cutting short my days.
²⁴ But I cried to him, "O my God, who lives
forever,
don't take my life while I am so young!
²⁵ Long ago you laid the foundation of the
earth
and made the heavens with your hands.
²⁶ They will perish, but you remain forever;
they will wear out like old clothing.
You will change them like a garment
and discard them.
²⁷ But you are always the same;
you will live forever.
²⁸ The children of your people
will live in security.
Their children's children
will thrive in your presence."

103 *A psalm of David.*

¹ Let all that I am praise the LORD;
with my whole heart, I will praise his
holy name.
² Let all that I am praise the LORD;
may I never forget the good things he
does for me.
³ He forgives all my sins
and heals all my diseases.
⁴ He redeems me from death
and crowns me with love and tender
mercies.
⁵ He fills my life with good things.
My youth is renewed like the eagle's!

⁶ The LORD gives righteousness
and justice to all who are treated unfairly.
⁷ He revealed his character to Moses
and his deeds to the people of Israel.
⁸ The LORD is compassionate and
merciful,
slow to get angry and filled with
unfailing love.

102:13 Hebrew *Zion;* also in 102:16.

⁹ He will not constantly accuse us,
nor remain angry forever.
¹⁰ He does not punish us for all our sins;
he does not deal harshly with us, as we
deserve.
¹¹ For his unfailing love toward those who
fear him
is as great as the height of the heavens
above the earth.
¹² He has removed our sins as far from us
as the east is from the west.
¹³ The Lord is like a father to his children,
tender and compassionate to those
who fear him.
¹⁴ For he knows how weak we are;
he remembers we are only dust.
¹⁵ Our days on earth are like grass;
like wildflowers, we bloom and die.
¹⁶ The wind blows, and we are gone—
as though we had never been here.
¹⁷ But the love of the Lord remains forever
with those who fear him.
His salvation extends to the children's
children
¹⁸ of those who are faithful to his
covenant,
of those who obey his commandments!

¹⁹ The Lord has made the heavens his
throne;
from there he rules over everything.

²⁰ Praise the Lord, you angels,
you mighty ones who carry out his
plans,
listening for each of his commands.
²¹ Yes, praise the Lord, you armies of
angels
who serve him and do his will!
²² Praise the Lord, everything he has
created,
everything in all his kingdom.

Let all that I am praise the Lord.

104

¹ Let all that I am praise the
Lord.

O Lord my God, how great you are!
You are robed with honor and majesty.
² You are dressed in a robe of light.
You stretch out the starry curtain of the
heavens;

³ you lay out the rafters of your home in
the rain clouds.
You make the clouds your chariot;
you ride upon the wings of the wind.
⁴ The winds are your messengers;
flames of fire are your servants.*
⁵ You placed the world on its foundation
so it would never be moved.
⁶ You clothed the earth with floods of
water,
water that covered even the mountains.
⁷ At your command, the water fled;
at the sound of your thunder, it
hurried away.
⁸ Mountains rose and valleys sank
to the levels you decree.
⁹ Then you set a firm boundary for the
seas,
so they would never again cover the
earth.

¹⁰ You make springs pour water into the
ravines,
so streams gush down from the
mountains.
¹¹ They provide water for all the animals,
and the wild donkeys quench their
thirst.
¹² The birds nest beside the streams
and sing among the branches of the
trees.
¹³ You send rain on the mountains from
your heavenly home,
and you fill the earth with the fruit of
your labor.
¹⁴ You cause grass to grow for the livestock
and plants for people to use.
You allow them to produce food from
the earth—
¹⁵ wine to make them glad,
olive oil to soothe their skin,
and bread to give them strength.
¹⁶ The trees of the Lord are well cared for—
the cedars of Lebanon that he planted.
¹⁷ There the birds make their nests,
and the storks make their homes in
the cypresses.
¹⁸ High in the mountains live the wild
goats,
and the rocks form a refuge for the
hyraxes.*

104:4 Greek version reads *He sends his angels like the winds, / his servants like flames of fire.* Compare Heb 1:7.   **104:18** Or *coneys,* or *rock badgers.*

¹⁹ You made the moon to mark the seasons,
  and the sun knows when to set.
²⁰ You send the darkness, and it becomes
  night,
  when all the forest animals prowl about.
²¹ Then the young lions roar for their prey,
  stalking the food provided by God.
²² At dawn they slink back
  into their dens to rest.
²³ Then people go off to their work,
  where they labor until evening.

²⁴ O LORD, what a variety of things you
  have made!
  In wisdom you have made them all.
  The earth is full of your creatures.
²⁵ Here is the ocean, vast and wide,
  teeming with life of every kind,
  both large and small.
²⁶ See the ships sailing along,
  and Leviathan,* which you made to
  play in the sea.

²⁷ They all depend on you
  to give them food as they need it.
²⁸ When you supply it, they gather it.
  You open your hand to feed them,
  and they are richly satisfied.
²⁹ But if you turn away from them, they
  panic.
  When you take away their breath,
  they die and turn again to dust.
³⁰ When you give them your breath,* life is
  created,
  and you renew the face of the earth.

³¹ May the glory of the LORD continue
  forever!
  The LORD takes pleasure in all he has
  made!
³² The earth trembles at his glance;
  the mountains smoke at his touch.

³³ I will sing to the LORD as long as I live.
  I will praise my God to my last breath!
³⁴ May all my thoughts be pleasing to him,
  for I rejoice in the LORD.
³⁵ Let all sinners vanish from the face of
  the earth;
  let the wicked disappear forever.

  Let all that I am praise the LORD.

  Praise the LORD!

105

¹ Give thanks to the LORD and
  proclaim his greatness.
  Let the whole world know what he has
  done.
² Sing to him; yes, sing his praises.
  Tell everyone about his wonderful
  deeds.
³ Exult in his holy name;
  rejoice, you who worship the LORD.
⁴ Search for the LORD and for his
  strength;
  continually seek him.
⁵ Remember the wonders he has
  performed,
  his miracles, and the rulings he has
  given,
⁶ you children of his servant Abraham,
  you descendants of Jacob, his chosen
  ones.

⁷ He is the LORD our God.
  His justice is seen throughout the land.
⁸ He always stands by his covenant—
  the commitment he made to a
  thousand generations.
⁹ This is the covenant he made with
  Abraham
  and the oath he swore to Isaac.
¹⁰ He confirmed it to Jacob as a decree,
  and to the people of Israel as a never-
  ending covenant:
¹¹ "I will give you the land of Canaan
  as your special possession."

¹² He said this when they were few in
  number,
  a tiny group of strangers in Canaan.
¹³ They wandered from nation to nation,
  from one kingdom to another.
¹⁴ Yet he did not let anyone oppress them.
  He warned kings on their behalf:
¹⁵ "Do not touch my chosen people,
  and do not hurt my prophets."

¹⁶ He called for a famine on the land of
  Canaan,
  cutting off its food supply.
¹⁷ Then he sent someone to Egypt ahead of
  them—
  Joseph, who was sold as a slave.
¹⁸ They bruised his feet with fetters
  and placed his neck in an iron collar.

104:26 The identification of Leviathan is disputed, ranging from an earthly creature to a mythical sea monster in ancient literature.
104:30 Or *When you send your Spirit.*

¹⁹ Until the time came to fulfill his dreams,*
   the LORD tested Joseph's character.
²⁰ Then Pharaoh sent for him and set him
   free;
   the ruler of the nation opened his
   prison door.
²¹ Joseph was put in charge of all the king's
   household;
   he became ruler over all the king's
   possessions.
²² He could instruct the king's aides as he
   pleased
   and teach the king's advisers.

²³ Then Israel arrived in Egypt;
   Jacob lived as a foreigner in the land
   of Ham.
²⁴ And the LORD multiplied the people of
   Israel
   until they became too mighty for their
   enemies.
²⁵ Then he turned the Egyptians against
   the Israelites,
   and they plotted against the LORD's
   servants.

²⁶ But the LORD sent his servant Moses,
   along with Aaron, whom he had
   chosen.
²⁷ They performed miraculous signs
   among the Egyptians,
   and wonders in the land of Ham.
²⁸ The LORD blanketed Egypt in darkness,
   for they had defied his commands to
   let his people go.
²⁹ He turned their water into blood,
   poisoning all the fish.
³⁰ Then frogs overran the land
   and even invaded the king's bedrooms.
³¹ When the LORD spoke, flies descended
   on the Egyptians,
   and gnats swarmed across Egypt.
³² He sent them hail instead of rain,
   and lightning flashed over the land.
³³ He ruined their grapevines and fig trees
   and shattered all the trees.
³⁴ He spoke, and hordes of locusts came—
   young locusts beyond number.
³⁵ They ate up everything green in the land,
   destroying all the crops in their fields.
³⁶ Then he killed the oldest son in each
   Egyptian home,
   the pride and joy of each family.

³⁷ The LORD brought his people out of
   Egypt, loaded with silver and gold;
   and not one among the tribes of Israel
   even stumbled.
³⁸ Egypt was glad when they were gone,
   for they feared them greatly.
³⁹ The LORD spread a cloud above them as
   a covering
   and gave them a great fire to light the
   darkness.
⁴⁰ They asked for meat, and he sent them
   quail;
   he satisfied their hunger with
   manna—bread from heaven.
⁴¹ He split open a rock, and water gushed
   out
   to form a river through the dry
   wasteland.
⁴² For he remembered his sacred promise
   to his servant Abraham.
⁴³ So he brought his people out of Egypt
   with joy,
   his chosen ones with rejoicing.
⁴⁴ He gave his people the lands of pagan
   nations,
   and they harvested crops that others
   had planted.
⁴⁵ All this happened so they would follow
   his decrees
   and obey his instructions.

   Praise the LORD!

106 ¹ Praise the LORD!

   Give thanks to the LORD, for he is good!
   His faithful love endures forever.
² Who can list the glorious miracles of the
   LORD?
   Who can ever praise him enough?
³ There is joy for those who deal justly
   with others
   and always do what is right.

⁴ Remember me, LORD, when you show
   favor to your people;
   come near and rescue me.
⁵ Let me share in the prosperity of your
   chosen ones.
   Let me rejoice in the joy of your people;
   let me praise you with those who are
   your heritage.

105:19 Hebrew *his word.*

Gratitude

The Struggle to Be Grateful

PSALM 106:1–12

We know that God has given us so much: our bodies and souls, reason and senses, material possessions and relationships. Yet with all that God richly provides us daily, many of us still struggle to be grateful.

Perhaps the problem is that we think too highly of ourselves. Margaret Visser studied cultural differences in showing thanks as she prepared her book *The Gift of Thanks: The Roots and Rituals of Gratitude.* The Japanese sometimes accept gifts by saying, "I'm sorry." The subtext, Visser explains, is *I am fully aware of my debt to you. I can never repay it.*

There's a lesson in that expression. In Luke 7:36–50 Simon the Pharisee hosts a dinner party for Jesus. A sinful woman with a bad reputation shows up, gets near Jesus, and washes his feet with her tears and anoints him with perfume. When Simon grumbles, Jesus tells a story about two debtors. One has a small debt, the other a large debt. Neither is able to repay, and the lender forgives both debts. The lesson: the greater the forgiveness, the greater the thankfulness.

We have trouble being grateful because we fail to acknowledge our sinfulness and debt. Isn't that why we complain about every slight from family or friends?

The truth is that we have so many things to be thankful for, including family, home, work, play, food, drink, and everything else that goes into daily life. But the God who provides these things has given us an even better gift: himself.

God has revealed himself to us, giving us his Word, granting us faith and the Holy Spirit, hearing our prayers, and forgiving our sins. So rejoice and receive the gifts of God, confessing him and his goodness. Or as the psalmist says, "Give thanks to the LORD, for he is good! His faithful love endures forever" (Psalm 106:1).

—Mollie Ziegler Hemingway

For more on gratitude, see reading at Psalm 136.

⁶ Like our ancestors, we have sinned.
  We have done wrong! We have acted
    wickedly!
⁷ Our ancestors in Egypt
    were not impressed by the LORD's
    miraculous deeds.
  They soon forgot his many acts of
    kindness to them.
  Instead, they rebelled against him at
    the Red Sea.*
⁸ Even so, he saved them—
    to defend the honor of his name
    and to demonstrate his mighty power.

⁹ He commanded the Red Sea* to dry up.
    He led Israel across the sea as if it
      were a desert.
¹⁰ So he rescued them from their enemies
    and redeemed them from their foes.
¹¹ Then the water returned and covered
      their enemies;
    not one of them survived.
¹² Then his people believed his promises.
    Then they sang his praise.

¹³ Yet how quickly they forgot what he had
      done!
    They wouldn't wait for his counsel!

106:7 Hebrew *at the sea, the sea of reeds.*   **106:9** Hebrew *sea of reeds;* also in 106:22.

¹⁴ In the wilderness their desires ran wild,
    testing God's patience in that dry
    wasteland.
¹⁵ So he gave them what they asked for,
    but he sent a plague along with it.
¹⁶ The people in the camp were jealous of
    Moses
    and envious of Aaron, the LORD's holy
    priest.
¹⁷ Because of this, the earth opened up;
    it swallowed Dathan
    and buried Abiram and the other
    rebels.
¹⁸ Fire fell upon their followers;
    a flame consumed the wicked.

¹⁹ The people made a calf at Mount Sinai*;
    they bowed before an image made of
    gold.
²⁰ They traded their glorious God
    for a statue of a grass-eating bull.
²¹ They forgot God, their savior,
    who had done such great things in
    Egypt—
²² such wonderful things in the land of
    Ham,
    such awesome deeds at the Red Sea.
²³ So he declared he would destroy them.
    But Moses, his chosen one, stepped
    between the LORD and the people.
    He begged him to turn from his anger
    and not destroy them.

²⁴ The people refused to enter the pleasant
    land,
    for they wouldn't believe his promise
    to care for them.
²⁵ Instead, they grumbled in their tents
    and refused to obey the LORD.
²⁶ Therefore, he solemnly swore
    that he would kill them in the
    wilderness,
²⁷ that he would scatter their descendants
    among the nations,
    exiling them to distant lands.

²⁸ Then our ancestors joined in the
    worship of Baal at Peor;
    they even ate sacrifices offered to the
    dead!
²⁹ They angered the LORD with all these
    things,
    so a plague broke out among them.

³⁰ But Phinehas had the courage to
    intervene,
    and the plague was stopped.
³¹ So he has been regarded as a righteous
    man
    ever since that time.

³² At Meribah, too, they angered the LORD,
    causing Moses serious trouble.
³³ They made Moses angry,*
    and he spoke foolishly.

³⁴ Israel failed to destroy the nations in the
    land,
    as the LORD had commanded them.
³⁵ Instead, they mingled among the pagans
    and adopted their evil customs.
³⁶ They worshiped their idols,
    which led to their downfall.
³⁷ They even sacrificed their sons
    and their daughters to the demons.
³⁸ They shed innocent blood,
    the blood of their sons and
    daughters.
    By sacrificing them to the idols of
    Canaan,
    they polluted the land with murder.
³⁹ They defiled themselves by their evil
    deeds,
    and their love of idols was adultery in
    the LORD's sight.

⁴⁰ That is why the LORD's anger burned
    against his people,
    and he abhorred his own special
    possession.
⁴¹ He handed them over to pagan nations,
    and they were ruled by those who
    hated them.
⁴² Their enemies crushed them
    and brought them under their cruel
    power.
⁴³ Again and again he rescued them,
    but they chose to rebel against him,
    and they were finally destroyed by
    their sin.
⁴⁴ Even so, he pitied them in their distress
    and listened to their cries.
⁴⁵ He remembered his covenant with them
    and relented because of his unfailing
    love.
⁴⁶ He even caused their captors
    to treat them with kindness.

106:19 Hebrew *at Horeb*, another name for Sinai. **106:33** Hebrew *They embittered his spirit.*

⁴⁷ Save us, O LORD our God!
    Gather us back from among the
        nations,
so we can thank your holy name
    and rejoice and praise you.

⁴⁸ Praise the LORD, the God of Israel,
    who lives from everlasting to
        everlasting!
Let all the people say, "Amen!"

Praise the LORD!

BOOK FIVE (Psalms 107–150)

107 ¹ Give thanks to the LORD, for he
    is good!
His faithful love endures forever.
² Has the LORD redeemed you? Then
    speak out!
Tell others he has redeemed you from
    your enemies.
³ For he has gathered the exiles from
    many lands,
from east and west,
from north and south.

⁴ Some wandered in the wilderness,
    lost and homeless.
⁵ Hungry and thirsty,
    they nearly died.
⁶ "LORD, help!" they cried in their trouble,
    and he rescued them from their
        distress.
⁷ He led them straight to safety,
    to a city where they could live.
⁸ Let them praise the LORD for his great
    love
and for the wonderful things he has
    done for them.
⁹ For he satisfies the thirsty
    and fills the hungry with good things.

¹⁰ Some sat in darkness and deepest
    gloom,
imprisoned in iron chains of misery.
¹¹ They rebelled against the words of God,
    scorning the counsel of the Most
        High.
¹² That is why he broke them with hard
    labor;
they fell, and no one was there to help
    them.
¹³ "LORD, help!" they cried in their trouble,
    and he saved them from their distress.

¹⁴ He led them from the darkness and
    deepest gloom;
he snapped their chains.
¹⁵ Let them praise the LORD for his great
    love
and for the wonderful things he has
    done for them.
¹⁶ For he broke down their prison gates of
    bronze;
he cut apart their bars of iron.

¹⁷ Some were fools; they rebelled
    and suffered for their sins.
¹⁸ They couldn't stand the thought of food,
    and they were knocking on death's
        door.
¹⁹ "LORD, help!" they cried in their trouble,
    and he saved them from their distress.
²⁰ He sent out his word and healed them,
    snatching them from the door of death.
²¹ Let them praise the LORD for his great
    love
and for the wonderful things he has
    done for them.
²² Let them offer sacrifices of thanksgiving
    and sing joyfully about his glorious
        acts.

²³ Some went off to sea in ships,
    plying the trade routes of the world.
²⁴ They, too, observed the LORD's power in
    action,
his impressive works on the deepest
    seas.
²⁵ He spoke, and the winds rose,
    stirring up the waves.
²⁶ Their ships were tossed to the heavens
    and plunged again to the depths;
the sailors cringed in terror.
²⁷ They reeled and staggered like drunkards
    and were at their wits' end.
²⁸ "LORD, help!" they cried in their trouble,
    and he saved them from their distress.
²⁹ He calmed the storm to a whisper
    and stilled the waves.
³⁰ What a blessing was that stillness
    as he brought them safely into harbor!
³¹ Let them praise the LORD for his great
    love
and for the wonderful things he has
    done for them.
³² Let them exalt him publicly before the
    congregation
and before the leaders of the nation.

33 He changes rivers into deserts,
  and springs of water into dry, thirsty
    land.
34 He turns the fruitful land into salty
    wastelands,
  because of the wickedness of those
    who live there.
35 But he also turns deserts into pools of
    water,
  the dry land into springs of water.
36 He brings the hungry to settle there
  and to build their cities.
37 They sow their fields, plant their vineyards,
  and harvest their bumper crops.
38 How he blesses them!
  They raise large families there,
  and their herds of livestock increase.

39 When they decrease in number and
    become impoverished
  through oppression, trouble, and
    sorrow,
40 the LORD pours contempt on their
    princes,
  causing them to wander in trackless
    wastelands.
41 But he rescues the poor from trouble
  and increases their families like flocks
    of sheep.
42 The godly will see these things and be
    glad,
  while the wicked are struck silent.
43 Those who are wise will take all this to
    heart;
  they will see in our history the faithful
    love of the LORD.

108 A song. A psalm of David.

1 My heart is confident in you, O God;
  no wonder I can sing your praises with
    all my heart!
2 Wake up, lyre and harp!
  I will wake the dawn with my song.
3 I will thank you, LORD, among all the
    people.
  I will sing your praises among the
    nations.
4 For your unfailing love is higher than the
    heavens.
  Your faithfulness reaches to the
    clouds.

5 Be exalted, O God, above the highest
    heavens.
  May your glory shine over all the
    earth.

6 Now rescue your beloved people.
  Answer and save us by your power.
7 God has promised this by his holiness*:
  "I will divide up Shechem with joy.
  I will measure out the valley of
    Succoth.
8 Gilead is mine,
  and Manasseh, too.
  Ephraim, my helmet, will produce my
    warriors,
  and Judah, my scepter, will produce
    my kings.
9 But Moab, my washbasin, will become
    my servant,
  and I will wipe my feet on Edom
  and shout in triumph over Philistia."

10 Who will bring me into the fortified
    city?
  Who will bring me victory over
    Edom?
11 Have you rejected us, O God?
  Will you no longer march with our
    armies?
12 Oh, please help us against our enemies,
  for all human help is useless.
13 With God's help we will do mighty
    things,
  for he will trample down our foes.

109 For the choir director: A psalm of David.

1 O God, whom I praise,
  don't stand silent and aloof
2 while the wicked slander me
  and tell lies about me.
3 They surround me with hateful words
  and fight against me for no reason.
4 I love them, but they try to destroy me
    with accusations
  even as I am praying for them!
5 They repay evil for good,
  and hatred for my love.

6 They say,* "Get an evil person to turn
    against him.
  Send an accuser to bring him to trial.

108:7 Or *in his sanctuary.*   **109:6** Hebrew lacks *They say.*

⁷ When his case comes up for judgment,
   let him be pronounced guilty.
   Count his prayers as sins.
⁸ Let his years be few;
   let someone else take his position.
⁹ May his children become fatherless,
   and his wife a widow.
¹⁰ May his children wander as beggars
   and be driven from their ruined
   homes.
¹¹ May creditors seize his entire estate,
   and strangers take all he has earned.
¹² Let no one be kind to him;
   let no one pity his fatherless children.
¹³ May all his offspring die.
   May his family name be blotted out in
   a single generation.
¹⁴ May the LORD never forget the sins of
   his fathers;
   may his mother's sins never be erased
   from the record.
¹⁵ May the LORD always remember these
   sins,
   and may his name disappear from
   human memory.
¹⁶ For he refused all kindness to others;
   he persecuted the poor and needy,
   and he hounded the brokenhearted to
   death.
¹⁷ He loved to curse others;
   now you curse him.
   He never blessed others;
   now don't you bless him.
¹⁸ Cursing is as natural to him as his
   clothing,
   or the water he drinks,
   or the rich food he eats.
¹⁹ Now may his curses return and cling to
   him like clothing;
   may they be tied around him like a
   belt."
²⁰ May those curses become the LORD's
   punishment
   for my accusers who speak evil of me.
²¹ But deal well with me, O Sovereign
   LORD,
   for the sake of your own reputation!
   Rescue me
   because you are so faithful and good.
²² For I am poor and needy,
   and my heart is full of pain.

²³ I am fading like a shadow at dusk;
   I am brushed off like a locust.
²⁴ My knees are weak from fasting,
   and I am skin and bones.
²⁵ I am a joke to people everywhere;
   when they see me, they shake their
   heads in scorn.
²⁶ Help me, O LORD my God!
   Save me because of your unfailing
   love.
²⁷ Let them see that this is your doing,
   that you yourself have done it, LORD.
²⁸ Then let them curse me if they like,
   but you will bless me!
   When they attack me, they will be
   disgraced!
   But I, your servant, will go right on
   rejoicing!
²⁹ May my accusers be clothed with
   disgrace;
   may their humiliation cover them like
   a cloak.
³⁰ But I will give repeated thanks to the
   LORD,
   praising him to everyone.
³¹ For he stands beside the needy,
   ready to save them from those who
   condemn them.

110 *A psalm of David.*

¹ The LORD said to my Lord,
   "Sit in the place of honor at my right
   hand
until I humble your enemies,
   making them a footstool under your
   feet."

² The LORD will extend your powerful
   kingdom from Jerusalem*;
   you will rule over your enemies.
³ When you go to war,
   your people will serve you willingly.
You are arrayed in holy garments,
   and your strength will be renewed
   each day like the morning dew.

⁴ The LORD has taken an oath and will not
   break his vow:
   "You are a priest forever in the order
   of Melchizedek."

110:2 Hebrew *Zion.*

Afraid of the Right Things
PSALM 111

Faith

We need to be afraid of the right things.

We taught our children to be careful with matches and to be respectful of open fire; fear of house and forest fires prompts sensible precautions. We also taught the children never to run into the street without first carefully looking both ways. A proper fear of cars is also legitimate—as are fears of accepting rides from strangers, using illegal drugs, not wearing helmets when riding motorcycles, breaking the law, and dishonoring one's parents or country.

There is one grand, noble fear we are taught from Genesis to Revelation. It is the fear of the Lord. This is not about "being scared" of God (though there is a hint of that). Biblical fear of the Lord is a reverential trust in God—not only a fear of offending but also a loving to the point that we would not want to offend. Consider how Scripture describes this proper "fear" of God:

Those who fear the LORD are secure; he will be a refuge for their children. (Proverbs 14:26)

Fear of the LORD is the foundation of true wisdom. (Psalm 111:10)

Oh, that they would always have hearts like this, that they might fear me and obey all my commands! If they did, they and their descendants would prosper forever. (Deuteronomy 5:29)

Eugene Peterson reminds us of the purpose of this faithful fear, this reverential trust, in *A Long Obedience in the Same Direction*: "To guard against all such blasphemous chumminess with the Almighty, the Bible talks of the fear of the LORD—not to scare us but to bring us to awesome attention before the overwhelming grandeur of God."

We live in a world racked by anxieties. All the bad news surrounding us clamors for our attention, tempting us to worry and cower. But God reassures his church in Revelation 2:10, even as they look at hardships coming their way, "Don't be afraid of what you are about to suffer." We are to fear only the Lord. It is the fear of God that puts all other fears in proper perspective.

—*Ruth Bell Graham*

For more on faith, see reading at Jeremiah 29:10–14.

---

⁵ The Lord stands at your right hand to
    protect you.
  He will strike down many kings when
    his anger erupts.
⁶ He will punish the nations
    and fill their lands with corpses;
  he will shatter heads over the whole
    earth.

⁷ But he himself will be refreshed from
    brooks along the way.
  He will be victorious.

111 *¹ Praise the LORD!

  I will thank the LORD with all my heart
    as I meet with his godly people.

---

111 This psalm is a Hebrew acrostic poem; after the introductory note of praise, each line begins with a successive letter of the Hebrew alphabet.

² How amazing are the deeds of the LORD!
All who delight in him should ponder
them.
³ Everything he does reveals his glory and
majesty.
His righteousness never fails.
⁴ He causes us to remember his wonderful
works.
How gracious and merciful is our
LORD!
⁵ He gives food to those who fear him;
he always remembers his covenant.
⁶ He has shown his great power to his
people
by giving them the lands of other
nations.
⁷ All he does is just and good,
and all his commandments are
trustworthy.
⁸ They are forever true,
to be obeyed faithfully and with
integrity.
⁹ He has paid a full ransom for his
people.
He has guaranteed his covenant with
them forever.
What a holy, awe-inspiring name he
has!
¹⁰ Fear of the LORD is the foundation of
true wisdom.
All who obey his commandments will
grow in wisdom.

Praise him forever!

112 *¹ Praise the LORD!

How joyful are those who fear the LORD
and delight in obeying his commands.
² Their children will be successful
everywhere;
an entire generation of godly people
will be blessed.
³ They themselves will be wealthy,
and their good deeds will last forever.
⁴ Light shines in the darkness for the
godly.
They are generous, compassionate,
and righteous.
⁵ Good comes to those who lend money
generously
and conduct their business fairly.

⁶ Such people will not be overcome by evil.
Those who are righteous will be long
remembered.
⁷ They do not fear bad news;
they confidently trust the LORD to
care for them.
⁸ They are confident and fearless
and can face their foes triumphantly.
⁹ They share freely and give generously to
those in need.
Their good deeds will be remembered
forever.
They will have influence and honor.
¹⁰ The wicked will see this and be
infuriated.
They will grind their teeth in anger;
they will slink away, their hopes
thwarted.

113 ¹ Praise the LORD!

Yes, give praise, O servants of the LORD.
Praise the name of the LORD!
² Blessed be the name of the LORD
now and forever.
³ Everywhere—from east to west—
praise the name of the LORD.
⁴ For the LORD is high above the nations;
his glory is higher than the heavens.

⁵ Who can be compared with the LORD
our God,
who is enthroned on high?
⁶ He stoops to look down
on heaven and on earth.
⁷ He lifts the poor from the dust
and the needy from the garbage dump.
⁸ He sets them among princes,
even the princes of his own people!
⁹ He gives the childless woman a family,
making her a happy mother.

Praise the LORD!

114 ¹ When the Israelites escaped from
Egypt—
when the family of Jacob left that
foreign land—
² the land of Judah became God's sanctuary,
and Israel became his kingdom.

³ The Red Sea* saw them coming and
hurried out of their way!

---

112 This psalm is a Hebrew acrostic poem; after the introductory note of praise, each line begins with a successive letter of the Hebrew alphabet. **114:3** Hebrew *the sea;* also in 114:5.

Celebration through the Psalms

PSALM 113

G ive thanks to the LORD for he is good! His faithful love endures forever" (Psalm 118:1).

Can you imagine a large crowd of people echoing out these words together? Can you picture a family reciting them around the table? From biblical times to today, the Psalms have served as a liturgy of celebration for God's people.

Psalms 113-118 (called the *Hallel*) and Psalm 136 (sometimes called the Great Hallel) were recited during Old Testament festivals and are still a part of Orthodox Jewish celebrations. These psalms recount God's rescue of his people from Egypt, describe his loving-kindness, and proclaim his promise of salvation.

Many of the poems and songs we find in the Book of Psalms served as corporate prayers of celebration and praise in biblical times, as God's people together declared truths about God's work as Creator and his miraculous works throughout history. Psalms 8, 19, 22, 46, 48, 67, 75, and 96 are just a few examples of these powerful songs that both remind us of God's goodness and prod us to respond in worship and celebration.

Like God's people in biblical times, we too can turn to Psalms to find words for our own practice of celebration. Alone or with others, we can answer the psalmist's call: "Each day proclaim the good news that he saves. Publish his glorious deeds among the nations. Tell everyone about the amazing things he does. Great is the LORD!" (96:2-4).

—*Kelli B. Trujillo*

For more on celebration, see reading at Psalm 126.

The water of the Jordan River turned
away.
4 The mountains skipped like rams,
the hills like lambs!
5 What's wrong, Red Sea, that made you
hurry out of their way?
What happened, Jordan River, that
you turned away?
6 Why, mountains, did you skip like rams?
Why, hills, like lambs?

7 Tremble, O earth, at the presence of the
Lord,
at the presence of the God of Jacob.
8 He turned the rock into a pool of
water;
yes, a spring of water flowed from
solid rock.

115 1 Not to us, O LORD, not to us,
but to your name goes all the
glory
for your unfailing love and faithfulness.
2 Why let the nations say,
"Where is their God?"
3 Our God is in the heavens,
and he does as he wishes.
4 Their idols are merely things of silver
and gold,
shaped by human hands.
5 They have mouths but cannot speak,
and eyes but cannot see.
6 They have ears but cannot hear,
and noses but cannot smell.
7 They have hands but cannot feel,
and feet but cannot walk,
and throats but cannot make a sound.

An Uncluttered Soul

PSALM 116:7

There is a show playing on cable TV called *Hoarders*. It looks inside the lives of people who can't part with their material "stuff"; they're out of control and on the verge of crisis, because they've acquired a literal mound of possessions and refuse to part with any of it.

Although my home doesn't look like that and I don't collect things to that extent, sometimes I think my inner life is like that: filled with "stuff."

For so many of us, our lives are so crammed, crazy-busy, and chaotic that it's tough just to slow down and take life more simply—to weed out the distractions, noise, and "stuff" and be content with less. It's difficult to set ourselves apart to focus solely on Jesus and who he's created each of us to be. Instead we just keep cramming it all into our homes, our schedules, our souls. We end up overpromising and underdelivering in so many areas. And as we cram in, we squeeze out our ability to hear God clearly and follow his plan for us.

But when we're able to throw off the excess stuff, noise, and distractions in our lives, we're better able to get our priorities in order. We focus on Christ and, somehow, all those other things don't really matter.

True, deep-rooted simplicity is about a lot more than just uncluttering our closets; it's a practice of uncluttering our souls. It's a way of life that makes choices and sets boundaries so our souls have space to rest in God (Psalm 116:7). It's learning how to say no to those things that don't fit in with the basic core of our calling and being. We choose to live lives that are slower, simpler, and down sized—and ultimately more joy filled, peaceful, and God honoring.

—Ginger Kolbaba

For more on simplicity, see reading at Proverbs 15:16.

---

⁸ And those who make idols are just like them,
   as are all who trust in them.

⁹ O Israel, trust the LORD!
   He is your helper and your shield.
¹⁰ O priests, descendants of Aaron, trust the LORD!
   He is your helper and your shield.
¹¹ All you who fear the LORD, trust the LORD!
   He is your helper and your shield.

¹² The LORD remembers us and will bless us.
   He will bless the people of Israel
   and bless the priests, the descendants of Aaron.

¹³ He will bless those who fear the LORD,
   both great and lowly.
¹⁴ May the LORD richly bless
   both you and your children.
¹⁵ May you be blessed by the LORD,
   who made heaven and earth.
¹⁶ The heavens belong to the LORD,
   but he has given the earth to all humanity.
¹⁷ The dead cannot sing praises to the LORD,
   for they have gone into the silence of the grave.
¹⁸ But we can praise the LORD
   both now and forever!

Praise the LORD!

116

¹ I love the LORD because he hears my voice
and my prayer for mercy.
² Because he bends down to listen,
I will pray as long as I have breath!
³ Death wrapped its ropes around me;
the terrors of the grave* overtook me.
I saw only trouble and sorrow.
⁴ Then I called on the name of the LORD:
"Please, LORD, save me!"
⁵ How kind the LORD is! How good he is!
So merciful, this God of ours!
⁶ The LORD protects those of childlike faith;
I was facing death, and he saved me.
⁷ Let my soul be at rest again,
for the LORD has been good to me.
⁸ He has saved me from death,
my eyes from tears,
my feet from stumbling.
⁹ And so I walk in the LORD's presence
as I live here on earth!
¹⁰ I believed in you, so I said,
"I am deeply troubled, LORD."
¹¹ In my anxiety I cried out to you,
"These people are all liars!"
¹² What can I offer the LORD
for all he has done for me?
¹³ I will lift up the cup of salvation
and praise the LORD's name for saving me.
¹⁴ I will keep my promises to the LORD
in the presence of all his people.

¹⁵ The LORD cares deeply
when his loved ones die.
¹⁶ O LORD, I am your servant;
yes, I am your servant, born into your household;
you have freed me from my chains.
¹⁷ I will offer you a sacrifice of thanksgiving
and call on the name of the LORD.
¹⁸ I will fulfill my vows to the LORD
in the presence of all his people—
¹⁹ in the house of the LORD
in the heart of Jerusalem.

Praise the LORD!

117

¹ Praise the LORD, all you nations.
Praise him, all you people of the earth.

² For he loves us with unfailing love;
the LORD's faithfulness endures forever.

Praise the LORD!

118

¹ Give thanks to the LORD, for he is good!
His faithful love endures forever.

² Let all Israel repeat:
"His faithful love endures forever."
³ Let Aaron's descendants, the priests, repeat:
"His faithful love endures forever."
⁴ Let all who fear the LORD repeat:
"His faithful love endures forever."

⁵ In my distress I prayed to the LORD,
and the LORD answered me and set me free.
⁶ The LORD is for me, so I will have no fear.
What can mere people do to me?
⁷ Yes, the LORD is for me; he will help me.
I will look in triumph at those who hate me.
⁸ It is better to take refuge in the LORD
than to trust in people.
⁹ It is better to take refuge in the LORD
than to trust in princes.

¹⁰ Though hostile nations surrounded me,
I destroyed them all with the authority of the LORD.
¹¹ Yes, they surrounded and attacked me,
but I destroyed them all with the authority of the LORD.
¹² They swarmed around me like bees;
they blazed against me like a crackling fire.
But I destroyed them all with the authority of the LORD.
¹³ My enemies did their best to kill me,
but the LORD rescued me.
¹⁴ The LORD is my strength and my song;
he has given me victory.
¹⁵ Songs of joy and victory are sung in the camp of the godly.
The strong right arm of the LORD has done glorious things!
¹⁶ The strong right arm of the LORD is raised in triumph.

116:3 Hebrew *of Sheol.*

The strong right arm of the LORD has
done glorious things!
[17] I will not die; instead, I will live
to tell what the LORD has done.
[18] The LORD has punished me severely,
but he did not let me die.

[19] Open for me the gates where the
righteous enter,
and I will go in and thank the LORD.
[20] These gates lead to the presence of the
LORD,
and the godly enter there.
[21] I thank you for answering my prayer
and giving me victory!

[22] The stone that the builders rejected
has now become the cornerstone.
[23] This is the LORD's doing,
and it is wonderful to see.
[24] This is the day the LORD has made.
We will rejoice and be glad in it.
[25] Please, LORD, please save us.
Please, LORD, please give us success.
[26] Bless the one who comes in the name of
the LORD.
We bless you from the house of the
LORD.
[27] The LORD is God, shining upon us.
Take the sacrifice and bind it with
cords on the altar.
[28] You are my God, and I will praise you!
You are my God, and I will exalt you!

[29] Give thanks to the LORD, for he is good!
His faithful love endures forever.

Aleph

119

[*] [1] Joyful are people of integrity,
who follow the instructions of
the LORD.
[2] Joyful are those who obey his laws
and search for him with all their
hearts.
[3] They do not compromise with evil,
and they walk only in his paths.
[4] You have charged us
to keep your commandments
carefully.
[5] Oh, that my actions would consistently
reflect your decrees!
[6] Then I will not be ashamed

when I compare my life with your
commands.
[7] As I learn your righteous regulations,
I will thank you by living as I should!
[8] I will obey your decrees.
Please don't give up on me!

Beth

[9] How can a young person stay pure?
By obeying your word.
[10] I have tried hard to find you—
don't let me wander from your
commands.
[11] I have hidden your word in my heart,
that I might not sin against you.
[12] I praise you, O LORD;
teach me your decrees.
[13] I have recited aloud
all the regulations you have given us.
[14] I have rejoiced in your laws
as much as in riches.
[15] I will study your commandments
and reflect on your ways.
[16] I will delight in your decrees
and not forget your word.

Gimel

[17] Be good to your servant,
that I may live and obey your word.
[18] Open my eyes to see
the wonderful truths in your
instructions.
[19] I am only a foreigner in the land.
Don't hide your commands from me!
[20] I am always overwhelmed
with a desire for your regulations.
[21] You rebuke the arrogant;
those who wander from your
commands are cursed.
[22] Don't let them scorn and insult me,
for I have obeyed your laws.
[23] Even princes sit and speak against me,
but I will meditate on your decrees.
[24] Your laws please me;
they give me wise advice.

Daleth

[25] I lie in the dust;
revive me by your word.
[26] I told you my plans, and you answered.
Now teach me your decrees.
[27] Help me understand the meaning of
your commandments,

---

119 This psalm is a Hebrew acrostic poem; there are twenty-two stanzas, one for each successive letter of the Hebrew alphabet. Each of the
eight verses within each stanza begins with the Hebrew letter named in its heading.

and I will meditate on your wonderful
   deeds.
²⁸ I weep with sorrow;
   encourage me by your word.
²⁹ Keep me from lying to myself;
   give me the privilege of knowing your
      instructions.
³⁰ I have chosen to be faithful;
   I have determined to live by your
      regulations.
³¹ I cling to your laws.
   Lᴏʀᴅ, don't let me be put to shame!
³² I will pursue your commands,
   for you expand my understanding.

He
³³ Teach me your decrees, O Lᴏʀᴅ;
   I will keep them to the end.
³⁴ Give me understanding and I will obey
      your instructions;
   I will put them into practice with all
      my heart.
³⁵ Make me walk along the path of your
      commands,
   for that is where my happiness is
      found.
³⁶ Give me an eagerness for your laws
   rather than a love for money!
³⁷ Turn my eyes from worthless things,
   and give me life through your word.*
³⁸ Reassure me of your promise,
   made to those who fear you.
³⁹ Help me abandon my shameful ways;
   for your regulations are good.
⁴⁰ I long to obey your commandments!
   Renew my life with your goodness.

Waw
⁴¹ Lᴏʀᴅ, give me your unfailing love,
   the salvation that you promised me.
⁴² Then I can answer those who taunt me,
   for I trust in your word.
⁴³ Do not snatch your word of truth
      from me,
   for your regulations are my only hope.
⁴⁴ I will keep on obeying your instructions
   forever and ever.
⁴⁵ I will walk in freedom,
   for I have devoted myself to your
      commandments.
⁴⁶ I will speak to kings about your laws,
   and I will not be ashamed.

⁴⁷ How I delight in your commands!
   How I love them!
⁴⁸ I honor and love your commands.
   I meditate on your decrees.

Zayin
⁴⁹ Remember your promise to me;
   it is my only hope.
⁵⁰ Your promise revives me;
   it comforts me in all my troubles.
⁵¹ The proud hold me in utter contempt,
   but I do not turn away from your
      instructions.
⁵² I meditate on your age-old regulations;
   O Lᴏʀᴅ, they comfort me.
⁵³ I become furious with the wicked,
   because they reject your instructions.
⁵⁴ Your decrees have been the theme of my
      songs
   wherever I have lived.
⁵⁵ I reflect at night on who you are, O Lᴏʀᴅ;
   therefore, I obey your instructions.
⁵⁶ This is how I spend my life:
   obeying your commandments.

Heth
⁵⁷ Lᴏʀᴅ, you are mine!
   I promise to obey your words!
⁵⁸ With all my heart I want your blessings.
   Be merciful as you promised.
⁵⁹ I pondered the direction of my life,
   and I turned to follow your laws.
⁶⁰ I will hurry, without delay,
   to obey your commands.
⁶¹ Evil people try to drag me into sin,
   but I am firmly anchored to your
      instructions.
⁶² I rise at midnight to thank you
   for your just regulations.
⁶³ I am a friend to anyone who fears you—
   anyone who obeys your
      commandments.
⁶⁴ O Lᴏʀᴅ, your unfailing love fills the
      earth;
   teach me your decrees.

Teth
⁶⁵ You have done many good things for me,
      Lᴏʀᴅ,
   just as you promised.
⁶⁶ I believe in your commands;
   now teach me good judgment and
      knowledge.

119:37 Some manuscripts read *in your ways.*

Hiding God's Word in My Heart

PSALM 119:9–16

"Keep a low profile," I was warned before I entered a country known for its religious persecution. So the last thing I expected was an invitation to visit a secret house church.

Sticking close to my guide and translator, I followed in a dizzying dash along the city streets, ducking into alleyways and courtyards, until we finally eased through the back door of a simple two-room house. I followed through the closet-sized kitchen to a room furnished with a single table and two chairs. "Fifty people worship here on Sundays," the young woman told me.

Fifty crowded into so small a room!

"They come quietly, one at a time. They know how to gather without attracting attention." They whispered their prayers, the translator told me, and soundlessly mouthed the songs. Making a joyful noise was not a privilege afforded them.

A little gray-haired lady—the owner of the house—shuffled in and sat at the table. She pulled a folded paper from her pocket and carefully smoothed it out. Then she took out a pencil and looked at me with eager anticipation.

"What does she want?" I asked.

"She's waiting for you to recite chapters from the Bible," the translator said. "She will write out the words, and we will memorize them. Then we can share them with other house churches."

Chapters of the Bible? I thought. Well, I did know some psalms. . . .

"Start with Romans," the translator encouraged. "We don't have any of Romans."

Recite chapters from Romans? She had to be kidding!

"I don't know any chapters from Romans," I admitted.

"Oh," the translator said. "You don't have it either?"

"Well . . . yes . . . I have it," I stammered. "I have several copies at my home. I have it on my computer too. I *have* it, but I don't *know* it. . . ."

The translator stared at me, then she repeated what I'd said to the little old lady. The lady fixed me with a gaze of shocked disbelief and poignant disappointment. She folded up her paper and put it and the pencil back into her pocket. Then she stood and quietly walked out of the room.

My favorite chapter of the Bible is Romans 8. If I'd known that chapter by heart, imagine what it would have meant to those believers who've experienced so much persecution! I could have said, "Yet what we suffer now is nothing compared to the glory he will reveal to us later" (Romans 8:18).

And I could have shared the encouragement: "And we know that God causes everything to work together for the good of those who love God and are called according to his purpose for them" (8:28).

I could have joyfully proclaimed:

> Can anything ever separate us from Christ's love? Does it mean he no longer loves us if we have trouble or calamity, or are persecuted, or hungry, or destitute, or in danger, or threatened with death? . . . No, despite all these things, overwhelming victory is ours through Christ who loved us. And I am convinced that nothing can ever separate us from God's love. Neither death nor life, neither angels nor demons, neither our fears for today nor our worries about tomorrow—not even the powers of hell can separate us from God's love. No power in the sky above or in the earth below—indeed, nothing in all creation will ever be able to separate us from the love of God that is revealed in Christ Jesus our Lord. (8:35, 37–39)

I couldn't say any of that, though, because I didn't memorize Romans 8 until after I'd returned home.

But that day, I made a life-changing decision. Standing in that small house, I determined that never again would someone ask me to share Scripture with them only to have me mumble, "I *have* it, but I don't *know* it."

Now Scripture memorization has become a central part of my spiritual life. I have a small notebook in which I record all the passages I want to memorize. Some of them I've already committed to memory, others I'm working on, and some I'm revisiting because I need to refresh my memory.

Sometimes when I start to recite a portion of Scripture, I stumble and make mistakes, but I've learned it doesn't matter. I'm not learning these passages for a performance; I'm memorizing them so that the Holy Spirit can call the right Scripture to mind when I need it. He cannot bring back what I never knew. But what is hidden in my heart can never be erased (Psalm 119:11).

—Kay Marshall Strom

For more on Bible study and meditation, see reading at Song of Songs 7:10–13.

⁶⁷ I used to wander off until you
disciplined me;
but now I closely follow your word.
⁶⁸ You are good and do only good;
teach me your decrees.
⁶⁹ Arrogant people smear me with lies,
but in truth I obey your
commandments with all my heart.
⁷⁰ Their hearts are dull and stupid,
but I delight in your instructions.
⁷¹ My suffering was good for me,
for it taught me to pay attention to
your decrees.
⁷² Your instructions are more valuable to me
than millions in gold and silver.

Yodh

⁷³ You made me; you created me.
Now give me the sense to follow your
commands.
⁷⁴ May all who fear you find in me a cause
for joy,
for I have put my hope in your word.
⁷⁵ I know, O LORD, that your regulations
are fair;
you disciplined me because I needed it.
⁷⁶ Now let your unfailing love comfort me,
just as you promised me, your servant.
⁷⁷ Surround me with your tender mercies
so I may live,
for your instructions are my delight.
⁷⁸ Bring disgrace upon the arrogant people
who lied about me;
meanwhile, I will concentrate on your
commandments.
⁷⁹ Let me be united with all who fear you,
with those who know your laws.
⁸⁰ May I be blameless in keeping your
decrees;
then I will never be ashamed.

Kaph

⁸¹ I am worn out waiting for your rescue,
but I have put my hope in your word.
⁸² My eyes are straining to see your
promises come true.
When will you comfort me?
⁸³ I am shriveled like a wineskin in the
smoke,
but I have not forgotten to obey your
decrees.
⁸⁴ How long must I wait?
When will you punish those who
persecute me?

⁸⁵ These arrogant people who hate your
instructions
have dug deep pits to trap me.
⁸⁶ All your commands are trustworthy.
Protect me from those who hunt me
down without cause.
⁸⁷ They almost finished me off,
but I refused to abandon your
commandments.
⁸⁸ In your unfailing love, spare my life;
then I can continue to obey your laws.

Lamedh

⁸⁹ Your eternal word, O LORD,
stands firm in heaven.
⁹⁰ Your faithfulness extends to every
generation,
as enduring as the earth you created.
⁹¹ Your regulations remain true to this day,
for everything serves your plans.
⁹² If your instructions hadn't sustained me
with joy,
I would have died in my misery.
⁹³ I will never forget your commandments,
for by them you give me life.
⁹⁴ I am yours; rescue me!
For I have worked hard at obeying
your commandments.
⁹⁵ Though the wicked hide along the way
to kill me,
I will quietly keep my mind on your
laws.
⁹⁶ Even perfection has its limits,
but your commands have no limit.

Mem

⁹⁷ Oh, how I love your instructions!
I think about them all day long.
⁹⁸ Your commands make me wiser than my
enemies,
for they are my constant guide.
⁹⁹ Yes, I have more insight than my
teachers,
for I am always thinking of your laws.
¹⁰⁰ I am even wiser than my elders,
for I have kept your commandments.
¹⁰¹ I have refused to walk on any evil path,
so that I may remain obedient to your
word.
¹⁰² I haven't turned away from your
regulations,
for you have taught me well.
¹⁰³ How sweet your words taste to me;
they are sweeter than honey.

104 Your commandments give me
   understanding;
   no wonder I hate every false way of
   life.

Nun

105 Your word is a lamp to guide my feet
   and a light for my path.
106 I've promised it once, and I'll promise it
   again:
   I will obey your righteous regulations.
107 I have suffered much, O LORD;
   restore my life again as you promised.
108 LORD, accept my offering of praise,
   and teach me your regulations.
109 My life constantly hangs in the balance,
   but I will not stop obeying your
   instructions.
110 The wicked have set their traps for me,
   but I will not turn from your
   commandments.
111 Your laws are my treasure;
   they are my heart's delight.
112 I am determined to keep your decrees
   to the very end.

Samekh

113 I hate those with divided loyalties,
   but I love your instructions.
114 You are my refuge and my shield;
   your word is my source of hope.
115 Get out of my life, you evil-minded
   people,
   for I intend to obey the commands of
   my God.
116 LORD, sustain me as you promised, that
   I may live!
   Do not let my hope be crushed.
117 Sustain me, and I will be rescued;
   then I will meditate continually on
   your decrees.
118 But you have rejected all who stray from
   your decrees.
   They are only fooling themselves.
119 You skim off the wicked of the earth like
   scum;
   no wonder I love to obey your laws!
120 I tremble in fear of you;
   I stand in awe of your regulations.

Ayin

121 Don't leave me to the mercy of my
   enemies,
   for I have done what is just and right.

122 Please guarantee a blessing for me.
   Don't let the arrogant oppress me!
123 My eyes strain to see your rescue,
   to see the truth of your promise fulfilled.
124 I am your servant; deal with me in
   unfailing love,
   and teach me your decrees.
125 Give discernment to me, your servant;
   then I will understand your laws.
126 LORD, it is time for you to act,
   for these evil people have violated
   your instructions.
127 Truly, I love your commands
   more than gold, even the finest gold.
128 Each of your commandments is right.
   That is why I hate every false way.

Pe

129 Your laws are wonderful.
   No wonder I obey them!
130 The teaching of your word gives light,
   so even the simple can understand.
131 I pant with expectation,
   longing for your commands.
132 Come and show me your mercy,
   as you do for all who love your name.
133 Guide my steps by your word,
   so I will not be overcome by evil.
134 Ransom me from the oppression of evil
   people;
   then I can obey your commandments.
135 Look upon me with love;
   teach me your decrees.
136 Rivers of tears gush from my eyes
   because people disobey your
   instructions.

Tsadhe

137 O LORD, you are righteous,
   and your regulations are fair.
138 Your laws are perfect
   and completely trustworthy.
139 I am overwhelmed with indignation,
   for my enemies have disregarded your
   words.
140 Your promises have been thoroughly
   tested;
   that is why I love them so much.
141 I am insignificant and despised,
   but I don't forget your
   commandments.
142 Your justice is eternal,
   and your instructions are perfectly
   true.

Submission

Relationship That Leads to Life

PSALM 119:129–144

My husband and I are trying to get our kids to consistently do their chores. We've tried threats and rewards but worry that our extrinsic motivators are holding our kids back from learning to obey simply because it's the right thing to do. "Gee," we long to hear them say, "my folks love me and know what's best for me, so I better pick up that broom and chip in."

Our struggle with our kids got us thinking about God's struggle with us. Surely he wants us to do the right things for the right reasons. As his people, do we behave "Christianly" because of extrinsic or intrinsic factors?

I once spoke at a family camp that had been meeting for years. One morning a seminary graduate shared his story with the group. David had weathered a crisis of faith when his father—a sternly religious man and prominent church leader—had been exposed in chronic sexual sin. David said that healing had come slowly and that, looking back, he realized the Christianity of his upbringing had overemphasized "morality" in place of "relationship."

It sounded to me like David's dad might have benefited from a little *more* emphasis on obeying God's moral standards. And I worried that David's take was not what the group needed to hear; two affairs had fractured their community in recent years. To me, it seemed they were suffering from too much relationship and too little morality.

I remember my reaction now with chagrin. I've since seen individuals and church communities with a robust focus on morality fall countless times. I get David's point: an emphasis on holy living without a genuine, life-changing relationship with a holy God can lead to rigid legalism on the one hand or secret sin on the other—and often it leads to both.

I also know Christians who emphasize relationship—and God's unearnable, inexhaustible love—yet neglect obedience. I've seen them, too, have catastrophic moral falls. Such failings do not disqualify us for God's forgiveness, but they often have shattering consequences.

So what works? When it comes to shaping character and behavior, is it better to focus on obedience to God's law or dwelling in his grace?

Psalm 119 is a love song to God's law, which seems odd. My friend Steve Bell says he never understood such passion for a moral code until he thought about children playing near the edge of a cliff. Without a fence, the children are always in danger, never able to relax. But if a barrier is installed, they can play freely and without fear. God's law *is* God's grace. It's a safety fence that brings incredible freedom.

Of course it's only a matter of time until a kid starts to wonder what's on the other side of the fence. If she doesn't know or trust the fence builder, she might suspect that the barrier is holding her back from bigger fun. So she hops the fence, a lemming for false liberty. Humanity has an extensive track record on this front.

Fortunately there's more to the story. God's law is not only a safety fence; it's also a mirror that shows us we can't live up to his standards without his help. Jesus comes not to abolish the Law but to finally fulfill it (Matthew 5:17). Yet rather than submit to God's guidance, many of us keep hopping the fence. Why? Partly because we still don't really know and trust the fence builder.

God doesn't expect moral obedience in the absence of relationship. The first line of the Ten Commandments is not, "You must not have any other God but me," but, "I am the LORD your God, who rescued you from the land of Egypt, the place of your slavery" (Exodus 20:2). God defines the relationship first, then describes a life lived in its context.

Psychologists warn that extrinsic motivators for morality erode intrinsic ones. When our preachers thunder warnings about living right to avoid God's wrath or earn his favor, we run the risk of drowning out that still, small voice that beckons us to live out the holiness given us solely by our Father's grace.

Conversely, when the message is that our behavior doesn't matter, that God's grace is unmerited and therefore moral obedience is not a major issue, we seem not to know our Father at all.

In the end, it isn't morality *versus* relationship. It's submission to God's moral expectations *because* of relationship. If we know our Father loves us, and we love him, we'll trust whatever he asks of us. We won't need the threats and rewards that can skew real faith toward pharisaism. We'll just pick up our brooms and chip in.

—*Carolyn Arends*

For more on submission, see reading at Isaiah 64:8.

143 As pressure and stress bear down on me,
   I find joy in your commands.
144 Your laws are always right;
   help me to understand them so I may
   live.

Qoph

145 I pray with all my heart; answer me,
   LORD!
   I will obey your decrees.
146 I cry out to you; rescue me,
   that I may obey your laws.
147 I rise early, before the sun is up;
   I cry out for help and put my hope in
   your words.
148 I stay awake through the night,
   thinking about your promise.
149 In your faithful love, O LORD, hear my
   cry;
   let me be revived by following your
   regulations.
150 Lawless people are coming to attack me;
   they live far from your instructions.
151 But you are near, O LORD,
   and all your commands are true.
152 I have known from my earliest days
   that your laws will last forever.

Resh

153 Look upon my suffering and rescue me,
   for I have not forgotten your
   instructions.
154 Argue my case; take my side!
   Protect my life as you promised.
155 The wicked are far from rescue,
   for they do not bother with your
   decrees.
156 LORD, how great is your mercy;
   let me be revived by following your
   regulations.
157 Many persecute and trouble me,
   yet I have not swerved from your
   laws.
158 Seeing these traitors makes me sick at
   heart,
   because they care nothing for your
   word.
159 See how I love your commandments,
   LORD.
   Give back my life because of your
   unfailing love.
160 The very essence of your words is truth;
   all your just regulations will stand
   forever.

Shin

161 Powerful people harass me without
   cause,
   but my heart trembles only at your
   word.
162 I rejoice in your word
   like one who discovers a great
   treasure.
163 I hate and abhor all falsehood,
   but I love your instructions.
164 I will praise you seven times a day
   because all your regulations are just.
165 Those who love your instructions have
   great peace
   and do not stumble.
166 I long for your rescue, LORD,
   so I have obeyed your commands.
167 I have obeyed your laws,
   for I love them very much.
168 Yes, I obey your commandments and
   laws
   because you know everything I do.

Taw

169 O LORD, listen to my cry;
   give me the discerning mind you
   promised.
170 Listen to my prayer;
   rescue me as you promised.
171 Let praise flow from my lips,
   for you have taught me your
   decrees.
172 Let my tongue sing about your word,
   for all your commands are right.
173 Give me a helping hand,
   for I have chosen to follow your
   commandments.
174 O LORD, I have longed for your rescue,
   and your instructions are my
   delight.
175 Let me live so I can praise you,
   and may your regulations help me.
176 I have wandered away like a lost
   sheep;
   come and find me,
   for I have not forgotten your
   commands.

120 *A song for pilgrims ascending to Jerusalem.*

1 I took my troubles to the LORD;
   I cried out to him, and he answered
   my prayer.

Sabbath & Rest

Rest That Leads to Worship

PSALM 121

Under doctor's orders after a major surgery, I was to take six weeks to do absolutely *nothing*. The adjustment from busyness to rest was difficult at first, but this "prescription" ended up working wonders for both my body and soul in a surprising way: rest led freely and naturally into worship and gratitude.

One morning as I looked out at my front yard, rather than noticing the yard work I needed to do, I simply thought: *Lord, there's a new day out there—and I'm alive to enjoy it!* It was a natural song of praise for the basics of life that I'd been too distracted to notice in my "normal" life dominated by work, commitments, and a drive to accomplish more.

A bird song. Roses in the garden. Dinner from a friend. A cup of hot tea from my husband. In my period of forced rest, I took notice of these good gifts—and I thanked God for them. I always knew, for example, that I had a sycamore tree in my backyard, but I'd never paid it attention. Now I looked at the color of its bark, the shape of its leaves. My "time out" turned up the volume on all my senses. I was able to tune in to the beauty and blessings of the world around me and, more important, to connect with my heavenly Father.

Rather than focusing on my normal preoccupations, I thought about God often. I talked to him, I noticed his love. Like a camera lens zooming in and focusing on an object, I rediscovered a spiritual posture of restful worship.

We need not wait for bed-rest orders, illnesses, or other crises that force us to rest: God invites us into a pattern of rest *today*. We can choose to have a frame of mind dominated by busyness and a schedule controlled by commitments, or we can settle into a healthy, restful pace that allows us to enjoy life, to sigh with delight at God's beauty, to notice and celebrate his many daily blessings.

—*Ruth Senter*

For more on Sabbath and rest, see reading at Psalm 127:1-2.

² Rescue me, O Lord, from liars
and from all deceitful people.
³ O deceptive tongue, what will God do to you?
How will he increase your punishment?
⁴ You will be pierced with sharp arrows
and burned with glowing coals.

⁵ How I suffer in far-off Meshech.
It pains me to live in distant Kedar.
⁶ I am tired of living
among people who hate peace.
⁷ I search for peace;
but when I speak of peace, they want war!

121 *A song for pilgrims ascending to Jerusalem.*

¹ I look up to the mountains—
does my help come from there?
² My help comes from the Lord,
who made heaven and earth!

³ He will not let you stumble;
the one who watches over you will not slumber.
⁴ Indeed, he who watches over Israel
never slumbers or sleeps.

⁵ The Lord himself watches over you!
The Lord stands beside you as your protective shade.

⁶ The sun will not harm you by day,
   nor the moon at night.
⁷ The LORD keeps you from all harm
   and watches over your life.
⁸ The LORD keeps watch over you as you
      come and go,
   both now and forever.

122 *A song for pilgrims ascending to Jerusalem. A psalm of David.*

¹ I was glad when they said to me,
   "Let us go to the house of the LORD."
² And now here we are,
   standing inside your gates,
      O Jerusalem.
³ Jerusalem is a well-built city;
   its seamless walls cannot be breached.
⁴ All the tribes of Israel—the LORD's
      people—
   make their pilgrimage here.
   They come to give thanks to the name of
      the LORD,
   as the law requires of Israel.
⁵ Here stand the thrones where judgment
      is given,
   the thrones of the dynasty of David.

⁶ Pray for peace in Jerusalem.
   May all who love this city prosper.
⁷ O Jerusalem, may there be peace within
      your walls
   and prosperity in your palaces.
⁸ For the sake of my family and friends, I
      will say,
   "May you have peace."
⁹ For the sake of the house of the LORD
      our God,
   I will seek what is best for you,
      O Jerusalem.

123 *A song for pilgrims ascending to Jerusalem.*

¹ I lift my eyes to you,
   O God, enthroned in heaven.
² We keep looking to the LORD our God
      for his mercy,
   just as servants keep their eyes on
      their master,
   as a slave girl watches her mistress for
      the slightest signal.
³ Have mercy on us, LORD, have mercy,
   for we have had our fill of contempt.

⁴ We have had more than our fill of the
      scoffing of the proud
   and the contempt of the arrogant.

124 *A song for pilgrims ascending to Jerusalem. A psalm of David.*

¹ What if the LORD had not been on our
      side?
   Let all Israel repeat:
² What if the LORD had not been on our
      side
   when people attacked us?
³ They would have swallowed us alive
   in their burning anger.
⁴ The waters would have engulfed us;
   a torrent would have
      overwhelmed us.
⁵ Yes, the raging waters of their fury
   would have overwhelmed our very
      lives.

⁶ Praise the LORD,
   who did not let their teeth tear us
      apart!
⁷ We escaped like a bird from a hunter's
      trap.
   The trap is broken, and we are free!
⁸ Our help is from the LORD,
   who made heaven and earth.

125 *A song for pilgrims ascending to Jerusalem.*

¹ Those who trust in the LORD are as
      secure as Mount Zion;
   they will not be defeated but will
      endure forever.
² Just as the mountains surround
      Jerusalem,
   so the LORD surrounds his people,
      both now and forever.
³ The wicked will not rule the land of the
      godly,
   for then the godly might be tempted
      to do wrong.
⁴ O LORD, do good to those who are
      good,
   whose hearts are in tune with you.
⁵ But banish those who turn to crooked
      ways, O LORD.
   Take them away with those who do
      evil.

May Israel have peace!

The Holiness of Laughter

PSALM 126

R ecently my daughter Bethany brought home a Sunday-school craft. She had cut out and colored pictures of children engaged in different acts of worship and glued them onto a sheet.

"Praying! Giving! Reading the Bible!" she shouted as I pointed to each scene.

I saved the best picture for last—a boy with his mouth open wide in song.

"Laughing!" said Bethany, when I pointed to the boy with the open mouth.

I stood corrected.

Laughter *is* a form of worship. A good laugh is a release—even if only for a moment—from worry, strife, and self. It is a sudden, often unbidden confession that someway, somehow, all is well, or at least there is a hope that it can be.

Trinitarian theologians use the word *perichoresis* to describe the happy fellowship of the Father, Son, and Spirit. Their relationship is often pictured as a tireless and joyful divine dance. I can't think about that holy dance without remembering all the times when my husband and I would twirl and spin our toddlers around until they were helpless with soundless laughter. We'd all end up laughing until we were all worn out with gladness. We could have quoted the psalmist as we held our aching sides on the family room floor: "We were filled with laughter, and we sang for joy. . . . The LORD has done amazing things for us! What joy!" (Psalm 126:2-3).

Laughter is the kind of sacrifice of praise that puts our insides right. The old cliché is true: laughter is a medicine that reminds us that our sickness will one day be healed and we shall be whole and holy. Until then, laughter is the Elmer's Glue that attaches us to the goodness that inhabits this world, and to the gladness that hints at the world to come.

—*Carolyn Arends*

For more on celebration, see reading at Ecclesiastes 11:7–12:2.

126 *A song for pilgrims ascending to Jerusalem.*

1 When the LORD brought back his exiles
　　to Jerusalem,*
　　it was like a dream!
2 We were filled with laughter,
　　and we sang for joy.
　And the other nations said,
　　"What amazing things the LORD has
　　　done for them."
3 Yes, the LORD has done amazing things
　　for us!
　　What joy!

4 Restore our fortunes, LORD,
　　as streams renew the desert.
5 Those who plant in tears
　　will harvest with shouts of joy.
6 They weep as they go to plant their
　　seed,
　　but they sing as they return with the
　　harvest.

127 *A song for pilgrims ascending to Jerusalem. A psalm of Solomon.*

1 Unless the LORD builds a house,
　　the work of the builders is wasted.

126:1 Hebrew *Zion.*

Addicted to Productivity

PSALM 127:1-2

The image of a dark, overcrowded closet comes to me periodically as a picture of my life. All manner of things are jammed in haphazardly, and everything is apt to topple perilously into a heap when the door is opened.

I am a productive, organized, and fast-moving person; I accomplish a lot in a short time. This is one of my strengths—and almost surely my greatest weakness. It's a weakness because I so quickly turn my capacity for productivity into an idol. My completed to-do list feels so gratifying that it's easy to find my worth in what I get done instead of in God.

This addiction to busyness makes us feel important. Psalm 127:1-2 warns against this mind-set: "Unless the LORD builds a house, the work of the builders is wasted. . . . It is useless for you to work so hard from early morning until late at night, anxiously working for food to eat; for God gives rest to his loved ones." In other words, we're kidding ourselves when we think we're building our lives and holding it all together. God is ultimately our Provider, and we'd do well to live within a mind-set that's dependent upon him rather than foolishly dependent on ourselves.

Instead of wedging more and more into our time, with our lives becoming like the crowded closet, we can rest well knowing that God wants to rescue us from this overwhelming and claustrophobic way of being. He wants to bring us out into a bright, open, spacious place and to simply experience his delight in us (Psalm 18:19).

We come to this beautiful place of rest not merely by trimming our schedules, but also by realigning our hearts. Should we still work hard? Certainly. But we work with a mind-set of humility that gives God the credit. We refuse to idolize our productivity. And we invite God to lead us in how we spend our time, conscientiously choosing to do what God directs, not more, not less.

—Susan Arico

For more on Sabbath and rest, see reading at Proverbs 31:10-31.

Unless the LORD protects a city,
    guarding it with sentries will do no
        good.
2 It is useless for you to work so hard
    from early morning until late at
        night,
anxiously working for food to eat;
    for God gives rest to his loved ones.

3 Children are a gift from the LORD;
    they are a reward from him.
4 Children born to a young man
    are like arrows in a warrior's hands.
5 How joyful is the man whose quiver is
    full of them!

He will not be put to shame when he
    confronts his accusers at the city
        gates.

128 *A song for pilgrims ascending to Jerusalem.*

1 How joyful are those who fear the
    LORD—
    all who follow his ways!
2 You will enjoy the fruit of your labor.
    How joyful and prosperous you will be!
3 Your wife will be like a fruitful
        grapevine,
    flourishing within your home.

Your children will be like vigorous young
olive trees
as they sit around your table.
⁴ That is the LORD's blessing
for those who fear him.

⁵ May the LORD continually bless you
from Zion.
May you see Jerusalem prosper as long
as you live.
⁶ May you live to enjoy your
grandchildren.
May Israel have peace!

129
*A song for pilgrims ascending to
Jerusalem.*

¹ From my earliest youth my enemies have
persecuted me.
Let all Israel repeat this:
² From my earliest youth my enemies have
persecuted me,
but they have never defeated me.
³ My back is covered with cuts,
as if a farmer had plowed long
furrows.
⁴ But the LORD is good;
he has cut me free from the ropes of
the ungodly.

⁵ May all who hate Jerusalem*
be turned back in shameful defeat.
⁶ May they be as useless as grass on a
rooftop,
turning yellow when only half grown,
⁷ ignored by the harvester,
despised by the binder.
⁸ And may those who pass by
refuse to give them this blessing:
"The LORD bless you;
we bless you in the LORD's name."

130
*A song for pilgrims ascending to
Jerusalem.*

¹ From the depths of despair, O LORD,
I call for your help.
² Hear my cry, O Lord.
Pay attention to my prayer.

³ LORD, if you kept a record of our sins,
who, O Lord, could ever survive?
⁴ But you offer forgiveness,
that we might learn to fear you.

⁵ I am counting on the LORD;
yes, I am counting on him.
I have put my hope in his word.
⁶ I long for the Lord
more than sentries long for the dawn,
yes, more than sentries long for the
dawn.

⁷ O Israel, hope in the LORD;
for with the LORD there is unfailing
love.
His redemption overflows.
⁸ He himself will redeem Israel
from every kind of sin.

131
*A song for pilgrims ascending to
Jerusalem. A psalm of David.*

¹ LORD, my heart is not proud;
my eyes are not haughty.
I don't concern myself with matters too
great
or too awesome for me to grasp.
² Instead, I have calmed and quieted myself,
like a weaned child who no longer
cries for its mother's milk.
Yes, like a weaned child is my soul
within me.

³ O Israel, put your hope in the LORD—
now and always.

132
*A song for pilgrims ascending to
Jerusalem.*

¹ LORD, remember David
and all that he suffered.
² He made a solemn promise to the LORD.
He vowed to the Mighty One of Israel,*
³ "I will not go home;
I will not let myself rest.
⁴ I will not let my eyes sleep
nor close my eyelids in slumber
⁵ until I find a place to build a house for
the LORD,
a sanctuary for the Mighty One of
Israel."

⁶ We heard that the Ark was in Ephrathah;
then we found it in the distant
countryside of Jaar.
⁷ Let us go to the sanctuary of the LORD;
let us worship at the footstool of his
throne.

129:5 Hebrew *Zion.*   **132:2** Hebrew *of Jacob;* also in 132:5. See note on 44:4.

Silence as Prayer

PSALM 131

It seems natural to connect prayer and words. Prayer is often supplication, a heart begging for comfort. Prayer is often praise, lifted up to God. In using words, we have a clear sense of what we want to accomplish.

But silence before God is also a form of prayer.

Christian Taizé communities stop three times a day to bring all believers into prayer. Any Bible study, chatter, or work stops as the bell tolls, beckoning everyone into the church for long periods of silence interspersed with Scripture reading. They take the oldest prayer book, Psalms, as their guide, and find three main forms of prayer. One cries out for help, another brings praise and thanksgiving to God, but the third kind of prayer Taizé communities seek to cultivate does neither. It is the prayer of silence. The prayer of a calmed and quieted soul (Psalm 131:2).

—*Catherine Bowler*

For more on silence, see reading at Proverbs 10:19–21.

8 Arise, O LORD, and enter your resting
place,
along with the Ark, the symbol of your
power.
9 May your priests be clothed in
godliness;
may your loyal servants sing for joy.
10 For the sake of your servant David,
do not reject the king you have
anointed.
11 The LORD swore an oath to David
with a promise he will never take
back:
"I will place one of your descendants
on your throne.
12 If your descendants obey the terms of
my covenant
and the laws that I teach them,
then your royal line
will continue forever and ever."
13 For the LORD has chosen
Jerusalem*;
he has desired it for his home.
14 "This is my resting place forever," he
said.
"I will live here, for this is the home I
desired.

15 I will bless this city and make it
prosperous;
I will satisfy its poor with food.
16 I will clothe its priests with godliness;
its faithful servants will sing for joy.
17 Here I will increase the power of David;
my anointed one will be a light for my
people.
18 I will clothe his enemies with shame,
but he will be a glorious king."

133 A song for pilgrims ascending to Jerusalem. A psalm of David.

1 How wonderful and pleasant it is
when brothers live together in
harmony!
2 For harmony is as precious as the
anointing oil
that was poured over Aaron's head,
that ran down his beard
and onto the border of his robe.
3 Harmony is as refreshing as the dew
from Mount Hermon
that falls on the mountains of Zion.
And there the LORD has pronounced his
blessing,
even life everlasting.

132:13 Hebrew Zion.

Community

Living in Harmony
PSALM 133

Without fail, I hear the word *harmony* and my mind goes right back to me at nine years old: I'm standing in front of our TV, watching Paul McCartney and Stevie Wonder bumbling along in the back of a wagon, lip-synching their hit song, "Ebony and Ivory."

In the song Paul and Stevie lament that ebony and ivory can "live together in perfect harmony" on a piano keyboard, but ask, "Oh, Lord, why can't we?"

It's a fair enough question—with a pretty easy answer. Consider that keyboard: the black and white keys don't necessarily live in perfect harmony. Yes, the F-sharp and G will sit there nicely, causing no trouble—until they're agitated. Play them at the same time and it's not harmony you'll hear. Instead you'll hear a creepy, dissonant-sounding clank.

It's the same with us. We can get along fine until one of us opens her mouth, expresses an idea, or reveals a background, bias, or point of view that differs from our own. Suddenly that person is a little too close, a little too different, and things get clanky.

And yet, as Christians, the call is clear: "Live in harmony with each other," Romans 12:16 says.

It's a lovely and difficult proposition, in music and in life. "How wonderful and pleasant it is," David wrote, "when brothers live together in harmony!" (Psalm 133:1). To truly live in harmony means our differences must play together nicely. In music this means notes need intervals—space in between them. In life this means we give one another space too. Space to be who we are. Space to live as God created us. Space to see and value—not clank and bicker about—the God-given and God-reflecting differences in one another. But this space isn't about distance or separation. This harmony-creating space is otherwise known as grace.

—*Caryn Rivadeneira*

For more on community, see reading at Ecclesiastes 4:9–12.

134

A song for pilgrims ascending to Jerusalem.

¹ Oh, praise the LORD, all you servants of the LORD,
you who serve at night in the house of the LORD.
² Lift up holy hands in prayer,
and praise the LORD.

³ May the LORD, who made heaven and earth,
bless you from Jerusalem.*

135

¹ Praise the LORD!

Praise the name of the LORD!
Praise him, you who serve the LORD,
² you who serve in the house of the LORD,
in the courts of the house of our God.

³ Praise the LORD, for the LORD is good;
celebrate his lovely name with music.
⁴ For the LORD has chosen Jacob for himself,
Israel for his own special treasure.

134:3 Hebrew *Zion.*

⁵ I know the greatness of the Lord—
    that our Lord is greater than any other
        god.
⁶ The Lord does whatever pleases him
    throughout all heaven and earth,
    and on the seas and in their depths.
⁷ He causes the clouds to rise over the
        whole earth.
    He sends the lightning with the rain
    and releases the wind from his
        storehouses.

⁸ He destroyed the firstborn in each
        Egyptian home,
    both people and animals.
⁹ He performed miraculous signs and
        wonders in Egypt
    against Pharaoh and all his people.
¹⁰ He struck down great nations
    and slaughtered mighty kings—
¹¹ Sihon king of the Amorites,
    Og king of Bashan,
    and all the kings of Canaan.
¹² He gave their land as an inheritance,
    a special possession to his people Israel.

¹³ Your name, O Lord, endures forever;
    your fame, O Lord, is known to every
        generation.
¹⁴ For the Lord will give justice to his
        people
    and have compassion on his servants.

¹⁵ The idols of the nations are merely
        things of silver and gold,
    shaped by human hands.
¹⁶ They have mouths but cannot speak,
    and eyes but cannot see.
¹⁷ They have ears but cannot hear,
    and noses but cannot smell.
¹⁸ And those who make idols are just like
        them,
    as are all who trust in them.

¹⁹ O Israel, praise the Lord!
    O priests—descendants of Aaron—
        praise the Lord!
²⁰ O Levites, praise the Lord!
    All you who fear the Lord, praise the
        Lord!
²¹ The Lord be praised from Zion,
    for he lives here in Jerusalem.

Praise the Lord!

136

¹ Give thanks to the Lord, for he
    is good!
    His faithful love endures forever.
² Give thanks to the God of gods.
    His faithful love endures forever.
³ Give thanks to the Lord of lords.
    His faithful love endures forever.

⁴ Give thanks to him who alone does
    mighty miracles.
    His faithful love endures forever.
⁵ Give thanks to him who made the
    heavens so skillfully.
    His faithful love endures forever.
⁶ Give thanks to him who placed the earth
    among the waters.
    His faithful love endures forever.
⁷ Give thanks to him who made the
    heavenly lights—
    His faithful love endures forever.
⁸ the sun to rule the day,
    His faithful love endures forever.
⁹ and the moon and stars to rule the
    night.
    His faithful love endures forever.

¹⁰ Give thanks to him who killed the
    firstborn of Egypt.
    His faithful love endures forever.
¹¹ He brought Israel out of Egypt.
    His faithful love endures forever.
¹² He acted with a strong hand and
    powerful arm.
    His faithful love endures forever.
¹³ Give thanks to him who parted the Red
    Sea.*
    His faithful love endures forever.
¹⁴ He led Israel safely through,
    His faithful love endures forever.
¹⁵ but he hurled Pharaoh and his army into
    the Red Sea.
    His faithful love endures forever.
¹⁶ Give thanks to him who led his people
    through the wilderness.
    His faithful love endures forever.
¹⁷ Give thanks to him who struck down
    mighty kings.
    His faithful love endures forever.
¹⁸ He killed powerful kings—
    His faithful love endures forever.
¹⁹ Sihon king of the Amorites,
    His faithful love endures forever.

136:13 Hebrew *sea of reeds;* also in 136:15.

Gratitude Driven by Love

PSALM 136

Psalm 136 offers a healthy perspective on gratitude. It's a psalm written after Israel's return from exile in Babylon some four hundred years after King David lived. It was written for the worship service in the rebuilt Jewish temple. Today the psalm is used by Jewish people as they celebrate Passover. Each line is followed by the same refrain: "His faithful love endures forever." Select singers sing the first line, and the congregation sings the refrain.

Our lives overflow with gratitude when we're convinced God loves us. The Hebrew verb for *give thanks* conveys the idea of verbally acknowledging something; this thankfulness is more than just an attitude. The refrain, "His faithful love endures forever," forms the basis for this command to thank God. The Hebrew word for *love* here is *hesed*, often translated as *steadfast love*, or covenant love. God's steadfast love is forever; it's not temporary or conditional.

The person convinced of the loyal love of God has a heart that naturally overflows with gratitude. A saying goes, "Gratitude can turn an ordinary meal into a feast, a house into a home, and a stranger into a friend." A life of gratitude is a life well lived.

—Timothy Peck, with JoHannah Reardon

For more on gratitude, see reading at Ezekiel 11:18-20.

²⁰ and Og king of Bashan.
His faithful love endures forever.
²¹ God gave the land of these kings as an inheritance—
His faithful love endures forever.
²² a special possession to his servant Israel.
His faithful love endures forever.

²³ He remembered us in our weakness.
His faithful love endures forever.
²⁴ He saved us from our enemies.
His faithful love endures forever.
²⁵ He gives food to every living thing.
His faithful love endures forever.
²⁶ Give thanks to the God of heaven.
His faithful love endures forever.

137 ¹ Beside the rivers of Babylon, we sat and wept
as we thought of Jerusalem.*
² We put away our harps,
hanging them on the branches of poplar trees.

³ For our captors demanded a song from us.
Our tormentors insisted on a joyful hymn:
"Sing us one of those songs of Jerusalem!"
⁴ But how can we sing the songs of the LORD
while in a pagan land?

⁵ If I forget you, O Jerusalem,
let my right hand forget how to play the harp.
⁶ May my tongue stick to the roof of my mouth
if I fail to remember you,
if I don't make Jerusalem my greatest joy.

⁷ O LORD, remember what the Edomites did
on the day the armies of Babylon captured Jerusalem.
"Destroy it!" they yelled.

137:1 Hebrew *Zion;* also in 137:3.

"Level it to the ground!"
⁸ O Babylon, you will be destroyed.
    Happy is the one who pays you back
    for what you have done to us.
⁹ Happy is the one who takes your babies
    and smashes them against the rocks!

138 *A psalm of David.*

¹ I give you thanks, O LORD, with all my
    heart;
    I will sing your praises before the gods.
² I bow before your holy Temple as I
    worship.
    I praise your name for your unfailing
    love and faithfulness;
    for your promises are backed
    by all the honor of your name.
³ As soon as I pray, you answer me;
    you encourage me by giving me
    strength.

⁴ Every king in all the earth will thank you,
    LORD,
    for all of them will hear your words.
⁵ Yes, they will sing about the LORD's
    ways,
    for the glory of the LORD is very great.
⁶ Though the LORD is great, he cares for
    the humble,
    but he keeps his distance from the
    proud.

⁷ Though I am surrounded by troubles,
    you will protect me from the anger of
    my enemies.
    You reach out your hand,
    and the power of your right hand
    saves me.
⁸ The LORD will work out his plans for my
    life—
    for your faithful love, O LORD,
    endures forever.
    Don't abandon me, for you made me.

139 *For the choir director: A psalm of David.*

¹ O LORD, you have examined my heart
    and know everything about me.
² You know when I sit down or stand up.
    You know my thoughts even when I'm
    far away.

³ You see me when I travel
    and when I rest at home.
    You know everything I do.
⁴ You know what I am going to say
    even before I say it, LORD.
⁵ You go before me and follow me.
    You place your hand of blessing on my
    head.
⁶ Such knowledge is too wonderful for me,
    too great for me to understand!

⁷ I can never escape from your Spirit!
    I can never get away from your
    presence!
⁸ If I go up to heaven, you are there;
    if I go down to the grave,* you are
    there.
⁹ If I ride the wings of the morning,
    if I dwell by the farthest oceans,
¹⁰ even there your hand will guide me,
    and your strength will support me.
¹¹ I could ask the darkness to hide me
    and the light around me to become
    night—
¹² but even in darkness I cannot hide
    from you.
    To you the night shines as bright as day.
    Darkness and light are the same to
    you.

¹³ You made all the delicate, inner parts of
    my body
    and knit me together in my mother's
    womb.
¹⁴ Thank you for making me so
    wonderfully complex!
    Your workmanship is marvelous—
    how well I know it.
¹⁵ You watched me as I was being formed
    in utter seclusion,
    as I was woven together in the dark of
    the womb.
¹⁶ You saw me before I was born.
    Every day of my life was recorded in
    your book.
    Every moment was laid out
    before a single day had passed.

¹⁷ How precious are your thoughts about
    me,* O God.
    They cannot be numbered!
¹⁸ I can't even count them;
    they outnumber the grains of sand!

139:8 Hebrew *to Sheol.*   **139:17** Or *How precious to me are your thoughts.*

Confession

Examen
PSALM 139

"Thank you, God, for Christopher," I begin, as I always do.

"Hmm," two-year-old Christopher sighs in agreement.

"Thanks for your peace. I felt it in my office today while I worked."

"Mmm." Christopher's eyelids flutter and then close. His breathing quiets.

"Help me to be patient with Jeff's job transition. I know that you know what we need. Help me let go of my frustration. Help me release Jeff into your care. He belongs to you. I'm so grateful for that."

And just like that, crumpled bed sheets become an altar, and Christopher and I are doing *examen* together. The simplicity of this way of praying pulls me in. The wonder of the prayer lies in that moment I realize that God is present, and his Spirit waits to guide me in remembering the day with all its good and bad, and to receive my confessions and my thanks.

Ignatius of Loyola developed the examen or "examination of conscience" in the *Spiritual Exercises* he wrote in 1522–1524. In examen we "go over [the day] hour by hour, or period by period, commencing at the hour [we rise], and continuing up to the [present] hour," honestly evaluating how well we have honored Christ in thoughts, words, and actions. Ignatius taught that our prayer of self-examination should begin with gratitude and praise, continue in dependence upon God's grace, include recognition and confession of sin, and conclude with a declaration of our reliance upon God to do what's right. Examen is one way we can pray like David: "Search me, O God, and know my heart; test me and know my anxious thoughts. Point out anything in me that offends you" (Psalm 139:23–24).

Recognizing and confessing sin can lead us into joy and peace; celebrating God's constant presence can usher us into gratitude. Practicing examen is a way to take sin seriously, as well as an avenue to see and celebrate God's faithful presence during each moment. As we pay attention to our lives with God in prayer, we experience the peace and joy of David as he wrote, "O LORD, you have examined my heart and know everything about me" (Psalm 139:1).

—Renee James and Kelli B. Trujillo

For more on confession, see reading at Isaiah 64:9.

And when I wake up,
    you are still with me!

19 O God, if only you would destroy the
        wicked!
    Get out of my life, you
        murderers!
20 They blaspheme you;
    your enemies misuse your name.
21 O LORD, shouldn't I hate those who hate
        you?

Shouldn't I despise those who oppose
    you?

22 Yes, I hate them with total hatred,
    for your enemies are my enemies.

23 Search me, O God, and know my heart;
    test me and know my anxious thoughts.
24 Point out anything in me that offends
        you,
    and lead me along the path of
        everlasting life.

Service

What You Were Created For

PSALM 139:13–16

My grandson loves video games. If given the opportunity, he will stay up all night and forget to eat, hoping to get to the next level. After all, who isn't perpetually optimistic when it comes to careening a motorcycle between cars on an iPhone or facing down Bowser in the final castle of a Mario game? We work hard to put forth our best effort. We pick ourselves up and start again when we fail, and when we achieve, we are jubilant and energized.

In her book, *Reality Is Broken*, Jane McGonigal contends that thousands are being drawn to the world of video games by the intoxicating experience of achieving victory against all odds. Bored with real life, they join forces online to triumph over imaginary enemies. They work for hours alongside comrades and allies, not for money, but for the joy of solving problems, grasping new concepts, and saving the virtual world from those who seek to destroy it.

Perhaps we could learn from the gaming world when it comes to the way we think of and approach service. We call people to faith in Christ and then ask them to sit docilely through church "services." We recruit them to usher or work in the nursery, but are we really challenging people to use their unique abilities in service? Are we urging them to take up the cross to follow Jesus down the path of self-sacrifice?

Frankly, I think many Christians are flat-out bored.

Yet when we were woven together in our mothers' wombs (Psalm 139:13), God prepared good works, in advance, for us to do (Ephesians 2:10). We were created to serve. It is our reason for being. Just as you were specially designed with a DNA that would result in the color of your skin, eyes, and hair, God has given you a job to do. Your service in the world is a natural outflow of the Creator's good work within you.

In *Wishful Thinking* Frederick Buechner says, "The place God calls you to is the place where your deep gladness and the world's deep hunger meet." Your place of service should be a place of gladness. There is no greater thrill than to work hard in places of the world's deep hunger—to give of ourselves in a cause that is bigger than ourselves with an effort that stretches us and brings out our best.

I've seen churches come alive when they finally get outside their walls and participate in acts of service. I saw parishioners at a church in Florida join forces to build a mission house for Habitat for Missionaries. They worked hard and then fasted and prayed that the house would sell. The epic pleasure on their faces when the pastor announced the house had sold in the first five minutes was palpable and would rival the face of any virtual game victor!

My daughter, who has been in the church for twenty-seven years, claims that her most profound church experience was when she sang and danced in praise with women at a homeless shelter. It was in that place, where battered women praised God in the midst of their pain, that she experienced the presence of God most powerfully.

Recently my friend Adam left his lucrative job on the commodities trading floor to build affordable housing in a metropolitan city. He becomes animated with passion as he talks about the history of housing discrimination in America. His wife told him, "Your heart has been broken for the people living in poverty in Chicago. You think about it all the time, you dream about it, how to fight it, how to solve it." Adam has caught the service bug and will never be the same.

Michael Chitwood, who organizes marathon runners for World Vision throughout the US and in Africa, told me, "I was afraid God was going to call me to a way of life that I couldn't live up to. If I obeyed I would be miserable. If I didn't obey I would be miserable. What I didn't understand was that God would indeed break my heart, but I would never want to go back to the way things were."

So what is it for you? What do *you* care about? What breaks *your* heart? What makes your blood boil? What would you stay up all night to do? Your deep gladness will erupt when you choose to obey, to go to the broken places of the world to do the good works created in advance for you to do.

—*Arloa Sutter*

For more on service, see reading at Proverbs 29:23.

140

For the choir director: A psalm of David.

¹ O LORD, rescue me from evil people.
    Protect me from those who are violent,
² those who plot evil in their hearts
    and stir up trouble all day long.
³ Their tongues sting like a snake;
    the venom of a viper drips from their
        lips.   *Interlude*

⁴ O LORD, keep me out of the hands of the
        wicked.
    Protect me from those who are
        violent,
    for they are plotting against me.
⁵ The proud have set a trap to catch me;
    they have stretched out a net;
    they have placed traps all along the
        way.   *Interlude*

⁶ I said to the LORD, "You are my God!"
    Listen, O LORD, to my cries for mercy!
⁷ O Sovereign LORD, the strong one who
        rescued me,
    you protected me on the day of battle.
⁸ LORD, do not let evil people have their
        way.
    Do not let their evil schemes succeed,
    or they will become proud.   *Interlude*

⁹ Let my enemies be destroyed
    by the very evil they have planned
        for me.
¹⁰ Let burning coals fall down on their heads.
    Let them be thrown into the fire
    or into watery pits from which they
        can't escape.
¹¹ Don't let liars prosper here in our land.
    Cause great disasters to fall on the
        violent.

¹² But I know the LORD will help those
        they persecute;
    he will give justice to the poor.
¹³ Surely righteous people are praising
        your name;
    the godly will live in your presence.

141

A psalm of David.

¹ O LORD, I am calling to you. Please
        hurry!
    Listen when I cry to you for help!

² Accept my prayer as incense offered to
        you,
    and my upraised hands as an evening
        offering.
³ Take control of what I say, O LORD,
    and guard my lips.
⁴ Don't let me drift toward evil
    or take part in acts of wickedness.
    Don't let me share in the delicacies
    of those who do wrong.

⁵ Let the godly strike me!
    It will be a kindness!
    If they correct me, it is soothing
        medicine.
    Don't let me refuse it.

    But I pray constantly
    against the wicked and their deeds.
⁶ When their leaders are thrown down
        from a cliff,
    the wicked will listen to my words and
        find them true.
⁷ Like rocks brought up by a plow,
    the bones of the wicked will lie
        scattered without burial.*

⁸ I look to you for help, O Sovereign
        LORD.
    You are my refuge; don't let them
        kill me.
⁹ Keep me from the traps they have set
        for me,
    from the snares of those who do
        wrong.
¹⁰ Let the wicked fall into their own nets,
    but let me escape.

142

A psalm* of David, regarding his experience in the cave. A prayer.

¹ I cry out to the LORD;
    I plead for the LORD's mercy.
² I pour out my complaints before him
    and tell him all my troubles.
³ When I am overwhelmed,
    you alone know the way I should turn.
    Wherever I go,
    my enemies have set traps for me.
⁴ I look for someone to come and help me,
    but no one gives me a passing thought!
    No one will help me;
    no one cares a bit what happens to me.

141:7 Hebrew *scattered at the mouth of Sheol.*   **142:TITLE** Hebrew *maskil.* This may be a literary or musical term.

⁵ Then I pray to you, O LORD.
  I say, "You are my place of refuge.
  You are all I really want in life.
⁶ Hear my cry,
  for I am very low.
Rescue me from my persecutors,
  for they are too strong for me.
⁷ Bring me out of prison
  so I can thank you.
The godly will crowd around me,
  for you are good to me."

143 A psalm of David.

¹ Hear my prayer, O LORD;
  listen to my plea!
  Answer me because you are faithful
    and righteous.
² Don't put your servant on trial,
  for no one is innocent before you.
³ My enemy has chased me.
  He has knocked me to the ground
  and forces me to live in darkness like
    those in the grave.
⁴ I am losing all hope;
  I am paralyzed with fear.
⁵ I remember the days of old.
  I ponder all your great works
  and think about what you have done.
⁶ I lift my hands to you in prayer.
  I thirst for you as parched land thirsts
    for rain.   *Interlude*

⁷ Come quickly, LORD, and answer me,
  for my depression deepens.
Don't turn away from me,
  or I will die.
⁸ Let me hear of your unfailing love each
    morning,
  for I am trusting you.
Show me where to walk,
  for I give myself to you.
⁹ Rescue me from my enemies, LORD;
  I run to you to hide me.
¹⁰ Teach me to do your will,
  for you are my God.
May your gracious Spirit lead me forward
  on a firm footing.
¹¹ For the glory of your name, O LORD,
  preserve my life.
  Because of your faithfulness, bring me
    out of this distress.

¹² In your unfailing love, silence all my
    enemies
  and destroy all my foes,
  for I am your servant.

144 A psalm of David.

¹ Praise the LORD, who is my rock.
  He trains my hands for war
  and gives my fingers skill for battle.
² He is my loving ally and my fortress,
  my tower of safety, my rescuer.
He is my shield, and I take refuge in him.
  He makes the nations* submit to me.

³ O LORD, what are human beings that
    you should notice them,
  mere mortals that you should think
    about them?
⁴ For they are like a breath of air;
  their days are like a passing shadow.

⁵ Open the heavens, LORD, and come down.
  Touch the mountains so they billow
    smoke.
⁶ Hurl your lightning bolts and scatter
    your enemies!
  Shoot your arrows and confuse them!
⁷ Reach down from heaven and rescue me;
  rescue me from deep waters,
  from the power of my enemies.
⁸ Their mouths are full of lies;
  they swear to tell the truth, but they
    lie instead.

⁹ I will sing a new song to you, O God!
  I will sing your praises with a ten-
    stringed harp.
¹⁰ For you grant victory to kings!
  You rescued your servant David from
    the fatal sword.
¹¹ Save me!
  Rescue me from the power of my
    enemies.
Their mouths are full of lies;
  they swear to tell the truth, but they
    lie instead.

¹² May our sons flourish in their youth
  like well-nurtured plants.
May our daughters be like graceful
    pillars,
  carved to beautify a palace.

144:2 Some manuscripts read *my people.*

¹³ May our barns be filled
with crops of every kind.
May the flocks in our fields multiply by
the thousands,
even tens of thousands,
¹⁴ and may our oxen be loaded down
with produce.
May there be no enemy breaking
through our walls,
no going into captivity,
no cries of alarm in our town squares.
¹⁵ Yes, joyful are those who live like this!
Joyful indeed are those whose God is
the LORD.

145* A psalm of praise of David.

¹ I will exalt you, my God and King,
and praise your name forever and ever.
² I will praise you every day;
yes, I will praise you forever.
³ Great is the LORD! He is most worthy of
praise!
No one can measure his greatness.

⁴ Let each generation tell its children of
your mighty acts;
let them proclaim your power.
⁵ I will meditate* on your majestic,
glorious splendor
and your wonderful miracles.
⁶ Your awe-inspiring deeds will be on
every tongue;
I will proclaim your greatness.
⁷ Everyone will share the story of your
wonderful goodness;
they will sing with joy about your
righteousness.

⁸ The LORD is merciful and
compassionate,
slow to get angry and filled with
unfailing love.
⁹ The LORD is good to everyone.
He showers compassion on all his
creation.
¹⁰ All of your works will thank you, LORD,
and your faithful followers will praise
you.
¹¹ They will speak of the glory of your
kingdom;

they will give examples of your power.
¹² They will tell about your mighty deeds
and about the majesty and glory of
your reign.
¹³ For your kingdom is an everlasting
kingdom.
You rule throughout all generations.

The LORD always keeps his promises;
he is gracious in all he does.*
¹⁴ The LORD helps the fallen
and lifts those bent beneath their
loads.
¹⁵ The eyes of all look to you in hope;
you give them their food as they
need it.
¹⁶ When you open your hand,
you satisfy the hunger and thirst of
every living thing.
¹⁷ The LORD is righteous in everything he
does;
he is filled with kindness.
¹⁸ The LORD is close to all who call on him,
yes, to all who call on him in truth.
¹⁹ He grants the desires of those who fear
him;
he hears their cries for help and
rescues them.
²⁰ The LORD protects all those who love him,
but he destroys the wicked.

²¹ I will praise the LORD,
and may everyone on earth bless his
holy name
forever and ever.

146 ¹ Praise the LORD!

Let all that I am praise the LORD.
² I will praise the LORD as long as I live.
I will sing praises to my God with my
dying breath.

³ Don't put your confidence in powerful
people;
there is no help for you there.
⁴ When they breathe their last, they
return to the earth,
and all their plans die with them.
⁵ But joyful are those who have the God of
Israel* as their helper,
whose hope is in the LORD their God.

---

145 This psalm is a Hebrew acrostic poem; each verse (including 13b) begins with a successive letter of the Hebrew alphabet.   **145:5** Some manuscripts read *They will speak.*   **145:13** The last two lines of 145:13 are not found in many of the ancient manuscripts.   **146:5** Hebrew *of Jacob.* See note on 44:4.

6 He made heaven and earth,
   the sea, and everything in them.
   He keeps every promise forever.
7 He gives justice to the oppressed
   and food to the hungry.
   The LORD frees the prisoners.
8   The LORD opens the eyes of the blind.
   The LORD lifts up those who are
      weighed down.
   The LORD loves the godly.
9 The LORD protects the foreigners
      among us.
   He cares for the orphans and
      widows,
   but he frustrates the plans of the
      wicked.
10 The LORD will reign forever.
   He will be your God, O Jerusalem,*
      throughout the generations.

   Praise the LORD!

147 ¹ Praise the LORD!

   How good to sing praises to our God!
   How delightful and how fitting!
2 The LORD is rebuilding Jerusalem
   and bringing the exiles back to Israel.
3 He heals the brokenhearted
   and bandages their wounds.
4 He counts the stars
   and calls them all by name.
5 How great is our Lord! His power is
      absolute!
   His understanding is beyond
      comprehension!
6 The LORD supports the humble,
   but he brings the wicked down into
      the dust.

7 Sing out your thanks to the LORD;
   sing praises to our God with a harp.
8 He covers the heavens with clouds,
   provides rain for the earth,
   and makes the grass grow in mountain
      pastures.
9 He gives food to the wild animals
   and feeds the young ravens when they
      cry.
10 He takes no pleasure in the strength of a
      horse
   or in human might.

11 No, the LORD's delight is in those who
      fear him,
   those who put their hope in his
      unfailing love.

12 Glorify the LORD, O Jerusalem!
   Praise your God, O Zion!
13 For he has strengthened the bars of your
      gates
   and blessed your children within your
      walls.
14 He sends peace across your nation
   and satisfies your hunger with the
      finest wheat.
15 He sends his orders to the world—
   how swiftly his word flies!
16 He sends the snow like white wool;
   he scatters frost upon the ground like
      ashes.
17 He hurls the hail like stones.*
   Who can stand against his freezing
      cold?
18 Then, at his command, it all melts.
   He sends his winds, and the ice
      thaws.
19 He has revealed his words to Jacob,
   his decrees and regulations to Israel.
20 He has not done this for any other
      nation;
   they do not know his regulations.

   Praise the LORD!

148 ¹ Praise the LORD!

   Praise the LORD from the heavens!
   Praise him from the skies!
2 Praise him, all his angels!
   Praise him, all the armies of heaven!
3 Praise him, sun and moon!
   Praise him, all you twinkling stars!
4 Praise him, skies above!
   Praise him, vapors high above the
      clouds!
5 Let every created thing give praise to the
      LORD,
   for he issued his command, and they
      came into being.
6 He set them in place forever and ever.
   His decree will never be revoked.

7 Praise the LORD from the earth,
   you creatures of the ocean depths,

146:10 Hebrew *Zion*.   **147:17** Hebrew *like bread crumbs*.

Worship

Worship Can Change Us
PSALM 148

I used to feel as though I didn't "get" worship. But when I had a health scare and had to go through an agonizing waiting process for test results, I began to worship. At first I intentionally spent time in worship because I hoped it might persuade God to keep me around longer. But the process changed me.

I turned to Psalms and read them out loud. When I came to praise psalms, I *praised* them out loud. When I came to ones where David's heart was breaking, I wept along with him. And I began to sing and to say what I believed to be true, despite the frightening health situation I faced.

The more I got to know God, the more I saw that his perfect love casts out fear (1 John 4:18). It doesn't mean that everything changes, but it means that I developed a bigger picture of who God is. Through the waiting and worshiping, I realized that no matter what the test results, I was blessed.

Thankfully, the results came back okay. But the process of waiting, and learning to worship, made an impact on my life. Worship is now a significant part of my daily life, because I know it's the only way I can live in this world.

—*Sheila Walsh*

For more on worship, see reading at Psalm 150.

---

⁸ fire and hail, snow and clouds,*
  wind and weather that obey him,
⁹ mountains and all hills,
  fruit trees and all cedars,
¹⁰ wild animals and all livestock,
  small scurrying animals and birds,
¹¹ kings of the earth and all people,
  rulers and judges of the earth,
¹² young men and young women,
  old men and children.

¹³ Let them all praise the name of the LORD.
  For his name is very great;
  his glory towers over the earth and
    heaven!
¹⁴ He has made his people strong,
  honoring his faithful ones—
  the people of Israel who are close to
    him.

Praise the LORD!

149
¹ Praise the LORD!

Sing to the LORD a new song.
  Sing his praises in the assembly of the
    faithful.

² O Israel, rejoice in your Maker.
  O people of Jerusalem,* exult in your
    King.
³ Praise his name with dancing,
  accompanied by tambourine and
    harp.
⁴ For the LORD delights in his people;
  he crowns the humble with victory.
⁵ Let the faithful rejoice that he honors
    them.
  Let them sing for joy as they lie on
    their beds.

⁶ Let the praises of God be in their
    mouths,
  and a sharp sword in their hands—
⁷ to execute vengeance on the nations
  and punishment on the peoples,
⁸ to bind their kings with shackles
  and their leaders with iron chains,
⁹ to execute the judgment written against
    them.

148:8 Or *mist,* or *smoke.*   **149:2** Hebrew *Zion.*

In Awe of God's Creation

PSALM 150

I've been known to run for the moon: straight out across the fields to that flock of geese flying right through that luminous milky pearl. "The heavens proclaim the glory of God" (Psalm 19:1). On a beautiful, moonlit night, how can one *not* desire to run out and worship?

Nature itself draws us into worship. Not worship of the wind in the pines or snow falling on hemlocks or a moon over harvested wheat, but worship of the Creator of beauty himself. God reveals the weight of his glory through the looking glass of nature. This is, in fact, a means of deep *theology*—study of God—as we step outside, look up, breathe deeply, and worship. It's a response to the miraculous daily invitation to see and enjoy the revelation of God's glory right outside the front door.

"Just ask the animals, and they will teach you. Ask the birds of the sky, and they will tell you," remarked Job as he spoke of God's sovereignty over all living things (Job 12:7). And indeed the created world *does* tell us about God—pointing us to him (Romans 1:20) and teaching us how to respond. It's from a laid-low head of wheat or from the wind rustling glory through dried grass that I learn how to worship God alone. Like the trees of the field, I clap my hands (Isaiah 55:12) and join everything that has breath (Psalm 150:6) in worshiping him. We cannot help but praise him and say, "Holy, Holy, Holy. . . . The whole earth is filled with his glory!" (Isaiah 6:3).

This is how to pay tribute to God: pay attention to his glory everywhere. Worship is the life-song of a soul gazing on God, the witnessing of geese-song gliding up into glory.

—Ann Voskamp

For more on worship, see reading at Isaiah 6:1-7.

This is the glorious privilege of his
   faithful ones.

Praise the LORD!

150 ¹ Praise the LORD!

Praise God in his sanctuary;
   praise him in his mighty heaven!
² Praise him for his mighty works;
   praise his unequaled greatness!

³ Praise him with a blast of the ram's horn;
   praise him with the lyre and harp!
⁴ Praise him with the tambourine and
   dancing;
   praise him with strings and flutes!
⁵ Praise him with a clash of cymbals;
   praise him with loud clanging cymbals.
⁶ Let everything that breathes sing praises
   to the LORD!

Praise the LORD!

Introduction to

Proverbs

Background

Proverbs is an excellent example of ancient Wisdom Literature. While Wisdom Literature is a staple of Near Eastern cultures (written examples in Egypt date from 2700 B.C.), the Book of Proverbs is unique in that it attributes wisdom to its source: God.

In Hebrew and Greek, the Book of Proverbs is called Proverbs of Solomon (the first words of chapter 1). The Latin title is Book of Proverbs. The Hebrew word translated as *proverb* often connotes a similitude. The Latin term *pro verba* ("proverb") refers to the reduction of many thoughts into a few memorable words.

Solomon is cited as the book's author or compiler three times: Proverbs 1:1; 10:1; 25:1. (First Kings 4:32 credits Solomon with composing "some 3,000 proverbs.") But others contributed: wise men, possibly drawing or patterning some proverbs from the Wisdom of Amenemope, an ancient document written between 1000 and 600 B.C. (22:17–24:34); Agur, an oracle (30:1–33); and Lemuel, a king and oracle (31:1–9).

Message

The aim of the Book of Proverbs can be found in this passage: The purpose of these proverbs "is to teach people wisdom and discipline, to help them understand the insights of the wise. Their purpose is to teach people to live disciplined and successful lives, to help them do what is right, just, and fair. These proverbs will give insight to the simple, knowledge and discernment to the young" (1:2–4).

Time

Solomon's proverbs were undoubtedly written before he descended into idolatry. Others were assembled by Hezekiah's scribes (25:1), likely during Hezekiah's reign of Judah more than two centuries later (715–686 B.C.).

Outline

Proverbs

1 The Purpose of Proverbs

These are the proverbs of Solomon, David's son, king of Israel.

² Their purpose is to teach people wisdom and discipline,
   to help them understand the insights of the wise.
³ Their purpose is to teach people to live disciplined and successful lives,
   to help them do what is right, just, and fair.
⁴ These proverbs will give insight to the simple,
   knowledge and discernment to the young.

⁵ Let the wise listen to these proverbs and become even wiser.
   Let those with understanding receive guidance
⁶ by exploring the meaning in these proverbs and parables,
   the words of the wise and their riddles.

⁷ Fear of the LORD is the foundation of true knowledge,
   but fools despise wisdom and discipline.

A Father's Exhortation: Acquire Wisdom

⁸ My child,* listen when your father corrects you.
   Don't neglect your mother's instruction.
⁹ What you learn from them will crown you with grace
   and be a chain of honor around your neck.

¹⁰ My child, if sinners entice you,
   turn your back on them!
¹¹ They may say, "Come and join us.
   Let's hide and kill someone!
   Just for fun, let's ambush the innocent!
¹² Let's swallow them alive, like the grave*;
   let's swallow them whole, like those who go down to the pit of death.
¹³ Think of the great things we'll get!
   We'll fill our houses with all the stuff we take.
¹⁴ Come, throw in your lot with us;
   we'll all share the loot."

¹⁵ My child, don't go along with them!
   Stay far away from their paths.
¹⁶ They rush to commit evil deeds.
   They hurry to commit murder.
¹⁷ If a bird sees a trap being set,
   it knows to stay away.
¹⁸ But these people set an ambush for themselves;
   they are trying to get themselves killed.
¹⁹ Such is the fate of all who are greedy for money;
   it robs them of life.

1:8 Hebrew *My son;* also in 1:10, 15.   **1:12** Hebrew *like Sheol.*

Mentoring

Desiring to Change

PROVERBS 1

There's an old joke that asks how many psychiatrists it takes to change a light bulb. The answer: one, if the light bulb wants to be changed.

To effectively mentor someone—or to *be* mentored—requires that the mentoree sincerely seeks to grow and change. This person may not know what specifically needs to change, but she should be someone who hungers to do things God's way, whatever that takes.

Mentors shouldn't be motivated by a desire to personally change the mentoree—but a good mentor should desire to see *God* change the mentoree just as much as the mentor is constantly seeking God's renewing and transforming work in her own life (Ephesians 4:22–32). Henry Blackaby's premise in his book *Experiencing God* is to look for what God is doing and join him. That's especially true in mentoring.

If a person is resistant to God, then nothing a mentor can say or do is going to make any difference in that person's life. But a mentoree who is surrendered to God—or who is seeking to know God more—will benefit greatly from mentoring as God works through the process to transform her life.

—*JoHannah Reardon*

For more on mentoring, see reading at Proverbs 13:20.

Wisdom Shouts in the Streets

20 Wisdom shouts in the streets.
    She cries out in the public square.
21 She calls to the crowds along the main
      street,
    to those gathered in front of the city
      gate:
22 "How long, you simpletons,
    will you insist on being simpleminded?
How long will you mockers relish your
      mocking?
    How long will you fools hate
      knowledge?
23 Come and listen to my counsel.
    I'll share my heart with you
    and make you wise.

24 "I called you so often, but you wouldn't
      come.
    I reached out to you, but you paid no
      attention.
25 You ignored my advice
    and rejected the correction I offered.
26 So I will laugh when you are in trouble!
    I will mock you when disaster
      overtakes you—

27 when calamity overtakes you like a
      storm,
    when disaster engulfs you like a
      cyclone,
    and anguish and distress overwhelm
      you.
28 "When they cry for help, I will not
      answer.
    Though they anxiously search for me,
      they will not find me.
29 For they hated knowledge
    and chose not to fear the LORD.
30 They rejected my advice
    and paid no attention when I
      corrected them.
31 Therefore, they must eat the bitter fruit
      of living their own way,
    choking on their own schemes.
32 For simpletons turn away from me—to
      death.
    Fools are destroyed by their own
      complacency.
33 But all who listen to me will live in
      peace,
    untroubled by fear of harm."

2 The Benefits of Wisdom

[1] My child,* listen to what I say,
and treasure my commands.
[2] Tune your ears to wisdom,
and concentrate on understanding.
[3] Cry out for insight,
and ask for understanding.
[4] Search for them as you would for silver;
seek them like hidden treasures.
[5] Then you will understand what it means
to fear the LORD,
and you will gain knowledge of God.
[6] For the LORD grants wisdom!
From his mouth come knowledge and
understanding.
[7] He grants a treasure of common sense to
the honest.
He is a shield to those who walk with
integrity.
[8] He guards the paths of the just
and protects those who are faithful to
him.
[9] Then you will understand what is right,
just, and fair,
and you will find the right way to go.
[10] For wisdom will enter your heart,
and knowledge will fill you with joy.
[11] Wise choices will watch over you.
Understanding will keep you safe.
[12] Wisdom will save you from evil people,
from those whose words are twisted.
[13] These men turn from the right way
to walk down dark paths.
[14] They take pleasure in doing wrong,
and they enjoy the twisted ways of
evil.
[15] Their actions are crooked,
and their ways are wrong.
[16] Wisdom will save you from the immoral
woman,
from the seductive words of the
promiscuous woman.
[17] She has abandoned her husband
and ignores the covenant she made
before God.
[18] Entering her house leads to death;
it is the road to the grave.*
[19] The man who visits her is doomed.
He will never reach the paths of life.
[20] Follow the steps of good men instead,
and stay on the paths of the righteous.
[21] For only the godly will live in the land,
and those with integrity will remain
in it.
[22] But the wicked will be removed from the
land,
and the treacherous will be uprooted.

3 Trusting in the LORD

[1] My child,* never forget the things I
have taught you.
Store my commands in your heart.
[2] If you do this, you will live many years,
and your life will be satisfying.
[3] Never let loyalty and kindness leave
you!
Tie them around your neck as a
reminder.
Write them deep within your heart.
[4] Then you will find favor with both God
and people,
and you will earn a good reputation.
[5] Trust in the LORD with all your heart;
do not depend on your own
understanding.
[6] Seek his will in all you do,
and he will show you which path to
take.
[7] Don't be impressed with your own
wisdom.
Instead, fear the LORD and turn away
from evil.
[8] Then you will have healing for your body
and strength for your bones.
[9] Honor the LORD with your wealth
and with the best part of everything
you produce.
[10] Then he will fill your barns with grain,
and your vats will overflow with good
wine.
[11] My child, don't reject the LORD's
discipline,
and don't be upset when he corrects
you.
[12] For the LORD corrects those he loves,
just as a father corrects a child in
whom he delights.*

2:1 Hebrew My son. 2:18 Hebrew to the spirits of the dead. 3:1 Hebrew My son; also in 3:11, 21. 3:12 Greek version reads And he punishes those he accepts as his children. Compare Heb 12:6.

¹³ Joyful is the person who finds wisdom,
the one who gains understanding.
¹⁴ For wisdom is more profitable than
silver,
and her wages are better than gold.
¹⁵ Wisdom is more precious than rubies;
nothing you desire can compare with
her.
¹⁶ She offers you long life in her right hand,
and riches and honor in her left.
¹⁷ She will guide you down delightful paths;
all her ways are satisfying.
¹⁸ Wisdom is a tree of life to those who
embrace her;
happy are those who hold her tightly.

¹⁹ By wisdom the LORD founded the earth;
by understanding he created the
heavens.
²⁰ By his knowledge the deep fountains of
the earth burst forth,
and the dew settles beneath the night
sky.

²¹ My child, don't lose sight of common
sense and discernment.
Hang on to them,
²² for they will refresh your soul.
They are like jewels on a necklace.
²³ They keep you safe on your way,
and your feet will not stumble.
²⁴ You can go to bed without fear;
you will lie down and sleep soundly.
²⁵ You need not be afraid of sudden
disaster
or the destruction that comes upon
the wicked,
²⁶ for the LORD is your security.
He will keep your foot from being
caught in a trap.

²⁷ Do not withhold good from those who
deserve it
when it's in your power to help them.
²⁸ If you can help your neighbor now, don't
say,
"Come back tomorrow, and then I'll
help you."

²⁹ Don't plot harm against your neighbor,
for those who live nearby trust you.
³⁰ Don't pick a fight without reason,
when no one has done you harm.

³¹ Don't envy violent people
or copy their ways.
³² Such wicked people are detestable to the
LORD,
but he offers his friendship to the godly.

³³ The LORD curses the house of the
wicked,
but he blesses the home of the upright.

³⁴ The LORD mocks the mockers
but is gracious to the humble.*

³⁵ The wise inherit honor,
but fools are put to shame!

4 A Father's Wise Advice

¹ My children,* listen when your father
corrects you.
Pay attention and learn good
judgment,
² for I am giving you good guidance.
Don't turn away from my instructions.
³ For I, too, was once my father's son,
tenderly loved as my mother's only
child.

⁴ My father taught me,
"Take my words to heart.
Follow my commands, and you will
live.
⁵ Get wisdom; develop good judgment.
Don't forget my words or turn away
from them.
⁶ Don't turn your back on wisdom, for she
will protect you.
Love her, and she will guard you.
⁷ Getting wisdom is the wisest thing you
can do!
And whatever else you do, develop
good judgment.
⁸ If you prize wisdom, she will make you
great.
Embrace her, and she will honor you.
⁹ She will place a lovely wreath on your
head;
she will present you with a beautiful
crown."

¹⁰ My child,* listen to me and do as I say,
and you will have a long, good life.
¹¹ I will teach you wisdom's ways
and lead you in straight paths.

3:34 Greek version reads *The LORD opposes the proud / but favors the humble.* Compare Jas 4:6; 1 Pet 5:5. **4:1** Hebrew *My sons.*
4:10 Hebrew *My son;* also in 4:20.

Hearing God's Whispers

PROVERBS 3:32

Contemplation

When the soul is strong and we operate from a quiet center, God doesn't need a megaphone to get our attention. We can hear his whispers.

Proverbs 3:32 tells us that God is intimate with the upright and takes them into his confidence, offering them friendship. The question isn't whether God is speaking to us. He sends us messages all the time—through creation, his Word, people, and events. Frederick Buechner put it this way in his book *Listening to Your Life*: "There is no chance thing through which God cannot speak—even the walk from the house to the garage that you have walked ten thousand times before, even the moments when you cannot believe there is a God who speaks at all anywhere."

There's one thing I hope I never get over as long as I live: that the awesome Creator of the universe is choosing to speak to me—not just once in a blue moon, but most of the time! Sometimes he wants to encourage and comfort me. Sometimes he needs to convict me about a sin I've committed and to guide me to confess. Sometimes he wants to give me an idea. Sometimes he just wants me to remember I am treasured.

I shudder to think how many messages I've missed. How mindful is your heart to the presence of God? Are you quick to listen? Are you attentive to his promptings? How is your hearing?

—Nancy Beach

For more on contemplation, see reading at Isaiah 30:18-21.

¹² When you walk, you won't be held back;
  when you run, you won't stumble.
¹³ Take hold of my instructions; don't let them go.
  Guard them, for they are the key to life.

¹⁴ Don't do as the wicked do,
  and don't follow the path of evildoers.
¹⁵ Don't even think about it; don't go that way.
  Turn away and keep moving.
¹⁶ For evil people can't sleep until they've done their evil deed for the day.
  They can't rest until they've caused someone to stumble.
¹⁷ They eat the food of wickedness
  and drink the wine of violence!

¹⁸ The way of the righteous is like the first gleam of dawn,
  which shines ever brighter until the full light of day.

¹⁹ But the way of the wicked is like total darkness.
  They have no idea what they are stumbling over.

²⁰ My child, pay attention to what I say.
  Listen carefully to my words.
²¹ Don't lose sight of them.
  Let them penetrate deep into your heart,
²² for they bring life to those who find them,
  and healing to their whole body.

²³ Guard your heart above all else,
  for it determines the course of your life.

²⁴ Avoid all perverse talk;
  stay away from corrupt speech.

²⁵ Look straight ahead,
  and fix your eyes on what lies before you.

26 Mark out a straight path for your feet;
stay on the safe path.
27 Don't get sidetracked;
keep your feet from following evil.

5 Avoid Immoral Women

1 My son, pay attention to my
wisdom;
listen carefully to my wise counsel.
2 Then you will show discernment,
and your lips will express what you've
learned.
3 For the lips of an immoral woman are as
sweet as honey,
and her mouth is smoother than oil.
4 But in the end she is as bitter as poison,
as dangerous as a double-edged
sword.
5 Her feet go down to death;
her steps lead straight to the grave.*
6 For she cares nothing about the path to
life.
She staggers down a crooked trail and
doesn't realize it.

7 So now, my sons, listen to me.
Never stray from what I am about to
say:
8 Stay away from her!
Don't go near the door of her house!
9 If you do, you will lose your honor
and will lose to merciless people all
you have achieved.
10 Strangers will consume your wealth,
and someone else will enjoy the fruit
of your labor.
11 In the end you will groan in anguish
when disease consumes your body.
12 You will say, "How I hated discipline!
If only I had not ignored all the
warnings!
13 Oh, why didn't I listen to my teachers?
Why didn't I pay attention to my
instructors?
14 I have come to the brink of utter ruin,
and now I must face public disgrace."

15 Drink water from your own well—
share your love only with your wife.*
16 Why spill the water of your springs in
the streets,
having sex with just anyone?*

17 You should reserve it for yourselves.
Never share it with strangers.
18 Let your wife be a fountain of blessing
for you.
Rejoice in the wife of your youth.
19 She is a loving deer, a graceful doe.
Let her breasts satisfy you always.
May you always be captivated by her
love.
20 Why be captivated, my son, by an
immoral woman,
or fondle the breasts of a promiscuous
woman?
21 For the LORD sees clearly what a man
does,
examining every path he takes.
22 An evil man is held captive by his own
sins;
they are ropes that catch and hold
him.
23 He will die for lack of self-control;
he will be lost because of his great
foolishness.

6 Lessons for Daily Life

1 My child,* if you have put up security
for a friend's debt
or agreed to guarantee the debt of a
stranger—
2 if you have trapped yourself by your
agreement
and are caught by what you said—
3 follow my advice and save yourself,
for you have placed yourself at your
friend's mercy.
Now swallow your pride;
go and beg to have your name erased.
4 Don't put it off; do it now!
Don't rest until you do.
5 Save yourself like a gazelle escaping from
a hunter,
like a bird fleeing from a net.
6 Take a lesson from the ants, you
lazybones.
Learn from their ways and become
wise!
7 Though they have no prince
or governor or ruler to make them
work,

5:5 Hebrew to Sheol.   5:15 Hebrew Drink water from your own cistern, / flowing water from your own well.   5:16 Hebrew Why spill your springs
in the streets, / your streams in the city squares?   6:1 Hebrew My son.

8 they labor hard all summer,
gathering food for the winter.
9 But you, lazybones, how long will you
sleep?
When will you wake up?
10 A little extra sleep, a little more slumber,
a little folding of the hands to rest—
11 then poverty will pounce on you like a
bandit;
scarcity will attack you like an armed
robber.

12 What are worthless and wicked people
like?
They are constant liars,
13 signaling their deceit with a wink of the
eye,
a nudge of the foot, or the wiggle of
fingers.
14 Their perverted hearts plot evil,
and they constantly stir up trouble.
15 But they will be destroyed suddenly,
broken in an instant beyond all hope
of healing.

16 There are six things the LORD hates—
no, seven things he detests:
17 haughty eyes,
a lying tongue,
hands that kill the innocent,
18 a heart that plots evil,
feet that race to do wrong,
19 a false witness who pours out lies,
a person who sows discord in a family.

20 My son, obey your father's commands,
and don't neglect your mother's
instruction.
21 Keep their words always in your heart.
Tie them around your neck.
22 When you walk, their counsel will lead
you.
When you sleep, they will protect you.
When you wake up, they will advise
you.
23 For their command is a lamp
and their instruction a light;
their corrective discipline
is the way to life.
24 It will keep you from the immoral
woman,
from the smooth tongue of a
promiscuous woman.

25 Don't lust for her beauty.
Don't let her coy glances seduce you.
26 For a prostitute will bring you to poverty,*
but sleeping with another man's wife
will cost you your life.
27 Can a man scoop a flame into his lap
and not have his clothes catch on fire?
28 Can he walk on hot coals
and not blister his feet?
29 So it is with the man who sleeps with
another man's wife.
He who embraces her will not go
unpunished.

30 Excuses might be found for a thief
who steals because he is starving.
31 But if he is caught, he must pay back
seven times what he stole,
even if he has to sell everything in his
house.
32 But the man who commits adultery is an
utter fool,
for he destroys himself.
33 He will be wounded and disgraced.
His shame will never be erased.
34 For the woman's jealous husband will be
furious,
and he will show no mercy when he
takes revenge.
35 He will accept no compensation,
nor be satisfied with a payoff of any
size.

7 Another Warning about Immoral Women

1 Follow my advice, my son;
always treasure my commands.
2 Obey my commands and live!
Guard my instructions as you guard
your own eyes.*
3 Tie them on your fingers as a reminder.
Write them deep within your heart.
4 Love wisdom like a sister;
make insight a beloved member of
your family.
5 Let them protect you from an affair with
an immoral woman,
from listening to the flattery of a
promiscuous woman.

6 While I was at the window of my house,
looking through the curtain,

6:26 Hebrew *to a loaf of bread.* 7:2 Hebrew *as the pupil of your eye.*

⁷ I saw some naive young men,
and one in particular who lacked
common sense.
⁸ He was crossing the street near the
house of an immoral woman,
strolling down the path by her house.
⁹ It was at twilight, in the evening,
as deep darkness fell.
¹⁰ The woman approached him,
seductively dressed and sly of heart.
¹¹ She was the brash, rebellious type,
never content to stay at home.
¹² She is often in the streets and markets,
soliciting at every corner.
¹³ She threw her arms around him and
kissed him,
and with a brazen look she said,
¹⁴ "I've just made my peace offerings
and fulfilled my vows.
¹⁵ You're the one I was looking for!
I came out to find you, and here you
are!
¹⁶ My bed is spread with beautiful
blankets,
with colored sheets of Egyptian linen.
¹⁷ I've perfumed my bed
with myrrh, aloes, and cinnamon.
¹⁸ Come, let's drink our fill of love until
morning.
Let's enjoy each other's caresses,
¹⁹ for my husband is not home.
He's away on a long trip.
²⁰ He has taken a wallet full of money with
him
and won't return until later this
month.*"
²¹ So she seduced him with her pretty
speech
and enticed him with her flattery.
²² He followed her at once,
like an ox going to the slaughter.
He was like a stag caught in a trap,
²³ awaiting the arrow that would pierce
its heart.
He was like a bird flying into a snare,
little knowing it would cost him his
life.
²⁴ So listen to me, my sons,
and pay attention to my words.
²⁵ Don't let your hearts stray away toward
her.

Don't wander down her wayward
path.
²⁶ For she has been the ruin of many;
many men have been her victims.
²⁷ Her house is the road to the grave.*
Her bedroom is the den of death.

8 Wisdom Calls for a Hearing

¹ Listen as Wisdom calls out!
Hear as understanding raises her
voice!
² On the hilltop along the road,
she takes her stand at the crossroads.
³ By the gates at the entrance to the town,
on the road leading in, she cries
aloud,
⁴ "I call to you, to all of you!
I raise my voice to all people.
⁵ You simple people, use good judgment.
You foolish people, show some
understanding.
⁶ Listen to me! For I have important
things to tell you.
Everything I say is right,
⁷ for I speak the truth
and detest every kind of deception.
⁸ My advice is wholesome.
There is nothing devious or crooked
in it.
⁹ My words are plain to anyone with
understanding,
clear to those with knowledge.
¹⁰ Choose my instruction rather than
silver,
and knowledge rather than pure gold.
¹¹ For wisdom is far more valuable than
rubies.
Nothing you desire can compare
with it.
¹² "I, Wisdom, live together with good
judgment.
I know where to discover knowledge
and discernment.
¹³ All who fear the LORD will hate evil.
Therefore, I hate pride and arrogance,
corruption and perverse speech.
¹⁴ Common sense and success belong
to me.
Insight and strength are mine.
¹⁵ Because of me, kings reign,
and rulers make just decrees.

7:20 Hebrew *until the moon is full.*   **7:27** Hebrew *to Sheol.*

¹⁶ Rulers lead with my help,
   and nobles make righteous
      judgments.*
¹⁷ "I love all who love me.
   Those who search will surely find me.
¹⁸ I have riches and honor,
   as well as enduring wealth and justice.
¹⁹ My gifts are better than gold, even the
      purest gold,
   my wages better than sterling silver!
²⁰ I walk in righteousness,
   in paths of justice.
²¹ Those who love me inherit wealth.
   I will fill their treasuries.

²² "The LORD formed me from the
      beginning,
   before he created anything else.
²³ I was appointed in ages past,
   at the very first, before the earth
      began.
²⁴ I was born before the oceans were
      created,
   before the springs bubbled forth their
      waters.
²⁵ Before the mountains were formed,
   before the hills, I was born—
²⁶ before he had made the earth and fields
   and the first handfuls of soil.
²⁷ I was there when he established the
      heavens,
   when he drew the horizon on the
      oceans.
²⁸ I was there when he set the clouds
      above,
   when he established springs deep in
      the earth.
²⁹ I was there when he set the limits of the
      seas,
   so they would not spread beyond their
      boundaries.
   And when he marked off the earth's
      foundations,
³⁰   I was the architect at his side.
   I was his constant delight,
      rejoicing always in his presence.
³¹ And how happy I was with the world he
      created;
   how I rejoiced with the human family!

³² "And so, my children,* listen to me,
   for all who follow my ways are joyful.

³³ Listen to my instruction and be wise.
   Don't ignore it.
³⁴ Joyful are those who listen to me,
   watching for me daily at my gates,
   waiting for me outside my home!
³⁵ For whoever finds me finds life
   and receives favor from the LORD.
³⁶ But those who miss me injure
      themselves.
   All who hate me love death."

9 ¹ Wisdom has built her house;
      she has carved its seven columns.
² She has prepared a great banquet,
   mixed the wines, and set the table.
³ She has sent her servants to invite
      everyone to come.
   She calls out from the heights
      overlooking the city.
⁴ "Come in with me," she urges the
      simple.
   To those who lack good judgment, she
      says,
⁵ "Come, eat my food,
   and drink the wine I have mixed.
⁶ Leave your simple ways behind, and
      begin to live;
   learn to use good judgment."

⁷ Anyone who rebukes a mocker will get
      an insult in return.
   Anyone who corrects the wicked will
      get hurt.
⁸ So don't bother correcting mockers;
   they will only hate you.
   But correct the wise,
      and they will love you.
⁹ Instruct the wise,
   and they will be even wiser.
   Teach the righteous,
      and they will learn even more.

¹⁰ Fear of the LORD is the foundation of
      wisdom.
   Knowledge of the Holy One results in
      good judgment.

¹¹ Wisdom will multiply your days
   and add years to your life.
¹² If you become wise, you will be the one
      to benefit.
   If you scorn wisdom, you will be the
      one to suffer.

8:16 Some Hebrew manuscripts and Greek version read *and nobles are judges over the earth.*   **8:32** Hebrew *my sons.*

Folly Calls for a Hearing

13 The woman named Folly is brash.
  She is ignorant and doesn't know it.
14 She sits in her doorway
  on the heights overlooking the city.
15 She calls out to men going by
  who are minding their own business.
16 "Come in with me," she urges the simple.
  To those who lack good judgment, she says,
17 "Stolen water is refreshing;
  food eaten in secret tastes the best!"
18 But little do they know that the dead are there.
  Her guests are in the depths of the grave.*

10 The Proverbs of Solomon

The proverbs of Solomon:

A wise child* brings joy to a father;
  a foolish child brings grief to a mother.

2 Tainted wealth has no lasting value,
  but right living can save your life.

3 The LORD will not let the godly go hungry,
  but he refuses to satisfy the craving of the wicked.

4 Lazy people are soon poor;
  hard workers get rich.

5 A wise youth harvests in the summer,
  but one who sleeps during harvest is a disgrace.

6 The godly are showered with blessings;
  the words of the wicked conceal violent intentions.

7 We have happy memories of the godly,
  but the name of a wicked person rots away.

8 The wise are glad to be instructed,
  but babbling fools fall flat on their faces.

9 People with integrity walk safely,
  but those who follow crooked paths will slip and fall.

10 People who wink at wrong cause trouble,
  but a bold reproof promotes peace.*

11 The words of the godly are a life-giving fountain;
  the words of the wicked conceal violent intentions.

12 Hatred stirs up quarrels,
  but love makes up for all offenses.

13 Wise words come from the lips of people with understanding,
  but those lacking sense will be beaten with a rod.

14 Wise people treasure knowledge,
  but the babbling of a fool invites disaster.

15 The wealth of the rich is their fortress;
  the poverty of the poor is their destruction.

16 The earnings of the godly enhance their lives,
  but evil people squander their money on sin.

17 People who accept discipline are on the pathway to life,
  but those who ignore correction will go astray.

18 Hiding hatred makes you a liar;
  slandering others makes you a fool.

19 Too much talk leads to sin.
  Be sensible and keep your mouth shut.

20 The words of the godly are like sterling silver;
  the heart of a fool is worthless.

21 The words of the godly encourage many,
  but fools are destroyed by their lack of common sense.

22 The blessing of the LORD makes a person rich,
  and he adds no sorrow with it.

23 Doing wrong is fun for a fool,
  but living wisely brings pleasure to the sensible.

24 The fears of the wicked will be fulfilled;
  the hopes of the godly will be granted.

25 When the storms of life come, the wicked are whirled away,

9:18 Hebrew in Sheol. 10:1 Hebrew son; also in 10:1b. 10:10 As in Greek version; Hebrew reads but babbling fools fall flat on their faces.

but the godly have a lasting
foundation.

²⁶ Lazy people irritate their employers,
like vinegar to the teeth or smoke in
the eyes.

²⁷ Fear of the LORD lengthens one's life,
but the years of the wicked are cut
short.

²⁸ The hopes of the godly result in
happiness,
but the expectations of the wicked
come to nothing.

²⁹ The way of the LORD is a stronghold to
those with integrity,
but it destroys the wicked.

³⁰ The godly will never be disturbed,
but the wicked will be removed from
the land.

³¹ The mouth of the godly person gives
wise advice,
but the tongue that deceives will be
cut off.

³² The lips of the godly speak helpful
words,
but the mouth of the wicked speaks
perverse words.

11 ¹ The LORD detests the use of
dishonest scales,
but he delights in accurate weights.

² Pride leads to disgrace,
but with humility comes wisdom.

³ Honesty guides good people;
dishonesty destroys treacherous
people.

⁴ Riches won't help on the day of
judgment,
but right living can save you from
death.

⁵ The godly are directed by honesty;
the wicked fall beneath their load of
sin.

⁶ The godliness of good people rescues
them;
the ambition of treacherous people
traps them.

⁷ When the wicked die, their hopes die
with them,
for they rely on their own feeble
strength.

⁸ The godly are rescued from trouble,
and it falls on the wicked instead.

⁹ With their words, the godless destroy
their friends,
but knowledge will rescue the
righteous.

¹⁰ The whole city celebrates when the godly
succeed;
they shout for joy when the wicked
die.

¹¹ Upright citizens are good for a city and
make it prosper,
but the talk of the wicked tears it
apart.

¹² It is foolish to belittle one's neighbor;
a sensible person keeps quiet.

¹³ A gossip goes around telling secrets,
but those who are trustworthy can
keep a confidence.

¹⁴ Without wise leadership, a nation falls;
there is safety in having many advisers.

¹⁵ There's danger in putting up security for
a stranger's debt;
it's safer not to guarantee another
person's debt.

¹⁶ A gracious woman gains respect,
but ruthless men gain only wealth.

¹⁷ Your kindness will reward you,
but your cruelty will destroy you.

¹⁸ Evil people get rich for the moment,
but the reward of the godly will last.

¹⁹ Godly people find life;
evil people find death.

²⁰ The LORD detests people with crooked
hearts,
but he delights in those with integrity.

²¹ Evil people will surely be punished,
but the children of the godly will go
free.

²² A beautiful woman who lacks discretion
is like a gold ring in a pig's snout.

Why We Need Silence

PROVERBS 10:19-21

When I started practicing silence, I lasted ten minutes, eventually twenty, then a half hour. Then someone led me into an all-day silence and solitude retreat. I'd never experienced an all-day time of silence, so it was daunting.

The morning felt similar to what I'd done on my own. But when it came time for lunch, we were also to eat in silence. As I sat alone with my food in the retreat house dining room, I fell to pieces. I started to weep, and I wondered, *What is happening to me?*

Because none of us were allowed to talk, nobody could come and try to fix me. All I could do was be by myself with God; he was my companion for lunch. In my tears I became aware of the weight of Christian expectations on me—of being a good Christian, a good neighbor, a good mother, a good wife, a good person in ministry, a good leader.

I realized that my Christian life had become a heavy weight. The tears were purely tears of relief that I didn't have to go into this lunch and talk to somebody, that I didn't have to figure out a social interaction, that nothing was expected of me. I didn't have to do anything but allow someone to serve me lunch in the presence of God.

I knew this was ridiculous; somehow my Christian life had gotten to the point that, when I was allowed to be quiet and be served, I became an emotional wreck. In silence I became aware of the level of exhaustion I never knew existed within me. The realization was profound.

Silence is the time when we withdraw from our addiction to noise, words, and activity. And so in silence we withdraw from our own inner compulsions, not just the expectations of other people, but from our addiction to our own thoughts and words. We develop a rhythm of silence and word.

Dietrich Bonhoeffer says right words come out of right silence, and right silence comes out of right words—an interplay between silence and word. Scripture also tells us that "Too much talk leads to sin." What's the solution to that? "Be sensible and keep your mouth shut" (Proverbs 10:19). We choose to shut our mouths every so often, so that we can hear a word from the Lord. One of the reasons we don't hear a word from the Lord and yet long for one is that we never stop the flow of our own words. How are we going to hear something from God if we're always talking?

Silence challenges us on every level of our being. When we're silent, we have to face ourselves. We might notice our own discomfort and anxiety, and we don't want to do that. We feel if we can just fill up the time, we don't have to face our true selves.

The human psyche is good at distracting us and finding ways to keep us from being aware of those things we'd rather not be aware of—our loneliness, emptiness, relationships that aren't working, questions that make us uncomfortable. That's one reason why silence before God makes us uncomfortable—because we have to face what's real and what's not real between us and God. We have to face our questions, our loneliness, our brokenness. Silence, in a sense, starves the ego; the normal things the ego loves to feed on aren't there anymore, and now we're just *me*—a soul in God's presence.

In our culture we tend to evaluate everything—even our encounters with God, which is a travesty. We come into periods of silence and say, *Okay, God, I'm giving you my full, undivided attention.* And then when we end the time of silence, we evaluate it. We may even judge it and say, "I didn't get anything out of that."

But think for a moment about being with your spouse in a time of intimacy. Would you look back on it, evaluate it, and say, "That didn't do anything for me"? That would cheapen your relationship and your moment together. We don't do that with a person we love; we just receive the time for what it is and are grateful for it.

That's the way I see silence—a time to be with God intimately, and, whatever it is, we're grateful for it. It's meaningful because we're with the One we enjoy and love.

—*Ruth Haley Barton*

For more on silence, see reading at Proverbs 21:23-24.

23 The godly can look forward to a reward,
while the wicked can expect only
judgment.

24 Give freely and become more wealthy;
be stingy and lose everything.

25 The generous will prosper;
those who refresh others will
themselves be refreshed.

26 People curse those who hoard their grain,
but they bless the one who sells in
time of need.

27 If you search for good, you will find favor;
but if you search for evil, it will find
you!

28 Trust in your money and down you go!
But the godly flourish like leaves in
spring.

29 Those who bring trouble on their
families inherit the wind.
The fool will be a servant to the wise.

30 The seeds of good deeds become a tree
of life;
a wise person wins friends.*

31 If the righteous are rewarded here on
earth,
what will happen to wicked sinners?*

12 1 To learn, you must love discipline;
it is stupid to hate correction.

2 The LORD approves of those who are
good,
but he condemns those who plan
wickedness.

3 Wickedness never brings stability,
but the godly have deep roots.

4 A worthy wife is a crown for her husband,
but a disgraceful woman is like cancer
in his bones.

5 The plans of the godly are just;
the advice of the wicked is
treacherous.

6 The words of the wicked are like a
murderous ambush,
but the words of the godly save lives.

7 The wicked die and disappear,
but the family of the godly stands firm.

8 A sensible person wins admiration,
but a warped mind is despised.

9 Better to be an ordinary person with a
servant
than to be self-important but have no
food.

10 The godly care for their animals,
but the wicked are always cruel.

11 A hard worker has plenty of food,
but a person who chases fantasies has
no sense.

12 Thieves are jealous of each other's loot,
but the godly are well rooted and bear
their own fruit.

13 The wicked are trapped by their own
words,
but the godly escape such trouble.

14 Wise words bring many benefits,
and hard work brings rewards.

15 Fools think their own way is right,
but the wise listen to others.

16 A fool is quick-tempered,
but a wise person stays calm when
insulted.

17 An honest witness tells the truth;
a false witness tells lies.

18 Some people make cutting remarks,
but the words of the wise bring healing.

19 Truthful words stand the test of time,
but lies are soon exposed.

20 Deceit fills hearts that are plotting evil;
joy fills hearts that are planning peace!

21 No harm comes to the godly,
but the wicked have their fill of
trouble.

22 The LORD detests lying lips,
but he delights in those who tell the
truth.

23 The wise don't make a show of their
knowledge,
but fools broadcast their foolishness.

11:30 Or *and those who win souls are wise.*   **11:31** Greek version reads *If the righteous are barely saved, / what will happen to godless sinners?*
Compare 1 Pet 4:18.

²⁴ Work hard and become a leader;
    be lazy and become a slave.

²⁵ Worry weighs a person down;
    an encouraging word cheers a
      person up.

²⁶ The godly give good advice to their
    friends;*
    the wicked lead them astray.

²⁷ Lazy people don't even cook the game
    they catch,
    but the diligent make use of
      everything they find.

²⁸ The way of the godly leads to life;
    that path does not lead to death.

13

¹ A wise child accepts a parent's
    discipline;*
    a mocker refuses to listen to correction.

² Wise words will win you a good meal,
    but treacherous people have an
      appetite for violence.

³ Those who control their tongue will have
    a long life;
    opening your mouth can ruin
      everything.

⁴ Lazy people want much but get little,
    but those who work hard will prosper.

⁵ The godly hate lies;
    the wicked cause shame and disgrace.

⁶ Godliness guards the path of the
    blameless,
    but the evil are misled by sin.

⁷ Some who are poor pretend to be rich;
    others who are rich pretend to be
      poor.

⁸ The rich can pay a ransom for their lives,
    but the poor won't even get
      threatened.

⁹ The life of the godly is full of light and
    joy,
    but the light of the wicked will be
      snuffed out.

¹⁰ Pride leads to conflict;
    those who take advice are wise.

¹¹ Wealth from get-rich-quick schemes
    quickly disappears;
    wealth from hard work grows over time.

¹² Hope deferred makes the heart sick,
    but a dream fulfilled is a tree of life.

¹³ People who despise advice are asking for
    trouble;
    those who respect a command will
      succeed.

¹⁴ The instruction of the wise is like a life-
    giving fountain;
    those who accept it avoid the snares
      of death.

¹⁵ A person with good sense is respected;
    a treacherous person is headed for
      destruction.*

¹⁶ Wise people think before they act;
    fools don't—and even brag about their
      foolishness.

¹⁷ An unreliable messenger stumbles into
    trouble,
    but a reliable messenger brings healing.

¹⁸ If you ignore criticism, you will end in
    poverty and disgrace;
    if you accept correction, you will be
      honored.

¹⁹ It is pleasant to see dreams come true,
    but fools refuse to turn from evil to
      attain them.

²⁰ Walk with the wise and become wise;
    associate with fools and get in trouble.

²¹ Trouble chases sinners,
    while blessings reward the righteous.

²² Good people leave an inheritance to
    their grandchildren,
    but the sinner's wealth passes to the
      godly.

²³ A poor person's farm may produce
    much food,
    but injustice sweeps it all away.

²⁴ Those who spare the rod of discipline
    hate their children.
    Those who love their children care
      enough to discipline them.

12:26 Or *The godly are cautious in friendship;* or *The godly are freed from evil.* The meaning of the Hebrew is uncertain. **13:1** Hebrew *A wise son accepts his father's discipline.* **13:15** As in Greek version; Hebrew reads *the way of the treacherous is lasting.*

Unofficial Mentors

PROVERBS 13:20

Mentoring

I've never had a mentor," I used to tell friends as they'd talk about teachers or church leaders who'd poured into their lives or guided them through tough decisions. I'm pretty self-sufficient; it's not in my nature to talk about a problem or decision with many others.

But lately I've begun to see the mentors that *do* populate my life. I sat across the table from one of them at a restaurant recently. She's my former boss, and every so often we get together to catch up. I left the three-hour dinner feeling so grateful for her. While probably neither she nor I would give her the title of "mentor" over "friend," it struck me that she was indeed a mentor to me and has been for the past nine years. Even now when I don't see her for long stretches of time, she remembers details of my life, encourages me, and speaks truth.

I love this kind of mentoring; it's not something planned or decided ahead of time. It just *happens*. It's an organic, natural extension of a person's care and concern for another person. I've found it to be a beautiful, tangible expression of God's commandment to love our neighbor as ourselves (Matthew 22:37-39). Proverbs 13:20 says: "Walk with the wise and become wise; associate with fools and get in trouble"—and it's been a privilege to walk through life with wise friends, unofficial mentors. Their examples inspire me; their presence, words, and listening ears encourage me. Though I'll probably never be the type to seek out a formal mentoring relationship with someone, I will continue to be open to the women in my life who know me. I need these older, wiser voices in my life. It is through these relationships that I learn about myself, draw nearer to God, and find encouragement and support.

—*Rachel Jay*

For more on mentoring, see reading at John 1:35-44.

25 The godly eat to their hearts' content,
    but the belly of the wicked goes hungry.

14 1 A wise woman builds her home,
    but a foolish woman tears it
    down with her own hands.

2 Those who follow the right path fear the
    LORD;
    those who take the wrong path despise
    him.

3 A fool's proud talk becomes a rod that
    beats him,
    but the words of the wise keep them
    safe.

4 Without oxen a stable stays clean,
    but you need a strong ox for a large
    harvest.

5 An honest witness does not lie;
    a false witness breathes lies.

6 A mocker seeks wisdom and never finds it,
    but knowledge comes easily to those
    with understanding.

7 Stay away from fools,
    for you won't find knowledge on their
    lips.

8 The prudent understand where they are
    going,
    but fools deceive themselves.

9 Fools make fun of guilt,
    but the godly acknowledge it and seek
    reconciliation.

10 Each heart knows its own bitterness,
    and no one else can fully share its joy.

11 The house of the wicked will be
destroyed,
but the tent of the godly will flourish.

12 There is a path before each person that
seems right,
but it ends in death.

13 Laughter can conceal a heavy heart,
but when the laughter ends, the grief
remains.

14 Backsliders get what they deserve;
good people receive their reward.

15 Only simpletons believe everything
they're told!
The prudent carefully consider their
steps.

16 The wise are cautious* and avoid danger;
fools plunge ahead with reckless
confidence.

17 Short-tempered people do foolish things,
and schemers are hated.

18 Simpletons are clothed with
foolishness,*
but the prudent are crowned with
knowledge.

19 Evil people will bow before good people;
the wicked will bow at the gates of the
godly.

20 The poor are despised even by their
neighbors,
while the rich have many "friends."

21 It is a sin to belittle one's neighbor;
blessed are those who help the poor.

22 If you plan to do evil, you will be lost;
if you plan to do good, you will receive
unfailing love and faithfulness.

23 Work brings profit,
but mere talk leads to poverty!

24 Wealth is a crown for the wise;
the effort of fools yields only
foolishness.

25 A truthful witness saves lives,
but a false witness is a traitor.

26 Those who fear the LORD are secure;
he will be a refuge for their children.

27 Fear of the LORD is a life-giving fountain;
it offers escape from the snares of
death.

28 A growing population is a king's glory;
a prince without subjects has nothing.

29 People with understanding control their
anger;
a hot temper shows great foolishness.

30 A peaceful heart leads to a healthy body;
jealousy is like cancer in the bones.

31 Those who oppress the poor insult their
Maker,
but helping the poor honors him.

32 The wicked are crushed by disaster,
but the godly have a refuge when they
die.

33 Wisdom is enshrined in an
understanding heart;
wisdom is not* found among fools.

34 Godliness makes a nation great,
but sin is a disgrace to any people.

35 A king rejoices in wise servants
but is angry with those who disgrace
him.

15 1 A gentle answer deflects anger,
but harsh words make tempers
flare.

2 The tongue of the wise makes knowledge
appealing,
but the mouth of a fool belches out
foolishness.

3 The LORD is watching everywhere,
keeping his eye on both the evil and
the good.

4 Gentle words are a tree of life;
a deceitful tongue crushes the spirit.

5 Only a fool despises a parent's*
discipline;
whoever learns from correction is
wise.

6 There is treasure in the house of the
godly,
but the earnings of the wicked bring
trouble.

14:16 Hebrew *The wise fear.* 14:18 Or *inherit foolishness.* 14:33 As in Greek and Syriac versions; Hebrew lacks *not.* 15:5 Hebrew *father's.*

The Benefits of Losing

PROVERBS 15:16

One frigid January day years ago, I stood across the street in the warmth of our neighbor's living room with my three young sons, watching as thick, acrid smoke billowed from our rented bungalow's windows.

Our house was on fire . . . and we lost nearly everything we owned.

Somehow that smoldering wreck of a home became the start of a new life for us—a life that would prize simplicity over stuff. In losing everything, we gained a freedom I could have never imagined. I was beginning to grasp the paradox of the apostle Paul's words, "I once thought these things were valuable, but now I consider them worthless because of what Christ has done" (Philippians 3:7).

I didn't experience this inverse reality overnight. At first I grieved the loss of my stuff with an intensity that surprised me. I began to understand what Corrie ten Boom meant when she said, "Hold everything in your hands lightly, otherwise it hurts when God pries your fingers open."

But as I loosened my grip and slowly moved beyond the pain of letting go of everything that seemed so important, I began to see the value in this forced austerity program. Losing had its benefits. We were forced, through our loss, to experience a profound truth: "Better to have little, with fear for the Lord, than to have great treasure and inner turmoil" (Proverbs 15:16). The same principle is repeated in Proverbs 16:8, "Better to have little, with godliness." We had lost our possessions—and that loss hurt. But it put into perspective for us what we *did* have: God himself.

—Marian V. Liautaud

For more on simplicity, see reading at Proverbs 28:6–27.

7 The lips of the wise give good advice;
   the heart of a fool has none to give.

8 The Lord detests the sacrifice of the wicked,
   but he delights in the prayers of the upright.

9 The Lord detests the way of the wicked,
   but he loves those who pursue godliness.

10 Whoever abandons the right path will be severely disciplined;
   whoever hates correction will die.

11 Even Death and Destruction* hold no secrets from the Lord.
   How much more does he know the human heart!

12 Mockers hate to be corrected,
   so they stay away from the wise.

13 A glad heart makes a happy face;
   a broken heart crushes the spirit.

14 A wise person is hungry for knowledge,
   while the fool feeds on trash.

15 For the despondent, every day brings trouble;
   for the happy heart, life is a continual feast.

16 Better to have little, with fear for the Lord,
   than to have great treasure and inner turmoil.

15:11 Hebrew *Sheol* and *Abaddon*.

¹⁷ A bowl of vegetables with someone you love
is better than steak with someone you hate.

¹⁸ A hot-tempered person starts fights;
a cool-tempered person stops them.

¹⁹ A lazy person's way is blocked with briers,
but the path of the upright is an open highway.

²⁰ Sensible children bring joy to their father;
foolish children despise their mother.

²¹ Foolishness brings joy to those with no sense;
a sensible person stays on the right path.

²² Plans go wrong for lack of advice;
many advisers bring success.

²³ Everyone enjoys a fitting reply;
it is wonderful to say the right thing at the right time!

²⁴ The path of life leads upward for the wise;
they leave the grave* behind.

²⁵ The LORD tears down the house of the proud,
but he protects the property of widows.

²⁶ The LORD detests evil plans,
but he delights in pure words.

²⁷ Greed brings grief to the whole family,
but those who hate bribes will live.

²⁸ The heart of the godly thinks carefully before speaking;
the mouth of the wicked overflows with evil words.

²⁹ The LORD is far from the wicked,
but he hears the prayers of the righteous.

³⁰ A cheerful look brings joy to the heart;
good news makes for good health.

³¹ If you listen to constructive criticism,
you will be at home among the wise.

³² If you reject discipline, you only harm yourself;
but if you listen to correction, you grow in understanding.

³³ Fear of the LORD teaches wisdom;
humility precedes honor.

16

¹ We can make our own plans,
but the LORD gives the right answer.

² People may be pure in their own eyes,
but the LORD examines their motives.

³ Commit your actions to the LORD,
and your plans will succeed.

⁴ The LORD has made everything for his own purposes,
even the wicked for a day of disaster.

⁵ The LORD detests the proud;
they will surely be punished.

⁶ Unfailing love and faithfulness make atonement for sin.
By fearing the LORD, people avoid evil.

⁷ When people's lives please the LORD,
even their enemies are at peace with them.

⁸ Better to have little, with godliness,
than to be rich and dishonest.

⁹ We can make our plans,
but the LORD determines our steps.

¹⁰ The king speaks with divine wisdom;
he must never judge unfairly.

¹¹ The LORD demands accurate scales and balances;
he sets the standards for fairness.

¹² A king detests wrongdoing,
for his rule is built on justice.

¹³ The king is pleased with words from righteous lips;
he loves those who speak honestly.

¹⁴ The anger of the king is a deadly threat;
the wise will try to appease it.

¹⁵ When the king smiles, there is life;
his favor refreshes like a spring rain.

---

¹⁶ How much better to get wisdom than gold,
and good judgment than silver!

¹⁷ The path of the virtuous leads away from
evil;
whoever follows that path is safe.

¹⁸ Pride goes before destruction,
and haughtiness before a fall.

¹⁹ Better to live humbly with the poor
than to share plunder with the proud.

²⁰ Those who listen to instruction will
prosper;
those who trust the LORD will be joyful.

²¹ The wise are known for their
understanding,
and pleasant words are persuasive.

²² Discretion is a life-giving fountain to
those who possess it,
but discipline is wasted on fools.

²³ From a wise mind comes wise speech;
the words of the wise are persuasive.

²⁴ Kind words are like honey—
sweet to the soul and healthy for the
body.

²⁵ There is a path before each person that
seems right,
but it ends in death.

²⁶ It is good for workers to have an appetite;
an empty stomach drives them on.

²⁷ Scoundrels create trouble;
their words are a destructive blaze.

²⁸ A troublemaker plants seeds of strife;
gossip separates the best of friends.

²⁹ Violent people mislead their companions,
leading them down a harmful path.

³⁰ With narrowed eyes, people plot evil;
with a smirk, they plan their mischief.

³¹ Gray hair is a crown of glory;
it is gained by living a godly life.

³² Better to be patient than powerful;
better to have self-control than to
conquer a city.

³³ We may throw the dice,*
but the LORD determines how they fall.

17 ¹ Better a dry crust eaten in peace
than a house filled with feasting—
and conflict.

² A wise servant will rule over the master's
disgraceful son
and will share the inheritance of the
master's children.

³ Fire tests the purity of silver and gold,
but the LORD tests the heart.

⁴ Wrongdoers eagerly listen to gossip;
liars pay close attention to slander.

⁵ Those who mock the poor insult their
Maker;
those who rejoice at the misfortune of
others will be punished.

⁶ Grandchildren are the crowning glory of
the aged;
parents* are the pride of their
children.

⁷ Eloquent words are not fitting for a fool;
even less are lies fitting for a ruler.

⁸ A bribe is like a lucky charm;
whoever gives one will prosper!

⁹ Love prospers when a fault is forgiven,
but dwelling on it separates close
friends.

¹⁰ A single rebuke does more for a person
of understanding
than a hundred lashes on the back of
a fool.

¹¹ Evil people are eager for rebellion,
but they will be severely punished.

¹² It is safer to meet a bear robbed of her
cubs
than to confront a fool caught in
foolishness.

¹³ If you repay good with evil,
evil will never leave your house.

¹⁴ Starting a quarrel is like opening a
floodgate,
so stop before a dispute breaks out.

¹⁵ Acquitting the guilty and condemning
the innocent—
both are detestable to the LORD.

16:33 Hebrew *We may cast lots.*   **17:6** Hebrew *fathers.*

¹⁶ It is senseless to pay tuition to educate a
fool,
since he has no heart for learning.

¹⁷ A friend is always loyal,
and a brother is born to help in time
of need.

¹⁸ It's poor judgment to guarantee another
person's debt
or put up security for a friend.

¹⁹ Anyone who loves to quarrel loves sin;
anyone who trusts in high walls invites
disaster.

²⁰ The crooked heart will not prosper;
the lying tongue tumbles into trouble.

²¹ It is painful to be the parent of a fool;
there is no joy for the father of a rebel.

²² A cheerful heart is good medicine,
but a broken spirit saps a person's
strength.

²³ The wicked take secret bribes
to pervert the course of justice.

²⁴ Sensible people keep their eyes glued on
wisdom,
but a fool's eyes wander to the ends of
the earth.

²⁵ Foolish children* bring grief to their father
and bitterness to the one who gave
them birth.

²⁶ It is wrong to punish the godly for being
good
or to flog leaders for being honest.

²⁷ A truly wise person uses few words;
a person with understanding is
even-tempered.

²⁸ Even fools are thought wise when they
keep silent;
with their mouths shut, they seem
intelligent.

18

¹ Unfriendly people care only about
themselves;
they lash out at common sense.

² Fools have no interest in understanding;
they only want to air their own
opinions.

³ Doing wrong leads to disgrace,
and scandalous behavior brings
contempt.

⁴ Wise words are like deep waters;
wisdom flows from the wise like a
bubbling brook.

⁵ It is not right to acquit the guilty
or deny justice to the innocent.

⁶ Fools' words get them into constant
quarrels;
they are asking for a beating.

⁷ The mouths of fools are their ruin;
they trap themselves with their lips.

⁸ Rumors are dainty morsels
that sink deep into one's heart.

⁹ A lazy person is as bad as
someone who destroys things.

¹⁰ The name of the LORD is a strong fortress;
the godly run to him and are safe.

¹¹ The rich think of their wealth as a strong
defense;
they imagine it to be a high wall of
safety.

¹² Haughtiness goes before destruction;
humility precedes honor.

¹³ Spouting off before listening to the facts
is both shameful and foolish.

¹⁴ The human spirit can endure a sick body,
but who can bear a crushed spirit?

¹⁵ Intelligent people are always ready to
learn.
Their ears are open for knowledge.

¹⁶ Giving a gift can open doors;
it gives access to important people!

¹⁷ The first to speak in court sounds right—
until the cross-examination begins.

¹⁸ Flipping a coin* can end arguments;
it settles disputes between powerful
opponents.

¹⁹ An offended friend is harder to win back
than a fortified city.
Arguments separate friends like a gate
locked with bars.

17:25 Hebrew *A foolish son.*   **18:18** Hebrew *Casting lots.*

Hospitality

Hospitality through Listening

PROVERBS 18:20-21

Words and often the absence thereof can be a powerful ministry to those we welcome into our homes and lives. Scripture has much to say about the power of words in our practice of hospitality. They can wield pain or bring healing. Proverbs 16:24 tells us, "Kind words are like honey—sweet to the soul and healthy for the body," while Proverbs 18:21 profoundly states, "The tongue can bring death or life." We all know this to be true—we've spoken or been on the receiving end of painful, damaging words. We've also been profoundly ministered to by words of hope, truth, encouragement, or kindness.

The absence of words can also minister; listening itself can be a profound act of hospitality. Scripture implores us to be people who are "quick to listen, slow to speak" (James 1:19). This not only paves the way for wisdom and prudence in our speech, but it also creates space in which others can open up, can verbally lay down burdens, or can experience the joy of telling their own stories.

Listening goes much deeper than nodding our heads in assent of what we're hearing. We need to listen for the movement of the Holy Spirit. We need to focus in such a way that our own agenda gets put on the back burner and all distractions are set aside. We need to follow Jesus' model of asking engaging and meaningful questions. If we could see Jesus speaking to the woman at the well, for example, I believe we'd see him sitting and leaning forward as he listened to her story (John 4). I imagine Jesus listened with his whole being.

That's what I felt like one August night as a ten-year-old. I can still picture myself sitting on the stairs, eavesdropping on a conversation between my father and Rob, a young man who had just returned home from his tour of military duty in Vietnam. It was a beautiful picture of mutual hospitality. Rob's ministering words flowed to my father (and to my eavesdropping ears). My father's hospitality came in the form of listening.

"Reverend Fore," Rob said, "I want you to know that I faked all those times I pretended to be asleep as I sat in the balcony listening to you preach when I was in high school. I heard every word. On more than one occasion, when you gave the invitation to commit my life to Christ, I resisted God with everything in me." Rob went on to tell his story of rebellion against God. He spoke of his fear while serving in Vietnam and finally of his surrender to Jesus, when he couldn't resist anymore.

The words flowed for at least two hours. As Rob got up to leave, I raced down the stairs and into the kitchen. I asked my mom if I could give Rob a loaf of homemade bread that she had baked that day. I had been given a gift in Rob's words. I remember saying to Rob, "I want to give you something. I was listening in, and your story was amazing. Here's some of Mom's homemade bread."

We had opened our home, our hearts, and our ears, and Rob gifted us with the hospitality of ministering words. The listening and the speaking—they were both acts of ministry. And I continue to experience the ministry of hospitable words today. In fact, some of the most significant experiences I've had of receiving hospitality as an adult have not been at someone's home or around a dinner table; they've been coffee-shop moments with friends who have welcomed me with loving and wise words or who have ministered by listening as I poured out my heart.

—Anita Lustrea

For more on hospitality, see reading at Matthew 10:10.

²⁰ Wise words satisfy like a good meal;
   the right words bring satisfaction.

²¹ The tongue can bring death or life;
   those who love to talk will reap the
   consequences.

²² The man who finds a wife finds a
   treasure,
   and he receives favor from the LORD.

²³ The poor plead for mercy;
   the rich answer with insults.

²⁴ There are "friends" who destroy each
   other,
   but a real friend sticks closer than a
   brother.

19 ¹ Better to be poor and honest
   than to be dishonest and a fool.

² Enthusiasm without knowledge is no
   good;
   haste makes mistakes.

³ People ruin their lives by their own
   foolishness
   and then are angry at the LORD.

⁴ Wealth makes many "friends";
   poverty drives them all away.

⁵ A false witness will not go unpunished,
   nor will a liar escape.

⁶ Many seek favors from a ruler;
   everyone is the friend of a person who
   gives gifts!

⁷ The relatives of the poor despise them;
   how much more will their friends
   avoid them!
   Though the poor plead with them,
   their friends are gone.

⁸ To acquire wisdom is to love oneself;
   people who cherish understanding
   will prosper.

⁹ A false witness will not go unpunished,
   and a liar will be destroyed.

¹⁰ It isn't right for a fool to live in luxury
   or for a slave to rule over princes!

¹¹ Sensible people control their temper;
   they earn respect by overlooking
   wrongs.

¹² The king's anger is like a lion's roar,
   but his favor is like dew on the grass.

¹³ A foolish child* is a calamity to a father;
   a quarrelsome wife is as annoying as
   constant dripping.

¹⁴ Fathers can give their sons an
   inheritance of houses and wealth,
   but only the LORD can give an
   understanding wife.

¹⁵ Lazy people sleep soundly,
   but idleness leaves them hungry.

¹⁶ Keep the commandments and keep your
   life;
   despising them leads to death.

¹⁷ If you help the poor, you are lending to
   the LORD—
   and he will repay you!

¹⁸ Discipline your children while there is
   hope.
   Otherwise you will ruin their lives.

¹⁹ Hot-tempered people must pay the
   penalty.
   If you rescue them once, you will have
   to do it again.

²⁰ Get all the advice and instruction you
   can,
   so you will be wise the rest of your life.

²¹ You can make many plans,
   but the LORD's purpose will prevail.

²² Loyalty makes a person attractive.
   It is better to be poor than dishonest.

²³ Fear of the LORD leads to life,
   bringing security and protection from
   harm.

²⁴ Lazy people take food in their hand
   but don't even lift it to their mouth.

²⁵ If you punish a mocker, the
   simpleminded will learn a lesson;
   if you correct the wise, they will be all
   the wiser.

²⁶ Children who mistreat their father or
   chase away their mother
   are an embarrassment and a public
   disgrace.

19:13 Hebrew *son;* also in 19:27.

27 If you stop listening to instruction, my
child,
you will turn your back on knowledge.

28 A corrupt witness makes a mockery of
justice;
the mouth of the wicked gulps down
evil.

29 Punishment is made for mockers,
and the backs of fools are made to be
beaten.

20 1 Wine produces mockers; alcohol
leads to brawls.
Those led astray by drink cannot be
wise.

2 The king's fury is like a lion's roar;
to rouse his anger is to risk your life.

3 Avoiding a fight is a mark of honor;
only fools insist on quarreling.

4 Those too lazy to plow in the right
season
will have no food at the harvest.

5 Though good advice lies deep within the
heart,
a person with understanding will draw
it out.

6 Many will say they are loyal friends,
but who can find one who is truly
reliable?

7 The godly walk with integrity;
blessed are their children who follow
them.

8 When a king sits in judgment, he weighs
all the evidence,
distinguishing the bad from the
good.

9 Who can say, "I have cleansed my heart;
I am pure and free from sin"?

10 False weights and unequal measures*—
the LORD detests double standards of
every kind.

11 Even children are known by the way they
act,
whether their conduct is pure, and
whether it is right.

12 Ears to hear and eyes to see—
both are gifts from the LORD.

13 If you love sleep, you will end in poverty.
Keep your eyes open, and there will be
plenty to eat!

14 The buyer haggles over the price, saying,
"It's worthless,"
then brags about getting a bargain!

15 Wise words are more valuable
than much gold and many rubies.

16 Get security from someone who
guarantees a stranger's debt.
Get a deposit if he does it for
foreigners.*

17 Stolen bread tastes sweet,
but it turns to gravel in the mouth.

18 Plans succeed through good counsel;
don't go to war without wise advice.

19 A gossip goes around telling secrets,
so don't hang around with chatterers.

20 If you insult your father or mother,
your light will be snuffed out in total
darkness.

21 An inheritance obtained too early in life
is not a blessing in the end.

22 Don't say, "I will get even for this wrong."
Wait for the LORD to handle the
matter.

23 The LORD detests double standards;
he is not pleased by dishonest scales.

24 The LORD directs our steps,
so why try to understand everything
along the way?

25 Don't trap yourself by making a rash
promise to God
and only later counting the cost.

26 A wise king scatters the wicked like
wheat,
then runs his threshing wheel over
them.

27 The LORD's light penetrates the human
spirit,*
exposing every hidden motive.

20:10 Hebrew *A stone and a stone, an ephah and an ephah.*   20:16 An alternate reading in the Masoretic Text is *for a promiscuous woman.*
20:27 Or *The human spirit is the LORD's light.*

²⁸ Unfailing love and faithfulness protect
the king;
his throne is made secure through
love.

²⁹ The glory of the young is their strength;
the gray hair of experience is the
splendor of the old.

³⁰ Physical punishment cleanses away evil;*
such discipline purifies the heart.

21

¹ The king's heart is like a stream of
water directed by the LORD;
he guides it wherever he pleases.

² People may be right in their own eyes,
but the LORD examines their heart.

³ The LORD is more pleased when we do
what is right and just
than when we offer him sacrifices.

⁴ Haughty eyes, a proud heart,
and evil actions are all sin.

⁵ Good planning and hard work lead to
prosperity,
but hasty shortcuts lead to poverty.

⁶ Wealth created by a lying tongue
is a vanishing mist and a deadly trap.*

⁷ The violence of the wicked sweeps them
away,
because they refuse to do what is just.

⁸ The guilty walk a crooked path;
the innocent travel a straight road.

⁹ It's better to live alone in the corner of
an attic
than with a quarrelsome wife in a
lovely home.

¹⁰ Evil people desire evil;
their neighbors get no mercy from
them.

¹¹ If you punish a mocker, the
simpleminded become wise;
if you instruct the wise, they will be all
the wiser.

¹² The Righteous One* knows what is going
on in the homes of the wicked;
he will bring disaster on them.

¹³ Those who shut their ears to the cries of
the poor
will be ignored in their own time of
need.

¹⁴ A secret gift calms anger;
a bribe under the table pacifies fury.

¹⁵ Justice is a joy to the godly,
but it terrifies evildoers.

¹⁶ The person who strays from common
sense
will end up in the company of the
dead.

¹⁷ Those who love pleasure become poor;
those who love wine and luxury will
never be rich.

¹⁸ The wicked are punished in place of the
godly,
and traitors in place of the honest.

¹⁹ It's better to live alone in the desert
than with a quarrelsome, complaining
wife.

²⁰ The wise have wealth and luxury,
but fools spend whatever they get.

²¹ Whoever pursues righteousness and
unfailing love
will find life, righteousness, and
honor.

²² The wise conquer the city of the strong
and level the fortress in which they
trust.

²³ Watch your tongue and keep your
mouth shut,
and you will stay out of trouble.

²⁴ Mockers are proud and haughty;
they act with boundless arrogance.

²⁵ Despite their desires, the lazy will come
to ruin,
for their hands refuse to work.

²⁶ Some people are always greedy for more,
but the godly love to give!

²⁷ The sacrifice of an evil person is
detestable,
especially when it is offered with
wrong motives.

20:30 The meaning of the Hebrew is uncertain.   **21:6** As in Greek version; Hebrew reads *mist for those who seek death.*   **21:12** Or *The righteous man.*

A Fast from Talking

PROVERBS 21:23–24

I'm an interrupter. In nearly every conversation, I find it's all I can do to keep my mouth shut long enough for the other person to finish her sentence. And then *bam!* I'm ready to offer my brilliant insight.

Having become more aware of this nasty habit, I've been trying to find ways to hear less of myself. The solution, it turns out, is silence.

This means more than waiting my turn in a conversation. It means listening with no intention of talking when others finish. It means not chiming in on every Facebook thread that catches my eye. It means recognizing that the more I talk, the less I have to say. It means giving the Holy Spirit some breathing space and quiet time in which to do his work in me.

This isn't easy. Like any kind of fasting, this limitation on my words takes tremendous effort and discipline. And yet, like a good fast should, it has made me more aware of the places where God is still working on me—in this case my pride and insecurity.

I've long admired people who sit at the edges of conversation only to chime in with one mind-blowing observation. And I've come to see that those people have learned the fine art of silence. They know that God's wisdom shines through when we put our words away and allow God's Spirit to speak.

—Carla Barnhill

For more on silence, see reading at Ecclesiastes 3:1–8.

---

²⁸ A false witness will be cut off,
   but a credible witness will be allowed
      to speak.

²⁹ The wicked bluff their way through,
   but the virtuous think before they act.

³⁰ No human wisdom or understanding or
      plan
   can stand against the LORD.

³¹ The horse is prepared for the day of
      battle,
   but the victory belongs to the LORD.

22 ¹ Choose a good reputation over
      great riches;
   being held in high esteem is better
      than silver or gold.

² The rich and poor have this in common:
   The LORD made them both.

³ A prudent person foresees danger and
      takes precautions.
   The simpleton goes blindly on and
      suffers the consequences.

⁴ True humility and fear of the LORD
   lead to riches, honor, and long life.

⁵ Corrupt people walk a thorny,
      treacherous road;
   whoever values life will avoid it.

⁶ Direct your children onto the right path,
   and when they are older, they will not
      leave it.

⁷ Just as the rich rule the poor,
   so the borrower is servant to the lender.

⁸ Those who plant injustice will harvest
      disaster,
   and their reign of terror will come to
      an end.*

22:8 The Greek version includes an additional proverb: *God blesses a man who gives cheerfully, / but his worthless deeds will come to an end.* Compare 2 Cor 9:7.

⁹ Blessed are those who are generous,
   because they feed the poor.

¹⁰ Throw out the mocker, and fighting
   goes, too.
   Quarrels and insults will disappear.

¹¹ Whoever loves a pure heart and
   gracious speech
   will have the king as a friend.

¹² The LORD preserves those with
   knowledge,
   but he ruins the plans of the
   treacherous.

¹³ The lazy person claims, "There's a lion
   out there!
   If I go outside, I might be killed!"

¹⁴ The mouth of an immoral woman is a
   dangerous trap;
   those who make the LORD angry will
   fall into it.

¹⁵ A youngster's heart is filled with
   foolishness,
   but physical discipline will drive it far
   away.

¹⁶ A person who gets ahead by oppressing
   the poor
   or by showering gifts on the rich will
   end in poverty.

Sayings of the Wise

¹⁷ Listen to the words of the wise;
   apply your heart to my
   instruction.

¹⁸ For it is good to keep these sayings in
   your heart
   and always ready on your lips.

¹⁹ I am teaching you today—yes, you—
   so you will trust in the LORD.

²⁰ I have written thirty sayings* for you,
   filled with advice and knowledge.

²¹ In this way, you may know the truth
   and take an accurate report to those
   who sent you.

²² Don't rob the poor just because you
   can,
   or exploit the needy in court.

²³ For the LORD is their defender.
   He will ruin anyone who ruins
   them.

²⁴ Don't befriend angry people
   or associate with hot-tempered
   people,

²⁵ or you will learn to be like them
   and endanger your soul.

²⁶ Don't agree to guarantee another
   person's debt
   or put up security for someone else.

²⁷ If you can't pay it,
   even your bed will be snatched from
   under you.

²⁸ Don't cheat your neighbor by moving
   the ancient boundary markers
   set up by previous generations.

²⁹ Do you see any truly competent
   workers?
   They will serve kings
   rather than working for ordinary
   people.

23

¹ While dining with a ruler,
   pay attention to what is put
   before you.

² If you are a big eater,
   put a knife to your throat;

³ don't desire all the delicacies,
   for he might be trying to trick you.

⁴ Don't wear yourself out trying to get
   rich.
   Be wise enough to know when to quit.

⁵ In the blink of an eye wealth disappears,
   for it will sprout wings
   and fly away like an eagle.

⁶ Don't eat with people who are stingy;
   don't desire their delicacies.

⁷ They are always thinking about how
   much it costs.*
   "Eat and drink," they say, but they
   don't mean it.

⁸ You will throw up what little you've
   eaten,
   and your compliments will be wasted.

⁹ Don't waste your breath on fools,
   for they will despise the wisest advice.

¹⁰ Don't cheat your neighbor by moving
   the ancient boundary markers;
   don't take the land of defenseless
   orphans.

22:20 Or *excellent sayings;* the meaning of the Hebrew is uncertain.   **23:7** The meaning of the Hebrew is uncertain.

¹¹ For their Redeemer* is strong;
    he himself will bring their charges
        against you.

¹² Commit yourself to instruction;
    listen carefully to words of knowledge.

¹³ Don't fail to discipline your children.
    They won't die if you spank them.
¹⁴ Physical discipline
    may well save them from death.*

¹⁵ My child,* if your heart is wise,
    my own heart will rejoice!
¹⁶ Everything in me will celebrate
    when you speak what is right.

¹⁷ Don't envy sinners,
    but always continue to fear the LORD.
¹⁸ You will be rewarded for this;
    your hope will not be disappointed.

¹⁹ My child, listen and be wise:
    Keep your heart on the right course.
²⁰ Do not carouse with drunkards
    or feast with gluttons,
²¹ for they are on their way to poverty,
    and too much sleep clothes them in
        rags.

²² Listen to your father, who gave you life,
    and don't despise your mother when
        she is old.
²³ Get the truth and never sell it;
    also get wisdom, discipline, and good
        judgment.
²⁴ The father of godly children has cause
    for joy.
    What a pleasure to have children who
        are wise.*
²⁵ So give your father and mother joy!
    May she who gave you birth be happy.

²⁶ O my son, give me your heart.
    May your eyes take delight in
        following my ways.
²⁷ A prostitute is a dangerous trap;
    a promiscuous woman is as dangerous
        as falling into a narrow well.
²⁸ She hides and waits like a robber,
    eager to make more men unfaithful.

²⁹ Who has anguish? Who has sorrow?
    Who is always fighting? Who is always
        complaining?

Who has unnecessary bruises? Who
    has bloodshot eyes?
³⁰ It is the one who spends long hours in
    the taverns,
    trying out new drinks.
³¹ Don't gaze at the wine, seeing how red
    it is,
    how it sparkles in the cup, how
        smoothly it goes down.
³² For in the end it bites like a poisonous
    snake;
    it stings like a viper.
³³ You will see hallucinations,
    and you will say crazy things.
³⁴ You will stagger like a sailor tossed at sea,
    clinging to a swaying mast.
³⁵ And you will say, "They hit me, but I
    didn't feel it.
    I didn't even know it when they beat
        me up.
    When will I wake up
        so I can look for another drink?"

24

¹ Don't envy evil people
    or desire their company.
² For their hearts plot violence,
    and their words always stir up trouble.

³ A house is built by wisdom
    and becomes strong through good
        sense.
⁴ Through knowledge its rooms are filled
    with all sorts of precious riches and
        valuables.

⁵ The wise are mightier than the strong,*
    and those with knowledge grow
        stronger and stronger.
⁶ So don't go to war without wise guidance;
    victory depends on having many
        advisers.

⁷ Wisdom is too lofty for fools.
    Among leaders at the city gate, they
        have nothing to say.

⁸ A person who plans evil
    will get a reputation as a troublemaker.
⁹ The schemes of a fool are sinful;
    everyone detests a mocker.

¹⁰ If you fail under pressure,
    your strength is too small.

23:11 Or *redeemer.*   **23:14** Hebrew *from Sheol.*   **23:15** Hebrew *My son;* also in 23:19.   **23:24** Hebrew *to have a wise son.*   **24:5** As in Greek
version; Hebrew reads *A wise man is strength.*

¹¹ Rescue those who are unjustly sentenced
    to die;
  save them as they stagger to their
    death.
¹² Don't excuse yourself by saying, "Look,
    we didn't know."
  For God understands all hearts, and
    he sees you.
  He who guards your soul knows you
    knew.
  He will repay all people as their
    actions deserve.

¹³ My child,* eat honey, for it is good,
  and the honeycomb is sweet to the
    taste.
¹⁴ In the same way, wisdom is sweet to
    your soul.
  If you find it, you will have a bright
    future,
  and your hopes will not be cut short.

¹⁵ Don't wait in ambush at the home of the
    godly,
  and don't raid the house where the
    godly live.
¹⁶ The godly may trip seven times, but they
    will get up again.
  But one disaster is enough to
    overthrow the wicked.

¹⁷ Don't rejoice when your enemies fall;
  don't be happy when they stumble.
¹⁸ For the LORD will be displeased with you
  and will turn his anger away from
    them.

¹⁹ Don't fret because of evildoers;
  don't envy the wicked.
²⁰ For evil people have no future;
  the light of the wicked will be snuffed
    out.

²¹ My child, fear the LORD and the king.
  Don't associate with rebels,
²²   for disaster will hit them suddenly.
  Who knows what punishment will come
    from the LORD and the king?

More Sayings of the Wise

²³ Here are some further sayings of the wise:

  It is wrong to show favoritism when
    passing judgment.

²⁴ A judge who says to the wicked, "You are
    innocent,"
  will be cursed by many people and
    denounced by the nations.
²⁵ But it will go well for those who convict
    the guilty;
  rich blessings will be showered on
    them.

²⁶ An honest answer
  is like a kiss of friendship.

²⁷ Do your planning and prepare your
    fields
  before building your house.

²⁸ Don't testify against your neighbors
    without cause;
  don't lie about them.
²⁹ And don't say, "Now I can pay them back
    for what they've done to me!
  I'll get even with them!"

³⁰ I walked by the field of a lazy person,
  the vineyard of one with no common
    sense.
³¹ I saw that it was overgrown with
    nettles.
  It was covered with weeds,
  and its walls were broken down.
³² Then, as I looked and thought about it,
  I learned this lesson:
³³ A little extra sleep, a little more slumber,
  a little folding of the hands to rest—
³⁴ then poverty will pounce on you like a
    bandit;
  scarcity will attack you like an armed
    robber.

25 More Proverbs of Solomon

These are more proverbs of Solomon, collected by the advisers of King Hezekiah of Judah.

² It is God's privilege to conceal things
  and the king's privilege to discover
    them.

³ No one can comprehend the height of
    heaven, the depth of the earth,
  or all that goes on in the king's mind!

⁴ Remove the impurities from silver,
  and the sterling will be ready for the
    silversmith.

24:13 Hebrew *My son;* also in 24:21.

⁵ Remove the wicked from the king's court,
    and his reign will be made secure by justice.

⁶ Don't demand an audience with the king
    or push for a place among the great.
⁷ It's better to wait for an invitation to the head table
    than to be sent away in public disgrace.

Just because you've seen something,
⁸   don't be in a hurry to go to court.
For what will you do in the end
    if your neighbor deals you a shameful defeat?

⁹ When arguing with your neighbor,
    don't betray another person's secret.
¹⁰ Others may accuse you of gossip,
    and you will never regain your good reputation.

¹¹ Timely advice is lovely,
    like golden apples in a silver basket.

¹² To one who listens, valid criticism
    is like a gold earring or other gold jewelry.

¹³ Trustworthy messengers refresh like snow in summer.
    They revive the spirit of their employer.

¹⁴ A person who promises a gift but doesn't give it
    is like clouds and wind that bring no rain.

¹⁵ Patience can persuade a prince,
    and soft speech can break bones.

¹⁶ Do you like honey?
    Don't eat too much, or it will make you sick!

¹⁷ Don't visit your neighbors too often,
    or you will wear out your welcome.

¹⁸ Telling lies about others
    is as harmful as hitting them with an ax,
wounding them with a sword,
    or shooting them with a sharp arrow.

¹⁹ Putting confidence in an unreliable person in times of trouble
    is like chewing with a broken tooth or walking on a lame foot.

²⁰ Singing cheerful songs to a person with a heavy heart
    is like taking someone's coat in cold weather
    or pouring vinegar in a wound.*

²¹ If your enemies are hungry, give them food to eat.
    If they are thirsty, give them water to drink.
²² You will heap burning coals of shame on their heads,
    and the LORD will reward you.

²³ As surely as a north wind brings rain,
    so a gossiping tongue causes anger!

²⁴ It's better to live alone in the corner of an attic
    than with a quarrelsome wife in a lovely home.

²⁵ Good news from far away
    is like cold water to the thirsty.

²⁶ If the godly give in to the wicked,
    it's like polluting a fountain or muddying a spring.

²⁷ It's not good to eat too much honey,
    and it's not good to seek honors for yourself.

²⁸ A person without self-control
    is like a city with broken-down walls.

26

¹ Honor is no more associated with fools
    than snow with summer or rain with harvest.

² Like a fluttering sparrow or a darting swallow,
    an undeserved curse will not land on its intended victim.

³ Guide a horse with a whip, a donkey with a bridle,
    and a fool with a rod to his back!

⁴ Don't answer the foolish arguments of fools,

25:20 As in Greek version; Hebrew reads *pouring vinegar on soda.*

or you will become as foolish as they are.

5 Be sure to answer the foolish arguments of fools,
or they will become wise in their own estimation.

6 Trusting a fool to convey a message
is like cutting off one's feet or drinking poison!

7 A proverb in the mouth of a fool
is as useless as a paralyzed leg.

8 Honoring a fool
is as foolish as tying a stone to a slingshot.

9 A proverb in the mouth of a fool
is like a thorny branch brandished by a drunk.

10 An employer who hires a fool or a bystander
is like an archer who shoots at random.

11 As a dog returns to its vomit,
so a fool repeats his foolishness.

12 There is more hope for fools
than for people who think they are wise.

13 The lazy person claims, "There's a lion on the road!
Yes, I'm sure there's a lion out there!"

14 As a door swings back and forth on its hinges,
so the lazy person turns over in bed.

15 Lazy people take food in their hand
but don't even lift it to their mouth.

16 Lazy people consider themselves smarter
than seven wise counselors.

17 Interfering in someone else's argument
is as foolish as yanking a dog's ears.

18 Just as damaging
as a madman shooting a deadly weapon
19 is someone who lies to a friend
and then says, "I was only joking."

20 Fire goes out without wood,
and quarrels disappear when gossip stops.

21 A quarrelsome person starts fights
as easily as hot embers light charcoal
or fire lights wood.

22 Rumors are dainty morsels
that sink deep into one's heart.

23 Smooth* words may hide a wicked heart,
just as a pretty glaze covers a clay pot.

24 People may cover their hatred with pleasant words,
but they're deceiving you.
25 They pretend to be kind, but don't believe them.
Their hearts are full of many evils.*
26 While their hatred may be concealed by trickery,
their wrongdoing will be exposed in public.

27 If you set a trap for others,
you will get caught in it yourself.
If you roll a boulder down on others,
it will crush you instead.

28 A lying tongue hates its victims,
and flattering words cause ruin.

27 1 Don't brag about tomorrow,
since you don't know what the day will bring.

2 Let someone else praise you, not your own mouth—
a stranger, not your own lips.

3 A stone is heavy and sand is weighty,
but the resentment caused by a fool is even heavier.

4 Anger is cruel, and wrath is like a flood,
but jealousy is even more dangerous.

5 An open rebuke
is better than hidden love!

6 Wounds from a sincere friend
are better than many kisses from an enemy.

7 A person who is full refuses honey,
but even bitter food tastes sweet to the hungry.

26:23 As in Greek version; Hebrew reads *Burning.*   26:25 Hebrew *seven evils.*

8 A person who strays from home
　　is like a bird that strays from its nest.

9 The heartfelt counsel of a friend
　　is as sweet as perfume and incense.

10 Never abandon a friend—
　　either yours or your father's.
　When disaster strikes, you won't have to
　　ask your brother for assistance.
　　It's better to go to a neighbor than to a
　　brother who lives far away.

11 Be wise, my child,* and make my heart
　　glad.
　　Then I will be able to answer my critics.

12 A prudent person foresees danger and
　　takes precautions.
　　The simpleton goes blindly on and
　　suffers the consequences.

13 Get security from someone who
　　guarantees a stranger's debt.
　　Get a deposit if he does it for
　　foreigners.*

14 A loud and cheerful greeting early in the
　　morning
　　will be taken as a curse!

15 A quarrelsome wife is as annoying
　　as constant dripping on a rainy day.

16 Stopping her complaints is like trying to
　　stop the wind
　　or trying to hold something with
　　greased hands.

17 As iron sharpens iron,
　　so a friend sharpens a friend.

18 As workers who tend a fig tree are
　　allowed to eat the fruit,
　　so workers who protect their
　　employer's interests will be
　　rewarded.

19 As a face is reflected in water,
　　so the heart reflects the real person.

20 Just as Death and Destruction* are never
　　satisfied,
　　so human desire is never satisfied.

21 Fire tests the purity of silver and gold,
　　but a person is tested by being
　　praised.*

22 You cannot separate fools from their
　　foolishness,
　　even though you grind them like grain
　　with mortar and pestle.

23 Know the state of your flocks,
　　and put your heart into caring for your
　　herds,

24 for riches don't last forever,
　　and the crown might not be passed to
　　the next generation.

25 After the hay is harvested and the new
　　crop appears
　　and the mountain grasses are
　　gathered in,

26 your sheep will provide wool for
　　clothing,
　　and your goats will provide the price
　　of a field.

27 And you will have enough goats' milk for
　　yourself,
　　your family, and your servant girls.

28

1 The wicked run away when no one
　　is chasing them,
　but the godly are as bold as lions.

2 When there is moral rot within a nation,
　　its government topples easily.
　　But wise and knowledgeable leaders
　　bring stability.

3 A poor person who oppresses the poor
　　is like a pounding rain that destroys
　　the crops.

4 To reject the law is to praise the
　　wicked;
　　to obey the law is to fight them.

5 Evil people don't understand justice,
　　but those who follow the LORD
　　understand completely.

6 Better to be poor and honest
　　than to be dishonest and rich.

7 Young people who obey the law are wise;
　　those with wild friends bring shame to
　　their parents.*

8 Income from charging high interest
　　rates
　　will end up in the pocket of someone
　　who is kind to the poor.

27:11 Hebrew my son. 　27:13 As in Greek and Latin versions (see also 20:16); Hebrew reads for a promiscuous woman. 　27:20 Hebrew Sheol and Abaddon. 　27:21 Or by flattery. 　28:7 Hebrew their father.

⁹ God detests the prayers
   of a person who ignores the law.

¹⁰ Those who lead good people along an
   evil path
   will fall into their own trap,
   but the honest will inherit good
   things.

¹¹ Rich people may think they are wise,
   but a poor person with discernment
   can see right through them.

¹² When the godly succeed, everyone is glad.
   When the wicked take charge, people
   go into hiding.

¹³ People who conceal their sins will not
   prosper,
   but if they confess and turn from
   them, they will receive mercy.

¹⁴ Blessed are those who fear to do wrong,*
   but the stubborn are headed for
   serious trouble.

Q&A — Spiritual and Material Simplicity

PROVERBS 28:6-27

Does the amount of stuff I own or the balance in my checkbook really matter? After all, isn't simplicity essentially a matter of the heart?

In the middle of Jesus' teachings about how we are to relate to money and possessions comes this dramatic warning: "No one can serve two masters. . . . You cannot serve both God and money" (Matthew 6:24).

In different ages and in different spiritual traditions, Christians have offered different answers to the problem of money and material possessions. Some have freed themselves through vows of extreme poverty by giving it all away and then living on the grace of God and the generosity of other Christians. Others have emphasized personal industriousness and the responsible management of its rewards. And still others have advocated striving for a "simple lifestyle."

We must realize that physical solutions (such as giving it away, managing it well, or simplifying) are only *partial* solutions. But so are solely spiritual solutions—such as practicing "simplicity of heart" without recognizing the very real spiritual danger of accumulating wealth and possessions. Those who affect an inner attitude of detachment—claiming to be beyond money's power while simultaneously embracing our culture's "normal" lifestyle of consumerism, materialism, and the drive for more—are simply fooling themselves. Money and wealth—this is a spiritual power and a physical reality. It must be dealt with on both the physical *and* spiritual levels.

—David Neff

For more on simplicity, see reading at Ecclesiastes 2:18-26.

28:14 Or *those who fear the LORD;* Hebrew reads *those who fear.*

15 A wicked ruler is as dangerous to the
poor
as a roaring lion or an attacking bear.

16 A ruler with no understanding will
oppress his people,
but one who hates corruption will
have a long life.

17 A murderer's tormented conscience will
drive him into the grave.
Don't protect him!

18 The blameless will be rescued from
harm,
but the crooked will be suddenly
destroyed.

19 A hard worker has plenty of food,
but a person who chases fantasies
ends up in poverty.

20 The trustworthy person will get a rich
reward,
but a person who wants quick riches
will get into trouble.

21 Showing partiality is never good,
yet some will do wrong for a mere
piece of bread.

22 Greedy people try to get rich quick
but don't realize they're headed for
poverty.

23 In the end, people appreciate honest
criticism
far more than flattery.

24 Anyone who steals from his father and
mother
and says, "What's wrong with that?"
is no better than a murderer.

25 Greed causes fighting;
trusting the LORD leads to
prosperity.

26 Those who trust their own insight are
foolish,
but anyone who walks in wisdom is
safe.

27 Whoever gives to the poor will lack
nothing,
but those who close their eyes to
poverty will be cursed.

28 When the wicked take charge, people go
into hiding.
When the wicked meet disaster, the
godly flourish.

29 1 Whoever stubbornly refuses to
accept criticism
will suddenly be destroyed beyond
recovery.

2 When the godly are in authority, the
people rejoice.
But when the wicked are in power,
they groan.

3 The man who loves wisdom brings joy to
his father,
but if he hangs around with
prostitutes, his wealth is wasted.

4 A just king gives stability to his nation,
but one who demands bribes
destroys it.

5 To flatter friends
is to lay a trap for their feet.

6 Evil people are trapped by sin,
but the righteous escape, shouting for
joy.

7 The godly care about the rights of the
poor;
the wicked don't care at all.

8 Mockers can get a whole town agitated,
but the wise will calm anger.

9 If a wise person takes a fool to court,
there will be ranting and ridicule but
no satisfaction.

10 The bloodthirsty hate blameless people,
but the upright seek to help them.*

11 Fools vent their anger,
but the wise quietly hold it back.

12 If a ruler pays attention to liars,
all his advisers will be wicked.

13 The poor and the oppressor have this in
common—
the LORD gives sight to the eyes of both.

14 If a king judges the poor fairly,
his throne will last forever.

29:10 Or The bloodthirsty hate blameless people, / and they seek to kill the upright; Hebrew reads The bloodthirsty hate blameless people; / as for the upright, they seek their life.

¹⁵ To discipline a child produces
 wisdom,
 but a mother is disgraced by an
 undisciplined child.

¹⁶ When the wicked are in authority, sin
 flourishes,
 but the godly will live to see their
 downfall.

¹⁷ Discipline your children, and they will
 give you peace of mind
 and will make your heart glad.

¹⁸ When people do not accept divine
 guidance, they run wild.
 But whoever obeys the law is joyful.

¹⁹ Words alone will not discipline a
 servant;
 the words may be understood, but
 they are not heeded.

²⁰ There is more hope for a fool
 than for someone who speaks without
 thinking.

²¹ A servant pampered from childhood
 will become a rebel.

²² An angry person starts fights;
 a hot-tempered person commits all
 kinds of sin.

²³ Pride ends in humiliation,
 while humility brings honor.

²⁴ If you assist a thief, you only hurt
 yourself.
 You are sworn to tell the truth, but
 you dare not testify.

²⁵ Fearing people is a dangerous trap,
 but trusting the LORD means safety.

²⁶ Many seek the ruler's favor,
 but justice comes from the LORD.

²⁷ The righteous despise the unjust;
 the wicked despise the godly.

30 The Sayings of Agur

The sayings of Agur son of Jakeh
contain this message.*

I am weary, O God;
 I am weary and worn out, O God.*

² I am too stupid to be human,
 and I lack common sense.

³ I have not mastered human wisdom,
 nor do I know the Holy One.

⁴ Who but God goes up to heaven and
 comes back down?
 Who holds the wind in his fists?
 Who wraps up the oceans in his cloak?
 Who has created the whole wide
 world?
 What is his name—and his son's name?
 Tell me if you know!

⁵ Every word of God proves true.
 He is a shield to all who come to him
 for protection.

⁶ Do not add to his words,
 or he may rebuke you and expose you
 as a liar.

⁷ O God, I beg two favors from you;
 let me have them before I die.

⁸ First, help me never to tell a lie.
 Second, give me neither poverty nor
 riches!
 Give me just enough to satisfy my
 needs.

⁹ For if I grow rich, I may deny you and
 say, "Who is the LORD?"
 And if I am too poor, I may steal and
 thus insult God's holy name.

¹⁰ Never slander a worker to the employer,
 or the person will curse you, and you
 will pay for it.

¹¹ Some people curse their father
 and do not thank their mother.

¹² They are pure in their own eyes,
 but they are filthy and unwashed.

¹³ They look proudly around,
 casting disdainful glances.

¹⁴ They have teeth like swords
 and fangs like knives.
 They devour the poor from the earth
 and the needy from among humanity.

¹⁵ The leech has two suckers
 that cry out, "More, more!"*

There are three things that are never
 satisfied—
 no, four that never say, "Enough!":

30:1a Or son of Jakeh from Massa; or son of Jakeh, an oracle.   **30:1b** The Hebrew can also be translated The man declares this to Ithiel, / to Ithiel and to Ucal.   **30:15** Hebrew two daughters who cry out, "Give, give!"

¹⁶ the grave,*
    the barren womb,
    the thirsty desert,
    the blazing fire.

¹⁷ The eye that mocks a father
    and despises a mother's instructions
  will be plucked out by ravens of the
      valley
    and eaten by vultures.

¹⁸ There are three things that amaze me—
    no, four things that I don't understand:
¹⁹ how an eagle glides through the sky,
    how a snake slithers on a rock,
    how a ship navigates the ocean,
    how a man loves a woman.

²⁰ An adulterous woman consumes a man,
    then wipes her mouth and says,
      "What's wrong with that?"

Q&A { The Prescription for Pride: Service }

PROVERBS 29:23

I struggle with pride—and I am trying to overcome it. What can I do?

It is important to distinguish "training" from "trying." I might *try* very hard to win a marathon race, but if I have not trained, I will not even finish, not to mention win. On the day of the race, no amount of trying will make up for the failure to train. It is the *training* that will enable me to participate effectively in the race. The same is true in the spiritual life.

I can never defeat pride by "trying." Direct assault against pride will only make me proud of my humility! No, I must train. But what do I do?

Well, as I read the great writers on the soul—Saint Benedict's "Twelve Steps of Humility," for example—I discover that they call me to deal with pride by training in service. Why? Because service takes us through the many little deaths of going beyond ourselves. A mother, for example, dies to her desire to watch a favorite TV show in order to play with her children and read to them before bed. Or a husband dies to a promotion that would mean relocating so that his wife can continue to advance in her chosen vocation.

These are little deaths, to be sure. But each one takes us beyond ourselves, and God uses these simple acts of service to work a miracle in us. "Me" and "mine" give way to "we" and "ours." We come to see ourselves as part of a whole. The spiritual discipline of service can nurture in us a proper perspective toward others, ourselves, and God.

—*Richard J. Foster*

For more on service, see reading at Matthew 13:33-35, 44-46.

30:16 Hebrew *Sheol.*

21 There are three things that make the
    earth tremble—
    no, four it cannot endure:
22 a slave who becomes a king,
    an overbearing fool who prospers,
23   a bitter woman who finally gets a
    husband,
    a servant girl who supplants her
    mistress.

24 There are four things on earth that are
    small but unusually wise:
25 Ants—they aren't strong,
    but they store up food all summer.
26 Hyraxes*—they aren't powerful,
    but they make their homes among the
    rocks.
27 Locusts—they have no king,
    but they march in formation.
28 Lizards—they are easy to catch,
    but they are found even in kings'
    palaces.

29 There are three things that walk with
    stately stride—
    no, four that strut about:
30 the lion, king of animals, who won't turn
    aside for anything,
31   the strutting rooster,
    the male goat,
    a king as he leads his army.

32 If you have been a fool by being proud or
    plotting evil,
    cover your mouth in shame.

33 As the beating of cream yields butter
    and striking the nose causes bleeding,
    so stirring up anger causes quarrels.

31 The Sayings of King Lemuel

The sayings of King Lemuel contain
this message,* which his mother taught him.

2 O my son, O son of my womb,
    O son of my vows,
3 do not waste your strength on women,
    on those who ruin kings.

4 It is not for kings, O Lemuel, to guzzle
    wine.
    Rulers should not crave alcohol.
5 For if they drink, they may forget the law
    and not give justice to the oppressed.

6 Alcohol is for the dying,
    and wine for those in bitter distress.
7 Let them drink to forget their poverty
    and remember their troubles no more.

8 Speak up for those who cannot speak for
    themselves;
    ensure justice for those being crushed.
9 Yes, speak up for the poor and helpless,
    and see that they get justice.

A Wife of Noble Character

10*Who can find a virtuous and capable
    wife?
    She is more precious than rubies.
11 Her husband can trust her,
    and she will greatly enrich his life.
12 She brings him good, not harm,
    all the days of her life.

13 She finds wool and flax
    and busily spins it.
14 She is like a merchant's ship,
    bringing her food from afar.
15 She gets up before dawn to prepare
    breakfast for her household
    and plan the day's work for her servant
    girls.

16 She goes to inspect a field and buys it;
    with her earnings she plants a vineyard.
17 She is energetic and strong,
    a hard worker.
18 She makes sure her dealings are profitable;
    her lamp burns late into the night.

19 Her hands are busy spinning thread,
    her fingers twisting fiber.
20 She extends a helping hand to the poor
    and opens her arms to the needy.
21 She has no fear of winter for her
    household,
    for everyone has warm* clothes.

22 She makes her own bedspreads.
    She dresses in fine linen and purple
    gowns.
23 Her husband is well known at the city
    gates,
    where he sits with the other civic
    leaders.
24 She makes belted linen garments
    and sashes to sell to the merchants.

30:26 Or Coneys, or Rock badgers. **31:1** Or of Lemuel, king of Massa; or of King Lemuel, an oracle. **31:10** Verses 10-31 comprise a Hebrew acrostic poem; each verse begins with a successive letter of the Hebrew alphabet. **31:21** As in Greek and Latin versions; Hebrew reads scarlet.

25 She is clothed with strength and dignity,
and she laughs without fear of the
future.
26 When she speaks, her words are wise,
and she gives instructions with
kindness.
27 She carefully watches everything in her
household
and suffers nothing from laziness.
28 Her children stand and bless her.
Her husband praises her:

29 "There are many virtuous and capable
women in the world,
but you surpass them all!"

30 Charm is deceptive, and beauty does not
last;
but a woman who fears the LORD will
be greatly praised.
31 Reward her for all she has
done.
Let her deeds publicly declare her
praise.

A Woman of Virtue: Living within Healthy Limits

PROVERBS 31:10-31

Proverbs 31 presents a daunting example of a woman of character. Her life reflects the fruit and gifts of God's Spirit, which is to say she is praised not just for her doing and producing, but also for her being. This woman's life is not driven by success or the need to please, but by virtue. She is trustworthy, generous, caring, prepared, and remarkably industrious.

It's easy to read this woman's accomplishments and feel intimidated, perhaps even disheartened. But before getting discouraged about how unlike the Proverbs 31 woman you are, remember that this woman lived millennia ago when the world ran by a natural daily rhythm. Seasons determined what food was available. Market days coincided with harvests, caravans, and ships that were in port. People traveled by foot, and Sunday was a rest day. This woman didn't own a watch or live by a 24/7 pace. When it was dark, everyone went to bed. Though verse 15 describes her as an early riser, we can assume she still got plenty of rest. After all, oil lamps hardly supplied the kind of light that allowed for working all night long. We misunderstand the passage if we think she's trying to "do it all." Busyness was not the Proverbs 31 woman's badge of honor. For all her doing, she lived a life within healthy rhythms and limits.

Our overoptioned world hoodwinks us into thinking we can go everywhere, do everything, know everyone, and have it all. But every life has limits. Saying yes to one thing inevitably means we're saying no to something else—to family time, space for quietness with God, and rest.

Living in sanity and spiritual health isn't simply about industry; it's about honoring our limits and embracing healthy margins. Without space for rest, recreation, hobbies, love making, and authentic communication, we will remain human doings rather than human beings.

God has given us enough time in each day to be who he created us to be and do what he wants us to do. The Proverbs 31 woman lived a *full* life, but a life within limits. God was honored—and so was she.

—Adele Ahlberg Calhoun

For more on Sabbath and rest, see reading at Jeremiah 6:16.

Introduction to

Ecclesiastes

Background

The title of Ecclesiastes is derived from the Greek word *ekklesia* ("assembly, congregation, church") and means "preacher." The Hebrew title, *Qoheleth,* has the same meaning.

King Solomon is the presumed author. He is a man who has it all: wisdom, wealth, accomplishment, and possessions. Yet he determines that all of these are meaningless—"completely meaningless!" (1:2)—apart from knowing God.

Message

Ecclesiastes shows the emptiness of life apart from a relationship with God. *Meaningless* is a key word in Ecclesiastes. The author, who is now an old man, once sought pleasure through his wealth, wives, idolatry, and position. He has come to the conclusion that God has placed a hunger in us to know who we are and where we fit in the universe.

Time

The Book of Ecclesiastes was probably written circa 935 B.C.

Outline

Ecclesiastes

1 These are the words of the Teacher,* King David's son, who ruled in Jerusalem.

Everything Is Meaningless

²"Everything is meaningless," says the Teacher, "completely meaningless!"

³What do people get for all their hard work under the sun? ⁴Generations come and generations go, but the earth never changes. ⁵The sun rises and the sun sets, then hurries around to rise again. ⁶The wind blows south, and then turns north. Around and around it goes, blowing in circles. ⁷Rivers run into the sea, but the sea is never full. Then the water returns again to the rivers and flows out again to the sea. ⁸Everything is wearisome beyond description. No matter how much we see, we are never satisfied. No matter how much we hear, we are not content.

⁹History merely repeats itself. It has all been done before. Nothing under the sun is truly new. ¹⁰Sometimes people say, "Here is something new!" But actually it is old; nothing is ever truly new. ¹¹We don't remember what happened in the past, and in future generations, no one will remember what we are doing now.

The Teacher Speaks: The Futility of Wisdom

¹²I, the Teacher, was king of Israel, and I lived in Jerusalem. ¹³I devoted myself to search for understanding and to explore by wisdom everything being done under heaven. I soon discovered that God has dealt a tragic existence to the human race. ¹⁴I observed everything going on under the sun, and really, it is all meaningless—like chasing the wind.

¹⁵ What is wrong cannot be made right.
    What is missing cannot be recovered.

¹⁶I said to myself, "Look, I am wiser than any of the kings who ruled in Jerusalem before me. I have greater wisdom and knowledge than any of them." ¹⁷So I set out to learn everything from wisdom to madness and folly. But I learned firsthand that pursuing all this is like chasing the wind.

¹⁸ The greater my wisdom, the greater my grief.
    To increase knowledge only increases sorrow.

2 The Futility of Pleasure

I said to myself, "Come on, let's try pleasure. Let's look for the 'good things' in life." But I found that this, too, was meaningless. ²So I said, "Laughter is silly. What good does it do to seek pleasure?" ³After much thought, I decided to cheer myself with wine. And while still seeking wisdom, I clutched at foolishness. In this way, I tried to experience the only happiness most people find during their brief life in this world.

⁴I also tried to find meaning by building huge homes for myself and by

---

1:1 Hebrew *Qoheleth*; this term is rendered "the Teacher" throughout this book.

planting beautiful vineyards. [5] I made gardens and parks, filling them with all kinds of fruit trees. [6] I built reservoirs to collect the water to irrigate my many flourishing groves. [7] I bought slaves, both men and women, and others were born into my household. I also owned large herds and flocks, more than any of the kings who had lived in Jerusalem before me. [8] I collected great sums of silver and gold, the treasure of many kings and provinces. I hired wonderful singers, both men and women, and had many beautiful concubines. I had everything a man could desire!

[9] So I became greater than all who had lived in Jerusalem before me, and my wisdom never failed me. [10] Anything I wanted, I would take. I denied myself no pleasure. I even found great pleasure in hard work, a reward for all my labors. [11] But as I looked at everything I had worked so hard to accomplish, it was all so meaningless—like chasing the wind. There was nothing really worthwhile anywhere.

The Wise and the Foolish

[12] So I decided to compare wisdom with foolishness and madness (for who can do this better than I, the king?*). [13] I thought, "Wisdom is better than foolishness, just as light is better than darkness. [14] For the wise can see where they are going, but fools walk in the dark." Yet I saw that the wise and the foolish share the same fate. [15] Both will die. So I said to myself, "Since I will end up the same as the fool, what's the value of all my wisdom? This is all so meaningless!" [16] For the wise and the foolish both die. The wise will not be remembered any longer than the fool. In the days to come, both will be forgotten.

[17] So I came to hate life because everything done here under the sun is so troubling. Everything is meaningless—like chasing the wind.

The Futility of Work

[18] I came to hate all my hard work here on earth, for I must leave to others everything I have earned. [19] And who can tell whether my successors will be wise or foolish? Yet

they will control everything I have gained by my skill and hard work under the sun. How meaningless! [20] So I gave up in despair, questioning the value of all my hard work in this world.

[21] Some people work wisely with knowledge and skill, then must leave the fruit of their efforts to someone who hasn't worked for it. This, too, is meaningless, a great tragedy. [22] So what do people get in this life for all their hard work and anxiety? [23] Their days of labor are filled with pain and grief; even at night their minds cannot rest. It is all meaningless.

[24] So I decided there is nothing better than to enjoy food and drink and to find satisfaction in work. Then I realized that these pleasures are from the hand of God. [25] For who can eat or enjoy anything apart from him?* [26] God gives wisdom, knowledge, and joy to those who please him. But if a sinner becomes wealthy, God takes the wealth away and gives it to those who please him. This, too, is meaningless—like chasing the wind.

A Time for Everything

3 [1] For everything there is a season,
  a time for every activity under heaven.

[2] A time to be born and a time to die.
  A time to plant and a time to harvest.
[3] A time to kill and a time to heal.
  A time to tear down and a time to
  build up.
[4] A time to cry and a time to laugh.
  A time to grieve and a time to dance.
[5] A time to scatter stones and a time to
  gather stones.
  A time to embrace and a time to turn
  away.
[6] A time to search and a time to quit
  searching.
  A time to keep and a time to throw
  away.
[7] A time to tear and a time to mend.
  A time to be quiet and a time to speak.
[8] A time to love and a time to hate.
  A time for war and a time for peace.

[9] What do people really get for all their hard work? [10] I have seen the burden God has placed on us all. [11] Yet God has made

---

2:12 The meaning of the Hebrew is uncertain.   **2:25** As in Greek and Syriac versions; Hebrew reads *apart from me*?

The Rhythm of Silence and Speech

ECCLESIASTES 3:1-8

Alternating silence and speech is the very rhythm of God, as old and deep in the nature of things as creation itself. According to Genesis, God breaks the cosmic silence with a creative word, but he does this only during the days. At nightfall and on the Sabbath, God falls silent. Correspondingly, there is for us, the creatures of God, a natural rhythm not only of work and rest but also of sound and silence. "For everything there is a season," says the author of Ecclesiastes, "a time to be quiet and a time to speak" (3:1, 7).

But who knows how to tell time in this matter? Who knows when to speak up and when to keep still? Who knows when silence is golden and when it is lazy or even cowardly? The wise know these things. Wise people discern the deep grain and pattern of God's world and try to live in ways that go with the grain. These are people whose speech emerges from, and then reenters, a thoughtful and disciplined silence. These are people whose silence offers a roomy and welcoming harbor for the speech of others.

Saints listen for the sounds and silences of God. They quiet themselves into a kind of absorbency, a readiness to hear the Word of God and also the voice of God and even some of the silences of God. The silences of God—mysterious, exasperating, consoling, pregnant with meaning—require our trust at least as much as does the Word of God. God does not talk all the time, and God's silence is as emphatic as his speech.

To be a faithful creature of God is to learn something of God's rhythm of silence and sound and silence, to respect and trust it, and then to imitate God by speaking and listening from the context that is as old as the world.

—*Cornelius Plantinga, Jr.*

For more on silence, see reading at Luke 8:40-48.

everything beautiful for its own time. He has planted eternity in the human heart, but even so, people cannot see the whole scope of God's work from beginning to end. [12]So I concluded there is nothing better than to be happy and enjoy ourselves as long as we can. [13]And people should eat and drink and enjoy the fruits of their labor, for these are gifts from God.

[14]And I know that whatever God does is final. Nothing can be added to it or taken from it. God's purpose is that people should fear him. [15]What is happening now has happened before, and what will happen in the future has happened before, because God makes the same things happen over and over again.

The Injustices of Life

[16]I also noticed that under the sun there is evil in the courtroom. Yes, even the courts of law are corrupt! [17]I said to myself, "In due season God will judge everyone, both good and bad, for all their deeds."

[18]I also thought about the human condition—how God proves to people that they are like animals. [19]For people and animals share the same fate—both breathe*

3:19 Or *both have the same spirit.*

Simplicity

On Pace and Perspective

ECCLESIASTES 2:18-26

It's said that "busy" is the new "fine." It's become a positive response to the casual question, "How are you?" We equate being busy with being fulfilled—having a life that bursts with projects and parties, options and obligations. We think that being busy means we're important . . . and being important means we're satisfied.

But the unchecked life of busyness creates a chaotic inner world. We end up living at a breakneck pace, tumbling around like we've been tossed in a clothes dryer, tangled and unsure of our direction.

Life in the clothes dryer gets stifling. We find ourselves rushing from one obligation to the next, only to discover we've outrun our joy. Everything begins to feel like work. Resting makes us anxious, and nothing feels satisfying. We lose the feeling of accomplishment in our work. We forget to celebrate. And we miss sacred moments in our preoccupation with the next thing. As Henri Nouwen noted in *Making All Things New*, "The great paradox of our time is that many of us are busy and bored at the same time. While running from one event to the next, we wonder in our innermost selves if anything is really happening."

When the "innermost self" cannot be ignored, we think about ways to stop the chaos. We wonder if we need to board the next plane to Ireland or quit our jobs or change churches. We remember well-meaning women telling us that life is about "abiding" and "resting" with Christ and feel awash with shame, wondering if we are living with purpose, wondering why "no" seems to have become an unspoken curse word in our vocabulary.

The spiritual discipline of simplicity is important because it's about making peace with our pace and perspective. The simple life isn't about exiting from the complicated world we live in. Scripture certainly acknowledges this reality; Jesus promises to give us rest (Matthew 11:28), but Paul tells us to "run with endurance the race God has set before us" (Hebrews 12:1). Perhaps what we need is not just less to do, but the understanding of *why* we do what we do. If pace is the speed at which we live, then perspective is the engine that fuels our pace. So how do we find a perspective that orders our lives around something beyond the tyranny of the to-do list?

In Ecclesiastes, King Solomon takes a hard look at his perspective on life. After working very hard and finding great pleasure in his work, Solomon becomes disillusioned. He feels the despair of mortality, realizing that he cannot control the ultimate outcomes of his life. "So what do people get in this life for all their hard work and anxiety?" he asks. "Their days of labor are filled with pain and grief; even at night their minds cannot rest" (2:22–23). He then slips in a clue about pace and perspective. Solomon concludes, "There is nothing better than to enjoy food and drink and to *find satisfaction* in work. Then I realized that these pleasures are from the hand of God" (2:24, emphasis added).

How can we find true satisfaction in this life?

Our pace may be sometimes slow, sometimes quick. But that pace can become deliberate and "simple" when our perspective is fixed on the "one thing worth being concerned about" (Luke 10:42): ordering our life around Christ. This inner focus of the soul upon Christ then expresses itself in our outer world and our daily choices. My perspective is concerned with how I live with joy, not what I accomplish. My energies shift toward how I love those I encounter each day, not my to-do list. My life can be complicated and full, but as I seek him God will chart my path and direct me when to stop and rest (Psalm 139:3).

God does not leave us to figure out our pace alone; rather, he invites us to keep checking our perspective. Am I asking God first before I say yes or no? Do I believe that God will provide me with strength to complete the tasks he's given me, even when I feel overwhelmed? Is my pace truly God-driven and not self-driven? In answering these questions with God, we find courage to connect more deeply to the primary fuel that drives our pace.

Life is about both celebration and endurance—about savoring each moment and running the race. There is a time for everything, and checking our perspective allows us to wholeheartedly pursue the "one thing" even as we thrive in many things.

—Nicole Unice

For more on simplicity, see reading at Ecclesiastes 5:10–6:9.

and both must die. So people have no real advantage over the animals. How meaningless! [20]Both go to the same place—they came from dust and they return to dust. [21]For who can prove that the human spirit goes up and the spirit of animals goes down into the earth? [22]So I saw that there is nothing better for people than to be happy in their work. That is why we are here! No one will bring us back from death to enjoy life after we die.

4 Again, I observed all the oppression that takes place under the sun. I saw the tears of the oppressed, with no one to comfort them. The oppressors have great power, and their victims are helpless. [2]So I concluded that the dead are better off than the living. [3]But most fortunate of all are those who are not yet born. For they have not seen all the evil that is done under the sun.

[4]Then I observed that most people are motivated to success because they envy their neighbors. But this, too, is meaningless—like chasing the wind.

[5] "Fools fold their idle hands,
    leading them to ruin."

[6]And yet,

"Better to have one handful with
    quietness
than two handfuls with hard work
    and chasing the wind."

The Advantages of Companionship

[7]I observed yet another example of something meaningless under the sun. [8]This is the case of a man who is all alone, without a child or a brother, yet who works hard to gain as much wealth as he can. But then he asks himself, "Who am I working for? Why am I giving up so much pleasure now?" It is all so meaningless and depressing.

[9]Two people are better off than one, for they can help each other succeed. [10]If one person falls, the other can reach out and help. But someone who falls alone is in real trouble. [11]Likewise, two people lying close together can keep each other warm. But how can one be warm alone? [12]A person standing alone can be attacked and defeated, but two can stand back-to-back and conquer. Three are even better, for a triple-braided cord is not easily broken.

The Futility of Political Power

[13]It is better to be a poor but wise youth than an old and foolish king who refuses all advice. [14]Such a youth could rise from poverty and succeed. He might even become king, though he has been in prison. [15]But then everyone rushes to the side of yet another youth* who replaces him. [16]Endless crowds stand around him,* but then another generation grows up and rejects him, too. So it is all meaningless—like chasing the wind.

5 Approaching God with Care

[1]*As you enter the house of God, keep your ears open and your mouth shut. It is evil to make mindless offerings to God. [2]*Don't make rash promises, and don't be hasty in bringing matters before God. After all, God is in heaven, and you are here on earth. So let your words be few.

[3]Too much activity gives you restless dreams; too many words make you a fool.

[4]When you make a promise to God, don't delay in following through, for God takes no pleasure in fools. Keep all the promises you make to him. [5]It is better to say nothing than to make a promise and not keep it. [6]Don't let your mouth make you sin. And don't defend yourself by telling the Temple messenger that the promise you made was a mistake. That would make God angry, and he might wipe out everything you have achieved.

[7]Talk is cheap, like daydreams and other useless activities. Fear God instead.

The Futility of Wealth

[8]Don't be surprised if you see a poor person being oppressed by the powerful and if justice is being miscarried throughout the land. For every official is under orders from higher up, and matters of justice get lost in red tape and bureaucracy. [9]Even the king milks the land for his own profit!*

[10]Those who love money will never have

4:15 Hebrew *the second youth.* **4:16** Hebrew *There is no end to all the people, to all those who are before them.* **5:1** Verse 5:1 is numbered 4:17 in Hebrew text. **5:2** Verses 5:2-20 are numbered 5:1-19 in Hebrew text. **5:9** The meaning of the Hebrew in verses 8 and 9 is uncertain.

Community

Who's On Your Team?

ECCLESIASTES 4:9–12

I magine yourself kneeling at the blocks, ready to start a relay race. Who's in this relay with you? Who's going to get the baton on your second and third legs? Who's your anchor?

For me it's been many of the wrong people.

I'm in a race against a swift and powerful opponent who knows my weaknesses and strengths and who knows my running mates aren't ready. The second-leg person isn't in proper shape for a race of this magnitude; her faith weakens every time she hits a hurdle. Beaten down by life and marital struggles, my third leg gossips and criticizes to get by; she's not even ready for a jog in the park. My anchor is rooted in the Word, but the Word isn't rooted in her; she's self-righteous, judgmental, and hypocritical. The enemy will catch up with her because of her conduct, attitude, and character.

My team is alarmingly unprepared for victory. So I have to blow the whistle, or I might be forced to forfeit the whole thing.

Part of our journey includes separating from the people, places, or things that hold us back—anything that brings a false sense of happiness, peace, or comfort. Our enemy knows our weaknesses and wants to keep us from finishing "the race God has set before us" (Hebrews 12:1) by surrounding us with those who will drag us down and keep us distracted, living in the past.

Do you feel drained, robbed, or stagnant around those closest to you? If so, they're forfeiting *your* race.

Don't throw them away with last night's garbage, but be courageous and recognize who or what is holding you back from winning the race. Ecclesiastes 4:9–10 says, "Two people are better off than one, for they can help each other succeed. If one person falls, the other can reach out and help. But someone who falls alone is in real trouble." You need a strong team surrounding you in this spiritual race. If you love God, you're already in the winner's circle, so work to build a team that will help fight the good fight—one that won't dig up the good seeds that have been planted or plunder all you've worked for. Build a team that the enemy will tremble over!

—*Doña Jackson*

For more on community, see reading at Daniel 1.

enough. How meaningless to think that wealth brings true happiness! [11] The more you have, the more people come to help you spend it. So what good is wealth—except perhaps to watch it slip through your fingers!

[12] People who work hard sleep well, whether they eat little or much. But the rich seldom get a good night's sleep.

[13] There is another serious problem I have seen under the sun. Hoarding riches harms the saver. [14] Money is put into risky investments that turn sour, and everything is lost. In the end, there is nothing left to pass on to one's children. [15] We all come to the end of our lives as naked and empty-handed as on the day we were born. We can't take our riches with us.

[16] And this, too, is a very serious problem. People leave this world no better off than when they came. All their hard work

is for nothing—like working for the wind. [17]Throughout their lives, they live under a cloud—frustrated, discouraged, and angry.

[18]Even so, I have noticed one thing, at least, that is good. It is good for people to eat, drink, and enjoy their work under the sun during the short life God has given them, and to accept their lot in life. [19]And it is a good thing to receive wealth from God and the good health to enjoy it. To enjoy your work and accept your lot in life—this is indeed a gift from God. [20]God keeps such people so busy enjoying life that they take no time to brood over the past.

6 There is another serious tragedy I have seen under the sun, and it weighs heavily on humanity. [2]God gives some

Q&A
Is It Wrong to Want Possessions?

ECCLESIASTES 5:10–6:9

I want to practice simplicity, but I love having the latest technological gadget, new car, and better wardrobe. Is it wrong to want—and enjoy—possessions?

G. K. Chesterton once said that when a man knocks on the door of a brothel, he's really looking for God. Perhaps today he might say, when a person goes to the mall to shop, she's really looking for God. What drives us to buy, consume, and accumulate more? Often it's an attempt to satisfy an inner emptiness.

Material things are not inherently evil. God made the world and all that is in it, and what God made is good. We need things not only to survive but to thrive and enjoy life as God intended. The problem is what we do with material things and the importance we place on them. Saint Augustine said that sin is an inordinate desire for the relative good. In other words, sin can be giving too much emphasis to something that is good but not ultimate, thereby displacing better things in our lives, such as relationships with people and, above all else, our relationship with God.

Money and material possessions don't make us content or bring us satisfaction. In fact, they can make us *more* unhappy and anxious. The preacher of Ecclesiastes understood this (5:10–6:9). While the mere laborer seems blessed by good sleep, the wealthy person is sleepless and anxious about what he has or still wants. The awareness that our possessions can so quickly be taken from us makes us even more likely to hang on to what we have, despite the fact that we've come into the world with nothing and will leave that way when we die. Ecclesiastes recognizes that material possessions come from God, but they can't ultimately satisfy; only the God who provides for us can.

—*Richard A. Kauffman*

For more on simplicity, see reading at Amos 3:14–4:1.

people great wealth and honor and everything they could ever want, but then he doesn't give them the chance to enjoy these things. They die, and someone else, even a stranger, ends up enjoying their wealth! This is meaningless—a sickening tragedy.

³A man might have a hundred children and live to be very old. But if he finds no satisfaction in life and doesn't even get a decent burial, it would have been better for him to be born dead. ⁴His birth would have been meaningless, and he would have ended in darkness. He wouldn't even have had a name, ⁵and he would never have seen the sun or known of its existence. Yet he would have had more peace than in growing up to be an unhappy man. ⁶He might live a thousand years twice over but still not find contentment. And since he must die like everyone else—well, what's the use?

⁷All people spend their lives scratching for food, but they never seem to have enough. ⁸So are wise people really better off than fools? Do poor people gain anything by being wise and knowing how to act in front of others?

⁹Enjoy what you have rather than desiring what you don't have. Just dreaming about nice things is meaningless—like chasing the wind.

The Future—Determined and Unknown

¹⁰Everything has already been decided. It was known long ago what each person would be. So there's no use arguing with God about your destiny.

¹¹The more words you speak, the less they mean. So what good are they?

¹²In the few days of our meaningless lives, who knows how our days can best be spent? Our lives are like a shadow. Who can tell what will happen on this earth after we are gone?

7 Wisdom for Life

¹ A good reputation is more valuable
   than costly perfume.
And the day you die is better than the
   day you are born.
² Better to spend your time at funerals
   than at parties.

After all, everyone dies—
   so the living should take this to
   heart.
³ Sorrow is better than laughter,
   for sadness has a refining influence
   on us.
⁴ A wise person thinks a lot about death,
   while a fool thinks only about having a
   good time.

⁵ Better to be criticized by a wise person
   than to be praised by a fool.
⁶ A fool's laughter is quickly gone,
   like thorns crackling in a fire.
   This also is meaningless.

⁷ Extortion turns wise people into fools,
   and bribes corrupt the heart.

⁸ Finishing is better than starting.
   Patience is better than pride.

⁹ Control your temper,
   for anger labels you a fool.

¹⁰ Don't long for "the good old days."
   This is not wise.

¹¹ Wisdom is even better when you have
   money.
   Both are a benefit as you go through
   life.
¹² Wisdom and money can get you almost
   anything,
   but only wisdom can save your life.

¹³ Accept the way God does things,
   for who can straighten what he has
   made crooked?
¹⁴ Enjoy prosperity while you can,
   but when hard times strike, realize
   that both come from God.
   Remember that nothing is certain in
   this life.

The Limits of Human Wisdom

¹⁵I have seen everything in this meaningless life, including the death of good young people and the long life of wicked people. ¹⁶So don't be too good or too wise! Why destroy yourself? ¹⁷On the other hand, don't be too wicked either. Don't be a fool! Why die before your time? ¹⁸Pay attention to these instructions, for anyone who fears God will avoid both extremes.*

7:18 Or will follow them both.

¹⁹One wise person is stronger than ten leading citizens of a town!

²⁰Not a single person on earth is always good and never sins.

²¹Don't eavesdrop on others—you may hear your servant curse you. ²²For you know how often you yourself have cursed others.

²³I have always tried my best to let wisdom guide my thoughts and actions. I said to myself, "I am determined to be wise." But it didn't work. ²⁴Wisdom is always distant and difficult to find. ²⁵I searched everywhere, determined to find wisdom and to understand the reason for things. I was determined to prove to myself that wickedness is stupid and that foolishness is madness.

²⁶I discovered that a seductive woman* is a trap more bitter than death. Her passion is a snare, and her soft hands are chains. Those who are pleasing to God will escape her, but sinners will be caught in her snare.

²⁷"This is my conclusion," says the Teacher. "I discovered this after looking at the matter from every possible angle. ²⁸Though I have searched repeatedly, I have not found what I was looking for. Only one out of a thousand men is virtuous, but not one woman! ²⁹But I did find this: God created people to be virtuous, but they have each turned to follow their own downward path."

8 ¹ How wonderful to be wise,
    to analyze and interpret things.
Wisdom lights up a person's face,
    softening its harshness.

Obedience to the King

²Obey the king since you vowed to God that you would. ³Don't try to avoid doing your duty, and don't stand with those who plot evil, for the king can do whatever he wants. ⁴His command is backed by great power. No one can resist or question it. ⁵Those who obey him will not be punished. Those who are wise will find a time and a way to do what is right, ⁶for there is a time and a way for everything, even when a person is in trouble.

⁷Indeed, how can people avoid what they don't know is going to happen? ⁸None of us can hold back our spirit from departing. None of us has the power to prevent the day of our death. There is no escaping that obligation, that dark battle. And in the face of death, wickedness will certainly not rescue the wicked.

The Wicked and the Righteous

⁹I have thought deeply about all that goes on here under the sun, where people have the power to hurt each other. ¹⁰I have seen wicked people buried with honor. Yet they were the very ones who frequented the Temple and are now praised* in the same city where they committed their crimes! This, too, is meaningless. ¹¹When a crime is not punished quickly, people feel it is safe to do wrong. ¹²But even though a person sins a hundred times and still lives a long time, I know that those who fear God will be better off. ¹³The wicked will not prosper, for they do not fear God. Their days will never grow long like the evening shadows.

¹⁴And this is not all that is meaningless in our world. In this life, good people are often treated as though they were wicked, and wicked people are often treated as though they were good. This is so meaningless!

¹⁵So I recommend having fun, because there is nothing better for people in this world than to eat, drink, and enjoy life. That way they will experience some happiness along with all the hard work God gives them under the sun.

¹⁶In my search for wisdom and in my observation of people's burdens here on earth, I discovered that there is ceaseless activity, day and night. ¹⁷I realized that no one can discover everything God is doing under the sun. Not even the wisest people discover everything, no matter what they claim.

9 Death Comes to All

This, too, I carefully explored: Even though the actions of godly and wise people are in God's hands, no one knows whether God will show them favor. ²The same destiny ultimately awaits everyone, whether righteous or wicked, good or bad,*

7:26 Hebrew *a woman.* 8:10 As in some Hebrew manuscripts and Greek version; many Hebrew manuscripts read *and are forgotten.*
9:2 As in Greek and Syriac versions and Latin Vulgate; Hebrew lacks *or bad.*

ceremonially clean or unclean, religious or irreligious. Good people receive the same treatment as sinners, and people who make promises to God are treated like people who don't.

³It seems so tragic that everyone under the sun suffers the same fate. That is why people are not more careful to be good. Instead, they choose their own mad course, for they have no hope. There is nothing ahead but death anyway. ⁴There is hope only for the living. As they say, "It's better to be a live dog than a dead lion!"

⁵The living at least know they will die, but the dead know nothing. They have no further reward, nor are they remembered. ⁶Whatever they did in their lifetime—loving, hating, envying—is all long gone. They no longer play a part in anything here on earth. ⁷So go ahead. Eat your food with joy, and drink your wine with a happy heart, for God approves of this! ⁸Wear fine clothes, with a splash of cologne!

⁹Live happily with the woman you love through all the meaningless days of life that God has given you under the sun. The wife God gives you is your reward for all your earthly toil. ¹⁰Whatever you do, do well. For when you go to the grave,* there will be no work or planning or knowledge or wisdom.

¹¹I have observed something else under the sun. The fastest runner doesn't always win the race, and the strongest warrior doesn't always win the battle. The wise sometimes go hungry, and the skillful are not necessarily wealthy. And those who are educated don't always lead successful lives. It is all decided by chance, by being in the right place at the right time.

¹²People can never predict when hard times might come. Like fish in a net or birds in a trap, people are caught by sudden tragedy.

Thoughts on Wisdom and Folly

¹³Here is another bit of wisdom that has impressed me as I have watched the way our world works. ¹⁴There was a small town with only a few people, and a great king came with his army and besieged it. ¹⁵A poor, wise man knew how to save the town,

and so it was rescued. But afterward no one thought to thank him. ¹⁶So even though wisdom is better than strength, those who are wise will be despised if they are poor. What they say will not be appreciated for long.

¹⁷ Better to hear the quiet words of a wise person
   than the shouts of a foolish king.
¹⁸ Better to have wisdom than weapons of war,
   but one sinner can destroy much that is good.

10 ¹ As dead flies cause even a bottle of perfume to stink,
   so a little foolishness spoils great wisdom and honor.

² A wise person chooses the right road;
   a fool takes the wrong one.

³ You can identify fools
   just by the way they walk down the street!

⁴ If your boss is angry at you, don't quit!
   A quiet spirit can overcome even great mistakes.

The Ironies of Life

⁵There is another evil I have seen under the sun. Kings and rulers make a grave mistake ⁶when they give great authority to foolish people and low positions to people of proven worth. ⁷I have even seen servants riding horseback like princes—and princes walking like servants!

⁸ When you dig a well,
   you might fall in.
   When you demolish an old wall,
   you could be bitten by a snake.
⁹ When you work in a quarry,
   stones might fall and crush you.
   When you chop wood,
   there is danger with each stroke of your ax.

¹⁰ Using a dull ax requires great strength,
   so sharpen the blade.
   That's the value of wisdom;
   it helps you succeed.

¹¹ If a snake bites before you charm it,
    what's the use of being a snake
        charmer?

¹² Wise words bring approval,
    but fools are destroyed by their own
        words.

¹³ Fools base their thoughts on foolish
        assumptions,
    so their conclusions will be wicked
        madness;
¹⁴   they chatter on and on.

No one really knows what is going to
        happen;
    no one can predict the future.

¹⁵ Fools are so exhausted by a little work
    that they can't even find their way
        home.

¹⁶ What sorrow for the land ruled by a
        servant,*
    the land whose leaders feast in the
        morning.

¹⁷ Happy is the land whose king is a noble
        leader
    and whose leaders feast at the proper
        time
    to gain strength for their work, not to
        get drunk.

¹⁸ Laziness leads to a sagging roof;
    idleness leads to a leaky house.

¹⁹ A party gives laughter,
    wine gives happiness,
    and money gives everything!

²⁰ Never make light of the king, even in
        your thoughts.
    And don't make fun of the powerful,
        even in your own bedroom.
    For a little bird might deliver your
        message
    and tell them what you said.

11 The Uncertainties of Life

¹ Send your grain across the seas,
    and in time, profits will flow back to
        you.*
² But divide your investments among
    many places,*
for you do not know what risks might
        lie ahead.

³ When clouds are heavy, the rains come
        down.
    Whether a tree falls north or south, it
        stays where it falls.

⁴ Farmers who wait for perfect weather
        never plant.
    If they watch every cloud, they never
        harvest.

⁵Just as you cannot understand the path of the wind or the mystery of a tiny baby growing in its mother's womb,* so you cannot understand the activity of God, who does all things.

⁶Plant your seed in the morning and keep busy all afternoon, for you don't know if profit will come from one activity or another—or maybe both.

Advice for Young and Old

⁷Light is sweet; how pleasant to see a new day dawning.

⁸When people live to be very old, let them rejoice in every day of life. But let them also remember there will be many dark days. Everything still to come is meaningless.

⁹Young people,* it's wonderful to be young! Enjoy every minute of it. Do everything you want to do; take it all in. But remember that you must give an account to God for everything you do. ¹⁰So refuse to worry, and keep your body healthy. But remember that youth, with a whole life before you, is meaningless.

12 Don't let the excitement of youth cause you to forget your Creator. Honor him in your youth before you grow old and say, "Life is not pleasant anymore." ²Remember him before the light of the sun, moon, and stars is dim to your old eyes, and rain clouds continually darken your sky. ³Remember him before your legs—the guards of your house—start to tremble; and before your shoulders—the strong men—stoop. Remember him before your teeth—your few remaining servants—stop grinding; and before your eyes—the

---

10:16 Or *a child.*   **11:1** Or *Give generously, / for your gifts will return to you later.* Hebrew reads *Throw your bread on the waters, / for after many days you will find it again.*   **11:2** Hebrew *among seven or even eight.*   **11:5** Some manuscripts read *Just as you cannot understand how breath comes to a tiny baby in its mother's womb.*   **11:9** Hebrew *Young man.*

Connecting Our Pleasure with God

ECCLESIASTES 11:7–12:2

Celebration

S ometimes we forget the reality that pleasure comes from a good God who loves us deeply. When the church teaches a glum faith of responsibility, a faith devoid of joy; when the pulpit treats pleasure like some kind of spiritual leprosy; when people of faith speak as though they are antisex, antihumor, antifun, antianything that brings pleasure, we risk fostering the kind of devotion that the Bible shockingly and without reservation rejects.

The fact that we are children of God—and that Jesus urges us to become like children (Matthew 18:3)—points us toward a certain demeanor, a certain delight, a certain trust in God's goodness that should characterize our faith.

Connecting our pleasure with God—even seeing pleasure as a legitimate and blessed pathway to worship—builds our souls and strengthens our devotion. Pleasure divorced from God leads to pain and misery; but looking at our pleasures as a way to please God can slowly begin to shape and transform what it is that we take pleasure in.

—Gary Thomas

For more on celebration, see reading at Zephaniah 3:15–17.

---

women looking through the windows—see dimly.

⁴Remember him before the door to life's opportunities is closed and the sound of work fades. Now you rise at the first chirping of the birds, but then all their sounds will grow faint.

⁵Remember him before you become fearful of falling and worry about danger in the streets; before your hair turns white like an almond tree in bloom, and you drag along without energy like a dying grasshopper, and the caperberry no longer inspires sexual desire. Remember him before you near the grave, your everlasting home, when the mourners will weep at your funeral.

⁶Yes, remember your Creator now while you are young, before the silver cord of life snaps and the golden bowl is broken. Don't wait until the water jar is smashed at the spring and the pulley is broken at the well. ⁷For then the dust will return to the earth, and the spirit will return to God who gave it.

Concluding Thoughts about the Teacher

⁸"Everything is meaningless," says the Teacher, "completely meaningless."

⁹Keep this in mind: The Teacher was considered wise, and he taught the people everything he knew. He listened carefully to many proverbs, studying and classifying them. ¹⁰The Teacher sought to find just the right words to express truths clearly.*

¹¹The words of the wise are like cattle prods—painful but helpful. Their collected sayings are like a nail-studded stick with which a shepherd* drives the sheep.

¹²But, my child,* let me give you some further advice: Be careful, for writing books is endless, and much study wears you out.

¹³That's the whole story. Here now is my final conclusion: Fear God and obey his commands, for this is everyone's duty. ¹⁴God will judge us for everything we do, including every secret thing, whether good or bad.

12:10 Or sought to write what was upright and true.   **12:11** Or one shepherd.   **12:12** Hebrew my son.

Introduction to

Song of Songs

Background

Is the Song of Songs an allegory about the love of Christ for the church? A love story penned by a king? Theologians believe that the story is both literal truth as well as symbolic of the people of Israel as God's bride (see also Hosea 2:19–20) and the church as the bride of Christ (see also Revelation 21:9).

Solomon is believed to be the author of this book, categorized as Wisdom Literature; in the text he is mentioned seven times (1:1, 5; 3:7, 9, 11; 8:11–12) and identified as the groom. The book takes its title from the first verse: "This is Solomon's song of songs."

Message

The book weaves a love story and a portrait of God's love for his people. Other Old and New Testament Scriptures also use the picture of husband and wife to describe this relationship: "For your Creator will be your husband; the LORD of Heaven's Armies is his name! He is your Redeemer, the Holy One of Israel, the God of all the earth" (Isaiah 54:5; see also 62:5; Jeremiah 2:2; 3:14, 20; 31:32; Ezekiel 16:32, 35; Hosea 2); "And I saw the holy city, the new Jerusalem, coming down from God out of heaven like a bride beautifully dressed for her husband" (Revelation 21:2; see also 22:17).

Time

The Song of Songs was probably written around 965 B.C., early in Solomon's reign.

Outline

Song of Songs

1 This is Solomon's song of songs, more wonderful than any other.

*Young Woman**

2 Kiss me and kiss me again,
   for your love is sweeter than wine.
3 How fragrant your cologne;
   your name is like its spreading fragrance.
   No wonder all the young women love you!
4 Take me with you; come, let's run!
   The king has brought me into his bedroom.

Young Women of Jerusalem

How happy we are for you, O king.
   We praise your love even more than wine.

Young Woman

How right they are to adore you.

5 I am dark but beautiful,
   O women of Jerusalem—
dark as the tents of Kedar,
   dark as the curtains of Solomon's tents.
6 Don't stare at me because I am dark—
   the sun has darkened my skin.
My brothers were angry with me;
   they forced me to care for their vineyards,
   so I couldn't care for myself—my own vineyard.

7 Tell me, my love, where are you leading your flock today?
   Where will you rest your sheep at noon?
For why should I wander like a prostitute*
   among your friends and their flocks?

Young Man

8 If you don't know, O most beautiful woman,
   follow the trail of my flock,
   and graze your young goats by the shepherds' tents.
9 You are as exciting, my darling,
   as a mare among Pharaoh's stallions.
10 How lovely are your cheeks;
   your earrings set them afire!
How lovely is your neck,
   enhanced by a string of jewels.
11 We will make for you earrings of gold
   and beads of silver.

1:1 The headings identifying the speakers are not in the original text, though the Hebrew usually gives clues by means of the gender of the person speaking.   **1:7** Hebrew *like a veiled woman.*

Young Woman

¹² The king is lying on his couch,
    enchanted by the fragrance of my
      perfume.
¹³ My lover is like a sachet of myrrh
    lying between my breasts.
¹⁴ He is like a bouquet of sweet henna
    blossoms
      from the vineyards of En-gedi.

Young Man

¹⁵ How beautiful you are, my darling,
    how beautiful!
    Your eyes are like doves.

Young Woman

¹⁶ You are so handsome, my love,
    pleasing beyond words!
    The soft grass is our bed;
¹⁷   fragrant cedar branches are the beams
    of our house,
    and pleasant smelling firs are the
      rafters.

Young Woman

2¹ I am the spring crocus blooming on
    the Sharon Plain,*
    the lily of the valley.

Young Man

² Like a lily among thistles
    is my darling among young women.

Young Woman

³ Like the finest apple tree in the orchard
    is my lover among other young men.
    I sit in his delightful shade
    and taste his delicious fruit.
⁴ He escorts me to the banquet hall;
    it's obvious how much he loves me.
⁵ Strengthen me with raisin cakes,
    refresh me with apples,
    for I am weak with love.
⁶ His left arm is under my head,
    and his right arm embraces me.
⁷ Promise me, O women of Jerusalem,
    by the gazelles and wild deer,
    not to awaken love until the time is
      right.*

⁸ Ah, I hear my lover coming!
    He is leaping over the mountains,
    bounding over the hills.

⁹ My lover is like a swift gazelle
    or a young stag.
    Look, there he is behind the wall,
    looking through the window,
    peering into the room.

¹⁰ My lover said to me,
    "Rise up, my darling!
    Come away with me, my fair one!
¹¹ Look, the winter is past,
    and the rains are over and gone.
¹² The flowers are springing up,
    the season of singing birds* has
      come,
    and the cooing of turtledoves fills the
      air.
¹³ The fig trees are forming young fruit,
    and the fragrant grapevines are
      blossoming.
    Rise up, my darling!
    Come away with me, my fair
      one!"

Young Man

¹⁴ My dove is hiding behind the rocks,
    behind an outcrop on the cliff.
    Let me see your face;
    let me hear your voice.
    For your voice is pleasant,
    and your face is lovely.

Young Women of Jerusalem

¹⁵ Catch all the foxes,
    those little foxes,
    before they ruin the vineyard of love,
    for the grapevines are blossoming!

Young Woman

¹⁶ My lover is mine, and I am his.
    He browses among the lilies.
¹⁷ Before the dawn breezes blow
    and the night shadows flee,
    return to me, my love, like a gazelle
    or a young stag on the rugged
      mountains.*

Young Woman

3¹ One night as I lay in bed, I yearned for
    my lover.
    I yearned for him, but he did not
      come.
² So I said to myself, "I will get up and
    roam the city,

2:1 Traditionally rendered *I am the rose of Sharon. Sharon Plain* is a region in the coastal plain of Palestine.   2:7 Or *not to awaken love until it is ready.*   2:12 Or *the season of pruning vines.*   2:17 Or *on the hills of Bether.*

searching in all its streets and
squares.
I will search for the one I love."
So I searched everywhere but did not
find him.
³ The watchmen stopped me as they made
their rounds,
and I asked, "Have you seen the one I
love?"
⁴ Then scarcely had I left them
when I found my love!
I caught and held him tightly,
then I brought him to my mother's
house,
into my mother's bed, where I had
been conceived.

⁵ Promise me, O women of
Jerusalem,
by the gazelles and wild deer,
not to awaken love until the time is
right.*

Young Women of Jerusalem
⁶ Who is this sweeping in from the
wilderness
like a cloud of smoke?
Who is it, fragrant with myrrh and
frankincense
and every kind of spice?
⁷ Look, it is Solomon's carriage,
surrounded by sixty heroic men,
the best of Israel's soldiers.
⁸ They are all skilled swordsmen,
experienced warriors.
Each wears a sword on his thigh,
ready to defend the king against an
attack in the night.
⁹ King Solomon's carriage is built
of wood imported from Lebanon.
¹⁰ Its posts are silver,
its canopy gold;
its cushions are purple.
It was decorated with love
by the young women of Jerusalem.

Young Woman
¹¹ Come out to see King Solomon,
young women of Jerusalem.*
He wears the crown his mother gave
him on his wedding day,
his most joyous day.

Young Man
4 ¹ You are beautiful, my darling,
beautiful beyond words.
Your eyes are like doves
behind your veil.
Your hair falls in waves,
like a flock of goats winding down the
slopes of Gilead.
² Your teeth are as white as sheep,
recently shorn and freshly washed.
Your smile is flawless,
each tooth matched with its twin.*
³ Your lips are like scarlet ribbon;
your mouth is inviting.
Your cheeks are like rosy pomegranates
behind your veil.
⁴ Your neck is as beautiful as the tower of
David,
jeweled with the shields of a thousand
heroes.
⁵ Your breasts are like two fawns,
twin fawns of a gazelle grazing among
the lilies.
⁶ Before the dawn breezes blow
and the night shadows flee,
I will hurry to the mountain of myrrh
and to the hill of frankincense.
⁷ You are altogether beautiful, my darling,
beautiful in every way.

⁸ Come with me from Lebanon, my bride,
come with me from Lebanon.
Come down* from Mount Amana,
from the peaks of Senir and Hermon,
where the lions have their dens
and leopards live among the hills.

⁹ You have captured my heart,
my treasure,* my bride.
You hold it hostage with one glance of
your eyes,
with a single jewel of your necklace.
¹⁰ Your love delights me,
my treasure, my bride.
Your love is better than wine,
your perfume more fragrant than
spices.
¹¹ Your lips are as sweet as nectar, my bride.
Honey and milk are under your
tongue.
Your clothes are scented
like the cedars of Lebanon.

3:5 Or not to awaken love until it is ready.   **3:11** Hebrew of Zion.   **4:2** Hebrew Not one is missing; each has a twin.   **4:8** Or Look down.
4:9 Hebrew my sister; also in 4:10, 12.

¹² You are my private garden, my treasure,
my bride;
a secluded spring, a hidden fountain.
¹³ Your thighs shelter a paradise of
pomegranates
with rare spices—
henna with nard,
¹⁴ nard and saffron,
fragrant calamus and cinnamon,
with all the trees of frankincense, myrrh,
and aloes,
and every other lovely spice.
¹⁵ You are a garden fountain,
a well of fresh water
streaming down from Lebanon's
mountains.

Young Woman
¹⁶ Awake, north wind!
Rise up, south wind!
Blow on my garden
and spread its fragrance all around.
Come into your garden, my love;
taste its finest fruits.

Young Man
5 ¹ I have entered my garden, my
treasure,* my bride!
I gather myrrh with my spices
and eat honeycomb with my honey.
I drink wine with my milk.

Young Women of Jerusalem
Oh, lover and beloved, eat and drink!
Yes, drink deeply of your love!

Young Woman
² I slept, but my heart was awake,
when I heard my lover knocking and
calling:
"Open to me, my treasure, my darling,
my dove, my perfect one.
My head is drenched with dew,
my hair with the dampness of the
night."
³ But I responded,
"I have taken off my robe.
Should I get dressed again?
I have washed my feet.
Should I get them soiled?"
⁴ My lover tried to unlatch the door,
and my heart thrilled within me.

⁵ I jumped up to open the door for my love,
and my hands dripped with perfume.
My fingers dripped with lovely myrrh
as I pulled back the bolt.
⁶ I opened to my lover,
but he was gone!
My heart sank.
I searched for him
but could not find him anywhere.
I called to him,
but there was no reply.
⁷ The night watchmen found me
as they made their rounds.
They beat and bruised me
and stripped off my veil,
those watchmen on the walls.

⁸ Make this promise, O women of
Jerusalem—
If you find my lover,
tell him I am weak with love.

Young Women of Jerusalem
⁹ Why is your lover better than all others,
O woman of rare beauty?
What makes your lover so special
that we must promise this?

Young Woman
¹⁰ My lover is dark and dazzling,
better than ten thousand others!
¹¹ His head is finest gold,
his wavy hair is black as a raven.
¹² His eyes sparkle like doves
beside springs of water;
they are set like jewels
washed in milk.
¹³ His cheeks are like gardens of spices
giving off fragrance.
His lips are like lilies,
perfumed with myrrh.
¹⁴ His arms are like rounded bars of gold,
set with beryl.
His body is like bright ivory,
glowing with lapis lazuli.
¹⁵ His legs are like marble pillars
set in sockets of finest gold.
His posture is stately,
like the noble cedars of Lebanon.
¹⁶ His mouth is sweetness itself;
he is desirable in every way.
Such, O women of Jerusalem,
is my lover, my friend.

5:1 Hebrew *my sister;* also in 5:2.

Young Women of Jerusalem

6 ¹ Where has your lover gone,
O woman of rare beauty?
Which way did he turn
so we can help you find him?

Young Woman

² My lover has gone down to his garden,
to his spice beds,
to browse in the gardens
and gather the lilies.
³ I am my lover's, and my lover is mine.
He browses among the lilies.

Young Man

⁴ You are beautiful, my darling,
like the lovely city of Tirzah.
Yes, as beautiful as Jerusalem,
as majestic as an army with billowing
banners.
⁵ Turn your eyes away,
for they overpower me.
Your hair falls in waves,
like a flock of goats winding down the
slopes of Gilead.
⁶ Your teeth are as white as sheep
that are freshly washed.
Your smile is flawless,
each tooth matched with its twin.*
⁷ Your cheeks are like rosy pomegranates
behind your veil.

⁸ Even among sixty queens
and eighty concubines
and countless young women,
⁹ I would still choose my dove, my perfect
one—
the favorite of her mother,
dearly loved by the one who bore her.
The young women see her and praise her;
even queens and royal concubines
sing her praises:
¹⁰ "Who is this, arising like the dawn,
as fair as the moon,
as bright as the sun,
as majestic as an army with billowing
banners?"

Young Woman

¹¹ I went down to the grove of walnut trees
and out to the valley to see the new
spring growth,
to see whether the grapevines had
budded
or the pomegranates were in bloom.
¹² Before I realized it,
my strong desires had taken me to the
chariot of a noble man.*

Young Women of Jerusalem

¹³*Return, return to us, O maid of Shulam.
Come back, come back, that we may
see you again.

Young Man

Why do you stare at this young woman
of Shulam,
as she moves so gracefully between
two lines of dancers?*

7 *¹ How beautiful are your sandaled feet,
O queenly maiden.
Your rounded thighs are like jewels,
the work of a skilled craftsman.
² Your navel is perfectly formed
like a goblet filled with mixed wine.
Between your thighs lies a mound of
wheat
bordered with lilies.
³ Your breasts are like two fawns,
twin fawns of a gazelle.
⁴ Your neck is as beautiful as an ivory
tower.
Your eyes are like the sparkling pools in
Heshbon
by the gate of Bath-rabbim.
Your nose is as fine as the tower of
Lebanon
overlooking Damascus.
⁵ Your head is as majestic as Mount
Carmel,
and the sheen of your hair radiates
royalty.
The king is held captive by its
tresses.
⁶ Oh, how beautiful you are!
How pleasing, my love, how full of
delights!
⁷ You are slender like a palm tree,
and your breasts are like its clusters of
fruit.
⁸ I said, "I will climb the palm tree
and take hold of its fruit."

6:6 Hebrew *Not one is missing; each has a twin.* **6:12** Or *to the royal chariots of my people, or to the chariots of Amminadab.* The meaning of the Hebrew is uncertain. **6:13a** Verse 6:13 is numbered 7:1 in Hebrew text. **6:13b** Or *as you would at the movements of two armies?* or *as you would at the dance of Mahanaim?* The meaning of the Hebrew is uncertain. **7:1** Verses 7:1-13 are numbered 7:2-14 in Hebrew text.

Listening to the Text

SONG OF SONGS 7:10-13

In high school I was very involved in poetry. You cannot read a poem quickly. There's too much going on. There are rhythms and alliterations. You have to read poetry slow, slow, slow to absorb it all. That's how I began reading and praying psalms as a student, because I realized they were poems.

Reading poetry has taught me how to approach Scripture. The first time you read a poem, you usually don't understand it. You've got to read it ten times or more. You've got to listen to it—and that listening process is fluid.

Most of us have never been taught to read and listen reflectively. For example, when we use the word *study*—such as in "Bible study groups"—people think the goal is to master information. They think the Bible is something you try to understand and explain. Further, when you've spent twelve, fourteen, or eighteen years in school, your habits form in a nonreflective way. After all, it's not a school's job to make us reflective. We're there to learn information; we need to pass examinations and be able to read and retain. But is that really how we want to approach Scripture?

It seems to me that we need to break the stronghold that academic scholarship can have over how we approach the Bible. I do think Bible dictionaries, concordances, commentaries, and other Bible study tools are useful—but we need to make sure they don't get in the way of really *listening* to the text. Often it's as if we don't trust ourselves to encounter God's Word without the aid of study tools. When we make everything academic rather than reflective, we lose something.

—*Eugene Peterson*

For more on Bible study and meditation, see reading at Isaiah 31:4.

May your breasts be like grape clusters,
and the fragrance of your breath like
apples.
9 May your kisses be as exciting as the
best wine,
flowing gently over lips and teeth.*

Young Woman
10 I am my lover's,
and he claims me as his own.
11 Come, my love, let us go out to the
fields
and spend the night among the
wildflowers.*
12 Let us get up early and go to the
vineyards
to see if the grapevines have budded,

if the blossoms have opened,
and if the pomegranates have
bloomed.
There I will give you my love.
13 There the mandrakes give off their
fragrance,
and the finest fruits are at our door,
new delights as well as old,
which I have saved for you, my lover.

Young Woman
8 1 Oh, I wish you were my brother,
who nursed at my mother's
breasts.
Then I could kiss you no matter who was
watching,
and no one would criticize me.

7:9 As in Greek and Syriac versions and Latin Vulgate; Hebrew reads *over lips of sleepers.*   **7:11** Or *in the villages.*

² I would bring you to my childhood home,
and there you would teach me.*
I would give you spiced wine to drink,
my sweet pomegranate wine.
³ Your left arm would be under my head,
and your right arm would embrace me.

⁴ Promise me, O women of Jerusalem,
not to awaken love until the time is
right.*

Young Women of Jerusalem
⁵ Who is this sweeping in from the desert,
leaning on her lover?

Young Woman
I aroused you under the apple tree,
where your mother gave you birth,
where in great pain she delivered you.
⁶ Place me like a seal over your heart,
like a seal on your arm.
For love is as strong as death,
its jealousy* as enduring as the grave.*
Love flashes like fire,
the brightest kind of flame.
⁷ Many waters cannot quench love,
nor can rivers drown it.
If a man tried to buy love
with all his wealth,
his offer would be utterly scorned.

The Young Woman's Brothers
⁸ We have a little sister
too young to have breasts.
What will we do for our sister
if someone asks to marry her?

⁹ If she is a virgin, like a wall,
we will protect her with a silver
tower.
But if she is promiscuous, like a
swinging door,
we will block her door with a cedar
bar.

Young Woman
¹⁰ I was a virgin, like a wall;
now my breasts are like towers.
When my lover looks at me,
he is delighted with what he sees.

¹¹ Solomon has a vineyard at Baal-hamon,
which he leases out to tenant
farmers.
Each of them pays a thousand pieces of
silver*
for harvesting its fruit.
¹² But my vineyard is mine to give,
and Solomon need not pay a thousand
pieces of silver.
But I will give two hundred pieces
to those who care for its vines.

Young Man
¹³ O my darling, lingering in the gardens,
your companions are fortunate to hear
your voice.
Let me hear it, too!

Young Woman
¹⁴ Come away, my love! Be like a gazelle
or a young stag on the mountains of
spices.

8:2 Or *there she will teach me;* or *there she bore me.*   **8:4** Or *not to awaken love until it is ready.*   **8:6a** Or *its passion.*   **8:6b** Hebrew as *Sheol.*
8:11 Hebrew *1,000 shekels of silver.*

Introduction to
Isaiah

Background

Isaiah is the first of the major biblical books of prophecy. Isaiah, who is believed to be the author, was known in the royal court of the southern kingdom of Judah. Like Moses, he was well educated. He had a prophetess wife and at least two sons (7:3; 8:3). As a prophet and a writer, he is mentioned in the historical record of 2 Chronicles (26:22; 32:20, 32). Isaiah is quoted in the New Testament more than any other Old Testament prophet (see Matthew 3:3; 12:17–21; Luke 3:4–6; 4:17–19; John 12:38–41; Acts 8:28, 32–33; Romans 9:27–29; 10:16–21).

In Hebrew Isaiah means "Yahweh is salvation."

Message

The format of Isaiah shows why it is called a "miniature Bible." The first thirty-nine chapters of Isaiah have a theme of judgment, which is a prominent theme throughout the Old Testament. Even so, stern warnings are interspersed with comfort and the promise of the Messiah, including reference to a child named Immanuel (7:14). The final twenty-seven chapters of Isaiah reflect the message of the New Testament: hope found in the coming Savior. Isaiah's prophetic description of the Suffering Servant is the highlight of the book. Isaiah ends with prophecies of the future restoration of Zion, when all things will be made new.

Time

Isaiah lived during the time of the divided kingdoms of Israel and Judah. During his lifetime the northern kingdom of Israel fell to the Assyrians. Isaiah's ministry extended over the reign of five Judean kings, starting in 740 B.C. at the end of Uzziah's reign, through the reigns of Jotham, Ahaz, and Hezekiah, and ending in about 680 B.C. during the reign of Manasseh (686–642 B.C.). Tradition, supported by Hebrews 11:37, says Isaiah was killed—"sawed in half"—by Manasseh.

Outline

Isaiah

1 These are the visions that Isaiah son of Amoz saw concerning Judah and Jerusalem. He saw these visions during the years when Uzziah, Jotham, Ahaz, and Hezekiah were kings of Judah.*

A Message for Rebellious Judah

² Listen, O heavens! Pay attention, earth!
   This is what the LORD says:
"The children I raised and cared for
   have rebelled against me.
³ Even an ox knows its owner,
   and a donkey recognizes its master's care—
but Israel doesn't know its master.
   My people don't recognize my care for them."
⁴ Oh, what a sinful nation they are—
   loaded down with a burden of guilt.
They are evil people,
   corrupt children who have rejected the LORD.
They have despised the Holy One of Israel
   and turned their backs on him.

⁵ Why do you continue to invite punishment?
   Must you rebel forever?
Your head is injured,
   and your heart is sick.
⁶ You are battered from head to foot—
   covered with bruises, welts, and infected wounds—
   without any soothing ointments or bandages.
⁷ Your country lies in ruins,
   and your towns are burned.
Foreigners plunder your fields before your eyes
   and destroy everything they see.
⁸ Beautiful Jerusalem* stands abandoned
   like a watchman's shelter in a vineyard,
like a lean-to in a cucumber field after the harvest,
   like a helpless city under siege.
⁹ If the LORD of Heaven's Armies
   had not spared a few of us,*
we would have been wiped out like Sodom,
   destroyed like Gomorrah.

¹⁰ Listen to the LORD, you leaders of "Sodom."
   Listen to the law of our God, people of "Gomorrah."
¹¹ "What makes you think I want all your sacrifices?"
   says the LORD.

1:1 These kings reigned from 792 to 686 B.C.   **1:8** Hebrew *The daughter of Zion.*   **1:9** Greek version reads *a few of our children.* Compare Rom 9:29.

"I am sick of your burnt offerings of rams
and the fat of fattened cattle.
I get no pleasure from the blood
of bulls and lambs and goats.
¹² When you come to worship me,
who asked you to parade through my
courts with all your ceremony?
¹³ Stop bringing me your meaningless gifts;
the incense of your offerings
disgusts me!
As for your celebrations of the new
moon and the Sabbath
and your special days for fasting—
they are all sinful and false.
I want no more of your pious meetings.
¹⁴ I hate your new moon celebrations and
your annual festivals.
They are a burden to me. I cannot
stand them!
¹⁵ When you lift up your hands in prayer, I
will not look.
Though you offer many prayers, I will
not listen,
for your hands are covered with the
blood of innocent victims.
¹⁶ Wash yourselves and be clean!
Get your sins out of my sight.
Give up your evil ways.
¹⁷ Learn to do good.
Seek justice.
Help the oppressed.
Defend the cause of orphans.
Fight for the rights of widows.

¹⁸ "Come now, let's settle this,"
says the LORD.
"Though your sins are like scarlet,
I will make them as white as snow.
Though they are red like crimson,
I will make them as white as wool.
¹⁹ If you will only obey me,
you will have plenty to eat.
²⁰ But if you turn away and refuse to listen,
you will be devoured by the sword of
your enemies.
I, the LORD, have spoken!"

Unfaithful Jerusalem

²¹ See how Jerusalem, once so faithful,
has become a prostitute.
Once the home of justice and
righteousness,
she is now filled with murderers.

²² Once like pure silver,
you have become like worthless slag.
Once so pure,
you are now like watered-down wine.
²³ Your leaders are rebels,
the companions of thieves.
All of them love bribes
and demand payoffs,
but they refuse to defend the cause of
orphans
or fight for the rights of widows.

²⁴ Therefore, the Lord, the LORD of
Heaven's Armies,
the Mighty One of Israel, says,
"I will take revenge on my enemies
and pay back my foes!
²⁵ I will raise my fist against you.
I will melt you down and skim off your
slag.
I will remove all your impurities.
²⁶ Then I will give you good judges again
and wise counselors like you used to
have.
Then Jerusalem will again be called the
Home of Justice
and the Faithful City."

²⁷ Zion will be restored by justice;
those who repent will be revived by
righteousness.
²⁸ But rebels and sinners will be completely
destroyed,
and those who desert the LORD will be
consumed.

²⁹ You will be ashamed of your idol worship
in groves of sacred oaks.
You will blush because you worshiped
in gardens dedicated to idols.
³⁰ You will be like a great tree with
withered leaves,
like a garden without water.
³¹ The strongest among you will disappear
like straw;
their evil deeds will be the spark that
sets it on fire.
They and their evil works will burn up
together,
and no one will be able to put out the
fire.

2 The LORD's Future Reign

This is a vision that Isaiah son of Amoz
saw concerning Judah and Jerusalem:

2 In the last days, the mountain of the
LORD's house
will be the highest of all—
the most important place on earth.
It will be raised above the other hills,
and people from all over the world will
stream there to worship.

3 People from many nations will come and
say,
"Come, let us go up to the mountain of
the LORD,
to the house of Jacob's God.
There he will teach us his ways,
and we will walk in his paths."

Q&A { Responding to Injustice }

ISAIAH 1:17

Accounts of injustice—slavery, sex-trafficking, oppressive poverty—feel so overwhelming. What can *I* do?

As we seek to respond to slavery and other immense injustices in the world, we need to reflect on three key questions.

First, does our sense of mission reflect God's passion for the world beyond our borders? We hear "for God loved the world so much," but often we don't think much about the world he loves. Focused on ministering to those around us, we don't have enough left over for "the uttermost parts of the earth"—that broader world for which God also "gave his one and only Son." We need a sense of mission that aligns with God's global love. So we must develop our global awareness, reading about and asking God to give us his heart for the people, cultures, and nations who populate this planet.

Second, will we do the work of justice? Millions of poor people in developing countries are suffering under an epidemic of violence—domestic abuse, sexual violence, slavery, illegal detention, police abuse, land seizures, and extortion. They aren't crying out for a sermon, food, medicine, housing, or microloans. In due course they may. But *right now* they're crying out for someone to restrain the hand of the oppressor. They're crying out for the ministry of justice. You can give goods and services to the poor in Christ's name, but if you haven't worked to restrain the hand of their oppressors, you haven't done much significant or sustainable. One way to help is to give to and participate in justice organizations, such as International Justice Mission.

Finally, will our response reflect the God of justice? Ultimately, protecting victims of violence and slavery is the work of God's kingdom. It is the Lord who commands us, "Seek justice. Help the oppressed. Defend the cause of orphans. Fight for the rights of widows" (Isaiah 1:17), and it is almighty God who promises to go with us as we declare to the pharaohs of this world, "Let my people go" (Exodus 5:1). Our faith is in the God of justice—our actions should be motivated by the character of the God we know and love.

—*Gary Haugen*

For more on justice, see reading at Isaiah 10:1–3.

For the Lord's teaching will go out from
    Zion;
  his word will go out from Jerusalem.
4 The Lord will mediate between nations
    and will settle international disputes.
They will hammer their swords into
    plowshares
  and their spears into pruning hooks.
Nation will no longer fight against
    nation,
  nor train for war anymore.

A Warning of Judgment

5 Come, descendants of Jacob,
  let us walk in the light of the Lord!
6 For the Lord has rejected his people,
  the descendants of Jacob,
because they have filled their land with
    practices from the East
  and with sorcerers, as the
    Philistines do.
They have made alliances with
    pagans.
7 Israel is full of silver and gold;
  there is no end to its treasures.
Their land is full of warhorses;
  there is no end to its chariots.
8 Their land is full of idols;
  the people worship things they have
    made
  with their own hands.
9 So now they will be humbled,
  and all will be brought low—
  do not forgive them.
10 Crawl into caves in the rocks.
  Hide in the dust
from the terror of the Lord
  and the glory of his majesty.
11 Human pride will be brought down,
  and human arrogance will be
    humbled.
Only the Lord will be exalted
  on that day of judgment.

12 For the Lord of Heaven's Armies
  has a day of reckoning.
He will punish the proud and mighty
  and bring down everything that is
    exalted.
13 He will cut down the tall cedars of
    Lebanon
  and all the mighty oaks of Bashan.

14 He will level all the high mountains
  and all the lofty hills.
15 He will break down every high tower
  and every fortified wall.
16 He will destroy all the great trading
    ships*
  and every magnificent vessel.
17 Human pride will be humbled,
  and human arrogance will be brought
    down.
Only the Lord will be exalted
  on that day of judgment.

18 Idols will completely disappear.
19 When the Lord rises to shake the earth,
  his enemies will crawl into holes in the
    ground.
They will hide in caves in the rocks
  from the terror of the Lord
  and the glory of his majesty.
20 On that day of judgment they will
    abandon the gold and silver idols
  they made for themselves to worship.
They will leave their gods to the rodents
    and bats,
21 while they crawl away into caverns
  and hide among the jagged rocks in
    the cliffs.
They will try to escape the terror of the
    Lord
  and the glory of his majesty
  as he rises to shake the earth.
22 Don't put your trust in mere humans.
  They are as frail as breath.
  What good are they?

3 Judgment against Judah

1 The Lord, the Lord of Heaven's
    Armies,
  will take away from Jerusalem and
    Judah
everything they depend on:
  every bit of bread
  and every drop of water,
2 all their heroes and soldiers,
  judges and prophets,
  fortune-tellers and elders,
3 army officers and high officials,
  advisers, skilled craftsmen, and
    astrologers.

4 I will make boys their leaders,
  and toddlers their rulers.

2:16 Hebrew *every ship of Tarshish.*

5 People will oppress each other—
man against man,
neighbor against neighbor.
Young people will insult their elders,
and vulgar people will sneer at the
honorable.

6 In those days a man will say to his
brother,
"Since you have a coat, you be our
leader!
Take charge of this heap of ruins!"
7 But he will reply,
"No! I can't help.
I don't have any extra food or clothes.
Don't put me in charge!"

8 For Jerusalem will stumble,
and Judah will fall,
because they speak out against the LORD
and refuse to obey him.
They provoke him to his face.
9 The very look on their faces gives them
away.
They display their sin like the people
of Sodom
and don't even try to hide it.
They are doomed!
They have brought destruction upon
themselves.

10 Tell the godly that all will be well for
them.
They will enjoy the rich reward they
have earned!
11 But the wicked are doomed,
for they will get exactly what they
deserve.

12 Childish leaders oppress my people,
and women rule over them.
O my people, your leaders mislead you;
they send you down the wrong road.

13 The LORD takes his place in court
and presents his case against his
people!
14 The LORD comes forward to pronounce
judgment
on the elders and rulers of his people:
"You have ruined Israel, my vineyard.
Your houses are filled with things
stolen from the poor.

15 How dare you crush my people,
grinding the faces of the poor into the
dust?"
demands the Lord, the LORD of
Heaven's Armies.

A Warning to Jerusalem

16 The LORD says, "Beautiful Zion* is
haughty:
craning her elegant neck,
flirting with her eyes,
walking with dainty steps,
tinkling her ankle bracelets.
17 So the Lord will send scabs on her
head;
the LORD will make beautiful Zion
bald."

18 On that day of judgment
the Lord will strip away everything
that makes her beautiful:
ornaments, headbands, crescent
necklaces,
19   earrings, bracelets, and veils;
20 scarves, ankle bracelets, sashes,
perfumes, and charms;
21 rings, jewels,
22   party clothes, gowns, capes, and
purses;
23 mirrors, fine linen garments,
head ornaments, and shawls.

24 Instead of smelling of sweet perfume,
she will stink.
She will wear a rope for a sash,
and her elegant hair will fall out.
She will wear rough burlap instead of
rich robes.
Shame will replace her beauty.*
25 The men of the city will be killed with
the sword,
and her warriors will die in battle.
26 The gates of Zion will weep and mourn.
The city will be like a ravaged woman,
huddled on the ground.

4 In that day so few men will be left that
seven women will fight for each man,
saying, "Let us all marry you! We will provide our own food and clothing. Only let us
take your name so we won't be mocked as
old maids."

3:16 Or The women of Zion (with corresponding changes to plural forms through verse 24); Hebrew reads The daughters of Zion; also in 3:17.
3:24 As in Dead Sea Scrolls; Masoretic Text reads robes / because instead of beauty.

A Promise of Restoration

2 But in that day, the branch* of the Lord
will be beautiful and glorious;
the fruit of the land will be the pride and
glory
of all who survive in Israel.
3 All who remain in Zion
will be a holy people—
those who survive the destruction of
Jerusalem
and are recorded among the living.
4 The Lord will wash the filth from
beautiful Zion*
and cleanse Jerusalem of its
bloodstains
with the hot breath of fiery judgment.
5 Then the Lord will provide shade for
Mount Zion
and all who assemble there.
He will provide a canopy of cloud during
the day
and smoke and flaming fire at night,
covering the glorious land.
6 It will be a shelter from daytime heat
and a hiding place from storms and
rain.

5 A Song about the Lord's Vineyard

1 Now I will sing for the one I love
a song about his vineyard:
My beloved had a vineyard
on a rich and fertile hill.
2 He plowed the land, cleared its stones,
and planted it with the best vines.
In the middle he built a watchtower
and carved a winepress in the nearby
rocks.
Then he waited for a harvest of sweet
grapes,
but the grapes that grew were bitter.

3 Now, you people of Jerusalem and
Judah,
you judge between me and my
vineyard.
4 What more could I have done for my
vineyard
that I have not already done?
When I expected sweet grapes,
why did my vineyard give me bitter
grapes?

5 Now let me tell you
what I will do to my vineyard:
I will tear down its hedges
and let it be destroyed.
I will break down its walls
and let the animals trample it.
6 I will make it a wild place
where the vines are not pruned and
the ground is not hoed,
a place overgrown with briers and
thorns.
I will command the clouds
to drop no rain on it.

7 The nation of Israel is the vineyard of the
Lord of Heaven's Armies.
The people of Judah are his pleasant
garden.
He expected a crop of justice,
but instead he found oppression.
He expected to find righteousness,
but instead he heard cries of violence.

Judah's Guilt and Judgment

8 What sorrow for you who buy up house
after house and field after field,
until everyone is evicted and you live
alone in the land.
9 But I have heard the Lord of Heaven's
Armies
swear a solemn oath:
"Many houses will stand deserted;
even beautiful mansions will be
empty.
10 Ten acres* of vineyard will not produce
even six gallons* of wine.
Ten baskets of seed will yield only one
basket* of grain."

11 What sorrow for those who get up early
in the morning
looking for a drink of alcohol
and spend long evenings drinking wine
to make themselves flaming drunk.
12 They furnish wine and lovely music at
their grand parties—
lyre and harp, tambourine and flute—
but they never think about the Lord
or notice what he is doing.

13 So my people will go into exile far away
because they do not know me.

4:2 Or the Branch. 4:4 Or from the women of Zion; Hebrew reads from the daughters of Zion. 5:10a Hebrew A ten yoke, that is, the area of
land plowed by ten teams of oxen in one day. 5:10b Hebrew a bath [21 liters]. 5:10c Hebrew A homer [5 bushels or 182 liters] of seed will
yield only an ephah [20 quarts or 22 liters].

Those who are great and honored will
  starve,
  and the common people will die of
    thirst.
¹⁴ The grave* is licking its lips in
  anticipation,
  opening its mouth wide.
The great and the lowly
  and all the drunken mob will be
    swallowed up.
¹⁵ Humanity will be destroyed, and people
  brought down;
  even the arrogant will lower their eyes
    in humiliation.
¹⁶ But the LORD of Heaven's Armies will be
  exalted by his justice.
  The holiness of God will be displayed
    by his righteousness.
¹⁷ In that day lambs will find good
  pastures,
  and fattened sheep and young goats*
    will feed among the ruins.

¹⁸ What sorrow for those who drag their
  sins behind them
  with ropes made of lies,
  who drag wickedness behind them like
    a cart!
¹⁹ They even mock God and say,
  "Hurry up and do something!
  We want to see what you can do.
Let the Holy One of Israel carry out his
    plan,
  for we want to know what it is."

²⁰ What sorrow for those who say
  that evil is good and good is evil,
  that dark is light and light is dark,
  that bitter is sweet and sweet is bitter.
²¹ What sorrow for those who are wise in
  their own eyes
  and think themselves so clever.
²² What sorrow for those who are heroes at
  drinking wine
  and boast about all the alcohol they
    can hold.
²³ They take bribes to let the wicked go free,
  and they punish the innocent.

²⁴ Therefore, just as fire licks up stubble
  and dry grass shrivels in the flame,
  so their roots will rot
  and their flowers wither.

For they have rejected the law of the
  LORD of Heaven's Armies;
  they have despised the word of the
    Holy One of Israel.
²⁵ That is why the LORD's anger burns
  against his people,
  and why he has raised his fist to crush
    them.
The mountains tremble,
  and the corpses of his people litter the
    streets like garbage.
But even then the LORD's anger is not
  satisfied.
  His fist is still poised to strike!

²⁶ He will send a signal to distant nations
  far away
  and whistle to those at the ends of the
    earth.
  They will come racing toward
    Jerusalem.
²⁷ They will not get tired or stumble.
  They will not stop for rest or sleep.
Not a belt will be loose,
  not a sandal strap broken.
²⁸ Their arrows will be sharp
  and their bows ready for battle.
Sparks will fly from their horses' hooves,
  and the wheels of their chariots will
    spin like a whirlwind.
²⁹ They will roar like lions,
  like the strongest of lions.
Growling, they will pounce on their
    victims and carry them off,
  and no one will be there to rescue
    them.
³⁰ They will roar over their victims on that
  day of destruction
  like the roaring of the sea.
If someone looks across the land,
  only darkness and distress will be
    seen;
  even the light will be darkened by
    clouds.

6 Isaiah's Cleansing and Call

It was in the year King Uzziah died*
that I saw the Lord. He was sitting on a
lofty throne, and the train of his robe filled
the Temple. ²Attending him were mighty
seraphim, each having six wings. With two
wings they covered their faces, with two

5:14 Hebrew *Sheol.*   **5:17** As in Greek version; Hebrew reads *and strangers.*   **6:1** King Uzziah died in 740 B.C.

The Humility of True Worship

ISAIAH 6:1-7

True worship treasures God's presence. God welcomes those into his presence who want him. The quest may be one of desperation or of delight, of frantic need or of a loving hunger for fellowship, but the motivation is clear—and so is his pleasure with it.

As we focus on God's presence and glory in worship, our hearts are humbled. We're stunned by his greatness and our smallness. Our pride shrinks, his glory shines. We see ourselves as we truly are. "It's all over!" Isaiah cries. "I am doomed, for I am a sinful man" (6:5). This self-discovery—and humility—was an instinctive response for Isaiah upon entering into God's glorious presence.

Isaiah says, "I have seen the King" (6:5) with neither apology nor arrogance; it was a breakthrough of grace that produced a breakup of pride. Isaiah, a member of the cultural, educated elite of Judah, demonstrates a childlike humility and teachability. His cry, without a vestige of style-consciousness, reveals an unreserved availability to God.

As we focus on God's presence in worship, may we learn to respond in the humility of Isaiah. Only this will help us view God afresh and pave the way to deeply felt confession and purification.

—Jack Hayford

For more on worship, see reading at Lamentations 3:16-24.

they covered their feet, and with two they flew. ³They were calling out to each other,

"Holy, holy, holy is the LORD of Heaven's Armies!
The whole earth is filled with his glory!"

⁴Their voices shook the Temple to its foundations, and the entire building was filled with smoke.

⁵Then I said, "It's all over! I am doomed, for I am a sinful man. I have filthy lips, and I live among a people with filthy lips. Yet I have seen the King, the LORD of Heaven's Armies."

⁶Then one of the seraphim flew to me with a burning coal he had taken from the altar with a pair of tongs. ⁷He touched my lips with it and said, "See, this coal has touched your lips. Now your guilt is removed, and your sins are forgiven."

⁸Then I heard the Lord asking, "Whom should I send as a messenger to this people? Who will go for us?"

I said, "Here I am. Send me."

⁹And he said, "Yes, go, and say to this people,

'Listen carefully, but do not understand.
Watch closely, but learn nothing.'
¹⁰ Harden the hearts of these people.
Plug their ears and shut their eyes.
That way, they will not see with their eyes,
nor hear with their ears,
nor understand with their hearts
and turn to me for healing."*

6:9-10 Greek version reads *And he said, "Go and say to this people, / 'When you hear what I say, you will not understand. / When you see what I do, you will not comprehend.' / For the hearts of these people are hardened, / and their ears cannot hear, and they have closed their eyes— / so their eyes cannot see, / and their ears cannot hear, / and their hearts cannot understand, / and they cannot turn to me and let me heal them."* Compare Matt 13:14-15; Mark 4:12; Luke 8:10; Acts 28:26-27.

¹¹Then I said, "Lord, how long will this go on?"

And he replied,

"Until their towns are empty,
their houses are deserted,
and the whole country is a wasteland;
¹² until the LORD has sent everyone away,
and the entire land of Israel lies
deserted.
¹³ If even a tenth—a remnant—survive,
it will be invaded again and burned.
But as a terebinth or oak tree leaves a
stump when it is cut down,
so Israel's stump will be a holy seed."

7 A Message for Ahaz

When Ahaz, son of Jotham and grandson of Uzziah, was king of Judah, King Rezin of Syria* and Pekah son of Remaliah, the king of Israel, set out to attack Jerusalem. However, they were unable to carry out their plan.

²The news had come to the royal court of Judah: "Syria is allied with Israel* against us!" So the hearts of the king and his people trembled with fear, like trees shaking in a storm.

³Then the LORD said to Isaiah, "Take your son Shear-jashub* and go out to meet King Ahaz. You will find him at the end of the aqueduct that feeds water into the upper pool, near the road leading to the field where cloth is washed.* ⁴Tell him to stop worrying. Tell him he doesn't need to fear the fierce anger of those two burned-out embers, King Rezin of Syria and Pekah son of Remaliah. ⁵Yes, the kings of Syria and Israel are plotting against him, saying, ⁶'We will attack Judah and capture it for ourselves. Then we will install the son of Tabeel as Judah's king.' ⁷But this is what the Sovereign LORD says:

"This invasion will never happen;
it will never take place;
⁸ for Syria is no stronger than its capital,
Damascus,
and Damascus is no stronger than its
king, Rezin.
As for Israel, within sixty-five years
it will be crushed and completely
destroyed.
⁹ Israel is no stronger than its capital,
Samaria,
and Samaria is no stronger than its
king, Pekah son of Remaliah.
Unless your faith is firm,
I cannot make you stand firm."

The Sign of Immanuel

¹⁰Later, the LORD sent this message to King Ahaz: ¹¹"Ask the LORD your God for a sign of confirmation, Ahaz. Make it as difficult as you want—as high as heaven or as deep as the place of the dead.*"

¹²But the king refused. "No," he said, "I will not test the LORD like that."

¹³Then Isaiah said, "Listen well, you royal family of David! Isn't it enough to exhaust human patience? Must you exhaust the patience of my God as well? ¹⁴All right then, the Lord himself will give you the sign. Look! The virgin* will conceive a child! She will give birth to a son and will call him Immanuel (which means 'God is with us'). ¹⁵By the time this child is old enough to choose what is right and reject what is wrong, he will be eating yogurt* and honey. ¹⁶For before the child is that old, the lands of the two kings you fear so much will both be deserted.

¹⁷"Then the LORD will bring things on you, your nation, and your family unlike anything since Israel broke away from Judah. He will bring the king of Assyria upon you!"

¹⁸In that day the LORD will whistle for the army of southern Egypt and for the army of Assyria. They will swarm around you like flies and bees. ¹⁹They will come in vast hordes and settle in the fertile areas and also in the desolate valleys, caves, and thorny places. ²⁰In that day the Lord will hire a "razor" from beyond the Euphrates River*—the king of Assyria—and use it to shave off everything: your land, your crops, and your people.*

²¹In that day a farmer will be fortunate to have a cow and two sheep or goats left. ²²Nevertheless, there will be enough milk

---

7:1 Hebrew *Aram;* also in 7:2, 4; 5, 8.   7:2 Hebrew *Ephraim,* referring to the northern kingdom of Israel; also in 7:5, 8, 9, 17.   7:3a *Shear-jashub* means "A remnant will return."   7:3b Or *bleached.*   7:11 Hebrew *as deep as Sheol.*   7:14 Or *young woman.*   7:15 Or *curds;* also in 7:22.
7:20a Hebrew *the river.*   7:20b Hebrew *shave off the head, the hair of the legs, and the beard.*

for everyone because so few people will be left in the land. They will eat their fill of yogurt and honey. 23 In that day the lush vineyards, now worth 1,000 pieces of silver,* will become patches of briers and thorns. 24 The entire land will become a vast expanse of briers and thorns, a hunting ground overrun by wildlife. 25 No one will go to the fertile hillsides where the gardens once grew, for briers and thorns will cover them. Cattle, sheep, and goats will graze there.

8 The Coming Assyrian Invasion

Then the LORD said to me, "Make a large signboard and clearly write this name on it: Maher-shalal-hash-baz.*" 2 I asked Uriah the priest and Zechariah son of Jeberekiah, both known as honest men, to witness my doing this.

3 Then I slept with my wife, and she became pregnant and gave birth to a son. And the LORD said, "Call him Maher-shalal-hash-baz. 4 For before this child is old enough to say 'Papa' or 'Mama,' the king of Assyria will carry away both the abundance of Damascus and the riches of Samaria."

5 Then the LORD spoke to me again and said, 6 "My care for the people of Judah is like the gently flowing waters of Shiloah, but they have rejected it. They are rejoicing over what will happen to* King Rezin and King Pekah.* 7 Therefore, the Lord will overwhelm them with a mighty flood from the Euphrates River*—the king of Assyria and all his glory. This flood will overflow all its channels 8 and sweep into Judah until it is chin deep. It will spread its wings, submerging your land from one end to the other, O Immanuel.

9 "Huddle together, you nations, and be terrified.
   Listen, all you distant lands.
   Prepare for battle, but you will be crushed!
   Yes, prepare for battle, but you will be crushed!
10 Call your councils of war, but they will be worthless.
   Develop your strategies, but they will not succeed.
   For God is with us!*"

A Call to Trust the LORD

11 The LORD has given me a strong warning not to think like everyone else does. He said,

12 "Don't call everything a conspiracy, like they do,
   and don't live in dread of what frightens them.
13 Make the LORD of Heaven's Armies holy in your life.
   He is the one you should fear.
   He is the one who should make you tremble.
14   He will keep you safe.
   But to Israel and Judah
   he will be a stone that makes people stumble,
   a rock that makes them fall.
   And for the people of Jerusalem
   he will be a trap and a snare.
15 Many will stumble and fall,
   never to rise again.
   They will be snared and captured."

16 Preserve the teaching of God;
   entrust his instructions to those who follow me.
17 I will wait for the LORD,
   who has turned away from the descendants of Jacob.
   I will put my hope in him.

18 I and the children the LORD has given me serve as signs and warnings to Israel from the LORD of Heaven's Armies who dwells in his Temple on Mount Zion.

19 Someone may say to you, "Let's ask the mediums and those who consult the spirits of the dead. With their whisperings and mutterings, they will tell us what to do." But shouldn't people ask God for guidance? Should the living seek guidance from the dead?

20 Look to God's instructions and teachings! People who contradict his word are completely in the dark. 21 They will go from one place to another, weary and hungry. And because they are hungry, they will rage and curse their king and their God. They will look up to heaven 22 and down at the earth, but wherever they look, there will be

---

7:23 Hebrew *1,000 shekels of silver*, about 25 pounds or 11.4 kilograms in weight.   8:1 *Maher-shalal-hash-baz* means "Swift to plunder and quick to carry away."   8:6a Or *They are rejoicing because of*.   8:6b Hebrew *and the son of Remaliah*.   8:7 Hebrew *the river*.   8:10 Hebrew *Immanuel!*

Pursuing Present and Future Peace
ISAIAH 9:1–7

Isaiah's vision of the "last days" recorded in Isaiah 2:1–4 is a beautiful, idyllic image: people of all nations stream to the Lord's mountain to worship, inviting one another to walk in obedience. Rather than wars that have so long ravaged this planet, "The LORD will mediate between nations" (2:4). Isaiah's next words have been captured in song and poetry, echoed in the finale of *Les Misérables,* in classic spirituals, and even in the poems of antiwar demonstrations: "They will hammer their swords into plowshares and their spears into pruning hooks. Nation will no longer fight against nation, nor train for war anymore" (2:4). From instruments of death to tools of cultivation; from images of violence to flourishing vibrance. From lives ended to new life begun. When God finally rules—when the corruption of sin is finally wiped out—peace will reign. This is the promise of God. This is our future hope.

This promise speaks to our deepest longings. We weren't created for war, bloodshed, and violence. We were made to be people of peace—peace with God, peace with one another.

And this promise in Isaiah links to the Messiah, the prophesied "Prince of Peace" (9:6). Isaiah tells us, "His government and its peace will never end. He will rule with fairness and justice from the throne of his ancestor David for all eternity" (9:7). This child who was born to us—who was given for us on the Cross, who rose and ascended to heaven—will one day return to fulfill Isaiah's vision.

So as we align our lives with this hope, we diligently pursue reconciliation with God and others. We fix our eyes on this glorious future while we live in the present, living as people of vibrant peace in a world of contagious violence.

—*Kelli B. Trujillo*

For more on reconciliation, see reading at Matthew 5:3–10.

---

trouble and anguish and dark despair. They will be thrown out into the darkness.

9 Hope in the Messiah

1*Nevertheless, that time of darkness and despair will not go on forever. The land of Zebulun and Naphtali will be humbled, but there will be a time in the future when Galilee of the Gentiles, which lies along the road that runs between the Jordan and the sea, will be filled with glory.

2* The people who walk in darkness
will see a great light.
For those who live in a land of deep
darkness,*
a light will shine.
3 You will enlarge the nation of Israel,
and its people will rejoice.
They will rejoice before you
as people rejoice at the harvest
and like warriors dividing the
plunder.

9:1 Verse 9:1 is numbered 8:23 in Hebrew text. **9:2a** Verses 9:2-21 are numbered 9:1-20 in Hebrew text. **9:2b** Greek version reads *a land where death casts its shadow.* Compare Matt 4:16.

⁴ For you will break the yoke of their
    slavery
  and lift the heavy burden from their
    shoulders.
  You will break the oppressor's rod,
    just as you did when you destroyed the
      army of Midian.
⁵ The boots of the warrior
    and the uniforms bloodstained by war
  will all be burned.
  They will be fuel for the fire.

⁶ For a child is born to us,
    a son is given to us.
  The government will rest on his
    shoulders.
  And he will be called:
  Wonderful Counselor,* Mighty God,
    Everlasting Father, Prince of Peace.
⁷ His government and its peace
    will never end.
  He will rule with fairness and justice from
    the throne of his ancestor David
    for all eternity.
  The passionate commitment of the
    LORD of Heaven's Armies
    will make this happen!

The LORD's Anger against Israel

⁸ The Lord has spoken out against Jacob;
    his judgment has fallen upon Israel.
⁹ And the people of Israel* and Samaria,
    who spoke with such pride and
      arrogance,
  will soon know it.
¹⁰ They said, "We will replace the broken
      bricks of our ruins with finished
      stone,
    and replant the felled sycamore-fig
      trees with cedars."

¹¹ But the LORD will bring Rezin's enemies
      against Israel
    and stir up all their foes.
¹² The Syrians* from the east and the
      Philistines from the west
    will bare their fangs and devour Israel.
  But even then the LORD's anger will not
    be satisfied.
  His fist is still poised to strike.

¹³ For after all this punishment, the people
    will still not repent.

They will not seek the LORD of
    Heaven's Armies.
¹⁴ Therefore, in a single day the LORD will
      destroy both the head and the tail,
    the noble palm branch and the lowly
      reed.
¹⁵ The leaders of Israel are the head,
    and the lying prophets are the tail.
¹⁶ For the leaders of the people have misled
      them.
  They have led them down the path of
    destruction.
¹⁷ That is why the Lord takes no pleasure
      in the young men
    and shows no mercy even to the
      widows and orphans.
  For they are all wicked hypocrites,
    and they all speak foolishness.
  But even then the LORD's anger will not
    be satisfied.
  His fist is still poised to strike.

¹⁸ This wickedness is like a brushfire.
    It burns not only briers and thorns
  but also sets the forests ablaze.
    Its burning sends up clouds of
      smoke.
¹⁹ The land will be blackened
    by the fury of the LORD of Heaven's
      Armies.
  The people will be fuel for the fire,
    and no one will spare even his own
      brother.
²⁰ They will attack their neighbor on the
      right
    but will still be hungry.
  They will devour their neighbor on the
      left
    but will not be satisfied.
  In the end they will even eat their own
      children.*
²¹ Manasseh will feed on Ephraim,
    Ephraim will feed on Manasseh,
    and both will devour Judah.
  But even then the LORD's anger will not
    be satisfied.
  His fist is still poised to strike.

10 ¹ What sorrow awaits the unjust
      judges
    and those who issue unfair laws.

9:6 Or *Wonderful, Counselor.*   9:9 Hebrew *of Ephraim,* referring to the northern kingdom of Israel.   9:12 Hebrew *Arameans.*   9:20 Or *eat their own arms.*

From Impasse to Action

ISAIAH 10:1-3

News of suffering and injustice can overwhelm and immobilize us. Though we care deeply, "We feel like deer frozen by headlights," writes Gary Haugen in *Good News about Injustice*. "Instead of energizing us for action, the overwhelming injustice in our world actually makes us feel numb."

All of us, at one time or other, find ourselves here. Dr. Viji Cammauf hit her moment of overwhelmed paralysis after watching a film about a child-bride who endured savage abuse. For three days Viji wept in despair until finally, she asked herself, *What am I going to do about it?* She rallied others and eventually led the way for a children's home to be built in Kondamangalam, India.

Viji was able to move from impasse to action by . . .

Starting small. Taking a cue from one of her role models, Amy Carmichael, Viji focused on the importance of one child at a time. "When you hear about the millions who are homeless or orphaned, it seems like an overwhelming number that you cannot do anything about," says Viji. "But if you start with one, that makes a big difference in the life of that one child."

Relying on God's power. Early on Viji learned human effort is not enough to change the world. As an idealistic teenager, she joined Gandhi's Freedom Fighters on a month-long journey across her native country. Yet even as a young pre-Christian, Viji says, "I realized we could not change India just through the teachings of a human being." Viji's confidence today rests in knowing God's vibrant power is at work.

Persevering. In her ministry Viji has faced all sorts of problems with government red tape. When faced with such challenges, Viji says, "You keep moving in the direction God has given you. You don't give up. If God has given you a promise, hold on to that, and persevere."

Meaningful action begins with transforming our despair about injustice into imaginative solutions. It begins with the question, *What am I going to do about it?* Then, with finding the courage to take that first small step.

—*Karen Keen*

For more on justice, see reading at Isaiah 58:6-12.

2 They deprive the poor of justice
and deny the rights of the needy
among my people.
They prey on widows
and take advantage of orphans.
3 What will you do when I punish you,
when I send disaster upon you from a
distant land?
To whom will you turn for help?
Where will your treasures be
safe?

4 You will stumble along as prisoners
or lie among the dead.
But even then the LORD's anger will not
be satisfied.
His fist is still poised to strike.

Judgment against Assyria

5 "What sorrow awaits Assyria, the rod of
my anger.
I use it as a club to express my
anger.

⁶ I am sending Assyria against a godless
  nation,
    against a people with whom I am
      angry.
  Assyria will plunder them,
    trampling them like dirt beneath its
      feet.
⁷ But the king of Assyria will not
    understand that he is my tool;
  his mind does not work that way.
  His plan is simply to destroy,
    to cut down nation after nation.
⁸ He will say,
  'Each of my princes will soon be a
    king.
⁹ We destroyed Calno just as we did
    Carchemish.
  Hamath fell before us as Arpad did.
  And we destroyed Samaria just as we
    did Damascus.
¹⁰ Yes, we have finished off many a
    kingdom
  whose gods were greater than those in
    Jerusalem and Samaria.
¹¹ So we will defeat Jerusalem and her gods,
  just as we destroyed Samaria with
    hers.'"

¹² After the Lord has used the king of
Assyria to accomplish his purposes on
Mount Zion and in Jerusalem, he will
turn against the king of Assyria and punish him—for he is proud and arrogant. ¹³ He
boasts,

  "By my own powerful arm I have done
    this.
  With my own shrewd wisdom I
    planned it.
  I have broken down the defenses of
    nations
    and carried off their treasures.
  I have knocked down their kings like
    a bull.
¹⁴ I have robbed their nests of riches
  and gathered up kingdoms as a farmer
    gathers eggs.
  No one can even flap a wing against me
    or utter a peep of protest."

¹⁵ But can the ax boast greater power than
  the person who uses it?

  Is the saw greater than the person who
    saws?
  Can a rod strike unless a hand moves it?
  Can a wooden cane walk by itself?
¹⁶ Therefore, the Lord, the LORD of
    Heaven's Armies,
  will send a plague among Assyria's
    proud troops,
  and a flaming fire will consume its
    glory.
¹⁷ The LORD, the Light of Israel, will be a
    fire;
  the Holy One will be a flame.
  He will devour the thorns and briers
    with fire,
  burning up the enemy in a single
    night.
¹⁸ The LORD will consume Assyria's glory
  like a fire consumes a forest in a
    fruitful land;
  it will waste away like sick people in a
    plague.
¹⁹ Of all that glorious forest, only a few
    trees will survive—
  so few that a child could count them!

Hope for the LORD's People

²⁰ In that day the remnant left in Israel,
  the survivors in the house of Jacob,
  will no longer depend on allies
    who seek to destroy them.
  But they will faithfully trust the LORD,
    the Holy One of Israel.
²¹ A remnant will return;*
  yes, the remnant of Jacob will return
    to the Mighty God.
²² But though the people of Israel are as
    numerous
  as the sand of the seashore,
  only a remnant of them will return.
  The LORD has rightly decided to
    destroy his people.
²³ Yes, the Lord, the LORD of Heaven's
    Armies,
  has already decided to destroy the
    entire land.*

²⁴ So this is what the Lord, the LORD of
Heaven's Armies, says: "O my people in
Zion, do not be afraid of the Assyrians
when they oppress you with rod and club as

10:21 Hebrew *Shear-jashub;* see 7:3; 8:18.   10:22-23 Greek version reads *only a remnant of them will be saved. / For he will carry out his
sentence quickly and with finality and righteousness; / for God will carry out his sentence upon all the world with finality.* Compare Rom 9:27-28.

the Egyptians did long ago. [25]In a little while my anger against you will end, and then my anger will rise up to destroy them." [26]The LORD of Heaven's Armies will lash them with his whip, as he did when Gideon triumphed over the Midianites at the rock of Oreb, or when the LORD's staff was raised to drown the Egyptian army in the sea.

[27] In that day the LORD will end the
bondage of his people.
He will break the yoke of slavery
and lift it from their shoulders.*

[28] Look, the Assyrians are now at Aiath.
They are passing through Migron
and are storing their equipment at
Micmash.
[29] They are crossing the pass
and are camping at Geba.
Fear strikes the town of Ramah.
All the people of Gibeah, the
hometown of Saul,
are running for their lives.
[30] Scream in terror,
you people of Gallim!
Shout out a warning to Laishah.
Oh, poor Anathoth!
[31] There go the people of Madmenah, all
fleeing.
The citizens of Gebim are trying to
hide.
[32] The enemy stops at Nob for the rest of
that day.
He shakes his fist at beautiful Mount
Zion, the mountain of Jerusalem.

[33] But look! The Lord, the LORD of
Heaven's Armies,
will chop down the mighty tree of
Assyria with great power!
He will cut down the proud.
That lofty tree will be brought down.
[34] He will cut down the forest trees with
an ax.
Lebanon will fall to the Mighty One.*

11 A Branch from David's Line

[1] Out of the stump of David's family*
will grow a shoot—
yes, a new Branch bearing fruit from
the old root.

[2] And the Spirit of the LORD will rest on
him—
the Spirit of wisdom and
understanding,
the Spirit of counsel and might,
the Spirit of knowledge and the fear of
the LORD.
[3] He will delight in obeying the LORD.
He will not judge by appearance
nor make a decision based on hearsay.
[4] He will give justice to the poor
and make fair decisions for the
exploited.
The earth will shake at the force of his
word,
and one breath from his mouth will
destroy the wicked.
[5] He will wear righteousness like a belt
and truth like an undergarment.

[6] In that day the wolf and the lamb will
live together;
the leopard will lie down with the
baby goat.
The calf and the yearling will be safe
with the lion,
and a little child will lead them all.
[7] The cow will graze near the bear.
The cub and the calf will lie down
together.
The lion will eat hay like a cow.
[8] The baby will play safely near the hole of
a cobra.
Yes, a little child will put its hand in a
nest of deadly snakes without harm.
[9] Nothing will hurt or destroy in all my
holy mountain,
for as the waters fill the sea,
so the earth will be filled with people
who know the LORD.

[10] In that day the heir to David's throne*
will be a banner of salvation to all the
world.
The nations will rally to him,
and the land where he lives will be a
glorious place.*
[11] In that day the Lord will reach out his
hand a second time
to bring back the remnant of his
people—

10:27 As in Greek version; Hebrew reads *The yoke will be broken, / for you have grown so fat.* **10:34** Or *with an ax / as even the mighty trees of Lebanon fall.* **11:1** Hebrew *the stump of the line of Jesse.* Jesse was King David's father. **11:10a** Hebrew *the root of Jesse.* **11:10b** Greek version reads *In that day the heir to David's throne* [literally *the root of Jesse*] *will come, / and he will rule over the Gentiles. / They will place their hopes on him.* Compare Rom 15:12.

those who remain in Assyria and
northern Egypt;
in southern Egypt, Ethiopia,* and Elam;
in Babylonia,* Hamath, and all the
distant coastlands.
12 He will raise a flag among the nations
and assemble the exiles of Israel.
He will gather the scattered people of
Judah
from the ends of the earth.

13 Then at last the jealousy between Israel*
and Judah will end.
They will not be rivals anymore.
14 They will join forces to swoop down on
Philistia to the west.
Together they will attack and plunder
the nations to the east.
They will occupy the lands of Edom and
Moab,
and Ammon will obey them.
15 The LORD will make a dry path through
the gulf of the Red Sea.*
He will wave his hand over the
Euphrates River,*
sending a mighty wind to divide it into
seven streams
so it can easily be crossed on foot.
16 He will make a highway for the remnant
of his people,
the remnant coming from Assyria,
just as he did for Israel long ago
when they returned from Egypt.

12 Songs of Praise for Salvation

1 In that day you will sing:
"I will praise you, O LORD!
You were angry with me, but not any
more.
Now you comfort me.
2 See, God has come to save me.
I will trust in him and not be afraid.
The LORD GOD is my strength and my
song;
he has given me victory."

3 With joy you will drink deeply
from the fountain of salvation!
4 In that wonderful day you will sing:
"Thank the LORD! Praise his name!
Tell the nations what he has done.
Let them know how mighty he is!

5 Sing to the LORD, for he has done
wonderful things.
Make known his praise around the
world.
6 Let all the people of Jerusalem* shout his
praise with joy!
For great is the Holy One of Israel who
lives among you."

13 A Message about Babylon

Isaiah son of Amoz received this message concerning the destruction of Babylon:

2 "Raise a signal flag on a bare hilltop.
Call up an army against Babylon.
Wave your hand to encourage them
as they march into the palaces of the
high and mighty.
3 I, the LORD, have dedicated these
soldiers for this task.
Yes, I have called mighty warriors to
express my anger,
and they will rejoice when I am
exalted."

4 Hear the noise on the mountains!
Listen, as the vast armies march!
It is the noise and shouting of many
nations.
The LORD of Heaven's Armies has
called this army together.
5 They come from distant countries,
from beyond the farthest horizons.
They are the LORD's weapons to carry
out his anger.
With them he will destroy the whole
land.

6 Scream in terror, for the day of the LORD
has arrived—
the time for the Almighty to destroy.
7 Every arm is paralyzed with fear.
Every heart melts,
8 and people are terrified.
Pangs of anguish grip them,
like those of a woman in labor.
They look helplessly at one another,
their faces aflame with fear.

9 For see, the day of the LORD is coming—
the terrible day of his fury and fierce
anger.

11:11a Hebrew in Pathros, Cush.   11:11b Hebrew in Shinar.   11:13 Hebrew Ephraim, referring to the northern kingdom of Israel.
11:15a Hebrew will destroy the tongue of the sea of Egypt.   11:15b Hebrew the river.   12:6 Hebrew Zion.

The land will be made desolate,
and all the sinners destroyed with it.
¹⁰ The heavens will be black above them;
the stars will give no light.
The sun will be dark when it rises,
and the moon will provide no light.

¹¹ "I, the LORD, will punish the world for
its evil
and the wicked for their sin.
I will crush the arrogance of the proud
and humble the pride of the mighty.
¹² I will make people scarcer than gold—
more rare than the fine gold of
Ophir.
¹³ For I will shake the heavens.
The earth will move from its place
when the LORD of Heaven's Armies
displays his wrath
in the day of his fierce anger."

¹⁴ Everyone in Babylon will run about like
a hunted gazelle,
like sheep without a shepherd.
They will try to find their own people
and flee to their own land.
¹⁵ Anyone who is captured will be cut
down—
run through with a sword.
¹⁶ Their little children will be dashed to
death before their eyes.
Their homes will be sacked, and their
wives will be raped.

¹⁷ "Look, I will stir up the Medes against
Babylon.
They cannot be tempted by silver
or bribed with gold.
¹⁸ The attacking armies will shoot down
the young men with arrows.
They will have no mercy on helpless
babies
and will show no compassion for
children."

¹⁹ Babylon, the most glorious of kingdoms,
the flower of Chaldean pride,
will be devastated like Sodom and
Gomorrah
when God destroyed them.
²⁰ Babylon will never be inhabited again.
It will remain empty for generation
after generation.

Nomads will refuse to camp there,
and shepherds will not bed down their
sheep.
²¹ Desert animals will move into the ruined
city,
and the houses will be haunted by
howling creatures.
Owls will live among the ruins,
and wild goats will go there to dance.
²² Hyenas will howl in its fortresses,
and jackals will make dens in its
luxurious palaces.
Babylon's days are numbered;
its time of destruction will soon arrive.

14 A Taunt for Babylon's King

But the LORD will have mercy on the
descendants of Jacob. He will choose Israel
as his special people once again. He will
bring them back to settle once again in their
own land. And people from many different nations will come and join them there
and unite with the people of Israel.* ²The
nations of the world will help the LORD's
people to return, and those who come to
live in their land will serve them. Those
who captured Israel will themselves be captured, and Israel will rule over its enemies.

³ In that wonderful day when the LORD
gives his people rest from sorrow and fear,
from slavery and chains, ⁴you will taunt the
king of Babylon. You will say,

"The mighty man has been destroyed.
Yes, your insolence* is ended.
⁵ For the LORD has crushed your wicked
power
and broken your evil rule.
⁶ You struck the people with endless
blows of rage
and held the nations in your angry
grip
with unrelenting tyranny.
⁷ But finally the earth is at rest and quiet.
Now it can sing again!
⁸ Even the trees of the forest—
the cypress trees and the cedars of
Lebanon—
sing out this joyous song:
'Since you have been cut down,
no one will come now to cut us down!'

14:1 Hebrew *the house of Jacob*. The names "Jacob" and "Israel" are often interchanged throughout the Old Testament, referring sometimes to the individual patriarch and sometimes to the nation.   **14:4** As in Dead Sea Scrolls; the meaning of the Masoretic Text is uncertain.

⁹ "In the place of the dead* there is
  excitement
    over your arrival.
The spirits of world leaders and mighty
    kings long dead
  stand up to see you.
¹⁰ With one voice they all cry out,
  'Now you are as weak as we are!
¹¹ Your might and power were buried with
    you.*
  The sound of the harp in your palace
    has ceased.
  Now maggots are your sheet,
    and worms your blanket.'

¹² "How you are fallen from heaven,
    O shining star, son of the morning!
You have been thrown down to the
    earth,
  you who destroyed the nations of the
    world.
¹³ For you said to yourself,
  'I will ascend to heaven and set my
    throne above God's stars.
I will preside on the mountain of the
    gods
  far away in the north.*
¹⁴ I will climb to the highest heavens
  and be like the Most High.'
¹⁵ Instead, you will be brought down to the
    place of the dead,
  down to its lowest depths.
¹⁶ Everyone there will stare at you and ask,
  'Can this be the one who shook the earth
    and made the kingdoms of the world
    tremble?
¹⁷ Is this the one who destroyed the world
    and made it into a wasteland?
  Is this the king who demolished the
    world's greatest cities
    and had no mercy on his prisoners?'

¹⁸ "The kings of the nations lie in stately
    glory,
  each in his own tomb,
¹⁹ but you will be thrown out of your grave
    like a worthless branch.
  Like a corpse trampled underfoot,
    you will be dumped into a mass grave
    with those killed in battle.
  You will descend to the pit.
²⁰ You will not be given a proper burial,

for you have destroyed your nation
  and slaughtered your people.
The descendants of such an evil person
  will never again receive honor.
²¹ Kill this man's children!
  Let them die because of their father's
    sins!
They must not rise and conquer the earth,
  filling the world with their cities."

²² This is what the Lord of Heaven's
    Armies says:
  "I, myself, have risen against Babylon!
I will destroy its children and its
    children's children,"
  says the Lord.
²³ "I will make Babylon a desolate place of
    owls,
  filled with swamps and marshes.
I will sweep the land with the broom of
    destruction.
  I, the Lord of Heaven's Armies, have
    spoken!"

A Message about Assyria

²⁴ The Lord of Heaven's Armies has sworn
this oath:

  "It will all happen as I have planned.
    It will be as I have decided.
²⁵ I will break the Assyrians when they are
    in Israel;
  I will trample them on my mountains.
My people will no longer be their slaves
    nor bow down under their heavy
    loads.
²⁶ I have a plan for the whole earth,
  a hand of judgment upon all the
    nations.
²⁷ The Lord of Heaven's Armies has
    spoken—
  who can change his plans?
When his hand is raised,
  who can stop him?"

A Message about Philistia

²⁸ This message came to me the year King
Ahaz died:*

²⁹ Do not rejoice, you Philistines,
  that the rod that struck you is broken—
    that the king who attacked you is
    dead.

14:9 Hebrew *Sheol;* also in 14:15.   **14:11** Hebrew *were brought down to Sheol.*   **14:13** Or *on the heights of Zaphon.*   **14:28** King Ahaz died in
715 b.c.

For from that snake a more poisonous
snake will be born,
a fiery serpent to destroy you!
[30] I will feed the poor in my pasture;
the needy will lie down in peace.
But as for you, I will wipe you out with
famine
and destroy the few who remain.
[31] Wail at the gates! Weep in the cities!
Melt with fear, you Philistines!
A powerful army comes like smoke from
the north.
Each soldier rushes forward eager to
fight.

[32] What should we tell the Philistine messengers? Tell them,

"The LORD has built Jerusalem*;
its walls will give refuge to his
oppressed people."

15 A Message about Moab

This message came to me concerning
Moab:

In one night the town of Ar will be
leveled,
and the city of Kir will be
destroyed.
[2] Your people will go to their temple in
Dibon to mourn.
They will go to their sacred shrines to
weep.
They will wail for the fate of Nebo and
Medeba,
shaving their heads in sorrow and
cutting off their beards.
[3] They will wear burlap as they wander
the streets.
From every home and public
square will come the sound of
wailing.
[4] The people of Heshbon and Elealeh will
cry out;
their voices will be heard as far away
as Jahaz!
The bravest warriors of Moab will cry
out in utter terror.
They will be helpless with fear.

[5] My heart weeps for Moab.
Its people flee to Zoar and Eglath-
shelishiyah.

Weeping, they climb the road to Luhith.
Their cries of distress can be heard all
along the road to Horonaim.
[6] Even the waters of Nimrim are dried up!
The grassy banks are scorched.
The tender plants are gone;
nothing green remains.
[7] The people grab their possessions
and carry them across the Ravine of
Willows.
[8] A cry of distress echoes through the
land of Moab
from one end to the other—
from Eglaim to Beer-elim.
[9] The stream near Dibon* runs red with
blood,
but I am still not finished with Dibon!
Lions will hunt down the survivors—
both those who try to escape
and those who remain behind.

16

[1] Send lambs from Sela as tribute
to the ruler of the land.
Send them through the desert
to the mountain of beautiful Zion.
[2] The women of Moab are left like
homeless birds
at the shallow crossings of the Arnon
River.
[3] "Help us," they cry.
"Defend us against our enemies.
Protect us from their relentless
attack.
Do not betray us now that we have
escaped.
[4] Let our refugees stay among you.
Hide them from our enemies until the
terror is past."

When oppression and destruction have
ended
and enemy raiders have disappeared,
[5] then God will establish one of David's
descendants as king.
He will rule with mercy and truth.
He will always do what is just
and be eager to do what is right.

[6] We have heard about proud Moab—
about its pride and arrogance and
rage.
But all that boasting has disappeared.

14:32 Hebrew *Zion.* 15:9 As in Dead Sea Scrolls, some Greek manuscripts, and Latin Vulgate; Masoretic Text reads *Dimon;* also in 15:9b.

7 The entire land of Moab weeps.
    Yes, everyone in Moab mourns
for the cakes of raisins from Kir-hareseth.
    They are all gone now.
8 The farms of Heshbon are abandoned;
    the vineyards at Sibmah are deserted.
The rulers of the nations have broken
        down Moab—
    that beautiful grapevine.
Its tendrils spread north as far as the
        town of Jazer
    and trailed eastward into the
        wilderness.
Its shoots reached so far west
    that they crossed over the Dead Sea.*

9 So now I weep for Jazer and the
        vineyards of Sibmah;
    my tears will flow for Heshbon and
        Elealeh.
There are no more shouts of joy
    over your summer fruits and harvest.
10 Gone now is the gladness,
    gone the joy of harvest.
There will be no singing in the
        vineyards,
    no more happy shouts,
no treading of grapes in the winepresses.
    I have ended all their harvest joys.
11 My heart's cry for Moab is like a lament
        on a harp.
    I am filled with anguish for Kir-
        hareseth.*
12 The people of Moab will worship at their
        pagan shrines,
    but it will do them no good.
They will cry to the gods in their
        temples,
    but no one will be able to save them.

13 The Lord has already said these things
about Moab in the past. 14 But now the
Lord says, "Within three years, counting
each day,* the glory of Moab will be ended.
From its great population, only a few of its
people will be left alive."

17 A Message about Damascus and Israel

This message came to me concerning Damascus:

"Look, the city of Damascus will
    disappear!
    It will become a heap of ruins.
2 The towns of Aroer will be deserted.
    Flocks will graze in the streets and lie
        down undisturbed,
    with no one to chase them away.
3 The fortified towns of Israel* will also be
        destroyed,
    and the royal power of Damascus will
        end.
All that remains of Syria*
    will share the fate of Israel's departed
        glory,"
    declares the Lord of Heaven's Armies.

4 "In that day Israel's* glory will grow dim;
    its robust body will waste away.
5 The whole land will look like a grainfield
    after the harvesters have gathered the
        grain.
It will be desolate,
    like the fields in the valley of Rephaim
        after the harvest.
6 Only a few of its people will be left,
    like stray olives left on a tree after the
        harvest.
Only two or three remain in the highest
        branches,
    four or five scattered here and there
        on the limbs,"
    declares the Lord, the God of Israel.

7 Then at last the people will look to their
        Creator
    and turn their eyes to the Holy One of
        Israel.
8 They will no longer look to their idols
        for help
    or worship what their own hands have
        made.
They will never again bow down to their
    Asherah poles
    or worship at the pagan shrines they
        have built.
9 Their largest cities will be like a deserted
        forest,
    like the land the Hivites and Amorites
        abandoned*
when the Israelites came here so long ago.
    It will be utterly desolate.

16:8 Hebrew *the sea.* **16:11** Hebrew *Kir-heres,* a variant spelling of Kir-hareseth. **16:14** Hebrew *Within three years, as a servant bound by contract would count them.* **17:3a** Hebrew *of Ephraim,* referring to the northern kingdom of Israel. **17:3b** Hebrew *Aram.* **17:4** Hebrew *Jacob's.* See note on 14:1. **17:9** As in Greek version; Hebrew reads *like places of the wood and the highest bough.*

¹⁰ Why? Because you have turned from the
God who can save you.
You have forgotten the Rock who can
hide you.
So you may plant the finest grapevines
and import the most expensive
seedlings.
¹¹ They may sprout on the day you set
them out;
yes, they may blossom on the very
morning you plant them,
but you will never pick any grapes from
them.
Your only harvest will be a load of
grief and unrelieved pain.

¹² Listen! The armies of many nations
roar like the roaring of the sea.
Hear the thunder of the mighty forces
as they rush forward like thundering
waves.
¹³ But though they thunder like breakers
on a beach,
God will silence them, and they will
run away.
They will flee like chaff scattered by the
wind,
like a tumbleweed whirling before a
storm.
¹⁴ In the evening Israel waits in terror,
but by dawn its enemies are dead.
This is the just reward of those who
plunder us,
a fitting end for those who destroy us.

18 A Message about Ethiopia

¹ Listen, Ethiopia*—land of fluttering
sails*
that lies at the headwaters of the Nile,
² that sends ambassadors
in swift boats down the river.

Go, swift messengers!
Take a message to a tall, smooth-skinned
people,
who are feared far and wide
for their conquests and destruction,
and whose land is divided by rivers.

³ All you people of the world,
everyone who lives on the earth—
when I raise my battle flag on the
mountain, look!
When I blow the ram's horn, listen!

⁴ For the LORD has told me this:
"I will watch quietly from my dwelling
place—
as quietly as the heat rises on a
summer day,
or as the morning dew forms during
the harvest."
⁵ Even before you begin your attack,
while your plans are ripening like
grapes,
the LORD will cut off your new growth
with pruning shears.
He will snip off and discard your
spreading branches.
⁶ Your mighty army will be left dead in the
fields
for the mountain vultures and wild
animals.
The vultures will tear at the corpses all
summer.
The wild animals will gnaw at the
bones all winter.

⁷ At that time the LORD of Heaven's
Armies will receive gifts
from this land divided by rivers,
from this tall, smooth-skinned
people,
who are feared far and wide for their
conquests and destruction.
They will bring the gifts to Jerusalem,*
where the LORD of Heaven's Armies
dwells.

19 A Message about Egypt

This message came to me concerning
Egypt:

Look! The LORD is advancing against
Egypt,
riding on a swift cloud.
The idols of Egypt tremble.
The hearts of the Egyptians melt with
fear.

² "I will make Egyptian fight against
Egyptian—
brother against brother,
neighbor against neighbor,
city against city,
province against province.
³ The Egyptians will lose heart,
and I will confuse their plans.

18:1a Hebrew *Cush.* **18:1b** Or *land of many locusts;* Hebrew reads *land of whirring wings.* **18:7** Hebrew *to Mount Zion.*

They will plead with their idols for
wisdom
and call on spirits, mediums, and
those who consult the spirits of the
dead.
⁴ I will hand Egypt over
to a hard, cruel master.
A fierce king will rule them,"
says the Lord, the LORD of Heaven's
Armies.

⁵ The waters of the Nile will fail to rise
and flood the fields.
The riverbed will be parched and dry.
⁶ The canals of the Nile will dry up,
and the streams of Egypt will stink
with rotting reeds and rushes.
⁷ All the greenery along the riverbank
and all the crops along the river
will dry up and blow away.
⁸ The fishermen will lament for lack of
work.
Those who cast hooks into the Nile
will groan,
and those who use nets will lose heart.
⁹ There will be no flax for the harvesters,
no thread for the weavers.
¹⁰ They will be in despair,
and all the workers will be sick at
heart.

¹¹ What fools are the officials of Zoan!
Their best counsel to the king of Egypt
is stupid and wrong.
Will they still boast to Pharaoh of their
wisdom?
Will they dare brag about all their wise
ancestors?
¹² Where are your wise counselors,
Pharaoh?
Let them tell you what God plans,
what the LORD of Heaven's Armies is
going to do to Egypt.
¹³ The officials of Zoan are fools,
and the officials of Memphis* are
deluded.
The leaders of the people
have led Egypt astray.
¹⁴ The LORD has sent a spirit of foolishness
on them,
so all their suggestions are wrong.
They cause Egypt to stagger
like a drunk in his vomit.

¹⁵ There is nothing Egypt can do.
All are helpless—
the head and the tail,
the noble palm branch and the lowly
reed.

¹⁶ In that day the Egyptians will be as
weak as women. They will cower in fear
beneath the upraised fist of the LORD of
Heaven's Armies. ¹⁷ Just to speak the name
of Israel will terrorize them, for the LORD
of Heaven's Armies has laid out his plans
against them.

¹⁸ In that day five of Egypt's cities will follow the LORD of Heaven's Armies. They
will even begin to speak Hebrew, the language of Canaan. One of these cities will be
Heliopolis, the City of the Sun.*

¹⁹ In that day there will be an altar to the
LORD in the heart of Egypt, and there will
be a monument to the LORD at its border.
²⁰ It will be a sign and a witness that the
LORD of Heaven's Armies is worshiped in
the land of Egypt. When the people cry
to the LORD for help against those who
oppress them, he will send them a savior who will rescue them. ²¹ The LORD will
make himself known to the Egyptians. Yes,
they will know the LORD and will give their
sacrifices and offerings to him. They will
make a vow to the LORD and will keep it.
²² The LORD will strike Egypt, and then he
will bring healing. For the Egyptians will
turn to the LORD, and he will listen to their
pleas and heal them.

²³ In that day Egypt and Assyria will be
connected by a highway. The Egyptians and
Assyrians will move freely between their
lands, and they will both worship God.
²⁴ And Israel will be their ally. The three will
be together, and Israel will be a blessing to
them. ²⁵ For the LORD of Heaven's Armies
will say, "Blessed be Egypt, my people.
Blessed be Assyria, the land I have made.
Blessed be Israel, my special possession!"

20 A Message about Egypt and Ethiopia

In the year when King Sargon of Assyria
sent his commander in chief to capture
the Philistine city of Ashdod,* ²the LORD
told Isaiah son of Amoz, "Take off the bur-

19:13 Hebrew *Noph.*   **19:18** Or *will be the City of Destruction.*   **20:1** Ashdod was captured by Assyria in 711 B.C.

lap you have been wearing, and remove your sandals." Isaiah did as he was told and walked around naked and barefoot.

³ Then the LORD said, "My servant Isaiah has been walking around naked and barefoot for the last three years. This is a sign—a symbol of the terrible troubles I will bring upon Egypt and Ethiopia.* ⁴ For the king of Assyria will take away the Egyptians and Ethiopians* as prisoners. He will make them walk naked and barefoot, both young and old, their buttocks bared, to the shame of Egypt. ⁵ Then the Philistines will be thrown into panic, for they counted on the power of Ethiopia and boasted of their allies in Egypt! ⁶ They will say, 'If this can happen to Egypt, what chance do we have? We were counting on Egypt to protect us from the king of Assyria.'"

21 A Message about Babylon

This message came to me concerning Babylon—the desert by the sea*:

Disaster is roaring down on you from
    the desert,
    like a whirlwind sweeping in from the
      Negev.
² I see a terrifying vision:
    I see the betrayer betraying,
    the destroyer destroying.
Go ahead, you Elamites and Medes,
    attack and lay siege.
I will make an end
    to all the groaning Babylon caused.
³ My stomach aches and burns with pain.
    Sharp pangs of anguish are upon me,
    like those of a woman in labor.
I grow faint when I hear what God is
    planning;
    I am too afraid to look.
⁴ My mind reels and my heart races.
    I longed for evening to come,
    but now I am terrified of the dark.

⁵ Look! They are preparing a great feast.
    They are spreading rugs for people to
      sit on.
    Everyone is eating and drinking.
But quick! Grab your shields and prepare
    for battle.
    You are being attacked!

⁶ Meanwhile, the Lord said to me,
    "Put a watchman on the city wall.
    Let him shout out what he sees.
⁷ He should look for chariots
    drawn by pairs of horses,
    and for riders on donkeys and
      camels.
    Let the watchman be fully alert."

⁸ Then the watchman* called out,
    "Day after day I have stood on the
      watchtower, my lord.
    Night after night I have remained at
      my post.
⁹ Now at last—look!
Here comes a man in a chariot
    with a pair of horses!"
Then the watchman said,
    "Babylon is fallen, fallen!
All the idols of Babylon
    lie broken on the ground!"
¹⁰ O my people, threshed and
    winnowed,
    I have told you everything the LORD of
      Heaven's Armies has said,
    everything the God of Israel has
      told me.

A Message about Edom

¹¹ This message came to me concerning Edom*:

Someone from Edom* keeps calling
    to me,
    "Watchman, how much longer until
      morning?
    When will the night be over?"
¹² The watchman replies,
    "Morning is coming, but night will soon
      return.
    If you wish to ask again, then come
      back and ask."

A Message about Arabia

¹³ This message came to me concerning Arabia:

O caravans from Dedan,
    hide in the deserts of Arabia.
¹⁴ O people of Tema,
    bring water to these thirsty people,
    food to these weary refugees.

20:3 Hebrew *Cush*; also in 20:5.   **20:4** Hebrew *Cushites*.   **21:1** Hebrew *concerning the desert by the sea*.   **21:8** As in Dead Sea Scrolls and Syriac version; Masoretic Text reads *a lion*.   **21:11a** Hebrew *Dumah*, which means "silence" or "stillness." It is a wordplay on the word *Edom*. **21:11b** Hebrew *Seir*, another name for Edom.

¹⁵ They have fled from the sword,
　from the drawn sword,
from the bent bow
　and the terrors of battle.

¹⁶ The Lord said to me, "Within a year, counting each day,* all the glory of Kedar will come to an end. ¹⁷ Only a few of its courageous archers will survive. I, the LORD, the God of Israel, have spoken!"

22 A Message about Jerusalem

This message came to me concerning Jerusalem—the Valley of Vision*:

What is happening?
　Why is everyone running to the
　　rooftops?
² The whole city is in a terrible uproar.
　What do I see in this reveling city?
Bodies are lying everywhere,
　killed not in battle but by famine and
　　disease.
³ All your leaders have fled.
　They surrendered without resistance.
The people tried to slip away,
　but they were captured, too.
⁴ That's why I said, "Leave me alone to
　　weep;
　do not try to comfort me.
Let me cry for my people
　as I watch them being destroyed."

⁵ Oh, what a day of crushing defeat!
　What a day of confusion and terror
brought by the Lord, the LORD of
　　Heaven's Armies,
　upon the Valley of Vision!
The walls of Jerusalem have been broken,
　and cries of death echo from the
　　mountainsides.
⁶ Elamites are the archers,
　with their chariots and charioteers.
　The men of Kir hold up the shields.
⁷ Chariots fill your beautiful valleys,
　and charioteers storm your gates.
⁸ Judah's defenses have been stripped away.
　You run to the armory* for your
　　weapons.
⁹ You inspect the breaks in the walls of
　　Jerusalem.*
　You store up water in the lower pool.

¹⁰ You survey the houses and tear some
　　down
　for stone to strengthen the walls.
¹¹ Between the city walls, you build a
　　reservoir
　for water from the old pool.
But you never ask for help from the One
　who did all this.
You never considered the One who
　planned this long ago.

¹² At that time the Lord, the LORD of
　　Heaven's Armies,
　called you to weep and mourn.
He told you to shave your heads in
　　sorrow for your sins
　and to wear clothes of burlap to show
　　your remorse.
¹³ But instead, you dance and play;
　you slaughter cattle and kill sheep.
You feast on meat and drink wine.
You say, "Let's feast and drink,
　for tomorrow we die!"

¹⁴ The LORD of Heaven's Armies has revealed this to me: "Till the day you die, you will never be forgiven for this sin." That is the judgment of the Lord, the LORD of Heaven's Armies.

A Message for Shebna

¹⁵ This is what the Lord, the LORD of Heaven's Armies, said to me: "Confront Shebna, the palace administrator, and give him this message:

¹⁶ "Who do you think you are,
　and what are you doing here,
building a beautiful tomb for yourself—
　a monument high up in the rock?
¹⁷ For the LORD is about to hurl you away,
　mighty man.
　He is going to grab you,
¹⁸ crumple you into a ball,
　and toss you away into a distant,
　　barren land.
There you will die,
　and your glorious chariots will be
　　broken and useless.
You are a disgrace to your master!

¹⁹ "Yes, I will drive you out of office," says the LORD. "I will pull you down from your

---

21:16 Hebrew *Within a year, as a servant bound by contract would count it.* Some ancient manuscripts read *Within three years,* as in 16:14. **22:1** Hebrew *concerning the Valley of Vision.* **22:8** Hebrew *to the House of the Forest;* see 1 Kgs 7:2-5. **22:9** Hebrew *the city of David.*

high position. ²⁰ And then I will call my servant Eliakim son of Hilkiah to replace you. ²¹ I will dress him in your royal robes and will give him your title and your authority. And he will be a father to the people of Jerusalem and Judah. ²² I will give him the key to the house of David—the highest position in the royal court. When he opens doors, no one will be able to close them; when he closes doors, no one will be able to open them. ²³ He will bring honor to his family name, for I will drive him firmly in place like a nail in the wall. ²⁴ They will give him great responsibility, and he will bring honor to even the lowliest members of his family.*”

²⁵ But the Lord of Heaven's Armies also says: “The time will come when I will pull out the nail that seemed so firm. It will come out and fall to the ground. Everything it supports will fall with it. I, the Lord, have spoken!”

23 A Message about Tyre

This message came to me concerning Tyre:

Weep, O ships of Tarshish,
for the harbor and houses of Tyre are
gone!
The rumors you heard in Cyprus*
are all true.
² Mourn in silence, you people of the
coast
and you merchants of Sidon.
Your traders crossed the sea,
³ sailing over deep waters.
They brought you grain from Egypt*
and harvests from along the Nile.
You were the marketplace of the world.
⁴ But now you are put to shame, city of
Sidon,
for Tyre, the fortress of the sea, says,
“Now I am childless;
I have no sons or daughters.”
⁵ When Egypt hears the news about Tyre,
there will be great sorrow.
⁶ Send word now to Tarshish!
Wail, you people who live in distant
lands!

⁷ Is this silent ruin all that is left of your
once joyous city?
What a long history was yours!
Think of all the colonists you sent to
distant places.

⁸ Who has brought this disaster on Tyre,
that great creator of kingdoms?
Her traders were all princes,
her merchants were nobles.
⁹ The Lord of Heaven's Armies has
done it
to destroy your pride
and bring low all earth's nobility.

¹⁰ Come, people of Tarshish,
sweep over the land like the flooding
Nile,
for Tyre is defenseless.*
¹¹ The Lord held out his hand over the
sea
and shook the kingdoms of the
earth.
He has spoken out against Phoenicia,*
ordering that her fortresses be
destroyed.
¹² He says, “Never again will you rejoice,
O daughter of Sidon, for you have
been crushed.
Even if you flee to Cyprus,
you will find no rest.”

¹³ Look at the land of Babylonia*—
the people of that land are gone!
The Assyrians have handed Babylon
over
to the wild animals of the desert.
They have built siege ramps against its
walls,
torn down its palaces,
and turned it to a heap of rubble.

¹⁴ Wail, O ships of Tarshish,
for your harbor is destroyed!

¹⁵ For seventy years, the length of a king's life, Tyre will be forgotten. But then the city will come back to life as in the song about the prostitute:

¹⁶ Take a harp and walk the streets,
you forgotten harlot.
Make sweet melody and sing your songs
so you will be remembered again.

22:24 Hebrew *They will hang on him all the glory of his father's house: its offspring and offshoots, all its lesser vessels, from the bowls to all the jars.* 23:1 Hebrew *Kittim;* also in 23:12. 23:3 Hebrew *from Shihor,* a branch of the Nile River. 23:10 The meaning of the Hebrew in this verse is uncertain. 23:11 Hebrew *Canaan.* 23:13 Or *Chaldea.*

¹⁷Yes, after seventy years the LORD will revive Tyre. But she will be no different than she was before. She will again be a prostitute to all kingdoms around the world. ¹⁸But in the end her profits will be given to the LORD. Her wealth will not be hoarded but will provide good food and fine clothing for the LORD's priests.

24 Destruction of the Earth

¹ Look! The LORD is about to
destroy the earth
and make it a vast wasteland.
He devastates the surface of the earth
and scatters the people.
² Priests and laypeople,
servants and masters,
maids and mistresses,
buyers and sellers,
lenders and borrowers,
bankers and debtors—none will be
spared.
³ The earth will be completely emptied
and looted.
The LORD has spoken!

⁴ The earth mourns and dries up,
and the crops waste away and wither.
Even the greatest people on earth
waste away.
⁵ The earth suffers for the sins of its
people,
for they have twisted God's
instructions,
violated his laws,
and broken his everlasting covenant.
⁶ Therefore, a curse consumes the earth.
Its people must pay the price for their
sin.
They are destroyed by fire,
and only a few are left alive.
⁷ The grapevines waste away,
and there is no new wine.
All the merrymakers sigh and mourn.
⁸ The cheerful sound of tambourines is
stilled;
the happy cries of celebration are
heard no more.
The melodious chords of the harp are
silent.
⁹ Gone are the joys of wine and song;
alcoholic drink turns bitter in the
mouth.

¹⁰ The city writhes in chaos;
every home is locked to keep out
intruders.
¹¹ Mobs gather in the streets, crying out
for wine.
Joy has turned to gloom.
Gladness has been banished from the
land.
¹² The city is left in ruins,
its gates battered down.
¹³ Throughout the earth the story is the
same—
only a remnant is left,
like the stray olives left on the tree
or the few grapes left on the vine after
harvest.

¹⁴ But all who are left shout and sing for
joy.
Those in the west praise the LORD's
majesty.
¹⁵ In eastern lands, give glory to the LORD.
In the lands beyond the sea, praise the
name of the LORD, the God of Israel.
¹⁶ We hear songs of praise from the ends of
the earth,
songs that give glory to the Righteous
One!

But my heart is heavy with grief.
Weep for me, for I wither away.
Deceit still prevails,
and treachery is everywhere.
¹⁷ Terror and traps and snares will be your
lot,
you people of the earth.
¹⁸ Those who flee in terror will fall into a
trap,
and those who escape the trap will be
caught in a snare.

Destruction falls like rain from the
heavens;
the foundations of the earth shake.
¹⁹ The earth has broken up.
It has utterly collapsed;
it is violently shaken.
²⁰ The earth staggers like a drunk.
It trembles like a tent in a storm.
It falls and will not rise again,
for the guilt of its rebellion is very
heavy.

²¹ In that day the LORD will punish the
gods in the heavens

and the proud rulers of the nations on
earth.
22 They will be rounded up and put in
prison.
They will be shut up in prison
and will finally be punished.
23 Then the glory of the moon will wane,
and the brightness of the sun will fade,
for the LORD of Heaven's Armies will
rule on Mount Zion.
He will rule in great glory in
Jerusalem,
in the sight of all the leaders of his
people.

25 Praise for Judgment and Salvation

1 O LORD, I will honor and praise
your name,
for you are my God.
You do such wonderful things!
You planned them long ago,
and now you have accomplished them.
2 You turn mighty cities into heaps of
ruins.
Cities with strong walls are turned to
rubble.
Beautiful palaces in distant lands
disappear
and will never be rebuilt.
3 Therefore, strong nations will declare
your glory;
ruthless nations will fear you.

4 But you are a tower of refuge to the
poor, O LORD,
a tower of refuge to the needy in
distress.
You are a refuge from the storm
and a shelter from the heat.
For the oppressive acts of ruthless
people
are like a storm beating against a wall,
5 or like the relentless heat of the desert.
But you silence the roar of foreign
nations.
As the shade of a cloud cools
relentless heat,
so the boastful songs of ruthless
people are stilled.

6 In Jerusalem,* the LORD of Heaven's
Armies
will spread a wonderful feast
for all the people of the world.

It will be a delicious banquet
with clear, well-aged wine and choice
meat.
7 There he will remove the cloud of
gloom,
the shadow of death that hangs over
the earth.
8 He will swallow up death forever!*
The Sovereign LORD will wipe away
all tears.
He will remove forever all insults and
mockery
against his land and people.
The LORD has spoken!

9 In that day the people will proclaim,
"This is our God!
We trusted in him, and he saved us!
This is the LORD, in whom we trusted.
Let us rejoice in the salvation he
brings!"
10 For the LORD's hand of blessing will rest
on Jerusalem.
But Moab will be crushed.
It will be like straw trampled down
and left to rot.
11 God will push down Moab's people
as a swimmer pushes down water with
his hands.
He will end their pride
and all their evil works.
12 The high walls of Moab will be
demolished.
They will be brought down to the
ground,
down into the dust.

26 A Song of Praise to the LORD

In that day, everyone in the land of
Judah will sing this song:

Our city is strong!
We are surrounded by the walls of
God's salvation.
2 Open the gates to all who are righteous;
allow the faithful to enter.
3 You will keep in perfect peace
all who trust in you,
all whose thoughts are fixed on you!
4 Trust in the LORD always,
for the LORD GOD is the eternal
Rock.

25:6 Hebrew *On this mountain;* also in 25:10.   25:8 Greek version reads *Death is swallowed up in victory.* Compare 1 Cor 15:54.

What Am I Truly Hungering For?

ISAIAH 26:8–9

During the Lenten season, Christians often abstain from a particular "vice" as a way of realigning themselves spiritually. Some fast from chocolate, television, or ungodly patterns of behavior or thought. These are all worthy endeavors, and engaging in these kinds of fasts can give us a small taste of what it means to experience self-denial. However, it's equally important to recognize that the things we desire may actually be expressions of a deeper yearning, a spiritual hunger for God himself. The prophet Isaiah depicts this idea when he says, "Our heart's desire is to glorify your name. All night long I search for you; in the morning I earnestly seek for God" (Isaiah 26:8–9). In Psalm 42:1–2 the sons of Korah write, "As the deer longs for streams of water, so I long for you, O God. I thirst for God, the living God."

In *The Problem of Pain*, C. S. Lewis writes, "There have been times when I think we do not desire heaven but more often I find myself wondering whether, in our heart of hearts, we have ever desired anything else." As we engage in fasting and experience hunger pangs both literal and figurative, it's helpful to ask ourselves, *What am I truly hungering for?* It might not be chocolate after all.

—Helen Lee

For more on fasting, see reading at Daniel 10:3.

5 He humbles the proud
   and brings down the arrogant city.
   He brings it down to the dust.
6 The poor and oppressed trample it
      underfoot,
   and the needy walk all over it.

7 But for those who are righteous,
   the way is not steep and rough.
   You are a God who does what is right,
   and you smooth out the path ahead of
      them.
8 LORD, we show our trust in you by
      obeying your laws;
   our heart's desire is to glorify your
      name.
9 All night long I search for you;
   in the morning I earnestly seek for
      God.
   For only when you come to judge the
      earth
   will people learn what is right.
10 Your kindness to the wicked
   does not make them do good.

Although others do right, the wicked
      keep doing wrong
   and take no notice of the LORD's
      majesty.
11 O LORD, they pay no attention to your
      upraised fist.
   Show them your eagerness to defend
      your people.
   Then they will be ashamed.
   Let your fire consume your enemies.

12 LORD, you will grant us peace;
   all we have accomplished is really
      from you.
13 O LORD our God, others have ruled us,
   but you alone are the one we worship.
14 Those we served before are dead and
      gone.
   Their departed spirits will never
      return!
   You attacked them and destroyed them,
   and they are long forgotten.
15 O LORD, you have made our nation great;
   yes, you have made us great.

You have extended our borders,
and we give you the glory!

[16] LORD, in distress we searched for you.
We prayed beneath the burden of your
discipline.
[17] Just as a pregnant woman
writhes and cries out in pain as she
gives birth,
so were we in your presence, LORD.
[18] We, too, writhe in agony,
but nothing comes of our suffering.
We have not given salvation to the earth,
nor brought life into the world.
[19] But those who die in the LORD will live;
their bodies will rise again!
Those who sleep in the earth
will rise up and sing for joy!
For your life-giving light will fall like dew
on your people in the place of the dead!

Restoration for Israel

[20] Go home, my people,
and lock your doors!
Hide yourselves for a little while
until the LORD's anger has passed.
[21] Look! The LORD is coming from heaven
to punish the people of the earth for
their sins.
The earth will no longer hide those who
have been killed.
They will be brought out for all to see.

27 In that day the LORD will take his terrible, swift sword and punish Leviathan,* the swiftly moving serpent, the coiling, writhing serpent. He will kill the dragon of the sea.

[2] "In that day,
sing about the fruitful vineyard.
[3] I, the LORD, will watch over it,
watering it carefully.
Day and night I will watch so no one can
harm it.
[4] My anger will be gone.
If I find briers and thorns growing,
I will attack them;
I will burn them up—
[5] unless they turn to me for help.
Let them make peace with me;
yes, let them make peace with me."

[6] The time is coming when Jacob's
descendants will take root.
Israel will bud and blossom
and fill the whole earth with fruit!

[7] Has the LORD struck Israel
as he struck her enemies?
Has he punished her
as he punished them?
[8] No, but he exiled Israel to call her to
account.
She was exiled from her land
as though blown away in a storm from
the east.
[9] The LORD did this to purge Israel's*
wickedness,
to take away all her sin.
As a result, all the pagan altars will be
crushed to dust.
No Asherah pole or pagan shrine will
be left standing.
[10] The fortified towns will be silent and
empty,
the houses abandoned, the streets
overgrown with weeds.
Calves will graze there,
chewing on twigs and branches.
[11] The people are like the dead branches of
a tree,
broken off and used for kindling
beneath the cooking pots.
Israel is a foolish and stupid nation,
for its people have turned away from
God.
Therefore, the one who made them
will show them no pity or mercy.

[12] Yet the time will come when the LORD will gather them together like handpicked grain. One by one he will gather them—from the Euphrates River* in the east to the Brook of Egypt in the west. [13] In that day the great trumpet will sound. Many who were dying in exile in Assyria and Egypt will return to Jerusalem to worship the LORD on his holy mountain.

28 A Message about Samaria
[1] What sorrow awaits the proud city
of Samaria—
the glorious crown of the drunks of
Israel.*

27:1 The identification of Leviathan is disputed, ranging from an earthly creature to a mythical sea monster in ancient literature. **27:9** Hebrew *Jacob's*. See note on 14:1. **27:12** Hebrew *the river*. **28:1** Hebrew *What sorrow awaits the crowning glory of the drunks of Ephraim*, referring to Samaria, capital of the northern kingdom of Israel.

It sits at the head of a fertile valley,
  but its glorious beauty will fade like a
    flower.
It is the pride of a people
  brought down by wine.
2 For the Lord will send a mighty army
    against it.
  Like a mighty hailstorm and a
    torrential rain,
they will burst upon it like a surging
    flood
  and smash it to the ground.
3 The proud city of Samaria—
  the glorious crown of the drunks of
    Israel*—
will be trampled beneath its enemies'
    feet.
4 It sits at the head of a fertile valley,
  but its glorious beauty will fade like a
    flower.
Whoever sees it will snatch it up,
  as an early fig is quickly picked and
    eaten.

5 Then at last the Lord of Heaven's
    Armies
  will himself be Israel's glorious crown.
He will be the pride and joy
  of the remnant of his people.
6 He will give a longing for justice
  to their judges.
He will give great courage
  to their warriors who stand at the
    gates.

7 Now, however, Israel is led by drunks
  who reel with wine and stagger with
    alcohol.
The priests and prophets stagger with
    alcohol
  and lose themselves in wine.
They reel when they see visions
  and stagger as they render decisions.
8 Their tables are covered with vomit;
  filth is everywhere.
9 "Who does the Lord think we are?" they
    ask.
  "Why does he speak to us like this?
Are we little children,
  just recently weaned?
10 He tells us everything over and over—

one line at a time,
  one line at a time,
a little here,
  and a little there!"
11 So now God will have to speak to his
    people
  through foreign oppressors who speak
    a strange language!
12 God has told his people,
  "Here is a place of rest;
  let the weary rest here.
This is a place of quiet rest."
  But they would not listen.
13 So the Lord will spell out his message
    for them again,
one line at a time,
  one line at a time,
a little here,
  and a little there,
so that they will stumble and fall.
  They will be injured, trapped, and
    captured.

14 Therefore, listen to this message from
    the Lord,
  you scoffing rulers in Jerusalem.
15 You boast, "We have struck a bargain to
    cheat death
  and have made a deal to dodge the
    grave.*
The coming destruction can never
    touch us,
  for we have built a strong refuge made
    of lies and deception."
16 Therefore, this is what the Sovereign
    Lord says:
"Look! I am placing a foundation stone
    in Jerusalem,*
  a firm and tested stone.
It is a precious cornerstone that is safe to
    build on.
  Whoever believes need never be
    shaken.*
17 I will test you with the measuring line of
    justice
  and the plumb line of righteousness.
Since your refuge is made of lies,
  a hailstorm will knock it down.
Since it is made of deception,
  a flood will sweep it away.

28:3 Hebrew *The crowning glory of the drunks of Ephraim*; see note on 28:1.   28:15 Hebrew *Sheol*; also in 28:18.   28:16a Hebrew *in Zion*.
28:16b Greek version reads *Look! I am placing a stone in the foundation of Jerusalem* [literally *Zion*], / *a precious cornerstone for its foundation,*
chosen for great honor. / *Anyone who trusts in him will never be disgraced.* Compare Rom 9:33; 1 Pet 2:6.

¹⁸ I will cancel the bargain you made to
  cheat death,
    and I will overturn your deal to dodge
    the grave.
When the terrible enemy sweeps
  through,
    you will be trampled into the ground.
¹⁹ Again and again that flood will come,
  morning after morning,
day and night,
  until you are carried away."

This message will bring terror to your
  people.
²⁰ The bed you have made is too short to
  lie on.
    The blankets are too narrow to cover
    you.
²¹ The LORD will come as he did against
    the Philistines at Mount Perazim
    and against the Amorites at Gibeon.
He will come to do a strange thing;
  he will come to do an unusual deed:
²² For the Lord, the LORD of Heaven's
    Armies,
    has plainly said that he is determined
    to crush the whole land.
So scoff no more,
  or your punishment will be even
  greater.

²³ Listen to me;
  listen, and pay close attention.
²⁴ Does a farmer always plow and never
  sow?
    Is he forever cultivating the soil and
    never planting?
²⁵ Does he not finally plant his seeds—
    black cumin, cumin, wheat, barley,
    and emmer wheat—
each in its proper way,
  and each in its proper place?
²⁶ The farmer knows just what to do,
  for God has given him understanding.
²⁷ A heavy sledge is never used to thresh
    black cumin;
    rather, it is beaten with a light stick.
A threshing wheel is never rolled on
    cumin;
    instead, it is beaten lightly with a
    flail.
²⁸ Grain for bread is easily crushed,
  so he doesn't keep on pounding it.

He threshes it under the wheels of a cart,
  but he doesn't pulverize it.
²⁹ The LORD of Heaven's Armies is a
  wonderful teacher,
    and he gives the farmer great wisdom.

29 A Message about Jerusalem

¹ "What sorrow awaits Ariel,* the
    City of David.
Year after year you celebrate your
  feasts.
² Yet I will bring disaster upon you,
  and there will be much weeping and
  sorrow.
For Jerusalem will become what her
  name Ariel means—
    an altar covered with blood.
³ I will be your enemy,
  surrounding Jerusalem and attacking
  its walls.
I will build siege towers
  and destroy it.
⁴ Then deep from the earth you will speak;
  from low in the dust your words will
  come.
Your voice will whisper from the ground
  like a ghost conjured up from the grave.

⁵ "But suddenly, your ruthless enemies
    will be crushed
  like the finest of dust.
Your many attackers will be driven away
  like chaff before the wind.
Suddenly, in an instant,
⁶   I, the LORD of Heaven's Armies, will
    act for you
with thunder and earthquake and great
  noise,
    with whirlwind and storm and
    consuming fire.
⁷ All the nations fighting against
    Jerusalem*
  will vanish like a dream!
Those who are attacking her walls
  will vanish like a vision in the night.
⁸ A hungry person dreams of eating
  but wakes up still hungry.
A thirsty person dreams of drinking
  but is still faint from thirst when
  morning comes.
So it will be with your enemies,
  with those who attack Mount Zion."

29:1 *Ariel* sounds like a Hebrew term that means "hearth" or "altar."   29:7 Hebrew *Ariel.*

9 Are you amazed and incredulous?
    Don't you believe it?
Then go ahead and be blind.
    You are stupid, but not from wine!
    You stagger, but not from liquor!
10 For the LORD has poured out on you a
        spirit of deep sleep.
    He has closed the eyes of your
        prophets and visionaries.

11 All the future events in this vision are
like a sealed book to them. When you give
it to those who can read, they will say, "We
can't read it because it is sealed." 12 When
you give it to those who cannot read, they
will say, "We don't know how to read."

13 And so the Lord says,
    "These people say they are mine.
They honor me with their lips,
    but their hearts are far from me.
And their worship of me
    is nothing but man-made rules
        learned by rote.*
14 Because of this, I will once again
        astound these hypocrites
    with amazing wonders.
The wisdom of the wise will pass away,
    and the intelligence of the intelligent
        will disappear."

15 What sorrow awaits those who try to
        hide their plans from the LORD,
    who do their evil deeds in the dark!
"The LORD can't see us," they say.
    "He doesn't know what's going on!"
16 How foolish can you be?
    He is the Potter, and he is certainly
        greater than you, the clay!
Should the created thing say of the one
        who made it,
    "He didn't make me"?
Does a jar ever say,
    "The potter who made me is
        stupid"?

17 Soon—and it will not be very long—
    the forests of Lebanon will become a
        fertile field,
    and the fertile field will yield bountiful
        crops.
18 In that day the deaf will hear words read
    from a book,

and the blind will see through the
        gloom and darkness.
19 The humble will be filled with fresh joy
        from the LORD.
    The poor will rejoice in the Holy One
        of Israel.
20 The scoffer will be gone,
    the arrogant will disappear,
    and those who plot evil will be killed.
21 Those who convict the innocent
    by their false testimony will disappear.
A similar fate awaits those who use
        trickery to pervert justice
    and who tell lies to destroy the
        innocent.

22 That is why the LORD, who redeemed
Abraham, says to the people of Israel,*

"My people will no longer be ashamed
    or turn pale with fear.
23 For when they see their many children
    and all the blessings I have given
        them,
they will recognize the holiness of the
        Holy One of Israel.
    They will stand in awe of the God of
        Jacob.
24 Then the wayward will gain
        understanding,
    and complainers will accept
        instruction.

30 Judah's Worthless Treaty with Egypt

1 "What sorrow awaits my rebellious
        children,"
    says the LORD.
"You make plans that are contrary to
        mine.
    You make alliances not directed by my
        Spirit,
    thus piling up your sins.
2 For without consulting me,
    you have gone down to Egypt for help.
You have put your trust in Pharaoh's
        protection.
    You have tried to hide in his shade.
3 But by trusting Pharaoh, you will be
        humiliated,
    and by depending on him, you will be
        disgraced.

29:13 Greek version reads *Their worship is a farce, / for they teach man-made ideas as commands from God.* Compare Mark 7:7. 29:22 Hebrew
of Jacob. See note on 14:1.

⁴ For though his power extends to Zoan
 and his officials have arrived in Hanes,
⁵ all who trust in him will be ashamed.
 He will not help you.
 Instead, he will disgrace you."

⁶ This message came to me concerning the animals in the Negev:

The caravan moves slowly
 across the terrible desert to Egypt—
donkeys weighed down with riches
 and camels loaded with treasure—
 all to pay for Egypt's protection.
They travel through the wilderness,
 a place of lionesses and lions,
 a place where vipers and poisonous
 snakes live.
All this, and Egypt will give you nothing
 in return.
⁷ Egypt's promises are worthless!
Therefore, I call her Rahab—
 the Harmless Dragon.*

A Warning for Rebellious Judah

⁸ Now go and write down these words.
 Write them in a book.
They will stand until the end of time
 as a witness
⁹ that these people are stubborn rebels
 who refuse to pay attention to the
 LORD's instructions.
¹⁰ They tell the seers,
 "Stop seeing visions!"
They tell the prophets,
 "Don't tell us what is right.
Tell us nice things.
 Tell us lies.
¹¹ Forget all this gloom.
 Get off your narrow path.
Stop telling us about your
 'Holy One of Israel.'"

¹² This is the reply of the Holy One of Israel:

"Because you despise what I tell you
 and trust instead in oppression and
 lies,
¹³ calamity will come upon you suddenly—
 like a bulging wall that bursts and
 falls.
In an instant it will collapse
 and come crashing down.

¹⁴ You will be smashed like a piece of
 pottery—
 shattered so completely that
there won't be a piece big enough
 to carry coals from a fireplace
 or a little water from the well."

¹⁵ This is what the Sovereign LORD,
 the Holy One of Israel, says:
"Only in returning to me
 and resting in me will you be saved.
In quietness and confidence is your
 strength.
But you would have none of it.
¹⁶ You said, 'No, we will get our help from
 Egypt.
They will give us swift horses for
 riding into battle.'
But the only swiftness you are going to
 see
 is the swiftness of your enemies
 chasing you!
¹⁷ One of them will chase a thousand of
 you.
 Five of them will make all of you flee.
You will be left like a lonely flagpole on
 a hill
 or a tattered banner on a distant
 mountaintop."

Blessings for the LORD's People

¹⁸ So the LORD must wait for you to come
 to him
 so he can show you his love and
 compassion.
For the LORD is a faithful God.
 Blessed are those who wait for his
 help.

¹⁹ O people of Zion, who live in Jerusalem,
 you will weep no more.
He will be gracious if you ask for help.
 He will surely respond to the sound of
 your cries.
²⁰ Though the Lord gave you adversity for
 food
 and suffering for drink,
he will still be with you to teach you.
 You will see your teacher with your
 own eyes.
²¹ Your own ears will hear him.
 Right behind you a voice will say,

30:7 Hebrew *Rahab who sits still.* Rahab is the name of a mythical sea monster that represents chaos in ancient literature. The name is used here as a poetic name for Egypt.

"This is the way you should go,"
whether to the right or to the left.
[22] Then you will destroy all your silver idols
and your precious gold images.
You will throw them out like filthy rags,
saying to them, "Good riddance!"

[23] Then the LORD will bless you with rain at planting time. There will be wonderful harvests and plenty of pastureland for your livestock. [24] The oxen and donkeys that till the ground will eat good grain, its chaff blown away by the wind. [25] In that day, when your enemies are slaughtered and the towers fall, there will be streams of water flowing down every mountain and hill. [26] The moon will be as bright as the sun, and the sun will be seven times brighter—like the light of seven days in one! So it will be

Q&A — Discerning God's Voice

ISAIAH 30:18-21

Contemplation

How can I discern if I'm really hearing God's voice?

In Isaiah God makes an incredible promise to his people: "Your own ears will hear him. Right behind you a voice will say, 'This is the way you should go'" (Isaiah 30:21). Wouldn't it be amazing if we heard God this clearly?

Learning to hear and recognize God's voice is something I've wrestled with since I was a girl. People talk about a relationship with Jesus, and that implies communication: talking and listening. But what does that mean? How do I live that out? I studied the Scriptures and asked people, "*How* do you hear from God?" And one of the things I heard over and over is that many experience God's voice as a thought that's a little brighter than most.

We must always be careful to maintain an attitude of humility as we try to discern God's voice. Scripture should be the foundation and filter for anything God says. If what we think God is telling us doesn't line up with God's Word, then we know it isn't from him. In addition, we should look for a sense of peace. In Philippians 4:7 Paul wrote that God's peace will guard our hearts and minds. We also need to ask whether what we heard was blanketed in love. A bitter, cutting voice is not from God.

Often God is diligently and persistently communicating to us in various ways; I call these messages "sacred echoes." For example, a sacred echo can be a moment when we're reading the Bible, and it comes alive. Then we go to church, and the pastor is teaching on that same story or passage. Later that week we go to lunch with friends, and that same topic pops up in the conversation. Finally, we realize that maybe God is at work, trying to get our attention! God *is* speaking to us through the Holy Spirit as Isaiah promised. As we're attentive to life with a listening spirit, we'll recognize the sacred echoes in our lives.

—*Margaret Feinberg*

For more on contemplation, see reading at Isaiah 51:12-16.

when the LORD begins to heal his people
and cure the wounds he gave them.

²⁷ Look! The LORD is coming from far
away,
burning with anger,
surrounded by thick, rising smoke.
His lips are filled with fury;
his words consume like fire.
²⁸ His hot breath pours out like a flood
up to the neck of his enemies.
He will sift out the proud nations for
destruction.
He will bridle them and lead them
away to ruin.
²⁹ But the people of God will sing a song of
joy,
like the songs at the holy festivals.
You will be filled with joy,
as when a flutist leads a group of
pilgrims
to Jerusalem, the mountain of the LORD—
to the Rock of Israel.
³⁰ And the LORD will make his majestic
voice heard.
He will display the strength of his
mighty arm.
It will descend with devouring flames,
with cloudbursts, thunderstorms, and
huge hailstones.
³¹ At the LORD's command, the Assyrians
will be shattered.
He will strike them down with his
royal scepter.
³² And as the LORD strikes them with his
rod of punishment,
his people will celebrate with
tambourines and harps.
Lifting his mighty arm, he will fight
the Assyrians.
³³ Topheth—the place of burning—
has long been ready for the Assyrian
king;
the pyre is piled high with wood.
The breath of the LORD, like fire from a
volcano,
will set it ablaze.

31 The Futility of Relying on Egypt

¹ What sorrow awaits those who look
to Egypt for help,
trusting their horses, chariots, and
charioteers

and depending on the strength of
human armies
instead of looking to the LORD,
the Holy One of Israel.
² In his wisdom, the LORD will send great
disaster;
he will not change his mind.
He will rise against the wicked
and against their helpers.
³ For these Egyptians are mere humans,
not God!
Their horses are puny flesh, not
mighty spirits!
When the LORD raises his fist against
them,
those who help will stumble,
and those being helped will fall.
They will all fall down and die
together.

⁴But this is what the LORD has told me:

"When a strong young lion
stands growling over a sheep it has
killed,
it is not frightened by the shouts and
noise
of a whole crowd of shepherds.
In the same way, the LORD of Heaven's
Armies
will come down and fight on Mount
Zion.
⁵ The LORD of Heaven's Armies will hover
over Jerusalem
and protect it like a bird protecting its
nest.
He will defend and save the city;
he will pass over it and rescue it."

⁶Though you are such wicked rebels, my
people, come and return to the LORD. ⁷I
know the glorious day will come when each
of you will throw away the gold idols and
silver images your sinful hands have made.

⁸ "The Assyrians will be destroyed,
but not by the swords of men.
The sword of God will strike them,
and they will panic and flee.
The strong young Assyrians
will be taken away as captives.
⁹ Even the strongest will quake with
terror,
and princes will flee when they see
your battle flags,"

Gnawing on Scripture

ISAIAH 31:4

When my pit bull works on her bone, she holds it between her crossed front paws, sucking and chewing and rumbling away. Totally engrossed, she'll pause only to raise an eyebrow when one of my kids walks by. *Unless you've got bacon or we're going for a walk, back off,* she seems to say. Then with a low rumble, she gets back to that bone.

While I've long enjoyed watching my dog do this, until I read Eugene Peterson's *Eat This Book,* I never applied any spiritual significance to her gnarling and gnawing.

As it happens, Peterson shares my love of dogs and their crazy bone-chewing. But he caught the spiritual significance. While reading Isaiah 31:4 ("When a strong young lion stands growling over a sheep it has killed . . ."), he realized *hagah,* the Hebrew word for *growl* in this instance, is more often translated as *meditate.* Psalm 63:6, "I lie awake thinking of you, meditating on you through the night," according to Peterson, uses hagah.

"'Meditate' is far too tame a word for what is being signified," writes Peterson. "When Isaiah's lion and my dog meditated they chewed and swallowed, using teeth and tongue, stomach and intestines."

You don't have to love dogs (or lions) to appreciate the beauty and power of this as it relates to how we might hagah on the Word of God. In fact, those of us who get sleepy thinking about traditional meditation welcome this image. Instead of quiet and passive reflection, it's an invitation to grapple with Scripture so we might know and savor it better.

—*Caryn Rivadeneira*

For more on Bible study and meditation, see reading at Matthew 4:4.

says the LORD, whose fire burns in Zion,
whose flame blazes from Jerusalem.

32 Israel's Ultimate Deliverance

¹ Look, a righteous king is coming!
And honest princes will rule under him.
² Each one will be like a shelter from the wind
and a refuge from the storm,
like streams of water in the desert
and the shadow of a great rock in a parched land.
³ Then everyone who has eyes will be able to see the truth,
and everyone who has ears will be able to hear it.

⁴ Even the hotheads will be full of sense and understanding.
Those who stammer will speak out plainly.
⁵ In that day ungodly fools will not be heroes.
Scoundrels will not be respected.
⁶ For fools speak foolishness
and make evil plans.
They practice ungodliness
and spread false teachings about the LORD.
They deprive the hungry of food
and give no water to the thirsty.
⁷ The smooth tricks of scoundrels are evil.
They plot crooked schemes.

They lie to convict the poor,
even when the cause of the poor is just.
⁸ But generous people plan to do what is
generous,
and they stand firm in their generosity.

⁹ Listen, you women who lie around in
ease.
Listen to me, you who are so smug.
¹⁰ In a short time—just a little more than a
year—
you careless ones will suddenly begin
to care.
For your fruit crops will fail,
and the harvest will never take place.
¹¹ Tremble, you women of ease;
throw off your complacency.
Strip off your pretty clothes,
and put on burlap to show your grief.
¹² Beat your breasts in sorrow for your
bountiful farms
and your fruitful grapevines.
¹³ For your land will be overgrown with
thorns and briers.
Your joyful homes and happy towns
will be gone.
¹⁴ The palace and the city will be deserted,
and busy towns will be empty.
Wild donkeys will frolic and flocks will
graze
in the empty forts* and watchtowers
¹⁵ until at last the Spirit is poured out
on us from heaven.
Then the wilderness will become a fertile
field,
and the fertile field will yield bountiful
crops.
¹⁶ Justice will rule in the wilderness
and righteousness in the fertile field.
¹⁷ And this righteousness will bring peace.
Yes, it will bring quietness and
confidence forever.
¹⁸ My people will live in safety, quietly at
home.
They will be at rest.
¹⁹ Even if the forest should be destroyed
and the city torn down,
²⁰ the LORD will greatly bless his people.
Wherever they plant seed, bountiful
crops will spring up.

Their cattle and donkeys will graze
freely.

33 A Message about Assyria

¹ What sorrow awaits you Assyrians,
who have destroyed others*
but have never been destroyed
yourselves.
You betray others,
but you have never been betrayed.
When you are done destroying,
you will be destroyed.
When you are done betraying,
you will be betrayed.
² But LORD, be merciful to us,
for we have waited for you.
Be our strong arm each day
and our salvation in times of trouble.
³ The enemy runs at the sound of your
voice.
When you stand up, the nations flee!
⁴ Just as caterpillars and locusts strip the
fields and vines,
so the fallen army of Assyria will be
stripped!
⁵ Though the LORD is very great and lives
in heaven,
he will make Jerusalem* his home of
justice and righteousness.
⁶ In that day he will be your sure
foundation,
providing a rich store of salvation,
wisdom, and knowledge.
The fear of the LORD will be your
treasure.
⁷ But now your brave warriors weep in
public.
Your ambassadors of peace cry in
bitter disappointment.
⁸ Your roads are deserted;
no one travels them anymore.
The Assyrians have broken their peace
treaty
and care nothing for the promises they
made before witnesses.*
They have no respect for anyone.
⁹ The land of Israel wilts in mourning.
Lebanon withers with shame.
The plain of Sharon is now a wilderness.

32:14 Hebrew *the Ophel.* **33:1** Hebrew *What sorrow awaits you, O destroyer.* The Hebrew text does not specifically name Assyria as the
object of the prophecy in this chapter. **33:5** Hebrew *Zion;* also in 33:14. **33:8** As in Dead Sea Scrolls; Masoretic Text reads *care nothing for
the cities.*

Bashan and Carmel have been
plundered.

¹⁰ But the LORD says: "Now I will stand up.
Now I will show my power and might.
¹¹ You Assyrians produce nothing but dry
grass and stubble.
Your own breath will turn to fire and
consume you.
¹² Your people will be burned up
completely,
like thornbushes cut down and tossed
in a fire.
¹³ Listen to what I have done, you nations
far away!
And you that are near, acknowledge
my might!"

¹⁴ The sinners in Jerusalem shake with fear.
Terror seizes the godless.
"Who can live with this devouring fire?"
they cry.
"Who can survive this all-consuming
fire?"
¹⁵ Those who are honest and fair,
who refuse to profit by fraud,
who stay far away from bribes,
who refuse to listen to those who plot
murder,
who shut their eyes to all enticement
to do wrong—
¹⁶ these are the ones who will dwell on
high.
The rocks of the mountains will be
their fortress.
Food will be supplied to them,
and they will have water in abundance.

¹⁷ Your eyes will see the king in all his
splendor,
and you will see a land that stretches
into the distance.
¹⁸ You will think back to this time of terror,
asking,
"Where are the Assyrian officers
who counted our towers?
Where are the bookkeepers
who recorded the plunder taken from
our fallen city?"
¹⁹ You will no longer see these fierce,
violent people
with their strange, unknown language.

²⁰ Instead, you will see Zion as a place of
holy festivals.
You will see Jerusalem, a city quiet and
secure.
It will be like a tent whose ropes are taut
and whose stakes are firmly fixed.
²¹ The LORD will be our Mighty One.
He will be like a wide river of
protection
that no enemy can cross,
that no enemy ship can sail upon.
²² For the LORD is our judge,
our lawgiver, and our king.
He will care for us and save us.
²³ The enemies' sails hang loose
on broken masts with useless tackle.
Their treasure will be divided by the
people of God.
Even the lame will take their share!
²⁴ The people of Israel will no longer say,
"We are sick and helpless,"
for the LORD will forgive their sins.

34 A Message for the Nations

¹ Come here and listen, O nations of
the earth.
Let the world and everything in it hear
my words.
² For the LORD is enraged against the
nations.
His fury is against all their armies.
He will completely destroy* them,
dooming them to slaughter.
³ Their dead will be left unburied,
and the stench of rotting bodies will
fill the land.
The mountains will flow with their
blood.
⁴ The heavens above will melt away
and disappear like a rolled-up scroll.
The stars will fall from the sky
like withered leaves from a grapevine,
or shriveled figs from a fig tree.

⁵ And when my sword has finished its
work in the heavens,
it will fall upon Edom,
the nation I have marked for
destruction.
⁶ The sword of the LORD is drenched with
blood
and covered with fat—

34:2 The Hebrew term used here refers to the complete consecration of things or people to the LORD, either by destroying them or by giving them as an offering; similarly in 34:5.

with the blood of lambs and goats,
  with the fat of rams prepared for
    sacrifice.
Yes, the LORD will offer a sacrifice in the
    city of Bozrah.
  He will make a mighty slaughter in
    Edom.
⁷ Even men as strong as wild oxen will
    die—
  the young men alongside the veterans.
The land will be soaked with blood
  and the soil enriched with fat.

⁸ For it is the day of the LORD's revenge,
  the year when Edom will be paid back
    for all it did to Israel.*
⁹ The streams of Edom will be filled with
    burning pitch,
  and the ground will be covered with
    fire.
¹⁰ This judgment on Edom will never end;
  the smoke of its burning will rise
    forever.
The land will lie deserted from
  generation to generation.
  No one will live there anymore.
¹¹ It will be haunted by the desert owl and
    the screech owl,
  the great owl and the raven.*
For God will measure that land
  carefully;
  he will measure it for chaos and
    destruction.
¹² It will be called the Land of Nothing,
  and all its nobles will soon be gone.*
¹³ Thorns will overrun its palaces;
  nettles and thistles will grow in its
    forts.
The ruins will become a haunt for jackals
  and a home for owls.
¹⁴ Desert animals will mingle there with
    hyenas,
  their howls filling the night.
Wild goats will bleat at one another
  among the ruins,
  and night creatures* will come there
    to rest.
¹⁵ There the owl will make her nest and lay
    her eggs.
  She will hatch her young and cover
    them with her wings.

And the buzzards will come,
  each one with its mate.
¹⁶ Search the book of the LORD,
  and see what he will do.
Not one of these birds and animals will
  be missing,
  and none will lack a mate,
for the LORD has promised this.
  His Spirit will make it all come true.
¹⁷ He has surveyed and divided the land
  and deeded it over to those
    creatures.
They will possess it forever,
  from generation to generation.

35 Hope for Restoration

¹ Even the wilderness and desert will
  be glad in those days.
The wasteland will rejoice and
  blossom with spring crocuses.
² Yes, there will be an abundance of
    flowers
  and singing and joy!
The deserts will become as green as the
  mountains of Lebanon,
  as lovely as Mount Carmel or the plain
    of Sharon.
There the LORD will display his glory,
  the splendor of our God.
³ With this news, strengthen those who
    have tired hands,
  and encourage those who have weak
    knees.
⁴ Say to those with fearful hearts,
  "Be strong, and do not fear,
for your God is coming to destroy your
    enemies.
  He is coming to save you."

⁵ And when he comes, he will open the
    eyes of the blind
  and unplug the ears of the deaf.
⁶ The lame will leap like a deer,
  and those who cannot speak will sing
    for joy!
Springs will gush forth in the
  wilderness,
  and streams will water the wasteland.
⁷ The parched ground will become a pool,
  and springs of water will satisfy the
    thirsty land.

34:8 Hebrew to Zion. 34:11 The identification of some of these birds is uncertain. 34:12 The meaning of the Hebrew is uncertain.
34:14 Hebrew Lilith, possibly a reference to a mythical demon of the night.

Marsh grass and reeds and rushes will
flourish
where desert jackals once lived.
8 And a great road will go through that
once deserted land.
It will be named the Highway of
Holiness.
Evil-minded people will never travel
on it.
It will be only for those who walk in
God's ways;
fools will never walk there.
9 Lions will not lurk along its course,
nor any other ferocious beasts.
There will be no other dangers.
Only the redeemed will walk on it.
10 Those who have been ransomed by the
LORD will return.
They will enter Jerusalem* singing,
crowned with everlasting joy.
Sorrow and mourning will disappear,
and they will be filled with joy and
gladness.

36 Assyria Invades Judah

In the fourteenth year of King Hezekiah's reign,* King Sennacherib of Assyria came to attack the fortified towns of Judah and conquered them. 2 Then the king of Assyria sent his chief of staff* from Lachish with a huge army to confront King Hezekiah in Jerusalem. The Assyrians took up a position beside the aqueduct that feeds water into the upper pool, near the road leading to the field where cloth is washed.* 3 These are the officials who went out to meet with them: Eliakim son of Hilkiah, the palace administrator; Shebna the court secretary; and Joah son of Asaph, the royal historian.

Sennacherib Threatens Jerusalem

4 Then the Assyrian king's chief of staff told them to give this message to Hezekiah:

"This is what the great king of Assyria says: What are you trusting in that makes you so confident? 5 Do you think that mere words can substitute for military skill and strength? Who are you counting on, that you have rebelled against me? 6 On Egypt? If you lean on Egypt, it will be like a reed that splinters beneath your weight and pierces your hand. Pharaoh, the king of Egypt, is completely unreliable!

7 "But perhaps you will say to me, 'We are trusting in the LORD our God!' But isn't he the one who was insulted by Hezekiah? Didn't Hezekiah tear down his shrines and altars and make everyone in Judah and Jerusalem worship only at the altar here in Jerusalem?

8 "I'll tell you what! Strike a bargain with my master, the king of Assyria. I will give you 2,000 horses if you can find that many men to ride on them! 9 With your tiny army, how can you think of challenging even the weakest contingent of my master's troops, even with the help of Egypt's chariots and charioteers? 10 What's more, do you think we have invaded your land without the LORD's direction? The LORD himself told us, 'Attack this land and destroy it!'"

11 Then Eliakim, Shebna, and Joah said to the Assyrian chief of staff, "Please speak to us in Aramaic, for we understand it well. Don't speak in Hebrew,* for the people on the wall will hear."

12 But Sennacherib's chief of staff replied, "Do you think my master sent this message only to you and your master? He wants all the people to hear it, for when we put this city under siege, they will suffer along with you. They will be so hungry and thirsty that they will eat their own dung and drink their own urine."

13 Then the chief of staff stood and shouted in Hebrew to the people on the wall, "Listen to this message from the great king of Assyria! 14 This is what the king says: Don't let Hezekiah deceive you. He will never be able to rescue you. 15 Don't let him fool you into trusting in the LORD by saying, 'The LORD will surely rescue us. This city will never fall into the hands of the Assyrian king!'

16 "Don't listen to Hezekiah! These are the terms the king of Assyria is offering: Make peace with me—open the gates and come

---

35:10 Hebrew *Zion.* 36:1 The fourteenth year of Hezekiah's reign was 701 B.C. 36:2a Or *the rabshakeh;* also in 36:4, 11, 12, 22. 36:2b Or *bleached.* 36:11 Hebrew *in the dialect of Judah;* also in 36:13.

out. Then each of you can continue eating from your own grapevine and fig tree and drinking from your own well. [17] Then I will arrange to take you to another land like this one—a land of grain and new wine, bread and vineyards.

[18] "Don't let Hezekiah mislead you by saying, 'The LORD will rescue us!' Have the gods of any other nations ever saved their people from the king of Assyria? [19] What happened to the gods of Hamath and Arpad? And what about the gods of Sepharvaim? Did any god rescue Samaria from my power? [20] What god of any nation has ever been able to save its people from my power? So what makes you think that the LORD can rescue Jerusalem from me?"

[21] But the people were silent and did not utter a word because Hezekiah had commanded them, "Do not answer him."

[22] Then Eliakim son of Hilkiah, the palace administrator; Shebna the court secretary; and Joah son of Asaph, the royal historian, went back to Hezekiah. They tore their clothes in despair, and they went in to see the king and told him what the Assyrian chief of staff had said.

37 Hezekiah Seeks the LORD's Help

When King Hezekiah heard their report, he tore his clothes and put on burlap and went into the Temple of the LORD. [2] And he sent Eliakim the palace administrator, Shebna the court secretary, and the leading priests, all dressed in burlap, to the prophet Isaiah son of Amoz. [3] They told him, "This is what King Hezekiah says: Today is a day of trouble, insults, and disgrace. It is like when a child is ready to be born, but the mother has no strength to deliver the baby. [4] But perhaps the LORD your God has heard the Assyrian chief of staff,* sent by the king to defy the living God, and will punish him for his words. Oh, pray for those of us who are left!"

[5] After King Hezekiah's officials delivered the king's message to Isaiah, [6] the prophet replied, "Say to your master, 'This is what the LORD says: Do not be disturbed by this blasphemous speech against me from the Assyrian king's messengers. [7] Listen! I

myself will move against him,* and the king will receive a message that he is needed at home. So he will return to his land, where I will have him killed with a sword.'"

[8] Meanwhile, the Assyrian chief of staff left Jerusalem and went to consult the king of Assyria, who had left Lachish and was attacking Libnah.

[9] Soon afterward King Sennacherib received word that King Tirhakah of Ethiopia* was leading an army to fight against him. Before leaving to meet the attack, he sent messengers back to Hezekiah in Jerusalem with this message:

[10] "This message is for King Hezekiah of Judah. Don't let your God, in whom you trust, deceive you with promises that Jerusalem will not be captured by the king of Assyria. [11] You know perfectly well what the kings of Assyria have done wherever they have gone. They have completely destroyed everyone who stood in their way! Why should you be any different? [12] Have the gods of other nations rescued them—such nations as Gozan, Haran, Rezeph, and the people of Eden who were in Tel-assar? My predecessors destroyed them all! [13] What happened to the king of Hamath and the king of Arpad? What happened to the kings of Sepharvaim, Hena, and Ivvah?"

[14] After Hezekiah received the letter from the messengers and read it, he went up to the LORD's Temple and spread it out before the LORD. [15] And Hezekiah prayed this prayer before the LORD: [16] "O LORD of Heaven's Armies, God of Israel, you are enthroned between the mighty cherubim! You alone are God of all the kingdoms of the earth. You alone created the heavens and the earth. [17] Bend down, O LORD, and listen! Open your eyes, O LORD, and see! Listen to Sennacherib's words of defiance against the living God.

[18] "It is true, LORD, that the kings of Assyria have destroyed all these nations. [19] And they have thrown the gods of these nations into the fire and burned them. But of course the Assyrians could destroy them! They were not gods at all—only idols of

---

37:4 Or *the rabshakeh;* also in 37:8.   **37:7** Hebrew *I will put a spirit in him.*   **37:9** Hebrew *of Cush.*

wood and stone shaped by human hands. [20] Now, O Lord our God, rescue us from his power; then all the kingdoms of the earth will know that you alone, O Lord, are God.*"

Isaiah Predicts Judah's Deliverance

[21] Then Isaiah son of Amoz sent this message to Hezekiah: "This is what the Lord, the God of Israel, says: Because you prayed about King Sennacherib of Assyria, [22] the Lord has spoken this word against him:

"The virgin daughter of Zion
despises you and laughs at you.
The daughter of Jerusalem
shakes her head in derision as you flee.

[23] "Whom have you been defying and
ridiculing?
Against whom did you raise your
voice?
At whom did you look with such
haughty eyes?
It was the Holy One of Israel!
[24] By your messengers you have defied the
Lord.
You have said, 'With my many chariots
I have conquered the highest
mountains—
yes, the remotest peaks of Lebanon.
I have cut down its tallest cedars
and its finest cypress trees.
I have reached its farthest heights
and explored its deepest forests.
[25] I have dug wells in many foreign lands*
and refreshed myself with their water.
With the sole of my foot,
I stopped up all the rivers of Egypt!'

[26] "But have you not heard?
I decided this long ago.
Long ago I planned it,
and now I am making it happen.
I planned for you to crush fortified cities
into heaps of rubble.
[27] That is why their people have so little
power
and are so frightened and confused.
They are as weak as grass,
as easily trampled as tender green
shoots.

They are like grass sprouting on a
housetop,
scorched* before it can grow lush and
tall.

[28] "But I know you well—
where you stay
and when you come and go.
I know the way you have raged
against me.
[29] And because of your raging against me
and your arrogance, which I have
heard for myself,
I will put my hook in your nose
and my bit in your mouth.
I will make you return
by the same road on which you
came."

[30] Then Isaiah said to Hezekiah, "Here is the proof that what I say is true:

"This year you will eat only what grows
up by itself,
and next year you will eat what springs
up from that.
But in the third year you will plant crops
and harvest them;
you will tend vineyards and eat their
fruit.
[31] And you who are left in Judah,
who have escaped the ravages of the
siege,
will put roots down in your own soil
and grow up and flourish.
[32] For a remnant of my people will spread
out from Jerusalem,
a group of survivors from Mount
Zion.
The passionate commitment of the
Lord of Heaven's Armies
will make this happen!

[33] "And this is what the Lord says about the king of Assyria:

"'His armies will not enter Jerusalem.
They will not even shoot an arrow
at it.
They will not march outside its gates
with their shields
nor build banks of earth against its
walls.

37:20 As in Dead Sea Scrolls (see also 2 Kgs 19:19); Masoretic Text reads *you alone are the Lord.*   37:25 As in Dead Sea Scrolls (see also 2 Kgs 19:24); Masoretic Text lacks *in many foreign lands.*   37:27 As in Dead Sea Scrolls and some Greek manuscripts (see also 2 Kgs 19:26); most Hebrew manuscripts read *like a terraced field.*

34 The king will return to his own
    country
    by the same road on which he came.
He will not enter this city,'
    says the LORD.
35 'For my own honor and for the sake of
    my servant David,
    I will defend this city and protect it.'"

36 That night the angel of the LORD went out to the Assyrian camp and killed 185,000 Assyrian soldiers. When the surviving Assyrians* woke up the next morning, they found corpses everywhere. 37 Then King Sennacherib of Assyria broke camp and returned to his own land. He went home to his capital of Nineveh and stayed there.

38 One day while he was worshiping in the temple of his god Nisroch, his sons Adrammelech and Sharezer killed him with their swords. They then escaped to the land of Ararat, and another son, Esarhaddon, became the next king of Assyria.

38 Hezekiah's Sickness and Recovery

About that time Hezekiah became deathly ill, and the prophet Isaiah son of Amoz went to visit him. He gave the king this message: "This is what the LORD says: 'Set your affairs in order, for you are going to die. You will not recover from this illness.'"

2 When Hezekiah heard this, he turned his face to the wall and prayed to the LORD, 3 "Remember, O LORD, how I have always been faithful to you and have served you single-mindedly, always doing what pleases you." Then he broke down and wept bitterly.

4 Then this message came to Isaiah from the LORD: 5 "Go back to Hezekiah and tell him, 'This is what the LORD, the God of your ancestor David, says: I have heard your prayer and seen your tears. I will add fifteen years to your life, 6 and I will rescue you and this city from the king of Assyria. Yes, I will defend this city.

7 "'And this is the sign from the LORD to prove that he will do as he promised: 8 I will cause the sun's shadow to move ten steps backward on the sundial* of Ahaz!'" So the shadow on the sundial moved backward ten steps.

Hezekiah's Poem of Praise

9 When King Hezekiah was well again, he wrote this poem:

10 I said, "In the prime of my life,
    must I now enter the place of the
      dead?*
    Am I to be robbed of the rest of my
      years?"
11 I said, "Never again will I see the LORD
    GOD
    while still in the land of the living.
Never again will I see my friends
    or be with those who live in this
      world.
12 My life has been blown away
    like a shepherd's tent in a storm.
It has been cut short,
    as when a weaver cuts cloth from a
      loom.
    Suddenly, my life was over.
13 I waited patiently all night,
    but I was torn apart as though by
      lions.
    Suddenly, my life was over.
14 Delirious, I chattered like a swallow or a
    crane,
    and then I moaned like a mourning
      dove.
My eyes grew tired of looking to heaven
    for help.
    I am in trouble, Lord. Help me!"

15 But what could I say?
    For he himself sent this sickness.
Now I will walk humbly throughout my
    years
    because of this anguish I have felt.
16 Lord, your discipline is good,
    for it leads to life and health.
You restore my health
    and allow me to live!
17 Yes, this anguish was good for me,
    for you have rescued me from death
    and forgiven all my sins.
18 For the dead* cannot praise you;
    they cannot raise their voices in
      praise.
Those who go down to the grave
    can no longer hope in your
      faithfulness.
19 Only the living can praise you as I do
    today.

37:36 Hebrew *When they.*   **38:8** Hebrew *the steps.*   **38:10** Hebrew *enter the gates of Sheol?*   **38:18** Hebrew *Sheol.*

Each generation tells of your
faithfulness to the next.
²⁰ Think of it—the LORD is ready to
heal me!
I will sing his praises with instruments
every day of my life
in the Temple of the LORD.

²¹Isaiah had said to Hezekiah's servants, "Make an ointment from figs and spread it over the boil, and Hezekiah will recover." ²²And Hezekiah had asked, "What sign will prove that I will go to the Temple of the LORD?"

39 Envoys from Babylon

Soon after this, Merodach-baladan son of Baladan, king of Babylon, sent Hezekiah his best wishes and a gift. He had heard that Hezekiah had been very sick and that he had recovered. ²Hezekiah was delighted with the Babylonian envoys and showed them everything in his treasure-houses— the silver, the gold, the spices, and the aromatic oils. He also took them to see his armory and showed them everything in his royal treasuries! There was nothing in his palace or kingdom that Hezekiah did not show them.

³Then Isaiah the prophet went to King Hezekiah and asked him, "What did those men want? Where were they from?"

Hezekiah replied, "They came from the distant land of Babylon."

⁴"What did they see in your palace?" asked Isaiah.

"They saw everything," Hezekiah replied. "I showed them everything I own—all my royal treasuries."

⁵Then Isaiah said to Hezekiah, "Listen to this message from the LORD of Heaven's Armies: ⁶'The time is coming when everything in your palace—all the treasures stored up by your ancestors until now— will be carried off to Babylon. Nothing will be left,' says the LORD. ⁷'Some of your very own sons will be taken away into exile. They will become eunuchs who will serve in the palace of Babylon's king.'"

⁸Then Hezekiah said to Isaiah, "This message you have given me from the LORD is good." For the king was thinking, "At least there will be peace and security during my lifetime."

40 Comfort for God's People

¹ "Comfort, comfort my people," says your God.
² "Speak tenderly to Jerusalem.
Tell her that her sad days are gone
and her sins are pardoned.
Yes, the LORD has punished her twice
over
for all her sins."

³ Listen! It's the voice of someone
shouting,
"Clear the way through the wilderness
for the LORD!
Make a straight highway through the
wasteland
for our God!
⁴ Fill in the valleys,
and level the mountains and hills.
Straighten the curves,
and smooth out the rough places.
⁵ Then the glory of the LORD will be
revealed,
and all people will see it together.
The LORD has spoken!"*

⁶ A voice said, "Shout!"
I asked, "What should I shout?"

"Shout that people are like the grass.
Their beauty fades as quickly
as the flowers in a field.
⁷ The grass withers and the flowers fade
beneath the breath of the LORD.
And so it is with people.
⁸ The grass withers and the flowers fade,
but the word of our God stands
forever."

⁹ O Zion, messenger of good news,
shout from the mountaintops!
Shout it louder, O Jerusalem.*
Shout, and do not be afraid.
Tell the towns of Judah,
"Your God is coming!"
¹⁰ Yes, the Sovereign LORD is coming in
power.

40:3-5 Greek version reads *He is a voice shouting in the wilderness, / "Prepare the way for the LORD's coming! / Clear a road for our God! / Fill in the valleys, / and level the mountains and hills. / And then the glory of the LORD will be revealed, / and all people will see the salvation sent from God. / The LORD has spoken!"* Compare Matt 3:3; Mark 1:3; Luke 3:4-6. **40:9** Or *O messenger of good news, shout to Zion from the mountaintops! Shout it louder to Jerusalem.*

He will rule with a powerful arm.
See, he brings his reward with him as
he comes.
[11] He will feed his flock like a shepherd.
He will carry the lambs in his arms,
holding them close to his heart.
He will gently lead the mother sheep
with their young.

The LORD Has No Equal

[12] Who else has held the oceans in his
hand?
Who has measured off the heavens
with his fingers?
Who else knows the weight of the
earth
or has weighed the mountains and
hills on a scale?
[13] Who is able to advise the Spirit of the
LORD?*
Who knows enough to give him
advice or teach him?
[14] Has the LORD ever needed anyone's
advice?
Does he need instruction about what
is good?
Did someone teach him what is right
or show him the path of justice?

[15] No, for all the nations of the world
are but a drop in the bucket.
They are nothing more
than dust on the scales.
He picks up the whole earth
as though it were a grain of sand.
[16] All the wood in Lebanon's forests
and all Lebanon's animals would not
be enough
to make a burnt offering worthy of our
God.
[17] The nations of the world are worth
nothing to him.
In his eyes they count for less than
nothing—
mere emptiness and froth.

[18] To whom can you compare God?
What image can you find to resemble
him?
[19] Can he be compared to an idol formed
in a mold,
overlaid with gold, and decorated with
silver chains?

[20] Or if people are too poor for that,
they might at least choose wood that
won't decay
and a skilled craftsman
to carve an image that won't fall down!

[21] Haven't you heard? Don't you
understand?
Are you deaf to the words of God—
the words he gave before the world
began?
Are you so ignorant?
[22] God sits above the circle of the earth.
The people below seem like
grasshoppers to him!
He spreads out the heavens like a curtain
and makes his tent from them.
[23] He judges the great people of the world
and brings them all to nothing.
[24] They hardly get started, barely taking
root,
when he blows on them and they
wither.
The wind carries them off like chaff.

[25] "To whom will you compare me?
Who is my equal?" asks the Holy One.

[26] Look up into the heavens.
Who created all the stars?
He brings them out like an army, one
after another,
calling each by its name.
Because of his great power and
incomparable strength,
not a single one is missing.
[27] O Jacob, how can you say the LORD does
not see your troubles?
O Israel, how can you say God ignores
your rights?
[28] Have you never heard?
Have you never understood?
The LORD is the everlasting God,
the Creator of all the earth.
He never grows weak or weary.
No one can measure the depths of his
understanding.
[29] He gives power to the weak
and strength to the powerless.
[30] Even youths will become weak and tired,
and young men will fall in exhaustion.
[31] But those who trust in the LORD will
find new strength.

40:13 Greek version reads *Who can know the LORD's thoughts?* Compare Rom 11:34; 1 Cor 2:16.

They will soar high on wings like
    eagles.
They will run and not grow weary.
    They will walk and not faint.

41 God's Help for Israel

1 "Listen in silence before me, you
    lands beyond the sea.
Bring your strongest arguments.
Come now and speak.
    The court is ready for your case.

2 "Who has stirred up this king from the
    east,
    rightly calling him to God's service?
Who gives this man victory over many
    nations
    and permits him to trample their
    kings underfoot?
With his sword, he reduces armies to
    dust.
    With his bow, he scatters them like
    chaff before the wind.
3 He chases them away and goes on
    safely,
    though he is walking over unfamiliar
    ground.
4 Who has done such mighty deeds,
    summoning each new generation from
    the beginning of time?
It is I, the LORD, the First and the Last.
    I alone am he."

5 The lands beyond the sea watch in fear.
    Remote lands tremble and mobilize
    for war.
6 The idol makers encourage one another,
    saying to each other, "Be strong!"
7 The carver encourages the goldsmith,
    and the molder helps at the anvil.
    "Good," they say. "It's coming along
    fine."
Carefully they join the parts together,
    then fasten the thing in place so it
    won't fall over.

8 "But as for you, Israel my servant,
    Jacob my chosen one,
    descended from Abraham my friend,
9 I have called you back from the ends of
    the earth,
    saying, 'You are my servant.'
For I have chosen you
    and will not throw you away.

10 Don't be afraid, for I am with you.
    Don't be discouraged, for I am your
    God.
I will strengthen you and help you.
    I will hold you up with my victorious
    right hand.

11 "See, all your angry enemies lie there,
    confused and humiliated.
Anyone who opposes you will die
    and come to nothing.
12 You will look in vain
    for those who tried to conquer you.
Those who attack you
    will come to nothing.
13 For I hold you by your right hand—
    I, the LORD your God.
And I say to you,
    'Don't be afraid. I am here to help you.
14 Though you are a lowly worm, O Jacob,
    don't be afraid, people of Israel, for I
    will help you.
I am the LORD, your Redeemer.
    I am the Holy One of Israel.'
15 You will be a new threshing instrument
    with many sharp teeth.
You will tear your enemies apart,
    making chaff of mountains.
16 You will toss them into the air,
    and the wind will blow them all away;
    a whirlwind will scatter them.
Then you will rejoice in the LORD.
    You will glory in the Holy One of Israel.

17 "When the poor and needy search for
    water and there is none,
    and their tongues are parched from
    thirst,
then I, the LORD, will answer them.
    I, the God of Israel, will never
    abandon them.
18 I will open up rivers for them on the
    high plateaus.
    I will give them fountains of water in
    the valleys.
I will fill the desert with pools of water.
    Rivers fed by springs will flow across
    the parched ground.
19 I will plant trees in the barren desert—
    cedar, acacia, myrtle, olive, cypress, fir,
    and pine.
20 I am doing this so all who see this
    miracle
    will understand what it means—

that it is the LORD who has done this,
   the Holy One of Israel who created it.

21 "Present the case for your idols,"
   says the LORD.
"Let them show what they can do,"
   says the King of Israel.*
22 "Let them try to tell us what happened
    long ago
  so that we may consider the evidence.
Or let them tell us what the future holds,
  so we can know what's going to
    happen.
23 Yes, tell us what will occur in the days
    ahead.
  Then we will know you are gods.
In fact, do anything—good or bad!
  Do something that will amaze and
    frighten us.
24 But no! You are less than nothing and
    can do nothing at all.
  Those who choose you pollute
    themselves.

25 "But I have stirred up a leader who will
    come from the north.
  I have called him by name from the
    east.
I will give him victory over kings and
    princes.
  He will trample them as a potter
    treads on clay.

26 "Who told you from the beginning
    that this would happen?
Who predicted this,
  making you admit that he was right?
  No one said a word!
27 I was the first to tell Zion,
   'Look! Help is on the way!'*
I will send Jerusalem a messenger with
    good news.
28 Not one of your idols told you this.
  Not one gave any answer when I
    asked.
29 See, they are all foolish, worthless things.
  All your idols are as empty as the wind.

42 The LORD's Chosen Servant

1 "Look at my servant, whom I
    strengthen.
  He is my chosen one, who pleases me.

I have put my Spirit upon him.
  He will bring justice to the nations.
2 He will not shout
  or raise his voice in public.
3 He will not crush the weakest reed
  or put out a flickering candle.
  He will bring justice to all who have
    been wronged.
4 He will not falter or lose heart
  until justice prevails throughout the
    earth.
  Even distant lands beyond the sea will
    wait for his instruction.*"

5 God, the LORD, created the heavens and
    stretched them out.
  He created the earth and everything
    in it.
He gives breath to everyone,
  life to everyone who walks the earth.
And it is he who says,
6 "I, the LORD, have called you to
    demonstrate my righteousness.
  I will take you by the hand and guard
    you,
and I will give you to my people, Israel,
  as a symbol of my covenant with
    them.
And you will be a light to guide the
    nations.
7 You will open the eyes of the blind.
You will free the captives from prison,
  releasing those who sit in dark
    dungeons.

8 "I am the LORD; that is my name!
  I will not give my glory to anyone
    else,
  nor share my praise with carved idols.
9 Everything I prophesied has come true,
  and now I will prophesy again.
I will tell you the future before it
    happens."

A Song of Praise to the LORD

10 Sing a new song to the LORD!
  Sing his praises from the ends of the
    earth!
Sing, all you who sail the seas,
  all you who live in distant coastlands.
11 Join in the chorus, you desert towns;
  let the villages of Kedar rejoice!

41:21 Hebrew *the King of Jacob.* See note on 14:1.   41:27 Or *'Look! They are coming home.'*   42:4 Greek version reads *And his name will be the hope of all the world.* Compare Matt 12:21.

Let the people of Sela sing for joy;
    shout praises from the mountaintops!
¹² Let the whole world glorify the LORD;
    let it sing his praise.
¹³ The LORD will march forth like a mighty
       hero;
    he will come out like a warrior, full of
       fury.
He will shout his battle cry
    and crush all his enemies.

¹⁴ He will say, "I have long been silent;
    yes, I have restrained myself.
But now, like a woman in labor,
    I will cry and groan and pant.
¹⁵ I will level the mountains and hills
    and blight all their greenery.
I will turn the rivers into dry land
    and will dry up all the pools.
¹⁶ I will lead blind Israel down a new path,
    guiding them along an unfamiliar
      way.
I will brighten the darkness before them
    and smooth out the road ahead of
      them.
Yes, I will indeed do these things;
    I will not forsake them.
¹⁷ But those who trust in idols,
    who say, 'You are our gods,'
    will be turned away in shame.

Israel's Failure to Listen and See

¹⁸ "Listen, you who are deaf!
    Look and see, you blind!
¹⁹ Who is as blind as my own people, my
      servant?
    Who is as deaf as my messenger?
Who is as blind as my chosen people,
    the servant of the LORD?
²⁰ You see and recognize what is right
    but refuse to act on it.
You hear with your ears,
    but you don't really listen."

²¹ Because he is righteous,
    the LORD has exalted his glorious
      law.
²² But his own people have been robbed
    and plundered,
    enslaved, imprisoned, and trapped.
They are fair game for anyone
    and have no one to protect them,
    no one to take them back home.

²³ Who will hear these lessons from the
    past
    and see the ruin that awaits you in the
      future?
²⁴ Who allowed Israel to be robbed and
    hurt?
    It was the LORD, against whom we
      sinned,
for the people would not walk in his path,
    nor would they obey his law.
²⁵ Therefore, he poured out his fury on
    them
    and destroyed them in battle.
They were enveloped in flames,
    but they still refused to understand.
They were consumed by fire,
    but they did not learn their lesson.

43 The Savior of Israel

¹ But now, O Jacob, listen to the
    LORD who created you.
O Israel, the one who formed you says,
"Do not be afraid, for I have ransomed
    you.
    I have called you by name; you are
      mine.
² When you go through deep waters,
    I will be with you.
When you go through rivers of difficulty,
    you will not drown.
When you walk through the fire of
      oppression,
    you will not be burned up;
    the flames will not consume you.
³ For I am the LORD, your God,
    the Holy One of Israel, your Savior.
I gave Egypt as a ransom for your
    freedom;
    I gave Ethiopia* and Seba in your
      place.
⁴ Others were given in exchange for you.
    I traded their lives for yours
because you are precious to me.
    You are honored, and I love you.

⁵ "Do not be afraid, for I am with you.
    I will gather you and your children
      from east and west.
⁶ I will say to the north and south,
    'Bring my sons and daughters back to
    Israel
    from the distant corners of the earth.

43:3 Hebrew Cush.

⁷ Bring all who claim me as their God,
    for I have made them for my glory.
    It was I who created them.'"

⁸ Bring out the people who have eyes but
        are blind,
    who have ears but are deaf.
⁹ Gather the nations together!
    Assemble the peoples of the world!
    Which of their idols has ever foretold
        such things?
    Which can predict what will happen
        tomorrow?
    Where are the witnesses of such
        predictions?
    Who can verify that they spoke the
        truth?

¹⁰ "But you are my witnesses, O Israel!"
        says the LORD.
    "You are my servant.
    You have been chosen to know me,
        believe in me,
    and understand that I alone am God.
    There is no other God—
        there never has been, and there never
        will be.
¹¹ I, yes I, am the LORD,
    and there is no other Savior.
¹² First I predicted your rescue,
    then I saved you and proclaimed it to
        the world.
    No foreign god has ever done this.
    You are witnesses that I am the only
        God,"
    says the LORD.
¹³ "From eternity to eternity I am God.
    No one can snatch anyone out of my
        hand.
    No one can undo what I have done."

The LORD's Promise of Victory

¹⁴ This is what the LORD says—your Redeemer, the Holy One of Israel:

    "For your sakes I will send an army
        against Babylon,
    forcing the Babylonians* to flee in
        those ships they are so proud of.
¹⁵ I am the LORD, your Holy One,
    Israel's Creator and King.
¹⁶ I am the LORD, who opened a way
        through the waters,
    making a dry path through the sea.

¹⁷ I called forth the mighty army of Egypt
    with all its chariots and horses.
    I drew them beneath the waves, and they
        drowned,
    their lives snuffed out like a
        smoldering candlewick.

¹⁸ "But forget all that—
    it is nothing compared to what I am
        going to do.
¹⁹ For I am about to do something new.
    See, I have already begun! Do you not
        see it?
    I will make a pathway through the
        wilderness.
    I will create rivers in the dry
        wasteland.
²⁰ The wild animals in the fields will
        thank me,
    the jackals and owls, too,
    for giving them water in the desert.
    Yes, I will make rivers in the dry
        wasteland
    so my chosen people can be refreshed.
²¹ I have made Israel for myself,
    and they will someday honor me
        before the whole world.

²² "But, dear family of Jacob, you refuse to
        ask for my help.
    You have grown tired of me, O Israel!
²³ You have not brought me sheep or goats
        for burnt offerings.
    You have not honored me with
        sacrifices,
    though I have not burdened and wearied
        you
    with requests for grain offerings and
        frankincense.
²⁴ You have not brought me fragrant
        calamus
    or pleased me with the fat from
        sacrifices.
    Instead, you have burdened me with
        your sins
    and wearied me with your faults.

²⁵ "I—yes, I alone—will blot out your sins
        for my own sake
    and will never think of them again.
²⁶ Let us review the situation together,
    and you can present your case to
        prove your innocence.

43:14 Or Chaldeans.

Forgiveness

Understanding Forgiveness
ISAIAH 43:14–25

Jesus was unequivocal on this point: as his followers, we are required to forgive those who sin against us (Matthew 6:15). But what if we don't feel like we've forgiven them? How do we know, then, if we've truly forgiven? The Holy Spirit, thank God, often enables people to forgive even though they are not sure how they did it. But forgiving, and knowing that we've truly forgiven, comes easier when we understand the realities of forgiveness:

Forgiveness is a redemptive response to having been wronged and wounded. This is simple but important. Only those who have wronged and wounded us are candidates for forgiveness. If they injure us accidentally, we excuse them. We only *forgive* the ones we blame.

Forgiveness requires three basic actions. First, we surrender our right to get even. Every victim is sure that the victimizer deserves to suffer at least as much as he made us suffer. But that isn't necessarily so. "The wages of sin [wronging God] is death" (Romans 6:23), but the payment was made through the death of God's own Son. The blood of Christ covers all our sins, but each of us must do personal business with God in order to experience his forgiveness. When we forgive, therefore, we place the outcome of the matter in God's hands and often choose to live with the scales unbalanced.

Second, we rediscover the humanity of our wrongdoer. When we have been badly injured and clearly wronged, we make an instant caricature of the person who did it to us. We define him totally by the one wrong he did. If he betrayed us, his total being is reduced to his betrayal. When we forgive, we rediscover that the person who wronged us is a complex, weak, confused, fragile person, not all that different from us. This is what God does. Our sin hid our faces from him; now, forgiven, we shine like sparkling jewels before him.

And third, we wish our wrongdoer well. We not only surrender our right to revenge against him; we desire good things to happen to him. We bless him. Unnatural? Too much to ask of us? Perhaps. And yet this is how God forgives us; he not only surrenders his right to see us punished, he also graces us with whatever blessing is right for us.

Forgiving takes time. God can forgive in a single breath. But we need time. Just before he died, C. S. Lewis wrote: "I think I have *at last* forgiven the cruel schoolmaster who so darkened my youth. I had done it many times before, but this time I think I have really done it." Maybe, had he lived longer, he would have had to do it again.

Forgiving does not require forgetting. True, God said through Isaiah (43:25), "I—yes, I alone—will blot out your sins . . . and will never think of them again." But does God have amnesia? Does God not remember that Peter denied his Lord? Or does he treat Peter and all other forgiven people *as if* he cannot remember what they did? On a human level, it's futile to try to forget; the more we try to forget, the more we remember. But we can dethrone the memory; we can refuse to let it control our lives. We can detoxify the memory; we can purge its poison from our souls. But we do well not to worry about forgetting. Sufficient unto the day is forgiving.

Ideally forgiving leads to reconciliation. But we often have to put up with less than the ideal. Sometimes the forgiven person will not want to be reunited with us; he may not care a fig for our grace. Besides, though he is forgiven, he may not be changed. If he's reunited with us, he's likely to clobber us again. Forgiving happens in our hearts. There can be no reunion without forgiving, but there can be forgiving without reunion. An offender who has violated a law will need to endure the just judicial consequences. But even as that happens, the offended person can pray and seek full reconciliation on the other side of justice.

Forgiving comes naturally to the forgiven. Nothing enables us to forgive like knowing in our hearts that we have been forgiven. This is probably why Jesus taught us to pray, "Forgive us our sins, [but only] as we have forgiven those who sin against us" (Matthew 6:12). Jesus implies that it is unthinkable for a forgiven person to refuse to forgive. If we do refuse, he says later, we have no claim on God's forgiveness. But remember, he does not expect *perfect* forgiving; he is the only expert at it. We're just poor, imperfect sinners trying our hardest to treat others as he treats us.

—Lewis B. Smedes

For more on forgiveness, see reading at Ezekiel 37:1–14.

²⁷ From the very beginning, your first
ancestor sinned against me;
all your leaders broke my laws.
²⁸ That is why I have disgraced your
priests;
I have decreed complete destruction*
for Jacob
and shame for Israel.

44

¹ "But now, listen to me, Jacob my
servant,
Israel my chosen one.
² The LORD who made you and helps you
says:
Do not be afraid, O Jacob, my servant,
O dear Israel,* my chosen one.
³ For I will pour out water to quench your
thirst
and to irrigate your parched
fields.
And I will pour out my Spirit on your
descendants,
and my blessing on your children.
⁴ They will thrive like watered grass,
like willows on a riverbank.
⁵ Some will proudly claim, 'I belong to the
LORD.'
Others will say, 'I am a descendant of
Jacob.'
Some will write the LORD's name on
their hands
and will take the name of Israel as
their own."

The Foolishness of Idols

⁶ This is what the LORD says—Israel's King
and Redeemer, the LORD of Heaven's
Armies:

"I am the First and the Last;
there is no other God.
⁷ Who is like me?
Let him step forward and prove to you
his power.
Let him do as I have done since ancient
times
when I established a people and
explained its future.
⁸ Do not tremble; do not be afraid.
Did I not proclaim my purposes for
you long ago?

You are my witnesses—is there any
other God?
No! There is no other Rock—not one!"

⁹ How foolish are those who manufacture
idols.
These prized objects are really
worthless.
The people who worship idols don't
know this,
so they are all put to shame.
¹⁰ Who but a fool would make his own
god—
an idol that cannot help him one bit?
¹¹ All who worship idols will be disgraced
along with all these craftsmen—mere
humans—
who claim they can make a god.
They may all stand together,
but they will stand in terror and
shame.
¹² The blacksmith stands at his forge to
make a sharp tool,
pounding and shaping it with all his
might.
His work makes him hungry and weak.
It makes him thirsty and faint.
¹³ Then the wood-carver measures a block
of wood
and draws a pattern on it.
He works with chisel and plane
and carves it into a human figure.
He gives it human beauty
and puts it in a little shrine.
¹⁴ He cuts down cedars;
he selects the cypress and the oak;
he plants the pine in the forest
to be nourished by the rain.
¹⁵ Then he uses part of the wood to make a
fire.
With it he warms himself and bakes
his bread.
Then—yes, it's true—he takes the rest
of it
and makes himself a god to worship!
He makes an idol
and bows down in front of it!
¹⁶ He burns part of the tree to roast his
meat
and to keep himself warm.
He says, "Ah, that fire feels good."

43:28 The Hebrew term used here refers to the complete consecration of things or people to the LORD, either by destroying them or by giving them as an offering. 44:2 Hebrew *Jeshurun*, a term of endearment for Israel.

17 Then he takes what's left
    and makes his god: a carved idol!
He falls down in front of it,
    worshiping and praying to it.
"Rescue me!" he says.
    "You are my god!"

18 Such stupidity and ignorance!
    Their eyes are closed, and they cannot
        see.
    Their minds are shut, and they cannot
        think.
19 The person who made the idol never
        stops to reflect,
    "Why, it's just a block of wood!
I burned half of it for heat
    and used it to bake my bread and roast
        my meat.
How can the rest of it be a god?
    Should I bow down to worship a piece
        of wood?"
20 The poor, deluded fool feeds on ashes.
    He trusts something that can't help
        him at all.
Yet he cannot bring himself to ask,
    "Is this idol that I'm holding in my
        hand a lie?"

Restoration for Jerusalem

21 "Pay attention, O Jacob,
    for you are my servant, O Israel.
I, the Lord, made you,
    and I will not forget you.
22 I have swept away your sins like a cloud.
    I have scattered your offenses like the
        morning mist.
Oh, return to me,
    for I have paid the price to set you
        free."

23 Sing, O heavens, for the Lord has done
        this wondrous thing.
    Shout for joy, O depths of the earth!
Break into song,
    O mountains and forests and every
        tree!
For the Lord has redeemed Jacob
    and is glorified in Israel.

24 This is what the Lord says—
    your Redeemer and Creator:
"I am the Lord, who made all things.
    I alone stretched out the heavens.

Who was with me
    when I made the earth?
25 I expose the false prophets as liars
    and make fools of fortune-tellers.
I cause the wise to give bad advice,
    thus proving them to be fools.
26 But I carry out the predictions of my
        prophets!
    By them I say to Jerusalem, 'People
        will live here again,'
and to the towns of Judah, 'You will be
        rebuilt;
    I will restore all your ruins!'
27 When I speak to the rivers and say, 'Dry
        up!'
    they will be dry.
28 When I say of Cyrus, 'He is my
        shepherd,'
    he will certainly do as I say.
He will command, 'Rebuild Jerusalem';
    he will say, 'Restore the Temple.'"

45 Cyrus, the Lord's Chosen One

1 This is what the Lord says to
        Cyrus, his anointed one,
    whose right hand he will empower.
Before him, mighty kings will be
        paralyzed with fear.
    Their fortress gates will be opened,
        never to shut again.
2 This is what the Lord says:

"I will go before you, Cyrus,
    and level the mountains.*
I will smash down gates of bronze
    and cut through bars of iron.
3 And I will give you treasures hidden in
        the darkness—
    secret riches.
I will do this so you may know that I am
        the Lord,
    the God of Israel, the one who calls
        you by name.

4 "And why have I called you for this
        work?
    Why did I call you by name when you
        did not know me?
It is for the sake of Jacob my servant,
    Israel my chosen one.
5 I am the Lord;
    there is no other God.

45:2 As in Dead Sea Scrolls and Greek version; Masoretic Text reads the swellings.

I have equipped you for battle,
 though you don't even know me,
6 so all the world from east to west
 will know there is no other God.
I am the LORD, and there is no other.
7   I create the light and make the
 darkness.
I send good times and bad times.
 I, the LORD, am the one who does
 these things.

8 "Open up, O heavens,
 and pour out your righteousness.
Let the earth open wide
 so salvation and righteousness can
 sprout up together.
 I, the LORD, created them.

9 "What sorrow awaits those who argue
 with their Creator.
Does a clay pot argue with its
 maker?
Does the clay dispute with the one who
 shapes it, saying,
'Stop, you're doing it wrong!'
Does the pot exclaim,
'How clumsy can you be?'
10 How terrible it would be if a newborn
 baby said to its father,
'Why was I born?'
or if it said to its mother,
'Why did you make me this way?'"

11 This is what the LORD says—
 the Holy One of Israel and your
 Creator:
"Do you question what I do for my
 children?
Do you give me orders about the work
 of my hands?
12 I am the one who made the earth
 and created people to live on it.
With my hands I stretched out the
 heavens.
All the stars are at my command.
13 I will raise up Cyrus to fulfill my
 righteous purpose,
 and I will guide his actions.
He will restore my city and free my
 captive people—
 without seeking a reward!
I, the LORD of Heaven's Armies, have
 spoken!"

Future Conversion of Gentiles

14 This is what the LORD says:

"You will rule the Egyptians,
 the Ethiopians,* and the Sabeans.
They will come to you with all their
 merchandise,
 and it will all be yours.
They will follow you as prisoners in
 chains.
They will fall to their knees in front of
 you and say,
'God is with you, and he is the only God.
There is no other.'"

15 Truly, O God of Israel, our Savior,
 you work in mysterious ways.
16 All craftsmen who make idols will be
 humiliated.
They will all be disgraced together.
17 But the LORD will save the people of
 Israel
 with eternal salvation.
Throughout everlasting ages,
 they will never again be humiliated
 and disgraced.

18 For the LORD is God,
 and he created the heavens and
 earth
 and put everything in place.
He made the world to be lived in,
 not to be a place of empty chaos.
"I am the LORD," he says,
 "and there is no other.
19 I publicly proclaim bold promises.
 I do not whisper obscurities in some
 dark corner.
I would not have told the people of
 Israel* to seek me
 if I could not be found.
I, the LORD, speak only what is true
 and declare only what is right.

20 "Gather together and come,
 you fugitives from surrounding
 nations.
What fools they are who carry around
 their wooden idols
 and pray to gods that cannot save!
21 Consult together, argue your case.
 Get together and decide what to say.
Who made these things known so long
 ago?

45:14 Hebrew *Cushites.*   45:19 Hebrew *of Jacob.* See note on 14:1.

What idol ever told you they would
happen?
Was it not I, the LORD?
For there is no other God but me,
a righteous God and Savior.
There is none but me.
22 Let all the world look to me for
salvation!
For I am God; there is no other.
23 I have sworn by my own name;
I have spoken the truth,
and I will never go back on my word:
Every knee will bend to me,
and every tongue will confess
allegiance to me.*"
24 The people will declare,
"The LORD is the source of all my
righteousness and strength."
And all who were angry with him
will come to him and be ashamed.
25 In the LORD all the generations of Israel
will be justified,
and in him they will boast.

46 Babylon's False Gods

1 Bel and Nebo, the gods of
Babylon,
bow as they are lowered to the
ground.
They are being hauled away on ox carts.
The poor beasts stagger under the
weight.
2 Both the idols and their owners are
bowed down.
The gods cannot protect the people,
and the people cannot protect the gods.
They go off into captivity together.

3 "Listen to me, descendants of Jacob,
all you who remain in Israel.
I have cared for you since you were
born.
Yes, I carried you before you were
born.
4 I will be your God throughout your
lifetime—
until your hair is white with age.
I made you, and I will care for you.
I will carry you along and save you.

5 "To whom will you compare me?
Who is my equal?

6 Some people pour out their silver and
gold
and hire a craftsman to make a god
from it.
Then they bow down and worship it!
7 They carry it around on their
shoulders,
and when they set it down, it stays
there.
It can't even move!
And when someone prays to it, there is
no answer.
It can't rescue anyone from trouble.

8 "Do not forget this! Keep it in mind!
Remember this, you guilty ones.
9 Remember the things I have done in the
past.
For I alone am God!
I am God, and there is none like me.
10 Only I can tell you the future
before it even happens.
Everything I plan will come to pass,
for I do whatever I wish.
11 I will call a swift bird of prey from the
east—
a leader from a distant land to come
and do my bidding.
I have said what I would do,
and I will do it.

12 "Listen to me, you stubborn people
who are so far from doing right.
13 For I am ready to set things right,
not in the distant future, but right
now!
I am ready to save Jerusalem*
and show my glory to Israel.

47 Prediction of Babylon's Fall

1 "Come down, virgin daughter of
Babylon, and sit in the dust.
For your days of sitting on a throne
have ended.
O daughter of Babylonia,* never again
will you be
the lovely princess, tender and
delicate.
2 Take heavy millstones and grind flour.
Remove your veil, and strip off your
robe.
Expose yourself to public view.

³ You will be naked and burdened with
    shame.
  I will take vengeance against you
    without pity."

⁴ Our Redeemer, whose name is the LORD
    of Heaven's Armies,
  is the Holy One of Israel.

⁵ "O beautiful Babylon, sit now in
    darkness and silence.
  Never again will you be known as the
    queen of kingdoms.

⁶ For I was angry with my chosen people
  and punished them by letting them fall
    into your hands.
  But you, Babylon, showed them no
    mercy.
  You oppressed even the elderly.

⁷ You said, 'I will reign forever as queen of
    the world!'
  You did not reflect on your actions
  or think about their consequences.

⁸ "Listen to this, you pleasure-loving
    kingdom,
  living at ease and feeling secure.
  You say, 'I am the only one, and there is
    no other.
  I will never be a widow or lose my
    children.'

⁹ Well, both these things will come upon
    you in a moment:
  widowhood and the loss of your
    children.
  Yes, these calamities will come upon
    you,
  despite all your witchcraft and magic.

¹⁰ "You felt secure in your wickedness.
  'No one sees me,' you said.
  But your 'wisdom' and 'knowledge' have
    led you astray,
  and you said, 'I am the only one, and
    there is no other.'

¹¹ So disaster will overtake you,
  and you won't be able to charm it
    away.
  Calamity will fall upon you,
  and you won't be able to buy your way
    out.
  A catastrophe will strike you
    suddenly,
  one for which you are not
    prepared.

¹² "Now use your magical charms!
  Use the spells you have worked at all
    these years!
  Maybe they will do you some good.
  Maybe they can make someone afraid
    of you.

¹³ All the advice you receive has made you
    tired.
  Where are all your astrologers,
  those stargazers who make predictions
    each month?
  Let them stand up and save you from
    what the future holds.

¹⁴ But they are like straw burning in a
    fire;
  they cannot save themselves from the
    flame.
  You will get no help from them at all;
  their hearth is no place to sit for
    warmth.

¹⁵ And all your friends,
  those with whom you've done
    business since childhood,
  will go their own ways,
  turning a deaf ear to your cries.

48 God's Stubborn People

¹ "Listen to me, O family of Jacob,
  you who are called by the name of
    Israel
  and born into the family of Judah.
Listen, you who take oaths in the name
    of the LORD
  and call on the God of Israel.
You don't keep your promises,
² even though you call yourself the holy
    city
  and talk about depending on the God of
    Israel,
  whose name is the LORD of Heaven's
    Armies.

³ Long ago I told you what was going to
    happen.
  Then suddenly I took action,
  and all my predictions came true.

⁴ For I know how stubborn and obstinate
    you are.
  Your necks are as unbending as iron.
  Your heads are as hard as bronze.

⁵ That is why I told you what would
    happen;
  I told you beforehand what I was
    going to do.

Then you could never say, 'My idols
did it.
My wooden image and metal god
commanded it to happen!'
[6] You have heard my predictions and seen
them fulfilled,
but you refuse to admit it.
Now I will tell you new things,
secrets you have not yet heard.
[7] They are brand new, not things from the
past.
So you cannot say, 'We knew that all
the time!'

[8] "Yes, I will tell you of things that are
entirely new,
things you never heard of before.
For I know so well what traitors you are.
You have been rebels from birth.
[9] Yet for my own sake and for the honor of
my name,
I will hold back my anger and not wipe
you out.
[10] I have refined you, but not as silver is
refined.
Rather, I have refined you in the
furnace of suffering.
[11] I will rescue you for my sake—
yes, for my own sake!
I will not let my reputation be tarnished,
and I will not share my glory with
idols!

Freedom from Babylon

[12] "Listen to me, O family of Jacob,
Israel my chosen one!
I alone am God,
the First and the Last.
[13] It was my hand that laid the foundations
of the earth,
my right hand that spread out the
heavens above.
When I call out the stars,
they all appear in order."

[14] Have any of your idols ever told you
this?
Come, all of you, and listen:
The LORD has chosen Cyrus as his ally.
He will use him to put an end to the
empire of Babylon
and to destroy the Babylonian*
armies.

[15] "I have said it: I am calling Cyrus!
I will send him on this errand and will
help him succeed.
[16] Come closer, and listen to this.
From the beginning I have told you
plainly what would happen."

And now the Sovereign LORD and his
Spirit
have sent me with this message.

[17] This is what the LORD says—
your Redeemer, the Holy One of
Israel:
"I am the LORD your God,
who teaches you what is good for you
and leads you along the paths you
should follow.
[18] Oh, that you had listened to my
commands!
Then you would have had peace
flowing like a gentle river
and righteousness rolling over you like
waves in the sea.
[19] Your descendants would have been like
the sands along the seashore—
too many to count!
There would have been no need for your
destruction,
or for cutting off your family name."

[20] Yet even now, be free from your
captivity!
Leave Babylon and the Babylonians.*
Sing out this message!
Shout it to the ends of the earth!
The LORD has redeemed his servants,
the people of Israel.*
[21] They were not thirsty
when he led them through the
desert.
He divided the rock,
and water gushed out for them to
drink.
[22] "But there is no peace for the wicked,"
says the LORD.

49 The LORD's Servant Commissioned
[1] Listen to me, all you in distant
lands!
Pay attention, you who are far away!
The LORD called me before my birth;
from within the womb he called me
by name.

48:14 Or *Chaldean.*   48:20a Or *the Chaldeans.*   48:20b Hebrew *his servant, Jacob.* See note on 14:1.

2 He made my words of judgment as sharp
as a sword.
He has hidden me in the shadow of his
hand.
I am like a sharp arrow in his quiver.

3 He said to me, "You are my servant,
Israel,
and you will bring me glory."

4 I replied, "But my work seems so useless!
I have spent my strength for nothing
and to no purpose.
Yet I leave it all in the LORD's hand;
I will trust God for my reward."

5 And now the LORD speaks—
the one who formed me in my
mother's womb to be his servant,
who commissioned me to bring Israel
back to him.
The LORD has honored me,
and my God has given me strength.
6 He says, "You will do more than restore
the people of Israel to me.
I will make you a light to the Gentiles,
and you will bring my salvation to the
ends of the earth."

7 The LORD, the Redeemer
and Holy One of Israel,
says to the one who is despised and
rejected by the nations,
to the one who is the servant of rulers:
"Kings will stand at attention when you
pass by.
Princes will also bow low
because of the LORD, the faithful one,
the Holy One of Israel, who has
chosen you."

Promises of Israel's Restoration

8 This is what the LORD says:

"At just the right time, I will respond to
you.*
On the day of salvation I will help you.
I will protect you and give you to the
people
as my covenant with them.
Through you I will reestablish the land
of Israel
and assign it to its own people again.

9 I will say to the prisoners, 'Come out in
freedom,'
and to those in darkness, 'Come into
the light.'
They will be my sheep, grazing in green
pastures
and on hills that were previously bare.
10 They will neither hunger nor thirst.
The searing sun will not reach them
anymore.
For the LORD in his mercy will lead
them;
he will lead them beside cool waters.
11 And I will make my mountains into level
paths for them.
The highways will be raised above the
valleys.
12 See, my people will return from far
away,
from lands to the north and west,
and from as far south as Egypt.*"

13 Sing for joy, O heavens!
Rejoice, O earth!
Burst into song, O mountains!
For the LORD has comforted his people
and will have compassion on them in
their suffering.

14 Yet Jerusalem* says, "The LORD has
deserted us;
the Lord has forgotten us."

15 "Never! Can a mother forget her nursing
child?
Can she feel no love for the child she
has borne?
But even if that were possible,
I would not forget you!
16 See, I have written your name on the
palms of my hands.
Always in my mind is a picture of
Jerusalem's walls in ruins.
17 Soon your descendants will come back,
and all who are trying to destroy you
will go away.
18 Look around you and see,
for all your children will come back to
you.
As surely as I live," says the LORD,
"they will be like jewels or bridal
ornaments for you to display.

49:8 Greek version reads *I heard you.* Compare 2 Cor 6:2.   **49:12** As in Dead Sea Scrolls, which read *from the region of Aswan,* which is in
southern Egypt. Masoretic Text reads *from the region of Sinim.*   **49:14** Hebrew *Zion.*

¹⁹ "Even the most desolate parts of your
abandoned land
will soon be crowded with your
people.
Your enemies who enslaved you
will be far away.
²⁰ The generations born in exile will return
and say,
'We need more room! It's crowded
here!'
²¹ Then you will think to yourself,
'Who has given me all these
descendants?
For most of my children were killed,
and the rest were carried away into
exile.
I was left here all alone.
Where did all these people come
from?
Who bore these children?
Who raised them for me?'"

²² This is what the Sovereign LORD says:
"See, I will give a signal to the godless
nations.
They will carry your little sons back to
you in their arms;
they will bring your daughters on their
shoulders.
²³ Kings and queens will serve you
and care for all your needs.
They will bow to the earth before you
and lick the dust from your feet.
Then you will know that I am the LORD.
Those who trust in me will never be
put to shame."

²⁴ Who can snatch the plunder of war from
the hands of a warrior?
Who can demand that a tyrant* let his
captives go?
²⁵ But the LORD says,
"The captives of warriors will be
released,
and the plunder of tyrants will be
retrieved.
For I will fight those who fight you,
and I will save your children.
²⁶ I will feed your enemies with their own
flesh.
They will be drunk with rivers of their
own blood.

All the world will know that I, the LORD,
am your Savior and your Redeemer,
the Mighty One of Israel.*"

50 This is what the LORD says:
"Was your mother sent away because I
divorced her?
Did I sell you as slaves to my
creditors?
No, you were sold because of your sins.
And your mother, too, was taken
because of your sins.
² Why was no one there when I came?
Why didn't anyone answer when I
called?
Is it because I have no power to rescue?
No, that is not the reason!
For I can speak to the sea and make it
dry up!
I can turn rivers into deserts covered
with dying fish.
³ I dress the skies in darkness,
covering them with clothes of
mourning."

The LORD's Obedient Servant

⁴ The Sovereign LORD has given me his
words of wisdom,
so that I know how to comfort the
weary.
Morning by morning he wakens me
and opens my understanding to his
will.
⁵ The Sovereign LORD has spoken to me,
and I have listened.
I have not rebelled or turned away.
⁶ I offered my back to those who beat me
and my cheeks to those who pulled
out my beard.
I did not hide my face
from mockery and spitting.

⁷ Because the Sovereign LORD helps me,
I will not be disgraced.
Therefore, I have set my face like a stone,
determined to do his will.
And I know that I will not be put to
shame.
⁸ He who gives me justice is near.
Who will dare to bring charges against
me now?

49:24 As in Dead Sea Scrolls, Syriac version, and Latin Vulgate (also see 49:25); Masoretic Text reads *a righteous person*. **49:26** Hebrew of *Jacob*. See note on 14:1.

Where are my accusers?
Let them appear!
⁹ See, the Sovereign LORD is on my side!
Who will declare me guilty?
All my enemies will be destroyed
like old clothes that have been eaten
by moths!

¹⁰ Who among you fears the LORD
and obeys his servant?
If you are walking in darkness,
without a ray of light,
trust in the LORD
and rely on your God.
¹¹ But watch out, you who live in your own
light
and warm yourselves by your own fires.
This is the reward you will receive
from me:
You will soon fall down in great
torment.

51 A Call to Trust the LORD
¹ "Listen to me, all who hope for
deliverance—
all who seek the LORD!
Consider the rock from which you were
cut,
the quarry from which you were
mined.
² Yes, think about Abraham, your
ancestor,
and Sarah, who gave birth to your
nation.
Abraham was only one man when I
called him.
But when I blessed him, he became a
great nation."

³ The LORD will comfort Israel* again
and have pity on her ruins.
Her desert will blossom like Eden,
her barren wilderness like the garden
of the LORD.
Joy and gladness will be found there.
Songs of thanksgiving will fill the air.

⁴ "Listen to me, my people.
Hear me, Israel,
for my law will be proclaimed,
and my justice will become a light to
the nations.

⁵ My mercy and justice are coming soon.
My salvation is on the way.
My strong arm will bring justice to the
nations.
All distant lands will look to me
and wait in hope for my powerful arm.
⁶ Look up to the skies above,
and gaze down on the earth below.
For the skies will disappear like smoke,
and the earth will wear out like a piece
of clothing.
The people of the earth will die like flies,
but my salvation lasts forever.
My righteous rule will never end!

⁷ "Listen to me, you who know right from
wrong,
you who cherish my law in your hearts.
Do not be afraid of people's scorn,
nor fear their insults.
⁸ For the moth will devour them as it
devours clothing.
The worm will eat at them as it eats
wool.
But my righteousness will last forever.
My salvation will continue from
generation to generation."

⁹ Wake up, wake up, O LORD! Clothe
yourself with strength!
Flex your mighty right arm!
Rouse yourself as in the days of old
when you slew Egypt, the dragon of
the Nile.*
¹⁰ Are you not the same today,
the one who dried up the sea,
making a path of escape through the
depths
so that your people could cross over?
¹¹ Those who have been ransomed by the
LORD will return.
They will enter Jerusalem* singing,
crowned with everlasting joy.
Sorrow and mourning will disappear,
and they will be filled with joy and
gladness.

¹² "I, yes I, am the one who comforts you.
So why are you afraid of mere
humans,
who wither like the grass and
disappear?

51:3 Hebrew *Zion;* also in 51:16.   51:9 Hebrew *You slew Rahab; you pierced the dragon.* Rahab is the name of a mythical sea monster that represents chaos in ancient literature. The name is used here as a poetic name for Egypt.   51:11 Hebrew *Zion.*

¹³ Yet you have forgotten the LORD, your
Creator,
the one who stretched out the sky like
a canopy
and laid the foundations of the earth.
Will you remain in constant dread of
human oppressors?
Will you continue to fear the anger of
your enemies?
Where is their fury and anger now?
It is gone!
¹⁴ Soon all you captives will be released!
Imprisonment, starvation, and death
will not be your fate!
¹⁵ For I am the LORD your God,
who stirs up the sea, causing its waves
to roar.
My name is the LORD of Heaven's
Armies.
¹⁶ And I have put my words in your mouth
and hidden you safely in my hand.
I stretched out* the sky like a canopy
and laid the foundations of the earth.
I am the one who says to Israel,
'You are my people!'"

¹⁷ Wake up, wake up, O Jerusalem!
You have drunk the cup of the LORD's
fury.
You have drunk the cup of terror,
tipping out its last drops.
¹⁸ Not one of your children is left alive
to take your hand and guide you.
¹⁹ These two calamities have fallen on you:
desolation and destruction, famine
and war.
And who is left to sympathize with you?
Who is left to comfort you?*
²⁰ For your children have fainted and lie in
the streets,
helpless as antelopes caught in a net.
The LORD has poured out his fury;
God has rebuked them.

²¹ But now listen to this, you afflicted ones
who sit in a drunken stupor,
though not from drinking wine.
²² This is what the Sovereign LORD,
your God and Defender, says:
"See, I have taken the terrible cup from
your hands.
You will drink no more of my fury.

²³ Instead, I will hand that cup to your
tormentors,
those who said, 'We will trample you
into the dust
and walk on your backs.'"

52 Deliverance for Jerusalem

¹ Wake up, wake up, O Zion!
Clothe yourself with strength.
Put on your beautiful clothes, O holy
city of Jerusalem,
for unclean and godless people will
enter your gates no longer.
² Rise from the dust, O Jerusalem.
Sit in a place of honor.
Remove the chains of slavery from your
neck,
O captive daughter of Zion.
³ For this is what the LORD says:
"When I sold you into exile,
I received no payment.
Now I can redeem you
without having to pay for you."

⁴ This is what the Sovereign LORD says:
"Long ago my people chose to live in Egypt.
Now they are oppressed by Assyria. ⁵ What
is this?" asks the LORD. "Why are my people
enslaved again? Those who rule them shout
in exultation. My name is blasphemed all
day long.* ⁶ But I will reveal my name to
my people, and they will come to know its
power. Then at last they will recognize that
I am the one who speaks to them."

⁷ How beautiful on the mountains
are the feet of the messenger who
brings good news,
the good news of peace and salvation,
the news that the God of Israel*
reigns!
⁸ The watchmen shout and sing
with joy,
for before their very eyes
they see the LORD returning to
Jerusalem.*
⁹ Let the ruins of Jerusalem break into
joyful song,
for the LORD has comforted his
people.
He has redeemed Jerusalem.

51:16 As in Syriac version (see also 51:13); Hebrew reads *planted.* **51:19** As in Dead Sea Scrolls and Greek, Latin, and Syriac versions;
Masoretic Text reads *How can I comfort you?* **52:5** Greek version reads *The Gentiles continually blaspheme my name because of you.* Compare
Rom 2:24. **52:7** Hebrew *of Zion.* **52:8** Hebrew *to Zion.*

Contemplation

When I Consider the Heavens . . .

ISAIAH 51:12–16

Several years ago I had a crisis of faith. It began with a television program I saw about supermassive black holes (the size of an entire solar system) that are in the center of every galaxy. On the show the scientists described how these black holes have caused them to rethink physics and even the space-time continuum. Summing up, several scientists said, "If, as it now seems, every single galaxy has a black hole at its heart, this can't be a coincidence."

My thoughts went right to God, our amazing Creator.

But then the screen exploded with images of all these multicolored, multishaped, multigaseous galaxies. The vastness of what I saw overwhelmed me; I was bowled over by the size and power and strength of my Creator. And in that instant, I felt thrust into my own black hole that was dark and desperate.

How could this cosmos-spinning God possibly know or care about me?

I thought of Thomas Jefferson's belief that God was like a watchmaker: he wound up the universe (or, in our case, the earth and life on it) and then let it run its course without his interference while he was off creating other worlds. It seemed more plausible to me in that moment. I never stopped believing in God; I just began to think that God was so giant that he would never be personally involved in my insignificant, irrelevant life.

I walked through life in a spiritual daze; eventually my sense of confusion about God became so overwhelming that finally I began daily and purposefully to sit quietly, just focusing on him. Ironically it was in my crisis of faith that I discovered the spiritual discipline of contemplation.

Every day I sat with my hands open, looking up to the heavens and asking God to show up—if he was, in fact, who I'd always believed him to be. And the longer I sat, clearing my mind of the doubts and arguments, the more I realized he *was* showing up. Over the course of several months, I continued awakening to God's presence. And he began to press upon my mind irrefutable truths. He reminded me that although he created supermassive black holes, he also created amoebas. And male parasitic wasps, which measure only 139 micrometers in length. He created microbiology with all its clear and direct order.

Through my contemplation God helped me realize that if he cared enough to create such order with the most microscopic things, then isn't it possible that he *does* have a personal interest in me? That maybe Jesus' words were true: "What is the price of five sparrows—two copper coins? Yet God does not forget a single one of them. And the very hairs on your head are all numbered. So don't be afraid; you are more valuable to God than a whole flock of sparrows" (Luke 12:6-7).

Those times of contemplation moved me through my faith crisis. Now those times of contemplation have become times of worship, abandon, awakening, awe. They center me back to remembering how awesome our Creator is, that I *can* do all things through Christ who gives me strength, that nothing *is* impossible for God to handle.

Contemplation helps set my perspective of God aright—he's not my buddy that may or may not be able to handle the problems in my life or the country or the world. He's Creator God who made everything from nothing. Who raises people from the dead. Who opens wombs. Who gives sight to the blind. Who organizes and orders the massive, incomprehensible universe—from the microscopic to the outer edges of all existence. And who gave his only Son for me because he loves me.

When I practice contemplation, I ask God, "When I look at the night sky and see the work of your fingers—the moon and the stars you have set in place—what are mere mortals that you should think about them, human beings that you should care for them?" (Psalm 8:3-4; "When I consider the heavens, . . ." says the King James Version).

And he answers, "I, yes I, am the one who comforts you. . . . I have put my words in your mouth and hidden you safely in my hand. I stretched out the sky like a canopy and laid the foundations of the earth. I am the one who says to Israel, 'You are my people!'" (Isaiah 51:12, 16).

I'm still in awe of how awesomely vast and mammoth and ordered and creative our God is. But now in contemplation, I open my heart with abandon and invite our great God to abide with me, to awaken me to his work in my life and the world around me, and to remind me that absolutely nothing is impossible for him to accomplish in and through insignificant, irrelevant, loved me.

—*Ginger Kolbaba*

For more on contemplation, see reading at Jeremiah 23:23-24.

¹⁰ The LORD has demonstrated his holy
power
before the eyes of all the nations.
All the ends of the earth will see
the victory of our God.

¹¹ Get out! Get out and leave your
captivity,
where everything you touch is unclean.
Get out of there and purify yourselves,
you who carry home the sacred
objects of the LORD.

¹² You will not leave in a hurry,
running for your lives.
For the LORD will go ahead of you;
yes, the God of Israel will protect you
from behind.

The LORD's Suffering Servant

¹³ See, my servant will prosper;
he will be highly exalted.

¹⁴ But many were amazed when they saw
him.*
His face was so disfigured he seemed
hardly human,
and from his appearance, one would
scarcely know he was a man.

¹⁵ And he will startle* many nations.
Kings will stand speechless in his
presence.
For they will see what they had not been
told;
they will understand what they had
not heard about.*

53

¹ Who has believed our message?
To whom has the LORD revealed
his powerful arm?

² My servant grew up in the LORD's
presence like a tender green shoot,
like a root in dry ground.
There was nothing beautiful or majestic
about his appearance,
nothing to attract us to him.

³ He was despised and rejected—
a man of sorrows, acquainted with
deepest grief.
We turned our backs on him and looked
the other way.
He was despised, and we did not care.

⁴ Yet it was our weaknesses he carried;
it was our sorrows* that weighed him
down.
And we thought his troubles were a
punishment from God,
a punishment for his own sins!

⁵ But he was pierced for our rebellion,
crushed for our sins.
He was beaten so we could be whole.
He was whipped so we could be
healed.

⁶ All of us, like sheep, have strayed
away.
We have left God's paths to follow our
own.
Yet the LORD laid on him
the sins of us all.

⁷ He was oppressed and treated harshly,
yet he never said a word.
He was led like a lamb to the
slaughter.
And as a sheep is silent before the
shearers,
he did not open his mouth.

⁸ Unjustly condemned,
he was led away.*
No one cared that he died without
descendants,
that his life was cut short in
midstream.*
But he was struck down
for the rebellion of my people.

⁹ He had done no wrong
and had never deceived anyone.
But he was buried like a criminal;
he was put in a rich man's grave.

¹⁰ But it was the LORD's good plan to crush
him
and cause him grief.
Yet when his life is made an offering for
sin,
he will have many descendants.
He will enjoy a long life,
and the LORD's good plan will prosper
in his hands.

¹¹ When he sees all that is accomplished by
his anguish,
he will be satisfied.

52:14 As in Syriac version; Hebrew reads *you.*   **52:15a** Or *cleanse.*   **52:15b** Greek version reads *Those who have never been told about him
will see, / and those who have never heard about him will understand.* Compare Rom 15:21.   **53:4** Or *Yet it was our sicknesses he carried; / it was our
diseases.*   **53:8a** Greek version reads *He was humiliated and received no justice.* Compare Acts 8:33.   **53:8b** Or *As for his contemporaries, /
who cared that his life was cut short in midstream?* Greek version reads *Who can speak of his descendants? / For his life was taken from the earth.*
Compare Acts 8:33.

And because of his experience,
my righteous servant will make it
possible
for many to be counted righteous,
for he will bear all their sins.
¹² I will give him the honors of a victorious
soldier,
because he exposed himself to death.
He was counted among the rebels.
He bore the sins of many and
interceded for rebels.

54 Future Glory for Jerusalem

¹ "Sing, O childless woman,
you who have never given birth!
Break into loud and joyful song,
O Jerusalem,
you who have never been in labor.
For the desolate woman now has more
children
than the woman who lives with her
husband,"
says the LORD.
² "Enlarge your house; build an addition.
Spread out your home, and spare no
expense!
³ For you will soon be bursting at the
seams.
Your descendants will occupy other
nations
and resettle the ruined cities.

⁴ "Fear not; you will no longer live in
shame.
Don't be afraid; there is no more
disgrace for you.
You will no longer remember the shame
of your youth
and the sorrows of widowhood.
⁵ For your Creator will be your husband;
the LORD of Heaven's Armies is his
name!
He is your Redeemer, the Holy One of
Israel,
the God of all the earth.
⁶ For the LORD has called you back from
your grief—
as though you were a young wife
abandoned by her husband,"
says your God.
⁷ "For a brief moment I abandoned you,
but with great compassion I will take
you back.

⁸ In a burst of anger I turned my face away
for a little while.
But with everlasting love I will have
compassion on you,"
says the LORD, your Redeemer.

⁹ "Just as I swore in the time of Noah
that I would never again let a flood
cover the earth,
so now I swear
that I will never again be angry and
punish you.
¹⁰ For the mountains may move
and the hills disappear,
but even then my faithful love for you
will remain.
My covenant of blessing will never be
broken,"
says the LORD, who has mercy on you.

¹¹ "O storm-battered city,
troubled and desolate!
I will rebuild you with precious jewels
and make your foundations from lapis
lazuli.
¹² I will make your towers of sparkling rubies,
your gates of shining gems,
and your walls of precious stones.
¹³ I will teach all your children,
and they will enjoy great peace.
¹⁴ You will be secure under a government
that is just and fair.
Your enemies will stay far away.
You will live in peace,
and terror will not come near.
¹⁵ If any nation comes to fight you,
it is not because I sent them.
Whoever attacks you will go down in
defeat.

¹⁶ "I have created the blacksmith
who fans the coals beneath the forge
and makes the weapons of destruction.
And I have created the armies that
destroy.
¹⁷ But in that coming day
no weapon turned against you will
succeed.
You will silence every voice
raised up to accuse you.
These benefits are enjoyed by the
servants of the LORD;
their vindication will come from me.
I, the LORD, have spoken!

55 Invitation to the Lord's Salvation

¹ "Is anyone thirsty?
  Come and drink—
  even if you have no money!
Come, take your choice of wine or
    milk—
  it's all free!
² Why spend your money on food that
    does not give you strength?
Why pay for food that does you no
    good?
Listen to me, and you will eat what is
    good.
  You will enjoy the finest food.

³ "Come to me with your ears wide open.
  Listen, and you will find life.
I will make an everlasting covenant with
    you.

Q&A — Time Alone versus Engagement with the World

ISAIAH 55

Solitude

What makes solitude so important? Doesn't God call us to engage with our world?

Solitude is the most foundational of the disciplines of abstinence. Many Christians have a passion for engagement with the world, and that's good. But as Blaise Pascal said, we would solve the world's problems if we just learned to sit in our room alone. Solitude is essential for right engagement.

I appreciate Dietrich Bonhoeffer's comments in *Life Together*, in which he emphasized the idea that you can't be with people in a right way without also knowing how to be alone. And of course you can't be alone unless you've learned to be with people. Solitude teaches us to live in the presence of God so that we can be with people in a way that helps them rather than manipulates them.

Solitude also teaches us how to love God's ways; in time alone we learn the cosmic patience of God, for instance. In Isaiah 55:8 God tells us, "My thoughts are nothing like your thoughts. . . . And my ways are far beyond anything you could imagine." The passage goes on to describe how God's mysterious ways are like the rain that comes down and waters the earth. It descends and disappears, and then up comes life. It's that type of patience.

In solitude I unhook myself from the compulsion to climb and push and shove. When I was pastoring, I'd go off for solitude and worry about what was happening and how people were doing and whether they'd get along without me. And of course the great fear is that they'll get along quite well! But you learn that's okay. And that God's in charge. With regular times of solitude, you begin to learn that, truly, God's got the whole world in his hands.

—*Richard J. Foster*

For more on solitude, see reading at Jeremiah 1:4–5.

I will give you all the unfailing love I
promised to David.
⁴ See how I used him to display my power
among the peoples.
I made him a leader among the
nations.
⁵ You also will command nations you do
not know,
and peoples unknown to you will
come running to obey,
because I, the LORD your God,
the Holy One of Israel, have made you
glorious."

⁶ Seek the LORD while you can find him.
Call on him now while he is near.
⁷ Let the wicked change their ways
and banish the very thought of doing
wrong.
Let them turn to the LORD that he may
have mercy on them.
Yes, turn to our God, for he will
forgive generously.

⁸ "My thoughts are nothing like your
thoughts," says the LORD.
"And my ways are far beyond anything
you could imagine.
⁹ For just as the heavens are higher than
the earth,
so my ways are higher than your ways
and my thoughts higher than your
thoughts.

¹⁰ "The rain and snow come down from the
heavens
and stay on the ground to water the
earth.
They cause the grain to grow,
producing seed for the farmer
and bread for the hungry.
¹¹ It is the same with my word.
I send it out, and it always produces
fruit.
It will accomplish all I want it to,
and it will prosper everywhere I
send it.
¹² You will live in joy and peace.
The mountains and hills will burst into
song,
and the trees of the field will clap their
hands!
¹³ Where once there were thorns, cypress
trees will grow.

Where nettles grew, myrtles will
sprout up.
These events will bring great honor to
the LORD's name;
they will be an everlasting sign of his
power and love."

56 Blessings for All Nations

This is what the LORD says:

"Be just and fair to all.
Do what is right and good,
for I am coming soon to rescue you
and to display my righteousness
among you.
² Blessed are all those
who are careful to do this.
Blessed are those who honor my
Sabbath days of rest
and keep themselves from doing
wrong.

³ "Don't let foreigners who commit
themselves to the LORD say,
'The LORD will never let me be part of
his people.'
And don't let the eunuchs say,
'I'm a dried-up tree with no children
and no future.'
⁴ For this is what the LORD says:
I will bless those eunuchs
who keep my Sabbath days holy
and who choose to do what
pleases me
and commit their lives to me.
⁵ I will give them—within the walls of my
house—
a memorial and a name
far greater than sons and daughters
could give.
For the name I give them is an
everlasting one.
It will never disappear!

⁶ "I will also bless the foreigners who
commit themselves to the LORD,
who serve him and love his name,
who worship him and do not desecrate
the Sabbath day of rest,
and who hold fast to my covenant.
⁷ I will bring them to my holy mountain of
Jerusalem
and will fill them with joy in my house
of prayer.

I will accept their burnt offerings and
sacrifices,
because my Temple will be called a
house of prayer for all nations.
⁸ For the Sovereign LORD,
who brings back the outcasts of Israel,
says:
I will bring others, too,
besides my people Israel."

Sinful Leaders Condemned

⁹ Come, wild animals of the field!
Come, wild animals of the forest!
Come and devour my people!
¹⁰ For the leaders of my people—
the LORD's watchmen, his shepherds—
are blind and ignorant.
They are like silent watchdogs
that give no warning when danger
comes.
They love to lie around, sleeping and
dreaming.
¹¹ Like greedy dogs, they are never
satisfied.
They are ignorant shepherds,
all following their own path
and intent on personal gain.
¹² "Come," they say, "let's get some wine
and have a party.
Let's all get drunk.
Then tomorrow we'll do it again
and have an even bigger party!"

57 ¹ Good people pass away;
the godly often die before their
time.
But no one seems to care or wonder
why.
No one seems to understand
that God is protecting them from the
evil to come.
² For those who follow godly paths
will rest in peace when they die.

Idolatrous Worship Condemned

³ "But you—come here, you witches'
children,
you offspring of adulterers and
prostitutes!
⁴ Whom do you mock,
making faces and sticking out your
tongues?
You children of sinners and liars!
⁵ You worship your idols with great
passion
beneath the oaks and under every
green tree.
You sacrifice your children down in the
valleys,
among the jagged rocks in the cliffs.
⁶ Your gods are the smooth stones in the
valleys.
You worship them with liquid
offerings and grain offerings.
They, not I, are your inheritance.
Do you think all this makes me happy?
⁷ You have committed adultery on every
high mountain.
There you have worshiped idols
and have been unfaithful to me.
⁸ You have put pagan symbols
on your doorposts and behind your
doors.
You have left me
and climbed into bed with these
detestable gods.
You have committed yourselves to
them.
You love to look at their naked bodies.
⁹ You have given olive oil to Molech*
with many gifts of perfume.
You have traveled far,
even into the world of the dead,*
to find new gods to love.
¹⁰ You grew weary in your search,
but you never gave up.
Desire gave you renewed strength,
and you did not grow weary.

¹¹ "Are you afraid of these idols?
Do they terrify you?
Is that why you have lied to me
and forgotten me and my words?
Is it because of my long silence
that you no longer fear me?
¹² Now I will expose your so-called good
deeds.
None of them will help you.
¹³ Let's see if your idols can save you
when you cry to them for help.
Why, a puff of wind can knock them
down!
If you just breathe on them, they fall
over!

57:9a Or to the king.   **57:9b** Hebrew into Sheol.

But whoever trusts in me will inherit the
land
and possess my holy mountain."

God Forgives the Repentant

14 God says, "Rebuild the road!
Clear away the rocks and stones
so my people can return from
captivity."
15 The high and lofty one who lives in
eternity,
the Holy One, says this:
"I live in the high and holy place
with those whose spirits are contrite
and humble.
I restore the crushed spirit of the
humble
and revive the courage of those with
repentant hearts.
16 For I will not fight against you forever;
I will not always be angry.
If I were, all people would pass away—
all the souls I have made.
17 I was angry,
so I punished these greedy people.
I withdrew from them,
but they kept going on their own
stubborn way.
18 I have seen what they do,
but I will heal them anyway!
I will lead them.
I will comfort those who mourn,
19   bringing words of praise to their lips.
May they have abundant peace, both
near and far,"
says the LORD, who heals them.
20 "But those who still reject me are like
the restless sea,
which is never still
but continually churns up mud and dirt.
21 There is no peace for the wicked,"
says my God.

58 True and False Worship

1 "Shout with the voice of a trumpet
blast.
Shout aloud! Don't be timid.
Tell my people Israel* of their sins!
2   Yet they act so pious!
They come to the Temple every day
and seem delighted to learn all
about me.

They act like a righteous nation
that would never abandon the laws of
its God.
They ask me to take action on their
behalf,
pretending they want to be near me.
3 'We have fasted before you!' they say.
'Why aren't you impressed?
We have been very hard on ourselves,
and you don't even notice it!'

"I will tell you why!" I respond.
"It's because you are fasting to please
yourselves.
Even while you fast,
you keep oppressing your workers.
4 What good is fasting
when you keep on fighting and
quarreling?
This kind of fasting
will never get you anywhere with me.
5 You humble yourselves
by going through the motions of
penance,
bowing your heads
like reeds bending in the wind.
You dress in burlap
and cover yourselves with ashes.
Is this what you call fasting?
Do you really think this will please the
LORD?

6 "No, this is the kind of fasting I want:
Free those who are wrongly imprisoned;
lighten the burden of those who work
for you.
Let the oppressed go free,
and remove the chains that bind people.
7 Share your food with the hungry,
and give shelter to the homeless.
Give clothes to those who need them,
and do not hide from relatives who
need your help.

8 "Then your salvation will come like the
dawn,
and your wounds will quickly heal.
Your godliness will lead you forward,
and the glory of the LORD will protect
you from behind.
9 Then when you call, the LORD will
answer.
'Yes, I am here,' he will quickly reply.

58:1 Hebrew *Jacob*. See note on 14:1.

Envisioning a Just Church
ISAIAH 58:6-12

A mos 5 and Isaiah 58 present us with chilling images. In both cases God is calling out his people—they worship, they fast, but God will not listen. Through Amos he says, "Away with your noisy hymns of praise! I will not listen to the music of your harps. Instead, I want to see a mighty flood of justice, an endless river of righteous living" (5:23-24). Through Isaiah God proclaims, "This is the kind of fasting I want: Free those who are wrongly imprisoned; lighten the burden of those who work for you. Let the oppressed go free, and remove the chains that bind people. Share your food with the hungry, and give shelter to the homeless" (58:6-7).

When we read passages like these, we can't help but wonder, *What would God say to my church today?*

And we can't help but dream, *What might it look like for my church to answer God's call to justice?*

Justice isn't a "project" for the church; it's a passion of God. As our congregations grow to understand that God is just and that God seeks justice, we can respond with action. When the joy of our worship songs is tied to the joy of our love, when the saving grace of Jesus Christ reveals God's suffering and redeeming heart for a world filled with oppression, alienation, and deprivation, then the Good News we proclaim and live is a true reflection of the God we name in our worship.

Food bags for the homeless assembled on Sunday? Anti-sex-trafficking concerts by our youth group? Adopting an underserved neighborhood school and loving the kids and parents? Prayer for effective public justice systems in nations without the rule of law? All this and far more can be ways our church communities can live out the saving love of Jesus Christ.

—Mark Labberton

For more on justice, see reading at Isaiah 61.

"Remove the heavy yoke of
oppression.
Stop pointing your finger and
spreading vicious rumors!
¹⁰ Feed the hungry,
and help those in trouble.
Then your light will shine out from the
darkness,
and the darkness around you will be as
bright as noon.
¹¹ The LORD will guide you continually,
giving you water when you are dry
and restoring your strength.
You will be like a well-watered garden,
like an ever-flowing spring.

¹² Some of you will rebuild the deserted
ruins of your cities.
Then you will be known as a rebuilder
of walls
and a restorer of homes.

¹³ "Keep the Sabbath day holy.
Don't pursue your own interests on
that day,
but enjoy the Sabbath
and speak of it with delight as the
LORD's holy day.
Honor the Sabbath in everything you do
on that day,
and don't follow your own desires or
talk idly.

¹⁴ Then the LORD will be your delight.
I will give you great honor
and satisfy you with the inheritance I
promised to your ancestor Jacob.
I, the LORD, have spoken!"

59 Warnings against Sin

¹ Listen! The LORD's arm is not too
weak to save you,
nor is his ear too deaf to hear you call.
² It's your sins that have cut you off from
God.
Because of your sins, he has turned
away
and will not listen anymore.
³ Your hands are the hands of murderers,
and your fingers are filthy with sin.
Your lips are full of lies,
and your mouth spews corruption.

⁴ No one cares about being fair and
honest.
The people's lawsuits are based on lies.
They conceive evil deeds
and then give birth to sin.
⁵ They hatch deadly snakes
and weave spiders' webs.
Whoever falls into their webs will die,
and there's danger even in getting near
them.
⁶ Their webs can't be made into clothing,
and nothing they do is productive.
All their activity is filled with sin,
and violence is their trademark.
⁷ Their feet run to do evil,
and they rush to commit murder.
They think only about sinning.
Misery and destruction always follow
them.
⁸ They don't know where to find peace
or what it means to be just and good.
They have mapped out crooked roads,
and no one who follows them knows a
moment's peace.

⁹ So there is no justice among us,
and we know nothing about right living.
We look for light but find only darkness.
We look for bright skies but walk in
gloom.
¹⁰ We grope like the blind along a wall,
feeling our way like people without
eyes.
Even at brightest noontime,
we stumble as though it were dark.
Among the living,
we are like the dead.
¹¹ We growl like hungry bears;
we moan like mournful doves.
We look for justice, but it never comes.
We look for rescue, but it is far away
from us.
¹² For our sins are piled up before God
and testify against us.
Yes, we know what sinners we are.
¹³ We know we have rebelled and have
denied the LORD.
We have turned our backs on our God.
We know how unfair and oppressive we
have been,
carefully planning our deceitful lies.
¹⁴ Our courts oppose the righteous,
and justice is nowhere to be found.
Truth stumbles in the streets,
and honesty has been outlawed.
¹⁵ Yes, truth is gone,
and anyone who renounces evil is
attacked.

The LORD looked and was displeased
to find there was no justice.
¹⁶ He was amazed to see that no one
intervened
to help the oppressed.
So he himself stepped in to save them
with his strong arm,
and his justice sustained him.
¹⁷ He put on righteousness as his body
armor
and placed the helmet of salvation on
his head.
He clothed himself with a robe of
vengeance
and wrapped himself in a cloak of
divine passion.
¹⁸ He will repay his enemies for their evil
deeds.
His fury will fall on his foes.
He will pay them back even to the
ends of the earth.
¹⁹ In the west, people will respect the name
of the LORD;
in the east, they will glorify him.
For he will come like a raging flood tide
driven by the breath of the LORD.*

59:19 Or *When the enemy comes like a raging flood tide, / the Spirit of the LORD will drive him back.*

20 "The Redeemer will come to
Jerusalem
to buy back those in Israel
who have turned from their sins,"*
says the LORD.

21 "And this is my covenant with them,"
says the LORD. "My Spirit will not leave
them, and neither will these words I have
given you. They will be on your lips and on
the lips of your children and your children's
children forever. I, the LORD, have spoken!

60 Future Glory for Jerusalem

1 "Arise, Jerusalem! Let your light
shine for all to see.
For the glory of the LORD rises to
shine on you.
2 Darkness as black as night covers all the
nations of the earth,
but the glory of the LORD rises and
appears over you.
3 All nations will come to your light;
mighty kings will come to see your
radiance.

4 "Look and see, for everyone is coming
home!
Your sons are coming from distant
lands;
your little daughters will be carried
home.
5 Your eyes will shine,
and your heart will thrill with joy,
for merchants from around the world
will come to you.
They will bring you the wealth of
many lands.
6 Vast caravans of camels will converge on
you,
the camels of Midian and Ephah.
The people of Sheba will bring gold and
frankincense
and will come worshiping the LORD.
7 The flocks of Kedar will be given to
you,
and the rams of Nebaioth will be
brought for my altars.
I will accept their offerings,
and I will make my Temple
glorious.

8 "And what do I see flying like clouds to
Israel,
like doves to their nests?
9 They are ships from the ends of the
earth,
from lands that trust in me,
led by the great ships of Tarshish.
They are bringing the people of Israel
home from far away,
carrying their silver and gold.
They will honor the LORD your God,
the Holy One of Israel,
for he has filled you with splendor.

10 "Foreigners will come to rebuild your
towns,
and their kings will serve you.
For though I have destroyed you in my
anger,
I will now have mercy on you through
my grace.
11 Your gates will stay open day and night
to receive the wealth of many lands.
The kings of the world will be led as
captives
in a victory procession.
12 For the nations that refuse to serve you
will be destroyed.

13 "The glory of Lebanon will be yours—
the forests of cypress, fir, and pine—
to beautify my sanctuary.
My Temple will be glorious!
14 The descendants of your tormentors
will come and bow before you.
Those who despised you
will kiss your feet.
They will call you the City of the LORD,
and Zion of the Holy One of Israel.

15 "Though you were once despised and
hated,
with no one traveling through you,
I will make you beautiful forever,
a joy to all generations.
16 Powerful kings and mighty nations
will satisfy your every need,
as though you were a child
nursing at the breast of a queen.
You will know at last that I, the LORD,
am your Savior and your Redeemer,
the Mighty One of Israel.*

59:20 Hebrew *The Redeemer will come to Zion / to buy back those in Jacob / who have turned from their sins.* Greek version reads *The one who rescues will come on behalf of Zion, / and he will turn Jacob away from ungodliness.* Compare Rom 11:26. **60:16** Hebrew *of Jacob.* See note on 14:1.

¹⁷ I will exchange your bronze for gold,
    your iron for silver,
your wood for bronze,
    and your stones for iron.
I will make peace your leader
    and righteousness your ruler.
¹⁸ Violence will disappear from your land;
    the desolation and destruction of war
      will end.
Salvation will surround you like city walls,
    and praise will be on the lips of all
      who enter there.

¹⁹ "No longer will you need the sun to
    shine by day,
    nor the moon to give its light by night,
for the LORD your God will be your
    everlasting light,
    and your God will be your glory.
²⁰ Your sun will never set;
    your moon will not go down.
For the LORD will be your everlasting
    light.
    Your days of mourning will come to
      an end.
²¹ All your people will be righteous.
    They will possess their land forever,
for I will plant them there with my own
    hands
    in order to bring myself glory.
²² The smallest family will become a
    thousand people,
    and the tiniest group will become a
      mighty nation.
    At the right time, I, the LORD, will
      make it happen."

61 Good News for the Oppressed

¹ The Spirit of the Sovereign LORD is
    upon me,
    for the LORD has anointed me
to bring good news to the poor.
He has sent me to comfort the
    brokenhearted
    and to proclaim that captives will be
      released
    and prisoners will be freed.*
² He has sent me to tell those who mourn
    that the time of the LORD's favor has
      come,*
    and with it, the day of God's anger
      against their enemies.

³ To all who mourn in Israel,*
    he will give a crown of beauty for ashes,
a joyous blessing instead of mourning,
    festive praise instead of despair.
In their righteousness, they will be like
    great oaks
    that the LORD has planted for his own
      glory.

⁴ They will rebuild the ancient ruins,
    repairing cities destroyed long ago.
They will revive them,
    though they have been deserted for
      many generations.
⁵ Foreigners will be your servants.
    They will feed your flocks
and plow your fields
    and tend your vineyards.
⁶ You will be called priests of the LORD,
    ministers of our God.
You will feed on the treasures of the
    nations
    and boast in their riches.
⁷ Instead of shame and dishonor,
    you will enjoy a double share of honor.
You will possess a double portion of
    prosperity in your land,
    and everlasting joy will be yours.

⁸ "For I, the LORD, love justice.
    I hate robbery and wrongdoing.
I will faithfully reward my people for
    their suffering
    and make an everlasting covenant
      with them.
⁹ Their descendants will be recognized
    and honored among the nations.
Everyone will realize that they are a
    people
    the LORD has blessed."

¹⁰ I am overwhelmed with joy in the LORD
    my God!
    For he has dressed me with the
    clothing of salvation
    and draped me in a robe of
    righteousness.
I am like a bridegroom in his wedding
    suit
    or a bride with her jewels.
¹¹ The Sovereign LORD will show his
    justice to the nations of the world.
    Everyone will praise him!

61:1 Greek version reads *and the blind will see.* Compare Luke 4:18. **61:2** Or *to proclaim the acceptable year of the LORD.* **61:3** Hebrew *in Zion.*

The Messiah's Justice Mission

ISAIAH 61

When we think about God as a God of justice, we might be inclined to think about the final Judgment Day, in which God metes out his "just" rewards and punishments according to how we lived. And we who have chosen to follow Christ will "justly" be given our promised reward of eternal life.

But in Isaiah 61 we see a broader and deeper description of what justice actually entails: good news to the poor, comfort to the brokenhearted, freedom for the captives. Verse 8 specifically says, "For I, the LORD, love justice. I hate robbery and wrongdoing."

The word *justice* in the original Greek and Hebrew (*dikaiosune; tsedhaqah*) is actually the same word that is also often translated as *righteousness*. Justice, in other words, means making all that is wrong in our world right, which includes eradicating the injustice of poverty, eliminating spiritual captivity, and healing those who have been hurt by others.

While Jesus is the only one who can bring about true and complete justice, he calls us to partner with him in this mission so that his will is done on earth as it is in heaven. In what ways will you join him?

—*Helen Lee*

For more on justice, see reading at Jeremiah 22:1–5.

His righteousness will be like a garden in
  early spring,
  with plants springing up everywhere.

62 Isaiah's Prayer for Jerusalem

¹ Because I love Zion,
  I will not keep still.
Because my heart yearns for Jerusalem,
  I cannot remain silent.
I will not stop praying for her
  until her righteousness shines like the
  dawn,
  and her salvation blazes like a burning
  torch.
² The nations will see your righteousness.
  World leaders will be blinded by your
  glory.
And you will be given a new name
  by the LORD's own mouth.
³ The LORD will hold you in his hand for
  all to see—

a splendid crown in the hand
  of God.
⁴ Never again will you be called "The
  Forsaken City"*
  or "The Desolate Land."*
Your new name will be "The City of
  God's Delight"*
  and "The Bride of God,"*
for the LORD delights in you
  and will claim you as his bride.
⁵ Your children will commit themselves to
  you, O Jerusalem,
  just as a young man commits himself
  to his bride.
Then God will rejoice over you
  as a bridegroom rejoices over his
  bride.

⁶ O Jerusalem, I have posted watchmen
  on your walls;
  they will pray day and night,
  continually.

62:4a Hebrew *Azubah*, which means "forsaken."   **62:4b** Hebrew *Shemamah*, which means "desolate."   **62:4c** Hebrew *Hephzibah*, which means "my delight is in her."   **62:4d** Hebrew *Beulah*, which means "married."

Take no rest, all you who pray to the
Lord.
7 Give the Lord no rest until he
completes his work,
until he makes Jerusalem the pride of
the earth.
8 The Lord has sworn to Jerusalem by his
own strength:
"I will never again hand you over to
your enemies.
Never again will foreign warriors come
and take away your grain and new wine.
9 You raised the grain, and you will eat it,
praising the Lord.
Within the courtyards of the Temple,
you yourselves will drink the wine you
have pressed."

10 Go out through the gates!
Prepare the highway for my people to
return!
Smooth out the road; pull out the
boulders;
raise a flag for all the nations to see.
11 The Lord has sent this message to every
land:
"Tell the people of Israel,*
'Look, your Savior is coming.
See, he brings his reward with him as
he comes.'"
12 They will be called "The Holy People"
and "The People Redeemed by the
Lord."
And Jerusalem will be known as "The
Desirable Place"
and "The City No Longer Forsaken."

63 Judgment against the Lord's Enemies

1 Who is this who comes from Edom,
from the city of Bozrah,
with his clothing stained red?
Who is this in royal robes,
marching in his great strength?

"It is I, the Lord, announcing your
salvation!
It is I, the Lord, who has the power to
save!"

2 Why are your clothes so red,
as if you have been treading out
grapes?

3 "I have been treading the winepress
alone;
no one was there to help me.
In my anger I have trampled my enemies
as if they were grapes.
In my fury I have trampled my foes.
Their blood has stained my clothes.
4 For the time has come for me to avenge
my people,
to ransom them from their
oppressors.
5 I was amazed to see that no one
intervened
to help the oppressed.
So I myself stepped in to save them with
my strong arm,
and my wrath sustained me.
6 I crushed the nations in my anger
and made them stagger and fall to the
ground,
spilling their blood upon the earth."

Praise for Deliverance

7 I will tell of the Lord's unfailing love.
I will praise the Lord for all he has
done.
I will rejoice in his great goodness to
Israel,
which he has granted according to his
mercy and love.
8 He said, "They are my very own people.
Surely they will not betray me again."
And he became their Savior.
9 In all their suffering he also suffered,
and he personally* rescued them.
In his love and mercy he redeemed them.
He lifted them up and carried them
through all the years.
10 But they rebelled against him
and grieved his Holy Spirit.
So he became their enemy
and fought against them.

11 Then they remembered those days of old
when Moses led his people out of
Egypt.
They cried out, "Where is the one who
brought Israel through the sea,
with Moses as their shepherd?
Where is the one who sent his Holy
Spirit
to be among his people?

62:11 Hebrew *Tell the daughter of Zion.*   **63:9** Hebrew *and the angel of his presence.*

¹² Where is the one whose power was
    displayed
    when Moses lifted up his hand—
the one who divided the sea before
    them,
    making himself famous forever?
¹³ Where is the one who led them through
    the bottom of the sea?
    They were like fine stallions
    racing through the desert, never
    stumbling.
¹⁴ As with cattle going down into a
    peaceful valley,
    the Spirit of the LORD gave them rest.
You led your people, LORD,
    and gained a magnificent reputation."

Prayer for Mercy and Pardon

¹⁵ LORD, look down from heaven;
    look from your holy, glorious home,
    and see us.
Where is the passion and the might
    you used to show on our behalf?
    Where are your mercy and
    compassion now?
¹⁶ Surely you are still our Father!
    Even if Abraham and Jacob* would
    disown us,
    LORD, you would still be our Father.
You are our Redeemer from ages past.
¹⁷ LORD, why have you allowed us to turn
    from your path?
    Why have you given us stubborn
    hearts so we no longer fear you?
Return and help us, for we are your
    servants,
    the tribes that are your special
    possession.
¹⁸ How briefly your holy people possessed
    your holy place,
    and now our enemies have
    destroyed it.
¹⁹ Sometimes it seems as though we never
    belonged to you,
    as though we had never been known
    as your people.

64 ¹*Oh, that you would burst from
        the heavens and come down!
How the mountains would quake in
    your presence!

²*As fire causes wood to burn
    and water to boil,
your coming would make the nations
    tremble.
    Then your enemies would learn the
    reason for your fame!
³ When you came down long ago,
    you did awesome deeds beyond our
    highest expectations.
    And oh, how the mountains quaked!
⁴ For since the world began,
    no ear has heard
and no eye has seen a God like you,
    who works for those who wait for him!
⁵ You welcome those who gladly do good,
    who follow godly ways.
But you have been very angry with us,
    for we are not godly.
We are constant sinners;
    how can people like us be saved?
⁶ We are all infected and impure with sin.
    When we display our righteous deeds,
    they are nothing but filthy rags.
Like autumn leaves, we wither and fall,
    and our sins sweep us away like the
    wind.
⁷ Yet no one calls on your name
    or pleads with you for mercy.
Therefore, you have turned away from us
    and turned us over* to our sins.

⁸ And yet, O LORD, you are our Father.
    We are the clay, and you are the potter.
    We all are formed by your hand.
⁹ Don't be so angry with us, LORD.
    Please don't remember our sins
    forever.
Look at us, we pray,
    and see that we are all your people.
¹⁰ Your holy cities are destroyed.
    Zion is a wilderness;
    yes, Jerusalem is a desolate ruin.
¹¹ The holy and beautiful Temple
    where our ancestors praised you
has been burned down,
    and all the things of beauty are
    destroyed.
¹² After all this, LORD, must you still refuse
    to help us?
    Will you continue to be silent and
    punish us?

63:16 Hebrew *Israel*. See note on 14:1.   **64:1** In the Hebrew text this verse is included in 63:19.   **64:2** Verses 64:2-12 are numbered 64:1-11 in Hebrew text.   **64:7** As in Greek, Syriac, and Aramaic versions; Hebrew reads *melted us.*

Pottery in God's Hands

ISAIAH 64:8

In Isaiah 64:8 we read, "O LORD, you are our Father. We are the clay, and you are the potter. We all are formed by your hand." His hands formed the pot. And he has a plan for each of us.

Psalm 139 tells me that his eyes saw me before I was even formed. Every detail of this pot is written in his book. I've been on his mind. I'm marvelously made for a purpose.

Once we seek what God has in mind for us, then he begins to make us a vessel fit for glory. But we must be pliable. As the Potter works the clay, he continually wets it. If he doesn't, it gets dry and becomes a misshapen lump, good for nothing.

Isn't it an incredible thing, then, that even though we're just little dust creatures, we shake a little dust fist in the face of the Lord, Creator and Potter, and say that he knows nothing? Instead, we need to submit to the Potter and let him make us into the kind of vessel that will be useful.

We're formed to carry Christ, our treasure, who has come within our vessels through our submissive hearts. As we submit to the Potter, we discover and live our true purpose and value.

—*Jill Briscoe*

For more on submission, see reading at Jeremiah 7:23.

65 Judgment and Final Salvation

The LORD says,

"I was ready to respond, but no one
    asked for help.
I was ready to be found, but no one
    was looking for me.
I said, 'Here I am, here I am!'
    to a nation that did not call on my
    name.*
2 All day long I opened my arms to a
    rebellious people.*
But they follow their own evil
    paths
and their own crooked schemes.
3 All day long they insult me to my face
    by worshiping idols in their sacred
    gardens.
They burn incense on pagan altars.
4 At night they go out among the graves,
    worshiping the dead.

They eat the flesh of pigs
    and make stews with other forbidden
    foods.
5 Yet they say to each other,
    'Don't come too close or you will defile
    me!
I am holier than you!'
These people are a stench in my
    nostrils,
    an acrid smell that never goes away.

6 "Look, my decree is written out* in front
    of me:
I will not stand silent;
    I will repay them in full!
Yes, I will repay them—
7 both for their own sins
    and for those of their ancestors,"
    says the LORD.
"For they also burned incense on the
    mountains

65:1 Or to a nation that did not bear my name.   65:1-2 Greek version reads I was found by people who were not looking for me. / I showed myself to those who were not asking for me. / All day long I opened my arms to them, / but they were disobedient and rebellious. Compare Rom 10:20-21.
65:6 Or their sins are written out; Hebrew reads it stands written.

Confessions of the Well Behaved

"I'm sorry, Mom."

"For what?"

"What I did."

"What did you do?"

"You know."

"Yeah, but you need to say it."

My well-behaved, highly responsible, perfectionist firstborn is a great kid. She makes good choices, is obedient, a brilliant student, and genuinely concerned with doing the right thing. Like the stereotypical firstborn, she thinks rules are important and likes to follow them. And she's extremely hard on herself when she fails. Since she was a toddler, it's been easy for her to apologize and painfully difficult for her to say what she did wrong—to name her sin and shortcomings.

Parenting this girl for nearly ten years has taught me a lot about myself and my relationship with God. Recently I learned something about confession: the people most in need of confession are often the most well behaved.

Many of us, without thinking about it, probably believe that the people who most need confession are the ones who have done the worst things, like murderers. These are people we place in a different category from the rest of us. While we occasionally "mess up," the ones who need to confess are burdened with the guilt of *really* bad deeds—of honest-to-goodness sin that God probably has to exert himself to forgive.

This kind of thinking reveals the true nature of confession and why we all need it. Confession's primary purpose is not to set us straight, give other people satisfaction in our shame, or make it easier for God to forgive us. It's to show us our sin. To show us who we are, in comparison not to others but to our perfect, holy God. And to help us understand the undeserved grace he extends every single time. We who most need to see our own sin are the ones most tempted to think we're not that bad.

This is why God, in his wisdom, gave us the law—the requirements and prohibitions we slam into when we try to go our own way. Paul tells us, "God's law was given so that all people could see how sinful they were. But as people sinned more and more, God's wonderful grace became more abundant. So just as sin ruled over all people and brought them to death,

───────────── { ❖ } ─────────────

now God's wonderful grace rules instead, giving us right standing with God and resulting in eternal life through Jesus Christ our Lord" (Romans 5:20–21). The law exists to show us our sin so we can understand and accept God's grace—and be changed by it. Without a shameful and repentant acknowledgment of who we are, grace is just a nice name for a pretty girl.

When my well-behaved daughter can't bring herself to say what she did wrong, she doesn't have to fully face her sin and shortcomings. But unless she does, she won't fully see her need for Christ either. And she won't see the brightness of the light of his grace cutting through her own cloud of sin.

So when my daughter apologizes, I require her to describe her behavior. And then I forgive her effusively. And I remind her that God does the same when she confesses to him. I ask her to do this hard work for the good of her heart and soul—so she can live in the assurance of forgiveness and grace that really mean something. Not to get lost in her sin, but to be truly found by the most astounding truth possible.

My daughter and I have a lot in common. I'm a perfectionist too, and I spend a lot of energy trying to be good enough to merit God's love and favor. I often live as if my chief calling in life is to avoid confession.

On the contrary, while God calls us to holiness, he won't be fooled. There's no avoiding the need to confess. Even our attempts at good behavior are fraught with sin and the suggestion that what we do is as good as what God does. We need to believe this: "We are all infected and impure with sin. When we display our righteous deeds, they are nothing but filthy rags" (Isaiah 64:6).

In the process of trying to help my daughter experience grace in contrast to her sin, I've realized how much I need this lesson myself. *I* need to confess constantly, with shocking honesty and complete disregard for how I stack up against others. I need to remember that confession is for *me*. And then accept and embrace the undeserved and yet freely given grace God wraps around me, his child.

—Amy Simpson

For more on confession, see reading at Zechariah 10:1–8.

and insulted me on the hills.
I will pay them back in full!

8 "But I will not destroy them all,"
    says the LORD.
"For just as good grapes are found
    among a cluster of bad ones
    (and someone will say, 'Don't throw
    them all away—
some of those grapes are good!'),
so I will not destroy all Israel.
    For I still have true servants there.
9 I will preserve a remnant of the people
    of Israel*
    and of Judah to possess my land.
Those I choose will inherit it,
    and my servants will live there.
10 The plain of Sharon will again be filled
    with flocks
for my people who have searched
    for me,
    and the valley of Achor will be a place
    to pasture herds.

11 "But because the rest of you have
    forsaken the LORD
    and have forgotten his Temple,
and because you have prepared feasts to
    honor the god of Fate
    and have offered mixed wine to the
    god of Destiny,
12 now I will 'destine' you for the sword.
    All of you will bow down before the
    executioner.
For when I called, you did not answer.
    When I spoke, you did not listen.
You deliberately sinned—before my very
    eyes—
    and chose to do what you know I
    despise."

13 Therefore, this is what the Sovereign
    LORD says:
"My servants will eat,
    but you will starve.
My servants will drink,
    but you will be thirsty.
My servants will rejoice,
    but you will be sad and ashamed.
14 My servants will sing for joy,
    but you will cry in sorrow and despair.
15 Your name will be a curse word among
    my people,

for the Sovereign LORD will destroy
    you
    and will call his true servants by
    another name.
16 All who invoke a blessing or take an oath
    will do so by the God of truth.
For I will put aside my anger
    and forget the evil of earlier days.

17 "Look! I am creating new heavens and a
    new earth,
    and no one will even think about the
    old ones anymore.
18 Be glad; rejoice forever in my creation!
    And look! I will create Jerusalem as a
    place of happiness.
    Her people will be a source of joy.
19 I will rejoice over Jerusalem
    and delight in my people.
And the sound of weeping and crying
    will be heard in it no more.

20 "No longer will babies die when only a
    few days old.
    No longer will adults die before they
    have lived a full life.
No longer will people be considered old
    at one hundred!
    Only the cursed will die that young!
21 In those days people will live in the
    houses they build
    and eat the fruit of their own
    vineyards.
22 Unlike the past, invaders will not take
    their houses
    and confiscate their vineyards.
For my people will live as long as trees,
    and my chosen ones will have time to
    enjoy their hard-won gains.
23 They will not work in vain,
    and their children will not be doomed
    to misfortune.
For they are people blessed by the LORD,
    and their children, too, will be blessed.
24 I will answer them before they even call
    to me.
    While they are still talking about their
    needs,
    I will go ahead and answer their
    prayers!
25 The wolf and the lamb will feed together.
    The lion will eat hay like a cow.
    But the snakes will eat dust.

65:9 Hebrew *remnant of Jacob*. See note on 14:1.

In those days no one will be hurt or
destroyed on my holy mountain.
I, the LORD, have spoken!"

66

This is what the LORD says:

"Heaven is my throne,
and the earth is my footstool.
Could you build me a temple as good as
that?
Could you build me such a resting
place?
² My hands have made both heaven and
earth;
they and everything in them are
mine.*
I, the LORD, have spoken!

"I will bless those who have humble and
contrite hearts,
who tremble at my word.
³ But those who choose their own ways—
delighting in their detestable sins—
will not have their offerings accepted.
When such people sacrifice a bull,
it is no more acceptable than a human
sacrifice.
When they sacrifice a lamb,
it's as though they had sacrificed a
dog!
When they bring an offering of grain,
they might as well offer the blood of
a pig.
When they burn frankincense,
it's as if they had blessed an idol.
⁴ I will send them great trouble—
all the things they feared.
For when I called, they did not answer.
When I spoke, they did not listen.
They deliberately sinned before my very
eyes
and chose to do what they know I
despise."

⁵ Hear this message from the LORD,
all you who tremble at his words:
"Your own people hate you
and throw you out for being loyal to
my name.
'Let the LORD be honored!' they scoff.
'Be joyful in him!'
But they will be put to shame.

⁶ What is all the commotion in the city?
What is that terrible noise from the
Temple?
It is the voice of the LORD
taking vengeance against his enemies.

⁷ "Before the birth pains even begin,
Jerusalem gives birth to a son.
⁸ Who has ever seen anything as strange
as this?
Who ever heard of such a thing?
Has a nation ever been born in a single
day?
Has a country ever come forth in a
mere moment?
But by the time Jerusalem's* birth pains
begin,
her children will be born.
⁹ Would I ever bring this nation to the
point of birth
and then not deliver it?" asks the
LORD.
"No! I would never keep this nation
from being born,"
says your God.

¹⁰ "Rejoice with Jerusalem!
Be glad with her, all you who love her
and all you who mourn for her.
¹¹ Drink deeply of her glory
even as an infant drinks at its mother's
comforting breasts."

¹² This is what the LORD says:
"I will give Jerusalem a river of peace
and prosperity.
The wealth of the nations will flow to
her.
Her children will be nursed at her
breasts,
carried in her arms, and held on her
lap.
¹³ I will comfort you there in Jerusalem
as a mother comforts her child."

¹⁴ When you see these things, your heart
will rejoice.
You will flourish like the grass!
Everyone will see the LORD's hand of
blessing on his servants—
and his anger against his enemies.
¹⁵ See, the LORD is coming with fire,
and his swift chariots roar like a
whirlwind.

66:2 As in Greek, Latin, and Syriac versions; Hebrew reads *these things are*. 66:8 Hebrew *Zion's*.

He will bring punishment with the fury
  of his anger
  and the flaming fire of his hot rebuke.
¹⁶ The LORD will punish the world by fire
  and by his sword.
He will judge the earth,
  and many will be killed by him.

¹⁷ "Those who 'consecrate' and 'purify' themselves in a sacred garden with its idol in the center—feasting on pork and rats and other detestable meats—will come to a terrible end," says the LORD.

¹⁸ "I can see what they are doing, and I know what they are thinking. So I will gather all nations and peoples together, and they will see my glory. ¹⁹ I will perform a sign among them. And I will send those who survive to be messengers to the nations— to Tarshish, to the Libyans* and Lydians* (who are famous as archers), to Tubal and Greece,* and to all the lands beyond the sea that have not heard of my fame or seen my glory. There they will declare my glory to the nations. ²⁰ They will bring the remnant of your people back from every nation.

They will bring them to my holy mountain in Jerusalem as an offering to the LORD. They will ride on horses, in chariots and wagons, and on mules and camels," says the LORD. ²¹ "And I will appoint some of them to be my priests and Levites. I, the LORD, have spoken!

²² "As surely as my new heavens and earth
  will remain,
  so will you always be my people,
with a name that will never
  disappear,"
  says the LORD.
²³ "All humanity will come to worship me
  from week to week
  and from month to month.
²⁴ And as they go out, they will see
  the dead bodies of those who have
  rebelled against me.
For the worms that devour them will
  never die,
  and the fire that burns them will never
  go out.
All who pass by
  will view them with utter horror."

66:19a As in some Greek manuscripts, which read Put [that is, Libya]; Hebrew reads Pul. 66:19b Hebrew Lud. 66:19c Hebrew Javan.

Introduction to
Jeremiah

Background

Jeremiah has the distinction of being known as the "Weeping Prophet." He had a long and difficult ministry and lived during the most soul-wrenching period in Judah's history: the fall of Jerusalem in 586 B.C.

In Hebrew, Jeremiah might mean "Yahweh throws" or "Yahweh establishes, appoints, or sends." In Greek, Jeremiah is *Hieremias*.

Message

A steady moral decline occurs in Judah during the reigns of four idolatrous kings that succeed King Josiah, who is on the throne when Jeremiah first receives his prophetic call (1:2). The kings' apostasy leads God to carry out the ultimate disciplinary action of permitting his people to be conquered by an enemy nation. Jeremiah has the unenviable task of predicting God's judgment, calling the nation to repentance, and observing God's judgment firsthand. But there is good news also: eventually the nation will be restored. Yet Jeremiah's words are continually ignored or disputed. The prophet also suffers beatings and imprisonment for being God's spokesman.

Time

Jeremiah's ministry began in about 627 B.C. and lasted until around 580 B.C. In chapter 43 we find Jeremiah exiled in Egypt, still speaking forth the "message from the LORD"; tradition claims he was stoned to death in Egypt.

Outline

Jeremiah

1 These are the words of Jeremiah son of Hilkiah, one of the priests from the town of Anathoth in the land of Benjamin. ²The LORD first gave messages to Jeremiah during the thirteenth year of the reign of Josiah son of Amon, king of Judah.* ³The LORD's messages continued throughout the reign of King Jehoiakim, Josiah's son, until the eleventh year of the reign of King Zedekiah, another of Josiah's sons. In August* of that eleventh year the people of Jerusalem were taken away as captives.

Jeremiah's Call and First Visions

⁴The LORD gave me this message:

⁵ "I knew you before I formed you in your mother's womb.
   Before you were born I set you apart
   and appointed you as my prophet to the nations."

⁶"O Sovereign LORD," I said, "I can't speak for you! I'm too young!"

⁷The LORD replied, "Don't say, 'I'm too young,' for you must go wherever I send you and say whatever I tell you. ⁸And don't be afraid of the people, for I will be with you and will protect you. I, the LORD, have spoken!" ⁹Then the LORD reached out and touched my mouth and said,

"Look, I have put my words in your mouth!
¹⁰ Today I appoint you to stand up
   against nations and kingdoms.
Some you must uproot and tear down,
   destroy and overthrow.
Others you must build up
   and plant."

¹¹Then the LORD said to me, "Look, Jeremiah! What do you see?"

And I replied, "I see a branch from an almond tree."

¹²And the LORD said, "That's right, and it means that I am watching,* and I will certainly carry out all my plans."

¹³Then the LORD spoke to me again and asked, "What do you see now?"

And I replied, "I see a pot of boiling water, spilling from the north."

¹⁴"Yes," the LORD said, "for terror from the north will boil out on the people of this land. ¹⁵Listen! I am calling the armies of the kingdoms of the north to come to Jerusalem. I, the LORD, have spoken!

"They will set their thrones
   at the gates of the city.
They will attack its walls
   and all the other towns of Judah.

1:2 The thirteenth year of Josiah's reign was 627 B.C.   **1:3** Hebrew *In the fifth month,* of the ancient Hebrew lunar calendar. A number of events in Jeremiah can be cross-checked with dates in surviving Babylonian records and related accurately to our modern calendar. The fifth month in the eleventh year of Zedekiah's reign occurred within the months of August and September 586 B.C. Also see 52:12 and the note there.   **1:12** The Hebrew word for "watching" (*shoqed*) sounds like the word for "almond tree" (*shaqed*).

Solitude — Created to Commune with God

JEREMIAH 1:4–5

An essential secret to being an effective Christian is to cultivate the habit of solitude. Pulling back from our network of relationships and commitments gives us the chance to slow our pace, clear our head, and give top priority to our relationship with God—who created us primarily to be in communion with him. When our soul is quieted, it's easier to remember the astonishing truth that Christ breathes his life and love into us when we open our hearts to him.

Practicing solitude not only helps us reconnect with God; it also helps us reconnect with ourselves. You'll be better able to ask yourself important questions, such as *What am I doing with my life? Am I resisting God in some area? Am I using my talents for him or for others? Am I becoming more loving, more giving?* Whether you spend time walking alone through a forest preserve or sitting by yourself in your car, office, kitchen, or restaurant, in solitude you'll be better able to ponder these weighty issues.

The *when, how,* and *where* of your alone times aren't important; you and God can determine those matters. At first being alone may feel awkward and unnatural, particularly in our noise-filled, frenetic culture. But once you cultivate it, you won't want to live without it.

—Bill Hybels

For more on solitude, see reading at Jeremiah 15:10–21.

---

¹⁶ I will pronounce judgment
on my people for all their evil—
for deserting me and burning incense to
other gods.
Yes, they worship idols made with
their own hands!

¹⁷ "Get up and prepare for action.
Go out and tell them everything I tell
you to say.
Do not be afraid of them,
or I will make you look foolish in front
of them.
¹⁸ For see, today I have made you strong
like a fortified city that cannot be
captured,
like an iron pillar or a bronze wall.
You will stand against the whole
land—
the kings, officials, priests, and people
of Judah.
¹⁹ They will fight you, but they will
fail.

For I am with you, and I will take care
of you.
I, the LORD, have spoken!"

2 The LORD's Case against His People

The LORD gave me another message. He said, ²"Go and shout this message to Jerusalem. This is what the LORD says:

"I remember how eager you were to
please me
as a young bride long ago,
how you loved me and followed me
even through the barren wilderness.
³ In those days Israel was holy to the LORD,
the first of his children.*
All who harmed his people were
declared guilty,
and disaster fell on them.
I, the LORD, have spoken!"

⁴Listen to the word of the LORD, people of Jacob—all you families of Israel! ⁵This is what the LORD says:

2:3 Hebrew *the firstfruits of his harvest.*

"What did your ancestors find wrong
    with me
  that led them to stray so far from me?
They worshiped worthless idols,
  only to become worthless themselves.
⁶ They did not ask, 'Where is the LORD
  who brought us safely out of Egypt
and led us through the barren
    wilderness—
  a land of deserts and pits,
a land of drought and death,
  where no one lives or even travels?'

⁷ "And when I brought you into a fruitful
    land
  to enjoy its bounty and goodness,
you defiled my land and
  corrupted the possession I had
    promised you.
⁸ The priests did not ask,
  'Where is the LORD?'
Those who taught my word ignored me,
  the rulers turned against me,
and the prophets spoke in the name of
    Baal,
  wasting their time on worthless idols.
⁹ Therefore, I will bring my case against
    you,"
  says the LORD.
"I will even bring charges against your
    children's children
  in the years to come.

¹⁰ "Go west and look in the land of
    Cyprus*;
  go east and search through the land of
    Kedar.
Has anyone ever heard of anything
  as strange as this?
¹¹ Has any nation ever traded its gods for
    new ones,
  even though they are not gods at all?
Yet my people have exchanged their
    glorious God*
  for worthless idols!
¹² The heavens are shocked at such a thing
  and shrink back in horror and dismay,"
  says the LORD.
¹³ "For my people have done two evil
    things:
They have abandoned me—
  the fountain of living water.

And they have dug for themselves
    cracked cisterns
  that can hold no water at all!

The Results of Israel's Sin

¹⁴ "Why has Israel become a slave?
  Why has he been carried away as
    plunder?
¹⁵ Strong lions have roared against him,
  and the land has been destroyed.
The towns are now in ruins,
  and no one lives in them anymore.
¹⁶ Egyptians, marching from their cities of
    Memphis* and Tahpanhes,
  have destroyed Israel's glory and
    power.
¹⁷ And you have brought this upon
    yourselves
  by rebelling against the LORD your
    God,
  even though he was leading you on
    the way!

¹⁸ "What have you gained by your alliances
    with Egypt
  and your covenants with Assyria?
What good to you are the streams of the
    Nile*
  or the waters of the Euphrates River?*
¹⁹ Your wickedness will bring its own
    punishment.
  Your turning from me will shame you.
You will see what an evil, bitter thing
    it is
  to abandon the LORD your God and
    not to fear him.
I, the Lord, the LORD of Heaven's
    Armies, have spoken!

²⁰ "Long ago I broke the yoke that
    oppressed you
  and tore away the chains of your
    slavery,
but still you said,
  'I will not serve you.'
On every hill and under every green
    tree,
  you have prostituted yourselves by
    bowing down to idols.
²¹ But I was the one who planted you,
  choosing a vine of the purest stock—
  the very best.

2:10 Hebrew *Kittim.*   **2:11** Hebrew *their glory.*   **2:16** Hebrew *Noph.*   **2:18a** Hebrew of *Shihor,* a branch of the Nile River.   **2:18b** Hebrew *the river?*

How did you grow into this corrupt
wild vine?
²² No amount of soap or lye can make you
clean.
I still see the stain of your guilt.
I, the Sovereign Lord, have spoken!

Israel, an Unfaithful Wife

²³ "You say, 'That's not true!
I haven't worshiped the images of Baal!'
But how can you say that?
Go and look in any valley in the land!
Face the awful sins you have done.
You are like a restless female camel
desperately searching for a mate.
²⁴ You are like a wild donkey,
sniffing the wind at mating time.
Who can restrain her lust?
Those who desire her don't need to
search,
for she goes running to them!
²⁵ When will you stop running?
When will you stop panting after
other gods?
But you say, 'Save your breath.
I'm in love with these foreign gods,
and I can't stop loving them now!'

²⁶ "Israel is like a thief
who feels shame only when he gets
caught.
They, their kings, officials, priests, and
prophets—
all are alike in this.
²⁷ To an image carved from a piece of
wood they say,
'You are my father.'
To an idol chiseled from a block of stone
they say,
'You are my mother.'
They turn their backs on me,
but in times of trouble they cry out
to me,
'Come and save us!'
²⁸ But why not call on these gods you have
made?
When trouble comes, let them save
you if they can!
For you have as many gods
as there are towns in Judah.
²⁹ Why do you accuse me of doing wrong?
You are the ones who have rebelled,"
says the Lord.

³⁰ "I have punished your children,
but they did not respond to my
discipline.
You yourselves have killed your prophets
as a lion kills its prey.

³¹ "O my people, listen to the words of the
Lord!
Have I been like a desert to Israel?
Have I been to them a land of darkness?
Why then do my people say, 'At last we
are free from God!
We don't need him anymore!'
³² Does a young woman forget her jewelry?
Does a bride hide her wedding dress?
Yet for years on end
my people have forgotten me.

³³ "How you plot and scheme to win your
lovers.
Even an experienced prostitute could
learn from you!
³⁴ Your clothing is stained with the blood
of the innocent and the poor,
though you didn't catch them breaking
into your houses!
³⁵ And yet you say,
'I have done nothing wrong.
Surely God isn't angry with me!'
But now I will punish you severely
because you claim you have not
sinned.
³⁶ First here, then there—
you flit from one ally to another asking
for help.
But your new friends in Egypt will let
you down,
just as Assyria did before.
³⁷ In despair, you will be led into exile
with your hands on your heads,
for the Lord has rejected the nations
you trust.
They will not help you at all.

3 ¹ "If a man divorces a woman
and she goes and marries someone
else,
he will not take her back again,
for that would surely corrupt the land.
But you have prostituted yourself with
many lovers,
so why are you trying to come back
to me?"
says the Lord.

2 "Look at the shrines on every hilltop.
  Is there any place you have not been
    defiled
  by your adultery with other gods?
You sit like a prostitute beside the road
    waiting for a customer.
  You sit alone like a nomad in the
    desert.
You have polluted the land with your
    prostitution
  and your wickedness.
3 That's why even the spring rains have
    failed.
  For you are a brazen prostitute and
    completely shameless.
4 Yet you say to me,
  'Father, you have been my guide since
    my youth.
5 Surely you won't be angry forever!
  Surely you can forget about it!'
So you talk,
  but you keep on doing all the evil you
    can."

Judah Follows Israel's Example

6 During the reign of King Josiah, the LORD said to me, "Have you seen what fickle Israel has done? Like a wife who commits adultery, Israel has worshiped other gods on every hill and under every green tree. 7 I thought, 'After she has done all this, she will return to me.' But she did not return, and her faithless sister Judah saw this. 8 She saw that I divorced faithless Israel because of her adultery. But that treacherous sister Judah had no fear, and now she, too, has left me and given herself to prostitution. 9 Israel treated it all so lightly—she thought nothing of committing adultery by worshiping idols made of wood and stone. So now the land has been polluted. 10 But despite all this, her faithless sister Judah has never sincerely returned to me. She has only pretended to be sorry. I, the LORD, have spoken!"

Hope for Wayward Israel

11 Then the LORD said to me, "Even faithless Israel is less guilty than treacherous Judah! 12 Therefore, go and give this message to Israel.* This is what the LORD says:

"O Israel, my faithless people,
  come home to me again,
for I am merciful.
  I will not be angry with you forever.
13 Only acknowledge your guilt.
  Admit that you rebelled against the
    LORD your God
and committed adultery against him
  by worshiping idols under every green
    tree.
Confess that you refused to listen to my
    voice.
  I, the LORD, have spoken!

14 "Return home, you wayward children,"
    says the LORD,
  "for I am your master.
I will bring you back to the land of
    Israel*—
  one from this town and two from that
    family—
  from wherever you are scattered.
15 And I will give you shepherds after my
    own heart,
  who will guide you with knowledge
    and understanding.

16 "And when your land is once more filled with people," says the LORD, "you will no longer wish for 'the good old days' when you possessed the Ark of the LORD's Covenant. You will not miss those days or even remember them, and there will be no need to rebuild the Ark. 17 In that day Jerusalem will be known as 'The Throne of the LORD.' All nations will come there to honor the LORD. They will no longer stubbornly follow their own evil desires. 18 In those days the people of Judah and Israel will return together from exile in the north. They will return to the land I gave their ancestors as an inheritance forever.

19 "I thought to myself,
  'I would love to treat you as my own
    children!'
I wanted nothing more than to give you
    this beautiful land—
  the finest possession in the world.
I looked forward to your calling me
    'Father,'
  and I wanted you never to turn
    from me.

3:12 Hebrew *toward the north.* 3:14 Hebrew *to Zion.*

²⁰ But you have been unfaithful to me, you
people of Israel!
You have been like a faithless wife who
leaves her husband.
I, the Lord, have spoken."

²¹ Voices are heard high on the windswept
mountains,
the weeping and pleading of Israel's
people.
For they have chosen crooked paths
and have forgotten the Lord their God.

²² "My wayward children," says the Lord,
"come back to me, and I will heal your
wayward hearts."

"Yes, we're coming," the people reply,
"for you are the Lord our God.
²³ Our worship of idols on the hills
and our religious orgies on the
mountains
are a delusion.
Only in the Lord our God
will Israel ever find salvation.
²⁴ From childhood we have watched
as everything our ancestors worked
for—
their flocks and herds, their sons and
daughters—
was squandered on a delusion.
²⁵ Let us now lie down in shame
and cover ourselves with dishonor,
for we and our ancestors have sinned
against the Lord our God.
From our childhood to this day
we have never obeyed him."

4 ¹ "O Israel," says the Lord,
"if you wanted to return to me, you
could.
You could throw away your detestable
idols
and stray away no more.
² Then when you swear by my name,
saying,
'As surely as the Lord lives,'
you could do so
with truth, justice, and righteousness.
Then you would be a blessing to the
nations of the world,
and all people would come and praise
my name."

Coming Judgment against Judah

³ This is what the Lord says to the people of
Judah and Jerusalem:

"Plow up the hard ground of your hearts!
Do not waste your good seed among
thorns.
⁴ O people of Judah and Jerusalem,
surrender your pride and power.
Change your hearts before the Lord,*
or my anger will burn like an
unquenchable fire
because of all your sins.

⁵ "Shout to Judah, and broadcast to
Jerusalem!
Tell them to sound the alarm
throughout the land:
'Run for your lives!
Flee to the fortified cities!'
⁶ Raise a signal flag as a warning for
Jerusalem*:
'Flee now! Do not delay!'
For I am bringing terrible destruction
upon you
from the north."

⁷ A lion stalks from its den,
a destroyer of nations.
It has left its lair and is headed your way.
It's going to devastate your land!
Your towns will lie in ruins,
with no one living in them anymore.
⁸ So put on clothes of mourning
and weep with broken hearts,
for the fierce anger of the Lord
is still upon us.

⁹ "In that day," says the Lord,
"the king and the officials will tremble
in fear.
The priests will be struck with horror,
and the prophets will be appalled."

¹⁰ Then I said, "O Sovereign Lord,
the people have been deceived by
what you said,
for you promised peace for Jerusalem.
But the sword is held at their throats!"

¹¹ The time is coming when the Lord will
say
to the people of Jerusalem,
"My dear people, a burning wind is
blowing in from the desert,

4:4 Hebrew *Circumcise yourselves to the Lord, and take away the foreskins of your heart.* **4:6** Hebrew *Zion.*

and it's not a gentle breeze useful for
   winnowing grain.
¹² It is a roaring blast sent by me!
   Now I will pronounce your
      destruction!"

¹³ Our enemy rushes down on us like
      storm clouds!
   His chariots are like whirlwinds.
   His horses are swifter than eagles.
   How terrible it will be, for we are
      doomed!
¹⁴ O Jerusalem, cleanse your heart
   that you may be saved.
   How long will you harbor
   your evil thoughts?
¹⁵ Your destruction has been announced
   from Dan and the hill country of
      Ephraim.

¹⁶ "Warn the surrounding nations
   and announce this to Jerusalem:
   The enemy is coming from a distant
      land,
   raising a battle cry against the towns
      of Judah.
¹⁷ They surround Jerusalem like watchmen
      around a field,
   for my people have rebelled against
      me,"
   says the LORD.
¹⁸ "Your own actions have brought this
      upon you.
   This punishment is bitter, piercing you
      to the heart!"

Jeremiah Weeps for His People

¹⁹ My heart, my heart—I writhe in pain!
   My heart pounds within me! I cannot
      be still.
   For I have heard the blast of enemy
      trumpets
   and the roar of their battle cries.
²⁰ Waves of destruction roll over the land,
      until it lies in complete desolation.
   Suddenly my tents are destroyed;
      in a moment my shelters are
      crushed.
²¹ How long must I see the battle flags
   and hear the trumpets of war?

²² "My people are foolish
   and do not know me," says the LORD.

"They are stupid children
   who have no understanding.
   They are clever enough at doing wrong,
   but they have no idea how to do right!"

Jeremiah's Vision of Coming Disaster

²³ I looked at the earth, and it was empty
      and formless.
   I looked at the heavens, and there was
      no light.
²⁴ I looked at the mountains and hills,
   and they trembled and shook.
²⁵ I looked, and all the people were gone.
   All the birds of the sky had flown
      away.
²⁶ I looked, and the fertile fields had
      become a wilderness.
   The towns lay in ruins,
   crushed by the LORD's fierce anger.

²⁷ This is what the LORD says:
   "The whole land will be ruined,
   but I will not destroy it completely.
²⁸ The earth will mourn
   and the heavens will be draped in
      black
   because of my decree against my people.
   I have made up my mind and will not
      change it."

²⁹ At the noise of charioteers and archers,
   the people flee in terror.
   They hide in the bushes
   and run for the mountains.
   All the towns have been abandoned—
   not a person remains!
³⁰ What are you doing,
   you who have been plundered?
   Why do you dress up in beautiful
      clothing
   and put on gold jewelry?
   Why do you brighten your eyes with
      mascara?
   Your primping will do you no good!
   The allies who were your lovers
   despise you and seek to kill you.

³¹ I hear a cry, like that of a woman in labor,
   the groans of a woman giving birth to
      her first child.
   It is beautiful Jerusalem*
   gasping for breath and crying out,
   "Help! I'm being murdered!"

4:31 Hebrew *the daughter of Zion.*

5 The Sins of Judah

¹ "Run up and down every street in
Jerusalem," says the LORD.
"Look high and low; search
throughout the city!
If you can find even one just and honest
person,
I will not destroy the city.
² But even when they are under oath,
saying, 'As surely as the LORD lives,'
they are still telling lies!"

³ LORD, you are searching for honesty.
You struck your people,
but they paid no attention.
You crushed them,
but they refused to be corrected.
They are determined, with faces set like
stone;
they have refused to repent.

⁴ Then I said, "But what can we expect
from the poor?
They are ignorant.
They don't know the ways of the LORD.
They don't understand God's laws.
⁵ So I will go and speak to their leaders.
Surely they know the ways of the
LORD
and understand God's laws."
But the leaders, too, as one man,
had thrown off God's yoke
and broken his chains.
⁶ So now a lion from the forest will attack
them;
a wolf from the desert will pounce on
them.
A leopard will lurk near their towns,
tearing apart any who dare to venture
out.
For their rebellion is great,
and their sins are many.

⁷ "How can I pardon you?
For even your children have turned
from me.
They have sworn by gods that are not
gods at all!
I fed my people until they were full.
But they thanked me by committing
adultery
and lining up at the brothels.
⁸ They are well-fed, lusty stallions,
each neighing for his neighbor's wife.

⁹ Should I not punish them for this?" says
the LORD.
"Should I not avenge myself against
such a nation?

¹⁰ "Go down the rows of the vineyards and
destroy the grapevines,
leaving a scattered few alive.
Strip the branches from the vines,
for these people do not belong to the
LORD.
¹¹ The people of Israel and Judah
are full of treachery against me,"
says the LORD.
¹² "They have lied about the LORD
and said, 'He won't bother us!
No disasters will come upon us.
There will be no war or famine.
¹³ God's prophets are all windbags
who don't really speak for him.
Let their predictions of disaster fall on
themselves!'"

¹⁴ Therefore, this is what the LORD God of
Heaven's Armies says:

"Because the people are talking like this,
my messages will flame out of your
mouth
and burn the people like kindling
wood.
¹⁵ O Israel, I will bring a distant nation
against you,"
says the LORD.
"It is a mighty nation,
an ancient nation,
a people whose language you do not
know,
whose speech you cannot understand.
¹⁶ Their weapons are deadly;
their warriors are mighty.
¹⁷ They will devour the food of your
harvest;
they will devour your sons and
daughters.
They will devour your flocks and herds;
they will devour your grapes and figs.
And they will destroy your fortified
towns,
which you think are so safe.

¹⁸ "Yet even in those days I will not blot
you out completely," says the LORD. ¹⁹ "And
when your people ask, 'Why did the LORD
our God do all this to us?' you must reply,

'You rejected him and gave yourselves to foreign gods in your own land. Now you will serve foreigners in a land that is not your own.'

A Warning for God's People

20 "Make this announcement to Israel,*
and say this to Judah:

21 Listen, you foolish and senseless people,
with eyes that do not see
and ears that do not hear.

22 Have you no respect for me?
Why don't you tremble in my
presence?
I, the LORD, define the ocean's sandy
shoreline
as an everlasting boundary that the
waters cannot cross.
The waves may toss and roar,
but they can never pass the
boundaries I set.

23 But my people have stubborn and
rebellious hearts.
They have turned away and
abandoned me.

24 They do not say from the heart,
'Let us live in awe of the LORD our God,
for he gives us rain each spring and fall,
assuring us of a harvest when the time
is right.'

25 Your wickedness has deprived you of
these wonderful blessings.
Your sin has robbed you of all these
good things.

26 "Among my people are wicked men
who lie in wait for victims like a
hunter hiding in a blind.
They continually set traps
to catch people.

27 Like a cage filled with birds,
their homes are filled with evil plots.
And now they are great and rich.

28 They are fat and sleek,
and there is no limit to their wicked
deeds.
They refuse to provide justice to orphans
and deny the rights of the poor.

29 Should I not punish them for this?" says
the LORD.
"Should I not avenge myself against
such a nation?

30 A horrible and shocking thing
has happened in this land—

31 the prophets give false prophecies,
and the priests rule with an iron hand.
Worse yet, my people like it that way!
But what will you do when the end
comes?

6 Jerusalem's Last Warning

1 "Run for your lives, you people of
Benjamin!
Get out of Jerusalem!
Sound the alarm in Tekoa!
Send up a signal at Beth-hakkerem!
A powerful army is coming from the
north,
coming with disaster and destruction.

2 O Jerusalem,* you are my beautiful and
delicate daughter—
but I will destroy you!

3 Enemies will surround you, like
shepherds camped around the city.
Each chooses a place for his troops to
devour.

4 They shout, 'Prepare for battle!
Attack at noon!'
'No, it's too late; the day is fading,
and the evening shadows are falling.'

5 'Well then, let's attack at night
and destroy her palaces!'"

6 This is what the LORD of Heaven's
Armies says:
"Cut down the trees for battering rams.
Build siege ramps against the walls of
Jerusalem.
This is the city to be punished,
for she is wicked through and through.

7 She spouts evil like a fountain.
Her streets echo with the sounds of
violence and destruction.
I always see her sickness and sores.

8 Listen to this warning, Jerusalem,
or I will turn from you in disgust.
Listen, or I will turn you into a heap of
ruins,
a land where no one lives."

9 This is what the LORD of Heaven's
Armies says:
"Even the few who remain in Israel
will be picked over again,

5:20 Hebrew to the house of Jacob. The names "Jacob" and "Israel" are often interchanged throughout the Old Testament, referring sometimes to the individual patriarch and sometimes to the nation. 6:2 Hebrew Daughter of Zion.

A Benefit of Obedience

JEREMIAH 6:16

Sabbath & Rest

In our culture, relaxation and freedom are a natural pair. We picture rest as a time to kick back and do *whatever we want*.

But God presents us with an opposite image of rest; in Scripture we see that true rest is tied inextricably to obedience. When Jesus promised his followers, "You will find rest for your souls," his promise was directly connected to a charge, "Let me teach you" (Matthew 11:29). Jesus was reiterating an invitation that God issued to his people through the prophet Jeremiah: "Stop at the crossroads and look around. Ask for the old, godly way, and walk in it. Travel its path, and you will find rest for your souls" (Jeremiah 6:16).

Rest is found not in following our own whims in life. Instead, true rest is found in submitting to God's will, in obeying his direction. It is when we place our trust in God and align ourselves to the "old, godly way" that we find both rest and renewed strength. We are refreshed and empowered to "soar high on wings like eagles," to "run and not grow weary," to "walk and not faint" (Isaiah 40:31).

—*Kelli B. Trujillo*

For more on Sabbath and rest, see reading at Jeremiah 17:19–26.

as when a harvester checks each vine a
  second time
  to pick the grapes that were missed."

Judah's Constant Rebellion

10 To whom can I give warning?
  Who will listen when I speak?
  Their ears are closed,
  and they cannot hear.
  They scorn the word of the LORD.
  They don't want to listen at all.
11 So now I am filled with the LORD's fury.
  Yes, I am tired of holding it in!

"I will pour out my fury on children
  playing in the streets
  and on gatherings of young men,
on husbands and wives
  and on those who are old and gray.
12 Their homes will be turned over to their
  enemies,
  as will their fields and their wives.
For I will raise my powerful fist
  against the people of this land,"
  says the LORD.
13 "From the least to the greatest,
  their lives are ruled by greed.
From prophets to priests,
  they are all frauds.

14 They offer superficial treatments
  for my people's mortal wound.
They give assurances of peace
  when there is no peace.
15 Are they ashamed of their disgusting
  actions?
  Not at all—they don't even know how
  to blush!
  Therefore, they will lie among the
  slaughtered.
  They will be brought down when I
  punish them,"
  says the LORD.

Judah Rejects the LORD's Way

16 This is what the LORD says:
  "Stop at the crossroads and look
  around.
  Ask for the old, godly way, and walk
  in it.
  Travel its path, and you will find rest for
  your souls.
  But you reply, 'No, that's not the road
  we want!'
17 I posted watchmen over you who said,
  'Listen for the sound of the alarm.'
  But you replied,
  'No! We won't pay attention!'

18 "Therefore, listen to this, all you nations.
    Take note of my people's situation.
19 Listen, all the earth!
    I will bring disaster on my people.
    It is the fruit of their own schemes,
      because they refuse to listen to me.
    They have rejected my word.
20 There's no use offering me sweet
      frankincense from Sheba.
    Keep your fragrant calamus imported
      from distant lands!
    I will not accept your burnt offerings.
    Your sacrifices have no pleasing aroma
      for me."

21 Therefore, this is what the LORD says:
    "I will put obstacles in my people's
      path.
    Fathers and sons will both fall over them.
    Neighbors and friends will die
      together."

An Invasion from the North

22 This is what the LORD says:
    "Look! A great army coming from the
      north!
    A great nation is rising against you
      from far-off lands.
23 They are armed with bows and spears.
    They are cruel and show no mercy.
    They sound like a roaring sea
      as they ride forward on horses.
    They are coming in battle formation,
      planning to destroy you, beautiful
      Jerusalem.*"

24 We have heard reports about the enemy,
      and we wring our hands in fright.
    Pangs of anguish have gripped us,
      like those of a woman in labor.
25 Don't go out to the fields!
    Don't travel on the roads!
    The enemy's sword is everywhere
      and terrorizes us at every turn!
26 Oh, my people, dress yourselves in burlap
      and sit among the ashes.
    Mourn and weep bitterly, as for the loss
      of an only son.
    For suddenly the destroying armies
      will be upon you!

27 "Jeremiah, I have made you a tester of
      metals,*

that you may determine the quality of
      my people.
28 They are the worst kind of rebel,
      full of slander.
    They are as hard as bronze and iron,
      and they lead others into corruption.
29 The bellows fiercely fan the flames
      to burn out the corruption.
    But it does not purify them,
      for the wickedness remains.
30 I will label them 'Rejected Silver,'
      for I, the LORD, am discarding them."

7 Jeremiah Speaks at the Temple

The LORD gave another message to Jeremiah. He said, 2 "Go to the entrance of the LORD's Temple, and give this message to the people: 'O Judah, listen to this message from the LORD! Listen to it, all of you who worship here! 3 This is what the LORD of Heaven's Armies, the God of Israel, says:

"'Even now, if you quit your evil ways, I will let you stay in your own land. 4 But don't be fooled by those who promise you safety simply because the LORD's Temple is here. They chant, "The LORD's Temple is here! The LORD's Temple is here!" 5 But I will be merciful only if you stop your evil thoughts and deeds and start treating each other with justice; 6 only if you stop exploiting foreigners, orphans, and widows; only if you stop your murdering; and only if you stop harming yourselves by worshiping idols. 7 Then I will let you stay in this land that I gave to your ancestors to keep forever.

8 "'Don't be fooled into thinking that you will never suffer because the Temple is here. It's a lie! 9 Do you really think you can steal, murder, commit adultery, lie, and burn incense to Baal and all those other new gods of yours, 10 and then come here and stand before me in my Temple and chant, "We are safe!"—only to go right back to all those evils again? 11 Don't you yourselves admit that this Temple, which bears my name, has become a den of thieves? Surely I see all the evil going on there. I, the LORD, have spoken!

12 "'Go now to the place at Shiloh where I once put the Tabernacle that bore my name. See what I did there because of all the wickedness of my people, the Israelites. 13 While

---

6:23 Hebrew *daughter of Zion.*   **6:27** As in Greek version; Hebrew reads *a tester of my people a fortress.*

you were doing these wicked things, says the Lord, I spoke to you about it repeatedly, but you would not listen. I called out to you, but you refused to answer. ¹⁴So just as I destroyed Shiloh, I will now destroy this Temple that bears my name, this Temple that you trust in for help, this place that I gave to you and your ancestors. ¹⁵And I will send you out of my sight into exile, just as I did your relatives, the people of Israel.*'

Judah's Persistent Idolatry

¹⁶"Pray no more for these people, Jeremiah. Do not weep or pray for them, and don't beg me to help them, for I will not listen to you. ¹⁷Don't you see what they are doing throughout the towns of Judah and in the streets of Jerusalem? ¹⁸No wonder I am so angry! Watch how the children gather wood and the fathers build sacrificial fires. See how the women knead dough and make cakes to offer to the Queen of Heaven. And they pour out liquid offerings to their other idol gods! ¹⁹Am I the one they are hurting?" asks the Lord. "Most of all, they hurt themselves, to their own shame."

²⁰So this is what the Sovereign Lord says: "I will pour out my terrible fury on this place. Its people, animals, trees, and crops will be consumed by the unquenchable fire of my anger."

²¹This is what the Lord of Heaven's Armies, the God of Israel, says: "Take your burnt offerings and your other sacrifices and eat them yourselves! ²²When I led your ancestors out of Egypt, it was not burnt offerings and sacrifices I wanted from them. ²³This is what I told them: 'Obey me, and I will be your God, and you will be my people. Do everything as I say, and all will be well!' ²⁴But my people would not listen to me. They kept doing whatever they wanted, following the stubborn desires of their evil hearts. They went backward instead of forward. ²⁵From the day your ancestors left Egypt until now, I have continued to send my servants, the prophets—day in and day out. ²⁶But my people have not listened to me or even tried to hear. They have been stubborn and sinful—even worse than their ancestors. ²⁷"Tell them all this, but do not expect

them to listen. Shout out your warnings, but do not expect them to respond. ²⁸Say to them, 'This is the nation whose people will not obey the Lord their God and who refuse to be taught. Truth has vanished from among them; it is no longer heard on their lips. ²⁹Shave your head in mourning, and weep alone on the mountains. For the Lord has rejected and forsaken this generation that has provoked his fury.'

The Valley of Slaughter

³⁰"The people of Judah have sinned before my very eyes," says the Lord. "They have set up their abominable idols right in the Temple that bears my name, defiling it. ³¹They have built pagan shrines at Topheth, the garbage dump in the valley of Ben-Hinnom, and there they burn their sons and daughters in the fire. I have never commanded such a horrible deed; it never even crossed my mind to command such a thing! ³²So beware, for the time is coming," says the Lord, "when that garbage dump will no longer be called Topheth or the valley of Ben-Hinnom, but the Valley of Slaughter. They will bury the bodies in Topheth until there is no more room for them. ³³The bodies of my people will be food for the vultures and wild animals, and no one will be left to scare them away. ³⁴I will put an end to the happy singing and laughter in the streets of Jerusalem. The joyful voices of bridegrooms and brides will no longer be heard in the towns of Judah. The land will lie in complete desolation.

8 "In that day," says the Lord, "the enemy will break open the graves of the kings and officials of Judah, and the graves of the priests, prophets, and common people of Jerusalem. ²They will spread out their bones on the ground before the sun, moon, and stars—the gods my people have loved, served, and worshiped. Their bones will not be gathered up again or buried but will be scattered on the ground like manure. ³And the people of this evil nation who survive will wish to die rather than live where I will send them. I, the Lord of Heaven's Armies, have spoken!

7:15 Hebrew *of Ephraim*, referring to the northern kingdom of Israel.

Deception by False Prophets

4"Jeremiah, say to the people, 'This is what the LORD says:

"'When people fall down, don't they get up again?

When they discover they're on the wrong road, don't they turn back?
5 Then why do these people stay on their self-destructive path?
Why do the people of Jerusalem refuse to turn back?

Q&A

When Submission Brings Pain

JEREMIAH 7:23

Some Scriptures promise that God will reward obedience. But what about times when submitting to God's will leads to pain and difficulty?

In Jeremiah 7:23 God promises his people, "Obey me, and I will be your God, and you will be my people. Do everything as I say, and all will be well!" This is one of several passages of Scripture that describe the benefits of obedience. When we submit to God, we see him more fully, resulting in holiness and deeper peace. Psalm 103 gives us a taste of submission's benefits: forgiveness, healing, redemption, love, compassion, and satisfaction.

What's not listed among these blessings are ease and comfort. When you obey God by relying on his wisdom and not your own, your way doesn't get easier. Often submission means giving up the need to know *why*. Job's journey, for instance, reminds us simply to let God be God. Job's difficulties resulted in Job saying to God, "I had only heard about you before, but now I have seen you with my own eyes" (Job 42:5). Somehow through all the pain he endured, we can see that submission to God brought Job deeper intimacy with God.

A key aspect of submitting to God is deciding to "agree with him about all things—even those you cannot understand," as François Fénelon put it. Depending on our own understanding of a situation comes more naturally to us (Proverbs 3:5). It's easy to agree with something we understand, but God's ways and thoughts are higher than ours (as the heavens are higher than the earth— Isaiah 55:9). Even when we don't understand what God is doing—and even when the results of submission are pain—we're to trust God and agree with him.

When we submit ourselves to God, we get more of him. We give up something fundamental to who we are and what we ultimately want out of life, but in return we get a deeper love and understanding of our Father. We're able to face even a difficult road ahead with a sense of renewed joy and purpose, because we know that the Lord's love is with those who fear him (Psalm 103:17).

—Beatrice Rusu

For more on submission, see reading at Luke 1:26–38.

They cling tightly to their lies
and will not turn around.
⁶ I listen to their conversations
and don't hear a word of truth.
Is anyone sorry for doing wrong?
Does anyone say, "What a terrible
thing I have done"?
No! All are running down the path of sin
as swiftly as a horse galloping into
battle!
⁷ Even the stork that flies across the sky
knows the time of her migration,
as do the turtledove, the swallow, and
the crane.*
They all return at the proper time each
year.
But not my people!
They do not know the LORD's laws.

⁸ "'How can you say, "We are wise
because we have the word of the
LORD,"
when your teachers have twisted it by
writing lies?
⁹ These wise teachers will fall
into the trap of their own foolishness,
for they have rejected the word of the
LORD.
Are they so wise after all?
¹⁰ I will give their wives to others
and their farms to strangers.
From the least to the greatest,
their lives are ruled by greed.
Yes, even my prophets and priests are
like that.
They are all frauds.
¹¹ They offer superficial treatments
for my people's mortal wound.
They give assurances of peace
when there is no peace.
¹² Are they ashamed of these disgusting
actions?
Not at all—they don't even know how
to blush!
Therefore, they will lie among the
slaughtered.
They will be brought down when I
punish them,
says the LORD.
¹³ I will surely consume them.
There will be no more harvests of figs
and grapes.

Their fruit trees will all die.
Whatever I gave them will soon be
gone.
I, the LORD, have spoken!'

¹⁴ "Then the people will say,
'Why should we wait here to die?
Come, let's go to the fortified towns and
die there.
For the LORD our God has decreed
our destruction
and has given us a cup of poison to drink
because we sinned against the LORD.
¹⁵ We hoped for peace, but no peace came.
We hoped for a time of healing, but
found only terror.'

¹⁶ "The snorting of the enemies' warhorses
can be heard
all the way from the land of Dan in the
north!
The neighing of their stallions makes the
whole land tremble.
They are coming to devour the land
and everything in it—
cities and people alike.
¹⁷ I will send these enemy troops among
you
like poisonous snakes you cannot
charm.
They will bite you, and you will die.
I, the LORD, have spoken!"

Jeremiah Weeps for Sinful Judah

¹⁸ My grief is beyond healing;
my heart is broken.
¹⁹ Listen to the weeping of my people;
it can be heard all across the land.
"Has the LORD abandoned Jerusalem?*"
the people ask.
"Is her King no longer there?"

"Oh, why have they provoked my anger
with their carved idols
and their worthless foreign gods?" says
the LORD.

²⁰ "The harvest is finished,
and the summer is gone," the people
cry,
"yet we are not saved!"

²¹ I hurt with the hurt of my people.
I mourn and am overcome with grief.

8:7 The identification of some of these birds is uncertain.   8:19 Hebrew *Zion?*

²² Is there no medicine in Gilead?
    Is there no physician there?
Why is there no healing
    for the wounds of my people?

9 ¹*If only my head were a pool of water
    and my eyes a fountain of tears,
I would weep day and night
    for all my people who have been
    slaughtered.
²*Oh, that I could go away and forget my
    people
    and live in a travelers' shack in the
    desert.
For they are all adulterers—
    a pack of treacherous liars.

Judgment for Disobedience

³ "My people bend their tongues like bows
    to shoot out lies.
They refuse to stand up for the truth.
    They only go from bad to worse.
They do not know me,"
    says the LORD.

⁴ "Beware of your neighbor!
    Don't even trust your brother!
For brother takes advantage of brother,
    and friend slanders friend.
⁵ They all fool and defraud each other;
    no one tells the truth.
With practiced tongues they tell lies;
    they wear themselves out with all their
    sinning.
⁶ They pile lie upon lie
    and utterly refuse to acknowledge me,"
    says the LORD.

⁷ Therefore, this is what the LORD of
    Heaven's Armies says:
"See, I will melt them down in a
    crucible
    and test them like metal.
What else can I do with my people?*
⁸   For their tongues shoot lies like
    poisoned arrows.
They speak friendly words to their
    neighbors
    while scheming in their heart to kill
    them.
⁹ Should I not punish them for this?" says
    the LORD.

"Should I not avenge myself against
    such a nation?"

¹⁰ I will weep for the mountains
    and wail for the wilderness pastures.
For they are desolate and empty of life;
    the lowing of cattle is heard no more;
    the birds and wild animals have all
    fled.

¹¹ "I will make Jerusalem into a heap of
    ruins," says the LORD.
"It will be a place haunted by jackals.
The towns of Judah will be ghost towns,
    with no one living in them."

¹²Who is wise enough to understand all this? Who has been instructed by the LORD and can explain it to others? Why has the land been so ruined that no one dares to travel through it?

¹³The LORD replies, "This has happened because my people have abandoned my instructions; they have refused to obey what I said. ¹⁴Instead, they have stubbornly followed their own desires and worshiped the images of Baal, as their ancestors taught them. ¹⁵So now, this is what the LORD of Heaven's Armies, the God of Israel, says: Look! I will feed them with bitterness and give them poison to drink. ¹⁶I will scatter them around the world, in places they and their ancestors never heard of, and even there I will chase them with the sword until I have destroyed them completely."

Weeping in Jerusalem

¹⁷ This is what the LORD of Heaven's
    Armies says:
"Consider all this, and call for the
    mourners.
Send for the women who mourn at
    funerals.
¹⁸ Quick! Begin your weeping!
    Let the tears flow from your eyes.
¹⁹ Hear the people of Jerusalem* crying in
    despair,
    'We are ruined! We are completely
    humiliated!
We must leave our land,
    because our homes have been torn
    down.'"

9:1 Verse 9:1 is numbered 8:23 in Hebrew text.   **9:2** Verses 9:2-26 are numbered 9:1-25 in Hebrew text.   **9:7** Hebrew *with the daughter of my people?* Greek version reads *with the evil daughter of my people?*   **9:19** Hebrew *Zion.*

²⁰ Listen, you women, to the words of the
LORD;
    open your ears to what he has to say.
Teach your daughters to wail;
    teach one another how to lament.
²¹ For death has crept in through our
        windows
    and has entered our mansions.
It has killed off the flower of our youth:
    Children no longer play in the streets,
    and young men no longer gather in
        the squares.

²² This is what the LORD says:
"Bodies will be scattered across the fields
    like clumps of manure,
    like bundles of grain after the
        harvest.
No one will be left to bury them."

²³ This is what the LORD says:
"Don't let the wise boast in their
        wisdom,
    or the powerful boast in their power,
    or the rich boast in their riches.
²⁴ But those who wish to boast
    should boast in this alone:
that they truly know me and understand
        that I am the LORD
who demonstrates unfailing love
and who brings justice and
        righteousness to the earth,
and that I delight in these things.
    I, the LORD, have spoken!

²⁵ "A time is coming," says the LORD,
"when I will punish all those who are circumcised in body but not in spirit—²⁶ the
Egyptians, Edomites, Ammonites, Moabites, the people who live in the desert in
remote places,* and yes, even the people of
Judah. And like all these pagan nations, the
people of Israel also have uncircumcised
hearts."

10 Idolatry Brings Destruction
Hear the word that the LORD speaks
to you, O Israel! ² This is what the LORD
says:

"Do not act like the other nations,
    who try to read their future in the
        stars.
Do not be afraid of their predictions,
    even though other nations are terrified
        by them.
³ Their ways are futile and foolish.
    They cut down a tree, and a craftsman
        carves an idol.
⁴ They decorate it with gold and silver
    and then fasten it securely with
        hammer and nails
    so it won't fall over.
⁵ Their gods are like
    helpless scarecrows in a cucumber
        field!
They cannot speak,
    and they need to be carried because
        they cannot walk.
Do not be afraid of such gods,
    for they can neither harm you nor do
        you any good."

⁶ LORD, there is no one like you!
    For you are great, and your name is
        full of power.
⁷ Who would not fear you, O King of
        nations?
    That title belongs to you alone!
Among all the wise people of the earth
    and in all the kingdoms of the world,
    there is no one like you.

⁸ People who worship idols are stupid and
        foolish.
    The things they worship are made of
        wood!
⁹ They bring beaten sheets of silver from
        Tarshish
    and gold from Uphaz,
and they give these materials to skillful
        craftsmen
    who make their idols.
Then they dress these gods in royal blue
        and purple robes
    made by expert tailors.
¹⁰ But the LORD is the only true God.
    He is the living God and the
        everlasting King!
The whole earth trembles at his anger.
    The nations cannot stand up to his
        wrath.

¹¹ Say this to those who worship other
gods: "Your so-called gods, who did not
make the heavens and earth, will vanish

9:26 Or *in the desert and clip the corners of their hair.*

from the earth and from under the heavens."*

¹² But God made the earth by his power,
and he preserves it by his wisdom.
With his own understanding
he stretched out the heavens.
¹³ When he speaks in the thunder,
the heavens roar with rain.
He causes the clouds to rise over the earth.
He sends the lightning with the rain
and releases the wind from his
storehouses.
¹⁴ The whole human race is foolish and has
no knowledge!
The craftsmen are disgraced by the
idols they make,
for their carefully shaped works are a
fraud.
These idols have no breath or power.
¹⁵ Idols are worthless; they are ridiculous
lies!
On the day of reckoning they will all
be destroyed.
¹⁶ But the God of Israel* is no idol!
He is the Creator of everything that
exists,
including Israel, his own special
possession.
The LORD of Heaven's Armies is his
name!

The Coming Destruction

¹⁷ Pack your bags and prepare to leave;
the siege is about to begin.
¹⁸ For this is what the LORD says:
"Suddenly, I will fling out
all you who live in this land.
I will pour great troubles upon you,
and at last you will feel my anger."

¹⁹ My wound is severe,
and my grief is great.
My sickness is incurable,
but I must bear it.
²⁰ My home is gone,
and no one is left to help me rebuild it.
My children have been taken away,
and I will never see them again.
²¹ The shepherds of my people have lost
their senses.

They no longer seek wisdom from the
LORD.
Therefore, they fail completely,
and their flocks are scattered.
²² Listen! Hear the terrifying roar of great
armies
as they roll down from the north.
The towns of Judah will be destroyed
and become a haunt for jackals.

Jeremiah's Prayer

²³ I know, LORD, that our lives are not our
own.
We are not able to plan our own course.
²⁴ So correct me, LORD, but please be
gentle.
Do not correct me in anger, for I
would die.
²⁵ Pour out your wrath on the nations that
refuse to acknowledge you—
on the peoples that do not call upon
your name.
For they have devoured your people
Israel*;
they have devoured and consumed
them,
making the land a desolate wilderness.

11 Judah's Broken Covenant

The LORD gave another message to
Jeremiah. He said, ²"Remind the people
of Judah and Jerusalem about the terms
of my covenant with them. ³Say to them,
'This is what the LORD, the God of Israel,
says: Cursed is anyone who does not obey
the terms of my covenant! ⁴For I said to
your ancestors when I brought them out
of the iron-smelting furnace of Egypt, "If
you obey me and do whatever I command
you, then you will be my people, and I will
be your God." ⁵I said this so I could keep
my promise to your ancestors to give you
a land flowing with milk and honey—the
land you live in today.'"

Then I replied, "Amen, LORD! May it be
so."

⁶Then the LORD said, "Broadcast this
message in the streets of Jerusalem. Go
from town to town throughout the land and
say, 'Remember the ancient covenant, and

10:11 The original text of this verse is in Aramaic.　**10:16** Hebrew *the Portion of Jacob.* See note on 5:20.　**10:25** Hebrew *devoured Jacob.* See note on 5:20.

do everything it requires. ⁷For I solemnly warned your ancestors when I brought them out of Egypt, "Obey me!" I have repeated this warning over and over to this day, ⁸but your ancestors did not listen or even pay attention. Instead, they stubbornly followed their own evil desires. And because they refused to obey, I brought upon them all the curses described in this covenant.'"

⁹Again the LORD spoke to me and said, "I have discovered a conspiracy against me among the people of Judah and Jerusalem. ¹⁰They have returned to the sins of their forefathers. They have refused to listen to me and are worshiping other gods. Israel and Judah have both broken the covenant I made with their ancestors. ¹¹Therefore, this is what the LORD says: I am going to bring calamity upon them, and they will not escape. Though they beg for mercy, I will not listen to their cries. ¹²Then the people of Judah and Jerusalem will pray to their idols and burn incense before them. But the idols will not save them when disaster strikes! ¹³Look now, people of Judah; you have as many gods as you have towns. You have as many altars of shame—altars for burning incense to your god Baal—as there are streets in Jerusalem.

¹⁴"Pray no more for these people, Jeremiah. Do not weep or pray for them, for I will not listen to them when they cry out to me in distress.

¹⁵ "What right do my beloved people have
to come to my Temple,
when they have done so many
immoral things?
Can their vows and sacrifices prevent
their destruction?
They actually rejoice in doing evil!
¹⁶ I, the LORD, once called them a thriving
olive tree,
beautiful to see and full of good fruit.
But now I have sent the fury of their
enemies
to burn them with fire,
leaving them charred and broken.

¹⁷"I, the LORD of Heaven's Armies, who planted this olive tree, have ordered it destroyed. For the people of Israel and Judah have done evil, arousing my anger by burning incense to Baal."

A Plot against Jeremiah

¹⁸Then the LORD told me about the plots my enemies were making against me. ¹⁹I was like a lamb being led to the slaughter. I had no idea that they were planning to kill me! "Let's destroy this man and all his words," they said. "Let's cut him down, so his name will be forgotten forever."

²⁰ O LORD of Heaven's Armies,
you make righteous judgments,
and you examine the deepest thoughts
and secrets.
Let me see your vengeance against them,
for I have committed my cause to you.

²¹This is what the LORD says about the men of Anathoth who wanted me dead. They had said, "We will kill you if you do not stop prophesying in the LORD's name." ²²So this is what the LORD of Heaven's Armies says about them: "I will punish them! Their young men will die in battle, and their boys and girls will starve to death. ²³Not one of these plotters from Anathoth will survive, for I will bring disaster upon them when their time of punishment comes."

12 Jeremiah Questions the LORD's Justice

¹ LORD, you always give me justice
when I bring a case before you.
So let me bring you this complaint:
Why are the wicked so prosperous?
Why are evil people so happy?
² You have planted them,
and they have taken root and
prospered.
Your name is on their lips,
but you are far from their hearts.
³ But as for me, LORD, you know my
heart.
You see me and test my thoughts.
Drag these people away like sheep to be
butchered!
Set them aside to be
slaughtered!

⁴ How long must this land mourn?
Even the grass in the fields has
withered.
The wild animals and birds have
disappeared
because of the evil in the land.

For the people have said,
"The LORD doesn't see what's ahead
for us!"

The LORD's Reply to Jeremiah

[5] "If racing against mere men makes you
tired,
how will you race against horses?
If you stumble and fall on open ground,
what will you do in the thickets near
the Jordan?
[6] Even your brothers, members of your
own family,
have turned against you.
They plot and raise complaints against
you.
Do not trust them,
no matter how pleasantly they speak.

[7] "I have abandoned my people, my
special possession.
I have surrendered my dearest ones to
their enemies.
[8] My chosen people have roared at me like
a lion of the forest,
so I have treated them with contempt.
[9] My chosen people act like speckled
vultures,*
but they themselves are surrounded
by vultures.
Bring on the wild animals to pick their
corpses clean!

[10] "Many rulers have ravaged my vineyard,
trampling down the vines
and turning all its beauty into a barren
wilderness.
[11] They have made it an empty wasteland;
I hear its mournful cry.
The whole land is desolate,
and no one even cares.
[12] On all the bare hilltops,
destroying armies can be seen.
The sword of the LORD devours people
from one end of the nation to the other.
No one will escape!
[13] My people have planted wheat
but are harvesting thorns.
They have worn themselves out,
but it has done them no good.
They will harvest a crop of shame
because of the fierce anger of the
LORD."

A Message for Israel's Neighbors

[14] Now this is what the LORD says: "I will
uproot from their land all the evil nations
reaching out for the possession I gave my
people Israel. And I will uproot Judah from
among them. [15] But afterward I will return
and have compassion on all of them. I will
bring them home to their own lands again,
each nation to its own possession. [16] And
if these nations truly learn the ways of my
people, and if they learn to swear by my
name, saying, 'As surely as the LORD lives'
(just as they taught my people to swear by
the name of Baal), then they will be given a
place among my people. [17] But any nation
who refuses to obey me will be uprooted
and destroyed. I, the LORD, have spoken!"

13 Jeremiah's Linen Loincloth

This is what the LORD said to me: "Go
and buy a linen loincloth and put it on, but
do not wash it." [2] So I bought the loincloth
as the LORD directed me, and I put it on.

[3] Then the LORD gave me another mes-
sage: [4] "Take the linen loincloth you are
wearing, and go to the Euphrates River.*
Hide it there in a hole in the rocks." [5] So
I went and hid it by the Euphrates as the
LORD had instructed me.

[6] A long time afterward the LORD said
to me, "Go back to the Euphrates and get
the loincloth I told you to hide there." [7] So I
went to the Euphrates and dug it out of the
hole where I had hidden it. But now it was
rotting and falling apart. The loincloth was
good for nothing.

[8] Then I received this message from the
LORD: [9] "This is what the LORD says: This
shows how I will rot away the pride of
Judah and Jerusalem. [10] These wicked people refuse to listen to me. They stubbornly
follow their own desires and worship other
gods. Therefore, they will become like
this loincloth—good for nothing! [11] As a
loincloth clings to a man's waist, so I created Judah and Israel to cling to me, says
the LORD. They were to be my people, my
pride, my glory—an honor to my name. But
they would not listen to me.

[12] "So tell them, 'This is what the LORD,
the God of Israel, says: May all your jars be

12:9 Or *speckled hyenas.*   **13:4** Hebrew *Perath;* also in 13:5, 6, 7.

filled with wine.' And they will reply, 'Of course! Jars are made to be filled with wine!'

¹³ "Then tell them, 'No, this is what the LORD means: I will fill everyone in this land with drunkenness—from the king sitting on David's throne to the priests and the prophets, right down to the common people of Jerusalem. ¹⁴ I will smash them against each other, even parents against children, says the LORD. I will not let my pity or mercy or compassion keep me from destroying them.'"

A Warning against Pride

¹⁵ Listen and pay attention!
Do not be arrogant, for the LORD has spoken.
¹⁶ Give glory to the LORD your God before it is too late.
Acknowledge him before he brings darkness upon you,
causing you to stumble and fall on the darkening mountains.
For then, when you look for light, you will find only terrible darkness and gloom.
¹⁷ And if you still refuse to listen, I will weep alone because of your pride.
My eyes will overflow with tears, because the LORD's flock will be led away into exile.

¹⁸ Say to the king and his mother,
"Come down from your thrones and sit in the dust,
for your glorious crowns will soon be snatched from your heads."
¹⁹ The towns of the Negev will close their gates,
and no one will be able to open them.
The people of Judah will be taken away as captives.
All will be carried into exile.

²⁰ Open up your eyes and see the armies marching down from the north!
Where is your flock—
your beautiful flock—
that he gave you to care for?

²¹ What will you say when the LORD takes the allies you have cultivated
and appoints them as your rulers?
Pangs of anguish will grip you,
like those of a woman in labor!
²² You may ask yourself,
"Why is all this happening to me?"
It is because of your many sins!
That is why you have been stripped
and raped by invading armies.
²³ Can an Ethiopian* change the color of his skin?
Can a leopard take away its spots?
Neither can you start doing good,
for you have always done evil.

²⁴ "I will scatter you like chaff
that is blown away by the desert winds.
²⁵ This is your allotment,
the portion I have assigned to you,"
says the LORD,
"for you have forgotten me,
putting your trust in false gods.
²⁶ I myself will strip you
and expose you to shame.
²⁷ I have seen your adultery and lust,
and your disgusting idol worship out in the fields and on the hills.
What sorrow awaits you, Jerusalem!
How long before you are pure?"

14 Judah's Terrible Drought

This message came to Jeremiah from the LORD, explaining why he was holding back the rain:

² "Judah wilts;
commerce at the city gates grinds to a halt.
All the people sit on the ground in mourning,
and a great cry rises from Jerusalem.
³ The nobles send servants to get water,
but all the wells are dry.
The servants return with empty pitchers, confused and desperate,
covering their heads in grief.
⁴ The ground is parched
and cracked for lack of rain.
The farmers are deeply troubled;
they, too, cover their heads.

13:23 Hebrew *a Cushite.*

⁵ Even the doe abandons her newborn
    fawn
  because there is no grass in the field.
⁶ The wild donkeys stand on the bare hills
    panting like thirsty jackals.
  They strain their eyes looking for grass,
    but there is none to be found."

⁷ The people say, "Our wickedness has
    caught up with us, LORD,
  but help us for the sake of your own
    reputation.
  We have turned away from you
    and sinned against you again and
    again.
⁸ O Hope of Israel, our Savior in times of
    trouble,
  why are you like a stranger to us?
  Why are you like a traveler passing
    through the land,
  stopping only for the night?
⁹ Are you also confused?
  Is our champion helpless to save us?
  You are right here among us, LORD.
  We are known as your people.
  Please don't abandon us now!"

¹⁰ So this is what the LORD says to his
    people:
  "You love to wander far from me
    and do not restrain yourselves.
  Therefore, I will no longer accept you as
    my people.
  Now I will remember all your
    wickedness
    and will punish you for your sins."

The LORD Forbids Jeremiah to Intercede

¹¹ Then the LORD said to me, "Do not pray
for these people anymore. ¹² When they fast,
I will pay no attention. When they present
their burnt offerings and grain offerings to
me, I will not accept them. Instead, I will
devour them with war, famine, and disease."

¹³ Then I said, "O Sovereign LORD, their
prophets are telling them, 'All is well—no
war or famine will come. The LORD will
surely send you peace.'"

¹⁴ Then the LORD said, "These prophets are telling lies in my name. I did not
send them or tell them to speak. I did not
give them any messages. They prophesy

of visions and revelations they have never
seen or heard. They speak foolishness made
up in their own lying hearts. ¹⁵ Therefore,
this is what the LORD says: I will punish
these lying prophets, for they have spoken in my name even though I never sent
them. They say that no war or famine will
come, but they themselves will die by war
and famine! ¹⁶ As for the people to whom
they prophesy—their bodies will be thrown
out into the streets of Jerusalem, victims of
famine and war. There will be no one left
to bury them. Husbands, wives, sons, and
daughters—all will be gone. For I will pour
out their own wickedness on them. ¹⁷ Now,
Jeremiah, say this to them:

"Night and day my eyes overflow with
    tears.
  I cannot stop weeping,
  for my virgin daughter—my precious
    people—
    has been struck down
    and lies mortally wounded.
¹⁸ If I go out into the fields,
  I see the bodies of people slaughtered
    by the enemy.
  If I walk the city streets,
  I see people who have died of
    starvation.
  The prophets and priests continue with
    their work,
    but they don't know what they're
    doing."

A Prayer for Healing

¹⁹ LORD, have you completely rejected
    Judah?
  Do you really hate Jerusalem?*
  Why have you wounded us past all hope
    of healing?
  We hoped for peace, but no peace
    came.
  We hoped for a time of healing, but
    found only terror.
²⁰ LORD, we confess our wickedness
    and that of our ancestors, too.
  We all have sinned against you.
²¹ For the sake of your reputation, LORD,
    do not abandon us.
  Do not disgrace your own glorious
    throne.

14:19 Hebrew *Zion?*

Please remember us,
    and do not break your covenant
        with us.

²² Can any of the worthless foreign gods
        send us rain?
    Does it fall from the sky by itself?
    No, you are the one, O LORD our God!
    Only you can do such things.
    So we will wait for you to help us.

15 Judah's Inevitable Doom

Then the LORD said to me, "Even if Moses and Samuel stood before me pleading for these people, I wouldn't help them. Away with them! Get them out of my sight! ²And if they say to you, 'But where can we go?' tell them, 'This is what the LORD says:

"'Those who are destined for death, to death;
    those who are destined for war, to war;
    those who are destined for famine, to famine;
    those who are destined for captivity, to captivity.'

³"I will send four kinds of destroyers against them," says the LORD. "I will send the sword to kill, the dogs to drag away, the vultures to devour, and the wild animals to finish up what is left. ⁴Because of the wicked things Manasseh son of Hezekiah, king of Judah, did in Jerusalem, I will make my people an object of horror to all the kingdoms of the earth.

⁵ "Who will feel sorry for you, Jerusalem?
    Who will weep for you?
    Who will even bother to ask how you are?
⁶ You have abandoned me
    and turned your back on me,"
    says the LORD.
"Therefore, I will raise my fist to destroy you.
    I am tired of always giving you another chance.
⁷ I will winnow you like grain at the gates of your cities
    and take away the children you hold dear.
    I will destroy my own people,

because they refuse to change their evil ways.
⁸ There will be more widows
    than the grains of sand on the seashore.
    At noontime I will bring a destroyer
    against the mothers of young men.
    I will cause anguish and terror
        to come upon them suddenly.
⁹ The mother of seven grows faint and
        gasps for breath;
    her sun has gone down while it is still day.
    She sits childless now,
        disgraced and humiliated.
    And I will hand over those who are left
        to be killed by the enemy.
    I, the LORD, have spoken!"

Jeremiah's Complaint

¹⁰Then I said,

"What sorrow is mine, my mother.
    Oh, that I had died at birth!
    I am hated everywhere I go.
    I am neither a lender who threatens to foreclose
    nor a borrower who refuses to pay—
    yet they all curse me."

¹¹The LORD replied,

"I will take care of you, Jeremiah.
    Your enemies will ask you to plead on their behalf
    in times of trouble and distress.
¹² Can a man break a bar of iron from the north,
    or a bar of bronze?
¹³ At no cost to them,
    I will hand over your wealth and treasures
    as plunder to your enemies,
    for sin runs rampant in your land.
¹⁴ I will tell your enemies to take you
    as captives to a foreign land.
    For my anger blazes like a fire
    that will burn forever.*"

¹⁵Then I said,

"LORD, you know what's happening to me.
    Please step in and help me. Punish my persecutors!

15:14 As in some Hebrew manuscripts (see also 17:4); most Hebrew manuscripts read *will burn against you.*

Learning from Hermits

Solitude

JEREMIAH 15:10-21

I once thought of hermits as shaggy recluses notable mainly for their self-obsession and dearth of social skills. But as I've learned more about hermits, I've come to be challenged and inspired by their practice. For example, Saint Anthony of Egypt, the famous Desert Father, chose the hermitic life in deliberate contrast to his upper-crust upbringing. After twenty years of not seeing another human face, Anthony emerged healthy, balanced, and full of sage advice.

Solitude rips off all masks and breaks needless dependence on material goods. Henry David Thoreau, who perfected a peculiarly American blend of asceticism, love of nature, and self-reliance, insisted in *Walden*, "I never found the companion that was so companionable as solitude."

It surprises me that, amid the moral upheaval of our culture, the church has not responded again with a great movement toward solitude. Elijah, Moses, and Jacob met God alone. The apostle Paul, John the Baptist, and Jesus himself escaped to the wilderness for spiritual nourishment. What might happen, in the church and in our very souls, if every Christian took a two-hour nature walk each weekend, without speaking? Or if we observed a day of being alone? How might we better learn to love God and humanity?

—*Philip Yancey*

For more on solitude, see reading at Lamentations 3:22-28.

Please give me time; don't let me die
    young.
  It's for your sake that I am suffering.
¹⁶ When I discovered your words, I
    devoured them.
  They are my joy and my heart's
    delight,
for I bear your name,
  O Lord God of Heaven's Armies.
¹⁷ I never joined the people in their merry
    feasts.
  I sat alone because your hand was
    on me.
  I was filled with indignation at their
    sins.
¹⁸ Why then does my suffering
    continue?
  Why is my wound so incurable?
Your help seems as uncertain as a
    seasonal brook,
  like a spring that has gone dry."

¹⁹ This is how the Lord responds:

"If you return to me, I will restore you
  so you can continue to serve me.

If you speak good words rather than
    worthless ones,
  you will be my spokesman.
You must influence them;
  do not let them influence you!
²⁰ They will fight against you like an
    attacking army,
  but I will make you as secure as a
    fortified wall of bronze.
They will not conquer you,
  for I am with you to protect and
    rescue you.
I, the Lord, have spoken!
²¹ Yes, I will certainly keep you safe from
    these wicked men.
  I will rescue you from their cruel
    hands."

16 Jeremiah Forbidden to Marry

The Lord gave me another message. He said, ²"Do not get married or have children in this place. ³For this is what the Lord says about the children born here in this city and about their mothers and fathers: ⁴They will die from terrible diseases. No one will mourn for them or bury them, and they will lie scattered on the ground like manure. They will die from war and famine, and their bodies will be food for the vultures and wild animals."

Judah's Coming Punishment

⁵This is what the LORD says: "Do not go to funerals to mourn and show sympathy for these people, for I have removed my protection and peace from them. I have taken away my unfailing love and my mercy. ⁶Both the great and the lowly will die in this land. No one will bury them or mourn for them. Their friends will not cut themselves in sorrow or shave their heads in sadness. ⁷No one will offer a meal to comfort those who mourn for the dead—not even at the death of a mother or father. No one will send a cup of wine to console them.

⁸"And do not go to their feasts and parties. Do not eat and drink with them at all. ⁹For this is what the LORD of Heaven's Armies, the God of Israel, says: In your own lifetime, before your very eyes, I will put an end to the happy singing and laughter in this land. The joyful voices of bridegrooms and brides will no longer be heard.

¹⁰"When you tell the people all these things, they will ask, 'Why has the LORD decreed such terrible things against us? What have we done to deserve such treatment? What is our sin against the LORD our God?'

¹¹"Then you will give them the LORD's reply: 'It is because your ancestors were unfaithful to me. They worshiped other gods and served them. They abandoned me and did not obey my word. ¹²And you are even worse than your ancestors! You stubbornly follow your own evil desires and refuse to listen to me. ¹³So I will throw you out of this land and send you into a foreign land where you and your ancestors have never been. There you can worship idols day and night—and I will grant you no favors!'

Hope despite the Disaster

¹⁴"But the time is coming," says the LORD, "when people who are taking an oath will no longer say, 'As surely as the LORD lives, who rescued the people of Israel from the land of Egypt.' ¹⁵Instead, they will say, 'As surely as the LORD lives, who brought the people of Israel back to their own land from the land of the north and from all the countries to which he had exiled them.' For I will bring them back to this land that I gave their ancestors.

¹⁶"But now I am sending for many fishermen who will catch them," says the LORD. "I am sending for hunters who will hunt them down in the mountains, hills, and caves. ¹⁷I am watching them closely, and I see every sin. They cannot hope to hide from me. ¹⁸I will double their punishment for all their sins, because they have defiled my land with lifeless images of their detestable gods and have filled my territory with their evil deeds."

Jeremiah's Prayer of Confidence

¹⁹ LORD, you are my strength and fortress,
　　my refuge in the day of trouble!
Nations from around the world
　　will come to you and say,
"Our ancestors left us a foolish heritage,
　　for they worshiped worthless idols.
²⁰ Can people make their own gods?
　　These are not real gods at all!"

²¹ The LORD says,
"Now I will show them my power;
　　now I will show them my might.
At last they will know and understand
　　that I am the LORD.

17 Judah's Sin and Punishment

¹ "The sin of Judah
　　is inscribed with an iron chisel—
engraved with a diamond point on their
　　stony hearts
　　and on the corners of their altars.
² Even their children go to worship
　　at their pagan altars and Asherah
　　　poles,
　　beneath every green tree
　　and on every high hill.
³ So I will hand over my holy
　　　mountain—
　　along with all your wealth and
　　　treasures
　　and your pagan shrines—
as plunder to your enemies,
　　for sin runs rampant in your land.

⁴ The wonderful possession I have
reserved for you
will slip from your hands.
I will tell your enemies to take you
as captives to a foreign land.
For my anger blazes like a fire
that will burn forever.”

Wisdom from the LORD

⁵ This is what the LORD says:
“Cursed are those who put their trust in
mere humans,
who rely on human strength
and turn their hearts away from the
LORD.
⁶ They are like stunted shrubs in the
desert,
with no hope for the future.
They will live in the barren wilderness,
in an uninhabited salty land.

⁷ “But blessed are those who trust in the
LORD
and have made the LORD their hope
and confidence.
⁸ They are like trees planted along a
riverbank,
with roots that reach deep into the
water.
Such trees are not bothered by the heat
or worried by long months of drought.
Their leaves stay green,
and they never stop producing fruit.

⁹ “The human heart is the most deceitful
of all things,
and desperately wicked.
Who really knows how bad it is?
¹⁰ But I, the LORD, search all hearts
and examine secret motives.
I give all people their due rewards,
according to what their actions
deserve.”

Jeremiah's Trust in the LORD

¹¹ Like a partridge that hatches eggs she
has not laid,
so are those who get their wealth by
unjust means.
At midlife they will lose their riches;
in the end, they will become poor old
fools.
¹² But we worship at your throne—
eternal, high, and glorious!

¹³ O LORD, the hope of Israel,
all who turn away from you will be
disgraced.
They will be buried in the dust of the
earth,
for they have abandoned the LORD,
the fountain of living water.

¹⁴ O LORD, if you heal me, I will be truly
healed;
if you save me, I will be truly saved.
My praises are for you alone!
¹⁵ People scoff at me and say,
“What is this ‘message from the LORD’
you talk about?
Why don't your predictions come
true?”
¹⁶ LORD, I have not abandoned my job
as a shepherd for your people.
I have not urged you to send disaster.
You have heard everything I've said.
¹⁷ LORD, don't terrorize me!
You alone are my hope in the day of
disaster.
¹⁸ Bring shame and dismay on all who
persecute me,
but don't let me experience shame and
dismay.
Bring a day of terror on them.
Yes, bring double destruction upon
them!

Observing the Sabbath

¹⁹ This is what the LORD said to me: “Go and
stand in the gates of Jerusalem, first in the
gate where the king goes in and out, and
then in each of the other gates. ²⁰ Say to all
the people, ‘Listen to this message from the
LORD, you kings of Judah and all you people of Judah and everyone living in Jerusalem. ²¹ This is what the LORD says: Listen to
my warning! Stop carrying on your trade at
Jerusalem's gates on the Sabbath day. ²² Do
not do your work on the Sabbath, but make
it a holy day. I gave this command to your
ancestors, ²³ but they did not listen or obey.
They stubbornly refused to pay attention or
accept my discipline.
²⁴ “‘But if you obey me, says the LORD,
and do not carry on your trade at the gates
or work on the Sabbath day, and if you keep
it holy, ²⁵ then kings and their officials will
go in and out of these gates forever. There

will always be a descendant of David sitting on the throne here in Jerusalem. Kings and their officials will always ride in and out among the people of Judah in chariots and on horses, and this city will remain forever. [26] And from all around Jerusalem, from the towns of Judah and Benjamin, from the western foothills* and the hill country and the Negev, the people will come with their

burnt offerings and sacrifices. They will bring their grain offerings, frankincense, and thanksgiving offerings to the LORD's Temple.

[27] "But if you do not listen to me and refuse to keep the Sabbath holy, and if on the Sabbath day you bring loads of merchandise through the gates of Jerusalem just as on other days, then I will set fire to

Q&A | Navigating Sabbath and Responsibilities
Sabbath & Rest
JEREMIAH 17:19-26

How can I navigate my commitment to family and other responsibilities with my desire to honor the Sabbath?

During a particularly busy time in my life, I was injured in an accident. I was riding my bike and was hit by a van. Though I was seriously bruised and emotionally traumatized, I still continued to live at a harried pace. One of my best friends challenged me: "Ruth, you know you really could take a break. You *did* just get run over by a car." She helped me realize a profound truth about my lifestyle: I could even get run over by a truck, and I still wasn't willing to stop and rest!

God brought Sabbath keeping to mind, but I didn't want to open the inevitable can of worms I knew I'd face if I really grappled with it. *How would we deal with my daughter's soccer games? My husband's work? My overbusy life?* I couldn't imagine a day where I just rested—in which I simply delighted in God's good gifts to me. But I sensed God saying, *Yes, you can. Let's work on it together.*

How my family and I keep the Sabbath continues to be a work in progress. But as I make it a priority to focus my Sundays on rest and time with God, I've realized that this is the rhythm God intended for his people. In the Old Testament God directed his people to work for six days and then rest on the seventh—in a sense, it was a way of giving the seventh day back to God like a tithe of one's time. Later in the New Testament Jesus taught his disciples to rest even from the good work of ministry. God knows that even our most noble passions—even good work done in his name—can wear us out. Left to ourselves, we would never know when to stop.

—*Ruth Haley Barton*

For more on Sabbath and rest, see reading at Ezekiel 20:1-20.

these gates. The fire will spread to the palaces, and no one will be able to put out the roaring flames.'"

18 The Potter and the Clay

The LORD gave another message to Jeremiah. He said, ²"Go down to the potter's shop, and I will speak to you there." ³So I did as he told me and found the potter working at his wheel. ⁴But the jar he was making did not turn out as he had hoped, so he crushed it into a lump of clay again and started over.

⁵Then the LORD gave me this message: ⁶"O Israel, can I not do to you as this potter has done to his clay? As the clay is in the potter's hand, so are you in my hand. ⁷If I announce that a certain nation or kingdom is to be uprooted, torn down, and destroyed, ⁸but then that nation renounces its evil ways, I will not destroy it as I had planned. ⁹And if I announce that I will plant and build up a certain nation or kingdom, ¹⁰but then that nation turns to evil and refuses to obey me, I will not bless it as I said I would.

¹¹"Therefore, Jeremiah, go and warn all Judah and Jerusalem. Say to them, 'This is what the LORD says: I am planning disaster for you instead of good. So turn from your evil ways, each of you, and do what is right.'"

¹²But the people replied, "Don't waste your breath. We will continue to live as we want to, stubbornly following our own evil desires."

¹³So this is what the LORD says:

"Has anyone ever heard of such a thing,
    even among the pagan nations?
My virgin daughter Israel
    has done something terrible!
¹⁴ Does the snow ever disappear from the
        mountaintops of Lebanon?
    Do the cold streams flowing from
        those distant mountains ever run
        dry?
¹⁵ But my people are not so reliable, for
        they have deserted me;
    they burn incense to worthless idols.
They have stumbled off the ancient
        highways
    and walk in muddy paths.

¹⁶ Therefore, their land will become
        desolate,
    a monument to their stupidity.
All who pass by will be astonished
    and will shake their heads in
        amazement.
¹⁷ I will scatter my people before their
        enemies
    as the east wind scatters dust.
And in all their trouble I will turn my
        back on them
    and refuse to notice their distress."

A Plot against Jeremiah

¹⁸Then the people said, "Come on, let's plot a way to stop Jeremiah. We have plenty of priests and wise men and prophets. We don't need him to teach the word and give us advice and prophecies. Let's spread rumors about him and ignore what he says."

¹⁹ LORD, hear me and help me!
    Listen to what my enemies are saying.
²⁰ Should they repay evil for good?
    They have dug a pit to kill me,
though I pleaded for them
    and tried to protect them from your
        anger.
²¹ So let their children starve!
    Let them die by the sword!
Let their wives become childless
        widows.
    Let their old men die in a plague,
    and let their young men be killed in
        battle!
²² Let screaming be heard from their
        homes
    as warriors come suddenly upon them.
For they have dug a pit for me
    and have hidden traps along my path.
²³ LORD, you know all about their
        murderous plots against me.
    Don't forgive their crimes and blot out
        their sins.
Let them die before you.
    Deal with them in your anger.

19 Jeremiah's Shattered Jar

This is what the LORD said to me: "Go and buy a clay jar. Then ask some of the leaders of the people and of the priests to follow you. ²Go out through the Gate of Broken Pots to the garbage dump in the valley of

Ben-Hinnom, and give them this message. ³Say to them, 'Listen to this message from the LORD, you kings of Judah and citizens of Jerusalem! This is what the LORD of Heaven's Armies, the God of Israel, says: I will bring a terrible disaster on this place, and the ears of those who hear about it will ring!

⁴"For Israel has forsaken me and turned this valley into a place of wickedness. The people burn incense to foreign gods—idols never before acknowledged by this generation, by their ancestors, or by the kings of Judah. And they have filled this place with the blood of innocent children. ⁵They have built pagan shrines to Baal, and there they burn their sons as sacrifices to Baal. I have never commanded such a horrible deed; it never even crossed my mind to command such a thing! ⁶So beware, for the time is coming, says the LORD, when this garbage dump will no longer be called Topheth or the valley of Ben-Hinnom, but the Valley of Slaughter.

⁷"For I will upset the careful plans of Judah and Jerusalem. I will allow the people to be slaughtered by invading armies, and I will leave their dead bodies as food for the vultures and wild animals. ⁸I will reduce Jerusalem to ruins, making it a monument to their stupidity. All who pass by will be astonished and will gasp at the destruction they see there. ⁹I will see to it that your enemies lay siege to the city until all the food is gone. Then those trapped inside will eat their own sons and daughters and friends. They will be driven to utter despair.'

¹⁰"As these men watch you, Jeremiah, smash the jar you brought. ¹¹Then say to them, 'This is what the LORD of Heaven's Armies says: As this jar lies shattered, so I will shatter the people of Judah and Jerusalem beyond all hope of repair. They will bury the bodies here in Topheth, the garbage dump, until there is no more room for them. ¹²This is what I will do to this place and its people, says the LORD. I will cause this city to become defiled like Topheth. ¹³Yes, all the houses in Jerusalem, including the palace of Judah's kings, will become like Topheth—all the houses where you burned incense on the rooftops to your star gods,

and where liquid offerings were poured out to your idols.'"

¹⁴Then Jeremiah returned from Topheth, the garbage dump where he had delivered this message, and he stopped in front of the Temple of the LORD. He said to the people there, ¹⁵"This is what the LORD of Heaven's Armies, the God of Israel, says: 'I will bring disaster upon this city and its surrounding towns as I promised, because you have stubbornly refused to listen to me.'"

20 Jeremiah and Pashhur

Now Pashhur son of Immer, the priest in charge of the Temple of the LORD, heard what Jeremiah was prophesying. ²So he arrested Jeremiah the prophet and had him whipped and put in stocks at the Benjamin Gate of the LORD's Temple.

³The next day, when Pashhur finally released him, Jeremiah said, "Pashhur, the LORD has changed your name. From now on you are to be called 'The Man Who Lives in Terror.'* ⁴For this is what the LORD says: 'I will send terror upon you and all your friends, and you will watch as they are slaughtered by the swords of the enemy. I will hand the people of Judah over to the king of Babylon. He will take them captive to Babylon or run them through with the sword. ⁵And I will let your enemies plunder Jerusalem. All the famed treasures of the city—the precious jewels and gold and silver of your kings—will be carried off to Babylon. ⁶As for you, Pashhur, you and all your household will go as captives to Babylon. There you will die and be buried, you and all your friends to whom you prophesied that everything would be all right.'"

Jeremiah's Complaint

⁷ O LORD, you misled me,
and I allowed myself to be misled.
You are stronger than I am,
and you overpowered me.
Now I am mocked every day;
everyone laughs at me.
⁸ When I speak, the words burst out.
"Violence and destruction!" I shout.
So these messages from the LORD
have made me a household joke.

20:3 Hebrew *Magor-missabib*, which means "surrounded by terror"; also in 20:10.

⁹ But if I say I'll never mention the Lord
or speak in his name,
his word burns in my heart like a fire.
It's like a fire in my bones!
I am worn out trying to hold it in!
I can't do it!
¹⁰ I have heard the many rumors
about me.
They call me "The Man Who Lives in
Terror."
They threaten, "If you say anything, we
will report it."
Even my old friends are watching me,
waiting for a fatal slip.
"He will trap himself," they say,
"and then we will get our revenge on
him."

¹¹ But the Lord stands beside me like a
great warrior.
Before him my persecutors will
stumble.
They cannot defeat me.
They will fail and be thoroughly
humiliated.
Their dishonor will never be forgotten.

¹² O Lord of Heaven's Armies,
you test those who are righteous,
and you examine the deepest thoughts
and secrets.
Let me see your vengeance against them,
for I have committed my cause to you.

¹³ Sing to the Lord!
Praise the Lord!
For though I was poor and needy,
he rescued me from my oppressors.

¹⁴ Yet I curse the day I was born!
May no one celebrate the day of my
birth.
¹⁵ I curse the messenger who told my
father,
"Good news—you have a son!"
¹⁶ Let him be destroyed like the cities of
old
that the Lord overthrew without
mercy.
Terrify him all day long with battle
shouts,
¹⁷ because he did not kill me at birth.
Oh, that I had died in my mother's
womb,
that her body had been my grave!

¹⁸ Why was I ever born?
My entire life has been filled
with trouble, sorrow, and shame.

21 No Deliverance from Babylon

The Lord spoke through Jeremiah when King Zedekiah sent Pashhur son of Malkijah and Zephaniah son of Maaseiah, the priest, to speak with him. They begged Jeremiah, ²"Please speak to the Lord for us and ask him to help us. King Nebuchadnezzar* of Babylon is attacking Judah. Perhaps the Lord will be gracious and do a mighty miracle as he has done in the past. Perhaps he will force Nebuchadnezzar to withdraw his armies."

³Jeremiah replied, "Go back to King Zedekiah and tell him, ⁴'This is what the Lord, the God of Israel, says: I will make your weapons useless against the king of Babylon and the Babylonians* who are outside your walls attacking you. In fact, I will bring your enemies right into the heart of this city. ⁵I myself will fight against you with a strong hand and a powerful arm, for I am very angry. You have made me furious! ⁶I will send a terrible plague upon this city, and both people and animals will die. ⁷And after all that, says the Lord, I will hand over King Zedekiah, his staff, and everyone else in the city who survives the disease, war, and famine. I will hand them over to King Nebuchadnezzar of Babylon and to their other enemies. He will slaughter them and show them no mercy, pity, or compassion.'

⁸"Tell all the people, 'This is what the Lord says: Take your choice of life or death! ⁹Everyone who stays in Jerusalem will die from war, famine, or disease, but those who go out and surrender to the Babylonians will live. Their reward will be life! ¹⁰For I have decided to bring disaster and not good upon this city, says the Lord. It will be handed over to the king of Babylon, and he will reduce it to ashes.'

Judgment on Judah's Kings

¹¹"Say to the royal family of Judah, 'Listen to this message from the Lord! ¹²This is what the Lord says to the dynasty of David:

" 'Give justice each morning to the
people you judge!
Help those who have been robbed;
rescue them from their
oppressors.
Otherwise, my anger will burn like an
unquenchable fire
because of all your sins.
¹³ I will personally fight against the people
in Jerusalem,
that mighty fortress—
the people who boast, "No one can
touch us here.
No one can break in here."
¹⁴ And I myself will punish you for your
sinfulness,
says the LORD.
I will light a fire in your forests
that will burn up everything around
you.' "

22 A Message for Judah's Kings

This is what the LORD said to me:
"Go over and speak directly to the king of
Judah. Say to him, ²'Listen to this message
from the LORD, you king of Judah, sitting
on David's throne. Let your attendants and
your people listen, too. ³This is what the
LORD says: Be fair-minded and just. Do
what is right! Help those who have been
robbed; rescue them from their oppressors.
Quit your evil deeds! Do not mistreat foreigners, orphans, and widows. Stop murdering the innocent! ⁴If you obey me, there
will always be a descendant of David sitting on the throne here in Jerusalem. The
king will ride through the palace gates in
chariots and on horses, with his parade of
attendants and subjects. ⁵But if you refuse
to pay attention to this warning, I swear by
my own name, says the LORD, that this palace will become a pile of rubble.' "

A Message about the Palace

⁶Now this is what the LORD says concerning Judah's royal palace:

"I love you as much as fruitful Gilead
and the green forests of Lebanon.
But I will turn you into a desert,
with no one living within your walls.

⁷ I will call for wreckers,
who will bring out their tools to
dismantle you.
They will tear out all your fine cedar beams
and throw them on the fire.

⁸"People from many nations will pass by
the ruins of this city and say to one another,
'Why did the LORD destroy such a great
city?' ⁹And the answer will be, 'Because
they violated their covenant with the LORD
their God by worshiping other gods.' "

A Message about Jehoahaz

¹⁰ Do not weep for the dead king or mourn
his loss.
Instead, weep for the captive king
being led away!
For he will never return to see his
native land again.

¹¹For this is what the LORD says about Jehoahaz,* who succeeded his father, King Josiah,
and was taken away as a captive: "He will
never return. ¹²He will die in a distant land
and will never again see his own country."

A Message about Jehoiakim

¹³ And the LORD says, "What sorrow
awaits Jehoiakim,*
who builds his palace with forced labor.*
He builds injustice into its walls,
for he makes his neighbors work for
nothing.
He does not pay them for their labor.
¹⁴ He says, 'I will build a magnificent palace
with huge rooms and many windows.
I will panel it throughout with fragrant
cedar
and paint it a lovely red.'
¹⁵ But a beautiful cedar palace does not
make a great king!
Your father, Josiah, also had plenty to
eat and drink.
But he was just and right in all his
dealings.
That is why God blessed him.
¹⁶ He gave justice and help to the poor and
needy,
and everything went well for him.
Isn't that what it means to know me?"
says the LORD.

22:11 Hebrew *Shallum*, another name for Jehoahaz.   **22:13a** The brother and successor of the exiled Jehoahaz. See 22:18.   **22:13b** Hebrew *by unrighteousness.*

Orphans, Widows, and . . . Us

JEREMIAH 22:1-5

At first read Jeremiah 22:3 offers a clear-enough directive: "Do not mistreat foreigners, orphans, and widows," the Lord himself tells us. And we nod along. Of course, most of us would never think of mistreating a foreigner, an orphan, or a widow!

But while we may understand *mistreat* as intentional physical or mental cruelty, it can include much more: ostracizing, ignoring, allowing injustice, failing to show love. And while certainly we understand *foreigners, widows,* and *orphans* in their literal sense, because these three are grouped together we must consider a broader meaning. In Old Testament times, this trio had something in common: they lacked rights and financial means, their survival was utterly dependent upon the kindness and mercy of others, and they were often marginalized and mistreated. God was telling his people (and now us) to offer kindness, justice, and mercy. And he reiterated this theme throughout Scripture. In fact, Deuteronomy alone contains nearly a dozen specific regulations about ensuring justice for widows and orphans.

Who in *our* lives are we ignoring and forgetting? Who needs justice? On the streets where we live, at the schools our kids attend, at the places we work—who among us is desperately in need of an advocate?

Maybe it's the people mentioned in this passage: a widow, an orphan, a recent immigrant. But maybe it's a single mom, working so hard and never getting a break. Maybe it's a bullied kid, scared of that walk to school. Maybe it's someone who just doesn't fit in to your community and feels alone.

There are lots of possibilities. We all are surrounded by people who are in a desperate state—emotionally or physically—who feel as though their survival is dependent on the kindness, mercy, and justice of another. They need our advocacy—our willingness to step up and fight for them, to defend them, and to "speak up for those who cannot speak for themselves; ensure justice for those being crushed" (Proverbs 31:8). Yet how many times do we "mistreat" them by not noticing? How might we treat them justly instead?

—Caryn Rivadeneira

For more on justice, see reading at Daniel 12:1-3.

---

¹⁷ "But you! You have eyes only for greed
　　and dishonesty!
　You murder the innocent,
　oppress the poor, and reign
　　ruthlessly."

¹⁸ Therefore, this is what the LORD says about Jehoiakim, son of King Josiah:

"The people will not mourn for him,
　　crying to one another,
　'Alas, my brother! Alas, my sister!'

His subjects will not mourn for him,
　　crying,
　'Alas, our master is dead! Alas, his
　　splendor is gone!'

¹⁹ He will be buried like a dead donkey—
　　dragged out of Jerusalem and dumped
　　outside the gates!

²⁰ Weep for your allies in Lebanon.
　Shout for them in Bashan.
　Search for them in the regions east of
　　the river.*

22:20 Or *in Abarim.*

See, they are all destroyed.
Not one is left to help you.
²¹ I warned you when you were
      prosperous,
    but you replied, 'Don't bother me.'
You have been that way since
      childhood—
    you simply will not obey me!
²² And now the wind will blow away your
      allies.
    All your friends will be taken away as
      captives.
    Surely then you will see your
      wickedness and be ashamed.
²³ It may be nice to live in a beautiful
      palace
    paneled with wood from the cedars of
      Lebanon,
    but soon you will groan with pangs of
      anguish—
    anguish like that of a woman in
      labor.

A Message for Jehoiachin

²⁴ "As surely as I live," says the Lord, "I will abandon you, Jehoiachin* son of Jehoiakim, king of Judah. Even if you were the signet ring on my right hand, I would pull you off. ²⁵ I will hand you over to those who seek to kill you, those you so desperately fear—to King Nebuchadnezzar* of Babylon and the mighty Babylonian* army. ²⁶ I will expel you and your mother from this land, and you will die in a foreign country, not in your native land. ²⁷ You will never again return to the land you yearn for.

²⁸ "Why is this man Jehoiachin like a
      discarded, broken jar?
    Why are he and his children to be
      exiled to a foreign land?
²⁹ O earth, earth, earth!
    Listen to this message from the
      Lord!
³⁰ This is what the Lord says:
    'Let the record show that this man
      Jehoiachin was childless.
    He is a failure,
    for none of his children will succeed him
      on the throne of David
    to rule over Judah.'

23 The Righteous Descendant

¹ "What sorrow awaits the leaders of my people—the shepherds of my sheep—for they have destroyed and scattered the very ones they were expected to care for," says the Lord.

² Therefore, this is what the Lord, the God of Israel, says to these shepherds: "Instead of caring for my flock and leading them to safety, you have deserted them and driven them to destruction. Now I will pour out judgment on you for the evil you have done to them. ³ But I will gather together the remnant of my flock from the countries where I have driven them. I will bring them back to their own sheepfold, and they will be fruitful and increase in number. ⁴ Then I will appoint responsible shepherds who will care for them, and they will never be afraid again. Not a single one will be lost or missing. I, the Lord, have spoken!

⁵ "For the time is coming,"
      says the Lord,
    "when I will raise up a righteous
      descendant*
      from King David's line.
    He will be a King who rules with
      wisdom.
    He will do what is just and right
      throughout the land.
⁶ And this will be his name:
      'The Lord Is Our Righteousness.'*
    In that day Judah will be saved,
      and Israel will live in safety.

⁷ "In that day," says the Lord, "when people are taking an oath, they will no longer say, 'As surely as the Lord lives, who rescued the people of Israel from the land of Egypt.' ⁸ Instead, they will say, 'As surely as the Lord lives, who brought the people of Israel back to their own land from the land of the north and from all the countries to which he had exiled them.' Then they will live in their own land."

Judgment on False Prophets

⁹ My heart is broken because of the false
      prophets,
    and my bones tremble.

22:24 Hebrew *Coniah,* a variant spelling of Jehoiachin; also 22:28. **22:25a** Hebrew *Nebuchadrezzar,* a variant spelling of Nebuchadnezzar. **22:25b** Or *Chaldean.* **23:5** Hebrew *a righteous branch.* **23:6** Hebrew *Yahweh Tsidqenu.*

I stagger like a drunkard,
  like someone overcome by wine,
because of the holy words
  the LORD has spoken against them.
¹⁰ For the land is full of adultery,
  and it lies under a curse.
The land itself is in mourning—
  its wilderness pastures are dried up.
For they all do evil
  and abuse what power they have.

¹¹ "Even the priests and prophets
  are ungodly, wicked men.
I have seen their despicable acts
  right here in my own Temple,"
  says the LORD.
¹² "Therefore, the paths they take
  will become slippery.
They will be chased through the dark,
  and there they will fall.
For I will bring disaster upon them
  at the time fixed for their punishment.
I, the LORD, have spoken!

¹³ "I saw that the prophets of Samaria were
  terribly evil,
  for they prophesied in the name of
  Baal
  and led my people of Israel into sin.
¹⁴ But now I see that the prophets of
  Jerusalem are even worse!
They commit adultery and love
  dishonesty.
They encourage those who are doing evil
  so that no one turns away from their
  sins.
These prophets are as wicked
  as the people of Sodom and
  Gomorrah once were."

¹⁵ Therefore, this is what the LORD of Heaven's Armies says concerning the prophets:

"I will feed them with bitterness
  and give them poison to drink.
For it is because of Jerusalem's prophets
  that wickedness has filled this land."

¹⁶ This is what the LORD of Heaven's Armies says to his people:

"Do not listen to these prophets when
  they prophesy to you,
  filling you with futile hopes.
They are making up everything they say.
They do not speak for the LORD!

¹⁷ They keep saying to those who despise
  my word,
  'Don't worry! The LORD says you will
  have peace!'
And to those who stubbornly follow
  their own desires,
  they say, 'No harm will come your
  way!'

¹⁸ "Have any of these prophets been in the
  LORD's presence
to hear what he is really saying?
Has even one of them cared enough
  to listen?
¹⁹ Look! The LORD's anger bursts out like a
  storm,
  a whirlwind that swirls down on the
  heads of the wicked.
²⁰ The anger of the LORD will not
  diminish
  until it has finished all he has
  planned.
In the days to come
  you will understand all this very
  clearly.

²¹ "I have not sent these prophets,
  yet they run around claiming to speak
  for me.
I have given them no message,
  yet they go on prophesying.
²² If they had stood before me and listened
  to me,
  they would have spoken my words,
  and they would have turned my people
  from their evil ways and deeds.
²³ Am I a God who is only close at hand?"
  says the LORD.
"No, I am far away at the same time.
²⁴ Can anyone hide from me in a secret
  place?
  Am I not everywhere in all the
  heavens and earth?"
  says the LORD.

²⁵ "I have heard these prophets say, 'Listen to the dream I had from God last night.' And then they proceed to tell lies in my name. ²⁶ How long will this go on? If they are prophets, they are prophets of deceit, inventing everything they say. ²⁷ By telling these false dreams, they are trying to get my people to forget me, just as their ancestors did by worshiping the idols of Baal.

Contemplation

Practicing the Presence of God

JEREMIAH 23:23–24

"God go with you as you go," I said to the visiting missionary before he left.

"That is what we always need," he responded, looking me in the eye. "An awareness of the Lord—that alone comforts, convicts, kindles."

His words spoke deeply into my heart, echoing A. W. Tozer: "The Presence of God is the central fact of Christianity. At the heart of the Christian message is God Himself waiting for His redeemed children to push into conscious awareness of His Presence."

We intellectually know this is true—but *how* do we push into a constant awareness of the presence of God?

Brother Lawrence, a humble cook who connected with God in the kitchen four hundred years ago, penned letters to a friend that now make up the book *The Practice of the Presence of God.* "We should establish ourselves in a sense of God's presence by continually conversing with him," he wrote. Brother Lawrence believed as David did: "I can never get away from your presence!" (Psalm 139:7). He knew that God is "everywhere in all the heavens and the earth" (Jeremiah 23:24). God's amazing, powerful, beloved presence was right there in the kitchen, as Brother Lawrence washed dishes or quartered potatoes, transforming normal routine moments into soul-sustaining encounters with the Almighty.

The same is true for *our* kitchens—and our workplaces, neighborhood sidewalks, city streets, front stoops. Every place we go, God is present. Even when our minds may be necessarily occupied with other thoughts, Brother Lawrence taught, we can still remain connected with God's presence. "It is the *heart*," he wrote, "whose attention we must carefully focus on God."

The Word-God (John 1:1) becomes present to us as we live in this endless interchange of words with him—reading his Word; listening in our hearts for his words to us; responding with hushed, awed words of our own. Isn't this what it means to pray without ceasing (1 Thessalonians 5:17) as we live in constant connection to his presence? We "go with God" as we open our hearts to this stunning reality of his miraculous, moment-by-moment presence.

—Ann Voskamp

For more on contemplation, see reading at Luke 2:19, 51.

---

28 "Let these false prophets tell their dreams,
   but let my true messengers faithfully proclaim my every word.
   There is a difference between straw and grain!
29 Does not my word burn like fire?" says the LORD.

"Is it not like a mighty hammer that smashes a rock to pieces?

30 "Therefore," says the LORD, "I am against these prophets who steal messages from each other and claim they are from me. 31 I am against these smooth-tongued prophets who say, 'This prophecy is from the LORD!' 32 I am against these false

prophets. Their imaginary dreams are fla-grant lies that lead my people into sin. I did not send or appoint them, and they have no message at all for my people. I, the LORD, have spoken!

False Prophecies and False Prophets

33 "Suppose one of the people or one of the prophets or priests asks you, 'What proph-ecy has the LORD burdened you with now?' You must reply, 'You are the burden!* The LORD says he will abandon you!'

34 "If any prophet, priest, or anyone else says, 'I have a prophecy from the LORD,' I will punish that person along with his entire family. 35 You should keep asking each other, 'What is the LORD's answer?' or 'What is the LORD saying?' 36 But stop using this phrase, 'prophecy from the LORD.' For people are using it to give authority to their own ideas, turning upside down the words of our God, the living God, the LORD of Heaven's Armies.

37 "This is what you should say to the prophets: 'What is the LORD's answer?' or 'What is the LORD saying?' 38 But suppose they respond, 'This is a prophecy from the LORD!' Then you should say, 'This is what the LORD says: Because you have used this phrase, "prophecy from the LORD," even though I warned you not to use it, 39 I will forget you completely.* I will expel you from my presence, along with this city that I gave to you and your ancestors. 40 And I will make you an object of ridicule, and your name will be infamous throughout the ages.'"

24 Good and Bad Figs

After King Nebuchadnezzar* of Babylon exiled Jehoiachin* son of Jehoia-kim, king of Judah, to Babylon along with the officials of Judah and all the craftsmen and artisans, the LORD gave me this vision. I saw two baskets of figs placed in front of the LORD's Temple in Jerusalem. 2 One bas-ket was filled with fresh, ripe figs, while the other was filled with bad figs that were too rotten to eat.

3 Then the LORD said to me, "What do you see, Jeremiah?"

I replied, "Figs, some very good and some very bad, too rotten to eat."

4 Then the LORD gave me this message: 5 "This is what the LORD, the God of Israel, says: The good figs represent the exiles I sent from Judah to the land of the Babylonians.* 6 I will watch over and care for them, and I will bring them back here again. I will build them up and not tear them down. I will plant them and not uproot them. 7 I will give them hearts that recognize me as the LORD. They will be my people, and I will be their God, for they will return to me whole-heartedly.

8 "But the bad figs," the LORD said, "rep-resent King Zedekiah of Judah, his offi-cials, all the people left in Jerusalem, and those who live in Egypt. I will treat them like bad figs, too rotten to eat. 9 I will make them an object of horror and a symbol of evil to every nation on earth. They will be disgraced and mocked, taunted and cursed, wherever I scatter them. 10 And I will send war, famine, and disease until they have vanished from the land of Israel, which I gave to them and their ancestors."

25 Seventy Years of Captivity

This message for all the people of Judah came to Jeremiah from the LORD during the fourth year of Jehoiakim's reign over Judah.* This was the year when King Nebuchadnezzar* of Babylon began his reign.

2 Jeremiah the prophet said to all the peo-ple in Judah and Jerusalem, 3 "For the past twenty-three years—from the thirteenth year of the reign of Josiah son of Amon,* king of Judah, until now—the LORD has been giving me his messages. I have faith-fully passed them on to you, but you have not listened.

4 "Again and again the LORD has sent you his servants, the prophets, but you have not listened or even paid attention. 5 Each time the message was this: 'Turn from the evil road you are traveling and from the

---

23:33 As in Greek version and Latin Vulgate; Hebrew reads *What burden?*   23:39 Some Hebrew manuscripts and Greek version read *I will surely lift you up.*   24:1a Hebrew *Nebuchadrezzar,* a variant spelling of Nebuchadnezzar.   24:1b Hebrew *Jeconiah,* a variant spelling of Jehoiachin.   24:5 Or *Chaldeans.*   25:1a The fourth year of Jehoiakim's reign and the accession year of Nebuchadnezzar's reign was 605 B.C. 25:1b Hebrew *Nebuchadrezzar,* a variant spelling of Nebuchadnezzar; also in 25:9.   25:3 The thirteenth year of Josiah's reign was 627 B.C.

evil things you are doing. Only then will I let you live in this land that the LORD gave to you and your ancestors forever. ⁶Do not provoke my anger by worshiping idols you made with your own hands. Then I will not harm you.'

⁷"But you would not listen to me," says the LORD. "You made me furious by worshiping idols you made with your own hands, bringing on yourselves all the disasters you now suffer. ⁸And now the LORD of Heaven's Armies says: Because you have not listened to me, ⁹I will gather together all the armies of the north under King Nebuchadnezzar of Babylon, whom I have appointed as my deputy. I will bring them all against this land and its people and against the surrounding nations. I will completely destroy* you and make you an object of horror and contempt and a ruin forever. ¹⁰I will take away your happy singing and laughter. The joyful voices of bridegrooms and brides will no longer be heard. Your millstones will fall silent, and the lights in your homes will go out. ¹¹This entire land will become a desolate wasteland. Israel and her neighboring lands will serve the king of Babylon for seventy years.

¹²"Then, after the seventy years of captivity are over, I will punish the king of Babylon and his people for their sins," says the LORD. "I will make the country of the Babylonians* a wasteland forever. ¹³I will bring upon them all the terrors I have promised in this book—all the penalties announced by Jeremiah against the nations. ¹⁴Many nations and great kings will enslave the Babylonians, just as they enslaved my people. I will punish them in proportion to the suffering they cause my people."

The Cup of the LORD's Anger

¹⁵This is what the LORD, the God of Israel, said to me: "Take from my hand this cup filled to the brim with my anger, and make all the nations to whom I send you drink from it. ¹⁶When they drink from it, they will stagger, crazed by the warfare I will send against them."

¹⁷So I took the cup of anger from the LORD and made all the nations drink from it—every nation to which the LORD sent me. ¹⁸I went to Jerusalem and the other towns of Judah, and their kings and officials drank from the cup. From that day until this, they have been a desolate ruin, an object of horror, contempt, and cursing. ¹⁹I gave the cup to Pharaoh, king of Egypt, his attendants, his officials, and all his people, ²⁰along with all the foreigners living in that land. I also gave it to all the kings of the land of Uz and the kings of the Philistine cities of Ashkelon, Gaza, Ekron, and what remains of Ashdod. ²¹Then I gave the cup to the nations of Edom, Moab, and Ammon, ²²and the kings of Tyre and Sidon, and the kings of the regions across the sea. ²³I gave it to Dedan, Tema, and Buz, and to the people who live in distant places.* ²⁴I gave it to the kings of Arabia, the kings of the nomadic tribes of the desert, ²⁵and to the kings of Zimri, Elam, and Media. ²⁶And I gave it to the kings of the northern countries, far and near, one after the other—all the kingdoms of the world. And finally, the king of Babylon* himself drank from the cup of the LORD's anger.

²⁷Then the LORD said to me, "Now tell them, 'This is what the LORD of Heaven's Armies, the God of Israel, says: Drink from this cup of my anger. Get drunk and vomit; fall to rise no more, for I am sending terrible wars against you.' ²⁸And if they refuse to accept the cup, tell them, 'The LORD of Heaven's Armies says: You have no choice but to drink from it. ²⁹I have begun to punish Jerusalem, the city that bears my name. Now should I let you go unpunished? No, you will not escape disaster. I will call for war against all the nations of the earth. I, the LORD of Heaven's Armies, have spoken!'

³⁰"Now prophesy all these things, and say to them,

" 'The LORD will roar against his own land
      from his holy dwelling in heaven.
He will shout like those who tread
      grapes;
he will shout against everyone on
      earth.

25:9 The Hebrew term used here refers to the complete consecration of things or people to the LORD, either by destroying them or by giving them as an offering. **25:12** Or *Chaldeans.* **25:23** Or *who clip the corners of their hair.* **25:26** Hebrew *of Sheshach,* a code name for Babylon.

³¹ His cry of judgment will reach the ends
of the earth,
for the LORD will bring his case
against all the nations.
He will judge all the people of the earth,
slaughtering the wicked with the
sword.
I, the LORD, have spoken!'"

³² This is what the LORD of Heaven's
Armies says:
"Look! Disaster will fall upon nation
after nation!
A great whirlwind of fury is rising
from the most distant corners of the
earth!"

³³ In that day those the LORD has slaughtered will fill the earth from one end to the
other. No one will mourn for them or gather
up their bodies to bury them. They will be
scattered on the ground like manure.

³⁴ Weep and moan, you evil shepherds!
Roll in the dust, you leaders of the
flock!
The time of your slaughter has arrived;
you will fall and shatter like a fragile
vase.
³⁵ You will find no place to hide;
there will be no way to escape.
³⁶ Listen to the frantic cries of the
shepherds.
The leaders of the flock are wailing in
despair,
for the LORD is ruining their pastures.
³⁷ Peaceful meadows will be turned into a
wasteland
by the LORD's fierce anger.
³⁸ He has left his den like a strong lion
seeking its prey,
and their land will be made desolate
by the sword of the enemy
and the LORD's fierce anger.

26 Jeremiah's Escape from Death

This message came to Jeremiah from
the LORD early in the reign of Jehoiakim
son of Josiah,* king of Judah. ²"This is what
the LORD says: Stand in the courtyard in
front of the Temple of the LORD, and make
an announcement to the people who have
come there to worship from all over Judah.
Give them my entire message; include every
word. ³Perhaps they will listen and turn
from their evil ways. Then I will change my
mind about the disaster I am ready to pour
out on them because of their sins.

⁴"Say to them, 'This is what the LORD
says: If you will not listen to me and obey
my word I have given you, ⁵and if you will
not listen to my servants, the prophets—for
I sent them again and again to warn you,
but you would not listen to them—⁶then
I will destroy this Temple as I destroyed
Shiloh, the place where the Tabernacle
was located. And I will make Jerusalem an
object of cursing in every nation on earth.'"

⁷The priests, the prophets, and all the
people listened to Jeremiah as he spoke
in front of the LORD's Temple. ⁸But when
Jeremiah had finished his message, saying
everything the LORD had told him to say,
the priests and prophets and all the people at the Temple mobbed him. "Kill him!"
they shouted. ⁹"What right do you have
to prophesy in the LORD's name that this
Temple will be destroyed like Shiloh? What
do you mean, saying that Jerusalem will be
destroyed and left with no inhabitants?"
And all the people threatened him as he
stood in front of the Temple.

¹⁰When the officials of Judah heard what
was happening, they rushed over from the
palace and sat down at the New Gate of
the Temple to hold court. ¹¹The priests and
prophets presented their accusations to the
officials and the people. "This man should
die!" they said. "You have heard with your
own ears what a traitor he is, for he has
prophesied against this city."

¹²Then Jeremiah spoke to the officials and
the people in his own defense. "The LORD
sent me to prophesy against this Temple
and this city," he said. "The LORD gave me
every word that I have spoken. ¹³But if you
stop your sinning and begin to obey the
LORD your God, he will change his mind
about this disaster that he has announced
against you. ¹⁴As for me, I am in your
hands—do with me as you think best. ¹⁵But
if you kill me, rest assured that you will be
killing an innocent man! The responsibility for such a deed will lie on you, on this
city, and on every person living in it. For it

26:1 The first year of Jehoiakim's reign was 608 B.C.

is absolutely true that the LORD sent me to speak every word you have heard."

¹⁶Then the officials and the people said to the priests and prophets, "This man does not deserve the death sentence, for he has spoken to us in the name of the LORD our God."

¹⁷Then some of the wise old men stood and spoke to all the people assembled there. ¹⁸They said, "Remember when Micah of Moresheth prophesied during the reign of King Hezekiah of Judah. He told the people of Judah,

'This is what the LORD of Heaven's
    Armies says:
Mount Zion will be plowed like an open
    field;
Jerusalem will be reduced to ruins!
A thicket will grow on the heights
    where the Temple now stands.'*

¹⁹But did King Hezekiah and the people kill him for saying this? No, they turned from their sins and worshiped the LORD. They begged him for mercy. Then the LORD changed his mind about the terrible disaster he had pronounced against them. So we are about to do ourselves great harm."

²⁰At this time Uriah son of Shemaiah from Kiriath-jearim was also prophesying for the LORD. And he predicted the same terrible disaster against the city and nation as Jeremiah did. ²¹When King Jehoiakim and the army officers and officials heard what he was saying, the king sent someone to kill him. But Uriah heard about the plan and escaped in fear to Egypt. ²²Then King Jehoiakim sent Elnathan son of Acbor to Egypt along with several other men to capture Uriah. ²³They took him prisoner and brought him back to King Jehoiakim. The king then killed Uriah with a sword and had him buried in an unmarked grave.

²⁴Nevertheless, Ahikam son of Shaphan stood up for Jeremiah and persuaded the court not to turn him over to the mob to be killed.

27 Jeremiah Wears an Ox Yoke

This message came to Jeremiah from the LORD early in the reign of Zedekiah* son of Josiah, king of Judah.

²This is what the LORD said to me: "Make a yoke, and fasten it on your neck with leather straps. ³Then send messages to the kings of Edom, Moab, Ammon, Tyre, and Sidon through their ambassadors who have come to see King Zedekiah in Jerusalem. ⁴Give them this message for their masters: 'This is what the LORD of Heaven's Armies, the God of Israel, says: ⁵With my great strength and powerful arm I made the earth and all its people and every animal. I can give these things of mine to anyone I choose. ⁶Now I will give your countries to King Nebuchadnezzar of Babylon, who is my servant. I have put everything, even the wild animals, under his control. ⁷All the nations will serve him, his son, and his grandson until his time is up. Then many nations and great kings will conquer and rule over Babylon. ⁸So you must submit to Babylon's king and serve him; put your neck under Babylon's yoke! I will punish any nation that refuses to be his slave, says the LORD. I will send war, famine, and disease upon that nation until Babylon has conquered it.

⁹"'Do not listen to your false prophets, fortune-tellers, interpreters of dreams, mediums, and sorcerers who say, "The king of Babylon will not conquer you." ¹⁰They are all liars, and their lies will lead to your being driven out of your land. I will drive you out and send you far away to die. ¹¹But the people of any nation that submits to the king of Babylon will be allowed to stay in their own country to farm the land as usual. I, the LORD, have spoken!'"

¹²Then I repeated this same message to King Zedekiah of Judah. "If you want to live, submit to the yoke of the king of Babylon and his people. ¹³Why do you insist on dying—you and your people? Why should you choose war, famine, and disease, which the LORD will bring against every nation that refuses to submit to Babylon's king? ¹⁴Do not listen to the false prophets who keep telling you, 'The king of Babylon will not conquer you.' They are liars. ¹⁵This is what the LORD says: 'I have not sent these prophets! They are telling you lies in my name, so I will drive you from this land. You will all die—you and all these prophets, too.'"

26:18 Mic 3:12.   27:1 As in some Hebrew manuscripts and Syriac version (see also 27:3, 12); most Hebrew manuscripts read *Jehoiakim*.

[16]Then I spoke to the priests and the people and said, "This is what the LORD says: 'Do not listen to your prophets who claim that soon the gold articles taken from my Temple will be returned from Babylon. It is all a lie! [17]Do not listen to them. Surrender to the king of Babylon, and you will live. Why should this whole city be destroyed? [18]If they really are prophets and speak the LORD's messages, let them pray to the LORD of Heaven's Armies. Let them pray that the articles remaining in the LORD's Temple and in the king's palace and in the palaces of Jerusalem will not be carried away to Babylon!'

[19]"For the LORD of Heaven's Armies has spoken about the pillars in front of the Temple, the great bronze basin called the Sea, the water carts, and all the other ceremonial articles. [20]King Nebuchadnezzar of Babylon left them here when he exiled Jehoiachin* son of Jehoiakim, king of Judah, to Babylon, along with all the other nobles of Judah and Jerusalem. [21]Yes, this is what the LORD of Heaven's Armies, the God of Israel, says about the precious things still in the Temple and in the palace of Judah's king: [22]'They will all be carried away to Babylon and will stay there until I send for them,' says the LORD. 'Then I will bring them back to Jerusalem again.'"

Jeremiah Condemns Hananiah

28 One day in late summer* of that same year—the fourth year of the reign of Zedekiah, king of Judah—Hananiah son of Azzur, a prophet from Gibeon, addressed me publicly in the Temple while all the priests and people listened. He said, [2]"This is what the LORD of Heaven's Armies, the God of Israel, says: 'I will remove the yoke of the king of Babylon from your necks. [3]Within two years I will bring back all the Temple treasures that King Nebuchadnezzar carried off to Babylon. [4]And I will bring back Jehoiachin* son of Jehoiakim, king of Judah, and all the other captives that were taken to Babylon. I will surely break the yoke that the king of Babylon has put on your necks. I, the LORD, have spoken!'"

[5]Jeremiah responded to Hananiah as they stood in front of all the priests and people at the Temple. [6]He said, "Amen! May your prophecies come true! I hope the LORD does everything you say. I hope he does bring back from Babylon the treasures of this Temple and all the captives. [7]But listen now to the solemn words I speak to you in the presence of all these people. [8]The ancient prophets who preceded you and me spoke against many nations, always warning of war, disaster, and disease. [9]So a prophet who predicts peace must show he is right. Only when his predictions come true can we know that he is really from the LORD."

[10]Then Hananiah the prophet took the yoke off Jeremiah's neck and broke it in pieces. [11]And Hananiah said again to the crowd that had gathered, "This is what the LORD says: 'Just as this yoke has been broken, within two years I will break the yoke of oppression from all the nations now subject to King Nebuchadnezzar of Babylon.'" With that, Jeremiah left the Temple area.

[12]Soon after this confrontation with Hananiah, the LORD gave this message to Jeremiah: [13]"Go and tell Hananiah, 'This is what the LORD says: You have broken a wooden yoke, but you have replaced it with a yoke of iron. [14]The LORD of Heaven's Armies, the God of Israel, says: I have put a yoke of iron on the necks of all these nations, forcing them into slavery under King Nebuchadnezzar of Babylon. I have put everything, even the wild animals, under his control.'"

[15]Then Jeremiah the prophet said to Hananiah, "Listen, Hananiah! The LORD has not sent you, but the people believe your lies. [16]Therefore, this is what the LORD says: 'You must die. Your life will end this very year because you have rebelled against the LORD.'"

[17]Two months later* the prophet Hananiah died.

A Letter to the Exiles

29 Jeremiah wrote a letter from Jerusalem to the elders, priests, prophets, and all the people who had been exiled to Babylon

---

27:20 Hebrew *Jeconiah,* a variant spelling of Jehoiachin. **28:1** Hebrew *In the fifth month,* of the ancient Hebrew lunar calendar. The fifth month in the fourth year of Zedekiah's reign occurred within the months of August and September 593 B.C. Also see note on 1:3. **28:4** Hebrew *Jeconiah,* a variant spelling of Jehoiachin. **28:17** Hebrew *In the seventh month of that same year.* See 28:1 and the note there.

by King Nebuchadnezzar. ²This was after King Jehoiachin,* the queen mother, the court officials, the other officials of Judah, and all the craftsmen and artisans had been deported from Jerusalem. ³He sent the letter with Elasah son of Shaphan and Gemariah son of Hilkiah when they went to Babylon as King Zedekiah's ambassadors to Nebuchadnezzar. This is what Jeremiah's letter said:

⁴This is what the LORD of Heaven's Armies, the God of Israel, says to all the captives he has exiled to Babylon from Jerusalem: ⁵"Build homes, and plan to stay. Plant gardens, and eat the food they produce. ⁶Marry and have children. Then find spouses for them so that you may have many grandchildren. Multiply! Do not dwindle away! ⁷And work for the peace and prosperity of the city where I sent you into exile. Pray to the LORD for it, for its welfare will determine your welfare."

⁸This is what the LORD of Heaven's Armies, the God of Israel, says: "Do not let your prophets and fortune-tellers who are with you in the land of Babylon trick you. Do not listen to their dreams, ⁹because they are telling you lies in my name. I have not sent them," says the LORD.

¹⁰This is what the LORD says: "You will be in Babylon for seventy years. But then I will come and do for you all the good things I have promised, and I will bring you home again. ¹¹For I know the plans I have for you," says the LORD. "They are plans for good and not for disaster, to give you a future and a hope. ¹²In those days when you pray, I will listen. ¹³If you look for me wholeheartedly, you will find me. ¹⁴I will be found by you," says the LORD. "I will end your captivity and restore your fortunes. I will gather you out of the nations where I sent you and will bring you home again to your own land."

¹⁵You claim that the LORD has raised up prophets for you in Babylon. ¹⁶But this is what the LORD says about the king who sits on David's throne and all those still living here in Jerusalem—your relatives who were not exiled to Babylon. ¹⁷This is what the LORD of Heaven's Armies says: "I will send war, famine, and disease upon them and make them like bad figs, too rotten to eat. ¹⁸Yes, I will pursue them with war, famine, and disease, and I will scatter them around the world. In every nation where I send them, I will make them an object of damnation, horror, contempt, and mockery. ¹⁹For they refuse to listen to me, though I have spoken to them repeatedly through the prophets I sent. And you who are in exile have not listened either," says the LORD.

²⁰Therefore, listen to this message from the LORD, all you captives there in Babylon. ²¹This is what the LORD of Heaven's Armies, the God of Israel, says about your prophets—Ahab son of Kolaiah and Zedekiah son of Maaseiah—who are telling you lies in my name: "I will turn them over to Nebuchadnezzar* for execution before your eyes. ²²Their terrible fate will become proverbial, so that the Judean exiles will curse someone by saying, 'May the LORD make you like Zedekiah and Ahab, whom the king of Babylon burned alive!' ²³For these men have done terrible things among my people. They have committed adultery with their neighbors' wives and have lied in my name, saying things I did not command. I am a witness to this. I, the LORD, have spoken."

A Message for Shemaiah

²⁴The LORD sent this message to Shemaiah the Nehelamite in Babylon: ²⁵"This is what the LORD of Heaven's Armies, the God of Israel, says: You wrote a letter on your own authority to Zephaniah son of Maaseiah, the priest, and you sent copies to the other priests and people in Jerusalem. You wrote to Zephaniah,

²⁶"The LORD has appointed you to replace Jehoiada as the priest in charge of the house of the LORD. You are responsible to put into stocks and neck irons any crazy man who claims

---

29:2 Hebrew *Jeconiah*, a variant spelling of Jehoiachin.   **29:21** Hebrew *Nebuchadrezzar*, a variant spelling of Nebuchadnezzar.

to be a prophet. ²⁷ So why have you done nothing to stop Jeremiah from Anathoth, who pretends to be a prophet among you? ²⁸ Jeremiah sent a letter here to Babylon, predicting that our captivity will be a long one. He said, 'Build homes, and plan to stay. Plant gardens, and eat the food they produce.'"

²⁹ But when Zephaniah the priest received Shemaiah's letter, he took it to Jeremiah and read it to him. ³⁰ Then the LORD gave this message to Jeremiah: ³¹ "Send an open letter to all the exiles in Babylon. Tell them, 'This is what the LORD says concerning Shemaiah the Nehelamite: Since he has prophesied to you when I did not send him

Q&A — Unshakable Faith

JEREMIAH 29:10–14

How do I hold on to my faith during intense heartache?

After the death of my two young children during a three-month period—and after several years of reflection—I've come to see aspects of God's character and of Christian faith in much sharper focus. One realization I've had is that faith is more intentional.

It's like the classical distinction between virtue and innocence. Virtue, unlike innocence, has successfully passed a point of temptation. Perhaps a similar distinction can be found in faith—innocent faith can trust God because it hasn't seen the abyss; virtuous faith has known the terror and chooses to trust God. Even as a child, I loved to read, and I quickly learned that I'd most likely be confused during a novel's opening chapters. New characters were introduced. Disparate, seemingly random events took place. Subplots were complicated and didn't make sense in relation to the main plot.

But I kept reading. Why? Because I knew that the author would weave them all together by the book's end. Eventually each element would be meaningful.

At times such faith has to be a conscious choice.

Even when I can't explain why a chromosomal abnormality develops in my son, which prevents him from living more than two minutes . . .

Even when I can't fathom why our daughter has to endure two years of severe and profound retardation and continual seizures . . .

I choose to trust that before the book closes, the Author will make things clear. And to remember his words through the prophet: "'For I know the plans I have for you,' says the LORD. 'They are plans for good and not for disaster, to give you a future and a hope'" (Jeremiah 29:11).

Clinging to that promise, even when the weight of sorrow makes our knees buckle, makes faith intentional and, I trust, unshakable.

—Marshall Shelley

For more on faith, see reading at Daniel 4:34–37.

and has tricked you into believing his lies, [32]I will punish him and his family. None of his descendants will see the good things I will do for my people, for he has incited you to rebel against me. I, the LORD, have spoken!'"

30 Promises of Deliverance

The LORD gave another message to Jeremiah. He said, [2]"This is what the LORD, the God of Israel, says: Write down for the record everything I have said to you, Jeremiah. [3]For the time is coming when I will restore the fortunes of my people of Israel and Judah. I will bring them home to this land that I gave to their ancestors, and they will possess it again. I, the LORD, have spoken!"

[4]This is the message the LORD gave concerning Israel and Judah. [5]This is what the LORD says:

"I hear cries of fear;
  there is terror and no peace.
[6] Now let me ask you a question:
  Do men give birth to babies?
Then why do they stand there, ashen-faced,
  hands pressed against their sides
  like a woman in labor?
[7] In all history there has never been such a
    time of terror.
  It will be a time of trouble for my
    people Israel.*
  Yet in the end they will be saved!
[8] For in that day,"
  says the LORD of Heaven's Armies,
"I will break the yoke from their necks
  and snap their chains.
Foreigners will no longer be their
  masters.
[9] For my people will serve the LORD
    their God
and their king descended from David—
  the king I will raise up for them.

[10] "So do not be afraid, Jacob, my servant;
  do not be dismayed, Israel,"
  says the LORD.
"For I will bring you home again from
    distant lands,
  and your children will return from
    their exile.

Israel will return to a life of peace and
    quiet,
  and no one will terrorize them.
[11] For I am with you and will save you,"
  says the LORD.
"I will completely destroy the nations
    where I have scattered you,
  but I will not completely destroy you.
I will discipline you, but with justice;
  I cannot let you go unpunished."

[12] This is what the LORD says:
"Your injury is incurable—
  a terrible wound.
[13] There is no one to help you
  or to bind up your injury.
  No medicine can heal you.
[14] All your lovers—your allies—have left
    you
  and do not care about you anymore.
I have wounded you cruelly,
  as though I were your enemy.
For your sins are many,
  and your guilt is great.
[15] Why do you protest your punishment—
    this wound that has no cure?
I have had to punish you
  because your sins are many
  and your guilt is great.

[16] "But all who devour you will be
    devoured,
  and all your enemies will be sent into
    exile.
All who plunder you will be plundered,
  and all who attack you will be
    attacked.
[17] I will give you back your health
  and heal your wounds," says the LORD.
"For you are called an outcast—
  'Jerusalem* for whom no one cares.'"

[18] This is what the LORD says:
"When I bring Israel home again from
    captivity
  and restore their fortunes,
Jerusalem will be rebuilt on its ruins,
  and the palace reconstructed as
    before.
[19] There will be joy and songs of
    thanksgiving,
  and I will multiply my people, not
    diminish them;

30:7 Hebrew *Jacob;* also in 30:10b, 18. See note on 5:20. **30:17** Hebrew *Zion.*

I will honor them, not despise them.
²⁰ Their children will prosper as they did
long ago.
I will establish them as a nation before me,
and I will punish anyone who hurts
them.
²¹ They will have their own ruler again,
and he will come from their own people.
I will invite him to approach me," says
the LORD,
"for who would dare to come unless
invited?
²² You will be my people,
and I will be your God."

²³ Look! The LORD's anger bursts out like a
storm,
a driving wind that swirls down on the
heads of the wicked.
²⁴ The fierce anger of the LORD will not
diminish
until it has finished all he has planned.
In the days to come
you will understand all this.

31 Hope for Restoration

"In that day," says the LORD, "I will
be the God of all the families of Israel, and
they will be my people. ² This is what the
LORD says:

"Those who survive the coming
destruction
will find blessings even in the barren
land,
for I will give rest to the people of
Israel."

³ Long ago the LORD said to Israel:
"I have loved you, my people, with an
everlasting love.
With unfailing love I have drawn you
to myself.
⁴ I will rebuild you, my virgin Israel.
You will again be happy
and dance merrily with your
tambourines.
⁵ Again you will plant your vineyards on
the mountains of Samaria
and eat from your own gardens there.
⁶ The day will come when watchmen will
shout
from the hill country of Ephraim,

'Come, let us go up to Jerusalem*
to worship the LORD our God.'"

⁷ Now this is what the LORD says:
"Sing with joy for Israel.*
Shout for the greatest of nations!
Shout out with praise and joy:
'Save your people, O LORD,
the remnant of Israel!'
⁸ For I will bring them from the north
and from the distant corners of the
earth.
I will not forget the blind and lame,
the expectant mothers and women in
labor.
A great company will return!
⁹ Tears of joy will stream down their
faces,
and I will lead them home with great
care.
They will walk beside quiet streams
and on smooth paths where they will
not stumble.
For I am Israel's father,
and Ephraim is my oldest child.

¹⁰ "Listen to this message from the LORD,
you nations of the world;
proclaim it in distant coastlands:
The LORD, who scattered his people,
will gather them and watch over them
as a shepherd does his flock.
¹¹ For the LORD has redeemed Israel
from those too strong for them.
¹² They will come home and sing songs of
joy on the heights of Jerusalem.
They will be radiant because of the
LORD's good gifts—
the abundant crops of grain, new wine,
and olive oil,
and the healthy flocks and herds.
Their life will be like a watered garden,
and all their sorrows will be gone.
¹³ The young women will dance for joy,
and the men—old and young—will
join in the celebration.
I will turn their mourning into joy.
I will comfort them and exchange
their sorrow for rejoicing.
¹⁴ The priests will enjoy abundance,
and my people will feast on my good
gifts.
I, the LORD, have spoken!"

31:6 Hebrew *Zion;* also in 31:12. **31:7** Hebrew *Jacob;* also in 31:11. See note on 5:20.

Messy, Costly, Dirty Ministry

JEREMIAH 31:1–14

In a visit with Brooklyn Tabernacle pastor Jim Cymbala, Jim shared with me what he believed was the number-one sin in our country. "Pastors and leaders are not on their knees crying out to God, 'Bring us the drug-addicted, the prostitutes, the destitute, the gang leaders. Bring us those with AIDS; bring us the people nobody else wants, whom only you can heal, and let us love them in your name until they are whole.'"

I was utterly convicted. I had never prayed, not once, for God to bring such people to my church. So I went home and repented. I stopped sinning. I began to cry out for "those nobody wanted."

And God brought them.

I found out *why* nobody wants them: they're messy, costly, and dirty. They swear at you, lie to you, steal from you. Worse, they make you love them and then often break your heart. It reminds me of a scene from the film *Entertaining Angels*, the story of Dorothy Day and her ministry during the Depression. Dorothy was praying before a life-sized crucifix. "Why," she asked Jesus, "did you have to wear such a revolting disguise, covered in vomit, smelling of urine, dressed in rags, cussing?"

But when God brings messy people, it makes you real. You realize you're dealing with a magnitude of sin that bromides and platitudes are powerless against. It reminds you of how desperate you are for God to work powerfully. Ministering to sex-trade workers and crack-addicts is like being called out of the boat to walk on the water: you've never been here before, and unless Jesus is with you, ready to catch you when you fall, you are going to sink all the way down.

Some days I wish things were tidy again. But if ministry and mess are inseparable, I'll take them both.

—*Mark Buchanan*

For more on outreach, see reading at Matthew 10:28–33.

Rachel's Sadness Turns to Joy

¹⁵This is what the LORD says:

"A cry is heard in Ramah—
    deep anguish and bitter weeping.
Rachel weeps for her children,
    refusing to be comforted—
    for her children are gone."

¹⁶ But now this is what the LORD says:
"Do not weep any longer,
    for I will reward you," says the LORD.

"Your children will come back to you
    from the distant land of the
    enemy.
¹⁷ There is hope for your future," says the
    LORD.
"Your children will come again to their
    own land.
¹⁸ I have heard Israel* saying,
'You disciplined me severely,
    like a calf that needs training for the
    yoke.

31:18 Hebrew *Ephraim*, referring to the northern kingdom of Israel; also in 31:20.

Turn me again to you and restore me,
for you alone are the LORD my
God.
19 I turned away from God,
but then I was sorry.
I kicked myself for my stupidity!
I was thoroughly ashamed of all I did
in my younger days.'

20 "Is not Israel still my son,
my darling child?" says the LORD.
"I often have to punish him,
but I still love him.
That's why I long for him
and surely will have mercy on him.
21 Set up road signs;
put up guideposts.
Mark well the path
by which you came.
Come back again, my virgin Israel;
return to your towns here.
22 How long will you wander,
my wayward daughter?
For the LORD will cause something new
to happen—
Israel will embrace her God.*"

23 This is what the LORD of Heaven's
Armies, the God of Israel, says: "When I
bring them back from captivity, the people
of Judah and its towns will again say, 'The
LORD bless you, O righteous home, O holy
mountain!' 24 Townspeople and farmers and
shepherds alike will live together in peace
and happiness. 25 For I have given rest to the
weary and joy to the sorrowing."

26 At this, I woke up and looked around.
My sleep had been very sweet.

27 "The day is coming," says the LORD,
"when I will greatly increase the human
population and the number of animals here
in Israel and Judah. 28 In the past I deliberately uprooted and tore down this nation.
I overthrew it, destroyed it, and brought
disaster upon it. But in the future I will just
as deliberately plant it and build it up. I, the
LORD, have spoken!

29 "The people will no longer quote this
proverb:

'The parents have eaten sour grapes,
but their children's mouths pucker at
the taste.'

30 All people will die for their own sins—
those who eat the sour grapes will be the
ones whose mouths will pucker.

31 "The day is coming," says the LORD,
"when I will make a new covenant with the
people of Israel and Judah. 32 This covenant
will not be like the one I made with their
ancestors when I took them by the hand
and brought them out of the land of Egypt.
They broke that covenant, though I loved
them as a husband loves his wife," says the
LORD.

33 "But this is the new covenant I will
make with the people of Israel on that day,"
says the LORD. "I will put my instructions
deep within them, and I will write them on
their hearts. I will be their God, and they
will be my people. 34 And they will not need
to teach their neighbors, nor will they need
to teach their relatives, saying, 'You should
know the LORD.' For everyone, from the
least to the greatest, will know me already,"
says the LORD. "And I will forgive their
wickedness, and I will never again remember their sins."

35 It is the LORD who provides the sun to
light the day
and the moon and stars to light the
night,
and who stirs the sea into roaring
waves.
His name is the LORD of Heaven's
Armies,
and this is what he says:
36 "I am as likely to reject my people Israel
as I am to abolish the laws of nature!"
37 This is what the LORD says:
"Just as the heavens cannot be measured
and the foundations of the earth
cannot be explored,
so I will not consider casting them away
for the evil they have done.
I, the LORD, have spoken!

38 "The day is coming," says the LORD,
"when all Jerusalem will be rebuilt for me,
from the Tower of Hananel to the Corner
Gate. 39 A measuring line will be stretched
out over the hill of Gareb and across to
Goah. 40 And the entire area—including the
graveyard and ash dump in the valley, and
all the fields out to the Kidron Valley on the

31:22 Hebrew *a woman will surround a man.*

east as far as the Horse Gate—will be holy to the LORD. The city will never again be captured or destroyed."

32 Jeremiah's Land Purchase

The following message came to Jeremiah from the LORD in the tenth year of the reign of Zedekiah,* king of Judah. This was also the eighteenth year of the reign of King Nebuchadnezzar.* ²Jerusalem was then under siege from the Babylonian army, and Jeremiah was imprisoned in the courtyard of the guard in the royal palace. ³King Zedekiah had put him there, asking why he kept giving this prophecy: "This is what the LORD says: 'I am about to hand this city over to the king of Babylon, and he will take it. ⁴King Zedekiah will be captured by the Babylonians* and taken to meet the king of Babylon face to face. ⁵He will take Zedekiah to Babylon, and I will deal with him there,' says the LORD. 'If you fight against the Babylonians, you will never succeed.'"

⁶At that time the LORD sent me a message. He said, ⁷"Your cousin Hanamel son of Shallum will come and say to you, 'Buy my field at Anathoth. By law you have the right to buy it before it is offered to anyone else.'"

⁸Then, just as the LORD had said he would, my cousin Hanamel came and visited me in the prison. He said, "Please buy my field at Anathoth in the land of Benjamin. By law you have the right to buy it before it is offered to anyone else, so buy it for yourself." Then I knew that the message I had heard was from the LORD.

⁹So I bought the field at Anathoth, paying Hanamel seventeen pieces* of silver for it. ¹⁰I signed and sealed the deed of purchase before witnesses, weighed out the silver, and paid him. ¹¹Then I took the sealed deed and an unsealed copy of the deed, which contained the terms and conditions of the purchase, ¹²and I handed them to Baruch son of Neriah and grandson of Mahseiah. I did all this in the presence of my cousin Hanamel, the witnesses who had signed the deed, and all the men of Judah who were there in the courtyard of the guardhouse.

¹³Then I said to Baruch as they all listened, ¹⁴"This is what the LORD of Heaven's Armies, the God of Israel, says: 'Take both this sealed deed and the unsealed copy, and put them into a pottery jar to preserve them for a long time.' ¹⁵For this is what the LORD of Heaven's Armies, the God of Israel, says: 'Someday people will again own property here in this land and will buy and sell houses and vineyards and fields.'"

Jeremiah's Prayer

¹⁶Then after I had given the papers to Baruch, I prayed to the LORD:

¹⁷"O Sovereign LORD! You made the heavens and earth by your strong hand and powerful arm. Nothing is too hard for you! ¹⁸You show unfailing love to thousands, but you also bring the consequences of one generation's sin upon the next. You are the great and powerful God, the LORD of Heaven's Armies. ¹⁹You have all wisdom and do great and mighty miracles. You see the conduct of all people, and you give them what they deserve. ²⁰You performed miraculous signs and wonders in the land of Egypt—things still remembered to this day! And you have continued to do great miracles in Israel and all around the world. You have made your name famous to this day.

²¹"You brought Israel out of Egypt with mighty signs and wonders, with a strong hand and powerful arm, and with overwhelming terror. ²²You gave the people of Israel this land that you had promised their ancestors long before—a land flowing with milk and honey. ²³Our ancestors came and conquered it and lived in it, but they refused to obey you or follow your word. They have not done anything you commanded. That is why you have sent this terrible disaster upon them.

²⁴"See how the siege ramps have been built against the city walls! Through war, famine, and disease, the city will be handed over to the Babylonians, who will conquer it. Everything has

---

32:1a The tenth year of Zedekiah's reign and the eighteenth year of Nebuchadnezzar's reign was 587 B.C.   **32:1b** Hebrew *Nebuchadrezzar*, a variant spelling of Nebuchadnezzar; also in 32:28.   **32:4** Or *Chaldeans*; also in 32:5, 24, 25, 28, 29, 43.   **32:9** Hebrew *17 shekels*, about 7 ounces or 194 grams in weight.

happened just as you said. 25 And yet, O Sovereign LORD, you have told me to buy the field—paying good money for it before these witnesses—even though the city will soon be handed over to the Babylonians."

A Prediction of Jerusalem's Fall

26 Then this message came to Jeremiah from the LORD: 27 "I am the LORD, the God of all the peoples of the world. Is anything too hard for me? 28 Therefore, this is what the LORD says: I will hand this city over to the Babylonians and to Nebuchadnezzar, king of Babylon, and he will capture it. 29 The Babylonians outside the walls will come in and set fire to the city. They will burn down all these houses where the people provoked my anger by burning incense to Baal on the rooftops and by pouring out liquid offerings to other gods. 30 Israel and Judah have done nothing but wrong since their earliest days. They have infuriated me with all their evil deeds," says the LORD. 31 "From the time this city was built until now, it has done nothing but anger me, so I am determined to get rid of it.

32 "The sins of Israel and Judah—the sins of the people of Jerusalem, the kings, the officials, the priests, and the prophets—have stirred up my anger. 33 My people have turned their backs on me and have refused to return. Even though I diligently taught them, they would not receive instruction or obey. 34 They have set up their abominable idols right in my own Temple, defiling it. 35 They have built pagan shrines to Baal in the valley of Ben-Hinnom, and there they sacrifice their sons and daughters to Molech. I have never commanded such a horrible deed; it never even crossed my mind to command such a thing. What an incredible evil, causing Judah to sin so greatly!

A Promise of Restoration

36 "Now I want to say something more about this city. You have been saying, 'It will fall to the king of Babylon through war, famine, and disease.' But this is what the LORD, the God of Israel, says: 37 I will certainly bring my people back again from all the countries where I will scatter them in my fury. I will bring them back to this very city and let them live in peace and safety. 38 They will be my people, and I will be their God. 39 And I will give them one heart and one purpose: to worship me forever, for their own good and for the good of all their descendants. 40 And I will make an everlasting covenant with them: I will never stop doing good for them. I will put a desire in their hearts to worship me, and they will never leave me. 41 I will find joy doing good for them and will faithfully and wholeheartedly replant them in this land.

42 "This is what the LORD says: Just as I have brought all these calamities on them, so I will do all the good I have promised them. 43 Fields will again be bought and sold in this land about which you now say, 'It has been ravaged by the Babylonians, a desolate land where people and animals have all disappeared.' 44 Yes, fields will once again be bought and sold—deeds signed and sealed and witnessed—in the land of Benjamin and here in Jerusalem, in the towns of Judah and in the hill country, in the foothills of Judah* and in the Negev, too. For someday I will restore prosperity to them. I, the LORD, have spoken!"

33 Promises of Peace and Prosperity

While Jeremiah was still confined in the courtyard of the guard, the LORD gave him this second message: 2 "This is what the LORD says—the LORD who made the earth, who formed and established it, whose name is the LORD: 3 Ask me and I will tell you remarkable secrets you do not know about things to come. 4 For this is what the LORD, the God of Israel, says: You have torn down the houses of this city and even the king's palace to get materials to strengthen the walls against the siege ramps and swords of the enemy. 5 You expect to fight the Babylonians,* but the men of this city are already as good as dead, for I have determined to destroy them in my terrible anger. I have abandoned them because of all their wickedness.

6 "Nevertheless, the time will come when

32:44 Hebrew *the Shephelah.* **33:5** Or *Chaldeans.*

I will heal Jerusalem's wounds and give it prosperity and true peace. ⁷I will restore the fortunes of Judah and Israel and rebuild their towns. ⁸I will cleanse them of their sins against me and forgive all their sins of rebellion. ⁹Then this city will bring me joy, glory, and honor before all the nations of the earth! The people of the world will see all the good I do for my people, and they will tremble with awe at the peace and prosperity I provide for them.

¹⁰"This is what the LORD says: You have said, 'This is a desolate land where people and animals have all disappeared.' Yet in the empty streets of Jerusalem and Judah's other towns, there will be heard once more ¹¹the sounds of joy and laughter. The joyful voices of bridegrooms and brides will be heard again, along with the joyous songs of people bringing thanksgiving offerings to the LORD. They will sing,

'Give thanks to the LORD of Heaven's
	Armies,
	for the LORD is good.
His faithful love endures forever!'

For I will restore the prosperity of this land to what it was in the past, says the LORD.

¹²"This is what the LORD of Heaven's Armies says: This land—though it is now desolate and has no people and animals—will once more have pastures where shepherds can lead their flocks. ¹³Once again shepherds will count their flocks in the towns of the hill country, the foothills of Judah,* the Negev, the land of Benjamin, the vicinity of Jerusalem, and all the towns of Judah. I, the LORD, have spoken!

¹⁴"The day will come, says the LORD, when I will do for Israel and Judah all the good things I have promised them.

¹⁵ "In those days and at that time
	I will raise up a righteous descendant*
		from King David's line.
	He will do what is just and right
		throughout the land.
¹⁶ In that day Judah will be saved,
	and Jerusalem will live in
		safety.
	And this will be its name:
	'The LORD Is Our Righteousness.'*

¹⁷For this is what the LORD says: David will have a descendant sitting on the throne of Israel forever. ¹⁸And there will always be Levitical priests to offer burnt offerings and grain offerings and sacrifices to me."

¹⁹Then this message came to Jeremiah from the LORD: ²⁰"This is what the LORD says: If you can break my covenant with the day and the night so that one does not follow the other, ²¹only then will my covenant with my servant David be broken. Only then will he no longer have a descendant to reign on his throne. The same is true for my covenant with the Levitical priests who minister before me. ²²And as the stars of the sky cannot be counted and the sand on the seashore cannot be measured, so I will multiply the descendants of my servant David and the Levites who minister before me."

²³The LORD gave another message to Jeremiah. He said, ²⁴"Have you noticed what people are saying?—'The LORD chose Judah and Israel and then abandoned them!' They are sneering and saying that Israel is not worthy to be counted as a nation. ²⁵But this is what the LORD says: I would no more reject my people than I would change my laws that govern night and day, earth and sky. ²⁶I will never abandon the descendants of Jacob or David, my servant, or change the plan that David's descendants will rule the descendants of Abraham, Isaac, and Jacob. Instead, I will restore them to their land and have mercy on them."

34 A Warning for Zedekiah

King Nebuchadnezzar of Babylon came with all the armies from the kingdoms he ruled, and he fought against Jerusalem and the towns of Judah. At that time this message came to Jeremiah from the LORD: ²"Go to King Zedekiah of Judah, and tell him, 'This is what the LORD, the God of Israel, says: I am about to hand this city over to the king of Babylon, and he will burn it down. ³You will not escape his grasp but will be captured and taken to meet the king of Babylon face to face. Then you will be exiled to Babylon.

⁴"'But listen to this promise from the LORD, O Zedekiah, king of Judah. This is

---

33:13 Hebrew *the Shephelah.*   **33:15** Hebrew *a righteous branch.*   **33:16** Hebrew *Yahweh Tsidqenu.*

what the LORD says: You will not be killed in war ⁵but will die peacefully. People will burn incense in your memory, just as they did for your ancestors, the kings who preceded you. They will mourn for you, crying, "Alas, our master is dead!" This I have decreed, says the LORD.'"

⁶So Jeremiah the prophet delivered the message to King Zedekiah of Judah. ⁷At this time the Babylonian army was besieging Jerusalem, Lachish, and Azekah—the only fortified cities of Judah not yet captured.

Freedom for Hebrew Slaves

⁸This message came to Jeremiah from the LORD after King Zedekiah made a covenant with the people, proclaiming freedom for the slaves. ⁹He had ordered all the people to free their Hebrew slaves—both men and women. No one was to keep a fellow Judean in bondage. ¹⁰The officials and all the people had obeyed the king's command, ¹¹but later they changed their minds. They took back the men and women they had freed, forcing them to be slaves again.

¹²So the LORD gave them this message through Jeremiah: ¹³"This is what the LORD, the God of Israel, says: I made a covenant with your ancestors long ago when I rescued them from their slavery in Egypt. ¹⁴I told them that every Hebrew slave must be freed after serving six years. But your ancestors paid no attention to me. ¹⁵Recently you repented and did what was right, following my command. You freed your slaves and made a solemn covenant with me in the Temple that bears my name. ¹⁶But now you have shrugged off your oath and defiled my name by taking back the men and women you had freed, forcing them to be slaves once again.

¹⁷"Therefore, this is what the LORD says: Since you have not obeyed me by setting your countrymen free, I will set you free to be destroyed by war, disease, and famine. You will be an object of horror to all the nations of the earth. ¹⁸Because you have broken the terms of our covenant, I will cut you apart just as you cut apart the calf when you walked between its halves to solemnize your vows. ¹⁹Yes, I will cut you

apart, whether you are officials of Judah or Jerusalem, court officials, priests, or common people—for you have broken your oath. ²⁰I will give you to your enemies, and they will kill you. Your bodies will be food for the vultures and wild animals.

²¹"I will hand over King Zedekiah of Judah and his officials to the army of the king of Babylon. And although Babylon's king has left Jerusalem for a while, ²²I will call the Babylonian armies back again. They will fight against this city and will capture it and burn it down. I will see to it that all the towns of Judah are destroyed, with no one living there."

35 The Faithful Recabites

This is the message the LORD gave Jeremiah when Jehoiakim son of Josiah was king of Judah: ²"Go to the settlement where the families of the Recabites live, and invite them to the LORD's Temple. Take them into one of the inner rooms, and offer them some wine."

³So I went to see Jaazaniah son of Jeremiah and grandson of Habazziniah and all his brothers and sons—representing all the Recabite families. ⁴I took them to the Temple, and we went into the room assigned to the sons of Hanan son of Igdaliah, a man of God. This room was located next to the one used by the Temple officials, directly above the room of Maaseiah son of Shallum, the Temple gatekeeper.

⁵I set cups and jugs of wine before them and invited them to have a drink, ⁶but they refused. "No," they said, "we don't drink wine, because our ancestor Jehonadab* son of Recab gave us this command: 'You and your descendants must never drink wine. ⁷And do not build houses or plant crops or vineyards, but always live in tents. If you follow these commands, you will live long, good lives in the land.' ⁸So we have obeyed him in all these things. We have never had a drink of wine to this day, nor have our wives, our sons, or our daughters. ⁹We haven't built houses or owned vineyards or farms or planted crops. ¹⁰We have lived in tents and have fully obeyed all the commands of Jehonadab, our ancestor. ¹¹But

---

35:6 Hebrew *Jonadab*, a variant spelling of Jehonadab; also in 35:10, 14, 16, 18, 19. See 2 Kgs 10:15.

when King Nebuchadnezzar* of Babylon attacked this country, we were afraid of the Babylonian and Syrian* armies. So we decided to move to Jerusalem. That is why we are here."

12 Then the LORD gave this message to Jeremiah: 13 "This is what the LORD of Heaven's Armies, the God of Israel, says: Go and say to the people in Judah and Jerusalem, 'Come and learn a lesson about how to obey me. 14 The Recabites do not drink wine to this day because their ancestor Jehonadab told them not to. But I have spoken to you again and again, and you refuse to obey me. 15 Time after time I sent you prophets, who told you, "Turn from your wicked ways, and start doing things right. Stop worshiping other gods so that you might live in peace here in the land I have given to you and your ancestors." But you would not listen to me or obey me. 16 The descendants of Jehonadab son of Recab have obeyed their ancestor completely, but you have refused to listen to me.'

17 "Therefore, this is what the LORD God of Heaven's Armies, the God of Israel, says: 'Because you refuse to listen or answer when I call, I will send upon Judah and Jerusalem all the disasters I have threatened.'"

18 Then Jeremiah turned to the Recabites and said, "This is what the LORD of Heaven's Armies, the God of Israel, says: 'You have obeyed your ancestor Jehonadab in every respect, following all his instructions.' 19 Therefore, this is what the LORD of Heaven's Armies, the God of Israel, says: 'Jehonadab son of Recab will always have descendants who serve me.'"

36 Baruch Reads the LORD's Messages

During the fourth year that Jehoiakim son of Josiah was king in Judah,* the LORD gave this message to Jeremiah: 2 "Get a scroll, and write down all my messages against Israel, Judah, and the other nations. Begin with the first message back in the days of Josiah, and write down every message, right up to the present time. 3 Perhaps the people of Judah will repent when they hear again all the terrible things I have planned for them. Then I will be able to forgive their sins and wrongdoings."

4 So Jeremiah sent for Baruch son of Neriah, and as Jeremiah dictated all the prophecies that the LORD had given him, Baruch wrote them on a scroll. 5 Then Jeremiah said to Baruch, "I am a prisoner here and unable to go to the Temple. 6 So you go to the Temple on the next day of fasting, and read the messages from the LORD that I have had you write on this scroll. Read them so the people who are there from all over Judah will hear them. 7 Perhaps even yet they will turn from their evil ways and ask the LORD's forgiveness before it is too late. For the LORD has threatened them with his terrible anger."

8 Baruch did as Jeremiah told him and read these messages from the LORD to the people at the Temple. 9 He did this on a day of sacred fasting held in late autumn,* during the fifth year of the reign of Jehoiakim son of Josiah. People from all over Judah had come to Jerusalem to attend the services at the Temple on that day. 10 Baruch read Jeremiah's words on the scroll to all the people. He stood in front of the Temple room of Gemariah, son of Shaphan the secretary. This room was just off the upper courtyard of the Temple, near the New Gate entrance.

11 When Micaiah son of Gemariah and grandson of Shaphan heard the messages from the LORD, 12 he went down to the secretary's room in the palace where the administrative officials were meeting. Elishama the secretary was there, along with Delaiah son of Shemaiah, Elnathan son of Acbor, Gemariah son of Shaphan, Zedekiah son of Hananiah, and all the other officials. 13 When Micaiah told them about the messages Baruch was reading to the people, 14 the officials sent Jehudi son of Nethaniah, grandson of Shelemiah and great-grandson of Cushi, to ask Baruch to come and read the messages to them, too. So Baruch took the scroll and went to them. 15 "Sit down and read the scroll to us," the officials said, and Baruch did as they requested.

35:11a Hebrew *Nebuchadrezzar*, a variant spelling of Nebuchadnezzar.   35:11b Or *Chaldean and Aramean.*   36:1 The fourth year of Jehoiakim's reign was 605 B.C.   36:9 Hebrew *in the ninth month,* of the ancient Hebrew lunar calendar (also in 36:22). The ninth month in the fifth year of Jehoiakim's reign occurred within the months of November and December 604 B.C. Also see note on 1:3.

¹⁶When they heard all the messages, they looked at one another in alarm. "We must tell the king what we have heard," they said to Baruch. ¹⁷"But first, tell us how you got these messages. Did they come directly from Jeremiah?"

¹⁸So Baruch explained, "Jeremiah dictated them, and I wrote them down in ink, word for word, on this scroll."

¹⁹"You and Jeremiah should both hide," the officials told Baruch. "Don't tell anyone where you are!" ²⁰Then the officials left the scroll for safekeeping in the room of Elishama the secretary and went to tell the king what had happened.

King Jehoiakim Burns the Scroll

²¹The king sent Jehudi to get the scroll. Jehudi brought it from Elishama's room and read it to the king as all his officials stood by. ²²It was late autumn, and the king was in a winterized part of the palace, sitting in front of a fire to keep warm. ²³Each time Jehudi finished reading three or four columns, the king took a knife and cut off that section of the scroll. He then threw it into the fire, section by section, until the whole scroll was burned up. ²⁴Neither the king nor his attendants showed any signs of fear or repentance at what they heard. ²⁵Even when Elnathan, Delaiah, and Gemariah begged the king not to burn the scroll, he wouldn't listen.

²⁶Then the king commanded his son Jerahmeel, Seraiah son of Azriel, and Shelemiah son of Abdeel to arrest Baruch and Jeremiah. But the LORD had hidden them.

Jeremiah Rewrites the Scroll

²⁷After the king had burned the scroll on which Baruch had written Jeremiah's words, the LORD gave Jeremiah another message. He said, ²⁸"Get another scroll, and write everything again just as you did on the scroll King Jehoiakim burned. ²⁹Then say to the king, 'This is what the LORD says: You burned the scroll because it said the king of Babylon would destroy this land and empty it of people and animals. ³⁰Now this is what the LORD says about King Jehoiakim of Judah: He will have no

heirs to sit on the throne of David. His dead body will be thrown out to lie unburied—exposed to the heat of the day and the frost of the night. ³¹I will punish him and his family and his attendants for their sins. I will pour out on them and on all the people of Jerusalem and Judah all the disasters I promised, for they would not listen to my warnings.'"

³²So Jeremiah took another scroll and dictated again to his secretary, Baruch. He wrote everything that had been on the scroll King Jehoiakim had burned in the fire. Only this time he added much more!

37 Zedekiah Calls for Jeremiah

Zedekiah son of Josiah succeeded Jehoiachin* son of Jehoiakim as the king of Judah. He was appointed by King Nebuchadnezzar* of Babylon. ²But neither King Zedekiah nor his attendants nor the people who were left in the land listened to what the LORD said through Jeremiah.

³Nevertheless, King Zedekiah sent Jehucal son of Shelemiah, and Zephaniah the priest, son of Maaseiah, to ask Jeremiah, "Please pray to the LORD our God for us." ⁴Jeremiah had not yet been imprisoned, so he could come and go among the people as he pleased.

⁵At this time the army of Pharaoh Hophra* of Egypt appeared at the southern border of Judah. When the Babylonian* army heard about it, they withdrew from their siege of Jerusalem.

⁶Then the LORD gave this message to Jeremiah: ⁷"This is what the LORD, the God of Israel, says: The king of Judah sent you to ask me what is going to happen. Tell him, 'Pharaoh's army is about to return to Egypt, though he came here to help you. ⁸Then the Babylonians* will come back and capture this city and burn it to the ground.'

⁹"This is what the LORD says: Do not fool yourselves into thinking that the Babylonians are gone for good. They aren't! ¹⁰Even if you were to destroy the entire Babylonian army, leaving only a handful of wounded survivors, they would still stagger from their tents and burn this city to the ground!"

37:1a Hebrew *Coniah*, a variant spelling of Jehoiachin. **37:1b** Hebrew *Nebuchadrezzar*, a variant spelling of Nebuchadnezzar.
37:5a Hebrew *army of Pharaoh*; see 44:30. **37:5b** Or *Chaldean*; also in 37:10, 11. **37:8** Or *Chaldeans*; also in 37:9, 13.

Jeremiah Is Imprisoned

¹¹ When the Babylonian army left Jerusalem because of Pharaoh's approaching army, ¹² Jeremiah started to leave the city on his way to the territory of Benjamin, to claim his share of the property among his relatives there.* ¹³ But as he was walking through the Benjamin Gate, a sentry arrested him and said, "You are defecting to the Babylonians!" The sentry making the arrest was Irijah son of Shelemiah, grandson of Hananiah.

¹⁴ "That's not true!" Jeremiah protested. "I had no intention of doing any such thing." But Irijah wouldn't listen, and he took Jeremiah before the officials. ¹⁵ They were furious with Jeremiah and had him flogged and imprisoned in the house of Jonathan the secretary. Jonathan's house had been converted into a prison. ¹⁶ Jeremiah was put into a dungeon cell, where he remained for many days.

¹⁷ Later King Zedekiah secretly requested that Jeremiah come to the palace, where the king asked him, "Do you have any messages from the LORD?"

"Yes, I do!" said Jeremiah. "You will be defeated by the king of Babylon."

¹⁸ Then Jeremiah asked the king, "What crime have I committed? What have I done against you, your attendants, or the people that I should be imprisoned like this? ¹⁹ Where are your prophets now who told you the king of Babylon would not attack you or this land? ²⁰ Listen, my lord the king, I beg you. Don't send me back to the dungeon in the house of Jonathan the secretary, for I will die there."

²¹ So King Zedekiah commanded that Jeremiah not be returned to the dungeon. Instead, he was imprisoned in the courtyard of the guard in the royal palace. The king also commanded that Jeremiah be given a loaf of fresh bread every day as long as there was any left in the city. So Jeremiah was put in the palace prison.

38 Jeremiah in a Cistern

Now Shephatiah son of Mattan, Gedaliah son of Pashhur, Jehucal* son of Shelemiah, and Pashhur son of Malkijah heard what Jeremiah had been telling the people. He had been saying, ²"This is what the LORD says: 'Everyone who stays in Jerusalem will die from war, famine, or disease, but those who surrender to the Babylonians* will live. Their reward will be life. They will live!' ³ The LORD also says: 'The city of Jerusalem will certainly be handed over to the army of the king of Babylon, who will capture it.'"

⁴ So these officials went to the king and said, "Sir, this man must die! That kind of talk will undermine the morale of the few fighting men we have left, as well as that of all the people. This man is a traitor!"

⁵ King Zedekiah agreed. "All right," he said. "Do as you like. I can't stop you."

⁶ So the officials took Jeremiah from his cell and lowered him by ropes into an empty cistern in the prison yard. It belonged to Malkijah, a member of the royal family. There was no water in the cistern, but there was a thick layer of mud at the bottom, and Jeremiah sank down into it.

⁷ But Ebed-melech the Ethiopian,* an important court official, heard that Jeremiah was in the cistern. At that time the king was holding court at the Benjamin Gate, ⁸ so Ebed-melech rushed from the palace to speak with him. ⁹ "My lord the king," he said, "these men have done a very evil thing in putting Jeremiah the prophet into the cistern. He will soon die of hunger, for almost all the bread in the city is gone."

¹⁰ So the king told Ebed-melech, "Take thirty of my men with you, and pull Jeremiah out of the cistern before he dies."

¹¹ So Ebed-melech took the men with him and went to a room in the palace beneath the treasury, where he found some old rags and discarded clothing. He carried these to the cistern and lowered them to Jeremiah on a rope. ¹² Ebed-melech called down to Jeremiah, "Put these rags under your armpits to protect you from the ropes." Then when Jeremiah was ready, ¹³ they pulled him out. So Jeremiah was returned to the courtyard of the guard—the palace prison—where he remained.

37:12 Hebrew *to separate from there in the midst of the people.*   **38:1** Hebrew *Jucal,* a variant spelling of Jehucal; see 37:3.   **38:2** Or *Chaldeans;* also in 38:18, 19, 23.   **38:7** Hebrew *the Cushite.*

Zedekiah Questions Jeremiah

[14] One day King Zedekiah sent for Jeremiah and had him brought to the third entrance of the LORD's Temple. "I want to ask you something," the king said. "And don't try to hide the truth."

[15] Jeremiah said, "If I tell you the truth, you will kill me. And if I give you advice, you won't listen to me anyway."

[16] So King Zedekiah secretly promised him, "As surely as the LORD our Creator lives, I will not kill you or hand you over to the men who want you dead."

[17] Then Jeremiah said to Zedekiah, "This is what the LORD God of Heaven's Armies, the God of Israel, says: 'If you surrender to the Babylonian officers, you and your family will live, and the city will not be burned down. [18] But if you refuse to surrender, you will not escape! This city will be handed over to the Babylonians, and they will burn it to the ground.'"

[19] "But I am afraid to surrender," the king said, "for the Babylonians may hand me over to the Judeans who have defected to them. And who knows what they will do to me!"

[20] Jeremiah replied, "You won't be handed over to them if you choose to obey the LORD. Your life will be spared, and all will go well for you. [21] But if you refuse to surrender, this is what the LORD has revealed to me: [22] All the women left in your palace will be brought out and given to the officers of the Babylonian army. Then the women will taunt you, saying,

'What fine friends you have!
    They have betrayed and misled you.
When your feet sank in the mud,
    they left you to your fate!'

[23] All your wives and children will be led out to the Babylonians, and you will not escape. You will be seized by the king of Babylon, and this city will be burned down."

[24] Then Zedekiah said to Jeremiah, "Don't tell anyone you told me this, or you will die! [25] My officials may hear that I spoke to you, and they may say, 'Tell us what you and the king were talking about. If you don't tell us, we will kill you.' [26] If this happens, just tell them you begged me not to send you back to Jonathan's dungeon, for fear you would die there."

[27] Sure enough, it wasn't long before the king's officials came to Jeremiah and asked him why the king had called for him. But Jeremiah followed the king's instructions, and they left without finding out the truth. No one had overheard the conversation between Jeremiah and the king. [28] And Jeremiah remained a prisoner in the courtyard of the guard until the day Jerusalem was captured.

39 The Fall of Jerusalem

In January* of the ninth year of King Zedekiah's reign, King Nebuchadnezzar* came with his army to besiege Jerusalem. [2] Two and a half years later, on July 18* in the eleventh year of Zedekiah's reign, the Babylonians broke through the wall, and the city fell. [3] All the officers of the Babylonian army came in and sat in triumph at the Middle Gate: Nergal-sharezer of Samgar, and Nebo-sarsekim,* a chief officer, and Nergal-sharezer, the king's adviser, and all the other officers.

[4] When King Zedekiah and all the soldiers saw that the Babylonians had broken into the city, they fled. They waited for nightfall and then slipped through the gate between the two walls behind the king's garden and headed toward the Jordan Valley.*

[5] But the Babylonian* troops chased the king and caught him on the plains of Jericho. They took him to King Nebuchadnezzar of Babylon, who was at Riblah in the land of Hamath. There the king of Babylon pronounced judgment upon Zedekiah. [6] He made Zedekiah watch as they slaughtered his sons and all the nobles of Judah. [7] Then they gouged out Zedekiah's eyes, bound him in bronze chains, and led him away to Babylon.

[8] Meanwhile, the Babylonians burned Jerusalem, including the palace, and tore down the walls of the city. [9] Then Nebuzar-

---

39:1a Hebrew *in the tenth month,* of the ancient Hebrew lunar calendar. A number of events in Jeremiah can be cross-checked with dates in surviving Babylonian records and related accurately to our modern calendar. This event occurred on January 15, 588 B.C.; see 52:4a and the note there.   **39:1b** Hebrew *Nebuchadrezzar,* a variant spelling of Nebuchadnezzar; also in 39:11.   **39:2** Hebrew *On the ninth day of the fourth month.* This day was July 18, 586 B.C.; also see note on 39:1a.   **39:3** Or *Nergal-sharezer, Samgar-nebo, Sarsekim.*   **39:4** Hebrew *the Arabah.*   **39:5** Or *Chaldean;* similarly in 39:8.

adan, the captain of the guard, sent to Babylon the rest of the people who remained in the city as well as those who had defected to him. [10] But Nebuzaradan left a few of the poorest people in Judah, and he assigned them vineyards and fields to care for.

Jeremiah Remains in Judah

[11] King Nebuchadnezzar had told Nebuzaradan, the captain of the guard, to find Jeremiah. [12] "See that he isn't hurt," he said. "Look after him well, and give him anything he wants." [13] So Nebuzaradan, the captain of the guard; Nebushazban, a chief officer; Nergal-sharezer, the king's adviser; and the other officers of Babylon's king [14] sent messengers to bring Jeremiah out of the prison. They put him under the care of Gedaliah son of Ahikam and grandson of Shaphan, who took him back to his home. So Jeremiah stayed in Judah among his own people.

[15] The LORD had given the following message to Jeremiah while he was still in prison: [16] "Say to Ebed-melech the Ethiopian,* 'This is what the LORD of Heaven's Armies, the God of Israel, says: I will do to this city everything I have threatened. I will send disaster, not prosperity. You will see its destruction, [17] but I will rescue you from those you fear so much. [18] Because you trusted me, I will give you your life as a reward. I will rescue you and keep you safe. I, the LORD, have spoken!'"

40 The LORD gave a message to Jeremiah after Nebuzaradan, the captain of the guard, had released him at Ramah. He had found Jeremiah bound in chains among all the other captives of Jerusalem and Judah who were being sent to exile in Babylon.

[2] The captain of the guard called for Jeremiah and said, "The LORD your God has brought this disaster on this land, [3] just as he said he would. For these people have sinned against the LORD and disobeyed him. That is why it happened. [4] But I am going to take off your chains and let you go. If you want to come with me to Babylon, you are welcome. I will see that you

are well cared for. But if you don't want to come, you may stay here. The whole land is before you—go wherever you like. [5] If you decide to stay, then return to Gedaliah son of Ahikam and grandson of Shaphan. He has been appointed governor of Judah by the king of Babylon. Stay there with the people he rules. But it's up to you; go wherever you like."

Then Nebuzaradan, the captain of the guard, gave Jeremiah some food and money and let him go. [6] So Jeremiah returned to Gedaliah son of Ahikam at Mizpah, and he lived in Judah with the few who were still left in the land.

Gedaliah Governs in Judah

[7] The leaders of the Judean guerrilla bands in the countryside heard that the king of Babylon had appointed Gedaliah son of Ahikam as governor over the poor people who were left behind in Judah—the men, women, and children who hadn't been exiled to Babylon. [8] So they went to see Gedaliah at Mizpah. These included: Ishmael son of Nethaniah, Johanan and Jonathan sons of Kareah, Seraiah son of Tanhumeth, the sons of Ephai the Netophathite, Jezaniah son of the Maacathite, and all their men.

[9] Gedaliah vowed to them that the Babylonians* meant them no harm. "Don't be afraid to serve them. Live in the land and serve the king of Babylon, and all will go well for you," he promised. [10] "As for me, I will stay at Mizpah to represent you before the Babylonians who come to meet with us. Settle in the towns you have taken, and live off the land. Harvest the grapes and summer fruits and olives, and store them away."

[11] When the Judeans in Moab, Ammon, Edom, and the other nearby countries heard that the king of Babylon had left a few people in Judah and that Gedaliah was the governor, [12] they began to return to Judah from the places to which they had fled. They stopped at Mizpah to meet with Gedaliah and then went into the Judean countryside to gather a great harvest of grapes and other crops.

39:16 Hebrew *the Cushite.*   **40:9** Or *Chaldeans;* also in 40:10.

A Plot against Gedaliah

¹³ Soon after this, Johanan son of Kareah and the other guerrilla leaders came to Gedaliah at Mizpah. ¹⁴ They said to him, "Did you know that Baalis, king of Ammon, has sent Ishmael son of Nethaniah to assassinate you?" But Gedaliah refused to believe them.

¹⁵ Later Johanan had a private conference with Gedaliah and volunteered to kill Ishmael secretly. "Why should we let him come and murder you?" Johanan asked. "What will happen then to the Judeans who have returned? Why should the few of us who are still left be scattered and lost?"

¹⁶ But Gedaliah said to Johanan, "I forbid you to do any such thing, for you are lying about Ishmael."

41 The Murder of Gedaliah

But in midautumn,* Ishmael son of Nethaniah and grandson of Elishama, who was a member of the royal family and had been one of the king's high officials, went to Mizpah with ten men to meet Gedaliah. While they were eating together, ² Ishmael and his ten men suddenly jumped up, drew their swords, and killed Gedaliah, whom the king of Babylon had appointed governor. ³ Ishmael also killed all the Judeans and the Babylonian* soldiers who were with Gedaliah at Mizpah.

⁴ The next day, before anyone had heard about Gedaliah's murder, ⁵ eighty men arrived from Shechem, Shiloh, and Samaria to worship at the Temple of the LORD. They had shaved off their beards, torn their clothes, and cut themselves, and had brought along grain offerings and frankincense. ⁶ Ishmael left Mizpah to meet them, weeping as he went. When he reached them, he said, "Oh, come and see what has happened to Gedaliah!"

⁷ But as soon as they were all inside the town, Ishmael and his men killed all but ten of them and threw their bodies into a cistern. ⁸ The other ten had talked Ishmael into letting them go by promising to bring him their stores of wheat, barley, olive oil, and honey that they had hidden away. ⁹ The cistern where Ishmael dumped the bodies of the men he murdered was the large one dug by King Asa when he fortified Mizpah to protect himself against King Baasha of Israel. Ishmael son of Nethaniah filled it with corpses.

¹⁰ Then Ishmael made captives of the king's daughters and the other people who had been left under Gedaliah's care in Mizpah by Nebuzaradan, the captain of the guard. Taking them with him, he started back toward the land of Ammon.

¹¹ But when Johanan son of Kareah and the other guerrilla leaders heard about Ishmael's crimes, ¹² they took all their men and set out to stop him. They caught up with him at the large pool near Gibeon. ¹³ The people Ishmael had captured shouted for joy when they saw Johanan and the other guerrilla leaders. ¹⁴ And all the captives from Mizpah escaped and began to help Johanan. ¹⁵ Meanwhile, Ishmael and eight of his men escaped from Johanan into the land of Ammon.

¹⁶ Then Johanan son of Kareah and the other guerrilla leaders took all the people they had rescued in Gibeon—the soldiers, women, children, and court officials* whom Ishmael had captured after he killed Gedaliah. ¹⁷ They took them all to the village of Geruth-kimham near Bethlehem, where they prepared to leave for Egypt. ¹⁸ They were afraid of what the Babylonians* would do when they heard that Ishmael had killed Gedaliah, the governor appointed by the Babylonian king.

42 Warning to Stay in Judah

Then all the guerrilla leaders, including Johanan son of Kareah and Jezaniah* son of Hoshaiah, and all the people, from the least to the greatest, approached ² Jeremiah the prophet. They said, "Please pray to the LORD your God for us. As you can see, we are only a tiny remnant compared to what we were before. ³ Pray that the LORD your God will show us what to do and where to go."

⁴ "All right," Jeremiah replied. "I will pray to the LORD your God, as you have asked,

---

41:1 Hebrew *in the seventh month*, of the ancient Hebrew lunar calendar. This month occurred within the months of October and November 586 B.C.; also see note on 39:1a. **41:3** Or *Chaldean*. **41:16** Or *eunuchs*. **41:18** Or *Chaldeans*. **42:1** Greek version reads *Azariah*; compare 43:2.

and I will tell you everything he says. I will hide nothing from you."

⁵Then they said to Jeremiah, "May the LORD your God be a faithful witness against us if we refuse to obey whatever he tells us to do! ⁶Whether we like it or not, we will obey the LORD our God to whom we are sending you with our plea. For if we obey him, everything will turn out well for us."

⁷Ten days later the LORD gave his reply to Jeremiah. ⁸So he called for Johanan son of Kareah and the other guerrilla leaders, and for all the people, from the least to the greatest. ⁹He said to them, "You sent me to the LORD, the God of Israel, with your request, and this is his reply: ¹⁰'Stay here in this land. If you do, I will build you up and not tear you down; I will plant you and not uproot you. For I am sorry about all the punishment I have had to bring upon you. ¹¹Do not fear the king of Babylon anymore,' says the LORD. 'For I am with you and will save you and rescue you from his power. ¹²I will be merciful to you by making him kind, so he will let you stay here in your land.'

¹³"But if you refuse to obey the LORD your God, and if you say, 'We will not stay here; ¹⁴instead, we will go to Egypt where we will be free from war, the call to arms, and hunger,' ¹⁵then hear the LORD's message to the remnant of Judah. This is what the LORD of Heaven's Armies, the God of Israel, says: 'If you are determined to go to Egypt and live there, ¹⁶the very war and famine you fear will catch up to you, and you will die there. ¹⁷That is the fate awaiting every one of you who insists on going to live in Egypt. Yes, you will die from war, famine, and disease. None of you will escape the disaster I will bring upon you there.'

¹⁸"This is what the LORD of Heaven's Armies, the God of Israel, says: 'Just as my anger and fury have been poured out on the people of Jerusalem, so they will be poured out on you when you enter Egypt. You will be an object of damnation, horror, cursing, and mockery. And you will never see your homeland again.'

¹⁹"Listen, you remnant of Judah. The LORD has told you: 'Do not go to Egypt!' Don't forget this warning I have given you

today. ²⁰For you were not being honest when you sent me to pray to the LORD your God for you. You said, 'Just tell us what the LORD our God says, and we will do it!' ²¹And today I have told you exactly what he said, but you will not obey the LORD your God any better now than you have in the past. ²²So you can be sure that you will die from war, famine, and disease in Egypt, where you insist on going."

43 Jeremiah Taken to Egypt

When Jeremiah had finished giving this message from the LORD their God to all the people, ²Azariah son of Hoshaiah and Johanan son of Kareah and all the other proud men said to Jeremiah, "You lie! The LORD our God hasn't forbidden us to go to Egypt! ³Baruch son of Neriah has convinced you to say this, because he wants us to stay here and be killed by the Babylonians* or be carried off into exile."

⁴So Johanan and the other guerrilla leaders and all the people refused to obey the LORD's command to stay in Judah. ⁵Johanan and the other leaders took with them all the people who had returned from the nearby countries to which they had fled. ⁶In the crowd were men, women, and children, the king's daughters, and all those whom Nebuzaradan, the captain of the guard, had left with Gedaliah. The prophet Jeremiah and Baruch were also included. ⁷The people refused to obey the voice of the LORD and went to Egypt, going as far as the city of Tahpanhes.

⁸Then at Tahpanhes, the LORD gave another message to Jeremiah. He said, ⁹"While the people of Judah are watching, take some large rocks and bury them under the pavement stones at the entrance of Pharaoh's palace here in Tahpanhes. ¹⁰Then say to the people of Judah, 'This is what the LORD of Heaven's Armies, the God of Israel, says: I will certainly bring my servant Nebuchadnezzar,* king of Babylon, here to Egypt. I will set his throne over these stones that I have hidden. He will spread his royal canopy over them. ¹¹And when he comes, he will destroy the land of Egypt. He will bring death to those destined for

---

43:3 Or *Chaldeans.* **43:10** Hebrew *Nebuchadrezzar,* a variant spelling of Nebuchadnezzar.

death, captivity to those destined for captivity, and war to those destined for war. ¹²He will set fire to the temples of Egypt's gods; he will burn the temples and carry the idols away as plunder. He will pick clean the land of Egypt as a shepherd picks fleas from his cloak. And he himself will leave unharmed. ¹³He will break down the sacred pillars standing in the temple of the sun* in Egypt, and he will burn down the temples of Egypt's gods.'"

44

Judgment for Idolatry

This is the message Jeremiah received concerning the Judeans living in northern Egypt in the cities of Migdol, Tahpanhes, and Memphis,* and in southern Egypt* as well: ²"This is what the LORD of Heaven's Armies, the God of Israel, says: You saw the calamity I brought on Jerusalem and all the towns of Judah. They now lie deserted and in ruins. ³They provoked my anger with all their wickedness. They burned incense and worshiped other gods—gods that neither they nor you nor any of your ancestors had ever even known.

⁴"Again and again I sent my servants, the prophets, to plead with them, 'Don't do these horrible things that I hate so much.' ⁵But my people would not listen or turn back from their wicked ways. They kept on burning incense to these gods. ⁶And so my fury boiled over and fell like fire on the towns of Judah and into the streets of Jerusalem, and they are still a desolate ruin today.

⁷"And now the LORD God of Heaven's Armies, the God of Israel, asks you: Why are you destroying yourselves? For not one of you will survive—not a man, woman, or child among you who has come here from Judah, not even the babies in your arms. ⁸Why provoke my anger by burning incense to the idols you have made here in Egypt? You will only destroy yourselves and make yourselves an object of cursing and mockery for all the nations of the earth. ⁹Have you forgotten the sins of your ancestors, the sins of the kings and queens of Judah, and the sins you and your wives committed in Judah and Jerusalem? ¹⁰To this very hour

you have shown no remorse or reverence. No one has chosen to follow my word and the decrees I gave to you and your ancestors before you.

¹¹"Therefore, this is what the LORD of Heaven's Armies, the God of Israel, says: I am determined to destroy every one of you! ¹²I will take this remnant of Judah—those who were determined to come here and live in Egypt—and I will consume them. They will fall here in Egypt, killed by war and famine. All will die, from the least to the greatest. They will be an object of damnation, horror, cursing, and mockery. ¹³I will punish them in Egypt just as I punished them in Jerusalem, by war, famine, and disease. ¹⁴Of that remnant who fled to Egypt, hoping someday to return to Judah, there will be no survivors. Even though they long to return home, only a handful will do so."

¹⁵Then all the women present and all the men who knew that their wives had burned incense to idols—a great crowd of all the Judeans living in northern Egypt and southern Egypt*—answered Jeremiah, ¹⁶"We will not listen to your messages from the LORD! ¹⁷We will do whatever we want. We will burn incense and pour out liquid offerings to the Queen of Heaven just as much as we like—just as we, and our ancestors, and our kings and officials have always done in the towns of Judah and in the streets of Jerusalem. For in those days we had plenty to eat, and we were well off and had no troubles! ¹⁸But ever since we quit burning incense to the Queen of Heaven and stopped worshiping her with liquid offerings, we have been in great trouble and have been dying from war and famine."

¹⁹"Besides," the women added, "do you suppose that we were burning incense and pouring out liquid offerings to the Queen of Heaven, and making cakes marked with her image, without our husbands knowing it and helping us? Of course not!"

²⁰Then Jeremiah said to all of them, men and women alike, who had given him that answer, ²¹"Do you think the LORD did not know that you and your ancestors, your kings and officials, and all the people were burning incense to idols in the towns of

---

43:13 Or in *Heliopolis.*   44:1a Hebrew *Noph.*   44:1b Hebrew *in Pathros.*   44:15 Hebrew *in Egypt, in Pathros.*

Judah and in the streets of Jerusalem? ²²It was because the LORD could no longer bear all the disgusting things you were doing that he made your land an object of cursing—a desolate ruin without inhabitants—as it is today. ²³All these terrible things happened to you because you have burned incense to idols and sinned against the LORD. You have refused to obey him and have not followed his instructions, his decrees, and his laws."

²⁴Then Jeremiah said to them all, including the women, "Listen to this message from the LORD, all you citizens of Judah who live in Egypt. ²⁵This is what the LORD of Heaven's Armies, the God of Israel, says: 'You and your wives have said, "We will keep our promises to burn incense and pour out liquid offerings to the Queen of Heaven," and you have proved by your actions that you meant it. So go ahead and carry out your promises and vows to her!'

²⁶"But listen to this message from the LORD, all you Judeans now living in Egypt: 'I have sworn by my great name,' says the LORD, 'that my name will no longer be spoken by any of the Judeans in the land of Egypt. None of you may invoke my name or use this oath: "As surely as the Sovereign LORD lives." ²⁷For I will watch over you to bring you disaster and not good. Everyone from Judah who is now living in Egypt will suffer war and famine until all of you are dead. ²⁸Only a small number will escape death and return to Judah from Egypt. Then all those who came to Egypt will find out whose words are true—mine or theirs!

²⁹"'And this is the proof I give you,' says the LORD, 'that all I have threatened will happen to you and that I will punish you here.' ³⁰This is what the LORD says: 'I will turn Pharaoh Hophra, king of Egypt, over to his enemies who want to kill him, just as I turned King Zedekiah of Judah over to King Nebuchadnezzar* of Babylon.'"

45 A Message for Baruch

The prophet Jeremiah gave a message to Baruch son of Neriah in the fourth year of the reign of Jehoiakim son of Josiah,* after Baruch had written down everything Jeremiah had dictated to him. He said, ²"This is what the LORD, the God of Israel, says to you, Baruch: ³You have said, 'I am overwhelmed with trouble! Haven't I had enough pain already? And now the LORD has added more! I am worn out from sighing and can find no rest.'

⁴"Baruch, this is what the LORD says: 'I will destroy this nation that I built. I will uproot what I planted. ⁵Are you seeking great things for yourself? Don't do it! I will bring great disaster upon all these people; but I will give you your life as a reward wherever you go. I, the LORD, have spoken!'"

46 Messages for the Nations

The following messages were given to Jeremiah the prophet from the LORD concerning foreign nations.

Messages about Egypt

²This message concerning Egypt was given in the fourth year of the reign of Jehoiakim son of Josiah, the king of Judah, on the occasion of the battle of Carchemish* when Pharaoh Neco, king of Egypt, and his army were defeated beside the Euphrates River by King Nebuchadnezzar* of Babylon.

³ "Prepare your shields,
   and advance into battle!
⁴ Harness the horses,
   and mount the stallions.
 Take your positions.
   Put on your helmets.
 Sharpen your spears,
   and prepare your armor.
⁵ But what do I see?
   The Egyptian army flees in terror.
 The bravest of its fighting men run
   without a backward glance.
 They are terrorized at every turn,"
   says the LORD.
⁶ "The swiftest runners cannot flee;
   the mightiest warriors cannot escape.
 By the Euphrates River to the north,
   they stumble and fall.

⁷ "Who is this, rising like the Nile at
      floodtime,
   overflowing all the land?

44:30 Hebrew *Nebuchadrezzar*, a variant spelling of Nebuchadnezzar.   45:1 The fourth year of Jehoiakim's reign was 605 B.C.   46:2a This event occurred in 605 B.C., during the fourth year of Jehoiakim's reign (according to the calendar system in which the new year begins in the spring).   46:2b Hebrew *Nebuchadrezzar*, a variant spelling of Nebuchadnezzar; also in 46:13, 26.

8 It is the Egyptian army,
overflowing all the land,
boasting that it will cover the earth like
a flood,
destroying cities and their people.
9 Charge, you horses and chariots;
attack, you mighty warriors of Egypt!
Come, all you allies from Ethiopia,
Libya, and Lydia*
who are skilled with the shield and
bow!
10 For this is the day of the Lord, the LORD
of Heaven's Armies,
a day of vengeance on his enemies.
The sword will devour until it is
satisfied,
yes, until it is drunk with your
blood!
The Lord, the LORD of Heaven's Armies,
will receive a sacrifice today
in the north country beside the
Euphrates River.

11 "Go up to Gilead to get medicine,
O virgin daughter of Egypt!
But your many treatments
will bring you no healing.
12 The nations have heard of your shame.
The earth is filled with your cries of
despair.
Your mightiest warriors will run into
each other
and fall down together."

13 Then the LORD gave the prophet Jeremiah this message about King Nebuchadnezzar's plans to attack Egypt.

14 "Shout it out in Egypt!
Publish it in the cities of Migdol,
Memphis,* and Tahpanhes!
Mobilize for battle,
for the sword will devour everyone
around you.
15 Why have your warriors fallen?
They cannot stand, for the LORD has
knocked them down.
16 They stumble and fall over each other
and say among themselves,
'Come, let's go back to our people,
to the land of our birth.
Let's get away from the sword of the
enemy!'

17 There they will say,
'Pharaoh, the king of Egypt, is a
loudmouth
who missed his opportunity!'

18 "As surely as I live," says the King,
whose name is the LORD of Heaven's
Armies,
"one is coming against Egypt
who is as tall as Mount Tabor,
or as Mount Carmel by the sea!
19 Pack up! Get ready to leave for exile,
you citizens of Egypt!
The city of Memphis will be destroyed,
without a single inhabitant.
20 Egypt is as sleek as a beautiful young cow,
but a horsefly from the north is on its
way!
21 Egypt's mercenaries have become like
fattened calves.
They, too, will turn and run,
for it is a day of great disaster for Egypt,
a time of great punishment.
22 Egypt flees, silent as a serpent gliding
away.
The invading army marches in;
they come against her with axes like
woodsmen.
23 They will cut down her people like
trees," says the LORD,
"for they are more numerous than
locusts.
24 Egypt will be humiliated;
she will be handed over to people
from the north."

25 The LORD of Heaven's Armies, the God of Israel, says: "I will punish Amon, the god of Thebes,* and all the other gods of Egypt. I will punish its rulers and Pharaoh, too, and all who trust in him. 26 I will hand them over to those who want them killed—to King Nebuchadnezzar of Babylon and his army. But afterward the land will recover from the ravages of war. I, the LORD, have spoken!

27 "But do not be afraid, Jacob, my servant;
do not be dismayed, Israel.
For I will bring you home again from
distant lands,
and your children will return from
their exile.

Israel* will return to a life of peace and
quiet,
and no one will terrorize them.
²⁸ Do not be afraid, Jacob, my servant,
for I am with you," says the LORD.
"I will completely destroy the nations to
which I have exiled you,
but I will not completely destroy you.
I will discipline you, but with justice;
I cannot let you go unpunished."

47 A Message about Philistia

This is the LORD's message to the
prophet Jeremiah concerning the Philistines of Gaza, before it was captured by the
Egyptian army. ²This is what the LORD says:

"A flood is coming from the north
to overflow the land.
It will destroy the land and everything
in it—
cities and people alike.
People will scream in terror,
and everyone in the land will wail.
³ Hear the clatter of stallions' hooves
and the rumble of wheels as the
chariots rush by.
Terrified fathers run madly,
without a backward glance at their
helpless children.

⁴ "The time has come for the Philistines to
be destroyed,
along with their allies from Tyre and
Sidon.
Yes, the LORD is destroying the remnant
of the Philistines,
those colonists from the island of
Crete.*
⁵ Gaza will be humiliated, its head shaved
bald;
Ashkelon will lie silent.
You remnant from the Mediterranean
coast,*
how long will you lament and
mourn?

⁶ "Now, O sword of the LORD,
when will you be at rest again?
Go back into your sheath;
rest and be still.

⁷ "But how can it be still
when the LORD has sent it on a
mission?
For the city of Ashkelon
and the people living along the sea
must be destroyed."

48 A Message about Moab

This message was given concerning
Moab. This is what the LORD of Heaven's
Armies, the God of Israel, says:

"What sorrow awaits the city of Nebo;
it will soon lie in ruins.
The city of Kiriathaim will be humiliated
and captured;
the fortress will be humiliated and
broken down.
² No one will ever brag about Moab again,
for in Heshbon there is a plot to
destroy her.
'Come,' they say, 'we will cut her off from
being a nation.'
The town of Madmen,* too, will be
silenced;
the sword will follow you there.
³ Listen to the cries from Horonaim,
cries of devastation and great
destruction.
⁴ All Moab is destroyed.
Her little ones will cry out.*
⁵ Her refugees weep bitterly,
climbing the slope to Luhith.
They cry out in terror,
descending the slope to
Horonaim.
⁶ Flee for your lives!
Hide* in the wilderness!
⁷ Because you have trusted in your wealth
and skill,
you will be taken captive.
Your god Chemosh, with his priests and
officials,
will be hauled off to distant lands!

⁸ "All the towns will be destroyed,
and no one will escape—
either on the plateaus or in the valleys,
for the LORD has spoken.
⁹ Oh, that Moab had wings
so she could fly away,*

46:27 Hebrew Jacob. See note on 5:20.   47:4 Hebrew from Caphtor.   47:5 Hebrew the plain.   48:2 Madmen sounds like the Hebrew word for "silence"; it should not be confused with the English word madmen.   48:4 Greek version reads Her cries are heard as far away as Zoar.   48:6 Or Hide like a wild donkey; or Hide like a juniper shrub; or Be like [the town of] Aroer. The meaning of the Hebrew is uncertain.   48:9 Or Put salt on Moab, / for she will be laid waste.

for her towns will be left empty,
with no one living in them.
¹⁰ Cursed are those who refuse to do the
Lord's work,
who hold back their swords from
shedding blood!

¹¹ "From his earliest history, Moab has
lived in peace,
never going into exile.
He is like wine that has been allowed to
settle.
He has not been poured from flask to
flask,
and he is now fragrant and smooth.
¹² But the time is coming soon," says the
Lord,
"when I will send men to pour him
from his jar.
They will pour him out,
then shatter the jar!
¹³ At last Moab will be ashamed of his idol
Chemosh,
as the people of Israel were ashamed
of their gold calf at Bethel.*

¹⁴ "You used to boast, 'We are heroes,
mighty men of war.'
¹⁵ But now Moab and his towns will be
destroyed.
His most promising youth are doomed
to slaughter,"
says the King, whose name is the
Lord of Heaven's Armies.
¹⁶ "Destruction is coming fast for Moab;
calamity threatens ominously.
¹⁷ You friends of Moab,
weep for him and cry!
See how the strong scepter is broken,
how the beautiful staff is shattered!

¹⁸ "Come down from your glory
and sit in the dust, you people of
Dibon,
for those who destroy Moab will shatter
Dibon, too.
They will tear down all your
towers.
¹⁹ You people of Aroer,
stand beside the road and watch.
Shout to those who flee from Moab,
'What has happened there?'

²⁰ "And the reply comes back,
'Moab lies in ruins, disgraced;
weep and wail!
Tell it by the banks of the Arnon River:
Moab has been destroyed!'
²¹ Judgment has been poured out on the
towns of the plateau—
on Holon and Jahaz* and Mephaath,
²² on Dibon and Nebo and
Beth-diblathaim,
²³ on Kiriathaim and Beth-gamul and
Beth-meon,
²⁴ on Kerioth and Bozrah—
all the towns of Moab, far and near.

²⁵ "The strength of Moab has ended.
His arm has been broken," says the
Lord.
²⁶ "Let him stagger and fall like a drunkard,
for he has rebelled against the Lord.
Moab will wallow in his own vomit,
ridiculed by all.
²⁷ Did you not ridicule the people of Israel?
Were they caught in the company of
thieves
that you should despise them as
you do?

²⁸ "You people of Moab,
flee from your towns and live in the
caves.
Hide like doves that nest
in the clefts of the rocks.
²⁹ We have all heard of the pride of Moab,
for his pride is very great.
We know of his lofty pride,
his arrogance, and his haughty heart.
³⁰ I know about his insolence,"
says the Lord,
"but his boasts are empty—
as empty as his deeds.
³¹ So now I wail for Moab;
yes, I will mourn for Moab.
My heart is broken for the men of
Kir-hareseth.*

³² "You people of Sibmah, rich in
vineyards,
I will weep for you even more than I
did for Jazer.
Your spreading vines once reached as far
as the Dead Sea,*

but the destroyer has stripped you bare!
He has harvested your grapes and
summer fruits.
³³ Joy and gladness are gone from fruitful
Moab.
The presses yield no wine.
No one treads the grapes with shouts of
joy.
There is shouting, yes, but not of joy.

³⁴"Instead, their awful cries of terror can be heard from Heshbon clear across to Ele-aleh and Jahaz; from Zoar all the way to Horonaim and Eglath-shelishiyah. Even the waters of Nimrim are dried up now. ³⁵"I will put an end to Moab," says the LORD, "for the people offer sacrifices at the pagan shrines and burn incense to their false gods. ³⁶My heart moans like a flute for Moab and Kir-hareseth, for all their wealth has disappeared. ³⁷The people shave their heads and beards in mourning. They slash their hands and put on clothes made of burlap. ³⁸There is crying and sorrow in every Moabite home and on every street. For I have smashed Moab like an old, unwanted jar. ³⁹How it is shattered! Hear the wailing! See the shame of Moab! It has become an object of ridicule, an example of ruin to all its neighbors."

⁴⁰This is what the LORD says:

"Look! The enemy swoops down like an
eagle,
spreading his wings over Moab.
⁴¹ Its cities will fall,
and its strongholds will be seized.
Even the mightiest warriors will be in
anguish
like a woman in labor.
⁴² Moab will no longer be a nation,
for it has boasted against the LORD.

⁴³ "Terror and traps and snares will be your
lot,
O Moab," says the LORD.
⁴⁴ "Those who flee in terror will fall into a
trap,
and those who escape the trap will
step into a snare.
I will see to it that you do not get away,
for the time of your judgment has come,"
says the LORD.

⁴⁵ "The people flee as far as Heshbon
but are unable to go on.
For a fire comes from Heshbon,
King Sihon's ancient home,
to devour the entire land
with all its rebellious people.
⁴⁶ "O Moab, they weep for you!
The people of the god Chemosh are
destroyed!
Your sons and your daughters
have been taken away as captives.
⁴⁷ But I will restore the fortunes of Moab
in days to come.
I, the LORD, have spoken!"

This is the end of Jeremiah's prophecy concerning Moab.

49 A Message about Ammon

This message was given concerning the Ammonites. This is what the LORD says:

"Are there no descendants of Israel
to inherit the land of Gad?
Why are you, who worship Molech,*
living in its towns?
² In the days to come," says the LORD,
"I will sound the battle cry against
your city of Rabbah.
It will become a desolate heap of ruins,
and the neighboring towns will be
burned.
Then Israel will take back the land
you took from her," says the LORD.

³ "Cry out, O Heshbon,
for the town of Ai is destroyed.
Weep, O people of Rabbah!
Put on your clothes of mourning.
Weep and wail, hiding in the hedges,
for your god Molech, with his priests
and officials,
will be hauled off to distant lands.
⁴ You are proud of your fertile valleys,
but they will soon be ruined.
You trusted in your wealth,
you rebellious daughter,
and thought no one could ever harm
you.
⁵ But look! I will bring terror upon you,"
says the Lord, the LORD of Heaven's
Armies.

49:1 Hebrew *Malcam*, a variant spelling of Molech; also in 49:3.

"Your neighbors will chase you from
your land,
and no one will help your exiles as
they flee.
⁶ But I will restore the fortunes of the
Ammonites
in days to come.
I, the LORD, have spoken."

Messages about Edom

⁷ This message was given concerning Edom.
This is what the LORD of Heaven's Armies
says:

"Is there no wisdom in Teman?
Is no one left to give wise counsel?
⁸ Turn and flee!
Hide in deep caves, you people of
Dedan!
For when I bring disaster on Edom,*
I will punish you, too!
⁹ Those who harvest grapes
always leave a few for the poor.
If thieves came at night,
they would not take everything.
¹⁰ But I will strip bare the land
of Edom,
and there will be no place left to
hide.
Its children, its brothers, and its
neighbors
will all be destroyed,
and Edom itself will be no more.
¹¹ But I will protect the orphans who
remain among you.
Your widows, too, can depend on me
for help."

¹² And this is what the LORD says: "If the
innocent must suffer, how much more must
you! You will not go unpunished! You must
drink this cup of judgment! ¹³ For I have
sworn by my own name," says the LORD,
"that Bozrah will become an object of horror and a heap of ruins; it will be mocked
and cursed. All its towns and villages will
be desolate forever."

¹⁴ I have heard a message from the LORD
that an ambassador was sent to the
nations to say,
"Form a coalition against Edom,
and prepare for battle!"

¹⁵ The LORD says to Edom,
"I will cut you down to size among the
nations.
You will be despised by all.
¹⁶ You have been deceived
by the fear you inspire in others
and by your own pride.
You live in a rock fortress
and control the mountain heights.
But even if you make your nest among
the peaks with the eagles,
I will bring you crashing down,"
says the LORD.

¹⁷ "Edom will be an object of horror.
All who pass by will be appalled
and will gasp at the destruction they
see there.
¹⁸ It will be like the destruction of Sodom
and Gomorrah
and their neighboring towns," says the
LORD.
"No one will live there;
no one will inhabit it.
¹⁹ I will come like a lion from the thickets
of the Jordan,
leaping on the sheep in the pasture.
I will chase Edom from its land,
and I will appoint the leader of my
choice.
For who is like me, and who can
challenge me?
What ruler can oppose my will?"

²⁰ Listen to the LORD's plans against Edom
and the people of Teman.
Even the little children will be dragged
off like sheep,
and their homes will be destroyed.
²¹ The earth will shake with the noise of
Edom's fall,
and its cry of despair will be heard all
the way to the Red Sea.*
²² Look! The enemy swoops down like an
eagle,
spreading his wings over Bozrah.
Even the mightiest warriors will be in
anguish
like a woman in labor.

A Message about Damascus

²³ This message was given concerning Damascus. This is what the LORD says:

49:8 Hebrew *Esau*; also in 49:10.   49:21 Hebrew *sea of reeds.*

"The towns of Hamath and Arpad are
    struck with fear,
  for they have heard the news of their
    destruction.
Their hearts are troubled
    like a wild sea in a raging storm.
²⁴ Damascus has become feeble,
    and all her people turn to flee.
  Fear, anguish, and pain have gripped her
    as they grip a woman in labor.
²⁵ That famous city, a city of joy,
    will be forsaken!
²⁶ Her young men will fall in the streets
    and die.
  Her soldiers will all be killed,"
    says the LORD of Heaven's Armies.
²⁷ "And I will set fire to the walls of
    Damascus
    that will burn up the palaces of Ben-
    hadad."

A Message about Kedar and Hazor

²⁸ This message was given concerning Kedar
and the kingdoms of Hazor, which were
attacked by King Nebuchadnezzar* of Babylon. This is what the LORD says:

"Advance against Kedar!
    Destroy the warriors from the East!
²⁹ Their flocks and tents will be captured,
    and their household goods and camels
    will be taken away.
  Everywhere shouts of panic will be heard:
    'We are terrorized at every turn!'
³⁰ Run for your lives," says the LORD.
    "Hide yourselves in deep caves, you
    people of Hazor,
  for King Nebuchadnezzar of Babylon
    has plotted against you
    and is preparing to destroy you.

³¹ "Go up and attack that complacent
    nation,"
    says the LORD.
  "Its people live alone in the desert
    without walls or gates.
³² Their camels and other livestock will all
    be yours.
  I will scatter to the winds these people
    who live in remote places.*
  I will bring calamity upon them
    from every direction," says the LORD.

³³ "Hazor will be inhabited by jackals,
    and it will be desolate forever.
  No one will live there;
    no one will inhabit it."

A Message about Elam

³⁴ This message concerning Elam came to
the prophet Jeremiah from the LORD at the
beginning of the reign of King Zedekiah of
Judah. ³⁵ This is what the LORD of Heaven's
Armies says:

"I will destroy the archers of Elam—
    the best of their forces.
³⁶ I will bring enemies from all directions,
    and I will scatter the people of Elam to
    the four winds.
  They will be exiled to countries
    around the world.
³⁷ I myself will go with Elam's enemies to
    shatter it.
  In my fierce anger, I will bring great
    disaster
  upon the people of Elam," says the
    LORD.
  "Their enemies will chase them with the
    sword
    until I have destroyed them
    completely.
³⁸ I will set my throne in Elam," says the
    LORD,
  "and I will destroy its king and
    officials.
³⁹ But I will restore the fortunes of Elam
    in days to come.
  I, the LORD, have spoken!"

A Message about Babylon

50 The LORD gave Jeremiah the
prophet this message concerning Babylon
and the land of the Babylonians.* ² This is
what the LORD says:

"Tell the whole world,
    and keep nothing back.
  Raise a signal flag
    to tell everyone that Babylon will fall!
  Her images and idols* will be shattered.
    Her gods Bel and Marduk will be
    utterly disgraced.
³ For a nation will attack her from the
    north

49:28 Hebrew *Nebuchadrezzar*, a variant spelling of Nebuchadnezzar; also in 49:30. **49:32** Or *who clip the corners of their hair.* **50:1** Or *Chaldeans;* also in 50:8, 25, 35, 45. **50:2** The Hebrew term (literally *round things*) probably alludes to dung.

and bring such destruction that no
one will live there again.
Everything will be gone;
both people and animals will flee.

Hope for Israel and Judah

⁴ "In those coming days,"
says the LORD,
"the people of Israel will return home
together with the people of Judah.
They will come weeping
and seeking the LORD their God.
⁵ They will ask the way to Jerusalem*
and will start back home again.
They will bind themselves to the LORD
with an eternal covenant that will
never be forgotten.

⁶ "My people have been lost sheep.
Their shepherds have led them astray
and turned them loose in the
mountains.
They have lost their way
and can't remember how to get back
to the sheepfold.
⁷ All who found them devoured them.
Their enemies said,
'We did nothing wrong in attacking
them,
for they sinned against the LORD,
their true place of rest,
and the hope of their ancestors.'

⁸ "But now, flee from Babylon!
Leave the land of the Babylonians.
Like male goats at the head of the flock,
lead my people home again.
⁹ For I am raising up an army
of great nations from the north.
They will join forces to attack Babylon,
and she will be captured.
The enemies' arrows will go straight to
the mark;
they will not miss!
¹⁰ Babylonia* will be looted
until the attackers are glutted with
loot.
I, the LORD, have spoken!

Babylon's Sure Fall

¹¹ "You rejoice and are glad,
you who plundered my chosen people.

You frisk about like a calf in a meadow
and neigh like a stallion.
¹² But your homeland* will be
overwhelmed
with shame and disgrace.
You will become the least of nations—
a wilderness, a dry and desolate land.
¹³ Because of the LORD's anger,
Babylon will become a deserted
wasteland.
All who pass by will be horrified
and will gasp at the destruction they
see there.

¹⁴ "Yes, prepare to attack Babylon,
all you surrounding nations.
Let your archers shoot at her; spare no
arrows.
For she has sinned against the LORD.
¹⁵ Shout war cries against her from every
side.
Look! She surrenders!
Her walls have fallen.
It is the LORD's vengeance,
so take vengeance on her.
Do to her as she has done to others!
¹⁶ Take from Babylon all those who plant
crops;
send all the harvesters away.
Because of the sword of the enemy,
everyone will run away and rush back
to their own lands.

Hope for God's People

¹⁷ "The Israelites are like sheep
that have been scattered by lions.
First the king of Assyria ate them up.
Then King Nebuchadnezzar* of
Babylon cracked their bones."
¹⁸ Therefore, this is what the LORD of
Heaven's Armies,
the God of Israel, says:
"Now I will punish the king of Babylon
and his land,
just as I punished the king of Assyria.
¹⁹ And I will bring Israel home again to its
own land,
to feed in the fields of Carmel and
Bashan,
and to be satisfied once more
in the hill country of Ephraim and
Gilead.

50:5 Hebrew *Zion;* also in 50:28.   **50:10** Or *Chaldea.*   **50:12** Hebrew *your mother.*   **50:17** Hebrew *Nebuchadrezzar,* a variant spelling of
Nebuchadnezzar.

20 In those days," says the LORD,
"no sin will be found in Israel or in
Judah,
for I will forgive the remnant I
preserve.

The LORD's Judgment on Babylon

21 "Go up, my warriors, against the land of
Merathaim
and against the people of Pekod.
Pursue, kill, and completely destroy*
them,
as I have commanded you," says the
LORD.
22 "Let the battle cry be heard in the land,
a shout of great destruction.
23 Babylon, the mightiest hammer in all the
earth,
lies broken and shattered.
Babylon is desolate among the
nations!
24 Listen, Babylon, for I have set a trap for
you.
You are caught, for you have fought
against the LORD.
25 The LORD has opened his armory
and brought out weapons to vent his
fury.
The terror that falls upon the
Babylonians
will be the work of the Sovereign
LORD of Heaven's Armies.
26 Yes, come against her from distant
lands.
Break open her granaries.
Crush her walls and houses into heaps
of rubble.
Destroy her completely, and leave
nothing!
27 Destroy even her young bulls—
it will be terrible for them, too!
Slaughter them all!
For Babylon's day of reckoning has
come.
28 Listen to the people who have escaped
from Babylon,
as they tell in Jerusalem
how the LORD our God has taken
vengeance
against those who destroyed his
Temple.

29 "Send out a call for archers to come to
Babylon.
Surround the city so none can
escape.
Do to her as she has done to others,
for she has defied the LORD, the Holy
One of Israel.
30 Her young men will fall in the streets
and die.
Her soldiers will all be killed,"
says the LORD.
31 "See, I am your enemy, you arrogant
people,"
says the Lord, the LORD of Heaven's
Armies.
"Your day of reckoning has arrived—
the day when I will punish you.
32 O land of arrogance, you will stumble
and fall,
and no one will raise you up.
For I will light a fire in the cities of
Babylon
that will burn up everything around
them."

33 This is what the LORD of Heaven's
Armies says:
"The people of Israel and Judah have
been wronged.
Their captors hold them and refuse to
let them go.
34 But the one who redeems them is
strong.
His name is the LORD of Heaven's
Armies.
He will defend them
and give them rest again in Israel.
But for the people of Babylon
there will be no rest!

35 "The sword of destruction will strike the
Babylonians,"
says the LORD.
"It will strike the people of Babylon—
her officials and wise men, too.
36 The sword will strike her wise
counselors,
and they will become fools.
The sword will strike her mightiest
warriors,
and panic will seize them.

50:21 The Hebrew term used here refers to the complete consecration of things or people to the LORD, either by destroying them or by giving them as an offering.

³⁷ The sword will strike her horses and
  chariots
    and her allies from other lands,
    and they will all become like women.
  The sword will strike her treasures,
    and they all will be plundered.
³⁸ The sword will even strike her water
  supply,
    causing it to dry up.
  And why? Because the whole land is
  filled with idols,
    and the people are madly in love with
    them.

³⁹ "Soon Babylon will be inhabited by
  desert animals and hyenas.
    It will be a home for owls.
  Never again will people live there;
    it will lie desolate forever.
⁴⁰ I will destroy it as I* destroyed Sodom
  and Gomorrah
    and their neighboring towns," says the
    LORD.
  "No one will live there;
    no one will inhabit it.

⁴¹ "Look! A great army is coming from the
  north.
    A great nation and many kings
    are rising against you from far-off
    lands.
⁴² They are armed with bows and spears.
  They are cruel and show no mercy.
  As they ride forward on horses,
    they sound like a roaring sea.
  They are coming in battle formation,
    planning to destroy you, Babylon.
⁴³ The king of Babylon has heard reports
  about the enemy,
    and he is weak with fright.
  Pangs of anguish have gripped him,
    like those of a woman in labor.

⁴⁴ "I will come like a lion from the thickets
  of the Jordan,
    leaping on the sheep in the pasture.
  I will chase Babylon from its land,
    and I will appoint the leader of my
    choice.
  For who is like me, and who can
    challenge me?
  What ruler can oppose my will?"

⁴⁵ Listen to the LORD's plans against
  Babylon
    and the land of the Babylonians.
  Even the little children will be dragged
  off like sheep,
    and their homes will be destroyed.
⁴⁶ The earth will shake with the shout,
  "Babylon has been taken!"
    and its cry of despair will be heard
    around the world.

51 ¹ This is what the LORD says:
  "I will stir up a destroyer against
  Babylon
    and the people of Babylonia.*
² Foreigners will come and winnow her,
    blowing her away as chaff.
  They will come from every side
    to rise against her in her day of
    trouble.
³ Don't let the archers put on their armor
  or draw their bows.
  Don't spare even her best soldiers!
    Let her army be completely
    destroyed.*
⁴ They will fall dead in the land of the
  Babylonians,*
    slashed to death in her streets.
⁵ For the LORD of Heaven's Armies
  has not abandoned Israel and Judah.
  He is still their God,
    even though their land was filled
    with sin
  against the Holy One of Israel."

⁶ Flee from Babylon! Save yourselves!
    Don't get trapped in her punishment!
  It is the LORD's time for vengeance;
    he will repay her in full.
⁷ Babylon has been a gold cup in the
  LORD's hands,
    a cup that made the whole earth
    drunk.
  The nations drank Babylon's wine,
    and it drove them all mad.
⁸ But suddenly Babylon, too, has fallen.
  Weep for her.
  Give her medicine.
    Perhaps she can yet be healed.
⁹ We would have helped her if we could,
    but nothing can save her now.

Let her go; abandon her.
    Return now to your own land.
For her punishment reaches to the
    heavens;
    it is so great it cannot be measured.
10 The LORD has vindicated us.
    Come, let us announce in Jerusalem*
    everything the LORD our God has done.

11 Sharpen the arrows!
    Lift up the shields!*
For the LORD has inspired the kings of
    the Medes
    to march against Babylon and destroy
    her.
This is his vengeance against those
    who desecrated his Temple.
12 Raise the battle flag against Babylon!
    Reinforce the guard and station the
    watchmen.
Prepare an ambush,
    for the LORD will fulfill all his plans
    against Babylon.
13 You are a city by a great river,
    a great center of commerce,
but your end has come.
    The thread of your life is cut.
14 The LORD of Heaven's Armies has taken
    this vow
and has sworn to it by his own name:
"Your cities will be filled with enemies,
like fields swarming with locusts,
and they will shout in triumph over
    you."

A Hymn of Praise to the LORD

15 The LORD made the earth by his power,
    and he preserves it by his wisdom.
With his own understanding
    he stretched out the heavens.
16 When he speaks in the thunder,
    the heavens are filled with water.
He causes the clouds to rise over the
    earth.
    He sends the lightning with the rain
and releases the wind from his
    storehouses.

17 The whole human race is foolish and has
    no knowledge!
    The craftsmen are disgraced by the
    idols they make,

for their carefully shaped works are a
    fraud.
    These idols have no breath or power.
18 Idols are worthless; they are ridiculous
    lies!
    On the day of reckoning they will all
    be destroyed.
19 But the God of Israel* is no idol!
    He is the Creator of everything that
    exists,
including his people, his own special
    possession.
    The LORD of Heaven's Armies is his
    name!

Babylon's Great Punishment

20 "You* are my battle-ax and sword,"
    says the LORD.
"With you I will shatter nations
    and destroy many kingdoms.
21 With you I will shatter armies—
    destroying the horse and rider,
    the chariot and charioteer.
22 With you I will shatter men and
    women,
    old people and children,
    young men and maidens.
23 With you I will shatter shepherds and
    flocks,
    farmers and oxen,
    captains and officers.

24 "I will repay Babylon
    and the people of Babylonia*
for all the wrong they have done
    to my people in Jerusalem," says the
    LORD.

25 "Look, O mighty mountain, destroyer of
    the earth!
    I am your enemy," says the LORD.
"I will raise my fist against you,
    to knock you down from the
    heights.
When I am finished,
    you will be nothing but a heap of
    burnt rubble.
26 You will be desolate forever.
    Even your stones will never again be
    used for building.
You will be completely wiped out,"
    says the LORD.

51:10 Hebrew *Zion;* also in 51:24.   **51:11** Greek version reads *Fill up the quivers.*   **51:19** Hebrew *the Portion of Jacob.* See note on 5:20.
51:20 Possibly Cyrus, whom God used to conquer Babylon. Compare Isa 44:28; 45:1.   **51:24** Or *Chaldea;* also in 51:35.

27 Raise a signal flag to the nations.
　　Sound the battle cry!
Mobilize them all against Babylon.
　　Prepare them to fight against her!
Bring out the armies of Ararat, Minni,
　　and Ashkenaz.
　　Appoint a commander,
　　and bring a multitude of horses like
　　　swarming locusts!
28 Bring against her the armies of the
　　nations—
　　led by the kings of the Medes
　　and all their captains and officers.

29 The earth trembles and writhes in pain,
　　for everything the LORD has planned
　　　against Babylon stands unchanged.
Babylon will be left desolate without a
　　single inhabitant.
30 　Her mightiest warriors no longer fight.
They stay in their barracks, their courage
　　gone.
　　They have become like women.
The invaders have burned the houses
　　and broken down the city gates.
31 The news is passed from one runner to
　　the next
　　as the messengers hurry to tell the king
　　that his city has been captured.
32 All the escape routes are blocked.
　　The marshes have been set aflame,
　　and the army is in a panic.

33 This is what the LORD of Heaven's
　　Armies,
　　the God of Israel, says:
"Babylon is like wheat on a threshing
　　floor,
　　about to be trampled.
In just a little while
　　her harvest will begin."

34 "King Nebuchadnezzar* of Babylon has
　　eaten and crushed us
　　and drained us of strength.
He has swallowed us like a great
　　monster
　　and filled his belly with our riches.
He has thrown us out of our own
　　country.
35 Make Babylon suffer as she made us
　　suffer,"
　　say the people of Zion.

"Make the people of Babylonia pay for
　　spilling our blood,"
　　says Jerusalem.

The LORD's Vengeance on Babylon

36 This is what the LORD says to Jerusalem:

"I will be your lawyer to plead your case,
　　and I will avenge you.
I will dry up her river,
　　as well as her springs,
37 and Babylon will become a heap of ruins,
　　haunted by jackals.
She will be an object of horror and
　　contempt,
　　a place where no one lives.
38 Her people will roar together like strong
　　lions.
　　They will growl like lion cubs.
39 And while they lie inflamed with all their
　　wine,
　　I will prepare a different kind of feast
　　for them.
I will make them drink until they fall
　　asleep,
　　and they will never wake up again,"
　　says the LORD.
40 "I will bring them down
　　like lambs to the slaughter,
　　like rams and goats to be sacrificed.

41 "How Babylon* is fallen—
　　great Babylon, praised throughout the
　　earth!
Now she has become an object of horror
　　among the nations.
42 The sea has risen over Babylon;
　　she is covered by its crashing waves.
43 Her cities now lie in ruins;
　　she is a dry wasteland
　　where no one lives or even passes by.
44 And I will punish Bel, the god of
　　Babylon,
　　and make him vomit up all he has
　　eaten.
The nations will no longer come and
　　worship him.
　　The wall of Babylon has fallen!

A Message for the Exiles

45 "Come out, my people, flee from Babylon.
　　Save yourselves! Run from the LORD's
　　fierce anger.

51:34 Hebrew *Nebuchadrezzar*, a variant spelling of Nebuchadnezzar. 　51:41 Hebrew *Sheshach*, a code name for Babylon.

⁴⁶ But do not panic; don't be afraid
    when you hear the first rumor of
        approaching forces.
    For rumors will keep coming year by
        year.
    Violence will erupt in the land
        as the leaders fight against each other.
⁴⁷ For the time is surely coming
    when I will punish this great city and
        all her idols.
    Her whole land will be disgraced,
        and her dead will lie in the streets.
⁴⁸ Then the heavens and earth will rejoice,
    for out of the north will come
        destroying armies
    against Babylon," says the LORD.
⁴⁹ "Just as Babylon killed the people of
        Israel
    and others throughout the world,
        so must her people be killed.
⁵⁰ Get out, all you who have escaped the
        sword!
    Do not stand and watch—flee while
        you can!
    Remember the LORD, though you are in
        a far-off land,
    and think about your home in
        Jerusalem."

⁵¹ "We are ashamed," the people say.
    "We are insulted and disgraced
    because the LORD's Temple
        has been defiled by foreigners."

⁵² "Yes," says the LORD, "but the time is
        coming
    when I will destroy Babylon's idols.
    The groans of her wounded people
        will be heard throughout the land.
⁵³ Though Babylon reaches as high as the
        heavens
    and makes her fortifications incredibly
        strong,
    I will still send enemies to plunder her.
    I, the LORD, have spoken!

Babylon's Complete Destruction

⁵⁴ "Listen! Hear the cry of Babylon,
    the sound of great destruction from
        the land of the Babylonians.
⁵⁵ For the LORD is destroying Babylon.
    He will silence her loud voice.

Waves of enemies pound against her;
    the noise of battle rings through the
        city.
⁵⁶ Destroying armies come against
        Babylon.
    Her mighty men are captured,
    and their weapons break in their
        hands.
    For the LORD is a God who gives just
        punishment;
    he always repays in full.
⁵⁷ I will make her officials and wise men
        drunk,
    along with her captains, officers, and
        warriors.
    They will fall asleep
        and never wake up again!"
    says the King, whose name is
        the LORD of Heaven's Armies.

⁵⁸ This is what the LORD of Heaven's
        Armies says:
    "The thick walls of Babylon will be
        leveled to the ground,
    and her massive gates will be burned.
    The builders from many lands have
        worked in vain,
    for their work will be destroyed by
        fire!"

Jeremiah's Message Sent to Babylon

⁵⁹ The prophet Jeremiah gave this message to Seraiah son of Neriah and grandson of Mahseiah, a staff officer, when Seraiah went to Babylon with King Zedekiah of Judah. This was during the fourth year of Zedekiah's reign.* ⁶⁰ Jeremiah had recorded on a scroll all the terrible disasters that would soon come upon Babylon—all the words written here. ⁶¹ He said to Seraiah, "When you get to Babylon, read aloud everything on this scroll. ⁶² Then say, 'LORD, you have said that you will destroy Babylon so that neither people nor animals will remain here. She will lie empty and abandoned forever.' ⁶³ When you have finished reading the scroll, tie it to a stone and throw it into the Euphrates River. ⁶⁴ Then say, 'In this same way Babylon and her people will sink, never again to rise, because of the disasters I will bring upon her.'"

This is the end of Jeremiah's messages.

51:59 The fourth year of Zedekiah's reign was 593 B.C.

52 The Fall of Jerusalem

Zedekiah was twenty-one years old when he became king, and he reigned in Jerusalem eleven years. His mother was Hamutal, the daughter of Jeremiah from Libnah. [2] But Zedekiah did what was evil in the LORD's sight, just as Jehoiakim had done. [3] These things happened because of the LORD's anger against the people of Jerusalem and Judah, until he finally banished them from his presence and sent them into exile.

Zedekiah rebelled against the king of Babylon. [4] So on January 15,* during the ninth year of Zedekiah's reign, King Nebuchadnezzar* of Babylon led his entire army against Jerusalem. They surrounded the city and built siege ramps against its walls. [5] Jerusalem was kept under siege until the eleventh year of King Zedekiah's reign.

[6] By July 18 in the eleventh year of Zedekiah's reign,* the famine in the city had become very severe, and the last of the food was entirely gone. [7] Then a section of the city wall was broken down, and all the soldiers fled. Since the city was surrounded by the Babylonians,* they waited for nightfall. Then they slipped through the gate between the two walls behind the king's garden and headed toward the Jordan Valley.*

[8] But the Babylonian troops chased King Zedekiah and caught him on the plains of Jericho, for his men had all deserted him and scattered. [9] They took him to the king of Babylon at Riblah in the land of Hamath. There the king of Babylon pronounced judgment upon Zedekiah. [10] He made Zedekiah watch as they slaughtered his sons and all the other officials of Judah. [11] Then they gouged out Zedekiah's eyes, bound him in bronze chains, and led him away to Babylon. Zedekiah remained there in prison until the day of his death.

The Temple Destroyed

[12] On August 17 of that year,* which was the nineteenth year of King Nebuchadnezzar's reign, Nebuzaradan, the captain of the guard and an official of the Babylonian king, arrived in Jerusalem. [13] He burned down the Temple of the LORD, the royal palace, and all the houses of Jerusalem. He destroyed all the important buildings* in the city. [14] Then he supervised the entire Babylonian* army as they tore down the walls of Jerusalem on every side. [15] Nebuzaradan, the captain of the guard, then took as exiles some of the poorest of the people, the rest of the people who remained in the city, the defectors who had declared their allegiance to the king of Babylon, and the rest of the craftsmen. [16] But Nebuzaradan allowed some of the poorest people to stay behind in Judah to care for the vineyards and fields.

[17] The Babylonians broke up the bronze pillars in front of the LORD's Temple, the bronze water carts, and the great bronze basin called the Sea, and they carried all the bronze away to Babylon. [18] They also took all the ash buckets, shovels, lamp snuffers, basins, dishes, and all the other bronze articles used for making sacrifices at the Temple. [19] Nebuzaradan, the captain of the guard, also took the small bowls, incense burners, basins, pots, lampstands, dishes, bowls used for liquid offerings, and all the other articles made of pure gold or silver.

[20] The weight of the bronze from the two pillars, the Sea with the twelve bronze oxen beneath it, and the water carts was too great to be measured. These things had been made for the LORD's Temple in the days of King Solomon. [21] Each of the pillars was 27 feet tall and 18 feet in circumference.* They were hollow, with walls 3 inches thick.* [22] The bronze capital on top of each pillar was 7½ feet* high and was decorated with a network of bronze pomegranates all the way around. [23] There were 96 pomegranates on the sides, and a total of 100 on the network around the top.

[24] Nebuzaradan, the captain of the guard, took with him as prisoners Seraiah the high priest, Zephaniah the priest of the second rank, and the three chief gatekeepers.

52:4a Hebrew *on the tenth day of the tenth month,* of the ancient Hebrew lunar calendar. A number of events in Jeremiah can be cross-checked with dates in surviving Babylonian records and related accurately to our modern calendar. This day was January 15, 588 B.C. **52:4b** Hebrew *Nebuchadrezzar,* a variant spelling of Nebuchadnezzar; also in 52:12, 28, 29, 30. **52:6** Hebrew *By the ninth day of the fourth month* [in the eleventh year of Zedekiah's reign]. This day was July 18, 586 B.C.; also see note on 52:4a. **52:7a** Or *the Chaldeans;* similarly in 52:8, 17. **52:7b** Hebrew *the Arabah.* **52:12** Hebrew *On the tenth day of the fifth month,* of the ancient Hebrew lunar calendar. This day was August 17, 586 B.C.; also see note on 52:4a. **52:13** Or *destroyed the houses of all the important people.* **52:14** Or *Chaldean.* **52:21a** Hebrew *18 cubits* [8.1 meters] *tall and 12 cubits* [5.4 meters] *in circumference.* **52:21b** Hebrew *4 fingers thick* [8 centimeters]. **52:22** Hebrew *5 cubits* [2.3 meters].

⁴⁶ But do not panic; don't be afraid
    when you hear the first rumor of
        approaching forces.
    For rumors will keep coming year by
        year.
    Violence will erupt in the land
        as the leaders fight against each other.
⁴⁷ For the time is surely coming
    when I will punish this great city and
        all her idols.
    Her whole land will be disgraced,
        and her dead will lie in the streets.
⁴⁸ Then the heavens and earth will rejoice,
    for out of the north will come
        destroying armies
    against Babylon," says the LORD.
⁴⁹ "Just as Babylon killed the people of
        Israel
    and others throughout the world,
        so must her people be killed.
⁵⁰ Get out, all you who have escaped the
        sword!
    Do not stand and watch—flee while
        you can!
    Remember the LORD, though you are in
        a far-off land,
    and think about your home in
        Jerusalem."
⁵¹ "We are ashamed," the people say.
    "We are insulted and disgraced
        because the LORD's Temple
    has been defiled by foreigners."
⁵² "Yes," says the LORD, "but the time is
        coming
    when I will destroy Babylon's idols.
    The groans of her wounded people
        will be heard throughout the land.
⁵³ Though Babylon reaches as high as the
        heavens
    and makes her fortifications incredibly
        strong,
    I will still send enemies to plunder her.
        I, the LORD, have spoken!

Babylon's Complete Destruction

⁵⁴ "Listen! Hear the cry of Babylon,
    the sound of great destruction from
        the land of the Babylonians.
⁵⁵ For the LORD is destroying Babylon.
    He will silence her loud voice.

    Waves of enemies pound against her;
        the noise of battle rings through the
            city.
⁵⁶ Destroying armies come against
        Babylon.
    Her mighty men are captured,
        and their weapons break in their
            hands.
    For the LORD is a God who gives just
        punishment;
    he always repays in full.
⁵⁷ I will make her officials and wise men
        drunk,
    along with her captains, officers, and
        warriors.
    They will fall asleep
        and never wake up again!"
    says the King, whose name is
        the LORD of Heaven's Armies.

⁵⁸ This is what the LORD of Heaven's
        Armies says:
    "The thick walls of Babylon will be
        leveled to the ground,
    and her massive gates will be burned.
    The builders from many lands have
        worked in vain,
    for their work will be destroyed by
        fire!"

Jeremiah's Message Sent to Babylon

⁵⁹ The prophet Jeremiah gave this message
to Seraiah son of Neriah and grandson of
Mahseiah, a staff officer, when Seraiah went
to Babylon with King Zedekiah of Judah.
This was during the fourth year of Zedekiah's reign.* ⁶⁰ Jeremiah had recorded on
a scroll all the terrible disasters that would
soon come upon Babylon—all the words
written here. ⁶¹ He said to Seraiah, "When
you get to Babylon, read aloud everything
on this scroll. ⁶² Then say, 'LORD, you have
said that you will destroy Babylon so that
neither people nor animals will remain
here. She will lie empty and abandoned
forever.' ⁶³ When you have finished reading the scroll, tie it to a stone and throw it
into the Euphrates River. ⁶⁴ Then say, 'In this
same way Babylon and her people will sink,
never again to rise, because of the disasters
I will bring upon her.'"
This is the end of Jeremiah's messages.

51:59 The fourth year of Zedekiah's reign was 593 B.C.

52 The Fall of Jerusalem

Zedekiah was twenty-one years old when he became king, and he reigned in Jerusalem eleven years. His mother was Hamutal, the daughter of Jeremiah from Libnah. ²But Zedekiah did what was evil in the LORD's sight, just as Jehoiakim had done. ³These things happened because of the LORD's anger against the people of Jerusalem and Judah, until he finally banished them from his presence and sent them into exile.

Zedekiah rebelled against the king of Babylon. ⁴So on January 15,* during the ninth year of Zedekiah's reign, King Nebuchadnezzar* of Babylon led his entire army against Jerusalem. They surrounded the city and built siege ramps against its walls. ⁵Jerusalem was kept under siege until the eleventh year of King Zedekiah's reign.

⁶By July 18 in the eleventh year of Zedekiah's reign,* the famine in the city had become very severe, and the last of the food was entirely gone. ⁷Then a section of the city wall was broken down, and all the soldiers fled. Since the city was surrounded by the Babylonians,* they waited for nightfall. Then they slipped through the gate between the two walls behind the king's garden and headed toward the Jordan Valley.*

⁸But the Babylonian troops chased King Zedekiah and caught him on the plains of Jericho, for his men had all deserted him and scattered. ⁹They took him to the king of Babylon at Riblah in the land of Hamath. There the king of Babylon pronounced judgment upon Zedekiah. ¹⁰He made Zedekiah watch as they slaughtered his sons and all the other officials of Judah. ¹¹Then they gouged out Zedekiah's eyes, bound him in bronze chains, and led him away to Babylon. Zedekiah remained there in prison until the day of his death.

The Temple Destroyed

¹²On August 17 of that year,* which was the nineteenth year of King Nebuchadnezzar's reign, Nebuzaradan, the captain of the guard and an official of the Babylonian king, arrived in Jerusalem. ¹³He burned down the Temple of the LORD, the royal palace, and all the houses of Jerusalem. He destroyed all the important buildings* in the city. ¹⁴Then he supervised the entire Babylonian* army as they tore down the walls of Jerusalem on every side. ¹⁵Nebuzaradan, the captain of the guard, then took as exiles some of the poorest of the people, the rest of the people who remained in the city, the defectors who had declared their allegiance to the king of Babylon, and the rest of the craftsmen. ¹⁶But Nebuzaradan allowed some of the poorest people to stay behind in Judah to care for the vineyards and fields.

¹⁷The Babylonians broke up the bronze pillars in front of the LORD's Temple, the bronze water carts, and the great bronze basin called the Sea, and they carried all the bronze away to Babylon. ¹⁸They also took all the ash buckets, shovels, lamp snuffers, basins, dishes, and all the other bronze articles used for making sacrifices at the Temple. ¹⁹Nebuzaradan, the captain of the guard, also took the small bowls, incense burners, basins, pots, lampstands, dishes, bowls used for liquid offerings, and all the other articles made of pure gold or silver.

²⁰The weight of the bronze from the two pillars, the Sea with the twelve bronze oxen beneath it, and the water carts was too great to be measured. These things had been made for the LORD's Temple in the days of King Solomon. ²¹Each of the pillars was 27 feet tall and 18 feet in circumference.* They were hollow, with walls 3 inches thick.* ²²The bronze capital on top of each pillar was 7½ feet* high and was decorated with a network of bronze pomegranates all the way around. ²³There were 96 pomegranates on the sides, and a total of 100 on the network around the top.

²⁴Nebuzaradan, the captain of the guard, took with him as prisoners Seraiah the high priest, Zephaniah the priest of the second rank, and the three chief gatekeepers.

52:4a Hebrew *on the tenth day of the tenth month,* of the ancient Hebrew lunar calendar. A number of events in Jeremiah can be cross-checked with dates in surviving Babylonian records and related accurately to our modern calendar. This day was January 15, 588 B.C. 52:4b Hebrew *Nebuchadrezzar,* a variant spelling of Nebuchadnezzar; also in 52:12, 28, 29, 30. 52:6 Hebrew *By the ninth day of the fourth month* [in the eleventh year of Zedekiah's reign]. This day was July 18, 586 B.C.; also see note on 52:4a. 52:7a Or *the Chaldeans;* similarly in 52:8, 17. 52:7b Hebrew *the Arabah.* 52:12 Hebrew *On the tenth day of the fifth month,* of the ancient Hebrew lunar calendar. This day was August 17, 586 B.C.; also see note on 52:4a. 52:13 Or *destroyed the houses of all the important people.* 52:14 Or *Chaldean.* 52:21a Hebrew *18 cubits* [8.1 meters] *tall and 12 cubits* [5.4 meters] *in circumference.* 52:21b Hebrew *4 fingers thick* [8 centimeters]. 52:22 Hebrew *5 cubits* [2.3 meters].

Lamentations

Sorrow in Jerusalem

1 *¹ Jerusalem, once so full of people,
    is now deserted.
She who was once great among the nations
    now sits alone like a widow.
Once the queen of all the earth,
    she is now a slave.

² She sobs through the night;
    tears stream down her cheeks.
Among all her lovers,
    there is no one left to comfort her.
All her friends have betrayed her
    and become her enemies.

³ Judah has been led away into captivity,
    oppressed with cruel slavery.
She lives among foreign nations
    and has no place of rest.
Her enemies have chased her down,
    and she has nowhere to turn.

⁴ The roads to Jerusalem* are in mourning,
    for crowds no longer come to celebrate the
      festivals.
The city gates are silent,
    her priests groan,
her young women are crying—
    how bitter is her fate!

⁵ Her oppressors have become her masters,
    and her enemies prosper,
for the LORD has punished Jerusalem
    for her many sins.
Her children have been captured
    and taken away to distant lands.

⁶ All the majesty of beautiful Jerusalem*
    has been stripped away.
Her princes are like starving deer
    searching for pasture.
They are too weak to run
    from the pursuing enemy.

---

1 Each of the first four chapters of this book is an acrostic, laid out in the order of the Hebrew alphabet. The first word of each verse begins with a successive Hebrew letter. Chapters 1, 2, and 4 have one verse for each of the 22 Hebrew letters. Chapter 3 contains 22 stanzas of three verses each. Though chapter 5 has 22 verses, it is not an acrostic. **1:4** Hebrew *Zion*; also in 1:17. **1:6** Hebrew *of the daughter of Zion.*

⁷ In the midst of her sadness and
  wandering,
    Jerusalem remembers her ancient
    splendor.
But now she has fallen to her enemy,
  and there is no one to help her.
Her enemy struck her down
  and laughed as she fell.

⁸ Jerusalem has sinned greatly,
  so she has been tossed away like a
  filthy rag.
All who once honored her now despise
  her,
    for they have seen her stripped naked
    and humiliated.
All she can do is groan
  and hide her face.

⁹ She defiled herself with immorality
  and gave no thought to her future.
Now she lies in the gutter
  with no one to lift her out.
"Lord, see my misery," she cries.
  "The enemy has triumphed."

¹⁰ The enemy has plundered her
  completely,
    taking every precious thing she
    owns.
She has seen foreigners violate her
  sacred Temple,
    the place the Lord had forbidden
    them to enter.

¹¹ Her people groan as they search for
  bread.
    They have sold their treasures for food
    to stay alive.
"O Lord, look," she mourns,
  "and see how I am despised.

¹² "Does it mean nothing to you, all you
  who pass by?
    Look around and see if there is any
    suffering like mine,
which the Lord brought on me
  when he erupted in fierce anger.

¹³ "He has sent fire from heaven that burns
  in my bones.
    He has placed a trap in my path and
    turned me back.
He has left me devastated,
  racked with sickness all day long.

¹⁴ "He wove my sins into ropes
  to hitch me to a yoke of captivity.
The Lord sapped my strength and
  turned me over to my enemies;
    I am helpless in their hands.

¹⁵ "The Lord has treated my mighty men
  with contempt.
At his command a great army has come
  to crush my young warriors.
The Lord has trampled his beloved
  city*
    like grapes are trampled in a
    winepress.

¹⁶ "For all these things I weep;
  tears flow down my cheeks.
No one is here to comfort me;
  any who might encourage me are far
  away.
My children have no future,
  for the enemy has conquered us."

¹⁷ Jerusalem reaches out for help,
  but no one comforts her.
Regarding his people Israel,*
  the Lord has said,
"Let their neighbors be their enemies!
  Let them be thrown away like a filthy
  rag!"

¹⁸ "The Lord is right," Jerusalem says,
  "for I rebelled against him.
Listen, people everywhere;
  look upon my anguish and despair,
for my sons and daughters
  have been taken captive to distant
  lands.

¹⁹ "I begged my allies for help,
  but they betrayed me.
My priests and leaders
  starved to death in the city,
even as they searched for food
  to save their lives.

²⁰ "Lord, see my anguish!
  My heart is broken
and my soul despairs,
  for I have rebelled against you.
In the streets the sword kills,
  and at home there is only death.

²¹ "Others heard my groans,
  but no one turned to comfort me.

1:15 Hebrew *the virgin daughter of Judah.* 1:17 Hebrew *Jacob.* The names "Jacob" and "Israel" are often interchanged throughout the Old Testament, referring sometimes to the individual patriarch and sometimes to the nation.

When my enemies heard about my
    troubles,
    they were happy to see what you had
        done.
Oh, bring the day you promised,
    when they will suffer as I have suffered.

²² "Look at all their evil deeds, LORD.
        Punish them,
    as you have punished me
        for all my sins.
My groans are many,
    and I am sick at heart."

2 God's Anger at Sin

¹ The Lord in his anger
    has cast a dark shadow over beautiful
        Jerusalem.*
The fairest of Israel's cities lies in the
        dust,
    thrown down from the heights of
        heaven.
In his day of great anger,
    the Lord has shown no mercy even to
        his Temple.*

² Without mercy the Lord has destroyed
    every home in Israel.*
In his anger he has broken down
    the fortress walls of beautiful
        Jerusalem.*
He has brought them to the ground,
    dishonoring the kingdom and its
        rulers.

³ All the strength of Israel
    vanishes beneath his fierce anger.
The Lord has withdrawn his protection
    as the enemy attacks.
He consumes the whole land of Israel
    like a raging fire.

⁴ He bends his bow against his people,
    as though he were their enemy.
His strength is used against them
    to kill their finest youth.
His fury is poured out like fire
    on beautiful Jerusalem.*

⁵ Yes, the Lord has vanquished Israel
    like an enemy.
He has destroyed her palaces
    and demolished her fortresses.

He has brought unending sorrow and
        tears
    upon beautiful Jerusalem.

⁶ He has broken down his Temple
    as though it were merely a garden
        shelter.
The LORD has blotted out all memory
    of the holy festivals and Sabbath days.
Kings and priests fall together
    before his fierce anger.

⁷ The Lord has rejected his own altar;
    he despises his own sanctuary.
He has given Jerusalem's palaces
    to her enemies.
They shout in the LORD's Temple
    as though it were a day of
        celebration.

⁸ The LORD was determined
    to destroy the walls of beautiful
        Jerusalem.
He made careful plans for their
        destruction,
    then did what he had planned.
Therefore, the ramparts and walls
    have fallen down before him.

⁹ Jerusalem's gates have sunk into the
        ground.
    He has smashed their locks and bars.
Her kings and princes have been exiled
    to distant lands;
    her law has ceased to exist.
Her prophets receive
    no more visions from the LORD.

¹⁰ The leaders of beautiful Jerusalem
    sit on the ground in silence.
They are clothed in burlap
    and throw dust on their heads.
The young women of Jerusalem
    hang their heads in shame.

¹¹ I have cried until the tears no longer
        come;
    my heart is broken.
My spirit is poured out in agony
    as I see the desperate plight of my
        people.
Little children and tiny babies
    are fainting and dying in the streets.

2:1a Hebrew *the daughter of Zion;* also in 2:8, 10, 18.   2:1b Hebrew *his footstool.*   2:2a Hebrew *Jacob;* also in 2:3b. See note on 1:17.
2:2b Hebrew *the daughter of Judah;* also in 2:5.   2:4 Hebrew *on the tent of the daughter of Zion.*

[12] They cry out to their mothers,
 "We need food and drink!"
Their lives ebb away in the streets
 like the life of a warrior wounded in
 battle.
They gasp for life
 as they collapse in their mothers'
 arms.

[13] What can I say about you?
 Who has ever seen such sorrow?
O daughter of Jerusalem,
 to what can I compare your anguish?
O virgin daughter of Zion,
 how can I comfort you?
For your wound is as deep as the sea.
 Who can heal you?

[14] Your prophets have said
 so many foolish things, false to the
 core.
They did not save you from exile
 by pointing out your sins.
Instead, they painted false pictures,
 filling you with false hope.

[15] All who pass by jeer at you.
 They scoff and insult beautiful
 Jerusalem,* saying,
"Is this the city called 'Most Beautiful in
 All the World'
 and 'Joy of All the Earth'?"

[16] All your enemies mock you.
 They scoff and snarl and say,
"We have destroyed her at last!
 We have long waited for this day,
 and it is finally here!"

[17] But it is the LORD who did just as he
 planned.
He has fulfilled the promises of
 disaster
he made long ago.
He has destroyed Jerusalem without
 mercy.
He has caused her enemies to gloat
 over her
and has given them power over her.

[18] Cry aloud* before the Lord,
 O walls of beautiful Jerusalem!
Let your tears flow like a river
 day and night.

Give yourselves no rest;
 give your eyes no relief.

[19] Rise during the night and cry out.
 Pour out your hearts like water to the
 Lord.
Lift up your hands to him in prayer,
 pleading for your children,
for in every street
 they are faint with hunger.

[20] "O LORD, think about this!
 Should you treat your own people this
 way?
Should mothers eat their own children,
 those they once bounced on their
 knees?
Should priests and prophets be killed
 within the Lord's Temple?

[21] "See them lying in the streets—
 young and old,
boys and girls,
 killed by the swords of the enemy.
You have killed them in your anger,
 slaughtering them without mercy.

[22] "You have invited terrors from all
 around,
 as though you were calling them to a
 day of feasting.
In the day of the LORD's anger,
 no one has escaped or survived.
The enemy has killed all the children
 whom I carried and raised."

3 Hope in the LORD's Faithfulness

[1] I am the one who has seen the
 afflictions
 that come from the rod of the LORD's
 anger.
[2] He has led me into darkness,
 shutting out all light.
[3] He has turned his hand against me
 again and again, all day long.

[4] He has made my skin and flesh grow old.
 He has broken my bones.
[5] He has besieged and surrounded me
 with anguish and distress.
[6] He has buried me in a dark place,
 like those long dead.

[7] He has walled me in, and I cannot escape.
 He has bound me in heavy chains.

2:15 Hebrew *the daughter of Jerusalem.* 2:18 Hebrew *Their heart cried.*

Worship during Suffering

LAMENTATIONS 3:16-24

"Caught up amidst a whirlwind of pain and confusion," Matt and Beth Redman write in *Blessed Be Your Name*, "the decision to cry out, 'Yet I will praise you' is a costly act of devotion. . . . Times will come when worship meets suffering. And these moments shape what kind of worshipers we become."

Indeed they do. Especially since when we suffer, our first instinct is not to worship the God who could have spared us our pain but chose not to. So often we then choose to become fair-weather worshipers. Sure, we'll praise God when the times are good, when life rolls our way. But when the weather turns, when times tighten and worry rises, we pull back our praise.

But we miss something lovely and essential when we do this: we miss the opportunity to become come-what-may worshipers. We miss the opportunity to trust God when he doesn't seem trustworthy and to believe in his goodness when he doesn't seem good. We miss the opportunity to believe his promises and to love and adore him in all things, at all times.

In Lamentations Jeremiah wrote, "The thought of my suffering and homelessness is bitter beyond words. . . . Yet I still dare to hope when I remember this: The faithful love of the LORD never ends! His mercies never cease. Great is his faithfulness; his mercies begin afresh each morning" (3:19, 21-23).

Even battling bitterness, Jeremiah dared to hope in the goodness and faithfulness of God. Even in his pain, Jeremiah experienced the joy of one of the most important truths we can grasp—that God's faithfulness never ends, no matter how things seem to us!

Jeremiah chose to be a come-what-may worshiper; he chose to worship God in every situation. Instead of backing away from God because of his suffering, he moved in closer, allowing his suffering to mingle right into his worship. In doing so Jeremiah gave us one of the loveliest, most intimate moments in Scripture—a moment we can emulate in our own worship during times of suffering.

—*Caryn Rivadeneira*

For more on worship, see reading at Acts 17:18-34.

⁸ And though I cry and shout,
    he has shut out my prayers.
⁹ He has blocked my way with a high stone wall;
    he has made my road crooked.

¹⁰ He has hidden like a bear or a lion,
    waiting to attack me.
¹¹ He has dragged me off the path and torn me in pieces,
    leaving me helpless and devastated.
¹² He has drawn his bow
    and made me the target for his arrows.

¹³ He shot his arrows
    deep into my heart.
¹⁴ My own people laugh at me.
    All day long they sing their mocking songs.
¹⁵ He has filled me with bitterness
    and given me a bitter cup of sorrow to drink.
¹⁶ He has made me chew on gravel.
    He has rolled me in the dust.
¹⁷ Peace has been stripped away,
    and I have forgotten what prosperity is.

¹⁸ I cry out, "My splendor is gone!
  Everything I had hoped for from the
  LORD is lost!"

¹⁹ The thought of my suffering and
  homelessness
  is bitter beyond words.*

²⁰ I will never forget this awful time,
  as I grieve over my loss.

²¹ Yet I still dare to hope
  when I remember this:

²² The faithful love of the LORD never
  ends!*
  His mercies never cease.

²³ Great is his faithfulness;
  his mercies begin afresh each
  morning.

²⁴ I say to myself, "The LORD is my
  inheritance;
  therefore, I will hope in him!"

²⁵ The LORD is good to those who depend
  on him,
  to those who search for him.

²⁶ So it is good to wait quietly
  for salvation from the LORD.

²⁷ And it is good for people to submit at an
  early age
  to the yoke of his discipline:

²⁸ Let them sit alone in silence
  beneath the LORD's demands.

²⁹ Let them lie face down in the dust,
  for there may be hope at last.

³⁰ Let them turn the other cheek to those
  who strike them
  and accept the insults of their
  enemies.

³¹ For no one is abandoned
  by the Lord forever.

³² Though he brings grief, he also shows
  compassion
  because of the greatness of his
  unfailing love.

³³ For he does not enjoy hurting people
  or causing them sorrow.

³⁴ If people crush underfoot
  all the prisoners of the land,

³⁵ if they deprive others of their rights
  in defiance of the Most High,

³⁶ if they twist justice in the courts—
  doesn't the Lord see all these things?

³⁷ Who can command things to happen
  without the Lord's permission?

³⁸ Does not the Most High
  send both calamity and good?

³⁹ Then why should we, mere humans,
  complain
  when we are punished for our sins?

⁴⁰ Instead, let us test and examine our
  ways.
  Let us turn back to the LORD.

⁴¹ Let us lift our hearts and hands
  to God in heaven and say,

⁴² "We have sinned and rebelled,
  and you have not forgiven us.

⁴³ "You have engulfed us with your anger,
  chased us down,
  and slaughtered us without mercy.

⁴⁴ You have hidden yourself in a cloud
  so our prayers cannot reach you.

⁴⁵ You have discarded us as refuse and
  garbage
  among the nations.

⁴⁶ "All our enemies
  have spoken out against us.

⁴⁷ We are filled with fear,
  for we are trapped, devastated, and
  ruined."

⁴⁸ Tears stream from my eyes
  because of the destruction of my
  people!

⁴⁹ My tears flow endlessly;
  they will not stop

⁵⁰ until the LORD looks down
  from heaven and sees.

⁵¹ My heart is breaking
  over the fate of all the women of
  Jerusalem.

⁵² My enemies, whom I have never
  harmed,
  hunted me down like a bird.

⁵³ They threw me into a pit
  and dropped stones on me.

⁵⁴ The water rose over my head,
  and I cried out, "This is the end!"

⁵⁵ But I called on your name, LORD,
  from deep within the pit.

⁵⁶ You heard me when I cried, "Listen to
  my pleading!
  Hear my cry for help!"

3:19 Or *is wormwood and gall.*   **3:22** As in Syriac version; Hebrew reads *of the LORD keeps us from destruction.*

⁵⁷ Yes, you came when I called;
   you told me, "Do not fear."

⁵⁸ Lord, you are my lawyer! Plead my
      case!
   For you have redeemed my life.
⁵⁹ You have seen the wrong they have done
      to me, LORD.
   Be my judge, and prove me right.
⁶⁰ You have seen the vengeful plots
   my enemies have laid against me.

⁶¹ LORD, you have heard the vile names
      they call me.

You know all about the plans they
      have made.
⁶² My enemies whisper and mutter
   as they plot against me all day long.
⁶³ Look at them! Whether they sit or stand,
   I am the object of their mocking
      songs.

⁶⁴ Pay them back, LORD,
   for all the evil they have done.
⁶⁵ Give them hard and stubborn hearts,
   and then let your curse fall on
      them!

Q&A
Weaving Solitude into Everyday Life
LAMENTATIONS 3:22–28

How often should I practice solitude? Hours or days alone don't seem possible or realistic in my life right now.

I think about solitude in two categories: I need brief periods of solitude on a regular basis—preferably each day, even at intervals during the day. But I also need extended periods of solitude—a half day, a day, or a few days—and this is possible only at greater intervals.

When I go into solitude, I withdraw from conversation, people, noise, media, and the constant barrage of stimulation. I try to begin my days by praying over the day's schedule—meetings I'll attend, tasks I must perform, people I'll be with—and placing them all in God's hands. Through the day I try to take five-minute breaks, close the door to my office, and remind myself that one day the office will be gone and I'll still belong to God.

At the end of the day, I like to review the day with God: to go over the events to see what he might be saying to me through them, and to hand over to him any anxieties or regrets. One of the great benefits of this exercise is that you begin to learn from your days.

But in addition to these daily moments of solitude and reflection, I believe I also need extended times alone. How often or long these times alone with God may be will vary for each person. Prioritizing opportunities for longer periods of time alone will require relentless perseverance. I've learned that unless I pull my calendar out and write down well in advance when I am committed to times of solitude, it simply won't happen.

—*John Ortberg*

For more on solitude, see reading at Matthew 26:36–39.

⁶⁶ Chase them down in your anger,
    destroying them beneath the Lord's
        heavens.

4 God's Anger Satisfied

¹ How the gold has lost its luster!
    Even the finest gold has become dull.
The sacred gemstones
    lie scattered in the streets!

² See how the precious children of
        Jerusalem,*
    worth their weight in fine gold,
are now treated like pots of clay
    made by a common potter.

³ Even the jackals feed their young,
    but not my people Israel.
They ignore their children's cries,
    like ostriches in the desert.

⁴ The parched tongues of their little ones
    stick to the roofs of their mouths in
        thirst.
The children cry for bread,
    but no one has any to give them.

⁵ The people who once ate the richest
        foods
    now beg in the streets for anything
        they can get.
Those who once wore the finest clothes
    now search the garbage dumps for
        food.

⁶ The guilt* of my people
    is greater than that of Sodom,
where utter disaster struck in a moment
    and no hand offered help.

⁷ Our princes once glowed with health—
    brighter than snow, whiter than milk.
Their faces were as ruddy as rubies,
    their appearance like fine jewels.*

⁸ But now their faces are blacker than
        soot.
    No one recognizes them in the streets.
Their skin sticks to their bones;
    it is as dry and hard as wood.

⁹ Those killed by the sword are better off
    than those who die of hunger.
Starving, they waste away
    for lack of food from the fields.

¹⁰ Tenderhearted women
    have cooked their own children.
They have eaten them
    to survive the siege.

¹¹ But now the anger of the Lord is
        satisfied.
    His fierce anger has been poured out.
He started a fire in Jerusalem*
    that burned the city to its foundations.

¹² Not a king in all the earth—
    no one in all the world—
would have believed that an enemy
    could march through the gates of
        Jerusalem.

¹³ Yet it happened because of the sins of
        her prophets
    and the sins of her priests,
who defiled the city
    by shedding innocent blood.

¹⁴ They wandered blindly
    through the streets,
so defiled by blood
    that no one dared touch them.

¹⁵ "Get away!" the people shouted at them.
    "You're defiled! Don't touch us!"
So they fled to distant lands
    and wandered among foreign nations,
    but none would let them stay.

¹⁶ The Lord himself has scattered them,
    and he no longer helps them.
People show no respect for the priests
    and no longer honor the leaders.

¹⁷ We looked in vain for our allies
    to come and save us,
but we were looking to nations
    that could not help us.

¹⁸ We couldn't go into the streets
    without danger to our lives.
Our end was near; our days were
        numbered.
    We were doomed!

¹⁹ Our enemies were swifter than eagles in
        flight.
    If we fled to the mountains, they
        found us.
If we hid in the wilderness,
    they were waiting for us there.

4:2 Hebrew precious sons of Zion.   4:6 Or punishment.   4:7 Hebrew like lapis lazuli.   4:11 Hebrew in Zion.

²⁰ Our king—the LORD's anointed, the very
   life of our nation—
   was caught in their snares.
We had thought that his shadow
   would protect us against any nation
   on earth!

²¹ Are you rejoicing in the land of Uz,
   O people of Edom?
But you, too, must drink from the cup of
   the LORD's anger.
   You, too, will be stripped naked in
   your drunkenness.

²² O beautiful Jerusalem,* your
   punishment will end;
   you will soon return from exile.
But Edom, your punishment is just
   beginning;
   soon your many sins will be exposed.

5 Prayer for Restoration

¹ LORD, remember what has happened
   to us.
   See how we have been disgraced!
² Our inheritance has been turned over to
   strangers,
   our homes to foreigners.
³ We are orphaned and fatherless.
   Our mothers are widowed.
⁴ We have to pay for water to drink,
   and even firewood is expensive.
⁵ Those who pursue us are at our heels;
   we are exhausted but are given no rest.
⁶ We submitted to Egypt and Assyria
   to get enough food to survive.
⁷ Our ancestors sinned, but they have died—
   and we are suffering the punishment
   they deserved!
⁸ Slaves have now become our masters;
   there is no one left to rescue us.

⁹ We hunt for food at the risk of our lives,
   for violence rules the countryside.
¹⁰ The famine has blackened our skin
   as though baked in an oven.
¹¹ Our enemies rape the women in
   Jerusalem*
   and the young girls in all the towns of
   Judah.
¹² Our princes are being hanged by their
   thumbs,
   and our elders are treated with
   contempt.
¹³ Young men are led away to work at
   millstones,
   and boys stagger under heavy loads of
   wood.
¹⁴ The elders no longer sit in the city gates;
   the young men no longer dance and
   sing.
¹⁵ Joy has left our hearts;
   our dancing has turned to mourning.
¹⁶ The garlands have* fallen from our
   heads.
   Weep for us because we have sinned.
¹⁷ Our hearts are sick and weary,
   and our eyes grow dim with tears.
¹⁸ For Jerusalem* is empty and desolate,
   a place haunted by jackals.
¹⁹ But LORD, you remain the same
   forever!
   Your throne continues from
   generation to generation.
²⁰ Why do you continue to forget us?
   Why have you abandoned us for so
   long?
²¹ Restore us, O LORD, and bring us back
   to you again!
   Give us back the joys we once had!
²² Or have you utterly rejected us?
   Are you angry with us still?

4:22 Hebrew *O daughter of Zion.*   **5:11** Hebrew *in Zion.*   **5:16** Or *The crown has.*   **5:18** Hebrew *Mount Zion.*

Introduction to

Ezekiel

Background

Ezekiel lives and serves in a turbulent time. When the Babylonians defeat the Egyptians in 605 B.C., the king of Judah (Jehoiakim) swears allegiance to Nebuchadnezzar. But after the Babylonians fail to defeat the Egyptians, Jehoiakim switches sides. The invading army of Nebuchadnezzar moves against Jerusalem during the short reign of Jehoiachin in 597 B.C., taking captive the priest-prophet Ezekiel and many others. Ezekiel prophesies the destruction of Judah. He also prophesies against the future enemies of Israel, proclaiming that God will defend his people.

Most scholars believe that Ezekiel is the author of this book. In Hebrew, Ezekiel means "God strengthens." The name is particularly apt, considering the circumstances of living through captivity.

Message

Ezekiel has one of the most unusual ministries of any prophet. He has the task of acting out some of the judgments to come, as shown in 24:15–27, where he is warned of his wife's imminent death and given mourning instructions. Throughout the Book of Ezekiel, the visionary prophet is guided by the Spirit of God as he prophesies through the darkest days in the history of his people.

While the exiles hope for immediate relief from judgment, Ezekiel has the thankless task of speaking an opposing word. Like Jeremiah, Ezekiel preaches about God's judgment on Judah, but also the hope of restoration. His vision of "dry bones" coming to life (37:1–14) has spoken hope to God's people for millennia. The most prominent images throughout the book are the temple, God's departure from it, and his return to it.

Time

Like Daniel several years earlier, Ezekiel was taken to Babylon—in 597 B.C., before Jerusalem's destruction. In Babylon, Ezekiel prophesied from 592 B.C. until at least 570 and died in about 560.

Outline

Ezekiel

1 A Vision of Living Beings

On July 31* of my thirtieth year,* while I was with the Judean exiles beside the Kebar River in Babylon, the heavens were opened and I saw visions of God. ²This happened during the fifth year of King Jehoiachin's captivity. ³(The LORD gave this message to Ezekiel son of Buzi, a priest, beside the Kebar River in the land of the Babylonians,* and he felt the hand of the LORD take hold of him.)

⁴As I looked, I saw a great storm coming from the north, driving before it a huge cloud that flashed with lightning and shone with brilliant light. There was fire inside the cloud, and in the middle of the fire glowed something like gleaming amber.* ⁵From the center of the cloud came four living beings that looked human, ⁶except that each had four faces and four wings. ⁷Their legs were straight, and their feet had hooves like those of a calf and shone like burnished bronze. ⁸Under each of their four wings I could see human hands. So each of the four beings had four faces and four wings. ⁹The wings of each living being touched the wings of the beings beside it. Each one moved straight forward in any direction without turning around.

¹⁰Each had a human face in the front, the face of a lion on the right side, the face of an ox on the left side, and the face of an eagle at the back. ¹¹Each had two pairs of outstretched wings—one pair stretched out to touch the wings of the living beings on either side of it, and the other pair covered its body. ¹²They went in whatever direction the spirit chose, and they moved straight forward in any direction without turning around.

¹³The living beings looked like bright coals of fire or brilliant torches, and lightning seemed to flash back and forth among them. ¹⁴And the living beings darted to and fro like flashes of lightning.

¹⁵As I looked at these beings, I saw four wheels touching the ground beside them, one wheel belonging to each. ¹⁶The wheels sparkled as if made of beryl. All four wheels looked alike and were made the same; each wheel had a second wheel turning crosswise within it. ¹⁷The beings could move in any of the four directions they faced, without turning as they moved. ¹⁸The rims of the four wheels were tall and frightening, and they were covered with eyes all around.

¹⁹When the living beings moved, the wheels moved with them. When they flew upward, the wheels went up, too. ²⁰The spirit of the living beings was in the wheels. So wherever the spirit went, the wheels and the living beings also went. ²¹When the beings moved, the wheels moved. When the beings stopped, the wheels stopped. When the beings flew upward, the wheels rose up, for the spirit of the living beings was in the wheels.

²²Spread out above them was a surface like the sky, glittering like crystal. ²³Beneath this surface the wings of each living being stretched out to touch the others' wings, and each had two wings covering its body. ²⁴As they flew, their wings sounded to me like waves crashing against the shore or like the

---

1:1a Hebrew *On the fifth day of the fourth month,* of the ancient Hebrew lunar calendar. A number of dates in Ezekiel can be cross-checked with dates in surviving Babylonian records and related accurately to our modern calendar. This event occurred on July 31, 593 B.C. **1:1b** Or *in the thirtieth year.* **1:3** Or *Chaldeans.* **1:4** Or *like burnished metal;* also in 1:27.

voice of the Almighty* or like the shouting of a mighty army. When they stopped, they let down their wings. ²⁵ As they stood with wings lowered, a voice spoke from beyond the crystal surface above them.

²⁶ Above this surface was something that looked like a throne made of blue lapis lazuli. And on this throne high above was a figure whose appearance resembled a man. ²⁷ From what appeared to be his waist up, he looked like gleaming amber, flickering like a fire. And from his waist down, he looked like a burning flame, shining with splendor. ²⁸ All around him was a glowing halo, like a rainbow shining in the clouds on a rainy day. This is what the glory of the LORD looked like to me. When I saw it, I fell face down on the ground, and I heard someone's voice speaking to me.

2 Ezekiel's Call and Commission

"Stand up, son of man," said the voice. "I want to speak with you." ² The Spirit came into me as he spoke, and he set me on my feet. I listened carefully to his words. ³ "Son of man," he said, "I am sending you to the nation of Israel, a rebellious nation that has rebelled against me. They and their ancestors have been rebelling against me to this very day. ⁴ They are a stubborn and hard-hearted people. But I am sending you to say to them, 'This is what the Sovereign LORD says!' ⁵ And whether they listen or refuse to listen—for remember, they are rebels—at least they will know they have had a prophet among them.

⁶ "Son of man, do not fear them or their words. Don't be afraid even though their threats surround you like nettles and briers and stinging scorpions. Do not be dismayed by their dark scowls, even though they are rebels. ⁷ You must give them my messages whether they listen or not. But they won't listen, for they are completely rebellious! ⁸ Son of man, listen to what I say to you. Do not join them in their rebellion. Open your mouth, and eat what I give you."

⁹ Then I looked and saw a hand reaching out to me. It held a scroll, ¹⁰ which he unrolled. And I saw that both sides were covered with funeral songs, words of sorrow, and pronouncements of doom.

3

The voice said to me, "Son of man, eat what I am giving you—eat this scroll! Then go and give its message to the people of Israel." ² So I opened my mouth, and he fed me the scroll. ³ "Fill your stomach with this," he said. And when I ate it, it tasted as sweet as honey in my mouth.

⁴ Then he said, "Son of man, go to the people of Israel and give them my messages. ⁵ I am not sending you to a foreign people whose language you cannot understand. ⁶ No, I am not sending you to people with strange and difficult speech. If I did, they would listen! ⁷ But the people of Israel won't listen to you any more than they listen to me! For the whole lot of them are hard-hearted and stubborn. ⁸ But look, I have made you as obstinate and hard-hearted as they are. ⁹ I have made your forehead as hard as the hardest rock! So don't be afraid of them or fear their angry looks, even though they are rebels."

¹⁰ Then he added, "Son of man, let all my words sink deep into your own heart first. Listen to them carefully for yourself. ¹¹ Then go to your people in exile and say to them, 'This is what the Sovereign LORD says!' Do this whether they listen to you or not."

¹² Then the Spirit lifted me up, and I heard a loud rumbling sound behind me. (May the glory of the LORD be praised in his place!)* ¹³ It was the sound of the wings of the living beings as they brushed against each other and the rumbling of their wheels beneath them.

¹⁴ The Spirit lifted me up and took me away. I went in bitterness and turmoil, but the LORD's hold on me was strong. ¹⁵ Then I came to the colony of Judean exiles in Tel-abib, beside the Kebar River. I was overwhelmed and sat among them for seven days.

A Watchman for Israel

¹⁶ After seven days the LORD gave me a message. He said, ¹⁷ "Son of man, I have appointed you as a watchman for Israel. Whenever you receive a message from me, warn people immediately. ¹⁸ If I warn the wicked, saying, 'You are under the penalty of death,' but you fail to deliver the warning,

---

1:24 Hebrew *Shaddai*. **3:12** A possible reading for this verse is *Then the Spirit lifted me up, and as the glory of the LORD rose from its place, I heard a loud rumbling sound behind me.*

they will die in their sins. And I will hold you responsible for their deaths. ¹⁹ If you warn them and they refuse to repent and keep on sinning, they will die in their sins. But you will have saved yourself because you obeyed me.

²⁰ "If righteous people turn away from their righteous behavior and ignore the obstacles I put in their way, they will die. And if you do not warn them, they will die in their sins. None of their righteous acts will be remembered, and I will hold you responsible for their deaths. ²¹ But if you warn righteous people not to sin and they listen to you and do not sin, they will live, and you will have saved yourself, too."

²² Then the LORD took hold of me and said, "Get up and go out into the valley, and I will speak to you there." ²³ So I got up and went, and there I saw the glory of the LORD, just as I had seen in my first vision by the Kebar River. And I fell face down on the ground.

²⁴ Then the Spirit came into me and set me on my feet. He spoke to me and said, "Go to your house and shut yourself in. ²⁵ There, son of man, you will be tied with ropes so you cannot go out among the people. ²⁶ And I will make your tongue stick to the roof of your mouth so that you will be speechless and unable to rebuke them, for they are rebels. ²⁷ But when I give you a message, I will loosen your tongue and let you speak. Then you will say to them, 'This is what the Sovereign LORD says!' Those who choose to listen will listen, but those who refuse will refuse, for they are rebels.

4 A Sign of the Coming Siege

"And now, son of man, take a large clay brick and set it down in front of you. Then draw a map of the city of Jerusalem on it. ² Show the city under siege. Build a wall around it so no one can escape. Set up the enemy camp, and surround the city with siege ramps and battering rams. ³ Then take an iron griddle and place it between you and the city. Turn toward the city and demonstrate how harsh the siege will be against Jerusalem. This will be a warning to the people of Israel.

⁴ "Now lie on your left side and place the

sins of Israel on yourself. You are to bear their sins for the number of days you lie there on your side. ⁵ I am requiring you to bear Israel's sins for 390 days—one day for each year of their sin. ⁶ After that, turn over and lie on your right side for 40 days—one day for each year of Judah's sin.

⁷ "Meanwhile, keep staring at the siege of Jerusalem. Lie there with your arm bared and prophesy her destruction. ⁸ I will tie you up with ropes so you won't be able to turn from side to side until the days of your siege have been completed.

⁹ "Now go and get some wheat, barley, beans, lentils, millet, and emmer wheat, and mix them together in a storage jar. Use them to make bread for yourself during the 390 days you will be lying on your side. ¹⁰ Ration this out to yourself, eight ounces* of food for each day, and eat it at set times. ¹¹ Then measure out a jar* of water for each day, and drink it at set times. ¹² Prepare and eat this food as you would barley cakes. While all the people are watching, bake it over a fire using dried human dung as fuel and then eat the bread." ¹³ Then the LORD said, "This is how Israel will eat defiled bread in the Gentile lands to which I will banish them!"

¹⁴ Then I said, "O Sovereign LORD, must I be defiled by using human dung? For I have never been defiled before. From the time I was a child until now I have never eaten any animal that died of sickness or was killed by other animals. I have never eaten any meat forbidden by the law."

¹⁵ "All right," the LORD said. "You may bake your bread with cow dung instead of human dung." ¹⁶ Then he told me, "Son of man, I will make food very scarce in Jerusalem. It will be weighed out with great care and eaten fearfully. The water will be rationed out drop by drop, and the people will drink it with dismay. ¹⁷ Lacking food and water, people will look at one another in terror, and they will waste away under their punishment.

5 A Sign of the Coming Judgment

"Son of man, take a sharp sword and use it as a razor to shave your head and beard. Use a scale to weigh the hair into three

---

4:10 Hebrew *20 shekels* [228 grams].   **4:11** Hebrew *⅙ of a hin* [about 1 pint or 0.6 liters].

equal parts. ²Place a third of it at the center of your map of Jerusalem. After acting out the siege, burn it there. Scatter another third across your map and chop it with a sword. Scatter the last third to the wind, for I will scatter my people with the sword. ³Keep just a bit of the hair and tie it up in your robe. ⁴Then take some of these hairs out and throw them into the fire, burning them up. A fire will then spread from this remnant and destroy all of Israel.

⁵"This is what the Sovereign LORD says: This is an illustration of what will happen to Jerusalem. I placed her at the center of the nations, ⁶but she has rebelled against my regulations and decrees and has been even more wicked than the surrounding nations. She has refused to obey the regulations and decrees I gave her to follow.

⁷"Therefore, this is what the Sovereign LORD says: You people have behaved worse than your neighbors and have refused to obey my decrees and regulations. You have not even lived up to the standards of the nations around you. ⁸Therefore, I myself, the Sovereign LORD, am now your enemy. I will punish you publicly while all the nations watch. ⁹Because of your detestable idols, I will punish you like I have never punished anyone before or ever will again. ¹⁰Parents will eat their own children, and children will eat their parents. I will punish you and scatter to the winds the few who survive.

¹¹"As surely as I live, says the Sovereign LORD, I will cut you off completely. I will show you no pity at all because you have defiled my Temple with your vile images and detestable sins. ¹²A third of your people will die in the city from disease and famine. A third of them will be slaughtered by the enemy outside the city walls. And I will scatter a third to the winds, chasing them with my sword. ¹³Then at last my anger will be spent, and I will be satisfied. And when my fury against them has subsided, all Israel will know that I, the LORD, have spoken to them in my jealous anger.

¹⁴"So I will turn you into a ruin, a mockery in the eyes of the surrounding nations and to all who pass by. ¹⁵You will become an object of mockery and taunting and horror. You will be a warning to all the nations around you. They will see what happens when the LORD punishes a nation in anger and rebukes it, says the LORD.

¹⁶"I will shower you with the deadly arrows of famine to destroy you. The famine will become more and more severe until every crumb of food is gone. ¹⁷And along with the famine, wild animals will attack you and rob you of your children. Disease and war will stalk your land, and I will bring the sword of the enemy against you. I, the LORD, have spoken!"

6 Judgment against Israel's Mountains

Again a message came to me from the LORD: ²"Son of man, turn and face the mountains of Israel and prophesy against them. ³Proclaim this message from the Sovereign LORD against the mountains of Israel. This is what the Sovereign LORD says to the mountains and hills and to the ravines and valleys: I am about to bring war upon you, and I will smash your pagan shrines. ⁴All your altars will be demolished, and your places of worship will be destroyed. I will kill your people in front of your idols.* ⁵I will lay your corpses in front of your idols and scatter your bones around your altars. ⁶Wherever you live there will be desolation, and I will destroy your pagan shrines. Your altars will be demolished, your idols will be smashed, your places of worship will be torn down, and all the religious objects you have made will be destroyed. ⁷The place will be littered with corpses, and you will know that I alone am the LORD.

⁸"But I will let a few of my people escape destruction, and they will be scattered among the nations of the world. ⁹Then when they are exiled among the nations, they will remember me. They will recognize how hurt I am by their unfaithful hearts and lustful eyes that long for their idols. Then at last they will hate themselves for all their detestable sins. ¹⁰They will know that I alone am the LORD and that I was serious when I said I would bring this calamity on them.

¹¹"This is what the Sovereign LORD says:

6:4 The Hebrew term (literally *round things*) probably alludes to dung; also in 6:5, 6, 9, 13.

Clap your hands in horror, and stamp your feet. Cry out because of all the detestable sins the people of Israel have committed. Now they are going to die from war and famine and disease. ¹²Disease will strike down those who are far away in exile. War will destroy those who are nearby. And anyone who survives will be killed by famine. So at last I will spend my fury on them. ¹³They will know that I am the LORD when their dead lie scattered among their idols and altars on every hill and mountain and under every green tree and every great shade tree—the places where they offered sacrifices to their idols. ¹⁴I will crush them and make their cities desolate from the wilderness in the south to Riblah* in the north. Then they will know that I am the LORD."

7 The Coming of the End

Then this message came to me from the LORD: ²"Son of man, this is what the Sovereign LORD says to Israel:

"The end is here!
    Wherever you look—
east, west, north, or south—
    your land is finished.
³ No hope remains,
    for I will unleash my anger against
        you.
I will call you to account
    for all your detestable sins.
⁴ I will turn my eyes away and show no
        pity.
I will repay you for all your detestable
        sins.
Then you will know that I am the LORD.

⁵ "This is what the Sovereign LORD says:
Disaster after disaster
    is coming your way!
⁶ The end has come.
    It has finally arrived.
    Your final doom is waiting!
⁷ O people of Israel, the day of your
        destruction is dawning.
The time has come; the day of trouble
        is near.
Shouts of anguish will be heard on the
        mountains,
    not shouts of joy.

⁸ Soon I will pour out my fury on you
    and unleash my anger against you.
I will call you to account
    for all your detestable sins.
⁹ I will turn my eyes away and show no pity.
    I will repay you for all your detestable
        sins.
Then you will know that it is I, the LORD,
    who is striking the blow.

¹⁰ "The day of judgment is here;
    your destruction awaits!
The people's wickedness and pride
    have blossomed to full flower.
¹¹ Their violence has grown into a rod
    that will beat them for their
        wickedness.
None of these proud and wicked people
    will survive.
All their wealth and prestige will be
    swept away.
¹² Yes, the time has come;
    the day is here!
Buyers should not rejoice over bargains,
    nor sellers grieve over losses,
for all of them will fall
    under my terrible anger.
¹³ Even if the merchants survive,
    they will never return to their
        business.
For what God has said applies to
        everyone—
    it will not be changed!
Not one person whose life is twisted by
        sin
    will ever recover.

The Desolation of Israel

¹⁴ "The trumpet calls Israel's army to
        mobilize,
    but no one listens,
    for my fury is against them all.
¹⁵ There is war outside the city
    and disease and famine within.
Those outside the city walls
    will be killed by enemy swords.
Those inside the city
    will die of famine and disease.
¹⁶ The survivors who escape to the
        mountains
    will moan like doves, weeping for their
        sins.

6:14 As in some Hebrew manuscripts; most Hebrew manuscripts read *Diblah*.

¹⁷ Their hands will hang limp,
    their knees will be weak as water.
¹⁸ They will dress themselves in burlap;
    horror and shame will cover them.
They will shave their heads
    in sorrow and remorse.

¹⁹ "They will throw their money in the
    streets,
    tossing it out like worthless trash.
Their silver and gold won't save them
    on that day of the LORD's anger.
It will neither satisfy nor feed them,
    for their greed can only trip
    them up.
²⁰ They were proud of their beautiful
    jewelry
    and used it to make detestable idols
    and vile images.
Therefore, I will make all their wealth
    disgusting to them.
²¹ I will give it as plunder to foreigners,
    to the most wicked of nations,
    and they will defile it.
²² I will turn my eyes from them
    as these robbers invade and defile my
    treasured land.

²³ "Prepare chains for my people,
    for the land is bloodied by terrible
    crimes.
Jerusalem is filled with violence.
²⁴ I will bring the most ruthless of nations
    to occupy their homes.
I will break down their proud fortresses
    and defile their sanctuaries.
²⁵ Terror and trembling will overcome my
    people.
They will look for peace but not
    find it.
²⁶ Calamity will follow calamity;
    rumor will follow rumor.
They will look in vain
    for a vision from the prophets.
They will receive no teaching from the
    priests
    and no counsel from the leaders.
²⁷ The king and the prince will stand
    helpless,
    weeping in despair,
and the people's hands
    will tremble with fear.

I will bring on them
    the evil they have done to others,
and they will receive the punishment
    they so richly deserve.
Then they will know that I am the
    LORD."

8 Idolatry in the Temple

Then on September 17,* during the sixth year of King Jehoiachin's captivity, while the leaders of Judah were in my home, the Sovereign LORD took hold of me. ²I saw a figure that appeared to be a man. From what appeared to be his waist down, he looked like a burning flame. From the waist up he looked like gleaming amber.* ³He reached out what seemed to be a hand and took me by the hair. Then the Spirit lifted me up into the sky and transported me to Jerusalem in a vision from God. I was taken to the north gate of the inner courtyard of the Temple, where there is a large idol that has made the LORD very jealous. ⁴Suddenly, the glory of the God of Israel was there, just as I had seen it before in the valley.

⁵Then the LORD said to me, "Son of man, look toward the north." So I looked, and there to the north, beside the entrance to the gate near the altar, stood the idol that had made the LORD so jealous.

⁶"Son of man," he said, "do you see what they are doing? Do you see the detestable sins the people of Israel are committing to drive me from my Temple? But come, and you will see even more detestable sins than these!" ⁷Then he brought me to the door of the Temple courtyard, where I could see a hole in the wall. ⁸He said to me, "Now, son of man, dig into the wall." So I dug into the wall and found a hidden doorway.

⁹"Go in," he said, "and see the wicked and detestable sins they are committing in there!" ¹⁰So I went in and saw the walls engraved with all kinds of crawling animals and detestable creatures. I also saw the various idols* worshiped by the people of Israel. ¹¹Seventy leaders of Israel were standing there with Jaazaniah son of Shaphan in the center. Each of them held an incense burner, from which a cloud of incense rose above their heads.

8:1 Hebrew *on the fifth day of the sixth month,* of the ancient Hebrew lunar calendar. This event occurred on September 17, 592 B.C.; also see note on 1:1. **8:2** Or *like burnished metal.* **8:10** The Hebrew term (literally *round things*) probably alludes to dung.

¹²Then the LORD said to me, "Son of man, have you seen what the leaders of Israel are doing with their idols in dark rooms? They are saying, 'The LORD doesn't see us; he has deserted our land!'" ¹³Then the LORD added, "Come, and I will show you even more detestable sins than these!"

¹⁴He brought me to the north gate of the LORD's Temple, and some women were sitting there, weeping for the god Tammuz. ¹⁵"Have you seen this?" he asked. "But I will show you even more detestable sins than these!"

¹⁶Then he brought me into the inner courtyard of the LORD's Temple. At the entrance to the sanctuary, between the entry room and the bronze altar, there were about twenty-five men with their backs to the sanctuary of the LORD. They were facing east, bowing low to the ground, worshiping the sun!

¹⁷"Have you seen this, son of man?" he asked. "Is it nothing to the people of Judah that they commit these detestable sins, leading the whole nation into violence, thumbing their noses at me, and provoking my anger? ¹⁸Therefore, I will respond in fury. I will neither pity nor spare them. And though they cry for mercy, I will not listen."

9 The Slaughter of Idolaters

Then the LORD thundered, "Bring on the men appointed to punish the city! Tell them to bring their weapons with them!" ²Six men soon appeared from the upper gate that faces north, each carrying a deadly weapon in his hand. With them was a man dressed in linen, who carried a writer's case at his side. They all went into the Temple courtyard and stood beside the bronze altar.

³Then the glory of the God of Israel rose up from between the cherubim, where it had rested, and moved to the entrance of the Temple. And the LORD called to the man dressed in linen who was carrying the writer's case. ⁴He said to him, "Walk through the streets of Jerusalem and put a mark on the foreheads of all who weep and sigh because of the detestable sins being committed in their city."

⁵Then I heard the LORD say to the other men, "Follow him through the city and kill everyone whose forehead is not marked. Show no mercy; have no pity! ⁶Kill them all—old and young, girls and women and little children. But do not touch anyone with the mark. Begin right here at the Temple." So they began by killing the seventy leaders.

⁷"Defile the Temple!" the LORD commanded. "Fill its courtyards with corpses. Go!" So they went and began killing throughout the city.

⁸While they were out killing, I was all alone. I fell face down on the ground and cried out, "O Sovereign LORD! Will your fury against Jerusalem wipe out everyone left in Israel?"

⁹Then he said to me, "The sins of the people of Israel and Judah are very, very great. The entire land is full of murder; the city is filled with injustice. They are saying, 'The LORD doesn't see it! The LORD has abandoned the land!' ¹⁰So I will not spare them or have any pity on them. I will fully repay them for all they have done."

¹¹Then the man in linen clothing, who carried the writer's case, reported back and said, "I have done as you commanded."

10 The LORD's Glory Leaves the Temple

In my vision I saw what appeared to be a throne of blue lapis lazuli above the crystal surface over the heads of the cherubim. ²Then the LORD spoke to the man in linen clothing and said, "Go between the whirling wheels beneath the cherubim, and take a handful of burning coals and scatter them over the city." He did this as I watched.

³The cherubim were standing at the south end of the Temple when the man went in, and the cloud of glory filled the inner courtyard. ⁴Then the glory of the LORD rose up from above the cherubim and went over to the door of the Temple. The Temple was filled with this cloud of glory, and the courtyard glowed brightly with the glory of the LORD. ⁵The moving wings of the cherubim sounded like the voice of God Almighty* and could be heard even in the outer courtyard.

10:5 Hebrew *El-Shaddai.*

⁶The Lord said to the man in linen clothing, "Go between the cherubim and take some burning coals from between the wheels." So the man went in and stood beside one of the wheels. ⁷Then one of the cherubim reached out his hand and took some live coals from the fire burning among them. He put the coals into the hands of the man in linen clothing, and the man took them and went out. ⁸(All the cherubim had what looked like human hands under their wings.)

⁹I looked, and each of the four cherubim had a wheel beside him, and the wheels sparkled like beryl. ¹⁰All four wheels looked alike and were made the same; each wheel had a second wheel turning crosswise within it. ¹¹The cherubim could move in any of the four directions they faced, without turning as they moved. They went straight in the direction they faced, never turning aside. ¹²Both the cherubim and the wheels were covered with eyes. The cherubim had eyes all over their bodies, including their hands, their backs, and their wings. ¹³I heard someone refer to the wheels as "the whirling wheels." ¹⁴Each of the four cherubim had four faces: the first was the face of an ox,* the second was a human face, the third was the face of a lion, and the fourth was the face of an eagle.

¹⁵Then the cherubim rose upward. These were the same living beings I had seen beside the Kebar River. ¹⁶When the cherubim moved, the wheels moved with them. When they lifted their wings to fly, the wheels stayed beside them. ¹⁷When the cherubim stopped, the wheels stopped. When they flew upward, the wheels rose up, for the spirit of the living beings was in the wheels.

¹⁸Then the glory of the Lord moved out from the door of the Temple and hovered above the cherubim. ¹⁹And as I watched, the cherubim flew with their wheels to the east gate of the Lord's Temple. And the glory of the God of Israel hovered above them.

²⁰These were the same living beings I had seen beneath the God of Israel when I was by the Kebar River. I knew they were cherubim, ²¹for each had four faces and four wings and what looked like human hands under their wings. ²²And their faces were just like the faces of the beings I had seen at the Kebar, and they traveled straight ahead, just as the others had.

11 Judgment on Israel's Leaders

Then the Spirit lifted me and brought me to the east gateway of the Lord's Temple, where I saw twenty-five prominent men of the city. Among them were Jaazaniah son of Azzur and Pelatiah son of Benaiah, who were leaders among the people.

²The Spirit said to me, "Son of man, these are the men who are planning evil and giving wicked counsel in this city. ³They say to the people, 'Is it not a good time to build houses? This city is like an iron pot. We are safe inside it like meat in a pot.*' ⁴Therefore, son of man, prophesy against them loudly and clearly."

⁵Then the Spirit of the Lord came upon me, and he told me to say, "This is what the Lord says to the people of Israel: I know what you are saying, for I know every thought that comes into your minds. ⁶You have murdered many in this city and filled its streets with the dead.

⁷"Therefore, this is what the Sovereign Lord says: This city is an iron pot all right, but the pieces of meat are the victims of your injustice. As for you, I will soon drag you from this pot. ⁸I will bring on you the sword of war you so greatly fear, says the Sovereign Lord. ⁹I will drive you out of Jerusalem and hand you over to foreigners, who will carry out my judgments against you. ¹⁰You will be slaughtered all the way to the borders of Israel. I will execute judgment on you, and you will know that I am the Lord. ¹¹No, this city will not be an iron pot for you, and you will not be like meat safe inside it. I will judge you even to the borders of Israel, ¹²and you will know that I am the Lord. For you have refused to obey my decrees and regulations; instead, you have copied the standards of the nations around you."

¹³While I was still prophesying, Pelatiah son of Benaiah suddenly died. Then I fell face down on the ground and cried out,

---

10:14 Hebrew *the face of a cherub*; compare 1:10.   11:3 Hebrew *This city is the pot, and we are the meat.*

Deliberately Choosing Contentment

EZEKIEL 11:18-20

Once, while on a sabbatical, I had a life-altering conversation with my friend Dallas Willard.

"You must arrange to live with deep contentment, joy, and confidence in your everyday experience of life with God," Dallas challenged me. Those words are now on a sign that hangs in my office. I see it every day, and I think about those words several times every hour.

It sounded easy when I was on sabbatical. Then I came back to real life—to work, to bills, to relationship challenges and frustrations. Fostering contentment in everyday life is a difficult task; it's a conscious choice.

I now have come to believe that my main job is to live with deep contentment, joy, and confidence in my everyday experience of life with God. Everything else is job number two. Trying to live out this commitment has led me to another critical realization: there is a large difference between having deep contentment in my everyday experience with God and being in a good mood.

When I first talked with Dallas, I was hoping to live in "Good Mood Land," but being in a good mood is an episodic emotional experience. It is often unavailable. But being deeply contented with God in my everyday life is a focused attitude. It is *always* available.

—*John Ortberg*

For more on gratitude, see reading at Haggai 1:1-10.

"O Sovereign LORD, are you going to kill everyone in Israel?"

Hope for Exiled Israel

¹⁴Then this message came to me from the LORD: ¹⁵"Son of man, the people still left in Jerusalem are talking about you and your relatives and all the people of Israel who are in exile. They are saying, 'Those people are far away from the LORD, so now he has given their land to us!'

¹⁶"Therefore, tell the exiles, 'This is what the Sovereign LORD says: Although I have scattered you in the countries of the world, I will be a sanctuary to you during your time in exile. ¹⁷I, the Sovereign LORD, will gather you back from the nations where you have been scattered, and I will give you the land of Israel once again.'

¹⁸"When the people return to their homeland, they will remove every trace of their vile images and detestable idols. ¹⁹And I will give them singleness of heart and put a new spirit within them. I will take away their stony, stubborn heart and give them a tender, responsive heart,* ²⁰so they will obey my decrees and regulations. Then they will truly be my people, and I will be their God. ²¹But as for those who long for vile images and detestable idols, I will repay them fully for their sins. I, the Sovereign LORD, have spoken!"

The LORD's Glory Leaves Jerusalem

²²Then the cherubim lifted their wings and rose into the air with their wheels beside them, and the glory of the God of Israel hovered above them. ²³Then the glory of the LORD went up from the city and stopped above the mountain to the east.

11:19 Hebrew *a heart of flesh.*

²⁴Afterward the Spirit of God carried me back again to Babylonia,* to the people in exile there. And so ended the vision of my visit to Jerusalem. ²⁵And I told the exiles everything the LORD had shown me.

12 Signs of the Coming Exile

Again a message came to me from the LORD: ²"Son of man, you live among rebels who have eyes but refuse to see. They have ears but refuse to hear. For they are a rebellious people.

³"So now, son of man, pretend you are being sent into exile. Pack the few items an exile could carry, and leave your home to go somewhere else. Do this right in front of the people so they can see you. For perhaps they will pay attention to this, even though they are such rebels. ⁴Bring your baggage outside during the day so they can watch you. Then in the evening, as they are watching, leave your house as captives do when they begin a long march to distant lands. ⁵Dig a hole through the wall while they are watching and go out through it. ⁶As they watch, lift your pack to your shoulders and walk away into the night. Cover your face so you cannot see the land you are leaving. For I have made you a sign for the people of Israel."

⁷So I did as I was told. In broad daylight I brought my pack outside, filled with the things I might carry into exile. Then in the evening while the people looked on, I dug through the wall with my hands and went out into the night with my pack on my shoulder.

⁸The next morning this message came to me from the LORD: ⁹"Son of man, these rebels, the people of Israel, have asked you what all this means. ¹⁰Say to them, 'This is what the Sovereign LORD says: These actions contain a message for King Zedekiah in Jerusalem* and for all the people of Israel.' ¹¹Explain that your actions are a sign to show what will soon happen to them, for they will be driven into exile as captives.

¹²"Even Zedekiah will leave Jerusalem at night through a hole in the wall, taking only what he can carry with him. He will cover his face, and his eyes will not see the land he is leaving. ¹³Then I will throw my net over him and capture him in my snare. I will bring him to Babylon, the land of the Babylonians,* though he will never see it, and he will die there. ¹⁴I will scatter his servants and warriors to the four winds and send the sword after them. ¹⁵And when I scatter them among the nations, they will know that I am the LORD. ¹⁶But I will spare a few of them from death by war, famine, or disease, so they can confess all their detestable sins to their captors. Then they will know that I am the LORD."

¹⁷Then this message came to me from the LORD: ¹⁸"Son of man, tremble as you eat your food. Shake with fear as you drink your water. ¹⁹Tell the people, 'This is what the Sovereign LORD says concerning those living in Israel and Jerusalem: They will eat their food with trembling and sip their water in despair, for their land will be stripped bare because of their violence. ²⁰The cities will be destroyed and the farmland made desolate. Then you will know that I am the LORD.'"

A New Proverb for Israel

²¹Again a message came to me from the LORD: ²²"Son of man, you've heard that proverb they quote in Israel: 'Time passes, and prophecies come to nothing.' ²³Tell the people, 'This is what the Sovereign LORD says: I will put an end to this proverb, and you will soon stop quoting it.' Now give them this new proverb to replace the old one: 'The time has come for every prophecy to be fulfilled!'

²⁴"There will be no more false visions and flattering predictions in Israel. ²⁵For I am the LORD! If I say it, it will happen. There will be no more delays, you rebels of Israel. I will fulfill my threat of destruction in your own lifetime. I, the Sovereign LORD, have spoken!"

²⁶Then this message came to me from the LORD: ²⁷"Son of man, the people of Israel are saying, 'He's talking about the distant future. His visions won't come true for a long, long time.' ²⁸Therefore, tell them, 'This is what the Sovereign LORD says: No more delay! I will now do everything I have

threatened. I, the Sovereign LORD, have spoken!'"

13 Judgment against False Prophets

Then this message came to me from the LORD: ²"Son of man, prophesy against the false prophets of Israel who are inventing their own prophecies. Say to them, 'Listen to the word of the LORD. ³This is what the Sovereign LORD says: What sorrow awaits the false prophets who are following their own imaginations and have seen nothing at all!'

⁴"O people of Israel, these prophets of yours are like jackals digging in the ruins. ⁵They have done nothing to repair the breaks in the walls around the nation. They have not helped it to stand firm in battle on the day of the LORD. ⁶Instead, they have told lies and made false predictions. They say, 'This message is from the LORD,' even though the LORD never sent them. And yet they expect him to fulfill their prophecies! ⁷Can your visions be anything but false if you claim, 'This message is from the LORD,' when I have not even spoken to you?

⁸"Therefore, this is what the Sovereign LORD says: Because what you say is false and your visions are a lie, I will stand against you, says the Sovereign LORD. ⁹I will raise my fist against all the prophets who see false visions and make lying predictions, and they will be banished from the community of Israel. I will blot their names from Israel's record books, and they will never again set foot in their own land. Then you will know that I am the Sovereign LORD.

¹⁰"This will happen because these evil prophets deceive my people by saying, 'All is peaceful' when there is no peace at all! It's as if the people have built a flimsy wall, and these prophets are trying to reinforce it by covering it with whitewash! ¹¹Tell these whitewashers that their wall will soon fall down. A heavy rainstorm will undermine it; great hailstones and mighty winds will knock it down. ¹²And when the wall falls, the people will cry out, 'What happened to your whitewash?'

¹³"Therefore, this is what the Sovereign LORD says: I will sweep away your whitewashed wall with a storm of indignation, with a great flood of anger, and with hailstones of fury. ¹⁴I will break down your wall right to its foundation, and when it falls, it will crush you. Then you will know that I am the LORD. ¹⁵At last my anger against the wall and those who covered it with whitewash will be satisfied. Then I will say to you: 'The wall and those who whitewashed it are both gone. ¹⁶They were lying prophets who claimed peace would come to Jerusalem when there was no peace. I, the Sovereign LORD, have spoken!'

Judgment against False Women Prophets

¹⁷"Now, son of man, speak out against the women who prophesy from their own imaginations. ¹⁸This is what the Sovereign LORD says: What sorrow awaits you women who are ensnaring the souls of my people, young and old alike. You tie magic charms on their wrists and furnish them with magic veils. Do you think you can trap others without bringing destruction on yourselves? ¹⁹You bring shame on me among my people for a few handfuls of barley or a piece of bread. By lying to my people who love to listen to lies, you kill those who should not die, and you promise life to those who should not live.

²⁰"This is what the Sovereign LORD says: I am against all your magic charms, which you use to ensnare my people like birds. I will tear them from your arms, setting my people free like birds set free from a cage. ²¹I will tear off the magic veils and save my people from your grasp. They will no longer be your victims. Then you will know that I am the LORD. ²²You have discouraged the righteous with your lies, but I didn't want them to be sad. And you have encouraged the wicked by promising them life, even though they continue in their sins. ²³Because of all this, you will no longer talk of seeing visions that you never saw, nor will you make predictions. For I will rescue my people from your grasp. Then you will know that I am the LORD."

14 The Idolatry of Israel's Leaders

Then some of the leaders of Israel visited me, and while they were sitting with me, ²this message came to me from the LORD: ³"Son of man, these leaders have set up idols* in their hearts. They have embraced things that will make them fall into sin. Why should I listen to their requests? ⁴Tell them, 'This is what the Sovereign LORD says: The people of Israel have set up idols in their hearts and fallen into sin, and then they go to a prophet asking for a message. So I, the LORD, will give them the kind of answer their great idolatry deserves. ⁵I will do this to capture the minds and hearts of all my people who have turned from me to worship their detestable idols.'

⁶"Therefore, tell the people of Israel, 'This is what the Sovereign LORD says: Repent and turn away from your idols, and stop all your detestable sins. ⁷I, the LORD, will answer all those, both Israelites and foreigners, who reject me and set up idols in their hearts and so fall into sin, and who then come to a prophet asking for my advice. ⁸I will turn against such people and make a terrible example of them, eliminating them from among my people. Then you will know that I am the LORD.

⁹"'And if a prophet is deceived into giving a message, it is because I, the LORD, have deceived that prophet. I will lift my fist against such prophets and cut them off from the community of Israel. ¹⁰False prophets and those who seek their guidance will all be punished for their sins. ¹¹In this way, the people of Israel will learn not to stray from me, polluting themselves with sin. They will be my people, and I will be their God. I, the Sovereign LORD, have spoken!'"

The Certainty of the LORD's Judgment

¹²Then this message came to me from the LORD: ¹³"Son of man, suppose the people of a country were to sin against me, and I lifted my fist to crush them, cutting off their food supply and sending a famine to destroy both people and animals. ¹⁴Even if Noah, Daniel, and Job were there, their righteousness would save no one but themselves, says the Sovereign LORD.

¹⁵"Or suppose I were to send wild animals to invade the country, kill the people, and make the land too desolate and dangerous to pass through. ¹⁶As surely as I live, says the Sovereign LORD, even if those three men were there, they wouldn't be able to save their own sons or daughters. They alone would be saved, but the land would be made desolate.

¹⁷"Or suppose I were to bring war against the land, and I sent enemy armies to destroy both people and animals. ¹⁸As surely as I live, says the Sovereign LORD, even if those three men were there, they wouldn't be able to save their own sons or daughters. They alone would be saved.

¹⁹"Or suppose I were to pour out my fury by sending an epidemic into the land, and the disease killed people and animals alike. ²⁰As surely as I live, says the Sovereign LORD, even if Noah, Daniel, and Job were there, they wouldn't be able to save their own sons or daughters. They alone would be saved by their righteousness.

²¹"Now this is what the Sovereign LORD says: How terrible it will be when all four of these dreadful punishments fall upon Jerusalem—war, famine, wild animals, and disease—destroying all her people and animals. ²²Yet there will be survivors, and they will come here to join you as exiles in Babylon. You will see with your own eyes how wicked they are, and then you will feel better about what I have done to Jerusalem. ²³When you meet them and see their behavior, you will understand that these things are not being done to Israel without cause. I, the Sovereign LORD, have spoken!"

15 Jerusalem—a Useless Vine

Then this message came to me from the LORD: ²"Son of man, how does a grapevine compare to a tree? Is a vine's wood as useful as the wood of a tree? ³Can its wood be used for making things, like pegs to hang up pots and pans? ⁴No, it can only be used for fuel, and even as fuel, it burns too quickly. ⁵Vines are useless both before and after being put into the fire!

⁶"And this is what the Sovereign LORD says: The people of Jerusalem are like grapevines growing among the trees of the forest. Since they are useless, I have thrown them on the fire to be burned. ⁷And I will

---

14:3 The Hebrew term (literally *round things*) probably alludes to dung; also in 14:4, 5, 6, 7.

see to it that if they escape from one fire, they will fall into another. When I turn against them, you will know that I am the LORD. [8]And I will make the land desolate because my people have been unfaithful to me. I, the Sovereign LORD, have spoken!"

16 Jerusalem—an Unfaithful Wife

Then another message came to me from the LORD: [2]"Son of man, confront Jerusalem with her detestable sins. [3]Give her this message from the Sovereign LORD: You are nothing but a Canaanite! Your father was an Amorite and your mother a Hittite. [4]On the day you were born, no one cared about you. Your umbilical cord was not cut, and you were never washed, rubbed with salt, and wrapped in cloth. [5]No one had the slightest interest in you; no one pitied you or cared for you. On the day you were born, you were unwanted, dumped in a field and left to die.

[6]"But I came by and saw you there, helplessly kicking about in your own blood. As you lay there, I said, 'Live!' [7]And I helped you to thrive like a plant in the field. You grew up and became a beautiful jewel. Your breasts became full, and your body hair grew, but you were still naked. [8]And when I passed by again, I saw that you were old enough for love. So I wrapped my cloak around you to cover your nakedness and declared my marriage vows. I made a covenant with you, says the Sovereign LORD, and you became mine.

[9]"Then I bathed you and washed off your blood, and I rubbed fragrant oils into your skin. [10]I gave you expensive clothing of fine linen and silk, beautifully embroidered, and sandals made of fine goatskin leather. [11]I gave you lovely jewelry, bracelets, beautiful necklaces, [12]a ring for your nose, earrings for your ears, and a lovely crown for your head. [13]And so you were adorned with gold and silver. Your clothes were made of fine linen and were beautifully embroidered. You ate the finest foods—choice flour, honey, and olive oil—and became more beautiful than ever. You looked like a queen, and so you were! [14]Your fame soon spread throughout the world because of your beauty. I dressed you in my splendor and perfected your beauty, says the Sovereign LORD.

[15]"But you thought your fame and beauty were your own. So you gave yourself as a prostitute to every man who came along. Your beauty was theirs for the asking. [16]You used the lovely things I gave you to make shrines for idols, where you played the prostitute. Unbelievable! How could such a thing ever happen? [17]You took the very jewels and gold and silver ornaments I had given you and made statues of men and worshiped them. This is adultery against me! [18]You used the beautifully embroidered clothes I gave you to dress your idols. Then you used my special oil and my incense to worship them. [19]Imagine it! You set before them as a sacrifice the choice flour, olive oil, and honey I had given you, says the Sovereign LORD.

[20]"Then you took your sons and daughters—the children you had borne to me—and sacrificed them to your gods. Was your prostitution not enough? [21]Must you also slaughter my children by sacrificing them to idols? [22]In all your years of adultery and detestable sin, you have not once remembered the days long ago when you lay naked in a field, kicking about in your own blood.

[23]"What sorrow awaits you, says the Sovereign LORD. In addition to all your other wickedness, [24]you built a pagan shrine and put altars to idols in every town square. [25]On every street corner you defiled your beauty, offering your body to every passerby in an endless stream of prostitution. [26]Then you added lustful Egypt to your lovers, provoking my anger with your increasing promiscuity. [27]That is why I struck you with my fist and reduced your boundaries. I handed you over to your enemies, the Philistines, and even they were shocked by your lewd conduct. [28]You have prostituted yourself with the Assyrians, too. It seems you can never find enough new lovers! And after your prostitution there, you still were not satisfied. [29]You added to your lovers by embracing Babylonia,* the land of merchants, but you still weren't satisfied.

[30]"What a sick heart you have, says the

16:29 Or Chaldea.

Sovereign LORD, to do such things as these, acting like a shameless prostitute. ³¹You build your pagan shrines on every street corner and your altars to idols in every square. In fact, you have been worse than a prostitute, so eager for sin that you have not even demanded payment. ³²Yes, you are an adulterous wife who takes in strangers instead of her own husband. ³³Prostitutes charge for their services—but not you! You give gifts to your lovers, bribing them to come and have sex with you. ³⁴So you are the opposite of other prostitutes. You pay your lovers instead of their paying you!

Judgment on Jerusalem's Prostitution

³⁵"Therefore, you prostitute, listen to this message from the LORD! ³⁶This is what the Sovereign LORD says: Because you have poured out your lust and exposed yourself in prostitution to all your lovers, and because you have worshiped detestable idols,* and because you have slaughtered your children as sacrifices to your gods, ³⁷this is what I am going to do. I will gather together all your allies—the lovers with whom you have sinned, both those you loved and those you hated—and I will strip you naked in front of them so they can stare at you. ³⁸I will punish you for your murder and adultery. I will cover you with blood in my jealous fury. ³⁹Then I will give you to these many nations who are your lovers, and they will destroy you. They will knock down your pagan shrines and the altars to your idols. They will strip you and take your beautiful jewels, leaving you stark naked. ⁴⁰They will band together in a mob to stone you and cut you up with swords. ⁴¹They will burn your homes and punish you in front of many women. I will stop your prostitution and end your payments to your many lovers.

⁴²"Then at last my fury against you will be spent, and my jealous anger will subside. I will be calm and will not be angry with you anymore. ⁴³But first, because you have not remembered your youth but have angered me by doing all these evil things, I will fully repay you for all of your sins, says the Sovereign LORD. For you have added lewd acts to all your detestable sins. ⁴⁴Everyone who makes up proverbs will say of you, 'Like mother, like daughter.' ⁴⁵For your mother loathed her husband and her children, and so do you. And you are exactly like your sisters, for they despised their husbands and their children. Truly your mother was a Hittite and your father an Amorite.

⁴⁶"Your older sister was Samaria, who lived with her daughters in the north. Your younger sister was Sodom, who lived with her daughters in the south. ⁴⁷But you have not merely sinned as they did. You quickly surpassed them in corruption. ⁴⁸As surely as I live, says the Sovereign LORD, Sodom and her daughters were never as wicked as you and your daughters. ⁴⁹Sodom's sins were pride, gluttony, and laziness, while the poor and needy suffered outside her door. ⁵⁰She was proud and committed detestable sins, so I wiped her out, as you have seen.*

⁵¹"Even Samaria did not commit half your sins. You have done far more detestable things than your sisters ever did. They seem righteous compared to you. ⁵²Shame on you! Your sins are so terrible that you make your sisters seem righteous, even virtuous.

⁵³"But someday I will restore the fortunes of Sodom and Samaria, and I will restore you, too. ⁵⁴Then you will be truly ashamed of everything you have done, for your sins make them feel good in comparison. ⁵⁵Yes, your sisters, Sodom and Samaria, and all their people will be restored, and at that time you also will be restored. ⁵⁶In your proud days you held Sodom in contempt. ⁵⁷But now your greater wickedness has been exposed to all the world, and you are the one who is scorned—by Edom* and all her neighbors and by Philistia. ⁵⁸This is your punishment for all your lewdness and detestable sins, says the LORD.

⁵⁹"Now this is what the Sovereign LORD says: I will give you what you deserve, for you have taken your solemn vows lightly by breaking your covenant. ⁶⁰Yet I will remember the covenant I made with you when you were young, and I will establish an everlasting covenant with you. ⁶¹Then you will remember with shame all the evil you have

---

16:36 The Hebrew term (literally *round things*) probably alludes to dung.   **16:50** As in a few Hebrew manuscripts and Greek version; Masoretic Text reads *as I have seen*.   **16:57** As in many Hebrew manuscripts and Syriac version; Masoretic Text reads *Aram*.

done. I will make your sisters, Samaria and Sodom, to be your daughters, even though they are not part of our covenant. 62 And I will reaffirm my covenant with you, and you will know that I am the LORD. 63 You will remember your sins and cover your mouth in silent shame when I forgive you of all that you have done. I, the Sovereign LORD, have spoken!"

17 A Story of Two Eagles

Then this message came to me from the LORD: 2 "Son of man, give this riddle, and tell this story to the people of Israel. 3 Give them this message from the Sovereign LORD:

"A great eagle with broad wings and long feathers,
    covered with many-colored plumage,
    came to Lebanon.
He seized the top of a cedar tree
4   and plucked off its highest branch.
He carried it away to a city filled with merchants.
    He planted it in a city of traders.
5 He also took a seedling from the land
    and planted it in fertile soil.
He placed it beside a broad river,
    where it could grow like a willow tree.
6 It took root there and
    grew into a low, spreading vine.
Its branches turned up toward the eagle,
    and its roots grew down into the ground.
It produced strong branches
    and put out shoots.
7 But then another great eagle came
    with broad wings and full plumage.
So the vine now sent its roots and branches
    toward him for water,
8 even though it was already planted in good soil
    and had plenty of water
so it could grow into a splendid vine
    and produce rich leaves and luscious fruit.

9 "So now the Sovereign LORD asks:
Will this vine grow and prosper?
No! I will pull it up, roots and all!
I will cut off its fruit
    and let its leaves wither and die.
I will pull it up easily
    without a strong arm or a large army.
10 But when the vine is transplanted,
    will it thrive?
No, it will wither away
    when the east wind blows against it.
It will die in the same good soil
    where it had grown so well."

The Riddle Explained

11 Then this message came to me from the LORD: 12 "Say to these rebels of Israel: Don't you understand the meaning of this riddle of the eagles? The king of Babylon came to Jerusalem, took away her king and princes, and brought them to Babylon. 13 He made a treaty with a member of the royal family and forced him to take an oath of loyalty. He also exiled Israel's most influential leaders, 14 so Israel would not become strong again and revolt. Only by keeping her treaty with Babylon could Israel survive.

15 "Nevertheless, this man of Israel's royal family rebelled against Babylon, sending ambassadors to Egypt to request a great army and many horses. Can Israel break her sworn treaties like that and get away with it? 16 No! For as surely as I live, says the Sovereign LORD, the king of Israel will die in Babylon, the land of the king who put him in power and whose treaty he disregarded and broke. 17 Pharaoh and all his mighty army will fail to help Israel when the king of Babylon lays siege to Jerusalem again and destroys many lives. 18 For the king of Israel disregarded his treaty and broke it after swearing to obey; therefore, he will not escape.

19 "So this is what the Sovereign LORD says: As surely as I live, I will punish him for breaking my covenant and disregarding the solemn oath he made in my name. 20 I will throw my net over him and capture him in my snare. I will bring him to Babylon and put him on trial for this treason against me. 21 And all his best warriors* will be killed in battle, and those who survive will be scattered to the four winds. Then you will know that I, the LORD, have spoken.

17:21 Or *his fleeing warriors.* The meaning of the Hebrew is uncertain.

²²"This is what the Sovereign LORD says: I will take a branch from the top of a tall cedar, and I will plant it on the top of Israel's highest mountain. ²³It will become a majestic cedar, sending forth its branches and producing seed. Birds of every sort will nest in it, finding shelter in the shade of its branches. ²⁴And all the trees will know that it is I, the LORD, who cuts the tall tree down and makes the short tree grow tall. It is I who makes the green tree wither and gives the dead tree new life. I, the LORD, have spoken, and I will do what I said!"

18 The Justice of a Righteous God

Then another message came to me from the LORD: ²"Why do you quote this proverb concerning the land of Israel: 'The parents have eaten sour grapes, but their children's mouths pucker at the taste'? ³As surely as I live, says the Sovereign LORD, you will not quote this proverb anymore in Israel. ⁴For all people are mine to judge—both parents and children alike. And this is my rule: The person who sins is the one who will die.

⁵"Suppose a certain man is righteous and does what is just and right. ⁶He does not feast in the mountains before Israel's idols* or worship them. He does not commit adultery or have intercourse with a woman during her menstrual period. ⁷He is a merciful creditor, not keeping the items given as security by poor debtors. He does not rob the poor but instead gives food to the hungry and provides clothes for the needy. ⁸He grants loans without interest, stays away from injustice, is honest and fair when judging others, ⁹and faithfully obeys my decrees and regulations. Anyone who does these things is just and will surely live, says the Sovereign LORD.

¹⁰"But suppose that man has a son who grows up to be a robber or murderer and refuses to do what is right. ¹¹And that son does all the evil things his father would never do—he worships idols on the mountains, commits adultery, ¹²oppresses the poor and helpless, steals from debtors by refusing to let them redeem their security, worships idols, commits detestable sins, ¹³and lends money at excessive interest. Should such a sinful person live? No! He must die and must take full blame.

¹⁴"But suppose that sinful son, in turn, has a son who sees his father's wickedness and decides against that kind of life. ¹⁵This son refuses to worship idols on the mountains and does not commit adultery. ¹⁶He does not exploit the poor, but instead is fair to debtors and does not rob them. He gives food to the hungry and provides clothes for the needy. ¹⁷He helps the poor,* does not lend money at interest, and obeys all my regulations and decrees. Such a person will not die because of his father's sins; he will surely live. ¹⁸But the father will die for his many sins—for being cruel, robbing people, and doing what was clearly wrong among his people.

¹⁹"'What?' you ask. 'Doesn't the child pay for the parent's sins?' No! For if the child does what is just and right and keeps my decrees, that child will surely live. ²⁰The person who sins is the one who will die. The child will not be punished for the parent's sins, and the parent will not be punished for the child's sins. Righteous people will be rewarded for their own righteous behavior, and wicked people will be punished for their own wickedness. ²¹But if wicked people turn away from all their sins and begin to obey my decrees and do what is just and right, they will surely live and not die. ²²All their past sins will be forgotten, and they will live because of the righteous things they have done.

²³"Do you think that I like to see wicked people die? says the Sovereign LORD. Of course not! I want them to turn from their wicked ways and live. ²⁴However, if righteous people turn from their righteous behavior and start doing sinful things and act like other sinners, should they be allowed to live? No, of course not! All their righteous acts will be forgotten, and they will die for their sins.

²⁵"Yet you say, 'The Lord isn't doing what's right!' Listen to me, O people of Israel. Am I the one not doing what's right, or is it you? ²⁶When righteous people turn from their righteous behavior and start doing sinful

---

18:6 The Hebrew term (literally *round things*) probably alludes to dung; also in 18:12, 15.   **18:17** Greek version reads *He refuses to do evil.*

things, they will die for it. Yes, they will die because of their sinful deeds. ²⁷And if wicked people turn from their wickedness, obey the law, and do what is just and right, they will save their lives. ²⁸They will live because they thought it over and decided to turn from their sins. Such people will not die. ²⁹And yet the people of Israel keep saying, 'The Lord isn't doing what's right!' O people of Israel, it is you who are not doing what's right, not I.

³⁰"Therefore, I will judge each of you, O people of Israel, according to your actions, says the Sovereign LORD. Repent, and turn from your sins. Don't let them destroy you! ³¹Put all your rebellion behind you, and find yourselves a new heart and a new spirit. For why should you die, O people of Israel? ³²I don't want you to die, says the Sovereign LORD. Turn back and live!

19 A Funeral Song for Israel's Kings

"Sing this funeral song for the princes of Israel:

² "What is your mother?
  A lioness among lions!
She lay down among the young lions
  and reared her cubs.
³ She raised one of her cubs
  to become a strong young lion.
He learned to hunt and devour prey,
  and he became a man-eater.
⁴ Then the nations heard about him,
  and he was trapped in their pit.
They led him away with hooks
  to the land of Egypt.

⁵ "When the lioness saw
  that her hopes for him were gone,
she took another of her cubs
  and taught him to be a strong young
  lion.
⁶ He prowled among the other lions
  and stood out among them in his
  strength.
He learned to hunt and devour prey,
  and he, too, became a man-eater.
⁷ He demolished fortresses*
  and destroyed their towns and cities.
Their farms were desolated,
  and their crops were destroyed.

The land and its people trembled in fear
  when they heard him roar.
⁸ Then the armies of the nations attacked
  him,
  surrounding him from every direction.
They threw a net over him
  and captured him in their pit.
⁹ With hooks, they dragged him into a
  cage
  and brought him before the king of
  Babylon.
They held him in captivity,
  so his voice could never again be
  heard
  on the mountains of Israel.

¹⁰ "Your mother was like a vine
  planted by the water's edge.
It had lush, green foliage
  because of the abundant water.
¹¹ Its branches became strong—
  strong enough to be a ruler's scepter.
It grew very tall,
  towering above all others.
It stood out because of its height
  and its many lush branches.
¹² But the vine was uprooted in fury
  and thrown down to the ground.
The desert wind dried up its fruit
  and tore off its strong branches,
so that it withered
  and was destroyed by fire.
¹³ Now the vine is transplanted to the
  wilderness,
  where the ground is hard and dry.
¹⁴ A fire has burst out from its branches
  and devoured its fruit.
Its remaining limbs are not
  strong enough to be a ruler's scepter.

"This is a funeral song, and it will be used in a funeral."

20 The Rebellion of Israel

On August 14,* during the seventh year of King Jehoiachin's captivity, some of the leaders of Israel came to request a message from the LORD. They sat down in front of me to wait for his reply. ²Then this message came to me from the LORD: ³"Son of man, tell the leaders of Israel, 'This is what the Sovereign LORD says: How dare you

---

19:7 As in Greek version; Hebrew reads *He knew widows.* **20:1** Hebrew *In the fifth month, on the tenth day,* of the ancient Hebrew lunar calendar. This day was August 14, 591 B.C.; also see note on 1:1.

come to ask me for a message? As surely as I live, says the Sovereign Lord, I will tell you nothing!'

⁴"Son of man, bring charges against them and condemn them. Make them realize how detestable the sins of their ancestors really were. ⁵Give them this message from the Sovereign Lord: When I chose Israel—when I revealed myself to the descendants of Jacob in Egypt—I took a solemn oath that I, the Lord, would be their God. ⁶I took a solemn oath that day that I would bring them out of Egypt to a land I had discovered and explored for them—a good land, a land flowing with milk and honey, the best of all lands anywhere. ⁷Then I said to them, 'Each of you, get rid of the vile images you are so obsessed with. Do not defile yourselves with the idols* of Egypt, for I am the Lord your God.'

⁸"But they rebelled against me and would not listen. They did not get rid of the vile images they were obsessed with, or forsake the idols of Egypt. Then I threatened to pour out my fury on them to satisfy my anger while they were still in Egypt. ⁹But I didn't do it, for I acted to protect the honor of my name. I would not allow shame to be brought on my name among the surrounding nations who saw me reveal myself by bringing the Israelites out of Egypt. ¹⁰So I brought them out of Egypt and led them into the wilderness. ¹¹There I gave them my decrees and regulations so they could find life by keeping them. ¹²And I gave them my Sabbath days of rest as a sign between them and me. It was to remind them that I am the Lord, who had set them apart to be holy.

¹³"But the people of Israel rebelled against me, and they refused to obey my decrees there in the wilderness. They wouldn't obey my regulations even though obedience would have given them life. They also violated my Sabbath days. So I threatened to pour out my fury on them, and I made plans to utterly consume them in the wilderness. ¹⁴But again I held back in order to protect the honor of my name before the nations who had seen my power in bringing Israel out of Egypt. ¹⁵But I took a solemn

oath against them in the wilderness. I swore I would not bring them into the land I had given them, a land flowing with milk and honey, the most beautiful place on earth. ¹⁶For they had rejected my regulations, refused to follow my decrees, and violated my Sabbath days. Their hearts were given to their idols. ¹⁷Nevertheless, I took pity on them and held back from destroying them in the wilderness.

¹⁸"Then I warned their children not to follow in their parents' footsteps, defiling themselves with their idols. ¹⁹'I am the Lord your God,' I told them. 'Follow my decrees, pay attention to my regulations, ²⁰and keep my Sabbath days holy, for they are a sign to remind you that I am the Lord your God.'

²¹"But their children, too, rebelled against me. They refused to keep my decrees and follow my regulations, even though obedience would have given them life. And they also violated my Sabbath days. So again I threatened to pour out my fury on them in the wilderness. ²²Nevertheless, I withdrew my judgment against them to protect the honor of my name before the nations that had seen my power in bringing them out of Egypt. ²³But I took a solemn oath against them in the wilderness. I swore I would scatter them among all the nations ²⁴because they did not obey my regulations. They scorned my decrees by violating my Sabbath days and longing for the idols of their ancestors. ²⁵I gave them over to worthless decrees and regulations that would not lead to life. ²⁶I let them pollute themselves* with the very gifts I had given them, and I allowed them to give their firstborn children as offerings to their gods—so I might devastate them and remind them that I alone am the Lord.

Judgment and Restoration

²⁷"Therefore, son of man, give the people of Israel this message from the Sovereign Lord: Your ancestors continued to blaspheme and betray me, ²⁸for when I brought them into the land I had promised them, they offered sacrifices on every high hill and under every green tree they saw! They

---

20:7 The Hebrew term (literally *round things*) probably alludes to dung; also in 20:8, 16, 18, 24, 31, 39.   **20:25-26** Or *I gave them worthless decrees and regulations. . . . I polluted them.*

Sabbath & Rest

The Ignored Commandment

EZEKIEL 20:1–20

When I was growing up, Sunday was distinct from all the other weekdays. My family and I would go to church, then come home and have a nice meal. Then we just hung out. I'd read, listen to music, or take a nap. It was slower, quieter. More relaxing.

When I became an adult, Sundays became church, then errands and e-mail and laundry and work preparing for the next workweek. I never took a day off.

God has something to say about that schedule that I and so many others keep. The fourth commandment says to keep the Sabbath (Deuteronomy 5:12–15)—to unplug completely and do no work. To focus on God and allow ourselves to be rejuvenated.

The history of God's people in Scripture reveals that often God's people neglected this commandment. Nehemiah railed against a pattern of work on the Sabbath (Nehemiah 13:15–22). God spoke through Ezekiel to confront his people on their Sabbath disobedience (Ezekiel 20:1–26), declaring, "You . . . violate my Sabbath days of rest" (22:8).

We also often break the Sabbath commandment—and brag about it. I've had conversations where we complain about all the work we have to do and how we don't have time to take off.

Of course we don't brag about breaking other commandments: "I'm planning to steal something." Or, "I think I'll take God's name in vain." Or, "I'm going to go commit adultery."

Maybe we break the Sabbath commandment because we're more comfortable with working than with stopping? Maybe because honoring the Sabbath requires a humility—an acknowledgment that says, *God rested after his work, but I'm exempt. I just have too much to do.*

J. R. R. Tolkien writes in *The Fellowship of the Ring,* "The future, good or ill, was not forgotten, but ceased to have power over the present." That's the promise of celebrating Sabbath. We turn to God in obedience, trusting him with our schedules and responsibilities, enjoying his blessings of delight, rest, and play. We discover—and live within—the true freedom offered by the fourth commandment.

—*Ginger Kolbaba*

For more on Sabbath and rest, see reading at Ezekiel 46:1–3.

roused my fury as they offered up sacrifices to their gods. They brought their perfumes and incense and poured out their liquid offerings to them. ²⁹I said to them, 'What is this high place where you are going?' (This kind of pagan shrine has been called Bamah—'high place'—ever since.)

³⁰"Therefore, give the people of Israel this message from the Sovereign LORD: Do you plan to pollute yourselves just as your ancestors did? Do you intend to keep prostituting yourselves by worshiping vile images? ³¹For when you offer gifts to them and give your little children to be burned as sacrifices,* you continue to pollute yourselves with idols to this day. Should I allow

20:31 Or *and make your little children pass through the fire.*

you to ask for a message from me, O people of Israel? As surely as I live, says the Sovereign LORD, I will tell you nothing.

³² "You say, 'We want to be like the nations all around us, who serve idols of wood and stone.' But what you have in mind will never happen. ³³ As surely as I live, says the Sovereign LORD, I will rule over you with an iron fist in great anger and with awesome power. ³⁴ And in anger I will reach out with my strong hand and powerful arm, and I will bring you back* from the lands where you are scattered. ³⁵ I will bring you into the wilderness of the nations, and there I will judge you face to face. ³⁶ I will judge you there just as I did your ancestors in the wilderness after bringing them out of Egypt, says the Sovereign LORD. ³⁷ I will examine you carefully and hold you to the terms of the covenant. ³⁸ I will purge you of all those who rebel and revolt against me. I will bring them out of the countries where they are in exile, but they will never enter the land of Israel. Then you will know that I am the LORD.

³⁹ "As for you, O people of Israel, this is what the Sovereign LORD says: Go right ahead and worship your idols, but sooner or later you will obey me and will stop bringing shame on my holy name by worshiping idols. ⁴⁰ For on my holy mountain, the great mountain of Israel, says the Sovereign LORD, the people of Israel will someday worship me, and I will accept them. There I will require that you bring me all your offerings and choice gifts and sacrifices. ⁴¹ When I bring you home from exile, you will be like a pleasing sacrifice to me. And I will display my holiness through you as all the nations watch. ⁴² Then when I have brought you home to the land I promised with a solemn oath to give to your ancestors, you will know that I am the LORD. ⁴³ You will look back on all the ways you defiled yourselves and will hate yourselves because of the evil you have done. ⁴⁴ You will know that I am the LORD, O people of Israel, when I have honored my name by treating you mercifully in spite of your wickedness. I, the Sovereign LORD, have spoken!"

Judgment against the Negev

⁴⁵ *Then this message came to me from the LORD: ⁴⁶ "Son of man, turn and face the south* and speak out against it; prophesy against the brushlands of the Negev. ⁴⁷ Tell the southern wilderness, 'This is what the Sovereign LORD says: Hear the word of the LORD! I will set you on fire, and every tree, both green and dry, will be burned. The terrible flames will not be quenched and will scorch everything from south to north. ⁴⁸ And everyone in the world will see that I, the LORD, have set this fire. It will not be put out.'"

⁴⁹ Then I said, "O Sovereign LORD, they are saying of me, 'He only talks in riddles!'"

21 The LORD's Sword of Judgment

¹ *Then this message came to me from the LORD: ² "Son of man, turn and face Jerusalem and prophesy against Israel and her sanctuaries. ³ Tell her, 'This is what the LORD says: I am your enemy, O Israel, and I am about to unsheath my sword to destroy your people—the righteous and the wicked alike. ⁴ Yes, I will cut off both the righteous and the wicked! I will draw my sword against everyone in the land from south to north. ⁵ Everyone in the world will know that I am the LORD. My sword is in my hand, and it will not return to its sheath until its work is finished.'

⁶ "Son of man, groan before the people! Groan before them with bitter anguish and a broken heart. ⁷ When they ask why you are groaning, tell them, 'I groan because of the terrifying news I have heard. When it comes true, the boldest heart will melt with fear; all strength will disappear. Every spirit will faint; strong knees will become as weak as water. And the Sovereign LORD says: It is coming! It's on its way!'"

⁸ Then the LORD said to me, ⁹ "Son of man, give the people this message from the Lord:

"A sword, a sword
  is being sharpened and polished.
¹⁰ It is sharpened for terrible slaughter
  and polished to flash like lightning!
Now will you laugh?
  Those far stronger than you have
  fallen beneath its power!*

20:34 Greek version reads *I will welcome you.* Compare 2 Cor 6:17.   **20:45** Verses 20:45-49 are numbered 21:1-5 in Hebrew text.
20:46 Hebrew *toward Teman.*   **21:1** Verses 21:1-32 are numbered 21:6-37 in Hebrew text.   **21:10** The meaning of the Hebrew is uncertain.

¹¹ Yes, the sword is now being sharpened
and polished;
it is being prepared for the
executioner.

¹² "Son of man, cry out and wail;
pound your thighs in anguish,
for that sword will slaughter my people
and their leaders—
everyone will die!
¹³ It will put them all to the test.
What chance do they have?*
says the Sovereign LORD.

¹⁴ "Son of man, prophesy to them
and clap your hands.
Then take the sword and brandish it
twice,
even three times,
to symbolize the great massacre,
the great massacre facing them on
every side.
¹⁵ Let their hearts melt with terror,
for the sword glitters at every gate.
It flashes like lightning
and is polished for slaughter!
¹⁶ O sword, slash to the right,
then slash to the left,
wherever you will,
wherever you want.
¹⁷ I, too, will clap my hands,
and I will satisfy my fury.
I, the LORD, have spoken!"

Omens for Babylon's King

¹⁸ Then this message came to me from the
LORD: ¹⁹ "Son of man, make a map and
trace two routes on it for the sword of Babylon's king to follow. Put a signpost on the
road that comes out of Babylon where the
road forks into two—²⁰ one road going to
Ammon and its capital, Rabbah, and the
other to Judah and fortified Jerusalem.
²¹ The king of Babylon now stands at the
fork, uncertain whether to attack Jerusalem
or Rabbah. He calls his magicians to look
for omens. They cast lots by shaking arrows
from the quiver. They inspect the livers of
animal sacrifices. ²² The omen in his right
hand says, 'Jerusalem!' With battering
rams his soldiers will go against the gates,
shouting for the kill. They will put up siege

towers and build ramps against the walls.
²³ The people of Jerusalem will think it is a
false omen, because of their treaty with the
Babylonians. But the king of Babylon will
remind the people of their rebellion. Then
he will attack and capture them.

²⁴ "Therefore, this is what the Sovereign
LORD says: Again and again you remind me
of your sin and your guilt. You don't even
try to hide it! In everything you do, your
sins are obvious for all to see. So now the
time of your punishment has come!

²⁵ "O you corrupt and wicked prince of
Israel, your final day of reckoning is here!
²⁶ This is what the Sovereign LORD says:

"Take off your jeweled crown,
for the old order changes.
Now the lowly will be exalted,
and the mighty will be brought down.
²⁷ Destruction! Destruction!
I will surely destroy the kingdom.
And it will not be restored until the one
appears
who has the right to judge it.
Then I will hand it over to him.

A Message for the Ammonites

²⁸ "And now, son of man, prophesy con-
cerning the Ammonites and their mockery.
Give them this message from the Sovereign
LORD:

"A sword, a sword
is drawn for your slaughter.
It is polished to destroy,
flashing like lightning!
²⁹ Your prophets have given false visions,
and your fortune-tellers have told lies.
The sword will fall on the necks of the
wicked
for whom the day of final reckoning
has come.

³⁰ "Now return the sword to its sheath,
for in your own country,
the land of your birth,
I will pass judgment upon you.
³¹ I will pour out my fury on you
and blow on you with the fire of my
anger.
I will hand you over to cruel men
who are skilled in destruction.

21:13 The meaning of the Hebrew is uncertain.

³²You will be fuel for the fire,
and your blood will be spilled in your
own land.
You will be utterly wiped out,
your memory lost to history,
for I, the LORD, have spoken!"

22 The Sins of Jerusalem

Now this message came to me from
the LORD: ²"Son of man, are you ready to
judge Jerusalem? Are you ready to judge
this city of murderers? Publicly denounce
her detestable sins, ³and give her this message from the Sovereign LORD: O city of
murderers, doomed and damned—city
of idols,* filthy and foul—⁴you are guilty
because of the blood you have shed. You are
defiled because of the idols you have made.
Your day of destruction has come! You have
reached the end of your years. I will make
you an object of mockery throughout the
world. ⁵O infamous city, filled with confusion, you will be mocked by people far and
near.

⁶"Every leader in Israel who lives within
your walls is bent on murder. ⁷Fathers and
mothers are treated with contempt. Foreigners are forced to pay for protection.
Orphans and widows are wronged and
oppressed among you. ⁸You despise my
holy things and violate my Sabbath days of
rest. ⁹People accuse others falsely and send
them to their death. You are filled with idol
worshipers and people who do obscene
things. ¹⁰Men sleep with their fathers' wives
and have intercourse with women who are
menstruating. ¹¹Within your walls live men
who commit adultery with their neighbors' wives, who defile their daughters-in-
law, or who rape their own sisters. ¹²There
are hired murderers, loan racketeers, and
extortioners everywhere. They never even
think of me and my commands, says the
Sovereign LORD.

¹³"But now I clap my hands in indignation over your dishonest gain and bloodshed. ¹⁴How strong and courageous will
you be in my day of reckoning? I, the LORD,
have spoken, and I will do what I said. ¹⁵I
will scatter you among the nations and
purge you of your wickedness. ¹⁶And when

I have been dishonored among the nations
because of you,* you will know that I am
the LORD."

The LORD's Refining Furnace

¹⁷Then this message came to me from the
LORD: ¹⁸"Son of man, the people of Israel
are the worthless slag that remains after silver is smelted. They are the dross that is left
over—a useless mixture of copper, tin, iron,
and lead. ¹⁹So tell them, 'This is what the
Sovereign LORD says: Because you are all
worthless slag, I will bring you to my cruci-
ble in Jerusalem. ²⁰Just as copper, iron, lead,
and tin are melted down in a furnace, I will
melt you down in the heat of my fury. ²¹I
will gather you together and blow the fire
of my anger upon you, ²²and you will melt
like silver in fierce heat. Then you will know
that I, the LORD, have poured out my fury
on you.'"

The Sins of Israel's Leaders

²³Again a message came to me from the
LORD: ²⁴"Son of man, give the people of
Israel this message: In the day of my indignation, you will be like a polluted land, a
land without rain. ²⁵Your princes* plot con-
spiracies just as lions stalk their prey. They
devour innocent people, seizing treasures
and extorting wealth. They make many
widows in the land. ²⁶Your priests have violated my instructions and defiled my holy
things. They make no distinction between
what is holy and what is not. And they do
not teach my people the difference between
what is ceremonially clean and unclean.
They disregard my Sabbath days so that I
am dishonored among them. ²⁷Your leaders are like wolves who tear apart their victims. They actually destroy people's lives
for money! ²⁸And your prophets cover up
for them by announcing false visions and
making lying predictions. They say, 'My
message is from the Sovereign LORD,' when
the LORD hasn't spoken a single word to
them. ²⁹Even common people oppress the
poor, rob the needy, and deprive foreigners
of justice.

³⁰"I looked for someone who might
rebuild the wall of righteousness that

22:3 The Hebrew term (literally *round things*) probably alludes to dung; also in 22:4.   **22:16** Or *when you have been dishonored among the nations.*   **22:25** As in Greek version; Hebrew reads *prophets.*

Standing in the Gap

EZEKIEL 22:30

Prayer

After I offered to pray in her stead as she walked through a period of deep doubt, a friend told me, "You understand sorrow." I offered to pray on her behalf not only because I do understand her sorrow, but also because I understand the importance of having others take our prayers before God when we can't.

Ezekiel 22:30 offers a beautiful image for us to consider as we intercede for others in prayer. It says, "I looked for someone who might rebuild the wall of righteousness that guards the land. I searched for someone to stand in the gap in the wall so I wouldn't have to destroy the land, but I found no one."

Standing in the gap between someone and God is exactly what intercessory prayer is all about. When there is a gap in a loved one's faith or in her words or her energy, we stand in the gap and prayerfully offer what we have *for her.*

Jesus did this when he prayed for the soldiers as they gambled for his clothes: "Father, forgive them, for they don't know what they are doing" (Luke 23:34). Job also did this when he prayed for his misguided friends (Job 42:7-10).

Intercessory prayer requires understanding—not judging—another person's gaps and being ready to pray when we see them. We can pray privately—without the person knowing—or we can simply let friends or loved ones know that we understand that prayer is hard for them and that we will pray on their behalf.

But intercessory prayer also requires that we understand our own weaknesses—that we're aware of our own gaps with God. This self-awareness enables us to truly understand the joy and mercy of having another go to God when we cannot.

—*Caryn Rivadeneira*

For more on prayer, see reading at Luke 5:17-26.

guards the land. I searched for someone to stand in the gap in the wall so I wouldn't have to destroy the land, but I found no one. [31] So now I will pour out my fury on them, consuming them with the fire of my anger. I will heap on their heads the full penalty for all their sins. I, the Sovereign LORD, have spoken!"

23 The Adultery of Two Sisters

This message came to me from the LORD: [2] "Son of man, once there were two sisters who were daughters of the same mother. [3] They became prostitutes in Egypt. Even as young girls, they allowed men to fondle their breasts. [4] The older girl was named Oholah, and her sister was Oholibah. I married them, and they bore me sons and daughters. I am speaking of Samaria and Jerusalem, for Oholah is Samaria and Oholibah is Jerusalem.

[5] "Then Oholah lusted after other lovers instead of me, and she gave her love to the Assyrian officers. [6] They were all attractive young men, captains and commanders dressed in handsome blue, charioteers driving their horses. [7] And so she prostituted herself with the most desirable men of Assyria, worshiping their idols* and defiling herself. [8] For when she left Egypt,

---

23:7 The Hebrew term (literally *round things*) probably alludes to dung; also in 23:30, 37, 39, 49.

she did not leave her spirit of prostitution behind. She was still as lewd as in her youth, when the Egyptians slept with her, fondled her breasts, and used her as a prostitute.

9"And so I handed her over to her Assyrian lovers, whom she desired so much. 10They stripped her, took away her children as their slaves, and then killed her. After she received her punishment, her reputation was known to every woman in the land.

11"Yet even though Oholibah saw what had happened to Oholah, her sister, she followed right in her footsteps. And she was even more depraved, abandoning herself to her lust and prostitution. 12She fawned over all the Assyrian officers—those captains and commanders in handsome uniforms, those charioteers driving their horses—all of them attractive young men. 13I saw the way she was going, defiling herself just like her older sister.

14"Then she carried her prostitution even further. She fell in love with pictures that were painted on a wall—pictures of Babylonian* military officers, outfitted in striking red uniforms. 15Handsome belts encircled their waists, and flowing turbans crowned their heads. They were dressed like chariot officers from the land of Babylonia.* 16When she saw these paintings, she longed to give herself to them, so she sent messengers to Babylonia to invite them to come to her. 17So they came and committed adultery with her, defiling her in the bed of love. After being defiled, however, she rejected them in disgust.

18"In the same way, I became disgusted with Oholibah and rejected her, just as I had rejected her sister, because she flaunted herself before them and gave herself to satisfy their lusts. 19Yet she turned to even greater prostitution, remembering her youth when she was a prostitute in Egypt. 20She lusted after lovers with genitals as large as a donkey's and emissions like those of a horse. 21And so, Oholibah, you relived your former days as a young girl in Egypt, when you first allowed your breasts to be fondled.

The Lord's Judgment of Oholibah

22"Therefore, Oholibah, this is what the Sovereign Lord says: I will send your lovers against you from every direction—those very nations from which you turned away in disgust. 23For the Babylonians will come with all the Chaldeans from Pekod and Shoa and Koa. And all the Assyrians will come with them—handsome young captains, commanders, chariot officers, and other high-ranking officers, all riding their horses. 24They will all come against you from the north* with chariots, wagons, and a great army prepared for attack. They will take up positions on every side, surrounding you with men armed with shields and helmets. And I will hand you over to them for punishment so they can do with you as they please. 25I will turn my jealous anger against you, and they will deal harshly with you. They will cut off your nose and ears, and any survivors will then be slaughtered by the sword. Your children will be taken away as captives, and everything that is left will be burned. 26They will strip you of your beautiful clothes and jewels. 27In this way, I will put a stop to the lewdness and prostitution you brought from Egypt. You will never again cast longing eyes on those things or fondly remember your time in Egypt.

28"For this is what the Sovereign Lord says: I will surely hand you over to your enemies, to those you loathe, those you rejected. 29They will treat you with hatred and rob you of all you own, leaving you stark naked. The shame of your prostitution will be exposed to all the world. 30You brought all this on yourself by prostituting yourself to other nations, defiling yourself with all their idols. 31Because you have followed in your sister's footsteps, I will force you to drink the same cup of terror she drank.

32"Yes, this is what the Sovereign Lord says:

"You will drink from your sister's cup of
    terror,
  a cup that is large and deep.
It is filled to the brim
  with scorn and derision.
33 Drunkenness and anguish will fill you,
    for your cup is filled to the brim with
      distress and desolation,
    the same cup your sister Samaria
      drank.

23:14 Or Chaldean.   23:15 Or Chaldea; also in 23:16.   23:24 As in Greek version; the meaning of the Hebrew is uncertain.

34 You will drain that cup of terror
  to the very bottom.
Then you will smash it to pieces
  and beat your breast in anguish.
I, the Sovereign LORD, have spoken!

35 "And because you have forgotten me and turned your back on me, this is what the Sovereign LORD says: You must bear the consequences of all your lewdness and prostitution."

The LORD's Judgment on Both Sisters

36 The LORD said to me, "Son of man, you must accuse Oholah and Oholibah of all their detestable sins. 37 They have committed both adultery and murder—adultery by worshiping idols and murder by burning as sacrifices the children they bore to me. 38 Furthermore, they have defiled my Temple and violated my Sabbath day! 39 On the very day that they sacrificed their children to their idols, they boldly came into my Temple to worship! They came in and defiled my house.

40 "You sisters sent messengers to distant lands to get men. Then when they arrived, you bathed yourselves, painted your eyelids, and put on your finest jewels for them. 41 You sat with them on a beautifully embroidered couch and put my incense and my special oil on a table that was spread before you. 42 From your room came the sound of many men carousing. They were lustful men and drunkards* from the wilderness, who put bracelets on your wrists and beautiful crowns on your heads. 43 Then I said, 'If they really want to have sex with old worn-out prostitutes like these, let them!' 44 And that is what they did. They had sex with Oholah and Oholibah, these shameless prostitutes. 45 But righteous people will judge these sister cities for what they really are—adulterers and murderers.

46 "Now this is what the Sovereign LORD says: Bring an army against them and hand them over to be terrorized and plundered. 47 For their enemies will stone them and kill them with swords. They will butcher their sons and daughters and burn their homes. 48 In this way, I will put an end to lewdness and idolatry in the land, and my judgment will be a warning to others not to follow their wicked example. 49 You will be fully repaid for all your prostitution—your worship of idols. Yes, you will suffer the full penalty. Then you will know that I am the Sovereign LORD."

24

The Sign of the Cooking Pot

On January 15,* during the ninth year of King Jehoiachin's captivity, this message came to me from the LORD: 2 "Son of man, write down today's date, because on this very day the king of Babylon is beginning his attack against Jerusalem. 3 Then give these rebels an illustration with this message from the Sovereign LORD:

"Put a pot on the fire,
  and pour in some water.
4 Fill it with choice pieces of meat—
  the rump and the shoulder
  and all the most tender cuts.
5 Use only the best sheep from the flock,
  and heap fuel on the fire beneath the
    pot.
Bring the pot to a boil,
  and cook the bones along with the
    meat.

6 "Now this is what the Sovereign LORD
    says:
What sorrow awaits Jerusalem,
  the city of murderers!
She is a cooking pot
  whose corruption can't be cleaned
    out.
Take the meat out in random order,
  for no piece is better than another.
7 For the blood of her murders
  is splashed on the rocks.
It isn't even spilled on the ground,
  where the dust could cover it!
8 So I will splash her blood on a rock
  for all to see,
an expression of my anger
  and vengeance against her.

9 "This is what the Sovereign LORD says:
What sorrow awaits Jerusalem,
  the city of murderers!
  I myself will pile up the fuel beneath
    her.

23:42 Or *Sabeans.* 24:1 Hebrew *On the tenth day of the tenth month,* of the ancient Hebrew lunar calendar. This event occurred on January 15, 588 B.C.; also see note on 1:1.

¹⁰ Yes, heap on the wood!
  Let the fire roar to make the pot boil.
  Cook the meat with many spices,
    and afterward burn the bones.
¹¹ Now set the empty pot on the coals.
    Heat it red hot!
    Burn away the filth and corruption.
¹² But it's hopeless;
    the corruption can't be cleaned out.
    So throw it into the fire.
¹³ Your impurity is your lewdness
    and the corruption of your idolatry.
  I tried to cleanse you,
    but you refused.
  So now you will remain in your filth
    until my fury against you has been
    satisfied.

¹⁴"I, the LORD, have spoken! The time has come, and I won't hold back. I will not change my mind, and I will have no pity on you. You will be judged on the basis of all your wicked actions, says the Sovereign LORD."

The Death of Ezekiel's Wife

¹⁵Then this message came to me from the LORD: ¹⁶"Son of man, with one blow I will take away your dearest treasure. Yet you must not show any sorrow at her death. Do not weep; let there be no tears. ¹⁷Groan silently, but let there be no wailing at her grave. Do not uncover your head or take off your sandals. Do not perform the usual rituals of mourning or accept any food brought to you by consoling friends."

¹⁸So I proclaimed this to the people the next morning, and in the evening my wife died. The next morning I did everything I had been told to do. ¹⁹Then the people asked, "What does all this mean? What are you trying to tell us?"

²⁰So I said to them, "A message came to me from the LORD, ²¹and I was told to give this message to the people of Israel. This is what the Sovereign LORD says: I will defile my Temple, the source of your security and pride, the place your heart delights in. Your sons and daughters whom you left behind in Judea will be slaughtered by the sword. ²²Then you will do as Ezekiel has done. You will not mourn in public or console yourselves by eating the food brought by

friends. ²³Your heads will remain covered, and your sandals will not be taken off. You will not mourn or weep, but you will waste away because of your sins. You will mourn privately for all the evil you have done. ²⁴Ezekiel is an example for you; you will do just as he has done. And when that time comes, you will know that I am the Sovereign LORD."

²⁵Then the LORD said to me, "Son of man, on the day I take away their stronghold—their joy and glory, their heart's desire, their dearest treasure—I will also take away their sons and daughters. ²⁶And on that day a survivor from Jerusalem will come to you in Babylon and tell you what has happened. ²⁷And when he arrives, your voice will suddenly return so you can talk to him, and you will be a symbol for these people. Then they will know that I am the LORD."

25 A Message for Ammon

Then this message came to me from the LORD: ²"Son of man, turn and face the land of Ammon and prophesy against its people. ³Give the Ammonites this message from the Sovereign LORD: Hear the word of the Sovereign LORD! Because you cheered when my Temple was defiled, mocked Israel in her desolation, and laughed at Judah as she went away into exile, ⁴I will allow nomads from the eastern deserts to overrun your country. They will set up their camps among you and pitch their tents on your land. They will harvest all your fruit and drink the milk from your livestock. ⁵And I will turn the city of Rabbah into a pasture for camels, and all the land of the Ammonites into a resting place for sheep and goats. Then you will know that I am the LORD.

⁶"This is what the Sovereign LORD says: Because you clapped and danced and cheered with glee at the destruction of my people, ⁷I will raise my fist of judgment against you. I will give you as plunder to many nations. I will cut you off from being a nation and destroy you completely. Then you will know that I am the LORD.

A Message for Moab

⁸"This is what the Sovereign LORD says: Because the people of Moab have said that

Judah is just like all the other nations, ⁹I will open up their eastern flank and wipe out their glorious frontier towns—Beth-jeshimoth, Baal-meon, and Kiriathaim. ¹⁰And I will hand Moab over to nomads from the eastern deserts, just as I handed over Ammon. Yes, the Ammonites will no longer be counted among the nations. ¹¹In the same way, I will bring my judgment down on the Moabites. Then they will know that I am the LORD.

A Message for Edom

¹²"This is what the Sovereign LORD says: The people of Edom have sinned greatly by avenging themselves against the people of Judah. ¹³Therefore, says the Sovereign LORD, I will raise my fist of judgment against Edom. I will wipe out its people and animals with the sword. I will make a wasteland of everything from Teman to Dedan. ¹⁴I will accomplish this by the hand of my people of Israel. They will carry out my vengeance with anger, and Edom will know that this vengeance is from me. I, the Sovereign LORD, have spoken!

A Message for Philistia

¹⁵"This is what the Sovereign LORD says: The people of Philistia have acted against Judah out of bitter revenge and long-standing contempt. ¹⁶Therefore, this is what the Sovereign LORD says: I will raise my fist of judgment against the land of the Philistines. I will wipe out the Kerethites and utterly destroy the people who live by the sea. ¹⁷I will execute terrible vengeance against them to punish them for what they have done. And when I have inflicted my revenge, they will know that I am the LORD."

26 A Message for Tyre

On February 3, during the twelfth year of King Jehoiachin's captivity,* this message came to me from the LORD: ²"Son of man, Tyre has rejoiced over the fall of Jerusalem, saying, 'Ha! She who was the gateway to the rich trade routes to the east has been broken, and I am the heir! Because she has been made desolate, I will become wealthy!'

³"Therefore, this is what the Sovereign LORD says: I am your enemy, O Tyre, and I will bring many nations against you, like the waves of the sea crashing against your shoreline. ⁴They will destroy the walls of Tyre and tear down its towers. I will scrape away its soil and make it a bare rock! ⁵It will be just a rock in the sea, a place for fishermen to spread their nets, for I have spoken, says the Sovereign LORD. Tyre will become the prey of many nations, ⁶and its mainland villages will be destroyed by the sword. Then they will know that I am the LORD.

⁷"This is what the Sovereign LORD says: From the north I will bring King Nebuchadnezzar* of Babylon against Tyre. He is king of kings and brings his horses, chariots, charioteers, and great army. ⁸First he will destroy your mainland villages. Then he will attack you by building a siege wall, constructing a ramp, and raising a roof of shields against you. ⁹He will pound your walls with battering rams and demolish your towers with sledgehammers. ¹⁰The hooves of his horses will choke the city with dust, and the noise of the charioteers and chariot wheels will shake your walls as they storm through your broken gates. ¹¹His horsemen will trample through every street in the city. They will butcher your people, and your strong pillars will topple.

¹²"They will plunder all your riches and merchandise and break down your walls. They will destroy your lovely homes and dump your stones and timbers and even your dust into the sea. ¹³I will stop the music of your songs. No more will the sound of harps be heard among your people. ¹⁴I will make your island a bare rock, a place for fishermen to spread their nets. You will never be rebuilt, for I, the LORD, have spoken. Yes, the Sovereign LORD has spoken!

The Effect of Tyre's Destruction

¹⁵"This is what the Sovereign LORD says to Tyre: The whole coastline will tremble at the sound of your fall, as the screams of the

---

26:1 Hebrew *In the eleventh year, on the first day of the month,* of the ancient Hebrew lunar calendar year. Since an element is missing in the date formula here, scholars have reconstructed this probable reading: *In the eleventh [month of the twelfth] year, on the first day of the month.* This reading would put this message on February 3, 585 B.C.; also see note on 1:1. 26:7 Hebrew *Nebuchadrezzar,* a variant spelling of Nebuchadnezzar.

wounded echo in the continuing slaughter. [16]All the seaport rulers will step down from their thrones and take off their royal robes and beautiful clothing. They will sit on the ground trembling with horror at your destruction. [17]Then they will wail for you, singing this funeral song:

"O famous island city,
once ruler of the sea,
how you have been destroyed!
Your people, with their naval power,
once spread fear around the world.
[18] Now the coastlands tremble at your fall.
The islands are dismayed as you
disappear.

[19]"This is what the Sovereign Lord says: I will make Tyre an uninhabited ruin, like many others. I will bury you beneath the terrible waves of enemy attack. Great seas will swallow you. [20]I will send you to the pit to join those who descended there long ago. Your city will lie in ruins, buried beneath the earth, like those in the pit who have entered the world of the dead. You will have no place of respect here in the land of the living. [21]I will bring you to a terrible end, and you will exist no more. You will be looked for, but you will never again be found. I, the Sovereign Lord, have spoken!"

27 The End of Tyre's Glory

Then this message came to me from the Lord: [2]"Son of man, sing a funeral song for Tyre, [3]that mighty gateway to the sea, the trading center of the world. Give Tyre this message from the Sovereign Lord:

"You boasted, O Tyre,
'My beauty is perfect!'
[4] You extended your boundaries into the
sea.
Your builders made your beauty
perfect.
[5] You were like a great ship
built of the finest cypress from Senir.*
They took a cedar from Lebanon
to make a mast for you.
[6] They carved your oars
from the oaks of Bashan.

Your deck of pine from the coasts of
Cyprus*
was inlaid with ivory.
[7] Your sails were made of Egypt's finest
linen,
and they flew as a banner above you.
You stood beneath blue and purple
awnings
made bright with dyes from the coasts
of Elishah.
[8] Your oarsmen came from Sidon and
Arvad;
your helmsmen were skilled men from
Tyre itself.
[9] Wise old craftsmen from Gebal did the
caulking.
Ships from every land came with
goods to barter for your trade.

[10]"Men from distant Persia, Lydia, and Libya* served in your great army. They hung their shields and helmets on your walls, giving you great honor. [11]Men from Arvad and Helech stood on your walls. Your towers were manned by men from Gammad. Their shields hung on your walls, completing your beauty.

[12]"Tarshish sent merchants to buy your wares in exchange for silver, iron, tin, and lead. [13]Merchants from Greece,* Tubal, and Meshech brought slaves and articles of bronze to trade with you.

[14] "From Beth-togarmah came riding horses, chariot horses, and mules, all in exchange for your goods. [15]Merchants came to you from Dedan.* Numerous coastlands were your captive markets; they brought payment in ivory tusks and ebony wood.

[16]"Syria* sent merchants to buy your rich variety of goods. They traded turquoise, purple dyes, embroidery, fine linen, and jewelry of coral and rubies. [17]Judah and Israel traded for your wares, offering wheat from Minnith, figs,* honey, olive oil, and balm.

[18] "Damascus sent merchants to buy your rich variety of goods, bringing wine from Helbon and white wool from Zahar. [19]Greeks from Uzal* came to trade for your merchandise. Wrought iron, cassia, and fragrant calamus were bartered for your wares.

27:5 Or *Hermon*.   27:6 Hebrew *Kittim*.   27:10 Hebrew *Paras, Lud, and Put*.   27:13 Hebrew *Javan*.   27:15 Greek version reads *Rhodes*.
27:16 Hebrew *Aram;* some manuscripts read *Edom*.   27:17 The meaning of the Hebrew is uncertain.   27:19 Hebrew *Vedan and Javan from Uzal*. The meaning of the Hebrew is uncertain.

²⁰"Dedan sent merchants to trade their expensive saddle blankets with you. ²¹The Arabians and the princes of Kedar sent merchants to trade lambs and rams and male goats in exchange for your goods. ²²The merchants of Sheba and Raamah came with all kinds of spices, jewels, and gold in exchange for your wares.

²³"Haran, Canneh, Eden, Sheba, Asshur, and Kilmad came with their merchandise, too. ²⁴They brought choice fabrics to trade—blue cloth, embroidery, and multicolored carpets rolled up and bound with cords. ²⁵The ships of Tarshish were your ocean caravans. Your island warehouse was filled to the brim!

The Destruction of Tyre

²⁶ "But look! Your oarsmen
    have taken you into stormy seas!
A mighty eastern gale
    has wrecked you in the heart of the
      sea!
²⁷ Everything is lost—
    your riches and wares,
your sailors and pilots,
    your ship builders, merchants, and
      warriors.
On the day of your ruin,
    everyone on board sinks into the
      depths of the sea.
²⁸ Your cities by the sea tremble
    as your pilots cry out in terror.
²⁹ All the oarsmen abandon their ships;
    the sailors and pilots on shore come to
      stand on the beach.
³⁰ They cry aloud over you
    and weep bitterly.
They throw dust on their heads
    and roll in ashes.
³¹ They shave their heads in grief for you
    and dress themselves in burlap.
They weep for you with bitter anguish
    and deep mourning.
³² As they wail and mourn over you,
    they sing this sad funeral song:
'Was there ever such a city as Tyre,
    now silent at the bottom of the sea?
³³ The merchandise you traded
    satisfied the desires of many nations.
Kings at the ends of the earth
    were enriched by your trade.

³⁴ Now you are a wrecked ship,
    broken at the bottom of the sea.
All your merchandise and crew
    have gone down with you.
³⁵ All who live along the coastlands
    are appalled at your terrible fate.
Their kings are filled with horror
    and look on with twisted faces.
³⁶ The merchants among the nations
    shake their heads at the sight of you,*
for you have come to a horrible end
    and will exist no more.'"

28 A Message for Tyre's King

Then this message came to me from the LORD: ²"Son of man, give the prince of Tyre this message from the Sovereign LORD:

"In your great pride you claim, 'I am a
    god!
I sit on a divine throne in the heart of
    the sea.'
But you are only a man and not a god,
    though you boast that you are a god.
³ You regard yourself as wiser than Daniel
    and think no secret is hidden from
      you.
⁴ With your wisdom and understanding
    you have amassed great wealth—
gold and silver for your treasuries.
⁵ Yes, your wisdom has made you very
    rich,
and your riches have made you very
    proud.

⁶ "Therefore, this is what the Sovereign
    LORD says:
Because you think you are as wise as a
    god,
⁷   I will now bring against you a foreign
    army,
    the terror of the nations.
They will draw their swords against your
    marvelous wisdom
    and defile your splendor!
⁸ They will bring you down to the pit,
    and you will die in the heart of the sea,
    pierced with many wounds.
⁹ Will you then boast, 'I am a god!'
    to those who kill you?
To them you will be no god
    but merely a man!

27:36 Hebrew *hiss at you.*

¹⁰ You will die like an outcast*
 at the hands of foreigners.
 I, the Sovereign Lord, have spoken!"

¹¹ Then this further message came to me
from the Lord: ¹² "Son of man, sing this
funeral song for the king of Tyre. Give him
this message from the Sovereign Lord:

"You were the model of perfection,
 full of wisdom and exquisite in beauty.
¹³ You were in Eden,
 the garden of God.
Your clothing was adorned with every
 precious stone*—
 red carnelian, pale-green peridot,
 white moonstone,
 blue-green beryl, onyx, green jasper,
 blue lapis lazuli, turquoise, and
 emerald—
all beautifully crafted for you
 and set in the finest gold.
They were given to you
 on the day you were created.
¹⁴ I ordained and anointed you
 as the mighty angelic guardian.*
You had access to the holy mountain of
 God
 and walked among the stones of fire.

¹⁵ "You were blameless in all you did
 from the day you were created
 until the day evil was found in you.
¹⁶ Your rich commerce led you to violence,
 and you sinned.
So I banished you in disgrace
 from the mountain of God.
I expelled you, O mighty guardian,
 from your place among the stones of
 fire.
¹⁷ Your heart was filled with pride
 because of all your beauty.
Your wisdom was corrupted
 by your love of splendor.
So I threw you to the ground
 and exposed you to the curious gaze
 of kings.
¹⁸ You defiled your sanctuaries
 with your many sins and your
 dishonest trade.
So I brought fire out from within you,
 and it consumed you.

I reduced you to ashes on the ground
 in the sight of all who were watching.
¹⁹ All who knew you are appalled at your
 fate.
You have come to a terrible end,
 and you will exist no more."

A Message for Sidon

²⁰ Then another message came to me from
the Lord: ²¹ "Son of man, turn and face the
city of Sidon and prophesy against it. ²² Give
the people of Sidon this message from the
Sovereign Lord:

"I am your enemy, O Sidon,
 and I will reveal my glory by what I do
 to you.
When I bring judgment against you
 and reveal my holiness among you,
everyone watching will know
 that I am the Lord.
²³ I will send a plague against you,
 and blood will be spilled in your streets.
The attack will come from every direction,
 and your people will lie slaughtered
 within your walls.
Then everyone will know
 that I am the Lord.
²⁴ No longer will Israel's scornful neighbors
 prick and tear at her like briers and
 thorns.
For then they will know
 that I am the Sovereign Lord.

Restoration for Israel

²⁵ "This is what the Sovereign Lord says:
The people of Israel will again live in their
own land, the land I gave my servant Jacob.
For I will gather them from the distant lands
where I have scattered them. I will reveal to
the nations of the world my holiness among
my people. ²⁶ They will live safely in Israel
and build homes and plant vineyards. And
when I punish the neighboring nations
that treated them with contempt, they will
know that I am the Lord their God."

29 A Message for Egypt

On January 7,* during the tenth year
of King Jehoiachin's captivity, this message
came to me from the Lord: ² "Son of man,

28:10 Hebrew *will die the death of the uncircumcised.* **28:13** The identification of some of these gemstones is uncertain. **28:14** Hebrew *guardian cherub;* similarly in 28:16. **29:1** Hebrew *On the twelfth day of the tenth month,* of the ancient Hebrew lunar calendar. This event occurred on January 7, 587 B.C.; also see note on 1:1.

turn and face Egypt and prophesy against Pharaoh the king and all the people of Egypt. ³Give them this message from the Sovereign Lord:

"I am your enemy, O Pharaoh, king of
    Egypt—
  you great monster, lurking in the
    streams of the Nile.
For you have said, 'The Nile River is
    mine;
  I made it for myself.'
⁴ I will put hooks in your jaws
  and drag you out on the land
  with fish sticking to your scales.
⁵ I will leave you and all your fish
  stranded in the wilderness to die.
You will lie unburied on the open
    ground,
  for I have given you as food to the wild
    animals and birds.
⁶ All the people of Egypt will know that I
    am the Lord,
  for to Israel you were just a staff made
    of reeds.
⁷ When Israel leaned on you,
  you splintered and broke
  and stabbed her in the armpit.
When she put her weight on you, you
    gave way,
  and her back was thrown out of joint.

⁸"Therefore, this is what the Sovereign Lord says: I will bring an army against you, O Egypt, and destroy both people and animals. ⁹The land of Egypt will become a desolate wasteland, and the Egyptians will know that I am the Lord.

"Because you said, 'The Nile River is mine; I made it,' ¹⁰I am now the enemy of both you and your river. I will make the land of Egypt a totally desolate wasteland, from Migdol to Aswan, as far south as the border of Ethiopia.* ¹¹For forty years not a soul will pass that way, neither people nor animals. It will be completely uninhabited. ¹²I will make Egypt desolate, and it will be surrounded by other desolate nations. Its cities will be empty and desolate for forty years, surrounded by other ruined cities. I will scatter the Egyptians to distant lands.

¹³"But this is what the Sovereign Lord also says: At the end of the forty years I will bring the Egyptians home again from the nations to which they have been scattered. ¹⁴I will restore the prosperity of Egypt and bring its people back to the land of Pathros in southern Egypt from which they came. But Egypt will remain an unimportant, minor kingdom. ¹⁵It will be the lowliest of all the nations, never again great enough to rise above its neighbors.

¹⁶"Then Israel will no longer be tempted to trust in Egypt for help. Egypt's shattered condition will remind Israel of how sinful she was to trust Egypt in earlier days. Then Israel will know that I am the Sovereign Lord."

Nebuchadnezzar to Conquer Egypt

¹⁷On April 26, the first day of the new year,* during the twenty-seventh year of King Jehoiachin's captivity, this message came to me from the Lord: ¹⁸"Son of man, the army of King Nebuchadnezzar* of Babylon fought so hard against Tyre that the warriors' heads were rubbed bare and their shoulders were raw and blistered. Yet Nebuchadnezzar and his army won no plunder to compensate them for all their work. ¹⁹Therefore, this is what the Sovereign Lord says: I will give the land of Egypt to Nebuchadnezzar, king of Babylon. He will carry off its wealth, plundering everything it has so he can pay his army. ²⁰Yes, I have given him the land of Egypt as a reward for his work, says the Sovereign Lord, because he was working for me when he destroyed Tyre.

²¹"And the day will come when I will cause the ancient glory of Israel to revive,* and then, Ezekiel, your words will be respected. Then they will know that I am the Lord."

30 A Sad Day for Egypt

This is another message that came to me from the Lord: ²"Son of man, prophesy and give this message from the Sovereign Lord:

"Weep and wail
  for that day,

³ for the terrible day is almost here—
   the day of the LORD!
It is a day of clouds and gloom,
   a day of despair for the nations.
⁴ A sword will come against Egypt,
   and those who are slaughtered will
      cover the ground.
Its wealth will be carried away
   and its foundations destroyed.
The land of Ethiopia* will be ravished.
⁵   Ethiopia, Libya, Lydia, all Arabia,*
and all their other allies
   will be destroyed in that war.

⁶ "For this is what the LORD says:
All of Egypt's allies will fall,
   and the pride of her power will end.
From Migdol to Aswan*
   they will be slaughtered by the sword,
   says the Sovereign LORD.
⁷ Egypt will be desolate,
   surrounded by desolate nations,
and its cities will be in ruins,
   surrounded by other ruined cities.
⁸ And the people of Egypt will know that I
      am the LORD
when I have set Egypt on fire
   and destroyed all their allies.
⁹ At that time I will send swift messengers
      in ships
   to terrify the complacent Ethiopians.
Great panic will come upon them
   on that day of Egypt's certain
      destruction.
Watch for it!
   It is sure to come!

¹⁰ "For this is what the Sovereign LORD
      says:
By the power of King Nebuchadnezzar*
   of Babylon,
   I will destroy the hordes of Egypt.
¹¹ He and his armies—the most ruthless of
      all—
   will be sent to demolish the land.
They will make war against Egypt
   until slaughtered Egyptians cover the
      ground.
¹² I will dry up the Nile River
   and sell the land to wicked men.

I will destroy the land of Egypt and
      everything in it
   by the hands of foreigners.
I, the LORD, have spoken!

¹³ "This is what the Sovereign LORD says:
I will smash the idols* of Egypt
   and the images at Memphis.*
There will be no rulers left in Egypt;
   terror will sweep the land.
¹⁴ I will destroy southern Egypt,*
   set fire to Zoan,
   and bring judgment against Thebes.*
¹⁵ I will pour out my fury on Pelusium,*
   the strongest fortress of Egypt,
and I will stamp out
   the hordes of Thebes.
¹⁶ Yes, I will set fire to all Egypt!
   Pelusium will be racked with pain;
Thebes will be torn apart;
   Memphis will live in constant terror.
¹⁷ The young men of Heliopolis and
      Bubastis* will die in battle,
   and the women* will be taken away as
      slaves.
¹⁸ When I come to break the proud
      strength of Egypt,
   it will be a dark day for Tahpanhes,
      too.
A dark cloud will cover Tahpanhes,
   and its daughters will be led away as
      captives.
¹⁹ And so I will greatly punish Egypt,
   and they will know that I am the
      LORD."

The Broken Arms of Pharaoh

²⁰ On April 29,* during the eleventh year
of King Jehoiachin's captivity, this message came to me from the LORD: ²¹ "Son of
man, I have broken the arm of Pharaoh, the
king of Egypt. His arm has not been put
in a cast so that it may heal. Neither has
it been bound up with a splint to make it
strong enough to hold a sword. ²²Therefore,
this is what the Sovereign LORD says: I am
the enemy of Pharaoh, the king of Egypt! I
will break both of his arms—the good arm
along with the broken one—and I will make

30:4 Hebrew *Cush;* similarly in 30:9.   **30:5** Hebrew *Cush, Put, Lud, all Arabia, Cub. Cub* is otherwise unknown and may be another spelling for *Lub* (Libya).   **30:6** Hebrew *to Syene.*   **30:10** Hebrew *Nebuchadrezzar,* a variant spelling of Nebuchadnezzar.   **30:13a** The Hebrew term (literally *round things*) probably alludes to dung.   **30:13b** Hebrew *Noph;* also in 30:16.   **30:14a** Hebrew *Pathros.*   **30:14b** Hebrew *No;* also in 30:15, 16.   **30:15** Hebrew *Sin;* also in 30:16.   **30:17a** Hebrew *of Awen and Pi-beseth.*   **30:17b** Or *and her cities.*   **30:20** Hebrew *On the seventh day of the first month,* of the ancient Hebrew lunar calendar. This event occurred on April 29, 587 B.C.; also see note on 1:1.

his sword clatter to the ground. ²³I will scatter the Egyptians to many lands throughout the world. ²⁴I will strengthen the arms of Babylon's king and put my sword in his hand. But I will break the arms of Pharaoh, king of Egypt, and he will lie there mortally wounded, groaning in pain. ²⁵I will strengthen the arms of the king of Babylon, while the arms of Pharaoh fall useless to his sides. And when I put my sword in the hand of Babylon's king and he brings it against the land of Egypt, Egypt will know that I am the Lord. ²⁶I will scatter the Egyptians among the nations, dispersing them throughout the earth. Then they will know that I am the Lord."

31 Egypt Compared to Fallen Assyria

On June 21,* during the eleventh year of King Jehoiachin's captivity, this message came to me from the Lord: ²"Son of man, give this message to Pharaoh, king of Egypt, and all his hordes:

"To whom would you compare your
greatness?
³ You are like mighty Assyria,
which was once like a cedar of
Lebanon,
with beautiful branches that cast deep
forest shade
and with its top high among the
clouds.
⁴ Deep springs watered it
and helped it to grow tall and
luxuriant.
The water flowed around it like a river,
streaming to all the trees nearby.
⁵ This great tree towered high,
higher than all the other trees
around it.
It prospered and grew long thick
branches
because of all the water at its roots.
⁶ The birds nested in its branches,
and in its shade all the wild animals
gave birth.
All the great nations of the world
lived in its shadow.
⁷ It was strong and beautiful,
with wide-spreading branches,

for its roots went deep
into abundant water.
⁸ No other cedar in the garden of God
could rival it.
No cypress had branches to equal it;
no plane tree had boughs to compare.
No tree in the garden of God
came close to it in beauty.
⁹ Because I made this tree so beautiful,
and gave it such magnificent foliage,
it was the envy of all the other trees of
Eden,
the garden of God.

¹⁰"Therefore, this is what the Sovereign Lord says: Because Egypt* became proud and arrogant, and because it set itself so high above the others, with its top reaching to the clouds, ¹¹I will hand it over to a mighty nation that will destroy it as its wickedness deserves. I have already discarded it. ¹²A foreign army—the terror of the nations—has cut it down and left it fallen on the ground. Its branches are scattered across the mountains and valleys and ravines of the land. All those who lived in its shadow have gone away and left it lying there.

¹³ "The birds roost on its fallen trunk,
and the wild animals lie among its
branches.
¹⁴ Let the tree of no other nation
proudly exult in its own prosperity,
though it be higher than the clouds
and it be watered from the depths.
For all are doomed to die,
to go down to the depths of the earth.
They will land in the pit
along with everyone else on earth.

¹⁵"This is what the Sovereign Lord says: When Assyria went down to the grave,* I made the deep springs mourn. I stopped its rivers and dried up its abundant water. I clothed Lebanon in black and caused the trees of the field to wilt. ¹⁶I made the nations shake with fear at the sound of its fall, for I sent it down to the grave with all the others who descend to the pit. And all the other proud trees of Eden, the most beautiful and the best of Lebanon, the ones

---

31:1 Hebrew *On the first day of the third month,* of the ancient Hebrew lunar calendar. This event occurred on June 21, 587 b.c.; also see note on 1:1.   31:10 Hebrew *you.*   31:15 Hebrew *to Sheol;* also in 31:16, 17.

whose roots went deep into the water, took comfort to find it there with them in the depths of the earth. ¹⁷Its allies, too, were all destroyed and had passed away. They had gone down to the grave—all those nations that had lived in its shade.

¹⁸ "O Egypt, to which of the trees of Eden will you compare your strength and glory? You, too, will be brought down to the depths with all these other nations. You will lie there among the outcasts* who have died by the sword. This will be the fate of Pharaoh and all his hordes. I, the Sovereign LORD, have spoken!"

32 A Warning for Pharaoh

On March 3,* during the twelfth year of King Jehoiachin's captivity, this message came to me from the LORD: ²"Son of man, mourn for Pharaoh, king of Egypt, and give him this message:

"You think of yourself as a strong young lion among the nations,
    but you are really just a sea monster,
heaving around in your own rivers,
    stirring up mud with your feet.
³ Therefore, this is what the Sovereign
        LORD says:
I will send many people
    to catch you in my net
    and haul you out of the water.
⁴ I will leave you stranded on the land to die.
    All the birds of the heavens will land on you,
and the wild animals of the whole earth
    will gorge themselves on you.
⁵ I will scatter your flesh on the hills
    and fill the valleys with your bones.
⁶ I will drench the earth with your gushing blood
    all the way to the mountains,
    filling the ravines to the brim.
⁷ When I blot you out,
    I will veil the heavens and darken the stars.
I will cover the sun with a cloud,
    and the moon will not give you its light.

⁸ I will darken the bright stars overhead
    and cover your land in darkness.
    I, the Sovereign LORD, have spoken!

⁹ "I will disturb many hearts when I bring news of your downfall to distant nations you have never seen. ¹⁰Yes, I will shock many lands, and their kings will be terrified at your fate. They will shudder in fear for their lives as I brandish my sword before them on the day of your fall. ¹¹For this is what the Sovereign LORD says:

"The sword of the king of Babylon
    will come against you.
¹² I will destroy your hordes with the
        swords of mighty warriors—
    the terror of the nations.
They will shatter the pride of Egypt,
    and all its hordes will be destroyed.
¹³ I will destroy all your flocks and herds
    that graze beside the streams.
Never again will people or animals
    muddy those waters with their feet.
¹⁴ Then I will let the waters of Egypt
        become calm again,
    and they will flow as smoothly as olive oil,
    says the Sovereign LORD.
¹⁵ And when I destroy Egypt
    and strip you of everything you own
and strike down all your people,
    then you will know that I am the
        LORD.
¹⁶ Yes, this is the funeral song
    they will sing for Egypt.
Let all the nations mourn.
    Let them mourn for Egypt and its hordes.
    I, the Sovereign LORD, have spoken!"

Egypt Falls into the Pit

¹⁷On March 17,* during the twelfth year, another message came to me from the LORD: ¹⁸"Son of man, weep for the hordes of Egypt and for the other mighty nations.* For I will send them down to the world below in company with those who descend to the pit. ¹⁹Say to them,

---

31:18 Hebrew *among the uncircumcised.* **32:1** Hebrew *On the first day of the twelfth month,* of the ancient Hebrew lunar calendar. This event occurred on March 3, 585 B.C.; also see note on 1:1. **32:17** Hebrew *On the fifteenth day of the month,* presumably in the twelfth month of the ancient Hebrew lunar calendar (see 32:1). This would put this message at the end of King Jehoiachin's twelfth year of captivity, on March 17, 585 B.C.; also see note on 1:1. Greek version reads *On the fifteenth day of the first month,* which would put this message on April 27, 586 B.C., at the beginning of Jehoiachin's twelfth year. **32:18** The meaning of the Hebrew is uncertain.

'O Egypt, are you lovelier than the other nations?

No! So go down to the pit and lie there among the outcasts.'*

²⁰The Egyptians will fall with the many who have died by the sword, for the sword is drawn against them. Egypt and its hordes will be dragged away to their judgment. ²¹Down in the grave* mighty leaders will mockingly welcome Egypt and its allies, saying, 'They have come down; they lie among the outcasts, hordes slaughtered by the sword.'

²²"Assyria lies there surrounded by the graves of its army, those who were slaughtered by the sword. ²³Their graves are in the depths of the pit, and they are surrounded by their allies. They struck terror in the hearts of people everywhere, but now they have been slaughtered by the sword.

²⁴"Elam lies there surrounded by the graves of all its hordes, those who were slaughtered by the sword. They struck terror in the hearts of people everywhere, but now they have descended as outcasts to the world below. Now they lie in the pit and share the shame of those who have gone before them. ²⁵They have a resting place among the slaughtered, surrounded by the graves of all their hordes. Yes, they terrorized the nations while they lived, but now they lie in shame with others in the pit, all of them outcasts, slaughtered by the sword.

²⁶"Meshech and Tubal are there, surrounded by the graves of all their hordes. They once struck terror in the hearts of people everywhere. But now they are outcasts, all slaughtered by the sword. ²⁷They are not buried in honor like their fallen heroes, who went down to the grave* with their weapons—their shields covering their bodies* and their swords beneath their heads. Their guilt rests upon them because they brought terror to everyone while they were still alive.

²⁸"You too, Egypt, will lie crushed and broken among the outcasts, all slaughtered by the sword.

²⁹"Edom is there with its kings and princes. Mighty as they were, they also lie among those slaughtered by the sword, with the outcasts who have gone down to the pit.

³⁰"All the princes of the north and the Sidonians are there with others who have died. Once a terror, they have been put to shame. They lie there as outcasts with others who were slaughtered by the sword. They share the shame of all who have descended to the pit.

³¹"When Pharaoh and his entire army arrive, he will take comfort that he is not alone in having his hordes killed, says the Sovereign LORD. ³²Although I have caused his terror to fall upon all the living, Pharaoh and his hordes will lie there among the outcasts who were slaughtered by the sword. I, the Sovereign LORD, have spoken!"

33 Ezekiel as Israel's Watchman

Once again a message came to me from the LORD: ²"Son of man, give your people this message: 'When I bring an army against a country, the people of that land choose one of their own to be a watchman. ³When the watchman sees the enemy coming, he sounds the alarm to warn the people. ⁴Then if those who hear the alarm refuse to take action, it is their own fault if they die. ⁵They heard the alarm but ignored it, so the responsibility is theirs. If they had listened to the warning, they could have saved their lives. ⁶But if the watchman sees the enemy coming and doesn't sound the alarm to warn the people, he is responsible for their captivity. They will die in their sins, but I will hold the watchman responsible for their deaths.'

⁷"Now, son of man, I am making you a watchman for the people of Israel. Therefore, listen to what I say and warn them for me. ⁸If I announce that some wicked people are sure to die and you fail to tell them to change their ways, then they will die in their sins, and I will hold you responsible for their deaths. ⁹But if you warn them to repent and they don't repent, they will die in their sins, but you will have saved yourself.

The Watchman's Message

¹⁰"Son of man, give the people of Israel this message: You are saying, 'Our sins are heavy

32:19 Hebrew *the uncircumcised;* also in 32:21, 24, 25, 26, 28, 29, 30, 32.　**32:21** Hebrew *in Sheol.*　**32:27a** Hebrew *to Sheol.*　**32:27b** The meaning of the Hebrew is uncertain.

upon us; we are wasting away! How can we survive?' ¹¹As surely as I live, says the Sovereign LORD, I take no pleasure in the death of wicked people. I only want them to turn from their wicked ways so they can live. Turn! Turn from your wickedness, O people of Israel! Why should you die?

¹²"Son of man, give your people this message: The righteous behavior of righteous people will not save them if they turn to sin, nor will the wicked behavior of wicked people destroy them if they repent and turn from their sins. ¹³When I tell righteous people that they will live, but then they sin, expecting their past righteousness to save them, then none of their righteous acts will be remembered. I will destroy them for their sins. ¹⁴And suppose I tell some wicked people that they will surely die, but then they turn from their sins and do what is just and right. ¹⁵For instance, they might give back a debtor's security, return what they have stolen, and obey my life-giving laws, no longer doing what is evil. If they do this, then they will surely live and not die. ¹⁶None of their past sins will be brought up again, for they have done what is just and right, and they will surely live.

¹⁷"Your people are saying, 'The Lord isn't doing what's right,' but it is they who are not doing what's right. ¹⁸For again I say, when righteous people turn away from their righteous behavior and turn to evil, they will die. ¹⁹But if wicked people turn from their wickedness and do what is just and right, they will live. ²⁰O people of Israel, you are saying, 'The Lord isn't doing what's right.' But I judge each of you according to your deeds."

Explanation of Jerusalem's Fall

²¹On January 8,* during the twelfth year of our captivity, a survivor from Jerusalem came to me and said, "The city has fallen!" ²²The previous evening the LORD had taken hold of me and given me back my voice. So I was able to speak when this man arrived the next morning.

²³Then this message came to me from the LORD: ²⁴"Son of man, the scattered remnants of Judah living among the ruined cities keep saying, 'Abraham was only one man, yet he gained possession of the entire land. We are many; surely the land has been given to us as a possession.' ²⁵So tell these people, 'This is what the Sovereign LORD says: You eat meat with blood in it, you worship idols,* and you murder the innocent. Do you really think the land should be yours? ²⁶Murderers! Idolaters! Adulterers! Should the land belong to you?'

²⁷"Say to them, 'This is what the Sovereign LORD says: As surely as I live, those living in the ruins will die by the sword. And I will send wild animals to eat those living in the open fields. Those hiding in the forts and caves will die of disease. ²⁸I will completely destroy the land and demolish her pride. Her arrogant power will come to an end. The mountains of Israel will be so desolate that no one will even travel through them. ²⁹When I have completely destroyed the land because of their detestable sins, then they will know that I am the LORD.'

³⁰"Son of man, your people talk about you in their houses and whisper about you at the doors. They say to each other, 'Come on, let's go hear the prophet tell us what the LORD is saying!' ³¹So my people come pretending to be sincere and sit before you. They listen to your words, but they have no intention of doing what you say. Their mouths are full of lustful words, and their hearts seek only after money. ³²You are very entertaining to them, like someone who sings love songs with a beautiful voice or plays fine music on an instrument. They hear what you say, but they don't act on it! ³³But when all these terrible things happen to them—as they certainly will—then they will know a prophet has been among them."

34 The Shepherds of Israel

Then this message came to me from the LORD: ²"Son of man, prophesy against the shepherds, the leaders of Israel. Give them this message from the Sovereign LORD: What sorrow awaits you shepherds who feed yourselves instead of your flocks. Shouldn't shepherds feed their sheep? ³You drink the milk, wear the wool, and butcher the best animals, but you let your

---

33:21 Hebrew *On the fifth day of the tenth month,* of the ancient Hebrew lunar calendar. This event occurred on January 8, 585 B.C.; also see note on 1:1.   **33:25** The Hebrew term (literally *round things*) probably alludes to dung.

flocks starve. ⁴You have not taken care of the weak. You have not tended the sick or bound up the injured. You have not gone looking for those who have wandered away and are lost. Instead, you have ruled them with harshness and cruelty. ⁵So my sheep have been scattered without a shepherd, and they are easy prey for any wild animal. ⁶They have wandered through all the mountains and all the hills, across the face of the earth, yet no one has gone to search for them.

⁷"Therefore, you shepherds, hear the word of the LORD: ⁸As surely as I live, says the Sovereign LORD, you abandoned my flock and left them to be attacked by every wild animal. And though you were my shepherds, you didn't search for my sheep when they were lost. You took care of yourselves and left the sheep to starve. ⁹Therefore, you shepherds, hear the word of the LORD. ¹⁰This is what the Sovereign LORD says: I now consider these shepherds my enemies, and I will hold them responsible for what has happened to my flock. I will take away their right to feed the flock, and I will stop them from feeding themselves. I will rescue my flock from their mouths; the sheep will no longer be their prey.

The Good Shepherd

¹¹"For this is what the Sovereign LORD says: I myself will search and find my sheep. ¹²I will be like a shepherd looking for his scattered flock. I will find my sheep and rescue them from all the places where they were scattered on that dark and cloudy day. ¹³I will bring them back home to their own land of Israel from among the peoples and nations. I will feed them on the mountains of Israel and by the rivers and in all the places where people live. ¹⁴Yes, I will give them good pastureland on the high hills of Israel. There they will lie down in pleasant places and feed in the lush pastures of the hills. ¹⁵I myself will tend my sheep and give them a place to lie down in peace, says the Sovereign LORD. ¹⁶I will search for my lost ones who strayed away, and I will bring them safely home again. I will bandage the injured and strengthen the weak. But I will destroy those who are fat and powerful. I will feed them, yes—feed them justice!

¹⁷"And as for you, my flock, this is what the Sovereign LORD says to his people: I will judge between one animal of the flock and another, separating the sheep from the goats. ¹⁸Isn't it enough for you to keep the best of the pastures for yourselves? Must you also trample down the rest? Isn't it enough for you to drink clear water for yourselves? Must you also muddy the rest with your feet? ¹⁹Why must my flock eat what you have trampled down and drink water you have fouled?

²⁰"Therefore, this is what the Sovereign LORD says: I will surely judge between the fat sheep and the scrawny sheep. ²¹For you fat sheep pushed and butted and crowded my sick and hungry flock until you scattered them to distant lands. ²²So I will rescue my flock, and they will no longer be abused. I will judge between one animal of the flock and another. ²³And I will set over them one shepherd, my servant David. He will feed them and be a shepherd to them. ²⁴And I, the LORD, will be their God, and my servant David will be a prince among my people. I, the LORD, have spoken!

The Lord's Covenant of Peace

²⁵"I will make a covenant of peace with my people and drive away the dangerous animals from the land. Then they will be able to camp safely in the wildest places and sleep in the woods without fear. ²⁶I will bless my people and their homes around my holy hill. And in the proper season I will send the showers they need. There will be showers of blessing. ²⁷The orchards and fields of my people will yield bumper crops, and everyone will live in safety. When I have broken their chains of slavery and rescued them from those who enslaved them, then they will know that I am the LORD. ²⁸They will no longer be prey for other nations, and wild animals will no longer devour them. They will live in safety, and no one will frighten them.

²⁹"And I will make their land famous for its crops, so my people will never again suffer from famines or the insults of foreign nations. ³⁰In this way, they will know that I, the LORD their God, am with them. And they will know that they, the people of Israel, are my people, says the Sovereign

LORD. ³¹You are my flock, the sheep of my pasture. You are my people, and I am your God. I, the Sovereign LORD, have spoken!"

35 A Message for Edom

Again a message came to me from the LORD: ²"Son of man, turn and face Mount Seir, and prophesy against its people. ³Give them this message from the Sovereign LORD:

"I am your enemy, O Mount Seir,
    and I will raise my fist against you
    to destroy you completely.
⁴ I will demolish your cities
    and make you desolate.
Then you will know that I am the LORD.

⁵"Your eternal hatred for the people of Israel led you to butcher them when they were helpless, when I had already punished them for all their sins. ⁶As surely as I live, says the Sovereign LORD, since you show no distaste for blood, I will give you a bloodbath of your own. Your turn has come! ⁷I will make Mount Seir utterly desolate, killing off all who try to escape and any who return. ⁸I will fill your mountains with the dead. Your hills, your valleys, and your ravines will be filled with people slaughtered by the sword. ⁹I will make you desolate forever. Your cities will never be rebuilt. Then you will know that I am the LORD.

¹⁰"For you said, 'The lands of Israel and Judah will be ours. We will take possession of them. What do we care that the LORD is there!' ¹¹Therefore, as surely as I live, says the Sovereign LORD, I will pay back your angry deeds with my own. I will punish you for all your acts of anger, envy, and hatred. And I will make myself known to Israel* by what I do to you. ¹²Then you will know that I, the LORD, have heard every contemptuous word you spoke against the mountains of Israel. For you said, 'They are desolate; they have been given to us as food to eat!' ¹³In saying that, you boasted proudly against me, and I have heard it all!

¹⁴"This is what the Sovereign LORD says: The whole world will rejoice when I make you desolate. ¹⁵You rejoiced at the desolation of Israel's territory. Now I will rejoice at yours! You will be wiped out, you people of Mount Seir and all who live in Edom! Then you will know that I am the LORD.

36 Restoration for Israel

"Son of man, prophesy to Israel's mountains. Give them this message: O mountains of Israel, hear the word of the LORD! ²This is what the Sovereign LORD says: Your enemies have taunted you, saying, 'Aha! Now the ancient heights belong to us!' ³Therefore, son of man, give the mountains of Israel this message from the Sovereign LORD: Your enemies have attacked you from all directions, making you the property of many nations and the object of much mocking and slander. ⁴Therefore, O mountains of Israel, hear the word of the Sovereign LORD. He speaks to the hills and mountains, ravines and valleys, and to ruined wastes and long-deserted cities that have been destroyed and mocked by the surrounding nations. ⁵This is what the Sovereign LORD says: My jealous anger burns against these nations, especially Edom, because they have shown utter contempt for me by gleefully taking my land for themselves as plunder.

⁶"Therefore, prophesy to the hills and mountains, the ravines and valleys of Israel. This is what the Sovereign LORD says: I am furious that you have suffered shame before the surrounding nations. ⁷Therefore, this is what the Sovereign LORD says: I have taken a solemn oath that those nations will soon have their own shame to endure.

⁸"But the mountains of Israel will produce heavy crops of fruit for my people—for they will be coming home again soon! ⁹See, I care about you, and I will pay attention to you. Your ground will be plowed and your crops planted. ¹⁰I will greatly increase the population of Israel, and the ruined cities will be rebuilt and filled with people. ¹¹I will increase not only the people, but also your animals. O mountains of Israel, I will bring people to live on you once again. I will make you even more prosperous than you were before. Then you will know that I am the LORD. ¹²I will cause my people to walk

on you once again, and you will be their territory. You will never again rob them of their children.

¹³"This is what the Sovereign LORD says: The other nations taunt you, saying, 'Israel is a land that devours its own people and robs them of their children!' ¹⁴But you will never again devour your people or rob them of their children, says the Sovereign LORD. ¹⁵I will not let you hear those other nations insult you, and you will no longer be mocked by them. You will not be a land that causes its nation to fall, says the Sovereign LORD."

¹⁶Then this further message came to me from the LORD: ¹⁷"Son of man, when the people of Israel were living in their own land, they defiled it by the evil way they lived. To me their conduct was as unclean as a woman's menstrual cloth. ¹⁸They polluted the land with murder and the worship of idols,* so I poured out my fury on them. ¹⁹I scattered them to many lands to punish them for the evil way they had lived. ²⁰But when they were scattered among the nations, they brought shame on my holy name. For the nations said, 'These are the people of the LORD, but he couldn't keep them safe in his own land!' ²¹Then I was concerned for my holy name, on which my people brought shame among the nations.

²²"Therefore, give the people of Israel this message from the Sovereign LORD: I am bringing you back, but not because you deserve it. I am doing it to protect my holy name, on which you brought shame while you were scattered among the nations. ²³I will show how holy my great name is—the name on which you brought shame among the nations. And when I reveal my holiness through you before their very eyes, says the Sovereign LORD, then the nations will know that I am the LORD. ²⁴For I will gather you up from all the nations and bring you home again to your land.

²⁵"Then I will sprinkle clean water on you, and you will be clean. Your filth will be washed away, and you will no longer worship idols. ²⁶And I will give you a new heart, and I will put a new spirit in you. I will take out your stony, stubborn heart and give you

a tender, responsive heart.* ²⁷And I will put my Spirit in you so that you will follow my decrees and be careful to obey my regulations.

²⁸"And you will live in Israel, the land I gave your ancestors long ago. You will be my people, and I will be your God. ²⁹I will cleanse you of your filthy behavior. I will give you good crops of grain, and I will send no more famines on the land. ³⁰I will give you great harvests from your fruit trees and fields, and never again will the surrounding nations be able to scoff at your land for its famines. ³¹Then you will remember your past sins and despise yourselves for all the detestable things you did. ³²But remember, says the Sovereign LORD, I am not doing this because you deserve it. O my people of Israel, you should be utterly ashamed of all you have done!

³³"This is what the Sovereign LORD says: When I cleanse you from your sins, I will repopulate your cities, and the ruins will be rebuilt. ³⁴The fields that used to lie empty and desolate in plain view of everyone will again be farmed. ³⁵And when I bring you back, people will say, 'This former wasteland is now like the Garden of Eden! The abandoned and ruined cities now have strong walls and are filled with people!' ³⁶Then the surrounding nations that survive will know that I, the LORD, have rebuilt the ruins and replanted the wasteland. For I, the LORD, have spoken, and I will do what I say.

³⁷"This is what the Sovereign LORD says: I am ready to hear Israel's prayers and to increase their numbers like a flock. ³⁸They will be as numerous as the sacred flocks that fill Jerusalem's streets at the time of her festivals. The ruined cities will be crowded with people once more, and everyone will know that I am the LORD."

37 A Valley of Dry Bones

The LORD took hold of me, and I was carried away by the Spirit of the LORD to a valley filled with bones. ²He led me all around among the bones that covered the valley floor. They were scattered everywhere across the ground and were

---

36:18 The Hebrew term (literally *round things*) probably alludes to dung; also in 36:25.   **36:26** Hebrew *a heart of flesh.*

completely dried out. ³Then he asked me, "Son of man, can these bones become living people again?"

"O Sovereign LORD," I replied, "you alone know the answer to that."

⁴Then he said to me, "Speak a prophetic message to these bones and say, 'Dry bones, listen to the word of the LORD! ⁵This is what the Sovereign LORD says: Look! I am going to put breath into you and make you live again! ⁶I will put flesh and muscles on you and cover you with skin. I will put breath into you, and you will come to life. Then you will know that I am the LORD.'"

⁷So I spoke this message, just as he told me. Suddenly as I spoke, there was a rattling noise all across the valley. The bones of each body came together and attached themselves as complete skeletons. ⁸Then as I watched, muscles and flesh formed over the bones. Then skin formed to cover their bodies, but they still had no breath in them.

⁹Then he said to me, "Speak a prophetic message to the winds, son of man. Speak a prophetic message and say, 'This is what the Sovereign LORD says: Come, O breath, from the four winds! Breathe into these dead bodies so they may live again.'"

¹⁰So I spoke the message as he commanded me, and breath came into their bodies. They all came to life and stood up on their feet—a great army.

¹¹Then he said to me, "Son of man, these bones represent the people of Israel. They are saying, 'We have become old, dry bones—all hope is gone. Our nation is finished.' ¹²Therefore, prophesy to them and say, 'This is what the Sovereign LORD says: O my people, I will open your graves of exile and cause you to rise again. Then I will bring you back to the land of Israel. ¹³When this happens, O my people, you will know that I am the LORD. ¹⁴I will put my Spirit in you, and you will live again and return home to your own land. Then you will know that I, the LORD, have spoken, and I have done what I said. Yes, the LORD has spoken!'"

Reunion of Israel and Judah

¹⁵Again a message came to me from the LORD: ¹⁶"Son of man, take a piece of wood and carve on it these words: 'This represents Judah and its allied tribes.' Then take another piece and carve these words on it: 'This represents Ephraim and the northern tribes of Israel.'* ¹⁷Now hold them together in your hand as if they were one piece of wood. ¹⁸When your people ask you what your actions mean, ¹⁹say to them, 'This is what the Sovereign LORD says: I will take Ephraim and the northern tribes and join them to Judah. I will make them one piece of wood in my hand.'

²⁰"Then hold out the pieces of wood you have inscribed, so the people can see them. ²¹And give them this message from the Sovereign LORD: I will gather the people of Israel from among the nations. I will bring them home to their own land from the places where they have been scattered. ²²I will unify them into one nation on the mountains of Israel. One king will rule them all; no longer will they be divided into two nations or into two kingdoms. ²³They will never again pollute themselves with their idols* and vile images and rebellion, for I will save them from their sinful backsliding. I will cleanse them. Then they will truly be my people, and I will be their God.

²⁴"My servant David will be their king, and they will have only one shepherd. They will obey my regulations and be careful to keep my decrees. ²⁵They will live in the land I gave my servant Jacob, the land where their ancestors lived. They and their children and their grandchildren after them will live there forever, generation after generation. And my servant David will be their prince forever. ²⁶And I will make a covenant of peace with them, an everlasting covenant. I will give them their land and increase their numbers,* and I will put my Temple among them forever. ²⁷I will make my home among them. I will be their God, and they will be my people. ²⁸And when my Temple is among them forever, the nations will know that I am the LORD, who makes Israel holy."

38 A Message for Gog

This is another message that came to me from the LORD: ²"Son of man, turn and face Gog of the land of Magog, the prince

---

37:16 Hebrew *This is Ephraim's wood, representing Joseph and all the house of Israel.*   37:23 The Hebrew term (literally *round things*) probably alludes to dung.   37:26 Hebrew reads *I will give them and increase their numbers;* Greek version lacks the entire phrase.

Forgiveness Frees Us to Worship

EZEKIEL 37:1-14

It was an unbelievably peaceful and vibrant evening as I went for a hike in the woods on the New England coast. The moon, the tide, the birdsongs—the beauty was stunning. All of creation seemed to be joining together in a cosmic chorus, an exquisite dance—but somehow *without me*. The more I listened and watched, the more it seemed like worship. And yet I was clearly on the outside—wanting in and yet standing against it in rebellion. The stars shone around me, while inside I felt flat and cold.

How could I enter back into God's presence with this enchanted symphony of the creation around me? The answer came to me clearly: I was to choose life, to join the dance, by *forgiving*. I was holding on to a grudge that I was unwilling to forgive. That unwillingness isolated me, somehow separating me from true worship.

Whether I bent my knees or my legs were broken for me that night, I don't know. But I fell to the wet earth, forehead down in mud and snow. I began by asking for mercy for myself . . . and I began to forgive.

Bitterness is like saltwater at high tide, forcing us to shrink back, to retreat into safe places and sorrow. But Someone changed the tide for me that evening on the ocean. He welcomed me back in. I rose and joined that symphony of worship, of gratitude, of life.

When his light and love flood us, they shift the boundaries of our being. Our hearts get bigger. Our minds begin to heal. I was grafted into the tree of life, brought into the land of the living.

I was finally free to join in the cosmic song of worship.

—Kelly Monroe Kullberg

For more on forgiveness, see reading at Hosea 3.

who rules over the nations of Meshech and Tubal, and prophesy against him. ³Give him this message from the Sovereign LORD: Gog, I am your enemy! ⁴I will turn you around and put hooks in your jaws to lead you out with your whole army—your horses and charioteers in full armor and a great horde armed with shields and swords. ⁵Persia, Ethiopia, and Libya* will join you, too, with all their weapons. ⁶Gomer and all its armies will also join you, along with the armies of Beth-togarmah from the distant north, and many others.

⁷"Get ready; be prepared! Keep all the armies around you mobilized, and take command of them. ⁸A long time from now you will be called into action. In the distant future you will swoop down on the land of Israel, which will be enjoying peace after recovering from war and after its people have returned from many lands to the mountains of Israel. ⁹You and all your allies—a vast and awesome army—will roll down on them like a storm and cover the land like a cloud.

¹⁰"This is what the Sovereign LORD says: At that time evil thoughts will come to your mind, and you will devise a wicked scheme. ¹¹You will say, 'Israel is an unprotected land filled with unwalled villages! I

38:5 Hebrew *Paras, Cush,* and *Put.*

will march against her and destroy these people who live in such confidence! ¹²I will go to those formerly desolate cities that are now filled with people who have returned from exile in many nations. I will capture vast amounts of plunder, for the people are rich with livestock and other possessions now. They think the whole world revolves around them!' ¹³But Sheba and Dedan and the merchants of Tarshish will ask, 'Do you really think the armies you have gathered can rob them of silver and gold? Do you think you can drive away their livestock and seize their goods and carry off plunder?'

¹⁴"Therefore, son of man, prophesy against Gog. Give him this message from the Sovereign LORD: When my people are living in peace in their land, then you will rouse yourself.* ¹⁵You will come from your homeland in the distant north with your vast cavalry and your mighty army, ¹⁶and you will attack my people Israel, covering their land like a cloud. At that time in the distant future, I will bring you against my land as everyone watches, and my holiness will be displayed by what happens to you, Gog. Then all the nations will know that I am the LORD.

¹⁷"This is what the Sovereign LORD asks: Are you the one I was talking about long ago, when I announced through Israel's prophets that in the future I would bring you against my people? ¹⁸But this is what the Sovereign LORD says: When Gog invades the land of Israel, my fury will boil over! ¹⁹In my jealousy and blazing anger, I promise a mighty shaking in the land of Israel on that day. ²⁰All living things—the fish in the sea, the birds of the sky, the animals of the field, the small animals that scurry along the ground, and all the people on earth—will quake in terror at my presence. Mountains will be thrown down; cliffs will crumble; walls will fall to the earth. ²¹I will summon the sword against you on all the hills of Israel, says the Sovereign LORD. Your men will turn their swords against each other. ²²I will punish you and your armies with disease and bloodshed; I will send torrential rain, hailstones, fire, and burning sulfur! ²³In this way, I will show my greatness and holiness, and I will make myself known to all the nations of the world. Then they will know that I am the LORD.

39 The Slaughter of Gog's Hordes

"Son of man, prophesy against Gog. Give him this message from the Sovereign LORD: I am your enemy, O Gog, ruler of the nations of Meshech and Tubal. ²I will turn you around and drive you toward the mountains of Israel, bringing you from the distant north. ³I will knock the bow from your left hand and the arrows from your right hand, and I will leave you helpless. ⁴You and your army and your allies will all die on the mountains. I will feed you to the vultures and wild animals. ⁵You will fall in the open fields, for I have spoken, says the Sovereign LORD. ⁶And I will rain down fire on Magog and on all your allies who live safely on the coasts. Then they will know that I am the LORD.

⁷"In this way, I will make known my holy name among my people of Israel. I will not let anyone bring shame on it. And the nations, too, will know that I am the LORD, the Holy One of Israel. ⁸That day of judgment will come, says the Sovereign LORD. Everything will happen just as I have declared it.

⁹"Then the people in the towns of Israel will go out and pick up your small and large shields, bows and arrows, javelins and spears, and they will use them for fuel. There will be enough to last them seven years! ¹⁰They won't need to cut wood from the fields or forests, for these weapons will give them all the fuel they need. They will plunder those who planned to plunder them, and they will rob those who planned to rob them, says the Sovereign LORD.

¹¹"And I will make a vast graveyard for Gog and his hordes in the Valley of the Travelers, east of the Dead Sea.* It will block the way of those who travel there, and they will change the name of the place to the Valley of Gog's Hordes. ¹²It will take seven months for the people of Israel to bury the bodies and cleanse the land. ¹³Everyone in Israel will help, for it will be a glorious victory for

---

38:14 As in Greek version; Hebrew reads *then you will know.* **39:11** Hebrew *the sea.*

Israel when I demonstrate my glory on that day, says the Sovereign LORD.

¹⁴"After seven months, teams of men will be appointed to search the land for skeletons to bury, so the land will be made clean again. ¹⁵Whenever bones are found, a marker will be set up so the burial crews will take them to be buried in the Valley of Gog's Hordes. ¹⁶(There will be a town there named Hamonah, which means 'horde.') And so the land will finally be cleansed.

¹⁷"And now, son of man, this is what the Sovereign LORD says: Call all the birds and wild animals. Say to them: Gather together for my great sacrificial feast. Come from far and near to the mountains of Israel, and there eat flesh and drink blood! ¹⁸Eat the flesh of mighty men and drink the blood of princes as though they were rams, lambs, goats, and bulls—all fattened animals from Bashan! ¹⁹Gorge yourselves with flesh until you are glutted; drink blood until you are drunk. This is the sacrificial feast I have prepared for you. ²⁰Feast at my banquet table—feast on horses and charioteers, on mighty men and all kinds of valiant warriors, says the Sovereign LORD.

²¹"In this way, I will demonstrate my glory to the nations. Everyone will see the punishment I have inflicted on them and the power of my fist when I strike. ²²And from that time on the people of Israel will know that I am the LORD their God. ²³The nations will then know why Israel was sent away to exile—it was punishment for sin, for they were unfaithful to their God. Therefore, I turned away from them and let their enemies destroy them. ²⁴I turned my face away and punished them because of their defilement and their sins.

Restoration for God's People

²⁵"So now, this is what the Sovereign LORD says: I will end the captivity of my people*; I will have mercy on all Israel, for I jealously guard my holy reputation! ²⁶They will accept responsibility for* their past shame and unfaithfulness after they come home to live in peace in their own land, with no one to bother them. ²⁷When I bring them home from the lands of their enemies, I will display my holiness among them for all the nations to see. ²⁸Then my people will know that I am the LORD their God, because I sent them away to exile and brought them home again. I will leave none of my people behind. ²⁹And I will never again turn my face from them, for I will pour out my Spirit upon the people of Israel. I, the Sovereign LORD, have spoken!"

40 The New Temple Area

On April 28,* during the twenty-fifth year of our captivity—fourteen years after the fall of Jerusalem—the LORD took hold of me. ²In a vision from God he took me to the land of Israel and set me down on a very high mountain. From there I could see toward the south what appeared to be a city. ³As he brought me nearer, I saw a man whose face shone like bronze standing beside a gateway entrance. He was holding in his hand a linen measuring cord and a measuring rod.

⁴He said to me, "Son of man, watch and listen. Pay close attention to everything I show you. You have been brought here so I can show you many things. Then you will return to the people of Israel and tell them everything you have seen."

The East Gateway

⁵I could see a wall completely surrounding the Temple area. The man took a measuring rod that was 10½ feet* long and measured the wall, and the wall was 10½ feet* thick and 10½ feet high.

⁶Then he went over to the eastern gateway. He climbed the steps and measured the threshold of the gateway; it was 10½ feet front to back.* ⁷There were guard alcoves on each side built into the gateway passage. Each of these alcoves was 10½ feet square, with a distance between them of 8¾ feet* along the passage wall. The gateway's inner threshold, which led to the entry room at the inner end of the gateway passage, was 10½ feet front to back. ⁸He also

39:25 Hebrew of Jacob. 39:26 A few Hebrew manuscripts read They will forget. 40:1 Hebrew At the beginning of the year, on the tenth day of the month, of the ancient Hebrew lunar calendar. This event occurred on April 28, 573 B.C.; also see note on 1:1. 40:5a Hebrew 6 long cubits [3.2 meters], each being a cubit [18 inches or 45 centimeters] and a handbreadth [3 inches or 8 centimeters] in length. 40:5b Hebrew 1 rod [3.2 meters]; also in 40:5c, 7. 40:6 As in Greek version, which reads 1 rod [3.2 meters] deep; Hebrew reads 1 rod deep, and 1 threshold, 1 rod deep. 40:7 Hebrew 5 cubits [2.7 meters]; also in 40:48.

measured the entry room of the gateway.* [9] It was 14 feet* across, with supporting columns 3½ feet* thick. This entry room was at the inner end of the gateway structure, facing toward the Temple.

[10] There were three guard alcoves on each side of the gateway passage. Each had the same measurements, and the dividing walls separating them were also identical. [11] The man measured the gateway entrance, which was 17½ feet* wide at the opening and 22¾ feet* wide in the gateway passage. [12] In front of each of the guard alcoves was a 21-inch* curb. The alcoves themselves were 10½ feet* on each side.

[13] Then he measured the entire width of the gateway, measuring the distance between the back walls of facing guard alcoves; this distance was 43¾ feet.* [14] He measured the dividing walls all along the inside of the gateway up to the entry room of the gateway; this distance was 105 feet.* [15] The full length of the gateway passage was 87½ feet* from one end to the other. [16] There were recessed windows that narrowed inward through the walls of the guard alcoves and their dividing walls. There were also windows in the entry room. The surfaces of the dividing walls were decorated with carved palm trees.

The Outer Courtyard

[17] Then the man brought me through the gateway into the outer courtyard of the Temple. A stone pavement ran along the walls of the courtyard, and thirty rooms were built against the walls, opening onto the pavement. [18] This pavement flanked the gates and extended out from the walls into the courtyard the same distance as the gateway entrance. This was the lower pavement. [19] Then the man measured across the Temple's outer courtyard between the outer and inner gateways; the distance was 175 feet.*

The North Gateway

[20] The man measured the gateway on the north just like the one on the east. [21] Here,
too, there were three guard alcoves on each side, with dividing walls and an entry room. All the measurements matched those of the east gateway. The gateway passage was 87½ feet long and 43¾ feet wide between the back walls of facing guard alcoves. [22] The windows, the entry room, and the palm tree decorations were identical to those in the east gateway. There were seven steps leading up to the gateway entrance, and the entry room was at the inner end of the gateway passage. [23] Here on the north side, just as on the east, there was another gateway leading to the Temple's inner courtyard directly opposite this outer gateway. The distance between the two gateways was 175 feet.

The South Gateway

[24] Then the man took me around to the south gateway and measured its various parts, and they were exactly the same as in the others. [25] It had windows along the walls as the others did, and there was an entry room where the gateway passage opened into the outer courtyard. And like the others, the gateway passage was 87½ feet long and 43¾ feet wide between the back walls of facing guard alcoves. [26] This gateway also had a stairway of seven steps leading up to it, and an entry room at the inner end, and palm tree decorations along the dividing walls. [27] And here again, directly opposite the outer gateway, was another gateway that led into the inner courtyard. The distance between the two gateways was 175 feet.

Gateways to the Inner Courtyard

[28] Then the man took me to the south gateway leading into the inner courtyard. He measured it, and it had the same measurements as the other gateways. [29] Its guard alcoves, dividing walls, and entry room were the same size as those in the others. It also had windows along its walls and in the entry room. And like the others, the gateway passage was 87½ feet long and 43¾

40:8 Many Hebrew manuscripts add which faced inward toward the Temple; it was 1 rod [10.5 feet or 3.2 meters] deep. 9Then he measured the entry room of the gateway. 40:9a Hebrew 8 cubits [4.2 meters]. 40:9b Hebrew 2 cubits [1.1 meters]. 40:11a Hebrew 10 cubits [5.3 meters]. 40:11b Hebrew 13 cubits [6.9 meters]. 40:12a Hebrew 1 cubit [53 centimeters]. 40:12b Hebrew 6 cubits [3.2 meters]. 40:13 Hebrew 25 cubits [13.3 meters]; also in 40:21, 25, 29, 30, 33, 36. 40:14 Hebrew 60 cubits [31.8 meters]. Greek version reads 20 cubits [35 feet or 10.6 meters]. The meaning of the Hebrew in this verse is uncertain. 40:15 Hebrew 50 cubits [26.5 meters]; also in 40:21, 25, 29, 33, 36. 40:19 Hebrew 100 cubits [53 meters]; also in 40:23, 27, 47.

feet wide. ³⁰(The entry rooms of the gateways leading into the inner courtyard were 14 feet* across and 43¾ feet wide.) ³¹The entry room to the south gateway faced into the outer courtyard. It had palm tree decorations on its columns, and there were eight steps leading to its entrance.

³²Then he took me to the east gateway leading to the inner courtyard. He measured it, and it had the same measurements as the other gateways. ³³Its guard alcoves, dividing walls, and entry room were the same size as those of the others, and there were windows along the walls and in the entry room. The gateway passage measured 87½ feet long and 43¾ feet wide. ³⁴Its entry room faced into the outer courtyard. It had palm tree decorations on its columns, and there were eight steps leading to its entrance.

³⁵Then he took me around to the north gateway leading to the inner courtyard. He measured it, and it had the same measurements as the other gateways. ³⁶The guard alcoves, dividing walls, and entry room of this gateway had the same measurements as in the others and the same window arrangements. The gateway passage measured 87½ feet long and 43¾ feet wide. ³⁷Its entry room faced into the outer courtyard, and it had palm tree decorations on the columns. There were eight steps leading to its entrance.

Rooms for Preparing Sacrifices

³⁸A door led from the entry room of one of the inner gateways into a side room, where the meat for sacrifices was washed. ³⁹On each side of this entry room were two tables, where the sacrificial animals were slaughtered for the burnt offerings, sin offerings, and guilt offerings. ⁴⁰Outside the entry room, on each side of the stairs going up to the north entrance, were two more tables. ⁴¹So there were eight tables in all—four inside and four outside—where the sacrifices were cut up and prepared.

⁴²There were also four tables of finished stone for preparation of the burnt offerings, each 31½ inches square and 21 inches high.* On these tables were placed the butchering knives and other implements for slaughtering the sacrificial animals. ⁴³There were hooks, each 3 inches* long, fastened to the foyer walls. The sacrificial meat was laid on the tables.

Rooms for the Priests

⁴⁴Inside the inner courtyard were two rooms,* one beside the north gateway, facing south, and the other beside the south* gateway, facing north. ⁴⁵And the man said to me, "The room beside the north inner gate is for the priests who supervise the Temple maintenance. ⁴⁶The room beside the south inner gate is for the priests in charge of the altar—the descendants of Zadok—for they alone of all the Levites may approach the LORD to minister to him."

The Inner Courtyard and Temple

⁴⁷Then the man measured the inner courtyard, and it was a square, 175 feet wide and 175 feet across. The altar stood in the courtyard in front of the Temple. ⁴⁸Then he brought me to the entry room of the Temple. He measured the walls on either side of the opening to the entry room, and they were 8¾ feet thick. The entrance itself was 24½ feet wide, and the walls on each side of the entrance were an additional 5¼ feet long.* ⁴⁹The entry room was 35 feet* wide and 21 feet* deep. There were ten steps leading up to it, with a column on each side.

41 After that, the man brought me into the sanctuary of the Temple. He measured the walls on either side of its doorway, and they were 10½ feet* thick. ²The doorway was 17½ feet* wide, and the walls on each side of it were 8¾ feet* long. The sanctuary itself was 70 feet long and 35 feet wide.*

³Then he went beyond the sanctuary into

40:30 As in 40:9, which reads 8 cubits [14 feet or 4.2 meters]; here the Hebrew reads 5 cubits [8¾ feet or 2.7 meters]. Some Hebrew manuscripts and the Greek version lack this entire verse. **40:42** Hebrew 1½ cubits [80 centimeters] long and 1½ cubits wide and 1 cubit [53 centimeters] high. **40:43** Hebrew a handbreadth [8 centimeters]. **40:44a** As in Greek version; Hebrew reads rooms for singers. **40:44b** As in Greek version; Hebrew reads east. **40:48** As in Greek version, which reads The entrance was 14 cubits [7.4 meters] wide, and the walls of the entrance were 3 cubits [1.6 meters] on each side; Hebrew lacks 14 cubits wide, and the walls of the entrance were. **40:49a** Hebrew 20 cubits [10.6 meters]. **40:49b** As in Greek version, which reads 12 cubits [21 feet or 6.4 meters]; Hebrew reads 11 cubits [19¼ feet or 5.8 meters]. **41:1** Hebrew 6 cubits [3.2 meters]; also in 41:3, 5. **41:2a** Hebrew 10 cubits [5.3 meters]. **41:2b** Hebrew 5 cubits [2.7 meters]; also in 41:9, 11. **41:2c** Hebrew 40 cubits [21.2 meters] long and 20 cubits [10.6 meters] wide.

the inner room. He measured the walls on either side of its entrance, and they were 3½ feet* thick. The entrance was 10½ feet wide, and the walls on each side of the entrance were 12¼ feet* long. ⁴The inner room of the sanctuary was 35 feet* long and 35 feet wide. "This," he told me, "is the Most Holy Place."

⁵Then he measured the wall of the Temple, and it was 10½ feet thick. There was a row of rooms along the outside wall; each room was 7 feet* wide. ⁶These side rooms were built in three levels, one above the other, with thirty rooms on each level. The supports for these side rooms rested on exterior ledges on the Temple wall; they did not extend into the wall. ⁷Each level was wider than the one below it, corresponding to the narrowing of the Temple wall as it rose higher. A stairway led up from the bottom level through the middle level to the top level.

⁸I saw that the Temple was built on a terrace, which provided a foundation for the side rooms. This terrace was 10½ feet* high. ⁹The outer wall of the Temple's side rooms was 8¾ feet thick. This left an open area between these side rooms ¹⁰and the row of rooms along the outer wall of the inner courtyard. This open area was 35 feet wide, and it went all the way around the Temple. ¹¹Two doors opened from the side rooms into the terrace yard, which was 8¾ feet wide. One door faced north and the other south.

¹²A large building stood on the west, facing the Temple courtyard. It was 122½ feet wide and 157½ feet long, and its walls were 8¾ feet* thick. ¹³Then the man measured the Temple, and it was 175 feet* long. The courtyard around the building, including its walls, was an additional 175 feet in length. ¹⁴The inner courtyard to the east of the Temple was also 175 feet wide. ¹⁵The building to the west, including its two walls, was also 175 feet wide.

The sanctuary, the inner room, and the entry room of the Temple ¹⁶were all paneled with wood, as were the frames of the recessed windows. The inner walls of the Temple were paneled with wood above and below the windows. ¹⁷The space above the door leading into the inner room, and its walls inside and out, were also paneled. ¹⁸All the walls were decorated with carvings of cherubim, each with two faces, and there was a carving of a palm tree between each of the cherubim. ¹⁹One face—that of a man—looked toward the palm tree on one side. The other face—that of a young lion—looked toward the palm tree on the other side. The figures were carved all along the inside of the Temple, ²⁰from the floor to the top of the walls, including the outer wall of the sanctuary.

²¹There were square columns at the entrance to the sanctuary, and the ones at the entrance of the Most Holy Place were similar. ²²There was an altar made of wood, 5¼ feet high and 3½ feet across.* Its corners, base, and sides were all made of wood. "This," the man told me, "is the table that stands in the LORD's presence."

²³Both the sanctuary and the Most Holy Place had double doorways, ²⁴each with two swinging doors. ²⁵The doors leading into the sanctuary were decorated with carved cherubim and palm trees, just as on the walls. And there was a wooden roof at the front of the entry room to the Temple. ²⁶On both sides of the entry room were recessed windows decorated with carved palm trees. The side rooms along the outside wall also had roofs.

42 Rooms for the Priests

Then the man led me out of the Temple courtyard by way of the north gateway. We entered the outer courtyard and came to a group of rooms against the north wall of the inner courtyard. ²This structure, whose entrance opened toward the north, was 175 feet* long and 87½ feet* wide. ³One block of rooms overlooked the 35-foot* width of the inner courtyard. Another block of rooms looked out onto the pavement of the outer courtyard. The two blocks were built three levels high and stood across

41:3a Hebrew *2 cubits* [1.1 meters].   **41:3b** Hebrew *7 cubits* [3.7 meters].   **41:4** Hebrew *20 cubits* [10.6 meters]; also in 41:4b, 10.   **41:5** Hebrew *4 cubits* [2.1 meters].   **41:8** Hebrew *1 rod, 6 cubits* [3.2 meters].   **41:12** Hebrew *70 cubits* [37.1 meters] *wide and 90 cubits* [47.7 meters] *long, and its walls were 5 cubits* [2.7 meters] *thick.*   **41:13** Hebrew *100 cubits* [53 meters]; also in 41:13b, 14, 15.   **41:22** Hebrew *3 cubits* [1.6 meters] *high and 2 cubits* [1.1 meters] *across.*   **42:2a** Hebrew *100 cubits* [53 meters]; also in 42:8.   **42:2b** Hebrew *50 cubits* [26.5 meters]; also in 42:7, 8.   **42:3** Hebrew *20-cubit* [10.6-meter].

from each other. ⁴Between the two blocks of rooms ran a walkway 17½ feet* wide. It extended the entire 175 feet of the complex,* and all the doors faced north. ⁵Each of the two upper levels of rooms was narrower than the one beneath it because the upper levels had to allow space for walkways in front of them. ⁶Since there were three levels and they did not have supporting columns as in the courtyards, each of the upper levels was set back from the level beneath it. ⁷There was an outer wall that separated the rooms from the outer courtyard; it was 87½ feet long. ⁸This wall added length to the outer block of rooms, which extended for only 87½ feet, while the inner block— the rooms toward the Temple—extended for 175 feet. ⁹There was an eastern entrance from the outer courtyard to these rooms.

¹⁰On the south* side of the Temple there were two blocks of rooms just south of the inner courtyard between the Temple and the outer courtyard. These rooms were arranged just like the rooms on the north. ¹¹There was a walkway between the two blocks of rooms just like the complex on the north side of the Temple. This complex of rooms was the same length and width as the other one, and it had the same entrances and doors. The dimensions of each were identical. ¹²So there was an entrance in the wall facing the doors of the inner block of rooms, and another on the east at the end of the interior walkway.

¹³Then the man told me, "These rooms that overlook the Temple from the north and south are holy. Here the priests who offer sacrifices to the LORD will eat the most holy offerings. And because these rooms are holy, they will be used to store the sacred offerings—the grain offerings, sin offerings, and guilt offerings. ¹⁴When the priests leave the sanctuary, they must not go directly to the outer courtyard. They must first take off the clothes they wore while ministering, because these clothes are holy. They must put on other clothes before entering the parts of the building complex open to the public."

¹⁵When the man had finished measuring the inside of the Temple area, he led me out through the east gateway to measure the entire perimeter. ¹⁶He measured the east side with his measuring rod, and it was 875 feet long.* ¹⁷Then he measured the north side, and it was also 875 feet. ¹⁸The south side was also 875 feet, ¹⁹and the west side was also 875 feet. ²⁰So the area was 875 feet on each side with a wall all around it to separate what was holy from what was common.

43 The LORD's Glory Returns

After this, the man brought me back around to the east gateway. ²Suddenly, the glory of the God of Israel appeared from the east. The sound of his coming was like the roar of rushing waters, and the whole landscape shone with his glory. ³This vision was just like the others I had seen, first by the Kebar River and then when he came to destroy Jerusalem. I fell face down on the ground. ⁴And the glory of the LORD came into the Temple through the east gateway.

⁵Then the Spirit took me up and brought me into the inner courtyard, and the glory of the LORD filled the Temple. ⁶And I heard someone speaking to me from within the Temple, while the man who had been measuring stood beside me. ⁷The LORD said to me, "Son of man, this is the place of my throne and the place where I will rest my feet. I will live here forever among the people of Israel. They and their kings will not defile my holy name any longer by their adulterous worship of other gods or by honoring the relics of their kings who have died. ⁸They put their idol altars right next to mine with only a wall between them and me. They defiled my holy name by such detestable sin, so I consumed them in my anger. ⁹Now let them stop worshiping other gods and honoring the relics of their kings, and I will live among them forever.

¹⁰"Son of man, describe to the people of Israel the Temple I have shown you, so they will be ashamed of all their sins. Let them study its plan, ¹¹and they will be ashamed* of what they have done. Describe to them all the specifications of the Temple—including

---

42:4a Hebrew *10 cubits* [5.3 meters].   **42:4b** As in Greek and Syriac versions, which read *Its length was 100 cubits* [53 meters]; Hebrew reads *and a passage 1 cubit* [18 inches or 53 centimeters] *wide*.   **42:10** As in Greek version; Hebrew reads *east*.   **42:16** As in 45:2 and in Greek version at 42:17, which reads *500 cubits* [265 meters]; Hebrew reads *500 rods* [5,250 feet or 1,590 meters]; similarly in 42:17, 18, 19, 20.   **43:11** As in Greek version; Hebrew reads *if they are ashamed*.

its entrances and exits—and everything else about it. Tell them about its decrees and laws. Write down all these specifications and decrees as they watch so they will be sure to remember and follow them. ¹²And this is the basic law of the Temple: absolute holiness! The entire top of the mountain where the Temple is built is holy. Yes, this is the basic law of the Temple.

The Altar

¹³ "These are the measurements of the altar*: There is a gutter all around the altar 21 inches deep and 21 inches wide,* with a curb 9 inches* wide around its edge. And this is the height* of the altar: ¹⁴From the gutter the altar rises 3½ feet* to a lower ledge that surrounds the altar and is 21 inches* wide. From the lower ledge the altar rises 7 feet* to the upper ledge that is also 21 inches wide. ¹⁵The top of the altar, the hearth, rises another 7 feet higher, with a horn rising up from each of the four corners. ¹⁶The top of the altar is square, measuring 21 feet by 21 feet.* ¹⁷The upper ledge also forms a square, measuring 24½ feet by 24½ feet,* with a 21-inch gutter and a 10½-inch curb* all around the edge. There are steps going up the east side of the altar."

¹⁸Then he said to me, "Son of man, this is what the Sovereign LORD says: These will be the regulations for the burning of offerings and the sprinkling of blood when the altar is built. ¹⁹At that time, the Levitical priests of the family of Zadok, who minister before me, are to be given a young bull for a sin offering, says the Sovereign LORD. ²⁰You will take some of its blood and smear it on the four horns of the altar, the four corners of the upper ledge, and the curb that runs around that ledge. This will cleanse and make atonement for the altar. ²¹Then take the young bull for the sin offering and burn it at the appointed place outside the Temple area.

²²"On the second day, sacrifice as a sin offering a young male goat that has no physical defects. Then cleanse and make atonement for the altar again, just as you did with the young bull. ²³When you have finished the cleansing ceremony, offer another young bull that has no defects and a perfect ram from the flock. ²⁴You are to present them to the LORD, and the priests are to sprinkle salt on them and offer them as a burnt offering to the LORD.

²⁵"Every day for seven days a male goat, a young bull, and a ram from the flock will be sacrificed as a sin offering. None of these animals may have physical defects of any kind. ²⁶Do this each day for seven days to cleanse and make atonement for the altar, thus setting it apart for holy use. ²⁷On the eighth day, and on each day afterward, the priests will sacrifice on the altar the burnt offerings and peace offerings of the people. Then I will accept you. I, the Sovereign LORD, have spoken!"

44 The Prince, Levites, and Priests

Then the man brought me back to the east gateway in the outer wall of the Temple area, but it was closed. ²And the LORD said to me, "This gate must remain closed; it will never again be opened. No one will ever open it and pass through, for the LORD, the God of Israel, has entered here. Therefore, it must always remain shut. ³Only the prince himself may sit inside this gateway to feast in the LORD's presence. But he may come and go only through the entry room of the gateway."

⁴Then the man brought me through the north gateway to the front of the Temple. I looked and saw that the glory of the LORD filled the Temple of the LORD, and I fell face down on the ground.

⁵And the LORD said to me, "Son of man, take careful notice. Use your eyes and ears, and listen to everything I tell you about the regulations concerning the LORD's Temple. Take careful note of the procedures for using the Temple's entrances and exits. ⁶And give these rebels, the people of Israel, this message from the Sovereign LORD: O people of Israel, enough of your detestable sins! ⁷You have brought uncircumcised foreign-

---

43:13a Hebrew *measurements of the altar in long cubits, each being a cubit* [18 inches or 45 centimeters] *and a handbreadth* [3 inches or 8 centimeters] *in length.* 43:13b Hebrew *a cubit* [53 centimeters] *deep and a cubit wide.* 43:13c Hebrew *1 span* [23 centimeters]. 43:13d As in Greek version; Hebrew reads *base.* 43:14a Hebrew *2 cubits* [1.1 meters]. 43:14b Hebrew *1 cubit* [53 centimeters]; also in 43:14d. 43:14c Hebrew *4 cubits* [2.1 meters]; also in 43:15. 43:16 Hebrew *12 cubits* [6.4 meters] *long and 12 cubits wide.* 43:17a Hebrew *14 cubits* [7.4 meters] *long and 14 cubits wide.* 43:17b Hebrew *a gutter of 1 cubit* [53 centimeters] *and a curb of ½ a cubit* [27 centimeters].

ers into my sanctuary—people who have no heart for God. In this way, you defiled my Temple even as you offered me my food, the fat and blood of sacrifices. In addition to all your other detestable sins, you have broken my covenant. [8] Instead of safeguarding my sacred rituals, you have hired foreigners to take charge of my sanctuary.

[9] "So this is what the Sovereign LORD says: No foreigners, including those who live among the people of Israel, will enter my sanctuary if they have not been circumcised and have not surrendered themselves to the LORD. [10] And the men of the tribe of Levi who abandoned me when Israel strayed away from me to worship idols* must bear the consequences of their unfaithfulness. [11] They may still be Temple guards and gatekeepers, and they may slaughter the animals brought for burnt offerings and be present to help the people. [12] But they encouraged my people to worship idols, causing Israel to fall into deep sin. So I have taken a solemn oath that they must bear the consequences for their sins, says the Sovereign LORD. [13] They may not approach me to minister as priests. They may not touch any of my holy things or the holy offerings, for they must bear the shame of all the detestable sins they have committed. [14] They are to serve as the Temple caretakers, taking charge of the maintenance work and performing general duties.

[15] "However, the Levitical priests of the family of Zadok continued to minister faithfully in the Temple when Israel abandoned me for idols. These men will serve as my ministers. They will stand in my presence and offer the fat and blood of the sacrifices, says the Sovereign LORD. [16] They alone will enter my sanctuary and approach my table to serve me. They will fulfill all my requirements.

[17] "When they enter the gateway to the inner courtyard, they must wear only linen clothing. They must wear no wool while on duty in the inner courtyard or in the Temple itself. [18] They must wear linen turbans and linen undergarments. They must not wear anything that would cause them to perspire. [19] When they return to the outer courtyard where the people are, they must take off the clothes they wear while ministering to me. They must leave them in the sacred rooms and put on other clothes so they do not endanger anyone by transmitting holiness to them through this clothing.

[20] "They must neither shave their heads nor let their hair grow too long. Instead, they must trim it regularly. [21] The priests must not drink wine before entering the inner courtyard. [22] They may choose their wives only from among the virgins of Israel or the widows of the priests. They may not marry other widows or divorced women. [23] They will teach my people the difference between what is holy and what is common, what is ceremonially clean and unclean.

[24] "They will serve as judges to resolve any disagreements among my people. Their decisions must be based on my regulations. And the priests themselves must obey my instructions and decrees at all the sacred festivals, and see to it that the Sabbaths are set apart as holy days.

[25] "A priest must not defile himself by being in the presence of a dead person unless it is his father, mother, child, brother, or unmarried sister. In such cases it is permitted. [26] Even then, he can return to his Temple duties only after being ceremonially cleansed and then waiting for seven days. [27] The first day he returns to work and enters the inner courtyard and the sanctuary, he must offer a sin offering for himself, says the Sovereign LORD.

[28] "The priests will not have any property or possession of land, for I alone am their special possession. [29] Their food will come from the gifts and sacrifices brought to the Temple by the people—the grain offerings, the sin offerings, and the guilt offerings. Whatever anyone sets apart* for the LORD will belong to the priests. [30] The first of the ripe fruits and all the gifts brought to the LORD will go to the priests. The first samples of each grain harvest and the first of your flour must also be given to the priests so the LORD will bless your homes. [31] The priests may not eat meat from any bird or animal that dies a natural death or that dies after being attacked by another animal.

45 Division of the Land

"When you divide the land among the tribes of Israel, you must set aside a section for the LORD as his holy portion. This piece of land will be 8⅓ miles long and 6⅔ miles wide.* The entire area will be holy. ²A section of this land, measuring 875 feet by 875 feet,* will be set aside for the Temple. An additional strip of land 87½ feet* wide is to be left empty all around it. ³Within the larger sacred area, measure out a portion of land 8⅓ miles long and 3⅓ miles wide.* Within it the sanctuary of the Most Holy Place will be located. ⁴This area will be holy, set aside for the priests who minister to the LORD in the sanctuary. They will use it for their homes, and my Temple will be located within it. ⁵The strip of sacred land next to it, also 8⅓ miles long and 3⅓ miles wide, will be a living area for the Levites who work at the Temple. It will be their possession and a place for their towns.*

⁶"Adjacent to the larger sacred area will be a section of land 8⅓ miles long and 1⅔ miles wide.* This will be set aside for a city where anyone in Israel can live.

⁷"Two special sections of land will be set apart for the prince. One section will share a border with the east side of the sacred lands and city, and the second section will share a border on the west side. Then the far eastern and western borders of the prince's lands will line up with the eastern and western boundaries of the tribal areas. ⁸These sections of land will be the prince's allotment. Then my princes will no longer oppress and rob my people; they will assign the rest of the land to the people, giving an allotment to each tribe.

Rules for the Princes

⁹"For this is what the Sovereign LORD says: Enough, you princes of Israel! Stop your violence and oppression and do what is just and right. Quit robbing and cheating my people out of their land. Stop expelling them from their homes, says the Sovereign LORD. ¹⁰Use only honest weights and scales and honest measures, both dry and liquid.* ¹¹The homer* will be your standard unit for measuring volume. The ephah and the bath* will each measure one-tenth of a homer. ¹²The standard unit for weight will be the silver shekel.* One shekel will consist of twenty gerahs, and sixty shekels will be equal to one mina.*

Special Offerings and Celebrations

¹³"You must give this tax to the prince: one bushel of wheat or barley for every 60* you harvest, ¹⁴one percent of your olive oil,* ¹⁵and one sheep or goat for every 200 in your flocks in Israel. These will be the grain offerings, burnt offerings, and peace offerings that will make atonement for the people who bring them, says the Sovereign LORD. ¹⁶All the people of Israel must join in bringing these offerings to the prince. ¹⁷The prince will be required to provide offerings that are given at the religious festivals, the new moon celebrations, the Sabbath days, and all other similar occasions. He will provide the sin offerings, burnt offerings, grain offerings, liquid offerings, and peace offerings to purify the people of Israel, making them right with the LORD.*

¹⁸"This is what the Sovereign LORD says: In early spring, on the first day of each new year,* sacrifice a young bull with no defects to purify the Temple. ¹⁹The priest will take blood from this sin offering and put it on the doorposts of the Temple, the four corners of the upper ledge of the altar, and the gateposts at the entrance to the inner courtyard. ²⁰Do this also on the seventh day of the new year for anyone who has sinned through error or ignorance. In this way, you will purify* the Temple.

²¹"On the fourteenth day of the first month,* you must celebrate the Passover.

45:1 As in Greek version, which reads 25,000 cubits [13.3 kilometers] long and 20,000 cubits [10.6 kilometers] wide; Hebrew reads 25,000 cubits long and 10,000 cubits [3⅓ miles or 5.3 kilometers] wide. Compare 45:3, 5; 48:9.   45:2a Hebrew 500 cubits [265 meters] by 500 cubits, a square.   45:2b Hebrew 50 cubits [26.5 meters].   45:3 Hebrew 25,000 cubits [13.3 kilometers] long and 10,000 cubits [5.3 kilometers] wide; also in 45:5.   45:5 As in Greek version; Hebrew reads They will have as their possession 20 rooms.   45:6 Hebrew 25,000 cubits [13.3 kilometers] long and 5,000 cubits [2.65 kilometers] wide.   45:10 Hebrew use honest scales, an honest ephah, and an honest bath. 45:11a The homer measures about 40 gallons or 182 liters.   45:11b The ephah is a dry measure; the bath is a liquid measure.   45:12a The shekel weighs about 0.4 ounces or 11 grams.   45:12b Elsewhere the mina is equated to 50 shekels.   45:13 Hebrew ⅙ of an ephah from each homer of wheat and ⅙ of an ephah from each homer of barley.   45:14 Hebrew the portion of oil, measured by the bath, is ¹⁄₁₀₀ of a bath from each cor, which consists of 10 baths or 1 homer, for 10 baths are equivalent to a homer.   45:17 Or to make atonement for the people of Israel.   45:18 Hebrew On the first day of the first month, of the Hebrew calendar. This day in the ancient Hebrew lunar calendar occurred in March or April.   45:20 Or will make atonement for.   45:21 This day in the ancient Hebrew lunar calendar occurred in late March, April, or early May.

Sacred Selfishness
and Calling

EZEKIEL 46:1–3

One of my mentors often reminds me, "You have all the time you need to do the things that God has called you to do." But I tend to doubt her. I often feel that I have *anything but* all the time I need!

The truth is that none of us has all the time we need to do everything everyone else wants us to do, or even to do the things we think we want to do. In order to have all the time we truly need, we must begin by listening to the call of God.

One spiritual practice that has helped me slow down and listen—to really live out this all-the-time-you-need philosophy—is the practice of Sabbath keeping. Taking one day a week to rest actually has made me more productive and given me clarity about God's specific calling in my life.

I believe God has called me to his purposes: to be a leader in my church, my family, my neighborhood; to be compassionate, mindful, and kind. And if I want to answer that call, then I need to figure out the best way to live. Along with giving my best efforts to the ministries, work, and relationships God has put before me, I must also prioritize time to rest. Times in which I withdraw from people and their demands. Times in which I allow myself to spend time with Jesus, to respond to his invitation, "Let's go off by ourselves to a quiet place and rest awhile" (Mark 6:31). In these moments of what I call "sacred selfishness," I let Jesus attend to my deepest needs: for quiet, peace, and intimacy with him. Sabbath keeping is a spiritual practice that enables us to recover our lives—to clarify our sense of calling as we step away from a hectic, harried schedule.

—*Keri Wyatt Kent*

For more on Sabbath and rest, see reading at Matthew 19:13–15.

This festival will last for seven days. The bread you eat during that time must be made without yeast. [22] On the day of Passover the prince will provide a young bull as a sin offering for himself and the people of Israel. [23] On each of the seven days of the feast he will prepare a burnt offering to the LORD, consisting of seven young bulls and seven rams without defects. A male goat will also be given each day for a sin offering. [24] The prince will provide a basket of flour as a grain offering and a gallon of olive oil* with each young bull and ram.

[25] "During the seven days of the Festival of Shelters, which occurs every year in early autumn,* the prince will provide these same sacrifices for the sin offering, the burnt offering, and the grain offering, along with the required olive oil.

46 "This is what the Sovereign LORD says: The east gateway of the inner courtyard will be closed during the six workdays each week, but it will be open on Sabbath days and the days of new moon celebrations. [2] The prince will enter the entry room of the gateway from the outside. Then he will stand by the gatepost while the priest offers his burnt offering and peace offering. He will bow down in worship inside the gateway passage and then go back out the way he came. The

---

45:24 Hebrew *an ephah* [20 quarts or 22 liters] *of flour . . . and a hin* [3.8 liters] *of olive oil.*   **45:25** Hebrew *the festival which begins on the fifteenth day of the seventh month* (see Lev 23:34). This day in the ancient Hebrew lunar calendar occurred in late September, October, or early November.

gateway will not be closed until evening. ³The common people will bow down and worship the Lᴏʀᴅ in front of this gateway on Sabbath days and the days of new moon celebrations.

⁴"Each Sabbath day the prince will present to the Lᴏʀᴅ a burnt offering of six lambs and one ram, all with no defects. ⁵He will present a grain offering of a basket of choice flour to go with the ram and whatever amount of flour he chooses to go with each lamb, and he is to offer one gallon of olive oil* for each basket of flour. ⁶At the new moon celebrations, he will bring one young bull, six lambs, and one ram, all with no defects. ⁷With the young bull he must bring a basket of choice flour for a grain offering. With the ram he must bring another basket of flour. And with each lamb he is to bring whatever amount of flour he chooses to give. With each basket of flour he must offer one gallon of olive oil.

⁸"The prince must enter the gateway through the entry room, and he must leave the same way. ⁹But when the people come in through the north gateway to worship the Lᴏʀᴅ during the religious festivals, they must leave by the south gateway. And those who entered through the south gateway must leave by the north gateway. They must never leave by the same gateway they came in, but must always use the opposite gateway. ¹⁰The prince will enter and leave with the people on these occasions.

¹¹"So at the special feasts and sacred festivals, the grain offering will be a basket of choice flour with each young bull, another basket of flour with each ram, and as much flour as the prince chooses to give with each lamb. Give one gallon of olive oil with each basket of flour. ¹²When the prince offers a voluntary burnt offering or peace offering to the Lᴏʀᴅ, the east gateway to the inner courtyard will be opened for him, and he will offer his sacrifices as he does on Sabbath days. Then he will leave, and the gateway will be shut behind him.

¹³"Each morning you must sacrifice a one-year-old lamb with no defects as a burnt offering to the Lᴏʀᴅ. ¹⁴With the lamb, a grain offering must also be given to the Lᴏʀᴅ—about three quarts of flour with a third of a gallon of olive oil* to moisten the choice flour. This will be a permanent law for you. ¹⁵The lamb, the grain offering, and the olive oil must be given as a daily sacrifice every morning without fail.

¹⁶"This is what the Sovereign Lᴏʀᴅ says: If the prince gives a gift of land to one of his sons as his inheritance, it will belong to him and his descendants forever. ¹⁷But if the prince gives a gift of land from his inheritance to one of his servants, the servant may keep it only until the Year of Jubilee, which comes every fiftieth year.* At that time the land will return to the prince. But when the prince gives gifts to his sons, those gifts will be permanent. ¹⁸And the prince may never take anyone's property by force. If he gives property to his sons, it must be from his own land, for I do not want any of my people unjustly evicted from their property."

The Temple Kitchens

¹⁹In my vision, the man brought me through the entrance beside the gateway and led me to the sacred rooms assigned to the priests, which faced toward the north. He showed me a place at the extreme west end of these rooms. ²⁰He explained, "This is where the priests will cook the meat from the guilt offerings and sin offerings and bake the flour from the grain offerings into bread. They will do it here to avoid carrying the sacrifices through the outer courtyard and endangering the people by transmitting holiness to them."

²¹Then he brought me back to the outer courtyard and led me to each of its four corners. In each corner I saw an enclosure. ²²Each of these enclosures was 70 feet long and 52½ feet wide,* surrounded by walls. ²³Along the inside of these walls was a ledge of stone with fireplaces under the ledge all the way around. ²⁴The man said to me, "These are the kitchens to be used by the Temple assistants to boil the sacrifices offered by the people."

46:5 Hebrew *an ephah* [20 quarts or 22 liters] *of choice flour . . . a hin* [3.8 liters] *of olive oil;* similarly in 46:7, 11. 46:14 Hebrew ⅙ *of an ephah* [3.7 liters] *of flour with* ⅓ *of a hin* [1.3 liters] *of olive oil.* 46:17 Hebrew *until the Year of Release;* see Lev 25:8-17. 46:22 Hebrew *40 cubits* [21.2 meters] *long and 30 cubits* [15.9 meters] *wide.*

47 The River of Healing

In my vision, the man brought me back to the entrance of the Temple. There I saw a stream flowing east from beneath the door of the Temple and passing to the right of the altar on its south side. ²The man brought me outside the wall through the north gateway and led me around to the eastern entrance. There I could see the water flowing out through the south side of the east gateway.

³Measuring as he went, he took me along the stream for 1,750 feet* and then led me across. The water was up to my ankles. ⁴He measured off another 1,750 feet and led me across again. This time the water was up to my knees. After another 1,750 feet, it was up to my waist. ⁵Then he measured another 1,750 feet, and the river was too deep to walk across. It was deep enough to swim in, but too deep to walk through.

⁶He asked me, "Have you been watching, son of man?" Then he led me back along the riverbank. ⁷When I returned, I was surprised by the sight of many trees growing on both sides of the river. ⁸Then he said to me, "This river flows east through the desert into the valley of the Dead Sea.* The waters of this stream will make the salty waters of the Dead Sea fresh and pure. ⁹There will be swarms of living things wherever the water of this river flows. Fish will abound in the Dead Sea, for its waters will become fresh. Life will flourish wherever this water flows. ¹⁰Fishermen will stand along the shores of the Dead Sea. All the way from En-gedi to En-eglaim, the shores will be covered with nets drying in the sun. Fish of every kind will fill the Dead Sea, just as they fill the Mediterranean.* ¹¹But the marshes and swamps will not be purified; they will still be salty. ¹²Fruit trees of all kinds will grow along both sides of the river. The leaves of these trees will never turn brown and fall, and there will always be fruit on their branches. There will be a new crop every month, for they are watered by the river flowing from the Temple. The fruit will be for food and the leaves for healing."

Boundaries for the Land

¹³This is what the Sovereign LORD says: "Divide the land in this way for the twelve tribes of Israel: The descendants of Joseph will be given two shares of land.* ¹⁴Otherwise each tribe will receive an equal share. I took a solemn oath and swore that I would give this land to your ancestors, and it will now come to you as your possession.

¹⁵"These are the boundaries of the land: The northern border will run from the Mediterranean toward Hethlon, then on through Lebo-hamath to Zedad; ¹⁶then it will run to Berothah and Sibraim, which are on the border between Damascus and Hamath, and finally to Hazer-hatticon, on the border of Hauran. ¹⁷So the northern border will run from the Mediterranean to Hazar-enan, on the border between Hamath to the north and Damascus to the south.

¹⁸"The eastern border starts at a point between Hauran and Damascus and runs south along the Jordan River between Israel and Gilead, past the Dead Sea* and as far south as Tamar.* This will be the eastern border.

¹⁹"The southern border will go west from Tamar to the waters of Meribah at Kadesh* and then follow the course of the Brook of Egypt to the Mediterranean. This will be the southern border.

²⁰"On the west side, the Mediterranean itself will be your border from the southern border to the point where the northern border begins, opposite Lebohamath.

²¹"Divide the land within these boundaries among the tribes of Israel. ²²Distribute the land as an allotment for yourselves and for the foreigners who have joined you and are raising their families among you. They will be like native-born Israelites to you and will receive an allotment among the tribes. ²³These foreigners are to be given land within the territory of the tribe with whom they now live. I, the Sovereign LORD, have spoken!

47:3 Hebrew 1,000 cubits [530 meters]; also in 47:4, 5. **47:8** Hebrew the sea. **47:10** Hebrew the great sea; also in 47:15, 17, 19, 20.
47:13 It was important to retain twelve portions of land. Since Levi had no portion, the descendants of Joseph's sons, Ephraim and Manasseh, received land as two tribes. **47:18a** Hebrew the eastern sea. **47:18b** As in Greek version; Hebrew reads you will measure. **47:19** Hebrew waters of Meribath-kadesh.

48 Division of the Land

"Here is the list of the tribes of Israel and the territory each is to receive. The territory of Dan is in the extreme north. Its boundary line follows the Hethlon road to Lebo-hamath and then runs on to Hazar-enan on the border of Damascus, with Hamath to the north. Dan's territory extends all the way across the land of Israel from east to west.

2 "Asher's territory lies south of Dan's and also extends from east to west. 3 Naphtali's land lies south of Asher's, also extending from east to west. 4 Then comes Manasseh south of Naphtali, and its territory also extends from east to west. 5 South of Manasseh is Ephraim, 6 and then Reuben, 7 and then Judah, all of whose boundaries extend from east to west.

8 "South of Judah is the land set aside for a special purpose. It will be 8⅓ miles* wide and will extend as far east and west as the tribal territories, with the Temple at the center.

9 "The area set aside for the LORD's Temple will be 8⅓ miles long and 6⅔ miles wide.* 10 For the priests there will be a strip of land measuring 8⅓ miles long by 3⅓ miles wide,* with the LORD's Temple at the center. 11 This area is set aside for the ordained priests, the descendants of Zadok who served me faithfully and did not go astray with the people of Israel and the rest of the Levites. 12 It will be their special portion when the land is distributed, the most sacred land of all. Next to the priests' territory will lie the land where the other Levites will live.

13 "The land allotted to the Levites will be the same size and shape as that belonging to the priests—8⅓ miles long and 3⅓ miles wide. Together these portions of land will measure 8⅓ miles long by 6⅔ miles wide.* 14 None of this special land may ever be sold or traded or used by others, for it belongs to the LORD; it is set apart as holy.

15 "An additional strip of land 8⅓ miles long by 1⅔ miles wide,* south of the sacred Temple area, will be allotted for public use—homes, pasturelands, and common lands, with a city at the center. 16 The city will measure 1½ miles* on each side—north, south, east, and west. 17 Open lands will surround the city for 150 yards* in every direction. 18 Outside the city there will be a farming area that stretches 3⅓ miles to the east and 3⅓ miles to the west* along the border of the sacred area. This farmland will produce food for the people working in the city. 19 Those who come from the various tribes to work in the city may farm it. 20 This entire area—including the sacred lands and the city—is a square that measures 8⅓ miles* on each side.

21 "The areas that remain, to the east and to the west of the sacred lands and the city, will belong to the prince. Each of these areas will be 8⅓ miles wide, extending in opposite directions to the eastern and western borders of Israel, with the sacred lands and the sanctuary of the Temple in the center. 22 So the prince's land will include everything between the territories allotted to Judah and Benjamin, except for the areas set aside for the sacred lands and the city.

23 "These are the territories allotted to the rest of the tribes. Benjamin's territory lies just south of the prince's lands, and it extends across the entire land of Israel from east to west. 24 South of Benjamin's territory lies that of Simeon, also extending across the land from east to west. 25 Next is the territory of Issachar with the same eastern and western boundaries.

26 "Then comes the territory of Zebulun, which also extends across the land from east to west. 27 The territory of Gad is just south of Zebulun with the same borders to the east and west. 28 The southern border of Gad runs from Tamar to the waters of Meribah at Kadesh* and then follows the Brook of Egypt to the Mediterranean.*

29 "These are the allotments that will be set aside for each tribe's exclusive possession. I, the Sovereign LORD, have spoken!

48:8 Hebrew 25,000 cubits [13.3 kilometers].   **48:9** As in one Greek manuscript and the Greek reading in 45:1: 25,000 cubits [13.3 kilometers] long and 20,000 cubits [10.6 kilometers] wide; Hebrew reads 25,000 cubits long and 10,000 cubits [3¾ miles or 5.3 kilometers] wide. Similarly in 48:13b. Compare 45:1-5; 48:10-13.   **48:10** Hebrew 25,000 cubits [13.3 kilometers] long by 10,000 cubits [5.3 kilometers] wide; also in 48:13a.   **48:13** See note on 48:9.   **48:15** Hebrew 25,000 cubits [13.3 kilometers] long by 5,000 cubits [2.65 kilometers] wide.   **48:16** Hebrew 4,500 cubits [2.4 kilometers]; also in 48:30, 32, 33, 34.   **48:17** Hebrew 250 cubits [133 meters].   **48:18** Hebrew 10,000 cubits [5.3 kilometers] to the east and 10,000 cubits to the west.   **48:20** Hebrew 25,000 cubits [13.3 kilometers]; also in 48:21.   **48:28a** Hebrew waters of Meribath-kadesh.   **48:28b** Hebrew the great sea.

The Gates of the City

[30]"These will be the exits to the city: On the north wall, which is 1½ miles long, [31]there will be three gates, each one named after a tribe of Israel. The first will be named for Reuben, the second for Judah, and the third for Levi. [32]On the east wall, also 1½ miles long, the gates will be named for Joseph, Benjamin, and Dan. [33]The south wall, also 1½ miles long, will have gates named for Simeon, Issachar, and Zebulun. [34]And on the west wall, also 1½ miles long, the gates will be named for Gad, Asher, and Naphtali.

[35]"The distance around the entire city will be 6 miles.* And from that day the name of the city will be 'The LORD Is There.'*"

48:35a Hebrew *18,000 cubits* [9.6 kilometers].　　48:35b Hebrew *Yahweh Shammah*.

Introduction to

Daniel

Background

Daniel's life summarizes the exile of the people of Judah. Having been taken as a teen to Babylon nearly twenty years before the fall of Jerusalem, Daniel saw kings rise and fall throughout the decades he spent away from home. The common thread through the reigns of these non-Hebrew kings is the wisdom of Daniel, which comes from God.

   Daniel is the Greek form of a Hebrew name meaning "God is my judge." Several passages in the book point to Daniel as the author: the first-person account, starting in 7:2; and the words of 12:4: "But you, Daniel, keep this prophecy a secret; seal up the book until the time of the end." Jesus also attributed the book to Daniel (see Matthew 24:15).

Message

The Book of Daniel is a mixture of historical narrative and apocalyptic or symbolic literature. God's sovereignty is the theme of this book. While Daniel and his friends are the spoils of war and serve in the palace, God has other plans for his men. This is evident when Daniel's colleagues are saved in the midst of a "blazing furnace" (3:6) and when Daniel survives a night in the den of lions. These men are to be God's representatives—towers of faithfulness—in a permissive society. Having served as a trusted administrator through the reigns of conquerors Nebuchadnezzar, Belshazzar, and Darius, Daniel knows that ultimately God is in control. Much of the Book of Daniel recounts dreams and visions—some given to kings and some to Daniel about world kingdoms and end times.

Time

Although the books of Esther and Ezekiel precede the Book of Daniel in the Bible, some of the events of Daniel predate Ezekiel's time and certainly all of Esther's era. Daniel and his three friends, Hananiah, Mishael, and Azariah (Shadrach, Meshach, and Abednego), along with thousands of citizens of Judah, were taken captive to Babylon in 605 B.C., before the fall of Jerusalem in 586.

Outline

Daniel

1 Daniel in Nebuchadnezzar's Court

During the third year of King Jehoiakim's reign in Judah,* King Nebuchadnezzar of Babylon came to Jerusalem and besieged it. ²The Lord gave him victory over King Jehoiakim of Judah and permitted him to take some of the sacred objects from the Temple of God. So Nebuchadnezzar took them back to the land of Babylonia* and placed them in the treasure-house of his god.

³Then the king ordered Ashpenaz, his chief of staff, to bring to the palace some of the young men of Judah's royal family and other noble families, who had been brought to Babylon as captives. ⁴"Select only strong, healthy, and good-looking young men," he said. "Make sure they are well versed in every branch of learning, are gifted with knowledge and good judgment, and are suited to serve in the royal palace. Train these young men in the language and literature of Babylon.*" ⁵The king assigned them a daily ration of food and wine from his own kitchens. They were to be trained for three years, and then they would enter the royal service.

⁶Daniel, Hananiah, Mishael, and Azariah were four of the young men chosen, all from the tribe of Judah. ⁷The chief of staff renamed them with these Babylonian names:

Daniel was called Belteshazzar.
Hananiah was called Shadrach.
Mishael was called Meshach.
Azariah was called Abednego.

⁸But Daniel was determined not to defile himself by eating the food and wine given to them by the king. He asked the chief of staff for permission not to eat these unacceptable foods. ⁹Now God had given the chief of staff both respect and affection for Daniel. ¹⁰But he responded, "I am afraid of my lord the king, who has ordered that you eat this food and wine. If you become pale and thin compared to the other youths your age, I am afraid the king will have me beheaded."

¹¹Daniel spoke with the attendant who had been appointed by the chief of staff to look after Daniel, Hananiah, Mishael, and Azariah. ¹²"Please test us for ten days on a diet of vegetables and water," Daniel said. ¹³"At the end of the ten days, see how we look compared to the other young men who are eating the king's food. Then make your decision in light of what you see." ¹⁴The attendant agreed to Daniel's suggestion and tested them for ten days.

¹⁵At the end of the ten days, Daniel and his three friends looked healthier and better nourished than the young men who had been eating the food assigned by the king. ¹⁶So after that, the attendant fed them only vegetables instead of the food and wine provided for the others.

¹⁷God gave these four young men an unusual aptitude for understanding every aspect of literature and wisdom. And God gave Daniel the special ability

---

1:1 This event occurred in 605 B.C., during the third year of Jehoiakim's reign (according to the calendar system in which the new year begins in the spring). **1:2** Hebrew *the land of Shinar.* **1:4** Or *of the Chaldeans.*

Community

Life-Changing Community

DANIEL 1

reedom. It was the wonderful, overwhelming feeling I used to have when the organ postlude began, ending another week's church service. To me, nothing was worse than the stifling boredom of my church experience. It was the same every week: get up, argue with my family about going to church, arrive late, doodle on the bulletin for an hour, stand up, sit down, and then shoot out the front door dodging anyone who wanted to "visit" after the service. I put nothing in; I got nothing out. I knew no one. I was very happily a church outsider.

So no one was more surprised than me when years later, despite Sunday after Sunday of empty church attendance, I finally had a relationship with God and couldn't get enough church! How did God change my stubborn mind? While he used several influential individuals and teachable moments to cause me to commit my life to him, he brought the real change through a women's small group that I fell into.

To get me into church, all it took was one friend. She was outgoing, interesting, and we liked the same music; so I said yes when she invited me to attend a small party with her church friends. I enjoyed myself and decided to join my friend at her next small-group meeting. The next week I went back. And the week after and the week after. After a few months I couldn't imagine myself *not* attending. I realized that although I was a Christian in some sense of the word, I had lacked a connection to the body of Christ and his community, which left me feeling lonely and defeated. I'd heard about the early church described in Acts 2:42-47—those initial believers who were a tight-knit community and who thrived on service to God through aggressive kindness—but I'd never actually experienced that type of community. Although it scared and intimidated me, I knew that my heart longed for that kind of connection with other believers.

So I took the risk of "doing life together" with this small band of believers, and I found community. In that group I began to discover that God wants us to be *real* with one another. Every one of us desires to be known for who we truly are—and loved anyway. But it's a risk. In our meetings, I often experienced that "holy discomfort" when I felt the nudge to confess something deeper and darker than I'd have liked to admit. Sharing shortcomings and past mistakes was fine; I could appear humble by admitting those. But last year I was pressed to admit something to my group that brought fear to my soul. What if they judged me, shunned me, or kicked me out? I finally took the step of admitting a current, private struggle. Instead of gasping in horror at my godlessness, the others listened, prayed, and helped me understand where God was in all of this. Friendships were deepened as my group helped me navigate that tough time.

I've also discovered the value of having a place in which to ask and wrestle through honest questions. In a close-knit community, our discussions can go on divine tangents, and I've learned a lot in these discussions about theological issues and various cultural ideas. In that first small group, members of our group had different views on the theology of predestination; so instead of discussing that night's planned topic, we spent the whole evening in a rousing conversation about this complex topic. Our healthy dialogue spurred me on to do more research on the subject as I grew to solidify what I believe and why.

God has shown me that the way to truly know his heart and to live biblically is to pursue life in community. Healthy, Christ-focused community must be about more than feel-good therapy sessions or social gatherings. Consider the challenge of Micah 6:8, which describes the tasks of God's people: "The LORD has told you what is good, and this is what he requires of you: to do what is right, to love mercy, and to walk humbly with your God." These are action words, focused not on puffing ourselves up but reaching out. Practicing the discipline of community means we equip one another to engage in church ministry and local service because we're motivated by real encounters with the living God.

The vehicle God has used so many times throughout my life to fill that void of community is a group of like-minded people simply doing life together. Spiritual and physical needs can be met, which equip us to go out and share the gospel message with others. This is how the body of Christ is supposed to operate.

—*Hollie Baker-Lutz*

For more on community, see reading at Acts 2:42–47.

to interpret the meanings of visions and dreams.

¹⁸When the training period ordered by the king was completed, the chief of staff brought all the young men to King Nebuchadnezzar. ¹⁹The king talked with them, and no one impressed him as much as Daniel, Hananiah, Mishael, and Azariah. So they entered the royal service. ²⁰Whenever the king consulted them in any matter requiring wisdom and balanced judgment, he found them ten times more capable than any of the magicians and enchanters in his entire kingdom.

²¹Daniel remained in the royal service until the first year of the reign of King Cyrus.*

2 Nebuchadnezzar's Dream

One night during the second year of his reign,* Nebuchadnezzar had such disturbing dreams that he couldn't sleep. ²He called in his magicians, enchanters, sorcerers, and astrologers,* and he demanded that they tell him what he had dreamed. As they stood before the king, ³he said, "I have had a dream that deeply troubles me, and I must know what it means."

⁴Then the astrologers answered the king in Aramaic,* "Long live the king! Tell us the dream, and we will tell you what it means."

⁵But the king said to the astrologers, "I am serious about this. If you don't tell me what my dream was and what it means, you will be torn limb from limb, and your houses will be turned into heaps of rubble! ⁶But if you tell me what I dreamed and what the dream means, I will give you many wonderful gifts and honors. Just tell me the dream and what it means!"

⁷They said again, "Please, Your Majesty. Tell us the dream, and we will tell you what it means."

⁸The king replied, "I know what you are doing! You're stalling for time because you know I am serious when I say, ⁹'If you don't tell me the dream, you are doomed.' So you have conspired to tell me lies, hoping I will change my mind. But tell me the dream, and then I'll know that you can tell me what it means."

¹⁰The astrologers replied to the king, "No one on earth can tell the king his dream! And no king, however great and powerful, has ever asked such a thing of any magician, enchanter, or astrologer! ¹¹The king's demand is impossible. No one except the gods can tell you your dream, and they do not live here among people."

¹²The king was furious when he heard this, and he ordered that all the wise men of Babylon be executed. ¹³And because of the king's decree, men were sent to find and kill Daniel and his friends.

¹⁴When Arioch, the commander of the king's guard, came to kill them, Daniel handled the situation with wisdom and discretion. ¹⁵He asked Arioch, "Why has the king issued such a harsh decree?" So Arioch told him all that had happened. ¹⁶Daniel went at once to see the king and requested more time to tell the king what the dream meant.

¹⁷Then Daniel went home and told his friends Hananiah, Mishael, and Azariah what had happened. ¹⁸He urged them to ask the God of heaven to show them his mercy by telling them the secret, so they would not be executed along with the other wise men of Babylon. ¹⁹That night the secret was revealed to Daniel in a vision. Then Daniel praised the God of heaven. ²⁰He said,

"Praise the name of God forever and
        ever,
    for he has all wisdom and power.
²¹ He controls the course of world events;
    he removes kings and sets up other
        kings.
He gives wisdom to the wise
    and knowledge to the scholars.
²² He reveals deep and mysterious things
    and knows what lies hidden in
        darkness,
    though he is surrounded by light.
²³ I thank and praise you, God of my
        ancestors,
    for you have given me wisdom and
        strength.
You have told me what we asked of you
    and revealed to us what the king
        demanded."

1:21 Cyrus began his reign (over Babylon) in 539 B.C.   2:1 The second year of Nebuchadnezzar's reign was 603 B.C.   2:2 Or Chaldeans; also in 2:4, 5, 10.   2:4 The original text from this point through chapter 7 is in Aramaic.

Daniel Interprets the Dream

24 Then Daniel went in to see Arioch, whom the king had ordered to execute the wise men of Babylon. Daniel said to him, "Don't kill the wise men. Take me to the king, and I will tell him the meaning of his dream."

25 Arioch quickly took Daniel to the king and said, "I have found one of the captives from Judah who will tell the king the meaning of his dream!"

26 The king said to Daniel (also known as Belteshazzar), "Is this true? Can you tell me what my dream was and what it means?"

27 Daniel replied, "There are no wise men, enchanters, magicians, or fortune-tellers who can reveal the king's secret. 28 But there is a God in heaven who reveals secrets, and he has shown King Nebuchadnezzar what will happen in the future. Now I will tell you your dream and the visions you saw as you lay on your bed.

29 "While Your Majesty was sleeping, you dreamed about coming events. He who reveals secrets has shown you what is going to happen. 30 And it is not because I am wiser than anyone else that I know the secret of your dream, but because God wants you to understand what was in your heart.

31 "In your vision, Your Majesty, you saw standing before you a huge, shining statue of a man. It was a frightening sight. 32 The head of the statue was made of fine gold. Its chest and arms were silver, its belly and thighs were bronze, 33 its legs were iron, and its feet were a combination of iron and baked clay. 34 As you watched, a rock was cut from a mountain, but not by human hands. It struck the feet of iron and clay, smashing them to bits. 35 The whole statue was crushed into small pieces of iron, clay, bronze, silver, and gold. Then the wind blew them away without a trace, like chaff on a threshing floor. But the rock that knocked the statue down became a great mountain that covered the whole earth.

36 "That was the dream. Now we will tell the king what it means. 37 Your Majesty, you are the greatest of kings. The God of heaven has given you sovereignty, power, strength, and honor. 38 He has made you the ruler over all the inhabited world and has put even the wild animals and birds under your control. You are the head of gold.

39 "But after your kingdom comes to an end, another kingdom, inferior to yours, will rise to take your place. After that kingdom has fallen, yet a third kingdom, represented by bronze, will rise to rule the world. 40 Following that kingdom, there will be a fourth one, as strong as iron. That kingdom will smash and crush all previous empires, just as iron smashes and crushes everything it strikes. 41 The feet and toes you saw were a combination of iron and baked clay, showing that this kingdom will be divided. Like iron mixed with clay, it will have some of the strength of iron. 42 But while some parts of it will be as strong as iron, other parts will be as weak as clay. 43 This mixture of iron and clay also shows that these kingdoms will try to strengthen themselves by forming alliances with each other through intermarriage. But they will not hold together, just as iron and clay do not mix.

44 "During the reigns of those kings, the God of heaven will set up a kingdom that will never be destroyed or conquered. It will crush all these kingdoms into nothingness, and it will stand forever. 45 That is the meaning of the rock cut from the mountain, though not by human hands, that crushed to pieces the statue of iron, bronze, clay, silver, and gold. The great God was showing the king what will happen in the future. The dream is true, and its meaning is certain."

Nebuchadnezzar Rewards Daniel

46 Then King Nebuchadnezzar threw himself down before Daniel and worshiped him, and he commanded his people to offer sacrifices and burn sweet incense before him. 47 The king said to Daniel, "Truly, your God is the greatest of gods, the Lord over kings, a revealer of mysteries, for you have been able to reveal this secret."

48 Then the king appointed Daniel to a high position and gave him many valuable gifts. He made Daniel ruler over the whole province of Babylon, as well as chief over all his wise men. 49 At Daniel's request, the king appointed Shadrach, Meshach, and Abednego to be in charge of all the affairs of the province of Babylon, while Daniel remained in the king's court.

3 Nebuchadnezzar's Gold Statue

King Nebuchadnezzar made a gold statue ninety feet tall and nine feet wide* and set it up on the plain of Dura in the province of Babylon. [2] Then he sent messages to the high officers, officials, governors, advisers, treasurers, judges, magistrates, and all the provincial officials to come to the dedication of the statue he had set up. [3] So all these officials* came and stood before the statue King Nebuchadnezzar had set up.

[4] Then a herald shouted out, "People of all races and nations and languages, listen to the king's command! [5] When you hear the sound of the horn, flute, zither, lyre, harp, pipes, and other musical instruments,* bow to the ground to worship King Nebuchadnezzar's gold statue. [6] Anyone who refuses to obey will immediately be thrown into a blazing furnace."

[7] So at the sound of the musical instruments,* all the people, whatever their race or nation or language, bowed to the ground and worshiped the gold statue that King Nebuchadnezzar had set up.

[8] But some of the astrologers* went to the king and informed on the Jews. [9] They said to King Nebuchadnezzar, "Long live the king! [10] You issued a decree requiring all the people to bow down and worship the gold statue when they hear the sound of the horn, flute, zither, lyre, harp, pipes, and other musical instruments. [11] That decree also states that those who refuse to obey must be thrown into a blazing furnace. [12] But there are some Jews—Shadrach, Meshach, and Abednego—whom you have put in charge of the province of Babylon. They pay no attention to you, Your Majesty. They refuse to serve your gods and do not worship the gold statue you have set up."

[13] Then Nebuchadnezzar flew into a rage and ordered that Shadrach, Meshach, and Abednego be brought before him. When they were brought in, [14] Nebuchadnezzar said to them, "Is it true, Shadrach, Meshach, and Abednego, that you refuse to serve my gods or to worship the gold statue I have set up? [15] I will give you one more chance to bow down and worship the statue I have made when you hear the sound of the musical instruments.* But if you refuse, you will be thrown immediately into the blazing furnace. And then what god will be able to rescue you from my power?"

[16] Shadrach, Meshach, and Abednego replied, "O Nebuchadnezzar, we do not need to defend ourselves before you. [17] If we are thrown into the blazing furnace, the God whom we serve is able to save us. He will rescue us from your power, Your Majesty. [18] But even if he doesn't, we want to make it clear to you, Your Majesty, that we will never serve your gods or worship the gold statue you have set up."

The Blazing Furnace

[19] Nebuchadnezzar was so furious with Shadrach, Meshach, and Abednego that his face became distorted with rage. He commanded that the furnace be heated seven times hotter than usual. [20] Then he ordered some of the strongest men of his army to bind Shadrach, Meshach, and Abednego and throw them into the blazing furnace. [21] So they tied them up and threw them into the furnace, fully dressed in their pants, turbans, robes, and other garments. [22] And because the king, in his anger, had demanded such a hot fire in the furnace, the flames killed the soldiers as they threw the three men in. [23] So Shadrach, Meshach, and Abednego, securely tied, fell into the roaring flames.

[24] But suddenly, Nebuchadnezzar jumped up in amazement and exclaimed to his advisers, "Didn't we tie up three men and throw them into the furnace?"

"Yes, Your Majesty, we certainly did," they replied.

[25] "Look!" Nebuchadnezzar shouted. "I see four men, unbound, walking around in the fire unharmed! And the fourth looks like a god*!"

[26] Then Nebuchadnezzar came as close as he could to the door of the flaming furnace and shouted: "Shadrach, Meshach, and

---

3:1 Aramaic 60 cubits [27 meters] tall and 6 cubits [2.7 meters] wide.   **3:3** Aramaic the high officers, officials, governors, advisers, treasurers, judges, magistrates, and all the provincial officials.   **3:5** The identification of some of these musical instruments is uncertain.   **3:7** Aramaic the horn, flute, zither, lyre, harp, and other musical instruments.   **3:8** Aramaic Chaldeans.   **3:15** Aramaic the horn, flute, zither, lyre, harp, pipes, and other musical instruments.   **3:25** Aramaic like a son of the gods.

Abednego, servants of the Most High God, come out! Come here!"

So Shadrach, Meshach, and Abednego stepped out of the fire. ²⁷ Then the high officers, officials, governors, and advisers crowded around them and saw that the fire had not touched them. Not a hair on their heads was singed, and their clothing was not scorched. They didn't even smell of smoke!

²⁸ Then Nebuchadnezzar said, "Praise to the God of Shadrach, Meshach, and Abednego! He sent his angel to rescue his servants who trusted in him. They defied the king's command and were willing to die rather than serve or worship any god except their own God. ²⁹ Therefore, I make this decree: If any people, whatever their race or nation or language, speak a word against the God of Shadrach, Meshach, and Abednego, they will be torn limb from limb, and their houses will be turned into heaps of rubble. There is no other god who can rescue like this!"

³⁰ Then the king promoted Shadrach, Meshach, and Abednego to even higher positions in the province of Babylon.

4 Nebuchadnezzar's Dream about a Tree

¹ *King Nebuchadnezzar sent this message to the people of every race and nation and language throughout the world:

"Peace and prosperity to you!

² "I want you all to know about the miraculous signs and wonders the Most High God has performed for me.

³ How great are his signs,
   how powerful his wonders!
His kingdom will last forever,
   his rule through all generations.

⁴ *"I, Nebuchadnezzar, was living in my palace in comfort and prosperity. ⁵ But one night I had a dream that frightened me; I saw visions that terrified me as I lay in my bed. ⁶ So I issued an order calling in all the wise men of Babylon, so they could tell me what my dream meant. ⁷ When all the magicians, enchanters, astrologers,* and fortune-tellers came in, I told them the dream, but they could not tell me what it meant. ⁸ At last Daniel came in before me, and I told him the dream. (He was named Belteshazzar after my god, and the spirit of the holy gods is in him.)

⁹ "I said to him, 'Belteshazzar, chief of the magicians, I know that the spirit of the holy gods is in you and that no mystery is too great for you to solve. Now tell me what my dream means.

¹⁰ "'While I was lying in my bed, this is what I dreamed. I saw a large tree in the middle of the earth. ¹¹ The tree grew very tall and strong, reaching high into the heavens for all the world to see. ¹² It had fresh green leaves, and it was loaded with fruit for all to eat. Wild animals lived in its shade, and birds nested in its branches. All the world was fed from this tree.

¹³ "'Then as I lay there dreaming, I saw a messenger,* a holy one, coming down from heaven. ¹⁴ The messenger shouted,

"Cut down the tree and lop off its
   branches!
Shake off its leaves and scatter its
   fruit!
Chase the wild animals from its shade
   and the birds from its branches.
¹⁵ But leave the stump and the roots in
   the ground,
   bound with a band of iron and
   bronze
   and surrounded by tender grass.
Now let him be drenched with the
   dew of heaven,
   and let him live with the wild
   animals among the plants of the
   field.
¹⁶ For seven periods of time,
   let him have the mind of a wild
   animal
   instead of the mind of a human.
¹⁷ For this has been decreed by the
   messengers*;
   it is commanded by the holy ones,
so that everyone may know
   that the Most High rules over the
   kingdoms of the world.

4:1 Verses 4:1-3 are numbered 3:31-33 in Aramaic text.   4:4 Verses 4:4-37 are numbered 4:1-34 in Aramaic text.   4:7 Or *Chaldeans.*
4:13 Aramaic *a watcher;* also in 4:23.   4:17 Aramaic *the watchers.*

He gives them to anyone he chooses—
even to the lowliest of people."

¹⁸"'Belteshazzar, that was the dream that I, King Nebuchadnezzar, had. Now tell me what it means, for none of the wise men of my kingdom can do so. But you can tell me because the spirit of the holy gods is in you.'

Daniel Explains the Dream

¹⁹"Upon hearing this, Daniel (also known as Belteshazzar) was overcome for a time, frightened by the meaning of the dream. Then the king said to him, 'Belteshazzar, don't be alarmed by the dream and what it means.'

"Belteshazzar replied, 'I wish the events foreshadowed in this dream would happen to your enemies, my lord, and not to you! ²⁰The tree you saw was growing very tall and strong, reaching high into the heavens for all the world to see. ²¹It had fresh green leaves and was loaded with fruit for all to eat. Wild animals lived in its shade, and birds nested in its branches. ²²That tree, Your Majesty, is you. For you have grown strong and great; your greatness reaches up to heaven, and your rule to the ends of the earth.

²³"'Then you saw a messenger, a holy one, coming down from heaven and saying, "Cut down the tree and destroy it. But leave the stump and the roots in the ground, bound with a band of iron and bronze and surrounded by tender grass. Let him be drenched with the dew of heaven. Let him live with the animals of the field for seven periods of time."

²⁴"'This is what the dream means, Your Majesty, and what the Most High has declared will happen to my lord the king. ²⁵You will be driven from human society, and you will live in the fields with the wild animals. You will eat grass like a cow, and you will be drenched with the dew of heaven. Seven periods of time will pass while you live this way, until you learn that the Most High rules over the kingdoms of the world and gives them to anyone he chooses. ²⁶But the stump and roots of the tree were left

in the ground. This means that you will receive your kingdom back again when you have learned that heaven rules.

²⁷"'King Nebuchadnezzar, please accept my advice. Stop sinning and do what is right. Break from your wicked past and be merciful to the poor. Perhaps then you will continue to prosper.'

The Dream's Fulfillment

²⁸"But all these things did happen to King Nebuchadnezzar. ²⁹Twelve months later he was taking a walk on the flat roof of the royal palace in Babylon. ³⁰As he looked out across the city, he said, 'Look at this great city of Babylon! By my own mighty power, I have built this beautiful city as my royal residence to display my majestic splendor.'

³¹"While these words were still in his mouth, a voice called down from heaven, 'O King Nebuchadnezzar, this message is for you! You are no longer ruler of this kingdom. ³²You will be driven from human society. You will live in the fields with the wild animals, and you will eat grass like a cow. Seven periods of time will pass while you live this way, until you learn that the Most High rules over the kingdoms of the world and gives them to anyone he chooses.'

³³"That same hour the judgment was fulfilled, and Nebuchadnezzar was driven from human society. He ate grass like a cow, and he was drenched with the dew of heaven. He lived this way until his hair was as long as eagles' feathers and his nails were like birds' claws.

Nebuchadnezzar Praises God

³⁴"After this time had passed, I, Nebuchadnezzar, looked up to heaven. My sanity returned, and I praised and worshiped the Most High and honored the one who lives forever.

His rule is everlasting,
    and his kingdom is eternal.
³⁵ All the people of the earth
    are nothing compared to him.
He does as he pleases
    among the angels of heaven
    and among the people of the earth.

Trusting God's Blueprint
DANIEL 4:34-37

In high school I took pride in my ability to play chess. I studied techniques, won most of my matches, and then put the game aside for twenty years. Then I met a truly fine chess player who had been perfecting his skills long after high school.

When we played a few matches, I learned what it is like to play against a master. Although I had complete freedom to make any move I wished, I soon reached the conclusion that none of my strategies mattered much. His superior skill guaranteed that my purposes inevitably ended up serving his own.

Perhaps God engages our universe, his own creation, in much the same way. Consider what the humbled Nebuchadnezzar declared: "All the people of the earth are nothing compared to him. He does as he pleases. . . . No one can stop him" (Daniel 4:35). And listen to how God describes himself: "Only I can tell you the future before it even happens. Everything I plan will come to pass, for I do whatever I wish" (Isaiah 46:10). Like a master player in a chess match, God grants us freedom to rebel against the original design, but even as we do so we end up ironically serving his eventual goal of restoration.

If I accept that blueprint, it transforms how I view both good and bad things that happen. Good things, such as health, talent, and money, I can present to God as offerings to serve his purposes. And bad things too—disability, poverty, family dysfunction, failures—can be redeemed as the instruments that drive me to God.

A skeptic might accuse me of flagrant rationalization, arguing backwards to make evidence fit a prior conclusion. Yes, exactly. A Christian begins with the conclusion that a good God will restore creation to its original design and sees all history as proceeding toward that end. When a Grand Master plays a chess amateur, victory is assured no matter how the board may look at any given moment. In a miracle of grace, even our personal failures can become tools in God's hands.

—Philip Yancey

For more on faith, see reading at Habakkuk 1:2-4.

No one can stop him or say to him,
'What do you mean by doing these
   things?'

[36] "When my sanity returned to me, so did my honor and glory and kingdom. My advisers and nobles sought me out, and I was restored as head of my kingdom, with even greater honor than before.

[37] "Now I, Nebuchadnezzar, praise and glorify and honor the King of heaven. All his acts are just and true, and he is able to humble the proud."

5 The Writing on the Wall
Many years later King Belshazzar gave a great feast for 1,000 of his nobles, and he drank wine with them. [2] While Belshazzar was drinking the wine, he gave orders to bring in the gold and silver cups that his predecessor,* Nebuchadnezzar, had

5:2 Aramaic *father*; also in 5:11, 13, 18.

taken from the Temple in Jerusalem. He wanted to drink from them with his nobles, his wives, and his concubines. ³So they brought these gold cups taken from the Temple, the house of God in Jerusalem, and the king and his nobles, his wives, and his concubines drank from them. ⁴While they drank from them they praised their idols made of gold, silver, bronze, iron, wood, and stone.

⁵Suddenly, they saw the fingers of a human hand writing on the plaster wall of the king's palace, near the lampstand. The king himself saw the hand as it wrote, ⁶and his face turned pale with fright. His knees knocked together in fear and his legs gave way beneath him.

⁷The king shouted for the enchanters, astrologers,* and fortune-tellers to be brought before him. He said to these wise men of Babylon, "Whoever can read this writing and tell me what it means will be dressed in purple robes of royal honor and will have a gold chain placed around his neck. He will become the third highest ruler in the kingdom!"

⁸But when all the king's wise men had come in, none of them could read the writing or tell him what it meant. ⁹So the king grew even more alarmed, and his face turned pale. His nobles, too, were shaken.

¹⁰But when the queen mother heard what was happening, she hurried to the banquet hall. She said to Belshazzar, "Long live the king! Don't be so pale and frightened. ¹¹There is a man in your kingdom who has within him the spirit of the holy gods. During Nebuchadnezzar's reign, this man was found to have insight, understanding, and wisdom like that of the gods. Your predecessor, the king—your predecessor King Nebuchadnezzar—made him chief over all the magicians, enchanters, astrologers, and fortune-tellers of Babylon. ¹²This man Daniel, whom the king named Belteshazzar, has exceptional ability and is filled with divine knowledge and understanding. He can interpret dreams, explain riddles, and solve difficult problems. Call for Daniel, and he will tell you what the writing means."

Daniel Explains the Writing

¹³So Daniel was brought in before the king. The king asked him, "Are you Daniel, one of the exiles brought from Judah by my predecessor, King Nebuchadnezzar? ¹⁴I have heard that you have the spirit of the gods within you and that you are filled with insight, understanding, and wisdom. ¹⁵My wise men and enchanters have tried to read the words on the wall and tell me their meaning, but they cannot do it. ¹⁶I am told that you can give interpretations and solve difficult problems. If you can read these words and tell me their meaning, you will be clothed in purple robes of royal honor, and you will have a gold chain placed around your neck. You will become the third highest ruler in the kingdom."

¹⁷Daniel answered the king, "Keep your gifts or give them to someone else, but I will tell you what the writing means. ¹⁸Your Majesty, the Most High God gave sovereignty, majesty, glory, and honor to your predecessor, Nebuchadnezzar. ¹⁹He made him so great that people of all races and nations and languages trembled before him in fear. He killed those he wanted to kill and spared those he wanted to spare. He honored those he wanted to honor and disgraced those he wanted to disgrace. ²⁰But when his heart and mind were puffed up with arrogance, he was brought down from his royal throne and stripped of his glory. ²¹He was driven from human society. He was given the mind of a wild animal, and he lived among the wild donkeys. He ate grass like a cow, and he was drenched with the dew of heaven, until he learned that the Most High God rules over the kingdoms of the world and appoints anyone he desires to rule over them.

²²"You are his successor,* O Belshazzar, and you knew all this, yet you have not humbled yourself. ²³For you have proudly defied the Lord of heaven and have had these cups from his Temple brought before you. You and your nobles and your wives and concubines have been drinking wine from them while praising gods of silver, gold, bronze, iron, wood, and stone—gods that neither see nor hear nor know any-

5:7 Or *Chaldeans;* also in 5:11.   5:22 Aramaic *son.*

thing at all. But you have not honored the God who gives you the breath of life and controls your destiny! ²⁴So God has sent this hand to write this message.

²⁵"This is the message that was written: MENE, MENE, TEKEL, and PARSIN. ²⁶This is what these words mean:

Mene means 'numbered'—God has numbered the days of your reign and has brought it to an end.
²⁷ Tekel means 'weighed'—you have been weighed on the balances and have not measured up.
²⁸ Parsin* means 'divided'—your kingdom has been divided and given to the Medes and Persians."

²⁹Then at Belshazzar's command, Daniel was dressed in purple robes, a gold chain was hung around his neck, and he was proclaimed the third highest ruler in the kingdom. ³⁰That very night Belshazzar, the Babylonian* king, was killed.*

³¹*And Darius the Mede took over the kingdom at the age of sixty-two.

6 Daniel in the Lions' Den

¹*Darius the Mede decided to divide the kingdom into 120 provinces, and he appointed a high officer to rule over each province. ²The king also chose Daniel and two others as administrators to supervise the high officers and protect the king's interests. ³Daniel soon proved himself more capable than all the other administrators and high officers. Because of Daniel's great ability, the king made plans to place him over the entire empire.

⁴Then the other administrators and high officers began searching for some fault in the way Daniel was handling government affairs, but they couldn't find anything to criticize or condemn. He was faithful, always responsible, and completely trustworthy. ⁵So they concluded, "Our only chance of finding grounds for accusing Daniel will be in connection with the rules of his religion."

⁶So the administrators and high officers went to the king and said, "Long live King Darius! ⁷We are all in agreement— we administrators, officials, high officers, advisers, and governors—that the king should make a law that will be strictly enforced. Give orders that for the next thirty days any person who prays to anyone, divine or human—except to you, Your Majesty—will be thrown into the den of lions. ⁸And now, Your Majesty, issue and sign this law so it cannot be changed, an official law of the Medes and Persians that cannot be revoked." ⁹So King Darius signed the law.

¹⁰But when Daniel learned that the law had been signed, he went home and knelt down as usual in his upstairs room, with its windows open toward Jerusalem. He prayed three times a day, just as he had always done, giving thanks to his God. ¹¹Then the officials went together to Daniel's house and found him praying and asking for God's help. ¹²So they went straight to the king and reminded him about his law. "Did you not sign a law that for the next thirty days any person who prays to anyone, divine or human—except to you, Your Majesty—will be thrown into the den of lions?"

"Yes," the king replied, "that decision stands; it is an official law of the Medes and Persians that cannot be revoked."

¹³Then they told the king, "That man Daniel, one of the captives from Judah, is ignoring you and your law. He still prays to his God three times a day."

¹⁴Hearing this, the king was deeply troubled, and he tried to think of a way to save Daniel. He spent the rest of the day looking for a way to get Daniel out of this predicament.

¹⁵In the evening the men went together to the king and said, "Your Majesty, you know that according to the law of the Medes and the Persians, no law that the king signs can be changed."

¹⁶So at last the king gave orders for Daniel to be arrested and thrown into the den of lions. The king said to him, "May your God, whom you serve so faithfully, rescue you."

¹⁷A stone was brought and placed over the mouth of the den. The king sealed the stone with his own royal seal and the seals

of his nobles, so that no one could rescue Daniel. ¹⁸Then the king returned to his palace and spent the night fasting. He refused his usual entertainment and couldn't sleep at all that night.

¹⁹Very early the next morning, the king got up and hurried out to the lions' den. ²⁰When he got there, he called out in anguish, "Daniel, servant of the living God! Was your God, whom you serve so faithfully, able to rescue you from the lions?"

²¹Daniel answered, "Long live the king! ²²My God sent his angel to shut the lions' mouths so that they would not hurt me, for I have been found innocent in his sight. And I have not wronged you, Your Majesty."

²³The king was overjoyed and ordered that Daniel be lifted from the den. Not a scratch was found on him, for he had trusted in his God.

²⁴Then the king gave orders to arrest the men who had maliciously accused Daniel. He had them thrown into the lions' den, along with their wives and children. The lions leaped on them and tore them apart before they even hit the floor of the den.

²⁵Then King Darius sent this message to the people of every race and nation and language throughout the world:

"Peace and prosperity to you!

²⁶"I decree that everyone throughout my kingdom should tremble with fear before the God of Daniel.

For he is the living God,
and he will endure forever.
His kingdom will never be destroyed,
and his rule will never end.
²⁷ He rescues and saves his people;
he performs miraculous signs and
wonders
in the heavens and on earth.
He has rescued Daniel
from the power of the lions."

²⁸So Daniel prospered during the reign of Darius and the reign of Cyrus the Persian.*

7 Daniel's Vision of Four Beasts

Earlier, during the first year of King Belshazzar's reign in Babylon,* Daniel had a dream and saw visions as he lay in his bed. He wrote down the dream, and this is what he saw.

²In my vision that night, I, Daniel, saw a great storm churning the surface of a great sea, with strong winds blowing from every direction. ³Then four huge beasts came up out of the water, each different from the others.

⁴The first beast was like a lion with eagles' wings. As I watched, its wings were pulled off, and it was left standing with its two hind feet on the ground, like a human being. And it was given a human mind.

⁵Then I saw a second beast, and it looked like a bear. It was rearing up on one side, and it had three ribs in its mouth between its teeth. And I heard a voice saying to it, "Get up! Devour the flesh of many people!"

⁶Then the third of these strange beasts appeared, and it looked like a leopard. It had four bird's wings on its back, and it had four heads. Great authority was given to this beast.

⁷Then in my vision that night, I saw a fourth beast—terrifying, dreadful, and very strong. It devoured and crushed its victims with huge iron teeth and trampled their remains beneath its feet. It was different from any of the other beasts, and it had ten horns.

⁸As I was looking at the horns, suddenly another small horn appeared among them. Three of the first horns were torn out by the roots to make room for it. This little horn had eyes like human eyes and a mouth that was boasting arrogantly.

⁹ I watched as thrones were put in place
and the Ancient One* sat down to
judge.
His clothing was as white as snow,
his hair like purest wool.
He sat on a fiery throne
with wheels of blazing fire,
¹⁰ and a river of fire was pouring out,
flowing from his presence.
Millions of angels ministered to him;
many millions stood to attend him.
Then the court began its session,
and the books were opened.

6:28 Or *of Darius, that is, the reign of Cyrus the Persian.* **7:1** The first year of Belshazzar's reign (who was co-regent with his father, Nabonidus) was 556 B.C. (or perhaps as late as 553 B.C.). **7:9** Aramaic *an Ancient of Days;* also in 7:13, 22.

¹¹I continued to watch because I could hear the little horn's boastful speech. I kept watching until the fourth beast was killed and its body was destroyed by fire. ¹²The other three beasts had their authority taken from them, but they were allowed to live a while longer.*

¹³As my vision continued that night, I saw someone like a son of man* coming with the clouds of heaven. He approached the Ancient One and was led into his presence. ¹⁴He was given authority, honor, and sovereignty over all the nations of the world, so that people of every race and nation and language would obey him. His rule is eternal—it will never end. His kingdom will never be destroyed.

The Vision Is Explained

¹⁵I, Daniel, was troubled by all I had seen, and my visions terrified me. ¹⁶So I approached one of those standing beside the throne and asked him what it all meant. He explained it to me like this: ¹⁷"These four huge beasts represent four kingdoms that will arise from the earth. ¹⁸But in the end, the holy people of the Most High will be given the kingdom, and they will rule forever and ever."

¹⁹Then I wanted to know the true meaning of the fourth beast, the one so different from the others and so terrifying. It had devoured and crushed its victims with iron teeth and bronze claws, trampling their remains beneath its feet. ²⁰I also asked about the ten horns on the fourth beast's head and the little horn that came up afterward and destroyed three of the other horns. This horn had seemed greater than the others, and it had human eyes and a mouth that was boasting arrogantly. ²¹As I watched, this horn was waging war against God's holy people and was defeating them, ²²until the Ancient One—the Most High—came and judged in favor of his holy people. Then the time arrived for the holy people to take over the kingdom.

²³Then he said to me, "This fourth beast is the fourth world power that will rule the earth. It will be different from all the others. It will devour the whole world, tram-pling and crushing everything in its path. ²⁴Its ten horns are ten kings who will rule that empire. Then another king will arise, different from the other ten, who will subdue three of them. ²⁵He will defy the Most High and oppress the holy people of the Most High. He will try to change their sacred festivals and laws, and they will be placed under his control for a time, times, and half a time.

²⁶"But then the court will pass judgment, and all his power will be taken away and completely destroyed. ²⁷Then the sovereignty, power, and greatness of all the kingdoms under heaven will be given to the holy people of the Most High. His kingdom will last forever, and all rulers will serve and obey him."

²⁸That was the end of the vision. I, Daniel, was terrified by my thoughts and my face was pale with fear, but I kept these things to myself.

8 Daniel's Vision of a Ram and Goat

¹*During the third year of King Belshazzar's reign, I, Daniel, saw another vision, following the one that had already appeared to me. ²In this vision I was at the fortress of Susa, in the province of Elam, standing beside the Ulai River.*

³As I looked up, I saw a ram with two long horns standing beside the river.* One of the horns was longer than the other, even though it had grown later than the other one. ⁴The ram butted everything out of his way to the west, to the north, and to the south, and no one could stand against him or help his victims. He did as he pleased and became very great.

⁵While I was watching, suddenly a male goat appeared from the west, crossing the land so swiftly that he didn't even touch the ground. This goat, which had one very large horn between its eyes, ⁶headed toward the two-horned ram that I had seen standing beside the river, rushing at him in a rage. ⁷The goat charged furiously at the ram and struck him, breaking off both his horns. Now the ram was helpless, and the goat knocked him down and trampled him. No one could rescue the ram from the goat's power.

7:12 Aramaic *for a season and a time.*　**7:13** Or *like a Son of Man.*　**8:1** The original text from this point through chapter 12 is in Hebrew. See note at 2:4.　**8:2** Or *the Ulai Gate;* also in 8:16.　**8:3** Or *the gate;* also in 8:6.

⁸The goat became very powerful. But at the height of his power, his large horn was broken off. In the large horn's place grew four prominent horns pointing in the four directions of the earth. ⁹Then from one of the prominent horns came a small horn whose power grew very great. It extended toward the south and the east and toward the glorious land of Israel. ¹⁰Its power reached to the heavens, where it attacked the heavenly army, throwing some of the heavenly beings and some of the stars to the ground and trampling them. ¹¹It even challenged the Commander of heaven's army by canceling the daily sacrifices offered to him and by destroying his Temple. ¹²The army of heaven was restrained from responding to this rebellion. So the daily sacrifice was halted, and truth was overthrown. The horn succeeded in everything it did.*

¹³Then I heard two holy ones talking to each other. One of them asked, "How long will the events of this vision last? How long will the rebellion that causes desecration stop the daily sacrifices? How long will the Temple and heaven's army be trampled on?"

¹⁴The other replied, "It will take 2,300 evenings and mornings; then the Temple will be made right again."

Gabriel Explains the Vision

¹⁵As I, Daniel, was trying to understand the meaning of this vision, someone who looked like a man stood in front of me. ¹⁶And I heard a human voice calling out from the Ulai River, "Gabriel, tell this man the meaning of his vision."

¹⁷As Gabriel approached the place where I was standing, I became so terrified that I fell with my face to the ground. "Son of man," he said, "you must understand that the events you have seen in your vision relate to the time of the end."

¹⁸While he was speaking, I fainted and lay there with my face to the ground. But Gabriel roused me with a touch and helped me to my feet. ¹⁹Then he said, "I am here to tell you what will happen later in the time of wrath. What you have seen pertains to the very end of time. ²⁰The two-horned ram represents the

kings of Media and Persia. ²¹The shaggy male goat represents the king of Greece,* and the large horn between his eyes represents the first king of the Greek Empire. ²²The four prominent horns that replaced the one large horn show that the Greek Empire will break into four kingdoms, but none as great as the first.

²³"At the end of their rule, when their sin is at its height, a fierce king, a master of intrigue, will rise to power. ²⁴He will become very strong, but not by his own power. He will cause a shocking amount of destruction and succeed in everything he does. He will destroy powerful leaders and devastate the holy people. ²⁵He will be a master of deception and will become arrogant; he will destroy many without warning. He will even take on the Prince of princes in battle, but he will be broken, though not by human power.

²⁶"This vision about the 2,300 evenings and mornings* is true. But none of these things will happen for a long time, so keep this vision a secret."

²⁷Then I, Daniel, was overcome and lay sick for several days. Afterward I got up and performed my duties for the king, but I was greatly troubled by the vision and could not understand it.

9 Daniel's Prayer for His People

It was the first year of the reign of Darius the Mede, the son of Ahasuerus, who became king of the Babylonians.* ²During the first year of his reign, I, Daniel, learned from reading the word of the LORD, as revealed to Jeremiah the prophet, that Jerusalem must lie desolate for seventy years.* ³So I turned to the Lord God and pleaded with him in prayer and fasting. I also wore rough burlap and sprinkled myself with ashes.

⁴I prayed to the LORD my God and confessed:

"O Lord, you are a great and awesome God! You always fulfill your covenant and keep your promises of unfailing love to those who love you and obey your commands. ⁵But we have sinned and done wrong. We have rebelled against

---

8:11-12 The meaning of the Hebrew for these verses is uncertain. 8:21 Hebrew of Javan. 8:26 Hebrew about the evenings and mornings; compare 8:14. 9:1 Or the Chaldeans. 9:2 See Jer 25:11-12; 29:10.

you and scorned your commands and regulations. [6]We have refused to listen to your servants the prophets, who spoke on your authority to our kings and princes and ancestors and to all the people of the land.

[7]"Lord, you are in the right; but as you see, our faces are covered with shame. This is true of all of us, including the people of Judah and Jerusalem and all Israel, scattered near and far, wherever you have driven us because of our disloyalty to you. [8]O LORD, we and our kings, princes, and ancestors are covered with shame because we have sinned against you. [9]But the Lord our God is merciful and forgiving, even though we have rebelled against him. [10]We have not obeyed the LORD our God, for we have not followed the instructions he gave us through his servants the prophets. [11]All Israel has disobeyed your instruction and turned away, refusing to listen to your voice.

"So now the solemn curses and judgments written in the Law of Moses, the servant of God, have been poured down on us because of our sin. [12]You have kept your word and done to us and our rulers exactly as you warned. Never has there been such a disaster as happened in Jerusalem. [13]Every curse written against us in the Law of Moses has come true. Yet we have refused to seek mercy from the LORD our God by turning from our sins and recognizing his truth. [14]Therefore, the LORD has brought upon us the disaster he prepared. The LORD our God was right to do all of these things, for we did not obey him.

[15]"O Lord our God, you brought lasting honor to your name by rescuing your people from Egypt in a great display of power. But we have sinned and are full of wickedness. [16]In view of all your faithful mercies, Lord, please turn your furious anger away from your city Jerusalem, your holy mountain. All the neighboring nations mock Jerusalem and your people because of our sins and the sins of our ancestors.

[17]"O our God, hear your servant's prayer! Listen as I plead. For your own sake, Lord, smile again on your desolate sanctuary.

[18]"O my God, lean down and listen to me. Open your eyes and see our despair. See how your city—the city that bears your name—lies in ruins. We make this plea, not because we deserve help, but because of your mercy.

[19]"O Lord, hear. O Lord, forgive. O Lord, listen and act! For your own sake, do not delay, O my God, for your people and your city bear your name."

Gabriel's Message about the Anointed One

[20]I went on praying and confessing my sin and the sin of my people, pleading with the LORD my God for Jerusalem, his holy mountain. [21]As I was praying, Gabriel, whom I had seen in the earlier vision, came swiftly to me at the time of the evening sacrifice. [22]He explained to me, "Daniel, I have come here to give you insight and understanding. [23]The moment you began praying, a command was given. And now I am here to tell you what it was, for you are very precious to God. Listen carefully so that you can understand the meaning of your vision.

[24]"A period of seventy sets of seven* has been decreed for your people and your holy city to finish their rebellion, to put an end to their sin, to atone for their guilt, to bring in everlasting righteousness, to confirm the prophetic vision, and to anoint the Most Holy Place.* [25]Now listen and understand! Seven sets of seven plus sixty-two sets of seven* will pass from the time the command is given to rebuild Jerusalem until a ruler—the Anointed One*—comes. Jerusalem will be rebuilt with streets and strong defenses,* despite the perilous times.

[26]"After this period of sixty-two sets of seven,* the Anointed One will be killed, appearing to have accomplished nothing, and a ruler will arise whose armies will destroy the city and the Temple. The end will come with a flood, and war and its miseries are decreed from that time to the very end. [27]The ruler will make a treaty with the

---

9:24a Hebrew seventy sevens.   **9:24b** Or the Most Holy One.   **9:25a** Hebrew Seven sevens plus sixty-two sevens.   **9:25b** Or an anointed one; similarly in 9:26. Hebrew reads a messiah.   **9:25c** Or and a moat, or and trenches.   **9:26** Hebrew After sixty-two sevens.

people for a period of one set of seven,* but after half this time, he will put an end to the sacrifices and offerings. And as a climax to all his terrible deeds,* he will set up a sacrilegious object that causes desecration,* until the fate decreed for this defiler is finally poured out on him."

10 Daniel's Vision of a Messenger

In the third year of the reign of King Cyrus of Persia,* Daniel (also known as Belteshazzar) had another vision. He understood that the vision concerned events certain to happen in the future—times of war and great hardship.

²When this vision came to me, I, Daniel, had been in mourning for three whole weeks. ³All that time I had eaten no rich food. No meat or wine crossed my lips, and I used no fragrant lotions until those three weeks had passed.

⁴On April 23,* as I was standing on the bank of the great Tigris River, ⁵I looked up and saw a man dressed in linen clothing, with a belt of pure gold around his waist. ⁶His body looked like a precious gem. His face flashed like lightning, and his eyes flamed like torches. His arms and feet shone like polished bronze, and his voice roared like a vast multitude of people.

⁷Only I, Daniel, saw this vision. The men with me saw nothing, but they were suddenly terrified and ran away to hide. ⁸So I was left there all alone to see this amazing vision. My strength left me, my face grew deathly pale, and I felt very weak. ⁹Then I heard the man speak, and when I heard the sound of his voice, I fainted and lay there with my face to the ground.

¹⁰Just then a hand touched me and lifted me, still trembling, to my hands and knees. ¹¹And the man said to me, "Daniel, you are very precious to God, so listen carefully to what I have to say to you. Stand up, for I have been sent to you." When he said this to me, I stood up, still trembling.

¹²Then he said, "Don't be afraid, Dan-iel. Since the first day you began to pray for understanding and to humble yourself before your God, your request has been heard in heaven. I have come in answer to your prayer. ¹³But for twenty-one days the spirit prince* of the kingdom of Persia blocked my way. Then Michael, one of the archangels,* came to help me, and I left him there with the spirit prince of the kingdom of Persia.* ¹⁴Now I am here to explain what will happen to your people in the future, for this vision concerns a time yet to come."

¹⁵While he was speaking to me, I looked down at the ground, unable to say a word. ¹⁶Then the one who looked like a man* touched my lips, and I opened my mouth and began to speak. I said to the one standing in front of me, "I am filled with anguish because of the vision I have seen, my lord, and I am very weak. ¹⁷How can someone like me, your servant, talk to you, my lord? My strength is gone, and I can hardly breathe."

¹⁸Then the one who looked like a man touched me again, and I felt my strength returning. ¹⁹"Don't be afraid," he said, "for you are very precious to God. Peace! Be encouraged! Be strong!"

As he spoke these words to me, I suddenly felt stronger and said to him, "Please speak to me, my lord, for you have strengthened me."

²⁰He replied, "Do you know why I have come? Soon I must return to fight against the spirit prince of the kingdom of Persia, and after that the spirit prince of the kingdom of Greece* will come. ²¹Meanwhile, I will tell you what is written in the Book of Truth. (No one helps me against these spirit princes except Michael, your spirit prince.* ¹¹:¹I have been standing beside Michael* to support and strengthen him since the first year of the reign of Darius the Mede.)

11 Kings of the South and North

²"Now then, I will reveal the truth to you. Three more Persian kings will reign,

---

9:27a Hebrew *for one seven.*   9:27b Hebrew *And on the wing of abominations;* the meaning of the Hebrew is uncertain.   9:27c Hebrew *an abomination of desolation.*   10:1 The third year of Cyrus's reign was 536 B.C.   10:4 Hebrew *On the twenty-fourth day of the first month,* of the ancient Hebrew lunar calendar. This date in the book of Daniel can be cross-checked with dates in surviving Persian records and can be related accurately to our modern calendar. This event occurred on April 23, 536 B.C.   10:13a Hebrew *the prince;* also in 10:13c, 20.   10:13b Hebrew *the chief princes.*   10:13c As in one Greek version; Hebrew reads *and I was left there with the kings of Persia.* The meaning of the Hebrew is uncertain.   10:16 As in most manuscripts of the Masoretic Text; one manuscript of the Masoretic Text and one Greek version read *Then something that looked like a human hand.*   10:20 Hebrew *of Javan.*   10:21 Hebrew *against these except Michael, your prince.*   11:1 Hebrew *him.*

to be succeeded by a fourth, far richer than the others. He will use his wealth to stir up everyone to fight against the kingdom of Greece.*

3 "Then a mighty king will rise to power who will rule with great authority and accomplish everything he sets out to do. 4 But at the height of his power, his kingdom will be broken apart and divided into four parts. It will not be ruled by the king's descendants, nor will the kingdom hold the authority it once had. For his empire will be uprooted and given to others.

5 "The king of the south will increase in power, but one of his own officials will become more powerful than he and will rule his kingdom with great strength.

6 "Some years later an alliance will be formed between the king of the north and the king of the south. The daughter of the king of the south will be given in marriage to the king of the north to secure the alliance, but she will lose her influence over him, and so will her father. She will be abandoned along with her supporters. 7 But when one of her relatives* becomes king of the south, he will raise an army and enter the fortress of the king of the north and defeat him. 8 When he returns to Egypt, he will carry back their idols with him, along with priceless articles of gold and silver. For some years afterward he will leave the king of the north alone.

9 "Later the king of the north will invade the realm of the king of the south but will soon return to his own land. 10 However, the sons of the king of the north will assemble a mighty army that will advance like a flood and carry the battle as far as the enemy's fortress.

11 "Then, in a rage, the king of the south will rally against the vast forces assembled by the king of the north and will defeat them. 12 After the enemy army is swept away, the king of the south will be filled with pride and will execute many thousands of his enemies. But his success will be short lived.

13 "A few years later the king of the north will return with a fully equipped army far greater than before. 14 At that time there will be a general uprising against the king of the south. Violent men among your own people will join them in fulfillment of this vision, but they will not succeed. 15 Then the king of the north will come and lay siege to a fortified city and capture it. The best troops of the south will not be able to stand in the face of the onslaught.

16 "The king of the north will march onward unopposed; none will be able to stop him. He will pause in the glorious land of Israel,* intent on destroying it. 17 He will make plans to come with the might of his entire kingdom and will form an alliance with the king of the south. He will give him a daughter in marriage in order to overthrow the kingdom from within, but his plan will fail.

18 "After this, he will turn his attention to the coastland and conquer many cities. But a commander from another land will put an end to his insolence and cause him to retreat in shame. 19 He will take refuge in his own fortresses but will stumble and fall and be seen no more.

20 "His successor will send out a tax collector to maintain the royal splendor. But after a very brief reign, he will die, though not from anger or in battle.

21 "The next to come to power will be a despicable man who is not in line for royal succession. He will slip in when least expected and take over the kingdom by flattery and intrigue. 22 Before him great armies will be swept away, including a covenant prince. 23 With deceitful promises, he will make various alliances. He will become strong despite having only a handful of followers. 24 Without warning he will enter the richest areas of the land. Then he will distribute among his followers the plunder and wealth of the rich—something his predecessors had never done. He will plot the overthrow of strongholds, but this will last for only a short while.

25 "Then he will stir up his courage and raise a great army against the king of the south. The king of the south will go to battle with a mighty army, but to no avail, for there will be plots against him. 26 His own household will cause his downfall. His army

---

11:2 Hebrew *of Javan.*   **11:7** Hebrew *a branch from her roots.*   **11:16** Hebrew *the glorious land.*

Fasting

The Daniel Fast
DANIEL 10:3

A few Mondays ago, I inhaled deeply as the warm, earthy scent of brewing coffee wafted gently over several rows of cubicles and wandered toward my nose. I can usually smell coffee brewing, but on this particular day the scent was so strong I could almost see it meandering around the corner and swirling around me, like in a scene from a cartoon.

I stepped over to my desk and flipped open a small black notebook I'd placed next to my keyboard. Uncapping a pen, I wrote the first thing that came to mind: "8:15. Smelling coffee. ARRGH."

That Monday was Day 1 of a ten-day Daniel fast my church was participating in. Inspired by Daniel 10:3, in which Daniel determines to forgo "rich food" to demonstrate humility before the Lord and to gain understanding, our pastors called us to eat simple foods for ten days and to add additional prayer and Bible study to our daily routines. Refined foods, sugar, dairy, and yeast were out, in favor of fruits, vegetables, whole grains, and nuts. Also on the "no" list? Caffeine.

The journal I kept during the first couple of days records my adjustment to the routine in stream-of-consciousness style.

Early that morning I jotted a quick prayer. Because I've restricted myself from particular kinds or amounts of food before, I needed help focusing on the spiritual purpose of this fast, rather than any physical benefits that might accompany the healthier diet. I didn't want to diet when the calling was to fast.

Around 8:30 I noted that I was responding to some minor interruptions with more irritation than I normally would have. I was challenged by the thought that my pleasant demeanor might actually reflect a sated tongue rather than a contented soul.

Mid-morning I'd started to think about how, by challenging my routine choices, the fast was building some spiritual muscle. "I'm wondering now about my capacity to do hard things," I wrote. "Have I let that part of me atrophy?"

By 3:45 Monday afternoon, I'd already tired of oatmeal, apples, and lentil soup. I opened the notebook again: "burrito with shredded chicken and sour cream. I sure hope I start having more spiritual thoughts soon."

Before the fast began, a friend and I prayerfully decided to increase our intake of Scripture. For me that meant unearthing some Bible CDs I had and listening to them during a leg of my long daily commute. As I slid one into the CD player, I recognized my resistance to this change—and realized I often rely on "preprocessed" spiritual insight. My preference is often for music in which someone else has done the hard spiritual work of connecting with God or for programs in which someone else reflects on his or her interpretation of Scripture and what it means for our lives. Listening to the texts without this kind of mediation was challenging for me. I prayed that God would allow me to crave "unprocessed" encounters with him and with Scripture in the same way I was experiencing physical cravings for a tall, skim vanilla latte.

Although I was pleased when our fast ended nine days later, I was also grateful for the experience and for the connections it helped me make between my physical and spiritual lives. The challenge of fasting by food type helped me to think more deeply about issues of physical and spiritual satiety and to explore the parallels between the pleasure of processed foods and the fleeting satisfaction they provide. I continued to pray for a "fasting" mentality versus a "dieting" mind-set. And as time went on, I enjoyed my unmediated encounters with the Bible more than I had before. Even though it was challenging, fasting helped me realize more about myself than I'd ever have imagined.

—LaTonya Taylor

For more on fasting, see reading at Joel 2:12-13.

will be swept away, and many will be killed. ²⁷ Seeking nothing but each other's harm, these kings will plot against each other at the conference table, attempting to deceive each other. But it will make no difference, for the end will come at the appointed time.

²⁸ "The king of the north will then return home with great riches. On the way he will set himself against the people of the holy covenant, doing much damage before continuing his journey.

²⁹ "Then at the appointed time he will once again invade the south, but this time the result will be different. ³⁰ For warships from western coastlands* will scare him off, and he will withdraw and return home. But he will vent his anger against the people of the holy covenant and reward those who forsake the covenant.

³¹ "His army will take over the Temple fortress, pollute the sanctuary, put a stop to the daily sacrifices, and set up the sacrilegious object that causes desecration.* ³² He will flatter and win over those who have violated the covenant. But the people who know their God will be strong and will resist him.

³³ "Wise leaders will give instruction to many, but these teachers will die by fire and sword, or they will be jailed and robbed. ³⁴ During these persecutions, little help will arrive, and many who join them will not be sincere. ³⁵ And some of the wise will fall victim to persecution. In this way, they will be refined and cleansed and made pure until the time of the end, for the appointed time is still to come.

³⁶ "The king will do as he pleases, exalting himself and claiming to be greater than every god, even blaspheming the God of gods. He will succeed, but only until the time of wrath is completed. For what has been determined will surely take place. ³⁷ He will have no respect for the gods of his ancestors, or for the god loved by women, or for any other god, for he will boast that he is greater than them all. ³⁸ Instead of these, he will worship the god of fortresses—a god his ancestors never knew—and lavish on him gold, silver, precious stones, and expensive gifts. ³⁹ Claiming this foreign god's help, he

will attack the strongest fortresses. He will honor those who submit to him, appointing them to positions of authority and dividing the land among them as their reward.*

⁴⁰ "Then at the time of the end, the king of the south will attack the king of the north. The king of the north will storm out with chariots, charioteers, and a vast navy. He will invade various lands and sweep through them like a flood. ⁴¹ He will enter the glorious land of Israel,* and many nations will fall, but Moab, Edom, and the best part of Ammon will escape. ⁴² He will conquer many countries, and even Egypt will not escape. ⁴³ He will gain control over the gold, silver, and treasures of Egypt, and the Libyans and Ethiopians* will be his servants.

⁴⁴ "But then news from the east and the north will alarm him, and he will set out in great anger to destroy and obliterate many. ⁴⁵ He will stop between the glorious holy mountain and the sea and will pitch his royal tents. But while he is there, his time will suddenly run out, and no one will help him.

12 The Time of the End

"At that time Michael, the archangel* who stands guard over your nation, will arise. Then there will be a time of anguish greater than any since nations first came into existence. But at that time every one of your people whose name is written in the book will be rescued. ² Many of those whose bodies lie dead and buried will rise up, some to everlasting life and some to shame and everlasting disgrace. ³ Those who are wise will shine as bright as the sky, and those who lead many to righteousness will shine like the stars forever. ⁴ But you, Daniel, keep this prophecy a secret; seal up the book until the time of the end, when many will rush here and there, and knowledge will increase."

⁵ Then I, Daniel, looked and saw two others standing on opposite banks of the river. ⁶ One of them asked the man dressed in linen, who was now standing above the river, "How long will it be until these shocking events are over?"

⁷ The man dressed in linen, who was standing above the river, raised both his

---

11:30 Hebrew *from Kittim.* **11:31** Hebrew *the abomination of desolation.* **11:39** Or *at a price.* **11:41** Hebrew *the glorious land.* **11:43** Hebrew *Cushites.* **12:1** Hebrew *the great prince.*

Ultimate Justice

DANIEL 12:1-3

Heaven puts our vision of justice in perspective. You can't talk about paradise—the time-place where everything is right—without talking about the way things will be *put* right. That means we can't talk about heaven without talking about the resurrection of the body and the Last Judgment.

Our individual memories and our community stories are full of injustices—both those we suffer and those we perpetrate. In this life there is no undoing those injustices. There can be forgiveness and reconciliation and even restitution, but we cannot recover lost lives and lost opportunities.

Scripture's earliest clear teaching of the resurrection of the dead (Daniel 12:1-3) follows a prophecy about God's people suffering unjust persecution. How will God put things right? Through a general resurrection and a judgment: "Many of those whose bodies lie dead and buried will rise up, some to everlasting life and some to shame and everlasting disgrace" (12:2).

"Faith in the Last Judgment," Pope Benedict writes in *Saved in Hope,* is "first and foremost hope." He calls "the question of justice . . . the strongest argument in favor of faith in eternal life." It is morally inconceivable "that the injustice of history should be the final word," he says, and when we face that "the necessity for Christ's return and for new life become fully convincing."

Christians talk now more about justice than ever. God is on an intergalactic justice mission, and we are God's agents, charged with bringing about a limited and relative justice. But lest the overwhelming task make us weary, our heavenly hope keeps it in perspective. The restoration of justice is ultimately God's task.

The Christian's future, the world's justice, and the believer's bliss are the where and when of everything and everyone being in perfect concord with God. A taste of that is available now through our work—the fullness will come in God's time by God's power.

—David Neff

For more on justice, see reading at Hosea 12:6.

hands toward heaven and took a solemn oath by the One who lives forever, saying, "It will go on for a time, times, and half a time. When the shattering of the holy people has finally come to an end, all these things will have happened."

[8] I heard what he said, but I did not understand what he meant. So I asked, "How will all this finally end, my lord?"

[9] But he said, "Go now, Daniel, for what I have said is kept secret and sealed until the time of the end. [10] Many will be purified, cleansed, and refined by these trials. But the wicked will continue in their wickedness, and none of them will understand. Only those who are wise will know what it means.

[11] "From the time the daily sacrifice is stopped and the sacrilegious object that causes desecration* is set up to be worshiped, there will be 1,290 days. [12] And blessed are those who wait and remain until the end of the 1,335 days!

[13] "As for you, go your way until the end. You will rest, and then at the end of the days, you will rise again to receive the inheritance set aside for you."

12:11 Hebrew *the abomination of desolation.*

Introduction to

Hosea

Background

The Book of Hosea features a love story with a thorn in it: a faithful husband; an adulterous wife. While these descriptions fit Hosea and Gomer respectively, they also fit God and Israel. Told to "Go and marry a prostitute" (1:2), Hosea's subsequent marriage became a symbol of God's love for his adulterous people.

The name Hosea, like Joshua and Jesus, means "salvation." Hosea is believed to be the author of this book. Hosea is the first of twelve books referred to as the Minor Prophets, "minor" referring to the length of the texts.

Message

Hosea, like many other prophets, calls the nation to repentance. The names of Hosea's children reflect God's messages to his people: Jezreel (1:4) means "God scatters"; Lo-ruhamah (1:6), "not loved"; and Lo-ammi (1:9), "not my people." Judgment is coming. Since Israel broke the covenant with God, he scatters his wayward people. Yet there is hope, as expressed in the first chapter: "Yet the time will come when Israel's people will be like the sands of the seashore—too many to count! Then, at the place where they were told, 'You are not my people,' it will be said, 'You are children of the living God'" (1:10).

Time

The prophet Hosea's ministry spanned four decades, circa 755–710 B.C. He prophesied in the northern kingdom of Israel at the time of Amos, and was a contemporary of Isaiah and Micah in Judah.

Outline

I. Gomer, the Symbol of Israel

A. The family of Hosea	1:1–11
B. God judges Israel	2:1–13
C. Gomer is redeemed	3:1–3
D. Israel is redeemed	2:14–23; 3:4–5

II. Judgment and Mercy

A. Israel to be punished	4:1–7:16
B. Reaping the whirlwind	8:1–9:9
C. Israel's apostasy	9:10–11:7
D. God's mercy triumphs	11:8–14:9

Hosea

1 The LORD gave this message to Hosea son of Beeri during the years when Uzziah, Jotham, Ahaz, and Hezekiah were kings of Judah, and Jeroboam son of Jehoash* was king of Israel.

Hosea's Wife and Children

²When the LORD first began speaking to Israel through Hosea, he said to him, "Go and marry a prostitute,* so that some of her children will be conceived in prostitution. This will illustrate how Israel has acted like a prostitute by turning against the LORD and worshiping other gods."

³So Hosea married Gomer, the daughter of Diblaim, and she became pregnant and gave Hosea a son. ⁴And the LORD said, "Name the child Jezreel, for I am about to punish King Jehu's dynasty to avenge the murders he committed at Jezreel. In fact, I will bring an end to Israel's independence. ⁵I will break its military power in the Jezreel Valley."

⁶Soon Gomer became pregnant again and gave birth to a daughter. And the LORD said to Hosea, "Name your daughter Lo-ruhamah—'Not loved'—for I will no longer show love to the people of Israel or forgive them. ⁷But I will show love to the people of Judah. I will free them from their enemies—not with weapons and armies or horses and charioteers, but by my power as the LORD their God."

⁸After Gomer had weaned Lo-ruhamah, she again became pregnant and gave birth to a second son. ⁹And the LORD said, "Name him Lo-ammi—'Not my people'—for Israel is not my people, and I am not their God.

¹⁰*"Yet the time will come when Israel's people will be like the sands of the seashore—too many to count! Then, at the place where they were told, 'You are not my people,' it will be said, 'You are children of the living God.' ¹¹Then the people of Judah and Israel will unite together. They will choose one leader for themselves, and they will return from exile together. What a day that will be—the day of Jezreel*—when God will again plant his people in his land.

²:¹*"In that day you will call your brothers Ammi—'My people.' And you will call your sisters Ruhamah—'The ones I love.'

Charges against an Unfaithful Wife

2 ² "But now bring charges against Israel—your mother—
for she is no longer my wife,
and I am no longer her husband.
Tell her to remove the prostitute's makeup from her face
and the clothing that exposes her breasts.
³ Otherwise, I will strip her as naked
as she was on the day she was born.
I will leave her to die of thirst,
as in a dry and barren wilderness.

1:1 Hebrew *Joash,* a variant spelling of Jehoash. **1:2** Or *a promiscuous woman.* **1:10** Verses 1:10-11 are numbered 2:1-2 in Hebrew text. **1:11** *Jezreel* means "God plants." **2:1** Verses 2:1-23 are numbered 2:3-25 in Hebrew text.

⁴ And I will not love her children,
  for they were conceived in
    prostitution.
⁵ Their mother is a shameless prostitute
  and became pregnant in a shameful
    way.
She said, 'I'll run after other lovers
  and sell myself to them for food and
    water,
for clothing of wool and linen,
  and for olive oil and drinks.'

⁶ "For this reason I will fence her in with
    thornbushes.
  I will block her path with a wall
    to make her lose her way.
⁷ When she runs after her lovers,
  she won't be able to catch them.
She will search for them
  but not find them.
Then she will think,
'I might as well return to my husband,
  for I was better off with him than I am
    now.'
⁸ She doesn't realize it was I who gave her
    everything she has—
  the grain, the new wine, the olive oil;
I even gave her silver and gold.
  But she gave all my gifts to Baal.

⁹ "But now I will take back the ripened
    grain and new wine
  I generously provided each harvest
    season.
I will take away the wool and linen
    clothing
  I gave her to cover her nakedness.
¹⁰ I will strip her naked in public,
  while all her lovers look on.
No one will be able
  to rescue her from my hands.
¹¹ I will put an end to her annual festivals,
  her new moon celebrations, and her
    Sabbath days—
  all her appointed festivals.
¹² I will destroy her grapevines and fig
    trees,
  things she claims her lovers gave her.
I will let them grow into tangled
    thickets,
  where only wild animals will eat the
    fruit.

¹³ I will punish her for all those times
  when she burned incense to her
    images of Baal,
when she put on her earrings and jewels
  and went out to look for her lovers
but forgot all about me,"
  says the LORD.

The LORD's Love for Unfaithful Israel

¹⁴ "But then I will win her back once again.
  I will lead her into the desert
  and speak tenderly to her there.
¹⁵ I will return her vineyards to her
  and transform the Valley of Trouble*
    into a gateway of hope.
She will give herself to me there,
  as she did long ago when she was
    young,
  when I freed her from her captivity in
    Egypt.
¹⁶ When that day comes," says the LORD,
  "you will call me 'my husband'
  instead of 'my master.'*
¹⁷ O Israel, I will wipe the many names of
    Baal from your lips,
  and you will never mention them again.
¹⁸ On that day I will make a covenant
  with all the wild animals and the birds
    of the sky
and the animals that scurry along the
    ground
  so they will not harm you.
I will remove all weapons of war from
    the land,
  all swords and bows,
so you can live unafraid
  in peace and safety.
¹⁹ I will make you my wife forever,
  showing you righteousness and
    justice,
  unfailing love and compassion.
²⁰ I will be faithful to you and make you
    mine,
  and you will finally know me as the
    LORD.

²¹ "In that day, I will answer,"
  says the LORD.
"I will answer the sky as it pleads for
    clouds.
  And the sky will answer the earth with
    rain.

2:15 Hebrew *valley of Achor.*   2:16 Hebrew *'my baal.'*

What Forgiveness Isn't

HOSEA 3

Forgiveness can be hard work—but its difficulty is doubled when we misunderstand what forgiveness really means. When we face the task of forgiving, we must seek God's help in discerning the truth from a lie.

One common myth about forgiveness is that *forgiving means the offender didn't really hurt you.* "Forgiveness is a redemptive response to having been wronged and wounded," wrote author Lewis B. Smedes. Choosing to forgive must involve acknowledging the pain and hurt caused by the other's wrong—but this choice is what can begin the process of healing.

We also misunderstand forgiveness when we think it means that *the forgiven offender should face no consequences.* When we choose to forgive someone, our forgiveness doesn't "let him off the hook." Consider the example of Pope John Paul II who, in December 1983, visited Mehmet Ali Agca in the Rebibbia prison in Rome. Two years earlier Agca had shot the pope in the chest. After much agony John Paul recovered, and now he looked Agca in the eye, extended his hand, and said, "I forgive you." But even though the pope forgave him, Agca still faced the consequences of his crime and served out his lengthy prison sentence.

The decision to forgive an offender is probably the hardest choice we can ever make—but we must make that decision with an accurate understanding of what true forgiveness is. God is our model. He directly acknowledges our wrongs and allows us to face the natural consequences of our sin, but he also seeks reconciliation and healing for us far beyond what we deserve. May we learn to forgive others the way God has forgiven us (Ephesians 4:32).

—*Denise George*

For more on forgiveness, see reading at Hosea 11:1-11.

²² Then the earth will answer the thirsty cries
    of the grain, the grapevines, and the olive trees.
And they in turn will answer,
    'Jezreel'—'God plants!'
²³ At that time I will plant a crop of Israelites
    and raise them for myself.
I will show love
    to those I called 'Not loved.'*
And to those I called 'Not my people,'*
    I will say, 'Now you are my people.'
And they will reply, 'You are our God!' "

3 Hosea's Wife Is Redeemed

Then the LORD said to me, "Go and love your wife again, even though she* commits adultery with another lover. This will illustrate that the LORD still loves Israel, even though the people have turned to other gods and love to worship them.*"

²So I bought her back for fifteen pieces of silver* and five bushels of barley and a measure of wine.* ³Then I said to her, "You must live in my house for many days and stop your prostitution. During this time, you will not have sexual relations with anyone, not even with me.*"

2:23a Hebrew *Lo-ruhamah;* see 1:6.   **2:23b** Hebrew *Lo-ammi;* see 1:9.   **3:1a** Or *Go and love a woman who.*   **3:1b** Hebrew *love their raisin cakes.* **3:2a** Hebrew *15 shekels of silver,* about 6 ounces or 171 grams in weight.   **3:2b** As in Greek version, which reads *a homer of barley and a wineskin full of wine;* Hebrew reads *a homer* [5 bushels or 182 liters] *of barley and a lethech* [2.5 bushels or 91 liters] *of barley.*   **3:3** Or *and I will live with you.*

[4]This shows that Israel will go a long time without a king or prince, and without sacrifices, sacred pillars, priests,* or even idols! [5]But afterward the people will return and devote themselves to the Lord their God and to David's descendant, their king.* In the last days, they will tremble in awe of the Lord and of his goodness.

The Lord's Case against Israel

4 [1]Hear the word of the Lord, O people of Israel!

The Lord has brought charges against you, saying:

"There is no faithfulness, no kindness,
no knowledge of God in your land.
[2]You make vows and break them;
you kill and steal and commit adultery.
There is violence everywhere—
one murder after another.
[3]That is why your land is in mourning,
and everyone is wasting away.
Even the wild animals, the birds of the sky,
and the fish of the sea are disappearing.

[4]"Don't point your finger at someone else
and try to pass the blame!
My complaint, you priests,
is with you.*
[5]So you will stumble in broad daylight,
and your false prophets will fall with you in the night.
And I will destroy Israel, your mother.
[6]My people are being destroyed
because they don't know me.
Since you priests refuse to know me,
I refuse to recognize you as my priests.
Since you have forgotten the laws of your God,
I will forget to bless your children.
[7]The more priests there are,
the more they sin against me.
They have exchanged the glory of God
for the shame of idols.*

[8]"When the people bring their sin offerings,
the priests get fed.
So the priests are glad when the people sin!
[9]'And what the priests do, the people also do.'
So now I will punish both priests and people
for their wicked deeds.
[10]They will eat and still be hungry.
They will play the prostitute and gain nothing from it,
for they have deserted the Lord
[11]to worship other gods.

"Wine has robbed my people
of their understanding.
[12]They ask a piece of wood for advice!
They think a stick can tell them the future!
Longing after idols
has made them foolish.
They have played the prostitute,
serving other gods and deserting their God.
[13]They offer sacrifices to idols on the mountaintops.
They go up into the hills to burn incense
in the pleasant shade of oaks, poplars, and terebinth trees.

"That is why your daughters turn to prostitution,
and your daughters-in-law commit adultery.
[14]But why should I punish them
for their prostitution and adultery?
For your men are doing the same thing,
sinning with whores and shrine prostitutes.
O foolish people! You refuse to understand,
so you will be destroyed.

[15]"Though you, Israel, are a prostitute,
may Judah avoid such guilt.
Do not join the false worship at Gilgal or Beth-aven,*
even though they take oaths there in the Lord's name.

3:4 Hebrew *ephod*, the vest worn by the priest. 3:5 Hebrew *to David their king.* 4:4 Hebrew *Your people are like those with a complaint against the priests.* 4:7 As in Syriac version and an ancient Hebrew tradition; Masoretic Text reads *I will turn their glory into shame.* 4:15 *Beth-aven* means "house of wickedness"; it is being used as another name for Bethel, which means "house of God."

¹⁶ Israel is stubborn,
    like a stubborn heifer.
So should the LORD feed her
    like a lamb in a lush pasture?
¹⁷ Leave Israel* alone,
    because she is married to idolatry.
¹⁸ When the rulers of Israel finish their
        drinking,
    off they go to find some prostitutes.
    They love shame more than honor.*
¹⁹ So a mighty wind will sweep them away.
    Their sacrifices to idols will bring
        them shame.

5 The Failure of Israel's Leaders

¹ "Hear this, you priests.
    Pay attention, you leaders of Israel.
Listen, you members of the royal family.
    Judgment has been handed down
        against you.
For you have led the people into a snare
    by worshiping the idols at Mizpah and
        Tabor.
² You have dug a deep pit to trap them at
    Acacia Grove.*
    But I will settle with you for what you
        have done.
³ I know what you are like, O Ephraim.
    You cannot hide yourself from me,
        O Israel.
You have left me as a prostitute leaves
    her husband;
    you are utterly defiled.
⁴ Your deeds won't let you return to your
        God.
    You are a prostitute through and
        through,
    and you do not know the LORD.
⁵ "The arrogance of Israel testifies against
        her;
    Israel and Ephraim will stumble under
        their load of guilt.
    Judah, too, will fall with them.
⁶ When they come with their flocks and
        herds
    to offer sacrifices to the LORD,
they will not find him,
    because he has withdrawn from them.

⁷ They have betrayed the honor of the
    LORD,
    bearing children that are not his.
    Now their false religion will devour
        them
    along with their wealth.*
⁸ "Sound the alarm in Gibeah!
    Blow the trumpet in Ramah!
Raise the battle cry in Beth-aven*!
    Lead on into battle, O warriors of
        Benjamin!
⁹ One thing is certain, Israel*:
    On your day of punishment,
    you will become a heap of rubble.

¹⁰ "The leaders of Judah have become like
        thieves.*
    So I will pour my anger on them like a
        waterfall.
¹¹ The people of Israel will be crushed and
        broken by my judgment
    because they are determined to
        worship idols.*
¹² I will destroy Israel as a moth consumes
        wool.
    I will make Judah as weak as rotten
        wood.
¹³ "When Israel and Judah saw how sick
        they were,
    Israel turned to Assyria—
    to the great king there—
    but he could neither help nor cure
        them.
¹⁴ I will be like a lion to Israel,
    like a strong young lion to Judah.
I will tear them to pieces!
I will carry them off,
    and no one will be left to rescue them.
¹⁵ Then I will return to my place
    until they admit their guilt and turn
        to me.
For as soon as trouble comes,
    they will earnestly search for me."

6 A Call to Repentance

¹ "Come, let us return to the LORD.
    He has torn us to pieces;
    now he will heal us.

4:17 Hebrew *Ephraim*, referring to the northern kingdom of Israel.   **4:18** As in Greek version; the meaning of the Hebrew is uncertain.
5:2 Hebrew *at Shittim*. The meaning of the Hebrew for this sentence is uncertain.   **5:7** The meaning of the Hebrew is uncertain.
5:8 *Beth-aven* means "house of wickedness"; it is being used as another name for Bethel, which means "house of God."   **5:9** Hebrew
Ephraim, referring to the northern kingdom of Israel; also in 5:11, 12, 13, 14.   **5:10** Hebrew *like those who move a boundary marker*.
5:11 Or *determined to follow human commands*. The meaning of the Hebrew is uncertain.

Caring for Creation

HOSEA 4:3

There are some things for which words cannot do justice—sights, smells, and sounds that make the heart come alive, that renew our passions, and that whisper to us of the presence of a good God.

On the southern route into Yosemite National Park, the road winds through a tunnel of trees before rounding a bend and giving way to a view known as Inspiration Point. There, just beyond the old stagecoach stop of Wawona, cars pull over to the side and people emerge to gaze silently at the vista, a majestic sweep of the valley with views of El Capitan, Bridal Veil Falls, and Half Dome. It's awe inspiring.

Just south of Carmel, California, Highway 1 winds down the spine of the West Coast in one of the most beautiful drives in the world, the Big Sur. People journey from all over the world to see where the Pacific Ocean crashes into the sheer cliffs of the Santa Lucia Mountains.

I could fill this page with descriptions of magnificent sights and experiences in our natural world. There's so much beauty, and God's glory is in all of it. Romans 1:20 tells us creation points us to God, and that we "can clearly see his invisible qualities—his eternal power and divine nature" through the world he's made. Psalm 19 tells us the earth proclaims the glory of God and the work of his hands. When we preserve creation, we preserve a form of God's testimony to us—evidence for seekers and spiritual formation for believers.

But this is only one of many reasons conservation of natural resources is important from a Christian perspective. When we take action to protect the earth God gave us, we also serve the poor, the importance of which is discussed throughout the Bible. Environmental decay results in dirty air, toxic water, soil erosion, and the depletion of species, all of which impact poor people first and hardest.

And then there's the simple command God gave. In Genesis 1 the refrain "it was good" follows God's creation of sunlight and stars, willow trees and orchids, red-winged blackbirds and white-tailed deer. What God created is a gift to us, and in verse 15 he commands us to take care of it. The Fall made that directive more difficult, but there's been no release from this caretaking mandate.

Romans 8:19–22 tells us creation groans and waits to be liberated from its bondage to decay, and Hosea 4:3 paints the picture of the direct impact our sins have on creation: "That is why your land is in mourning, and everyone is wasting away. Even the wild animals, the birds of the sky, and the fish of the sea are disappearing."

It's true that environmental issues are often associated with politics of the sort many Christians oppose. But this doesn't have to be the case. Christians can, and perhaps should, be at the forefront of efforts to preserve God's creation. Perhaps just like Jesus' resurrected body was recognizable but new, the new heaven and new earth promised to us (2 Peter 3:13) is from the template of this earth we now know.

So recycle! And do it with your children, teaching the next generation to value God's creation along the way. Turn off the lights when you leave a room. Consider buying a fuel-efficient car. Research and get involved in ways that support environmental causes and are in line with biblical values. And the next time you witness a sight that makes your heart come alive, that renews your passion, that whispers to you of the presence of a good God—remember that God created what you're looking at in order for you to have just such a response.

—*Nancy Ortberg*

For more on stewardship, see reading at Malachi 3:6-12.

He has injured us;
 now he will bandage our wounds.
² In just a short time he will restore us,
 so that we may live in his presence.
³ Oh, that we might know the LORD!
 Let us press on to know him.
He will respond to us as surely as the
 arrival of dawn
 or the coming of rains in early spring."

⁴ "O Israel* and Judah,
 what should I do with you?" asks the
 LORD.
"For your love vanishes like the morning
 mist
 and disappears like dew in the
 sunlight.
⁵ I sent my prophets to cut you to pieces—
 to slaughter you with my words,
 with judgments as inescapable as light.
⁶ I want you to show love,*
 not offer sacrifices.
I want you to know me*
 more than I want burnt offerings.
⁷ But like Adam,* you broke my covenant
 and betrayed my trust.

⁸ "Gilead is a city of sinners,
 tracked with footprints of blood.
⁹ Priests form bands of robbers,
 waiting in ambush for their victims.
They murder travelers along the road to
 Shechem
 and practice every kind of sin.
¹⁰ Yes, I have seen something horrible in
 Ephraim and Israel:
My people are defiled by prostituting
 themselves with other gods!

¹¹ "O Judah, a harvest of punishment is
 also waiting for you,
 though I wanted to restore the
 fortunes of my people.

7 Israel's Love for Wickedness

¹ "I want to heal Israel,* but its sins are
 too great.
 Samaria is filled with liars.
Thieves are on the inside
 and bandits on the outside!
² Its people don't realize
 that I am watching them.

Their sinful deeds are all around them,
 and I see them all.

³ "The people entertain the king with their
 wickedness,
 and the princes laugh at their lies.
⁴ They are all adulterers,
 always aflame with lust.
They are like an oven that is kept hot
 while the baker is kneading the
 dough.
⁵ On royal holidays, the princes get drunk
 with wine,
 carousing with those who mock them.
⁶ Their hearts are like an oven
 blazing with intrigue.
Their plot smolders* through the night,
 and in the morning it breaks out like a
 raging fire.
⁷ Burning like an oven,
 they consume their leaders.
They kill their kings one after another,
 and no one cries to me for help.

⁸ "The people of Israel mingle with
 godless foreigners,
 making themselves as worthless as a
 half-baked cake!
⁹ Worshiping foreign gods has sapped
 their strength,
 but they don't even know it.
Their hair is gray,
 but they don't realize they're old and
 weak.
¹⁰ Their arrogance testifies against them,
 yet they don't return to the LORD their
 God
 or even try to find him.

¹¹ "The people of Israel have become like
 silly, witless doves,
 first calling to Egypt, then flying to
 Assyria for help.
¹² But as they fly about,
 I will throw my net over them
and bring them down like a bird from
 the sky.
 I will punish them for all the evil
 they do.*

¹³ "What sorrow awaits those who have
 deserted me!

6:4 Hebrew *Ephraim*, referring to the northern kingdom of Israel.   6:6a Greek version translates this Hebrew term as *to show mercy*. Compare
Matt 9:13; 12:7.   6:6b Hebrew *to know God*.   6:7 Or *But at Adam*.   7:1 Hebrew *Ephraim*, referring to the northern kingdom of Israel; also in
7:8, 11.   7:6 Hebrew *Their baker sleeps*.   7:12 Hebrew *I will punish them because of what was reported against them in the assembly*.

Let them die, for they have rebelled
against me.
I wanted to redeem them,
but they have told lies about me.
[14] They do not cry out to me with sincere
hearts.
Instead, they sit on their couches and
wail.
They cut themselves,* begging foreign
gods for grain and new wine,
and they turn away from me.
[15] I trained them and made them strong,
yet now they plot evil against me.
[16] They look everywhere except to the
Most High.
They are as useless as a crooked bow.
Their leaders will be killed by their
enemies
because of their insolence toward me.
Then the people of Egypt
will laugh at them.

8 Israel Harvests the Whirlwind

[1] "Sound the alarm!
The enemy descends like an eagle on
the people of the LORD,
for they have broken my covenant
and revolted against my law.
[2] Now Israel pleads with me,
'Help us, for you are our God!'
[3] But it is too late.
The people of Israel have rejected what
is good,
and now their enemies will chase after
them.
[4] The people have appointed kings
without my consent,
and princes without my knowledge.
By making idols for themselves from
their silver and gold,
they have brought about their own
destruction.
[5] "O Samaria, I reject this calf—
this idol you have made.
My fury burns against you.
How long will you be incapable of
innocence?
[6] This calf you worship, O Israel,
was crafted by your own hands!
It is not God!
Therefore, it must be smashed to bits.

[7] "They have planted the wind
and will harvest the whirlwind.
The stalks of grain wither
and produce nothing to eat.
And even if there is any grain,
foreigners will eat it.
[8] The people of Israel have been
swallowed up;
they lie among the nations like an old
discarded pot.
[9] Like a wild donkey looking for a mate,
they have gone up to Assyria.
The people of Israel* have sold
themselves—
sold themselves to many lovers.
[10] But though they have sold themselves to
many allies,
I will now gather them together for
judgment.
Then they will writhe
under the burden of the great king.

[11] "Israel has built many altars to take away
sin,
but these very altars became places for
sinning!
[12] Even though I gave them all my laws,
they act as if those laws don't apply to
them.
[13] The people of Israel love their rituals of
sacrifice,
but to me their sacrifices are all
meaningless.
I will hold my people accountable for
their sins,
and I will punish them.
They will return to Egypt.
[14] Israel has forgotten its Maker and built
great palaces,
and Judah has fortified its cities.
Therefore, I will send down fire on their
cities
and will burn up their fortresses."

9 Hosea Announces Israel's Punishment

[1] O people of Israel,
do not rejoice as other nations do.
For you have been unfaithful to your God,
hiring yourselves out like prostitutes,
worshiping other gods on every
threshing floor.

7:14 As in Greek version; Hebrew reads *They gather together.* **8:9** Hebrew *Ephraim,* referring to the northern kingdom of Israel; also in 8:11.

² So now your harvests will be too small
    to feed you.
  There will be no grapes for making
    new wine.
³ You may no longer stay here in the
    Lord's land.
  Instead, you will return to Egypt,
and in Assyria you will eat food
    that is ceremonially unclean.
⁴ There you will make no offerings of wine
    to the Lord.
  None of your sacrifices there will
    please him.
They will be unclean, like food touched
    by a person in mourning.
  All who present such sacrifices will be
    defiled.
They may eat this food themselves,
  but they may not offer it to the Lord.
⁵ What then will you do on festival days?
  How will you observe the Lord's
    festivals?
⁶ Even if you escape destruction from
    Assyria,
  Egypt will conquer you, and
    Memphis* will bury you.
Nettles will take over your treasures of
    silver;
  thistles will invade your ruined homes.
⁷ The time of Israel's punishment has
    come;
  the day of payment is here.
  Soon Israel will know this all too well.
Because of your great sin and hostility,
  you say, "The prophets are crazy
  and the inspired men are fools!"
⁸ The prophet is a watchman over Israel*
    for my God,
  yet traps are laid for him wherever he
    goes.
  He faces hostility even in the house of
    God.
⁹ The things my people do are as depraved
  as what they did in Gibeah long ago.
God will not forget.
  He will surely punish them for their
    sins.
¹⁰ The Lord says, "O Israel, when I first
    found you,
  it was like finding fresh grapes in the
    desert.

When I saw your ancestors,
  it was like seeing the first ripe figs of
    the season.
But then they deserted me for Baal-peor,
  giving themselves to that shameful
    idol.
Soon they became vile,
  as vile as the god they worshiped.
¹¹ The glory of Israel will fly away like a bird,
  for your children will not be born
or grow in the womb
  or even be conceived.
¹² Even if you do have children who
    grow up,
  I will take them from you.
It will be a terrible day when I turn away
  and leave you alone.
¹³ I have watched Israel become as
    beautiful as Tyre.
  But now Israel will bring out her
    children for slaughter."

¹⁴ O Lord, what should I request for your
    people?
  I will ask for wombs that don't give
    birth
  and breasts that give no milk.

¹⁵ The Lord says, "All their wickedness
    began at Gilgal;
  there I began to hate them.
I will drive them from my land
  because of their evil actions.
I will love them no more
  because all their leaders are rebels.
¹⁶ The people of Israel are struck down.
  Their roots are dried up,
  and they will bear no more fruit.
And if they give birth,
  I will slaughter their beloved children."

¹⁷ My God will reject the people of Israel
  because they will not listen or obey.
They will be wanderers,
  homeless among the nations.

10 The Lord's Judgment against Israel

¹ How prosperous Israel is—
a luxuriant vine loaded with fruit.
But the richer the people get,
  the more pagan altars they build.
The more bountiful their harvests,
  the more beautiful their sacred pillars.

9:6 Memphis was the capital of northern Egypt.   9:8 Hebrew *Ephraim*, referring to the northern kingdom of Israel; also in 9:11, 13, 16.

² The hearts of the people are fickle;
  they are guilty and must be punished.
The LORD will break down their altars
  and smash their sacred pillars.
³ Then they will say, "We have no king
  because we didn't fear the LORD.
But even if we had a king,
  what could he do for us anyway?"
⁴ They spout empty words
  and make covenants they don't intend
    to keep.
So injustice springs up among them
  like poisonous weeds in a farmer's field.

⁵ The people of Samaria tremble in fear
  for what might happen to their calf
    idol at Beth-aven.*
The people mourn and the priests wail,
  because its glory will be stripped away.*
⁶ This idol will be carted away to Assyria,
  a gift to the great king there.
Ephraim will be ridiculed and Israel will
    be shamed,
  because its people have trusted in this
    idol.
⁷ Samaria and its king will be cut off;
  they will float away like driftwood on
    an ocean wave.
⁸ And the pagan shrines of Aven,* the
    place of Israel's sin, will crumble.
Thorns and thistles will grow up
    around their altars.
They will beg the mountains, "Bury us!"
  and plead with the hills, "Fall on us!"

⁹ The LORD says, "O Israel, ever since
    Gibeah,
  there has been only sin and more sin!
You have made no progress whatsoever.
  Was it not right that the wicked men
    of Gibeah were attacked?
¹⁰ Now whenever it fits my plan,
  I will attack you, too.
I will call out the armies of the nations
  to punish you for your multiplied sins.

¹¹ "Israel* is like a trained heifer treading
    out the grain—
  an easy job she loves.
But I will put a heavy yoke on her
  tender neck.

I will force Judah to pull the plow
  and Israel* to break up the hard ground.
¹² I said, 'Plant the good seeds of
    righteousness,
  and you will harvest a crop of love.
Plow up the hard ground of your hearts,
  for now is the time to seek the LORD,
that he may come
  and shower righteousness upon you.'

¹³ "But you have cultivated wickedness
  and harvested a thriving crop of sins.
You have eaten the fruit of lies—
  trusting in your military might,
believing that great armies
  could make your nation safe.
¹⁴ Now the terrors of war
  will rise among your people.
All your fortifications will fall,
  just as when Shalman destroyed Beth-
    arbel.
Even mothers and children
  were dashed to death there.
¹⁵ You will share that fate, Bethel,
  because of your great wickedness.
When the day of judgment dawns,
  the king of Israel will be completely
    destroyed.

11 The LORD's Love for Israel

¹ "When Israel was a child, I loved
    him,
  and I called my son out of Egypt.
² But the more I* called to him,
  the farther he moved from me,
offering sacrifices to the images of Baal
  and burning incense to idols.
³ I myself taught Israel* how to walk,
  leading him along by the hand.
But he doesn't know or even care
  that it was I who took care of him.
⁴ I led Israel along
  with my ropes of kindness and love.
I lifted the yoke from his neck,
  and I myself stooped to feed him.

⁵ "But since my people refuse to return
    to me,
  they will return to Egypt
and will be forced to serve Assyria.

10:5a Beth-aven means "house of wickedness"; it is being used as another name for Bethel, which means "house of God." 10:5b Or will be taken away into exile. 10:8 Aven is a reference to Beth-aven; see 10:5a and the note there. 10:11a Hebrew Ephraim, referring to the northern kingdom of Israel. 10:11b Hebrew Jacob. The names "Jacob" and "Israel" are often interchanged throughout the Old Testament, referring sometimes to the individual patriarch and sometimes to the nation. 11:2 As in Greek version; Hebrew reads they. 11:3 Hebrew Ephraim, referring to the northern kingdom of Israel; also in 11:8, 9, 12.

Forgiveness

To Make the Unjust Person Just

HOSEA 11:1–11

Over and over we see God's people breaking God's law—yet God continually maintains his covenant with them. In Hosea we see God saying, "Oh, how can I give you up, Israel? How can I let you go?" (11:8). Why? Because God is bound to Israel with a bond of love. God's commitment and covenant are irrevocable. God's relationship with his people takes priority. All sorts of things can happen within a relationship, but relationship is forever; the commitment to the other is eternal. And because this eternal commitment is there, it leads God (and anyone who is in relationship) to suffering on account of the other who has done wrong.

A different way of making the same point would be to say that, at its core, the Christian faith is not about justice—it's about *justification*. There's a world of difference between the two. If Christian faith was primarily about justice, it would focus on the enforcement of justice in relationships between people and between God and humankind. But it's *not* about that. The Christian faith is about justification of the ungodly; it's about showing grace to the one who has done wrong and seeking to make that person and that relationship *just* again.

This is the Christian—the Christlike—way of dealing with being wronged: in a sense, we seek to justify one another when wrong has been done. In our human way, we need to seek to make the unjust person just and thereby create just peace between us. This is what Paul meant when he summarized the whole teaching of Romans by applying it to the relationship between Christians. He instructs, "Accept each other just as Christ has accepted you" (15:7). We are to make the pattern of divine action toward us a pattern of our actions toward the other.

—*Miroslav Volf*

For more on forgiveness, see reading at Mark 11:25.

6 War will swirl through their cities;
   their enemies will crash through their
      gates.
They will destroy them,
   trapping them in their own evil plans.
7 For my people are determined to
      desert me.
They call me the Most High,
   but they don't truly honor me.

8 "Oh, how can I give you up, Israel?
   How can I let you go?
How can I destroy you like Admah
   or demolish you like Zeboiim?
My heart is torn within me,
   and my compassion overflows.

9 No, I will not unleash my fierce anger.
   I will not completely destroy Israel,
for I am God and not a mere mortal.
   I am the Holy One living among you,
   and I will not come to destroy.
10 For someday the people will follow me.
   I, the LORD, will roar like a lion.
And when I roar,
   my people will return trembling from
      the west.
11 Like a flock of birds, they will come from
      Egypt.
   Trembling like doves, they will return
      from Assyria.
And I will bring them home again,"
   says the LORD.

Charges against Israel and Judah

12 *Israel surrounds me with lies and deceit,
but Judah still obeys God
and is faithful to the Holy One.*

12 1* The people of Israel* feed on the
wind;
they chase after the east wind all day
long.
They pile up lies and violence;
they are making an alliance with Assyria
while sending olive oil to buy support
from Egypt.

2 Now the Lord is bringing charges
against Judah.
He is about to punish Jacob* for all his
deceitful ways,
and pay him back for all he has done.

3 Even in the womb,
Jacob struggled with his brother;
when he became a man,
he even fought with God.

4 Yes, he wrestled with the angel and won.
He wept and pleaded for a blessing
from him.
There at Bethel he met God face to face,
and God spoke to him*—

5 the Lord God of Heaven's Armies,
the Lord is his name!

6 So now, come back to your God.
Act with love and justice,
and always depend on him.

7 But no, the people are like crafty merchants
selling from dishonest scales—
they love to cheat.

8 Israel boasts, "I am rich!
I've made a fortune all by myself!
No one has caught me cheating!
My record is spotless!"

9 "But I am the Lord your God,
who rescued you from slavery in Egypt.
And I will make you live in tents again,
as you do each year at the Festival of
Shelters.*

10 I sent my prophets to warn you
with many visions and parables."

11 But the people of Gilead are worthless
because of their idol worship.
And in Gilgal, too, they sacrifice bulls;
their altars are lined up like the heaps
of stone
along the edges of a plowed field.

12 Jacob fled to the land of Aram,
and there he* earned a wife by tending
sheep.

13 Then by a prophet
the Lord brought Jacob's descendants*
out of Egypt;
and by that prophet
they were protected.

14 But the people of Israel
have bitterly provoked the Lord,
so their Lord will now sentence them to
death
in payment for their sins.

13 The Lord's Anger against Israel
1 When the tribe of Ephraim spoke,
the people shook with fear,
for that tribe was important in Israel.
But the people of Ephraim sinned by
worshiping Baal
and thus sealed their destruction.

2 Now they continue to sin by making
silver idols,
images shaped skillfully with human
hands.
"Sacrifice to these," they cry,
"and kiss the calf idols!"

3 Therefore, they will disappear like the
morning mist,
like dew in the morning sun,
like chaff blown by the wind,
like smoke from a chimney.

4 "I have been the Lord your God
ever since I brought you out of Egypt.
You must acknowledge no God but me,
for there is no other savior.

5 I took care of you in the wilderness,
in that dry and thirsty land.

6 But when you had eaten and were
satisfied,
you became proud and forgot me.

7 So now I will attack you like a lion,
like a leopard that lurks along the road.

8 Like a bear whose cubs have been taken
away,
I will tear out your heart.

11:12a Verse 11:12 is numbered 12:1 in Hebrew text. **11:12b** Or *and Judah is unruly against God, the faithful Holy One.* The meaning of the Hebrew is uncertain. **12:1a** Verses 12:1-14 are numbered 12:2-15 in Hebrew text. **12:1b** Hebrew *Ephraim,* referring to the northern kingdom of Israel; also in 12:8, 14. **12:2** *Jacob* sounds like the Hebrew word for "deceiver." **12:4** As in Greek and Syriac versions; Hebrew reads *to us.* **12:9** Hebrew *as in the days of your appointed feast.* **12:12** Hebrew *Israel.* See note on 10:11b. **12:13** Hebrew *brought Israel.* See note on 10:11b.

What's It Got to Do with Me?

HOSEA 12:6

Several months ago, within the span of about two weeks, I received two separate e-mails that were so disturbing they made me feel physically ill. Both depicted atrocities—one against an African man; the other against a litter of puppies.

Then while watching the news last week, I saw a video of a girl in a McDonald's restaurant who was beaten to the point that she went into convulsions. No one stepped in to help. Everyone just watched the girl curled in a corner having a seizure. Even the "videographer" didn't stop recording to care for or aid the victim.

As I watched these videos, my first thoughts were, *Why didn't anybody stop this? Why didn't anybody help? Where's the justice?*

And then I thought about the old saying "Ignorance is bliss." I realized there is truth to that saying! It's easier, less messy, to look the other way. To go about our business and think, *What's it got to do with me?*

If you're like me, you can see those injustices on the nightly news or on the Internet and wonder what you would do if you were on the scene. Would you act? Or would you stay on the sidelines, in shock, paralyzed and unable—or unwilling—to step in?

I've done both.

When I lived in Chicago, I rode public transportation everywhere. One day I noticed a man standing close behind a woman wearing a backpack. She wore earphones and was oblivious to what was going on around her. I watched the man quietly unzip her backpack and slide his hand inside. My jaw dropped. I looked around to see if anyone else saw—several people were watching him too!

And very quickly I felt a righteous indignation swell up from deep within me. I became angry. And in the next moment, I stepped over to him, grabbed the arm that was now fully into the backpack, and said loudly, "I wouldn't do that if I were you, mister."

He was shocked! A twenty-something, sweet, little girl had just taken him on! He pulled his hand out but didn't say anything. And as soon as the next stop arrived, he jumped off that train as though it were on fire.

I looked around again. Everybody saw and heard (except for the potential victim who was still clueless). But nobody else acted.

Before I get too smug about my superhero role in fighting justice, though, I think back on the many times when I didn't act. The time when I was walking down the street and saw a man get mugged and I simply moved to the other side of the street and kept my head down. The time when classmates made fun of an "undesirable" and I didn't speak up. And I'm ashamed. Yes, ignorance is bliss.

When I watch the news now, I pray for God to grow in me a righteous indignation about the right things and a willingness and ability to step out and do something. To call it wrong—whether it's someone being mugged or an elderly woman being cheated or an animal being mistreated or . . .

God doesn't call his followers to be ignorant of what's going on in the world. He calls us to get out of our comfort zones and move into the world with eyes wide open. If we're to be genuine in our faith, then we must heed and act on God's words in Hosea 12:6, "Act with love and justice, and always depend on him."

As Christ-followers we have powerful weapons to change the world. You and I have a lot more influence and muscle than we realize. But we have to start using them.

Injustice can be overwhelming. Just listening to the news each night can throw me into a paralyzed state, unsure where even to begin.

Those are the moments when I've learned to pray, "What do you want me to do, Lord?" And then as I wait for his answer, I pray for the strength and courage to be obedient and for wisdom to say and do as he leads, when and how he leads.

If at the end of our lives God asks us, "Did you live justly? Did you do everything in your power to fight against injustice and oppression, obediently rising to the call to make a difference in the lives of the oppressed and hurting?" may you and I be able to look at God and answer truthfully, "Yes, Lord. Yes."

—*Ginger Kolbaba*

For more on justice, see reading at Amos 5:21–24.

I will devour you like a hungry lioness
　　and mangle you like a wild animal.

9 "You are about to be destroyed, O Israel—
　　yes, by me, your only helper.
10 Now where is* your king?
　　Let him save you!
Where are all the leaders of the land,
　　the king and the officials you
　　demanded of me?
11 In my anger I gave you kings,
　　and in my fury I took them away.

12 "Ephraim's guilt has been collected,
　　and his sin has been stored up for
　　punishment.
13 Pain has come to the people
　　like the pain of childbirth,
but they are like a child
　　who resists being born.
The moment of birth has arrived,
　　but they stay in the womb!

14 "Should I ransom them from the grave*?
　　Should I redeem them from death?
O death, bring on your terrors!
　　O grave, bring on your plagues!*
For I will not take pity on them.
15 Ephraim was the most fruitful of all his
　　brothers,
　　but the east wind—a blast from the
　　Lord—
will arise in the desert.
All their flowing springs will run dry,
　　and all their wells will disappear.
Every precious thing they own
　　will be plundered and carried away.
16*The people of Samaria
　　must bear the consequences of their
　　guilt
　　because they rebelled against their God.
They will be killed by an invading army,
　　their little ones dashed to death
　　against the ground,
　　their pregnant women ripped open by
　　swords."

14 **Healing for the Repentant**
1*Return, O Israel, to the Lord your
　　God,
　　for your sins have brought you down.

2 Bring your confessions, and return to
　　the Lord.
Say to him,
"Forgive all our sins and graciously
　　receive us,
　　so that we may offer you our
　　praises.*
3 Assyria cannot save us,
　　nor can our warhorses.
Never again will we say to the idols we
　　have made,
　　'You are our gods.'
No, in you alone
　　do the orphans find mercy."

4 The Lord says,
"Then I will heal you of your
　　faithlessness;
　　my love will know no bounds,
　　for my anger will be gone forever.
5 I will be to Israel
　　like a refreshing dew from heaven.
Israel will blossom like the lily;
　　it will send roots deep into the soil
　　like the cedars in Lebanon.
6 Its branches will spread out like
　　beautiful olive trees,
　　as fragrant as the cedars of
　　Lebanon.
7 My people will again live under my
　　shade.
They will flourish like grain and
　　blossom like grapevines.
They will be as fragrant as the wines of
　　Lebanon.

8 "O Israel,* stay away from idols!
　　I am the one who answers your
　　prayers and cares for you.
I am like a tree that is always green;
　　all your fruit comes from me."

9 Let those who are wise understand these
　　things.
　　Let those with discernment listen
　　carefully.
The paths of the Lord are true and
　　right,
　　and righteous people live by walking
　　in them.
But in those paths sinners stumble
　　and fall.

13:10 As in Greek and Syriac versions and Latin Vulgate; Hebrew reads *I will be.*　　13:14a Hebrew *Sheol;* also in 13:14b.　　13:14b Greek version reads *O death, where is your punishment? / O grave* [Hades], *where is your sting?* Compare 1 Cor 15:55.　　13:16 Verse 16 is numbered 14:1 in Hebrew text.　　14:1 Verses 14:1-9 are numbered 14:2-10 in Hebrew text.　　14:2 As in Greek and Syriac versions, which read *may repay the fruit of our lips;* Hebrew reads *may repay the bulls of our lips.*　　14:8 Hebrew *Ephraim,* referring to the northern kingdom of Israel.

Introduction to
Joel

Background

The list of blessings and curses recorded in Deuteronomy includes this curse for disobedience: "Swarms of insects will destroy your trees and crops" (28:42). Joel mentions this pestilence in Judah as a sign of the "day of the LORD" (2:1).

The Hebrew form of the name Joel means "Yahweh is God." While Joel is mentioned in the first sentence, there is no further introduction than the name of Joel's father, Pethuel, whose name means "persuaded of God." The frequent remarks about Zion and the temple indicate that Joel may have lived close to Jerusalem while he served as a prophet to Judah.

Message

Joel prophesies the threat of judgment ("the day of the LORD") and the promise of subsequent restoration. Repentance is encouraged for "leaders of the people" (1:2), "drunkards" (1:5), "farmers" and "vine growers" (1:11), "priests," and those who "serve before the altar" (1:13) before the coming Day of the Lord. "'Don't tear your clothing in your grief; but tear your hearts.' Return to the LORD your God, for he is merciful and compassionate, slow to get angry and filled with unfailing love. He is eager to relent and not punish" (2:13).

Time

Although no specific time period is mentioned in Joel, some scholars think that it was written after 722 B.C., following the destruction of Samaria. Others favor 835 B.C. for Joel's ministry, making him a contemporary of Elisha. The foreign nations Joel discusses were more prominent in the ninth century than the eighth century. Furthermore, Joel's message seems closer to that of earlier prophets, such as Hosea, Amos, and Micah, than to postexilic prophets, such as Haggai and Zechariah.

Outline

Joel

1 The LORD gave this message to Joel son of Pethuel.

Mourning over the Locust Plague

² Hear this, you leaders of the people.
  Listen, all who live in the land.
In all your history,
  has anything like this happened before?
³ Tell your children about it in the years to come,
  and let your children tell their children.
  Pass the story down from generation to generation.
⁴ After the cutting locusts finished eating the crops,
  the swarming locusts took what was left!
After them came the hopping locusts,
  and then the stripping locusts,* too!

⁵ Wake up, you drunkards, and weep!
  Wail, all you wine-drinkers!
All the grapes are ruined,
  and all your sweet wine is gone.
⁶ A vast army of locusts* has invaded my land,
  a terrible army too numerous to count.
Its teeth are like lions' teeth,
  its fangs like those of a lioness.
⁷ It has destroyed my grapevines
  and ruined my fig trees,
stripping their bark and destroying it,
  leaving the branches white and bare.

⁸ Weep like a bride dressed in black,
  mourning the death of her husband.
⁹ For there is no grain or wine
  to offer at the Temple of the LORD.
So the priests are in mourning.
  The ministers of the LORD are weeping.
¹⁰ The fields are ruined,
  the land is stripped bare.
The grain is destroyed,
  the grapes have shriveled,
  and the olive oil is gone.

¹¹ Despair, all you farmers!
  Wail, all you vine growers!
Weep, because the wheat and barley—
  all the crops of the field—are ruined.

1:4 The precise identification of the four kinds of locusts mentioned here is uncertain.　**1:6** Hebrew *A nation.*

¹² The grapevines have dried up,
    and the fig trees have withered.
The pomegranate trees, palm trees, and
        apple trees—
    all the fruit trees—have dried up.
    And the people's joy has dried up with
        them.

¹³ Dress yourselves in burlap and weep,
        you priests!
    Wail, you who serve before the
        altar!
Come, spend the night in burlap,
    you ministers of my God.
For there is no grain or wine
    to offer at the Temple of your God.

¹⁴ Announce a time of fasting;
    call the people together for a solemn
        meeting.
Bring the leaders
    and all the people of the land
into the Temple of the Lord your
        God,
    and cry out to him there.

¹⁵ The day of the Lord is near,
    the day when destruction comes from
        the Almighty.
    How terrible that day will be!

¹⁶ Our food disappears before our very
        eyes.
    No joyful celebrations are held in the
        house of our God.

¹⁷ The seeds die in the parched ground,
    and the grain crops fail.
The barns stand empty,
    and granaries are abandoned.

¹⁸ How the animals moan with hunger!
    The herds of cattle wander about
        confused,
    because they have no pasture.
    The flocks of sheep and goats bleat in
        misery.

¹⁹ Lord, help us!
    The fire has consumed the wilderness
        pastures,
    and flames have burned up all the
        trees.

²⁰ Even the wild animals cry out to you
    because the streams have dried up,
    and fire has consumed the wilderness
        pastures.

2 Locusts Invade like an Army

¹ Sound the alarm in Jerusalem*!
    Raise the battle cry on my holy
        mountain!
Let everyone tremble in fear
    because the day of the Lord is
        upon us.

² It is a day of darkness and gloom,
    a day of thick clouds and deep
        blackness.
Suddenly, like dawn spreading across the
        mountains,
    a great and mighty army appears.
Nothing like it has been seen before
    or will ever be seen again.

³ Fire burns in front of them,
    and flames follow after them.
Ahead of them the land lies
    as beautiful as the Garden of Eden.
Behind them is nothing but desolation;
    not one thing escapes.

⁴ They look like horses;
    they charge forward like warhorses.*

⁵ Look at them as they leap along the
        mountaintops.
Listen to the noise they make—like
    the rumbling of chariots,
like the roar of fire sweeping across a
        field of stubble,
    or like a mighty army moving into
        battle.

⁶ Fear grips all the people;
    every face grows pale with terror.

⁷ The attackers march like warriors
    and scale city walls like soldiers.
Straight forward they march,
    never breaking rank.

⁸ They never jostle each other;
    each moves in exactly the right
        position.
They break through defenses
    without missing a step.

⁹ They swarm over the city
    and run along its walls.
They enter all the houses,
    climbing like thieves through the
        windows.

¹⁰ The earth quakes as they advance,
    and the heavens tremble.
The sun and moon grow dark,
    and the stars no longer shine.

Fasting

What Our Brokenness Feels Like

JOEL 2:12-13

For those of us with legalist leanings, it's easy to misunderstand the words of Joel 2:12-13 as an ultimatum from God, as if he's conditioning his mercy on a "penance" of fasting, weeping, and mourning: "'Turn to me now, while there is time. Give me your hearts. Come with fasting, weeping, and mourning.' . . . [The LORD] is eager to relent and not punish."

But a couple of clues in Scripture tell us otherwise. Isaiah 58:5 says, "You humble yourselves by going through the motions of penance, bowing your heads like reeds bending in the wind. You dress in burlap and cover yourselves with ashes. Is this what you call fasting? Do you really think this will please the LORD?"

The middle of Joel 2:13 tells us that as well. "Don't tear your clothing in your grief, but tear your hearts instead." This offers the truth of what God wants from us when we turn to him, when we seek his grace.

God wants us to know the depth of our sins—and let our hearts break over them—so that we can truly grasp the depth of his love for us in seeking to redeem and restore us. This isn't about punishment or penance but about understanding sin with our bodies, minds, and souls.

In her book *Craving Grace,* Lisa Velthouse writes, "Part of what's so incredible about fasting and other spiritual disciplines is the way they put physicality on faith. They tie our understanding of God to everyday tangibility, creating a connection between bodily habit—eating, perhaps—and soul."

When we fast, when we deprive ourselves from the food we desire, we not only learn to lean more on God, but we are reminded physically of what our brokenness feels like. Our stomach pains reflect how our hearts ought to feel when we consider our sin.

This is the role that fasting can help play in our repentance. In fasting we recognize the need we have for God in our lives—to fill us, to nourish us, and to heal our brokenness.

—*Caryn Rivadeneira*

For more on fasting, see reading at Jonah 3.

[11] The LORD is at the head of the column.
He leads them with a shout.
This is his mighty army,
and they follow his orders.
The day of the LORD is an awesome,
terrible thing.
Who can possibly survive?

A Call to Repentance

[12] That is why the LORD says,
"Turn to me now, while there is time.

Give me your hearts.
Come with fasting, weeping, and mourning.
[13] Don't tear your clothing in your grief,
but tear your hearts instead."
Return to the LORD your God,
for he is merciful and compassionate,
slow to get angry and filled with unfailing love.
He is eager to relent and not punish.

¹⁴ Who knows? Perhaps he will give you a reprieve,
> sending you a blessing instead of this curse.
> Perhaps you will be able to offer grain and wine
> to the LORD your God as before.

¹⁵ Blow the ram's horn in Jerusalem!
> Announce a time of fasting;
> call the people together
> for a solemn meeting.
¹⁶ Gather all the people—
> the elders, the children, and even the babies.
> Call the bridegroom from his quarters
> and the bride from her private room.
¹⁷ Let the priests, who minister in the LORD's presence,
> stand and weep between the entry room to the Temple and the altar.
> Let them pray, "Spare your people, LORD!
> Don't let your special possession become an object of mockery.
> Don't let them become a joke for unbelieving foreigners who say,
> 'Has the God of Israel left them?'"

The LORD's Promise of Restoration

¹⁸ Then the LORD will pity his people
> and jealously guard the honor of his land.
¹⁹ The LORD will reply,
> "Look! I am sending you grain and new wine and olive oil,
> enough to satisfy your needs.
> You will no longer be an object of mockery
> among the surrounding nations.
²⁰ I will drive away these armies from the north.
> I will send them into the parched wastelands.
> Those in the front will be driven into the Dead Sea,
> and those at the rear into the Mediterranean.*
> The stench of their rotting bodies will rise over the land."

Surely the LORD has done great things!
²¹   Don't be afraid, my people.
> Be glad now and rejoice,
> for the LORD has done great things.
²² Don't be afraid, you animals of the field,
> for the wilderness pastures will soon be green.
> The trees will again be filled with fruit;
> fig trees and grapevines will be loaded down once more.
²³ Rejoice, you people of Jerusalem!
> Rejoice in the LORD your God!
> For the rain he sends demonstrates his faithfulness.
> Once more the autumn rains will come,
> as well as the rains of spring.
²⁴ The threshing floors will again be piled high with grain,
> and the presses will overflow with new wine and olive oil.

²⁵ The LORD says, "I will give you back what you lost
> to the swarming locusts, the hopping locusts,
> the stripping locusts, and the cutting locusts.*
> It was I who sent this great destroying army against you.
²⁶ Once again you will have all the food you want,
> and you will praise the LORD your God,
> who does these miracles for you.
> Never again will my people be disgraced.
²⁷ Then you will know that I am among my people Israel,
> that I am the LORD your God, and there is no other.
> Never again will my people be disgraced.

The LORD's Promise of His Spirit

²⁸* "Then, after doing all those things,
> I will pour out my Spirit upon all people.
> Your sons and daughters will prophesy.
> Your old men will dream dreams,
> and your young men will see visions.

2:20 Hebrew *into the eastern sea, . . . into the western sea.*   **2:25** The precise identification of the four kinds of locusts mentioned here is uncertain.   **2:28** Verses 2:28-32 are numbered 3:1-5 in Hebrew text.

²⁹ In those days I will pour out my Spirit
even on servants—men and women
alike.
³⁰ And I will cause wonders in the heavens
and on the earth—
blood and fire and columns of smoke.
³¹ The sun will become dark,
and the moon will turn blood red
before that great and terrible* day of
the LORD arrives.
³² But everyone who calls on the name of
the LORD
will be saved,
for some on Mount Zion in Jerusalem
will escape,
just as the LORD has said.
These will be among the survivors
whom the LORD has called.

3 **Judgment against Enemy Nations**
¹* "At the time of those events," says the
LORD,
"when I restore the prosperity of
Judah and Jerusalem,
² I will gather the armies of the world
into the valley of Jehoshaphat.*
There I will judge them
for harming my people, my special
possession,
for scattering my people among the
nations,
and for dividing up my land.
³ They threw dice* to decide which of my
people
would be their slaves.
They traded boys to obtain prostitutes
and sold girls for enough wine to get
drunk.

⁴ "What do you have against me, Tyre
and Sidon and you cities of Philistia? Are
you trying to take revenge on me? If you
are, then watch out! I will strike swiftly and
pay you back for everything you have done.
⁵ You have taken my silver and gold and all
my precious treasures, and have carried
them off to your pagan temples. ⁶ You have
sold the people of Judah and Jerusalem to
the Greeks,* so they could take them far
from their homeland.
⁷ "But I will bring them back from all the

places to which you sold them, and I will
pay you back for everything you have done.
⁸ I will sell your sons and daughters to the
people of Judah, and they will sell them to
the people of Arabia,* a nation far away. I,
the LORD, have spoken!"

⁹ Say to the nations far and wide:
"Get ready for war!
Call out your best warriors.
Let all your fighting men advance for
the attack.
¹⁰ Hammer your plowshares into swords
and your pruning hooks into spears.
Train even your weaklings to be
warriors.
¹¹ Come quickly, all you nations
everywhere.
Gather together in the valley."

And now, O LORD, call out your warriors!

¹² "Let the nations be called to arms.
Let them march to the valley of
Jehoshaphat.
There I, the LORD, will sit
to pronounce judgment on them all.
¹³ Swing the sickle,
for the harvest is ripe.*
Come, tread the grapes,
for the winepress is full.
The storage vats are overflowing
with the wickedness of these people."

¹⁴ Thousands upon thousands are waiting
in the valley of decision.
There the day of the LORD will soon
arrive.
¹⁵ The sun and moon will grow dark,
and the stars will no longer shine.
¹⁶ The LORD's voice will roar from Zion
and thunder from Jerusalem,
and the heavens and the earth will
shake.
But the LORD will be a refuge for his
people,
a strong fortress for the people of
Israel.

Blessings for God's People
¹⁷ "Then you will know that I, the LORD
your God,
live in Zion, my holy mountain.

2:31 Greek version reads *glorious.* **3:1** Verses 3:1-21 are numbered 4:1-21 in Hebrew text. **3:2** *Jehoshaphat* means "the LORD judges."
3:3 Hebrew *They cast lots.* **3:6** Hebrew *to the peoples of Javan.* **3:8** Hebrew *to the Sabeans.* **3:13** Greek version reads *for the harvest time
has come.* Compare Mark 4:29.

Jerusalem will be holy forever,
and foreign armies will never conquer
her again.

¹⁸ In that day the mountains will drip with
sweet wine,
and the hills will flow with milk.
Water will fill the streambeds of
Judah,
and a fountain will burst forth from
the LORD's Temple,
watering the arid valley of acacias.*

¹⁹ But Egypt will become a wasteland
and Edom will become a wilderness,

because they attacked the people of
Judah
and killed innocent people in their
land.

²⁰ "But Judah will be filled with people
forever,
and Jerusalem will endure through all
generations.

²¹ I will pardon my people's crimes,
which I have not yet pardoned;
and I, the LORD, will make my home
in Jerusalem* with my people."

Introduction to
Amos

Background

A false sense of security, complacency, and optimism pervade the northern kingdom of Israel at the time of Amos. Many people maintain a luxurious lifestyle, even as the poor suffer (4:1; 5:11–12; 8:4–6). Idolatry and corruption abound (5:10, 12–13; 6:12). Amos is sent with a message: God's judgment of their sins is about to take place.

Amos is generally believed to be the author of this book. His name means "burden" or "burden-bearer." His hometown is the rural village of Tekoa (1:1), some twelve miles south of Jerusalem in Judah. Since he is from the southern kingdom and opposes practices in Israel, Amos is unpopular among the people of the northern kingdom (7:10–13).

Message

Israel and Judah are at peace with each other and are both experiencing economic and political success. Amos's message, primarily directed to the northern kingdom, reveals distressing developments. Immorality and injustice are increasing. Amos proclaims a clarion call for righteous living and justice; God will judge Israel because "they sell honorable people for silver and poor people for a pair of sandals" (2:6). The strength of the nation of Israel and the weakness of potential rivals such as Assyria, Babylon, and Egypt give Israel a false sense of security; they ignore Amos's prophetic warning of destruction and exile and fall to the Assyrians in 722 B.C.

Time

The phrase "when Uzziah was king of Judah" and the mention of an earthquake (1:1; see also Zechariah 14:5) place Amos's ministry between 767 and 753 B.C. during the reigns of Uzziah (767–739 B.C.) and Jeroboam II, king of Israel (782–753 B.C.). Amos spoke two years before the earthquake (1:1).

Outline

Amos

1 This message was given to Amos, a shepherd from the town of Tekoa in Judah. He received this message in visions two years before the earthquake, when Uzziah was king of Judah and Jeroboam II, the son of Jehoash,* was king of Israel.

² This is what he saw and heard:

"The LORD's voice will roar from Zion
and thunder from Jerusalem!
The lush pastures of the shepherds will dry up;
the grass on Mount Carmel will wither and die."

God's Judgment on Israel's Neighbors

³ This is what the LORD says:

"The people of Damascus have sinned again and again,*
and I will not let them go unpunished!
They beat down my people in Gilead
as grain is threshed with iron sledges.
⁴ So I will send down fire on King Hazael's palace,
and the fortresses of King Ben-hadad will be destroyed.
⁵ I will break down the gates of Damascus
and slaughter the people in the valley of Aven.
I will destroy the ruler in Beth-eden,
and the people of Aram will go as captives to Kir,"
says the LORD.

⁶ This is what the LORD says:

"The people of Gaza have sinned again and again,
and I will not let them go unpunished!
They sent whole villages into exile,
selling them as slaves to Edom.
⁷ So I will send down fire on the walls of Gaza,
and all its fortresses will be destroyed.
⁸ I will slaughter the people of Ashdod
and destroy the king of Ashkelon.
Then I will turn to attack Ekron,
and the few Philistines still left will be killed,"
says the Sovereign LORD.

⁹ This is what the LORD says:

"The people of Tyre have sinned again and again,
and I will not let them go unpunished!
They broke their treaty of brotherhood with Israel,
selling whole villages as slaves to Edom.

1:1 Hebrew *Joash,* a variant spelling of Jehoash.   **1:3** Hebrew *have committed three sins, even four;* also in 1:6, 9, 11, 13.

[10] So I will send down fire on the walls of Tyre,
and all its fortresses will be destroyed."

[11] This is what the Lord says:

"The people of Edom have sinned again and again,
and I will not let them go unpunished!
They chased down their relatives, the Israelites, with swords,
showing them no mercy.
In their rage, they slashed them continually
and were unrelenting in their anger.
[12] So I will send down fire on Teman,
and the fortresses of Bozrah will be destroyed."

[13] This is what the Lord says:

"The people of Ammon have sinned again and again,
and I will not let them go unpunished!
When they attacked Gilead to extend their borders,
they ripped open pregnant women with their swords.
[14] So I will send down fire on the walls of Rabbah,
and all its fortresses will be destroyed.
The battle will come upon them with shouts,
like a whirlwind in a mighty storm.
[15] And their king* and his princes will go into exile together,"
says the Lord.

2 This is what the Lord says:

"The people of Moab have sinned again and again,*
and I will not let them go unpunished!
They desecrated the bones of Edom's king,
burning them to ashes.
[2] So I will send down fire on the land of Moab,
and all the fortresses in Kerioth will be destroyed.
The people will fall in the noise of battle,
as the warriors shout and the ram's horn sounds.

[3] And I will destroy their king
and slaughter all their princes,"
says the Lord.

God's Judgment on Judah and Israel

[4] This is what the Lord says:

"The people of Judah have sinned again and again,
and I will not let them go unpunished!
They have rejected the instruction of the Lord,
refusing to obey his decrees.
They have been led astray by the same lies
that deceived their ancestors.
[5] So I will send down fire on Judah,
and all the fortresses of Jerusalem will be destroyed."

[6] This is what the Lord says:

"The people of Israel have sinned again and again,
and I will not let them go unpunished!
They sell honorable people for silver
and poor people for a pair of sandals.
[7] They trample helpless people in the dust
and shove the oppressed out of the way.
Both father and son sleep with the same woman,
corrupting my holy name.
[8] At their religious festivals,
they lounge in clothing their debtors put up as security.
In the house of their gods,*
they drink wine bought with unjust fines.

[9] "But as my people watched,
I destroyed the Amorites,
though they were as tall as cedars
and as strong as oaks.
I destroyed the fruit on their branches
and dug out their roots.
[10] It was I who rescued you from Egypt
and led you through the desert for forty years,
so you could possess the land of the Amorites.
[11] I chose some of your sons to be prophets
and others to be Nazirites.

1:15 Hebrew *malcam*, possibly referring to their god Molech.   **2:1** Hebrew *have committed three sins, even four;* also in 2:4, 6.   **2:8** Or *their God.*

Can you deny this, my people of Israel?"
    asks the LORD.

12 "But you caused the Nazirites to sin by
    making them drink wine,
    and you commanded the prophets,
    'Shut up!'

13 "So I will make you groan
    like a wagon loaded down with
    sheaves of grain.

14 Your fastest runners will not get away.
    The strongest among you will become
    weak.
   Even mighty warriors will be unable to
    save themselves.

15   The archers will not stand their ground.
   The swiftest runners won't be fast
    enough to escape.
   Even those riding horses won't be able
    to save themselves.

16 On that day the most courageous of your
    fighting men
    will drop their weapons and run for
    their lives,"
    says the LORD.

3 Listen to this message that the LORD
    has spoken against you, O people of
Israel and Judah—against the entire family
I rescued from Egypt:

2 "From among all the families on the earth,
    I have been intimate with you alone.
   That is why I must punish you
    for all your sins."

Witnesses against Guilty Israel

3 Can two people walk together
    without agreeing on the direction?

4 Does a lion ever roar in a thicket
    without first finding a victim?
   Does a young lion growl in its den
    without first catching its prey?

5 Does a bird ever get caught in a trap
    that has no bait?
   Does a trap spring shut
    when there's nothing to catch?

6 When the ram's horn blows a warning,
    shouldn't the people be alarmed?
   Does disaster come to a city
    unless the LORD has planned it?

7 Indeed, the Sovereign LORD never does
    anything
    until he reveals his plans to his
    servants the prophets.

8 The lion has roared—
    so who isn't frightened?
   The Sovereign LORD has spoken—
    so who can refuse to proclaim his
    message?

9 Announce this to the leaders of
    Philistia*
    and to the great ones of Egypt:
   "Take your seats now on the hills around
    Samaria,
    and witness the chaos and oppression
    in Israel."

10 "My people have forgotten how to do
    right,"
    says the LORD.
   "Their fortresses are filled with wealth
    taken by theft and violence.

11 Therefore," says the Sovereign LORD,
    "an enemy is coming!
   He will surround them and shatter their
    defenses.
   Then he will plunder all their fortresses."

12 This is what the LORD says:

   "A shepherd who tries to rescue a sheep
    from a lion's mouth
    will recover only two legs or a piece of
    an ear.
   So it will be for the Israelites in Samaria
    lying on luxurious beds,
    and for the people of Damascus
    reclining on couches.*

13 "Now listen to this, and announce it
throughout all Israel,*" says the Lord, the
LORD God of Heaven's Armies.

14 "On the very day I punish Israel for its sins,
    I will destroy the pagan altars at Bethel.
   The horns of the altar will be cut off
    and fall to the ground.

15 And I will destroy the beautiful homes
    of the wealthy—
    their winter mansions and their
    summer houses, too—
   all their palaces filled with ivory,"
    says the LORD.

3:9 Hebrew *Ashdod.*   **3:12** The meaning of the Hebrew in this sentence is uncertain.   **3:13** Hebrew *the house of Jacob.* The names "Jacob"
and "Israel" are often interchanged throughout the Old Testament, referring sometimes to the individual patriarch and sometimes to the
nation.

4 Israel's Failure to Learn

¹ Listen to me, you fat cows*
    living in Samaria,
you women who oppress the poor
    and crush the needy,
and who are always calling to your
    husbands,
    "Bring us another drink!"

² The Sovereign LORD has sworn this by
    his holiness:
"The time will come when you will be
    led away
    with hooks in your noses.
Every last one of you will be dragged
    away
    like a fish on a hook!"

The Women of Israel:
Lives of Materialism and Luxury

AMOS 3:14—4:1

God called the prophet Amos to challenge his people in Israel. While they unjustly trampled upon the poor, they lived self-focused lives of profound luxury. Amos's striking imagery describes God's people lounging around on luxurious beds and couches (3:12), feasting (2:6), enjoying the affluence of owning both winter mansions and summer homes (3:15), wearing expensive clothing and sandals (2:6, 8), and being obsessed with building wealth (2:6; 8:6).

God had particularly harsh words for some of the women: "Listen to me, you fat cows living in Samaria, you women who oppress the poor and crush the needy, and who are always calling to your husbands, 'Bring us another drink!'" (4:1).

This was more than just name calling. Amos was making a specific reference to the cows of Bashan, a lush and fertile region in Transjordan, famous for its pampered and plump cattle. "The prophet's condemnation is leveled specifically against the uppity upper-class women of Northern Israel, [and their] incessant demand[s] upon their husbands," explains commentator Shalom M. Paul. Their "main purpose in life is to tend to their own self-indulgence, irrespective of the cost."

Look at any popular women's magazine: our culture is driven by this same obsession with comfort, luxury, more, more, more. As Christians we know there's more to life than possessions, yet we may still be guilty of buying into the "fat cow" mentality. We may not even realize that the cancer of consumerism, greed, and self-centeredness has crept in, slowly threatening our spiritual vitality.

As we practice simplicity, we seek to counter the spiritual dangers of materialism and obsession with personal comfort. We prayerfully and intentionally ask, "How much is enough?" We discern truth from lies in our culture's messages about what we need to be happy. We invite God to help us find contentment in him rather than the accumulation of physical comforts. We proclaim by the way we relate to material possessions what we believe is important in life: obedience to God, rather our own comfort; a rich relationship with him, rather than fleeting material luxury.

—Kelli B. Trujillo

For more on simplicity, see reading at John 10:1–10.

4:1 Hebrew you cows of Bashan.

3 You will be led out through the ruins of
the wall;
you will be thrown from your
fortresses,*"
says the LORD.

4 "Go ahead and offer sacrifices to the
idols at Bethel.
Keep on disobeying at Gilgal.
Offer sacrifices each morning,
and bring your tithes every three days.
5 Present your bread made with yeast
as an offering of thanksgiving.
Then give your extra voluntary offerings
so you can brag about it everywhere!
This is the kind of thing you Israelites
love to do,"
says the Sovereign LORD.

6 "I brought hunger to every city
and famine to every town.
But still you would not return to me,"
says the LORD.

7 "I kept the rain from falling
when your crops needed it the most.
I sent rain on one town
but withheld it from another.
Rain fell on one field,
while another field withered away.
8 People staggered from town to town
looking for water,
but there was never enough.
But still you would not return to me,"
says the LORD.

9 "I struck your farms and vineyards with
blight and mildew.
Locusts devoured all your fig and olive
trees.
But still you would not return to me,"
says the LORD.

10 "I sent plagues on you
like the plagues I sent on Egypt long
ago.
I killed your young men in war
and led all your horses away.*
The stench of death filled the air!
But still you would not return to me,"
says the LORD.

11 "I destroyed some of your cities,
as I destroyed* Sodom and Gomorrah.

Those of you who survived
were like charred sticks pulled from
a fire.
But still you would not return to me,"
says the LORD.

12 "Therefore, I will bring upon you all the
disasters I have announced.
Prepare to meet your God in
judgment, you people of Israel!"

13 For the LORD is the one who shaped the
mountains,
stirs up the winds, and reveals his
thoughts to mankind.
He turns the light of dawn into
darkness
and treads on the heights of the earth.
The LORD God of Heaven's Armies is
his name!

5 A Call to Repentance

Listen, you people of Israel! Listen to
this funeral song I am singing:

2 "The virgin Israel has fallen,
never to rise again!
She lies abandoned on the ground,
with no one to help her up."

3 The Sovereign LORD says:

"When a city sends a thousand men to
battle,
only a hundred will return.
When a town sends a hundred,
only ten will come back alive."

4 Now this is what the LORD says to the family of Israel:

"Come back to me and live!
5 Don't worship at the pagan altars at
Bethel;
don't go to the shrines at Gilgal or
Beersheba.
For the people of Gilgal will be dragged
off into exile,
and the people of Bethel will be
reduced to nothing."
6 Come back to the LORD and live!
Otherwise, he will roar through Israel*
like a fire,
devouring you completely.

4:3 Or thrown out toward Harmon, possibly a reference to Mount Hermon.   4:10 Or and slaughtered your captured horses.   4:11 Hebrew as
when God destroyed.   5:6 Hebrew the house of Joseph.

Your gods in Bethel
won't be able to quench the flames.
⁷ You twist justice, making it a bitter pill
for the oppressed.
You treat the righteous like dirt.

⁸ It is the LORD who created the stars,
the Pleiades and Orion.
He turns darkness into morning
and day into night.
He draws up water from the oceans
and pours it down as rain on the land.
The LORD is his name!
⁹ With blinding speed and power he
destroys the strong,
crushing all their defenses.

¹⁰ How you hate honest judges!
How you despise people who tell the
truth!
¹¹ You trample the poor,
stealing their grain through taxes and
unfair rent.
Therefore, though you build beautiful
stone houses,
you will never live in them.
Though you plant lush vineyards,
you will never drink wine from them.
¹² For I know the vast number of your sins
and the depth of your rebellions.
You oppress good people by taking
bribes
and deprive the poor of justice in the
courts.
¹³ So those who are smart keep their
mouths shut,
for it is an evil time.

¹⁴ Do what is good and run from evil
so that you may live!
Then the LORD God of Heaven's Armies
will be your helper,
just as you have claimed.
¹⁵ Hate evil and love what is good;
turn your courts into true halls of
justice.
Perhaps even yet the LORD God of
Heaven's Armies
will have mercy on the remnant of his
people.*

¹⁶ Therefore, this is what the Lord, the LORD
God of Heaven's Armies, says:

"There will be crying in all the public
squares
and mourning in every street.
Call for the farmers to weep with you,
and summon professional mourners
to wail.
¹⁷ There will be wailing in every vineyard,
for I will destroy them all,"
says the LORD.

Warning of Coming Judgment

¹⁸ What sorrow awaits you who say,
"If only the day of the LORD were here!"
You have no idea what you are wishing for.
That day will bring darkness, not light.
¹⁹ In that day you will be like a man who
runs from a lion—
only to meet a bear.
Escaping from the bear, he leans his
hand against a wall in his house—
and he's bitten by a snake.
²⁰ Yes, the day of the LORD will be dark and
hopeless,
without a ray of joy or hope.

²¹ "I hate all your show and pretense—
the hypocrisy of your religious
festivals and solemn assemblies.
²² I will not accept your burnt offerings
and grain offerings.
I won't even notice all your choice
peace offerings.
²³ Away with your noisy hymns of praise!
I will not listen to the music of your
harps.
²⁴ Instead, I want to see a mighty flood of
justice,
an endless river of righteous living.

²⁵ "Was it to me you were bringing sacrifices and offerings during the forty years in the wilderness, Israel? ²⁶ No, you served your pagan gods—Sakkuth your king god and Kaiwan your star god—the images you made for yourselves. ²⁷ So I will send you into exile, to a land east of Damascus,*" says the LORD, whose name is the God of Heaven's Armies.

6 ¹ What sorrow awaits you who lounge in luxury in Jerusalem,* and you who feel secure in Samaria!

5:15 Hebrew *the remnant of Joseph.* **5:26-27** Greek version reads *No, you carried your pagan gods—the shrine of Molech, the star of your god Rephan, and the images you made for yourselves. So I will send you into exile, to a land east of Damascus.* Compare Acts 7:43. **6:1** Hebrew *in Zion.*

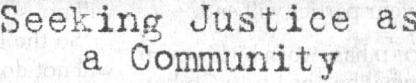

Seeking Justice as a Community

AMOS 5:21–24

Living out the principles of biblical justice is easier said than done. Especially since our world is more complex than the world in which these words from Amos 5:24 were written: "I want to see a mighty flood of justice, an endless river of righteous living."

Although it's possible to be a seeker of justice by myself, I've found it's a lot harder and a lot less joyful. How we are called to live out biblical justice boils down to the Holy Spirit speaking to us individually, as well as through community conversations.

Often God uses the community of believers to help us wrestle with and understand what biblical justice is and what we can do to be a part of the solution.

As I try to figure out how to live justly in my middle-class, comfortable, suburban lifestyle, I've started meeting monthly with friends to read books on justice and kingdom living in general and discuss what that looks like. We've tried to hold one another accountable for how we think God is nudging us, because we know we can't do it alone. Being in community like this means asking the hard questions, trying to pin down answers that relate to me as well as the others, and then celebrating as a group what God is doing.

Beyond just talking and dreaming of justice, we also act justly. Those actions, when we experience them in community, produce a profound effect on everyone involved. The more who work together toward something, the greater the change. Living justly—and seeking what this means in community—brings us more in touch with God and God's care and love for people. It also brings us in touch with the way every single person is made in God's image.

—*Kara Powell*

For more on justice, see reading at Micah 6:6-8.

You are famous and popular in Israel,
  and people go to you for help.
² But go over to Calneh
  and see what happened there.
Then go to the great city of Hamath
  and down to the Philistine city of Gath.
You are no better than they were,
  and look at how they were destroyed.
³ You push away every thought of coming
    disaster,
  but your actions only bring the day of
    judgment closer.
⁴ How terrible for you who sprawl on
    ivory beds
and lounge on your couches,
  eating the meat of tender lambs from
    the flock
  and of choice calves fattened in the
    stall.
⁵ You sing trivial songs to the sound of the
    harp
  and fancy yourselves to be great
    musicians like David.
⁶ You drink wine by the bowlful
  and perfume yourselves with fragrant
    lotions.
You care nothing about the ruin of
    your nation.*

6:6 Hebrew *of Joseph*.

⁷ Therefore, you will be the first to be led
  away as captives.
Suddenly, all your parties will end.

⁸ The Sovereign LORD has sworn by his own
name, and this is what he, the LORD God of
Heaven's Armies, says:

  "I despise the arrogance of Israel,*
    and I hate their fortresses.
  I will give this city
    and everything in it to their enemies."

⁹ (If there are ten men left in one house,
they will all die. ¹⁰ And when a relative
who is responsible to dispose of the dead*
goes into the house to carry out the bodies, he will ask the last survivor, "Is anyone
else with you?" When the person begins to
swear, "No, by . . . ," he will interrupt and
say, "Stop! Don't even mention the name of
the LORD.")

¹¹ When the LORD gives the command,
  homes both great and small will be
    smashed to pieces.

¹² Can horses gallop over boulders?
  Can oxen be used to plow them?
But that's how foolish you are when you
    turn justice into poison
  and the sweet fruit of righteousness
    into bitterness.

¹³ And you brag about your conquest of
    Lo-debar.*
  You boast, "Didn't we take Karnaim*
    by our own strength?"

¹⁴ "O people of Israel, I am about to bring
    an enemy nation against you,"
  says the LORD God of Heaven's
    Armies.
"They will oppress you throughout your
    land—
  from Lebo-hamath in the north
    to the Arabah Valley in the south."

7 A Vision of Locusts

The Sovereign LORD showed me a
vision. I saw him preparing to send a vast
swarm of locusts over the land. This was
after the king's share had been harvested
from the fields and as the main crop was
coming up. ² In my vision the locusts ate

every green plant in sight. Then I said,
"O Sovereign LORD, please forgive us or we
will not survive, for Israel* is so small."

³ So the LORD relented from this plan. "I
will not do it," he said.

A Vision of Fire

⁴ Then the Sovereign LORD showed me
another vision. I saw him preparing to punish his people with a great fire. The fire had
burned up the depths of the sea and was
devouring the entire land. ⁵ Then I said,
"O Sovereign LORD, please stop or we will
not survive, for Israel is so small."

⁶ Then the LORD relented from this plan,
too. "I will not do that either," said the Sovereign LORD.

A Vision of a Plumb Line

⁷ Then he showed me another vision. I saw
the Lord standing beside a wall that had
been built using a plumb line. He was using
a plumb line to see if it was still straight.
⁸ And the LORD said to me, "Amos, what do
you see?"

I answered, "A plumb line."

And the Lord replied, "I will test my people with this plumb line. I will no longer
ignore all their sins. ⁹ The pagan shrines
of your ancestors* will be ruined, and the
temples of Israel will be destroyed; I will
bring the dynasty of King Jeroboam to a
sudden end."

Amos and Amaziah

¹⁰ Then Amaziah, the priest of Bethel, sent a
message to Jeroboam, king of Israel: "Amos
is hatching a plot against you right here on
your very doorstep! What he is saying is
intolerable. ¹¹ He is saying, 'Jeroboam will
soon be killed, and the people of Israel will
be sent away into exile.'"

¹² Then Amaziah sent orders to Amos:
"Get out of here, you prophet! Go on back
to the land of Judah, and earn your living by
prophesying there! ¹³ Don't bother us with
your prophecies here in Bethel. This is the
king's sanctuary and the national place of
worship!"

¹⁴ But Amos replied, "I'm not a professional prophet, and I was never trained to

---

6:8 Hebrew *Jacob*. See note on 3:13.   **6:10** Or *to burn the dead*. The meaning of the Hebrew is uncertain.   **6:13a** *Lo-debar* means "nothing."
6:13b *Karnaim* means "horns," a term that symbolizes strength.   **7:2** Hebrew *Jacob*; also in 7:5. See note on 3:13.   **7:9** Hebrew *of Isaac*.

be one.* I'm just a shepherd, and I take care of sycamore-fig trees. [15]But the LORD called me away from my flock and told me, 'Go and prophesy to my people in Israel.' [16]Now then, listen to this message from the LORD:

"You say,
'Don't prophesy against Israel.
  Stop preaching against my people.*'
[17] But this is what the LORD says:
'Your wife will become a prostitute in
    this city,
  and your sons and daughters will be
    killed.
Your land will be divided up,
  and you yourself will die in a foreign
    land.
And the people of Israel will certainly
    become captives in exile,
  far from their homeland.'"

8 A Vision of Ripe Fruit

Then the Sovereign LORD showed me another vision. In it I saw a basket filled with ripe fruit. [2]"What do you see, Amos?" he asked.

I replied, "A basket full of ripe fruit."

Then the LORD said, "Like this fruit, Israel is ripe for punishment! I will not delay their punishment again. [3]In that day the singing in the Temple will turn to wailing. Dead bodies will be scattered everywhere. They will be carried out of the city in silence. I, the Sovereign LORD, have spoken!"

[4] Listen to this, you who rob the poor
    and trample down the needy!
[5] You can't wait for the Sabbath day to be
    over
  and the religious festivals to end
    so you can get back to cheating the
      helpless.
You measure out grain with dishonest
    measures
  and cheat the buyer with dishonest
    scales.*
[6] And you mix the grain you sell
    with chaff swept from the floor.
Then you enslave poor people
    for one piece of silver or a pair of
      sandals.

[7] Now the LORD has sworn this oath
    by his own name, the Pride of Israel*:
"I will never forget
    the wicked things you have done!
[8] The earth will tremble for your deeds,
    and everyone will mourn.
The ground will rise like the Nile River
    at floodtime;
  it will heave up, then sink again.

[9] "In that day," says the Sovereign LORD,
"I will make the sun go down at noon
    and darken the earth while it is still day.
[10] I will turn your celebrations into times
    of mourning
  and your singing into weeping.
You will wear funeral clothes
    and shave your heads to show your
      sorrow—
as if your only son had died.
    How very bitter that day will be!

[11] "The time is surely coming," says the
    Sovereign LORD,
"when I will send a famine on the
    land—
not a famine of bread or water
  but of hearing the words of the LORD.
[12] People will stagger from sea to sea
    and wander from border to border*
searching for the word of the LORD,
    but they will not find it.
[13] Beautiful girls and strong young men
    will grow faint in that day,
  thirsting for the LORD's word.
[14] And those who swear by the shameful
    idols of Samaria—
who take oaths in the name of the god
    of Dan
  and make vows in the name of the god
    of Beersheba*—
they will all fall down,
    never to rise again."

9 A Vision of God at the Altar

Then I saw a vision of the Lord standing beside the altar. He said,

"Strike the tops of the Temple columns,
    so that the foundation will shake.
Bring down the roof
    on the heads of the people below.

7:14 Or *I'm not a prophet nor the son of a prophet.*   7:16 Hebrew *against the house of Isaac.*   8:5 Hebrew *You make the ephah* [a unit for measuring grain] *small and the shekel* [a unit of weight] *great, and you deal falsely by using deceitful balances.*   8:7 Hebrew *the pride of Jacob.* See note on 3:13.   8:12 Hebrew *from north to east.*   8:14 Hebrew *the way of Beersheba.*

I will kill with the sword those who
   survive.
   No one will escape!

2 "Even if they dig down to the place of the
   dead,*
   I will reach down and pull them up.
   Even if they climb up into the heavens,
   I will bring them down.
3 Even if they hide at the very top of
   Mount Carmel,
   I will search them out and capture
   them.
   Even if they hide at the bottom of the
   ocean,
   I will send the sea serpent after them
   to bite them.
4 Even if their enemies drive them into
   exile,
   I will command the sword to kill them
   there.
   I am determined to bring disaster upon
   them
   and not to help them."

5 The Lord, the LORD of Heaven's Armies,
   touches the land and it melts,
   and all its people mourn.
   The ground rises like the Nile River at
   floodtime,
   and then it sinks again.
6 The LORD's home reaches up to the
   heavens,
   while its foundation is on the earth.
   He draws up water from the oceans
   and pours it down as rain on the land.
   The LORD is his name!

7 "Are you Israelites more important to
   me
   than the Ethiopians?*" asks the LORD.
   "I brought Israel out of Egypt,
   but I also brought the Philistines from
   Crete*
   and led the Arameans out of Kir.
8 "I, the Sovereign LORD,
   am watching this sinful nation of
   Israel.

I will destroy it
   from the face of the earth.
   But I will never completely destroy the
   family of Israel,*"
   says the LORD.
9 "For I will give the command
   and will shake Israel along with the
   other nations
   as grain is shaken in a sieve,
   yet not one true kernel will be lost.
10 But all the sinners will die by the
   sword—
   all those who say, 'Nothing bad will
   happen to us.'

A Promise of Restoration

11 "In that day I will restore the fallen
   house* of David.
   I will repair its damaged walls.
   From the ruins I will rebuild it
   and restore its former glory.
12 And Israel will possess what is left of
   Edom
   and all the nations I have called to be
   mine.*"
   The LORD has spoken,
   and he will do these things.

13 "The time will come," says the LORD,
   "when the grain and grapes will grow
   faster
   than they can be harvested.
   Then the terraced vineyards on the hills
   of Israel
   will drip with sweet wine!
14 I will bring my exiled people of Israel
   back from distant lands,
   and they will rebuild their ruined cities
   and live in them again.
   They will plant vineyards and gardens;
   they will eat their crops and drink
   their wine.
15 I will firmly plant them there
   in their own land.
   They will never again be uprooted
   from the land I have given them,"
   says the LORD your God.

9:2 Hebrew to Sheol.   9:7a Hebrew the Cushites?   9:7b Hebrew Caphtor.   9:8 Hebrew the house of Jacob. See note on 3:13.   9:11a Or
kingdom; Hebrew reads tent.   9:11b-12 Greek version reads and restore its former glory, / so that the rest of humanity, including the Gentiles— /
all those I have called to be mine—might seek me. Compare Acts 15:16-17.

Introduction to
Obadiah

Background

The indictment against Edom in the Book of Obadiah relates to a story that began in Genesis 25. The Edomites were the descendants of Esau, brother of Jacob. Obadiah prophesies against Edom. Because they have helped a foreign nation invade Jerusalem, Edom will be destroyed and their land possessed by the people of Israel.

Obadiah in Hebrew means "worshiper [or servant] of Yahweh."

Message

Moses declared in Numbers 32:23, "Be sure that your sin will find you out." Edom's sins over the centuries finally resulted in its destruction. They refused to let the Hebrews pass through on the way from Egypt to Canaan (Numbers 20:14–21) and fought against King Saul (1 Samuel 14:47). They served Israel during the time of David (2 Samuel 8:14) but gained freedom during the reign of Jehoram of Judah (2 Kings 8:20–22). Later, the Assyrians and Babylonians would rule over them. After settling in southern Palestine and becoming known as the Idumeans, tensions still existed between them and the Jews. The Idumeans joined in the ill-fated Jewish rebellion against Rome (A.D. 66–70). This marked the end of the Idumean people as a nation, thus fulfilling the words of Obadiah.

Time

Scholars have a variety of theories concerning the time of Obadiah. Verses 10–14 describe Edom's involvement in an attack on Jerusalem. Yet this is not the incident in 926 B.C. when Shishak of Egypt plundered the temple and the palace of Rehoboam (1 Kings 14:25–26). At that point, Edom was under the control of Judah.

Edom's revolt against Judah (2 Kings 8:20–22; 2 Chronicles 21:8–10) during the time of Jehoram (848–841 B.C.) is another possibility. Still another is 586 B.C., when Nebuchadnezzar's army destroyed Judah and Jerusalem (2 Kings 24:1–25:30); the Edomites were indicted for their participation (Psalm 137:7; Lamentations 4:21–22). However, 848–841 B.C. fits best.

Outline

Obadiah

This is the vision that the Sovereign LORD revealed to Obadiah concerning the land of Edom.

Edom's Judgment Announced

We have heard a message from the LORD
    that an ambassador was sent to the nations to say,
"Get ready, everyone!
    Let's assemble our armies and attack Edom!"

² The LORD says to Edom,
"I will cut you down to size among the nations;
    you will be greatly despised.
³ You have been deceived by your own pride
    because you live in a rock fortress
    and make your home high in the mountains.
'Who can ever reach us way up here?'
    you ask boastfully.
⁴ But even if you soar as high as eagles
    and build your nest among the stars,
I will bring you crashing down,"
    says the LORD.

⁵ "If thieves came at night and robbed you
    (what a disaster awaits you!),
    they would not take everything.
Those who harvest grapes
    always leave a few for the poor.
    But your enemies will wipe you out completely!
⁶ Every nook and cranny of Edom*
    will be searched and looted.
    Every treasure will be found and taken.

⁷ "All your allies will turn against you.
    They will help to chase you from your land.
They will promise you peace
    while plotting to deceive and destroy you.
Your trusted friends will set traps for you,
    and you won't even know about it.
⁸ At that time not a single wise person
    will be left in the whole land of Edom,"
    says the LORD.
"For on the mountains of Edom
    I will destroy everyone who has understanding.
⁹ The mightiest warriors of Teman
    will be terrified,

---

6 Hebrew *Esau*; also in 8b, 9, 18, 19, 21.

and everyone on the mountains of Edom
will be cut down in the slaughter.

Reasons for Edom's Punishment

10 "Because of the violence you did
to your close relatives in Israel,*
you will be filled with shame
and destroyed forever.
11 When they were invaded,
you stood aloof, refusing to help them.
Foreign invaders carried off their wealth
and cast lots to divide up Jerusalem,
but you acted like one of Israel's
enemies.

12 "You should not have gloated
when they exiled your relatives to
distant lands.
You should not have rejoiced
when the people of Judah suffered
such misfortune.
You should not have spoken arrogantly
in that terrible time of trouble.
13 You should not have plundered the land
of Israel
when they were suffering such
calamity.
You should not have gloated over their
destruction
when they were suffering such
calamity.
You should not have seized their wealth
when they were suffering such
calamity.
14 You should not have stood at the
crossroads,
killing those who tried to escape.
You should not have captured the
survivors
and handed them over in their terrible
time of trouble.

Edom Destroyed, Israel Restored

15 "The day is near when I, the LORD,
will judge all godless nations!

As you have done to Israel,
so it will be done to you.
All your evil deeds
will fall back on your own heads.
16 Just as you swallowed up my people
on my holy mountain,
so you and the surrounding nations
will swallow the punishment I pour
out on you.
Yes, all you nations will drink and stagger
and disappear from history.

17 "But Jerusalem* will become a refuge for
those who escape;
it will be a holy place.
And the people of Israel* will come back
to reclaim their inheritance.
18 The people of Israel will be a raging fire,
and Edom a field of dry stubble.
The descendants of Joseph will be a
flame
roaring across the field, devouring
everything.
There will be no survivors in Edom.
I, the LORD, have spoken!

19 "Then my people living in the Negev
will occupy the mountains of Edom.
Those living in the foothills of Judah*
will possess the Philistine plains
and take over the fields of Ephraim
and Samaria.
And the people of Benjamin
will occupy the land of Gilead.
20 The exiles of Israel will return to their
land
and occupy the Phoenician coast as far
north as Zarephath.
The captives from Jerusalem exiled in
the north*
will return home and resettle the
towns of the Negev.
21 Those who have been rescued* will go
up to* Mount Zion in Jerusalem
to rule over the mountains of Edom.
And the LORD himself will be king!"

10 Hebrew your brother Jacob. The names "Jacob" and "Israel" are often interchanged throughout the Old Testament, referring sometimes to the individual patriarch and sometimes to the nation.   17a Hebrew Mount Zion.   17b Hebrew house of Jacob; also in 18. See note on 10.   19 Hebrew the Shephelah.   20 Hebrew in Sepharad.   21a As in Greek and Syriac versions; Hebrew reads Rescuers.   21b Or from.

Introduction to

Jonah

Background

Called by God to prophesy destruction to Nineveh, the capital city of the Assyrians, Jonah runs away, toward Tarshish, and ends up in the belly of a great fish. Yet God's will prevails. The recalcitrant prophet goes to Nineveh and finally delivers God's message. The people of Nineveh are receptive and repent.

Traditionally, this book has been ascribed to Jonah the son of Amittai (1:1). He also appears in 2 Kings 14:25 as the one who prophesied about the restoration of the boundaries of Israel during the reign of Jeroboam II.

Message

The Book of Jonah is the story of God's incredible mercy and forgiveness. A resentful Jonah refuses to deliver God's message of destruction, knowing that God is merciful and will forgive. The Assyrians' well-deserved reputation for violence caused Israel to see them as a wicked people who were a political threat, even if the nation was not as powerful as it once was.

Time

Jonah's ministry likely took place during the reign of Jeroboam II (782–753 B.C.), after Elisha.

The revival that Jonah describes probably happened during the rule of Ashurdan III (773–755 B.C.). It was short-lived, for Assyria destroyed Samaria, Israel, in 722 B.C. Assyria fell to Babylon in 612 B.C.

Outline

Jonah

1
Jonah Runs from the Lord

The Lord gave this message to Jonah son of Amittai: ²"Get up and go to the great city of Nineveh. Announce my judgment against it because I have seen how wicked its people are."

³But Jonah got up and went in the opposite direction to get away from the Lord. He went down to the port of Joppa, where he found a ship leaving for Tarshish. He bought a ticket and went on board, hoping to escape from the Lord by sailing to Tarshish.

⁴But the Lord hurled a powerful wind over the sea, causing a violent storm that threatened to break the ship apart. ⁵Fearing for their lives, the desperate sailors shouted to their gods for help and threw the cargo overboard to lighten the ship.

But all this time Jonah was sound asleep down in the hold. ⁶So the captain went down after him. "How can you sleep at a time like this?" he shouted. "Get up and pray to your god! Maybe he will pay attention to us and spare our lives."

⁷Then the crew cast lots to see which of them had offended the gods and caused the terrible storm. When they did this, the lots identified Jonah as the culprit. ⁸"Why has this awful storm come down on us?" they demanded. "Who are you? What is your line of work? What country are you from? What is your nationality?"

⁹Jonah answered, "I am a Hebrew, and I worship the Lord, the God of heaven, who made the sea and the land."

¹⁰The sailors were terrified when they heard this, for he had already told them he was running away from the Lord. "Oh, why did you do it?" they groaned. ¹¹And since the storm was getting worse all the time, they asked him, "What should we do to you to stop this storm?"

¹²"Throw me into the sea," Jonah said, "and it will become calm again. I know that this terrible storm is all my fault."

¹³Instead, the sailors rowed even harder to get the ship to the land. But the stormy sea was too violent for them, and they couldn't make it. ¹⁴Then they cried out to the Lord, Jonah's God. "O Lord," they pleaded, "don't make us die for this man's sin. And don't hold us responsible for his death. O Lord, you have sent this storm upon him for your own good reasons."

¹⁵Then the sailors picked Jonah up and threw him into the raging sea, and the storm stopped at once! ¹⁶The sailors were awestruck by the Lord's great power, and they offered him a sacrifice and vowed to serve him.

¹⁷*Now the Lord had arranged for a great fish to swallow Jonah. And Jonah was inside the fish for three days and three nights.

2
Jonah's Prayer

¹*Then Jonah prayed to the Lord his God from inside the fish. ²He said,

"I cried out to the Lord in my great trouble,
and he answered me.

1:17 Verse 1:17 is numbered 2:1 in Hebrew text.　　**2:1** Verses 2:1-10 are numbered 2:2-11 in Hebrew text.

I called to you from the land of the
dead,*
and LORD, you heard me!
³ You threw me into the ocean depths,
and I sank down to the heart of the
sea.
The mighty waters engulfed me;
I was buried beneath your wild and
stormy waves.
⁴ Then I said, 'O LORD, you have driven
me from your presence.
Yet I will look once more toward your
holy Temple.'
⁵ "I sank beneath the waves,
and the waters closed over me.
Seaweed wrapped itself around my
head.
⁶ I sank down to the very roots of the
mountains.
I was imprisoned in the earth,
whose gates lock shut forever.
But you, O LORD my God,
snatched me from the jaws of death!
⁷ As my life was slipping away,
I remembered the LORD.
And my earnest prayer went out to you
in your holy Temple.
⁸ Those who worship false gods
turn their backs on all God's mercies.
⁹ But I will offer sacrifices to you with
songs of praise,
and I will fulfill all my vows.
For my salvation comes from the
LORD alone."

¹⁰ Then the LORD ordered the fish to spit
Jonah out onto the beach.

3 Jonah Goes to Nineveh

Then the LORD spoke to Jonah a second time: ²"Get up and go to the great city
of Nineveh, and deliver the message I have
given you."

³ This time Jonah obeyed the LORD's command and went to Nineveh, a city so large
that it took three days to see it all.* ⁴On the
day Jonah entered the city, he shouted to
the crowds: "Forty days from now Nineveh will be destroyed!" ⁵ The people of Nineveh believed God's message, and from the
greatest to the least, they declared a fast
and put on burlap to show their sorrow.

⁶ When the king of Nineveh heard what
Jonah was saying, he stepped down from
his throne and took off his royal robes. He
dressed himself in burlap and sat on a heap
of ashes. ⁷ Then the king and his nobles sent
this decree throughout the city:

"No one, not even the animals from
your herds and flocks, may eat or drink
anything at all. ⁸ People and animals alike
must wear garments of mourning, and
everyone must pray earnestly to God.
They must turn from their evil ways
and stop all their violence. ⁹ Who can
tell? Perhaps even yet God will change
his mind and hold back his fierce anger
from destroying us."

¹⁰ When God saw what they had done and
how they had put a stop to their evil ways,
he changed his mind and did not carry out
the destruction he had threatened.

4 Jonah's Anger at the LORD's Mercy

This change of plans greatly upset
Jonah, and he became very angry. ²So he
complained to the LORD about it: "Didn't
I say before I left home that you would do
this, LORD? That is why I ran away to Tarshish! I knew that you are a merciful and
compassionate God, slow to get angry and
filled with unfailing love. You are eager to
turn back from destroying people. ³Just kill
me now, LORD! I'd rather be dead than alive
if what I predicted will not happen."

⁴ The LORD replied, "Is it right for you to
be angry about this?"

⁵ Then Jonah went out to the east side
of the city and made a shelter to sit under
as he waited to see what would happen
to the city. ⁶ And the LORD God arranged
for a leafy plant to grow there, and soon it
spread its broad leaves over Jonah's head,
shading him from the sun. This eased his
discomfort, and Jonah was very grateful for
the plant.

⁷ But God also arranged for a worm!
The next morning at dawn the worm ate
through the stem of the plant so that it
withered away. ⁸ And as the sun grew hot,
God arranged for a scorching east wind to
blow on Jonah. The sun beat down on his

2:2 Hebrew *from Sheol.*   3:3 Hebrew *a great city to God, of three days' journey.*

A Holy Diet?

JONAH 3

On a Sunday morning one of our elders challenged the church to take a day to fast. After the service I stopped to talk to a group of women. Several of them said, "Sure, I'll fast. Why not? I might lose some weight." I had to admit the same thought had crossed my mind. I knew we were fasting as a church to examine our lives before God, but why not slip the pounds off too—two birds with one stone?

But deep down the idea bothered me. I wouldn't imagine Paul and Silas, for example, fasting in order to attain some physical ideal! Our culture is so obsessed with losing weight that we can have trouble fasting with the right motives. Those of us who are overweight want to fast primarily to jump-start our efforts to lose a few pounds. And the fewer number of us who struggle with eating disorders use fasting as a way to validate our dysfunctional relationship with food.

Scripture outlines several reasons to fast, including repentance that leads to change (Jonah 3:5-10), asking God to change his course—although this is a request, not a guarantee (2 Samuel 12:13-23)—and preparation for ministry (Acts 13:2-3). Weight loss is definitely *not* among the biblical reasons to fast.

Rather than a means of losing weight, fasting is about gaining strength of soul and character. I've learned to fast with the right motive. I take time to determine my reason and then search the Scriptures to make sure it's biblical. I enter the fast prayerfully and devoutly, letting Christ work in and through me as a result of the fast. And when I'm tempted with the reward of potential weight loss, I face that squarely. Because fasting in order to connect with an almighty, glorious God is far more thrilling (and eternal) than losing a few pounds.

—*JoHannah Reardon*

For more on fasting, see reading at Matthew 6:16-18.

---

head until he grew faint and wished to die. "Death is certainly better than living like this!" he exclaimed.

⁹Then God said to Jonah, "Is it right for you to be angry because the plant died?"

"Yes," Jonah retorted, "even angry enough to die!"

¹⁰Then the LORD said, "You feel sorry about the plant, though you did nothing to put it there. It came quickly and died quickly. ¹¹But Nineveh has more than 120,000 people living in spiritual darkness,* not to mention all the animals. Shouldn't I feel sorry for such a great city?"

4:11 Hebrew *people who don't know their right hand from their left.*

Introduction to

Micah

Background

The opening verse of Micah identifies the prophet's hometown as Moresheth, likely Moresheth-gath (1:14) on the border of Judah and Philistia, twenty-five miles southwest of Jerusalem. He speaks to conditions in both kingdoms, Israel and Judah.

Micah focuses his complaints on the injustices of the land and the sufferings of the poor at the hands of the rich, a message similar to that of the prophet Amos. Jeremiah 26:17–19 refers to Micah, as King Hezekiah repented after hearing Micah's message.

Micaia is a shortened form of the Hebrew name *Michayahu*, which means "who is like Yahweh?"

Message

God calls Micah to preach a message of God's hatred of sin and the love he has for his people. In the trial scene of chapter 6, God puts his people on trial for sin, declares them guilty, and assigns them a punishment of destruction and exile. However, God also promises to pardon their sin (7:18–20), using their punishment as a way of purifying his people and drawing them back to himself.

The Book of Micah also has a description of a coming time of peace and prosperity when the Messiah will shepherd his people and rule over the whole world (4:1–5:9).

God promises to rescue a remnant of his people from captivity (2:12; 4:10) just as he had brought them out of Egypt (6:4).

Time

Micah prophesied during the reigns of three kings of Judah: Jotham, Ahaz, and Hezekiah (1:1). Micah predicts the fall of Samaria (1:6), an additional indication that his ministry started before Assyria took Israel into captivity in 722 B.C.

A number of religious changes happened during the reign of Hezekiah (715–686 B.C.), in part in response to Micah's condemnation of the rampant idolatry and immorality in the land (Jeremiah 26:18). These factors indicate that Micah likely prophesied from 735 B.C. to 710 B.C., making his ministry contemporaneous with Isaiah's to Judah and Hosea's to Israel.

Outline

Micah

1 The LORD gave this message to Micah of Moresheth during the years when Jotham, Ahaz, and Hezekiah were kings of Judah. The visions he saw concerned both Samaria and Jerusalem.

Grief over Samaria and Jerusalem

² Attention! Let all the people of the world listen!
　　Let the earth and everything in it hear.
　The Sovereign LORD is making accusations against you;
　　the Lord speaks from his holy Temple.
³ Look! The LORD is coming!
　　He leaves his throne in heaven
　　and tramples the heights of the earth.
⁴ The mountains melt beneath his feet
　　and flow into the valleys
　like wax in a fire,
　　like water pouring down a hill.
⁵ And why is this happening?
　　Because of the rebellion of Israel*—
　　yes, the sins of the whole nation.
　Who is to blame for Israel's rebellion?
　　Samaria, its capital city!
　Where is the center of idolatry in Judah?
　　In Jerusalem, its capital!

⁶ "So I, the LORD, will make the city of Samaria
　　a heap of ruins.
　Her streets will be plowed up
　　for planting vineyards.
　I will roll the stones of her walls into the valley below,
　　exposing her foundations.
⁷ All her carved images will be smashed.
　　All her sacred treasures will be burned.
　These things were bought with the money
　　earned by her prostitution,
　and they will now be carried away
　　to pay prostitutes elsewhere."

⁸ Therefore, I will mourn and lament.
　　I will walk around barefoot and naked.
　I will howl like a jackal
　　and moan like an owl.
⁹ For my people's wound
　　is too deep to heal.

1:5 Hebrew *Jacob;* also in 1:5b. The names "Jacob" and "Israel" are often interchanged throughout the Old Testament, referring sometimes to the individual patriarch and sometimes to the nation.

It has reached into Judah,
even to the gates of Jerusalem.

[10] Don't tell our enemies in Gath*;
don't weep at all.
You people in Beth-leaphrah,*
roll in the dust to show your despair.
[11] You people in Shaphir,*
go as captives into exile—naked and
ashamed.
The people of Zaanan*
dare not come outside their walls.
The people of Beth-ezel* mourn,
for their house has no support.
[12] The people of Maroth* anxiously wait
for relief,
but only bitterness awaits them
as the LORD's judgment reaches
even to the gates of Jerusalem.

[13] Harness your chariot horses and flee,
you people of Lachish.*
You were the first city in Judah
to follow Israel in her rebellion,
and you led Jerusalem* into sin.
[14] Send farewell gifts to Moresheth-gath*;
there is no hope of saving it.
The town of Aczib*
has deceived the kings of Israel.
[15] O people of Mareshah,*
I will bring a conqueror to capture
your town.
And the leaders* of Israel
will go to Adullam.

[16] Oh, people of Judah, shave your heads in
sorrow,
for the children you love will be
snatched away.
Make yourselves as bald as a vulture,
for your little ones will be exiled to
distant lands.

2 Judgment against Wealthy Oppressors

[1] What sorrow awaits you who lie awake
at night,
thinking up evil plans.
You rise at dawn and hurry to carry
them out,
simply because you have the power to
do so.
[2] When you want a piece of land,
you find a way to seize it.
When you want someone's house,
you take it by fraud and violence.
You cheat a man of his property,
stealing his family's inheritance.

[3] But this is what the LORD says:
"I will reward your evil with evil;
you won't be able to pull your neck out
of the noose.
You will no longer walk around proudly,
for it will be a terrible time."

[4] In that day your enemies will make fun
of you
by singing this song of despair about
you:
"We are finished,
completely ruined!
God has confiscated our land,
taking it from us.
He has given our fields
to those who betrayed us.*"
[5] Others will set your boundaries then,
and the LORD's people will have no say
in how the land is divided.

True and False Prophets

[6] "Don't say such things,"
the people respond.*
"Don't prophesy like that.
Such disasters will never come our
way!"

[7] Should you talk that way, O family of
Israel?*
Will the LORD's Spirit have patience
with such behavior?
If you would do what is right,
you would find my words comforting.
[8] Yet to this very hour
my people rise against me like an
enemy!
You steal the shirts right off the backs
of those who trusted you,
making them as ragged as men
returning from battle.

1:10a Gath sounds like the Hebrew term for "tell."   1:10b Beth-leaphrah means "house of dust."   1:11a Shaphir means "pleasant."
1:11b Zaanan sounds like the Hebrew term for "come out."   1:11c Beth-ezel means "adjoining house."   1:12 Maroth sounds like the Hebrew
term for "bitter."   1:13a Lachish sounds like the Hebrew term for "team of horses."   1:13b Hebrew the daughter of Zion.   1:14a Moresheth
sounds like the Hebrew term for "gift" or "dowry."   1:14b Aczib means "deception."   1:15a Mareshah sounds like the Hebrew term for
"conqueror."   1:15b Hebrew the glory.   2:4 Or to those who took us captive.   2:6 Or the prophets respond; Hebrew reads they prophesy.
2:7 Hebrew O house of Jacob? See note on 1:5a.

⁹ You have evicted women from their
  pleasant homes
    and forever stripped their children of
    all that God would give them.
¹⁰ Up! Begone!
  This is no longer your land and home,
  for you have filled it with sin
    and ruined it completely.
¹¹ Suppose a prophet full of lies would say
    to you,
  "I'll preach to you the joys of wine and
    alcohol!"
  That's just the kind of prophet you
    would like!

Hope for Restoration

¹² "Someday, O Israel, I will gather you;
  I will gather the remnant who are left.
  I will bring you together again like sheep
    in a pen,
    like a flock in its pasture.
  Yes, your land will again
    be filled with noisy crowds!
¹³ Your leader will break out
    and lead you out of exile,
  out through the gates of the enemy
    cities,
    back to your own land.
  Your king will lead you;
    the LORD himself will guide you."

3 Judgment against Israel's Leaders

¹ I said, "Listen, you leaders of Israel!
  You are supposed to know right from
    wrong,
² but you are the very ones
    who hate good and love evil.
  You skin my people alive
    and tear the flesh from their bones.
³ Yes, you eat my people's flesh,
    strip off their skin,
    and break their bones.
  You chop them up
    like meat for the cooking pot.
⁴ Then you beg the LORD for help in times
    of trouble!
    Do you really expect him to answer?
  After all the evil you have done,
    he won't even look at you!"
⁵ This is what the LORD says:
  "You false prophets are leading my
    people astray!

You promise peace for those who give
    you food,
  but you declare war on those who
    refuse to feed you.
⁶ Now the night will close around you,
    cutting off all your visions.
  Darkness will cover you,
    putting an end to your predictions.
  The sun will set for you prophets,
    and your day will come to an end.
⁷ Then you seers will be put to shame,
    and you fortune-tellers will be
    disgraced.
  And you will cover your faces
    because there is no answer from
    God."

⁸ But as for me, I am filled with
    power—
    with the Spirit of the LORD.
  I am filled with justice and strength
    to boldly declare Israel's sin and
    rebellion.
⁹ Listen to me, you leaders of Israel!
    You hate justice and twist all that is
    right.
¹⁰ You are building Jerusalem
    on a foundation of murder and
    corruption.
¹¹ You rulers make decisions based on
    bribes;
    you priests teach God's laws only for
    a price;
  you prophets won't prophesy unless you
    are paid.
    Yet all of you claim to depend on the
    LORD.
  "No harm can come to us," you say,
    "for the LORD is here among us."
¹² Because of you, Mount Zion will be
    plowed like an open field;
  Jerusalem will be reduced to ruins!
  A thicket will grow on the heights
    where the Temple now stands.

4 The LORD's Future Reign

¹ In the last days, the mountain of the
    LORD's house
  will be the highest of all—
    the most important place on earth.
  It will be raised above the other hills,
    and people from all over the world will
    stream there to worship.

² People from many nations will come and
say,
"Come, let us go up to the mountain of
the LORD,
to the house of Jacob's God.
There he will teach us his ways,
and we will walk in his paths."
For the LORD's teaching will go out from
Zion;
his word will go out from Jerusalem.
³ The LORD will mediate between peoples
and will settle disputes between strong
nations far away.
They will hammer their swords into
plowshares
and their spears into pruning hooks.
Nation will no longer fight against
nation,
nor train for war anymore.
⁴ Everyone will live in peace and
prosperity,
enjoying their own grapevines and fig
trees,
for there will be nothing to fear.
The LORD of Heaven's Armies
has made this promise!
⁵ Though the nations around us follow
their idols,
we will follow the LORD our God
forever and ever.

Israel's Return from Exile

⁶ "In that coming day," says the LORD,
"I will gather together those who are
lame,
those who have been exiles,
and those whom I have filled with grief.
⁷ Those who are weak will survive as a
remnant;
those who were exiles will become a
strong nation.
Then I, the LORD, will rule from
Jerusalem*
as their king forever."
⁸ As for you, Jerusalem,
the citadel of God's people,*
your royal might and power
will come back to you again.
The kingship will be restored
to my precious Jerusalem.

⁹ But why are you now screaming in
terror?
Have you no king to lead you?
Have your wise people all died?
Pain has gripped you like a woman in
childbirth.
¹⁰ Writhe and groan like a woman in labor,
you people of Jerusalem,*
for now you must leave this city
to live in the open country.
You will soon be sent in exile
to distant Babylon.
But the LORD will rescue you there;
he will redeem you from the grip of
your enemies.

¹¹ Now many nations have gathered
against you.
"Let her be desecrated," they say.
"Let us see the destruction of
Jerusalem.*"
¹² But they do not know the LORD's
thoughts
or understand his plan.
These nations don't know
that he is gathering them together
to be beaten and trampled
like sheaves of grain on a threshing
floor.
¹³ "Rise up and crush the nations,
O Jerusalem!"*
says the LORD.
"For I will give you iron horns and
bronze hooves,
so you can trample many nations to
pieces.
You will present their stolen riches to
the LORD,
their wealth to the LORD of all the
earth."

5 ¹* Mobilize! Marshal your troops!
The enemy is laying siege to
Jerusalem.
They will strike Israel's leader
in the face with a rod.

A Ruler from Bethlehem

²* But you, O Bethlehem Ephrathah,
are only a small village among all the
people of Judah.

4:7 Hebrew *Mount Zion.* 4:8 Hebrew *As for you, Migdal-eder, / the Ophel of the daughter of Zion.* 4:10 Hebrew *O daughter of Zion.*
4:11 Hebrew *of Zion.* 4:13 Hebrew *"Rise up and thresh, O daughter of Zion."* 5:1 Verse 5:1 is numbered 4:14 in Hebrew text. 5:2 Verses
5:2-15 are numbered 5:1-14 in Hebrew text.

Yet a ruler of Israel will come from you,
    one whose origins are from the distant
    past.
³ The people of Israel will be abandoned
    to their enemies
    until the woman in labor gives birth.
Then at last his fellow countrymen
    will return from exile to their own
    land.
⁴ And he will stand to lead his flock with
    the Lord's strength,
    in the majesty of the name of the
    Lord his God.
Then his people will live there
    undisturbed,
    for he will be highly honored around
    the world.
⁵   And he will be the source of peace.

When the Assyrians invade our land
    and break through our defenses,
we will appoint seven rulers to watch
    over us,
    eight princes to lead us.
⁶ They will rule Assyria with drawn
    swords
    and enter the gates of the land of
    Nimrod.
He will rescue us from the Assyrians
    when they pour over the borders to
    invade our land.

The Remnant Purified

⁷ Then the remnant left in Israel*
    will take their place among the
    nations.
They will be like dew sent by the Lord
    or like rain falling on the grass,
which no one can hold back
    and no one can restrain.
⁸ The remnant left in Israel
    will take their place among the
    nations.
They will be like a lion among the
    animals of the forest,
    like a strong young lion among flocks
    of sheep and goats,
pouncing and tearing as they go
    with no rescuer in sight.
⁹ The people of Israel will stand up to
    their foes,
    and all their enemies will be wiped out.

¹⁰ "In that day," says the Lord,
    "I will slaughter your horses
    and destroy your chariots.
¹¹ I will tear down your walls
    and demolish your defenses.
¹² I will put an end to all witchcraft,
    and there will be no more fortune-
    tellers.
¹³ I will destroy all your idols and sacred
    pillars,
    so you will never again worship the
    work of your own hands.
¹⁴ I will abolish your idol shrines with their
    Asherah poles
    and destroy your pagan cities.
¹⁵ I will pour out my vengeance
    on all the nations that refuse to obey
    me."

6 **The Lord's Case against Israel**
Listen to what the Lord is saying:

"Stand up and state your case
    against me.
    Let the mountains and hills be called
    to witness your complaints.
² And now, O mountains,
    listen to the Lord's complaint!
He has a case against his people.
    He will bring charges against Israel.

³ "O my people, what have I done to you?
    What have I done to make you tired
    of me?
    Answer me!
⁴ For I brought you out of Egypt
    and redeemed you from slavery.
I sent Moses, Aaron, and Miriam to
    help you.
⁵ Don't you remember, my people,
    how King Balak of Moab tried to have
    you cursed
    and how Balaam son of Beor blessed
    you instead?
And remember your journey from
    Acacia Grove* to Gilgal,
    when I, the Lord, did everything I
    could
    to teach you about my faithfulness."

⁶ What can we bring to the Lord?
    What kind of offerings should we give
    him?

5:7 Hebrew *in Jacob;* also in 5:8. See note on 1:5a. **6:5** Hebrew *Shittim.*

Moving from "Charity" to Justice

MICAH 6:6–8

Musician Sara Groves has long championed ministries of compassion and justice, but it wasn't until a personal visit to Rwanda that she really started to "get it."

Sara often prided herself on her charity work, and she felt her trip to Africa would allow her to offer her heart of charity. But she discovered a huge difference between justice and charity. God broke her heart to see the tremendous injustice of life there.

On another trip to Rwanda, Groves, her husband, and her son Kirby visited the home of Ann Marie, a widow with five children ages ten to nineteen. Their mud-brick dwelling, about ten by twelve feet, had a thatched roof and a fire pit for cooking. The family slept on a straw mat on the dirt floor.

Crowded into the house, the Groves family listened to Ann Marie's story of raising her family in a nation still struggling to get back on its feet fifteen years after genocide.

Later Groves asked her then eight-year-old son, "What room in our house is this size?"

"Our bathroom," Kirby replied.

Groves began to weep. Later she explained in an interview with *Thought Quotient*, "As a mom, I can't imagine trying to raise my whole family in my bathroom. It was a vivid lesson in justice. I thought, *This is not acceptable. This is an injustice, and this is where we begin.*"

Spiritual fervency can easily mingle with impure motives—like pride masking itself as virtuous compassion or exemplary faith. In our efforts to live justly, like Groves, we must seek to discern between self-congratulatory "charity" (in which we give ourselves a spiritual pat on the back for our efforts) and the sincere work of justice—which, as Micah 6:8 stresses, ought to be accompanied with a love of mercy and constant humility before God.

—*Mark Moring*

For more on justice, see reading at Zechariah 8.

Should we bow before God
  with offerings of yearling calves?
⁷ Should we offer him thousands of rams
  and ten thousand rivers of olive oil?
Should we sacrifice our firstborn
    children
  to pay for our sins?

⁸ No, O people, the LORD has told you
  what is good,
  and this is what he requires of you:

to do what is right, to love mercy,
  and to walk humbly with your
    God.

Israel's Guilt and Punishment

⁹ Fear the LORD if you are wise!
  His voice calls to everyone in
    Jerusalem:
"The armies of destruction are
    coming;
  the LORD is sending them.*

6:9 Hebrew *"Listen to the rod. / Who appointed it?"*

¹⁰ What shall I say about the homes of the wicked
  filled with treasures gained by cheating?
What about the disgusting practice
  of measuring out grain with dishonest measures?*
¹¹ How can I tolerate your merchants
  who use dishonest scales and weights?
¹² The rich among you have become wealthy
  through extortion and violence.
Your citizens are so used to lying
  that their tongues can no longer tell the truth.

¹³ "Therefore, I will wound you!
  I will bring you to ruin for all your sins.
¹⁴ You will eat but never have enough.
  Your hunger pangs and emptiness will remain.
And though you try to save your money,
  it will come to nothing in the end.
You will save a little,
  but I will give it to those who conquer you.
¹⁵ You will plant crops
  but not harvest them.
You will press your olives
  but not get enough oil to anoint yourselves.
You will trample the grapes
  but get no juice to make your wine.
¹⁶ You keep only the laws of evil King Omri;
  you follow only the example of wicked King Ahab!
Therefore, I will make an example of you,
  bringing you to complete ruin.
You will be treated with contempt,
  mocked by all who see you."

7 Misery Turned to Hope
¹ How miserable I am!
I feel like the fruit picker after the harvest
  who can find nothing to eat.
Not a cluster of grapes or a single early fig
  can be found to satisfy my hunger.

² The godly people have all disappeared;
  not one honest person is left on the earth.
They are all murderers,
  setting traps even for their own brothers.
³ Both their hands are equally skilled at doing evil!
  Officials and judges alike demand bribes.
The people with influence get what they want,
  and together they scheme to twist justice.
⁴ Even the best of them is like a brier;
  the most honest is as dangerous as a hedge of thorns.
But your judgment day is coming swiftly now.
  Your time of punishment is here, a time of confusion.
⁵ Don't trust anyone—
  not your best friend or even your wife!
⁶ For the son despises his father.
  The daughter defies her mother.
The daughter-in-law defies her mother-in-law.
  Your enemies are right in your own household!

⁷ As for me, I look to the LORD for help.
  I wait confidently for God to save me,
  and my God will certainly hear me.
⁸ Do not gloat over me, my enemies!
  For though I fall, I will rise again.
Though I sit in darkness,
  the LORD will be my light.
⁹ I will be patient as the LORD punishes me,
  for I have sinned against him.
But after that, he will take up my case
  and give me justice for all I have suffered from my enemies.
The LORD will bring me into the light,
  and I will see his righteousness.
¹⁰ Then my enemies will see that the LORD is on my side.
  They will be ashamed that they taunted me, saying,
"So where is the LORD—
  that God of yours?"

6:10 Hebrew *of using the short ephah?* The ephah was a unit for measuring grain.

With my own eyes I will see their
 downfall;
   they will be trampled like mud in the
 streets.

[11] In that day, Israel, your cities will be
 rebuilt,
   and your borders will be extended.
[12] People from many lands will come and
 honor you—
   from Assyria all the way to the towns
 of Egypt,
   from Egypt all the way to the Euphrates
 River,*
   and from distant seas and
 mountains.
[13] But the land* will become empty and
 desolate
   because of the wickedness of those
 who live there.

The Lord's Compassion on Israel

[14] O Lord, protect your people with your
 shepherd's staff;
   lead your flock, your special
 possession.
Though they live alone in a thicket
   on the heights of Mount Carmel,*
let them graze in the fertile pastures of
 Bashan and Gilead
   as they did long ago.

[15] "Yes," says the Lord,
   "I will do mighty miracles for you,

like those I did when I rescued you
 from slavery in Egypt."

[16] All the nations of the world will stand
 amazed
   at what the Lord will do for you.
They will be embarrassed
   at their feeble power.
They will cover their mouths in silent awe,
   deaf to everything around them.
[17] Like snakes crawling from their holes,
   they will come out to meet the Lord
 our God.
They will fear him greatly,
   trembling in terror at his presence.

[18] Where is another God like you,
   who pardons the guilt of the remnant,
   overlooking the sins of his special
 people?
You will not stay angry with your people
 forever,
   because you delight in showing
 unfailing love.
[19] Once again you will have compassion
 on us.
   You will trample our sins under your
 feet
   and throw them into the depths of the
 ocean!
[20] You will show us your faithfulness and
 unfailing love
   as you promised to our ancestors
 Abraham and Jacob long ago.

7:12 Hebrew *the river.*   **7:13** Or *earth.*   **7:14** Or *surrounded by a fruitful land.*

Introduction to

Nahum

Background

After the revival inspired by Jonah's ministry in Nineveh, Assyria quickly returns
to its cruel ways, destroying Samaria in 722 B.C. Assyria then sets its sights on
Judah, and Sennacherib attacks Jerusalem in 701 B.C. Only by turning to God
is King Hezekiah able to save the city (2 Kings 18:13–19:27; 2 Chronicles 32:1–
23), even while Assyria takes some people into exile. Under King Esarhaddon
(r. 681–669 B.C.), Judah becomes subject to Assyria. The early years of the reign of
Ashurbanipal (669–633 B.C.) mark the peak of Assyria's power, demonstrated by
its capture of Thebes.

While the prophet Nahum is believed to be the author of this book, the only
biblical information about him appears in 1:1, where his hometown (Elkosh) is
identified. The Hebrew name *Nahum* means "comfort, consolation."

Message

Like the prophet Obadiah, who focused on one nation, Nahum's message focuses
on a foreign nation—Assyria. While the prophet's message may seem stern, it
comforts the people by proclaiming that God will destroy the cruel Assyrians who
conquered the northern kingdom of Israel and elicited fear in Judah. Assyria was at
the height of its influence at the time of Nahum's prophecy. The city of Nineveh had
fortifications that would allow it to withstand a twenty-year siege. While Nahum's
prophecy of its destruction (1:8; 3:13–15) may have been difficult to envision at that
time, it would come to pass less than fifty years later. The Tigris River overflowed,
the floodwaters destroyed parts of the immense wall, and the Babylonians invaded
through the holes in the wall, plundering the city and setting it on fire.

Time

Nahum wrote sometime before 612 B.C. The vivid description of the fall of Thebes
(3:8–10) points to Nahum writing shortly after this event (circa 664 B.C.). The
absence of discussion of the restoration of Thebes indicates that Nahum wrote
between its fall and its restoration in 654 B.C.

Nahum proclaims the fall of Nineveh as a future event. Since chapter 1 does not
note the king during whose reign Nahum prophesies, a date of 663–654 B.C. places
Nahum's ministry during the reign of Manasseh of Judah.

Outline

Nahum

1 This message concerning Nineveh came as a vision to Nahum, who lived in Elkosh.

The LORD's Anger against Nineveh

² The LORD is a jealous God,
   filled with vengeance and rage.
He takes revenge on all who oppose him
   and continues to rage against his enemies!
³ The LORD is slow to get angry, but his power is great,
   and he never lets the guilty go unpunished.
He displays his power in the whirlwind and the storm.
   The billowing clouds are the dust beneath his feet.
⁴ At his command the oceans dry up,
   and the rivers disappear.
The lush pastures of Bashan and Carmel fade,
   and the green forests of Lebanon wither.
⁵ In his presence the mountains quake,
   and the hills melt away;
the earth trembles,
   and its people are destroyed.
⁶ Who can stand before his fierce anger?
   Who can survive his burning fury?
His rage blazes forth like fire,
   and the mountains crumble to dust in his presence.

⁷ The LORD is good,
   a strong refuge when trouble comes.
He is close to those who trust in him.
⁸ But he will sweep away his enemies
   in an overwhelming flood.
He will pursue his foes
   into the darkness of night.

⁹ Why are you scheming against the LORD?
   He will destroy you with one blow;
   he won't need to strike twice!
¹⁰ His enemies, tangled like thornbushes
   and staggering like drunks,
   will be burned up like dry stubble in a field.
¹¹ Who is this wicked counselor of yours
   who plots evil against the LORD?

¹² This is what the LORD says:
   "Though the Assyrians have many allies,
      they will be destroyed and disappear.
   O my people, I have punished you before,
      but I will not punish you again.

¹³ Now I will break the yoke of bondage
from your neck
and tear off the chains of Assyrian
oppression."

¹⁴ And this is what the LORD says
concerning the Assyrians in
Nineveh:
"You will have no more children to carry
on your name.
I will destroy all the idols in the
temples of your gods.
I am preparing a grave for you
because you are despicable!"

¹⁵* Look! A messenger is coming over the
mountains with good news!
He is bringing a message of peace.
Celebrate your festivals, O people of
Judah,
and fulfill all your vows,
for your wicked enemies will never
invade your land again.
They will be completely destroyed!

2 The Fall of Nineveh

¹* Your enemy is coming to crush you,
Nineveh.
Man the ramparts! Watch the
roads!
Prepare your defenses! Call out your
forces!

² Even though the destroyer has destroyed
Judah,
the LORD will restore its honor.
Israel's vine has been stripped of
branches,
but he will restore its splendor.

³ Shields flash red in the sunlight!
See the scarlet uniforms of the valiant
troops!
Watch as their glittering chariots move
into position,
with a forest of spears waving above
them.*

⁴ The chariots race recklessly along the
streets
and rush wildly through the
squares.
They flash like firelight
and move as swiftly as lightning.

⁵ The king shouts to his officers;
they stumble in their haste,
rushing to the walls to set up their
defenses.
⁶ The river gates have been torn open!
The palace is about to collapse!
⁷ Nineveh's exile has been decreed,
and all the servant girls mourn its
capture.
They moan like doves
and beat their breasts in sorrow.
⁸ Nineveh is like a leaking water reservoir!
The people are slipping away.
"Stop, stop!" someone shouts,
but no one even looks back.
⁹ Loot the silver!
Plunder the gold!
There's no end to Nineveh's treasures—
its vast, uncounted wealth.
¹⁰ Soon the city is plundered, empty, and
ruined.
Hearts melt and knees shake.
The people stand aghast,
their faces pale and trembling.

¹¹ Where now is that great Nineveh,
that den filled with young lions?
It was a place where people—like lions
and their cubs—
walked freely and without fear.
¹² The lion tore up meat for his cubs
and strangled prey for his mate.
He filled his den with prey,
his caverns with his plunder.

¹³ "I am your enemy!"
says the LORD of Heaven's Armies.
"Your chariots will soon go up in smoke.
Your young men* will be killed in
battle.
Never again will you plunder conquered
nations.
The voices of your proud messengers
will be heard no more."

3 The LORD's Judgment against Nineveh

¹ What sorrow awaits Nineveh,
the city of murder and lies!
She is crammed with wealth
and is never without victims.
² Hear the crack of whips,
the rumble of wheels!

1:15 Verse 1:15 is numbered 2:1 in Hebrew text.   **2:1** Verses 2:1-13 are numbered 2:2-14 in Hebrew text.   **2:3** Greek and Syriac versions read
into position, / the horses whipped into a frenzy.   **2:13** Hebrew *young lions.*

Horses' hooves pound,
and chariots clatter wildly.
³ See the flashing swords and glittering
spears
as the charioteers charge past!
There are countless casualties,
heaps of bodies—
so many bodies that
people stumble over them.
⁴ All this because Nineveh,
the beautiful and faithless city,
mistress of deadly charms,
enticed the nations with her beauty.
She taught them all her magic,
enchanting people everywhere.

⁵ "I am your enemy!"
says the LORD of Heaven's Armies.
"And now I will lift your skirts
and show all the earth your nakedness
and shame.
⁶ I will cover you with filth
and show the world how vile you
really are.
⁷ All who see you will shrink back and say,
'Nineveh lies in ruins.
Where are the mourners?'
Does anyone regret your
destruction?"

⁸ Are you any better than the city of
Thebes,*
situated on the Nile River, surrounded
by water?
She was protected by the river on all
sides,
walled in by water.
⁹ Ethiopia* and the land of Egypt
gave unlimited assistance.
The nations of Put and Libya
were among her allies.
¹⁰ Yet Thebes fell,
and her people were led away as
captives.
Her babies were dashed to death
against the stones of the streets.
Soldiers threw dice* to get Egyptian
officers as servants.
All their leaders were bound in chains.

¹¹ And you, Nineveh, will also stagger like
a drunkard.

You will hide for fear of the attacking
enemy.
¹² All your fortresses will fall.
They will be devoured like the ripe figs
that fall into the mouths
of those who shake the trees.
¹³ Your troops will be as weak
and helpless as women.
The gates of your land will be opened
wide to the enemy
and set on fire and burned.
¹⁴ Get ready for the siege!
Store up water!
Strengthen the defenses!
Go into the pits to trample clay,
and pack it into molds,
making bricks to repair the walls.

¹⁵ But the fire will devour you;
the sword will cut you down.
The enemy will consume you like
locusts,
devouring everything they see.
There will be no escape,
even if you multiply like swarming
locusts.
¹⁶ Your merchants have multiplied
until they outnumber the stars.
But like a swarm of locusts,
they strip the land and fly away.
¹⁷ Your guards* and officials are also like
swarming locusts
that crowd together in the hedges on
a cold day.
But like locusts that fly away when the
sun comes up,
all of them will fly away and disappear.

¹⁸ Your shepherds are asleep, O Assyrian
king;
your princes lie dead in the dust.
Your people are scattered across the
mountains
with no one to gather them together.
¹⁹ There is no healing for your wound;
your injury is fatal.
All who hear of your destruction
will clap their hands for joy.
Where can anyone be found
who has not suffered from your
continual cruelty?

3:8 Hebrew *No-amon*; also in 3:10.   3:9 Hebrew *Cush*.   3:10 Hebrew *They cast lots*.   3:17 Or *princes*.

Introduction to
Habakkuk

Background

The Babylonians replaced the Assyrians as the dominant nation in the region. Babylon's power begins to increase through the rule of Nabopolassar (626–605 B.C.), and it destroys Nineveh, Assyria's capital, in 612 B.C. Habakkuk may have lived to witness the fall of Jerusalem to Babylon in 586 B.C.

The only biblical references to the prophet Habakkuk are in this book (1:1; 3:1). The Hebrew name *Habakkuk* means "embrace."

Message

The format of Habakkuk differs from the other prophetic books in that it consists of a dialogue between God and the prophet, instead of a proclamation from the prophet to the nation. The questions in this book have been asked by many people through the ages. How can God, who is too pure to look on evil, allow evil to continue? When Habakkuk asks this very question of God, God declares that he will punish Israel for its sin through the Babylonians. Rather than satisfying Habakkuk's desire for justice, this answer only intensifies it. Yet God calls Habakkuk to have faith in God's actions even when the prophet does not understand them, for "the righteous will live by their faithfulness to God" (2:4).

Time

While the list of sins in 1:2–4 leads some scholars to believe that Habakkuk prophesied during the reign of Manasseh (686–642 B.C.) or Amon (642–640 B.C.), a date during either of these reigns seems unlikely, because the Assyrians continued to control Babylon when these kings ruled. A date in Jehoiakim's rule (609–597 B.C.) seems more likely, as Jehoiakim's leadership took the nation away from the reforms of Josiah, reflecting the behaviors listed in 1:2–4. A probable date for the book is circa 607 B.C., causing Habakkuk's ministry to overlap with that of Jeremiah.

Outline

Habakkuk

1 This is the message that the prophet Habakkuk received in a vision.

Habakkuk's Complaint

2 How long, O LORD, must I call for help?
　　But you do not listen!
"Violence is everywhere!" I cry,
　　but you do not come to save.
3 Must I forever see these evil deeds?
　　Why must I watch all this misery?
Wherever I look,
　　I see destruction and violence.
I am surrounded by people
　　who love to argue and fight.
4 The law has become paralyzed,
　　and there is no justice in the courts.
The wicked far outnumber the righteous,
　　so that justice has become perverted.

The LORD's Reply

5 The LORD replied,

"Look around at the nations;
　　look and be amazed!*
For I am doing something in your own day,
　　something you wouldn't believe
　　even if someone told you about it.
6 I am raising up the Babylonians,*
　　a cruel and violent people.
They will march across the world
　　and conquer other lands.
7 They are notorious for their cruelty
　　and do whatever they like.
8 Their horses are swifter than cheetahs*
　　and fiercer than wolves at dusk.
Their charioteers charge from far away.
　　Like eagles, they swoop down to devour their prey.

9 "On they come, all bent on violence.
　　Their hordes advance like a desert wind,
　　sweeping captives ahead of them like sand.
10 They scoff at kings and princes
　　and scorn all their fortresses.
They simply pile ramps of earth
　　against their walls and capture them!

1:5 Greek version reads *Look, you mockers; / look and be amazed and die.* Compare Acts 13:41.　**1:6** Or *Chaldeans.*
1:8 Or *leopards.*

Questioning God

HABAKKUK 1:2–4

Babylon conquered Jerusalem, demolished the temple of God, and took the Israelites captive. In the midst of this disaster, Habakkuk cried out to God from a broken, doubting heart. "How long, O LORD, must I call for help? But you do not listen!" (1:2). Why wasn't God answering his prayers for help? Why didn't God save his people from injustice and violence? Why did the wicked appear to prevail?

We too can have the same questions. Habakkuk didn't understand what God was doing, and sometimes neither do we. No human can fully know or understand the mind of God (Romans 11:33–35). Further, God doesn't need to explain himself to us, for he is God.

Habakkuk, whose name means to "embrace" or "wrestle," spiritually and emotionally wrestled with God, voicing his questions and seeking answers. Like Habakkuk, though we will never fully understand God's ways, the very act of wrestling with God draws us nearer to him because we are interacting with him. Each time we wrestle with God in our despair or fear, we come to know and understand God a little better.

It's doubtful that Habakkuk liked God's answers to his questions, but somehow through the process he made his peace with God. Despite his fear of coming disaster, he chose to trust God's plan: "I am filled with awe by your amazing works. . . . I will rejoice in the LORD! I will be joyful in the God of my salvation! The Sovereign LORD is my strength!" Habakkuk proclaimed (3:2, 18–19). Even with unanswered questions, Habakkuk had a new understanding of God's sovereign purposes and everlasting love.

Though at times life feels so dark that we cannot see the way, we can be assured God will guide us. Through the darkness, this intimacy with God will transform our quaking questions into unswerving hope. Like Habakkuk, the one who wrestled with God and emerged with an unwavering faith no longer dependent on circumstance, we will learn to more deeply trust our gentle Savior who understands our sorrow and pain.

—*Julie Kloster*

For more on faith, see reading at Mark 9:14–29.

---

¹¹ They sweep past like the wind
　　and are gone.
But they are deeply guilty,
　　for their own strength is their god."

Habakkuk's Second Complaint

¹² O LORD my God, my Holy One, you
　　who are eternal—
surely you do not plan to wipe us
　　out?
O LORD, our Rock, you have sent these
　　Babylonians to correct us,
to punish us for our many sins.

¹³ But you are pure and cannot stand the
　　sight of evil.
Will you wink at their treachery?
Should you be silent while the wicked
swallow up people more righteous
　　than they?

¹⁴ Are we only fish to be caught and
　　killed?
Are we only sea creatures that have no
　　leader?

¹⁵ Must we be strung up on their hooks
　　and caught in their nets while they
　　rejoice and celebrate?

¹⁶ Then they will worship their nets
and burn incense in front of them.
"These nets are the gods who have made
us rich!"
they will claim.
¹⁷ Will you let them get away with this
forever?
Will they succeed forever in their
heartless conquests?

2 ¹ I will climb up to my watchtower
and stand at my guardpost.
There I will wait to see what the LORD
says
and how he* will answer my
complaint.

The LORD's Second Reply
² Then the LORD said to me,

"Write my answer plainly on tablets,
so that a runner can carry the correct
message to others.
³ This vision is for a future time.
It describes the end, and it will be
fulfilled.
If it seems slow in coming, wait
patiently,
for it will surely take place.
It will not be delayed.
⁴ "Look at the proud!
They trust in themselves, and their
lives are crooked.
But the righteous will live by their
faithfulness to God.*
⁵ Wealth* is treacherous,
and the arrogant are never at rest.
They open their mouths as wide as the
grave,*
and like death, they are never satisfied.
In their greed they have gathered up
many nations
and swallowed many peoples.

⁶ "But soon their captives will taunt them.
They will mock them, saying,
'What sorrow awaits you thieves!
Now you will get what you deserve!
You've become rich by extortion,
but how much longer can this go on?'

⁷ Suddenly, your debtors will take action.
They will turn on you and take all you
have,
while you stand trembling and
helpless.
⁸ Because you have plundered many
nations,
now all the survivors will plunder
you.
You committed murder throughout the
countryside
and filled the towns with violence.

⁹ "What sorrow awaits you who build big
houses
with money gained dishonestly!
You believe your wealth will buy
security,
putting your family's nest beyond the
reach of danger.
¹⁰ But by the murders you committed,
you have shamed your name and
forfeited your lives.
¹¹ The very stones in the walls cry out
against you,
and the beams in the ceilings echo the
complaint.

¹² "What sorrow awaits you who build
cities
with money gained through murder
and corruption!
¹³ Has not the LORD of Heaven's Armies
promised
that the wealth of nations will turn to
ashes?
They work so hard,
but all in vain!
¹⁴ For as the waters fill the sea,
the earth will be filled with an
awareness
of the glory of the LORD.

¹⁵ "What sorrow awaits you who make
your neighbors drunk!
You force your cup on them
so you can gloat over their shameful
nakedness.
¹⁶ But soon it will be your turn to be
disgraced.
Come, drink and be exposed!*

2:1 As in Syriac version; Hebrew reads *I*.   **2:3b-4** Greek version reads *If the vision is delayed, wait patiently, / for it will surely come and not delay. / 4I will take no pleasure in anyone who turns away. / But the righteous person will live by my faith.* Compare Rom 1:17; Gal 3:11; Heb 10:37-38.   **2:5a** As in Dead Sea Scroll 1QpHab; other Hebrew manuscripts read *Wine*.   **2:5b** Hebrew as *Sheol*.   **2:16** Dead Sea Scrolls and Greek and Syriac versions read *and stagger!*

Drink from the cup of the LORD's
    judgment,
and all your glory will be turned to
    shame.
¹⁷ You cut down the forests of Lebanon.
    Now you will be cut down.
You destroyed the wild animals,
    so now their terror will be yours.
You committed murder throughout the
    countryside
and filled the towns with violence.

¹⁸ "What good is an idol carved by man,
    or a cast image that deceives you?
How foolish to trust in your own
    creation—
a god that can't even talk!
¹⁹ What sorrow awaits you who say to
    wooden idols,
    'Wake up and save us!'
To speechless stone images you say,
    'Rise up and teach us!'
Can an idol tell you what to do?
They may be overlaid with gold and
    silver,
but they are lifeless inside.
²⁰ But the LORD is in his holy Temple.
    Let all the earth be silent before him.'

3 Habakkuk's Prayer

This prayer was sung by the prophet
Habakkuk*:

² I have heard all about you, LORD.
    I am filled with awe by your amazing
    works.
In this time of our deep need,
    help us again as you did in years
    gone by.
And in your anger,
    remember your mercy.

³ I see God moving across the deserts
    from Edom,*
the Holy One coming from Mount
    Paran.*
His brilliant splendor fills the heavens,
    and the earth is filled with his praise.
⁴ His coming is as brilliant as the
    sunrise.
Rays of light flash from his hands,
    where his awesome power is hidden.

⁵ Pestilence marches before him;
    plague follows close behind.
⁶ When he stops, the earth shakes.
    When he looks, the nations tremble.
He shatters the everlasting mountains
    and levels the eternal hills.
    He is the Eternal One!
⁷ I see the people of Cushan in distress,
    and the nation of Midian trembling in
    terror.

⁸ Was it in anger, LORD, that you struck
    the rivers
    and parted the sea?
Were you displeased with them?
    No, you were sending your chariots of
    salvation!
⁹ You brandished your bow
    and your quiver of arrows.
    You split open the earth with flowing
    rivers.
¹⁰ The mountains watched and trembled.
    Onward swept the raging waters.
The mighty deep cried out,
    lifting its hands to the LORD.
¹¹ The sun and moon stood still in the sky
    as your brilliant arrows flew
    and your glittering spear flashed.

¹² You marched across the land in anger
    and trampled the nations in your
    fury.
¹³ You went out to rescue your chosen
    people,
    to save your anointed ones.
You crushed the heads of the wicked
    and stripped their bones from head
    to toe.
¹⁴ With his own weapons,
    you destroyed the chief of those
who rushed out like a whirlwind,
    thinking Israel would be easy prey.
¹⁵ You trampled the sea with your horses,
    and the mighty waters piled high.

¹⁶ I trembled inside when I heard this;
    my lips quivered with fear.
My legs gave way beneath me,*
    and I shook in terror.
I will wait quietly for the coming day
    when disaster will strike the people
    who invade us.

3:1 Hebrew adds *according to shigionoth*, probably indicating the musical setting for the prayer.   **3:3a** Hebrew *Teman*.   **3:3b** Hebrew adds *selah;* also in 3:9, 13. The meaning of this Hebrew term is uncertain; it is probably a musical or literary term.   **3:16** Hebrew *Decay entered my bones.*

¹⁷ Even though the fig trees have no blossoms,
    and there are no grapes on the vines;
even though the olive crop fails,
    and the fields lie empty and barren;
even though the flocks die in the fields,
    and the cattle barns are empty,
¹⁸ yet I will rejoice in the LORD!
    I will be joyful in the God of my salvation!
¹⁹ The Sovereign LORD is my strength!
    He makes me as surefooted as a deer,*
    able to tread upon the heights.

(For the choir director: This prayer is to be accompanied by stringed instruments.)

3:19 Or *He gives me the speed of a deer.*

Introduction to
Zephaniah

Background

The first verse of Zephaniah attributes the book to the prophet and also boasts an ancestry to the fourth generation. Zephaniah's great-great-grandfather is King Hezekiah of Judah, making Zephaniah the only prophet with royal ancestry.

The Hebrew name for Zephaniah means "Yahweh hides" or "Yahweh has hidden." Born during the reign of the evil king Manasseh, young Zephaniah may have been hidden from the king.

Message

During the reigns of Manasseh and Amon, the people of Judah worship other gods and defile God's holy places. Zephaniah speaks about the coming Day of the Lord when the wrath of God will come upon Judah and all the nations of the earth. Afterward, God will rejoice over a purified remnant that he will return to the land.

Under the leadership of King Josiah, the nation turns toward God; it seems that Judah listens to Zephaniah's call. Their repentance is short-lived, however, as the people forget Zephaniah's message and experience the reality of the judgment about which he spoke when Jerusalem falls to Babylon in 586 B.C.

Time

Zephaniah prophesied during the reign of Josiah (640–609 B.C.), probably before Josiah's great reform of 621 B.C. Zephaniah was a contemporary of Jeremiah.

Outline

Zephaniah

1 The LORD gave this message to Zephaniah when Josiah son of Amon was king of Judah. Zephaniah was the son of Cushi, son of Gedaliah, son of Amariah, son of Hezekiah.

Coming Judgment against Judah

² "I will sweep away everything
   from the face of the earth," says the LORD.
³ "I will sweep away people and animals alike.
   I will sweep away the birds of the sky and the fish in the sea.
I will reduce the wicked to heaps of rubble,*
   and I will wipe humanity from the face of the earth," says the LORD.
⁴ "I will crush Judah and Jerusalem with my fist
   and destroy every last trace of their Baal worship.
I will put an end to all the idolatrous priests,
   so that even the memory of them will disappear.
⁵ For they go up to their roofs
   and bow down to the sun, moon, and stars.
They claim to follow the LORD,
   but then they worship Molech,* too.
⁶ And I will destroy those who used to worship me
   but now no longer do.
They no longer ask for the LORD's guidance
   or seek my blessings."

⁷ Stand in silence in the presence of the Sovereign LORD,
   for the awesome day of the LORD's judgment is near.
The LORD has prepared his people for a great slaughter
   and has chosen their executioners.*
⁸ "On that day of judgment,"
   says the LORD,
"I will punish the leaders and princes of Judah
   and all those following pagan customs.
⁹ Yes, I will punish those who participate in pagan worship ceremonies,
   and those who fill their masters' houses with violence and deceit.

¹⁰ "On that day," says the LORD,
   "a cry of alarm will come from the Fish Gate
and echo throughout the New Quarter of the city.*
   And a great crash will sound from the hills.
¹¹ Wail in sorrow, all you who live in the market area,
   for all the merchants and traders will be destroyed.

¹² "I will search with lanterns in Jerusalem's darkest corners
   to punish those who sit complacent in their sins.

1:3 The meaning of the Hebrew is uncertain. **1:5** Hebrew *Malcam*, a variant spelling of Molech; or it could possibly mean *their king.* **1:7** Hebrew *has prepared a sacrifice and sanctified his guests.* **1:10** Or *the Second Quarter*, a newer section of Jerusalem. Hebrew reads *the Mishneh.*

They think the LORD will do nothing to
 them,
   either good or bad.
13 So their property will be plundered,
   their homes will be ransacked.
They will build new homes
   but never live in them.
They will plant vineyards
   but never drink wine from them.

14 "That terrible day of the LORD is near.
   Swiftly it comes—
a day of bitter tears,
   a day when even strong men will cry
     out.
15 It will be a day when the LORD's anger is
     poured out—
   a day of terrible distress and anguish,
a day of ruin and desolation,
   a day of darkness and gloom,
   a day of clouds and blackness,
16   a day of trumpet calls and battle cries.
Down go the walled cities
   and the strongest battlements!

17 "Because you have sinned against the
     LORD,
   I will make you grope around like the
     blind.
Your blood will be poured into the dust,
   and your bodies will lie rotting on the
     ground."

18 Your silver and gold will not save you
   on that day of the LORD's anger.
For the whole land will be devoured
   by the fire of his jealousy.
He will make a terrifying end
   of all the people on earth.*

2 A Call to Repentance
1 Gather together—yes, gather
     together,
   you shameless nation.
2 Gather before judgment begins,
   before your time to repent is blown
     away like chaff.
Act now, before the fierce fury of the
     LORD falls
   and the terrible day of the LORD's
     anger begins.
3 Seek the LORD, all who are humble,
   and follow his commands.

Seek to do what is right
   and to live humbly.
Perhaps even yet the LORD will protect
     you—
   protect you from his anger on that day
     of destruction.

Judgment against Philistia
4 Gaza and Ashkelon will be abandoned,
   Ashdod and Ekron torn down.
5 And what sorrow awaits you Philistines*
   who live along the coast and in the
     land of Canaan,
   for this judgment is against you, too!
The LORD will destroy you
   until not one of you is left.
6 The Philistine coast will become a
     wilderness pasture,
   a place of shepherd camps
   and enclosures for sheep and goats.
7 The remnant of the tribe of Judah will
     pasture there.
   They will rest at night in the
     abandoned houses in Ashkelon.
For the LORD their God will visit his
     people in kindness
   and restore their prosperity again.

Judgment against Moab and Ammon
8 "I have heard the taunts of the Moabites
   and the insults of the Ammonites,
mocking my people
   and invading their borders.
9 Now, as surely as I live,"
   says the LORD of Heaven's Armies, the
     God of Israel,
"Moab and Ammon will be destroyed—
   destroyed as completely as Sodom and
     Gomorrah.
Their land will become a place of
     stinging nettles,
   salt pits, and eternal desolation.
The remnant of my people will plunder
     them
   and take their land."

10 They will receive the wages of their
     pride,
   for they have scoffed at the people of
     the LORD of Heaven's Armies.
11 The LORD will terrify them
   as he destroys all the gods in the land.

1:18 Or the people living in the land. 2:5 Hebrew Kerethites.

Then nations around the world will
worship the LORD,
each in their own land.

Judgment against Ethiopia and Assyria

12 "You Ethiopians* will also be
slaughtered
by my sword," says the LORD.

13 And the LORD will strike the lands of the
north with his fist,
destroying the land of Assyria.
He will make its great capital, Nineveh, a
desolate wasteland,
parched like a desert.
14 The proud city will become a pasture for
flocks and herds,
and all sorts of wild animals will settle
there.
The desert owl and screech owl will
roost on its ruined columns,
their calls echoing through the gaping
windows.
Rubble will block all the doorways,
and the cedar paneling will be exposed
to the weather.
15 This is the boisterous city,
once so secure.
"I am the greatest!" it boasted.
"No other city can compare with me!"
But now, look how it has become an
utter ruin,
a haven for wild animals.
Everyone passing by will laugh in
derision
and shake a defiant fist.

3 Jerusalem's Rebellion and Redemption

1 What sorrow awaits rebellious, polluted
Jerusalem,
the city of violence and crime!
2 No one can tell it anything;
it refuses all correction.
It does not trust in the LORD
or draw near to its God.
3 Its leaders are like roaring lions
hunting for their victims.
Its judges are like ravenous wolves at
evening time,
who by dawn have left no trace of
their prey.

4 Its prophets are arrogant liars seeking
their own gain.
Its priests defile the Temple by
disobeying God's instructions.
5 But the LORD is still there in the city,
and he does no wrong.
Day by day he hands down justice,
and he does not fail.
But the wicked know no shame.

6 "I have wiped out many nations,
devastating their fortress walls and
towers.
Their streets are now deserted;
their cities lie in silent ruin.
There are no survivors—
none at all.
7 I thought, 'Surely they will have
reverence for me now!
Surely they will listen to my warnings.
Then I won't need to strike again,
destroying their homes.'
But no, they get up early
to continue their evil deeds.
8 Therefore, be patient," says the LORD.
"Soon I will stand and accuse these
evil nations.
For I have decided to gather the
kingdoms of the earth
and pour out my fiercest anger and
fury on them.
All the earth will be devoured
by the fire of my jealousy.

9 "Then I will purify the speech of all
people,
so that everyone can worship the
LORD together.
10 My scattered people who live beyond
the rivers of Ethiopia*
will come to present their offerings.
11 On that day you will no longer need to
be ashamed,
for you will no longer be rebels
against me.
I will remove all proud and arrogant
people from among you.
There will be no more haughtiness on
my holy mountain.
12 Those who are left will be the lowly and
humble,
for it is they who trust in the name of
the LORD.

2:12 Hebrew Cushites.   3:10 Hebrew Cush.

Celebration

Our Celebrating God
ZEPHANIAH 3:15-17

Tucked away in the short book of Zephaniah we discover an amazing glimpse into the character of God. Most of Zephaniah contains a stunning description of God's coming judgment upon his people in Judah. But along with his prediction of an imminent day of judgment, Zephaniah also describes an amazing, hopeful future when "the LORD himself, the King of Israel, will live among you!" (3:15).

Zephaniah's words point us to the Incarnation, when in the person of Christ, God himself would take on flesh and live among his people. John 1:14 puts it this way: "The Word became human and made his home among us." Zephaniah's prophecies reiterate this theme: "The LORD your God is living among you. He is a mighty savior" (3:17).

Not only is he the mighty Savior and King, but Zephaniah also reveals that he is a *celebrating* God; "He will take delight in you with gladness. . . . He will rejoice over you with joyful songs" (3:17). Do you often picture God this way? Overflowing with gladness? Singing songs of rejoicing? And all of it driven by his delight in his people?

If we're honest, most of us would admit that we seldom focus on this side of God—this joyful, celebrating part of his character. We affirm his omniscience. We worship him in his holiness. His grace we accept and rest in. But his celebratory heart? His joy? Why do we overlook it? Perhaps it doesn't seem important enough in the scheme of weighty theological ideas. Or perhaps in our own insecurity it's too difficult to swallow the idea that it's his love for *us* that's the cause of his joy.

Invite God to help you know this joyful, delighting side of his character. Ask him to help you enter into his celebration.

—Kelli B. Trujillo

For more on celebration, see reading at Luke 10:17-20.

---

¹³ The remnant of Israel will do no wrong;
    they will never tell lies or deceive one
      another.
  They will eat and sleep in safety,
    and no one will make them afraid."

¹⁴ Sing, O daughter of Zion;
    shout aloud, O Israel!
  Be glad and rejoice with all your heart,
    O daughter of Jerusalem!
¹⁵ For the LORD will remove his hand of
      judgment
  and will disperse the armies of your
    enemy.

And the LORD himself, the King of Israel,
    will live among you!
At last your troubles will be over,
    and you will never again fear disaster.
¹⁶ On that day the announcement to
    Jerusalem will be,
  "Cheer up, Zion! Don't be afraid!
¹⁷ For the LORD your God is living among
    you.
  He is a mighty savior.
  He will take delight in you with gladness.
    With his love, he will calm all your fears.*
  He will rejoice over you with joyful
    songs."

3:17 Or *He will be silent in his love.* Greek and Syriac versions read *He will renew you with his love.*

18 "I will gather you who mourn for the
appointed festivals;
you will be disgraced no more.*
19 And I will deal severely with all who
have oppressed you.
I will save the weak and helpless ones;
I will bring together
those who were chased away.
I will give glory and fame to my former
exiles,
wherever they have been mocked and
shamed.
20 On that day I will gather you together
and bring you home again.
I will give you a good name, a name of
distinction,
among all the nations of the earth,
as I restore your fortunes before their
very eyes.
I, the LORD, have spoken!"

Introduction to
Haggai

Background

King Cyrus has issued a decree allowing Jews to return from Babylon (now in the hands of Persia) and rebuild Jerusalem. Their governor is a descendant of David, Zerubbabel, who is mentioned in the genealogy of Jesus (Matthew 1:12). At first, the returning exiles are eager to undertake the task. However, their enthusiasm ebbs and, sixteen years later, in the reign of King Darius, the temple is still not rebuilt (although their houses are, 1:4).

Haggai is one of the Jews who returns to Jerusalem under the leadership of Zerubbabel. Haggai may have been around seventy-five years old at the time of his ministry in 520 B.C. and would have remembered the first temple (2:3). He has a brief ministry, prophesying for about two years. The name Haggai means "festive."

Message

Through Haggai, God challenges the people to regain proper priorities and resume work on the temple. Promises also accompany this challenge: God will reward the obedience of the people with blessings that surpass the glory of Israel before the exile (2:6–9, 18–23). Haggai ends with a word about Zerubbabel, who spearheaded the completion of the temple: that he is a "signet ring" or a guarantee that a Messiah will come through the lineage of David.

Time

Based on the information in the text, hooking prophecies to the reign of Darius the Great, Haggai's preaching took place on four days in the last four months of 520 B.C. The prophet Zechariah was a contemporary of Haggai and began his ministry between Haggai's second and third messages. The temple, sometimes called Zerubbabel's temple, was completed in 516 B.C.

Outline

Haggai

1 A Call to Rebuild the Temple

On August 29* of the second year of King Darius's reign, the LORD gave a message through the prophet Haggai to Zerubbabel son of Shealtiel, governor of Judah, and to Jeshua* son of Jehozadak, the high priest.

2 "This is what the LORD of Heaven's Armies says: The people are saying, 'The time has not yet come to rebuild the house of the LORD.'"

3 Then the LORD sent this message through the prophet Haggai: 4 "Why are you living in luxurious houses while my house lies in ruins? 5 This is what the LORD of Heaven's Armies says: Look at what's happening to you! 6 You have planted much but harvest little. You eat but are not satisfied. You drink but are still thirsty. You put on clothes but cannot keep warm. Your wages disappear as though you were putting them in pockets filled with holes!

7 "This is what the LORD of Heaven's Armies says: Look at what's happening to you! 8 Now go up into the hills, bring down timber, and rebuild my house. Then I will take pleasure in it and be honored, says the LORD. 9 You hoped for rich harvests, but they were poor. And when you brought your harvest home, I blew it away. Why? Because my house lies in ruins, says the LORD of Heaven's Armies, while all of you are busy building your own fine houses. 10 It's because of you that the heavens withhold the dew and the earth produces no crops. 11 I have called for a drought on your fields and hills—a drought to wither the grain and grapes and olive trees and all your other crops, a drought to starve you and your livestock and to ruin everything you have worked so hard to get."

Obedience to God's Call

12 Then Zerubbabel son of Shealtiel, and Jeshua son of Jehozadak, the high priest, and the whole remnant of God's people began to obey the message from the LORD their God. When they heard the words of the prophet Haggai, whom the LORD their God had sent, the people feared the LORD. 13 Then Haggai, the LORD's messenger, gave the people this message from the LORD: "I am with you, says the LORD!"

14 So the LORD sparked the enthusiasm of Zerubbabel son of Shealtiel, governor of Judah, and the enthusiasm of Jeshua son of Jehozadak, the high priest, and the enthusiasm of the whole remnant of God's people. They began to work on the house of their God, the LORD of Heaven's Armies, 15 on September 21* of the second year of King Darius's reign.

2 The New Temple's Diminished Splendor

Then on October 17 of that same year,* the LORD sent another message through the prophet Haggai. 2 "Say this to Zerubbabel son of Shealtiel, gover-

---

1:1a Hebrew *On the first day of the sixth month,* of the ancient Hebrew lunar calendar. A number of dates in Haggai can be cross-checked with dates in surviving Persian records and related accurately to our modern calendar. This event occurred on August 29, 520 B.C.   **1:1b** Hebrew *Joshua,* a variant spelling of Jeshua; also in 1:12, 14.   **1:15** Hebrew *on the twenty-fourth day of the sixth month,* of the ancient Hebrew lunar calendar. This event occurred on September 21, 520 B.C.; also see note on 1:1a.   **2:1** Hebrew *on the twenty-first day of the seventh month,* of the ancient Hebrew lunar calendar. This event (in the second year of Darius's reign) occurred on October 17, 520 B.C.; also see note on 1:1a.

Fighting Discontent

HAGGAI 1:1–10

Gratitude

Never satisfied. Never enough. Always looking for more, hungering for what's next. Chronic discontent is a spiritual disease plaguing our culture, but it's not an exclusively modern phenomenon. Consider this passage in Haggai, spoken after the Israelites had returned from their exile to find the temple in ruins. They intended to rebuild it . . . but had their *own* places to fix and fields to replant first.

"Look at what's happening to you!" God said through the prophet. "You have planted much but harvest little. You eat but are not satisfied. You drink but are still thirsty. You put on clothes but cannot keep warm. Your wages disappear as though you were putting them in pockets filled with holes!" (1:5–6).

The Israelites, to quote a much later poet, can't get no satisfaction. God tells them that life is a treadmill of diminishing returns because they have neglected the temple, and the only way to enjoy the sort of productive, satisfying existence he intends for them is to spend time in that holy place once more.

Throughout Scripture God continually develops the concept of the temple as the place he meets with his people. By the time of the New Testament, it's clear that the temple is now inside of us. So I read Haggai and begin to understand: satisfaction comes only when I spend intentional time with God. It comes when that original longing for God—a desire that's been mutated into a thousand splintering directions—gets redirected back to him.

We, like the culture around us, can live lives driven by a perpetual sense of discontent, or we can choose a different perspective. The truth we must recognize is that the desire for fullness, wellness, wholeness, productivity, security, and satisfaction is ultimately a desire for Jesus. All substitutes merely intensify the hunger.

—*Carolyn Arends*

For more on gratitude, see reading at Matthew 20:1–16.

nor of Judah, and to Jeshua* son of Jehozadak, the high priest, and to the remnant of God's people there in the land: ³'Does anyone remember this house—this Temple—in its former splendor? How, in comparison, does it look to you now? It must seem like nothing at all! ⁴But now the LORD says: Be strong, Zerubbabel. Be strong, Jeshua son of Jehozadak, the high priest. Be strong, all you people still left in the land. And now get to work, for I am with you, says the LORD of Heaven's Armies. ⁵My Spirit remains among you, just as I promised when you came out of Egypt. So do not be afraid.'

⁶"For this is what the LORD of Heaven's Armies says: In just a little while I will again shake the heavens and the earth, the oceans and the dry land. ⁷I will shake all the nations, and the treasures of all the nations will be brought to this Temple. I will fill this place with glory, says the LORD of Heaven's Armies. ⁸The silver is mine, and the gold is mine, says the LORD of Heaven's Armies. ⁹The future glory of this Temple will be greater than its past glory, says the LORD of Heaven's Armies. And in this place I will bring peace. I, the LORD of Heaven's Armies, have spoken!"

2:2 Hebrew *Joshua*, a variant spelling of Jeshua; also in 2:4.

Blessings Promised for Obedience

[10] On December 18* of the second year of King Darius's reign, the LORD sent this message to the prophet Haggai: [11] "This is what the LORD of Heaven's Armies says. Ask the priests this question about the law: [12] If one of you is carrying some meat from a holy sacrifice in his robes and his robe happens to brush against some bread or stew, wine or olive oil, or any other kind of food, will it also become holy?'"

The priests replied, "No."

[13] Then Haggai asked, "If someone becomes ceremonially unclean by touching a dead person and then touches any of these foods, will the food be defiled?"

And the priests answered, "Yes."

[14] Then Haggai responded, "That is how it is with this people and this nation, says the LORD. Everything they do and everything they offer is defiled by their sin. [15] Look at what was happening to you before you began to lay the foundation of the LORD's Temple. [16] When you hoped for a twenty-bushel crop, you harvested only ten. When you expected to draw fifty gallons from the winepress, you found only twenty. [17] I sent blight and mildew and hail to destroy everything you worked so hard to produce. Even so, you refused to return to me, says the LORD.

[18] "Think about this eighteenth day of December, the day* when the foundation of the LORD's Temple was laid. Think carefully. [19] I am giving you a promise now while the seed is still in the barn.* You have not yet harvested your grain, and your grapevines, fig trees, pomegranates, and olive trees have not yet produced their crops. But from this day onward I will bless you."

Promises for Zerubbabel

[20] On that same day, December 18,* the LORD sent this second message to Haggai: [21] "Tell Zerubbabel, the governor of Judah, that I am about to shake the heavens and the earth. [22] I will overthrow royal thrones and destroy the power of foreign kingdoms. I will overturn their chariots and riders. The horses will fall, and their riders will kill each other.

[23] "But when this happens, says the LORD of Heaven's Armies, I will honor you, Zerubbabel son of Shealtiel, my servant. I will make you like a signet ring on my finger, says the LORD, for I have chosen you. I, the LORD of Heaven's Armies, have spoken!"

2:10 Hebrew *On the twenty-fourth day of the ninth month,* of the ancient Hebrew lunar calendar (similarly in 2:18). This event occurred on December 18, 520 B.C.; also see note on 1:1a. 2:18 Or *On this eighteenth day of December, think about the day.* 2:19 Hebrew *Is the seed yet in the barn?* 2:20 Hebrew *On the twenty-fourth day of the [ninth] month;* see note on 2:10.

Introduction to
Zechariah

Background

Prophets such as Isaiah, Jeremiah, and Ezekiel had prophesied of a remnant returning to their homeland after the exile. The Jews who return from Babylon to Jerusalem most likely expect the promise to be fulfilled immediately. Instead, they still live under foreign rule and experience economic hardships. Out of discouragement, they stop rebuilding the temple. Haggai and Zechariah speak to this situation, challenging the people to finish the temple and worship their God.

Like the prophets Ezekiel and Jeremiah, Zechariah, the son of Berekiah and grandson of Iddo (1:1, 7), is a priest. Zechariah's name means "Yahweh remembers" or "Yahweh has remembered." Born in Babylon, Zechariah moves to Jerusalem with Iddo as part of the group of returnees led by Zerubbabel and Jeshua the high priest (Nehemiah 12:4). When he begins his ministry in 520 B.C., Zechariah is considered a young man (2:4). He is mentioned by name in the Book of Ezra (5:1; 6:14). According to Matthew 23:35, Zechariah was murdered.

Message

Zechariah is considered the most messianic book of the Old Testament—and one of the most difficult to understand. By relating visions—some apocalyptic—proclaiming messages, and delivering "burdens," he draws the people to repentance, encourages them to rebuild the temple, looks to the coming Messiah's rejection and triumph, and describes how God will defeat the nations and cleanse his people through the Messiah. A coronation scene (6:9–15) of the priest Jeshua is viewed as a messianic passage.

Time

Some of Zechariah's ministry can be pinpointed by dates given in relation to the reign of King Darius: November 520 B.C. (1:1), February 519 B.C. (1:7), and December 518 B.C. (7:1). (See also the introduction to the Book of Haggai.) Scholars tentatively give 510 B.C. as the end of Zechariah's ministry, but chapters 9–14 may have been written even later. Zechariah most likely served longer than his contemporary Haggai.

Outline

Zechariah

1
A Call to Return to the Lord

In November* of the second year of King Darius's reign, the Lord gave this message to the prophet Zechariah son of Berekiah and grandson of Iddo:

²"I, the Lord, was very angry with your ancestors. ³Therefore, say to the people, 'This is what the Lord of Heaven's Armies says: Return to me, and I will return to you, says the Lord of Heaven's Armies.' ⁴Don't be like your ancestors who would not listen or pay attention when the earlier prophets said to them, 'This is what the Lord of Heaven's Armies says: Turn from your evil ways, and stop all your evil practices.'

⁵"Where are your ancestors now? They and the prophets are long dead. ⁶But everything I said through my servants the prophets happened to your ancestors, just as I said. As a result, they repented and said, 'We have received what we deserved from the Lord of Heaven's Armies. He has done what he said he would do.'"

A Man among the Myrtle Trees

⁷Three months later, on February 15,* the Lord sent another message to the prophet Zechariah son of Berekiah and grandson of Iddo.

⁸In a vision during the night, I saw a man sitting on a red horse that was standing among some myrtle trees in a small valley. Behind him were riders on red, brown, and white horses. ⁹I asked the angel who was talking with me, "My lord, what do these horses mean?"

"I will show you," the angel replied.

¹⁰The rider standing among the myrtle trees then explained, "They are the ones the Lord has sent out to patrol the earth."

¹¹Then the other riders reported to the angel of the Lord, who was standing among the myrtle trees, "We have been patrolling the earth, and the whole earth is at peace."

¹²Upon hearing this, the angel of the Lord prayed this prayer: "O Lord of Heaven's Armies, for seventy years now you have been angry with Jerusalem and the towns of Judah. How long until you again show mercy to them?" ¹³And the Lord spoke kind and comforting words to the angel who talked with me.

¹⁴Then the angel said to me, "Shout this message for all to hear: 'This is what the Lord of Heaven's Armies says: My love for Jerusalem and Mount Zion is passionate and strong. ¹⁵But I am very angry with the other nations that are now enjoying peace and security. I was only a little angry with my people, but the nations inflicted harm on them far beyond my intentions.

¹⁶"'Therefore, this is what the Lord says: I have returned to show mercy to Jerusalem. My Temple will be rebuilt, says the Lord of Heaven's Armies, and measurements will be taken for the reconstruction of Jerusalem.*'

1:1 Hebrew *In the eighth month.* A number of dates in Zechariah can be cross-checked with dates in surviving Persian records and related accurately to our modern calendar. This month of the ancient Hebrew lunar calendar occurred within the months of October and November 520 b.c.   **1:7** Hebrew *On the twenty-fourth day of the eleventh month, the month of Shebat, in the second year of Darius.* This event occurred on February 15, 519 b.c.; also see note on 1:1.   **1:16** Hebrew *and the measuring line will be stretched out over Jerusalem.*

[17]"Say this also: 'This is what the LORD of Heaven's Armies says: The towns of Israel will again overflow with prosperity, and the LORD will again comfort Zion and choose Jerusalem as his own.'"

Four Horns and Four Blacksmiths

[18]*Then I looked up and saw four animal horns. [19]"What are these?" I asked the angel who was talking with me.

He replied, "These horns represent the nations that scattered Judah, Israel, and Jerusalem."

[20]Then the LORD showed me four blacksmiths. [21]"What are these men coming to do?" I asked.

The angel replied, "These four horns—these nations—scattered and humbled Judah. Now these blacksmiths have come to terrify those nations and throw them down and destroy them."

2 Future Prosperity of Jerusalem

[1]*When I looked again, I saw a man with a measuring line in his hand. [2]"Where are you going?" I asked.

He replied, "I am going to measure Jerusalem, to see how wide and how long it is."

[3]Then the angel who was with me went to meet a second angel who was coming toward him. [4]The other angel said, "Hurry, and say to that young man, 'Jerusalem will someday be so full of people and livestock that there won't be room enough for everyone! Many will live outside the city walls. [5]Then I, myself, will be a protective wall of fire around Jerusalem, says the LORD. And I will be the glory inside the city!'"

The Exiles Are Called Home

[6]The LORD says, "Come away! Flee from Babylon in the land of the north, for I have scattered you to the four winds. [7]Come away, people of Zion, you who are exiled in Babylon!"

[8]After a period of glory, the LORD of Heaven's Armies sent me* against the nations who plundered you. For he said, "Anyone who harms you harms my most precious possession.* [9]I will raise my fist

to crush them, and their own slaves will plunder them." Then you will know that the LORD of Heaven's Armies has sent me.

[10]The LORD says, "Shout and rejoice, O beautiful Jerusalem,* for I am coming to live among you. [11]Many nations will join themselves to the LORD on that day, and they, too, will be my people. I will live among you, and you will know that the LORD of Heaven's Armies sent me to you. [12]The land of Judah will be the LORD's special possession in the holy land, and he will once again choose Jerusalem to be his own city. [13]Be silent before the LORD, all humanity, for he is springing into action from his holy dwelling."

3 Cleansing for the High Priest

Then the angel showed me Jeshua* the high priest standing before the angel of the LORD. The Accuser, Satan,* was there at the angel's right hand, making accusations against Jeshua. [2]And the LORD said to Satan, "I, the LORD, reject your accusations, Satan. Yes, the LORD, who has chosen Jerusalem, rebukes you. This man is like a burning stick that has been snatched from the fire."

[3]Jeshua's clothing was filthy as he stood there before the angel. [4]So the angel said to the others standing there, "Take off his filthy clothes." And turning to Jeshua he said, "See, I have taken away your sins, and now I am giving you these fine new clothes."

[5]Then I said, "They should also place a clean turban on his head." So they put a clean priestly turban on his head and dressed him in new clothes while the angel of the LORD stood by.

[6]Then the angel of the LORD spoke very solemnly to Jeshua and said, [7]"This is what the LORD of Heaven's Armies says: If you follow my ways and carefully serve me, then you will be given authority over my Temple and its courtyards. I will let you walk among these others standing here.

[8]"Listen to me, O Jeshua the high priest, and all you other priests. You are symbols of things to come. Soon I am going to bring my servant, the Branch. [9]Now look at

---

1:18 Verses 1:18-21 are numbered 2:1-4 in Hebrew text.   **2:1** Verses 2:1-13 are numbered 2:5-17 in Hebrew text.   **2:8a** The meaning of the Hebrew is uncertain.   **2:8b** Hebrew *Anyone who touches you touches the pupil of his eye.*   **2:10** Hebrew *O daughter of Zion.*   **3:1a** Hebrew *Joshua,* a variant spelling of Jeshua; also in 3:3, 4, 6, 8, 9.   **3:1b** Hebrew *The satan;* similarly in 3:2.

the jewel I have set before Jeshua, a single stone with seven facets.* I will engrave an inscription on it, says the LORD of Heaven's Armies, and I will remove the sins of this land in a single day.

¹⁰ "And on that day, says the LORD of Heaven's Armies, each of you will invite your neighbor to sit with you peacefully under your own grapevine and fig tree."

4 A Lampstand and Two Olive Trees

Then the angel who had been talking with me returned and woke me, as though I had been asleep. ²"What do you see now?" he asked.

I answered, "I see a solid gold lampstand with a bowl of oil on top of it. Around the bowl are seven lamps, each having seven spouts with wicks. ³And I see two olive trees, one on each side of the bowl." ⁴Then I asked the angel, "What are these, my lord? What do they mean?"

⁵"Don't you know?" the angel asked.

"No, my lord," I replied.

⁶Then he said to me, "This is what the LORD says to Zerubbabel: It is not by force nor by strength, but by my Spirit, says the LORD of Heaven's Armies. ⁷Nothing, not even a mighty mountain, will stand in Zerubbabel's way; it will become a level plain before him! And when Zerubbabel sets the final stone of the Temple in place, the people will shout: 'May God bless it! May God bless it!'*"

⁸Then another message came to me from the LORD: ⁹"Zerubbabel is the one who laid the foundation of this Temple, and he will complete it. Then you will know that the LORD of Heaven's Armies has sent me. ¹⁰Do not despise these small beginnings, for the LORD rejoices to see the work begin, to see the plumb line in Zerubbabel's hand."

(The seven lamps* represent the eyes of the LORD that search all around the world.)

¹¹Then I asked the angel, "What are these two olive trees on each side of the lampstand, ¹²and what are the two olive branches that pour out golden oil through two gold tubes?"

¹³"Don't you know?" he asked.

"No, my lord," I replied.

¹⁴Then he said to me, "They represent the two heavenly beings who stand in the court of the Lord of all the earth."

5 A Flying Scroll

I looked up again and saw a scroll flying through the air.

²"What do you see?" the angel asked.

"I see a flying scroll," I replied. "It appears to be about 30 feet long and 15 feet wide.*"

³Then he said to me, "This scroll contains the curse that is going out over the entire land. One side of the scroll says that those who steal will be banished from the land; the other side says that those who swear falsely will be banished from the land. ⁴And this is what the LORD of Heaven's Armies says: I am sending this curse into the house of every thief and into the house of everyone who swears falsely using my name. And my curse will remain in that house and completely destroy it—even its timbers and stones."

A Woman in a Basket

⁵Then the angel who was talking with me came forward and said, "Look up and see what's coming."

⁶"What is it?" I asked.

He replied, "It is a basket for measuring grain,* and it's filled with the sins* of everyone throughout the land."

⁷Then the heavy lead cover was lifted off the basket, and there was a woman sitting inside it. ⁸The angel said, "The woman's name is Wickedness," and he pushed her back into the basket and closed the heavy lid again.

⁹Then I looked up and saw two women flying toward us, gliding on the wind. They had wings like a stork, and they picked up the basket and flew into the sky.

¹⁰"Where are they taking the basket?" I asked the angel.

¹¹He replied, "To the land of Babylonia,* where they will build a temple for the basket. And when the temple is ready, they will set the basket there on its pedestal."

3:9 Hebrew seven eyes.   **4:7** Hebrew 'Grace, grace to it.'   **4:10** Or The seven facets (see 3:9); Hebrew reads These seven.   **5:2** Hebrew 20 cubits [9 meters] long and 10 cubits [4.5 meters] wide.   **5:6a** Hebrew an ephah [20 quarts or 22 liters]; also in 5:7, 8, 9, 10, 11.   **5:6b** As in Greek version; Hebrew reads the appearance.   **5:11** Hebrew the land of Shinar.

6 Four Chariots

Then I looked up again and saw four chariots coming from between two bronze mountains. [2] The first chariot was pulled by red horses, the second by black horses, [3] the third by white horses, and the fourth by powerful dappled-gray horses. [4] "And what are these, my lord?" I asked the angel who was talking with me.

[5] The angel replied, "These are the four spirits* of heaven who stand before the Lord of all the earth. They are going out to do his work. [6] The chariot with black horses is going north, the chariot with white horses is going west,* and the chariot with dappled-gray horses is going south."

[7] The powerful horses were eager to set out to patrol the earth. And the Lord said, "Go and patrol the earth!" So they left at once on their patrol.

[8] Then the Lord summoned me and said, "Look, those who went north have vented the anger of my Spirit* there in the land of the north."

The Crowning of Jeshua

[9] Then I received another message from the Lord: [10] "Heldai, Tobijah, and Jedaiah will bring gifts of silver and gold from the Jews exiled in Babylon. As soon as they arrive, meet them at the home of Josiah son of Zephaniah. [11] Accept their gifts, and make a crown* from the silver and gold. Then put the crown on the head of Jeshua* son of Jehozadak, the high priest. [12] Tell him, 'This is what the Lord of Heaven's Armies says: Here is the man called the Branch. He will branch out from where he is and build the Temple of the Lord. [13] Yes, he will build the Temple of the Lord. Then he will receive royal honor and will rule as king from his throne. He will also serve as priest from his throne,* and there will be perfect harmony between his two roles.'

[14] "The crown will be a memorial in the Temple of the Lord to honor those who gave it—Heldai,* Tobijah, Jedaiah, and Josiah* son of Zephaniah."

[15] People will come from distant lands to rebuild the Temple of the Lord. And when this happens, you will know that my messages have been from the Lord of Heaven's Armies. All this will happen if you carefully obey what the Lord your God says.

7 A Call to Justice and Mercy

On December 7* of the fourth year of King Darius's reign, another message came to Zechariah from the Lord. [2] The people of Bethel had sent Sharezer and Regemmelech,* along with their attendants, to seek the Lord's favor. [3] They were to ask this question of the prophets and the priests at the Temple of the Lord of Heaven's Armies: "Should we continue to mourn and fast each summer on the anniversary of the Temple's destruction,* as we have done for so many years?"

[4] The Lord of Heaven's Armies sent me this message in reply: [5] "Say to all your people and your priests, 'During these seventy years of exile, when you fasted and mourned in the summer and in early autumn,* was it really for me that you were fasting? [6] And even now in your holy festivals, aren't you eating and drinking just to please yourselves? [7] Isn't this the same message the Lord proclaimed through the prophets in years past when Jerusalem and the towns of Judah were bustling with people, and the Negev and the foothills of Judah* were well populated?'"

[8] Then this message came to Zechariah from the Lord: [9] "This is what the Lord of Heaven's Armies says: Judge fairly, and show mercy and kindness to one another. [10] Do not oppress widows, orphans, foreigners, and the poor. And do not scheme against each other.

[11] "Your ancestors refused to listen to this message. They stubbornly turned away and put their fingers in their ears to keep

---

6:5 Or the four winds.   6:6 Hebrew is going after them.   6:8 Hebrew have given my Spirit rest.   6:11a As in Greek and Syriac versions; Hebrew reads crowns.   6:11b Hebrew Joshua, a variant spelling of Jeshua.   6:13 Or There will be a priest by his throne.   6:14a As in Syriac version (compare 6:10); Hebrew reads Helem.   6:14b As in Syriac version (compare 6:10); Hebrew reads Hen.   7:1 Hebrew On the fourth day of the ninth month, the month of Kislev, of the ancient Hebrew lunar calendar. This event occurred on December 7, 518 B.C.; also see note on 1:1.   7:2 Or Bethel-sharezer had sent Regemmelech.   7:3 Hebrew mourn and fast in the fifth month. The Temple had been destroyed in the fifth month of the ancient Hebrew lunar calendar (August 586 B.C.); see 2 Kgs 25:8.   7:5 Hebrew fasted and mourned in the fifth and seventh months. The fifth month of the ancient Hebrew lunar calendar usually occurs within the months of July and August. The seventh month usually occurs within the months of September and October; both the Day of Atonement and the Festival of Shelters were celebrated in the seventh month.   7:7 Hebrew the Shephelah.

from hearing. ¹²They made their hearts as hard as stone, so they could not hear the instructions or the messages that the Lord of Heaven's Armies had sent them by his Spirit through the earlier prophets. That is why the Lord of Heaven's Armies was so angry with them.

¹³"Since they refused to listen when I called to them, I would not listen when they called to me, says the Lord of Heaven's Armies. ¹⁴As with a whirlwind, I scattered them among the distant nations, where they lived as strangers. Their land became so desolate that no one even traveled through it. They turned their pleasant land into a desert."

8 Promised Blessings for Jerusalem

Then another message came to me from the Lord of Heaven's Armies: ²"This is what the Lord of Heaven's Armies says: My love for Mount Zion is passionate and strong; I am consumed with passion for Jerusalem!

³"And now the Lord says: I am returning to Mount Zion, and I will live in Jerusalem. Then Jerusalem will be called the Faithful City; the mountain of the Lord of Heaven's Armies will be called the Holy Mountain.

⁴"This is what the Lord of Heaven's Armies says: Once again old men and women will walk Jerusalem's streets with their canes and will sit together in the city squares. ⁵And the streets of the city will be filled with boys and girls at play.

⁶"This is what the Lord of Heaven's Armies says: All this may seem impossible to you now, a small remnant of God's people. But is it impossible for me? says the Lord of Heaven's Armies.

⁷"This is what the Lord of Heaven's Armies says: You can be sure that I will rescue my people from the east and from the west. ⁸I will bring them home again to live safely in Jerusalem. They will be my people, and I will be faithful and just toward them as their God.

⁹"This is what the Lord of Heaven's Armies says: Be strong and finish the task! Ever since the laying of the foundation of the Temple of the Lord of Heaven's Armies, you have heard what the prophets have been saying about completing the building. ¹⁰Before the work on the Temple began, there were no jobs and no money to hire people or animals. No traveler was safe from the enemy, for there were enemies on all sides. I had turned everyone against each other.

¹¹"But now I will not treat the remnant of my people as I treated them before, says the Lord of Heaven's Armies. ¹²For I am planting seeds of peace and prosperity among you. The grapevines will be heavy with fruit. The earth will produce its crops, and the heavens will release the dew. Once more I will cause the remnant in Judah and Israel to inherit these blessings. ¹³Among the other nations, Judah and Israel became symbols of a cursed nation. But no longer! Now I will rescue you and make you both a symbol and a source of blessing. So don't be afraid. Be strong, and get on with rebuilding the Temple!

¹⁴"For this is what the Lord of Heaven's Armies says: I was determined to punish you when your ancestors angered me, and I did not change my mind, says the Lord of Heaven's Armies. ¹⁵But now I am determined to bless Jerusalem and the people of Judah. So don't be afraid. ¹⁶But this is what you must do: Tell the truth to each other. Render verdicts in your courts that are just and that lead to peace. ¹⁷Don't scheme against each other. Stop your love of telling lies that you swear are the truth. I hate all these things, says the Lord."

¹⁸Here is another message that came to me from the Lord of Heaven's Armies. ¹⁹"This is what the Lord of Heaven's Armies says: The traditional fasts and times of mourning you have kept in early summer, midsummer, autumn, and winter* are now ended. They will become festivals of joy and celebration for the people of Judah. So love truth and peace.

²⁰"This is what the Lord of Heaven's Armies says: People from nations and cities around the world will travel to Jerusalem. ²¹The people of one city will say to the peo-

---

8:19 Hebrew *in the fourth, fifth, seventh, and tenth months.* The fourth month of the ancient Hebrew lunar calendar usually occurs within the months of June and July. The fifth month usually occurs within the months of July and August. The seventh month usually occurs within the months of September and October. The tenth month usually occurs within the months of December and January.

ple of another, 'Come with us to Jerusalem to ask the LORD to bless us. Let's worship the LORD of Heaven's Armies. I'm determined to go.' ²²Many peoples and powerful nations will come to Jerusalem to seek the LORD of Heaven's Armies and to ask for his blessing.

²³"This is what the LORD of Heaven's Armies says: In those days ten men from different nations and languages of the world will clutch at the sleeve of one Jew. And they will say, 'Please let us walk with you, for we have heard that God is with you.'"

9 Judgment against Israel's Enemies

This is the message* from the LORD against the land of Aram* and the city of Damascus, for the eyes of humanity, including all the tribes of Israel, are on the LORD.

²Doom is certain for Hamath,
near Damascus,
and for the cities of Tyre and Sidon,
though they are so clever.
³Tyre has built a strong fortress
and has made silver and gold
as plentiful as dust in the streets!
⁴But now the Lord will strip away Tyre's
possessions
and hurl its fortifications into the sea,
and it will be burned to the ground.
⁵The city of Ashkelon will see Tyre fall
and will be filled with fear.
Gaza will shake with terror,
as will Ekron, for their hopes will be
dashed.
Gaza's king will be killed,
and Ashkelon will be deserted.
⁶Foreigners will occupy the city of
Ashdod.
I will destroy the pride of the
Philistines.
⁷I will grab the bloody meat from their
mouths
and snatch the detestable sacrifices
from their teeth.
Then the surviving Philistines will
worship our God
and become like a clan in Judah.*
The Philistines of Ekron will join my
people,
as the ancient Jebusites once did.

⁸I will guard my Temple
and protect it from invading armies.
I am watching closely to ensure
that no more foreign oppressors
overrun my people's land.

Zion's Coming King

⁹Rejoice, O people of Zion!*
Shout in triumph, O people of
Jerusalem!
Look, your king is coming to you.
He is righteous and victorious,*
yet he is humble, riding on a donkey—
riding on a donkey's colt.
¹⁰I will remove the battle chariots from
Israel*
and the warhorses from Jerusalem.
I will destroy all the weapons used in
battle,
and your king will bring peace to the
nations.
His realm will stretch from sea to sea
and from the Euphrates River* to the
ends of the earth.*
¹¹Because of the covenant I made with
you,
sealed with blood,
I will free your prisoners
from death in a waterless dungeon.
¹²Come back to the place of safety,
all you prisoners who still have
hope!
I promise this very day
that I will repay two blessings for each
of your troubles.
¹³Judah is my bow,
and Israel is my arrow.
Jerusalem* is my sword,
and like a warrior, I will brandish it
against the Greeks.*

¹⁴The LORD will appear above his people;
his arrows will fly like lightning!
The Sovereign LORD will sound the
ram's horn
and attack like a whirlwind from the
southern desert.
¹⁵The LORD of Heaven's Armies will
protect his people,
and they will defeat their enemies by
hurling great stones.

9:1a Hebrew An Oracle: The message. 9:1b Hebrew land of Hadrach. 9:7 Hebrew and will become a leader in Judah. 9:9a Hebrew O daughter of Zion! 9:9b Hebrew and is being vindicated. 9:10a Hebrew Ephraim, referring to the northern kingdom of Israel; also in 9:13. 9:10b Hebrew the river. 9:10c Or the end of the land. 9:13a Hebrew Zion. 9:13b Hebrew the sons of Javan.

Justice and Evangelism
ZECHARIAH 8

There's a biblical prophecy I've freshly discovered. I eagerly await its fulfillment and am doing whatever I can, whatever I must, to hasten it. The prophecy is in Zechariah 8. It begins with a vision of what a community looks like when God reigns within it. But here's how the chapter ends; here is the vision's crescendo: "This is what the LORD of Heaven's Armies says: In those days ten men from different nations and languages of the world will clutch at the sleeve of one Jew. And they will say, 'Please let us walk with you, for we have heard that God is with you'" (8:23).

That's evangelism. Good news is embodied. It is a way of life, a thing plain for all to see. The evangelized, not the evangelists, do all the talking: let us go with you! The lost take the initiative. And the lost come from every tribe and tongue and nation.

This is the dream of every church—for God's life among us to be so obvious, so fragrant, so magnetic, so contagious, that all peoples clamor for the privilege of joining. Rather than us grabbing hold of people, people grab hold of us. Rather than us telling anyone, "God is with us," they tell one another that.

All these things happen "in those days," which refers to a promise God makes at the beginning of Zechariah 8: "I am returning to Mount Zion, and I will live in Jerusalem" (8:3). This vision is a description of what happens in, to, and through God's people when God dwells in their midst.

Several things happen in this vision, but let me draw out one: there is a breaking of ethnic, cultural, and political divides through an in-breaking of the gospel. "People from nations and cities around the world will travel to Jerusalem . . . [saying], 'Come with us to Jerusalem to ask the LORD to bless us. Let's worship the LORD of Heaven's Armies. I'm determined to go.' Many peoples and powerful nations will come to Jerusalem to seek the LORD" (8:20-22).

Good News, the gospel, is for all nations. It embraces and welcomes all languages—Urdu speakers and Inuit and Norwegians and remote tribes tucked in the folds of Burmese mountain jungles. It's for the homeless under the bridges of Los Angeles, the untouchables in the streets of Calcutta, the drug addicted in sweaty apartments not far from where you live. It's for rich people who live atop hills and poor people who live in ditches. It's for the old man in his lonely room, the teenage girl struggling with her identity, the single mom wondering where the next meal's coming from. It's for the discouraged dentist, the confused mill-worker, the weary postman. It's for everyone, everywhere.

This is evangelism Bible-style. This is evangelism that is cross-cultural, transpolitical, multiethnic, intergenerational, class defying, and wildly bountiful.

And natural. No one strategizes. No one takes classes for this. It's just that a people who live with God in their midst evoke, simply and powerfully, far and wide, curiosity about God. A community like that makes others envious in the best sense: they want what we have (Romans 11:13–14). When God's ways become our ways, we become attractive and compelling to the world.

But stop.

God asks us to do something before he releases any of this: he asks us to *do justly*.

"But this is what you must do: Tell the truth to each other. Render verdicts in your courts that are just and that lead to peace. Don't scheme against each other. Stop your love of telling lies that you swear are the truth. I hate all these things, says the LORD" (8:16–17).

A crucial shift in Zechariah 8 happens midway through. It's announced by the phrase, "But this is what you must do." Up until this moment, Zechariah 8 has been a litany of things God promises to do. Right after this moment, it continues with things God promises to do. But inserted in the middle of the prophecy is something God requires us to do.

Act justly.

God hates injustice. He hates deceit. Unless we deal fairly and honestly with one another, unless we have a bone-deep commitment to justice and truth, all the good God intends to do for us and through us gets undone by us.

We have a passion for sharing God's truth with the lost—for helping friends, neighbors, loved ones, our communities to come to see, know, and love God. But as we hold on to this hope, we must also understand that God requires us to do justly. For if we are not living out the redemptive, just, and whole Christian life, it can be hard to recommend it to other folks.

—*Mark Buchanan*

They will shout in battle as though
    drunk with wine.
They will be filled with blood like a
    bowl,
    drenched with blood like the corners
    of the altar.
16 On that day the LORD their God will
    rescue his people,
    just as a shepherd rescues his sheep.
They will sparkle in his land
    like jewels in a crown.
17 How wonderful and beautiful they
    will be!
    The young men will thrive on
    abundant grain,
    and the young women will flourish on
    new wine.

10 The LORD Will Restore His People

1 Ask the LORD for rain in the
    spring,
    for he makes the storm clouds.
And he will send showers of rain
    so every field becomes a lush pasture.
2 Household gods give worthless advice,
    fortune-tellers predict only lies,
    and interpreters of dreams pronounce
    falsehoods that give no comfort.
So my people are wandering like lost
    sheep;
    they are attacked because they have
    no shepherd.

3 "My anger burns against your shepherds,
    and I will punish these leaders.*
For the LORD of Heaven's Armies has
    arrived
    to look after Judah, his flock.
He will make them strong and glorious,
    like a proud warhorse in battle.
4 From Judah will come the cornerstone,
    the tent peg,
    the bow for battle,
    and all the rulers.
5 They will be like mighty warriors in
    battle,
    trampling their enemies in the mud
    under their feet.
Since the LORD is with them as they
    fight,
    they will overthrow even the enemy's
    horsemen.

6 "I will strengthen Judah and save Israel*;
    I will restore them because of my
    compassion.
It will be as though I had never rejected
    them,
    for I am the LORD their God, who will
    hear their cries.
7 The people of Israel* will become like
    mighty warriors,
    and their hearts will be made happy as
    if by wine.
Their children, too, will see it and be
    glad;
    their hearts will rejoice in the LORD.
8 When I whistle to them, they will come
    running,
    for I have redeemed them.
From the few who are left,
    they will grow as numerous as they
    were before.
9 Though I have scattered them like seeds
    among the nations,
    they will still remember me in distant
    lands.
They and their children will survive
    and return again to Israel.
10 I will bring them back from Egypt
    and gather them from Assyria.
I will resettle them in Gilead and
    Lebanon
    until there is no more room for them
    all.
11 They will pass safely through the sea of
    distress,*
    for the waves of the sea will be held
    back,
    and the waters of the Nile will dry up.
The pride of Assyria will be crushed,
    and the rule of Egypt will end.
12 By my power* I will make my people
    strong,
    and by my authority they will go
    wherever they wish.
I, the LORD, have spoken!"

11 1 Open your doors, Lebanon,
    so that fire may devour your cedar
    forests.
2 Weep, you cypress trees, for all the
    ruined cedars;
    the most majestic ones have fallen.

10:3 Or these male goats. 10:6 Hebrew save the house of Joseph. 10:7 Hebrew of Ephraim. 10:11 Or the sea of Egypt, referring to the Red
Sea. 10:12 Hebrew In the LORD.

Confession

Why Can't I Shake My Sins?

ZECHARIAH 10:1–6

Why do persistent sins stubbornly remain, despite all our best efforts to turn away from them? Some classic Christian texts have provided me with an unexpected answer.

François Fénelon, a Christian spiritual adviser in the 1600s, wrote a letter that included a phrase that stopped me in my tracks: "Sometimes [God] leaves people with certain unconquerable imperfections . . ."

Really? *God* does this? What good end could God possibly have for leaving unconquered areas in our lives?

Fénelon continued, ". . . in order to deprive them of all inward self-satisfaction. . . . Self-reliance, even in the matter of curing one's faults, fosters a hidden conceit."

In other words, we may be concerned about our "unconquerable imperfections," while God is more concerned about our pride. To stab our pride, he may leave those imperfections, for a time, to make us humble—to cause us to throw ourselves, in frustration, upon God.

Even faults that stubbornly remain can be used by God for our good, says Fénelon: "Let us profit by the faults we have committed, through the humble consciousness of our weakness, without discouragement."

Francis de Sales concurs with this idea in *Introduction to the Devout Life*: "For the furtherance of humility, it is needful that we sometimes find ourselves worsted in this spiritual battle." According to de Sales, our persistent failings bring us "abjection" (humility), and that's spiritually beneficial as long as we persevere.

While striving for holiness, we must not underestimate the value of humility. As Peter of Damaskos wrote in the *Philokalia*: if "you sin out of habit even when you do not want to, show humility like the tax collector (Luke 18:13); this is enough to ensure your salvation."

So when struggling with persistent sin, take heart. God is at work, and even your persistent failings may work to your good and his glory. Let yourself be humbled by your falls.

—*Kevin A. Miller*

For more on confession, see reading at Mark 1:15.

Weep, you oaks of Bashan,
  for the thick forests have been cut down.
3 Listen to the wailing of the shepherds,
  for their rich pastures are destroyed.
Hear the young lions roaring,
  for their thickets in the Jordan Valley
    are ruined.

The Good and Evil Shepherds

4 This is what the LORD my God says: "Go and care for the flock that is intended for slaughter. 5 The buyers slaughter their sheep without remorse. The sellers say, 'Praise the LORD! Now I'm rich!' Even the shepherds have no compassion for them. 6 Likewise, I will no longer have pity on the people of the land," says the LORD. "I will let them fall into each other's hands and into the hands of their king. They will turn the land into a wilderness, and I will not rescue them."

7 So I cared for the flock intended for slaughter—the flock that was oppressed.

Then I took two shepherd's staffs and named one Favor and the other Union. ⁸I got rid of their three evil shepherds in a single month.

But I became impatient with these sheep, and they hated me, too. ⁹So I told them, "I won't be your shepherd any longer. If you die, you die. If you are killed, you are killed. And let those who remain devour each other!"

¹⁰Then I took my staff called Favor and cut it in two, showing that I had revoked the covenant I had made with all the nations. ¹¹That was the end of my covenant with them. The suffering flock was watching me, and they knew that the LORD was speaking through my actions.

¹²And I said to them, "If you like, give me my wages, whatever I am worth; but only if you want to." So they counted out for my wages thirty pieces of silver.

¹³And the LORD said to me, "Throw it to the potter*"—this magnificent sum at which they valued me! So I took the thirty coins and threw them to the potter in the Temple of the LORD.

¹⁴Then I took my other staff, Union, and cut it in two, showing that the bond of unity between Judah and Israel was broken.

¹⁵Then the LORD said to me, "Go again and play the part of a worthless shepherd. ¹⁶This illustrates how I will give this nation a shepherd who will not care for those who are dying, nor look after the young,* nor heal the injured, nor feed the healthy. Instead, this shepherd will eat the meat of the fattest sheep and tear off their hooves.

¹⁷ "What sorrow awaits this worthless
     shepherd
  who abandons the flock!
The sword will cut his arm
  and pierce his right eye.
His arm will become useless,
  and his right eye completely blind."

12 Future Deliverance for Jerusalem

This* message concerning the fate of Israel came from the LORD: "This message is from the LORD, who stretched out the heavens, laid the foundations of the earth, and formed the human spirit. ²I will make Jerusalem like an intoxicating drink that makes the nearby nations stagger when they send their armies to besiege Jerusalem and Judah. ³On that day I will make Jerusalem an immovable rock. All the nations will gather against it to try to move it, but they will only hurt themselves.

⁴"On that day," says the LORD, "I will cause every horse to panic and every rider to lose his nerve. I will watch over the people of Judah, but I will blind all the horses of their enemies. ⁵And the clans of Judah will say to themselves, 'The people of Jerusalem have found strength in the LORD of Heaven's Armies, their God.'

⁶"On that day I will make the clans of Judah like a flame that sets a woodpile ablaze or like a burning torch among sheaves of grain. They will burn up all the neighboring nations right and left, while the people living in Jerusalem remain secure.

⁷"The LORD will give victory to the rest of Judah first, before Jerusalem, so that the people of Jerusalem and the royal line of David will not have greater honor than the rest of Judah. ⁸On that day the LORD will defend the people of Jerusalem; the weakest among them will be as mighty as King David! And the royal descendants will be like God, like the angel of the LORD who goes before them! ⁹For on that day I will begin to destroy all the nations that come against Jerusalem.

¹⁰"Then I will pour out a spirit* of grace and prayer on the family of David and on the people of Jerusalem. They will look on me whom they have pierced and mourn for him as for an only son. They will grieve bitterly for him as for a firstborn son who has died. ¹¹The sorrow and mourning in Jerusalem on that day will be like the great mourning for Hadad-rimmon in the valley of Megiddo.

¹²"All Israel will mourn, each clan by itself, and with the husbands separate from their wives. The clan of David will mourn alone, as will the clan of Nathan, ¹³the clan of Levi, and the clan of Shimei. ¹⁴Each of the surviving clans from Judah will mourn separately, and with the husbands separate from their wives.

11:13 Syriac version reads *into the treasury;* also in 11:13b. Compare Matt 27:6-10.   11:16 Or *the scattered.*   12:1 Hebrew *An Oracle: This.*
12:10 Or *the Spirit.*

13 A Fountain of Cleansing

"On that day a fountain will be opened for the dynasty of David and for the people of Jerusalem, a fountain to cleanse them from all their sins and impurity.

2 "And on that day," says the LORD of Heaven's Armies, "I will erase idol worship throughout the land, so that even the names of the idols will be forgotten. I will remove from the land both the false prophets and the spirit of impurity that came with them. 3 If anyone continues to prophesy, his own father and mother will tell him, 'You must die, for you have prophesied lies in the name of the LORD.' And as he prophesies, his own father and mother will stab him.

4 "On that day people will be ashamed to claim the prophetic gift. No one will pretend to be a prophet by wearing prophet's clothes. 5 He will say, 'I'm no prophet; I'm a farmer. I began working for a farmer as a boy.' 6 And if someone asks, 'Then what about those wounds on your chest?*' he will say, 'I was wounded at my friends' house!'

The Scattering of the Sheep

7 "Awake, O sword, against my shepherd,
   the man who is my partner,"
      says the LORD of Heaven's Armies.
   "Strike down the shepherd,
      and the sheep will be scattered,
      and I will turn against the lambs.
8 Two-thirds of the people in the land
      will be cut off and die," says the LORD.
   "But one-third will be left in the land.
9 I will bring that group through the fire
      and make them pure.
   I will refine them like silver
      and purify them like gold.
   They will call on my name,
      and I will answer them.
   I will say, 'These are my people,'
      and they will say, 'The LORD is our
         God.'"

14 The LORD Will Rule the Earth

Watch, for the day of the LORD is coming when your possessions will be plundered right in front of you! 2 I will gather all the nations to fight against Jerusalem. The city will be taken, the houses looted, and the women raped. Half the population will be taken into captivity, and the rest will be left among the ruins of the city.

3 Then the LORD will go out to fight against those nations, as he has fought in times past. 4 On that day his feet will stand on the Mount of Olives, east of Jerusalem. And the Mount of Olives will split apart, making a wide valley running from east to west. Half the mountain will move toward the north and half toward the south. 5 You will flee through this valley, for it will reach across to Azal.* Yes, you will flee as you did from the earthquake in the days of King Uzziah of Judah. Then the LORD my God will come, and all his holy ones with him.*

6 On that day the sources of light will no longer shine,* 7 yet there will be continuous day! Only the LORD knows how this could happen. There will be no normal day and night, for at evening time it will still be light.

8 On that day life-giving waters will flow out from Jerusalem, half toward the Dead Sea and half toward the Mediterranean,* flowing continuously in both summer and winter.

9 And the LORD will be king over all the earth. On that day there will be one LORD— his name alone will be worshiped.

10 All the land from Geba, north of Judah, to Rimmon, south of Jerusalem, will become one vast plain. But Jerusalem will be raised up in its original place and will be inhabited all the way from the Benjamin Gate over to the site of the old gate, then to the Corner Gate, and from the Tower of Hananel to the king's winepresses. 11 And Jerusalem will be filled, safe at last, never again to be cursed and destroyed.

12 And the LORD will send a plague on all the nations that fought against Jerusalem. Their people will become like walking corpses, their flesh rotting away. Their eyes will rot in their sockets, and their tongues will rot in their mouths. 13 On that day they will be terrified, stricken by the

---

13:6 Hebrew *wounds between your hands?* **14:5a** The meaning of the Hebrew is uncertain. **14:5b** As in Greek version; Hebrew reads *with you.* **14:6** Hebrew *there will be no light, no cold or frost.* The meaning of the Hebrew is uncertain. **14:8** Hebrew *half toward the eastern sea and half toward the western sea.*

LORD with great panic. They will fight their neighbors hand to hand. [14]Judah, too, will be fighting at Jerusalem. The wealth of all the neighboring nations will be captured—great quantities of gold and silver and fine clothing. [15]This same plague will strike the horses, mules, camels, donkeys, and all the other animals in the enemy camps.

[16]In the end, the enemies of Jerusalem who survive the plague will go up to Jerusalem each year to worship the King, the LORD of Heaven's Armies, and to celebrate the Festival of Shelters. [17]Any nation in the world that refuses to come to Jerusalem to worship the King, the LORD of Heaven's Armies, will have no rain. [18]If the people of Egypt refuse to attend the festival, the LORD will punish them with the same plague that he sends on the other nations who refuse to go. [19]Egypt and the other nations will all be punished if they don't go to celebrate the Festival of Shelters.

[20]On that day even the harness bells of the horses will be inscribed with these words: HOLY TO THE LORD. And the cooking pots in the Temple of the LORD will be as sacred as the basins used beside the altar. [21]In fact, every cooking pot in Jerusalem and Judah will be holy to the LORD of Heaven's Armies. All who come to worship will be free to use any of these pots to boil their sacrifices. And on that day there will no longer be traders* in the Temple of the LORD of Heaven's Armies.

Introduction to
Malachi

Background

Malachi is the last of the Old Testament prophets; his name is not mentioned elsewhere in the Bible. According to a Jewish tradition, Malachi was a Levite who was part of the "Great Synagogue," which gathered and protected the Old Testament. Malachi means "my messenger."

At the time of Malachi, the people are discouraged by corrupt priests and have a complacent attitude about their relationship with God. Malachi writes to condemn their behavior.

Message

The book starts with a strong statement of God's love for his people. It continues with God asking his priests for the honor due him—in sacrifices and in teaching. God then reproaches his people for their unfaithfulness to one another, particularly in terms of divorce, intermarriage with idolaters, and violence. After an interlude warning of judgment—"a blazing fire that refines" (3:2), the prophecy turns to questions of the people robbing God by failing to bring "tithes into the storehouse" (3:10). Does one serve God in vain? No. God will punish the wicked and reward the righteous. Malachi ends with a promise of Elijah as a forerunner of the coming Lord.

Time

Malachi's ministry was about a century after the other postexilic prophets (Haggai and Zechariah). The use of the Persian term for governor (*pechah*) in 1:8 shows that Malachi was written when Persia controlled Judah (539–333 B.C.), possibly when Nehemiah was deployed temporarily back to Persia; this term also appears in Nehemiah 5:14 and Haggai. Four hundred years of silence passed between the time of Malachi and the events recorded in the New Testament.

Outline

Malachi

1 This is the message* that the LORD gave to Israel through the prophet Malachi.*

The LORD's Love for Israel

²"I have always loved you," says the LORD.

But you retort, "Really? How have you loved us?"

And the LORD replies, "This is how I showed my love for you: I loved your ancestor Jacob, ³but I rejected his brother, Esau, and devastated his hill country. I turned Esau's inheritance into a desert for jackals."

⁴Esau's descendants in Edom may say, "We have been shattered, but we will rebuild the ruins."

But the LORD of Heaven's Armies replies, "They may try to rebuild, but I will demolish them again. Their country will be known as 'The Land of Wickedness,' and their people will be called 'The People with Whom the LORD Is Forever Angry.' ⁵When you see the destruction for yourselves, you will say, 'Truly, the LORD's greatness reaches far beyond Israel's borders!'"

Unworthy Sacrifices

⁶The LORD of Heaven's Armies says to the priests: "A son honors his father, and a servant respects his master. If I am your father and master, where are the honor and respect I deserve? You have shown contempt for my name!

"But you ask, 'How have we ever shown contempt for your name?'

⁷"You have shown contempt by offering defiled sacrifices on my altar.

"Then you ask, 'How have we defiled the sacrifices?*'

"You defile them by saying the altar of the LORD deserves no respect. ⁸When you give blind animals as sacrifices, isn't that wrong? And isn't it wrong to offer animals that are crippled and diseased? Try giving gifts like that to your governor, and see how pleased he is!" says the LORD of Heaven's Armies.

⁹"Go ahead, beg God to be merciful to you! But when you bring that kind of offering, why should he show you any favor at all?" asks the LORD of Heaven's Armies.

¹⁰"How I wish one of you would shut the Temple doors so that these worthless sacrifices could not be offered! I am not pleased with you," says the LORD of Heaven's Armies, "and I will not accept your offerings. ¹¹But my name is honored* by people of other nations from morning till night. All around the world they offer* sweet incense and pure offerings in honor of my name. For my name is great among the nations," says the LORD of Heaven's Armies.

¹²"But you dishonor my name with your actions. By bringing contemptible food, you are saying it's all right to defile the Lord's table. ¹³You say, 'It's too hard to serve the LORD,' and you turn up your noses at my commands," says the LORD of Heaven's Armies. "Think of it! Animals that are stolen and crippled and sick are being presented as offerings! Should I accept from you such offerings as these?" asks the LORD.

1:1a Hebrew *An Oracle: The message.* **1:1b** *Malachi* means "my messenger." **1:7** As in Greek version; Hebrew reads *defiled you?* **1:11a** Or *will be honored.* **1:11b** Or *will offer.*

¹⁴"Cursed is the cheat who promises to give a fine ram from his flock but then sacrifices a defective one to the Lord. For I am a great king," says the LORD of Heaven's Armies, "and my name is feared among the nations!

2 A Warning to the Priests

"Listen, you priests—this command is for you! ²Listen to me and make up your minds to honor my name," says the LORD of Heaven's Armies, "or I will bring a terrible curse against you. I will curse even the blessings you receive. Indeed, I have already cursed them, because you have not taken my warning to heart. ³I will punish your descendants and splatter your faces with the manure from your festival sacrifices, and I will throw you on the manure pile. ⁴Then at last you will know it was I who sent you this warning so that my covenant with the Levites can continue," says the LORD of Heaven's Armies.

⁵"The purpose of my covenant with the Levites was to bring life and peace, and that is what I gave them. This required reverence from them, and they greatly revered me and stood in awe of my name. ⁶They passed on to the people the truth of the instructions they received from me. They did not lie or cheat; they walked with me, living good and righteous lives, and they turned many from lives of sin.

⁷"The words of a priest's lips should preserve knowledge of God, and people should go to him for instruction, for the priest is the messenger of the LORD of Heaven's Armies. ⁸But you priests have left God's paths. Your instructions have caused many to stumble into sin. You have corrupted the covenant I made with the Levites," says the LORD of Heaven's Armies. ⁹"So I have made you despised and humiliated in the eyes of all the people. For you have not obeyed me but have shown favoritism in the way you carry out my instructions."

A Call to Faithfulness

¹⁰Are we not all children of the same Father? Are we not all created by the same God? Then why do we betray each other, violating the covenant of our ancestors?

¹¹Judah has been unfaithful, and a detestable thing has been done in Israel and in Jerusalem. The men of Judah have defiled the LORD's beloved sanctuary by marrying women who worship idols. ¹²May the LORD cut off from the nation of Israel* every last man who has done this and yet brings an offering to the LORD of Heaven's Armies.

¹³Here is another thing you do. You cover the LORD's altar with tears, weeping and groaning because he pays no attention to your offerings and doesn't accept them with pleasure. ¹⁴You cry out, "Why doesn't the LORD accept my worship?" I'll tell you why! Because the LORD witnessed the vows you and your wife made when you were young. But you have been unfaithful to her, though she remained your faithful partner, the wife of your marriage vows.

¹⁵Didn't the LORD make you one with your wife? In body and spirit you are his.* And what does he want? Godly children from your union. So guard your heart; remain loyal to the wife of your youth. ¹⁶"For I hate divorce!" says the LORD, the God of Israel. "To divorce your wife is to overwhelm her with cruelty,*" says the LORD of Heaven's Armies. "So guard your heart; do not be unfaithful to your wife."

¹⁷You have wearied the LORD with your words.

"How have we wearied him?" you ask.

You have wearied him by saying that all who do evil are good in the LORD's sight, and he is pleased with them. You have wearied him by asking, "Where is the God of justice?"

3 The Coming Day of Judgment

"Look! I am sending my messenger, and he will prepare the way before me. Then the Lord you are seeking will suddenly come to his Temple. The messenger of the covenant, whom you look for so eagerly, is surely coming," says the LORD of Heaven's Armies. ²"But who will be able to endure it when he comes? Who will be able to stand and face him when he appears? For he will be like a

---

2:12 Hebrew *from the tents of Jacob.* The names "Jacob" and "Israel" are often interchanged throughout the Old Testament, referring sometimes to the individual patriarch and sometimes to the nation. **2:15** Or *Didn't the one LORD make us and preserve our life and breath?* or *Didn't the one LORD make her, both flesh and spirit?* The meaning of the Hebrew is uncertain. **2:16** Hebrew *to cover one's garment with violence.*

Stewardship

Tithing?

MALACHI 3:6-12

Malachi was the last of the Old Testament prophets and ministered during a time of moral and spiritual apathy in Israel. During Malachi's ministry Israel was a shell of its former self—politically, morally, and spiritually—and God told them why. "Should people cheat God? Yet you have cheated me! . . . You have cheated me of the tithes and offerings due to me" (3:8). Israelites who didn't bring tithes and offerings were robbing God. Malachi identified this giving problem as the root—and the cure—of the nation's deceit, debauchery, and immorality.

The tithe referred to in this passage was the fundamental giving unit of the Old Testament—one-tenth of a person's income (Leviticus 27:30). It was used to fund the temple and provide for the Levites; "offerings" in Malachi 3:8 referred to gifts over and above the tithe.

Tithes are not mentioned in the New Testament for three reasons: our giving is now inspired by love, not law; tithing was the accepted starting point; and tithing was too limited for the New Testament writers. First Corinthians 16:1–2 implies that Christians were expected to give proportionately, in keeping with their income.

Regardless of which percentage you decide to give—10 percent, less, or more—make sure you are giving what God is asking of you. This is the only area in the Bible where God asks us to test him (Malachi 3:10). God promises to reward our faith and obedience with an outpouring of blessing.

If you're not in the habit of giving regularly to your church and other needs, it's time to start. If you have been giving but sense it's less than God desires, prayerfully consider what he's asking of you. If you want to live a life that counts, you have to give sacrificially.

—*Bryan Wilkerson, with JoHannah Reardon*

For more on stewardship, see reading at Mark 12:41–44.

blazing fire that refines metal, or like a strong soap that bleaches clothes. ³He will sit like a refiner of silver, burning away the dross. He will purify the Levites, refining them like gold and silver, so that they may once again offer acceptable sacrifices to the LORD. ⁴Then once more the LORD will accept the offerings brought to him by the people of Judah and Jerusalem, as he did in the past.

⁵"At that time I will put you on trial. I am eager to witness against all sorcerers and adulterers and liars. I will speak against those who cheat employees of their wages, who oppress widows and orphans, or who deprive the foreigners living among you of justice, for these people do not fear me," says the LORD of Heaven's Armies.

A Call to Repentance

⁶"I am the LORD, and I do not change. That is why you descendants of Jacob are not already destroyed. ⁷Ever since the days of your ancestors, you have scorned my decrees and failed to obey them. Now return to me, and I will return to you," says the LORD of Heaven's Armies.

"But you ask, 'How can we return when we have never gone away?'

8 "Should people cheat God? Yet you have cheated me!

"But you ask, 'What do you mean? When did we ever cheat you?'

"You have cheated me of the tithes and offerings due to me. 9 You are under a curse, for your whole nation has been cheating me. 10 Bring all the tithes into the storehouse so there will be enough food in my Temple. If you do," says the LORD of Heaven's Armies, "I will open the windows of heaven for you. I will pour out a blessing so great you won't have enough room to take it in! Try it! Put me to the test! 11 Your crops will be abundant, for I will guard them from insects and disease.* Your grapes will not fall from the vine before they are ripe," says the LORD of Heaven's Armies. 12 "Then all nations will call you blessed, for your land will be such a delight," says the LORD of Heaven's Armies.

13 "You have said terrible things about me," says the LORD.

"But you say, 'What do you mean? What have we said against you?'

14 "You have said, 'What's the use of serving God? What have we gained by obeying his commands or by trying to show the LORD of Heaven's Armies that we are sorry for our sins? 15 From now on we will call the arrogant blessed. For those who do evil get rich, and those who dare God to punish them suffer no harm.'"

The LORD's Promise of Mercy

16 Then those who feared the LORD spoke with each other, and the LORD listened to what they said. In his presence, a scroll of remembrance was written to record the names of those who feared him and always thought about the honor of his name.

17 "They will be my people," says the LORD of Heaven's Armies. "On the day when I act in judgment, they will be my own special treasure. I will spare them as a father spares an obedient child. 18 Then you will again see the difference between the righteous and the wicked, between those who serve God and those who do not."

4 The Coming Day of Judgment

1 *The LORD of Heaven's Armies says, "The day of judgment is coming, burning like a furnace. On that day the arrogant and the wicked will be burned up like straw. They will be consumed—roots, branches, and all.

2 "But for you who fear my name, the Sun of Righteousness will rise with healing in his wings.* And you will go free, leaping with joy like calves let out to pasture. 3 On the day when I act, you will tread upon the wicked as if they were dust under your feet," says the LORD of Heaven's Armies.

4 "Remember to obey the Law of Moses, my servant—all the decrees and regulations that I gave him on Mount Sinai* for all Israel.

5 "Look, I am sending you the prophet Elijah before the great and dreadful day of the LORD arrives. 6 His preaching will turn the hearts of fathers to their children, and the hearts of children to their fathers. Otherwise I will come and strike the land with a curse."

3:11 Hebrew *from the devourer.*   **4:1** Verses 4:1-6 are numbered 3:19-24 in Hebrew text.   **4:2** Or *the sun of righteousness will rise with healing in its wings.*   **4:4** Hebrew *Horeb,* another name for Sinai.

The
New
Testament

Introduction to

Matthew

Background

Matthew's gospel bridges the Old Testament and the New Testament, linking the prophecies of the coming Messiah and their fulfillment in Jesus Christ. It is the first of the three synoptic Gospels (with Mark and Luke), so called because of their similarities.

Matthew, whose name means "gift of the Lord," was surnamed Levi (Mark 2:14; Luke 5:27). He was the son of Alphaeus (Mark 2:14) and worked as a tax collector in Capernaum for the Roman government—an unpopular profession among the people of Israel. Yet Jesus called Matthew to follow him. Matthew left his profession behind, becoming one of Jesus' chosen twelve. After the Gospels, Matthew is mentioned only once, in Acts 1:13.

Message

Matthew repeatedly quotes the Old Testament to show that Jesus is the one who was spoken of by the ancient writers. Even his opening lines, a genealogy beginning with Abraham, show that Matthew wrote to a Jewish audience to present overwhelming evidence of Jesus' kingship: "the Kingdom of God has arrived among you" (12:28). Jesus' genealogy, baptism, messages, miracles, death, and resurrection point to the conclusion that he is the promised Messiah. Matthew includes an extensive version of Jesus' Sermon on the Mount (5:1–7:29)—much of it explaining the kingdom of God—and his teaching on end times (24:1–25:46). Matthew's gospel ends with a command and challenge to go into the world and make disciples; the gospel is not for Jews alone but for all people. But that mandate is not the last word. The final statement is the assuring, "I am with you always, even to the end of the age" (28:20).

Time

Matthew wrote his gospel between A.D. 58 and 68. The expressions "is still called" (27:8) and "they still tell it today" (28:15) indicate a substantial period of time between the events in the book and the time they were written down. The Olivet Discourse (24:1–25:46) anticipated the destruction of Jerusalem in A.D. 70.

Outline

Matthew

1 The Ancestors of Jesus the Messiah

This is a record of the ancestors of Jesus the Messiah, a descendant of David* and of Abraham:

2 Abraham was the father of Isaac.
Isaac was the father of Jacob.
Jacob was the father of Judah and his brothers.
3 Judah was the father of Perez and Zerah (whose mother was Tamar).
Perez was the father of Hezron.
Hezron was the father of Ram.*
4 Ram was the father of Amminadab.
Amminadab was the father of Nahshon.
Nahshon was the father of Salmon.
5 Salmon was the father of Boaz (whose mother was Rahab).
Boaz was the father of Obed (whose mother was Ruth).
Obed was the father of Jesse.
6 Jesse was the father of King David.
David was the father of Solomon (whose mother was Bathsheba, the widow of Uriah).
7 Solomon was the father of Rehoboam.
Rehoboam was the father of Abijah.
Abijah was the father of Asa.*
8 Asa was the father of Jehoshaphat.
Jehoshaphat was the father of Jehoram.*
Jehoram was the father* of Uzziah.
9 Uzziah was the father of Jotham.
Jotham was the father of Ahaz.
Ahaz was the father of Hezekiah.
10 Hezekiah was the father of Manasseh.
Manasseh was the father of Amon.*
Amon was the father of Josiah.
11 Josiah was the father of Jehoiachin* and his brothers (born at the time of the exile to Babylon).
12 After the Babylonian exile:
Jehoiachin was the father of Shealtiel.
Shealtiel was the father of Zerubbabel.
13 Zerubbabel was the father of Abiud.
Abiud was the father of Eliakim.
Eliakim was the father of Azor.
14 Azor was the father of Zadok.
Zadok was the father of Akim.

1:1 Greek *Jesus the Messiah, son of David.*   1:3 Greek *Aram,* a variant spelling of Ram; also in 1:4. See 1 Chr 2:9-10.   1:7 Greek *Asaph,* a variant spelling of Asa; also in 1:8. See 1 Chr 3:10.   1:8a Greek *Joram,* a variant spelling of Jehoram; also in 1:8b. See 1 Kgs 22:50 and note at 1 Chr 3:11.   1:8b Or *ancestor;* also in 1:11.   1:10 Greek *Amos,* a variant spelling of Amon; also in 1:10b. See 1 Chr 3:14.   1:11 Greek *Jeconiah,* a variant spelling of Jehoiachin; also in 1:12. See 2 Kgs 24:6 and note at 1 Chr 3:16.

Akim was the father of Eliud.
¹⁵ Eliud was the father of Eleazar.
Eleazar was the father of Matthan.
Matthan was the father of Jacob.
¹⁶ Jacob was the father of Joseph, the
husband of Mary.
Mary gave birth to Jesus, who is called
the Messiah.

¹⁷ All those listed above include fourteen generations from Abraham to David, fourteen from David to the Babylonian exile, and fourteen from the Babylonian exile to the Messiah.

The Birth of Jesus the Messiah

¹⁸ This is how Jesus the Messiah was born. His mother, Mary, was engaged to be married to Joseph. But before the marriage took place, while she was still a virgin, she became pregnant through the power of the Holy Spirit. ¹⁹ Joseph, her fiancé, was a good man and did not want to disgrace her publicly, so he decided to break the engagement* quietly.

²⁰ As he considered this, an angel of the Lord appeared to him in a dream. "Joseph, son of David," the angel said, "do not be afraid to take Mary as your wife. For the child within her was conceived by the Holy Spirit. ²¹ And she will have a son, and you are to name him Jesus,* for he will save his people from their sins."

²² All of this occurred to fulfill the Lord's message through his prophet:

²³ "Look! The virgin will conceive a child!
She will give birth to a son,
and they will call him Immanuel,*
which means 'God is with us.'"

²⁴ When Joseph woke up, he did as the angel of the Lord commanded and took Mary as his wife. ²⁵ But he did not have sexual relations with her until her son was born. And Joseph named him Jesus.

2 Visitors from the East

Jesus was born in Bethlehem in Judea, during the reign of King Herod. About that time some wise men* from eastern lands arrived in Jerusalem, asking, ² "Where is the newborn king of the Jews? We saw his star as it rose,* and we have come to worship him."

³ King Herod was deeply disturbed when he heard this, as was everyone in Jerusalem. ⁴ He called a meeting of the leading priests and teachers of religious law and asked, "Where is the Messiah supposed to be born?"

⁵ "In Bethlehem in Judea," they said, "for this is what the prophet wrote:

⁶ 'And you, O Bethlehem in the land of Judah,
are not least among the ruling cities*
of Judah,
for a ruler will come from you
who will be the shepherd for my
people Israel.'*"

⁷ Then Herod called for a private meeting with the wise men, and he learned from them the time when the star first appeared. ⁸ Then he told them, "Go to Bethlehem and search carefully for the child. And when you find him, come back and tell me so that I can go and worship him, too!"

⁹ After this interview the wise men went their way. And the star they had seen in the east guided them to Bethlehem. It went ahead of them and stopped over the place where the child was. ¹⁰ When they saw the star, they were filled with joy! ¹¹ They entered the house and saw the child with his mother, Mary, and they bowed down and worshiped him. Then they opened their treasure chests and gave him gifts of gold, frankincense, and myrrh.

¹² When it was time to leave, they returned to their own country by another route, for God had warned them in a dream not to return to Herod.

The Escape to Egypt

¹³ After the wise men were gone, an angel of the Lord appeared to Joseph in a dream. "Get up! Flee to Egypt with the child and his mother," the angel said. "Stay there until I tell you to return, because Herod is going to search for the child to kill him."

¹⁴ That night Joseph left for Egypt with the child and Mary, his mother, ¹⁵ and they

1:19 Greek *to divorce her.* **1:21** *Jesus* means "The LORD saves." **1:23** Isa 7:14; 8:8, 10 (Greek version). **2:1** Or *royal astrologers*; Greek reads *magi*; also in 2:7, 16. **2:2** Or *star in the east.* **2:6a** Greek *the rulers.* **2:6b** Mic 5:2; 2 Sam 5:2.

stayed there until Herod's death. This fulfilled what the Lord had spoken through the prophet: "I called my Son out of Egypt."*

16 Herod was furious when he realized that the wise men had outwitted him. He sent soldiers to kill all the boys in and around Bethlehem who were two years old and under, based on the wise men's report of the star's first appearance. 17 Herod's brutal action fulfilled what God had spoken through the prophet Jeremiah:

18 "A cry was heard in Ramah—
    weeping and great mourning.
Rachel weeps for her children,
    refusing to be comforted,
    for they are dead."*

The Return to Nazareth

19 When Herod died, an angel of the Lord appeared in a dream to Joseph in Egypt. 20 "Get up!" the angel said. "Take the child and his mother back to the land of Israel, because those who were trying to kill the child are dead."

21 So Joseph got up and returned to the land of Israel with Jesus and his mother. 22 But when he learned that the new ruler of Judea was Herod's son Archelaus, he was afraid to go there. Then, after being warned in a dream, he left for the region of Galilee. 23 So the family went and lived in a town called Nazareth. This fulfilled what the prophets had said: "He will be called a Nazarene."

3 John the Baptist Prepares the Way

In those days John the Baptist came to the Judean wilderness and began preaching. His message was, 2 "Repent of your sins and turn to God, for the Kingdom of Heaven is near.*" 3 The prophet Isaiah was speaking about John when he said,

"He is a voice shouting in the wilderness,
'Prepare the way for the LORD's coming!
    Clear the road for him!'"*

4 John's clothes were woven from coarse camel hair, and he wore a leather belt around his waist. For food he ate locusts and wild honey. 5 People from Jerusalem and from all of Judea and all over the Jordan

Valley went out to see and hear John. 6 And when they confessed their sins, he baptized them in the Jordan River.

7 But when he saw many Pharisees and Sadducees coming to watch him baptize,* he denounced them. "You brood of snakes!" he exclaimed. "Who warned you to flee God's coming wrath? 8 Prove by the way you live that you have repented of your sins and turned to God. 9 Don't just say to each other, 'We're safe, for we are descendants of Abraham.' That means nothing, for I tell you, God can create children of Abraham from these very stones. 10 Even now the ax of God's judgment is poised, ready to sever the roots of the trees. Yes, every tree that does not produce good fruit will be chopped down and thrown into the fire.

11 "I baptize with* water those who repent of their sins and turn to God. But someone is coming soon who is greater than I am—so much greater that I'm not worthy even to be his slave and carry his sandals. He will baptize you with the Holy Spirit and with fire.* 12 He is ready to separate the chaff from the wheat with his winnowing fork. Then he will clean up the threshing area, gathering the wheat into his barn but burning the chaff with never-ending fire."

The Baptism of Jesus

13 Then Jesus went from Galilee to the Jordan River to be baptized by John. 14 But John tried to talk him out of it. "I am the one who needs to be baptized by you," he said, "so why are you coming to me?"

15 But Jesus said, "It should be done, for we must carry out all that God requires.*" So John agreed to baptize him.

16 After his baptism, as Jesus came up out of the water, the heavens were opened* and he saw the Spirit of God descending like a dove and settling on him. 17 And a voice from heaven said, "This is my dearly loved Son, who brings me great joy."

4 The Temptation of Jesus

Then Jesus was led by the Spirit into the wilderness to be tempted there by the devil. 2 For forty days and forty nights he fasted and became very hungry.

2:15 Hos 11:1. 2:18 Jer 31:15. 3:2 Or has come, or is coming soon. 3:3 Isa 40:3 (Greek version). 3:7 Or coming to be baptized. 3:11a Or in. 3:11b Or in the Holy Spirit and in fire. 3:15 Or for we must fulfill all righteousness. 3:16 Some manuscripts read opened to him.

A Steady Stream of Spiritual Nourishment

MATTHEW 4:4

Bible Study & Meditation

Out of the blue, I found myself dealing with a difficult issue I thought had long ago been resolved. Despite my best efforts to handle the problem well, it just wouldn't go away. I slowly realized that part of the problem was that I was spiritually malnourished. Though I have countless spiritual resources (Bibles, faith-oriented books, Christian music), I'd mistaken being *surrounded* by them with actually being *fed* by them.

As a result my soul had withered in a land of plenty. I didn't have the strength to speak God's truth to my heart or to stand firm in spiritual battle, the way Paul instructed Christians (Ephesians 6:10-17). I wondered: *what if I fed my body at the same frequency I've been taking in spiritual food?* I imagined my physical body shrunken and emaciated. I pictured my limbs spindly and my cheeks hollow. I imagined myself struggling through the basic tasks of my day, like climbing stairs or walking uphill. It would be difficult—if not impossible—to move through my daily routine with strength and vigor in that state.

Startled, I realized that God was giving me insight into the condition of my heart; I was fooling myself if I thought I could handle difficulties and temptation from a position of spiritual malnourishment. God gently revealed my need for humility, repentance, and recommitment to the nourishing spiritual practices I'd neglected. "People do not live by bread alone; rather, we live by every word that comes from the mouth of the LORD" (Deuteronomy 8:3); I needed to be truly fed by the Word of God. Now, more than ever, I am mindful of my need for that steady stream of spiritual nourishment.

—LaTonya Taylor

For more on Bible study and meditation, see reading at John 8:1-11.

³During that time the devil* came and said to him, "If you are the Son of God, tell these stones to become loaves of bread."

⁴But Jesus told him, "No! The Scriptures say,

'People do not live by bread alone,
    but by every word that comes from
    the mouth of God.'*"

⁵Then the devil took him to the holy city, Jerusalem, to the highest point of the Temple, ⁶and said, "If you are the Son of God, jump off! For the Scriptures say,

'He will order his angels to protect you.
And they will hold you up with their
    hands

so you won't even hurt your foot on a stone.'*"

⁷Jesus responded, "The Scriptures also say, 'You must not test the LORD your God.'*"

⁸Next the devil took him to the peak of a very high mountain and showed him all the kingdoms of the world and their glory. ⁹"I will give it all to you," he said, "if you will kneel down and worship me."

¹⁰"Get out of here, Satan," Jesus told him. "For the Scriptures say,

'You must worship the LORD your God
    and serve only him.'*"

¹¹Then the devil went away, and angels came and took care of Jesus.

4:3 Greek *the tempter.*   **4:4** Deut 8:3.   **4:6** Ps 91:11-12.   **4:7** Deut 6:16.   **4:10** Deut 6:13.

The Ministry of Jesus Begins

12 When Jesus heard that John had been arrested, he left Judea and returned to Galilee. 13 He went first to Nazareth, then left there and moved to Capernaum, beside the Sea of Galilee, in the region of Zebulun and Naphtali. 14 This fulfilled what God said through the prophet Isaiah:

15 "In the land of Zebulun and of Naphtali,
    beside the sea, beyond the Jordan
      River,
    in Galilee where so many Gentiles live,
16 the people who sat in darkness
    have seen a great light.
  And for those who lived in the land
    where death casts its shadow,
  a light has shined."*

17 From then on Jesus began to preach, "Repent of your sins and turn to God, for the Kingdom of Heaven is near.*"

The First Disciples

18 One day as Jesus was walking along the shore of the Sea of Galilee, he saw two brothers—Simon, also called Peter, and Andrew—throwing a net into the water, for they fished for a living. 19 Jesus called out to them, "Come, follow me, and I will show you how to fish for people!" 20 And they left their nets at once and followed him.

21 A little farther up the shore he saw two other brothers, James and John, sitting in a boat with their father, Zebedee, repairing their nets. And he called them to come, too. 22 They immediately followed him, leaving the boat and their father behind.

Crowds Follow Jesus

23 Jesus traveled throughout the region of Galilee, teaching in the synagogues and announcing the Good News about the Kingdom. And he healed every kind of disease and illness. 24 News about him spread as far as Syria, and people soon began bringing to him all who were sick. And whatever their sickness or disease, or if they were demon possessed or epileptic or paralyzed—he healed them all. 25 Large crowds followed him wherever he went— people from Galilee, the Ten Towns,* Jeru-

salem, from all over Judea, and from east of the Jordan River.

5 The Sermon on the Mount

One day as he saw the crowds gathering, Jesus went up on the mountainside and sat down. His disciples gathered around him, 2 and he began to teach them.

The Beatitudes

3 "God blesses those who are poor and
    realize their need for him,*
  for the Kingdom of Heaven is theirs.
4 God blesses those who mourn,
    for they will be comforted.
5 God blesses those who are humble,
    for they will inherit the whole earth.
6 God blesses those who hunger and thirst
    for justice,*
  for they will be satisfied.
7 God blesses those who are merciful,
    for they will be shown mercy.
8 God blesses those whose hearts are
    pure,
  for they will see God.
9 God blesses those who work for peace,
    for they will be called the children of
      God.
10 God blesses those who are persecuted
    for doing right,
  for the Kingdom of Heaven is theirs.

11 "God blesses you when people mock you and persecute you and lie about you* and say all sorts of evil things against you because you are my followers. 12 Be happy about it! Be very glad! For a great reward awaits you in heaven. And remember, the ancient prophets were persecuted in the same way.

Teaching about Salt and Light

13 "You are the salt of the earth. But what good is salt if it has lost its flavor? Can you make it salty again? It will be thrown out and trampled underfoot as worthless.

14 "You are the light of the world—like a city on a hilltop that cannot be hidden. 15 No one lights a lamp and then puts it under a basket. Instead, a lamp is placed on a stand, where it gives light to everyone in

---

4:15-16 Isa 9:1-2 (Greek version).   4:17 Or has come, or is coming soon.   4:25 Greek Decapolis.   5:3 Greek poor in spirit.   5:6 Or for righteousness.   5:11 Some manuscripts do not include and lie about you.

the house. ¹⁶In the same way, let your good deeds shine out for all to see, so that everyone will praise your heavenly Father.

Teaching about the Law

¹⁷"Don't misunderstand why I have come. I did not come to abolish the law of Moses or the writings of the prophets. No, I came to accomplish their purpose. ¹⁸I tell you the truth, until heaven and earth disappear, not even the smallest detail of God's law will disappear until its purpose is achieved. ¹⁹So if you ignore the least commandment and teach others to do the same, you will be called the least in the Kingdom of Heaven. But anyone who obeys God's laws and teaches them will be called great in the Kingdom of Heaven.

²⁰"But I warn you—unless your righteousness is better than the righteousness of the teachers of religious law and the Pharisees, you will never enter the Kingdom of Heaven!

Teaching about Anger

²¹"You have heard that our ancestors were told, 'You must not murder. If you commit murder, you are subject to judgment.'* ²²But I say, if you are even angry with someone,* you are subject to judgment! If you call someone an idiot,* you are in danger of being brought before the court. And if you curse someone,* you are in danger of the fires of hell.*

²³"So if you are presenting a sacrifice* at the altar in the Temple and you suddenly remember that someone has something against you, ²⁴leave your sacrifice there at the altar. Go and be reconciled to that person. Then come and offer your sacrifice to God.

²⁵"When you are on the way to court with your adversary, settle your differences quickly. Otherwise, your accuser may hand you over to the judge, who will hand you over to an officer, and you will be thrown into prison. ²⁶And if that happens, you surely won't be free again until you have paid the last penny.*

Teaching about Adultery

²⁷"You have heard the commandment that says, 'You must not commit adultery.'* ²⁸But I say, anyone who even looks at a woman with lust has already committed adultery with her in his heart. ²⁹So if your eye—even your good eye*—causes you to lust, gouge it out and throw it away. It is better for you to lose one part of your body than for your whole body to be thrown into hell. ³⁰And if your hand—even your stronger hand*—causes you to sin, cut it off and throw it away. It is better for you to lose one part of your body than for your whole body to be thrown into hell.

Teaching about Divorce

³¹"You have heard the law that says, 'A man can divorce his wife by merely giving her a written notice of divorce.'* ³²But I say that a man who divorces his wife, unless she has been unfaithful, causes her to commit adultery. And anyone who marries a divorced woman also commits adultery.

Teaching about Vows

³³"You have also heard that our ancestors were told, 'You must not break your vows; you must carry out the vows you make to the LORD.'* ³⁴But I say, do not make any vows! Do not say, 'By heaven!' because heaven is God's throne. ³⁵And do not say, 'By the earth!' because the earth is his footstool. And do not say, 'By Jerusalem!' for Jerusalem is the city of the great King. ³⁶Do not even say, 'By my head!' for you can't turn one hair white or black. ³⁷Just say a simple, 'Yes, I will,' or 'No, I won't.' Anything beyond this is from the evil one.

Teaching about Revenge

³⁸"You have heard the law that says the punishment must match the injury: 'An eye for an eye, and a tooth for a tooth.'* ³⁹But I say, do not resist an evil person! If someone slaps you on the right cheek, offer the other cheek also. ⁴⁰If you are sued in court and your shirt is taken from you, give your coat, too. ⁴¹If a soldier demands that you

5:21 Exod 20:13; Deut 5:17.   5:22a Some manuscripts add without cause.   5:22b Greek uses an Aramaic term of contempt: If you say to your brother, 'Raca.'   5:22c Greek if you say, 'You fool.'   5:22d Greek Gehenna; also in 5:29, 30.   5:23 Greek gift; also in 5:24.   5:26 Greek the last kodrantes [i.e., quadrans].   5:27 Exod 20:14; Deut 5:18.   5:29 Greek your right eye.   5:30 Greek your right hand.   5:31 Deut 24:1.   5:33 Num 30:2.   5:38 Greek the law that says: 'An eye for an eye and a tooth for a tooth.' Exod 21:24; Lev 24:20; Deut 19:21.

Reconciliation

Our Shalom Vocation

MATTHEW 5:3–10

I loathe confrontation. I am sometimes called a "peacemaker," but the truth is that I have always been easily pacified by a counterfeit peace that is really more about not making waves than about right relationship. At the other extreme, I've watched assertive friends make pseudopeace by the sheer force of their persuasive personalities.

Neither the passive nor the aggressive route brings the kind of peace Jesus had in mind when he said, "God blesses those who work for peace" (Matthew 5:9). Real peace is not just about the ceasing of conflict (between relatives, ethnic groups, or nations); it's also about dealing with underlying causes. Be it the Middle East or the middle of my family room, there are forces of evil at work, manifesting themselves as greed, ego, insecurity, and sometimes aggression.

The problems are infinitely complex; my default response is to shrug my shoulders in low-grade despair. But I know better. I know that Jesus not only desires peace, he *is* peace. And he wants us to be not only its recipients but also its agents.

There is a scene in *Monty Python's Life of Brian* in which Jesus is delivering his Sermon on the Mount. A woman at the back can't quite hear, and when Jesus intones, "Blessed are the peacemakers," she asks, "What's so special about the cheesemakers?" To which her husband replies, "Well, obviously it's not meant to be taken literally; it refers to any manufacturers of dairy products."

It's a ridiculous exchange, but given the context in which Jesus delivered his sermon, I doubt his audience would have found "peacemakers" any less absurd than "cheesemakers." For centuries the Israelites had been promised a messiah to rescue them from a long line of oppressors. When Jesus started teaching, healing, and even resurrecting people, hopes must have soared. I can imagine Jesus clearing his throat, the locals holding their breath as they waited to hear his plan for overturning Roman rule. What a shock it must have been when he opened with, "Congratulations when you are poor in spirit," built to a focus on making peace, and closed with, "How wonderful when you are persecuted."

Jesus' audience was getting a crash course on one of his core messages: the kingdom of God is near—breaking in, alive, active—and it's nothing like you think. Two thousand years later we have cross-stitched Jesus' words and hung them docilely on our walls, but his real message is no less counterintuitive or shocking.

The Beatitudes recorded in Matthew 5:3–12 are not a tame to-do list of "be-attitudes." They are descriptions of what happens when the kingdom breaks into—and revolutionizes—a person's life. And each of the first six beatitudes builds toward the seventh: kingdom people will be peacemakers.

Shalom, the Hebrew word for peace, has expansive connotations. It means "harmony, wholeness, and right relationship with God, others, self, and the earth." Isaiah offers prophetic pictures of shalom: the wolf lying with the lamb, weapons turned into farming tools, deserts blooming. Fourteenth-century theologian Julian of Norwich must have glimpsed shalom when she said, "All shall be well, and all shall be well, and all manner of thing shall be well."

Jesus promises that kingdom people will be not just shalom lovers or even shalom keepers, but shalom *makers*. God wants to include his children in the family business. Peacemaking is a mandate each of us is called to live out inside our own skin and circumstances, whether we work for the United Nations or not.

When I think of shalom, I picture a nineteenth-century Russian priest named Father John of Kronstadt. Most of his fellow clergymen refused to visit the villages that surrounded their cathedrals—chronic poverty had fostered a debauched despair that made the rural areas treacherous. But Father John would enter the slums and get down in the gutters. He would find some guy sleeping off whatever he had done the night before; he would cup his chin, look him in the eyes, and say, "This is beneath your dignity. You were created to house the fullness of God." Wherever Father John went, revival broke out, because people discovered who—and whose—they were. Shalom is contagious.

Preacher, homemaker, cheesemaker—whatever our vocations, we are here for a reason. God's kingdom is at hand, breaking in, offering the job opportunity of a lifetime. We get to help him make shalom. Anything less is beneath our dignity.

—*Carolyn Arends*

For more on reconciliation, see reading at Luke 15:11–32.

carry his gear for a mile,* carry it two miles. 42 Give to those who ask, and don't turn away from those who want to borrow.

Teaching about Love for Enemies

43 "You have heard the law that says, 'Love your neighbor'* and hate your enemy. 44 But I say, love your enemies!* Pray for those who persecute you! 45 In that way, you will be acting as true children of your Father in heaven. For he gives his sunlight to both the evil and the good, and he sends rain on the just and the unjust alike. 46 If you love only those who love you, what reward is there for that? Even corrupt tax collectors do that much. 47 If you are kind only to your friends,* how are you different from anyone else? Even pagans do that. 48 But you are to be perfect, even as your Father in heaven is perfect.

6 Teaching about Giving to the Needy

"Watch out! Don't do your good deeds publicly, to be admired by others, for you will lose the reward from your Father in heaven. 2 When you give to someone in need, don't do as the hypocrites do—blowing trumpets in the synagogues and streets to call attention to their acts of charity! I tell you the truth, they have received all the reward they will ever get. 3 But when you give to someone in need, don't let your left hand know what your right hand is doing. 4 Give your gifts in private, and your Father, who sees everything, will reward you.

Teaching about Prayer and Fasting

5 "When you pray, don't be like the hypocrites who love to pray publicly on street corners and in the synagogues where everyone can see them. I tell you the truth, that is all the reward they will ever get. 6 But when you pray, go away by yourself, shut the door behind you, and pray to your Father in private. Then your Father, who sees everything, will reward you.

7 "When you pray, don't babble on and on as people of other religions do. They think their prayers are answered merely by repeating their words again and again. 8 Don't be like them, for your Father knows exactly what you need even before you ask him! 9 Pray like this:

Our Father in heaven,
may your name be kept holy.
10 May your Kingdom come soon.
May your will be done on earth,
as it is in heaven.
11 Give us today the food we need,*
12 and forgive us our sins,
as we have forgiven those who sin
against us.
13 And don't let us yield to temptation,*
but rescue us from the evil one.*

14 "If you forgive those who sin against you, your heavenly Father will forgive you. 15 But if you refuse to forgive others, your Father will not forgive your sins.

16 "And when you fast, don't make it obvious, as the hypocrites do, for they try to look miserable and disheveled so people will admire them for their fasting. I tell you the truth, that is the only reward they will ever get. 17 But when you fast, comb your hair and wash your face. 18 Then no one will notice that you are fasting, except your Father, who knows what you do in private. And your Father, who sees everything, will reward you.

Teaching about Money and Possessions

19 "Don't store up treasures here on earth, where moths eat them and rust destroys them, and where thieves break in and steal. 20 Store your treasures in heaven, where moths and rust cannot destroy, and thieves do not break in and steal. 21 Wherever your treasure is, there the desires of your heart will also be.

22 "Your eye is a lamp that provides light for your body. When your eye is good, your whole body is filled with light. 23 But when your eye is bad, your whole body is filled with darkness. And if the light you think you have is actually darkness, how deep that darkness is!

24 "No one can serve two masters. For you will hate one and love the other; you will be devoted to one and despise the other. You cannot serve both God and money.

5:41 Greek *milion* [4,854 feet or 1,478 meters]. 5:43 Lev 19:18. 5:44 Some manuscripts add *Bless those who curse you. Do good to those who hate you.* Compare Luke 6:27-28. 5:47 Greek *your brothers.* 6:11 Or *Give us today our food for the day;* or *Give us today our food for tomorrow.* 6:13a Or *And keep us from being tested.* 6:13b Or *from evil.* Some manuscripts add *For yours is the kingdom and the power and the glory forever. Amen.*

²⁵"That is why I tell you not to worry about everyday life—whether you have enough food and drink, or enough clothes to wear. Isn't life more than food, and your body more than clothing? ²⁶Look at the birds. They don't plant or harvest or store food in barns, for your heavenly Father feeds them. And aren't you far more valuable to him than they are? ²⁷Can all your worries add a single moment to your life?

²⁸"And why worry about your clothing? Look at the lilies of the field and how they grow. They don't work or make their clothing, ²⁹yet Solomon in all his glory was not dressed as beautifully as they are. ³⁰And if God cares so wonderfully for wildflowers that are here today and thrown into the fire tomorrow, he will certainly care for you. Why do you have so little faith?

³¹"So don't worry about these things, saying, 'What will we eat? What will we drink? What will we wear?' ³²These things dominate the thoughts of unbelievers, but your heavenly Father already knows all your needs. ³³Seek the Kingdom of God* above all else, and live righteously, and he will give you everything you need.

³⁴"So don't worry about tomorrow, for tomorrow will bring its own worries. Today's trouble is enough for today.

7 Do Not Judge Others

"Do not judge others, and you will not be judged. ²For you will be treated as you treat others.* The standard you use in judging is the standard by which you will be judged.*

³"And why worry about a speck in your friend's eye* when you have a log in your own? ⁴How can you think of saying to your friend,* 'Let me help you get rid of that speck in your eye,' when you can't see past the log in your own eye? ⁵Hypocrite! First get rid of the log in your own eye; then you will see well enough to deal with the speck in your friend's eye.

⁶"Don't waste what is holy on people who are unholy.* Don't throw your pearls to pigs! They will trample the pearls, then turn and attack you.

Effective Prayer

⁷"Keep on asking, and you will receive what you ask for. Keep on seeking, and you will find. Keep on knocking, and the door will be opened to you. ⁸For everyone who asks, receives. Everyone who seeks, finds. And to everyone who knocks, the door will be opened.

⁹"You parents—if your children ask for a loaf of bread, do you give them a stone instead? ¹⁰Or if they ask for a fish, do you give them a snake? Of course not! ¹¹So if you sinful people know how to give good gifts to your children, how much more will your heavenly Father give good gifts to those who ask him.

The Golden Rule

¹²"Do to others whatever you would like them to do to you. This is the essence of all that is taught in the law and the prophets.

The Narrow Gate

¹³"You can enter God's Kingdom only through the narrow gate. The highway to hell* is broad, and its gate is wide for the many who choose that way. ¹⁴But the gateway to life is very narrow and the road is difficult, and only a few ever find it.

The Tree and Its Fruit

¹⁵"Beware of false prophets who come disguised as harmless sheep but are really vicious wolves. ¹⁶You can identify them by their fruit, that is, by the way they act. Can you pick grapes from thornbushes, or figs from thistles? ¹⁷A good tree produces good fruit, and a bad tree produces bad fruit. ¹⁸A good tree can't produce bad fruit, and a bad tree can't produce good fruit. ¹⁹So every tree that does not produce good fruit is chopped down and thrown into the fire. ²⁰Yes, just as you can identify a tree by its fruit, so you can identify people by their actions.

True Disciples

²¹"Not everyone who calls out to me, 'Lord! Lord!' will enter the Kingdom of Heaven. Only those who actually do the will of my Father in heaven will enter. ²²On judgment

---

6:33 Some manuscripts do not include *of God.*   **7:2a** Or *For God will judge you as you judge others.*   **7:2b** Or *The measure you give will be the measure you get back.*   **7:3** Greek *your brother's eye; also in 7:5.*   **7:4** Greek *your brother.*   **7:6** Greek *Don't give the sacred to dogs.*   **7:13** Greek *The road that leads to destruction.*

Fasting

Why Fast?
MATTHEW 6:16–18

Over the past few decades, a prevailing philosophy in culture and within the church has grown, which says it's a positive virtue to satisfy absolutely every human passion. Is it any wonder that fasting has become a neglected spiritual discipline? And when fasting *is* practiced, it's usually either to lose weight or for political pressure; its function is either vanity or manipulation. True biblical fasting receives little attention in many of our churches.

But the biblical tradition tells a different story. The list of biblical fasters runs like a "who's who" of Scripture:
- Moses on several occasions
- David on several occasions
- Elijah after his victory over Jezebel
- Ezra when he was mourning Israel's faithlessness
- Nehemiah when he was preparing for the trip back to Israel
- Esther when God's people were threatened with extermination
- Daniel on numerous occasions
- The people of Nineveh, including the cattle, involuntarily no doubt
- Jesus when he began his public ministry
- Paul at the point of his conversion
- The Christians at Antioch when they sent off Paul and Barnabas on their mission endeavor
- Paul and others when they appointed elders in all of the churches

Not only that, but many of the great Christians throughout church history have fasted—such as Martin Luther, John Calvin, John Knox, John Wesley, Jonathan Edwards, Teresa of Avila.

The central idea in fasting is the voluntary denial of an otherwise normal function for the sake of intense spiritual activity. This may mean fasting from food, or it may include other forms of fasting, such as fasting from other people, from the media, or from certain activities and pleasures. In a fast we set these normal functions aside in order to concentrate on God and his purposes.

Why should we fast? First, we fast because of an urging or prompting, a sense of call, or a sense of rightness. We have heard the call from Yahweh, the voice of the Lord, and we must obey. In the Sermon on the Mount, Jesus said, "When you give . . . When you pray . . . And when you fast . . ." (Matthew 6:1–18). He did not say, "*If* you give . . . *If* you pray . . . And *if* you fast." It has always amazed me that we will unquestionably accept giving as a Christian discipline and yet we resist or ignore fasting. There's at least as much evidence for fasting in the New Testament as there is for giving. Perhaps we do this because in an affluent culture it can involve far less sacrifice to give money than to fast.

Second, we fast because it reveals the things that control us. We often cover up what is inside of us with food and other good things, but in fasting these things come to the surface. One of the first things I learned about myself through fasting was my lust for good feelings. I was hungry and I didn't feel good, and pretty soon I began to realize that I would do just about anything in order to feel good. There's nothing wrong with feeling good—but that urge ought not control us. Pride, fear, hostility, bitterness, anger, self-centeredness—all these feelings and issues tend to come to the surface when we fast.

Third, we fast because there's an urgent need. Sometimes drastic situations demand a drastic response, such as intense fasting as part of our prayer for a crisis or difficulty. A spiritually disciplined person will know when a situation requires the intense supplication of fasting.

The ability to have the power to do what needs to be done when it needs to be done is crucial in all of life, but it is never more central than in our spiritual lives. Fasting is a critical discipline for the life of the spirit—through fasting we respond in obedience to God's urgings, we come to know ourselves (and our sins) more fully, and we turn to God in complete reliance as we seek his will in difficult situations.

—*Richard J. Foster*

For more on fasting, see reading at John 6:35-59.

day many will say to me, 'Lord! Lord! We prophesied in your name and cast out demons in your name and performed many miracles in your name.' 23 But I will reply, 'I never knew you. Get away from me, you who break God's laws.'

Building on a Solid Foundation

24 "Anyone who listens to my teaching and follows it is wise, like a person who builds a house on solid rock. 25 Though the rain comes in torrents and the floodwaters rise and the winds beat against that house, it won't collapse because it is built on bedrock. 26 But anyone who hears my teaching and doesn't obey it is foolish, like a person who builds a house on sand. 27 When the rains and floods come and the winds beat against that house, it will collapse with a mighty crash."

28 When Jesus had finished saying these things, the crowds were amazed at his teaching, 29 for he taught with real authority—quite unlike their teachers of religious law.

8 Jesus Heals a Man with Leprosy

Large crowds followed Jesus as he came down the mountainside. 2 Suddenly, a man with leprosy approached him and knelt before him. "Lord," the man said, "if you are willing, you can heal me and make me clean."

3 Jesus reached out and touched him. "I am willing," he said. "Be healed!" And instantly the leprosy disappeared. 4 Then Jesus said to him, "Don't tell anyone about this. Instead, go to the priest and let him examine you. Take along the offering required in the law of Moses for those who have been healed of leprosy.* This will be a public testimony that you have been cleansed."

The Faith of a Roman Officer

5 When Jesus returned to Capernaum, a Roman officer* came and pleaded with him, 6 "Lord, my young servant* lies in bed, paralyzed and in terrible pain."

7 Jesus said, "I will come and heal him."

8 But the officer said, "Lord, I am not worthy to have you come into my home. Just say the word from where you are, and my servant will be healed. 9 I know this because I am under the authority of my superior officers, and I have authority over my soldiers. I only need to say, 'Go,' and they go, or 'Come,' and they come. And if I say to my slaves, 'Do this,' they do it."

10 When Jesus heard this, he was amazed. Turning to those who were following him, he said, "I tell you the truth, I haven't seen faith like this in all Israel! 11 And I tell you this, that many Gentiles will come from all over the world—from east and west—and sit down with Abraham, Isaac, and Jacob at the feast in the Kingdom of Heaven. 12 But many Israelites—those for whom the Kingdom was prepared—will be thrown into outer darkness, where there will be weeping and gnashing of teeth."

13 Then Jesus said to the Roman officer, "Go back home. Because you believed, it has happened." And the young servant was healed that same hour.

Jesus Heals Many People

14 When Jesus arrived at Peter's house, Peter's mother-in-law was sick in bed with a high fever. 15 But when Jesus touched her hand, the fever left her. Then she got up and prepared a meal for him.

16 That evening many demon-possessed people were brought to Jesus. He cast out the evil spirits with a simple command, and he healed all the sick. 17 This fulfilled the word of the Lord through the prophet Isaiah, who said,

> "He took our sicknesses
> and removed our diseases."*

The Cost of Following Jesus

18 When Jesus saw the crowd around him, he instructed his disciples to cross to the other side of the lake.

19 Then one of the teachers of religious law said to him, "Teacher, I will follow you wherever you go."

20 But Jesus replied, "Foxes have dens to live in, and birds have nests, but the Son of Man* has no place even to lay his head."

21 Another of his disciples said, "Lord, first let me return home and bury my father."

8:4 See Lev 14:2-32. **8:5** Greek *a centurion;* similarly in 8:8, 13. **8:6** Or *child;* also in 8:13. **8:17** Isa 53:4. **8:20** "Son of Man" is a title Jesus used for himself.

22But Jesus told him, "Follow me now. Let the spiritually dead bury their own dead.*"

Jesus Calms the Storm

23Then Jesus got into the boat and started across the lake with his disciples. 24Suddenly, a fierce storm struck the lake, with waves breaking into the boat. But Jesus was sleeping. 25The disciples went and woke him up, shouting, "Lord, save us! We're going to drown!"

26Jesus responded, "Why are you afraid? You have so little faith!" Then he got up and rebuked the wind and waves, and suddenly there was a great calm.

27The disciples were amazed. "Who is this man?" they asked. "Even the winds and waves obey him!"

Jesus Heals Two Demon-Possessed Men

28When Jesus arrived on the other side of the lake, in the region of the Gadarenes,* two men who were possessed by demons met him. They lived in a cemetery and were so violent that no one could go through that area.

29They began screaming at him, "Why are you interfering with us, Son of God? Have you come here to torture us before God's appointed time?"

30There happened to be a large herd of pigs feeding in the distance. 31So the demons begged, "If you cast us out, send us into that herd of pigs."

32"All right, go!" Jesus commanded them. So the demons came out of the men and entered the pigs, and the whole herd plunged down the steep hillside into the lake and drowned in the water.

33The herdsmen fled to the nearby town, telling everyone what happened to the demon-possessed men. 34Then the entire town came out to meet Jesus, but they begged him to go away and leave them alone.

9 Jesus Heals a Paralyzed Man

Jesus climbed into a boat and went back across the lake to his own town. 2Some people brought to him a paralyzed man on a mat. Seeing their faith, Jesus said to the paralyzed man, "Be encouraged, my child! Your sins are forgiven."

3But some of the teachers of religious law said to themselves, "That's blasphemy! Does he think he's God?"

4Jesus knew* what they were thinking, so he asked them, "Why do you have such evil thoughts in your hearts? 5Is it easier to say 'Your sins are forgiven,' or 'Stand up and walk'? 6So I will prove to you that the Son of Man* has the authority on earth to forgive sins." Then Jesus turned to the paralyzed man and said, "Stand up, pick up your mat, and go home!"

7And the man jumped up and went home! 8Fear swept through the crowd as they saw this happen. And they praised God for sending a man with such great authority.*

Jesus Calls Matthew

9As Jesus was walking along, he saw a man named Matthew sitting at his tax collector's booth. "Follow me and be my disciple," Jesus said to him. So Matthew got up and followed him.

10Later, Matthew invited Jesus and his disciples to his home as dinner guests, along with many tax collectors and other disreputable sinners. 11But when the Pharisees saw this, they asked his disciples, "Why does your teacher eat with such scum?*"

12When Jesus heard this, he said, "Healthy people don't need a doctor—sick people do." 13Then he added, "Now go and learn the meaning of this Scripture: 'I want you to show mercy, not offer sacrifices.'* For I have come to call not those who think they are righteous, but those who know they are sinners."

A Discussion about Fasting

14One day the disciples of John the Baptist came to Jesus and asked him, "Why don't your disciples fast* like we do and the Pharisees do?"

15Jesus replied, "Do wedding guests mourn while celebrating with the groom? Of course not. But someday the groom will be taken away from them, and then they will fast.

8:22 Greek *Let the dead bury their own dead.* **8:28** Other manuscripts read *Gerasenes;* still others read *Gergesenes.* Compare Mark 5:1; Luke 8:26. **9:4** Some manuscripts read *saw.* **9:6** "Son of Man" is a title Jesus used for himself. **9:8** Greek *for giving such authority to human beings.* **9:11** Greek *with tax collectors and sinners?* **9:13** Hos 6:6 (Greek version). **9:14** Some manuscripts read *fast often.*

[16] "Besides, who would patch old clothing with new cloth? For the new patch would shrink and rip away from the old cloth, leaving an even bigger tear than before.

[17] "And no one puts new wine into old wineskins. For the old skins would burst from the pressure, spilling the wine and ruining the skins. New wine is stored in new wineskins so that both are preserved."

Jesus Heals in Response to Faith

[18] As Jesus was saying this, the leader of a synagogue came and knelt before him. "My daughter has just died," he said, "but you can bring her back to life again if you just come and lay your hand on her."

[19] So Jesus and his disciples got up and went with him. [20] Just then a woman who had suffered for twelve years with constant bleeding came up behind him. She touched the fringe of his robe, [21] for she thought, "If I can just touch his robe, I will be healed."

[22] Jesus turned around, and when he saw her he said, "Daughter, be encouraged! Your faith has made you well." And the woman was healed at that moment.

[23] When Jesus arrived at the official's home, he saw the noisy crowd and heard the funeral music. [24] "Get out!" he told them. "The girl isn't dead; she's only asleep." But the crowd laughed at him. [25] After the crowd was put outside, however, Jesus went in and took the girl by the hand, and she stood up! [26] The report of this miracle swept through the entire countryside.

Jesus Heals the Blind

[27] After Jesus left the girl's home, two blind men followed along behind him, shouting, "Son of David, have mercy on us!"

[28] They went right into the house where he was staying, and Jesus asked them, "Do you believe I can make you see?"

"Yes, Lord," they told him, "we do."

[29] Then he touched their eyes and said, "Because of your faith, it will happen." [30] Then their eyes were opened, and they could see! Jesus sternly warned them, "Don't tell anyone about this." [31] But instead, they went out and spread his fame all over the region.

[32] When they left, a demon-possessed man who couldn't speak was brought to Jesus. [33] So Jesus cast out the demon, and then the man began to speak. The crowds were amazed. "Nothing like this has ever happened in Israel!" they exclaimed.

[34] But the Pharisees said, "He can cast out demons because he is empowered by the prince of demons."

The Need for Workers

[35] Jesus traveled through all the towns and villages of that area, teaching in the synagogues and announcing the Good News about the Kingdom. And he healed every kind of disease and illness. [36] When he saw the crowds, he had compassion on them because they were confused and helpless, like sheep without a shepherd. [37] He said to his disciples, "The harvest is great, but the workers are few. [38] So pray to the Lord who is in charge of the harvest; ask him to send more workers into his fields."

10 Jesus Sends Out the Twelve Apostles

Jesus called his twelve disciples together and gave them authority to cast out evil* spirits and to heal every kind of disease and illness. [2] Here are the names of the twelve apostles:

first, Simon (also called Peter),
then Andrew (Peter's brother),
James (son of Zebedee),
John (James's brother),
[3] Philip,
Bartholomew,
Thomas,
Matthew (the tax collector),
James (son of Alphaeus),
Thaddaeus,*
[4] Simon (the zealot*),
Judas Iscariot (who later betrayed him).

[5] Jesus sent out the twelve apostles with these instructions: "Don't go to the Gentiles or the Samaritans, [6] but only to the people of Israel—God's lost sheep. [7] Go and announce to them that the Kingdom of Heaven is near.* [8] Heal the sick, raise the dead, cure those with leprosy, and cast out demons. Give as freely as you have received!

10:1 Greek *unclean.* **10:3** Other manuscripts read *Lebbaeus;* still others read *Lebbaeus who is called Thaddaeus.* **10:4** Greek *the Cananean,* an Aramaic term for Jewish nationalists. **10:7** Or *has come,* or *is coming soon.*

Receiving Hospitality
MATTHEW 10:10

Many people see hospitality as an outward spiritual discipline—such as giving food or providing shelter. But if you're practicing biblical hospitality, you're also open to receiving what others offer (Matthew 10:10; Luke 10:7). My faith has been strengthened as I've received hospitality, heard others' stories, and shared their lives. Receiving the hospitality of others can also push against our self-righteousness. It takes us out of control and puts us in touch with our own neediness.

One of the things that surprised me most as I started to study hospitality in the Bible was how fluid that role is. Jesus did some of his best hospitality ministry when he was *receiving* hospitality, staying in the homes of Pharisees and tax collectors, for instance. For many of us, receiving hospitality is more difficult than giving. One of the greatest gifts we can give to others when they are offering hospitality is to allow them to host us and allow God to bless them in that way.

—Michele Hershberger

For more on hospitality, see reading at Matthew 25:31-46.

⁹"Don't take any money in your money belts—no gold, silver, or even copper coins. ¹⁰Don't carry a traveler's bag with a change of clothes and sandals or even a walking stick. Don't hesitate to accept hospitality, because those who work deserve to be fed.

¹¹"Whenever you enter a city or village, search for a worthy person and stay in his home until you leave town. ¹²When you enter the home, give it your blessing. ¹³If it turns out to be a worthy home, let your blessing stand; if it is not, take back the blessing. ¹⁴If any household or town refuses to welcome you or listen to your message, shake its dust from your feet as you leave. ¹⁵I tell you the truth, the wicked cities of Sodom and Gomorrah will be better off than such a town on the judgment day.

¹⁶"Look, I am sending you out as sheep among wolves. So be as shrewd as snakes and harmless as doves. ¹⁷But beware! For you will be handed over to the courts and will be flogged with whips in the synagogues. ¹⁸You will stand trial before governors and kings because you are my followers. But this will be your opportunity to tell the rulers and other unbeliev-ers about me.* ¹⁹When you are arrested, don't worry about how to respond or what to say. God will give you the right words at the right time. ²⁰For it is not you who will be speaking—it will be the Spirit of your Father speaking through you.

²¹"A brother will betray his brother to death, a father will betray his own child, and children will rebel against their parents and cause them to be killed. ²²And all nations will hate you because you are my followers.* But everyone who endures to the end will be saved. ²³When you are persecuted in one town, flee to the next. I tell you the truth, the Son of Man* will return before you have reached all the towns of Israel.

²⁴"Students* are not greater than their teacher, and slaves are not greater than their master. ²⁵Students are to be like their teacher, and slaves are to be like their master. And since I, the master of the household, have been called the prince of demons,* the members of my household will be called by even worse names!

²⁶"But don't be afraid of those who threaten you. For the time is coming when

10:18 Or *But this will be your testimony against the rulers and other unbelievers.* 10:22 Greek *on account of my name.* 10:23 "Son of Man" is a title Jesus used for himself. 10:24 Or *Disciples.* 10:25 Greek *Beelzeboul;* other manuscripts read *Beezeboul;* Latin version reads *Beelzebub.*

everything that is covered will be revealed, and all that is secret will be made known to all. ²⁷ What I tell you now in the darkness, shout abroad when daybreak comes. What I whisper in your ear, shout from the housetops for all to hear!

²⁸ "Don't be afraid of those who want to kill your body; they cannot touch your soul. Fear only God, who can destroy both soul and body in hell.* ²⁹ What is the price of two sparrows—one copper coin*? But not a single sparrow can fall to the ground without your Father knowing it. ³⁰ And the very hairs on your head are all numbered. ³¹ So don't be afraid; you are more valuable to God than a whole flock of sparrows.

³² "Everyone who acknowledges me publicly here on earth, I will also acknowledge

Q&A — Going Incognito

MATTHEW 10:28-33

Outreach

What role should our Christian identity play in public?

Not long ago I came across an article that made me recoil upon reading it. However, as the days wore on, I wondered if there wasn't some wisdom in the words that initially horrified me.

In his book, *Secret Faith in the Public Square*, theologian Jonathan Malesic says that Christians should keep quiet about our Christian identity when in public. Why? Because we tend to proclaim our faith thinking it will benefit us somehow materially.

Malesic isn't suggesting that we should stop *acting* like Christians, but simply stop identifying ourselves as such. After all, whether it's candidates running for office, businesspeople networking at church, or someone who writes for the Christian "market," we can easily become guilty of using our Christian identity to gain material benefit—to attract followers, sell tickets, fill seats, generate votes, sell books, gain friends.

In our public Christian witness, we must be willing to ask ourselves continually: *what do I hope to gain by publicly aligning myself with Jesus?* Are we compromising our Christian practice by gaining "Christian notoriety"?

I don't believe we should keep quiet about our faith for many reasons, not the least of which is that when Jesus sent out the disciples, he made clear that acknowledging Jesus publicly is tied to acknowledgment in heaven (Matthew 10:32). But I do believe that as we publicly identify ourselves with Christ, we ought to be continually aware of the temptation to "use" our faith for selfish gain. As we witness publicly of our faith, we must rely on God to help us develop and maintain pure motives for doing so.

—*Caryn Rivadeneira*

For more on outreach, see reading at Mark 1:40-45.

10:28 Greek *Gehenna*.   **10:29** Greek *one assarion* [i.e., one "as," a Roman coin equal to ¹⁄₁₆ of a denarius].

Receiving Hospitality
MATTHEW 10:10

Many people see hospitality as an outward spiritual discipline—such as giving food or providing shelter. But if you're practicing biblical hospitality, you're also open to receiving what others offer (Matthew 10:10; Luke 10:7). My faith has been strengthened as I've received hospitality, heard others' stories, and shared their lives. Receiving the hospitality of others can also push against our self-righteousness. It takes us out of control and puts us in touch with our own neediness.

One of the things that surprised me most as I started to study hospitality in the Bible was how fluid that role is. Jesus did some of his best hospitality ministry when he was *receiving* hospitality, staying in the homes of Pharisees and tax collectors, for instance. For many of us, receiving hospitality is more difficult than giving. One of the greatest gifts we can give to others when they are offering hospitality is to allow them to host us and allow God to bless them in that way.

—Michele Hershberger

For more on hospitality, see reading at Matthew 25:31-46.

---

⁹"Don't take any money in your money belts—no gold, silver, or even copper coins. ¹⁰Don't carry a traveler's bag with a change of clothes and sandals or even a walking stick. Don't hesitate to accept hospitality, because those who work deserve to be fed.

¹¹"Whenever you enter a city or village, search for a worthy person and stay in his home until you leave town. ¹²When you enter the home, give it your blessing. ¹³If it turns out to be a worthy home, let your blessing stand; if it is not, take back the blessing. ¹⁴If any household or town refuses to welcome you or listen to your message, shake its dust from your feet as you leave. ¹⁵I tell you the truth, the wicked cities of Sodom and Gomorrah will be better off than such a town on the judgment day.

¹⁶"Look, I am sending you out as sheep among wolves. So be as shrewd as snakes and harmless as doves. ¹⁷But beware! For you will be handed over to the courts and will be flogged with whips in the synagogues. ¹⁸You will stand trial before governors and kings because you are my followers. But this will be your opportunity to tell the rulers and other unbeliev-ers about me.* ¹⁹When you are arrested, don't worry about how to respond or what to say. God will give you the right words at the right time. ²⁰For it is not you who will be speaking—it will be the Spirit of your Father speaking through you.

²¹"A brother will betray his brother to death, a father will betray his own child, and children will rebel against their parents and cause them to be killed. ²²And all nations will hate you because you are my followers.* But everyone who endures to the end will be saved. ²³When you are per-secuted in one town, flee to the next. I tell you the truth, the Son of Man* will return before you have reached all the towns of Israel.

²⁴"Students* are not greater than their teacher, and slaves are not greater than their master. ²⁵Students are to be like their teacher, and slaves are to be like their master. And since I, the master of the house-hold, have been called the prince of demons,* the members of my household will be called by even worse names!

²⁶"But don't be afraid of those who threaten you. For the time is coming when

---

10:18 Or *But this will be your testimony against the rulers and other unbelievers.* **10:22** Greek *on account of my name.* **10:23** "Son of Man" is a title Jesus used for himself. **10:24** Or *Disciples.* **10:25** Greek *Beelzeboul;* other manuscripts read *Beezeboul;* Latin version reads *Beelzebub.*

everything that is covered will be revealed, and all that is secret will be made known to all. ²⁷ What I tell you now in the darkness, shout abroad when daybreak comes. What I whisper in your ear, shout from the housetops for all to hear!

²⁸ "Don't be afraid of those who want to kill your body; they cannot touch your soul. Fear only God, who can destroy both soul and body in hell.* ²⁹ What is the price of two sparrows—one copper coin*? But not a single sparrow can fall to the ground without your Father knowing it. ³⁰ And the very hairs on your head are all numbered. ³¹ So don't be afraid; you are more valuable to God than a whole flock of sparrows.

³² "Everyone who acknowledges me publicly here on earth, I will also acknowledge

Q&A — Going Incognito
MATTHEW 10:28-33
Outreach

What role should our Christian identity play in public?

Not long ago I came across an article that made me recoil upon reading it. However, as the days wore on, I wondered if there wasn't some wisdom in the words that initially horrified me.

In his book, *Secret Faith in the Public Square,* theologian Jonathan Malesic says that Christians should keep quiet about our Christian identity when in public. Why? Because we tend to proclaim our faith thinking it will benefit us somehow materially.

Malesic isn't suggesting that we should stop *acting* like Christians, but simply stop identifying ourselves as such. After all, whether it's candidates running for office, businesspeople networking at church, or someone who writes for the Christian "market," we can easily become guilty of using our Christian identity to gain material benefit—to attract followers, sell tickets, fill seats, generate votes, sell books, gain friends.

In our public Christian witness, we must be willing to ask ourselves continually: *what do I hope to gain by publicly aligning myself with Jesus?* Are we compromising our Christian practice by gaining "Christian notoriety"?

I don't believe we should keep quiet about our faith for many reasons, not the least of which is that when Jesus sent out the disciples, he made clear that acknowledging Jesus publicly is tied to acknowledgment in heaven (Matthew 10:32). But I do believe that as we publicly identify ourselves with Christ, we ought to be continually aware of the temptation to "use" our faith for selfish gain. As we witness publicly of our faith, we must rely on God to help us develop and maintain pure motives for doing so.

—*Caryn Rivadeneira*

For more on outreach, see reading at Mark 1:40-45.

10:28 Greek *Gehenna.*   10:29 Greek *one assarion* [i.e., one "as," a Roman coin equal to 1/16 of a denarius].

¹⁹ He will not fight or shout
　　or raise his voice in public.
²⁰ He will not crush the weakest reed
　　or put out a flickering candle.
　　Finally he will cause justice to be
　　　victorious.
²¹ And his name will be the hope
　　of all the world."*

Jesus and the Prince of Demons

²² Then a demon-possessed man, who was blind and couldn't speak, was brought to Jesus. He healed the man so that he could both speak and see. ²³ The crowd was amazed and asked, "Could it be that Jesus is the Son of David, the Messiah?"

²⁴ But when the Pharisees heard about the miracle, they said, "No wonder he can cast out demons. He gets his power from Satan,* the prince of demons."

²⁵ Jesus knew their thoughts and replied, "Any kingdom divided by civil war is doomed. A town or family splintered by feuding will fall apart. ²⁶ And if Satan is casting out Satan, he is divided and fighting against himself. His own kingdom will not survive. ²⁷ And if I am empowered by Satan, what about your own exorcists? They cast out demons, too, so they will condemn you for what you have said. ²⁸ But if I am casting out demons by the Spirit of God, then the Kingdom of God has arrived among you. ²⁹ For who is powerful enough to enter the house of a strong man like Satan and plunder his goods? Only someone even stronger—someone who could tie him up and then plunder his house.

³⁰ "Anyone who isn't with me opposes me, and anyone who isn't working with me is actually working against me.

³¹ "So I tell you, every sin and blasphemy can be forgiven—except blasphemy against the Holy Spirit, which will never be forgiven. ³² Anyone who speaks against the Son of Man can be forgiven, but anyone who speaks against the Holy Spirit will never be forgiven, either in this world or in the world to come.

³³ "A tree is identified by its fruit. If a tree is good, its fruit will be good. If a tree is bad, its fruit will be bad. ³⁴ You brood of snakes! How could evil men like you speak what is good and right? For whatever is in your heart determines what you say. ³⁵ A good person produces good things from the treasury of a good heart, and an evil person produces evil things from the treasury of an evil heart. ³⁶ And I tell you this, you must give an account on judgment day for every idle word you speak. ³⁷ The words you say will either acquit you or condemn you."

The Sign of Jonah

³⁸ One day some teachers of religious law and Pharisees came to Jesus and said, "Teacher, we want you to show us a miraculous sign to prove your authority."

³⁹ But Jesus replied, "Only an evil, adulterous generation would demand a miraculous sign; but the only sign I will give them is the sign of the prophet Jonah. ⁴⁰ For as Jonah was in the belly of the great fish for three days and three nights, so will the Son of Man be in the heart of the earth for three days and three nights.

⁴¹ "The people of Nineveh will stand up against this generation on judgment day and condemn it, for they repented of their sins at the preaching of Jonah. Now someone greater than Jonah is here—but you refuse to repent. ⁴² The queen of Sheba* will also stand up against this generation on judgment day and condemn it, for she came from a distant land to hear the wisdom of Solomon. Now someone greater than Solomon is here—but you refuse to listen.

⁴³ "When an evil* spirit leaves a person, it goes into the desert, seeking rest but finding none. ⁴⁴ Then it says, 'I will return to the person I came from.' So it returns and finds its former home empty, swept, and in order. ⁴⁵ Then the spirit finds seven other spirits more evil than itself, and they all enter the person and live there. And so that person is worse off than before. That will be the experience of this evil generation."

The True Family of Jesus

⁴⁶ As Jesus was speaking to the crowd, his mother and brothers stood outside, asking to speak to him. ⁴⁷ Someone told Jesus,

---

12:18-21 Isa 42:1-4 (Greek version for 42:4).　**12:24** Greek *Beelzeboul*; also in 12:27. Other manuscripts read *Beezeboul*; Latin version reads *Beelzebub*.　**12:42** Greek *The queen of the south.*　**12:43** Greek *unclean.*

"Your mother and your brothers are outside, and they want to speak to you."*

48Jesus asked, "Who is my mother? Who are my brothers?" 49Then he pointed to his disciples and said, "Look, these are my mother and brothers. 50Anyone who does the will of my Father in heaven is my brother and sister and mother!"

13 Parable of the Farmer Scattering Seed

Later that same day Jesus left the house and sat beside the lake. 2A large crowd soon gathered around him, so he got into a boat. Then he sat there and taught as the people stood on the shore. 3He told many stories in the form of parables, such as this one:

"Listen! A farmer went out to plant some seeds. 4As he scattered them across his field, some seeds fell on a footpath, and the birds came and ate them. 5Other seeds fell on shallow soil with underlying rock. The seeds sprouted quickly because the soil was shallow. 6But the plants soon wilted under the hot sun, and since they didn't have deep roots, they died. 7Other seeds fell among thorns that grew up and choked out the tender plants. 8Still other seeds fell on fertile soil, and they produced a crop that was thirty, sixty, and even a hundred times as much as had been planted! 9Anyone with ears to hear should listen and understand."

10His disciples came and asked him, "Why do you use parables when you talk to the people?"

11He replied, "You are permitted to understand the secrets* of the Kingdom of Heaven, but others are not. 12To those who listen to my teaching, more understanding will be given, and they will have an abundance of knowledge. But for those who are not listening, even what little understanding they have will be taken away from them. 13That is why I use these parables,

For they look, but they don't really see.
They hear, but they don't really listen
or understand.

14This fulfills the prophecy of Isaiah that says,

'When you hear what I say,
you will not understand.
When you see what I do,
you will not comprehend.
15 For the hearts of these people are
hardened,
and their ears cannot hear,
and they have closed their eyes—
so their eyes cannot see,
and their ears cannot hear,
and their hearts cannot understand,
and they cannot turn to me
and let me heal them.'*

16"But blessed are your eyes, because they see; and your ears, because they hear. 17I tell you the truth, many prophets and righteous people longed to see what you see, but they didn't see it. And they longed to hear what you hear, but they didn't hear it.

18"Now listen to the explanation of the parable about the farmer planting seeds: 19The seed that fell on the footpath represents those who hear the message about the Kingdom and don't understand it. Then the evil one comes and snatches away the seed that was planted in their hearts. 20The seed on the rocky soil represents those who hear the message and immediately receive it with joy. 21But since they don't have deep roots, they don't last long. They fall away as soon as they have problems or are persecuted for believing God's word. 22The seed that fell among the thorns represents those who hear God's word, but all too quickly the message is crowded out by the worries of this life and the lure of wealth, so no fruit is produced. 23The seed that fell on good soil represents those who truly hear and understand God's word and produce a harvest of thirty, sixty, or even a hundred times as much as had been planted!"

Parable of the Wheat and Weeds

24Here is another story Jesus told: "The Kingdom of Heaven is like a farmer who planted good seed in his field. 25But that night as the workers slept, his enemy came and planted weeds among the wheat, then slipped away. 26When the crop began to grow and produce grain, the weeds also grew.

12:47 Some manuscripts do not include verse 47. Compare Mark 3:32 and Luke 8:20.   13:11 Greek *the mysteries*.   13:14-15 Isa 6:9-10 (Greek version).

Kingdom Service

MATTHEW 13:33–35, 44–46

I grew up thinking God's kingdom meant heaven—a place we'd go in the future if we were "in" with Jesus. Yet Jesus often said, "The Kingdom of God is near you" or "among you" (Luke 10:9; 17:20–21). He described this kingdom with word pictures: it's like a seed or a bit of yeast or a hidden treasure (Matthew 13)—small inanimate things that effect great change in the *here and now*. The kingdom of heaven isn't only a place we go when we die; it's a movement we're part of *today*. It's living in the presence of God forever, starting right now.

Jesus taught that his disciples would be known by their sacrificial love for one another and for God (John 13:35). How do we show that love? By serving and ministering to the hungry, the sick, the prisoner; by extending hospitality to strangers and outcasts (Matthew 25:35–36). This is what it is to live *in* the kingdom right now: to live in the way of Jesus, responding to his teachings and example of love and service. We experience the kingdom of heaven on earth when we recognize God's presence here with us and serve him as if he really is our King.

And we can start to serve right where we are. As Will and Lisa Samson note in their book *Justice in the Burbs*, "Wherever you are, that is where the kingdom of God is at work."

—*Keri Wyatt Kent*

For more on service, see reading at John 5:1–15.

---

²⁷"The farmer's workers went to him and said, 'Sir, the field where you planted that good seed is full of weeds! Where did they come from?'

²⁸"'An enemy has done this!' the farmer exclaimed.

"'Should we pull out the weeds?' they asked.

²⁹"'No,' he replied, 'you'll uproot the wheat if you do. ³⁰Let both grow together until the harvest. Then I will tell the harvesters to sort out the weeds, tie them into bundles, and burn them, and to put the wheat in the barn.'"

Parable of the Mustard Seed

³¹ Here is another illustration Jesus used: "The Kingdom of Heaven is like a mustard seed planted in a field. ³²It is the smallest of all seeds, but it becomes the largest of garden plants; it grows into a tree, and birds come and make nests in its branches."

Parable of the Yeast

³³Jesus also used this illustration: "The Kingdom of Heaven is like the yeast a woman used in making bread. Even though she put only a little yeast in three measures of flour, it permeated every part of the dough."

³⁴ Jesus always used stories and illustrations like these when speaking to the crowds. In fact, he never spoke to them without using such parables. ³⁵This fulfilled what God had spoken through the prophet:

"I will speak to you in parables.
I will explain things hidden since the creation of the world.*"

Parable of the Wheat and Weeds Explained

³⁶ Then, leaving the crowds outside, Jesus went into the house. His disciples said, "Please explain to us the story of the weeds in the field."

13:35 Some manuscripts do not include *of the world.* Ps 78:2.

37 Jesus replied, "The Son of Man* is the farmer who plants the good seed. 38 The field is the world, and the good seed represents the people of the Kingdom. The weeds are the people who belong to the evil one. 39 The enemy who planted the weeds among the wheat is the devil. The harvest is the end of the world,* and the harvesters are the angels.

40 "Just as the weeds are sorted out and burned in the fire, so it will be at the end of the world. 41 The Son of Man will send his angels, and they will remove from his Kingdom everything that causes sin and all who do evil. 42 And the angels will throw them into the fiery furnace, where there will be weeping and gnashing of teeth. 43 Then the righteous will shine like the sun in their Father's Kingdom. Anyone with ears to hear should listen and understand!

Parables of the Hidden Treasure and the Pearl

44 "The Kingdom of Heaven is like a treasure that a man discovered hidden in a field. In his excitement, he hid it again and sold everything he owned to get enough money to buy the field.

45 "Again, the Kingdom of Heaven is like a merchant on the lookout for choice pearls. 46 When he discovered a pearl of great value, he sold everything he owned and bought it!

Parable of the Fishing Net

47 "Again, the Kingdom of Heaven is like a fishing net that was thrown into the water and caught fish of every kind. 48 When the net was full, they dragged it up onto the shore, sat down, and sorted the good fish into crates, but threw the bad ones away. 49 That is the way it will be at the end of the world. The angels will come and separate the wicked people from the righteous, 50 throwing the wicked into the fiery furnace, where there will be weeping and gnashing of teeth. 51 Do you understand all these things?"

"Yes," they said, "we do."

52 Then he added, "Every teacher of religious law who becomes a disciple in the Kingdom of Heaven is like a homeowner who brings from his storeroom new gems of truth as well as old."

Jesus Rejected at Nazareth

53 When Jesus had finished telling these stories and illustrations, he left that part of the country. 54 He returned to Nazareth, his hometown. When he taught there in the synagogue, everyone was amazed and said, "Where does he get this wisdom and the power to do miracles?" 55 Then they scoffed, "He's just the carpenter's son, and we know Mary, his mother, and his brothers—James, Joseph,* Simon, and Judas. 56 All his sisters live right here among us. Where did he learn all these things?" 57 And they were deeply offended and refused to believe in him.

Then Jesus told them, "A prophet is honored everywhere except in his own hometown and among his own family." 58 And so he did only a few miracles there because of their unbelief.

14

The Death of John the Baptist

When Herod Antipas, the ruler of Galilee,* heard about Jesus, 2 he said to his advisers, "This must be John the Baptist raised from the dead! That is why he can do such miracles."

3 For Herod had arrested and imprisoned John as a favor to his wife Herodias (the former wife of Herod's brother Philip). 4 John had been telling Herod, "It is against God's law for you to marry her." 5 Herod wanted to kill John, but he was afraid of a riot, because all the people believed John was a prophet.

6 But at a birthday party for Herod, Herodias's daughter performed a dance that greatly pleased him, 7 so he promised with a vow to give her anything she wanted. 8 At her mother's urging, the girl said, "I want the head of John the Baptist on a tray!" 9 Then the king regretted what he had said; but because of the vow he had made in front of his guests, he issued the necessary orders. 10 So John was beheaded in the prison, 11 and his head was brought on a

13:37 "Son of Man" is a title Jesus used for himself.   13:39 Or the age; also in 13:40, 49.   13:55 Other manuscripts read Joses; still others read John.   14:1 Greek Herod the tetrarch. Herod Antipas was a son of King Herod and was ruler over Galilee.

tray and given to the girl, who took it to her mother. ¹²Later, John's disciples came for his body and buried it. Then they went and told Jesus what had happened.

Jesus Feeds Five Thousand

¹³As soon as Jesus heard the news, he left in a boat to a remote area to be alone. But the crowds heard where he was headed and followed on foot from many towns. ¹⁴Jesus saw the huge crowd as he stepped from the boat, and he had compassion on them and healed their sick.

¹⁵That evening the disciples came to him and said, "This is a remote place, and it's already getting late. Send the crowds away so they can go to the villages and buy food for themselves."

¹⁶But Jesus said, "That isn't necessary—you feed them."

¹⁷"But we have only five loaves of bread and two fish!" they answered.

¹⁸"Bring them here," he said. ¹⁹Then he told the people to sit down on the grass. Jesus took the five loaves and two fish, looked up toward heaven, and blessed them. Then, breaking the loaves into pieces, he gave the bread to the disciples, who distributed it to the people. ²⁰They all ate as much as they wanted, and afterward, the disciples picked up twelve baskets of leftovers. ²¹About 5,000 men were fed that day, in addition to all the women and children!

Jesus Walks on Water

²²Immediately after this, Jesus insisted that his disciples get back into the boat and cross to the other side of the lake, while he sent the people home. ²³After sending them home, he went up into the hills by himself to pray. Night fell while he was there alone.

²⁴Meanwhile, the disciples were in trouble far away from land, for a strong wind had risen, and they were fighting heavy waves. ²⁵About three o'clock in the morning* Jesus came toward them, walking on the water. ²⁶When the disciples saw him walking on the water, they were terrified. In their fear, they cried out, "It's a ghost!"

²⁷But Jesus spoke to them at once. "Don't be afraid," he said. "Take courage. I am here!*"

²⁸Then Peter called to him, "Lord, if it's really you, tell me to come to you, walking on the water."

²⁹"Yes, come," Jesus said.

So Peter went over the side of the boat and walked on the water toward Jesus. ³⁰But when he saw the strong* wind and the waves, he was terrified and began to sink. "Save me, Lord!" he shouted.

³¹Jesus immediately reached out and grabbed him. "You have so little faith," Jesus said. "Why did you doubt me?"

³²When they climbed back into the boat, the wind stopped. ³³Then the disciples worshiped him. "You really are the Son of God!" they exclaimed.

³⁴After they had crossed the lake, they landed at Gennesaret. ³⁵When the people recognized Jesus, the news of his arrival spread quickly throughout the whole area, and soon people were bringing all their sick to be healed. ³⁶They begged him to let the sick touch at least the fringe of his robe, and all who touched him were healed.

15 Jesus Teaches about Inner Purity

Some Pharisees and teachers of religious law now arrived from Jerusalem to see Jesus. They asked him, ²"Why do your disciples disobey our age-old tradition? For they ignore our tradition of ceremonial hand washing before they eat."

³Jesus replied, "And why do you, by your traditions, violate the direct commandments of God? ⁴For instance, God says, 'Honor your father and mother,'* and 'Anyone who speaks disrespectfully of father or mother must be put to death.'* ⁵But you say it is all right for people to say to their parents, 'Sorry, I can't help you. For I have vowed to give to God what I would have given to you.' ⁶In this way, you say they don't need to honor their parents.* And so you cancel the word of God for the sake of your own tradition. ⁷You hypocrites! Isaiah was right when he prophesied about you, for he wrote,

14:25 Greek In the fourth watch of the night. 14:27 Or The 'I AM' is here; Greek reads I am. See Exod 3:14. 14:30 Some manuscripts do not include strong. 15:4a Exod 20:12; Deut 5:16. 15:4b Exod 21:17 (Greek version); Lev 20:9 (Greek version). 15:6 Greek their father; other manuscripts read their father or their mother.

8 'These people honor me with their lips,
    but their hearts are far from me.
9 Their worship is a farce,
    for they teach man-made ideas as
      commands from God.'*"

10 Then Jesus called to the crowd to come and hear. "Listen," he said, "and try to understand. 11 It's not what goes into your mouth that defiles you; you are defiled by the words that come out of your mouth."

12 Then the disciples came to him and asked, "Do you realize you offended the Pharisees by what you just said?"

13 Jesus replied, "Every plant not planted by my heavenly Father will be uprooted, 14 so ignore them. They are blind guides leading the blind, and if one blind person guides another, they will both fall into a ditch."

15 Then Peter said to Jesus, "Explain to us the parable that says people aren't defiled by what they eat."

16 "Don't you understand yet?" Jesus asked. 17 "Anything you eat passes through the stomach and then goes into the sewer. 18 But the words you speak come from the heart—that's what defiles you. 19 For from the heart come evil thoughts, murder, adultery, all sexual immorality, theft, lying, and slander. 20 These are what defile you. Eating with unwashed hands will never defile you."

The Faith of a Gentile Woman

21 Then Jesus left Galilee and went north to the region of Tyre and Sidon. 22 A Gentile* woman who lived there came to him, pleading, "Have mercy on me, O Lord, Son of David! For my daughter is possessed by a demon that torments her severely."

23 But Jesus gave her no reply, not even a word. Then his disciples urged him to send her away. "Tell her to go away," they said. "She is bothering us with all her begging."

24 Then Jesus said to the woman, "I was sent only to help God's lost sheep—the people of Israel."

25 But she came and worshiped him, pleading again, "Lord, help me!"

26 Jesus responded, "It isn't right to take food from the children and throw it to the dogs."

27 She replied, "That's true, Lord, but even dogs are allowed to eat the scraps that fall beneath their masters' table."

28 "Dear woman," Jesus said to her, "your faith is great. Your request is granted." And her daughter was instantly healed.

Jesus Heals Many People

29 Jesus returned to the Sea of Galilee and climbed a hill and sat down. 30 A vast crowd brought to him people who were lame, blind, crippled, those who couldn't speak, and many others. They laid them before Jesus, and he healed them all. 31 The crowd was amazed! Those who hadn't been able to speak were talking, the crippled were made well, the lame were walking, and the blind could see again! And they praised the God of Israel.

Jesus Feeds Four Thousand

32 Then Jesus called his disciples and told them, "I feel sorry for these people. They have been here with me for three days, and they have nothing left to eat. I don't want to send them away hungry, or they will faint along the way."

33 The disciples replied, "Where would we get enough food here in the wilderness for such a huge crowd?"

34 Jesus asked, "How much bread do you have?"

They replied, "Seven loaves, and a few small fish."

35 So Jesus told all the people to sit down on the ground. 36 Then he took the seven loaves and the fish, thanked God for them, and broke them into pieces. He gave them to the disciples, who distributed the food to the crowd.

37 They all ate as much as they wanted. Afterward, the disciples picked up seven large baskets of leftover food. 38 There were 4,000 men who were fed that day, in addition to all the women and children. 39 Then Jesus sent the people home, and he got into a boat and crossed over to the region of Magadan.

16 Leaders Demand a Miraculous Sign

One day the Pharisees and Sadducees came to test Jesus, demanding that he show them a miraculous sign from heaven to prove his authority.

15:8-9 Isa 29:13 (Greek version).   15:22 Greek Canaanite.

The Confidence to Wrestle
MATTHEW 15:21-28

Acceptance

We don't know her name. All we know is that this Gentile woman desperately needed help for her sick child. As Matthew 15:21-28 records, she went directly to Jesus—and received a decidedly less-than-warm reception. At first he refused to help, but she courageously argued her case.

Talk about confidence! In a world of strict ethnic and gender divisions, she shouldn't have *dared* to speak so directly to this Jewish man (or even to approach him at all!). Yet despite the cultural taboos barring her way, this self-assured woman went toe to toe with Jesus.

Why? Because she believed Jesus was "Lord" and had the power to save her child.

So even when the disciples dismissed her, even when Jesus himself insulted her (using the common euphemism referring to Gentiles as "dogs"), she boldly persisted.

She knew who she was—a Gentile woman—but she wasn't about to let that stop her. Her spirit was undaunted; she wouldn't give up.

Her encounter with Jesus echoes Jacob's strange wrestling bout with God (Genesis 32:22-32). He was alone when a mysterious visitor came and grappled with him all night; as they wrestled, Jacob insisted, "I will not let you go unless you bless me" (32:26). Jacob was a man defined by his past: he'd deceived his father, betrayed his brother, and was now on the run from his father-in-law. But this wrestling match became a turning point: God changed his name from *Jacob* (which sounds in Hebrew like "deceiver") to *Israel* ("God fights"). With a new name and future before him, Jacob declared, "I have seen God face to face" (32:30).

Jacob dared. He grappled. He persisted.

And so did this determined Gentile mother: she was ready to wrestle with God in this verbal bout with Jesus.

Jesus' response? He answered her tenderly, commended her for her faith, and healed her child.

Will *you* grapple with God in determination and faith to receive his blessing? Invite God to give you a faith characterized by self-assurance, courageous boldness, and confidence.

—*Kelli B. Trujillo*

For more on acceptance, see reading at John 21:15-23.

[2]He replied, "You know the saying, 'Red sky at night means fair weather tomorrow; [3]red sky in the morning means foul weather all day.' You know how to interpret the weather signs in the sky, but you don't know how to interpret the signs of the times!* [4]Only an evil, adulterous generation would demand a miraculous sign, but the only sign I will give them is the sign of the prophet Jonah.*" Then Jesus left them and went away.

16:2-3 Several manuscripts do not include any of the words in 16:2-3 after *He replied.* **16:4** Greek *the sign of Jonah.*

Yeast of the Pharisees and Sadducees

⁵Later, after they crossed to the other side of the lake, the disciples discovered they had forgotten to bring any bread. ⁶"Watch out!" Jesus warned them. "Beware of the yeast of the Pharisees and Sadducees."

⁷At this they began to argue with each other because they hadn't brought any bread. ⁸Jesus knew what they were saying, so he said, "You have so little faith! Why are you arguing with each other about having no bread? ⁹Don't you understand even yet? Don't you remember the 5,000 I fed with five loaves, and the baskets of leftovers you picked up? ¹⁰Or the 4,000 I fed with seven loaves, and the large baskets of leftovers you picked up? ¹¹Why can't you understand that I'm not talking about bread? So again I say, 'Beware of the yeast of the Pharisees and Sadducees.'"

¹²Then at last they understood that he wasn't speaking about the yeast in bread, but about the deceptive teaching of the Pharisees and Sadducees.

Peter's Declaration about Jesus

¹³When Jesus came to the region of Caesarea Philippi, he asked his disciples, "Who do people say that the Son of Man is?"*

¹⁴"Well," they replied, "some say John the Baptist, some say Elijah, and others say Jeremiah or one of the other prophets."

¹⁵Then he asked them, "But who do you say I am?"

¹⁶Simon Peter answered, "You are the Messiah,* the Son of the living God."

¹⁷Jesus replied, "You are blessed, Simon son of John,* because my Father in heaven has revealed this to you. You did not learn this from any human being. ¹⁸Now I say to you that you are Peter (which means 'rock'),* and upon this rock I will build my church, and all the powers of hell* will not conquer it. ¹⁹And I will give you the keys of the Kingdom of Heaven. Whatever you forbid* on earth will be forbidden in heaven, and whatever you permit* on earth will be permitted in heaven."

²⁰Then he sternly warned the disciples not to tell anyone that he was the Messiah.

Jesus Predicts His Death

²¹From then on Jesus* began to tell his disciples plainly that it was necessary for him to go to Jerusalem, and that he would suffer many terrible things at the hands of the elders, the leading priests, and the teachers of religious law. He would be killed, but on the third day he would be raised from the dead.

²²But Peter took him aside and began to reprimand him* for saying such things. "Heaven forbid, Lord," he said. "This will never happen to you!"

²³Jesus turned to Peter and said, "Get away from me, Satan! You are a dangerous trap to me. You are seeing things merely from a human point of view, not from God's."

²⁴Then Jesus said to his disciples, "If any of you wants to be my follower, you must turn from your selfish ways, take up your cross, and follow me. ²⁵If you try to hang on to your life, you will lose it. But if you give up your life for my sake, you will save it. ²⁶And what do you benefit if you gain the whole world but lose your own soul?* Is anything worth more than your soul? ²⁷For the Son of Man will come with his angels in the glory of his Father and will judge all people according to their deeds. ²⁸And I tell you the truth, some standing here right now will not die before they see the Son of Man coming in his Kingdom."

17 The Transfiguration

Six days later Jesus took Peter and the two brothers, James and John, and led them up a high mountain to be alone. ²As the men watched, Jesus' appearance was transformed so that his face shone like the sun, and his clothes became as white as light. ³Suddenly, Moses and Elijah appeared and began talking with Jesus.

⁴Peter exclaimed, "Lord, it's wonderful for us to be here! If you want, I'll make three shelters as memorials*—one for you, one for Moses, and one for Elijah."

⁵But even as he spoke, a bright cloud overshadowed them, and a voice from the cloud said, "This is my dearly loved Son, who brings me great joy. Listen to him." ⁶The dis-

16:13 "Son of Man" is a title Jesus used for himself.　**16:16** Or the Christ. Messiah (a Hebrew term) and Christ (a Greek term) both mean "the anointed one."　**16:17** Greek Simon bar-Jonah; see John 1:42; 21:15-17.　**16:18a** Greek that you are Peter.　**16:18b** Greek and the gates of Hades.　**16:19a** Or bind, or lock.　**16:19b** Or loose, or open.　**16:21** Some manuscripts read Jesus the Messiah.　**16:22** Or began to correct him.　**16:26** Or your self? also in 16:26b.　**17:4** Greek three tabernacles.

ciples were terrified and fell face down on the ground.

⁷Then Jesus came over and touched them. "Get up," he said. "Don't be afraid." ⁸And when they looked up, Moses and Elijah were gone, and they saw only Jesus.

⁹As they went back down the mountain, Jesus commanded them, "Don't tell anyone what you have seen until the Son of Man* has been raised from the dead."

¹⁰Then his disciples asked him, "Why do the teachers of religious law insist that Elijah must return before the Messiah comes?*"

¹¹Jesus replied, "Elijah is indeed coming first to get everything ready. ¹²But I tell you, Elijah has already come, but he wasn't recognized, and they chose to abuse him. And in the same way they will also make the Son of Man suffer." ¹³Then the disciples realized he was talking about John the Baptist.

Jesus Heals a Demon-Possessed Boy

¹⁴At the foot of the mountain, a large crowd was waiting for them. A man came and knelt before Jesus and said, ¹⁵"Lord, have mercy on my son. He has seizures and suffers terribly. He often falls into the fire or into the water. ¹⁶So I brought him to your disciples, but they couldn't heal him."

¹⁷Jesus said, "You faithless and corrupt people! How long must I be with you? How long must I put up with you? Bring the boy here to me." ¹⁸Then Jesus rebuked the demon in the boy, and it left him. From that moment the boy was well.

¹⁹Afterward the disciples asked Jesus privately, "Why couldn't we cast out that demon?"

²⁰"You don't have enough faith," Jesus told them. "I tell you the truth, if you had faith even as small as a mustard seed, you could say to this mountain, 'Move from here to there,' and it would move. Nothing would be impossible.*"

Jesus Again Predicts His Death

²²After they gathered again in Galilee, Jesus told them, "The Son of Man is going to be betrayed into the hands of his enemies.

²³He will be killed, but on the third day he will be raised from the dead." And the disciples were filled with grief.

Payment of the Temple Tax

²⁴On their arrival in Capernaum, the collectors of the Temple tax* came to Peter and asked him, "Doesn't your teacher pay the Temple tax?"

²⁵"Yes, he does," Peter replied. Then he went into the house.

But before he had a chance to speak, Jesus asked him, "What do you think, Peter?* Do kings tax their own people or the people they have conquered?*"

²⁶"They tax the people they have conquered," Peter replied.

"Well, then," Jesus said, "the citizens are free! ²⁷However, we don't want to offend them, so go down to the lake and throw in a line. Open the mouth of the first fish you catch, and you will find a large silver coin.* Take it and pay the tax for both of us."

18 The Greatest in the Kingdom

About that time the disciples came to Jesus and asked, "Who is greatest in the Kingdom of Heaven?"

²Jesus called a little child to him and put the child among them. ³Then he said, "I tell you the truth, unless you turn from your sins and become like little children, you will never get into the Kingdom of Heaven. ⁴So anyone who becomes as humble as this little child is the greatest in the Kingdom of Heaven.

⁵"And anyone who welcomes a little child like this on my behalf* is welcoming me. ⁶But if you cause one of these little ones who trusts in me to fall into sin, it would be better for you to have a large millstone tied around your neck and be drowned in the depths of the sea.

⁷"What sorrow awaits the world, because it tempts people to sin. Temptations are inevitable, but what sorrow awaits the person who does the tempting. ⁸So if your hand or foot causes you to sin, cut it off and throw it away. It's better to enter eternal life with only one hand or one foot than to be

---

17:9 "Son of Man" is a title Jesus used for himself.   **17:10** Greek that Elijah must come first?   **17:20** Some manuscripts add verse 21, But this kind of demon won't leave except by prayer and fasting. Compare Mark 9:29.   **17:24** Greek the two-drachma [tax]; also in 17:24b. See Exod 30:13-16; Neh 10:32-33.   **17:25a** Greek Simon?   **17:25b** Greek their sons or others?   **17:27** Greek a stater [a Greek coin equivalent to four drachmas].   **18:5** Greek in my name.

thrown into eternal fire with both of your hands and feet. ⁹And if your eye causes you to sin, gouge it out and throw it away. It's better to enter eternal life with only one eye than to have two eyes and be thrown into the fire of hell.*

¹⁰"Beware that you don't look down on any of these little ones. For I tell you that in heaven their angels are always in the presence of my heavenly Father.*

Parable of the Lost Sheep

¹²"If a man has a hundred sheep and one of them wanders away, what will he do? Won't he leave the ninety-nine others on the hills and go out to search for the one that is lost? ¹³And if he finds it, I tell you the truth, he will rejoice over it more than over the ninety-nine that didn't wander away! ¹⁴In the same way, it is not my heavenly Father's will that even one of these little ones should perish.

Correcting Another Believer

¹⁵"If another believer* sins against you,* go privately and point out the offense. If the other person listens and confesses it, you have won that person back. ¹⁶But if you are unsuccessful, take one or two others with you and go back again, so that everything you say may be confirmed by two or three witnesses. ¹⁷If the person still refuses to listen, take your case to the church. Then if he or she won't accept the church's decision, treat that person as a pagan or a corrupt tax collector.

¹⁸"I tell you the truth, whatever you forbid* on earth will be forbidden in heaven, and whatever you permit* on earth will be permitted in heaven.

¹⁹"I also tell you this: If two of you agree here on earth concerning anything you ask, my Father in heaven will do it for you. ²⁰For where two or three gather together as my followers,* I am there among them."

Parable of the Unforgiving Debtor

²¹Then Peter came to him and asked, "Lord, how often should I forgive someone* who sins against me? Seven times?"

²²"No, not seven times," Jesus replied, "but seventy times seven!*

²³"Therefore, the Kingdom of Heaven can be compared to a king who decided to bring his accounts up to date with servants who had borrowed money from him. ²⁴In the process, one of his debtors was brought in who owed him millions of dollars.* ²⁵He couldn't pay, so his master ordered that he be sold—along with his wife, his children, and everything he owned—to pay the debt.

²⁶"But the man fell down before his master and begged him, 'Please, be patient with me, and I will pay it all.' ²⁷Then his master was filled with pity for him, and he released him and forgave his debt.

²⁸"But when the man left the king, he went to a fellow servant who owed him a few thousand dollars.* He grabbed him by the throat and demanded instant payment.

²⁹"His fellow servant fell down before him and begged for a little more time. 'Be patient with me, and I will pay it,' he pleaded. ³⁰But his creditor wouldn't wait. He had the man arrested and put in prison until the debt could be paid in full.

³¹"When some of the other servants saw this, they were very upset. They went to the king and told him everything that had happened. ³²Then the king called in the man he had forgiven and said, 'You evil servant! I forgave you that tremendous debt because you pleaded with me. ³³Shouldn't you have mercy on your fellow servant, just as I had mercy on you?' ³⁴Then the angry king sent the man to prison to be tortured until he had paid his entire debt.

³⁵"That's what my heavenly Father will do to you if you refuse to forgive your brothers and sisters* from your heart."

19 Discussion about Divorce and Marriage

When Jesus had finished saying these things, he left Galilee and went down to the region of Judea east of the Jordan River. ²Large crowds followed him there, and he healed their sick.

³Some Pharisees came and tried to trap him with this question: "Should a man be

---

18:9 Greek *the Gehenna of fire.*   **18:10** Some manuscripts add verse 11, *And the Son of Man came to save those who are lost.* Compare Luke 19:10.
18:15a Greek *If your brother.*   **18:15b** Some manuscripts do not include *against you.*   **18:18a** Or *bind, or lock.*   **18:18b** Or *loose, or open.*
18:20 Greek *gather together in my name.*   **18:21** Greek *my brother.*   **18:22** Or *seventy-seven times.*   **18:24** Greek *10,000 talents* [375 tons or 340 metric tons of silver].   **18:28** Greek *100 denarii.* A denarius was equivalent to a laborer's full day's wage.   **18:35** Greek *your brother.*

allowed to divorce his wife for just any reason?"

[4] "Haven't you read the Scriptures?" Jesus replied. "They record that from the beginning 'God made them male and female.'* [5] And he said, "'This explains why a man leaves his father and mother and is joined to his wife, and the two are united into one.'* [6] Since they are no longer two but one, let no one split apart what God has joined together."

[7] "Then why did Moses say in the law that a man could give his wife a written notice of divorce and send her away?"* they asked.

[8] Jesus replied, "Moses permitted divorce only as a concession to your hard hearts, but it was not what God had originally intended. [9] And I tell you this, whoever divorces his wife and marries someone else commits adultery—unless his wife has been unfaithful.*"

[10] Jesus' disciples then said to him, "If this is the case, it is better not to marry!"

[11] "Not everyone can accept this statement," Jesus said. "Only those whom God helps. [12] Some are born as eunuchs, some have been made eunuchs by others, and some choose not to marry* for the sake of the Kingdom of Heaven. Let anyone accept this who can."

Jesus Blesses the Children

[13] One day some parents brought their children to Jesus so he could lay his hands on them and pray for them. But the disciples scolded the parents for bothering him.

[14] But Jesus said, "Let the children come to me. Don't stop them! For the Kingdom of Heaven belongs to those who are like these children." [15] And he placed his hands on their heads and blessed them before he left.

The Rich Man

[16] Someone came to Jesus with this question: "Teacher,* what good deed must I do to have eternal life?"

[17] "Why ask me about what is good?" Jesus replied. "There is only One who is good. But to answer your question—if you

want to receive eternal life, keep* the commandments."

[18] "Which ones?" the man asked.

And Jesus replied: "'You must not murder. You must not commit adultery. You must not steal. You must not testify falsely. [19] Honor your father and mother. Love your neighbor as yourself.'*"

[20] "I've obeyed all these commandments," the young man replied. "What else must I do?"

[21] Jesus told him, "If you want to be perfect, go and sell all your possessions and give the money to the poor, and you will have treasure in heaven. Then come, follow me."

[22] But when the young man heard this, he went away sad, for he had many possessions.

[23] Then Jesus said to his disciples, "I tell you the truth, it is very hard for a rich person to enter the Kingdom of Heaven. [24] I'll say it again—it is easier for a camel to go through the eye of a needle than for a rich person to enter the Kingdom of God!"

[25] The disciples were astounded. "Then who in the world can be saved?" they asked.

[26] Jesus looked at them intently and said, "Humanly speaking, it is impossible. But with God everything is possible."

[27] Then Peter said to him, "We've given up everything to follow you. What will we get?"

[28] Jesus replied, "I assure you that when the world is made new* and the Son of Man* sits upon his glorious throne, you who have been my followers will also sit on twelve thrones, judging the twelve tribes of Israel. [29] And everyone who has given up houses or brothers or sisters or father or mother or children or property, for my sake, will receive a hundred times as much in return and will inherit eternal life. [30] But many who are the greatest now will be least important then, and those who seem least important now will be the greatest then.*

20 Parable of the Vineyard Workers

"For the Kingdom of Heaven is like the landowner who went out early one

---

19:4 Gen 1:27; 5:2.   19:5 Gen 2:24.   19:7 See Deut 24:1.   19:9 Some manuscripts add And anyone who marries a divorced woman commits adultery. Compare Matt 5:32.   19:12 Greek and some make themselves eunuchs.   19:16 Some manuscripts read Good Teacher.   19:17 Some manuscripts read continue to keep.   19:18-19 Exod 20:12-16; Deut 5:16-20; Lev 19:18.   19:28a Or in the regeneration.   19:28b "Son of Man" is a title Jesus used for himself.   19:30 Greek But many who are first will be last; and the last, first.

Sabbath & Rest

Play!
MATTHEW 19:13–15

When you want to show my one-year-old nephew, Henry, a good time, all you have to do is say, "Boo!" If you get the cadence right, building up to the "boo" repeatedly in a rhythmic flow, Henry will collapse in spasms of unbridled laughter. Henry doesn't need to observe the Sabbath; he already lives there. He works hard—building vocabulary, developing mobility, eating crayons, laughing at aunts—and rests whenever the need for a nap seizes him. He doesn't yet reside in what the Greeks called *chronos* (chronological) time; to Henry, the ticking of a clock is just another element of rhythm in the music of his life.

Henry is still operating in *kairos*—the elastic, eternal present of God's time. The "boo" game goes on so endlessly because Henry has all the time in the universe. We grown-ups aren't so fortunate.

Sabbath is, among other things, an invitation to periodically step out of the relentless stream of chronos in the hope of catching a whiff of kairos. It's a willingness to see time as a gift that need not be managed or maximized but simply enjoyed. In fact, one of the telltale ways we know we've entered into kairos is the fact that when we do, we lose track of time altogether.

For many of us, this happens most readily when we are at play. If we desire to live within God's time on the Sabbath, we may have to consider the spiritual practices of snowboarding, Scrabble, or sandcastle building. We may need, as Jesus so famously suggested, to become like children again (Matthew 19:14; Mark 10:14).

Certainly Sabbath time is well used in meditation and contemplation—but play can also be a spiritual act of worship. Recreation might just be a missing piece of the puzzle in the re-creation of you.

—Carolyn Arends

For more on Sabbath and rest, see reading at Mark 6:30–32.

---

morning to hire workers for his vineyard. ²He agreed to pay the normal daily wage* and sent them out to work.

³"At nine o'clock in the morning he was passing through the marketplace and saw some people standing around doing nothing. ⁴So he hired them, telling them he would pay them whatever was right at the end of the day. ⁵So they went to work in the vineyard. At noon and again at three o'clock he did the same thing.

⁶"At five o'clock that afternoon he was in town again and saw some more people standing around. He asked them, 'Why haven't you been working today?'

⁷"They replied, 'Because no one hired us.'

"The landowner told them, 'Then go out and join the others in my vineyard.'

⁸"That evening he told the foreman to call the workers in and pay them, beginning with the last workers first. ⁹When those hired at five o'clock were paid, each received a full day's wage. ¹⁰When those hired first came to get their pay, they assumed they would receive more. But they, too, were paid a day's wage. ¹¹When they received their pay, they protested to the owner, ¹²'Those people worked only one hour, and yet you've paid them just as much as you paid us who worked all day in the scorching heat.'

20:2 Greek *a denarius*, the payment for a full day's labor; similarly in 20:9, 10, 13.

13"He answered one of them, 'Friend, I haven't been unfair! Didn't you agree to work all day for the usual wage? 14Take your money and go. I wanted to pay this last worker the same as you. 15Is it against the law for me to do what I want with my money? Should you be jealous because I am kind to others?'

16"So those who are last now will be first then, and those who are first will be last."

Jesus Again Predicts His Death

17As Jesus was going up to Jerusalem, he took the twelve disciples aside privately and told them what was going to happen to him. 18"Listen," he said, "we're going up to Jerusalem, where the Son of Man* will be betrayed to the leading priests and the teachers of religious law. They will sentence him to die. 19Then they will hand him over to the Romans* to be mocked, flogged with a whip, and crucified. But on the third day he will be raised from the dead."

Jesus Teaches about Serving Others

20Then the mother of James and John, the sons of Zebedee, came to Jesus with her sons. She knelt respectfully to ask a favor. 21"What is your request?" he asked.

She replied, "In your Kingdom, please let my two sons sit in places of honor next to you, one on your right and the other on your left."

22But Jesus answered by saying to them, "You don't know what you are asking! Are you able to drink from the bitter cup of suffering I am about to drink?"

"Oh yes," they replied, "we are able!"

23Jesus told them, "You will indeed drink from my bitter cup. But I have no right to say who will sit on my right or my left. My Father has prepared those places for the ones he has chosen."

24When the ten other disciples heard what James and John had asked, they were indignant. 25But Jesus called them together and said, "You know that the rulers in this world lord it over their people, and officials flaunt their authority over those under them. 26But among you it will be different. Whoever wants to be a leader among you must be your servant, 27and whoever wants to be first among you must become your slave. 28For even the Son of Man came not to be served but to serve others and to give his life as a ransom for many."

Jesus Heals Two Blind Men

29As Jesus and the disciples left the town of Jericho, a large crowd followed behind. 30Two blind men were sitting beside the road. When they heard that Jesus was coming that way, they began shouting, "Lord, Son of David, have mercy on us!"

31"Be quiet!" the crowd yelled at them.

But they only shouted louder, "Lord, Son of David, have mercy on us!"

32When Jesus heard them, he stopped and called, "What do you want me to do for you?"

33"Lord," they said, "we want to see!" 34Jesus felt sorry for them and touched their eyes. Instantly they could see! Then they followed him.

21 Jesus' Triumphant Entry

As Jesus and the disciples approached Jerusalem, they came to the town of Bethphage on the Mount of Olives. Jesus sent two of them on ahead. 2"Go into the village over there," he said. "As soon as you enter it, you will see a donkey tied there, with its colt beside it. Untie them and bring them to me. 3If anyone asks what you are doing, just say, 'The Lord needs them,' and he will immediately let you take them."

4This took place to fulfill the prophecy that said,

5 "Tell the people of Jerusalem,*
    'Look, your King is coming to you.
He is humble, riding on a donkey—
    riding on a donkey's colt.'"*

6The two disciples did as Jesus commanded. 7They brought the donkey and the colt to him and threw their garments over the colt, and he sat on it.* 8Most of the crowd spread their garments on the road ahead of him, and others cut branches from the trees and spread them on the road. 9Jesus was in the center of the procession, and the people all around him were shouting,

---

20:18 "Son of Man" is a title Jesus used for himself.   20:19 Greek the Gentiles.   21:5a Greek Tell the daughter of Zion. Isa 62:11.
21:5b Zech 9:9.   21:7 Greek over them, and he sat on them.

Gratitude

When Our Focus Is Off

MATTHEW 20:1–16

My ten-year-old daughter wants a mobile phone. She knows she's not getting one anytime soon, but she keeps asking anyway. When I ask her why she wants a phone, she basically says, "Because everyone else has one." (When I ask her who "everyone else" is, she can name only a few people, but that's beside the point.) When I ask what important purposes her phone would serve that the family phone doesn't, she pretty much draws a blank. She just wants to have what other people have. She's so like the rest of us.

I'm as guilty of me-too-ism as the next person, and as I've paid attention, I've noticed three activities in particular fuel my sense of discontentment: watching TV, watching my neighbors, and taking even one step inside a mall. Plus I'm surrounded by people to whom I constantly compare myself, because I want to keep up.

Cue the spiritual discipline of expressing gratitude. This actually may be one of the most difficult spiritual disciplines to exercise with consistency and authenticity. And yet every moment that we let God's Spirit lead us to focus on his goodness is a transformative moment for us.

Jesus' parable in Matthew 20 illustrates what happens to us when we focus on what other people have. In the parable of the vineyard workers, a landowner hires men to work in his vineyard, agreeing on a price for their work. A few hours later, he finds more workers and sends them to his vineyard. He does this again a few hours later, and again. And finally at five o'clock (one hour before "quitting time"), he hires more workers and sends them into the vineyard.

When the time comes to pay the workers, the laborers who began working first are shocked when the landowner pays every worker the same wage. He pays them the wage they had agreed to, but when they see that the men who worked only one hour receive the same amount, it doesn't seem like enough for themselves. The landowner's response: "Friend, I haven't been unfair! Didn't you agree to work all day for the usual wage? Take your money and go. I wanted to pay this last worker the same as you. Is it against the law for me to do what I want with my money? Should you be jealous because I am kind to others?" (20:13–15). Ugh. I think I recognize myself here.

Jesus told this parable as an illustration of the kingdom of heaven. And what a fitting illustration of how we tend to respond to others' blessings. Rather than focusing on how God has blessed us, we want more money, more impressive gifts and talents, and more comfortable circumstances.

Many of us tend to live as if we believe we never have enough. We deserve more, better, and easier. We *need* what other people have. These beliefs are built on lies and pave a path to misery. Gratitude, on the other hand, changes our focus from our neighbors to God. From what we don't have to what God has done. From our desires to our blessings. Gratitude can even move us to focus on—and meet—others' needs, especially if we take the step of purposely spending time with people who have less than we do. God can overwhelm us with a sense of his goodness. And that sounds a lot like contentment to me.

—Amy Simpson

For more on gratitude, see reading at Ephesians 5:20.

"Praise God* for the Son of David!
Blessings on the one who comes in the
name of the Lord!
Praise God in highest heaven!"*

¹⁰ The entire city of Jerusalem was in an uproar as he entered. "Who is this?" they asked.

¹¹ And the crowds replied, "It's Jesus, the prophet from Nazareth in Galilee."

Jesus Clears the Temple

¹² Jesus entered the Temple and began to drive out all the people buying and selling animals for sacrifice. He knocked over the tables of the money changers and the chairs of those selling doves. ¹³ He said to them, "The Scriptures declare, 'My Temple will be called a house of prayer,' but you have turned it into a den of thieves!"*

¹⁴ The blind and the lame came to him in the Temple, and he healed them. ¹⁵ The leading priests and the teachers of religious law saw these wonderful miracles and heard even the children in the Temple shouting, "Praise God for the Son of David."

But the leaders were indignant. ¹⁶ They asked Jesus, "Do you hear what these children are saying?"

"Yes," Jesus replied. "Haven't you ever read the Scriptures? For they say, 'You have taught children and infants to give you praise.'*" ¹⁷ Then he returned to Bethany, where he stayed overnight.

Jesus Curses the Fig Tree

¹⁸ In the morning, as Jesus was returning to Jerusalem, he was hungry, ¹⁹ and he noticed a fig tree beside the road. He went over to see if there were any figs, but there were only leaves. Then he said to it, "May you never bear fruit again!" And immediately the fig tree withered up.

²⁰ The disciples were amazed when they saw this and asked, "How did the fig tree wither so quickly?"

²¹ Then Jesus told them, "I tell you the truth, if you have faith and don't doubt, you can do things like this and much more. You can even say to this mountain, 'May you be lifted up and thrown into the sea,' and it will

happen. ²² You can pray for anything, and if you have faith, you will receive it."

The Authority of Jesus Challenged

²³ When Jesus returned to the Temple and began teaching, the leading priests and elders came up to him. They demanded, "By what authority are you doing all these things? Who gave you the right?"

²⁴ "I'll tell you by what authority I do these things if you answer one question," Jesus replied. ²⁵ "Did John's authority to baptize come from heaven, or was it merely human?"

They talked it over among themselves. "If we say it was from heaven, he will ask us why we didn't believe John. ²⁶ But if we say it was merely human, we'll be mobbed because the people believe John was a prophet." ²⁷ So they finally replied, "We don't know."

And Jesus responded, "Then I won't tell you by what authority I do these things.

Parable of the Two Sons

²⁸ "But what do you think about this? A man with two sons told the older boy, 'Son, go out and work in the vineyard today.' ²⁹ The son answered, 'No, I won't go,' but later he changed his mind and went anyway. ³⁰ Then the father told the other son, 'You go,' and he said, 'Yes, sir, I will.' But he didn't go.

³¹ "Which of the two obeyed his father?"

They replied, "The first."*

Then Jesus explained his meaning: "I tell you the truth, corrupt tax collectors and prostitutes will get into the Kingdom of God before you do. ³² For John the Baptist came and showed you the right way to live, but you didn't believe him, while tax collectors and prostitutes did. And even when you saw this happening, you refused to believe him and repent of your sins.

Parable of the Evil Farmers

³³ "Now listen to another story. A certain landowner planted a vineyard, built a wall around it, dug a pit for pressing out the grape juice, and built a lookout tower. Then he leased the vineyard to tenant farmers

---

21:9a Greek *Hosanna*, an exclamation of praise that literally means "save now"; also in 21:9b, 15.   **21:9b** Pss 118:25-26; 148:1.   **21:13** Isa 56:7; Jer 7:11.   **21:16** Ps 8:2.   **21:29-31** Other manuscripts read *"The second."* In still other manuscripts the first son says "Yes" but does nothing, the second son says "No" but then repents and goes, and the answer to Jesus' question is that the second son obeyed his father.

and moved to another country. ³⁴At the time of the grape harvest, he sent his servants to collect his share of the crop. ³⁵But the farmers grabbed his servants, beat one, killed one, and stoned another. ³⁶So the landowner sent a larger group of his servants to collect for him, but the results were the same.

³⁷"Finally, the owner sent his son, thinking, 'Surely they will respect my son.'

³⁸"But when the tenant farmers saw his son coming, they said to one another, 'Here comes the heir to this estate. Come on, let's kill him and get the estate for ourselves!' ³⁹So they grabbed him, dragged him out of the vineyard, and murdered him.

⁴⁰"When the owner of the vineyard returns," Jesus asked, "what do you think he will do to those farmers?"

⁴¹The religious leaders replied, "He will put the wicked men to a horrible death and lease the vineyard to others who will give him his share of the crop after each harvest."

⁴²Then Jesus asked them, "Didn't you ever read this in the Scriptures?

'The stone that the builders rejected
    has now become the cornerstone.
This is the LORD's doing,
    and it is wonderful to see.'*

⁴³I tell you, the Kingdom of God will be taken away from you and given to a nation that will produce the proper fruit. ⁴⁴Anyone who stumbles over that stone will be broken to pieces, and it will crush anyone it falls on.*"

⁴⁵When the leading priests and Pharisees heard this parable, they realized he was telling the story against them—they were the wicked farmers. ⁴⁶They wanted to arrest him, but they were afraid of the crowds, who considered Jesus to be a prophet.

22 Parable of the Great Feast

Jesus also told them other parables. He said, ²"The Kingdom of Heaven can be illustrated by the story of a king who prepared a great wedding feast for his son. ³When the banquet was ready, he sent his servants to notify those who were invited. But they all refused to come!

⁴"So he sent other servants to tell them, 'The feast has been prepared. The bulls and fattened cattle have been killed, and everything is ready. Come to the banquet!' ⁵But the guests he had invited ignored them and went their own way, one to his farm, another to his business. ⁶Others seized his messengers and insulted them and killed them.

⁷"The king was furious, and he sent out his army to destroy the murderers and burn their town. ⁸And he said to his servants, 'The wedding feast is ready, and the guests I invited aren't worthy of the honor. ⁹Now go out to the street corners and invite everyone you see.' ¹⁰So the servants brought in everyone they could find, good and bad alike, and the banquet hall was filled with guests.

¹¹"But when the king came in to meet the guests, he noticed a man who wasn't wearing the proper clothes for a wedding. ¹²'Friend,' he asked, 'how is it that you are here without wedding clothes?' But the man had no reply. ¹³Then the king said to his aides, 'Bind his hands and feet and throw him into the outer darkness, where there will be weeping and gnashing of teeth.'

¹⁴"For many are called, but few are chosen."

Taxes for Caesar

¹⁵Then the Pharisees met together to plot how to trap Jesus into saying something for which he could be arrested. ¹⁶They sent some of their disciples, along with the supporters of Herod, to meet with him. "Teacher," they said, "we know how honest you are. You teach the way of God truthfully. You are impartial and don't play favorites. ¹⁷Now tell us what you think about this: Is it right to pay taxes to Caesar or not?"

¹⁸But Jesus knew their evil motives. "You hypocrites!" he said. "Why are you trying to trap me? ¹⁹Here, show me the coin used for the tax." When they handed him a Roman coin,* ²⁰he asked, "Whose picture and title are stamped on it?"

²¹"Caesar's," they replied.

"Well, then," he said, "give to Caesar what belongs to Caesar, and give to God what belongs to God."

21:42 Ps 118:22-23.   21:44 This verse is not included in some early manuscripts. Compare Luke 20:18.   22:19 Greek *a denarius.*

²²His reply amazed them, and they went away.

Discussion about Resurrection

²³That same day Jesus was approached by some Sadducees—religious leaders who say there is no resurrection from the dead. They posed this question: ²⁴"Teacher, Moses said, 'If a man dies without children, his brother should marry the widow and have a child who will carry on the brother's name.'* ²⁵Well, suppose there were seven brothers. The oldest one married and then died without children, so his brother married the widow. ²⁶But the second brother also died, and the third brother married her. This continued with all seven of them. ²⁷Last of all, the woman also died. ²⁸So tell us, whose wife will she be in the resurrection? For all seven were married to her."

²⁹Jesus replied, "Your mistake is that you don't know the Scriptures, and you don't know the power of God. ³⁰For when the dead rise, they will neither marry nor be given in marriage. In this respect they will be like the angels in heaven.

³¹"But now, as to whether there will be a resurrection of the dead—haven't you ever read about this in the Scriptures? Long after Abraham, Isaac, and Jacob had died, God said,* ³²'I am the God of Abraham, the God of Isaac, and the God of Jacob.'* So he is the God of the living, not the dead."

³³When the crowds heard him, they were astounded at his teaching.

The Most Important Commandment

³⁴But when the Pharisees heard that he had silenced the Sadducees with his reply, they met together to question him again. ³⁵One of them, an expert in religious law, tried to trap him with this question: ³⁶"Teacher, which is the most important commandment in the law of Moses?"

³⁷Jesus replied, "'You must love the LORD your God with all your heart, all your soul, and all your mind.'* ³⁸This is the first and greatest commandment. ³⁹A second is equally important: 'Love your neighbor as yourself.'* ⁴⁰The entire law and all

the demands of the prophets are based on these two commandments."

Whose Son Is the Messiah?

⁴¹Then, surrounded by the Pharisees, Jesus asked them a question: ⁴²"What do you think about the Messiah? Whose son is he?"

They replied, "He is the son of David."

⁴³Jesus responded, "Then why does David, speaking under the inspiration of the Spirit, call the Messiah 'my Lord'? For David said,

⁴⁴ 'The LORD said to my Lord,
  Sit in the place of honor at my right
    hand
    until I humble your enemies beneath
      your feet.'*

⁴⁵Since David called the Messiah 'my Lord,' how can the Messiah be his son?"

⁴⁶No one could answer him. And after that, no one dared to ask him any more questions.

23 Jesus Criticizes the Religious Leaders

Then Jesus said to the crowds and to his disciples, ²"The teachers of religious law and the Pharisees are the official interpreters of the law of Moses.* ³So practice and obey whatever they tell you, but don't follow their example. For they don't practice what they teach. ⁴They crush people with unbearable religious demands and never lift a finger to ease the burden.

⁵"Everything they do is for show. On their arms they wear extra wide prayer boxes with Scripture verses inside, and they wear robes with extra long tassels.* ⁶And they love to sit at the head table at banquets and in the seats of honor in the synagogues. ⁷They love to receive respectful greetings as they walk in the marketplaces, and to be called 'Rabbi.'*

⁸"Don't let anyone call you 'Rabbi,' for you have only one teacher, and all of you are equal as brothers and sisters.* ⁹And don't address anyone here on earth as 'Father,' for only God in heaven is your spiritual Father. ¹⁰And don't let anyone call you 'Teacher,'

22:24 Deut 25:5-6. **22:31** Greek read about this? God said. **22:32** Exod 3:6. **22:37** Deut 6:5. **22:39** Lev 19:18. **22:44** Ps 110:1.
23:2 Greek and the Pharisees sit in the seat of Moses. **23:5** Greek They enlarge their phylacteries and lengthen their tassels. **23:7** Rabbi, from Aramaic, means "master" or "teacher." **23:8** Greek brothers.

for you have only one teacher, the Messiah. ¹¹The greatest among you must be a servant. ¹²But those who exalt themselves will be humbled, and those who humble themselves will be exalted.

¹³"What sorrow awaits you teachers of religious law and you Pharisees. Hypocrites! For you shut the door of the Kingdom of Heaven in people's faces. You won't go in yourselves, and you don't let others enter either.*

¹⁵"What sorrow awaits you teachers of religious law and you Pharisees. Hypocrites! For you cross land and sea to make one convert, and then you turn that person into twice the child of hell* you yourselves are!

¹⁶"Blind guides! What sorrow awaits you! For you say that it means nothing to swear 'by God's Temple,' but that it is binding to swear 'by the gold in the Temple.' ¹⁷Blind fools! Which is more important—the gold or the Temple that makes the gold sacred? ¹⁸And you say that to swear 'by the altar' is not binding, but to swear 'by the gifts on the altar' is binding. ¹⁹How blind! For which is more important—the gift on the altar or the altar that makes the gift sacred? ²⁰When you swear 'by the altar,' you are swearing by it and by everything on it. ²¹And when you swear 'by the Temple,' you are swearing by it and by God, who lives in it. ²²And when you swear 'by heaven,' you are swearing by the throne of God and by God, who sits on the throne.

²³"What sorrow awaits you teachers of religious law and you Pharisees. Hypocrites! For you are careful to tithe even the tiniest income from your herb gardens,* but you ignore the more important aspects of the law—justice, mercy, and faith. You should tithe, yes, but do not neglect the more important things. ²⁴Blind guides! You strain your water so you won't accidentally swallow a gnat, but you swallow a camel!*

²⁵"What sorrow awaits you teachers of religious law and you Pharisees. Hypocrites! For you are so careful to clean the outside of the cup and the dish, but inside you are filthy—full of greed and self-indul-gence! ²⁶You blind Pharisee! First wash the inside of the cup and the dish,* and then the outside will become clean, too.

²⁷"What sorrow awaits you teachers of religious law and you Pharisees. Hypocrites! For you are like whitewashed tombs—beautiful on the outside but filled on the inside with dead people's bones and all sorts of impurity. ²⁸Outwardly you look like righteous people, but inwardly your hearts are filled with hypocrisy and lawlessness.

²⁹"What sorrow awaits you teachers of religious law and you Pharisees. Hypocrites! For you build tombs for the prophets your ancestors killed, and you decorate the monuments of the godly people your ancestors destroyed. ³⁰Then you say, 'If we had lived in the days of our ancestors, we would never have joined them in killing the prophets.'

³¹"But in saying that, you testify against yourselves that you are indeed the descendants of those who murdered the prophets. ³²Go ahead and finish what your ancestors started. ³³Snakes! Sons of vipers! How will you escape the judgment of hell?

³⁴"Therefore, I am sending you prophets and wise men and teachers of religious law. But you will kill some by crucifixion, and you will flog others with whips in your synagogues, chasing them from city to city. ³⁵As a result, you will be held responsible for the murder of all godly people of all time—from the murder of righteous Abel to the murder of Zechariah son of Berekiah, whom you killed in the Temple between the sanctuary and the altar. ³⁶I tell you the truth, this judgment will fall on this very generation.

Jesus Grieves over Jerusalem

³⁷"O Jerusalem, Jerusalem, the city that kills the prophets and stones God's messengers! How often I have wanted to gather your children together as a hen protects her chicks beneath her wings, but you wouldn't let me. ³⁸And now, look, your house is abandoned and desolate.* ³⁹For I tell you

---

23:13 Some manuscripts add verse 14, *What sorrow awaits you teachers of religious law and you Pharisees. Hypocrites! You shamelessly cheat widows out of their property and then pretend to be pious by making long prayers in public. Because of this, you will be severely punished.* Compare Mark 12:40 and Luke 20:47. **23:15** Greek *of Gehenna;* also in 23:33. **23:23** Greek *tithe the mint, the dill, and the cumin.* **23:24** See Lev 11:4, 23, where gnats and camels are both forbidden as food. **23:26** Some manuscripts do not include *and the dish.* **23:38** Some manuscripts do not include *and desolate.*

this, you will never see me again until you say, 'Blessings on the one who comes in the name of the LORD!'*"

24 Jesus Foretells the Future

As Jesus was leaving the Temple grounds, his disciples pointed out to him the various Temple buildings. ²But he responded, "Do you see all these buildings? I tell you the truth, they will be completely demolished. Not one stone will be left on top of another!"

³Later, Jesus sat on the Mount of Olives. His disciples came to him privately and said, "Tell us, when will all this happen? What sign will signal your return and the end of the world?*"

⁴Jesus told them, "Don't let anyone mislead you, ⁵for many will come in my name, claiming, 'I am the Messiah.' They will deceive many. ⁶And you will hear of wars and threats of wars, but don't panic. Yes, these things must take place, but the end won't follow immediately. ⁷Nation will go to war against nation, and kingdom against kingdom. There will be famines and earthquakes in many parts of the world. ⁸But all this is only the first of the birth pains, with more to come.

⁹"Then you will be arrested, persecuted, and killed. You will be hated all over the world because you are my followers.* ¹⁰And many will turn away from me and betray and hate each other. ¹¹And many false prophets will appear and will deceive many people. ¹²Sin will be rampant everywhere, and the love of many will grow cold. ¹³But the one who endures to the end will be saved. ¹⁴And the Good News about the Kingdom will be preached throughout the whole world, so that all nations* will hear it; and then the end will come.

¹⁵"The day is coming when you will see what Daniel the prophet spoke about—the sacrilegious object that causes desecration* standing in the Holy Place." (Reader, pay attention!) ¹⁶"Then those in Judea must flee to the hills. ¹⁷A person out on the deck of a roof must not go down into the house to pack. ¹⁸A person out in the field must not

return even to get a coat. ¹⁹How terrible it will be for pregnant women and for nursing mothers in those days. ²⁰And pray that your flight will not be in winter or on the Sabbath. ²¹For there will be greater anguish than at any time since the world began. And it will never be so great again. ²²In fact, unless that time of calamity is shortened, not a single person will survive. But it will be shortened for the sake of God's chosen ones.

²³"Then if anyone tells you, 'Look, here is the Messiah,' or 'There he is,' don't believe it. ²⁴For false messiahs and false prophets will rise up and perform great signs and wonders so as to deceive, if possible, even God's chosen ones. ²⁵See, I have warned you about this ahead of time.

²⁶"So if someone tells you, 'Look, the Messiah is out in the desert,' don't bother to go and look. Or, 'Look, he is hiding here,' don't believe it! ²⁷For as the lightning flashes in the east and shines to the west, so it will be when the Son of Man* comes. ²⁸Just as the gathering of vultures shows there is a carcass nearby, so these signs indicate that the end is near.*

²⁹"Immediately after the anguish of those days,

the sun will be darkened,
the moon will give no light,
the stars will fall from the sky,
and the powers in the heavens will be shaken.*

³⁰And then at last, the sign that the Son of Man is coming will appear in the heavens, and there will be deep mourning among all the peoples of the earth. And they will see the Son of Man coming on the clouds of heaven with power and great glory.* ³¹And he will send out his angels with the mighty blast of a trumpet, and they will gather his chosen ones from all over the world*—from the farthest ends of the earth and heaven.

³²"Now learn a lesson from the fig tree. When its branches bud and its leaves begin to sprout, you know that summer is near. ³³In the same way, when you see all these things, you can know his return is very near,

---

23:39 Ps 118:26.   **24:3** Or *the age?*   **24:9** Greek *on account of my name.*   **24:14** Or *all peoples.*   **24:15** Greek *the abomination of desolation.*
See Dan 9:27; 11:31; 12:11.   **24:27** "Son of Man" is a title Jesus used for himself.   **24:28** Greek *Wherever the carcass is, the vultures gather.*
24:29 See Isa 13:10; 34:4; Joel 2:10.   **24:30** See Dan 7:13.   **24:31** Greek *from the four winds.*

right at the door. [34]I tell you the truth, this generation* will not pass from the scene until all these things take place. [35]Heaven and earth will disappear, but my words will never disappear.

[36]"However, no one knows the day or hour when these things will happen, not even the angels in heaven or the Son himself.* Only the Father knows.

[37]"When the Son of Man returns, it will be like it was in Noah's day. [38]In those days before the flood, the people were enjoying banquets and parties and weddings right up to the time Noah entered his boat. [39]People didn't realize what was going to happen until the flood came and swept them all away. That is the way it will be when the Son of Man comes.

[40]"Two men will be working together in the field; one will be taken, the other left. [41]Two women will be grinding flour at the mill; one will be taken, the other left.

[42]"So you, too, must keep watch! For you don't know what day your Lord is coming. [43]Understand this: If a homeowner knew exactly when a burglar was coming, he would keep watch and not permit his house to be broken into. [44]You also must be ready all the time, for the Son of Man will come when least expected.

[45]"A faithful, sensible servant is one to whom the master can give the responsibility of managing his other household servants and feeding them. [46]If the master returns and finds that the servant has done a good job, there will be a reward. [47]I tell you the truth, the master will put that servant in charge of all he owns. [48]But what if the servant is evil and thinks, 'My master won't be back for a while,' [49]and he begins beating the other servants, partying, and getting drunk? [50]The master will return unannounced and unexpected, [51]and he will cut the servant to pieces and assign him a place with the hypocrites. In that place there will be weeping and gnashing of teeth.

25 Parable of the Ten Bridesmaids

"Then the Kingdom of Heaven will be like ten bridesmaids* who took their lamps and went to meet the bridegroom. [2]Five of them were foolish, and five were wise. [3]The five who were foolish didn't take enough olive oil for their lamps, [4]but the other five were wise enough to take along extra oil. [5]When the bridegroom was delayed, they all became drowsy and fell asleep.

[6]"At midnight they were roused by the shout, 'Look, the bridegroom is coming! Come out and meet him!'

[7]"All the bridesmaids got up and prepared their lamps. [8]Then the five foolish ones asked the others, 'Please give us some of your oil because our lamps are going out.'

[9]"But the others replied, 'We don't have enough for all of us. Go to a shop and buy some for yourselves.'

[10]"But while they were gone to buy oil, the bridegroom came. Then those who were ready went in with him to the marriage feast, and the door was locked. [11]Later, when the other five bridesmaids returned, they stood outside, calling, 'Lord! Lord! Open the door for us!'

[12]"But he called back, 'Believe me, I don't know you!'

[13]"So you, too, must keep watch! For you do not know the day or hour of my return.

Parable of the Three Servants

[14]"Again, the Kingdom of Heaven can be illustrated by the story of a man going on a long trip. He called together his servants and entrusted his money to them while he was gone. [15]He gave five bags of silver* to one, two bags of silver to another, and one bag of silver to the last—dividing it in proportion to their abilities. He then left on his trip. [16]"The servant who received the five bags of silver began to invest the money and earned five more. [17]The servant with two bags of silver also went to work and earned two more. [18]But the servant who received the one bag of silver dug a hole in the ground and hid the master's money.

[19]"After a long time their master returned from his trip and called them to give an account of how they had used his money. [20]The servant to whom he had entrusted the five bags of silver came forward with five more and said, 'Master, you gave me

five bags of silver to invest, and I have earned five more.'

²¹ "The master was full of praise. 'Well done, my good and faithful servant. You have been faithful in handling this small amount, so now I will give you many more responsibilities. Let's celebrate together!*'

²² "The servant who had received the two bags of silver came forward and said, 'Master, you gave me two bags of silver to invest, and I have earned two more.'

²³ "The master said, 'Well done, my good and faithful servant. You have been faithful in handling this small amount, so now I will give you many more responsibilities. Let's celebrate together!'

²⁴ "Then the servant with the one bag of silver came and said, 'Master, I knew you were a harsh man, harvesting crops you didn't plant and gathering crops you didn't cultivate. ²⁵ I was afraid I would lose your money, so I hid it in the earth. Look, here is your money back.'

²⁶ "But the master replied, 'You wicked and lazy servant! If you knew I harvested crops I didn't plant and gathered crops I didn't cultivate, ²⁷ why didn't you deposit my money in the bank? At least I could have gotten some interest on it.'

²⁸ "Then he ordered, 'Take the money from this servant, and give it to the one with the ten bags of silver. ²⁹ To those who use well what they are given, even more will be given, and they will have an abundance. But from those who do nothing, even what little they have will be taken away. ³⁰ Now throw this useless servant into outer darkness, where there will be weeping and gnashing of teeth.'

The Final Judgment

³¹ "But when the Son of Man* comes in his glory, and all the angels with him, then he will sit upon his glorious throne. ³² All the nations* will be gathered in his presence, and he will separate the people as a shepherd separates the sheep from the goats. ³³ He will place the sheep at his right hand and the goats at his left.

³⁴ "Then the King will say to those on his right, 'Come, you who are blessed by my Father, inherit the Kingdom prepared for you from the creation of the world. ³⁵ For I was hungry, and you fed me. I was thirsty, and you gave me a drink. I was a stranger, and you invited me into your home. ³⁶ I was naked, and you gave me clothing. I was sick, and you cared for me. I was in prison, and you visited me.'

³⁷ "Then these righteous ones will reply, 'Lord, when did we ever see you hungry and feed you? Or thirsty and give you something to drink? ³⁸ Or a stranger and show you hospitality? Or naked and give you clothing? ³⁹ When did we ever see you sick or in prison and visit you?'

⁴⁰ "And the King will say, 'I tell you the truth, when you did it to one of the least of these my brothers and sisters,* you were doing it to me!'

⁴¹ "Then the King will turn to those on the left and say, 'Away with you, you cursed ones, into the eternal fire prepared for the devil and his demons.* ⁴² For I was hungry, and you didn't feed me. I was thirsty, and you didn't give me a drink. ⁴³ I was a stranger, and you didn't invite me into your home. I was naked, and you didn't give me clothing. I was sick and in prison, and you didn't visit me.'

⁴⁴ "Then they will reply, 'Lord, when did we ever see you hungry or thirsty or a stranger or naked or sick or in prison, and not help you?'

⁴⁵ "And he will answer, 'I tell you the truth, when you refused to help the least of these my brothers and sisters, you were refusing to help me.'

⁴⁶ "And they will go away into eternal punishment, but the righteous will go into eternal life."

26 The Plot to Kill Jesus

When Jesus had finished saying all these things, he said to his disciples, ² "As you know, Passover begins in two days, and the Son of Man* will be handed over to be crucified."

³ At that same time the leading priests and elders were meeting at the residence of Caiaphas, the high priest, ⁴ plotting how to capture Jesus secretly and kill him. ⁵ "But

---

25:21 Greek *Enter into the joy of your master* [or *your Lord*]; also in 25:23.   **25:31** "Son of Man" is a title Jesus used for himself.   **25:32** Or *peoples.*   **25:40** Greek *my brothers.*   **25:41** Greek *his angels.*   **26:2** "Son of Man" is a title Jesus used for himself.

not during the Passover celebration," they agreed, "or the people may riot."

Jesus Anointed at Bethany

⁶ Meanwhile, Jesus was in Bethany at the home of Simon, a man who had previously had leprosy. ⁷ While he was eating,* a woman came in with a beautiful alabaster jar of expensive perfume and poured it over his head.

⁸ The disciples were indignant when they saw this. "What a waste!" they said. ⁹ "It could have been sold for a high price and the money given to the poor."

Q&A — What Is Biblical Hospitality?

MATTHEW 25:31–46

When I think of hospitality, I think of being a good hostess at a dinner party. But is that true biblical hospitality?

While hospitality involves physically interacting and sometimes sharing food and lodging, it's much more than that. Jesus described how, in the final judgment, he will say to the righteous, "I was a stranger, and you invited me into your home" (Matthew 25:35), and to the unrighteous, "I was a stranger, and you didn't invite me into your home" (Matthew 25:43). Hospitality, in a sense, is being willing to see Christ in others. It's the intentional practice of putting yourself in a situation to both receive Christ in others and extend Christ's love to others. It's as much about attitude as it is about food.

We are not all obligated nor should we even attempt to do the fancy dinners or big to-dos that people mistake for hospitality. In fact, sometimes people can go so overboard with getting ready for guests that it becomes merely showing off rather than hospitality.

But we *are* called to be ready to welcome and love the stranger. The "stranger" may literally be someone we don't know, but more often it may be someone we do know who God brings our way for us to care for, listen to, nurture, and bless.

In hospitality we say, *I will trust Jesus and not be afraid; I will share who I really am*. Everybody can do that. Part of hospitality is sheer presence. Because we're doing it in the name of Jesus, we are simply with people, and then Jesus is with those people. And what seems so simple—for example, sharing a peanut butter sandwich and being with somebody—can give that person hope at just the right time.

—Michele Hershberger

For more on hospitality, see reading at Luke 10:25–37.

26:7 Or reclining.

¹⁰But Jesus, aware of this, replied, "Why criticize this woman for doing such a good thing to me? ¹¹You will always have the poor among you, but you will not always have me. ¹²She has poured this perfume on me to prepare my body for burial. ¹³I tell you the truth, wherever the Good News is preached throughout the world, this woman's deed will be remembered and discussed."

Judas Agrees to Betray Jesus

¹⁴Then Judas Iscariot, one of the twelve disciples, went to the leading priests ¹⁵and asked, "How much will you pay me to betray Jesus to you?" And they gave him thirty pieces of silver. ¹⁶From that time on, Judas began looking for an opportunity to betray Jesus.

The Last Supper

¹⁷On the first day of the Festival of Unleavened Bread, the disciples came to Jesus and asked, "Where do you want us to prepare the Passover meal for you?"

¹⁸"As you go into the city," he told them, "you will see a certain man. Tell him, 'The Teacher says: My time has come, and I will eat the Passover meal with my disciples at your house.'" ¹⁹So the disciples did as Jesus told them and prepared the Passover meal there.

²⁰When it was evening, Jesus sat down at the table* with the twelve disciples.* ²¹While they were eating, he said, "I tell you the truth, one of you will betray me."

²²Greatly distressed, each one asked in turn, "Am I the one, Lord?"

²³He replied, "One of you who has just eaten from this bowl with me will betray me. ²⁴For the Son of Man must die, as the Scriptures declared long ago. But how terrible it will be for the one who betrays him. It would be far better for that man if he had never been born!"

²⁵Judas, the one who would betray him, also asked, "Rabbi, am I the one?"

And Jesus told him, "You have said it."

²⁶As they were eating, Jesus took some bread and blessed it. Then he broke it in pieces and gave it to the disciples, saying, "Take this and eat it, for this is my body."

²⁷And he took a cup of wine and gave thanks to God for it. He gave it to them and said, "Each of you drink from it, ²⁸for this is my blood, which confirms the covenant* between God and his people. It is poured out as a sacrifice to forgive the sins of many. ²⁹Mark my words—I will not drink wine again until the day I drink it new with you in my Father's Kingdom."

³⁰Then they sang a hymn and went out to the Mount of Olives.

Jesus Predicts Peter's Denial

³¹On the way, Jesus told them, "Tonight all of you will desert me. For the Scriptures say,

'God will strike* the Shepherd,
    and the sheep of the flock will be
        scattered.'

³²But after I have been raised from the dead, I will go ahead of you to Galilee and meet you there."

³³Peter declared, "Even if everyone else deserts you, I will never desert you."

³⁴Jesus replied, "I tell you the truth, Peter—this very night, before the rooster crows, you will deny three times that you even know me."

³⁵"No!" Peter insisted. "Even if I have to die with you, I will never deny you!" And all the other disciples vowed the same.

Jesus Prays in Gethsemane

³⁶Then Jesus went with them to the olive grove called Gethsemane, and he said, "Sit here while I go over there to pray." ³⁷He took Peter and Zebedee's two sons, James and John, and he became anguished and distressed. ³⁸He told them, "My soul is crushed with grief to the point of death. Stay here and keep watch with me."

³⁹He went on a little farther and bowed with his face to the ground, praying, "My Father! If it is possible, let this cup of suffering be taken away from me. Yet I want your will to be done, not mine."

⁴⁰Then he returned to the disciples and found them asleep. He said to Peter, "Couldn't you watch with me even one hour? ⁴¹Keep watch and pray, so that you will not

---

26:20a Or *Jesus reclined.*   **26:20b** Some manuscripts read *the Twelve.*   **26:28** Some manuscripts read *the new covenant.*   **26:31** Greek *I will strike.* Zech 13:7.

Solitude for Extroverts
MATTHEW 26:36-39

Solitude

An extrovert is often described as someone who gets recharged by being around other people. If this description holds true, it's not much of a stretch to assume that most true extroverts shudder at the spiritual discipline of solitude.

Yet an extrovert has as much to gain from solitude as an introvert. So how can an extrovert make solitude more palatable? Maybe even desirable?

First, we can remember that the goal of solitude is not to be alone. The goal is to be with *God*. A triune God at that! A God who is a community within himself. Solitude is you, the Father, the Son, and the Holy Spirit. While we may be retreating from other humans, we're turning toward the miraculous three-in-one fellowship of the triune God.

Second, we can find motivation in the truth that God longs to be with us as much as extroverts long to be with other people. While God doesn't "need" us to recharge, he clearly loves it when we take the time to notice his presence and hang out with him. In our lives filled with noise and people vying for our attention, our solitude tells God that he is enough, that his company suffices.

And third, we can look at how Jesus practiced solitude in the Garden of Gethsemane: "Then Jesus went with [his disciples] to the olive grove called Gethsemane, and he said, 'Sit here while I go over there to pray.' He took Peter and Zebedee's two sons, James and John. . . . He told them, 'My soul is crushed with grief to the point of death. Stay here and keep watch with me'" (Matthew 26:36-38). His practice of solitude was couched within his practice of community.

"Sit here while I go over there to pray" is an encouraging model of solitude for extroverts. Solitude doesn't have to be an agonizing forty days in a desert or a lonely weekend at a silent retreat. Sometimes it can simply mean being a few steps from our waiting friends while we seek God.

—*Caryn Rivadeneira*

For more on solitude, see reading at Mark 14:32-42.

---

give in to temptation. For the spirit is willing, but the body is weak!"

[42] Then Jesus left them a second time and prayed, "My Father! If this cup cannot be taken away* unless I drink it, your will be done." [43] When he returned to them again, he found them sleeping, for they couldn't keep their eyes open.

[44] So he went to pray a third time, saying the same things again. [45] Then he came to the disciples and said, "Go ahead and sleep. Have your rest. But look—the time has come. The Son of Man is betrayed into the hands of sinners. [46] Up, let's be going. Look, my betrayer is here!"

Jesus Is Betrayed and Arrested

[47] And even as Jesus said this, Judas, one of the twelve disciples, arrived with a crowd of men armed with swords and clubs. They had been sent by the leading priests and elders of the people. [48] The traitor, Judas, had given them a prearranged signal: "You will know which one to arrest when I greet

26:42 Greek *If this cannot pass.*

him with a kiss." ⁴⁹So Judas came straight to Jesus. "Greetings, Rabbi!" he exclaimed and gave him the kiss.

⁵⁰Jesus said, "My friend, go ahead and do what you have come for."

Then the others grabbed Jesus and arrested him. ⁵¹But one of the men with Jesus pulled out his sword and struck the high priest's slave, slashing off his ear.

⁵²"Put away your sword," Jesus told him. "Those who use the sword will die by the sword. ⁵³Don't you realize that I could ask my Father for thousands* of angels to protect us, and he would send them instantly? ⁵⁴But if I did, how would the Scriptures be fulfilled that describe what must happen now?"

⁵⁵Then Jesus said to the crowd, "Am I some dangerous revolutionary, that you come with swords and clubs to arrest me? Why didn't you arrest me in the Temple? I was there teaching every day. ⁵⁶But this is all happening to fulfill the words of the prophets as recorded in the Scriptures." At that point, all the disciples deserted him and fled.

Jesus before the Council

⁵⁷Then the people who had arrested Jesus led him to the home of Caiaphas, the high priest, where the teachers of religious law and the elders had gathered. ⁵⁸Meanwhile, Peter followed him at a distance and came to the high priest's courtyard. He went in and sat with the guards and waited to see how it would all end.

⁵⁹Inside, the leading priests and the entire high council* were trying to find witnesses who would lie about Jesus, so they could put him to death. ⁶⁰But even though they found many who agreed to give false witness, they could not use anyone's testimony. Finally, two men came forward ⁶¹who declared, "This man said, 'I am able to destroy the Temple of God and rebuild it in three days.'"

⁶²Then the high priest stood up and said to Jesus, "Well, aren't you going to answer these charges? What do you have to say for yourself?" ⁶³But Jesus remained silent. Then the high priest said to him, "I demand in the name of the living God—tell us if you are the Messiah, the Son of God."

⁶⁴Jesus replied, "You have said it. And in the future you will see the Son of Man seated in the place of power at God's right hand* and coming on the clouds of heaven."*

⁶⁵Then the high priest tore his clothing to show his horror and said, "Blasphemy! Why do we need other witnesses? You have all heard his blasphemy. ⁶⁶What is your verdict?"

"Guilty!" they shouted. "He deserves to die!"

⁶⁷Then they began to spit in Jesus' face and beat him with their fists. And some slapped him, ⁶⁸jeering, "Prophesy to us, you Messiah! Who hit you that time?"

Peter Denies Jesus

⁶⁹Meanwhile, Peter was sitting outside in the courtyard. A servant girl came over and said to him, "You were one of those with Jesus the Galilean."

⁷⁰But Peter denied it in front of everyone. "I don't know what you're talking about," he said.

⁷¹Later, out by the gate, another servant girl noticed him and said to those standing around, "This man was with Jesus of Nazareth.*"

⁷²Again Peter denied it, this time with an oath. "I don't even know the man," he said.

⁷³A little later some of the other bystanders came over to Peter and said, "You must be one of them; we can tell by your Galilean accent."

⁷⁴Peter swore, "A curse on me if I'm lying—I don't know the man!" And immediately the rooster crowed.

⁷⁵Suddenly, Jesus' words flashed through Peter's mind: "Before the rooster crows, you will deny three times that you even know me." And he went away, weeping bitterly.

27 Judas Hangs Himself

Very early in the morning the leading priests and the elders of the people met again to lay plans for putting Jesus to death.

26:53 Greek *twelve legions.* 26:59 Greek *the Sanhedrin.* 26:64a Greek *seated at the right hand of the power.* See Ps 110:1. 26:64b See Dan 7:13. 26:71 Or *Jesus the Nazarene.*

² Then they bound him, led him away, and took him to Pilate, the Roman governor.

³ When Judas, who had betrayed him, realized that Jesus had been condemned to die, he was filled with remorse. So he took the thirty pieces of silver back to the leading priests and the elders. ⁴ "I have sinned," he declared, "for I have betrayed an innocent man."

"What do we care?" they retorted. "That's your problem."

⁵ Then Judas threw the silver coins down in the Temple and went out and hanged himself.

⁶ The leading priests picked up the coins. "It wouldn't be right to put this money in the Temple treasury," they said, "since it was payment for murder."* ⁷ After some discussion they finally decided to buy the potter's field, and they made it into a cemetery for foreigners. ⁸ That is why the field is still called the Field of Blood. ⁹ This fulfilled the prophecy of Jeremiah that says,

"They took* the thirty pieces of silver—
the price at which he was valued by
the people of Israel,
¹⁰ and purchased the potter's field,
as the LORD directed.*"

Jesus' Trial before Pilate

¹¹ Now Jesus was standing before Pilate, the Roman governor. "Are you the king of the Jews?" the governor asked him.

Jesus replied, "You have said it."

¹² But when the leading priests and the elders made their accusations against him, Jesus remained silent. ¹³ "Don't you hear all these charges they are bringing against you?" Pilate demanded. ¹⁴ But Jesus made no response to any of the charges, much to the governor's surprise.

¹⁵ Now it was the governor's custom each year during the Passover celebration to release one prisoner to the crowd—anyone they wanted. ¹⁶ This year there was a notorious prisoner, a man named Barabbas.* ¹⁷ As the crowds gathered before Pilate's house that morning, he asked them, "Which one do you want me to release to you—Barabbas, or Jesus who is called the Messiah?"

¹⁸ (He knew very well that the religious leaders had arrested Jesus out of envy.)

¹⁹ Just then, as Pilate was sitting on the judgment seat, his wife sent him this message: "Leave that innocent man alone. I suffered through a terrible nightmare about him last night."

²⁰ Meanwhile, the leading priests and the elders persuaded the crowd to ask for Barabbas to be released and for Jesus to be put to death. ²¹ So the governor asked again, "Which of these two do you want me to release to you?"

The crowd shouted back, "Barabbas!"

²² Pilate responded, "Then what should I do with Jesus who is called the Messiah?"

They shouted back, "Crucify him!"

²³ "Why?" Pilate demanded. "What crime has he committed?"

But the mob roared even louder, "Crucify him!"

²⁴ Pilate saw that he wasn't getting anywhere and that a riot was developing. So he sent for a bowl of water and washed his hands before the crowd, saying, "I am innocent of this man's blood. The responsibility is yours!"

²⁵ And all the people yelled back, "We will take responsibility for his death—we and our children!"*

²⁶ So Pilate released Barabbas to them. He ordered Jesus flogged with a lead-tipped whip, then turned him over to the Roman soldiers to be crucified.

The Soldiers Mock Jesus

²⁷ Some of the governor's soldiers took Jesus into their headquarters* and called out the entire regiment. ²⁸ They stripped him and put a scarlet robe on him. ²⁹ They wove thorn branches into a crown and put it on his head, and they placed a reed stick in his right hand as a scepter. Then they knelt before him in mockery and taunted, "Hail! King of the Jews!" ³⁰ And they spit on him and grabbed the stick and struck him on the head with it. ³¹ When they were finally tired of mocking him, they took off the robe and put his own clothes on him again. Then they led him away to be crucified.

27:6 Greek since it is the price for blood. **27:9** Or I took. **27:9-10** Greek as the LORD directed me. Zech 11:12-13; Jer 32:6-9. **27:16** Some manuscripts read Jesus Barabbas; also in 27:17. **27:25** Greek "His blood be on us and on our children." **27:27** Or into the Praetorium.

The Crucifixion

³²Along the way, they came across a man named Simon, who was from Cyrene,* and the soldiers forced him to carry Jesus' cross. ³³And they went out to a place called Golgotha (which means "Place of the Skull"). ³⁴The soldiers gave him wine mixed with bitter gall, but when he had tasted it, he refused to drink it.

³⁵After they had nailed him to the cross, the soldiers gambled for his clothes by throwing dice.* ³⁶Then they sat around and kept guard as he hung there. ³⁷A sign was fastened above Jesus' head, announcing the charge against him. It read: "This is Jesus, the King of the Jews." ³⁸Two revolutionaries* were crucified with him, one on his right and one on his left.

³⁹The people passing by shouted abuse, shaking their heads in mockery. ⁴⁰"Look at you now!" they yelled at him. "You said you were going to destroy the Temple and rebuild it in three days. Well then, if you are the Son of God, save yourself and come down from the cross!"

⁴¹The leading priests, the teachers of religious law, and the elders also mocked Jesus. ⁴²"He saved others," they scoffed, "but he can't save himself! So he is the King of Israel, is he? Let him come down from the cross right now, and we will believe in him! ⁴³He trusted God, so let God rescue him now if he wants him! For he said, 'I am the Son of God.'" ⁴⁴Even the revolutionaries who were crucified with him ridiculed him in the same way.

The Death of Jesus

⁴⁵At noon, darkness fell across the whole land until three o'clock. ⁴⁶At about three o'clock, Jesus called out with a loud voice, *"Eli, Eli,* lema sabachthani?"* which means "My God, my God, why have you abandoned me?"*

⁴⁷Some of the bystanders misunderstood and thought he was calling for the prophet Elijah. ⁴⁸One of them ran and filled a sponge with sour wine, holding it up to him on a reed stick so he could drink. ⁴⁹But the rest said, "Wait! Let's see whether Elijah comes to save him."*

⁵⁰Then Jesus shouted out again, and he released his spirit. ⁵¹At that moment the curtain in the sanctuary of the Temple was torn in two, from top to bottom. The earth shook, rocks split apart, ⁵²and tombs opened. The bodies of many godly men and women who had died were raised from the dead. ⁵³They left the cemetery after Jesus' resurrection, went into the holy city of Jerusalem, and appeared to many people.

⁵⁴The Roman officer* and the other soldiers at the crucifixion were terrified by the earthquake and all that had happened. They said, "This man truly was the Son of God!"

⁵⁵And many women who had come from Galilee with Jesus to care for him were watching from a distance. ⁵⁶Among them were Mary Magdalene, Mary (the mother of James and Joseph), and the mother of James and John, the sons of Zebedee.

The Burial of Jesus

⁵⁷As evening approached, Joseph, a rich man from Arimathea who had become a follower of Jesus, ⁵⁸went to Pilate and asked for Jesus' body. And Pilate issued an order to release it to him. ⁵⁹Joseph took the body and wrapped it in a long sheet of clean linen cloth. ⁶⁰He placed it in his own new tomb, which had been carved out of the rock. Then he rolled a great stone across the entrance and left. ⁶¹Both Mary Magdalene and the other Mary were sitting across from the tomb and watching.

The Guard at the Tomb

⁶²The next day, on the Sabbath,* the leading priests and Pharisees went to see Pilate. ⁶³They told him, "Sir, we remember what that deceiver once said while he was still alive: 'After three days I will rise from the dead.' ⁶⁴So we request that you seal the tomb until the third day. This will prevent his disciples from coming and stealing his body and then telling everyone he was raised from the dead! If that happens, we'll be worse off than we were at first."

⁶⁵Pilate replied, "Take guards and secure

27:32 Cyrene was a city in northern Africa.   **27:35** Greek by casting lots. A few late manuscripts add This fulfilled the word of the prophet: "They divided my garments among themselves and cast lots for my robe." See Ps 22:18.   **27:38** Or criminals; also in 27:44.   **27:46a** Some manuscripts read Eloi, Eloi.   **27:46b** Ps 22:1.   **27:49** Some manuscripts add And another took a spear and pierced his side, and out flowed water and blood. Compare John 19:34.   **27:54** Greek The centurion.   **27:62** Or On the next day, which is after the Preparation.

it the best you can." [66] So they sealed the tomb and posted guards to protect it.

28 The Resurrection

Early on Sunday morning,* as the new day was dawning, Mary Magdalene and the other Mary went out to visit the tomb.

[2] Suddenly there was a great earthquake! For an angel of the Lord came down from heaven, rolled aside the stone, and sat on it. [3] His face shone like lightning, and his clothing was as white as snow. [4] The guards shook with fear when they saw him, and they fell into a dead faint.

[5] Then the angel spoke to the women. "Don't be afraid!" he said. "I know you are looking for Jesus, who was crucified. [6] He isn't here! He is risen from the dead, just as he said would happen. Come, see where his body was lying. [7] And now, go quickly and tell his disciples that he has risen from the dead, and he is going ahead of you to Galilee. You will see him there. Remember what I have told you."

[8] The women ran quickly from the tomb. They were very frightened but also filled with great joy, and they rushed to give the disciples the angel's message. [9] And as they went, Jesus met them and greeted them. And they ran to him, grasped his feet, and worshiped him. [10] Then Jesus said to them, "Don't be afraid! Go tell my brothers to leave for Galilee, and they will see me there."

The Report of the Guard

[11] As the women were on their way, some of the guards went into the city and told the leading priests what had happened. [12] A meeting with the elders was called, and they decided to give the soldiers a large bribe. [13] They told the soldiers, "You must say, 'Jesus' disciples came during the night while we were sleeping, and they stole his body.' [14] If the governor hears about it, we'll stand up for you so you won't get in trouble." [15] So the guards accepted the bribe and said what they were told to say. Their story spread widely among the Jews, and they still tell it today.

The Great Commission

[16] Then the eleven disciples left for Galilee, going to the mountain where Jesus had told them to go. [17] When they saw him, they worshiped him—but some of them doubted!

[18] Jesus came and told his disciples, "I have been given all authority in heaven and on earth. [19] Therefore, go and make disciples of all the nations,* baptizing them in the name of the Father and the Son and the Holy Spirit. [20] Teach these new disciples to obey all the commands I have given you. And be sure of this: I am with you always, even to the end of the age."

28:1 Greek *After the Sabbath, on the first day of the week.*   **28:19** Or *all peoples.*

Introduction to

Mark

Background

Mark was written to a Gentile audience to explain that Jesus was the Son of God. The early church attested that Mark wrote this gospel. Since Mark's readers probably knew little about Old Testament theology or Jewish traditions, he emphasized different topics than did Matthew, omitting the genealogy of Jesus, fulfillments of Old Testament prophecy, and references to the Jewish law and certain Jewish customs.

After the resurrection of Jesus, Mark (also called John Mark or John) was a companion of Peter and Paul. Peter was Mark's primary source of information on the life of Jesus. In his first epistle, Peter refers to him as "my son" (1 Peter 5:13).

Mark accompanied Barnabas and Paul on their first missionary journey (Acts 13:5). Mark left that trip early, which led to an argument between Paul and Barnabas on the second journey. Mark and Paul later reconciled (2 Timothy 4:11).

Message

Mark's gospel is the shortest of the four Gospels. It includes no nativity narrative and only a short resurrection account. Though Mark frequently refers to Jesus as a teacher, the text gives more attention to his miracles than his parables or discourses. Mark highlights eighteen miracles, demonstrating Jesus' power, authority, and compassion. Though the Gospel opens with a declaration that Jesus is "the Son of God" and the same testimony is given by a Roman officer at the crucifixion, in Mark's gospel Jesus often tells people to keep secret his life-changing miracles.

Mark shows Jesus as a Suffering Servant whose death is his ultimate act of service. At his death the veil in the temple was "torn in two" (15:38), providing open access to God through the atoning work of Christ.

Time

Mark's gospel seems to be the earliest written account of Jesus' life and ministry. The destruction of the temple is mentioned only prophetically (13:2), so it should be dated before A.D. 70, when the prophecy was fulfilled by the Romans. The probable date for this book is A.D. 55–65. Tradition says it was written in Rome, the final home of Peter and Paul.

Outline

Mark

1

John the Baptist Prepares the Way

¹This is the Good News about Jesus the Messiah, the Son of God.* It began ²just as the prophet Isaiah had written:

> "Look, I am sending my messenger ahead of you,
> and he will prepare your way.*
> ³ He is a voice shouting in the wilderness,
> 'Prepare the way for the Lord's coming!
> Clear the road for him!'*"

⁴This messenger was John the Baptist. He was in the wilderness and preached that people should be baptized to show that they had repented of their sins and turned to God to be forgiven. ⁵All of Judea, including all the people of Jerusalem, went out to see and hear John. And when they confessed their sins, he baptized them in the Jordan River. ⁶His clothes were woven from coarse camel hair, and he wore a leather belt around his waist. For food he ate locusts and wild honey.

⁷John announced: "Someone is coming soon who is greater than I am—so much greater that I'm not even worthy to stoop down like a slave and untie the straps of his sandals. ⁸I baptize you with* water, but he will baptize you with the Holy Spirit!"

The Baptism and Temptation of Jesus

⁹One day Jesus came from Nazareth in Galilee, and John baptized him in the Jordan River. ¹⁰As Jesus came up out of the water, he saw the heavens splitting apart and the Holy Spirit descending on him* like a dove. ¹¹And a voice from heaven said, "You are my dearly loved Son, and you bring me great joy."

¹²The Spirit then compelled Jesus to go into the wilderness, ¹³where he was tempted by Satan for forty days. He was out among the wild animals, and angels took care of him.

¹⁴Later on, after John was arrested, Jesus went into Galilee, where he preached God's Good News.* ¹⁵"The time promised by God has come at last!" he announced. "The Kingdom of God is near! Repent of your sins and believe the Good News!"

The First Disciples

¹⁶One day as Jesus was walking along the shore of the Sea of Galilee, he saw Simon* and his brother Andrew throwing a net into the water, for they fished for a living. ¹⁷Jesus called out to them, "Come, follow me, and I will show you how to fish for people!" ¹⁸And they left their nets at once and followed him.

¹⁹A little farther up the shore Jesus saw Zebedee's sons, James and John, in a boat repairing their nets. ²⁰He called them at once, and they also followed him,

---

1:1 Some manuscripts do not include *the Son of God*. 1:2 Mal 3:1. 1:3 Isa 40:3 (Greek version). 1:8 Or *in;* also in 1:8b. 1:10 Or *toward him,* or *into him.* 1:14 Some manuscripts read *the Good News of the Kingdom of God.* 1:16 *Simon* is called "Peter" in 3:16 and thereafter.

leaving their father, Zebedee, in the boat with the hired men.

Jesus Casts Out an Evil Spirit

²¹ Jesus and his companions went to the town of Capernaum. When the Sabbath day came, he went into the synagogue and began to teach. ²² The people were amazed at his teaching, for he taught with real authority—quite unlike the teachers of religious law.

²³ Suddenly, a man in the synagogue who was possessed by an evil* spirit began shouting, ²⁴ "Why are you interfering with

Q&A — Course Corrections

MARK 1:15

If I've already been forgiven when I became a Christian, why is ongoing repentance so important?

To see the kingdom of God, you must repent. Jesus' inaugural address was exactly that. "The time promised by God has come at last!" he said. "The Kingdom of God is near! Repent of your sins and believe the Good News!" (Mark 1:15).

Jesus connects repentance with both his kingdom and his gospel. At the church where I pastor, we talk a lot about both—the kingdom and the gospel. And so we talk often about repentance as well. It is, after all, the narrow door into the big kingdom (Luke 13:24).

But I don't take the fire-and-brimstone approach—scowling, thundering, finger waving. I doubt Jesus struck that pose. Jesus' message isn't, "Repent, because hell looms close." His message is, "Repent, because the kingdom is near." There's a world of difference between the two. In Jesus' hands repentance is an invitation, not a threat. It's a promise, not a curse. It's good news, not bad. Repentance often involves sorrow. But it's sorrow that quickly turns to gladness because repentance is the gift of starting fresh. It's the doorway into life abundant, life anew, and life eternal. Repentance means that what I've done and who I am no longer need define me. My past is not my destiny, if I so choose.

So almost weekly I ask people to repent. I ask them to change their minds, which is literally what repentance means. I invite them to see things God's way. To align themselves, stem to stern, with God's purposes. Initially that alignment is violent and dramatic, a 180-degree turn. But thereafter it's mostly course corrections; 15 degrees here, 5 degrees there. But every turn, by whatever degree, is good news. Every turn moves us closer to where we want to be.

—Mark Buchanan

For more on confession, see reading at Luke 7:36–50.

1:23 Greek *unclean;* also in 1:26, 27.

us, Jesus of Nazareth? Have you come to destroy us? I know who you are—the Holy One of God!"

²⁵ Jesus cut him short. "Be quiet! Come out of the man," he ordered. ²⁶ At that, the evil spirit screamed, threw the man into a convulsion, and then came out of him.

²⁷ Amazement gripped the audience, and they began to discuss what had happened. "What sort of new teaching is this?" they asked excitedly. "It has such authority! Even evil spirits obey his orders!" ²⁸ The news about Jesus spread quickly throughout the entire region of Galilee.

Jesus Heals Many People

²⁹ After Jesus left the synagogue with James and John, they went to Simon and Andrew's home. ³⁰ Now Simon's mother-in-law was sick in bed with a high fever. They told Jesus about her right away. ³¹ So he went to her bedside, took her by the hand, and helped her sit up. Then the fever left her, and she prepared a meal for them.

³² That evening after sunset, many sick and demon-possessed people were brought to Jesus. ³³ The whole town gathered at the door to watch. ³⁴ So Jesus healed many people who were sick with various diseases, and he cast out many demons. But because the demons knew who he was, he did not allow them to speak.

Jesus Preaches in Galilee

³⁵ Before daybreak the next morning, Jesus got up and went out to an isolated place to pray. ³⁶ Later Simon and the others went out to find him. ³⁷ When they found him, they said, "Everyone is looking for you."

³⁸ But Jesus replied, "We must go on to other towns as well, and I will preach to them, too. That is why I came." ³⁹ So he traveled throughout the region of Galilee, preaching in the synagogues and casting out demons.

Jesus Heals a Man with Leprosy

⁴⁰ A man with leprosy came and knelt in front of Jesus, begging to be healed. "If you are willing, you can heal me and make me clean," he said.

⁴¹ Moved with compassion,* Jesus reached out and touched him. "I am willing," he said. "Be healed!" ⁴² Instantly the leprosy disappeared, and the man was healed. ⁴³ Then Jesus sent him on his way with a stern warning: ⁴⁴ "Don't tell anyone about this. Instead, go to the priest and let him examine you. Take along the offering required in the law of Moses for those who have been healed of leprosy.* This will be a public testimony that you have been cleansed."

⁴⁵ But the man went and spread the word, proclaiming to everyone what had happened. As a result, large crowds soon surrounded Jesus, and he couldn't publicly enter a town anywhere. He had to stay out in the secluded places, but people from everywhere kept coming to him.

2 Jesus Heals a Paralyzed Man

When Jesus returned to Capernaum several days later, the news spread quickly that he was back home. ² Soon the house where he was staying was so packed with visitors that there was no more room, even outside the door. While he was preaching God's word to them, ³ four men arrived carrying a paralyzed man on a mat. ⁴ They couldn't bring him to Jesus because of the crowd, so they dug a hole through the roof above his head. Then they lowered the man on his mat, right down in front of Jesus. ⁵ Seeing their faith, Jesus said to the paralyzed man, "My child, your sins are forgiven."

⁶ But some of the teachers of religious law who were sitting there thought to themselves, ⁷ "What is he saying? This is blasphemy! Only God can forgive sins!"

⁸ Jesus knew immediately what they were thinking, so he asked them, "Why do you question this in your hearts? ⁹ Is it easier to say to the paralyzed man 'Your sins are forgiven,' or 'Stand up, pick up your mat, and walk'? ¹⁰ So I will prove to you that the Son of Man* has the authority on earth to forgive sins." Then Jesus turned to the paralyzed man and said, ¹¹ "Stand up, pick up your mat, and go home!"

¹² And the man jumped up, grabbed his mat, and walked out through the stunned

---

1:41 Some manuscripts read *Moved with anger.*   **1:44** See Lev 14:2-32.   **2:10** "Son of Man" is a title Jesus used for himself.

The Hands and Feet of Jesus

MARK 1:40-45

Outreach

A leper approached Jesus and begged to be made clean. The law said lepers couldn't have contact with nonlepers. They had to cry out, "Unclean!" and stay outside the village. But when this leper came to Jesus and said, "If you are willing, you can heal me and make me clean" (Mark 1:40), Jesus didn't turn away.

To everyone's amazement, Jesus reached out to touch this man who hadn't been touched in years. Jesus didn't have to do that; he could have healed the man through the spoken word. But instead, he reached out his hand to touch the man, then said, "I am willing. . . . Be healed!" (1:41). Was Jesus infected by leprosy? No, it was the other way around! Jesus was so full of life and health that he "infected" the leper with the Good News of the kingdom of God. Jesus was more contagious with God's power and love than the leper was with his disease.

If the Spirit of God lives inside you, you're like that. You can be a contagious Christian who infects others with God's power and love as well. Take a look at your hands for a moment. How often are they extended in service to someone who's far from God?

Both your words and your actions pair up to form your proclamation. What is your life proclaiming? The kingdom of God never has spread primarily through preachers speaking to unconnected strangers. It's never spread primarily through the mass media. God's kingdom is spread by the same method it's been spread for two thousand years: through Christ-followers who reach beyond their circle of Christian friends, develop meaningful relationships, and bring people to Christ—one life at a time.

—John Ortberg

For more on outreach, see reading at Mark 5:1-20.

onlookers. They were all amazed and praised God, exclaiming, "We've never seen anything like this before!"

Jesus Calls Levi (Matthew)

¹³Then Jesus went out to the lakeshore again and taught the crowds that were coming to him. ¹⁴As he walked along, he saw Levi son of Alphaeus sitting at his tax collector's booth. "Follow me and be my disciple," Jesus said to him. So Levi got up and followed him.

¹⁵Later, Levi invited Jesus and his disciples to his home as dinner guests, along with many tax collectors and other disreputable sinners. (There were many people of this kind among Jesus' followers.)

¹⁶But when the teachers of religious law who were Pharisees* saw him eating with tax collectors and other sinners, they asked his disciples, "Why does he eat with such scum?*"

¹⁷When Jesus heard this, he told them, "Healthy people don't need a doctor—sick people do. I have come to call not those who think they are righteous, but those who know they are sinners."

A Discussion about Fasting

¹⁸Once when John's disciples and the Pharisees were fasting, some people came to Jesus and asked, "Why don't your disciples fast like John's disciples and the Pharisees do?"

2:16a Greek *the scribes of the Pharisees.* 2:16b Greek *with tax collectors and sinners?*

¹⁹ Jesus replied, "Do wedding guests fast while celebrating with the groom? Of course not. They can't fast while the groom is with them. ²⁰But someday the groom will be taken away from them, and then they will fast.

²¹ "Besides, who would patch old clothing with new cloth? For the new patch would shrink and rip away from the old cloth, leaving an even bigger tear than before.

²² "And no one puts new wine into old wineskins. For the wine would burst the wineskins, and the wine and the skins would both be lost. New wine calls for new wineskins."

A Discussion about the Sabbath

²³ One Sabbath day as Jesus was walking through some grainfields, his disciples began breaking off heads of grain to eat. ²⁴But the Pharisees said to Jesus, "Look, why are they breaking the law by harvesting grain on the Sabbath?"

²⁵ Jesus said to them, "Haven't you ever read in the Scriptures what David did when he and his companions were hungry? ²⁶He went into the house of God (during the days when Abiathar was high priest) and broke the law by eating the sacred loaves of bread that only the priests are allowed to eat. He also gave some to his companions."

²⁷ Then Jesus said to them, "The Sabbath was made to meet the needs of people, and not people to meet the requirements of the Sabbath. ²⁸So the Son of Man is Lord, even over the Sabbath!"

3 Jesus Heals on the Sabbath

Jesus went into the synagogue again and noticed a man with a deformed hand. ²Since it was the Sabbath, Jesus' enemies watched him closely. If he healed the man's hand, they planned to accuse him of working on the Sabbath.

³ Jesus said to the man with the deformed hand, "Come and stand in front of everyone." ⁴Then he turned to his critics and asked, "Does the law permit good deeds on the Sabbath, or is it a day for doing evil? Is this a day to save life or to destroy it?" But they wouldn't answer him.

⁵ He looked around at them angrily and was deeply saddened by their hard hearts. Then he said to the man, "Hold out your hand." So the man held out his hand, and it was restored! ⁶At once the Pharisees went away and met with the supporters of Herod to plot how to kill Jesus.

Crowds Follow Jesus

⁷ Jesus went out to the lake with his disciples, and a large crowd followed him. They came from all over Galilee, Judea, ⁸Jerusalem, Idumea, from east of the Jordan River, and even from as far north as Tyre and Sidon. The news about his miracles had spread far and wide, and vast numbers of people came to see him.

⁹ Jesus instructed his disciples to have a boat ready so the crowd would not crush him. ¹⁰He had healed many people that day, so all the sick people eagerly pushed forward to touch him. ¹¹And whenever those possessed by evil* spirits caught sight of him, the spirits would throw them to the ground in front of him shrieking, "You are the Son of God!" ¹²But Jesus sternly commanded the spirits not to reveal who he was.

Jesus Chooses the Twelve Apostles

¹³ Afterward Jesus went up on a mountain and called out the ones he wanted to go with him. And they came to him. ¹⁴Then he appointed twelve of them and called them his apostles.* They were to accompany him, and he would send them out to preach, ¹⁵giving them authority to cast out demons. ¹⁶These are the twelve he chose:

Simon (whom he named Peter),
¹⁷ James and John (the sons of Zebedee, but Jesus nicknamed them "Sons of Thunder"*),
¹⁸ Andrew,
Philip,
Bartholomew,
Matthew,
Thomas,
James (son of Alphaeus),
Thaddaeus,
Simon (the zealot*),
¹⁹ Judas Iscariot (who later betrayed him).

3:11 Greek *unclean;* also in 3:30. **3:14** Some manuscripts do not include *and called them his apostles.* **3:17** Greek *whom he named Boanerges, which means Sons of Thunder.* **3:18** Greek *the Cananean,* an Aramaic term for Jewish nationalists.

Jesus and the Prince of Demons

²⁰One time Jesus entered a house, and the crowds began to gather again. Soon he and his disciples couldn't even find time to eat. ²¹When his family heard what was happening, they tried to take him away. "He's out of his mind," they said.

²²But the teachers of religious law who had arrived from Jerusalem said, "He's possessed by Satan,* the prince of demons. That's where he gets the power to cast out demons."

²³Jesus called them over and responded with an illustration. "How can Satan cast out Satan?" he asked. ²⁴"A kingdom divided by civil war will collapse. ²⁵Similarly, a family splintered by feuding will fall apart. ²⁶And if Satan is divided and fights against himself, how can he stand? He would never survive. ²⁷Let me illustrate this further. Who is powerful enough to enter the house of a strong man like Satan and plunder his goods? Only someone even stronger—someone who could tie him up and then plunder his house.

²⁸"I tell you the truth, all sin and blasphemy can be forgiven, ²⁹but anyone who blasphemes the Holy Spirit will never be forgiven. This is a sin with eternal consequences." ³⁰He told them this because they were saying, "He's possessed by an evil spirit."

The True Family of Jesus

³¹Then Jesus' mother and brothers came to see him. They stood outside and sent word for him to come out and talk with them. ³²There was a crowd sitting around Jesus, and someone said, "Your mother and your brothers* are outside asking for you."

³³Jesus replied, "Who is my mother? Who are my brothers?" ³⁴Then he looked at those around him and said, "Look, these are my mother and brothers. ³⁵Anyone who does God's will is my brother and sister and mother."

4 Parable of the Farmer Scattering Seed

Once again Jesus began teaching by the lakeshore. A very large crowd soon gathered around him, so he got into a boat. Then he sat in the boat while all the people remained on the shore. ²He taught them by telling many stories in the form of parables, such as this one:

³"Listen! A farmer went out to plant some seed. ⁴As he scattered it across his field, some of the seed fell on a footpath, and the birds came and ate it. ⁵Other seed fell on shallow soil with underlying rock. The seed sprouted quickly because the soil was shallow. ⁶But the plant soon wilted under the hot sun, and since it didn't have deep roots, it died. ⁷Other seed fell among thorns that grew up and choked out the tender plants so they produced no grain. ⁸Still other seeds fell on fertile soil, and they sprouted, grew, and produced a crop that was thirty, sixty, and even a hundred times as much as had been planted!" ⁹Then he said, "Anyone with ears to hear should listen and understand."

¹⁰Later, when Jesus was alone with the twelve disciples and with the others who were gathered around, they asked him what the parables meant.

¹¹He replied, "You are permitted to understand the secret* of the Kingdom of God. But I use parables for everything I say to outsiders, ¹²so that the Scriptures might be fulfilled:

'When they see what I do,
    they will learn nothing.
When they hear what I say,
    they will not understand.
Otherwise, they will turn to me
    and be forgiven.'*"

¹³Then Jesus said to them, "If you can't understand the meaning of this parable, how will you understand all the other parables? ¹⁴The farmer plants seed by taking God's word to others. ¹⁵The seed that fell on the footpath represents those who hear the message, only to have Satan come at once and take it away. ¹⁶The seed on the rocky soil represents those who hear the message and immediately receive it with joy. ¹⁷But since they don't have deep roots, they don't last long. They fall away as soon as they have problems or are persecuted for believing God's word. ¹⁸The seed that fell among the thorns represents others who

---

3:22 Greek *Beelzeboul;* other manuscripts read *Beezeboul;* Latin version reads *Beelzebub.*   **3:32** Some manuscripts add *and sisters.*
4:11 Greek *mystery.*   **4:12** Isa 6:9-10 (Greek version).

hear God's word, [19]but all too quickly the message is crowded out by the worries of this life, the lure of wealth, and the desire for other things, so no fruit is produced. [20]And the seed that fell on good soil represents those who hear and accept God's word and produce a harvest of thirty, sixty, or even a hundred times as much as had been planted!"

Parable of the Lamp

[21]Then Jesus asked them, "Would anyone light a lamp and then put it under a basket or under a bed? Of course not! A lamp is placed on a stand, where its light will shine. [22]For everything that is hidden will eventually be brought into the open, and every secret will be brought to light. [23]Anyone with ears to hear should listen and understand."

[24]Then he added, "Pay close attention to what you hear. The closer you listen, the more understanding you will be given*— and you will receive even more. [25]To those who listen to my teaching, more understanding will be given. But for those who are not listening, even what little understanding they have will be taken away from them."

Parable of the Growing Seed

[26]Jesus also said, "The Kingdom of God is like a farmer who scatters seed on the ground. [27]Night and day, while he's asleep or awake, the seed sprouts and grows, but he does not understand how it happens. [28]The earth produces the crops on its own. First a leaf blade pushes through, then the heads of wheat are formed, and finally the grain ripens. [29]And as soon as the grain is ready, the farmer comes and harvests it with a sickle, for the harvest time has come."

Parable of the Mustard Seed

[30]Jesus said, "How can I describe the Kingdom of God? What story should I use to illustrate it? [31]It is like a mustard seed planted in the ground. It is the smallest of all seeds, [32]but it becomes the largest of all garden plants; it grows long branches, and birds can make nests in its shade."

[33]Jesus used many similar stories and illustrations to teach the people as much as they could understand. [34]In fact, in his public ministry he never taught without using parables; but afterward, when he was alone with his disciples, he explained everything to them.

Jesus Calms the Storm

[35]As evening came, Jesus said to his disciples, "Let's cross to the other side of the lake." [36]So they took Jesus in the boat and started out, leaving the crowds behind (although other boats followed). [37]But soon a fierce storm came up. High waves were breaking into the boat, and it began to fill with water.

[38]Jesus was sleeping at the back of the boat with his head on a cushion. The disciples woke him up, shouting, "Teacher, don't you care that we're going to drown?"

[39]When Jesus woke up, he rebuked the wind and said to the waves, "Silence! Be still!" Suddenly the wind stopped, and there was a great calm. [40]Then he asked them, "Why are you afraid? Do you still have no faith?"

[41]The disciples were absolutely terrified. "Who is this man?" they asked each other. "Even the wind and waves obey him!"

5 Jesus Heals a Demon-Possessed Man

So they arrived at the other side of the lake, in the region of the Gerasenes.* [2]When Jesus climbed out of the boat, a man possessed by an evil* spirit came out from a cemetery to meet him. [3]This man lived among the burial caves and could no longer be restrained, even with a chain. [4]Whenever he was put into chains and shackles— as he often was—he snapped the chains from his wrists and smashed the shackles. No one was strong enough to subdue him. [5]Day and night he wandered among the burial caves and in the hills, howling and cutting himself with sharp stones.

[6]When Jesus was still some distance away, the man saw him, ran to meet him, and bowed low before him. [7]With a shriek, he screamed, "Why are you interfering with me, Jesus, Son of the Most High God? In the name of God, I beg you, don't

---

4:24 Or *The measure you give will be the measure you get back.*   **5:1** Other manuscripts read *Gadarenes;* still others read *Gergesenes.* See Matt 8:28; Luke 8:26.   **5:2** Greek *unclean;* also in 5:8, 13.

torture me!" ⁸For Jesus had already said to the spirit, "Come out of the man, you evil spirit."

⁹Then Jesus demanded, "What is your name?"

And he replied, "My name is Legion, because there are many of us inside this man." ¹⁰Then the evil spirits begged him again and again not to send them to some distant place.

¹¹There happened to be a large herd of pigs feeding on the hillside nearby. ¹²"Send us into those pigs," the spirits begged. "Let us enter them."

¹³So Jesus gave them permission. The evil spirits came out of the man and entered the pigs, and the entire herd of about 2,000 pigs plunged down the steep hillside into the lake and drowned in the water.

¹⁴The herdsmen fled to the nearby town and the surrounding countryside, spreading the news as they ran. People rushed out to see what had happened. ¹⁵A crowd soon gathered around Jesus, and they saw the man who had been possessed by the legion of demons. He was sitting there fully clothed and perfectly sane, and they were all afraid. ¹⁶Then those who had seen what happened told the others about the demon-possessed man and the pigs. ¹⁷And the crowd began pleading with Jesus to go away and leave them alone.

¹⁸As Jesus was getting into the boat, the man who had been demon possessed begged to go with him. ¹⁹But Jesus said, "No, go home to your family, and tell them everything the Lord has done for you and how merciful he has been." ²⁰So the man started off to visit the Ten Towns* of that region and began to proclaim the great things Jesus had done for him; and everyone was amazed at what he told them.

Jesus Heals in Response to Faith

²¹Jesus got into the boat again and went back to the other side of the lake, where a large crowd gathered around him on the shore. ²²Then a leader of the local synagogue, whose name was Jairus, arrived. When he saw Jesus, he fell at his feet, ²³pleading fervently with him. "My little daughter is dying," he said. "Please come and lay your hands on her; heal her so she can live."

²⁴Jesus went with him, and all the people followed, crowding around him. ²⁵A woman in the crowd had suffered for twelve years with constant bleeding. ²⁶She had suffered a great deal from many doctors, and over the years she had spent everything she had to pay them, but she had gotten no better. In fact, she had gotten worse. ²⁷She had heard about Jesus, so she came up behind him through the crowd and touched his robe. ²⁸For she thought to herself, "If I can just touch his robe, I will be healed." ²⁹Immediately the bleeding stopped, and she could feel in her body that she had been healed of her terrible condition.

³⁰Jesus realized at once that healing power had gone out from him, so he turned around in the crowd and asked, "Who touched my robe?"

³¹His disciples said to him, "Look at this crowd pressing around you. How can you ask, 'Who touched me?'"

³²But he kept on looking around to see who had done it. ³³Then the frightened woman, trembling at the realization of what had happened to her, came and fell to her knees in front of him and told him what she had done. ³⁴And he said to her, "Daughter, your faith has made you well. Go in peace. Your suffering is over."

³⁵While he was still speaking to her, messengers arrived from the home of Jairus, the leader of the synagogue. They told him, "Your daughter is dead. There's no use troubling the Teacher now."

³⁶But Jesus overheard* them and said to Jairus, "Don't be afraid. Just have faith."

³⁷Then Jesus stopped the crowd and wouldn't let anyone go with him except Peter, James, and John (the brother of James). ³⁸When they came to the home of the synagogue leader, Jesus saw much commotion and weeping and wailing. ³⁹He went inside and asked, "Why all this commotion and weeping? The child isn't dead; she's only asleep."

⁴⁰The crowd laughed at him. But he made them all leave, and he took the girl's father and mother and his three disciples into the

---

5:20 Greek *Decapolis.*   **5:36** Or *ignored.*

Changing the World from Your Doorstep

Outreach

MARK 5:1-20

Recently I felt convicted that God wanted me to minister where I live—right in my neighborhood. I began by inviting families with kids to come over and play in our yard. The first night eleven kids came with their parents. Now, over time, it's grown into a group of fourteen families who regularly meet to play—and also to explore spiritual matters.

I used to think I had to go somewhere to have a vibrant ministry—but now I see things differently. I can relate a bit to the demon-possessed man Jesus healed in Mark 5. This man wanted to follow him to the ends of the earth—but Jesus told him instead to go back to his village and share the Good News.

God has shown me that staying put in my "village" means I should deliberately invest in the people on my path—those who walk to school with me, put the garbage out at the same time I do, and ride bikes on the street. God surprised me with his mission calling in my life. How might he be calling you to change the world from your doorstep?

—*Heather Holleman*

For more on outreach, see reading at Acts 9:36-43.

---

room where the girl was lying. [41] Holding her hand, he said to her, *"Talitha koum,"* which means "Little girl, get up!" [42] And the girl, who was twelve years old, immediately stood up and walked around! They were overwhelmed and totally amazed. [43] Jesus gave them strict orders not to tell anyone what had happened, and then he told them to give her something to eat.

Jesus Rejected at Nazareth

6 Jesus left that part of the country and returned with his disciples to Nazareth, his hometown. [2] The next Sabbath he began teaching in the synagogue, and many who heard him were amazed. They asked, "Where did he get all this wisdom and the power to perform such miracles?" [3] Then they scoffed, "He's just a carpenter, the son of Mary* and the brother of James, Joseph,* Judas, and Simon. And his sisters live right here among us." They were deeply offended and refused to believe in him.

[4] Then Jesus told them, "A prophet is honored everywhere except in his own home-

town and among his relatives and his own family." [5] And because of their unbelief, he couldn't do any miracles among them except to place his hands on a few sick people and heal them. [6] And he was amazed at their unbelief.

Jesus Sends Out the Twelve Disciples

Then Jesus went from village to village, teaching the people. [7] And he called his twelve disciples together and began sending them out two by two, giving them authority to cast out evil* spirits. [8] He told them to take nothing for their journey except a walking stick—no food, no traveler's bag, no money.* [9] He allowed them to wear sandals but not to take a change of clothes.

[10] "Wherever you go," he said, "stay in the same house until you leave town. [11] But if any place refuses to welcome you or listen to you, shake its dust from your feet as you leave to show that you have abandoned those people to their fate."

[12] So the disciples went out, telling everyone they met to repent of their sins and turn

---

6:3a Some manuscripts read *He's just the son of the carpenter and of Mary.* **6:3b** Most manuscripts read *Joses;* see Matt 13:55. **6:7** Greek *unclean.* **6:8** Greek *no copper coins in their money belts.*

to God. [13] And they cast out many demons and healed many sick people, anointing them with olive oil.

The Death of John the Baptist

[14] Herod Antipas, the king, soon heard about Jesus, because everyone was talking about him. Some were saying,* "This must be John the Baptist raised from the dead. That is why he can do such miracles." [15] Others said, "He's the prophet Elijah." Still others said, "He's a prophet like the other great prophets of the past."

[16] When Herod heard about Jesus, he said, "John, the man I beheaded, has come back from the dead."

[17] For Herod had sent soldiers to arrest and imprison John as a favor to Herodias. She had been his brother Philip's wife, but Herod had married her. [18] John had been telling Herod, "It is against God's law for you to marry your brother's wife." [19] So Herodias bore a grudge against John and wanted to kill him. But without Herod's approval she was powerless, [20] for Herod respected John; and knowing that he was a good and holy man, he protected him. Herod was greatly disturbed whenever he talked with John, but even so, he liked to listen to him.

[21] Herodias's chance finally came on Herod's birthday. He gave a party for his high government officials, army officers, and the leading citizens of Galilee. [22] Then his daughter, also named Herodias,* came in and performed a dance that greatly pleased Herod and his guests. "Ask me for anything you like," the king said to the girl, "and I will give it to you." [23] He even vowed, "I will give you whatever you ask, up to half my kingdom!"

[24] She went out and asked her mother, "What should I ask for?"

Her mother told her, "Ask for the head of John the Baptist!"

[25] So the girl hurried back to the king and told him, "I want the head of John the Baptist, right now, on a tray!"

[26] Then the king deeply regretted what he had said; but because of the vows he had made in front of his guests, he couldn't refuse her. [27] So he immediately sent an executioner to the prison to cut off John's head and bring it to him. The soldier beheaded John in the prison, [28] brought his head on a tray, and gave it to the girl, who took it to her mother. [29] When John's disciples heard what had happened, they came to get his body and buried it in a tomb.

Jesus Feeds Five Thousand

[30] The apostles returned to Jesus from their ministry tour and told him all they had done and taught. [31] Then Jesus said, "Let's go off by ourselves to a quiet place and rest awhile." He said this because there were so many people coming and going that Jesus and his apostles didn't even have time to eat.

[32] So they left by boat for a quiet place, where they could be alone. [33] But many people recognized them and saw them leaving, and people from many towns ran ahead along the shore and got there ahead of them. [34] Jesus saw the huge crowd as he stepped from the boat, and he had compassion on them because they were like sheep without a shepherd. So he began teaching them many things.

[35] Late in the afternoon his disciples came to him and said, "This is a remote place, and it's already getting late. [36] Send the crowds away so they can go to the nearby farms and villages and buy something to eat."

[37] But Jesus said, "You feed them."

"With what?" they asked. "We'd have to work for months to earn enough money* to buy food for all these people!"

[38] "How much bread do you have?" he asked. "Go and find out."

They came back and reported, "We have five loaves of bread and two fish."

[39] Then Jesus told the disciples to have the people sit down in groups on the green grass. [40] So they sat down in groups of fifty or a hundred. [41] Jesus took the five loaves and two fish, looked up toward heaven, and blessed them. Then, breaking the loaves into pieces, he kept giving the bread to the disciples so they could distribute it to the people. He also divided the fish for everyone to share.

6:14 Some manuscripts read *He was saying.*   6:22 Some manuscripts read *the daughter of Herodias herself.*   6:37 Greek *It would take 200 denarii.* A denarius was equivalent to a laborer's full day's wage.

A Steady Rhythm

MARK 6:30-32

Sabbath & Rest

Jesus understood how quickly our passions, even the most noble, can wear us out if we're not careful. Early in his ministry, he began to teach the disciples about establishing sane rhythms of work and rest.

In Mark 6 Jesus commissioned the disciples for ministry and gave them the authority to cast out demons, preach the gospel, and heal the sick. They went on their first ministry excursion and returned excited about their newfound power and influence. They crowded around Jesus to report all they had done.

But Jesus didn't seem to have much time for their ministry reports. Immediately he invited them, "Let's go off by ourselves to a quiet place and rest awhile" (Mark 6:31). He seemed more concerned about helping them establish a rhythm that would sustain them in ministry than allowing them to be overly enamored by ministry success, which can lead to a compulsion to do more without ceasing.

When we keep pushing forward without taking adequate time for rest, our way of life may seem heroic, but a frenetic quality comes to our work that lacks true effectiveness. We lose the ability to be fully present to God and to other people. And we lose the ability to discern what is really needed in our situation.

The result can be "sloppy desperation," a mental and spiritual state in which we're just trying to get it all done. And this prevents us from the quality of presence that delivers true insight and enables us to minister effectively to others.

Yet when we are rested—both physically and spiritually—we bring steady, alert attention to our ministry to others. We have discernment to determine what God needs us to do in response to ministry opportunity, and we have the energy and creativity to carry it out.

—Ruth Haley Barton

For more on Sabbath and rest, see reading at John 20:1-18.

---

[42] They all ate as much as they wanted, [43] and afterward, the disciples picked up twelve baskets of leftover bread and fish. [44] A total of 5,000 men and their families were fed from those loaves!

Jesus Walks on Water

[45] Immediately after this, Jesus insisted that his disciples get back into the boat and head across the lake to Bethsaida, while he sent the people home. [46] After telling everyone good-bye, he went up into the hills by himself to pray.

[47] Late that night, the disciples were in their boat in the middle of the lake, and Jesus was alone on land. [48] He saw that they were in serious trouble, rowing hard and struggling against the wind and waves. About three o'clock in the morning* Jesus came toward them, walking on the water. He intended to go past them, [49] but when they saw him walking on the water, they cried out in terror, thinking he was a ghost. [50] They were all terrified when they saw him.

But Jesus spoke to them at once. "Don't be afraid," he said. "Take courage! I am

6:48 Greek *About the fourth watch of the night.*

here!*" ⁵¹ Then he climbed into the boat, and the wind stopped. They were totally amazed, ⁵² for they still didn't understand the significance of the miracle of the loaves. Their hearts were too hard to take it in.

⁵³ After they had crossed the lake, they landed at Gennesaret. They brought the boat to shore ⁵⁴ and climbed out. The people recognized Jesus at once, ⁵⁵ and they ran throughout the whole area, carrying sick people on mats to wherever they heard he was. ⁵⁶ Wherever he went—in villages, cities, or the countryside—they brought the sick out to the marketplaces. They begged him to let the sick touch at least the fringe of his robe, and all who touched him were healed.

Jesus Teaches about Inner Purity

7 One day some Pharisees and teachers of religious law arrived from Jerusalem to see Jesus. ² They noticed that some of his disciples failed to follow the Jewish ritual of hand washing before eating. ³ (The Jews, especially the Pharisees, do not eat until they have poured water over their cupped hands,* as required by their ancient traditions. ⁴ Similarly, they don't eat anything from the market until they immerse their hands* in water. This is but one of many traditions they have clung to—such as their ceremonial washing of cups, pitchers, and kettles.*)

⁵ So the Pharisees and teachers of religious law asked him, "Why don't your disciples follow our age-old tradition? They eat without first performing the hand-washing ceremony."

⁶ Jesus replied, "You hypocrites! Isaiah was right when he prophesied about you, for he wrote,

'These people honor me with their lips,
    but their hearts are far from me.
⁷ Their worship is a farce,
    for they teach man-made ideas as
        commands from God.'*

⁸ For you ignore God's law and substitute your own tradition."

⁹ Then he said, "You skillfully sidestep God's law in order to hold on to your own tradition. ¹⁰ For instance, Moses gave you this law from God: 'Honor your father and mother,'* and 'Anyone who speaks disrespectfully of father or mother must be put to death.'* ¹¹ But you say it is all right for people to say to their parents, 'Sorry, I can't help you. For I have vowed to give to God what I would have given to you.'* ¹² In this way, you let them disregard their needy parents. ¹³ And so you cancel the word of God in order to hand down your own tradition. And this is only one example among many others."

¹⁴ Then Jesus called to the crowd to come and hear. "All of you listen," he said, "and try to understand. ¹⁵ It's not what goes into your body that defiles you; you are defiled by what comes from your heart.*"

¹⁷ Then Jesus went into a house to get away from the crowd, and his disciples asked him what he meant by the parable he had just used. ¹⁸ "Don't you understand either?" he asked. "Can't you see that the food you put into your body cannot defile you? ¹⁹ Food doesn't go into your heart, but only passes through the stomach and then goes into the sewer." (By saying this, he declared that every kind of food is acceptable in God's eyes.)

²⁰ And then he added, "It is what comes from inside that defiles you. ²¹ For from within, out of a person's heart, come evil thoughts, sexual immorality, theft, murder, ²² adultery, greed, wickedness, deceit, lustful desires, envy, slander, pride, and foolishness. ²³ All these vile things come from within; they are what defile you."

The Faith of a Gentile Woman

²⁴ Then Jesus left Galilee and went north to the region of Tyre.* He didn't want anyone to know which house he was staying in, but he couldn't keep it a secret. ²⁵ Right away a woman who had heard about him came and fell at his feet. Her little girl was possessed by an evil* spirit, ²⁶ and she begged him to cast out the demon from her daughter.

6:50 Or *The 'I AM' is here;* Greek reads *I am.* See Exod 3:14. **7:3** Greek *have washed with the fist.* **7:4a** Some manuscripts read *sprinkle themselves.* **7:4b** Some manuscripts add *and dining couches.* **7:7** Isa 29:13 (Greek version). **7:10a** Exod 20:12; Deut 5:16. **7:10b** Exod 21:17 (Greek version); Lev 20:9 (Greek version). **7:11** Greek *'What I would have given to you is Corban'* (that is, a gift). **7:15** Some manuscripts add verse 16, *Anyone with ears to hear should listen and understand.* Compare 4:9, 23. **7:24** Some manuscripts add *and Sidon.* **7:25** Greek *unclean.*

Since she was a Gentile, born in Syrian Phoenicia, ²⁷Jesus told her, "First I should feed the children—my own family, the Jews.* It isn't right to take food from the children and throw it to the dogs."

²⁸She replied, "That's true, Lord, but even the dogs under the table are allowed to eat the scraps from the children's plates."

²⁹"Good answer!" he said. "Now go home, for the demon has left your daughter." ³⁰And when she arrived home, she found her little girl lying quietly in bed, and the demon was gone.

Jesus Heals a Deaf Man

³¹Jesus left Tyre and went up to Sidon before going back to the Sea of Galilee and the region of the Ten Towns.* ³²A deaf man with a speech impediment was brought to him, and the people begged Jesus to lay his hands on the man to heal him.

³³Jesus led him away from the crowd so they could be alone. He put his fingers into the man's ears. Then, spitting on his own fingers, he touched the man's tongue. ³⁴Looking up to heaven, he sighed and said, "*Ephphatha*," which means, "Be opened!" ³⁵Instantly the man could hear perfectly, and his tongue was freed so he could speak plainly!

³⁶Jesus told the crowd not to tell anyone, but the more he told them not to, the more they spread the news. ³⁷They were completely amazed and said again and again, "Everything he does is wonderful. He even makes the deaf to hear and gives speech to those who cannot speak."

8 Jesus Feeds Four Thousand

About this time another large crowd had gathered, and the people ran out of food again. Jesus called his disciples and told them, ²"I feel sorry for these people. They have been here with me for three days, and they have nothing left to eat. ³If I send them home hungry, they will faint along the way. For some of them have come a long distance."

⁴His disciples replied, "How are we supposed to find enough food to feed them out here in the wilderness?"

⁵Jesus asked, "How much bread do you have?"

"Seven loaves," they replied.

⁶So Jesus told all the people to sit down on the ground. Then he took the seven loaves, thanked God for them, and broke them into pieces. He gave them to his disciples, who distributed the bread to the crowd. ⁷A few small fish were found, too, so Jesus also blessed these and told the disciples to distribute them.

⁸They ate as much as they wanted. Afterward, the disciples picked up seven large baskets of leftover food. ⁹There were about 4,000 people in the crowd that day, and Jesus sent them home after they had eaten. ¹⁰Immediately after this, he got into a boat with his disciples and crossed over to the region of Dalmanutha.

Pharisees Demand a Miraculous Sign

¹¹When the Pharisees heard that Jesus had arrived, they came and started to argue with him. Testing him, they demanded that he show them a miraculous sign from heaven to prove his authority.

¹²When he heard this, he sighed deeply in his spirit and said, "Why do these people keep demanding a miraculous sign? I tell you the truth, I will not give this generation any such sign." ¹³So he got back into the boat and left them, and he crossed to the other side of the lake.

Yeast of the Pharisees and Herod

¹⁴But the disciples had forgotten to bring any food. They had only one loaf of bread with them in the boat. ¹⁵As they were crossing the lake, Jesus warned them, "Watch out! Beware of the yeast of the Pharisees and of Herod."

¹⁶At this they began to argue with each other because they hadn't brought any bread. ¹⁷Jesus knew what they were saying, so he said, "Why are you arguing about having no bread? Don't you know or understand even yet? Are your hearts too hard to take it in? ¹⁸'You have eyes—can't you see? You have ears—can't you hear?'* Don't you remember anything at all? ¹⁹When I fed the 5,000 with five loaves of bread, how many

---

7:27 Greek *Let the children eat first.*   **7:31** Greek *Decapolis.*   **8:18** Jer 5:21.

baskets of leftovers did you pick up afterward?"

"Twelve," they said.

²⁰"And when I fed the 4,000 with seven loaves, how many large baskets of leftovers did you pick up?"

"Seven," they said.

²¹"Don't you understand yet?" he asked them.

Jesus Heals a Blind Man

²²When they arrived at Bethsaida, some people brought a blind man to Jesus, and they begged him to touch the man and heal him. ²³Jesus took the blind man by the hand and led him out of the village. Then, spitting on the man's eyes, he laid his hands on him and asked, "Can you see anything now?"

²⁴The man looked around. "Yes," he said, "I see people, but I can't see them very clearly. They look like trees walking around."

²⁵Then Jesus placed his hands on the man's eyes again, and his eyes were opened. His sight was completely restored, and he could see everything clearly. ²⁶Jesus sent him away, saying, "Don't go back into the village on your way home."

Peter's Declaration about Jesus

²⁷Jesus and his disciples left Galilee and went up to the villages near Caesarea Philippi. As they were walking along, he asked them, "Who do people say I am?"

²⁸"Well," they replied, "some say John the Baptist, some say Elijah, and others say you are one of the other prophets."

²⁹Then he asked them, "But who do you say I am?"

Peter replied, "You are the Messiah.*"

³⁰But Jesus warned them not to tell anyone about him.

Jesus Predicts His Death

³¹Then Jesus began to tell them that the Son of Man* must suffer many terrible things and be rejected by the elders, the leading priests, and the teachers of religious law. He would be killed, but three days later he would rise from the dead. ³²As he talked

about this openly with his disciples, Peter took him aside and began to reprimand him for saying such things.*

³³Jesus turned around and looked at his disciples, then reprimanded Peter. "Get away from me, Satan!" he said. "You are seeing things merely from a human point of view, not from God's."

³⁴Then, calling the crowd to join his disciples, he said, "If any of you wants to be my follower, you must turn from your selfish ways, take up your cross, and follow me. ³⁵If you try to hang on to your life, you will lose it. But if you give up your life for my sake and for the sake of the Good News, you will save it. ³⁶And what do you benefit if you gain the whole world but lose your own soul?* ³⁷Is anything worth more than your soul? ³⁸If anyone is ashamed of me and my message in these adulterous and sinful days, the Son of Man will be ashamed of that person when he returns in the glory of his Father with the holy angels."

9 Jesus went on to say, "I tell you the truth, some standing here right now will not die before they see the Kingdom of God arrive in great power!"

The Transfiguration

²Six days later Jesus took Peter, James, and John, and led them up a high mountain to be alone. As the men watched, Jesus' appearance was transformed, ³and his clothes became dazzling white, far whiter than any earthly bleach could ever make them. ⁴Then Elijah and Moses appeared and began talking with Jesus.

⁵Peter exclaimed, "Rabbi, it's wonderful for us to be here! Let's make three shelters as memorials*—one for you, one for Moses, and one for Elijah." ⁶He said this because he didn't really know what else to say, for they were all terrified.

⁷Then a cloud overshadowed them, and a voice from the cloud said, "This is my dearly loved Son. Listen to him." ⁸Suddenly, when they looked around, Moses and Elijah were gone, and they saw only Jesus with them.

⁹As they went back down the mountain, he told them not to tell anyone what they

---

8:29 Or the Christ. Messiah (a Hebrew term) and Christ (a Greek term) both mean "the anointed one."   **8:31** "Son of Man" is a title Jesus used for himself.   **8:32** Or began to correct him.   **8:36** Or your self? also in 8:37.   **9:5** Greek three tabernacles.

Moving from Doubt to Certainty
MARK 9:14-29

Christians may walk through periods of doubt, and we ought to be honest about those struggles. But at the same time, we need to be careful of glorifying doubt or even reveling in it. Instead, as Scripture encourages us, our aim ought to be to hold fast to a faith that's grounded in certainty.

Consider what Martin Luther wrote in his *Preface to Romans*: "Faith is a living, unshakable confidence in God's grace." In a 1525 debate with Erasmus, who praised doubt and accused Luther of seeking certainty, he said, "To take no pleasure in assertions is not the mark of a Christian heart; indeed, one must delight in assertions to be a Christian at all. . . . Take away assertion, and you take away Christianity." Luther pointed to the words of Paul, who so often called for full assurance (Colossians 2:2), or the highest degree of certainty and conviction.

"The Holy Spirit is no skeptic, and the things he has written in our hearts are not doubts or opinions, but assertions—surer and more certain than sense and life itself," Luther said.

Does that mean that with the knowledge of the life, death, and resurrection of Christ, we won't face doubts? Hardly. Scripture is full of stories of people, from Eve (Genesis 3) to Thomas (John 20), who doubted the promises of God. But just because it's human to doubt, and we all do it, does not mean it should be celebrated so much as endured.

Shortly after the Transfiguration, in which Jesus shone with the glory of his divine nature, he came upon an anxious father. When the father asked Jesus to deliver his son from demonic possession, Jesus told him, "Anything is possible if a person believes." The father responded, "I do believe, but help me overcome my unbelief!" (Mark 9:23-24). Jesus cast out the demon. What a beautiful reminder of how Jesus delivers us from a world of despair and doubt.

—*Mollie Ziegler Hemingway*

For more on faith, see reading at John 11:1-44.

---

had seen until the Son of Man* had risen from the dead. ¹⁰So they kept it to themselves, but they often asked each other what he meant by "rising from the dead."

¹¹Then they asked him, "Why do the teachers of religious law insist that Elijah must return before the Messiah comes?*"

¹²Jesus responded, "Elijah is indeed coming first to get everything ready. Yet why do the Scriptures say that the Son of Man must suffer greatly and be treated with utter contempt? ¹³But I tell you, Elijah has already come, and they chose to abuse him, just as the Scriptures predicted."

Jesus Heals a Demon-Possessed Boy

¹⁴When they returned to the other disciples, they saw a large crowd surrounding them, and some teachers of religious law were arguing with them. ¹⁵When the crowd saw Jesus, they were overwhelmed with awe, and they ran to greet him.

9:9 "Son of Man" is a title Jesus used for himself.   9:11 Greek *that Elijah must come first?*

¹⁶"What is all this arguing about?" Jesus asked.

¹⁷One of the men in the crowd spoke up and said, "Teacher, I brought my son so you could heal him. He is possessed by an evil spirit that won't let him talk. ¹⁸And whenever this spirit seizes him, it throws him violently to the ground. Then he foams at the mouth and grinds his teeth and becomes rigid.* So I asked your disciples to cast out the evil spirit, but they couldn't do it."

¹⁹Jesus said to them,* "You faithless people! How long must I be with you? How long must I put up with you? Bring the boy to me."

²⁰So they brought the boy. But when the evil spirit saw Jesus, it threw the child into a violent convulsion, and he fell to the ground, writhing and foaming at the mouth.

²¹"How long has this been happening?" Jesus asked the boy's father.

He replied, "Since he was a little boy. ²²The spirit often throws him into the fire or into water, trying to kill him. Have mercy on us and help us, if you can."

²³"What do you mean, 'If I can'?" Jesus asked. "Anything is possible if a person believes."

²⁴The father instantly cried out, "I do believe, but help me overcome my unbelief!"

²⁵When Jesus saw that the crowd of onlookers was growing, he rebuked the evil* spirit. "Listen, you spirit that makes this boy unable to hear and speak," he said. "I command you to come out of this child and never enter him again!"

²⁶Then the spirit screamed and threw the boy into another violent convulsion and left him. The boy appeared to be dead. A murmur ran through the crowd as people said, "He's dead." ²⁷But Jesus took him by the hand and helped him to his feet, and he stood up.

²⁸Afterward, when Jesus was alone in the house with his disciples, they asked him, "Why couldn't we cast out that evil spirit?"

²⁹Jesus replied, "This kind can be cast out only by prayer.*"

Jesus Again Predicts His Death

³⁰Leaving that region, they traveled through Galilee. Jesus didn't want anyone to know he was there, ³¹for he wanted to spend more time with his disciples and teach them. He said to them, "The Son of Man is going to be betrayed into the hands of his enemies. He will be killed, but three days later he will rise from the dead." ³²They didn't understand what he was saying, however, and they were afraid to ask him what he meant.

The Greatest in the Kingdom

³³After they arrived at Capernaum and settled in a house, Jesus asked his disciples, "What were you discussing out on the road?" ³⁴But they didn't answer, because they had been arguing about which of them was the greatest. ³⁵He sat down, called the twelve disciples over to him, and said, "Whoever wants to be first must take last place and be the servant of everyone else."

³⁶Then he put a little child among them. Taking the child in his arms, he said to them, ³⁷"Anyone who welcomes a little child like this on my behalf* welcomes me, and anyone who welcomes me welcomes not only me but also my Father who sent me."

Using the Name of Jesus

³⁸John said to Jesus, "Teacher, we saw someone using your name to cast out demons, but we told him to stop because he wasn't in our group."

³⁹"Don't stop him!" Jesus said. "No one who performs a miracle in my name will soon be able to speak evil of me. ⁴⁰Anyone who is not against us is for us. ⁴¹If anyone gives you even a cup of water because you belong to the Messiah, I tell you the truth, that person will surely be rewarded.

⁴²"But if you cause one of these little ones who trusts in me to fall into sin, it would be better for you to be thrown into the sea with a large millstone hung around your neck. ⁴³If your hand causes you to sin, cut it off. It's better to enter eternal life with only one hand than to go into the unquenchable fires of hell* with two hands.* ⁴⁵If your

---

9:18 Or becomes weak.   9:19 Or said to his disciples.   9:25 Greek unclean.   9:29 Some manuscripts read by prayer and fasting.   9:37 Greek in my name.   9:43a Greek Gehenna; also in 9:45, 47.   9:43b Some manuscripts add verse 44, 'where the maggots never die and the fire never goes out.' See 9:48.

foot causes you to sin, cut it off. It's better to enter eternal life with only one foot than to be thrown into hell with two feet.* [47] And if your eye causes you to sin, gouge it out. It's better to enter the Kingdom of God with only one eye than to have two eyes and be thrown into hell, [48] 'where the maggots never die and the fire never goes out.'*

[49] "For everyone will be tested with fire.* [50] Salt is good for seasoning. But if it loses its flavor, how do you make it salty again? You must have the qualities of salt among yourselves and live in peace with each other."

10 Discussion about Divorce and Marriage

Then Jesus left Capernaum and went down to the region of Judea and into the area east of the Jordan River. Once again crowds gathered around him, and as usual he was teaching them.

[2] Some Pharisees came and tried to trap him with this question: "Should a man be allowed to divorce his wife?"

[3] Jesus answered them with a question: "What did Moses say in the law about divorce?"

[4] "Well, he permitted it," they replied. "He said a man can give his wife a written notice of divorce and send her away."*

[5] But Jesus responded, "He wrote this commandment only as a concession to your hard hearts. [6] But 'God made them male and female'* from the beginning of creation. [7] 'This explains why a man leaves his father and mother and is joined to his wife,* [8] and the two are united into one.'* Since they are no longer two but one, [9] let no one split apart what God has joined together."

[10] Later, when he was alone with his disciples in the house, they brought up the subject again. [11] He told them, "Whoever divorces his wife and marries someone else commits adultery against her. [12] And if a woman divorces her husband and marries someone else, she commits adultery."

Jesus Blesses the Children

[13] One day some parents brought their children to Jesus so he could touch and bless them. But the disciples scolded the parents for bothering him.

[14] When Jesus saw what was happening, he was angry with his disciples. He said to them, "Let the children come to me. Don't stop them! For the Kingdom of God belongs to those who are like these children. [15] I tell you the truth, anyone who doesn't receive the Kingdom of God like a child will never enter it." [16] Then he took the children in his arms and placed his hands on their heads and blessed them.

The Rich Man

[17] As Jesus was starting out on his way to Jerusalem, a man came running up to him, knelt down, and asked, "Good Teacher, what must I do to inherit eternal life?"

[18] "Why do you call me good?" Jesus asked. "Only God is truly good. [19] But to answer your question, you know the commandments: 'You must not murder. You must not commit adultery. You must not steal. You must not testify falsely. You must not cheat anyone. Honor your father and mother.'*"

[20] "Teacher," the man replied, "I've obeyed all these commandments since I was young."

[21] Looking at the man, Jesus felt genuine love for him. "There is still one thing you haven't done," he told him. "Go and sell all your possessions and give the money to the poor, and you will have treasure in heaven. Then come, follow me."

[22] At this the man's face fell, and he went away sad, for he had many possessions.

[23] Jesus looked around and said to his disciples, "How hard it is for the rich to enter the Kingdom of God!" [24] This amazed them. But Jesus said again, "Dear children, it is very hard* to enter the Kingdom of God. [25] In fact, it is easier for a camel to go through the eye of a needle than for a rich person to enter the Kingdom of God!"

[26] The disciples were astounded. "Then who in the world can be saved?" they asked.

[27] Jesus looked at them intently and said, "Humanly speaking, it is impossible. But not with God. Everything is possible with God."

9:45 Some manuscripts add verse 46, 'where the maggots never die and the fire never goes out.' See 9:48.   **9:48** Isa 66:24.   **9:49** Greek salted with fire; other manuscripts add and every sacrifice will be salted with salt.   **10:4** See Deut 24:1.   **10:6** Gen 1:27; 5:2.   **10:7** Some manuscripts do not include and is joined to his wife.   **10:7-8** Gen 2:24.   **10:19** Exod 20:12-16; Deut 5:16-20.   **10:24** Some manuscripts read very hard for those who trust in riches.

28 Then Peter began to speak up. "We've given up everything to follow you," he said. 29 "Yes," Jesus replied, "and I assure you that everyone who has given up house or brothers or sisters or mother or father or children or property, for my sake and for the Good News, 30 will receive now in return a hundred times as many houses, brothers, sisters, mothers, children, and property—along with persecution. And in the world to come that person will have eternal life. 31 But many who are the greatest now will be least important then, and those who seem least important now will be the greatest then.*"

Jesus Again Predicts His Death

32 They were now on the way up to Jerusalem, and Jesus was walking ahead of them. The disciples were filled with awe, and the people following behind were overwhelmed with fear. Taking the twelve disciples aside, Jesus once more began to describe everything that was about to happen to him. 33 "Listen," he said, "we're going up to Jerusalem, where the Son of Man* will be betrayed to the leading priests and the teachers of religious law. They will sentence him to die and hand him over to the Romans.* 34 They will mock him, spit on him, flog him with a whip, and kill him, but after three days he will rise again."

Jesus Teaches about Serving Others

35 Then James and John, the sons of Zebedee, came over and spoke to him. "Teacher," they said, "we want you to do us a favor."

36 "What is your request?" he asked.

37 They replied, "When you sit on your glorious throne, we want to sit in places of honor next to you, one on your right and the other on your left."

38 But Jesus said to them, "You don't know what you are asking! Are you able to drink from the bitter cup of suffering I am about to drink? Are you able to be baptized with the baptism of suffering I must be baptized with?"

39 "Oh yes," they replied, "we are able!"

Then Jesus told them, "You will indeed drink from my bitter cup and be baptized with my baptism of suffering. 40 But I have no right to say who will sit on my right or my left. God has prepared those places for the ones he has chosen."

41 When the ten other disciples heard what James and John had asked, they were indignant. 42 So Jesus called them together and said, "You know that the rulers in this world lord it over their people, and officials flaunt their authority over those under them. 43 But among you it will be different. Whoever wants to be a leader among you must be your servant, 44 and whoever wants to be first among you must be the slave of everyone else. 45 For even the Son of Man came not to be served but to serve others and to give his life as a ransom for many."

Jesus Heals Blind Bartimaeus

46 Then they reached Jericho, and as Jesus and his disciples left town, a large crowd followed him. A blind beggar named Bartimaeus (son of Timaeus) was sitting beside the road. 47 When Bartimaeus heard that Jesus of Nazareth was nearby, he began to shout, "Jesus, Son of David, have mercy on me!"

48 "Be quiet!" many of the people yelled at him.

But he only shouted louder, "Son of David, have mercy on me!"

49 When Jesus heard him, he stopped and said, "Tell him to come here."

So they called the blind man. "Cheer up," they said. "Come on, he's calling you!" 50 Bartimaeus threw aside his coat, jumped up, and came to Jesus.

51 "What do you want me to do for you?" Jesus asked.

"My rabbi,*" the blind man said, "I want to see!"

52 And Jesus said to him, "Go, for your faith has healed you." Instantly the man could see, and he followed Jesus down the road.*

11 Jesus' Triumphant Entry

As Jesus and his disciples approached Jerusalem, they came to the towns of Bethphage and Bethany on the Mount of Olives. Jesus sent two of them on ahead. 2 "Go into

---

10:31 Greek But many who are first will be last; and the last, first.   10:33a "Son of Man" is a title Jesus used for himself.   10:33b Greek the Gentiles.   10:51 Greek uses the Hebrew term Rabboni.   10:52 Or on the way.

that village over there," he told them. "As soon as you enter it, you will see a young donkey tied there that no one has ever ridden. Untie it and bring it here. ³If anyone asks, 'What are you doing?' just say, 'The Lord needs it and will return it soon.'"

⁴The two disciples left and found the colt standing in the street, tied outside the front door. ⁵As they were untying it, some bystanders demanded, "What are you doing, untying that colt?" ⁶They said what Jesus had told them to say, and they were permitted to take it. ⁷Then they brought the colt to Jesus and threw their garments over it, and he sat on it.

⁸Many in the crowd spread their garments on the road ahead of him, and others spread leafy branches they had cut in the fields. ⁹Jesus was in the center of the procession, and the people all around him were shouting,

"Praise God!*
    Blessings on the one who comes in the
        name of the Lord!
¹⁰ Blessings on the coming Kingdom of our
        ancestor David!
    Praise God in highest heaven!"*

¹¹So Jesus came to Jerusalem and went into the Temple. After looking around carefully at everything, he left because it was late in the afternoon. Then he returned to Bethany with the twelve disciples.

Jesus Curses the Fig Tree

¹²The next morning as they were leaving Bethany, Jesus was hungry. ¹³He noticed a fig tree in full leaf a little way off, so he went over to see if he could find any figs. But there were only leaves because it was too early in the season for fruit. ¹⁴Then Jesus said to the tree, "May no one ever eat your fruit again!" And the disciples heard him say it.

Jesus Clears the Temple

¹⁵When they arrived back in Jerusalem, Jesus entered the Temple and began to drive out the people buying and selling animals for sacrifices. He knocked over the tables of the money changers and the chairs of those selling doves, ¹⁶and he stopped everyone from using the Temple as a marketplace.* ¹⁷He said to them, "The Scriptures declare, 'My Temple will be called a house of prayer for all nations,' but you have turned it into a den of thieves."*

¹⁸When the leading priests and teachers of religious law heard what Jesus had done, they began planning how to kill him. But they were afraid of him because the people were so amazed at his teaching.

¹⁹That evening Jesus and the disciples left* the city.

²⁰The next morning as they passed by the fig tree he had cursed, the disciples noticed it had withered from the roots up. ²¹Peter remembered what Jesus had said to the tree on the previous day and exclaimed, "Look, Rabbi! The fig tree you cursed has withered and died!"

²²Then Jesus said to the disciples, "Have faith in God. ²³I tell you the truth, you can say to this mountain, 'May you be lifted up and thrown into the sea,' and it will happen. But you must really believe it will happen and have no doubt in your heart. ²⁴I tell you, you can pray for anything, and if you believe that you've received it, it will be yours. ²⁵But when you are praying, first forgive anyone you are holding a grudge against, so that your Father in heaven will forgive your sins, too.*"

The Authority of Jesus Challenged

²⁷Again they entered Jerusalem. As Jesus was walking through the Temple area, the leading priests, the teachers of religious law, and the elders came up to him. ²⁸They demanded, "By what authority are you doing all these things? Who gave you the right to do them?"

²⁹"I'll tell you by what authority I do these things if you answer one question," Jesus replied. ³⁰"Did John's authority to baptize come from heaven, or was it merely human? Answer me!"

³¹They talked it over among themselves. "If we say it was from heaven, he will ask why we didn't believe John. ³²But do we

11:9 Greek Hosanna, an exclamation of praise that literally means "save now"; also in 11:10.   11:9-10 Pss 118:25-26; 148:1.   11:16 Or from carrying merchandise through the Temple.   11:17 Isa 56:7; Jer 7:11.   11:19 Greek they left; other manuscripts read he left.   11:25 Some manuscripts add verse 26, But if you refuse to forgive, your Father in heaven will not forgive your sins. Compare Matt 6:15.

Throwing Away Resentment
MARK 11:25

What did Jesus mean by forgiveness? What, exactly, does he expect us to do in response to his challenge to forgive if we have anything against anyone (Mark 11:25)?

Three Greek words are usually translated as *forgive*. One speaks about having an attitude of mercy or love (as in Ephesians 4:32: being tenderhearted and forgiving one another). Another word describes the cancellation of an obligation (as in Luke 6:37: forgive and you will be forgiven). But the word Jesus uses in Mark 11 is the most common and the most vigorous New Testament word for forgiveness. Literally it means "to release, to hurl away, to free yourself from something." The Jews of Jesus' day picked up this term to describe what happened in the Law when sacrifices were offered in the temple to cover the sins of God's people. Jesus uses this word to describe the obligation of his disciples when anyone has wronged them.

To forgive, as Jesus intended the word, means willingly to throw away our resentment at being wronged. This entails not just containing or restraining our resentment, but letting go of it entirely so we can be truly free of its influence.

—*Allen C. Gueizo*

For more on forgiveness, see reading at Luke 17:1-10.

---

dare say it was merely human?" For they were afraid of what the people would do, because everyone believed that John was a prophet. [33] So they finally replied, "We don't know."

And Jesus responded, "Then I won't tell you by what authority I do these things."

12 Parable of the Evil Farmers

Then Jesus began teaching them with stories: "A man planted a vineyard. He built a wall around it, dug a pit for pressing out the grape juice, and built a lookout tower. Then he leased the vineyard to tenant farmers and moved to another country. [2] At the time of the grape harvest, he sent one of his servants to collect his share of the crop. [3] But the farmers grabbed the servant, beat him up, and sent him back empty-handed. [4] The owner then sent another servant, but they insulted him and beat him over the head. [5] The next servant he sent was killed. Others he sent were either beaten or killed, [6] until there was only one left—his son

whom he loved dearly. The owner finally sent him, thinking, 'Surely they will respect my son.'

[7] "But the tenant farmers said to one another, 'Here comes the heir to this estate. Let's kill him and get the estate for ourselves!' [8] So they grabbed him and murdered him and threw his body out of the vineyard.

[9] "What do you suppose the owner of the vineyard will do?" Jesus asked. "I'll tell you—he will come and kill those farmers and lease the vineyard to others. [10] Didn't you ever read this in the Scriptures?

'The stone that the builders rejected
    has now become the cornerstone.
[11] This is the LORD's doing,
    and it is wonderful to see.'*"

[12] The religious leaders* wanted to arrest Jesus because they realized he was telling the story against them—they were the wicked farmers. But they were afraid of the crowd, so they left him and went away.

12:10-11 Ps 118:22-23. **12:12** Greek *They*.

Taxes for Caesar

¹³ Later the leaders sent some Pharisees and supporters of Herod to trap Jesus into saying something for which he could be arrested. ¹⁴ "Teacher," they said, "we know how honest you are. You are impartial and don't play favorites. You teach the way of God truthfully. Now tell us—is it right to pay taxes to Caesar or not? ¹⁵ Should we pay them, or shouldn't we?"

Jesus saw through their hypocrisy and said, "Why are you trying to trap me? Show me a Roman coin,* and I'll tell you." ¹⁶ When they handed it to him, he asked, "Whose picture and title are stamped on it?"

"Caesar's," they replied.

¹⁷ "Well, then," Jesus said, "give to Caesar what belongs to Caesar, and give to God what belongs to God."

His reply completely amazed them.

Discussion about Resurrection

¹⁸ Then Jesus was approached by some Sadducees—religious leaders who say there is no resurrection from the dead. They posed this question: ¹⁹ "Teacher, Moses gave us a law that if a man dies, leaving a wife without children, his brother should marry the widow and have a child who will carry on the brother's name.* ²⁰ Well, suppose there were seven brothers. The oldest one married and then died without children. ²¹ So the second brother married the widow, but he also died without children. Then the third brother married her. ²² This continued with all seven of them, and still there were no children. Last of all, the woman also died. ²³ So tell us, whose wife will she be in the resurrection? For all seven were married to her."

²⁴ Jesus replied, "Your mistake is that you don't know the Scriptures, and you don't know the power of God. ²⁵ For when the dead rise, they will neither marry nor be given in marriage. In this respect they will be like the angels in heaven.

²⁶ "But now, as to whether the dead will be raised—haven't you ever read about this in the writings of Moses, in the story of the burning bush? Long after Abraham, Isaac, and Jacob had died, God said to Moses,* 'I am the God of Abraham, the God of Isaac, and the God of Jacob.'* ²⁷ So he is the God of the living, not the dead. You have made a serious error."

The Most Important Commandment

²⁸ One of the teachers of religious law was standing there listening to the debate. He realized that Jesus had answered well, so he asked, "Of all the commandments, which is the most important?"

²⁹ Jesus replied, "The most important commandment is this: 'Listen, O Israel! The LORD our God is the one and only LORD. ³⁰ And you must love the LORD your God with all your heart, all your soul, all your mind, and all your strength.'* ³¹ The second is equally important: 'Love your neighbor as yourself.'* No other commandment is greater than these."

³² The teacher of religious law replied, "Well said, Teacher. You have spoken the truth by saying that there is only one God and no other. ³³ And I know it is important to love him with all my heart and all my understanding and all my strength, and to love my neighbor as myself. This is more important than to offer all of the burnt offerings and sacrifices required in the law."

³⁴ Realizing how much the man understood, Jesus said to him, "You are not far from the Kingdom of God." And after that, no one dared to ask him any more questions.

Whose Son Is the Messiah?

³⁵ Later, as Jesus was teaching the people in the Temple, he asked, "Why do the teachers of religious law claim that the Messiah is the son of David? ³⁶ For David himself, speaking under the inspiration of the Holy Spirit, said,

'The LORD said to my Lord,
Sit in the place of honor at my right
    hand
    until I humble your enemies beneath
        your feet.'*

³⁷ Since David himself called the Messiah 'my Lord,' how can the Messiah be his son?" The large crowd listened to him with great delight.

12:15 Greek a denarius.   12:19 See Deut 25:5-6.   12:26a Greek in the story of the bush? God said to him.   12:26b Exod 3:6.   12:29-30 Deut 6:4-5.   12:31 Lev 19:18.   12:36 Ps 110:1.

³⁸ Jesus also taught: "Beware of these teachers of religious law! For they like to parade around in flowing robes and receive respectful greetings as they walk in the marketplaces. ³⁹ And how they love the seats of honor in the synagogues and the head table at banquets. ⁴⁰ Yet they shamelessly cheat widows out of their property and then pretend to be pious by making long prayers in public. Because of this, they will be more severely punished."

The Widow's Offering

⁴¹ Jesus sat down near the collection box in the Temple and watched as the crowds dropped in their money. Many rich people put in large amounts. ⁴² Then a poor widow came and dropped in two small coins.*

⁴³ Jesus called his disciples to him and said, "I tell you the truth, this poor widow has given more than all the others who are making contributions. ⁴⁴ For they gave a tiny part of their surplus, but she, poor

A Poor Widow:
Giving All to God
MARK 12:41-44

When Jesus sat in the outer court of the temple with his disciples and watched the crowd putting their money into the collection box, he found the environment rich for teaching about faith, trust, and stewardship (Mark 12:41-44). Jesus observed people putting in both large and small sums of money. But it was one poor widow who caught his eye. After her meager gift—equivalent to pocket change—he declared that her offering was great because it came out of poverty. Jesus recognized that she gave "everything she had to live on" (12:44)—she gave her *all*.

Just before he observed this widow, Jesus was debating the teachers of the Law on the greatest commandment, and spoke about what it means to offer God everything. Love the Lord with *all* of yourself, Jesus taught. With all of the heart, the soul, the mind, the strength (Mark 12:29-31).

The poor widow was living an active expression of that "all." A rich man may give mountains compared to this poor woman. But when she gave all—as small as that might be to the world—she actually gave *more*. She showed us that it takes sacrifice to give much, but it takes absolute trust in God's provision to give all.

How often do I look for ways to give "enough" rather than opportunities to give "all"? The kind of radical faith in action that this widow displayed is a picture of what it truly means to give generously and sacrificially. When God asks us to give, it's not out of his need, but out of ours. Giving is a tangible way we express the truth that all we have comes from God's hand. Giving is an active expression of trust.

Our *all* isn't calculated in comparison to others; it's not about how much they give or how much we have compared to someone else. Rather, giving our *all* is an expression of our hearts. Perhaps the example of the widow came to mind when C. S. Lewis wrote in *Mere Christianity*: "I am afraid the only safe rule is to give more than we can spare."

—*Nicole Unice*

For more on stewardship, see reading at 2 Corinthians 8:2-4.

12:42 Greek *two lepta, which is a kodrantes* [i.e., a quadrans].

as she is, has given everything she had to live on."

13 Jesus Foretells the Future

As Jesus was leaving the Temple that day, one of his disciples said, "Teacher, look at these magnificent buildings! Look at the impressive stones in the walls."

² Jesus replied, "Yes, look at these great buildings. But they will be completely demolished. Not one stone will be left on top of another!"

³ Later, Jesus sat on the Mount of Olives across the valley from the Temple. Peter, James, John, and Andrew came to him privately and asked him, ⁴ "Tell us, when will all this happen? What sign will show us that these things are about to be fulfilled?"

⁵ Jesus replied, "Don't let anyone mislead you, ⁶ for many will come in my name, claiming, 'I am the Messiah.'* They will deceive many. ⁷ And you will hear of wars and threats of wars, but don't panic. Yes, these things must take place, but the end won't follow immediately. ⁸ Nation will go to war against nation, and kingdom against kingdom. There will be earthquakes in many parts of the world, as well as famines. But this is only the first of the birth pains, with more to come.

⁹ "When these things begin to happen, watch out! You will be handed over to the local councils and beaten in the synagogues. You will stand trial before governors and kings because you are my followers. But this will be your opportunity to tell them about me.* ¹⁰ For the Good News must first be preached to all nations.* ¹¹ But when you are arrested and stand trial, don't worry in advance about what to say. Just say what God tells you at that time, for it is not you who will be speaking, but the Holy Spirit.

¹² "A brother will betray his brother to death, a father will betray his own child, and children will rebel against their parents and cause them to be killed. ¹³ And everyone will hate you because you are my followers.* But the one who endures to the end will be saved.

¹⁴ "The day is coming when you will see the sacrilegious object that causes desecration* standing where he* should not be." (Reader, pay attention!) "Then those in Judea must flee to the hills. ¹⁵ A person out on the deck of a roof must not go down into the house to pack. ¹⁶ A person out in the field must not return even to get a coat. ¹⁷ How terrible it will be for pregnant women and for nursing mothers in those days. ¹⁸ And pray that your flight will not be in winter. ¹⁹ For there will be greater anguish in those days than at any time since God created the world. And it will never be so great again. ²⁰ In fact, unless the Lord shortens that time of calamity, not a single person will survive. But for the sake of his chosen ones he has shortened those days.

²¹ "Then if anyone tells you, 'Look, here is the Messiah,' or 'There he is,' don't believe it. ²² For false messiahs and false prophets will rise up and perform signs and wonders so as to deceive, if possible, even God's chosen ones. ²³ Watch out! I have warned you about this ahead of time!

²⁴ "At that time, after the anguish of those days,

the sun will be darkened,
the moon will give no light,
²⁵ the stars will fall from the sky,
and the powers in the heavens will be shaken.*

²⁶ Then everyone will see the Son of Man* coming on the clouds with great power and glory.* ²⁷ And he will send out his angels to gather his chosen ones from all over the world*—from the farthest ends of the earth and heaven.

²⁸ "Now learn a lesson from the fig tree. When its branches bud and its leaves begin to sprout, you know that summer is near. ²⁹ In the same way, when you see all these things taking place, you can know that his return is very near, right at the door. ³⁰ I tell you the truth, this generation* will not pass from the scene before all these things take place. ³¹ Heaven and earth will disappear, but my words will never disappear.

³² "However, no one knows the day or hour when these things will happen, not

13:6 Greek claiming, 'I am.' 13:9 Or But this will be your testimony against them. 13:10 Or all peoples. 13:13 Greek on account of my name. 13:14a Greek the abomination of desolation. See Dan 9:27; 11:31; 12:11. 13:14b Or it. 13:24-25 See Isa 13:10; 34:4; Joel 2:10. 13:26a "Son of Man" is a title Jesus used for himself. 13:26b See Dan 7:13. 13:27 Greek from the four winds. 13:30 Or this age, or this nation.

even the angels in heaven or the Son himself. Only the Father knows. ³³And since you don't know when that time will come, be on guard! Stay alert*!

³⁴"The coming of the Son of Man can be illustrated by the story of a man going on a long trip. When he left home, he gave each of his slaves instructions about the work they were to do, and he told the gatekeeper to watch for his return. ³⁵You, too, must keep watch! For you don't know when the master of the household will return—in the evening, at midnight, before dawn, or at daybreak. ³⁶Don't let him find you sleeping when he arrives without warning. ³⁷I say to you what I say to everyone: Watch for him!"

14 Jesus Anointed at Bethany

It was now two days before Passover and the Festival of Unleavened Bread. The leading priests and the teachers of religious law were still looking for an opportunity to capture Jesus secretly and kill him. ²"But not during the Passover celebration," they agreed, "or the people may riot."

³Meanwhile, Jesus was in Bethany at the home of Simon, a man who had previously had leprosy. While he was eating,* a woman came in with a beautiful alabaster jar of expensive perfume made from essence of nard. She broke open the jar and poured the perfume over his head.

⁴Some of those at the table were indignant. "Why waste such expensive perfume?" they asked. ⁵"It could have been sold for a year's wages* and the money given to the poor!" So they scolded her harshly.

⁶But Jesus replied, "Leave her alone. Why criticize her for doing such a good thing to me? ⁷You will always have the poor among you, and you can help them whenever you want to. But you will not always have me. ⁸She has done what she could and has anointed my body for burial ahead of time. ⁹I tell you the truth, wherever the Good News is preached throughout the world, this woman's deed will be remembered and discussed."

Judas Agrees to Betray Jesus

¹⁰Then Judas Iscariot, one of the twelve disciples, went to the leading priests to arrange to betray Jesus to them. ¹¹They were delighted when they heard why he had come, and they promised to give him money. So he began looking for an opportunity to betray Jesus.

The Last Supper

¹²On the first day of the Festival of Unleavened Bread, when the Passover lamb is sacrificed, Jesus' disciples asked him, "Where do you want us to go to prepare the Passover meal for you?"

¹³So Jesus sent two of them into Jerusalem with these instructions: "As you go into the city, a man carrying a pitcher of water will meet you. Follow him. ¹⁴At the house he enters, say to the owner, 'The Teacher asks: Where is the guest room where I can eat the Passover meal with my disciples?' ¹⁵He will take you upstairs to a large room that is already set up. That is where you should prepare our meal." ¹⁶So the two disciples went into the city and found everything just as Jesus had said, and they prepared the Passover meal there.

¹⁷In the evening Jesus arrived with the twelve disciples.* ¹⁸As they were at the table* eating, Jesus said, "I tell you the truth, one of you eating with me here will betray me."

¹⁹Greatly distressed, each one asked in turn, "Am I the one?"

²⁰He replied, "It is one of you twelve who is eating from this bowl with me. ²¹For the Son of Man* must die, as the Scriptures declared long ago. But how terrible it will be for the one who betrays him. It would be far better for that man if he had never been born!"

²²As they were eating, Jesus took some bread and blessed it. Then he broke it in pieces and gave it to the disciples, saying, "Take it, for this is my body."

²³And he took a cup of wine and gave thanks to God for it. He gave it to them, and they all drank from it. ²⁴And he said to them, "This is my blood, which confirms the covenant* between God and his people. It is poured out as a sacrifice for many. ²⁵I tell you the truth, I will not drink wine again until the day I drink it new in the Kingdom of God."

13:33 Some manuscripts add *and pray.* **14:3** Or *reclining.* **14:5** Greek *for 300 denarii. A denarius was equivalent to a laborer's full day's wage.* **14:17** Greek *the Twelve.* **14:18** Or *As they reclined.* **14:21** "Son of Man" is a title Jesus used for himself. **14:24** Some manuscripts read *the new covenant.*

Dark Solitude

MARK 14:32–42

Solitude

I have a friend who simply cannot be alone. She spends plenty of time on her own, but she avoids being truly alone for more than a few hours at a time. It is, she says, simply more than she can bear.

Like so many of us, my friend has issues in her life she doesn't want to think about. It's not so much that she ignores them—she is well aware of them—but she finds that when she's alone for too long, the pain of those issues moves from a low-grade simmer to a full-on boil. And she doesn't like it.

For some of us, solitude can be more than uncomfortable; it can be searingly painful. Cecil Murphey describes such an experience when, during a routine morning run, "sadness came over me—a deep, depressive melancholy. The tears began to flow and I couldn't figure out why. I was sobbing." As he ran his mind flooded with agonizing memories of physical and sexual abuse. "I had never experienced such inner pain," he writes in *When a Man You Love Was Abused*. Solitude magnified his anguish, shining a bright light on dark scenes from his life.

Jesus too waded through a period of painful solitude. As he faced the Cross— the physical and spiritual pain he knew he was about to bear—he wrestled with agony, fear, and temptation. He was "deeply troubled and distressed," and he told his closest friends, "My soul is crushed with grief to the point of death" (Mark 14:33–34). Yet he still pressed on into solitude so that he could be alone with his Father.

Busyness, noisiness, crowdedness—all of these help us avoid inner struggles, tuck away hidden pain, turn down the volume on inner cries. But theses noises and distractions also push aside the healing work God longs to do in us, work that can sometimes only take place in our solitude, even when it's painful. Jesus, who also experienced anguish in solitude, is with you, even as you feel "crushed with grief."

—Carla Barnhill

For more on solitude, see reading at John 6:15.

---

[26] Then they sang a hymn and went out to the Mount of Olives.

Jesus Predicts Peter's Denial

[27] On the way, Jesus told them, "All of you will desert me. For the Scriptures say,

'God will strike* the Shepherd,
    and the sheep will be scattered.'

[28] But after I am raised from the dead, I will go ahead of you to Galilee and meet you there."

[29] Peter said to him, "Even if everyone else deserts you, I never will."

[30] Jesus replied, "I tell you the truth, Peter—this very night, before the rooster crows twice, you will deny three times that you even know me."

[31] "No!" Peter declared emphatically. "Even if I have to die with you, I will never deny you!" And all the others vowed the same.

Jesus Prays in Gethsemane

[32] They went to the olive grove called Gethsemane, and Jesus said, "Sit here while I go and pray." [33] He took Peter, James, and John with him, and he became deeply troubled

---

14:27 Greek *I will strike.* Zech 13:7.

and distressed. ³⁴He told them, "My soul is crushed with grief to the point of death. Stay here and keep watch with me."

³⁵He went on a little farther and fell to the ground. He prayed that, if it were possible, the awful hour awaiting him might pass him by. ³⁶"Abba, Father,"* he cried out, "everything is possible for you. Please take this cup of suffering away from me. Yet I want your will to be done, not mine."

³⁷Then he returned and found the disciples asleep. He said to Peter, "Simon, are you asleep? Couldn't you watch with me even one hour? ³⁸Keep watch and pray, so that you will not give in to temptation. For the spirit is willing, but the body is weak."

³⁹Then Jesus left them again and prayed the same prayer as before. ⁴⁰When he returned to them again, he found them sleeping, for they couldn't keep their eyes open. And they didn't know what to say.

⁴¹When he returned to them the third time, he said, "Go ahead and sleep. Have your rest. But no—the time has come. The Son of Man is betrayed into the hands of sinners. ⁴²Up, let's be going. Look, my betrayer is here!"

Jesus Is Betrayed and Arrested

⁴³And immediately, even as Jesus said this, Judas, one of the twelve disciples, arrived with a crowd of men armed with swords and clubs. They had been sent by the leading priests, the teachers of religious law, and the elders. ⁴⁴The traitor, Judas, had given them a prearranged signal: "You will know which one to arrest when I greet him with a kiss. Then you can take him away under guard." ⁴⁵As soon as they arrived, Judas walked up to Jesus. "Rabbi!" he exclaimed, and gave him the kiss.

⁴⁶Then the others grabbed Jesus and arrested him. ⁴⁷But one of the men with Jesus pulled out his sword and struck the high priest's slave, slashing off his ear.

⁴⁸Jesus asked them, "Am I some dangerous revolutionary, that you come with swords and clubs to arrest me? ⁴⁹Why didn't you arrest me in the Temple? I was there among you teaching every day. But these things are happening to fulfill what the Scriptures say about me."

⁵⁰Then all his disciples deserted him and ran away. ⁵¹One young man following behind was clothed only in a long linen shirt. When the mob tried to grab him, ⁵²he slipped out of his shirt and ran away naked.

Jesus before the Council

⁵³They took Jesus to the high priest's home where the leading priests, the elders, and the teachers of religious law had gathered. ⁵⁴Meanwhile, Peter followed him at a distance and went right into the high priest's courtyard. There he sat with the guards, warming himself by the fire.

⁵⁵Inside, the leading priests and the entire high council* were trying to find evidence against Jesus, so they could put him to death. But they couldn't find any. ⁵⁶Many false witnesses spoke against him, but they contradicted each other. ⁵⁷Finally, some men stood up and gave this false testimony: ⁵⁸"We heard him say, 'I will destroy this Temple made with human hands, and in three days I will build another, made without human hands.'" ⁵⁹But even then they didn't get their stories straight!

⁶⁰Then the high priest stood up before the others and asked Jesus, "Well, aren't you going to answer these charges? What do you have to say for yourself?" ⁶¹But Jesus was silent and made no reply. Then the high priest asked him, "Are you the Messiah, the Son of the Blessed One?"

⁶²Jesus said, "I Am.* And you will see the Son of Man seated in the place of power at God's right hand* and coming on the clouds of heaven.*"

⁶³Then the high priest tore his clothing to show his horror and said, "Why do we need other witnesses? ⁶⁴You have all heard his blasphemy. What is your verdict?"

"Guilty!" they all cried. "He deserves to die!"

⁶⁵Then some of them began to spit at him, and they blindfolded him and beat him with his fists. "Prophesy to us," they jeered. And the guards slapped him as they took him away.

14:36 *Abba* is an Aramaic term for "father." **14:55** Greek *the Sanhedrin.* **14:62a** Or *The 'I Am' is here; or I am the LORD.* See Exod 3:14. **14:62b** Greek *at the right hand of the power.* See Ps 110:1. **14:62c** See Dan 7:13.

Peter Denies Jesus

⁶⁶Meanwhile, Peter was in the courtyard below. One of the servant girls who worked for the high priest came by ⁶⁷and noticed Peter warming himself at the fire. She looked at him closely and said, "You were one of those with Jesus of Nazareth.*"

⁶⁸But Peter denied it. "I don't know what you're talking about," he said, and he went out into the entryway. Just then, a rooster crowed.*

⁶⁹When the servant girl saw him standing there, she began telling the others, "This man is definitely one of them!" ⁷⁰But Peter denied it again.

A little later some of the other bystanders confronted Peter and said, "You must be one of them, because you are a Galilean."

⁷¹Peter swore, "A curse on me if I'm lying—I don't know this man you're talking about!" ⁷²And immediately the rooster crowed the second time.

Suddenly, Jesus' words flashed through Peter's mind: "Before the rooster crows twice, you will deny three times that you even know me." And he broke down and wept.

15 Jesus' Trial before Pilate

Very early in the morning the leading priests, the elders, and the teachers of religious law—the entire high council*— met to discuss their next step. They bound Jesus, led him away, and took him to Pilate, the Roman governor.

²Pilate asked Jesus, "Are you the king of the Jews?"

Jesus replied, "You have said it."

³Then the leading priests kept accusing him of many crimes, ⁴and Pilate asked him, "Aren't you going to answer them? What about all these charges they are bringing against you?" ⁵But Jesus said nothing, much to Pilate's surprise.

⁶Now it was the governor's custom each year during the Passover celebration to release one prisoner—anyone the people requested. ⁷One of the prisoners at that time was Barabbas, a revolutionary who had committed murder in an uprising. ⁸The crowd went to Pilate and asked him to release a prisoner as usual.

⁹"Would you like me to release to you this 'King of the Jews'?" Pilate asked. ¹⁰(For he realized by now that the leading priests had arrested Jesus out of envy.) ¹¹But at this point the leading priests stirred up the crowd to demand the release of Barabbas instead of Jesus. ¹²Pilate asked them, "Then what should I do with this man you call the king of the Jews?"

¹³They shouted back, "Crucify him!"

¹⁴"Why?" Pilate demanded. "What crime has he committed?"

But the mob roared even louder, "Crucify him!"

¹⁵So to pacify the crowd, Pilate released Barabbas to them. He ordered Jesus flogged with a lead-tipped whip, then turned him over to the Roman soldiers to be crucified.

The Soldiers Mock Jesus

¹⁶The soldiers took Jesus into the courtyard of the governor's headquarters (called the Praetorium) and called out the entire regiment. ¹⁷They dressed him in a purple robe, and they wove thorn branches into a crown and put it on his head. ¹⁸Then they saluted him and taunted, "Hail! King of the Jews!" ¹⁹And they struck him on the head with a reed stick, spit on him, and dropped to their knees in mock worship. ²⁰When they were finally tired of mocking him, they took off the purple robe and put his own clothes on him again. Then they led him away to be crucified.

The Crucifixion

²¹A passerby named Simon, who was from Cyrene,* was coming in from the countryside just then, and the soldiers forced him to carry Jesus' cross. (Simon was the father of Alexander and Rufus.) ²²And they brought Jesus to a place called Golgotha (which means "Place of the Skull"). ²³They offered him wine drugged with myrrh, but he refused it.

²⁴Then the soldiers nailed him to the cross. They divided his clothes and threw dice* to decide who would get each piece. ²⁵It was nine o'clock in the morning when they crucified him. ²⁶A sign announced the charge against him. It read, "The King of the Jews."

14:67 Or *Jesus the Nazarene.*   14:68 Some manuscripts do not include *Just then, a rooster crowed.*   15:1 Greek *the Sanhedrin;* also in 15:43.
15:21 *Cyrene* was a city in northern Africa.   15:24 Greek *cast lots.* See Ps 22:18.

27 Two revolutionaries* were crucified with him, one on his right and one on his left.*

29 The people passing by shouted abuse, shaking their heads in mockery. "Ha! Look at you now!" they yelled at him. "You said you were going to destroy the Temple and rebuild it in three days. 30 Well then, save yourself and come down from the cross!"

31 The leading priests and teachers of religious law also mocked Jesus. "He saved others," they scoffed, "but he can't save himself! 32 Let this Messiah, this King of Israel, come down from the cross so we can see it and believe him!" Even the men who were crucified with Jesus ridiculed him.

The Death of Jesus

33 At noon, darkness fell across the whole land until three o'clock. 34 Then at three o'clock Jesus called out with a loud voice, *"Eloi, Eloi, lema sabachthani?"* which means "My God, my God, why have you abandoned me?"*

35 Some of the bystanders misunderstood and thought he was calling for the prophet Elijah. 36 One of them ran and filled a sponge with sour wine, holding it up to him on a reed stick so he could drink. "Wait!" he said. "Let's see whether Elijah comes to take him down!"

37 Then Jesus uttered another loud cry and breathed his last. 38 And the curtain in the sanctuary of the Temple was torn in two, from top to bottom.

39 When the Roman officer* who stood facing him* saw how he had died, he exclaimed, "This man truly was the Son of God!"

40 Some women were there, watching from a distance, including Mary Magdalene, Mary (the mother of James the younger and of Joseph*), and Salome. 41 They had been followers of Jesus and had cared for him while he was in Galilee. Many other women who had come with him to Jerusalem were also there.

The Burial of Jesus

42 This all happened on Friday, the day of preparation,* the day before the Sabbath. As evening approached, 43 Joseph of Arimathea took a risk and went to Pilate and asked for Jesus' body. (Joseph was an honored member of the high council, and he was waiting for the Kingdom of God to come.) 44 Pilate couldn't believe that Jesus was already dead, so he called for the Roman officer and asked if he had died yet. 45 The officer confirmed that Jesus was dead, so Pilate told Joseph he could have the body. 46 Joseph bought a long sheet of linen cloth. Then he took Jesus' body down from the cross, wrapped it in the cloth, and laid it in a tomb that had been carved out of the rock. Then he rolled a stone in front of the entrance. 47 Mary Magdalene and Mary the mother of Joseph saw where Jesus' body was laid.

16 The Resurrection

Saturday evening, when the Sabbath ended, Mary Magdalene, Mary the mother of James, and Salome went out and purchased burial spices so they could anoint Jesus' body. 2 Very early on Sunday morning,* just at sunrise, they went to the tomb. 3 On the way they were asking each other, "Who will roll away the stone for us from the entrance to the tomb?" 4 But as they arrived, they looked up and saw that the stone, which was very large, had already been rolled aside.

5 When they entered the tomb, they saw a young man clothed in a white robe sitting on the right side. The women were shocked, 6 but the angel said, "Don't be alarmed. You are looking for Jesus of Nazareth,* who was crucified. He isn't here! He is risen from the dead! Look, this is where they laid his body. 7 Now go and tell his disciples, including Peter, that Jesus is going ahead of you to Galilee. You will see him there, just as he told you before he died."

8 The women fled from the tomb, trembling and bewildered, and they said nothing to anyone because they were too frightened.*

15:27a Or *Two criminals.* 15:27b Some manuscripts add verse 28, *And the Scripture was fulfilled that said, "He was counted among those who were rebels."* See Isa 53:12; also compare Luke 22:37. 15:34 Ps 22:1. 15:39a Greek *the centurion;* similarly in 15:44, 45. 15:39b Some manuscripts add *heard his cry and.* 15:40 Greek *Joses;* also in 15:47. See Matt 27:56. 15:42 Greek *It was the day of preparation.* 16:2 Greek *on the first day of the week;* also in 16:9. 16:6 Or *Jesus the Nazarene.* 16:8 The most reliable early manuscripts of the Gospel of Mark end at verse 8. Other manuscripts include various endings to the Gospel. A few include both the "shorter ending" and the "longer ending." The majority of manuscripts include the "longer ending" immediately after verse 8.

[Shorter Ending of Mark]

Then they briefly reported all this to Peter and his companions. Afterward Jesus himself sent them out from east to west with the sacred and unfailing message of salvation that gives eternal life. Amen.

[Longer Ending of Mark]

[9] After Jesus rose from the dead early on Sunday morning, the first person who saw him was Mary Magdalene, the woman from whom he had cast out seven demons. [10] She went to the disciples, who were grieving and weeping, and told them what had happened. [11] But when she told them that Jesus was alive and she had seen him, they didn't believe her.

[12] Afterward he appeared in a different form to two of his followers who were walking from Jerusalem into the country. [13] They rushed back to tell the others, but no one believed them.

[14] Still later he appeared to the eleven disciples as they were eating together. He rebuked them for their stubborn unbelief because they refused to believe those who had seen him after he had been raised from the dead.*

[15] And then he told them, "Go into all the world and preach the Good News to everyone. [16] Anyone who believes and is baptized will be saved. But anyone who refuses to believe will be condemned. [17] These miraculous signs will accompany those who believe: They will cast out demons in my name, and they will speak in new languages.* [18] They will be able to handle snakes with safety, and if they drink anything poisonous, it won't hurt them. They will be able to place their hands on the sick, and they will be healed."

[19] When the Lord Jesus had finished talking with them, he was taken up into heaven and sat down in the place of honor at God's right hand. [20] And the disciples went everywhere and preached, and the Lord worked through them, confirming what they said by many miraculous signs.

16:14 Some early manuscripts add: *And they excused themselves, saying, "This age of lawlessness and unbelief is under Satan, who does not permit God's truth and power to conquer the evil [unclean] spirits. Therefore, reveal your justice now." This is what they said to Christ. And Christ replied to them, "The period of years of Satan's power has been fulfilled, but other dreadful things will happen soon. And I was handed over to death for those who have sinned, so that they may return to the truth and sin no more, and so they may inherit the spiritual, incorruptible, and righteous glory in heaven."* **16:17** Or *new tongues;* some manuscripts do not include *new.*

Introduction to

Luke

Background

Luke, the gospel writer, was a physician, and the only Gentile contributor to the New Testament. Luke translates many Aramaic terms into their Greek equivalents and explains Jewish customs and geography to make Jesus more understandable to his Greek audience. Luke was also a faithful traveling companion of Paul. Paul refers to him as "Luke, the beloved doctor" (Colossians 4:14).

Luke was not an eyewitness to the events of Jesus' life. Yet being a careful historian, he used eyewitness testimony to record his gospel. The Book of Acts, also written by Luke, is a continuation of the gospel account. Both books are addressed to Theophilus, a name that means "lover of God."

Message

A skilled storyteller, Luke penned the most complete account of Jesus' ancestry, birth, life, death, and resurrection. His genealogical account goes back to Adam, emphasizing Jesus' connection to the whole human race. Luke refers to Jesus as the Son of Man, a title used by the prophet Ezekiel. Only Luke's gospel contains the birth narratives of John the Baptist and Jesus.

The reading of Isaiah 61:1–2 (4:18–19) signals Jesus' fulfillment of that prophecy and the start of his public ministry. Luke presents Jesus as someone interested in the physical and spiritual needs of the poor, the grieving, the lost, and the sick; as a physician Luke includes details of Jesus' healing miracles. Many of his stories feature women, with their needs presented in a sympathetic light. Luke emphasizes Jesus' reliance on prayer and the work of the Holy Spirit. The book that started with gladsome birth announcements ends with the disciples worshiping "with great joy" (24:52) awaiting Pentecost.

Time

Luke's gospel was probably written in the early A.D. 60s. Having been with Paul during his Roman imprisonment (2 Timothy 4:11), Luke may have traveled to Palestine to gather information from eyewitnesses of Jesus' ministry.

Outline

Luke

1 Introduction

Many people have set out to write accounts about the events that have been fulfilled among us. ²They used the eyewitness reports circulating among us from the early disciples.* ³Having carefully investigated everything from the beginning, I also have decided to write a careful account for you, most honorable Theophilus, ⁴so you can be certain of the truth of everything you were taught.

The Birth of John the Baptist Foretold

⁵When Herod was king of Judea, there was a Jewish priest named Zechariah. He was a member of the priestly order of Abijah, and his wife, Elizabeth, was also from the priestly line of Aaron. ⁶Zechariah and Elizabeth were righteous in God's eyes, careful to obey all of the Lord's commandments and regulations. ⁷They had no children because Elizabeth was unable to conceive, and they were both very old.

⁸One day Zechariah was serving God in the Temple, for his order was on duty that week. ⁹As was the custom of the priests, he was chosen by lot to enter the sanctuary of the Lord and burn incense. ¹⁰While the incense was being burned, a great crowd stood outside, praying.

¹¹While Zechariah was in the sanctuary, an angel of the Lord appeared to him, standing to the right of the incense altar. ¹²Zechariah was shaken and overwhelmed with fear when he saw him. ¹³But the angel said, "Don't be afraid, Zechariah! God has heard your prayer. Your wife, Elizabeth, will give you a son, and you are to name him John. ¹⁴You will have great joy and gladness, and many will rejoice at his birth, ¹⁵for he will be great in the eyes of the Lord. He must never touch wine or other alcoholic drinks. He will be filled with the Holy Spirit, even before his birth.* ¹⁶And he will turn many Israelites to the Lord their God. ¹⁷He will be a man with the spirit and power of Elijah. He will prepare the people for the coming of the Lord. He will turn the hearts of the fathers to their children,* and he will cause those who are rebellious to accept the wisdom of the godly."

¹⁸Zechariah said to the angel, "How can I be sure this will happen? I'm an old man now, and my wife is also well along in years."

¹⁹Then the angel said, "I am Gabriel! I stand in the very presence of God. It was he who sent me to bring you this good news! ²⁰But now, since you didn't believe what I said, you will be silent and unable to speak until the child is born. For my words will certainly be fulfilled at the proper time."

²¹Meanwhile, the people were waiting for Zechariah to come out of the sanctuary, wondering why he was taking so long. ²²When he finally did come out, he couldn't speak to them. Then they realized from his gestures and his silence that he must have seen a vision in the sanctuary.

²³When Zechariah's week of service in the Temple was over, he returned home. ²⁴Soon afterward his wife, Elizabeth, became pregnant and went into seclusion for five months. ²⁵"How kind the Lord is!" she exclaimed. "He has

---

1:2 Greek *from those who from the beginning were servants of the word.* **1:15** Or *even from birth.* **1:17** See Mal 4:5-6.

taken away my disgrace of having no children."

The Birth of Jesus Foretold

26 In the sixth month of Elizabeth's pregnancy, God sent the angel Gabriel to Nazareth, a village in Galilee, 27 to a virgin named Mary. She was engaged to be married to a man named Joseph, a descendant of King David. 28 Gabriel appeared to her and said, "Greetings, favored woman! The Lord is with you!*"

29 Confused and disturbed, Mary tried to think what the angel could mean. 30 "Don't be afraid, Mary," the angel told her, "for you have found favor with God! 31 You will conceive and give birth to a son, and you will name him Jesus. 32 He will be very great and will be called the Son of the Most High. The Lord God will give him the throne of his ancestor David. 33 And he will reign over Israel* forever; his Kingdom will never end!"

34 Mary asked the angel, "But how can this happen? I am a virgin."

Mary: Yes to Shame and Glory
LUKE 1:26-38

Mary's life was forever changed as she said yes to God's stunning decision that she was to carry, give birth to, and parent the Son of God. Her submission to God's plan would bring hope and joy to her life, but there was as much pain as there was promise in that moment when Mary said her unmistakable yes and became a mother-to-be.

Mary said yes without knowing all that parenthood would involve, but with trust that God knew, and that he was the Parent who loved her. Mary's calling was to bear not only her own pain but her son's, feeling his anguish as intensely as all mothers before or since have felt with their children.

When Mary and Joseph presented their new infant son in the Jerusalem temple, elderly Simeon spoke prophetic words about Jesus, then turned to fix his piercing eyes on Mary. He uttered words of foreboding: "a sword will pierce your very soul" (Luke 2:35). With his soul's eyes, Simeon saw the link between Christ's rejection and Mary's own anguish, and from then on, the sword of his remembered words pierced and penetrated her.

We can only imagine Mary's agony when she stood at the foot of the cross and watched Jesus suffer and die (John 19:25-27). "I am the Lord's servant" (Luke 1:38), that long-ago surrender, seems easy compared with this silent, "Lord, here is my son."

Mary learned one of the lessons I am just beginning to understand—that pain is a fire that purges; that it works in us what no amount of pleasure can accomplish; that it is best not to dodge pain but to let it hurt, and to live through it to the other side. To submit, in obedience, to God's call—even the call to suffer.

May we learn from Mary the courage to say yes to God, especially as we are faced with challenges that seem impossible, outrageous, or that lead us down a path of purging pain.

—Luci Shaw

For more on submission, see reading at Romans 13:1-6.

1:28 Some manuscripts add *Blessed are you among women.*   **1:33** Greek *over the house of Jacob.*

[35] The angel replied, "The Holy Spirit will come upon you, and the power of the Most High will overshadow you. So the baby to be born will be holy, and he will be called the Son of God. [36] What's more, your relative Elizabeth has become pregnant in her old age! People used to say she was barren, but she has conceived a son and is now in her sixth month. [37] For nothing is impossible with God.*"

[38] Mary responded, "I am the Lord's servant. May everything you have said about me come true." And then the angel left her.

Mary Visits Elizabeth

[39] A few days later Mary hurried to the hill country of Judea, to the town [40] where Zechariah lived. She entered the house and greeted Elizabeth. [41] At the sound of Mary's greeting, Elizabeth's child leaped within her, and Elizabeth was filled with the Holy Spirit.

[42] Elizabeth gave a glad cry and exclaimed to Mary, "God has blessed you above all women, and your child is blessed. [43] Why am I so honored, that the mother of my Lord should visit me? [44] When I heard your greeting, the baby in my womb jumped for joy. [45] You are blessed because you believed that the Lord would do what he said."

The Magnificat: Mary's Song of Praise

[46] Mary responded,

"Oh, how my soul praises the Lord.
[47]   How my spirit rejoices in God my
            Savior!
[48] For he took notice of his lowly servant
            girl,
        and from now on all generations will
            call me blessed.
[49] For the Mighty One is holy,
        and he has done great things for me.
[50] He shows mercy from generation to
            generation
        to all who fear him.
[51] His mighty arm has done tremendous
            things!
        He has scattered the proud and
            haughty ones.
[52] He has brought down princes from their
            thrones
        and exalted the humble.

[53] He has filled the hungry with good
            things
        and sent the rich away with empty
            hands.
[54] He has helped his servant Israel
        and remembered to be merciful.
[55] For he made this promise to our
            ancestors,
        to Abraham and his children
            forever."

[56] Mary stayed with Elizabeth about three months and then went back to her own home.

The Birth of John the Baptist

[57] When it was time for Elizabeth's baby to be born, she gave birth to a son. [58] And when her neighbors and relatives heard that the Lord had been very merciful to her, everyone rejoiced with her.

[59] When the baby was eight days old, they all came for the circumcision ceremony. They wanted to name him Zechariah, after his father. [60] But Elizabeth said, "No! His name is John!"

[61] "What?" they exclaimed. "There is no one in all your family by that name." [62] So they used gestures to ask the baby's father what he wanted to name him. [63] He motioned for a writing tablet, and to everyone's surprise he wrote, "His name is John." [64] Instantly Zechariah could speak again, and he began praising God.

[65] Awe fell upon the whole neighborhood, and the news of what had happened spread throughout the Judean hills. [66] Everyone who heard about it reflected on these events and asked, "What will this child turn out to be?" For the hand of the Lord was surely upon him in a special way.

Zechariah's Prophecy

[67] Then his father, Zechariah, was filled with the Holy Spirit and gave this prophecy:

[68] "Praise the Lord, the God of
            Israel,
        because he has visited and redeemed
            his people.
[69] He has sent us a mighty Savior*
        from the royal line of his servant
            David,

1:37 Some manuscripts read *For the word of God will never fail.*   **1:69** Greek *has raised up a horn of salvation for us.*

70 just as he promised
through his holy prophets long ago.
71 Now we will be saved from our enemies
and from all who hate us.
72 He has been merciful to our ancestors
by remembering his sacred
covenant—
73 the covenant he swore with an oath
to our ancestor Abraham.
74 We have been rescued from our enemies
so we can serve God without fear,
75 in holiness and righteousness
for as long as we live.

76 "And you, my little son,
will be called the prophet of the Most
High,
because you will prepare the way for
the Lord.
77 You will tell his people how to find
salvation
through forgiveness of their sins.
78 Because of God's tender mercy,
the morning light from heaven is
about to break upon us,*
79 to give light to those who sit in darkness
and in the shadow of death,
and to guide us to the path of peace."

80 John grew up and became strong in spirit. And he lived in the wilderness until he began his public ministry to Israel.

2 The Birth of Jesus

At that time the Roman emperor, Augustus, decreed that a census should be taken throughout the Roman Empire. 2 (This was the first census taken when Quirinius was governor of Syria.) 3 All returned to their own ancestral towns to register for this census. 4 And because Joseph was a descendant of King David, he had to go to Bethlehem in Judea, David's ancient home. He traveled there from the village of Nazareth in Galilee. 5 He took with him Mary, his fiancée, who was now obviously pregnant.

6 And while they were there, the time came for her baby to be born. 7 She gave birth to her first child, a son. She wrapped him snugly in strips of cloth and laid him in a manger, because there was no lodging available for them.

The Shepherds and Angels

8 That night there were shepherds staying in the fields nearby, guarding their flocks of sheep. 9 Suddenly, an angel of the Lord appeared among them, and the radiance of the Lord's glory surrounded them. They were terrified, 10 but the angel reassured them. "Don't be afraid!" he said. "I bring you good news that will bring great joy to all people. 11 The Savior—yes, the Messiah, the Lord—has been born today in Bethlehem, the city of David! 12 And you will recognize him by this sign: You will find a baby wrapped snugly in strips of cloth, lying in a manger."

13 Suddenly, the angel was joined by a vast host of others—the armies of heaven—praising God and saying,

14 "Glory to God in highest heaven,
and peace on earth to those with
whom God is pleased."

15 When the angels had returned to heaven, the shepherds said to each other, "Let's go to Bethlehem! Let's see this thing that has happened, which the Lord has told us about."

16 They hurried to the village and found Mary and Joseph. And there was the baby, lying in the manger. 17 After seeing him, the shepherds told everyone what had happened and what the angel had said to them about this child. 18 All who heard the shepherds' story were astonished, 19 but Mary kept all these things in her heart and thought about them often. 20 The shepherds went back to their flocks, glorifying and praising God for all they had heard and seen. It was just as the angel had told them.

Jesus Is Presented in the Temple

21 Eight days later, when the baby was circumcised, he was named Jesus, the name given him by the angel even before he was conceived.

22 Then it was time for their purification offering, as required by the law of Moses after the birth of a child; so his parents took him to Jerusalem to present him to the Lord. 23 The law of the Lord says, "If a woman's first child is a boy, he must be ded-

---

1:78 Or the Morning Light from Heaven is about to visit us.

"He is a voice shouting in the wilderness,
'Prepare the way for the LORD's coming!
Clear the road for him!
[5] The valleys will be filled,
and the mountains and hills made
level.
The curves will be straightened,
and the rough places made smooth.
[6] And then all people will see
the salvation sent from God.'"*

[7] When the crowds came to John for baptism, he said, "You brood of snakes! Who warned you to flee God's coming wrath? [8] Prove by the way you live that you have repented of your sins and turned to God. Don't just say to each other, 'We're safe, for we are descendants of Abraham.' That means nothing, for I tell you, God can create children of Abraham from these very stones. [9] Even now the ax of God's judgment is poised, ready to sever the roots of the trees. Yes, every tree that does not produce good fruit will be chopped down and thrown into the fire."

[10] The crowds asked, "What should we do?"

[11] John replied, "If you have two shirts, give one to the poor. If you have food, share it with those who are hungry."

[12] Even corrupt tax collectors came to be baptized and asked, "Teacher, what should we do?"

[13] He replied, "Collect no more taxes than the government requires."

[14] "What should we do?" asked some soldiers.

John replied, "Don't extort money or make false accusations. And be content with your pay."

[15] Everyone was expecting the Messiah to come soon, and they were eager to know whether John might be the Messiah. [16] John answered their questions by saying, "I baptize you with* water; but someone is coming soon who is greater than I am—so much greater that I'm not even worthy to be his slave and untie the straps of his sandals. He will baptize you with the Holy Spirit and with fire.* [17] He is ready to separate the chaff from the wheat with his winnowing fork. Then he will clean up the threshing area,

gathering the wheat into his barn but burning the chaff with never-ending fire." [18] John used many such warnings as he announced the Good News to the people.

[19] John also publicly criticized Herod Antipas, the ruler of Galilee,* for marrying Herodias, his brother's wife, and for many other wrongs he had done. [20] So Herod put John in prison, adding this sin to his many others.

The Baptism of Jesus

[21] One day when the crowds were being baptized, Jesus himself was baptized. As he was praying, the heavens opened, [22] and the Holy Spirit, in bodily form, descended on him like a dove. And a voice from heaven said, "You are my dearly loved Son, and you bring me great joy.*"

The Ancestors of Jesus

[23] Jesus was about thirty years old when he began his public ministry.

Jesus was known as the son of Joseph.
Joseph was the son of Heli.
[24] Heli was the son of Matthat.
Matthat was the son of Levi.
Levi was the son of Melki.
Melki was the son of Jannai.
Jannai was the son of Joseph.
[25] Joseph was the son of Mattathias.
Mattathias was the son of Amos.
Amos was the son of Nahum.
Nahum was the son of Esli.
Esli was the son of Naggai.
[26] Naggai was the son of Maath.
Maath was the son of Mattathias.
Mattathias was the son of Semein.
Semein was the son of Josech.
Josech was the son of Joda.
[27] Joda was the son of Joanan.
Joanan was the son of Rhesa.
Rhesa was the son of Zerubbabel.
Zerubbabel was the son of Shealtiel.
Shealtiel was the son of Neri.
[28] Neri was the son of Melki.
Melki was the son of Addi.
Addi was the son of Cosam.
Cosam was the son of Elmadam.
Elmadam was the son of Er.

3:4-6 Isa 40:3-5 (Greek version). 3:16a Or in. 3:16b Or in the Holy Spirit and in fire. 3:19 Greek Herod the tetrarch. 3:22 Some manuscripts read my Son, and today I have become your Father.

²⁹ Er was the son of Joshua.
Joshua was the son of Eliezer.
Eliezer was the son of Jorim.
Jorim was the son of Matthat.
Matthat was the son of Levi.
³⁰ Levi was the son of Simeon.
Simeon was the son of Judah.
Judah was the son of Joseph.
Joseph was the son of Jonam.
Jonam was the son of Eliakim.
³¹ Eliakim was the son of Melea.
Melea was the son of Menna.
Menna was the son of Mattatha.
Mattatha was the son of Nathan.
Nathan was the son of David.
³² David was the son of Jesse.
Jesse was the son of Obed.
Obed was the son of Boaz.
Boaz was the son of Salmon.*
Salmon was the son of Nahshon.
³³ Nahshon was the son of Amminadab.
Amminadab was the son of Admin.
Admin was the son of Arni.*
Arni was the son of Hezron.
Hezron was the son of Perez.
Perez was the son of Judah.
³⁴ Judah was the son of Jacob.
Jacob was the son of Isaac.
Isaac was the son of Abraham.
Abraham was the son of Terah.
Terah was the son of Nahor.
³⁵ Nahor was the son of Serug.
Serug was the son of Reu.
Reu was the son of Peleg.
Peleg was the son of Eber.
Eber was the son of Shelah.
³⁶ Shelah was the son of Cainan.
Cainan was the son of Arphaxad.
Arphaxad was the son of Shem.
Shem was the son of Noah.
Noah was the son of Lamech.
³⁷ Lamech was the son of Methuselah.
Methuselah was the son of Enoch.
Enoch was the son of Jared.
Jared was the son of Mahalalel.
Mahalalel was the son of Kenan.
³⁸ Kenan was the son of Enosh.*
Enosh was the son of Seth.
Seth was the son of Adam.
Adam was the son of God.

4 The Temptation of Jesus

Then Jesus, full of the Holy Spirit, returned from the Jordan River. He was led by the Spirit in the wilderness,* ²where he was tempted by the devil for forty days. Jesus ate nothing all that time and became very hungry.

³ Then the devil said to him, "If you are the Son of God, tell this stone to become a loaf of bread."

⁴ But Jesus told him, "No! The Scriptures say, 'People do not live by bread alone.'*"

⁵ Then the devil took him up and revealed to him all the kingdoms of the world in a moment of time. ⁶"I will give you the glory of these kingdoms and authority over them," the devil said, "because they are mine to give to anyone I please. ⁷I will give it all to you if you will worship me."

⁸ Jesus replied, "The Scriptures say,

'You must worship the LORD your God
    and serve only him.'*"

⁹ Then the devil took him to Jerusalem, to the highest point of the Temple, and said, "If you are the Son of God, jump off! ¹⁰For the Scriptures say,

'He will order his angels to protect and
    guard you.
¹¹ And they will hold you up with their
    hands
    so you won't even hurt your foot on a
        stone.'*"

¹² Jesus responded, "The Scriptures also say, 'You must not test the LORD your God.'*"

¹³ When the devil had finished tempting Jesus, he left him until the next opportunity came.

Jesus Rejected at Nazareth

¹⁴ Then Jesus returned to Galilee, filled with the Holy Spirit's power. Reports about him spread quickly through the whole region. ¹⁵ He taught regularly in their synagogues and was praised by everyone.

¹⁶ When he came to the village of Nazareth, his boyhood home, he went as usual to the synagogue on the Sabbath and stood

---

3:32 Greek *Sala*, a variant spelling of Salmon; also in 3:32b. See Ruth 4:20. **3:33** Some manuscripts read *Amminadab was the son of Aram. Arni* and *Aram* are alternate spellings of Ram. See 1 Chr 2:9-10. **3:38** Greek *Enos*, a variant spelling of Enosh; also in 3:38b. See Gen 5:6. **4:1** Some manuscripts read *into the wilderness.* **4:4** Deut 8:3. **4:8** Deut 6:13. **4:10-11** Ps 91:11-12. **4:12** Deut 6:16.

up to read the Scriptures. ¹⁷ The scroll of Isaiah the prophet was handed to him. He unrolled the scroll and found the place where this was written:

¹⁸ "The Spirit of the LORD is upon me,
for he has anointed me to bring Good News to the poor.
He has sent me to proclaim that captives will be released,
that the blind will see,
that the oppressed will be set free,
¹⁹ and that the time of the LORD's favor has come.*"

²⁰ He rolled up the scroll, handed it back to the attendant, and sat down. All eyes in the synagogue looked at him intently. ²¹ Then he began to speak to them. "The Scripture you've just heard has been fulfilled this very day!"

²² Everyone spoke well of him and was amazed by the gracious words that came from his lips. "How can this be?" they asked. "Isn't this Joseph's son?"

²³ Then he said, "You will undoubtedly quote me this proverb: 'Physician, heal yourself'—meaning, 'Do miracles here in your hometown like those you did in Capernaum.' ²⁴ But I tell you the truth, no prophet is accepted in his own hometown.

²⁵ "Certainly there were many needy widows in Israel in Elijah's time, when the heavens were closed for three and a half years, and a severe famine devastated the land. ²⁶ Yet Elijah was not sent to any of them. He was sent instead to a foreigner—a widow of Zarephath in the land of Sidon. ²⁷ And there were many lepers in Israel in the time of the prophet Elisha, but the only one healed was Naaman, a Syrian."

²⁸ When they heard this, the people in the synagogue were furious. ²⁹ Jumping up, they mobbed him and forced him to the edge of the hill on which the town was built. They intended to push him over the cliff, ³⁰ but he passed right through the crowd and went on his way.

Jesus Casts Out a Demon

³¹ Then Jesus went to Capernaum, a town in Galilee, and taught there in the synagogue every Sabbath day. ³² There, too, the people were amazed at his teaching, for he spoke with authority.

³³ Once when he was in the synagogue, a man possessed by a demon—an evil* spirit—began shouting at Jesus, ³⁴ "Go away! Why are you interfering with us, Jesus of Nazareth? Have you come to destroy us? I know who you are—the Holy One of God!"

³⁵ Jesus cut him short. "Be quiet! Come out of the man," he ordered. At that, the demon threw the man to the floor as the crowd watched; then it came out of him without hurting him further.

³⁶ Amazed, the people exclaimed, "What authority and power this man's words possess! Even evil spirits obey him, and they flee at his command!" ³⁷ The news about Jesus spread through every village in the entire region.

Jesus Heals Many People

³⁸ After leaving the synagogue that day, Jesus went to Simon's home, where he found Simon's mother-in-law very sick with a high fever. "Please heal her," everyone begged. ³⁹ Standing at her bedside, he rebuked the fever, and it left her. And she got up at once and prepared a meal for them.

⁴⁰ As the sun went down that evening, people throughout the village brought sick family members to Jesus. No matter what their diseases were, the touch of his hand healed every one. ⁴¹ Many were possessed by demons; and the demons came out at his command, shouting, "You are the Son of God!" But because they knew he was the Messiah, he rebuked them and refused to let them speak.

Jesus Continues to Preach

⁴² Early the next morning Jesus went out to an isolated place. The crowds searched everywhere for him, and when they finally found him, they begged him not to leave them. ⁴³ But he replied, "I must preach the Good News of the Kingdom of God in other towns, too, because that is why I was sent." ⁴⁴ So he continued to travel around, preaching in synagogues throughout Judea.*

5 The First Disciples

One day as Jesus was preaching on the shore of the Sea of Galilee,* great crowds pressed in on him to listen to the word of God. [2] He noticed two empty boats at the water's edge, for the fishermen had left them and were washing their nets. [3] Stepping into one of the boats, Jesus asked Simon,* its owner, to push it out into the water. So he sat in the boat and taught the crowds from there.

[4] When he had finished speaking, he said to Simon, "Now go out where it is deeper, and let down your nets to catch some fish."

[5] "Master," Simon replied, "we worked hard all last night and didn't catch a thing. But if you say so, I'll let the nets down again." [6] And this time their nets were so full of fish they began to tear! [7] A shout for help brought their partners in the other boat, and soon both boats were filled with fish and on the verge of sinking.

[8] When Simon Peter realized what had happened, he fell to his knees before Jesus and said, "Oh, Lord, please leave me—I'm too much of a sinner to be around you." [9] For he was awestruck by the number of fish they had caught, as were the others with him. [10] His partners, James and John, the sons of Zebedee, were also amazed.

Jesus replied to Simon, "Don't be afraid! From now on you'll be fishing for people!" [11] And as soon as they landed, they left everything and followed Jesus.

Jesus Heals a Man with Leprosy

[12] In one of the villages, Jesus met a man with an advanced case of leprosy. When the man saw Jesus, he bowed with his face to the ground, begging to be healed. "Lord," he said, "if you are willing, you can heal me and make me clean."

[13] Jesus reached out and touched him. "I am willing," he said. "Be healed!" And instantly the leprosy disappeared. [14] Then Jesus instructed him not to tell anyone what had happened. He said, "Go to the priest and let him examine you. Take along the offering required in the law of Moses for those who have been healed of leprosy.* This will be a public testimony that you have been cleansed."

[15] But despite Jesus' instructions, the report of his power spread even faster, and vast crowds came to hear him preach and to be healed of their diseases. [16] But Jesus often withdrew to the wilderness for prayer.

Jesus Heals a Paralyzed Man

[17] One day while Jesus was teaching, some Pharisees and teachers of religious law were sitting nearby. (It seemed that these men showed up from every village in all Galilee and Judea, as well as from Jerusalem.) And the Lord's healing power was strongly with Jesus.

[18] Some men came carrying a paralyzed man on a sleeping mat. They tried to take him inside to Jesus, [19] but they couldn't reach him because of the crowd. So they went up to the roof and took off some tiles. Then they lowered the sick man on his mat down into the crowd, right in front of Jesus. [20] Seeing their faith, Jesus said to the man, "Young man, your sins are forgiven."

[21] But the Pharisees and teachers of religious law said to themselves, "Who does he think he is? That's blasphemy! Only God can forgive sins!"

[22] Jesus knew what they were thinking, so he asked them, "Why do you question this in your hearts? [23] Is it easier to say 'Your sins are forgiven,' or 'Stand up and walk'? [24] So I will prove to you that the Son of Man* has the authority on earth to forgive sins." Then Jesus turned to the paralyzed man and said, "Stand up, pick up your mat, and go home!"

[25] And immediately, as everyone watched, the man jumped up, picked up his mat, and went home praising God. [26] Everyone was gripped with great wonder and awe, and they praised God, exclaiming, "We have seen amazing things today!"

Jesus Calls Levi (Matthew)

[27] Later, as Jesus left the town, he saw a tax collector named Levi sitting at his tax collector's booth. "Follow me and be my disciple," Jesus said to him. [28] So Levi got up, left everything, and followed him.

[29] Later, Levi held a banquet in his home with Jesus as the guest of honor. Many of Levi's fellow tax collectors and other guests

---

5:1 Greek *Lake Gennesaret,* another name for the Sea of Galilee.   5:3 *Simon* is called "Peter" in 6:14 and thereafter.   5:14 See Lev 14:2-32.
5:24 "Son of Man" is a title Jesus used for himself.

A Model for Intercessory Prayer

LUKE 5:17-26

The scene described in Luke 5:17-26 is filled with spectacular images; we can picture the crowd of eager, anxious people, pressing in, trying to get through the door of a house. Many of them sick, some with walking sticks, some very old, babies and children crying, holding on to their parents' hands as the crowds push forward. The air is hot, thick, and dusty. The noise level is climbing.

And we see Jesus, standing inside this crowded house, calmly attending to the throng.

At the outer edges of the crowd, we see four men, each carrying a corner of the stretcher that's holding his paralyzed friend. The four men see that walking through the front door with their friend on a stretcher simply isn't an option. The crowds won't allow it. Not to be dissuaded, they carry their friend to the roof, through which they boldly punch a hole, and lower their friend down, right in front of Jesus. And Jesus proceeds to forgive this paralyzed man of his sins and heal him of his paralysis, in front of the Pharisees and everybody.

This account can serve as a model for us of the purpose and focus of intercessory prayer. In a basic sense, intercession is about deeply loving and caring for others and bringing them directly to Jesus in prayer. We can bring our friends to Jesus in prayer and in full faith leave them there, knowing that he will do exactly what he knows is best.

Interceding for others is a way of loving them, deeply and meaningfully. This gift takes on real meaning when I consider that one day I will likely have my own turn as the paralytic on the stretcher. I will covet and rely on the prayers of others—the friends who, I hope, will with bold determination place me right at the feet of Jesus in prayer.

—*Tracy Balzer*

For more on prayer, see reading at Luke 11:1-13.

also ate with them. [30]But the Pharisees and their teachers of religious law complained bitterly to Jesus' disciples, "Why do you eat and drink with such scum?*"

[31]Jesus answered them, "Healthy people don't need a doctor—sick people do. [32]I have come to call not those who think they are righteous, but those who know they are sinners and need to repent."

A Discussion about Fasting

[33]One day some people said to Jesus, "John the Baptist's disciples fast and pray regularly, and so do the disciples of the Pharisees. Why are your disciples always eating and drinking?"

[34]Jesus responded, "Do wedding guests fast while celebrating with the groom? Of course not. [35]But someday the groom will be taken away from them, and then they will fast."

[36]Then Jesus gave them this illustration: "No one tears a piece of cloth from a new garment and uses it to patch an old garment. For then the new garment would be ruined, and the new patch wouldn't even match the old garment.

5:30 Greek *with tax collectors and sinners?*

37 "And no one puts new wine into old wineskins. For the new wine would burst the wineskins, spilling the wine and ruining the skins. 38 New wine must be stored in new wineskins. 39 But no one who drinks the old wine seems to want the new wine. 'The old is just fine,' they say."

A Discussion about the Sabbath

6 One Sabbath day as Jesus was walking through some grainfields, his disciples broke off heads of grain, rubbed off the husks in their hands, and ate the grain. 2 But some Pharisees said, "Why are you breaking the law by harvesting grain on the Sabbath?"

3 Jesus replied, "Haven't you read in the Scriptures what David did when he and his companions were hungry? 4 He went into the house of God and broke the law by eating the sacred loaves of bread that only the priests can eat. He also gave some to his companions." 5 And Jesus added, "The Son of Man* is Lord, even over the Sabbath."

Jesus Heals on the Sabbath

6 On another Sabbath day, a man with a deformed right hand was in the synagogue while Jesus was teaching. 7 The teachers of religious law and the Pharisees watched Jesus closely. If he healed the man's hand, they planned to accuse him of working on the Sabbath.

8 But Jesus knew their thoughts. He said to the man with the deformed hand, "Come and stand in front of everyone." So the man came forward. 9 Then Jesus said to his critics, "I have a question for you. Does the law permit good deeds on the Sabbath, or is it a day for doing evil? Is this a day to save life or to destroy it?"

10 He looked around at them one by one and then said to the man, "Hold out your hand." So the man held out his hand, and it was restored! 11 At this, the enemies of Jesus were wild with rage and began to discuss what to do with him.

Jesus Chooses the Twelve Apostles

12 One day soon afterward Jesus went up on a mountain to pray, and he prayed to God all night. 13 At daybreak he called together all of his disciples and chose twelve of them to be apostles. Here are their names:

14 Simon (whom he named Peter),
   Andrew (Peter's brother),
   James,
   John,
   Philip,
   Bartholomew,
15 Matthew,
   Thomas,
   James (son of Alphaeus),
   Simon (who was called the zealot),
16 Judas (son of James),
   Judas Iscariot (who later betrayed him).

Crowds Follow Jesus

17 When they came down from the mountain, the disciples stood with Jesus on a large, level area, surrounded by many of his followers and by the crowds. There were people from all over Judea and from Jerusalem and from as far north as the seacoasts of Tyre and Sidon. 18 They had come to hear him and to be healed of their diseases; and those troubled by evil* spirits were healed. 19 Everyone tried to touch him, because healing power went out from him, and he healed everyone.

The Beatitudes

20 Then Jesus turned to his disciples and said,

"God blesses you who are poor,
   for the Kingdom of God is yours.
21 God blesses you who are hungry now,
   for you will be satisfied.
God blesses you who weep now,
   for in due time you will laugh.

22 What blessings await you when people hate you and exclude you and mock you and curse you as evil because you follow the Son of Man. 23 When that happens, be happy! Yes, leap for joy! For a great reward awaits you in heaven. And remember, their ancestors treated the ancient prophets that same way.

Sorrows Foretold

24 "What sorrow awaits you who are rich,
   for you have your only happiness now.

6:5 "Son of Man" is a title Jesus used for himself.   6:18 Greek *unclean*.

25 What sorrow awaits you who are fat and
    prosperous now,
      for a time of awful hunger awaits you.
    What sorrow awaits you who laugh now,
      for your laughing will turn to
        mourning and sorrow.
26 What sorrow awaits you who are praised
      by the crowds,
      for their ancestors also praised false
        prophets.

Love for Enemies

27 "But to you who are willing to listen, I say,
love your enemies! Do good to those who
hate you. 28 Bless those who curse you. Pray
for those who hurt you. 29 If someone slaps
you on one cheek, offer the other cheek
also. If someone demands your coat, offer
your shirt also. 30 Give to anyone who asks;
and when things are taken away from you,
don't try to get them back. 31 Do to others as
you would like them to do to you.

32 "If you love only those who love you,
why should you get credit for that? Even sinners love those who love them! 33 And if you
do good only to those who do good to you,
why should you get credit? Even sinners do
that much! 34 And if you lend money only to
those who can repay you, why should you
get credit? Even sinners will lend to other
sinners for a full return.

35 "Love your enemies! Do good to them.
Lend to them without expecting to be
repaid. Then your reward from heaven will
be very great, and you will truly be acting
as children of the Most High, for he is kind
to those who are unthankful and wicked.
36 You must be compassionate, just as your
Father is compassionate.

Do Not Judge Others

37 "Do not judge others, and you will not be
judged. Do not condemn others, or it will
all come back against you. Forgive others,
and you will be forgiven. 38 Give, and you
will receive. Your gift will return to you
in full—pressed down, shaken together to
make room for more, running over, and
poured into your lap. The amount you give
will determine the amount you get back.*"

39 Then Jesus gave the following illustration: "Can one blind person lead another?
Won't they both fall into a ditch? 40 Students* are not greater than their teacher.
But the student who is fully trained will
become like the teacher.

41 "And why worry about a speck in
your friend's eye* when you have a log in
your own? 42 How can you think of saying,
'Friend,* let me help you get rid of that
speck in your eye,' when you can't see past
the log in your own eye? Hypocrite! First
get rid of the log in your own eye; then you
will see well enough to deal with the speck
in your friend's eye.

The Tree and Its Fruit

43 "A good tree can't produce bad fruit, and
a bad tree can't produce good fruit. 44 A tree
is identified by its fruit. Figs are never gathered from thornbushes, and grapes are not
picked from bramble bushes. 45 A good person produces good things from the treasury of a good heart, and an evil person
produces evil things from the treasury of an
evil heart. What you say flows from what is
in your heart.

Building on a Solid Foundation

46 "So why do you keep calling me 'Lord,
Lord!' when you don't do what I say? 47 I
will show you what it's like when someone
comes to me, listens to my teaching, and
then follows it. 48 It is like a person building
a house who digs deep and lays the foundation on solid rock. When the floodwaters
rise and break against that house, it stands
firm because it is well built. 49 But anyone
who hears and doesn't obey is like a person
who builds a house without a foundation.
When the floods sweep down against that
house, it will collapse into a heap of ruins."

7 The Faith of a Roman Officer

When Jesus had finished saying all this
to the people, he returned to Capernaum.
2 At that time the highly valued slave of a
Roman officer* was sick and near death.
3 When the officer heard about Jesus, he
sent some respected Jewish elders to ask
him to come and heal his slave. 4 So they
earnestly begged Jesus to help the man. "If

6:38 Or *The measure you give will be the measure you get back.*   **6:40** Or *Disciples.*   **6:41** Greek *your brother's eye;* also in 6:42.   **6:42** Greek *Brother.*   **7:2** Greek *a centurion;* similarly in 7:6.

anyone deserves your help, he does," they said, ⁵"for he loves the Jewish people and even built a synagogue for us."

⁶So Jesus went with them. But just before they arrived at the house, the officer sent some friends to say, "Lord, don't trouble yourself by coming to my home, for I am not worthy of such an honor. ⁷I am not even worthy to come and meet you. Just say the word from where you are, and my servant will be healed. ⁸I know this because I am under the authority of my superior officers, and I have authority over my soldiers. I only need to say, 'Go,' and they go, or 'Come,' and they come. And if I say to my slaves, 'Do this,' they do it."

⁹When Jesus heard this, he was amazed. Turning to the crowd that was following him, he said, "I tell you, I haven't seen faith like this in all Israel!" ¹⁰And when the officer's friends returned to his house, they found the slave completely healed.

Jesus Raises a Widow's Son

¹¹Soon afterward Jesus went with his disciples to the village of Nain, and a large crowd followed him. ¹²A funeral procession was coming out as he approached the village gate. The young man who had died was a widow's only son, and a large crowd from the village was with her. ¹³When the Lord saw her, his heart overflowed with compassion. "Don't cry!" he said. ¹⁴Then he walked over to the coffin and touched it, and the bearers stopped. "Young man," he said, "I tell you, get up." ¹⁵Then the dead boy sat up and began to talk! And Jesus gave him back to his mother.

¹⁶Great fear swept the crowd, and they praised God, saying, "A mighty prophet has risen among us," and "God has visited his people today." ¹⁷And the news about Jesus spread throughout Judea and the surrounding countryside.

Jesus and John the Baptist

¹⁸The disciples of John the Baptist told John about everything Jesus was doing. So John called for two of his disciples, ¹⁹and he sent them to the Lord to ask him, "Are you the Messiah we've been expecting,* or should we keep looking for someone else?"

²⁰John's two disciples found Jesus and said to him, "John the Baptist sent us to ask, 'Are you the Messiah we've been expecting, or should we keep looking for someone else?'"

²¹At that very time, Jesus cured many people of their diseases, illnesses, and evil spirits, and he restored sight to many who were blind. ²²Then he told John's disciples, "Go back to John and tell him what you have seen and heard—the blind see, the lame walk, the lepers are cured, the deaf hear, the dead are raised to life, and the Good News is being preached to the poor. ²³And tell him, 'God blesses those who do not turn away because of me.*'"

²⁴After John's disciples left, Jesus began talking about him to the crowds. "What kind of man did you go into the wilderness to see? Was he a weak reed, swayed by every breath of wind? ²⁵Or were you expecting to see a man dressed in expensive clothes? No, people who wear beautiful clothes and live in luxury are found in palaces. ²⁶Were you looking for a prophet? Yes, and he is more than a prophet. ²⁷John is the man to whom the Scriptures refer when they say,

'Look, I am sending my messenger
    ahead of you,
  and he will prepare your way before
    you.'*

²⁸I tell you, of all who have ever lived, none is greater than John. Yet even the least person in the Kingdom of God is greater than he is!"

²⁹When they heard this, all the people—even the tax collectors—agreed that God's way was right,* for they had been baptized by John. ³⁰But the Pharisees and experts in religious law rejected God's plan for them, for they had refused John's baptism.

³¹"To what can I compare the people of this generation?" Jesus asked. "How can I describe them? ³²They are like children playing a game in the public square. They complain to their friends,

'We played wedding songs,
    and you didn't dance,
  so we played funeral songs,
    and you didn't weep.'

7:19 Greek *Are you the one who is coming?* Also in 7:20.   **7:23** Or *who are not offended by me.*   **7:27** Mal 3:1.   **7:29** Or *praised God for his justice.*

³³For John the Baptist didn't spend his time eating bread or drinking wine, and you say, 'He's possessed by a demon.' ³⁴The Son of Man,* on the other hand, feasts and drinks, and you say, 'He's a glutton and a drunkard, and a friend of tax collectors and other sinners!' ³⁵But wisdom is shown to be right by the lives of those who follow it.*"

Jesus Anointed by a Sinful Woman

³⁶One of the Pharisees asked Jesus to have dinner with him, so Jesus went to his home and sat down to eat.* ³⁷When a certain immoral woman from that city heard he was eating there, she brought a beautiful alabaster jar filled with expensive perfume. ³⁸Then she knelt behind him at his feet, weeping. Her tears fell on his feet, and she wiped them off with her hair. Then she kept kissing his feet and putting perfume on them.

³⁹When the Pharisee who had invited him saw this, he said to himself, "If this man were a prophet, he would know what kind of woman is touching him. She's a sinner!"

Jesus' Anointer: Wordless Repentance
LUKE 7:36–50

She made a decision; she resolved what to do. It scared her, but it was the only way she could be free. So when Jesus arrived at Simon's house for dinner that night, she was already there. The guests arrayed themselves around the low table, reclining on cushions, while she took her place behind Jesus, standing near his feet.

She might not have been the only uninvited guest that night; it wasn't uncommon for interested outsiders to stand alongside at a feast, listening to the conversation. The host, Simon the Pharisee, didn't seem shocked that she was there.

But then she started to weep. Her tears left streaks in the dust covering Christ's feet. With her long hair she wiped them, then kissed them reverently, with gratitude. From an alabaster jar she poured out perfume—possibly myrrh—anointing his feet and filling the room with fragrance.

What did her actions mean? In a sense she was making a confession though she used no words. Words would not be necessary; everyone in the room knew her reputation. But she did need to express her repentance. Like an artist, she made each action an eloquent expression of sorrow and gratitude, and Jesus identified the crowning motivation as love.

What does it take to know you have been forgiven? An unwillingness to look closely at sins because "they're forgiven anyway" can cause a sense of distance in your relationship with God. Naming sins—recognizing them, owning them—is an indispensable first step in grasping the cost of salvation. The woman who expressed her sorrow over sin and her gratitude for Christ's forgiveness that day heard Jesus speak these words: "Your sins are forgiven. . . . Your faith has saved you; go in peace" (Luke 7:48, 50). As we too come before Christ in repentance, as we gratefully receive his forgiveness, as we worship him for his grace, we also can live in Christ's peace.

—*Frederica Mathewes-Green*

For more on confession, see reading at Romans 5:6–11.

7:34 "Son of Man" is a title Jesus used for himself. **7:35** Or *But wisdom is justified by all her children.* **7:36** Or *and reclined.*

⁴⁰Then Jesus answered his thoughts. "Simon," he said to the Pharisee, "I have something to say to you."

"Go ahead, Teacher," Simon replied.

⁴¹Then Jesus told him this story: "A man loaned money to two people—500 pieces of silver* to one and 50 pieces to the other. ⁴²But neither of them could repay him, so he kindly forgave them both, canceling their debts. Who do you suppose loved him more after that?"

⁴³Simon answered, "I suppose the one for whom he canceled the larger debt."

"That's right," Jesus said. ⁴⁴Then he turned to the woman and said to Simon, "Look at this woman kneeling here. When I entered your home, you didn't offer me water to wash the dust from my feet, but she has washed them with her tears and wiped them with her hair. ⁴⁵You didn't greet me with a kiss, but from the time I first came in, she has not stopped kissing my feet. ⁴⁶You neglected the courtesy of olive oil to anoint my head, but she has anointed my feet with rare perfume.

⁴⁷"I tell you, her sins—and they are many—have been forgiven, so she has shown me much love. But a person who is forgiven little shows only little love." ⁴⁸Then Jesus said to the woman, "Your sins are forgiven."

⁴⁹The men at the table said among themselves, "Who is this man, that he goes around forgiving sins?"

⁵⁰And Jesus said to the woman, "Your faith has saved you; go in peace."

8 Women Who Followed Jesus

Soon afterward Jesus began a tour of the nearby towns and villages, preaching and announcing the Good News about the Kingdom of God. He took his twelve disciples with him, ²along with some women who had been cured of evil spirits and diseases. Among them were Mary Magdalene, from whom he had cast out seven demons; ³Joanna, the wife of Chuza, Herod's business manager; Susanna; and many others who were contributing from their own resources to support Jesus and his disciples.

Parable of the Farmer Scattering Seed

⁴One day Jesus told a story in the form of a parable to a large crowd that had gathered from many towns to hear him: ⁵"A farmer went out to plant his seed. As he scattered it across his field, some seed fell on a footpath, where it was stepped on, and the birds ate it. ⁶Other seed fell among rocks. It began to grow, but the plant soon wilted and died for lack of moisture. ⁷Other seed fell among thorns that grew up with it and choked out the tender plants. ⁸Still other seed fell on fertile soil. This seed grew and produced a crop that was a hundred times as much as had been planted!" When he had said this, he called out, "Anyone with ears to hear should listen and understand."

⁹His disciples asked him what this parable meant. ¹⁰He replied, "You are permitted to understand the secrets* of the Kingdom of God. But I use parables to teach the others so that the Scriptures might be fulfilled:

'When they look, they won't really see.
  When they hear, they won't
    understand.'*

¹¹"This is the meaning of the parable: The seed is God's word. ¹²The seeds that fell on the footpath represent those who hear the message, only to have the devil come and take it away from their hearts and prevent them from believing and being saved. ¹³The seeds on the rocky soil represent those who hear the message and receive it with joy. But since they don't have deep roots, they believe for a while, then they fall away when they face temptation. ¹⁴The seeds that fell among the thorns represent those who hear the message, but all too quickly the message is crowded out by the cares and riches and pleasures of this life. And so they never grow into maturity. ¹⁵And the seeds that fell on the good soil represent honest, good-hearted people who hear God's word, cling to it, and patiently produce a huge harvest.

Parable of the Lamp

¹⁶"No one lights a lamp and then covers it with a bowl or hides it under a bed. A lamp is placed on a stand, where its light can be

---

7:41 Greek *500 denarii. A denarius was equivalent to a laborer's full day's wage.* 8:10a Greek *mysteries.* 8:10b Isa 6:9 (Greek version).

seen by all who enter the house. [17]For all that is secret will eventually be brought into the open, and everything that is concealed will be brought to light and made known to all.

[18]"So pay attention to how you hear. To those who listen to my teaching, more understanding will be given. But for those who are not listening, even what they think they understand will be taken away from them."

The True Family of Jesus

[19]Then Jesus' mother and brothers came to see him, but they couldn't get to him because of the crowd. [20]Someone told Jesus, "Your mother and your brothers are outside, and they want to see you."

[21]Jesus replied, "My mother and my brothers are all those who hear God's word and obey it."

Jesus Calms the Storm

[22]One day Jesus said to his disciples, "Let's cross to the other side of the lake." So they got into a boat and started out. [23]As they sailed across, Jesus settled down for a nap. But soon a fierce storm came down on the lake. The boat was filling with water, and they were in real danger.

[24]The disciples went and woke him up, shouting, "Master, Master, we're going to drown!"

When Jesus woke up, he rebuked the wind and the raging waves. Suddenly the storm stopped and all was calm. [25]Then he asked them, "Where is your faith?"

The disciples were terrified and amazed. "Who is this man?" they asked each other. "When he gives a command, even the wind and waves obey him!"

Jesus Heals a Demon-Possessed Man

[26]So they arrived in the region of the Gerasenes,* across the lake from Galilee. [27]As Jesus was climbing out of the boat, a man who was possessed by demons came out to meet him. For a long time he had been homeless and naked, living in a cemetery outside the town.

[28]As soon as he saw Jesus, he shrieked and fell down in front of him. Then he screamed, "Why are you interfering with me, Jesus, Son of the Most High God? Please, I beg you, don't torture me!" [29]For Jesus had already commanded the evil* spirit to come out of him. This spirit had often taken control of the man. Even when he was placed under guard and put in chains and shackles, he simply broke them and rushed out into the wilderness, completely under the demon's power.

[30]Jesus demanded, "What is your name?"

"Legion," he replied, for he was filled with many demons. [31]The demons kept begging Jesus not to send them into the bottomless pit.*

[32]There happened to be a large herd of pigs feeding on the hillside nearby, and the demons begged him to let them enter into the pigs.

So Jesus gave them permission. [33]Then the demons came out of the man and entered the pigs, and the entire herd plunged down the steep hillside into the lake and drowned.

[34]When the herdsmen saw it, they fled to the nearby town and the surrounding countryside, spreading the news as they ran. [35]People rushed out to see what had happened. A crowd soon gathered around Jesus, and they saw the man who had been freed from the demons. He was sitting at Jesus' feet, fully clothed and perfectly sane, and they were all afraid. [36]Then those who had seen what happened told the others how the demon-possessed man had been healed. [37]And all the people in the region of the Gerasenes begged Jesus to go away and leave them alone, for a great wave of fear swept over them.

So Jesus returned to the boat and left, crossing back to the other side of the lake. [38]The man who had been freed from the demons begged to go with him. But Jesus sent him home, saying, [39]"No, go back to your family, and tell them everything God has done for you." So he went all through the town proclaiming the great things Jesus had done for him.

Jesus Heals in Response to Faith

[40]On the other side of the lake the crowds welcomed Jesus, because they had been

8:26 Other manuscripts read *Gadarenes*; still others read *Gergesenes*; also in 8:37. See Matt 8:28; Mark 5:1. **8:29** Greek *unclean*. **8:31** Or *the abyss*, or *the underworld*.

Without Words

LUKE 8:40-48

T welve years of bleeding, money gone on doctors who could not help, and getting worse by the day, this woman we see in Mark 5 and Luke 8 was desperate. She'd likely already tried everything she could think of.

I'm much the same way. I go through every open door trying to solve my problems, chasing each lead with hope that this one thing will make my life better, more bearable. I'm always looking for another way to fix everything. And, like this woman, I most often end up poorer and depleted.

But reaching that place of utter need causes me to cease striving. I'm too tired and confused to keep searching for a solution. So I do what this woman did. I become quiet. I quit talking, even to God, and in silence I throw my needs at Christ's feet, too exhausted to form words.

That sounds unspiritual, but it is the most spiritual thing I can do. Jesus has been waiting for me to come to the end of myself, to see that he is the one more thing I've been seeking. And like this woman, I find that when I am silent in his presence, my true needs are met.

—*JoHannah Reardon*

For more on silence, see reading at Luke 10:38-42.

waiting for him. [41] Then a man named Jairus, a leader of the local synagogue, came and fell at Jesus' feet, pleading with him to come home with him. [42] His only daughter,* who was about twelve years old, was dying.

As Jesus went with him, he was surrounded by the crowds. [43] A woman in the crowd had suffered for twelve years with constant bleeding,* and she could find no cure. [44] Coming up behind Jesus, she touched the fringe of his robe. Immediately, the bleeding stopped.

[45] "Who touched me?" Jesus asked.

Everyone denied it, and Peter said, "Master, this whole crowd is pressing up against you."

[46] But Jesus said, "Someone deliberately touched me, for I felt healing power go out from me." [47] When the woman realized that she could not stay hidden, she began to tremble and fell to her knees in front of him. The whole crowd heard her explain why she had touched him and that she had been immediately healed. [48] "Daughter," he said to her, "your faith has made you well. Go in peace."

[49] While he was still speaking to her, a messenger arrived from the home of Jairus, the leader of the synagogue. He told him, "Your daughter is dead. There's no use troubling the Teacher now."

[50] But when Jesus heard what had happened, he said to Jairus, "Don't be afraid. Just have faith, and she will be healed."

[51] When they arrived at the house, Jesus wouldn't let anyone go in with him except Peter, John, James, and the little girl's father and mother. [52] The house was filled with people weeping and wailing, but he said, "Stop the weeping! She isn't dead; she's only asleep."

[53] But the crowd laughed at him because they all knew she had died. [54] Then Jesus took her by the hand and said in a loud voice, "My child, get up!" [55] And at that moment her life* returned, and she immediately stood up! Then Jesus told them to give her something to eat. [56] Her parents

---

8:42 Or His only child, a daughter. **8:43** Some manuscripts add *having spent everything she had on doctors.* **8:55** Or *her spirit.*

were overwhelmed, but Jesus insisted that they not tell anyone what had happened.

9 Jesus Sends Out the Twelve Disciples

One day Jesus called together his twelve disciples* and gave them power and authority to cast out all demons and to heal all diseases. ²Then he sent them out to tell everyone about the Kingdom of God and to heal the sick. ³"Take nothing for your journey," he instructed them. "Don't take a walking stick, a traveler's bag, food, money,* or even a change of clothes. ⁴Wherever you go, stay in the same house until you leave town. ⁵And if a town refuses to welcome you, shake its dust from your feet as you leave to show that you have abandoned those people to their fate."

⁶So they began their circuit of the villages, preaching the Good News and healing the sick.

Herod's Confusion

⁷When Herod Antipas, the ruler of Galilee,* heard about everything Jesus was doing, he was puzzled. Some were saying that John the Baptist had been raised from the dead. ⁸Others thought Jesus was Elijah or one of the other prophets risen from the dead.

⁹"I beheaded John," Herod said, "so who is this man about whom I hear such stories?" And he kept trying to see him.

Jesus Feeds Five Thousand

¹⁰When the apostles returned, they told Jesus everything they had done. Then he slipped quietly away with them toward the town of Bethsaida. ¹¹But the crowds found out where he was going, and they followed him. He welcomed them and taught them about the Kingdom of God, and he healed those who were sick.

¹²Late in the afternoon the twelve disciples came to him and said, "Send the crowds away to the nearby villages and farms, so they can find food and lodging for the night. There is nothing to eat here in this remote place."

¹³But Jesus said, "You feed them."

"But we have only five loaves of bread and two fish," they answered. "Or are you expecting us to go and buy enough food for this whole crowd?" ¹⁴For there were about 5,000 men there.

Jesus replied, "Tell them to sit down in groups of about fifty each." ¹⁵So the people all sat down. ¹⁶Jesus took the five loaves and two fish, looked up toward heaven, and blessed them. Then, breaking the loaves into pieces, he kept giving the bread and fish to the disciples so they could distribute it to the people. ¹⁷They all ate as much as they wanted, and afterward, the disciples picked up twelve baskets of leftovers!

Peter's Declaration about Jesus

¹⁸One day Jesus left the crowds to pray alone. Only his disciples were with him, and he asked them, "Who do people say I am?"

¹⁹"Well," they replied, "some say John the Baptist, some say Elijah, and others say you are one of the other ancient prophets risen from the dead."

²⁰Then he asked them, "But who do you say I am?"

Peter replied, "You are the Messiah* sent from God!"

Jesus Predicts His Death

²¹Jesus warned his disciples not to tell anyone who he was. ²²"The Son of Man* must suffer many terrible things," he said. "He will be rejected by the elders, the leading priests, and the teachers of religious law. He will be killed, but on the third day he will be raised from the dead."

²³Then he said to the crowd, "If any of you wants to be my follower, you must turn from your selfish ways, take up your cross daily, and follow me. ²⁴If you try to hang on to your life, you will lose it. But if you give up your life for my sake, you will save it. ²⁵And what do you benefit if you gain the whole world but are yourself lost or destroyed? ²⁶If anyone is ashamed of me and my message, the Son of Man will be ashamed of that person when he returns in his glory and in the glory of the Father and the holy angels. ²⁷I tell you the truth, some

---

9:1 Greek *the Twelve;* other manuscripts read *the twelve apostles.*   **9:3** Or *silver coins.*   **9:7** Greek *Herod the tetrarch.* Herod Antipas was a son of King Herod and was ruler over Galilee.   **9:20** Or *the Christ. Messiah* (a Hebrew term) and *Christ* (a Greek term) both mean "the anointed one."   **9:22** "Son of Man" is a title Jesus used for himself.

standing here right now will not die before they see the Kingdom of God."

The Transfiguration

28 About eight days later Jesus took Peter, John, and James up on a mountain to pray. 29 And as he was praying, the appearance of his face was transformed, and his clothes became dazzling white. 30 Suddenly, two men, Moses and Elijah, appeared and began talking with Jesus. 31 They were glorious to see. And they were speaking about his exodus from this world, which was about to be fulfilled in Jerusalem.

32 Peter and the others had fallen asleep. When they woke up, they saw Jesus' glory and the two men standing with him. 33 As Moses and Elijah were starting to leave, Peter, not even knowing what he was saying, blurted out, "Master, it's wonderful for us to be here! Let's make three shelters as memorials*—one for you, one for Moses, and one for Elijah." 34 But even as he was saying this, a cloud overshadowed them, and terror gripped them as the cloud covered them.

35 Then a voice from the cloud said, "This is my Son, my Chosen One.* Listen to him." 36 When the voice finished, Jesus was there alone. They didn't tell anyone at that time what they had seen.

Jesus Heals a Demon-Possessed Boy

37 The next day, after they had come down the mountain, a large crowd met Jesus. 38 A man in the crowd called out to him, "Teacher, I beg you to look at my son, my only child. 39 An evil spirit keeps seizing him, making him scream. It throws him into convulsions so that he foams at the mouth. It batters him and hardly ever leaves him alone. 40 I begged your disciples to cast out the spirit, but they couldn't do it."

41 Jesus said, "You faithless and corrupt people! How long must I be with you and put up with you?" Then he said to the man, "Bring your son here."

42 As the boy came forward, the demon knocked him to the ground and threw him into a violent convulsion. But Jesus rebuked the evil* spirit and healed the boy. Then he gave him back to his father. 43 Awe gripped the people as they saw this majestic display of God's power.

Jesus Again Predicts His Death

While everyone was marveling at everything he was doing, Jesus said to his disciples, 44 "Listen to me and remember what I say. The Son of Man is going to be betrayed into the hands of his enemies." 45 But they didn't know what he meant. Its significance was hidden from them, so they couldn't understand it, and they were afraid to ask him about it.

The Greatest in the Kingdom

46 Then his disciples began arguing about which of them was the greatest. 47 But Jesus knew their thoughts, so he brought a little child to his side. 48 Then he said to them, "Anyone who welcomes a little child like this on my behalf* welcomes me, and anyone who welcomes me also welcomes my Father who sent me. Whoever is the least among you is the greatest."

Using the Name of Jesus

49 John said to Jesus, "Master, we saw someone using your name to cast out demons, but we told him to stop because he isn't in our group."

50 But Jesus said, "Don't stop him! Anyone who is not against you is for you."

Opposition from Samaritans

51 As the time drew near for him to ascend to heaven, Jesus resolutely set out for Jerusalem. 52 He sent messengers ahead to a Samaritan village to prepare for his arrival. 53 But the people of the village did not welcome Jesus because he was on his way to Jerusalem. 54 When James and John saw this, they said to Jesus, "Lord, should we call down fire from heaven to burn them up*?" 55 But Jesus turned and rebuked them.* 56 So they went on to another village.

The Cost of Following Jesus

57 As they were walking along, someone said to Jesus, "I will follow you wherever you go."

9:33 Greek three tabernacles.   9:35 Some manuscripts read This is my dearly loved Son.   9:42 Greek unclean.   9:48 Greek in my name.
9:54 Some manuscripts add as Elijah did.   9:55 Some manuscripts add an expanded conclusion to verse 55 and an additional sentence in verse 56: And he said, "You don't realize what your hearts are like. 56 For the Son of Man has not come to destroy people's lives, but to save them."

Celebration

The True Cause of Our Happiness

LUKE 10:17-20

One night at family devotions my husband asked our boys, "Are you happy in the Lord?"

"Yes," our thirteen-year-old said.

"Why are you happy?" Bob asked.

"Because I'm in cross-country running and it's fun," my son answered.

"Could you be happy if you weren't in cross-country?"

"Yes. Because I have lots of friends," he replied.

"Could you be happy if you didn't have lots of friends?"

Our son didn't answer.

Being happy in the Lord, Bob and I had learned, isn't getting everything we want when we want it. It's an elusive and indescribable sense that all is well, regardless of our circumstances.

When the seventy-two disciples Jesus had sent out on a ministry tour returned elated with their results, he told them, "Don't rejoice because evil spirits obey you; rejoice because your names are registered in heaven" (Luke 10:20). It was as if Jesus had asked them, "Could you be 'happy' serving me if the demons *hadn't* submitted to you?"

God blesses us with many delights to enjoy in our lives: family, friends, talents, hobbies, good food, the beauty of nature, and so on. But there will be moments when those external sources of joy are stripped away—times when the obvious reasons for happiness are gone. In those stark moments, life is boiled down to the basics—to the elemental truths at the core of who we are. When all else fades from view, we see with a new clarity that the ultimate source of our happiness and delight is Christ himself.

—*Wendy Murray*

For more on celebration, see reading at John 19:17-37.

---

[58] But Jesus replied, "Foxes have dens to live in, and birds have nests, but the Son of Man has no place even to lay his head."

[59] He said to another person, "Come, follow me."

The man agreed, but he said, "Lord, first let me return home and bury my father."

[60] But Jesus told him, "Let the spiritually dead bury their own dead!* Your duty is to go and preach about the Kingdom of God."

[61] Another said, "Yes, Lord, I will follow you, but first let me say good-bye to my family."

[62] But Jesus told him, "Anyone who puts a hand to the plow and then looks back is not fit for the Kingdom of God."

10 Jesus Sends Out His Disciples

The Lord now chose seventy-two* other disciples and sent them ahead in pairs to all the towns and places he planned to visit. [2] These were his instructions to them:

9:60 Greek *Let the dead bury their own dead.* **10:1** Some manuscripts read *seventy;* also in 10:17.

Scary Hospitality
LUKE 10:25-37

In New Testament times, Jews and Samaritans hated one another, or as John understated it in John 4:9, "Jews refuse to have anything to do with Samaritans." But in Jesus' parable, an injured Jewish man is completely disregarded by his own people (Luke 10:25-37). Instead, his enemy, a Samaritan, is the one who extends his hand, bandages him, and pays the hotel and medical fees.

The Greek word for hospitality is *philoxenia,* which means "showing brotherly love (*phileo*) to strangers (*xenia*)." We see the Samaritan showing this kind of hospitality to the injured man. He knows the man is a Jew and is well aware that he probably holds the same prejudices against him as the rest of the Jews. Yet the Samaritan takes a risk and demonstrates philoxenia.

This story convicts me. How often do *I* reach out to someone who may hate me because of my religious, cultural, or racial baggage? How often is my inaction motivated by fear? What prejudices may blind me from seeing a stranger as my neighbor whom I am called to love?

The radical kind of hospitality Jesus calls us to can be scary, risky, and uncomfortable. His parable compels us to consider the question: who is my neighbor? And then to love that person—stranger, enemy, or friend—as we love ourselves.

—Joy-Elizabeth Lawrence

For more on hospitality, see reading at Luke 14:7-24.

"The harvest is great, but the workers are few. So pray to the Lord who is in charge of the harvest; ask him to send more workers into his fields. ³Now go, and remember that I am sending you out as lambs among wolves. ⁴Don't take any money with you, nor a traveler's bag, nor an extra pair of sandals. And don't stop to greet anyone on the road.

⁵"Whenever you enter someone's home, first say, 'May God's peace be on this house.' ⁶If those who live there are peaceful, the blessing will stand; if they are not, the blessing will return to you. ⁷Don't move around from home to home. Stay in one place, eating and drinking what they provide. Don't hesitate to accept hospitality, because those who work deserve their pay.

⁸"If you enter a town and it welcomes you, eat whatever is set before you. ⁹Heal the sick, and tell them, 'The Kingdom of God is near you now.' ¹⁰But if a town refuses to welcome you, go out into its streets and say, ¹¹'We wipe even the dust of your town from our feet to show that we have abandoned you to your fate. And know this—the Kingdom of God is near!' ¹²I assure you, even wicked Sodom will be better off than such a town on judgment day.

¹³"What sorrow awaits you, Korazin and Bethsaida! For if the miracles I did in you had been done in wicked Tyre and Sidon, their people would have repented of their sins long ago, clothing themselves in burlap and throwing ashes on their heads to show their remorse. ¹⁴Yes, Tyre and Sidon will be better off on judgment day than you. ¹⁵And you people of Capernaum, will you be honored in heaven? No, you will go down to the place of the dead.*"

¹⁶Then he said to the disciples, "Anyone who accepts your message is also accepting me. And anyone who rejects you is

rejecting me. And anyone who rejects me is rejecting God, who sent me."

[17] When the seventy-two disciples returned, they joyfully reported to him, "Lord, even the demons obey us when we use your name!"

[18] "Yes," he told them, "I saw Satan fall from heaven like lightning! [19] Look, I have given you authority over all the power of the enemy, and you can walk among snakes and scorpions and crush them. Nothing will injure you. [20] But don't rejoice because evil spirits obey you; rejoice because your names are registered in heaven."

Jesus' Prayer of Thanksgiving

[21] At that same time Jesus was filled with the joy of the Holy Spirit, and he said, "O Father, Lord of heaven and earth, thank you for hiding these things from those who think themselves wise and clever, and for revealing them to the childlike. Yes, Father, it pleased you to do it this way.

[22] "My Father has entrusted everything to me. No one truly knows the Son except the Father, and no one truly knows the Father except the Son and those to whom the Son chooses to reveal him."

[23] Then when they were alone, he turned

Mary of Bethany: Quiet at Christ's Feet

LUKE 10:38-42

We all know the story well. When Jesus arrived at Martha's home in Bethany, she and her sister, Mary, welcomed him in. In a spirit of hospitality, Martha did what was expected: she got to work preparing a meal for her guest. Mary did the unexpected. Rather than joining her sister in the necessary work, she chose something of greater necessity: she sat at Jesus' feet and attentively listened to him.

In that familiar act, Mary seized the moment, shifting her focus from the necessary external to-dos to the internal soul-priority of *listening* to Jesus. This, for us too, is the essence of the disciplines of silence and contemplation: a drawing away from external demands, an internal soul-attention, a heart in repose, listening to Jesus with eager anticipation.

Too often we think that to correctly practice silence and contemplation, we have to get everything "just right"—that it requires a change of circumstance or scenery. Yet Mary of Bethany shows us that it requires, rather, a change of attitude and attention—that in the midst of a busy household, Mary focused her mind and attention on Christ.

And what were the rewards to those disciplines? A deep passion and worship of the Savior. Just days before Jesus' death, again Mary did the unexpected. And once more, she takes a posture of repose, at Jesus' feet. Her actions reflect the richness of her spiritual life, filled with faith and overflowing with love. "Then Mary took a twelve-ounce jar of expensive perfume made from essence of nard, and she anointed Jesus' feet with it, wiping his feet with her hair" (John 12:3).

Mary poetically demonstrates the beauty of being with Jesus. Her example draws us away from our own external distractions, compelling us to do the unexpected: to choose being over doing, to embrace silence over productivity. Mary invites us into the possibility that if we stop to listen, we might truly hear what God is trying to say. And maybe if we hear, we will understand. And maybe if we understand, we will love. And maybe if we love, we will keep listening.

—Amie Hollmann

to the disciples and said, "Blessed are the eyes that see what you have seen. [24] I tell you, many prophets and kings longed to see what you see, but they didn't see it. And they longed to hear what you hear, but they didn't hear it."

The Most Important Commandment

[25] One day an expert in religious law stood up to test Jesus by asking him this question: "Teacher, what should I do to inherit eternal life?"

[26] Jesus replied, "What does the law of Moses say? How do you read it?"

[27] The man answered, "'You must love the LORD your God with all your heart, all your soul, all your strength, and all your mind.' And, 'Love your neighbor as yourself.'"*

[28] "Right!" Jesus told him. "Do this and you will live!"

[29] The man wanted to justify his actions, so he asked Jesus, "And who is my neighbor?"

Parable of the Good Samaritan

[30] Jesus replied with a story: "A Jewish man was traveling from Jerusalem down to Jericho, and he was attacked by bandits. They stripped him of his clothes, beat him up, and left him half dead beside the road.

[31] "By chance a priest came along. But when he saw the man lying there, he crossed to the other side of the road and passed him by. [32] A Temple assistant* walked over and looked at him lying there, but he also passed by on the other side.

[33] "Then a despised Samaritan came along, and when he saw the man, he felt compassion for him. [34] Going over to him, the Samaritan soothed his wounds with olive oil and wine and bandaged them. Then he put the man on his own donkey and took him to an inn, where he took care of him. [35] The next day he handed the innkeeper two silver coins,* telling him, 'Take care of this man. If his bill runs higher than this, I'll pay you the next time I'm here.'

[36] "Now which of these three would you say was a neighbor to the man who was attacked by bandits?" Jesus asked.

[37] The man replied, "The one who showed him mercy."

Then Jesus said, "Yes, now go and do the same."

Jesus Visits Martha and Mary

[38] As Jesus and the disciples continued on their way to Jerusalem, they came to a certain village where a woman named Martha welcomed him into her home. [39] Her sister, Mary, sat at the Lord's feet, listening to what he taught. [40] But Martha was distracted by the big dinner she was preparing. She came to Jesus and said, "Lord, doesn't it seem unfair to you that my sister just sits here while I do all the work? Tell her to come and help me."

[41] But the Lord said to her, "My dear Martha, you are worried and upset over all these details! [42] There is only one thing worth being concerned about. Mary has discovered it, and it will not be taken away from her."

11 Teaching about Prayer

Once Jesus was in a certain place praying. As he finished, one of his disciples came to him and said, "Lord, teach us to pray, just as John taught his disciples."

[2] Jesus said, "This is how you should pray:*

"Father, may your name be kept holy.
    May your Kingdom come soon.
[3] Give us each day the food we
        need,*
[4] and forgive us our sins,
        as we forgive those who sin
            against us.
    And don't let us yield to temptation.*"

[5] Then, teaching them more about prayer, he used this story: "Suppose you went to a friend's house at midnight, wanting to borrow three loaves of bread. You say to him, [6] 'A friend of mine has just arrived for a visit, and I have nothing for him to eat.' [7] And suppose he calls out from his bedroom, 'Don't bother me. The door is locked for the night, and my family and I are all in bed. I

10:27 Deut 6:5; Lev 19:18. **10:32** Greek *A Levite.* **10:35** Greek *two denarii.* A denarius was equivalent to a laborer's full day's wage. **11:2** Some manuscripts add additional phrases from the Lord's Prayer as it reads in Matt 6:9-13. **11:3** Or *Give us each day our food for the day;* or *Give us each day our food for tomorrow.* **11:4** Or *And keep us from being tested.*

Praying like Jesus
LUKE 11:1-13

Prayer

Alone on a mountainside, before the sun warms the sky, Jesus prays. With a crowd gathered and his hands raised, Jesus prays. In agony, as his friends fall asleep around him, Jesus prays.

In the Gospels we see Jesus pray more often than we hear him talk about prayer. We listen to his words in groans and whispers spoken to the Father, interwoven throughout his ministry. The emotions and locations change, but Jesus models a constant connection with the Father.

In the Sermon on the Mount, Jesus helps us understand how we are to pray (Matthew 6:5-15). He says not, "If you pray," but rather, "When you pray," asserting that prayer is a given. For the Christ-follower, prayer is to be a natural part of the fabric of our daily lives.

In his teaching on prayer in Matthew, Jesus provides a model, telling his followers to "pray like this" (6:9). The prayer he offers as our example pushes us out of our inclination to focus on our individual interests and instead roots us squarely in community: "Our Father . . ." In his prayer Jesus invites us to welcome God's kingdom and grow in forgiveness as we forgive.

The Lord's Prayer does not limit us—rather, it offers us a starting point. In prayer we can remember that our needs seem to be endless, but God's grace is limitless. He knows what we need, and he longs to answer us. As the Lord's Prayer patterns for us, God can help us see with an eternal perspective as we choose to pray about what matters most and not just focus on our individual wish lists.

Before the sun comes up. After the sun goes down. On our knees. On our faces. Heads bowed. Hands lifted. In a quiet moment alone. Surrounded by joyous worshipers. Wherever we are. However we feel. Our prayers continue. We are kept in communion with "Our Father." And together we seek God's kingdom until the final "amen."

—Amie Hollmann

For more on prayer, see reading at Luke 18:1-8.

---

can't help you.' ⁸But I tell you this—though he won't do it for friendship's sake, if you keep knocking long enough, he will get up and give you whatever you need because of your shameless persistence.*

⁹"And so I tell you, keep on asking, and you will receive what you ask for. Keep on seeking, and you will find. Keep on knocking, and the door will be opened to you. ¹⁰For everyone who asks, receives. Everyone who seeks, finds. And to everyone who knocks, the door will be opened.

¹¹"You fathers—if your children ask* for a fish, do you give them a snake instead? ¹²Or if they ask for an egg, do you give them a scorpion? Of course not! ¹³So if you sinful people know how to give good gifts to your children, how much more will your heavenly Father give the Holy Spirit to those who ask him."

Jesus and the Prince of Demons

¹⁴One day Jesus cast out a demon from a man who couldn't speak, and when the

---

11:8 Or *in order to avoid shame, so his reputation won't be damaged.* **11:11** Some manuscripts add *for bread, do you give them a stone? Or [if they ask].*

demon was gone, the man began to speak. The crowds were amazed, [15] but some of them said, "No wonder he can cast out demons. He gets his power from Satan,* the prince of demons." [16] Others, trying to test Jesus, demanded that he show them a miraculous sign from heaven to prove his authority.

[17] He knew their thoughts, so he said, "Any kingdom divided by civil war is doomed. A family splintered by feuding will fall apart. [18] You say I am empowered by Satan. But if Satan is divided and fighting against himself, how can his kingdom survive? [19] And if I am empowered by Satan, what about your own exorcists? They cast out demons, too, so they will condemn you for what you have said. [20] But if I am casting out demons by the power of God,* then the Kingdom of God has arrived among you. [21] For when a strong man like Satan is fully armed and guards his palace, his possessions are safe—[22] until someone even stronger attacks and overpowers him, strips him of his weapons, and carries off his belongings.

[23] "Anyone who isn't with me opposes me, and anyone who isn't working with me is actually working against me.

[24] "When an evil* spirit leaves a person, it goes into the desert, searching for rest. But when it finds none, it says, 'I will return to the person I came from.' [25] So it returns and finds that its former home is all swept and in order. [26] Then the spirit finds seven other spirits more evil than itself, and they all enter the person and live there. And so that person is worse off than before."

[27] As he was speaking, a woman in the crowd called out, "God bless your mother—the womb from which you came, and the breasts that nursed you!"

[28] Jesus replied, "But even more blessed are all who hear the word of God and put it into practice."

The Sign of Jonah

[29] As the crowd pressed in on Jesus, he said, "This evil generation keeps asking me to show them a miraculous sign. But the only sign I will give them is the sign of Jonah.

[30] What happened to him was a sign to the people of Nineveh that God had sent him. What happens to the Son of Man* will be a sign to these people that he was sent by God.

[31] "The queen of Sheba* will stand up against this generation on judgment day and condemn it, for she came from a distant land to hear the wisdom of Solomon. Now someone greater than Solomon is here—but you refuse to listen. [32] The people of Nineveh will also stand up against this generation on judgment day and condemn it, for they repented of their sins at the preaching of Jonah. Now someone greater than Jonah is here—but you refuse to repent.

Receiving the Light

[33] "No one lights a lamp and then hides it or puts it under a basket.* Instead, a lamp is placed on a stand, where its light can be seen by all who enter the house.

[34] "Your eye is a lamp that provides light for your body. When your eye is good, your whole body is filled with light. But when it is bad, your body is filled with darkness. [35] Make sure that the light you think you have is not actually darkness. [36] If you are filled with light, with no dark corners, then your whole life will be radiant, as though a floodlight were filling you with light."

Jesus Criticizes the Religious Leaders

[37] As Jesus was speaking, one of the Pharisees invited him home for a meal. So he went in and took his place at the table.* [38] His host was amazed to see that he sat down to eat without first performing the hand-washing ceremony required by Jewish custom. [39] Then the Lord said to him, "You Pharisees are so careful to clean the outside of the cup and the dish, but inside you are filthy—full of greed and wickedness! [40] Fools! Didn't God make the inside as well as the outside? [41] So clean the inside by giving gifts to the poor, and you will be clean all over.

[42] "What sorrow awaits you Pharisees! For you are careful to tithe even the tiniest income from your herb gardens,* but

---

11:15 Greek *Beelzeboul;* also in 11:18, 19. Other manuscripts read *Beezeboul;* Latin version reads *Beelzebub.* **11:20** Greek *by the finger of God.* **11:24** Greek *unclean.* **11:30** "Son of Man" is a title Jesus used for himself. **11:31** Greek *The queen of the south.* **11:33** Some manuscripts do not include *or puts it under a basket.* **11:37** Or *and reclined.* **11:42** Greek *tithe the mint, the rue, and every herb.*

you ignore justice and the love of God. You should tithe, yes, but do not neglect the more important things.

43 "What sorrow awaits you Pharisees! For you love to sit in the seats of honor in the synagogues and receive respectful greetings as you walk in the marketplaces. 44 Yes, what sorrow awaits you! For you are like hidden graves in a field. People walk over them without knowing the corruption they are stepping on."

45 "Teacher," said an expert in religious law, "you have insulted us, too, in what you just said."

46 "Yes," said Jesus, "what sorrow also awaits you experts in religious law! For you crush people with unbearable religious demands, and you never lift a finger to ease the burden. 47 What sorrow awaits you! For you build monuments for the prophets your own ancestors killed long ago. 48 But in fact, you stand as witnesses who agree with what your ancestors did. They killed the prophets, and you join in their crime by building the monuments! 49 This is what God in his wisdom said about you:* 'I will send prophets and apostles to them, but they will kill some and persecute the others.'

50 "As a result, this generation will be held responsible for the murder of all God's prophets from the creation of the world— 51 from the murder of Abel to the murder of Zechariah, who was killed between the altar and the sanctuary. Yes, it will certainly be charged against this generation.

52 "What sorrow awaits you experts in religious law! For you remove the key to knowledge from the people. You don't enter the Kingdom yourselves, and you prevent others from entering."

53 As Jesus was leaving, the teachers of religious law and the Pharisees became hostile and tried to provoke him with many questions. 54 They wanted to trap him into saying something they could use against him.

12 A Warning against Hypocrisy

Meanwhile, the crowds grew until thousands were milling about and stepping on each other. Jesus turned first to his disciples and warned them, "Beware of the yeast of the Pharisees—their hypocrisy. 2 The time is coming when everything that is covered up will be revealed, and all that is secret will be made known to all. 3 Whatever you have said in the dark will be heard in the light, and what you have whispered behind closed doors will be shouted from the housetops for all to hear!

4 "Dear friends, don't be afraid of those who want to kill your body; they cannot do any more to you after that. 5 But I'll tell you whom to fear. Fear God, who has the power to kill you and then throw you into hell.* Yes, he's the one to fear.

6 "What is the price of five sparrows—two copper coins*? Yet God does not forget a single one of them. 7 And the very hairs on your head are all numbered. So don't be afraid; you are more valuable to God than a whole flock of sparrows.

8 "I tell you the truth, everyone who acknowledges me publicly here on earth, the Son of Man* will also acknowledge in the presence of God's angels. 9 But anyone who denies me here on earth will be denied before God's angels. 10 Anyone who speaks against the Son of Man can be forgiven, but anyone who blasphemes the Holy Spirit will not be forgiven.

11 "And when you are brought to trial in the synagogues and before rulers and authorities, don't worry about how to defend yourself or what to say, 12 for the Holy Spirit will teach you at that time what needs to be said."

Parable of the Rich Fool

13 Then someone called from the crowd, "Teacher, please tell my brother to divide our father's estate with me."

14 Jesus replied, "Friend, who made me a judge over you to decide such things as that?" 15 Then he said, "Beware! Guard against every kind of greed. Life is not measured by how much you own."

16 Then he told them a story: "A rich man had a fertile farm that produced fine crops. 17 He said to himself, 'What should I do? I don't have room for all my crops.' 18 Then he said, 'I know! I'll tear down my barns

---

11:49 Greek *Therefore, the wisdom of God said.* 12:5 Greek *Gehenna.* 12:6 Greek *two assaria* [Roman coins equal to 1/16 of a denarius]. 12:8 "Son of Man" is a title Jesus used for himself.

and build bigger ones. Then I'll have room enough to store all my wheat and other goods. [19] And I'll sit back and say to myself, "My friend, you have enough stored away for years to come. Now take it easy! Eat, drink, and be merry!"'

[20] "But God said to him, 'You fool! You will die this very night. Then who will get everything you worked for?'

[21] "Yes, a person is a fool to store up earthly wealth but not have a rich relationship with God."

Teaching about Money and Possessions

[22] Then, turning to his disciples, Jesus said, "That is why I tell you not to worry about everyday life—whether you have enough food to eat or enough clothes to wear. [23] For life is more than food, and your body more than clothing. [24] Look at the ravens. They don't plant or harvest or store food in barns, for God feeds them. And you are far more valuable to him than any birds! [25] Can all your worries add a single moment to your life? [26] And if worry can't accomplish a little thing like that, what's the use of worrying over bigger things?

[27] "Look at the lilies and how they grow. They don't work or make their clothing, yet Solomon in all his glory was not dressed as beautifully as they are. [28] And if God cares so wonderfully for flowers that are here today and thrown into the fire tomorrow, he will certainly care for you. Why do you have so little faith?

[29] "And don't be concerned about what to eat and what to drink. Don't worry about such things. [30] These things dominate the thoughts of unbelievers all over the world, but your Father already knows your needs. [31] Seek the Kingdom of God above all else, and he will give you everything you need.

[32] "So don't be afraid, little flock. For it gives your Father great happiness to give you the Kingdom.

[33] "Sell your possessions and give to those in need. This will store up treasure for you in heaven! And the purses of heaven never get old or develop holes. Your treasure will be safe; no thief can steal it and no moth can destroy it. [34] Wherever your treasure is, there the desires of your heart will also be.

Be Ready for the Lord's Coming

[35] "Be dressed for service and keep your lamps burning, [36] as though you were waiting for your master to return from the wedding feast. Then you will be ready to open the door and let him in the moment he arrives and knocks. [37] The servants who are ready and waiting for his return will be rewarded. I tell you the truth, he himself will seat them, put on an apron, and serve them as they sit and eat! [38] He may come in the middle of the night or just before dawn.* But whenever he comes, he will reward the servants who are ready.

[39] "Understand this: If a homeowner knew exactly when a burglar was coming, he would not permit his house to be broken into. [40] You also must be ready all the time, for the Son of Man will come when least expected."

[41] Peter asked, "Lord, is that illustration just for us or for everyone?"

[42] And the Lord replied, "A faithful, sensible servant is one to whom the master can give the responsibility of managing his other household servants and feeding them. [43] If the master returns and finds that the servant has done a good job, there will be a reward. [44] I tell you the truth, the master will put that servant in charge of all he owns. [45] But what if the servant thinks, 'My master won't be back for a while,' and he begins beating the other servants, partying, and getting drunk? [46] The master will return unannounced and unexpected, and he will cut the servant in pieces and banish him with the unfaithful.

[47] "And a servant who knows what the master wants, but isn't prepared and doesn't carry out those instructions, will be severely punished. [48] But someone who does not know, and then does something wrong, will be punished only lightly. When someone has been given much, much will be required in return; and when someone has been entrusted with much, even more will be required.

Jesus Causes Division

[49] "I have come to set the world on fire, and I wish it were already burning! [50] I have a terrible baptism of suffering ahead of me, and I am under a heavy burden until it is

---

12:38 Greek *in the second or third watch.*

accomplished. ⁵¹Do you think I have come to bring peace to the earth? No, I have come to divide people against each other! ⁵²From now on families will be split apart, three in favor of me, and two against—or two in favor and three against.

⁵³ 'Father will be divided against son
    and son against father;
mother against daughter
    and daughter against mother;
and mother-in-law against
        daughter-in-law
    and daughter-in-law against
        mother-in-law.'*"

⁵⁴Then Jesus turned to the crowd and said, "When you see clouds beginning to form in the west, you say, 'Here comes a shower.' And you are right. ⁵⁵When the south wind blows, you say, 'Today will be a scorcher.' And it is. ⁵⁶You fools! You know how to interpret the weather signs of the earth and sky, but you don't know how to interpret the present times.

⁵⁷"Why can't you decide for yourselves what is right? ⁵⁸When you are on the way to court with your accuser, try to settle the matter before you get there. Otherwise, your accuser may drag you before the judge, who will hand you over to an officer, who will throw you into prison. ⁵⁹And if that happens, you won't be free again until you have paid the very last penny.*"

13 A Call to Repentance

About this time Jesus was informed that Pilate had murdered some people from Galilee as they were offering sacrifices at the Temple. ²"Do you think those Galileans were worse sinners than all the other people from Galilee?" Jesus asked. "Is that why they suffered? ³Not at all! And you will perish, too, unless you repent of your sins and turn to God. ⁴And what about the eighteen people who died when the tower in Siloam fell on them? Were they the worst sinners in Jerusalem? ⁵No, and I tell you again that unless you repent, you will perish, too."

Parable of the Barren Fig Tree

⁶Then Jesus told this story: "A man planted a fig tree in his garden and came again and again to see if there was any fruit on it, but he was always disappointed. ⁷Finally, he said to his gardener, 'I've waited three years, and there hasn't been a single fig! Cut it down. It's just taking up space in the garden.'

⁸"The gardener answered, 'Sir, give it one more chance. Leave it another year, and I'll give it special attention and plenty of fertilizer. ⁹If we get figs next year, fine. If not, then you can cut it down.'"

Jesus Heals on the Sabbath

¹⁰One Sabbath day as Jesus was teaching in a synagogue, ¹¹he saw a woman who had been crippled by an evil spirit. She had been bent double for eighteen years and was unable to stand up straight. ¹²When Jesus saw her, he called her over and said, "Dear woman, you are healed of your sickness!" ¹³Then he touched her, and instantly she could stand straight. How she praised God!

¹⁴But the leader in charge of the synagogue was indignant that Jesus had healed her on the Sabbath day. "There are six days of the week for working," he said to the crowd. "Come on those days to be healed, not on the Sabbath."

¹⁵But the Lord replied, "You hypocrites! Each of you works on the Sabbath day! Don't you untie your ox or your donkey from its stall on the Sabbath and lead it out for water? ¹⁶This dear woman, a daughter of Abraham, has been held in bondage by Satan for eighteen years. Isn't it right that she be released, even on the Sabbath?"

¹⁷This shamed his enemies, but all the people rejoiced at the wonderful things he did.

Parable of the Mustard Seed

¹⁸Then Jesus said, "What is the Kingdom of God like? How can I illustrate it? ¹⁹It is like a tiny mustard seed that a man planted in a garden; it grows and becomes a tree, and the birds make nests in its branches."

Parable of the Yeast

²⁰He also asked, "What else is the Kingdom of God like? ²¹It is like the yeast a woman used in making bread. Even though she put only a little yeast in three measures of flour, it permeated every part of the dough."

12:53 Mic 7:6.   12:59 Greek last lepton [the smallest Jewish coin].

The Narrow Door

22 Jesus went through the towns and villages, teaching as he went, always pressing on toward Jerusalem. 23 Someone asked him, "Lord, will only a few be saved?"

He replied, 24 "Work hard to enter the narrow door to God's Kingdom, for many will try to enter but will fail. 25 When the master of the house has locked the door, it will be too late. You will stand outside knocking and pleading, 'Lord, open the door for us!' But he will reply, 'I don't know you or where you come from.' 26 Then you will say, 'But we ate and drank with you, and you taught in our streets.' 27 And he will reply, 'I tell you, I don't know you or where you come from. Get away from me, all you who do evil.'

28 "There will be weeping and gnashing of teeth, for you will see Abraham, Isaac, Jacob, and all the prophets in the Kingdom of God, but you will be thrown out. 29 And people will come from all over the world—from east and west, north and south—to take their places in the Kingdom of God. 30 And note this: Some who seem least important now will be the greatest then, and some who are the greatest now will be least important then.*"

Jesus Grieves over Jerusalem

31 At that time some Pharisees said to him, "Get away from here if you want to live! Herod Antipas wants to kill you!"

32 Jesus replied, "Go tell that fox that I will keep on casting out demons and healing people today and tomorrow; and the third day I will accomplish my purpose. 33 Yes, today, tomorrow, and the next day I must proceed on my way. For it wouldn't do for a prophet of God to be killed except in Jerusalem!

34 "O Jerusalem, Jerusalem, the city that kills the prophets and stones God's messengers! How often I have wanted to gather your children together as a hen protects her chicks beneath her wings, but you wouldn't let me. 35 And now, look, your house is abandoned. And you will never see me again until you say, 'Blessings on the one who comes in the name of the Lord!'*"

Jesus Heals on the Sabbath

14 One Sabbath day Jesus went to eat dinner in the home of a leader of the Pharisees, and the people were watching him closely. 2 There was a man there whose arms and legs were swollen.* 3 Jesus asked the Pharisees and experts in religious law, "Is it permitted in the law to heal people on the Sabbath day, or not?" 4 When they refused to answer, Jesus touched the sick man and healed him and sent him away. 5 Then he turned to them and said, "Which of you doesn't work on the Sabbath? If your son* or your cow falls into a pit, don't you rush to get him out?" 6 Again they could not answer.

Jesus Teaches about Humility

7 When Jesus noticed that all who had come to the dinner were trying to sit in the seats of honor near the head of the table, he gave them this advice: 8 "When you are invited to a wedding feast, don't sit in the seat of honor. What if someone who is more distinguished than you has also been invited? 9 The host will come and say, 'Give this person your seat.' Then you will be embarrassed, and you will have to take whatever seat is left at the foot of the table!

10 "Instead, take the lowest place at the foot of the table. Then when your host sees you, he will come and say, 'Friend, we have a better place for you!' Then you will be honored in front of all the other guests. 11 For those who exalt themselves will be humbled, and those who humble themselves will be exalted."

12 Then he turned to his host. "When you put on a luncheon or a banquet," he said, "don't invite your friends, brothers, relatives, and rich neighbors. For they will invite you back, and that will be your only reward. 13 Instead, invite the poor, the crippled, the lame, and the blind. 14 Then at the resurrection of the righteous, God will reward you for inviting those who could not repay you."

Parable of the Great Feast

15 Hearing this, a man sitting at the table with Jesus exclaimed, "What a blessing it

---

13:30 Greek Some are last who will be first, and some are first who will be last. 13:35 Ps 118:26. 14:2 Or who had dropsy. 14:5 Some manuscripts read donkey.

Hospitality in Worship

LUKE 14:7–24

I once heard theologian Robert Webber tell a story about hospitality in the context of church worship. He visited an unfamiliar church while traveling. When it was time for the choir to sing, the choir director turned to the congregation and taught them their parts—soprano, alto, tenor, bass. Webber claimed that in the course of the opening song, guided by the choir at the front, he went from being a stranger to someone who belonged. He felt welcomed into that community's worship.

Hospitality matters because every time we worship together, we are drawn not only into our particular community but also into the community of angels and saints who are always praising God. Even better, we are reminded that we are included in the circle of fellowship among the Father, Son, and Spirit. The Son is the true worship leader who helps us express our thanks to the Father, the phenomenally hospitable God who invites us to make ourselves at home with him.

Jesus emphasized this inclusive nature of the kingdom of God when he described a great heavenly feast in which society's outcasts are welcome at the table (Luke 14:15–24). Beyond the symbolism of this parable, Jesus challenged his real-life dinner host to literally "invite the poor, the crippled, the lame, and the blind" into his home, rather than just his "friends, brothers, relatives, and rich neighbors" (14:12–13).

Church is powerful when it embodies this heavenly inclusion. When church is like that, it becomes the home away from home where we offer one another a place to reunite, be fed, commune, wash, rest, and receive what we need for the road ahead.

—*Carolyn Arends*

For more on hospitality, see reading at Acts 4:32–37.

---

will be to attend a banquet* in the Kingdom of God!"

¹⁶ Jesus replied with this story: "A man prepared a great feast and sent out many invitations. ¹⁷ When the banquet was ready, he sent his servant to tell the guests, 'Come, the banquet is ready.' ¹⁸ But they all began making excuses. One said, 'I have just bought a field and must inspect it. Please excuse me.' ¹⁹ Another said, 'I have just bought five pairs of oxen, and I want to try them out. Please excuse me.' ²⁰ Another said, 'I now have a wife, so I can't come.'

²¹ "The servant returned and told his master what they had said. His master was furious and said, 'Go quickly into the streets and alleys of the town and invite the poor, the crippled, the blind, and the lame.' ²² After the servant had done this, he reported, 'There is still room for more.' ²³ So his master said, 'Go out into the country lanes and behind the hedges and urge anyone you find to come, so that the house will be full. ²⁴ For none of those I first invited will get even the smallest taste of my banquet.'"

The Cost of Being a Disciple

²⁵ A large crowd was following Jesus. He turned around and said to them, ²⁶ "If you want to be my disciple, you must hate everyone else by comparison—your father and mother, wife and children, brothers and sisters—yes, even your own life. Otherwise,

14:15 Greek *to eat bread.*

you cannot be my disciple. ²⁷And if you do not carry your own cross and follow me, you cannot be my disciple.

²⁸"But don't begin until you count the cost. For who would begin construction of a building without first calculating the cost to see if there is enough money to finish it? ²⁹Otherwise, you might complete only the foundation before running out of money, and then everyone would laugh at you. ³⁰They would say, 'There's the person who started that building and couldn't afford to finish it!'

³¹"Or what king would go to war against another king without first sitting down with his counselors to discuss whether his army of 10,000 could defeat the 20,000 soldiers marching against him? ³²And if he can't, he will send a delegation to discuss terms of peace while the enemy is still far away. ³³So you cannot become my disciple without giving up everything you own.

³⁴"Salt is good for seasoning. But if it loses its flavor, how do you make it salty again? ³⁵Flavorless salt is good neither for the soil nor for the manure pile. It is thrown away. Anyone with ears to hear should listen and understand!"

15 Parable of the Lost Sheep

Tax collectors and other notorious sinners often came to listen to Jesus teach. ²This made the Pharisees and teachers of religious law complain that he was associating with such sinful people—even eating with them!

³So Jesus told them this story: ⁴"If a man has a hundred sheep and one of them gets lost, what will he do? Won't he leave the ninety-nine others in the wilderness and go to search for the one that is lost until he finds it? ⁵And when he has found it, he will joyfully carry it home on his shoulders. ⁶When he arrives, he will call together his friends and neighbors, saying, 'Rejoice with me because I have found my lost sheep.' ⁷In the same way, there is more joy in heaven over one lost sinner who repents and returns to God than over ninety-nine others who are righteous and haven't strayed away!

Parable of the Lost Coin

⁸"Or suppose a woman has ten silver coins* and loses one. Won't she light a lamp and sweep the entire house and search carefully until she finds it? ⁹And when she finds it, she will call in her friends and neighbors and say, 'Rejoice with me because I have found my lost coin.' ¹⁰In the same way, there is joy in the presence of God's angels when even one sinner repents."

Parable of the Lost Son

¹¹To illustrate the point further, Jesus told them this story: "A man had two sons. ¹²The younger son told his father, 'I want my share of your estate now before you die.' So his father agreed to divide his wealth between his sons.

¹³"A few days later this younger son packed all his belongings and moved to a distant land, and there he wasted all his money in wild living. ¹⁴About the time his money ran out, a great famine swept over the land, and he began to starve. ¹⁵He persuaded a local farmer to hire him, and the man sent him into his fields to feed the pigs. ¹⁶The young man became so hungry that even the pods he was feeding the pigs looked good to him. But no one gave him anything.

¹⁷"When he finally came to his senses, he said to himself, 'At home even the hired servants have food enough to spare, and here I am dying of hunger! ¹⁸I will go home to my father and say, "Father, I have sinned against both heaven and you, ¹⁹and I am no longer worthy of being called your son. Please take me on as a hired servant."'

²⁰"So he returned home to his father. And while he was still a long way off, his father saw him coming. Filled with love and compassion, he ran to his son, embraced him, and kissed him. ²¹His son said to him, 'Father, I have sinned against both heaven and you, and I am no longer worthy of being called your son.*'

²²"But his father said to the servants, 'Quick! Bring the finest robe in the house and put it on him. Get a ring for his finger and sandals for his feet. ²³And kill the calf we have been fattening. We must celebrate with a feast, ²⁴for this son of mine was dead

---

15:8 Greek *ten drachmas.* A drachma was the equivalent of a full day's wage.   **15:21** Some manuscripts add *Please take me on as a hired servant.*

and has now returned to life. He was lost, but now he is found.' So the party began.

25 "Meanwhile, the older son was in the fields working. When he returned home, he heard music and dancing in the house, 26 and he asked one of the servants what was going on. 27 'Your brother is back,' he was told, 'and your father has killed the fattened calf. We are celebrating because of his safe return.'

28 "The older brother was angry and wouldn't go in. His father came out and begged him, 29 but he replied, 'All these years I've slaved for you and never once refused to do a single thing you told me to. And in all that time you never gave me even one young goat for a feast with my friends. 30 Yet when this son of yours comes back after squandering your money on prostitutes, you celebrate by killing the fattened calf!'

31 "His father said to him, 'Look, dear son, you have always stayed by me, and everything I have is yours. 32 We had to celebrate

Q&A — The Theology of Embrace

Reconciliation

LUKE 15:11–32

How can we balance grace and justice in our efforts to reconcile with others?

One of the best portrayals of what lies at the core of Christian faith is this amazing story of the Lost Son, which is an expression of what God did for us on the Cross. The open arms of the father in this parable are a picture of who God is, how God has acted toward sinful humanity—and also how we ought to act toward those who have sinned against us.

This parable has significant implications for how we relate to one another in situations of conflict, enmity, wrongdoing, suffering. The basic challenge in all human conflict is the same one identified in the story of this prodigal: the relationship between justice and peace, liberation and reconciliation, law and grace. Do you call first for justice, then peace? First liberation, then reconciliation? Or is it the other way around?

In Jesus' parable we see that the primacy was given to grace, embrace, reconciliation. At the center of Christian faith lies this theology of embrace: the father will not give up his relationship with his lost son in spite of his son's wrongdoing. When that son returns, the father runs toward him without having heard a single word from that son. He shows his son grace and acceptance because the prodigal was and is and remained his son even through the wrongdoing.

That is what we see on the Cross. The significance of the Crucifixion is not only what God does for us; consistently throughout the New Testament the Crucifixion is portrayed as the pattern that we are to follow.

—Miroslav Volf

For more on reconciliation, see reading at John 4:4–42.

this happy day. For your brother was dead and has come back to life! He was lost, but now he is found!'"

16 Parable of the Shrewd Manager

Jesus told this story to his disciples: "There was a certain rich man who had a manager handling his affairs. One day a report came that the manager was wasting his employer's money. ²So the employer called him in and said, 'What's this I hear about you? Get your report in order, because you are going to be fired.'

³"The manager thought to himself, 'Now what? My boss has fired me. I don't have the strength to dig ditches, and I'm too proud to beg. ⁴Ah, I know how to ensure that I'll have plenty of friends who will give me a home when I am fired.'

⁵"So he invited each person who owed money to his employer to come and discuss the situation. He asked the first one, 'How much do you owe him?' ⁶The man replied, 'I owe him 800 gallons of olive oil.' So the manager told him, 'Take the bill and quickly change it to 400 gallons.*'

⁷"'And how much do you owe my employer?' he asked the next man. 'I owe him 1,000 bushels of wheat,' was the reply. 'Here,' the manager said, 'take the bill and change it to 800 bushels.*'

⁸"The rich man had to admire the dishonest rascal for being so shrewd. And it is true that the children of this world are more shrewd in dealing with the world around them than are the children of the light. ⁹Here's the lesson: Use your worldly resources to benefit others and make friends. Then, when your earthly possessions are gone, they will welcome you to an eternal home.*

¹⁰"If you are faithful in little things, you will be faithful in large ones. But if you are dishonest in little things, you won't be honest with greater responsibilities. ¹¹And if you are untrustworthy about worldly wealth, who will trust you with the true riches of heaven? ¹²And if you are not faithful with other people's things, why should you be trusted with things of your own?

¹³"No one can serve two masters. For you will hate one and love the other; you will be devoted to one and despise the other. You cannot serve both God and money."

¹⁴The Pharisees, who dearly loved their money, heard all this and scoffed at him. ¹⁵Then he said to them, "You like to appear righteous in public, but God knows your hearts. What this world honors is detestable in the sight of God.

¹⁶"Until John the Baptist, the law of Moses and the messages of the prophets were your guides. But now the Good News of the Kingdom of God is preached, and everyone is eager to get in.* ¹⁷But that doesn't mean that the law has lost its force. It is easier for heaven and earth to disappear than for the smallest point of God's law to be overturned.

¹⁸"For example, a man who divorces his wife and marries someone else commits adultery. And anyone who marries a woman divorced from her husband commits adultery."

Parable of the Rich Man and Lazarus

¹⁹Jesus said, "There was a certain rich man who was splendidly clothed in purple and fine linen and who lived each day in luxury. ²⁰At his gate lay a poor man named Lazarus who was covered with sores. ²¹As Lazarus lay there longing for scraps from the rich man's table, the dogs would come and lick his open sores.

²²"Finally, the poor man died and was carried by the angels to be with Abraham.* The rich man also died and was buried, ²³and his soul went to the place of the dead.* There, in torment, he saw Abraham in the far distance with Lazarus at his side.

²⁴"The rich man shouted, 'Father Abraham, have some pity! Send Lazarus over here to dip the tip of his finger in water and cool my tongue. I am in anguish in these flames.'

²⁵"But Abraham said to him, 'Son, remember that during your lifetime you had everything you wanted, and Lazarus had nothing. So now he is here being comforted, and you are in anguish. ²⁶And besides, there is a great chasm separating us. No one can cross over to you from here, and no one can cross over to us from there.'

16:6 Greek *100 baths . . . 50 [baths].* **16:7** Greek *100 korous . . . 80 [korous].* **16:9** Or *you will be welcomed into eternal homes.* **16:16** Or *everyone is urged to enter in.* **16:22** Greek *into Abraham's bosom.* **16:23** Greek *to Hades.*

27 "Then the rich man said, 'Please, Father Abraham, at least send him to my father's home. 28 For I have five brothers, and I want him to warn them so they don't end up in this place of torment.'

29 "But Abraham said, 'Moses and the prophets have warned them. Your brothers can read what they wrote.'

30 "The rich man replied, 'No, Father Abraham! But if someone is sent to them from the dead, then they will repent of their sins and turn to God.'

31 "But Abraham said, 'If they won't listen to Moses and the prophets, they won't listen even if someone rises from the dead.'"

17 Teachings about Forgiveness and Faith

One day Jesus said to his disciples, "There will always be temptations to sin, but what sorrow awaits the person who does the tempting! 2 It would be better to be thrown into the sea with a millstone hung around your neck than to cause one of these little ones to fall into sin. 3 So watch yourselves!

"If another believer* sins, rebuke that person; then if there is repentance, forgive. 4 Even if that person wrongs you seven times a day and each time turns again and asks forgiveness, you must forgive."

5 The apostles said to the Lord, "Show us how to increase our faith."

6 The Lord answered, "If you had faith even as small as a mustard seed, you could say to this mulberry tree, 'May you be uprooted and thrown into the sea,' and it would obey you!

7 "When a servant comes in from plowing or taking care of sheep, does his master say, 'Come in and eat with me'? 8 No, he says, 'Prepare my meal, put on your apron, and serve me while I eat. Then you can eat later.' 9 And does the master thank the servant for doing what he was told to do? Of course not. 10 In the same way, when you obey me you should say, 'We are unworthy servants who have simply done our duty.'"

Ten Healed of Leprosy

11 As Jesus continued on toward Jerusalem, he reached the border between Galilee and Samaria. 12 As he entered a village there, ten lepers stood at a distance, 13 crying out, "Jesus, Master, have mercy on us!"

14 He looked at them and said, "Go show yourselves to the priests."* And as they went, they were cleansed of their leprosy.

15 One of them, when he saw that he was healed, came back to Jesus, shouting, "Praise God!" 16 He fell to the ground at Jesus' feet, thanking him for what he had done. This man was a Samaritan.

17 Jesus asked, "Didn't I heal ten men? Where are the other nine? 18 Has no one returned to give glory to God except this foreigner?" 19 And Jesus said to the man, "Stand up and go. Your faith has healed you.*"

The Coming of the Kingdom

20 One day the Pharisees asked Jesus, "When will the Kingdom of God come?"

Jesus replied, "The Kingdom of God can't be detected by visible signs.* 21 You won't be able to say, 'Here it is!' or 'It's over there!' For the Kingdom of God is already among you.*"

22 Then he said to his disciples, "The time is coming when you will long to see the day when the Son of Man returns,* but you won't see it. 23 People will tell you, 'Look, there is the Son of Man,' or 'Here he is,' but don't go out and follow them. 24 For as the lightning flashes and lights up the sky from one end to the other, so it will be on the day when the Son of Man comes. 25 But first the Son of Man must suffer terribly* and be rejected by this generation.

26 "When the Son of Man returns, it will be like it was in Noah's day. 27 In those days, the people enjoyed banquets and parties and weddings right up to the time Noah entered his boat and the flood came and destroyed them all.

28 "And the world will be as it was in the days of Lot. People went about their daily business—eating and drinking, buying and selling, farming and building—29 until the morning Lot left Sodom. Then fire and burning sulfur rained down from heaven and destroyed them all. 30 Yes, it will be

---

17:3 Greek If your brother. 17:14 See Lev 14:2-32. 17:19 Or Your faith has saved you. 17:20 Or by your speculations. 17:21 Or is within you, or is in your grasp. 17:22 Or long for even one day with the Son of Man. "Son of Man" is a title Jesus used for himself. 17:25 Or suffer many things.

'business as usual' right up to the day when the Son of Man is revealed. ³¹On that day a person out on the deck of a roof must not go down into the house to pack. A person out in the field must not return home. ³²Remember what happened to Lot's wife! ³³If you cling to your life, you will lose it, and if you let your life go, you will save it. ³⁴That night two people will be asleep in one bed; one will be taken, the other left. ³⁵Two women will be grinding flour together at the mill; one will be taken, the other left.*"

³⁷"Where will this happen, Lord?"* the disciples asked.

Jesus replied, "Just as the gathering of vultures shows there is a carcass nearby, so these signs indicate that the end is near."*

Q&A — Forgiving the Unrepentant

LUKE 17:1–10

How can I forgive someone who has done something horrific—and who is unrepentant?

Still forgive. Why? Forgiveness isn't so much a word spoken, an action performed, or a feeling felt, as it is an embodied way of life in an ever-deepening friendship with God and with others. As such, a Christian account of forgiveness ought not simply be focused on an absolution of guilt; rather, it ought to be focused on the reconciliation of brokenness, the restoration of communion—with God, with one another, and with the whole Creation.

Each of us lives in the midst of particular sins and specific instances of brokenness. And each of us must choose how we will respond. Living a life of holiness and learning the ways of God sometimes mean letting go of our need for justice and instead embracing a world that groans in anticipation of the day when it, and we, will be redeemed. When we choose to forgive, it's a way of recognizing our own brokenness—and accepting with humility that God alone is good.

When Jesus called his disciples to this radical standard of forgiveness, they recognized how far beyond their natural abilities this kind of forgiveness was; they immediately responded, "Show us how to increase our faith" (Luke 17:5).

So when I face someone's horrific wrongdoing or complete lack of repentance, I'm left with a question: who am I to say I won't forgive, when I know forgiveness doesn't mean to condone another's actions or to absolve them—since God alone can absolve? I am no better than the apostles who rightly understood the challenge that was before them. With them, I can only reply, "Increase my faith, dear Lord."

—Christine A. Scheller

For more on forgiveness, see reading at Luke 23:32–43.

17:35 Some manuscripts add verse 36, *Two men will be working in the field; one will be taken, the other left.* Compare Matt 24:40.
17:37a Greek *"Where, Lord?"* **17:37b** Greek *"Wherever the carcass is, the vultures gather."*

Waiting for an Answer

LUKE 18:1–8

Prayer

Waiting for an answer to prayer is painful. We don't understand why God doesn't act when we so clearly see what he should do.

Jesus told a parable about a persistent widow, explaining that we "should always pray and never give up" (Luke 18:1). In this society widows were some of the most helpless people, often having no one to advocate for them. The judge was this widow's only hope for justice, so she banged on his door until he answered her request.

We too are helpless in so many ways. Our prayer requests are about things over which we have no control. We have nowhere to turn, so we bang on God's door because we know deep down that only he can help us. Yet God often waits to answer, and we may need to return to him in prayer again and again. When we don't understand why he waits, we can trust that he sees from the perspective of eternity, he knows what is best, and his timing is perfect.

Although at times waiting for God's answer may seem simply too hard, Jesus reminds us, "Never give up!" We can trust that God *will* answer—not because he's tired of our knocking, but simply because it's time.

—Linda Taylor

For more on prayer, see reading at 1 Thessalonians 5:16–17.

18 Parable of the Persistent Widow

One day Jesus told his disciples a story to show that they should always pray and never give up. [2] "There was a judge in a certain city," he said, "who neither feared God nor cared about people. [3] A widow of that city came to him repeatedly, saying, 'Give me justice in this dispute with my enemy.' [4] The judge ignored her for a while, but finally he said to himself, 'I don't fear God or care about people, [5] but this woman is driving me crazy. I'm going to see that she gets justice, because she is wearing me out with her constant requests!'"

[6] Then the Lord said, "Learn a lesson from this unjust judge. [7] Even he rendered a just decision in the end. So don't you think God will surely give justice to his chosen people who cry out to him day and night? Will he keep putting them off? [8] I tell you, he will grant justice to them quickly! But when the Son of Man* returns, how many will he find on the earth who have faith?"

Parable of the Pharisee and Tax Collector

[9] Then Jesus told this story to some who had great confidence in their own righteousness and scorned everyone else: [10] "Two men went to the Temple to pray. One was a Pharisee, and the other was a despised tax collector. [11] The Pharisee stood by himself and prayed this prayer*: 'I thank you, God, that I am not a sinner like everyone else. For I don't cheat, I don't sin, and I don't commit adultery. I'm certainly not like that tax collector! [12] I fast twice a week, and I give you a tenth of my income.'

[13] "But the tax collector stood at a distance and dared not even lift his eyes to heaven as he prayed. Instead, he beat his chest in sorrow, saying, 'O God, be merciful to me, for I am a sinner.' [14] I tell you, this sinner, not the Pharisee, returned home justified before God. For those who exalt themselves will be humbled, and those who humble themselves will be exalted."

18:8 "Son of Man" is a title Jesus used for himself.　　**18:11** Some manuscripts read *stood and prayed this prayer to himself.*

Jesus Blesses the Children

¹⁵One day some parents brought their little children to Jesus so he could touch and bless them. But when the disciples saw this, they scolded the parents for bothering him.

¹⁶Then Jesus called for the children and said to the disciples, "Let the children come to me. Don't stop them! For the Kingdom of God belongs to those who are like these children. ¹⁷I tell you the truth, anyone who doesn't receive the Kingdom of God like a child will never enter it."

The Rich Man

¹⁸Once a religious leader asked Jesus this question: "Good Teacher, what should I do to inherit eternal life?"

¹⁹"Why do you call me good?" Jesus asked him. "Only God is truly good. ²⁰But to answer your question, you know the commandments: 'You must not commit adultery. You must not murder. You must not steal. You must not testify falsely. Honor your father and mother.'*"

²¹The man replied, "I've obeyed all these commandments since I was young."

²²When Jesus heard his answer, he said, "There is still one thing you haven't done. Sell all your possessions and give the money to the poor, and you will have treasure in heaven. Then come, follow me."

²³But when the man heard this he became very sad, for he was very rich.

²⁴When Jesus saw this,* he said, "How hard it is for the rich to enter the Kingdom of God! ²⁵In fact, it is easier for a camel to go through the eye of a needle than for a rich person to enter the Kingdom of God!"

²⁶Those who heard this said, "Then who in the world can be saved?"

²⁷He replied, "What is impossible for people is possible with God."

²⁸Peter said, "We've left our homes to follow you."

²⁹"Yes," Jesus replied, "and I assure you that everyone who has given up house or wife or brothers or parents or children, for the sake of the Kingdom of God, ³⁰will be repaid many times over in this life, and will have eternal life in the world to come."

Jesus Again Predicts His Death

³¹Taking the twelve disciples aside, Jesus said, "Listen, we're going up to Jerusalem, where all the predictions of the prophets concerning the Son of Man will come true. ³²He will be handed over to the Romans,* and he will be mocked, treated shamefully, and spit upon. ³³They will flog him with a whip and kill him, but on the third day he will rise again."

³⁴But they didn't understand any of this. The significance of his words was hidden from them, and they failed to grasp what he was talking about.

Jesus Heals a Blind Beggar

³⁵As Jesus approached Jericho, a blind beggar was sitting beside the road. ³⁶When he heard the noise of a crowd going past, he asked what was happening. ³⁷They told him that Jesus the Nazarene* was going by. ³⁸So he began shouting, "Jesus, Son of David, have mercy on me!"

³⁹"Be quiet!" the people in front yelled at him.

But he only shouted louder, "Son of David, have mercy on me!"

⁴⁰When Jesus heard him, he stopped and ordered that the man be brought to him. As the man came near, Jesus asked him, ⁴¹"What do you want me to do for you?"

"Lord," he said, "I want to see!"

⁴²And Jesus said, "All right, receive your sight! Your faith has healed you." ⁴³Instantly the man could see, and he followed Jesus, praising God. And all who saw it praised God, too.

19 Jesus and Zacchaeus

Jesus entered Jericho and made his way through the town. ²There was a man there named Zacchaeus. He was the chief tax collector in the region, and he had become very rich. ³He tried to get a look at Jesus, but he was too short to see over the crowd. ⁴So he ran ahead and climbed a sycamore-fig tree beside the road, for Jesus was going to pass that way.

⁵When Jesus came by, he looked up at Zacchaeus and called him by name. "Zacchaeus!" he said. "Quick, come down! I must be a guest in your home today."

18:20 Exod 20:12-16; Deut 5:16-20.   **18:24** Some manuscripts read *When Jesus saw how sad the man was.*   **18:32** Greek *the Gentiles.*
18:37 Or *Jesus of Nazareth.*

⁶Zacchaeus quickly climbed down and took Jesus to his house in great excitement and joy. ⁷But the people were displeased. "He has gone to be the guest of a notorious sinner," they grumbled.

⁸Meanwhile, Zacchaeus stood before the Lord and said, "I will give half my wealth to the poor, Lord, and if I have cheated people on their taxes, I will give them back four times as much!"

⁹Jesus responded, "Salvation has come to this home today, for this man has shown himself to be a true son of Abraham. ¹⁰For the Son of Man* came to seek and save those who are lost."

Parable of the Ten Servants

¹¹The crowd was listening to everything Jesus said. And because he was nearing Jerusalem, he told them a story to correct the impression that the Kingdom of God would begin right away. ¹²He said, "A nobleman was called away to a distant empire to be crowned king and then return. ¹³Before he left, he called together ten of his servants and divided among them ten pounds of silver,* saying, 'Invest this for me while I am gone.' ¹⁴But his people hated him and sent a delegation after him to say, 'We do not want him to be our king.'

¹⁵"After he was crowned king, he returned and called in the servants to whom he had given the money. He wanted to find out what their profits were. ¹⁶The first servant reported, 'Master, I invested your money and made ten times the original amount!'

¹⁷"'Well done!' the king exclaimed. 'You are a good servant. You have been faithful with the little I entrusted to you, so you will be governor of ten cities as your reward.'

¹⁸"The next servant reported, 'Master, I invested your money and made five times the original amount.'

¹⁹"'Well done!' the king said. 'You will be governor over five cities.'

²⁰"But the third servant brought back only the original amount of money and said, 'Master, I hid your money and kept it safe. ²¹I was afraid because you are a hard man to deal with, taking what isn't yours and harvesting crops you didn't plant.'

²²"'You wicked servant!' the king roared. 'Your own words condemn you. If you knew that I'm a hard man who takes what isn't mine and harvests crops I didn't plant, ²³why didn't you deposit my money in the bank? At least I could have gotten some interest on it.'

²⁴"Then, turning to the others standing nearby, the king ordered, 'Take the money from this servant, and give it to the one who has ten pounds.'

²⁵"'But, master,' they said, 'he already has ten pounds!'

²⁶"'Yes,' the king replied, 'and to those who use well what they are given, even more will be given. But from those who do nothing, even what little they have will be taken away. ²⁷And as for these enemies of mine who didn't want me to be their king— bring them in and execute them right here in front of me.'"

Jesus' Triumphant Entry

²⁸After telling this story, Jesus went on toward Jerusalem, walking ahead of his disciples. ²⁹As he came to the towns of Bethphage and Bethany on the Mount of Olives, he sent two disciples ahead. ³⁰"Go into that village over there," he told them. "As you enter it, you will see a young donkey tied there that no one has ever ridden. Untie it and bring it here. ³¹If anyone asks, 'Why are you untying that colt?' just say, 'The Lord needs it.'"

³²So they went and found the colt, just as Jesus had said. ³³And sure enough, as they were untying it, the owners asked them, "Why are you untying that colt?"

³⁴And the disciples simply replied, "The Lord needs it." ³⁵So they brought the colt to Jesus and threw their garments over it for him to ride on.

³⁶As he rode along, the crowds spread out their garments on the road ahead of him. ³⁷When he reached the place where the road started down the Mount of Olives, all of his followers began to shout and sing as they walked along, praising God for all the wonderful miracles they had seen.

³⁸ "Blessings on the King who comes in the
    name of the Lord!
  Peace in heaven, and glory in highest
    heaven!"*

19:10 "Son of Man" is a title Jesus used for himself.   19:13 Greek *ten minas;* one mina was worth about three months' wages.   19:38 Pss 118:26; 148:1.

³⁹But some of the Pharisees among the crowd said, "Teacher, rebuke your followers for saying things like that!"

⁴⁰He replied, "If they kept quiet, the stones along the road would burst into cheers!"

Jesus Weeps over Jerusalem

⁴¹But as he came closer to Jerusalem and saw the city ahead, he began to weep. ⁴²"How I wish today that you of all people would understand the way to peace. But now it is too late, and peace is hidden from your eyes. ⁴³Before long your enemies will build ramparts against your walls and encircle you and close in on you from every side. ⁴⁴They will crush you into the ground, and your children with you. Your enemies will not leave a single stone in place, because you did not accept your opportunity for salvation."

Jesus Clears the Temple

⁴⁵Then Jesus entered the Temple and began to drive out the people selling animals for sacrifices. ⁴⁶He said to them, "The Scriptures declare, 'My Temple will be a house of prayer,' but you have turned it into a den of thieves."*

⁴⁷After that, he taught daily in the Temple, but the leading priests, the teachers of religious law, and the other leaders of the people began planning how to kill him. ⁴⁸But they could think of nothing, because all the people hung on every word he said.

20 **The Authority of Jesus Challenged**
One day as Jesus was teaching the people and preaching the Good News in the Temple, the leading priests, the teachers of religious law, and the elders came up to him. ²They demanded, "By what authority are you doing all these things? Who gave you the right?"

³"Let me ask you a question first," he replied. ⁴"Did John's authority to baptize come from heaven, or was it merely human?"

⁵They talked it over among themselves. "If we say it was from heaven, he will ask why we didn't believe John. ⁶But if we say it was merely human, the people will stone us because they are convinced John was a prophet." ⁷So they finally replied that they didn't know.

⁸And Jesus responded, "Then I won't tell you by what authority I do these things."

Parable of the Evil Farmers

⁹Now Jesus turned to the people again and told them this story: "A man planted a vineyard, leased it to tenant farmers, and moved to another country to live for several years. ¹⁰At the time of the grape harvest, he sent one of his servants to collect his share of the crop. But the farmers attacked the servant, beat him up, and sent him back empty-handed. ¹¹So the owner sent another servant, but they also insulted him, beat him up, and sent him away empty-handed. ¹²A third man was sent, and they wounded him and chased him away.

¹³"'What will I do?' the owner asked himself. 'I know! I'll send my cherished son. Surely they will respect him.'

¹⁴"But when the tenant farmers saw his son, they said to each other, 'Here comes the heir to this estate. Let's kill him and get the estate for ourselves!' ¹⁵So they dragged him out of the vineyard and murdered him.

"What do you suppose the owner of the vineyard will do to them?" Jesus asked. ¹⁶"I'll tell you—he will come and kill those farmers and lease the vineyard to others."

"How terrible that such a thing should ever happen," his listeners protested.

¹⁷Jesus looked at them and said, "Then what does this Scripture mean?

'The stone that the builders rejected
has now become the cornerstone.'*

¹⁸Everyone who stumbles over that stone will be broken to pieces, and it will crush anyone it falls on."

¹⁹The teachers of religious law and the leading priests wanted to arrest Jesus immediately because they realized he was telling the story against them—they were the wicked farmers. But they were afraid of the people's reaction.

Taxes for Caesar

²⁰Watching for their opportunity, the leaders sent spies pretending to be honest men.

They tried to get Jesus to say something that could be reported to the Roman governor so he would arrest Jesus. ²¹"Teacher," they said, "we know that you speak and teach what is right and are not influenced by what others think. You teach the way of God truthfully. ²²Now tell us—is it right for us to pay taxes to Caesar or not?"

²³He saw through their trickery and said, ²⁴"Show me a Roman coin.* Whose picture and title are stamped on it?"

"Caesar's," they replied.

²⁵"Well then," he said, "give to Caesar what belongs to Caesar, and give to God what belongs to God."

²⁶So they failed to trap him by what he said in front of the people. Instead, they were amazed by his answer, and they became silent.

Discussion about Resurrection

²⁷Then Jesus was approached by some Sadducees—religious leaders who say there is no resurrection from the dead. ²⁸They posed this question: "Teacher, Moses gave us a law that if a man dies, leaving a wife but no children, his brother should marry the widow and have a child who will carry on the brother's name.* ²⁹Well, suppose there were seven brothers. The oldest one married and then died without children. ³⁰So the second brother married the widow, but he also died. ³¹Then the third brother married her. This continued with all seven of them, who died without children. ³²Finally, the woman also died. ³³So tell us, whose wife will she be in the resurrection? For all seven were married to her!"

³⁴Jesus replied, "Marriage is for people here on earth. ³⁵But in the age to come, those worthy of being raised from the dead will neither marry nor be given in marriage. ³⁶And they will never die again. In this respect they will be like angels. They are children of God and children of the resurrection.

³⁷"But now, as to whether the dead will be raised—even Moses proved this when he wrote about the burning bush. Long after Abraham, Isaac, and Jacob had died, he referred to the Lord* as 'the God of Abraham, the God of Isaac, and the God of Jacob.'* ³⁸So he is the God of the living, not the dead, for they are all alive to him."

³⁹"Well said, Teacher!" remarked some of the teachers of religious law who were standing there. ⁴⁰And then no one dared to ask him any more questions.

Whose Son Is the Messiah?

⁴¹Then Jesus presented them with a question. "Why is it," he asked, "that the Messiah is said to be the son of David? ⁴²For David himself wrote in the book of Psalms:

'The LORD said to my Lord,
Sit in the place of honor at my right hand
⁴³ until I humble your enemies,
making them a footstool under your feet.'*

⁴⁴Since David called the Messiah 'Lord,' how can the Messiah be his son?"

⁴⁵Then, with the crowds listening, he turned to his disciples and said, ⁴⁶"Beware of these teachers of religious law! For they like to parade around in flowing robes and love to receive respectful greetings as they walk in the marketplaces. And how they love the seats of honor in the synagogues and the head table at banquets. ⁴⁷Yet they shamelessly cheat widows out of their property and then pretend to be pious by making long prayers in public. Because of this, they will be severely punished."

21 The Widow's Offering

While Jesus was in the Temple, he watched the rich people dropping their gifts in the collection box. ²Then a poor widow came by and dropped in two small coins.*

³"I tell you the truth," Jesus said, "this poor widow has given more than all the rest of them. ⁴For they have given a tiny part of their surplus, but she, poor as she is, has given everything she has."

Jesus Foretells the Future

⁵Some of his disciples began talking about the majestic stonework of the Temple and the memorial decorations on the walls. But Jesus said, ⁶"The time is coming when

20:24 Greek a denarius. 20:28 See Deut 25:5-6. 20:37a Greek when he wrote about the bush. He referred to the Lord. 20:37b Exod 3:6. 20:42-43 Ps 110:1. 21:2 Greek two lepta [the smallest of Jewish coins].

all these things will be completely demolished. Not one stone will be left on top of another!"

7 "Teacher," they asked, "when will all this happen? What sign will show us that these things are about to take place?"

8 He replied, "Don't let anyone mislead you, for many will come in my name, claiming, 'I am the Messiah,'* and saying, 'The time has come!' But don't believe them. 9 And when you hear of wars and insurrections, don't panic. Yes, these things must take place first, but the end won't follow immediately." 10 Then he added, "Nation will go to war against nation, and kingdom against kingdom. 11 There will be great earthquakes, and there will be famines and plagues in many lands, and there will be terrifying things and great miraculous signs from heaven.

12 "But before all this occurs, there will be a time of great persecution. You will be dragged into synagogues and prisons, and you will stand trial before kings and governors because you are my followers. 13 But this will be your opportunity to tell them about me.* 14 So don't worry in advance about how to answer the charges against you, 15 for I will give you the right words and such wisdom that none of your opponents will be able to reply or refute you! 16 Even those closest to you—your parents, brothers, relatives, and friends—will betray you. They will even kill some of you. 17 And everyone will hate you because you are my followers.* 18 But not a hair of your head will perish! 19 By standing firm, you will win your souls.

20 "And when you see Jerusalem surrounded by armies, then you will know that the time of its destruction has arrived. 21 Then those in Judea must flee to the hills. Those in Jerusalem must get out, and those out in the country should not return to the city. 22 For those will be days of God's vengeance, and the prophetic words of the Scriptures will be fulfilled. 23 How terrible it will be for pregnant women and for nursing mothers in those days. For there will be disaster in the land and great anger against this people. 24 They will be killed by the sword or sent away as captives to all the nations of the world. And Jerusalem will be trampled down by the Gentiles until the period of the Gentiles comes to an end.

25 "And there will be strange signs in the sun, moon, and stars. And here on earth the nations will be in turmoil, perplexed by the roaring seas and strange tides. 26 People will be terrified at what they see coming upon the earth, for the powers in the heavens will be shaken. 27 Then everyone will see the Son of Man* coming on a cloud with power and great glory.* 28 So when all these things begin to happen, stand and look up, for your salvation is near!"

29 Then he gave them this illustration: "Notice the fig tree, or any other tree. 30 When the leaves come out, you know without being told that summer is near. 31 In the same way, when you see all these things taking place, you can know that the Kingdom of God is near. 32 I tell you the truth, this generation will not pass from the scene until all these things have taken place. 33 Heaven and earth will disappear, but my words will never disappear.

34 "Watch out! Don't let your hearts be dulled by carousing and drunkenness, and by the worries of this life. Don't let that day catch you unaware, 35 like a trap. For that day will come upon everyone living on the earth. 36 Keep alert at all times. And pray that you might be strong enough to escape these coming horrors and stand before the Son of Man."

37 Every day Jesus went to the Temple to teach, and each evening he returned to spend the night on the Mount of Olives. 38 The crowds gathered at the Temple early each morning to hear him.

22 Judas Agrees to Betray Jesus

The Festival of Unleavened Bread, which is also called Passover, was approaching. 2 The leading priests and teachers of religious law were plotting how to kill Jesus, but they were afraid of the people's reaction.

3 Then Satan entered into Judas Iscariot, who was one of the twelve disciples, 4 and he went to the leading priests and captains of the Temple guard to discuss the best way to

---

21:8 Greek claiming, 'I am.' 21:13 Or This will be your testimony against them. 21:17 Greek on account of my name. 21:27a "Son of Man" is a title Jesus used for himself. 21:27b See Dan 7:13.

betray Jesus to them. [5] They were delighted, and they promised to give him money. [6] So he agreed and began looking for an opportunity to betray Jesus so they could arrest him when the crowds weren't around.

The Last Supper

[7] Now the Festival of Unleavened Bread arrived, when the Passover lamb is sacrificed. [8] Jesus sent Peter and John ahead and said, "Go and prepare the Passover meal, so we can eat it together."

[9] "Where do you want us to prepare it?" they asked him.

[10] He replied, "As soon as you enter Jerusalem, a man carrying a pitcher of water will meet you. Follow him. At the house he enters, [11] say to the owner, 'The Teacher asks: Where is the guest room where I can eat the Passover meal with my disciples?' [12] He will take you upstairs to a large room that is already set up. That is where you should prepare our meal." [13] They went off to the city and found everything just as Jesus had said, and they prepared the Passover meal there.

[14] When the time came, Jesus and the apostles sat down together at the table.* [15] Jesus said, "I have been very eager to eat this Passover meal with you before my suffering begins. [16] For I tell you now that I won't eat this meal again until its meaning is fulfilled in the Kingdom of God."

[17] Then he took a cup of wine and gave thanks to God for it. Then he said, "Take this and share it among yourselves. [18] For I will not drink wine again until the Kingdom of God has come."

[19] He took some bread and gave thanks to God for it. Then he broke it in pieces and gave it to the disciples, saying, "This is my body, which is given for you. Do this to remember me."

[20] After supper he took another cup of wine and said, "This cup is the new covenant between God and his people—an agreement confirmed with my blood, which is poured out as a sacrifice for you.*

[21] "But here at this table, sitting among us as a friend, is the man who will betray me. [22] For it has been determined that the Son of Man* must die. But what sorrow awaits the one who betrays him." [23] The disciples began to ask each other which of them would ever do such a thing.

[24] Then they began to argue among themselves about who would be the greatest among them. [25] Jesus told them, "In this world the kings and great men lord it over their people, yet they are called 'friends of the people.' [26] But among you it will be different. Those who are the greatest among you should take the lowest rank, and the leader should be like a servant. [27] Who is more important, the one who sits at the table or the one who serves? The one who sits at the table, of course. But not here! For I am among you as one who serves.

[28] "You have stayed with me in my time of trial. [29] And just as my Father has granted me a Kingdom, I now grant you the right [30] to eat and drink at my table in my Kingdom. And you will sit on thrones, judging the twelve tribes of Israel.

Jesus Predicts Peter's Denial

[31] "Simon, Simon, Satan has asked to sift each of you like wheat. [32] But I have pleaded in prayer for you, Simon, that your faith should not fail. So when you have repented and turned to me again, strengthen your brothers."

[33] Peter said, "Lord, I am ready to go to prison with you, and even to die with you."

[34] But Jesus said, "Peter, let me tell you something. Before the rooster crows tomorrow morning, you will deny three times that you even know me."

[35] Then Jesus asked them, "When I sent you out to preach the Good News and you did not have money, a traveler's bag, or an extra pair of sandals, did you need anything?"

"No," they replied.

[36] "But now," he said, "take your money and a traveler's bag. And if you don't have a sword, sell your cloak and buy one! [37] For the time has come for this prophecy about me to be fulfilled: 'He was counted among the rebels.'* Yes, everything written about me by the prophets will come true."

[38] "Look, Lord," they replied, "we have two swords among us."

"That's enough," he said.

22:14 Or reclined together.   **22:19-20** Some manuscripts do not include 22:19b-20, which is given for you . . . which is poured out as a sacrifice for you.   **22:22** "Son of Man" is a title Jesus used for himself.   **22:37** Isa 53:12.

Jesus Prays on the Mount of Olives

³⁹ Then, accompanied by the disciples, Jesus left the upstairs room and went as usual to the Mount of Olives. ⁴⁰ There he told them, "Pray that you will not give in to temptation."

⁴¹ He walked away, about a stone's throw, and knelt down and prayed, ⁴² "Father, if you are willing, please take this cup of suffering away from me. Yet I want your will to be done, not mine." ⁴³ Then an angel from heaven appeared and strengthened him. ⁴⁴ He prayed more fervently, and he was in such agony of spirit that his sweat fell to the ground like great drops of blood.*

⁴⁵ At last he stood up again and returned to the disciples, only to find them asleep, exhausted from grief. ⁴⁶ "Why are you sleeping?" he asked them. "Get up and pray, so that you will not give in to temptation."

Jesus Is Betrayed and Arrested

⁴⁷ But even as Jesus said this, a crowd approached, led by Judas, one of the twelve disciples. Judas walked over to Jesus to greet him with a kiss. ⁴⁸ But Jesus said, "Judas, would you betray the Son of Man with a kiss?"

⁴⁹ When the other disciples saw what was about to happen, they exclaimed, "Lord, should we fight? We brought the swords!" ⁵⁰ And one of them struck at the high priest's slave, slashing off his right ear.

⁵¹ But Jesus said, "No more of this." And he touched the man's ear and healed him.

⁵² Then Jesus spoke to the leading priests, the captains of the Temple guard, and the elders who had come for him. "Am I some dangerous revolutionary," he asked, "that you come with swords and clubs to arrest me? ⁵³ Why didn't you arrest me in the Temple? I was there every day. But this is your moment, the time when the power of darkness reigns."

Peter Denies Jesus

⁵⁴ So they arrested him and led him to the high priest's home. And Peter followed at a distance. ⁵⁵ The guards lit a fire in the middle of the courtyard and sat around it, and Peter joined them there. ⁵⁶ A servant girl noticed him in the firelight and began staring at him. Finally she said, "This man was one of Jesus' followers!"

⁵⁷ But Peter denied it. "Woman," he said, "I don't even know him!"

⁵⁸ After a while someone else looked at him and said, "You must be one of them!"

"No, man, I'm not!" Peter retorted.

⁵⁹ About an hour later someone else insisted, "This must be one of them, because he is a Galilean, too."

⁶⁰ But Peter said, "Man, I don't know what you are talking about." And immediately, while he was still speaking, the rooster crowed.

⁶¹ At that moment the Lord turned and looked at Peter. Suddenly, the Lord's words flashed through Peter's mind: "Before the rooster crows tomorrow morning, you will deny three times that you even know me." ⁶² And Peter left the courtyard, weeping bitterly.

⁶³ The guards in charge of Jesus began mocking and beating him. ⁶⁴ They blindfolded him and said, "Prophesy to us! Who hit you that time?" ⁶⁵ And they hurled all sorts of terrible insults at him.

Jesus before the Council

⁶⁶ At daybreak all the elders of the people assembled, including the leading priests and the teachers of religious law. Jesus was led before this high council,* ⁶⁷ and they said, "Tell us, are you the Messiah?"

But he replied, "If I tell you, you won't believe me. ⁶⁸ And if I ask you a question, you won't answer. ⁶⁹ But from now on the Son of Man will be seated in the place of power at God's right hand.*"

⁷⁰ They all shouted, "So, are you claiming to be the Son of God?"

And he replied, "You say that I am."

⁷¹ "Why do we need other witnesses?" they said. "We ourselves heard him say it."

23 Jesus' Trial before Pilate

Then the entire council took Jesus to Pilate, the Roman governor. ² They began to state their case: "This man has been leading our people astray by telling them not to pay their taxes to the Roman government and by claiming he is the Messiah, a king."

22:43-44 Verses 43 and 44 are not included in many ancient manuscripts. **22:66** Greek *before their Sanhedrin.* **22:69** See Ps 110:1.

³So Pilate asked him, "Are you the king of the Jews?"

Jesus replied, "You have said it."

⁴Pilate turned to the leading priests and to the crowd and said, "I find nothing wrong with this man!"

⁵Then they became insistent. "But he is causing riots by his teaching wherever he goes—all over Judea, from Galilee to Jerusalem!"

⁶"Oh, is he a Galilean?" Pilate asked. ⁷When they said that he was, Pilate sent him to Herod Antipas, because Galilee was under Herod's jurisdiction, and Herod happened to be in Jerusalem at the time.

⁸Herod was delighted at the opportunity to see Jesus, because he had heard about him and had been hoping for a long time to see him perform a miracle. ⁹He asked Jesus question after question, but Jesus refused to answer. ¹⁰Meanwhile, the leading priests and the teachers of religious law stood there shouting their accusations. ¹¹Then Herod and his soldiers began mocking and ridiculing Jesus. Finally, they put a royal robe on him and sent him back to Pilate. ¹²(Herod and Pilate, who had been enemies before, became friends that day.)

¹³Then Pilate called together the leading priests and other religious leaders, along with the people, ¹⁴and he announced his verdict. "You brought this man to me, accusing him of leading a revolt. I have examined him thoroughly on this point in your presence and find him innocent. ¹⁵Herod came to the same conclusion and sent him back to us. Nothing this man has done calls for the death penalty. ¹⁶So I will have him flogged, and then I will release him."*

¹⁸Then a mighty roar rose from the crowd, and with one voice they shouted, "Kill him, and release Barabbas to us!" ¹⁹(Barabbas was in prison for taking part in an insurrection in Jerusalem against the government, and for murder.) ²⁰Pilate argued with them, because he wanted to release Jesus. ²¹But they kept shouting, "Crucify him! Crucify him!"

²²For the third time he demanded, "Why? What crime has he committed? I have found no reason to sentence him to death. So I will have him flogged, and then I will release him."

²³But the mob shouted louder and louder, demanding that Jesus be crucified, and their voices prevailed. ²⁴So Pilate sentenced Jesus to die as they demanded. ²⁵As they had requested, he released Barabbas, the man in prison for insurrection and murder. But he turned Jesus over to them to do as they wished.

The Crucifixion

²⁶As they led Jesus away, a man named Simon, who was from Cyrene,* happened to be coming in from the countryside. The soldiers seized him and put the cross on him and made him carry it behind Jesus. ²⁷A large crowd trailed behind, including many grief-stricken women. ²⁸But Jesus turned and said to them, "Daughters of Jerusalem, don't weep for me, but weep for yourselves and for your children. ²⁹For the days are coming when they will say, 'Fortunate indeed are the women who are childless, the wombs that have not borne a child and the breasts that have never nursed.' ³⁰People will beg the mountains, 'Fall on us,' and plead with the hills, 'Bury us.'* ³¹For if these things are done when the tree is green, what will happen when it is dry?*"

³²Two others, both criminals, were led out to be executed with him. ³³When they came to a place called The Skull,* they nailed him to the cross. And the criminals were also crucified—one on his right and one on his left.

³⁴Jesus said, "Father, forgive them, for they don't know what they are doing."* And the soldiers gambled for his clothes by throwing dice.*

³⁵The crowd watched and the leaders scoffed. "He saved others," they said, "let him save himself if he is really God's Messiah, the Chosen One." ³⁶The soldiers mocked him, too, by offering him a drink of sour wine. ³⁷They called out to him, "If you are the King

---

23:16 Some manuscripts add verse 17, *Now it was necessary for him to release one prisoner to them during the Passover celebration.* Compare Matt 27:15; Mark 15:6; John 18:39.   23:26 *Cyrene* was a city in northern Africa.   23:30 Hos 10:8.   23:31 Or *If these things are done to me, the living tree, what will happen to you, the dry tree?*   23:33 Sometimes rendered *Calvary,* which comes from the Latin word for "skull."   23:34a This sentence is not included in many ancient manuscripts.   23:34b Greek *by casting lots.* See Ps 22:18.

of the Jews, save yourself!" [38] A sign was fastened above him with these words: "This is the King of the Jews."

[39] One of the criminals hanging beside him scoffed, "So you're the Messiah, are you? Prove it by saving yourself—and us, too, while you're at it!"

[40] But the other criminal protested, "Don't you fear God even when you have been sentenced to die? [41] We deserve to die for our crimes, but this man hasn't done anything wrong." [42] Then he said, "Jesus, remember me when you come into your Kingdom."

[43] And Jesus replied, "I assure you, today you will be with me in paradise."

The Death of Jesus

[44] By this time it was about noon, and darkness fell across the whole land until three o'clock. [45] The light from the sun was gone.

Q&A | Moving beyond Resentment
LUKE 23:32-43

I can't shake my anger or the feeling that the other person *deserves* my resentment. How can I honestly forgive?

Someone once said that staying angry is like taking poison and waiting for the other person to die.

The worst effect of self-righteous anger is the inner damage it can do. It distorts your clarity about your own sinfulness and undermines your humility. Jesus told us to love our enemies and demonstrated it by asking his Father to forgive his murderers (Matthew 5:43-48; Luke 23:34). One way of dealing with our inner sense of guilt is to locate somebody worse than us and condemn him. The alternative is repentance and preferring others above ourselves.

Think about the weeping woman who wiped Jesus' feet with her hair (Luke 7:36-50). Her repentance broadened her heart to receive and express much love. She was more whole and blessed than the Pharisee who judged her. A modern-day equivalent might be an urbane young person who judges a backward-thinking racist. That racist who repents in tears will return home forgiven and justified, while the smug guy—who says, "Well, it's about time," but feels vaguely disappointed inside—does not (Luke 18:9-14). Self-righteous angry people can't afford to be humble. Their peace is fragile. But we can love and forgive them all the same.

The illusion is that we have to fight against our enemies. But in reality our opponents are not our enemies. We have an Enemy, who wants to destroy both our opponent and us. He will entice us to hatred and self-righteousness, even in doing what we think is the work of God. There is only one way to defeat him: to love our enemies instead.

—*Frederica Mathewes-Green*

For more on forgiveness, see reading at 1 Corinthians 6:4-7.

And suddenly, the curtain in the sanctuary of the Temple was torn down the middle. ⁴⁶Then Jesus shouted, "Father, I entrust my spirit into your hands!"* And with those words he breathed his last.

⁴⁷When the Roman officer* overseeing the execution saw what had happened, he worshiped God and said, "Surely this man was innocent.*" ⁴⁸And when all the crowd that came to see the crucifixion saw what had happened, they went home in deep sorrow.* ⁴⁹But Jesus' friends, including the women who had followed him from Galilee, stood at a distance watching.

The Burial of Jesus

⁵⁰Now there was a good and righteous man named Joseph. He was a member of the Jewish high council, ⁵¹but he had not agreed with the decision and actions of the other religious leaders. He was from the town of Arimathea in Judea, and he was waiting for the Kingdom of God to come. ⁵²He went to Pilate and asked for Jesus' body. ⁵³Then he took the body down from the cross and wrapped it in a long sheet of linen cloth and laid it in a new tomb that had been carved out of rock. ⁵⁴This was done late on Friday afternoon, the day of preparation,* as the Sabbath was about to begin.

⁵⁵As his body was taken away, the women from Galilee followed and saw the tomb where his body was placed. ⁵⁶Then they went home and prepared spices and ointments to anoint his body. But by the time they were finished the Sabbath had begun, so they rested as required by the law.

24 The Resurrection

But very early on Sunday morning* the women went to the tomb, taking the spices they had prepared. ²They found that the stone had been rolled away from the entrance. ³So they went in, but they didn't find the body of the Lord Jesus. ⁴As they stood there puzzled, two men suddenly appeared to them, clothed in dazzling robes.

⁵The women were terrified and bowed with their faces to the ground. Then the men asked, "Why are you looking among the dead for someone who is alive? ⁶He isn't here! He is risen from the dead! Remember what he told you back in Galilee, ⁷that the Son of Man* must be betrayed into the hands of sinful men and be crucified, and that he would rise again on the third day."

⁸Then they remembered that he had said this. ⁹So they rushed back from the tomb to tell his eleven disciples—and everyone else—what had happened. ¹⁰It was Mary Magdalene, Joanna, Mary the mother of James, and several other women who told the apostles what had happened. ¹¹But the story sounded like nonsense to the men, so they didn't believe it. ¹²However, Peter jumped up and ran to the tomb to look. Stooping, he peered in and saw the empty linen wrappings; then he went home again, wondering what had happened.

The Walk to Emmaus

¹³That same day two of Jesus' followers were walking to the village of Emmaus, seven miles* from Jerusalem. ¹⁴As they walked along they were talking about everything that had happened. ¹⁵As they talked and discussed these things, Jesus himself suddenly came and began walking with them. ¹⁶But God kept them from recognizing him.

¹⁷He asked them, "What are you discussing so intently as you walk along?"

They stopped short, sadness written across their faces. ¹⁸Then one of them, Cleopas, replied, "You must be the only person in Jerusalem who hasn't heard about all the things that have happened there the last few days."

¹⁹"What things?" Jesus asked.

"The things that happened to Jesus, the man from Nazareth," they said. "He was a prophet who did powerful miracles, and he was a mighty teacher in the eyes of God and all the people. ²⁰But our leading priests and other religious leaders handed him over to be condemned to death, and they crucified him. ²¹We had hoped he was the Messiah who had come to rescue Israel. This all happened three days ago.

²²"Then some women from our group

23:46 Ps 31:5.   23:47a Greek the centurion.   23:47b Or righteous.   23:48 Greek went home beating their breasts.   23:54 Greek It was the day of preparation.   24:1 Greek But on the first day of the week, very early in the morning.   24:7 "Son of Man" is a title Jesus used for himself.   24:13 Greek 60 stadia [11.1 kilometers].

Time Well Wasted

LUKE 24:13-35

Most of us don't waste enough time.

Don't get me wrong; there's good wasting, and there's bad wasting. Bad time wasting is the hang-around/watch-TV/perform-random-online-search kind that leaves you with less life than you started with.

The good kind of time wasting will actually lead you to be more connected with God and more full of life. But it's difficult to engage in, because there are always more pressing matters. This isn't really wasting time, of course, but our culture makes it feel as though it is.

One important form of time wasting is musing or listening. Here I mentally and emotionally bring before God what I'm concerned about. Often it involves either family or ministry. I'm worried about one of my children. I'm concerned about my staff. I'm unsure about a ministry at our church.

I spread these out before God, and then I listen. This listening is a form of prayer, but it's prayer that involves thinking and imagination and asking questions. Often at the beginning I'll ask God for wisdom regarding next steps to take. I might write some ideas. Sometimes this musing will lead to plans. Other times my period of contemplation is simply a time of letting go of all outcomes and experiencing the freedom God wants to give.

—John Ortberg

For more on contemplation, see reading at 2 Corinthians 3:18.

---

of his followers were at his tomb early this morning, and they came back with an amazing report. [23] They said his body was missing, and they had seen angels who told them Jesus is alive! [24] Some of our men ran out to see, and sure enough, his body was gone, just as the women had said."

[25] Then Jesus said to them, "You foolish people! You find it so hard to believe all that the prophets wrote in the Scriptures. [26] Wasn't it clearly predicted that the Messiah would have to suffer all these things before entering his glory?" [27] Then Jesus took them through the writings of Moses and all the prophets, explaining from all the Scriptures the things concerning himself.

[28] By this time they were nearing Emmaus and the end of their journey. Jesus acted as if he were going on, [29] but they begged him, "Stay the night with us, since it is getting late." So he went home with them. [30] As they sat down to eat,* he took the bread and blessed it. Then he broke it and gave it to them. [31] Suddenly, their eyes were opened, and they recognized him. And at that moment he disappeared!

[32] They said to each other, "Didn't our hearts burn within us as he talked with us on the road and explained the Scriptures to us?" [33] And within the hour they were on their way back to Jerusalem. There they found the eleven disciples and the others who had gathered with them, [34] who said, "The Lord has really risen! He appeared to Peter.*"

Jesus Appears to the Disciples

[35] Then the two from Emmaus told their story of how Jesus had appeared to them as they were walking along the road, and how they had recognized him as he was breaking the bread. [36] And just as they were telling about it, Jesus himself was suddenly

---

24:30 Or *As they reclined.*   **24:34** Greek *Simon.*

standing there among them. "Peace be with you," he said. ³⁷But the whole group was startled and frightened, thinking they were seeing a ghost!

³⁸"Why are you frightened?" he asked. "Why are your hearts filled with doubt? ³⁹Look at my hands. Look at my feet. You can see that it's really me. Touch me and make sure that I am not a ghost, because ghosts don't have bodies, as you see that I do." ⁴⁰As he spoke, he showed them his hands and his feet.

⁴¹Still they stood there in disbelief, filled with joy and wonder. Then he asked them, "Do you have anything here to eat?" ⁴²They gave him a piece of broiled fish, ⁴³and he ate it as they watched.

⁴⁴Then he said, "When I was with you before, I told you that everything written about me in the law of Moses and the prophets and in the Psalms must be fulfilled." ⁴⁵Then he opened their minds to under-stand the Scriptures. ⁴⁶And he said, "Yes, it was written long ago that the Messiah would suffer and die and rise from the dead on the third day. ⁴⁷It was also written that this message would be proclaimed in the authority of his name to all the nations,* beginning in Jerusalem: 'There is forgiveness of sins for all who repent.' ⁴⁸You are witnesses of all these things.

⁴⁹"And now I will send the Holy Spirit, just as my Father promised. But stay here in the city until the Holy Spirit comes and fills you with power from heaven."

The Ascension

⁵⁰Then Jesus led them to Bethany, and lifting his hands to heaven, he blessed them. ⁵¹While he was blessing them, he left them and was taken up to heaven. ⁵²So they worshiped him and then returned to Jerusalem filled with great joy. ⁵³And they spent all of their time in the Temple, praising God.

24:47 Or all peoples.

Background

The author of John's gospel refers to himself as the disciple "Jesus loved" (see 13:23; 21:20, 24). This disciple is believed to be John, one of three fishermen who formed Jesus' inner circle. John and his brother, James, the sons of Zebedee and Salome, were called the "Sons of Thunder" (Mark 3:17) by Jesus because of their fiery temperaments. Having been an ardent follower of John the Baptist, John was among Jesus' original disciples. As he died Jesus entrusted his own mother to John's care. John played a prominent role in the early church, as evidenced in the Book of Acts and in the writing of his epistles and visionary Book of Revelation.

Message

It seems John addresses the Gospel to a wide audience, both Jewish and Gentile. Whereas the first three Gospels focus on events in the life of Jesus, John emphasizes the meaning behind those events. John's gospel is not so much biographical as it is a theological argument; John uses every event, miracle, and title to show that Jesus is God. Before Jesus took on flesh, he was "with God" and "was God" from "the beginning" (1:1). John does not relate Jesus' parables as much as extended accounts of his encounters: a miracle at a wedding, Nicodemus coming by night, the conversion of the Samaritan woman, and the raising of Lazarus. John shows Jesus giving metaphoric discourses: "I am the bread of life" (6:35); "I am the light of the world" (8:12); "I am the good shepherd" (10:11). Jesus' discourses to and prayer for his disciples have edified and heartened the church of Christ throughout the ages. Toward the end of the book, John reveals his purpose for writing: "These are written so that you may continue to believe that Jesus is the Messiah, the Son of God, and that by believing in him you will have life by the power of his name" (20:31).

Time

The probable range for the writing of this gospel is A.D. 60–90. It was written after the synoptic Gospels, but before John's three epistles and Revelation. John was one of the last surviving eyewitnesses of Jesus' earthly ministry. Tradition says that John wrote this gospel in Ephesus.

Outline

John

1. Prologue: Christ, the Eternal Word

¹ In the beginning the Word already existed.
The Word was with God,
and the Word was God.
² He existed in the beginning with God.
³ God created everything through him,
and nothing was created except through him.
⁴ The Word gave life to everything that was created,*
and his life brought light to everyone.
⁵ The light shines in the darkness,
and the darkness can never extinguish it.*

⁶God sent a man, John the Baptist,* ⁷to tell about the light so that everyone might believe because of his testimony. ⁸John himself was not the light; he was simply a witness to tell about the light. ⁹The one who is the true light, who gives light to everyone, was coming into the world.

¹⁰He came into the very world he created, but the world didn't recognize him. ¹¹He came to his own people, and even they rejected him. ¹²But to all who believed him and accepted him, he gave the right to become children of God. ¹³They are reborn—not with a physical birth resulting from human passion or plan, but a birth that comes from God.

¹⁴So the Word became human* and made his home among us. He was full of unfailing love and faithfulness.* And we have seen his glory, the glory of the Father's one and only Son.

¹⁵John testified about him when he shouted to the crowds, "This is the one I was talking about when I said, 'Someone is coming after me who is far greater than I am, for he existed long before me.'"

¹⁶From his abundance we have all received one gracious blessing after another.* ¹⁷For the law was given through Moses, but God's unfailing love and faithfulness came through Jesus Christ. ¹⁸No one has ever seen God. But the unique One, who is himself God,* is near to the Father's heart. He has revealed God to us.

The Testimony of John the Baptist

¹⁹This was John's testimony when the Jewish leaders sent priests and Temple assistants* from Jerusalem to ask John, "Who are you?" ²⁰He came right out and said, "I am not the Messiah."

²¹"Well then, who are you?" they asked. "Are you Elijah?"

"No," he replied.

"Are you the Prophet we are expecting?"*

"No."

1:3-4 Or and nothing that was created was created except through him. The Word gave life to everything.   **1:5** Or and the darkness has not understood it.   **1:6** Greek a man named John.   **1:14a** Greek became flesh.   **1:14b** Or grace and truth; also in 1:17.   **1:16** Or received the grace of Christ rather than the grace of the law; Greek reads received grace upon grace.   **1:18** Some manuscripts read But the one and only Son.   **1:19** Greek and Levites.   **1:21** Greek Are you the Prophet? See Deut 18:15, 18; Mal 4:5-6.

22 "Then who are you? We need an answer for those who sent us. What do you have to say about yourself?"

23 John replied in the words of the prophet Isaiah:

"I am a voice shouting in the wilderness,
    'Clear the way for the LORD's
        coming!' "*

24 Then the Pharisees who had been sent 25 asked him, "If you aren't the Messiah or Elijah or the Prophet, what right do you have to baptize?"

26 John told them, "I baptize with* water, but right here in the crowd is someone you do not recognize. 27 Though his ministry follows mine, I'm not even worthy to be his slave and untie the straps of his sandal."

28 This encounter took place in Bethany, an area east of the Jordan River, where John was baptizing.

Jesus, the Lamb of God

29 The next day John saw Jesus coming toward him and said, "Look! The Lamb of God who takes away the sin of the world! 30 He is the one I was talking about when I said, 'A man is coming after me who is far greater than I am, for he existed long before me.' 31 I did not recognize him as the Messiah, but I have been baptizing with water so that he might be revealed to Israel."

32 Then John testified, "I saw the Holy Spirit descending like a dove from heaven and resting upon him. 33 I didn't know he was the one, but when God sent me to baptize with water, he told me, 'The one on whom you see the Spirit descend and rest is the one who will baptize with the Holy Spirit.' 34 I saw this happen to Jesus, so I testify that he is the Chosen One of God.*"

The First Disciples

35 The following day John was again standing with two of his disciples. 36 As Jesus walked by, John looked at him and declared, "Look! There is the Lamb of God!" 37 When John's two disciples heard this, they followed Jesus.

38 Jesus looked around and saw them following. "What do you want?" he asked them.

They replied, "Rabbi" (which means "Teacher"), "where are you staying?"

39 "Come and see," he said. It was about four o'clock in the afternoon when they went with him to the place where he was staying, and they remained with him the rest of the day.

40 Andrew, Simon Peter's brother, was one of these men who heard what John said and then followed Jesus. 41 Andrew went to find his brother, Simon, and told him, "We have found the Messiah" (which means "Christ"*).

42 Then Andrew brought Simon to meet Jesus. Looking intently at Simon, Jesus said, "Your name is Simon, son of John—but you will be called Cephas" (which means "Peter"*).

43 The next day Jesus decided to go to Galilee. He found Philip and said to him, "Come, follow me." 44 Philip was from Bethsaida, Andrew and Peter's hometown.

45 Philip went to look for Nathanael and told him, "We have found the very person Moses* and the prophets wrote about! His name is Jesus, the son of Joseph from Nazareth."

46 "Nazareth!" exclaimed Nathanael. "Can anything good come from Nazareth?"

"Come and see for yourself," Philip replied.

47 As they approached, Jesus said, "Now here is a genuine son of Israel—a man of complete integrity."

48 "How do you know about me?" Nathanael asked.

Jesus replied, "I could see you under the fig tree before Philip found you."

49 Then Nathanael exclaimed, "Rabbi, you are the Son of God—the King of Israel!"

50 Jesus asked him, "Do you believe this just because I told you I had seen you under the fig tree? You will see greater things than this." 51 Then he said, "I tell you the truth, you will all see heaven open and the angels of God going up and down on the Son of Man, the one who is the stairway between heaven and earth.*"

1:23 Isa 40:3. 1:26 Or in; also in 1:31, 33. 1:34 Some manuscripts read the Son of God. 1:41 Messiah (a Hebrew term) and Christ (a Greek term) both mean "the anointed one." 1:42 The names Cephas (from Aramaic) and Peter (from Greek) both mean "rock." 1:45 Greek Moses in the law. 1:51 Greek going up and down on the Son of Man; see Gen 28:10-17. "Son of Man" is a title Jesus used for himself.

2 The Wedding at Cana

The next day* there was a wedding celebration in the village of Cana in Galilee. Jesus' mother was there, ²and Jesus and his disciples were also invited to the celebration. ³The wine supply ran out during the festivities, so Jesus' mother told him, "They have no more wine."

⁴"Dear woman, that's not our problem," Jesus replied. "My time has not yet come."

⁵But his mother told the servants, "Do whatever he tells you."

⁶Standing nearby were six stone water jars, used for Jewish ceremonial washing. Each could hold twenty to thirty gallons.* ⁷Jesus told the servants, "Fill the jars with water." When the jars had been filled, ⁸he said, "Now dip some out, and take it to the master of ceremonies." So the servants followed his instructions.

⁹When the master of ceremonies tasted the water that was now wine, not knowing where it had come from (though, of course, the servants knew), he called the bridegroom over. ¹⁰"A host always serves the best wine first," he said. "Then, when everyone has had a lot to drink, he brings out the less expensive wine. But you have kept the best until now!"

¹¹This miraculous sign at Cana in Galilee was the first time Jesus revealed his glory. And his disciples believed in him.

¹²After the wedding he went to Capernaum for a few days with his mother, his brothers, and his disciples.

Jesus Clears the Temple

¹³It was nearly time for the Jewish Passover celebration, so Jesus went to Jerusalem. ¹⁴In the Temple area he saw merchants selling cattle, sheep, and doves for sacrifices; he also saw dealers at tables exchanging foreign money. ¹⁵Jesus made a whip from some ropes and chased them all out of the Temple. He drove out the sheep and cattle, scattered the money changers' coins over the floor, and turned over their tables. ¹⁶Then, going over to the people who sold doves, he told them, "Get these things out of here. Stop turning my Father's house into a marketplace!"

¹⁷Then his disciples remembered this prophecy from the Scriptures: "Passion for God's house will consume me."*

¹⁸But the Jewish leaders demanded, "What are you doing? If God gave you authority to do this, show us a miraculous sign to prove it."

¹⁹"All right," Jesus replied. "Destroy this temple, and in three days I will raise it up."

²⁰"What!" they exclaimed. "It has taken forty-six years to build this Temple, and you can rebuild it in three days?" ²¹But when Jesus said "this temple," he meant his own body. ²²After he was raised from the dead, his disciples remembered he had said this, and they believed both the Scriptures and what Jesus had said.

Jesus and Nicodemus

²³Because of the miraculous signs Jesus did in Jerusalem at the Passover celebration, many began to trust in him. ²⁴But Jesus didn't trust them, because he knew human nature. ²⁵No one needed to tell him what mankind is really like.

3 There was a man named Nicodemus, a Jewish religious leader who was a Pharisee. ²After dark one evening, he came to speak with Jesus. "Rabbi," he said, "we all know that God has sent you to teach us. Your miraculous signs are evidence that God is with you."

³Jesus replied, "I tell you the truth, unless you are born again,* you cannot see the Kingdom of God."

⁴"What do you mean?" exclaimed Nicodemus. "How can an old man go back into his mother's womb and be born again?"

⁵Jesus replied, "I assure you, no one can enter the Kingdom of God without being born of water and the Spirit.* ⁶Humans can reproduce only human life, but the Holy Spirit gives birth to spiritual life.* ⁷So don't be surprised when I say, 'You* must be born again.' ⁸The wind blows wherever it wants. Just as you can hear the wind but can't tell where it comes from or where it is going, so you can't explain how people are born of the Spirit."

2:1 Greek *On the third day;* see 1:35, 43. **2:6** Greek *2 or 3 measures* [75 to 113 liters]. **2:17** Or *"Concern for God's house will be my undoing."* Ps 69:9. **3:3** Or *born from above;* also in 3:7. **3:5** Or *and spirit.* The Greek word for *Spirit* can also be translated *wind;* see 3:8. **3:6** Greek *what is born of the Spirit is spirit.* **3:7** The Greek word for *you* is plural; also in 3:12.

Becoming a Mentored Disciple

JOHN 1:35-44

In a culture captivated by grandiosity, it's not surprising that people often overestimate their abilities. The illusion of superiority is everywhere. A study at the University of Nebraska found that 68 percent of the faculty rate their teaching ability to be in the top 25 percent. The vast majority of students at Stanford claim their academic performance is above the median. Studies like these expose our pretense and a deep need to appear larger than life. Still, most of us would agree that character and authenticity depend on an awareness of both our strengths and limitations. People of character can lay down their need to be on top. They are not attached to a grandiose image of who they are. They know how to follow, how to learn, and how to admit they are wrong.

The first thing Jesus said to his would-be disciples was, "Follow me" (John 1:43). It was the last thing he said to them as well (John 21:19, 22). But following another's lead doesn't come to us automatically. It begins with admitting to ourselves that we *need* help—help from God and help from others. Jesus continually looked for people who were teachable enough to have ears to hear and eyes to see. He wanted followers who could be mentored. Mentorees are people who know at least some of what they *don't* know; this awareness forges a desire to learn from and follow the lead of another. A teachable heart is one that can let go of its need to be in control and let someone else guide, correct, instruct, and nurture.

Being wide open to the guidance of another person shapes us in profound ways. When I had young children, each week I took my ignorance and my questions about child rearing to a friend who was fifteen years older than I. Sometimes she answered my questions with questions; sometimes she gave guidance and advice. For thirteen years she poured her wisdom and experience into my eager ears, and when we moved away, my husband and children rued the loss of my mentor. She had loved me into becoming a better wife and mother. I have appreciated being mentored by those ahead of me in life, but I have also received mentoring from peers in ministry and even from my children. After all, they all know things I don't yet know. And they all have an awareness of me that could help me in my journey.

There are no self-made people. We are all shaped by our relationships, for good or ill. Yet sometimes people treat their spiritual journey as a solo flight; they like the independence of listening to God on their own and charting their own course. This is not what the first Jesus-followers did; they kept company with Jesus and with one another.

The disciples had both their good and bad moments as mentorees. The questions they asked Jesus could lead them deeper into God, truth, and self-awareness; their resistance to what Jesus said could lead them to clam up, talk behind his back, and "correct" his leadership. Still, the disciples let themselves be mentored and shaped in ways that confounded their plans and agendas. They remained open to Jesus' example and words, even when Jesus' teachings sanded away their egos and pretenses. In the process, they discovered they were loved not for what they knew and got right, but in their utter humanness, to the very end.

Jesus was the perfect mentor—but he couldn't teach those who wouldn't follow and be mentored. Like the disciples we need mentoring—and we need to *realize* that truth. Lay down your need to pontificate, prognosticate, or otherwise be the expert, and invite Jesus to mentor you. Receiving mentoring from Jesus, and from him through others, is an antidote to grandiosity. It is your answer to his call, "Follow me."

—*Adele Ahlberg Calhoun*

For more on mentoring, see reading at Acts 18:24–28.

⁹"How are these things possible?" Nicodemus asked.

¹⁰Jesus replied, "You are a respected Jewish teacher, and yet you don't understand these things? ¹¹I assure you, we tell you what we know and have seen, and yet you won't believe our testimony. ¹²But if you don't believe me when I tell you about earthly things, how can you possibly believe if I tell you about heavenly things? ¹³No one has ever gone to heaven and returned. But the Son of Man* has come down from heaven. ¹⁴And as Moses lifted up the bronze snake on a pole in the wilderness, so the Son of Man must be lifted up, ¹⁵so that everyone who believes in him will have eternal life.*

¹⁶"For God loved the world so much that he gave his one and only Son, so that everyone who believes in him will not perish but have eternal life. ¹⁷God sent his Son into the world not to judge the world, but to save the world through him.

¹⁸"There is no judgment against anyone who believes in him. But anyone who does not believe in him has already been judged for not believing in God's one and only Son. ¹⁹And the judgment is based on this fact: God's light came into the world, but people loved the darkness more than the light, for their actions were evil. ²⁰All who do evil hate the light and refuse to go near it for fear their sins will be exposed. ²¹But those who do what is right come to the light so others can see that they are doing what God wants.*"

John the Baptist Exalts Jesus

²²Then Jesus and his disciples left Jerusalem and went into the Judean countryside. Jesus spent some time with them there, baptizing people. ²³At this time John the Baptist was baptizing at Aenon, near Salim, because there was plenty of water there; and people kept coming to him for baptism. ²⁴(This was before John was thrown into prison.) ²⁵A debate broke out between John's disciples and a certain Jew* over ceremonial cleansing. ²⁶So John's disciples came to him and said, "Rabbi, the man you met on the other side of the Jordan River, the one you identified as the Messiah, is also baptizing people. And everybody is going to him instead of coming to us."

²⁷John replied, "No one can receive anything unless God gives it from heaven. ²⁸You yourselves know how plainly I told you, 'I am not the Messiah. I am only here to prepare the way for him.' ²⁹It is the bridegroom who marries the bride, and the best man is simply glad to stand with him and hear his vows. Therefore, I am filled with joy at his success. ³⁰He must become greater and greater, and I must become less and less.

³¹"He has come from above and is greater than anyone else. We are of the earth, and we speak of earthly things, but he has come from heaven and is greater than anyone else.* ³²He testifies about what he has seen and heard, but how few believe what he tells them! ³³Anyone who accepts his testimony can affirm that God is true. ³⁴For he is sent by God. He speaks God's words, for God gives him the Spirit without limit. ³⁵The Father loves his Son and has put everything into his hands. ³⁶And anyone who believes in God's Son has eternal life. Anyone who doesn't obey the Son will never experience eternal life but remains under God's angry judgment."

Jesus and the Samaritan Woman

4 Jesus* knew the Pharisees had heard that he was baptizing and making more disciples than John ²(though Jesus himself didn't baptize them—his disciples did). ³So he left Judea and returned to Galilee.

⁴He had to go through Samaria on the way. ⁵Eventually he came to the Samaritan village of Sychar, near the field that Jacob gave to his son Joseph. ⁶Jacob's well was there; and Jesus, tired from the long walk, sat wearily beside the well about noontime. ⁷Soon a Samaritan woman came to draw water, and Jesus said to her, "Please give me a drink." ⁸He was alone at the time because his disciples had gone into the village to buy some food.

⁹The woman was surprised, for Jews

3:13 Some manuscripts add *who lives in heaven.* "Son of Man" is a title Jesus used for himself.   **3:15** Or *everyone who believes will have eternal life in him.*   **3:21** Or *can see God at work in what he is doing.*   **3:25** Some manuscripts read *some Jews.*   **3:31** Some manuscripts do not include *and is greater than anyone else.*   **4:1** Some manuscripts read *The Lord.*

refuse to have anything to do with Samaritans.* She said to Jesus, "You are a Jew, and I am a Samaritan woman. Why are you asking me for a drink?"

¹⁰Jesus replied, "If you only knew the gift God has for you and who you are speaking to, you would ask me, and I would give you living water."

¹¹"But sir, you don't have a rope or a bucket," she said, "and this well is very deep. Where would you get this living water? ¹²And besides, do you think you're greater than our ancestor Jacob, who gave us this well? How can you offer better water than he and his sons and his animals enjoyed?"

¹³Jesus replied, "Anyone who drinks this water will soon become thirsty again. ¹⁴But those who drink the water I give will never be thirsty again. It becomes a fresh, bubbling spring within them, giving them eternal life."

¹⁵"Please, sir," the woman said, "give me this water! Then I'll never be thirsty again, and I won't have to come here to get water."

¹⁶"Go and get your husband," Jesus told her.

¹⁷"I don't have a husband," the woman replied.

Jesus said, "You're right! You don't have a husband—¹⁸for you have had five husbands, and you aren't even married to the man you're living with now. You certainly spoke the truth!"

¹⁹"Sir," the woman said, "you must be a prophet. ²⁰So tell me, why is it that you Jews insist that Jerusalem is the only place of worship, while we Samaritans claim it is here at Mount Gerizim,* where our ancestors worshiped?"

²¹Jesus replied, "Believe me, dear woman, the time is coming when it will no longer matter whether you worship the Father on this mountain or in Jerusalem. ²²You Samaritans know very little about the one you worship, while we Jews know all about him, for salvation comes through the Jews. ²³But the time is coming—indeed it's here now—when true worshipers will worship the Father in spirit and in truth. The Father is looking for those who will worship him that way. ²⁴For God is Spirit, so those who worship him must worship in spirit and in truth."

²⁵The woman said, "I know the Messiah is coming—the one who is called Christ. When he comes, he will explain everything to us."

²⁶Then Jesus told her, "I Am the Messiah!"*

²⁷Just then his disciples came back. They were shocked to find him talking to a woman, but none of them had the nerve to ask, "What do you want with her?" or "Why are you talking to her?" ²⁸The woman left her water jar beside the well and ran back to the village, telling everyone, ²⁹"Come and see a man who told me everything I ever did! Could he possibly be the Messiah?" ³⁰So the people came streaming from the village to see him.

³¹Meanwhile, the disciples were urging Jesus, "Rabbi, eat something."

³²But Jesus replied, "I have a kind of food you know nothing about."

³³"Did someone bring him food while we were gone?" the disciples asked each other.

³⁴Then Jesus explained: "My nourishment comes from doing the will of God, who sent me, and from finishing his work. ³⁵You know the saying, 'Four months between planting and harvest.' But I say, wake up and look around. The fields are already ripe* for harvest. ³⁶The harvesters are paid good wages, and the fruit they harvest is people brought to eternal life. What joy awaits both the planter and the harvester alike! ³⁷You know the saying, 'One plants and another harvests.' And it's true. ³⁸I sent you to harvest where you didn't plant; others had already done the work, and now you will get to gather the harvest."

Many Samaritans Believe

³⁹Many Samaritans from the village believed in Jesus because the woman had said, "He told me everything I ever did!" ⁴⁰When they came out to see him, they begged him to stay in their village. So he stayed for two days, ⁴¹long enough for many more to hear his message and believe. ⁴²Then they said to the woman, "Now we believe, not just because of what you told us, but because we

---

4:9 Some manuscripts do not include this sentence. **4:20** Greek *on this mountain.* **4:26** Or *"The 'I Am' is here"*; or *"I am the Lord"*; Greek reads *"I am, the one speaking to you."* See Exod 3:14. **4:35** Greek *white.*

have heard him ourselves. Now we know that he is indeed the Savior of the world."

Jesus Heals an Official's Son

⁴³ At the end of the two days, Jesus went on to Galilee. ⁴⁴ He himself had said that a prophet is not honored in his own hometown. ⁴⁵ Yet the Galileans welcomed him, for they had been in Jerusalem at the Passover celebration and had seen everything he did there.

⁴⁶ As he traveled through Galilee, he came

The Samaritan Woman:
Inviting Others to Reconcile with God
JOHN 4:4-42

What a vivid character she is, the "woman at the well"! From her conversation with Jesus we can see that she is bold and intelligent, but her past behavior—a "home-wrecker" perhaps, seducing married men and destabilizing families—would have made her unwelcome in the community. So she comes to draw water at the hottest hour of the day, when no one else is around.

There she encounters Jesus, who crosses strict gender and ethnic barriers by initiating a conversation with her. He asks her for a drink of water, then he offers her something mysterious: *living water* and *eternal life*.

Next Jesus details her past. She must have been taken aback by his knowledge: "Sir . . . you must be a prophet" (John 4:19). She deftly changes the subject, asking whether he thinks Samaria or Jerusalem is the proper place to worship.

Instead of pontificating on this culturally controversial question, Jesus speaks about worship in terms so profound she must have been baffled. She falls back on a diplomatic standby: "When [the Messiah] comes, he will explain everything to us" (4:25).

"I AM the Messiah!" Jesus says to her (4:26).

I can picture her opening her mouth to reply, then closing it, then staring at him steadily for some seconds, as if seeing him for the first time. She puts down her water jar—it might slow her down—and hikes back to the city as fast as she can.

Though she was probably used to avoiding her fellow-villagers, now she seeks them out, saying to everyone she meets, "Come and see a man who told me everything I ever did!" Her unsavory past, the cause of that estrangement, is now the first thing she brings up. Her brokenness has become her bold witness! "Could he possibly be the Messiah?" she asks (4:29). Perhaps her honesty disarmed them. Despite longstanding alienation, they listened. They went to see for themselves and believed.

In Jesus' kindness, this woman tasted the sweet living water of reconciliation with God— and she immediately responded by telling others the phenomenal good news. Reconciled, she became a reconciler. Eastern Christian tradition records her name as *Photini*, which means "light-bearer." The light that she received, and bore to others, had the power to tear down walls and forge bonds of reconciliation—in our day just as in hers.

—Frederica Mathewes-Green

For more on reconciliation, see reading at Acts 10.

to Cana, where he had turned the water into wine. There was a government official in nearby Capernaum whose son was very sick. ⁴⁷When he heard that Jesus had come from Judea to Galilee, he went and begged Jesus to come to Capernaum to heal his son, who was about to die.

⁴⁸Jesus asked, "Will you never believe in me unless you see miraculous signs and wonders?"

⁴⁹The official pleaded, "Lord, please come now before my little boy dies."

⁵⁰Then Jesus told him, "Go back home. Your son will live!" And the man believed what Jesus said and started home.

⁵¹While the man was on his way, some of his servants met him with the news that his son was alive and well. ⁵²He asked them when the boy had begun to get better, and they replied, "Yesterday afternoon at one o'clock his fever suddenly disappeared!" ⁵³Then the father realized that that was the very time Jesus had told him, "Your son will live." And he and his entire household believed in Jesus. ⁵⁴This was the second miraculous sign Jesus did in Galilee after coming from Judea.

Jesus Heals a Lame Man

5 Afterward Jesus returned to Jerusalem for one of the Jewish holy days. ²Inside the city, near the Sheep Gate, was the pool of Bethesda,* with five covered porches. ³Crowds of sick people—blind, lame, or paralyzed—lay on the porches.* ⁵One of the men lying there had been sick for thirty-eight years. ⁶When Jesus saw him and knew he had been ill for a long time, he asked him, "Would you like to get well?"

⁷"I can't, sir," the sick man said, "for I have no one to put me into the pool when the water bubbles up. Someone else always gets there ahead of me."

⁸Jesus told him, "Stand up, pick up your mat, and walk!"

⁹Instantly, the man was healed! He rolled up his sleeping mat and began walking! But this miracle happened on the Sabbath, ¹⁰so the Jewish leaders objected. They said to the man who was cured, "You can't work

on the Sabbath! The law doesn't allow you to carry that sleeping mat!"

¹¹But he replied, "The man who healed me told me, 'Pick up your mat and walk.'"

¹²"Who said such a thing as that?" they demanded.

¹³The man didn't know, for Jesus had disappeared into the crowd. ¹⁴But afterward Jesus found him in the Temple and told him, "Now you are well; so stop sinning, or something even worse may happen to you." ¹⁵Then the man went and told the Jewish leaders that it was Jesus who had healed him.

Jesus Claims to Be the Son of God

¹⁶So the Jewish leaders began harassing* Jesus for breaking the Sabbath rules. ¹⁷But Jesus replied, "My Father is always working, and so am I." ¹⁸So the Jewish leaders tried all the harder to find a way to kill him. For he not only broke the Sabbath, he called God his Father, thereby making himself equal with God.

¹⁹So Jesus explained, "I tell you the truth, the Son can do nothing by himself. He does only what he sees the Father doing. Whatever the Father does, the Son also does. ²⁰For the Father loves the Son and shows him everything he is doing. In fact, the Father will show him how to do even greater works than healing this man. Then you will truly be astonished. ²¹For just as the Father gives life to those he raises from the dead, so the Son gives life to anyone he wants. ²²In addition, the Father judges no one. Instead, he has given the Son absolute authority to judge, ²³so that everyone will honor the Son, just as they honor the Father. Anyone who does not honor the Son is certainly not honoring the Father who sent him.

²⁴"I tell you the truth, those who listen to my message and believe in God who sent me have eternal life. They will never be condemned for their sins, but they have already passed from death into life.

²⁵"And I assure you that the time is coming, indeed it's here now, when the dead will hear my voice—the voice of the Son

---

5:2 Other manuscripts read *Beth-zatha;* still others read *Bethsaida.* **5:3** Some manuscripts add an expanded conclusion to verse 3 and all of verse 4: *waiting for a certain movement of the water,* ⁴*for an angel of the Lord came from time to time and stirred up the water. And the first person to step in after the water was stirred was healed of whatever disease he had.* **5:16** Or *persecuting.*

of God. And those who listen will live. [26] The Father has life in himself, and he has granted that same life-giving power to his Son. [27] And he has given him authority to judge everyone because he is the Son of Man.* [28] Don't be so surprised! Indeed, the time is coming when all the dead in their graves will hear the voice of God's Son, [29] and they will rise again. Those who have done good will rise to experience eternal life, and those who have continued in evil will rise to experience judgment. [30] I can do nothing on my own. I judge as God tells me. Therefore, my judgment is just, because I carry out the will of the one who sent me, not my own will.

Q&A [Feeling Pressured to Serve?]

JOHN 5:1-15

When is it okay to say no to a service opportunity?

Service can get complicated. God calls us to serve—but what that looks like means facing several important questions. *Why* do we serve others? Is there a limit to what we can—and should—give? Is there an art to the spiritual discipline of meeting needs? How can we determine what God is calling *us* to do—and the work he may have in mind for others?

We know that compassion is a central focus of our faith. Whenever the Gospels mention Jesus' compassion, he takes action. He does something with his feelings. He teaches, heals, feeds, and prays for the people who seek his care. But *he doesn't meet every need.*

At the pool in Jerusalem, Jesus healed the paralytic (John 5)—but how many crippled bodies and broken souls did he step over?

At the village of Nain, Jesus raised the young son of a widow from the dead (Luke 7)—but how many funerals did he attend as a mourner?

On the hillside by the Sea of Galilee, Jesus fed thousands (Matthew 14)—but how many hungry beggars did he walk by in his life?

Jesus taught, healed, fed, and prayed. But while Jesus took on flesh, he didn't do it all. In some miraculous way, Jesus experienced the humanness of seeing and experiencing unmet needs in a world crying out for help.

Perhaps we too may need to walk by some opportunities to serve in order to do some other ministry God has uniquely wired us to do. Our individual efforts can come together to form a glorious picture of the beauty and diversity of the body of Christ working in unity.

—Nicole Unice

For more on service, see reading at John 13:1-17.

5:27 "Son of Man" is a title Jesus used for himself.

Witnesses to Jesus

[31]"If I were to testify on my own behalf, my testimony would not be valid. [32]But someone else is also testifying about me, and I assure you that everything he says about me is true. [33]In fact, you sent investigators to listen to John the Baptist, and his testimony about me was true. [34]Of course, I have no need of human witnesses, but I say these things so you might be saved. [35]John was like a burning and shining lamp, and you were excited for a while about his message. [36]But I have a greater witness than John—my teachings and my miracles. The Father gave me these works to accomplish, and they prove that he sent me. [37]And the Father who sent me has testified about me himself. You have never heard his voice or seen him face to face, [38]and you do not have his message in your hearts, because you do not believe me—the one he sent to you.

[39]"You search the Scriptures because you think they give you eternal life. But the Scriptures point to me! [40]Yet you refuse to come to me to receive this life.

[41]"Your approval means nothing to me, [42]because I know you don't have God's love within you. [43]For I have come to you in my Father's name, and you have rejected me. Yet if others come in their own name, you gladly welcome them. [44]No wonder you can't believe! For you gladly honor each other, but you don't care about the honor that comes from the one who alone is God.*

[45]"Yet it isn't I who will accuse you before the Father. Moses will accuse you! Yes, Moses, in whom you put your hopes. [46]If you really believed Moses, you would believe me, because he wrote about me. [47]But since you don't believe what he wrote, how will you believe what I say?"

Jesus Feeds Five Thousand

6 After this, Jesus crossed over to the far side of the Sea of Galilee, also known as the Sea of Tiberias. [2]A huge crowd kept following him wherever he went, because they saw his miraculous signs as he healed the sick. [3]Then Jesus climbed a hill and sat down with his disciples around him. [4](It was nearly time for the Jewish Passover celebration.) [5]Jesus soon saw a huge crowd of people coming to look for him. Turning to Philip, he asked, "Where can we buy bread to feed all these people?" [6]He was testing Philip, for he already knew what he was going to do.

[7]Philip replied, "Even if we worked for months, we wouldn't have enough money* to feed them!"

[8]Then Andrew, Simon Peter's brother, spoke up. [9]"There's a young boy here with five barley loaves and two fish. But what good is that with this huge crowd?"

[10]"Tell everyone to sit down," Jesus said. So they all sat down on the grassy slopes. (The men alone numbered about 5,000.) [11]Then Jesus took the loaves, gave thanks to God, and distributed them to the people. Afterward he did the same with the fish. And they all ate as much as they wanted. [12]After everyone was full, Jesus told his disciples, "Now gather the leftovers, so that nothing is wasted." [13]So they picked up the pieces and filled twelve baskets with scraps left by the people who had eaten from the five barley loaves.

[14]When the people saw him* do this miraculous sign, they exclaimed, "Surely, he is the Prophet we have been expecting!"* [15]When Jesus saw that they were ready to force him to be their king, he slipped away into the hills by himself.

Jesus Walks on Water

[16]That evening Jesus' disciples went down to the shore to wait for him. [17]But as darkness fell and Jesus still hadn't come back, they got into the boat and headed across the lake toward Capernaum. [18]Soon a gale swept down upon them, and the sea grew very rough. [19]They had rowed three or four miles* when suddenly they saw Jesus walking on the water toward the boat. They were terrified, [20]but he called out to them, "Don't be afraid. I am here!"* [21]Then they were eager to let him in the boat, and immediately they arrived at their destination!

5:44 Some manuscripts read *from the only One*. **6:7** Greek *Two hundred denarii would not be enough*. A denarius was equivalent to a laborer's full day's wage. **6:14a** Some manuscripts read *Jesus*. **6:14b** See Deut 18:15, 18; Mal 4:5-6. **6:19** Greek *25 or 30 stadia* [4.6 or 5.5 kilometers]. **6:20** Or *The 'I Am' is here*; Greek reads *I am*. See Exod 3:14.

Solitude

Time Alone

JOHN 6:15

R ichard Foster, in his classic *Celebration of Discipline,* writes, "If we possess inward solitude we do not fear being alone, for we know that we are not alone. . . . In the midst of noise and confusion we are settled into a deep inner silence. Whether alone or among people, we always carry with us a portable sanctuary of the heart."

Don't you want that kind of peace and inner strength? In Scripture Christ makes clear that he desires it for us as well. But rather than peace, most people walk around carrying tremendous burdens. And many of us are so busy and distracted in our whirlwind world that we don't even recognize— let alone unload—those burdens. God can help us, and times of solitude can help create the right atmosphere for God's work. To experience the kind of peace that comes from inward solitude, we must practice being physically alone with God, forcing ourselves to tune in to his presence, releasing the burdens we needn't bear, until that tuned-in state becomes natural and normative.

We need solitude because when we're with other people, we're always relating to them—whether we're talking or not—verbally, nonverbally, and mentally. If we're conscious of others' presence, we are relating to them and it is impossible to be only with God.

When we spend time in solitude, we have no one to relate to but ourselves and God. We can reconnect with God one-on-one, and we gain a fresh perspective on life. As we depend on God alone for relationship during those times, we grow closer to him.

The Bible gives us a striking example of someone who practiced solitude: Jesus. Jesus often spent time by himself, praying, relating to God the Father. John 6:15 provides one such example.

John 21:25 tells us that if everything Jesus did on earth were written down, the world would not be large enough to contain all the volumes describing his deeds. How interesting that among the select activities that are recorded for us are multiple occasions in which Jesus spent time in solitude! This emphasis by the Gospel writers implies that this was a regular and profoundly important habit for Jesus.

In the Gospels, Jesus' times in solitude are often paired with his powerful acts of ministry. For example, right after his time of solitude John 6:15, Jesus famously walked on water. The practice of solitude—taking time alone with God—can similarly build our faith and strengthen us to minister to others, and face life's challenges.

Of course if we're unaccustomed to solitude, as soon as we're alone, we start hearing sounds we don't usually hear, and this may make us quite uncomfortable. We hear our own internal voices. We notice anxieties, fears, wishes, and desires that the voices of others and our frenetic pace usually drown out. Many people believe they can't truly be with God until those inner sounds are quiet, so they try to silence these sounds when they're alone only to find they can concentrate on nothing else. This presents great frustration. It's better to relax and let those voices speak their piece. We need to hear them in God's presence to put them in perspective. As we turn our attention to God and let him sort us out, the din will become quieter. With further practice, we can hear another new sound—God's voice breaking through the din.

To get started, try fifteen minutes of solitude. This may seem like a long time. Stick it out and see what happens. You don't have to be still or even silent. Pray, listen to God, ask God to guide your thoughts, move around, talk aloud, or even sing quietly.

Later challenge yourself to continue to practice. Think of God inviting you to spend time with him, away from the distractions and distortions of human society. Set an appointment with him. Where and when might God want you to spend time alone with him? In your bedroom in the morning? In a church near your workplace in the middle of the day? In a closet in your house? In the park after you drop off the kids at school?

Through the practice of solitude, we can reconnect with God one on one. Solitude builds faith by forcing us to depend on God for relationship—and for the truth about life. It is possible to incorporate the spiritual discipline of solitude into your life. You can get away by yourself even if it's for just five minutes a day, and that time of solitude with God can have a big impact in your life—as it did for Jesus.

—*Amy Simpson*

Jesus, the Bread of Life

²²The next day the crowd that had stayed on the far shore saw that the disciples had taken the only boat, and they realized Jesus had not gone with them. ²³Several boats from Tiberias landed near the place where the Lord had blessed the bread and the people had eaten. ²⁴So when the crowd saw that neither Jesus nor his disciples were there, they got into the boats and went across to Capernaum to look for him. ²⁵They found him on the other side of the lake and asked, "Rabbi, when did you get here?"

²⁶Jesus replied, "I tell you the truth, you want to be with me because I fed you, not because you understood the miraculous signs. ²⁷But don't be so concerned about perishable things like food. Spend your energy seeking the eternal life that the Son of Man* can give you. For God the Father has given me the seal of his approval."

²⁸They replied, "We want to perform God's works, too. What should we do?"

²⁹Jesus told them, "This is the only work God wants from you: Believe in the one he has sent."

³⁰They answered, "Show us a miraculous sign if you want us to believe in you. What can you do? ³¹After all, our ancestors ate manna while they journeyed through the wilderness! The Scriptures say, 'Moses gave them bread from heaven to eat.'*"

³²Jesus said, "I tell you the truth, Moses didn't give you bread from heaven. My Father did. And now he offers you the true bread from heaven. ³³The true bread of God is the one who comes down from heaven and gives life to the world."

³⁴"Sir," they said, "give us that bread every day."

³⁵Jesus replied, "I am the bread of life. Whoever comes to me will never be hungry again. Whoever believes in me will never be thirsty. ³⁶But you haven't believed in me even though you have seen me. ³⁷However, those the Father has given me will come to me, and I will never reject them. ³⁸For I have come down from heaven to do the will of God who sent me, not to do my own will. ³⁹And this is the will of God, that I should not lose even one of all those he has given

me, but that I should raise them up at the last day. ⁴⁰For it is my Father's will that all who see his Son and believe in him should have eternal life. I will raise them up at the last day."

⁴¹Then the people* began to murmur in disagreement because he had said, "I am the bread that came down from heaven." ⁴²They said, "Isn't this Jesus, the son of Joseph? We know his father and mother. How can he say, 'I came down from heaven'?"

⁴³But Jesus replied, "Stop complaining about what I said. ⁴⁴For no one can come to me unless the Father who sent me draws them to me, and at the last day I will raise them up. ⁴⁵As it is written in the Scriptures,* 'They will all be taught by God.' Everyone who listens to the Father and learns from him comes to me. ⁴⁶(Not that anyone has ever seen the Father; only I, who was sent from God, have seen him.)

⁴⁷"I tell you the truth, anyone who believes has eternal life. ⁴⁸Yes, I am the bread of life! ⁴⁹Your ancestors ate manna in the wilderness, but they all died. ⁵⁰Anyone who eats the bread from heaven, however, will never die. ⁵¹I am the living bread that came down from heaven. Anyone who eats this bread will live forever; and this bread, which I will offer so the world may live, is my flesh."

⁵²Then the people began arguing with each other about what he meant. "How can this man give us his flesh to eat?" they asked.

⁵³So Jesus said again, "I tell you the truth, unless you eat the flesh of the Son of Man and drink his blood, you cannot have eternal life within you. ⁵⁴But anyone who eats my flesh and drinks my blood has eternal life, and I will raise that person at the last day. ⁵⁵For my flesh is true food, and my blood is true drink. ⁵⁶Anyone who eats my flesh and drinks my blood remains in me, and I in him. ⁵⁷I live because of the living Father who sent me; in the same way, anyone who feeds on me will live because of me. ⁵⁸I am the true bread that came down from heaven. Anyone who eats this bread will not die as your ancestors did (even though they ate the manna) but will live forever."

6:27 "Son of Man" is a title Jesus used for himself.   **6:31** Exod 16:4; Ps 78:24.   **6:41** Greek *Jewish people;* also in 6:52.   **6:45** Greek *in the prophets.* Isa 54:13.

⁵⁹He said these things while he was teaching in the synagogue in Capernaum.

Many Disciples Desert Jesus

⁶⁰Many of his disciples said, "This is very hard to understand. How can anyone accept it?"

⁶¹Jesus was aware that his disciples were complaining, so he said to them, "Does this offend you? ⁶²Then what will you think if you see the Son of Man ascend to heaven again?

⁶³The Spirit alone gives eternal life. Human effort accomplishes nothing. And the very words I have spoken to you are spirit and life. ⁶⁴But some of you do not believe me." (For Jesus knew from the beginning which ones didn't believe, and he knew who would betray him.) ⁶⁵Then he said, "That is why I said that people can't come to me unless the Father gives them to me."

⁶⁶At this point many of his disciples turned away and deserted him. ⁶⁷Then

Q&A [Fasting like the Early Church?]
Fasting

JOHN 6:35-59

I know fasting was regularly practiced throughout biblical times. But what role did it play in the early church?

In church history early Christians made it a habit to fast together. The earliest existing Christian document outside Scripture is the *Didache*, or the *Teaching of the Twelve Apostles* (dates vary; but it may have been written as early as A.D. 70). The *Didache* reminds believers that the Jews fast on Tuesdays and Thursdays. (Remember the Pharisee in Luke 18:12, who proclaimed, "I fast twice a week"?) But the *Didache* does not say, "So avoid that fasting foolishness, because we don't need it." No, this earliest church-discipline text instructs that Christians should fast as well, but on Wednesdays (the day of Judas's betrayal) and Fridays (the day of the Crucifixion).

Regular fasting is a valuable practice on its own, and it can also strengthen and undergird our practice of many other spiritual disciplines. In *The Spirit of the Disciplines,* Dallas Willard writes, "Since food has the pervasive place it does in our lives, the effects of fasting will be diffused throughout our personality. In the midst of all our needs and wants, we experience the contentment of the child that has been weaned from its mother's breast" (Psalm 131:2).

This psalm used to puzzle me; I've seen the contentment of a *nursing* child and wondered why the psalmist didn't use that image. Why a weaned child instead? But I believe the point is this: the weaned child has learned to be satisfied with another food. We do not live by bread alone (Deuteronomy 8:3; Matthew 4:4; Luke 4:4). The earliest believers embodied this truth through their practice of twice-weekly fasting. How can fasting help you seek deeper contentment in Christ and strengthen your own spiritual self-discipline?

—Frederica Mathewes-Green

Jesus turned to the Twelve and asked, "Are you also going to leave?"

⁶⁸Simon Peter replied, "Lord, to whom would we go? You have the words that give eternal life. ⁶⁹We believe, and we know you are the Holy One of God.*"

⁷⁰Then Jesus said, "I chose the twelve of you, but one is a devil." ⁷¹He was speaking of Judas, son of Simon Iscariot, one of the Twelve, who would later betray him.

7 Jesus and His Brothers

After this, Jesus traveled around Galilee. He wanted to stay out of Judea, where the Jewish leaders were plotting his death. ²But soon it was time for the Jewish Festival of Shelters, ³and Jesus' brothers said to him, "Leave here and go to Judea, where your followers can see your miracles! ⁴You can't become famous if you hide like this! If you can do such wonderful things, show yourself to the world!" ⁵For even his brothers didn't believe in him.

⁶Jesus replied, "Now is not the right time for me to go, but you can go anytime. ⁷The world can't hate you, but it does hate me because I accuse it of doing evil. ⁸You go on. I'm not going* to this festival, because my time has not yet come." ⁹After saying these things, Jesus remained in Galilee.

Jesus Teaches Openly at the Temple

¹⁰But after his brothers left for the festival, Jesus also went, though secretly, staying out of public view. ¹¹The Jewish leaders tried to find him at the festival and kept asking if anyone had seen him. ¹²There was a lot of grumbling about him among the crowds. Some argued, "He's a good man," but others said, "He's nothing but a fraud who deceives the people." ¹³But no one had the courage to speak favorably about him in public, for they were afraid of getting in trouble with the Jewish leaders.

¹⁴Then, midway through the festival, Jesus went up to the Temple and began to teach. ¹⁵The people* were surprised when they heard him. "How does he know so much when he hasn't been trained?" they asked.

¹⁶So Jesus told them, "My message is not my own; it comes from God who sent me. ¹⁷Anyone who wants to do the will of God will know whether my teaching is from God or is merely my own. ¹⁸Those who speak for themselves want glory only for themselves, but a person who seeks to honor the one who sent him speaks truth, not lies. ¹⁹Moses gave you the law, but none of you obeys it! In fact, you are trying to kill me."

²⁰The crowd replied, "You're demon possessed! Who's trying to kill you?"

²¹Jesus replied, "I did one miracle on the Sabbath, and you were amazed. ²²But you work on the Sabbath, too, when you obey Moses' law of circumcision. (Actually, this tradition of circumcision began with the patriarchs, long before the law of Moses.) ²³For if the correct time for circumcising your son falls on the Sabbath, you go ahead and do it so as not to break the law of Moses. So why should you be angry with me for healing a man on the Sabbath? ²⁴Look beneath the surface so you can judge correctly."

Is Jesus the Messiah?

²⁵Some of the people who lived in Jerusalem started to ask each other, "Isn't this the man they are trying to kill? ²⁶But here he is, speaking in public, and they say nothing to him. Could our leaders possibly believe that he is the Messiah? ²⁷But how could he be? For we know where this man comes from. When the Messiah comes, he will simply appear; no one will know where he comes from."

²⁸While Jesus was teaching in the Temple, he called out, "Yes, you know me, and you know where I come from. But I'm not here on my own. The one who sent me is true, and you don't know him. ²⁹But I know him because I come from him, and he sent me to you." ³⁰Then the leaders tried to arrest him; but no one laid a hand on him, because his time* had not yet come.

³¹Many among the crowds at the Temple believed in him. "After all," they said, "would you expect the Messiah to do more miraculous signs than this man has done?"

³²When the Pharisees heard that the crowds were whispering such things, they

---

6:69 Other manuscripts read *you are the Christ, the Holy One of God;* still others read *you are the Christ, the Son of God;* and still others read *you are the Christ, the Son of the living God.*   **7:8** Some manuscripts read *not yet going.*   **7:15** Greek *Jewish people.*   **7:30** Greek *his hour.*

and the leading priests sent Temple guards to arrest Jesus. ³³But Jesus told them, "I will be with you only a little longer. Then I will return to the one who sent me. ³⁴You will search for me but not find me. And you cannot go where I am going."

³⁵The Jewish leaders were puzzled by this statement. "Where is he planning to go?" they asked. "Is he thinking of leaving the country and going to the Jews in other lands?* Maybe he will even teach the Greeks! ³⁶What does he mean when he says, 'You will search for me but not find me,' and 'You cannot go where I am going'?"

Jesus Promises Living Water

³⁷On the last day, the climax of the festival, Jesus stood and shouted to the crowds, "Anyone who is thirsty may come to me! ³⁸Anyone who believes in me may come and drink! For the Scriptures declare, 'Rivers of living water will flow from his heart.'* ³⁹(When he said "living water," he was speaking of the Spirit, who would be given to everyone believing in him. But the Spirit had not yet been given,* because Jesus had not yet entered into his glory.)

Division and Unbelief

⁴⁰When the crowds heard him say this, some of them declared, "Surely this man is the Prophet we've been expecting."* ⁴¹Others said, "He is the Messiah." Still others said, "But he can't be! Will the Messiah come from Galilee? ⁴²For the Scriptures clearly state that the Messiah will be born of the royal line of David, in Bethlehem, the village where King David was born."* ⁴³So the crowd was divided about him. ⁴⁴Some even wanted him arrested, but no one laid a hand on him.

⁴⁵When the Temple guards returned without having arrested Jesus, the leading priests and Pharisees demanded, "Why didn't you bring him in?"

⁴⁶"We have never heard anyone speak like this!" the guards responded.

⁴⁷"Have you been led astray, too?" the Pharisees mocked. ⁴⁸"Is there a single one of us rulers or Pharisees who believes in him? ⁴⁹This foolish crowd follows him, but they are ignorant of the law. God's curse is on them!"

⁵⁰Then Nicodemus, the leader who had met with Jesus earlier, spoke up. ⁵¹"Is it legal to convict a man before he is given a hearing?" he asked.

⁵²They replied, "Are you from Galilee, too? Search the Scriptures and see for yourself—no prophet ever comes* from Galilee!"

[*The most ancient Greek manuscripts do not include John 7:53–8:11.*]

⁵³Then the meeting broke up, and everybody went home.

8 A Woman Caught in Adultery

Jesus returned to the Mount of Olives, ²but early the next morning he was back again at the Temple. A crowd soon gathered, and he sat down and taught them. ³As he was speaking, the teachers of religious law and the Pharisees brought a woman who had been caught in the act of adultery. They put her in front of the crowd.

⁴"Teacher," they said to Jesus, "this woman was caught in the act of adultery. ⁵The law of Moses says to stone her. What do you say?"

⁶They were trying to trap him into saying something they could use against him, but Jesus stooped down and wrote in the dust with his finger. ⁷They kept demanding an answer, so he stood up again and said, "All right, but let the one who has never sinned throw the first stone!" ⁸Then he stooped down again and wrote in the dust.

⁹When the accusers heard this, they slipped away one by one, beginning with the oldest, until only Jesus was left in the middle of the crowd with the woman. ¹⁰Then Jesus stood up again and said to the woman, "Where are your accusers? Didn't even one of them condemn you?"

¹¹"No, Lord," she said.

And Jesus said, "Neither do I. Go and sin no more."

7:35 Or *the Jews who live among the Greeks?* **7:37-38** Or *"Let anyone who is thirsty come to me and drink.* ³⁸*For the Scriptures declare, 'Rivers of living water will flow from the heart of anyone who believes in me.'"* **7:39** Some manuscripts read *But as yet there was no Spirit.* Still others read *But as yet there was no Holy Spirit.* **7:40** See Deut 18:15, 18; Mal 4:5-6. **7:42** See Mic 5:2. **7:52** Some manuscripts read *the prophet does not come.*

Imagine Yourself in the Gospel Story

JOHN 8:1–11

Have you ever read a biography or a great novel and felt so swept up in the story that the book's characters became real to you? As you read their story, you felt you actually were spending time with them?

Gospel meditation—what I'd call "being there"—has traditionally been called the Ignatian method, after Saint Ignatius of Loyola (1491–1556). He instructed his followers to spend time with Jesus by imagining themselves in the gospel story.

David Benner, author of *The Gift of Being Yourself*, writes, "Gospel meditation provides an opportunity to enter specific moments in Jesus' life and thereby share his experience. Shared experience is the core of any friendship."

To begin this practice of devotional reading, choose a passage from one of the Gospels. Read it slowly. Daydream about it, imagining you're there. Perhaps you're a bystander watching Jesus or the person talking to Jesus. Try playing various roles in the scene. Use your imagination to add details. Put yourself into the story through your five senses: what do you see, hear, feel, taste, and smell? By being there, you're spending time with Jesus.

—Keri Wyatt Kent

For more on Bible study and meditation, see reading at John 15:1–7.

Jesus, the Light of the World

[12] Jesus spoke to the people once more and said, "I am the light of the world. If you follow me, you won't have to walk in darkness, because you will have the light that leads to life."

[13] The Pharisees replied, "You are making those claims about yourself! Such testimony is not valid."

[14] Jesus told them, "These claims are valid even though I make them about myself. For I know where I came from and where I am going, but you don't know this about me. [15] You judge me by human standards, but I do not judge anyone. [16] And if I did, my judgment would be correct in every respect because I am not alone. The Father* who sent me is with me. [17] Your own law says that if two people agree about something, their witness is accepted as fact.* [18] I am one witness, and my Father who sent me is the other."

[19] "Where is your father?" they asked.

Jesus answered, "Since you don't know who I am, you don't know who my Father is. If you knew me, you would also know my Father." [20] Jesus made these statements while he was teaching in the section of the Temple known as the Treasury. But he was not arrested, because his time* had not yet come.

The Unbelieving People Warned

[21] Later Jesus said to them again, "I am going away. You will search for me but will die in your sin. You cannot come where I am going."

[22] The people* asked, "Is he planning to commit suicide? What does he mean, 'You cannot come where I am going'?"

8:16 Some manuscripts read *The One.*   **8:17** See Deut 19:15.   **8:20** Greek *his hour.*   **8:22** Greek *Jewish people*; also in 8:31, 48, 52, 57.

²³Jesus continued, "You are from below; I am from above. You belong to this world; I do not. ²⁴That is why I said that you will die in your sins; for unless you believe that I Aᴍ who I claim to be,* you will die in your sins."

²⁵"Who are you?" they demanded.

Jesus replied, "The one I have always claimed to be.* ²⁶I have much to say about you and much to condemn, but I won't. For I say only what I have heard from the one who sent me, and he is completely truthful." ²⁷But they still didn't understand that he was talking about his Father.

²⁸So Jesus said, "When you have lifted up the Son of Man on the cross, then you will understand that I Aᴍ he.* I do nothing on my own but say only what the Father taught me. ²⁹And the one who sent me is with me—he has not deserted me. For I always do what pleases him." ³⁰Then many who heard him say these things believed in him.

Jesus and Abraham

³¹Jesus said to the people who believed in him, "You are truly my disciples if you remain faithful to my teachings. ³²And you will know the truth, and the truth will set you free."

³³"But we are descendants of Abraham," they said. "We have never been slaves to anyone. What do you mean, 'You will be set free'?"

³⁴Jesus replied, "I tell you the truth, everyone who sins is a slave of sin. ³⁵A slave is not a permanent member of the family, but a son is part of the family forever. ³⁶So if the Son sets you free, you are truly free. ³⁷Yes, I realize that you are descendants of Abraham. And yet some of you are trying to kill me because there's no room in your hearts for my message. ³⁸I am telling you what I saw when I was with my Father. But you are following the advice of your father."

³⁹"Our father is Abraham!" they declared.

"No," Jesus replied, "for if you were really the children of Abraham, you would follow his example.* ⁴⁰Instead, you are trying to kill me because I told you the truth, which I heard from God. Abraham never did such a thing. ⁴¹No, you are imitating your real father."

They replied, "We aren't illegitimate children! God himself is our true Father."

⁴²Jesus told them, "If God were your Father, you would love me, because I have come to you from God. I am not here on my own, but he sent me. ⁴³Why can't you understand what I am saying? It's because you can't even hear me! ⁴⁴For you are the children of your father the devil, and you love to do the evil things he does. He was a murderer from the beginning. He has always hated the truth, because there is no truth in him. When he lies, it is consistent with his character; for he is a liar and the father of lies. ⁴⁵So when I tell the truth, you just naturally don't believe me! ⁴⁶Which of you can truthfully accuse me of sin? And since I am telling you the truth, why don't you believe me? ⁴⁷Anyone who belongs to God listens gladly to the words of God. But you don't listen because you don't belong to God."

⁴⁸The people retorted, "You Samaritan devil! Didn't we say all along that you were possessed by a demon?"

⁴⁹"No," Jesus said, "I have no demon in me. For I honor my Father—and you dishonor me. ⁵⁰And though I have no wish to glorify myself, God is going to glorify me. He is the true judge. ⁵¹I tell you the truth, anyone who obeys my teaching will never die!"

⁵²The people said, "Now we know you are possessed by a demon. Even Abraham and the prophets died, but you say, 'Anyone who obeys my teaching will never die!' ⁵³Are you greater than our father Abraham? He died, and so did the prophets. Who do you think you are?"

⁵⁴Jesus answered, "If I want glory for myself, it doesn't count. But it is my Father who will glorify me. You say, 'He is our God,*' ⁵⁵but you don't even know him. I know him. If I said otherwise, I would be as great a liar as you! But I do know him and obey him. ⁵⁶Your father Abraham rejoiced as he looked forward to my coming. He saw it and was glad."

8:24 Greek *unless you believe that I am.* See Exod 3:14.   **8:25** Or *Why do I speak to you at all?*   **8:28** Greek *When you have lifted up the Son of Man, then you will know that I am.* "Son of Man" is a title Jesus used for himself.   **8:39** Some manuscripts read *if you are really the children of Abraham, follow his example.*   **8:54** Some manuscripts read *your God.*

57 The people said, "You aren't even fifty years old. How can you say you have seen Abraham?*"

58 Jesus answered, "I tell you the truth, before Abraham was even born, I Am!*" 59 At that point they picked up stones to throw at him. But Jesus was hidden from them and left the Temple.

9 Jesus Heals a Man Born Blind

As Jesus was walking along, he saw a man who had been blind from birth. 2 "Rabbi," his disciples asked him, "why was this man born blind? Was it because of his own sins or his parents' sins?"

3 "It was not because of his sins or his parents' sins," Jesus answered. "This happened so the power of God could be seen in him. 4 We must quickly carry out the tasks assigned us by the one who sent us.* The night is coming, and then no one can work. 5 But while I am here in the world, I am the light of the world."

6 Then he spit on the ground, made mud with the saliva, and spread the mud over the blind man's eyes. 7 He told him, "Go wash yourself in the pool of Siloam" (Siloam means "sent"). So the man went and washed and came back seeing!

8 His neighbors and others who knew him as a blind beggar asked each other, "Isn't this the man who used to sit and beg?" 9 Some said he was, and others said, "No, he just looks like him!"

But the beggar kept saying, "Yes, I am the same one!"

10 They asked, "Who healed you? What happened?"

11 He told them, "The man they call Jesus made mud and spread it over my eyes and told me, 'Go to the pool of Siloam and wash yourself.' So I went and washed, and now I can see!"

12 "Where is he now?" they asked.

"I don't know," he replied.

13 Then they took the man who had been blind to the Pharisees, 14 because it was on the Sabbath that Jesus had made the mud and healed him. 15 The Pharisees asked the man all about it. So he told them, "He put the mud over my eyes, and when I washed it away, I could see!"

16 Some of the Pharisees said, "This man Jesus is not from God, for he is working on the Sabbath." Others said, "But how could an ordinary sinner do such miraculous signs?" So there was a deep division of opinion among them.

17 Then the Pharisees again questioned the man who had been blind and demanded, "What's your opinion about this man who healed you?"

The man replied, "I think he must be a prophet."

18 The Jewish leaders still refused to believe the man had been blind and could now see, so they called in his parents. 19 They asked them, "Is this your son? Was he born blind? If so, how can he now see?"

20 His parents replied, "We know this is our son and that he was born blind, 21 but we don't know how he can see or who healed him. Ask him. He is old enough to speak for himself." 22 His parents said this because they were afraid of the Jewish leaders, who had announced that anyone saying Jesus was the Messiah would be expelled from the synagogue. 23 That's why they said, "He is old enough. Ask him."

24 So for the second time they called in the man who had been blind and told him, "God should get the glory for this,* because we know this man Jesus is a sinner."

25 "I don't know whether he is a sinner," the man replied. "But I know this: I was blind, and now I can see!"

26 "But what did he do?" they asked. "How did he heal you?"

27 "Look!" the man exclaimed. "I told you once. Didn't you listen? Why do you want to hear it again? Do you want to become his disciples, too?"

28 Then they cursed him and said, "You are his disciple, but we are disciples of Moses! 29 We know God spoke to Moses, but we don't even know where this man comes from."

30 "Why, that's very strange!" the man replied. "He healed my eyes, and yet you don't know where he comes from? 31 We

---

8:57 Some manuscripts read How can you say Abraham has seen you? 8:58 Or before Abraham was even born, I have always been alive; Greek reads before Abraham was, I am. See Exod 3:14. 9:4 Other manuscripts read I must quickly carry out the tasks assigned me by the one who sent me; still others read We must quickly carry out the tasks assigned us by the one who sent me. 9:24 Or Give glory to God, not to Jesus; Greek reads Give glory to God.

know that God doesn't listen to sinners, but he is ready to hear those who worship him and do his will. ³²Ever since the world began, no one has been able to open the eyes of someone born blind. ³³If this man were not from God, he couldn't have done it."

³⁴"You were born a total sinner!" they answered. "Are you trying to teach us?" And they threw him out of the synagogue.

Spiritual Blindness

³⁵When Jesus heard what had happened, he found the man and asked, "Do you believe in the Son of Man?*"

³⁶The man answered, "Who is he, sir? I want to believe in him."

³⁷"You have seen him," Jesus said, "and he is speaking to you!"

³⁸"Yes, Lord, I believe!" the man said. And he worshiped Jesus.

³⁹Then Jesus told him,* "I entered this world to render judgment—to give sight to the blind and to show those who think they see* that they are blind."

⁴⁰Some Pharisees who were standing nearby heard him and asked, "Are you saying we're blind?"

⁴¹"If you were blind, you wouldn't be guilty," Jesus replied. "But you remain guilty because you claim you can see.

10 The Good Shepherd and His Sheep

"I tell you the truth, anyone who sneaks over the wall of a sheepfold, rather than going through the gate, must surely be a thief and a robber! ²But the one who enters through the gate is the shepherd of the sheep. ³The gatekeeper opens the gate for him, and the sheep recognize his voice and come to him. He calls his own sheep by name and leads them out. ⁴After he has gathered his own flock, he walks ahead of them, and they follow him because they know his voice. ⁵They won't follow a stranger; they will run from him because they don't know his voice."

⁶Those who heard Jesus use this illustration didn't understand what he meant, ⁷so he explained it to them: "I tell you the truth, I am the gate for the sheep. ⁸All who

came before me* were thieves and robbers. But the true sheep did not listen to them. ⁹Yes, I am the gate. Those who come in through me will be saved.* They will come and go freely and will find good pastures. ¹⁰The thief's purpose is to steal and kill and destroy. My purpose is to give them a rich and satisfying life.

¹¹"I am the good shepherd. The good shepherd sacrifices his life for the sheep. ¹²A hired hand will run when he sees a wolf coming. He will abandon the sheep because they don't belong to him and he isn't their shepherd. And so the wolf attacks them and scatters the flock. ¹³The hired hand runs away because he's working only for the money and doesn't really care about the sheep.

¹⁴"I am the good shepherd; I know my own sheep, and they know me, ¹⁵just as my Father knows me and I know the Father. So I sacrifice my life for the sheep. ¹⁶I have other sheep, too, that are not in this sheepfold. I must bring them also. They will listen to my voice, and there will be one flock with one shepherd.

¹⁷"The Father loves me because I sacrifice my life so I may take it back again. ¹⁸No one can take my life from me. I sacrifice it voluntarily. For I have the authority to lay it down when I want to and also to take it up again. For this is what my Father has commanded."

¹⁹When he said these things, the people* were again divided in their opinions about him. ²⁰Some said, "He's demon possessed and out of his mind. Why listen to a man like that?" ²¹Others said, "This doesn't sound like a man possessed by a demon! Can a demon open the eyes of the blind?"

Jesus Claims to Be the Son of God

²²It was now winter, and Jesus was in Jerusalem at the time of Hanukkah, the Festival of Dedication. ²³He was in the Temple, walking through the section known as Solomon's Colonnade. ²⁴The people surrounded him and asked, "How long are you going to keep us in suspense? If you are the Messiah, tell us plainly."

9:35 Some manuscripts read *the Son of God?* "Son of Man" is a title Jesus used for himself.   **9:38-39a** Some manuscripts do not include *"Yes, Lord, I believe!" the man said. And he worshiped Jesus. Then Jesus told him.*   **9:39b** Greek *those who see.*   **10:8** Some manuscripts do not include *before me.*   **10:9** Or *will find safety.*   **10:19** Greek *Jewish people;* also in 10:24, 31.

Abundant Simplicity
JOHN 10:1-10

In a basic sense, the Christian virtue of simplicity challenges us to own less. Biblical examples of giving away wealth and possessions abound, from Old Testament teachings on tithing to Jesus telling the rich young man to "sell all your possessions and give the money to the poor" (Mark 10:21). But does a strict understanding of material simplicity—spending and owning less—always lead to spiritual and emotional enrichment?

I once lived in meager financial circumstances—but instead of flourishing in this period of simplicity, I ended up feeling resentful. Even the most mundane purchases turned into occasions for anxiety and guilt. Scrutinizing every purchase didn't free me from material concerns to make room for spiritual ones. It just made me cranky.

Yet Jesus said that he came that we might have a rich, satisfying, abundant life (John 10:10). I believe that Christians should strive for *abundant simplicity*. Abundant simplicity does not mean agonizing over every purchase or merely adhering to an austere number of possessions. Gratitude, contentment, and acceptance of life as it is, even when it does not conform to our preferences, are also virtues. Abundant simplicity is about paying attention—to what we want and need; what we have and buy; what we spend, save, and give; and our relationship with our bank accounts and material objects. We're able to honestly ask ourselves: when do money and things enhance our lives, and when do they tempt us to envy, anxiety, fear, pride, or selfishness?

Simplicity doesn't always mean spending less, and it doesn't always mean having less. Our practice of simplicity should be interwoven with our gratitude for God's good gifts, our faithful stewardship of the money and possessions he's given us, our generous giving to those in need, and a sense of freedom to respond joyfully to God's leading.

—*Ellen Painter Dollar*

For more on simplicity, see reading at 1 Corinthians 7:29-31.

---

²⁵Jesus replied, "I have already told you, and you don't believe me. The proof is the work I do in my Father's name. ²⁶But you don't believe me because you are not my sheep. ²⁷My sheep listen to my voice; I know them, and they follow me. ²⁸I give them eternal life, and they will never perish. No one can snatch them away from me, ²⁹for my Father has given them to me, and he is more powerful than anyone else.* No one can snatch them from the Father's hand. ³⁰The Father and I are one."

³¹Once again the people picked up stones to kill him. ³²Jesus said, "At my Father's direction I have done many good works. For which one are you going to stone me?"

³³They replied, "We're stoning you not for any good work, but for blasphemy! You, a mere man, claim to be God."

³⁴Jesus replied, "It is written in your own Scriptures* that God said to certain leaders of the people, 'I say, you are gods!'* ³⁵And you know that the Scriptures cannot be altered. So if those people who received

---

10:29 Other manuscripts read *for what my Father has given me is more powerful than anything;* still others read *for regarding that which my Father has given me, he is greater than all.* **10:34a** Greek *your own law.* **10:34b** Ps 82:6.

God's message were called 'gods,' ³⁶why do you call it blasphemy when I say, 'I am the Son of God'? After all, the Father set me apart and sent me into the world. ³⁷Don't believe me unless I carry out my Father's work. ³⁸But if I do his work, believe in the evidence of the miraculous works I have done, even if you don't believe me. Then you will know and understand that the Father is in me, and I am in the Father."

³⁹Once again they tried to arrest him, but he got away and left them. ⁴⁰He went beyond the Jordan River near the place where John was first baptizing and stayed there awhile. ⁴¹And many followed him. "John didn't perform miraculous signs," they remarked to one another, "but everything he said about this man has come true." ⁴²And many who were there believed in Jesus.

11 The Raising of Lazarus

A man named Lazarus was sick. He lived in Bethany with his sisters, Mary and Martha. ²This is the Mary who later poured the expensive perfume on the Lord's feet and wiped them with her hair.* Her brother, Lazarus, was sick. ³So the two sisters sent a message to Jesus telling him, "Lord, your dear friend is very sick."

⁴But when Jesus heard about it he said, "Lazarus's sickness will not end in death. No, it happened for the glory of God so that the Son of God will receive glory from this." ⁵So although Jesus loved Martha, Mary, and Lazarus, ⁶he stayed where he was for the next two days. ⁷Finally, he said to his disciples, "Let's go back to Judea."

⁸But his disciples objected. "Rabbi," they said, "only a few days ago the people* in Judea were trying to stone you. Are you going there again?"

⁹Jesus replied, "There are twelve hours of daylight every day. During the day people can walk safely. They can see because they have the light of this world. ¹⁰But at night there is danger of stumbling because they have no light." ¹¹Then he said, "Our friend Lazarus has fallen asleep, but now I will go and wake him up."

¹²The disciples said, "Lord, if he is sleep-ing, he will soon get better!" ¹³They thought Jesus meant Lazarus was simply sleeping, but Jesus meant Lazarus had died.

¹⁴So he told them plainly, "Lazarus is dead. ¹⁵And for your sakes, I'm glad I wasn't there, for now you will really believe. Come, let's go see him."

¹⁶Thomas, nicknamed the Twin,* said to his fellow disciples, "Let's go, too—and die with Jesus."

¹⁷When Jesus arrived at Bethany, he was told that Lazarus had already been in his grave for four days. ¹⁸Bethany was only a few miles* down the road from Jerusalem, ¹⁹and many of the people had come to console Martha and Mary in their loss. ²⁰When Martha got word that Jesus was coming, she went to meet him. But Mary stayed in the house. ²¹Martha said to Jesus, "Lord, if only you had been here, my brother would not have died. ²²But even now I know that God will give you whatever you ask."

²³Jesus told her, "Your brother will rise again."

²⁴"Yes," Martha said, "he will rise when everyone else rises, at the last day."

²⁵Jesus told her, "I am the resurrection and the life.* Anyone who believes in me will live, even after dying. ²⁶Everyone who lives in me and believes in me will never ever die. Do you believe this, Martha?"

²⁷"Yes, Lord," she told him. "I have always believed you are the Messiah, the Son of God, the one who has come into the world from God." ²⁸Then she returned to Mary. She called Mary aside from the mourners and told her, "The Teacher is here and wants to see you." ²⁹So Mary immediately went to him.

³⁰Jesus had stayed outside the village, at the place where Martha met him. ³¹When the people who were at the house consoling Mary saw her leave so hastily, they assumed she was going to Lazarus's grave to weep. So they followed her there. ³²When Mary arrived and saw Jesus, she fell at his feet and said, "Lord, if only you had been here, my brother would not have died."

³³When Jesus saw her weeping and saw the other people wailing with her, a deep anger welled up within him,* and he was

---

11:2 This incident is recorded in chapter 12. **11:8** Greek *Jewish people;* also in 11:19, 31, 33, 36, 45, 54. **11:16** Greek *Thomas, who was called Didymus.* **11:18** Greek *was about 15 stadia* [about 2.8 kilometers]. **11:25** Some manuscripts do not include *and the life.* **11:33** Or *he was angry in his spirit.*

deeply troubled. ³⁴"Where have you put him?" he asked them.

They told him, "Lord, come and see." ³⁵Then Jesus wept. ³⁶The people who were standing nearby said, "See how much he loved him!" ³⁷But some said, "This man healed a blind man. Couldn't he have kept Lazarus from dying?"

³⁸Jesus was still angry as he arrived at the tomb, a cave with a stone rolled across its entrance. ³⁹"Roll the stone aside," Jesus told them.

But Martha, the dead man's sister, pro-

tested, "Lord, he has been dead for four days. The smell will be terrible."

⁴⁰Jesus responded, "Didn't I tell you that you would see God's glory if you believe?" ⁴¹So they rolled the stone aside. Then Jesus looked up to heaven and said, "Father, thank you for hearing me. ⁴²You always hear me, but I said it out loud for the sake of all these people standing here, so that they will believe you sent me." ⁴³Then Jesus shouted, "Lazarus, come out!" ⁴⁴And the dead man came out, his hands and feet bound in graveclothes, his face wrapped in

Martha: Bold Faith

JOHN 11:1-44

Poor Martha—she's gone down in history as the woman we *shouldn't* be like. Her sister, Mary, is held up as the shining example of the one who chose to listen to Jesus in sharp contrast to Martha, relegated to the role of a woman who's too worried about dinner.

But there's much more to Martha's story than the snapshot recorded in Luke 10:38–42. Her life is not defined by that moment of distraction. Rather than someone who's too busy for Jesus, we instead see in Martha a woman with a profoundly close friendship with Jesus and with a stunning degree of faith.

In John 11 Martha's beloved brother had just died. In this place of great grief, she ran to Jesus when she heard he was on his way to their home, honestly expressing her heartache: "Lord, if only you had been here, my brother would not have died." Now listen to this profound expression of faith: "But even now I know that God will give you whatever you ask" (11:21–22).

Martha then went on boldly to declare something even more profound. Jesus asked her, "Everyone who lives in me and believes in me will never ever die. Do you believe this, Martha?"

"'Yes, Lord,' she told him. 'I have always believed *you are the Messiah, the Son of God,* the one who has come into the world from God'" (11:26–27, italics added).

When so few people truly recognized Jesus as the Christ—when even his *disciples* were having a hard time grasping this truth—Martha proclaimed boldly her conviction that Jesus was the Son of God! Her statement of belief is just as daring and significant as Peter's famous declaration, when Jesus asked him, "But who do you say I am?" and Peter answered, "You are the Messiah, the Son of the living God" (Matthew 16:15–16).

May we, like Martha, have the courage to proclaim boldly with our words and our lives our unswerving belief that Jesus *is* the Messiah, the Son of the living God.

—JoHannah Reardon

For more on faith, see reading at John 14:6.

a headcloth. Jesus told them, "Unwrap him and let him go!"

The Plot to Kill Jesus

[45] Many of the people who were with Mary believed in Jesus when they saw this happen. [46] But some went to the Pharisees and told them what Jesus had done. [47] Then the leading priests and Pharisees called the high council* together. "What are we going to do?" they asked each other. "This man certainly performs many miraculous signs. [48] If we allow him to go on like this, soon everyone will believe in him. Then the Roman army will come and destroy both our Temple* and our nation."

[49] Caiaphas, who was high priest at that time,* said, "You don't know what you're talking about! [50] You don't realize that it's better for you that one man should die for the people than for the whole nation to be destroyed."

[51] He did not say this on his own; as high priest at that time he was led to prophesy that Jesus would die for the entire nation. [52] And not only for that nation, but to bring together and unite all the children of God scattered around the world.

[53] So from that time on, the Jewish leaders began to plot Jesus' death. [54] As a result, Jesus stopped his public ministry among the people and left Jerusalem. He went to a place near the wilderness, to the village of Ephraim, and stayed there with his disciples.

[55] It was now almost time for the Jewish Passover celebration, and many people from all over the country arrived in Jerusalem several days early so they could go through the purification ceremony before Passover began. [56] They kept looking for Jesus, but as they stood around in the Temple, they said to each other, "What do you think? He won't come for Passover, will he?" [57] Meanwhile, the leading priests and Pharisees had publicly ordered that anyone seeing Jesus must report it immediately so they could arrest him.

12 Jesus Anointed at Bethany

Six days before the Passover celebration began, Jesus arrived in Bethany, the home of Lazarus—the man he had raised from the dead. [2] A dinner was prepared in Jesus' honor. Martha served, and Lazarus was among those who ate* with him. [3] Then Mary took a twelve-ounce jar* of expensive perfume made from essence of nard, and she anointed Jesus' feet with it, wiping his feet with her hair. The house was filled with the fragrance.

[4] But Judas Iscariot, the disciple who would soon betray him, said, [5] "That perfume was worth a year's wages.* It should have been sold and the money given to the poor." [6] Not that he cared for the poor—he was a thief, and since he was in charge of the disciples' money, he often stole some for himself.

[7] Jesus replied, "Leave her alone. She did this in preparation for my burial. [8] You will always have the poor among you, but you will not always have me."

[9] When all the people* heard of Jesus' arrival, they flocked to see him and also to see Lazarus, the man Jesus had raised from the dead. [10] Then the leading priests decided to kill Lazarus, too, [11] for it was because of him that many of the people had deserted them* and believed in Jesus.

Jesus' Triumphant Entry

[12] The next day, the news that Jesus was on the way to Jerusalem swept through the city. A large crowd of Passover visitors [13] took palm branches and went down the road to meet him. They shouted,

"Praise God!*
Blessings on the one who comes in the
    name of the LORD!
Hail to the King of Israel!"*

[14] Jesus found a young donkey and rode on it, fulfilling the prophecy that said:

[15] "Don't be afraid, people of Jerusalem.*
Look, your King is coming,
    riding on a donkey's colt."*

11:47 Greek the *Sanhedrin.*   **11:48** Or *our position;* Greek reads *our place.*   **11:49** Greek *that year;* also in 11:51.   **12:2** Or *who reclined.*   **12:3** Greek *took 1 litra* [327 grams].   **12:5** Greek *worth 300 denarii.* A denarius was equivalent to a laborer's full day's wage.   **12:9** Greek *Jewish people;* also in 12:11.   **12:11** Or *had deserted their traditions;* Greek reads *had deserted.*   **12:13a** Greek *Hosanna,* an exclamation of praise adapted from a Hebrew expression that means "save now."   **12:13b** Ps 118:25-26; Zeph 3:15.   **12:15a** Greek *daughter of Zion.*   **12:15b** Zech 9:9.

¹⁶His disciples didn't understand at the time that this was a fulfillment of prophecy. But after Jesus entered into his glory, they remembered what had happened and realized that these things had been written about him.

¹⁷Many in the crowd had seen Jesus call Lazarus from the tomb, raising him from the dead, and they were telling others* about it. ¹⁸That was the reason so many went out to meet him—because they had heard about this miraculous sign. ¹⁹Then the Pharisees said to each other, "There's nothing we can do. Look, everyone* has gone after him!"

Jesus Predicts His Death

²⁰Some Greeks who had come to Jerusalem for the Passover celebration ²¹paid a visit to Philip, who was from Bethsaida in Galilee. They said, "Sir, we want to meet Jesus." ²²Philip told Andrew about it, and they went together to ask Jesus.

²³Jesus replied, "Now the time has come for the Son of Man* to enter into his glory. ²⁴I tell you the truth, unless a kernel of wheat is planted in the soil and dies, it remains alone. But its death will produce many new kernels—a plentiful harvest of new lives. ²⁵Those who love their life in this world will lose it. Those who care nothing for their life in this world will keep it for eternity. ²⁶Anyone who wants to be my disciple must follow me, because my servants must be where I am. And the Father will honor anyone who serves me.

²⁷"Now my soul is deeply troubled. Should I pray, 'Father, save me from this hour'? But this is the very reason I came! ²⁸Father, bring glory to your name."

Then a voice spoke from heaven, saying, "I have already brought glory to my name, and I will do so again." ²⁹When the crowd heard the voice, some thought it was thunder, while others declared an angel had spoken to him.

³⁰Then Jesus told them, "The voice was for your benefit, not mine. ³¹The time for judging this world has come, when Satan, the ruler of this world, will be cast out. ³²And when I am lifted up from the earth, I will draw everyone to myself." ³³He said this to indicate how he was going to die.

³⁴The crowd responded, "We understood from Scripture* that the Messiah would live forever. How can you say the Son of Man will die? Just who is this Son of Man, anyway?"

³⁵Jesus replied, "My light will shine for you just a little longer. Walk in the light while you can, so the darkness will not overtake you. Those who walk in the darkness cannot see where they are going. ³⁶Put your trust in the light while there is still time; then you will become children of the light."

After saying these things, Jesus went away and was hidden from them.

The Unbelief of the People

³⁷But despite all the miraculous signs Jesus had done, most of the people still did not believe in him. ³⁸This is exactly what Isaiah the prophet had predicted:

"LORD, who has believed our message?
    To whom has the LORD revealed his
        powerful arm?"*

³⁹But the people couldn't believe, for as Isaiah also said,

⁴⁰ "The Lord has blinded their eyes
    and hardened their hearts—
so that their eyes cannot see,
    and their hearts cannot understand,
    and they cannot turn to me
    and have me heal them."*

⁴¹Isaiah was referring to Jesus when he said this, because he saw the future and spoke of the Messiah's glory. ⁴²Many people did believe in him, however, including some of the Jewish leaders. But they wouldn't admit it for fear that the Pharisees would expel them from the synagogue. ⁴³For they loved human praise more than the praise of God.

⁴⁴Jesus shouted to the crowds, "If you trust me, you are trusting not only me, but also God who sent me. ⁴⁵For when you see me, you are seeing the one who sent me. ⁴⁶I have come as a light to shine in this dark world, so that all who put their trust in me will no longer remain in the dark. ⁴⁷I will not judge those who hear me but don't obey me, for I have come to save the world

---

12:17 Greek were testifying.   12:19 Greek the world.   12:23 "Son of Man" is a title Jesus used for himself.   12:34 Greek from the law.
12:38 Isa 53:1.   12:40 Isa 6:10.

Service

Jesus-Style Service

JOHN 13:1–17

I am *not* your servant!"

These are the words I half grunted, half spoke to one of my kids yesterday as I got on my hands and knees to pick up the crumpled pieces of dry pasta he'd decided to deposit on the floor rather than in the garbage can.

Then a thought struck me: *I sure hope Jesus didn't hear me say that!*

Unfortunately this attitude toward servanthood extends well beyond my feelings about cleaning the floor. Most of the time, serving others just rubs me the wrong way. Sure, if it's some sort of extra-meaningful service project (where you can nearly *hear* the soundtrack of inspirational feel-good music as you work and feel an exhilarating rush, sensing how great you are for doing this), then it's not too hard. But what about real service? The kind Jesus talked about? The kind that involves getting no credit? The kind that may not be accompanied by any feelings other than a waging battle against your selfish impulses? The kind that may even involve serious germs or really bad smells?

Remember when Jesus knelt down and washed the disciples' feet? We know this was a humble thing to do, but from our modern-day perspective we may not realize how culturally radical Jesus' act really was. This job was normally reserved for servants and slaves. In fact, it was considered to be so lowly that it was usually set aside for Gentile slaves—those who were on the very bottom rung of Jewish society. That's why Peter responded so dramatically at first, absolutely refusing to let Jesus demean himself in that way (John 13:8).

"I have given you an example to follow. Do as I have done to you," Jesus said (13:15). He called his disciples—and he calls us—into a life that's willing to do bottom-rung, lowly, distasteful, and even repulsive acts of service. This *is* a call to the hard stuff. But in those on-your-knees-on-the-kitchen-floor moments, we're answering that call as we serve in Jesus' name.

—*Kelli B. Trujillo*

For more on service, see reading at Acts 6:1-7.

and not to judge it. [48] But all who reject me and my message will be judged on the day of judgment by the truth I have spoken. [49] I don't speak on my own authority. The Father who sent me has commanded me what to say and how to say it. [50] And I know his commands lead to eternal life; so I say whatever the Father tells me to say."

13 Jesus Washes His Disciples' Feet

Before the Passover celebration, Jesus knew that his hour had come to leave this world and return to his Father. He had loved his disciples during his ministry on earth, and now he loved them to the very end.* [2] It was time for supper, and the devil had already prompted Judas,* son of Simon Iscariot, to betray Jesus. [3] Jesus knew that the Father had given him authority over everything and that he had come from God and would return to God. [4] So he got up from the table, took off his robe, wrapped a towel around his waist, [5] and poured water into a basin. Then he began to wash the disciples' feet, drying them with the towel he had around him.

13:1 Or *he showed them the full extent of his love.*   **13:2** Or *the devil had already intended for Judas.*

⁶When Jesus came to Simon Peter, Peter said to him, "Lord, are you going to wash my feet?"

⁷Jesus replied, "You don't understand now what I am doing, but someday you will."

⁸"No," Peter protested, "you will never ever wash my feet!"

Jesus replied, "Unless I wash you, you won't belong to me."

⁹Simon Peter exclaimed, "Then wash my hands and head as well, Lord, not just my feet!"

¹⁰Jesus replied, "A person who has bathed all over does not need to wash, except for the feet,* to be entirely clean. And you disciples are clean, but not all of you." ¹¹For Jesus knew who would betray him. That is what he meant when he said, "Not all of you are clean."

¹²After washing their feet, he put on his robe again and sat down and asked, "Do you understand what I was doing? ¹³You call me 'Teacher' and 'Lord,' and you are right, because that's what I am. ¹⁴And since I, your Lord and Teacher, have washed your feet, you ought to wash each other's feet. ¹⁵I have given you an example to follow. Do as I have done to you. ¹⁶I tell you the truth, slaves are not greater than their master. Nor is the messenger more important than the one who sends the message. ¹⁷Now that you know these things, God will bless you for doing them.

Jesus Predicts His Betrayal

¹⁸"I am not saying these things to all of you; I know the ones I have chosen. But this fulfills the Scripture that says, 'The one who eats my food has turned against me.'* ¹⁹I tell you this beforehand, so that when it happens you will believe that I AM the Messiah.* ²⁰I tell you the truth, anyone who welcomes my messenger is welcoming me, and anyone who welcomes me is welcoming the Father who sent me."

²¹Now Jesus was deeply troubled,* and he exclaimed, "I tell you the truth, one of you will betray me!"

²²The disciples looked at each other, wondering whom he could mean. ²³The disciple Jesus loved was sitting next to Jesus at the table.* ²⁴Simon Peter motioned to him to ask, "Who's he talking about?" ²⁵So that disciple leaned over to Jesus and asked, "Lord, who is it?"

²⁶Jesus responded, "It is the one to whom I give the bread I dip in the bowl." And when he had dipped it, he gave it to Judas, son of Simon Iscariot. ²⁷When Judas had eaten the bread, Satan entered into him. Then Jesus told him, "Hurry and do what you're going to do." ²⁸None of the others at the table knew what Jesus meant. ²⁹Since Judas was their treasurer, some thought Jesus was telling him to go and pay for the food or to give some money to the poor. ³⁰So Judas left at once, going out into the night.

Jesus Predicts Peter's Denial

³¹As soon as Judas left the room, Jesus said, "The time has come for the Son of Man* to enter into his glory, and God will be glorified because of him. ³²And since God receives glory because of the Son,* he will soon give glory to the Son. ³³Dear children, I will be with you only a little longer. And as I told the Jewish leaders, you will search for me, but you can't come where I am going. ³⁴So now I am giving you a new commandment: Love each other. Just as I have loved you, you should love each other. ³⁵Your love for one another will prove to the world that you are my disciples."

³⁶Simon Peter asked, "Lord, where are you going?"

And Jesus replied, "You can't go with me now, but you will follow me later."

³⁷"But why can't I come now, Lord?" he asked. "I'm ready to die for you."

³⁸Jesus answered, "Die for me? I tell you the truth, Peter—before the rooster crows tomorrow morning, you will deny three times that you even know me.

14

Jesus, the Way to the Father

"Don't let your hearts be troubled. Trust in God, and trust also in me. ²There is more than enough room in my Father's home.* If this were not so, would I have told you that I am going to prepare a place

---

13:10 Some manuscripts do not include *except for the feet.*   13:18 Ps 41:9.   13:19 Or *that the 'I AM' has come; or that I am the LORD;* Greek reads *that I am.* See Exod 3:14.   13:21 Greek *was troubled in his spirit.*   13:23 Greek *was reclining on Jesus' bosom.* The "disciple Jesus loved" was probably John.   13:31 "Son of Man" is a title Jesus used for himself.   13:32 Some manuscripts do not include *And since God receives glory because of the Son.*   14:2a Or *There are many rooms in my Father's house.*

for you?* ³When everything is ready, I will come and get you, so that you will always be with me where I am. ⁴And you know the way to where I am going."

⁵"No, we don't know, Lord," Thomas said. "We have no idea where you are going, so how can we know the way?"

⁶Jesus told him, "I am the way, the truth, and the life. No one can come to the Father except through me. ⁷If you had really known me, you would know who my Father is.* From now on, you do know him and have seen him!"

⁸Philip said, "Lord, show us the Father, and we will be satisfied."

⁹Jesus replied, "Have I been with you all this time, Philip, and yet you still don't know who I am? Anyone who has seen me has seen the Father! So why are you asking me to show him to you? ¹⁰Don't you believe that I am in the Father and the Father is in me? The words I speak are not my own, but my Father who lives in me does his work through me. ¹¹Just believe that I am in the Father and the Father is in me. Or at least believe because of the work you have seen me do.

¹²"I tell you the truth, anyone who believes in me will do the same works I have done, and even greater works, because I am going to be with the Father. ¹³You can ask for anything in my name, and I will do it, so that the Son can bring glory to the Father. ¹⁴Yes, ask me for anything in my name, and I will do it!

Jesus Promises the Holy Spirit

¹⁵"If you love me, obey* my commandments. ¹⁶And I will ask the Father, and he will give you another Advocate,* who will never leave you. ¹⁷He is the Holy Spirit, who leads into all truth. The world cannot receive him, because it isn't looking for him and doesn't recognize him. But you know him, because he lives with you now and later will be in you.* ¹⁸No, I will not abandon you as orphans—I will come to you. ¹⁹Soon the world will no longer see me, but you will see me. Since I live, you also will

live. ²⁰When I am raised to life again, you will know that I am in my Father, and you are in me, and I am in you. ²¹Those who accept my commandments and obey them are the ones who love me. And because they love me, my Father will love them. And I will love them and reveal myself to each of them."

²²Judas (not Judas Iscariot, but the other disciple with that name) said to him, "Lord, why are you going to reveal yourself only to us and not to the world at large?"

²³Jesus replied, "All who love me will do what I say. My Father will love them, and we will come and make our home with each of them. ²⁴Anyone who doesn't love me will not obey me. And remember, my words are not my own. What I am telling you is from the Father who sent me. ²⁵I am telling you these things now while I am still with you. ²⁶But when the Father sends the Advocate as my representative—that is, the Holy Spirit—he will teach you everything and will remind you of everything I have told you.

²⁷"I am leaving you with a gift—peace of mind and heart. And the peace I give is a gift the world cannot give. So don't be troubled or afraid. ²⁸Remember what I told you: I am going away, but I will come back to you again. If you really loved me, you would be happy that I am going to the Father, who is greater than I am. ²⁹I have told you these things before they happen so that when they do happen, you will believe.

³⁰"I don't have much more time to talk to you, because the ruler of this world approaches. He has no power over me, ³¹but I will do what the Father requires of me, so that the world will know that I love the Father. Come, let's be going.

15 Jesus, the True Vine

"I am the true grapevine, and my Father is the gardener. ²He cuts off every branch of mine that doesn't produce fruit, and he prunes the branches that do bear fruit so they will produce even more. ³You have already been pruned and purified by

---

14:2b Or *If this were not so, I would have told you that I am going to prepare a place for you.* Some manuscripts read *If this were not so, I would have told you. I am going to prepare a place for you.*   **14:7** Some manuscripts read *If you have really known me, you will know who my Father is.*   **14:15** Other manuscripts read *you will obey;* still others read *you should obey.*   **14:16** Or *Comforter,* or *Encourager,* or *Counselor.* Greek reads *Paraclete;* also in 14:26.   **14:17** Some manuscripts read *and is in you.*

Untidy, Mysterious Faith

JOHN 14:6

I love office supply stores. I'm most drawn to the bins, sorters, and all manner of organizational aids in Aisle 7. They glisten with shiny plastic promise, reminding me I am just one astute purchase away from transforming the paper-riddled chaos of my life into structured bliss.

Recently I found just the thing, a two-foot black box with an open front divided into eight sections. I used my label maker to give each compartment its purpose, happily imagining soccer notices and utility bills lying obediently in their designated places. I labeled one of the compartments "Seminary." I've begun chipping away at a master's degree with a concentration in spiritual theology. I long for more structure, not only in my office but also in my faith.

I've been searching for frameworks, outlines, contexts; ways to more thoroughly understand what I believe. The studies I've chosen emphasize systematic theology. The very word *systematic* gives me that Aisle-7 rush. I can hardly wait to be organized!

"Do you think," asked my friend Barbara, who happens to be a theology professor, "that part of you is looking for control?" I stared at her blankly. No, part of me isn't looking for control. *All* of me is looking for control. I hate chaos and uncertainty. I am deeply bothered by doctrinal divisions within even the small confines of my own church tradition.

And honestly, I really don't like it when God behaves unpredictably, when he seems to be as much about mystery as he is about revelation, and when he refuses to fit into the slots I have labeled for him.

Faith would be much tidier if God could be contained within mutually agreed upon doctrinal positions. Scripture would be much more manageable if it were pure exposition, if there weren't all those sprawling narratives, wistful poems, and cryptic apocalyptic visions. Why didn't God give us his Word in sermon points that spell out catchy acronyms? Why is it all so messy? Even our most precise expositor, the apostle Paul, holds revelation and mystery in tension. In Ephesians 1:9 he proclaims, "God has now revealed to us his mysterious plan regarding Christ, a plan to fulfill his own good pleasure."

But for all the time Paul spends explaining things, he still has the nerve to celebrate everything he can't understand about God. "Oh, how great are God's riches and wisdom and knowledge! How impossible it is for us to understand his decisions and his ways! 'For who can know the LORD's thoughts? . . .' All glory to him forever!" (Romans 11:33–34, 36).

This, I'm beginning to understand, is my challenge: to immerse myself in all that has been revealed about God while celebrating all that is mystery. We have a God who both transcends our messy lives and incarnates himself in them. That reality is hard to organize, but it's the best news there is.

There's a story, often credited to E. Stanley Jones, about a missionary who gets lost in the jungle. He comes upon a village in the middle of the trees and asks a resident to lead him out. The local agrees, and for an hour he walks ahead of the missionary, clearing a way through the foliage with a machete.

Eventually the missionary asks, "Are you sure we are going the right way? Isn't there a path somewhere?" The villager smiles. "Friend, I *am* the path."

"I am the way, the truth, and the life," Jesus tells us (John 14:6); "I Am Who I Am," declares Yahweh (Exodus 3:14). My ideas about God are not the path. My church tradition, helpful as it is in pointing to him, is not the path. I plan to spend the rest of my life learning the best terminology we have for our understanding of what God has done and is doing, but the terms are not the path. Only God is. Only he can lead me through the jungle that is my life and into the boundless adventure of life with him. Praise God, there is not a thing in Aisle 7—or in the universe—that can contain him.

—*Carolyn Arends*

For more on faith, see reading at Hebrews 11:1-2.

the message I have given you. ⁴Remain in me, and I will remain in you. For a branch cannot produce fruit if it is severed from the vine, and you cannot be fruitful unless you remain in me.

⁵"Yes, I am the vine; you are the branches. Those who remain in me, and I in them, will produce much fruit. For apart from me you can do nothing. ⁶Anyone who does not remain in me is thrown away like a useless branch and withers. Such branches are gathered into a pile to be burned. ⁷But

if you remain in me and my words remain in you, you may ask for anything you want, and it will be granted! ⁸When you produce much fruit, you are my true disciples. This brings great glory to my Father.

⁹"I have loved you even as the Father has loved me. Remain in my love. ¹⁰When you obey my commandments, you remain in my love, just as I obey my Father's commandments and remain in his love. ¹¹I have told you these things so that you will be filled with my joy. Yes, your joy will over-

Q&A — Making Time for God's Word
JOHN 15:1-7

Bible Study & Meditation

How do I find time to study Scripture when I'm so busy?

Years ago I was meditating on John 15:5 where Jesus says, "I am the vine; you are the branches. Those who remain in me, and I in them, will produce much fruit. For apart from me you can do nothing." Some translations use the word *abide*.

I realized, Lord, I don't want to live my life doing nothing. If I need to abide in you in order to live a fruitful life, then that's what I want to do the rest of my life.

I can connect with Jesus in this way by consistently, daily, making time to sit with my Bible reading plan and let God speak to my heart. I want to read his Word as his child, not simply to gain knowledge—and that's what makes the difference.

When I'm busy and feel tempted to neglect reading Scripture, I ask myself, *How much do I love Jesus?* If I love him, I can't imagine not spending time with him every day. In fact, to read through the Bible every year takes no longer than fifteen minutes a day if you read three to four chapters.

As we grow in Christ, reading his Word becomes such a part of life that it's like eating. Just as I love to eat—and must eat daily to give strength and energy to my body—I should have that same delight in feeding my spirit. But here's what's interesting: when we eat physically, we become satisfied; when we eat spiritually, we become more hungry. Also, when we don't eat physically, we become hungry; when we don't eat spiritually, we lose our appetite.

—Cynthia Heald

For more on Bible study and meditation, see reading at 2 Timothy 3:16.

flow! ¹²This is my commandment: Love each other in the same way I have loved you. ¹³There is no greater love than to lay down one's life for one's friends. ¹⁴You are my friends if you do what I command. ¹⁵I no longer call you slaves, because a master doesn't confide in his slaves. Now you are my friends, since I have told you everything the Father told me. ¹⁶You didn't choose me. I chose you. I appointed you to go and produce lasting fruit, so that the Father will give you whatever you ask for, using my name. ¹⁷This is my command: Love each other.

The World's Hatred

¹⁸"If the world hates you, remember that it hated me first. ¹⁹The world would love you as one of its own if you belonged to it, but you are no longer part of the world. I chose you to come out of the world, so it hates you. ²⁰Do you remember what I told you? 'A slave is not greater than the master.' Since they persecuted me, naturally they will persecute you. And if they had listened to me, they would listen to you. ²¹They will do all this to you because of me, for they have rejected the one who sent me. ²²They would not be guilty if I had not come and spoken to them. But now they have no excuse for their sin. ²³Anyone who hates me also hates my Father. ²⁴If I hadn't done such miraculous signs among them that no one else could do, they would not be guilty. But as it is, they have seen everything I did, yet they still hate me and my Father. ²⁵This fulfills what is written in their Scriptures*: 'They hated me without cause.'

²⁶"But I will send you the Advocate*—the Spirit of truth. He will come to you from the Father and will testify all about me. ²⁷And you must also testify about me because you have been with me from the beginning of my ministry.

16

"I have told you these things so that you won't abandon your faith. ²For you will be expelled from the synagogues, and the time is coming when those who kill you will think they are doing a holy service for God. ³This is because they have never

known the Father or me. ⁴Yes, I'm telling you these things now, so that when they happen, you will remember my warning. I didn't tell you earlier because I was going to be with you for a while longer.

The Work of the Holy Spirit

⁵"But now I am going away to the one who sent me, and not one of you is asking where I am going. ⁶Instead, you grieve because of what I've told you. ⁷But in fact, it is best for you that I go away, because if I don't, the Advocate* won't come. If I do go away, then I will send him to you. ⁸And when he comes, he will convict the world of its sin, and of God's righteousness, and of the coming judgment. ⁹The world's sin is that it refuses to believe in me. ¹⁰Righteousness is available because I go to the Father, and you will see me no more. ¹¹Judgment will come because the ruler of this world has already been judged.

¹²"There is so much more I want to tell you, but you can't bear it now. ¹³When the Spirit of truth comes, he will guide you into all truth. He will not speak on his own but will tell you what he has heard. He will tell you about the future. ¹⁴He will bring me glory by telling you whatever he receives from me. ¹⁵All that belongs to the Father is mine; this is why I said, 'The Spirit will tell you whatever he receives from me.'

Sadness Will Be Turned to Joy

¹⁶"In a little while you won't see me anymore. But a little while after that, you will see me again."

¹⁷Some of the disciples asked each other, "What does he mean when he says, 'In a little while you won't see me, but then you will see me,' and 'I am going to the Father'? ¹⁸And what does he mean by 'a little while'? We don't understand."

¹⁹Jesus realized they wanted to ask him about it, so he said, "Are you asking yourselves what I meant? I said in a little while you won't see me, but a little while after that you will see me again. ²⁰I tell you the truth, you will weep and mourn over what is going to happen to me, but the world will rejoice. You will grieve, but your grief will

---

15:25 Greek *in their law.* Pss 35:19; 69:4. **15:26** Or *Comforter*, or *Encourager*, or *Counselor.* Greek reads *Paraclete.* **16:7** Or *Comforter*, or *Encourager*, or *Counselor.* Greek reads *Paraclete.*

suddenly turn to wonderful joy. ²¹It will be like a woman suffering the pains of labor. When her child is born, her anguish gives way to joy because she has brought a new baby into the world. ²²So you have sorrow now, but I will see you again; then you will rejoice, and no one can rob you of that joy. ²³At that time you won't need to ask me for anything. I tell you the truth, you will ask the Father directly, and he will grant your request because you use my name. ²⁴You haven't done this before. Ask, using my name, and you will receive, and you will have abundant joy.

²⁵"I have spoken of these matters in figures of speech, but soon I will stop speaking figuratively and will tell you plainly all about the Father. ²⁶Then you will ask in my name. I'm not saying I will ask the Father on your behalf, ²⁷for the Father himself loves you dearly because you love me and believe that I came from God.* ²⁸Yes, I came from the Father into the world, and now I will leave the world and return to the Father."

²⁹Then his disciples said, "At last you are speaking plainly and not figuratively. ³⁰Now we understand that you know everything, and there's no need to question you. From this we believe that you came from God."

³¹Jesus asked, "Do you finally believe? ³²But the time is coming—indeed it's here now—when you will be scattered, each one going his own way, leaving me alone. Yet I am not alone because the Father is with me. ³³I have told you all this so that you may have peace in me. Here on earth you will have many trials and sorrows. But take heart, because I have overcome the world."

17 The Prayer of Jesus

After saying all these things, Jesus looked up to heaven and said, "Father, the hour has come. Glorify your Son so he can give glory back to you. ²For you have given him authority over everyone. He gives eternal life to each one you have given him. ³And this is the way to have eternal life— to know you, the only true God, and Jesus Christ, the one you sent to earth. ⁴I brought glory to you here on earth by completing the work you gave me to do. ⁵Now, Father,

bring me into the glory we shared before the world began.

⁶"I have revealed you* to the ones you gave me from this world. They were always yours. You gave them to me, and they have kept your word. ⁷Now they know that everything I have is a gift from you, ⁸for I have passed on to them the message you gave me. They accepted it and know that I came from you, and they believe you sent me.

⁹"My prayer is not for the world, but for those you have given me, because they belong to you. ¹⁰All who are mine belong to you, and you have given them to me, so they bring me glory. ¹¹Now I am departing from the world; they are staying in this world, but I am coming to you. Holy Father, you have given me your name;* now protect them by the power of your name so that they will be united just as we are. ¹²During my time here, I protected them by the power of the name you gave me.* I guarded them so that not one was lost, except the one headed for destruction, as the Scriptures foretold.

¹³"Now I am coming to you. I told them many things while I was with them in this world so they would be filled with my joy. ¹⁴I have given them your word. And the world hates them because they do not belong to the world, just as I do not belong to the world. ¹⁵I'm not asking you to take them out of the world, but to keep them safe from the evil one. ¹⁶They do not belong to this world any more than I do. ¹⁷Make them holy by your truth; teach them your word, which is truth. ¹⁸Just as you sent me into the world, I am sending them into the world. ¹⁹And I give myself as a holy sacrifice for them so they can be made holy by your truth.

²⁰"I am praying not only for these disciples but also for all who will ever believe in me through their message. ²¹I pray that they will all be one, just as you and I are one—as you are in me, Father, and I am in you. And may they be in us so that the world will believe you sent me.

²²"I have given them the glory you gave me, so they may be one as we are one. ²³I am in them and you are in me. May they experience such perfect unity that the world will

---

16:27 Some manuscripts read *from the Father.*   **17:6** Greek *have revealed your name;* also in 17:26.   **17:11** Some manuscripts read *you have given me these [disciples].*   **17:12** Some manuscripts read *I protected those you gave me, by the power of your name.*

know that you sent me and that you love them as much as you love me. ²⁴Father, I want these whom you have given me to be with me where I am. Then they can see all the glory you gave me because you loved me even before the world began!

²⁵"O righteous Father, the world doesn't know you, but I do; and these disciples know you sent me. ²⁶I have revealed you to them, and I will continue to do so. Then your love for me will be in them, and I will be in them."

18 Jesus Is Betrayed and Arrested

After saying these things, Jesus crossed the Kidron Valley with his disciples and entered a grove of olive trees. ²Judas, the betrayer, knew this place, because Jesus had often gone there with his disciples. ³The leading priests and Pharisees had given Judas a contingent of Roman soldiers and Temple guards to accompany him. Now with blazing torches, lanterns, and weapons, they arrived at the olive grove.

⁴Jesus fully realized all that was going to happen to him, so he stepped forward to meet them. "Who are you looking for?" he asked.

⁵"Jesus the Nazarene,"* they replied.

"I Am he,"* Jesus said. (Judas, who betrayed him, was standing with them.) ⁶As Jesus said "I Am he," they all drew back and fell to the ground! ⁷Once more he asked them, "Who are you looking for?"

And again they replied, "Jesus the Nazarene."

⁸"I told you that I Am he," Jesus said. "And since I am the one you want, let these others go." ⁹He did this to fulfill his own statement: "I did not lose a single one of those you have given me."*

¹⁰Then Simon Peter drew a sword and slashed off the right ear of Malchus, the high priest's slave. ¹¹But Jesus said to Peter, "Put your sword back into its sheath. Shall I not drink from the cup of suffering the Father has given me?"

Jesus at the High Priest's House

¹²So the soldiers, their commanding officer, and the Temple guards arrested Jesus and tied him up. ¹³First they took him to Annas, the father-in-law of Caiaphas, the high priest at that time.* ¹⁴Caiaphas was the one who had told the other Jewish leaders, "It's better that one man should die for the people."

Peter's First Denial

¹⁵Simon Peter followed Jesus, as did another of the disciples. That other disciple was acquainted with the high priest, so he was allowed to enter the high priest's courtyard with Jesus. ¹⁶Peter had to stay outside the gate. Then the disciple who knew the high priest spoke to the woman watching at the gate, and she let Peter in. ¹⁷The woman asked Peter, "You're not one of that man's disciples, are you?"

"No," he said, "I am not."

¹⁸Because it was cold, the household servants and the guards had made a charcoal fire. They stood around it, warming themselves, and Peter stood with them, warming himself.

The High Priest Questions Jesus

¹⁹Inside, the high priest began asking Jesus about his followers and what he had been teaching them. ²⁰Jesus replied, "Everyone knows what I teach. I have preached regularly in the synagogues and the Temple, where the people* gather. I have not spoken in secret. ²¹Why are you asking me this question? Ask those who heard me. They know what I said."

²²Then one of the Temple guards standing nearby slapped Jesus across the face. "Is that the way to answer the high priest?" he demanded.

²³Jesus replied, "If I said anything wrong, you must prove it. But if I'm speaking the truth, why are you beating me?"

²⁴Then Annas bound Jesus and sent him to Caiaphas, the high priest.

Peter's Second and Third Denials

²⁵Meanwhile, as Simon Peter was standing by the fire warming himself, they asked him again, "You're not one of his disciples, are you?"

He denied it, saying, "No, I am not."

18:5a Or *Jesus of Nazareth;* also in 18:7.   **18:5b** Or *"The 'I Am' is here";* or *"I am the Lord";* Greek reads *I am;* also in 18:6, 8. See Exod 3:14.
18:9 See John 6:39 and 17:12.   **18:13** Greek *that year.*   **18:20** Greek *Jewish people;* also in 18:38.

²⁶But one of the household slaves of the high priest, a relative of the man whose ear Peter had cut off, asked, "Didn't I see you out there in the olive grove with Jesus?" ²⁷Again Peter denied it. And immediately a rooster crowed.

Jesus' Trial before Pilate

²⁸Jesus' trial before Caiaphas ended in the early hours of the morning. Then he was taken to the headquarters of the Roman governor.* His accusers didn't go inside because it would defile them, and they wouldn't be allowed to celebrate the Passover. ²⁹So Pilate, the governor, went out to them and asked, "What is your charge against this man?"

³⁰"We wouldn't have handed him over to you if he weren't a criminal!" they retorted.

³¹"Then take him away and judge him by your own law," Pilate told them.

"Only the Romans are permitted to execute someone," the Jewish leaders replied. ³²(This fulfilled Jesus' prediction about the way he would die.*)

³³Then Pilate went back into his headquarters and called for Jesus to be brought to him. "Are you the king of the Jews?" he asked him.

³⁴Jesus replied, "Is this your own question, or did others tell you about me?"

³⁵"Am I a Jew?" Pilate retorted. "Your own people and their leading priests brought you to me for trial. Why? What have you done?"

³⁶Jesus answered, "My Kingdom is not an earthly kingdom. If it were, my followers would fight to keep me from being handed over to the Jewish leaders. But my Kingdom is not of this world."

³⁷Pilate said, "So you are a king?"

Jesus responded, "You say I am a king. Actually, I was born and came into the world to testify to the truth. All who love the truth recognize that what I say is true."

³⁸"What is truth?" Pilate asked. Then he went out again to the people and told them, "He is not guilty of any crime. ³⁹But you have a custom of asking me to release one prisoner each year at Passover. Would you like me to release this 'King of the Jews'?"

⁴⁰But they shouted back, "No! Not this man. We want Barabbas!" (Barabbas was a revolutionary.)

19 Jesus Sentenced to Death

Then Pilate had Jesus flogged with a lead-tipped whip. ²The soldiers wove a crown of thorns and put it on his head, and they put a purple robe on him. ³"Hail! King of the Jews!" they mocked, as they slapped him across the face.

⁴Pilate went outside again and said to the people, "I am going to bring him out to you now, but understand clearly that I find him not guilty." ⁵Then Jesus came out wearing the crown of thorns and the purple robe. And Pilate said, "Look, here is the man!"

⁶When they saw him, the leading priests and Temple guards began shouting, "Crucify him! Crucify him!"

"Take him yourselves and crucify him," Pilate said. "I find him not guilty."

⁷The Jewish leaders replied, "By our law he ought to die because he called himself the Son of God."

⁸When Pilate heard this, he was more frightened than ever. ⁹He took Jesus back into the headquarters* again and asked him, "Where are you from?" But Jesus gave no answer. ¹⁰"Why don't you talk to me?" Pilate demanded. "Don't you realize that I have the power to release you or crucify you?"

¹¹Then Jesus said, "You would have no power over me at all unless it were given to you from above. So the one who handed me over to you has the greater sin."

¹²Then Pilate tried to release him, but the Jewish leaders shouted, "If you release this man, you are no 'friend of Caesar.'* Anyone who declares himself a king is a rebel against Caesar."

¹³When they said this, Pilate brought Jesus out to them again. Then Pilate sat down on the judgment seat on the platform that is called the Stone Pavement (in Hebrew, *Gabbatha*). ¹⁴It was now about noon on the day of preparation for the Passover. And Pilate said to the people,* "Look, here is your king!"

¹⁵"Away with him," they yelled. "Away with him! Crucify him!"

18:28 Greek *to the Praetorium;* also in 18:33.   18:32 See John 12:32-33.   19:9 Greek *the Praetorium.*   19:12 "Friend of Caesar" is a technical term that refers to an ally of the emperor.   19:14 Greek *Jewish people;* also in 19:20.

Celebration

Celebrate the Crucifixion?

JOHN 19:17-37

Our hearts long for the great joy of Easter—the deep *hallelujah* we experience as we celebrate Resurrection Sunday. But our natural, almost instinctive celebration of the freedom of Resurrection Sunday can be truly understood only when we first face the darkness of Good Friday, the Crucifixion.

How can we possibly "celebrate" Good Friday? It's so ugly, so gruesome, so deeply sad and bleak. We look upon the Cross and face our Savior dying, entering the blackness of our communal and individual sin as a crowd mocks and points.

But our hearts need Good Friday. If we don't dwell on the reality of the Cross, we cannot fully comprehend the wonder of Christ's victory over death and hell. Theologian Jeremy Begbie says that Easter doesn't negate Good Friday, but, in fact, it affirms and strengthens the power of the Cross. The celebration we experience on Easter Sunday is infused with a richness because we know what the Crucifixion required. We realize again our deep need for Christ to destroy death and sin. Our hearts ache and yearn for his victory.

Celebration is often deeper when we've witnessed darkness first—yet we don't remain in that darkness. Even during the bleak Good Fridays of our lives, there is always the promise of Easter dawn.

—*Bonnie McMaken*

For more on celebration, see reading at 1 Corinthians 16:5-18.

"What? Crucify your king?" Pilate asked.

"We have no king but Caesar," the leading priests shouted back.

[16] Then Pilate turned Jesus over to them to be crucified.

The Crucifixion

So they took Jesus away. [17] Carrying the cross by himself, he went to the place called Place of the Skull (in Hebrew, *Golgotha*). [18] There they nailed him to the cross. Two others were crucified with him, one on either side, with Jesus between them. [19] And Pilate posted a sign on the cross that read, "Jesus of Nazareth,* the King of the Jews." [20] The place where Jesus was crucified was near the city, and the sign was written in Hebrew, Latin, and Greek, so that many people could read it.

[21] Then the leading priests objected and said to Pilate, "Change it from 'The King of the Jews' to 'He said, I am King of the Jews.'"

[22] Pilate replied, "No, what I have written, I have written."

[23] When the soldiers had crucified Jesus, they divided his clothes among the four of them. They also took his robe, but it was seamless, woven in one piece from top to bottom. [24] So they said, "Rather than tearing it apart, let's throw dice* for it." This fulfilled the Scripture that says, "They divided my garments among themselves and threw dice for my clothing."* So that is what they did.

[25] Standing near the cross were Jesus' mother, and his mother's sister, Mary (the wife of Clopas), and Mary Magdalene. [26] When Jesus saw his mother standing there beside the disciple he loved, he said to her, "Dear woman, here is your son." [27] And he said to this disciple, "Here is your mother."

19:19 Or *Jesus the Nazarene.*   **19:24a** Greek *cast lots.*   **19:24b** Ps 22:18.

And from then on this disciple took her into his home.

The Death of Jesus

[28] Jesus knew that his mission was now finished, and to fulfill Scripture he said, "I am thirsty."* [29] A jar of sour wine was sitting there, so they soaked a sponge in it, put it on a hyssop branch, and held it up to his lips. [30] When Jesus had tasted it, he said, "It is finished!" Then he bowed his head and released his spirit.

[31] It was the day of preparation, and the Jewish leaders didn't want the bodies hanging there the next day, which was the Sabbath (and a very special Sabbath, because it was the Passover). So they asked Pilate to hasten their deaths by ordering that their legs be broken. Then their bodies could be taken down. [32] So the soldiers came and broke the legs of the two men crucified with Jesus. [33] But when they came to Jesus, they saw that he was already dead, so they didn't break his legs. [34] One of the soldiers, however, pierced his side with a spear, and immediately blood and water flowed out. [35] (This report is from an eyewitness giving an accurate account. He speaks the truth so that you also can believe.*) [36] These things happened in fulfillment of the Scriptures that say, "Not one of his bones will be broken,"* [37] and "They will look on the one they pierced."*

The Burial of Jesus

[38] Afterward Joseph of Arimathea, who had been a secret disciple of Jesus (because he feared the Jewish leaders), asked Pilate for permission to take down Jesus' body. When Pilate gave permission, Joseph came and took the body away. [39] With him came Nicodemus, the man who had come to Jesus at night. He brought about seventy-five pounds* of perfumed ointment made from myrrh and aloes. [40] Following Jewish burial custom, they wrapped Jesus' body with the spices in long sheets of linen cloth. [41] The place of crucifixion was near a garden, where there was a new tomb, never used before. [42] And so, because it was the day of preparation for the Jewish Passover* and since the tomb was close at hand, they laid Jesus there.

20 The Resurrection

Early on Sunday morning,* while it was still dark, Mary Magdalene came to the tomb and found that the stone had been rolled away from the entrance. [2] She ran and found Simon Peter and the other disciple, the one whom Jesus loved. She said, "They have taken the Lord's body out of the tomb, and we don't know where they have put him!"

[3] Peter and the other disciple started out for the tomb. [4] They were both running, but the other disciple outran Peter and reached the tomb first. [5] He stooped and looked in and saw the linen wrappings lying there, but he didn't go in. [6] Then Simon Peter arrived and went inside. He also noticed the linen wrappings lying there, [7] while the cloth that had covered Jesus' head was folded up and lying apart from the other wrappings. [8] Then the disciple who had reached the tomb first also went in, and he saw and believed—[9] for until then they still hadn't understood the Scriptures that said Jesus must rise from the dead. [10] Then they went home.

Jesus Appears to Mary Magdalene

[11] Mary was standing outside the tomb crying, and as she wept, she stooped and looked in. [12] She saw two white-robed angels, one sitting at the head and the other at the foot of the place where the body of Jesus had been lying. [13] "Dear woman, why are you crying?" the angels asked her.

"Because they have taken away my Lord," she replied, "and I don't know where they have put him."

[14] She turned to leave and saw someone standing there. It was Jesus, but she didn't recognize him. [15] "Dear woman, why are you crying?" Jesus asked her. "Who are you looking for?"

She thought he was the gardener. "Sir," she said, "if you have taken him away, tell me where you have put him, and I will go and get him."

[16] "Mary!" Jesus said.

19:28 See Pss 22:15; 69:21.　19:35 Some manuscripts read can continue to believe.　19:36 Exod 12:46; Num 9:12; Ps 34:20.　19:37 Zech 12:10.　19:39 Greek 100 litras [32.7 kilograms].　19:42 Greek because of the Jewish day of preparation.　20:1 Greek On the first day of the week.

She turned to him and cried out, "Rabboni!" (which is Hebrew for "Teacher").

¹⁷"Don't cling to me," Jesus said, "for I haven't yet ascended to the Father. But go find my brothers and tell them, 'I am ascending to my Father and your Father, to my God and your God.'"

¹⁸Mary Magdalene found the disciples and told them, "I have seen the Lord!" Then she gave them his message.

Mary Magdalene: Meeting the Risen Lord

JOHN 20:1–18

It was a Sunday when Mary Magdalene made the early morning walk to Jesus' tomb. She likely had more than spices on her mind.

Jesus had stilled her inner storm; he'd freed her from the demons that had once made chaos her everyday normal (Mark 16:9). But now he was dead. Hearing her sandals slap along the path on her way to the tomb where his dead body lay, did she wonder if evil had somehow won?

Finding the tomb empty, seeking a male disciple to help her, watching them dash about and then leave her weeping alone at the maw of the mountain, Mary was depleted.

Wiped.

Drawn.

Lifeless. Like the Teacher she had followed.

Mary's bewilderment grew when a man began to speak behind her. She didn't recognize him at first, until she heard him say, "Mary!"

Whirling around, she cried, "Rabboni!"

Mary sank down, clinging to the Source of her sanity, her soul's Emancipator, her beloved Teacher (Matthew 28:9). The Messiah who freed her didn't demand she stand on her own; he let Mary collapse. He allowed her, for that moment, simply to enjoy his presence. We can picture the spices rolling from her hands, her day's intentions disappearing, as she found her soul's replenishment and purpose in Jesus' presence.

We can only imagine what Mary felt on that Resurrection Sunday—that first "Lord's Day" that Christians now mark, week after week, as the moment of glorious victory over sin and death. Jesus' nearness sustained and emboldened her; her weeping was transformed into courage as she proclaimed Christ's resurrection: "I have seen the Lord!" (John 20:18).

Mary's Resurrection Sunday encounter can shape and form our understanding of the Sabbath. We may come to the Sabbath wiped out, exhausted, or perhaps even weeping. But in the Sabbath we can encounter the risen Lord. We can enjoy his presence. Our souls can be replenished and emboldened to live in obedience. The remaining days of the week our lives can proclaim, "I have seen the Lord!"

—Jonalyn Fincher

For more on Sabbath and rest, see reading at Colossians 2:16–17.

Jesus Appears to His Disciples

¹⁹ That Sunday evening* the disciples were meeting behind locked doors because they were afraid of the Jewish leaders. Suddenly, Jesus was standing there among them! "Peace be with you," he said. ²⁰ As he spoke, he showed them the wounds in his hands and his side. They were filled with joy when they saw the Lord! ²¹ Again he said, "Peace be with you. As the Father has sent me, so I am sending you." ²² Then he breathed on them and said, "Receive the Holy Spirit. ²³ If you forgive anyone's sins, they are forgiven. If you do not forgive them, they are not forgiven."

Jesus Appears to Thomas

²⁴ One of the twelve disciples, Thomas (nicknamed the Twin),* was not with the others when Jesus came. ²⁵ They told him, "We have seen the Lord!"

But he replied, "I won't believe it unless I see the nail wounds in his hands, put my fingers into them, and place my hand into the wound in his side."

²⁶ Eight days later the disciples were together again, and this time Thomas was with them. The doors were locked; but suddenly, as before, Jesus was standing among them. "Peace be with you," he said. ²⁷ Then he said to Thomas, "Put your finger here, and look at my hands. Put your hand into the wound in my side. Don't be faithless any longer. Believe!"

²⁸ "My Lord and my God!" Thomas exclaimed.

²⁹ Then Jesus told him, "You believe because you have seen me. Blessed are those who believe without seeing me."

Purpose of the Book

³⁰ The disciples saw Jesus do many other miraculous signs in addition to the ones recorded in this book. ³¹ But these are written so that you may continue to believe* that Jesus is the Messiah, the Son of God, and that by believing in him you will have life by the power of his name.

21 Epilogue: Jesus Appears to Seven Disciples

Later, Jesus appeared again to the disciples beside the Sea of Galilee.* This is how it happened. ² Several of the disciples were there—Simon Peter, Thomas (nicknamed the Twin),* Nathanael from Cana in Galilee, the sons of Zebedee, and two other disciples.

³ Simon Peter said, "I'm going fishing."

"We'll come, too," they all said. So they went out in the boat, but they caught nothing all night.

⁴ At dawn Jesus was standing on the beach, but the disciples couldn't see who he was. ⁵ He called out, "Fellows,* have you caught any fish?"

"No," they replied.

⁶ Then he said, "Throw out your net on the right-hand side of the boat, and you'll get some!" So they did, and they couldn't haul in the net because there were so many fish in it.

⁷ Then the disciple Jesus loved said to Peter, "It's the Lord!" When Simon Peter heard that it was the Lord, he put on his tunic (for he had stripped for work), jumped into the water, and headed to shore. ⁸ The others stayed with the boat and pulled the loaded net to the shore, for they were only about a hundred yards* from shore. ⁹ When they got there, they found breakfast waiting for them—fish cooking over a charcoal fire, and some bread.

¹⁰ "Bring some of the fish you've just caught," Jesus said. ¹¹ So Simon Peter went aboard and dragged the net to the shore. There were 153 large fish, and yet the net hadn't torn.

¹² "Now come and have some breakfast!" Jesus said. None of the disciples dared to ask him, "Who are you?" They knew it was the Lord. ¹³ Then Jesus served them the bread and the fish. ¹⁴ This was the third time Jesus had appeared to his disciples since he had been raised from the dead.

¹⁵ After breakfast Jesus asked Simon Peter, "Simon son of John, do you love me more than these?*"

"Yes, Lord," Peter replied, "you know I love you."

"Then feed my lambs," Jesus told him.

¹⁶ Jesus repeated the question: "Simon son of John, do you love me?"

"Yes, Lord," Peter said, "you know I love you."

"Then take care of my sheep," Jesus said.

¹⁷ A third time he asked him, "Simon son of John, do you love me?"

Peter was hurt that Jesus asked the question a third time. He said, "Lord, you know everything. You know that I love you."

Jesus said, "Then feed my sheep.

¹⁸ "I tell you the truth, when you were young, you were able to do as you liked; you dressed yourself and went wherever you wanted to go. But when you are old, you will stretch out your hands, and others* will dress you and take you where you don't want to go." ¹⁹ Jesus said this to let him know by what kind of death he would glorify God. Then Jesus told him, "Follow me."

²⁰ Peter turned around and saw behind them the disciple Jesus loved—the one

Q&A — Hearing God's Call — Acceptance

JOHN 21:15-23

How can I discover what God wants me to do with my life?

Pay attention to who God made you to be. What are you good at? What do you love to do? Before he met Christ, the apostle Paul was an activist and a zealot—an articulate *opponent* of the church. When he met Christ, he continued to be an activist and a zealot, but he changed for whom he worked. Acts 9:20 says he at once began to preach in the synagogues that Jesus is the Son of God. He didn't change who he was by design, but he did change the lordship in his life.

Noticing what you're not good at is also valuable. We only have so many yeses we can give, so don't spend them on what you don't do well. I know I shouldn't say yes to volunteering in the church nursery. The kids agree!

We each have a unique design. Don't get caught in the comparison trap. In John 21, right after Jesus says three times to Peter to feed and take care of his sheep, Peter looks at John the disciple and says, "What about him, Lord?" (21:21). It's as if he's saying, "Yeah, I heard what your calling for me is, but before I decide, I'd like to hear about John, compare callings, and then decide."

Jesus' reply is direct: "What is that to you? As for you, follow me" (21:22).

So while I'm no help in the nursery, I've found things I *am* good at: teaching and leading. These are my spiritual gifts and a large part of my calling.

Finally, remember that God's calling for your life goes way beyond what you *do*. It's who you are, where you belong, who and how you love. A life lived operating in the gifts God has given us—and mindful of meeting the needs of others—beautifully reflects the person of God.

—Nancy Ortberg

For more on acceptance, see reading at Galatians 3:28.

21:18 Some manuscripts read *and another one.*

who had leaned over to Jesus during supper and asked, "Lord, who will betray you?" 21 Peter asked Jesus, "What about him, Lord?"

22 Jesus replied, "If I want him to remain alive until I return, what is that to you? As for you, follow me." 23 So the rumor spread among the community of believers* that this disciple wouldn't die. But that isn't what Jesus said at all. He only said, "If I want him to remain alive until I return, what is that to you?"

24 This disciple is the one who testifies to these events and has recorded them here. And we know that his account of these things is accurate.

25 Jesus also did many other things. If they were all written down, I suppose the whole world could not contain the books that would be written.

21:23 Greek *the brothers.*

Introduction to
Acts

Background

Acts, also known as the Acts of the Apostles, details how the disciples fulfilled the Great Commission (Matthew 28:19–20). "Acts," *Praxeis* in Greek, is a title used in Greek literature for accounts of great deeds of notable men. In this case, the spotlight is on specific notables, Peter and Paul—and the Holy Spirit.

Luke, a physician and historian, is the acknowledged author of Acts and the Gospel of Luke. Both documents are addressed to a particular Gentile, Theophilus. Luke was noted for his careful investigative procedures (Luke 1:1–4). It is likely he had opportunities to interview apostles Peter and John in Jerusalem for the information used in chapters 1–12. As a close companion of the apostle Paul, Luke was an eyewitness of many of the events recorded in chapters 13–28.

Message

This narrative book recounts the tumultuous history of the early church. The arrival of the Holy Spirit at Pentecost, a fulfillment of the gift promised by the Father (1:4), gives the apostles the power to carry out the Great Commission. In chapter 2 Peter preaches a powerful evangelistic sermon, just one of the several public gospel proclamations—others by Stephen and Paul—recounted by Luke. There is nothing secret about this faith. Yet the book is more than speeches; it is a high-action story of faithful witness in the face of persecution as the apostles and other believers claim the power of the Spirit in sharing the spiritually liberating message of salvation in Christ.

A high point of this narrative is the conversion of the Pharisee Saul, who becomes the great apostle Paul. Luke chronicles Paul's missionary journeys, his trials, his appeal to Caesar, and his passage to Rome. Even there, under house arrest, he "boldly" proclaimed and taught (28:31).

Time

Because Acts ends with Paul awaiting trial in Rome, Luke probably wrote the text around A.D. 62 before the outcome of the trial.

Outline

Acts

1 The Promise of the Holy Spirit

In my first book* I told you, Theophilus, about everything Jesus began to do and teach [2]until the day he was taken up to heaven after giving his chosen apostles further instructions through the Holy Spirit. [3]During the forty days after his crucifixion, he appeared to the apostles from time to time, and he proved to them in many ways that he was actually alive. And he talked to them about the Kingdom of God.

[4]Once when he was eating with them, he commanded them, "Do not leave Jerusalem until the Father sends you the gift he promised, as I told you before. [5]John baptized with* water, but in just a few days you will be baptized with the Holy Spirit."

The Ascension of Jesus

[6]So when the apostles were with Jesus, they kept asking him, "Lord, has the time come for you to free Israel and restore our kingdom?"

[7]He replied, "The Father alone has the authority to set those dates and times, and they are not for you to know. [8]But you will receive power when the Holy Spirit comes upon you. And you will be my witnesses, telling people about me everywhere—in Jerusalem, throughout Judea, in Samaria, and to the ends of the earth."

[9]After saying this, he was taken up into a cloud while they were watching, and they could no longer see him. [10]As they strained to see him rising into heaven, two white-robed men suddenly stood among them. [11]"Men of Galilee," they said, "why are you standing here staring into heaven? Jesus has been taken from you into heaven, but someday he will return from heaven in the same way you saw him go!"

Matthias Replaces Judas

[12]Then the apostles returned to Jerusalem from the Mount of Olives, a distance of half a mile.* [13]When they arrived, they went to the upstairs room of the house where they were staying.

Here are the names of those who were present: Peter, John, James, Andrew, Philip, Thomas, Bartholomew, Matthew, James (son of Alphaeus), Simon (the Zealot), and Judas (son of James). [14]They all met together and were constantly united in prayer, along with Mary the mother of Jesus, several other women, and the brothers of Jesus.

[15]During this time, when about 120 believers* were together in one place, Peter stood up and addressed them. [16]"Brothers," he said, "the Scriptures had to be fulfilled concerning Judas, who guided those who arrested Jesus. This was predicted long ago by the Holy Spirit, speaking through King David. [17]Judas was one of us and shared in the ministry with us."

[18](Judas had bought a field with the money he received for his treachery. Falling headfirst there, his body split open, spilling out all his intestines. [19]The

---

1:1 The reference is to the Gospel of Luke. **1:5** Or *in*; also in 1:5b. **1:12** Greek *a Sabbath day's journey.* **1:15** Greek *brothers.*

news of his death spread to all the people of Jerusalem, and they gave the place the Aramaic name *Akeldama*, which means "Field of Blood.")

²⁰Peter continued, "This was written in the book of Psalms, where it says, 'Let his home become desolate, with no one living in it.' It also says, 'Let someone else take his position.'*

²¹"So now we must choose a replacement for Judas from among the men who were with us the entire time we were traveling with the Lord Jesus—²²from the time he was baptized by John until the day he was taken from us. Whoever is chosen will join us as a witness of Jesus' resurrection."

²³So they nominated two men: Joseph called Barsabbas (also known as Justus) and Matthias. ²⁴Then they all prayed, "O Lord, you know every heart. Show us which of these men you have chosen ²⁵as an apostle to replace Judas in this ministry, for he has deserted us and gone where he belongs." ²⁶Then they cast lots, and Matthias was selected to become an apostle with the other eleven.

2 The Holy Spirit Comes

On the day of Pentecost* all the believers were meeting together in one place. ²Suddenly, there was a sound from heaven like the roaring of a mighty windstorm, and it filled the house where they were sitting. ³Then, what looked like flames or tongues of fire appeared and settled on each of them. ⁴And everyone present was filled with the Holy Spirit and began speaking in other languages,* as the Holy Spirit gave them this ability.

⁵At that time there were devout Jews from every nation living in Jerusalem. ⁶When they heard the loud noise, everyone came running, and they were bewildered to hear their own languages being spoken by the believers. ⁷They were completely amazed. "How can this be?" they exclaimed. "These people are all from Galilee, ⁸and yet we hear them speaking in our own native languages! ⁹Here we are—Parthians, Medes, Elamites, people from Mesopotamia, Judea, Cappadocia, Pontus, the province of Asia, ¹⁰Phrygia, Pamphylia, Egypt, and the areas of Libya around Cyrene, visitors from Rome ¹¹(both Jews and converts to Judaism), Cretans, and Arabs. And we all hear these people speaking in our own languages about the wonderful things God has done!" ¹²They stood there amazed and perplexed. "What can this mean?" they asked each other.

¹³But others in the crowd ridiculed them, saying, "They're just drunk, that's all!"

Peter Preaches to the Crowd

¹⁴Then Peter stepped forward with the eleven other apostles and shouted to the crowd, "Listen carefully, all of you, fellow Jews and residents of Jerusalem! Make no mistake about this. ¹⁵These people are not drunk, as some of you are assuming. Nine o'clock in the morning is much too early for that. ¹⁶No, what you see was predicted long ago by the prophet Joel:

¹⁷ 'In the last days,' God says,
  'I will pour out my Spirit upon all
    people.
  Your sons and daughters will prophesy.
    Your young men will see visions,
    and your old men will dream dreams.
¹⁸ In those days I will pour out my Spirit
    even on my servants—men and
      women alike—
    and they will prophesy.
¹⁹ And I will cause wonders in the heavens
      above
    and signs on the earth below—
    blood and fire and clouds of smoke.
²⁰ The sun will become dark,
    and the moon will turn blood red
    before that great and glorious day of
      the LORD arrives.
²¹ But everyone who calls on the name of
      the LORD
    will be saved.'*

²²"People of Israel, listen! God publicly endorsed Jesus the Nazarene* by doing powerful miracles, wonders, and signs through him, as you well know. ²³But God knew what would happen, and his prearranged plan was carried out when Jesus

---

1:20 Pss 69:25; 109:8. **2:1** The Festival of Pentecost came 50 days after Passover (when Jesus was crucified). **2:4** Or *in other tongues.*
2:17-21 Joel 2:28-32. **2:22** Or *Jesus of Nazareth.*

was betrayed. With the help of lawless Gentiles, you nailed him to a cross and killed him. ²⁴But God released him from the horrors of death and raised him back to life, for death could not keep him in its grip. ²⁵King David said this about him:

'I see that the LORD is always with me.
I will not be shaken, for he is right beside me.
²⁶ No wonder my heart is glad,
and my tongue shouts his praises!
My body rests in hope.
²⁷ For you will not leave my soul among the dead*
or allow your Holy One to rot in the grave.
²⁸ You have shown me the way of life,
and you will fill me with the joy of your presence.'*

²⁹"Dear brothers, think about this! You can be sure that the patriarch David wasn't referring to himself, for he died and was buried, and his tomb is still here among us. ³⁰But he was a prophet, and he knew God had promised with an oath that one of David's own descendants would sit on his throne. ³¹David was looking into the future and speaking of the Messiah's resurrection. He was saying that God would not leave him among the dead or allow his body to rot in the grave.

³²"God raised Jesus from the dead, and we are all witnesses of this. ³³Now he is exalted to the place of highest honor in heaven, at God's right hand. And the Father, as he had promised, gave him the Holy Spirit to pour out upon us, just as you see and hear today. ³⁴For David himself never ascended into heaven, yet he said,

'The LORD said to my Lord,
"Sit in the place of honor at my right hand
³⁵ until I humble your enemies,
making them a footstool under your feet."'*

³⁶"So let everyone in Israel know for certain that God has made this Jesus, whom you crucified, to be both Lord and Messiah!"

³⁷Peter's words pierced their hearts, and they said to him and to the other apostles, "Brothers, what should we do?"

³⁸Peter replied, "Each of you must repent of your sins and turn to God, and be baptized in the name of Jesus Christ for the forgiveness of your sins. Then you will receive the gift of the Holy Spirit. ³⁹This promise is to you, and to your children, and even to the Gentiles*—all who have been called by the Lord our God." ⁴⁰Then Peter continued preaching for a long time, strongly urging all his listeners, "Save yourselves from this crooked generation!"

⁴¹Those who believed what Peter said were baptized and added to the church that day—about 3,000 in all.

The Believers Form a Community

⁴²All the believers devoted themselves to the apostles' teaching, and to fellowship, and to sharing in meals (including the Lord's Supper*), and to prayer.

⁴³A deep sense of awe came over them all, and the apostles performed many miraculous signs and wonders. ⁴⁴And all the believers met together in one place and shared everything they had. ⁴⁵They sold their property and possessions and shared the money with those in need. ⁴⁶They worshiped together at the Temple each day, met in homes for the Lord's Supper, and shared their meals with great joy and generosity*—⁴⁷all the while praising God and enjoying the goodwill of all the people. And each day the Lord added to their fellowship those who were being saved.

Peter Heals a Crippled Beggar

3 Peter and John went to the Temple one afternoon to take part in the three o'clock prayer service. ²As they approached the Temple, a man lame from birth was being carried in. Each day he was put beside the Temple gate, the one called the Beautiful Gate, so he could beg from the people going into the Temple. ³When he saw Peter and John about to enter, he asked them for some money.

⁴Peter and John looked at him intently, and Peter said, "Look at us!" ⁵The lame man looked at them eagerly, expecting some

---

2:27 Greek *in Hades;* also in 2:31.   2:25-28 Ps 16:8-11 (Greek version).   2:34-35 Ps 110:1.   2:39 *Or and to people far in the future;* Greek reads *and to those far away.*   2:42 Greek *the breaking of bread;* also in 2:46.   2:46 *Or and sincere hearts.*

money. ⁶But Peter said, "I don't have any silver or gold for you. But I'll give you what I have. In the name of Jesus Christ the Nazarene,* get up and* walk!"

⁷Then Peter took the lame man by the right hand and helped him up. And as he did, the man's feet and ankles were instantly healed and strengthened. ⁸He jumped up, stood on his feet, and began to walk! Then, walking, leaping, and praising God, he went into the Temple with them.

⁹All the people saw him walking and heard him praising God. ¹⁰When they realized he was the lame beggar they had seen so often at the Beautiful Gate, they were absolutely astounded! ¹¹They all rushed out in amazement to Solomon's Colonnade, where the man was holding tightly to Peter and John.

Peter Preaches in the Temple

¹²Peter saw his opportunity and addressed the crowd. "People of Israel," he said, "what

Q&A The Family of God

ACTS 2:42-47

What can we learn from the early church about true Christian community?

The early Christians in Acts and in the first centuries of Christianity had a markedly different perspective on how "church" works than do we modern-day, individualistic readers. Jesus' early followers were convinced that the group came first—that I as an individual will become all God wants me to be only when I begin to view my goals, desires, and relational needs as secondary to what God is doing through his people, the local church. The group, not the individual, took priority in a believer's life.

Consider, for example, the teachings of Cyprian (bishop of Carthage, circa 250) about the Lord's Prayer (Matthew 6:9-13; Luke 11:2-4): "We do not say: 'My Father, who art in heaven,' nor 'Give me this day my bread,' nor does each one ask that only his debt be forgiven him and that he be led not into temptation and that he be delivered from evil for himself alone. Our prayer is public and common, and when we pray, we pray not for one but for the whole people, because we, the whole people, are one."

Early Christian communities, moreover, represented a specific kind of group: they functioned as a family. Kinship language (*brother, sister, Father, child, inheritance*) permeates the New Testament. Family is the dominant metaphor for the church in the writings of the church fathers. Spiritual formation occurs primarily in the context of community. If we're really serious about spiritual formation, then we must become really serious about creating church communities that act like real families.

—*Joseph H. Hellerman*

For more on community, see reading at 1 Corinthians 13.

3:6a Or *Jesus Christ of Nazareth.*   **3:6b** Some manuscripts do not include *get up and.*

is so surprising about this? And why stare at us as though we had made this man walk by our own power or godliness? ¹³For it is the God of Abraham, Isaac, and Jacob—the God of all our ancestors—who has brought glory to his servant Jesus by doing this. This is the same Jesus whom you handed over and rejected before Pilate, despite Pilate's decision to release him. ¹⁴You rejected this holy, righteous one and instead demanded the release of a murderer. ¹⁵You killed the author of life, but God raised him from the dead. And we are witnesses of this fact!

¹⁶"Through faith in the name of Jesus, this man was healed—and you know how crippled he was before. Faith in Jesus' name has healed him before your very eyes.

¹⁷"Friends,* I realize that what you and your leaders did to Jesus was done in ignorance. ¹⁸But God was fulfilling what all the prophets had foretold about the Messiah— that he must suffer these things. ¹⁹Now repent of your sins and turn to God, so that your sins may be wiped away. ²⁰Then times of refreshment will come from the presence of the Lord, and he will again send you Jesus, your appointed Messiah. ²¹For he must remain in heaven until the time for the final restoration of all things, as God promised long ago through his holy prophets. ²²Moses said, 'The LORD your God will raise up for you a Prophet like me from among your own people. Listen carefully to everything he tells you.'* ²³Then Moses said, 'Anyone who will not listen to that Prophet will be completely cut off from God's people.'*

²⁴"Starting with Samuel, every prophet spoke about what is happening today. ²⁵You are the children of those prophets, and you are included in the covenant God promised to your ancestors. For God said to Abraham, 'Through your descendants* all the families on earth will be blessed.' ²⁶When God raised up his servant, Jesus, he sent him first to you people of Israel, to bless you by turning each of you back from your sinful ways."

4 Peter and John before the Council

While Peter and John were speaking to the people, they were confronted by the priests, the captain of the Temple guard, and some of the Sadducees. ²These leaders were very disturbed that Peter and John were teaching the people that through Jesus there is a resurrection of the dead. ³They arrested them and, since it was already evening, put them in jail until morning. ⁴But many of the people who heard their message believed it, so the number of believers now totaled about 5,000 men, not counting women and children.*

⁵The next day the council of all the rulers and elders and teachers of religious law met in Jerusalem. ⁶Annas the high priest was there, along with Caiaphas, John, Alexander, and other relatives of the high priest. ⁷They brought in the two disciples and demanded, "By what power, or in whose name, have you done this?"

⁸Then Peter, filled with the Holy Spirit, said to them, "Rulers and elders of our people, ⁹are we being questioned today because we've done a good deed for a crippled man? Do you want to know how he was healed? ¹⁰Let me clearly state to all of you and to all the people of Israel that he was healed by the powerful name of Jesus Christ the Nazarene,* the man you crucified but whom God raised from the dead. ¹¹For Jesus is the one referred to in the Scriptures, where it says,

'The stone that you builders rejected
    has now become the cornerstone.'*

¹²There is salvation in no one else! God has given no other name under heaven by which we must be saved."

¹³The members of the council were amazed when they saw the boldness of Peter and John, for they could see that they were ordinary men with no special training in the Scriptures. They also recognized them as men who had been with Jesus. ¹⁴But since they could see the man who had been healed standing right there among them, there was nothing the council could say. ¹⁵So they ordered Peter and John out of the council chamber* and conferred among themselves.

¹⁶"What should we do with these men?" they asked each other. "We can't deny that

---

3:17 Greek *Brothers.*   **3:22** Deut 18:15.   **3:23** Deut 18:19; Lev 23:29.   **3:25** Greek *your seed;* see Gen 12:3; 22:18.   **4:4** Greek *5,000 adult males.*   **4:10** Or *Jesus Christ of Nazareth.*   **4:11** Ps 118:22.   **4:15** Greek *the Sanhedrin.*

they have performed a miraculous sign, and everybody in Jerusalem knows about it. [17] But to keep them from spreading their propaganda any further, we must warn them not to speak to anyone in Jesus' name again." [18] So they called the apostles back in and commanded them never again to speak or teach in the name of Jesus.

[19] But Peter and John replied, "Do you think God wants us to obey you rather than him? [20] We cannot stop telling about everything we have seen and heard."

[21] The council then threatened them further, but they finally let them go because they didn't know how to punish them without starting a riot. For everyone was praising God [22] for this miraculous sign—the healing of a man who had been lame for more than forty years.

The Believers Pray for Courage

[23] As soon as they were freed, Peter and John returned to the other believers and told them what the leading priests and elders had said. [24] When they heard the report, all the believers lifted their voices together in prayer to God: "O Sovereign Lord, Creator of heaven and earth, the sea, and everything in them—[25] you spoke long ago by the Holy Spirit through our ancestor David, your servant, saying,

'Why were the nations so angry?
  Why did they waste their time with
    futile plans?
[26] The kings of the earth prepared for battle;
  the rulers gathered together
against the LORD
  and against his Messiah.'*

[27] "In fact, this has happened here in this very city! For Herod Antipas, Pontius Pilate the governor, the Gentiles, and the people of Israel were all united against Jesus, your holy servant, whom you anointed. [28] But everything they did was determined beforehand according to your will. [29] And now, O Lord, hear their threats, and give us, your servants, great boldness in preaching your word. [30] Stretch out your hand with healing power; may miraculous signs and wonders be done through the name of your holy servant Jesus."

[31] After this prayer, the meeting place shook, and they were all filled with the Holy Spirit. Then they preached the word of God with boldness.

The Believers Share Their Possessions

[32] All the believers were united in heart and mind. And they felt that what they owned was not their own, so they shared everything they had. [33] The apostles testified powerfully to the resurrection of the Lord Jesus, and God's great blessing was upon them all. [34] There were no needy people among them, because those who owned land or houses would sell them [35] and bring the money to the apostles to give to those in need.

[36] For instance, there was Joseph, the one the apostles nicknamed Barnabas (which means "Son of Encouragement"). He was from the tribe of Levi and came from the island of Cyprus. [37] He sold a field he owned and brought the money to the apostles.

5 Ananias and Sapphira

But there was a certain man named Ananias who, with his wife, Sapphira, sold some property. [2] He brought part of the money to the apostles, claiming it was the full amount. With his wife's consent, he kept the rest.

[3] Then Peter said, "Ananias, why have you let Satan fill your heart? You lied to the Holy Spirit, and you kept some of the money for yourself. [4] The property was yours to sell or not sell, as you wished. And after selling it, the money was also yours to give away. How could you do a thing like this? You weren't lying to us but to God!"

[5] As soon as Ananias heard these words, he fell to the floor and died. Everyone who heard about it was terrified. [6] Then some young men got up, wrapped him in a sheet, and took him out and buried him.

[7] About three hours later his wife came in, not knowing what had happened. [8] Peter asked her, "Was this the price you and your husband received for your land?"

"Yes," she replied, "that was the price."

[9] And Peter said, "How could the two of you even think of conspiring to test the Spirit of the Lord like this? The young men

---

4:25-26 Or his anointed one; or his Christ. Ps 2:1-2.

Hospitality

All God's Stuff
ACTS 4:32-37

I've known people who have returned from short-term missions trips to undeveloped countries humbled by the enthusiastic, sacrificial, and generous hospitality of the poor people they encountered. Some of these missionaries, to their dismay, were given the only bed in the house, while family members slept on mats!

The contrast with our culture of selfishness is stunning. Most of us have the means to extend hospitality without depriving ourselves. We have guest rooms or foldout sofas; we have shelves filled with food we can whip into a meal on short notice. Yet we're stingy with our goods and our space; and when we do share, it's seldom sacrificial giving.

A young minister recently told me, rather ruefully, that his wife would give anything away. If she learned that someone needed something, she'd just hand it over—a blanket, an electric mixer, food in the refrigerator. Her actions were disconcerting and inconvenient for the family. But her reasoning was simple: "It's all God's stuff."

I've thought about that little sentence many times since. How do I respond when I see someone who needs a meal, a place to sit, or something more? When I'm given an opportunity to give or to invite in, it comes back to me: "It's all God's stuff."

—Marilyn Chandler McEntyre

For more on hospitality, see reading at Acts 16:11-15.

who buried your husband are just outside the door, and they will carry you out, too."

¹⁰ Instantly, she fell to the floor and died. When the young men came in and saw that she was dead, they carried her out and buried her beside her husband. ¹¹ Great fear gripped the entire church and everyone else who heard what had happened.

The Apostles Heal Many

¹² The apostles were performing many miraculous signs and wonders among the people. And all the believers were meeting regularly at the Temple in the area known as Solomon's Colonnade. ¹³ But no one else dared to join them, even though all the people had high regard for them. ¹⁴ Yet more and more people believed and were brought to the Lord—crowds of both men and women. ¹⁵ As a result of the apostles' work, sick people were brought out into the streets on beds and mats so that Peter's shadow might fall across some of them as he went by. ¹⁶ Crowds came from the villages around Jerusalem, bringing their sick and those possessed by evil* spirits, and they were all healed.

The Apostles Meet Opposition

¹⁷ The high priest and his officials, who were Sadducees, were filled with jealousy. ¹⁸ They arrested the apostles and put them in the public jail. ¹⁹ But an angel of the Lord came at night, opened the gates of the jail, and brought them out. Then he told them, ²⁰ "Go to the Temple and give the people this message of life!"

²¹ So at daybreak the apostles entered the Temple, as they were told, and immediately began teaching.

When the high priest and his officials arrived, they convened the high council*—the full assembly of the elders of Israel. Then they sent for the apostles to be brought from the jail for trial. [22] But when the Temple guards went to the jail, the men were gone. So they returned to the council and reported, [23] "The jail was securely locked, with the guards standing outside, but when we opened the gates, no one was there!"

[24] When the captain of the Temple guard and the leading priests heard this, they were perplexed, wondering where it would all end. [25] Then someone arrived with startling news: "The men you put in jail are standing in the Temple, teaching the people!"

[26] The captain went with his Temple guards and arrested the apostles, but without violence, for they were afraid the people would stone them. [27] Then they brought the apostles before the high council, where the high priest confronted them. [28] "Didn't we tell you never again to teach in this man's name?" he demanded. "Instead, you have filled all Jerusalem with your teaching about him, and you want to make us responsible for his death!"

[29] But Peter and the apostles replied, "We must obey God rather than any human authority. [30] The God of our ancestors raised Jesus from the dead after you killed him by hanging him on a cross.* [31] Then God put him in the place of honor at his right hand as Prince and Savior. He did this so the people of Israel would repent of their sins and be forgiven. [32] We are witnesses of these things and so is the Holy Spirit, who is given by God to those who obey him."

[33] When they heard this, the high council was furious and decided to kill them. [34] But one member, a Pharisee named Gamaliel, who was an expert in religious law and respected by all the people, stood up and ordered that the men be sent outside the council chamber for a while. [35] Then he said to his colleagues, "Men of Israel, take care what you are planning to do to these men! [36] Some time ago there was that fellow Theudas, who pretended to be someone great. About 400 others joined him, but he was killed, and all his followers went their various ways. The whole movement came to nothing. [37] After him, at the time of the census, there was Judas of Galilee. He got people to follow him, but he was killed, too, and all his followers were scattered.

[38] "So my advice is, leave these men alone. Let them go. If they are planning and doing these things merely on their own, it will soon be overthrown. [39] But if it is from God, you will not be able to overthrow them. You may even find yourselves fighting against God!"

[40] The others accepted his advice. They called in the apostles and had them flogged. Then they ordered them never again to speak in the name of Jesus, and they let them go.

[41] The apostles left the high council rejoicing that God had counted them worthy to suffer disgrace for the name of Jesus.* [42] And every day, in the Temple and from house to house, they continued to teach and preach this message: "Jesus is the Messiah."

6 Seven Men Chosen to Serve

But as the believers* rapidly multiplied, there were rumblings of discontent. The Greek-speaking believers complained about the Hebrew-speaking believers, saying that their widows were being discriminated against in the daily distribution of food.

[2] So the Twelve called a meeting of all the believers. They said, "We apostles should spend our time teaching the word of God, not running a food program. [3] And so, brothers, select seven men who are well respected and are full of the Spirit and wisdom. We will give them this responsibility. [4] Then we apostles can spend our time in prayer and teaching the word."

[5] Everyone liked this idea, and they chose the following: Stephen (a man full of faith and the Holy Spirit), Philip, Procorus, Nicanor, Timon, Parmenas, and Nicolas of Antioch (an earlier convert to the Jewish faith). [6] These seven were presented to the apostles, who prayed for them as they laid their hands on them.

[7] So God's message continued to spread. The number of believers greatly increased in Jerusalem, and many of the Jewish priests were converted, too.

5:21 Greek *Sanhedrin*; also in 5:27, 41.   **5:30** Greek *on a tree.*   **5:41** Greek *for the name.*   **6:1** Greek *disciples*; also in 6:2, 7.

Serving behind the Scenes
ACTS 6:1-7

God could have gained maximum notice for his Son by sending him to Rome, Milan, Carthage, or Alexandria—at least Jerusalem. Instead, he sent his Son to a village so boorish that the locals quipped, "Can anything good come from Nazareth?" (John 1:46).

But rather than trying to overcome this disadvantage, Jesus seeks to avoid the big show. He tells a man he's healed from a disfiguring case of leprosy, "Don't tell anyone about this" (Mark 1:44). When he feeds an entire convention with one sack lunch, it's his grand moment: the people want to make him king. He walks away (John 6:15).

The thought of being hidden—unnoticed and overlooked—slays us. Let's be honest: it can be very hard to serve when our service goes unnoticed.

But true service *is* often hidden. This truth gives us wisdom: when certain gifts rightly attract attention, we won't make the fatal mistake of thinking that being known is better. Enjoyable, yes, and necessary, sometimes, but spiritually hazardous. The fact we still long to be noticed is evidence enough that it would only harm us spiritually.

If we're hidden, we're not forgotten by God. He places us, as Oswald Chambers writes, "where we may bring him the most glory, and we are no judges of where that is."

—Kevin A. Miller

For more on service, see reading at Acts 8:26-40.

Stephen Is Arrested

⁸Stephen, a man full of God's grace and power, performed amazing miracles and signs among the people. ⁹But one day some men from the Synagogue of Freed Slaves, as it was called, started to debate with him. They were Jews from Cyrene, Alexandria, Cilicia, and the province of Asia. ¹⁰None of them could stand against the wisdom and the Spirit with which Stephen spoke.

¹¹So they persuaded some men to lie about Stephen, saying, "We heard him blaspheme Moses, and even God." ¹²This roused the people, the elders, and the teachers of religious law. So they arrested Stephen and brought him before the high council.*

¹³The lying witnesses said, "This man is always speaking against the holy Temple and against the law of Moses. ¹⁴We have heard him say that this Jesus of Nazareth* will destroy the Temple and change the customs Moses handed down to us."

¹⁵At this point everyone in the high council stared at Stephen, because his face became as bright as an angel's.

7 Stephen Addresses the Council

Then the high priest asked Stephen, "Are these accusations true?"

²This was Stephen's reply: "Brothers and fathers, listen to me. Our glorious God appeared to our ancestor Abraham in Mesopotamia before he settled in Haran.* ³God told him, 'Leave your native land and your relatives, and come into the land that I will show you.'* ⁴So Abraham left the land of the Chaldeans and lived in Haran until his father died. Then God brought him here to the land where you now live.

⁵"But God gave him no inheritance here,

6:12 Greek *Sanhedrin;* also in 6:15. **6:14** Or *Jesus the Nazarene.* **7:2** *Mesopotamia* was the region now called Iraq. *Haran* was a city in what is now called Syria. **7:3** Gen 12:1.

not even one square foot of land. God did promise, however, that eventually the whole land would belong to Abraham and his descendants—even though he had no children yet. ⁶God also told him that his descendants would live in a foreign land, where they would be oppressed as slaves for 400 years. ⁷'But I will punish the nation that enslaves them,' God said, 'and in the end they will come out and worship me here in this place.'*

⁸"God also gave Abraham the covenant of circumcision at that time. So when Abraham became the father of Isaac, he circumcised him on the eighth day. And the practice was continued when Isaac became the father of Jacob, and when Jacob became the father of the twelve patriarchs of the Israelite nation.

⁹"These patriarchs were jealous of their brother Joseph, and they sold him to be a slave in Egypt. But God was with him ¹⁰and rescued him from all his troubles. And God gave him favor before Pharaoh, king of Egypt. God also gave Joseph unusual wisdom, so that Pharaoh appointed him governor over all of Egypt and put him in charge of the palace.

¹¹"But a famine came upon Egypt and Canaan. There was great misery, and our ancestors ran out of food. ¹²Jacob heard that there was still grain in Egypt, so he sent his sons—our ancestors—to buy some. ¹³The second time they went, Joseph revealed his identity to his brothers,* and they were introduced to Pharaoh. ¹⁴Then Joseph sent for his father, Jacob, and all his relatives to come to Egypt, seventy-five persons in all. ¹⁵So Jacob went to Egypt. He died there, as did our ancestors. ¹⁶Their bodies were taken to Shechem and buried in the tomb Abraham had bought for a certain price from Hamor's sons in Shechem.

¹⁷"As the time drew near when God would fulfill his promise to Abraham, the number of our people in Egypt greatly increased. ¹⁸But then a new king came to the throne of Egypt who knew nothing about Joseph. ¹⁹This king exploited our people and oppressed them, forcing parents to abandon their newborn babies so they would die.

²⁰"At that time Moses was born—a beautiful child in God's eyes. His parents cared for him at home for three months. ²¹When they had to abandon him, Pharaoh's daughter adopted him and raised him as her own son. ²²Moses was taught all the wisdom of the Egyptians, and he was powerful in both speech and action.

²³"One day when Moses was forty years old, he decided to visit his relatives, the people of Israel. ²⁴He saw an Egyptian mistreating an Israelite. So Moses came to the man's defense and avenged him, killing the Egyptian. ²⁵Moses assumed his fellow Israelites would realize that God had sent him to rescue them, but they didn't.

²⁶"The next day he visited them again and saw two men of Israel fighting. He tried to be a peacemaker. 'Men,' he said, 'you are brothers. Why are you fighting each other?'

²⁷"But the man in the wrong pushed Moses aside. 'Who made you a ruler and judge over us?' he asked. ²⁸'Are you going to kill me as you killed that Egyptian yesterday?' ²⁹When Moses heard that, he fled the country and lived as a foreigner in the land of Midian. There his two sons were born.

³⁰"Forty years later, in the desert near Mount Sinai, an angel appeared to Moses in the flame of a burning bush. ³¹When Moses saw it, he was amazed at the sight. As he went to take a closer look, the voice of the Lord called out to him, ³²'I am the God of your ancestors—the God of Abraham, Isaac, and Jacob.' Moses shook with terror and did not dare to look.

³³"Then the Lord said to him, 'Take off your sandals, for you are standing on holy ground. ³⁴I have certainly seen the oppression of my people in Egypt. I have heard their groans and have come down to rescue them. Now go, for I am sending you back to Egypt.'*

³⁵"So God sent back the same man his people had previously rejected when they demanded, 'Who made you a ruler and judge over us?' Through the angel who appeared to him in the burning bush, God sent Moses to be their ruler and savior. ³⁶And by means of many wonders and

7:5-7 Gen 12:7; 15:13-14; Exod 3:12.   7:13 Other manuscripts read *Joseph was recognized by his brothers.*   7:31-34 Exod 3:5-10.

miraculous signs, he led them out of Egypt, through the Red Sea, and through the wilderness for forty years.

[37] "Moses himself told the people of Israel, 'God will raise up for you a Prophet like me from among your own people.'* [38] Moses was with our ancestors, the assembly of God's people in the wilderness, when the angel spoke to him at Mount Sinai. And there Moses received life-giving words to pass on to us.*

[39] "But our ancestors refused to listen to Moses. They rejected him and wanted to return to Egypt. [40] They told Aaron, 'Make us some gods who can lead us, for we don't know what has become of this Moses, who brought us out of Egypt.' [41] So they made an idol shaped like a calf, and they sacrificed to it and celebrated over this thing they had made. [42] Then God turned away from them and abandoned them to serve the stars of heaven as their gods! In the book of the prophets it is written,

'Was it to me you were bringing
    sacrifices and offerings
during those forty years in the
    wilderness, Israel?
[43] No, you carried your pagan gods—
    the shrine of Molech,
    the star of your god Rephan,
    and the images you made to worship
        them.
So I will send you into exile
    as far away as Babylon.'*

[44] "Our ancestors carried the Tabernacle* with them through the wilderness. It was constructed according to the plan God had shown to Moses. [45] Years later, when Joshua led our ancestors in battle against the nations that God drove out of this land, the Tabernacle was taken with them into their new territory. And it stayed there until the time of King David.

[46] "David found favor with God and asked for the privilege of building a permanent Temple for the God of Jacob.* [47] But it was Solomon who actually built it. [48] However, the Most High doesn't live in temples made by human hands. As the prophet says,

[49] 'Heaven is my throne,
    and the earth is my footstool.
Could you build me a temple as good as
    that?'
    asks the LORD.
'Could you build me such a resting
    place?
[50] Didn't my hands make both heaven
    and earth?'*

[51] "You stubborn people! You are heathen* at heart and deaf to the truth. Must you forever resist the Holy Spirit? That's what your ancestors did, and so do you! [52] Name one prophet your ancestors didn't persecute! They even killed the ones who predicted the coming of the Righteous One—the Messiah whom you betrayed and murdered. [53] You deliberately disobeyed God's law, even though you received it from the hands of angels."

[54] The Jewish leaders were infuriated by Stephen's accusation, and they shook their fists at him in rage.* [55] But Stephen, full of the Holy Spirit, gazed steadily into heaven and saw the glory of God, and he saw Jesus standing in the place of honor at God's right hand. [56] And he told them, "Look, I see the heavens opened and the Son of Man standing in the place of honor at God's right hand!"

[57] Then they put their hands over their ears and began shouting. They rushed at him [58] and dragged him out of the city and began to stone him. His accusers took off their coats and laid them at the feet of a young man named Saul.*

[59] As they stoned him, Stephen prayed, "Lord Jesus, receive my spirit." [60] He fell to his knees, shouting, "Lord, don't charge them with this sin!" And with that, he died.

8 Saul was one of the witnesses, and he agreed completely with the killing of Stephen.

Persecution Scatters the Believers

A great wave of persecution began that day, sweeping over the church in Jerusalem; and all the believers except the apostles were scattered through the regions of Judea

---

7:37 Deut 18:15. **7:38** Some manuscripts read *to you.* **7:42-43** Amos 5:25-27 (Greek version). **7:44** Greek *the tent of witness.*
7:46 Some manuscripts read *the house of Jacob.* **7:49-50** Isa 66:1-2. **7:51** Greek *uncircumcised.* **7:54** Greek *they were grinding their teeth against him.* **7:58** *Saul* is later called Paul; see 13:9.

and Samaria. ²(Some devout men came and buried Stephen with great mourning.) ³But Saul was going everywhere to destroy the church. He went from house to house, dragging out both men and women to throw them into prison.

Philip Preaches in Samaria

⁴But the believers who were scattered preached the Good News about Jesus wherever they went. ⁵Philip, for example, went to the city of Samaria and told the people there about the Messiah. ⁶Crowds listened intently to Philip because they were eager to hear his message and see the miraculous signs he did. ⁷Many evil* spirits were cast out, screaming as they left their victims. And many who had been paralyzed or lame were healed. ⁸So there was great joy in that city.

⁹A man named Simon had been a sorcerer there for many years, amazing the people of Samaria and claiming to be someone great. ¹⁰Everyone, from the least to the greatest, often spoke of him as "the Great One—the Power of God." ¹¹They listened closely to him because for a long time he had astounded them with his magic.

¹²But now the people believed Philip's message of Good News concerning the Kingdom of God and the name of Jesus Christ. As a result, many men and women were baptized. ¹³Then Simon himself believed and was baptized. He began following Philip wherever he went, and he was amazed by the signs and great miracles Philip performed.

¹⁴When the apostles in Jerusalem heard that the people of Samaria had accepted God's message, they sent Peter and John there. ¹⁵As soon as they arrived, they prayed for these new believers to receive the Holy Spirit. ¹⁶The Holy Spirit had not yet come upon any of them, for they had only been baptized in the name of the Lord Jesus. ¹⁷Then Peter and John laid their hands upon these believers, and they received the Holy Spirit.

¹⁸When Simon saw that the Spirit was given when the apostles laid their hands on people, he offered them money to buy this power. ¹⁹"Let me have this power, too," he exclaimed, "so that when I lay my hands on people, they will receive the Holy Spirit!"

²⁰But Peter replied, "May your money be destroyed with you for thinking God's gift can be bought! ²¹You can have no part in this, for your heart is not right with God. ²²Repent of your wickedness and pray to the Lord. Perhaps he will forgive your evil thoughts, ²³for I can see that you are full of bitter jealousy and are held captive by sin."

²⁴"Pray to the Lord for me," Simon exclaimed, "that these terrible things you've said won't happen to me!"

²⁵After testifying and preaching the word of the Lord in Samaria, Peter and John returned to Jerusalem. And they stopped in many Samaritan villages along the way to preach the Good News.

Philip and the Ethiopian Eunuch

²⁶As for Philip, an angel of the Lord said to him, "Go south* down the desert road that runs from Jerusalem to Gaza." ²⁷So he started out, and he met the treasurer of Ethiopia, a eunuch of great authority under the Kandake, the queen of Ethiopia. The eunuch had gone to Jerusalem to worship, ²⁸and he was now returning. Seated in his carriage, he was reading aloud from the book of the prophet Isaiah.

²⁹The Holy Spirit said to Philip, "Go over and walk along beside the carriage."

³⁰Philip ran over and heard the man reading from the prophet Isaiah. Philip asked, "Do you understand what you are reading?"

³¹The man replied, "How can I, unless someone instructs me?" And he urged Philip to come up into the carriage and sit with him.

³²The passage of Scripture he had been reading was this:

"He was led like a sheep to the slaughter.
    And as a lamb is silent before the
        shearers,
    he did not open his mouth.
³³ He was humiliated and received no
        justice.
    Who can speak of his descendants?
    For his life was taken from the earth."*

8:7 Greek *unclean*.　**8:26** Or *Go at noon*.　**8:32-33** Isa 53:7-8 (Greek version).

Responding to Holy Invitations

ACTS 8:26–40

Rushing out of my local grocery store parking lot, I check my watch. I'm running late. While calculating whether I can make it through a yellow light, I spot a thin, weathered man standing on the median. Without enough time to accelerate past or enough space to switch lanes, I reluctantly pull up beside him.

Before I even read his cardboard sign, my pulse quickens with trepidation. Should I look at him? Should I roll down the window? Should I offer him food? No matter what response I choose, I'm uncomfortable with the whole situation. Yet I'm beginning to suspect my discomfort may be a sort of holy invitation.

Moments of discomfort as we observe people in need may in fact be God's Spirit nudging us to pray—and maybe also to action. "Most people dismiss these promptings as foolish," explains Bruce Main, author of *Holy Hunches: Responding to the Promptings of God*. Yet what "moves people into acts of service . . . is this intuitive sense. It is not enough to have our hearts fill with compassion. . . . We really need to convert these feelings into an appropriate response." Our faithful response springs from noticing what moves God's heart.

That day I slowed my minivan to a stop beside the median man, pawed through my groceries, and pulled out some peanut butter jars. Rolling down the window, I asked the man if he liked chunky or smooth. "Chunky," he said, reaching for the small token of care.

I wish I could say I no longer feel anxious when I encounter strangers in need, but I do. But I've come to recognize that feeling as the Holy Spirit's invitation to see and serve.

—Margot Starbuck

For more on service, see reading at Philippians 2:6-8.

³⁴The eunuch asked Philip, "Tell me, was the prophet talking about himself or someone else?" ³⁵So beginning with this same Scripture, Philip told him the Good News about Jesus.

³⁶As they rode along, they came to some water, and the eunuch said, "Look! There's some water! Why can't I be baptized?"* ³⁸He ordered the carriage to stop, and they went down into the water, and Philip baptized him.

³⁹When they came up out of the water, the Spirit of the Lord snatched Philip away. The eunuch never saw him again but went on his way rejoicing. ⁴⁰Meanwhile, Philip found himself farther north at the town of Azotus. He preached the Good News there and in every town along the way until he came to Caesarea.

9 Saul's Conversion

Meanwhile, Saul was uttering threats with every breath and was eager to kill the Lord's followers.* So he went to the high priest. ²He requested letters addressed to the synagogues in Damascus, asking for their cooperation in the arrest of any followers of the Way he found there. He

---

8:36 Some manuscripts add verse 37, *"You can,"* Philip answered, *"if you believe with all your heart." And the eunuch replied, "I believe that Jesus Christ is the Son of God."* **9:1** Greek *disciples*.

wanted to bring them—both men and women—back to Jerusalem in chains.

³As he was approaching Damascus on this mission, a light from heaven suddenly shone down around him. ⁴He fell to the ground and heard a voice saying to him, "Saul! Saul! Why are you persecuting me?"

⁵"Who are you, lord?" Saul asked.

And the voice replied, "I am Jesus, the one you are persecuting! ⁶Now get up and go into the city, and you will be told what you must do."

⁷The men with Saul stood speechless, for they heard the sound of someone's voice but saw no one! ⁸Saul picked himself up off the ground, but when he opened his eyes he was blind. So his companions led him by the hand to Damascus. ⁹He remained there blind for three days and did not eat or drink.

¹⁰Now there was a believer* in Damascus named Ananias. The Lord spoke to him in a vision, calling, "Ananias!"

"Yes, Lord!" he replied.

¹¹The Lord said, "Go over to Straight Street, to the house of Judas. When you get there, ask for a man from Tarsus named Saul. He is praying to me right now. ¹²I have shown him a vision of a man named Ananias coming in and laying hands on him so he can see again."

¹³"But Lord," exclaimed Ananias, "I've heard many people talk about the terrible things this man has done to the believers* in Jerusalem! ¹⁴And he is authorized by the leading priests to arrest everyone who calls upon your name."

¹⁵But the Lord said, "Go, for Saul is my chosen instrument to take my message to the Gentiles and to kings, as well as to the people of Israel. ¹⁶And I will show him how much he must suffer for my name's sake."

¹⁷So Ananias went and found Saul. He laid his hands on him and said, "Brother Saul, the Lord Jesus, who appeared to you on the road, has sent me so that you might regain your sight and be filled with the Holy Spirit." ¹⁸Instantly something like scales fell from Saul's eyes, and he regained his sight. Then he got up and was baptized. ¹⁹Afterward he ate some food and regained his strength.

Saul in Damascus and Jerusalem

Saul stayed with the believers* in Damascus for a few days. ²⁰And immediately he began preaching about Jesus in the synagogues, saying, "He is indeed the Son of God!"

²¹All who heard him were amazed. "Isn't this the same man who caused such devastation among Jesus' followers in Jerusalem?" they asked. "And didn't he come here to arrest them and take them in chains to the leading priests?"

²²Saul's preaching became more and more powerful, and the Jews in Damascus couldn't refute his proofs that Jesus was indeed the Messiah. ²³After a while some of the Jews plotted together to kill him. ²⁴They were watching for him day and night at the city gate so they could murder him, but Saul was told about their plot. ²⁵So during the night, some of the other believers* lowered him in a large basket through an opening in the city wall.

²⁶When Saul arrived in Jerusalem, he tried to meet with the believers, but they were all afraid of him. They did not believe he had truly become a believer! ²⁷Then Barnabas brought him to the apostles and told them how Saul had seen the Lord on the way to Damascus and how the Lord had spoken to Saul. He also told them that Saul had preached boldly in the name of Jesus in Damascus.

²⁸So Saul stayed with the apostles and went all around Jerusalem with them, preaching boldly in the name of the Lord. ²⁹He debated with some Greek-speaking Jews, but they tried to murder him. ³⁰When the believers* heard about this, they took him down to Caesarea and sent him away to Tarsus, his hometown.

³¹The church then had peace throughout Judea, Galilee, and Samaria, and it became stronger as the believers lived in the fear of the Lord. And with the encouragement of the Holy Spirit, it also grew in numbers.

Peter Heals Aeneas and Raises Dorcas

³²Meanwhile, Peter traveled from place to place, and he came down to visit the believers in the town of Lydda. ³³There he met a man named Aeneas, who had been

---

9:10 Greek disciple; also in 9:26, 36.   **9:13** Greek God's holy people; also in 9:32, 41.   **9:19** Greek disciples; also in 9:26, 38.   **9:25** Greek his disciples.   **9:30** Greek brothers.

paralyzed and bedridden for eight years. ³⁴Peter said to him, "Aeneas, Jesus Christ heals you! Get up, and roll up your sleeping mat!" And he was healed instantly. ³⁵Then the whole population of Lydda and Sharon saw Aeneas walking around, and they turned to the Lord.

³⁶There was a believer in Joppa named Tabitha (which in Greek is Dorcas*). She was always doing kind things for others and helping the poor. ³⁷About this time she became ill and died. Her body was washed for burial and laid in an upstairs room. ³⁸But the believers had heard that Peter was nearby at Lydda, so they sent two men to beg him, "Please come as soon as possible!" ³⁹So Peter returned with them; and as soon as he arrived, they took him to the upstairs room. The room was filled with widows who were weeping and showing him the coats and other clothes Dorcas had made for them. ⁴⁰But Peter asked

Tabitha: The Witness of Kindness

ACTS 9:36-43

I n Acts 9:36-43 we see a portrait of how the world-altering Good News of Jesus changed one woman . . . and her world. Tabitha (also called Dorcas) was a new convert to the way of Jesus. Tabitha believed the Good News was about much more than just getting saved and into heaven; it meant bringing the peace, goodness, love, and forgiveness of Jesus into Roman culture where worshiping him was illegal. Though the dream of the kingdom of God put her life in danger, that dream exploded in Tabitha's heart. In just a few short words, Scripture describes Tabitha's compelling new way of life: "She was always doing kind things for others and helping the poor" (9:36).

Was she rich or poor? Married or widowed? Important or unknown? We don't know much about Tabitha—except that she was energized by the reality that she had a part to play in bringing God's peaceable kingdom to Joppa. Her talents existed for a cause beyond her own comfort: her sewing could be for others; her love could be for widows (9:39). Her life could shine with Jesus in every conversation.

Tabitha must have given Jesus her all, because when she died it was as though a light went out in the neighborhood and everyone was in shock. Even Peter was sent an urgent message, "Please come as soon as possible!" (9:38).

As soon as Peter arrived, he was bombarded by the story of Tabitha's compelling witness—her ministry of kindness to those in need. We might think that the finale of this story was when Peter prayed for dead Tabitha to "get up" . . . and she did (9:40). Certainly Tabitha's rising from the dead is amazing. But the true finale is that news of Tabitha's life, death, and life "spread through the whole town, and many believed in the Lord" (9:42). Tabitha used her life and her gifts to minister to others—and God used Tabitha's life to turn Joppa upside down.

How can your life do the same? How will you live a testimony of kindness and ministry to those in need?

—Adele Ahlberg Calhoun

For more on outreach, see reading at Acts 15:36-40.

9:36 The names *Tabitha* in Aramaic and *Dorcas* in Greek both mean "gazelle."

them all to leave the room; then he knelt and prayed. Turning to the body he said, "Get up, Tabitha." And she opened her eyes! When she saw Peter, she sat up! [41] He gave her his hand and helped her up. Then he called in the widows and all the believers, and he presented her to them alive.

[42] The news spread through the whole town, and many believed in the Lord. [43] And Peter stayed a long time in Joppa, living with Simon, a tanner of hides.

10 Cornelius Calls for Peter

In Caesarea there lived a Roman army officer* named Cornelius, who was a captain of the Italian Regiment. [2] He was a devout, God-fearing man, as was everyone in his household. He gave generously to the poor and prayed regularly to God. [3] One afternoon about three o'clock, he had a vision in which he saw an angel of God coming toward him. "Cornelius!" the angel said.

[4] Cornelius stared at him in terror. "What is it, sir?" he asked the angel.

And the angel replied, "Your prayers and gifts to the poor have been received by God as an offering! [5] Now send some men to Joppa, and summon a man named Simon Peter. [6] He is staying with Simon, a tanner who lives near the seashore."

[7] As soon as the angel was gone, Cornelius called two of his household servants and a devout soldier, one of his personal attendants. [8] He told them what had happened and sent them off to Joppa.

Peter Visits Cornelius

[9] The next day as Cornelius's messengers were nearing the town, Peter went up on the flat roof to pray. It was about noon, [10] and he was hungry. But while a meal was being prepared, he fell into a trance. [11] He saw the sky open, and something like a large sheet was let down by its four corners. [12] In the sheet were all sorts of animals, reptiles, and birds. [13] Then a voice said to him, "Get up, Peter; kill and eat them."

[14] "No, Lord," Peter declared. "I have never eaten anything that our Jewish laws have declared impure and unclean.*"

[15] But the voice spoke again: "Do not call something unclean if God has made it clean." [16] The same vision was repeated three times. Then the sheet was suddenly pulled up to heaven.

[17] Peter was very perplexed. What could the vision mean? Just then the men sent by Cornelius found Simon's house. Standing outside the gate, [18] they asked if a man named Simon Peter was staying there.

[19] Meanwhile, as Peter was puzzling over the vision, the Holy Spirit said to him, "Three men have come looking for you. [20] Get up, go downstairs, and go with them without hesitation. Don't worry, for I have sent them."

[21] So Peter went down and said, "I'm the man you are looking for. Why have you come?"

[22] They said, "We were sent by Cornelius, a Roman officer. He is a devout and God-fearing man, well respected by all the Jews. A holy angel instructed him to summon you to his house so that he can hear your message." [23] So Peter invited the men to stay for the night. The next day he went with them, accompanied by some of the brothers from Joppa.

[24] They arrived in Caesarea the following day. Cornelius was waiting for them and had called together his relatives and close friends. [25] As Peter entered his home, Cornelius fell at his feet and worshiped him. [26] But Peter pulled him up and said, "Stand up! I'm a human being just like you!" [27] So they talked together and went inside, where many others were assembled.

[28] Peter told them, "You know it is against our laws for a Jewish man to enter a Gentile home like this or to associate with you. But God has shown me that I should no longer think of anyone as impure or unclean. [29] So I came without objection as soon as I was sent for. Now tell me why you sent for me."

[30] Cornelius replied, "Four days ago I was praying in my house about this same time, three o'clock in the afternoon. Suddenly, a man in dazzling clothes was standing in front of me. [31] He told me, 'Cornelius, your prayer has been heard, and your gifts to the poor have been noticed by God! [32] Now

10:1 Greek a centurion; similarly in 10:22. 10:14 Greek anything common and unclean.

Reconciliation in and through Grace

ACTS 10

During a lecture my African American friend Spencer—whose father had been beaten bloody in a Mississippi jail cell in 1970—once suggested we change the way we pursue justice. "Although we must continue to speak on behalf of those who are oppressed and warn oppressors," he said, "my willingness to forgive them is not dependent on how they respond. Being able to extend grace and to forgive sets us free. We no longer need to spend precious emotional energy thinking about the day oppressors will get what they deserve."

Spencer's words that night were not received with thunderous applause. But just three days later, at age forty-four, my dear friend Spencer died of a heart attack. Afterward many told me they were now taking his words *very* seriously.

But what does it mean to pursue racial reconciliation in and through *grace*?

First, it means to recognize that reconciliation is God's gift; it does not begin with our activism. In the realm of racial reconciliation, the language of sociology, marketing, and rights often dominates our talk. The message is: *Our country is changing demographically; therefore, the church must change. Everyone should share in power. Now let's go out and make it happen.*

Such visions don't say enough about God's desires and God's power. Second Corinthians 5 offers a far more beautiful and radical vision: we are God's new creation in Christ and are becoming his ambassadors of reconciliation (5:16–21).

Reconciliation has already begun with the work of Christ (2 Corinthians 5:19). And God invites us on the journey of reconciliation, the same journey that the early church was on: a journey that includes interruptions (Pentecost, Acts 2), a reconciliation among social divides (Peter's discovery that the gospel is for Gentiles, Acts 10), dismantling discrimination (against Greek widows, Acts 6:1–6), a new intimacy (the church in Antioch, Acts 11:19–26), speaking to injustice (Paul confronting Peter, Galatians 2:11–14) and, especially the Holy Spirit—not Peter or Paul—being the central actor.

Second, reconciliation through grace means working for justice with a spirit of mercy. Even during the grip of South African apartheid, with no guarantee that justice would win, Desmond Tutu preached "no future without forgiveness." And Nelson Mandela, from his imprisonment through his presidency, strove for a future of blacks and whites living together. Different ethnic communities have different captivities, and all are in need of the conversion that grace and the new creation make possible.

Without grace, we can miss seeing the possibility of reconciliation. Bitterness can blind an African American from imagining why her church should bother building relationships with whites who "don't get it." Legalism can prevent a white Christian from listening to the painful story of a Mexican who crossed the border illegally to feed his family. In everyday situations like these, a lack of grace is tearing Christians apart.

At the same time, a major challenge is seeing the depth of racial, ethnic, and cultural brokenness. Grace calls us first to slow down and start with God's gift of lament: to see, name, and feel the brokenness. Only when we experience lament, feel helpless, and let go of control can we open up to our need for God and God's gifts—the only things that can rescue us from our alienation. Getting God's love into our bones gives us a holy boldness and mercy to take the time to see what's going on in our communities and institutions—the residue, the powers, and the imaginations that exclude others or lead to self-sufficiency.

Third, conversion by grace takes time and does not leave us standing complacently where we are. Grace not only takes time but also *gives us time* to pursue reconciliation, not with desperation but by embracing long-term practices and disciplines that in the light of God's love become "graces" through which we and our institutions can be converted.

Finally, pursuing reconciliation in grace means to journey toward holiness. Reconciliation is not an event or achievement but a journey that forms the fruit of the Holy Spirit in us—love, joy, peace, patience, kindness, goodness, faithfulness, gentleness, and self-control. Grace insists that segregation in the intimate places of our lives is not normal, inevitable, or acceptable—and that reconciliation is *beautiful*. When knit and transformed together in visible friendship and common mission for the sake of the gospel, we not only become like Christ, we are also joined into Christ.

—Chris Rice

For more on reconciliation, see reading at 2 Corinthians 5:18–19.

send messengers to Joppa, and summon a man named Simon Peter. He is staying in the home of Simon, a tanner who lives near the seashore.' ³³So I sent for you at once, and it was good of you to come. Now we are all here, waiting before God to hear the message the Lord has given you."

The Gentiles Hear the Good News

³⁴Then Peter replied, "I see very clearly that God shows no favoritism. ³⁵In every nation he accepts those who fear him and do what is right. ³⁶This is the message of Good News for the people of Israel—that there is peace with God through Jesus Christ, who is Lord of all. ³⁷You know what happened throughout Judea, beginning in Galilee, after John began preaching his message of baptism. ³⁸And you know that God anointed Jesus of Nazareth with the Holy Spirit and with power. Then Jesus went around doing good and healing all who were oppressed by the devil, for God was with him.

³⁹"And we apostles are witnesses of all he did throughout Judea and in Jerusalem. They put him to death by hanging him on a cross,* ⁴⁰but God raised him to life on the third day. Then God allowed him to appear, ⁴¹not to the general public,* but to us whom God had chosen in advance to be his witnesses. We were those who ate and drank with him after he rose from the dead. ⁴²And he ordered us to preach everywhere and to testify that Jesus is the one appointed by God to be the judge of all—the living and the dead. ⁴³He is the one all the prophets testified about, saying that everyone who believes in him will have their sins forgiven through his name."

The Gentiles Receive the Holy Spirit

⁴⁴Even as Peter was saying these things, the Holy Spirit fell upon all who were listening to the message. ⁴⁵The Jewish believers* who came with Peter were amazed that the gift of the Holy Spirit had been poured out on the Gentiles, too. ⁴⁶For they heard them speaking in other tongues* and praising God.

Then Peter asked, ⁴⁷"Can anyone object

to their being baptized, now that they have received the Holy Spirit just as we did?" ⁴⁸So he gave orders for them to be baptized in the name of Jesus Christ. Afterward Cornelius asked him to stay with them for several days.

11 Peter Explains His Actions

Soon the news reached the apostles and other believers* in Judea that the Gentiles had received the word of God. ²But when Peter arrived back in Jerusalem, the Jewish believers* criticized him. ³"You entered the home of Gentiles* and even ate with them!" they said.

⁴Then Peter told them exactly what had happened. ⁵"I was in the town of Joppa," he said, "and while I was praying, I went into a trance and saw a vision. Something like a large sheet was let down by its four corners from the sky. And it came right down to me. ⁶When I looked inside the sheet, I saw all sorts of tame and wild animals, reptiles, and birds. ⁷And I heard a voice say, 'Get up, Peter; kill and eat them.'

⁸"'No, Lord,' I replied. 'I have never eaten anything that our Jewish laws have declared impure or unclean.*'

⁹"But the voice from heaven spoke again: 'Do not call something unclean if God has made it clean.' ¹⁰This happened three times before the sheet and all it contained was pulled back up to heaven.

¹¹"Just then three men who had been sent from Caesarea arrived at the house where we were staying. ¹²The Holy Spirit told me to go with them and not to worry that they were Gentiles. These six brothers here accompanied me, and we soon entered the home of the man who had sent for us. ¹³He told us how an angel had appeared to him in his home and had told him, 'Send messengers to Joppa, and summon a man named Simon Peter. ¹⁴He will tell you how you and everyone in your household can be saved!'

¹⁵"As I began to speak," Peter continued, "the Holy Spirit fell on them, just as he fell on us at the beginning. ¹⁶Then I thought of the Lord's words when he said, 'John baptized with* water, but you will be baptized

---

10:39 Greek *on a tree.* 10:41 Greek *the people.* 10:45 Greek *The faithful ones of the circumcision.* 10:46 Or *in other languages.* 11:1 Greek *brothers.* 11:2 Greek *those of the circumcision.* 11:3 Greek *of uncircumcised men.* 11:8 Greek *anything common or unclean.* 11:16 Or *in;* also in 11:16b.

with the Holy Spirit.' [17] And since God gave these Gentiles the same gift he gave us when we believed in the Lord Jesus Christ, who was I to stand in God's way?"

[18] When the others heard this, they stopped objecting and began praising God. They said, "We can see that God has also given the Gentiles the privilege of repenting of their sins and receiving eternal life."

The Church in Antioch of Syria

[19] Meanwhile, the believers who had been scattered during the persecution after Stephen's death traveled as far as Phoenicia, Cyprus, and Antioch of Syria. They preached the word of God, but only to Jews. [20] However, some of the believers who went to Antioch from Cyprus and Cyrene began preaching to the Gentiles* about the Lord Jesus. [21] The power of the Lord was with them, and a large number of these Gentiles believed and turned to the Lord.

[22] When the church at Jerusalem heard what had happened, they sent Barnabas to Antioch. [23] When he arrived and saw this evidence of God's blessing, he was filled with joy, and he encouraged the believers to stay true to the Lord. [24] Barnabas was a good man, full of the Holy Spirit and strong in faith. And many people were brought to the Lord.

[25] Then Barnabas went on to Tarsus to look for Saul. [26] When he found him, he brought him back to Antioch. Both of them stayed there with the church for a full year, teaching large crowds of people. (It was at Antioch that the believers* were first called Christians.)

[27] During this time some prophets traveled from Jerusalem to Antioch. [28] One of them named Agabus stood up in one of the meetings and predicted by the Spirit that a great famine was coming upon the entire Roman world. (This was fulfilled during the reign of Claudius.) [29] So the believers in Antioch decided to send relief to the brothers and sisters* in Judea, everyone giving as much as they could. [30] This they did, entrusting their gifts to Barnabas and Saul

to take to the elders of the church in Jerusalem.

12 James Is Killed and Peter Is Imprisoned

About that time King Herod Agrippa* began to persecute some believers in the church. [2] He had the apostle James (John's brother) killed with a sword. [3] When Herod saw how much this pleased the Jewish people, he also arrested Peter. (This took place during the Passover celebration.*) [4] Then he imprisoned him, placing him under the guard of four squads of four soldiers each. Herod intended to bring Peter out for public trial after the Passover. [5] But while Peter was in prison, the church prayed very earnestly for him.

Peter's Miraculous Escape from Prison

[6] The night before Peter was to be placed on trial, he was asleep, fastened with two chains between two soldiers. Others stood guard at the prison gate. [7] Suddenly, there was a bright light in the cell, and an angel of the Lord stood before Peter. The angel struck him on the side to awaken him and said, "Quick! Get up!" And the chains fell off his wrists. [8] Then the angel told him, "Get dressed and put on your sandals." And he did. "Now put on your coat and follow me," the angel ordered.

[9] So Peter left the cell, following the angel. But all the time he thought it was a vision. He didn't realize it was actually happening. [10] They passed the first and second guard posts and came to the iron gate leading to the city, and this opened for them all by itself. So they passed through and started walking down the street, and then the angel suddenly left him.

[11] Peter finally came to his senses. "It's really true!" he said. "The Lord has sent his angel and saved me from Herod and from what the Jewish leaders* had planned to do to me!"

[12] When he realized this, he went to the home of Mary, the mother of John Mark, where many were gathered for prayer. [13] He knocked at the door in the gate, and a servant girl named Rhoda came to open

---

11:20 Greek *the Hellenists* (i.e., those who speak Greek); other manuscripts read *the Greeks*.   **11:26** Greek *disciples;* also in 11:29.
11:29 Greek *the brothers.*   **12:1** Greek *Herod the king.* He was the nephew of Herod Antipas and a grandson of Herod the Great.   **12:3** Greek *the days of unleavened bread.*   **12:11** Or *the Jewish people.*

it. [14] When she recognized Peter's voice, she was so overjoyed that, instead of opening the door, she ran back inside and told everyone, "Peter is standing at the door!"

[15] "You're out of your mind!" they said. When she insisted, they decided, "It must be his angel."

[16] Meanwhile, Peter continued knocking. When they finally opened the door and saw him, they were amazed. [17] He motioned for them to quiet down and told them how the Lord had led him out of prison. "Tell James and the other brothers what happened," he said. And then he went to another place.

[18] At dawn there was a great commotion among the soldiers about what had happened to Peter. [19] Herod Agrippa ordered a thorough search for him. When he couldn't be found, Herod interrogated the guards and sentenced them to death. Afterward Herod left Judea to stay in Caesarea for a while.

The Death of Herod Agrippa

[20] Now Herod was very angry with the people of Tyre and Sidon. So they sent a delegation to make peace with him because their cities were dependent upon Herod's country for food. The delegates won the support of Blastus, Herod's personal assistant, [21] and an appointment with Herod was granted. When the day arrived, Herod put on his royal robes, sat on his throne, and made a speech to them. [22] The people gave him a great ovation, shouting, "It's the voice of a god, not of a man!"

[23] Instantly, an angel of the Lord struck Herod with a sickness, because he accepted the people's worship instead of giving the glory to God. So he was consumed with worms and died.

[24] Meanwhile, the word of God continued to spread, and there were many new believers.

[25] When Barnabas and Saul had finished their mission to Jerusalem, they returned,* taking John Mark with them.

13 Barnabas and Saul Are Commissioned

Among the prophets and teachers of the church at Antioch of Syria were Barnabas, Simeon (called "the black man"*), Lucius (from Cyrene), Manaen (the childhood companion of King Herod Antipas*), and Saul. [2] One day as these men were worshiping the Lord and fasting, the Holy Spirit said, "Dedicate Barnabas and Saul for the special work to which I have called them." [3] So after more fasting and prayer, the men laid their hands on them and sent them on their way.

Paul's First Missionary Journey

[4] So Barnabas and Saul were sent out by the Holy Spirit. They went down to the seaport of Seleucia and then sailed for the island of Cyprus. [5] There, in the town of Salamis, they went to the Jewish synagogues and preached the word of God. John Mark went with them as their assistant.

[6] Afterward they traveled from town to town across the entire island until finally they reached Paphos, where they met a Jewish sorcerer, a false prophet named Bar-Jesus. [7] He had attached himself to the governor, Sergius Paulus, who was an intelligent man. The governor invited Barnabas and Saul to visit him, for he wanted to hear the word of God. [8] But Elymas, the sorcerer (as his name means in Greek), interfered and urged the governor to pay no attention to what Barnabas and Saul said. He was trying to keep the governor from believing.

[9] Saul, also known as Paul, was filled with the Holy Spirit, and he looked the sorcerer in the eye. [10] Then he said, "You son of the devil, full of every sort of deceit and fraud, and enemy of all that is good! Will you never stop perverting the true ways of the Lord? [11] Watch now, for the Lord has laid his hand of punishment upon you, and you will be struck blind. You will not see the sunlight for some time." Instantly mist and darkness came over the man's eyes, and he began groping around begging for someone to take his hand and lead him.

[12] When the governor saw what had happened, he became a believer, for he was astonished at the teaching about the Lord.

Paul Preaches in Antioch of Pisidia

[13] Paul and his companions then left Paphos by ship for Pamphylia, landing at the port

---

12:25 Or *mission, they returned to Jerusalem.* Other manuscripts read *mission, they returned from Jerusalem;* still others read *mission, they returned from Jerusalem to Antioch.* **13:1a** Greek *who was called Niger.* **13:1b** Greek *Herod the tetrarch.*

town of Perga. There John Mark left them and returned to Jerusalem. ¹⁴But Paul and Barnabas traveled inland to Antioch of Pisidia.*

On the Sabbath they went to the synagogue for the services. ¹⁵After the usual readings from the books of Moses* and the prophets, those in charge of the service sent them this message: "Brothers, if you have any word of encouragement for the people, come and give it."

¹⁶So Paul stood, lifted his hand to quiet them, and started speaking. "Men of Israel," he said, "and you God-fearing Gentiles, listen to me.

¹⁷"The God of this nation of Israel chose our ancestors and made them multiply and grow strong during their stay in Egypt. Then with a powerful arm he led them out of their slavery. ¹⁸He put up with them* through forty years of wandering in the wilderness. ¹⁹Then he destroyed seven nations in Canaan and gave their land to Israel as an inheritance. ²⁰All this took about 450 years.

"After that, God gave them judges to rule until the time of Samuel the prophet. ²¹Then the people begged for a king, and God gave them Saul son of Kish, a man of the tribe of Benjamin, who reigned for forty years. ²²But God removed Saul and replaced him with David, a man about whom God said, 'I have found David son of Jesse, a man after my own heart. He will do everything I want him to do.'*

²³"And it is one of King David's descendants, Jesus, who is God's promised Savior of Israel! ²⁴Before he came, John the Baptist preached that all the people of Israel needed to repent of their sins and turn to God and be baptized. ²⁵As John was finishing his ministry he asked, 'Do you think I am the Messiah? No, I am not! But he is coming soon—and I'm not even worthy to be his slave and untie the sandals on his feet.'

²⁶"Brothers—you sons of Abraham, and also you God-fearing Gentiles—this message of salvation has been sent to us! ²⁷The people in Jerusalem and their leaders did not recognize Jesus as the one the prophets had spoken about. Instead, they condemned him, and in doing this they fulfilled the prophets' words that are read every Sabbath. ²⁸They found no legal reason to execute him, but they asked Pilate to have him killed anyway.

²⁹"When they had done all that the prophecies said about him, they took him down from the cross* and placed him in a tomb. ³⁰But God raised him from the dead! ³¹And over a period of many days he appeared to those who had gone with him from Galilee to Jerusalem. They are now his witnesses to the people of Israel.

³²"And now we are here to bring you this Good News. The promise was made to our ancestors, ³³and God has now fulfilled it for us, their descendants, by raising Jesus. This is what the second psalm says about Jesus:

'You are my Son.
    Today I have become your Father.*'

³⁴For God had promised to raise him from the dead, not leaving him to rot in the grave. He said, 'I will give you the sacred blessings I promised to David.'* ³⁵Another psalm explains it more fully: 'You will not allow your Holy One to rot in the grave.'* ³⁶This is not a reference to David, for after David had done the will of God in his own generation, he died and was buried with his ancestors, and his body decayed. ³⁷No, it was a reference to someone else—someone whom God raised and whose body did not decay.

³⁸*"Brothers, listen! We are here to proclaim that through this man Jesus there is forgiveness for your sins. ³⁹Everyone who believes in him is declared right with God—something the law of Moses could never do. ⁴⁰Be careful! Don't let the prophets' words apply to you. For they said,

⁴¹ 'Look, you mockers,
    be amazed and die!
For I am doing something in your own
    day,
    something you wouldn't believe
    even if someone told you about it.'*"

⁴²As Paul and Barnabas left the synagogue that day, the people begged them to speak

---

13:13-14 *Pamphylia* and *Pisidia* were districts in what is now Turkey.   **13:15** Greek *from the law.*   **13:18** Some manuscripts read *He cared for them;* compare Deut 1:31.   **13:22** 1 Sam 13:14.   **13:29** Greek *from the tree.*   **13:33** Or *Today I reveal you as my Son.* Ps 2:7.   **13:34** Isa 55:3.
13:35 Ps 16:10.   **13:38** English translations divide verses 38 and 39 in various ways.   **13:41** Hab 1:5 (Greek version).

about these things again the next week. 43 Many Jews and devout converts to Judaism followed Paul and Barnabas, and the two men urged them to continue to rely on the grace of God.

Paul Turns to the Gentiles

44 The following week almost the entire city turned out to hear them preach the word of the Lord. 45 But when some of the Jews saw the crowds, they were jealous; so they slandered Paul and argued against whatever he said.

46 Then Paul and Barnabas spoke out boldly and declared, "It was necessary that we first preach the word of God to you Jews. But since you have rejected it and judged yourselves unworthy of eternal life, we will offer it to the Gentiles. 47 For the Lord gave us this command when he said,

'I have made you a light to the Gentiles,
    to bring salvation to the farthest
        corners of the earth.'*"

48 When the Gentiles heard this, they were very glad and thanked the Lord for his message; and all who were chosen for eternal life became believers. 49 So the Lord's message spread throughout that region. 50 Then the Jews stirred up the influential religious women and the leaders of the city, and they incited a mob against Paul and Barnabas and ran them out of town. 51 So they shook the dust from their feet as a sign of rejection and went to the town of Iconium. 52 And the believers* were filled with joy and with the Holy Spirit.

14 Paul and Barnabas in Iconium

The same thing happened in Iconium.* Paul and Barnabas went to the Jewish synagogue and preached with such power that a great number of both Jews and Greeks became believers. 2 Some of the Jews, however, spurned God's message and poisoned the minds of the Gentiles against Paul and Barnabas. 3 But the apostles stayed there a long time, preaching boldly about the grace of the Lord. And the Lord proved their message was true by giving them power to do miraculous signs and wonders.

4 But the people of the town were divided in their opinion about them. Some sided with the Jews, and some with the apostles. 5 Then a mob of Gentiles and Jews, along with their leaders, decided to attack and stone them. 6 When the apostles learned of it, they fled to the region of Lycaonia—to the towns of Lystra and Derbe and the surrounding area. 7 And there they preached the Good News.

Paul and Barnabas in Lystra and Derbe

8 While they were at Lystra, Paul and Barnabas came upon a man with crippled feet. He had been that way from birth, so he had never walked. He was sitting 9 and listening as Paul preached. Looking straight at him, Paul realized he had faith to be healed. 10 So Paul called to him in a loud voice, "Stand up!" And the man jumped to his feet and started walking.

11 When the crowd saw what Paul had done, they shouted in their local dialect, "These men are gods in human form!" 12 They decided that Barnabas was the Greek god Zeus and that Paul was Hermes, since he was the chief speaker. 13 Now the temple of Zeus was located just outside the town. So the priest of the temple and the crowd brought bulls and wreaths of flowers to the town gates, and they prepared to offer sacrifices to the apostles.

14 But when the apostles Barnabas and Paul heard what was happening, they tore their clothing in dismay and ran out among the people, shouting, 15 "Friends,* why are you doing this? We are merely human beings—just like you! We have come to bring you the Good News that you should turn from these worthless things and turn to the living God, who made heaven and earth, the sea, and everything in them. 16 In the past he permitted all the nations to go their own ways, 17 but he never left them without evidence of himself and his goodness. For instance, he sends you rain and good crops and gives you food and joyful hearts." 18 But even with these words, Paul and Barnabas could scarcely restrain the people from sacrificing to them.

19 Then some Jews arrived from Antioch

13:47 Isa 49:6. 13:52 Greek the disciples. 14:1 Iconium, as well as Lystra and Derbe (14:6), were towns in what is now Turkey. 14:15 Greek Men.

and Iconium and won the crowds to their side. They stoned Paul and dragged him out of town, thinking he was dead. ²⁰But as the believers* gathered around him, he got up and went back into the town. The next day he left with Barnabas for Derbe.

Paul and Barnabas Return to Antioch of Syria

²¹After preaching the Good News in Derbe and making many disciples, Paul and Barnabas returned to Lystra, Iconium, and Antioch of Pisidia, ²²where they strengthened the believers. They encouraged them to continue in the faith, reminding them that we must suffer many hardships to enter the Kingdom of God. ²³Paul and Barnabas also appointed elders in every church. With prayer and fasting, they turned the elders over to the care of the Lord, in whom they had put their trust. ²⁴Then they traveled back through Pisidia to Pamphylia. ²⁵They preached the word in Perga, then went down to Attalia.

²⁶Finally, they returned by ship to Antioch of Syria, where their journey had begun. The believers there had entrusted them to the grace of God to do the work they had now completed. ²⁷Upon arriving in Antioch, they called the church together and reported everything God had done through them and how he had opened the door of faith to the Gentiles, too. ²⁸And they stayed there with the believers for a long time.

15 The Council at Jerusalem

While Paul and Barnabas were at Antioch of Syria, some men from Judea arrived and began to teach the believers*: "Unless you are circumcised as required by the law of Moses, you cannot be saved." ²Paul and Barnabas disagreed with them, arguing vehemently. Finally, the church decided to send Paul and Barnabas to Jerusalem, accompanied by some local believers, to talk to the apostles and elders about this question. ³The church sent the delegates to Jerusalem, and they stopped along the way in Phoenicia and Samaria to visit the believers. They told them—much to everyone's joy—that the Gentiles, too, were being converted.

⁴When they arrived in Jerusalem, Barnabas and Paul were welcomed by the whole church, including the apostles and elders. They reported everything God had done through them. ⁵But then some of the believers who belonged to the sect of the Pharisees stood up and insisted, "The Gentile converts must be circumcised and required to follow the law of Moses."

⁶So the apostles and elders met together to resolve this issue. ⁷At the meeting, after a long discussion, Peter stood and addressed them as follows: "Brothers, you all know that God chose me from among you some time ago to preach to the Gentiles so that they could hear the Good News and believe. ⁸God knows people's hearts, and he confirmed that he accepts Gentiles by giving them the Holy Spirit, just as he did to us. ⁹He made no distinction between us and them, for he cleansed their hearts through faith. ¹⁰So why are you now challenging God by burdening the Gentile believers* with a yoke that neither we nor our ancestors were able to bear? ¹¹We believe that we are all saved the same way, by the undeserved grace of the Lord Jesus."

¹²Everyone listened quietly as Barnabas and Paul told about the miraculous signs and wonders God had done through them among the Gentiles.

¹³When they had finished, James stood and said, "Brothers, listen to me. ¹⁴Peter* has told you about the time God first visited the Gentiles to take from them a people for himself. ¹⁵And this conversion of Gentiles is exactly what the prophets predicted. As it is written:

¹⁶ 'Afterward I will return
　　and restore the fallen house* of David.
I will rebuild its ruins
　　and restore it,
¹⁷ so that the rest of humanity might seek
　　the LORD,
　　including the Gentiles—
　　all those I have called to be mine.
The LORD has spoken—
¹⁸　he who made these things known so
　　long ago.'*

14:20 Greek *disciples;* also in 14:22, 28.　**15:1** Greek *brothers;* also in 15:3, 23, 32, 33, 36, 40.　**15:10** Greek *disciples.*　**15:14** Greek *Symeon.*
15:16 Or *kingdom;* Greek reads *tent.*　**15:16-18** Amos 9:11-12 (Greek version); Isa 45:21.

¹⁹"And so my judgment is that we should not make it difficult for the Gentiles who are turning to God. ²⁰Instead, we should write and tell them to abstain from eating food offered to idols, from sexual immorality, from eating the meat of strangled animals, and from consuming blood. ²¹For these laws of Moses have been preached in Jewish synagogues in every city on every Sabbath for many generations."

The Letter for Gentile Believers

²²Then the apostles and elders together with the whole church in Jerusalem chose delegates, and they sent them to Antioch of Syria with Paul and Barnabas to report on this decision. The men chosen were two of the church leaders*—Judas (also called Barsabbas) and Silas. ²³This is the letter they took with them:

"This letter is from the apostles and elders, your brothers in Jerusalem. It is written to the Gentile believers in Antioch, Syria, and Cilicia. Greetings!

²⁴"We understand that some men from here have troubled you and upset you with their teaching, but we did not send them! ²⁵So we decided, having come to complete agreement, to send you official representatives, along with our beloved Barnabas and Paul, ²⁶who have risked their lives for the name of our Lord Jesus Christ. ²⁷We are sending Judas and Silas to confirm what we have decided concerning your question.

²⁸"For it seemed good to the Holy Spirit and to us to lay no greater burden on you than these few requirements: ²⁹You must abstain from eating food offered to idols, from consuming blood or the meat of strangled animals, and from sexual immorality. If you do this, you will do well. Farewell."

³⁰The messengers went at once to Antioch, where they called a general meeting of the believers and delivered the letter. ³¹And there was great joy throughout the church that day as they read this encouraging message.

³²Then Judas and Silas, both being prophets, spoke at length to the believers, encouraging and strengthening their faith. ³³They stayed for a while, and then the believers sent them back to the church in Jerusalem with a blessing of peace.* ³⁵Paul and Barnabas stayed in Antioch. They and many others taught and preached the word of the Lord there.

Paul and Barnabas Separate

³⁶After some time Paul said to Barnabas, "Let's go back and visit each city where we previously preached the word of the Lord, to see how the new believers are doing." ³⁷Barnabas agreed and wanted to take along John Mark. ³⁸But Paul disagreed strongly, since John Mark had deserted them in Pamphylia and had not continued with them in their work. ³⁹Their disagreement was so sharp that they separated. Barnabas took John Mark with him and sailed for Cyprus. ⁴⁰Paul chose Silas, and as he left, the believers entrusted him to the Lord's gracious care. ⁴¹Then he traveled throughout Syria and Cilicia, strengthening the churches there.

16 Paul's Second Missionary Journey

Paul went first to Derbe and then to Lystra, where there was a young disciple named Timothy. His mother was a Jewish believer, but his father was a Greek. ²Timothy was well thought of by the believers* in Lystra and Iconium, ³so Paul wanted him to join them on their journey. In deference to the Jews of the area, he arranged for Timothy to be circumcised before they left, for everyone knew that his father was a Greek. ⁴Then they went from town to town, instructing the believers to follow the decisions made by the apostles and elders in Jerusalem. ⁵So the churches were strengthened in their faith and grew larger every day.

A Call from Macedonia

⁶Next Paul and Silas traveled through the area of Phrygia and Galatia, because the Holy Spirit had prevented them from preaching the word in the province of Asia at that time. ⁷Then coming to the borders of Mysia, they headed north for the province of Bithynia,* but again the Spirit of Jesus

---

15:22 Greek *were leaders among the brothers.*   15:33 Some manuscripts add verse 34, *But Silas decided to stay there.*   16:2 Greek *brothers;* also in 16:40.   16:6-7 *Phrygia, Galatia, Asia, Mysia,* and *Bithynia* were all districts in what is now Turkey.

When Christians Behave Badly

ACTS 15:36-40

Outreach

Watch the news and it won't take long before you see a headline about a self-proclaimed Christian doing something atrocious, cruel, ridiculous, offensive, hypocritical, or just plain embarrassing. News stories like those instinctively drive me to disassociate myself. *Well, I'm certainly not like "those Christians"!*

But lately the stories of "those Christians" have made me uncomfortable, because they've challenged me to consider my own life. Might I, too, be unknowingly buying into or projecting some of those same mistaken ideas and behaviors sometimes associated with Christianity?

How often have *I* been guilty of treating non-Christians as if they are morally or ethically inferior to believers? How might *I* be falling into the trap of viewing some sins as worse than others? How might *I* be communicating the idea that Christians earn a "spiritual rank" through works? Might *I* be guilty of an unteachable, superior attitude—thinking I've "arrived" spiritually?

I wonder how many people have noticed my bad attitudes, bad facial expressions, and maybe even bad actions, and said, "*That's* how Christians behave? I don't want to be like them." I'm actually grateful for the latest embarrassing news I've recently heard about obnoxious behavior by self-proclaimed Christians—because their bad behavior has helped me recognize behavior *I* need to change. The next time I read a story or hear a conversation about "those Christian jerks," I'll try not to nod smugly in agreement. Instead I'll listen carefully. After all, they might just be talking about me.

—*Holly Vicente Robaina*

For more on outreach, see reading at Acts 23:1-11.

did not allow them to go there. ⁸So instead, they went on through Mysia to the seaport of Troas.

⁹That night Paul had a vision: A man from Macedonia in northern Greece was standing there, pleading with him, "Come over to Macedonia and help us!" ¹⁰So we* decided to leave for Macedonia at once, having concluded that God was calling us to preach the Good News there.

Lydia of Philippi Believes in Jesus

¹¹We boarded a boat at Troas and sailed straight across to the island of Samothrace, and the next day we landed at Neapolis. ¹²From there we reached Philippi, a major city of that district of Macedonia and a Roman colony. And we stayed there several days.

¹³On the Sabbath we went a little way outside the city to a riverbank, where we thought people would be meeting for prayer, and we sat down to speak with some women who had gathered there. ¹⁴One of them was Lydia from Thyatira, a merchant of expensive purple cloth, who worshiped God. As she listened to us, the Lord opened her heart, and she accepted what Paul was saying. ¹⁵She was baptized along with other members of her household, and she asked us to be her guests. "If you agree that I am a true believer in the Lord," she said, "come

---

16:10 Luke, the writer of this book, here joined Paul and accompanied him on his journey.

and stay at my home." And she urged us until we agreed.

Paul and Silas in Prison

¹⁶One day as we were going down to the place of prayer, we met a demon-possessed slave girl. She was a fortune-teller who earned a lot of money for her masters. ¹⁷She followed Paul and the rest of us, shouting, "These men are servants of the Most High God, and they have come to tell you how to be saved."

¹⁸This went on day after day until Paul got so exasperated that he turned and said to the demon within her, "I command you in the name of Jesus Christ to come out of her." And instantly it left her.

¹⁹Her masters' hopes of wealth were now shattered, so they grabbed Paul and Silas and dragged them before the authorities at the marketplace. ²⁰"The whole city is in an uproar because of these Jews!" they shouted to the city officials. ²¹"They are teaching

Lydia: An Outpouring of Hospitality

ACTS 16:11-15

Lydia was a successful businesswoman in Philippi—a dealer in the renowned purple-dyed cloth of the region. She was likely prominent, well known, and respected in her city (Acts 17:4, 12). Rather than participate in the dominant pagan worship of her culture, Lydia "worshiped God" (Acts 16:14) as a Gentile convert to Judaism.

When Paul and Silas sat with Lydia and her friends near the riverbank outside their city, God "opened her heart" (16:14) to the gospel and she believed. She and her entire household committed their lives to Christ and were baptized.

Lydia's *immediate* response to her new life in Christ was to urge Paul and Silas to be her guests. She suddenly viewed her home and possessions in a different light—as resources that could be used by God to help build his church. She saw a need as she looked at Paul and his travel-worn missionary team, and she instinctively sought to meet it.

Scripture doesn't tell us that Lydia prepared a fabulous meal for Paul and his team (though she might have), or that her home was perfectly decorated for guests (though it could have been). Rather, Lydia's hospitality was expressed in her sincere openness to God; she exemplified a readiness to use her home and possessions to minister to those in need.

Lydia's hospitality extended beyond Paul and Silas to encompass the entire new and growing Christian community in Philippi. Scholars believe that her house served as home-base for the Philippian church for quite some time. Paul and Silas returned to Lydia's house after they were imprisoned (Acts 16:40) and possibly many more times (Acts 20:1, 6; 1 Timothy 1:3) to visit and encourage the Christians there.

Perhaps what's so compelling about Lydia's hospitality is its instantaneous quality, resulting directly from her new faith in Jesus. Hospitality was an immediate fruit in Lydia's life—and it should similarly be evident in ours. When we believe in Christ, something changes in us: our eyes see the needs of others, our hearts begin to care as God cares, and our homes become places of ministry.

—*Kelli B. Trujillo*

For more on hospitality, see reading at Romans 12:10-13.

customs that are illegal for us Romans to practice."

²²A mob quickly formed against Paul and Silas, and the city officials ordered them stripped and beaten with wooden rods. ²³They were severely beaten, and then they were thrown into prison. The jailer was ordered to make sure they didn't escape. ²⁴So the jailer put them into the inner dungeon and clamped their feet in the stocks.

²⁵Around midnight Paul and Silas were praying and singing hymns to God, and the other prisoners were listening. ²⁶Suddenly, there was a massive earthquake, and the prison was shaken to its foundations. All the doors immediately flew open, and the chains of every prisoner fell off! ²⁷The jailer woke up to see the prison doors wide open. He assumed the prisoners had escaped, so he drew his sword to kill himself. ²⁸But Paul shouted to him, "Stop! Don't kill yourself! We are all here!"

²⁹The jailer called for lights and ran to the dungeon and fell down trembling before Paul and Silas. ³⁰Then he brought them out and asked, "Sirs, what must I do to be saved?"

³¹They replied, "Believe in the Lord Jesus and you will be saved, along with everyone in your household." ³²And they shared the word of the Lord with him and with all who lived in his household. ³³Even at that hour of the night, the jailer cared for them and washed their wounds. Then he and everyone in his household were immediately baptized. ³⁴He brought them into his house and set a meal before them, and he and his entire household rejoiced because they all believed in God.

³⁵The next morning the city officials sent the police to tell the jailer, "Let those men go!" ³⁶So the jailer told Paul, "The city officials have said you and Silas are free to leave. Go in peace."

³⁷But Paul replied, "They have publicly beaten us without a trial and put us in prison—and we are Roman citizens. So now they want us to leave secretly? Certainly not! Let them come themselves to release us!"

³⁸When the police reported this, the city officials were alarmed to learn that Paul and Silas were Roman citizens. ³⁹So they came to the jail and apologized to them. Then they brought them out and begged them to leave the city. ⁴⁰When Paul and Silas left the prison, they returned to the home of Lydia. There they met with the believers and encouraged them once more. Then they left town.

17 Paul Preaches in Thessalonica

Paul and Silas then traveled through the towns of Amphipolis and Apollonia and came to Thessalonica, where there was a Jewish synagogue. ²As was Paul's custom, he went to the synagogue service, and for three Sabbaths in a row he used the Scriptures to reason with the people. ³He explained the prophecies and proved that the Messiah must suffer and rise from the dead. He said, "This Jesus I'm telling you about is the Messiah." ⁴Some of the Jews who listened were persuaded and joined Paul and Silas, along with many God-fearing Greek men and quite a few prominent women.*

⁵But some of the Jews were jealous, so they gathered some troublemakers from the marketplace to form a mob and start a riot. They attacked the home of Jason, searching for Paul and Silas so they could drag them out to the crowd.* ⁶Not finding them there, they dragged out Jason and some of the other believers* instead and took them before the city council. "Paul and Silas have caused trouble all over the world," they shouted, "and now they are here disturbing our city, too. ⁷And Jason has welcomed them into his home. They are all guilty of treason against Caesar, for they profess allegiance to another king, named Jesus."

⁸The people of the city, as well as the city council, were thrown into turmoil by these reports. ⁹So the officials forced Jason and the other believers to post bond, and then they released them.

Paul and Silas in Berea

¹⁰That very night the believers sent Paul and Silas to Berea. When they arrived

---

17:4 Some manuscripts read *quite a few of the wives of the leading men.* **17:5** Or *the city council.* **17:6** Greek *brothers;* also in 17:10, 14.

there, they went to the Jewish synagogue. [11] And the people of Berea were more open-minded than those in Thessalonica, and they listened eagerly to Paul's message. They searched the Scriptures day after day to see if Paul and Silas were teaching the truth. [12] As a result, many Jews believed, as did many of the prominent Greek women and men.

[13] But when some Jews in Thessalonica learned that Paul was preaching the word of God in Berea, they went there and stirred up trouble. [14] The believers acted at once, sending Paul on to the coast, while Silas and Timothy remained behind. [15] Those escorting Paul went with him all the way to Athens; then they returned to Berea with instructions for Silas and Timothy to hurry and join him.

Paul Preaches in Athens

[16] While Paul was waiting for them in Athens, he was deeply troubled by all the idols he saw everywhere in the city. [17] He went to the synagogue to reason with the Jews and the God-fearing Gentiles, and he spoke daily in the public square to all who happened to be there.

[18] He also had a debate with some of the Epicurean and Stoic philosophers. When he told them about Jesus and his resurrection, they said, "What's this babbler trying to say with these strange ideas he's picked up?" Others said, "He seems to be preaching about some foreign gods."

[19] Then they took him to the high council of the city.* "Come and tell us about this new teaching," they said. [20] "You are saying some rather strange things, and we want to know what it's all about." [21] (It should be explained that all the Athenians as well as the foreigners in Athens seemed to spend all their time discussing the latest ideas.)

[22] So Paul, standing before the council,* addressed them as follows: "Men of Athens, I notice that you are very religious in every way, [23] for as I was walking along I saw your many shrines. And one of your altars had this inscription on it: 'To an Unknown

God.' This God, whom you worship without knowing, is the one I'm telling you about.

[24] "He is the God who made the world and everything in it. Since he is Lord of heaven and earth, he doesn't live in man-made temples, [25] and human hands can't serve his needs—for he has no needs. He himself gives life and breath to everything, and he satisfies every need. [26] From one man* he created all the nations throughout the whole earth. He decided beforehand when they should rise and fall, and he determined their boundaries.

[27] "His purpose was for the nations to seek after God and perhaps feel their way toward him and find him—though he is not far from any one of us. [28] For in him we live and move and exist. As some of your* own poets have said, 'We are his offspring.' [29] And since this is true, we shouldn't think of God as an idol designed by craftsmen from gold or silver or stone.

[30] "God overlooked people's ignorance about these things in earlier times, but now he commands everyone everywhere to repent of their sins and turn to him. [31] For he has set a day for judging the world with justice by the man he has appointed, and he proved to everyone who this is by raising him from the dead."

[32] When they heard Paul speak about the resurrection of the dead, some laughed in contempt, but others said, "We want to hear more about this later." [33] That ended Paul's discussion with them, [34] but some joined him and became believers. Among them were Dionysius, a member of the council,* a woman named Damaris, and others with them.

18 Paul Meets Priscilla and Aquila in Corinth

Then Paul left Athens and went to Corinth.* [2] There he became acquainted with a Jew named Aquila, born in Pontus, who had recently arrived from Italy with his wife, Priscilla. They had left Italy when Claudius Caesar deported all Jews from Rome. [3] Paul lived and worked with them, for they were tentmakers* just as he was.

17:19 Or the most learned society of philosophers in the city. Greek reads the Areopagus.   17:22 Traditionally rendered standing in the middle of Mars Hill; Greek reads standing in the middle of the Areopagus.   17:26 Greek From one; other manuscripts read From one blood.   17:28 Some manuscripts read our.   17:34 Greek an Areopagite.   18:1 Athens and Corinth were major cities in Achaia, the region in the southern portion of the Greek peninsula.   18:3 Or leatherworkers.

Does God Need Our Worship?
ACTS 17:16–34

Does God need our love and praise? Is he lonely? And are we an important piece of the puzzle for him to be fulfilled within himself?

No. God is perfect, complete, and entirely self-existent. There is no deficiency within his inner being.

Paul addressed this issue on the Areopagus in Athens in his debate with philosophers who believed God needed the world. Paul pointed out that God is the Creator of the world and "human hands can't serve his needs—for he has no needs. He himself gives life and breath to everything, and he satisfies every need" (Acts 17:25). Paul believed that God has no inner unmet needs because he is the Source of all things. To put it in the form of a mathematical equation, one can say that God minus the world equals God, but the world minus God equals zero. As Søren Kierkegaard once remarked with irony, it would be embarrassing if, after having created the world, God should become dependent upon it.

Why then did God create the world if he did not need it? The biblical answer is that God was motivated by love and not by inner need (John 3:16; 1 John 4:8). It is the nature of love to give and to share, and creation reflects the superabundance and overflowing nature of God as love.

Because God is love, he desires our worship. As a father loves his children, God derives infinite joy when we praise and worship him. It is not just for our sake that God wants to be worshiped; he takes delight in our worship (Proverbs 15:8).

—*Laurence W. Wood*

For more on worship, see reading at Philippians 4:2–9.

⁴Each Sabbath found Paul at the synagogue, trying to convince the Jews and Greeks alike. ⁵And after Silas and Timothy came down from Macedonia, Paul spent all his time preaching the word. He testified to the Jews that Jesus was the Messiah. ⁶But when they opposed and insulted him, Paul shook the dust from his clothes and said, "Your blood is upon your own heads—I am innocent. From now on I will go preach to the Gentiles."

⁷Then he left and went to the home of Titius Justus, a Gentile who worshiped God and lived next door to the synagogue. ⁸Crispus, the leader of the synagogue, and everyone in his household believed in the Lord. Many others in Corinth also heard Paul, became believers, and were baptized.

⁹One night the Lord spoke to Paul in a vision and told him, "Don't be afraid! Speak out! Don't be silent! ¹⁰For I am with you, and no one will attack and harm you, for many people in this city belong to me." ¹¹So Paul stayed there for the next year and a half, teaching the word of God.

¹²But when Gallio became governor of Achaia, some Jews rose up together against Paul and brought him before the governor for judgment. ¹³They accused Paul of "persuading people to worship God in ways that are contrary to our law."

¹⁴But just as Paul started to make his defense, Gallio turned to Paul's accusers and said, "Listen, you Jews, if this were a case involving some wrongdoing or a serious crime, I would have a reason to accept

your case. ¹⁵But since it is merely a question of words and names and your Jewish law, take care of it yourselves. I refuse to judge such matters." ¹⁶And he threw them out of the courtroom.

¹⁷The crowd* then grabbed Sosthenes, the leader of the synagogue, and beat him right there in the courtroom. But Gallio paid no attention.

Paul Returns to Antioch of Syria

¹⁸Paul stayed in Corinth for some time after that, then said good-bye to the brothers and sisters* and went to nearby Cenchrea. There he shaved his head according to Jewish custom, marking the end of a vow. Then he set sail for Syria, taking Priscilla and Aquila with him.

¹⁹They stopped first at the port of Ephesus, where Paul left the others behind. While he was there, he went to the synagogue to reason with the Jews. ²⁰They asked him to stay longer, but he declined. ²¹As he left, however, he said, "I will come back later,* God willing." Then he set sail from Ephesus. ²²The next stop was at the port of Caesarea. From there he went up and visited the church at Jerusalem* and then went back to Antioch.

²³After spending some time in Antioch, Paul went back through Galatia and Phrygia, visiting and strengthening all the believers.*

Apollos Instructed at Ephesus

²⁴Meanwhile, a Jew named Apollos, an eloquent speaker who knew the Scriptures well, had arrived in Ephesus from Alexandria in Egypt. ²⁵He had been taught the way of the Lord, and he taught others about Jesus with an enthusiastic spirit* and with accuracy. However, he knew only about John's baptism. ²⁶When Priscilla and Aquila heard him preaching boldly in the synagogue, they took him aside and explained the way of God even more accurately.

²⁷Apollos had been thinking about going to Achaia, and the brothers and sisters in Ephesus encouraged him to go. They wrote to the believers in Achaia, asking them to welcome him. When he arrived there, he proved to be of great benefit to those who, by God's grace, had believed. ²⁸He refuted the Jews with powerful arguments in public debate. Using the Scriptures, he explained to them that Jesus was the Messiah.

19 Paul's Third Missionary Journey

While Apollos was in Corinth, Paul traveled through the interior regions until he reached Ephesus, on the coast, where he found several believers.* ²"Did you receive the Holy Spirit when you believed?" he asked them.

"No," they replied, "we haven't even heard that there is a Holy Spirit."

³"Then what baptism did you experience?" he asked.

And they replied, "The baptism of John."

⁴Paul said, "John's baptism called for repentance from sin. But John himself told the people to believe in the one who would come later, meaning Jesus."

⁵As soon as they heard this, they were baptized in the name of the Lord Jesus. ⁶Then when Paul laid his hands on them, the Holy Spirit came on them, and they spoke in other tongues* and prophesied. ⁷There were about twelve men in all.

Paul Ministers in Ephesus

⁸Then Paul went to the synagogue and preached boldly for the next three months, arguing persuasively about the Kingdom of God. ⁹But some became stubborn, rejecting his message and publicly speaking against the Way. So Paul left the synagogue and took the believers with him. Then he held daily discussions at the lecture hall of Tyrannus. ¹⁰This went on for the next two years, so that people throughout the province of Asia—both Jews and Greeks—heard the word of the Lord.

¹¹God gave Paul the power to perform unusual miracles. ¹²When handkerchiefs or aprons that had merely touched his skin were placed on sick people, they were healed of their diseases, and evil spirits were expelled.

¹³A group of Jews was traveling from town to town casting out evil spirits. They

---

18:17 Greek *Everyone;* other manuscripts read *All the Greeks.* **18:18** Greek *brothers;* also in 18:27. **18:21** Some manuscripts read *"I must by all means be at Jerusalem for the upcoming festival, but I will come back later."* **18:22** Greek *the church.* **18:23** Greek *disciples;* also in 18:27. **18:25** Or *with enthusiasm in the Spirit.* **19:1** Greek *disciples;* also in 19:9, 30. **19:6** Or *in other languages.*

tried to use the name of the Lord Jesus in their incantation, saying, "I command you in the name of Jesus, whom Paul preaches, to come out!" [14]Seven sons of Sceva, a leading priest, were doing this. [15]But one time when they tried it, the evil spirit replied, "I know Jesus, and I know Paul, but who are you?" [16]Then the man with the evil spirit leaped on them, overpowered them, and attacked them with such violence that they fled from the house, naked and battered.

[17]The story of what happened spread quickly all through Ephesus, to Jews and Greeks alike. A solemn fear descended on the city, and the name of the Lord Jesus was greatly honored. [18]Many who became believers confessed their sinful practices. [19]A number of them who had been practicing sorcery brought their incantation books and burned them at a public bonfire. The value of the books was several million dollars.* [20]So the message about

Priscilla: Invested in Others

ACTS 18:24–28

The New Testament church's Priscilla was a woman who devoted her life to disciple making. She and her husband, Aquila, were a Jewish couple who moved to Corinth after being expelled from Rome. Priscilla and Aquila worked alongside Paul in planting the church in Corinth; then they moved to Ephesus and built the church there while Paul continued on to Antioch. One unusual thing about this couple is that twice in Acts (18:18, 26) and in two of Paul's letters (Romans 16:3; 2 Timothy 4:19), Priscilla is named *first*, before her husband. This indicates that Priscilla had a profound and significant role as she and Aquila labored together for the cause of Christ.

Acts 18:24–28 gives us a snapshot of their ministry. They met Apollos, an enthusiastic believer with persuasive teaching gifts, but whose understanding of some key theological issues was incomplete. Priscilla and Aquila worked with Apollos, meeting with him to explain "the way of God even more accurately" (18:26). They took a man of talent and heart and led him into greater understanding and spiritual maturity. As a result of their investment and mentorship in his life, Apollos grew to become a significant apologist for the early church (18:28).

Priscilla is a model of the power of disciple making: she exercised her gift of leadership and used it to pass on the truth of Christ to other men and women. She saw potential in leaders like Apollos and invested heavily in them. She hosted a church in her home (Romans 16:5). Scripture paints a picture of her as someone who not only led by example but also got involved in others' lives—who walked alongside her brothers and sisters, helping them grow as Jesus' disciples.

Paul acknowledged the fruit of her work when he declared that "all of the Gentile churches" were grateful for the ministry of Priscilla and Aquila (Romans 16:4). Like Priscilla, may we too live as women who walk alongside others and point them toward the way of Christ.

—*Nicole Unice*

For more on mentoring, see reading at Romans 1:8–12.

19:19 Greek *50,000 pieces of silver,* each of which was the equivalent of a day's wage.

the Lord spread widely and had a powerful effect.

²¹ Afterward Paul felt compelled by the Spirit* to go over to Macedonia and Achaia before going to Jerusalem. "And after that," he said, "I must go on to Rome!" ²² He sent his two assistants, Timothy and Erastus, ahead to Macedonia while he stayed awhile longer in the province of Asia.

The Riot in Ephesus

²³ About that time, serious trouble developed in Ephesus concerning the Way. ²⁴ It began with Demetrius, a silversmith who had a large business manufacturing silver shrines of the Greek goddess Artemis.* He kept many craftsmen busy. ²⁵ He called them together, along with others employed in similar trades, and addressed them as follows:

"Gentlemen, you know that our wealth comes from this business. ²⁶ But as you have seen and heard, this man Paul has persuaded many people that handmade gods aren't really gods at all. And he's done this not only here in Ephesus but throughout the entire province! ²⁷ Of course, I'm not just talking about the loss of public respect for our business. I'm also concerned that the temple of the great goddess Artemis will lose its influence and that Artemis—this magnificent goddess worshiped throughout the province of Asia and all around the world—will be robbed of her great prestige!"

²⁸ At this their anger boiled, and they began shouting, "Great is Artemis of the Ephesians!" ²⁹ Soon the whole city was filled with confusion. Everyone rushed to the amphitheater, dragging along Gaius and Aristarchus, who were Paul's traveling companions from Macedonia. ³⁰ Paul wanted to go in, too, but the believers wouldn't let him. ³¹ Some of the officials of the province, friends of Paul, also sent a message to him, begging him not to risk his life by entering the amphitheater.

³² Inside, the people were all shouting, some one thing and some another. Everything was in confusion. In fact, most of them didn't even know why they were there.

³³ The Jews in the crowd pushed Alexander forward and told him to explain the situation. He motioned for silence and tried to speak. ³⁴ But when the crowd realized he was a Jew, they started shouting again and kept it up for about two hours: "Great is Artemis of the Ephesians! Great is Artemis of the Ephesians!"

³⁵ At last the mayor was able to quiet them down enough to speak. "Citizens of Ephesus," he said. "Everyone knows that Ephesus is the official guardian of the temple of the great Artemis, whose image fell down to us from heaven. ³⁶ Since this is an undeniable fact, you should stay calm and not do anything rash. ³⁷ You have brought these men here, but they have stolen nothing from the temple and have not spoken against our goddess.

³⁸ "If Demetrius and the craftsmen have a case against them, the courts are in session and the officials can hear the case at once. Let them make formal charges. ³⁹ And if there are complaints about other matters, they can be settled in a legal assembly. ⁴⁰ I am afraid we are in danger of being charged with rioting by the Roman government, since there is no cause for all this commotion. And if Rome demands an explanation, we won't know what to say." ⁴¹*Then he dismissed them, and they dispersed.

20 Paul Goes to Macedonia and Greece

When the uproar was over, Paul sent for the believers* and encouraged them. Then he said good-bye and left for Macedonia. ² While there, he encouraged the believers in all the towns he passed through. Then he traveled down to Greece, ³ where he stayed for three months. He was preparing to sail back to Syria when he discovered a plot by some Jews against his life, so he decided to return through Macedonia.

⁴ Several men were traveling with him. They were Sopater son of Pyrrhus from Berea; Aristarchus and Secundus from Thessalonica; Gaius from Derbe; Timothy; and Tychicus and Trophimus from the province of Asia. ⁵ They went on ahead and waited for us at Troas. ⁶ After the Passover*

19:21 Or decided in his spirit.   19:24 Artemis is otherwise known as Diana.   19:41 Some translations include verse 41 as part of verse 40.
20:1 Greek disciples.   20:6 Greek the days of unleavened bread.

ended, we boarded a ship at Philippi in Macedonia and five days later joined them in Troas, where we stayed a week.

Paul's Final Visit to Troas

⁷On the first day of the week, we gathered with the local believers to share in the Lord's Supper.* Paul was preaching to them, and since he was leaving the next day, he kept talking until midnight. ⁸The upstairs room where we met was lighted with many flickering lamps. ⁹As Paul spoke on and on, a young man named Eutychus, sitting on the windowsill, became very drowsy. Finally, he fell sound asleep and dropped three stories to his death below. ¹⁰Paul went down, bent over him, and took him into his arms. "Don't worry," he said, "he's alive!" ¹¹Then they all went back upstairs, shared in the Lord's Supper,* and ate together. Paul continued talking to them until dawn, and then he left. ¹²Meanwhile, the young man was taken home unhurt, and everyone was greatly relieved.

Paul Meets the Ephesian Elders

¹³Paul went by land to Assos, where he had arranged for us to join him, while we traveled by ship. ¹⁴He joined us there, and we sailed together to Mitylene. ¹⁵The next day we sailed past the island of Kios. The following day we crossed to the island of Samos, and* a day later we arrived at Miletus.

¹⁶Paul had decided to sail on past Ephesus, for he didn't want to spend any more time in the province of Asia. He was hurrying to get to Jerusalem, if possible, in time for the Festival of Pentecost. ¹⁷But when we landed at Miletus, he sent a message to the elders of the church at Ephesus, asking them to come and meet him.

¹⁸When they arrived he declared, "You know that from the day I set foot in the province of Asia until now ¹⁹I have done the Lord's work humbly and with many tears. I have endured the trials that came to me from the plots of the Jews. ²⁰I never shrank back from telling you what you needed to hear, either publicly or in your homes. ²¹I

have had one message for Jews and Greeks alike—the necessity of repenting from sin and turning to God, and of having faith in our Lord Jesus.

²²"And now I am bound by the Spirit* to go to Jerusalem. I don't know what awaits me, ²³except that the Holy Spirit tells me in city after city that jail and suffering lie ahead. ²⁴But my life is worth nothing to me unless I use it for finishing the work assigned me by the Lord Jesus—the work of telling others the Good News about the wonderful grace of God.

²⁵"And now I know that none of you to whom I have preached the Kingdom will ever see me again. ²⁶I declare today that I have been faithful. If anyone suffers eternal death, it's not my fault,* ²⁷for I didn't shrink from declaring all that God wants you to know.

²⁸"So guard yourselves and God's people. Feed and shepherd God's flock—his church, purchased with his own blood*—over which the Holy Spirit has appointed you as elders.* ²⁹I know that false teachers, like vicious wolves, will come in among you after I leave, not sparing the flock. ³⁰Even some men from your own group will rise up and distort the truth in order to draw a following. ³¹Watch out! Remember the three years I was with you—my constant watch and care over you night and day, and my many tears for you.

³²"And now I entrust you to God and the message of his grace that is able to build you up and give you an inheritance with all those he has set apart for himself.

³³"I have never coveted anyone's silver or gold or fine clothes. ³⁴You know that these hands of mine have worked to supply my own needs and even the needs of those who were with me. ³⁵And I have been a constant example of how you can help those in need by working hard. You should remember the words of the Lord Jesus: 'It is more blessed to give than to receive.'"

³⁶When he had finished speaking, he knelt and prayed with them. ³⁷They all cried as they embraced and kissed him good-bye. ³⁸They were sad most of all because he had

---

20:7 Greek to break bread. 20:11 Greek broke the bread. 20:15 Some manuscripts read and having stayed at Trogyllium. 20:22 Or by my spirit, or by an inner compulsion; Greek reads by the spirit. 20:26 Greek I am innocent of the blood of all. 20:28a Or with the blood of his own [Son]. 20:28b Greek overseers.

said that they would never see him again. Then they escorted him down to the ship.

21 Paul's Journey to Jerusalem

After saying farewell to the Ephesian elders, we sailed straight to the island of Cos. The next day we reached Rhodes and then went to Patara. ²There we boarded a ship sailing for Phoenicia. ³We sighted the island of Cyprus, passed it on our left, and landed at the harbor of Tyre, in Syria, where the ship was to unload its cargo.

⁴We went ashore, found the local believers,* and stayed with them a week. These believers prophesied through the Holy Spirit that Paul should not go on to Jerusalem. ⁵When we returned to the ship at the end of the week, the entire congregation, including women* and children, left the city and came down to the shore with us. There we knelt, prayed, ⁶and said our farewells. Then we went aboard, and they returned home.

⁷The next stop after leaving Tyre was Ptolemais, where we greeted the brothers and sisters* and stayed for one day. ⁸The next day we went on to Caesarea and stayed at the home of Philip the Evangelist, one of the seven men who had been chosen to distribute food. ⁹He had four unmarried daughters who had the gift of prophecy.

¹⁰Several days later a man named Agabus, who also had the gift of prophecy, arrived from Judea. ¹¹He came over, took Paul's belt, and bound his own feet and hands with it. Then he said, "The Holy Spirit declares, 'So shall the owner of this belt be bound by the Jewish leaders in Jerusalem and turned over to the Gentiles.'" ¹²When we heard this, we and the local believers all begged Paul not to go on to Jerusalem.

¹³But he said, "Why all this weeping? You are breaking my heart! I am ready not only to be jailed at Jerusalem but even to die for the sake of the Lord Jesus." ¹⁴When it was clear that we couldn't persuade him, we gave up and said, "The Lord's will be done."

Paul Arrives at Jerusalem

¹⁵After this we packed our things and left for Jerusalem. ¹⁶Some believers from Caesarea accompanied us, and they took us to the home of Mnason, a man originally from Cyprus and one of the early believers. ¹⁷When we arrived, the brothers and sisters in Jerusalem welcomed us warmly.

¹⁸The next day Paul went with us to meet with James, and all the elders of the Jerusalem church were present. ¹⁹After greeting them, Paul gave a detailed account of the things God had accomplished among the Gentiles through his ministry.

²⁰After hearing this, they praised God. And then they said, "You know, dear brother, how many thousands of Jews have also believed, and they all follow the law of Moses very seriously. ²¹But the Jewish believers here in Jerusalem have been told that you are teaching all the Jews who live among the Gentiles to turn their backs on the laws of Moses. They've heard that you teach them not to circumcise their children or follow other Jewish customs. ²²What should we do? They will certainly hear that you have come.

²³"Here's what we want you to do. We have four men here who have completed their vow. ²⁴Go with them to the Temple and join them in the purification ceremony, paying for them to have their heads ritually shaved. Then everyone will know that the rumors are all false and that you yourself observe the Jewish laws.

²⁵"As for the Gentile believers, they should do what we already told them in a letter: They should abstain from eating food offered to idols, from consuming blood or the meat of strangled animals, and from sexual immorality."

Paul Is Arrested

²⁶So Paul went to the Temple the next day with the other men. They had already started the purification ritual, so he publicly announced the date when their vows would end and sacrifices would be offered for each of them.

²⁷The seven days were almost ended when some Jews from the province of Asia saw Paul in the Temple and roused a mob against him. They grabbed him, ²⁸yelling, "Men of Israel, help us! This is the man who preaches against our people everywhere and tells everybody to disobey the Jewish laws. He speaks against the Temple—and

21:4 Greek disciples; also in 21:16.   21:5 Or wives.   21:7 Greek brothers; also in 21:17.

even defiles this holy place by bringing in Gentiles.*" ²⁹(For earlier that day they had seen him in the city with Trophimus, a Gentile from Ephesus,* and they assumed Paul had taken him into the Temple.)

³⁰The whole city was rocked by these accusations, and a great riot followed. Paul was grabbed and dragged out of the Temple, and immediately the gates were closed behind him. ³¹As they were trying to kill him, word reached the commander of the Roman regiment that all Jerusalem was in an uproar. ³²He immediately called out his soldiers and officers* and ran down among the crowd. When the mob saw the commander and the troops coming, they stopped beating Paul.

³³Then the commander arrested him and ordered him bound with two chains. He asked the crowd who he was and what he had done. ³⁴Some shouted one thing and some another. Since he couldn't find out the truth in all the uproar and confusion, he ordered that Paul be taken to the fortress. ³⁵As Paul reached the stairs, the mob grew so violent the soldiers had to lift him to their shoulders to protect him. ³⁶And the crowd followed behind, shouting, "Kill him, kill him!"

Paul Speaks to the Crowd

³⁷As Paul was about to be taken inside, he said to the commander, "May I have a word with you?"

"Do you know Greek?" the commander asked, surprised. ³⁸"Aren't you the Egyptian who led a rebellion some time ago and took 4,000 members of the Assassins out into the desert?"

³⁹"No," Paul replied, "I am a Jew and a citizen of Tarsus in Cilicia, which is an important city. Please, let me talk to these people." ⁴⁰The commander agreed, so Paul stood on the stairs and motioned to the people to be quiet. Soon a deep silence enveloped the crowd, and he addressed them in their own language, Aramaic.*

22 "Brothers and esteemed fathers," Paul said, "listen to me as I offer my defense." ²When they heard him speaking in their own language,* the silence was even greater.

³Then Paul said, "I am a Jew, born in Tarsus, a city in Cilicia, and I was brought up and educated here in Jerusalem under Gamaliel. As his student, I was carefully trained in our Jewish laws and customs. I became very zealous to honor God in everything I did, just like all of you today. ⁴And I persecuted the followers of the Way, hounding some to death, arresting both men and women and throwing them in prison. ⁵The high priest and the whole council of elders can testify that this is so. For I received letters from them to our Jewish brothers in Damascus, authorizing me to bring the Christians from there to Jerusalem, in chains, to be punished.

⁶"As I was on the road, approaching Damascus about noon, a very bright light from heaven suddenly shone down around me. ⁷I fell to the ground and heard a voice saying to me, 'Saul, Saul, why are you persecuting me?'

⁸"'Who are you, lord?' I asked.

"And the voice replied, 'I am Jesus the Nazarene,* the one you are persecuting.' ⁹The people with me saw the light but didn't understand the voice speaking to me.

¹⁰"I asked, 'What should I do, Lord?'

"And the Lord told me, 'Get up and go into Damascus, and there you will be told everything you are to do.'

¹¹"I was blinded by the intense light and had to be led by the hand to Damascus by my companions. ¹²A man named Ananias lived there. He was a godly man, deeply devoted to the law, and well regarded by all the Jews of Damascus. ¹³He came and stood beside me and said, 'Brother Saul, regain your sight.' And that very moment I could see him!

¹⁴"Then he told me, 'The God of our ancestors has chosen you to know his will and to see the Righteous One and hear him speak. ¹⁵For you are to be his witness, telling everyone what you have seen and heard. ¹⁶What are you waiting for? Get up and be baptized. Have your sins washed away by calling on the name of the Lord.'

¹⁷"After I returned to Jerusalem, I was

21:28 Greek Greeks. **21:29** Greek Trophimus, the Ephesian. **21:32** Greek centurions. **21:40** Or Hebrew. **22:2** Greek in Aramaic, or in Hebrew. **22:8** Or Jesus of Nazareth.

praying in the Temple and fell into a trance. ¹⁸ I saw a vision of Jesus* saying to me, 'Hurry! Leave Jerusalem, for the people here won't accept your testimony about me.'

¹⁹ "'But Lord,' I argued, 'they certainly know that in every synagogue I imprisoned and beat those who believed in you. ²⁰ And I was in complete agreement when your witness Stephen was killed. I stood by and kept the coats they took off when they stoned him.'

²¹ "But the Lord said to me, 'Go, for I will send you far away to the Gentiles!'"

²² The crowd listened until Paul said that word. Then they all began to shout, "Away with such a fellow! He isn't fit to live!" ²³ They yelled, threw off their coats, and tossed handfuls of dust into the air.

Paul Reveals His Roman Citizenship

²⁴ The commander brought Paul inside and ordered him lashed with whips to make him confess his crime. He wanted to find out why the crowd had become so furious. ²⁵ When they tied Paul down to lash him, Paul said to the officer* standing there, "Is it legal for you to whip a Roman citizen who hasn't even been tried?"

²⁶ When the officer heard this, he went to the commander and asked, "What are you doing? This man is a Roman citizen!"

²⁷ So the commander went over and asked Paul, "Tell me, are you a Roman citizen?"

"Yes, I certainly am," Paul replied.

²⁸ "I am, too," the commander muttered, "and it cost me plenty!"

Paul answered, "But I am a citizen by birth!"

²⁹ The soldiers who were about to interrogate Paul quickly withdrew when they heard he was a Roman citizen, and the commander was frightened because he had ordered him bound and whipped.

Paul before the High Council

³⁰ The next day the commander ordered the leading priests into session with the Jewish high council.* He wanted to find out what the trouble was all about, so he released Paul to have him stand before them.

23 Gazing intently at the high council,* Paul began: "Brothers, I have always lived before God with a clear conscience!"

² Instantly Ananias the high priest commanded those close to Paul to slap him on the mouth. ³ But Paul said to him, "God will slap you, you corrupt hypocrite!* What kind of judge are you to break the law yourself by ordering me struck like that?"

⁴ Those standing near Paul said to him, "Do you dare to insult God's high priest?"

⁵ "I'm sorry, brothers. I didn't realize he was the high priest," Paul replied, "for the Scriptures say, 'You must not speak evil of any of your rulers.'*"

⁶ Paul realized that some members of the high council were Sadducees and some were Pharisees, so he shouted, "Brothers, I am a Pharisee, as were my ancestors! And I am on trial because my hope is in the resurrection of the dead!"

⁷ This divided the council—the Pharisees against the Sadducees—⁸ for the Sadducees say there is no resurrection or angels or spirits, but the Pharisees believe in all of these. ⁹ So there was a great uproar. Some of the teachers of religious law who were Pharisees jumped up and began to argue forcefully. "We see nothing wrong with him," they shouted. "Perhaps a spirit or an angel spoke to him." ¹⁰ As the conflict grew more violent, the commander was afraid they would tear Paul apart. So he ordered his soldiers to go and rescue him by force and take him back to the fortress.

¹¹ That night the Lord appeared to Paul and said, "Be encouraged, Paul. Just as you have been a witness to me here in Jerusalem, you must preach the Good News in Rome as well."

The Plan to Kill Paul

¹² The next morning a group of Jews* got together and bound themselves with an oath not to eat or drink until they had killed Paul. ¹³ There were more than forty of them in the conspiracy. ¹⁴ They went to the leading priests and elders and told them, "We have bound ourselves with an oath to eat nothing until we have killed Paul. ¹⁵ So you and the high council should ask the com-

---

22:18 Greek *him.* **22:25** Greek *the centurion;* also in 22:26. **22:30** Greek *Sanhedrin.* **23:1** Greek *Sanhedrin;* also in 23:6, 15, 20, 28. **23:3** Greek *you whitewashed wall.* **23:5** Exod 22:28. **23:12** Greek *the Jews.*

Living Missionally

ACTS 23:1–11

Our family has been reading biographies of past missionary heroes, such as Cameron Townsend (founder of Wycliffe Bible Translators) and Amy Carmichael (missionary in India who rescued thousands of children). My kids have been inspired by these stories and will often respond by saying, "I want to be a missionary someday!"

In response to these heartfelt and innocent expressions of commitment I say, "That's wonderful! But you are actually called to be a missionary right here and now."

It's easy to think of missionaries as those people who have been given the high and noble task of taking the gospel to the far reaches of the globe. But in fact the Great Commandments (Matthew 22:36–40) and the Great Commission (Matthew 28:18–20) are not restricted to missionaries. They are intended for *every* Christ-follower, professional missionary or not. We are all called to love God and others, then to be his witnesses and disciple makers to the ends of the earth.

This calling has nothing to do with giftedness, although some in the church have been given a unique role as evangelists. Although we may feel as though the mandate to be "missional" in our lifestyle is daunting, we must remember that the work God calls us to is not ours alone; we take on the challenge in partnership with God himself.

—Helen Lee

For more on outreach, see reading at Acts 23:1-11.

---

mander to bring Paul back to the council again. Pretend you want to examine his case more fully. We will kill him on the way."

¹⁶ But Paul's nephew—his sister's son—heard of their plan and went to the fortress and told Paul. ¹⁷ Paul called for one of the Roman officers* and said, "Take this young man to the commander. He has something important to tell him."

¹⁸ So the officer did, explaining, "Paul, the prisoner, called me over and asked me to bring this young man to you because he has something to tell you."

¹⁹ The commander took his hand, led him aside, and asked, "What is it you want to tell me?"

²⁰ Paul's nephew told him, "Some Jews are going to ask you to bring Paul before the high council tomorrow, pretending they want to get some more information. ²¹ But don't do it! There are more than forty men hiding along the way ready to ambush him. They have vowed not to eat or drink anything until they have killed him. They are ready now, just waiting for your consent."

²² "Don't let anyone know you told me this," the commander warned the young man.

Paul Is Sent to Caesarea

²³ Then the commander called two of his officers and ordered, "Get 200 soldiers ready to leave for Caesarea at nine o'clock tonight. Also take 200 spearmen and 70 mounted troops. ²⁴ Provide horses for Paul to ride, and

---

23:17 Greek *centurions*; also in 23:23.

get him safely to Governor Felix." ²⁵Then he wrote this letter to the governor:

²⁶"From Claudius Lysias, to his Excellency, Governor Felix: Greetings!

²⁷"This man was seized by some Jews, and they were about to kill him when I arrived with the troops. When I learned that he was a Roman citizen, I removed him to safety. ²⁸Then I took him to their high council to try to learn the basis of the accusations against him. ²⁹I soon discovered the charge was something regarding their religious law—certainly nothing worthy of imprisonment or death. ³⁰But when I was informed of a plot to kill him, I immediately sent him on to you. I have told his accusers to bring their charges before you."

³¹So that night, as ordered, the soldiers took Paul as far as Antipatris. ³²They returned to the fortress the next morning, while the mounted troops took him on to Caesarea. ³³When they arrived in Caesarea, they presented Paul and the letter to Governor Felix. ³⁴He read it and then asked Paul what province he was from. "Cilicia," Paul answered.

³⁵"I will hear your case myself when your accusers arrive," the governor told him. Then the governor ordered him kept in the prison at Herod's headquarters.*

24 Paul Appears before Felix

Five days later Ananias, the high priest, arrived with some of the Jewish elders and the lawyer* Tertullus, to present their case against Paul to the governor. ²When Paul was called in, Tertullus presented the charges against Paul in the following address to the governor:

"You have provided a long period of peace for us Jews and with foresight have enacted reforms for us. ³For all of this, Your Excellency, we are very grateful to you. ⁴But I don't want to bore you, so please give me your attention for only a moment. ⁵We have found this man to be a troublemaker who is constantly stirring up riots among the Jews all over the world. He is a ring-

leader of the cult known as the Nazarenes. ⁶Furthermore, he was trying to desecrate the Temple when we arrested him.* ⁸You can find out the truth of our accusations by examining him yourself." ⁹Then the other Jews chimed in, declaring that everything Tertullus said was true.

¹⁰The governor then motioned for Paul to speak. Paul said, "I know, sir, that you have been a judge of Jewish affairs for many years, so I gladly present my defense before you. ¹¹You can quickly discover that I arrived in Jerusalem no more than twelve days ago to worship at the Temple. ¹²My accusers never found me arguing with anyone in the Temple, nor stirring up a riot in any synagogue or on the streets of the city. ¹³These men cannot prove the things they accuse me of doing.

¹⁴"But I admit that I follow the Way, which they call a cult. I worship the God of our ancestors, and I firmly believe the Jewish law and everything written in the prophets. ¹⁵I have the same hope in God that these men have, that he will raise both the righteous and the unrighteous. ¹⁶Because of this, I always try to maintain a clear conscience before God and all people.

¹⁷"After several years away, I returned to Jerusalem with money to aid my people and to offer sacrifices to God. ¹⁸My accusers saw me in the Temple as I was completing a purification ceremony. There was no crowd around me and no rioting. ¹⁹But some Jews from the province of Asia were there—and they ought to be here to bring charges if they have anything against me! ²⁰Ask these men here what crime the Jewish high council* found me guilty of, ²¹except for the one time I shouted out, 'I am on trial before you today because I believe in the resurrection of the dead!'"

²²At that point Felix, who was quite familiar with the Way, adjourned the hearing and said, "Wait until Lysias, the garrison commander, arrives. Then I will decide the case." ²³He ordered an officer* to keep Paul in custody but to give him some freedom and allow his friends to visit him and take care of his needs.

23:35 Greek Herod's Praetorium. 24:1 Greek some elders and an orator. 24:6 Some manuscripts add an expanded conclusion to verse 6, all of verse 7, and an additional phrase in verse 8: We would have judged him by our law, ⁷but Lysias, the commander of the garrison, came and violently took him away from us, ⁸commanding his accusers to come before you. 24:20 Greek Sanhedrin. 24:23 Greek a centurion.

²⁴A few days later Felix came back with his wife, Drusilla, who was Jewish. Sending for Paul, they listened as he told them about faith in Christ Jesus. ²⁵As he reasoned with them about righteousness and self-control and the coming day of judgment, Felix became frightened. "Go away for now," he replied. "When it is more convenient, I'll call for you again." ²⁶He also hoped that Paul would bribe him, so he sent for him quite often and talked with him.

²⁷After two years went by in this way, Felix was succeeded by Porcius Festus. And because Felix wanted to gain favor with the Jewish people, he left Paul in prison.

25 Paul Appears before Festus

Three days after Festus arrived in Caesarea to take over his new responsibilities, he left for Jerusalem, ²where the leading priests and other Jewish leaders met with him and made their accusations against Paul. ³They asked Festus as a favor to transfer Paul to Jerusalem (planning to ambush and kill him on the way). ⁴But Festus replied that Paul was at Caesarea and he himself would be returning there soon. ⁵So he said, "Those of you in authority can return with me. If Paul has done anything wrong, you can make your accusations."

⁶About eight or ten days later Festus returned to Caesarea, and on the following day he took his seat in court and ordered that Paul be brought in. ⁷When Paul arrived, the Jewish leaders from Jerusalem gathered around and made many serious accusations they couldn't prove.

⁸Paul denied the charges. "I am not guilty of any crime against the Jewish laws or the Temple or the Roman government," he said.

⁹Then Festus, wanting to please the Jews, asked him, "Are you willing to go to Jerusalem and stand trial before me there?"

¹⁰But Paul replied, "No! This is the official Roman court, so I ought to be tried right here. You know very well I am not guilty of harming the Jews. ¹¹If I have done something worthy of death, I don't refuse to die. But if I am innocent, no one has a right to turn me over to these men to kill me. I appeal to Caesar!"

¹²Festus conferred with his advisers and then replied, "Very well! You have appealed to Caesar, and to Caesar you will go!"

¹³A few days later King Agrippa arrived with his sister, Bernice,* to pay their respects to Festus. ¹⁴During their stay of several days, Festus discussed Paul's case with the king. "There is a prisoner here," he told him, "whose case was left for me by Felix. ¹⁵When I was in Jerusalem, the leading priests and Jewish elders pressed charges against him and asked me to condemn him. ¹⁶I pointed out to them that Roman law does not convict people without a trial. They must be given an opportunity to confront their accusers and defend themselves.

¹⁷"When his accusers came here for the trial, I didn't delay. I called the case the very next day and ordered Paul brought in. ¹⁸But the accusations made against him weren't any of the crimes I expected. ¹⁹Instead, it was something about their religion and a dead man named Jesus, who Paul insists is alive. ²⁰I was at a loss to know how to investigate these things, so I asked him whether he would be willing to stand trial on these charges in Jerusalem. ²¹But Paul appealed to have his case decided by the emperor. So I ordered that he be held in custody until I could arrange to send him to Caesar."

²²"I'd like to hear the man myself," Agrippa said.

And Festus replied, "You will—tomorrow!"

Paul Speaks to Agrippa

²³So the next day Agrippa and Bernice arrived at the auditorium with great pomp, accompanied by military officers and prominent men of the city. Festus ordered that Paul be brought in. ²⁴Then Festus said, "King Agrippa and all who are here, this is the man whose death is demanded by all the Jews, both here and in Jerusalem. ²⁵But in my opinion he has done nothing deserving death. However, since he appealed his case to the emperor, I have decided to send him to Rome.

²⁶"But what shall I write the emperor? For there is no clear charge against him. So

25:13 Greek *Agrippa the king and Bernice arrived.*

I have brought him before all of you, and especially you, King Agrippa, so that after we examine him, I might have something to write. ²⁷For it makes no sense to send a prisoner to the emperor without specifying the charges against him!"

26 Then Agrippa said to Paul, "You may speak in your defense."

So Paul, gesturing with his hand, started his defense: ²"I am fortunate, King Agrippa, that you are the one hearing my defense today against all these accusations made by the Jewish leaders, ³for I know you are an expert on all Jewish customs and controversies. Now please listen to me patiently!

⁴"As the Jewish leaders are well aware, I was given a thorough Jewish training from my earliest childhood among my own people and in Jerusalem. ⁵If they would admit it, they know that I have been a member of the Pharisees, the strictest sect of our religion. ⁶Now I am on trial because of my hope in the fulfillment of God's promise made to our ancestors. ⁷In fact, that is why the twelve tribes of Israel zealously worship God night and day, and they share the same hope I have. Yet, Your Majesty, they accuse me for having this hope! ⁸Why does it seem incredible to any of you that God can raise the dead?

⁹"I used to believe that I ought to do everything I could to oppose the very name of Jesus the Nazarene.* ¹⁰Indeed, I did just that in Jerusalem. Authorized by the leading priests, I caused many believers* there to be sent to prison. And I cast my vote against them when they were condemned to death. ¹¹Many times I had them punished in the synagogues to get them to curse Jesus.* I was so violently opposed to them that I even chased them down in foreign cities.

¹²"One day I was on such a mission to Damascus, armed with the authority and commission of the leading priests. ¹³About noon, Your Majesty, as I was on the road, a light from heaven brighter than the sun shone down on me and my companions. ¹⁴We all fell down, and I heard a voice saying to me in Aramaic,* 'Saul, Saul, why are you persecuting me? It is useless for you to fight against my will.*'

¹⁵"'Who are you, lord?' I asked.

"And the Lord replied, 'I am Jesus, the one you are persecuting. ¹⁶Now get to your feet! For I have appeared to you to appoint you as my servant and witness. You are to tell the world what you have seen and what I will show you in the future. ¹⁷And I will rescue you from both your own people and the Gentiles. Yes, I am sending you to the Gentiles ¹⁸to open their eyes, so they may turn from darkness to light and from the power of Satan to God. Then they will receive forgiveness for their sins and be given a place among God's people, who are set apart by faith in me.'

¹⁹"And so, King Agrippa, I obeyed that vision from heaven. ²⁰I preached first to those in Damascus, then in Jerusalem and throughout all Judea, and also to the Gentiles, that all must repent of their sins and turn to God—and prove they have changed by the good things they do. ²¹Some Jews arrested me in the Temple for preaching this, and they tried to kill me. ²²But God has protected me right up to this present time so I can testify to everyone, from the least to the greatest. I teach nothing except what the prophets and Moses said would happen—²³that the Messiah would suffer and be the first to rise from the dead, and in this way announce God's light to Jews and Gentiles alike."

²⁴Suddenly, Festus shouted, "Paul, you are insane. Too much study has made you crazy!"

²⁵But Paul replied, "I am not insane, Most Excellent Festus. What I am saying is the sober truth. ²⁶And King Agrippa knows about these things. I speak boldly, for I am sure these events are all familiar to him, for they were not done in a corner! ²⁷King Agrippa, do you believe the prophets? I know you do—"

²⁸Agrippa interrupted him. "Do you think you can persuade me to become a Christian so quickly?"*

²⁹Paul replied, "Whether quickly or not, I pray to God that both you and everyone here in this audience might become the same as I am, except for these chains."

26:9 Or *Jesus of Nazareth.* **26:10** Greek *many of God's holy people.* **26:11** Greek *to blaspheme.* **26:14a** Or *Hebrew.* **26:14b** Greek *It is hard for you to kick against the oxgoads.* **26:28** Or *"A little more, and your arguments would make me a Christian."*

³⁰Then the king, the governor, Bernice, and all the others stood and left. ³¹As they went out, they talked it over and agreed, "This man hasn't done anything to deserve death or imprisonment."

³²And Agrippa said to Festus, "He could have been set free if he hadn't appealed to Caesar."

27 Paul Sails for Rome

When the time came, we set sail for Italy. Paul and several other prisoners were placed in the custody of a Roman officer* named Julius, a captain of the Imperial Regiment. ²Aristarchus, a Macedonian from Thessalonica, was also with us. We left on a ship whose home port was Adramyttium on the northwest coast of the province of Asia;* it was scheduled to make several stops at ports along the coast of the province.

³The next day when we docked at Sidon, Julius was very kind to Paul and let him go ashore to visit with friends so they could provide for his needs. ⁴Putting out to sea from there, we encountered strong headwinds that made it difficult to keep the ship on course, so we sailed north of Cyprus between the island and the mainland. ⁵Keeping to the open sea, we passed along the coast of Cilicia and Pamphylia, landing at Myra, in the province of Lycia. ⁶There the commanding officer found an Egyptian ship from Alexandria that was bound for Italy, and he put us on board.

⁷We had several days of slow sailing, and after great difficulty we finally neared Cnidus. But the wind was against us, so we sailed across to Crete and along the sheltered coast of the island, past the cape of Salmone. ⁸We struggled along the coast with great difficulty and finally arrived at Fair Havens, near the town of Lasea. ⁹We had lost a lot of time. The weather was becoming dangerous for sea travel because it was so late in the fall,* and Paul spoke to the ship's officers about it.

¹⁰"Men," he said, "I believe there is trouble ahead if we go on—shipwreck, loss of cargo, and danger to our lives as well."

¹¹But the officer in charge of the prisoners listened more to the ship's captain and the owner than to Paul. ¹²And since Fair Havens was an exposed harbor—a poor place to spend the winter—most of the crew wanted to go on to Phoenix, farther up the coast of Crete, and spend the winter there. Phoenix was a good harbor with only a southwest and northwest exposure.

The Storm at Sea

¹³When a light wind began blowing from the south, the sailors thought they could make it. So they pulled up anchor and sailed close to the shore of Crete. ¹⁴But the weather changed abruptly, and a wind of typhoon strength (called a "northeaster") burst across the island and blew us out to sea. ¹⁵The sailors couldn't turn the ship into the wind, so they gave up and let it run before the gale.

¹⁶We sailed along the sheltered side of a small island named Cauda,* where with great difficulty we hoisted aboard the lifeboat being towed behind us. ¹⁷Then the sailors bound ropes around the hull of the ship to strengthen it. They were afraid of being driven across to the sandbars of Syrtis off the African coast, so they lowered the sea anchor to slow the ship and were driven before the wind.

¹⁸The next day, as gale-force winds continued to batter the ship, the crew began throwing the cargo overboard. ¹⁹The following day they even took some of the ship's gear and threw it overboard. ²⁰The terrible storm raged for many days, blotting out the sun and the stars, until at last all hope was gone.

²¹No one had eaten for a long time. Finally, Paul called the crew together and said, "Men, you should have listened to me in the first place and not left Crete. You would have avoided all this damage and loss. ²²But take courage! None of you will lose your lives, even though the ship will go down. ²³For last night an angel of the God to whom I belong and whom I serve stood beside me, ²⁴and he said, 'Don't be afraid, Paul, for you will surely stand trial before

---

27:1 Greek *centurion;* similarly in 27:6, 11, 31, 43.   **27:2** *Asia* was a Roman province in what is now western Turkey.   **27:9** Greek *because the fast was now already gone by.* This fast was associated with the Day of Atonement (*Yom Kippur*), which occurred in late September or early October.   **27:16** Some manuscripts read *Clauda.*

Rethinking Evangelism: Joining God in His Work

ACTS 28:17–31

I was a guest musician at a church, engaged in the familiar liturgies of a preservice prayer huddle. One person prayed for the congregation's safety in inclement weather, another for the technical aspects of the service, and a third kindly remembered my family back home.

When my turn came, I must have used a phrase like, "God, we invite you here among us." I clearly recall the minister's prayer, which followed mine: "We know we do not have to request your presence, because there is nowhere you are not. So we celebrate the fact that you are already here with us now."

My head stayed bowed, but my face burned. *This guy is correcting my theology with his prayer!*

Throughout the evening I found myself mentally defending my choice of words. *Of course I know God is everywhere—I've read Psalm 139! I was requesting an extra measure of his presence, an outpouring of his Spirit. Or if you want to be more precise (and clearly you do), I was praying that God would help us to be open to him. Aren't we just arguing semantics?*

I never articulated any of these thoughts to the minister. But the dialogue I've had with him in my head ever since has gradually refined my thinking—a case of iron sharpening particularly dull iron. I now believe that pastor's gentle correction was necessary.

In the Gospels Jesus makes a simple proclamation with seismic implications: "Repent . . . for the Kingdom of Heaven is near" (Matthew 4:17). For those of us who grew up in the hot, scary shadows of brimstone pulpits, the command to repent causes an involuntary shudder. But the Greek word is *metanoeite*, which is more invitation than threat. It means "change your mind" or "reconsider."

Reconsider what? According to Jesus, everything you thought you knew about reality. Why? Because the kingdom of heaven is near.

Most of us think of heaven as somewhere out there, the place where God watches from a distance and we will one day join him. But when Jesus describes the invisible (but very real) realm that God inhabits, he lets us know it's not only out there but also as near as the atmosphere surrounding our bodies and the air we breathe.

The minister at that church was calling me to repent—to reconsider what I thought I knew about reality and the way God pervades it. I don't have to invoke God's presence. I only have to attend to it.

This change of heart and mind significantly alters the way I approach evangelism. It's not about my effort, my strategizing, or my plan; it's not about having watertight apologetic arguments, a persuasive demeanor, or impeccable timing. I don't have to give a nonbeliever something I have that she doesn't. I need only invite her to open herself to what God is already doing all around her.

God is here. God is at work. God's kingdom is present in the life of my friend.

The other day I was trying to describe this shift in my understanding to my friend Roy Salmond. He ran to pull out an article he'd read in *Time* magazine more than a decade ago. It's an eloquent piece called "The Game of Catch" by Roger Rosenblatt, about baseball, parenthood, and the wordless communication between a father and son tossing the ball around. While the article is in no way religious, one thought in particular has permanently changed Roy's view of life with God.

"They do not call it a game of *throw*," Roy quoted, grinning. "They call it *catch*."

Oddly enough I understood exactly what he meant. Spiritually speaking I've been preoccupied with throwing the ball; this turns out to be a case in which it would be better to receive than to give.

God is the initiator. We love because he first loved us. We're here because he thought of us and welcomed us into his world. Yes, he stands at the door to our hearts and knocks, but we need only let him in. We don't have to summon him from another country or galaxy. The kingdom of God is already near.

Repent. It's time to play catch.

—Carolyn Arends

For more on outreach, see reading at Romans 15:14–19.

Caesar! What's more, God in his goodness has granted safety to everyone sailing with you.' ²⁵So take courage! For I believe God. It will be just as he said. ²⁶But we will be shipwrecked on an island."

The Shipwreck

²⁷About midnight on the fourteenth night of the storm, as we were being driven across the Sea of Adria,* the sailors sensed land was near. ²⁸They dropped a weighted line and found that the water was 120 feet deep. But a little later they measured again and found it was only 90 feet deep.* ²⁹At this rate they were afraid we would soon be driven against the rocks along the shore, so they threw out four anchors from the back of the ship and prayed for daylight.

³⁰Then the sailors tried to abandon the ship; they lowered the lifeboat as though they were going to put out anchors from the front of the ship. ³¹But Paul said to the commanding officer and the soldiers, "You will all die unless the sailors stay aboard." ³²So the soldiers cut the ropes to the lifeboat and let it drift away.

³³Just as day was dawning, Paul urged everyone to eat. "You have been so worried that you haven't touched food for two weeks," he said. ³⁴"Please eat something now for your own good. For not a hair of your heads will perish." ³⁵Then he took some bread, gave thanks to God before them all, and broke off a piece and ate it. ³⁶Then everyone was encouraged and began to eat—³⁷all 276 of us who were on board. ³⁸After eating, the crew lightened the ship further by throwing the cargo of wheat overboard.

³⁹When morning dawned, they didn't recognize the coastline, but they saw a bay with a beach and wondered if they could get to shore by running the ship aground. ⁴⁰So they cut off the anchors and left them in the sea. Then they lowered the rudders, raised the foresail, and headed toward shore. ⁴¹But they hit a shoal and ran the ship aground too soon. The bow of the ship stuck fast, while the stern was repeatedly smashed by the force of the waves and began to break apart.

⁴²The soldiers wanted to kill the prisoners to make sure they didn't swim ashore and escape. ⁴³But the commanding officer wanted to spare Paul, so he didn't let them carry out their plan. Then he ordered all who could swim to jump overboard first and make for land. ⁴⁴The others held on to planks or debris from the broken ship.* So everyone escaped safely to shore.

28 Paul on the Island of Malta

Once we were safe on shore, we learned that we were on the island of Malta. ²The people of the island were very kind to us. It was cold and rainy, so they built a fire on the shore to welcome us.

³As Paul gathered an armful of sticks and was laying them on the fire, a poisonous snake, driven out by the heat, bit him on the hand. ⁴The people of the island saw it hanging from his hand and said to each other, "A murderer, no doubt! Though he escaped the sea, justice will not permit him to live." ⁵But Paul shook off the snake into the fire and was unharmed. ⁶The people waited for him to swell up or suddenly drop dead. But when they had waited a long time and saw that he wasn't harmed, they changed their minds and decided he was a god.

⁷Near the shore where we landed was an estate belonging to Publius, the chief official of the island. He welcomed us and treated us kindly for three days. ⁸As it happened, Publius's father was ill with fever and dysentery. Paul went in and prayed for him, and laying his hands on him, he healed him. ⁹Then all the other sick people on the island came and were healed. ¹⁰As a result we were showered with honors, and when the time came to sail, people supplied us with everything we would need for the trip.

Paul Arrives at Rome

¹¹It was three months after the shipwreck that we set sail on another ship that had wintered at the island—an Alexandrian ship with the twin gods* as its figurehead. ¹²Our first stop was Syracuse,* where we stayed three days. ¹³From there we sailed across to Rhegium.* A day later a south wind began

---

27:27 The *Sea of Adria* includes the central portion of the Mediterranean.   **27:28** Greek *20 fathoms . . . 15 fathoms* [37 meters . . . 27 meters].   **27:44** Or *or were helped by members of the ship's crew.*   **28:11** The *twin gods* were the Roman gods Castor and Pollux.   **28:12** *Syracuse* was on the island of Sicily.   **28:13** *Rhegium* was on the southern tip of Italy.

blowing, so the following day we sailed up the coast to Puteoli. [14]There we found some believers,* who invited us to spend a week with them. And so we came to Rome.

[15]The brothers and sisters* in Rome had heard we were coming, and they came to meet us at the Forum* on the Appian Way. Others joined us at The Three Taverns.* When Paul saw them, he was encouraged and thanked God.

[16]When we arrived in Rome, Paul was permitted to have his own private lodging, though he was guarded by a soldier.

Paul Preaches at Rome under Guard

[17]Three days after Paul's arrival, he called together the local Jewish leaders. He said to them, "Brothers, I was arrested in Jerusalem and handed over to the Roman government, even though I had done nothing against our people or the customs of our ancestors. [18]The Romans tried me and wanted to release me, because they found no cause for the death sentence. [19]But when the Jewish leaders protested the decision, I felt it necessary to appeal to Caesar, even though I had no desire to press charges against my own people. [20]I asked you to come here today so we could get acquainted and so I could explain to you that I am bound with this chain because I believe that the hope of Israel—the Messiah—has already come."

[21]They replied, "We have had no letters from Judea or reports against you from anyone who has come here. [22]But we want to hear what you believe, for the only thing we know about this movement is that it is denounced everywhere."

[23]So a time was set, and on that day a large number of people came to Paul's lodging. He explained and testified about the Kingdom of God and tried to persuade them about Jesus from the Scriptures. Using the law of Moses and the books of the prophets, he spoke to them from morning until evening. [24]Some were persuaded by the things he said, but others did not believe. [25]And after they had argued back and forth among themselves, they left with this final word from Paul: "The Holy Spirit was right when he said to your ancestors through Isaiah the prophet,

[26]'Go and say to this people:
When you hear what I say,
    you will not understand.
When you see what I do,
    you will not comprehend.
[27]For the hearts of these people are
    hardened,
    and their ears cannot hear,
    and they have closed their eyes—
so their eyes cannot see,
    and their ears cannot hear,
    and their hearts cannot understand,
and they cannot turn to me
    and let me heal them.'*

[28]So I want you to know that this salvation from God has also been offered to the Gentiles, and they will accept it."*

[30]For the next two years, Paul lived in Rome at his own expense.* He welcomed all who visited him, [31]boldly proclaiming the Kingdom of God and teaching about the Lord Jesus Christ. And no one tried to stop him.

28:14 Greek *brothers.*   **28:15a** Greek *brothers.*   **28:15b** *The Forum* was about 43 miles (70 kilometers) from Rome.   **28:15c** *The Three Taverns* was about 35 miles (57 kilometers) from Rome.   **28:26-27** Isa 6:9-10 (Greek version).   **28:28** Some manuscripts add verse 29, *And when he had said these words, the Jews departed, greatly disagreeing with each other.*   **28:30** Or *in his own rented quarters.*

Introduction to

Romans

Background

In the first century, Rome was the Western world's greatest city. When Paul wrote this letter, he had not yet visited the church there. The church at Rome may have been begun by "strangers" in Jerusalem at Pentecost, converted in response to Peter's speech (Acts 2:10). From early on, the Epistle to the Romans was attributed to Paul. Paul dictated this epistle to his scribe, Tertius, who wrote his own greeting at the end (16:22).

Message

Romans is Paul's longest epistle, laying out a systematic treatise that theologically explains the gospel message of salvation as a gift of God provided through Jesus Christ, received by faith alone. Writing to a capital city obsessed with power, Paul emphasizes God's power to save. In chapters 1–11 Paul lays out the story of humanity, covering the sinfulness of Jews and Gentiles alike, God's righteousness, and God's love and forgiveness. Paul describes the freedom available only in Christ. Paul gives a shortened recounting of the story of Israel, demonstrating God's righteousness and saving power. In chapters 12–16 Paul shows how a believer's faith can be applied in the world. Having faith in Christ is more than theological knowledge; it is about living in the fullness of Christ in our everyday lives.

Time

Paul wrote the Epistle to the Romans in A.D. 57 while on his third missionary journey, more than likely while in Corinth (Acts 20:2–3).

Outline

Romans

1 Greetings from Paul

This letter is from Paul, a slave of Christ Jesus, chosen by God to be an apostle and sent out to preach his Good News. ²God promised this Good News long ago through his prophets in the holy Scriptures. ³The Good News is about his Son. In his earthly life he was born into King David's family line, ⁴and he was shown to be* the Son of God when he was raised from the dead by the power of the Holy Spirit.* He is Jesus Christ our Lord. ⁵Through Christ, God has given us the privilege* and authority as apostles to tell Gentiles everywhere what God has done for them, so that they will believe and obey him, bringing glory to his name.

⁶And you are included among those Gentiles who have been called to belong to Jesus Christ. ⁷I am writing to all of you in Rome who are loved by God and are called to be his own holy people.

May God our Father and the Lord Jesus Christ give you grace and peace.

God's Good News

⁸Let me say first that I thank my God through Jesus Christ for all of you, because your faith in him is being talked about all over the world. ⁹God knows how often I pray for you. Day and night I bring you and your needs in prayer to God, whom I serve with all my heart* by spreading the Good News about his Son.

¹⁰One of the things I always pray for is the opportunity, God willing, to come at last to see you. ¹¹For I long to visit you so I can bring you some spiritual gift that will help you grow strong in the Lord. ¹²When we get together, I want to encourage you in your faith, but I also want to be encouraged by yours.

¹³I want you to know, dear brothers and sisters,* that I planned many times to visit you, but I was prevented until now. I want to work among you and see spiritual fruit, just as I have seen among other Gentiles. ¹⁴For I have a great sense of obligation to people in both the civilized world and the rest of the world,* to the educated and uneducated alike. ¹⁵So I am eager to come to you in Rome, too, to preach the Good News.

¹⁶For I am not ashamed of this Good News about Christ. It is the power of God at work, saving everyone who believes—the Jew first and also the Gentile.* ¹⁷This Good News tells us how God makes us right in his sight. This is accomplished from start to finish by faith. As the Scriptures say, "It is through faith that a righteous person has life."*

God's Anger at Sin

¹⁸But God shows his anger from heaven against all sinful, wicked people who suppress the truth by their wickedness.* ¹⁹They know the truth about God because he has made it obvious to them. ²⁰For ever since the world was created, people have seen the earth and sky. Through everything God made, they can clearly see his invisible qualities—his eternal power and divine nature. So they have no excuse for not knowing God.

1:4a Or and was designated.　**1:4b** Or by the Spirit of holiness; or in the new realm of the Spirit.　**1:5** Or the grace.　**1:9** Or in my spirit.　**1:13** Greek brothers.　**1:14** Greek to Greeks and barbarians.　**1:16** Greek also the Greek.　**1:17** Or "The righteous will live by faith." Hab 2:4.　**1:18** Or who, by their wickedness, prevent the truth from being known.

²¹ Yes, they knew God, but they wouldn't worship him as God or even give him thanks. And they began to think up foolish ideas of what God was like. As a result, their minds became dark and confused. ²² Claiming to be wise, they instead became utter fools. ²³ And instead of worshiping the glorious, ever-living God, they worshiped idols made to look like mere people and birds and animals and reptiles.

²⁴ So God abandoned them to do whatever shameful things their hearts desired. As a result, they did vile and degrading things with each other's bodies. ²⁵ They traded the truth about God for a lie. So they worshiped and served the things God created instead of the Creator himself, who is worthy of eternal praise! Amen. ²⁶ That is why God abandoned them to their shameful desires. Even the women turned against the natural way to have sex and instead indulged in sex with each other. ²⁷ And the men, instead of having normal sexual relations with women, burned with lust for

Q&A
We Need Each Other
ROMANS 1:8-12

Mentoring

Why is it important to talk with another person about our relationship with God?

Many Christians set aside a quiet time to be with God and pray. But we often hesitate to talk with someone else about it, partly because of our awareness of intimacy with God and a sense of privacy. But we also hesitate because we feel spiritually inadequate. Yet with a mentor, spiritual director, or close spiritual friend, we have a place to say, "I'm an ordinary person, but I have an extraordinary God, and it's okay to be just who I am, to ask God to be a part of the conversation, and to talk to another person about that."

There are many stages in our spiritual lives—times of learning and serving; seasons of doubt; periods of boredom or mediocrity; seasons of heightened awareness of God's love and a growing trust in him; times of running away because we're angry, hurt, disappointed, or afraid.

Sharing our journey with a spiritual director or mentor can help us pay more attention to how we're responding to God as we move through these different stages. Such a person can help us notice grace in ways we might have missed. We see the spiritual power of this type of intimate fellowship in Paul's longing to spend time with the Christians in Rome (Romans 1:8-12), which he knew would result in profound spiritual empowerment and mutual encouragement in their faith.

Speaking with someone about our spiritual life helps us notice what's going on and helps us offer our hearts to God, to ask God for grace, mercy, assistance, or even to speak about our heart-hardness and lack of desire. We cannot see many things about ourselves; that's why we need each other.

—Jeannette Bakke

For more on mentoring, see reading at 1 Corinthians 10:31-11:2.

each other. Men did shameful things with other men, and as a result of this sin, they suffered within themselves the penalty they deserved.

²⁸ Since they thought it foolish to acknowledge God, he abandoned them to their foolish thinking and let them do things that should never be done. ²⁹ Their lives became full of every kind of wickedness, sin, greed, hate, envy, murder, quarreling, deception, malicious behavior, and gossip. ³⁰ They are backstabbers, haters of God, insolent, proud, and boastful. They invent new ways of sinning, and they disobey their parents. ³¹ They refuse to understand, break their promises, are heartless, and have no mercy. ³² They know God's justice requires that those who do these things deserve to die, yet they do them anyway. Worse yet, they encourage others to do them, too.

2 God's Judgment of Sin

You may think you can condemn such people, but you are just as bad, and you have no excuse! When you say they are wicked and should be punished, you are condemning yourself, for you who judge others do these very same things. ²And we know that God, in his justice, will punish anyone who does such things. ³Since you judge others for doing these things, why do you think you can avoid God's judgment when you do the same things? ⁴Don't you see how wonderfully kind, tolerant, and patient God is with you? Does this mean nothing to you? Can't you see that his kindness is intended to turn you from your sin?

⁵But because you are stubborn and refuse to turn from your sin, you are storing up terrible punishment for yourself. For a day of anger is coming, when God's righteous judgment will be revealed. ⁶He will judge everyone according to what they have done. ⁷He will give eternal life to those who keep on doing good, seeking after the glory and honor and immortality that God offers. ⁸But he will pour out his anger and wrath on those who live for themselves, who refuse to obey the truth and instead live lives of wickedness. ⁹There will be trouble and calamity

for everyone who keeps on doing what is evil—for the Jew first and also for the Gentile.* ¹⁰But there will be glory and honor and peace from God for all who do good—for the Jew first and also for the Gentile. ¹¹For God does not show favoritism.

¹²When the Gentiles sin, they will be destroyed, even though they never had God's written law. And the Jews, who do have God's law, will be judged by that law when they fail to obey it. ¹³For merely listening to the law doesn't make us right with God. It is obeying the law that makes us right in his sight. ¹⁴Even Gentiles, who do not have God's written law, show that they know his law when they instinctively obey it, even without having heard it. ¹⁵They demonstrate that God's law is written in their hearts, for their own conscience and thoughts either accuse them or tell them they are doing right. ¹⁶And this is the message I proclaim—that the day is coming when God, through Christ Jesus, will judge everyone's secret life.

The Jews and the Law

¹⁷You who call yourselves Jews are relying on God's law, and you boast about your special relationship with him. ¹⁸You know what he wants; you know what is right because you have been taught his law. ¹⁹You are convinced that you are a guide for the blind and a light for people who are lost in darkness. ²⁰You think you can instruct the ignorant and teach children the ways of God. For you are certain that God's law gives you complete knowledge and truth.

²¹Well then, if you teach others, why don't you teach yourself? You tell others not to steal, but do you steal? ²²You say it is wrong to commit adultery, but do you commit adultery? You condemn idolatry, but do you use items stolen from pagan temples?* ²³You are so proud of knowing the law, but you dishonor God by breaking it. ²⁴No wonder the Scriptures say, "The Gentiles blaspheme the name of God because of you."*

²⁵ The Jewish ceremony of circumcision has value only if you obey God's law. But if you don't obey God's law, you are

---

2:9 Greek *also for the Greek;* also in 2:10.　2:22 Greek *do you steal from temples?*　2:24 Isa 52:5 (Greek version).

no better off than an uncircumcised Gentile. ²⁶ And if the Gentiles obey God's law, won't God declare them to be his own people? ²⁷ In fact, uncircumcised Gentiles who keep God's law will condemn you Jews who are circumcised and possess God's law but don't obey it.

²⁸ For you are not a true Jew just because you were born of Jewish parents or because you have gone through the ceremony of circumcision. ²⁹ No, a true Jew is one whose heart is right with God. And true circumcision is not merely obeying the letter of the law; rather, it is a change of heart produced by God's Spirit. And a person with a changed heart seeks praise* from God, not from people.

3 God Remains Faithful

Then what's the advantage of being a Jew? Is there any value in the ceremony of circumcision? ² Yes, there are great benefits! First of all, the Jews were entrusted with the whole revelation of God.*

³ True, some of them were unfaithful; but just because they were unfaithful, does that mean God will be unfaithful? ⁴ Of course not! Even if everyone else is a liar, God is true. As the Scriptures say about him,

"You will be proved right in what you say,
and you will win your case in court."*

⁵ "But," some might say, "our sinfulness serves a good purpose, for it helps people see how righteous God is. Isn't it unfair, then, for him to punish us?" (This is merely a human point of view.) ⁶ Of course not! If God were not entirely fair, how would he be qualified to judge the world? ⁷ "But," someone might still argue, "how can God condemn me as a sinner if my dishonesty highlights his truthfulness and brings him more glory?" ⁸ And some people even slander us by claiming that we say, "The more we sin, the better it is!" Those who say such things deserve to be condemned.

All People Are Sinners

⁹ Well then, should we conclude that we Jews are better than others? No, not at all, for we have already shown that all people, whether Jews or Gentiles,* are under the power of sin. ¹⁰ As the Scriptures say,

"No one is righteous—
not even one.
¹¹ No one is truly wise;
no one is seeking God.
¹² All have turned away;
all have become useless.
No one does good,
not a single one."*
¹³ "Their talk is foul, like the stench from an open grave.
Their tongues are filled with lies."*
"Snake venom drips from their lips."*
¹⁴ "Their mouths are full of cursing and bitterness."*
¹⁵ "They rush to commit murder.
¹⁶ Destruction and misery always follow them.
¹⁷ They don't know where to find peace."*
¹⁸ "They have no fear of God at all."*

¹⁹ Obviously, the law applies to those to whom it was given, for its purpose is to keep people from having excuses, and to show that the entire world is guilty before God. ²⁰ For no one can ever be made right with God by doing what the law commands. The law simply shows us how sinful we are.

Christ Took Our Punishment

²¹ But now God has shown us a way to be made right with him without keeping the requirements of the law, as was promised in the writings of Moses* and the prophets long ago. ²² We are made right with God by placing our faith in Jesus Christ. And this is true for everyone who believes, no matter who we are.

²³ For everyone has sinned; we all fall short of God's glorious standard. ²⁴ Yet God, with undeserved kindness, declares that we are righteous. He did this through Christ Jesus when he freed us from the penalty for our sins. ²⁵ For God presented Jesus as the sacrifice for sin. People are made right with God when they believe that Jesus sacrificed his life, shedding his blood. This sacrifice shows that God was being fair when

---

2:29 Or receives praise. 3:2 Greek the oracles of God. 3:4 Ps 51:4 (Greek version). 3:9 Greek or Greeks. 3:10-12 Pss 14:1-3; 53:1-3 (Greek version). 3:13 Pss 5:9 (Greek version); 140:3. 3:14 Ps 10:7 (Greek version). 3:15-17 Isa 59:7-8. 3:18 Ps 36:1. 3:21 Greek in the law.

he held back and did not punish those who sinned in times past, ²⁶for he was looking ahead and including them in what he would do in this present time. God did this to demonstrate his righteousness, for he himself is fair and just, and he declares sinners to be right in his sight when they believe in Jesus.

²⁷Can we boast, then, that we have done anything to be accepted by God? No, because our acquittal is not based on obeying the law. It is based on faith. ²⁸So we are made right with God through faith and not by obeying the law.

²⁹After all, is God the God of the Jews only? Isn't he also the God of the Gentiles? Of course he is. ³⁰There is only one God, and he makes people right with himself only by faith, whether they are Jews or Gentiles.* ³¹Well then, if we emphasize faith, does this mean that we can forget about the law? Of course not! In fact, only when we have faith do we truly fulfill the law.

4 The Faith of Abraham

¹Abraham was, humanly speaking, the founder of our Jewish nation. What did he discover about being made right with God? ²If his good deeds had made him acceptable to God, he would have had something to boast about. But that was not God's way. ³For the Scriptures tell us, "Abraham believed God, and God counted him as righteous because of his faith."*

⁴When people work, their wages are not a gift, but something they have earned. ⁵But people are counted as righteous, not because of their work, but because of their faith in God who forgives sinners. ⁶David also spoke of this when he described the happiness of those who are declared righteous without working for it:

⁷ "Oh, what joy for those
   whose disobedience is forgiven,
   whose sins are put out of sight.
⁸ Yes, what joy for those
   whose record the Lord has cleared of
      sin."*

⁹Now, is this blessing only for the Jews, or is it also for uncircumcised Gentiles?* Well, we have been saying that Abraham was counted as righteous by God because of his faith. ¹⁰But how did this happen? Was he counted as righteous only after he was circumcised, or was it before he was circumcised? Clearly, God accepted Abraham before he was circumcised!

¹¹Circumcision was a sign that Abraham already had faith and that God had already accepted him and declared him to be righteous—even before he was circumcised. So Abraham is the spiritual father of those who have faith but have not been circumcised. They are counted as righteous because of their faith. ¹²And Abraham is also the spiritual father of those who have been circumcised, but only if they have the same kind of faith Abraham had before he was circumcised.

¹³Clearly, God's promise to give the whole earth to Abraham and his descendants was based not on his obedience to God's law, but on a right relationship with God that comes by faith. ¹⁴If God's promise is only for those who obey the law, then faith is not necessary and the promise is pointless. ¹⁵For the law always brings punishment on those who try to obey it. (The only way to avoid breaking the law is to have no law to break!)

¹⁶So the promise is received by faith. It is given as a free gift. And we are all certain to receive it, whether or not we live according to the law of Moses, if we have faith like Abraham's. For Abraham is the father of all who believe. ¹⁷That is what the Scriptures mean when God told him, "I have made you the father of many nations."* This happened because Abraham believed in the God who brings the dead back to life and who creates new things out of nothing.

¹⁸Even when there was no reason for hope, Abraham kept hoping—believing that he would become the father of many nations. For God had said to him, "That's how many descendants you will have!"* ¹⁹And Abraham's faith did not weaken, even though, at about 100 years of age, he figured his body was as good as dead—and so was Sarah's womb. ²⁰Abraham never wavered in believing

---

3:30 Greek *whether they are circumcised or uncircumcised.* **4:3** Gen 15:6. **4:7-8** Ps 32:1-2 (Greek version). **4:9** Greek *is this blessing only for the circumcised, or is it also for the uncircumcised?* **4:17** Gen 17:5. **4:18** Gen 15:5.

Confession

About the Way Things Really Are

ROMANS 5:6-11

The word *confession* has always had a double meaning for Christians. It means to acknowledge sins, yes. But it is also a synonym for professing faith. Thus many creedal statements in church history have been called "confessions," like the Lutheran Augsburg Confession, that church's statement of faith.

Confession is not primarily about the relief of getting things off our chest—although it often has that effect, thank God. Confession is speaking with God and others about reality, about the way things are. And the way things are is like this: "When we were utterly helpless" and "while we were still sinners"—long before we knew that reality and experienced its pain—God loved us and died for us (Romans 5:6, 8). In the moment of confession, we acknowledge our sin, yes, but more important, we acknowledge that his love prompted us to speak about our sin—already forgiven sin!—so that we can participate in the new life he offers us.

—*Mark Galli*

For more on confession, see reading at Romans 12:1-5.

God's promise. In fact, his faith grew stronger, and in this he brought glory to God. [21] He was fully convinced that God is able to do whatever he promises. [22] And because of Abraham's faith, God counted him as righteous. [23] And when God counted him as righteous, it wasn't just for Abraham's benefit. It was recorded [24] for our benefit, too, assuring us that God will also count us as righteous if we believe in him, the one who raised Jesus our Lord from the dead. [25] He was handed over to die because of our sins, and he was raised to life to make us right with God.

5 Faith Brings Joy

Therefore, since we have been made right in God's sight by faith, we have peace with God because of what Jesus Christ our Lord has done for us. [2] Because of our faith, Christ has brought us into this place of undeserved privilege where we now stand, and we confidently and joyfully look forward to sharing God's glory.

[3] We can rejoice, too, when we run into problems and trials, for we know that they help us develop endurance. [4] And endurance develops strength of character, and character strengthens our confident hope of salvation. [5] And this hope will not lead to disappointment. For we know how dearly God loves us, because he has given us the Holy Spirit to fill our hearts with his love.

[6] When we were utterly helpless, Christ came at just the right time and died for us sinners. [7] Now, most people would not be willing to die for an upright person, though someone might perhaps be willing to die for a person who is especially good. [8] But God showed his great love for us by sending Christ to die for us while we were still sinners. [9] And since we have been made right in God's sight by the blood of Christ, he will certainly save us from God's condemnation. [10] For since our friendship with God was restored by the death of his Son while we were still his enemies, we will certainly be saved through the life of his Son. [11] So now we can rejoice in our wonderful new relationship with God because our Lord Jesus Christ has made us friends of God.

Adam and Christ Contrasted

[12] When Adam sinned, sin entered the world. Adam's sin brought death, so death

spread to everyone, for everyone sinned. [13]Yes, people sinned even before the law was given. But it was not counted as sin because there was not yet any law to break. [14]Still, everyone died—from the time of Adam to the time of Moses—even those who did not disobey an explicit commandment of God, as Adam did. Now Adam is a symbol, a representation of Christ, who was yet to come. [15]But there is a great difference between Adam's sin and God's gracious gift. For the sin of this one man, Adam, brought death to many. But even greater is God's wonderful grace and his gift of forgiveness to many through this other man, Jesus Christ. [16]And the result of God's gracious gift is very different from the result of that one man's sin. For Adam's sin led to condemnation, but God's free gift leads to our being made right with God, even though we are guilty of many sins. [17]For the sin of this one man, Adam, caused death to rule over many. But even greater is God's wonderful grace and his gift of righteousness, for all who receive it will live in triumph over sin and death through this one man, Jesus Christ.

[18]Yes, Adam's one sin brings condemnation for everyone, but Christ's one act of righteousness brings a right relationship with God and new life for everyone. [19]Because one person disobeyed God, many became sinners. But because one other person obeyed God, many will be made righteous.

[20]God's law was given so that all people could see how sinful they were. But as people sinned more and more, God's wonderful grace became more abundant. [21]So just as sin ruled over all people and brought them to death, now God's wonderful grace rules instead, giving us right standing with God and resulting in eternal life through Jesus Christ our Lord.

6 Sin's Power Is Broken

Well then, should we keep on sinning so that God can show us more and more of his wonderful grace? [2]Of course not! Since we have died to sin, how can we continue to live in it? [3]Or have you forgotten that when we were joined with Christ Jesus in bap-

tism, we joined him in his death? [4]For we died and were buried with Christ by baptism. And just as Christ was raised from the dead by the glorious power of the Father, now we also may live new lives.

[5]Since we have been united with him in his death, we will also be raised to life as he was. [6]We know that our old sinful selves were crucified with Christ so that sin might lose its power in our lives. We are no longer slaves to sin. [7]For when we died with Christ we were set free from the power of sin. [8]And since we died with Christ, we know we will also live with him. [9]We are sure of this because Christ was raised from the dead, and he will never die again. Death no longer has any power over him. [10]When he died, he died once to break the power of sin. But now that he lives, he lives for the glory of God. [11]So you also should consider yourselves to be dead to the power of sin and alive to God through Christ Jesus.

[12]Do not let sin control the way you live;* do not give in to sinful desires. [13]Do not let any part of your body become an instrument of evil to serve sin. Instead, give yourselves completely to God, for you were dead, but now you have new life. So use your whole body as an instrument to do what is right for the glory of God. [14]Sin is no longer your master, for you no longer live under the requirements of the law. Instead, you live under the freedom of God's grace.

[15]Well then, since God's grace has set us free from the law, does that mean we can go on sinning? Of course not! [16]Don't you realize that you become the slave of whatever you choose to obey? You can be a slave to sin, which leads to death, or you can choose to obey God, which leads to righteous living. [17]Thank God! Once you were slaves of sin, but now you wholeheartedly obey this teaching we have given you. [18]Now you are free from your slavery to sin, and you have become slaves to righteous living.

[19]Because of the weakness of your human nature, I am using the illustration of slavery to help you understand all this. Previously, you let yourselves be slaves to impurity and lawlessness, which led ever deeper into sin. Now you must give yourselves to be slaves

---

6:12 Or *Do not let sin reign in your body, which is subject to death.*

to righteous living so that you will become holy. ²⁰When you were slaves to sin, you were free from the obligation to do right. ²¹And what was the result? You are now ashamed of the things you used to do, things that end in eternal doom. ²²But now you are free from the power of sin and have become slaves of God. Now you do those things that lead to holiness and result in eternal life. ²³For the wages of sin is death, but the free gift of God is eternal life through Christ Jesus our Lord.

7 No Longer Bound to the Law

Now, dear brothers and sisters*—you who are familiar with the law—don't you know that the law applies only while a person is living? ²For example, when a woman marries, the law binds her to her husband as long as he is alive. But if he dies, the laws of marriage no longer apply to her. ³So while her husband is alive, she would be committing adultery if she married another man. But if her husband dies, she is free from that law and does not commit adultery when she remarries.

⁴So, my dear brothers and sisters, this is the point: You died to the power of the law when you died with Christ. And now you are united with the one who was raised from the dead. As a result, we can produce a harvest of good deeds for God. ⁵When we were controlled by our old nature,* sinful desires were at work within us, and the law aroused these evil desires that produced a harvest of sinful deeds, resulting in death. ⁶But now we have been released from the law, for we died to it and are no longer captive to its power. Now we can serve God, not in the old way of obeying the letter of the law, but in the new way of living in the Spirit.

God's Law Reveals Our Sin

⁷Well then, am I suggesting that the law of God is sinful? Of course not! In fact, it was the law that showed me my sin. I would never have known that coveting is wrong if the law had not said, "You must not covet."* ⁸But sin used this command to arouse all kinds of covetous desires within me! If there were no law, sin would not have that power. ⁹At one time I lived without understanding the law. But when I learned the command not to covet, for instance, the power of sin came to life, ¹⁰and I died. So I discovered that the law's commands, which were supposed to bring life, brought spiritual death instead. ¹¹Sin took advantage of those commands and deceived me; it used the commands to kill me. ¹²But still, the law itself is holy, and its commands are holy and right and good.

¹³But how can that be? Did the law, which is good, cause my death? Of course not! Sin used what was good to bring about my condemnation to death. So we can see how terrible sin really is. It uses God's good commands for its own evil purposes.

Struggling with Sin

¹⁴So the trouble is not with the law, for it is spiritual and good. The trouble is with me, for I am all too human, a slave to sin. ¹⁵I don't really understand myself, for I want to do what is right, but I don't do it. Instead, I do what I hate. ¹⁶But if I know that what I am doing is wrong, this shows that I agree that the law is good. ¹⁷So I am not the one doing wrong; it is sin living in me that does it.

¹⁸And I know that nothing good lives in me, that is, in my sinful nature.* I want to do what is right, but I can't. ¹⁹I want to do what is good, but I don't. I don't want to do what is wrong, but I do it anyway. ²⁰But if I do what I don't want to do, I am not really the one doing wrong; it is sin living in me that does it.

²¹I have discovered this principle of life—that when I want to do what is right, I inevitably do what is wrong. ²²I love God's law with all my heart. ²³But there is another power* within me that is at war with my mind. This power makes me a slave to the sin that is still within me. ²⁴Oh, what a miserable person I am! Who will free me from this life that is dominated by sin and death? ²⁵Thank God! The answer is in Jesus Christ our Lord. So you see how it is: In my mind I really want to obey God's law, but because of my sinful nature I am a slave to sin.

7:1 Greek *brothers;* also in 7:4. **7:5** Greek *When we were in the flesh.* **7:7** Exod 20:17; Deut 5:21. **7:18** Greek *my flesh;* also in 7:25. **7:23** Greek *law;* also in 7:23b.

8 Life in the Spirit

So now there is no condemnation for those who belong to Christ Jesus. ²And because you belong to him, the power* of the life-giving Spirit has freed you* from the power of sin that leads to death. ³The law of Moses was unable to save us because of the weakness of our sinful nature.* So God did what the law could not do. He sent his own Son in a body like the bodies we sinners have. And in that body God declared an end to sin's control over us by giving his Son as a sacrifice for our sins. ⁴He did this so that the just requirement of the law would be fully satisfied for us, who no longer follow our sinful nature but instead follow the Spirit.

⁵Those who are dominated by the sinful nature think about sinful things, but those who are controlled by the Holy Spirit think about things that please the Spirit. ⁶So letting your sinful nature control your mind leads to death. But letting the Spirit control your mind leads to life and peace. ⁷For the sinful nature is always hostile to God. It never did obey God's laws, and it never will. ⁸That's why those who are still under the control of their sinful nature can never please God.

⁹But you are not controlled by your sinful nature. You are controlled by the Spirit if you have the Spirit of God living in you. (And remember that those who do not have the Spirit of Christ living in them do not belong to him at all.) ¹⁰And Christ lives within you, so even though your body will die because of sin, the Spirit gives you life* because you have been made right with God. ¹¹The Spirit of God, who raised Jesus from the dead, lives in you. And just as God raised Christ Jesus from the dead, he will give life to your mortal bodies by this same Spirit living within you.

¹²Therefore, dear brothers and sisters,* you have no obligation to do what your sinful nature urges you to do. ¹³For if you live by its dictates, you will die. But if through the power of the Spirit you put to death the deeds of your sinful nature,* you will live.

¹⁴For all who are led by the Spirit of God are children* of God.

¹⁵So you have not received a spirit that makes you fearful slaves. Instead, you received God's Spirit when he adopted you as his own children.* Now we call him, "Abba, Father."* ¹⁶For his Spirit joins with our spirit to affirm that we are God's children. ¹⁷And since we are his children, we are his heirs. In fact, together with Christ we are heirs of God's glory. But if we are to share his glory, we must also share his suffering.

The Future Glory

¹⁸Yet what we suffer now is nothing compared to the glory he will reveal to us later. ¹⁹For all creation is waiting eagerly for that future day when God will reveal who his children really are. ²⁰Against its will, all creation was subjected to God's curse. But with eager hope, ²¹the creation looks forward to the day when it will join God's children in glorious freedom from death and decay. ²²For we know that all creation has been groaning as in the pains of childbirth right up to the present time. ²³And we believers also groan, even though we have the Holy Spirit within us as a foretaste of future glory, for we long for our bodies to be released from sin and suffering. We, too, wait with eager hope for the day when God will give us our full rights as his adopted children,* including the new bodies he has promised us. ²⁴We were given this hope when we were saved. (If we already have something, we don't need to hope* for it. ²⁵But if we look forward to something we don't yet have, we must wait patiently and confidently.)

²⁶And the Holy Spirit helps us in our weakness. For example, we don't know what God wants us to pray for. But the Holy Spirit prays for us with groanings that cannot be expressed in words. ²⁷And the Father who knows all hearts knows what the Spirit is saying, for the Spirit pleads for us believers* in harmony with God's own will. ²⁸And we know that God causes everything to

---

8:2a Greek *the law;* also in 8:2b.   **8:2b** Some manuscripts read *me.*   **8:3** Greek *our flesh;* similarly in 8:4, 5, 6, 7, 8, 9, 12.   **8:10** Or *your spirit is alive.*   **8:12** Greek *brothers;* also in 8:29.   **8:13** Greek *deeds of the body.*   **8:14** Greek *sons;* also in 8:19.   **8:15a** Greek *you received a spirit of sonship.*   **8:15b** *Abba* is an Aramaic term for "father."   **8:23** Greek *wait anxiously for sonship.*   **8:24** Some manuscripts read *wait.*   **8:27** Greek *for God's holy people.*

work together* for the good of those who love God and are called according to his purpose for them. ²⁹For God knew his people in advance, and he chose them to become like his Son, so that his Son would be the firstborn* among many brothers and sisters. ³⁰And having chosen them, he called them to come to him. And having called them, he gave them right standing with himself. And having given them right standing, he gave them his glory.

Nothing Can Separate Us from God's Love

³¹What shall we say about such wonderful things as these? If God is for us, who can ever be against us? ³²Since he did not spare even his own Son but gave him up for us all, won't he also give us everything else? ³³Who dares accuse us whom God has chosen for his own? No one—for God himself has given us right standing with himself. ³⁴Who then will condemn us? No one—for Christ Jesus died for us and was raised to life for us, and he is sitting in the place of honor at God's right hand, pleading for us.

³⁵Can anything ever separate us from Christ's love? Does it mean he no longer loves us if we have trouble or calamity, or are persecuted, or hungry, or destitute, or in danger, or threatened with death? ³⁶(As the Scriptures say, "For your sake we are killed every day; we are being slaughtered like sheep."*) ³⁷No, despite all these things, overwhelming victory is ours through Christ, who loved us.

³⁸And I am convinced that nothing can ever separate us from God's love. Neither death nor life, neither angels nor demons,* neither our fears for today nor our worries about tomorrow—not even the powers of hell can separate us from God's love. ³⁹No power in the sky above or in the earth below—indeed, nothing in all creation will ever be able to separate us from the love of God that is revealed in Christ Jesus our Lord.

9 God's Selection of Israel

With Christ as my witness, I speak with utter truthfulness. My conscience and the Holy Spirit confirm it. ²My heart is filled with bitter sorrow and unending grief ³for my people, my Jewish brothers and sisters.* I would be willing to be forever cursed—cut off from Christ!—if that would save them. ⁴They are the people of Israel, chosen to be God's adopted children.* God revealed his glory to them. He made covenants with them and gave them his law. He gave them the privilege of worshiping him and receiving his wonderful promises. ⁵Abraham, Isaac, and Jacob are their ancestors, and Christ himself was an Israelite as far as his human nature is concerned. And he is God, the one who rules over everything and is worthy of eternal praise! Amen.*

⁶Well then, has God failed to fulfill his promise to Israel? No, for not all who are born into the nation of Israel are truly members of God's people! ⁷Being descendants of Abraham doesn't make them truly Abraham's children. For the Scriptures say, "Isaac is the son through whom your descendants will be counted,"* though Abraham had other children, too. ⁸This means that Abraham's physical descendants are not necessarily children of God. Only the children of the promise are considered to be Abraham's children. ⁹For God had promised, "I will return about this time next year, and Sarah will have a son."*

¹⁰This son was our ancestor Isaac. When he married Rebekah, she gave birth to twins.* ¹¹But before they were born, before they had done anything good or bad, she received a message from God. (This message shows that God chooses people according to his own purposes; ¹²he calls people, but not according to their good or bad works.) She was told, "Your older son will serve your younger son."* ¹³In the words of the Scriptures, "I loved Jacob, but I rejected Esau."*

¹⁴Are we saying, then, that God was unfair? Of course not! ¹⁵For God said to Moses,

"I will show mercy to anyone I choose,
and I will show compassion to anyone
I choose."*

8:28 Some manuscripts read And we know that everything works together. 8:29 Or would be supreme. 8:36 Ps 44:22. 8:38 Greek nor rulers. 9:3 Greek my brothers. 9:4 Greek chosen for sonship. 9:5 Or May God, the one who rules over everything, be praised forever. Amen. 9:7 Gen 21:12. 9:9 Gen 18:10, 14. 9:10 Greek she conceived children through this one man. 9:12 Gen 25:23. 9:13 Mal 1:2-3. 9:15 Exod 33:19.

[16] So it is God who decides to show mercy. We can neither choose it nor work for it.

[17] For the Scriptures say that God told Pharaoh, "I have appointed you for the very purpose of displaying my power in you and to spread my fame throughout the earth."* [18] So you see, God chooses to show mercy to some, and he chooses to harden the hearts of others so they refuse to listen.

[19] Well then, you might say, "Why does God blame people for not responding? Haven't they simply done what he makes them do?"

[20] No, don't say that. Who are you, a mere human being, to argue with God? Should the thing that was created say to the one who created it, "Why have you made me like this?" [21] When a potter makes jars out of clay, doesn't he have a right to use the same lump of clay to make one jar for decoration and another to throw garbage into? [22] In the same way, even though God has the right to show his anger and his power, he is very patient with those on whom his anger falls, who are destined for destruction. [23] He does this to make the riches of his glory shine even brighter on those to whom he shows mercy, who were prepared in advance for glory. [24] And we are among those whom he selected, both from the Jews and from the Gentiles.

[25] Concerning the Gentiles, God says in the prophecy of Hosea,

"Those who were not my people,
    I will now call my people.
And I will love those
    whom I did not love before."*

[26] And,

"Then, at the place where they were told,
    'You are not my people,'
there they will be called
    'children of the living God.'"*

[27] And concerning Israel, Isaiah the prophet cried out,

"Though the people of Israel are as
        numerous as the sand of the
        seashore,
    only a remnant will be saved.

[28] For the LORD will carry out his sentence
        upon the earth
    quickly and with finality."*

[29] And Isaiah said the same thing in another place:

"If the LORD of Heaven's Armies
    had not spared a few of our children,
we would have been wiped out like
        Sodom,
    destroyed like Gomorrah."*

Israel's Unbelief

[30] What does all this mean? Even though the Gentiles were not trying to follow God's standards, they were made right with God. And it was by faith that this took place. [31] But the people of Israel, who tried so hard to get right with God by keeping the law, never succeeded. [32] Why not? Because they were trying to get right with God by keeping the law* instead of by trusting in him. They stumbled over the great rock in their path. [33] God warned them of this in the Scriptures when he said,

"I am placing a stone in Jerusalem* that
        makes people stumble,
    a rock that makes them fall.
But anyone who trusts in him
    will never be disgraced."*

10 Dear brothers and sisters,* the longing of my heart and my prayer to God is for the people of Israel to be saved. [2] I know what enthusiasm they have for God, but it is misdirected zeal. [3] For they don't understand God's way of making people right with himself. Refusing to accept God's way, they cling to their own way of getting right with God by trying to keep the law. [4] For Christ has already accomplished the purpose for which the law was given.* As a result, all who believe in him are made right with God.

Salvation Is for Everyone

[5] For Moses writes that the law's way of making a person right with God requires obedience to all of its commands.* [6] But faith's way of getting right with God says,

---

9:17 Exod 9:16 (Greek version).   **9:25** Hos 2:23.   **9:26** Greek sons of the living God. Hos 1:10.   **9:27-28** Isa 10:22-23 (Greek version).
9:29 Isa 1:9.   **9:32** Greek by works.   **9:33a** Greek in Zion.   **9:33b** Isa 8:14; 28:16 (Greek version).   **10:1** Greek Brothers.   **10:4** Or For Christ is the end of the law.   **10:5** See Lev 18:5.

"Don't say in your heart, 'Who will go up to heaven?' (to bring Christ down to earth). ⁷And don't say, 'Who will go down to the place of the dead?' (to bring Christ back to life again)." ⁸In fact, it says,

"The message is very close at hand;
it is on your lips and in your heart."*

And that message is the very message about faith that we preach: ⁹If you confess with your mouth that Jesus is Lord and believe in your heart that God raised him from the dead, you will be saved. ¹⁰For it is by believing in your heart that you are made right with God, and it is by confessing with your mouth that you are saved. ¹¹As the Scriptures tell us, "Anyone who trusts in him will never be disgraced."* ¹²Jew and Gentile* are the same in this respect. They have the same Lord, who gives generously to all who call on him. ¹³For "Everyone who calls on the name of the LORD will be saved."*

¹⁴But how can they call on him to save them unless they believe in him? And how can they believe in him if they have never heard about him? And how can they hear about him unless someone tells them? ¹⁵And how will anyone go and tell them without being sent? That is why the Scriptures say, "How beautiful are the feet of messengers who bring good news!"*

¹⁶But not everyone welcomes the Good News, for Isaiah the prophet said, "LORD, who has believed our message?"* ¹⁷So faith comes from hearing, that is, hearing the Good News about Christ. ¹⁸But I ask, have the people of Israel actually heard the message? Yes, they have:

"The message has gone throughout the earth,
and the words to all the world."*

¹⁹But I ask, did the people of Israel really understand? Yes, they did, for even in the time of Moses, God said,

"I will rouse your jealousy through people who are not even a nation.
I will provoke your anger through the foolish Gentiles."*

²⁰And later Isaiah spoke boldly for God, saying,

"I was found by people who were not looking for me.
I showed myself to those who were not asking for me."*

²¹But regarding Israel, God said,

"All day long I opened my arms to them,
but they were disobedient and rebellious."*

11 God's Mercy on Israel

I ask, then, has God rejected his own people, the nation of Israel? Of course not! I myself am an Israelite, a descendant of Abraham and a member of the tribe of Benjamin.

²No, God has not rejected his own people, whom he chose from the very beginning. Do you realize what the Scriptures say about this? Elijah the prophet complained to God about the people of Israel and said, ³"LORD, they have killed your prophets and torn down your altars. I am the only one left, and now they are trying to kill me, too."*

⁴And do you remember God's reply? He said, "No, I have 7,000 others who have never bowed down to Baal!"*

⁵It is the same today, for a few of the people of Israel* have remained faithful because of God's grace—his undeserved kindness in choosing them. ⁶And since it is through God's kindness, then it is not by their good works. For in that case, God's grace would not be what it really is—free and undeserved.

⁷So this is the situation: Most of the people of Israel have not found the favor of God they are looking for so earnestly. A few have—the ones God has chosen—but the hearts of the rest were hardened. ⁸As the Scriptures say,

"God has put them into a deep sleep.
To this day he has shut their eyes so they do not see,
and closed their ears so they do not hear."*

10:6-8 Deut 30:12-14. **10:11** Isa 28:16 (Greek version). **10:12** Greek and Greek. **10:13** Joel 2:32. **10:15** Isa 52:7. **10:16** Isa 53:1.
10:18 Ps 19:4. **10:19** Deut 32:21. **10:20** Isa 65:1 (Greek version). **10:21** Isa 65:2 (Greek version). **11:3** 1 Kgs 19:10, 14. **11:4** 1 Kgs 19:18.
11:5 Greek for a remnant. **11:8** Isa 29:10; Deut 29:4.

⁹Likewise, David said,

"Let their bountiful table become a
snare,
a trap that makes them think all is well.
Let their blessings cause them to
stumble,
and let them get what they deserve.
¹⁰ Let their eyes go blind so they cannot
see,
and let their backs be bent forever."*

¹¹ Did God's people stumble and fall beyond recovery? Of course not! They were disobedient, so God made salvation available to the Gentiles. But he wanted his own people to become jealous and claim it for themselves. ¹²Now if the Gentiles were enriched because the people of Israel turned down God's offer of salvation, think how much greater a blessing the world will share when they finally accept it.

¹³I am saying all this especially for you Gentiles. God has appointed me as the apostle to the Gentiles. I stress this, ¹⁴for I want somehow to make the people of Israel jealous of what you Gentiles have, so I might save some of them. ¹⁵For since their rejection meant that God offered salvation to the rest of the world, their acceptance will be even more wonderful. It will be life for those who were dead! ¹⁶And since Abraham and the other patriarchs were holy, their descendants will also be holy—just as the entire batch of dough is holy because the portion given as an offering is holy. For if the roots of the tree are holy, the branches will be, too.

¹⁷But some of these branches from Abraham's tree—some of the people of Israel—have been broken off. And you Gentiles, who were branches from a wild olive tree, have been grafted in. So now you also receive the blessing God has promised Abraham and his children, sharing in the rich nourishment from the root of God's special olive tree. ¹⁸But you must not brag about being grafted in to replace the branches that were broken off. You are just a branch, not the root.

¹⁹"Well," you may say, "those branches were broken off to make room for me." ²⁰Yes, but remember—those branches were broken off because they didn't believe in Christ, and you are there because you do believe. So don't think highly of yourself, but fear what could happen. ²¹For if God did not spare the original branches, he won't* spare you either.

²²Notice how God is both kind and severe. He is severe toward those who disobeyed, but kind to you if you continue to trust in his kindness. But if you stop trusting, you also will be cut off. ²³And if the people of Israel turn from their unbelief, they will be grafted in again, for God has the power to graft them back into the tree. ²⁴You, by nature, were a branch cut from a wild olive tree. So if God was willing to do something contrary to nature by grafting you into his cultivated tree, he will be far more eager to graft the original branches back into the tree where they belong.

God's Mercy Is for Everyone

²⁵I want you to understand this mystery, dear brothers and sisters,* so that you will not feel proud about yourselves. Some of the people of Israel have hard hearts, but this will last only until the full number of Gentiles comes to Christ. ²⁶And so all Israel will be saved. As the Scriptures say,

"The one who rescues will come from
Jerusalem,*
and he will turn Israel* away from
ungodliness.
²⁷ And this is my covenant with them,
that I will take away their sins."*

²⁸Many of the people of Israel are now enemies of the Good News, and this benefits you Gentiles. Yet they are still the people he loves because he chose their ancestors Abraham, Isaac, and Jacob. ²⁹For God's gifts and his call can never be withdrawn. ³⁰Once, you Gentiles were rebels against God, but when the people of Israel rebelled against him, God was merciful to you instead. ³¹Now they are the rebels, and God's mercy has come to you so that they, too, will share* in God's mercy. ³²For God

---

11:9-10 Ps 69:22-23 (Greek version). **11:21** Some manuscripts read *perhaps he won't.* **11:25** Greek *brothers.* **11:26a** Greek *from Zion.*
11:26b Greek *Jacob.* **11:26-27** Isa 59:20-21; 27:9 (Greek version). **11:31** Other manuscripts read *will now share;* still others read *will someday share.*

Hospitality

Inviting In, Reaching Out
ROMANS 12:10-13

Love, devotion, enthusiasm, rejoicing, patience, eagerness: these are the virtues that Paul calls us to in Romans 12:10-13. They weave together to create a portrait of the demeanor that should characterize our lives. Hospitality is an essential part of this picture: "When God's people are in need, be ready to help them. Always be eager to practice hospitality." It's a way of living transparently in our interactions with others as we reveal the things we hope for, are afflicted with, and have spiritual fervor for, and practice those things with joy, patience, and faithfulness. It's about serving others with honor and loving others above ourselves. It's creating a safe place for people to come and share life with us. And we hope, then, that sharing our real lives with others will draw them closer to Christ.

How powerfully would we influence our neighborhood, apartment building, book club, or workout class if we devoted ourselves to them in love, being generous with our time and things? Would the world look at Christians differently? God has called us to be hospitable and to live transparently—continually inviting people into our homes and our lives—so that others might feel welcomed into a spiritual family with God the Father.

—Lindsey Learn

For more on hospitality, see reading at 1 Peter 4:7-11.

---

has imprisoned everyone in disobedience so he could have mercy on everyone.

³³Oh, how great are God's riches and wisdom and knowledge! How impossible it is for us to understand his decisions and his ways!

³⁴ For who can know the LORD's
thoughts?
Who knows enough to give him
advice?*
³⁵ And who has given him so much
that he needs to pay it back?*

³⁶ For everything comes from him and exists by his power and is intended for his glory. All glory to him forever! Amen.

12 A Living Sacrifice to God
And so, dear brothers and sisters,* I plead with you to give your bodies to God because of all he has done for you. Let them be a living and holy sacrifice—the kind he will find acceptable. This is truly the way

to worship him.* ²Don't copy the behavior and customs of this world, but let God transform you into a new person by changing the way you think. Then you will learn to know God's will for you, which is good and pleasing and perfect.

³Because of the privilege and authority* God has given me, I give each of you this warning: Don't think you are better than you really are. Be honest in your evaluation of yourselves, measuring yourselves by the faith God has given us.* ⁴Just as our bodies have many parts and each part has a special function, ⁵so it is with Christ's body. We are many parts of one body, and we all belong to each other.

⁶In his grace, God has given us different gifts for doing certain things well. So if God has given you the ability to prophesy, speak out with as much faith as God has given you. ⁷If your gift is serving others, serve them well. If you are a teacher, teach well. ⁸If your gift is to encourage others, be

---

11:34 Isa 40:13 (Greek version). **11:35** See Job 41:11. **12:1a** Greek *brothers*. **12:1b** Or *This is your spiritual worship;* or *This is your reasonable service.* **12:3a** Or *Because of the grace;* compare 1:5. **12:3b** Or *by the faith God has given you;* or *by the standard of our God-given faith.*

encouraging. If it is giving, give generously. If God has given you leadership ability, take the responsibility seriously. And if you have a gift for showing kindness to others, do it gladly.

9 Don't just pretend to love others. Really love them. Hate what is wrong. Hold tightly to what is good. 10 Love each other with genuine affection,* and take delight in honoring each other. 11 Never be lazy, but work hard and serve the Lord enthusiastically.* 12 Rejoice in our confident hope. Be patient in trouble, and keep on praying. 13 When God's people are in need, be ready to help them. Always be eager to practice hospitality.

14 Bless those who persecute you. Don't curse them; pray that God will bless them. 15 Be happy with those who are happy, and weep with those who weep. 16 Live in harmony with each other. Don't be too proud to enjoy the company of ordinary people. And don't think you know it all!

17 Never pay back evil with more evil. Do things in such a way that everyone can see you are honorable. 18 Do all that you can to live in peace with everyone.

19 Dear friends, never take revenge. Leave that to the righteous anger of God. For the Scriptures say,

"I will take revenge;
  I will pay them back,"*
  says the Lord.

20 Instead,

"If your enemies are hungry, feed them.
  If they are thirsty, give them
    something to drink.
  In doing this, you will heap
    burning coals of shame on their heads."*

21 Don't let evil conquer you, but conquer evil by doing good.

13 Respect for Authority

Everyone must submit to governing authorities. For all authority comes from God, and those in positions of authority have been placed there by God. 2 So anyone who rebels against authority is rebelling against what God has instituted, and they will be punished. 3 For the authorities do not strike fear in people who are doing right, but in those who are doing wrong. Would you like to live without fear of the authorities? Do what is right, and they will honor you. 4 The authorities are God's servants, sent for your good. But if you are doing wrong, of course you should be afraid, for they have the power to punish you. They are God's servants, sent for the very purpose of punishing those who do what is wrong. 5 So you must submit to them, not only to avoid punishment, but also to keep a clear conscience.

6 Pay your taxes, too, for these same reasons. For government workers need to be paid. They are serving God in what they do. 7 Give to everyone what you owe them: Pay your taxes and government fees to those who collect them, and give respect and honor to those who are in authority.

Love Fulfills God's Requirements

8 Owe nothing to anyone—except for your obligation to love one another. If you love your neighbor, you will fulfill the requirements of God's law. 9 For the commandments say, "You must not commit adultery. You must not murder. You must not steal. You must not covet."* These—and other such commandments—are summed up in this one commandment: "Love your neighbor as yourself."* 10 Love does no wrong to others, so love fulfills the requirements of God's law.

11 This is all the more urgent, for you know how late it is; time is running out. Wake up, for our salvation is nearer now than when we first believed. 12 The night is almost gone; the day of salvation will soon be here. So remove your dark deeds like dirty clothes, and put on the shining armor of right living. 13 Because we belong to the day, we must live decent lives for all to see. Don't participate in the darkness of wild parties and drunkenness, or in sexual promiscuity and immoral living, or in quarreling and jealousy. 14 Instead, clothe yourself with the presence of the Lord Jesus Christ. And don't let yourself think about ways to indulge your evil desires.

12:10 Greek with brotherly love. **12:11** Or but serve the Lord with a zealous spirit; or but let the Spirit excite you as you serve the Lord. **12:19** Deut 32:35. **12:20** Prov 25:21-22. **13:9a** Exod 20:13-15, 17. **13:9b** Lev 19:18.

Whatever Happened to Repentance?

ROMANS 12:1-5

Jesus often spoke words of comfort such as, "Come to me, all of you who are weary and carry heavy burdens, and I will give you rest" (Matthew 11:28). But more frequently he challenged his hearers, urging them to turn to God in humility and admit their sins. In fact, Jesus' very first instruction was "Repent" (Mark 1:15). From then on, this call to repentance was Jesus' most consistent message. In fact, even when told of a tragedy that caused many deaths, rather than speaking consoling words, he repeated this difficult theme: "Unless you repent, you will perish, too" (Luke 13:5).

We love the comfort sayings of Jesus. We repeat them often; we even print them on refrigerator magnets. But we mostly ignore his teachings on repentance. This says more about us than it does about Jesus.

When we start believing that consolation is the main reason Jesus came, we forget the hard part of the Good News. But what's wrong with us required much more than a hug; it required the Cross. We'd rather feel as if we're victims of a cruel world than admit we are contributors to the world's cruelty, lost sinners who perversely love our lostness, clinging to our treasured sins like a drowning man to an anvil.

The Lord does not love us for our good parts and pass over the rest. He died for the bad parts and will not rest until they are put right. We must stop thinking of God as infinitely indulgent. We must grapple with the scary and exhilarating truth that he is infinitely holy and that he wants the same for us.

A good place to start is with the word *repentance*, or the Greek *metanoia*, meaning a change of mind. (The Hebrew word is *shub*, which means to change from the wrong to the right path.) *Metanoia* is a compound word; "meta" denotes transformation. *Metamorphosis* is a change of shape; *metanoia* is a change of the nous, or the innermost consciousness, a region that lies below rational thought and emotion. Paul urged believers to be transformed by renewing their minds [Greek, *nous*] (Romans 12:2), and the devotional classic *The Shepherd* (A.D. 140) says, "Repentance is great understanding." Repentance is not blubbering and self-loathing. It is insight.

The insight is about our true condition. We begin to see our fallen inclinations the way God does and realize how deep-rooted is the rottenness in our hearts. His is like the eye of a surgeon, which sees through to the sickness deepest within. There's no other way for us to be healed. It's when the surgeon says, "All we can do is keep him comfortable," that you're really in trouble.

Some will object, "But I already hate myself; I feel ashamed and like a failure all the time." That miserable feeling can be pride with a twist: we have an unreasonably inflated idea of how wonderful we can be and find the inevitable failures crushing. God's assessment of our abilities is more accurate to begin with, so he doesn't share our surprised dismay. Repentance, "great understanding," replaces our distorted self-image with God's perspective.

Other times the wash of self-hatred is due to feelings of hopelessness. We all have committed a million wrongs, large and small. We can get stuck there, aware that God forgives us but unable to apply that fact, and aware that we're bound to continue to fail. It seems like there's no solution, so we sit in the garbage pile feeling miserable.

This isn't repentance; this is despair. The early church differentiated between the two, perceiving that healthy repentance is vigorous and clear minded, while despair is debilitating and in fact sinful. A fifth-century Egyptian monk named Isaiah warned against the kind of sadness that "sets off numerous diabolical mechanisms until your strength is sapped. The sadness according to God, on the other hand, is joy. . . . It says to the soul, 'Do not be afraid! Up! Return!' God knows that man is weak, and strengthens him."

"Sadness according to God," repentance, is joy. Initially we fear looking squarely at our sins, lest we get overwhelmed. But the reverse turns out to be true. The more we see the depth of our sin, the more we realize the height of God's love. The constant companion of repentance is gratitude; seeing our sin becomes, paradoxically, an opportunity for joy.

Then we are free indeed: free from any need to hide, to conceal or impress, to make excuses for ourselves, to demand our fair share. Free to love God with abandon, free to love others without bargaining and conditions. Free to love even those who hurt us, because ultimately nothing can hurt us. Knowing our sin, we pray for all other sinners, asking God to show them the mercy he has given so abundantly to us.

—*Frederica Mathewes-Green*

For more on confession, see reading at Hebrews 3:12–15.

14 The Danger of Criticism

Accept other believers who are weak in faith, and don't argue with them about what they think is right or wrong. [2] For instance, one person believes it's all right to eat anything. But another believer with a sensitive conscience will eat only vegetables. [3] Those who feel free to eat anything must not look down on those who don't. And those who don't eat certain foods must not condemn those who do, for God has accepted them. [4] Who are you to condemn someone else's servants? Their own master will judge whether they stand or fall. And with the Lord's help, they will stand and receive his approval.

[5] In the same way, some think one day is more holy than another day, while others think every day is alike. You should each be fully convinced that whichever day you choose is acceptable. [6] Those who worship the Lord on a special day do it to honor

---

Q&A — Submitting to Difficult Leaders?

ROMANS 13:1–6

How do I practice submission if the person I'm submitting to is difficult, makes poor choices, or doesn't earn my respect?

We don't submit to authority because the person is smarter, more capable, or knows best. We do it because Scripture tells us that all authority is put in place by God (Romans 13:1; 1 Peter 2:13). Our submission to earthly authority flows out of our submission to God. The only way we can submit gladly to unfair or inept authority is out of our desire to submit to God and please him.

Submission bears good fruit in our lives and character—and, conversely, an attitude of rebellion bears bad fruit. For example, when I failed to submit to a challenging boss, it bore the fruit of criticism, gossip, and hard feelings. God has used difficult leaders to teach me that often I come up with all kinds of criticism to justify why I shouldn't be expected to submit to that person. Over time, however, my refusal to submit to a difficult person is ultimately hardness toward God. It's as if I'm saying, *God, you haven't done right by me to put me in this situation.*

Submission doesn't mean that you never speak up. But it does mean you resist speaking *against* a person, and you treat him or her with respect. You interact with the person in a way that's blameless.

We resist disrespecting the other person, because it's the right thing to do, and we'll never regret it. And we trust God to bear good fruit in the situation and in us. No matter what's true about someone else, our response should be determined by whether we're willing to submit to the Lord in the situation and trust him with the results. Submission is ultimately about giving ourselves over to the goodness of God.

—Nancy Guthrie

For more on submission, see reading at Ephesians 5:21–33.

him. Those who eat any kind of food do so to honor the Lord, since they give thanks to God before eating. And those who refuse to eat certain foods also want to please the Lord and give thanks to God. [7] For we don't live for ourselves or die for ourselves. [8] If we live, it's to honor the Lord. And if we die, it's to honor the Lord. So whether we live or die, we belong to the Lord. [9] Christ died and rose again for this very purpose—to be Lord both of the living and of the dead.

[10] So why do you condemn another believer*? Why do you look down on another believer? Remember, we will all stand before the judgment seat of God. [11] For the Scriptures say,

"'As surely as I live,' says the LORD,
'every knee will bend to me,
  and every tongue will confess and give
    praise to God.*'"

[12] Yes, each of us will give a personal account to God. [13] So let's stop condemning each other. Decide instead to live in such a way that you will not cause another believer to stumble and fall.

[14] I know and am convinced on the authority of the Lord Jesus that no food, in and of itself, is wrong to eat. But if someone believes it is wrong, then for that person it is wrong. [15] And if another believer is distressed by what you eat, you are not acting in love if you eat it. Don't let your eating ruin someone for whom Christ died. [16] Then you will not be criticized for doing something you believe is good. [17] For the Kingdom of God is not a matter of what we eat or drink, but of living a life of goodness and peace and joy in the Holy Spirit. [18] If you serve Christ with this attitude, you will please God, and others will approve of you, too. [19] So then, let us aim for harmony in the church and try to build each other up.

[20] Don't tear apart the work of God over what you eat. Remember, all foods are acceptable, but it is wrong to eat something if it makes another person stumble. [21] It is better not to eat meat or drink wine or do anything else if it might cause another believer to stumble. [22] You may believe there's nothing wrong with what you are doing, but keep it between yourself and God. Blessed are those who don't feel guilty for doing something they have decided is right. [23] But if you have doubts about whether or not you should eat something, you are sinning if you go ahead and do it. For you are not following your convictions. If you do anything you believe is not right, you are sinning.

15 Living to Please Others

We who are strong must be considerate of those who are sensitive about things like this. We must not just please ourselves. [2] We should help others do what is right and build them up in the Lord. [3] For even Christ didn't live to please himself. As the Scriptures say, "The insults of those who insult you, O God, have fallen on me."* [4] Such things were written in the Scriptures long ago to teach us. And the Scriptures give us hope and encouragement as we wait patiently for God's promises to be fulfilled.

[5] May God, who gives this patience and encouragement, help you live in complete harmony with each other, as is fitting for followers of Christ Jesus. [6] Then all of you can join together with one voice, giving praise and glory to God, the Father of our Lord Jesus Christ.

[7] Therefore, accept each other just as Christ has accepted you so that God will be given glory. [8] Remember that Christ came as a servant to the Jews* to show that God is true to the promises he made to their ancestors. [9] He also came so that the Gentiles might give glory to God for his mercies to them. That is what the psalmist meant when he wrote:

"For this, I will praise you among the
    Gentiles;
  I will sing praises to your name."*

[10] And in another place it is written,

"Rejoice with his people,
  you Gentiles."*

[11] And yet again,

"Praise the LORD, all you Gentiles.
  Praise him, all you people of the
    earth."*

14:10 Greek *your brother*; also in 14:10b, 13, 15, 21.　**14:11** Or *confess allegiance to God.* Isa 49:18; 45:23 (Greek version).　**15:3** Greek *who insult you have fallen on me.* Ps 69:9.　**15:8** Greek *servant of circumcision.*　**15:9** Ps 18:49.　**15:10** Deut 32:43.　**15:11** Ps 117:1.

Proclaiming a Robust Gospel

ROMANS 15:14–19

Have we settled for a "little gospel"? Have we presented a small, personalized, simplistic message to our unbelieving culture? A miniaturized version of truth that cannot address the real problems of our world?

God calls us to share the whole, complete gospel—rather than a shrunken down, packaged, and incomplete version of it. As we share the gospel with friends and loved ones, we must remember several key ideas.

The gospel deals with a serious problem. Genesis 1–3 teaches us that humans are made in God's image and likeness. These image-bearers were in utter union with God, at home with themselves, in communion with one another, and in harmony with the world around them. When Eve, with her husband in tow, chose to eat of the wrong tree, the image was cracked in each of these four directions: God-alienation, self-shame, other-blame, and Eden-expulsion. Sin results not only in alienation from God, which is paramount, but also in shame of the self, blame and antagonism toward others, and banishment from the world as God made it to be. The rest of the Bible, from Genesis 4 to Revelation 22, is about these cracked image-bearers being restored to union with God, freed from shame, placed in communion with others, and offered to the world. This is not just about each individual's personal struggle with sin. Any gospel that does not expand the "problem" of Genesis 3 to these larger cosmic dimensions is not complete.

The gospel has a grand vision. A "little" gospel promises me personal salvation and eternal life. But the whole, big, and robust gospel doesn't stop there. It also promises a new society and a new creation. When Jesus stood to read Isaiah 61 in the synagogue at Nazareth, then sat down and declared that this prophetic vision was now coming to pass through him, there was more than personal redemption at work. God's kingdom, the society where God's will is established and lived, was now officially at work in his followers. That society was overturning the injustices and exclusions of the empire and establishing an inclusive and just alternative. We find this in Jesus' opening words (Luke 4:18-19) and the Beatitudes (Luke 6:20-23). This vision for a just society led to the radical practices of generosity and hospitality in the Jerusalem churches (Acts 2:42-47). Any gospel that is not announcing a new society at work in the world, what the apostle Paul called the church, is simply not a robust gospel.

The gospel demands not only faith but everything. Christian faith inherently involves repentance, trust, surrender, commitment, and obedience. Paul said that his intent in preaching the gospel is "so that they will believe and *obey* him" (Romans 1:5, italics added). Jesus called his disciples to surrender themselves to him in self-denial so they could follow him (Mark 8:34–38). The gospel summons each of us to respond in repentance, trust, surrender, commitment, and obedience. The gospel calls for a wholehearted, full-life response.

The gospel involves the work of God's Spirit. How often do we talk about the Spirit of God in our witness to others? To our shame, the Spirit has often been defined out of the gospel. But notice these words from Paul: "Yet I dare not boast about anything except what Christ has done through me, bringing the Gentiles to God by my message and by the way I worked among them. They were convinced by the power of miraculous signs and wonders and by *the power of God's Spirit*. In this way, I have fully presented *the Good News of Christ*" (Romans 15:18–19, italics added). Paul also wrote: "And now you Gentiles have also heard the truth, the Good News that God saves you. And when you believed in Christ, he identified you as his own *by giving you the Holy Spirit*, whom he promised long ago" (Ephesians 1:13, italics added). Jesus, too, said, "But if I am casting out demons *by the Spirit of God*, then the Kingdom of God has arrived among you" (Matthew 12:28, italics added). The gospel is animated by God's powerful Spirit, and its result is Spirit-empowerment for new living.

In Scripture we find a gospel that is much bigger than many of us have dared to believe: the gospel is the story of the work of the triune God to completely restore broken image-bearers in the context of the community of faith (through the life, death, and resurrection of Jesus Christ and the gift of the Pentecostal Spirit), to union with God and communion with others for the good of the world. This is the gospel—the whole, robust gospel—that we are called to proclaim.

—Scot McKnight

For more on outreach, see reading at 2 Corinthians 12:9–10.

¹²And in another place Isaiah said,

"The heir to David's throne* will come,
and he will rule over the Gentiles.
They will place their hope on him."*

¹³I pray that God, the source of hope, will fill you completely with joy and peace because you trust in him. Then you will overflow with confident hope through the power of the Holy Spirit.

Paul's Reason for Writing

¹⁴I am fully convinced, my dear brothers and sisters,* that you are full of goodness. You know these things so well you can teach each other all about them. ¹⁵Even so, I have been bold enough to write about some of these points, knowing that all you need is this reminder. For by God's grace, ¹⁶I am a special messenger from Christ Jesus to you Gentiles. I bring you the Good News so that I might present you as an acceptable offering to God, made holy by the Holy Spirit. ¹⁷So I have reason to be enthusiastic about all Christ Jesus has done through me in my service to God. ¹⁸Yet I dare not boast about anything except what Christ has done through me, bringing the Gentiles to God by my message and by the way I worked among them. ¹⁹They were convinced by the power of miraculous signs and wonders and by the power of God's Spirit.* In this way, I have fully presented the Good News of Christ from Jerusalem all the way to Illyricum.*

²⁰My ambition has always been to preach the Good News where the name of Christ has never been heard, rather than where a church has already been started by someone else. ²¹I have been following the plan spoken of in the Scriptures, where it says,

"Those who have never been told about
him will see,
and those who have never heard of
him will understand."*

²²In fact, my visit to you has been delayed so long because I have been preaching in these places.

Paul's Travel Plans

²³But now I have finished my work in these regions, and after all these long years of waiting, I am eager to visit you. ²⁴I am planning to go to Spain, and when I do, I will stop off in Rome. And after I have enjoyed your fellowship for a little while, you can provide for my journey.

²⁵But before I come, I must go to Jerusalem to take a gift to the believers* there. ²⁶For you see, the believers in Macedonia and Achaia* have eagerly taken up an offering for the poor among the believers in Jerusalem. ²⁷They were glad to do this because they feel they owe a real debt to them. Since the Gentiles received the spiritual blessings of the Good News from the believers in Jerusalem, they feel the least they can do in return is to help them financially. ²⁸As soon as I have delivered this money and completed this good deed of theirs, I will come to see you on my way to Spain. ²⁹And I am sure that when I come, Christ will richly bless our time together.

³⁰Dear brothers and sisters, I urge you in the name of our Lord Jesus Christ to join in my struggle by praying to God for me. Do this because of your love for me, given to you by the Holy Spirit. ³¹Pray that I will be rescued from those in Judea who refuse to obey God. Pray also that the believers there will be willing to accept the donation* I am taking to Jerusalem. ³²Then, by the will of God, I will be able to come to you with a joyful heart, and we will be an encouragement to each other.

³³And now may God, who gives us his peace, be with you all. Amen.*

16 Paul Greets His Friends

I commend to you our sister Phoebe, who is a deacon in the church in Cenchrea. ²Welcome her in the Lord as one who is worthy of honor among God's people. Help her in whatever she needs, for she has been helpful to many, and especially to me.

³Give my greetings to Priscilla and Aquila, my co-workers in the ministry of Christ Jesus. ⁴In fact, they once risked their lives

---

15:12a Greek *The root of Jesse.* David was the son of Jesse.   15:12b Isa 11:10 (Greek version).   15:14 Greek *brothers;* also in 15:30.   15:19a Other manuscripts read *the Spirit;* still others read *the Holy Spirit.*   15:19b *Illyricum* was a region northeast of Italy.   15:21 Isa 52:15 (Greek version).   15:25 Greek *God's holy people;* also in 15:26, 31.   15:26 *Macedonia* and *Achaia* were the northern and southern regions of Greece.   15:31 Greek *the ministry;* other manuscripts read *the gift.*   15:33 Some manuscripts do not include *Amen.* One very early manuscript places 16:25-27 here.

for me. I am thankful to them, and so are all the Gentile churches. [5]Also give my greetings to the church that meets in their home.

Greet my dear friend Epenetus. He was the first person from the province of Asia to become a follower of Christ. [6]Give my greetings to Mary, who has worked so hard for your benefit. [7]Greet Andronicus and Junia,* my fellow Jews,* who were in prison with me. They are highly respected among the apostles and became followers of Christ before I did. [8]Greet Ampliatus, my dear friend in the Lord. [9]Greet Urbanus, our co-worker in Christ, and my dear friend Stachys.

[10]Greet Apelles, a good man whom Christ approves. And give my greetings to the believers from the household of Aristobulus. [11]Greet Herodion, my fellow Jew.* Greet the Lord's people from the household of Narcissus. [12]Give my greetings to Tryphena and Tryphosa, the Lord's workers, and to dear Persis, who has worked so hard for the Lord. [13]Greet Rufus, whom the Lord picked out to be his very own; and also his dear mother, who has been a mother to me.

[14]Give my greetings to Asyncritus, Phlegon, Hermes, Patrobas, Hermas, and the brothers and sisters* who meet with them. [15]Give my greetings to Philologus, Julia, Nereus and his sister, and to Olympas and all the believers* who meet with them. [16]Greet each other in Christian love.* All the churches of Christ send you their greetings.

Paul's Final Instructions

[17]And now I make one more appeal, my dear brothers and sisters. Watch out for people who cause divisions and upset people's faith by teaching things contrary to what you have been taught. Stay away from them. [18]Such people are not serving Christ our Lord; they are serving their own personal interests. By smooth talk and glowing words they deceive innocent people. [19]But everyone knows that you are obedient to the Lord. This makes me very happy. I want you to be wise in doing right and to stay innocent of any wrong. [20]The God of peace will soon crush Satan under your feet. May the grace of our Lord Jesus* be with you.

[21]Timothy, my fellow worker, sends you his greetings, as do Lucius, Jason, and Sosipater, my fellow Jews.

[22]I, Tertius, the one writing this letter for Paul, send my greetings, too, as one of the Lord's followers.

[23]Gaius says hello to you. He is my host and also serves as host to the whole church. Erastus, the city treasurer, sends you his greetings, and so does our brother Quartus.*

[25]Now all glory to God, who is able to make you strong, just as my Good News says. This message about Jesus Christ has revealed his plan for you Gentiles, a plan kept secret from the beginning of time. [26]But now as the prophets* foretold and as the eternal God has commanded, this message is made known to all Gentiles everywhere, so that they too might believe and obey him. [27]All glory to the only wise God, through Jesus Christ, forever. Amen.

16:7a *Junia* is a feminine name. Some late manuscripts accent the word so it reads *Junias,* a masculine name; still others read *Julia* (feminine). **16:7b** Or *compatriots;* also in 16:21. **16:11** Or *compatriot.* **16:14** Greek *brothers;* also in 16:17. **16:15** Greek *all of God's holy people.* **16:16** Greek *with a sacred kiss.* **16:20** Some manuscripts read *Lord Jesus Christ.* **16:23** Some manuscripts add verse 24, *May the grace of our Lord Jesus Christ be with you all. Amen.* Still others add this sentence after verse 27. **16:26** Greek *the prophetic writings.*

Introduction to
1 Corinthians

Background

The city of Corinth was a major seaport and the capital of Achaia, in Greece. Two-thirds of the city's population were slaves. Corinth boasted many temples, the most famous being to Aphrodite, goddess of love; because of the temple's prostitutes, the city was identified with its immorality. The city also had a Jewish community, evidenced by archaeological remains of a synagogue. The author of 1 Corinthians is attested to in the book's first two verses: "This letter is from Paul, chosen by the will of God to be an apostle of Christ Jesus, and from our brother Sosthenes. I am writing to God's church in Corinth." Paul is also cited as the author in 16:21.

Message

Paul feels responsible for the Corinthian church, since he helped found it while on his second missionary journey (Acts 18:1–17). When Paul writes 1 Corinthians, the church is struggling with disunity, immorality, and the general difficulty of living as godly believers in a secular culture. Paul encourages them in unity in and through Christ. He confronts sin in the church community and comments about the advisability of marriage. He advocates freedom in Christ, lived out responsibly for the sake of the larger community. Toward the end of the admonishing text, Paul gives a critical teaching about the celebration of the Lord's Supper, and the church as a body with many members or parts, each with its specific function. Buried in this teaching is the often-cited chapter (13:1–13) on the virtue of love, or charity. Yet another memorable passage draws the reader's hope to the Resurrection and the resurrected Christ: "But thank God! He gives us victory over sin and death through our Lord Jesus Christ" (15:57).

Time

Paul's first letter to the believers in Corinth was written in Ephesus (16:8) circa A.D. 55.

Outline

1 Corinthians

1 Greetings from Paul

This letter is from Paul, chosen by the will of God to be an apostle of Christ Jesus, and from our brother Sosthenes.

²I am writing to God's church in Corinth,* to you who have been called by God to be his own holy people. He made you holy by means of Christ Jesus,* just as he did for all people everywhere who call on the name of our Lord Jesus Christ, their Lord and ours.

³May God our Father and the Lord Jesus Christ give you grace and peace.

Paul Gives Thanks to God

⁴I always thank my God for you and for the gracious gifts he has given you, now that you belong to Christ Jesus. ⁵Through him, God has enriched your church in every way—with all of your eloquent words and all of your knowledge. ⁶This confirms that what I told you about Christ is true. ⁷Now you have every spiritual gift you need as you eagerly wait for the return of our Lord Jesus Christ. ⁸He will keep you strong to the end so that you will be free from all blame on the day when our Lord Jesus Christ returns. ⁹God will do this, for he is faithful to do what he says, and he has invited you into partnership with his Son, Jesus Christ our Lord.

Divisions in the Church

¹⁰I appeal to you, dear brothers and sisters,* by the authority of our Lord Jesus Christ, to live in harmony with each other. Let there be no divisions in the church. Rather, be of one mind, united in thought and purpose. ¹¹For some members of Chloe's household have told me about your quarrels, my dear brothers and sisters. ¹²Some of you are saying, "I am a follower of Paul." Others are saying, "I follow Apollos," or "I follow Peter,*" or "I follow only Christ."

¹³Has Christ been divided into factions? Was I, Paul, crucified for you? Were any of you baptized in the name of Paul? Of course not! ¹⁴I thank God that I did not baptize any of you except Crispus and Gaius, ¹⁵for now no one can say they were baptized in my name. ¹⁶(Oh yes, I also baptized the household of Stephanas, but I don't remember baptizing anyone else.) ¹⁷For Christ didn't send me to baptize, but to preach the Good News—and not with clever speech, for fear that the cross of Christ would lose its power.

The Wisdom of God

¹⁸The message of the cross is foolish to those who are headed for destruction! But we who are being saved know it is the very power of God. ¹⁹As the Scriptures say,

"I will destroy the wisdom of the wise
    and discard the intelligence of the intelligent."*

1:2a *Corinth* was the capital city of Achaia, the southern region of the Greek peninsula.   **1:2b** Or *because you belong to Christ Jesus.*   **1:10** Greek *brothers;* also in 1:11, 26.   **1:12** Greek *Cephas.*   **1:19** Isa 29:14.

²⁰So where does this leave the philosophers, the scholars, and the world's brilliant debaters? God has made the wisdom of this world look foolish. ²¹Since God in his wisdom saw to it that the world would never know him through human wisdom, he has used our foolish preaching to save those who believe. ²²It is foolish to the Jews, who ask for signs from heaven. And it is foolish to the Greeks, who seek human wisdom. ²³So when we preach that Christ was crucified, the Jews are offended and the Gentiles say it's all nonsense.

²⁴But to those called by God to salvation, both Jews and Gentiles,* Christ is the power of God and the wisdom of God. ²⁵This foolish plan of God is wiser than the wisest of human plans, and God's weakness is stronger than the greatest of human strength.

²⁶Remember, dear brothers and sisters, that few of you were wise in the world's eyes or powerful or wealthy* when God called you. ²⁷Instead, God chose things the world considers foolish in order to shame those who think they are wise. And he chose things that are powerless to shame those who are powerful. ²⁸God chose things despised by the world,* things counted as nothing at all, and used them to bring to nothing what the world considers important. ²⁹As a result, no one can ever boast in the presence of God.

³⁰God has united you with Christ Jesus. For our benefit God made him to be wisdom itself. Christ made us right with God; he made us pure and holy, and he freed us from sin. ³¹Therefore, as the Scriptures say, "If you want to boast, boast only about the LORD."*

2 Paul's Message of Wisdom

When I first came to you, dear brothers and sisters,* I didn't use lofty words and impressive wisdom to tell you God's secret plan.* ²For I decided that while I was with you I would forget everything except Jesus Christ, the one who was crucified. ³I came to you in weakness—timid and trembling. ⁴And my message and my preaching were very plain. Rather than using clever and persuasive speeches, I relied only on the power of the Holy Spirit. ⁵I did this so you would trust not in human wisdom but in the power of God.

⁶Yet when I am among mature believers, I do speak with words of wisdom, but not the kind of wisdom that belongs to this world or to the rulers of this world, who are soon forgotten. ⁷No, the wisdom we speak of is the mystery of God*—his plan that was previously hidden, even though he made it for our ultimate glory before the world began. ⁸But the rulers of this world have not understood it; if they had, they would not have crucified our glorious Lord. ⁹That is what the Scriptures mean when they say,

"No eye has seen, no ear has heard,
    and no mind has imagined
what God has prepared
    for those who love him."*

¹⁰But* it was to us that God revealed these things by his Spirit. For his Spirit searches out everything and shows us God's deep secrets. ¹¹No one can know a person's thoughts except that person's own spirit, and no one can know God's thoughts except God's own Spirit. ¹²And we have received God's Spirit (not the world's spirit), so we can know the wonderful things God has freely given us.

¹³When we tell you these things, we do not use words that come from human wisdom. Instead, we speak words given to us by the Spirit, using the Spirit's words to explain spiritual truths.* ¹⁴But people who aren't spiritual* can't receive these truths from God's Spirit. It all sounds foolish to them and they can't understand it, for only those who are spiritual can understand what the Spirit means. ¹⁵Those who are spiritual can evaluate all things, but they themselves cannot be evaluated by others. ¹⁶For,

"Who can know the LORD's thoughts?
    Who knows enough to teach him?"*

But we understand these things, for we have the mind of Christ.

1:24 Greek and Greeks.   1:26 Or high born.   1:28 Or God chose those who are low born.   1:31 Jer 9:24.   2:1a Greek brothers.   2:1b Greek God's mystery; other manuscripts read God's testimony.   2:7 Greek But we speak God's wisdom in a mystery.   2:9 Isa 64:4.   2:10 Some manuscripts read For.   2:13 Or explaining spiritual truths in spiritual language; or explaining spiritual truths to spiritual people.   2:14 Or who don't have the Spirit; or who have only physical life.   2:16 Isa 40:13 (Greek version).

3 Paul and Apollos, Servants of Christ

Dear brothers and sisters,* when I was with you I couldn't talk to you as I would to spiritual people.* I had to talk as though you belonged to this world or as though you were infants in the Christian life.* ²I had to feed you with milk, not with solid food, because you weren't ready for anything stronger. And you still aren't ready, ³for you are still controlled by your sinful nature. You are jealous of one another and quarrel with each other. Doesn't that prove you are controlled by your sinful nature? Aren't you living like people of the world? ⁴When one of you says, "I am a follower of Paul," and another says, "I follow Apollos," aren't you acting just like people of the world?

⁵After all, who is Apollos? Who is Paul? We are only God's servants through whom you believed the Good News. Each of us did the work the Lord gave us. ⁶I planted the seed in your hearts, and Apollos watered it, but it was God who made it grow. ⁷It's not important who does the planting, or who does the watering. What's important is that God makes the seed grow. ⁸The one who plants and the one who waters work together with the same purpose. And both will be rewarded for their own hard work. ⁹For we are both God's workers. And you are God's field. You are God's building.

¹⁰Because of God's grace to me, I have laid the foundation like an expert builder. Now others are building on it. But whoever is building on this foundation must be very careful. ¹¹For no one can lay any foundation other than the one we already have—Jesus Christ.

¹²Anyone who builds on that foundation may use a variety of materials—gold, silver, jewels, wood, hay, or straw. ¹³But on the judgment day, fire will reveal what kind of work each builder has done. The fire will show if a person's work has any value. ¹⁴If the work survives, that builder will receive a reward. ¹⁵But if the work is burned up, the builder will suffer great loss. The builder will be saved, but like someone barely escaping through a wall of flames.

¹⁶Don't you realize that all of you together are the temple of God and that the Spirit of God lives in* you? ¹⁷God will destroy anyone who destroys this temple. For God's temple is holy, and you are that temple.

¹⁸Stop deceiving yourselves. If you think you are wise by this world's standards, you need to become a fool to be truly wise. ¹⁹For the wisdom of this world is foolishness to God. As the Scriptures say,

"He traps the wise
in the snare of their own cleverness."*

²⁰And again,

"The LORD knows the thoughts of the wise;
he knows they are worthless."*

²¹So don't boast about following a particular human leader. For everything belongs to you—²²whether Paul or Apollos or Peter,* or the world, or life and death, or the present and the future. Everything belongs to you, ²³and you belong to Christ, and Christ belongs to God.

4 Paul's Relationship with the Corinthians

So look at Apollos and me as mere servants of Christ who have been put in charge of explaining God's mysteries. ²Now, a person who is put in charge as a manager must be faithful. ³As for me, it matters very little how I might be evaluated by you or by any human authority. I don't even trust my own judgment on this point. ⁴My conscience is clear, but that doesn't prove I'm right. It is the Lord himself who will examine me and decide.

⁵So don't make judgments about anyone ahead of time—before the Lord returns. For he will bring our darkest secrets to light and will reveal our private motives. Then God will give to each one whatever praise is due.

⁶Dear brothers and sisters,* I have used Apollos and myself to illustrate what I've been saying. If you pay attention to what I have quoted from the Scriptures,* you won't be proud of one of your leaders at the expense of another. ⁷For what gives you the right to make such a judgment? What do

you have that God hasn't given you? And if everything you have is from God, why boast as though it were not a gift?

⁸You think you already have everything you need. You think you are already rich. You have begun to reign in God's kingdom without us! I wish you really were reigning already, for then we would be reigning with you. ⁹Instead, I sometimes think God has put us apostles on display, like prisoners of war at the end of a victor's parade, condemned to die. We have become a spectacle to the entire world—to people and angels alike.

¹⁰Our dedication to Christ makes us look like fools, but you claim to be so wise in Christ! We are weak, but you are so powerful! You are honored, but we are ridiculed. ¹¹Even now we go hungry and thirsty, and we don't have enough clothes to keep warm. We are often beaten and have no home. ¹²We work wearily with our own hands to earn our living. We bless those who curse us. We are patient with those who abuse us. ¹³We appeal gently when evil things are said about us. Yet we are treated like the world's garbage, like everybody's trash—right up to the present moment.

¹⁴I am not writing these things to shame you, but to warn you as my beloved children. ¹⁵For even if you had ten thousand others to teach you about Christ, you have only one spiritual father. For I became your father in Christ Jesus when I preached the Good News to you. ¹⁶So I urge you to imitate me.

¹⁷That's why I have sent Timothy, my beloved and faithful child in the Lord. He will remind you of how I follow Christ Jesus, just as I teach in all the churches wherever I go.

¹⁸Some of you have become arrogant, thinking I will not visit you again. ¹⁹But I will come—and soon—if the Lord lets me, and then I'll find out whether these arrogant people just give pretentious speeches or whether they really have God's power. ²⁰For the Kingdom of God is not just a lot of talk; it is living by God's power. ²¹Which

do you choose? Should I come with a rod to punish you, or should I come with love and a gentle spirit?

5 Paul Condemns Spiritual Pride

I can hardly believe the report about the sexual immorality going on among you—something that even pagans don't do. I am told that a man in your church is living in sin with his stepmother.* ²You are so proud of yourselves, but you should be mourning in sorrow and shame. And you should remove this man from your fellowship.

³Even though I am not with you in person, I am with you in the Spirit.* And as though I were there, I have already passed judgment on this man ⁴in the name of the Lord Jesus. You must call a meeting of the church.* I will be present with you in spirit, and so will the power of our Lord Jesus. ⁵Then you must throw this man out and hand him over to Satan so that his sinful nature will be destroyed* and he himself* will be saved on the day the Lord* returns.

⁶Your boasting about this is terrible. Don't you realize that this sin is like a little yeast that spreads through the whole batch of dough? ⁷Get rid of the old "yeast" by removing this wicked person from among you. Then you will be like a fresh batch of dough made without yeast, which is what you really are. Christ, our Passover Lamb, has been sacrificed for us.* ⁸So let us celebrate the festival, not with the old bread* of wickedness and evil, but with the new bread* of sincerity and truth.

⁹When I wrote to you before, I told you not to associate with people who indulge in sexual sin. ¹⁰But I wasn't talking about unbelievers who indulge in sexual sin, or are greedy, or cheat people, or worship idols. You would have to leave this world to avoid people like that. ¹¹I meant that you are not to associate with anyone who claims to be a believer* yet indulges in sexual sin, or is greedy, or worships idols, or is abusive, or is a drunkard, or cheats people. Don't even eat with such people.

5:1 Greek his father's wife.   **5:3** Or in spirit.   **5:4** Or In the name of the Lord Jesus, you must call a meeting of the church.   **5:5a** Or so that his body will be destroyed; Greek reads for the destruction of the flesh.   **5:5b** Greek and the spirit.   **5:5c** Other manuscripts read the Lord Jesus; still others read our Lord Jesus Christ.   **5:7** Greek has been sacrificed.   **5:8a** Greek not with old leaven.   **5:8b** Greek but with unleavened [bread].   **5:11** Greek a brother.

Praying for Those Who Hurt Us

1 CORINTHIANS 6:4–7

Forgiveness

When a friend betrayed me, I felt blindsided and deeply hurt. In the middle of my struggle, I sensed God drawing me to prayer. It began with prayers about how I could handle my hurt feelings, but eventually it turned into prayer for the woman who'd hurt me.

Every time I thought of her, I felt prompted to pray for her even though painful emotions remained. I focused my Bible reading and worship on Christ's death. In my prayers, over and over, I mentally pictured the offense nailed to the cross.

Then God caught me by surprise. I saw my offender in a store, and God prompted me to initiate a conversation with her. As we spoke God led me to hug her. I struggled, but chose to obey, and silently breathed a prayer for her as we embraced. I felt a supernatural freedom in that moment—in some quiet way, God triumphed in my life as he helped me show her his unconditional love.

Scripture calls us to forgive—and to *pray* for those who hurt us (Matthew 5:44; Romans 12:14). Although emotionally it can feel impossible, perhaps it's in those difficult prayers that the miracle of true forgiveness begins.

—Sherryl Stone

For more on forgiveness, see reading at Galatians 5:22–23.

---

¹²It isn't my responsibility to judge outsiders, but it certainly is your responsibility to judge those inside the church who are sinning. ¹³God will judge those on the outside; but as the Scriptures say, "You must remove the evil person from among you."*

6 Avoiding Lawsuits with Christians

When one of you has a dispute with another believer, how dare you file a lawsuit and ask a secular court to decide the matter instead of taking it to other believers*! ²Don't you realize that someday we believers will judge the world? And since you are going to judge the world, can't you decide even these little things among yourselves? ³Don't you realize that we will judge angels? So you should surely be able to resolve ordinary disputes in this life. ⁴If you have legal disputes about such matters, why go to outside judges who are not respected by the church? ⁵I am saying this to shame you. Isn't there anyone in all the church who is wise enough to decide these issues? ⁶But instead, one believer* sues another—right in front of unbelievers!

⁷Even to have such lawsuits with one another is a defeat for you. Why not just accept the injustice and leave it at that? Why not let yourselves be cheated? ⁸Instead, you yourselves are the ones who do wrong and cheat even your fellow believers.*

⁹Don't you realize that those who do wrong will not inherit the Kingdom of God? Don't fool yourselves. Those who indulge in sexual sin, or who worship idols, or commit adultery, or are male prostitutes, or practice homosexuality, ¹⁰or are thieves, or greedy people, or drunkards, or are abusive, or cheat people—none of these will inherit the Kingdom of God. ¹¹Some of you were once like that. But you were cleansed; you were made holy; you were made right with God by calling on the name of the Lord Jesus Christ and by the Spirit of our God.

5:13 Deut 17:7. **6:1** Greek *God's holy people;* also in 6:2. **6:6** Greek *one brother.* **6:8** Greek *even the brothers.*

Avoiding Sexual Sin

¹²You say, "I am allowed to do anything"—but not everything is good for you. And even though "I am allowed to do anything," I must not become a slave to anything. ¹³You say, "Food was made for the stomach, and the stomach for food." (This is true, though someday God will do away with both of them.) But you can't say that our bodies were made for sexual immorality. They were made for the Lord, and the Lord cares about our bodies. ¹⁴And God will raise us from the dead by his power, just as he raised our Lord from the dead.

¹⁵Don't you realize that your bodies are actually parts of Christ? Should a man take his body, which is part of Christ, and join it to a prostitute? Never! ¹⁶And don't you realize that if a man joins himself to a prostitute, he becomes one body with her? For the Scriptures say, "The two are united into one."* ¹⁷But the person who is joined to the Lord is one spirit with him.

¹⁸Run from sexual sin! No other sin so clearly affects the body as this one does. For sexual immorality is a sin against your own body. ¹⁹Don't you realize that your body is the temple of the Holy Spirit, who lives in you and was given to you by God? You do not belong to yourself, ²⁰for God bought you with a high price. So you must honor God with your body.

7 Instruction on Marriage

Now regarding the questions you asked in your letter. Yes, it is good to abstain from sexual relations.* ²But because there is so much sexual immorality, each man should have his own wife, and each woman should have her own husband.

³The husband should fulfill his wife's sexual needs, and the wife should fulfill her husband's needs. ⁴The wife gives authority over her body to her husband, and the husband gives authority over his body to his wife.

⁵Do not deprive each other of sexual relations, unless you both agree to refrain from sexual intimacy for a limited time so you can give yourselves more completely to prayer. Afterward, you should come together again so that Satan won't be able to tempt you because of your lack of self-control. ⁶I say this as a concession, not as a command. ⁷But I wish everyone were single, just as I am. Yet each person has a special gift from God, of one kind or another.

⁸So I say to those who aren't married and to widows—it's better to stay unmarried, just as I am. ⁹But if they can't control themselves, they should go ahead and marry. It's better to marry than to burn with lust.

¹⁰But for those who are married, I have a command that comes not from me, but from the Lord.* A wife must not leave her husband. ¹¹But if she does leave him, let her remain single or else be reconciled to him. And the husband must not leave his wife.

¹²Now, I will speak to the rest of you, though I do not have a direct command from the Lord. If a Christian man* has a wife who is not a believer and she is willing to continue living with him, he must not leave her. ¹³And if a Christian woman has a husband who is not a believer and he is willing to continue living with her, she must not leave him. ¹⁴For the Christian wife brings holiness to her marriage, and the Christian husband* brings holiness to his marriage. Otherwise, your children would not be holy, but now they are holy. ¹⁵(But if the husband or wife who isn't a believer insists on leaving, let them go. In such cases the Christian husband or wife* is no longer bound to the other, for God has called you* to live in peace.) ¹⁶Don't you wives realize that your husbands might be saved because of you? And don't you husbands realize that your wives might be saved because of you?

¹⁷Each of you should continue to live in whatever situation the Lord has placed you, and remain as you were when God first called you. This is my rule for all the churches. ¹⁸For instance, a man who was circumcised before he became a believer should not try to reverse it. And the man who was uncircumcised when he became a believer should not be circumcised now. ¹⁹For it makes no difference whether or not a man has been circumcised. The important thing is to keep God's commandments. ²⁰Yes, each of you should remain as you

6:16 Gen 2:24.   7:1 Or to live a celibate life; Greek reads It is good for a man not to touch a woman.   7:10 See Matt 5:32; 19:9; Mark 10:11-12; Luke 16:18.   7:12 Greek a brother.   7:14 Greek the brother.   7:15a Greek the brother or sister.   7:15b Some manuscripts read us.

Live like the Time Is Short

1 CORINTHIANS 7:29–31

The poet Mary Oliver asks, "Tell me, what is it you plan to do with your one wild and precious life?" It's a startling question to consider. Am I focusing on what's really important? Or is my one wild and precious life being lived overstretched, overcomplicated, and overcommitted?

The apostle Paul reminded the Corinthian Christians, "The time that remains is very short.... For this world as we know it will soon pass away" (1 Corinthians 7:29, 31). His words urge me to think about what's really important. What would I do if I knew I didn't have a lot of time left? This question draws me to the heart of simplicity.

I turn off my cell phone and stop checking my e-mail for a few hours. I go for a walk in the park—in the sun, rain, wind, or snow—and use my five senses to see, smell, feel, taste, and hear the natural world around me. I let the dishes soak in the sink for an evening and snuggle with my daughter on the couch. I sit in the dark on my back porch, marveling at the Big Dipper.

So much of the time we surround ourselves with white noise. God wants to talk to us, to linger with us, but we have to make a quiet space for him to come in. Simplicity is making that room, cutting out the things that clamor for attention, if only for a little while. When I die, I want to know I've paid attention to this "one wild and precious life" God's given me. True simplicity is a way to begin.

—Cindy Crosby

For more on simplicity, see reading at 1 Thessalonians 4:11–12.

---

were when God called you. ²¹ Are you a slave? Don't let that worry you—but if you get a chance to be free, take it. ²² And remember, if you were a slave when the Lord called you, you are now free in the Lord. And if you were free when the Lord called you, you are now a slave of Christ. ²³ God paid a high price for you, so don't be enslaved by the world.* ²⁴ Each of you, dear brothers and sisters,* should remain as you were when God first called you.

²⁵ Now regarding your question about the young women who are not yet married. I do not have a command from the Lord for them. But the Lord in his mercy has given me wisdom that can be trusted, and I will share it with you. ²⁶ Because of the present crisis,* I think it is best to remain as you are. ²⁷ If you have a wife, do not seek to end the marriage. If you do not have a wife, do not seek to get married. ²⁸ But if you do get married, it is not a sin. And if a young woman gets married, it is not a sin. However, those who get married at this time will have troubles, and I am trying to spare you those problems.

²⁹ But let me say this, dear brothers and sisters: The time that remains is very short. So from now on, those with wives should not focus only on their marriage. ³⁰ Those who weep or who rejoice or who buy things should not be absorbed by their weeping or their joy or their possessions. ³¹ Those who use the things of the world should not become attached to them. For this world as we know it will soon pass away.

³² I want you to be free from the concerns of this life. An unmarried man can spend his time doing the Lord's work and thinking how to please him. ³³ But a married man

7:23 Greek *don't become slaves of people.* **7:24** Greek *brothers;* also in 7:29. **7:26** Or *the pressures of life.*

has to think about his earthly responsibilities and how to please his wife. ³⁴His interests are divided. In the same way, a woman who is no longer married or has never been married can be devoted to the Lord and holy in body and in spirit. But a married woman has to think about her earthly responsibilities and how to please her husband. ³⁵I am saying this for your benefit, not to place restrictions on you. I want you to do whatever will help you serve the Lord best, with as few distractions as possible.

³⁶But if a man thinks that he's treating his fiancée improperly and will inevitably give in to his passion, let him marry her as he wishes. It is not a sin. ³⁷But if he has decided firmly not to marry and there is no urgency and he can control his passion, he does well not to marry. ³⁸So the person who marries his fiancée does well, and the person who doesn't marry does even better.

³⁹A wife is bound to her husband as long as he lives. If her husband dies, she is free to marry anyone she wishes, but only if he loves the Lord.* ⁴⁰But in my opinion it would be better for her to stay single, and I think I am giving you counsel from God's Spirit when I say this.

8 Food Sacrificed to Idols

Now regarding your question about food that has been offered to idols. Yes, we know that "we all have knowledge" about this issue. But while knowledge makes us feel important, it is love that strengthens the church. ²Anyone who claims to know all the answers doesn't really know very much. ³But the person who loves God is the one whom God recognizes.*

⁴So, what about eating meat that has been offered to idols? Well, we all know that an idol is not really a god and that there is only one God. ⁵There may be so-called gods both in heaven and on earth, and some people actually worship many gods and many lords. ⁶But we know that there is only one God, the Father, who created everything, and we live for him. And there is only one Lord, Jesus Christ, through whom God made everything and through whom we have been given life.

⁷However, not all believers know this. Some are accustomed to thinking of idols as being real, so when they eat food that has been offered to idols, they think of it as the worship of real gods, and their weak consciences are violated. ⁸It's true that we can't win God's approval by what we eat. We don't lose anything if we don't eat it, and we don't gain anything if we do.

⁹But you must be careful so that your freedom does not cause others with a weaker conscience to stumble. ¹⁰For if others see you—with your "superior knowledge"—eating in the temple of an idol, won't they be encouraged to violate their conscience by eating food that has been offered to an idol? ¹¹So because of your superior knowledge, a weak believer* for whom Christ died will be destroyed. ¹²And when you sin against other believers* by encouraging them to do something they believe is wrong, you are sinning against Christ. ¹³So if what I eat causes another believer to sin, I will never eat meat again as long as I live—for I don't want to cause another believer to stumble.

9 Paul Gives Up His Rights

Am I not as free as anyone else? Am I not an apostle? Haven't I seen Jesus our Lord with my own eyes? Isn't it because of my work that you belong to the Lord? ²Even if others think I am not an apostle, I certainly am to you. You yourselves are proof that I am the Lord's apostle.

³This is my answer to those who question my authority.* ⁴Don't we have the right to live in your homes and share your meals? ⁵Don't we have the right to bring a Christian wife with us as the other apostles and the Lord's brothers do, and as Peter* does? ⁶Or is it only Barnabas and I who have to work to support ourselves?

⁷What soldier has to pay his own expenses? What farmer plants a vineyard and doesn't have the right to eat some of its fruit? What shepherd cares for a flock of sheep and isn't allowed to drink some of the milk? ⁸Am I expressing merely a human opinion, or does the law say the same thing? ⁹For the law of Moses says, "You must not

---

7:39 Greek *but only in the Lord.*   **8:3** Some manuscripts read *the person who loves God has full knowledge.*   **8:11** Greek *brother;* also in 8:13.
8:12 Greek *brothers.*   **9:3** Greek *those who examine me.*   **9:5** Greek *Cephas.*

muzzle an ox to keep it from eating as it treads out the grain."* Was God thinking only about oxen when he said this? ¹⁰Wasn't he actually speaking to us? Yes, it was written for us, so that the one who plows and the one who threshes the grain might both expect a share of the harvest.

¹¹ Since we have planted spiritual seed among you, aren't we entitled to a harvest of physical food and drink? ¹²If you support others who preach to you, shouldn't we have an even greater right to be supported? But we have never used this right. We would rather put up with anything than be an obstacle to the Good News about Christ.

¹³Don't you realize that those who work in the temple get their meals from the offerings brought to the temple? And those who serve at the altar get a share of the sacrificial offerings. ¹⁴In the same way, the Lord ordered that those who preach the Good News should be supported by those who benefit from it. ¹⁵Yet I have never used any of these rights. And I am not writing this to suggest that I want to start now. In fact, I would rather die than lose my right to boast about preaching without charge. ¹⁶ Yet preaching the Good News is not something I can boast about. I am compelled by God to do it. How terrible for me if I didn't preach the Good News!

¹⁷If I were doing this on my own initiative, I would deserve payment. But I have no choice, for God has given me this sacred trust. ¹⁸What then is my pay? It is the opportunity to preach the Good News without charging anyone. That's why I never demand my rights when I preach the Good News.

¹⁹Even though I am a free man with no master, I have become a slave to all people to bring many to Christ. ²⁰When I was with the Jews, I lived like a Jew to bring the Jews to Christ. When I was with those who follow the Jewish law, I too lived under that law. Even though I am not subject to the law, I did this so I could bring to Christ those who are under the law. ²¹When I am with the Gentiles who do not follow the Jewish law,* I too live apart from that law

so I can bring them to Christ. But I do not ignore the law of God; I obey the law of Christ.

²²When I am with those who are weak, I share their weakness, for I want to bring the weak to Christ. Yes, I try to find common ground with everyone, doing everything I can to save some. ²³I do everything to spread the Good News and share in its blessings.

²⁴Don't you realize that in a race everyone runs, but only one person gets the prize? So run to win! ²⁵All athletes are disciplined in their training. They do it to win a prize that will fade away, but we do it for an eternal prize. ²⁶So I run with purpose in every step. I am not just shadowboxing. ²⁷I discipline my body like an athlete, training it to do what it should. Otherwise, I fear that after preaching to others I myself might be disqualified.

10 Lessons from Israel's Idolatry

I don't want you to forget, dear brothers and sisters,* about our ancestors in the wilderness long ago. All of them were guided by a cloud that moved ahead of them, and all of them walked through the sea on dry ground. ²In the cloud and in the sea, all of them were baptized as followers of Moses. ³All of them ate the same spiritual food, ⁴and all of them drank the same spiritual water. For they drank from the spiritual rock that traveled with them, and that rock was Christ. ⁵Yet God was not pleased with most of them, and their bodies were scattered in the wilderness.

⁶These things happened as a warning to us, so that we would not crave evil things as they did, ⁷or worship idols as some of them did. As the Scriptures say, "The people celebrated with feasting and drinking, and they indulged in pagan revelry."* ⁸And we must not engage in sexual immorality as some of them did, causing 23,000 of them to die in one day.

⁹Nor should we put Christ* to the test, as some of them did and then died from snakebites. ¹⁰And don't grumble as some of them did, and then were destroyed by the angel of death. ¹¹These things happened to

---

9:9 Deut 25:4.   **9:21** Greek those without the law.   **10:1** Greek brothers.   **10:7** Exod 32:6.   **10:9** Some manuscripts read the Lord.

them as examples for us. They were written down to warn us who live at the end of the age.

¹²If you think you are standing strong, be careful not to fall. ¹³The temptations in your life are no different from what others experience. And God is faithful. He will not allow the temptation to be more than you can stand. When you are tempted, he will show you a way out so that you can endure.

¹⁴So, my dear friends, flee from the worship of idols. ¹⁵You are reasonable people. Decide for yourselves if what I am saying is true. ¹⁶When we bless the cup at the Lord's Table, aren't we sharing in the blood of Christ? And when we break the bread, aren't we sharing in the body of Christ? ¹⁷And though we are many, we all eat from one loaf of bread, showing that we are one body. ¹⁸Think about the people of Israel. Weren't they united by eating the sacrifices at the altar?

¹⁹What am I trying to say? Am I saying that food offered to idols has some significance, or that idols are real gods? ²⁰No, not at all. I am saying that these sacrifices are offered to demons, not to God. And I don't want you to participate with demons. ²¹You cannot drink from the cup of the Lord and from the cup of demons, too. You cannot eat at the Lord's Table and at the table of demons, too. ²²What? Do we dare to rouse the Lord's jealousy? Do you think we are stronger than he is?

²³You say, "I am allowed to do anything"*—but not everything is good for you. You say, "I am allowed to do anything"—but not everything is beneficial. ²⁴Don't be concerned for your own good but for the good of others.

²⁵So you may eat any meat that is sold in the marketplace without raising questions of conscience. ²⁶For "the earth is the LORD's, and everything in it."*

²⁷If someone who isn't a believer asks you home for dinner, accept the invitation if you want to. Eat whatever is offered to you without raising questions of conscience. ²⁸(But suppose someone tells you,

"This meat was offered to an idol." Don't eat it, out of consideration for the conscience of the one who told you. ²⁹It might not be a matter of conscience for you, but it is for the other person.) For why should my freedom be limited by what someone else thinks? ³⁰If I can thank God for the food and enjoy it, why should I be condemned for eating it?

³¹So whether you eat or drink, or whatever you do, do it all for the glory of God. ³²Don't give offense to Jews or Gentiles* or the church of God. ³³I, too, try to please everyone in everything I do. I don't just do what is best for me; I do what is best for others so that many may be saved. ¹¹:¹And you should imitate me, just as I imitate Christ.

11 Instructions for Public Worship

²I am so glad that you always keep me in your thoughts, and that you are following the teachings I passed on to you. ³But there is one thing I want you to know: The head of every man is Christ, the head of woman is man, and the head of Christ is God.* ⁴A man dishonors his head* if he covers his head while praying or prophesying. ⁵But a woman dishonors her head* if she prays or prophesies without a covering on her head, for this is the same as shaving her head. ⁶Yes, if she refuses to wear a head covering, she should cut off all her hair! But since it is shameful for a woman to have her hair cut or her head shaved, she should wear a covering.*

⁷A man should not wear anything on his head when worshiping, for man is made in God's image and reflects God's glory. And woman reflects man's glory. ⁸For the first man didn't come from woman, but the first woman came from man. ⁹And man was not made for woman, but woman was made for man. ¹⁰For this reason, and because the angels are watching, a woman should wear a covering on her head to show she is under authority.*

¹¹But among the Lord's people, women are not independent of men, and men are

---

10:23 Greek *All things are lawful; also in 10:23b.* **10:26** Ps 24:1. **10:32** Greek *or Greeks.* **11:3** Or *to know: The source of every man is Christ, the source of woman is man, and the source of Christ is God.* Or *to know: Every man is responsible to Christ, a woman is responsible to her husband, and Christ is responsible to God.* **11:4** Or *dishonors Christ.* **11:5** Or *dishonors her husband.* **11:6** Or *should have long hair.* **11:10** Greek *should have an authority on her head.*

Stones That Speak
1 CORINTHIANS 10:31–11:2

Mentoring

Every summer I take a solo backpack trip. My biggest fear is getting lost. To bolster my courage, I have a waterproof map and two compasses. But a compass isn't much help if you've lost your trail—and instinct will take you only so far.

When my instincts fail, I look for cairns; small piles of stones that other hikers leave in critical places along the path to show the way. Cairns are built by the first backpackers on the trails during the season. After guessing at the wrong path, they eventually find the right way across. So they backtrack and build cairns to show future hikers the trail.

The spiritual life is also full of cairns—signposts that show us the way ahead. Sometimes these cairns are people whose words or example help us find our bearings through our spiritual journey. For me, one cairn was a wise older woman whose life and work I admire. I whined to her about an issue I was struggling with. She spoke simple but illuminating words of truth—words that both encouraged and convicted me. Because I respected her, when she said something challenging, I listened. Her words helped me see the direction to go.

This woman and many others have been spiritual cairns for me—cairns that were in the right place, at the right time, and helped me move forward on my spiritual journey. They remind me of Paul who consciously made his life be a cairn for other believers along the path, inviting them to "imitate me, just as I imitate Christ" (1 Corinthians 11:1). Sometimes they've been people who've journeyed by my side; other times just a moment with them—a glimpse of their God-honoring lives—has set me along the right path.

It's up to me to pay attention and find the cairns God has placed along my path to point the way. I know I'll still get lost sometimes. But as I take each step forward, I'm comforted to know I'll find someone has been there first and marked the pathway to home.

—Cindy Crosby

For more on mentoring, see reading at 2 Corinthians 1:3–4.

not independent of women. [12] For although the first woman came from man, every other man was born from a woman, and everything comes from God.

[13] Judge for yourselves. Is it right for a woman to pray to God in public without covering her head? [14] Isn't it obvious that it's disgraceful for a man to have long hair? [15] And isn't long hair a woman's pride and joy? For it has been given to her as a covering. [16] But if anyone wants to argue about this, I simply say that we have no other custom than this, and neither do God's other churches.

Order at the Lord's Supper

[17] But in the following instructions, I cannot praise you. For it sounds as if more harm than good is done when you meet together. [18] First, I hear that there are divisions among you when you meet as a church, and to some extent I believe it. [19] But, of course, there must be divisions among you so that you who have God's approval will be recognized!

[20] When you meet together, you are not really interested in the Lord's Supper. [21] For some of you hurry to eat your own meal without sharing with others. As a result,

some go hungry while others get drunk. [22] What? Don't you have your own homes for eating and drinking? Or do you really want to disgrace God's church and shame the poor? What am I supposed to say? Do you want me to praise you? Well, I certainly will not praise you for this!

[23] For I pass on to you what I received from the Lord himself. On the night when he was betrayed, the Lord Jesus took some bread [24] and gave thanks to God for it. Then he broke it in pieces and said, "This is my body, which is given for you.* Do this to remember me." [25] In the same way, he took the cup of wine after supper, saying, "This cup is the new covenant between God and his people—an agreement confirmed with my blood. Do this to remember me as often as you drink it." [26] For every time you eat this bread and drink this cup, you are announcing the Lord's death until he comes again.

[27] So anyone who eats this bread or drinks this cup of the Lord unworthily is guilty of sinning against* the body and blood of the Lord. [28] That is why you should examine yourself before eating the bread and drinking the cup. [29] For if you eat the bread or drink the cup without honoring the body of Christ,* you are eating and drinking God's judgment upon yourself. [30] That is why many of you are weak and sick and some have even died.

[31] But if we would examine ourselves, we would not be judged by God in this way. [32] Yet when we are judged by the Lord, we are being disciplined so that we will not be condemned along with the world.

[33] So, my dear brothers and sisters,* when you gather for the Lord's Supper, wait for each other. [34] If you are really hungry, eat at home so you won't bring judgment upon yourselves when you meet together. I'll give you instructions about the other matters after I arrive.

12 Spiritual Gifts
Now, dear brothers and sisters,* regarding your question about the special abilities the Spirit gives us. I don't want you to misunderstand this. [2] You know that when you were still pagans, you were led astray and swept along in worshiping speechless idols. [3] So I want you to know that no one speaking by the Spirit of God will curse Jesus, and no one can say Jesus is Lord, except by the Holy Spirit.

[4] There are different kinds of spiritual gifts, but the same Spirit is the source of them all. [5] There are different kinds of service, but we serve the same Lord. [6] God works in different ways, but it is the same God who does the work in all of us.

[7] A spiritual gift is given to each of us so we can help each other. [8] To one person the Spirit gives the ability to give wise advice*; to another the same Spirit gives a message of special knowledge.* [9] The same Spirit gives great faith to another, and to someone else the one Spirit gives the gift of healing. [10] He gives one person the power to perform miracles, and another the ability to prophesy. He gives someone else the ability to discern whether a message is from the Spirit of God or from another spirit. Still another person is given the ability to speak in unknown languages,* while another is given the ability to interpret what is being said. [11] It is the one and only Spirit who distributes all these gifts. He alone decides which gift each person should have.

One Body with Many Parts
[12] The human body has many parts, but the many parts make up one whole body. So it is with the body of Christ. [13] Some of us are Jews, some are Gentiles,* some are slaves, and some are free. But we have all been baptized into one body by one Spirit, and we all share the same Spirit.*

[14] Yes, the body has many different parts, not just one part. [15] If the foot says, "I am not a part of the body because I am not a hand," that does not make it any less a part of the body. [16] And if the ear says, "I am not part of the body because I am not an eye," would that make it any less a part of the body? [17] If the whole body were an eye, how would you hear? Or if your whole body were an ear, how would you smell anything?

[18] But our bodies have many parts, and

11:24 Greek which is for you; other manuscripts read which is broken for you. 11:27 Or is responsible for. 11:29 Greek the body; other manuscripts read the Lord's body. 11:33 Greek brothers. 12:1 Greek brothers. 12:8a Or gives a word of wisdom. 12:8b Or gives a word of knowledge. 12:10 Or in various tongues; also in 12:28, 30. 12:13a Greek some are Greeks. 12:13b Greek we were all given one Spirit to drink.

God has put each part just where he wants it. [19]How strange a body would be if it had only one part! [20]Yes, there are many parts, but only one body. [21]The eye can never say to the hand, "I don't need you." The head can't say to the feet, "I don't need you."

[22]In fact, some parts of the body that seem weakest and least important are actually the most necessary. [23]And the parts we regard as less honorable are those we clothe with the greatest care. So we carefully protect those parts that should not be seen, [24]while the more honorable parts do not require this special care. So God has put the body together such that extra honor and care are given to those parts that have less dignity. [25]This makes for harmony among the members, so that all the members care for each other. [26]If one part suffers, all the parts suffer with it, and if one part is honored, all the parts are glad.

[27]All of you together are Christ's body, and each of you is a part of it. [28]Here are some of the parts God has appointed for the church:

> first are apostles,
> second are prophets,
> third are teachers,
> then those who do miracles,
> those who have the gift of healing,
> those who can help others,
> those who have the gift of leadership,
> those who speak in unknown languages.

[29]Are we all apostles? Are we all prophets? Are we all teachers? Do we all have the power to do miracles? [30]Do we all have the gift of healing? Do we all have the ability to speak in unknown languages? Do we all have the ability to interpret unknown languages? Of course not! [31]So you should earnestly desire the most helpful gifts.

But now let me show you a way of life that is best of all.

13 Love Is the Greatest

If I could speak all the languages of earth and of angels, but didn't love others, I would only be a noisy gong or a clanging cymbal. [2]If I had the gift of prophecy, and if I understood all of God's secret plans and possessed all knowledge, and if I had such faith that I could move mountains, but didn't love others, I would be nothing. [3]If I gave everything I have to the poor and even sacrificed my body, I could boast about it;* but if I didn't love others, I would have gained nothing.

[4]Love is patient and kind. Love is not jealous or boastful or proud [5]or rude. It does not demand its own way. It is not irritable, and it keeps no record of being wronged. [6]It does not rejoice about injustice but rejoices whenever the truth wins out. [7]Love never gives up, never loses faith, is always hopeful, and endures through every circumstance.

[8]Prophecy and speaking in unknown languages* and special knowledge will become useless. But love will last forever! [9]Now our knowledge is partial and incomplete, and even the gift of prophecy reveals only part of the whole picture! [10]But when the time of perfection comes, these partial things will become useless.

[11]When I was a child, I spoke and thought and reasoned as a child. But when I grew up, I put away childish things. [12]Now we see things imperfectly, like puzzling reflections in a mirror, but then we will see everything with perfect clarity.* All that I know now is partial and incomplete, but then I will know everything completely, just as God now knows me completely.

[13]Three things will last forever—faith, hope, and love—and the greatest of these is love.

14 Tongues and Prophecy

Let love be your highest goal! But you should also desire the special abilities the Spirit gives—especially the ability to prophesy. [2]For if you have the ability to speak in tongues,* you will be talking only to God, since people won't be able to understand you. You will be speaking by the power of the Spirit,* but it will all be mysterious. [3]But one who prophesies strengthens others, encourages them, and comforts them. [4]A person who speaks in tongues is strengthened personally, but one who speaks a word of prophecy strengthens the entire church.

13:3 Some manuscripts read *sacrificed my body to be burned.* **13:8** Or *in tongues.* **13:12** Greek *see face to face.* **14:2a** Or *in unknown languages;* also in 14:4, 5, 13, 14, 18, 22, 26, 27, 28, 39. **14:2b** Or *speaking in your spirit.*

Q&A

To Know and Be Known

1 CORINTHIANS 13

I want to have close Christian friends, but I'm afraid of getting hurt. What can I do?

When I was a little girl, friendships were abundant, easy, and simple—but now the world is different. Despite technological advances that allow us constantly to network and communicate, we're an increasingly isolated, anonymous culture. Many of us hardly know our neighbors and have merely peripheral relationships with co-workers. The social landscape has become disturbingly bleak.

Christians are not immune to this trend; like the culture at large, we often live lonely lives. As we clip through each day at a frenetic pace, we hardly have the time or emotional energy needed to go deeper in our relationships with Christian friends or even with our spouses. This lack of investment in community spins us into an ever-deepening cycle of loneliness and isolation.

From the beginning of time, God declared that it wasn't good for the first human to be alone (Genesis 2:18). Though he was already in relationship with God, Adam also had a fundamental need for companionship. This same need for human connection lives on in each of us; we long to know and be known— to be understood and loved both by God and by others. But from Adam and Eve's first conflict until now, our efforts to sustain close relationships— marriages, friendships, familial bonds—are fraught with missteps, misunderstandings, mistakes, and misplaced expectations. We get it wrong; we hurt others or are hurt by them. Inevitably, we end up feeling lonely.

Yet rather than surrender to this hurt, disappointment, or loneliness, God calls us to press on—to turn *toward* deeper community rather than to self-protectively turn away. Christian community is certainly not some mythic, idealized state of relational bliss; even the truest Christian friendship, the most tight-knit small group, or the most committed marriage will have its problems. And ultimately our deepest soul longings will only find fulfillment in God. Yet God invites us to experience a glimmer of this satisfaction on earth as we choose vulnerability over anonymity, serving others over self-protection, and lives that are intimately and intricately connected with others rather than the "safe" but barren existence of isolation.

As we choose to practice community, we discover a strange joy. It's messy, it can hurt, and it won't completely fulfill our deepest soul needs—but we find a hopeful togetherness that God intended. *Together* we long for the full oneness we'll experience as we join the community of saints in God's truly satisfying presence for eternity.

—*Kelli B. Trujillo*

For more on community, see reading at Colossians 1:18.

⁵I wish you could all speak in tongues, but even more I wish you could all prophesy. For prophecy is greater than speaking in tongues, unless someone interprets what you are saying so that the whole church will be strengthened.

⁶Dear brothers and sisters,* if I should come to you speaking in an unknown language,* how would that help you? But if I bring you a revelation or some special knowledge or prophecy or teaching, that will be helpful. ⁷Even lifeless instruments like the flute or the harp must play the notes clearly, or no one will recognize the melody. ⁸And if the bugler doesn't sound a clear call, how will the soldiers know they are being called to battle?

⁹It's the same for you. If you speak to people in words they don't understand, how will they know what you are saying? You might as well be talking into empty space.

¹⁰There are many different languages in the world, and every language has meaning. ¹¹But if I don't understand a language, I will be a foreigner to someone who speaks it, and the one who speaks it will be a foreigner to me. ¹²And the same is true for you. Since you are so eager to have the special abilities the Spirit gives, seek those that will strengthen the whole church.

¹³So anyone who speaks in tongues should pray also for the ability to interpret what has been said. ¹⁴For if I pray in tongues, my spirit is praying, but I don't understand what I am saying.

¹⁵Well then, what shall I do? I will pray in the spirit,* and I will also pray in words I understand. I will sing in the spirit, and I will also sing in words I understand. ¹⁶For if you praise God only in the spirit, how can those who don't understand you praise God along with you? How can they join you in giving thanks when they don't understand what you are saying? ¹⁷You will be giving thanks very well, but it won't strengthen the people who hear you.

¹⁸I thank God that I speak in tongues more than any of you. ¹⁹But in a church meeting I would rather speak five understandable words to help others than ten thousand words in an unknown language.

²⁰Dear brothers and sisters, don't be childish in your understanding of these things. Be innocent as babies when it comes to evil, but be mature in understanding matters of this kind. ²¹It is written in the Scriptures*:

"I will speak to my own people
    through strange languages
    and through the lips of foreigners.
But even then, they will not listen to me,"*
    says the LORD.

²²So you see that speaking in tongues is a sign, not for believers, but for unbelievers. Prophecy, however, is for the benefit of believers, not unbelievers. ²³Even so, if unbelievers or people who don't understand these things come into your church meeting and hear everyone speaking in an unknown language, they will think you are crazy. ²⁴But if all of you are prophesying, and unbelievers or people who don't understand these things come into your meeting, they will be convicted of sin and judged by what you say. ²⁵As they listen, their secret thoughts will be exposed, and they will fall to their knees and worship God, declaring, "God is truly here among you."

A Call to Orderly Worship

²⁶Well, my brothers and sisters, let's summarize. When you meet together, one will sing, another will teach, another will tell some special revelation God has given, one will speak in tongues, and another will interpret what is said. But everything that is done must strengthen all of you.

²⁷No more than two or three should speak in tongues. They must speak one at a time, and someone must interpret what they say. ²⁸But if no one is present who can interpret, they must be silent in your church meeting and speak in tongues to God privately.

²⁹Let two or three people prophesy, and let the others evaluate what is said. ³⁰But if someone is prophesying and another person receives a revelation from the Lord, the one who is speaking must stop. ³¹In this way, all who prophesy will have a turn to speak, one after the other, so that everyone will learn and be encouraged. ³²Remember

---

14:6a Greek *brothers;* also in 14:20, 26, 39. **14:6b** Or *in tongues;* also in 14:19, 23. **14:15** Or *in the Spirit;* also in 14:15b, 16. **14:21a** Greek *in the law.* **14:21b** Isa 28:11-12.

that people who prophesy are in control of their spirit and can take turns. ³³For God is not a God of disorder but of peace, as in all the meetings of God's holy people.*

³⁴Women should be silent during the church meetings. It is not proper for them to speak. They should be submissive, just as the law says. ³⁵If they have any questions, they should ask their husbands at home, for it is improper for women to speak in church meetings.*

³⁶Or do you think God's word originated with you Corinthians? Are you the only ones to whom it was given? ³⁷If you claim to be a prophet or think you are spiritual, you should recognize that what I am saying is a command from the Lord himself. ³⁸But if you do not recognize this, you yourself will not be recognized.*

³⁹So, my dear brothers and sisters, be eager to prophesy, and don't forbid speaking in tongues. ⁴⁰But be sure that everything is done properly and in order.

15 The Resurrection of Christ

Let me now remind you, dear brothers and sisters,* of the Good News I preached to you before. You welcomed it then, and you still stand firm in it. ²It is this Good News that saves you if you continue to believe the message I told you—unless, of course, you believed something that was never true in the first place.*

³I passed on to you what was most important and what had also been passed on to me. Christ died for our sins, just as the Scriptures said. ⁴He was buried, and he was raised from the dead on the third day, just as the Scriptures said. ⁵He was seen by Peter* and then by the Twelve. ⁶After that, he was seen by more than 500 of his followers* at one time, most of whom are still alive, though some have died. ⁷Then he was seen by James and later by all the apostles. ⁸Last of all, as though I had been born at the wrong time, I also saw him. ⁹For I am the least of all the apostles. In fact, I'm not even worthy to be called an apostle after the way I persecuted God's church.

¹⁰But whatever I am now, it is all because God poured out his special favor on me— and not without results. For I have worked harder than any of the other apostles; yet it was not I but God who was working through me by his grace. ¹¹So it makes no difference whether I preach or they preach, for we all preach the same message you have already believed.

The Resurrection of the Dead

¹²But tell me this—since we preach that Christ rose from the dead, why are some of you saying there will be no resurrection of the dead? ¹³For if there is no resurrection of the dead, then Christ has not been raised either. ¹⁴And if Christ has not been raised, then all our preaching is useless, and your faith is useless. ¹⁵And we apostles would all be lying about God—for we have said that God raised Christ from the grave. But that can't be true if there is no resurrection of the dead. ¹⁶And if there is no resurrection of the dead, then Christ has not been raised. ¹⁷And if Christ has not been raised, then your faith is useless and you are still guilty of your sins. ¹⁸In that case, all who have died believing in Christ are lost! ¹⁹And if our hope in Christ is only for this life, we are more to be pitied than anyone in the world.

²⁰But in fact, Christ has been raised from the dead. He is the first of a great harvest of all who have died.

²¹So you see, just as death came into the world through a man, now the resurrection from the dead has begun through another man. ²²Just as everyone dies because we all belong to Adam, everyone who belongs to Christ will be given new life. ²³But there is an order to this resurrection: Christ was raised as the first of the harvest; then all who belong to Christ will be raised when he comes back.

²⁴After that the end will come, when he will turn the Kingdom over to God the Father, having destroyed every ruler and authority and power. ²⁵For Christ must reign until he humbles all his enemies beneath his feet. ²⁶And the last enemy to be destroyed is death. ²⁷For the Scriptures say, "God has put all things under his author-

---

14:33 The phrase *as in all the meetings of God's holy people* could instead be joined to the beginning of 14:34.   **14:35** Some manuscripts place verses 34-35 after 14:40.   **14:38** Some manuscripts read *If you are ignorant of this, stay in your ignorance.*   **15:1** Greek *brothers;* also in 15:31, 50, 58.   **15:2** Or *unless you never believed it in the first place.*   **15:5** Greek *Cephas.*   **15:6** Greek *the brothers.*

ity."* (Of course, when it says "all things are under his authority," that does not include God himself, who gave Christ his authority.) ²⁸Then, when all things are under his authority, the Son will put himself under God's authority, so that God, who gave his Son authority over all things, will be utterly supreme over everything everywhere.

²⁹If the dead will not be raised, what point is there in people being baptized for those who are dead? Why do it unless the dead will someday rise again?

³⁰And why should we ourselves risk our lives hour by hour? ³¹For I swear, dear brothers and sisters, that I face death daily. This is as certain as my pride in what Christ Jesus our Lord has done in you. ³²And what value was there in fighting wild beasts— those people of Ephesus*—if there will be no resurrection from the dead? And if there is no resurrection, "Let's feast and drink, for tomorrow we die!"* ³³Don't be fooled by those who say such things, for "bad company corrupts good character." ³⁴Think carefully about what is right, and stop sinning. For to your shame I say that some of you don't know God at all.

The Resurrection Body

³⁵But someone may ask, "How will the dead be raised? What kind of bodies will they have?" ³⁶What a foolish question! When you put a seed into the ground, it doesn't grow into a plant unless it dies first. ³⁷And what you put in the ground is not the plant that will grow, but only a bare seed of wheat or whatever you are planting. ³⁸Then God gives it the new body he wants it to have. A different plant grows from each kind of seed. ³⁹Similarly there are different kinds of flesh—one kind for humans, another for animals, another for birds, and another for fish.

⁴⁰There are also bodies in the heavens and bodies on the earth. The glory of the heavenly bodies is different from the glory of the earthly bodies. ⁴¹The sun has one kind of glory, while the moon and stars each have another kind. And even the stars differ from each other in their glory.

⁴²It is the same way with the resurrection of the dead. Our earthly bodies are planted in the ground when we die, but they will be raised to live forever. ⁴³Our bodies are buried in brokenness, but they will be raised in glory. They are buried in weakness, but they will be raised in strength. ⁴⁴They are buried as natural human bodies, but they will be raised as spiritual bodies. For just as there are natural bodies, there are also spiritual bodies.

⁴⁵The Scriptures tell us, "The first man, Adam, became a living person."* But the last Adam—that is, Christ—is a life-giving Spirit. ⁴⁶What comes first is the natural body, then the spiritual body comes later. ⁴⁷Adam, the first man, was made from the dust of the earth, while Christ, the second man, came from heaven. ⁴⁸Earthly people are like the earthly man, and heavenly people are like the heavenly man. ⁴⁹Just as we are now like the earthly man, we will someday be like* the heavenly man.

⁵⁰What I am saying, dear brothers and sisters, is that our physical bodies cannot inherit the Kingdom of God. These dying bodies cannot inherit what will last forever.

⁵¹But let me reveal to you a wonderful secret. We will not all die, but we will all be transformed! ⁵²It will happen in a moment, in the blink of an eye, when the last trumpet is blown. For when the trumpet sounds, those who have died will be raised to live forever. And we who are living will also be transformed. ⁵³For our dying bodies must be transformed into bodies that will never die; our mortal bodies must be transformed into immortal bodies.

⁵⁴Then, when our dying bodies have been transformed into bodies that will never die,* this Scripture will be fulfilled:

"Death is swallowed up in victory.*
⁵⁵O death, where is your victory?
   O death, where is your sting?*"

⁵⁶For sin is the sting that results in death, and the law gives sin its power. ⁵⁷But thank God! He gives us victory over sin and death through our Lord Jesus Christ.

⁵⁸So, my dear brothers and sisters, be

15:27 Ps 8:6.   15:32a Greek *fighting wild beasts in Ephesus.*   15:32b Isa 22:13.   15:45 Gen 2:7.   15:49 Some manuscripts read *let us be like.*   15:54a Some manuscripts add *and our mortal bodies have been transformed into immortal bodies.*   15:54b Isa 25:8.   15:55 Hos 13:14 (Greek version).

strong and immovable. Always work enthusiastically for the Lord, for you know that nothing you do for the Lord is ever useless.

16 The Collection for Jerusalem

Now regarding your question about the money being collected for God's people in Jerusalem. You should follow the same procedure I gave to the churches in Galatia.

²On the first day of each week, you should each put aside a portion of the money you have earned. Don't wait until I get there and then try to collect it all at once. ³When I come, I will write letters of recommendation for the messengers you choose to deliver your gift to Jerusalem. ⁴And if it seems appropriate for me to go along, they can travel with me.

Q&A — What Is Celebration?

Celebration

1 CORINTHIANS 16:5-18

What is celebration? Isn't it more than throwing parties?

Many of us gravitate toward ideas like discipline, sacrifice, and suffering in a way that Christ suffered, but we're somehow uncomfortable with the idea of deep joy. Yet when we look at the biblical pattern of festivals, feasts, and psalms, we see rejoicing people relishing the deep gladness of being alive and of being one of God's children. God made an extraordinary world for us to live in! To deny the beauty of that—to miss out on truly experiencing it and celebrating it—is a real loss, especially for Christians.

Celebration, at its core, is the practice of choosing to be truly present in the moments in our lives. Jesus didn't live at a pace in which he was so preoccupied with his agenda that he didn't connect with what was happening in the lives of the people around him. And he wasn't so bent out of shape about what was wrong in the world that he couldn't stop and notice what was good. Enjoying a wedding feast, sitting with Mary listening at his feet, spending time with children—in all these moments and many more, Jesus was present to the sacred things happening in everyday life.

Yes, celebration can involve going out to eat, fireworks, candles on a cake, loud music, and laughter. But more than that, it's about being present to what is, noticing the good that still exists even in the middle of the broken. It's choosing hope. It's trusting that you'll find something beautiful, redemptive, and sacred even when it looks like that's an impossible task. Life is wild, chaotic, beautiful, and sacred all at the same time. I've learned that celebrating in the midst of that wildness and chaos makes the beauty and the sacredness much clearer. That's one of God's greatest gifts.

—*Shauna Niequist*

For more on celebration, see reading at 1 John 1:1-7.

Paul's Final Instructions

⁵I am coming to visit you after I have been to Macedonia,* for I am planning to travel through Macedonia. ⁶Perhaps I will stay awhile with you, possibly all winter, and then you can send me on my way to my next destination. ⁷This time I don't want to make just a short visit and then go right on. I want to come and stay awhile, if the Lord will let me. ⁸In the meantime, I will be staying here at Ephesus until the Festival of Pentecost. ⁹There is a wide-open door for a great work here, although many oppose me.

¹⁰When Timothy comes, don't intimidate him. He is doing the Lord's work, just as I am. ¹¹Don't let anyone treat him with contempt. Send him on his way with your blessing when he returns to me. I expect him to come with the other believers.*

¹²Now about our brother Apollos—I urged him to visit you with the other believers, but he was not willing to go right now. He will see you later when he has the opportunity.

¹³Be on guard. Stand firm in the faith. Be courageous.* Be strong. ¹⁴And do everything with love.

¹⁵You know that Stephanas and his household were the first of the harvest of believers in Greece,* and they are spending their lives in service to God's people. I urge you, dear brothers and sisters,* ¹⁶to submit to them and others like them who serve with such devotion. ¹⁷I am very glad that Stephanas, Fortunatus, and Achaicus have come here. They have been providing the help you weren't here to give me. ¹⁸They have been a wonderful encouragement to me, as they have been to you. You must show your appreciation to all who serve so well.

Paul's Final Greetings

¹⁹The churches here in the province of Asia* send greetings in the Lord, as do Aquila and Priscilla* and all the others who gather in their home for church meetings. ²⁰All the brothers and sisters here send greetings to you. Greet each other with Christian love.*

²¹HERE IS MY GREETING IN MY OWN HANDWRITING—PAUL.

²²If anyone does not love the Lord, that person is cursed. Our Lord, come!*

²³May the grace of the Lord Jesus be with you.

²⁴My love to all of you in Christ Jesus.*

16:5 Macedonia was in the northern region of Greece.   16:11 Greek with the brothers; also in 16:12.   16:13 Greek Be men.   16:15a Greek in Achaia, the southern region of the Greek peninsula.   16:15b Greek brothers; also in 16:20.   16:19a Asia was a Roman province in what is now western Turkey.   16:19b Greek Prisca.   16:20 Greek with a sacred kiss.   16:22 From Aramaic, Marana tha. Some manuscripts read Maran atha, "Our Lord has come."   16:24 Some manuscripts add Amen.

Introduction to
2 Corinthians

Background

Paul is the acknowledged writer of 1 and 2 Corinthians. Paul no doubt wrote one or two other letters to the church in Corinth that have not survived. Paul writes this letter in anticipation of his third visit to the church community in Corinth (12:14; 13:1). He writes that his second visit had not gone well (2:1), but his greeting and encouragements of chapter 1 indicate that he is somewhat reconciled with the community. Because of the influence of false teachers over the believers in Corinth, Paul feels the need to defend his ministry against those who question his authority as an apostle. (See also the introduction to 1 Corinthians.)

Message

At the beginning of this very personal letter, Paul describes the comfort a believer can access in times of trouble. He uses strong images to describe the life of a Christian: we are a "Christ-like fragrance rising up to God" (2:15–16); we are a "letter from Christ. . . . This 'letter' is written not with pen and ink, but with the Spirit of the living God" (3:3). In our "fragile clay jars" we have the treasure of God's light (4:7). In Christ we are each "a new person" (5:17). We are "Christ's ambassadors" (5:20). Despite his hardships, Paul writes of his joy. He commends the church in Corinth for their generosity to others and encourages them to continue their financial support of those in need. Paul reminds his readers that his authority ultimately comes from God, responding directly to undermining opposition he has received. He urges the Corinthian believers to stay true to the gospel and the Savior in whom they initially believed and to avoid those opposed to Christ. The format of Paul's final blessing is uniquely Trinitarian.

Time

Second Corinthians was written in late A.D. 56, while Paul was in Macedonia (2:13; 7:5).

Outline

2 Corinthians

Greetings from Paul

1 This letter is from Paul, chosen by the will of God to be an apostle of Christ Jesus, and from our brother Timothy.

I am writing to God's church in Corinth and to all of his holy people throughout Greece.*

²May God our Father and the Lord Jesus Christ give you grace and peace.

God Offers Comfort to All

³All praise to God, the Father of our Lord Jesus Christ. God is our merciful Father and the source of all comfort. ⁴He comforts us in all our troubles so that we can comfort others. When they are troubled, we will be able to give them the same comfort God has given us. ⁵For the more we suffer for Christ, the more God will shower us with his comfort through Christ. ⁶Even when we are weighed down with troubles, it is for your comfort and salvation! For when we ourselves are comforted, we will certainly comfort you. Then you can patiently endure the same things we suffer. ⁷We are confident that as you share in our sufferings, you will also share in the comfort God gives us.

⁸We think you ought to know, dear brothers and sisters,* about the trouble we went through in the province of Asia. We were crushed and overwhelmed beyond our ability to endure, and we thought we would never live through it. ⁹In fact, we expected to die. But as a result, we stopped relying on ourselves and learned to rely only on God, who raises the dead. ¹⁰And he did rescue us from mortal danger, and he will rescue us again. We have placed our confidence in him, and he will continue to rescue us. ¹¹And you are helping us by praying for us. Then many people will give thanks because God has graciously answered so many prayers for our safety.

Paul's Change of Plans

¹²We can say with confidence and a clear conscience that we have lived with a God-given holiness* and sincerity in all our dealings. We have depended on God's grace, not on our own human wisdom. That is how we have conducted ourselves before the world, and especially toward you. ¹³Our letters have been straightforward, and there is nothing written between the lines and nothing you can't understand. I hope someday you will fully understand us, ¹⁴even if you don't understand us now. Then on the day when the Lord Jesus* returns, you will be proud of us in the same way we are proud of you.

¹⁵Since I was so sure of your understanding and trust, I wanted to give you a double blessing by visiting you twice—¹⁶first on my way to Macedonia and again when I returned from Macedonia.* Then you could send me on my way to Judea.

¹⁷You may be asking why I changed my plan. Do you think I make my plans carelessly? Do you think I am like people of the world who say "Yes" when they

---

1:1 Greek *Achaia*, the southern region of the Greek peninsula. **1:8** Greek *brothers*. **1:12** Some manuscripts read *honesty*.
1:14 Some manuscripts read *our Lord Jesus*. **1:16** *Macedonia* was in the northern region of Greece.

The Other Side of the Table
2 CORINTHIANS 1:3-4

I was a nervous wreck, anxious, depressed, and burned out. When I could take no more pain on my own, I reached out for someone. Jean was a co-worker who had trained and befriended me. She was classy, confident, and twenty years my senior. Each week we'd go for sandwiches or coffee. She'd listen and ask lots of questions. She'd share her experiences, encouraging me through the lessons she'd learned. Then she'd direct me to helpful Scriptures. She inspired me simply by being there, healthy and joyful.

Of all our conversations, I remember most her saying, "Someday, you'll be on the other side of the table. You'll be doing what I'm doing—recounting your experiences to help someone else, even though you'll have put them long behind you."

At the time I was convinced I'd never put my tough times behind me. I could see no light ahead. But she'd been there too. And she was right. Now, years later, I've been on the other side of the table many times. And I pass on her encouragement to those I talk to: "Someday you'll be on the other side of the table."

Jean's words expressed a truth that she'd learned over the years about how God goes before us, sometimes clearing a way with the footsteps of others. Second Corinthians 1:3-4 puts it like this: God "comforts us in all our troubles so that we can comfort others. When they are troubled, we will be able to give them the same comfort God has given us."

—Janine Petry

For more on mentoring, see reading at Galatians 4:17-20.

really mean "No"? ¹⁸As surely as God is faithful, our word to you does not waver between "Yes" and "No." ¹⁹For Jesus Christ, the Son of God, does not waver between "Yes" and "No." He is the one whom Silas,* Timothy, and I preached to you, and as God's ultimate "Yes," he always does what he says. ²⁰For all of God's promises have been fulfilled in Christ with a resounding "Yes!" And through Christ, our "Amen" (which means "Yes") ascends to God for his glory.

²¹It is God who enables us, along with you, to stand firm for Christ. He has commissioned us, ²²and he has identified us as his own by placing the Holy Spirit in our hearts as the first installment that guarantees everything he has promised us.

²³Now I call upon God as my witness that I am telling the truth. The reason I didn't return to Corinth was to spare you from a severe rebuke. ²⁴But that does not mean we want to dominate you by telling you how to put your faith into practice. We want to work together with you so you will be full of joy, for it is by your own faith that you stand firm.

2 So I decided that I would not bring you grief with another painful visit. ²For if I cause you grief, who will make me glad? Certainly not someone I have grieved. ³That is why I wrote to you as I did, so that when I do come, I won't be grieved by the very ones who ought to give me the greatest joy. Surely you all know that my joy comes from your being joyful. ⁴I wrote that letter in great anguish,

1:19 Greek *Silvanus.*

with a troubled heart and many tears. I didn't want to grieve you, but I wanted to let you know how much love I have for you.

Forgiveness for the Sinner

⁵I am not overstating it when I say that the man who caused all the trouble hurt all of you more than he hurt me. ⁶Most of you opposed him, and that was punishment enough. ⁷Now, however, it is time to forgive and comfort him. Otherwise he may be overcome by discouragement. ⁸So I urge you now to reaffirm your love for him.

⁹I wrote to you as I did to test you and see if you would fully comply with my instructions. ¹⁰When you forgive this man, I forgive him, too. And when I forgive whatever needs to be forgiven, I do so with Christ's authority for your benefit, ¹¹so that Satan will not outsmart us. For we are familiar with his evil schemes.

¹²When I came to the city of Troas to preach the Good News of Christ, the Lord opened a door of opportunity for me. ¹³But I had no peace of mind because my dear brother Titus hadn't yet arrived with a report from you. So I said good-bye and went on to Macedonia to find him.

Ministers of the New Covenant

¹⁴But thank God! He has made us his captives and continues to lead us along in Christ's triumphal procession. Now he uses us to spread the knowledge of Christ everywhere, like a sweet perfume. ¹⁵Our lives are a Christ-like fragrance rising up to God. But this fragrance is perceived differently by those who are being saved and by those who are perishing. ¹⁶To those who are perishing, we are a dreadful smell of death and doom. But to those who are being saved, we are a life-giving perfume. And who is adequate for such a task as this?

¹⁷You see, we are not like the many hucksters* who preach for personal profit. We preach the word of God with sincerity and with Christ's authority, knowing that God is watching us.

3 Are we beginning to praise ourselves again? Are we like others, who need to bring you letters of recommendation, or who ask you to write such letters on their behalf? Surely not! ²The only letter of recommendation we need is you yourselves. Your lives are a letter written in our* hearts; everyone can read it and recognize our good work among you. ³Clearly, you are a letter from Christ showing the result of our ministry among you. This "letter" is written not with pen and ink, but with the Spirit of the living God. It is carved not on tablets of stone, but on human hearts.

⁴We are confident of all this because of our great trust in God through Christ. ⁵It is not that we think we are qualified to do anything on our own. Our qualification comes from God. ⁶He has enabled us to be ministers of his new covenant. This is a covenant not of written laws, but of the Spirit. The old written covenant ends in death; but under the new covenant, the Spirit gives life.

The Glory of the New Covenant

⁷The old way,* with laws etched in stone, led to death, though it began with such glory that the people of Israel could not bear to look at Moses' face. For his face shone with the glory of God, even though the brightness was already fading away. ⁸Shouldn't we expect far greater glory under the new way, now that the Holy Spirit is giving life? ⁹If the old way, which brings condemnation, was glorious, how much more glorious is the new way, which makes us right with God! ¹⁰In fact, that first glory was not glorious at all compared with the overwhelming glory of the new way. ¹¹So if the old way, which has been replaced, was glorious, how much more glorious is the new, which remains forever!

¹²Since this new way gives us such confidence, we can be very bold. ¹³We are not like Moses, who put a veil over his face so the people of Israel would not see the glory, even though it was destined to fade away. ¹⁴But the people's minds were hardened, and to this day whenever the old covenant is being read, the same veil covers their minds so they cannot understand the truth. And this veil can be removed only by believing in Christ. ¹⁵Yes, even today when they read Moses' writings, their hearts are covered

A Heart Open to God

2 CORINTHIANS 3:18

I remember sitting quietly on a swing with my grandmother as we tried to identify birds landing nearby. I watched my dad stand over his garden in silence, studying some bit of plant life in this hand. I saw my mom bending over her journal late at night, taking long pauses during the writing. They showed me from a young age that a good life included time for quiet and thoughtfulness.

I followed their example: I'd go outdoors early on summer mornings to watch how the sun slowly lit up the clover. Or I'd sit under the willow tree and feel how soft and alive the earth was. Sometimes contemplation happened while I rode my bike, traveling the country roads just to notice the color of the soybean fields or how the breeze smelled or to linger at the place where a perfect spider web glittered with dewdrops. These times of contemplation brought me happiness; the ability to stop and absorb the ordinary beauties of life maintained within me a core of gratefulness and hope.

Contemplation can be described as silence, thoughtfulness, meditation, prayer, or concentration. But for me, a chief attribute of contemplation is an open heart. When I walk into my day saying yes to God and to the world God has created, an act as mundane as riding the train to work is transformed into deep and joyous prayer.

I live in the city now—there's not a bean field in sight. But still, the sun makes its way gradually and gloriously over the urban landscape. If I can cease busyness and still my overactive thoughts, I will feel that glory slip over me too. And my heart will respond with gratitude. My will can more freely conform itself to what is holy and good. Contemplation allows me to notice how graced my life truly is.

—Vinita Hampton Wright

For more on contemplation, see reading at Revelation 2:4.

with that veil, and they do not understand. [16] But whenever someone turns to the Lord, the veil is taken away. [17] For the Lord is the Spirit, and wherever the Spirit of the Lord is, there is freedom. [18] So all of us who have had that veil removed can see and reflect the glory of the Lord. And the Lord—who is the Spirit—makes us more and more like him as we are changed into his glorious image.

4 Treasure in Fragile Clay Jars

Therefore, since God in his mercy has given us this new way,* we never give up. [2] We reject all shameful deeds and under-handed methods. We don't try to trick anyone or distort the word of God. We tell the truth before God, and all who are honest know this.

[3] If the Good News we preach is hidden behind a veil, it is hidden only from people who are perishing. [4] Satan, who is the god of this world, has blinded the minds of those who don't believe. They are unable to see the glorious light of the Good News. They don't understand this message about the glory of Christ, who is the exact likeness of God.

[5] You see, we don't go around preaching about ourselves. We preach that Jesus Christ is Lord, and we ourselves are your

4:1 Or *ministry.*

servants for Jesus' sake. ⁶For God, who said, "Let there be light in the darkness," has made this light shine in our hearts so we could know the glory of God that is seen in the face of Jesus Christ.

⁷We now have this light shining in our hearts, but we ourselves are like fragile clay jars containing this great treasure.* This makes it clear that our great power is from God, not from ourselves.

⁸We are pressed on every side by troubles, but we are not crushed. We are perplexed, but not driven to despair. ⁹We are hunted down, but never abandoned by God. We get knocked down, but we are not destroyed. ¹⁰Through suffering, our bodies continue to share in the death of Jesus so that the life of Jesus may also be seen in our bodies.

¹¹Yes, we live under constant danger of death because we serve Jesus, so that the life of Jesus will be evident in our dying bodies. ¹²So we live in the face of death, but this has resulted in eternal life for you.

¹³But we continue to preach because we have the same kind of faith the psalmist had when he said, "I believed in God, so I spoke."* ¹⁴We know that God, who raised the Lord Jesus,* will also raise us with Jesus and present us to himself together with you. ¹⁵All of this is for your benefit. And as God's grace reaches more and more people, there will be great thanksgiving, and God will receive more and more glory.

¹⁶That is why we never give up. Though our bodies are dying, our spirits are* being renewed every day. ¹⁷For our present troubles are small and won't last very long. Yet they produce for us a glory that vastly outweighs them and will last forever! ¹⁸So we don't look at the troubles we can see now; rather, we fix our gaze on things that cannot be seen. For the things we see now will soon be gone, but the things we cannot see will last forever.

5 New Bodies

For we know that when this earthly tent we live in is taken down (that is, when we die and leave this earthly body), we will have a house in heaven, an eternal body made for us by God himself and not by human hands. ²We grow weary in our present bodies, and we long to put on our heavenly bodies like new clothing. ³For we will put on heavenly bodies; we will not be spirits without bodies.* ⁴While we live in these earthly bodies, we groan and sigh, but it's not that we want to die and get rid of these bodies that clothe us. Rather, we want to put on our new bodies so that these dying bodies will be swallowed up by life. ⁵God himself has prepared us for this, and as a guarantee he has given us his Holy Spirit.

⁶So we are always confident, even though we know that as long as we live in these bodies we are not at home with the Lord. ⁷For we live by believing and not by seeing. ⁸Yes, we are fully confident, and we would rather be away from these earthly bodies, for then we will be at home with the Lord. ⁹So whether we are here in this body or away from this body, our goal is to please him. ¹⁰For we must all stand before Christ to be judged. We will each receive whatever we deserve for the good or evil we have done in this earthly body.

We Are God's Ambassadors

¹¹Because we understand our fearful responsibility to the Lord, we work hard to persuade others. God knows we are sincere, and I hope you know this, too. ¹²Are we commending ourselves to you again? No, we are giving you a reason to be proud of us,* so you can answer those who brag about having a spectacular ministry rather than having a sincere heart. ¹³If it seems we are crazy, it is to bring glory to God. And if we are in our right minds, it is for your benefit. ¹⁴Either way, Christ's love controls us.* Since we believe that Christ died for all, we also believe that we have all died to our old life.* ¹⁵He died for everyone so that those who receive his new life will no longer live for themselves. Instead, they will live for Christ, who died and was raised for them.

¹⁶So we have stopped evaluating others from a human point of view. At one time we thought of Christ merely from a human point of view. How differently we know him

---

4:7 Greek *We now have this treasure in clay jars.*   **4:13** Ps 116:10.   **4:14** Some manuscripts read *who raised Jesus.*   **4:16** Greek *our inner being is.*
5:3 Greek *we will not be naked.*   **5:12** Some manuscripts read *proud of yourselves.*   **5:14a** Or *urges us on.*   **5:14b** Greek *Since one died for all, then all died.*

now! [17] This means that anyone who belongs to Christ has become a new person. The old life is gone; a new life has begun!

[18] And all of this is a gift from God, who brought us back to himself through Christ. And God has given us this task of reconciling people to him. [19] For God was in Christ, reconciling the world to himself, no longer counting people's sins against them. And he gave us this wonderful message of reconciliation. [20] So we are Christ's ambassadors; God is making his appeal through us.

We speak for Christ when we plead, "Come back to God!" [21] For God made Christ, who never sinned, to be the offering for our sin,* so that we could be made right with God through Christ.

6 As God's partners,* we beg you not to accept this marvelous gift of God's kindness and then ignore it. [2] For God says,

"At just the right time, I heard you.
On the day of salvation, I helped you."*

Q&A — Racial Reconciliation
2 CORINTHIANS 5:18–19

How important is it for us to pursue racial reconciliation?

Consider 2 Corinthians 5:18-19. Our commitment to reconciliation must be rooted in what we understand about God and his Word. As we study Scripture, we can't help but grapple with questions about reconciliation: Is the kingdom of God really made up of people who are different from one another, but they still get along? Have we really been entrusted with the ministry of reconciliation? And if we have, what does that mean?

Many of us seem to treat reconciliation like an elective, as if it's an optional part of the Christian life. We'll put effort into worship, evangelism, missions, or youth ministry, yet fundamentally we may not truly believe reconciliation—particularly racial reconciliation—is something we're called to. But it is at the core of what Christianity is all about! Christ came so we could be reconciled, not only to him but to one another as well.

We often make the mistake of talking about only one type of reconciliation: people being reconciled to God. We preach about it; we proclaim it to the world around us. But we must understand that it's only *one* axis of the truth. Reconciliation with God is the vertical axis—but in the same act of crucifixion and resurrection, we were also reconciled to *one another*. And it's that horizontal axis—true reconciliation across ethnic, gender, cultural, and economic divisions—that causes us to become people of the Cross (Galatians 3:28; Colossians 3:11).

—*Brenda Salter McNeil*

For more on reconciliation, see reading at Galatians 6:1–3.

5:21 Or *to become sin itself.*   **6:1** Or *As we work together.*   **6:2** Isa 49:8 (Greek version).

Indeed, the "right time" is now. Today is the day of salvation.

Paul's Hardships

³ We live in such a way that no one will stumble because of us, and no one will find fault with our ministry. ⁴ In everything we do, we show that we are true ministers of God. We patiently endure troubles and hardships and calamities of every kind. ⁵ We have been beaten, been put in prison, faced angry mobs, worked to exhaustion, endured sleepless nights, and gone without food. ⁶ We prove ourselves by our purity, our understanding, our patience, our kindness, by the Holy Spirit within us,* and by our sincere love. ⁷ We faithfully preach the truth. God's power is working in us. We use the weapons of righteousness in the right hand for attack and the left hand for defense. ⁸ We serve God whether people honor us or despise us, whether they slander us or praise us. We are honest, but they call us impostors. ⁹ We are ignored, even though we are well known. We live close to death, but we are still alive. We have been beaten, but we have not been killed. ¹⁰ Our hearts ache, but we always have joy. We are poor, but we give spiritual riches to others. We own nothing, and yet we have everything.

¹¹ Oh, dear Corinthian friends! We have spoken honestly with you, and our hearts are open to you. ¹² There is no lack of love on our part, but you have withheld your love from us. ¹³ I am asking you to respond as if you were my own children. Open your hearts to us!

The Temple of the Living God

¹⁴ Don't team up with those who are unbelievers. How can righteousness be a partner with wickedness? How can light live with darkness? ¹⁵ What harmony can there be between Christ and the devil*? How can a believer be a partner with an unbeliever? ¹⁶ And what union can there be between God's temple and idols? For we are the temple of the living God. As God said:

"I will live in them
and walk among them.

I will be their God,
and they will be my people."*
¹⁷ Therefore, come out from among unbelievers,
and separate yourselves from them,
says the LORD.
Don't touch their filthy things,
and I will welcome you.*
¹⁸ And I will be your Father,
and you will be my sons and daughters,
says the LORD Almighty.*"

7 Because we have these promises, dear friends, let us cleanse ourselves from everything that can defile our body or spirit. And let us work toward complete holiness because we fear God.

² Please open your hearts to us. We have not done wrong to anyone, nor led anyone astray, nor taken advantage of anyone. ³ I'm not saying this to condemn you. I said before that you are in our hearts, and we live or die together with you. ⁴ I have the highest confidence in you, and I take great pride in you. You have greatly encouraged me and made me happy despite all our troubles.

Paul's Joy at the Church's Repentance

⁵ When we arrived in Macedonia, there was no rest for us. We faced conflict from every direction, with battles on the outside and fear on the inside. ⁶ But God, who encourages those who are discouraged, encouraged us by the arrival of Titus. ⁷ His presence was a joy, but so was the news he brought of the encouragement he received from you. When he told us how much you long to see me, and how sorry you are for what happened, and how loyal you are to me, I was filled with joy!

⁸ I am not sorry that I sent that severe letter to you, though I was sorry at first, for I know it was painful to you for a little while. ⁹ Now I am glad I sent it, not because it hurt you, but because the pain caused you to repent and change your ways. It was the kind of sorrow God wants his people to have, so you were not harmed by us in any way. ¹⁰ For the kind of sorrow God wants us to experience leads

6:6 Or *by our holiness of spirit.* **6:15** Greek *Beliar;* various other manuscripts render this proper name of the devil as *Belian, Beliab,* or *Belial.* **6:16** Lev 26:12; Ezek 37:27. **6:17** Isa 52:11; Ezek 20:34 (Greek version). **6:18** 2 Sam 7:14.

us away from sin and results in salvation. There's no regret for that kind of sorrow. But worldly sorrow, which lacks repentance, results in spiritual death.

¹¹ Just see what this godly sorrow produced in you! Such earnestness, such concern to clear yourselves, such indignation, such alarm, such longing to see me, such zeal, and such a readiness to punish wrong. You showed that you have done everything necessary to make things right. ¹² My purpose, then, was not to write about who did the wrong or who was wronged. I wrote to you so that in the sight of God you could see for yourselves how loyal you are to us. ¹³ We have been greatly encouraged by this.

In addition to our own encouragement, we were especially delighted to see how happy Titus was about the way all of you welcomed him and set his mind* at ease. ¹⁴ I had told him how proud I was of you— and you didn't disappoint me. I have always told you the truth, and now my boasting to Titus has also proved true! ¹⁵ Now he cares for you more than ever when he remembers the way all of you obeyed him and welcomed him with such fear and deep respect. ¹⁶ I am very happy now because I have complete confidence in you.

8 A Call to Generous Giving

Now I want you to know, dear brothers and sisters,* what God in his kindness has done through the churches in Macedonia. ² They are being tested by many troubles, and they are very poor. But they are also filled with abundant joy, which has overflowed in rich generosity.

³ For I can testify that they gave not only what they could afford, but far more. And they did it of their own free will. ⁴ They begged us again and again for the privilege of sharing in the gift for the believers in Jerusalem.* ⁵ They even did more than we had hoped, for their first action was to give themselves to the Lord and to us, just as God wanted them to do.

⁶ So we have urged Titus, who encouraged your giving in the first place, to return to you and encourage you to finish this ministry of giving. ⁷ Since you excel in so many

ways—in your faith, your gifted speakers, your knowledge, your enthusiasm, and your love from us*—I want you to excel also in this gracious act of giving.

⁸ I am not commanding you to do this. But I am testing how genuine your love is by comparing it with the eagerness of the other churches.

⁹ You know the generous grace of our Lord Jesus Christ. Though he was rich, yet for your sakes he became poor, so that by his poverty he could make you rich.

¹⁰ Here is my advice: It would be good for you to finish what you started a year ago. Last year you were the first who wanted to give, and you were the first to begin doing it. ¹¹ Now you should finish what you started. Let the eagerness you showed in the beginning be matched now by your giving. Give in proportion to what you have. ¹² Whatever you give is acceptable if you give it eagerly. And give according to what you have, not what you don't have. ¹³ Of course, I don't mean your giving should make life easy for others and hard for yourselves. I only mean that there should be some equality. ¹⁴ Right now you have plenty and can help those who are in need. Later, they will have plenty and can share with you when you need it. In this way, things will be equal. ¹⁵ As the Scriptures say,

"Those who gathered a lot had nothing left over,
  and those who gathered only a little had enough."*

Titus and His Companions

¹⁶ But thank God! He has given Titus the same enthusiasm for you that I have. ¹⁷ Titus welcomed our request that he visit you again. In fact, he himself was very eager to go and see you. ¹⁸ We are also sending another brother with Titus. All the churches praise him as a preacher of the Good News. ¹⁹ He was appointed by the churches to accompany us as we take the offering to Jerusalem*—a service that glorifies the Lord and shows our eagerness to help.

²⁰ We are traveling together to guard against any criticism for the way we are

7:13 Greek his spirit. 8:1 Greek brothers. 8:4 Greek for God's holy people. 8:7 Some manuscripts read your love for us. 8:15 Exod 16:18.
8:19 See 1 Cor 16:3-4.

handling this generous gift. ²¹We are careful to be honorable before the Lord, but we also want everyone else to see that we are honorable.

²²We are also sending with them another of our brothers who has proven himself many times and has shown on many occasions how eager he is. He is now even more enthusiastic because of his great confidence in you. ²³If anyone asks about Titus, say that he is my partner who works with me to help you. And the brothers with him have been sent by the churches,* and they bring honor to Christ. ²⁴So show them your love, and prove to all the churches that our boasting about you is justified.

9 The Collection for Christians in Jerusalem

I really don't need to write to you about this ministry of giving for the believers in Jerusalem.* ²For I know how eager you are

Q&A — Giving When Times Are Tough

2 CORINTHIANS 9

Stewardship

I know giving to the church and to others is important, but what about when I'm in the middle of a financial crisis?

Generosity is a condition of the heart. As resources come into the hands of a generous person, she can't help giving them away. It's second nature. A lifestyle of generosity should not stop when times are hard. If anything, tithing when income is low reinforces gratitude and trust, as it reminds the giver that God can use even the smallest gift to accomplish his will. It also reminds me that I am always dependent on God for my sustenance, whether I have savings in the bank and a regular paycheck or not. This is where Christian community can be most apparent, in encouraging and supporting one another to live out generosity in tough times.

Living a generous lifestyle is not an obligation but rather an opportunity. It is something I *get* to do for God's kingdom, not something I *have* to do. As Paul says in 2 Corinthians 9:7–8, "You must each decide in your heart how much to give. And don't give reluctantly or in response to pressure. 'For God loves a person who gives cheerfully.' And God will generously provide all you need. Then you will always have everything you need and plenty left over to share with others."

During tough financial times, rather than retreat from Christian community because of feelings of shame, it is more important than ever to talk to pastors, leaders, and friends who can provide loving community and accountability as you seek to be a faithful steward.

—*Jim Sheppard*

For more on stewardship, see reading at Philippians 2:14–18.

8:23 Greek *are apostles of the churches.*   **9:1** Greek *about the offering for God's holy people.*

Stewardship

The Calling
of True
Stewardship

2 CORINTHIANS 8:2–4

Our world operates on a consumerist vision of the "good life" in which the early bird catches the worm; there's no such thing as a free lunch; what's mine is mine; and the one with the most toys wins!

These phrases are 180 degrees off from God's value system. They point to the reality that the more we have, the more we seem to want. As a child I had one pair of tennis shoes at a time. The luxury of having two pair never occurred to me. Now I have three different kinds of sneakers. And sometimes I don't think I have enough. Don't I *need* a pair with stronger soles for hiking?

God intends for each of us to be stewards of his gifts. Not all that long ago, large estates were entailed to male heirs. The property never really belonged to the heir; it wasn't his to sell. Stewarding the estate's resources and productivity for the next generation was his calling. Similarly, stewardship is a vocation—a calling from God in our lives. This calling means that everything I have and am is given to me in trust, to steward for kingdom purposes.

Still, being a steward has not come naturally to me. The phrase *we can't afford that* has shaped my heart into what a counselor called "deprivation neurosis." I fear not having enough for later. Not to put too fine a point on it, but stewarding my resources can make me nervous. Giving now can leave so much less for later; and sacrifice to the point of doing without certain things is a stretch for me. But I don't want to trust God *less* the more I have.

So when I am aware of any reticence to give, I try to take a deep breath and reclaim the vocation of steward rather than consumer. The earth I garden belongs to God. The house I have is God's house. The food I eat and commodities I buy can support those who steward God's creation. Stewardship is not a 10-percent tip I give to God that lets me then spend everything else as I wish. Stewardship is about *everything* God's given to me. And my model for it is Jesus—who didn't "tithe" just 10 percent of his life and blood. He stewarded all he was for the glory of God. And he has taught me to pray, "Your kingdom come—*in me*. Your will be done *by me* on earth as it is in heaven" (Matthew 6:10). Offering myself and my resources to God daily is the calling of true stewardship. Stewards risk that they can't out-give God. Stewards find their vocation shelters them from having a heart like the Grinch's: ten sizes too small.

No one needs a full bank account to be a steward. Jesus saw that people in all walks of life could be God-honoring stewards: a poor widow with two pennies (Mark 12:41–44); a boy with a sack lunch of bread and fish (John 6:9); a tax collector who gave away half of what he had (Luke 19:8); someone willing to make room in a stable (Luke 2:7); share a donkey (Mark 11:2–3); provide a tomb (Mark 15:46); and make a meal (Matthew 26:18).

There are always people who need something we steward for God: time, money, gifts, talents, cars, airline miles, hotel credits, houses, and on. Will we share? Will we invite God to use these resources for his purposes, not ours?

Paul wrote of how the church in Macedonia stewarded God's gifts. "They are being tested by many troubles, and they are very poor. But they are also filled with abundant joy, which has overflowed in rich generosity. For I can testify that they gave not only what they could afford but far more. And they did it of their own free will. They begged us again and again for the privilege of sharing in the gift for the believers in Jerusalem" (2 Corinthians 8:2–4).

These folks weren't thinking about how much they had to give not to look selfish or cheap. They had discovered that stewarding God's gifts draws us into the life of Jesus. It grows our hearts and nourishes our souls at the same time it offers God's gifts to the world. Could anything be a happier proposition than this? I don't need *more* to be a generous steward of the grace and gifts of heaven. I already have more than I deserve. And if I will shoulder the calling and honor of being a steward, Jesus' generosity not "deprivation neurosis" will define my giving and change my heart.

—*Adele Ahlberg Calhoun*

For more on stewardship, see reading at 2 Corinthians 9.

to help, and I have been boasting to the churches in Macedonia that you in Greece* were ready to send an offering a year ago. In fact, it was your enthusiasm that stirred up many of the Macedonian believers to begin giving.

³But I am sending these brothers to be sure you really are ready, as I have been telling them, and that your money is all collected. I don't want to be wrong in my boasting about you. ⁴We would be embarrassed—not to mention your own embarrassment—if some Macedonian believers came with me and found that you weren't ready after all I had told them! ⁵So I thought I should send these brothers ahead of me to make sure the gift you promised is ready. But I want it to be a willing gift, not one given grudgingly.

⁶Remember this—a farmer who plants only a few seeds will get a small crop. But the one who plants generously will get a generous crop. ⁷You must each decide in your heart how much to give. And don't give reluctantly or in response to pressure. "For God loves a person who gives cheerfully."* ⁸And God will generously provide all you need. Then you will always have everything you need and plenty left over to share with others. ⁹As the Scriptures say,

"They share freely and give generously to
　　the poor.
Their good deeds will be remembered
　　forever."*

¹⁰For God is the one who provides seed for the farmer and then bread to eat. In the same way, he will provide and increase your resources and then produce a great harvest of generosity* in you.

¹¹Yes, you will be enriched in every way so that you can always be generous. And when we take your gifts to those who need them, they will thank God. ¹²So two good things will result from this ministry of giving—the needs of the believers in Jerusalem* will be met, and they will joyfully express their thanks to God.

¹³As a result of your ministry, they will give glory to God. For your generosity to them and to all believers will prove that you are obedient to the Good News of Christ. ¹⁴And they will pray for you with deep affection because of the overflowing grace God has given to you. ¹⁵Thank God for this gift* too wonderful for words!

10 Paul Defends His Authority

Now I, Paul, appeal to you with the gentleness and kindness of Christ—though I realize you think I am timid in person and bold only when I write from far away. ²Well, I am begging you now so that when I come I won't have to be bold with those who think we act from human motives.

³We are human, but we don't wage war as humans do. ⁴*We use God's mighty weapons, not worldly weapons, to knock down the strongholds of human reasoning and to destroy false arguments. ⁵We destroy every proud obstacle that keeps people from knowing God. We capture their rebellious thoughts and teach them to obey Christ. ⁶And after you have become fully obedient, we will punish everyone who remains disobedient.

⁷Look at the obvious facts.* Those who say they belong to Christ must recognize that we belong to Christ as much as they do. ⁸I may seem to be boasting too much about the authority given to us by the Lord. But our authority builds you up; it doesn't tear you down. So I will not be ashamed of using my authority.

⁹I'm not trying to frighten you by my letters. ¹⁰For some say, "Paul's letters are demanding and forceful, but in person he is weak, and his speeches are worthless!" ¹¹Those people should realize that our actions when we arrive in person will be as forceful as what we say in our letters from far away.

¹²Oh, don't worry; we wouldn't dare say that we are as wonderful as these other men who tell you how important they are! But they are only comparing themselves with each other, using themselves as the standard of measurement. How ignorant! ¹³We will not boast about things done outside our area of authority. We will boast

9:2 Greek in Achaia, the southern region of the Greek peninsula. Macedonia was in the northern region of Greece.　9:7 See footnote on Prov 22:8.　9:9 Ps 112:9.　9:10 Greek righteousness.　9:12 Greek of God's holy people.　9:15 Greek his gift.　10:4 English translations divide verses 4 and 5 in various ways.　10:7 Or You look at things only on the basis of appearance.

only about what has happened within the boundaries of the work God has given us, which includes our working with you. [14]We are not reaching beyond these boundaries when we claim authority over you, as if we had never visited you. For we were the first to travel all the way to Corinth with the Good News of Christ.

[15]Nor do we boast and claim credit for the work someone else has done. Instead, we hope that your faith will grow so that the boundaries of our work among you will be extended. [16]Then we will be able to go and preach the Good News in other places far beyond you, where no one else is working. Then there will be no question of our boasting about work done in someone else's territory. [17]As the Scriptures say, "If you want to boast, boast only about the LORD."*

[18]When people commend themselves, it doesn't count for much. The important thing is for the Lord to commend them.

11 Paul and the False Apostles

I hope you will put up with a little more of my foolishness. Please bear with me. [2]For I am jealous for you with the jealousy of God himself. I promised you as a pure bride* to one husband—Christ. [3]But I fear that somehow your pure and undivided devotion to Christ will be corrupted, just as Eve was deceived by the cunning ways of the serpent. [4]You happily put up with whatever anyone tells you, even if they preach a different Jesus than the one we preach, or a different kind of Spirit than the one you received, or a different kind of gospel than the one you believed.

[5]But I don't consider myself inferior in any way to these "super apostles" who teach such things. [6]I may be unskilled as a speaker, but I'm not lacking in knowledge. We have made this clear to you in every possible way.

[7]Was I wrong when I humbled myself and honored you by preaching God's Good News to you without expecting anything in return? [8]I "robbed" other churches by accepting their contributions so I could serve you at no cost. [9]And when I was with

you and didn't have enough to live on, I did not become a financial burden to anyone. For the brothers who came from Macedonia brought me all that I needed. I have never been a burden to you, and I never will be. [10]As surely as the truth of Christ is in me, no one in all of Greece* will ever stop me from boasting about this. [11]Why? Because I don't love you? God knows that I do.

[12]But I will continue doing what I have always done. This will undercut those who are looking for an opportunity to boast that their work is just like ours. [13]These people are false apostles. They are deceitful workers who disguise themselves as apostles of Christ. [14]But I am not surprised! Even Satan disguises himself as an angel of light. [15]So it is no wonder that his servants also disguise themselves as servants of righteousness. In the end they will get the punishment their wicked deeds deserve.

Paul's Many Trials

[16]Again I say, don't think that I am a fool to talk like this. But even if you do, listen to me, as you would to a foolish person, while I also boast a little. [17]Such boasting is not from the Lord, but I am acting like a fool. [18]And since others boast about their human achievements, I will, too. [19]After all, you think you are so wise, but you enjoy putting up with fools! [20]You put up with it when someone enslaves you, takes everything you have, takes advantage of you, takes control of everything, and slaps you in the face. [21]I'm ashamed to say that we've been too "weak" to do that!

But whatever they dare to boast about— I'm talking like a fool again—I dare to boast about it, too. [22]Are they Hebrews? So am I. Are they Israelites? So am I. Are they descendants of Abraham? So am I. [23]Are they servants of Christ? I know I sound like a madman, but I have served him far more! I have worked harder, been put in prison more often, been whipped times without number, and faced death again and again. [24]Five different times the Jewish leaders gave me thirty-nine lashes. [25]Three times I was beaten with rods. Once I was

10:17 Jer 9:24. 11:2 Greek a virgin. 11:10 Greek Achaia, the southern region of the Greek peninsula.

stoned. Three times I was shipwrecked. Once I spent a whole night and a day adrift at sea. ²⁶I have traveled on many long journeys. I have faced danger from rivers and from robbers. I have faced danger from my own people, the Jews, as well as from the Gentiles. I have faced danger in the cities, in the deserts, and on the seas. And I have faced danger from men who claim to be believers but are not.* ²⁷I have worked hard and long, enduring many sleepless nights. I have been hungry and thirsty and have often gone without food. I have shivered in the cold, without enough clothing to keep me warm.

²⁸Then, besides all this, I have the daily burden of my concern for all the churches. ²⁹Who is weak without my feeling that weakness? Who is led astray, and I do not burn with anger?

³⁰If I must boast, I would rather boast about the things that show how weak I am. ³¹God, the Father of our Lord Jesus, who is worthy of eternal praise, knows I am not lying. ³²When I was in Damascus, the governor under King Aretas kept guards at the city gates to catch me. ³³I had to be lowered in a basket through a window in the city wall to escape from him.

12 Paul's Vision and His Thorn in the Flesh

This boasting will do no good, but I must go on. I will reluctantly tell about visions and revelations from the Lord. ²I* was caught up to the third heaven fourteen years ago. Whether I was in my body or out of my body, I don't know—only God knows. ³Yes, only God knows whether I was in my body or outside my body. But I do know ⁴that I was caught up* to paradise and heard things so astounding that they cannot be expressed in words, things no human is allowed to tell.

⁵That experience is worth boasting about, but I'm not going to do it. I will boast only about my weaknesses. ⁶If I wanted to boast, I would be no fool in doing so, because I would be telling the truth. But I won't do it, because I don't want anyone to give me credit beyond what they can see in my life

or hear in my message, ⁷even though I have received such wonderful revelations from God. So to keep me from becoming proud, I was given a thorn in my flesh, a messenger from Satan to torment me and keep me from becoming proud.

⁸Three different times I begged the Lord to take it away. ⁹Each time he said, "My grace is all you need. My power works best in weakness." So now I am glad to boast about my weaknesses, so that the power of Christ can work through me. ¹⁰That's why I take pleasure in my weaknesses, and in the insults, hardships, persecutions, and troubles that I suffer for Christ. For when I am weak, then I am strong.

Paul's Concern for the Corinthians

¹¹You have made me act like a fool—boasting like this.* You ought to be writing commendations for me, for I am not at all inferior to these "super apostles," even though I am nothing at all. ¹²When I was with you, I certainly gave you proof that I am an apostle. For I patiently did many signs and wonders and miracles among you. ¹³The only thing I failed to do, which I do in the other churches, was to become a financial burden to you. Please forgive me for this wrong!

¹⁴Now I am coming to you for the third time, and I will not be a burden to you. I don't want what you have—I want you. After all, children don't provide for their parents. Rather, parents provide for their children. ¹⁵I will gladly spend myself and all I have for you, even though it seems that the more I love you, the less you love me.

¹⁶Some of you admit I was not a burden to you. But others still think I was sneaky and took advantage of you by trickery. ¹⁷But how? Did any of the men I sent to you take advantage of you? ¹⁸When I urged Titus to visit you and sent our other brother with him, did Titus take advantage of you? No! For we have the same spirit and walk in each other's steps, doing things the same way.

¹⁹Perhaps you think we're saying these things just to defend ourselves. No, we tell you this as Christ's servants, and with

---

11:26 Greek *from false brothers.* **12:2** Greek *I know a man in Christ who.* **12:3-4** Greek *But I know such a man, ⁴that he was caught up.*
12:11 Some manuscripts do not include *boasting like this.*

Witnessing from Weakness

2 CORINTHIANS 12:9-10

Especially in a culture that so roundly criticizes Christians (not always without good reason), it's important for the world to see Christians as we really are, not as we often pretend to be. They need to see us as messed up, wounded, and hurting people who have found the great Hope and their ever-present Source of strength.

What might it be like for you to talk with friends or co-workers about the real mixture of joys and struggles in the Christian life? To speak with them of mighty ways God has moved, of huge disappointments, doubts, praise, unanswered prayers, your often rocky journeys through a life of faith?

If you were to share with your friends or co-workers the ways in which God has walked with you through difficult, stressful times, it might offer glimpses of how God could embolden their own lives. If they knew that you too went through seasons of doubt or confusion but were sustained by experiencing the Holy Spirit's work in your life, imagine the impact. And of course there's no better way to shine the irresistible grace that has saved wretches like us than to be willing to open up areas of struggle—and mercy—in our own lives.

Perhaps the strongest way one can witness is to give glory where glory is due.

—Caryn Rivadeneira

For more on outreach, see reading at 1 Peter 2:11-12.

God as our witness. Everything we do, dear friends, is to strengthen you. [20] For I am afraid that when I come I won't like what I find, and you won't like my response. I am afraid that I will find quarreling, jealousy, anger, selfishness, slander, gossip, arrogance, and disorderly behavior. [21] Yes, I am afraid that when I come again, God will humble me in your presence. And I will be grieved because many of you have not given up your old sins. You have not repented of your impurity, sexual immorality, and eagerness for lustful pleasure.

13 Paul's Final Advice

This is the third time I am coming to visit you (and as the Scriptures say, "The facts of every case must be established by the testimony of two or three witnesses"*). [2] I have already warned those who had been sinning when I was there on my second visit. Now I again warn them and all others, just as I did before, that next time I will not spare them.

[3] I will give you all the proof you want that Christ speaks through me. Christ is not weak when he deals with you; he is powerful among you. [4] Although he was crucified in weakness, he now lives by the power of God. We, too, are weak, just as Christ was, but when we deal with you we will be alive with him and will have God's power.

[5] Examine yourselves to see if your faith is genuine. Test yourselves. Surely you know that Jesus Christ is among you*; if not, you have failed the test of genuine faith. [6] As you test yourselves, I hope you will recognize that we have not failed the test of apostolic authority.

[7] We pray to God that you will not do what is wrong by refusing our correction. I hope we won't need to demonstrate our authority when we arrive. Do the right

13:1 Deut 19:15. 13:5 Or *in you.*

thing before we come—even if that makes it look like we have failed to demonstrate our authority. [8] For we cannot oppose the truth, but must always stand for the truth. [9] We are glad to seem weak if it helps show that you are actually strong. We pray that you will become mature.

[10] I am writing this to you before I come, hoping that I won't need to deal severely with you when I do come. For I want to use the authority the Lord has given me to strengthen you, not to tear you down.

Paul's Final Greetings

[11] Dear brothers and sisters,* I close my letter with these last words: Be joyful. Grow to maturity. Encourage each other. Live in harmony and peace. Then the God of love and peace will be with you.

[12] Greet each other with Christian love.* [13] All of God's people here send you their greetings.

[14]*May the grace of the Lord Jesus Christ, the love of God, and the fellowship of the Holy Spirit be with you all.

Introduction to

Galatians

Background

Galatia was a territory in the central part of Asia Minor that became a Roman province in 25 B.C. The Galatians were a migratory Celtic people who had moved from Gaul (France) to Asia Minor in the third century B.C. Their territory included the southern cities of Pisidian Antioch, Iconium, Lystra, and Derbe, in which Paul and Barnabas established churches on Paul's first missionary journey (Acts 13:13–14:23). The Epistle to the Galatians is addressed to people who had made a commitment to Christ but slipped back into old habits and practices—especially legalism. There is no doubt that Paul wrote this letter. "Listen! I, Paul, tell you this" (5:2; see also 1:1).

Message

Galatians weighs in on the controversy of justification by faith versus the gospel of works. Many Jewish believers needed help to determine how their new faith related to the practices of their old faith. Paul spends the early part of Galatians defending the gospel of grace the believers have recently accepted and defending his authority as an apostle from those who have attempted to undermine him. In chapters 3–4 Paul systematically outlines the gospel of grace. The final chapters explain the freedom found in Christ and the gospel of grace. Paul encourages the new believers to "follow the Spirit's leading" (5:25) and avoid "what your sinful nature craves" (5:16).

Time

There are two theories for the date of this letter. The first asserts that Paul wrote it between A.D. 53 and 56 either in Macedonia or Ephesus to cities north of those he visited while journeying with Barnabas. Paul may have visited this section of Galatia on his second missionary journey. The second argues that Paul wrote the book in Syrian Antioch circa A.D. 49 to the churches he and Barnabas had previously established in southern Galatia. If the southern Galatia theory is true, Galatians is one of the earliest books written in the New Testament Canon, just before the Council of Jerusalem (Acts 15:4–21).

Outline

Galatians

1 Greetings from Paul

This letter is from Paul, an apostle. I was not appointed by any group of people or any human authority, but by Jesus Christ himself and by God the Father, who raised Jesus from the dead.

²All the brothers and sisters* here join me in sending this letter to the churches of Galatia.

³May God our Father and the Lord Jesus Christ* give you grace and peace. ⁴Jesus gave his life for our sins, just as God our Father planned, in order to rescue us from this evil world in which we live. ⁵All glory to God forever and ever! Amen.

There Is Only One Good News

⁶I am shocked that you are turning away so soon from God, who called you to himself through the loving mercy of Christ.* You are following a different way that pretends to be the Good News ⁷but is not the Good News at all. You are being fooled by those who deliberately twist the truth concerning Christ.

⁸Let God's curse fall on anyone, including us or even an angel from heaven, who preaches a different kind of Good News than the one we preached to you. ⁹I say again what we have said before: If anyone preaches any other Good News than the one you welcomed, let that person be cursed.

¹⁰Obviously, I'm not trying to win the approval of people, but of God. If pleasing people were my goal, I would not be Christ's servant.

Paul's Message Comes from Christ

¹¹Dear brothers and sisters, I want you to understand that the gospel message I preach is not based on mere human reasoning. ¹²I received my message from no human source, and no one taught me. Instead, I received it by direct revelation from Jesus Christ.*

¹³You know what I was like when I followed the Jewish religion—how I violently persecuted God's church. I did my best to destroy it. ¹⁴I was far ahead of my fellow Jews in my zeal for the traditions of my ancestors.

¹⁵But even before I was born, God chose me and called me by his marvelous grace. Then it pleased him ¹⁶to reveal his Son to me* so that I would proclaim the Good News about Jesus to the Gentiles.

When this happened, I did not rush out to consult with any human being.* ¹⁷Nor did I go up to Jerusalem to consult with those who were apostles before I was. Instead, I went away into Arabia, and later I returned to the city of Damascus.

¹⁸Then three years later I went to Jerusalem to get to know Peter,* and I stayed with him for fifteen days. ¹⁹The only other apostle I met at that time was James, the Lord's brother. ²⁰I declare before God that what I am writing to you is not a lie.

1:2 Greek *brothers;* also in 1:11. **1:3** Some manuscripts read *God the Father and our Lord Jesus Christ.* **1:6** Some manuscripts read *through loving mercy.* **1:12** Or *by the revelation of Jesus Christ.* **1:16a** Or *in me.* **1:16b** Greek *with flesh and blood.* **1:18** Greek *Cephas.*

²¹After that visit I went north into the provinces of Syria and Cilicia. ²²And still the Christians in the churches in Judea didn't know me personally. ²³All they knew was that people were saying, "The one who used to persecute us is now preaching the very faith he tried to destroy!" ²⁴And they praised God because of me.

2 The Apostles Accept Paul

Then fourteen years later I went back to Jerusalem again, this time with Barnabas; and Titus came along, too. ²I went there because God revealed to me that I should go. While I was there I met privately with those considered to be leaders of the church and shared with them the message I had been preaching to the Gentiles. I wanted to make sure that we were in agreement, for fear that all my efforts had been wasted and I was running the race for nothing. ³And they supported me and did not even demand that my companion Titus be circumcised, though he was a Gentile.*

⁴Even that question came up only because of some so-called Christians there—false ones, really*—who were secretly brought in. They sneaked in to spy on us and take away the freedom we have in Christ Jesus. They wanted to enslave us and force us to follow their Jewish regulations. ⁵But we refused to give in to them for a single moment. We wanted to preserve the truth of the gospel message for you.

⁶And the leaders of the church had nothing to add to what I was preaching. (By the way, their reputation as great leaders made no difference to me, for God has no favorites.) ⁷Instead, they saw that God had given me the responsibility of preaching the gospel to the Gentiles, just as he had given Peter the responsibility of preaching to the Jews. ⁸For the same God who worked through Peter as the apostle to the Jews also worked through me as the apostle to the Gentiles.

⁹In fact, James, Peter,* and John, who were known as pillars of the church, recognized the gift God had given me, and they accepted Barnabas and me as their co-workers. They encouraged us to keep preaching to the Gentiles, while they continued their work with the Jews. ¹⁰Their only suggestion was that we keep on helping the poor, which I have always been eager to do.

Paul Confronts Peter

¹¹But when Peter came to Antioch, I had to oppose him to his face, for what he did was very wrong. ¹²When he first arrived, he ate with the Gentile Christians, who were not circumcised. But afterward, when some friends of James came, Peter wouldn't eat with the Gentiles anymore. He was afraid of criticism from these people who insisted on the necessity of circumcision. ¹³As a result, other Jewish Christians followed Peter's hypocrisy, and even Barnabas was led astray by their hypocrisy.

¹⁴When I saw that they were not following the truth of the gospel message, I said to Peter in front of all the others, "Since you, a Jew by birth, have discarded the Jewish laws and are living like a Gentile, why are you now trying to make these Gentiles follow the Jewish traditions?

¹⁵"You and I are Jews by birth, not 'sinners' like the Gentiles. ¹⁶Yet we know that a person is made right with God by faith in Jesus Christ, not by obeying the law. And we have believed in Christ Jesus, so that we might be made right with God because of our faith in Christ, not because we have obeyed the law. For no one will ever be made right with God by obeying the law."*

¹⁷But suppose we seek to be made right with God through faith in Christ and then we are found guilty because we have abandoned the law. Would that mean Christ has led us into sin? Absolutely not! ¹⁸Rather, I am a sinner if I rebuild the old system of law I already tore down. ¹⁹For when I tried to keep the law, it condemned me. So I died to the law—I stopped trying to meet all its requirements—so that I might live for God. ²⁰My old self has been crucified with Christ.* It is no longer I who live, but Christ lives in me. So I live in this earthly body by trusting in the Son of God, who loved me and gave himself for me. ²¹I do not treat the grace of God as meaningless. For if keeping the law could make us right with God, then there was no need for Christ to die.

2:3 Greek *a Greek.*   **2:4** Greek *some false brothers.*   **2:9** Greek *Cephas;* also in 2:11, 14.   **2:16** Some translators hold that the quotation extends through verse 14; others through verse 16; and still others through verse 21.   **2:20** Some English translations put this sentence in verse 19.

3 The Law and Faith in Christ

Oh, foolish Galatians! Who has cast an evil spell on you? For the meaning of Jesus Christ's death was made as clear to you as if you had seen a picture of his death on the cross. ²Let me ask you this one question: Did you receive the Holy Spirit by obeying the law of Moses? Of course not! You received the Spirit because you believed the message you heard about Christ. ³How foolish can you be? After starting your Christian lives in the Spirit, why are you now trying to become perfect by your own human effort? ⁴Have you experienced* so much for nothing? Surely it was not in vain, was it?

⁵I ask you again, does God give you the Holy Spirit and work miracles among you because you obey the law? Of course not! It is because you believe the message you heard about Christ.

⁶In the same way, "Abraham believed God, and God counted him as righteous because of his faith."* ⁷The real children of Abraham, then, are those who put their faith in God.

⁸What's more, the Scriptures looked forward to this time when God would declare the Gentiles to be righteous because of their faith. God proclaimed this good news to Abraham long ago when he said, "All nations will be blessed through you."* ⁹So all who put their faith in Christ share the same blessing Abraham received because of his faith.

¹⁰But those who depend on the law to make them right with God are under his curse, for the Scriptures say, "Cursed is everyone who does not observe and obey all the commands that are written in God's Book of the Law."* ¹¹So it is clear that no one can be made right with God by trying to keep the law. For the Scriptures say, "It is through faith that a righteous person has life."* ¹²This way of faith is very different from the way of law, which says, "It is through obeying the law that a person has life."*

¹³But Christ has rescued us from the curse pronounced by the law. When he was hung on the cross, he took upon himself the curse for our wrongdoing. For it is written in the Scriptures, "Cursed is everyone who is hung on a tree."* ¹⁴Through Christ Jesus, God has blessed the Gentiles with the same blessing he promised to Abraham, so that we who are believers might receive the promised* Holy Spirit through faith.

The Law and God's Promise

¹⁵Dear brothers and sisters,* here's an example from everyday life. Just as no one can set aside or amend an irrevocable agreement, so it is in this case. ¹⁶God gave the promises to Abraham and his child.* And notice that the Scripture doesn't say "to his children,*" as if it meant many descendants. Rather, it says "to his child"—and that, of course, means Christ. ¹⁷This is what I am trying to say: The agreement God made with Abraham could not be canceled 430 years later when God gave the law to Moses. God would be breaking his promise. ¹⁸For if the inheritance could be received by keeping the law, then it would not be the result of accepting God's promise. But God graciously gave it to Abraham as a promise.

¹⁹Why, then, was the law given? It was given alongside the promise to show people their sins. But the law was designed to last only until the coming of the child who was promised. God gave his law through angels to Moses, who was the mediator between God and the people. ²⁰Now a mediator is helpful if more than one party must reach an agreement. But God, who is one, did not use a mediator when he gave his promise to Abraham.

²¹Is there a conflict, then, between God's law and God's promises?* Absolutely not! If the law could give us new life, we could be made right with God by obeying it. ²²But the Scriptures declare that we are all prisoners of sin, so we receive God's promise of freedom only by believing in Jesus Christ.

God's Children through Faith

²³Before the way of faith in Christ was available to us, we were placed under guard by the law. We were kept in protective custody, so to speak, until the way of faith was revealed.

²⁴Let me put it another way. The law was our guardian until Christ came; it protected us until we could be made right with

---

3:4 Or *Have you suffered.* **3:6** Gen 15:6. **3:8** Gen 12:3; 18:18; 22:18. **3:10** Deut 27:26. **3:11** Hab 2:4. **3:12** Lev 18:5. **3:13** Deut 21:23 (Greek version). **3:14** Some manuscripts read *the blessing of the.* **3:15** Greek *Brothers.* **3:16a** Greek *seed;* also in 3:16c, 19. See notes on Gen 12:7 and 13:15. **3:16b** Greek *seeds.* **3:21** Some manuscripts read *and the promises?*

God through faith. ²⁵And now that the way of faith has come, we no longer need the law as our guardian.

²⁶For you are all children* of God through faith in Christ Jesus. ²⁷And all who have been united with Christ in baptism have put on Christ, like putting on new clothes.* ²⁸There is no longer Jew or Gentile,* slave or free, male and female. For you are all one in Christ Jesus. ²⁹And now that you belong to Christ, you are the true children* of Abraham. You are his heirs, and God's promise to Abraham belongs to you.

4 Think of it this way. If a father dies and leaves an inheritance for his young children, those children are not much better off than slaves until they grow up, even though they actually own everything their father had. ²They have to obey their guardians until they reach whatever age their father set. ³And that's the way it was with us before Christ came. We were like children; we were slaves to the basic spiritual principles* of this world.

⁴But when the right time came, God sent his Son, born of a woman, subject to the law. ⁵God sent him to buy freedom for us who were slaves to the law, so that he could adopt us as his very own children.* ⁶And because we* are his children, God has sent the Spirit of his Son into our hearts, prompting us to call out, "Abba, Father."* ⁷Now you are no longer a slave but God's own child.* And since you are his child, God has made you his heir.

Paul's Concern for the Galatians
⁸Before you Gentiles knew God, you were slaves to so-called gods that do not even exist. ⁹So now that you know God (or should I say, now that God knows you), why do you want to go back again and become slaves once more to the weak and useless spiritual principles of this world? ¹⁰You are trying to earn favor with God by observing certain days or months or seasons or years. ¹¹I fear for you. Perhaps all my hard work with you was for nothing. ¹²Dear brothers and sisters,* I plead with you to live as I do in free-

dom from these things, for I have become like you Gentiles—free from those laws.

You did not mistreat me when I first preached to you. ¹³Surely you remember that I was sick when I first brought you the Good News. ¹⁴But even though my condition tempted you to reject me, you did not despise me or turn me away. No, you took me in and cared for me as though I were an angel from God or even Christ Jesus himself. ¹⁵Where is that joyful and grateful spirit you felt then? I am sure you would have taken out your own eyes and given them to me if it had been possible. ¹⁶Have I now become your enemy because I am telling you the truth?

¹⁷Those false teachers are so eager to win your favor, but their intentions are not good. They are trying to shut you off from me so that you will pay attention only to them. ¹⁸If someone is eager to do good things for you, that's all right; but let them do it all the time, not just when I'm with you.

¹⁹Oh, my dear children! I feel as if I'm going through labor pains for you again, and they will continue until Christ is fully developed in your lives. ²⁰I wish I were with you right now so I could change my tone. But at this distance I don't know how else to help you.

Abraham's Two Children
²¹Tell me, you who want to live under the law, do you know what the law actually says? ²²The Scriptures say that Abraham had two sons, one from his slave wife and one from his freeborn wife.* ²³The son of the slave wife was born in a human attempt to bring about the fulfillment of God's promise. But the son of the freeborn wife was born as God's own fulfillment of his promise.

²⁴These two women serve as an illustration of God's two covenants. The first woman, Hagar, represents Mount Sinai where people received the law that enslaved them. ²⁵And now Jerusalem is just like Mount Sinai in Arabia,* because she and her children live in slavery to the law. ²⁶But the other woman, Sarah, represents the heavenly Jerusalem. She is the free woman, and she is our mother. ²⁷As Isaiah said,

---

3:26 Greek *sons.* **3:27** Greek *have put on Christ.* **3:28** Greek *Jew or Greek.* **3:29** Greek *seed.* **4:3** Or *powers;* also in 4:9. **4:5** Greek *sons;* also in 4:6. **4:6a** Greek *you.* **4:6b** *Abba* is an Aramaic term for "father." **4:7** Greek *son;* also in 4:7b. **4:12** Greek *brothers;* also in 4:28, 31. **4:22** See Gen 16:15; 21:2-3. **4:25** Greek *And Hagar, which is Mount Sinai in Arabia, is now like Jerusalem;* other manuscripts read *And Mount Sinai in Arabia is now like Jerusalem.*

Acceptance

Say Yes to God

GALATIANS 3:28

What are you worth?

Throughout history—and still today in some cultures—women were seen as property. So, for instance, if a woman was violated, legally her husband or father would receive compensation; she wouldn't. A woman's highest calling was to bear children. This was the world into which Jesus was born.

And yet Jesus taught and showed through his interactions with women that a woman's highest calling was not just to continue the species. Motherhood is a noble calling, but it is not the ultimate calling by which a woman is defined. Jesus showed that the highest calling—for both women and men, since they share a common mission—is to understand and do the will of God in whose image we were created.

That's what makes biblical history so wonderfully stunning juxtaposed against the rest of the world's history. Woven throughout Scripture—sometimes blatantly, often subtly—we see over and over the stories of women being called and used by God in mighty ways: as judges and prophets and military leaders and teachers *and* mothers. Miriam. Ruth. Deborah. Jael. Esther. Rahab. Hannah. The prophetess Huldah (2 Kings 22). Anna (Luke 2). Joanna. The many Marys. Phoebe. Priscilla. They said yes to God's purposes working in and through their lives.

But Jesus' story is, by far, the most amazing: one rabbi (who also happened to be God incarnate!) in a small country who brought the status of women right to the forefront—and changed history forever. Women were among his disciples. Mary of Bethany sat at his feet and listened to his teaching. In a day and culture when women were uneducated and not even allowed to participate in formal corporate worship, who were relegated to an outer courtyard in the temple, Mary sat at the Rabbi's feet to learn, and from learning, to follow in the Rabbi's footsteps. It was radical. It was shocking. It was awesome.

Jesus began the revolution, but then Paul formalized it.

During a visit to Israel, I stood by the ruins of an ancient synagogue and noticed steps running along the outside wall. I asked one of our tour leaders, Gary Burge, a Wheaton College New Testament professor, about it.

"Those steps would have gone to the second floor of the synagogue," he explained. "They were for the women. . . . They weren't allowed to worship with the men."

But, he went on to explain, "That's one reason Christianity was so revolutionary and radical. Paul brought women down into the service right alongside the men. Women were no longer second-class citizens in the kingdom. They were equals."

The New Testament church, unlike the culture around it, became desegregated. Paul brought women into the sanctuary, which told them, "You all have gifts and a purpose to fulfill in God's kingdom. You all need to work together." What a revolution!

All of a sudden the women in the early church went from being slaves, property, being good for birthing babies and not much else, to being side-by-side with the men. Paul told them, "There is no longer Jew or Gentile, slave or free, male or female. For you are all one in Christ Jesus" (Galatians 3:28). For the first time, they were hearing the good news: not only had Jesus died for their sins, he also had important work for them to do. He placed strengths within them that he wanted them to use. No longer did they have a "free pass" to get away with not doing kingdom work. They had a responsibility to step up to the plate and get 'er done.

God asks the same of us today.

So if we're serious about living in the fullness of who we are in Christ, if we truly understand the value God has placed on us, we must ask ourselves, *What has God prepared me for?* and *Am I living that out every day?*

Imagine how different the world would be if, throughout the centuries, women believers said yes to using their gifts—not the gifts they were told and believed they should have—but the ones God actually birthed within them. Imagine how different our culture, churches, and homes would be. Imagine how different our lives would be, how fulfilling, adventurous, and effective in God's kingdom!

Now is the time to continue the revolution that was started two thousand years ago. Now is the time to say yes to God—regardless of where we are, what church we attend, or what talents we have. And watch how he changes the world through and because of the unique, wonderful gifts he gave us, women.

—*Ginger Kolbaba*

For more on acceptance, see reading at Ephesians 4:1.

"Rejoice, O childless woman,
    you who have never given birth!
Break into a joyful shout,
    you who have never been in labor!
For the desolate woman now has more
    children

than the woman who lives with her
    husband!"*

28 And you, dear brothers and sisters,
are children of the promise, just like Isaac.
29 But you are now being persecuted by

Q&A — Mentoring toward Maturity

GALATIANS 4:17-20

What should we aim for as we mentor others? What should our "goal" look like?

As mentors our main goal should be to walk with a mentoree as she grows toward spiritual maturity.

There are two definitions of spiritual maturity: the first is engaging in behavior appropriate to the stage in which you are. A four-year-old is mature when he does everything that's reasonable for a four-year-old to do. We don't consider a four-year-old immature because he can't do what a twelve-year-old does. But if he doesn't do the things four-year-olds are capable of, then he's immature. So this kind of maturity is about living up to the capacities God has made possible for you.

The other definition has to do with qualities like those listed in Ephesians 4:7-16. A mature person is one who uses her spiritual gifts, builds the body, discerns truth from error, speaks the truth in love, and honors God in her relationships.

Spiritual maturity is an ongoing journey, in which we continually press toward the mark (Philippians 3:14); immaturity is complacency and self-satisfaction. Although only God knows the heart, we *can* observe whether someone, as a whole, cares deeply about the things God cares about. Does she have a genuine concern for the lost? For the poor? Does she speak the truth in love? Does she show discernment? Is she a praying person?

But while mentors can help someone become more mature, ultimately, it's not in our control. For example, Paul wrote letters, prayed, straightened out misunderstandings, and tried to reconcile relationships. However, Paul never said, "I am making you mature." Rather, he said Christ needs to be "fully developed" in our lives (Galatians 4:19). That's the Holy Spirit's work; as mentors, we seek to be colaborers with God.

—Roberta Hestenes

For more on mentoring, see reading at Titus 2:3-5.

4:27 Isa 54:1.

those who want you to keep the law, just as Ishmael, the child born by human effort, persecuted Isaac, the child born by the power of the Spirit.

³⁰But what do the Scriptures say about that? "Get rid of the slave and her son, for the son of the slave woman will not share the inheritance with the free woman's son."* ³¹So, dear brothers and sisters, we are not children of the slave woman; we are children of the free woman.

5 Freedom in Christ

So Christ has truly set us free. Now make sure that you stay free, and don't get tied up again in slavery to the law.

²Listen! I, Paul, tell you this: If you are counting on circumcision to make you right with God, then Christ will be of no benefit to you. ³I'll say it again. If you are trying to find favor with God by being circumcised, you must obey every regulation in the whole law of Moses. ⁴For if you are trying to make yourselves right with God by keeping the law, you have been cut off from Christ! You have fallen away from God's grace.

⁵But we who live by the Spirit eagerly wait to receive by faith the righteousness God has promised to us. ⁶For when we place our faith in Christ Jesus, there is no benefit in being circumcised or being uncircumcised. What is important is faith expressing itself in love.

⁷You were running the race so well. Who has held you back from following the truth? ⁸It certainly isn't God, for he is the one who called you to freedom. ⁹This false teaching is like a little yeast that spreads through the whole batch of dough! ¹⁰I am trusting the Lord to keep you from believing false teachings. God will judge that person, whoever he is, who has been confusing you.

¹¹Dear brothers and sisters,* if I were still preaching that you must be circumcised— as some say I do—why am I still being persecuted? If I were no longer preaching salvation through the cross of Christ, no one would be offended. ¹²I just wish that those troublemakers who want to mutilate you by circumcision would mutilate themselves.*

¹³For you have been called to live in freedom, my brothers and sisters. But don't use your freedom to satisfy your sinful nature. Instead, use your freedom to serve one another in love. ¹⁴For the whole law can be summed up in this one command: "Love your neighbor as yourself."* ¹⁵But if you are always biting and devouring one another, watch out! Beware of destroying one another.

Living by the Spirit's Power

¹⁶So I say, let the Holy Spirit guide your lives. Then you won't be doing what your sinful nature craves. ¹⁷The sinful nature wants to do evil, which is just the opposite of what the Spirit wants. And the Spirit gives us desires that are the opposite of what the sinful nature desires. These two forces are constantly fighting each other, so you are not free to carry out your good intentions. ¹⁸But when you are directed by the Spirit, you are not under obligation to the law of Moses.

¹⁹When you follow the desires of your sinful nature, the results are very clear: sexual immorality, impurity, lustful pleasures, ²⁰idolatry, sorcery, hostility, quarreling, jealousy, outbursts of anger, selfish ambition, dissension, division, ²¹envy, drunkenness, wild parties, and other sins like these. Let me tell you again, as I have before, that anyone living that sort of life will not inherit the Kingdom of God.

²²But the Holy Spirit produces this kind of fruit in our lives: love, joy, peace, patience, kindness, goodness, faithfulness, ²³gentleness, and self-control. There is no law against these things!

²⁴Those who belong to Christ Jesus have nailed the passions and desires of their sinful nature to his cross and crucified them there. ²⁵Since we are living by the Spirit, let us follow the Spirit's leading in every part of our lives. ²⁶Let us not become conceited, or provoke one another, or be jealous of one another.

6 We Harvest What We Plant

Dear brothers and sisters, if another believer* is overcome by some sin, you who are godly* should gently and humbly help that person back onto the right path. And

---

4:30 Gen 21:10. **5:11** Greek *Brothers;* similarly in 5:13. **5:12** Or *castrate themselves, or cut themselves off from you;* Greek reads *cut themselves off.* **5:14** Lev 19:18. **6:1a** Greek *Brothers, if a man.* **6:1b** Greek *spiritual.*

Forgiving versus Overlooking

GALATIANS 5:22-23

We sometimes mistake scenarios that merely ask us to be gracious with situations that truly require forgiveness. Everyday life is full of situations in which others may slight us unintentionally. Perhaps it's a disagreement with a co-worker about how to handle a problem, or maybe a friend forgets to give you a ride, or perhaps your husband accidentally leaves the grocery list behind and doesn't buy something you needed for dinner. How should we respond? With out-of-proportion frustration or resentment?

Rather than being overly sensitive or taking others' mistakes personally, we can foster attitudes of generous grace that naturally flow out of a Spirit-filled life (Galatians 5:22-23).

We need to have a clear understanding of when we need to forgive and when we may need just to "forget" something that isn't a big deal. Forgiveness is reserved for deep, serious hurts that result from the evil actions of others. We can *overlook* a friend forgetting to give us a ride; we must *forgive* the friend who lies to us.

So how can we know when a particular act crosses the line and requires forgiveness? Your own reaction is the best clue. If you can't shake feelings of hurt and anger, if you obsess over what happened, then forgiveness is called for. But first make sure you haven't misinterpreted a friend's actions or misunderstood what he or she said. If your friend forgot to pick you up because she was frazzled, and you interpret it to mean she doesn't care about you, then *your* thinking needs to be adjusted.

—Vinita Hampton Wright

For more on forgiveness, see reading at 1 John 3:19.

be careful not to fall into the same temptation yourself. [2] Share each other's burdens, and in this way obey the law of Christ. [3] If you think you are too important to help someone, you are only fooling yourself. You are not that important.

[4] Pay careful attention to your own work, for then you will get the satisfaction of a job well done, and you won't need to compare yourself to anyone else. [5] For we are each responsible for our own conduct.

[6] Those who are taught the word of God should provide for their teachers, sharing all good things with them.

[7] Don't be misled—you cannot mock the justice of God. You will always harvest what you plant. [8] Those who live only to satisfy their own sinful nature will harvest decay and death from that sinful nature. But those who live to please the Spirit will harvest everlasting life from the Spirit. [9] So let's not get tired of doing what is good. At just the right time we will reap a harvest of blessing if we don't give up. [10] Therefore, whenever we have the opportunity, we should do good to everyone—especially to those in the family of faith.

Paul's Final Advice

[11] NOTICE WHAT LARGE LETTERS I USE AS I WRITE THESE CLOSING WORDS IN MY OWN HANDWRITING.

[12] Those who are trying to force you to be circumcised want to look good to others. They don't want to be persecuted for teaching that the cross of Christ alone can save.

Reaching Out in Compassion

GALATIANS 6:1–3

Reconciliation

We must not mistake compassion for sentimentality—feeling sorry for someone and just trying to help her cheer up. Nor should we marry compassion with tolerance, the highest value of our age. That union results in the conclusion that we have no right to give direction to a lost soul; all we can do is provide reassurance, along with hand patting and hugs.

True Christian compassion means much more than that. The word traces back to a Latin root meaning "suffering with." In practice it means bearing one another's burdens and can include speaking a firm truth in love (Galatians 6:2; Ephesians 4:15). Those who practice true compassion find it demanding, sometimes difficult, always personal. There is no such thing as faceless compassion. We must suffer with others face to face, as Jesus did.

Didn't Jesus accept the people around him just as they were? Yes, but he loved them too much to leave them that way. Every life Jesus touched changed in a radical way, usually beginning with calling them to face themselves and their sin.

Our compassion for others grows out of our own awareness of need; the joy of the Christian life is knowing ourselves to be forgiven sinners. Cultivating that inner joy, by reflecting on our sins and the vastness of God's love, is the key to genuine compassion.

We are all lost sinners, by God's grace being prepared for lives in his holy presence. Those we see struggling in the mire alongside us cannot find salvation in our contempt or self-righteousness. But out of the depths of our own sinfulness and the heights of our joy at forgiveness, we can reach them with hope.

—Frederica Mathewes-Green

For more on outreach, see reading at James 3:17-18.

¹³ And even those who advocate circumcision don't keep the whole law themselves. They only want you to be circumcised so they can boast about it and claim you as their disciples.

¹⁴ As for me, may I never boast about anything except the cross of our Lord Jesus Christ. Because of that cross,* my interest in this world has been crucified, and the world's interest in me has also died. ¹⁵ It doesn't matter whether we have been cir-

cumcised or not. What counts is whether we have been transformed into a new creation. ¹⁶ May God's peace and mercy be upon all who live by this principle; they are the new people of God.*

¹⁷ From now on, don't let anyone trouble me with these things. For I bear on my body the scars that show I belong to Jesus.

¹⁸ Dear brothers and sisters,* may the grace of our Lord Jesus Christ be with your spirit. Amen.

6:14 Or *Because of him.*   **6:16** Greek *this principle, and upon the Israel of God.*   **6:18** Greek *Brothers.*

Introduction to

Ephesians

Background

A port city, Ephesus was one of the five major cities in the Roman Empire. The apostle Paul visited Ephesus at the end of his second missionary journey (Acts 18:19–21). During his third missionary journey, Paul remained in Ephesus for three years (Acts 19:1–41). On his way back to Jerusalem at the end of his third journey, Paul stopped in Ephesus to say goodbye to the elders of the church for what he knew would be the last time (Acts 20:17–38). He addresses this letter to "God's holy people in Ephesus, who are faithful followers of Christ Jesus" (1:1). Paul identifies himself as the author of Ephesians in 1:1, 3:1, and more indirectly throughout.

Message

This Pauline letter doesn't focus on any particular heresy, church problem, or dysfunction. Paul simply wants to encourage the churches in that region (now western Turkey). Paul's advice here is practical, and yet he repeatedly uses the phrases "heavenly realms" (1:3, 20; 2:6) and "heavenly places" (3:10; 6:12). His overriding theme is the relationship between Jesus exalted in his heavenly kingdom and the body of Christ—his church on earth. The fullness of the Spirit is available to the church united with Jesus as its head. Notably, Paul encourages believers to put on the armor of God—protection from the snares of the evil one.

Time

Ephesians was most likely written early in Paul's first Roman imprisonment (A.D. 60–62). He mentions his imprisonment in 3:1: "I, Paul, a prisoner of Christ Jesus for the benefit of you Gentiles . . ." (see also 4:1).

Outline

Ephesians

1 Greetings from Paul

This letter is from Paul, chosen by the will of God to be an apostle of Christ Jesus.

I am writing to God's holy people in Ephesus,* who are faithful followers of Christ Jesus.

²May God our Father and the Lord Jesus Christ give you grace and peace.

Spiritual Blessings

³All praise to God, the Father of our Lord Jesus Christ, who has blessed us with every spiritual blessing in the heavenly realms because we are united with Christ. ⁴Even before he made the world, God loved us and chose us in Christ to be holy and without fault in his eyes. ⁵God decided in advance to adopt us into his own family by bringing us to himself through Jesus Christ. This is what he wanted to do, and it gave him great pleasure. ⁶So we praise God for the glorious grace he has poured out on us who belong to his dear Son.* ⁷He is so rich in kindness and grace that he purchased our freedom with the blood of his Son and forgave our sins. ⁸He has showered his kindness on us, along with all wisdom and understanding.

⁹God has now revealed to us his mysterious plan regarding Christ, a plan to fulfill his own good pleasure. ¹⁰And this is the plan: At the right time he will bring everything together under the authority of Christ—everything in heaven and on earth. ¹¹Furthermore, because we are united with Christ, we have received an inheritance from God,* for he chose us in advance, and he makes everything work out according to his plan.

¹²God's purpose was that we Jews who were the first to trust in Christ would bring praise and glory to God. ¹³And now you Gentiles have also heard the truth, the Good News that God saves you. And when you believed in Christ, he identified you as his own* by giving you the Holy Spirit, whom he promised long ago. ¹⁴The Spirit is God's guarantee that he will give us the inheritance he promised and that he has purchased us to be his own people. He did this so we would praise and glorify him.

Paul's Prayer for Spiritual Wisdom

¹⁵Ever since I first heard of your strong faith in the Lord Jesus and your love for God's people everywhere,* ¹⁶I have not stopped thanking God for you. I pray for you constantly, ¹⁷asking God, the glorious Father of our Lord Jesus Christ, to give you spiritual wisdom* and insight so that you might grow in your knowledge of God. ¹⁸I pray that your hearts will be flooded with light so that you can understand the confident hope he has given to those he called—his holy people who are his rich and glorious inheritance.*

¹⁹I also pray that you will understand the incredible greatness of God's power

---

1:1 The most ancient manuscripts do not include *in Ephesus*.   **1:6** Greek *to us in the beloved*.   **1:11** Or *we have become God's inheritance*.   **1:13** Or *he put his seal on you*.   **1:15** Some manuscripts read *your faithfulness to the Lord Jesus and to God's people everywhere*.   **1:17** Or *to give you the Spirit of wisdom*.   **1:18** Or *called, and the rich and glorious inheritance he has given to his holy people*.

for us who believe him. This is the same mighty power ²⁰that raised Christ from the dead and seated him in the place of honor at God's right hand in the heavenly realms. ²¹Now he is far above any ruler or authority or power or leader or anything else—not only in this world but also in the world to come. ²²God has put all things under the authority of Christ and has made him head over all things for the benefit of the church. ²³And the church is his body; it is made full and complete by Christ, who fills all things everywhere with himself.

2 Made Alive with Christ

Once you were dead because of your disobedience and your many sins. ²You used to live in sin, just like the rest of the world, obeying the devil—the commander of the powers in the unseen world.* He is the spirit at work in the hearts of those who refuse to obey God. ³All of us used to live that way, following the passionate desires and inclinations of our sinful nature. By our very nature we were subject to God's anger, just like everyone else.

⁴But God is so rich in mercy, and he loved us so much, ⁵that even though we were dead because of our sins, he gave us life when he raised Christ from the dead. (It is only by God's grace that you have been saved!) ⁶For he raised us from the dead along with Christ and seated us with him in the heavenly realms because we are united with Christ Jesus. ⁷So God can point to us in all future ages as examples of the incredible wealth of his grace and kindness toward us, as shown in all he has done for us who are united with Christ Jesus.

⁸God saved you by his grace when you believed. And you can't take credit for this; it is a gift from God. ⁹Salvation is not a reward for the good things we have done, so none of us can boast about it. ¹⁰For we are God's masterpiece. He has created us anew in Christ Jesus, so we can do the good things he planned for us long ago.

Oneness and Peace in Christ

¹¹Don't forget that you Gentiles used to be outsiders. You were called "uncircumcised heathens" by the Jews, who were proud of their circumcision, even though it affected only their bodies and not their hearts. ¹²In those days you were living apart from Christ. You were excluded from citizenship among the people of Israel, and you did not know the covenant promises God had made to them. You lived in this world without God and without hope. ¹³But now you have been united with Christ Jesus. Once you were far away from God, but now you have been brought near to him through the blood of Christ.

¹⁴For Christ himself has brought peace to us. He united Jews and Gentiles into one people when, in his own body on the cross, he broke down the wall of hostility that separated us. ¹⁵He did this by ending the system of law with its commandments and regulations. He made peace between Jews and Gentiles by creating in himself one new people from the two groups. ¹⁶Together as one body, Christ reconciled both groups to God by means of his death on the cross, and our hostility toward each other was put to death.

¹⁷He brought this Good News of peace to you Gentiles who were far away from him, and peace to the Jews who were near. ¹⁸Now all of us can come to the Father through the same Holy Spirit because of what Christ has done for us.

A Temple for the Lord

¹⁹So now you Gentiles are no longer strangers and foreigners. You are citizens along with all of God's holy people. You are members of God's family. ²⁰Together, we are his house, built on the foundation of the apostles and the prophets. And the cornerstone is Christ Jesus himself. ²¹We are carefully joined together in him, becoming a holy temple for the Lord. ²²Through him you Gentiles are also being made part of this dwelling where God lives by his Spirit.

3 God's Mysterious Plan Revealed

When I think of all this, I, Paul, a prisoner of Christ Jesus for the benefit of you Gentiles* . . . ²assuming, by the way, that you know God gave me the special responsibility

---

2:2 Greek *obeying the commander of the power of the air.*   **3:1** Paul resumes this thought in verse 14: "When I think of all this, I fall to my knees and pray to the Father."

of extending his grace to you Gentiles. ³As I briefly wrote earlier, God himself revealed his mysterious plan to me. ⁴As you read what I have written, you will understand my insight into this plan regarding Christ. ⁵God did not reveal it to previous generations, but now by his Spirit he has revealed it to his holy apostles and prophets.

⁶And this is God's plan: Both Gentiles and Jews who believe the Good News share equally in the riches inherited by God's children. Both are part of the same body, and both enjoy the promise of blessings because they belong to Christ Jesus.* ⁷By God's grace and mighty power, I have been given the privilege of serving him by spreading this Good News.

⁸Though I am the least deserving of all God's people, he graciously gave me the privilege of telling the Gentiles about the endless treasures available to them in Christ. ⁹I was chosen to explain to everyone* this mysterious plan that God, the Creator of all things, had kept secret from the beginning.

¹⁰God's purpose in all this was to use the church to display his wisdom in its rich variety to all the unseen rulers and authorities in the heavenly places. ¹¹This was his eternal plan, which he carried out through Christ Jesus our Lord.

¹²Because of Christ and our faith in him,* we can now come boldly and confidently into God's presence. ¹³So please don't lose heart because of my trials here. I am suffering for you, so you should feel honored.

Paul's Prayer for Spiritual Growth

¹⁴When I think of all this, I fall to my knees and pray to the Father,* ¹⁵the Creator of everything in heaven and on earth.* ¹⁶I pray that from his glorious, unlimited resources he will empower you with inner strength through his Spirit. ¹⁷Then Christ will make his home in your hearts as you trust in him. Your roots will grow down into God's love and keep you strong. ¹⁸And may you have the power to understand, as all God's people should, how wide, how long, how high, and how deep his love is. ¹⁹May you experience the love of Christ, though it is too great to understand fully. Then you will be made complete with all the fullness of life and power that comes from God.

²⁰Now all glory to God, who is able, through his mighty power at work within us, to accomplish infinitely more than we might ask or think. ²¹Glory to him in the church and in Christ Jesus through all generations forever and ever! Amen.

4 Unity in the Body

Therefore I, a prisoner for serving the Lord, beg you to lead a life worthy of your calling, for you have been called by God. ²Always be humble and gentle. Be patient with each other, making allowance for each other's faults because of your love. ³Make every effort to keep yourselves united in the Spirit, binding yourselves together with peace. ⁴For there is one body and one Spirit, just as you have been called to one glorious hope for the future. ⁵There is one Lord, one faith, one baptism, ⁶and one God and Father, who is over all and in all and living through all.

⁷However, he has given each one of us a special gift* through the generosity of Christ. ⁸That is why the Scriptures say,

"When he ascended to the heights,
he led a crowd of captives
and gave gifts to his people."*

⁹Notice that it says "he ascended." This clearly means that Christ also descended to our lowly world.* ¹⁰And the same one who descended is the one who ascended higher than all the heavens, so that he might fill the entire universe with himself.

¹¹Now these are the gifts Christ gave to the church: the apostles, the prophets, the evangelists, and the pastors and teachers. ¹²Their responsibility is to equip God's people to do his work and build up the church, the body of Christ. ¹³This will continue until we all come to such unity in our faith and knowledge of God's Son that we will be mature in the Lord, measuring up to the full and complete standard of Christ.

¹⁴Then we will no longer be immature

3:6 Or because they are united with Christ Jesus. **3:9** Some manuscripts do not include to everyone. **3:12** Or Because of Christ's faithfulness.
3:14 Some manuscripts read the Father of our Lord Jesus Christ. **3:15** Or from whom every family in heaven and on earth takes its name.
4:7 Greek a grace. **4:8** Ps 68:18. **4:9** Or to the lowest parts of the earth.

Guard Your Calling

EPHESIANS 4:1

There is something sacred about being called. Paul reminds us, "Lead a life worthy of your calling, for you have been called by God" (Ephesians 4:1).

And a sense of calling needs desperately to be guarded.

Recently my daughter and I were rewatching the *Lord of the Rings* movies. On the last part of the journey through Mordor, Frodo turns to Sam and tells him how badly he wishes he did not have to be the one to carry the Ring. Being the Ring-Bearer was a difficult and dangerous role. He took it up voluntarily; he knew it was a worthy task. He understood in some dim way that he was suited for it—even his weakness was part of his gifting—and yet the cost of it wore him down.

Scholars sometimes speak of a distinctness that Christianity added to the idea of a vocation. The Greeks gloried in achievement; heroism was much to be aspired to. However, it was generally understood as a way to express the strength and greatness of the hero. The hero chose what army to lead and what battle to fight.

In the story of the Jesus movement, one's calling is not about achievement. From the history of Israel came the notion of a life not so much planned for glory as interrupted by God: "And the word of the LORD came to . . ." Having the word of the Lord come to you is a little like bearing the Ring; you may know it's a glorious and powerful thing, but the task can wear on you after a while.

In ancient Greece heroism was a chosen path. But in the Jesus story, it became a calling greater than oneself; both a glorious quest to be achieved and a spending of oneself for Something larger.

"But you have been chosen," Gandalf says to Frodo. "And you must therefore use such strength and hearts and wits as you have."

You have been chosen. You have been chosen, and gifted, by God to minister to others and influence your world. And this sense of having been called—the worthiness of it, the glorious goodness of a life lived beyond an individual's agenda—is a precious thing. It is sometimes subverted into grandiosity. It is perhaps more often lost in the ministry of the mundane. It needs to be accepted and guarded.

Calling matters—because the Caller matters.

A strong sense of call does not finally rest on being obsessed about what I'm doing. In fact, what I'm doing is—in a sense—a very small bit in a much larger picture. ("Because, Frodo Baggins, you're only a small hobbit after all.")

People with the strongest and healthiest sense of calling are not obsessed with their calling. They are preoccupied with the Caller. With a clear vision of a good, competent, and loving God before me, the significance of my own tiny part in his world is safely and manageably held.

We were made to live by inspiration, and callings can be maintained only if they are inspired. But inspiration can degenerate into merely human attempts at manipulating motivation. Visions can deteriorate into scenarios of my own success and recognition. I need an inspiration that is grounded in reality while thoroughly transcendent.

Elrond tells the Fellowship: "The road must be trod, but it will be very hard. And neither strength nor wisdom will carry us far upon it. This quest may be attempted by the weak with as much hope as the strong. Yet such is oft the course of deeds that move the wheels of the world: small hands do them because they must, while the eyes of the great are elsewhere."

The only true and lasting inspiration for life is genuine love for God and submitted gratitude that I get to be a part of the redemptive quest.

Guard your calling.

—*John Ortberg*

For more on acceptance, see reading at Philemon.

like children. We won't be tossed and blown about by every wind of new teaching. We will not be influenced when people try to trick us with lies so clever they sound like the truth. ¹⁵Instead, we will speak the truth in love, growing in every way more and more like Christ, who is the head of his body, the church. ¹⁶He makes the whole body fit together perfectly. As each part does its own special work, it helps the other parts grow, so that the whole body is healthy and growing and full of love.

Living as Children of Light

¹⁷With the Lord's authority I say this: Live no longer as the Gentiles do, for they are hopelessly confused. ¹⁸Their minds are full of darkness; they wander far from the life God gives because they have closed their minds and hardened their hearts against him. ¹⁹They have no sense of shame. They live for lustful pleasure and eagerly practice every kind of impurity.

²⁰But that isn't what you learned about Christ. ²¹Since you have heard about Jesus and have learned the truth that comes from him, ²²throw off your old sinful nature and your former way of life, which is corrupted by lust and deception. ²³Instead, let the Spirit renew your thoughts and attitudes. ²⁴Put on your new nature, created to be like God—truly righteous and holy.

²⁵So stop telling lies. Let us tell our neighbors the truth, for we are all parts of the same body. ²⁶And "don't sin by letting anger control you."* Don't let the sun go down while you are still angry, ²⁷for anger gives a foothold to the devil.

²⁸If you are a thief, quit stealing. Instead, use your hands for good hard work, and then give generously to others in need. ²⁹Don't use foul or abusive language. Let everything you say be good and helpful, so that your words will be an encouragement to those who hear them.

³⁰And do not bring sorrow to God's Holy Spirit by the way you live. Remember, he has identified you as his own,* guaranteeing that you will be saved on the day of redemption.

³¹Get rid of all bitterness, rage, anger, harsh words, and slander, as well as all types of evil behavior. ³²Instead, be kind to each other, tenderhearted, forgiving one another, just as God through Christ has forgiven you.

5 Living in the Light

Imitate God, therefore, in everything you do, because you are his dear children. ²Live a life filled with love, following the example of Christ. He loved us* and offered himself as a sacrifice for us, a pleasing aroma to God.

³Let there be no sexual immorality, impurity, or greed among you. Such sins have no place among God's people. ⁴Obscene stories, foolish talk, and coarse jokes—these are not for you. Instead, let there be thankfulness to God. ⁵You can be sure that no immoral, impure, or greedy person will inherit the Kingdom of Christ and of God. For a greedy person is an idolater, worshiping the things of this world.

⁶Don't be fooled by those who try to excuse these sins, for the anger of God will fall on all who disobey him. ⁷Don't participate in the things these people do. ⁸For once you were full of darkness, but now you have light from the Lord. So live as people of light! ⁹For this light within you produces only what is good and right and true.

¹⁰Carefully determine what pleases the Lord. ¹¹Take no part in the worthless deeds of evil and darkness; instead, expose them. ¹²It is shameful even to talk about the things that ungodly people do in secret. ¹³But their evil intentions will be exposed when the light shines on them, ¹⁴for the light makes everything visible. This is why it is said,

"Awake, O sleeper,
 rise up from the dead,
 and Christ will give you light."

Living by the Spirit's Power

¹⁵So be careful how you live. Don't live like fools, but like those who are wise. ¹⁶Make the most of every opportunity in these evil days. ¹⁷Don't act thoughtlessly, but understand what the Lord wants you to do. ¹⁸Don't be drunk with wine, because that will ruin your life. Instead, be filled with the Holy Spirit, ¹⁹singing psalms and hymns

---

4:26 Ps 4:4.   **4:30** Or *has put his seal on you.*   **5:2** Some manuscripts read *loved you.*

Submission in Marriage

EPHESIANS 5:21-33

T he word *submit* is surely one of the most difficult, disliked, and divisive words in the Bible. But Scripture clearly says, "Submit to one another out of reverence for Christ" (Ephesians 5:21). Paul illustrates how to submit by giving three examples from relationships in his day (5:22–6:9). In each example one person has more, and one person has far less, power.

In Paul's day a wife had no legal rights. Her husband could do whatever he wanted in legal affairs without her consent. Husbands also had the financial advantages and virtually all the education.

Paul speaks directly to this imbalance of power, saying, in effect, "In life, when you're in a place of less authority and power"—which in his day included wives, children, and slaves—"don't resist, resent, and rebel. Out of reverence for Christ, respect, honor, and work hard at pleasing the other person. And when you're in a place of more power"—which in Paul's day included husbands, parents, and slave masters—"don't lord it over the other person. Don't use them to make your life easier. Instead, use your power to benefit them."

Consider what this meant to those with less power. As author Jill Briscoe writes, "The Christian wife was about to be offered her first opportunity to have her husband ask her what she felt about selling their thirteen-year-old daughter into slavery. She'd never been asked before." The person with less power was now *empowered*.

Submission also benefits the person with more power. Richard Foster explains that "submission leads to liberty, the liberty to be able to let go of the terrible weight and burden of always needing to get my own way."

Paul asks husbands and wives to submit to each other in different ways, but in both cases submission says, in effect, "Use your power for the benefit of the other person." That was countercultural in Paul's day and is in ours as well. God didn't give us this doctrine of submission to put us into some sort of prison; he gave it to us to set us free.

—Kevin A. Miller

For more on submission, see reading at Hebrews 12:1-2.

and spiritual songs among yourselves, and making music to the Lord in your hearts. [20] And give thanks for everything to God the Father in the name of our Lord Jesus Christ.

Spirit-Guided Relationships: Wives and Husbands

[21] And further, submit to one another out of reverence for Christ.

[22] For wives, this means submit to your husbands as to the Lord. [23] For a husband is the head of his wife as Christ is the head of the church. He is the Savior of his body, the church. [24] As the church submits to Christ, so you wives should submit to your husbands in everything.

[25] For husbands, this means love your wives, just as Christ loved the church. He gave up his life for her [26] to make her holy and clean, washed by the cleansing of God's word.* [27] He did this to present her to

5:26 Greek *washed by water with the word.*

Gratitude

Gratefulness:
Impossible Duty or
Miraculous Gift?

EPHESIANS 5:20

When Paul summarizes the nature of the Christian life, and thus the fundamental activity of the church, he frames it in terms of gratefulness. "And now," he tells the Colossians, "just as you accepted Christ Jesus as your Lord, you must continue to follow him. Let your roots grow down into him, and let your lives be built on him. Then your faith will grow strong in the truth you were taught, and you will *overflow with thankfulness*" (2:6-7, italics added).

In the context of the church, then, gratefulness is the normal, expected lifestyle. In the context of the world in which we live, it is anything but that. Anyone with half an ounce of self-awareness recognizes how much we whine about what is missing in our lives, and how often we nurture what I call *thanks-killing* vices like anger, lust, and greed, and how often we're just indifferent to the many divine gifts showered upon us hour by hour.

So can a simple admonition like "be thankful" do the trick? Can something so deeply inbred in us as ungratefulness be whisked away with a simple command, one that seemingly can be simply obeyed with a tweaking of the will? Is thankfulness something we can conjure up like that?

Yes, at a certain level. For example, we've come up with verbal formulas to snap us out of ungrateful funks: "Look for the silver lining in the dark cloud"; "Look at the glass as half full, not half empty"; or the cliché par excellence, "Count your blessings." These clichés can help . . . for a while. But here's the truth of the matter: we can't keep it up. There are days when we just don't have the energy to count our blessings. And sometimes those days turn into weeks or even years. There are long stretches when we'd like to be thankful, but, frankly, we just don't give a rip.

Thanksgiving may sound easy at first, but under scrutiny it looks more and more impossible by the minute. And it doesn't get better when we look at the way Paul talks about it in Ephesians 5:20: "Give thanks for *everything* to God the Father . . ." (italics added).

This little phrase—*always for all things,* in the King James Version— reveals the utter inadequacy of all our human attempts to manufacture thanksgiving, whether through clichés or any other mood-altering activity. Be thankful always and for everything? Is he kidding? Even for my spouse and kids or roommates when they're driving me crazy? Even for my church when it fails to meet my spiritual needs? Even for my cancer, which is draining life from me?

This little phrase points out that it isn't from time to time that we get in sour moods, that once in a while we forget to be thankful, or that it's only a matter of willpower to get upbeat again. No, ungratefulness is a state of being, a sickness at the very core of souls, something that defines our personality; it's what theologians call original sin—a signal of something *desperately* wrong with us.

Thankful *always* and *for everything*? Are you crazy, Paul? It would take a miracle!

That's exactly what Paul believes it does take, and why he's bold enough to command thanksgiving. He believes the miracle is possible, and so he adds a phrase that suggests from whence the miracle comes: "Give thanks for everything to God the Father *in the name of our Lord Jesus Christ*" (italics added).

Jesus Christ is the Source of our hope. To live in gratefulness in the name of our Lord Jesus Christ is to recognize that the impossible possibility of gratefulness is granted to us again and again. There is no reason to despair.

Naturally our calling to live and breathe thanksgiving is high—so high as to be humanly impossible. So we will fall far short of it in this life, and fall short time and again. We will have moments when a pure and complete thanksgiving floods our souls, but most days we'll live in hope.

That means that when, unsurprisingly, we find ourselves wallowing in ungrateful-ness *again*, we will not get discouraged. Because at that moment, despite the fact that we do not yet thank God always and for everything in the name of our Lord Jesus Christ, we will remember that the Lord Jesus Christ has done something extraordinary in and for us, something that affects us in everything and for always.

—*Mark Galli*

For more on gratitude, see reading at James 1:2.

himself as a glorious church without a spot or wrinkle or any other blemish. Instead, she will be holy and without fault. [28]In the same way, husbands ought to love their wives as they love their own bodies. For a man who loves his wife actually shows love for himself. [29]No one hates his own body but feeds and cares for it, just as Christ cares for the church. [30]And we are members of his body.

[31]As the Scriptures say, "A man leaves his father and mother and is joined to his wife, and the two are united into one."* [32]This is a great mystery, but it is an illustration of the way Christ and the church are one. [33]So again I say, each man must love his wife as he loves himself, and the wife must respect her husband.

6 Children and Parents

Children, obey your parents because you belong to the Lord,* for this is the right thing to do. [2]"Honor your father and mother." This is the first commandment with a promise: [3]If you honor your father and mother, "things will go well for you, and you will have a long life on the earth."*

[4]Fathers, do not provoke your children to anger by the way you treat them. Rather, bring them up with the discipline and instruction that comes from the Lord.

Slaves and Masters

[5]Slaves, obey your earthly masters with deep respect and fear. Serve them sincerely as you would serve Christ. [6]Try to please them all the time, not just when they are watching you. As slaves of Christ, do the will of God with all your heart. [7]Work with enthusiasm, as though you were working for the Lord rather than for people. [8]Remember that the Lord will reward each one of us for the good we do, whether we are slaves or free.

[9]Masters, treat your slaves in the same way. Don't threaten them; remember, you both have the same Master in heaven, and he has no favorites.

The Whole Armor of God

[10]A final word: Be strong in the Lord and in his mighty power. [11]Put on all of God's armor so that you will be able to stand firm against all strategies of the devil. [12]For we* are not fighting against flesh-and-blood enemies, but against evil rulers and authorities of the unseen world, against mighty powers in this dark world, and against evil spirits in the heavenly places.

[13]Therefore, put on every piece of God's armor so you will be able to resist the enemy in the time of evil. Then after the battle you will still be standing firm. [14]Stand your ground, putting on the belt of truth and the body armor of God's righteousness. [15]For shoes, put on the peace that comes from the Good News so that you will be fully prepared.* [16]In addition to all of these, hold up the shield of faith to stop the fiery arrows of the devil.* [17]Put on salvation as your helmet, and take the sword of the Spirit, which is the word of God.

[18]Pray in the Spirit at all times and on every occasion. Stay alert and be persistent in your prayers for all believers everywhere.*

[19]And pray for me, too. Ask God to give me the right words so I can boldly explain God's mysterious plan that the Good News is for Jews and Gentiles alike.* [20]I am in chains now, still preaching this message as God's ambassador. So pray that I will keep on speaking boldly for him, as I should.

Final Greetings

[21]To bring you up to date, Tychicus will give you a full report about what I am doing and how I am getting along. He is a beloved brother and faithful helper in the Lord's work. [22]I have sent him to you for this very purpose—to let you know how we are doing and to encourage you.

[23]Peace be with you, dear brothers and sisters,* and may God the Father and the Lord Jesus Christ give you love with faithfulness. [24]May God's grace be eternally upon all who love our Lord Jesus Christ.

5:31 Gen 2:24. **6:1** Or *Children, obey your parents who belong to the Lord;* some manuscripts read simply *Children, obey your parents.*
6:2-3 Exod 20:12; Deut 5:16. **6:12** Some manuscripts read *you.* **6:15** Or *For shoes, put on the readiness to preach the Good News of peace with God.* **6:16** Greek *the evil one.* **6:18** Greek *all of God's holy people.* **6:19** Greek *explain the mystery of the Good News;* some manuscripts read simply *explain the mystery.* **6:23** Greek *brothers.*

This little phrase points out that it isn't from time to time that we get in sour moods, that once in a while we forget to be thankful, or that it's only a matter of willpower to get upbeat again. No, ungratefulness is a state of being, a sickness at the very core of souls, something that defines our personality; it's what theologians call original sin—a signal of something *desperately* wrong with us.

Thankful *always* and *for everything*? Are you crazy, Paul? It would take a miracle!

That's exactly what Paul believes it does take, and why he's bold enough to command thanksgiving. He believes the miracle is possible, and so he adds a phrase that suggests from whence the miracle comes: "Give thanks for everything to God the Father *in the name of our Lord Jesus Christ*" (italics added).

Jesus Christ is the Source of our hope. To live in gratefulness in the name of our Lord Jesus Christ is to recognize that the impossible possibility of gratefulness is granted to us again and again. There is no reason to despair.

Naturally our calling to live and breathe thanksgiving is high—so high as to be humanly impossible. So we will fall far short of it in this life, and fall short time and again. We will have moments when a pure and complete thanksgiving floods our souls, but most days we'll live in hope.

That means that when, unsurprisingly, we find ourselves wallowing in ungrateful-ness *again*, we will not get discouraged. Because at that moment, despite the fact that we do not yet thank God always and for everything in the name of our Lord Jesus Christ, we will remember that the Lord Jesus Christ has done something extraordinary in and for us, something that affects us in everything and for always.

—Mark Galli

For more on gratitude, see reading at James 1:2.

himself as a glorious church without a spot or wrinkle or any other blemish. Instead, she will be holy and without fault. ²⁸In the same way, husbands ought to love their wives as they love their own bodies. For a man who loves his wife actually shows love for himself. ²⁹No one hates his own body but feeds and cares for it, just as Christ cares for the church. ³⁰And we are members of his body.

³¹As the Scriptures say, "A man leaves his father and mother and is joined to his wife, and the two are united into one."* ³²This is a great mystery, but it is an illustration of the way Christ and the church are one. ³³So again I say, each man must love his wife as he loves himself, and the wife must respect her husband.

6 Children and Parents

Children, obey your parents because you belong to the Lord,* for this is the right thing to do. ²"Honor your father and mother." This is the first commandment with a promise: ³If you honor your father and mother, "things will go well for you, and you will have a long life on the earth."*

⁴Fathers, do not provoke your children to anger by the way you treat them. Rather, bring them up with the discipline and instruction that comes from the Lord.

Slaves and Masters

⁵Slaves, obey your earthly masters with deep respect and fear. Serve them sincerely as you would serve Christ. ⁶Try to please them all the time, not just when they are watching you. As slaves of Christ, do the will of God with all your heart. ⁷Work with enthusiasm, as though you were working for the Lord rather than for people. ⁸Remember that the Lord will reward each one of us for the good we do, whether we are slaves or free.

⁹Masters, treat your slaves in the same way. Don't threaten them; remember, you both have the same Master in heaven, and he has no favorites.

The Whole Armor of God

¹⁰A final word: Be strong in the Lord and in his mighty power. ¹¹Put on all of God's armor so that you will be able to stand firm against all strategies of the devil. ¹²For we* are not fighting against flesh-and-blood enemies, but against evil rulers and authorities of the unseen world, against mighty powers in this dark world, and against evil spirits in the heavenly places.

¹³Therefore, put on every piece of God's armor so you will be able to resist the enemy in the time of evil. Then after the battle you will still be standing firm. ¹⁴Stand your ground, putting on the belt of truth and the body armor of God's righteousness. ¹⁵For shoes, put on the peace that comes from the Good News so that you will be fully prepared.* ¹⁶In addition to all of these, hold up the shield of faith to stop the fiery arrows of the devil.* ¹⁷Put on salvation as your helmet, and take the sword of the Spirit, which is the word of God.

¹⁸Pray in the Spirit at all times and on every occasion. Stay alert and be persistent in your prayers for all believers everywhere.*

¹⁹And pray for me, too. Ask God to give me the right words so I can boldly explain God's mysterious plan that the Good News is for Jews and Gentiles alike.* ²⁰I am in chains now, still preaching this message as God's ambassador. So pray that I will keep on speaking boldly for him, as I should.

Final Greetings

²¹To bring you up to date, Tychicus will give you a full report about what I am doing and how I am getting along. He is a beloved brother and faithful helper in the Lord's work. ²²I have sent him to you for this very purpose—to let you know how we are doing and to encourage you.

²³Peace be with you, dear brothers and sisters,* and may God the Father and the Lord Jesus Christ give you love with faithfulness. ²⁴May God's grace be eternally upon all who love our Lord Jesus Christ.

5:31 Gen 2:24.   **6:1** Or *Children, obey your parents who belong to the Lord;* some manuscripts read simply *Children, obey your parents.*
6:2-3 Exod 20:12; Deut 5:16.   **6:12** Some manuscripts read *you.*   **6:15** Or *For shoes, put on the readiness to preach the Good News of peace with God.*   **6:16** Greek *the evil one.*   **6:18** Greek *all of God's holy people.*   **6:19** Greek *explain the mystery of the Good News;* some manuscripts read simply *explain the mystery.*   **6:23** Greek *brothers.*

Introduction to
Philippians

Background

Philippi was located in Macedonia (northern Greece). Philip II of Macedon (the father of Alexander the Great) renamed this city after himself. Paul, Silas, and Timothy visited this city during Paul's second missionary journey (Acts 16:12–40). They met Lydia and others as they worshiped beside the river. (The city did not have enough Jewish men to have a synagogue.) There they cast a demon out of a slave girl, were thrown into prison, had an earthquake free them, and saw the conversion of the jailer and his family. Paul's authorship is confirmed in the first verse: "This letter is from Paul and Timothy, slaves of Christ Jesus. I am writing to all of God's holy people in Philippi who belong to Christ Jesus, including the elders and deacons."

Message

Ironically, although the Epistle to the Philippians was written during Paul's imprisonment, it is known as the "joy letter," because he repeatedly refers to joy or rejoicing. Paul gives thanks for the generosity of the Philippian believers who have supported him financially at various hours of need, and he gives details of his current situation. Yet he is concerned that the work of Christ is being hindered by the lack of unity demonstrated within the church at Philippi. Paul wants the Philippian believers to imitate the humility of Christ. By humbling themselves, the believers will not only find unity within their ranks but also the complete joy that is found only in Christ.

Time

Paul probably wrote Philippians in A.D. 62 while imprisoned in Rome.

Outline

Philippians

1 Greetings from Paul

This letter is from Paul and Timothy, slaves of Christ Jesus.

I am writing to all of God's holy people in Philippi who belong to Christ Jesus, including the elders* and deacons.

²May God our Father and the Lord Jesus Christ give you grace and peace.

Paul's Thanksgiving and Prayer

³Every time I think of you, I give thanks to my God. ⁴Whenever I pray, I make my requests for all of you with joy, ⁵for you have been my partners in spreading the Good News about Christ from the time you first heard it until now. ⁶And I am certain that God, who began the good work within you, will continue his work until it is finally finished on the day when Christ Jesus returns.

⁷So it is right that I should feel as I do about all of you, for you have a special place in my heart. You share with me the special favor of God, both in my imprisonment and in defending and confirming the truth of the Good News. ⁸God knows how much I love you and long for you with the tender compassion of Christ Jesus.

⁹I pray that your love will overflow more and more, and that you will keep on growing in knowledge and understanding. ¹⁰For I want you to understand what really matters, so that you may live pure and blameless lives until the day of Christ's return. ¹¹May you always be filled with the fruit of your salvation—the righteous character produced in your life by Jesus Christ*—for this will bring much glory and praise to God.

Paul's Joy That Christ Is Preached

¹²And I want you to know, my dear brothers and sisters,* that everything that has happened to me here has helped to spread the Good News. ¹³For everyone here, including the whole palace guard,* knows that I am in chains because of Christ. ¹⁴And because of my imprisonment, most of the believers* here have gained confidence and boldly speak God's message* without fear.

¹⁵It's true that some are preaching out of jealousy and rivalry. But others preach about Christ with pure motives. ¹⁶They preach because they love me, for they know I have been appointed to defend the Good News. ¹⁷Those others do not have pure motives as they preach about Christ. They preach with selfish ambition, not sincerely, intending to make my chains more painful to me. ¹⁸But that doesn't matter. Whether their motives are false or genuine, the message about Christ is being preached either way, so I rejoice. And I will continue to rejoice. ¹⁹For I know that as you pray for me and the Spirit of Jesus Christ helps me, this will lead to my deliverance.

Paul's Life for Christ

²⁰For I fully expect and hope that I will never be ashamed, but that I will continue to be bold for Christ, as I have been in the past. And I trust that my life

1:1 Or *overseers; or bishops.*   **1:11** Greek *with the fruit of righteousness through Jesus Christ.*   **1:12** Greek *brothers.*   **1:13** Greek *including all the Praetorium.*   **1:14a** Greek *brothers in the Lord.*   **1:14b** Some manuscripts read *speak the message.*

Introduction to

Philippians

Background

Philippi was located in Macedonia (northern Greece). Philip II of Macedon (the father of Alexander the Great) renamed this city after himself. Paul, Silas, and Timothy visited this city during Paul's second missionary journey (Acts 16:12–40). They met Lydia and others as they worshiped beside the river. (The city did not have enough Jewish men to have a synagogue.) There they cast a demon out of a slave girl, were thrown into prison, had an earthquake free them, and saw the conversion of the jailer and his family. Paul's authorship is confirmed in the first verse: "This letter is from Paul and Timothy, slaves of Christ Jesus. I am writing to all of God's holy people in Philippi who belong to Christ Jesus, including the elders and deacons."

Message

Ironically, although the Epistle to the Philippians was written during Paul's imprisonment, it is known as the "joy letter," because he repeatedly refers to joy or rejoicing. Paul gives thanks for the generosity of the Philippian believers who have supported him financially at various hours of need, and he gives details of his current situation. Yet he is concerned that the work of Christ is being hindered by the lack of unity demonstrated within the church at Philippi. Paul wants the Philippian believers to imitate the humility of Christ. By humbling themselves, the believers will not only find unity within their ranks but also the complete joy that is found only in Christ.

Time

Paul probably wrote Philippians in A.D. 62 while imprisoned in Rome.

Outline

Philippians

1 Greetings from Paul

This letter is from Paul and Timothy, slaves of Christ Jesus.

I am writing to all of God's holy people in Philippi who belong to Christ Jesus, including the elders* and deacons.

²May God our Father and the Lord Jesus Christ give you grace and peace.

Paul's Thanksgiving and Prayer

³Every time I think of you, I give thanks to my God. ⁴Whenever I pray, I make my requests for all of you with joy, ⁵for you have been my partners in spreading the Good News about Christ from the time you first heard it until now. ⁶And I am certain that God, who began the good work within you, will continue his work until it is finally finished on the day when Christ Jesus returns.

⁷So it is right that I should feel as I do about all of you, for you have a special place in my heart. You share with me the special favor of God, both in my imprisonment and in defending and confirming the truth of the Good News. ⁸God knows how much I love you and long for you with the tender compassion of Christ Jesus.

⁹I pray that your love will overflow more and more, and that you will keep on growing in knowledge and understanding. ¹⁰For I want you to understand what really matters, so that you may live pure and blameless lives until the day of Christ's return. ¹¹May you always be filled with the fruit of your salvation—the righteous character produced in your life by Jesus Christ*—for this will bring much glory and praise to God.

Paul's Joy That Christ Is Preached

¹²And I want you to know, my dear brothers and sisters,* that everything that has happened to me here has helped to spread the Good News. ¹³For everyone here, including the whole palace guard,* knows that I am in chains because of Christ. ¹⁴And because of my imprisonment, most of the believers* here have gained confidence and boldly speak God's message* without fear.

¹⁵It's true that some are preaching out of jealousy and rivalry. But others preach about Christ with pure motives. ¹⁶They preach because they love me, for they know I have been appointed to defend the Good News. ¹⁷Those others do not have pure motives as they preach about Christ. They preach with selfish ambition, not sincerely, intending to make my chains more painful to me. ¹⁸But that doesn't matter. Whether their motives are false or genuine, the message about Christ is being preached either way, so I rejoice. And I will continue to rejoice. ¹⁹For I know that as you pray for me and the Spirit of Jesus Christ helps me, this will lead to my deliverance.

Paul's Life for Christ

²⁰For I fully expect and hope that I will never be ashamed, but that I will continue to be bold for Christ, as I have been in the past. And I trust that my life

---

1:1 Or *overseers; or bishops.*   **1:11** Greek *with the fruit of righteousness through Jesus Christ.*   **1:12** Greek *brothers.*   **1:13** Greek *including all the Praetorium.*   **1:14a** Greek *brothers in the Lord.*   **1:14b** Some manuscripts read *speak the message.*

will bring honor to Christ, whether I live or die. ²¹For to me, living means living for Christ, and dying is even better. ²²But if I live, I can do more fruitful work for Christ. So I really don't know which is better. ²³I'm torn between two desires: I long to go and be with Christ, which would be far better for me. ²⁴But for your sakes, it is better that I continue to live.

²⁵Knowing this, I am convinced that I will remain alive so I can continue to help all of you grow and experience the joy of your faith. ²⁶And when I come to you again, you will have even more reason to take pride in Christ Jesus because of what he is doing through me.

Live as Citizens of Heaven

²⁷Above all, you must live as citizens of heaven, conducting yourselves in a manner worthy of the Good News about Christ. Then, whether I come and see you again or only hear about you, I will know that you are standing together with one spirit and one purpose, fighting together for the faith, which is the Good News. ²⁸Don't be intimidated in any way by your enemies. This will be a sign to them that they are going to be destroyed, but that you are going to be saved, even by God himself. ²⁹For you have been given not only the privilege of trusting in Christ but also the privilege of suffering for him. ³⁰We are in this struggle together. You have seen my struggle in the past, and you know that I am still in the midst of it.

2 Have the Attitude of Christ

Is there any encouragement from belonging to Christ? Any comfort from his love? Any fellowship together in the Spirit? Are your hearts tender and compassionate? ²Then make me truly happy by agreeing wholeheartedly with each other, loving one another, and working together with one mind and purpose.

³Don't be selfish; don't try to impress others. Be humble, thinking of others as better than yourselves. ⁴Don't look out only for your own interests, but take an interest in others, too.

⁵You must have the same attitude that Christ Jesus had.

⁶ Though he was God,*
    he did not think of equality with God
    as something to cling to.
⁷ Instead, he gave up his divine
    privileges*;
    he took the humble position of a
    slave*
    and was born as a human being.
    When he appeared in human form,*
⁸   he humbled himself in obedience to
    God
    and died a criminal's death on a
    cross.

⁹ Therefore, God elevated him to the place
    of highest honor
    and gave him the name above all other
    names,
¹⁰ that at the name of Jesus every knee
    should bow,
    in heaven and on earth and under the
    earth,
¹¹ and every tongue confess that Jesus
    Christ is Lord,
    to the glory of God the Father.

Shine Brightly for Christ

¹²Dear friends, you always followed my instructions when I was with you. And now that I am away, it is even more important. Work hard to show the results of your salvation, obeying God with deep reverence and fear. ¹³For God is working in you, giving you the desire and the power to do what pleases him.

¹⁴Do everything without complaining and arguing, ¹⁵so that no one can criticize you. Live clean, innocent lives as children of God, shining like bright lights in a world full of crooked and perverse people. ¹⁶Hold firmly to the word of life; then, on the day of Christ's return, I will be proud that I did not run the race in vain and that my work was not useless. ¹⁷But I will rejoice even if I lose my life, pouring it out like a liquid offering to God,* just like your faithful service is an offering to God. And I want all of you to share that joy. ¹⁸Yes, you should rejoice, and I will share your joy.

2:6 Or *Being in the form of God.*   **2:7a** Greek *he emptied himself.*   **2:7b** Or *the form of a slave.*   **2:7c** Some English translations put this phrase in verse 8.   **2:17** Greek *I will rejoice even if I am to be poured out as a liquid offering.*

The Advent of Humility

PHILIPPIANS 2:6-8

Humility is crucial for Christians. We can receive Christ only through meekness and humility (Matthew 5:3, 5; 18:3-4). Scripture promises that it's true humility that leads to exaltation (Luke 14:11; 18:14). And God's Word admonishes us to "serve each other in humility" (1 Peter 5:5). Humility—and the joy we find through it—is the very dynamic of the Christian life.

The teaching seems simple and obvious. The problem is that it takes great humility to understand humility, and even more to resist the pride that comes so naturally with even a discussion of the subject.

Humility is a byproduct of belief in the gospel of Christ. In the gospel we have a confidence not based in our performance but in the love of God in Christ (Romans 3:22-24). Christ himself is our profound example of humility: "He gave up his divine privileges; he took the humble position of a slave and was born as a human being" (Philippians 2:7). Christ's humility is tied directly to his nature as a servant. Like him, we must strive to live in a way that links humility with the attitudes and actions of servanthood.

Gracious, self-forgetful humility should be one of the primary things that distinguishes Christian believers from the many other types of moral, decent people. But humility, which is a key differentiating mark of the Christian, is largely missing in the church. Nonbelievers, detecting the stench of sanctimony, turn away.

As we seek to reach out to those in our community, will they see in our actions and attitudes the humble servant's heart of Christ? We must remember that, to paraphrase an old song, they will know we are Christians by our graciousness.

—*Timothy Keller*

For more on service, see reading at 2 Timothy 1:3-7.

Paul Commends Timothy

¹⁹If the Lord Jesus is willing, I hope to send Timothy to you soon for a visit. Then he can cheer me up by telling me how you are getting along. ²⁰I have no one else like Timothy, who genuinely cares about your welfare. ²¹All the others care only for themselves and not for what matters to Jesus Christ. ²²But you know how Timothy has proved himself. Like a son with his father, he has served with me in preaching the Good News. ²³I hope to send him to you just as soon as I find out what is going to happen to me here. ²⁴And I have confidence from the Lord that I myself will come to see you soon.

Paul Commends Epaphroditus

²⁵Meanwhile, I thought I should send Epaphroditus back to you. He is a true brother, co-worker, and fellow soldier. And he was your messenger to help me in my need. ²⁶I am sending him because he has been longing to see you, and he was very distressed that you heard he was ill. ²⁷And he certainly was ill; in fact, he almost died. But God had mercy on him—and also on me, so that I would not have one sorrow after another.

²⁸So I am all the more anxious to send him back to you, for I know you will be glad to see him, and then I will not be so worried about you. ²⁹Welcome him with Christian

With All My Body

PHILIPPIANS 2:14–18

In my early twenties, I listened to an elderly man explain why he was going on a dangerous missions trip. "I'd rather wear out than rust out," he said.

Unfortunately that idea translated into my life as a sense that as Christians we're to serve and expend ourselves beyond our endurance. I found motivation for my furious pace of life from Philippians 2:17 in which Paul talks about being poured out as a drink offering for others. I pictured this life of dedicated service as giving, giving, and giving until my last ounce of physical strength was gone.

I now have a different perspective on this passage. I realize Paul was saying that if *God* poured him out as an offering, he'd count it joy. He didn't pour *himself* out as an offering. It was about obeying God's call, not trying to do it all.

Watching what we eat, getting enough exercise, and maintaining healthy sleep habits are in fact *spiritual* matters as we seek to be good stewards of the most basic thing we possess: our bodies.

Once, during a busy time in my life, my eating, exercise, and sleep habits went down the tubes. In fact, my doctor actually prescribed rest. He told me I had to say no to activities every other weekend so I could rest.

As stewards, maintaining physical health means saying no—and that no begins with asking God to lead us in how he wants us to invest our time. For me, that means regularly listening to God and examining myself in order to understand what it means to be his servant. Now I wholeheartedly throw myself into the direction he's led me, and say no to everything else. I'm using the talents God has blessed me with instead of trying to do everything that comes my way. That way I'll be rested and refreshed to be the best possible tool in God's hands.

—JoHannah Reardon

For more on stewardship, see reading at 1 Timothy 4:11–15.

---

love* and with great joy, and give him the honor that people like him deserve. [30] For he risked his life for the work of Christ, and he was at the point of death while doing for me what you couldn't do from far away.

3 The Priceless Value of Knowing Christ

Whatever happens, my dear brothers and sisters,* rejoice in the Lord. I never get tired of telling you these things, and I do it to safeguard your faith.

[2] Watch out for those dogs, those people who do evil, those mutilators who say you must be circumcised to be saved. [3] For we who worship by the Spirit of God* are the ones who are truly circumcised. We rely on what Christ Jesus has done for us. We put no confidence in human effort, [4] though I could have confidence in my own effort if anyone could. Indeed, if others have reason for confidence in their own efforts, I have even more!

[5] I was circumcised when I was eight days old. I am a pure-blooded citizen of Israel and a member of the tribe of Benjamin—a real Hebrew if there ever was one! I was a member of the Pharisees, who demand the strictest obedience to the Jewish law. [6] I was

---

2:29 Greek *in the Lord.*   **3:1** Greek *brothers;* also in 3:13, 17.   **3:3** Some manuscripts read *worship God in spirit;* one early manuscript reads *worship in spirit.*

Worship

Leftover Beauty

PHILIPPIANS 4:2–9

Even though the Fall introduced sin and deterioration into the world, everywhere we turn we get glimpses of God's original, perfect creation. Edith Schaeffer, in her book *Forever Music,* calls such beauty "leftover beauty." We can worship God by crediting him with everything that is good, true, or beautiful (Philippians 4:8).

God is behind all the order and harmony, all the perfection and beauty, all excellence and creativity. I think immediately of glorious mountain peaks that snag the clouds or reflect the sun, of forests of green that rise up after devastating fires, of tiny hummingbirds that lay jellybean eggs in the creeping fig outside my kitchen window.

But worshiping God for "leftover beauty" needn't stop with nature alone. Leftover beauty also includes acts of kindness from fallen human beings, the bits of creative living that are part of every person, and the almost supernatural beauty of art, music, and literature created by artists who honor the Giver of their gifts—and even by those who try to ignore him completely. It's true and inescapable. Ignorance, apathy, and even sin can't stop the glory of God from shining through.

Not long ago I sat in an audience mesmerized by eight loud, stomping, banging percussionists. It was a musical performance of rhythm and sounds made by trashcans, push brooms, rubber tubing, and cigarette lighters. *Where did this wonderful commotion come from?* I wondered. *Who came up with such a ridiculously splendid blend of noises?* I realized, with tears in my eyes, that God did. *He* made the minds that dreamed up this spectacle of creativity unlike anything I'd ever seen or heard. No one mentioned God; no one hinted at a Bible verse during the performance. Yet my heart stirred and leaped and rejoiced at what God did through these amazing performers.

Leftover beauty is what we can actually see of God. It's like finding the sweater your mother knit for your first day of kindergarten in the back of your closet, with her scent still part of the wool. The memory of her is strong enough to almost evoke her very presence and to remind you of her character.

Truly *all* our world is awash in the beauty of God's presence and echoes of his character. A large part of what God desires in our worship is that we look deeply and notice his presence in earth, sky, and man. God might be easier to worship if we could actually touch his skin, as could the early followers of Jesus. But by calling me his child, he's given me the freedom to touch, the eyes to see, and the heart to identify what's *come* from him—to peek under rocks and peel back corners and peer into souls for evidences of his glory. In response to my discoveries, I worship him and cling to what I know about him—that he's in control of it all, that he's capable of creating and moving mountains for me (or at least reducing them to molehills), that he's grander than my imagination.

So give me a soaring symphony that sings with rich cellos and deep French horns, and wild performers who stomp around stages with the creative energy of two-year-olds. Give me books in which every word seems chosen for that very place, and poetry that makes me weep with identification. Give me art that startles my eyes, that draws me in with realness, or abstraction that shouts wild joy.

And give me people in all their messy splendor! It's in them, even despite the brokenness of sin, that the leftover beauty cannot hide. In flawed and sinful—yet still beautiful—people I can see glimpses of the diversity and the magnificence that is God.

Praise you, mighty King, Lord of Lords, Creator of the purple grapes in my fruit bowl, so beautifully round and frosty cold. Praise you for Mozarts and Copelands and Sondheims, for "Twinkle, Twinkle, Little Star" and "A Mighty Fortress Is Our God." Praise you for Monets and Matisses—and for crayons and homemade valentines and refrigerator art. And praise you for the aspen leaves on the hillside, fluttering like confetti before my grateful eyes.

I wonder how long it will take until all the beauty and goodness is restored to life. But for now I'll wait. Right here and now I worship God for the leftovers.

—*Mary Jenson*

For more on worship, see reading at 1 Peter 1:1-2.

so zealous that I harshly persecuted the church. And as for righteousness, I obeyed the law without fault.

[7] I once thought these things were valuable, but now I consider them worthless because of what Christ has done. [8] Yes, everything else is worthless when compared with the infinite value of knowing Christ Jesus my Lord. For his sake I have discarded everything else, counting it all as garbage, so that I could gain Christ [9] and become one with him. I no longer count on my own righteousness through obeying the law; rather, I become righteous through faith in Christ.* For God's way of making us right with himself depends on faith. [10] I want to know Christ and experience the mighty power that raised him from the dead. I want to suffer with him, sharing in his death, [11] so that one way or another I will experience the resurrection from the dead!

Pressing toward the Goal

[12] I don't mean to say that I have already achieved these things or that I have already reached perfection. But I press on to possess that perfection for which Christ Jesus first possessed me. [13] No, dear brothers and sisters, I have not achieved it,* but I focus on this one thing: Forgetting the past and looking forward to what lies ahead, [14] I press on to reach the end of the race and receive the heavenly prize for which God, through Christ Jesus, is calling us.

[15] Let all who are spiritually mature agree on these things. If you disagree on some point, I believe God will make it plain to you. [16] But we must hold on to the progress we have already made.

[17] Dear brothers and sisters, pattern your lives after mine, and learn from those who follow our example. [18] For I have told you often before, and I say it again with tears in my eyes, that there are many whose conduct shows they are really enemies of the cross of Christ. [19] They are headed for destruction. Their god is their appetite, they brag about shameful things, and they think only about this life here on earth. [20] But we are citizens of heaven, where the Lord Jesus Christ lives. And we are eagerly waiting for

him to return as our Savior. [21] He will take our weak mortal bodies and change them into glorious bodies like his own, using the same power with which he will bring everything under his control.

4 Therefore, my dear brothers and sisters,* stay true to the Lord. I love you and long to see you, dear friends, for you are my joy and the crown I receive for my work.

Words of Encouragement

[2] Now I appeal to Euodia and Syntyche. Please, because you belong to the Lord, settle your disagreement. [3] And I ask you, my true partner,* to help these two women, for they worked hard with me in telling others the Good News. They worked along with Clement and the rest of my co-workers, whose names are written in the Book of Life.

[4] Always be full of joy in the Lord. I say it again—rejoice! [5] Let everyone see that you are considerate in all you do. Remember, the Lord is coming soon.

[6] Don't worry about anything; instead, pray about everything. Tell God what you need, and thank him for all he has done. [7] Then you will experience God's peace, which exceeds anything we can understand. His peace will guard your hearts and minds as you live in Christ Jesus.

[8] And now, dear brothers and sisters, one final thing. Fix your thoughts on what is true, and honorable, and right, and pure, and lovely, and admirable. Think about things that are excellent and worthy of praise. [9] Keep putting into practice all you learned and received from me—everything you heard from me and saw me doing. Then the God of peace will be with you.

Paul's Thanks for Their Gifts

[10] How I praise the Lord that you are concerned about me again. I know you have always been concerned for me, but you didn't have the chance to help me. [11] Not that I was ever in need, for I have learned how to be content with whatever I have. [12] I know how to live on almost nothing or with everything. I have learned the secret of living in every

---

3:9 Or through the faithfulness of Christ. **3:13** Some manuscripts read not yet achieved it. **4:1** Greek brothers; also in 4:8. **4:3** Or loyal Syzygus.

situation, whether it is with a full stomach or empty, with plenty or little. [13]For I can do everything through Christ,* who gives me strength. [14]Even so, you have done well to share with me in my present difficulty.

[15]As you know, you Philippians were the only ones who gave me financial help when I first brought you the Good News and then traveled on from Macedonia. No other church did this. [16]Even when I was in Thessalonica you sent help more than once. [17]I don't say this because I want a gift from you. Rather, I want you to receive a reward for your kindness.

[18]At the moment I have all I need—and more! I am generously supplied with the gifts you sent me with Epaphroditus. They are a sweet-smelling sacrifice that is acceptable and pleasing to God. [19]And this same God who takes care of me will supply all your needs from his glorious riches, which have been given to us in Christ Jesus.

[20]Now all glory to God our Father forever and ever! Amen.

Paul's Final Greetings

[21]Give my greetings to each of God's holy people—all who belong to Christ Jesus. The brothers who are with me send you their greetings. [22]And all the rest of God's people send you greetings, too, especially those in Caesar's household.

[23]May the grace of the Lord Jesus Christ be with your spirit.

4:13 Greek *through the one.*

Introduction to

Colossians

Background

Colosse was a small city about one hundred miles east of Ephesus. It had a large Jewish population, and the church there had been founded by Epaphras (1:7), a man whom Paul had led to Christ. As with his letter to the church in Rome, Paul wrote to the church in Colosse without having visited it. The epistle's personal information and its similarity with Ephesians and Philemon point to Paul's authorship (1:1, 23; 4:18). Some scholars have challenged Paul's authorship, arguing that the vocabulary is different from that used in Paul's other epistles, and that he was discussing a heresy that wasn't developed in the first century A.D. Nevertheless, these challenges are easily answered by Paul's wide use of vocabulary; also, there is evidence that the heresy was indeed forming and in early stages in Paul's day.

Message

Harmful heresy threatens the church at Colosse. Paul uses the truth of Christ to confront the false teaching and point out that the believers need Christ and Christ alone. Paul reminds the believers of the fullness found only in Christ, who existed before the foundation of the world. Chapter 1 includes an astounding hymn to Christ, showing his role as Creator, Redeemer, and as Sustainer of all things. As in many of his letters, Paul turns from theological issues to practical exhortation on how Christians should conduct themselves in daily circumstances. He asks for prayer for his ministry and closes with a poignant "Remember my chains. May God's grace be with you."

Time

Colossians was probably written in A.D. 60 or 61 during Paul's first Roman imprisonment. Tychicus and Onesimus (the converted slave Paul writes about in Philemon) delivered the letter to Colosse.

Outline

Colossians

1 Greetings from Paul

This letter is from Paul, chosen by the will of God to be an apostle of Christ Jesus, and from our brother Timothy.

²We are writing to God's holy people in the city of Colosse, who are faithful brothers and sisters* in Christ.

May God our Father give you grace and peace.

Paul's Thanksgiving and Prayer

³We always pray for you, and we give thanks to God, the Father of our Lord Jesus Christ. ⁴For we have heard of your faith in Christ Jesus and your love for all of God's people, ⁵which come from your confident hope of what God has reserved for you in heaven. You have had this expectation ever since you first heard the truth of the Good News.

⁶This same Good News that came to you is going out all over the world. It is bearing fruit everywhere by changing lives, just as it changed your lives from the day you first heard and understood the truth about God's wonderful grace.

⁷You learned about the Good News from Epaphras, our beloved co-worker. He is Christ's faithful servant, and he is helping us on your behalf.* ⁸He has told us about the love for others that the Holy Spirit has given you.

⁹So we have not stopped praying for you since we first heard about you. We ask God to give you complete knowledge of his will and to give you spiritual wisdom and understanding. ¹⁰Then the way you live will always honor and please the Lord, and your lives will produce every kind of good fruit. All the while, you will grow as you learn to know God better and better.

¹¹We also pray that you will be strengthened with all his glorious power so you will have all the endurance and patience you need. May you be filled with joy,* ¹²always thanking the Father. He has enabled you to share in the inheritance that belongs to his people, who live in the light. ¹³For he has rescued us from the kingdom of darkness and transferred us into the Kingdom of his dear Son, ¹⁴who purchased our freedom* and forgave our sins.

Christ Is Supreme

¹⁵ Christ is the visible image of the invisible God.
   He existed before anything was created and is supreme over all creation,*
¹⁶ for through him God created everything
      in the heavenly realms and on earth.
   He made the things we can see
      and the things we can't see—
   such as thrones, kingdoms, rulers, and authorities in the unseen world.
      Everything was created through him and for him.
¹⁷ He existed before anything else,
      and he holds all creation together.

1:2 Greek *faithful brothers.*   **1:7** Or *he is ministering on your behalf;* some manuscripts read *he is ministering on our behalf.*   **1:11** Or *all the patience and endurance you need with joy.*   **1:14** Some manuscripts add *with his blood.*   **1:15** Or *He is the firstborn of all creation.*

Community

The "We" We Want to Be

COLOSSIANS 1:18

I f I'm a member of a gym, it may not matter much to me what kind of shape other people are in. I'm interested in *my* fitness; I don't have a strong investment in the fitness of other people. In fact, I don't mind a little flab in the bodies working out around me. It makes me feel better by comparison. I use the fitness center to get my body in shape. The fitness center is a tool for individuals.

But the church is not a spiritual fitness center, and, for that matter, the church is not a tool.

The church is a body. It is *the* body. It is Christ's body (Colossians 1:18).

Ironically, when we think of spiritual formation purely in individual terms rather than within the context of community, those individuals will not grow well. God's design for spiritual formation is that it should take place within the church: we need membership in, submission to, and compassion for a community larger than our individual selves. If you love the body of Christ, you are concerned for the health of the whole body. It does no good to have a thriving kidney if the heart is a time bomb.

The body is an instructive metaphor. We're not simply a random assortment of individuals. We are greater than the sum of our parts. Together we form a new organism. Paul emphasizes this idea in 1 Corinthians 12, detailing how each part of the body is mutually dependent on the others. The body has a health or an illness beyond the function or dysfunction of the individuals. The body has certain patterns, habits, and tendencies that call out the best or the worst in those who make it up.

Thinking about the health of the body also has the advantage of reminding us that local churches are not simply "spiritual resource providers" that we shop around for like so many HMOs. The body doesn't so much exist for my sake as I exist for the sake of the body; together we are connected to the One who fills his body. Christ is the head of the church, Paul writes in Colossians 1:18, and "he holds the whole body together with its joints and ligaments, and it grows as God nourishes it" (Colossians 2:19). It is hard to sever yourself from a body but stay connected to the head. (Dis-membership can be as ugly spiritually as it can be physically.)

But Scripture emphasizes *both* the value of the individual as well as the importance of the collective body of Christ. The individual Christian and the corporate body help to define each other. In Eastern religions, a single human is sometimes compared to a drop in the ocean; when you die you simply go back into the great sea. But Christianity would not use this metaphor. Personhood has integrity; a person is a center of consciousness that will *not* lose her identity; the body must always honor the member just as the individual must honor the body. Paul wrote, "All of you together are Christ's body, and each of you is a part of it" (1 Corinthians 12:27). As we see ourselves within this body—as we situate ourselves within this unified, miraculously whole collection of different individuals—then we are able to do God's work in the world.

When I was growing up, we used to sing a song about the body in Sunday school.

Oh, be careful little eyes what you see,

Oh, be careful little eyes what you see,

For the Father up above is looking down in love,

So be careful little eyes what you see.

The following verses were "Be careful little hands what you do" and "Be careful little feet where you go."

I never liked that song. It sounded ominous, like the kind of Sunday-school song George Orwell would write.

But Richard Mouw suggested it could be interpreted another way. It could mean that little eyes should be careful to see what Jesus would see when he looks on our world; that little feet should go to those places of loneliness and suffering where his feet would go; that little hands should do the acts of love and compassion that his hands would do.

The body of Christ is beautiful when we all help one another be the eyes and feet and hands of the One we follow. We are part of the body at work—doing the work God has called us to, together with others. That's the "we" we want to be.

—*John Ortberg*

For more on community, see reading at Hebrews 10:24-25.

¹⁸ Christ is also the head of the church,
which is his body.
He is the beginning,
supreme over all who rise from the
dead.*
So he is first in everything.
¹⁹ For God in all his fullness
was pleased to live in Christ,
²⁰ and through him God reconciled
everything to himself.
He made peace with everything in
heaven and on earth
by means of Christ's blood on the cross.

²¹ This includes you who were once far away from God. You were his enemies, separated from him by your evil thoughts and actions. ²² Yet now he has reconciled you to himself through the death of Christ in his physical body. As a result, he has brought you into his own presence, and you are holy and blameless as you stand before him without a single fault.

²³ But you must continue to believe this truth and stand firmly in it. Don't drift away from the assurance you received when you heard the Good News. The Good News has been preached all over the world, and I, Paul, have been appointed as God's servant to proclaim it.

Paul's Work for the Church

²⁴ I am glad when I suffer for you in my body, for I am participating in the sufferings of Christ that continue for his body, the church. ²⁵ God has given me the responsibility of serving his church by proclaiming his entire message to you. ²⁶ This message was kept secret for centuries and generations past, but now it has been revealed to God's people. ²⁷ For God wanted them to know that the riches and glory of Christ are for you Gentiles, too. And this is the secret: Christ lives in you. This gives you assurance of sharing his glory.

²⁸ So we tell others about Christ, warning everyone and teaching everyone with all the wisdom God has given us. We want to present them to God, perfect* in their relationship to Christ. ²⁹ That's why I work and struggle so hard, depending on Christ's mighty power that works within me.

2 I want you to know how much I have agonized for you and for the church at Laodicea, and for many other believers who have never met me personally. ²I want them to be encouraged and knit together by strong ties of love. I want them to have complete confidence that they understand God's mysterious plan, which is Christ himself. ³In him lie hidden all the treasures of wisdom and knowledge.

⁴I am telling you this so no one will deceive you with well-crafted arguments. ⁵For though I am far away from you, my heart is with you. And I rejoice that you are living as you should and that your faith in Christ is strong.

Freedom from Rules and New Life in Christ

⁶And now, just as you accepted Christ Jesus as your Lord, you must continue to follow him. ⁷Let your roots grow down into him, and let your lives be built on him. Then your faith will grow strong in the truth you were taught, and you will overflow with thankfulness.

⁸Don't let anyone capture you with empty philosophies and high-sounding nonsense that come from human thinking and from the spiritual powers* of this world, rather than from Christ. ⁹For in Christ lives all the fullness of God in a human body.* ¹⁰So you also are complete through your union with Christ, who is the head over every ruler and authority.

¹¹When you came to Christ, you were "circumcised," but not by a physical procedure. Christ performed a spiritual circumcision—the cutting away of your sinful nature.* ¹²For you were buried with Christ when you were baptized. And with him you were raised to new life because you trusted the mighty power of God, who raised Christ from the dead.

¹³You were dead because of your sins and because your sinful nature was not yet cut away. Then God made you alive with Christ, for he forgave all our sins. ¹⁴He canceled the record of the charges against us and took it away by nailing it to the cross. ¹⁵In this way, he disarmed* the spiritual rulers and authorities. He shamed them publicly by his victory over them on the cross.

1:18 Or the firstborn from the dead.　**1:28** Or mature.　**2:8** Or the spiritual principles; also in 2:20.　**2:9** Or in him dwells all the completeness of the Godhead bodily.　**2:11** Greek the cutting away of the body of the flesh.　**2:15** Or he stripped off.

¹⁶So don't let anyone condemn you for what you eat or drink, or for not celebrating certain holy days or new moon ceremonies or Sabbaths. ¹⁷For these rules are only shadows of the reality yet to come. And Christ himself is that reality. ¹⁸Don't let anyone condemn you by insisting on pious self-denial or the worship of angels,* saying

Q&A — Why Sabbath on Sunday?
COLOSSIANS 2:16-17

When did the church switch the Sabbath from Saturday to Sunday?

No specific names or dates are associated with the church's shift from observing the holy day on Saturday to observing it on Sunday. At first, especially when many Christians were converted Jews, their holy day was Saturday. However, because the Resurrection and the beginning of Creation both occurred on the "first day" of the week (Sunday), the church soon observed that day instead. (More Gentiles were becoming Christians as well, which contributed to a desire to shake off Jewish customs.) By the end of the first century, Sunday worship was the norm. We can assume the change caused friction, for in Colossians 2:16 Paul admonishes, "So don't let anyone condemn you for what you eat or drink, or for not celebrating certain holy days or new moon ceremonies or Sabbaths."

Christians also significantly altered the observance of the day. In fact, by Jewish standards, Christians then and now don't keep the Sabbath at all. Rather than strictly adhering to Jewish practices, the early church observed Sunday Sabbaths with corporate worship. Significant hallmarks of the early Christian "Lord's Day" celebration, according to Justin Martyr (circa 100–circa 165), included readings from Scripture (particularly the Gospels), a sermon, communal prayer, and Communion.

The change from Saturday to Sunday wasn't necessarily an easy one for the young church. They aimed to welcome many kinds of believers—both Jewish and Gentile—without diluting their witness. This meant compromise: incorporating the Jewish principle of Sabbath rest while also beginning new and distinctly Christian practices in this weekly remembrance of Christ's resurrection. To make this harmonization of differences work, Christians needed to focus squarely on the reality of Christ rather than the form of their religious practices (Colossians 2:17).

In our Sabbath practice today, we can recognize the new covenant Jesus ushered in (Luke 22:20) as well as embrace the Sabbath principles of the Law, which Jesus came not to abolish but fulfill (Matthew 5:17).

—Elesha Coffman

For more on Sabbath and rest, see reading at Colossians 3:16-17.

2:18 Or *or worshiping with angels.*

they have had visions about these things. Their sinful minds have made them proud, [19]and they are not connected to Christ, the head of the body. For he holds the whole body together with its joints and ligaments, and it grows as God nourishes it.

[20]You have died with Christ, and he has set you free from the spiritual powers of this world. So why do you keep on following the rules of the world, such as, [21]"Don't handle! Don't taste! Don't touch!"? [22]Such rules are mere human teachings about things that deteriorate as we use them. [23]These rules may seem wise because they require strong devotion, pious self-denial, and severe bodily discipline. But they provide no help in conquering a person's evil desires.

3 Living the New Life

Since you have been raised to new life with Christ, set your sights on the realities of heaven, where Christ sits in the place of honor at God's right hand. [2]Think about the things of heaven, not the things of earth. [3]For you died to this life, and your real life is hidden with Christ in God. [4]And when Christ, who is your* life, is revealed to the whole world, you will share in all his glory.

[5]So put to death the sinful, earthly things lurking within you. Have nothing to do with sexual immorality, impurity, lust, and evil desires. Don't be greedy, for a greedy person is an idolater, worshiping the things of this world. [6]Because of these sins, the anger of God is coming.* [7]You used to do these things when your life was still part of this world. [8]But now is the time to get rid of anger, rage, malicious behavior, slander, and dirty language. [9]Don't lie to each other, for you have stripped off your old sinful nature and all its wicked deeds. [10]Put on your new nature, and be renewed as you learn to know your Creator and become like him. [11]In this new life, it doesn't matter if you are a Jew or a Gentile,* circumcised or uncircumcised, barbaric, uncivilized,* slave, or free. Christ is all that matters, and he lives in all of us.

[12]Since God chose you to be the holy people he loves, you must clothe yourselves with tenderhearted mercy, kindness, humility, gentleness, and patience. [13]Make allowance for each other's faults, and forgive anyone who offends you. Remember, the Lord forgave you, so you must forgive others. [14]Above all, clothe yourselves with love, which binds us all together in perfect harmony. [15]And let the peace that comes from Christ rule in your hearts. For as members of one body you are called to live in peace. And always be thankful.

[16]Let the message about Christ, in all its richness, fill your lives. Teach and counsel each other with all the wisdom he gives. Sing psalms and hymns and spiritual songs to God with thankful hearts. [17]And whatever you do or say, do it as a representative of the Lord Jesus, giving thanks through him to God the Father.

Instructions for Christian Households

[18]Wives, submit to your husbands, as is fitting for those who belong to the Lord.

[19]Husbands, love your wives and never treat them harshly.

[20]Children, always obey your parents, for this pleases the Lord. [21]Fathers, do not aggravate your children, or they will become discouraged.

[22]Slaves, obey your earthly masters in everything you do. Try to please them all the time, not just when they are watching you. Serve them sincerely because of your reverent fear of the Lord. [23]Work willingly at whatever you do, as though you were working for the Lord rather than for people. [24]Remember that the Lord will give you an inheritance as your reward, and that the Master you are serving is Christ.* [25]But if you do what is wrong, you will be paid back for the wrong you have done. For God has no favorites.

4 Masters, be just and fair to your slaves. Remember that you also have a Master—in heaven.

An Encouragement for Prayer

[2]Devote yourselves to prayer with an alert mind and a thankful heart. [3]Pray for us, too, that God will give us many opportunities to speak about his mysterious plan

---

3:4 Some manuscripts read *our.* **3:6** Some manuscripts read *is coming on all who disobey him.* **3:11a** Greek *a Greek.* **3:11b** Greek *Barbarian, Scythian.* **3:24** Or *and serve Christ as your Master.*

Filled Up to Be Poured Out

COLOSSIANS 3:16–17

Living in New York City, I rarely see the stars. Lights are always on somewhere, creating a hazy glow. In this 24/7 town, there is always someplace to be and something to do.

In the midst of our busy lives, we often forget about Sabbath. We squeeze Jesus into whatever moment we can find and don't take time to experience real rest and reflection.

"When we keep a Sabbath holy, we are practicing, for a day, the freedom that God intends for all people," writes Dorothy Bass in *Receiving the Day*. "We are trying on a new way of life as we begin to allow our weeks to be changed in response to God's promises."

God knows us better than we know ourselves. He knows we need an off button for the background noise that crowds out his voice. We need the renewal of community. We need the Holy Spirit. We might turn to the spa, the gym, or the TV for a quick fix, but God is our source and strength, sustaining us every day.

When we don't cram every minute with activity, it helps us see more clearly what matters. Sabbath is a time set apart to "let the message about Christ, in all its richness, fill your lives" (Colossians 3:16). We are filled up in the Sabbath to be poured out in service to others. Sabbath returns us to thankfulness, helping us recognize and rejoice in the larger reality that "the truth lives in us and will be with us forever" (2 John 1:2).

With our priorities back in check, the rhythm of our lives is renewed. We are refreshed and ready for the days ahead. To freely live out our purpose focused on God's promises. To be a vibrant light amid the haze. To shine brightly with love everywhere we go in everything we do.

—Amie Hollmann

---

concerning Christ. That is why I am here in chains. [4] Pray that I will proclaim this message as clearly as I should.

[5] Live wisely among those who are not believers, and make the most of every opportunity. [6] Let your conversation be gracious and attractive* so that you will have the right response for everyone.

Paul's Final Instructions and Greetings

[7] Tychicus will give you a full report about how I am getting along. He is a beloved brother and faithful helper who serves with me in the Lord's work. [8] I have sent him to you for this very purpose—to let you know how we are doing and to encourage you. [9] I am also sending Onesimus, a faithful and beloved brother, one of your own people. He and Tychicus will tell you everything that's happening here.

[10] Aristarchus, who is in prison with me, sends you his greetings, and so does Mark, Barnabas's cousin. As you were instructed before, make Mark welcome if he comes your way. [11] Jesus (the one we call Justus) also sends his greetings. These are the only Jewish believers among my co-workers; they are working with me here for the Kingdom of God. And what a comfort they have been!

[12] Epaphras, a member of your own fellowship and a servant of Christ Jesus, sends you his greetings. He always prays earnestly for

---

4:6 Greek *and seasoned with salt.*

you, asking God to make you strong and perfect, fully confident that you are following the whole will of God. ¹³I can assure you that he prays hard for you and also for the believers in Laodicea and Hierapolis.

¹⁴Luke, the beloved doctor, sends his greetings, and so does Demas. ¹⁵Please give my greetings to our brothers and sisters* at Laodicea, and to Nympha and the church that meets in her house.

¹⁶After you have read this letter, pass it on to the church at Laodicea so they can read it, too. And you should read the letter I wrote to them.

¹⁷And say to Archippus, "Be sure to carry out the ministry the Lord gave you."

¹⁸HERE IS MY GREETING IN MY OWN HANDWRITING—PAUL.

Remember my chains.

May God's grace be with you.

Introduction to

1 Thessalonians

Background

Thessalonica was one of the wealthiest trade centers of the Roman Empire, thanks to its position on the Via Egnatia, a main road from Rome to the eastern parts of the Empire. It was the largest city in and the capital of Macedonia. It also had a large Jewish population. Many Gentiles who had grown disenchanted with Greek paganism were attracted to the Jewish faith. As part of his apostolic ministry, Paul took these people under his spiritual wing. He ministered extensively to Gentiles who had come out of idolatry (1:9), working "night and day" (2:9) during his time in Thessalonica. While he was there, Paul received two offerings the Philippian believers sent to help him with living expenses. The personal details given in this letter mesh with those given in the Book of Acts, supporting Paul's authorship, credited in 1:1, with Silas and Timothy. Paul, Silas, and Timothy visited Thessalonica on Paul's second missionary journey, before writing this epistle.

Message

After Paul, Silas, and Timothy are forced out of Thessalonica (Acts 17:9–10), Paul is concerned about the progress of the believers' faith. In this letter, he notes that his previous visit "was not a failure" (2:1), and he offers words of encouragement, edification, and doctrine to assist the fledgling church to mature and develop. He commends the Thessalonian believers for remaining steadfast, exhorts them to excel—and to "never stop praying" (5:17)—and consoles them concerning their believing loved ones who have died. Christ's second coming surfaces throughout the epistle as a theme and will take a more prominent role in 2 Thessalonians.

Time

Paul wrote this epistle in A.D. 51. After Paul met Timothy in Athens (3:1–2), Paul sent Timothy to Thessalonica. Paul, now in Corinth (Acts 18:1–5), wrote this epistle in response to Timothy's good report concerning the Thessalonian church.

Outline

1 Thessalonians

1 Greetings from Paul

This letter is from Paul, Silas,* and Timothy.

We are writing to the church in Thessalonica, to you who belong to God the Father and the Lord Jesus Christ.

May God give you grace and peace.

The Faith of the Thessalonian Believers

2 We always thank God for all of you and pray for you constantly. 3 As we pray to our God and Father about you, we think of your faithful work, your loving deeds, and the enduring hope you have because of our Lord Jesus Christ.

4 We know, dear brothers and sisters,* that God loves you and has chosen you to be his own people. 5 For when we brought you the Good News, it was not only with words but also with power, for the Holy Spirit gave you full assurance* that what we said was true. And you know of our concern for you from the way we lived when we were with you. 6 So you received the message with joy from the Holy Spirit in spite of the severe suffering it brought you. In this way, you imitated both us and the Lord. 7 As a result, you have become an example to all the believers in Greece—throughout both Macedonia and Achaia.*

8 And now the word of the Lord is ringing out from you to people everywhere, even beyond Macedonia and Achaia, for wherever we go we find people telling us about your faith in God. We don't need to tell them about it, 9 for they keep talking about the wonderful welcome you gave us and how you turned away from idols to serve the living and true God. 10 And they speak of how you are looking forward to the coming of God's Son from heaven—Jesus, whom God raised from the dead. He is the one who has rescued us from the terrors of the coming judgment.

2 Paul Remembers His Visit

You yourselves know, dear brothers and sisters,* that our visit to you was not a failure. 2 You know how badly we had been treated at Philippi just before we came to you and how much we suffered there. Yet our God gave us the courage to declare his Good News to you boldly, in spite of great opposition. 3 So you can see we were not preaching with any deceit or impure motives or trickery.

4 For we speak as messengers approved by God to be entrusted with the Good News. Our purpose is to please God, not people. He alone examines the motives of our hearts. 5 Never once did we try to win you with flattery, as you well know. And God is our witness that we were not pretending to be your friends just to get your money! 6 As for human praise, we have never sought it from you or anyone else.

7 As apostles of Christ we certainly had a right to make some demands of you, but instead we were like children* among you. Or we were like a mother feed-

---

1:1 Greek *Silvanus*, the Greek form of the name.   1:4 Greek *brothers*.   1:5 Or *with the power of the Holy Spirit, so you can have full assurance*.   1:7 *Macedonia* and *Achaia* were the northern and southern regions of Greece.   2:1 Greek *brothers;* also in 2:9, 14, 17.   2:7 Some manuscripts read *we were gentle*.

ing and caring for her own children. ⁸We loved you so much that we shared with you not only God's Good News but our own lives, too.

⁹Don't you remember, dear brothers and sisters, how hard we worked among you? Night and day we toiled to earn a living so that we would not be a burden to any of you as we preached God's Good News to you. ¹⁰You yourselves are our witnesses—and so is God—that we were devout and honest and faultless toward all of you believers. ¹¹And you know that we treated each of you as a father treats his own children. ¹²We pleaded with you, encouraged you, and urged you to live your lives in a way that God would consider worthy. For he called you to share in his Kingdom and glory.

¹³Therefore, we never stop thanking God that when you received his message from us, you didn't think of our words as mere human ideas. You accepted what we said as the very word of God—which, of course, it is. And this word continues to work in you who believe.

¹⁴And then, dear brothers and sisters, you suffered persecution from your own countrymen. In this way, you imitated the believers in God's churches in Judea who, because of their belief in Christ Jesus, suffered from their own people, the Jews. ¹⁵For some of the Jews killed the prophets, and some even killed the Lord Jesus. Now they have persecuted us, too. They fail to please God and work against all humanity ¹⁶as they try to keep us from preaching the Good News of salvation to the Gentiles. By doing this, they continue to pile up their sins. But the anger of God has caught up with them at last.

Timothy's Good Report about the Church

¹⁷Dear brothers and sisters, after we were separated from you for a little while (though our hearts never left you), we tried very hard to come back because of our intense longing to see you again. ¹⁸We wanted very much to come to you, and I, Paul, tried again and again, but Satan prevented us. ¹⁹After all, what gives us hope and joy, and what will be our proud reward and crown

as we stand before our Lord Jesus when he returns? It is you! ²⁰Yes, you are our pride and joy.

3 Finally, when we could stand it no longer, we decided to stay alone in Athens, ²and we sent Timothy to visit you. He is our brother and God's co-worker* in proclaiming the Good News of Christ. We sent him to strengthen you, to encourage you in your faith, ³and to keep you from being shaken by the troubles you were going through. But you know that we are destined for such troubles. ⁴Even while we were with you, we warned you that troubles would soon come—and they did, as you well know. ⁵That is why, when I could bear it no longer, I sent Timothy to find out whether your faith was still strong. I was afraid that the tempter had gotten the best of you and that our work had been useless.

⁶But now Timothy has just returned, bringing us good news about your faith and love. He reports that you always remember our visit with joy and that you want to see us as much as we want to see you. ⁷So we have been greatly encouraged in the midst of our troubles and suffering, dear brothers and sisters,* because you have remained strong in your faith. ⁸It gives us new life to know that you are standing firm in the Lord.

⁹How we thank God for you! Because of you we have great joy as we enter God's presence. ¹⁰Night and day we pray earnestly for you, asking God to let us see you again to fill the gaps in your faith.

¹¹May God our Father and our Lord Jesus bring us to you very soon. ¹²And may the Lord make your love for one another and for all people grow and overflow, just as our love for you overflows. ¹³May he, as a result, make your hearts strong, blameless, and holy as you stand before God our Father when our Lord Jesus comes again with all his holy people. Amen.

4 **Live to Please God**
Finally, dear brothers and sisters,* we urge you in the name of the Lord Jesus to live in a way that pleases God, as we have

---

3:2 Other manuscripts read *and God's servant;* still others read *and a co-worker,* or *and a servant and co-worker for God,* or *and God's servant and our co-worker.* **3:7** Greek *brothers.* **4:1** Greek *brothers;* also in 4:10, 13.

A "Simple" Testimony

1 THESSALONIANS 4:11-12

Living in simplicity is countercultural in today's world. It involves choosing to wait, to abide, and to rest. Instead of rushing everywhere, a woman of simplicity is wise in what she says yes to, so she's not preoccupied, stressed, and always in turmoil.

Women of simplicity stand out because we're not rushing around. We say, "Thank you for asking, but I can't participate in that right now." We're at peace and flexible.

A friend had a flight canceled recently. As the poor, beleaguered airline employee tried to rebook everyone as they ranted and raved, my friend got to the counter and said, "I know this wasn't your fault. I feel for you and am sorry you're in this position." He put her in first class.

When we respond in a kind way or go through difficult times with peace, people notice. It opens the door for us to tell others we choose to live this way because we want to live a God-paced life. As 1 Peter 3:15 says, "If someone asks about your Christian hope, always be ready to explain it." In this way practicing simplicity helps us communicate the gospel to others; people are attracted to a centered, peace-filled life.

—*Cynthia Heald*

For more on simplicity, see reading at 2 Thessalonians 3:1-5.

taught you. You live this way already, and we encourage you to do so even more. ²For you remember what we taught you by the authority of the Lord Jesus.

³God's will is for you to be holy, so stay away from all sexual sin. ⁴Then each of you will control his own body* and live in holiness and honor—⁵not in lustful passion like the pagans who do not know God and his ways. ⁶Never harm or cheat a Christian brother in this matter by violating his wife,* for the Lord avenges all such sins, as we have solemnly warned you before. ⁷God has called us to live holy lives, not impure lives. ⁸Therefore, anyone who refuses to live by these rules is not disobeying human teaching but is rejecting God, who gives his Holy Spirit to you.

⁹But we don't need to write to you about the importance of loving each other,* for God himself has taught you to love one another. ¹⁰Indeed, you already show your love for all the believers* throughout Mac-

edonia. Even so, dear brothers and sisters, we urge you to love them even more.

¹¹Make it your goal to live a quiet life, minding your own business and working with your hands, just as we instructed you before. ¹²Then people who are not Christians will respect the way you live, and you will not need to depend on others.

The Hope of the Resurrection

¹³And now, dear brothers and sisters, we want you to know what will happen to the believers who have died* so you will not grieve like people who have no hope. ¹⁴For since we believe that Jesus died and was raised to life again, we also believe that when Jesus returns, God will bring back with him the believers who have died.

¹⁵We tell you this directly from the Lord: We who are still living when the Lord returns will not meet him ahead of those who have died.* ¹⁶For the Lord himself will come down from heaven with a commanding shout,

---

4:4 Or *will know how to take a wife for himself;* or *will learn to live with his own wife;* Greek reads *will know how to possess his own vessel.*
4:6 Greek *Never harm or cheat a brother in this matter.* **4:9** Greek *about brotherly love.* **4:10** Greek *the brothers.* **4:13** Greek *those who have fallen asleep; also in 4:14.* **4:15** Greek *those who have fallen asleep.*

with the voice of the archangel, and with the trumpet call of God. First, the Christians who have died* will rise from their graves. ¹⁷Then, together with them, we who are still alive and remain on the earth will be caught up in the clouds to meet the Lord in the air. Then we will be with the Lord forever. ¹⁸So encourage each other with these words.

5 Now concerning how and when all this will happen, dear brothers and sisters,* we don't really need to write you. ²For you know quite well that the day of the Lord's return will come unexpectedly, like a thief in the night. ³When people are saying, "Everything is peaceful and secure," then disaster will fall on them as suddenly as a pregnant woman's labor pains begin. And there will be no escape.

⁴But you aren't in the dark about these things, dear brothers and sisters, and you won't be surprised when the day of the Lord comes like a thief.* ⁵For you are all children of the light and of the day; we don't belong to darkness and night. ⁶So be on your guard, not asleep like the others. Stay alert and be clearheaded. ⁷Night is the time when people sleep and drinkers get drunk. ⁸But let us who live in the light be clearheaded, protected by the armor of faith and love, and wearing as our helmet the confidence of our salvation.

⁹For God chose to save us through our Lord Jesus Christ, not to pour out his anger on us. ¹⁰Christ died for us so that, whether we are dead or alive when he returns, we can live with him forever. ¹¹So encourage each other and build each other up, just as you are already doing.

Paul's Final Advice

¹²Dear brothers and sisters, honor those who are your leaders in the Lord's work. They work hard among you and give you spiritual guidance. ¹³Show them great respect and wholehearted love because of their work. And live peacefully with each other.

¹⁴Brothers and sisters, we urge you to warn those who are lazy. Encourage those who are timid. Take tender care of those who are weak. Be patient with everyone.

¹⁵See that no one pays back evil for evil, but always try to do good to each other and to all people.

¹⁶Always be joyful. ¹⁷Never stop praying. ¹⁸Be thankful in all circumstances, for this is God's will for you who belong to Christ Jesus.

¹⁹Do not stifle the Holy Spirit. ²⁰Do not scoff at prophecies, ²¹but test everything that is said. Hold on to what is good. ²²Stay away from every kind of evil.

Paul's Final Greetings

²³Now may the God of peace make you holy in every way, and may your whole spirit and soul and body be kept blameless until our Lord Jesus Christ comes again. ²⁴God will make this happen, for he who calls you is faithful.

²⁵Dear brothers and sisters, pray for us.

²⁶Greet all the brothers and sisters with Christian love.*

²⁷I command you in the name of the Lord to read this letter to all the brothers and sisters.

²⁸May the grace of our Lord Jesus Christ be with you.

4:16 Greek *the dead in Christ.* **5:1** Greek *brothers;* also in 5:4, 12, 14, 25, 26, 27. **5:4** Some manuscripts read *comes upon you as if you were thieves.* **5:26** Greek *with a holy kiss.*

Prayer

Pray without Ceasing

1 THESSALONIANS 5:16-17

Have you ever wondered what the apostle Paul was talking about when he wrote, "Always be joyful. Never stop praying" (1 Thessalonians 5:16-17)? How can a person pray constantly? Yet this wasn't the only time Paul urged his hearers to constant prayer.

In Romans he wrote, "Rejoice in our confident hope. Be patient in trouble, and keep on praying" (12:12). In Ephesians: "Pray in the Spirit at all times and on every occasion. Stay alert and be persistent in your prayers" (6:18). And in Colossians: "Devote yourselves to prayer with an alert mind and a thankful heart" (4:2).

If he took the trouble to say this to four different communities, he must have thought ongoing prayer was important—and *possible*. He wouldn't have urged his hearers to do something that was beyond their capability.

In the second through fifth centuries, men and women began going out into the deserts of Palestine and Egypt to devote themselves wholly to prayer.

These Desert Fathers and Mothers soon discerned that the reason it's difficult to be in such communion is the ceaseless flow of wandering thoughts: these were not the constructive thoughts used in problem solving, but old memories, desires, fears, criticism of others—any number of aimless thoughts that disrupt the mind and keep it unsettled.

The cure was a substitute single, simple thought of prayer. After experimenting with various short Scriptures and petitions, this form emerged: "Lord Jesus Christ, Son of God, have mercy on me, a sinner." It was called the Jesus Prayer.

The prayer is drawn from the Gospels, from passages where people called on Jesus for mercy: the ten lepers who cried, "Jesus, Master, have mercy on us!" (Luke 17:13), the Canaanite woman who said, "Have mercy on me, O Lord, Son of David!" (Matthew 15:22), and blind Bartimaeus, who said, "Jesus, Son of David, have mercy on me!" (Mark 10:47). In one of Jesus' parables, a tax collector "dared not even lift his eyes to heaven as he prayed. Instead, he beat his chest in sorrow, saying, 'O God, be merciful to me, for I am a sinner'" (Luke 18:13). These requests for mercy aren't like a criminal begging a judge for lenience, but of needy people asking for the Lord's tender mercy.

I've been saying the Jesus Prayer for fifteen years now and have found that it has greatly increased my ability to sense the presence and voice of the Lord. I wondered at first how it was possible to pray all the time when I had so many other things to think about and accomplish. I found that it works by using a layer of your awareness, not your entire awareness. It's like having a friend along as you go through your day. In this case the best of friends provides tranquility, perspective, love, patience, and good humor.

You too can begin a habit of praying constantly as you focus your mind and heart through the Jesus Prayer. Set aside a bit of time each day when you will do nothing but say the prayer—even just ten minutes a day. Sit quietly, close your eyes, and begin silently repeating the prayer. Discipline that hungry mind to keep gazing at the Lord. Deny it anything other than the words of the prayer to think about. As Paul said, "We capture their rebellious thoughts and teach them to obey Christ" (2 Corinthians 10:5). You will find this impossible at first, but gradually you will make headway.

The Jesus Prayer is not an end in itself, but a way of training the mind to remain always in Jesus' presence, no matter what else life brings. As you weave the Jesus Prayer into your life, you discover that at all times, the inner you rests in the presence of our Lord, the light that drives away all darkness.

—*Frederica Mathewes-Green*

For more on prayer, see reading at Revelation 21:3–5.

Introduction to
2 Thessalonians

Background

Paul, Silas, and Timothy established the church in Thessalonica but had to leave because of persecution (Acts 17:1–10). (See also the introduction to 1 Thessalonians.) The bearer of the first letter from Paul to the church in Thessalonica may have brought Paul an update on new developments at the church, prompting Paul's reply. The apostle's claims of authorship (1:1; 3:17) are supported by vocabulary, style, and doctrinal content that are congruent with his other writings.

Message

Paul writes 2 Thessalonians to correct a misunderstanding about the return of Christ. Facing persecution and thinking God's judgment has already begun, the believers are falling prey to false teaching. As a result, many of the believers stop working and are simply waiting for the Lord to suddenly appear. Paul admonishes them not to be idle and to "never get tired of doing good" (3:13). As in other epistles, he puts a high priority on prayer—his for the believers as well as theirs for him.

Time

First Thessalonians was written in A.D. 51, and 2 Thessalonians probably was written a few months later, while Paul remained in Corinth with Silas and Timothy.

Outline

2 Thessalonians

1 Greetings from Paul

This letter is from Paul, Silas,* and Timothy.

We are writing to the church in Thessalonica, to you who belong to God our Father and the Lord Jesus Christ.

²May God our Father* and the Lord Jesus Christ give you grace and peace.

Encouragement during Persecution

³Dear brothers and sisters,* we can't help but thank God for you, because your faith is flourishing and your love for one another is growing. ⁴We proudly tell God's other churches about your endurance and faithfulness in all the persecutions and hardships you are suffering. ⁵And God will use this persecution to show his justice and to make you worthy of his Kingdom, for which you are suffering. ⁶In his justice he will pay back those who persecute you.

⁷And God will provide rest for you who are being persecuted and also for us when the Lord Jesus appears from heaven. He will come with his mighty angels, ⁸in flaming fire, bringing judgment on those who don't know God and on those who refuse to obey the Good News of our Lord Jesus. ⁹They will be punished with eternal destruction, forever separated from the Lord and from his glorious power. ¹⁰When he comes on that day, he will receive glory from his holy people—praise from all who believe. And this includes you, for you believed what we told you about him.

¹¹So we keep on praying for you, asking our God to enable you to live a life worthy of his call. May he give you the power to accomplish all the good things your faith prompts you to do. ¹²Then the name of our Lord Jesus will be honored because of the way you live, and you will be honored along with him. This is all made possible because of the grace of our God and Lord, Jesus Christ.*

2 Events prior to the Lord's Second Coming

Now, dear brothers and sisters,* let us clarify some things about the coming of our Lord Jesus Christ and how we will be gathered to meet him. ²Don't be so easily shaken or alarmed by those who say that the day of the Lord has already begun. Don't believe them, even if they claim to have had a spiritual vision, a revelation, or a letter supposedly from us. ³Don't be fooled by what they say. For that day will not come until there is a great rebellion against God and the man of lawlessness* is revealed—the one who brings destruction.* ⁴He will exalt himself and defy everything that people call god and every object of worship. He will even sit in the temple of God, claiming that he himself is God.

⁵Don't you remember that I told you about all this when I was with you? ⁶And you know what is holding him back, for he can be revealed only when his time comes. ⁷For this lawlessness is already at work secretly, and it will remain secret until the one who is holding it back steps out of the way. ⁸Then

---

1:1 Greek *Silvanus*, the Greek form of the name. **1:2** Some manuscripts read *God the Father.* **1:3** Greek *Brothers.* **1:12** Or *of our God and our Lord Jesus Christ.* **2:1** Greek *brothers*; also in 2:13, 15. **2:3a** Some manuscripts read *the man of sin.* **2:3b** Greek *the son of destruction.*

A Path to Generosity

2 THESSALONIANS 3:1-5

As a young professor at Oxford University, John Wesley enjoyed relative financial prosperity and comfort. Then on a cold winter day, a chambermaid came to his door wearing only a thin linen gown. He reached into his pocket to give her money to buy a coat, but found he had too little left; he'd spent it all on his own wants. Immediately he felt convicted that God was not pleased with the way he'd spent his money.

So Wesley began a life committed to material simplicity; the less he spent on himself, the more he could give to the poor. He believed that with increasing income, what should rise is not the Christian's standard of living but the standard of giving. Even when Wesley's personal income rose into the thousands of pounds sterling, he lived simply (on about thirty pounds a year) and quickly gave away the surplus.

Wesley lived by three principles regarding money. "Gain all you can. Save all you can. Give all you can." For Wesley "save all you can" didn't mean saving money for oneself; it meant being thrifty and simple in one's expenditures. Wesley chose to go without the "normal" luxuries expected of a person of his station in life. In fact, he lived so simply that once the tax commission investigated his tax return; they couldn't believe a man with his income didn't own a large amount of silver tableware and other status symbols!

Though Wesley had no children, he believed Christians with families should provide first for their family's needs (1 Timothy 5:8). He also taught that believers should aim to pay off all their debts (Romans 13:8). But he felt strongly that all Christians—with or without families to provide for—should strive to live in simplicity, driven by the contentment they found in Christ (1 Timothy 5:8). Wesley believed that simplicity gave one the freedom and ability to seize every opportunity to do good for others (Galatians 6:10).

—Charles Edward White

For more on simplicity, see reading at 2 Peter 1:3-7.

the man of lawlessness will be revealed, but the Lord Jesus will kill him with the breath of his mouth and destroy him by the splendor of his coming.

[9] This man will come to do the work of Satan with counterfeit power and signs and miracles. [10] He will use every kind of evil deception to fool those on their way to destruction, because they refuse to love and accept the truth that would save them. [11] So God will cause them to be greatly deceived, and they will believe these lies. [12] Then they will be condemned for enjoying evil rather than believing the truth.

Believers Should Stand Firm

[13] As for us, we can't help but thank God for you, dear brothers and sisters loved by the Lord. We are always thankful that God chose you to be among the first* to experience salvation—a salvation that came through the Spirit who makes you holy and through your belief in the truth. [14] He called you to salvation when we told you the Good

2:13 Some manuscripts read *chose you from the very beginning.*

News; now you can share in the glory of our Lord Jesus Christ.

15 With all these things in mind, dear brothers and sisters, stand firm and keep a strong grip on the teaching we passed on to you both in person and by letter.

16 Now may our Lord Jesus Christ himself and God our Father, who loved us and by his grace gave us eternal comfort and a wonderful hope, 17 comfort you and strengthen you in every good thing you do and say.

3 Paul's Request for Prayer

Finally, dear brothers and sisters,* we ask you to pray for us. Pray that the Lord's message will spread rapidly and be honored wherever it goes, just as when it came to you. 2 Pray, too, that we will be rescued from wicked and evil people, for not everyone is a believer. 3 But the Lord is faithful; he will strengthen you and guard you from the evil one.* 4 And we are confident in the Lord that you are doing and will continue to do the things we commanded you. 5 May the Lord lead your hearts into a full understanding and expression of the love of God and the patient endurance that comes from Christ.

An Exhortation to Proper Living

6 And now, dear brothers and sisters, we give you this command in the name of our Lord Jesus Christ: Stay away from all believers* who live idle lives and don't follow the tradition they received* from us. 7 For you know that you ought to imitate us. We were not idle when we were with you. 8 We never accepted food from anyone without paying for it. We worked hard day and night so we would not be a burden to any of you. 9 We certainly had the right to ask you to feed us, but we wanted to give you an example to follow. 10 Even while we were with you, we gave you this command: "Those unwilling to work will not get to eat."

11 Yet we hear that some of you are living idle lives, refusing to work and meddling in other people's business. 12 We command such people and urge them in the name of the Lord Jesus Christ to settle down and work to earn their own living. 13 As for the rest of you, dear brothers and sisters, never get tired of doing good.

14 Take note of those who refuse to obey what we say in this letter. Stay away from them so they will be ashamed. 15 Don't think of them as enemies, but warn them as you would a brother or sister.*

Paul's Final Greetings

16 Now may the Lord of peace himself give you his peace at all times and in every situation. The Lord be with you all.

17 HERE IS MY GREETING IN MY OWN HANDWRITING—PAUL. I DO THIS IN ALL MY LETTERS TO PROVE THEY ARE FROM ME.

18 May the grace of our Lord Jesus Christ be with you all.

3:1 Greek brothers; also in 3:6, 13. **3:3** Or from evil. **3:6a** Greek from every brother. **3:6b** Some manuscripts read you received. **3:15** Greek as a brother.

Introduction to
1 Timothy

Background

The apostle Paul is recognized as the author of the Pastoral Epistles—1 Timothy, 2 Timothy, and Titus. Timothy and Titus exercised pastoral oversight over their respective churches. The events referred to in the Pastoral Epistles take place after those recounted in the Book of Acts. In his letters Paul mentions Timothy more than anyone else. It seems Timothy became a believer under the ministry of Paul at the town of Lystra, in modern-day Turkey (Acts 14:8–20; 16:1–3) during his second missionary journey. Paul refers to Timothy as his son in several epistles (1 Corinthians 4:17; 1 Timothy 1:2; 2 Timothy 1:2). Timothy was ordained to ministry (1 Timothy 4:14; 2 Timothy 1:6) and served as Paul's assistant in several cities, including during his house arrest in Rome.

Message

This first of two epistles to Timothy reads as a checklist of advice from a mature and wise apostle to a younger disciple. Paul instructs his charge to be watchful of false teachers and those only seeking after profit. He reminds Timothy not to let his youth get in the way of his mission, and to conduct himself as a bearer of the gospel's truth. Timothy, ministering in Ephesus, has several challenges to deal with: exposing false doctrines, setting parameters for public worship, and recruiting good leaders. In all things, Paul reminds Timothy to put God's virtues first: righteousness, godliness, faith, love, perseverance, and gentleness.

Time

After Paul was released from his prison in Rome (Acts 28:30), he likely wrote 1 Timothy at Philippi in Macedonia in A.D. 62 or 63 while Timothy ministered in Ephesus.

Outline

1 Timothy

1 Greetings from Paul

This letter is from Paul, an apostle of Christ Jesus, appointed by the command of God our Savior and Christ Jesus, who gives us hope.

²I am writing to Timothy, my true son in the faith.

May God the Father and Christ Jesus our Lord give you grace, mercy, and peace.

Warnings against False Teachings

³When I left for Macedonia, I urged you to stay there in Ephesus and stop those whose teaching is contrary to the truth. ⁴Don't let them waste their time in endless discussion of myths and spiritual pedigrees. These things only lead to meaningless speculations,* which don't help people live a life of faith in God.*

⁵The purpose of my instruction is that all believers would be filled with love that comes from a pure heart, a clear conscience, and genuine faith. ⁶But some people have missed this whole point. They have turned away from these things and spend their time in meaningless discussions. ⁷They want to be known as teachers of the law of Moses, but they don't know what they are talking about, even though they speak so confidently.

⁸We know that the law is good when used correctly. ⁹For the law was not intended for people who do what is right. It is for people who are lawless and rebellious, who are ungodly and sinful, who consider nothing sacred and defile what is holy, who kill their father or mother or commit other murders. ¹⁰The law is for people who are sexually immoral, or who practice homosexuality, or are slave traders,* liars, promise breakers, or who do anything else that contradicts the wholesome teaching ¹¹that comes from the glorious Good News entrusted to me by our blessed God.

Paul's Gratitude for God's Mercy

¹²I thank Christ Jesus our Lord, who has given me strength to do his work. He considered me trustworthy and appointed me to serve him, ¹³even though I used to blaspheme the name of Christ. In my insolence, I persecuted his people. But God had mercy on me because I did it in ignorance and unbelief. ¹⁴Oh, how generous and gracious our Lord was! He filled me with the faith and love that come from Christ Jesus.

¹⁵This is a trustworthy saying, and everyone should accept it: "Christ Jesus came into the world to save sinners"—and I am the worst of them all. ¹⁶But God had mercy on me so that Christ Jesus could use me as a prime example of his great patience with even the worst sinners. Then others will realize that they, too, can believe in him and receive eternal life. ¹⁷All honor and glory to God forever and ever! He is the eternal King, the unseen one who never dies; he alone is God. Amen.

1:4a Greek in myths and endless genealogies, which cause speculation. **1:4b** Greek a stewardship of God in faith. **1:10** Or kidnappers.

Timothy's Responsibility

[18] Timothy, my son, here are my instructions for you, based on the prophetic words spoken about you earlier. May they help you fight well in the Lord's battles. [19] Cling to your faith in Christ, and keep your conscience clear. For some people have deliberately violated their consciences; as a result, their faith has been shipwrecked. [20] Hymenaeus and Alexander are two examples. I threw them out and handed them over to Satan so they might learn not to blaspheme God.

2 Instructions about Worship

I urge you, first of all, to pray for all people. Ask God to help them; intercede on their behalf, and give thanks for them. [2] Pray this way for kings and all who are in authority so that we can live peaceful and quiet lives marked by godliness and dignity. [3] This is good and pleases God our Savior, [4] who wants everyone to be saved and to understand the truth. [5] For there is only one God and one Mediator who can reconcile God and humanity—the man Christ Jesus. [6] He gave his life to purchase freedom for everyone. This is the message God gave to the world at just the right time. [7] And I have been chosen as a preacher and apostle to teach the Gentiles this message about faith and truth. I'm not exaggerating—just telling the truth.

[8] In every place of worship, I want men to pray with holy hands lifted up to God, free from anger and controversy.

[9] And I want women to be modest in their appearance.* They should wear decent and appropriate clothing and not draw attention to themselves by the way they fix their hair or by wearing gold or pearls or expensive clothes. [10] For women who claim to be devoted to God should make themselves attractive by the good things they do.

[11] Women should learn quietly and submissively. [12] I do not let women teach men or have authority over them.* Let them listen quietly. [13] For God made Adam first, and afterward he made Eve. [14] And it was not Adam who was deceived by Satan.

The woman was deceived, and sin was the result. [15] But women will be saved through childbearing,* assuming they continue to live in faith, love, holiness, and modesty.

3 Leaders in the Church

This is a trustworthy saying: "If someone aspires to be an elder,* he desires an honorable position." [2] So an elder must be a man whose life is above reproach. He must be faithful to his wife.* He must exercise self-control, live wisely, and have a good reputation. He must enjoy having guests in his home, and he must be able to teach. [3] He must not be a heavy drinker* or be violent. He must be gentle, not quarrelsome, and not love money. [4] He must manage his own family well, having children who respect and obey him. [5] For if a man cannot manage his own household, how can he take care of God's church?

[6] An elder must not be a new believer, because he might become proud, and the devil would cause him to fall.* [7] Also, people outside the church must speak well of him so that he will not be disgraced and fall into the devil's trap.

[8] In the same way, deacons must be well respected and have integrity. They must not be heavy drinkers or dishonest with money. [9] They must be committed to the mystery of the faith now revealed and must live with a clear conscience. [10] Before they are appointed as deacons, let them be closely examined. If they pass the test, then let them serve as deacons.

[11] In the same way, their wives* must be respected and must not slander others. They must exercise self-control and be faithful in everything they do.

[12] A deacon must be faithful to his wife, and he must manage his children and household well. [13] Those who do well as deacons will be rewarded with respect from others and will have increased confidence in their faith in Christ Jesus.

The Truths of Our Faith

[14] I am writing these things to you now, even though I hope to be with you soon, [15] so that

---

2:9 Or to pray in modest apparel.   2:12 Or teach men or usurp their authority.   2:15 Or will be saved by accepting their role as mothers, or will be saved by the birth of the Child.   3:1 Or an overseer, or a bishop; also in 3:2, 6.   3:2 Or must have only one wife, or must be married only once; Greek reads must be the husband of one wife; also in 3:12.   3:3 Greek must not drink too much wine; similarly in 3:8.   3:6 Or he might fall into the same judgment as the devil.   3:11 Or the women deacons. The Greek word can be translated women or wives.

if I am delayed, you will know how people must conduct themselves in the household of God. This is the church of the living God, which is the pillar and foundation of the truth.

[16] Without question, this is the great mystery of our faith*:

Christ* was revealed in a human body
   and vindicated by the Spirit.*
He was seen by angels
   and announced to the nations.
He was believed in throughout the world
   and taken to heaven in glory.

4 Warnings against False Teachers

Now the Holy Spirit tells us clearly that in the last times some will turn away from the true faith; they will follow deceptive spirits and teachings that come from demons. [2] These people are hypocrites and liars, and their consciences are dead.* [3] They will say it is wrong to be married and wrong to eat certain foods. But God created those foods to be eaten with thanks by faithful people who know the truth. [4] Since everything God created is good, we should not reject any of it but receive it with thanks. [5] For we know it is made acceptable* by the word of God and prayer.

A Good Servant of Christ Jesus

[6] If you explain these things to the brothers and sisters,* Timothy, you will be a worthy servant of Christ Jesus, one who is nourished by the message of faith and the good teaching you have followed. [7] Do not waste time arguing over godless ideas and old wives' tales. Instead, train yourself to be godly. [8] "Physical training is good, but training for godliness is much better, promising benefits in this life and in the life to come." [9] This is a trustworthy saying, and everyone should accept it. [10] This is why we work hard and continue to struggle,* for our hope is in the living God, who is the Savior of all people and particularly of all believers.

[11] Teach these things and insist that everyone learn them. [12] Don't let anyone think less of you because you are young. Be an example to all believers in what you say, in the way

you live, in your love, your faith, and your purity. [13] Until I get there, focus on reading the Scriptures to the church, encouraging the believers, and teaching them.

[14] Do not neglect the spiritual gift you received through the prophecy spoken over you when the elders of the church laid their hands on you. [15] Give your complete attention to these matters. Throw yourself into your tasks so that everyone will see your progress. [16] Keep a close watch on how you live and on your teaching. Stay true to what is right for the sake of your own salvation and the salvation of those who hear you.

5 Advice about Widows, Elders, and Slaves

Never speak harshly to an older man,* but appeal to him respectfully as you would to your own father. Talk to younger men as you would to your own brothers. [2] Treat older women as you would your mother, and treat younger women with all purity as you would your own sisters.

[3] Take care of* any widow who has no one else to care for her. [4] But if she has children or grandchildren, their first responsibility is to show godliness at home and repay their parents by taking care of them. This is something that pleases God.

[5] Now a true widow, a woman who is truly alone in this world, has placed her hope in God. She prays night and day, asking God for his help. [6] But the widow who lives only for pleasure is spiritually dead even while she lives. [7] Give these instructions to the church so that no one will be open to criticism.

[8] But those who won't care for their relatives, especially those in their own household, have denied the true faith. Such people are worse than unbelievers.

[9] A widow who is put on the list for support must be a woman who is at least sixty years old and was faithful to her husband.* [10] She must be well respected by everyone because of the good she has done. Has she brought up her children well? Has she been kind to strangers and served other believers humbly?* Has she helped those who are in trouble? Has she always been ready to do good?

3:16a Or of godliness.   **3:16b** Greek He who; other manuscripts read God.   **3:16c** Or in his spirit.   **4:2** Greek are seared.   **4:5** Or made holy.
4:6 Greek brothers.   **4:10** Some manuscripts read continue to suffer.   **5:1** Or an elder.   **5:3** Or Honor.   **5:9** Greek was the wife of one husband.
5:10 Greek and washed the feet of God's holy people?

Stewardship of Time

1 TIMOTHY 4:11-15

The temptation to take on too much stalked God's people throughout Bible history. Moses rose to a position of power and leadership then found himself faced with the formidable task of single-handedly maintaining order and justice among the tribes of Israel (Exodus 18:13-26). The apostles drew many believers to the gospel then realized the job of helping an expanding congregation was more than they could handle (Acts 6:1-7).

How can you live as a good steward of your ministry and work opportunities as well as your time? Daily offer yourself, your activities, and the hours of your day to God, asking him to give you wisdom and discernment as you make decisions about which activities to accept, which to seek help with, and which to avoid. When you do, you'll find yourself willing to accept your God-given responsibilities (rather than self-imposed responsibilities) and make positive choices among your many options.

Jesus promised, "Seek the Kingdom of God above all else, and live righteously, and he will give you everything you need" (Matthew 6:33). With God as your first priority, instead of your tasks, your perspective on time shifts from yourself to him in three important ways. First, you recognize God has set time with limits, and he would never expect more from you than time allows. Second, your freedom from unhealthy competition and unrealistic goals allows you to put relationships ahead of achievements; delegate tasks to others; put certain dreams and desires on hold; say no when necessary to maintain balance in your life; and wholeheartedly focus on the path God has set out for you.

When we follow God's leading, not only does he make our path clear, but he also gives us the energy to enjoy our work, responsibilities, and activities to their fullest, because we've prioritized them and allowed a healthy balance between work and rest. Let God, the Giver of time, show you how to live—and enjoy—the time of your life.

—*Patricia Mitchell*

---

[11] The younger widows should not be on the list, because their physical desires will overpower their devotion to Christ and they will want to remarry. [12] Then they would be guilty of breaking their previous pledge. [13] And if they are on the list, they will learn to be lazy and will spend their time gossiping from house to house, meddling in other people's business and talking about things they shouldn't. [14] So I advise these younger widows to marry again, have children, and take care of their own homes. Then the enemy will not be able to say anything against them. [15] For I am afraid that some of them have already gone astray and now follow Satan.

[16] If a woman who is a believer has relatives who are widows, she must take care of them and not put the responsibility on the church. Then the church can care for the widows who are truly alone.

[17] Elders who do their work well should be respected and paid well,* especially those who work hard at both preaching and teaching. [18] For the Scripture says, "You must not muzzle an ox to keep it from eating as it treads out the grain." And in another place, "Those who work deserve their pay!"*

5:17 Greek *should be worthy of double honor.*   **5:18** Deut 25:4; Luke 10:7.

¹⁹Do not listen to an accusation against an elder unless it is confirmed by two or three witnesses. ²⁰Those who sin should be reprimanded in front of the whole church; this will serve as a strong warning to others.

²¹I solemnly command you in the presence of God and Christ Jesus and the highest angels to obey these instructions without taking sides or showing favoritism to anyone.

²²Never be in a hurry about appointing a church leader.* Do not share in the sins of others. Keep yourself pure.

²³Don't drink only water. You ought to drink a little wine for the sake of your stomach because you are sick so often.

²⁴Remember, the sins of some people are obvious, leading them to certain judgment. But there are others whose sins will not be revealed until later. ²⁵In the same way, the good deeds of some people are obvious. And the good deeds done in secret will someday come to light.

6 All slaves should show full respect for their masters so they will not bring shame on the name of God and his teaching. ²If the masters are believers, that is no excuse for being disrespectful. Those slaves should work all the harder because their efforts are helping other believers* who are well loved.

False Teaching and True Riches

Teach these things, Timothy, and encourage everyone to obey them. ³Some people may contradict our teaching, but these are the wholesome teachings of the Lord Jesus Christ. These teachings promote a godly life. ⁴Anyone who teaches something different is arrogant and lacks understanding. Such a person has an unhealthy desire to quibble over the meaning of words. This stirs up arguments ending in jealousy, division, slander, and evil suspicions. ⁵These people always cause trouble. Their minds are corrupt, and they have turned their backs on the truth. To them, a show of godliness is just a way to become wealthy.

⁶Yet true godliness with contentment is itself great wealth. ⁷After all, we brought nothing with us when we came into the world, and we can't take anything with us when we leave it. ⁸So if we have enough food and clothing, let us be content.

⁹But people who long to be rich fall into temptation and are trapped by many foolish and harmful desires that plunge them into ruin and destruction. ¹⁰For the love of money is the root of all kinds of evil. And some people, craving money, have wandered from the true faith and pierced themselves with many sorrows.

Paul's Final Instructions

¹¹But you, Timothy, are a man of God; so run from all these evil things. Pursue righteousness and a godly life, along with faith, love, perseverance, and gentleness. ¹²Fight the good fight for the true faith. Hold tightly to the eternal life to which God has called you, which you have confessed so well before many witnesses. ¹³And I charge you before God, who gives life to all, and before Christ Jesus, who gave a good testimony before Pontius Pilate, ¹⁴that you obey this command without wavering. Then no one can find fault with you from now until our Lord Jesus Christ comes again. ¹⁵For at just the right time Christ will be revealed from heaven by the blessed and only almighty God, the King of all kings and Lord of all lords. ¹⁶He alone can never die, and he lives in light so brilliant that no human can approach him. No human eye has ever seen him, nor ever will. All honor and power to him forever! Amen.

¹⁷Teach those who are rich in this world not to be proud and not to trust in their money, which is so unreliable. Their trust should be in God, who richly gives us all we need for our enjoyment. ¹⁸Tell them to use their money to do good. They should be rich in good works and generous to those in need, always being ready to share with others. ¹⁹By doing this they will be storing up their treasure as a good foundation for the future so that they may experience true life.

²⁰Timothy, guard what God has entrusted to you. Avoid godless, foolish discussions with those who oppose you with their so-called knowledge. ²¹Some people have wandered from the faith by following such foolishness.

May God's grace be with you all.

5:22 Greek *about the laying on of hands.*   **6:2** Greek *brothers.*

2 Timothy

Background

Second Timothy was written at the end of Paul's life. Sensing that he will soon be executed for his faith in Christ (4:6–8), he writes to Timothy, his son in the faith, a protégé, and a dear friend. At the conclusion of Acts, Paul was under house arrest, where visitors could come and go, and he had the hope of release. He did continue his ministry with additional travels, but now he is back in Rome, in a dank prison. He writes to his friend in Ephesus to tie up some loose ends and even to request that when Timothy visits, he bring along a coat and some special parchments (4:13). Acts 16:1 says that Timothy's father was Greek and his mother Jewish. Here in 2 Timothy we learn that his mother, named Eunice, raised him, along with his grandmother Lois, to know the Hebrew Scriptures (1:5; 3:15), which fortified his Christian faith.

Message

Paul's words are full of encouragement and instruction, despite the bleakness of the days ahead. He tells Timothy of his continual prayers and love for him, then reminds Timothy of his godly heritage and his responsibilities. Paul charges Timothy to remain steadfast in the faith, for only those who persevere in the things of God will be rewarded by God. There is also a warning against those who would attack Timothy for his teachings, men who desert the truth of God's Word to seek false doctrines. If ever a man had an example to follow, it was Timothy, for Paul remained true to the end despite the knowledge that he would die for what he believed.

Time

Paul wrote 2 Timothy in A.D. 67 during his second imprisonment, by the Roman emperor Nero. Paul hopes that Timothy can "get here before winter" (4:21). Timothy likely received Paul's letter from Tychicus at Ephesus (4:12).

Outline

2 Timothy

1 Greetings from Paul

This letter is from Paul, chosen by the will of God to be an apostle of Christ Jesus. I have been sent out to tell others about the life he has promised through faith in Christ Jesus.

²I am writing to Timothy, my dear son.

May God the Father and Christ Jesus our Lord give you grace, mercy, and peace.

Encouragement to Be Faithful

³Timothy, I thank God for you—the God I serve with a clear conscience, just as my ancestors did. Night and day I constantly remember you in my prayers. ⁴I long to see you again, for I remember your tears as we parted. And I will be filled with joy when we are together again.

⁵I remember your genuine faith, for you share the faith that first filled your grandmother Lois and your mother, Eunice. And I know that same faith continues strong in you. ⁶This is why I remind you to fan into flames the spiritual gift God gave you when I laid my hands on you. ⁷For God has not given us a spirit of fear and timidity, but of power, love, and self-discipline.

⁸So never be ashamed to tell others about our Lord. And don't be ashamed of me, either, even though I'm in prison for him. With the strength God gives you, be ready to suffer with me for the sake of the Good News. ⁹For God saved us and called us to live a holy life. He did this, not because we deserved it, but because that was his plan from before the beginning of time—to show us his grace through Christ Jesus. ¹⁰And now he has made all of this plain to us by the appearing of Christ Jesus, our Savior. He broke the power of death and illuminated the way to life and immortality through the Good News. ¹¹And God chose me to be a preacher, an apostle, and a teacher of this Good News.

¹²That is why I am suffering here in prison. But I am not ashamed of it, for I know the one in whom I trust, and I am sure that he is able to guard what I have entrusted to him* until the day of his return.

¹³Hold on to the pattern of wholesome teaching you learned from me—a pattern shaped by the faith and love that you have in Christ Jesus. ¹⁴Through the power of the Holy Spirit who lives within us, carefully guard the precious truth that has been entrusted to you.

¹⁵As you know, everyone from the province of Asia has deserted me—even Phygelus and Hermogenes.

¹⁶May the Lord show special kindness to Onesiphorus and all his family because he often visited and encouraged me. He was never ashamed of me because I was in chains. ¹⁷When he came to Rome, he searched everywhere until he found me. ¹⁸May the Lord show him special kindness on the day of Christ's return. And you know very well how helpful he was in Ephesus.

1:12 Or *what has been entrusted to me.*

Gifted for a Purpose
2 TIMOTHY 1:3–7

As a believer in Jesus, you have been miraculously gifted by the Holy Spirit; passages like 1 Corinthians 12–14, Romans 12, and 1 Peter 4 describe various spiritual gifts and how they should be used. Every spiritual gift reflects God's nature that you carry within you. And because your spiritual gift reflects God's design and direction for your life, you'll find great passion, joy, and satisfaction in expressing it.

Yet more important, our spiritual gifts are for a specific purpose. Paul puts it simply: "A spiritual gift is given to each of us so we can help each other" (1 Corinthians 12:7). Peter echoes this theme: "God has given each of you a gift from his great variety of spiritual gifts. Use them well to serve one another" (1 Peter 4:10). We are stewards—caretakers—of these gifts. Ultimately our gifts aren't about what they do for us—they're about what we do for others.

In 2 Timothy 1:6 Paul encourages Timothy to "fan into flames the spiritual gift God gave you." We develop and nurture our gifts as we use them—and we best use them in service to others as we seek to build the church (1 Corinthians 14:4, 12).

—Nancy Ortberg

2 A Good Soldier of Christ Jesus

Timothy, my dear son, be strong through the grace that God gives you in Christ Jesus. ²You have heard me teach things that have been confirmed by many reliable witnesses. Now teach these truths to other trustworthy people who will be able to pass them on to others.

³Endure suffering along with me, as a good soldier of Christ Jesus. ⁴Soldiers don't get tied up in the affairs of civilian life, for then they cannot please the officer who enlisted them. ⁵And athletes cannot win the prize unless they follow the rules. ⁶And hardworking farmers should be the first to enjoy the fruit of their labor. ⁷Think about what I am saying. The Lord will help you understand all these things.

⁸Always remember that Jesus Christ, a descendant of King David, was raised from the dead. This is the Good News I preach. ⁹And because I preach this Good News, I am suffering and have been chained like a criminal. But the word of God cannot be chained. ¹⁰So I am willing to endure anything if it will bring salvation and eternal glory in Christ Jesus to those God has chosen.

¹¹This is a trustworthy saying:

If we die with him,
we will also live with him.
¹² If we endure hardship,
we will reign with him.
If we deny him,
he will deny us.
¹³ If we are unfaithful,
he remains faithful,
for he cannot deny who he is.

¹⁴Remind everyone about these things, and command them in God's presence to stop fighting over words. Such arguments are useless, and they can ruin those who hear them.

An Approved Worker

¹⁵Work hard so you can present yourself to God and receive his approval. Be a good worker, one who does not need to be ashamed and who correctly explains the word of truth. ¹⁶Avoid worthless, foolish talk that only leads to more godless behavior. ¹⁷This kind of talk spreads like cancer,* as in the case of Hymenaeus and Philetus. ¹⁸They have left the path of truth, claim-

2:17 Greek gangrene.

ing that the resurrection of the dead has already occurred; in this way, they have turned some people away from the faith.

¹⁹But God's truth stands firm like a foundation stone with this inscription: "The LORD knows those who are his,"* and "All who belong to the LORD must turn away from evil."*

²⁰In a wealthy home some utensils are made of gold and silver, and some are made of wood and clay. The expensive utensils are used for special occasions, and the cheap ones are for everyday use. ²¹If you keep yourself pure, you will be a special utensil for honorable use. Your life will be clean, and you will be ready for the Master to use you for every good work.

²²Run from anything that stimulates youthful lusts. Instead, pursue righteous living, faithfulness, love, and peace. Enjoy the companionship of those who call on the Lord with pure hearts.

²³Again I say, don't get involved in foolish, ignorant arguments that only start fights. ²⁴A servant of the Lord must not quarrel but must be kind to everyone, be able to teach, and be patient with difficult people. ²⁵Gently instruct those who oppose the truth. Perhaps God will change those people's hearts, and they will learn the truth. ²⁶Then they will come to their senses and escape from the devil's trap. For they have been held captive by him to do whatever he wants.

3 The Dangers of the Last Days

You should know this, Timothy, that in the last days there will be very difficult times. ²For people will love only themselves and their money. They will be boastful and proud, scoffing at God, disobedient to their parents, and ungrateful. They will consider nothing sacred. ³They will be unloving and unforgiving; they will slander others and have no self-control. They will be cruel and hate what is good. ⁴They will betray their friends, be reckless, be puffed up with pride, and love pleasure rather than God. ⁵They will act religious, but they will reject the power that could make them godly. Stay away from people like that!

⁶They are the kind who work their way into people's homes and win the confidence of* vulnerable women who are burdened with the guilt of sin and controlled by various desires. ⁷(Such women are forever following new teachings, but they are never able to understand the truth.) ⁸These teachers oppose the truth just as Jannes and Jambres opposed Moses. They have depraved minds and a counterfeit faith. ⁹But they won't get away with this for long. Someday everyone will recognize what fools they are, just as with Jannes and Jambres.

Paul's Charge to Timothy

¹⁰But you, Timothy, certainly know what I teach, and how I live, and what my purpose in life is. You know my faith, my patience, my love, and my endurance. ¹¹You know how much persecution and suffering I have endured. You know all about how I was persecuted in Antioch, Iconium, and Lystra—but the Lord rescued me from all of it. ¹²Yes, and everyone who wants to live a godly life in Christ Jesus will suffer persecution. ¹³But evil people and impostors will flourish. They will deceive others and will themselves be deceived.

¹⁴But you must remain faithful to the things you have been taught. You know they are true, for you know you can trust those who taught you. ¹⁵You have been taught the holy Scriptures from childhood, and they have given you the wisdom to receive the salvation that comes by trusting in Christ Jesus. ¹⁶All Scripture is inspired by God and is useful to teach us what is true and to make us realize what is wrong in our lives. It corrects us when we are wrong and teaches us to do what is right. ¹⁷God uses it to prepare and equip his people to do every good work.

4

I solemnly urge you in the presence of God and Christ Jesus, who will someday judge the living and the dead when he appears to set up his Kingdom: ²Preach the word of God. Be prepared, whether the time is favorable or not. Patiently correct, rebuke, and encourage your people with good teaching.

2:19a Num 16:5. **2:19b** See Isa 52:11. **3:6** Greek *and take captive.*

The Discipline of "Convictability"

2 TIMOTHY 3:16

As I have grown older, I have come to appreciate the Bible for its devotional input into my life. When I found myself in one of my darkest moments more than twenty years ago, I remember fleeing to the Scripture to find healing for my broken heart. I chose to read Romans over and over until the book was semimemorized.

Paul's words leaped off the pages and into my fractured soul. I found things in each chapter that reframed the meaning of evil, grace, salvation, and restoration in ways I'd never appreciated before. More than once I found myself weeping, the tears staining the pages. I remember blurting out to my wife, Gail, that these chapters were like a life-ring being tossed out to a drowning swimmer and that I considered myself the swimmer going down for the third time.

Because I've had years to get acquainted with the Bible, many paragraphs from both testaments flood into my consciousness whenever I am feeling discouraged or distracted. I have tried to acquire what I call the discipline of "convictability," the willingness to let the Bible instruct me—even rebuke me—as its power, like that of the famed two-edged sword, cuts to my heart (Hebrews 4:12). Scripture, inspired by God, can "make us realize what is wrong in our lives. It corrects us when we are wrong and teaches us to do what is right" (2 Timothy 3:16).

I am haunted by the story Abraham Heschel told in one of his books—of a brilliant young Talmudic scholar who bragged to an old rebbe that he had "gone through the whole of the Talmud three times."

"Yes," the old man responded. "But how much of the Talmud has gone through you?"

And I wonder about that question for myself as I interact with Scripture. How deep has it gone? What difference has it made?

—Gordon MacDonald

For more on Bible study and meditation, see reading at Hebrews 4:12–13.

³For a time is coming when people will no longer listen to sound and wholesome teaching. They will follow their own desires and will look for teachers who will tell them whatever their itching ears want to hear. ⁴They will reject the truth and chase after myths.

⁵But you should keep a clear mind in every situation. Don't be afraid of suffering for the Lord. Work at telling others the Good News, and fully carry out the ministry God has given you.

⁶As for me, my life has already been poured out as an offering to God. The time of my death is near. ⁷I have fought the good fight, I have finished the race, and I have remained faithful. ⁸And now the prize awaits me—the crown of righteousness, which the Lord, the righteous Judge, will give me on the day of his return. And the prize is not just for me but for all who eagerly look forward to his appearing.

Paul's Final Words

⁹Timothy, please come as soon as you can. ¹⁰Demas has deserted me because he loves

the things of this life and has gone to Thessalonica. Crescens has gone to Galatia, and Titus has gone to Dalmatia. ¹¹Only Luke is with me. Bring Mark with you when you come, for he will be helpful to me in my ministry. ¹²I sent Tychicus to Ephesus. ¹³When you come, be sure to bring the coat I left with Carpus at Troas. Also bring my books, and especially my papers.*

¹⁴Alexander the coppersmith did me much harm, but the Lord will judge him for what he has done. ¹⁵Be careful of him, for he fought against everything we said.

¹⁶The first time I was brought before the judge, no one came with me. Everyone abandoned me. May it not be counted against them. ¹⁷But the Lord stood with me and gave me strength so that I might preach the Good News in its entirety for all the Gentiles to hear. And he rescued me from certain death.* ¹⁸Yes, and the Lord will deliver me from every evil attack and will bring me safely into his heavenly Kingdom. All glory to God forever and ever! Amen.

Paul's Final Greetings

¹⁹Give my greetings to Priscilla and Aquila and those living in the household of Onesiphorus. ²⁰Erastus stayed at Corinth, and I left Trophimus sick at Miletus.

²¹Do your best to get here before winter. Eubulus sends you greetings, and so do Pudens, Linus, Claudia, and all the brothers and sisters.*

²²May the Lord be with your spirit. And may his grace be with all of you.

Introduction to

Titus

Background

Titus was a Greek who was brought by Paul to Jerusalem (Galatians 2:1–3), where he became an example of Paul's mission to bring the gospel message to the Gentiles. Titus probably traveled with Paul on his third missionary journey years later; Paul sent him to Corinth, even entrusting him to deliver what we know as 2 Corinthians (see 2 Corinthians 7:6–8:23). Paul and Titus had ministered together in Crete, but Paul left Titus there to organize the church (1:5). Tradition says Titus became bishop of Crete. In the epistle Paul asks Titus to join him the next winter in Greece. Titus was with Paul when he was arrested and sent to prison a second time. At Paul's request Titus then left for Dalmatia (2 Timothy 4:10). At different times, Paul referred to Titus as his "dear brother" (2 Corinthians 2:13), his "partner" (2 Corinthians 8:23), and his "true son in the faith" (1:4).

Message

Paul begins with a doctrinal statement before detailing Titus's mission to organize the Cretan church and appoint elders. Paul lays out characteristics of qualified leaders, in marked contrast to characteristics of false teachers. He stresses the importance of teaching sound doctrine. His text forms a code of conduct for Titus and his followers, emphasizing good deeds and honorable behavior among the various groups that make up the churches, along with sound behavior in the world.

Time

Paul wrote his letter to Titus circa A.D. 63, on his journey to Rome. He sent the letter with his friends Zenas and Apollos, who he knew would be traveling to Crete (3:13). Paul's plans were to winter in the western Greek town of Nicopolis, and he asked Titus to join him there once a replacement for Titus (either Artemas or Tychicus) arrived in Crete (3:12).

Outline

Titus

1 Greetings from Paul

This letter is from Paul, a slave of God and an apostle of Jesus Christ. I have been sent to proclaim faith to* those God has chosen and to teach them to know the truth that shows them how to live godly lives. ²This truth gives them confidence that they have eternal life, which God—who does not lie—promised them before the world began. ³And now at just the right time he has revealed this message, which we announce to everyone. It is by the command of God our Savior that I have been entrusted with this work for him.

⁴I am writing to Titus, my true son in the faith that we share.

May God the Father and Christ Jesus our Savior give you grace and peace.

Titus's Work in Crete

⁵I left you on the island of Crete so you could complete our work there and appoint elders in each town as I instructed you. ⁶An elder must live a blameless life. He must be faithful to his wife,* and his children must be believers who don't have a reputation for being wild or rebellious. ⁷An elder* is a manager of God's household, so he must live a blameless life. He must not be arrogant or quick-tempered; he must not be a heavy drinker,* violent, or dishonest with money.

⁸Rather, he must enjoy having guests in his home, and he must love what is good. He must live wisely and be just. He must live a devout and disciplined life. ⁹He must have a strong belief in the trustworthy message he was taught; then he will be able to encourage others with wholesome teaching and show those who oppose it where they are wrong.

¹⁰For there are many rebellious people who engage in useless talk and deceive others. This is especially true of those who insist on circumcision for salvation. ¹¹They must be silenced, because they are turning whole families away from the truth by their false teaching. And they do it only for money. ¹²Even one of their own men, a prophet from Crete, has said about them, "The people of Crete are all liars, cruel animals, and lazy gluttons."* ¹³This is true. So reprimand them sternly to make them strong in the faith. ¹⁴They must stop listening to Jewish myths and the commands of people who have turned away from the truth.

¹⁵Everything is pure to those whose hearts are pure. But nothing is pure to those who are corrupt and unbelieving, because their minds and consciences are corrupted. ¹⁶Such people claim they know God, but they deny him by the way they live. They are detestable and disobedient, worthless for doing anything good.

2 Promote Right Teaching

As for you, Titus, promote the kind of living that reflects wholesome teaching. ²Teach the older men to exercise self-control, to be worthy of respect, and to live wisely. They must have sound faith and be filled with love and patience.

1:1 Or to strengthen the faith of. **1:6** Or must have only one wife, or must be married only once; Greek reads must be the husband of one wife. **1:7a** Or An overseer, or A bishop. **1:7b** Greek must not drink too much wine. **1:12** This quotation is from Epimenides of Knossos.

Mentoring

Biblical Female Mentors
TITUS 2:3-5

The Bible is filled with prominent relationships. There's Elijah and Elisha: Elijah placed his cloak over Elisha's shoulders, symbolically signaling the beginning of Elisha's prophetic apprenticeship (1 Kings 19:19-21). There's Jesus and his disciples, the ultimate model of intense mentoring: years together traveling, talking, life-shaping. And there's Paul and Timothy: Paul poured his life into Timothy and called Timothy to similarly mentor others (1 Timothy 4:6-16; 2 Timothy 2:2).

But the ones I really connect with are the female mentors. Consider the friendship of Naomi and Ruth. We can only imagine their heart-wrenching conversations as they traveled, in their grief, to a new home (Ruth 1). We can see Ruth's willingness to be guided by Naomi as she met and was eventually courted by Boaz (Ruth 3-4).

Then there's Mary, in her jumble of emotions as she carried the secret that she was miraculously pregnant. She went straight to her godly, older relative Elizabeth; when they met they immediately spoke profound spiritual truth to each other (Luke 1:39-56). Mary stayed with Elizabeth three months; undoubtedly they had many more worshipful, truth-proclaiming, and candid conversations as they sought to answer God's calling in their lives.

And finally there are the many women of the early church (Priscilla in Acts 18:26; Lydia in Acts 16:40; Phoebe in Romans 16:1-2; and others unnamed). Through the early church we see a clear model of older women intentionally investing in younger women: setting an example of godly character, teaching others, and training younger women in marriage and family matters (Titus 2:3-5). This model of spiritual growth required the willingness of older women to put time and effort into mentoring, and it also required that the younger women have a teachable spirit that was ready and open to receive the guidance of others.

Receiving the mentoring from those more spiritually mature, in return providing mentorship to those who are growing—this is the cycle of spiritual growth God put into motion for his people. Who will *you* invest in? Who will *you* listen to?

—Kelli B. Trujillo

For more on mentoring, see reading at 1 Peter 1:21-23.

³ Similarly, teach the older women to live in a way that honors God. They must not slander others or be heavy drinkers.* Instead, they should teach others what is good. ⁴ These older women must train the younger women to love their husbands and their children, ⁵ to live wisely and be pure, to work in their homes,* to do good, and to be submissive to their husbands. Then they will not bring shame on the word of God.

⁶ In the same way, encourage the young men to live wisely. ⁷ And you yourself must be an example to them by doing good works of every kind. Let everything you do reflect the integrity and seriousness of your teaching. ⁸ Teach the truth so that your teaching can't be criticized. Then those who oppose us will be ashamed and have nothing bad to say about us.

⁹ Slaves must always obey their masters and do their best to please them. They must not talk back ¹⁰ or steal, but must show themselves to be entirely trustworthy and good.

2:3 Greek *be enslaved to much wine.*   **2:5** Some manuscripts read *to care for their homes.*

Then they will make the teaching about God our Savior attractive in every way.

[11] For the grace of God has been revealed, bringing salvation to all people. [12] And we are instructed to turn from godless living and sinful pleasures. We should live in this evil world with wisdom, righteousness, and devotion to God, [13] while we look forward with hope to that wonderful day when the glory of our great God and Savior, Jesus Christ, will be revealed. [14] He gave his life to free us from every kind of sin, to cleanse us, and to make us his very own people, totally committed to doing good deeds.

[15] You must teach these things and encourage the believers to do them. You have the authority to correct them when necessary, so don't let anyone disregard what you say.

3 Do What Is Good

Remind the believers to submit to the government and its officers. They should be obedient, always ready to do what is good. [2] They must not slander anyone and must avoid quarreling. Instead, they should be gentle and show true humility to everyone.

[3] Once we, too, were foolish and disobedient. We were misled and became slaves to many lusts and pleasures. Our lives were full of evil and envy, and we hated each other.

[4] But—"When God our Savior revealed his kindness and love, [5] he saved us, not because of the righteous things we had done, but because of his mercy. He washed away our sins, giving us a new birth and new life through the Holy Spirit.* [6] He generously poured out the Spirit upon us through Jesus Christ our Savior. [7] Because of his grace he declared us righteous and gave us confidence that we will inherit eternal life." [8] This is a trustworthy saying, and I want you to insist on these teachings so that all who trust in God will devote themselves to doing good. These teachings are good and beneficial for everyone.

[9] Do not get involved in foolish discussions about spiritual pedigrees* or in quarrels and fights about obedience to Jewish laws. These things are useless and a waste of time. [10] If people are causing divisions among you, give a first and second warning. After that, have nothing more to do with them. [11] For people like that have turned away from the truth, and their own sins condemn them.

Paul's Final Remarks and Greetings

[12] I am planning to send either Artemas or Tychicus to you. As soon as one of them arrives, do your best to meet me at Nicopolis, for I have decided to stay there for the winter. [13] Do everything you can to help Zenas the lawyer and Apollos with their trip. See that they are given everything they need. [14] Our people must learn to do good by meeting the urgent needs of others; then they will not be unproductive.

[15] Everybody here sends greetings. Please give my greetings to the believers—all who love us.

May God's grace be with you all.

3:5 Greek *He saved us through the washing of regeneration and renewing of the Holy Spirit.*   **3:9** Or *spiritual genealogies.*

Introduction to
Philemon

Background

This letter addresses the personal concerns of two Christians, Philemon and Onesimus. Philemon lived in Colosse and was one of Paul's converts (Colossians 4:9). Onesimus, whose name means "useful," was a slave in Philemon's household. After stealing from his master, Onesimus escaped to Rome. Under Roman law, Philemon could have punished him by death if he was captured. At some point, Onesimus found Paul in Rome and became a believer.

Message

Paul, who refers to himself as being "a prisoner for preaching the Good News about Christ Jesus" (1:1, 9), is sending Onesimus back to the household of Philemon, appealing to Philemon to welcome Onesimus in the same way he would welcome Paul: not as a slave but as a fellow believer in Christ (1:15–17). Paul assures Philemon that he will pay any damages or debts Onesimus owes him, thus stepping in to intercede for Onesimus. Not only does Paul urge Philemon to act with Christ's love; he is also confident that love will carry the day: "I am confident as I write this letter that you will do what I ask and even more!" (1:21).

Time

Paul wrote the Epistle to Philemon when he was under house arrest in Rome in A.D. 60 or 61.

Outline

Philemon

Greetings from Paul

This letter is from Paul, a prisoner for preaching the Good News about Christ Jesus, and from our brother Timothy.

I am writing to Philemon, our beloved co-worker, ²and to our sister Apphia, and to our fellow soldier Archippus, and to the church that meets in your* house.

³May God our Father and the Lord Jesus Christ give you grace and peace.

Paul's Thanksgiving and Prayer

⁴I always thank my God when I pray for you, Philemon, ⁵because I keep hearing about your faith in the Lord Jesus and your love for all of God's people. ⁶And I am praying that you will put into action the generosity that comes from your faith as you understand and experience all the good things we have in Christ. ⁷Your love has given me much joy and comfort, my brother, for your kindness has often refreshed the hearts of God's people.

Paul's Appeal for Onesimus

⁸That is why I am boldly asking a favor of you. I could demand it in the name of Christ because it is the right thing for you to do. ⁹But because of our love, I prefer simply to ask you. Consider this as a request from me—Paul, an old man and now also a prisoner for the sake of Christ Jesus.*

¹⁰I appeal to you to show kindness to my child, Onesimus. I became his father in the faith while here in prison. ¹¹Onesimus* hasn't been of much use to you in the past, but now he is very useful to both of us. ¹²I am sending him back to you, and with him comes my own heart.

¹³I wanted to keep him here with me while I am in these chains for preaching the Good News, and he would have helped me on your behalf. ¹⁴But I didn't want to do anything without your consent. I wanted you to help because you were willing, not because you were forced. ¹⁵It seems you lost Onesimus for a little while so that you could have him back forever. ¹⁶He is no longer like a slave to you. He is more than a slave, for he is a beloved brother, especially to me. Now he will mean much more to you, both as a man and as a brother in the Lord.

¹⁷So if you consider me your partner, welcome him as you would welcome me. ¹⁸If he has wronged you in any way or owes you anything, charge it to me. ¹⁹I, PAUL, WRITE THIS WITH MY OWN HAND: I WILL REPAY IT. AND I WON'T MENTION THAT YOU OWE ME YOUR VERY SOUL!

²⁰Yes, my brother, please do me this favor* for the Lord's sake. Give me this encouragement in Christ.

²¹I am confident as I write this letter that you will do what I ask and even more! ²²One more thing—please prepare a guest room for me, for I am hoping

---

2 Throughout this letter, *you* and *your* are singular except in verses 3, 22, and 25.   **9** Or *a prisoner of Christ Jesus.*
11 *Onesimus* means "useful."   **20** Greek *onaimen,* a play on the name Onesimus.

Acceptance

The High Calling of Women
PHILEMON

Jesus used females as key figures in many of his parables and other teachings. Mary Magdalene, Martha, and her sister, Mary, were among Jesus' closest friends. Clearly, Jesus loved and valued women, making this visible by including their voices and experiences throughout his work.

This important role for women continued in the early church. Scripture records the examples of female evangelists (Mark 7:24-30; John 4:5-42; 20:17; Philippians 4:2-3); deacons (Romans 16:1-2); teachers (Acts 18:24-26; Colossians 3:16); leaders of house churches (Acts 16:13-15, 40; 18:1-3, 18, 24-26; Romans 16:3; 1 Corinthians 1:11; Colossians 4:15; Philemon 1:2; and 2 John 1:1); and women such as Mary, Junia, Tryphena, Tryphosa, and Persis who "worked so hard for the Lord" (Romans 16:6-7, 12).

And church history records examples of God using women in powerful ways to build his church. For example, the earliest Western translation of Scripture was the work of a fourth-century male-female translation team—Paula and Jerome. Jerome, a prominent early church leader, hailed Paula's mastery of Hebrew. In gratitude Jerome dedicated much of his work to her.

Macrina (330-379) was the older sister to Basil the Great and Gregory of Nyssa, and both credit her for their theological education. Insisting that humility and love are the fruit of scholarship, Basil (famous for his defense of the Nicene Creed) and Gregory (known for his theological understanding of the Holy Spirit) both called Macrina "teacher."

Hildegard of Bingen was celebrated for her learning, holiness, and unceasing service. She was a physician, composer, and political leader, and her counsel was sought by church leaders and kings. Hildegard revived the spiritual health of a church that had become morally and spiritually indifferent in the twelfth century.

Catherine of Siena worked tirelessly to oppose corruption and abuse of power in the fourteenth century. She demanded that bishops and popes lead righteous and humble lives. She cared for the victims of the plague and confronted the greed, corruption, and spiritual poverty of church leaders.

God has used women powerfully to build his church. How does he desire to use you today? Will you answer the call?

—Mimi Haddad

For more on acceptance, see reading at Hebrews 12:1-2.

that God will answer your prayers and let me return to you soon.

Paul's Final Greetings
²³ Epaphras, my fellow prisoner in Christ Jesus, sends you his greetings. ²⁴ So do Mark, Aristarchus, Demas, and Luke, my co-workers.

²⁵ May the grace of the Lord Jesus Christ be with your spirit.

Hebrews

Background

In the first century followers of Christ were often subject to persecution from their fellow citizens. Hebrews is a letter of encouragement to help Jewish believers in Christ who struggled in their newfound faith. The authorship of Hebrews is not as clear as that of other New Testament books. Eastern and Western churches debated between Paul, Barnabas, Luke, Apollos, or Clement as the book's author. From about the fourth century to the late 1800s, most Christians believed Paul to be the author. But this epistle does not bear Paul's usual salutation nor is it directed to a local church.

Message

To encourage believers who wonder whether Christianity is worth the pain of persecution, the writer discusses Christ's superiority to prophets, angels, Moses, and the high priests. For the writer, Christ is simply a better or greater way (1:4). He is over all and above all and deserves the believers' worship. He is the perfect fulfillment of the old covenant and the establisher of the new. The Book of Hebrews includes an Old Testament "hall of faith," commending men and women who walked with God and persevered in their faith, sometimes suffering persecution and death. Regardless of their trials, believers are called and equipped in Christ to become more like him each day. Christ alone—"the one who mediates the new covenant between God and people" (12:24)—is sufficient for salvation.

Time

Since the Epistle to the Hebrews does not mention the destruction of Jerusalem, which occurred in A.D. 70, it was probably written between A.D. 64 and 68.

Outline

Hebrews

1

Jesus Christ Is God's Son

Long ago God spoke many times and in many ways to our ancestors through the prophets. ²And now in these final days, he has spoken to us through his Son. God promised everything to the Son as an inheritance, and through the Son he created the universe. ³The Son radiates God's own glory and expresses the very character of God, and he sustains everything by the mighty power of his command. When he had cleansed us from our sins, he sat down in the place of honor at the right hand of the majestic God in heaven. ⁴This shows that the Son is far greater than the angels, just as the name God gave him is greater than their names.

The Son Is Greater Than the Angels

⁵For God never said to any angel what he said to Jesus:

"You are my Son.
  Today I have become your Father.*"

God also said,

"I will be his Father,
  and he will be my Son."*

⁶And when he brought his supreme* Son into the world, God said,*

"Let all of God's angels worship him."*

⁷Regarding the angels, he says,

"He sends his angels like the winds,
  his servants like flames of fire."*

⁸But to the Son he says,

"Your throne, O God, endures forever and ever.
  You rule with a scepter of justice.
⁹ You love justice and hate evil.
  Therefore, O God, your God has anointed you,
    pouring out the oil of joy on you more than on anyone else."*

¹⁰He also says to the Son,

"In the beginning, Lord, you laid the foundation of the earth
  and made the heavens with your hands.
¹¹ They will perish, but you remain forever.
  They will wear out like old clothing.
¹² You will fold them up like a cloak
  and discard them like old clothing.
But you are always the same;
  you will live forever."*

1:5a Or Today I reveal you as my Son. Ps 2:7.   **1:5b** 2 Sam 7:14.   **1:6a** Or firstborn.   **1:6b** Or when he again brings his supreme Son [or firstborn Son] into the world, God will say.   **1:6c** Deut 32:43.   **1:7** Ps 104:4 (Greek version).   **1:8-9** Ps 45:6-7.
1:10-12 Ps 102:25-27.

¹³And God never said to any of the angels,

"Sit in the place of honor at my right hand
until I humble your enemies,
making them a footstool under your
feet."*

¹⁴Therefore, angels are only servants—spirits sent to care for people who will inherit salvation.

2 A Warning against Drifting Away

So we must listen very carefully to the truth we have heard, or we may drift away from it. ²For the message God delivered through angels has always stood firm, and every violation of the law and every act of disobedience was punished. ³So what makes us think we can escape if we ignore this great salvation that was first announced by the Lord Jesus himself and then delivered to us by those who heard him speak? ⁴And God confirmed the message by giving signs and wonders and various miracles and gifts of the Holy Spirit whenever he chose.

Jesus, the Man

⁵And furthermore, it is not angels who will control the future world we are talking about. ⁶For in one place the Scriptures say,

"What are mere mortals that you should
think about them,
or a son of man* that you should care
for him?
⁷ Yet you made them only a little lower
than the angels
and crowned them with glory and
honor.*
⁸ You gave them authority over all things."*

Now when it says "all things," it means nothing is left out. But we have not yet seen all things put under their authority. ⁹What we do see is Jesus, who was given a position "a little lower than the angels"; and because he suffered death for us, he is now "crowned with glory and honor." Yes, by God's grace, Jesus tasted death for everyone. ¹⁰God, for whom and through whom everything was made, chose to bring many children into glory. And it was only right that he should

make Jesus, through his suffering, a perfect leader, fit to bring them into their salvation. ¹¹So now Jesus and the ones he makes holy have the same Father. That is why Jesus is not ashamed to call them his brothers and sisters.* ¹²For he said to God,

"I will proclaim your name to my
brothers and sisters.
I will praise you among your
assembled people."*

¹³He also said,

"I will put my trust in him,"
that is, "I and the children God has
given me."*

¹⁴Because God's children are human beings—made of flesh and blood—the Son also became flesh and blood. For only as a human being could he die, and only by dying could he break the power of the devil, who had* the power of death. ¹⁵Only in this way could he set free all who have lived their lives as slaves to the fear of dying.

¹⁶We also know that the Son did not come to help angels; he came to help the descendants of Abraham. ¹⁷Therefore, it was necessary for him to be made in every respect like us, his brothers and sisters,* so that he could be our merciful and faithful High Priest before God. Then he could offer a sacrifice that would take away the sins of the people. ¹⁸Since he himself has gone through suffering and testing, he is able to help us when we are being tested.

3 Jesus Is Greater Than Moses

And so, dear brothers and sisters who belong to God and* are partners with those called to heaven, think carefully about this Jesus whom we declare to be God's messenger* and High Priest. ²For he was faithful to God, who appointed him, just as Moses served faithfully when he was entrusted with God's entire* house.

³But Jesus deserves far more glory than Moses, just as a person who builds a house deserves more praise than the house itself. ⁴For every house has a builder, but the one who built everything is God.

1:13 Ps 110:1. **2:6** Or *the Son of Man.* **2:7** Some manuscripts add *You gave them charge of everything you made.* **2:6-8** Ps 8:4-6 (Greek version). **2:11** Greek *brothers;* also in 2:12. **2:12** Ps 22:22. **2:13** Isa 8:17-18. **2:14** Or *has.* **2:17** Greek *like the brothers.* **3:1a** Greek *And so, holy brothers who.* **3:1b** Greek *God's apostle.* **3:2** Some manuscripts do not include *entire.*

Confession

Taking "Little" Sins Seriously

HEBREWS 3:12–15

One night I stumbled across Hebrews 3:13: "Warn each other every day . . . so that none of you will be deceived by sin and hardened against God." No sooner had I closed my Bible than a scene from a few days earlier replayed in my mind. At the gas station, my gas cap was somehow lost. The attendant found one—a stainless steel cap—and asked me if it was mine. I hardly looked at it and said yes, but after he put it on my van, I realized it wasn't mine. I felt guilty but just let it slide.

Hebrews 3:13 convicted me: *I was a casualty of sin's deceitfulness.* The next day I returned to the gas station to apologize and give the attendant a new gas cap.

Although you may think I made a big deal over nothing, I knew that making excuses for my sin—though it was "small"—would harden me and callous my heart.

I've been through enough of those minor "gas cap" skirmishes against sin to know our struggle to be holy is a major battle. No matter how major or minor a sin seems, it still grieves God. When I was driving around with that gas cap and excusing my actions, the Spirit was trying to get through to me: *Joni, you're off course here. Are you listening? Do you care that this hurts me?*

If you're tired of your struggle against sin, if you're weary of its subtle deceit or the way it hardens your heart, don't give up. Instead, be ready and willing to confess, turn to God, and strive to be holy. Invite God to give you a sensitive conscience and a fresh love for the things that please and delight him. Holy living is demanding, but its rewards are precious.

—*Joni Eareckson Tada*

For more on confession, see reading at James 5:16.

---

⁵Moses was certainly faithful in God's house as a servant. His work was an illustration of the truths God would reveal later. ⁶But Christ, as the Son, is in charge of God's entire house. And we are God's house, if we keep our courage and remain confident in our hope in Christ.*

⁷That is why the Holy Spirit says,

"Today when you hear his voice,
⁸   don't harden your hearts
  as Israel did when they rebelled,
    when they tested me in the wilderness.
⁹ There your ancestors tested and tried my
      patience,
    even though they saw my miracles for
      forty years.

¹⁰ So I was angry with them, and I said,
  'Their hearts always turn away from me.
  They refuse to do what I tell them.'
¹¹ So in my anger I took an oath:
  'They will never enter my place of rest.'"*

¹²Be careful then, dear brothers and sisters.* Make sure that your own hearts are not evil and unbelieving, turning you away from the living God. ¹³You must warn each other every day, while it is still "today," so that none of you will be deceived by sin and hardened against God. ¹⁴For if we are faithful to the end, trusting God just as firmly as when we first believed, we will share in all that belongs to Christ. ¹⁵Remember what it says:

3:6 Some manuscripts add *faithful to the end.*   **3:7-11** Ps 95:7-11.   **3:12** Greek *brothers.*

"Today when you hear his voice,
    don't harden your hearts
    as Israel did when they rebelled."*

¹⁶And who was it who rebelled against God, even though they heard his voice? Wasn't it the people Moses led out of Egypt? ¹⁷And who made God angry for forty years? Wasn't it the people who sinned, whose corpses lay in the wilderness? ¹⁸And to whom was God speaking when he took an oath that they would never enter his rest? Wasn't it the people who disobeyed him? ¹⁹So we see that because of their unbelief they were not able to enter his rest.

4 Promised Rest for God's People

God's promise of entering his rest still stands, so we ought to tremble with fear that some of you might fail to experience it. ²For this good news—that God has prepared this rest—has been announced to us just as it was to them. But it did them no good because they didn't share the faith of those who listened to God.* ³For only we who believe can enter his rest. As for the others, God said,

"In my anger I took an oath:
    'They will never enter my place of rest,'"*

even though this rest has been ready since he made the world. ⁴We know it is ready because of the place in the Scriptures where it mentions the seventh day: "On the seventh day God rested from all his work."* ⁵But in the other passage God said, "They will never enter my place of rest."*

⁶So God's rest is there for people to enter, but those who first heard this good news failed to enter because they disobeyed God. ⁷So God set another time for entering his rest, and that time is today. God announced this through David much later in the words already quoted:

"Today when you hear his voice,
    don't harden your hearts."*

⁸Now if Joshua had succeeded in giving them this rest, God would not have spoken about another day of rest still to come. ⁹So there is a special rest* still waiting for the people of God. ¹⁰For all who have entered into God's rest have rested from their labors, just as God did after creating the world. ¹¹So let us do our best to enter that rest. But if we disobey God, as the people of Israel did, we will fall.

¹²For the word of God is alive and powerful. It is sharper than the sharpest two-edged sword, cutting between soul and spirit, between joint and marrow. It exposes our innermost thoughts and desires. ¹³Nothing in all creation is hidden from God. Everything is naked and exposed before his eyes, and he is the one to whom we are accountable.

Christ Is Our High Priest

¹⁴So then, since we have a great High Priest who has entered heaven, Jesus the Son of God, let us hold firmly to what we believe. ¹⁵This High Priest of ours understands our weaknesses, for he faced all of the same testings we do, yet he did not sin. ¹⁶So let us come boldly to the throne of our gracious God. There we will receive his mercy, and we will find grace to help us when we need it most.

5

Every high priest is a man chosen to represent other people in their dealings with God. He presents their gifts to God and offers sacrifices for their sins. ²And he is able to deal gently with ignorant and wayward people because he himself is subject to the same weaknesses. ³That is why he must offer sacrifices for his own sins as well as theirs.

⁴And no one can become a high priest simply because he wants such an honor. He must be called by God for this work, just as Aaron was. ⁵That is why Christ did not honor himself by assuming he could become High Priest. No, he was chosen by God, who said to him,

"You are my Son.
    Today I have become your Father.*"

⁶And in another passage God said to him,

"You are a priest forever in the order of Melchizedek."*

⁷While Jesus was here on earth, he offered prayers and pleadings, with a loud cry and tears, to the one who could

---

3:15 Ps 95:7-8.   **4:2** Some manuscripts read *they didn't combine what they heard with faith.*   **4:3** Ps 95:11.   **4:4** Gen 2:2.   **4:5** Ps 95:11.
4:7 Ps 95:7-8.   **4:9** Or *a Sabbath rest.*   **5:5** Or *Today I reveal you as my Son.* Ps 2:7.   **5:6** Ps 110:4.

rescue him from death. And God heard his prayers because of his deep reverence for God. [8]Even though Jesus was God's Son, he learned obedience from the things he suffered. [9]In this way, God qualified him as a perfect High Priest, and he became the source of eternal salvation for all those who obey him. [10]And God designated him to be a High Priest in the order of Melchizedek.

A Call to Spiritual Growth

[11]There is much more we would like to say about this, but it is difficult to explain, especially since you are spiritually dull and don't seem to listen. [12]You have been believers so long now that you ought to be teaching others. Instead, you need someone to teach you again the basic things about God's word.* You are like babies who need milk and can-

Q&A — Reigniting a Passion for Scripture

HEBREWS 4:12–13

Lately my time in the Bible has felt stale. How can I regain a passion for God's Word?

We've all had those moments in which we open our Bibles and read just because that's what we're "supposed to do." When we find ourselves with a lack of passion, we need to remember that the only way passion can be stirred within us is by the Holy Spirit. We cannot manufacture passion for God; only the Holy Spirit can do that.

When you're feeling passionless about God's Word, take that feeling of indifference to God as David did in Psalm 119:36–37: "Give me an eagerness for your laws . . . ! Turn my eyes from worthless things, and give me life through your word." David was saying, "I need you to give me some passion about your Word. It's not there on its own, God. I need you to revive my heart to your ways."

You can say the same things to God: *I can't make myself want to do what you're asking me to do right now. Create a passion in me for your Word and your ways; that's what I desire.*

I'd also challenge you to consider your mind-set as you approach God's Word. We get so used to approaching Scripture with familiarity and casualness that we forget that it's not just a historical book, but illuminated by the Holy Spirit. He causes it to become specific to our lives—living, active, and sharper than any two-edged sword (Hebrews 4:12). So don't approach it as something just to check off the list. Instead, try your best to come to the Scriptures with an expectant heart that you can and will hear the voice of God speaking clearly to you.

—*Priscilla Shirer*

For more on Bible study and meditation, see reading at James 1:22–25.

5:12 Or *about the oracles of God.*

not eat solid food. ¹³For someone who lives on milk is still an infant and doesn't know how to do what is right. ¹⁴Solid food is for those who are mature, who through training have the skill to recognize the difference between right and wrong.

6 So let us stop going over the basic teachings about Christ again and again. Let us go on instead and become mature in our understanding. Surely we don't need to start again with the fundamental importance of repenting from evil deeds* and placing our faith in God. ²You don't need further instruction about baptisms, the laying on of hands, the resurrection of the dead, and eternal judgment. ³And so, God willing, we will move forward to further understanding.

⁴For it is impossible to bring back to repentance those who were once enlightened—those who have experienced the good things of heaven and shared in the Holy Spirit, ⁵who have tasted the goodness of the word of God and the power of the age to come—⁶and who then turn away from God. It is impossible to bring such people back to repentance; by rejecting the Son of God, they themselves are nailing him to the cross once again and holding him up to public shame.

⁷When the ground soaks up the falling rain and bears a good crop for the farmer, it has God's blessing. ⁸But if a field bears thorns and thistles, it is useless. The farmer will soon condemn that field and burn it.

⁹Dear friends, even though we are talking this way, we really don't believe it applies to you. We are confident that you are meant for better things, things that come with salvation. ¹⁰For God is not unjust. He will not forget how hard you have worked for him and how you have shown your love to him by caring for other believers,* as you still do. ¹¹Our great desire is that you will keep on loving others as long as life lasts, in order to make certain that what you hope for will come true. ¹²Then you will not become spiritually dull and indifferent. Instead, you will follow the example of those who are going to inherit God's promises because of their faith and endurance.

God's Promises Bring Hope

¹³For example, there was God's promise to Abraham. Since there was no one greater to swear by, God took an oath in his own name, saying:

¹⁴ "I will certainly bless you,
    and I will multiply your descendants
      beyond number."*

¹⁵Then Abraham waited patiently, and he received what God had promised.

¹⁶Now when people take an oath, they call on someone greater than themselves to hold them to it. And without any question that oath is binding. ¹⁷God also bound himself with an oath, so that those who received the promise could be perfectly sure that he would never change his mind. ¹⁸So God has given both his promise and his oath. These two things are unchangeable because it is impossible for God to lie. Therefore, we who have fled to him for refuge can have great confidence as we hold to the hope that lies before us. ¹⁹This hope is a strong and trustworthy anchor for our souls. It leads us through the curtain into God's inner sanctuary. ²⁰Jesus has already gone in there for us. He has become our eternal High Priest in the order of Melchizedek.

7 Melchizedek Is Greater Than Abraham

This Melchizedek was king of the city of Salem and also a priest of God Most High. When Abraham was returning home after winning a great battle against the kings, Melchizedek met him and blessed him. ²Then Abraham took a tenth of all he had captured in battle and gave it to Melchizedek. The name Melchizedek means "king of justice," and king of Salem means "king of peace." ³There is no record of his father or mother or any of his ancestors—no beginning or end to his life. He remains a priest forever, resembling the Son of God.

⁴Consider then how great this Melchizedek was. Even Abraham, the great patriarch of Israel, recognized this by giving him a tenth of what he had taken in battle. ⁵Now the law of Moses required that the priests, who are descendants of Levi, must collect a tithe from the rest of the people of Israel,*

who are also descendants of Abraham. ⁶But Melchizedek, who was not a descendant of Levi, collected a tenth from Abraham. And Melchizedek placed a blessing upon Abraham, the one who had already received the promises of God. ⁷And without question, the person who has the power to give a blessing is greater than the one who is blessed.

⁸The priests who collect tithes are men who die, so Melchizedek is greater than they are, because we are told that he lives on. ⁹In addition, we might even say that these Levites—the ones who collect the tithe— paid a tithe to Melchizedek when their ancestor Abraham paid a tithe to him. ¹⁰For although Levi wasn't born yet, the seed from which he came was in Abraham's body when Melchizedek collected the tithe from him.

¹¹So if the priesthood of Levi, on which the law was based, could have achieved the perfection God intended, why did God need to establish a different priesthood, with a priest in the order of Melchizedek instead of the order of Levi and Aaron?*

¹²And if the priesthood is changed, the law must also be changed to permit it. ¹³For the priest we are talking about belongs to a different tribe, whose members have never served at the altar as priests. ¹⁴What I mean is, our Lord came from the tribe of Judah, and Moses never mentioned priests coming from that tribe.

Jesus Is like Melchizedek

¹⁵This change has been made very clear since a different priest, who is like Melchizedek, has appeared. ¹⁶Jesus became a priest, not by meeting the physical requirement of belonging to the tribe of Levi, but by the power of a life that cannot be destroyed. ¹⁷And the psalmist pointed this out when he prophesied,

"You are a priest forever in the order of
  Melchizedek."*

¹⁸Yes, the old requirement about the priesthood was set aside because it was weak and useless. ¹⁹For the law never made anything perfect. But now we have confidence in a better hope, through which we draw near to God.

²⁰This new system was established with a solemn oath. Aaron's descendants became priests without such an oath, ²¹but there was an oath regarding Jesus. For God said to him,

"The Lord has taken an oath and will
  not break his vow:
  'You are a priest forever.'"*

²²Because of this oath, Jesus is the one who guarantees this better covenant with God.

²³There were many priests under the old system, for death prevented them from remaining in office. ²⁴But because Jesus lives forever, his priesthood lasts forever. ²⁵Therefore he is able, once and forever, to save* those who come to God through him. He lives forever to intercede with God on their behalf.

²⁶He is the kind of high priest we need because he is holy and blameless, unstained by sin. He has been set apart from sinners and has been given the highest place of honor in heaven.* ²⁷Unlike those other high priests, he does not need to offer sacrifices every day. They did this for their own sins first and then for the sins of the people. But Jesus did this once for all when he offered himself as the sacrifice for the people's sins. ²⁸The law appointed high priests who were limited by human weakness. But after the law was given, God appointed his Son with an oath, and his Son has been made the perfect High Priest forever.

8 Christ Is Our High Priest

Here is the main point: We have a High Priest who sat down in the place of honor beside the throne of the majestic God in heaven. ²There he ministers in the heavenly Tabernacle,* the true place of worship that was built by the Lord and not by human hands.

³And since every high priest is required to offer gifts and sacrifices, our High Priest must make an offering, too. ⁴If he were here on earth, he would not even be a priest, since there already are priests who offer the gifts required by the law. ⁵They serve in a system of worship that is only a copy, a shadow of the real one in heaven. For when Moses was

---

getting ready to build the Tabernacle, God gave him this warning: "Be sure that you make everything according to the pattern I have shown you here on the mountain."*

⁶But now Jesus, our High Priest, has been given a ministry that is far superior to the old priesthood, for he is the one who mediates for us a far better covenant with God, based on better promises.

⁷If the first covenant had been faultless, there would have been no need for a second covenant to replace it. ⁸But when God found fault with the people, he said:

"The day is coming, says the LORD,
    when I will make a new covenant
    with the people of Israel and Judah.
⁹ This covenant will not be like the one
    I made with their ancestors
when I took them by the hand
    and led them out of the land of Egypt.
They did not remain faithful to my
        covenant,
    so I turned my back on them, says the
        LORD.
¹⁰ But this is the new covenant I will make
    with the people of Israel on that day,*
        says the LORD:
I will put my laws in their minds,
    and I will write them on their hearts.
I will be their God,
    and they will be my people.
¹¹ And they will not need to teach their
        neighbors,
    nor will they need to teach their
        relatives,*
    saying, 'You should know the LORD.'
For everyone, from the least to the
        greatest,
    will know me already.
¹² And I will forgive their wickedness,
    and I will never again remember their
        sins."*

¹³When God speaks of a "new" covenant, it means he has made the first one obsolete. It is now out of date and will soon disappear.

9 Old Rules about Worship

That first covenant between God and Israel had regulations for worship and a place of worship here on earth. ²There were two rooms in that Tabernacle.* In the first room were a lampstand, a table, and sacred loaves of bread on the table. This room was called the Holy Place. ³Then there was a curtain, and behind the curtain was the second room* called the Most Holy Place. ⁴In that room were a gold incense altar and a wooden chest called the Ark of the Covenant, which was covered with gold on all sides. Inside the Ark were a gold jar containing manna, Aaron's staff that sprouted leaves, and the stone tablets of the covenant. ⁵Above the Ark were the cherubim of divine glory, whose wings stretched out over the Ark's cover, the place of atonement. But we cannot explain these things in detail now.

⁶When these things were all in place, the priests regularly entered the first room* as they performed their religious duties. ⁷But only the high priest ever entered the Most Holy Place, and only once a year. And he always offered blood for his own sins and for the sins the people had committed in ignorance. ⁸By these regulations the Holy Spirit revealed that the entrance to the Most Holy Place was not freely open as long as the Tabernacle* and the system it represented were still in use.

⁹This is an illustration pointing to the present time. For the gifts and sacrifices that the priests offer are not able to cleanse the consciences of the people who bring them. ¹⁰For that old system deals only with food and drink and various cleansing ceremonies—physical regulations that were in effect only until a better system could be established.

Christ Is the Perfect Sacrifice

¹¹So Christ has now become the High Priest over all the good things that have come.* He has entered that greater, more perfect Tabernacle in heaven, which was not made by human hands and is not part of this created world. ¹²With his own blood—not the blood of goats and calves—he entered the Most Holy Place once for all time and secured our redemption forever.

¹³Under the old system, the blood of goats and bulls and the ashes of a young cow could cleanse people's bodies from

8:5 Exod 25:40; 26:30.   **8:10** Greek *after those days.*   **8:11** Greek *their brother.*   **8:8-12** Jer 31:31-34.   **9:2** Or *tent;* also in 9:11, 21.   **9:3** Greek *second tent.*   **9:6** Greek *first tent.*   **9:8** Or *the first room;* Greek reads *the first tent.*   **9:11** Some manuscripts read *that are about to come.*

ceremonial impurity. [14] Just think how much more the blood of Christ will purify our consciences from sinful deeds* so that we can worship the living God. For by the power of the eternal Spirit, Christ offered himself to God as a perfect sacrifice for our sins. [15] That is why he is the one who mediates a new covenant between God and people, so that all who are called can receive the eternal inheritance God has promised them. For Christ died to set them free from the penalty of the sins they had committed under that first covenant.

[16] Now when someone leaves a will,* it is necessary to prove that the person who made it is dead.* [17] The will goes into effect only after the person's death. While the person who made it is still alive, the will cannot be put into effect.

[18] That is why even the first covenant was put into effect with the blood of an animal. [19] For after Moses had read each of God's commandments to all the people, he took the blood of calves and goats,* along with water, and sprinkled both the book of God's law and all the people, using hyssop branches and scarlet wool. [20] Then he said, "This blood confirms the covenant God has made with you."* [21] And in the same way, he sprinkled blood on the Tabernacle and on everything used for worship. [22] In fact, according to the law of Moses, nearly everything was purified with blood. For without the shedding of blood, there is no forgiveness.

[23] That is why the Tabernacle and everything in it, which were copies of things in heaven, had to be purified by the blood of animals. But the real things in heaven had to be purified with far better sacrifices than the blood of animals.

[24] For Christ did not enter into a holy place made with human hands, which was only a copy of the true one in heaven. He entered into heaven itself to appear now before God on our behalf. [25] And he did not enter heaven to offer himself again and again, like the high priest here on earth who enters the Most Holy Place year after year with the blood of an animal. [26] If that had been necessary, Christ would have had to die again and again, ever since the world began. But now, once for all time, he has appeared at the end of the age* to remove sin by his own death as a sacrifice.

[27] And just as each person is destined to die once and after that comes judgment, [28] so also Christ died once for all time as a sacrifice to take away the sins of many people. He will come again, not to deal with our sins, but to bring salvation to all who are eagerly waiting for him.

10 Christ's Sacrifice Once for All

The old system under the law of Moses was only a shadow, a dim preview of the good things to come, not the good things themselves. The sacrifices under that system were repeated again and again, year after year, but they were never able to provide perfect cleansing for those who came to worship. [2] If they could have provided perfect cleansing, the sacrifices would have stopped, for the worshipers would have been purified once for all time, and their feelings of guilt would have disappeared.

[3] But instead, those sacrifices actually reminded them of their sins year after year. [4] For it is not possible for the blood of bulls and goats to take away sins. [5] That is why, when Christ* came into the world, he said to God,

"You did not want animal sacrifices or
    sin offerings.
But you have given me a body to offer.
[6] You were not pleased with burnt
    offerings
    or other offerings for sin.
[7] Then I said, 'Look, I have come to do
    your will, O God—
    as is written about me in the
    Scriptures.'"*

[8] First, Christ said, "You did not want animal sacrifices or sin offerings or burnt offerings or other offerings for sin, nor were you pleased with them" (though they are required by the law of Moses). [9] Then he said, "Look, I have come to do your will." He cancels the first covenant in order to put the second into effect. [10] For God's will was for us to be made holy by the sacrifice of the body of Jesus Christ, once for all time.

9:14 Greek *from dead works.* **9:16a** Or *covenant;* also in 9:17. **9:16b** Or *Now when someone makes a covenant, it is necessary to ratify it with the death of a sacrifice.* **9:19** Some manuscripts do not include *and goats.* **9:20** Exod 24:8. **9:26** Greek *the ages.* **10:5** Greek *he;* also in 10:8. **10:5-7** Ps 40:6-8 (Greek version).

¹¹Under the old covenant, the priest stands and ministers before the altar day after day, offering the same sacrifices again and again, which can never take away sins. ¹²But our High Priest offered himself to God as a single sacrifice for sins, good for all time. Then he sat down in the place of honor at God's right hand. ¹³There he waits until his enemies are humbled and made a footstool under his feet. ¹⁴For by that one offering he forever made perfect those who are being made holy.

¹⁵And the Holy Spirit also testifies that this is so. For he says,

¹⁶ "This is the new covenant I will make
    with my people on that day,* says the
    Lord:
I will put my laws in their hearts,
    and I will write them on their minds."*

¹⁷Then he says,

"I will never again remember
    their sins and lawless deeds."*

¹⁸And when sins have been forgiven, there is no need to offer any more sacrifices.

A Call to Persevere

¹⁹And so, dear brothers and sisters,* we can boldly enter heaven's Most Holy Place because of the blood of Jesus. ²⁰By his death,* Jesus opened a new and life-giving way through the curtain into the Most Holy Place. ²¹And since we have a great High Priest who rules over God's house, ²²let us go right into the presence of God with sincere hearts fully trusting him. For our guilty consciences have been sprinkled with Christ's blood to make us clean, and our bodies have been washed with pure water. ²³Let us hold tightly without wavering to the hope we affirm, for God can be trusted to keep his promise. ²⁴Let us think of ways to motivate one another to acts of love and good works. ²⁵And let us not neglect our meeting together, as some people do, but encourage one another, especially now that the day of his return is drawing near.

²⁶Dear friends, if we deliberately continue sinning after we have received knowledge of the truth, there is no longer any sacrifice that will cover these sins. ²⁷There is only the terrible expectation of God's judgment and the raging fire that will consume his enemies. ²⁸For anyone who refused to obey the law of Moses was put to death without mercy on the testimony of two or three witnesses. ²⁹Just think how much worse the punishment will be for those who have trampled on the Son of God, and have treated the blood of the covenant, which made us holy, as if it were common and unholy, and have insulted and disdained the Holy Spirit who brings God's mercy to us. ³⁰For we know the one who said,

"I will take revenge.
    I will pay them back."*

He also said,

"The Lord will judge his own people."*

³¹It is a terrible thing to fall into the hands of the living God.

³²Think back on those early days when you first learned about Christ.* Remember how you remained faithful even though it meant terrible suffering. ³³Sometimes you were exposed to public ridicule and were beaten, and sometimes you helped others who were suffering the same things. ³⁴You suffered along with those who were thrown into jail, and when all you owned was taken from you, you accepted it with joy. You knew there were better things waiting for you that will last forever.

³⁵So do not throw away this confident trust in the Lord. Remember the great reward it brings you! ³⁶Patient endurance is what you need now, so that you will continue to do God's will. Then you will receive all that he has promised.

³⁷ "For in just a little while,
    the Coming One will come and not
        delay.
³⁸ And my righteous ones will live by faith.*
    But I will take no pleasure in anyone
        who turns away."*

³⁹But we are not like those who turn away from God to their own destruction. We are the faithful ones, whose souls will be saved.

10:16a Greek *after those days.* 10:16b Jer 31:33a. 10:17 Jer 31:34b. 10:19 Greek *brothers.* 10:20 Greek *Through his flesh.* 10:30a Deut 32:35. 10:30b Deut 32:36. 10:32 Greek *when you were first enlightened.* 10:38 Or *my righteous ones will live by their faithfulness;* Greek reads *my righteous one will live by faith.* 10:37-38 Hab 2:3-4.

Called to One Another

HEBREWS 10:24–25

Throughout the New Testament, more than forty "one another" or "each other" commands instruct us on what Christian community should look like. "Love one another" (Romans 13:8). "Submit to one another" (Ephesians 5:21). "Teach and counsel each other" (Colossians 3:16). "Serve one another" (Galatians 5:13). "Let us think of ways to motivate one another to acts of love and good works" (Hebrews 10:24). These aren't merely warm-fuzzy, feel-good statements. They are challenging directives that call us out of selfishness, isolation, and pride. This radical "one another" mind-set is at the core of truly practicing the discipline of community.

The persecuted church exemplifies this biblical picture of community, observe Carl Moeller and David W. Hegg, the authors of *The Privilege of Persecution*, largely because the realities of extreme poverty and political persecution cause these Christians to work together as a matter of survival. Sticking together isn't an option; it's essential.

But it's a different situation for many of us; our circumstances usually don't force believers to commit to one home church. It's easy to pick up and leave if something or someone displeases us. We often think of joining in community as a personal choice rather than as a spiritual necessity. "Here's the dilemma: . . . To really practice the 'one anothers,' you have to be with one another. You have to be together in situations that you can't escape," the authors explain.

Affluence and freedom don't excuse the Western church from the biblical instruction to live in community. Neither does a self-centered desire to retain control over our time and energy. God calls us to live out Christlike love for "one another." As we obey these commands, we move toward a deeper holiness— and that's something we cannot do alone.

—Holly Vicente Robaina

For more on community, see reading at 2 John 1:1–6.

11 Great Examples of Faith

Faith is the confidence that what we hope for will actually happen; it gives us assurance about things we cannot see. ²Through their faith, the people in days of old earned a good reputation.

³By faith we understand that the entire universe was formed at God's command, that what we now see did not come from anything that can be seen.

⁴It was by faith that Abel brought a more acceptable offering to God than Cain did. Abel's offering gave evidence that he was a righteous man, and God showed his approval of his gifts. Although Abel is long dead, he still speaks to us by his example of faith.

⁵It was by faith that Enoch was taken up to heaven without dying—"he disappeared, because God took him."* For before he was taken up, he was known as a person who pleased God. ⁶And it is impossible to please God without faith. Anyone who wants to come to him must believe that God exists and that he rewards those who sincerely seek him.

⁷It was by faith that Noah built a large boat to save his family from the flood. He obeyed God, who warned him about things that had never happened before. By

11:5 Gen 5:24.

We of Little Faith
HEBREWS 11:1-2

Three times Jesus uses a phrase and a question: "You of little faith . . . why?"
- When a storm startles the disciples (Matthew 8)
- When Peter stumbles while trying to walk on water (Matthew 14)
- When the disciples wonder about not having enough bread (Matthew 16)

Jesus' words used to bother me; wasn't Jesus being hard on them? They were *trying*, after all. Why call their faith "little"? But in looking closer, I wonder if perhaps what we really see is Jesus showing the deepest tenderness.

Faith is a mystery—wild, strong, fierce, and beyond our understanding in so many ways. "Faith is the confidence that what we hope for will actually happen; it gives us assurance about things we cannot see," says Hebrews 11:1.

Doubt is a mystery too. Discouraging, deceptive, grasping our hearts in ways we don't fully comprehend. Until Jesus stops and asks us, *You of little faith . . . why?*

Perhaps rather than a rebuke, Jesus' words are an invitation—an opportunity to pause, to consider and unwrap the tendrils of doubt that have taken hold, to know them for what they are, and to remember the God who knows us.

Yes, *little faith.* Sometimes it's all we have. Perhaps that phrase isn't a demand or an accusation; perhaps it is a reminder that it's not ever about *our* faith, because we're all flawed and broken, prone to wander. After all, Jesus said even faith as tiny as a mustard seed can move mountains (Matthew 17:20).

Faith isn't really about what we can muster up, power through, or pretend we understand.

No, faith isn't really about us at all.

It's about who we place it in.

And we can place ours in the nail-scarred hands of One who knows how small we are and sees that not as an obstacle but an opportunity to show his bigness through us.

—Holley Gerth

For more on faith, see reading at 1 Peter 5:7.

his faith Noah condemned the rest of the world, and he received the righteousness that comes by faith.

[8] It was by faith that Abraham obeyed when God called him to leave home and go to another land that God would give him as his inheritance. He went without knowing where he was going. [9] And even when he reached the land God promised him, he lived there by faith—for he was like a foreigner, living in tents. And so did Isaac and Jacob, who inherited the same promise. [10] Abraham was confidently looking forward to a city with eternal foundations, a city designed and built by God.

[11] It was by faith that even Sarah was able to have a child, though she was barren and was too old. She believed* that God would

---

11:11 Or *It was by faith that he [Abraham] was able to have a child, even though Sarah was barren and he was too old. He believed.*

keep his promise. ¹²And so a whole nation came from this one man who was as good as dead—a nation with so many people that, like the stars in the sky and the sand on the seashore, there is no way to count them.

¹³All these people died still believing what God had promised them. They did not receive what was promised, but they saw it all from a distance and welcomed it. They agreed that they were foreigners and nomads here on earth. ¹⁴Obviously people who say such things are looking forward to a country they can call their own. ¹⁵If they had longed for the country they came from, they could have gone back. ¹⁶But they were looking for a better place, a heavenly homeland. That is why God is not ashamed to be called their God, for he has prepared a city for them.

¹⁷It was by faith that Abraham offered Isaac as a sacrifice when God was testing him. Abraham, who had received God's promises, was ready to sacrifice his only son, Isaac, ¹⁸even though God had told him, "Isaac is the son through whom your descendants will be counted."* ¹⁹Abraham reasoned that if Isaac died, God was able to bring him back to life again. And in a sense, Abraham did receive his son back from the dead.

²⁰It was by faith that Isaac promised blessings for the future to his sons, Jacob and Esau.

²¹It was by faith that Jacob, when he was old and dying, blessed each of Joseph's sons and bowed in worship as he leaned on his staff.

²²It was by faith that Joseph, when he was about to die, said confidently that the people of Israel would leave Egypt. He even commanded them to take his bones with them when they left.

²³It was by faith that Moses' parents hid him for three months when he was born. They saw that God had given them an unusual child, and they were not afraid to disobey the king's command.

²⁴It was by faith that Moses, when he grew up, refused to be called the son of Pharaoh's daughter. ²⁵He chose to share the oppression of God's people instead of enjoying the fleeting pleasures of sin. ²⁶He thought it was better to suffer for the sake of Christ than to own the treasures of Egypt, for he was looking ahead to his great reward. ²⁷It was by faith that Moses left the land of Egypt, not fearing the king's anger. He kept right on going because he kept his eyes on the one who is invisible. ²⁸It was by faith that Moses commanded the people of Israel to keep the Passover and to sprinkle blood on the doorposts so that the angel of death would not kill their firstborn sons.

²⁹It was by faith that the people of Israel went right through the Red Sea as though they were on dry ground. But when the Egyptians tried to follow, they were all drowned.

³⁰It was by faith that the people of Israel marched around Jericho for seven days, and the walls came crashing down.

³¹It was by faith that Rahab the prostitute was not destroyed with the people in her city who refused to obey God. For she had given a friendly welcome to the spies.

³²How much more do I need to say? It would take too long to recount the stories of the faith of Gideon, Barak, Samson, Jephthah, David, Samuel, and all the prophets. ³³By faith these people overthrew kingdoms, ruled with justice, and received what God had promised them. They shut the mouths of lions, ³⁴quenched the flames of fire, and escaped death by the edge of the sword. Their weakness was turned to strength. They became strong in battle and put whole armies to flight. ³⁵Women received their loved ones back again from death.

But others were tortured, refusing to turn from God in order to be set free. They placed their hope in a better life after the resurrection. ³⁶Some were jeered at, and their backs were cut open with whips. Others were chained in prisons. ³⁷Some died by stoning, some were sawed in half,* and others were killed with the sword. Some went about wearing skins of sheep and goats, destitute and oppressed and mistreated. ³⁸They were too good for this world, wandering over deserts and mountains, hiding in caves and holes in the ground.

³⁹All these people earned a good reputation because of their faith, yet none of them received all that God had promised. ⁴⁰For God had something better in mind for us, so that they would not reach perfection without us.

11:18 Gen 21:12. **11:37** Some manuscripts add *some were tested.*

Stretched in Scary Ways?

HEBREWS 12:1-2

The more I learn about God and his calling, the more I know my life is purposeful. I love Hebrews 12:1-2 where it talks about a race that's been marked out, which we're called to run; that nothing I encounter along the way is going to throw him off. I may make bad decisions; I may zig when I should zag, but my life is purposeful; I'm on a mission; God has me where he wants me. He takes me through experiences that shape me, that help me do more for his kingdom. This gives me a framework for my life.

It also stretches me in scary ways. There are situations where I need to show more courage, to step out and take a stand, to speak up because kingdom issues are at stake.

I don't think that comes easily when you've been conditioned to back away and not speak up. It creates battles within me because every once in a while I get confronted with a situation where the easy path is more appealing. I have to ask myself, *Is this what God wants me to do?* and take the harder route. But ultimately I know that's my race to run.

—*Carolyn Custis James*

12 God's Discipline Proves His Love

Therefore, since we are surrounded by such a huge crowd of witnesses to the life of faith, let us strip off every weight that slows us down, especially the sin that so easily trips us up. And let us run with endurance the race God has set before us. ²We do this by keeping our eyes on Jesus, the champion who initiates and perfects our faith.* Because of the joy* awaiting him, he endured the cross, disregarding its shame. Now he is seated in the place of honor beside God's throne. ³Think of all the hostility he endured from sinful people;* then you won't become weary and give up. ⁴After all, you have not yet given your lives in your struggle against sin.

⁵And have you forgotten the encouraging words God spoke to you as his children?* He said,

"My child,* don't make light of the
    LORD's discipline,
and don't give up when he corrects you.
⁶ For the LORD disciplines those he loves,
    and he punishes each one he accepts
    as his child."*

⁷As you endure this divine discipline, remember that God is treating you as his own children. Who ever heard of a child who is never disciplined by its father? ⁸If God doesn't discipline you as he does all of his children, it means that you are illegitimate and are not really his children at all. ⁹Since we respected our earthly fathers who disciplined us, shouldn't we submit even more to the discipline of the Father of our spirits, and live forever?*

¹⁰For our earthly fathers disciplined us for a few years, doing the best they knew how. But God's discipline is always good for us, so that we might share in his holiness. ¹¹No discipline is enjoyable while it is happening—it's painful! But afterward there will be a peaceful harvest of right living for those who are trained in this way.

¹²So take a new grip with your tired hands and strengthen your weak knees. ¹³Mark out a straight path for your feet so that those who are weak and lame will not fall but become strong.

12:2a Or *Jesus, the originator and perfecter of our faith.* **12:2b** Or *Instead of the joy.* **12:3** Some manuscripts read *Think of how people hurt themselves by opposing him.* **12:5a** Greek *sons;* also in 12:7, 8. **12:5b** Greek *son;* also in 12:6, 7. **12:5-6** Prov 3:11-12 (Greek version). **12:9** Or *and really live?*

Lessons from the Cross

HEBREWS 12:1-2

Beating, torture, mockery. Spikes driven through his wrists. Thorns shoved into his scalp.

The crushing weight of humanity's sin placed upon his shoulders.

The Cross.

Jesus knew what he was about to endure. He wrestled with what obedience to the Father entailed. And ultimately he chose to submit to the Father's will (Matthew 26:39). Though it was brutal and painful beyond our comprehension, "the wondrous cross," as hymnist Isaac Watts called it, became a meeting place of relinquishment, relief, and relationship.

Relinquishment. Jesus' obedience to the Cross meant relinquishment. He gave up heaven to come to earth; he gave up earth to take us to heaven. He surrendered his deity and was encapsulated in an infant's frame, coming into this world in physical pain and likely experiencing emotional pain we'll never understand. Then, in the act that resounds like a trumpet throughout the centuries, he relinquished his will. Christ released everything for our sake.

Unlike Christ, relinquishment for us means letting go of our self-will and sin. At the Cross, we relinquish through confession everything that gets in the way of our relationship with God. We face those sins, let go of them, and seek God's help in turning away from them in true repentance. When we stop blocking God's work by our sin, God releases his power in us and in our relationships, and the amazing can happen: forgiveness, healing, restoration, transformation.

Relief. Submission, says author and Bible teacher Kathi Macias, means to "come underneath in a safe place." Christ submitted to the Cross because he knew intimately the safest place for him to land was beneath the Father's will.

In this place of rest and relief, we are free from needing the upper hand, the smartest retort. What liberation from thinking the fate of everyone we love, of everything we touch, of all we oversee depends on us!

Janet Holm McHenry, author of *PrayerStreaming*, says, "When I examine my struggles in light of Christ's suffering on the cross, I'm then able—like the apostle Paul—to give thanks in all things. Suffering is our opportunity to identify with our Lord." As she identifies with Christ's suffering, she can more easily submit to her own suffering, bringing her unexpected relief. Suffering and submission present a gift we never expected: relationship.

--- { ❖ } ---

Relationship. Ultimately, submission to the Cross means relationship. But for Jesus, submission first meant abandonment. Our holy God severed his previously unbroken relationship with Jesus when Jesus acquired our sins. In the agony of that transition, darkness fell over the entire earth. The parting between Father and Son stole the sun from the sky. The pain each experienced is unimaginable.

Then Jesus cried out, "My God, my God, why have you abandoned me?" (Matthew 27:46). He endured that God-forsaken moment so we might never be forsaken by God. By severing his relationship with God, Christ secured for us God's eternal, irrevocable love. Hebrews 13:5 literally translates as, "I will never, no never, no never leave you or forsake you." This is the only time a triple negative occurs in Scripture.

At the Cross, because we relinquish our sin and the joke of our self-importance, we connect with God's unfailing love. Then, because sin no longer ruptures, our relationships come under the power of the Cross.

As Jesus looked ahead to the Cross, he also peered past the pain of submission to joy: his surrender to the Father's perfect will would bring us salvation. Scripture tells us, "Because of the joy awaiting him, he endured the cross" (Hebrews 12:2). *We're* part of the joy set before Jesus; he submitted to the Cross out of love for us. We show him our love by following his example of surrender and obedience.

—Jane Rubietta

For more on submission, see reading at Hebrews 13:17.

A Call to Listen to God

[14]Work at living in peace with everyone, and work at living a holy life, for those who are not holy will not see the Lord. [15]Look after each other so that none of you fails to receive the grace of God. Watch out that no poisonous root of bitterness grows up to trouble you, corrupting many. [16]Make sure that no one is immoral or godless like Esau, who traded his birthright as the firstborn son for a single meal. [17]You know that afterward, when he wanted his father's blessing, he was rejected. It was too late for repentance, even though he begged with bitter tears.

[18]You have not come to a physical mountain,* to a place of flaming fire, darkness, gloom, and whirlwind, as the Israelites did at Mount Sinai. [19]For they heard an awesome trumpet blast and a voice so terrible that they begged God to stop speaking. [20]They staggered back under God's command: "If even an animal touches the mountain, it must be stoned to death."* [21]Moses himself was so frightened at the sight that he said, "I am terrified and trembling."*

[22]No, you have come to Mount Zion, to the city of the living God, the heavenly Jerusalem, and to countless thousands of angels in a joyful gathering. [23]You have come to the assembly of God's firstborn children, whose names are written in heaven. You have come to God himself, who is the judge over all things. You have come to the spirits of the righteous ones in heaven who have now been made perfect. [24]You have come to Jesus, the one who mediates the new covenant between God and people, and to the sprinkled blood, which speaks of forgiveness instead of crying out for vengeance like the blood of Abel.

[25]Be careful that you do not refuse to listen to the One who is speaking. For if the people of Israel did not escape when they refused to listen to Moses, the earthly messenger, we will certainly not escape if we reject the One who speaks to us from heaven! [26]When God spoke from Mount Sinai his voice shook the earth, but now he makes another promise: "Once again I will shake not only the earth but the heavens also."* [27]This means that all of creation will be shaken and removed, so that only unshakable things will remain.

[28]Since we are receiving a Kingdom that is unshakable, let us be thankful and please God by worshiping him with holy fear and awe. [29]For our God is a devouring fire.

13 Concluding Words

Keep on loving each other as brothers and sisters.* [2]Don't forget to show hospitality to strangers, for some who have done this have entertained angels without realizing it! [3]Remember those in prison, as if you were there yourself. Remember also those being mistreated, as if you felt their pain in your own bodies.

[4]Give honor to marriage, and remain faithful to one another in marriage. God will surely judge people who are immoral and those who commit adultery.

[5]Don't love money; be satisfied with what you have. For God has said,

"I will never fail you.
　I will never abandon you."*

[6]So we can say with confidence,

"The LORD is my helper,
　so I will have no fear.
　What can mere people do to me?"*

[7]Remember your leaders who taught you the word of God. Think of all the good that has come from their lives, and follow the example of their faith.

[8]Jesus Christ is the same yesterday, today, and forever. [9]So do not be attracted by strange, new ideas. Your strength comes from God's grace, not from rules about food, which don't help those who follow them.

[10]We have an altar from which the priests in the Tabernacle* have no right to eat. [11]Under the old system, the high priest brought the blood of animals into the Holy Place as a sacrifice for sin, and the bodies of the animals were burned outside the camp. [12]So also Jesus suffered and died outside the city gates to make his people holy by means of his own blood. [13]So let us go out to him, outside the camp, and bear the disgrace he bore. [14]For this world is not our permanent

---

Submitting to Church Leaders

HEBREWS 13:17

The author of Hebrews writes: "Obey your spiritual leaders, and do what they say. Their work is to watch over your souls, and they are accountable to God" (13:17).

God clearly calls pastors and church leaders to a high standard of leadership, holy living, and pastoral care (1 Timothy 3:1–4:16). They are called to be concerned for our well-being and are keeping "watch over" us, always aware that they must give an account to the Ultimate Authority, and that they will be judged to a higher standard because of their position.

Hebrews asks us to bring a mind-set of submission into our sense of what it means to be part of the church. We recognize that God has placed church leaders in spiritual authority over us, and we make a conscious choice to follow, pray for, and obey our church leaders as they follow Christ (1 Corinthians 11:1).

God calls us to give our church leaders all the honor that is due them (1 Thessalonians 5:12), so that they can shepherd us "with joy" (Hebrews 13:17).

—*JoHannah Reardon*

---

home; we are looking forward to a home yet to come.

¹⁵ Therefore, let us offer through Jesus a continual sacrifice of praise to God, proclaiming our allegiance to his name. ¹⁶ And don't forget to do good and to share with those in need. These are the sacrifices that please God.

¹⁷ Obey your spiritual leaders, and do what they say. Their work is to watch over your souls, and they are accountable to God. Give them reason to do this with joy and not with sorrow. That would certainly not be for your benefit.

¹⁸ Pray for us, for our conscience is clear and we want to live honorably in everything we do. ¹⁹ And especially pray that I will be able to come back to you soon.

²⁰ Now may the God of peace—
who brought up from the dead our
Lord Jesus,

the great Shepherd of the sheep,
and ratified an eternal covenant with
his blood—
²¹ may he equip you with all you need
for doing his will.
May he produce in you,*
through the power of Jesus Christ,
every good thing that is pleasing to him.
All glory to him forever and ever!
Amen.

²²I urge you, dear brothers and sisters,* to pay attention to what I have written in this brief exhortation.

²³I want you to know that our brother Timothy has been released from jail. If he comes here soon, I will bring him with me to see you.

²⁴Greet all your leaders and all the believers there.* The believers from Italy send you their greetings.

²⁵May God's grace be with you all.

13:21 Some manuscripts read *in us.*   **13:22** Greek *brothers.*   **13:24** Greek *all of God's holy people.*

James

Background

The apostle John briefly recorded the relationship between Jesus and his brothers: "For even his brothers didn't believe in him" (John 7:5). Yet after Jesus' death and resurrection, a change occurred: James and Jude became believers. James became a bishop of the church at Jerusalem (Acts 15:13; see also Galatians 2:9) and is believed to be the writer of the Epistle of James, identified in 1:1. This epistle has been called the Proverbs of the New Testament because of its pithy style and pragmatic teaching. It does not have the personal tone of Paul's letters. It discusses the practical aspects of Christian conduct rather than doctrinal issues.

Message

James informs readers of Jewish descent about faith as it relates to trials, temptations, tests, the truth of God's Word, the tongue, wisdom, separation from the world, and submission to God. The letter echoes themes found in Matthew's extensive account of the Sermon on the Mount. For the spiritual life to work, faith must work. It is not enough to verbally say one has faith or intellectually claim to have faith; faith must be practically expressed every day in word and deed. Faith without works is dead, and a dead faith is worse than no faith at all.

Time

The Epistle of James was likely among the first books written in the New Testament. Scholars have proposed a date between A.D. 46 and 60; James, according to the Jewish historian Josephus, was martyred in A.D. 62.

Outline

James

1 Greetings from James

This letter is from James, a slave of God and of the Lord Jesus Christ.

I am writing to the "twelve tribes"—Jewish believers scattered abroad. Greetings!

Faith and Endurance

[2] Dear brothers and sisters,* when troubles come your way, consider it an opportunity for great joy. [3] For you know that when your faith is tested, your endurance has a chance to grow. [4] So let it grow, for when your endurance is fully developed, you will be perfect and complete, needing nothing.

[5] If you need wisdom, ask our generous God, and he will give it to you. He will not rebuke you for asking. [6] But when you ask him, be sure that your faith is in God alone. Do not waver, for a person with divided loyalty is as unsettled as a wave of the sea that is blown and tossed by the wind. [7] Such people should not expect to receive anything from the Lord. [8] Their loyalty is divided between God and the world, and they are unstable in everything they do.

[9] Believers who are* poor have something to boast about, for God has honored them. [10] And those who are rich should boast that God has humbled them. They will fade away like a little flower in the field. [11] The hot sun rises and the grass withers; the little flower droops and falls, and its beauty fades away. In the same way, the rich will fade away with all of their achievements.

[12] God blesses those who patiently endure testing and temptation. Afterward they will receive the crown of life that God has promised to those who love him. [13] And remember, when you are being tempted, do not say, "God is tempting me." God is never tempted to do wrong,* and he never tempts anyone else. [14] Temptation comes from our own desires, which entice us and drag us away. [15] These desires give birth to sinful actions. And when sin is allowed to grow, it gives birth to death.

[16] So don't be misled, my dear brothers and sisters. [17] Whatever is good and perfect comes down to us from God our Father, who created all the lights in the heavens.* He never changes or casts a shifting shadow.* [18] He chose to give birth to us by giving us his true word. And we, out of all creation, became his prized possession.*

Listening and Doing

[19] Understand this, my dear brothers and sisters: You must all be quick to listen, slow to speak, and slow to get angry. [20] Human anger* does not produce the righteousness* God desires. [21] So get rid of all the filth and evil in your lives, and humbly accept the word God has planted in your hearts, for it has the power to save your souls.

[22] But don't just listen to God's word. You must do what it says. Otherwise, you are only fooling yourselves. [23] For if you listen to the word and don't obey,

---

1:2 Greek *brothers;* also in 1:16, 19.   **1:9** Greek *The brother who is.*   **1:13** Or *God should not be put to a test by evil people.*
1:17a Greek *from above, from the Father of lights.*   **1:17b** Some manuscripts read *He never changes, as a shifting shadow does.*
1:18 Greek *we became a kind of firstfruit of his creatures.*   **1:20a** Greek *A man's anger.*   **1:20b** Or *the justice.*

it is like glancing at your face in a mirror. ²⁴You see yourself, walk away, and forget what you look like. ²⁵But if you look carefully into the perfect law that sets you free, and if you do what it says and don't forget what you heard, then God will bless you for doing it.

²⁶If you claim to be religious but don't control your tongue, you are fooling yourself, and your religion is worthless. ²⁷Pure and genuine religion in the sight of God the Father means caring for orphans and widows in their distress and refusing to let the world corrupt you.

Q&A — Gratitude in Suffering
JAMES 1:2

How can I be grateful when my life is full of pain?

"Dear brothers and sisters, when troubles come your way, consider it an opportunity for great joy" (James 1:2).

These words are hard to swallow, aren't they?

Trouble—loneliness, heartache, physical pain, family turmoil, betrayal, discouragement, persecution—cannot possibly be a reason for joy. This notion goes against every ounce of human logic, every honest fiber in our beings. We hate pain; it beats us down, leaving us raw or numb or scarred or cowering. It's certainly not something to celebrate or be thankful for . . . *is it*?

The early church knew something about pain—James himself would go on to suffer to the point of death, dying for his faith around A.D. 62. Yet he urged the church to gratefully celebrate their suffering because it produced endurance in their faith. Scripture also teaches us that pain can refine our focus and can help us be ever more aware of our total reliance upon God. But perhaps the most profound reason we can be grateful to God for the pain in our lives is found in 1 Peter 2:21, a passage quadriplegic Joni Eareckson Tada calls the "rule of thumb for any Christian struggling to understand God's purpose in hardship." Here Peter wrote, "God called you to do good, even if it means suffering, just as Christ suffered for you. He is your example, and you must follow in his steps."

When we suffer, we can be thankful that, in some strange way, we are privileged to experience just an ounce of the sufferings Christ endured for us. We can rejoice that we can follow in his steps to Calvary. Pain, if we let it, can lead us into deeper intimacy with Christ. Is there anything more deserving of our gratitude?

—Kelli B. Trujillo

For more on gratitude, see reading at Revelation 7:15–17.

Facing Who We Really Are

JAMES 1:22–25

Sometimes I don't want to read the Bible. It's not because I'm lazy or tired or too busy. It's not because I've given up my faith or I doubt the Bible's inerrancy.

It's because I know what it will say to me: it will speak truth into my life that I cannot ignore. It will point out my sins, shortcomings, and failings (2 Timothy 3:16). It will cut to the heart, exposing my "innermost thoughts and desires" (Hebrews 4:12). It will reveal the real me—and I will not like what I see.

There are many encouraging words in Scripture—beautiful and poetic lines that buoy our spirits and hang on flowery wall-plaques in countless kitchens and entry halls. But we come to Scripture not just for a pat on the back or an "'atta girl!" from God. When we come to the Word, we come to a dynamic text—alive, working in us through the Holy Spirit, speaking to us and engaging with our lives.

James urged the early church, "Don't just listen to God's word. You must do what it says. Otherwise, you are only fooling yourselves" (1:22). He went on to provide the example of someone looking in a mirror but then forgetting his own reflection; this foolish man represents Christians who come away from God's Word without responding in actions of obedience. "But," James says, "if you look carefully into the perfect law that sets you free, and if you do what it says and don't forget what you heard, then God will bless you for doing it" (1:25).

Like a mirror Scripture shows us, with painful accuracy, the parts of ourselves we may tend to overlook. We see our self-centered desires, light is shed on our hidden habits, and we're forced to face who we really are.

And we are invited—compelled—to respond.

If we read Scripture simply for platitudes that encourage us, we'll have to skip most of the text!

No, we read Scripture so we can change. If we expect something else, we're only fooling ourselves.

—*Kelli B. Trujillo*

2 A Warning against Prejudice

My dear brothers and sisters,* how can you claim to have faith in our glorious Lord Jesus Christ if you favor some people over others?

²For example, suppose someone comes into your meeting* dressed in fancy clothes and expensive jewelry, and another comes in who is poor and dressed in dirty clothes. ³If you give special attention and a good seat to the rich person, but you say to the poor one, "You can stand over there, or else sit on the floor"—well, ⁴doesn't this discrimination show that your judgments are guided by evil motives?

⁵Listen to me, dear brothers and sisters. Hasn't God chosen the poor in this world to be rich in faith? Aren't they the ones who will inherit the Kingdom he promised to those who love him? ⁶But you dishonor the poor! Isn't it the rich who oppress you and drag you into court? ⁷Aren't they the ones who slander Jesus Christ, whose noble name* you bear?

⁸Yes indeed, it is good when you obey

2:1 Greek *brothers;* also in 2:5, 14.   **2:2** Greek *your synagogue.*   **2:7** Greek *slander the noble name.*

the royal law as found in the Scriptures: "Love your neighbor as yourself."* ⁹But if you favor some people over others, you are committing a sin. You are guilty of breaking the law.

¹⁰For the person who keeps all of the laws except one is as guilty as a person who has broken all of God's laws. ¹¹For the same God who said, "You must not commit adultery," also said, "You must not murder."* So if you murder someone but do not commit adultery, you have still broken the law.

¹²So whatever you say or whatever you do, remember that you will be judged by the law that sets you free. ¹³There will be no mercy for those who have not shown mercy to others. But if you have been merciful, God will be merciful when he judges you.

Faith without Good Deeds Is Dead

¹⁴What good is it, dear brothers and sisters, if you say you have faith but don't show it by your actions? Can that kind of faith save anyone? ¹⁵Suppose you see a brother or sister who has no food or clothing, ¹⁶and you say, "Good-bye and have a good day; stay warm and eat well"—but then you don't give that person any food or clothing. What good does that do?

¹⁷So you see, faith by itself isn't enough. Unless it produces good deeds, it is dead and useless.

¹⁸Now someone may argue, "Some people have faith; others have good deeds." But I say, "How can you show me your faith if you don't have good deeds? I will show you my faith by my good deeds."

¹⁹You say you have faith, for you believe that there is one God.* Good for you! Even the demons believe this, and they tremble in terror. ²⁰How foolish! Can't you see that faith without good deeds is useless?

²¹Don't you remember that our ancestor Abraham was shown to be right with God by his actions when he offered his son Isaac on the altar? ²²You see, his faith and his actions worked together. His actions made his faith complete. ²³And so it happened just as the Scriptures say: "Abraham believed God, and God counted him as righteous because of his faith."* He was

even called the friend of God.* ²⁴So you see, we are shown to be right with God by what we do, not by faith alone.

²⁵Rahab the prostitute is another example. She was shown to be right with God by her actions when she hid those messengers and sent them safely away by a different road. ²⁶Just as the body is dead without breath,* so also faith is dead without good works.

3 Controlling the Tongue

Dear brothers and sisters,* not many of you should become teachers in the church, for we who teach will be judged more strictly. ²Indeed, we all make many mistakes. For if we could control our tongues, we would be perfect and could also control ourselves in every other way.

³We can make a large horse go wherever we want by means of a small bit in its mouth. ⁴And a small rudder makes a huge ship turn wherever the pilot chooses to go, even though the winds are strong. ⁵In the same way, the tongue is a small thing that makes grand speeches.

But a tiny spark can set a great forest on fire. ⁶And the tongue is a flame of fire. It is a whole world of wickedness, corrupting your entire body. It can set your whole life on fire, for it is set on fire by hell itself.*

⁷People can tame all kinds of animals, birds, reptiles, and fish, ⁸but no one can tame the tongue. It is restless and evil, full of deadly poison. ⁹Sometimes it praises our Lord and Father, and sometimes it curses those who have been made in the image of God. ¹⁰And so blessing and cursing come pouring out of the same mouth. Surely, my brothers and sisters, this is not right! ¹¹Does a spring of water bubble out with both fresh water and bitter water? ¹²Does a fig tree produce olives, or a grapevine produce figs? No, and you can't draw fresh water from a salty spring.*

True Wisdom Comes from God

¹³If you are wise and understand God's ways, prove it by living an honorable life, doing good works with the humility that comes from wisdom. ¹⁴But if you are bitterly jealous and there is selfish ambition in your

A Peacemaker like Francis

Reconciliation

JAMES 3:17-18

James 3:18 encourages us to be "peacemakers [who] will plant seeds of peace and reap a harvest of righteousness." Francis of Assisi was one such peacemaker.

Francis's hatred of conflict had an origin. In his younger years he had gone merrily off to war expecting honor and booty and ended up a POW in a hellhole. There he came face to face with cruelty and disease and discovered that combat was not a game. From that point forward he repudiated war and embraced peacemaking.

So it was not surprising that, when the "Christian movement" of his time (the Crusaders) marched off to the Middle East in hopes of annihilating Muslims, Francis traveled there himself, passed through enemy lines, and introduced himself to Malik-al-Kamil, the Muslim sultan of Egypt. While there, the two men spoke extensively of matters of faith and peace and became friends.

Francis's host listened carefully to the Christian message Francis shared with him. And not surprisingly, Francis returned the favor by listening to the sultan's Muslim convictions. Francis was not successful in his effort to make peace, and he did not convert the sultan. As a result the Crusaders got their war. But the fact that he *tried* to avert bloodshed says something significant. In contrast to the acceptance of violence that was normalized in the church during his time, Francis became known as a peacemaker. If he were to speak to us today, I can imagine him raising the topic of peacemaking and wondering why many modern Christians have so little to say about it. I can imagine him asking us, "Ought this not be an essential piece of your faith?"

—Gordon MacDonald

heart, don't cover up the truth with boasting and lying. ¹⁵For jealousy and selfishness are not God's kind of wisdom. Such things are earthly, unspiritual, and demonic. ¹⁶For wherever there is jealousy and selfish ambition, there you will find disorder and evil of every kind.

¹⁷But the wisdom from above is first of all pure. It is also peace loving, gentle at all times, and willing to yield to others. It is full of mercy and good deeds. It shows no favoritism and is always sincere. ¹⁸And those who are peacemakers will plant seeds of peace and reap a harvest of righteousness.*

4 Drawing Close to God

What is causing the quarrels and fights among you? Don't they come from the evil desires at war within you? ²You want what you don't have, so you scheme and kill to get it. You are jealous of what others have, but you can't get it, so you fight and wage war to take it away from them. Yet you don't have what you want because you don't ask God for it. ³And even when you ask, you don't get it because your motives are all wrong—you want only what will give you pleasure.

⁴You adulterers!* Don't you realize that friendship with the world makes you an enemy of God? I say it again: If you want to be a friend of the world, you make yourself an enemy of God. ⁵What do you think the Scriptures mean when they say that the spirit God has placed within us is filled with envy?* ⁶But he gives us even more grace

3:18 Or of good things, or of justice. **4:4** Greek You adulteresses! **4:5** Or that God longs jealously for the human spirit he has placed within us? or that the Holy Spirit, whom God has placed within us, opposes our envy?

to stand against such evil desires. As the Scriptures say,

"God opposes the proud
but favors the humble."*

[7]So humble yourselves before God. Resist the devil, and he will flee from you. [8]Come close to God, and God will come close to you. Wash your hands, you sinners; purify your hearts, for your loyalty is divided between God and the world. [9]Let there be tears for what you have done. Let there be sorrow and deep grief. Let there be sadness instead of laughter, and gloom instead of joy. [10]Humble yourselves before the Lord, and he will lift you up in honor.

Warning against Judging Others

[11]Don't speak evil against each other, dear brothers and sisters.* If you criticize and judge each other, then you are criticizing and judging God's law. But your job is to obey the law, not to judge whether it applies to you. [12]God alone, who gave the law, is the Judge. He alone has the power to save or to destroy. So what right do you have to judge your neighbor?

Warning about Self-Confidence

[13]Look here, you who say, "Today or tomorrow we are going to a certain town and will stay there a year. We will do business there and make a profit." [14]How do you know what your life will be like tomorrow? Your life is like the morning fog—it's here a little while, then it's gone. [15]What you ought to say is, "If the Lord wants us to, we will live and do this or that." [16]Otherwise you are boasting about your own plans, and all such boasting is evil.

[17]Remember, it is sin to know what you ought to do and then not do it.

5 Warning to the Rich

Look here, you rich people: Weep and groan with anguish because of all the terrible troubles ahead of you. [2]Your wealth is rotting away, and your fine clothes are moth-eaten rags. [3]Your gold and silver have become worthless. The very wealth you were counting on will eat away your flesh like fire. This treasure you have accumu-

lated will stand as evidence against you on the day of judgment. [4]For listen! Hear the cries of the field workers whom you have cheated of their pay. The wages you held back cry out against you. The cries of those who harvest your fields have reached the ears of the LORD of Heaven's Armies.

[5]You have spent your years on earth in luxury, satisfying your every desire. You have fattened yourselves for the day of slaughter. [6]You have condemned and killed innocent people,* who do not resist you.*

Patience and Endurance

[7]Dear brothers and sisters,* be patient as you wait for the Lord's return. Consider the farmers who patiently wait for the rains in the fall and in the spring. They eagerly look for the valuable harvest to ripen. [8]You, too, must be patient. Take courage, for the coming of the Lord is near.

[9]Don't grumble about each other, brothers and sisters, or you will be judged. For look—the Judge is standing at the door!

[10]For examples of patience in suffering, dear brothers and sisters, look at the prophets who spoke in the name of the Lord. [11]We give great honor to those who endure under suffering. For instance, you know about Job, a man of great endurance. You can see how the Lord was kind to him at the end, for the Lord is full of tenderness and mercy.

[12]But most of all, my brothers and sisters, never take an oath, by heaven or earth or anything else. Just say a simple yes or no, so that you will not sin and be condemned.

The Power of Prayer

[13]Are any of you suffering hardships? You should pray. Are any of you happy? You should sing praises. [14]Are any of you sick? You should call for the elders of the church to come and pray over you, anointing you with oil in the name of the Lord. [15]Such a prayer offered in faith will heal the sick, and the Lord will make you well. And if you have committed any sins, you will be forgiven.

[16]Confess your sins to each other and pray for each other so that you may be healed. The earnest prayer of a righteous

---

4:6 Prov 3:34 (Greek version). **4:11** Greek brothers. **5:6a** Or killed the Righteous One. **5:6b** Or Don't they resist you? or Doesn't God oppose you? or Aren't they now accusing you before God? **5:7** Greek brothers; also in 5:9, 10, 12, 19.

person has great power and produces wonderful results. ¹⁷Elijah was as human as we are, and yet when he prayed earnestly that no rain would fall, none fell for three and a half years! ¹⁸Then, when he prayed again, the sky sent down rain and the earth began to yield its crops.

Restore Wandering Believers

¹⁹My dear brothers and sisters, if someone among you wanders away from the truth and is brought back, ²⁰you can be sure that whoever brings the sinner back will save that person from death and bring about the forgiveness of many sins.

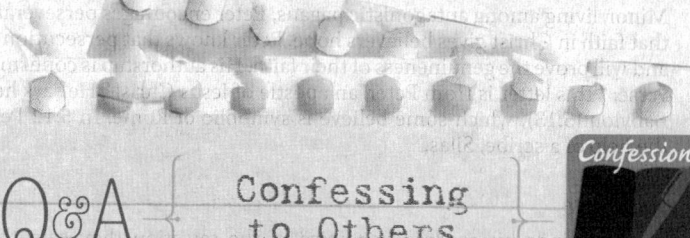

Q&A — Confessing to Others

JAMES 5:16

Why is it important to confess to other people? Isn't it enough to confess to God?

There's a clear biblical design for confessing our sins to God so we can reconcile with him and for confessing to others so that we can "share each other's burdens" (Galatians 6:2). When we share our failures with others, it also gives them the courage to confess their sins. James 5:16 directly commands us, "Confess your sins to each other." As we confess to others, and as we support one another in prayer, we can live whole and healed and experience true community.

It can be challenging, at first, to confess to other Christians. We may wonder whom we should confess to. I don't think it has to be someone in your small group or church; it just has to be someone you trust. Your spouse, friend, neighbor, pastor, counselor—somebody you're in relationship with to whom you can say, "This is where I'm screwing up, and this is where God's restoring me." Then you can celebrate that restoration together and be held accountable to your conscious decision to remedy those areas of brokenness.

God's Word calls us to spur on and encourage one another. Confession does that, ultimately pointing us back to Christ. It can be frightening to open up and be vulnerable with someone, but don't let fear stop you. It's scary, but ultimately it's worth it. The freedom that comes after you confess to others far outweighs any discomfort you might feel during the confession. I had to learn that—although painful—confessing my sins regularly to God and others allows Christ's power to rest on me. When we bring our sin into the light, God's glory shines. It shows a hurting world that there's grace and hope beyond brokenness.

—*Anne Jackson*

1 Peter

Background

Peter, one of Jesus' disciples, was present when Jesus said, "Here on earth you will have many trials and sorrows. But take heart, because I have overcome the world" (John 16:33). In writing to Jewish and Gentile Christians scattered throughout Asia Minor, living among antagonistic pagans, Peter encourages perseverance, knowing that faith in Christ gives believers hope. Peter knows that persecution is temporary and will prove the genuineness of their faith. His authorship is confirmed in the first verse: "This letter is from Peter, an apostle of Jesus Christ." He says he writes from Babylon (5:13), which some believe is symbolic of Rome. In 5:12 Peter mentions the help of a scribe, Silas.

Message

Peter reminds his readers to rejoice in the salvation they gain through God's grace. "The pure spiritual milk" (2:2) aids in spiritual growth. Peter exhorts his readers in practical matters—living honestly among nonbelievers, submitting to governmental leaders, loving fellow Christians, living peaceably in households. He gives direction for living faithfully in the face of persecution. He exhorts the older generation to be community leaders and the young to submit to their elders— all serving with humility. Final remarks include classic reminders: "Give all your worries and cares to God, for he cares about you.

"Stay alert! Watch out for your great enemy, the devil. He prowls around like a roaring lion, looking for someone to devour. Stand firm against him, and be strong in your faith" (5:7–9).

Time

Peter most likely wrote this letter from Rome between A.D. 60 and 64. Early nonbiblical writing indicates that Peter was crucified by Nero (who ruled from A.D. 54 to 68), probably between A.D. 64 and 66.

Outline

1 Peter

1

Greetings from Peter

This letter is from Peter, an apostle of Jesus Christ.

I am writing to God's chosen people who are living as foreigners in the provinces of Pontus, Galatia, Cappadocia, Asia, and Bithynia.* ²God the Father knew you and chose you long ago, and his Spirit has made you holy. As a result, you have obeyed him and have been cleansed by the blood of Jesus Christ.

May God give you more and more grace and peace.

The Hope of Eternal Life

³All praise to God, the Father of our Lord Jesus Christ. It is by his great mercy that we have been born again, because God raised Jesus Christ from the dead. Now we live with great expectation, ⁴and we have a priceless inheritance—an inheritance that is kept in heaven for you, pure and undefiled, beyond the reach of change and decay. ⁵And through your faith, God is protecting you by his power until you receive this salvation, which is ready to be revealed on the last day for all to see.

⁶So be truly glad.* There is wonderful joy ahead, even though you have to endure many trials for a little while. ⁷These trials will show that your faith is genuine. It is being tested as fire tests and purifies gold—though your faith is far more precious than mere gold. So when your faith remains strong through many trials, it will bring you much praise and glory and honor on the day when Jesus Christ is revealed to the whole world.

⁸You love him even though you have never seen him. Though you do not see him now, you trust him; and you rejoice with a glorious, inexpressible joy. ⁹The reward for trusting him will be the salvation of your souls.

¹⁰This salvation was something even the prophets wanted to know more about when they prophesied about this gracious salvation prepared for you. ¹¹They wondered what time or situation the Spirit of Christ within them was talking about when he told them in advance about Christ's suffering and his great glory afterward.

¹²They were told that their messages were not for themselves, but for you. And now this Good News has been announced to you by those who preached in the power of the Holy Spirit sent from heaven. It is all so wonderful that even the angels are eagerly watching these things happen.

A Call to Holy Living

¹³So think clearly and exercise self-control. Look forward to the gracious salvation that will come to you when Jesus Christ is revealed to the world. ¹⁴So you must live as God's obedient children. Don't slip back into your old ways of living to satisfy your own desires. You didn't know any better then. ¹⁵But now you must be holy in everything you do, just as God who chose you is holy. ¹⁶For the Scriptures say, "You must be holy because I am holy."*

1:1 *Pontus, Galatia, Cappadocia, Asia,* and *Bithynia* were Roman provinces in what is now Turkey. **1:6** Or *So you are truly glad.*
1:16 Lev 11:44-45; 19:2; 20:7.

¹⁷ And remember that the heavenly Father to whom you pray has no favorites. He will judge or reward you according to what you do. So you must live in reverent fear of him during your time as "foreigners in the land." ¹⁸ For you know that God paid a ransom to save you from the empty life you inherited from your ancestors. And the ransom he paid was not mere gold or silver. ¹⁹ It was the precious blood of Christ, the sinless, spotless Lamb of God. ²⁰ God chose him as your ransom long before the world began, but he has now revealed him to you in these last days.

Q&A — Flipping Worship on Its Head

1 PETER 1:1–2

What does it really mean to *worship* God?

Worship comes from an Old English term (*weorthscipe*) that means "worthiness" or "worth-ship." At its basic level, worship is ascribing worth to something and behaving toward it accordingly. Worship means saying *this* is the preeminent thing that I value; I'm going to take all the resources I have, everything that I am, and devote it to this thing that I give ultimate value to. For the Christian this means saying to God, *You are everything to me. I'm going to submit myself to you and bring everything I am to serve you.*

But we can't stop here, or our understanding of worship implies that it's all up to us—as if *we're* the ones who decide that God is valuable, and *we* find it within ourselves to serve God accordingly.

No, to really understand worship, we have to look at it from God's perspective. Throughout Scripture we see that God is the initiator with humanity. We love because he first loved us (1 John 4:19). We forgive because he forgave us (Ephesians 4:32). He always makes the first move, and the same is true with worship.

At the foundation of our faith is the understanding that God is triune—he's always been in relationship with himself: Father, Son, and Holy Spirit (2 Corinthians 13:14; Ephesians 2:18; 1 Peter 1:1–2). It's a divine, eternal dance among Father, Son, and Holy Spirit—loving one another, sharing mutual affection and admiration, sharing beauty and truth.

Worship means realizing that, through Christ's forgiveness, we're *part* of that mutual fellowship with our Trinitarian God. Worship is about us saying yes to that miraculous inclusion.

Worship *does* mean ascribing ultimate worth to God and aligning our lives accordingly. But even before that, worship means responding to the invitation from God to see who he is and to recognize our place in this circle of love and fellowship.

—*Carolyn Arends*

For more on worship, see reading at Revelation 4:8–11.

[21] Through Christ you have come to trust in God. And you have placed your faith and hope in God because he raised Christ from the dead and gave him great glory.

[22] You were cleansed from your sins when you obeyed the truth, so now you must show sincere love to each other as brothers and sisters.* Love each other deeply with all your heart.*

[23] For you have been born again, but not to a life that will quickly end. Your new life will last forever because it comes from the eternal, living word of God. [24] As the Scriptures say,

"People are like grass;
their beauty is like a flower in the field.
The grass withers and the flower fades.
[25] But the word of the Lord remains forever."*

And that word is the Good News that was preached to you.

2 So get rid of all evil behavior. Be done with all deceit, hypocrisy, jealousy, and all unkind speech. [2] Like newborn babies, you must crave pure spiritual milk so that you will grow into a full experience of salvation. Cry out for this nourishment, [3] now that you have had a taste of the Lord's kindness.

Living Stones for God's House

[4] You are coming to Christ, who is the living cornerstone of God's temple. He was rejected by people, but he was chosen by God for great honor.

[5] And you are living stones that God is building into his spiritual temple. What's more, you are his holy priests.* Through the mediation of Jesus Christ, you offer spiritual sacrifices that please God. [6] As the Scriptures say,

"I am placing a cornerstone in Jerusalem,*
chosen for great honor,
and anyone who trusts in him
will never be disgraced."*

[7] Yes, you who trust him recognize the honor God has given him. But for those who reject him,

"The stone that the builders rejected
has now become the cornerstone."*

[8] And,

"He is the stone that makes people stumble,
the rock that makes them fall."*

They stumble because they do not obey God's word, and so they meet the fate that was planned for them.

[9] But you are not like that, for you are a chosen people. You are royal priests,* a holy nation, God's very own possession. As a result, you can show others the goodness of God, for he called you out of the darkness into his wonderful light.

[10] "Once you had no identity as a people;
now you are God's people.
Once you received no mercy;
now you have received God's mercy."*

[11] Dear friends, I warn you as "temporary residents and foreigners" to keep away from worldly desires that wage war against your very souls. [12] Be careful to live properly among your unbelieving neighbors. Then even if they accuse you of doing wrong, they will see your honorable behavior, and they will give honor to God when he judges the world.*

Respecting People in Authority

[13] For the Lord's sake, respect all human authority—whether the king as head of state, [14] or the officials he has appointed. For the king has sent them to punish those who do wrong and to honor those who do right.

[15] It is God's will that your honorable lives should silence those ignorant people who make foolish accusations against you. [16] For you are free, yet you are God's slaves, so don't use your freedom as an excuse to do evil. [17] Respect everyone, and love your Christian brothers and sisters.* Fear God, and respect the king.

Slaves

[18] You who are slaves must accept the authority of your masters with all respect.* Do what they tell you—not only if they are

1:22a Greek must have brotherly love. **1:22b** Some manuscripts read with a pure heart. **1:24-25** Isa 40:6-8. **2:5** Greek holy priesthood. **2:6a** Greek in Zion. **2:6b** Isa 28:16 (Greek version). **2:7** Ps 118:22. **2:8** Isa 8:14. **2:9** Greek a royal priesthood. **2:10** Hos 1:6, 9; 2:23. **2:12** Or on the day of visitation. **2:17** Greek love the brotherhood. **2:18** Or because you fear God.

Mentoring

Why We Mentor
1 PETER 1:21-23

At the risk of sounding terribly simplistic, I believe the truest, most "proper" motivation for being a mentor is *love*. As a mentor you actually *care* about someone's spiritual development and are willing to come alongside her for a season of her journey. Sadly, though, this simple quality is a rare occurrence in our Christian communities today.

Sometimes, lacking this one core motivation, mentors will invest in others, but the outcomes can be disastrous, because—to be frank—their "ministry" is really all about *them*. Unhealthy motives for mentoring lurk below the surface, but they can be tempting to all of us when:

- We want to leave a legacy.
- We like being "the one" who is sought after in a community.
- We prefer meddling in other people's problems (especially at the neglect of our own).
- We have a need to teach—to be seen as an expert.
- We may be inclined toward codependency, where we create relationships that depend on us. (These unhealthy relationships don't actually help the other person gain maturity; they just cause the other person to "need" us.)
- We like the label. I recall meeting someone who boasted about an individual she was "mentoring," but I later discovered the supposed "mentoree" had no idea; they'd simply gotten together for a lunch meeting! In this case "mentor" was a self-assigned label of importance.

More common, though, are false motives not to be a mentor: I don't know the Bible well enough; I don't have enough time or energy; I can barely keep my own life together, so how can I mentor someone else? But even that kind of resistance reveals a deep misunderstanding of the true heart of mentoring: these excuses are still all about us.

True mentors reach out and into others' lives from a place of love. Pure and simple. Love—that's something we are all capable of doing!

Eight years ago a young woman scheduled an appointment with me to explain nervously why she'd like to meet with me on a regular basis; she wanted me to be her mentor. I was terrified at the prospect; too worried about my own inadequacies, too sure she was overly impressed with some characteristic she had misconstrued in my character, and, most of all, too fearful of getting involved in someone's life during a season that felt entirely overwhelming to me. So I politely said no. I told her I was honored by the request, but unfortunately I couldn't commit to that kind of relationship.

Sometime later a particular dilemma emerged in her life, and she asked if we could meet just to have coffee and see if I might have any insight into the situation. Now, with me, coffee is an entirely different prospect! And the focus of the particular concern probably made me more comfortable with this first conversation.

Now, some seven years later, April refers to me as her mentor. Over these years I have been invited into key areas of her life, ministry, and spiritual growth. And it's true that I am, or have become, a mentor in her life. I no longer resist that title, and we both laugh about how it actually came to be.

What I'd like to suggest to potential mentors is this: Forget the titles. Forget the label. Forget the role even. But *please* do this one thing: love the women in your life. Actually care. "You were cleansed from your sins when you obeyed the truth, so now you must show sincere love to each other as brothers and sisters. Love each other deeply with all your heart" (1 Peter 1:22). Out of our own spiritual growth, we're able to love deeply.

So listen attentively to their stories. When they ask for your input, share what God's taught you. Open up the rhythms of your life to them. Let them see you as a work in process; provide a safe place for them to describe what's broken or confusing or burning with passion inside them. Remind them of the truths in God's Word. For those who are young in their faith, perhaps you will be the one who introduces them to key truths in God's Word. Pray for them; pray with them.

Love is something that every one of us, at every stage of life's journey, can extend to others around us. This is core to how the body of Christ matures and grows: one person, one relationship, at a time.

—*Mindy Caliguire*

More than Words

1 PETER 2:11-12

Outreach

First Peter was written to believers scattered throughout the Roman Empire who were living through the early stages of Nero's persecution of Christians. This persecution grew in intensity over several years; some sources indicate that a massive fire in Rome was blamed on Christians (though it may have been started by Nero's own men), thus bringing the persecution to a fevered pitch. Church tradition records that Peter himself was executed around that time under Nero's regime.

So here in 1 Peter, we see Peter assessing the intensifying cultural pressure against Christianity and asking the church a critical question: what kind of witness would they be to a watching world? He warned the believers not to give their accusers any ammunition by doing wrong; instead, they should "keep away from worldly desires" (2:11) and should actively do good works in their community (2:12), embodying Jesus' teachings about caring for others, helping those in need, serving others with humility. Peter admonishes them that their witness to the way of Jesus must be one of both personal holiness and outward ministry.

We too ought to see our witness both in terms of what we "keep away" from as well as how we actively do good for others. We should be people of such vast compassion that we are the first on the frontlines to help, care, and meet needs in whatever ways we can.

Evangelism is more than just words; it is also our actions. And we do those good deeds in the name of Christ, no matter what the cost. Peter's audience faced persecution, and yet they were called to continue to do the good work of Christ. When we do that, unbelievers will take notice, and "they will give honor to God" (2:12).

—*Linda Taylor*

For more on outreach, see reading at 1 Peter 3:13-17.

---

kind and reasonable, but even if they are cruel. ¹⁹For God is pleased with you when you do what you know is right and patiently endure unfair treatment. ²⁰Of course, you get no credit for being patient if you are beaten for doing wrong. But if you suffer for doing good and endure it patiently, God is pleased with you.

²¹For God called you to do good, even if it means suffering, just as Christ suffered* for you. He is your example, and you must follow in his steps.

²² He never sinned,
 nor ever deceived anyone.*

²³ He did not retaliate when he was insulted,
 nor threaten revenge when he suffered.
He left his case in the hands of God,
 who always judges fairly.
²⁴ He personally carried our sins
 in his body on the cross
so that we can be dead to sin
 and live for what is right.
By his wounds
 you are healed.
²⁵ Once you were like sheep
 who wandered away.
But now you have turned to your
  Shepherd,
 the Guardian of your souls.

2:21 Some manuscripts read *died.*   **2:22** Isa 53:9.

3 Wives

In the same way, you wives must accept the authority of your husbands. Then, even if some refuse to obey the Good News, your godly lives will speak to them without any words. They will be won over [2]by observing your pure and reverent lives.

[3]Don't be concerned about the outward beauty of fancy hairstyles, expensive jewelry, or beautiful clothes. [4]You should clothe yourselves instead with the beauty that comes from within, the unfading beauty of a gentle and quiet spirit, which is so precious to God. [5]This is how the holy women of old made themselves beautiful. They trusted God and accepted the authority of their husbands. [6]For instance, Sarah obeyed her husband, Abraham, and called him her master. You are her daughters when you do what is right without fear of what your husbands might do.

Husbands

[7]In the same way, you husbands must give honor to your wives. Treat your wife with understanding as you live together. She may be weaker than you are, but she is your equal partner in God's gift of new life. Treat her as you should so your prayers will not be hindered.

All Christians

[8]Finally, all of you should be of one mind. Sympathize with each other. Love each other as brothers and sisters.* Be tenderhearted, and keep a humble attitude. [9]Don't repay evil for evil. Don't retaliate with insults when people insult you. Instead, pay them back with a blessing. That is what God has called you to do, and he will bless you for it. [10]For the Scriptures say,

"If you want to enjoy life
    and see many happy days,
keep your tongue from speaking evil
    and your lips from telling lies.
[11] Turn away from evil and do good.
    Search for peace, and work to
        maintain it.
[12] The eyes of the Lord watch over those
        who do right,
    and his ears are open to their prayers.

But the Lord turns his face
    against those who do evil."*

Suffering for Doing Good

[13]Now, who will want to harm you if you are eager to do good? [14]But even if you suffer for doing what is right, God will reward you for it. So don't worry or be afraid of their threats. [15]Instead, you must worship Christ as Lord of your life. And if someone asks about your Christian hope, always be ready to explain it. [16]But do this in a gentle and respectful way.* Keep your conscience clear. Then if people speak against you, they will be ashamed when they see what a good life you live because you belong to Christ. [17]Remember, it is better to suffer for doing good, if that is what God wants, than to suffer for doing wrong!

[18]Christ suffered* for our sins once for all time. He never sinned, but he died for sinners to bring you safely home to God. He suffered physical death, but he was raised to life in the Spirit.*

[19]So he went and preached to the spirits in prison—[20]those who disobeyed God long ago when God waited patiently while Noah was building his boat. Only eight people were saved from drowning in that terrible flood.* [21]And that water is a picture of baptism, which now saves you, not by removing dirt from your body, but as a response to God from* a clean conscience. It is effective because of the resurrection of Jesus Christ.

[22]Now Christ has gone to heaven. He is seated in the place of honor next to God, and all the angels and authorities and powers accept his authority.

4 Living for God

So then, since Christ suffered physical pain, you must arm yourselves with the same attitude he had, and be ready to suffer, too. For if you have suffered physically for Christ, you have finished with sin.* [2]You won't spend the rest of your lives chasing your own desires, but you will be anxious to do the will of God. [3]You have had enough in the past of the evil things that godless

---

3:8 Greek *Show brotherly love.*   **3:10-12** Ps 34:12-16.   **3:16** Some English translations put this sentence in verse 15.   **3:18a** Some manuscripts read *died.*   **3:18b** Or *in spirit.*   **3:20** Greek *saved through water.*   **3:21** Or *as an appeal to God for.*   **4:1** Or *For the one* [or *One*] *who has suffered physically has finished with sin.*

people enjoy—their immorality and lust, their feasting and drunkenness and wild parties, and their terrible worship of idols.

⁴Of course, your former friends are surprised when you no longer plunge into the flood of wild and destructive things they do. So they slander you. ⁵But remember that they will have to face God, who will judge everyone, both the living and the dead. ⁶That is why the Good News was preached to those who are now dead*—so although they were destined to die like all people,* they now live forever with God in the Spirit.*

⁷The end of the world is coming soon. Therefore, be earnest and disciplined in your prayers. ⁸Most important of all, con-

Q&A — Convicted Civility — Outreach
1 PETER 3:13-17

How can we stand for our Christian convictions without coming across as being judgmental or arrogant?

In a speech I heard several years ago, the Japanese-American theologian Kosuke Koyama put it nicely: we all have to decide whether we have a generous God or a stingy God. We Christians often give the impression that we have decided to be a spiritually stingy people. Many people in our society think of Christians primarily as "judgmental" types, hostile and mean-spirited toward those with whom we disagree.

Theologian Martin Marty once observed that people today who are civil often don't have strong convictions; conversely people who have strong convictions often are not civil. What we need, he said, is convicted civility.

It's easy to err on one side or the other; holding up both conviction and civility simultaneously takes constant effort. But the effort to keep this marriage together *needs* to be made. The proper antidote to relativism and universalism isn't a retreat into a stingy spirit. The apostle Peter teaches us that we must be clear in telling others about Christ, the hope that lies within us. But he adds that we must always do so "in a gentle and respectful way" (1 Peter 3:15-16).

How do we nurture a gentle and reverent spirit toward those with whom we disagree? We must remember that we serve a God whose generous, grace-filled ways are beyond our capacity to grasp; that divine, generous grace enables us to become gracious and humble in our demeanor toward others.

But that same generosity has been clearly displayed in the grace that sent our Savior to Calvary—an abundant grace that is greater than all our sin. Our bold proclamation of that overwhelming generosity must never be muted, even as we strive to show gentleness and respect to others.

—*Richard J. Mouw*

4:6a Greek *preached even to the dead.* 4:6b Or *so although people had judged them worthy of death.* 4:6c Or *in spirit.*

tinue to show deep love for each other, for love covers a multitude of sins. ⁹Cheerfully share your home with those who need a meal or a place to stay.

¹⁰God has given each of you a gift from his great variety of spiritual gifts. Use them well to serve one another. ¹¹Do you have the gift of speaking? Then speak as though God himself were speaking through you. Do you have the gift of helping others? Do it with all the strength and energy that God supplies. Then everything you do will bring glory to God through Jesus Christ. All glory and power to him forever and ever! Amen.

Suffering for Being a Christian

¹²Dear friends, don't be surprised at the fiery trials you are going through, as if

Q&A — Hospitality for Introverts
1 PETER 4:7-11

I find hospitality exhausting and intimidating. How can I practice hospitality when I'd rather just be alone?

As an introvert, the one thing I cannot live without is alone time. Whenever such time is crowded out of my life, I feel as if I'm being crushed in a vise, with so much pressure that I'm going to crack.

Extroverts may struggle with keeping their house clean and fixing edible meals as they consider hospitality, but they will often find ways to overcome that because they want to be with people. We introverts, on the other hand, usually look for ways to avoid people. We're the kind who look the other way when we see someone we know in the grocery store, because it means we'll have to talk to them. We don't enjoy going out of our way to meet new people and invite them into our living space.

Yet Scripture clearly commands us to practice hospitality (1 Peter 4:9). So how can we do so in a way that fits our God-given personality?

First, introverts can concentrate on reaching out to one or two people, rather than feeling pressured to continually make friends with everybody. For example, when my church service ends each Sunday, I seek out just one or two new people I'm getting to know.

Also, introverts can set boundaries. For example, my husband and I make an effort to communicate upfront a clear ending time for Bible studies or other gatherings we host in our home. Then if people stay longer, I say, "It's been lovely, but I've got to get some rest."

Hospitality will look different for introverts, but it can still be a powerful way God works in and through us. It's not just for the people person; it's even for those of us who would prefer to be alone.

—JoHannah Reardon

For more on hospitality, see reading at 3 John 1:5-8.

something strange were happening to you. [13]Instead, be very glad—for these trials make you partners with Christ in his suffering, so that you will have the wonderful joy of seeing his glory when it is revealed to all the world.

[14]So be happy when you are insulted for being a Christian,* for then the glorious Spirit of God* rests upon you.* [15]If you suffer, however, it must not be for murder, stealing, making trouble, or prying into other people's affairs. [16]But it is no shame to suffer for being a Christian. Praise God for the privilege of being called by his name! [17]For the time has come for judgment, and it must begin with God's household. And if judgment begins with us, what terrible fate awaits those who have never obeyed God's Good News? [18]And also,

"If the righteous are barely saved,
  what will happen to godless sinners?"*

[19]So if you are suffering in a manner that pleases God, keep on doing what is right, and trust your lives to the God who created you, for he will never fail you.

5 Advice for Elders and Young Men

And now, a word to you who are elders in the churches. I, too, am an elder and a witness to the sufferings of Christ. And I, too, will share in his glory when he is revealed to the whole world. As a fellow elder, I appeal to you: [2]Care for the flock that God has entrusted to you. Watch over it willingly, not grudgingly—not for what you will get out of it, but because you are eager to serve God. [3]Don't lord it over the people assigned to

Q&A   Worry versus Faith
1 PETER 5:7

I constantly worry about everything from my loved ones to the problems in the world. How can I stop?

Many of us are professional worriers. In fact, in a book by this title author Jerry Bridges calls worry a "respectable sin." It's so common among Christians that we allow it to become a normal part of our lives. Often even our prayers are shaped mostly by worry! We get on our knees not to commune with God but to handle damage control for him, to alert him to what's going on in this crazy world, and to suggest solutions.

With this simple directive, "I tell you not to worry . . ." (Matthew 6:25), Jesus calls us to trust him. To do so requires a certain emotional detachment, a conscious letting go of needing to control the outcome of every situation. Trust is a choice, the alternative to worry. It's not that we don't care; we do! But we intentionally "give all [our] worries and cares to God" (1 Peter 5:7), choosing to turn over our lives to him, one moment at a time.

—Keri Wyatt Kent

4:14a Greek for the name of Christ.   4:14b Or for the glory of God, which is his Spirit.   4:14c Some manuscripts add On their part he is blasphemed, but on your part he is glorified.   4:18 Prov 11:31 (Greek version).

your care, but lead them by your own good example. [4]And when the Great Shepherd appears, you will receive a crown of never-ending glory and honor.

[5]In the same way, you younger men must accept the authority of the elders. And all of you, serve each other in humility, for

"God opposes the proud
    but favors the humble."*

[6]So humble yourselves under the mighty power of God, and at the right time he will lift you up in honor. [7]Give all your worries and cares to God, for he cares about you.

[8]Stay alert! Watch out for your great enemy, the devil. He prowls around like a roaring lion, looking for someone to devour. [9]Stand firm against him, and be strong in your faith. Remember that your Christian brothers and sisters* all over the world are going through the same kind of suffering you are.

[10]In his kindness God called you to share in his eternal glory by means of Christ Jesus. So after you have suffered a little while, he will restore, support, and strengthen you, and he will place you on a firm foundation. [11]All power to him forever! Amen.

Peter's Final Greetings

[12]I have written and sent this short letter to you with the help of Silas,* whom I commend to you as a faithful brother. My purpose in writing is to encourage you and assure you that what you are experiencing is truly part of God's grace for you. Stand firm in this grace.

[13]Your sister church here in Babylon* sends you greetings, and so does my son Mark. [14]Greet each other with Christian love.*

Peace be with all of you who are in Christ.

5:5 Prov 3:34 (Greek version). **5:9** Greek *your brothers*. **5:12** Greek *Silvanus*. **5:13** Greek *The elect one in Babylon*. Babylon was probably symbolic for Rome. **5:14** Greek *with a kiss of love*.

Introduction to

2 Peter

Background

Peter wrote this letter in response to the false teachers prevalent in his time. Like 1 Peter, this epistle is not addressed to a single church. Its authorship has been questioned, one reason being the differences in the Greek vocabulary of 1 Peter compared to 2 Peter. But Peter dictated the first letter to a scribe (1 Peter 5:12), while the second letter does not mention a scribe. There is also some dispute because 2 Peter and Jude (a later book) are so similar in content. However, in 1:16–18 the author claims to have been present at the Transfiguration—witnessed only by the three disciples Peter, James, and John.

Message

Peter encourages his readers to add the following character traits to their faith: moral excellence, knowledge, self-control, patient endurance, godliness, brotherly affection, and love toward all (1:5–7)—a list not unlike the fruit of the Spirit (Galatians 5:22–23). Since the readers of Peter's epistle lived in a time of many heresies, Peter has harsh words for those who teach false doctrines and for those who fall prey to them. In a discussion of the last days, Peter avers that Christ will again appear. Believers must be prepared for his coming, making efforts to be "found living peaceful lives that are pure and blameless in his sight" (3:14).

Time

Second Peter was written after 1 Peter, just before his martyrdom, which occurred between A.D. 64 and 66.

Outline

2 Peter

1 Greetings from Peter

This letter is from Simon* Peter, a slave and apostle of Jesus Christ.

I am writing to you who share the same precious faith we have. This faith was given to you because of the justice and fairness* of Jesus Christ, our God and Savior.

²May God give you more and more grace and peace as you grow in your knowledge of God and Jesus our Lord.

Growing in Faith

³By his divine power, God has given us everything we need for living a godly life. We have received all of this by coming to know him, the one who called us to himself by means of his marvelous glory and excellence. ⁴And because of his glory and excellence, he has given us great and precious promises. These are the promises that enable you to share his divine nature and escape the world's corruption caused by human desires.

⁵In view of all this, make every effort to respond to God's promises. Supplement your faith with a generous provision of moral excellence, and moral excellence with knowledge, ⁶and knowledge with self-control, and self-control with patient endurance, and patient endurance with godliness, ⁷and godliness with brotherly affection, and brotherly affection with love for everyone.

⁸The more you grow like this, the more productive and useful you will be in your knowledge of our Lord Jesus Christ. ⁹But those who fail to develop in this way are shortsighted or blind, forgetting that they have been cleansed from their old sins.

¹⁰So, dear brothers and sisters,* work hard to prove that you really are among those God has called and chosen. Do these things, and you will never fall away. ¹¹Then God will give you a grand entrance into the eternal Kingdom of our Lord and Savior Jesus Christ.

Paying Attention to Scripture

¹²Therefore, I will always remind you about these things—even though you already know them and are standing firm in the truth you have been taught. ¹³And it is only right that I should keep on reminding you as long as I live.* ¹⁴For our Lord Jesus Christ has shown me that I must soon leave this earthly life,* ¹⁵so I will work hard to make sure you always remember these things after I am gone.

¹⁶For we were not making up clever stories when we told you about the powerful coming of our Lord Jesus Christ. We saw his majestic splendor with our own eyes ¹⁷when he received honor and glory from God the Father. The voice from the majestic glory of God said to him, "This is my dearly loved Son, who brings me great joy."* ¹⁸We ourselves heard that voice from heaven when we were with him on the holy mountain.

1:1a Greek *Symeon.*　**1:1b** Or *to you in the righteousness.*　**1:10** Greek *brothers.*　**1:13** Greek *as long as I am in this tent* [or *tabernacle*].　**1:14** Greek *I must soon put off my tent* [or *tabernacle*].　**1:17** Matt 17:5; Mark 9:7; Luke 9:35.

Centered Living

2 PETER 1:3–7

Simplicity sounds great—but how can we get started? What can it actually look like to live in Christ-centered simplicity in the reality of our complicated, postmodern lives?

We can discover a bit of the answer by looking at history and learning from the dynamic women who've gone before us. For example, consider Clare Offreduccio, who was the daughter of a wealthy count. Because of her faith, she chose to abandon her life of privilege and embrace material poverty. We know her today as Clare of Assisi—colleague of Francis—and she offers us this wisdom about living a life of simplicity: "Do not let the thought of Jesus leave your mind. Meditate constantly on the mysteries of the Cross."

That's what motivated many medieval Christian women to live lives of material simplicity, eschewing attachment to wealth or possessions. Their outer simplicity was motivated by an inner centeredness on Christ, which came through regular meditation on God's Word. These women regularly practiced the ancient discipline of *lectio divina* (Latin for "sacred reading/hearing"), memorized and chanted psalms, and read Scripture aloud with others. This time in Scripture led them into ever-deepening intimacy with God.

Grounded in this loving intimacy, their outward simplicity became a natural expression of their focus on Christ. The thirteenth-century German mystic Mechthild of Magdeburg knew that a "gentle and humble" heart always enjoys the happiness of simplicity: "Humble love comes only from holy simplicity. . . . Love that has discovered God's intimacy stuns the earth with its effortless kindness."

Mechthild knew that when our hearts are centered on God and his Word, we experience the inner simplicity of contentment and peace. Thus we're able to be at ease with our true selves, be more kind and loving toward others, and be undistracted by greed or the drive for material gain.

When we experience the depths of God's love for us through centeredness on his Word, we can't help but sing. As Hildegard of Bingen says, "Happy praises offered in simplicity and love lead the faithful to complete harmony. . . . So sing to God with joyful devotion, and don't stop."

—*Carmen Acevedo Butcher*

[19] Because of that experience, we have even greater confidence in the message proclaimed by the prophets. You must pay close attention to what they wrote, for their words are like a lamp shining in a dark place—until the Day dawns, and Christ the Morning Star shines* in your hearts. [20] Above all, you must realize that no prophecy in Scripture ever came from the prophet's own understanding,* [21] or from human initiative. No, those prophets were moved by the Holy Spirit, and they spoke from God.

2 The Danger of False Teachers

But there were also false prophets in Israel, just as there will be false teachers among you. They will cleverly teach destructive heresies and even deny the Master who bought them. In this way, they will bring sudden destruction on themselves. [2] Many will follow their evil teach-

---

1:19 Or *rises.*   **1:20** Or *is a matter of one's own interpretation.*

ing and shameful immorality. And because of these teachers, the way of truth will be slandered. ³In their greed they will make up clever lies to get hold of your money. But God condemned them long ago, and their destruction will not be delayed.

⁴For God did not spare even the angels who sinned. He threw them into hell,* in gloomy pits of darkness,* where they are being held until the day of judgment. ⁵And God did not spare the ancient world— except for Noah and the seven others in his family. Noah warned the world of God's righteous judgment. So God protected Noah when he destroyed the world of ungodly people with a vast flood. ⁶Later, God condemned the cities of Sodom and Gomorrah and turned them into heaps of ashes. He made them an example of what will happen to ungodly people. ⁷But God also rescued Lot out of Sodom because he was a righteous man who was sick of the shameful immorality of the wicked people around him. ⁸Yes, Lot was a righteous man who was tormented in his soul by the wickedness he saw and heard day after day. ⁹So you see, the Lord knows how to rescue godly people from their trials, even while keeping the wicked under punishment until the day of final judgment. ¹⁰He is especially hard on those who follow their own twisted sexual desire, and who despise authority.

These people are proud and arrogant, daring even to scoff at supernatural beings* without so much as trembling. ¹¹But the angels, who are far greater in power and strength, do not dare to bring from the Lord* a charge of blasphemy against those supernatural beings.

¹²These false teachers are like unthinking animals, creatures of instinct, born to be caught and destroyed. They scoff at things they do not understand, and like animals, they will be destroyed. ¹³Their destruction is their reward for the harm they have done. They love to indulge in evil pleasures in broad daylight. They are a disgrace and a stain among you. They delight in deception* even as they eat with you in your fellowship meals. ¹⁴They commit adultery with their

eyes, and their desire for sin is never satisfied. They lure unstable people into sin, and they are well trained in greed. They live under God's curse. ¹⁵They have wandered off the right road and followed the footsteps of Balaam son of Beor,* who loved to earn money by doing wrong. ¹⁶But Balaam was stopped from his mad course when his donkey rebuked him with a human voice.

¹⁷These people are as useless as dried-up springs or as mist blown away by the wind. They are doomed to blackest darkness. ¹⁸They brag about themselves with empty, foolish boasting. With an appeal to twisted sexual desires, they lure back into sin those who have barely escaped from a lifestyle of deception. ¹⁹They promise freedom, but they themselves are slaves of sin and corruption. For you are a slave to whatever controls you. ²⁰And when people escape from the wickedness of the world by knowing our Lord and Savior Jesus Christ and then get tangled up and enslaved by sin again, they are worse off than before. ²¹It would be better if they had never known the way to righteousness than to know it and then reject the command they were given to live a holy life. ²²They prove the truth of this proverb: "A dog returns to its vomit."* And another says, "A washed pig returns to the mud."

3 The Day of the Lord Is Coming

This is my second letter to you, dear friends, and in both of them I have tried to stimulate your wholesome thinking and refresh your memory. ²I want you to remember what the holy prophets said long ago and what our Lord and Savior commanded through your apostles.

³Most importantly, I want to remind you that in the last days scoffers will come, mocking the truth and following their own desires. ⁴They will say, "What happened to the promise that Jesus is coming again? From before the times of our ancestors, everything has remained the same since the world was first created."

⁵They deliberately forget that God made the heavens by the word of his command,

---

2:4a Greek *Tartarus.*   **2:4b** Some manuscripts read *in chains of gloom.*   **2:10** Greek *at glorious ones,* which are probably evil angels.
2:11 Other manuscripts read *to the Lord;* still others do not include this phrase at all.   **2:13** Some manuscripts read *in fellowship meals.*
2:15 Some manuscripts read *Bosor.*   **2:22** Prov 26:11.

and he brought the earth out from the water and surrounded it with water. [6] Then he used the water to destroy the ancient world with a mighty flood. [7] And by the same word, the present heavens and earth have been stored up for fire. They are being kept for the day of judgment, when ungodly people will be destroyed.

[8] But you must not forget this one thing, dear friends: A day is like a thousand years to the Lord, and a thousand years is like a day. [9] The Lord isn't really being slow about his promise, as some people think. No, he is being patient for your sake. He does not want anyone to be destroyed, but wants everyone to repent. [10] But the day of the Lord will come as unexpectedly as a thief. Then the heavens will pass away with a terrible noise, and the very elements themselves will disappear in fire, and the earth and everything on it will be found to deserve judgment.*

[11] Since everything around us is going to be destroyed like this, what holy and godly lives you should live, [12] looking forward to the day of God and hurrying it along. On that day, he will set the heavens on fire, and the elements will melt away in the flames. [13] But we are looking forward to the new heavens and new earth he has promised, a world filled with God's righteousness.

[14] And so, dear friends, while you are waiting for these things to happen, make every effort to be found living peaceful lives that are pure and blameless in his sight.

[15] And remember, our Lord's patience gives people time to be saved. This is what our beloved brother Paul also wrote to you with the wisdom God gave him—[16] speaking of these things in all of his letters. Some of his comments are hard to understand, and those who are ignorant and unstable have twisted his letters to mean something quite different, just as they do with other parts of Scripture. And this will result in their destruction.

Peter's Final Words

[17] I am warning you ahead of time, dear friends. Be on guard so that you will not be carried away by the errors of these wicked people and lose your own secure footing. [18] Rather, you must grow in the grace and knowledge of our Lord and Savior Jesus Christ.

All glory to him, both now and forever! Amen.

3:10 Other manuscripts read *will be burned up;* still others read *will be found destroyed.*

Introduction to

1 John

Background

First John, like many other letters in the New Testament, tackles the issue of false teaching. Heresy at its root is a denial of the gospel of Jesus Christ. Although the letter does not disclose its author, Greek and Latin church fathers consistently identified the author as the apostle John, the son of Zebedee and author of the Gospel of John. The letter includes no salutation; more than likely, John wrote this letter from Ephesus to send to the seven churches in Asia Minor.

Message

The apostle John is known as the "apostle of love" because of the emphasis on love in his writings. John shows his love for the recipients by addressing them as "dear children" (2:1, 28; 3:7, 18; 4:4; 5:21) and "dear friends" (3:2, 21; 4:1, 7, 11). Right in the first verse, John testifies to the physicality and divinity of Jesus, "who existed from the beginning. . . . We saw him with our own eyes and touched him with our own hands." He uses the image of light to describe God (1:5) and as an admonishment that believers should live "in the light" (1:7; 2:9). John's concern for the church also leads to the harsh words he uses for the false teachers (antichrists, 2:18–27) who are threatening the community. He calls for moral purity and exhorts readers to live and love as "children of God" (3:10; 5:2). John emphasizes the need to abide in Christ, who is the impetus of a believer's fellowship with God and others.

Time

The probable date of composition of this letter is between A.D. 85 and 95, as John appears to have written this after his gospel but before the persecution that occurred at the end of the reign of Emperor Domitian (A.D. 81–96).

Outline

1 John

1

Introduction

We proclaim to you the one who existed from the beginning,* whom we have heard and seen. We saw him with our own eyes and touched him with our own hands. He is the Word of life. ²This one who is life itself was revealed to us, and we have seen him. And now we testify and proclaim to you that he is the one who is eternal life. He was with the Father, and then he was revealed to us. ³We proclaim to you what we ourselves have actually seen and heard so that you may have fellowship with us. And our fellowship is with the Father and with his Son, Jesus Christ. ⁴We are writing these things so that you may fully share our joy.*

Living in the Light

⁵This is the message we heard from Jesus* and now declare to you: God is light, and there is no darkness in him at all. ⁶So we are lying if we say we have fellowship with God but go on living in spiritual darkness; we are not practicing the truth. ⁷But if we are living in the light, as God is in the light, then we have fellowship with each other, and the blood of Jesus, his Son, cleanses us from all sin.

⁸If we claim we have no sin, we are only fooling ourselves and not living in the truth. ⁹But if we confess our sins to him, he is faithful and just to forgive us our sins and to cleanse us from all wickedness. ¹⁰If we claim we have not sinned, we are calling God a liar and showing that his word has no place in our hearts.

2

My dear children, I am writing this to you so that you will not sin. But if anyone does sin, we have an advocate who pleads our case before the Father. He is Jesus Christ, the one who is truly righteous. ²He himself is the sacrifice that atones for our sins—and not only our sins but the sins of all the world.

³And we can be sure that we know him if we obey his commandments. ⁴If someone claims, "I know God," but doesn't obey God's commandments, that person is a liar and is not living in the truth. ⁵But those who obey God's word truly show how completely they love him. That is how we know we are living in him. ⁶Those who say they live in God should live their lives as Jesus did.

A New Commandment

⁷Dear friends, I am not writing a new commandment for you; rather it is an old one you have had from the very beginning. This old commandment—to love one another—is the same message you heard before. ⁸Yet it is also new. Jesus lived the truth of this commandment, and you also are living it. For the darkness is disappearing, and the true light is already shining.

⁹If anyone claims, "I am living in the light," but hates a Christian brother or sister,* that person is still living in darkness. ¹⁰Anyone who loves another brother or sister* is living in the light and does not cause others to stumble. ¹¹But anyone who hates another brother or sister is still living and walking in

---

1:1 Greek *What was from the beginning.*   **1:4** Or *so that our joy may be complete;* some manuscripts read *your joy.*   **1:5** Greek *from him.*   **2:9** Greek *hates his brother;* similarly in 2:11.   **2:10** Greek *loves his brother.*

darkness. Such a person does not know the way to go, having been blinded by the darkness.

¹² I am writing to you who are God's children
because your sins have been forgiven through Jesus.*
¹³ I am writing to you who are mature in the faith*
because you know Christ, who existed from the beginning.
I am writing to you who are young in the faith
because you have won your battle with the evil one.
¹⁴ I have written to you who are God's children
because you know the Father.
I have written to you who are mature in the faith
because you know Christ, who existed from the beginning.
I have written to you who are young in the faith
because you are strong.
God's word lives in your hearts,
and you have won your battle with the evil one.

Do Not Love This World

¹⁵Do not love this world nor the things it offers you, for when you love the world, you do not have the love of the Father in you. ¹⁶For the world offers only a craving for physical pleasure, a craving for everything we see, and pride in our achievements and possessions. These are not from the Father, but are from this world. ¹⁷And this world is fading away, along with everything that people crave. But anyone who does what pleases God will live forever.

Warning about Antichrists

¹⁸Dear children, the last hour is here. You have heard that the Antichrist is coming, and already many such antichrists have appeared. From this we know that the last hour has come. ¹⁹These people left our churches, but they never really belonged with us; otherwise they would have stayed with us. When they left, it proved that they did not belong with us.

²⁰But you are not like that, for the Holy One has given you his Spirit,* and all of you know the truth. ²¹So I am writing to you not because you don't know the truth but because you know the difference between truth and lies. ²²And who is a liar? Anyone who says that Jesus is not the Christ.* Anyone who denies the Father and the Son is an antichrist.* ²³Anyone who denies the Son doesn't have the Father, either. But anyone who acknowledges the Son has the Father also.

²⁴So you must remain faithful to what you have been taught from the beginning. If you do, you will remain in fellowship with the Son and with the Father. ²⁵And in this fellowship we enjoy the eternal life he promised us.

²⁶I am writing these things to warn you about those who want to lead you astray. ²⁷But you have received the Holy Spirit,* and he lives within you, so you don't need anyone to teach you what is true. For the Spirit* teaches you everything you need to know, and what he teaches is true—it is not a lie. So just as he has taught you, remain in fellowship with Christ.

Living as Children of God

²⁸And now, dear children, remain in fellowship with Christ so that when he returns, you will be full of courage and not shrink back from him in shame.

²⁹Since we know that Christ is righteous, we also know that all who do what is right are God's children.

3 See how very much our Father loves us, for he calls us his children, and that is what we are! But the people who belong to this world don't recognize that we are God's children because they don't know him. ²Dear friends, we are already God's children, but he has not yet shown us what we will be like when Christ appears. But we do know that we will be like him, for we will see him as he really is. ³And all who have this eager expectation will keep themselves pure, just as he is pure.

2:12 Greek *through his name.* **2:13** Or *to you fathers; also in 2:14.* **2:20** Greek *But you have an anointing from the Holy One.* **2:22a** Or *not the Messiah.* **2:22b** Or *the antichrist.* **2:27a** Greek *the anointing from him.* **2:27b** Greek *the anointing.*

Celebration

The Good, the Ordinary, the Delight

1 JOHN 1:1–7

Every good thing, no matter how trivial, can elicit delight. And delight is potent. Something of little significance provokes glee, and the spirit leaps. If you pay attention—and if you count all good things as coming from God—then the mundane can help you glimpse the Maker of all delight.

Momentous thrills—a wedding day, the birth of a child, reconciliation between hardened enemies, and a stunning answer to prayer when you're low on hope—point to God more noticeably. So do tragedies, mistakes, and sins. But I'm talking about delights that we encounter more frequently, those we have at our disposal and to which we have become accustomed—the terrain of the trivial, the minor, the normal, the everyday, the routine, even the boring. They too reside in the realm of providence.

People shudder, rightly, at what political theorist Hannah Arendt called the banality of evil—the idea that evil can become so normalized and ordinary that we cease to see it for what it is. As she pointed out, malevolence is good corrupted. If we don't take notice of and relish the uncorrupted goodness around us, then evil is likely to overwhelm us.

So let us give praise for the consoling ordinariness of goodness.

Ask the woman who anointed Jesus' feet with nard oil (Mark 14:1–9) and the widow who offered her two coins (Mark 12:41–44), and they'd tell you: God takes pleasure in the seemingly insignificant. Ask the hemorrhaging woman who touched Christ's robe amid a pressing crowd (Mark 5:25–34), and she'd tell you: the barely noticeable matters to him. Ask the wedding guests in Cana (John 2:1–11), and they'd tell you: God pays attention to details like wine chemistry, even when it doesn't seem to matter to anyone else. Finally, consult your body, and it will tell you (chances are, it already has, many times): God wants us to partake in all kinds of pleasures.

"Love, and do as you please," said Augustine in a sermon on 1 John. Folded into this advice is an implicit warning against addiction: you are not free to love God with all your heart, soul, strength, and mind when you're owned by pleasure. But when you experience enjoyment within the constraint of loving God, it can only be good.

Besides being enjoyable, everyday pleasures can be useful. During those darker times when I cannot bring myself to face God, I still cannot turn off delight. I am stuck with goodness. Sometimes, it seems as though all I have to hold on to is one small enjoyment. Something feels good, and no one can take it from me—sun rays on my face, a toddler's hand in mine, managing to tell the truth, a shower, a day without a headache, the five minutes I spend reading an article in *The Economist* that make my world both stranger and easier to grasp.

On those unguarded occasions when I can taste, see, feel, smell, and know that, in poet Gerard Manley Hopkins's words, "the world is charged with the grandeur of God," I revel a little. I notice. Something must have propelled the sun from behind the clouds. Some power must have suspended it in just the right spot.

Suddenly, without putting much thought into it, I find myself saying thank you. A lungful of marvel becomes a prayer of gratitude. Supposedly ordinary acts turn sacramental, with no effort on my part.

This too is worship: to receive all good things and to bow our heads in the knowledge that they come from God. To take whatever is lovely, splendid, pure, noble, and true—and to follow where it leads. To "taste and see that the LORD is good" (Psalm 34:8).

In her Pulitzer-winning study of nature's microcosm in a Blue Ridge Mountains valley, *Pilgrim at Tinker Creek*, Annie Dillard cautions against "taking leave of our senses," by which she means ceasing to marvel at the world around us. Our curiosity must be like that of children, she says, whose senses work overtime.

"Only children can hear the song of the male house mouse," she writes. "Only children keep their eyes open. The only thing they have got is sense; they have highly developed 'input systems,' admitting all data indiscriminately." If we must become like children to enter the kingdom of heaven, then something tells me that commonplace revelry is part of the package.

I know this for sure: goodness began at the very beginning. Before things turned bad, God declared all he had made to be unqualifiedly good (Genesis 1:31). Even our feelings of discontent cannot help but point us toward goodness: discontentment and longing remind that something's amiss from the way things ought to be.

When a fleeting delight promises a lasting one, we glimpse the goodness of God. Anything that does that is not ordinary.

—*Agnieszka Tennant*

[4]Everyone who sins is breaking God's law, for all sin is contrary to the law of God. [5]And you know that Jesus came to take away our sins, and there is no sin in him. [6]Anyone who continues to live in him will not sin. But anyone who keeps on sinning does not know him or understand who he is.

[7]Dear children, don't let anyone deceive you about this: When people do what is right, it shows that they are righteous, even as Christ is righteous. [8]But when people keep on sinning, it shows that they belong to the devil, who has been sinning since the beginning. But the Son of God came to destroy the works of the devil. [9]Those who have been born into God's family do not make a practice of sinning, because God's life* is in them. So they can't keep on sinning, because they are children of God. [10]So now we can tell who are children of God and who are children of the devil. Anyone who does not live righteously and does not love other believers* does not belong to God.

Love One Another

[11]This is the message you have heard from the beginning: We should love one another. [12]We must not be like Cain, who belonged to the evil one and killed his brother. And why did he kill him? Because Cain had been doing what was evil, and his brother had been doing what was righteous. [13]So don't be surprised, dear brothers and sisters,* if the world hates you.

[14]If we love our Christian brothers and sisters,* it proves that we have passed from death to life. But a person who has no love is still dead. [15]Anyone who hates another brother or sister* is really a murderer at heart. And you know that murderers don't have eternal life within them.

[16]We know what real love is because Jesus gave up his life for us. So we also ought to give up our lives for our brothers and sisters. [17]If someone has enough money to live well and sees a brother or sister* in need but shows no compassion—how can God's love be in that person?

[18]Dear children, let's not merely say that we love each other; let us show the truth by our actions. [19]Our actions will show that we belong to the truth, so we will be confident when we stand before God. [20]Even if we feel guilty, God is greater than our feelings, and he knows everything.

[21]Dear friends, if we don't feel guilty, we can come to God with bold confidence. [22]And we will receive from him whatever we ask because we obey him and do the things that please him.

[23]And this is his commandment: We must believe in the name of his Son, Jesus Christ, and love one another, just as he commanded us. [24]Those who obey God's commandments remain in fellowship with him, and he with them. And we know he lives in us because the Spirit he gave us lives in us.

4 Discerning False Prophets

[1]Dear friends, do not believe everyone who claims to speak by the Spirit. You must test them to see if the spirit they have comes from God. For there are many false prophets in the world. [2]This is how we know if they have the Spirit of God: If a person claiming to be a prophet* acknowledges that Jesus Christ came in a real body, that person has the Spirit of God. [3]But if someone claims to be a prophet and does not acknowledge the truth about Jesus, that person is not from God. Such a person has the spirit of the Antichrist, which you heard is coming into the world and indeed is already here.

[4]But you belong to God, my dear children. You have already won a victory over those people, because the Spirit who lives in you is greater than the spirit who lives in the world. [5]Those people belong to this world, so they speak from the world's viewpoint, and the world listens to them. [6]But we belong to God, and those who know God listen to us. If they do not belong to God, they do not listen to us. That is how we know if someone has the Spirit of truth or the spirit of deception.

Loving One Another

[7]Dear friends, let us continue to love one another, for love comes from God. Anyone

---

3:9 Greek *because his seed.*   **3:10** Greek *does not love his brother.*   **3:13** Greek *brothers.*   **3:14** Greek *the brothers;* similarly in 3:16.
3:15 Greek *hates his brother.*   **3:17** Greek *sees his brother.*   **4:2** Greek *If a spirit;* similarly in 4:3.

Forgiving Myself

1 JOHN 3:19

Forgiveness

I never understood people who couldn't forgive themselves until I became one of them. Souls eroded by guilt, lives haunted by regret, hearts consumed by failure . . . didn't they know that Jesus came to set them free?

The answer is yes. Most of us know—rationally speaking anyway—that at its core the Cross commands forgiveness. But when our same rational souls become overwhelmed by shame, guilt, or the pain of irreversible consequences, a perversion of the truth distorts reality: *my* sin is the *one* sin that Jesus' blood is incapable of covering.

In the midst of my struggle with self-forgiveness, a friend challenged me with a truth that I had long since shut out. She told me, "You are holding yourself to a higher standard than anyone else. You are a child of the light. You need to walk in the light."

With those simple words I was reminded that no matter what I had done I was, in fact, a child of the light (Ephesians 5:8). A new creation set free by the blood of the Lamb. "Forgiven" was not a status to which I needed to aspire; *it was who I already was.* And by choosing not to forgive myself, I was choosing not to believe the One who said, "I—yes, I alone—will blot out your sins for my own sake and will never think of them again" (Isaiah 43:25).

Self-forgiveness is a long, arduous journey. But when we finally live in its truth, new life awaits. Chains are broken. Dependence, gratitude, and grace permeate our hearts and redefine who we are. We understand, perhaps for the first time, our desperate need for a Savior, and we fall at his feet in worship because we know that in our unworthiness, we have finally found our worth.

Walk as a child of the light; be forgiven because you already are.

—Suanne Camfield

who loves is a child of God and knows God. [8] But anyone who does not love does not know God, for God is love.

[9] God showed how much he loved us by sending his one and only Son into the world so that we might have eternal life through him. [10] This is real love—not that we loved God, but that he loved us and sent his Son as a sacrifice to take away our sins. [11] Dear friends, since God loved us that much, we surely ought to love each other. [12] No one has ever seen God. But if we love each other, God lives in us, and his love is brought to full expression in us.

[13] And God has given us his Spirit as proof that we live in him and he in us. [14] Further-more, we have seen with our own eyes and now testify that the Father sent his Son to be the Savior of the world. [15] All who con-fess that Jesus is the Son of God have God living in them, and they live in God. [16] We know how much God loves us, and we have put our trust in his love.

God is love, and all who live in love live in God, and God lives in them. [17] And as we live in God, our love grows more perfect. So we will not be afraid on the day of judg-ment, but we can face him with confidence because we live like Jesus here in this world. [18] Such love has no fear, because perfect love expels all fear. If we are afraid, it is for fear of punishment, and this shows that we have not fully experienced his perfect love. [19] We love each other* because he loved us first.

[20] If someone says, "I love God," but hates a Christian brother or sister,* that person is a liar; for if we don't love people we can see, how can we love God, whom we cannot see? [21] And he has given us this command: Those who love God must also love their Christian brothers and sisters.*

5 Faith in the Son of God

Everyone who believes that Jesus is the Christ* has become a child of God. And everyone who loves the Father loves his children, too. [2] We know we love God's children if we love God and obey his commandments. [3] Loving God means keeping his commandments, and his commandments are not burdensome. [4] For every child of God defeats this evil world, and we achieve this victory through our faith. [5] And who can win this battle against the world? Only those who believe that Jesus is the Son of God.

[6] And Jesus Christ was revealed as God's Son by his baptism in water and by shedding his blood on the cross*—not by water only, but by water and blood. And the Spirit, who is truth, confirms it with his testimony. [7] So we have these three witnesses*—[8] the Spirit, the water, and the blood—and all three agree. [9] Since we believe human testimony, surely we can believe the greater testimony that comes from God. And God has testified about his Son. [10] All who believe in the Son of God know in their hearts that this testimony is true. Those who don't believe this are actually calling God a liar because they don't believe what God has testified about his Son.

[11] And this is what God has testified: He has given us eternal life, and this life is in his Son. [12] Whoever has the Son has life; whoever does not have God's Son does not have life.

Conclusion

[13] I have written this to you who believe in the name of the Son of God, so that you may know you have eternal life. [14] And we are confident that he hears us whenever we ask for anything that pleases him. [15] And since we know he hears us when we make our requests, we also know that he will give us what we ask for.

[16] If you see a Christian brother or sister* sinning in a way that does not lead to death, you should pray, and God will give that person life. But there is a sin that leads to death, and I am not saying you should pray for those who commit it. [17] All wicked actions are sin, but not every sin leads to death.

[18] We know that God's children do not make a practice of sinning, for God's Son holds them securely, and the evil one cannot touch them. [19] We know that we are children of God and that the world around us is under the control of the evil one.

[20] And we know that the Son of God has come, and he has given us understanding so that we can know the true God.* And now we live in fellowship with the true God because we live in fellowship with his Son, Jesus Christ. He is the only true God, and he is eternal life.

[21] Dear children, keep away from anything that might take God's place in your hearts.*

4:19 Greek *We love.* Other manuscripts read *We love God;* still others read *We love him.* **4:20** Greek *hates his brother.* **4:21** Greek *The one who loves God must also love his brother.* **5:1** Or *the Messiah.* **5:6** Greek *This is he who came by water and blood.* **5:7** A few very late manuscripts add *in heaven—the Father, the Word, and the Holy Spirit, and these three are one. And we have three witnesses on earth.* **5:16** Greek *a brother.* **5:20** Greek *the one who is true.* **5:21** Greek *keep yourselves from idols.*

Introduction to
2 John

Background

Like 1 John, 2 John deals with the issue of false teachers. Having departed from the community (1 John 2:19), these teachers now seek hospitality from the audience of 2 John (1:10). The author of 2 and 3 John refers to himself as "the elder" in verse 1. The second-century Christian writers Irenaeus and Clement of Alexandria believed that the apostle John wrote these letters. Second John is addressed to "the chosen lady and to her children" (1:1), which could be literal or metaphorical; one can similarly understand the reference to "the children of your sister" (1:13) either as the nieces and nephews of the woman or the members of another church.

Message

In this brief letter, John models and encourages the love Christians are to have for one another. He also demonstrates a great concern for knowing the truth and shows the intimate relationship between truth and love. While Christians are called to love one another, John advises believers to avoid giving hospitality or support to those who do not teach the truth "that Jesus Christ came in a real body" (1:7). The loving thing is to deny these teachers support, showing that they advocate a false gospel. Paul makes a similar point about the immoral behavior of professed Christians in 1 Corinthians 5:9–13.

Time

This letter is probably contemporaneous with or slightly later than 1 John, originating from Ephesus around A.D. 90.

Outline

2 John

Greetings

This letter is from John, the elder.*

I am writing to the chosen lady and to her children,* whom I love in the truth—as does everyone else who knows the truth—²because the truth lives in us and will be with us forever.

³Grace, mercy, and peace, which come from God the Father and from Jesus Christ—the Son of the Father—will continue to be with us who live in truth and love.

Live in the Truth

⁴How happy I was to meet some of your children and find them living according to the truth, just as the Father commanded.

⁵I am writing to remind you, dear friends,* that we should love one another. This is not a new commandment, but one we have had from the beginning. ⁶Love means doing what God has commanded us, and he has commanded us to love one another, just as you heard from the beginning.

⁷I say this because many deceivers have gone out into the world. They deny that Jesus Christ came* in a real body. Such a person is a deceiver and an antichrist. ⁸Watch out that you do not lose what we* have worked so hard to achieve. Be diligent so that you receive your full reward. ⁹Anyone who wanders away from this teaching has no relationship with God. But anyone who remains in the teaching of Christ has a relationship with both the Father and the Son.

¹⁰If anyone comes to your meeting and does not teach the truth about Christ, don't invite that person into your home or give any kind of encouragement. ¹¹Anyone who encourages such people becomes a partner in their evil work.

Conclusion

¹²I have much more to say to you, but I don't want to do it with paper and ink. For I hope to visit you soon and talk with you face to face. Then our joy will be complete.

¹³Greetings from the children of your sister,* chosen by God.

1a Greek *From the elder.*   **1b** Or *the church God has chosen and its members.*   **5** Greek *I urge you, lady.*   **7** Or *will come.*
8 Some manuscripts read *you.*   **13** Or *from the members of your sister church.*

Community on the Fringe
2 JOHN 1:1–6

Of all the spiritual disciplines, community building is the most difficult for me. Maybe it's because I've been burned one too many times by Christians. Sometimes it's their "well-meaning," but ignorant, comments. Sometimes it's their mean-spirited words and actions. So I've learned the art of community on the fringe. I show up, do my part, but never really allow myself to become too vulnerable—because I just don't want to get hurt anymore. And you can't get hurt when you aren't too invested.

I know other women who feel the same way. Their motto is that old saying, "Burn me once, shame on you. Burn me twice, shame on me." And that's how they practice living in community. On the fringe, never allowing life to get too messy—because that's too painful and takes too much energy—especially for introverted, people-pleasing, avoid-conflict-at-all costs women. Like me.

But while it's safe, I've found that practicing community on the fringe leaves me lonely and missing the joy of growing through conflict, of being stretched, challenged, and encouraged.

Jesus did community really well—which is amazing considering the men and women who continually did and said ignorant and hurtful things to him. But he kept diving in wholeheartedly—frustrated sometimes, definitely. But always centering his life and faith in the midst of other believers. And if Christ could do it and calls me to follow him, then I guess community on the fringe isn't all that God honoring after all.

In the times when it's easiest to withdraw from those who hurt us in community, maybe God is calling us to push in deeper, to become more invested—and to find the healing from the same source as the pain.

—Ginger Kolbaba

For more on community, see reading at Jude 1:17–25.

Introduction to
3 John

Background

The apostle John, identified as "the elder" in verse 1, sent itinerant teachers as part of his oversight of churches unnamed in this epistle. These teachers would stay in the homes of church members.

Message

Responding to a report received about a congregation, John compares and contrasts the conduct of three individuals: Gaius, Diotrephes, and Demetrius. Gaius is a humble servant of Christ, who has offered hospitality to the teachers whom John sent, recognizing them as brethren even though they are strangers (1:5). His conduct elicits great joy in John and causes John to pray for Gaius's health and well-being (1:2). In contrast, Diotrephes seizes control of a congregation and selfishly rejects the authority of John and the ministry of the teachers he sent. Diotrephes's opposition to John extends to spreading lies about John and excommunicating those who welcome the teachers. As a further contrast, John commends Demetrius of whom "everyone speaks highly . . . as does the truth itself" (1:12).

Time

The similarities in style and theme between 2 and 3 John indicate that John probably wrote them around the same time, likely A.D. 90, when he lived in Ephesus (the most prominent city in the region) and had oversight of the churches in Asia Minor.

Outline

3 John

Greetings

This letter is from John, the elder.*

I am writing to Gaius, my dear friend, whom I love in the truth.

²Dear friend, I hope all is well with you and that you are as healthy in body as you are strong in spirit. ³Some of the traveling teachers* recently returned and made me very happy by telling me about your faithfulness and that you are living according to the truth. ⁴I could have no greater joy than to hear that my children are following the truth.

Caring for the Lord's Workers

⁵Dear friend, you are being faithful to God when you care for the traveling teachers who pass through, even though they are strangers to you. ⁶They have told the church here of your loving friendship. Please continue providing for such teachers in a manner that pleases God. ⁷For they are traveling for the Lord,* and they accept nothing from people who are not believers.* ⁸So we ourselves should support them so that we can be their partners as they teach the truth.

⁹I wrote to the church about this, but Diotrephes, who loves to be the leader, refuses to have anything to do with us. ¹⁰When I come, I will report some of the things he is doing and the evil accusations he is making against us. Not only does he refuse to welcome the traveling teachers, he also tells others not to help them. And when they do help, he puts them out of the church.

¹¹Dear friend, don't let this bad example influence you. Follow only what is good. Remember that those who do good prove that they are God's children, and those who do evil prove that they do not know God.*

¹²Everyone speaks highly of Demetrius, as does the truth itself. We ourselves can say the same for him, and you know we speak the truth.

Conclusion

¹³I have much more to say to you, but I don't want to write it with pen and ink. ¹⁴For I hope to see you soon, and then we will talk face to face.

¹⁵*Peace be with you.

Your friends here send you their greetings. Please give my personal greetings to each of our friends there.

---

1 Greek *From the elder.*   **3** Greek *the brothers*; also in verses 5 and 10.   **7a** Greek *They went out on behalf of the Name.*
7b Greek *from Gentiles.*   **11** Greek *they have not seen God.*   **15** Some English translations combine verses 14 and 15 into verse 14.

Into Our Messy Lives

3 JOHN 1:5-8

I once decided to make a simple truffle recipe for some guests. To my horror, those truffles turned out to be the ugliest things ever. Instead of serving them, I took them to work and secretly placed them on the "free food" table. Hours later I heard a group of women say, "Who made these truffles? They're wonderful!" Stunned, I finally confessed.

Later God whispered to my heart, *You don't just do that with truffles.* He was right. I tend to hide anything I don't feel is "good enough." But what if the areas I feel inadequate about could actually become a blessing when offered to others?

As Lauren Winner says in her book *Mudhouse Sabbath*, "We aren't meant simply to invite people into our homes, but into our lives as well. . . . We aren't meant to rearrange our lives for our guests—we're meant to invite our guests to enter into our sometimes-messy lives." In hospitality God doesn't call us to impress people but rather to embrace them. Part of that involves a kind attitude, willingness to offer our time, and sharing who we really are.

Our messy lives—our day-to-day reality—can be a place of ministry. In hospitality we can invite others in, even into our hurts, insecurities, and shortcomings as we live within and express our reliance upon God's generous grace for all our not-good-enoughs. Perhaps that's the true heart of hospitality—simply having the courage to put who we are and all we have (even ugly truffles) on the table in love.

—Holley Gerth

Introduction to
Jude

Background

Jude was probably written to churches east of Judea. The epistle of Jude has some similarities to 2 Peter. The author of the epistle provides information about himself in verse 1: "Jude, a slave of Jesus Christ and a brother of James." Matthew 13:55 and Mark 6:3 indicate that Jesus had a brother named Judas, and Jude is a shortened form of Judas. Jude's brother James, a leader of the Jerusalem church (Acts 15:3–21; Galatians 2:9), wrote the epistle of James.

Message

The epistle of Jude deals with the subject of apostasy in a preventative way. Its advice: "Defend the faith that God has entrusted once for all time to his holy people" (1:3). Jude compares false teachers to Old Testament characters Cain, Balaam, and Korah and prophesies that they will face destruction. In making his case, Jude refers to extrabiblical traditions concerning the fallen angels, the archangel Michael, and Enoch. Those who accept false teaching will be judged. This judgment can be avoided as the believer grows in faith and looks with anticipation toward Christ's return. Believers can help those struggling to maintain their faith and recognize that God has the power to "keep [them] from falling away" (1:24).

Time

Even though he does not mention the fall of Jerusalem in A.D. 70, Jude probably wrote this letter between A.D. 66 and 80.

Outline

Jude

Greetings from Jude

This letter is from Jude, a slave of Jesus Christ and a brother of James.

I am writing to all who have been called by God the Father, who loves you and keeps you safe in the care of Jesus Christ.*

²May God give you more and more mercy, peace, and love.

The Danger of False Teachers

³Dear friends, I had been eagerly planning to write to you about the salvation we all share. But now I find that I must write about something else, urging you to defend the faith that God has entrusted once for all time to his holy people. ⁴I say this because some ungodly people have wormed their way into your churches, saying that God's marvelous grace allows us to live immoral lives. The condemnation of such people was recorded long ago, for they have denied our only Master and Lord, Jesus Christ.

⁵So I want to remind you, though you already know these things, that Jesus* first rescued the nation of Israel from Egypt, but later he destroyed those who did not remain faithful. ⁶And I remind you of the angels who did not stay within the limits of authority God gave them but left the place where they belonged. God has kept them securely chained in prisons of darkness, waiting for the great day of judgment. ⁷And don't forget Sodom and Gomorrah and their neighboring towns, which were filled with immorality and every kind of sexual perversion. Those cities were destroyed by fire and serve as a warning of the eternal fire of God's judgment.

⁸In the same way, these people—who claim authority from their dreams—live immoral lives, defy authority, and scoff at supernatural beings.* ⁹But even Michael, one of the mightiest of the angels,* did not dare accuse the devil of blasphemy, but simply said, "The Lord rebuke you!" (This took place when Michael was arguing with the devil about Moses' body.) ¹⁰But these people scoff at things they do not understand. Like unthinking animals, they do whatever their instincts tell them, and so they bring about their own destruction. ¹¹What sorrow awaits them! For they follow in the footsteps of Cain, who killed his brother. Like Balaam, they deceive people for money. And like Korah, they perish in their rebellion.

¹²When these people eat with you in your fellowship meals commemorating the Lord's love, they are like dangerous reefs that can shipwreck you.* They are like shameless shepherds who care only for themselves. They are like clouds blowing over the land without giving any rain. They are like trees in autumn that are doubly dead, for they bear no fruit and have been pulled up by the roots. ¹³They are like wild waves of the sea, churning up the foam of their shameful deeds. They are like wandering stars, doomed forever to blackest darkness.

¹⁴Enoch, who lived in the seventh generation after Adam, prophesied about

---

1 Or keeps you for Jesus Christ.   **5** As in the best manuscripts; various other manuscripts read [the] Lord, or God, or Christ; one reads God Christ.   **8** Greek at glorious ones, which are probably evil angels.   **9** Greek Michael, the archangel.   **12** Or they are contaminants among you; or they are stains.

Tempted to Leave

JUDE 1:17–25

Community

A number of years ago I withdrew from God's people.

Being involved in church seemed impossible because of family problems. My children had abandoned their faith. My husband's passion for God had cooled, and our marriage was taking such a hit that I wondered if it could survive much longer. My prayers seemed futile.

When I went to church, each time someone asked about my family, celebrated their children's godly lives, or talked about their wonderful marriages, pain and self-pity threatened to smother me.

No one else is suffering like me, I decided. *I'll just stay home.*

Yet the Lord continued to urge me to stay involved. Reluctantly I returned to church, and slowly I discovered God desired to use his people—even at their most imperfect—to help me navigate rough waters.

As I tentatively stepped back into my church community and mustered courage to open up, I noticed my honesty freed others to remove their my-life-is-perfect masks and share their heartaches as well. A sense of connection with others began to grow.

My honesty led others to minister to me—and I learned how to receive their counsel, hugs, prayers, wisdom from the Word, and at times their tears. As I humbled myself enough to listen, godly women helped me view my pain and hard times from God's perspective—a testing of my faith and a means to grow. Others helped me win the battle against fears, doubts, and unbelief.

Do people still unintentionally say things that hurt? Yes. But God has used those hurtful words too. They've made me more aware of times when *I've* said things without thinking; they've helped me become more compassionate toward and sensitive to noticing those who hurt.

When I'm feeling the worst emotionally and an inner voice shouts, *Stay home!* that's when I most *need* Christian fellowship. The voice telling me to stay home isn't God's, but the Enemy's. He wants to keep Christians isolated and hates when we bless and strengthen one another. God rejoices when we do.

—*Elaine Creasman*

these people. He said, "Listen! The Lord is coming with countless thousands of his holy ones [15]to execute judgment on the people of the world. He will convict every person of all the ungodly things they have done and for all the insults that ungodly sinners have spoken against him."*

[16]These people are grumblers and complainers, living only to satisfy their desires. They brag loudly about themselves, and they flatter others to get what they want.

A Call to Remain Faithful

[17]But you, my dear friends, must remember what the apostles of our Lord Jesus Christ said. [18]They told you that in the last times there would be scoffers whose purpose in life is to satisfy their ungodly desires. [19]These people are the ones who are creating divisions among you. They follow their natural instincts because they do not have God's Spirit in them.

[20]But you, dear friends, must build each other up in your most holy faith, pray in the

14-15 The quotation comes from intertestamental literature: Enoch 1:9.

power of the Holy Spirit,* ²¹and await the mercy of our Lord Jesus Christ, who will bring you eternal life. In this way, you will keep yourselves safe in God's love.

²²And you must show mercy to* those whose faith is wavering. ²³Rescue others by snatching them from the flames of judgment. Show mercy to still others,* but do so with great caution, hating the sins that contaminate their lives.*

A Prayer of Praise

²⁴Now all glory to God, who is able to keep you from falling away and will bring you with great joy into his glorious presence without a single fault. ²⁵All glory to him who alone is God, our Savior through Jesus Christ our Lord. All glory, majesty, power, and authority are his before all time, and in the present, and beyond all time! Amen.

---

20 Greek *pray in the Holy Spirit.* **22** Some manuscripts read *must reprove.* **22-23a** Some manuscripts have only two categories of people: (1) those whose faith is wavering and therefore need to be snatched from the flames of judgment, and (2) those who need to be shown mercy. **23b** Greek *with fear, hating even the clothing stained by the flesh.*

Introduction to

Revelation

Background

The Book of Revelation is apocalyptic. The original Greek title of this book referred to the "Apocalypse," meaning "unveiling" of things known to God. The book's symbolic imagery is meant to comfort—not confuse—its readers, facing persecution. The apostle John is widely believed to be the author of the book, the original title of which includes his name as the visionary. His name appears repeatedly in the first and concluding chapters. In chapter 1 John reveals his whereabouts, noting that he received the visions on Patmos, a very small Greek island to which he was exiled in his old age. A voice "like a trumpet blast" says, "Write in a book everything you see, and send it to the seven churches in the cities of Ephesus, Smyrna, Pergamum, Thyatira, Sardis, Philadelphia, and Laodicea" (1:9–11).

Message

Christians in the Roman Empire are experiencing increased persecution under the rule of Domitian. The first chapters, which detail strengths and weaknesses of the seven named churches in Asia, refer to the impending crackdown on believers who will not worship Caesar and to the "great time of testing that will come upon the whole world" (3:10). Beginning in chapter 4, John describes visions of heaven where the Lamb opens a series of seals, each revealing an aspect of peril and destruction. Persecution comes in the form of beasts, false prophets, and "the dragon" (12:9). The final battle between the forces of heaven led by the risen Christ and the forces of evil ends in a victory for the forces of heaven. When Christ returns to reign on earth for one thousand years, Satan will be bound and cast into the lake of fire. The book ends with a vision of the new heaven and new earth and the hope of the return of the risen Christ.

Time

Revelation was probably written toward the end of John's life, during his exile to the island of Patmos (A.D. 90–95).

Outline

Revelation

1 Prologue

This is a revelation from* Jesus Christ, which God gave him to show his servants the events that must soon* take place. He sent an angel to present this revelation to his servant John, ²who faithfully reported everything he saw. This is his report of the word of God and the testimony of Jesus Christ.

³God blesses the one who reads the words of this prophecy to the church, and he blesses all who listen to its message and obey what it says, for the time is near.

John's Greeting to the Seven Churches

⁴This letter is from John to the seven churches in the province of Asia.*

Grace and peace to you from the one who is, who always was, and who is still to come; from the sevenfold Spirit* before his throne; ⁵and from Jesus Christ. He is the faithful witness to these things, the first to rise from the dead, and the ruler of all the kings of the world.

All glory to him who loves us and has freed us from our sins by shedding his blood for us. ⁶He has made us a Kingdom of priests for God his Father. All glory and power to him forever and ever! Amen.

⁷ Look! He comes with the clouds of heaven.
And everyone will see him—
even those who pierced him.
And all the nations of the world
will mourn for him.
Yes! Amen!

⁸"I am the Alpha and the Omega—the beginning and the end,"* says the Lord God. "I am the one who is, who always was, and who is still to come—the Almighty One."

Vision of the Son of Man

⁹I, John, am your brother and your partner in suffering and in God's Kingdom and in the patient endurance to which Jesus calls us. I was exiled to the island of Patmos for preaching the word of God and for my testimony about Jesus. ¹⁰It was the Lord's Day, and I was worshiping in the Spirit.* Suddenly, I heard behind me a loud voice like a trumpet blast. ¹¹It said, "Write in a book* everything you see, and send it to the seven churches in the cities of Ephesus, Smyrna, Pergamum, Thyatira, Sardis, Philadelphia, and Laodicea."

¹²When I turned to see who was speaking to me, I saw seven gold lampstands. ¹³And standing in the middle of the lampstands was someone like the Son of Man.* He was wearing a long robe with a gold sash across his chest. ¹⁴His head and his hair were white like wool, as white as snow. And his eyes were like flames of fire. ¹⁵His feet were like polished bronze refined in a furnace, and his

---

1:1a Or of. 1:1b Or suddenly, or quickly. 1:4a Asia was a Roman province in what is now western Turkey. 1:4b Greek the seven spirits. 1:8 Greek I am the Alpha and the Omega, referring to the first and last letters of the Greek alphabet. 1:10 Or in spirit. 1:11 Or on a scroll. 1:13 Or like a son of man. See Dan 7:13. "Son of Man" is a title Jesus used for himself.

Seeking God in Our Busyness

REVELATION 2:4

Contemplation

Each of us has seasons that are extremely busy—the years caring for young children, periods in which our career is demanding, times of volunteering and relationship building that gobble up all possible "down time." The danger during these seasons is to buy into the idea that time with God must look a certain way—that it must mean an hour of intense daily study, for example. We begin to think that if we don't spend an hour, then it's not worth it to do anything at all—that our meager five or ten minutes is not enough. And then, all of a sudden, we get to a point at which we aren't even praying throughout the day. Our sense of guilt and failure over what we think time with God is *supposed* to be like—and how we aren't doing it—has driven us away from our passion for God.

But just because you're not spending long periods of time with your Bible open, a hot pot of coffee in front of you, and some candles for spiritual ambience, doesn't mean that you do not have passion!

During busy seasons when it's difficult to dive deep into Scripture, you can still go throughout your day seeking him. "I am with you always," Jesus promised (Matthew 28:20). While we're at the park with kids, at the office, running errands, in a meeting, or whatever it may be, we can still speak to him, listen to him, look around to see him; we can catch an awareness of his presence throughout the day.

You can live out your passion for God by intentionally engaging with God in your mind and heart as you go throughout the regular rhythms of your day. In fact, I think sometimes it takes *more passion* to be truly engaged with God all day than to spend an hour of quiet time in the morning.

—*Priscilla Shirer*

voice thundered like mighty ocean waves. [16]He held seven stars in his right hand, and a sharp two-edged sword came from his mouth. And his face was like the sun in all its brilliance.

[17]When I saw him, I fell at his feet as if I were dead. But he laid his right hand on me and said, "Don't be afraid! I am the First and the Last. [18]I am the living one. I died, but look—I am alive forever and ever! And I hold the keys of death and the grave.*

[19]"Write down what you have seen—both the things that are now happening and the things that will happen.* [20]This is the meaning of the mystery of the seven stars you saw in my right hand and the seven gold lampstands: The seven stars are the angels* of the seven churches, and the seven lampstands are the seven churches.

2 The Message to the Church in Ephesus

"Write this letter to the angel* of the church in Ephesus. This is the message from the one who holds the seven stars in his right hand, the one who walks among the seven gold lampstands:

[2]"I know all the things you do. I have seen your hard work and your patient endurance. I know you don't tolerate evil people. You have examined the claims of those who say they are apostles but are not. You have discovered they are liars. [3]You have patiently suffered for me without quitting.

[4]"But I have this complaint against you. You don't love me or each other as you did at first!* [5]Look how far you have

---

1:18 Greek *and Hades.*   **1:19** Or *what you have seen and what they mean—the things that have already begun to happen.*   **1:20** Or *the messengers.*   **2:1** Or *the messenger;* also in 2:8, 12, 18.   **2:4** Greek *You have lost your first love.*

fallen! Turn back to me and do the works you did at first. If you don't repent, I will come and remove your lampstand from its place among the churches. ⁶But this is in your favor: You hate the evil deeds of the Nicolaitans, just as I do.

⁷"Anyone with ears to hear must listen to the Spirit and understand what he is saying to the churches. To everyone who is victorious I will give fruit from the tree of life in the paradise of God.

The Message to the Church in Smyrna

⁸"Write this letter to the angel of the church in Smyrna. This is the message from the one who is the First and the Last, who was dead but is now alive:

⁹"I know about your suffering and your poverty—but you are rich! I know the blasphemy of those opposing you. They say they are Jews, but they are not, because their synagogue belongs to Satan. ¹⁰Don't be afraid of what you are about to suffer. The devil will throw some of you into prison to test you. You will suffer for ten days. But if you remain faithful even when facing death, I will give you the crown of life.

¹¹"Anyone with ears to hear must listen to the Spirit and understand what he is saying to the churches. Whoever is victorious will not be harmed by the second death.

The Message to the Church in Pergamum

¹²"Write this letter to the angel of the church in Pergamum. This is the message from the one with the sharp two-edged sword:

¹³"I know that you live in the city where Satan has his throne, yet you have remained loyal to me. You refused to deny me even when Antipas, my faithful witness, was martyred among you there in Satan's city.

¹⁴"But I have a few complaints against you. You tolerate some among you whose teaching is like that of Balaam, who showed Balak how to trip up the people of Israel. He taught them to sin by eating food offered to idols and by committing sexual sin. ¹⁵In a similar way, you have

some Nicolaitans among you who follow the same teaching. ¹⁶Repent of your sin, or I will come to you suddenly and fight against them with the sword of my mouth.

¹⁷"Anyone with ears to hear must listen to the Spirit and understand what he is saying to the churches. To everyone who is victorious I will give some of the manna that has been hidden away in heaven. And I will give to each one a white stone, and on the stone will be engraved a new name that no one understands except the one who receives it.

The Message to the Church in Thyatira

¹⁸"Write this letter to the angel of the church in Thyatira. This is the message from the Son of God, whose eyes are like flames of fire, whose feet are like polished bronze:

¹⁹"I know all the things you do. I have seen your love, your faith, your service, and your patient endurance. And I can see your constant improvement in all these things.

²⁰"But I have this complaint against you. You are permitting that woman—that Jezebel who calls herself a prophet—to lead my servants astray. She teaches them to commit sexual sin and to eat food offered to idols. ²¹I gave her time to repent, but she does not want to turn away from her immorality.

²²"Therefore, I will throw her on a bed of suffering,* and those who commit adultery with her will suffer greatly unless they repent and turn away from her evil deeds. ²³I will strike her children dead. Then all the churches will know that I am the one who searches out the thoughts and intentions of every person. And I will give to each of you whatever you deserve.

²⁴"But I also have a message for the rest of you in Thyatira who have not followed this false teaching ('deeper truths,' as they call them—depths of Satan, actually). I will ask nothing more of you ²⁵except that you hold tightly to what you have until I come. ²⁶To all who are victorious, who obey me to the very end,

To them I will give authority over all the nations.

2:22 Greek *a bed.*

²⁷ They will rule the nations with an iron rod
  and smash them like clay pots.*

²⁸ They will have the same authority I received from my Father, and I will also give them the morning star!

²⁹ "Anyone with ears to hear must listen to the Spirit and understand what he is saying to the churches.

3 The Message to the Church in Sardis

"Write this letter to the angel* of the church in Sardis. This is the message from the one who has the sevenfold Spirit* of God and the seven stars:

"I know all the things you do, and that you have a reputation for being alive— but you are dead. ² Wake up! Strengthen what little remains, for even what is left is almost dead. I find that your actions do not meet the requirements of my God. ³ Go back to what you heard and believed at first; hold to it firmly. Repent and turn to me again. If you don't wake up, I will come to you suddenly, as unexpected as a thief.

⁴ "Yet there are some in the church in Sardis who have not soiled their clothes with evil. They will walk with me in white, for they are worthy. ⁵ All who are victorious will be clothed in white. I will never erase their names from the Book of Life, but I will announce before my Father and his angels that they are mine.

⁶ "Anyone with ears to hear must listen to the Spirit and understand what he is saying to the churches.

The Message to the Church in Philadelphia

⁷ "Write this letter to the angel of the church in Philadelphia.

This is the message from the one who is holy and true,
  the one who has the key of David.
What he opens, no one can close;
  and what he closes, no one can open:*

⁸ "I know all the things you do, and I have opened a door for you that no one can close. You have little strength, yet you obeyed my word and did not deny me. ⁹ Look, I will force those who belong to Satan's synagogue—those liars who say they are Jews but are not—to come and bow down at your feet. They will acknowledge that you are the ones I love.

¹⁰ "Because you have obeyed my command to persevere, I will protect you from the great time of testing that will come upon the whole world to test those who belong to this world. ¹¹ I am coming soon.* Hold on to what you have, so that no one will take away your crown. ¹² All who are victorious will become pillars in the Temple of my God, and they will never have to leave it. And I will write on them the name of my God, and they will be citizens in the city of my God—the new Jerusalem that comes down from heaven from my God. And I will also write on them my new name.

¹³ "Anyone with ears to hear must listen to the Spirit and understand what he is saying to the churches.

The Message to the Church in Laodicea

¹⁴ "Write this letter to the angel of the church in Laodicea. This is the message from the one who is the Amen—the faithful and true witness, the beginning* of God's new creation:

¹⁵ "I know all the things you do, that you are neither hot nor cold. I wish that you were one or the other! ¹⁶ But since you are like lukewarm water, neither hot nor cold, I will spit you out of my mouth! ¹⁷ You say, 'I am rich. I have everything I want. I don't need a thing!' And you don't realize that you are wretched and miserable and poor and blind and naked. ¹⁸ So I advise you to buy gold from me—gold that has been purified by fire. Then you will be rich. Also buy white garments from me so you will not be shamed by your nakedness, and ointment for your eyes so you will be able to see. ¹⁹ I correct and discipline everyone I love. So be diligent and turn from your indifference.

²⁰ "Look! I stand at the door and knock. If you hear my voice and open the door,

---

2:26-27 Ps 2:8-9 (Greek Version).   **3:1a** Or *the messenger;* also in 3:7, 14.   **3:1b** Greek *the seven spirits.*   **3:7** Isa 22:22.   **3:11** Or *suddenly, or quickly.*   **3:14** Or *the ruler,* or *the source.*

I will come in, and we will share a meal together as friends. ²¹Those who are victorious will sit with me on my throne, just as I was victorious and sat with my Father on his throne.

²²"Anyone with ears to hear must listen to the Spirit and understand what he is saying to the churches."

4 Worship in Heaven

Then as I looked, I saw a door standing open in heaven, and the same voice I had heard before spoke to me like a trumpet blast. The voice said, "Come up here, and I will show you what must happen after this." ²And instantly I was in the Spirit,* and I saw a throne in heaven and someone sitting on it. ³The one sitting on the throne was as brilliant as gemstones—like jasper and carnelian. And the glow of an emerald circled his throne like a rainbow. ⁴Twenty-four thrones surrounded him, and twenty-four elders sat on them. They were all clothed in white and had gold crowns on their heads. ⁵From the throne came flashes of lightning and the rumble of thunder. And in front of the throne were seven torches with burning flames. This is the sevenfold Spirit* of God. ⁶In front of the throne was a shiny sea of glass, sparkling like crystal.

In the center and around the throne were four living beings, each covered with eyes, front and back. ⁷The first of these living beings was like a lion; the second was like an ox; the third had a human face; and the fourth was like an eagle in flight. ⁸Each of these living beings had six wings, and their wings were covered all over with eyes, inside and out. Day after day and night after night they keep on saying,

"Holy, holy, holy is the Lord God, the
    Almighty—
  the one who always was, who is, and
    who is still to come."

⁹Whenever the living beings give glory and honor and thanks to the one sitting on the throne (the one who lives forever and ever), ¹⁰the twenty-four elders fall down and worship the one sitting on the throne (the one who lives forever and ever). And they lay their crowns before the throne and say,

¹¹ "You are worthy, O Lord our God,
    to receive glory and honor and power.
For you created all things,
    and they exist because you created
      what you pleased."

5 The Lamb Opens the Scroll

Then I saw a scroll* in the right hand of the one who was sitting on the throne. There was writing on the inside and the outside of the scroll, and it was sealed with seven seals. ²And I saw a strong angel, who shouted with a loud voice: "Who is worthy to break the seals on this scroll and open it?" ³But no one in heaven or on earth or under the earth was able to open the scroll and read it.

⁴Then I began to weep bitterly because no one was found worthy to open the scroll and read it. ⁵But one of the twenty-four elders said to me, "Stop weeping! Look, the Lion of the tribe of Judah, the heir to David's throne,* has won the victory. He is worthy to open the scroll and its seven seals."

⁶Then I saw a Lamb that looked as if it had been slaughtered, but it was now standing between the throne and the four living beings and among the twenty-four elders. He had seven horns and seven eyes, which represent the sevenfold Spirit* of God that is sent out into every part of the earth. ⁷He stepped forward and took the scroll from the right hand of the one sitting on the throne. ⁸And when he took the scroll, the four living beings and the twenty-four elders fell down before the Lamb. Each one had a harp, and they held gold bowls filled with incense, which are the prayers of God's people. ⁹And they sang a new song with these words:

"You are worthy to take the scroll
    and break its seals and open it.
For you were slaughtered, and your
      blood has ransomed people for God
  from every tribe and language and
      people and nation.
¹⁰ And you have caused them to become
    a Kingdom of priests for our God.
  And they will reign* on the earth."

¹¹Then I looked again, and I heard the voices of thousands and millions of angels

---

4:2 Or *in spirit.* **4:5** Greek *They are the seven spirits.* **5:1** Or *book;* also in 5:2, 3, 4, 5, 7, 8, 9. **5:5** Greek *the root of David.* See Isa 11:10.
5:6 Greek *which are the seven spirits.* **5:10** Some manuscripts read *they are reigning.*

Joining the Eternal Song
REVELATION 4:8-11

Sometimes when I think of worship, an image comes to mind. I was about eleven years old, and our family was on vacation. One evening I was in the lake, waist deep. A wind danced upon the surface of the water; the sky was filled with stunning colors as the sun set. It was an incredible moment. I remember it so clearly because I got goose bumps. I had the sense that there was Something so much bigger than myself—Something that was good and true. It was that instinctive feeling in which everything in you says, *Yes!* and *Thank you!* I didn't fully understand it then, but I think everything in me was saying, *Holy!*

In Revelation 4 we see amazing heavenly creatures surrounding God's throne and singing, "Holy, holy, holy" (4:8). They've been doing it forever, and they'll do it forever. Every time our souls assent to that—when we agree and say, *Holy!*—we get to be part of that eternal song.

—Carolyn Arends

around the throne and of the living beings and the elders. ¹²And they sang in a mighty chorus:

"Worthy is the Lamb who was
slaughtered—
to receive power and riches
and wisdom and strength
and honor and glory and blessing."

¹³And then I heard every creature in heaven and on earth and under the earth and in the sea. They sang:

"Blessing and honor and glory and power
belong to the one sitting on the throne
and to the Lamb forever and ever."

¹⁴And the four living beings said, "Amen!" And the twenty-four elders fell down and worshiped the Lamb.

6 The Lamb Breaks the First Six Seals

As I watched, the Lamb broke the first of the seven seals on the scroll.* Then I heard one of the four living beings say with a voice like thunder, "Come!" ²I looked up and saw a white horse standing there. Its rider carried a bow, and a crown was placed on his head. He rode out to win many battles and gain the victory.

³When the Lamb broke the second seal, I heard the second living being say, "Come!" ⁴Then another horse appeared, a red one. Its rider was given a mighty sword and the authority to take peace from the earth. And there was war and slaughter everywhere.

⁵When the Lamb broke the third seal, I heard the third living being say, "Come!" I looked up and saw a black horse, and its rider was holding a pair of scales in his hand. ⁶And I heard a voice from among the four living beings say, "A loaf of wheat bread or three loaves of barley will cost a day's pay.* And don't waste* the olive oil and wine."

⁷When the Lamb broke the fourth seal, I heard the fourth living being say, "Come!" ⁸I looked up and saw a horse whose color was pale green. Its rider was named Death, and his companion was the Grave.* These two were given authority over one-fourth of the earth, to kill with the sword and famine and disease* and wild animals.

⁹When the Lamb broke the fifth seal, I saw under the altar the souls of all who had been martyred for the word of God and for being faithful in their testimony. ¹⁰They shouted to the Lord and said, "O Sovereign Lord, holy and true, how long before you judge the people who belong to this world and avenge our blood for what they have

6:1 Or *book.* 6:6a Greek *A choinix* [1 quart or 1 liter] *of wheat for a denarius, and 3 choinix of barley for a denarius.* A denarius was equivalent to a laborer's full day's wage. 6:6b Or *harm.* 6:8a Greek *was Hades.* 6:8b Greek *death.*

done to us?" ¹¹Then a white robe was given to each of them. And they were told to rest a little longer until the full number of their brothers and sisters*—their fellow servants of Jesus who were to be martyred—had joined them.

¹²I watched as the Lamb broke the sixth seal, and there was a great earthquake. The sun became as dark as black cloth, and the moon became as red as blood. ¹³Then the stars of the sky fell to the earth like green figs falling from a tree shaken by a strong wind. ¹⁴The sky was rolled up like a scroll, and all of the mountains and islands were moved from their places.

¹⁵Then everyone—the kings of the earth, the rulers, the generals, the wealthy, the powerful, and every slave and free person— all hid themselves in the caves and among the rocks of the mountains. ¹⁶And they cried to the mountains and the rocks, "Fall on us and hide us from the face of the one who sits on the throne and from the wrath of the Lamb. ¹⁷For the great day of their wrath has come, and who is able to survive?"

7 God's People Will Be Preserved

Then I saw four angels standing at the four corners of the earth, holding back the four winds so they did not blow on the earth or the sea, or even on any tree. ²And I saw another angel coming up from the east, carrying the seal of the living God. And he shouted to those four angels, who had been given power to harm land and sea, ³"Wait! Don't harm the land or the sea or the trees until we have placed the seal of God on the foreheads of his servants."

⁴And I heard how many were marked with the seal of God—144,000 were sealed from all the tribes of Israel:

⁵ from Judah	12,000
from Reuben	12,000
from Gad	12,000
⁶ from Asher	12,000
from Naphtali	12,000
from Manasseh	12,000
⁷ from Simeon	12,000
from Levi	12,000
from Issachar	12,000
⁸ from Zebulun	12,000
from Joseph	12,000
from Benjamin	12,000

Praise from the Great Crowd

⁹After this I saw a vast crowd, too great to count, from every nation and tribe and people and language, standing in front of the throne and before the Lamb. They were clothed in white robes and held palm branches in their hands. ¹⁰And they were shouting with a great roar,

"Salvation comes from our God who sits
    on the throne
    and from the Lamb!"

¹¹And all the angels were standing around the throne and around the elders and the four living beings. And they fell before the throne with their faces to the ground and worshiped God. ¹²They sang,

"Amen! Blessing and glory and wisdom
    and thanksgiving and honor
and power and strength belong to our
    God
    forever and ever! Amen."

¹³Then one of the twenty-four elders asked me, "Who are these who are clothed in white? Where did they come from?"

¹⁴And I said to him, "Sir, you are the one who knows."

Then he said to me, "These are the ones who died in* the great tribulation.* They have washed their robes in the blood of the Lamb and made them white.

¹⁵ "That is why they stand in front of God's
    throne
    and serve him day and night in his
        Temple.
And he who sits on the throne
    will give them shelter.
¹⁶ They will never again be hungry or
    thirsty;
    they will never be scorched by the
        heat of the sun.
¹⁷ For the Lamb on the throne*
    will be their Shepherd.
He will lead them to springs of
    life-giving water.
    And God will wipe every tear from
        their eyes."

6:11 Greek their brothers.   7:14a Greek who came out of.   7:14b Or the great suffering.   7:17 Greek on the center of the throne.

God Is the Giver

REVELATION 7:15–17

Come thou Fount of every blessing,
Tune my heart to sing thy grace.
Streams of mercy, never ceasing,
Call for songs of loudest praise.
—Robert Robinson, 1758

As the hymn "Come, Thou Fount" reminds me, God is the Fountain of life, the Giver of every blessing. He gives food (Psalm 145:15), provides clothes and shelter (Luke 12:27) and family and friends. He grants peace, joy, and love through knowing him (John 1:16).

Yet I often take God's blessings for granted. I may even take credit for earning those blessings. *My* hard work put food on the table. *My* ingenuity secured a pay raise. *My* bargaining skills netted that stylish new suit.

Sometimes I forget that my occupational abilities and creative capacities are also gifts from God. He is the Giver of all good things.

Not only do I frequently attribute God's blessings to my own capabilities, but I also sometimes spend more time searching for earthly rewards than seeking spiritual blessings. God's unlimited goodness longs to bestow gifts that will never be devalued by inflation. Riches that will never need paint or polish.

Yet when I start to think in terms of my work, talents, or capabilities, that's when I *most* need to stop and praise the "Fount of every blessing."

—*Sharla Fritz*

8 The Lamb Breaks the Seventh Seal

When the Lamb broke the seventh seal on the scroll,* there was silence throughout heaven for about half an hour. ²I saw the seven angels who stand before God, and they were given seven trumpets.

³Then another angel with a gold incense burner came and stood at the altar. And a great amount of incense was given to him to mix with the prayers of God's people as an offering on the gold altar before the throne. ⁴The smoke of the incense, mixed with the prayers of God's holy people, ascended up to God from the altar where the angel had poured them out. ⁵Then the angel filled the incense burner with fire from the altar and threw it down upon the earth; and thunder crashed, lightning flashed, and there was a terrible earthquake.

The First Four Trumpets

⁶Then the seven angels with the seven trumpets prepared to blow their mighty blasts.

⁷The first angel blew his trumpet, and hail and fire mixed with blood were thrown down on the earth. One-third of the earth was set on fire, one-third of the trees were burned, and all the green grass was burned.

⁸Then the second angel blew his trumpet, and a great mountain of fire was thrown into the sea. One-third of the water in the sea became blood, ⁹one-third of all things living in the sea died, and one-third of all the ships on the sea were destroyed.

¹⁰Then the third angel blew his trumpet, and a great star fell from the sky, burning like a torch. It fell on one-third of the rivers and on the springs of water. ¹¹The name of

8:1 Or *book.*

the star was Bitterness.* It made one-third of the water bitter, and many people died from drinking the bitter water.

¹²Then the fourth angel blew his trumpet, and one-third of the sun was struck, and one-third of the moon, and one-third of the stars, and they became dark. And one-third of the day was dark, and also one-third of the night.

¹³Then I looked, and I heard a single eagle crying loudly as it flew through the air, "Terror, terror, terror to all who belong to this world because of what will happen when the last three angels blow their trumpets."

9 The Fifth Trumpet Brings the First Terror

Then the fifth angel blew his trumpet, and I saw a star that had fallen to earth from the sky, and he was given the key to the shaft of the bottomless pit.* ²When he opened it, smoke poured out as though from a huge furnace, and the sunlight and air turned dark from the smoke.

³Then locusts came from the smoke and descended on the earth, and they were given power to sting like scorpions. ⁴They were told not to harm the grass or plants or trees, but only the people who did not have the seal of God on their foreheads. ⁵They were told not to kill them but to torture them for five months with pain like the pain of a scorpion sting. ⁶In those days people will seek death but will not find it. They will long to die, but death will flee from them!

⁷The locusts looked like horses prepared for battle. They had what looked like gold crowns on their heads, and their faces looked like human faces. ⁸They had hair like women's hair and teeth like the teeth of a lion. ⁹They wore armor made of iron, and their wings roared like an army of chariots rushing into battle. ¹⁰They had tails that stung like scorpions, and for five months they had the power to torment people. ¹¹Their king is the angel from the bottomless pit; his name in Hebrew is *Abaddon*, and in Greek, *Apollyon*—the Destroyer.

¹²The first terror is past, but look, two more terrors are coming!

The Sixth Trumpet Brings the Second Terror

¹³Then the sixth angel blew his trumpet, and I heard a voice speaking from the four horns of the gold altar that stands in the presence of God. ¹⁴And the voice said to the sixth angel who held the trumpet, "Release the four angels who are bound at the great Euphrates River." ¹⁵Then the four angels who had been prepared for this hour and day and month and year were turned loose to kill one-third of all the people on earth. ¹⁶I heard the size of their army, which was 200 million mounted troops.

¹⁷And in my vision, I saw the horses and the riders sitting on them. The riders wore armor that was fiery red and dark blue and yellow. The horses had heads like lions, and fire and smoke and burning sulfur billowed from their mouths. ¹⁸One-third of all the people on earth were killed by these three plagues—by the fire and smoke and burning sulfur that came from the mouths of the horses. ¹⁹Their power was in their mouths and in their tails. For their tails had heads like snakes, with the power to injure people.

²⁰But the people who did not die in these plagues still refused to repent of their evil deeds and turn to God. They continued to worship demons and idols made of gold, silver, bronze, stone, and wood—idols that can neither see nor hear nor walk! ²¹And they did not repent of their murders or their witchcraft or their sexual immorality or their thefts.

10 The Angel and the Small Scroll

Then I saw another mighty angel coming down from heaven, surrounded by a cloud, with a rainbow over his head. His face shone like the sun, and his feet were like pillars of fire. ²And in his hand was a small scroll* that had been opened. He stood with his right foot on the sea and his left foot on the land. ³And he gave a great shout like the roar of a lion. And when he shouted, the seven thunders answered.

⁴When the seven thunders spoke, I was about to write. But I heard a voice from heaven saying, "Keep secret* what the seven thunders said, and do not write it down."

8:11 Greek *Wormwood.*   **9:1** Or *the abyss,* or *the underworld;* also in 9:11.   **10:2** Or *book;* also in 10:8, 9, 10.   **10:4** Greek *Seal up.*

⁵Then the angel I saw standing on the sea and on the land raised his right hand toward heaven. ⁶He swore an oath in the name of the one who lives forever and ever, who created the heavens and everything in them, the earth and everything in it, and the sea and everything in it. He said, "There will be no more delay. ⁷When the seventh angel blows his trumpet, God's mysterious plan will be fulfilled. It will happen just as he announced it to his servants the prophets."

⁸Then the voice from heaven spoke to me again: "Go and take the open scroll from the hand of the angel who is standing on the sea and on the land."

⁹So I went to the angel and told him to give me the small scroll. "Yes, take it and eat it," he said. "It will be sweet as honey in your mouth, but it will turn sour in your stomach!" ¹⁰So I took the small scroll from the hand of the angel, and I ate it! It was sweet in my mouth, but when I swallowed it, it turned sour in my stomach.

¹¹Then I was told, "You must prophesy again about many peoples, nations, languages, and kings."

11 The Two Witnesses

Then I was given a measuring stick, and I was told, "Go and measure the Temple of God and the altar, and count the number of worshipers. ²But do not measure the outer courtyard, for it has been turned over to the nations. They will trample the holy city for 42 months. ³And I will give power to my two witnesses, and they will be clothed in burlap and will prophesy during those 1,260 days."

⁴These two prophets are the two olive trees and the two lampstands that stand before the Lord of all the earth. ⁵If anyone tries to harm them, fire flashes from their mouths and consumes their enemies. This is how anyone who tries to harm them must die. ⁶They have power to shut the sky so that no rain will fall for as long as they prophesy. And they have the power to turn the rivers and oceans into blood, and to strike the earth with every kind of plague as often as they wish.

⁷When they complete their testimony, the beast that comes up out of the bottomless pit* will declare war against them, and he will conquer them and kill them. ⁸And their bodies will lie in the main street of Jerusalem,* the city that is figuratively called "Sodom" and "Egypt," the city where their Lord was crucified. ⁹And for three and a half days, all peoples, tribes, languages, and nations will stare at their bodies. No one will be allowed to bury them. ¹⁰All the people who belong to this world will gloat over them and give presents to each other to celebrate the death of the two prophets who had tormented them.

¹¹But after three and a half days, God breathed life into them, and they stood up! Terror struck all who were staring at them. ¹²Then a loud voice from heaven called to the two prophets, "Come up here!" And they rose to heaven in a cloud as their enemies watched.

¹³At the same time there was a terrible earthquake that destroyed a tenth of the city. Seven thousand people died in that earthquake, and everyone else was terrified and gave glory to the God of heaven.

¹⁴The second terror is past, but look, the third terror is coming quickly.

The Seventh Trumpet Brings the Third Terror

¹⁵Then the seventh angel blew his trumpet, and there were loud voices shouting in heaven:

"The world has now become the
    Kingdom of our Lord and of his
    Christ,*
and he will reign forever and ever."

¹⁶The twenty-four elders sitting on their thrones before God fell with their faces to the ground and worshiped him. ¹⁷And they said,

"We give thanks to you, Lord God, the
    Almighty,
the one who is and who always was,
for now you have assumed your great
    power
and have begun to reign.
¹⁸ The nations were filled with wrath,
    but now the time of your wrath has
    come.

11:7 Or *the abyss,* or *the underworld.* **11:8** Greek *the great city.* **11:15** Or *his Messiah.*

It is time to judge the dead
and reward your servants the prophets,
as well as your holy people,
and all who fear your name,
from the least to the greatest.
It is time to destroy
all who have caused destruction on
the earth."

¹⁹Then, in heaven, the Temple of God was opened and the Ark of his covenant could be seen inside the Temple. Lightning flashed, thunder crashed and roared, and there was an earthquake and a terrible hailstorm.

12 The Woman and the Dragon

Then I witnessed in heaven an event of great significance. I saw a woman clothed with the sun, with the moon beneath her feet, and a crown of twelve stars on her head. ²She was pregnant, and she cried out because of her labor pains and the agony of giving birth.

³Then I witnessed in heaven another significant event. I saw a large red dragon with seven heads and ten horns, with seven crowns on his heads. ⁴His tail swept away one-third of the stars in the sky, and he threw them to the earth. He stood in front of the woman as she was about to give birth, ready to devour her baby as soon as it was born.

⁵She gave birth to a son who was to rule all nations with an iron rod. And her child was snatched away from the dragon and was caught up to God and to his throne. ⁶And the woman fled into the wilderness, where God had prepared a place to care for her for 1,260 days.

⁷Then there was war in heaven. Michael and his angels fought against the dragon and his angels. ⁸And the dragon lost the battle, and he and his angels were forced out of heaven. ⁹This great dragon—the ancient serpent called the devil, or Satan, the one deceiving the whole world—was thrown down to the earth with all his angels.

¹⁰Then I heard a loud voice shouting across the heavens,

"It has come at last—
salvation and power
and the Kingdom of our God,
and the authority of his Christ.*
For the accuser of our brothers and
sisters*
has been thrown down to earth—
the one who accuses them
before our God day and night.
¹¹And they have defeated him by the
blood of the Lamb
and by their testimony.
And they did not love their lives so
much
that they were afraid to die.
¹²Therefore, rejoice, O heavens!
And you who live in the heavens,
rejoice!
But terror will come on the earth and
the sea,
for the devil has come down to you in
great anger,
knowing that he has little time."

¹³When the dragon realized that he had been thrown down to the earth, he pursued the woman who had given birth to the male child. ¹⁴But she was given two wings like those of a great eagle so she could fly to the place prepared for her in the wilderness. There she would be cared for and protected from the dragon* for a time, times, and half a time.

¹⁵Then the dragon tried to drown the woman with a flood of water that flowed from his mouth. ¹⁶But the earth helped her by opening its mouth and swallowing the river that gushed out from the mouth of the dragon. ¹⁷And the dragon was angry at the woman and declared war against the rest of her children—all who keep God's commandments and maintain their testimony for Jesus.

¹⁸Then the dragon took his stand* on the shore beside the sea.

13 The Beast out of the Sea

Then I saw a beast rising up out of the sea. It had seven heads and ten horns, with ten crowns on its horns. And written on each head were names that blasphemed God. ²This beast looked like a leopard, but it had the feet of a bear and the mouth of a

---

12:10a Or *his Messiah.*   **12:10b** Greek *brothers.*   **12:14** Greek *the serpent;* also in 12:15. See 12:9.   **12:18** Greek *Then he took his stand;* some manuscripts read *Then I took my stand.* Some translations put this entire sentence into 13:1.

lion! And the dragon gave the beast his own power and throne and great authority.

³I saw that one of the heads of the beast seemed wounded beyond recovery—but the fatal wound was healed! The whole world marveled at this miracle and gave allegiance to the beast. ⁴They worshiped the dragon for giving the beast such power, and they also worshiped the beast. "Who is as great as the beast?" they exclaimed. "Who is able to fight against him?"

⁵Then the beast was allowed to speak great blasphemies against God. And he was given authority to do whatever he wanted for forty-two months. ⁶And he spoke terrible words of blasphemy against God, slandering his name and his dwelling—that is, those who dwell in heaven.* ⁷And the beast was allowed to wage war against God's holy people and to conquer them. And he was given authority to rule over every tribe and people and language and nation. ⁸And all the people who belong to this world worshiped the beast. They are the ones whose names were not written in the Book of Life before the world was made—the Book that belongs to the Lamb who was slaughtered.*

⁹ Anyone with ears to hear
    should listen and understand.
¹⁰ Anyone who is destined for prison
    will be taken to prison.
Anyone destined to die by the sword
    will die by the sword.

This means that God's holy people must endure persecution patiently and remain faithful.

The Beast out of the Earth

¹¹Then I saw another beast come up out of the earth. He had two horns like those of a lamb, but he spoke with the voice of a dragon. ¹²He exercised all the authority of the first beast. And he required all the earth and its people to worship the first beast, whose fatal wound had been healed. ¹³He did astounding miracles, even making fire flash down to earth from the sky while everyone was watching. ¹⁴And with all the miracles he was allowed to perform on behalf of the first beast, he deceived all the people who belong to this world. He ordered the people to make a great statue of the first beast, who was fatally wounded and then came back to life. ¹⁵He was then permitted to give life to this statue so that it could speak. Then the statue of the beast commanded that anyone refusing to worship it must die.

¹⁶He required everyone—small and great, rich and poor, free and slave—to be given a mark on the right hand or on the forehead. ¹⁷And no one could buy or sell anything without that mark, which was either the name of the beast or the number representing his name. ¹⁸Wisdom is needed here. Let the one with understanding solve the meaning of the number of the beast, for it is the number of a man.* His number is 666.*

14 The Lamb and the 144,000

Then I saw the Lamb standing on Mount Zion, and with him were 144,000 who had his name and his Father's name written on their foreheads. ²And I heard a sound from heaven like the roar of mighty ocean waves or the rolling of loud thunder. It was like the sound of many harpists playing together.

³This great choir sang a wonderful new song in front of the throne of God and before the four living beings and the twenty-four elders. No one could learn this song except the 144,000 who had been redeemed from the earth. ⁴They have kept themselves as pure as virgins,* following the Lamb wherever he goes. They have been purchased from among the people on the earth as a special offering* to God and to the Lamb. ⁵They have told no lies; they are without blame.

The Three Angels

⁶And I saw another angel flying through the sky, carrying the eternal Good News to proclaim to the people who belong to this world—to every nation, tribe, language, and people. ⁷"Fear God," he shouted. "Give glory to him. For the time has come when he will sit as judge. Worship him who made

---

the heavens, the earth, the sea, and all the springs of water."

⁸ Then another angel followed him through the sky, shouting, "Babylon is fallen—that great city is fallen—because she made all the nations of the world drink the wine of her passionate immorality."

⁹ Then a third angel followed them, shouting, "Anyone who worships the beast and his statue or who accepts his mark on the forehead or on the hand ¹⁰ must drink the wine of God's anger. It has been poured full strength into God's cup of wrath. And they will be tormented with fire and burning sulfur in the presence of the holy angels and the Lamb. ¹¹ The smoke of their torment will rise forever and ever, and they will have no relief day or night, for they have worshiped the beast and his statue and have accepted the mark of his name."

¹² This means that God's holy people must endure persecution patiently, obeying his commands and maintaining their faith in Jesus.

¹³ And I heard a voice from heaven saying, "Write this down: Blessed are those who die in the Lord from now on. Yes, says the Spirit, they are blessed indeed, for they will rest from their hard work; for their good deeds follow them!"

The Harvest of the Earth

¹⁴ Then I saw a white cloud, and seated on the cloud was someone like the Son of Man.* He had a gold crown on his head and a sharp sickle in his hand. ¹⁵ Then another angel came from the Temple and shouted to the one sitting on the cloud, "Swing the sickle, for the time of harvest has come; the crop on earth is ripe." ¹⁶ So the one sitting on the cloud swung his sickle over the earth, and the whole earth was harvested.

¹⁷ After that, another angel came from the Temple in heaven, and he also had a sharp sickle. ¹⁸ Then another angel, who had power to destroy with fire, came from the altar. He shouted to the angel with the sharp sickle, "Swing your sickle now to gather the clusters of grapes from the vines

of the earth, for they are ripe for judgment." ¹⁹ So the angel swung his sickle over the earth and loaded the grapes into the great winepress of God's wrath. ²⁰ The grapes were trampled in the winepress outside the city, and blood flowed from the winepress in a stream about 180 miles* long and as high as a horse's bridle.

15 The Song of Moses and of the Lamb

Then I saw in heaven another marvelous event of great significance. Seven angels were holding the seven last plagues, which would bring God's wrath to completion. ² I saw before me what seemed to be a glass sea mixed with fire. And on it stood all the people who had been victorious over the beast and his statue and the number representing his name. They were all holding harps that God had given them. ³ And they were singing the song of Moses, the servant of God, and the song of the Lamb:

"Great and marvelous are your
    works,
    O Lord God, the Almighty.
Just and true are your ways,
    O King of the nations.*
⁴ Who will not fear you, Lord,
    and glorify your name?
    For you alone are holy.
All nations will come and worship
    before you,
    for your righteous deeds have been
    revealed."

The Seven Bowls of the Seven Plagues

⁵ Then I looked and saw that the Temple in heaven, God's Tabernacle, was thrown wide open. ⁶ The seven angels who were holding the seven plagues came out of the Temple. They were clothed in spotless white linen* with gold sashes across their chests. ⁷ Then one of the four living beings handed each of the seven angels a gold bowl filled with the wrath of God, who lives forever and ever. ⁸ The Temple was filled with smoke from God's glory and power. No one could enter the Temple until the seven angels had completed pouring out the seven plagues.

14:14 Or *like a son of man.* See Dan 7:13. "Son of Man" is a title Jesus used for himself.   **14:20** Greek *1,600 stadia* [296 kilometers].
15:3 Some manuscripts read *King of the ages.*   **15:6** Other manuscripts read *white stone;* still others read *white [garments] made of linen.*

16

Then I heard a mighty voice from the Temple say to the seven angels, "Go your ways and pour out on the earth the seven bowls containing God's wrath."

[2] So the first angel left the Temple and poured out his bowl on the earth, and horrible, malignant sores broke out on everyone who had the mark of the beast and who worshiped his statue.

[3] Then the second angel poured out his bowl on the sea, and it became like the blood of a corpse. And everything in the sea died.

[4] Then the third angel poured out his bowl on the rivers and springs, and they became blood. [5] And I heard the angel who had authority over all water saying,

> "You are just, O Holy One, who is and
> who always was,
> because you have sent these
> judgments.
> [6] Since they shed the blood
> of your holy people and your
> prophets,
> you have given them blood to drink.
> It is their just reward."

[7] And I heard a voice from the altar,* saying,

> "Yes, O Lord God, the Almighty,
> your judgments are true and just."

[8] Then the fourth angel poured out his bowl on the sun, causing it to scorch everyone with its fire. [9] Everyone was burned by this blast of heat, and they cursed the name of God, who had control over all these plagues. They did not repent of their sins and turn to God and give him glory.

[10] Then the fifth angel poured out his bowl on the throne of the beast, and his kingdom was plunged into darkness. His subjects ground their teeth in anguish, [11] and they cursed the God of heaven for their pains and sores. But they did not repent of their evil deeds and turn to God.

[12] Then the sixth angel poured out his bowl on the great Euphrates River, and it dried up so that the kings from the east could march their armies toward the west without hindrance. [13] And I saw three evil* spirits that looked like frogs leap from the mouths of the dragon, the beast, and the false prophet. [14] They are demonic spirits who work miracles and go out to all the rulers of the world to gather them for battle against the Lord on that great judgment day of God the Almighty.

[15] "Look, I will come as unexpectedly as a thief! Blessed are all who are watching for me, who keep their clothing ready so they will not have to walk around naked and ashamed."

[16] And the demonic spirits gathered all the rulers and their armies to a place with the Hebrew name *Armageddon.**

[17] Then the seventh angel poured out his bowl into the air. And a mighty shout came from the throne in the Temple, saying, "It is finished!" [18] Then the thunder crashed and rolled, and lightning flashed. And a great earthquake struck—the worst since people were placed on the earth. [19] The great city of Babylon split into three sections, and the cities of many nations fell into heaps of rubble. So God remembered all of Babylon's sins, and he made her drink the cup that was filled with the wine of his fierce wrath. [20] And every island disappeared, and all the mountains were leveled. [21] There was a terrible hailstorm, and hailstones weighing as much as seventy-five pounds* fell from the sky onto the people below. They cursed God because of the terrible plague of the hailstorm.

17

The Great Prostitute

One of the seven angels who had poured out the seven bowls came over and spoke to me. "Come with me," he said, "and I will show you the judgment that is going to come on the great prostitute, who rules over many waters. [2] The kings of the world have committed adultery with her, and the people who belong to this world have been made drunk by the wine of her immorality."

[3] So the angel took me in the Spirit* into the wilderness. There I saw a woman sitting on a scarlet beast that had seven heads and ten horns, and blasphemies against God were written all over it. [4] The woman wore purple and scarlet clothing and beautiful jewelry made of gold and precious gems and

---

16:7 Greek *I heard the altar.*   **16:13** Greek *unclean.*   **16:16** Or *Harmagedon.*   **16:21** Greek *1 talent* [34 kilograms].   **17:3** Or *in spirit.*

pearls. In her hand she held a gold goblet full of obscenities and the impurities of her immorality. ⁵A mysterious name was written on her forehead: "Babylon the Great, Mother of All Prostitutes and Obscenities in the World." ⁶I could see that she was drunk—drunk with the blood of God's holy people who were witnesses for Jesus. I stared at her in complete amazement.

⁷"Why are you so amazed?" the angel asked. "I will tell you the mystery of this woman and of the beast with seven heads and ten horns on which she sits. ⁸The beast you saw was once alive but isn't now. And yet he will soon come up out of the bottomless pit* and go to eternal destruction. And the people who belong to this world, whose names were not written in the Book of Life before the world was made, will be amazed at the reappearance of this beast who had died.

⁹"This calls for a mind with understanding: The seven heads of the beast represent the seven hills where the woman rules. They also represent seven kings. ¹⁰Five kings have already fallen, the sixth now reigns, and the seventh is yet to come, but his reign will be brief.

¹¹"The scarlet beast that was, but is no longer, is the eighth king. He is like the other seven, and he, too, is headed for destruction. ¹²The ten horns of the beast are ten kings who have not yet risen to power. They will be appointed to their kingdoms for one brief moment to reign with the beast. ¹³They will all agree to give him their power and authority. ¹⁴Together they will go to war against the Lamb, but the Lamb will defeat them because he is Lord of all lords and King of all kings. And his called and chosen and faithful ones will be with him."

¹⁵Then the angel said to me, "The waters where the prostitute is ruling represent masses of people of every nation and language. ¹⁶The scarlet beast and his ten horns all hate the prostitute. They will strip her naked, eat her flesh, and burn her remains with fire. ¹⁷For God has put a plan into their minds, a plan that will carry out his purposes. They will agree to give their author-

ity to the scarlet beast, and so the words of God will be fulfilled. ¹⁸And this woman you saw in your vision represents the great city that rules over the kings of the world."

18 The Fall of Babylon

After all this I saw another angel come down from heaven with great authority, and the earth grew bright with his splendor. ²He gave a mighty shout:

"Babylon is fallen—that great city is fallen!
　She has become a home for demons.
She is a hideout for every foul* spirit,
　a hideout for every foul vulture
　and every foul and dreadful animal.*
³ For all the nations have fallen*
　because of the wine of her passionate
　　immorality.
The kings of the world
　have committed adultery with her.
Because of her desires for extravagant
　luxury,
　the merchants of the world have
　　grown rich."

⁴Then I heard another voice calling from heaven,

"Come away from her, my people.
　Do not take part in her sins,
　or you will be punished with her.
⁵ For her sins are piled as high as heaven,
　and God remembers her evil deeds.
⁶ Do to her as she has done to others.
　Double her penalty* for all her evil
　　deeds.
She brewed a cup of terror for others,
　so brew twice as much* for her.
⁷ She glorified herself and lived in luxury,
　so match it now with torment and
　　sorrow.
She boasted in her heart,
　'I am queen on my throne.
I am no helpless widow,
　and I have no reason to mourn.'
⁸ Therefore, these plagues will overtake
　her in a single day—
　death and mourning and famine.
She will be completely consumed by fire,
　for the Lord God who judges her is
　　mighty."

17:8 Or *the abyss,* or *the underworld.*　**18:2a** Greek *unclean;* also in each of the two following phrases.　**18:2b** Some manuscripts condense the last two lines to read *a hideout for every foul [unclean] and dreadful vulture.*　**18:3** Some manuscripts read *have drunk.*　**18:6a** Or *Give her an equal penalty.*　**18:6b** Or *brew just as much.*

⁹And the kings of the world who committed adultery with her and enjoyed her great luxury will mourn for her as they see the smoke rising from her charred remains. ¹⁰They will stand at a distance, terrified by her great torment. They will cry out,

"How terrible, how terrible for you,
    O Babylon, you great city!
In a single moment
    God's judgment came on you."

¹¹The merchants of the world will weep and mourn for her, for there is no one left to buy their goods. ¹²She bought great quantities of gold, silver, jewels, and pearls; fine linen, purple, silk, and scarlet cloth; things made of fragrant thyine wood, ivory goods, and objects made of expensive wood; and bronze, iron, and marble. ¹³She also bought cinnamon, spice, incense, myrrh, frankincense, wine, olive oil, fine flour, wheat, cattle, sheep, horses, chariots, and bodies—that is, human slaves.

¹⁴ "The fancy things you loved so much
    are gone," they cry.
"All your luxuries and splendor
    are gone forever,
    never to be yours again."

¹⁵The merchants who became wealthy by selling her these things will stand at a distance, terrified by her great torment. They will weep and cry out,

¹⁶ "How terrible, how terrible for that great
    city!
She was clothed in finest purple and
    scarlet linens,
    decked out with gold and precious
    stones and pearls!
¹⁷ In a single moment
    all the wealth of the city is gone!"

And all the captains of the merchant ships and their passengers and sailors and crews will stand at a distance. ¹⁸They will cry out as they watch the smoke ascend, and they will say, "Where is there another city as great as this?" ¹⁹And they will weep and throw dust on their heads to show their grief. And they will cry out,

"How terrible, how terrible for that great
    city!

The shipowners became wealthy
    by transporting her great wealth on
    the seas.
In a single moment it is all gone."

²⁰ Rejoice over her fate, O heaven
    and people of God and apostles and
    prophets!
For at last God has judged her
    for your sakes.

²¹Then a mighty angel picked up a boulder the size of a huge millstone. He threw it into the ocean and shouted,

"Just like this, the great city Babylon
    will be thrown down with violence
    and will never be found again.
²² The sound of harps, singers, flutes, and
    trumpets
    will never be heard in you again.
No craftsmen and no trades
    will ever be found in you again.
The sound of the mill
    will never be heard in you again.
²³ The light of a lamp
    will never shine in you again.
The happy voices of brides and
    grooms
    will never be heard in you again.
For your merchants were the greatest in
    the world,
    and you deceived the nations with
    your sorceries.
²⁴ In your* streets flowed the blood of the
    prophets and of God's holy
    people
    and the blood of people slaughtered
    all over the world."

19 Songs of Victory in Heaven

After this, I heard what sounded like a vast crowd in heaven shouting,

"Praise the LORD!*
    Salvation and glory and power belong
    to our God.
² His judgments are true and just.
    He has punished the great prostitute
who corrupted the earth with her
    immorality.
He has avenged the murder of his
    servants."

18:24 Greek *her.*   **19:1** Greek *Hallelujah;* also in 19:3, 4, 6. *Hallelujah* is the transliteration of a Hebrew term that means "Praise the LORD."

³ And again their voices rang out:

"Praise the LORD!
The smoke from that city ascends
forever and ever!"

⁴ Then the twenty-four elders and the four living beings fell down and worshiped God, who was sitting on the throne. They cried out, "Amen! Praise the LORD!"

⁵ And from the throne came a voice that said,

"Praise our God,
all his servants,
all who fear him,
from the least to the greatest."

⁶ Then I heard again what sounded like the shout of a vast crowd or the roar of mighty ocean waves or the crash of loud thunder:

"Praise the LORD!
For the Lord our God,* the Almighty,
reigns.
⁷ Let us be glad and rejoice,
and let us give honor to him.
For the time has come for the wedding
feast of the Lamb,
and his bride has prepared herself.
⁸ She has been given the finest of pure
white linen to wear."
For the fine linen represents the good
deeds of God's holy people.

⁹ And the angel said to me, "Write this: Blessed are those who are invited to the wedding feast of the Lamb." And he added, "These are true words that come from God."

¹⁰ Then I fell down at his feet to worship him, but he said, "No, don't worship me. I am a servant of God, just like you and your brothers and sisters* who testify about their faith in Jesus. Worship only God. For the essence of prophecy is to give a clear witness for Jesus.*"

The Rider on the White Horse

¹¹ Then I saw heaven opened, and a white horse was standing there. Its rider was named Faithful and True, for he judges fairly and wages a righteous war. ¹² His eyes were like flames of fire, and on his head were many crowns. A name was written on him that no one understood except himself. ¹³ He wore a robe dipped in blood, and his title was the Word of God. ¹⁴ The armies of heaven, dressed in the finest of pure white linen, followed him on white horses. ¹⁵ From his mouth came a sharp sword to strike down the nations. He will rule them with an iron rod. He will release the fierce wrath of God, the Almighty, like juice flowing from a winepress. ¹⁶ On his robe at his thigh* was written this title: King of all kings and Lord of all lords.

¹⁷ Then I saw an angel standing in the sun, shouting to the vultures flying high in the sky: "Come! Gather together for the great banquet God has prepared. ¹⁸ Come and eat the flesh of kings, generals, and strong warriors; of horses and their riders; and of all humanity, both free and slave, small and great."

¹⁹ Then I saw the beast and the kings of the world and their armies gathered together to fight against the one sitting on the horse and his army. ²⁰ And the beast was captured, and with him the false prophet who did mighty miracles on behalf of the beast—miracles that deceived all who had accepted the mark of the beast and who worshiped his statue. Both the beast and his false prophet were thrown alive into the fiery lake of burning sulfur. ²¹ Their entire army was killed by the sharp sword that came from the mouth of the one riding the white horse. And the vultures all gorged themselves on the dead bodies.

20 The Thousand Years

Then I saw an angel coming down from heaven with the key to the bottomless pit* and a heavy chain in his hand. ²He seized the dragon—that old serpent, who is the devil, Satan—and bound him in chains for a thousand years. ³ The angel threw him into the bottomless pit, which he then shut and locked so Satan could not deceive the nations anymore until the thousand years were finished. Afterward he must be released for a little while.

19:6 Some manuscripts read *the Lord God.*   **19:10a** Greek *brothers.*   **19:10b** Or *is the message confirmed by Jesus.*   **19:16** Or *On his robe and thigh.*   **20:1** Or *the abyss,* or *the underworld;* also in 20:3.

⁴Then I saw thrones, and the people sitting on them had been given the authority to judge. And I saw the souls of those who had been beheaded for their testimony about Jesus and for proclaiming the word of God. They had not worshiped the beast or his statue, nor accepted his mark on their foreheads or their hands. They all came to life again, and they reigned with Christ for a thousand years.

⁵This is the first resurrection. (The rest of the dead did not come back to life until the thousand years had ended.) ⁶Blessed and holy are those who share in the first resurrection. For them the second death holds no power, but they will be priests of God and of Christ and will reign with him a thousand years.

The Defeat of Satan

⁷When the thousand years come to an end, Satan will be let out of his prison. ⁸He will go out to deceive the nations—called Gog and Magog—in every corner of the earth. He will gather them together for battle—a mighty army, as numberless as sand along the seashore. ⁹And I saw them as they went up on the broad plain of the earth and surrounded God's people and the beloved city. But fire from heaven came down on the attacking armies and consumed them.

¹⁰Then the devil, who had deceived them, was thrown into the fiery lake of burning sulfur, joining the beast and the false prophet. There they will be tormented day and night forever and ever.

The Final Judgment

¹¹And I saw a great white throne and the one sitting on it. The earth and sky fled from his presence, but they found no place to hide. ¹²I saw the dead, both great and small, standing before God's throne. And the books were opened, including the Book of Life. And the dead were judged according to what they had done, as recorded in the books. ¹³The sea gave up its dead, and death and the grave* gave up their dead. And all were judged according to their deeds. ¹⁴Then death and the grave were thrown into the lake of fire. This lake of fire

is the second death. ¹⁵And anyone whose name was not found recorded in the Book of Life was thrown into the lake of fire.

21 The New Jerusalem

Then I saw a new heaven and a new earth, for the old heaven and the old earth had disappeared. And the sea was also gone. ²And I saw the holy city, the new Jerusalem, coming down from God out of heaven like a bride beautifully dressed for her husband.

³I heard a loud shout from the throne, saying, "Look, God's home is now among his people! He will live with them, and they will be his people. God himself will be with them.* ⁴He will wipe every tear from their eyes, and there will be no more death or sorrow or crying or pain. All these things are gone forever."

⁵And the one sitting on the throne said, "Look, I am making everything new!" And then he said to me, "Write this down, for what I tell you is trustworthy and true." ⁶And he also said, "It is finished! I am the Alpha and the Omega—the Beginning and the End. To all who are thirsty I will give freely from the springs of the water of life. ⁷All who are victorious will inherit all these blessings, and I will be their God, and they will be my children.

⁸"But cowards, unbelievers, the corrupt, murderers, the immoral, those who practice witchcraft, idol worshipers, and all liars—their fate is in the fiery lake of burning sulfur. This is the second death."

⁹Then one of the seven angels who held the seven bowls containing the seven last plagues came and said to me, "Come with me! I will show you the bride, the wife of the Lamb."

¹⁰So he took me in the Spirit* to a great, high mountain, and he showed me the holy city, Jerusalem, descending out of heaven from God. ¹¹It shone with the glory of God and sparkled like a precious stone—like jasper as clear as crystal. ¹²The city wall was broad and high, with twelve gates guarded by twelve angels. And the names of the twelve tribes of Israel were written on the gates. ¹³There were three gates on each side—east, north, south, and west.

20:13 Greek *and Hades;* also in 20:14.   **21:3** Some manuscripts read *God himself will be with them, their God.*   **21:10** Or *in spirit.*

Praying Scripture

REVELATION 21:3-5

Many years ago several young college students sat around the old oak table in Ruth Bell Graham's kitchen, listening to her stories. We were lonely and homesick. College life had been rougher than expected. Ruth talked to us frankly about bouts of loneliness and discouragement she'd battled during her life—she emphasized one particular incident that had laid her low.

"When I was thirteen," she said, "my parents, missionaries in China, enrolled me in boarding school in what is now Pyongyang, North Korea. It was a difficult parting, and on my last night home, I earnestly prayed that I would die." Ruth didn't die, but arriving in Korea, she succumbed to severe homesickness. Every night she buried her head in her pillow and cried herself to sleep. Finally in desperation, she went to her sister, Rosa, also enrolled at Pyongyang.

"I don't know what to tell you to do," Rosa replied bluntly, "unless you take some verse and put your own name in it. See if that helps."

Ruth told us how she then picked up her King James Bible and turned to a favorite chapter, Isaiah 53, and put her name in it: "He was wounded for Ruth's transgressions, he was bruised for Ruth's iniquities: the chastisement of Ruth's peace was upon him; and with his stripes Ruth is healed" (Isaiah 53:5).

"I claimed that verse and knew then," Ruth told us, "that I would make it."

Ruth went on to explain her habit of praying Scripture—of repeating to God the words of his promises and truths. This habit of personalizing Scripture passages and speaking them back to God in prayer formed an essential pattern in her spiritual life. "God loves to be reminded of his promises," Ruth told us. "He never rebukes us for asking too much."

—*Robert J. Morgan*

---

14 The wall of the city had twelve foundation stones, and on them were written the names of the twelve apostles of the Lamb.

15 The angel who talked to me held in his hand a gold measuring stick to measure the city, its gates, and its wall. 16 When he measured it, he found it was a square, as wide as it was long. In fact, its length and width and height were each 1,400 miles.* 17 Then he measured the walls and found them to be 216 feet thick* (according to the human standard used by the angel).

18 The wall was made of jasper, and the city was pure gold, as clear as glass. 19 The wall of the city was built on foundation stones inlaid with twelve precious stones:* the first was jasper, the second sapphire, the third agate, the fourth emerald, 20 the fifth onyx, the sixth carnelian, the seventh chrysolite, the eighth beryl, the ninth topaz, the tenth chrysoprase, the eleventh jacinth, the twelfth amethyst.

21 The twelve gates were made of pearls—each gate from a single pearl! And the main street was pure gold, as clear as glass.

22 I saw no temple in the city, for the Lord God Almighty and the Lamb are its temple. 23 And the city has no need of sun or moon, for the glory of God illuminates the city, and the Lamb is its light. 24 The nations

---

21:16 Greek *12,000 stadia* [2,220 kilometers].   **21:17** Greek *144 cubits* [65 meters].   **21:19** The identification of some of these gemstones is uncertain.

will walk in its light, and the kings of the world will enter the city in all their glory. ²⁵Its gates will never be closed at the end of day because there is no night there. ²⁶And all the nations will bring their glory and honor into the city. ²⁷Nothing evil* will be allowed to enter, nor anyone who practices shameful idolatry and dishonesty—but only those whose names are written in the Lamb's Book of Life.

22 Then the angel showed me a river with the water of life, clear as crystal, flowing from the throne of God and of the Lamb. ²It flowed down the center of the main street. On each side of the river grew a tree of life, bearing twelve crops of fruit,* with a fresh crop each month. The leaves were used for medicine to heal the nations.

³No longer will there be a curse upon anything. For the throne of God and of the Lamb will be there, and his servants will worship him. ⁴And they will see his face, and his name will be written on their foreheads. ⁵And there will be no night there—no need for lamps or sun—for the Lord God will shine on them. And they will reign forever and ever.

⁶Then the angel said to me, "Everything you have heard and seen is trustworthy and true. The Lord God, who inspires his prophets,* has sent his angel to tell his servants what will happen soon.*"

Jesus Is Coming

⁷"Look, I am coming soon! Blessed are those who obey the words of prophecy written in this book.*"

⁸I, John, am the one who heard and saw all these things. And when I heard and saw them, I fell down to worship at the feet of the angel who showed them to me. ⁹But he said, "No, don't worship me. I am a servant of God, just like you and your brothers the prophets, as well as all who obey what is written in this book. Worship only God!"

¹⁰Then he instructed me, "Do not seal up the prophetic words in this book, for the time is near. ¹¹Let the one who is doing harm continue to do harm; let the one who is vile continue to be vile; let the one who is righteous continue to live righteously; let the one who is holy continue to be holy."

¹²"Look, I am coming soon, bringing my reward with me to repay all people according to their deeds. ¹³I am the Alpha and the Omega, the First and the Last, the Beginning and the End."

¹⁴Blessed are those who wash their robes. They will be permitted to enter through the gates of the city and eat the fruit from the tree of life. ¹⁵Outside the city are the dogs—the sorcerers, the sexually immoral, the murderers, the idol worshipers, and all who love to live a lie.

¹⁶"I, Jesus, have sent my angel to give you this message for the churches. I am both the source of David and the heir to his throne.* I am the bright morning star."

¹⁷The Spirit and the bride say, "Come." Let anyone who hears this say, "Come." Let anyone who is thirsty come. Let anyone who desires drink freely from the water of life. ¹⁸And I solemnly declare to everyone who hears the words of prophecy written in this book: If anyone adds anything to what is written here, God will add to that person the plagues described in this book. ¹⁹And if anyone removes any of the words from this book of prophecy, God will remove that person's share in the tree of life and in the holy city that are described in this book.

²⁰He who is the faithful witness to all these things says, "Yes, I am coming soon!"

Amen! Come, Lord Jesus!

²¹May the grace of the Lord Jesus be with God's holy people.*

21:27 Or *ceremonially unclean.* **22:2** Or *twelve kinds of fruit.* **22:6a** Or *The Lord, the God of the spirits of the prophets.* **22:6b** Or *suddenly,* or *quickly;* also in 22:7, 12, 20. **22:7** Or *scroll;* also in 22:9, 10, 18, 19. **22:16** Greek *I am the root and offspring of David.* **22:21** Other manuscripts read *be with all;* still others read *be with all of God's holy people.* Some manuscripts add *Amen.*

How to Use This Bible in a Small Group Study

U sing study Bibles is like having a theology teacher available 24/7. And this *Everyday Matters Bible for Women* offers so many resources that it will not only enrich your spiritual life, but also help you share with others.

The supplemental content is broken into four categories: **Everyday Matters**, which are in-depth articles; **Everyday Profiles** of biblical women; **Everyday Q&A's**; and **Everyday Reflections**. For a basic tutorial on the features of the Bible and how to use them, refer to "How to Use This Bible," on page xxii. Here are some additional ideas for using the features effectively as you study together.

We suggest that each member of the group have her own copy of the *Everyday Matters Bible for Women*. This will allow her to prepare for the group session and fully participate in the group dynamics—looking at the page as your group discusses it.

As the leader or with your group, you'll need to decide how you want to approach the study, including its duration. This Bible highlights twenty-four spiritual practices. If you spend two weeks per spiritual practice, your study would last approximately a year. Four weekly sessions per discipline would spread the study out over two years. For an abbreviated study, you might decide to delve into only the Everyday Profiles, which would give you a view of most of the disciplines through the examples of particular women in the Bible. (A few disciplines include no profile; others include two.) Since there are twenty-five profiles, that study would last twenty-five sessions. Based on your group's needs, you may want to use one of the options above or choose your own.

At the beginning of each meeting, ask God to open your hearts and minds to hear how he would use the biblical content, the supplementary material, and the discussion to grow and shape you into the image of Christ. Then as you read or review each, discuss the cited Scripture, and then consider some of the following ideas:

Everyday Matters

The two-page Everyday Matters articles introduce major themes relevant to each spiritual discipline. Before you meet, ask the group to read one or both article(s) related to the spiritual practice you will be discussing. Request that they also look up any Scripture passages mentioned in the article(s). Ask the group to jot down any questions or insights that come to mind.

As the leader of the study, you will complete the same assignment. However, make sure you've listed enough questions to seed the discussion if the others in your group come unprepared.

Starter questions might include

- How did reading this article and Scripture passage affect your spirit?
- Do you identify with this article in your everyday life? How?
- What about this article *really matters* to you at this stage of life?
- In what ways could you apply the point of this article to your spiritual growth?

Also take time to look up other verses on the spiritual discipline you are discussing. (For suggestions see the Additional Scriptures of Note sections in the index.) Note any that seem particularly relevant to your group.

Everyday Profiles

The profiles in this Bible put the spotlight on biblical women who practiced or in some way reflected a specific discipline. Your group might want to focus on the women themselves. Each week one group member (or all) might research the woman profiled for a specific discipline. Acquaint your group with Bible reference sites such as Biblegateway.com, Biblos.com, Logos.com, or Olivetree.com. (Type in the woman's name and pick one or two verses that give insight into this woman's characteristics.)

When you meet, read the profile aloud and the cited Scripture. Did group members find other relevant Scripture about this woman (or women)? Discuss what you can learn from this biblical woman, asking,

- Why do you think this woman's story is in the Bible? Why does her story matter to us?
- What spiritual discipline did this woman best (or least) exhibit?
- Do you identify with this woman? Why or why not?
- What, if anything, did she do that you would like to avoid?
- What, if anything, did she do that you would like to emulate?
- How did her actions affect her relationship with others and with God?

Everyday Q&A's

The Everyday Q&A's delve into some deeper issues—subjects that may have more than one answer and that cause us all to scratch our heads at first. These articles can provide excellent material for small group discussions. Before meeting, ask your group members to read *just the question*, not the answer. Ask them to jot down what they think the answer is and any additional questions that come to mind. In your group time, look up any Scripture passages mentioned in the Q&A and any other relevant passages in the Additional Scriptures of Note section of the index or possibly found using the online search engines. When you have finished discussing the question, read the answer and take time to explore additional questions raised by group members.

Everyday Reflections

Use the shorter Everyday Reflections with all three of the above features. They will be invaluable for giving you and your group insight and further explanation of each of the subjects you are discussing. They will provide an answer key to help you teach with authority.

Apply What You Learn

These resources will give your group much to discuss for many weeks. But don't forget that the purpose of all Bible study is to apply what you learn, not simply to accumulate knowledge. So no matter what resource you use, end each group time with one or two ways you can put what you learned into action.

For example, if you studied the spiritual discipline of prayer, take a good amount of time to pray together as a group. Or if you studied hospitality, plan a way to practice that discipline as a group. At the end of each session, encourage each person to write down one way she can apply what she learned. And then in later group meetings, have your group members give updates on what they have done, what they learned, and how they would like to continue to grow in that practice.

This Bible can serve as your curriculum and your leader's guide. For deeper concentration on any discipline, see the For Further Reading section on page 1600. And if a particular author interests you, see the cross-references in About the Contributors on page 1587. All you have to do is a little upfront preparation, and your group members will be on their way to developing spiritual formation habits that will last a lifetime!

Index of Spiritual Practices

The additional Scripture passages listed for each discipline either specifically reference the discipline or are about the practice without actually using the name of it.

Acceptance

Everyday Matters
Galatians 3:28   Say Yes to God, by Ginger Kolbaba
Ephesians 4:1   Guard Your Calling, by John Ortberg

Everyday Profile
Genesis 2:18–3:20   Eve: The Self before Sin, by Kelli B. Trujillo

Everyday Q&A's
Genesis 2:18–22   The True Meaning of "Helper," by Carolyn Custis James
John 21:15–23   Hearing God's Call, by Nancy Ortberg

Everyday Reflections
Genesis 39:19–23   Your Calling May Change, by Kay Warren
Genesis 41:1–46   More Influence than You Realize, by Elisa Morgan
Exodus 4:1–17   When Fears Hold You Back, by Holly Vicente Robaina
Judges 6:11–16   Discover Your Calling, by Amy Boucher Pye
Nehemiah 1   The Dream Tucked Away in Your Heart, by Liz Curtis Higgs
Job 2:1–10   Purposeful Living in the Midst of Pain, by Katie Brazelton
Matthew 15:21–28   The Confidence to Wrestle, by Kelli B. Trujillo
Philemon   The High Calling of Women, by Mimi Haddad
Hebrews 12:1–2   Stretched in Scary Ways?, by Carolyn Custis James

Additional Scriptures of Note
Genesis 1:26–27
Exodus 3
Isaiah 6:1–8
Romans 6:1–14; 11:11–24; 12:1–8
1 Corinthians 12:1–11

2 Corinthians 4:1–18; 10:1–18
Galatians 1:11–24
Ephesians 2:1–22
2 Timothy 1:6

Bible Study and Meditation

Everyday Matters
Joshua 1:7–9   Meeting God in Scripture, by JoHannah Reardon
Psalm 119:9–16   Hiding God's Word in My Heart, by Kay Marshall Strom

Everyday Profile
2 Chronicles 34:22–29   Huldah: Leading Others to Obey God's Word, by Amie Hollmann

Everyday Q&A's

John 15:1-7	Making Time for God's Word, by Cynthia Heald
Hebrews 4:12-13	Reigniting a Passion for Scripture, by Priscilla Shirer

Everyday Reflections

Deuteronomy 28:1-14	When Scripture Doesn't Transform, by JoHannah Reardon
Nehemiah 8:1-8	Devoted Listening to Scripture, by Caryn Rivadeneira
Psalm 1	*Lectio Divina*, by Richard J. Foster and Carmen Acevedo Butcher
Psalm 19:7-10	Treating the Bible as Sacred, by Janice Sheridan
Song of Songs 7:10-13	Listening to the Text, by Eugene Peterson
Isaiah 31:4	Gnawing on Scripture, by Caryn Rivadeneira
Matthew 4:4	A Steady Stream of Spiritual Nourishment, by LaTonya Taylor
John 8:1-11	Imagine Yourself in the Gospel Story, by Keri Wyatt Kent
2 Timothy 3:16	The Discipline of "Convictability," by Gordon MacDonald
James 1:22-25	Facing Who We Really Are, by Kelli B. Trujillo
	Praying Scripture (see Prayer)
	Centered Living (see Simplicity)

Additional Scriptures of Note

Deuteronomy 4:1-14; 8:1-3	Luke 4:1-13
Nehemiah 8:1-18	Acts 8:26-39
Psalms 63:6; 119	1 Corinthians 15:27-28
Proverbs 30:5-6	2 Timothy 3:10-17
Isaiah 55:10-11	2 Peter 1:12-20
Matthew 4:1-11	

Celebration

Everyday Matters

Exodus 23:14-19	The Faith-Shaping Power of Festivals and Feasts, by L. L. Barkat
1 John 1:1-7	The Good, the Ordinary, the Delight, by Agnieszka Tennant

Everyday Profile

Ruth 4:13-18	Naomi: Celebration . . . Eventually, by Liz Curtis Higgs

Everyday Q&A's

Psalm 100	Joyful Living in a Dark World, by Mark Galli
1 Corinthians 16:5-18	What Is Celebration?, by Shauna Niequist

Everyday Reflections

Esther 9:20-32	Celebration and Worship, by Kelli B. Trujillo
Psalm 27:1-6	Joy Brings Strength, by George Rehberg
Psalm 113	Celebration through the Psalms, by Kelli B. Trujillo
Psalm 126	The Holiness of Laughter, by Carolyn Arends
Ecclesiastes 11:7-12:2	Connecting Our Pleasure with God, by Gary Thomas
Zephaniah 3:15-17	Our Celebrating God, by Kelli B. Trujillo

Jeremiah 23:23-24	Practicing the Presence of God, by Ann Voskamp
Luke 24:13-35	Time Well Wasted, by John Ortberg
2 Corinthians 3:18	A Heart Open to God, by Vinita Hampton Wright
Revelation 2:4	Seeking God in Our Busyness, by Priscilla Shirer
	Inner Conversation (see Prayer)

Additional Scriptures of Note

Joshua 1:6-9	Matthew 28:20
Psalms 8:3-4; 77:11-12; 121; 139:7-12	Luke 22:39-46
Isaiah 26:3; 55:3	Ephesians 1:15-23
Ezekiel 2:1-3:15	Philippians 4:7

Faith

Everyday Matters

| Job 38:25-33 | Choosing Hope, by Cindy Crosby |
| John 14:6 | Untidy, Mysterious Faith, by Carolyn Arends |

Everyday Profiles

| Genesis 18:9-15 | Sarah: Laughing Her Way to Hope, by Carla Barnhill |
| John 11:1-44 | Martha: Bold Faith, by JoHannah Reardon |

Everyday Q&A's

| Jeremiah 29:10-14 | Unshakable Faith, by Marshall Shelley |
| 1 Peter 5:7 | Worry versus Faith, by Keri Wyatt Kent |

Everyday Reflections

Exodus 2:1-10	Letting Go, by Kelli B. Trujillo
2 Kings 6:8-23	Expecting God to Act, by Ginger Kolbaba
1 Chronicles 16:34	Believing God Is Good, by Sara Groves
Psalm 42	Dark Nights of the Soul, by Sally Morgenthaler
Psalm 111	Afraid of the Right Things, by Ruth Bell Graham
Daniel 4:34-37	Trusting God's Blueprint, by Philip Yancey
Habakkuk 1:2-4	Questioning God, by Julie Kloster
Mark 9:14-29	Moving from Doubt to Certainty, by Mollie Ziegler Hemingway
Hebrews 11:1-2	We of Little Faith, by Holley Gerth
	Complain, Complain (see Gratitude)

Additional Scriptures of Note

Psalms 39:7; 56:3-4; 89	Colossians 3:1-4
Proverbs 3:3-6; 14:26	Hebrews 10:19-11:40
Ezekiel 37:1-14	James 2:14-26
Matthew 6:25-34; 15:21-28	1 Peter 1:3-9
Luke 17:5-10	1 John 5:1-12
2 Corinthians 5:1-10	Jude

Fasting

Everyday Matters
Daniel 10:3	The Daniel Fast, by LaTonya Taylor
Matthew 6:16–18	Why Fast?, by Richard J. Foster

Everyday Profile
Esther 4:7–5:2	Esther: Weakness That Leads to Strength, by Nicole Unice

Everyday Q&A's
Ezra 8:21–23	When Should We Fast?, by Alise Barrymore
John 6:35–59	Fasting like the Early Church?, by Frederica Mathewes-Green

Everyday Reflections
Leviticus 23:32	Rest and Self-Denial?, by Kelli B. Trujillo
Deuteronomy 8:1–5	A Clearer Focus, by Ben Patterson
2 Chronicles 20:1–9	Turning Off the News, by Ginger Kolbaba
Isaiah 26:8–9	What Am I Truly Hungering For?, by Helen Lee
Joel 2:12–13	What Our Brokenness Feels Like, by Caryn Rivadeneira
Jonah 3	A Holy Diet?, by JoHannah Reardon
	A Fast from Talking (see Silence)

Additional Scriptures of Note
Deuteronomy 9:18–19	Daniel 1:8–20; 9:3; 10:3
2 Samuel 12:15–23	Joel 2:12–13
Nehemiah 1:3–4	Matthew 4:1–2; 6:16–18; 9:14–17
Psalms 35; 42:1–2	Luke 2:36–38
Isaiah 58	Acts 13:1–3

Forgiveness

Everyday Matters
2 Samuel 18	Forgiving When It Seems Impossible, by Dianne Collard
Isaiah 43:14–25	Understanding Forgiveness, by Lewis B. Smedes

Everyday Profile
2 Kings 5:1–19	Naaman's Servant: Showing Kindness to Her Captor, by Nicole Unice

Everyday Q&A's
Luke 17:1–10	Forgiving the Unrepentant, by Christine A. Scheller
Luke 23:32–43	Moving beyond Resentment, by Frederica Mathewes-Green

Everyday Reflections
1 Samuel 25:23–38	Choosing Forgiveness over Bitterness, by Caryn Rivadeneira
Ezekiel 37:1–14	Forgiveness Frees Us to Worship, by Kelly Monroe Kullberg
Hosea 3	What Forgiveness Isn't, by Denise George
Hosea 11:1–11	To Make the Unjust Person Just, by Miroslav Volf
Mark 11:25	Throwing Away Resentment, by Allen C. Gueizo

Gratitude

Hospitality

Justice

Additional Scriptures of Note

Deuteronomy 10:17–19; 24:10–15

2 Samuel 9

Psalm 41

Proverbs 6:16–19; 11:1; 12:10; 13:23;
  28:27; 31:8

Ecclesiastes 4:1–3

Isaiah 1:17

Jeremiah 22:3

Ezekiel 45:9–12

Hosea 12:6

Amos 2:6–16; 5:23–24; 8:1–6

Micah 6:8

Zechariah 7; 8:16–17

Matthew 19:16–22

Philemon

Hebrews 13:15–16

James 1:27–2:13

Mentoring

Everyday Matters

John 1:35–44　　　Becoming a Mentored Disciple, by Adele Ahlberg Calhoun

1 Peter 1:21–23　　Why We Mentor, by Mindy Caliguire

Everyday Profile

Acts 18:24–28　　　Priscilla: Invested in Others, by Nicole Unice

Everyday Q&A's

Romans 1:8–12　　　　We Need Each Other, by Jeannette Bakke

Galatians 4:17–20　　Mentoring toward Maturity, by Roberta Hestenes

Everyday Reflections

Joshua 23　　　　　　　　Signs of Fruitful Mentoring, by Fred Smith

1 Samuel 3:1–14　　　　Mentors Help Us Hear God's Voice, by Priscilla Shirer

1 Samuel 23:15–29　　Spiritual Direction, by Jeannette Bakke

Proverbs 1　　　　　　　Desiring to Change, by JoHannah Reardon

Proverbs 13:20　　　　Unofficial Mentors, by Rachel Jay

1 Corinthians 10:31–11:2　Stones That Speak, by Cindy Crosby

2 Corinthians 1:3–4　The Other Side of the Table, by Janine Petry

Titus 2:3–5　　　　　　Biblical Female Mentors, by Kelli B. Trujillo

Additional Scriptures of Note

1 Kings 19:19–21

2 Kings 2:1–15

Proverbs 13:20; 18:24; 27:6

John 21:15–25

Acts 11:19–30

1 Timothy 4:1–16

2 Timothy 2:2

Hebrews 12:1–3

Outreach

Everyday Matters

Acts 28:17–31　　　Rethinking Evangelism: Joining God in His Work, by
　　　　　　　　　　　Carolyn Arends

Romans 15:14–19　Proclaiming a Robust Gospel, by Scot McKnight

Everyday Profiles

Acts 9:36–43　　　Tabitha: The Witness of Kindness, by Adele Ahlberg Calhoun

　　　　　　　　　*The Samaritan Woman: Inviting Others to Reconcile with God
　　　　　　　　　(see Reconciliation)*

Jeremiah 33:3
Daniel 6
Matthew 6:5-15; 18:20
Romans 12:12
Ephesians 6:18

Colossians 4:2-4
1 Thessalonians 5:16-18
1 Timothy 2:1-8
James 1:2-6; 5:13-18

Reconciliation

Everyday Matters

Matthew 5:3-10 — Our Shalom Vocation, by Carolyn Arends
Acts 10 — Reconciliation in and through Grace, by Chris Rice

Everyday Profile

John 4:4-42 — The Samaritan Woman: Inviting Others to Reconcile with God, by Frederica Mathewes-Green

Everyday Q&A's

Luke 15:11-32 — The Theology of Embrace, by Miroslav Volf
2 Corinthians 5:18-19 — Racial Reconciliation, by Brenda Salter McNeil

Everyday Reflections

Leviticus 16:20-25 — Atonement and Reconciliation, by Carla Barnhill
Leviticus 19:18 — Loving the "Other," by Holly Vicente Robaina
Isaiah 9:1-7 — Pursuing Present and Future Peace, by Kelli B. Trujillo
Galatians 6:1-3 — Reaching Out in Compassion, by Frederica Mathewes-Green
James 3:17-18 — A Peacemaker like Francis, by Gordon MacDonald

Additional Scriptures of Note

1 Samuel 25:1-35; 26:1-12
Proverbs 12:20; 24:17-18; 25:21-22
Isaiah 2:1-4; 65:17-25
Hosea 3
Matthew 5:43-48; 9:9-13

2 Corinthians 5:11-21
Ephesians 4:1-6
2 Timothy 2:23-26
1 John 2:9-14; 3:11-24

Sabbath and Rest

Everyday Matters

Exodus 33:12-14 — God Knows What We Need, by Jonalyn Fincher
Deuteronomy 5:12-15 — What Does It Mean to Keep the Sabbath Holy?, by Lauren F. Winner

Everyday Profiles

Proverbs 31:10-31 — A Woman of Virtue: Living within Healthy Limits, by Adele Ahlberg Calhoun
John 20:1-18 — Mary Magdalene: Meeting the Risen Lord, by Jonalyn Fincher

Service

Silence

Simplicity

Stewardship

Everyday Matters

Hosea 4:3 — Caring for Creation, by Nancy Ortberg

2 Corinthians 8:2-4 — The Calling of True Stewardship, by Adele Ahlberg Calhoun

Everyday Profiles

Mark 12:41-44 — A Poor Widow: Giving All to God, by Nicole Unice

A Woman of Virtue: Living within Healthy Limits (see Sabbath and Rest)

Everyday Q&A's

Psalm 24 — Stewardship and Entitlement, by Holly Vicente Robaina

2 Corinthians 9 — Giving When Times Are Tough, by Jim Sheppard

Everyday Reflections

Numbers 18:20-21 — Why 10 Percent?, by Collin Hansen

1 Chronicles 29:1-20 — "Little" Money Decisions, by Kara Powell

Psalm 50:7-15 — More than Caretakers, by Amy Simpson

Malachi 3:6-12 — Tithing?, by Bryan Wilkerson, with JoHannah Reardon

Philippians 2:14-18 — With All My Body, by JoHannah Reardon

1 Timothy 4:11-15 — Stewardship of Time, by Patricia Mitchell

All God's Stuff (see Hospitality)

A Path to Generosity (see Simplicity)

Additional Scriptures of Note

Genesis 1:27-31; 2:4-15

Numbers 18:8-32

Psalms 8; 104

Proverbs 3:9-10; 11:24-25; 13:11

Matthew 6:1-4; 25:14-30

Luke 16:1-15

1 Corinthians 16:1-2

2 Corinthians 8:1-15

1 Timothy 6:17-19

Hebrews 13:5-6

James 5:1-6

Submission

Everyday Matters

Psalm 119:129-144 — Relationship That Leads to Life, by Carolyn Arends

Hebrews 12:1-2 — Lessons from the Cross, by Jane Rubietta

Everyday Profiles

1 Kings 17 — The Widow of Zarephath: Ridiculous Obedience, by Joy-Elizabeth Lawrence

Luke 1:26-38 — Mary: Yes to Shame and Glory, by Luci Shaw

Everyday Q&A's

Jeremiah 7:23 — When Submission Brings Pain, by Beatrice Rusu

Romans 13:1-6 — Submitting to Difficult Leaders?, by Nancy Guthrie

Everyday Reflections

Genesis 22:1-18 — Submission for the Strong Willed, by John Ortberg

Additional Scriptures of Note

Worship

Everyday Matters

Everyday Profile

Everyday Q&A's

Everyday Reflections

Additional Scriptures of Note

About the
Contributors

Carolyn Arends is an award-winning Canadian singer-songwriter—recipient of two Gospel Music Association Dove awards. She is also the author of the critically acclaimed book *Wrestling with Angels* and a columnist for *Christianity Today* magazine. (See Job 20; Psalms 119:129–144; 126; Haggai 1:1–10; Matthew 5:3–10; 19:13–15; Luke 14:7–24; John 14:6; Acts 28:17–31; 1 Peter 1:1–2; Revelation 4:8–11.)

Susan Arico is founder of Pray Creek Consulting LLC, focusing largely on program development to benefit high-risk populations such as ex-prisoners, street children, and traumatized youth. (See Psalm 127:1–2.)

Greg Asimakoupoulos is senior pastor of Mercer Island Covenant Church in suburban Seattle. (See Genesis 18:1–8.)

Hollie Baker-Lutz writes about gender, justice, and culture. She is working on her master's degree in women's and gender studies at DePaul University. (See Daniel 1.)

Jeannette Bakke, a spiritual director, teaches spiritual direction at Bethel University and is the author of *Holy Invitations*. (See 1 Samuel 23:15–29; Romans 1:8–12.)

Tracy Balzer is the author of *Thin Places: An Evangelical Journey into Celtic Christianity* and *A Listening Life*. (See Psalms 73; 77:11–15; Luke 5:17–26.)

L. L. Barkat is a speaker and the author of *God in the Yard* and *Stone Crossings*. She is managing editor of TheHighCalling.org. (See Exodus 23:14–19.)

Carla Barnhill is a freelance editor and the author of *Blessings Every Day* and *The Myth of the Perfect Mother*. A former editor of *Christian Parenting Today* and associate editor of *Campus Life* magazines, she now guest blogs for GiftedforLeadership.com and is cofounder of the Mommy Revolution (themommyrevolution.wordpress.com). (See Genesis 18:9–15; Leviticus 16:20–25; Proverbs 21:23–24; Mark 14:32–42.)

Alise Barrymore is a cofounding pastor of the Emmaus Community in Chicago. She has also served as dean of university ministries and campus pastor at North Park University. (See Ezra 8:21–23.)

Ruth Haley Barton, a seasoned spiritual director, teacher, and retreat leader, is founder of the Transforming Center. She has served on the pastoral staff of Willow Creek Community Church in suburban Chicago. She is professor of spiritual transformation at Northern Seminary and the author of spiritual formation books and resources, including *Strengthening the Soul of Your Leadership*, *Sacred Rhythms*, and *Invitation to Solitude and Silence*. (See 1 Chronicles 17; Proverbs 10:19–21; Jeremiah 17:19–26; Mark 6:30–32.)

Nancy Beach is a speaker, visionary leader, and champion for the power of the arts and artists in the local church. She is the executive vice president for the arts at the Willow Creek Association and the author of *An Hour on Sunday*. (See Proverbs 3:32.)

Catherine Bowler is a professor who specializes in nineteenth- and twentieth-century North American religion. She is the author of *Global Pentecostal and Charismatic Healing*. (See Psalm 131.)

Katie Brazelton is a life coach and the author of the Pathway to Purpose for Women book series. She is also the founder of Life Purpose Coaching Centers, International®, which trains Christian men and women internationally to become Life Purpose Coaches and two-day-intensive Life Plan Facilitators. (See Job 2:1–10.)

Jill Briscoe, a well-known Bible teacher and the author of more than forty books, is executive editor for *Just Between Us*, a magazine of encouragement for ministry wives and women in leadership. She has served on the boards of World Relief and Christianity Today. She and her husband, Stuart, are ministers at large of Elmbrook Church, in Brookfield, Wisconsin. (See Isaiah 64:8.)

Mark Buchanan is pastor of New Life Community Baptist Church in Duncan, British Columbia. He has been published in numerous periodicals, including *Christianity Today* and *Books & Culture*, and is the author of several books, including *The Rest of God*. (See 2 Samuel 6:16–22; Jeremiah 31:1–14; Zechariah 8; Mark 1:15.)

Carmen Acevedo Butcher is a professor of English and scholar-in-residence at Shorter University in Rome, Georgia. She is the author or editor of numerous books, including *A Little Daily Wisdom: Christian Women Mystics* and *Hildegard of Bingen*. (See Job 42:1–5; Psalms 1; 46:10; 2 Peter 1:3–7.)

Adele Ahlberg Calhoun is copastor, with her husband, Doug, of Redeemer Community Church in Wellesley, Massachusetts. A trained spiritual director, she has taught courses at Wheaton College and Northern Baptist Theological Seminary. She is the author of *Spiritual Disciplines Handbook* and *Invitations from God*. (See Exodus 3:1–6; Proverbs 31:10–31; John 1:35–44; Acts 9:36-43; 2 Corinthians 8:2–4.)

Mindy Caliguire is the founder of Soul Care, a spiritual formation ministry, and director of transformation ministry for the Willow Creek Association. A frequent speaker and leadership consultant, she works with local churches and national organizations, including Seacoast Church, Renovaré, Spring Arbor University, and InterVarsity. Her books include *Discovering Soul Care*, *Soul Searching*, and *Simplicity*. (See 1 Kings 11:1–13; 1 Peter 1:21–23.)

Kathy Callahan-Howell is the pastor of Winton Community Free Methodist Church in Cincinnati and a published author of spiritual devotions and articles. (See Psalm 37:7.)

Suanne Camfield is a freelance writer, speaker, and editor. She is the blog manager for FullFill. com, a nonprofit effort focused on mobilizing women to invest their influence in the world for God's purposes. She has also written for *MomSense* and GiftedforLeadership.com. (See 1 John 3:19.)

Sally Clarkson is a speaker, discipler, and blogger (itakejoy.com). Her books include *Dancing with My Father*, *The Mission of Motherhood*, and *The Ministry of Motherhood*. (See 2 Samuel 22:47–51.)

Julie Clawson is the author of *Everyday Justice* and a blogger. She has been a church planter and has served as copastor of Via Christus Community Church in Yorkville, Illinois. (See Deuteronomy 24:17–21; Nehemiah 5.)

Elesha Coffman teaches history at Waynesburg University in Waynesburg, Pennsylvania. She is former editor of *Christian History* magazine. (See Colossians 2:16–17.)

Dianne Collard and her husband have been missionaries since 1986, serving in more than forty countries while living in Europe. Her role is multifaceted: preparing and directing the work of hundreds of missionaries; speaking at conferences throughout Europe, the United States, and Mexico; and directing the department of worship and the creative arts for an organization training European church planters. (See 2 Samuel 18.)

Elaine Creasman has been published in more than thirty Christian publications. She has served on the board of directors of Growth in Faith, an interdenominational women's ministry and as a prayer group leader for Moms in Touch and the Learning to Recognize God's Voice workshop. Elaine also works as a mental health tech on a psychiatric ward at a local hospital. (See Jude 1:17–25.)

Cindy Crosby is an editor, teacher, speaker, and naturalist. She is the author of six books, including *By Willoway Brook* and *Waiting for Morning.* She also has written for many periodicals and websites, including Kyria.com, *Books & Culture, Christian Century,* and *Christianity Today.* (See Genesis 45:1–15; 1 Kings 8:22–53; Job 38:25–33; Psalm 8; 1 Corinthians 7:29–31; 10:31–11:2.)

Marva Dawn is a teaching fellow in spiritual theology at Regent College in Vancouver, British Columbia. A scholar, she is also a popular preacher and speaker. She is the author of more than twenty books, including *Reaching Out without Dumbing Down, Keeping the Sabbath Wholly,* and *In the Beginning, GOD.* (See 2 Chronicles 29:25–36.)

Rebecca Konyndyk DeYoung is a professor of philosophy at Calvin College. She is the author of *Glittering Vices.* (See Psalm 51.)

Ellen Painter Dollar is a writer who focuses on Christian reproductive ethics and disability theology. (See John 10:1–10.)

Margaret Feinberg, author of books including *Scouting the Divine, Hungry for God,* and *Pursuing God's Love,* is a popular speaker at churches and conferences such as Catalyst and Thrive. (See Isaiah 30:18–21.)

Jonalyn Fincher is a philosopher, cultural critic, author, and speaker. She is cofounder, along with her husband, of Soulation (soulation.org). Her books include *Coffee Shop Conversations* and *Ruby Slippers.* (See Exodus 33:12–14; Joshua 2; John 20:1–18.)

Richard J. Foster, founder of Renovaré, is the author of *Celebration of Discipline, Freedom of Simplicity,* and *The Challenge of the Disciplined Life,* among others. (See Psalm 1; Proverbs 29:23; Isaiah 55; Matthew 6:16–18.)

Sharla Fritz is a speaker, singer, and the author of *Divine Design.* She serves in her church as pastor's wife, keyboardist, choir director, and Bible study leader. (See Revelation 7:15–17.)

Mark Galli, a former pastor, is senior managing editor of *Christianity Today.* He has also been an editor with *Leadership Journal* and *Christian History.* His books include *Jesus Mean and Wild* and *God Wins.* (See 1 Kings 19:9–13; Psalm 100; Romans 5:6–11; Ephesians 5:20.)

Denise George is the author of twenty-five books, including *What Pastors Wish Church Members Knew* and *God's Heart, God's Hands.* Her writing has appeared in *Redbook, Essence, Guideposts, Decision,* and *Christianity Today,* among others. She teaches at Beeson Divinity School, Samford University. (See Hosea 3.)

Holley Gerth, a writer for DaySpring and cofounder of (in)courage (incourage.me), is the author of *Rain on Me.* She is also a licensed counselor and a certified life coach. (See Hebrews 11:1–2; 3 John 1:5–8.)

Ruth Bell Graham (1920–2007) was the wife of evangelist Billy Graham. A gifted poet and writer, Ruth authored or coauthored fourteen books, including *Sitting by My Laughing Fire*, *Prodigals and Those Who Love Them*, and *One Wintry Night*. (See Psalm 111.)

Jennifer Grant, a journalist and editor, often freelances for the Chicago Tribune Media Group. (See 1 Samuel 15:22.)

Sara Groves is a renowned singer-songwriter, having been nominated for three Dove awards by the Gospel Music Association. She was named one of the best Christian music artists of 2005 and her album *Add to the Beauty* was named Album of the Year for 2005 by *CCM* magazine. (See 1 Chronicles 16:34.)

Allen C. Gueizo is Luce Professor of Civil War Era Studies at Gettysburg College, where he serves as director of the Civil War Era Studies Program. He is the author of *Edwards on the Will*. (See Mark 11:25.)

Nancy Guthrie, author of *Holding On to Hope,* is pursuing theological studies at Covenant Theological Seminary. She speaks regularly at women's retreats and evangelistic events nationally and internationally. (See Genesis 50:14–21; Romans 13:1–6.)

Mimi Haddad is president of Christians for Biblical Equality. She has contributed to eight books, including *Global Voices on Biblical Equality*. She is also an adjunct assistant professor at Bethel University and an adjunct professor at North Park Theological Seminary. (See Philemon.)

Collin Hansen is editorial director of the Gospel Coalition and a *Christianity Today* editor at large. He is the coauthor, with John Woodbridge, of *A God-Sized Vision*. (See Numbers 18:20–21.)

Gary Haugen is president and CEO of International Justice Mission. Until April 1997, Gary was a senior trial attorney with the Police Misconduct Task Force of the Civil Rights Division of the U.S. Department of Justice. (See Isaiah 1:17.)

Jack Hayford is president of The King's University (formerly The King's College and Seminary) in Los Angeles, which he founded in 1997. He is founding pastor of The Church on the Way in Van Nuys, California. He is the author (or coauthor) of more than one hundred books and has composed six hundred hymns and choruses, including the widely recorded "Majesty." (See Isaiah 6:1–7.)

Cynthia Heald is the author of numerous books and Bible studies, including *Becoming a Woman of Excellence, Intimacy with God,* and *Becoming a Woman of Freedom*. She speaks frequently for women's retreats and seminars nationally and internationally. (See Psalm 23; John 15:1–7; 1 Thessalonians 4:11–12.)

Joseph H. Hellerman is a professor of New Testament language and literature at Talbot School of Theology and is copastor at Oceanside Christian Fellowship in El Segundo, California. His books include *The Ancient Church as Family* and *Jesus and the People of God*. (See Acts 2:42–47.)

Mollie Ziegler Hemingway is a reporter for the *Federal Times* in Washington, D.C. She is the author of *Losing Our Religion*, a book on the changing shape of civil religion in America. (See Psalms 95; 106:1–12; Mark 9:14–29.)

Michele Hershberger is chair of the Bible and Religion Department at Hesston College. She is the author of *A Christian View of Hospitality* and *God's Story, Our Story*. (See Psalm 36:5–9; Matthew 10:10; 25:31–46.)

Roberta Hestenes is executive consultant at Koinonia Graduate School of Theology. An educator, lecturer, consultant, author, and ordained minister, she served as senior pastor of Solana Beach Presbyterian Church. She is a former president of Eastern College (now University) in St. David's, Pennsylvania. Prior to that, she was associate professor and director of Christian formation at Fuller Theological Seminary. She also had a long tenure on the board of World Vision. (See Galatians 4:17-20.)

Liz Curtis Higgs is a popular speaker and bestselling author of some thirty books, including *Embrace Grace*, winner of a 2007 Retailers Choice award, and *Bad Girls of the Bible*. She received an honorary doctorate from Georgetown College in 2010. (See Genesis 29:16-35; Ruth 4:13-18; Nehemiah 1.)

Heather Holleman is founder of Executive Writing Seminars. She writes regularly on her blog LivewithFlair.blogspot.com. (See Mark 5:1-20.)

Amie Hollmann lives with her pastor husband and son in New York City, where she enjoys capturing inspirations with her camera and pen. Her writing, illustrations, and photography have appeared in numerous magazines. She is a contributor to the *Live* devotional Bible for teens and the Good Question Bible Series. (See Exodus 1:15-22; 2 Chronicles 34:22-29; Psalm 34:9-10; Luke 10:38-42; 11:1-13; Colossians 3:16-17.)

Pam Howell works as a church solutions group specialist in the Chicago area. (See Exodus 19:10-20.)

Bill Hybels is the founding and senior pastor of Willow Creek Community Church in South Barrington, Illinois, and the chairman of the board of Willow Creek Association. He is a bestselling author of more than twenty books, including *Holy Discontent* and *The Power of a Whisper*. (See Jeremiah 1:4-5.)

Anne Jackson speaks at churches, colleges, and conventions. She is the author of *Mad Church Disease* and *Permission to Speak Freely*. She contributes to a number of magazines and blogs and is a Compassion International advocate. (See Joshua 7:1-22; James 5:16.)

Doña Jackson is founder of Sole to Sole, a program that helped raise more than fifty thousand dollars to provide shoes to children in Kenya and food through Kenya's school feeding programs. Doña and her husband, Bobby, an NBA point guard, work with low socioeconomic communities. She is the author of *I Will Survive*. (See Ecclesiastes 4:9-12.)

Carolyn Custis James is president of WhitbyForum ministry and the founder and president of the Synergy Women's Network, Inc. She is the author of *Lost Women of the Bible*, *The Gospel of Ruth*, and *Half the Church*. (See Genesis 2:18-22; Deuteronomy 17:1-13; Hebrews 12:1-2.)

Renee James directs communications for a women's mission organization in Canada. She is editor of *The Link & Visitor*, Canada's oldest magazine for Christian women. A gifted worship leader and public speaker, Renee is pursuing a master's in communications management. (See Psalm 139.)

Brenda Jank serves at a Christian retreat center in northeast Indiana, where she has launched ministries that introduce people to the rhythm of rest. As the mother of five, her passion for rest stems from a homegrown need to rediscover abundant life in the chaos of twenty-first-century living. (See Psalm 16.)

Rachel Jay is a freelance author and editor. (See Proverbs 13:20.)

Mary Jenson has published three books and works in partnership with her husband, Ron, on some of his writing endeavors. Together they speak at FamilyLife marriage conferences. Mary serves on the board of the San Diego Christian Writers Guild and works with Moms in Touch International. (See Philippians 4:2–9.)

Richard A. Kauffman is senior editor and book review editor for the *Christian Century*. He has also served as an editor at Mennonite Publishing House and *Christianity Today* and as administrative vice president and instructor in theology at Associated Mennonite Biblical Seminary. He has pastored several Mennonite congregations. He is the author of *An American in Persia*. (See Ecclesiastes 5:10–6:9.)

Karen Keen works in student affairs at the University of California, Santa Cruz. In 2004 she founded Campus Ministries Fellowship at UC Santa Cruz to unite campus Christian clubs in prayer and collaborative outreach. Through active involvement with the local chapter of the Veritas Forum, she has organized student dialogue on topics of faith and culture, including Palestinian-Israeli reconciliation and justice. (See Isaiah 10:1–3.)

Timothy Keller is the founding pastor of Redeemer Presbyterian Church in New York City. He is the author of numerous books, including *The Reason for God, The Prodigal God*, and *Counterfeit Gods*. (See Philippians 2:6–8.)

Keri Wyatt Kent, a regular contributor to several magazines, websites, and blogs, has written nine books, including *Rest, Listen,* and *Breathe.* At Willow Creek Community Church she has worshiped, taught, led groups, and volunteered for more than two decades. (See Ezekiel 46:1–3; Matthew 13:33-35, 44-46; John 8:1–11; 1 Peter 5:7.)

Julie Kloster is a regular contributor to ChristianBibleStudies.com. A fifth-grade teacher, she is also the author of *The Eternal Truths of Narnia*, a Bible study on The Chronicles of Narnia. (See Habakkuk 1:2–4.)

Ginger Kolbaba is a speaker, the founding editor of Kyria.com, and editor of discipleship resources for Christianity Today. She is former editor of *Today's Christian Woman* and *Marriage Partnership* magazines. She has written or contributed to twenty books, including *Desperate Pastors' Wives.* (See 1 Samuel 1; 2 Kings 6:8-23; 2 Chronicles 20:1-9; Job 12; Psalm 116:7; Isaiah 51:12-16; Ezekiel 20:1-20; Hosea 12:6; Galatians 3:28; 2 John 1:1-6.)

Kelly Monroe Kullberg is founder and director of project development of the Veritas Forum, an interactive forum addressing tough questions on college campuses across North America. She authored *Finding God beyond Harvard: The Quest for Veritas.* Since founding the first Veritas Forum at Harvard in 1992, she has traveled the country helping start forums in dozens of universities. For many years she also served as chaplain to the Harvard Graduate School Christian Fellowship. (See Ezekiel 37:1–14.)

Mark Labberton is the Lloyd John Ogilvie Associate Professor of Preaching and director of the Lloyd John Ogilvie Institute of Preaching at Fuller Theological Seminary. He is the author of *The Dangerous Act of Worship.* (See Isaiah 58:6-12.)

Joy-Elizabeth Lawrence is a writer, performer, theater publicist, and homemaker. She is a contributor to GiftedforLeadership.com, *Catapult* magazine, and various resources for Christianity Today. (See Genesis 16; Numbers 6:22-26; Judges 5; 1 Kings 17; Luke 10:25-37.)

Lindsey Learn is an assistant editor at Christianity Today and a contributing writer for Kyria. com. She is also a member of her church's communications team and heads its blog team. (See Romans 12:10-13.)

Helen Lee has been a journalist and contributing writer for *Christianity Today, Leadership Journal,* and *Today's Christian Woman.* She is the author of *The Missional Mom.* (See Isaiah 26:8-9; 61; Acts 23:1-11.)

Marian V. Liautaud is the managing editor for GiftedforLeadership.com. She works closely with some of the church's most trusted experts to develop management resources available on YourChurchResources.com and ChurchSafety.com. She has also written extensively for magazines, including *Christianity Today* and *Leadership Journal,* as well as *Today's Christian Woman* and *Marriage Partnership.* (See Proverbs 15:16.)

Anita Lustrea is a popular speaker at women's conferences and retreats, and cohost and producer of the award-winning *Midday Connection* radio broadcast. She is author of *What Women Tell Me* and coauthor of *Come to Our Table* and *Daily Seeds from Women Who Walk in Faith.* (See Proverbs 18:20-21.)

Gordon MacDonald is a seasoned pastor and author. A former chairman of World Relief, he is an editor at large for *Leadership Journal.* His books include *Who Stole My Church?, A Resilient Life,* and *Ordering Your Private World.* (See Genesis 4:1-7; 2 Timothy 3:16; James 3:17-18.)

Linda Manes is a freelance writer and mother of two. (See Exodus 16:1-18.)

Frederica Mathewes-Green is a wide-ranging author whose work has appeared in the *Washington Post, Smithsonian, Los Angeles Times, Books & Culture, Sojourners,* and the *Wall Street Journal.* She has published nine books, including *Facing East* and *The Illumined Heart.* (See Luke 7:36-50; 23:32-43; John 4:4-42; 6:35-59; Romans 12:1-5; Galatians 6:1-3; 1 Thessalonians 5:16-17.)

Marilyn Chandler McEntyre has taught at Princeton University, the College of New Jersey, Mills College, and Westmont College. She is the author of numerous books, including *Caring for Words in a Culture of Lies.* (See Acts 4:32-37.)

Scot McKnight is a New Testament scholar who has written widely on the historical Jesus, Christian spirituality, and the Emerging Church. He is the Karl A. Olsson Professor in Religious Studies at North Park University. One of Scot's more popular books, *The Jesus Creed,* won the *Christianity Today* book award for 2004 in the Christian living category. (See Romans 15:14-19.)

Bonnie McMaken, a worship leader at an evangelical Anglican church in the Chicago suburbs, is deeply committed to the study and practice of worship as spiritual discipline and celebration for individuals and the church body. (See John 19:17-37.)

Brenda Salter McNeil is founder and director of Salter McNeil & Associates, LLC, a racial and ethnic reconciliation training, consulting, and leadership development company based in Chicago. She is the coauthor of *The Heart of Racial Justice.* (See 2 Corinthians 5:18-19.)

Kevin A. Miller worked at Christianity Today for more than twenty years before venturing into full-time pastoral ministry. He is now the associate rector at Church of the Resurrection in Glen Ellyn, Illinois. He is the coauthor, with his wife, Karen, of *More than Me and You.* (See Zechariah 10:1-6; Acts 6:1-7; Ephesians 5:21-33.)

Patricia Mitchell is a freelance author. (See 1 Timothy 4:11-15.)

Elisa Morgan, former CEO of MOPS International, now serves as the ministry's president emerita. She served as the dean of women of Western Bible College (now Colorado Christian University) and on the board of Evangelical Council for Financial Accountability. She has authored more than fifteen books on mothering, spiritual formation, and evangelism—most recently *She Did What She Could.* (See Genesis 41:1-46.)

Robert J. Morgan, pastor of the Donelson Fellowship in Nashville, is the author of more than twenty books, including *Red Sea Rules* and *My All in All*. (See Revelation 21:3-5.)

Sally Morgenthaler is the author of *Worship Evangelism* and *Exploring the Worship Spectrum*. She has taught graduate courses at Yale University, Asbury Theological Seminary, and Fuller Theological Seminary, among others. (See Psalm 42.)

Mark Moring is senior associate editor of *Christianity Today*, where he covers topics including pop culture and justice issues. He has previously written for and edited other Christianity Today publications, principally *Campus Life*. (See Micah 6:6-8.)

Richard Mouw is president at Fuller Theological Seminary, where he also is a professor of Christian philosophy. He is the author of seventeen books, including *The God Who Commands, He Shines in All That's Fair*, and *Uncommon Decency*. (See 1 Peter 3:13-17.)

Wendy Murray is president and CEO of Ecco Qua Press. She is a veteran award-winning writer, having served across the globe as a reporter. She is an adjunct professor of writing at Gordon College. (See Luke 10:17-20.)

David Neff is editor in chief of *Christianity Today* and a vice president for Christianity Today. (See Proverbs 28:6-27; Daniel 12:1-3.)

Shauna Niequist is the author of two nonfiction books, *Cold Tangerines* and *Bittersweet*. (See 1 Corinthians 16:5-18.)

John Ortberg, pastor at Menlo Park Presbyterian Church in California, is a bestselling author of books including *If You Want to Walk on Water, You've Got to Get Out of the Boat* and *The Life You've Always Wanted*. He is a former teaching pastor at Willow Creek Community Church. (See Genesis 22:1-18; Exodus 19:10-20; Lamentations 3:22-28; Ezekiel 11:18-20; Mark 1:40-45; Luke 24:13-35; Ephesians 4:1; Colossians 1:18.)

Nancy Ortberg served as a teaching pastor for eight years at Willow Creek Community Church in South Barrington, Illinois. She is a founding partner of TeamWorx2, a business and leadership consultation firm that provides fast-paced, practical, and compelling sessions to leaders and their teams. She is the author of *Looking for God*. (See 2 Samuel 12:13-25; Hosea 4:3; John 21:15-23; 2 Timothy 1:3-7.)

Ben Patterson is campus pastor at Westmont College, a contributing editor to *Christianity Today, Leadership Journal*, and formerly a contributing editor and editorial writer with *The Wittenberg Door*. His books include *Serving God, Waiting, Deepening Your Conversation with God*, and *Muscular Faith*. He has served Presbyterian pastorates and also as dean of the chapel at Hope College. (See Deuteronomy 8:1-5.)

Lauretta Patterson ministers at Westmont College with her husband, Ben. She disciples small groups of students, leads women's Bible studies, and practices hospitality. (See Exodus 32:1-8.)

Timothy Peck is director of the chapel and a lecturer in the Haggard Graduate School of Theology at Azusa Pacific University. He preaches regularly at Christ Our King Church in Azusa, California. (See Psalm 136.)

Eugene Peterson has been the James M. Houston Professor of Spiritual Theology at Regent College. He also served as founding pastor of Christ Our King Presbyterian Church in Bel Air, Maryland. A prolific author, he is probably best known for *The Message*, his contemporary version of the Bible. (See Song of Songs 7:10-13.)

Janine Petry writes and edits for many publications, including those of Christianity Today and Focus on the Family. (See 2 Corinthians 1:3–4.)

Cornelius Plantinga Jr. was president of Calvin Theological Seminary from 2002 until 2011, when he stepped down to focus full time on speaking, preaching, and writing. Before joining the faculty at Calvin, he taught at Princeton Theological Seminary, Fuller Theological Seminary, and Regent College and pastored in the Christian Reformed Church. He is the author of *Engaging God's World* and *Not the Way It's Supposed to Be.* (See Ecclesiastes 3:1–8.)

Kara Powell is the executive director of the Fuller Youth Institute and a faculty member at Fuller Theological Seminary. She is the author or coauthor of numerous books and curriculum guides, including *Sticky Faith, Essential Leadership,* and *Deep Justice in a Broken World.* (See 1 Chronicles 29:1–20; Amos 5:21–24.)

Amy Boucher Pye is a freelance editor and writer. She now resides with her husband and children in a vicarage in London, England. (See Judges 6:11–16.)

Patricia Raybon is an award-winning author and journalist whose personal essays on faith, family, and race relations have been published in the *New York Times Magazine, Newsweek, USA Today, Chicago Tribune, Denver Post, Rocky Mountain News,* and Kyria.com. She is the author of two memoirs, *My First White Friend,* a winner of the Christopher Award, and *I Told the Mountain to Move,* a 2006 Book of the Year finalist in *Christianity Today*'s book awards competition. Her most recent book is *God's Greatest Blessings.* (See Psalm 91.)

JoHannah Reardon is a contributing editor for Kyria.com and the managing editor for ChristianBibleStudies.com. Besides writing, editing, and assigning Bible studies, she has ghostwritten two books, contributed to the *Couples' Devotional Bible,* and been published in magazines. (See Numbers 12; Deuteronomy 28:1–14; Joshua 1:7–9; 2 Kings 4:1–7; Psalms 62:1–2; 136; Proverbs 1; Jonah 3; Malachi 3:6–12; Luke 8:40–48; John 11:1–44; Philippians 2:14–18; Hebrews 13:17; 1 Peter 4:7–11.)

George Rehberg teaches Hebrew and is a freelance writer. (See Psalm 27:1–6.)

Chris Rice actively works toward racial reconciliation. His writings on the subject include *Reconciling All Things* and *More than Equals.* He is codirector of the Duke Divinity School Center for Reconciliation. (See Acts 10.)

Caryn Rivadeneira is the author of two books, *Mama's Got a Fake I.D.* and *Grumble Hallelujah.* A former managing editor of *Marriage Partnership, Christian Parenting Today,* and GiftedforLeadership.com, she now continues her work at Christianity Today as a contributing writer for Kyria.com. (See Judges 20:26–27; 1 Samuel 25:23–38; Nehemiah 8:1–8; Psalm 133; Isaiah 31:4; Jeremiah 22:1–5; Lamentations 3:16–24; Ezekiel 22:30; Joel 2:12–13; Matthew 10:28–33; 26:36–39; 2 Corinthians 12:9–10.)

Holly Vicente Robaina served on the staffs of *Campus Life* and *Today's Christian Woman* magazines. She is a regular contributor for Kyria.com and freelances for several print and online publications. (See Exodus 4:1–17; Leviticus 19:18; Psalm 24; Acts 15:36–40; Hebrews 10:24–25.)

Jane Rubietta speaks at women's events both nationally and internationally. Her books include *Come Along, Resting Place,* and *Grace Points.* (See Hebrews 12:1–2.)

Beatrice Rusu is the senior marketing coordinator for discipleship resources at Christianity Today. (See Jeremiah 7:23.)

Christine A. Scheller is a journalist and contributing editor at *Christianity Today*. She also writes for TheHighCalling.org and the Huffington Post. She is a member of the Religion Newswriters Association. (See Luke 17:1–10.)

Ruth Senter is a Bible teacher, conference speaker, editor, and the author of eleven books, including *Have We Really Come a Long Way?* Ruth has served as senior editor for *Campus Life* magazine, editor of *Partnership*, and contributing editor for *Today's Christian Woman*. (See Psalm 121.)

Luci Shaw was cofounder and later president of Harold Shaw Publishers and has been a writer in residence at Regent College, Vancouver, British Columbia. She has authored several nonfiction prose books, including *Water My Soul* and *The Crime of Living Cautiously*. (See Luke 1:26–38; 2:19, 51.)

Marshall Shelley is a vice president of Christianity Today and editor in chief of *Leadership Journal*. (See Jeremiah 29:10–14.)

Jim Sheppard is the CEO of Generis, a consulting firm devoted to expanding the generosity of churches and ministries. (See 2 Corinthians 9.)

Janice Sheridan, a mom and freelance writer, lives in Illinois. (See Psalm 19:7–10.)

Priscilla Shirer has been a conference speaker for major corporations, organizations, and Christian audiences around the world. She is now in full-time ministry to women. She is the author of *And We Are Changed, He Speaks to Me,* and *Discerning the Voice of God.* (See 1 Samuel 3:1–14; Hebrews 4:12–13; Revelation 2:4.)

Amy Simpson, former vice president and publisher for Kyria.com, now serves as managing editor for Kyria's ParentConnect and Marriage Partnership e-newsletters. She is the author of *Diving Deep.* (See Psalm 50:7–15; Isaiah 64:9; Matthew 20:1–16; John 6:15.)

Lewis B. Smedes (1921–2002) was a renowned author, ethicist, and theologian. He was a professor of theology and ethics at Fuller Theological Seminary for twenty-five years. He was the award-winning author of fifteen books, including *Forgive and Forget*. (See Isaiah 43:14–25.)

Fred Smith Sr. (1916–2007) was a behind-the-scenes adviser to ministry leaders, a mentor to business executives, and a leadership expert. He wrote numerous books, including *Breakfast with Fred.* (See Joshua 23.)

Margot Starbuck is the author of *The Girl in the Orange Dress* and *Small Things with Great Love*. She blogs for GiftedforLeadership.com, Her.meneutics.com, and TrueCampaign.com. She also partners as a speaker advocate with Compassion International. (See Acts 8:26–40.)

Sherryl Stone is the wife of the senior pastor of Ginger Creek Community Church in Aurora, Illinois. A part of the Sunday morning teaching team, she recently collaborated with a therapist and psychologist to develop a peer counseling and training ministry at Ginger Creek: the Guidance Support Ministry. (See 1 Corinthians 6:4–7.)

Kay Marshall Strom is a writer, traveler, speaker, and a fighter against injustice. She is the author of some forty books, including *Seeking Christ* and *Forgotten Girls*. (See Psalm 119:9–16.)

Arloa Sutter is founder of Breakthrough Urban Ministries, an organization in Chicago that partners with those affected by poverty to develop skills and open doors of opportunity. She is an associate pastor at River City Community Church and serves on the board of the Chicago Low-Income Housing Trust Fund. She is the author of *The Invisible*. (See Psalm 139:13–16.)

Joni Eareckson Tada is a bestselling author, artist, speaker, and an ardent disability advocate. She is the founder and CEO of Joni and Friends, a multifaceted outreach to the disability community. Her books include *Hope . . . the Best of Things* and *Place of Healing.* Her inspirational *Diamonds in the Dust* won the 2011 National Religious Broadcasters Radio Program of the Year award. (See Hebrews 3:12–15.)

LaTonya Taylor is a contributing writer for Kyria.com. Formerly an editor of *Ignite Your Faith, Christian College Guide, InTeen,* and *Young Adult Today* magazines, her writing credits also include publication in *Christianity Today, Today's Christian,* and *Today's Christian Woman.* (See Daniel 10:3; Matthew 4:4.)

Linda Taylor is editorial director at Livingstone, the publishing arm of eChristian, Inc. She is a speaker and author of several books including *Quiet Reflections of Hope* and *The Household Money Organizer.* (See Luke 18:1–8; 1 Peter 2:11–12.)

Agnieszka Tennant was an editor at large for *Christianity Today.* She is working toward her PhD at Northwestern University. (See 1 John 1:1–7.)

Gary Thomas is a pastor, speaker, and the author of several bestselling books, including *Sacred Pathways* and *Sacred Marriage.* (See Ecclesiastes 11:7–12:2.)

Becky Tirabassi is a motivational speaker and certified life coach. She is the author of *Sacred Obsession* and *Change Your Life,* among other popular works. (See 2 Kings 20:1–10.)

Kelli B. Trujillo is a contributing editor to Kyria.com and the author of several books, including the Flourishing Faith series and *The Busy Mom's Guide to Spiritual Survival.* As a freelance writer and editor, she has contributed to more than eighty Christian books, magazines, and online resources. (See Genesis 2:18–3:20; Exodus 2:1–10; Leviticus 23:32; Judges 13:1–13; 2 Kings 4:8–37; Esther 9:20–32; Psalms 29; 113; 139; Isaiah 9:1–7; Jeremiah 6:16; Amos 3:14–4:1; Zephaniah 3:15–17; Matthew 15:21–28; John 13:1–17; Acts 16:11–15; 1 Corinthians 13; Titus 2:3–5; James 1:2; 1:22–25.)

Nicole Unice has a master's in Christian counseling and is a contributing editor to GiftedforLeadership.com. (See 2 Kings 5:1–19; Esther 4:7–5:2; Ecclesiastes 2:18–26; Mark 12:41–44; John 5:1–15; Acts 18:24–28.)

Stephanie Voiland, who has written for numerous publications, is an editor for a major Christian publishing house. (See 1 Samuel 20.)

Miroslav Volf is the Henry B. Wright Professor of Systematic Theology at Yale Divinity School. A native of Croatia, he regularly teaches and lectures in central and eastern Europe. He is the author of *Allah: A Christian Response.* (See Hosea 11:1–11; Luke 15:11–32.)

Ann Voskamp is a writer for DaySpring's website (in)courage (incourage.me), a contributing editor to TheHighCalling.org, and the author of *One Thousand Gifts.* (See Psalm 150; Jeremiah 23:23–24.)

Sheila Walsh is a Bible teacher, vocalist, and bestselling author from Scotland with more than four million books sold. Her books include *Beautiful Things Happen When a Woman Trusts God* and *The Shelter of God's Promises.* (See Psalm 148.)

Kay Warren, wife of Rick Warren, pastor of Saddleback Church in southern California, founded P.E.A.C.E. Plan, an organization that challenges the worldwide church to take on not just AIDS but the global giants of spiritual darkness, lack of servant leaders, poverty, disease, and ignorance. Her recent book *Say Yes to God* addresses how each of us can find an area of compassionate service. (See Genesis 39:19–23; 2 Samuel 9.)

Charles Edward White is professor of Christian thought and history at Spring Arbor University in Michigan. (See 2 Thessalonians 3:1-5.)

Bryan Wilkerson is senior pastor at Grace Chapel in Lexington, Massachusetts, having previously served as senior pastor at Shelter Rock Church in Manhasset, New York. Bryan is a frequent contributor to PreachingToday.com and *Leadership Journal*. (See Malachi 3:6-12.)

Heather Gemmen Wilson writes and edits for various Christian publishing houses. She is the author of the Lydia Barnes series. (See Genesis 11:1-9; Deuteronomy 31:1-3; Psalm 55.)

Lauren F. Winner is the author of *Girl Meets God* and *Mudhouse Sabbath*. A former book editor for Beliefnet.com, she is a frequent contributor to *Books & Culture* and teaches at Duke Divinity School. (See Deuteronomy 5:12-15.)

Laurence W. Wood is the Frank Paul Morris Professor of Systematic Theology at Asbury Theological Seminary. He has also served in pastoral ministry and has authored five books, including *Designated Successor*. (See Acts 17:16-34.)

Vinita Hampton Wright writes fiction and nonfiction and is a book editor. Her most recent book, *Days of Deepening Friendship*, explores the spirituality of women's experience. She conducts workshops on creativity and spirituality as well as online retreats. (See 2 Corinthians 3:18; Galatians 5:22-23.)

Philip Yancey has written many award-winning titles, including *The Jesus I Never Knew* and *What's So Amazing about Grace?* (See 2 Samuel 24; Psalm 25; Jeremiah 15:10-21; Daniel 4:34-37.)

Joni Eareckson Tada is a bestselling author, artist, speaker, and an ardent disability advocate. She is the founder and CEO of Joni and Friends, a multifaceted outreach to the disability community. Her books include *Hope . . . the Best of Things* and *Place of Healing*. Her inspirational *Diamonds in the Dust* won the 2011 National Religious Broadcasters Radio Program of the Year award. (See Hebrews 3:12-15.)

LaTonya Taylor is a contributing writer for Kyria.com. Formerly an editor of *Ignite Your Faith*, *Christian College Guide*, *InTeen*, and *Young Adult Today* magazines, her writing credits also include publication in *Christianity Today*, *Today's Christian*, and *Today's Christian Woman*. (See Daniel 10:3; Matthew 4:4.)

Linda Taylor is editorial director at Livingstone, the publishing arm of eChristian, Inc. She is a speaker and author of several books including *Quiet Reflections of Hope* and *The Household Money Organizer*. (See Luke 18:1-8; 1 Peter 2:11-12.)

Agnieszka Tennant was an editor at large for *Christianity Today*. She is working toward her PhD at Northwestern University. (See 1 John 1:1-7.)

Gary Thomas is a pastor, speaker, and the author of several bestselling books, including *Sacred Pathways* and *Sacred Marriage.* (See Ecclesiastes 11:7–12:2.)

Becky Tirabassi is a motivational speaker and certified life coach. She is the author of *Sacred Obsession* and *Change Your Life*, among other popular works. (See 2 Kings 20:1-10.)

Kelli B. Trujillo is a contributing editor to Kyria.com and the author of several books, including the Flourishing Faith series and *The Busy Mom's Guide to Spiritual Survival*. As a freelance writer and· editor, she has contributed to more than eighty Christian books, magazines, and online resources. (See Genesis 2:18–3:20; Exodus 2:1-10; Leviticus 23:32; Judges 13:1-13; 2 Kings 4:8-37; Esther 9:20-32; Psalms 29; 113; 139; Isaiah 9:1-7; Jeremiah 6:16; Amos 3:14–4:1; Zephaniah 3:15-17; Matthew 15:21-28; John 13:1-17; Acts 16:11-15; 1 Corinthians 13; Titus 2:3-5; James 1:2; 1:22-25.)

Nicole Unice has a master's in Christian counseling and is a contributing editor to GiftedforLeadership.com. (See 2 Kings 5:1-19; Esther 4:7-5:2; Ecclesiastes 2:18-26; Mark 12:41-44; John 5:1-15; Acts 18:24-28.)

Stephanie Voiland, who has written for numerous publications, is an editor for a major Christian publishing house. (See 1 Samuel 20.)

Miroslav Volf is the Henry B. Wright Professor of Systematic Theology at Yale Divinity School. A native of Croatia, he regularly teaches and lectures in central and eastern Europe. He is the author of *Allah: A Christian Response*. (See Hosea 11:1-11; Luke 15:11-32.)

Ann Voskamp is a writer for DaySpring's website (in)courage (incourage.me), a contributing editor to TheHighCalling.org, and the author of *One Thousand Gifts*. (See Psalm 150; Jeremiah 23:23-24.)

Sheila Walsh is a Bible teacher, vocalist, and bestselling author from Scotland with more than four million books sold. Her books include *Beautiful Things Happen When a Woman Trusts God* and *The Shelter of God's Promises*. (See Psalm 148.)

Kay Warren, wife of Rick Warren, pastor of Saddleback Church in southern California, founded P.E.A.C.E. Plan, an organization that challenges the worldwide church to take on not just AIDS but the global giants of spiritual darkness, lack of servant leaders, poverty, disease, and ignorance. Her recent book *Say Yes to God* addresses how each of us can find an area of compassionate service. (See Genesis 39:19-23; 2 Samuel 9.)

Charles Edward White is professor of Christian thought and history at Spring Arbor University in Michigan. (See 2 Thessalonians 3:1–5.)

Bryan Wilkerson is senior pastor at Grace Chapel in Lexington, Massachusetts, having previously served as senior pastor at Shelter Rock Church in Manhasset, New York. Bryan is a frequent contributor to PreachingToday.com and *Leadership Journal*. (See Malachi 3:6–12.)

Heather Gemmen Wilson writes and edits for various Christian publishing houses. She is the author of the Lydia Barnes series. (See Genesis 11:1–9; Deuteronomy 31:1–3; Psalm 55.)

Lauren F. Winner is the author of *Girl Meets God* and *Mudhouse Sabbath*. A former book editor for Beliefnet.com, she is a frequent contributor to *Books & Culture* and teaches at Duke Divinity School. (See Deuteronomy 5:12–15.)

Laurence W. Wood is the Frank Paul Morris Professor of Systematic Theology at Asbury Theological Seminary. He has also served in pastoral ministry and has authored five books, including *Designated Successor*. (See Acts 17:16–34.)

Vinita Hampton Wright writes fiction and nonfiction and is a book editor. Her most recent book, *Days of Deepening Friendship*, explores the spirituality of women's experience. She conducts workshops on creativity and spirituality as well as online retreats. (See 2 Corinthians 3:18; Galatians 5:22–23.)

Philip Yancey has written many award-winning titles, including *The Jesus I Never Knew* and *What's So Amazing about Grace?* (See 2 Samuel 24; Psalm 25; Jeremiah 15:10–21; Daniel 4:34–37.)

Card, Michael. *A Sacred Sorrow*. Colorado Springs: NavPress, 2005.

Caussade, Jean-Pierre de. *The Sacrament of the Present Moment*. San Francisco: HarperSanFrancisco, 1982.

Chapman, Annie and Heidi Chapman Beal. *Entertaining Angels*. Eugene, OR: Harvest House, 2009.

ChristianBibleStudies.com. *How to Grow Spiritually*. http://biblestudies.stores.yahoo.net/howtogrsp.html

――――. *Pursuing Spiritual Formation*. http://biblestudies.stores.yahoo.net/puspfo.html

――――. *Soul Care for Women Leaders*. http://biblestudies.stores.yahoo.net/socaforwole.html

――――. *Spiritual Disciplines*. http://biblestudies.stores.yahoo.net/spdine.html

――――. *Spiritual Disciplines Assessment Pack*. http://biblestudies.stores.yahoo.net/spdiaspa.html

――――. *Spiritual Formation*. http://biblestudies.stores.yahoo.net/spfo.html

――――. *Spiritual Growth*. http://biblestudies.stores.yahoo.net/spgr.html

Christianity Today. *Crash Course on the Bible Series*. Cincinnati: Standard, 2009.

――――. *Good Questions on Right & Wrong*. Cincinnati: Standard, 2011.

Dawn, Marva. *Keeping the Sabbath Wholly*. Grand Rapids, MI: Eerdmans, 1989.

――――. *Reaching Out without Dumbing Down*. Grand Rapids, MI: Eerdmans, 1995.

de Sales, Francis. *Introduction to the Devout Life*. Mineola, NY: Dover, 2009.

Dillard, Annie. *Pilgrim at Tinker Creek*. New York: Harper, 2007.

Feinberg, Margaret. *Hungry for God: Hearing God's Voice in the Ordinary and the Everyday*. Grand Rapids, MI: Zondervan, 2011.

Fénelon, François de. *The Seeking Heart*. Jacksonville, FL: SeedSowers, 1992.

Fincher, Dale and Jonalyn Fincher. *Coffee Shop Conversations*. Grand Rapids, MI: Zondervan, 2010.

Foster, Richard J. *Celebration of Discipline*. Rev. ed. San Francisco: HarperSanFrancisco, 1988.

――――. *Freedom of Simplicity*. Rev. ed. San Francisco: HarperSanFrancisco, 2005.

――――. *Prayer: Finding the Heart's True Home*. San Francisco: HarperSanFrancisco, 1992.

Foster, Richard J. and Gayle D. Beebe. *Longing for God*. Downers Grove, IL: InterVarsity, 2009.

Fryling, Alice. *The Art of Spiritual Listening*. Colorado Springs: WaterBrook, 2003.

Gertrude the Great. *The Herald of Divine Love*. New York: Paulist, 1993.

Griffin, Emilie. *Wilderness Time: A Guide to Spiritual Retreat*. San Francisco: HarperSanFrancisco, 1997.

Guroian, Vigen. *The Fragrance of God*. Grand Rapids, MI: Eerdmans, 2006.

Heald, Cynthia. *Becoming a Woman of Simplicity*. Colorado Springs: NavPress, 2009.

Hybels, Lynne. *Nice Girls Don't Change the World*. Grand Rapids, MI: Zondervan, 2005.

James, Carolyn Custis. *Half the Church*. Grand Rapids, MI: Zondervan, 2010.

John of the Cross. *Dark Night of the Soul*. Radford, VA: Wilder, 2008.

Jones, E. Stanley. *The Christ of Every Road.* New York: Abingdon, 1930.

———. *Victorious Living.* Rev. ed. Minneapolis, MN: Summerside, 2010.

Lee, Helen. *The Missional Mom.* Chicago: Moody, 2011.

Lewis, C. S. *Letters to Malcolm: Chiefly on Prayer.* New York: Harcourt, Brace & World, 1964.

———. *Mere Christianity.* New York: HarperCollins, 1952.

———. *The Problem of Pain.* New York: HarperCollins, 1940.

Lockyer, Herbert. *All the Promises of the Bible.* Grand Rapids, MI: Zondervan, 1962.

Main, Bruce. *Holy Hunches: Responding to the Promptings of God.* Grand Rapids, MI: Baker, 2007.

Mains, Karen Burton. *Open Heart, Open Home.* Downers Grove, IL: InterVarsity, 1976.

Malesic, Jonathan. *Secret Faith in the Public Square: An Argument for the Concealment of Christian Identity.* Grand Rapids, MI: Brazos, 2009.

McHenry, Janet Holm. *Prayerstreaming.* Colorado Springs: WaterBrook, 2005.

McNeil, Brenda Salter. *A Credible Witness.* Downers Grove, IL: InterVarsity, 2008.

Miller, Paul E. *A Praying Life.* Colorado Springs: NavPress, 2009.

Moeller, Dr. Carl and David W. Hegg. *The Privilege of Persecution.* Chicago: Moody, 2011.

Mottola, Anthony. *The Spiritual Exercises of Saint Ignatius.* New York: Doubleday Dell, 1964.

Muggeridge, Malcolm. *Something Beautiful for God.* New York: Harper & Row, 1971.

Nee, Watchman. *The Normal Christian Life.* Carol Stream, IL: Tyndale, 1977.

Nouwen, Henri J. M. *Life of the Beloved.* New York: Crossroad, 1992.

———. *Reaching Out: The Three Movements of the Spiritual Life.* New York: Doubleday, 1975.

Ortberg, Nancy. *Looking for God.* Carol Stream, IL: Tyndale, 2008.

Patterson, Ben. *Muscular Faith.* Carol Stream, IL: Tyndale, 2011.

Peterson, Eugene. *Christ Plays in Ten Thousand Places: A Conversation in Spiritual Theology.* Grand Rapids, MI: Eerdmans, 2005.

———. *Eat This Book.* Grand Rapids, MI: Eerdmans, 2006.

———. *A Long Obedience in the Same Direction.* Downers Grove, IL: InterVarsity, 1980.

———. *Working the Angles: The Shape of Pastoral Integrity.* Grand Rapids, MI: Eerdmans, 1987.

Raybon, Patricia. *I Told the Mountain to Move.* Carol Stream, IL: SaltRiver, 2005.

———. *The One Year God's Great Blessings Devotional.* Carol Stream, IL: Tyndale, 2011.

Redman, Beth and Matt Redman. *Blessed Be Your Name.* Ventura, CA: Regal, 2005.

Samson, Lisa and Will Samson. *Justice in the Burbs.* Grand Rapids, MI: Baker, 2007.

Schaeffer, Edith. *Forever Music.* Nashville: Thomas Nelson, 1986.

Schaeffer, Francis. *True Spirituality.* Carol Stream, IL: Tyndale, 1979.

Shaw, Luci. *Life Path: Personal and Spiritual Growth through Journal Writing.* Portland, OR: Multnomah, 1991.

Shirer, Priscilla. *One in a Million: Journey to Your Promised Land.* Nashville: B&H, 2010.

Smedes, Lewis. *Forgive and Forget.* 2nd ed. San Francisco: HarperSanFrancisco, 2007.

Sutter, Arloa. *Compassion (Invisible Bible Study).* Indianapolis: Wesleyan Publishing House, 2011.

——. *Justice (Invisible Bible Study).* Indianapolis: Wesleyan Publishing House, 2011.

——. *The Invisible: What the Church Can Do to Find and Serve the Least of These.* Indianapolis: Wesleyan Publishing House, 2010.

Thomas, Gary. *Pure Pleasure: Why Do Christians Feel So Bad about Feeling Good?* Grand Rapids, MI: Zondervan, 2009.

——. *Sacred Pathways.* Grand Rapids, MI: Zondervan, 2000.

Tiegreen, Chris. *Fixing Abraham: How Taming Our Bible Heroes Blinds Us to the Wild Ways of God.* Carol Stream, IL: Tyndale, 2009.

Tolkien, J. R. R. *The Fellowship of the Ring.* New York: Random House, 1954.

Tozer, A. W. *The Pursuit of God.* Harrisburg, PA: Christian Publications, 1982.

Trujillo, Kelli B. *The Busy Mom's Guide to Spiritual Survival.* Indianapolis: Wesleyan Publishing House, 2007.

Velthouse, Lisa. *Craving Grace: A Story of Faith, Failure, and My Search for Sweetness.* Carol Stream, IL: Tyndale, 2011.

Visser, Margaret. *The Gift of Thanks: The Roots and Rituals of Gratitude.* New York: HarperCollins, 2008.

Voskamp, Ann. *One Thousand Gifts: A Dare to Live Fully Right Where You Are.* Grand Rapids, MI: Zondervan, 2010.

Willard, Dallas. *The Divine Conspiracy.* San Francisco: HarperSanFrancisco, 1998.

——. *Hearing God.* Downers Grove, IL: InterVarsity, 1999.

——. *The Spirit of the Disciplines.* San Francisco: HarperSanFrancisco, 1988.

Wilson, Heather Gemmen. *Startling Beauty.* Colorado Springs: David C. Cook, 2004.

Winner, Lauren. *Mudhouse Sabbath.* Brewster, MA: Paraclete Press, 2003.

Wright, Vinita Hampton. *Days of Deepening Friendship: For the Woman Who Wants Authentic Life with God.* Chicago: Loyola Press, 2009.